Current Biography

Cumulated Index 1940-2013

Current Biography

Cumulated Index 1940-2013

H. W. Wilson
A Division of EBSCO Information Services
Ipswich, Massachusetts
2014

GREY HOUSE PUBLISHING

Current Biography Cumulated Index, 1940-2013, published by Grey House Publishing, Inc., Amenia, NY under exclusive license from EBSCO Information Services, Inc.

International Standard Book Number: 978-1-61925-472-5

Library of Congress Catalog Card No. (40-27432)

Printed in the United States of America

TABLE OF CONTENTS

Prefatory Note   vi

Cumulated Index   1

Profession Index   273

PREFATORY NOTE

This edition covers the years from 1940 through 2013, and cumulates and supercedes the previous edition, *Current Biography Cumulated Index, 1940-2003*. The reader will need to only consult this index in order to locate a name that appeared in the previous 74 volumes of *Current Biography*.

The dates after the names indicate the monthly issue(s) and yearbooks containing the biographies and obituaries.

In addition to the alphabetical name index, this edition includes a Profession Index. The Profession Index lists the nearly 20,000 subjects by 849 professions – from AIDS activists to Zoologists. A subject is listed under as many professions as their biography profiles.

Current Biography

Cumulated Index 1940-2013

A

A-mei, Taiwanese pop singer, Jan 2002

AC\DC (Musical group), Mar 2005

Aalto, Alvar, Finnish architect, Apr 1948, *Obit* July 1976

Aaltonen, Waino, June 1954, *Obit* July 1966

Aamodt, Kjetil Andre, Norwegian skier, Jan 2002

Aandahl, Fred G., American governor, Sept 1958, *Obit* May 1966

Aaron, Hank, American baseball player, May 1958

Abacha, Sani, Nigerian dictator, Sept 1996, *Obit* Aug 1998

Abagnale, Frank, American security consultant and former con artist, Apr 2011

Abakanowicz, Magdalena, Polish sculptor, Jan 2001

Abbado, Claudio, Italian conductor, May 1973

Abbas, Ferhat, Algerian political leader, Mar 1961, *Obit* Feb 1986

Abbas, Mahmoud, Palestinian political leader, June 1999

Abbell, Maxwell, American accountant and lawyer, July 1951, *Obit* Sept 1957

Abbott and Costello, comedians, Oct 1941

Abbott, Berenice, American photographer, July 1942, *Obit* Feb 1992

Abbott, Bud, American comedian, Oct 1941, *Obit* June 1974

Abbott, Douglas, Canadian supreme court justice, June 1949

Abbott, Edith, American economist, Sept 1941, *Obit* Oct 1957

Abbott, Edwin Milton, American lawyer, *Obit* Jan 1941

Abbott, George, dramatist and producer, Apr 1940, Oct 1965, *Obit* Apr 1995

Abbott, Jim, American baseball player, Sept 1995

Abbott, Robert S., American newspaper publisher, *Obit* Mar 1940

Abdul Rahman, Malaysian head of state, Yrbk 1957, *Obit* May 1960

Abdul Rahman, Malaysian prime minister, Yrbk 1957, *Obit* Mar 1991

Abdul, Paula, American dancer, choreographer, singer and talent judge on television program, Sept 1991

Abdul-Jabbar, Kareem, American basketball player, July 1967, Feb 1997

Abdul-Razaq, Alhaji, Nigerian lawyer and government official, Jan 2005

Abdulhamid, Ammar, Syrian novelist, poet and essayist, Jan 2005

Abdullah, Yrbk 1947, *Obit* Sept 1955

Abdullah, Jan 2002

Abdullah, June 1948, *Obit* Sept 1951

Abdullah, Jan 2000

Abdullah, Achmed, British novelist and short story writer, *Obit* June 1945

Abdullah, Mohammad, Indian political leader, Nov 1952, *Obit* Jan 1983

Abe, Kobo, Japanese novelist, July 1989, *Obit* Mar 1993

Abe, Shinzo, Japanese prime minister, Jan 2006

Abel, I. W., American labor leader, Nov 1965, *Obit* Sept 1987

Abel, Jessica, American comic book writer and artist, Aug 2007

Abelson, Nat, American clothing industry executive, Nov 1957

Abelson, Philip H., American physicist and periodical editor, Oct 1965, *Obit* Yrbk 2004

Abend, Hallett, American journalist, Sept 1942, *Obit* Feb 1956

Abercrombie, Patrick, English architect, Apr 1946, *Obit* June 1957

Aberhart, William, Canadian evangelist and political leader, *Obit* July 1943

Abernathy, Ralph D., American clergyman and civil rights leader, July 1968, *Obit* June 1990

Aberra, Amsale, Ethiopian fashion designer, Jan 2005

Abetz, Otto, German diplomat, Feb 1941

Abiola, Hafsat, Nigerian dissident, Jan 2007

Abiola, Moshood Kashimawo, Nigerian political leader, Sept 1998, *Obit* Nov 1998

Abizaid, John P., American general, Oct 2003

Abouet, Marguerite, French comic book writer, Nov 2012

Abraham, F. Murray, American actor, Jan 1991

Abraham, John, Indian actor, Jan 2006

Abraham, Spencer, American Secretary of energy, May 2001

Abrahams, Peter, South African novelist and short story writer, Yrbk 1957

Abram, Morris B., American lawyer, Oct 1965, *Obit* July 2000

Abramovich, Roman, Russian energy industry executive and provincial governor, Jan 2004

Abrams, Benjamin, father of Robert Abrams, Sept 1954, *Obit* Oct 1967

Abrams, Charles, American city planner and lawyer, Feb 1969, *Obit* Apr 1970

Abrams, Creighton Williams, American general, Oct 1968, *Obit* Oct 1974

Abrams, Elliott, American diplomat and policy analyst, Aug 1988

Abrams, Floyd, American lawyer, July 1999

Abrams, Harry N., American publisher, June 1958, *Obit* Jan 1980

Abrams, J. J., American screenwriter and film director, July 2009

Abrams, Jonathan, Canadian Internet software developer and entrepreneur, Apr 2006

Abramson, Jill, American newspaper executive, Sept 2011

Abramson, Leslie, lawyer, June 1999

Abrikosov, Alexei A., Russian-American physicist, Jan 2007

Abril, Victoria, Spanish actress, Jan 2004

Abs, Hermann J., German banker, Oct 1970, *Obit* May 1994

Abts, Tomma, British painter, Jan 2007

Abu-Assad, Hany, Palestinian filmmaker and screenwriter, Jan 2006

Abumrad, Jad, American radio producer and personality, Sept 2012

Abzug, Bella, American congresswoman and feminist, July 1971, *Obit* June 1998

Ace, Goodman, radio and television author and actor, May 1948, *Obit* May 1982

Ace, Goodman; and Ace, Jane, May 1948

Ace, Jane, radio performer, May 1948, *Obit* Jan 1975

Achatz, Grant, American chef and restaurateur, Jan 2011

Achebe, Chinua, Nigerian novelist, Jan 1992, *Obit* Yrbk 2013

Achelis, Elisabeth, June 1954

Acheson, Albert R., American mechanical and electrical engineer, *Obit* Apr 1941

Acheson, Dean, American Secretary of state, Mar 1941, Feb 1949, *Obit* Nov 1971

Achmat, Zackie, South African AIDS activist, Jan 2003

Acker, Achille van, Belgian prime minister, May 1958, *Obit* Sept 1975

Ackerman, Carl William, journalist and college dean, Oct 1945, *Obit* Yrbk 1970

Ackerman, Diane, American poet, essayist, memoirist and nature writer, June 1997

Ackley, H. Gardner, American economist, diplomat and presidential adviser, Apr 1968, *Obit* May 1998

Ackroyd, Peter, English novelist, biographer, poet and literary critic, May 1993

Acland, Richard, British member of Parliament, Aug 1944

Acocella, Joan Ross, American dance critic, May 2007

Acosta, Carlos, Cuban ballet dancer, Jan 2004

Acuff, Roy, singer, June 1976, *Obit* Jan 1993

Adair, Frank E., American surgeon, May 1946, *Obit* Feb 1982

Adami, Edward Fenech, Maltese prime minister, Jan 2003

Adamic, Louis, author, Yrbk 1940, *Obit* Oct 1951

Adamowski, Timothee, Polish violinist, *Obit* May 1943

Adams, Alice, American short story writer, Aug 1989, *Obit* Aug 1999

Adams, Alva B., American senator, *Obit* Jan 1942

Adams, Ansel, American photographer, May 1977, *Obit* June 1984

Adams, Arthur S., American mechanical engineer and college president, Jan 1951

Adams, Brock, American Secretary of transportation and senator, July 1977, *Obit* Yrbk 2004

Adams, Diana, dancer and teacher, Apr 1954, *Obit* Mar 1993

Adams, Douglas, English science fiction writer and satirist, July 1993, *Obit* Sept 2001

Adams, Edie, American actress and singer, Feb 1954, *Obit* Yrbk 2008

Adams, Ernie, American football executive, Jan 2009

Adams, Eva Bertrand, government official, Sept 1962, *Obit* Oct 1991

Adams, Franklin P., humorist, July 1941, *Obit* May 1960

Adams, Gerry, Irish political leader, Sept 1994

Adams, Grantley Herbert, Barbadian prime minister, Sept 1958, *Obit* Jan 1972

Adams, Herbert, sculptor, *Obit* June 1945

Adams, James Truslow, historian, Nov 1941, *Obit* July 1949

Adams, John, American composer, May 1988

Adams, John Cranford, college president, Sept 1958, *Obit* Jan 1987

Adams, Joseph H., American inventor, philanthropist and nonfiction writer, *Obit* Apr 1941

Adams, Joseph Quincy, American Shakespearean scholar, *Obit* Yrbk 1946

Adams, Randolph Greenfield, librarian, Aug 1943

Adams, Richard, English fantasy novelist, Oct 1978

Adams, Roger, American chemist, June 1947, *Obit* Sept 1971

Adams, Sherman, American presidential adviser, Nov 1952, *Obit* Jan 1987

Adams, Stanley, American lyricist, Feb 1954, *Obit* Mar 1994

Adams, Thomas, British architect and urban planner, *Obit* Apr 1940

Adams, Yolanda, American gospel singer, Mar 2002

Adamson, Joy, Kenyan conservationist, writer and illustrator, Oct 1972, *Obit* Feb 1980

Addams, Charles, American cartoonist, Jan 1954, *Obit* Nov 1988

Addams, Clifford Isaac, *Obit* Jan 1943

Addario, Lynsey, American photojournalist, Apr 2013

Adderley, Cannonball, American jazz saxophonist, July 1961, *Obit* Oct 1975

Addington, David, American lawyer and vice-presidential aide, Jan 2007

Addington, Sarah, American children's author, *Obit* Yrbk 1940

Additon, Henrietta Silvis, American social worker, prison superintendent and police official, Sept 1940

Ade, George, American humorist, *Obit* July 1944

Ade, King Sunny, Nigerian pop musician, Nov 1994

Adebari, Rotimi, Nigerian-Irish mayor, Jan 2007

Adebimpe, Tunde, American singer, songwriter, and actor, Apr 2009

Adele, British singer, July 2009

Adelman, Kenneth L., diplomat and management consultant, July 1985

Adelson, Jay, American information technology executive, June 2012

Adenauer, Konrad, German statesman, July 1949, Apr 1958, *Obit* June 1967

Adjani, Isabelle, French actress, Jan 1990

Adkins, Bertha S., American educator and government official, May 1953, *Obit* Mar 1983

Adkins, Charles, American congressman, *Obit* May 1941

Adkinson, Burton W., American geographer and librarian, June 1959

Adler, Cyrus, college president, *Obit* May 1940

Adler, Guido, *Obit* May 1941

Adler, Harry Clay, American newspaper executive, *Obit* Apr 1940

Adler, Julius Ochs, American newspaper executive, June 1948, *Obit* Yrbk 1956

Adler, Kurt Herbert, opera director and conductor, Mar 1979, *Obit* Apr 1988

Adler, Larry, American harmonica player, Feb 1944, *Obit* Oct 2001

Adler, Mortimer J., American philosopher and educator, Apr 1940, Sept 1952, *Obit* Sept 2001

Adler, Renata, critic, journalist, novelist and short story writer, June 1984

Adler, Stella, American actress and drama teacher, Aug 1985, *Obit* Feb 1993

Adolfo, fashion designer, Nov 1972

Adoula, Cyrille, Congolese prime minister, Mar 1962

Adria, Ferran, Spanish chef and restaurateur, Jan 2006

Adrian, American costume and fashion designer, Feb 1941, *Obit* Nov 1959

Adrian, Edgar Douglas Adrian, British physiologist, Feb 1955, *Obit* Oct 1977

Adriano, Leite Ribeiro, Brazilian soccer player, Jan 2004

Adu, Freddy, Ghanaian-American soccer player, Jan 2005

Adzhubei, Aleksei I., Russian newspaper editor and son-in-law of Nikita Sergeevich Khrushchev, Sept 1964, *Obit* May 1993

Aerosmith (Musical group), July 2004

Affleck, Ben, American actor, Mar 1998

Affleck, Ben; and Damon, Matt, Mar 1998

Afro, Nov 1958

Aga Khan, Indian Islamic leader, May 1946, *Obit* Sept 1957

Aga Khan, Swiss Islamic leader and financier, Mar 1960, Jan 2004

Agacinski, Sylviane, Feb 2012

Agam, Yaacov, Israeli artist, Apr 1981

Agar, Herbert, author, poet and critic, Mar 1944, *Obit* Jan 1981

Agar, William, American geologist, May 1949, *Obit* July 1972

Agassi, Andre, American tennis player, Oct 1989

Agassi, Shai, Israeli entrepreneur, Sept 2010

Agatston, Arthur, American cardiologist, Mar 2007

Aghdashloo, Shohreh, Iranian actress, Jan 2005

Agnelli, Giovanni, Italian automobile executive, Jan 1972, *Obit* June 2003

Agnew, Spiro, American vice-president, Yrbk 1968, *Obit* Nov 1996

Agnon, Shmuel Yosef, Israeli novelist and short story writer, Mar 1967, *Obit* Apr 1970

Agresti, Alejandro, Argentine film director, Jan 2005

Aguilera, Christina, American singer, Aug 2000

Aguirre Cerda, Pedro, Chilean president, Jan 1941, *Obit* Jan 1941

Ahern, Bertie, Irish prime minister, July 1998

Aherne, Brian, English actor, Feb 1960, *Obit* Apr 1986

Ahlgren, Mildred Carlson, American newspaper columnist and organization official, July 1952

Ahmad, Mar 1956, *Obit* Nov 1962

Ahmadinejad, Mahmoud, Iranian president, Jan 2005

Ahmadu, Alhaji, Nigerian political leader, July 1957

Ahmed, Akbar S., Pakistani anthropologist, Jan 2005

Ahmed, Leila, Egyptian Islamist, Jan 2004

Ahn, Hyun-Soo, Korean speed skater, Jan 2006

Ahrents, Angela, American clothing industry executive, May 2012

Ai Wei Wei, Chinese artist and architect, Aug 2011

Aichi, Kiichi, Japanese statesman, July 1971, *Obit* Jan 1974

Aiello, Danny, American actor, June 1992

Aigner-Clark, Julie, American child development products company founder, Jan 2002

Aiken, Conrad, American poet, novelist, short story writer, critic and memoirist, May 1970, *Obit* Oct 1973

Aiken, George D., American senator, June 1947, *Obit* Feb 1985

Aiken, Howard Hathaway, American mathematician and computer scientist, Mar 1947, *Obit* May 1973

Aikman, Troy, American football player, May 1995

Ailes, Roger, American political campaign consultant and television news executive, Jan 1989

Ailes, Stephen, lawyer and secretary of the army, Jan 1965, *Obit* Oct 2001

Ailey, Alvin, American dancer and choreographer, Mar 1968, *Obit* Jan 1990

Ainsworth, William Newman, American bishop, *Obit* Aug 1942

Aitken, Doug, American multimedia artist, Apr 2007

Ajami, Fouad, Lebanese-American Islamic and Middle Eastern studies specialist, Feb 2007

Akalaitis, JoAnne, American actress, dramatist and director, Feb 1993

Akebono, American sumo wrestler, Aug 1999

Aked, Charles F., American clergyman, *Obit* Oct 1941

Akers, John F., computer industry executive, May 1988

Akers, Michelle, American soccer player, Nov 2004

Akhtar, Ayad, Aug 2013

Akihito, Apr 1959, Aug 1991

Akinola, Peter Jasper, Nigerian archbishop, Jan 2004

Akita, Masami, Japanese electronic musician, Jan 2006

Akon, Senegalese-American rap and rhythm and blues singer, Jan 2008

Aksenov, Vasilii Pavlovich, Russian novelist, Jan 1990, *Obit* Yrbk 2009

Al Thani, Hamad ibn Khalifa, July 2009

Al-Abnoudi, Attiyat, Egyptian documentary filmmaker, Jan 2005

Al-Baghdadi, Ahmad, Kuwaiti political scientist, Jan 2004

Al-Bashir, Omar, Sudanese head of state, Jan 2005

Al-Dari, Harith, Iraqi Islamic cleric and tribal leader, Jan 2007

Al-Emam, Mahassen, Jordanian journalist, Jan 2004

Al-Glawi, Thami al-Mezouari, Sept 1954, *Obit* Mar 1956

Al-Hassan, Seif al-Islam, Feb 1957

Al-Hilali, Ahmad Najib, July 1952, *Obit* Mar 1959

Al-Husseini, Faisal, Palestinian political leader, Jan 1998

Al-Jaafari, Ibrahim, Iraqi prime minister and physician, Jan 2006

Al-Jamali, Mohammed Fadhel, Iraqi prime minister, Jan 1954, *Obit* Aug 1997

Al-Jazairia, Warda, Algerian singer, Jan 2006

Al-Madfai, Ilham, Iraqi guitarist and songwriter, Jan 2004

Al-Maktoum, Mohammed bin Rashid, United Arab Emirates prime minister, Apr 2008

Al-Maliki, Nuri Kamal, Iraqi prime minister, Jan 2006

Al-Mubarak, Massouma, Kuwaiti cabinet member, Jan 2005

al-Mutawa, Naif, Kuwaiti businessman and comic book creator, May 2012

Al-Rajhi, Sulaiman Abdel-Aziz, Saudi Arabian financier, Jan 2006

Al-Sabah, Abdullah al-Salem, Kuwaiti ruler, July 1957, *Obit* Jan 1966

Al-Sabah, Jaber al-Ahmad al-Jaber, Aug 1988, *Obit* Yrbk 2006

Al-Sadr, Muqtada, Iraqi Islamic cleric, Jan 2007

Al-Sahir, Kazem, Iraqi singer, Jan 2003

Al-Said, Nuri, Iraqi prime minister, June 1955, *Obit* Oct 1958

Al-Shabibi, Sinan, Iraqi banker and economist, Jan 2005

Al-Sistani, Ali, Iraqi Islamic leader, Jan 2004

Al-Turabi, Hassan, Sudanese political leader, Jan 1999

Al-Yafi, Abdullah Aref, June 1956

Ala, Hussein, Iranian prime minister, May 1951, *Obit* Sept 1964

Alagna, Roberto, French opera singer, July 1997

Alaia, Azzedine, Tunisian fashion designer, Oct 1992

Alajalov, Constantin, American painter, illustrator and cartoonist, Jan 1942, *Obit* Jan 1988

Alanbrooke, Alan Francis Brooke, British field marshal, Jan 1941, *Obit* Sept 1963

Albanese, Licia, Italian opera singer, Mar 1946

Albarn, Damon, British singer, songwriter and keyboardist, Nov 2003

Albee, Edward, American dramatist, Feb 1963, Apr 1996

Albee, Fred H., May 1943, *Obit* Apr 1945

Alberghetti, Anna Maria, Italian singer, Jan 1955

Albers, Josef, German painter and printmaker, June 1962, *Obit* May 1976

Alberstein, Chava, Israeli singer, Jan 2003

Albert, Jan 2005

Albert, Carl, American congressman and Speaker of the House, June 1957, *Obit* June 2000

Albert, Eddie, American actor, Jan 1954, *Obit* Yrbk 2005

Alberti, Jules, American advertising executive, July 1959

Alberto, Alvaro, Brazilian chemist and United Nations official, Mar 1947

Albertson, Jack, American actor, Mar 1976, *Obit* Jan 1982

Albion, Robert Greenhalgh, historian, May 1954, *Obit* Oct 1983

Albright, Ivan Le Lorraine, American painter, Feb 1944, Yrbk 1969, *Obit* Jan 1984

Albright, Madeleine Korbel, American Secretary of state, May 1995, Apr 2000

Albright, Tenley, American figure skater and surgeon, Sept 1956

Albright, William Foxwell, American archaeologist and biblical scholar, Sept 1955

Alcock, Norman Z., Canadian physicist, Mar 1963

Alcorn, Hugh Meade, American lawyer and political party leader, May 1957, *Obit* Mar 1992

Alda, Alan, American actor and film director, Jan 1977

Aldredge, Theoni, American costume designer, Feb 1994, *Obit* Yrbk 2011

Aldrich, Chester Holmes, American architect, *Obit* Feb 1941

Aldrich, Richard, theatrical producer, June 1955, *Obit* June 1986

Aldrich, Richard S., American congressman, *Obit* Feb 1942

Aldrich, Winthrop Williams, American banker and diplomat, Oct 1940, Mar 1953, *Obit* Apr 1974

Aldridge, James, Australian author, Mar 1943

Aldridge, John W., American literary critic, Yrbk 1958

Aldrin, Buzz, American astronaut, Sept 1993

Alechinsky, Pierre, Belgian painter and lithographer, Sept 1988

Alegria, Ciro, Peruvian novelist, Yrbk 1941

Aleixandre, Vicente, Spanish poet, Mar 1978, *Obit* Mar 1985

Alekhine, Alexander, Russian chess player, *Obit* May 1946

Aleksievich, Svetlana, Belarusian journalist, Jan 2006

Aleksii, Mar 1953, *Obit* June 1970

Aleksii, Jan 2003, *Obit* Yrbk 2009

Aleman Valdez, Miguel, Mexican president, Sept 1946, *Obit* July 1983

Alessandri Rodriguez, Jorge, Chilean president, May 1959, *Obit* Oct 1986

Alexander, Albert, Yrbk 1940, *Obit* Feb 1965

Alexander, Archie Alphonse, American engineer and territorial governor, June 1955, *Obit* Mar 1958

Alexander, Christopher, British architect, Oct 2003

Alexander, Clifford, American Secretary of the army, Sept 1977

Alexander, Donald C., American lawyer and tax official, Yrbk 1974, *Obit* Yrbk 2009

Alexander, Franz, Austrian psychiatrist, Aug 1942, Sept 1960, *Obit* Apr 1964

Alexander, Harold Rupert Leofric George Alexander, British field marshal, Oct 1942, *Obit* Sept 1969

Alexander, Harry Held, American metallurgist, *Obit* Feb 1941

Alexander, Holmes Moss, columnist and author, Sept 1956

Alexander, Jane, American actress and government official, Feb 1977

Alexander, Jason, American actor, Jan 1998

Alexander, Lamar, American senator, July 1991

Alexander, Ruth, American economist and lecturer, Mar 1943

Alexander, Willis W., American banker and newspaper publisher, July 1969, *Obit* Jan 1986

Alexanderson, Ernst Fredrik Werner, Swedish electrical engineer and inventor, Sept 1955, *Obit* Aug 1975

Alexie, Sherman, American poet, novelist and screenwriter, Oct 1998

Alfonsin, Raul, Argentine president, July 1984, *Obit* Yrbk 2009

Alfonso, *Obit* Apr 1941

Alfrink, Bernard, May 1966, *Obit* Feb 1988

Alger, Ellice M., American ophthalmologist, *Obit* Apr 1945

Alhaji Ahmadu; Sardauna of Sokoto; Obafemi Awolowo; and Nnamdi Azikiwe, July 1957

Ali, Asaf, June 1947, *Obit* May 1953

Ali, Chaudhri Muhammad, Pakistani prime minister, Feb 1956

Ali, Laylah, American painter, July 2008

Ali, Mohammed, Pakistani prime minister and diplomat, Oct 1952, *Obit* Mar 1963

Ali, Muhammad, American boxer, Sept 1963, Nov 1978

Alia, Ramiz, Albanian president, Jan 1991, *Obit* Yrbk 2011

Alibek, Ken, Kazakh biological weapons expert, June 2002

Alinsky, Saul, American social activist, Nov 1968, *Obit* July 1972

Alioto, Joseph L., mayor, Sept 1969, *Obit* Apr 1998

Alito, Samuel A., American Supreme Court justice, Apr 2006

Aliyev, Heydar, Azerbaijani president, Sept 1999, *Obit* July 2004

Alkatiri, Mari, East Timorese prime minister, Jan 2006

Allan, John J., American Salvation Army leader, Jan 1950, *Obit* Jan 1961

Allawi, Iyad, Iraqi interim prime minister and neurologist, Jan 2004

Allee, Marjorie Hill, author, *Obit* June 1945

Allegro, John Marco, British paleographer and philologist, Yrbk 1970, *Obit* Apr 1988

Allen, Arthur Augustus, American ornithologist, Jan 1961, *Obit* Mar 1964

Allen, Betty, American opera singer, Nov 1990, *Obit* Yrbk 2009

Allen, Debbie, American dancer, actress and director, Feb 1987

Allen, Dick, American baseball player, May 1973

Allen, Edgar, American anatomist, *Obit* Mar 1943

Allen, Ethan, American baseball player and coach, Mar 1954, *Obit* Nov 1993

Allen, Florence Ellinwood, American judge, Feb 1941, July 1963, *Obit* Nov 1966

Allen, Frank A., American general, Mar 1945, *Obit* Jan 1980

Allen, Fred, comedian, Feb 1941, *Obit* May 1956

Allen, George, American football coach, Jan 1975, *Obit* Mar 1991

Allen, George E., American lawyer and government official, Mar 1946, *Obit* June 1973

Allen, George Venable, American diplomat, Nov 1948, *Obit* Oct 1970

Allen, Gracie, American comedienne, July 1940, Mar 1951, *Obit* Oct 1964

Allen, J. D., American jazz saxophonist, Nov 2010

Allen, James Edward, American government official and educator, June 1969, *Obit* Yrbk 1971

Allen, Jay, American journalist, Oct 1941, *Obit* Feb 1973

Allen, Joel Nott, American painter, *Obit* Mar 1940

Allen, Larry, American journalist, July 1942

Allen, Leo E., American congressman, June 1948, *Obit* Mar 1973

Allen, Lily, British pop singer and songwriter, Jan 2007

Allen, Marcus, American football player, Oct 1986

Allen, Marion Boyd, American painter, *Obit* Feb 1942

Allen, Martha F., American social worker and youth leader, Oct 1959

Allen, Mel, sportscaster, Oct 1950, *Obit* Aug 1996

Allen, Paul, American computer software executive and investor, July 1998

Allen, Peter, Australian singer and songwriter, Mar 1983, *Obit* Aug 1992

Allen, Ralph, Canadian periodical editor, July 1958, *Obit* Feb 1967

Allen, Ray, American basketball player, Jan 2009

Allen, Raymond B., college president and physician, Mar 1952, *Obit* May 1986

Allen, Rick, English drummer, Jan 2003

Allen, Robert Sharon, May 1941

Allen, Steve, American comedian and actor, July 1951, Mar 1982, *Obit* Jan 2001

Allen, Terry, Nov 1943, *Obit* Nov 1969

Allen, Tim, American comedian and actor, May 1995

Allen, Will, American urban farmer, Sept 2013

Allen, William L., Canadian labor leader, Sept 1953

Allen, William M., American aircraft industry executive, Mar 1953, *Obit* Jan 1986

Allen, Woody, American actor, filmmaker and screenwriter, Yrbk 1966, Sept 1979

Allende Gossens, Salvador, Chilean president, Sept 1971, *Obit* Nov 1973

Allende, Isabel, Chilean novelist, Feb 1988

Alley, Kirstie, American actress, July 1994

Alley, Rewi, New Zealand revolutionary, Oct 1943, *Obit* Feb 1988

Allilueva, Svetlana, daughter of Joseph Stalin, Oct 1968, *Obit* Yrbk 2012

Alliot-Marie, Michele, French cabinet member, Jan 2003

Allison, John Moore, American diplomat, Mar 1956, *Obit* Feb 1979

Allman, David B., American surgeon and medical association official, Feb 1958, *Obit* May 1971

Allon, Yigal, Israeli political leader, Sept 1975, *Obit* Apr 1980

Allott, Gordon, American senator, May 1955, *Obit* Apr 1989

Allport, Gordon, psychologist, Sept 1960, *Obit* Yrbk 1967

Allyn, Lewis B., American food chemist, *Obit* Jan 1940

Allyn, Stanley C., American cash register company executive, Mar 1956, *Obit* Yrbk 1970

Allyson, June, American actress, Jan 1952, *Obit* Yrbk 2006

Almada, Martin, Paraguayan educator, lawyer and human rights activist, Jan 2004

Almendros, Nestor, Cuban cinematographer and director, Nov 1989, *Obit* May 1992

Almirante, Giorgio, Italian political leader, Jan 1974, *Obit* July 1988

Almodovar, Pedro, Spanish film director, Sept 1990

Almond, Edward M., general, Mar 1951, *Obit* Aug 1979

Almond, J. Lindsay, American governor, Mar 1958, *Obit* June 1986

Alonso, Alicia, Cuban ballet dancer, July 1955, June 1977

Alou, Felipe, Dominican baseball player and manager, June 1999

Alou, Moises, American baseball player, Apr 1999

Alpert, George, railroad executive and lawyer, Sept 1961, *Obit* Oct 1988

Alpert, Herb, American trumpet player and composer, Jan 1967

Alphadi, Malian fashion designer, Jan 2004

Alphand, Herve, French diplomat, Nov 1951, *Obit* Mar 1994

Alsberg, Carl, American biochemist, *Obit* Yrbk 1940

Alsop, Joseph, American journalist, Oct 1952, *Obit* Oct 1989

Alsop, Joseph; and Alsop, Stewart, Oct 1952

Alsop, Stewart, American journalist, Oct 1952, *Obit* July 1974

Alstadt, W. R., American dentist, July 1958

Alston, Walter, baseball manager, June 1954, *Obit* Nov 1984

Altenburg, Alexander, American painter, *Obit* Mar 1940

Alter, George Elias, American lawyer and state attorney general, *Obit* Oct 1940

Alterman, Eric, American journalist, Feb 2007

Altizer, Thomas J. J., American theologian, June 1967

Altman, Robert, American motion picture director and producer, Feb 1974, *Obit* Yrbk 2007

Altmeyer, Arthur Joseph, American government official, Nov 1946, *Obit* Yrbk 1972

Alvarado, Elvia, Honduran human rights activist, Jan 2004

Alvarez Bravo, Manuel, Mexican photographer, Jan 1999, *Obit* Jan 2003

Alvarez Quintero, Joaquin, Spanish dramatist, *Obit* Aug 1944

Alvarez de Toledo, Luisa Isabel, Spanish novelist and social reformer, Apr 1972

Alvarez, Luis W., American physicist, May 1947, *Obit* Oct 1988

Alvarez, Walter C., American internist and physiologist, Sept 1953, *Obit* Aug 1978

Alvear, Marcelo Torcuato de, *Obit* May 1942

Alvtegen, Karin, Swedish novelist, Jan 2007

Alwaleed bin Talal al Saud, Saudi Arabian entrepreneur and financier, Jan 2006

Amado, Jorge, Brazilian novelist, Mar 1986, *Obit* Oct 2001

Amadou & Mariam (Musical group), Jan 2006

Amal'rik, Andrei, Russian essayist and historian, Apr 1974, *Obit* Jan 1981

Amalric, Mathieu, French actor, film director and screenwriter, Feb 2011

Amanpour, Christiane, British television reporter and moderator, Apr 1996

Amari, Raja, Tunisian screenwriter and motion picture director, Jan 2002

Amato, Giuliano, Italian prime minister, Sept 1993

Amato, Pasquale, Italian opera singer, *Obit* Oct 1942

Ambani, Anil, Indian telecommunications, textile and chemical conglomerate executive, Feb 2009

Ambani, Mukesh, Indian telecommunications, textile and chemical conglomerate executive, June 2009

Ambedkar, Bhimrao Ramji, Indian statesman and reformer, Nov 1951, *Obit* Feb 1957

Ambler, Eric, English mystery novelist, June 1975, *Obit* Jan 1999

Amdahl, Gene M., American electrical engineer and computer executive, Aug 1982

Ameche, Don, actor, May 1965, *Obit* Feb 1994

Amedeo, Italian air force officer and colonial administrator, *Obit* Apr 1942

Ameling, Elly, Dutch singer, Oct 1982

Amenabar, Alejandro, Spanish film director, Jan 2005

Amend, Bill, American cartoonist, Apr 2003

Amerasinghe, Hamilton Shirley, Sri Lankan diplomat, Mar 1977, *Obit* Feb 1981

Ameringer, Oscar, socialist leader, *Obit* Yrbk 1943

Amery, Leopold Charles Maurice Stennett, British cabinet member, July 1942, *Obit* Yrbk 1956

Ames, Amyas, investment banker and music patron, Apr 1972, *Obit* June 2000

Ames, Bruce N., American biochemist, Oct 1993

Ames, Jonathan, American novelist, humorist and columnist, Oct 2007

Ames, Joseph S., American physicist and university president, *Obit* Aug 1943

Ames, Louise Bates, child psychologist, Sept 1956, *Obit* Jan 1997

Amichai, Yehuda, Israeli poet, Feb 1998, *Obit* Jan 2001

Amies, Hardy, English fashion designer, Mar 1962, *Obit* Aug 2003

Amin, Idi, Ugandan general and president, Feb 1973, *Obit* Yrbk 2003

Amin, Samir, Egyptian economist, Aug 2012

Amini, Ali, Iranian prime minister, Jan 1962

Amis, Kingsley, English novelist, poet and critic, Yrbk 1958, Apr 1987, *Obit* Jan 1996

Amis, Martin, English novelist and short story writer, June 1990, Jan 2003

Amla, Hashim, South African cricket player, Jan 2006

Ammachi, Indian Hindu mystic, Jan 2003

Ammann, Karl, Swiss wildlife photographer, Jan 2002

Ammann, Othmar Hermann, American civil engineer, Jan 1963, *Obit* Nov 1965

Ammondt, Jukka, Finnish literary scholar and Elvis Presley impersonator, Jan 2002

Ammons, A. R., American poet, Feb 1982, *Obit* July 2001

Amoruso, Sophia, Sept 2013

Amory, Derick Heathcoat Amory, British textile industry executive and cabinet member, Apr 1958

Amos 'n' Andy (Radio program), Yrbk 1947

Amos, Tori, American singer and songwriter, Sept 1998

Amos, Wally, American baking industry executive, July 1995

Amram, David, American composer, conductor and French horn player, Nov 1969

Amsden, Charles Avery, American archaeologist, *Obit* Apr 1941

Amsterdam, Birdie, judge, Mar 1940, *Obit* Sept 1996

Amulree, William Warrender Mackenzie, British government official, *Obit* June 1942

Ananda Mahidol, *Obit* July 1946

Anastasio, Trey, American guitarist and songwriter, July 2003

Anders, William A., American astronaut and aerospace industry executive, Apr 1969

Andersen, Hendrik Christian, American sculptor, *Obit* Feb 1941

Andersen, Ib, Danish ballet dancer and director, Aug 1984

Anderson, Abraham Archibald, American painter, *Obit* Jan 1940

Anderson, Alexander E., American general, *Obit* Feb 1943

Anderson, Carl David, American physicist, Jan 1951, *Obit* Mar 1991

Anderson, Christopher, American magazine editor, Jan 2010

Anderson, Clinton P., American Secretary of agriculture and senator, June 1945, *Obit* Jan 1976

Anderson, Constance, youth leader, May 1948, *Obit* Apr 2001

Anderson, Don L., American geophysicist, Oct 2002

Anderson, Erica Kellner, Feb 1957, *Obit* Nov 1976

Anderson, Eugenie M., American diplomat, Jan 1950

Anderson, Frederick L., American general, May 1944, *Obit* Apr 1969

Anderson, Gaylord W., American physician, Feb 1953

Anderson, George Everett, American diplomat and journalist, *Obit* Apr 1940

Anderson, George Whelan, American admiral, Nov 1962, *Obit* May 1992

Anderson, H. Dewey, American economist, Jan 1950

Anderson, Howard R., American educator, Jan 1955

Anderson, Ian, British singer, flutist and songwriter, Feb 1998

Anderson, Jack, American newspaper columnist, June 1972, *Obit* Yrbk 2006

Anderson, John, American drama critic and playwright, *Obit* Sept 1943

Anderson, John Bayard, American congressman, Sept 1979

Anderson, John Crawford, American state supreme court justice, *Obit* Jan 1940

Anderson, John W., American merchant marine officer, July 1953

Anderson, Judith, English actress, Yrbk 1941, Feb 1961, *Obit* Mar 1992

Anderson, June, opera singer, May 1991

Anderson, Kenneth A. N., British general, Feb 1943, *Obit* July 1959

Anderson, Laurie, American performance artist and musician, July 1983

Anderson, Leroy, American composer, Sept 1952, *Obit* Aug 1975

Anderson, Lindsay, British motion picture and theatrical director, Nov 1975, *Obit* Nov 1994

Anderson, Marian, American opera singer, May 1940, Apr 1950, *Obit* June 1993

Anderson, Mary, American actress, *Obit* July 1940

Anderson, Mary, American labor leader and government official, Sept 1940, *Obit* Mar 1964

Anderson, Maxwell, American dramatist, Nov 1942, Sept 1953, *Obit* May 1959

Anderson, Ray C., American carpet industry executive, May 2005, *Obit* Yrbk 2012

Anderson, Reid, American jazz bassist, Oct 2011

Anderson, Robert, American dramatist and screenwriter, Sept 1954, *Obit* Yrbk 2009

Anderson, Robert Bernerd, American Secretary of the treasury, June 1953, *Obit* Oct 1989

Anderson, Robert Orville, American petroleum industry executive, Sept 1982, *Obit* Yrbk 2008

Anderson, Roy A., American aerospace executive, Aug 1983, *Obit* Mar 2004

Anderson, Samuel W., American investment banker and government official, June 1954, *Obit* Jan 1963

Anderson, Sherwood, American novelist and short story writer, *Obit* Apr 1941

Anderson, Sigurd, governor, Sept 1953, *Obit* Mar 1991

Anderson, Sparky, American baseball manager, Apr 1977, *Obit* Yrbk 2011

Anderson, Tom, American Internet executive, July 2007

Anderson, Victor E., American governor, Sept 1956, *Obit* Oct 1962

Anderson, Wes, American film director and screenwriter, May 2002

Anderson, William French, American geneticist, Oct 1994

Anderson, William Robert, American naval officer and congressman, Apr 1959, *Obit* Yrbk 2007

Anderson, Winston A., American biologist, Mar 2007

Andersson, Bibi, Swedish actress, Sept 1978

Ando, Tadao, Japanese architect, Jan 2000

Andrade, Victor, Bolivian diplomat, Feb 1953

Andre 3000, American rapper, Apr 2004

Andre, Carl, American sculptor, May 1986

Andreas, Dwayne O., food industry executive, Mar 1992

Andreessen, Marc, American computer programmer and software executive, June 1997

Andreessen, Marc; Clark, James H., June 1997

Andreotti, Giulio, Italian prime minister, Feb 1977, *Obit* Yrbk 2013

Andresen, August H., American congressman, Feb 1956, *Obit* Mar 1958

Andretti, Mario, American automobile racing driver, July 1968

Andreu Almazan, Juan, Mexican general and political leader, May 1940, *Obit* Yrbk 1965

Andrew, Mar 1987

Andrewes, William, British admiral, Sept 1952, *Obit* Jan 1975

Andrews, Anthony, English actor, June 1991

Andrews, Bert, American journalist, Sept 1948, *Obit* Oct 1953

Andrews, Charles McLean, American historian, *Obit* Oct 1943

Andrews, Charles O., American senator, *Obit* Nov 1946

Andrews, Dana, actor, Oct 1959, *Obit* Feb 1993

Andrews, Erin, American television sportscaster, Sept 2013

Andrews, Frank M., American general, Feb 1942, *Obit* June 1943

Andrews, John Bertram, economist, *Obit* Feb 1943

Andrews, Julie, English actress and singer, July 1956, Apr 1994

Andrews, Roy Chapman, American zoologist, explorer and museum director, Jan 1941, July 1953, *Obit* May 1960

Andrews, Stanley, June 1952

Andrews, T. Coleman, accountant and government official, Apr 1954

Andric, Ivo, Yugoslav novelist, short story writer and poet, Feb 1962, *Obit* May 1975

Andropov, Yuri, Soviet communist leader, May 1983, *Obit* Apr 1984

Andrus, Cecil D., governor, Aug 1977

Andr,s, Jos,, Spanish chef and restaurateur, June 2013

Angeles, Victoria de los, Spanish opera singer, Feb 1955, *Obit* Aug 2005

Angell, James Rowland, American psychologist and university president, Yrbk 1940, *Obit* Mar 1949

Angell, Marcia, American physician and medical writer, Nov 2005

Angell, Norman, English journalist and pacifist, May 1948, *Obit* Yrbk 1967

Angelopoulos, Theodoros, Greek film director and screenwriter, *Obit* Yrbk 2012

Angelopoulos-Daskalaki, Gianna, Greek Olympic executive, Jan 2004

Angelou, Maya, American poet and memoirist, June 1974, Feb 1994

Angier, Natalie, American science writer, Aug 1999

Angle, Paul McClelland, historian, July 1955, *Obit* Aug 1975

Angoff, Charles, American novelist and editor, Yrbk 1955, *Obit* July 1979

Anka, Paul, Canadian singer and songwriter, Feb 1964

Ann-Margret, American actress, singer and dancer, Sept 1975

Annan, Kofi, Ghanaian United Nations secretary-general, Mar 2000

Anne, Oct 1973

Annenberg, Walter H., American magazine and newspaper publisher, diplomat and philanthropist, Jan 1970, *Obit* Jan 2003

Annis, Edward R., Apr 1964

Anouilh, Jean, French dramatist, Apr 1954, *Obit* Nov 1987

Ansari, Anousheh, Iranian-American information technology executive, Jan 2005

Ansari, Aziz, American comedian and actor, Feb 2013

Anselmo, Giovanni, Italian artist, Jan 2003

Ansermet, Ernest, Swiss conductor, July 1949, *Obit* Apr 1969

Anslinger, Harry Jacob, government official, May 1948, *Obit* Jan 1976

Anspach, Charles L., American college president, Sept 1956

Antall, Jozsef, Hungarian prime minister, Sept 1990, *Obit* Feb 1994

Antes, Horst, German painter, etcher and sculptor, Feb 1986

Antheil, George, American composer, July 1954, *Obit* Apr 1959

Anthony, Carmelo, American basketball player, June 2005

Anthony, John J., American family and marriage counselor, Jan 1942, *Obit* Oct 1970

Antinori, Piero, Italian vintner, Jan 2006

Antinori, Severino, Italian physician, Jan 2002

Antoine, Polish hairstylist, June 1955, *Obit* Sept 1976

Antoine, Josephine, American opera singer, Aug 1944

Antonescu, Ion, Romanian dictator, Oct 1940, *Obit* July 1946

Antonioni, Michelangelo, Italian film director, Yrbk 1964, May 1993, *Obit* Yrbk 2007

Anu, Christine, Australian singer and actress, Jan 2003

Anuszkiewicz, Richard Joseph, Oct 1978

Aoki, Rocky, American restaurant chain executive, June 2005, *Obit* Yrbk 2008

Aouita, Said, Moroccan runner, May 1990

Aoun, Michel, Lebanese general and political leader, Mar 1990

Apgar, Virginia, American anesthesiologist, Feb 1968, *Obit* Oct 1974

Apl. de. Ap (Musician), American singer, Oct 2006

Appel, James Z., American physician and medical association official, Mar 1966, *Obit* Oct 1981

Appel, Karel, Dutch painter, Mar 1961, *Obit* Yrbk 2006

Appiah, Anthony, American professor of African-American studies, June 2002

Apple, Fiona, American singer and songwriter, Nov 2006

Apple, R. W., American journalist, Apr 1993, *Obit* Feb 2007

Applebaum, Anne, American journalist, Aug 2004

Appleton, Edward Dale, American publishing executive, *Obit* Mar 1942

Appleton, Edward Victor, British physicist, Sept 1945, *Obit* June 1965

Appleton, Robert, American publishing executive, *Obit* Mar 1945

Appley, Lawrence A., business consultant, July 1950, *Obit* June 1997

Appleyard, Rollo, British electrical engineer and inventor, *Obit* Apr 1943

Apted, Michael, British motion picture director, Feb 2000

Aquino, Corazon, Filipino president, Aug 1986, *Obit* Yrbk 2009

Arad, Michael, American architect, Oct 2013

Arafat, Yasir, Palestinian political leader, Mar 1971, Nov 1994, Jan 2002, *Obit* Feb 2005

Arakawa, Shizuka, Japanese figure skater, Jan 2006

Araki, Eikichi, Japanese diplomat, Oct 1952, *Obit* Apr 1959

Araki, Nobuyoshi, Japanese photographer, Jan 2003

Aramburu, Pedro Eugenio, Argentine president, Jan 1957, *Obit* Oct 1970

Aramburuzabala, Maria Asuncion, Mexican brewing executive, Jan 2002

Aranha, Oswaldo, Brazilian diplomat, Mar 1942, *Obit* Apr 1960

Aras, Tevfik Rustu, Turkish diplomat, June 1942

Araskog, Rand V., telecommunications executive, Nov 1991

Arau, Alfonso, Mexican motion picture director, Jan 2005

Arbenz Guzman, Jacobo, Guatemalan president, Sept 1953, *Obit* Mar 1971

Arcade Fire (Musical group), Jan 2007

Arcand, Denys, Canadian film director, Oct 1990

Arcaro, Eddie, American jockey, Sept 1958, *Obit* Jan 1998

Arce, Jose, Nov 1947, *Obit* Oct 1968

Arceneaux, Edgar, American artist, Aug 2008

Archambault, Louis, Sept 1959

Archer, Dennis, American mayor, Feb 1997

Archer, Glenn L., May 1949

Archer, Jeffrey, English novelist, Sept 1988

Archipenko, Alexander, Russian sculptor, Sept 1953, *Obit* Apr 1964

Arciniegas, German, Colombian historian, May 1954, *Obit* June 2000

Arco, Georg, German radio engineer, *Obit* Jan 1940

Arctic Monkeys (Musical group), Jan 2006

Ardalan, Ali Gholi, Iranian diplomat, Apr 1954

Arden, Elizabeth, American cosmetician, July 1957, *Obit* Yrbk 1966

Arden, Eve, actress, Sept 1953, *Obit* Jan 1991

Arden, John, English playwright and novelist, Sept 1988, *Obit* Yrbk 2012

Ardizzone, Edward, English painter, illustrator and author, May 1964, *Obit* Jan 1980

Ardrey, Robert, American playwright and screenwriter, July 1973, *Obit* Mar 1980

Areilza, Jose Maria de, Spanish diplomat and political leader, Apr 1955, *Obit* May 1998

Arellano, Gustavo, American journalist, Aug 2010

Arena, Bruce, American soccer coach, Sept 2010

Arenas, Gilbert, American basketball player, Feb 2009

Arends, Leslie Cornelius, American congressman, Feb 1948, *Obit* Sept 1985

Arendt, Hannah, German-American political philosopher, May 1959, *Obit* Feb 1976

Arens, Moshe, Israeli cabinet member, July 1989

Arfons, Art, American automobile racing driver, Feb 1970

Argentinita, Spanish dancer and choreographer, June 1942, *Obit* Oct 1945

Argento, Asia, Italian actress, Jan 2003

Argento, Dominick, composer, May 1977

Argerich, Martha, Argentine pianist, Sept 1999

Argeseanu, George, Romanian prime minister, *Obit* Jan 1941

Arias Navarro, Carlos, Spanish prime minister, Oct 1974, *Obit* Jan 1990

Arias Sanchez, Oscar, Costa Rican president, Aug 1987

Arias, Arnulfo, May 1941, *Obit* Sept 1988

Aristide, Jean-Bertrand, Haitian priest and president, May 1991

Ariyoshi, George R., governor, Jan 1985

Arkin, Alan, American actor, Oct 1967

Arledge, Roone, American television executive, Feb 1977, *Obit* Apr 2003

Arlen, Harold, American composer, July 1955, *Obit* June 1986

Arliss, George, English actor, *Obit* Mar 1946

Armand, Louis, French railroad executive, Sept 1957, *Obit* Oct 1971

Armand, Louis; Etzel, Franz; and Giordani, Francesco, Sept 1957

Armani, Giorgio, Italian fashion designer, Jan 1983

Armetta, Henry, American actor, *Obit* Nov 1945

Armey, Richard K., American political activist and former congressman, June 1995

Armfield, Neil, Australian theatrical director, Jan 2007

Armisen, Fred, American comedian and performance artist, Oct 2013

Armitage, Kenneth, English sculptor, Apr 1957, *Obit* May 2002

Armitage, Richard L., American government official, Oct 2003

Armour, Allison V., American botanist, *Obit* Apr 1941

Armour, Norman, American diplomat, Apr 1945, *Obit* Nov 1982

Armour, Richard Willard, philologist and poet, Nov 1958, *Obit* Apr 1989

Armstrong, Anne, American presidential adviser and diplomat, May 1976, *Obit* Yrbk 2008

Armstrong, Billie Joe, American singer and songwriter, Aug 2005

Armstrong, C. Michael, American telecommunications executive, June 1999

Armstrong, Charlotte, author, Yrbk 1946, *Obit* Sept 1969

Armstrong, David W., American youth leader, July 1949, *Obit* Mar 1963

Armstrong, Edwin Howard, American radio engineer and inventor, Apr 1940, *Obit* Mar 1954

Armstrong, George E., American physician and general, Apr 1952, *Obit* Aug 1979

Armstrong, Gillian, Australian film director, Aug 1995

Armstrong, Hamilton Fish, foreign policy expert and periodical editor, Jan 1948, *Obit* June 1973

Armstrong, Harry G., American physician and air force general, July 1951

Armstrong, J. Sinclair, banker, lawyer and government official, Mar 1958, *Obit* Mar 2001

Armstrong, Lance, American cyclist, Sept 1997

Armstrong, Louis, American trumpet player, Sept 1944, Apr 1966, *Obit* Sept 1971

Armstrong, Margaret Neilson, author, *Obit* Sept 1944

Armstrong, Neil, American astronaut, Oct 1969, *Obit* Yrbk 2012

Armstrong, Vic, British motion picture stunt coordinator, Aug 2003

Arnall, Ellis Gibbs, governor, Aug 1945, *Obit* Feb 1993

Arnault, Bernard, French manufacturing executive, June 1998

Arnaz, Desi, Cuban-American television producer, band leader and actor, Sept 1952, *Obit* Feb 1987

Arne, Sigrid, American journalist, Oct 1945

Arnesen, Liv, Norwegian teacher and cross-country skier, June 2001

Arness, James, American actor, Nov 1973, *Obit* Yrbk 2011

Arnett, Jeffrey Jensen, American psychologist, Feb 2011

Arnett, Peter, New Zealand television reporter, Nov 1991

Arno, Peter, cartoonist, Aug 1942, *Obit* Apr 1968

Arnold, Bion J., American electrical engineer, *Obit* Mar 1942

Arnold, Eddy, American country singer, Mar 1970, *Obit* Yrbk 2008

Arnold, Edwin G., American economic development consultant and foundation official, Sept 1947, *Obit* Jan 1961

Arnold, Eve, American photojournalist, Oct 2005, *Obit* Yrbk 2012

Arnold, George Stanleigh, American lawyer, *Obit* Mar 1942

Arnold, Henry Harley, American air force general, Feb 1942, *Obit* Feb 1950

Arnold, Thurman Wesley, American lawyer and government official, Jan 1940, *Obit* Yrbk 1969

Arnold, William R., American military chaplain and bishop, May 1942

Arnon, Daniel I., American plant physiologist, June 1955, *Obit* Mar 1995

Arnow, Harriette Louisa Simpson, American novelist and historian, Yrbk 1954, *Obit* May 1986

Arnstein, Daniel, American taxi executive, Mar 1942

Aroldingen, Karin von, German ballet dancer, Jan 1983

Aron, Raymond, French political philosopher and journalist, June 1954, *Obit* Jan 1984

Aronin, Jeffrey Ellis, Canadian architect, Jan 1955

Aronofsky, Darren, American screenwriter and director, Feb 2009

Aronson, J. Hugo, American governor, Feb 1954

Aronson, Jane, American pediatrician, Feb 2011

Aronson, Louis V., American inventor, manufacaturing executive and banker, *Obit* Yrbk 1940

Aronson, Naoum, Russian sculptor, *Obit* Nov 1943

Arp, Jean, French artist, poet and essayist, May 1954, *Obit* July 1966

Arpino, Gerald, American ballet dancer and choreographer, Oct 1970, *Obit* Yrbk 2008

Arquette, Cliff, June 1961, *Obit* Nov 1974

Arquette, Patricia, American actress, Oct 1997

Arrabal, Fernando, French-Spanish dramatist, Sept 1972

Arraras, Maria Celeste, Puerto Rican television news anchor, Aug 2002

Arrau, Claudio, Chilean pianist, Jan 1942, Nov 1986, *Obit* Aug 1991

Arriaga, Guillermo, Mexican novelist, short story writer and screenwriter, Jan 2007

Arrington, Michael, American Internet executive, July 2012

Arroyo del Rio, Carlos Alberto, Ecuadorian president, June 1942

Arroyo, Martina, American opera singer, Feb 1971

Arrupe, Pedro, Spanish priest, Feb 1970, *Obit* Apr 1991

Arsonval, Jacques Arsene d', French physiologist, *Obit* Feb 1941

Arsuaga, Juan Luis, Spanish paleontologist, Jan 2006

Arthur, *Obit* Mar 1942

Arthur, Bea, American actress, Yrbk 1973, *Obit* Yrbk 2009

Arthur, George, British army officer, *Obit* Mar 1946

Arthur, J. C., American botanist, *Obit* June 1942

Arthur, Jean, actress, Mar 1945, *Obit* Aug 1991

Artschwager, Richard, painter and sculptor, July 1990, *Obit* Yrbk 2013

Artzybasheff, Boris, author and illustrator, Oct 1945, *Obit* Sept 1965

Arzak, Juan Mari, Spanish chef and restaurateur, Jan 2007

Asahara, Shoko, Japanese cult leader, Jan 2003

Asakai, Koichiro, Japanese diplomat, Sept 1957

Asano, Tadanobu, Japanese actor, Jan 2007

Asashoryu, Mongolian sumo wrestler, Jan 2005

Ascher, Leo, Austrian composer, *Obit* Apr 1942

Ascoli, Max, American political scientist and magazine editor, Feb 1954, *Obit* Mar 1978

Asgeir Asgeirsson, Icelandic president, Sept 1952

Ash, Mary Kay, American cosmetics executive, May 1995, *Obit* Feb 2002

Ash, Roy, American presidential adviser and manufacturing executive, July 1968, *Obit* Yrbk 2012

Ashanti (Singer), American rhythm and blues singer, Jan 2003

Ashbery, John, American poet, Aug 1976

Ashbrook, John M., American congressman, Oct 1973, *Obit* June 1982

Ashcroft, John D., American Attorney general, Sept 1999

Ashcroft, Peggy, British actress, Sept 1963, Jan 1987, *Obit* Aug 1991

Ashdown, Paddy, British political leader, Oct 1992

Ashe, Arthur, American tennis player, Nov 1966, *Obit* Mar 1993

Ashford and Simpson, Apr 1997

Ashford, Nickolas, American singer and songwriter, Apr 1997, *Obit* Yrbk 2011

Ashida, Hitoshi, Japanese prime minister, June 1948, *Obit* Sept 1959

Ashkenazy, Vladimir, Russian pianist and conductor, July 1967

Ashley, Elizabeth, actress, Mar 1978

Ashley, Maurice, Jamaican-American chess player, Sept 1999

Ashley, Merrill, American ballet dancer, Nov 1981

Ashley, Thomas L., American lobbyist and congressman, May 1979, *Obit* Yrbk 2010

Ashmore, Harry S., American newspaper editor and foundation official, Sept 1958, *Obit* Apr 1998

Ashmun, Margaret Eliza, American children's author, *Obit* Apr 1940

Ashrawi, Hanan, Palestinian political leader, Mar 1992

Ashton, Frederick, British choreographer, May 1951, *Obit* Sept 1988

Ashwell, Rachel, British interior designer and home furnishings retailer, Oct 2004

Asimov, Isaac, American biochemist and science fiction writer, Yrbk 1953, Oct 1968, *Obit* May 1992

Askegard, Charles, American ballet dancer, Mar 2012

Askew, Reubin, governor, Apr 1973

Askey, E. Vincent, American surgeon, Feb 1961, *Obit* Feb 1975

Askwith, George Ranken Askwith, British labor mediator and government official, *Obit* July 1942

Asner, Edward, American actor, Aug 1978

Aspin, Les, American Secretary of defense, Feb 1986, *Obit* July 1995

Aspinall, Wayne N., American congressman, Apr 1968, *Obit* Nov 1983

Asquith, Margot, wife of British Prime Minister Herbert Henry Asquith, *Obit* Sept 1945

Assad, Hafez, Syrian president, July 1975, Apr 1992, *Obit* Aug 2000

Assange, Julian, Australian computer hacker and political activist, Mar 2011

Assis Chateaubriand, Brazilian newspaper and broadcasting executive, June 1957

Astaire, Fred, American dancer, singer and actor, Sept 1945, Apr 1964, *Obit* Aug 1987

Astin, Allen Varley, physicist, May 1956, *Obit* Apr 1984

Aston, Francis William, British chemist, *Obit* Jan 1946

Astor of Hever, John Jacob Astor, British newspaper publisher, May 1954, *Obit* Sept 1971

Astor, Brooke, American socialite and philanthropist, Jan 1987, *Obit* Yrbk 2007

Astor, Mary, American actress, Nov 1961, *Obit* Nov 1987

Astor, Nancy Witcher Langhorne, British member of Parliament, Nov 1940, *Obit* July 1964

Asturias, Miguel Angel, Guatemalan novelist, Oct 1968, *Obit* July 1974

Aswell, James, American novelist, Yrbk 1951, *Obit* Apr 1955

Ataman, Kutlug, Turkish video artist and film director, Jan 2006

Atcheson, George, American diplomat, Sept 1946, *Obit* Oct 1947

Athenagoras, Mar 1949, *Obit* Sept 1972

Atherton, Gertrude Franklin Horn, American novelist, Nov 1940, *Obit* Sept 1948

Atherton, Warren H., American army officer, lawyer and veterans organization official, Yrbk 1943, *Obit* May 1976

Athey, Susan, American economist, Sept 2007

Atholl, John George Stewart-Murray, British army officer and member of Parliament, *Obit* May 1942

Atkins, Chet, American guitarist and record industry executive, Jan 1975, *Obit* Sept 2001

Atkins, Eileen, English actress, Jan 2002

Atkinson, Brooks, American drama critic, Apr 1942, Feb 1961, *Obit* Mar 1984

Atkinson, Eleanor, author, *Obit* Jan 1943

Atkinson, Joseph Hampton, American air force general, May 1956

Atkinson, Kate, English novelist, Feb 2007

Atkinson, Oriana Torrey MacIlveen, author, Yrbk 1953, *Obit* Oct 1989

Attaway, William, American novelist, Yrbk 1941

Attenborough, David, British television producer and personality, Apr 1983

Attenborough, Richard, British actor and motion picture director, May 1984

Attlee, C. R., British prime minister, May 1940, Feb 1947, *Obit* Yrbk 1967

Attwood, William, diplomat, publisher and author, Jan 1968, *Obit* July 1989

Atwater, Lee, American presidential adviser, June 1989, *Obit* May 1991

Atwell, Wayne J., American anatomist, *Obit* May 1941

Atwill, Lionel, English actor, *Obit* June 1946

Atwood, Colleen, American costume designer, Oct 2010

Atwood, Donna, American figure skater, May 1954

Atwood, Margaret, Canadian novelist and poet, May 1984

Atyam, Angelina, Ugandan peace activist and children's rights advocate, Jan 2004

Aubrey, James T., American television and motion picture executive, Mar 1972, *Obit* Nov 1994

Auchincloss, Louis, American novelist, short story writer and lawyer, Yrbk 1954, Aug 1978, *Obit* Apr 2010

Auchinleck, Claude John Eyre, British field marshal, Feb 1942, *Obit* May 1981

Auden, W. H., Anglo-American poet, Sept 1971, *Obit* Nov 1973

Auel, Jean M., American novelist, Feb 1991

Auerbach, Dan, American singer and guitarist, Jan 2013

Auerbach, Red, American basketball executive, Feb 1969, *Obit* Yrbk 2007

Auerbach-Levy, William, painter and etcher, Feb 1948, *Obit* Sept 1964

Augenbraum, Harold, American literary scholar, Apr 2012

Auger, Arleen, American opera singer, Feb 1989, *Obit* Aug 1993

Aughinbaugh, William, American lawyer, physician and travel writer, *Obit* Feb 1941

Augstein, Rudolf, German magazine publisher, June 1966, *Obit* Jan 2003

Augustine, Norman R., aerospace executive, June 1998

Aulaire, Edgar Parin D'; and Aulaire, Ingri D', Aug 1940

Aulenti, Gae, Italian architect, Sept 1999, *Obit* Yrbk 2013

Aumann, Robert J., Israeli economist, Jan 2007

Aung San Suu Kyi, Burmese human rights activist, Feb 1992

Auriol, Jacqueline, French aviator, Sept 1953, *Obit* June 2000

Auriol, Vincent, French president, Mar 1947, *Obit* Feb 1966

Auster, Paul, American novelist, poet and essayist, Mar 1996

Austin, F. Britten, English novelist, dramatist and screenwriter, *Obit* May 1941

Austin, Herbert Austin, English automobile executive, *Obit* July 1941

Austin, Margretta, American diplomat, Feb 1954

Austin, Steve, American wrestler, Nov 2001

Austin, Tracy, American tennis player, May 1981

Austin, Warren Robinson, American senator and diplomat, Jan 1944, *Obit* Feb 1963

Austin, William Lane, American statistician, Apr 1940

Auteuil, Daniel, French actor, Jan 2007

Auth, Tony, American cartoonist, illustrator and children's author, Feb 2006

Automator (Musician), American recording producer, May 2007

Autry, Gene, American cowboy singer, actor and baseball executive, Yrbk 1947, *Obit* Jan 1999

Avedon, Richard, American photographer, Feb 1975, *Obit* Mar 2005

Avenol, Joseph, Jan 1940, *Obit* Oct 1952

Averoff-Tossizza, Evangelos, Greek political leader, May 1957, *Obit* Mar 1990

Avery, Milton, American painter, June 1958, *Obit* Feb 1965

Avery, Sewell, American manufacturing and retail executive, June 1944, *Obit* Jan 1961

Avila Camacho, Manuel, Mexican president, Sept 1940, *Obit* Yrbk 1956

Awolowo, Obafemi, Nigerian prime minister, July 1957, *Obit* July 1987

Ax, Emanuel, American pianist, Mar 1984

Axelrod, David, American presidential adviser, Apr 2009

Ayala, Eusebio, Paraguayan president, *Obit* July 1942

Ayala, Francisco, American geneticist, Oct 2012

Ayckbourn, Alan, English dramatist and theatrical director, Jan 1980

Aydelotte, Frank, educator, Oct 1941, Apr 1952, *Obit* Feb 1957

Ayer, A. J., British philosopher, May 1964, *Obit* Aug 1989

Ayers, William, American educator, Apr 2009

Aykroyd, Dan, Canadian actor, Jan 1992

Aylwin, Patricio, Chilean president, Aug 1990

Aymar, Luciana, Feb 2013

Ayres, Agnes, American actress, *Obit* Feb 1941

Ayres, Leonard Porter, May 1940, *Obit* Yrbk 1946

Ayub Khan, Mohammad, Pakistani president, Apr 1959, *Obit* June 1974

Azad, Abulkalam, Indian political leader, July 1942, *Obit* May 1958

Azana, Manuel, Spanish president, *Obit* Yrbk 1940

Azarenka, Victoria, Belarusian tennis player, Oct 2013

Azcona Hoyo, Jose, Honduran president, Feb 1988, *Obit* Yrbk 2006

Azikiwe, Nnamdi, Nigerian president, July 1957, *Obit* Aug 1996

Azimi, Abdul Salam, Afghan supreme court justice, Jan 2006

Aziz, Shaukat, Pakistani prime minister, Jan 2007

Aziz, Tariq, Iraqi cabinet member, May 1991

Azmi, Shabana, Indian actress, Jan 2002

Aznar, Jose Maria, Spanish prime minister, Jan 2002

Aznavour, Charles, French singer and songwriter, Feb 1968

Azuma, Tokuho, Japanese dancer, Apr 1954

Azzam, Abd al-Rahman, Egyptian diplomat, Apr 1947

B

Ba, Amadou Mahtar, Senegalese multi-media content service provider executive, Jan 2004

Babangida, Ibrahim, Nigerian general and head of state, Sept 1990

Babb, James Tinkham, American librarian, July 1955, *Obit* Oct 1968

Babbitt, Bruce E., American Secretary of the interior, Apr 1987

Babbitt, Milton, American composer, Sept 1962, *Obit* Yrbk 2011

Babson, Naomi Lane, American novelist and short story writer, Yrbk 1952

Babson, Roger W., statistician, Feb 1945, *Obit* May 1967

Babyface, American singer, songwriter and producer, July 1998

Baca-Flor, Carlos, Peruvian painter, *Obit* July 1941

Bacall, Lauren, American actress, Mar 1970

Baccaloni, Salvatore, Oct 1944, *Obit* Feb 1970

Bach, Reginald, British actor and theatrical director, *Obit* Feb 1941

Bach, Richard, American inspirational writer, Oct 1973

Bacharach, Bert, American fashion critic, Yrbk 1957

Bacharach, Burt, American composer, Oct 1970

Bachauer, Gina, Greek pianist, June 1954, *Obit* Sept 1977

Bachchan, Amitabh, Indian actor, Jan 2002

Bache, Harold L., American securities broker, May 1959

Bache, Jules Semon, financier and art collector, *Obit* May 1944

Bachelet, Michelle, Chilean president, Jan 2006

Bacher, Robert F., American physicist, Feb 1947, *Obit* Yrbk 2005

Bachrach, Elise Wald, American painter, *Obit* Mar 1940

Backe, John David, Apr 1978

Backman, Jules, Apr 1952, *Obit* June 1982

Backstrand, C. J., American manufacturing executive, Feb 1954, *Obit* Yrbk 1968

Backstreet Boys (Musical group), May 2000

Bacon, Charles L., American lawyer and veterans leader, May 1962

Bacon, Charles Reade, American newspaper editor and state librarian, *Obit* June 1943

Bacon, Francis, English painter, Feb 1957, Aug 1985, *Obit* June 1992

Bacon, George P., American physicist and college dean, *Obit* Nov 1941

Bacon, Leonard, poet, critic and translator, June 1941, *Obit* Mar 1954

Bacon, Peggy, American mystery writer and illustrator, Jan 1940, *Obit* Mar 1987

Bacon, Selden Daskam, sociologist, May 1952, *Obit* Feb 1993

Bad Plus (Musical group), Oct 2011

Bada, Angelo, Italian opera singer, *Obit* May 1941

Baden-Powell of Gilwell, Robert Stephenson Smyth Baden-Powell, English Boy Scouts founder, *Obit* Mar 1941

Baden-Powell, Olave St. Clair, British girls association founder, May 1946

Badger, Oscar C., American admiral, May 1949, *Obit* Feb 1959

Badillo, Herman, American municipal official and congressman, May 1971

Badinter, Elisabeth, French philosopher, Nov 2011

Badoglio, Pietro, Italian field marshal, Oct 1940, *Obit* Jan 1957

Badu, Erykah, American singer and songwriter, Apr 1998

Bae, Yong Joon, Korean actor, Jan 2005

Baehr, George, American physician and health insurance executive, May 1942

Baekeland, Leo Hendrik, Belgian-American chemist, *Obit* Apr 1944

Baer, William J., American painter, *Obit* Nov 1941

Baez, Joan, American folk singer and songwriter, Nov 1963

Bagayoko, Amadou, Malian singer and guitarist, Jan 2006

Bagger, Mianne, Danish golfer, Jan 2006

Baghdatis, Marcos, Cypriot tennis player, Jan 2006

Bagley, William Chandler, American educator, *Obit* July 1946

Bagnold, Enid, English novelist and dramatist, June 1964, *Obit* May 1981

Bagramyan, Ivan K., Soviet general, Yrbk 1944, *Obit* Jan 1983

Bagwell, Jeff, American baseball player, Aug 2000

Bahcall, John N., American astrophysicist, Apr 2000, *Obit* Yrbk 2007

Bailar, Benjamin F., American chemical industry executive and Postmaster general, July 1976

Bailar, John Christian, American chemist, July 1959

Bailey, Abe, South African financier and political leader, *Obit* Sept 1940

Bailey, Carolyn Sherwin, American children's author, Yrbk 1948

Bailey, Consuelo Northrop, American lawyer and state legislator, June 1954

Bailey, Donald Coleman, English civil engineer and inventor, Oct 1945, *Obit* July 1985

Bailey, F. Lee, lawyer, Yrbk 1967

Bailey, Glenda, American magazine editor, Oct 2001

Bailey, Guy W., American university president, *Obit* Yrbk 1940

Bailey, John Moran, American lawyer and political leader, June 1962, *Obit* June 1975

Bailey, Josiah W., American senator, Apr 1945, *Obit* Jan 1947

Bailey, L. H., American botanist, June 1948, *Obit* Mar 1955

Bailey, Pearl, American singer and actress, June 1955, Oct 1969, *Obit* Oct 1990

Bailey, Thomas L., American governor, *Obit* Yrbk 1946

Bailey, Vernon, American naturalist, *Obit* June 1942

Baillie, Hugh, American reporter and news agency executive, Feb 1946, *Obit* Mar 1966

Bainton, Roland Herbert, church historian, June 1962, *Obit* June 1984

Bair, Sheila C., American regulatory agency official, Feb 2010

Baird, Bil, puppeteer, Mar 1954, *Obit* May 1987

Baird, Bil; and Baird, Cora, Mar 1954

Baird, Cora, American puppeteer, Mar 1954, *Obit* Feb 1968

Baitz, Jon Robin, American dramatist, Aug 2004

Bajaj, Rahul, Indian automobile executive, Jan 2007

Baker, Anita, American singer, Apr 1989

Baker, Asa George, American publishing executive, *Obit* Oct 1940

Baker, Charles Whiting, American civil engineer, *Obit* Aug 1941

Baker, Dorothy, author, Yrbk 1943, *Obit* Sept 1968

Baker, Dusty, American baseball player and manager, Apr 2001

Baker, Frank, English author, Yrbk 1948

Baker, George, American cartoonist, Nov 1944, *Obit* Aug 1975

Baker, George Theodore, American airline executive, June 1953, *Obit* Jan 1964

Baker, Howard H., American senator and presidential adviser, Mar 1974, Aug 1987

Baker, James A., American Secretary of state, Feb 1982, Mar 2007

Baker, Janet, English opera singer, June 1971

Baker, John Hopkinson, American investment banker and conservationist, May 1949

Baker, Josephine, American actress, singer and dancer, July 1964, *Obit* June 1975

Baker, Louise, American novelist, short story writer and memoirist, Yrbk 1954

Baker, Melvin H., American constructon materials industry executive, Feb 1960

Baker, Mitchell, American Internet executive, Apr 2009

Baker, Nicholson, American novelist, Aug 1994

Baker, Nina Brown, American young adult author, Yrbk 1947, *Obit* Nov 1957

Baker, Phil, American comedian, accordionist and radio personality, Nov 1946, *Obit* Jan 1964

Baker, Ray Stannard, American journalist and biographer, Jan 1940, *Obit* Sept 1946

Baker, Rick, American makeup artist, Mar 1997

Baker, Roy, American lawyer, Nov 1948

Baker, Russell, American journalist and humorist, Mar 1980

Baker, Sara Josephine, American physician, *Obit* Apr 1945

Baker, Tom, British actor, Jan 2004

Bakiyev, Kurmanbek, Kirghiz president, Jan 2007

Bakke, E. Wight, Sept 1953, *Obit* Jan 1972

Bakker, Robert T., American paleontologist, Aug 1995

Bakoyianni, Dora, Greek mayor, Jan 2003

Bakri, Mohammad, Palestinian filmmaker and actor, Jan 2005

Bakshi, Ghulam Mohammad, June 1956, *Obit* Sept 1972

Bakshi, Ralph, American animator, Mar 1979

Bakula, Scott, American actor, Feb 2002

Balaban, Barney, American motion picture executive, Oct 1946, *Obit* Apr 1971

Balaguer, Joaquin, Dominican president, Nov 1966, *Obit* Yrbk 2002

Balanchine, George, Russian-American choreographer, Nov 1942, June 1954, *Obit* June 1983

Balbo, Italo, Italian air marshal, *Obit* Aug 1940

Balch, Emily Greene, American economist and pacifist, Jan 1947, *Obit* Mar 1961

Balchen, Bernt, aviator, Jan 1949, *Obit* Yrbk 1973

Baldauf, Sari, Finnish cellular telephone equipment industry executive, Jan 2004

Balderston, William, radio equipment industry executive, Sept 1949, *Obit* Oct 1983

Baldessari, John, American artist, June 1991

Baldomir, Alfredo, Uruguayan general and president, June 1942, *Obit* Mar 1948

Baldrige, Letitia, columnist, social secretary and public relations executive, Feb 1988, *Obit* Yrbk 2013

Baldrige, Malcolm, American Secretary of commerce, Aug 1982, *Obit* Sept 1987

Baldwin, Alec, American actor, July 1992

Baldwin, C. B., American political leader, Nov 1943

Baldwin, Hanson Weightman, journalist and military historian, Aug 1942, *Obit* Jan 1992

Baldwin, James, American novelist, playwright and essayist, Yrbk 1959, July 1964, *Obit* Jan 1988

Baldwin, Raymond Earl, American governor and senator, July 1946, *Obit* Nov 1986

Baldwin, Roger Nash, American civil rights leader, Jan 1940, *Obit* Oct 1981

Baldwin, Tammy, American congresswoman, June 2005

Baldwin, William H., American public relations executive and civil rights activist, Nov 1945

Balenciaga, Spanish fashion designer, May 1954, *Obit* May 1972

Balewa, Abubakar Tafawa, Nigerian prime minister, Sept 1961, *Obit* Feb 1966

Ball, Alan, American film and television screenwriter and producer, Sept 2011

Ball, George W., American diplomat, Feb 1962, *Obit* July 1994

Ball, Joseph H., American senator, Oct 1943, *Obit* Feb 1994

Ball, Lucille, American actress, Sept 1952, Jan 1978, *Obit* June 1989

Ball, Lucille; and Arnaz, Desi, Sept 1952

Ball, Robert M., American government official, Jan 1968, *Obit* Yrbk 2008

Ball, Stuart S., American retail executive, July 1952

Ball, William, theatrical director and producer, May 1974, *Obit* Oct 1991

Ball, Zachary, Yrbk 1953

Balladur, Edouard, French prime minister, Feb 1994

Ballantine, Ian, publisher, May 1954, *Obit* May 1995

Ballantine, Stuart, American radio engineer, *Obit* June 1944

Ballard, J. G., English novelist and short story writer, May 1988, *Obit* Yrbk 2009

Ballard, Kaye, American actress, singer and comedienne, Sept 1969

Ballard, Robert D., American oceanographer, June 1986

Ballesteros, Seve, Spanish golfer, Sept 1980, *Obit* Yrbk 2011

Balmain, Pierre, French fashion designer, July 1954, *Obit* Aug 1982

Balsom, Alison, Trumpeter, Mar 2012

Baltasar Kormakur, Icelandic actor, motion picture director and screenwriter, Jan 2003

Balthus, French painter, Nov 1979, *Obit* May 2001

Baltimore, David, American microbiologist, July 1983

Bamford, Maria, comedian, Jan 2012

Bampton, Rose, American opera singer, Mar 1940, *Obit* Yrbk 2007

Ban, Ki Moon, Korean diplomat and United Nations secretary-general, Jan 2007

Bana, Eric, Australian comedian and actor, Jan 2003

Bancroft, Ann, American adventurer, July 2000

Bancroft, Anne, American actress, June 1960, *Obit* Oct 2005

Banda, Enos, South African banker, Jan 2005

Banda, Hastings Kamuzu, Malawian president, Jan 1963, *Obit* Feb 1998

Banda, Joyce, Malawian entrepreneur, educator and social activist, Apr 2013

Bandaranaike, S. W. R. D., Sri Lankan prime minister, Sept 1956, *Obit* Nov 1959

Bandaranaike, Sirimavo, Sri Lankan prime minister, May 1961, *Obit* Jan 2001

Banderas, Antonio, Spanish actor, Mar 1997

Banerjee, Mamata, Indian political leader, Nov 2011

Banfield, Ashleigh, Canadian television newscaster, July 2002

Banfield, Edward C., American political scientist, May 1972, *Obit* Feb 2000

Banfield, Jillian Fiona, Australian geologist, Feb 2000

Bang, Abhay, Indian physician and public health scientist, Jan 2007

Bang, Rani, Indian gynecologist and public health scientist, Jan 2007

Bani-Sadr, Abu al-Hasan, Iranian president, Feb 1981

Bankhead, John Hollis, American senator, May 1943, *Obit* July 1946

Bankhead, Tallulah, American actress, July 1941, Jan 1953, *Obit* Feb 1969

Bankhead, William Brockman, American Speaker of the House, Oct 1940, *Obit* Oct 1940

Bankole, Isaach de, Ivorian actor, Jan 2004

Banks, Dennis, American Indian leader, June 1992

Banks, Ernie, American baseball player, May 1959

Banks, Russell, American novelist and short story writer, Jan 1992

Banks, Tyra, American model, actress and talk show host, Apr 2007

Banksy, English grafitti artist, Apr 2009

Banning, Kendall, American magazine editor, publisher and military writer, *Obit* Feb 1945

Banning, Margaret Culkin, author, May 1940, *Obit* Feb 1982

Bannister, Constance, American baby photographer, July 1955, *Obit* Yrbk 2005

Bannister, Roger, British neurologist and runner, Apr 1956

Bannow, Rudolph F., American manufacturing executive, Yrbk 1960, *Obit* Sept 1962

Banting, Frederick G., Canadian physician, *Obit* Apr 1941

Bantock, Granville, English composer, *Obit* Yrbk 1946

Banville, John, Irish novelist, May 1992

Banzer Suarez, Hugo, Bolivian president, Sept 1973, *Obit* Sept 2002

Banzhaf, John F., law professor, Yrbk 1973

Bao Dai, Nov 1949, *Obit* Oct 1997

Barad, Jill E., American toy industry executive, Sept 1995

Barak, Ehud, Israeli political leader, Aug 1997

Baraka, Imamu Amiri, American poet, playwright, essayist and short story writer, May 1970

Barber, Anthony, Jan 1971

Barber, Jerry, golfer, Apr 1962, *Obit* Nov 1994

Barber, Mary I., American dietician and home economist, July 1941, *Obit* Apr 1963

Barber, Patricia, American jazz singer and pianist, Sept 2007

Barber, Red, sportscaster, July 1943, *Obit* Jan 1993

Barber, Ronde, American football player, Oct 2003

Barber, Samuel, American composer, Sept 1944, Sept 1963, *Obit* Mar 1981

Barber, Tiki, American football player and television personality, Oct 2003

Barber, Tiki and Ronde, Oct 2003

Barbey, Daniel E., admiral, Jan 1945, *Obit* June 1969

Barbier, George W., American actor, *Obit* Aug 1945

Barbieri, Fedora, Italian opera singer, Feb 1957, *Obit* Aug 2003

Barbirolli, John, British conductor, Yrbk 1940, *Obit* Oct 1970

Barbosa, Leandro, Brazilian basketball player, June 2011

Barbour, Haley, American governor, Nov 1996

Barbour, Henry Gray, American pharmacologist, *Obit* Nov 1943

Barbour, Ralph Henry, author, *Obit* Apr 1944

Barbour, W. Warren, American senator, *Obit* Jan 1944

Barclay, McClelland, American illustrator, Sept 1940, *Obit* Yrbk 1946

Barco Vargas, Virgilio, Colombian president, Feb 1990, *Obit* Aug 1997

Bard, Mary, American novelist, essayist and memoirist, Yrbk 1956

Bardeen, John, American physicist and electrical engineer, Sept 1957, *Obit* Apr 1991

Bardem, Javier, Spanish actor, Jan 2002

Barden, Graham Arthur, American congressman, Sept 1949, *Obit* Mar 1967

Bardot, Brigitte, French actress, Jan 1960

Barenboim, Daniel, Israeli pianist and conductor, Apr 1969

Barfield, Tanya, American playwright, Mar 2011

Barker, Bob, American game show host, Nov 1999

Barker, Lewellys Franklin, American physician, *Obit* Sept 1943

Barker, Travis, American drummer, Aug 2002

Barkley, Alben William, American vice-president, May 1941, Jan 1949, *Obit* July 1956

Barkley, Charles, American basketball player, Oct 1991

Barlow, Howard, Jan 1940, July 1954, *Obit* Mar 1972

Barlow, Maude, Canadian environmentalist, Feb 2009

Barlow, Reginald, American actor, *Obit* Aug 1943

Barmak, Siddiq, Afghan motion picture director and screenwriter, Jan 2005

Barnard, Chester Irving, American telephone executive and foundation official, Mar 1945, *Obit* Sept 1961

Barnard, Christiaan, South African heart surgeon, May 1968, *Obit* Nov 2001

Barnard, Elinor M., American painter, *Obit* Apr 1942

Barnard, James Lynn, American political scientist, *Obit* Oct 1941

Barnes, Albert Coombs, American chemist and pharmaceutical executive, Mar 1945, *Obit* Sept 1951

Barnes, Brenda, American food industry executive, May 2006

Barnes, Clifford Webster, American clergyman and sociologist, *Obit* Nov 1944

Barnes, Clive, British dance and drama critic, Mar 1972, *Obit* Feb 2009

Barnes, Henry A., American traffic engineer, June 1955, *Obit* Nov 1968

Barnes, Julian, English novelist, short story writer and essayist, Mar 1988

Barnes, Margaret Campbell, English novelist, Yrbk 1953

Barnes, Roy E., American governor, Jan 2000

Barnes, Stanley N., American judge, Sept 1953

Barnes, Wendell B., government official and congressman, June 1957, *Obit* Aug 1985

Barnes, William R., American publisher and bookseller, *Obit* Mar 1945

Barnet, Will, American painter, June 1985, *Obit* Yrbk 2013

Barnett, Etta Moten, American singer and actress, Feb 2002

Barnett, Eugene Epperson, May 1941

Barnett, M. Robert, American journalist and foundation official, Jan 1950

Barnett, Ross Robert, American governor, Sept 1961, *Obit* Jan 1988

Barney, Matthew, American sculptor and installation and video artist, Aug 2003

Barney, Samuel E., American civil engineer, *Obit* Mar 1940

Barnhart, Clarence Lewis, lexicographer, Sept 1954, *Obit* Jan 1994

Barnouw, Erik, American sociologist, Nov 1940, *Obit* Oct 2001

Baron-Cohen, Sacha, British comedian, Jan 2003

Baron-Cohen, Simon, British psychologist, Jan 2006

Barr, Alfred Hamilton, American museum director, Jan 1961, *Obit* Oct 1981

Barr, John A., American lawyer and college dean, Jan 1961, *Obit* Mar 1979

Barr, Joseph W., American Secretary of the treasury, Jan 1968, *Obit* May 1996

Barr, Norman B., American clergyman, *Obit* May 1943

Barr, Roseanne, American comedienne, May 1989

Barr, Stringfellow, American college president and historian, Aug 1940, *Obit* Apr 1982

Barr, William P., American Attorney general, June 1992

Barratt, Arthur Sheridan, British air marshal, Jan 1941

Barrault, Jean-Louis, French actor and theatrical director, Mar 1953, *Obit* Mar 1994

Barrault, Jean-Louis; and Renaud, Madeleine, Mar 1953

Barre, Raymond, French prime minister, July 1977, *Obit* Yrbk 2007

Barrere, Camille, French diplomat, *Obit* Yrbk 1940

Barrere, Georges, *Obit* Aug 1944

Barrett, Clifton Waller, American shipping executive and book collector, Mar 1965

Barrett, Craig, American semiconductor industry executive, Mar 1999

Barrett, Edward W., journalist and college dean, Feb 1947, *Obit* Feb 1990

Barrett, Frank A., American senator and governor, July 1956, *Obit* July 1962

Barrett, William, professor of philosophy, Aug 1982, *Obit* Nov 1992

Barrett, Wilton Agnew, American film critic, *Obit* Mar 1940

Barrette, Antonio, Canadian provincial premier, July 1960, *Obit* Feb 1969

Barringer, Emily Dunning, physician, Mar 1940, *Obit* June 1961

Barringer, Paul B., American physician and college president, *Obit* Mar 1941

Barris, Chuck, American television producer and personality, Mar 2005

Barros Hurtado, Cesar, Argentine lawyer, sociologist and diplomat, Jan 1959

Barrow, Errol W., Barbadian prime minister, Sept 1968, *Obit* July 1987

Barry, Dave, American humorist, May 1998

Barry, John, English composer, Mar 2000, *Obit* Yrbk 2011

Barry, Lynda, American cartoonist and novelist, Nov 1994

Barry, Marion, American mayor, May 1987

Barry, Patrick, Irish-American bishop, *Obit* Sept 1940

Barry, Rick, American basketball player and sportscaster, Mar 1971

Barry, William Bernard, American congressman, *Obit* Yrbk 1946

Barrymore, Drew, American actress, Oct 1998

Barrymore, Ethel, actress, Mar 1941, *Obit* Sept 1959

Barrymore, John, American actor, *Obit* July 1942

Barrymore, Lionel, actor, July 1943, *Obit* Jan 1955

Barsamian, David, American radio program host, Mar 2007

Barshefsky, Charlene, American trade representative, Feb 2000

Barth, John, American novelist and essayist, May 1969

Barth, Karl, Swiss theologian, Nov 1962, *Obit* Feb 1969

Barthe, Richmond, American sculptor, July 1940, *Obit* May 1989

Barthelme, Donald, American short story writer and novelist, Mar 1976, *Obit* Sept 1989

Barthes, Roland, French literary critic, Feb 1979, *Obit* May 1980

Bartholomeos, Jan 2004

Bartiromo, Maria, American television reporter, Nov 2003

Bartlett, Bruce R., American economist and columnist, June 2006

Bartlett, Edward Lewis, American senator, June 1951, *Obit* Mar 1969

Bartlett, Jennifer, American painter, Nov 1985

Bartlett, Robert A., *Obit* June 1946

Bartok, Bela, Hungarian composer, Sept 1940, *Obit* Oct 1945

Bartol, William Cyrus, American mathematician, *Obit* Yrbk 1940

Bartoli, Cecilia, Italian opera singer, June 1992

Barton, Bruce, American advertising executive, religious writer and congressman, Feb 1961, *Obit* Oct 1967

Barton, George, American journalist and mystery writer, *Obit* Apr 1940

Barton, George A., American sportswriter, May 1953

Barton, Jacqueline K., American chemist, Sept 2006

Barton, Robert B. M., games industry executive, Apr 1959, *Obit* Apr 1995

Barton, William H., American astronomer and planetarium curator, *Obit* Aug 1944

Bartz, Carol A., American computer software executive, July 1999

Baruch, Bernard Mannes, American financier and presidential adviser, Aug 1941, July 1950, *Obit* Sept 1965

Baryshnikov, Mikhail, Russian-American ballet dancer, Feb 1975

Barzel, Rainer, German political leader, May 1967, *Obit* Yrbk 2006

Barzin, Leon, conductor, May 1951, *Obit* Aug 1999

Barzini, Luigi Giorgio, Italian journalist and author, July 1972, *Obit* May 1984

Barzun, Jacques, American historian, Sept 1964, *Obit* Yrbk 2013

Basdevant, Jules, French lawyer, diplomat and judge, Feb 1950, *Obit* Mar 1968

Basie, Count, American jazz pianist and band leader, June 1942, *Obit* June 1984

Basinger, Kim, American actress, Feb 1990

Baskin, Leonard, American sculptor and illustrator, May 1964, *Obit* Aug 2000

Bass, George Fletcher, American archaeologist, Mar 2000

Bass, Lance, American singer, Nov 2000

Bass, Robert M., investor, July 1989

Bassett, Angela, American actress, May 1996

Bassett, Sara Ware, American novelist, Yrbk 1956

Bassler, Bonnie L., American molecular biologist, Apr 2003

Bastianich, Joseph, American restaurateur and winemaker, June 2011

Batali, Mario, American chef and restaurateur, Apr 2011

Batcheller, Hiland Garfield, American steel industry executive, Apr 1949, *Obit* July 1961

Bateman, Jason, American actor, Oct 2005

Bates, Alan, English actor, Mar 1969, *Obit* Yrbk 2004

Bates, Blanche, American actress, *Obit* Feb 1942

Bates, Ernest Sutherland, biographer, historian and literary critic, Jan 1940

Bates, Granville, American actor, *Obit* Sept 1940

Bates, H. E., English short story writer and novelist, Sept 1944, *Obit* Mar 1974

Bates, Kathy, American actress, Sept 1991

Bates, Marston, zoologist, Apr 1956, *Obit* May 1974

Bates, Sanford, American penologist, Jan 1961, *Obit* Nov 1972

Bathgate, Andy, Canadian hockey player, Feb 1964

Batista y Zaldivar, Fulgencio, Cuban general and president, Sept 1940, Apr 1952, *Obit* Oct 1973

Batistuta, Gabriel, Argentine soccer player, Jan 2002

Batt, William L., American manufacturing executive, Feb 1942, *Obit* Mar 1965

Batt, William L., American government official, Sept 1962

Battle, John S., American lawyer and governor, Nov 1950, *Obit* June 1972

Battle, Kathleen, American opera singer, Nov 1984

Baudouin, Sept 1950, *Obit* Oct 1993

Baudrillard, Jean, French social theorist, June 1993, *Obit* Yrbk 2007

Baudrillart, Alfred, *Obit* July 1942

Bauer, Erwin A., photographer, Feb 1993

Bauer, Erwin A.; and Bauer, Peggy, Feb 1993

Bauer, Gary L., political activist, Jan 1999

Bauer, Hank, American baseball player and manager, Feb 1967

Bauer, Louis Hopewell, American cardiologist, Oct 1948, *Obit* Mar 1964

Bauer, Peggy, photographer, Feb 1993

Baulieu, Etienne-Emile, French biochemist, Nov 1995

Baum, Kurt, opera singer, Sept 1956, *Obit* Feb 1990

Baum, William W., Oct 1976

Baumbach, Noah, American film director and screenwriter, Oct 2010

Baumer, Marie, American screenwriter and novelist, Yrbk 1958

Baumgartner, Leona, American physician and public health official, Jan 1950, *Obit* Mar 1991

Baur, Bertha, American music teacher, *Obit* Nov 1940

Baur, Harry, French actor, *Obit* May 1943

Baur, John Ireland Howe, museum director, Yrbk 1969, *Obit* July 1987

Bausch, Edward, American optical equipment company executive, *Obit* Sept 1944

Bausch, Pina, German dancer, choreographer and director, Sept 1986, *Obit* Yrbk 2009

Bausch, William, *Obit* Yrbk 1944

Bautista, Jose, Dominican baseball player, Oct 2011

Bavetta, Dick, American basketball referee, Mar 2008

Bawer, Bruce, American critic, poet and essayist, July 2007

Bax, Arnold, English composer, Sept 1943, *Obit* Jan 1954

Baxter, Anne, actress, May 1972, *Obit* Feb 1986

Baxter, Frank C., American professor of English and television personality, Mar 1955

Baxter, James Phinney, American historian, July 1947, *Obit* Aug 1975

Bayar, Celal, Turkish president, July 1950, *Obit* Oct 1986

Bayard, Thomas Francis, American senator, *Obit* Sept 1942

Bayh, Birch, American senator and governor, June 1965

Bayh, Evan, American senator, Nov 1998

Bayne, Stephen F., Jan 1964, *Obit* Mar 1974

Bazelon, David L., American judge, Jan 1971, *Obit* Apr 1993

Bazin, Germain, French art historian and museum curator, Jan 1959, *Obit* July 1990

Bea, Augustin, Sept 1964, *Obit* Jan 1969

Beach, Amy Marcy Cheney, American composer and pianist, *Obit* Feb 1945

Beach, Edward Latimer, American naval officer, Oct 1960, *Obit* May 2003

Beachley, Layne, Australian surfer, Jan 2002

Beadle, George W., American geneticist and college president, Apr 1956, *Obit* Aug 1989

Beale, Howard, Australian cabinet member and diplomat, Mar 1959

Beall, J. Glenn, American senator, Apr 1955, *Obit* Mar 1971

Beall, Lester, American graphic designer, Nov 1949, *Obit* Sept 1969

Beals, Carleton, journalist, Yrbk 1942, *Obit* Aug 1979

Beals, Ralph Albert, librarian, Feb 1947, *Obit* Yrbk 1954

Beam, Jacob Dyneley, American diplomat, July 1959, *Obit* Oct 1993

Beam, Sam (Iron and Wine), American folk singer and songwriter, Mar 2013

Beame, Abraham D., American mayor, July 1974, *Obit* Apr 2001

Bean, Louis H., agricultural economist and public opinion analyst, Nov 1948, *Obit* Oct 1994

Bean, Orson, comedian, Feb 1967

Beane, Billy, American baseball executive, July 2005

Bear, Christopher, American drummer, Sept 2011

Beard, Charles A.; and Beard, Mary Ritter, Mar 1941

Beard, Charles Austin, American historian, Mar 1941, *Obit* Oct 1948

Beard, Charles E., American airline executive, July 1956, *Obit* Oct 1982

Beard, Daniel Carter, American children's author, illustrator and Boy Scouts founder, *Obit* Aug 1941

Beard, Frank, American golfer, May 1970

Beard, James, American chef, Yrbk 1964, *Obit* Mar 1985

Beard, James T., American mining engineer, *Obit* Yrbk 1942

Beard, Mary Ritter, historian and feminist, Mar 1941, *Obit* Yrbk 1959

Bearden, Bessye J., American political activist and civic leader, *Obit* Nov 1943

Bearden, Romare, American artist, Jan 1972, *Obit* May 1988

Beardsley, William S., American governor, June 1950, *Obit* Jan 1955

Beart, Emmanuelle, French actress, Jan 2002

Beaton, Cecil, English designer and photographer, Oct 1944, July 1962, *Obit* Mar 1980

Beatrice, *Obit* Yrbk 1944

Beatrix, May 1981

Beattie, Ann, American novelist and short story writer, Oct 1985

Beatty, Arthur, American professor of English, *Obit* Apr 1943

Beatty, Bessie, radio commentator and journalist, Jan 1944, *Obit* Apr 1947

Beatty, Jim, American runner, Jan 1963

Beatty, Warren, American actor, producer and director, May 1962, May 1988

Beau, Lucas Victor, air force general, June 1954, *Obit* Jan 1987

Beaulac, Willard Leon, diplomat, Sept 1958, *Obit* Oct 1990

Beauvoir, Simone de, French novelist and philosopher, Jan 1973, *Obit* June 1986

Beaux, Cecilia, American painter, *Obit* Nov 1942

Beaverbrook, Max Aitken, British newspaper publisher, July 1940, *Obit* Sept 1964

Beban, Gary J., football player and real estate executive, May 1970

Bebey, Francis, Cameroonian guitarist, composer and novelist, Apr 1994, *Obit* Sept 2001

Bebler, Ales, Yugoslav diplomat, Apr 1950

Bech, Joseph, Luxembourgian statesman, Feb 1950, *Obit* May 1975

Bechdel, Alison, American cartoonist and graphic novelist, July 2009

Bechtel, Stephen Davison, builder, Apr 1957, *Obit* May 1989

Beck, Bertram M., social worker, May 1961, *Obit* Sept 2000

Beck, Dave, American labor leader, May 1949, *Obit* Feb 1994

Beck, Jozef, Polish diplomat, *Obit* July 1944

Beck, Kent, American computer programmer, Jan 2007

Beck, Martin, American theater owner, *Obit* Jan 1941

Beck, Mildred Buchwalder, American social worker, June 1950

Beckenbauer, Franz, German soccer player and coach, Jan 2006

Becker, Boris, German tennis player, Feb 1987

Becker, Gary Stanley, American economist, Sept 1993

Becker, May Lamberton, author and editor, May 1941, *Obit* July 1958

Becker, Ralph E., lawyer and diplomat, Nov 1948, *Obit* Oct 1994

Becker, William Dee, American judge and mayor, *Obit* Sept 1943

Beckett, Josh, American baseball player, July 2011

Beckett, Samuel, Irish playwright and novelist, Feb 1970, *Obit* Feb 1990

Beckett, Wendy, English nun and art critic, Jan 1998

Beckham, David, British soccer player, Jan 2003

Beckinsale, Kate, English actress, Aug 2001

Beckman, Arnold O., American chemist, inventor and instrument industry executive, Jan 2002, *Obit* Yrbk 2004

Bedaux, Charles Eugene, French-American industrial engineer, *Obit* Apr 1944

Bede, J. Adam, American congressman, *Obit* June 1942

Bedford, Herbrand Arthur Russell, English zoologist, *Obit* Oct 1940

Bedford, Sybille, English novelist, Feb 1990, *Obit* Yrbk 2006

Beebe, Lucius Morris, journalist, Sept 1940, *Obit* Mar 1966

Beebe, William, American naturalist and author, July 1941, *Obit* Sept 1962

Beech, Olive Ann, American aircraft executive, June 1956, *Obit* Sept 1993

Beecham, Thomas, English conductor, Yrbk 1941, Jan 1951, *Obit* May 1961

Beeching, Richard, British physicist, government official and chemical industry executive, Sept 1963

Beecroft, John, American editor, Mar 1954, *Obit* Yrbk 1966

Beehler, Bruce McP., American ornithologist and conservationist, Aug 2006

Beene, Geoffrey, American fashion designer, Apr 1978, *Obit* Mar 2005

Beer, Thomas, author, *Obit* May 1940

Beers, Charlotte, American advertising executive and government official, June 1998

Beers, Clifford Whittingham, American mental hygienist, *Obit* Aug 1943

Beers, Rand, American foreign policy adviser, Oct 2004

Begaye, Kelsey, Navajo leader, Jan 2000

Begg, Alexander Swanson, American physician and college dean, *Obit* Nov 1940

Begg, Colin Luke, American physician, *Obit* Mar 1941

Begin, Menachem, Israeli prime minister, Oct 1977, *Obit* Apr 1992

Begley, Ed, American actor, Mar 1956, *Obit* June 1970

Begtrup, Bodil, Danish diplomat and United Nations official, Sept 1946

Behan, Brendan, Irish dramatist, Mar 1961, *Obit* May 1964

Behar, Ruth, American anthropologist, poet and filmmaker, May 2005

Behe, Michael J., American biochemist and intelligent design advocate, Feb 2006

Behn, Sosthenes, American telephone executive, Jan 1947, *Obit* Sept 1957

Behnisch, Stefan, German architect, Jan 2007

Behrens, Hildegard, German opera singer, Jan 1985, *Obit* Yrbk 2009

Behrman, Beatrice, American doll maker, Sept 1957

Behrman, S. N., dramatist, screenwriter and author, Feb 1943, *Obit* Nov 1973

Beinum, Eduard van, Apr 1955, *Obit* June 1959

Beirne, Joseph A., American labor leader, Mar 1946, *Obit* Oct 1974

Beiser, Maya, American cellist, May 2009

Beitz, Berthold, German steel executive, Feb 1973, *Obit* Yrbk 2013

Bejart, Maurice, French ballet dancer and choreographer, Mar 1971, *Obit* Yrbk 2008

Bekmambetov, Timur, Kazakhstani film director, Jan 2006

Bel Geddes, Barbara, American actress, July 1948, *Obit* Yrbk 2005

Belafonte, Harry, American singer and actor, Jan 1956

Belaunde Terry, Fernando, Peruvian president, July 1965, *Obit* Sept 2002

Belaunde, Victor Andres, Peruvian diplomat, Feb 1960, *Obit* Feb 1967

Belcher, Angela, American chemical engineer, July 2006

Belichick, Bill, American football coach, Sept 2002

Belkin, Samuel, American rabbi and college president, Nov 1952, *Obit* June 1976

Bell Burnell, Jocelyn, British astronomer, May 1995

Bell, Art, American radio talk show host, Apr 2000

Bell, Bernard Iddings, clergyman and educator, Apr 1953, *Obit* Yrbk 1959

Bell, Bert, American football commissioner, Sept 1950, *Obit* Yrbk 1959

Bell, Daniel, American sociologist, Yrbk 1973, *Obit* Yrbk 2011

Bell, Daniel W., American banker and government official, Oct 1946, *Obit* Nov 1971

Bell, David E., American economist and government official, June 1961, *Obit* Yrbk 2000

Bell, Derrick A., American law professor, Feb 1993, *Obit* Yrbk 2011

Bell, Edward Price, American journalist, *Obit* Nov 1943

Bell, Elliott V., economist, editor and publisher, Mar 1953, *Obit* Mar 1983

Bell, Griffin B., American Attorney general, June 1977, *Obit* Yrbk 2009

Bell, James A., American aerospace industry executive, July 2006

Bell, Joshua, American violinist, July 2000

Bell, Lawrence D., July 1942, *Obit* Jan 1957

Bell, Margaret Elizabeth, Yrbk 1952

Bell, Marilyn, Canadian swimmer, Sept 1956

Bell, Rob, American pastor, Mar 2013

Bell, Steve, British political cartoonist, Jan 2003

Bell, Terrel Howard, American Secretary of education, May 1976, *Obit* Sept 1996

Bell, Thomas M., *Obit* May 1941

Bellamann, Henry, author and poet, Sept 1942, *Obit* July 1945

Bellamy, Carol, American United Nations official, Oct 1999

Bellamy, Ralph, actor, Nov 1951, *Obit* Jan 1992

Belle, David, French actor and roof jumper, Jan 2007

Belli, Melvin M., American lawyer, July 1979, *Obit* Sept 1996

Bellmon, Henry, American governor and senator, July 1963, *Obit* Yrbk 2009

Bellow, Saul, American novelist, Feb 1965, Nov 1988, *Obit* Aug 2005

Bellucci, Monica, Italian actress, Jan 2003

Belluck, Pam, New York Times science writer and journalist, June 2012

Belluschi, Pietro, American architect, Feb 1959, *Obit* Apr 1994

Belmondo, Jean-Paul, French actor, Yrbk 1965

Belmont, Eleanor Robson, July 1944, *Obit* Jan 1980

Belmore, Alice, British actress, *Obit* Sept 1943

Belt, Guillermo, Cuban diplomat, Nov 1947, *Obit* Sept 1989

Belton, Sharon Sayles, American mayor, Jan 2001

Beltran, Pedro G., Peruvian newspaper publisher and statesman, Apr 1967, *Obit* Apr 1979

Belushi, Jim, American actor, Jan 1995

Belushi, John, American comedian, Jan 1980, *Obit* Apr 1982

Belyayev, Pavel, Soviet cosmonaut, July 1965, *Obit* Mar 1970

Bemelmans, Ludwig, American children's author and illustrator, Apr 1941, *Obit* Yrbk 1962

Bemis, Samuel Flagg, historian, June 1950, *Obit* Nov 1973

Ben Bella, Ahmed, Algerian president, Feb 1963, *Obit* Yrbk 2012

Ben and Jerry, Apr 1994

Ben-Gurion, David, Israeli prime minister, Oct 1947, Jan 1957, *Obit* Jan 1974

Ben-Zvi, Itzhak, Israeli president, Apr 1953, *Obit* June 1963

Benavente, Jacinto, Spanish dramatist, June 1953, *Obit* Sept 1954

Benavides, Oscar R., Peruvian president, *Obit* Aug 1945

Bench, Johnny, American baseball player, Oct 1971

Benchley, Belle Jennings, zoo director, Oct 1940

Benchley, Nathaniel, American novelist, short story writer and children's author, Sept 1953, *Obit* Feb 1982

Benchley, Peter, American novelist and journalist, July 1976, *Obit* June 2006

Benchley, Robert, humorist, Sept 1941, *Obit* Jan 1946

Bender, George H., American congressman and senator, Jan 1952, *Obit* Sept 1961

Bender, James F., speech educator and business consultant, May 1949, *Obit* Mar 1998

Bendetsen, Karl Robin, American paper industry executive, May 1952, *Obit* Sept 1989

Bendix, Vincent, American inventor and aircraft industry executive, *Obit* May 1945

Bendix, William, American actor, Sept 1948, *Obit* Feb 1965

Benedict, Apr 1986, Sept 2005

Benedict, Ruth, American anthropologist, May 1941, *Obit* Nov 1948

Benelli, Giovanni Cardinal, Sept 1977, *Obit* Jan 1983

Benes, Edvard, Czech statesman, Jan 1942, *Obit* Oct 1948

Benesh, Joan, British ballet dancer, choreographer and teacher, July 1957

Benesh, Rudolf, British mathematician, July 1957

Benesh, Rudolf; and Benesh, Joan, July 1957

Benet, Stephen Vincent, American poet, novelist and short story writer, *Obit* Apr 1943

Bengough, Percy R., Canadian labor leader, Apr 1951

Benigni, Roberto, Italian actor and filmmaker, June 1999

Benjamin, Regina, American Surgeon general, Jan 2010

Benjamin, William Evarts, American publisher, *Obit* Mar 1940

Benn, Tony, British member of Parliament, June 1965, Nov 1982

Bennett, H. S., anatomist, Apr 1966, *Obit* Oct 1992

Bennett, Henry Garland, American college president, Feb 1951, *Obit* Feb 1952

Bennett, Henry Gordon, Australian general, Mar 1942, *Obit* Oct 1962

Bennett, Hugh Hammond, American soil scientist, Yrbk 1946, *Obit* Oct 1960

Bennett, Ivan L., American military chaplain, Nov 1952, *Obit* Aug 1980

Bennett, James O'Donnell, American journalist, *Obit* Mar 1940

Bennett, James V., American penologist and prison official, Apr 1949, *Obit* Feb 1979

Bennett, John C., clergyman, ethicist and seminary president, Jan 1961, *Obit* July 1995

Bennett, John W. F., American civil engineer, *Obit* Oct 1943

Bennett, Lerone, American magazine editor and historian, Jan 2001

Bennett, Michael, American choreographer, Mar 1981, *Obit* Aug 1987

Bennett, Rawson, American admiral, Sept 1958, *Obit* Feb 1968

Bennett, Richard, American actor, *Obit* Yrbk 1944

Bennett, Richard Rodney, English composer, Mar 1992, *Obit* Yrbk 2013

Bennett, Robert LaFollette, American lawyer and government official, Sept 1967

Bennett, Robert Russell, American composer, arranger and conductor, Apr 1942, May 1962, *Obit* Oct 1981

Bennett, Tony, American singer, Mar 1965, June 1995

Bennett, W. A. C., Canadian political leader, May 1953, *Obit* May 1979

Bennett, Wallace F., American senator, Feb 1949, *Obit* Feb 1994

Bennett, William John, Canadian government official and energy industry executive, June 1954

Bennett, William John, American political commentator, Sept 1985

Bennington, Chester, American singer, Mar 2002

Benny, Jack, comedian, Aug 1941, Nov 1963, *Obit* Feb 1975

Benoit-Levy, Jean, Oct 1947, *Obit* Nov 1959

Benrimo, J. Harry, American dramatist, theatrical director and actor, *Obit* May 1942

Bensin, Basil M., American agriculturist, July 1948

Benson, Allan L., American socialist leader, *Obit* Oct 1940

Benson, E. F., English author, Mar 1940

Benson, Ezra Taft, American Secretary of agriculture and Mormon leader, Feb 1953, *Obit* Aug 1994

Benson, Francis Colgate, American surgeon and radiologist, *Obit* Apr 1941

Benson, John, American advertising executive, Apr 1940, *Obit* Nov 1962

Benson, Sally, American short story writer, dramatist and screenwriter, Aug 1941, *Obit* Sept 1972

Bensouda, Fatou, Gambian lawyer and international court prosecutor, Jan 2007

Bentley, Helen Delich, American congresswoman, Yrbk 1971

Bentley, Irene, American actress, *Obit* July 1940

Benton, Thomas Hart, American painter, Oct 1940, *Obit* Mar 1975

Benton, William, American senator, publisher and diplomat, Yrbk 1945, *Obit* May 1973

Bentsen, Lloyd, American Secretary of the treasury, Sept 1973, Apr 1993, *Obit* Oct 2006

Benyus, Janine M., American environmentalist, naturalist and science writer, Mar 2006

Benzer, Seymour, American biophysicist, May 2001, *Obit* Yrbk 2008

Beranek, Leo Leroy, American acoustic engineer, Mar 1963

Berding, Andrew H., American journalist and government official, Apr 1960

Beregovoy, Pierre Eugene, French prime minister, Feb 1993, *Obit* Feb 1993

Berelson, Bernard, American librarian and sociologist, July 1961, *Obit* Nov 1979

Berendsen, Carl August, New Zealand diplomat, Oct 1948, *Obit* Yrbk 1973

Berendt, John, American writer, Apr 1998

Beresford, Bruce, Australian film director, Mar 1993

Beresford-Kroeger, Diana, Irish botanist, Nov 2008

Berezovsky, Boris A., Russian financier and government official, Jan 2002, *Obit* Yrbk 2013

Berg, Elizabeth, American novelist and short story writer, Nov 1999

Berg, Ernst Julius, Swedish electrical engineer, *Obit* Nov 1941

Berg, Gertrude, American actress and radio scriptwriter, July 1941, Sept 1960, *Obit* Nov 1966

Berg, Hart O., American aviation and arms expert, *Obit* Feb 1942

Berg, Irving H., American clergyman and college dean, *Obit* Nov 1941

Berg, Patty, American golfer, Sept 1940, *Obit* Yrbk 2007

Berganza, Teresa, Spanish opera singer, Jan 1979

Berge, Pierre, French clothing industry executive, Jan 1990

Berge, Wendell, American lawyer and government official, Feb 1946, *Obit* Yrbk 1956

Bergen, Candice, American actress, Aug 1976

Bergen, Edgar, American ventriloquist and radio performer, May 1945, *Obit* Nov 1978

Bergen, John J., American financier, June 1961, *Obit* Feb 1981

Bergen, Polly, actress and singer, Sept 1958

Berger Perdomo, Oscar, Guatemalan president, Jan 2004

Berger, Meyer, newspaper reporter and columnist, Jan 1943, *Obit* Apr 1959

Berger, Peter L., American sociologist, Mar 1983

Berger, Sandy, American presidential adviser, Feb 1998

Berger, Thomas, author, June 1988

Bergeron, Tom, American television personality, Oct 2007

Berggrav, Eivind, Norwegian bishop, Oct 1950, *Obit* Mar 1959

Bergland, Bob, American Secretary of agriculture, Sept 1977

Bergman, Ingmar, Swedish film and theatrical director, Apr 1960, Oct 1981, *Obit* Sept 2007

Bergman, Ingrid, Swedish actress, Jan 1940, Sept 1965, *Obit* Oct 1982

Bergonzi, Carlo, Italian opera singer, Nov 1992

Bergquist, Kenneth P., American air force general, Mar 1961

Bergson, Henri, French philosopher, *Obit* Feb 1941

Bergson, Herbert A., American lawyer, Sept 1950

Beria, Lavrenti, Soviet intelligence official, Yrbk 1942, *Obit* Sept 1954

Berigan, Bunny, American jazz trumpet player, *Obit* July 1942

Berio, Luciano, Italian composer, Mar 1971, *Obit* Yrbk 2003

Beriosova, Svetlana, Lithuanian ballet dancer and teacher, Sept 1960, *Obit* Feb 1999

Berkeley, Busby, American choreographer and film director, Apr 1971, *Obit* May 1976

Berkner, Lloyd, Sept 1949, *Obit* Oct 1967

Berkson, Seymour, American news agency executive, Oct 1949, *Obit* Mar 1959

Berle, Adolf Augustus, American lawyer and diplomat, July 1940, June 1961, *Obit* Apr 1971

Berle, Milton, American comedian, June 1949, *Obit* Yrbk 2002

Berlin, Ellin, author and wife of Irving Berlin, Aug 1944, *Obit* Sept 1988

Berlin, Irving, American composer and lyricist, May 1942, May 1963, *Obit* Nov 1989

Berlin, Isaiah, British political philosopher, July 1964, *Obit* Jan 1998

Berlin, Steve, American keyboardist and saxophonist, Oct 2005

Berlinguer, Enrico, Italian communist leader, July 1976, *Obit* Aug 1984

Berlitz, Charles, American educator and writer on the paranormal, Feb 1957, *Obit* Yrbk 2004

Berlusconi, Silvio, Italian prime minister, Aug 1994

Berman, Chris, American television sportscaster, Aug 1998

Berman, Emile Zola, American lawyer, June 1972, *Obit* Aug 1981

Berman, Eugene, American painter, June 1965, *Obit* Feb 1973

Berman, Lazar, Russian pianist, Sept 1977, *Obit* Yrbk 2005

Bernadotte, Folke, Swedish diplomat, May 1945, *Obit* Nov 1948

Bernanke, Ben, American economist and Federal Reserve chairman, Mar 2006

Bernard, Emile, French painter, art critic and poet, *Obit* June 1941

Bernard, Michelle D., American journalist and political commentator, Sept 2011

Bernardin, Joseph L., Oct 1982, *Obit* Jan 1997

Bernardino, Minerva, Dominican feminist and diplomat, Mar 1950, *Obit* Nov 1998

Bernays, Edward L., American public relations consultant, Feb 1942, Sept 1960, *Obit* May 1995

Bernbach, William, American advertising executive, Mar 1967, *Obit* Nov 1982

Bernhard Leopold, June 1950, *Obit* Mar 2005

Bernhard, Sandra, American comedienne and actress, Sept 1990

Bernheim, Bertram M., American surgeon, Sept 1943

Bernie, Ben, American band leader, Yrbk 1941, *Obit* Yrbk 1943

Bernier, Rosamond, American art critic, Feb 1988

Bernstein, Carl, American journalist, Oct 1976

Bernstein, Elmer, American composer, June 2003

Bernstein, Leonard, American conductor and composer, Feb 1944, Feb 1960, *Obit* Nov 1990

Bernstein, Michelle, American chef and restaurateur, Nov 2013

Bernstein, Philip S., American rabbi, Nov 1951, *Obit* Feb 1986

Bernstein, Robert L., American publishing executive and human rights activist, July 1987

Bernstein, William, American investment adviser and neurologist, Nov 2009

Berra, Yogi, American baseball player and manager, May 1952

Berri, Claude, French actor, director and screenwriter, Mar 1989, *Obit* Yrbk 2009

Berri, Nabih, Lebanese political leader, Nov 1985

Berrigan, Daniel, American priest, poet and pacifist, Sept 1970

Berrigan, Philip, American peace activist, Feb 1976, *Obit* Mar 2003

Berry, Charles A., American flight surgeon, Apr 1969

Berry, Chuck, American singer and guitarist, Apr 1977

Berry, Edward Wilber, American paleontologist, *Obit* Oct 1945

Berry, George L., American labor leader, Jan 1948, *Obit* Jan 1949

Berry, Halle, American actress, May 1999

Berry, Martha, Apr 1940, *Obit* Apr 1942

Berry, Mary Frances, American historian, civil rights leader and government official, June 1999

Berry, Wendell, American poet and novelist, May 1986

Berryman, Guy, Scottish bassist, May 2004

Berryman, James Thomas, cartoonist, July 1950, *Obit* Oct 1971

Berryman, John, American poet and critic, May 1969, *Obit* Feb 1972

Bertolucci, Bernardo, Italian film director, July 1974

Berton, Pierre, Canadian journalist and historian, Oct 1991, *Obit* Yrbk 2005

Bertozzi, Carolyn R., American chemist, July 2003

Bertram, Adolf, *Obit* Aug 1945

Bertrand, Louis, French novelist and historian, *Obit* Feb 1942

Bervoets, Gene, Dutch actor, Jan 2002

Bess, Demaree, American journalist, Jan 1943, *Obit* Sept 1962

Bessmertnova, Natalia, Russian ballet dancer, Jan 1988, *Obit* Yrbk 2008

Bessmertnykh, Aleksandr A., Soviet diplomat, June 1991

Besson, Luc, French film director, Jan 2002

Best, Charles Herbert, Canadian physiologist, June 1957, *Obit* May 1978

Best, Edna, English actress, July 1954, *Obit* Nov 1974

Besteiro, Julian, Spanish socialist leader, *Obit* Nov 1940

Bestor, Arthur, American historian, Sept 1958, *Obit* Feb 1995

Bestor, Arthur E., American educator, *Obit* Mar 1944

Betancourt, Ingrid, Colombian political leader, Jan 2002

Betancourt, Romulo, Venezuelan president, May 1960, *Obit* Nov 1981

Betancur, Belisario, Colombian president, Apr 1985

Bethe, Hans, German-American physicist, Jan 1940, Apr 1950, *Obit* Aug 2005

Bethune, Gordon M., American airline executive, June 2001

Bethune, Mary Jane McLeod, American educator, Jan 1942, *Obit* July 1955

Betjeman, John, English poet and architectural historian, Mar 1973, *Obit* July 1984

Bettelheim, Bruno, American psychologist, July 1961, *Obit* May 1990

Bettis, Jerome, American football player, Aug 2006

Bettis, Valerie, dancer and choreographer, May 1953, *Obit* Nov 1982

Bettman, Gary, American lawyer and hockey commissioner, Mar 1999

Bettmann, Otto L., archivist, Nov 1961, *Obit* July 1998

Betts, Rome A., American medical association official, Mar 1949

Beuys, Joseph, German artist, July 1980, *Obit* Mar 1986

Bevan, Aneurin, British cabinet member, May 1943, *Obit* Oct 1960

Bevan, Arthur Dean, American surgeon, *Obit* Aug 1943

Beveridge, William Henry Beveridge, British economist, Jan 1943, *Obit* May 1963

Bevier, Isabel, home economist, *Obit* May 1942

Bevin, Ernest, British statesman, Sept 1940, June 1949, *Obit* May 1951

Bevis, Howard L., American university president, Jan 1940, Nov 1950, *Obit* June 1968

Bevis, Palmer, American public relations executive, Apr 1953

Bewkes, Jeffrey L., American mass media executive, Nov 2010

Beyen, J. W., Dutch banker, economist and diplomat, Feb 1953, *Obit* June 1976

Beyonce, American singer and actress, Aug 2001

Bezos, Jeffrey, American Internet and retail executive, June 1998

Bhabha, Homi Jehangir, Indian physicist, Sept 1956, *Obit* Feb 1966

Bhave, Vinoba, Indian mystic and social reformer, Sept 1953, *Obit* Jan 1983

Bhosle, Asha, Indian singer, Jan 2006

Bhumibol Adulyadej, July 1950

Bhutto, Benazir, Pakistani prime minister, July 1986, *Obit* Apr 2008

Bhutto, Zulfikar Ali, Pakistani president, Apr 1972, *Obit* May 1979

Biaggi, Mario, congressman, Jan 1986

Bialk, Elisa, author, Yrbk 1954, *Obit* May 1990

Bianchini, Gina, American Internet executive, Oct 2013

Bible, Alan, American senator, Feb 1957, *Obit* Oct 1988

Bible, Geoffrey C., American tobacco and food industry executive, Feb 2002

Bickel, George, American comedian and actor, *Obit* Aug 1941

Bidault, Georges, French statesman, May 1945, *Obit* Mar 1983

Biddle, Anthony Joseph Drexel, American general and diplomat, Mar 1941, *Obit* Jan 1962

Biddle, Francis, American Attorney general, Sept 1941, *Obit* Yrbk 1968

Biddle, George, American painter and sculptor, Feb 1942, *Obit* Jan 1974

Biddle, Katherine Garrison Chapin, poet, Oct 1943, *Obit* Jan 1984

Biden, Joseph R., American vice-president, Jan 1987, Mar 2009

Bieber, Owen, labor leader, Apr 1986

Biermann, Wolf, German poet, Jan 2003

Bierut, Boleslaw, Polish president, Sept 1949, *Obit* May 1956

Biffle, Leslie L., American presidential aide, Sept 1946, *Obit* May 1966

Big Boi, American rapper, Apr 2004

Bigart, Homer, American journalist, June 1951, *Obit* July 1991

Bigelow, Karl W., economist and educator, Feb 1949, *Obit* June 1980

Bigelow, Kathryn, American film director, Mar 2010

Bigelow, Robert T., American real estate executive and financier, Aug 2008

Bigelow, William P., American music teacher, *Obit* May 1941

Biggers, John D., American manufacturing executive, Sept 1941, *Obit* Feb 1974

Biggs, E. Power, organist, Nov 1950, *Obit* May 1977

Bikel, Theodore, American singer and actor, Mar 1960

Bilandic, Michael A., American mayor, Feb 1979, *Obit* Apr 2002

Bilbo, Theodore G., American senator, Apr 1943, *Obit* Oct 1947

Bildt, Carl, Swedish prime minister, Jan 1993

Biller, Moe, American labor leader, June 1987, *Obit* Yrbk 2004

Billingsley, Franny, American children's author, Aug 2012

Billingsley, Sherman, American nightclub owner, Feb 1946, *Obit* Yrbk 1966

Billington, James H., American historian and Librarian of Congress, May 1989

Billups, Chauncey, American basketball player, Feb 2011

Bimson, Carl A., American banker, Mar 1961

Binchy, Maeve, Irish novelist and short story writer, Nov 1995, *Obit* Yrbk 2012

Binder, Carroll, journalist, May 1951, *Obit* July 1956

Binder, Theodor, German physician and missionary, Sept 1964

Binet-Valmer, Jean, French novelist, *Obit* Sept 1940

Bing, Rudolf, British opera manager, Feb 1950, *Obit* Nov 1997

Bingham, Barry, American newspaper publisher, Sept 1949, *Obit* Sept 1988

Bingham, Hiram, American explorer and senator, Mar 1951, *Obit* Sept 1956

Bingham, Jonathan B., congressman, July 1954, *Obit* Aug 1986

Bingham, Millicent Todd, American geographer and conservationist, June 1961, *Obit* Jan 1969

Binkley, Robert Cedric, American historian, *Obit* May 1940

Binns, Joseph Patterson, American hotel executive, June 1954, *Obit* Mar 1981

Binyon, Laurence, English poet, dramatist and art critic, *Obit* Apr 1943

Birch, Reginald Bathurst, *Obit* Aug 1943

Bird, Caroline, July 1976

Bird, Larry, American basketball player and coach, June 1982

Bird, Rose Elizabeth, judge, May 1984, *Obit* May 2000

Bird, Will R., Canadian historian and short story writer, Sept 1954

Birdseye, Clarence, American inventor and frozen food industry executive, Mar 1946, *Obit* Yrbk 1957

Birdseye, Claude Hale, American topographer, *Obit* July 1941

Birdwell, Russell, July 1946, *Obit* Mar 1978

Birendra Bir Bikram Shah Deva, Aug 1975, *Obit* Sept 2001

Birge, Raymond T., American physicist, Mar 1940

Birkin, Jane, English actress, Jan 2002

Birmingham, Stephen, author, May 1974

Birnie, William A. H., American magazine editor, Sept 1952, *Obit* Oct 1979

Birren, Faber, industrial color consultant, May 1956, *Obit* Feb 1989

Bishop, Andre, American theatrical producer, July 1999

Bishop, Billy, Canadian air marshal, Sept 1941

Bishop, Elizabeth, American poet, Sept 1977, *Obit* Nov 1979

Bishop, Hazel, American chemist and cosmetics executive, Sept 1957, *Obit* Feb 1999

Bishop, Isabel, American painter, Oct 1977, *Obit* Apr 1988

Bishop, Jim, columnist and author, June 1969, *Obit* Sept 1987

Bishop, Joey, American comedian, Apr 1962, *Obit* Yrbk 2008

Bissell, Claude T., May 1959

Bissell, Clayton L., American air force general, Feb 1943

Bisset, Jacqueline, English actress, May 1977

Bisset, James, British ship captain, Yrbk 1946

Bitar, Salah al-Din, Syrian political leader, Feb 1958, *Obit* Sept 1980

Bittman, Mark, American food columnist and cookbook writer, Feb 2005

Bittner, Van A., American labor leader, Mar 1947, *Obit* Sept 1949

Bjoerndalen, Ole Einar, Norwegian biathlete, Jan 2003

Bjork, Icelandic singer, July 2001

Bjorling, Jussi, Swedish opera singer, Sept 1947, *Obit* Nov 1960

Black Eyed Peas (Musical group), Oct 2006

Black, Alexander, American photographer, *Obit* Jan 1940

Black, Cathleen, American school superintendent and former magazine executive, Jan 1998

Black, Clint, American country singer and songwriter, Aug 1994

Black, Conrad M., Canadian financier and newspaper publisher, Aug 1992

Black, Eugene Robert, American banking official, Jan 1950, *Obit* Apr 1992

Black, Hugo LaFayette, American Supreme Court justice, Sept 1941, May 1964, *Obit* Nov 1971

Black, Jack, American singer and actor, Feb 2002

Black, Karen, American actress, Mar 1976, *Obit* Yrbk 2013

Black, Michael Ian, American actor, Sept 2013

Black, Shirley Temple, American actress and diplomat, Oct 1945, Apr 1970

Black, William, coffee company executive, July 1964, *Obit* May 1983

Blackall, Frederick S., American manufacturing executive, Jan 1953

Blackburn, Elizabeth H., Australian molecular biologist, July 2001

Blackett, Patrick M. S., British physicist, Feb 1949, *Obit* Sept 1974

Blackfan, K. D., American pediatrician, *Obit* Jan 1942

Blackie, Ernest Morell, British bishop, *Obit* Apr 1943

Blackman, Cindy, American drummer, Oct 2010

Blackmun, Harry A., American Supreme Court justice, Oct 1970, *Obit* May 1999

Blackton, James Stuart, American film director and producer, *Obit* Oct 1941

Blackwell, Betsy Talbot, American magazine editor, June 1954, *Obit* Apr 1985

Blackwell, Earl, society leader and celebrity information service executive, Nov 1960, *Obit* May 1995

Blades, Ruben, Panamanian salsa singer, songwriter and actor, May 1986

Blaese, R. Michael, physician, Mar 2000

Blagonravov, A. A., Soviet rocket engineer, Feb 1958, *Obit* Apr 1975

Blahnik, Manolo, Spanish shoe designer, Jan 2004

Blaik, Earl Henry, football coach, Jan 1945, *Obit* July 1989

Blain, Daniel, American psychiatrist, Sept 1947

Blaine, David, American magician, Apr 2001

Blair, Bonnie, American speed skater, July 1992

Blair, David, British ballet dancer and choreographer, Jan 1961, *Obit* May 1976

Blair, David H., American tax official and lawyer, *Obit* Nov 1944

Blair, Dennis, American admiral and intelligence official, May 2010

Blair, James T., American governor, Apr 1958, *Obit* Sept 1962

Blair, Tony, British prime minister, Aug 1996, Jan 2005

Blaisdell, Thomas Charles, economist and government official, July 1949, *Obit* Feb 1989

Blake, Doris, Canadian journalist, Nov 1941

Blake, Edgar, American bishop, *Obit* July 1943

Blake, Eubie, American pianist and composer, Apr 1974, *Obit* Apr 1983

Blake, Eugene Carson, American clergyman and church leader, Sept 1955, *Obit* Oct 1985

Blake, Francis G., American physician, Jan 1943, *Obit* Mar 1952

Blake, James, American tennis player, Mar 2006

Blake, Robert, American actor, Oct 1975

Blake, Tiffany, American journalist, *Obit* Nov 1943

Blakely, Sara, American hosiery company executive, Jan 2013

Blakemore, Michael, Australian theatrical director, May 2001

Blaker, Richard, English author, *Obit* Mar 1940

Blakeslee, Albert Francis, American botanist, Oct 1941, *Obit* Jan 1955

Blakeslee, Francis D., American clergyman, educator and prohibitionist, *Obit* Nov 1942

Blakey, Art, American jazz drummer and band leader, Sept 1988, *Obit* Jan 1991

Blakey, Michael L., biological anthropologist, Sept 2000

Blalock, Alfred, American surgeon, Sept 1946, *Obit* Nov 1964

Blalock, Alfred; and Taussig, Helen B., Sept 1946

Blalock, Richard W., American youth organization official, May 1950

Blamey, Thomas Albert, Australian general, June 1942, *Obit* July 1951

Blanc, Mel, American animated cartoon voice specialist, June 1976, *Obit* Sept 1989

Blanch, Arnold, American painter, May 1940, Jan 1954, *Obit* Yrbk 1968

Blanchard, Doc, American football player and air force officer, Mar 1946, *Obit* Yrbk 2009

Blanchard, Hazel A., American school principal, June 1963

Blanche, Jacques-Emile, French painter, *Obit* Nov 1942

Blanchett, Cate, Australian actress, Aug 1999

Blanchfield, Florence Aby, American nurse and army officer, Sept 1943, *Obit* June 1971

Blancke, Harold, American chemical industry executive, June 1957

Blanco Galindo, Carlos, Bolivian president, *Obit* Nov 1943

Blanco, Kathleen, American governor, June 2004

Bland, Bobby Blue, singer, *Obit* Yrbk 2013

Blanda, George, American football player, Sept 1972, *Obit* Yrbk 2010

Blandford, John B., American government official, May 1942, *Obit* Mar 1972

Blanding, Don, American poet and illustrator, Jan 1957

Blanding, Sarah Gibson, college president, June 1946, *Obit* Apr 1985

Blandy, W. H. P., American admiral, Nov 1942, *Obit* Mar 1954

Blank, Theodor, Sept 1952, *Obit* July 1972

Blankenbuehler, Andy, American choreographer and dancer, Apr 2009

Blankenhorn, Herbert, German diplomat, Apr 1956

Blankfein, Lloyd C., American investment banker, Jan 2011

Blanton, Smiley, June 1956, *Obit* Jan 1967

Blass, Bill, American fashion designer, Sept 1966, *Obit* Nov 2002

Blatch, Harriot Eaton Stanton, American suffratist, *Obit* Jan 1941

Blatchford, Joseph H., Mar 1971

Blatchley, W. S., American entomologist and geologist, *Obit* July 1940

Blatnik, John A., American congressman, Feb 1958, *Obit* Feb 1992

Blattenberger, Raymond, American printing industry executive and government official, Mar 1958, *Obit* June 1971

Blatty, William Peter, American novelist, June 1974

Blau, Bela, American theatrical producer, *Obit* Yrbk 1940

Blaustein, Jacob, American petroleum industry executive and Jewish leader, Apr 1949, *Obit* Jan 1971

Blease, Coleman Livingston, American senator and governor, *Obit* Mar 1942

Bledsoe, Jules, American opera singer, actor and composer, *Obit* Sept 1943

Blegen, Judith, American opera singer, June 1977

Blier, Bertrand, French motion picture director, Oct 1988

Blind Boys of Alabama (Musical group), Oct 2001

Blink-182 (Musical group), Aug 2002

Bliss, A. Richard, American pharmacologist and college dean, *Obit* Oct 1941

Bliss, Anthony Addison, lawyer and opera manager, Apr 1979, *Obit* Nov 1991

Bliss, Henry Evelyn, librarian, Sept 1953, *Obit* Oct 1955

Bliss, Ray C., American political party leader, Jan 1966, *Obit* Oct 1981

Bliss, Raymond W., American surgeon and general, Jan 1951, *Obit* Jan 1966

Blitch, Iris Faircloth, congresswoman, Apr 1956, *Obit* Oct 1993

Blitzer, Wolf, American television news anchor, Feb 2007

Blitzstein, Marc, American dramatist and composer, July 1940, *Obit* Mar 1964

Bliven, Bruce, American magazine editor, Yrbk 1941, *Obit* July 1977

Blix, Hans, Swedish diplomat and United Nations official, Jan 2003

Bloch, Charles Edward, American publishing executive, *Obit* Oct 1940

Bloch, Claude Charles, American admiral, Feb 1942, *Obit* Yrbk 1967

Bloch, Ernest, American composer, Sept 1953, *Obit* Oct 1959

Bloch, Felix, Swiss-American physicist, Sept 1954, *Obit* Nov 1983

Block, Herbert, American editorial cartoonist, July 1954, *Obit* Jan 2002

Block, John R., American Secretary of agriculture, Apr 1982

Block, Joseph L., steel executive, June 1961, *Obit* Feb 1993

Block, Paul, American newspaper publisher, *Obit* Aug 1941

Blodgett, Katharine, American physicist, Jan 1940, May 1952, *Obit* Jan 1980

Blomfield, Reginald Theodore, British architect, *Obit* Feb 1943

Bloodworth-Thomason, Linda, American television scriptwriter and producer, Feb 1993

Bloom, Allan David, philosopher, Mar 1988, *Obit* Nov 1992

Bloom, Claire, English actress, May 1956

Bloom, Harold, American literary critic, Apr 1987

Bloom, Jeremy, American football player and skier, Sept 2013

Bloom, Orlando, English actor, Jan 2003

Bloom, Paul, June 2012

Bloom, Sol, American congressman, May 1943, *Obit* Mar 1949

Bloomberg, Michael, American mayor, June 1996, Mar 2002

Bloomgarden, Kermit, American theatrical producer, Yrbk 1958, *Obit* Nov 1976

Blough, Roger M., American steel industry executive, July 1955, *Obit* Jan 1986

Blough, Roy, economist, July 1950, *Obit* Sept 2000

Blount, Winton Malcolm, American construction executive and postmaster general, Apr 1969, *Obit* Jan 2003

Bloustein, Edward J., college president, Nov 1965, *Obit* Feb 1990

Blucher, Franz, German cabinet member, Jan 1956, *Obit* June 1959

Blue, Robert Donald, American governor, Yrbk 1948, *Obit* Feb 1990

Blue, Vida, baseball player, Mar 1972

Bluford, Guion S., American astronaut, Sept 1984

Blum, Leon, French statesman, Nov 1940, *Obit* May 1950

Blum, William, American journalist, May 2007

Blumberg, Baruch S., American physician and biochemist, Nov 1977, *Obit* Yrbk 2011

Blume, Judy, American young adult novelist, Apr 1980

Blume, Peter, American painter, Mar 1956, *Obit* Jan 1993

Blumenthal, George, American financier and museum and hospital administrator, *Obit* Yrbk 1941

Blumenthal, George, American theatrical producer, *Obit* Sept 1943

Blumenthal, Heston, British chef and restaurateur, Jan 2005

Blumenthal, Hugo, American investment banker and philanthropist, *Obit* Sept 1943

Blumenthal, W. Michael, American Secretary of the treasury, July 1977

Blumer, George Alder, American psychiatrist and hospital administrator, *Obit* Jan 1940

Blundell, Michael, British farmer and colonial leader, Mar 1954

Blunt, Katharine, home economist and nutritionist, Yrbk 1946, *Obit* Oct 1954

Blunt, Roy, American senator, Mar 2008

Blur (Musical group), Nov 2003

Bly, Robert, American poet, critic, editor and translator, Mar 1984, Mar 1993

Blythe, Stephanie, American opera singer, Aug 2004

Boardman, Mabel Thorp, Red Cross official, Aug 1944, *Obit* Apr 1946

Boas, Franz, American anthropologist, May 1940, *Obit* Feb 1943

Boateng, Ozwald, British fashion designer, Jan 2006

Boateng, Paul, British cabinet member, Jan 2002

Boatner, Haydon L., American general, July 1952

Bob and Ray, American comedians, Oct 1957

Bobst, Elmer Holmes, American pharmaceutical executive, Yrbk 1973, *Obit* Sept 1978

Bocelli, Andrea, Italian singer, Jan 2002

Bochco, Steven, American television scriptwriter and producer, May 1991

Bock, Fedor von, German field marshal, Oct 1942, *Obit* June 1945

Bocuse, Paul, French chef and restaurateur, Jan 1988

Bodansky, Meyer, American biochemist and pathologist, *Obit* Aug 1941

Bodanzky, Artur, *Obit* Jan 1940

Boe, Lars Wilhelm, American clergyman and college president, *Obit* Feb 1943

Boehner, John, American congressman and Speaker of the House, Apr 2006

Boerma, Addeke H., Dutch agronomist and United Nations official, Yrbk 1974

Boesak, Allan Aubrey, South African church official and human rights activist, Nov 1986

Boeschenstein, Harold, American manufacturing executive, Feb 1961, *Obit* Yrbk 1972

Boff, Leonardo, Brazilian theologian, Jan 1988

Bogarde, Dirk, English actor and author, July 1967, *Obit* July 1999

Bogart, Anne, theatrical director, Feb 1999

Bogart, Humphrey, American actor, May 1942, *Obit* Mar 1957

Bogdanovich, Peter, American film director and producer, June 1972

Bogert, George H., American painter, *Obit* Feb 1945

Boggiani, Tommaso Pio, *Obit* Apr 1942

Boggs, Charles Reid, American chemist and manufacturing executive, *Obit* Apr 1940

Boggs, Hale, American congressman and political leader, Apr 1958, *Obit* Mar 1973

Boggs, J. Caleb, American governor and senator, July 1956

Boggs, Wade, American baseball player, Aug 1990

Bogosian, Eric, American actor, playwright and monologist, Sept 1987

Boguslawski, Moissaye, American pianist, composer and teacher, *Obit* Oct 1944

Bogut, Andrew, Australian basketball player, Jan 2008

Bohan, Marc, French fashion designer, Apr 1965

Boheman, Erik, Swedish diplomat, Mar 1951

Bohlen, Charles E., American diplomat, June 1948, May 1960, *Obit* Feb 1974

Bohlen, Dieter, German pop singer, songwriter and producer, Jan 2006

Bohm, Karl, Austrian conductor, June 1968, *Obit* Oct 1981

Bohr, Niels Henrik David, Danish physicist, Sept 1945, *Obit* Jan 1963

Bohrod, Aaron, painter, Feb 1955, *Obit* June 1992

Boileau, Ethel, English author, *Obit* Mar 1942

Bois, Jules, *Obit* Aug 1943

Bois, Yve-Alain, French art historian, Jan 2005

Boissieu, Pierre de, Feb 1943, *Obit* Sept 1948

Boitano, Brian, American figure skater, Nov 1989

Bok, Curtis, American state supreme court justice, May 1954, *Obit* July 1962

Bok, Derek Curtis, college president, July 1971

Bok, Sissela, philosopher, Jan 1996

Bokassa, Apr 1978, *Obit* Jan 1997

Boland, Edward P., American congressman, Oct 1987, *Obit* Feb 2002

Boland, Frederick H., Irish United Nations official and diplomat, Feb 1961, *Obit* Feb 1986

Boland, Patrick J., American congressman, *Obit* July 1942

Bolcom, William, American composer and pianist, Apr 1990

Bolden, Charles, American astronaut and NASA official, July 2010

Boles, Ewing T., American investment banker, Apr 1953

Boles, Paul Darcy, author, Yrbk 1956, *Obit* June 1984

Bolger, Ray, American dancer, singer and actor, Aug 1942, *Obit* Mar 1987

Bolger, William F., postmaster general, Oct 1979, *Obit* Oct 1989

Boll, Heinrich, German novelist and short story writer, July 1972, *Obit* Sept 1985

Boll, Uwe, German film director, producer and screenwriter, Sept 2010

Bolles, Stephen, American newspaper editor and congressman, *Obit* Sept 1941

Bolling, Richard Walker, American congressman, Mar 1960, *Obit* July 1991

Bollinger, Lee C., American university president, Feb 2008

Bolotowsky, Ilya, American painter and sculptor, Apr 1975, *Obit* Jan 1982

Bolt, Richard H., American sound engineer, June 1954

Bolt, Robert, English dramatist and screenwriter, July 1963, *Obit* Apr 1995

Bolt, Usain, Jamaican runner, July 2009

Bolte, Charles G., author and publishing executive, Oct 1945, *Obit* May 1994

Bolte, Charles Lawrence, general, Jan 1954, *Obit* May 1989

Bolten, Josh, American presidential adviser, July 2006

Bolton, Frances Payne Bingham, American congresswoman, Mar 1940, Apr 1954, *Obit* May 1977

Bolton, John R., American diplomat, Feb 2006

Bolton, Michael, American singer and songwriter, Aug 1993

Bolz, Lothar, East German diplomat, Sept 1959, *Obit* Apr 1987

Bombeck, Erma, American humorist, Feb 1979, *Obit* June 1996

Bombieri, Enrico, Italian mathematician, Jan 2005

Bon Jovi, Jon, American singer and actor, Jan 1990

Bonaly, Surya, French figure skater, Jan 2002

Bonamassa, Joe, Apr 2013

Bonci, Alessandro, Italian opera singer, *Obit* Sept 1940

Bond, Edward, English dramatist, June 1978

Bond, Horace Mann, educator, Mar 1954

Bond, Jessie, English singer and actress, *Obit* Aug 1942

Bond, John, British banker, Jan 2005

Bond, Julian, American civil rights leader, Yrbk 1969, July 2001

Bonds, Barry, American baseball player, June 1994

Bonesteel, Charles H., American general, June 1942, *Obit* Sept 1964

Bong, Joon-Ho, Korean film director, Jan 2007

Bonham Carter, Helena, English actress, Jan 1998

Bonham, Milledge Louis, American historian, *Obit* Mar 1941

Bonine, Frederick N., American ophthalmologist, *Obit* Oct 1941

Bonino, Emma, Italian trade official, Jan 2006

Bonnell, John Sutherland, clergyman, June 1945, *Obit* Apr 1992

Bonner, Elena, Soviet physician and human rights activist, Apr 1987, *Obit* Yrbk 2011

Bonner, Herbert C., American congressman, July 1956, *Obit* Jan 1966

Bonner, Mary Graham, Yrbk 1950

Bonner, Paul Hyde, American novelist, Yrbk 1955, *Obit* Mar 1969

Bonnet, Henri, French diplomat, Feb 1945, *Obit* Feb 1979

Bonney, Therese, Feb 1944

Bono, Irish singer, Mar 1993

Bono, Sonny, American singer, songwriter and congressman, Feb 1974, *Obit* Mar 1998

Bonomi, Ivanhoe, Aug 1944, *Obit* May 1951

Bonomi, Maria, Brazilian artist, July 1960

Bonsal, Philip Wilson, diplomat, June 1959, *Obit* Sept 1995

Bonsal, Stephen, journalist, historian and biographer, Aug 1945, *Obit* July 1951

Bontecou, Lee, American sculptor, assemblage artist and printmaker, Mar 2004

Bontemps, Arna Wendell, American novelist, poet, biographer and children's author, Yrbk 1946, *Obit* July 1973

Bonynge, Richard, Australian conductor, Feb 1981

Booker, Cory, American mayor, Feb 2007

Booker, Edna Lee, American journalist, Apr 1940

Boone, J. T., American physician and admiral, Mar 1951, *Obit* June 1974

Boone, Pat, American singer and actor, July 1959

Boone, Richard, Feb 1964, *Obit* Mar 1981

Boorman, John, British film director, June 1988

Boorstin, Daniel J., American historian and Librarian of Congress, Sept 1968, Jan 1984, *Obit* Yrbk 2004

Boosler, Elayne, comedienne, May 1993

Booth, Arch N., Yrbk 1961

Booth, Ballington, American evangelist and social reformer, *Obit* Nov 1940

Booth, Evangeline C., English evangelist and Salvation Army leader, Feb 1941, *Obit* Sept 1950

Booth, Shirley, American actress, Nov 1942, Apr 1953, *Obit* Jan 1993

Borah, William Edgar, American senator, Jan 1940

Boras, Scott, American baseball agent, May 2009

Borberg, William, Nov 1952, *Obit* Sept 1958

Borch, Fred J., manufacturing executive, Oct 1971

Borcherds, Richard, English mathematician, Feb 1999

Bordaberry, Juan Maria, Uruguayan president, Apr 1975, *Obit* Yrbk 2011

Borden, Neil H., American marketing association executive and business teacher, May 1954

Bordes, Pierre-Louis, *Obit* Sept 1943

Boren, David L., American governor, senator and college president, Nov 1989

Borg, Bjorn, Swedish tennis player, Yrbk 1974

Borge, Victor, American pianist and comedian, Mar 1946, May 1993, *Obit* Mar 2001

Borges, Jorge Luis, Argentine short story writer and poet, Jan 1970, *Obit* Aug 1986

Borgese, Giuseppe Antonio, Italian-American novelist, Yrbk 1947, *Obit* Jan 1953

Borglum, Gutzon, American sculptor and painter, *Obit* Apr 1941

Borgnine, Ernest, American actor, Apr 1956, *Obit* Yrbk 2012

Boring, E. G., American psychologist, Mar 1962, *Obit* Sept 1968

Boris, Feb 1941, *Obit* Yrbk 1991

Boris Vladimirovitch, *Obit* Yrbk 1943

Borlaug, Norman, American plant pathologist and geneticist, July 1971, *Obit* Yrbk 2009

Borman, Frank, American astronaut and engineering executive, Mar 1969, Apr 1980

Born, Max, German physicist, May 1955, *Obit* Feb 1970

Borne, Mortimer, Apr 1954

Borno, Louis, *Obit* Sept 1942

Borodina, Olga, Russian opera singer, Feb 2002

Borofsky, Jonathan, American artist, July 1985

Boros, Julius, American golfer, Nov 1968, *Obit* Aug 1994

Borowitz, Andy, American humorist, July 2007

Borst, Lyle B., American nuclear physicist, July 1954, *Obit* Yrbk 2002

Bortz, Edward Leroy, physician, Sept 1947, *Obit* Apr 1970

Borysenko, Joan, psychologist and biologist, Oct 1996

Borzage, Frank, motion picture director, Yrbk 1946, *Obit* Sept 1962

Bosch, Carl, German chemist, *Obit* Jan 1940

Bosch, Juan, Dominican president, June 1963, *Obit* Feb 2002

Bosch, Robert, German manufacturing executive, *Obit* Apr 1942

Bose, Subhas Chandra, Indian political leader, June 1944, *Obit* Yrbk 1945

Bosh, Chris, American basketball player, Mar 2010

Boskin, Michael J., American economist and government official, Sept 1989

Bosone, Reva Zilpha Beck, congresswoman and judge, Jan 1949

Boss, Alan P., American astrophysicist, Apr 2010

Bosselaar, Laure-Anne, Belgian poet, Sept 2006

Bossy, Mike, Canadian hockey player, June 1981

Bostic, Onika, Trinidadian singer, Jan 2004

Bostridge, Ian, British classical singer, Jan 2006

Bostwick, Arthur Elmore, American librarian, *Obit* Apr 1942

Bosustow, Stephen, June 1958

Bosworth, Hobart, American actor, *Obit* Feb 1944

Botero, Fernando, Colombian painter and sculptor, Mar 1980

Botha, Pieter W., South African president, Sept 1979, *Obit* Yrbk 2007

Botha, R. F., South African diplomat, May 1984

Bothe, Walther Wilhelm, German physicist, May 1955, *Obit* Apr 1957

Bothwell, Jean, Yrbk 1946

Botin, Ana Patricia, Spanish banker, Jan 2005

Botstein, Leon, college president, Aug 1996

Botta, Mario, Swiss architect, Jan 2007

Botvinnik, M. M., Russian chess player, June 1965, *Obit* July 1995

Bouchard, Lucien, Canadian political leader, Apr 1999

Boucher, Anthony, American mystery and science fiction writer, June 1962, *Obit* June 1968

Boudreau, Lou, American baseball player and manager, Aug 1942, *Obit* Oct 2001

Boulanger, Nadia, French conductor and teacher, May 1962, *Obit* Jan 1980

Boulding, Kenneth Ewart, American economist and pacifist, Mar 1965, *Obit* May 1993

Boulez, Pierre, French composer and conductor, Mar 1969

Boult, Adrian Cedric, English conductor, Mar 1946, *Obit* Apr 1983

Boulud, Daniel, French chef and restaurateur, Jan 2005

Boumedienne, Houari, Algerian president, Jan 1971, *Obit* Feb 1979

Bourassa, Robert, Canadian economist and political leader, Sept 1976, *Obit* Jan 1997

Bourdain, Anthony, American chef, writer and television personality, Jan 2006

Bourdon, Rob, American drummer, Mar 2002

Bourgeois, Louise, American sculptor, Oct 1983, *Obit* Yrbk 2010

Bourges-Maunoury, Maurice, French political leader, July 1957

Bourguiba, Habib, Tunisian president, Sept 1955, *Obit* Aug 2000

Bourke-White, Margaret, American photographer, Jan 1940, *Obit* Oct 1971

Bourne, Jonathan, American senator, *Obit* Oct 1940

Bourne, Matthew, English dancer and choreographer, Jan 2005

Bourne, St. Clair, American documentary filmmaker, June 2000, *Obit* Mar 2008

Bouteflika, Abdelaziz, Algerian president, Feb 1976

Boutell, Clarence B., July 1946

Boutelle, Richard S., Sept 1951

Bouton, Jim, American baseball player and sportscaster, Oct 1971

Boutros-Ghali, Boutros, Egyptian diplomat and United Nations secretary-general, Apr 1992

Bova, Raoul, Italian actor, Jan 2004

Bove, Jose, French farmer, Jan 2002

Bovet, Daniel, Swiss-Italian pharmacologist, Jan 1958, *Obit* June 1992

Bowater, Eric Vansittart, English paper industry executive, Sept 1956, *Obit* Nov 1962

Bowden, Bobby, American football coach, Nov 1996

Bowden, Mark, American journalist, Jan 2002

Bowditch, Richard L., July 1953, *Obit* Nov 1959

Bowe, Riddick, American boxer, June 1996

Bowen, Catherine Drinker, American biographer, July 1944, *Obit* Yrbk 1973

Bowen, Ira S., astrophysicist, June 1951, *Obit* Apr 1973

Bowen, Otis R., American governor and Secretary of health and human services, Nov 1986, *Obit* Yrbk 2013

Bowen, William G., American college president and foundation official, May 1973

Bower, Bertha Muzzy, American novelist, *Obit* Sept 1940

Bowers, Claude Gernade, American journalist, historian and diplomat, Sept 1941, *Obit* Mar 1958

Bowers, Faubion, critic, Sept 1959, *Obit* May 2000

Bowes, Edward, radio performer, Mar 1941, *Obit* July 1946

Bowie, David, English singer and songwriter, Oct 1976, Nov 1994

Bowie, Edward Hall, *Obit* Sept 1943

Bowker, Albert H., American college administrator, Jan 1966, *Obit* Yrbk 2008

Bowles, Chester, American government official and diplomat, Sept 1943, Jan 1957, *Obit* July 1986

Bowles, Erskine, American presidential adviser, Aug 1998

Bowles, Paul, American composer, novelist, short story writer, poet and travel writer, Oct 1990, *Obit* Feb 2000

Bowman, George Ernest, American historian, *Obit* Nov 1941

Bowman, Isaiah, American geographer, Jan 1945, *Obit* Feb 1950

Bowman, Scotty, Canadian hockey coach, Jan 1999

Bowron, Fletcher, American mayor, Feb 1950, *Obit* Nov 1968

Boxer, Barbara, American senator, Apr 1994

Boxx, Shannon, American soccer player, May 2011

Boy George, British pop singer and songwriter, Oct 1985

Boyce, Westray Battle, Sept 1945, *Obit* Mar 1972

Boyd, Alan S., American Secretary of transportation and railroad executive, Mar 1965

Boyd, James, Mar 1949

Boyd, James, author, *Obit* Apr 1944

Boyd, John W., American farmers' association executive, Feb 2001

Boyd, Julian P., historian and librarian, June 1976, *Obit* Aug 1980

Boyd, Louise Arner, American explorer, Sept 1960, *Obit* Nov 1972

Boyd, Malcolm, American clergyman, gay rights activist and writer, Mar 1968

Boyd, Stephen, Irish actor, Yrbk 1961, *Obit* Aug 1977

Boyd, William, American actor, Mar 1950, *Obit* Nov 1972

Boyd-Orr, John Boyd Orr, Scottish agriculturist, June 1946, *Obit* Sept 1971

Boyer, Charles, French actor, Feb 1943, *Obit* Oct 1978

Boyer, Ernest L., American educator and foundation official, Jan 1988, *Obit* Feb 1996

Boyer, Harold Raymond, Feb 1952

Boyer, Ken, baseball player, Mar 1966, *Obit* Oct 1982

Boyer, Lucien, *Obit* Aug 1942

Boyer, Marion W., chemical engineer, Jan 1951, *Obit* Jan 1983

Boylan, Robert P., Apr 1950

Boyle, Hal, June 1945, *Obit* May 1974

Boyle, Kay, American novelist, short story writer and poet, June 1942, *Obit* Feb 1993

Boyle, T. Coraghessan, American novelist and short story writer, Jan 1991

Boyle, Tony, American labor leader, July 1970, *Obit* July 1985

Boyle, William Marshall, American political leader and lawyer, June 1949, *Obit* Nov 1961

Boylston, Helen Dore, author, July 1942, *Obit* Nov 1984

Bozize, Francois, Central African Republic general and president, Jan 2005

Brabazon of Tara, John Theodore Cuthbert Moore-Brabazon, British aviator and government official, May 1941

Brabeck-Letmathe, Peter, Austrian-Swiss food industry executive, Jan 2005

Bracco, Roberto, *Obit* June 1943

Brace, Gerald Warner, author, Yrbk 1947, *Obit* Sept 1978

Bracken, Brendan Bracken, British cabinet member, Yrbk 1941

Bracken, Eddie, American actor, Oct 1944, *Obit* Feb 2003

Brackett, Charles, American screenwriter and motion picture producer, Feb 1951, *Obit* Apr 1969

Brackman, Robert, painter, July 1953, *Obit* Sept 1980

Bradbury, James H., *Obit* Yrbk 1940

Bradbury, Norris Edwin, physicist, Apr 1949, *Obit* Nov 1997

Bradbury, Ray, American science fiction writer, June 1953, July 1982, *Obit* Yrbk 2012

Braddock, E. M., British labor leader and member of Parliament, July 1957, *Obit* Jan 1971

Brademas, John, American congressman and university president, May 1977

Braden, Spruille, American diplomat, Sept 1945, *Obit* Mar 1978

Bradford, Barbara Taylor, English novelist, Oct 1991

Bradford, Robert F., governor, Yrbk 1948, *Obit* May 1983

Bradlee, Benjamin C., American newspaper editor, Sept 1975

Bradley, Bill, American senator, July 1965, Sept 1982

Bradley, Bob, American soccer coach, Aug 2010

Bradley, David, American nonfiction author, surgeon and state legislator, Apr 1949

Bradley, Ed, American television reporter, May 1988, *Obit* Yrbk 2007

Bradley, Omar Nelson, American general, July 1943, *Obit* May 1981

Bradley, Pat, golfer, Feb 1994

Bradley, Preston, Mar 1956

Bradley, Raymond S., July 2012

Bradley, Tom, American lawyer and mayor, Nov 1973, Oct 1992, *Obit* Jan 1999

Bradshaw, John E., American philosopher, educator and writer, Apr 1993

Bradshaw, Lillian Moore, American library director, June 1970

Bradshaw, Terry, American football player, Apr 1979

Bradshaw, Thornton F., petroleum and electronics executive, June 1982, *Obit* Feb 1989

Brady, James S., American presidential press secretary and gun control activist, Oct 1991

Brady, Nicholas F., American Secretary of the treasury, Nov 1988

Brady, Sarah, American gun control activist and wife of James S. Brady, Oct 1996

Brady, Tom, American football player, Aug 2004

Brady, William Thomas, food industry executive, Jan 1961, *Obit* July 1984

Bragdon, Claude Fayette, American architect, *Obit* Oct 1946

Bragdon, Helen D., Feb 1951

Bragg, Rick, American journalist and memoirist, Apr 2002

Bragg, William Henry, British physicist, *Obit* Apr 1942

Brailowsky, Alexander, French pianist, June 1956, *Obit* June 1976

Braly, Angela F., American health insurance executive, Aug 2011

Bramah, Ernest, English author, *Obit* Sept 1942

Brameld, Theodore, professor of education, June 1967, *Obit* Jan 1988

Bramuglia, Juan Atilio, Argentine cabinet member, May 1949, *Obit* Nov 1962

Branagh, Kenneth, Irish actor and director, Apr 1997

Branch, Michelle, American singer and songwriter, May 2005

Brancusi, Constantin, Romanian sculptor, Sept 1955, *Obit* June 1957

Brand, Oscar, folklorist, June 1962

Brand, Russell, British comedian and actor, Jan 2011

Brandauer, Klaus Maria, Austrian actor, July 1990

Brandeis, Louis Dembitz, American Supreme Court justice, *Obit* Nov 1941

Brandenburg, William A., *Obit* Yrbk 1940

Brando, Marlon, American actor, Apr 1952, Mar 1974, *Obit* Yrbk 2004

Brandt, Bill, English photographer, Aug 1981, *Obit* Feb 1984

Brandt, Willy, German chancellor, June 1958, Yrbk 1973, *Obit* Nov 1992

Braniff, T. E., Apr 1952, *Obit* Mar 1954

Branly, Edouard, French physicist and inventor, *Obit* Apr 1940

Brannaman, Buck, American horse trainer and motivational speaker, Sept 2011

Brannaman, Ray H., Nov 1947

Brannan, Charles F., American Secretary of agriculture, Sept 1948

Bransome, Edward D., American truck company executive, Apr 1952

Branson, Richard, British financier, Feb 1995

Brantley, Ben, American drama critic, Aug 2011

Branzell, Karin, Swedish opera singer, Feb 1946, *Obit* Feb 1975

Braque, Georges, French painter, Nov 1949, *Obit* Oct 1963

Brattain, Walter Houser, American physicist, Sept 1957, *Obit* Nov 1987

Brauchitsch, Walther von, German field marshal, Mar 1940, *Obit* Yrbk 1948

Braudel, Fernand, French historian, Apr 1985, *Obit* Jan 1986

Braun, Werner, German microbiologist, June 1957, *Obit* Jan 1973

Bravo, Ellen, feminist, Aug 1997

Bravo, Rose Marie, American clothing industry executive, June 2004

Braxton, Toni, American singer, Sept 2000

Bray, Robert S., Feb 1966, *Obit* Feb 1975

Brazauskas, Algirdas, Lithuanian president and prime minister, Jan 2002, *Obit* Yrbk 2010

Brazelton, T. Berry, pediatrician, Oct 1993

Brazile, Donna, American political consultant, Mar 2006

Brazzi, Rossano, Italian actor, May 1961, *Obit* Mar 1995

Bream, Julian, English guitarist, Mar 1968

Breathitt, Edward T., American governor, July 1964, *Obit* Yrbk 2004

Breazeal, Cynthia, American electronics engineer and inventor, June 2011

Breckenridge, L. P., American mechanical engineer, *Obit* Oct 1940

Breckinridge, Aida de Costa, American social welfare leader, June 1954, *Obit* July 1962

Breech, Ernest, Sept 1955, *Obit* Aug 1978

Breedlove, Craig, American automobile racing driver, Sept 1966

Breen, Edward D., American electronics industry executive, July 2004

Breen, Joseph Ignatius, American motion picture censor and association executive, July 1950, *Obit* Jan 1966

Bregovic, Goran, Bosnian composer, Jan 2006

Breitmeyer, Philip, *Obit* Jan 1942

Brel, Jacques, French singer and songwriter, Mar 1971, *Obit* Nov 1978

Bremmer, Ian, American international relations specialist, Aug 2013

Brenan, Gerald, English author, poet and critic, July 1986, *Obit* Mar 1987

Brendel, Alfred, Austrian pianist, July 1977

Brenly, Bob, American baseball player and manager, Apr 2002

Brennan, Edward A., American retail executive, Nov 1990, *Obit* Yrbk 2008

Brennan, Francis, Oct 1967, *Obit* Sept 1968

Brennan, Peter J., American Secretary of labor, Apr 1973, *Obit* Jan 1997

Brennan, Walter, actor, May 1941, *Obit* Nov 1974

Brennan, William J., American Supreme Court justice, June 1957, *Obit* Oct 1997

Brenner, Charles H., forensic mathematician, Oct 2000

Brenner, David, American comedian, Mar 1987

Brenner, Frederic, French photographer, Jan 2004

Brenner, Sydney, British geneticist, Jan 2007

Brentano, Arthur, *Obit* Mar 1944

Brentano, Heinrich von, Feb 1955, *Obit* Jan 1965

Brenton, W. Harold, Jan 1953

Brereton, Lewis H., American general, Yrbk 1943, *Obit* Oct 1967

Breslin, Howard, Yrbk 1958, *Obit* July 1964

Breslin, Jimmy, American author and columnist, Yrbk 1973

Bressanutti, Daniel, Belgian rock musician, Jan 2006

Bresson, Robert, French film director, Jan 1971, *Obit* June 2000

Brett, George, American baseball player, July 1981

Brett, George H., American air force general, June 1942

Brett, George Platt, publisher, Yrbk 1948, *Obit* May 1984

Breuer, Lee, dramatist and director, Oct 1999

Breuer, Marcel, American architect and furniture designer, Sept 1941, June 1960, *Obit* Aug 1981

Brewer, Jan, American governor, Jan 2011

Brewer, Roy M., American labor leader, Sept 1953, *Obit* Yrbk 2006

Brewster, Benjamin, American bishop, *Obit* Mar 1941

Brewster, Chauncey B., American bishop, *Obit* June 1941

Brewster, Kingman, American college president and diplomat, May 1964, Sept 1979, *Obit* Jan 1989

Brewster, Owen, American senator, May 1947, *Obit* Feb 1962

Breyer, Stephen G., American Supreme Court justice, June 1996

Breytenbach, Breyten, South African poet and painter, June 1986

Brezhnev, Leonid Il'ich, Soviet communist leader, Jan 1963, Nov 1978, *Obit* Jan 1983

Brice, Fanny, American singer and comedian, June 1946, *Obit* July 1951

Brick, John, Yrbk 1953, *Obit* Yrbk 1973

Brickell, Herschel, Nov 1945, *Obit* July 1952

Bricker, John William, American senator and governor, Apr 1943, July 1956, *Obit* May 1986

Brickner, Richard M., Sept 1943

Brico, Antonia, conductor, Sept 1948, *Obit* Oct 1989

Bridge, Frank, English composer and conductor, *Obit* Mar 1941

Bridges, Harry, American labor leader, Nov 1940, May 1950, *Obit* May 1990

Bridges, Jeff, American actor, Mar 1991

Bridges, Lloyd, actor, July 1990, *Obit* May 1998

Bridges, Robert, *Obit* Nov 1941

Bridges, Styles, American governor and senator, Mar 1948, *Obit* Jan 1962

Bridgewater, Dee Dee, American jazz singer, Oct 2008

Bridgman, P. W., American physicist, Apr 1955, *Obit* Nov 1961

Brier, Bob, American Egyptologist, Sept 2002

Brier, Howard M., Yrbk 1951

Briggs, Ellis Ormsbee, diplomat, Apr 1965, *Obit* Apr 1976

Briggs, Eugene S., Oct 1948

Briggs, James E., June 1957, *Obit* Aug 1979

Brigham, Carl C., *Obit* Mar 1943

Brigham, Clarence Saunders, librarian, July 1959, *Obit* Oct 1963

Brill, Steven, American lawyer, journalist and television executive, Nov 1997

Brimmer, Andrew F., American economist and financial consultant, July 1968, *Obit* Yrbk 2012

Brin, Sergey, American Internet search engine executive, Oct 2001

Brin, Sergey; and Page, Larry, Oct 2001

Brind, Patrick, British admiral, Nov 1952, *Obit* Jan 1964

Briney, Nancy, Jan 1954

Brink, Carol Ryrie, American children's author, Yrbk 1946

Brinkley, Christie, American model, Feb 1994

Brinkley, David, American television newscaster and moderator, Mar 1960, Sept 1987, *Obit* Sept 2003

Brinkley, John Richard, American physician and swindler, *Obit* July 1942

Brinkley, Nell, *Obit* Yrbk 1944

Brinton, Crane, American historian, June 1959, *Obit* Nov 1968

Brinton, Howard H., American educator, July 1949, *Obit* Yrbk 1984

Briscoe, Connie, American romance novelist, Jan 2000

Briscoe, Robert, Irish member of Parliament and mayor, May 1957, *Obit* July 1969

Bristol, Arthur LeRoy, *Obit* June 1942

Bristol, Lee H., Sept 1962

Bristow, Gwen, author, Yrbk 1940, *Obit* Yrbk 1984

Bristow, Joseph Little, *Obit* Sept 1944

Brittan, Leon, British cabinet member and European Commission official, Aug 1994

Britten, Benjamin, English composer, Oct 1942, Apr 1961, *Obit* Feb 1977

Britton, Edgar C., Apr 1952, *Obit* Oct 1962

Bro, Marguerite Harmon, Yrbk 1952

Broadbent, Edward, Canadian political leader, May 1988

Broadhurst, Harry, May 1943

Brock, Lou, American baseball player, June 1975

Brock, William Emerson, American senator and Secretary of labor, May 1971

Brockmeier, Kevin, American novelist, short story writer and children's author, May 2010

Brode, Mildred H., Sept 1963

Brode, Wallace R., June 1958, *Obit* Oct 1974

Broder, David S., American columnist and political commentator, Sept 2010, *Obit* Yrbk 2011

Broder, Samuel, physician and government official, Aug 1992

Broderick, Matthew, American actor, May 1987

Brodeur, Martin, Canadian hockey player, Nov 2002

Brodie, Bernard B., American pharmacologist, Sept 1969, *Obit* May 1989

Brodkey, Harold, author, Apr 1989, *Obit* Apr 1996

Brodsky, Joseph, Russian poet, July 1982, *Obit* Apr 1996

Brody, Adrien, American actor, July 2003

Brody, Jane E., American columnist and nutritionist, Feb 1986

Broeg, Bob, American sportswriter, May 2002

Broemel, Carl, American rock guitarist and singer, Nov 2008

Brogan, Denis William, Scottish political scientist and historian, Yrbk 1947, *Obit* Feb 1974

Broglie, Louis de, French physicist, Sept 1955, *Obit* May 1987

Brokaw, Tom, American television news anchor, May 1981, Nov 2002

Brokenshire, Norman, May 1950, *Obit* June 1965

Brolin, Josh, American actor, Feb 2008

Bromfield, Louis, novelist, July 1944, *Obit* May 1956

Bromley, Dorothy Dunbar, journalist and feminist, Apr 1946, *Obit* Feb 1986

Bronfman, Edgar M., American liquor industry executive, July 1974

Bronfman, Edgar M., American recording industry executive, Oct 1995

Bronfman, Yefim, American pianist, Jan 2007

Bronk, Detlev Wulf, American college president and biophysicist, Oct 1949, *Obit* Jan 1976

Bronowski, Jacob, British mathematician, Sept 1958, *Obit* Oct 1974

Bronson, Charles, American actor, Mar 1975, *Obit* Mar 2004

Brook, Alexander, painter, Apr 1941, *Obit* Apr 1980

Brook, Peter, English director and dramatist, May 1961

Brooke, Edward, American senator, Apr 1967

Brooke-Popham, Robert, Oct 1941, *Obit* Jan 1954

Brookeborough, Basil Stanlake Brooke, Northern Ireland political leader, June 1948, *Obit* Oct 1973

Brookes, George S., Aug 1940

Brookhart, Smith W., American senator, *Obit* Jan 1945

Brookner, Anita, English novelist and art historian, Feb 1989

Brooks & Dunn (Musical group), Sept 2004

Brooks, Albert, American actor, director and screenwriter, Apr 1997

Brooks, Angela, American architect, Mar 1970

Brooks, C. Wayland, Sept 1947, *Obit* Mar 1957

Brooks, D. W., June 1951

Brooks, David, American journalist and political commentator, Apr 2004

Brooks, Diana D., American art dealer and auctioneer, June 1998

Brooks, Donald, American fashion and costume designer, Mar 1972, *Obit* Yrbk 2005

Brooks, Garth, American country singer, Mar 1992

Brooks, Geraldine, Australian journalist, Aug 2006

Brooks, Gwendolyn, American poet, June 1950, July 1977, *Obit* Feb 2001

Brooks, Jack, congressman, June 1992, *Obit* Yrbk 2013

Brooks, James, painter, Feb 1959, *Obit* May 1992

Brooks, James L., American screenwriter, director and producer, Apr 1998

Brooks, Kix, American country singer and songwriter, Sept 2004

Brooks, Louise, American actress, Apr 1984, *Obit* Oct 1985

Brooks, Matilda Moldenhauer, physiologist, Nov 1941

Brooks, Mel, American actor, writer, director and producer, Sept 1974

Brooks, Overton, June 1957, *Obit* Yrbk 1961

Brooks, Robert C., *Obit* Apr 1941

Brooks, Van Wyck, literary critic and biographer, June 1941, Sept 1960, *Obit* June 1963

Brooks, Vincent, American general, June 2003

Brophy, Thomas D'Arcy, Sept 1952, *Obit* Oct 1967

Brosio, Manlio, Italian diplomat, Sept 1955, *Obit* May 1980

Brosnan, Jim, American baseball player and sportswriter, Nov 1964

Brosnan, Pierce, Irish actor, Jan 1997

Brossard, Edgar Bernard, July 1954

Brothers, Joyce, psychologist, Apr 1971, *Obit* Yrbk 2013

Brough, Louise, American tennis player, June 1948

Broun, Heywood, American journalist, *Obit* Jan 1940

Brouwer, Dirk, Mar 1951, *Obit* Mar 1966

Browder, Earl, American communist leader, Oct 1944, *Obit* Sept 1973

Browdy, Benjamin G., July 1951

Brower, Charles H., advertising executive, Feb 1965, *Obit* Nov 1984

Brower, David, American conservationist, June 1973, *Obit* Feb 2001

Brown, A. Ten Eyck, *Obit* July 1940

Brown, Aaron, American television news anchor, Mar 2003

Brown, Albert Eger, Jan 1948

Brown, Alberta L., May 1958

Brown, Bobby, American singer, Apr 1991

Brown, Campbell, American television news anchor, Nov 2008

Brown, Carleton, *Obit* Aug 1941

Brown, Cecil, radio newscaster, Mar 1942, *Obit* Jan 1988

Brown, Charles Harvey, librarian, Aug 1941, *Obit* Mar 1960

Brown, Charles L., American telephone executive, Sept 1981, *Obit* Yrbk 2004

Brown, Charles R., admiral, July 1958

Brown, Chuck, band leader and songwriter, *Obit* Yrbk 2012

Brown, Clarence J., American congressman, Feb 1947, *Obit* Nov 1965

Brown, Claude, American memoirist and journalist, Nov 1967, *Obit* Apr 2002

Brown, Dan, American novelist, May 2004

Brown, David M., American coal executive and veterans' leader, June 1950

Brown, Dee Alexander, American historian and novelist, Aug 1979, *Obit* Mar 2003

Brown, Dustin, Jamaican tennis player, Oct 2010

Brown, Edmund G., American governor, Mar 1960, *Obit* Apr 1996

Brown, Francis Shunk, *Obit* Jan 1940

Brown, George Hay, marketing executive and consultant, Jan 1971

Brown, George S., American air force general, Oct 1975, *Obit* Feb 1979

Brown, Gilmor, July 1944

Brown, Gordon, British prime minister, Jan 2002

Brown, Harold, American Secretary of defense and physicist, Sept 1961, Oct 1977

Brown, Harrison Scott, American geochemist, July 1955, *Obit* Feb 1987

Brown, Helen Dawes, *Obit* Nov 1941

Brown, Helen Gurley, American magazine editor, Nov 1969, *Obit* Yrbk 2012

Brown, Irving, American labor leader, July 1951, *Obit* May 1989

Brown, J. Carter, American museum director, Apr 1976, *Obit* Yrbk 2002

Brown, James, American singer, Mar 1992, *Obit* Mar 2007

Brown, Jerry, American governor, Apr 1975

Brown, Jesse, American Secretary of veterans affairs, Nov 1993, *Obit* Yrbk 2002

Brown, Jim, American football player and actor, Sept 1964

Brown, Joe E., American actor, Feb 1945, *Obit* Sept 1973

Brown, John Franklin, *Obit* Mar 1940

Brown, John Mason, drama critic and biographer, Apr 1942, *Obit* May 1969

Brown, Junior, American country singer and guitarist, Nov 2004

Brown, Kwame, American basketball player, Feb 2002

Brown, Larry, American basketball coach, Apr 1996

Brown, Larry, American football player, Mar 1973

Brown, Lee Patrick, American mayor, Sept 2002

Brown, Lester Russell, American agriculturist and environmentalist, Jan 1993

Brown, Lewis H, Oct 1947, *Obit* Mar 1951

Brown, Newell, government official, Sept 1959, *Obit* Sept 2000

Brown, Perry J., Apr 1949

Brown, Prentiss M., American senator, Jan 1943, *Obit* Feb 1974

Brown, Rita Mae, American novelist, poet, essayist and screenwriter, Sept 1986

Brown, Robert McAfee, American theologian and human rights activist, May 1965, *Obit* Nov 2001

Brown, Ron, American Secretary of commerce, July 1989, *Obit* June 1996

Brown, Ronald K., American choreographer, May 2002

Brown, Scott, American senator, Aug 2010

Brown, Sterling Allen, American poet and literary critic, Aug 1982, *Obit* Apr 1989

Brown, Tina, British journalist and magazine editor, Feb 1990

Brown, Tony, American television talk show host and producer, Feb 1997

Brown, Trisha, American dancer and choreographer, Apr 1997

Brown, Troy, American football player, Oct 2007

Brown, Virginia Mae, lawyer and government official, July 1970, *Obit* May 1991

Brown, Willie Lewis, American mayor and political leader, Apr 1997

Brownback, Sam, American senator, Apr 2008

Browne, Coral, Australian actress, Yrbk 1959, *Obit* July 1991

Browne, E. John P., British petroleum industry executive, Jan 2002

Browne, Edward E., *Obit* Jan 1946

Browne, George Elmer, American painter, *Obit* Sept 1946

Browne, Jackson, American singer and songwriter, Oct 1989

Browne, Sidney Jane, *Obit* Oct 1941

Brownell, Herbert, American Attorney general, Aug 1944, Feb 1954, *Obit* July 1996

Brownell, Samuel Miller, educator, Feb 1954, *Obit* Jan 1991

Browner, Carol M., American environmentalist and government official, May 1994

Browning, Frederick, June 1943, *Obit* Apr 1965

Browning, John, American pianist, May 1969, *Obit* June 2003

Browning, Webster E., *Obit* June 1942

Brownlow, Kevin, English television producer and director, Mar 1992

Brownmiller, Susan, journalist and feminist, Jan 1978

Brownson, Charles B., July 1955

Brownson, Josephine, American children's author and social worker, Mar 1940

Broyhill, Joel T., American congressman, May 1974, *Obit* Feb 2007

Brubeck, Dave, American jazz pianist and composer, Mar 1956, Apr 1993, *Obit* Yrbk 2013

Bruce, David K. E., American diplomat, June 1949, Sept 1961, *Obit* Feb 1978

Bruce, Howard, Sept 1948, *Obit* Sept 1961

Bruce, James, diplomat, Jan 1949, *Obit* Sept 1980

Bruce, Louis Rooks, American government official, May 1972, *Obit* July 1989

Bruce, Robert Randolph, *Obit* Apr 1942

Bruce, William Cabell, author and senator, *Obit* June 1946

Brucker, Wilber M., American Secretary of the army, Sept 1955, *Obit* Yrbk 1968

Bruckheimer, Jerry, American film producer, Mar 1999

Bruckner, Henry, *Obit* June 1942

Brueggemann, Ingar, German family planning advocate, Nov 2001

Bruel, Patrick, French singer and actor, Jan 2007

Bruhn, Erik, Danish ballet dancer and director, Apr 1959, *Obit* May 1986

Bruijn, Inge de, Dutch swimmer, Jan 2004

Brule, Tyler, Canadian magazine publisher, Mar 2011

Brumel, Valerii, Russian high jumper, Apr 1963, *Obit* June 2003

Brunauer, Esther Caukin, American diplomat, Nov 1947, *Obit* Sept 1959

Brundage, Avery, American engineer and Olympics executive, Jan 1948, *Obit* Aug 1975

Brundage, Percival F., American accountant and government official, Apr 1957

Brundtland, Gro Harlem, Norwegian prime minister and international health official, Nov 1981

Bruner, Jerome Seymour, American psychologist and law professor, Oct 1984

Bruni-Sarkozy, Carla, Italian model, singer and wife of French president Nicolas Sarkozy, Jan 2007

Brunner, Edmund de Schweinitz, Sept 1958, *Obit* Feb 1974

Brunner, Jean Adam, Sept 1945, *Obit* June 1951

Bruns, Franklin R., May 1954

Brunsdale, Clarence Norman, governor and banker, Sept 1954

Brunson, Doyle, American poker player, Sept 2007

Brush, George de Forest, American painter, *Obit* June 1941

Brustein, Robert, American theatrical director and critic, Aug 1975

Brustlein, Daniel, American painter, Sept 1941

Bruton, John, Irish prime minister, Nov 1996

Bryan, Charles W., governor, *Obit* Apr 1945

Bryan, Ernest R., July 1950, *Obit* Feb 1955

Bryan, George Sands, *Obit* Feb 1944

Bryan, James E., American library director and consultant, June 1962

Bryan, Julien, American photographer and documentary filmmaker, July 1940, *Obit* Jan 1975

Bryant, Anita, American singer, Nov 1975

Bryant, Bear, American football coach, June 1980, *Obit* Mar 1983

Bryant, Benjamin, Nov 1943

Bryant, C. Farris, American governor, Sept 1961, *Obit* Yrbk 2002

Bryant, Gyude, Liberian businessman and interim leader, Jan 2005

Bryce, Elizabeth Marion, *Obit* Jan 1940

Bryce, Quentin, Australian governor general, Feb 2010

Brynner, Rock, American historian and novelist, Mar 2005

Brynner, Yul, American actor, Sept 1956, *Obit* Nov 1985

Bryson, David, American guitarist, Mar 2003

Bryson, Lyman, educator, Sept 1940, Sept 1951, *Obit* Feb 1960

Brzezinski, Mika, American television news anchor, July 2010

Brzezinski, Zbigniew, American political scientist and presidential adviser, Apr 1970

Buatta, Mario, American interior designer, May 1991

Buber, Martin, Israeli philosopher, June 1953, *Obit* July 1965

Bubka, Sergei, Ukrainian pole vaulter, July 1996

Buble, Michael, Canadian singer, May 2009

Buchan, John, Scottish novelist, historian and Governor General of Canada, Jan 1940

Buchanan, Edna, American journalist and novelist, Sept 1997

Buchanan, Frank, Feb 1951

Buchanan, Patrick, American political commentator, Aug 1985

Buchanan, Scott Milross, American college dean and educational consultant, Sept 1962, *Obit* May 1968

Buchanan, Thomas Drysdale, *Obit* Apr 1940

Buchanan, Wiley T., diplomat, Nov 1957, *Obit* Mar 1986

Bucher, Walter Herman, geologist, Feb 1957, *Obit* Apr 1965

Buchholz, Horst, German actor, Mar 1960, *Obit* Aug 2003

Buchman, Frank Nathan Daniel, missionary, Oct 1940, *Obit* Nov 1961

Buchwald, Art, American humorist, Jan 1960, *Obit* May 2007

Buck, Dorothea Dutcher, Sept 1947

Buck, Frank, big game hunter, June 1943, *Obit* Apr 1950

Buck, Gene, Feb 1941, *Obit* May 1957

Buck, Paul Herman, historian, July 1955, *Obit* Apr 1989

Buck, Pearl S., American novelist, July 1956, *Obit* Apr 1973

Buck, Solon Justus, historian and archivist, May 1947, *Obit* July 1962

Buckingham, Marcus, American management consultant, Aug 2006

Buckland, Jon, English guitarist, May 2004

Buckley, Christopher Taylor, American novelist, humorist and editor, Apr 1997

Buckley, George W., British manufacturing executive, Sept 2011

Buckley, James L., American senator and judge, Oct 1971

Buckley, Priscilla L., American magazine editor, Apr 2002, *Obit* Yrbk 2012

Buckley, William F., American magazine editor, columnist

and novelist, June 1962, Oct 1982, *Obit* June 2008

Buckmaster, Henrietta, Yrbk 1946, *Obit* June 1983

Buckner, Emory Roy, American lawyer, *Obit* May 1941

Buckner, Simon Bolivar, Oct 1942, *Obit* July 1945

Budd, Edward G., July 1949, *Obit* July 1971

Budd, Ralph, July 1940, *Obit* Mar 1962

Budennyi, Semen M., Soviet field marshal, Sept 1941, *Obit* Yrbk 1973

Budenz, Louis F., American newspaper editor, June 1951, *Obit* June 1972

Budge, Don, American tennis player, June 1941, *Obit* June 2000

Budge, Hamer H., American congressman and regulatory agency official, Yrbk 1970, *Obit* Yrbk 2003

Budington, William S., June 1964

Buechner, Frederick, American novelist and clergyman, Yrbk 1959

Buechner, Thomas S., American painter and museum director, Feb 1961, *Obit* Yrbk 2010

Buell, Raymond Leslie, *Obit* Apr 1946

Bueno, Maria, American tennis player, Apr 1965

Buergenthal, Thomas, American judge and human rights activist, Jan 2009

Buetow, Herbert P., Mar 1960, *Obit* Mar 1972

Buffet, Bernard, French painter, Apr 1959, *Obit* Feb 2000

Buffett, Jimmy, American singer and songwriter, Mar 1999

Buffett, Warren E., American financier, Nov 1987

Buffum, Charles A., *Obit* Sept 1941

Buford, John Lester, Apr 1956

Bugas, John S., automobile executive, Yrbk 1947, *Obit* Feb 1983

Bugher, John C., Apr 1953

Buitoni, Giovanni, June 1962, *Obit* Mar 1979

Bujones, Fernando, American ballet dancer, Jan 1976, *Obit* Yrbk 2006

Bukovskii, Vladimir Konstantinovich, Soviet dissident, Mar 1978

Bukowski, Charles, American poet, novelist and short story writer, Apr 1994, *Obit* Apr 1994

Buley, R. Carlyle, historian, July 1951, *Obit* June 1968

Bulgakov, Mikhail Afanas'evich, Russian novelist and dramatist, *Obit* Mar 1940

Bulganin, Nikolai Aleksandrovich, Soviet communist leader, Feb 1955, *Obit* Apr 1975

Bull, Johan, *Obit* Oct 1945

Bull, Odd, Nov 1968

Bullard, Edward Crisp, English geophysicist, Sept 1954, *Obit* May 1980

Bullins, Ed, American dramatist, May 1977

Bullis, Harry A., Oct 1946, *Obit* Jan 1964

Bullitt, William C., American diplomat, July 1940, *Obit* Apr 1967

Bullock, Sandra, American actress, Aug 1997

Bulosan, Carlos, American memoirist, poet and short story writer, Yrbk 1946, *Obit* Nov 1956

Bultmann, Rudolf Karl, German theologian, Jan 1972, *Obit* Sept 1976

Bumbry, Grace, American opera singer, Mar 1964

Bumiller, Elisabeth, American journalist, Sept 2008

Bumpers, Dale, American senator, Aug 1979

Bunau-Varilla, Philippe, *Obit* July 1940

Bunche, Ralph J., American diplomat, Feb 1948, *Obit* Jan 1972

Bundchen, Gisele, Brazilian model, Jan 2007

Bundesen, Herman N., Oct 1948, *Obit* Nov 1960

Bundy, McGeorge, American presidential adviser, Mar 1962, *Obit* Jan 1997

Bundy, William P., American international relations specialist, June 1964, *Obit* Feb 2001

Bunge, Alejandro E., *Obit* July 1943

Bunim, Mary-Ellis, American television producer, May 2002, *Obit* Yrbk 2004

Bunim, Mary-Ellis; and Murray, Jonathan, May 2002

Bunker, Ellsworth, American diplomat, Apr 1954, Mar 1978, *Obit* Nov 1984

Bunker, George M., Apr 1957

Bunshaft, Gordon, American architect, Mar 1989, *Obit* Oct 1990

Bunting, Earl, American manufacturing association official, Feb 1947

Bunting-Smith, Mary Ingraham, microbiologist and college president, June 1967, *Obit* Apr 1998

Bunton, Jaleel, American drummer, Apr 2009

Bunuel, Luis, Mexican film director, Mar 1965, *Obit* Sept 1983

Burbank, Daniel, Astronaut, Sept 2012

Burbidge, Eleanor Margaret, Anglo-American astronomer, Nov 2000

Burch, Tory, American fashion designer and philanthropist, Sept 2010

Burchard, John E., Apr 1958, *Obit* Mar 1976

Burchfield, Charles Ephraim, American painter, May 1942, May 1961, *Obit* Mar 1967

Burdell, Edwin S., Feb 1952

Burdett, Winston, radio reporters, Oct 1943, *Obit* July 1993

Burdick, Charles K., *Obit* Aug 1940

Burdick, Quentin, American senator, May 1963, *Obit* Nov 1992

Burdick, Usher L., American congressman, Apr 1952, *Obit* Nov 1960

Buress, Hannibal, American comedian, Aug 2012

Burford, Anne McGill, American regulatory agency official, Sept 1982, *Obit* Yrbk 2004

Burger, Warren E., American Chief Justice of the Supreme Court, Nov 1969, *Obit* Aug 1995

Burgess, Anthony, English novelist and critic, May 1972, *Obit* Jan 1994

Burgess, Carter Lane, American airline and machinery industry executive and diplomat, Apr 1957, *Obit* Yrbk 2002

Burgess, Robert Wilbur, July 1960, *Obit* July 1969

Burgess, Warren, June 1949, *Obit* Nov 1978

Burgin, William O., *Obit* May 1946

Burke, Arleigh A., American admiral, Sept 1955, *Obit* Mar 1996

Burke, Brian, American hockey executive, Mar 2013

Burke, Charles H., *Obit* May 1944

Burke, Edmund J., *Obit* Feb 1941

Burke, Edward Raymond, Sept 1940, *Obit* Yrbk 1968

Burke, James, British science historian, Jan 2005

Burke, Michael, sports executive, Apr 1972, *Obit* Mar 1987

Burke, Thomas, English author, *Obit* Oct 1945

Burke, Thomas A., July 1954, *Obit* Jan 1972

Burke, William R., July 1961

Burke, Yvonne Brathwaite, American lawyer and congresswoman, Oct 1975

Burleigh, George William, *Obit* Apr 1940

Burleigh, Harry T., American singer and composer, Aug 1941, *Obit* Oct 1949

Burliuk, David Davidovich, Russian painter and poet, Apr 1940, *Obit* Mar 1967

Burnet, Frank Macfarlane, Australian bacteriologist, May 1954, *Obit* Oct 1985

Burnett, Carol, American actress, Jan 1962, Nov 1990

Burnett, Charles, American film director and screenwriter, Sept 1995

Burnett, Erin, American television news anchor, Sept 2012

Burnett, Hallie Southgate, author and editor, Yrbk 1954, *Obit* Nov 1991

Burnett, Mark, British television producer, May 2001

Burnett, Whit, magazine editor and author, Apr 1941, *Obit* June 1973

Burney, Leroy E., surgeon general, July 1957, *Obit* Oct 1998

Burnham, Donald C., Nov 1968

Burnham, Forbes, Guyanese president, Nov 1966, *Obit* Oct 1985

Burnham, James, American political and social philosopher, Nov 1941, *Obit* Jan 1988

Burning Flames (Musical group), Jan 2004

Burns and Allen, Mar 1951

Burns, Alan, Sept 1953

Burns, Arthur F., American economist and diplomat, Sept 1953, Aug 1976, *Obit* Aug 1987

Burns, Cecil Delisle, *Obit* Mar 1942

Burns, E. L. M., Canadian general, Feb 1955

Burns, Edward, American television scriptwriter and former police officer, May 2008

Burns, Edward McNall, Feb 1954

Burns, Eveline M., American economist and government official, Nov 1960, *Obit* Jan 1986

Burns, George, American comedian, Mar 1951, July 1976, *Obit* May 1996

Burns, H. S. M., May 1954, *Obit* Yrbk 1971

Burns, J. A., *Obit* Oct 1940

Burns, James MacGregor, American biographer and historian, Yrbk 1962

Burns, John A., American governor, Feb 1972, *Obit* June 1975

Burns, John Lawrence, youth organization official, Apr 1960, *Obit* Nov 1996

Burns, Ken, American documentary filmmaker, May 1992

Burns, Ursula, American office equipment industry executive, Oct 2007

Burnside, Iain, Scottish pianist, Jan 2004

Burnside, Jay, Finnish drummer, Jan 2003

Burpee, David, Mar 1955, *Obit* Aug 1980

Burr, Donald C., American airline executive, Sept 1986

Burr, Henry, *Obit* May 1941

Burr, Raymond, actor, Sept 1961, *Obit* Nov 1993

Burri, Rene, Swiss photojournalist, Jan 2007

Burris, Roland W., American senator, June 2009

Burroughs, Augusten, American novelist and memoirist, Apr 2004

Burroughs, William S., American novelist, Nov 1971, *Obit* Nov 1997

Burrows, Abe, American composer, lyricist, playwright and theatrical director, Nov 1951, *Obit* July 1985

Burrows, James, American television director, Oct 2006

Burrows, Millar, July 1956, *Obit* July 1980

Burrows, Stephen, American fashion designer, Nov 2003

Burstyn, Ellen, American actress, June 1975

Burstyn, Mike, American actor and singer, May 2005

Burton, Alan C., Sept 1956

Burton, Charles Emerson, *Obit* Oct 1940

Burton, Dan, American congressman, Sept 1998

Burton, Harold Hitz, American senator and Supreme Court justice, Apr 1945, *Obit* Jan 1965

Burton, Jean, Yrbk 1948

Burton, LeVar, American actor, Mar 2000

Burton, Lewis William, *Obit* Yrbk 1940

Burton, Richard, Welsh actor, Yrbk 1960, *Obit* Sept 1984

Burton, Richard, *Obit* May 1940

Burton, Tim, American film director, July 1991

Burton, Virginia Lee, American children's author, Sept 1943, *Obit* Yrbk 1968

Burtsev, Vladimir L'vovich, Russian revolutionary and journalist, *Obit* Yrbk 1942

Burtt, Ben, American motion picture sound designer, editor and documentary filmmaker, May 2003

Burwash, Lachlin Taylor, *Obit* Feb 1941

Buscaglia, Leo F., educator and lecturer, Oct 1983, *Obit* Aug 1998

Buscemi, Steve, American actor and filmmaker, Apr 1999

Busch, August Anheuser, American brewing industry and baseball executive, July 1973, *Obit* Nov 1989

Busch, Carl, *Obit* Feb 1944

Busch, Charles, American playwright, actor and female impersonator, June 1995

Busch, Fritz, German conductor, Jan 1946, *Obit* Oct 1951

Bush, Barbara, wife of American president George Bush, Oct 1989

Bush, Dorothy Vredenburgh, American political party secretary, July 1948

Bush, George, American president, Jan 1972, Sept 1983

Bush, George W., American president, Apr 1997, Aug 2001

Bush, Jeb, American governor, Feb 1999

Bush, Kate, English singer and songwriter, Mar 1995

Bush, Laura, wife of American president George W. Bush, June 2001

Bush, Prescott S., American banker, senator and father of President George Bush, May 1942, Jan 1954, *Obit* Yrbk 1972

Bush, Vannevar, American electrical engineer and inventor, Sept 1940, May 1947, *Obit* Sept 1974

Bush, Wendell T., *Obit* Mar 1941

Bushnell, Asa S., July 1952, *Obit* May 1975

Bushnell, Candace, American advice columnist and novelist, Nov 2003

Busiek, Kurt, American comic book writer, Sept 2005

Bustamante, Alexander, Jamaican prime minister, May 1965, *Obit* Sept 1977

Butcher, Susan, American sled dog racer, June 1991, *Obit* Yrbk 2006

Butcher, Willard C., banker, July 1980, *Obit* Yrbk 2012

Buthelezi, Mangosuthu, South African Zulu statesman, Oct 1986

Butler of Saffron Walden, Richard Austen Butler, British cabinet member, May 1944, Sept 1964, *Obit* May 1982

Butler, Hugh, American senator, Feb 1950, *Obit* Sept 1954

Butler, John, American dancer and choreographer, June 1955, *Obit* Nov 1993

Butler, John Marshall, American senator, May 1954, *Obit* May 1978

Butler, Marie Joseph, American nun and educator, *Obit* Jan 1940

Butler, Nevile Montagu, Apr 1941

Butler, Nicholas Murray, American educator, Nov 1940, *Obit* Yrbk 1947

Butler, Paul M., American political party leader, May 1955, *Obit* Feb 1962

Butler, R. Paul, American astrophysicist, Nov 2002

Butler, Reg, Sept 1956

Butler, Robert N., American gerontologist and psychiatrist, Jan 1997, *Obit* Yrbk 2010

Butler, Sally, Yrbk 1946

Butler, Smedley D., American Marine corps general, *Obit* Aug 1940

Butler, Will, American bassist, guitarist and percussionist, Jan 2007

Butler, Win, American singer and songwriter, Jan 2007

Buttenwieser, Benjamin Joseph, investment banker, Nov 1950, *Obit* Mar 1992

Butterfield, Roger Place, journalist, Mar 1948, *Obit* Yrbk 1991

Butterworth, Brad, New Zealand yacht racer, Jan 2007

Butterworth, Charles, *Obit* July 1946

Button, Dick, American figure skater and sportscaster, Mar 1949

Buttons, Red, American comedian and actor, Sept 1958, *Obit* Yrbk 2006

Butts, Alfred, American architect and game inventor, July 1954, *Obit* June 1993

Butts, Calvin O., American clergyman and civic leader, Feb 1999

Butz, Earl, American Secretary of agriculture, July 1972, *Obit* Yrbk 2008

Buzzi-Peccia, Arturo, *Obit* Oct 1943

Byas, Hugh, Mar 1943, *Obit* Apr 1945

Byatt, A. S., English novelist, short story writer and literary critic, Sept 1991

Byers, Margaretta, Sept 1941

Byington, Spring, actress, Sept 1956, *Obit* Oct 1971

Bykovskii, Valerii Fedorovich, Soviet astronaut, Jan 1965

Byrd, Charlie, American jazz guitarist, Oct 1967, *Obit* Mar 2000

Byrd, Harry Flood, American senator, Apr 1942, Sept 1955, *Obit* Yrbk 1966

Byrd, Richard Evelyn, American admiral and explorer, Oct 1942, May 1956, *Obit* May 1957

Byrd, Robert C., American senator, Mar 1960, Feb 1978, *Obit* Sept 2010

Byrd, Sam, Nov 1942, *Obit* Jan 1956

Byrne, Brendan T., May 1974

Byrne, David, Scottish-American rock singer and songwriter, June 1985

Byrne, Gabriel, Irish actor, May 1999

Byrne, Jane, American mayor, Jan 1980

Byrne, John, Anglo-Canadian comic book artist and writer, Oct 2000

Byrnes, James Francis, American senator, Supreme Court justice and Secretary of state, June 1941, Oct 1951, *Obit* June 1972

Byrnes, John W., American congressman, Oct 1960, *Obit* Mar 1985

Byroade, Henry Alfred, diplomat, Feb 1952, *Obit* Mar 1994

Byron, Arthur, *Obit* Sept 1943

Byron, Don, American jazz clarinetist, Sept 2000

Byron, William D., *Obit* Apr 1941

C

C. K., Louis, American comedian, Feb 2010

Caan, James, American actor, May 1976

Caballe, Montserrat, Spanish opera singer, June 1967

Caballero, Maria Cristina, Colombian journalist, Jan 2004

Cabot, John M., American diplomat, Sept 1953, *Obit* Apr 1981

Cabot, Thomas D., chemical executive and philanthropist, June 1951, *Obit* Aug 1995

Cabrera, Miguel, Venezuelan baseball player, July 2009

Caccia, Harold Anthony, British diplomat, Feb 1957, *Obit* Jan 1991

Cacoyannis, Michael, Greek film and theatrical director, May 1966, *Obit* Yrbk 2011

Caddell, Patrick, public opinion analyst and presidential adviser, Nov 1979

Cadell, Elizabeth, English author, Yrbk 1951

Cadle, E. Howard, *Obit* Feb 1943

Cadmus, Paul, painter and printmaker, July 1942, *Obit* Mar 2000

Cadogan, Alexander, British diplomat, Oct 1944, *Obit* Sept 1968

Caesar, Sid, American comedian and actor, Apr 1951

Caetano, Adrian, Argentine film director and screenwriter, Jan 2003

Caetano, Marcello, Portuguese prime minister, Mar 1970, *Obit* Jan 1981

Cafe Filho, Joao, Jan 1955, *Obit* Apr 1970

Cafferty, Jack, American television newscaster, Oct 2008

Caffery, Jefferson, diplomat, Nov 1943, *Obit* June 1974

Caffrey, James J., June 1947, *Obit* May 1961

Cage, John, American composer, Sept 1961, *Obit* Sept 1992

Cage, Nicolas, American actor, Apr 1994

Cagney, James, American actor, Yrbk 1942, *Obit* May 1986

Cahill, Michael Harrison, *Obit* Apr 1940

Cahill, William Thomas, governor, June 1970, *Obit* Sept 1996

Cahn, Sammy, American lyricist, Nov 1974, *Obit* Mar 1993

Cai Yuanpei, Chinese educator, *Obit* Mar 1940

Caillaux, Joseph, French statesman, *Obit* Jan 1945

Cain, Harry P., American senator, Apr 1949, *Obit* May 1979

Cain, Herman, American restaurant chain executive, radio talk show host and political commentator, Oct 2011

Cain, James M., American novelist, Yrbk 1947, *Obit* Jan 1978

Caine, Michael, English actor, May 1968, Jan 1988

Cairns, Huntington, American lawyer, Nov 1940

Calagione, Sam, American brewing company executive, Jan 2013

Calatrava, Santiago, Spanish architect, Aug 1997

Calder, Alexander, American sculptor, Apr 1946, July 1966, *Obit* Jan 1977

Calder, Alexander Stirling, American sculptor, *Obit* Feb 1945

Calder, Nigel, English author, June 1986

Calder, Ritchie, Scottish author and journalist, Apr 1963, *Obit* May 1986

Calder, William M., *Obit* Apr 1945

Caldera, Rafael, Venezuelan president, July 1969, *Obit* Yrbk 2010

Calderon Guardia, Rafael Angel, Costa Rican president, June 1942, *Obit* Sept 1970

Calderon Hinojosa, Felipe, Mexican president, Jan 2006

Calderon, Sila M., Puerto Rican governor, Nov 2001

Calderone, Frank A., physician and public health official, July 1952, *Obit* Apr 1987

Calderone, Mary Steichen, sexologist, Nov 1967, *Obit* Jan 1999

Caldicott, Helen, American pediatrician and anti-nuclear activist, Oct 1983

Caldwell, Erskine, American novelist and short story writer, Oct 1940, *Obit* May 1987

Caldwell, Millard Fillmore, American governor, Nov 1948, *Obit* Feb 1985

Caldwell, Sarah, American opera director and conductor, Oct 1973, *Obit* Yrbk 2006

Caldwell, Sarah C., Jan 1953

Caldwell, Taylor, author, Jan 1940, *Obit* Oct 1985

Caldwell, William E., *Obit* May 1943

Caldwell, Zoe, Australian actress, Yrbk 1970

Calero, Adolfo, Nicaraguan rebel leader, Oct 1987, *Obit* Yrbk 2012

Calfee, John Edward, *Obit* Jan 1941

Calhern, Louis, July 1951, *Obit* July 1956

Calhoun, Jim, American basketball coach, May 2011

Califano, Joseph A., American Secretary of health, education and welfare, June 1977

Calisher, Hortense, American short story writer and novelist, Nov 1973, *Obit* Yrbk 2009

Calkins, Robert DeBlois, economist and foundation official, Oct 1952, *Obit* Sept 1992

Callaghan, Daniel J., American admiral, *Obit* Jan 1943

Callaghan, James, British prime minister, Feb 1968, *Obit* Yrbk 2005

Callahan, Harry M., American photographer, Nov 1984, *Obit* July 1999

Callahan, John, American cartoonist, Sept 1998, *Obit* Yrbk 2010

Callander, W. F., Oct 1948

Callas, Maria, American opera singer, Sept 1956, *Obit* Nov 1977

Calle, Sophie, French artist, May 2001

Callender, John Hancock, architect and editor, Sept 1955, *Obit* June 1995

Calleros, Juan, Mexican bassist, Jan 2005

Callery, Mary, July 1955

Calles, Plutarco Elias, Mexican president, *Obit* Nov 1945

Callow, John Michael, *Obit* Sept 1940

Calloway, Cab, American singer and band leader, Nov 1945, *Obit* Jan 1995

Calmy-Rey, Micheline, Swiss president, Jan 2007

Calve, Emma, French opera singer, *Obit* Mar 1942

Calverton, Victor Francis, American political writer, editor and literary critic, *Obit* Jan 1941

Calvin, Melvin, American biochemist, Apr 1962, *Obit* Mar 1997

Calvino, Italo, Italian novelist and short story writer, Feb 1984, *Obit* Nov 1985

Calvo-Sotelo y Bustelo, Leopoldo, Spanish prime minister, Aug 1981

Calwell, A. A., Oct 1947

Cam'Ron (Musician), American rapper, Feb 2011

Cam, Helen Maud, English medievalist, Sept 1948, *Obit* Apr 1968

Camac, Charles Nicoll Bancker, *Obit* Nov 1940

Camacho, Hector, boxer, *Obit* Yrbk 2013

Camara, Helder, Brazilian archbishop, July 1971, *Obit* Jan 2000

Cambiaso, Adolfo, Argentine polo player, Jan 2007

Cambridge, Godfrey, American actor and comedian, Mar 1969, *Obit* Feb 1977

Camby, Marcus, American basketball player, Jan 2000

Camden, Harry P., *Obit* Sept 1943

Cameron, Basil, English conductor, Apr 1943

Cameron, Charles S., Sept 1954

Cameron, David, British prime minister, Aug 2010

Cameron, Hugh, *Obit* Jan 1942

Cameron, James, Canadian film director, producer and screenwriter, Jan 1998

Camilla, Jan 2005

Camm, Sydney, English aircraft designer, Apr 1942, *Obit* Apr 1966

Cammerer, Arno B., *Obit* June 1941

Campa, Miguel Angel, Sept 1957, *Obit* Nov 1965

Campanella, Roy, American baseball player, June 1953, *Obit* Aug 1993

Campbell, Bebe Moore, American social critic and novelist, Apr 2000, *Obit* Yrbk 2007

Campbell, Ben Nighthorse, American senator, Oct 1994

Campbell, Bill, American mayor, July 1996

Campbell, Boyd, May 1956

Campbell, Bruce, American actor, May 2013

Campbell, Donald, British automobile and boat racer, Feb 1964, *Obit* Feb 1967

Campbell, Douglas, Canadian actor and theatrical director, June 1958, *Obit* Yrbk 2009

Campbell, E. Simms, Jan 1941, *Obit* Mar 1971

Campbell, Earl, American football player, Apr 1983

Campbell, Gerald, Mar 1941, *Obit* Sept 1964

Campbell, Glen, American singer and guitarist, July 1969

Campbell, Grace, Yrbk 1948, *Obit* July 1963

Campbell, Harold G., *Obit* Aug 1942

Campbell, Joseph, American mythologist, June 1984, *Obit* Jan 1988

Campbell, Malcolm, English automobile racing driver, Sept 1947, *Obit* Feb 1949

Campbell, Naomi, British model, Feb 1997

Campbell, Neve, Canadian actress, Jan 2000

Campbell, Patricia, Yrbk 1957

Campbell, Patrick, English actress, *Obit* May 1940

Campbell, Philip P., Speaker of the House, *Obit* July 1941

Campbell, Vivian, English guitarist and singer, Jan 2003

Campbell, Willis C., *Obit* June 1941

Campeau, Robert, Canadian real estate and retail executive, Mar 1989

Campinchi, Cesar, *Obit* Apr 1941

Campion, Jane, New Zealand film director, Apr 1994

Camplin, Alisa, Australian skier, Jan 2004

Campney, Ralph Osborne, Sept 1955, *Obit* Yrbk 1967

Campora, Giuseppe, Italian opera singer, July 1957

Campora, Hector Jose, Argentine political leader, Oct 1973, *Obit* Feb 1981

Camrose, William Ewert Berry, British newspaper publisher, Oct 1941, *Obit* Sept 1954

Canada, Geoffrey, American charitable organization official, Feb 2005

Canaday, John Edwin, art critic and author, May 1962, *Obit* Sept 1985

Canaday, Ward Murphey, Mar 1951, *Obit* Apr 1976

Canady, Alexa, neurosurgeon, Aug 2000

Canavan, Joseph J., *Obit* Yrbk 1940

Canby, Al H., *Obit* Yrbk 1940

Canby, Henry Seidel, literary critic, Sept 1942, *Obit* June 1961

Candau, Marcolino G., Brazilian physican and public health official, Sept 1954

Candee, Robert C., May 1944

Candela, Felix, Spanish architect, July 1960

Candler, Warren A., American bishop and college president, *Obit* Nov 1941

Candy, John, Canadian actor, Feb 1990, *Obit* May 1994

Canetti, Elias, Bulgarian novelist and dramatist, Jan 1983, *Obit* Oct 1994

Canfield, Cass, publisher, Apr 1954, *Obit* May 1986

Canham, Erwin Dain, newspaper editor, July 1945, Jan 1960, *Obit* Feb 1982

Caniff, Milton Arthur, cartoonist, Jan 1944, *Obit* May 1988

Canin, Ethan, American novelist, short story writer and physician, Aug 2001

Cannavaro, Fabio, Italian soccer player, Jan 2006

Cannon, Annie Jump, American astronomer, *Obit* June 1941

Cannon, Cavendish Welles, diplomat, July 1957, *Obit* Yrbk 1962

Cannon, Clarence, American congressman, Nov 1949, *Obit* July 1964

Cannon, Howard W., American senator, Feb 1960, *Obit* Sept 2002

Cannon, James, bishop, *Obit* Nov 1944

Cannon, LeGrand, author, Mar 1943

Cannon, Walter Bradford, American physiologist, *Obit* Nov 1945

Canovas del Castillo, Antonio, Sept 1962

Canseco, Jose, Cuban-American baseball player, Nov 1991

Cantinflas, Mexican comedian, June 1953, *Obit* June 1993

Canton, Allen A., *Obit* Apr 1940

Cantor, Eddie, singer and comedian, Nov 1941, May 1954, *Obit* Jan 1965

Cantu, Giuseppe, *Obit* Yrbk 1940

Cantwell, Maria, American senator, Feb 2005

Canty, Brendan, American drummer, Mar 2002

Cao, Joseph, American congressman, June 2009

Capa, Cornell, American photojournalist, July 2005, *Obit* Yrbk 2008

Capehart, H. E., American senator, Apr 1947, *Obit* Oct 1979

Caperton, William B., American admiral, *Obit* Feb 1942

Caplin, Mortimer Maxwell, American lawyer, Sept 1961

Capogrossi, Giuseppe, Yrbk 1957

Capote, Truman, American short story writer and novelist, Sept 1951, Mar 1968, *Obit* Oct 1984

Capp, Al, cartoonist, May 1947, *Obit* Jan 1980

Capper, Arthur, American senator and governor, Sept 1946, *Obit* Feb 1952

Capps, Lois, American congresswoman, Mar 2008

Capra, Frank, American motion picture director and producer, Apr 1948, *Obit* Oct 1991

Capriati, Jennifer, American tennis player, Nov 2001

Caputo, Philip, American journalist and novelist, Apr 1996

Caradon, Hugh Foot, British diplomat, Oct 1953, *Obit* Nov 1990

Caramanlis, Constantinos, Greek president, May 1956, Apr 1976, *Obit* July 1998

Caramanlis, Constantinos, Greek prime minister, Jan 2004

Caras, Roger A., environmentalist, journalist and animal rights activist, Apr 1988, *Obit* July 2001

Caraway, Hattie Wyatt, American senator, Mar 1945, *Obit* Jan 1951

Card, Andrew H., American presidential adviser, Nov 2003

Cardin, Pierre, French fashion designer, Mar 1965

Cardon, P. V., May 1954, *Obit* Yrbk 1965

Cardoso, Fernando Henrique, Brazilian president, Oct 1996

Carell, Steve, American comedian and actor, Feb 2007

Carew, Rod, American baseball player, Jan 1978

Carewe, Edwin, *Obit* Jan 1940

Carey, Charles Henry, *Obit* Oct 1941

Carey, Drew, American comedian and game show host, Mar 1998

Carey, Ernestine Gilbreth, American memoirist, May 1949, *Obit* Yrbk 2007

Carey, George, British archbishop, Aug 1991

Carey, Hugh L., American governor, Sept 1965, *Obit* Yrbk 2011

Carey, James B., American labor leader, Nov 1941, July 1951, *Obit* Nov 1973

Carey, Mariah, American singer, July 1992

Carey, Ron, American labor leader, May 1992, *Obit* Yrbk 2009

Carey, Walter F., Feb 1965

Carias Andino, Tiburcio, Honduran president, June 1942, *Obit* Feb 1970

Carl, Feb 1974

Carle, Eric, American illustrator and children's author, Nov 2013

Carle, Richard, *Obit* Aug 1941

Carlin, George, American comedian, Oct 1976, *Obit* Oct 2008

Carlino, Lewis John, dramatist and filmmaker, May 1983

Carlos, Wendy, American composer, Sept 2008

Carlsen, Magnus, Norwegian chess player, July 2013

Carlson, Anton Julius, physiologist, Jan 1948, *Obit* Nov 1956

Carlson, Evans F., American Marine corps general, Oct 1943, *Obit* June 1947

Carlson, Frank, American governor and senator, Apr 1949, *Obit* July 1987

Carlson, John F., *Obit* May 1945

Carlson, Margaret, American journalist, Nov 2003

Carlson, William S., college president, July 1952, *Obit* July 1994

Carlsson, Ingvar, Swedish prime minister, Feb 1988

Carlton, W. N. C., *Obit* Mar 1943

Carlucci, Frank Charles, American Secretary of defense, Oct 1981

Carlyle, A. J., *Obit* July 1943

Carmack, John, American software engineer and video game company executive, Mar 2000

Carmichael, Hoagy, American songwriter, May 1941, *Obit* Feb 1982

Carmichael, Oliver C., Jan 1946, *Obit* Yrbk 1966

Carmines, Al, American clergyman, composer, singer and actor, Sept 1972, *Obit* Yrbk 2005

Carmody, John M., American mining executive, labor mediator and government official, May 1940, *Obit* Jan 1964

Carmona, Antonio Oscar de Fragoso, Nov 1950, *Obit* May 1951

Carmona, Richard, American Surgeon general, Jan 2003

Carnegie, Dale, American self-improvement lecturer and writer, Yrbk 1941, Sept 1955

Carnegie, Dorothy, author and corporate training executive, Sept 1955, *Obit* Jan 1999

Carnegie, Hattie, fashion designer, Oct 1942, *Obit* May 1956

Carney, Art, American actor, Apr 1958, *Obit* Yrbk 2004

Carney, Patrick, American drummer, Jan 2013

Carney, Robert Bostwick, admiral, Oct 1951, *Obit* Aug 1990

Carnovsky, Morris, actor, Jan 1991

Caro, Anthony, English sculptor, Nov 1981

Caro, Robert A., American biographer, Jan 1984

Carol, Aug 1940, *Obit* May 1953

Caroline, Nov 1989

Caron, Leslie, French dancer and actress, Sept 1954

Carone, Nicolas, American painter and draughtsman, July 2006, *Obit* Yrbk 2010

Carpenter, Chris, American baseball player, Aug 2012

Carpenter, George L., Jan 1943, *Obit* May 1948

Carpenter, Henry Cort Harold, *Obit* Nov 1940

Carpenter, J. Henry, Feb 1943, *Obit* Sept 1954

Carpenter, John Alden, composer, May 1947, *Obit* May 1951

Carpenter, Lewis Van, *Obit* July 1940

Carpenter, Mary Chapin, American singer and songwriter, Feb 1994

Carpenter, Scott, American astronaut, Sept 1962

Carpentier, Marcel Maurice, Apr 1951

Carr, Alexander, *Obit* Yrbk 1946

Carr, Emma Perry, American chemist, Apr 1959

Carr, Kris, American actress, photographer and documentary filmmaker, May 2012

Carr, Robert, Jan 1973

Carr, Robert Kenneth, Apr 1961

Carr, Wilbur J., diplomat, *Obit* Aug 1942

Carr, William G., educator, Sept 1952, *Obit* May 1996

Carradine, Keith, American actor, Aug 1991

Carraway, Gertrude Sprague, Jan 1954

Carrel, Alexis, French surgeon and biologist, Mar 1940, *Obit* Yrbk 1944

Carreras, Jose, Spanish opera singer, June 1979

Carrero Blanco, Luis, Oct 1973, *Obit* Feb 1974

Carrey, Jim, Canadian comedian and actor, Feb 1996

Carrillo, Santiago, Spanish communist leader, June 1977, *Obit* Yrbk 2012

Carrington, Elaine, Feb 1944, *Obit* July 1958

Carrington, Peter Alexander Rupert Carington, British statesman, June 1971

Carroll, Cynthia, American mining executive, May 2011

Carroll, Diahann, American singer and actress, Sept 1962

Carroll, E. Jean, American advice columnist, July 2008

Carroll, James, American novelist, May 1997

Carroll, Jim, American poet and lyricist, Oct 1995, *Obit* Yrbk 2009

Carroll, John, painter, July 1955, *Obit* Jan 1960

Carroll, John A., American senator, May 1958, *Obit* Oct 1983

Carroll, Joseph Francis, American air force general, Apr 1962, *Obit* Mar 1991

Carroll, Madeleine, actress, Apr 1949, *Obit* Nov 1987

Carroll, Pat, actress, Aug 1980

Carroll, Thomas H., July 1962, *Obit* Oct 1964

Carroll, Vinnette, American actress, dramatist and theatrical director, Sept 1983, *Obit* Feb 2003

Carroll-Abbing, J. Patrick, priest and social worker, July 1967, *Obit* Nov 2001

Carruth, Hayden, American poet, Apr 1992, *Obit* Yrbk 2008

Carsey, Marcy, American television producer, Jan 1997

Carson, Anne, Canadian classicist, poet and essayist, May 2006

Carson, Benjamin, American neurosurgeon, May 1997

Carson, David, American graphic designer, July 2008

Carson, John Renshaw, *Obit* Yrbk 1940

Carson, Johnny, American television talk show host, Jan 1964, Apr 1982, *Obit* July 2005

Carson, Rachel, American marine biologist and environmentalist, Nov 1951, *Obit* June 1964

Carstens, Karl, German president, Apr 1980, *Obit* Aug 1992

Carter, Benny, American saxophonist, July 1987, *Obit* Oct 2003

Carter, Betty, American jazz singer, Mar 1982, *Obit* Jan 1999

Carter, Boake, radio commentator, Jan 1942, *Obit* Yrbk 1947

Carter, Don, American bowler, Mar 1963, *Obit* Yrbk 2012

Carter, Elliott, American composer, Nov 1960, *Obit* Yrbk 2013

Carter, Hodding, American journalist and government official, Aug 1981

Carter, Hodding, American newspaper editor and publisher, July 1946, *Obit* May 1972

Carter, Huntly, *Obit* May 1942

Carter, James, American jazz saxophonist, Feb 1997

Carter, Jimmy, American gospel singer, Oct 2001

Carter, Jimmy, American president, Sept 1971, Nov 1977

Carter, John, British bibliographer and rare book dealer, May 1959, *Obit* May 1975

Carter, John Franklin, journalist and author, Oct 1941, *Obit* Jan 1968

Carter, John Ridgely, *Obit* July 1944

Carter, Lillian, mother of American president Jimmy Carter, Jan 1978, *Obit* Jan 1984

Carter, Majora, American community activist and conservationist, Oct 2007, May 2013

Carter, Matthew, British typographer, Oct 2007

Carter, Nick, American singer, May 2000

Carter, Regina, American jazz violinist, Oct 2003

Carter, Rosalynn, wife of American president Jimmy Carter, Mar 1978

Carter, Rubin, American boxer and victim of false imprisonment, May 2000

Carter, Stephen L., American law professor, July 1997

Carter, Vince, American basketball player, Apr 2002

Cartier de Marchienne, Emile de, *Obit* July 1946

Cartier-Bresson, Henri, French photographer, Mar 1947, May 1976, Jan 2003, *Obit* Yrbk 2004

Cartland, Barbara, English romance novelist, Aug 1979, *Obit* Aug 2000

Carton de Wiart, Adrian, May 1940, *Obit* July 1963

Cartotto, Ercole, *Obit* Nov 1946

Cartwright, Morse A., Sept 1947, *Obit* June 1974

Carusi, Ugo, government official, Oct 1948, *Obit* Sept 1994

Carvel, Elbert N., June 1963

Carver, George Washington, American botanist, Nov 1940, *Obit* Feb 1943

Carver, Raymond, American short story writer and poet, Feb 1984, *Obit* Sept 1988

Carvey, Dana, American comedian and actor, June 1992

Carville, James, American political consultant and commentator, Mar 1993

Cary, Frank Taylor, American computer industry executive, Jan 1980, *Obit* May 2006

Cary, Joyce, Anglo-Irish novelist, Yrbk 1949, *Obit* June 1957

Cary, William L., American lawyer and regulatory agency official, Jan 1963, *Obit* Apr 1983

Casablancas, Julian, American singer and songwriter, Feb 2007

Casadesus, Robert, French pianist and composer, Jan 1945, *Obit* Nov 1972

Casals, Pablo, Spanish cellist, Nov 1950, Nov 1964, *Obit* Yrbk 1973

Casals, Rosie, tennis player and executive, Feb 1974

Case, Clifford Philip, American senator, Mar 1955, *Obit* Apr 1982

Case, Francis H., American senator and congressman, May 1946, *Obit* Sept 1962

Case, Frank, *Obit* July 1946

Case, Neko, American singer and songwriter, June 2013

Case, Steve, American mass media executive, Oct 1996

Casey, Bernie, actor, screenwriter and film director, July 1999

Casey, Edward Pearce, *Obit* Jan 1940

Casey, George W., American general, Mar 2006

Casey, Ralph E., Feb 1966

Casey, Richard Gardiner Casey, Australian governor-general, Jan 1940, *Obit* Aug 1976

Casey, Robert J., Mar 1943, *Obit* Jan 1963

Casey, William J., American intelligence official, Mar 1972, *Obit* June 1987

Cash, Johnny, American country singer and songwriter, Sept 1969, *Obit* Jan 2004

Cash, Rosanne, American country singer and songwriter, Oct 1991

Cashin, Bonnie, American fashion designer, May 1970, *Obit* June 2000

Cashman, Robert, Nov 1952

Caspary, Vera, author, dramatist and screenwriter, Yrbk 1947, *Obit* Aug 1987

Casper, Billy, American golfer, July 1966

Cassady, John H., Oct 1952, *Obit* Mar 1969

Cassavetes, John, American actor and film director, July 1969, *Obit* Mar 1989

Cassel, Karl Gustav, *Obit* Mar 1945

Cassidy, Claudia, drama and music critic, Sept 1955, *Obit* Oct 1996

Cassidy, Henry Clarence, journalist, Sept 1943

Cassini, Oleg, French-American fashion designer, July 1961, *Obit* Yrbk 2006

Castagna, Edwin, librarian, June 1964

Castagnetta, Grace, Feb 1954

Castelli, Leo, American art dealer, Aug 1984, *Obit* Jan 2000

Castelnau, Noel Marie Joseph Edouard de Curieres de, French general, *Obit* May 1944

Castelo Branco, Humberto de Alencar, Brazilian president, Feb 1965, *Obit* Oct 1967

Castiella, Fernando Maria, May 1958, *Obit* Feb 1977

Castillo Armas, Carlos, Guatemalan president, Jan 1955, *Obit* Sept 1957

Castillo Najera, Francisco, May 1946, *Obit* Feb 1955

Castillo, Ramon S., July 1941, *Obit* Yrbk 1944

Castle, Barbara, British socialist leader, Jan 1967, *Obit* Yrbk 2002

Castle, Lewis G., July 1958, *Obit* Sept 1960

Castro e Silva, Jose Machado de, *Obit* Aug 1943

Castro, Fidel, Cuban president, July 1958, July 1970, June 2001

Castro, Julian, American mayor, June 2013

Castro, Raul, Cuban president, Feb 1977

Caswell, Hollis L., college president, July 1956, *Obit* Sept 1989

Cat Power (Singer), American singer and songwriter, Oct 2007

Catchings, Tamika, American basketball player, Nov 2013

Cates, Clifton B., American Marine corps officer, Nov 1950, *Obit* Sept 1970

Cates, Gilbert, American film director, producer and college dean, Mar 1997, *Obit* Yrbk 2012

Catherine, Aug 2011

Catledge, Turner, American newspaper editor, July 1975, *Obit* July 1983

Catlett, Elizabeth, American sculptor and printmaker, May 1998, *Obit* Yrbk 2012

Catlin, Don H., American pharmacologist, Mar 2010

Catroux, Georges, May 1943, *Obit* Feb 1970

Catt, Carrie Chapman, American feminist and pacifist, Oct 1940, *Obit* Apr 1947

Cattani-Amadori, Federico, *Obit* May 1943

Cattell, James McKeen, psychologist, *Obit* Mar 1944

Catto, Thomas Sivewright Catto, English banker, Nov 1944

Catton, Bruce, journalist and author, Yrbk 1954, *Obit* Oct 1978

Cattrall, Kim, Anglo-Canadian actress, Jan 2003

Caturani, Michele Gaetano, *Obit* Mar 1940

Catz, Safra, American computer software executive, Jan 2008

Caudill, Rebecca, author, Yrbk 1950, *Obit* Jan 1986

Cauldwell, Leslie Giffen, *Obit* July 1941

Caulfield, Joan, actress, May 1954, *Obit* Aug 1991

Cauthen, Steve, American jockey, July 1977

Cavaco Silva, Anibal, Portuguese prime minister, Mar 1991

Cavallero, Ugo, *Obit* Oct 1943

Cavalli-Sforza, Luigi Luca, Italian geneticist, Aug 1997

Cavanagh, Jerome P., Apr 1968, *Obit* Jan 1980

Cavanagh, Tom, Canadian actor, June 2003

Cavanah, Frances, author and editor, Yrbk 1954

Cavanaugh, John J., Mar 1947, *Obit* Feb 1980

Cavanna, Betty, American young adult novelist, Yrbk 1950, *Obit* Oct 2001

Cavazos, Lauro Fred, American Secretary of education, Apr 1989

Cave, Nick, Australian singer and songwriter, June 2005

Cavero, Salvador, Peruvian vice-president, *Obit* Mar 1940

Cavert, Samuel McCrea, Jan 1951, *Obit* Mar 1977

Cavett, Dick, American television talk show host, Oct 1970

Cayton, Horace R., Jan 1946, *Obit* Mar 1970

Cazalet, Victor Alexander, *Obit* Aug 1943

Ceausescu, Nicolae, Romanian dictator, Nov 1967, *Obit* Feb 1990

Cecil, Mary, *Obit* Feb 1941

Cedras, Raoul, Haitian general, July 1995

Cedric the Entertainer, American comedian, Feb 2004

Cela, Camilo Jose, Spanish novelist, short story writer, essayist, travel writer and poet, June 1990, *Obit* Apr 2002

Celebrezze, Anthony J., American Secretary of health, education and welfare, Jan 1963, *Obit* Jan 1999

Celler, Emanuel, American congressman, Oct 1949, Nov 1966, *Obit* Mar 1981

Celmins, Vija, American painter, Jan 2005

Cenerazzo, Walter W., Sept 1955

Cepeda, Orlando, Puerto Rican baseball player, Oct 1968

Ceram, C. W., Jan 1957, *Obit* June 1972

Cerezo Arevalo, Vinicio, Guatemalan president, Mar 1987

Cerf, Bennett, American publisher, Nov 1941, Sept 1958, *Obit* Oct 1971

Cerf, Vinton G., American computer scientist, Sept 1998

Cernan, Eugene A., American astronaut and business consultant, May 1973

Cester, Chris, Australian drummer and singer, Jan 2005

Cester, Nic, Australian guitarist and singer, Jan 2005

Chaban-Delmas, Jacques, French prime minister, July 1958, *Obit* Feb 2001

Chabon, Michael, American novelist, Nov 2012

Chabrol, Claude, French film director, Jan 1975, *Obit* Yrbk 2010

Chaddock, Robert Emmet, *Obit* Yrbk 1940

Chadha, Gurinder, British motion picture director, Jan 2004

Chadli, Bendjedid, Algerian president, Apr 1991, *Obit* Yrbk 2012

Chadourne, Marc, *Obit* Feb 1941

Chadwick, Florence, American swimmer and stockbroker, Oct 1950, *Obit* May 1995

Chadwick, Helene, *Obit* Oct 1940

Chadwick, James, British physicist, Nov 1945, *Obit* Oct 1974

Chafee, John, American senator and governor, Nov 1969, *Obit* Jan 2000

Chafee, Lincoln, American senator, Jan 2004

Chafee, Zechariah, American law professor, Aug 1942, *Obit* Apr 1957

Chagall, Marc, Russian painter, Nov 1943, Nov 1960, *Obit* May 1985

Chagla, Mahomed Ali Currim, Indian diplomat, June 1959, *Obit* Jan 1984

Chaikin, Joseph, American theatrical director and actor, July 1981, *Obit* Yrbk 2003

Chaikin, Sol C., garment workers' union leader, Apr 1979, *Obit* June 1991

Chailly, Riccardo, Italian conductor, June 1991

Chain, Ernst Boris, British biochemist, Nov 1965, *Obit* Oct 1979

Chalk, O. Roy, American transportation and communications executive, Nov 1971, *Obit* Feb 1996

Chalmers, Philip O., *Obit* Mar 1946

Chambas, Mohamed Ibn, Ghanaian diplomat and international organization official, Jan 2003

Chamberlain, Francis L., July 1959

Chamberlain, John, journalist and critic, Apr 1940, *Obit* June 1995

Chamberlain, Neville, British prime minister, *Obit* Yrbk 1940

Chamberlain, Owen, American physicist, Mar 1960, *Obit* July 2006

Chamberlain, Paul M., *Obit* July 1940

Chamberlain, Richard, American actor, July 1963, Nov 1987

Chamberlain, Samuel, American photographer and artist, Sept 1954, *Obit* Mar 1975

Chamberlain, Wilt, American basketball player, June 1960, *Obit* Jan 2000

Chamberlin, Georgia Louise, *Obit* Oct 1943

Chambers, R. W., *Obit* June 1942

Chaminade, Cecile, French composer, *Obit* June 1944

Chamorro, Violeta Barrios de, Nicaraguan president, June 1990

Chamoun, Camille Nimer, Lebanese president, July 1956, *Obit* Sept 1987

Champion, George, banker, Apr 1961, *Obit* Jan 1998

Champion, Gower, American dancer, choreographer and theatrical director, Sept 1953, *Obit* Oct 1980

Champion, Gower; and Champion, Marge, Sept 1953

Champion, Marge, American dancer and choreographer, Sept 1953

Champion, Pierre, *Obit* Aug 1942

Champion, Will, English drummer, May 2004

Chan, Jackie, Chinese actor, Nov 1997

Chan, Margaret F. C., Chinese physician and public health official, Jan 2007

Chan, Paul, American video artist, Mar 2011

Chance, Dean, baseball player, July 1969

Chancellor, John, American television news anchor and commentator, Jan 1962, Nov 1988, *Obit* Sept 1996

Chandler, Dorothy Buffum, American newspaper publisher and patron of the arts, July 1957, *Obit* Sept 1997

Chandler, Dorothy Buffum; and Chandler, Norman, July 1957

Chandler, Happy, American governor, senator and baseball executive, Aug 1943, Sept 1956, *Obit* Aug 1991

Chandler, Norman, American newspaper publisher, July 1957, *Obit* Yrbk 1973

Chandler, Otis, American newspaper publisher, Nov 1968, *Obit* Yrbk 2006

Chandler, Raymond, American mystery novelist, Yrbk 1946, *Obit* June 1959

Chandos, Oliver Lyttelton, British manufacturing executive and cabinet member, Sept 1941, Jan 1953, *Obit* Mar 1972

Chandrasekhar, S., Indian economist and demographer, Oct 1969, *Obit* Sept 2001

Chandrasekhar, Subrahmanyan, American astrophysicist, Mar 1986, *Obit* Oct 1995

Chandy, Anna, Apr 1960

Chanel, Coco, French fashion designer and perfumer, Sept 1954, *Obit* Feb 1971

Chaney, John, American basketball coach, Mar 1999

Chang, David, American chef and restaurateur, Aug 2010

Chang, Gary, Chinese architect, Jan 2005

Chang, John M., June 1949, *Obit* July 1966

Chang, Juju, television reporter, Aug 2013

Chang, Michael, American tennis player, July 1997

Chang, Shan-tzu, *Obit* Yrbk 1940

Chang-Diaz, Franklin R., American astronaut and physicist, Aug 2011

Channing, Carol, American actress, Sept 1964

Channing, Stockard, American actress, Apr 1991

Chao, Elaine, American Secretary of labor, May 2001

Chao, Manu, French singer, Jan 2002

Chaon, Dan, American novelist and short story writer, Feb 2012

Chapin, Charles Value, American epidemiologist and public health official, *Obit* Mar 1941

Chapin, James, American painter, Mar 1940, *Obit* Sept 1975

Chapin, Schuyler, American municipal arts administrator, Feb 1974, *Obit* Yrbk 2009

Chaplin, Charlie, English actor, director and producer, Yrbk

1940, Mar 1961, *Obit* Feb 1978

Chaplin, Geraldine, actress, July 1979

Chapman, Albert Kinkade, photographic industry executive, Sept 1952, *Obit* Yrbk 1984

Chapman, Blanche, *Obit* Aug 1941

Chapman, Charles Frederic, American magazine editor and motorboat racer, May 1958, *Obit* Yrbk 1984

Chapman, Daniel A., Apr 1959

Chapman, Duane Lee, American bounty hunter, Mar 2005

Chapman, Frank Michler, American ornithologist, *Obit* Jan 1946

Chapman, Gilbert W., June 1957, *Obit* Feb 1980

Chapman, Helen B., Apr 1955

Chapman, Leonard F., American Marine corps general, July 1968, *Obit* Sept 2000

Chapman, Oscar L., American Secretary of the interior, Feb 1949, *Obit* Apr 1978

Chapman, Steven Curtis, American Christian rock singer and songwriter, Oct 2004

Chapman, Sydney, English geophysicist, July 1957, *Obit* Sept 1970

Chapman, Tracy, American singer and songwriter, Aug 1989

Chappedelaine, Louis de, *Obit* Jan 1940

Chappell, Tom, American personal care products industry executive, May 1994

Chappelle, Dave, American comedian and actor, June 2004

Charisse, Cyd, American dancer and actress, Jan 1954, *Obit* Yrbk 2008

Charles, May 1946, *Obit* July 1983

Charles, Nov 1969

Charles, Eugenia, Dominica prime minister, Oct 1986, *Obit* Yrbk 2006

Charles, Ezzard, American boxer, June 1949, *Obit* Aug 1975

Charles, Michael Ray, American painter, Oct 2005

Charles, Ray, American singer and pianist, Apr 1965, June 1992, *Obit* Yrbk 2004

Charles-Roux, Francois, Jan 1952, *Obit* Sept 1961

Charlesworth, James Clyde, Sept 1954, *Obit* Mar 1974

Charlot, Jean, American painter and illustrator, Sept 1945, *Obit* Yrbk 1984

Charlotte, Apr 1949, *Obit* Aug 1985

Charney, Dov, American t-shirt manufacturer, Sept 2009

Charnwood, Godfrey Rathbone Benson, English biographer, *Obit* Mar 1945

Charoen Sirivadhanabhakdi, Chinese-Thai liquor industry executive, Jan 2005

Charques, Dorothy, Yrbk 1958

Charriol, Philippe, French watch, jewelry and accessories manufacturer, Jan 2004

Charters, Spencer, *Obit* Mar 1943

Charyk, Joseph V., American government official and telecommunications executive, Yrbk 1970

Chase, Alison Becker, American choreographer, Nov 2006

Chase, Charley, actor, *Obit* Aug 1940

Chase, Chevy, American actor and comedian, Mar 1979

Chase, David, American television producer and scriptwriter, Mar 2001

Chase, Edna Woolman, magazine editor, Nov 1940, *Obit* June 1957

Chase, Harry Woodburn, June 1948, *Obit* June 1955

Chase, Ilka, May 1942, *Obit* Apr 1978

Chase, Joseph Cummings, May 1955

Chase, Lucia, American ballet dancer and manager, July 1947, Aug 1975, *Obit* Mar 1986

Chase, Mary, dramatist, Oct 1945, *Obit* Jan 1982

Chase, Mary Ellen, author, May 1940, *Obit* Oct 1973

Chase, Stuart, economist, Oct 1940, *Obit* Jan 1986

Chase, William C., Nov 1952

Chase, William Sheafe, *Obit* Sept 1940

Chasez, JC, American singer, Nov 2000

Chasins, Abram, American pianist and composer, Feb 1960, *Obit* Aug 1987

Chassagne, Regine, Canadian singer and instrumentalist, Jan 2007

Chast, Roz, American cartoonist, July 1997

Chastain, Madye Lee, Yrbk 1958

Chatel, Yves, *Obit* Yrbk 1944

Chatwin, Bruce, English memoirist, travel writer and novelist, Jan 1988, *Obit* Mar 1989

Chaudhry, Iftikhar Mohammad, Pakistani supreme court justice, Jan 2007

Chauncey, Henry, American educational testing service executive, July 1951, *Obit* Mar 2003

Chauvel, Jean, French diplomat, Oct 1950, *Obit* July 1979

Chauvin, Yves, French chemist, Jan 2007

Chavan, Yashwantrao Balwantrao, Apr 1963

Chavchavadze, George, Mar 1943, *Obit* Apr 1962

Chavez Frias, Hugo, Venezuelan president, May 2000

Chavez, Carlos, Mexican composer and conductor, May 1949, *Obit* Sept 1978

Chavez, Cesar, Mexican-American labor leader, Feb 1969, *Obit* June 1993

Chavez, Dennis, American senator, Mar 1946, *Obit* Jan 1963

Chavez, Hugo, Venezuelan president, *Obit* Yrbk 2013

Chavez, Julio Cesar, Mexican boxer, Apr 1999

Chavez, Linda, American policy scientist and commentator, Nov 1999

Chavez-Thompson, Linda, American labor leader, Mar 2000

Chavis, Benjamin F., American clergyman and civil rights leader, Jan 1994

Chayefsky, Paddy, American screenwriter and dramatist, Sept 1957, *Obit* Sept 1981

Cheadle, Don, American actor, Sept 1999

Cheatham, Kitty, *Obit* Feb 1946

Chee, Soon Juan, Singaporean political leader, Jan 2004

Cheeks, Maurice, American basketball player and coach, Feb 2004

Cheeky Girls (Musical group), Jan 2003

Cheever, John, American novelist and short story writer, Sept 1975, *Obit* Aug 1982

Chelf, Frank L., June 1952

Chen Cheng, Chinese general, Sept 1941, *Obit* Apr 1965

Chen Guidi, Chinese journalist, Jan 2005

Chen Peisi, Chinese actor and comedian, Jan 2004

Chen Yi, Chinese general, Oct 1959, *Obit* Feb 1972

Chen, Eugene, Chinese newspaper executive and diplomat, *Obit* July 1944

Chen, Joan, Chinese actress, Sept 1999

Chen, Shui-bian, Taiwanese president, Sept 2000

Chen, Steve S., American video sharing web site founder, Jan 2007

Chenault, Kenneth I., American financial services executive, June 1998

Cheney, Brainard, author, Yrbk 1959, *Obit* Mar 1990

Cheney, Liz, American lawyer, political activist and daughter of Vice-president Richard B. Cheney, Aug 2010

Cheney, Lynne V., American educator, novelist and government official, Oct 1992

Cheney, Richard B., American vice-president, Aug 1989, Jan 2002

Cheney, Russell, American painter, *Obit* Aug 1945

Chennault, Claire Lee, American general, Oct 1942, *Obit* Oct 1958

Cher, American singer and actress, Jan 1974, June 1991

Chereau, Patrice, French theatrical, opera and film director, Jan 1990

Cherkassky, Shura, American pianist, Oct 1990, *Obit* Mar 1996

Cherne, Leo, economist and humanitarian, Yrbk 1940, *Obit* Mar 1999

Chernenko, Konstantin Ustinovich, Soviet communist leader, Aug 1984, *Obit* May 1985

Cherniakhovskii, Ivan Danilovich, Oct 1944, *Obit* Apr 1945

Chernomyrdin, Viktor, Russian prime minister, Aug 1998, *Obit* Yrbk 2011

Cherry, Addie, American vaudeville actress, *Obit* Yrbk 1942

Cherry, Don, Canadian hockey coach and sportscaster, Jan 2004

Cherry, Francis Adams, American governor, July 1954, *Obit* Sept 1965

Chertoff, Michael, American Secretary of homeland security, Oct 2005

Cherwell, Frederick Alexander Lindemann, British physicist, Mar 1952, *Obit* Sept 1957

Cheshire, Leonard, British air force officer and social welfare leader, Jan 1962, *Obit* Sept 1992

Chesney, Kenny, American country singer, May 2004

Chesser, Elizabeth Sloan, *Obit* Mar 1940

Chester, Edmund, Mar 1941

Chestnut, Cyrus, American jazz pianist, July 2009

Chevalier, Elizabeth Pickett, Jan 1943

Chevalier, Maurice, French singer and actor, Jan 1948, Mar 1969, *Obit* Feb 1972

Chevrier, Lionel, June 1952

Chevrolet, Louis, American automobile executive and engineer, *Obit* Aug 1941

Chia, Sandro, Italian painter, June 1990

Chiang, Ching-kuo, Taiwanese president, Sept 1954, *Obit* Mar 1988

Chiang, Kai-shek, Chinese president, Jan 1940, May 1953, *Obit* May 1975

Chiang, Mei-ling, wife of Taiwanse president Chiang Kai-shek, May 1940, *Obit* Mar 2004

Chiappe, Jean, French government official, *Obit* Jan 1941

Chiari, Roberto F., Panamanian president, Feb 1961

Chiba, Sonny, Japanese martial artist and actor, Jan 2005

Chicago, Judy, American artist, Feb 1981

Chicherina, Julia, Russian pop singer, Jan 2006

Chichester, Francis, English cartographer and boat racer, Yrbk 1967, *Obit* Oct 1972

Chidlaw, Benjamin W., Mar 1955

Chieftains (Musical group), Mar 2004

Chifley, Joseph B., Aug 1945, *Obit* July 1951

Chihuly, Dale, American glass artist, Aug 1995

Child, Julia, American cook, Feb 1967, *Obit* Yrbk 2004

Childs, Lucinda, American dancer and choreographer, Apr 1984

Childs, Marquis William, journalist and author, Jan 1943, *Obit* Sept 1990

Childs, Richard Spencer, cleaning products industry executive and civic reformer, Sept 1955, *Obit* Jan 1979

Chiles, Lawton, senator and governor, Sept 1971, *Obit* Mar 1999

Chilingarov, Artur, Russian polar explorer, Jan 2007

Chillida, Eduardo, Spanish sculptor, Sept 1985, *Obit* Yrbk 2002

Chiluba, Frederick, Zambian president, May 1992, *Obit* Yrbk 2011

Chin, Frank, American novelist, essayist, playwright and short story writer, Mar 1999

Chinery-Hesse, Hermann, Ghanaian computer software executive, Jan 2003

Ching, Cyrus S., labor mediator, Jan 1948, *Obit* Feb 1968

Chinmoy, Sri, Indian guru, Apr 1976, *Obit* Yrbk 2008

Chiperfield, Robert B., Sept 1956, *Obit* May 1971

Chirac, Jacques, French president, June 1975, Apr 1993

Chisholm, Brock, Canadian psychistrist, July 1948, *Obit* Mar 1971

Chisholm, Shirley, American congresswoman, Oct 1969, *Obit* Apr 2005

Chissano, Joaquim Alberto, Mozambican president, Nov 1990

Chizmadzhev, IUrii Aleksandrovich, Russian physical chemist, Jan 2005

Cho, Fujio, Japanese automobile executive, Jan 2006

Cho, Margaret, American comedienne, Oct 2000

Chodorov, Edward, American dramatist and screenwriter, Apr 1944, *Obit* Nov 1988

Chomsky, Noam, American linguist and social critic, Oct 1970, Aug 1995

Chopra, Deepak, American physician and writer, Oct 1995

Chopra, Yash, Indian film director and producer, Jan 2006, *Obit* Yrbk 2013

Chotzinoff, Samuel, pianist, Apr 1940, *Obit* Apr 1964

Choudhury, Bikram, Indian yogi, Jan 2004

Chouinard, Yvon, American mail order sportswear company executive, June 1998

Chow, Stephen, Chinese actor, motion picture director and screenwriter, Jan 2003

Chow, Yun Fat, Chinese actor, May 1998

Chrebet, Wayne, American football player, Feb 1999

Chretien, Jean, Canadian prime minister, Apr 1990

Christenberry, Robert K., Mar 1952, *Obit* June 1973

Christensen, Hayden, Canadian actor, Jan 2005

Christian, Nov 1943, *Obit* May 1947

Christians, Mady, May 1945, *Obit* Yrbk 1951

Christie, Agatha, English mystery writer, Sept 1940, July 1964, *Obit* Mar 1976

Christie, J. Walter, *Obit* Feb 1944

Christie, Julie, English actress, Sept 1966

Christie, William, American harpsichordist and conductor, Jan 1992

Christison, Philip, British general, Nov 1945, *Obit* Feb 1994

Christman, Elizabeth, Jan 1947

Christo, Bulgarian artist, Mar 1977

Christofilos, Nicholas C., Nov 1965, *Obit* Nov 1972

Christopher, George, mayor, Feb 1958, *Obit* Yrbk 2000

Christopher, George T., Nov 1947, *Obit* July 1954

Christopher, Warren, American Secretary of state, June 1981, Nov 1995, *Obit* Yrbk 2011

Chrysler, Walter Percy, American automobile executive, *Obit* Oct 1940

Chryssa, American sculptor and painter, Nov 1978

Chu, Shen, *Obit* Aug 1943

Chu, Steven, American physicist and Secretary of energy, Mar 2009

Chuan Leekpai, Thai prime minister, Nov 1998

Chubb, L. Warrington, Feb 1947, *Obit* May 1952

Chuikov, Vasilii Ivanovich, Soviet general, May 1943, *Obit* May 1982

Chukwuogo-Roy, Chinwe, Nigerian painter, Jan 2007

Chun, Doo Hwan, Korean president, Mar 1981

Chung, Connie, American television newscaster, July 1989

Chung, Kyung-Wha, Korean violinist, Feb 2007

Chung, Myung-Whun, Korean pianist and conductor, Aug 1990

Church, Frank, American senator, Mar 1958, Mar 1978, *Obit* May 1984

Church, Marguerite Stitt, congresswoman, Feb 1951, *Obit* July 1990

Church, Sam, American labor leader, Oct 1981, *Obit* Yrbk 2009

Church, Samuel Harden, American railroad executive and foundation official, *Obit* Nov 1943

Churchill, Berton, *Obit* Yrbk 1940

Churchill, Caryl, English playwright, June 1985

Churchill, Clementine, wife of British Prime Minister Sir Winston Churchill, July 1953, *Obit* Mar 1978

Churchill, Edward D., American surgeon, Feb 1963

Churchill, Gordon, Sept 1958

Churchill, Randolph S., British journalist and biographer, Oct 1947, *Obit* Sept 1968

Churchill, Sarah, English actress and daughter of Winston Churchill, May 1955, *Obit* Jan 1983

Churchill, Winston, British statesman, July 1940, Mar 1942, July 1953, *Obit* Mar 1965

Churchland, Patricia Smith, Canadian philosopher, May 2003

Chute, B. J., author, Yrbk 1950, *Obit* Oct 1987

Chute, Charles Lionel, Sept 1949, *Obit* Jan 1954

Chute, Marchette Gaylord, biographer and literary historian, Yrbk 1950, *Obit* July 1994

Chwast, Seymour, American children's author, illustrator and graphic designer, Sept 1995

Ciano, Galeazzo, Italian diplomat, July 1940, *Obit* Feb 1944

Ciardi, John, American poet, translator and critic, Oct 1967, *Obit* May 1986

Cico, Carla, Italian telecommunications executive, Jan 2005

Cicognani, Amleto Giovanni, July 1951, *Obit* Feb 1974

Ciechanover, Aaron J., Israeli biochemist, Jan 2007

Ciller, Tansu, Turkish political leader, Sept 1994

Cimino, Michael, motion picture director, Jan 1981

Cink, Stewart, American golfer, Feb 2010

Ciocci, Jacob, American multi-media artist, Apr 2010

Ciocci, Jessica, American video and installation artist, Apr 2010

Cisler, Walker Lee, electric utility executive, Sept 1955, *Obit* Jan 1995

Cisneros, Henry, American urban development organization official, broadcasting executive and former Secretary of housing and urban development, Aug 1987

Citrine, Walter McLennan Citrine, English electric utility executive, Feb 1941, *Obit* Apr 1983

Civiletti, Benjamin, Feb 1980

Clague, Ewan, statistician and government official, July 1947, *Obit* June 1987

Claiborne, Craig, American food critic, Sept 1969, *Obit* Apr 2000

Claiborne, Liz, American fashion designer, June 1989, *Obit* Yrbk 2007

Claiborne, Loretta, American runner, July 1996

Clair, Rene, French motion picture director, Nov 1941, *Obit* May 1981

Claire, Ina, actress, May 1954, *Obit* Apr 1985

Clampitt, Amy, American poet, Feb 1992, *Obit* Nov 1994

Clancy, Tom, American novelist, Apr 1988

Clapp, Gordon R., Feb 1947, *Obit* June 1963

Clapp, Margaret, American biographer, historian and college president, June 1948, *Obit* June 1974

Clapp, Verner W., librarian, Mar 1959, *Obit* Sept 1972

Clapper, Olive Ewing, Sept 1946, *Obit* Jan 1969

Clapper, Raymond, American journalist and radio commentator, Mar 1940, *Obit* Mar 1944

Clapton, Eric, British guitarist and singer, June 1987

Claremont, Chris, American fantasy, science fiction and comic book writer, Sept 2003

Clark Kerr, Archibald John Kerr, Yrbk 1942, *Obit* Sept 1951

Clark, Bennett Champ, Nov 1941, *Obit* Sept 1954

Clark, Bobby, May 1949, *Obit* Apr 1960

Clark, Charles E., American judge, July 1959, *Obit* Mar 1964

Clark, Dick, American television personality and producer, May 1959, Jan 1987, *Obit* Yrbk 2012

Clark, Dorothy Park, American novelist, Yrbk 1957

Clark, Eleanor, novelist, travel essayist and children's author, May 1978, *Obit* Apr 1996

Clark, Eugenie, American oceanographer, Sept 1953

Clark, Evans, Sept 1947, *Obit* Nov 1970

Clark, Fred G., Oct 1949

Clark, Geoff, Australian boxer, football player and government official, Jan 2004

Clark, Georgia Neese, banker and government official, Sept 1949, *Obit* Feb 1996

Clark, Helen, New Zealand prime minister, Nov 2000

Clark, J. J., American admiral, Jan 1954, *Obit* Sept 1971

Clark, James H., American computer software executive, June 1997

Clark, Jim, Scottish automobile racing driver, Nov 1965, *Obit* June 1968

Clark, Joe, Canadian prime minister, Oct 1976

Clark, John, American labor leader, Apr 1952

Clark, John Davidson, Jan 1947

Clark, Joseph S., American senator, June 1952, *Obit* Mar 1990

Clark, Kenneth, British art historian and museum director, Sept 1963, *Obit* July 1983

Clark, Kenneth B., American psychologist, Sept 1964, *Obit* Sept 2005

Clark, Leonard Frances, Jan 1956, *Obit* Sept 1957

Clark, Marguerite, *Obit* Nov 1940

Clark, Mark W., American general, Nov 1942, *Obit* June 1984

Clark, Mary Higgins, American mystery novelist, Jan 1994

Clark, Paul F., Apr 1955, *Obit* Mar 1973

Clark, Petula, English singer, Feb 1970

Clark, Ramsey, American Attorney general and political activist, Oct 1967

Clark, Robert L., Nov 1952

Clark, Roy, American country singer and banjoist, June 1978

Clark, Sydney, Sept 1956

Clark, Tom C., American Supreme Court justice, July 1945, *Obit* Aug 1977

Clark, Wesley K., American general, July 1999

Clark, William Patrick, American Secretary of the interior, July 1982, *Obit* Yrbk 2013

Clarke, Arthur C., English science fiction writer, Oct 1966, *Obit* Yrbk 2008

Clarke, John Hessin, Supreme Court justice, *Obit* May 1945

Clarke, Kenneth H., British political leader, Jan 2002

Clarke, Martha, American dancer and choreographer, Jan 1989

Clarke, Richard A., American presidential aide and security consultant, May 2006

Clarke, Ron, May 1971

Clarke, Walter, American physician, May 1947, *Obit* Jan 1965

Clarkson, Kelly, American singer and contestant on reality TV show American idol, Sept 2006

Clarkson, Patricia, American actress, Aug 2005

Clash, Kevin, American muppeteer, June 2000

Clausen, A. W., banking official, Nov 1981

Claussen, Julia, *Obit* June 1941

Clavell, James, Australian-American novelist and screenwriter, Oct 1981, *Obit* Nov 1994

Claxton, Brooke, Yrbk 1947, *Obit* Sept 1960

Clay, Laura, American suffragist, *Obit* Aug 1941

Clay, Lucius D., American general, May 1945, June 1963, *Obit* June 1978

Clayburgh, Jill, American actress, Sept 1979, *Obit* Yrbk 2011

Clayton, Eva, American congresswoman, June 2000

Clayton, Horace R.; and Drake, St. Clair, Jan 1946

Clayton, P. B., May 1955, *Obit* Mar 1973

Clayton, William Lockhart, American cotton executive and government official, Apr 1944, *Obit* Mar 1966

Claytor, W. Graham, railroad executive, May 1979, *Obit* July 1994

Cleaver, Eldridge, American civil rights leader, Mar 1970, *Obit* July 1998

Cleese, John, English actor and humorist, Jan 1984

Clegg, Johnny, South African singer and songwriter, Jan 2005

Cleland, Max, American senator, Feb 1978

Clemens, Roger, American baseball player, Nov 1988, Aug 2003

Clemensen, Erik Christian, *Obit* July 1941

Clement, Frank Goad, American governor, July 1955, *Obit* Yrbk 1969

Clement, Jemaine, New Zealand comedian, Mar 2008

Clement, Martin W., Nov 1946, *Obit* Nov 1966

Clement, Paul D., American law professor, Oct 2012

Clement, Rufus E., American college president, June 1946, *Obit* Jan 1968

Clemente, Roberto, Puerto Rican baseball player, Feb 1972, *Obit* Feb 1973

Clements, Earle C., senator and governor, Sept 1955, *Obit* May 1985

Clendening, Logan, physician, *Obit* Mar 1945

Cleveland, Harlan, American diplomat and university president, Sept 1961, *Obit* Yrbk 2008

Cleveland, James, American clergyman and gospel singer, Aug 1985, *Obit* Apr 1991

Cliburn, Van, American pianist, Sept 1958, *Obit* Yrbk 2013

Clifford, Clark M., American presidential adviser, lawyer and Secretary of defense, Mar 1947, Sept 1968, *Obit* Jan 1999

Clifford, John, American ballet dancer and choreographer, Nov 1972

Clift, David Horace, librarian, June 1952, *Obit* Yrbk 1973

Clift, Montgomery, American actor, July 1954, *Obit* Sept 1966

Clijsters, Kim, Belgian tennis player, Jan 2004

Clinchy, Everett R., religious leader, Apr 1941, *Obit* Mar 1986

Cline, John Wesley, June 1951, *Obit* Sept 1974

Cline, Nels, American guitarist, Feb 2010

Clinton, Bill, American president, Apr 1988, Nov 1994

Clinton, George, American singer and songwriter, July 1993

Clinton, Hillary Rodham, American Secretary of state, Nov 1993, Jan 2002, Mar 2009

Clive, E. E., *Obit* July 1940

Cloninger, Kathy, American Girl Scouts official, Oct 2012

Clooney, George, American actor, July 2008

Clooney, Rosemary, American singer, Feb 1957, *Obit* Nov 2002

Close, Chuck, American painter, July 1983

Close, Glenn, American actress, Nov 1984

Clowes, Daniel, American comic book artist and writer, Jan 2002

Clurman, Harold, theatrical director and critic, Feb 1959, *Obit* Nov 1980

Clyburn, James E., American congressman, Oct 2001

Clyde, George D., July 1958, *Obit* May 1972

Coanda, Henri, July 1956, *Obit* Feb 1973

Coates, Gordon, *Obit* July 1943

Coates, John, *Obit* Oct 1941

Cobb, Geraldyn M., American aviator, Feb 1961

Cobb, Irvin S., American humorist, *Obit* Apr 1944

Cobb, Lee J., Feb 1960, *Obit* Apr 1976

Cobb, Ty, American baseball player, Sept 1951, *Obit* Oct 1961

Cobham, Charles John Lyttelton, Apr 1962

Coblentz, Stanton Arthur, American science fiction writer and poet, June 1954

Coblentz, William W., American physicist, Mar 1954, *Obit* Nov 1962

Cobo, Albert E., Nov 1951, *Obit* Yrbk 1958

Coburn, Charles, actor, June 1944, *Obit* Nov 1961

Coburn, James, American actor, June 1999, *Obit* Feb 2003

Coca, Imogene, American actress and comedienne, Apr 1951, *Obit* Sept 2001

Cochran, Charles Blake, English theatrical producer, Oct 1940, *Obit* Mar 1951

Cochran, H. Merle, Feb 1950, *Obit* Nov 1973

Cochran, Jacqueline, American aviator and cosmetics industry executive, Sept 1940, June 1963, *Obit* Oct 1980

Cochran, Johnnie, American lawyer, June 1999, *Obit* Oct 2005

Cochran, Thad, American senator, Apr 2002

Cochrane, Edward L., Mar 1951, *Obit* Jan 1960

Cock, Guillermo A., Peruvian archaeologist, Jan 2007

Cockburn, Bruce, Canadian singer and songwriter, Jan 2005

Cockcroft, John, British physicist, Nov 1948, *Obit* Nov 1967

Cocke, Charles Francis, Mar 1952

Cocke, Erle, army officer and veterans' leader, Jan 1951, *Obit* Sept 2000

Cocker, Jarvis, English rock singer, Nov 1998

Cockrell, Ewing, May 1951, *Obit* Apr 1962

Coco, James, actor, May 1974, *Obit* Apr 1987

Coddington, Grace, British fashion editor, Apr 2005

Codenys, Patrick, Belgian rock musician, Jan 2006

Cody, John Patrick, Nov 1965, *Obit* June 1982

Coe, Fred, television producer, Jan 1959, *Obit* June 1979

Coe, Sebastian, British runner, Nov 1980

Coe, Sue, Anglo-American painter and illustrator, Aug 1997

Coetzee, J. M., South African novelist, Jan 1987

Coffee, John M., Oct 1946

Coffin, Frank M., American judge, Apr 1959, *Obit* Yrbk 2010

Coffin, Haskell, *Obit* July 1941

Coffin, Henry S., clergyman and educator, Apr 1944, *Obit* Jan 1955

Coffin, William Sloane, American clergyman and pacifist, July 1968, Apr 1980, *Obit* Yrbk 2006

Coggan, Frederick Donald, English archbishop, July 1974, *Obit* Sept 2000

Coggeshall, Lowell T., college administrator and physician, Sept 1963, *Obit* Jan 1988

Cogswell, Charles N., *Obit* Feb 1942

Cohan, George M., American actor, dramatist, songwriter and producer, *Obit* Jan 1943

Cohen, Abby Joseph, American investment adviser, June 1998

Cohen, Alexander H., American theatrical producer, June 1965, *Obit* Aug 2000

Cohen, Arthur, author and publisher, Sept 1960, *Obit* Jan 1987

Cohen, Barbara, American poetry recorder, May 1957

Cohen, Barbara; and Roney, Marianne, May 1957

Cohen, Ben, American ice cream company executive, Apr 1994

Cohen, Benjamin, Chilean diplomat and United Nations official, May 1948, *Obit* May 1960

Cohen, Benjamin V., American government official and lawyer, Apr 1941, *Obit* Oct 1983

Cohen, Leonard, Canadian poet, novelist, singer and songwriter, June 1969

Cohen, Lyor, American recording industry executive, Aug 2012

Cohen, Manuel F., Apr 1967, *Obit* Aug 1977

Cohen, Richard, Nov 2007

Cohen, Rob, American motion picture director and producer, Nov 2002

Cohen, Roger, British journalist, May 2008

Cohen, Sasha, American figure skater, Feb 2006

Cohen, Wilbur Joseph, American Secretary of health, education and welfare, Sept 1968, *Obit* July 1987

Cohen, William S., American Secretary of defense, Apr 1982, Jan 1998

Cohn, Linda, American television sportscaster, Aug 2002

Cohn-Bendit, Daniel, German political activist, Jan 2003

Cohu, La Motte T., Apr 1951, *Obit* Nov 1968

Cointreau, Andre, French chef and cooking school administrator, Jan 2004

Coit, Margaret L., American biographer, June 1951

Coker, Elizabeth Boatwright, author, Yrbk 1959, *Obit* Nov 1993

Colbert, Claudette, American actress, Jan 1945, May 1964, *Obit* Oct 1996

Colbert, Edwin Harris, American paleontologist, Sept 1965, *Obit* Feb 2002

Colbert, Gregory, Canadian photographer and cinematographer, Sept 2005

Colbert, Lester Lum, automobile executive, Apr 1951, *Obit* Nov 1995

Colbert, Stephen, American comedian and actor, Nov 2006

Colby, Charles De Witt, *Obit* Nov 1941

Colby, Nathalie S., *Obit* July 1942

Colby, William E., American intelligence official, Jan 1975, *Obit* July 1996

Coldplay (Musical group), May 2004

Coldwell, M. J., Canadian member of Parliament, Sept 1943, *Obit* Oct 1974

Cole, Albert M., Jan 1954

Cole, David L., Jan 1949, *Obit* Mar 1978

Cole, Edward N., American automobile executive, July 1972, *Obit* July 1977

Cole, Jessie Duncan Savage, *Obit* Yrbk 1940

Cole, Johnnetta B., American anthropologist and museum director, Aug 1994

Cole, Juan R. I., American Middle Eastern studies specialist, Oct 2010

Cole, Nat King, American singer and pianist, Feb 1956, *Obit* Mar 1965

Cole, Natalie, American singer, Nov 1991

Cole, William Sterling, congressman, Mar 1954, *Obit* May 1987

Cole-Hamilton, J. B., *Obit* Sept 1945

Coleman, Cy, American composer, Aug 1990, *Obit* Feb 2005

Coleman, Georgia, diver, *Obit* Nov 1940

Coleman, J. P., American governor and judge, Sept 1956, *Obit* Nov 1991

Coleman, James Samuel, American sociologist, Oct 1970, *Obit* June 1995

Coleman, John R., Oct 1974

Coleman, John S., American manufacturing executive, Apr 1953, *Obit* July 1958

Coleman, Lonnie, Yrbk 1958, *Obit* Oct 1982

Coleman, Mary Sue, American university president, Feb 2007

Coleman, Norman, American senator, Sept 2004

Coleman, Ornette, American jazz saxophonist, June 1961

Coleman, Ronnie, American bodybuilder and policeman, Feb 2007

Coleman, Steve, American jazz saxophonist, July 2004

Coleman, William T., American Secretary of transportation, Mar 1976

Coleraine, Richard Kidston Law, Feb 1944

Coles, Robert, American psychiatrist, Nov 1969

Colicchio, Tom, American chef and restaurateur, Feb 2013

Colijn, Hendrikus, Dutch prime minister, *Obit* Jan 1945

Colina, Rafael de la, Jan 1951

Collen, Phil, English guitarist and singer, Jan 2003

Colles, H. C., *Obit* Apr 1943

Collet, John C., Feb 1946, *Obit* Feb 1956

Collier, Constance, July 1954, *Obit* June 1955

Collier, John, American anthropologist and government official, Mar 1941, *Obit* July 1968

Collier, Sophia, American television and Internet service executive, July 2002

Collier, William, American actor, *Obit* Mar 1944

Collina, Pierluigi, Italian soccer referee, Jan 2002

Collingwood, Charles, American radio and television reporter, June 1943, *Obit* Nov 1985

Collingwood, R. G., British philosopher and historian, *Obit* Mar 1943

Collins, Cardiss, American congresswoman, Feb 1997, *Obit* Yrbk 2013

Collins, Eddie, American actor, *Obit* Oct 1940

Collins, Gail, American columnist, Mar 1999

Collins, George Lewis, *Obit* Aug 1940

Collins, J. Lawton, American general, Nov 1949, *Obit* Oct 1987

Collins, Jackie, English novelist, July 2000

Collins, James Daniel, philosopher, Yrbk 1963

Collins, Jim, American business consultant, Aug 2003

Collins, Jimmy, baseball player, *Obit* Apr 1943

Collins, Joan, British actress, Jan 1984

Collins, John F., American mayor, Jan 1965, *Obit* Feb 1996

Collins, Judy, American singer and songwriter, Apr 1969

Collins, LeRoy, American governor, June 1956, Apr 1965, *Obit* May 1991

Collins, Lorin Cone, *Obit* Yrbk 1940

Collins, Martha Layne, governor, Jan 1986

Collins, Marva, American teacher, Nov 1986

Collins, Michael, American astronaut and aerospace consultant, May 1975

Collins, Patricia Hill, American sociologist, Mar 2003

Collins, Phil, English video artist, Jan 2007

Collins, Phil, British singer, songwriter and drummer, Nov 1986

Collins, Seaborn P., Apr 1955

Collins, Susan, American senator, May 2000

Collins, Suzanne, American young adult fantasy novelist, Sept 2012

Collison, Wilson, *Obit* July 1941

Collor de Mello, Fernando, Brazilian president, Mar 1990

Collyer, John L., Mar 1947

Colman, Ronald, English actor, July 1943, *Obit* Sept 1958

Colombo, Emilio, Apr 1971, *Obit* Yrbk 2013

Colquitt, Oscar Branch, *Obit* Mar 1940

Colson, Charles W., American lawyer, presidential aide and evangelist, *Obit* Yrbk 2012

Columbus, Chris, American film director and screenwriter, Nov 2001

Colville, Alex, Canadian painter, Mar 1985, *Obit* Yrbk 2013

Colvin, Mamie White, Yrbk 1944, *Obit* Jan 1956

Colvin, Shawn, singer, Mar 1999

Colwell, Eileen, British librarian, July 1963

Colwell, Rita R., American microbiologist, May 1999

Comaneci, Nadia, Romanian gymnast, Feb 1977

Combs, Bert Thomas, governor and lawyer, June 1960, *Obit* Feb 1992

Comden, Betty, American lyricist, librettist and screenwriter, Mar 1945, *Obit* Yrbk 2007

Comden, Betty; and Green, Adolph, Mar 1945

Comer, James P., professor of psychiatry, Aug 1991

Cometbus, Aaron, American magazine publisher and writer, Mar 2005

Comfort, Alex, English physician, novelist and poet, Sept 1974, *Obit* Aug 2000

Commager, Henry Steele, historian, Jan 1946, *Obit* May 1998

Common, American rapper, Feb 2012

Commoner, Barry, American biologist and environmentalist, Sept 1970, *Obit* Yrbk 2012

Como, Perry, American singer, Apr 1947, *Obit* July 2001

Companys y Jover, Luis, *Obit* Yrbk 1940

Compton, Arthur Holly, American physicist, Aug 1940, Sept 1958, *Obit* May 1962

Compton, Karl Taylor, Mar 1941, *Obit* Sept 1954

Compton, Wilson, Apr 1952, *Obit* May 1967

Conable, Barber B., American congressman and banking official, July 1984, *Obit* Yrbk 2004

Conant, James Bryant, American college president and diplomat, Mar 1941, Feb 1951, *Obit* Apr 1978

Concheso, Aurelio Fernandez, May 1942, *Obit* Jan 1956

Conde, Cristobal, Chilean-American computer software executive, Sept 2010

Condon, Eddie, American jazz guitarist, Oct 1944, *Obit* Oct 1973

Condon, Edward Uhler, American physicist and government official, Apr 1946, *Obit* May 1974

Condon, Frank, *Obit* Feb 1941

Condon, Richard, novelist, Feb 1989, *Obit* June 1996

Cone, David, American baseball player, Feb 1998

Cone, Fairfax, July 1966, *Obit* Aug 1977

Conerly, Charlie, football player, Apr 1960, *Obit* Apr 1996

Congdon, William, painter, May 1967, *Obit* July 1998

Conigliaro, Tony, baseball player, Feb 1971, *Obit* Apr 1990

Coningham, Arthur, British air marshal, Nov 1944, *Obit* Feb 1948

Conlee, Jenny, American keyboardist, Aug 2007

Conley, Eugene, July 1954, *Obit* Feb 1982

Conley, William Gustavus, *Obit* Yrbk 1940

Conn, Billy, American boxer, Aug 1941, *Obit* Aug 1993

Connah, Douglas John, *Obit* Oct 1941

Connally, John B., American governor, presidential adviser and Secretary of the treasury, July 1961, *Obit* Aug 1993

Connally, Tom, American senator, Yrbk 1941, Apr 1949, *Obit* Jan 1964

Conneff, Kevin, Irish bodhran player and singer, Mar 2004

Connell, Arthur J., Feb 1954

Connell, Karl, *Obit* Yrbk 1941

Connelly, Jennifer, American actress, June 2002

Connelly, Marc, dramatist, Nov 1969, *Obit* Feb 1981

Conner, Dennis, yacht racer, Nov 1987

Conner, Nadine, American opera singer, Jan 1955, *Obit* Aug 2003

Connerly, Ward, American business consultant and anti-affirmative action activist, Nov 2000

Connery, Lawrence J., *Obit* Yrbk 1941

Connery, Sean, Scottish actor, Jan 1966, June 1993

Conness, Robert, *Obit* Mar 1941

Connick, Harry, American pianist and singer, Nov 1990

Connolly, Cyril, English essayist, critic and editor, Yrbk 1947

Connolly, Maureen, American tennis player, Nov 1951, *Obit* Sept 1969

Connolly, Walter, actor, *Obit* July 1940

Connor, John T., American Secretary of commerce, Apr 1961, *Obit* Feb 2001

Connors, Jimmy, American tennis player, Sept 1975

Conover, Harry, Feb 1949, *Obit* Oct 1965

Conrad, Barnaby, author and painter, Sept 1959, *Obit* Yrbk 2013

Conrad, Pete, American astronaut, Yrbk 1965

Conroy, Pat, American novelist, Jan 1996

Conroy, Patrick Dominic, July 1954

Considine, Bob, columnist, Yrbk 1947, *Obit* Nov 1975

Constantine, Apr 1967

Conte, Nicola, Italian DJ and record producer, Jan 2005

Conti, Tom, Scottish actor, June 1985

Converse, Frederick Shepherd, composer, *Obit* Aug 1940

Conway, Gerry, English drummer, Sept 2005

Conway, Jill K., Australian historian and college president, June 1991

Conway, John Horton, British mathematician, Sept 2003

Conway, Tim, American comedian and actor, Apr 1981

Conyers, John, American congressman, Sept 1970

Coogan, Steve, English actor and comedian, Jan 2002

Cook, Barbara, American singer, Feb 1963

Cook, Donald, July 1954, *Obit* Yrbk 1961

Cook, Donald C., May 1952, *Obit* Feb 1982

Cook, Fannie, American novelist and painter, Yrbk 1946, *Obit* Oct 1949

Cook, Frederick Albert, American physician and explorer, *Obit* Sept 1940

Cook, Jamie, British rock singer, Jan 2006

Cook, Marlow W., Jan 1972

Cook, Murray, Australian actor and singer, Jan 2004

Cook, Richard, American motion picture executive, July 2003

Cook, Tim, American computer industry executive, Sept 2012

Cook, W. W., *Obit* Yrbk 1943

Cooke, Alistair, Anglo-American radio reporter and television personality, June 1952, May 1974, *Obit* Yrbk 2004

Cooke, Hope, author, Feb 1967

Cooke, Leslie E., June 1962, *Obit* Apr 1967

Cooke, Morris Llewellyn, American industrial engineer and government official, May 1950, *Obit* May 1960

Cooke, Terence James, Sept 1968, *Obit* Nov 1983

Cool, Tre, American drummer, Aug 2005

Cooley, Denton A., American cardiac surgeon, Jan 1976

Cooley, Harold D., American congressman, Mar 1951, *Obit* Mar 1974

Coolidge, Dane, author, *Obit* Sept 1940

Coolidge, Elizabeth Sprague, music patron, Aug 1941, *Obit* Jan 1954

Coolidge, William David, American physical chemist and inventor, June 1947, *Obit* Mar 1975

Coolio, American rapper, Aug 1998

Coon, Carleton Stevens, American anthropologist, Sept 1955, *Obit* July 1981

Cooney, Joan Ganz, American television executive, July 1970

Coons, Albert H., June 1960

Coontz, Stephanie, American historian, July 2003

Cooper, Anderson, American television news anchor and talk show host, June 2006

Cooper, Chris, American actor, July 2004

Cooper, Courtney Ryley, author, *Obit* Nov 1940

Cooper, Duff, British diplomat, Aug 1940, *Obit* Mar 1954

Cooper, Edwin, English architect, *Obit* Aug 1942

Cooper, Gary, American actor, Yrbk 1941, *Obit* July 1961

Cooper, Gladys, English actress, Feb 1956, *Obit* Jan 1972

Cooper, Gordon, American astronaut and aircraft industry executive, Sept 1963

Cooper, Irving S., neurosurgeon, Apr 1974, *Obit* Jan 1986

Cooper, Jere, American congressman, Mar 1955, *Obit* Feb 1958

Cooper, John Sherman, American senator and diplomat, June 1950, *Obit* Apr 1991

Cooper, Joseph David, Feb 1952

Cooper, Kent, journalist, Oct 1944, *Obit* Mar 1965

Cooper, Kyle, American graphic designer, Nov 2009

Cooper, Louise Field, author, Yrbk 1950, *Obit* Jan 1993

Cooper, R. Conrad, Jan 1960

Cooper-Dyke, Cynthia, American basketball player and coach, Aug 1998

Coover, Robert, American novelist, Feb 1991

Copeland, Benjamin, *Obit* Jan 1941

Copeland, Lammot Du Pont, chemical executive, May 1963

Copland, Aaron, American composer, Sept 1940, Mar 1951, *Obit* Yrbk 1991

Copperfield, David, American magician, July 1992

Coppers, George H., May 1952

Coppola, Francis Ford, American film director, May 1974, July 1991

Coppola, Sofia, American film director and screenwriter, Nov 2003

Cora, Cat, American chef and cookbook writer, Nov 2011

Corbett, Jim, British game hunter, May 1946, *Obit* June 1955

Corbijn, Anton, Dutch photographer, June 2006

Corcoran, Thomas, American lawyer, Mar 1940, *Obit* Feb 1982

Cordero, Angel, jockey, Oct 1975

Cordier, Andrew Wellington, Apr 1950, *Obit* Sept 1975

Cordier, Constant, *Obit* Mar 1940

Cordiner, Ralph, Jan 1951, *Obit* Jan 1974

Cordobes, Jan 1966

Cordon, Guy, American senator, Apr 1952, *Obit* July 1969

Corea, Chick, American jazz pianist, Oct 1988

Corea, Claude, Mar 1961, *Obit* Nov 1962

Corell, Hans, Swedish diplomat, lawyer and United Nations official, Jan 2003

Corella, Angel, Spanish ballet dancer, Mar 1999

Corelli, Franco, Italian opera singer, Feb 1964, *Obit* Mar 2004

Corey, Paul, American novelist, Yrbk 1940

Cori, Carl F., American biochemist, Yrbk 1947, *Obit* Feb 1985

Cori, Carl F.; and Cori, Gerty T., Yrbk 1947

Cori, Gerty Theresa, American biochemist, Yrbk 1947, *Obit* Jan 1958

Corman, Roger, American motion picture director, producer and screenwriter, Feb 1983

Cornelius, Don, American television program host and producer, *Obit* Yrbk 2012

Cornelius, John C., June 1960

Cornell, Katharine, American actress, May 1941, Mar 1952, *Obit* July 1974

Cornwell, Patricia Daniels, American mystery novelist, May 1997

Corrales, Raul, Cuban photographer, Jan 2003

Correa, Rafael, Ecuadorian president, Jan 2007

Correll, Charles J., Yrbk 1947, *Obit* Nov 1972

Corrigan, Joseph M., *Obit* Aug 1942

Corrigan, Mairead, Irish pacifist, Apr 1978

Corsaro, Frank, American theatrical director and drama teacher, Aug 1975

Corsi, Jerome R., American political writer, Nov 2008

Corson, Fred Pierce, bishop, May 1961, *Obit* Apr 1985

Cortazar, Julio, Argentine novelist, Feb 1974, *Obit* Apr 1984

Cortelyou, George Bruce, postmaster general and secretary of the treasury, *Obit* Yrbk 1940

Cortez, Jayne, American poet, *Obit* Yrbk 2013

Cortney, Philip, Jan 1958, *Obit* July 1971

Corwin, Norman, American radio and television scriptwriter and producer, Yrbk 1940, *Obit* Yrbk 2011

Cory, John Mackenzie, librarian, Sept 1949, *Obit* May 1988

Corzine, Jon S., American financial executive and former governor, Aug 2006

Cosby, Bill, American actor and comedian, Apr 1967, Oct 1986

Cosell, Howard, American sportscaster, Nov 1972, *Obit* July 1995

Cosgrave, Liam, Irish prime minister, June 1977

Cossiga, Francesco, Italian president, Jan 1981, *Obit* Yrbk 2010

Cost, March, Jan 1958, *Obit* Apr 1973

Costa e Silva, Arthur da, Sept 1967, *Obit* Feb 1970

Costa, Albert, Spanish tennis player, Jan 2002

Costa, Ronaldo da, Brazilian marathon runner, Jan 2002

Costa-Gavras, Greek-French motion picture director, Sept 1972

Costain, Thomas B., American novelist and editor, May 1953, *Obit* Yrbk 1965

Costanza, Midge, American presidential aide, June 1978, *Obit* Yrbk 2010

Costas, Bob, American sportscaster, Jan 1993

Costello, John A., Apr 1948, *Obit* Feb 1976

Costello, Lou, American comedian, Oct 1941, *Obit* May 1959

Costle, Douglas M., June 1980

Costner, Kevin, American actor and film director, June 1990

Cot, Pierre, French political leader, June 1944, *Obit* Oct 1977

Cothran, James W., Sept 1953

Cotler, Irwin, Canadian member of Parliament, Jan 2006

Cotrubas, Ileana, Oct 1981

Cotten, Joseph, American actor, July 1943, *Obit* Apr 1994

Cottenham, Mark Everard Pepys, *Obit* Sept 1943

Cotterell, Geoffrey, Yrbk 1954

Cotto, Miguel, Puerto Rican boxer, Feb 2008

Cotton, Joseph Bell, *Obit* Sept 1940

Cotton, Norris, American senator, Feb 1956, *Obit* May 1989

Cottrell, Dorothy, Yrbk 1955, *Obit* Sept 1957

Coty, Rene, French president, Apr 1954, *Obit* Jan 1963

Coudenhove-Kalergi, Richard Nicolaus, Austrian political philosopher and international organization official, Feb 1948, *Obit* Oct 1972

Coudert, Frederic Rene, American congressman, June 1941, *Obit* July 1972

Coughlin, Charles Edward, American priest and radio commentator, Sept 1940, *Obit* Jan 1980

Coughlin, Natalie, American swimmer, July 2012

Coughlin, Tom, American football coach, Aug 2008

Coulter, Ann, American television commentator, Sept 2003

Coulter, Calvin Brewster, *Obit* Jan 1940

Coulter, John B., June 1954

Counsell, Craig, American baseball player, Sept 2002

Counting Crows (Musical group), Mar 2003

Counts, George S., author and educator, Yrbk 1941, *Obit* Jan 1975

Couples, Fred, American golfer, July 1993

Courant, Richard, mathematician, Sept 1966, *Obit* Mar 1972

Couric, Katie, American television news anchor, Mar 1993, Apr 2008

Cournand, Andre F., American physician, Mar 1957, *Obit* Apr 1988

Courreges, Andre, French fashion designer, Jan 1970

Court, Margaret, Australian tennis player, Sept 1973

Courtenay, Tom, English actor, May 1964

Cousins, Frank, English labor leader, Feb 1960, *Obit* July 1986

Cousins, Margaret, author and editor, June 1954, *Obit* Oct 1996

Cousins, Norman, American magazine editor, writer and anti-nuclear activist, Aug 1943, Aug 1977, *Obit* Jan 1991

Cousteau, Fabien, Aquatic filmmaker and oceanographer, June 2012

Cousteau, Jacques Yves, French oceanographer, June 1953, Jan 1976, *Obit* Sept 1997

Cousy, Bob, American basketball player, Sept 1958

Coutts, Frederick, English evangelist, Mar 1964

Coutts, Russell, New Zealand boat racer, Jan 2003

Couve de Murville, Maurice, French diplomat and prime minister, Apr 1955, *Obit* June 2000

Covarrubias, Miguel, Mexican painter and caricaturist, July 1940, *Obit* Apr 1957

Covey, Stephen R., American business training consultant, Jan 1998, *Obit* Yrbk 2012

Cowan, Minna G., Feb 1948

Coward, Noel, English actor, dramatist and composer, Jan 1941, Mar 1962, *Obit* May 1973

Cowden, Howard A., Mar 1952

Cowdry, E. V., anatomist and gerontologist, Jan 1948

Cowell, Simon, British record producer and talent judge on television program, Jan 2004

Cowen, Joshua Lionel, American inventor and toy train manufacturer, Sept 1954, *Obit* Nov 1965

Cowher, Bill, American football coach, Nov 2006

Cowles, Fleur, American painter and magazine editor, Apr 1952, *Obit* Yrbk 2009

Cowles, Gardner, American publisher, June 1943, *Obit* Aug 1985

Cowles, John, American newspaper publisher, June 1954, *Obit* Apr 1983

Cowles, Virginia, author and journalist, May 1942, *Obit* Nov 1983

Cowley, Malcolm, American literary critic, philologist and poet, June 1979, *Obit* May 1989

Cox, Allyn, painter, July 1954, *Obit* Jan 1983

Cox, Archibald, American lawyer and special counsel in Watergate investigation, July 1961, *Obit* Yrbk 2004

Cox, Bobby, American baseball manager, Feb 1998

Cox, Brian, Scottish actor, Jan 2004

Cox, Christopher, American regulatory agency official, July 1999

Cox, E. Eugene, American congressman, Apr 1943, *Obit* Feb 1953

Cox, Harvey Gallagher, American theologian, Nov 1968

Cox, Herald R., Apr 1961

Cox, Lynne, American swimmer, Sept 2004

Cox, Margaret, British archaeologist, Jan 2006

Cox, Wally, Feb 1954, *Obit* Apr 1973

Coxe, Howard, *Obit* Jan 1941

Coy, Wayne, Mar 1948, *Obit* Yrbk 1958

Coyne, James E., July 1955

Coyne, Wayne, American guitarist, singer and songwriter, Oct 2002

Cozzens, James Gould, American novelist, June 1949, *Obit* Oct 1978

Crabtree, James W., *Obit* July 1945

Craft, Robert, American conductor, Mar 1984

Craig, Cleo F., Sept 1951, *Obit* June 1978

Craig, Daniel, British actor, Apr 2007

Craig, George North, governor, Feb 1950, *Obit* Feb 1993

Craig, Lyman C., Apr 1964, *Obit* Sept 1974

Craig, Malin, Mar 1944, *Obit* Aug 1945

Craig, May, journalist, June 1949, *Obit* Sept 1975

Craig, Walter Early, judge, June 1964, *Obit* Sept 1986

Craigavon, James Craig, Northern Ireland political leader, *Obit* Jan 1941

Craigie, Robert, British diplomat, July 1942, *Obit* July 1959

Crain, Jeanne, American actress, Nov 1951, *Obit* Yrbk 2004

Cram, Ralph Adams, American architect, Oct 1942, *Obit* Oct 1942

Cramer, Stuart Warren, *Obit* Aug 1940

Crandall, Martin, American keyboardist, June 2007

Crandall, Robert L., American airline executive, Nov 1992

Crane, Eva, British apiculturist, Aug 1993, *Obit* Yrbk 2007

Crane, Philip M., American congressman, May 1980

Cranko, John, South African dancer and choreographer, July 1970, *Obit* Sept 1973

Cranston, Alan, American senator, Feb 1950, Oct 1969, *Obit* Mar 2001

Cravath, Paul D., *Obit* Aug 1940

Craveiro Lopes, Francisco Higino, Mar 1956, *Obit* Nov 1964

Craven, Frank, *Obit* Oct 1945

Craven, Thomas, American art critic, Apr 1944, *Obit* Apr 1969

Crawford, Broderick, actor, Apr 1950, *Obit* June 1986

Crawford, Cheryl, American theatrical producer, Yrbk 1945, *Obit* Nov 1986

Crawford, Cindy, American model, Aug 1993

Crawford, Frederick C., defense industries executive, Feb 1943, *Obit* Feb 1995

Crawford, Joan, American actress, Jan 1946, Sept 1966, *Obit* July 1977

Crawford, Michael, English actor and singer, Jan 1992

Crawford, Morris Barker, *Obit* Yrbk 1940

Crawford, Phyllis, author, Nov 1940

Crawshaw, William Henry, *Obit* Aug 1940

Craxi, Bettino, Italian prime minister, Feb 1984, *Obit* June 2000

Creamer, Paula, American golfer, May 2011

Creasey, John, English novelist, Sept 1963, *Obit* July 1973

Creed (Musical group), May 2002

Creel, George, American newspaper editor and government official, June 1944, *Obit* Jan 1954

Creeley, Robert, American poet, novelist, short story writer and essayist, Oct 1988, *Obit* Yrbk 2005

Cregar, Laird, *Obit* Jan 1945

Crenshaw, Ben, American golfer, Sept 1985

Crenshaw, Kimberle Williams, American law professor, May 2011

Crerar, Henry Duncan Graham, Canadian general, Nov 1944, *Obit* May 1965

Cresap, Mark W., Oct 1959, *Obit* Sept 1963

Crespin, Regine, French opera singer, Sept 1979, *Obit* Yrbk 2007

Cresson, Edith, French prime minister, Sept 1991

Cresswell, Robert, American newspaper publisher, *Obit* Nov 1943

Cret, Paul Philippe, French-American architect, Nov 1942, *Obit* Nov 1945

Crewe, Albert, American physicist, Feb 1964, *Obit* Yrbk 2010

Crewe, Robert Offley Ashburton Crew-Milnes, *Obit* July 1945

Crews, Laura Hope, actress, *Obit* Jan 1943

Crichton, Michael, American novelist, screenwriter and film director, Apr 1976, Nov 1993, *Obit* Apr 2009

Crick, Francis, British biochemist, Mar 1983, *Obit* Yrbk 2004

Crider, John H., June 1949, *Obit* Sept 1966

Crile, George Washington, American surgeon, *Obit* Feb 1943

Cripps, C. A., *Obit* Aug 1941

Cripps, Richard Stafford, British statesman, July 1940, Apr 1948, *Obit* June 1952

Crisler, Herbert Orin, football coach, Feb 1948, *Obit* Oct 1982

Crispin, Edmund, English novelist and short story writer, Yrbk 1949

Criss, Peter, American drummer, Apr 1999

Crist, William E., Nov 1945

Cristiani, Alfredo, Salvadoran president, Jan 1990

Cristiano Ronaldo, Portuguese soccer player, Jan 2007

Critchley, Simon, British philosopher, Apr 2010

Crittenden, Danielle, Canadian journalist, July 2003

Croce, Benedetto, Italian philosopher, historian and critic, Jan 1944, *Obit* Jan 1953

Crocker, Chester A., American diplomat, July 1990

Crocker, Ryan, American diplomat, Oct 2007

Crockett, Lucy Herndon, Yrbk 1953

Croft, Arthur C., June 1952

Cromer, David, American theatrical director and actor, Sept 2011

Cromer, George Rowland Stanley Baring, English

banker and diplomat, May 1971, *Obit* May 1991

Crompton, Rookes Evelyn Bell, English electrical equipment industry executive, *Obit* Mar 1940

Cromwell, James, American actor, Aug 2005

Cromwell, James H. R., American financial executive, diplomat and developer, Mar 1940, *Obit* May 1990

Cronenberg, David, Canadian motion picture director, May 1992

Cronin, A. J., Scottish novelist and physician, July 1942, *Obit* Mar 1981

Cronin, Joe, American baseball player, manager and executive, Mar 1965, *Obit* Nov 1984

Cronkite, Walter, American television news anchor, Jan 1956, Nov 1975, *Obit* Sept 2009

Cronyn, Hume, Canadian actor, Mar 1956, June 1988, *Obit* Yrbk 2003

Croome, Rodney, Australian gay rights activist, Jan 2004

Crosbie, John Carnell, Canadian political leader, Jan 1990

Crosby, Bing, American singer and actor, Sept 1941, June 1953, *Obit* Jan 1978

Crosby, John, journalist, novelist and television critic, June 1953

Crosby, John O'Hea, American conductor and opera company manager, Nov 1981, *Obit* Yrbk 2003

Crosby, Robert, June 1954

Crosland, Anthony, British cabinet member, Sept 1963, *Obit* Apr 1977

Crosley, Powel, American baseball and automobile executive, June 1947, *Obit* June 1961

Cross, Ben, English actor, Aug 1984

Cross, Burton Melvin, governor, Apr 1954, *Obit* Jan 1999

Cross, Milton, Jan 1940, *Obit* Feb 1975

Cross, Ronald H., June 1941

Crossan, John Dominic, Irish theologian, May 2011

Crosser, Robert, Mar 1953, *Obit* Sept 1957

Crossfield, A. Scott, American aeronautical engineer, test pilot and consultant, Oct 1969, *Obit* Yrbk 2006

Crossley, Archibald M., public opinion analyst, Yrbk 1941, *Obit* July 1985

Crossman, R. H. S., British socialist leader, May 1947, *Obit* June 1974

Crouch, Stanley, American essayist and critic, Mar 1994

Crouse, Russel, dramatist, June 1941, *Obit* May 1966

Crow, Carl, American journalist, Oct 1941, *Obit* July 1945

Crow, John O., Mar 1969

Crow, Sheryl, American singer and songwriter, May 1998

Crowe, Cameron, American screenwriter and film director, Mar 1996

Crowe, Russell, Australian actor, May 2000

Crowe, William J., American admiral, July 1988, *Obit* Yrbk 2008

Crowell, T. Irving, *Obit* Mar 1942

Crowley, Candy, American television reporter, Jan 2011

Crowley, John J., priest, *Obit* Apr 1940

Crowley, Leo, American banker and government official, June 1943, *Obit* June 1972

Crown, Henry, financier, Jan 1972, *Obit* Oct 1990

Crownfield, Gertrude, *Obit* July 1945

Crowther, Bosley, motion picture critic, July 1957, *Obit* Apr 1981

Cruise, Tom, American actor, Apr 1987

Crum, Bartley C., lawyer, May 1947, *Obit* Feb 1960

Crumb, George, American composer, Yrbk 1979

Crumb, R., American cartoonist, Apr 1995

Crumit, Frank, *Obit* Oct 1943

Crump, N. R., Sept 1957

Cruyff, Johan, Dutch soccer player and manager, Nov 1981

Cruz, Celia, Cuban-American singer, July 1983, *Obit* Nov 2003

Cruz, Penelope, Spanish actress, July 2001

Cruz, Ted, American state solicitor general, May 2013

Cruze, James, motion picture director, *Obit* Sept 1942

Cruzen, Richard H., Mar 1947, *Obit* June 1970

Crystal, Billy, American comedian and actor, Feb 1987

Csaky, Stephen, *Obit* Mar 1941

Csonka, Larry, American football player, Feb 1977

Cuaron, Alfonso, Mexican film director, Jan 2003

Cuban, Mark, American broadcasting and basketball executive, Mar 2001

Cubberley, Ellwood Patterson, educator, *Obit* Nov 1941

Cudahy, John, diplomat, *Obit* Oct 1943

Cuevas, Jose Luis, Mexican illustrator and printmaker, Jan 1968

Cuevas, Manuel, Mexican-American costume designer, Jan 2005

Cugat, Xavier, band leader, May 1942, *Obit* Jan 1991

Cui Jian, Chinese rock musician, Jan 2002

Cukor, George, American motion picture director, Apr 1943, *Obit* Mar 1983

Culbertson, Ely, bridge player, May 1940, *Obit* Mar 1956

Culkin, Francis D., *Obit* Sept 1943

Cullberg, Birgit, Swedish ballet dancer and choreographer, Nov 1982, *Obit* Nov 1999

Cullen, Bill, television game show host, Jan 1960, *Obit* Sept 1990

Cullen, Countee, American poet, *Obit* Mar 1946

Cullen, Glenn Ernest, *Obit* May 1940

Cullen, Hugh Roy, petroleum executive, July 1955, *Obit* Sept 1957

Cullen, Thomas H., *Obit* Apr 1944

Cullis, Winifred C., Nov 1943, *Obit* Jan 1957

Cullman, Howard S., June 1951, *Obit* Sept 1972

Culpepper, Daunte, American football player, Sept 2007

Culshaw, John, British recording producer, June 1968, *Obit* June 1980

Culver, Essae Martha, American librarian, Sept 1940

Culver, John C., Nov 1979

Cummings, Elijah E., American congressman, Feb 2004

Cummings, Robert, actor, Jan 1956, *Obit* Feb 1991

Cuneo, John F., June 1950

Cunhal, Alvaro, Portuguese communist leader, Sept 1975, *Obit* Yrbk 2005

Cunningham of Hyndhope, Andrew Browne Cunningham, British admiral, May 1941, *Obit* Sept 1963

Cunningham, Alan, British general, June 1946, *Obit* Apr 1983

Cunningham, Bill, American photographer, Aug 2011

Cunningham, Graham, Sept 1949

Cunningham, Merce, American dancer and choreographer, May 1966, *Obit* Yrbk 2009

Cunningham, Michael, American novelist, July 1999

Cunningham, Phil, British guitarist and keyboardist, Jan 2006

Cunningham, Randall, American football player, Mar 1991

Cunningham, William Francis, *Obit* Jan 1941

Cunningham-Agee, Mary, American electronics industry executive, Nov 1984

Cuomo, Andrew, American governor, Oct 1998

Cuomo, Mario, American governor, Aug 1983

Curran, Charles Courtney, American painter, *Obit* Jan 1943

Curran, Charles E., American priest and theologian, Jan 1987

Curran, Joseph E., American labor leader, Apr 1945, *Obit* Oct 1981

Curran, Pearl G., *Obit* June 1941

Currie, Lauchlin Bernard, American economist, May 1941, *Obit* Mar 1994

Currie, Nancy, American astronaut, June 2002

Curry, Ann, American television newscaster, June 2004

Curry, John, English figure skater, July 1979, *Obit* June 1994

Curry, John Steuart, American painter, Apr 1941, *Obit* Oct 1946

Curry, Peggy Simson, author and poet, Yrbk 1958

Curtice, Harlow H., American automobile executive, Mar 1953, *Obit* Jan 1963

Curtin, Jane, actress, Jan 1997

Curtin, John, Australian prime minister, July 1941, *Obit* Aug 1945

Curtin, Phyllis, American opera singer and teacher, Sept 1964

Curtis, Ann, swimmer, June 1945, *Obit* Yrbk 2012

Curtis, Carl T., American senator, Sept 1954, *Obit* June 2000

Curtis, George V., *Obit* Oct 1943

Curtis, Heber D., American astronomer, *Obit* Mar 1942

Curtis, Jamie Lee, American actress, Nov 1998

Curtis, Thomas B., American congressman, Mar 1965, *Obit* Mar 1993

Curtis, Tony, American actor, May 1959, *Obit* Nov 2010

Curzon, Clifford, English pianist, May 1950, *Obit* Oct 1982

Cusack, Joan, American actress, July 1998

Cusack, John, American actor, June 1996

Cushing, Charles C. S., *Obit* Apr 1941

Cushing, Richard James, June 1952, *Obit* Yrbk 1970

Cushman, Robert Everton, American Marine Corps general, Nov 1972, *Obit* Apr 1985

Cussler, Clive, American novelist, Nov 2000

Custin, Mildred, retail executive, Nov 1967, *Obit* June 1997

Cuthbert, Margaret, May 1947, *Obit* Oct 1968

Cyrankiewicz, Jozef, Feb 1957

Czettel, Ladislas, Mar 1941, *Obit* Apr 1949

D

D'Amato, Alfonse, American senator, Sept 1983

D'Amboise, Jacques, American ballet dancer, choreographer and teacher, Sept 1964

D'Ambrosio, Ubiratan, Brazilian mathematician, Jan 2003

D'Angelo, American singer, May 2001

D'Antoni, Mike, American basketball coach, June 2009

D'Arcy, Martin Cyril, British priest and philosopher, Jan 1960, *Obit* Mar 1977

D'Aubuisson, Roberto, Salvadoran political leader, July 1983, *Obit* Apr 1992

D'Aulaire, Edgar Parin, author and illustrator, Aug 1940

D'Aulaire, Ingri, author and illustrator, Aug 1940

D'Harnoncourt, Rene, Sept 1952, *Obit* Oct 1968

D'Onofrio, Vincent, American actor, May 2004

D'Oyly Carte, Rupert, Feb 1948

D'Usseau, Arnaud, dramatist and screenwriter, Mar 1944, *Obit* Apr 1990

DMX, American rapper, Aug 2003

Dabney, Virginius, American newspaper editor and historian, Sept 1948, *Obit* Mar 1996

Dache, Lilly, French milliner, July 1941, *Obit* Mar 1990

Daddy G (Singer), English singer and DJ, June 2004

Dafoe, Allan Roy, *Obit* July 1943

Dafoe, John Wesley, *Obit* Feb 1944

Dafoe, Willem, American actor, Apr 1990

Daft, Doug, Australian beverage industry executive, May 2001

Dahanayake, Wijeyananda, Apr 1960

Dahlberg, Edwin T., clergyman, May 1958, *Obit* Oct 1986

Daladier, Edouard, French statesman, Apr 1940, *Obit* Yrbk 1970

Dalai Lama, Tibetan religious and political leader (deposed 1959), July 1951, June 1982

Dale, Benjamin James, *Obit* Sept 1943

Dale, Chester, American investment banker and art collector, Sept 1958, *Obit* Jan 1963

Dale, Clamma, Apr 1979

Dale, Jim, English actor, July 1981

Daley, Arthur, sportswriter, Sept 1956, *Obit* Feb 1974

Daley, Richard J., American mayor, Sept 1955, June 1976

Daley, Richard M., American mayor, Aug 1992

Daley, William, American presidential adviser, Mar 1998

Dali, Salvador, Spanish painter, Sept 1940, Apr 1951, *Obit* Mar 1989

Dallapiccola, Luigi, Italian composer, Feb 1966

Dallas, C. Donald, Apr 1949, *Obit* June 1959

Dallek, Robert, American historian, Sept 2007

Dallin, Cyrus Edwin, sculptor, *Obit* Jan 1945

Dalmia, Ramkrishna, Yrbk 1948

Dalrymple, Jean, theatrical producer, Sept 1953, *Obit* Feb 1999

Dalton, Charles, *Obit* Aug 1942

Dalton, Hugh Dalton, British cabinet member, Aug 1945, *Obit* Apr 1962

Dalton, Timothy, English actor, May 1988

Daluege, Kurt, German Nazi leader, *Obit* Yrbk 1946

Daly, Cahal B., Jan 2002, *Obit* Yrbk 2010

Daly, Carson, American video jockey and talk show host, Nov 2009

Daly, Chuck, American basketball coach, Apr 1991, *Obit* Yrbk 2009

Daly, James, Oct 1959, *Obit* Sept 1978

Daly, John Charles, radio reporter and television moderator, May 1948, *Obit* May 1991

Daly, Maureen, American young adult novelist, Jan 1946, *Obit* Yrbk 2006

Daly, Thomas A., *Obit* Mar 1941

Daly, Tyne, actress, Mar 1992

Dam, Henrik, Danish biochemist, Sept 1949, *Obit* June 1976

Damadian, Raymond, American physician and inventor, Jan 2000

Damasio, Antonio R., American neurobiologist, Oct 2007

Damaskenos, Nov 1945, *Obit* July 1949

Damerel, Donna, *Obit* Apr 1941

Damon, Lindsay Todd, *Obit* Jan 1940

Damon, Matt, American actor, Mar 1998

Damon, Ralph S., July 1949, *Obit* Mar 1956

Damrosch, Walter, American conductor and composer, Mar 1944, *Obit* Jan 1951

Dancer, Stanley, American harness racer, June 1973, *Obit* Yrbk 2005

Dandurand, Raoul, *Obit* Apr 1942

Dandy, Walter E., American neurosurgeon, *Obit* May 1946

Danforth, John C., American senator, Jan 1992

Danforth, William, *Obit* June 1941

Dangarembga, Tsitsi, Zimbabwean novelist and film director, Jan 2006

Dangerfield, George, American historian, Sept 1953, *Obit* Mar 1987

Dangerfield, Rodney, American comedian, *Obit* Feb 2005

Daniel, Clifton, American journalist, Mar 1966, *Obit* July 2000

Daniel, Dan, congressman, June 1957

Daniel, Price, American senator and governor, Jan 1956, *Obit* Oct 1988

Daniel, Robert Prentiss, May 1952, *Obit* Mar 1968

Daniel-Rops, Henri, Mar 1957, *Obit* Oct 1965

Daniell, Raymond, Mar 1944, *Obit* June 1969

Daniels, Arthur Hill, *Obit* Apr 1940

Daniels, Charles N., composer, *Obit* Mar 1943

Daniels, Farrington, July 1965, *Obit* Sept 1972

Daniels, Grace B., Sept 1959

Daniels, Jonathan, newspaper editor, Apr 1942, *Obit* Jan 1982

Daniels, Josephus, American Secretary of the navy and diplomat, Oct 1944, *Obit* Feb 1948

Daniels, Lee, American film director and producer, June 2010

Daniken, Erich von, Swiss author, May 1976

Danilova, Alexandra, Russian ballet dancer and teacher, July 1987, *Obit* Sept 1997

Dannay, Frederic, American mystery writer, July 1940, *Obit* Oct 1982

Danner, Blythe, American actress, Jan 1981

Danner, Louise Rutledge, *Obit* Nov 1943

Danson, Ted, American actor, Oct 1990

Danto, Arthur Coleman, American philosopher and art critic, Apr 1995

Daratista, Inul, Indonesian singer and dancer, Jan 2003

Dardel, Nils von, Swedish painter, *Obit* July 1943

Darden, Christopher, district attorney, Feb 1997

Darden, Colgate W., Sept 1948

Dardenne, Jean-Pierre, Belgian film director and screenwriter, May 2011

Dardenne, Luc, Belgian film director and screenwriter, May 2011

Dargan, Edwin Preston, *Obit* Feb 1941

Darin, Bobby, American singer and actor, Mar 1963, *Obit* Feb 1974

Darin, Ricardo, Argentine actor, Jan 2002

Daringer, Helen Fern, Yrbk 1951

Dark, Alvin, baseball manager, Mar 1975

Darkness (Musical group), Jan 2004

Darlan, Francois, French admiral, Mar 1941, *Obit* Feb 1943

Darling, Jay Norwood, American cartoonist and conservationist, July 1942, *Obit* Mar 1962

Darling, Sharon, American literacy advocate, May 2003

Darman, Richard, American presidential aide, May 1989, *Obit* Yrbk 2008

Darre, R. Walther, German Nazi leader, Nov 1941, *Obit* Jan 1957

Darrell, R. D., music critic, Sept 1955, *Obit* June 1988

Darrow, Whitney, cartoonist, Yrbk 1958, *Obit* Oct 1999

Dart, Justin Whitlock, drug industry executive, Nov 1946, *Obit* Mar 1984

Dart, Raymond A., South African anatomist, Sept 1966, *Obit* Jan 1989

Darwell, Jane, June 1941, *Obit* Oct 1967

Darwin, Leonard, *Obit* May 1943

Daschle, Thomas, American senator, Oct 1995

Dashiell, Willard, *Obit* June 1943

Dassault, Marcel, French aircraft executive and engineer, June 1970, *Obit* June 1986

Dassin, Jules, American film director, Mar 1971, *Obit* Yrbk 2008

Dati, Rachida, French lawyer and cabinet member, Apr 2009

Datsyuk, Pavel, Russian hockey player, Nov 2012

Daud Khan, Sardar Mohammed, Mar 1957

Daudet, Leon, French journalist, novelist and memoirist, *Obit* Aug 1942

Daugherty, Carroll Roop, economist, Oct 1949, *Obit* June 1988

Daugherty, Harry M., American Attorney general, *Obit* Yrbk 1941

Daugherty, James Henry, American children's author and illustrator, July 1940, *Obit* Apr 1974

Dauser, Sue S., Aug 1944

Dausset, Jean, French immunologist, May 1981, *Obit* Yrbk 2009

Davenport, Charles B., biologist and educator, *Obit* Apr 1944

Davenport, Eugene, *Obit* May 1941

Davenport, Marcia, novelist, Jan 1944, *Obit* Mar 1996

Davenport, Russell W., Jan 1944, *Obit* June 1954

Davey, Martin L., American governor, congressman and mayor, *Obit* May 1946

David, Donald K., Feb 1948, *Obit* June 1979

David, Edward E., physicist and engineer, May 1974

David, Hal, songwriter, Sept 1980, *Obit* Yrbk 2012

David, Larry, American comedian, television scriptwriter and producer, Aug 1998

Davidovich, Bella, Russian pianist, May 1989

Davidovitch, Ljuba, *Obit* Mar 1940

Davidson, Garrison Holt, general, June 1957, *Obit* Feb 1993

Davidson, Gordon, American theatrical director and producer, Apr 2005

Davidson, Irwin D., American congressman, Jan 1956

Davidson, Jo, American sculptor and engraver, Apr 1945, *Obit* Feb 1952

Davidson, John, singer and actor, Sept 1976

Davidson, John Frederick, admiral, Nov 1960, *Obit* Apr 1989

Davidson, Richard J., American neuroscientist, Aug 2004

Davidson, Roy E., Sept 1963, *Obit* Sept 1964

Davidson, William L., American physicist, July 1952

Davies, Clement, Oct 1950, *Obit* May 1962

Davies, Dennis Russell, conductor, May 1993

Davies, Ernest, May 1951

Davies, Joseph Edward, American lawyer and diplomat, Apr 1942, *Obit* July 1958

Davies, P. C. W., English physicist, Jan 2002

Davies, Peter Maxwell, English composer, Mar 1980

Davies, Robertson, Canadian novelist, playwright and critic, June 1975, *Obit* Mar 1996

Davies, Ronald N., American judge, Sept 1958, *Obit* June 1996

Davies, W. H., Welsh poet and author, *Obit* Nov 1940

Davies, Walford, *Obit* May 1941

Davis, Adelle, nutritionist, Jan 1973, *Obit* July 1974

Davis, Al, American football executive, July 1985, *Obit* Yrbk 2011

Davis, Andrew, British conductor, May 1983

Davis, Angela Yvonne, American political activist, Nov 1972

Davis, Anthony, American composer and pianist, May 1990

Davis, Archie K., May 1966

Davis, Artur, American congressman, Feb 2009

Davis, Benjamin O., American general, Yrbk 1942, *Obit* Jan 1971

Davis, Benjamin O., American air force general, Sept 1955, *Obit* Yrbk 2002

Davis, Bette, American actress, Oct 1941, Mar 1953, *Obit* Nov 1989

Davis, Chester Charles, American agricultural leader, banker and government official, July 1940, *Obit* Nov 1975

Davis, Clive, American recording executive, July 2000

Davis, Colin, British conductor, Nov 1968, *Obit* Yrbk 2013

Davis, Edward W., Sept 1955, *Obit* Feb 1974

Davis, Elmer, American radio commentator and short story writer, May 1940, *Obit* Sept 1958

Davis, Evelyn Y., American shareholders' rights activist, Oct 2007

Davis, Geena, American actress, Oct 1991

Davis, Gladys Rockmore, painter, Sept 1953, *Obit* Apr 1967

Davis, Glen, American basketball player, Nov 2010

Davis, Glenn W., American football player, Yrbk 1946, *Obit* Yrbk 2005

Davis, Gray, American governor, June 1999

Davis, Harvey N., July 1947, *Obit* Jan 1953

Davis, Herbert John, Jan 1940, *Obit* May 1967

Davis, J. Frank, *Obit* May 1942

Davis, James C., Apr 1957, *Obit* Feb 1982

Davis, Jess H., Jan 1956

Davis, Joan, comedienne and actress, June 1945, *Obit* Sept 1961

Davis, John William, American lawyer, congressman and

diplomat, Mar 1953, *Obit* May 1955

Davis, Jonathan M., governor, *Obit* Aug 1943

Davis, Joseph S., July 1947, *Obit* June 1975

Davis, Judy, Australian actress, Nov 1993

Davis, Mac, American country singer and songwriter, Aug 1980

Davis, Martin S., motion picture, television and publishing executive, Nov 1989, *Obit* Jan 2000

Davis, Meyer, June 1961, *Obit* June 1976

Davis, Miles, American jazz trumpet player and flugelhornist, June 1962, *Obit* Nov 1991

Davis, Nathanael V., American aluminum industry executive, Jan 1959, *Obit* Yrbk 2005

Davis, Norman Hezekiah, banker and diplomat, Jan 1940, *Obit* Aug 1944

Davis, Ossie, American actor and dramatist, Oct 1969, *Obit* Yrbk 2005

Davis, Patti, American novelist and daughter of President Ronald Reagan, Nov 1986

Davis, Peter, American film and television producer and director, Feb 1983

Davis, Robert, Yrbk 1949

Davis, Robert C., *Obit* Oct 1944

Davis, Robert H., dramatist and journalist, *Obit* Yrbk 1942

Davis, Roy H., Feb 1955, *Obit* Sept 1956

Davis, Sammy, American actor and singer, Sept 1956, July 1978, *Obit* July 1990

Davis, Shani, American speed skater, May 2006

Davis, Stuart, American painter, engraver and illustrator, Aug 1940, July 1964

Davis, Tobe Coller, Yrbk 1959, *Obit* Feb 1963

Davis, Wade, Canadian ethnobotanist, Jan 2003

Davis, Watson, Yrbk 1945, *Obit* Oct 1967

Davis, Westmoreland, *Obit* Oct 1942

Davis, William Ellsworth, Apr 1940

Davis, William G., Canadian political leader, May 1973

Davis, William H., June 1941, *Obit* Oct 1964

Davis, William Rhodes, Mar 1941, *Obit* Mar 1941

Davis-Kimball, Jeannine, American archaeologist, Feb 2006

Davison, F. Trubee, Yrbk 1945

Davison, Frederic Ellis, American general, Feb 1974

Dawdy, Shannon Lee, American archaeologist and anthropologist, Apr 2006

Dawes, Rufus Cutler, *Obit* Jan 1940

Dawkins, Richard, British zoologist, Aug 1997

Dawson of Penn, Bertrand Edward Dawson, English physician, *Obit* Apr 1945

Dawson, John A., investment banker, Sept 1952

Dawson, William, diplomat, Apr 1941, *Obit* Sept 1972

Dawson, William Levi, American congressman, Apr 1945, *Obit* Yrbk 1970

Day Lewis, C., Anglo-Irish poet, critic and mystery writer, Jan 1940, July 1969, *Obit* July 1972

Day, Albert M., biologist, Yrbk 1948

Day, Doris, American singer and actress, Apr 1954

Day, Dorothy, American journalist and social reformer, May 1962, *Obit* Jan 1981

Day, Edmund, Sept 1946, *Obit* Apr 1951

Day, James Edward, American postmaster general, May 1962, *Obit* Jan 1997

Day, Laraine, American actress, Sept 1953, *Obit* Yrbk 2008

Day, Pat, American jockey, Oct 1997

Day-Lewis, Daniel, Anglo-Irish actor, July 1990

Dayal, Rajeshwar, Feb 1961

Dayan, Moshe, Israeli general, Mar 1957, *Obit* Jan 1982

Dayan, Yael, Israeli author and daughter of Moshe Dayan, Apr 1997

De Angeli, Marguerite Lofft, American children's author and illustrator, Yrbk 1947

De Beck, Billy, cartoonist, *Obit* Jan 1943

De Benedetti, Carlo, Italian computer and telecommunications executive, May 1990

De Bono, Emilio, Italian field marshal, *Obit* Feb 1944

de Botton, Alain, English novelist and journalist, Sept 2013

De Branges, Louis, American mathematician, Nov 2005

De Casseres, Benjamin, essayist, critic and journalist, *Obit* Feb 1946

De Castro, Morris F., May 1950

De Chirico, Giorgio, Italian painter, Jan 1956, June 1972, *Obit* Jan 1979

De Creeft, Jose, sculptor, Yrbk 1942, *Obit* Yrbk 1991

De Forest, Lee, American radio engineer, May 1941, *Obit* Oct 1961

De Geer, Gerard, *Obit* Sept 1943

De Graff, Robert F., May 1943

De Hartog, Jan, Dutch novelist, Feb 1970, *Obit* Jan 2003

de Havilland, Olivia; and Fontaine, Joan, May 1944

De Havilland, Olivia, American actress, May 1944, Nov 1966

De Jong, David C., novelist, July 1944, *Obit* Nov 1967

De Kiewiet, C. W., college president and historian, July 1953, *Obit* Apr 1986

De Kleine, William, Apr 1941, *Obit* Yrbk 1958

De Klerk, Frederik Willem, South African president, Feb 1990

De Kooning, Elaine Marie Catherine, American painter, July 1982, *Obit* Mar 1989

De Kooning, Willem, American painter, June 1955, Sept 1984, *Obit* May 1997

De Kruif, Paul, author and bacteriologist, May 1942, July 1963, *Obit* Apr 1971

De La Hoya, Oscar, American boxer, Jan 1997

De Laurentiis, Dino, Italian film producer, May 1965, *Obit* Yrbk 2011

De Laurentiis, Giada, American chef and television personality, July 2013

De Lavallade, Carmen, American actress and dancer, Yrbk 1967

De Leath, Vaughn, *Obit* July 1943

De Lille, Patricia, South African political leader, Jan 2004

De Lima, Sigrid, novelist, Yrbk 1958, *Obit* Feb 2000

De Long, Emma J. Wotton, *Obit* Jan 1941

De Lorean, John Z., American automobile executive, Mar 1976, *Obit* Yrbk 2005

De Luca, Giuseppe, Italian opera singer, Mar 1947, *Obit* Oct 1950

De Luce, Daniel, June 1944

De Maiziere, Lothar, German political leader, Aug 1990

De Mille, Agnes, American choreographer, Oct 1943, Jan 1985, *Obit* Jan 1994

De Mille, Cecil B., American motion picture director and producer, May 1942, *Obit* Mar 1959

De Montebello, Philippe, American museum director, Apr 1981

De Niro, Robert, American actor, Aug 1976, May 1993

De Onis, Harriet, translator, Apr 1957, *Obit* May 1969

De Palma, Brian, American motion picture director, Sept 1982

De Paola, Tomie, American painter, illustrator and children's author, Feb 1999

De Pauw, Gommar A., May 1974

De Quay, Jan Eduard, Dutch prime minister, May 1963, *Obit* Aug 1985

De Rochemont, Louis, motion picture producer, Nov 1949, *Obit* Feb 1979

De Rochemont, Richard G., Oct 1945, *Obit* Sept 1982

De Roussy de Sales, Raoul, *Obit* Jan 1943

De Sapio, Carmine G., American political leader, Sept 1955, *Obit* Yrbk 2004

De Selincourt, Ernest, English editor and literary critic, *Obit* July 1943

De Seversky, Alexander P., Feb 1941, *Obit* Oct 1974

De Sherbinin, Betty, Yrbk 1948

De Sica, Vittorio, Italian motion picture director, July 1952, *Obit* Jan 1975

De Silva, Desmond, British barrister and United Nations war crimes prosecutor, Jan 2006

De Sylva, Buddy, songwriter and motion picture producer, Sept 1943, *Obit* Sept 1950

De Valera, Eamon, Irish statesman, Nov 1940, Sept 1951, *Obit* Oct 1975

De Valois, Ninette, English ballet dancer, choreographer and director, Yrbk 1949, *Obit* Aug 2001

De Varona, Donna, American sportscaster and swimmer, Aug 2003

De Voto, Bernard Augustine, American historian, literary critic and novelist, Sept 1943, *Obit* Jan 1956

De Vries, Peter, American novelist, Yrbk 1959, *Obit* Jan 1994

De Vry, Herman A., *Obit* May 1941

De Witt, John Lesesne, American general, July 1942

De Wohl, Louis, Yrbk 1955, *Obit* Oct 1961

De Wolfe, James P., Aug 1942, *Obit* Mar 1966

De la Renta, Oscar, Dominican fashion designer, Mar 1970

De la Torre, Lillian, author, Yrbk 1949, *Obit* Nov 1993

De, Shobha, Indian novelist, journalist and television personality, Jan 2005

DeBakey, Michael E., American surgeon and inventor, Mar 1964, *Obit* Yrbk 2008

DeBarge, El, American singer, June 2011

DeBusschere, Dave, American basketball executive and player, Oct 1973, *Obit* Yrbk 2003

DeCarava, Roy, American photographer, Aug 2008, *Obit* Yrbk 2009

DeCarlo, Dan, American comic book artist, Aug 2001, *Obit* Mar 2002

DeConcini, Dennis, American senator, Feb 1992

DeCoursey, Elbert, Sept 1954

DeGaetani, Jan, opera singer, Oct 1977

DeGeneres, Ellen, American comedienne and talk show host, Apr 1996

DeJong, Meindert, Dutch-American children's author, Yrbk 1952, *Obit* Sept 1991

DeLany, Walter S., admiral, Yrbk 1952

DeLauro, Rosa, American congresswoman, Mar 2000

DeLay, Tom, American congressman, May 1999

DeLillo, Don, American novelist, Jan 1989

DeLonge, Tom, American guitarist, Aug 2002

DeMarcus, Jay, American keyboardist and singer, Aug 2003

DeMille, Nelson, American novelist, Oct 2002

DeMott, Richard H., Feb 1951, *Obit* Nov 1968

DePreist, James, conductor, Oct 1990

DeVito, Danny, American actor and film director, Feb 1988

DeVries, William C., surgeon, Jan 1985

DeWolfe, Chris, American Internet executive, July 2007

Deakin, Arthur, English labor leader, Jan 1948, *Obit* June 1955

Deakins, Roger, British cinematographer, May 2001

Dean, Arthur Hobson, American lawyer and diplomat, Mar 1954, *Obit* Jan 1988

Dean, Dizzy, American baseball player and sportscaster, Sept 1951, *Obit* Sept 1974

Dean, Gordon E., American government official, Sept 1950, *Obit* Nov 1958

Dean, H. Trendley, June 1957, *Obit* July 1962

Dean, Howard, American governor and political party leader, Oct 2002

Dean, Jimmy, American singer, Yrbk 1965, *Obit* Aug 2010

Dean, Laura, dancer and choreographer, Oct 1988

Dean, Patrick, British diplomat, May 1961, *Obit* Jan 1995

Dean, Tacita, English installation artist, May 2010

Dean, Vera Micheles, international relations specialist, May 1943, *Obit* Yrbk 1972

Dean, William F., American general, Sept 1954, *Obit* Oct 1981

Deane, Seamus, Irish literary critic and poet, Jan 2007

Deane, Sidney N., *Obit* June 1943

Dearborn, Ned Harland, Jan 1947, *Obit* Oct 1962

Dearden, John, July 1969, *Obit* Sept 1988

Dearie, Blossom, American singer, Feb 1989, *Obit* Yrbk 2009

Deasy, Luere B., *Obit* Apr 1940

Deasy, Mary, Yrbk 1958

Deat, Marcel, French political leader, Jan 1942, *Obit* May 1955

Debbouze, Jamel, French comedian and actor, Jan 2005

Debeljak, Ales, Slovenian poet and critic, Jan 2007

Debray, Regis, French political philosopher, novelist and government official, June 1982

Debre, Michel, French prime minister, May 1959, *Obit* Oct 1996

Debus, Kurt H., rocket engineer and NASA official, Nov 1973, *Obit* Nov 1983

Debutts, Harry A., Apr 1953

Debye, Peter J. W., Dutch physical chemist, July 1963, *Obit* Jan 1967

Decemberists (Musical group), Aug 2007

Decker, George H., American general, Jan 1961

Decker, Karl, *Obit* Feb 1942

Decter, Midge, social critic, Apr 1982

Dee, Ruby, American actress, Nov 1970

Deen, Paula H., American cook, restaurateur and television personality, Mar 2010

Deer, Ada, Native American leader and government official, Sept 1994

Dees, Morris S., American lawyer, Jan 1995

Def Leppard (Musical group), Jan 2003

Defauw, Desire, Jan 1940, *Obit* Oct 1960

Defferre, Gaston, French cabinet member, Sept 1967, *Obit* June 1986

Deford, Frank, American sportswriter and novelist, Aug 1996

Dehler, Thomas, July 1955, *Obit* Oct 1967

Dehn, Adolf, Apr 1941, *Obit* July 1968

Deighton, Len, English novelist, Sept 1984

Del Monaco, Mario, Feb 1957, *Obit* Jan 1983

Del Ponte, Carla, Swiss war crimes prosecutor, Jan 2002

Del Toro, Benicio, American actor, Sept 2001

Del Tredici, David, American composer, Mar 1983

Delacorte, George T., American publisher and philanthropist, Nov 1965, *Obit* July 1991

Delafield, E. M., English novelist, *Obit* Jan 1944

Deland, Margaret Wade Campbell, author, *Obit* Mar 1945

Delaney, Frank, Irish novelist and broadcaster, Jan 2005

Delaney, Shelagh, English playwright and screenwriter, Apr 1962, *Obit* Yrbk 2012

Delanoe, Bertrand, French mayor, Jan 2002

Delany, Bessie, American dentist, Nov 1995, *Obit* Jan 1996

Delany, Sadie, American science teacher, Nov 1995, *Obit* Apr 1999

Delany, Sadie; and Delany, Bessie, Nov 1995

Delaunay, Sonia, French painter and fashion designer, Aug 1977, *Obit* Feb 1980

Delgado, Jose Manuel R., Spanish neurobiologist, Feb 1976

Delilah, American radio talk show host, Apr 2005

Dell, Robert Edward, *Obit* Sept 1940

Della Casa, Lisa, Swiss opera singer, July 1956, *Obit* Yrbk 2013

Della Chiesa, Vivian, American opera singer, Nov 1943

Della Femina, Jerry, American advertising executive,

restaurateur and grocery store owner, Nov 1979

Dellinger, David, American peace activist, Aug 1976, *Obit* Yrbk 2004

Dello Joio, Norman, American composer, Sept 1957, *Obit* Yrbk 2008

Dellums, Ronald V., American congressman, Sept 1972, Sept 1993

Delon, Alain, French actor, Apr 1964

Deloncle, Eugene, French political leader, *Obit* Feb 1944

Deloria, Vine, Native American leader, historian and philosopher, Sept 1974, *Obit* Yrbk 2006

Delors, Jacques, French economist and government official, June 1989

Delson, Brad, American guitarist, Mar 2002

Demand, Thomas C., German photographer, Mar 2010

Demarbre, Lee Gordon, Canadian film director, Jan 2003

Dementieva, Elena, Russian tennis player, Jan 2005

Demikhov, Vladimir P., Russian surgeon, June 1960, *Obit* Feb 1999

Deming, Dorothy, nurse and educator, May 1943

Deming, Edwin Willard, painter and sculptor, *Obit* Yrbk 1942

Deming, W. Edwards, American statistician and business consultant, Sept 1993, *Obit* Mar 1994

Demirel, Suleyman, Turkish prime minister, Feb 1980

Demme, Jonathan, American film director, Apr 1985

Dempsey, Jack, American boxer, Feb 1945, *Obit* July 1983

Dempsey, John Noel, governor, June 1961, *Obit* Sept 1989

Dempsey, Miles Christopher, Oct 1944, *Obit* July 1969

Dench, Judi, English actress, Jan 1999

Dendramis, Vassili, June 1947, *Obit* July 1956

Denebrink, Francis C., admiral, Feb 1956, *Obit* June 1987

Denenberg, Herbert S., Yrbk 1972

Deneuve, Catherine, French actress, Feb 1978

Denfeld, Louis E., American admiral, Yrbk 1947, *Obit* May 1972

Deng Xiaoping, Chinese communist leader, May 1976, June 1994, *Obit* Apr 1997

Denham, R. N., American regulatory agency official, Oct 1947, *Obit* Sept 1954

Dennehy, Brian, American actor, July 1991

Denning, Alfred Thompson Denning, British judge, July 1965, *Obit* June 1999

Dennis, Charles H., newspaper editor, *Obit* Nov 1943

Dennis, Eugene, American communist leader, May 1949, *Obit* Mar 1961

Dennis, Felix, British magazine publisher, Apr 2000

Dennis, Lawrence, American political writer and diplomat, Mar 1941, *Obit* Oct 1977

Dennis, Olive Wetzel, civil engineer, June 1941

Dennis, Patrick, American novelist, May 1959, *Obit* Feb 1977

Dennis, Sandy, actress, Jan 1969, *Obit* May 1992

Dennison, Robert L., Apr 1960, *Obit* May 1980

Denniston, Reynolds, *Obit* Mar 1943

Denny, Charles R., May 1947

Denny, Collins, *Obit* July 1943

Denny, George V., Sept 1940, Sept 1950, *Obit* Jan 1960

Densen-Gerber, Judianne, American lawyer and psychiatrist, Nov 1983, *Obit* July 2003

Densford, Katharine J., Feb 1947

Dent, Frederick B., American Secretary of commerce, Apr 1974

Denton, Jeremiah, American admiral and senator, May 1982

Denton, Nick, British journalist and Internet news service executive, Apr 2011

Denver, John, American singer and actor, Jan 1975, *Obit* Jan 1998

Depardieu, Gerard, French actor, Oct 1987

Depinet, Ned E., June 1950

Depp, Johnny, American actor, May 1991

Der Harootian, Koren, Jan 1955

Deripaska, Oleg, Russian aluminum industry executive, Jan 2006

Dern, Bruce, American actor, Oct 1978

Dern, Laura, American actress, Oct 1992

Derounian, Arthur, journalist, Oct 1943

Derrida, Jacques, French philosopher, July 1993, *Obit* Mar 2005

Dershowitz, Alan M., American lawyer, Sept 1986

Derthick, Lawrence Gridley, educator and government official, Apr 1957, *Obit* Mar 1993

Deruddere, Dominique, Belgian motion picture director, Jan 2003

Derwent, Clarence, Nov 1947, *Obit* Nov 1959

Derwinski, Edward J., American Secretary of veterans affairs, Aug 1991, *Obit* Yrbk 2012

Des Graz, Charles Louis, *Obit* Yrbk 1940

Des Portes, Fay Allen, *Obit* Nov 1944

Desai, Kiran, Indian novelist, Jan 2007

Desai, Morarji, Indian prime minister, Sept 1958, Jan 1978, *Obit* June 1995

Deschanel, Caleb, American cinematographer and film director, Feb 2008

Deschanel, Zooey, American actress, Aug 2012

Desmond-Hellman, Susan, American oncologist and biotechnology executive, Nov 2012

Desplat, Alexandre, French composer, June 2011

Desses, Jean, Jan 1956, *Obit* Oct 1970

Destiny's Child (Musical group), Aug 2001

Dett, Robert Nathaniel, composer, *Obit* Nov 1943

Deuba, Sher Bahadur, Nepalese prime minister, Jan 2002

Deuel, Wallace R., Aug 1942

Deukmejian, George, governor, June 1983

Deupree, Richard R., Apr 1946, *Obit* May 1974

Deutsch, Julius, Nov 1944, *Obit* Mar 1968

Deutsch, Linda, American court reporter, Apr 2007

Deutscher, Guy, Feb 2012

Devaney, John Patrick, *Obit* Nov 1941

Dever, Paul A., American governor, May 1949, *Obit* July 1958

Devereaux, William Charles, *Obit* Sept 1941

Devers, Gail, American runner and hurdler, July 1996

Devers, Jacob Loucks, general, Sept 1942, *Obit* Jan 1980

Deveshwar, Yogesh Chander, Indian tobacco company executive, Jan 2005

Devi, Mahasweta, Feb 2012

Devine, John M., American general, Jan 1948

Deviny, John J., Sept 1948, *Obit* Apr 1955

Devoe, Ralph G., Oct 1944, *Obit* Nov 1966

Devold, Kristin Krohn, Norwegian military official, Jan 2003

Dewart, William T., American newspaper publisher, *Obit* Mar 1944

Dewey, Charles Schuveldt, Jan 1949, *Obit* Feb 1981

Dewey, John, American philosopher and educator, Aug 1944, *Obit* July 1952

Dewey, Thomas E., American governor, July 1940, Sept 1944, *Obit* Apr 1971

Dewhurst, Colleen, actress, July 1974, *Obit* Oct 1991

Dewhurst, J. Frederic, Jan 1948, *Obit* July 1967

Dexheimer, W. A., Feb 1955

Dexter, John, English theatrical director, July 1976, *Obit* May 1990

Dhaliwal, Daljit, English television newscaster, Nov 2000

Dhalla, Ruby, Canadian member of Parliament, Jan 2006

Dhebar, Uchhrangrai Navalshankar, June 1955

Di Montezemolo, Luca Cordero, Italian automobile executive, Jan 2006

Di Suvero, Mark, sculptor, Nov 1979
DiCaprio, Leonardo, American actor, Mar 1997
DiCorcia, Philip-Lorca, American photographer, Apr 2008
DiFranco, Ani, American singer and songwriter, Aug 1997
DiMaggio, Joe, American baseball player, June 1941, July 1951, Obit May 1999
DiSalle, Michael V., American governor, Jan 1951, Obit Nov 1981
DiSpirito, Rocco, American chef and restaurateur, Feb 2012
Dial, Morse G., chemical executive, Mar 1956, Obit Jan 1983
Diamant, Gertrude, American novelist and nonfiction writer, Nov 1942
Diamond, David, American composer, Nov 1966, Obit Yrbk 2005
Diamond, Neil, American singer and songwriter, May 1981
Diamond, Peter, American economist, Nov 2012
Diana, Jan 1983, Obit Nov 1997
Diaz Ordaz, Gustavo, Mexican president, May 1965, Obit Sept 1979
Diaz, Cameron, American actress, Apr 2005
Dibelius, Friedrich Karl Otto, German bishop, May 1953, Obit Mar 1967
Dichter, Ernest, American psychologist and marketing research executive, Jan 1961, Obit Jan 1992
Dick, Charles, Obit May 1945
Dickerson, Debra, American journalist, Apr 2004
Dickerson, Ernest, American cinematographer and film director, July 2000
Dickerson, Nancy, American television reporter, Sept 1962, Obit Jan 1998
Dickerson, Roy E., Obit Apr 1944
Dickey, James, American poet and novelist, Apr 1968, Obit Mar 1997
Dickey, John Sloan, college president, Apr 1955, Obit Apr 1991
Dickey, R. A., American baseball player, Oct 2013

Dickinson, Amy, American freelance writer and advice columnist, Apr 2004
Dickinson, Angie, American actress, Feb 1981
Dickinson, Edwin Walter, American painter, Sept 1963, Obit Feb 1979
Dickinson, Lucy Jennings, Nov 1945
Dickinson, Luren D., Obit June 1943
Dickinson, Robert Latou, American gynecologist and obstetrician, Mar 1950, Obit Jan 1951
Dickinson, Willoughby Hyett Dickinson, British member of Parliament, Obit July 1943
Dickson, Lovat, Sept 1962
Dickson, Marguerite, Yrbk 1952, Obit Jan 1954
Diddley, Bo, American guitarist, singer and songwriter, June 1989, Obit Sept 2008
Diddy, American rapper, record producer and actor, Apr 1998
Didion, Joan, American novelist, essayist and journalist, Sept 1978
Diebenkorn, Richard, American painter, Yrbk 1971, Obit May 1993
Diebold, John, American management consultant, Mar 1967, Obit Yrbk 2006
Diefenbaker, John George, Canadian prime minister, May 1957, Obit Oct 1979
Diefendorf, Allen Ross, Obit Sept 1943
Diehl, Frances, Oct 1947
Dies, Martin, American lawyer and congressman, Apr 1940, Obit Jan 1973
Dieterich, William H., Obit Yrbk 1940
Dieterle, William, motion picture director, Sept 1943, Obit Feb 1973
Dietrich, Marlene, German-American actress, June 1953, Feb 1968, Obit June 1992
Dietz, David, author and journalist, Oct 1940, Obit Apr 1985
Dietz, Howard, American lyricist, Oct 1965, Obit Sept 1983

Diggs, Charles, American congressman, July 1957, Obit Nov 1998
Diggs, Taye, American actor, Aug 2011
Dike, Phil, Yrbk 1942
Dill, John Greer, British field marshal, Feb 1941, Obit Yrbk 1944
Dillard, Annie, American poet, critic and nature writer, Jan 1983
Dillard, James Hardy, Obit Sept 1940
Diller, Barry, American motion picture and television executive, Apr 1986
Diller, Phyllis, American comedienne, July 1967, Obit Yrbk 2012
Dillman, Bradford, actor, Jan 1960
Dillon, Douglas, American investment banker and Secretary of the treasury, Apr 1953, Obit May 2003
Dillon, Matt, American actor, May 1985
Dimechkie, Nadim, Feb 1960
Dimitrov, Georgi, Bulgarian prime minister, May 1949
Dimon, James, American investment banker, June 2004
Dine, Jim, American painter, June 1969
Dinehart, Alan, Obit Sept 1944
Dingell, John D., American congressman, Mar 1949, Obit Yrbk 1956
Dingell, John D., American congressman, Aug 1983
Diniz, Abilio, Brazilian supermarket and department store executive, Jan 2006
Dinkins, David, American mayor, Mar 1990
Dinklage, Peter, American actor, Apr 2013
Dinsmore, Charles Allen, Obit Oct 1941
Diogo, Luisa, Mozambican prime minister, Jan 2004
Dion, Stephane, Canadian political leader, Jan 2007
Dionne, E. J., American columnist and political commentator, May 2006
Dior, Christian, French fashion designer, Oct 1948, Obit Jan 1958

Diouf, El Hadji, Senegalese soccer player, Jan 2003

Dirie, Waris, Somali model and social activist, Jan 2005

Dirksen, Everett McKinley, American senator, Apr 1941, Sept 1957, *Obit* Nov 1969

Dirnt, Mike, American bassist and singer, Aug 2005

Disney, Anthea, English publishing executive, June 1998

Disney, Doris Miles, American novelist, Yrbk 1954

Disney, Walt, American animator and motion picture executive, Aug 1940, Apr 1952, *Obit* Feb 1967

Ditchy, Clair W., Mar 1954, *Obit* Oct 1967

Dith, Pran, Cambodian photojournalist, Oct 1996, *Obit* Yrbk 2008

Ditka, Mike, American football coach, Oct 1987

Ditmars, Raymond Lee, herpetologist, Sept 1940, *Obit* July 1942

Ditter, J. William, *Obit* Jan 1944

Divine, Frank H., *Obit* May 1941

Dix, Dorothy, American advice columnist, Jan 1940, *Obit* Feb 1952

Dix, William S., librarian, June 1969, *Obit* Apr 1978

Dixey, Henry E., *Obit* Apr 1943

Dixie Chicks (Musical group), July 2000

Dixit, Madhuri, Indian actress, Jan 2006

Dixon, Dean, conductor, Apr 1943, *Obit* Jan 1977

Dixon, Jeane, American astrologer and psychic, Feb 1973, *Obit* Mar 1997

Dixon, Owen, Australian judge and diplomat, Aug 1942

Dixon, Paul Rand, American regulatory agency official, Jan 1968

Dixon, Pierson, British diplomat, Sept 1954, *Obit* June 1965

Dixon, Thomas, American novelist, *Obit* May 1946

Dixon, Willie, American blues singer, May 1989, *Obit* Apr 1992

Djanira, Jan 1961

Djerassi, Carl, American chemist, Oct 2001

Djilas, Milovan, Yugoslav communist leader, memoirist and political writer, Sept 1958, *Obit* July 1995

Djokovic, Novak, Serbian tennis player, Apr 2012

Djuanda, Apr 1958, *Obit* Jan 1964

Djukanovic, Milo, Montenegrin president, Aug 2001

Doan, Leland I., American chemical industry executive, Oct 1952, *Obit* May 1974

Dobbie, William George Shedden, British general, July 1945

Dobbs, Lou, American television newscaster, Nov 2006

Dobbs, Mattiwilda, American opera singer, Sept 1955

Dobie, J. Frank, American folklorist, Yrbk 1945, *Obit* Nov 1964

Dobrynin, Anatoly F., Soviet diplomat, Sept 1962, *Obit* Yrbk 2010

Dobson, James C., American psychologist and social activist, Aug 1998

Dobson, William Alexander, *Obit* July 1943

Dobzhansky, Theodosius Grigorievich, American geneticist, Sept 1962, *Obit* Feb 1976

Docking, George, governor, June 1958, *Obit* Mar 1964

Doctorow, E. L., American novelist, July 1976

Dodd, Alvin E., Nov 1947, *Obit* July 1951

Dodd, Christopher J., American motion picture association executive and former senator, Oct 1989

Dodd, Norris E., Feb 1949, *Obit* Sept 1968

Dodd, Thomas, American senator, Sept 1959, *Obit* July 1971

Dodd, William Edward, historian and diplomat, *Obit* Mar 1940

Dodds, Gil, June 1947, *Obit* Apr 1977

Dodds, Harold W., Yrbk 1945, *Obit* Jan 1981

Dodge, Bayard, Feb 1948, *Obit* July 1972

Dodge, Charles, American composer, Aug 2007

Dodge, Cleveland E., Mar 1954, *Obit* Feb 1983

Dodge, David, author, Yrbk 1956

Dodge, John V., July 1960

Dodge, Joseph Morrell, American banker and government official, Nov 1947, *Obit* Jan 1965

Dodge, Raymond, *Obit* May 1942

Doe, Samuel Kanyon, Liberian president, May 1981, *Obit* Nov 1990

Doerr, Anthony, American short story writer and novelist, Oct 2011

Doerr, John, American financier, May 2009

Doherty, Henry Latham, American gas and electric utility executive, *Obit* Jan 1940

Doherty, Robert E., Sept 1949, *Obit* Yrbk 1950

Dohnanyi, Christoph von, German conductor, Oct 1985

Doi, Peter Tatsuo, Nov 1960

Doi, Takako, Japanese socialist leader, July 1992

Doig, Ivan, American western writer, Feb 2011

Doihara, Kenji, Mar 1942, *Obit* Feb 1949

Doisy, Edward Adelbert, American biochemist, Mar 1949, *Obit* Jan 1987

Dolan, Daniel Leo, Sept 1956

Dolan, Timothy Michael, American archbishop, Mar 2011

Dolbier, Maurice, author and literary critic, Yrbk 1956, *Obit* Jan 1994

Dolce & Gabbana, Jan 2005

Dolce, Domenico, Italian fashion designer, Jan 2005

Dolci, Danilo, Italian social reformer and author, Sept 1961, *Obit* Mar 1998

Dole, Elizabeth Hanford, American senator, June 1983, Jan 1997

Dole, Robert J., American senator, Apr 1972, Oct 1987

Dolin, Anton, English dancer and choreographer, Jan 1946, *Obit* Jan 1984

Doll, Richard, British epidemiologist, Jan 2002

Dollard, Charles, Yrbk 1948, *Obit* Apr 1977

Dolly, Jenny, *Obit* July 1941

Domagk, Gerhard, German bacteriologist, Mar 1958, *Obit* June 1964

Domenici, Pete, American senator, June 1982

Domingo, Placido, Spanish opera singer, Mar 1972

Dominguin, Spanish bullfighter, Mar 1972, *Obit* July 1996

Domini, Amy L., American investment manager, Nov 2005

Dominy, Nathaniel J., American anthropologist, Apr 2010

Doms, Keith, June 1971

Donahey, Vic, *Obit* May 1946

Donahue, Phil, American television talk show host, May 1980

Donald, Arnold, American food industry executive, Nov 2005

Donald, David Herbert, American historian and biographer, Sept 1961, *Obit* Yrbk 2009

Donald, W. H., July 1946

Donaldson, Jesse M., American postmaster general, Jan 1948, *Obit* May 1970

Donaldson, Sam, American television newscaster, Sept 1987

Donaldson, Simon K., English mathematician, Jan 2005

Donaldson, William, American regulatory agency official, June 2003

Donegan, Horace William Baden, bishop, July 1954, *Obit* Jan 1992

Dongen, Kees van, Dutch artist, Sept 1960, *Obit* July 1968

Donitz, Karl, German admiral, Nov 1942, *Obit* Feb 1981

Donleavy, J. P., Irish novelist, dramatist and short story writer, July 1979

Donlon, Mary H., July 1949, *Obit* May 1977

Donnell, Forrest C., American governor and senator, Sept 1949

Donnelly, Phil M., June 1956, *Obit* Nov 1961

Donnelly, Walter Joseph, diplomat, Sept 1952, *Obit* Jan 1971

Donner, Frederic Garrett, automobile executive, Jan 1959, *Obit* Apr 1987

Donoghue, Emma, Irish novelist and dramatist, Jan 2013

Donoghue, John P., American neuroscientist, May 2010

Donoso, Jose, Chilean novelist, Feb 1978, *Obit* Feb 1997

Donovan, Billy, American basketball coach, Feb 2007

Donovan, Carrie, American fashion editor, Sept 1999, *Obit* Feb 2002

Donovan, Hedley, journalist and magazine publishing executive, May 1965, *Obit* Oct 1990

Donovan, James B., American lawyer, June 1961, *Obit* Mar 1970

Donovan, Landon, American soccer player, June 2006

Donovan, Raymond James, American Secretary of labor, Jan 1982

Donovan, Shaun, American Secretary of housing and urban development, Mar 2009

Donovan, William J., American intelligence official and general, Mar 1941, Sept 1954, *Obit* Apr 1959

Dooley, Tom, American physician and missionary, July 1957, *Obit* Mar 1961

Doolittle, James Harold, American general, Aug 1942, Mar 1957, *Obit* Jan 1994

Dooyeweerd, Herman, Dutch philosopher, Sept 1958

Dorati, Antal, Hungarian conductor and composer, July 1948, *Obit* Jan 1989

Doriot, Jacques, French political leader and wartime collaborationist, Nov 1940

Dorman, Gerald D., June 1970

Dornay, Louis, *Obit* Sept 1940

Dornberger, Walter, Feb 1965, *Obit* Sept 1980

Dorough, Howie, American singer, May 2000

Dorpfeld, Wilhelm, German archaeologist, *Obit* Jan 1940

Dorris, Michael, American anthropologist and memoirist, Mar 1995, *Obit* June 1997

Dorsett, Tony, American football player, Apr 1980

Dorsey, Jimmy, band leader, Apr 1942, *Obit* Sept 1957

Dorsey, Jimmy; and Dorsey, Tommy, Apr 1942

Dorsey, Tommy, American band leader, Apr 1942, *Obit* Feb 1957

Dorticos Torrado, Osvaldo, Cuban president, Feb 1963, *Obit* Aug 1983

Dos Passos, John, American novelist, Aug 1940, *Obit* Nov 1970

Doster, James J., *Obit* Yrbk 1942

Doten, Carroll W., *Obit* Aug 1942

Doubilet, David, American underwater photographer, Mar 2003

Doubleday, Nelson, publisher and baseball executive, May 1987

Doudna, Jennifer A., American biochemist, Feb 2005

Dougherty, Dora, Mar 1963

Doughton, Robert L., American congressman, July 1942, *Obit* Yrbk 1955

Douglas of Kirtleside, William Sholto Douglas, British air marshal, June 1943, *Obit* Yrbk 1969

Douglas, Arthur F., Nov 1950, *Obit* May 1956

Douglas, Dave, American jazz trumpet player and composer, Mar 2006

Douglas, Denzil, Saint Kitts-Nevis prime minister, Jan 2007

Douglas, Donald Wills, aircraft executive, Nov 1941, Yrbk 1950, *Obit* Mar 1981

Douglas, Emily Taft, congresswoman, Apr 1945, *Obit* Mar 1994

Douglas, Emory, American illustrator, cartoonist and social activist, Feb 2010

Douglas, Helen Gahagan, American congresswoman, Sept 1944, *Obit* Aug 1980

Douglas, James Henderson, American Secretary of the air force, Sept 1957, *Obit* Apr 1988

Douglas, Jerry, American dobro guitar player, Aug 2004

Douglas, John E., American criminologist, July 2001

Douglas, Kirk, American actor, Mar 1952

Douglas, Lewis W., American government official, Mar 1947, *Obit* May 1974

Douglas, Marjory Stoneman, American short story writer, novelist and conservationist, July 1953, *Obit* July 1998

Douglas, Melvyn, actor, May 1942, *Obit* Sept 1981

Douglas, Michael, American actor and motion picture producer, Apr 1987

Douglas, Mike, American television talk show host, May 1968, *Obit* Yrbk 2007

Douglas, Paul H., American senator and economist, Apr 1949, *Obit* Nov 1976

Douglas, T. C., Canadian political leader, July 1957, *Obit* Apr 1986

Douglas, Walter Jules, American civil engineer, *Obit* Sept 1941

Douglas, William O., American Supreme Court justice, Oct 1941, Nov 1950, *Obit* Mar 1980

Doumbia, Mariam, Malian singer, Jan 2006

Douthat, Ross Gregory, American journalist, Aug 2009

Dove, Rita, American poet and short story writer, May 1994

Dover, Elmer, *Obit* Nov 1940

Dow, Willard H., Feb 1944, *Obit* May 1949

Dowd, Maureen, American newspaper columnist, Sept 1996

Dowding, Hugh Caswall Tremenheere Dowding, British air marshal, Nov 1940, *Obit* Apr 1970

Dowell, Anthony, English ballet dancer and manager, May 1971

Dowling, Eddie, Feb 1946, *Obit* Apr 1976

Dowling, Robert W., Oct 1952, *Obit* Nov 1973

Dowling, Walter, American diplomat, Mar 1963, *Obit* Sept 1977

Downes, Olin, music critic and historian, Mar 1943, *Obit* Oct 1955

Downey, Fairfax, author and historian, Yrbk 1949, *Obit* Aug 1990

Downey, James, American television comedy writer, June 2008

Downey, Morton, American singer, July 1949, *Obit* Jan 1986

Downey, Robert, American actor, Aug 1998

Downey, Sheridan, Oct 1949, *Obit* Jan 1962

Downs, Hugh, television personality, Mar 1965

Downs, Robert B., librarian, Jan 1941, June 1952, *Obit* Apr 1991

Doxiadis, Constantinos A., Greek architect, Sept 1964, *Obit* Sept 1975

Doyle, Adrian Conan, Sept 1954

Doyle, Christopher, Australian cinematographer, Jan 2006

Doyle, Roddy, Irish novelist, Oct 1997

Drabble, Margaret, English novelist and playwright, May 1981

Drabinsky, Garth, Canadian theatrical producer, Oct 1997

Drake, Alfred, actor and singer, Apr 1944, *Obit* Sept 1992

Drake, Bobby, American drummer, Sept 2010

Drake, Frank Donald, American astronomer, Jan 1963

Drake, James, American artist, July 2005

Drake, St. Clair, anthropologist and sociologist, Jan 1946, *Obit* Aug 1990

Drapeau, Jean, Canadian mayor, Yrbk 1967, *Obit* Oct 1999

Draper, Charles Stark, aeronautic and rocket engineer, Yrbk 1965, *Obit* Sept 1987

Draper, Dorothy, American interior designer, May 1941, *Obit* Apr 1969

Draper, Paul, dancer, Feb 1944, *Obit* Jan 1997

Draper, William Henry, banker and government official, Mar 1952, *Obit* Feb 1975

Drees, Willem, Dutch prime minister, Jan 1949, *Obit* July 1988

Dreiser, Theodore, American novelist, *Obit* Feb 1946

Drescher, Fran, American actress, Apr 1998

Dressen, Chuck, baseball player and manager, July 1951, *Obit* Nov 1966

Drew, Charles Richard, American surgeon, May 1944, *Obit* May 1950

Drew, Elizabeth, journalist, Oct 1979

Drew, George A., Canadian political leader, Yrbk 1948, *Obit* May 1984

Drexler, Clyde, American basketball player and coach, Jan 1996

Drexler, Jorge, Uruguayan singer and songwriter, Jan 2005

Drexler, Millard S., American clothing chain executive, Jan 1993

Dreyfus, Camille, May 1955, *Obit* Yrbk 1957

Dreyfus, Pierre, French automobile executive and cabinet member, July 1958, *Obit* Mar 1995

Dreyfuss, Henry, American industrial designer, May 1948, Oct 1959, *Obit* Yrbk 1972

Dreyfuss, Richard, American actor, Jan 1976

Driesch, Hans, German biologist and philosopher, *Obit* June 1941

Drinan, Robert F., American priest, lawyer and congressman, June 1971, *Obit* Yrbk 2007

Driscoll, Alfred E., American governor, Jan 1949, *Obit* May 1975

Driskell, David C., American painter and printmaker, Aug 2000

Drogba, Didier, Ivorian soccer player, July 2011

Drooker, Eric, American painter and graphic novelist, Feb 2011

Drossaerts, Arthur, *Obit* Oct 1940

Droste, Ed, American guitarist and singer, Sept 2011

Drouet, Bessie Clarke, *Obit* Oct 1940

Drozd, Steven, American drummer, guitarist and keyboardist, Oct 2002

Drozniak, Edward, July 1962, *Obit* Jan 1967

Drucker, Eugene, American violinist, July 2002

Drucker, Peter F., American management consultant and economist, May 1964, *Obit* Apr 2006

Druckman, Jacob, composer, May 1981, *Obit* Aug 1996

Drum, Hugh A., July 1941, *Obit* Nov 1951

Drummond, Roscoe, journalist, Nov 1949, *Obit* Nov 1983

Dryden, Hugh L., American physicist and NASA official, Apr 1959, *Obit* Jan 1966

Dryfoos, Orvil Eugene, American newspaper publisher, Jan 1962, *Obit* July 1963

Drysdale, Don, American baseball player and sportscaster, Feb 1965, *Obit* Sept 1993

Du Bois, Guy Pene, painter and critic, Oct 1946, *Obit* Oct 1958

Du Bois, Shirley Graham, American biographer, dramatist and composer, Oct 1946, *Obit* June 1977

Du Bois, W. E. B., American sociologist, historian and novelist, Jan 1940, *Obit* Oct 1963

Du Bose, Horace M., *Obit* Mar 1941

Du Fournet, Louis Rene Marie Charles Dartige, *Obit* Mar 1940

Du Jardin, Rosamond, Yrbk 1953

Du Maurier, Daphne, English novelist, short story writer and biographer, May 1940, *Obit* June 1989

Du Mont, Allen B., American electrical engineer and inventor, June 1946, *Obit* Jan 1966

Du Pont, Francis Irenee, *Obit* May 1942

Du Pont, Pierre S., American business executive, Sept 1940, *Obit* May 1954

Du Pre, Jacqueline, British cellist, May 1970, *Obit* Nov 1987

Du Puy, William Atherton, *Obit* Oct 1941

Du Toit, Natalie, South African swimmer, Jan 2005

Du Vigneaud, Vincent, American biochemist, Jan 1956, *Obit* Feb 1979

DuBridge, Lee A., college president and physicist, June 1948, *Obit* Mar 1994

Duany, Andres, American architect and urban planner, Jan 2006

Duarte Frutos, Nicanor, Paraguayan president, Jan 2004

Duarte, Jose Napoleon, Salvadoran president, Sept 1981, *Obit* Apr 1990

Dubcek, Alexander, Czech communist leader, Nov 1968

Dubilier, William, Sept 1957, *Obit* Oct 1969

Dubinsky, David, American labor leader, Yrbk 1942, June 1957, *Obit* Jan 1983

Dublin, Louis Israel, statistician, Oct 1942, *Obit* Yrbk 1991

Dubois, Eugene, Dutch anthropologist and paleontologist, *Obit* May 1941

Dubos, Rene Jules, American bacteriologist, Oct 1952, Jan 1973, *Obit* Apr 1982

Dubuc, Nancy, American television executive, May 2012

Dubuffet, Jean, French painter and sculptor, July 1962, *Obit* July 1985

Duchamp, Marcel, French painter, June 1960, *Obit* Yrbk 1968

Duchin, Eddy, pianist and band leader, Jan 1947, *Obit* Mar 1951

Duchin, Peter, band leader, Jan 1977

Duclos, Jacques, French communist leader, Feb 1946, *Obit* June 1975

Dudamel, Gustavo, Venezuelan conductor, Apr 2010

Dudley, Bide, *Obit* Feb 1944

Dudley, Robert, American petroleum industry executive, June 2011

Due-Gundersen, Gunnar, Feb 1959, *Obit* Aug 1979

Duerk, Alene, Sept 1973

Duesberg, Peter H., German molecular biologist, June 2004

Dufek, George J., Mar 1957

Duff, Hilary, American actress and singer, Feb 2006

Duff, James Henderson, senator and governor, Apr 1948, *Obit* Feb 1970

Duffey, Joseph D., college administrator, Mar 1971

Duffy, Bernard C., July 1952, *Obit* Nov 1972

Duffy, Edmund, cartoonist, Jan 1940, *Obit* Nov 1962

Duffy, James J., *Obit* Feb 1942

Duflo, Esther, French economist, Aug 2011

Dufy, Raoul, French painter, Mar 1951, *Obit* May 1953

Dugan, Alan, American poet, Nov 1990, *Obit* Yrbk 2004

Dugan, Raymond Smith, *Obit* Oct 1940

Duggan, Ervin S., public broadcasting executive, Oct 1998

Duggan, Laurence, May 1947, *Obit* Jan 1949

Duggar, Benjamin Minge, botanist, Nov 1952, *Obit* Nov 1956

Duisenberg, Willem, Dutch European banking official, Jan 2002, *Obit* CB Int 2006

Dujardin, Jean, Oct 2013

Dukakis, Michael, American governor, Feb 1978

Dukakis, Olympia, American actress, July 1991

Duke of Windsor; and Windsor, Wallis Warfield, Sept 1944

Duke, Angier Biddle, diplomat, Feb 1962, *Obit* July 1995

Duke, Annie, American poker player, Aug 2006

Duke, Patty, American actress, Sept 1963

Duke, Vernon, American composer, June 1941, *Obit* Mar 1969

Dullea, Keir, American actor, June 1970

Dulles, Allen Welsh, American diplomat and intelligence official, Mar 1949, *Obit* Mar 1969

Dulles, Eleanor Lansing, American memoirist and diplomat, Sept 1962, *Obit* Jan 1997

Dulles, John Foster, American Secretary of state, Aug 1944, Sept 1953, *Obit* July 1959

Dumas, Marlene, South African painter, Jan 2010

Dumas, Roland, French cabinet member, Oct 1990

Dunaway, Faye, American actress, Feb 1972

Dunbar, P. B., July 1949, *Obit* Nov 1968

Dunbar, Rudolph, Oct 1946

Duncan Smith, Iain, British political leader, Jan 2002

Duncan, Andrew Rae, July 1941, *Obit* May 1952

Duncan, Arne, American Secretary of education, Mar 2009

Duncan, Charles W., American Secretary of energy, Apr 1980

Duncan, David Douglas, American photojournalist, Nov 1968

Duncan, Malcolm, *Obit* June 1942

Duncan, Michael Clarke, actor, Aug 2000, *Obit* Yrbk 2012

Duncan, Patrick, South African governor-general, *Obit* Sept 1943

Duncan, Sandy, actress, Jan 1980

Duncan, Thomas W., Yrbk 1947

Duncan, Tim, American basketball player, Nov 1999

Duncan, Todd, singer and voice teacher, July 1942, *Obit* May 1998

Duncan-Sandys, Duncan Edwin Duncan-Sandys, British cabinet member, May 1952

Dungy, Tony, American football player and coach, Aug 2007

Dunham, Charles L., Mar 1966

Dunham, Franklin, Jan 1942, *Obit* Jan 1962

Dunham, Katherine, American dancer and choreographer, Mar 1941, *Obit* Yrbk 2006

Dunlap, John B., Yrbk 1951, *Obit* Feb 1965

Dunlop, John T., American economist, labor relations expert and Secretary of labor, Apr 1951, *Obit* Yrbk 2004

Dunmall, Paul, British jazz saxophonist, May 2011

Dunn, Gordon E., meteorologist, May 1966

Dunn, J. Allan, *Obit* May 1941

Dunn, James Clement, May 1943, *Obit* June 1979

Dunn, Jennifer, American congresswoman, Mar 1999, *Obit* Nov 2007

Dunn, Loula, Mar 1951

Dunn, Ronnie Gene, American country singer and songwriter, Sept 2004

Dunne, Dominick, American novelist, journalist and true-crime writer, May 1999, *Obit* Yrbk 2009

Dunne, Irene, American actress and singer, Aug 1945, *Obit* Nov 1990

Dunne, John Gregory, American novelist and screenwriter, June 1983, *Obit* Yrbk 2004

Dunning, John R., May 1948, *Obit* Oct 1975

Dunninger, Joseph, magician and mind reader, Sept 1944, *Obit* May 1975

Dunnock, Mildred, actress, Sept 1955, *Obit* Sept 1991

Dunst, Kirsten, American actress, Oct 2001

Dunton, Arnold Davidson, Canadian college president, Jan 1959, *Obit* Apr 1987

Dunwoody, Ann E., American general, Nov 2008

Duplessis, Maurice LeNoblet, Canadian provincial premier, Oct 1948, *Obit* Nov 1959

Duran, Roberto, Panamanian boxer, Sept 1980

Durang, Christopher, American dramatist, June 1987

Durant, Kevin, American basketball player, May 2010

Durant, William James, American historian, Sept 1964, *Obit* Jan 1982

Durante, Jimmy, comedian, Sept 1946, *Obit* Mar 1980

Duranty, Walter, Anglo-American journalist, Jan 1943, *Obit* Yrbk 1958

Duras, Marguerite, French novelist, screenwriter and film director, Nov 1985, *Obit* May 1996

Durbin, Deanna, American singer and actress, June 1941, *Obit* Yrbk 2013

Durbin, Richard J., American senator, Aug 2006

Durenberger, David, American senator, Oct 1988

Durgin, C. T., Sept 1954, *Obit* May 1965

Durham, Carl, American congressman, July 1957, *Obit* June 1974

Duritz, Adam, American singer and songwriter, Mar 2003

Durkin, Martin Patrick, American Secretary of labor, Feb 1953, *Obit* Jan 1956

Durning, Charles, American actor, Sept 1997, *Obit* Yrbk 2013

Durocher, Leo, baseball player and manager, Sept 1940, July 1950, *Obit* Nov 1991

Durrell, Gerald M., British naturalist and conservationist, May 1985, *Obit* Apr 1995

Durrell, Lawrence, English novelist, poet and travel writer, July 1963, *Obit* Jan 1991

Durrenmatt, Friedrich, Swiss novelist and dramatist, Feb 1959, *Obit* Apr 1991

Dusapin, Pascal, French composer, Jan 2007

Dusser de Barenne, Joannes Gregorius, *Obit* Aug 1940

Dutoit, Charles, Swiss conductor, Feb 1987

Dutra, Eurico Gaspar, Mar 1946, *Obit* Sept 1974

Dutton, Charles S., American actor and television director, Oct 2000

Dutton, Denis, American philosopher, Aug 2009, *Obit* Yrbk 2011

Dutton, Lawrence, American violist, July 2002

Duva, Lou, American boxing manager and promoter, Nov 1999

Duval, David, American golfer, Oct 1999

Duvalier, Francois, Haitian president, Sept 1958, *Obit* June 1971

Duvalier, Jean-Claude, Haitian president, June 1972

Duvall, Evelyn Ruth Millis, Oct 1947

Duvall, Robert, American actor and motion picture director, July 1977

Duvieusart, Jean, Sept 1950

Duvivier, Julien, French motion picture director, July 1943, *Obit* Jan 1968

Dwight, Edward J., American astronaut and sculptor, July 2007

Dwinell, Lane, governor, June 1956, *Obit* June 1997

Dworkin, Andrea, American feminist and writer, Oct 1994, *Obit* Yrbk 2005

Dworkin, Ronald Myles, American law professor, *Obit* Yrbk 2013

Dworshak, Henry C., American senator, congressman and newspaper publisher, Jan 1950, *Obit* Oct 1962

Dye, Marie, Yrbk 1948

Dyer, Gwynne, Canadian journalist and television documentary host, Jan 2006

Dyer-Bennet, Richard, singer, June 1944, *Obit* Feb 1992

Dyhrenfurth, Norman G., American mountaineer, Apr 1965

Dyke, Cornelius G., *Obit* June 1943

Dyke, Greg, British broadcasting executive, Jan 2002

Dykstra, Clarence A., American university president, Jan 1941, *Obit* June 1950

Dykstra, John, American automobile executive, Apr 1963, *Obit* May 1972

Dylan, Bob, American folk singer and songwriter, May 1965, Oct 1991

Dyson, Esther, American computer industry analyst, Aug 1997

Dyson, Freeman J., American physicist, Jan 1980

Dyson, Michael Eric, American social scientist, clergyman and writer, Oct 1997

E

Eady, Wilfrid, Oct 1947, *Obit* Feb 1962

Eagleburger, Lawrence S., American diplomat, Nov 1992, *Obit* Yrbk 2011

Eagleman, David, American neuroscientist, Jan 2012

Eagleton, Thomas F., American senator, Nov 1973, *Obit* Yrbk 2007

Eaker, Ira Clarence, general, Oct 1942, *Obit* Sept 1987

Eames, Charles, American furniture, interior and exhibit designer, Jan 1965, *Obit* Oct 1978

Eanes, Antonio dos Santos Ramalho, Portuguese president, Apr 1979

Earle, Steve, American country singer and guitarist, Oct 1998

Earle, Sylvia A., American marine botanist, May 1972, May 1992

Early, Gerald Lyn, American essayist, editor and poet, May 1995

Early, Stephen, American presidential press secretary, July 1941, Yrbk 1949, *Obit* Sept 1951

Early, William Ashby, Mar 1954

Earnhardt, Dale, American automobile racing driver, Jan 2007

Easley, Claudius M., American general, *Obit* July 1945

Eastland, James O., American senator, Jan 1949, *Obit* Apr 1986

Eastman, Howard, Guyanese-English boxer, Jan 2003

Eastman, Joseph B., July 1942, *Obit* May 1944

Eastman, Max, American poet, journalist and critic, Apr 1969, *Obit* Apr 1969

Eastwood, Clint, American actor and film director, Oct 1971, Mar 1989

Eaton, Charles A., American congressman, May 1945, *Obit* Mar 1953

Eaton, Cyrus, American financier, July 1948, *Obit* July 1979

Eban, Abba, Israeli diplomat, Oct 1948, May 1957, *Obit* Mar 2003

Ebbers, Bernard, American telecommunications executive, Feb 1998

Ebbott, Percy J., American banker, Oct 1954

Eberhart, Richard, American poet, Jan 1961, *Obit* Yrbk 2005

Eberle, Irmengarde, Yrbk 1946

Ebersol, Dick, American television executive, July 1996

Eberstadt, Ferdinand, investment banker, Yrbk 1942, *Obit* Jan 1970

Ebert, Roger, American film critic, Mar 1997, *Obit* Yrbk 2013

Eboue, Felix, French colonial governor, *Obit* July 1944

Ebsen, Buddy, American actor and dancer, Jan 1977, *Obit* Yrbk 2003

Eccles, David, British cabinet member, Jan 1952, *Obit* May 1999

Eccles, John C., Australian physiologist, Oct 1972, *Obit* July 1997

Eccles, Marriner S., American financier and Federal Reserve chairman, Apr 1941, *Obit* Feb 1978

Ecevit, Bulent, Turkish prime minister, Jan 1975, *Obit* Yrbk 2007

Echeverria Alvarez, Luis, Mexican president, Nov 1972

Echols, Oliver P., Yrbk 1947, *Obit* July 1954

Eckardt, Felix von, Jan 1956

Ecker, Frederick H., June 1948, *Obit* May 1964

Eckert, Robert, American toy industry executive, Mar 2003

Eckstein, Gustav, physiologist, May 1942, *Obit* Nov 1981

Eckstein, Otto, American economist, Feb 1967, *Obit* May 1984

Eckstine, Billy, American jazz singer, July 1952, *Obit* Apr 1993

Eco, Umberto, Italian semiotician and novelist, Apr 1985

Edberg, Stefan, Swedish tennis player, Jan 1994

Eddington, Arthur Stanley, British astronomer, Apr 1941, *Obit* Yrbk 1991

Eddins, William Frederick, American conductor and pianist, Feb 2002

Eddy, Manton S., general, Feb 1951, *Obit* June 1962

Eddy, Nelson, singer and actor, Feb 1943, *Obit* May 1967

Ede, James Chuter, May 1946, *Obit* Jan 1966

Edel, Leon, biographer, July 1963, *Obit* Nov 1997

Edelman, Gerald M., American biochemist, Apr 1995

Edelman, Marian Wright, American children's rights advocate, Sept 1992

Edelman, Maurice, Jan 1954, *Obit* Feb 1976

Eden, Anthony, British statesman, Yrbk 1940, Apr 1951, *Obit* Mar 1977

Edey, Birdsall Otis, *Obit* Aug 1940

Edge, Walter Evans, senator and governor, June 1945, *Obit* Jan 1957

Edgerton, Harold Eugene, American electrical engineer, Nov 1966, *Obit* Mar 1990

Edison, Charles, July 1940, *Obit* Oct 1969

Edman, Irwin, philosopher, July 1953, *Obit* Oct 1954

Edmonds, Walter D., American novelist and children's author, Sept 1942, *Obit* May 1998

Edwards, Blake, American film director, producer and screenwriter, Jan 1983, *Obit* Yrbk 2011

Edwards, Bob, American radio newscaster, Sept 2001

Edwards, Charles C., American surgeon and regulatory official, Oct 1973, *Obit* Yrbk 2011

Edwards, Clarence, Antiguan keyboardist and singer, Jan 2004

Edwards, David, Antiguan bassist, Jan 2004

Edwards, Don, American congressman, Mar 1983

Edwards, Douglas, radio and television newscaster, Aug 1988, *Obit* Jan 1991

Edwards, Gus, songwriter, *Obit* Yrbk 1945

Edwards, India, journalist and political activist, Sept 1949, *Obit* Mar 1990

Edwards, James Burrows, American dentist, governor and Secretary of energy, Nov 1982

Edwards, Joan, singer and composer, Oct 1953, *Obit* Oct 1981

Edwards, John, American senator and lawyer, Oct 2004

Edwards, John H., American congressman and government official, *Obit* Yrbk 1945

Edwards, Kathleen, Canadian singer and songwriter, Oct 2012

Edwards, Ralph, American television producer and

personality, July 1943, *Obit* Yrbk 2006

Edwards, Teresa, American basketball player, Mar 1998

Edwards, Toriano, Antiguan guitarist and singer, Jan 2004

Edwards, Vince, actor, Oct 1962, *Obit* May 1996

Edwards, Waldo B., American obstetrician, June 1943

Egan, Edward M., July 2001

Egan, Jennifer, American novelist, journalist and short story writer, Mar 2002

Egan, William Allen, American governor, Sept 1959, *Obit* July 1984

Egbert, Sherwood H., June 1963, *Obit* Oct 1969

Egeberg, Roger Olaf, government official, physician and college dean, Jan 1970, *Obit* Nov 1997

Eger, Ernst, Oct 1942

Eggers, Dave, American writer and publisher, July 2000

Eggerth, Marta, Austro-Hungarian singer and actress, Nov 1943

Eggleston, Edward Mason, *Obit* Mar 1941

Eggleston, William, American photographer, Feb 2002

Eghbal, Manouchehr, May 1959, *Obit* Feb 1978

Eglevsky, Andre, Feb 1953, *Obit* Feb 1978

Egloff, Gustav, Sept 1940

Egoyan, Atom, Canadian film director and screenwriter, May 1994

Ehlers, Vernon J., American congressman, Jan 2005

Ehrenburg, Ilya, Russian novelist, critic, memoirist and journalist, June 1966, *Obit* Nov 1967

Ehrenreich, Barbara, American feminist and social critic, Mar 1995

Ehricke, Krafft A., physicist and rocket engineer, June 1958, *Obit* Feb 1985

Ehrlich, Paul R., biologist, Sept 1970

Ehrlichman, John, American presidential adviser, Oct 1979, *Obit* Apr 1999

Ehrman, Bart D., American biblical scholar, Apr 2010

Eichelberger, Clark M., Jan 1947, *Obit* Mar 1980

Eichelberger, Robert L., American general, Jan 1943, *Obit* Yrbk 1961

Eicher, Edward C., May 1941, *Obit* Jan 1945

Eichheim, Henry, American violinist, conductor and composer, *Obit* Oct 1942

Eidmann, Frank Lewis, *Obit* Nov 1941

Eikenberry, Karl W., American general and diplomat, Mar 2010

Eiko, Japanese dancer and choreographer, May 2003

Eiko and Koma, May 2003

Eilshemius, Louis Michel, American painter, Apr 1940, *Obit* Feb 1942

Einaudi, Luigi, July 1948, *Obit* Jan 1962

Einem, Gottfried von, Austrian composer, July 1953, *Obit* Sept 1996

Einstein, Albert, German-American physicist, Nov 1941, May 1953, *Obit* June 1955

Eiseley, Loren C., American anthropologist and science writer, June 1960, *Obit* Sept 1977

Eisen, Gustavus A., *Obit* Yrbk 1940

Eisendrath, Maurice Nathan, May 1950, *Obit* Jan 1974

Eisenhower, Dwight D., American president, Aug 1942, Feb 1948, Sept 1957, *Obit* May 1969

Eisenhower, John S. D., army officer, diplomat and son of Dwight D. Eisenhower, July 1969

Eisenhower, Mamie Doud, wife of American president Dwight D. Eisenhower, May 1953, *Obit* Jan 1980

Eisenhower, Milton Stover, American college president, diplomat and government official, Yrbk 1946, *Obit* July 1985

Eisenman, Peter, American architect, Oct 1997

Eisenschiml, Otto, Austrian-American chemist and historian, Oct 1963, *Obit* Jan 1964

Eisenstaedt, Alfred, American photojournalist, Jan 1975, *Obit* Oct 1995

Eisenstein, Sergei, Russian theatrical and motion picture director, May 1946, *Obit* Mar 1948

Eisler, Hanns, German composer, May 1942, *Obit* Nov 1962

Eisner, Michael, American motion picture executive, Nov 1987

Eisner, Thomas, American entomologist, Mar 1993, *Obit* Yrbk 2011

Eisner, Will, American cartoonist and comic book publisher, Oct 1994, *Obit* May 2005

Ejiofor, Chiwetel, British actor, Jan 2004

Ejiro, Zeb, Nigerian motion picture producer and director, Jan 2002

Ek, Daniel, Swedish computer software executive, Mar 2012

Eklund, John M., labor leader and teacher, Yrbk 1949, *Obit* Mar 1997

Eklund, Sigvard, July 1962

Ekman, Carl Gustaf, *Obit* July 1945

El Baradei, Mohamed, Egyptian diplomat and international organization official, Jan 2003

El Juli, Spanish bullfighter, Jan 2002

El Mallakh, Kamal, Egyptian archaeologist, Oct 1954, *Obit* Jan 1988

El-Guerrouj, Hicham, Moroccan runner, Jan 2004

El-Khoury, Beshira, Yrbk 1951, *Obit* Feb 1964

El-Nahas, Mustafa, July 1951, *Obit* Nov 1965

El-Sayed, Karimat, Egyptian crystallographer, Jan 2004

El-Tahri, Jihan, French-Egyptian documentary filmmaker, Aug 2009

Elath, Eliahu, Israeli Zionist leader, Yrbk 1948, *Obit* Aug 1990

Elder, Albert L., Sept 1960

Elder, Lee, American golfer, Aug 1976

Elders, Joycelyn, American surgeon general, Mar 1994

Eldridge, Edward H., *Obit* June 1941

Eldridge, Florence, actress, Mar 1943, *Obit* Sept 1988

Eldridge, Roy, American trumpet player, Mar 1987, *Obit* Apr 1989

Elfman, Danny, American composer, Jan 2007

Elgin, Suzette Haden, American linguist, science fiction writer and poet, Aug 2006

Eliade, Mircea, Romanian religion historian and novelist, Nov 1985, *Obit* June 1986

Elias, Rosalind, Jan 1967

Eliasson, Jan, Swedish diplomat, Jan 2005

Elijah Muhammad, American Black Muslim leader, Jan 1971, *Obit* Apr 1975

Elion, Gertrude B., American biochemist, Mar 1995, *Obit* May 1999

Eliot, George Fielding, American journalist, Jan 1940, *Obit* June 1971

Eliot, Martha May, American pediatrician, Oct 1948, *Obit* Apr 1978

Eliot, T. S., American poet, critic and dramatist, Oct 1962, *Obit* Feb 1965

Eliot, Thomas Hopkinson, congressman, political scientist and dean, May 1942, *Obit* Jan 1992

Elisofon, Eliot, American photographer and painter, Jan 1972, *Obit* May 1973

Elizabeth, June 1944, June 1955, Jan 2002

Elizabeth, Aug 1981, *Obit* June 2002

Elizalde, Joaquin M., Feb 1948, *Obit* Mar 1965

Elizondo, Hector, American actor, Jan 1992

Elkin, Stanley, American novelist and short story writer, July 1987, *Obit* Aug 1995

Ellena, Jean-Claude, French perfumer, Jan 2005

Ellender, Allen J., American senator, July 1946, *Obit* Oct 1972

Ellerbee, Linda, American television newscaster, Oct 1986

Ellerman, Ferdinand, *Obit* Apr 1940

Elling, Kurt, American jazz singer, Jan 2005

Ellingson, Mark, college president, Sept 1957, *Obit* Apr 1993

Ellington, Buford, governor, Sept 1960, *Obit* May 1972

Ellington, Duke, American band leader and composer, Mar 1941, Jan 1970, *Obit* July 1974

Elliot, Kathleen Morrow, Mar 1940

Elliott, Bob, American comedian, Oct 1957

Elliott, Harriet Wiseman, college dean, July 1940, *Obit* Sept 1947

Elliott, Herb, Australian runner, July 1960

Elliott, Joe, English singer, Jan 2003

Elliott, John Lovejoy, social reformer, *Obit* June 1942

Elliott, Maxine, actress, Mar 1940

Elliott, Osborn, American journalist and college dean, Jan 1978, *Obit* Yrbk 2008

Elliott, Sean, basketball player, Apr 2001

Elliott, William Thompson, English theologian and canonist, *Obit* Aug 1940

Ellis, Albert, American psychologist, July 1994, *Obit* Yrbk 2007

Ellis, Bret Easton, American novelist, Nov 1994

Ellis, Carleton, *Obit* Mar 1941

Ellis, Elmer, college president, July 1962

Ellis, George, South African mathematician and astronomer, Jan 2006

Ellis, John Tracy, American priest and church historian, Mar 1990, *Obit* Jan 1993

Ellis, Monta, American basketball player, Feb 2008

Ellis, Perry, fashion designer, Jan 1986, *Obit* Jan 1986

Ellis, Ruth, American gay rights activist, *Obit* Apr 2000, Sept 2000

Ellison, Keith, American congressman, Apr 2007

Ellison, Lawrence J., American computer software executive, Jan 1998

Ellison, Ralph, American novelist and essayist, Oct

1968, June 1993, *Obit* June 1994

Elliston, Herbert, June 1949, *Obit* Mar 1957

Ellroy, James, American novelist, Apr 1998

Ells, Steve, American restaurant chain executive, May 2012

Ellsberg, Daniel, American peace activist, Yrbk 1973

Ellsberg, Edward, admiral, salvage engineer and author, Nov 1942, *Obit* Yrbk 1991

Elman, Mischa, American violinist, Oct 1945, *Obit* June 1967

Elo, Jorma, Finnish ballet dancer and choreographer, July 2009

Els, Ernie, South African golfer, Jan 2003

Elsenhans, Lynn Laverty, American petroleum company executive, July 2011

Elson, Arthur, Mar 1940

Elson, Edward L. R., clergyman, Nov 1967, *Obit* Nov 1993

Eltinge, Julian, *Obit* Apr 1941

Elvehjem, C. A., May 1948, *Obit* Oct 1962

Elway, John, American football player, Nov 1990

Ely, Paul, Oct 1954, *Obit* Mar 1975

Ely, Richard Theodore, American economist, *Obit* Nov 1943

Elytes, Odysseus, Greek poet, Sept 1980, *Obit* June 1996

Elzy, Ruby, *Obit* Aug 1943

Emanuel, Ariel, American talent agent, July 2009

Emanuel, Kerry A., American meteorologist, Jan 2007

Emanuel, Rahm, American mayor, Apr 1998, Mar 2009

Emanuel, Victor, American manufacturing executive, May 1951, *Obit* Jan 1961

Embree, Edwin R., Yrbk 1948, *Obit* Mar 1950

Emeny, Brooks, Nov 1947

Emerson String Quartet, July 2002

Emerson, Faye, American actress and television personality, Sept 1951, *Obit* May 1983

Emerson, Lee E., Oct 1953

Emerson, Roy, Australian tennis player, June 1965

Emerson, Victor Lee, *Obit* July 1941

Emery, Anne, author, Yrbk 1952

Emery, DeWitt, Oct 1946, *Obit* Oct 1955

Emin, Tracey, British performance artist, Nov 2009

Eminem, American rapper, Jan 2001

Emmerich, Roland, German film director, producer and screenwriter, Nov 2000

Emmerson, Louis Lincoln, *Obit* Mar 1941

Emmet of Amberley, Evelyn, Mar 1953

Emmet, William L., *Obit* Nov 1941

Emmons, Delos C., American general, Mar 1942, *Obit* Yrbk 1965

Emmons, Glenn L., Oct 1954

Empie, Paul C., Oct 1958

Emrich, Duncan, Mar 1955

Enckell, Carl J. A., Apr 1950, *Obit* June 1959

Endara, Guillermo, Panamanian president, Feb 1991, *Obit* Yrbk 2009

Endeley, E. M. L., July 1959

Enders, John F., American virologist, June 1955, *Obit* Jan 1986

Enders, John F.; Robbins, Frederick C.; and Weller, Thomas H., June 1955

Enders, Thomas, German aircraft industry executive, Mar 2011

Engel, Carl, musicologist and composer, *Obit* June 1944

Engel, Kurt, *Obit* Mar 1942

Engelbreit, Mary, American children's author, illustrator and magazine publisher, Oct 1999

Engibous, Thomas J., American semiconductor industry executive, Oct 2003

Engle, Clair, American senator, Mar 1957, *Obit* Oct 1964

Engle, Paul, American poet and college professor, June 1942, *Obit* May 1991

Englebright, Harry L., *Obit* July 1943

Engleman, J. O., *Obit* Nov 1943

English, Diane, television author and producer, June 1993

English, Todd, American chef and restaurateur, Jan 2012

Englund, Robert, actor, Mar 1990

Engstrom, Elmer W., electronics engineer and executive, Yrbk 1951, *Obit* Feb 1985

Enkhbayar, Nambaryn, Mongolian president, Jan 2007

Enright, Anne, Irish novelist and short story writer, Jan 2002

Enright, Elizabeth, American children's author and illustrator, Yrbk 1947, *Obit* Sept 1968

Enrique y Tarancon, Vicente, Oct 1972, *Obit* Feb 1995

Ensler, Eve, American dramatist, Aug 2002

Ensor, James, Belgian painter and engraver, *Obit* Feb 1943

Enters, Angna, dancer, painter and author, Jan 1940, June 1952, *Obit* Apr 1989

Entremont, Philippe, French pianist and conductor, Mar 1977

Enwezor, Okwui, Nigerian art critic and exhibition curator, Jan 2002

Ephron, Nora, American screenwriter and film director, Jan 1990, *Obit* Yrbk 2012

Epstein, Abraham, *Obit* June 1942

Epstein, Jacob, English sculptor and illustrator, July 1945, *Obit* Nov 1959

Epstein, Jason, American publishing executive, Aug 1990

Epstein, Joseph, American essayist, editor and critic, Mar 1990

Epstein, Samuel S., Anglo-American physician, Aug 2001

Epstein, Theo, American baseball executive, May 2004

Epworth, Paul, Aug 2013

Erdman, Jean, dancer, choreographer and teacher, Sept 1971

Erdogan, Recep Tayyip, Turkish prime minister, Jan 2003

Erdrich, Louise, American novelist and poet, Apr 1989

Erhard, Ludwig, German chancellor, Jan 1950, June 1964, *Obit* July 1977

Erhard, Werner, self-actualization educator, Apr 1977

Erickson, John Edward, *Obit* June 1946

Ericsson-Jackson, Aprille J., aerospace engineer, Mar 2001

Erikson, Erik H., American psychoanalyst, May 1971, *Obit* July 1994

Erikson, Leonard F., Oct 1953

Erkin, Feridun C., Jan 1952

Erlander, Tage F., Swedish prime minister, Oct 1947, *Obit* Aug 1985

Erlanger, Mitchell Louis, *Obit* Oct 1940

Ernst, Jimmy, painter, Mar 1966, *Obit* Apr 1984

Ernst, Max, German painter, Yrbk 1942, Oct 1961, *Obit* May 1976

Ernst, Morris, American lawyer and civil rights activist, Aug 1940, Feb 1961, *Obit* July 1976

Ershad, Hussain Mohammad, Bangladeshi prime minister, Nov 1984

Erskine, G. B., American Marine corps general, July 1946, *Obit* July 1973

Erskine, George, British general, Jan 1952, *Obit* Nov 1965

Erte, French painter, set and costume designer, Nov 1980, *Obit* June 1990

Ertegun, Mehmet Munir, *Obit* Jan 1945

Ervin, Sam J., American senator, Jan 1955, Oct 1973, *Obit* June 1985

Erving, Julius, American basketball player, May 1975

Esch, John J., *Obit* June 1941

Eschenbach, Christoph, German pianist and conductor, Aug 1989

Escoffery, Wayne, American jazz saxophonist and composer, Jan 2011

Eshelman, W. W., May 1960

Eshkol, Levi, Israeli prime minister, Oct 1963, *Obit* Apr 1969

Esiason, Boomer, American football player, Nov 1995

Espinoza Fuentes, Fernando, Ecuadorian biologist, Jan 2004

Espinoza, Alvaro, Chilean vintner, Jan 2004

Esposito, Phil, Canadian hockey player, May 1973

Espy, Mike, American Secretary of agriculture, Oct 1993

Estefan, Gloria, Cuban-American singer and songwriter, Oct 1995

Estern, Neil, American sculptor, Nov 2008

Estes, Eleanor, American librarian, children's author and illustrator, Yrbk 1946, *Obit* Sept 1988

Estes, Elliott M., American automobile executive, Jan 1979, *Obit* May 1988

Estes, Harlow, Mar 1941

Estes, Richard, American painter, Nov 1995

Estes, Simon, American opera singer, Aug 1986

Estigarribia, Jose Felix, Paraguayan field marshal and president, Mar 1940, *Obit* Mar 1940

Estrada, Joseph, Filipino president, Feb 2000

Eszterhas, Joe, American screenwriter, Apr 1998

Etheridge, Melissa, American singer and guitarist, May 1995

Etherington, Edwin D., stock exchange official and college president, Apr 1966, *Obit* Apr 2001

Ethridge, Mark Foster, American newspaper publisher and diplomat, Jan 1946, *Obit* June 1981

Eto'o, Samuel, Cameroonian soccer player, Feb 2013

Ettinger, Richard P., Yrbk 1951, *Obit* Apr 1971

Ettl, John, *Obit* Feb 1941

Etzel, Franz, German economist and cabinet member, Sept 1957

Etzioni, Amitai, American sociologist, Mar 1980

Euclide, Gregory, May 2013

Eugenides, Jeffrey, American novelist, Oct 2003

Eurich, Alvin C., educator, June 1949, *Obit* Aug 1987

Eustis, Helen, author, Yrbk 1955

Eustis, Oskar, American theatrical director and drama teacher, Oct 2002

Evanovich, Janet, American mystery novelist, Apr 2001

Evans, Alice Catherine, American bacteriologist, Oct 1943, *Obit* Oct 1975

Evans, Anne, *Obit* Feb 1941

Evans, Arthur John, British archaeologist, *Obit* Sept 1941

Evans, Bergen, Yrbk 1955, *Obit* Apr 1978

Evans, Chris, American actor, Aug 2013

Evans, Daniel Jackson, American senator and governor, Aug 1975

Evans, Donald L., American Secretary of commerce, Nov 2001

Evans, Edith, English actress, June 1956, *Obit* Jan 1977

Evans, Faith, American singer and songwriter, Feb 1999

Evans, Frank, British bullfighter, Jan 2005

Evans, Harold, British publishing executive, Apr 1985

Evans, Herbert McLean, endocrinologist and anatomist, July 1959, *Obit* Apr 1971

Evans, Hugh Ivan, Nov 1950, *Obit* July 1958

Evans, Janet, American swimmer, July 1996

Evans, Linda, American actress, Mar 1986

Evans, Luther Harris, American Librarian of Congress and United Nations official, Aug 1945, *Obit* Feb 1982

Evans, Maurice, English actor, May 1940, June 1961, *Obit* May 1989

Evans, Nancy, Internet service executive and editor, Mar 2000

Evans, Walker, American photographer, Sept 1971, *Obit* June 1975

Evaristti, Marco, Chilean installation artist, Jan 2007

Evatt, Harriet, Yrbk 1959

Evatt, Herbert Vere, Australian statesman, May 1942, *Obit* Jan 1966

Eve (Singer), American rapper and actress, July 2003

Everett, Percival L., American novelist, children's author and short story writer, Sept 2004

Everett, Rupert, English actor, Jan 2005

Evergood, Philip, American painter, Oct 1944, Oct 1960, *Obit* Apr 1973

Evers, Charles, American civil rights activist, mayor and brother of Medgar Evers, Apr 1969

Evers-Williams, Myrlie, civil rights leader and wife of Medgar Wiley Evers, Aug 1995

Everson, Kevin Jerome, American filmmaker and video artist, Nov 2011

Evert, Chris, American tennis player, Apr 1973

Eves, Reginald Grenville, Sept 1940, *Obit* Aug 1941

Evren, Kenan, Turkish president, Apr 1984

Ewbank, Weeb, football coach, June 1969, *Obit* Feb 1999

Ewell, Tom, actor, May 1961, *Obit* Nov 1994

Ewing, James, *Obit* July 1943

Ewing, Maria, American opera singer, Apr 1990

Ewing, Maurice, American geophysicist, Jan 1953, *Obit* June 1974

Ewing, Oscar R., American government official, July 1948, *Obit* Mar 1980

Ewing, Patrick, American basketball player, May 1991

Exeter, David George Brownlow Cecil, British hurdler and Olympic executive, Jan 1956

Exley, Frederick, novelist, Oct 1989, *Obit* Aug 1992

Exner, Max J., *Obit* Nov 1943

Exon, J. James, American senator, Nov 1996, *Obit* Yrbk 2005

Eyadema, Gnassingbe, Togolese president, Apr 2002, *Obit* Yrbk 2005

Eyde, Samuel, *Obit* Aug 1940

Eyler, John, American toy store chain executive, Aug 2000

Eyre, Chris, Native American motion picture director, May 2003

Eyre, Katherine Wigmore, Yrbk 1949, Yrbk 1957

Eyring, Henry, chemist, Oct 1961

Eysenck, H. J., German-British psychologist, Nov 1972, *Obit* Nov 1997

Eyskens, Gaston, Belgian prime minister, Nov 1949, *Obit* Feb 1988

Eytan, Walter, Israeli diplomat, Oct 1958, *Obit* Oct 2001

Eyuboglu, Bedri Rahmi, Turkish artist and poet, Sept 1954

Ezarik, Justine, American webcaster, Mar 2013

F

Faber, Joachim, German investment manager, Jan 2002

Faber, Sandra M., American astronomer, Apr 2002

Fabian, Robert, Apr 1954, *Obit* Aug 1978

Fabius, Laurent, French political leader, Feb 1985

Fabray, Nanette, comedienne, Jan 1956

Fabre, Jan, Belgian artist, Jan 2004

Fabregas, Cesc, Spanish soccer player, Jan 2006

Fabris, Enrico, Italian speed skater, Jan 2006

Fackenthal, Frank D., Feb 1949, *Obit* Nov 1968

Fadiman, Anne, American essayist and journalist, Aug 2005

Fadiman, Clifton, literary critic, editor and television moderator, May 1941, Oct 1955, *Obit* Sept 1999

Fagan, Garth, American dancer, director and choreographer, Aug 1998

Fager, Jeff, American television producer, Jan 2012

Fagerholm, Karl August, Finnish prime minister, Oct 1948, *Obit* July 1984

Fagg, Fred D., Feb 1956, *Obit* Jan 1982

Fagles, Robert, American translator, poet and literary scholar, Apr 2006, *Obit* Yrbk 2008

Fagnani, Charles P., *Obit* Mar 1941

Fahd, May 1979, *Obit* Yrbk 2005

Fahmy, Azza, Egyptian jewelry designer, Jan 2004

Fahy, Charles, American judge and solicitor general, Jan 1942, *Obit* Nov 1979

Faidley, Warren, American photographer and storm chaser, Feb 2008

Fairbank, John King, American Sinologist, Oct 1966, *Obit* Nov 1991

Fairbanks, Douglas, American actor, Jan 1940

Fairbanks, Douglas, American actor, Nov 1941, Feb 1956, *Obit* Aug 2000

Fairchild, Benjamin Lewis, *Obit* Yrbk 1946

Fairchild, David, American plant pathologist and explorer, July 1953, *Obit* Oct 1954

Fairchild, Henry Pratt, sociologist and economist, Yrbk 1942, *Obit* Yrbk 1957

Fairchild, John, American magazine publisher, June 1971

Fairclough, Ellen Louks, Canadian cabinet member, Oct 1957, *Obit* Yrbk 2005

Fairless, Benjamin F., American steel industry executive, June 1942, May 1957, *Obit* Feb 1962

Fairport Convention (Musical group), Sept 2005

Faisal, July 1955, *Obit* Oct 1958

Faisal, May 1966, *Obit* May 1975

Faith, Paloma, Aug 2013

Falco, Edie, American actress, Mar 2006

Faldo, Nick, English golfer, Sept 1992

Falk, Maurice, *Obit* Apr 1946

Falk, Peter, American actor, July 1972, *Obit* Yrbk 2011

Falkner, Roland Post, *Obit* Jan 1941

Fall, Albert B., American Secretary of the interior, *Obit* Jan 1945

Falla, Manuel de, Spanish composer, *Obit* Yrbk 1946

Fallaci, Oriana, Italian journalist and novelist, Feb 1977, *Obit* Yrbk 2007

Falldin, Thorbjorn, Swedish prime minister, May 1978

Fallin, Mary, American congresswoman, Mar 2011

Fallon, Jimmy, American comedian, actor and talk show host, July 2002

Fallon, William J., American admiral, July 2007

Fallows, James M., American journalist, Nov 1996

Falls, Robert, American theatrical director, Jan 2004

Fals, Iwan, Indonesian singer and songwriter, Jan 2002

Faludi, Susan, American journalist and feminist, Feb 1993

Falwell, Jerry, American evangelist, Jan 1981, *Obit* Aug 2007

Fanfani, Amintore, Italian prime minister, Oct 1958, *Obit* Mar 2000

Fang Lizhi, Chinese astrophysicist, Nov 1989, *Obit* Yrbk 2012

Fangmeier, Stefen, American special effects technician, Aug 2004

Fanning, Mick, Australian surfer, June 2013

Farah, Mar 1976

Farber, Sid, builder, Sept 1967, *Obit* May 1973

Farhi, Nicole, French fashion designer, Nov 2001

Faricy, William T., June 1948

Farina, Dennis, American actor, *Obit* Yrbk 2013

Farish, William Stamps, *Obit* Jan 1943

Farley, James Aloysius, American political leader, Sept 1944, *Obit* Aug 1976

Farley, Walter, American children's and young adult author, Yrbk 1949, *Obit* Feb 1990

Farmer, Guy, Feb 1955

Farmer, James, American civil rights leader, Feb 1964, *Obit* Sept 1999

Farmer, Paul, American physician, Feb 2004

Farmer-Paellmann, Deadria, American activist seeking reparations for slavery, Mar 2004

Farnsworth, Arthur, *Obit* Oct 1943

Farnsworth, Jerry, Oct 1954

Farny, George W., *Obit* Oct 1941

Farooq, Umar, Kashmiri Islamic leader, Jan 2002

Farouk, Oct 1942, *Obit* May 1965

Farrakhan, Louis, American Black Muslim leader, Apr 1992

Farrar, John, June 1954, *Obit* Jan 1975

Farrar, Margaret, crossword puzzle editor, July 1955, *Obit* Aug 1984

Farrell, Colin, Irish actor, Jan 2004

Farrell, Eileen, American singer, Feb 1961, *Obit* June 2002

Farrell, James T., American novelist and short story writer, Sept 1942, *Obit* Oct 1979

Farrell, Suzanne, American ballet dancer, Sept 1967

Farrelly, Bobby, American screenwriter and film director, Sept 2001

Farrelly, Peter, American screenwriter and film director, Sept 2001

Farrelly, Peter; and Farrelly, Bobby, Sept 2001

Farrington, Elizabeth Pruett, American newspaper publisher, June 1955, *Obit* Sept 1984

Farrington, Joseph Rider, American newspaper executive and congressman, May 1948, *Obit* Sept 1954

Farrow, Mia, American actress, Apr 1970

Fasanella, Ralph, painter, June 1975, *Obit* Mar 1998

Fascell, Dante B., congressman, Apr 1960, *Obit* Feb 1999

Fassbaender, Brigitte, German opera singer, June 1994

Fassbinder, Rainer Werner, German film director and producer, May 1977, *Obit* Aug 1982

Fassett, Kaffe, American textile designer, June 1995

Fast, Howard, American novelist and short story writer, Apr 1943, Apr 1991, *Obit* July 2003

Fatemi, Hossein, May 1953, *Obit* Jan 1955

Fath, Jacques, French fashion designer, Apr 1951, *Obit* Jan 1955

Fatone, Joey, American singer, Nov 2000

Fatt, Jeff, Australian actor and singer, Jan 2004

Fattah, Chaka, American congressman, Sept 2003

Faubus, Orval, American governor, Oct 1956, *Obit* Feb 1995

Fauci, Anthony S., American immunologist, Aug 1988

Fauley, Wilbur F., *Obit* Feb 1943

Faulk, Marshall, American football player, Jan 2003

Faulkner, Brian, prime minister of Northern Ireland, Feb 1972, *Obit* May 1977

Faulkner, Nancy, Yrbk 1956

Faulkner, William, American novelist, Jan 1951, *Obit* Sept 1962

Fauntroy, Walter E., American congressman, Feb 1979

Faure, Edgar, French statesman, Feb 1952, *Obit* May 1988

Faurot, Joseph A., *Obit* Jan 1943

Faussart, Celia, French singer, Jan 2003

Faussart, Helene, French singer, Jan 2003

Faust, Clarence H., Mar 1952, *Obit* Aug 1975

Faust, Drew Gilpin, American historian and college president, July 2007

Faust, Frederick, American western novelist, *Obit* July 1944

Fausto-Sterling, Anne, American biologist, Sept 2005

Faversham, William, *Obit* May 1940

Favre, Brett, American football player, Nov 1996

Favreau, Jon, American actor, screenwriter and film director, July 2010

Favreau, Jonathan, American speechwriter, May 2009

Fawcett, Edward, *Obit* Nov 1942

Fawcett, Farrah, American actress, Feb 1978, *Obit* Aug 2009

Fawcett, Joy, American soccer player, May 2004

Fawcett, Sherwood L., Yrbk 1972

Fawzi, Mahmoud, Yrbk 1951

Fay, Frank, Aug 1945, *Obit* Yrbk 1961

Fay, Martin, Irish fiddler, Mar 2004, *Obit* Yrbk 2013

Fay, Michael, American biologist and conservationist, Sept 2001

Feather, Vic, Mar 1973, *Obit* Sept 1976

Fechteler, William M., American admiral, Sept 1951, *Obit* Oct 1967

Federer, Roger, Swiss tennis player, Jan 2004

Fedorenko, Nikolai T., Yrbk 1967

Fedorova, Nina, Nov 1940

Fei Junlong, Chinese astronaut, Jan 2006

Feifel, Herman, American psychologist, Aug 1994, *Obit* Yrbk 2005

Feiffer, Jules, American cartoonist, children's author and dramatist, Oct 1961

Feingold, Russ, American senator, July 1998

Feininger, Andreas, American photographer, Oct 1957, *Obit* May 1999

Feininger, Lyonel, German painter and cartoonist, July 1955, *Obit* Mar 1956

Feinsinger, Nathan P., professor of law and labor mediator, May 1952, *Obit* Jan 1984

Feinstein, Dianne, American senator, June 1979, Aug 1995

Feinstein, John, American sportswriter, July 1998

Feinstein, Michael, American pianist and singer, Apr 1988

Feis, Herbert, historian, Oct 1961, *Obit* May 1972

Feist (Musician), Canadian singer and songwriter, June 2008

Feith, Douglas J., American military official, July 2008

Feld, Eliot, American choreographer and dance teacher, Oct 1971

Feld, Irvin, circus owner, Feb 1979, *Obit* Nov 1984

Feldmann, Markus, June 1956, *Obit* Jan 1959

Feldstein, Martin S., American economist and presidential adviser, May 1983

Feldt, Gloria A., American birth control advocate, July 2000

Feliciano, Jose, singer and guitarist, July 1969

Felix, Robert Hanna, psychiatrist, Apr 1957, *Obit* May 1990

Felker, Clay, American magazine founder and editor, Feb 1975, *Obit* Yrbk 2008

Feller, Abraham H., Nov 1946, *Obit* Jan 1953

Feller, Bob, American baseball player, Aug 1941, *Obit* Yrbk 2011

Fellini, Federico, Italian motion picture director, June 1957, Oct 1980, *Obit* Jan 1994

Fellows, George Emory, American historian and university president, *Obit* Mar 1942

Fellows, Harold E., Feb 1952, *Obit* May 1960

Fels, William C., Apr 1959, *Obit* Jan 1965

Felt, Harry D., Mar 1959

Felt, W. Mark, American FBI official and Watergate informant Deep Throat, Sept 2005, *Obit* Yrbk 2009

Feltin, Maurice, May 1954, *Obit* Nov 1975

Felton, Ralph A., Sept 1957

Feltsman, Vladimir, Russian pianist, Apr 1988

Feniger, Susan, American chef and restaurateur, Apr 2013

Fenimore-Cooper, Susan De Lancey, *Obit* Mar 1940

Fenton, George, English composer, July 2010

Fenty, Adrian, American mayor, Mar 2007

Fenwick, Millicent, American congresswoman, Apr 1977, *Obit* Nov 1992

Feoktistov, Konstantin Petrovich, Soviet astronaut and aerospace engineer, Nov 1967, *Obit* Yrbk 2010

Ferber, Herbert, American sculptor and painter, Nov 1960, *Obit* Oct 1991

Fergie, American singer, Oct 2006

Ferguson, Alex, Scottish soccer manager, June 2010

Ferguson, Craig, Scottish-American comedian, actor and talk show host, Jan 2005

Ferguson, Elsie, Feb 1944, *Obit* Jan 1962

Ferguson, Garland S., July 1949, *Obit* June 1963

Ferguson, Harriet, Jan 1947, *Obit* Feb 1966

Ferguson, Harry, Irish inventor, Mar 1956, *Obit* Jan 1961

Ferguson, Homer, American diplomat and senator, May 1943, *Obit* Mar 1983

Ferguson, Howard, *Obit* Apr 1946

Ferguson, James Edward, governor, *Obit* Nov 1944

Ferguson, Malcolm P., May 1957

Ferguson, Maynard, Canadian jazz trumpet player, Feb 1980, *Obit* Yrbk 2006

Ferguson, Niall, Scottish historian, July 2012

Fergusson, Erna, Yrbk 1955

Ferlinghetti, Lawrence, American poet, novelist, dramatist and publisher, June 1991

Fermi, Enrico, Italian-American physicist, Oct 1945, *Obit* Jan 1955

Fermi, Laura, wife of Enrico Fermi, May 1958

Fermor, Patrick Leigh, English travel writer and novelist, Yrbk 1955, *Obit* Yrbk 2011

Fernandel, Oct 1955, *Obit* Apr 1971

Fernandes, L. Esteves, Oct 1950

Fernandez de la Vega, Maria Teresa, Spanish vice-president, Jan 2007

Fernandez, Alejandro, Mexican singer, Jan 2005

Ferrari, Enzo, Italian automobile executive, May 1967, *Obit* Sept 1988

Ferraro, Geraldine A., American lawyer, congresswoman, political commentator and vice-presidential candidate, Sept 1984, *Obit* Yrbk 2011

Ferre, Gianfranco, Italian fashion designer, July 1991, *Obit* Yrbk 2007

Ferre, Luis A., Puerto Rican governor, Mar 1970, *Obit* Mar 2004

Ferrell, Will, American comedian and actor, Feb 2003

Ferren, John, American painter, July 1958, *Obit* Oct 1970

Ferrer, Jose, American actor and director, May 1944, *Obit* Mar 1992

Ferrer, Rafael, Puerto Rican artist, July 2001

Ferrera, America, American actress, Sept 2007

Ferrero, Gina Lombroso, *Obit* May 1944

Ferrero, Guglielmo, Italian historian and author, *Obit* Sept 1942

Ferrier, Kathleen, British opera singer, Oct 1951, *Obit* Yrbk 1953

Ferris, Harry Burr, *Obit* Yrbk 1940

Ferris, Joshua, American novelist, Oct 2010

Ferris, Scott, *Obit* July 1945

Ferris, Timothy, American journalist and science writer, Jan 2001

Ferriss, Hugh, July 1945, *Obit* Mar 1962

Festing, Francis, Feb 1945

Feuermann, Emanuel, *Obit* July 1942

Few, William Preston, college president, *Obit* Yrbk 1940

Fey, Tina, American actress and comedienne, Apr 2002

Feynman, Richard Phillips, American physicist, Oct 1955, Nov 1986, *Obit* Apr 1988

Fichandler, Zelda, American theatrical producer and director, June 1987

Fidrych, Mark, American baseball player, Mar 1978, *Obit* Yrbk 2009

Fiedler, Arthur, American conductor, Sept 1945, May 1977, *Obit* Sept 1979

Fiedler, Leslie A., American literary critic and novelist, Yrbk 1970, *Obit* Yrbk 2003

Field, Anthony, Australian actor and singer, Jan 2004

Field, Betty, Sept 1959, *Obit* Nov 1973

Field, Frederick Laurence, *Obit* Yrbk 1945

Field, Henry, anthropologist, Mar 1955, *Obit* Mar 1986

Field, Marshall, American department store executives and newspaper publisher, Apr 1941, Mar 1952, *Obit* Jan 1957

Field, Patricia, American fashion and costume designer, Nov 2010

Field, Rachel, American novelist, poet and children's author, *Obit* May 1942

Field, Sally, American actress, Oct 1979

Fielder, Prince, American baseball player, June 2008

Fielding, Gabriel, English novelist, poet and physician, Feb 1962, *Obit* Apr 1987

Fielding, Mantle, *Obit* May 1941

Fielding, Temple Hornaday, travel book author, Apr 1969, *Obit* July 1983

Fields, Dorothy, American lyricist and librettist, Feb 1958, *Obit* May 1974

Fields, Gracie, English actress and singer, Apr 1941, *Obit* Nov 1979

Fields, Herbert, Feb 1958

Fields, Herbert; and Fields, Dorothy, Feb 1958

Fields, Lew, comedian, *Obit* Sept 1941

Fields, Mark, American automobile executive, Apr 2005

Fields, Stanley, *Obit* June 1941

Fiene, Ernest, American painter and printmaker, Aug 1941

Fiennes, Ralph, British actor, Sept 1996

Fiennes, Ranulph, British explorer, Jan 2004

Fieri, Guy, American chef, restaurateur and television personality, Mar 2011

Fierstein, Harvey, American dramatist and actor, Feb 1984

Figgis, D. W., Nov 1948, *Obit* Jan 1965

Figl, Leopold, Apr 1948, *Obit* June 1965

Figo, Luis, Portuguese soccer player, Jan 2003

Figueiredo, Joao Baptista de Oliveira, Brazilian president, Jan 1980, *Obit* May 2000

Figueres Ferrer, Jose, Costa Rican president, Oct 1953, *Obit* Aug 1990

Figueroa, Ana, Chilean educator, diplomat and feminist, Feb 1952

Fili-Krushel, Patricia, television executive, Nov 1999

Filippenko, Alex, Oct 2013

Filmus, Tully, painter, Apr 1964, *Obit* June 1998

Filo, David, American Internet search engine executive, Oct 1997

Filo, David; Yang, Jerry, Co-founders of Yahoo! Inc., Oct 1997

Filov, Bogdan, Apr 1941

Finch, Caleb Ellicott, American neurobiologist, Sept 2004

Finch, Flora, *Obit* Jan 1940

Finch, Jennie, American softball player, Oct 2004

Finch, Peter, English actor, Sept 1972, *Obit* Mar 1977

Finch, Robert H., American secretary of health, education and welfare, Mar 1969, *Obit* Jan 1996

Finckel, David, American cellist and recording producer, July 2002

Fine, Benjamin, Mar 1961

Fine, John Sydney, governor, Sept 1951, *Obit* July 1978

Finet, Paul, Belgian labor leader, Sept 1951

Finger, Charles Joseph, American children's author, *Obit* Mar 1941

Fingesten, Peter, painter and art teacher, Oct 1954, *Obit* Oct 1987

Fini, Gianfranco, Italian political leader, Jan 2003

Finkelstein, Arthur, American political consultant, Nov 1999

Finkelstein, Louis, rabbi and educator, Nov 1940, Mar 1952, *Obit* Jan 1992

Finletter, Thomas K., American diplomat and government official, Jan 1948, *Obit* June 1980

Finley, Charles, American baseball executive, June 1974, *Obit* Apr 1996

Finley, David E., American museum administrator and historic preservationist, Feb 1951, *Obit* Apr 1977

Finley, John Huston, Mar 1940

Finley, Karen, performance artist, Sept 1998

Finn, Craig, American singer and songwriter, Sept 2010

Finn, William J., July 1940

Finnegan, Joseph F., Apr 1959, *Obit* Apr 1964

Finney, Albert, English actor, Oct 1963

Finney, Gertrude E., Yrbk 1957

Finscher, Ludwig, German musicologist, Jan 2007

Fiore, Mark, American cartoonist and animator, Apr 2011

Fiorina, Carly, American computer industry executive, Jan 2000

Fireman, Paul, American shoe company executive, Mar 1992

Firestone, Harvey S., July 1944, *Obit* July 1973

Firkusny, Rudolf, Czech pianist, Oct 1979, *Obit* Sept 1994

Firth, Colin, English actor, Mar 2004

Fischbacher, Siegfried, German magician and animal trainer, Jan 1998

Fischer, Bobby, American chess player, Oct 1963, May 1994, *Obit* Yrbk 2008

Fischer, Carlos L., Feb 1959

Fischer, Hans, German chemist, *Obit* May 1945

Fischer, Israel Frederick, judge and congressman, *Obit* Apr 1940

Fischer, John, May 1953, *Obit* Oct 1978

Fischer, John H., American college dean and president, July 1960, *Obit* Yrbk 2010

Fischer, Joschka, German political leader and diplomat, Jan 2002

Fischer, Louis, journalist and historian, May 1940, *Obit* Mar 1970

Fischer-Dieskau, Dietrich, German opera singer, Feb 1967, *Obit* Yrbk 2012

Fischl, Eric, American painter and sculptor, June 1986

Fish, Bert, *Obit* Sept 1943

Fish, Hamilton, American congressman, Jan 1941, *Obit* Mar 1991

Fish, Marie Poland, oceanographer, Oct 1941, *Obit* Apr 1989

Fishback, Margaret, copywriter and humorist, Apr 1941, *Obit* Nov 1985

Fishbein, Morris, American periodical editor and physician, May 1940, *Obit* Nov 1976

Fishburne, Laurence, American actor, Aug 1996

Fisher of Lambeth, Geoffrey Francis Fisher, British archbishop, Mar 1945, *Obit* Nov 1972

Fisher, Carrie, American actress and novelist, Feb 1991

Fisher, Clarence S., *Obit* Sept 1941

Fisher, Eddie, American singer, Oct 1954, *Obit* Yrbk 2010

Fisher, Fred, songwriter and composer, *Obit* Mar 1942

Fisher, Harry L., Oct 1954

Fisher, Helen E., American anthropologist and psychologist, Oct 2010

Fisher, John Stuchell, governor, *Obit* Aug 1940

Fisher, M. F. K., American food writer, Yrbk 1948, Sept 1983, *Obit* Aug 1992

Fisher, Sterling, Yrbk 1940

Fisher, Walter C., July 1950

Fisher, Welthy Honsinger, educator, Yrbk 1969, *Obit* Feb 1981

Fishman, Jon, American drummer, July 2003

Fisk, Jack, American motion picture production designer, June 2011

Fisk, James Brown, Jan 1959, *Obit* Oct 1981

Fisk, Robert, British journalist, Jan 2006

Fiske, Bradley A., *Obit* May 1942

Fiske, Charles, *Obit* Mar 1942

Fiske, James Porter, orthopedic surgeon and hospital administrator, *Obit* Yrbk 1941

Fister, George M., June 1963, *Obit* July 1976

Fitch, Aubrey, Oct 1945, *Obit* July 1978

Fitch, Robert Elliot, Apr 1962

Fittipaldi, Emerson, Brazilian automobile racing driver, Apr 1992

Fitz Gerald, Leslie M., Sept 1954

FitzGerald, Frances, American journalist, June 1987

FitzGerald, Garret, Irish prime minister, Aug 1984, *Obit* Yrbk 2011

Fitzgerald, Albert J., American labor leader, Oct 1948, *Obit* July 1982

Fitzgerald, Barry, Feb 1945, *Obit* Feb 1961

Fitzgerald, Cissy, *Obit* July 1941

Fitzgerald, Ed; and Fitzgerald, Pegeen, Apr 1947

Fitzgerald, Edward, radio talk show host, Apr 1947, *Obit* June 1982

Fitzgerald, Ella, American singer, Oct 1956, July 1990, *Obit* Aug 1996

Fitzgerald, F. Scott, American novelist and short story writer, *Obit* Feb 1941

Fitzgerald, Geraldine, Irish actress and director, Oct 1976, *Obit* Yrbk 2005

Fitzgerald, Patrick, American district attorney, Jan 2006

Fitzgerald, Pegeen, radio talk show host, Apr 1947, *Obit* Apr 1989

Fitzgerald, Robert, American poet and classicist, Sept 1976, *Obit* Mar 1985

Fitzgibbons, John, *Obit* Oct 1941

Fitzmaurice, George, *Obit* Aug 1940

Fitzpatrick, Daniel Robert, cartoonist, July 1941, *Obit* July 1969

Fitzpatrick, George L., *Obit* June 1941

Fitzroy, Edward Algernon, *Obit* Apr 1943

Fitzsimmons, Frank Edward, American labor leader, May 1971, *Obit* July 1981

Fitzwater, Marlin, American presidential press secretary, May 1988

Flack, Roberta, American singer, Nov 1973

Flagg, Fannie, American comedienne, actress and novelist, Nov 2006

Flagg, James Montgomery, painter and illustrator, Nov 1940, *Obit* Sept 1960

Flagstad, Kirsten, Norwegian opera singer, May 1947, *Obit* Jan 1963

Flaherty, Robert Joseph, American film director and explorer, Mar 1949, *Obit* Sept 1951

Flair, Ric, wrestler, Mar 2000

Flaming Lips (Musical group), Oct 2002

Flaming Sideburns (Musical group), Jan 2003

Flanagan, Edward Joseph, American priest and youth leader, Sept 1941, *Obit* June 1948

Flanagan, Tommy, American pianist, Apr 1995, *Obit* Mar 2002

Flanders, Michael, Jan 1970, *Obit* June 1975

Flanders, Ralph E., American senator, Jan 1948, *Obit* Apr 1970

Flandin, Pierre Etienne, French political leader, Jan 1941, *Obit* Oct 1958

Flannagan, John, American sculptor, *Obit* Mar 1942

Flanner, Janet, American journalist and novelist, May 1943, *Obit* Jan 1979

Flannery, Harry W., Oct 1943

Flansburgh, John, guitarist, Nov 1999

Flavin, Martin, dramatist and author, Yrbk 1943, *Obit* Feb 1968

Flay, Bobby, American chef and restaurateur, May 2008

Fleck, Alexander Fleck, Scottish chemical executive, Apr 1956, *Obit* Oct 1968

Fleck, Bela, American banjoist, Nov 1996

Fleck, Jack, golfer, Sept 1955

Fleeson, Doris, American newspaper columnist, May 1959, *Obit* Oct 1970

Fleischmann, Manly, lawyer, July 1951

Fleisher, Leon, American pianist and conductor, Jan 1971

Fleming, Alexander, British bacteriologist, Apr 1944, *Obit* May 1955

Fleming, Alexander; and Florey, Howard, Apr 1944

Fleming, Amalia Koutsouri, Greek legislator, Nov 1972, *Obit* Apr 1986

Fleming, Arthur Henry, *Obit* Sept 1940

Fleming, Berry, author, Yrbk 1953, *Obit* Nov 1989

Fleming, Donald M., Canadian cabinet member, Feb 1959, *Obit* Mar 1987

Fleming, Ian, English spy novelist, Jan 1964

Fleming, John A., May 1940, *Obit* Oct 1956

Fleming, John Ambrose, English electrical engineer, *Obit* May 1945

Fleming, Maureen, American dancer and choreographer, Mar 2010

Fleming, Peggy, American figure skater, July 1968

Fleming, Philip Bracken, Apr 1940, *Obit* Yrbk 1956

Fleming, Renee, American opera singer, May 1997

Fleming, Robben W., American university president, Yrbk 1970, *Obit* Yrbk 2010

Fleming, Sam M., June 1962

Flemming, Arthur S., American Secretary of health, education and welfare, June 1951, Apr 1960, *Obit* Nov 1996

Flesch, Carl, Hungarian violinist, *Obit* Jan 1945

Flesch, Rudolf Franz, American educational reformer, Apr 1948, *Obit* Nov 1986

Fletcher, Angus, Sept 1946, *Obit* Nov 1960

Fletcher, Arthur Allen, American civil rights leader and government official, Nov 1971, *Obit* Yrbk 2005

Fletcher, C. Scott, Feb 1953

Fletcher, Inglis, American children's author and novelist, Yrbk 1947, *Obit* July 1969

Fletcher, James C., American physicist and NASA official, May 1972, *Obit* Feb 1992

Flexner, Abraham, American educator, June 1941, *Obit* Nov 1959

Flexner, Bernard, *Obit* June 1945

Flexner, Jennie Maas, librarian, *Obit* Jan 1945

Flexner, Simon, American physician, *Obit* June 1946

Flickinger, Roy Caston, *Obit* Aug 1942

Flight of the Conchords, Mar 2008

Flikke, Julia O., July 1942

Flint, Keith, British singer and dancer, Oct 2009

Flood, Daniel J., American congressman, Aug 1978, *Obit* Aug 1994

Flore, Edward F., *Obit* Oct 1945

Florence, Fred F., June 1956, *Obit* Feb 1961

Florence, Tyler, American chef, Aug 2012

Flores Nano, Lourdes, Peruvian political leader, Jan 2006

Florey, Howard, Australian bacteriologist, Apr 1944, *Obit* Apr 1968

Florez, Juan Diego, Peruvian opera singer, Jan 2007

Florinsky, Michael T., Russian historian, Oct 1941, *Obit* Jan 1982

Florio, James J., governor, May 1990

Flory, Paul J., American chemist, Mar 1975, *Obit* Nov 1985

Flowers, Vonetta, American bobsledder, May 2006

Floyd, Carlisle, American composer, July 1960

Floyd, William, *Obit* Jan 1944

Flutie, Doug, American football player, Oct 1985

Fly, James L., lawyer, Sept 1940, *Obit* Feb 1966

Flynn, Edward J., American political leader, Sept 1940, *Obit* Oct 1953

Flynn, Elizabeth Gurley, American communist leader, Oct 1961, *Obit* Nov 1964

Flynn, Gillian, American television critic and novelist, Apr 2013

Flynn, Raymond, American mayor and diplomat, Oct 1993

Flynt, Larry, American magazine publisher, Sept 1999

Fo, Dario, Italian actor and dramatist, Nov 1986

Foakes-Jackson, F. J., *Obit* Jan 1942

Fodor, Eugene, American violinist, Apr 1976, *Obit* Yrbk 2011

Foer, Jonathan Safran, American novelist, Sept 2002

Foerster, Friedrich Wilhelm, July 1962, *Obit* Feb 1966

Fogarty, Anne, fashion designer, Oct 1958, *Obit* Mar 1980

Fogarty, John Edward, congressman, Apr 1964, *Obit* Mar 1967

Fogh Rasmussen, Anders, Danish prime minister, Jan 2004

Fokine, Michel, Russian ballet dancer and choreographer, *Obit* Oct 1942

Foley, Martha, author and magazine editor, Apr 1941, *Obit* Oct 1977

Foley, Martha; and Burnett, Whit, Apr 1941

Foley, Mick, American wrestler, Sept 2001

Foley, Raymond M., Oct 1949, *Obit* Apr 1975

Foley, Thomas S., American Speaker of the House, Sept 1989

Folger, A. D., *Obit* June 1941

Folkers, Karl August, American chemist, Oct 1962

Folkman, Judah, American surgeon, May 1998, *Obit* Yrbk 2008

Folks, Homer, Yrbk 1940

Follett, Ken, Welsh novelist, Jan 1990

Folliard, Edward T., journalist, Nov 1947, *Obit* Feb 1977

Followill, Caleb, American singer and guitarist, July 2010

Followill, Jared, American bassist, July 2010

Followill, Matthew, American guitarist, July 2010

Followill, Nathan, American drummer, July 2010

Folon, Jean Michel, Belgian painter and illustrator, Feb 1981, *Obit* Yrbk 2006

Folsom, Frank M., Feb 1949, *Obit* Mar 1970

Folsom, James Elisha, American governor, Sept 1949, *Obit* Jan 1988

Folsom, Marion Bayard, American Secretary of health, education and welfare, Jan 1950, *Obit* Nov 1976

Fonda, Bridget, American actress, Jan 1994

Fonda, Henry, American actor, Yrbk 1948, Nov 1974, *Obit* Sept 1982

Fonda, Jane, American actress, July 1964, June 1986

Fonda, Peter, American actor, Mar 1998

Foner, Eric, American historian, Aug 2004

Fong, Dennis, American computer game player and executive, Aug 2012

Fong, Hiram, American senator, Feb 1960, *Obit* Yrbk 2004

Fong-Torres, Ben, American music journalist, Aug 2001

Fontaine, Joan, American actress, May 1944

Fontana, Tom, American television producer and scriptwriter, Aug 2000

Fontanne, Lynn, Anglo-American actress, June 1941, *Obit* Sept 1983

Fonteyn, Margot, English ballet dancer, Yrbk 1949, Mar 1972, *Obit* Apr 1991

Foo, Sharin, Danish singer and bassist, Jan 2004

Foot, Michael, British political leader, Yrbk 1950, May 1981, *Obit* Yrbk 2010

Foote, H. W., *Obit* Mar 1942

Foote, Horton, American playwright, screenwriter and novelist, Aug 1986, *Obit* Yrbk 2009

Foote, Shelby, American novelist and historian, Apr 1991, *Obit* Yrbk 2005

Forand, Aime J., June 1960, *Obit* Mar 1972

Forbes, Bertie Charles, publisher, Mar 1950, *Obit* July 1954

Forbes, Guillaume, *Obit* July 1940

Forbes, John J., Apr 1952

Forbes, Kathryn, Yrbk 1944, *Obit* June 1966

Forbes, Malcolm S., American magazine publisher, May 1996

Forbes, Malcolm Stevenson, American magazine publisher and investment adviser, Feb 1975, *Obit* Apr 1990

Force, Juliana, museum director, Mar 1941, *Obit* Oct 1948

Ford, Benson, automobile executive, Feb 1952, *Obit* Sept 1978

Ford, Betty, wife of American president Gerald R. Ford, Sept 1975, *Obit* Yrbk 2011

Ford, Edsel Bryant, American automobile executive, *Obit* July 1943

Ford, Eileen, American model agent, Oct 1971

Ford, Frederick W., government official, Nov 1960, *Obit* Sept 1986

Ford, Gerald R., American president, Mar 1961, Nov 1975, *Obit* Feb 2007

Ford, Glenn, American actor, June 1959, *Obit* Yrbk 2007

Ford, Harold, American financial executive and political commentator, Nov 1999

Ford, Harrison, American actor, Sept 1984, June 2008

Ford, Henry, American automobile executive, Yrbk 1944, *Obit* May 1947

Ford, Henry, American automobile executive, Apr 1946, June 1978, *Obit* Nov 1987

Ford, John, American film director, Feb 1941, *Obit* Nov 1973

Ford, Richard, American novelist and short story writer, Sept 1995

Ford, Tennessee Ernie, singer, Mar 1958, *Obit* Jan 1992

Ford, Tom, American fashion designer, May 1998

Ford, W. W., *Obit* Aug 1941

Ford, Whitey, American baseball player, Apr 1962

Ford, Worthington C., American historian, editor and bibliographer, *Obit* Apr 1941

Foreman, Clark, Oct 1948, *Obit* Aug 1977

Foreman, George, American boxer, May 1974, Aug 1995

Foreman, Richard, American theatrical director and playwright, July 1988

Forgeard, Noel, French aircraft industry executive, Jan 2004

Forman, Milos, Czech film director, Yrbk 1971

Formell, Juan-Carlos, Cuban singer, songwriter and guitarist, Jan 2005

Fornos, Werner H., demographer and social reformer, July 1993

Forrest, Alan, *Obit* Sept 1941

Forrest, Vernon, American boxer, July 2002, *Obit* Yrbk 2009

Forrest, Wilbur S., May 1948, *Obit* May 1977

Forrestal, James V., American Secretary of defense, Feb 1942, Jan 1948, *Obit* July 1949

Forrester, Maureen, Canadian opera singer, July 1962, *Obit* Yrbk 2010

Forsberg, Peter, Swedish hockey player, Nov 2005

Forsee, Gary, American telecommunications executive, Oct 2005

Forssmann, Werner, German physician, Mar 1957, *Obit* Aug 1979

Forster, E. M., English novelist, short story writer and essayist, Apr 1964, *Obit* Sept 1970

Forster, Marc, Swiss film director, Jan 2007

Forster, Rudolph, *Obit* Aug 1943

Forsyth, Bill, Scottish motion picture director, Jan 1989

Forsyth, Cecil, *Obit* Feb 1942

Forsyth, Frederick, English journalist and novelist, May 1986

Forsyth, W. D., Apr 1952

Forsythe, John, American actor, May 1973, *Obit* Yrbk 2010

Forsythe, Robert S., *Obit* Aug 1941

Forsythe, William, American choreographer, ballet dancer and director, Feb 2003

Fortas, Abe, American Supreme Court justice, Feb 1966, *Obit* May 1982

Fortey, Richard A., British paleontologist, Sept 2005

Fortier, Paul-Andre, Canadian choreographer and dancer, Nov 2010

Fosdick, Harry Emerson, American clergyman, Oct 1940, *Obit* Nov 1969

Fosdick, Raymond Blaine, Feb 1945, *Obit* Sept 1972

Foss, Joe, American governor and firearms association executive, Oct 1955, *Obit* Yrbk 2003

Foss, Lukas, American composer, conductor and pianist, June 1966, *Obit* Yrbk 2009

Fosse, Bob, American director and choreographer, June 1972, *Obit* Nov 1987

Fossett, Steve, American stockbroker and balloonist, Apr 2005, *Obit* Yrbk 2008

Fossey, Dian, American primatologist, May 1985, *Obit* Feb 1986

Fossum, Karin, Norwegian novelist, Jan 2007

Foster, Jodie, American actress and film director, June 1981, Aug 1992

Foster, John S., Yrbk 1971

Foster, Maximilian, *Obit* Nov 1943

Foster, Norman, British architect, Sept 2000

Foster, Richard C., *Obit* Jan 1942

Foster, William C., American government official, Nov 1950

Foster, William Zebulon, American communist leader, July 1945, *Obit* Nov 1961

Fou Ts'ong, Chinese pianist, Jan 2003

Fougner, G. Selmer, journalist and wine critic, *Obit* May 1941

Fouilhoux, J. Andre, American architect, *Obit* July 1945

Fountain, Clarence, American gospel singer, Oct 2001

Fowler, Alfred, English astrophysicist, *Obit* Aug 1940

Fowler, Gene, author, Mar 1944, *Obit* Sept 1960

Fowler, Henry H., American Secretary of the treasury, Sept 1952, *Obit* May 2000

Fowler, Mark S., government official, Mar 1986

Fowler, R. M., Oct 1954

Fowler, William A., American physicist, Sept 1974, *Obit* May 1995

Fowler-Billings, Katharine Stevens, geologist, Jan 1940

Fowles, John, English novelist, Mar 1977, *Obit* Apr 2006

Fox Quesada, Vicente, Mexican president, May 2001

Fox, Carol, July 1978, *Obit* Sept 1981

Fox, Eytan, Israeli motion picture director, Jan 2004

Fox, Genevieve, Yrbk 1949, *Obit* Yrbk 1959

Fox, John McDill, *Obit* May 1940

Fox, Megan, American actress, Feb 2010

Fox, Michael J., Canadian actor, Nov 1987

Fox, Michael W., Feb 1977

Fox, Nellie, American baseball player, Mar 1960, *Obit* Feb 1976

Fox, Robert John, priest and social welfare leader, May 1970, *Obit* June 1984

Fox, Sidney, actress, *Obit* Jan 1943

Fox, Virgil, Jan 1964, *Obit* Jan 1981

Foxx, Jamie, American comedian and actor, May 2005

Foxx, Redd, American comedian, Yrbk 1972, *Obit* Jan 1992

Foyle, Gilbert, June 1954, *Obit* Jan 1972

Foyle, Gilbert; and Foyle, William Alfred, June 1954

Foyle, William Alfred, English bookseller, June 1954, *Obit* July 1963

Foyt, A. J., American automobile racing driver, Nov 1967

Fracci, Carla, Italian ballet dancer, Feb 1975

Fraga Iribarne, Manuel, Spanish political leader, May 1965, *Obit* Yrbk 2012

Frager, Malcolm, pianist, Apr 1967, *Obit* Aug 1991

Fraiture, Nikolai, American bassist, Feb 2007

Frakes, Jonathan, actor and motion picture director, July 1999

Frampton, Peter, English guitarist and singer, May 1978

Franca, Celia, Canadian ballet director and dancer, May 1956, *Obit* Yrbk 2007

Francescatti, Zino, French violinist, Oct 1947, *Obit* Nov 1991

Franchet d'Esperey, Louis Felix Marie Francois, French field marshal, *Obit* Sept 1942

Franciosa, Tony, American actor, July 1961, *Obit* Yrbk 2006

Francis, July 2013

Francis, Arlene, American television personality, May 1956, *Obit* Sept 2001

Francis, Clarence, food industry executive, Feb 1948, *Obit* Mar 1986

Francis, Connie, singer, July 1962

Francis, Dick, Welsh mystery novelist and jockey, Aug 1981, *Obit* May 2010

Francis, Emile, Apr 1968

Francis, Frank Chalton, British librarian, July 1959, *Obit* Apr 1989

Francis, Sam, American painter, Oct 1973, *Obit* Jan 1995

Francis-Williams, Edward Francis, English author and

journalist, Mar 1946, *Obit* Sept 1970

Francisco, Chilean television personality, Feb 2001

Franck, James, German-American physicist, May 1957, *Obit* July 1964

Franco, Francisco, Spanish dictator, Mar 1942, Mar 1954, *Obit* Jan 1976

Franco, James, American actor, Apr 2011

Franco, Julio, Dominican baseball player, Sept 2006

Francois-Poncet, Andre, Oct 1949, *Obit* Mar 1978

Francona, Terry, American baseball manager, July 2008

Frank, Anthony M., postmaster general, Aug 1991

Frank, Barney, American congressman, Apr 1995

Frank, Glenn, *Obit* Nov 1940

Frank, Hans, German jurist and Nazi leader, Mar 1941, *Obit* Nov 1946

Frank, Jerome N., American judge, Apr 1941, *Obit* Mar 1957

Frank, Lawrence K., social scientist, Jan 1958, *Obit* Nov 1968

Frank, Lawrence K.; and Frank, Mary, Jan 1958

Frank, Louis, *Obit* May 1941

Frank, Mary Hughes, Jan 1958

Frank, Reuven, American journalist and television executive, June 1973, *Obit* Yrbk 2006

Frank, Robert, Swiss-American photographer and film director, Aug 1997

Frank, Waldo David, American novelist and essayist, Nov 1940, *Obit* Mar 1967

Franke, William B., Sept 1959, *Obit* Aug 1979

Frankel, Bethenny, American chef, food service executive and participant in reality TV show Real housewives of New York City, Mar 2013

Frankel, Charles, philosopher and educator, Apr 1966, *Obit* July 1979

Frankel, Felice, American photographer, Apr 1998

Frankel, Max, newspaper editor, Apr 1987

Franken, Al, American senator, June 1999

Franken, Rose, novelist and playwright, Yrbk 1941, Yrbk 1947, *Obit* Aug 1988

Frankenheimer, John, American film director, Oct 1964, *Obit* Oct 2002

Frankensteen, Richard T., Yrbk 1945

Frankenthaler, Helen, American painter, Apr 1966, *Obit* Yrbk 2012

Frankfurter, Felix, American Supreme Court justice, June 1941, July 1957, *Obit* Apr 1965

Frankl, Viktor E., Austrian psychiatrist, July 1997, *Obit* Nov 1997

Franklin, Aretha, American singer, Yrbk 1968, May 1992

Franklin, Frederic, English ballet dancer and choreographer, Sept 1943, *Obit* Yrbk 2013

Franklin, Irene, actress, *Obit* Aug 1941

Franklin, John Hope, American historian, Oct 1963, *Obit* May 2009

Franklin, John M., Sept 1949, *Obit* Aug 1975

Franklin, Kirk, American gospel rap singer, Mar 2000

Franklin, Shirley, American mayor, Aug 2002

Franklin, Walter S., Feb 1950, *Obit* Oct 1972

Franks, Oliver Shewell Franks, British diplomat, Mar 1948, *Obit* Jan 1993

Franks, Tommy, American general, Jan 2002

Franz, Dennis, American actor, July 1995

Franzen, Jonathan, American novelist, Sept 2003

Frasconi, Antonio, Uruguayan painter and wood engraver, Mar 1972, *Obit* Yrbk 2013

Fraser, Antonia, English biographer, historian and novelist, Oct 1974

Fraser, Brad, Canadian dramatist, July 1995

Fraser, Brendan, American actor, Feb 2001

Fraser, Bruce, July 1943, *Obit* Apr 1981

Fraser, Douglas Andrew, American labor leader, Oct 1977, *Obit* Yrbk 2008

Fraser, Hugh Russell, June 1943

Fraser, I., Yrbk 1947

Fraser, Ian Forbes, American library director, June 1954

Fraser, James Earle, sculptor and medalist, July 1951, *Obit* Jan 1954

Fraser, Leon, *Obit* May 1945

Fraser, Malcolm, Australian prime minister, Mar 1976

Fraser, Peter, May 1942, *Obit* Jan 1951

Fraser, Robert, British television executive, Oct 1956

Fratellini, Paul, *Obit* Yrbk 1940

Frayn, Michael, English dramatist and novelist, Jan 1985

Frazer, James George, Scottish classicist and anthropologist, *Obit* July 1941

Frazer, Joseph W., Mar 1946, *Obit* Sept 1971

Frazer, Spaulding, *Obit* Apr 1940

Frazier, Edward Franklin, sociologist, July 1940

Frazier, Ian, American essayist and humorist, Aug 1996

Frazier, Joe, American boxer, Apr 1971, *Obit* Yrbk 2012

Frazier, Walt, American basketball player and sportscaster, Feb 1973

Frear, J. Allen, Oct 1954

Frears, Stephen, British motion picture director, Apr 1990, Jan 2004

Fred, Edwin Broun, bacteriologist and college president, Yrbk 1950

Fredenthal, David, Sept 1942, *Obit* Jan 1959

Frederick, Nov 1947, *Obit* Mar 1972

Frederick, John T., June 1941

Frederick, Pauline, American television reporter and commentator, Oct 1954, *Obit* July 1990

Frederika, Queen, consort of Paul I, King Of The Hellenes, Jan 1955, *Obit* Apr 1981

Fredman, Samuel, *Obit* June 1941

Freed, James Ingo, American architect, Nov 1994, *Obit* Yrbk 2006

Freed, Lynn, South African novelist, Jan 2002

Freedlander, Arthur R., *Obit* Aug 1940

Freedley, George, American theater historian and librarian, Sept 1947, *Obit* Nov 1967

Freedman, Benedict, Sept 1947, *Obit* Yrbk 2012

Freedman, Benedict; and Freedman, Nancy, Sept 1947

Freedman, Nancy, Sept 1947

Freeh, Louis J., American FBI director, May 1996

Freehafer, Edward G., librarian, June 1955, *Obit* Feb 1986

Freeman, Cathy, Australian runner, Jan 2002

Freeman, James Edward, American bishop, *Obit* July 1943

Freeman, John, June 1969

Freeman, Lucy, American journalist and nonfiction writer, Oct 1953, *Obit* Yrbk 2005

Freeman, Martin, British actor, Nov 2013

Freeman, Morgan, American actor, Feb 1991

Freeman, Orville L., American governor, Secretary of agriculture and magazine publishing executive, June 1956, *Obit* Yrbk 2003

Freeman, R. Austin, English physician and mystery writer, *Obit* Nov 1943

Frehley, Ace, American guitarist, Apr 1999

Frei Montalva, Eduardo, Chilean president, Apr 1965, *Obit* Mar 1982

Freilicher, Jane, American painter, Nov 1989

Freitag, Walter, Jan 1954, *Obit* Oct 1958

Fremantle, Francis Edward, *Obit* Oct 1943

French, Hollis, *Obit* Jan 1941

French, Marilyn, American novelist and critic, Sept 1992, *Obit* Yrbk 2009

French, Paul Comly, May 1951, *Obit* Sept 1960

French, Robert W., Oct 1959

Frere, Albert, Belgian financier, Jan 2002

Fresnay, Pierre, Feb 1959, *Obit* Feb 1975

Freston, Tom, American television executive, Aug 2003

Freud, Anna, British psychoanalyst, Apr 1979, *Obit* Mar 1983

Freud, Lucian, British painter, July 1988, *Obit* Yrbk 2011

Freund, Philip, Canadian novelist and short story writer, Yrbk 1948

Freundlich, Herbert, German chemist, *Obit* May 1941

Freyberg, Bernard Freyberg, Oct 1940, *Obit* Sept 1963

Frick, Ford, American baseball executive, May 1945, *Obit* June 1978

Frick, Wilhelm, German Nazi leader, Aug 1942, *Obit* Nov 1946

Friday, William Clyde, college president, Apr 1958, *Obit* Yrbk 2013

Friedan, Betty, American feminist, Nov 1970, Mar 1989, *Obit* May 2006

Friedkin, William, American motion picture director, June 1987

Friedlander, Lee, American photographer, May 2006

Friedman, Bruce Jay, American novelist, short story writer and dramatist, June 1972

Friedman, Herbert, American astrophysicist, Sept 1963, *Obit* Nov 2000

Friedman, Jane, American publisher, Mar 2001

Friedman, Kinky, American country singer, band leader, songwriter and mystery novelist, Feb 2012

Friedman, Milton, American economist, Oct 1969, *Obit* Yrbk 2007

Friedman, Thomas L., American newspaper columnist, Oct 1995

Friedman, Tom, American sculptor, Oct 2008

Friel, Brian, Irish short story writer and dramatist, June 1974

Friendly, Edwin S., American newspaper executive, July 1949, *Obit* Sept 1970

Friendly, Fred W., American broadcast news executive, Sept 1957, Aug 1987, *Obit* May 1998

Friis, Janus, Danish computer software engineer and executive, Jan 2007

Frings, Ketti, dramatist and screenwriter, Jan 1960, *Obit* Apr 1981

Frisch, Karl von, German zoologist, Feb 1974, *Obit* Yrbk 1983

Frisch, Max, Swiss architect, novelist and dramatist, Jan 1965, *Obit* June 1991

Frische, Carl A., Oct 1962

Frissell, Toni, photographer, June 1947, *Obit* June 1988

Frist, Bill, American surgeon and senator, Nov 2002

Froehlich, Jack E., July 1959

Froese, Edgar, German electronic musician, Jan 2005

Froese, Jerome, German keyboardist, Jan 2005

Frohman, Daniel, *Obit* Feb 1941

Frohnmayer, John E., lawyer and government official, Apr 1990

Fromm, Erich, American psychoanalyst and philosopher, Apr 1967, *Obit* May 1980

Frondizi, Arturo, Argentine president, Oct 1958, *Obit* June 1995

Front 242 (Musical group), Jan 2006

Frost, David, English talk show host, July 1969, *Obit* Yrbk 2013

Frost, Frances, Yrbk 1950, *Obit* Apr 1959

Frost, Leslie M., Canadian political leader, Oct 1953, *Obit* July 1973

Frost, Robert, American poet, Sept 1942, *Obit* Mar 1963

Frothingham, Channing, Mar 1948, *Obit* Nov 1959

Fruehauf, Roy, Feb 1953, *Obit* Jan 1966

Frum, David, Canadian journalist, June 2004

Fry, Christopher, English dramatist, Feb 1951, *Obit* Yrbk 2005

Fry, Franklin, June 1946, *Obit* Sept 1968

Fry, Kenneth D., Apr 1947

Fry, Stephen, English actor and novelist, Sept 1998

Frye, David, American impressionist, Mar 1975, *Obit* Yrbk 2011

Frye, Jack, Apr 1945, *Obit* Apr 1959

Frye, Northrop, Canadian literary critic, Aug 1983, *Obit* Mar 1991

Fryer, Jr., Roland G., American economist, May 2012

Fu Chengyu, Chinese petroleum company executive, Jan 2005

Fu Mingxia, Chinese diver, Jan 2002

Fu, Ping, Chinese computer software executive, Oct 2006

Fuchs, Elaine V., American cytologist, Jan 2011

Fuchs, Joseph, violinist, Oct 1962, *Obit* May 1997

Fuchs, Michael Joseph, cable television executive, Feb 1996

Fuchs, Vivian, English explorer, Oct 1958, *Obit* Jan 2000

Fudge, Ann M., American advertising executive, June 1998

Fuentes, Carlos, Mexican novelist, short story writer and essayist, Oct 1972, *Obit* Yrbk 2012

Fugard, Athol, South African dramatist, actor and director, June 1975

Fugazi (Musical group), Mar 2002

Fujii, Satoko, Japanese jazz pianist, June 2010

Fujimori, Alberto, Peruvian president, Nov 1990

Fujiyama, Aiichiro, Japanese cabinet member, Apr 1958, *Obit* May 1985

Fukuda, Takeo, Japanese prime minister, June 1974, *Obit* Sept 1995

Fukui, Toshihiko, Japanese banking official, Jan 2004

Fukuyama, Francis, American international relations specialist, June 2001

Fulani, Lenora, American psychologist and political activist, Mar 2000

Fulbright, J. William, American senator, Nov 1943, Oct 1955, *Obit* Apr 1995

Fulghum, Robert, clergyman and essayist, July 1994

Fuller, Alfred C., brush industry executive, Oct 1950, *Obit* Jan 1974

Fuller, Bonnie, American magazine editor, May 2000

Fuller, Charles, American dramatist, June 1989

Fuller, Charles E., evangelist, Yrbk 1951, *Obit* May 1968

Fuller, Clara Cornelia, *Obit* Yrbk 1940

Fuller, George Washington, *Obit* Yrbk 1940

Fuller, John L., Mar 1959

Fuller, Kathryn, conservationist and lawyer, Jan 1994

Fuller, Margaret H., American librarian, June 1959

Fuller, Millard, American lawyer and humanitarian, Apr 1995, *Obit* Yrbk 2009

Fuller, R. Buckminster, American engineer and architect, Jan 1960, Feb 1976, *Obit* Aug 1983

Fuller, S. R., May 1941, *Obit* Mar 1966

Fuller, Samuel, American film director, Aug 1992, *Obit* Jan 1998

Fuller, Walter Deane, American publishing executive, Mar 1941, *Obit* Jan 1965

Fulmer, Hampton Pitts, *Obit* Yrbk 1944

Fulton, E. D., Jan 1959

Funicello, Annette, American actress and singer, *Obit* Yrbk 2013

Funk, Casimir, biochemist, May 1945, *Obit* Jan 1968

Funk, Charles Earle, June 1947, *Obit* July 1957

Funk, Chris, American guitarist and thereminist, Aug 2007

Funk, Walther, German financier and cabinet member, Oct 1940, *Obit* Sept 1960

Funk, Wilfred, American publisher and lexicographer, Jan 1955, *Obit* July 1965

Funke, Cornelia Caroline, German illustrator and children's author, Jan 2007

Funston, Keith, American stock exchange official, July 1951, *Obit* July 1992

Funt, Allen, television producer and performer, Yrbk 1966, *Obit* Nov 1999

Fuoss, Robert M., Feb 1959, *Obit* Mar 1980

Fuqua, Stephen Ogden, Feb 1943

Furcolo, Foster, American governor, Jan 1958, *Obit* Sept 1995

Furey, Warren W., May 1950, *Obit* Jan 1959

Furman, N. Howell, Yrbk 1951, *Obit* Oct 1965

Furnas, Clifford Cook, Oct 1956, *Obit* June 1969

Furness, Betty, television commentator and consumer adviser, Feb 1968, *Obit* June 1994

Furse, Clara, British-Canadian stock exchange official, Jan 2006

Furtado, Jorge, Brazilian film director, Jan 2006

Furtado, Nelly, Canadian singer, songwriter and guitarist, Jan 2007

Furtseva, Ekaterina A., Soviet communist leader, June 1956, *Obit* Yrbk 1974

Furuta, Atsuya, Japanese baseball player, Jan 2005

Futter, Ellen Victoria, American college president and museum director, Oct 1985

Fyan, Loleta Dawson, librarian, Yrbk 1951

Fyfe, H. Hamilton, Yrbk 1940, *Obit* July 1951

G

G, Kenny, American saxophonist, Nov 1995

Gabbana, Stefano, Italian fashion designer, Jan 2005

Gabbard, Tulsi, July 2013

Gabin, Jean, French actor, June 1941, *Obit* Jan 1977

Gable, Clark, American actor, May 1945, *Obit* Jan 1961

Gable, Dan, wrestler and coach, Aug 1997

Gabo, Naum, Russian painter and sculptor, Apr 1972, *Obit* Oct 1977

Gabor, Dennis, British physicist, Oct 1972, *Obit* Apr 1979

Gabor, Eva, Hungarian actress, July 1968, *Obit* Sept 1995

Gabor, Zsa Zsa, Hungarian-American actress, Mar 1988

Gabriel, Peter, English singer and songwriter, Jan 1990

Gabriel, Roman, football player, Nov 1975

Gabrielson, Guy George, American lawyer, Oct 1949, *Obit* June 1976

Gaddis, William, American novelist, Nov 1987, *Obit* Mar 1999

Gades, Antonio, Spanish flamenco dancer and choreographer, Feb 1973, *Obit* Yrbk 2004

Gaer, Joseph, author, publishing executive and foundation official, Yrbk 1951

Gaffney, T. St. John, *Obit* Mar 1945

Gag, Wanda, American children's author and illustrator, *Obit* July 1946

Gagarin, Yuri, Soviet cosmonaut, Oct 1961, *Obit* May 1968

Gage, Nicholas, American journalist, Mar 1990

Gagliardi, John, American football coach, Jan 2008

Gagne, Eric, Canadian baseball player, June 2004

Gaillard, Felix, French prime minister, Feb 1958, *Obit* Oct 1970

Gaines, Donna, American sociologist, June 2006

Gaines, Ernest J., American novelist and short story writer, Mar 1994

Gainza Paz, Alberto, Argentine newspaper publisher, Apr 1951, *Obit* Feb 1978

Gaither, Frances, author, Yrbk 1950, *Obit* Jan 1956

Gaither, H. Rowan, American foundation official, May 1953, *Obit* June 1961

Gaitskell, Hugh, British cabinet member, June 1950, *Obit* Feb 1963

Gajdusek, Daniel Carleton, American virologist, June 1981, *Obit* Yrbk 2009

Galanos, James, American fashion designer, Sept 1970

Galard Terraube, Genevieve de, Oct 1954

Galassi, Jonathan, American editor, poet and translator, Sept 1999

Galbraith, James K., American economist, Feb 2006

Galbraith, John Kenneth, American economist, Mar 1959, May 1975, *Obit* Yrbk 2007

Galbraith, Paul, British guitarist, Jan 2007

Galdikas, Birute, Canadian primatologist, Mar 1995

Gale, Henry Gordon, *Obit* Jan 1943

Gale, Robert Peter, physician, Jan 1987

Galen, Clemens August von, *Obit* Apr 1946

Galinsky, Ellen, American educator and organization official, Oct 2003

Gallagher, Buell G., college president, May 1953, *Obit* Jan 1979

Gallagher, Ellen, American painter, Feb 2009

Gallagher, William J., *Obit* Oct 1946

Gallagher, William M., Oct 1953, *Obit* Nov 1975

Gallant, Mavis, Canadian short story writer and novelist, May 1990

Gallegos, Romulo, Venezuelan author and president, May 1948, *Obit* May 1969

Gallery, Daniel V., Apr 1966, *Obit* Mar 1977

Galli, Rosina, *Obit* Jan 1940

Galliano, John, British fashion designer, Oct 1996

Gallico, Paul, American novelist, short story writer and screenwriter, Apr 1946, *Obit* Sept 1976

Gallo, Fortune, Oct 1949, *Obit* May 1970

Gallo, Robert C., biochemist, Oct 1986

Galloway, George, British member of Parliament, Jan 2005

Galloway, Irene O., May 1953, *Obit* Feb 1963

Galloway, Joseph L., American journalist, Sept 2003

Gallup, George Horace, American public opinion analyst, Mar 1940, Yrbk 1952, *Obit* Sept 1984

Galtieri, Leopoldo Fortunato, Argentine general and president, Aug 1982, *Obit* Yrbk 2003

Galvin, Robert W., American electronics industry executive, Mar 1960, *Obit* Yrbk 2011

Galway, James, Irish flutist, June 1980

Gamble, Ralph A., Jan 1953, *Obit* May 1959

Gambling, John B., radio announcer, Mar 1950, *Obit* Jan 1975

Gambrell, E. Smythe, June 1956

Gamelin, Maurice Gustave, French general, Jan 1940, *Obit* July 1958

Gammons, Peter, American sportswriter, June 2011

Gamow, George, American physicist and science writer, Oct 1951, *Obit* Oct 1968

Gandhi, Indira, Indian prime minister, Oct 1959, June 1966, *Obit* Jan 1985

Gandhi, Mahatma, Indian nationalist leader, Yrbk 1942, *Obit* Feb 1948

Gandhi, Rajiv, Indian prime minister, Apr 1985, *Obit* July 1991

Gandhi, Sonia, Italian wife of Indian Prime Minister Rajiv Gandhi, May 1998

Gandolfini, James, American actor, Feb 2000, *Obit* Yrbk 2013

Gandy, Kim A., American feminist, Oct 2001

Ganfield, William Arthur, *Obit* Yrbk 1940

Gang, Jeanne, American architect, Aug 2012

Ganim, Sara, Aug 2013

Gannett, Frank Ernest, American newspaper publisher, Mar 1945, *Obit* Feb 1958

Gannett, Lewis Stiles, American journalist and literary critic, Aug 1941, *Obit* Mar 1966

Gannon, Robert I., Mar 1945, *Obit* May 1978

Ganso, Emil, *Obit* June 1941

Ganz, Bruno, Swiss actor, Jan 2006

Gao Zhisheng, Chinese lawyer and dissident, Jan 2007

Gaposchkin, Cecilia Helena Payne, astronomer, Yrbk 1957

Gara, Jeremy, Canadian drummer, Jan 2007

Garagiola, Joe, American sportscaster and baseball player, Jan 1976

Garand, John C., American design engineer and inventor, Aug 1945, *Obit* Apr 1974

Garbett, Cyril Forster, Feb 1951, *Obit* Mar 1956

Garbo, Greta, Swedish-American actress, Apr 1955, *Obit* June 1990

Garbus, Martin, American lawyer, Nov 2000

Garcia Bernal, Gael, Mexican actor, Jan 2003

Garcia Marquez, Gabriel, Colombian novelist and short story writer, July 1973, Jan 2002

Garcia Medina, Amalia, Mexican provincial governor, Jan 2004

Garcia Perez, Alan, Peruvian president, Nov 1985

Garcia, Carlos P., Filipino president, June 1957, *Obit* July 1971

Garcia, Cristina, American novelist and journalist, Aug 1999

Garcia, Jerry, American guitarist and singer, May 1990, *Obit* Oct 1995

Garcia, Sergio, Spanish golfer, Mar 2001

Garciaparra, Nomar, American baseball player, June 2000

Gardiner, James Garfield, Canadian cabinet member, June 1956, *Obit* Mar 1962

Gardiner, John Eliot, English conductor, Aug 1991

Gardiner, Robert, July 1975

Gardner, Arthur, Jan 1956, *Obit* June 1967

Gardner, Ava, American actress, Mar 1965, *Obit* Mar 1990

Gardner, Ed, Sept 1943, *Obit* Oct 1963

Gardner, Erle Stanley, American mystery novelist, June 1944, *Obit* Apr 1970

Gardner, Howard, American psychologist, Oct 1998

Gardner, John, American novelist, critic and translator, Oct 1978, *Obit* Nov 1982

Gardner, John William, American Secretary of health, education and welfare, Mar 1956, Mar 1976, *Obit* May 2002

Gardner, Lester Durand, Sept 1947, *Obit* Feb 1957

Gardner, Martin, American children's author and mathematician, Sept 1999, *Obit* Yrbk 2010

Gardner, Matthias B., June 1952

Gardner, O. Max, Jan 1947

Gardner, Rulon, American wrestler, Nov 2004

Garfield, Harry Augustus, American college president and son of President James A. Garfield, *Obit* Feb 1943

Garfield, John, actor, Apr 1948, *Obit* July 1952

Garfunkel, Art, American singer and actor, June 1974

Gargan, William, Jan 1969, *Obit* Apr 1979

Garland, Hamlin, American novelist and memoirist, Mar 1940

Garland, Judy, American singer and actress, Nov 1941, Yrbk 1952, *Obit* Sept 1969

Garn, Jake, senator, Aug 1985

Garner, Erroll, American jazz pianist, Sept 1959, *Obit* Mar 1977

Garner, Helen, Australian novelist, Jan 2007

Garner, James, American actor, Nov 1966

Garner, Jennifer, American actress, Apr 2008

Garnett, Kevin, American basketball player, Sept 1998

Garnsey, Elmer E., *Obit* Yrbk 1946

Garofalo, Janeane, American comedienne and actress, Mar 2005

Garratt, Geoffrey Theodore, *Obit* June 1942

Garreau, Roger, Apr 1950

Garrels, Anne, American television and radio reporter, Mar 2004

Garrels, Arthur, *Obit* Aug 1943

Garreton Merino, Manuel A., Chilean sociologist, Jan 2006

Garrison, Deborah, American poet and editor, Jan 2001

Garrison, Lloyd Kirkham, lawyer and reformer, June 1947, *Obit* Nov 1991

Garroway, Dave, American television personality, May 1952, *Obit* Sept 1982

Garson, Greer, Anglo-Irish actress, Sept 1942, *Obit* June 1996

Garst, Jonathan, Oct 1964

Garst, Roswell, agriculturist and banker, Apr 1964, *Obit* Jan 1978

Garst, Shannon, Yrbk 1947

Garth, Dave, political consultant, Jan 1981

Garth, David, Yrbk 1957

Gartner, Michael G., newspaper editor, May 1990

Garvey, Jane F., government official, Sept 2000

Garvey, Marcus, Jamaican-American civil rights activist, *Obit* Aug 1940

Garvin, Clifton Canter, petroleum executive, Nov 1980

Garwin, Richard, American physicist, Mar 1989

Gary, John, singer and songwriter, July 1967, *Obit* Mar 1998

Gary, Raymond, governor, Oct 1955, *Obit* Feb 1994

Gary, Willie, American lawyer, Apr 2001

Garza, Ed, American mayor, June 2002

Garzarelli, Elaine, American investment adviser, Sept 1995

Garzon, Baltasar, Spanish judge, Mar 2001

Gaselee, Stephen, *Obit* Aug 1943

Gaskin, Ina May, midwife, May 2001

Gasol, Pau, Spanish basketball player, Mar 2011

Gaspard, Patrick, American presidential aide, July 2010

Gasperi, Alcide de, Italian statesman, Yrbk 1946, *Obit* Oct 1954

Gass, Michelle, American coffee chain executive, Apr 2012

Gass, William H., American philosopher, novelist, short story writer and critic, Apr 1986

Gasser, Herbert Spencer, American physiologist, Oct 1945, *Obit* July 1963

Gassman, Vittorio, Italian actor and theatrical director, Oct 1964, *Obit* Oct 2000

Gassner, John, Jan 1947, *Obit* June 1967

Gaston, Cito, American baseball player and manager, Apr 1993

Gatch, Lee, Mar 1966, *Obit* Jan 1969

Gates, Bill, American computer software executive, May 1991

Gates, Henry Louis, American professor of African-American studies, Oct 1992

Gates, Melinda French, American philanthropist and wife of Bill Gates, Feb 2004

Gates, Ralph F., Sept 1947

Gates, Robert M., American Secretary of defense, Apr 1992, May 2007, Mar 2009

Gates, Thomas S., American Secretary of the navy, Sept 1957, *Obit* May 1983

Gates, William E., American archaeologist, *Obit* Jan 1940

Gatov, Elizabeth Rudel, Yrbk 1961

Gatti-Casazza, Giulio, opera director, *Obit* Oct 1940

Gaubatz, Lynn, bassoonist, Feb 2001

Gaud, William S., Jan 1969, *Obit* Feb 1978

Gaulle, Charles de, French president, Sept 1940, June 1949, Apr 1960, *Obit* Yrbk 1970

Gaultier, Jean-Paul, French fashion designer, Jan 1999

Gaumont, Leon, *Obit* Sept 1946

Gauss, Clarence Edward, diplomat, Jan 1941, *Obit* June 1960

Gauss, D. Christian, Apr 1945, *Obit* Yrbk 1951

Gauthier, Joseph Alexandre Georges, *Obit* Oct 1940

Gaver, Mary Virginia, American librarian, June 1966, *Obit* Mar 1992

Gavin, James Maurice, American general and diplomat, Feb 1945, Sept 1961, *Obit* Apr 1990

Gavin, John, American actor and diplomat, Sept 1962

Gavrilov, Andrei, Russian pianist, Oct 2000

Gavrilovic, Stoyan, May 1946, *Obit* Mar 1965

Gawande, Atul, American physician and medical writer, Mar 2005

Gay, Peter, American historian, Feb 1986

Gayatri Devi, Mar 1968, *Obit* Yrbk 2009

Gayda, Virginio, Sept 1940, *Obit* Sept 1943

Gayle, Crystal, singer, Mar 1986

Gayle, Helene D., American epidemiologist, Jan 2002

Gaylord, Robert M., Mar 1944

Gazzaniga, Michael S., American neuroscientist, Apr 1999

Gazzara, Ben, American actor, Nov 1967, *Obit* Yrbk 2012

Gbagbo, Laurent, Ivorian president, Jan 2004

Gbowee, Leymah, Liberian peace activist, Oct 2012

Gebel-Williams, Gunther, German animal trainer and circus owner, Yrbk 1971, *Obit* Oct 2001

Gebrselassie, Haile, Ethiopian runner, July 1999

Gedda, Nicolai, Swedish opera singer, Nov 1965

Geddes, Norman Bel, stage designer and producer, May 1940, *Obit* July 1958

Gedi, Ali Mohamed, Somalian prime minister, Jan 2007

Geer, Alpheus, *Obit* Oct 1941

Geffen, David, American recording and motion picture executive, Jan 1992

Geha, Marla, American astronomer, June 2010

Gehrig, Lou, American baseball player, Jan 1940, *Obit* July 1941

Gehrmann, Don, runner, Oct 1952

Gehry, Frank, American architect, June 1987

Geiger, Roy S., American Marine general, July 1945, *Obit* Mar 1947

Geijer, Arne, Swedish labor leader and member of Parliament, July 1964

Geis, Bernard, American publisher, Sept 1960, *Obit* Mar 2001

Geisel, Ernesto, Brazilian president, Aug 1975, *Obit* Nov 1996

Geithner, Timothy F., American Secretary of the treasury, Mar 2009

Gelb, Leslie H., American journalist, government official

and international relations specialist, Jan 2003

Geldof, Bob, Irish rock musician and humanitarian, Mar 1986

Geldzahler, Henry, art historian, critic and curator, Sept 1978, *Obit* Oct 1994

Gell-Mann, Murray, American physicist, Feb 1966, Oct 1998

Geller, Margaret J., American astrophysicist, June 1997

Geller, Uri, American psychic, Sept 1978

Gellhorn, Walter, professor of law, May 1967, *Obit* Feb 1996

Gemayel, Amin, Lebanese president, Mar 1983

Geneen, Harold S., American financier, Feb 1974, *Obit* Jan 1998

Genet, Jean, French dramatist, novelist and poet, Apr 1974, *Obit* June 1986

Gennaro, Peter, American dancer and choreographer, June 1964, *Obit* Feb 2001

Genscher, Hans Dietrich, German diplomat and political leader, June 1975

Gentele, Goran, Sept 1972

Genthe, Arnold, *Obit* Oct 1942

Geoffrey-Lloyd, Geoffrey William, British cabinet member, Feb 1956

George, Yrbk 1943, *Obit* Apr 1947

George, Mar 1942, *Obit* Mar 1952

George, *Obit* Oct 1942

George, Albert Bailey, *Obit* Apr 1940

George, Anju Bobby, Indian long jumper, Jan 2005

George, Elizabeth, American mystery novelist, Mar 2000

George, Harold L., Yrbk 1942

George, Manfred, German newspaper editor and writer, Oct 1965, *Obit* Feb 1966

George, Susan, American social scientist, July 2007

George, Walter F., American senator, June 1943, June 1955, *Obit* Oct 1957

George, Zelma Watson, sociologist and opera singer, Oct 1961, *Obit* Sept 1994

George-Brown, George Alfred George-Brown, British cabinet member, Yrbk 1963, *Obit* July 1985

Gephardt, Richard A., American congressman, Oct 1987

Gerard, Ralph W., May 1965, *Obit* Apr 1974

Geraud, Andre, Sept 1940, *Obit* Jan 1975

Gerberding, Julie, American physician and public health official, Sept 2004

Gerbner, George, American university dean and television critic, Aug 1983, *Obit* Yrbk 2006

Gere, Richard, American actor, Aug 1980

Gergen, David, American political commentator, Feb 1994

Gergiev, Valery, Russian conductor and opera director, Jan 1998

Gerhardsen, Einar, Norwegian prime minister, Mar 1949, *Obit* Nov 1987

Germond, Jack, American columnist and political commentator, July 2005

Gernreich, Rudi, American fashion designer, Yrbk 1968, *Obit* June 1985

Gerow, Leonard Townsend, Apr 1945, *Obit* Yrbk 1972

Gershwin, Ira, American lyricist, Jan 1956, *Obit* Oct 1983

Gerson, Michael, American presidential speechwriter, Feb 2002

Gerstacker, Carl A., American chemical executive, Oct 1961, *Obit* July 1995

Gerstenmaier, Eugen, German political leader, Feb 1958, *Obit* May 1986

Gerstner, Louis V., American computer industry executive, June 1991

Gerulaitis, Vitas, American tennis player, June 1979, *Obit* Nov 1994

Gervais, Ricky, British comedian, Jan 2006

Gervasi, Frank Henry, author and journalist, June 1942, *Obit* Mar 1990

Gerwig, Greta, American actress, June 2010

Gesell, Arnold Lucius, American psychologist, Nov 1940, *Obit* Sept 1961

Gessen, Keith, American magazine editor, novelist and critic, Sept 2008

Gessen, Masha, Russian journalist, Nov 2013

Gest, Morris, *Obit* July 1942

Getman, Frederick H., *Obit* Jan 1942

Getty, Estelle, American actress, Mar 1990, *Obit* Yrbk 2008

Getty, Gordon P., American petroleum executive and composer, Feb 1985

Getz, Stan, American jazz saxophonist, Apr 1971, *Obit* Aug 1991

Geyer, Georgie Anne, columnist, Aug 1986

Ghai, Subhash, Indian motion picture producer, Jan 2003

Gheerbrant, Alain, Feb 1959

Gheorghiu-Dej, Gheorghe, Romanian prime minister, Oct 1958, *Obit* May 1965

Ghermezian, Eskander, Canadian real estate developer, Jan 2004

Ghesquiere, Nicolas, French fashion designer, Jan 2011

Ghez, Andrea Mia, American astronomer, Nov 2010

Ghezali, Salima, Algerian newspaper editor, May 1998

Ghormley, Robert Lee, admiral, Oct 1942, *Obit* Oct 1958

Ghosn, Carlos, Brazilian-French automobile executive, Jan 2004

Ghostface Killah, American rapper, June 2008

Giacometti, Alberto, Swiss sculptor, Feb 1956, *Obit* Feb 1966

Giacomin, Eddie, Canadian hockey player, Mar 1968

Giamatti, A. Bartlett, American university president, literary scholar and baseball commissioner, Apr 1978, *Obit* Oct 1989

Giamatti, Paul, American actor, Sept 2005

Giannini, Amadeo Peter, American banker, Mar 1947, *Obit* July 1949

Giannini, Giancarlo, June 1979

Giannini, L. M., Nov 1950, *Obit* Oct 1952

Giannulli, Mossimo, American fashion designer and clothing executive, Feb 2003

Giauque, William Francis, American chemist, Jan 1950, *Obit* May 1982

Gibb, Barry, English singer and songwriter, Sept 1981

Gibbings, Robert, Irish travel writer and illustrator, Yrbk 1948, *Obit* Mar 1958

Gibbs, George, *Obit* July 1940

Gibbs, Joe, American football coach, Apr 1992

Gibbs, Lois, American environmentalist, Sept 1999

Gibbs, Robert, American presidential press secretary, Apr 2009

Gibbs, William Francis, naval architect, Apr 1944, *Obit* Nov 1967

Gibson, Althea, American tennis player, Oct 1957, *Obit* Feb 2004

Gibson, Bob, American baseball player, Yrbk 1968

Gibson, Charles, American television news anchor, Sept 2002

Gibson, Charles Dana, American illustrator and painter, *Obit* Feb 1945

Gibson, Ernest W., American governor and judge, July 1949, *Obit* Yrbk 1969

Gibson, Ernest Willard, American senator, *Obit* Aug 1940

Gibson, Hugh, diplomat, Jan 1953, *Obit* Feb 1955

Gibson, John W., Oct 1947

Gibson, Kenneth A., American mayor, May 1971

Gibson, Lois, American forensic artist, Mar 2008

Gibson, Mel, American actor and motion picture director, Apr 1984, Aug 2003

Gibson, Robert William, May 1969

Gibson, William, American dramatist, memoirist, poet and novelist, July 1983

Giddens, Anthony, British sociologist and college administrator, Apr 1998

Gideonse, Harry D., college president, May 1940, *Obit* May 1985

Gidney, Ray M., Oct 1953

Giegengack, A. E., Nov 1944, *Obit* Sept 1974

Gielgud, John, English actor, director and producer, Apr 1947, Feb 1984, *Obit* Aug 2000

Gierek, Edward, Polish communist leader, May 1971, *Obit* Oct 2001

Gieseking, Walter, German pianist, Oct 1956, *Obit* Jan 1957

Gifford, Chloe, Mar 1959

Gifford, Frank, American football player and sportscaster, May 1964, Jan 1995

Gifford, Kathie Lee, American singer and television personality, Nov 1994

Gifford, Sanford R., American ophthalmologist, *Obit* Apr 1944

Gifford, Walter Sherman, telephone executive, Jan 1945, *Obit* June 1966

Giffords, Gabrielle, American congresswoman, Mar 2012

Giger, H. R., Swiss painter, sculptor and scenic designer, Jan 2002

Gigli, Romeo, Italian fashion designer, Aug 1998

Gil Fortoul, Jose, *Obit* Aug 1943

Gil, Gilberto, Brazilian singer and songwriter, Jan 2003

Gilani, Yusuf Raza, Pakistani prime minister, Nov 2008

Gilbert and George, English artists, June 2009

Gilbert, George, *Obit* May 1943

Gilbert, Gillian, British guitarist, keyboardist and singer, Jan 2006

Gilbert, Martin, English historian, Feb 1991

Gilbert, Rod, Canadian hockey player and executive, July 1969

Gilbert, Walter, American molecular biologist and genetic engineering executive, Nov 1992

Gilbreth, Frank B., American journalist, memoirist and novelist, May 1949, *Obit* July 2001

Gilbreth, Frank B.; and Carey, Ernestine Gilbreth, May 1949

Gilbreth, Lillian Moller, American industrial engineer, May 1940, Sept 1951, *Obit* Feb 1972

Gilchrist, Brad, cartoonist, Jan 1999

Gilchrist, Guy, author, illustrator and cartoonist, Jan 1999

Gilchrist, Guy; and Gilchrist, Brad, Jan 1999

Gilchrist, Huntington, Apr 1949, *Obit* Mar 1975

Gilder, George F., American economist and forecaster, Oct 1981

Gilder, Robert F., American journalist and archaeologist, *Obit* Mar 1940

Gilder, Rosamond, American drama critic, Nov 1945, *Obit* Oct 1986

Gildersleeve, Virginia C., Aug 1941, *Obit* Sept 1965

Gilels, Emil, Russian pianist, Oct 1956, *Obit* Jan 1986

Giles, Barney McKinney, general, July 1944, *Obit* Aug 1984

Giles, Janice Holt, author, Yrbk 1958

Gill, Eric, English sculptor, engraver and typographer, *Obit* Jan 1941

Gillespie, Dizzy, American trumpet player, Apr 1957, Jan 1993, *Obit* Jan 1993

Gillespie, Louis J., *Obit* Mar 1941

Gillet, Louis, *Obit* Aug 1943

Gillette, Guy M., Sept 1946, *Obit* Apr 1973

Gillibrand, Kirsten, American senator, Oct 2013

Gilligan, Carol, American psychologist, May 1997

Gilligan, John J., American governor and congressman, May 1972, *Obit* Yrbk 2013

Gillingham, Charlie, American keyboardist, Mar 2003

Gillis, James M., priest, June 1956, *Obit* June 1957

Gillmore, Frank, *Obit* May 1943

Gilmore, Eddy, American journalist, June 1947, *Obit* Yrbk 1967

Gilmore, James S., governor, June 2001

Gilmore, John Washington, *Obit* Aug 1942

Gilmore, Melvin R., *Obit* Sept 1940

Gilmore, Voit, Feb 1962

Gilmour, John, British cabinet member, *Obit* Apr 1940

Gilpatric, Roswell L., American lawyer and government

official, Mar 1964, *Obit* May 1996

Gilroy, Frank Daniel, American playwright, screenwriter and filmmaker, Oct 1965

Gilruth, Robert R., American aerospace engineer and NASA official, Oct 1963, *Obit* Yrbk 2000

Gilyard, Keith, American sociolinguist, Oct 2011

Gimbel, Bernard F., Mar 1950, *Obit* Yrbk 1966

Gimbel, Peter, motion picture director and producer, Jan 1982, *Obit* Aug 1987

Gimlette, John, English travel writer and lawyer, Apr 2012

Ginastera, Alberto, Argentine composer, Jan 1971

Ginger, Lyman V., May 1958

Gingold, Hermione, English actress, Oct 1958, *Obit* July 1987

Gingrich, Arnold, magazine editor and book collector, Feb 1961, *Obit* Sept 1976

Gingrich, Newt, American political leader and former Speaker of the House, July 1989

Ginobili, Manu, Argentine basketball player, Apr 2011

Ginsberg, Allen, American poet, Apr 1970, Apr 1987, *Obit* June 1997

Ginsberg, Mitchell I., social worker and municipal official, June 1971, *Obit* May 1996

Ginsburg, Ruth Bader, American Supreme Court justice, Feb 1994

Ginzberg, Eli, American economist and educator, Mar 1966, *Obit* Yrbk 2003

Ginzburg, Natalia, Italian novelist, July 1990, *Obit* Nov 1991

Ginzburg, Vitalii L., Russian physicist, Jan 2007, *Obit* Yrbk 2010

Gioia, Ted, American jazz historian, Jan 2010

Giordani, Francesco, Sept 1957, *Obit* Mar 1961

Giordani, Marcello, Italian opera singer, May 2008

Giovanni, Nikki, American poet and essayist, Apr 1973

Gipson, Frederick Benjamin, author, Yrbk 1957

Gipson, Lawrence Henry, Oct 1954, *Obit* Nov 1971

Giral, Jose, May 1946

Girardi, Joe, American baseball player and manager, May 2008

Giraud, Henri, French general, Yrbk 1942, *Obit* Apr 1949

Giraudoux, Jean, French dramatist and novelist, *Obit* Mar 1944

Girdler, Tom M., American steel executive, Apr 1944, *Obit* Mar 1965

Giri, V. Mohini, Indian social activist, Jan 2007

Giri, V. V., Jan 1970, *Obit* Aug 1980

Giroud, Francoise, French journalist and cabinet member, Apr 1975, *Obit* July 2003

Giroux, Robert, American editor and publisher, Nov 1982, *Obit* Yrbk 2008

Giscard d'Estaing, Valery, French president, July 1967, Oct 1974

Gish, Dorothy, American actress, Aug 1944, *Obit* Sept 1968

Gish, Dorothy; and Gish, Lillian, Aug 1944

Gish, Lillian, American actress, Aug 1944, Aug 1978, *Obit* Apr 1993

Gitai, Amos, Israeli film director, Jan 2003

Giuliani, Rudolph W., American mayor and lawyer, Apr 1988, Jan 2008

Giulini, Carlo Maria, Italian conductor, Mar 1978, *Obit* Yrbk 2005

Givenchy, Hubert de, French fashion designer, May 1955

Givens, Willard E., Sept 1948, *Obit* July 1971

Gladstone, Brooke, American radio reporter, Jan 2009

Gladwell, Malcolm, Canadian business writer, June 2005

Gladwyn, Hubert Miles Gladwyn Jebb, British diplomat, Yrbk 1948

Glaser, Donald Arthur, American physicist, Mar 1961, *Obit* Yrbk 2013

Glaser, Milton, American illustrator and designer, May 1980

Glasgow, Ellen Anderson Gholson, American novelist, *Obit* Jan 1946

Glasper, Robert, American jazz pianist, Mar 2011

Glass, Bentley, American biologist, Apr 1966, *Obit* Yrbk 2005

Glass, Carter, American senator, Oct 1941, *Obit* June 1946

Glass, Philip, American composer, Mar 1981

Glasser, Ira, American civil rights activist, Jan 1986

Glavine, Tom, American baseball player, Oct 2006

Glazer, Nathan, American sociologist and educator, Yrbk 1970

Gleason, Clarence Willard, American classicist, *Obit* Yrbk 1942

Gleason, Jackie, American actor, Oct 1955, *Obit* Aug 1987

Gleason, John S., June 1958

Gleason, Thomas W., American labor leader, Oct 1965, *Obit* Mar 1993

Gleick, James, American science writer, July 2011

Glemp, Jozef, Sept 1982, *Obit* Yrbk 2013

Glenn, John, American astronaut and senator, June 1962, Mar 1976, Jan 1999

Glenn, Mary Willcox, *Obit* Yrbk 1940

Glennan, T. Keith, American NASA official, Oct 1950, *Obit* June 1995

Glennie, Evelyn, Scottish percussionist, July 1997

Glennon, John Joseph, *Obit* Apr 1946

Glicenstein, Enrico, *Obit* Feb 1943

Glintenkamp, H., *Obit* May 1946

Glover, Danny, American actor, Apr 1992

Glover, Savion, American tap dancer, Mar 1996

Glubb, John Bagot, British general, Sept 1951, *Obit* May 1986

Glucksmann, Andre, French philosopher, Jan 2006

Glueck, Eleanor Touroff, Oct 1957, *Obit* Nov 1972

Glueck, Nelson, rabbi, archaeologist and college president, Oct 1948, July 1969, *Obit* Mar 1971

Glueck, Sheldon, Oct 1957, *Obit* May 1980

Glueck, Sheldon; and Glueck, Eleanor T., Oct 1957

Glyn, Elinor, English novelist, *Obit* Nov 1943

Gmeiner, Hermann, Austrian social worker, May 1963, *Obit* June 1986

Gnassingbe, Faure, Togolese president, Jan 2005

Gobbi, Tito, Italian opera singer, Jan 1957, *Obit* May 1984

Gobel, George, comedian, Mar 1955, *Obit* Apr 1991

Godard, Jean Luc, French film director, May 1969, Oct 1993

Goddard, James L., American regulatory agency official, Oct 1968, *Obit* Yrbk 2010

Goddard, Paulette, American actress, *Obit* June 1990

Goddard, Robert Hutchings, American physicist, *Obit* Sept 1945

Godden, Rumer, English novelist and children's author, Aug 1976, *Obit* Jan 1999

Goddio, Franck, French marine archaeologist, Jan 2002

Godfrey, Arthur, radio and television personality, July 1948, *Obit* May 1983

Godunov, Alexander, Russian ballet dancer and actor, Feb 1983, *Obit* July 1995

Godwin, Gail, American novelist and short story writer, Oct 1995

Goebbels, Joseph, German Nazi leader, Sept 1941, *Obit* Yrbk 1991

Goeppert-Mayer, Maria, American physicist, June 1964, *Obit* Apr 1972

Goerne, Matthias, German opera singer, Jan 2006

Goertz, Arthemise, Yrbk 1953

Goetz, Delia, author and translator, Yrbk 1949, *Obit* Sept 1996

Goff, M. Lee, forensic entomologist, June 2001

Gogarty, Oliver St. John, Irish otolaryngologist, poet and novelist, July 1941, *Obit* Yrbk 1957

Goheen, Robert F., American college president, Jan 1958, *Obit* Yrbk 2008

Goizueta, Roberto C., American beverage industry executive, Aug 1996, *Obit* Jan 1998

Gold, Herbert, American novelist and short story writer, Yrbk 1955

Gold, Thomas, American astrophysicist, June 1966, *Obit* Yrbk 2004

Goldberg, wrestler, Apr 2001

Goldberg, Arthur J., American diplomat and Supreme Court justice, July 1949, July 1961, *Obit* Mar 1990

Goldberg, Michelle, American journalist, Jan 2012

Goldberg, Rube, cartoonist, Sept 1948, *Obit* Jan 1971

Goldberg, Whoopi, American actress, Mar 1985

Goldblum, Jeff, American actor, July 1997

Golden, Clinton S., Apr 1948, *Obit* Sept 1961

Golden, Harry Lewis, American newspaper publisher and essayist, Jan 1959, *Obit* Nov 1981

Golden, John, Mar 1944, *Obit* Sept 1955

Golden, Thelma, American museum curator, Sept 2001

Goldenson, Leonard H., radio and television executive, Sept 1957, *Obit* May 2000

Goldenweiser, Alexander A., American anthropologist, *Obit* Sept 1940

Goldin, Daniel, screenwriter, June 1993

Golding, Bruce, Jamaican prime minister, Mar 2008

Golding, William, English novelist, Mar 1964, *Obit* Aug 1993

Goldman, Edwin Franko, Sept 1942, *Obit* May 1956

Goldman, Emma, American anarchist, *Obit* Jan 1940

Goldman, Eric Frederick, American historian, July 1964, *Obit* Apr 1989

Goldman, Frank, Jan 1953, *Obit* Apr 1965

Goldman, Olive Mortimer Remington, Sept 1950

Goldman, William, American novelist and screenwriter, Jan 1995

Goldman-Rakic, Patricia S., American neuroscientist, Feb 2003

Goldmann, Nahum, Israeli Zionist leader, May 1957, *Obit* Oct 1982

Goldmark, Henry, *Obit* Mar 1941

Goldmark, Peter Carl, American physicist and television engineer, Nov 1940, Yrbk 1950, *Obit* Feb 1978

Goldovsky, Boris, Russian-American pianist, conductor and opera director, Yrbk 1966, *Obit* Aug 2001

Goldsborough, John Byron, *Obit* May 1943

Goldsborough, Phillips Lee, *Obit* Yrbk 1946

Goldsborough, T. Alan, June 1948, *Obit* July 1951

Goldschmidt, Neil E., American Secretary of transportation and governor, Aug 1980

Goldsman, Akiva, American screenwriter, Sept 2004

Goldsmith, James, English financier, Feb 1988, *Obit* Oct 1997

Goldsmith, Jerry, American composer, May 2001, *Obit* Yrbk 2004

Goldsmith, Lester Morris, Apr 1940

Goldstein, Israel, Zionist leader and rabbi, July 1946, *Obit* June 1986

Goldstein, Joseph Leonard, American physician, July 1987

Goldstine, Herman Heine, American mathematician and computer scientist, Nov 1952, *Obit* Yrbk 2004

Goldsworthy, Andy, English photographer and sculptor, Oct 2000

Goldthwait, Bobcat, American comedian, Sept 2010

Goldthwaite, Anne, American painter and printmaker, *Obit* Mar 1944

Goldwater, Barry M., American senator, May 1955, June 1978, *Obit* Aug 1998

Goldwater, S. S., American physician, hospital administrator and public health official, *Obit* Yrbk 1942

Goldwyn, Samuel, American motion picture producer, Jan 1944, *Obit* Mar 1974

Goler, George Washington, American physician, *Obit* Nov 1940

Golijov, Osvaldo, Argentine composer, Jan 2006

Golikov, Filipp Ivanovich, Soviet general, Apr 1943, *Obit* Sept 1980

Gollancz, Victor, British publisher, Oct 1963, *Obit* Apr 1967

Golschmann, Vladimir, Apr 1951, *Obit* May 1972

Golub, Leon Albert, American painter, Aug 1984, *Obit* Yrbk 2004

Goma y Tomas, Isidro, *Obit* Oct 1940

Gomes, Francisco da Costa, Portuguese president, May 1976

Gomes, Manuel Teixeira, *Obit* Yrbk 1941

Gomes, Marcelo, Brazilian ballet dancer, May 2007

Gomez, Jean-Jacques, French judge, Jan 2002

Gomez, Laureano, Colombian president, May 1950, *Obit* Sept 1965

Gomulka, Wladyslaw, Polish communist leader, Jan 1957, *Obit* Oct 1982

Gondry, Michel, French film director, May 2007

Gonzales, Alberto R., American Attorney general, Apr 2002

Gonzales, Pancho, American tennis player, Oct 1949, *Obit* Sept 1995

Gonzalez Inarritu, Alejandro, Mexican film director, Jan 2003

Gonzalez Videla, Gabriel, Cuban president, June 1950

Gonzalez, Alex, Mexican drummer, Jan 2005

Gonzalez, Cesar, Oct 1954

Gonzalez, Efren W., Jan 1971

Gonzalez, Felipe, Spanish prime minister, Jan 1978

Gonzalez, Henry B., American congressman, June 1964, Feb 1993, *Obit* Feb 2001

Gonzalez, Tony, American football player, Jan 2011

Good, Mary L., American chemist, Sept 2001

Good, Robert A., American physician, Mar 1972, *Obit* Yrbk 2003

Goodall, Jane, British primatologist, Nov 1967, Nov 1991

Goode, Richard, American pianist, Nov 1988

Goode, W. Wilson, American mayor, Oct 1985

Goodell, Charles E., American senator, Yrbk 1968, *Obit* Mar 1987

Gooden, Dwight, American baseball player, Apr 1986

Goodhart, Arthur L., American lawyer, July 1964, *Obit* Feb 1979

Goodloe, John D., Apr 1947

Goodman, Andrew, American department store executive, Apr 1975, *Obit* June 1993

Goodman, Benny, American clarinetist and band leader, Jan 1942, Oct 1962, *Obit* Aug 1986

Goodman, Bertram, May 1954

Goodman, Julian, Feb 1967, *Obit* Yrbk 2012

Goodman, Paul, American poet, novelist, essayist and dramatist, June 1968, *Obit* Oct 1972

Goodpaster, Andrew Jackson, American general, July 1969, *Obit* Yrbk 2005

Goodrich, Arthur, *Obit* Aug 1941

Goodrich, Frances, American dramatist and screenwriter, Oct 1956, *Obit* Apr 1984

Goodrich, Frances; and Hackett, Albert, Oct 1956

Goodrich, James P., *Obit* Oct 1940

Goodrich, Lloyd, museum director, May 1967, *Obit* May 1987

Goodrich, Marcus, author, Apr 1941, *Obit* Jan 1992

Goodson, Mark, television producer, May 1978, *Obit* Feb 1993

Goodspeed, Edgar Johnson, biblical scholar, Nov 1946, *Obit* Mar 1962

Goodwin, Doris Kearns, American historian and television commentator, Nov 1997

Goodwin, Harry, *Obit* Yrbk 1942

Goodwin, Richard N., American speechwriter and journalist, Yrbk 1968

Goodwin, Robert C., May 1951

Googe, George L., July 1947, *Obit* Yrbk 1961

Googoosh, Iranian singer and actress, May 2001

Goolagong, Evonne, Australian tennis player, Nov 1971

Goossens, Eugene, English conductor and composer, May 1945, *Obit* Sept 1962

Gopinath, Suhas, Indian information technology executive, July 2008

Gopnik, Adam, American essayist and art critic, Apr 2005

Gopnik, Alison, American psychologist, Jan 2007

Gorbach, Alfons, Oct 1961, *Obit* Oct 1972

Gorbachev, Mikhail, Soviet president, Aug 1985

Gorbachev, Raisa Maksimovna, wife of Soviet President Mikhail Gorbachev, May 1988, *Obit* Nov 1999

Gordimer, Nadine, South African novelist, Yrbk 1959, June 1980

Gordon, Bruce, American civil rights organization official, Oct 2005

Gordon, C. Henry, *Obit* Jan 1941

Gordon, Crawford, Canadian aircraft and steel executive, Mar 1958, *Obit* Mar 1967

Gordon, Cyrus Herzl, American biblical scholar and archaeologist, May 1963, *Obit* Aug 2001

Gordon, David, American choreographer, June 1994

Gordon, Donald, Oct 1950, *Obit* June 1969

Gordon, Dorothy, Jan 1955, *Obit* July 1970

Gordon, Ed, American television newscaster, July 2005

Gordon, Edmund W., American psychologist, June 2003

Gordon, Jaimy, American novelist, poet and short story writer, July 2011

Gordon, Jan, English author and illustrator, *Obit* Mar 1944

Gordon, Jeff, American automobile racing driver, Aug 2000

Gordon, John Sloan, *Obit* Yrbk 1940

Gordon, Kermit, economist, July 1963, *Obit* Aug 1976

Gordon, Leon, *Obit* Feb 1944

Gordon, Lincoln, American diplomat, Feb 1962, *Obit* Yrbk 2010

Gordon, Mary, American novelist, Nov 1981

Gordon, Max, Oct 1943, *Obit* Jan 1979

Gordon, Mike, American bassist, July 2003

Gordon, Ruth, actress and screenwriter, Apr 1943, Apr 1972, *Obit* Oct 1985

Gordon, Thomas S., American congressman, Apr 1957, *Obit* Apr 1959

Gordon, Wycliffe, American jazz trombonist, Sept 2009

Gordon-Levitt, Joseph, American actor, June 2011

Gordon-Reed, Annette, American law professor, biographer and historian, May 2009

Gordon-Walker, Patrick Chrestien Gordon Walker, Jan 1966

Gordy, Berry, American recording executive, July 1975

Gore, Al, American vice-president, June 1987

Gore, Albert A., American senator and father of Vice-President Albert Gore, Jr., Jan 1952, *Obit* Feb 1999

Gore, Tipper, wife of American vice-president Albert Gore, Jr., Oct 2000

Gorecki, Henryk, Polish composer, May 1994, *Obit* Yrbk 2011

Goren, Charles Henry, bridge player, Mar 1959, *Obit* July 1991

Gorey, Edward, American illustrator, children's author and designer, Nov 1976, *Obit* Aug 2000

Gorin, Igor, July 1942, *Obit* June 1982

Goring, Hermann, German Nazi leader, Aug 1941, *Obit* Nov 1946

Gork, Haydar, Oct 1956

Gorman, Herbert Sherman, author and literary critic, Mar 1940, *Obit* Jan 1955

Gorman, James P., Australian financial executive, June 2010

Gorman, R. C., American painter and sculptor, Jan 2001

Gorman, Thomas Francis Xavier, mental health official, Oct 1956, *Obit* July 1989

Gorme, Eydie, singer, Feb 1965, *Obit* Yrbk 2013

Gorrie, Jack Osborne, Mar 1952

Gort, John Standish Surtees Prendergast Vereker, British general, Oct 1940, *Obit* May 1946

Gorton, John Grey, Australian prime minister, July 1968, *Obit* Sept 2002

Gorton, Slade, senator, Aug 1993

Gosden, Freeman F., actor, Yrbk 1947, *Obit* Feb 1983

Goshorn, Clarence B., Mar 1950, *Obit* Jan 1951

Goss, Albert S., Mar 1945, *Obit* Yrbk 1950

Gossage, Rich, American baseball player, Aug 1984

Gossett, Louis, American actor, Nov 1990

Gossett, William T., lawyer and diplomat, July 1969, *Obit* Oct 1998

Gott, J. Richard, astrophysicist, Oct 1999

Gott, William Henry Ewart, *Obit* Oct 1942

Gottlieb, Adolph, American painter, Jan 1959, *Obit* Apr 1974

Gottlieb, Melvin, physicist, Jan 1974, *Obit* Mar 2001

Gottlieb, Robert Adams, American editor and publishing executive, Sept 1987

Gottwald, Klement, Czech president, Apr 1948, *Obit* Apr 1953

Goudge, Elizabeth, English novelist, children's author and short story writer, Sept 1940, *Obit* Aug 1984

Goudsmit, Samuel Abraham, American physicist, Oct 1954, *Obit* Feb 1979

Goudy, Frederic W., typographer, June 1941, *Obit* June 1947

Gough, Lewis K., Jan 1953, *Obit* Jan 1968

Gouin, Felix, French statesman, Mar 1946, *Obit* Oct 1979

Goulart, Joao Belchior Marques, Brazilian president, Sept 1962, *Obit* Feb 1977

Gould, Arthur R., *Obit* Sept 1946

Gould, Beatrice Blackmar, magazine editor, Nov 1947, *Obit* Apr 1989

Gould, Bruce, magazine editor, Nov 1947, *Obit* Oct 1989

Gould, Bruce; and Gould, Beatrice Blackmar, Nov 1947

Gould, Chester, American cartoonist, Sept 1971, *Obit* July 1985

Gould, Elliott, American actor, Feb 1971

Gould, Glenn, Canadian pianist, Oct 1960, *Obit* Nov 1982

Gould, Laurence McKinley, explorer and college president, Jan 1978, *Obit* Aug 1995

Gould, Morton, pianist and composer, Sept 1945, Jan 1968, *Obit* May 1996

Gould, Ronald, English labor leader and teacher, Nov 1952

Gould, Samuel B., educator, Jan 1958, *Obit* Sept 1997

Gould, Stephen Jay, American paleontologist and science writer, Sept 1982, *Obit* Aug 2002

Gould, Wayne, New Zealand judge, Jan 2006

Goulding, Ellie, British guitarist, singer and songwriter, Apr 2013

Goulding, Ray, American comedian, Oct 1957, *Obit* May 1990

Goulet, Robert, American singer and actor, Sept 1962, *Obit* Yrbk 2008

Goulian, Mehran, July 1968

Goussinsky, Vladimir, Russian financier, Jan 2002

Gove, Philip Babcock, Oct 1962, *Obit* Jan 1973

Gow, James Ellis, Mar 1944, *Obit* Mar 1952

Gowda, Sheela, Indian artist, Jan 2002

Gowdy, Curt, American television sportscaster, May 1967, *Obit* Yrbk 2006

Gower, Pauline, English aviator, Aug 1943, *Obit* Mar 1947

Gowers, Tim, English mathematician, Jan 2001

Gowon, Yakubu, Nigerian general and head of state, June 1970

Gows, James; and D'usseau, Arnaud, Mar 1944

Grace, Mar 1955, Oct 1977, *Obit* Nov 1982

Grace, Alonzo G., Jan 1950, *Obit* Yrbk 1971

Grace, Eugene G., American steel company executive, Apr 1941, *Obit* Oct 1960

Grace, J. Peter, chemical industry executive, Mar 1960, *Obit* June 1995

Grade, Lew, British film and television producer, Aug 1979, *Obit* Mar 1999

Grady, Henry Francis, American diplomat and trade expert, July 1947, *Obit* Nov 1957

Graebner, Clark, American tennis player, Feb 1970

Graebner, Walter, Aug 1943

Graf, Herbert, May 1942, *Obit* May 1973

Graf, Steffi, German tennis player, Feb 1989

Graff, Laurence, British jeweler, Sept 2011

Graffman, Gary, pianist, July 1970

Grafton, Samuel, columnist, Jan 1940, *Obit* Feb 1998

Grafton, Sue, American mystery novelist, Sept 1995

Graham, Billy, American evangelist, Apr 1951, Jan 1973

Graham, Bob, American senator, July 1986

Graham, Clarence R., librarian, Nov 1950

Graham, Donald E., American newspaper publisher, May 1998

Graham, Ed, British drummer, Jan 2004

Graham, Elinor, Yrbk 1952

Graham, Evarts A., American surgeon, Feb 1952, *Obit* May 1957

Graham, Frank Porter, college president and civil rights leader, May 1941, July 1951, *Obit* Apr 1972

Graham, Franklin, American evangelist and son of Billy Graham, May 2002

Graham, Gwethalyn, Canadian novelist, Jan 1945, *Obit* Jan 1966

Graham, Harry Chrysostom, Apr 1950

Graham, Horace F., *Obit* Jan 1942

Graham, John, architect, Oct 1962, *Obit* Apr 1991

Graham, Jorie, American poet, May 1997

Graham, Katharine, American newspaper publisher, Jan 1971, *Obit* Oct 2001

Graham, Martha, American dancer and choreographer, Feb 1944, June 1961, *Obit* May 1991

Graham, Philip Leslie, American newspaper publisher, Feb 1948, *Obit* Oct 1963

Graham, Sheilah, American gossip columnist, Oct 1969, *Obit* Jan 1989

Graham, Susan, American opera singer, Oct 2005

Graham, Virginia, radio and television talk show host, Oct 1956, *Obit* Mar 1999

Graham, Wallace Harry, physician and general, Feb 1947, *Obit* Mar 1996

Graham, Winston, English novelist, Yrbk 1955, *Obit* Yrbk 2003

Grahame-Smith, Seth, American screenwriter, Nov 2012

Gramm, Donald, opera singer, Nov 1975, *Obit* July 1983

Gramm, Phil, American senator and economist, May 1986

Grammer, Kelsey, American actor, May 1996

Granahan, Kathryn Elizabeth, congresswoman, Oct 1959, *Obit* Sept 1979

Granato, Cammi, American hockey player, Apr 1998

Grand, Sarah, English novelist and feminist, *Obit* July 1943

Granderson, LZ, Journalist and online columnist, Oct 2012

Grandes, Almudena, Spanish novelist, Jan 2006

Grandi, Dino, Italian political leader, July 1943, *Obit* July 1988

Grandin, Temple, American autistic animal scientist, July 1994

Grandjany, Marcel, May 1943, *Obit* Apr 1975

Granger, Clive W. J., British economist, Jan 2007, *Obit* Yrbk 2009

Granger, Lester Blackwell, civil rights leader, Apr 1946, *Obit* Mar 1976

Granger, Walter, *Obit* Oct 1941

Granholm, Jennifer M., American governor, Oct 2003

Granik, Samuel Theodore, Yrbk 1952, *Obit* Nov 1970

Grant, Cary, Anglo-American actor, Sept 1941, Nov 1965, *Obit* Jan 1987

Grant, Elihu, *Obit* Yrbk 1942

Grant, Gordon, June 1953, *Obit* July 1962

Grant, Heber J., *Obit* June 1945

Grant, Hugh, English actor, Sept 1995

Grant, Kay, Yrbk 1959

Grant, Lee, actress and director, Mar 1974

Grant, Robert, author and judge, *Obit* July 1940

Grantham, Alexander, May 1954

Grantley, John Richard Brinsley Norton, *Obit* Sept 1943

Granville, William Spencer Leveson-Gower, Sept 1950, *Obit* Sept 1953

Grappelli, Stephane, French jazz violinist, Aug 1988, *Obit* Feb 1998

Graser, Earle W., *Obit* June 1941

Grass, Gunter, German novelist, Oct 1964, July 1983

Grasso, Ella, American governor, May 1975, *Obit* Mar 1981

Grasso, Richard, American stock exchange official, Oct 2002

Grau San Martin, Ramon, Cuban president, Oct 1944, *Obit* Oct 1969

Grau, Shirley Ann, novelist and short story writer, Yrbk 1959

Grauer, Ben, Feb 1941, July 1959, *Obit* July 1977

Gravel, Mike, American senator, Jan 1972

Graves, Alvin C., American physicist, Yrbk 1952, *Obit* Oct 1965

Graves, Bibb, governor, *Obit* May 1942

Graves, Earl G., American magazine publishing executive, Aug 1997

Graves, Florence, American journalist, May 2005

Graves, Frederick Rogers, *Obit* July 1940

Graves, Michael, American architect and designer, Jan 1989

Graves, Morris, painter, July 1956, *Obit* Sept 2001

Graves, Nancy, American painter and sculptor, May 1981, *Obit* Jan 1996

Graves, Robert, English novelist and poet, May 1978, *Obit* Feb 1986

Graves, William Sidney, general, *Obit* Mar 1940

Gray, C. Boyden, American lawyer and presidential adviser, Aug 1989

Gray, Carl R., Mar 1948, *Obit* Feb 1956

Gray, David, British singer and songwriter, Jan 2004

Gray, F. Gary, American film director, Mar 2011

Gray, Gordon, American broadcasting executive and military official, Sept 1949, *Obit* Feb 1983

Gray, Hanna Holborn, American historian and college president, Mar 1979

Gray, Harold E., Feb 1969

Gray, Jim, American sportscaster, Jan 2011

Gray, L. Patrick, American FBI director, Sept 1972, *Obit* Yrbk 2005

Gray, Macy, American singer and songwriter, May 2000

Gray, Simon, English dramatist and novelist, June 1983, *Obit* Yrbk 2008

Gray, Spalding, American monologist, Sept 1986, *Obit* Yrbk 2004

Gray, William H., American congressman and college fund administrator, Feb 1988, *Obit* Yrbk 2013

Gray, William M., American meteorologist, Jan 2010

Grayson, C. Jackson, Sept 1972

Graziani, Rodolfo, Italian field marshal and colonial

administrator, Apr 1941, *Obit* Mar 1955

Greatbatch, Wilson, American biomedical engineer and inventor of pacemaker, *Obit* Yrbk 2012

Grebe, John J., Oct 1955

Grebenshikov, Boris, Russian singer, Jan 2002

Grechko, Andrei Antonovich, Soviet field marshal, Nov 1968, *Obit* June 1976

Greco, Jose, American dancer and choreographer, Mar 1952, *Obit* Mar 2001

Greco, Juliette, French singer, Jan 1992

Grede, William J., iron and steel executive, Feb 1952, *Obit* Aug 1989

Greeley, Andrew M., American sociologist, priest and novelist, Yrbk 1972, *Obit* Yrbk 2013

Greeley, Dana McLean, clergyman, civil rights leader and pacifist, Mar 1964, *Obit* Aug 1986

Green Day (Musical group), Aug 2005

Green, Adolph, American lyricist, librettist and screenwriter, Mar 1945, *Obit* Mar 2003

Green, Al, American gospel singer and clergyman, Feb 1996

Green, Constance McLaughlin, historian, Oct 1963

Green, Darrell, American football player, Jan 2001

Green, Dwight H., American governor, Apr 1948, *Obit* Apr 1958

Green, Edith, American congresswoman, May 1956, *Obit* June 1987

Green, Florence Topping, *Obit* June 1945

Green, Howard, Jan 1960

Green, Julien, American novelist, essayist and memoirist, Jan 1940, *Obit* Oct 1998

Green, Mark J., American lawyer, consumer rights advocate and municipal official, Feb 1988

Green, Martyn, June 1950, *Obit* Apr 1975

Green, Theodore Francis, American senator and

governor, Feb 1950, *Obit* June 1966

Green, Tim, American football player, sportscaster and novelist, Aug 2000

Green, Tom, Canadian comedian, Oct 2003

Green, William, American labor leader, Mar 1942, *Obit* Jan 1953

Greenaway, Emerson, librarian, July 1958, *Obit* June 1990

Greenaway, Peter, British film director, Feb 1991

Greenberg, Hank, American baseball player, June 1947, *Obit* Oct 1986

Greenberg, Jack, fast food industry executive, Nov 2001

Greenberg, Maurice R., American insurance executive, Nov 2000

Greenberg, Noah, conductor and musicologist, May 1964, *Obit* Feb 1966

Greenbie, Sydney, Sept 1941, *Obit* Sept 1960

Greene, Balcomb, painter, Nov 1965, *Obit* Jan 1991

Greene, Bob, American journalist, July 1995

Greene, Brian R., American physicist, Aug 2000

Greene, Frank Russell, *Obit* Jan 1940

Greene, Graham, English novelist, Oct 1969, *Obit* May 1991

Greene, Harold H., American judge, Aug 1985, *Obit* May 2000

Greene, Hugh, English radio and television executive, Sept 1963, *Obit* Apr 1987

Greene, Lorne, actor, Jan 1967, *Obit* Oct 1987

Greene, Nancy, Mar 1969

Greene, Wallace M., American Marine corps general, June 1965, *Obit* Aug 2003

Greenebaum, Leon C., Jan 1962, *Obit* May 1968

Greenewalt, Crawford H., American chemical industry executive, Jan 1949

Greenfield, Abraham Lincoln, *Obit* Sept 1941

Greenfield, Jerry, American ice cream company executive, Apr 1994

Greenfield, Susan, British neuroscientist, Jan 2003

Greenough, Carroll, *Obit* Oct 1941

Greenspan, Alan, American economist and Federal Reserve chairman, Yrbk 1974, Jan 1989

Greenstein, Jesse Leonard, American astrophysicist, Sept 1963, *Obit* Yrbk 2003

Greenstreet, Sydney, May 1943, *Obit* Mar 1954

Greenwald, Julie, American recording industry executive, Nov 2009

Greenway, Walter Burton, *Obit* Feb 1941

Greenwood, Allen, *Obit* Yrbk 1942

Greenwood, Arthur, Oct 1940, *Obit* Sept 1954

Greenwood, Colin, English bassist, June 2001

Greenwood, Joan, English actress, May 1954, *Obit* Apr 1987

Greenwood, Jonny, English guitarist, June 2001

Greer, Germaine, Australian feminist and writer, Nov 1971, Oct 1988

Gregg, Hugh, Jan 1954

Gregg, Milton F., Oct 1955

Gregorian, Vartan, American foundation official, Oct 1985

Gregory, Cynthia, American ballet dancer, May 1977

Gregory, David, American television reporter and moderator, Oct 2010

Gregory, Dick, American comedian, author and civil rights leader, June 1962

Gregory, Edmund B., Sept 1945, *Obit* Mar 1961

Gregory, Frederick Drew, American astronaut and NASA official, Oct 2005

Gregory, Menas S., *Obit* Jan 1942

Gregory, Paul, Apr 1956

Gregory, Wilton D., American archbishop, Mar 2002

Greider, Carol W., American molecular biologist, Feb 2008

Greiner, Markus, Physicist and educator, June 2012

Greinke, Zack, American baseball player, July 2010

Grenfell, Joyce, English actress, Mar 1958, *Obit* Feb 1980

Grenfell, Wilfred Thomason, British medical missionary, *Obit* Yrbk 1940

Gres, Alix, French fashion designer, June 1980, *Obit* Feb 1995

Gresley, Nigel, *Obit* May 1941

Gretzky, Wayne, Canadian hockey player and coach, Feb 1982

Grew, Joseph C., American diplomat, Feb 1941, *Obit* July 1965

Grewe, Wilhelm, Oct 1958

Grey, Clifford, *Obit* Nov 1941

Grey, J. D., clergyman, Sept 1952, *Obit* Sept 1985

Grey, Joel, American actor and singer, Jan 1973

Gribble, Harry Wagstaff, Sept 1945, *Obit* Apr 1981

Grieff, Joseph Nicholas, *Obit* Aug 1941

Grier, Pam, American actress, Feb 1998

Grier, Rosey, American football player and entertainer, Mar 1975

Griffey, Ken, American baseball player, Aug 1996

Griffies, Ethel, Jan 1968, *Obit* Nov 1975

Griffin, Bernard, Oct 1946, *Obit* Oct 1956

Griffin, Blake, American basketball player, Jan 2012

Griffin, John Douglas Morecroft, May 1957

Griffin, John Howard, American novelist and journalist, Nov 1960, *Obit* Nov 1980

Griffin, Kathy, American comedienne and actress, Sept 2008

Griffin, Marvin, American governor, June 1956, *Obit* Aug 1982

Griffin, Merv, American talk show host and television producer, Sept 1967, *Obit* Yrbk 2007

Griffin, Michael D., American NASA official, Aug 2005

Griffin, R. Allen, American newspaper publisher, Feb 1951

Griffin, Robert P., American senator, May 1960

Griffis, Stanton, investment banker and diplomat, Oct 1944, *Obit* Oct 1974

Griffith Joyner, Florence, American sprinter, Apr 1989, *Obit* Nov 1998

Griffith, Andy, American actor, May 1960, *Obit* Yrbk 2012

Griffith, Clark, baseball player, manager and executive, June 1950, *Obit* Jan 1956

Griffith, Ernest S., political scientist, Oct 1947, *Obit* Apr 1997

Griffith, J. P. Crozer, *Obit* Sept 1941

Griffith, Melanie, American actress, Oct 1990

Griffith, Nanci, American folk and country singer and songwriter, Feb 1998

Griffith, Paul H., American management consultant and military official, Jan 1947, *Obit* Feb 1975

Griffiths, Martha Wright, American congresswoman and state official, Oct 1955, *Obit* Yrbk 2003

Grigg, James, Apr 1942, *Obit* July 1964

Grigg, John, English journalist and biographer, Oct 1964, *Obit* Apr 2002

Grigorovich, Yuri, Russian choreographer and dance director, Sept 1975

Grimaud, Helene, French pianist, Jan 2007

Grimes, Tammy, actress, July 1962

Grimes, W. H., June 1947, *Obit* Mar 1972

Grimond, Jo, British political leader, Oct 1963, *Obit* Jan 1994

Grimshaw, Robert, *Obit* June 1941

Griner, Brittney, American basketball player, Mar 2013

Grisham, John, American lawyer and novelist, Sept 1993

Grissom, Gus, American astronaut, Nov 1965, *Obit* Mar 1967

Griswold, A. Whitney, American college president, Apr 1950, *Obit* June 1963

Griswold, Augustus H., *Obit* Mar 1940

Griswold, Dwight P., American senator, governor and diplomat, Yrbk 1947, *Obit* June 1954

Griswold, Erwin N., American solicitor general and law school dean, Oct 1956, *Obit* Jan 1995

Griswold, Oscar W., American general, Sept 1943, *Obit* Yrbk 1959

Grivas, Giorgios, Oct 1964, *Obit* Mar 1974

Grizodubova, Valentina S., Soviet aviator, Yrbk 1941, *Obit* July 1993

Grizzard, George, American actor, June 1976, *Obit* Yrbk 2008

Grizzly Bear (Musical group), Sept 2011

Groat, Dick, May 1961

Groban, Josh, American pop singer, Aug 2009

Grodin, Charles, American actor, Nov 1995

Groening, Matt, American cartoonist and animator, Sept 1990

Groenman, Frans Eyso Henricus, *Obit* Aug 1943

Grofe, Ferde, July 1940, *Obit* May 1972

Grogan, John J., Yrbk 1951

Grohl, Dave, American singer and guitarist, May 2002

Gromyko, Andrei Andreevich, Soviet diplomat, Oct 1943, Oct 1958, *Obit* Aug 1989

Gronchi, Giovanni, Oct 1955, *Obit* Jan 1979

Gronemeyer, Herbert, German singer and actor, Jan 2003

Groninger, Homer M., American general, Aug 1945

Gronouski, John A., American postmaster general, Jan 1966, *Obit* Mar 1996

Grooms, Red, American artist, Yrbk 1972

Groopman, Jerome E., American physician and medical writer, Oct 2004

Groot, Adriaan M. de, *Obit* Mar 1942

Gropius, Walter, American architect, Nov 1941, Mar 1952, *Obit* Sept 1969

Gropper, William, American cartoonist, painter and

illustrator, Mar 1940, *Obit* Mar 1977

Gros, Edmund L., *Obit* Yrbk 1942

Gross, Chaim, American sculptor, Nov 1941, Feb 1966, *Obit* July 1991

Gross, Charles P., Mar 1946, *Obit* Sept 1975

Gross, Ernest A., diplomat and lawyer, Feb 1951, *Obit* July 1999

Gross, H. R., American congressman, Jan 1964, *Obit* Oct 1987

Gross, Mason W., June 1969, *Obit* Jan 1978

Gross, Paul Magnus, chemist, May 1963, *Obit* June 1986

Gross, Robert E., Jan 1956, *Obit* Nov 1961

Gross, William H., American investment manager, July 2010

Grossinger, Jennie, American resort owner, Oct 1956, *Obit* Jan 1973

Grossman, Edith, American translator and literary scholar, Mar 2006

Grossman, Lev, American literary critic and novelist, Apr 2010

Grosvenor, Gilbert Hovey, magazine editor, Yrbk 1946, *Obit* Mar 1966

Grosvenor, Graham Bethune, American elevator manufacturing company and airline executive, *Obit* Yrbk 1943

Grosvenor, Melville Bell, periodical editor, Apr 1960, *Obit* June 1982

Grosz, George, American painter and cartoonist, Apr 1942, *Obit* Oct 1959

Grosz, Karoly, Hungarian prime minister, Sept 1988, *Obit* Mar 1996

Grotewohl, Otto, July 1950, *Obit* Nov 1964

Groth, John, illustrator and painter, Feb 1943, *Obit* Aug 1988

Grotowski, Jerzy, Polish theatrical director, Yrbk 1970, *Obit* Mar 1999

Grotzinger, John, Apr 2013

Grove, Andrew S., American semiconductor industry executive, Mar 1998

Groves, Ernest R., sociologist, June 1943, *Obit* Oct 1946

Groves, Ernest R.; and Groves, Gladys Hoagland, June 1943

Groves, Gladys Hoagland, June 1943, *Obit* Sept 1980

Groves, Leslie R., American general, Aug 1945, *Obit* Oct 1970

Gruber, Frank, American screenwriter and mystery novelist, Nov 1941, *Obit* Feb 1970

Gruber, Karl, Austrian diplomat, Feb 1947

Gruber, L. Franklin, *Obit* Feb 1942

Gruber, Lilli, Italian television news anchor and member of European parliament, Jan 2007

Gruber, Ruth, American journalist, photographer and humanitarian, June 2001

Gruber, Samuel H., American marine biologist, Aug 2004

Grubin, David, American documentary filmmaker, producer and screenwriter, Aug 2002

Gruen, Victor, American architect, Mar 1959, *Obit* Apr 1980

Gruenberg, Sidonie Matsner, May 1940, *Obit* May 1974

Gruening, Ernest, American territorial governor and senator, Yrbk 1946, July 1966, *Obit* Sept 1974

Gruenther, Alfred M., American general, Yrbk 1950, *Obit* July 1983

Grumman, Leroy R., aircraft executive, Aug 1945, *Obit* Jan 1983

Gruppe, Charles Paul, *Obit* Nov 1940

Grylls, Bear, British adventurer and television personality, Oct 2011

Grzimek, Bernhard, German zoo director and television performer, Mar 1973, *Obit* May 1987

Guardia, Ernesto de la, Panamanian president, Jan 1957

Guardia, Ricardo Adolfo de la, Panamanian president, May 1942, *Obit* Feb 1970

Guare, John, American dramatist, Aug 1982

Guarente, Leonard, American biologist, May 2007

Gubaidulina, Sofia Asgatovna, Russian composer, Oct 1999

Guccione, Bob, American magazine publisher, Aug 1994, *Obit* Yrbk 2010

Guedalla, Philip, English historian, *Obit* Feb 1945

Gueden, Hilde, Apr 1955

Guerard, Albert J., novelist and critic, Yrbk 1946, *Obit* Mar 2001

Guerlain, Jean-Paul, French perfumer, Jan 2006

Guerrero, Jose Gustavo, Jan 1947, *Obit* Jan 1959

Guerrero, Vladimir, Dominican baseball player, June 2006

Guest, Edgar A., American newspaper columnist, Sept 1941, *Obit* Nov 1959

Guevara, Ana, Mexican runner, Jan 2004

Guevara, Ernesto, Argentine-Cuban revolutionary, June 1963, *Obit* Yrbk 1967

Guffey, Joseph F., Mar 1944, *Obit* May 1959

Guggenheim, Davis, American film director, Nov 2009

Guggenheim, Florence Shloss, *Obit* July 1944

Guggenheim, Harry Frank, American mining executive, Oct 1956, *Obit* Mar 1971

Guggenheim, Peggy, American patron of the arts, Oct 1962, *Obit* Feb 1980

Guggenheimer, Minnie, Oct 1962, *Obit* June 1966

Guidry, Ron, American baseball player, May 1979

Guillaumat, Marie Louis Adolphe, *Obit* July 1940

Guillaume, Augustin, French general, Jan 1952

Guillaume, Robert, American actor, Apr 2000

Guillem, Sylvie, French ballet dancer and choreographer, Jan 2002

Guillen, Ozzie, Venezuelan baseball player and manager, May 2006

Guillermoprieto, Alma, Mexican journalist, Sept 2004

Guinan, Matthew, labor leader, Sept 1974, *Obit* May 1995

Guinier, Lani, American law teacher and civil rights activist, Jan 2004

Guinness, Alec, English actor, Oct 1950, Mar 1981, *Obit* Oct 2000

Guinness, Arthur, June 1948

Guinzburg, Harold K., July 1957, *Obit* Jan 1962

Guion, Connie M., Feb 1962

Guise, Jean d'Orleans, *Obit* Oct 1940

Guisewite, Cathy, cartoonist, Feb 1989

Guiterman, Arthur, poet, *Obit* Mar 1943

Gujral, Inder K., Indian prime minister, *Obit* Yrbk 2013

Gul, Abdullah, Turkish prime minister, Jan 2007

Gulick, Luther Halsey, American municipal official, June 1945, *Obit* Mar 1993

Gullander, W. P., Oct 1963

Gullar, Ferreira, Brazilian poet and art critic, Jan 2004

Gullion, Allen W., Feb 1943, *Obit* July 1946

Gulpilil, David, Australian actor, Jan 2003

Gumbel, Bryant, American television newscaster, July 1986

Gumbel, Greg, American television sportscaster, Sept 1996

Gumpert, Martin, Yrbk 1951

Gunn, Selskar M., *Obit* Sept 1944

Gunn, Thom, English poet, Nov 1988, *Obit* Yrbk 2004

Gunn, Tim, American clothing company executive, Oct 2009

Gunter, Julius Caldeen, *Obit* Yrbk 1940

Gunter, Ray, July 1967, *Obit* June 1977

Gunther, Franklin Mott, *Obit* Feb 1942

Gunther, John, journalist and author, Nov 1941, Feb 1961, *Obit* July 1970

Gupta, Mahabir P., Indian pharmacologist, Jan 2005

Gupta, Sanjay, American neurosurgeon and television reporter, Aug 2006

Guptill, Arthur L., Mar 1955, *Obit* May 1956

Gurdon, John Bertrand, British microbiologist, Jan 2007

Gurney, A. R., American dramatist, July 1986

Gurney, Chan, Oct 1950

Gursky, Andreas, German photographer, July 2001

Gurtner, Franz, German cabinet member, *Obit* Mar 1941

Gusmao, Xanana, East Timorese president, Jan 2002

Gustaf, Sept 1942, *Obit* Yrbk 1950

Gustaf, Yrbk 1950, *Obit* Nov 1973

Guston, Philip, American painter, Feb 1971, *Obit* July 1980

Guterson, David, American novelist and short story writer, Nov 1996

Guth, Alan H., physicist, Sept 1987

Guthman, Edwin O., American newspaper editor, June 1950, *Obit* Yrbk 2008

Guthrie, A. B., American novelist, short story writer and poet, July 1950, *Obit* July 1991

Guthrie, Arlo, American folk singer and songwriter, Feb 1982

Guthrie, Charles Ellsworth, *Obit* Sept 1940

Guthrie, Janet, American automobile racing driver, Oct 1978

Guthrie, Tyrone, British theatrical producer and director, July 1954, *Obit* July 1971

Guthrie, William Buck, *Obit* Yrbk 1940

Guthrie, Woody, American folk singer and songwriter, May 1963, *Obit* Yrbk 1967

Gutierrez, Gustavo, Peruvian priest and theologian, Jan 2004

Gutt, Camille, Apr 1948

Guttmacher, Alan Frank, physician, Oct 1965, *Obit* May 1974

Guy, Buddy, American blues guitarist, Feb 2000

Guy, Raymond F., May 1950

Guyer, Ulysses Samuel, *Obit* July 1943

Guzy, Carol, American photojournalist, Feb 2000

Gwathmey, Charles, American architect, Jan 1988, *Obit* Yrbk 2009

Gwathmey, James T., *Obit* Apr 1944

Gwathmey, Robert, American painter, Yrbk 1943, *Obit* Nov 1988

Gwenn, Edmund, Sept 1943, *Obit* Nov 1959

Gwynn, Tony, American baseball player, Oct 1996

Gyanendra Bir Bikram Shah, Jan 2005

Gygax, Gary, American game inventor, Mar 2007, *Obit* Yrbk 2008

H

Haack, Robert, stock exchange official, Mar 1969, *Obit* Aug 1992

Haacke, Hans, German artist, July 1987

Haagen-Smit, A. J., chemist, Mar 1966, *Obit* May 1977

Haakon, May 1940, *Obit* Yrbk 1957

Haas, Arthur E., *Obit* Apr 1941

Haas, Francis J., bishop, Aug 1943, *Obit* Oct 1953

Haas, Jonathan, American timpanist, June 2003

Haass, Richard, American international relations specialist, June 2010

Habash, George, Palestinian nationalist leader, Mar 1988, *Obit* Yrbk 2008

Habe, Hans, German author and journalist, Feb 1943, *Obit* Nov 1977

Haber, Heinz, Yrbk 1952

Habermas, Jurgen, German social philosopher, Jan 2007

Habib, Philip Charles, American diplomat, Sept 1981, *Obit* July 1992

Habibie, Bacharuddin Jusuf, Indonesian president, Oct 1998

Habre, Hissene, Chadian president, Aug 1987

Habsburg, Otto, German member of European Parliament, June 1941, *Obit* Yrbk 2011

Hacha, Emil, Yrbk 1942, *Obit* Sept 1945

Hackett, Albert, American dramatist and screenwriter, Oct 1956, *Obit* May 1995

Hackett, Buddy, American comedian, May 1965, *Obit* Oct 2003

Hackett, Charles, American opera singer, *Obit* Feb 1942

Hackett, Horatio B., *Obit* Nov 1941

Hackett, Walter, *Obit* Mar 1944

Hackl, Georg, German luge racer, Jan 2003

Hackman, Gene, American actor, July 1972

Hackworth, Green H., Jan 1958, *Obit* Sept 1973

Hadas, Moses, Mar 1960, *Obit* Nov 1966

Haddon, Alfred Cort, British anthropologist, *Obit* May 1940

Haddon, William, government official and physician, Feb 1969, *Obit* Apr 1985

Hadfield, Robert Abbott, *Obit* Nov 1940

Hadi Awang, Malaysian Islamic leader, Jan 2004

Hadid, Zaha M., Iraqi architect, Jan 2003

Hadley, Jerry, American opera singer, Nov 1991, *Obit* Yrbk 2007

Hadley, Stephen J., American national security adviser, Nov 2006

Hafezi, Parisa, Journalist and bureau chief for Reuters in Iran, Sept 2012

Haffajee, Ferial, South African newspaper editor, Jan 2004

Hafstad, Lawrence R., physicist, Oct 1956, *Obit* Jan 1994

Hagegard, Hakan, Swedish opera singer, May 1985

Hagel, Chuck, American senator, Aug 2004

Hagen, John P., astronomer, Oct 1957, *Obit* Nov 1990

Hagen, Uta, American actress, May 1944, Oct 1963, *Obit* Yrbk 2004

Hagens, Gunther von, German anatomist, Jan 2005

Hagerty, James C., American journalist and presidential aide, Mar 1953, *Obit* June 1981

Haggard, Merle, American country singer, Jan 1977

Haggard, William David, *Obit* Mar 1940

Haggis, Paul, Canadian screenwriter and film director, Aug 2006

Hagman, Larry, American actor, Sept 1980, *Obit* Yrbk 2013

Hagy, Ruth Geri, Oct 1957

Hahn, Emily, American novelist and biographer, July 1942, *Obit* Apr 1997

Hahn, Hilary, American violinist, Sept 2002

Hahn, Joseph, American DJ, Mar 2002

Hahn, Otto, German chemist, Mar 1951, *Obit* Oct 1968

Haig, Alexander Meigs, American general and Secretary of state, Jan 1973, Sept 1987, *Obit* Yrbk 2010

Haig-Brown, Roderick Langmere, Canadian naturalist, conservationist and author, Yrbk 1950

Haignere, Claudie, French astronaut and cabinet member, Jan 2003

Haile Selassie, Apr 1941, Oct 1954, *Obit* Oct 1975

Hailey, Arthur, Canadian novelist, Feb 1972, *Obit* Yrbk 2005

Hailsham of St. Marylebone, Quintin Hogg, British cabinet member, Sept 1957, *Obit* Feb 2002

Hainisch, Michael, *Obit* Mar 1940

Hair, Jay D., American zoologist and conservationist, Nov 1993, *Obit* Jan 2003

Haitink, Bernard, Dutch conductor, Nov 1977

Haji-Ioannou, Stelios, Greek shipping heir and entrepreneur, Jan 2007

Hakim, Christine, Indonesian actress and social activist, Jan 2003

Halaby, Najeeb E., American airline executive and regulatory agency official, Oct 1961, *Obit* Yrbk 2003

Halasz, Laszlo, Hungarian-American conductor and pianist, Jan 1949, *Obit* Feb 2002

Halberstam, David, American journalist, Apr 1973, *Obit* July 2007

Haldane, J. B. S., British geneticist, Nov 1940, *Obit* Jan 1965

Haldeman, H. R., American presidential adviser, Sept 1978, *Obit* Jan 1994

Hale, Arthur, *Obit* Mar 1940

Hale, Clara, American child benefactor, July 1985, *Obit* Feb 1993

Hale, Richard Walden, *Obit* Apr 1943

Haley, Alex, American biographer, historian and journalist, Jan 1977, *Obit* Mar 1992

Haley, Andrew G., lawyer, Oct 1955, *Obit* Nov 1966

Haley, Nikki, American governor, Feb 2011

Haley, William, English newspaper editor and broadcasting executive, Apr 1948, *Obit* Oct 1987

Halifax, Edward Frederick Lindley Wood, British statesman, Sept 1940, *Obit* Feb 1960

Halim, Mustafa ben, Libyan prime minister, Sept 1956

Hall, Arsenio, American comedian and talk show host, Sept 1989

Hall, Conrad L., American cinematographer, Aug 2000, *Obit* May 2003

Hall, Deidre, American actress, Nov 2002

Hall, Donald, American poet, essayist, critic and children's author, May 1984

Hall, Edward Twitchell, American anthropologist, Feb 1992, *Obit* Yrbk 2009

Hall, Florence L., Aug 1943

Hall, Floyd D., June 1970, *Obit* Yrbk 2012

Hall, Frank O., *Obit* Yrbk 1941

Hall, Frederick Lee, American judge and governor, Oct 1955, *Obit* May 1970

Hall, George A., American child welfare leader, *Obit* Nov 1941

Hall, George W., *Obit* Yrbk 1941

Hall, Gus, American communist leader, May 1973, *Obit* Jan 2001

Hall, James, actor, *Obit* July 1940

Hall, Josef Washington, journalist, historian and radio commentator, Yrbk 1944, *Obit* Jan 1961

Hall, Joyce Clyde, greeting card executive, May 1953, *Obit* Jan 1983

Hall, Leonard Wood, American congressman, July 1953, *Obit* July 1979

Hall, Paul, Feb 1966, *Obit* Aug 1980

Hall, Peter, British theatrical director, Feb 1962

Hall, Radclyffe, English novelist and poet, *Obit* Nov 1943

Hall, Raymond S., Oct 1953

Hall, Tex G., Native American leader, May 2005

Hall, William Edwin, Jan 1954, *Obit* Mar 1961

Halladay, Roy, American baseball player, Sept 2009

Hallahan, Patrick, American rock drummer, Nov 2008

Hallaren, Mary A., American army officer, Mar 1949, *Obit* Yrbk 2005

Halleck, Charles A., American congressman and political leader, Mar 1947, *Obit* Apr 1986

Halley, Rudolph, June 1953, *Obit* Jan 1957

Halligan, William J., Oct 1957

Hallinan, Vincent, American lawyer, Oct 1952, *Obit* Nov 1992

Halloran, Roy D., *Obit* Yrbk 1943

Hallstein, Walter, German diplomat, Oct 1953, *Obit* May 1982

Hallstrom, Lasse, Swedish motion picture director, Feb 2005

Hallyday, Johnny, French singer, Jan 2003

Halonen, Tarja, Finnish president, Jan 2006

Halpert, Edith Gregor, art dealer, July 1955, *Obit* Nov 1970

Halprin, Rose L., June 1950

Halsey, Edwin A., *Obit* Mar 1945

Halsey, Margaret, author, Nov 1944, *Obit* Apr 1997

Halsey, William Frederick, American admiral, Yrbk 1942, *Obit* Nov 1959

Halsman, Philippe, Latvian-American photographer, Mar 1960, *Obit* Aug 1979

Halston, American fashion designer, Yrbk 1972, *Obit* May 1990

Hamblet, Julia E., Oct 1953

Hambro, Carl Joachim, May 1940, *Obit* Feb 1965

Hamed, Naseem, English boxer, Oct 1998

Hamels, Cole, American baseball player, Nov 2011

Hamer, Dean H., geneticist, June 1997

Hamied, Yusuf K., Indian pharmaceutical executive, Jan 2004

Hamill, Dorothy, American figure skater, June 1976

Hamill, Pete, American journalist and novelist, Feb 1998

Hamilton, Alice, American physician, May 1946, *Obit* Nov 1970

Hamilton, Charles, American autograph dealer and handwriting expert, July 1976, *Obit* Feb 1997

Hamilton, Clayton Meeker, dramatist and critic, *Obit* Oct 1946

Hamilton, Cosmo, English author and dramatist, *Obit* Yrbk 1942

Hamilton, Edith, American classicist, Apr 1963

Hamilton, Gabrielle, American chef and restaurateur, May 2013

Hamilton, George Livingston, *Obit* Nov 1940

Hamilton, Hale, *Obit* July 1942

Hamilton, Josh, American baseball player, Apr 2011

Hamilton, Laird, American surfer, Aug 2005

Hamilton, Lee H., American congressman, Mar 1988

Hamilton, Lewis, British automobile racing driver, Jan 2007

Hamilton, Margaret, actress, Apr 1979, *Obit* July 1985

Hamilton, Scott, American figure skater, Apr 1985

Hamilton, Tom, American rock bassist, July 2004

Hamlin, Clarence Clark, American lawyer and

newspaper executive, *Obit* Yrbk 1940

Hamlin, Talbot Faulkner, Oct 1954, *Obit* Yrbk 1957

Hamlisch, Marvin, American composer and pianist, May 1976, *Obit* Yrbk 2012

Hamm, Jon, American actor, Mar 2013

Hamm, Mia, American soccer player, Sept 1999

Hamm, Morgan, American gymnast, Nov 2004

Hamm, Paul, American gymnast, Nov 2004

Hammarskjold, Dag, Swedish United Nations secretary-general, May 1953, *Obit* Nov 1961

Hammer (Musician), American rapper, Apr 1991

Hammer, Armand, American petroleum executive, June 1973, *Obit* Feb 1991

Hammer, Bonnie, American television executive, Apr 2006

Hammerstein, Oscar, American lyricist and librettist, Feb 1944, *Obit* Nov 1960

Hammerstein-Equord, Kurt, German general, *Obit* June 1943

Hammon, Becky, American basketball player, Jan 2003

Hammon, William McDowell, physician, Sept 1957, *Obit* Nov 1989

Hammond, Albert, American guitarist, Feb 2007

Hammond, Aubrey, English illustrator, *Obit* Apr 1940

Hammond, Caleb D., American map publisher and cartographer, Apr 1956, *Obit* Yrbk 2006

Hammond, E. Cuyler, biologist and statistician, June 1957, *Obit* Jan 1987

Hammond, Godfrey, Oct 1953, *Obit* Oct 1969

Hammond, Graeme M., *Obit* Yrbk 1944

Hammond, John, American recording industry executive, July 1979, *Obit* Aug 1987

Hammond, John Hays, July 1962, *Obit* Apr 1965

Hammons, David, American artist, May 2006

Hampden, Walter, American actor, May 1953, *Obit* Sept 1955

Hampshire, Susan, English actress and author, Jan 1974

Hampson, Thomas, American opera singer, Mar 1991

Hampton, Lionel, American band leader, Oct 1971, *Obit* Yrbk 2002

Han, Myeong Sook, Korean prime minister, Jan 2006

Han, Seung-Soo, Korean economist and diplomat, Jan 2002

Han, Suyin, Chinese novelist and physician, Yrbk 1957, *Obit* Yrbk 2013

Hancher, Virgil M., Feb 1957, *Obit* Mar 1965

Hancock, Florence, Nov 1948

Hancock, Graham, Scottish writer, Feb 2005

Hancock, Herbie, American jazz keyboardist and composer, Apr 1988

Hancock, John M., Apr 1949, *Obit* Yrbk 1957

Hancock, Joy Bright, naval officer, Feb 1949, *Obit* Oct 1986

Hancock, Trenton Doyle, American painter and performance artist, Apr 2006

Hand, Learned, American judge, Apr 1950, *Obit* Nov 1961

Handke, Peter, Austrian novelist and dramatist, Apr 1973

Handler, Chelsea, American comedian and actress, Oct 2010

Handler, Philip, biochemist, Feb 1964, *Obit* Feb 1982

Handley, Harold W., July 1960, *Obit* Nov 1972

Handlin, Oscar, American historian, July 1952, *Obit* Yrbk 2011

Handy, Thomas T., American general, Sept 1951, *Obit* June 1982

Handy, W. C., American composer and music publisher, Mar 1941, *Obit* June 1958

Haney, Fred, Jan 1967

Hanfmann, George Maxim Anossov, archaeologist, Oct 1967, *Obit* May 1986

Haniyeh, Ismail, Palestinian prime minister, Jan 2006

Hanks, Nancy, American government official, Sept 1971, *Obit* Mar 1983

Hanks, Tom, American actor, Apr 1989

Hanley, James Frederick, songwriter, *Obit* Apr 1942

Hanna, Edward Joseph, *Obit* Aug 1944

Hanna, William, American animator and producer, July 1983, *Obit* Sept 2001

Hannagan, Steve, publicist and sportswriter, Aug 1944, *Obit* Mar 1953

Hannah, Daryl, American actress, May 1990

Hannah, John A., American college president, Oct 1952, *Obit* Apr 1991

Hannan, Philip M., American archbishop, July 1968, *Obit* Yrbk 2011

Hannawald, Sven, German ski jumper, Jan 2002

Hannegan, Robert Emmet, American postmaster general, June 1944, *Obit* Nov 1949

Hannikainen, Tauno, July 1955, *Obit* Yrbk 1968

Hannity, Sean, American television moderator, Apr 2005

Hansberry, Lorraine, American dramatist, Sept 1959, *Obit* Feb 1965

Hansch, Theodor W., German physicist, Jan 2007

Hansell, Haywood S., air force general, Jan 1945, *Obit* Jan 1989

Hansen, Alvin Harvey, American economist, Sept 1945, *Obit* Aug 1975

Hansen, Carl F., Oct 1962

Hansen, Chris, American television reporter, June 2010

Hansen, Fred, pole vaulter, Yrbk 1965

Hansen, H. C., Mar 1956, *Obit* Apr 1960

Hansen, Harry, editor and critic, Yrbk 1942, *Obit* Yrbk 1991

Hansen, James E., American physicist, meteorologist and government official, May 1996

Hansen, Liane, American radio reporter and program host, May 2003

Hansenne, Marcel, Apr 1946

Hanson, Duane, American sculptor, Oct 1983, *Obit* Mar 1996

Hanson, Howard, American composer, Oct 1941, Sept 1966, *Obit* Apr 1981

Hanson, Ole, *Obit* Sept 1940

Hansson, Per Albin, Oct 1942, *Obit* Nov 1946

Hanus, Paul H., *Obit* Feb 1942

Harada, Tasuku, Japanese college teacher and president, *Obit* Mar 1940

Harbach, Otto, American librettist and lyricist, July 1950, *Obit* Mar 1963

Harber, W. Elmer, Mar 1951

Harbison, John, composer, Feb 1993

Harbord, James G., American general, Mar 1945, *Obit* Sept 1947

Harburg, E. Y., American lyricist, July 1980, *Obit* Apr 1981

Harcourt, Nic, American disc jockey, Oct 2005

Hard, Darlene, July 1964

Hardaway, Tim, American basketball player, July 1998

Harden, Arthur, British biochemist, *Obit* Aug 1940

Harden, Cecil Murray, congresswoman, Feb 1949, *Obit* Feb 1985

Harden, Marcia Gay, American actress, Sept 2001

Hardenbrook, Donald J., July 1962, *Obit* Aug 1976

Hardie, S. J. L., July 1951

Hardin, Clifford M., American Secretary of agriculture, May 1969, *Obit* Yrbk 2010

Hardin, Garrett James, American biologist, Sept 1974, *Obit* Apr 2004

Harding of Petherton, John Harding, British field marshal, Oct 1952

Harding, Margaret S., Apr 1947

Harding, Nelson, *Obit* Feb 1945

Hardwick, Chris, game show host, June 2012

Hardwick, Elizabeth, American novelist, short story writer, essayist and critic, Feb 1981, *Obit* Yrbk 2008

Hardwicke, Cedric, English actor, Oct 1949, *Obit* Oct 1964

Hardy, Ashley Kingsley, *Obit* Sept 1940

Hardy, Francoise, French singer, Jan 2005

Hardy, Porter, congressman, May 1957, *Obit* June 1995

Hare, David, English dramatist and theatrical director, Aug 1983

Hare, Raymond Arthur, American diplomat, July 1957, *Obit* May 1994

Harewood, George Henry Hubert Lascelles, English editor and writer on opera, Jan 1965, *Obit* Yrbk 2011

Hargis, Billy James, American clergyman, Mar 1972, *Obit* Yrbk 2005

Hargrave, Thomas J., Apr 1949, *Obit* Apr 1962

Hargrove, Marion, American novelist and humorist, June 1946, *Obit* Yrbk 2004

Hargrove, Roy, American jazz trumpet player, Apr 2000

Haring, Bernhard, German theologian, June 1969, *Obit* Sept 1998

Haring, Keith, American artist, Aug 1986, *Obit* Apr 1990

Harington, Charles, British general, *Obit* Yrbk 1940

Hariri, Saad, Lebanese telecommunications executive and political leader, Jan 2005

Harjo, Joy, American poet, Aug 2001

Harkin, Tom, American senator, Jan 1992

Harkins, Paul D., American general, Apr 1964

Harkness, Douglas S., Oct 1961

Harkness, Edward Stephen, Jan 1940

Harkness, Georgia Elma, theologian, Nov 1960

Harkness, Rebekah West, American composer, ballet manager and dance patron, Apr 1974, *Obit* Sept 1982

Harlan, John Marshall, American Supreme Court justice, May 1955, *Obit* Feb 1972

Harlan, Otis, *Obit* Jan 1940

Harlech, William David Ormsby Gore, British statesman and diplomat, Mar 1961, *Obit* Mar 1985

Harmon, Ernest N., American general and university president, Nov 1946, *Obit* Jan 1980

Harmon, Millard F., Yrbk 1942, *Obit* Apr 1945

Harnoncourt, Nikolaus, Austrian conductor, Jan 1991

Harnwell, Gaylord Probasco, June 1956

Harp, Edward B., Oct 1953

Harper, Alexander James, *Obit* Nov 1940

Harper, Ben, American singer and guitarist, Jan 2004

Harper, Bryce, American baseball player, May 2013

Harper, Marion, advertising executive, Mar 1961, *Obit* Feb 1990

Harper, Samuel Northrup, *Obit* Mar 1943

Harper, Stephen, Canadian prime minister, Jan 2006

Harper, Theodore Acland, *Obit* June 1942

Harper, Valerie, American actress, Feb 1975

Harrar, J. George, Jan 1964, *Obit* June 1982

Harrell, Lynn, cellist, Feb 1983

Harrelson, Ken, baseball player and executive, Apr 1970

Harrelson, Walter J., May 1959

Harrelson, Woody, American actor, Jan 1997

Harrer, Heinrich, Austrian mountaineer, Oct 1954, *Obit* Yrbk 2006

Harridge, William, baseball executive, Sept 1949, *Obit* June 1971

Harriman, Averell, American statesman, Apr 1941, Nov 1946, *Obit* Sept 1986

Harriman, E. Roland, Mar 1951, *Obit* Apr 1978

Harriman, Florence Jaffray Hurst, social welfare leader, Mar 1940, *Obit* Nov 1967

Harrington, David, violinist, Nov 1998

Harrington, Francis Clark, *Obit* Mar 1940

Harrington, Michael, American social critic and political activist, Jan 1969, Oct 1988, *Obit* Sept 1989

Harrington, Russell C., Apr 1956, *Obit* Oct 1971

Harris, Arthur Travers, British air marshal, Sept 1942, *Obit* May 1984

Harris, Barbara, American actress, Apr 1968

Harris, Barbara C., American bishop, June 1989

Harris, Bernice Kelly, novelist and dramatist, Yrbk 1949

Harris, Bucky, baseball manager, June 1948, *Obit* Jan 1978

Harris, Cyril M., American acoustic engineer, Feb 1977, *Obit* Yrbk 2011

Harris, E. Lynn, American novelist, June 1996, *Obit* Yrbk 2009

Harris, Emmylou, American singer, Oct 1994

Harris, Eva, American geneticist, Mar 2004

Harris, Franco, American football player, June 1976

Harris, Fred R., American senator, Jan 1968

Harris, Harwell Hamilton, American architect, Jan 1962, *Obit* Jan 1991

Harris, James Rendel, *Obit* Apr 1941

Harris, Jonathan, American artist and web designer, Oct 2013

Harris, Judith Rich, textbook author, Apr 1999

Harris, Julie, American actress, Feb 1956, Aug 1977, *Obit* Yrbk 2013

Harris, Louis, American public opinion analyst, May 1966

Harris, Mark, American novelist and memoirist, Yrbk 1959, *Obit* Yrbk 2007

Harris, Naomie, British actress, Sept 2012

Harris, Oren, American congressman and judge, May 1956

Harris, Patricia, American cabinet member, Yrbk 1965, *Obit* May 1985

Harris, Richard, Irish actor, May 1964, *Obit* Yrbk 2003

Harris, Rolf, Australian television personality, singer and cartoonist, Jan 2002

Harris, Rosemary, British actress, Sept 1967

Harris, Roy, composer, Aug 1940, *Obit* Nov 1979

Harris, Sam, American neuroscientist, Jan 2012

Harris, Sam H., American theatrical producer, *Obit* Aug 1941

Harris, Seymour Edwin, American economist, Feb 1965, *Obit* Yrbk 1974

Harris, Walter, June 1955

Harris, William, *Obit* Oct 1946

Harrison, Earl G., Aug 1943, *Obit* Oct 1955

Harrison, George, British singer and guitarist, Nov 1966, Jan 1989, *Obit* Mar 2002

Harrison, George M., Jan 1949, *Obit* Jan 1969

Harrison, Gilbert A., American magazine editor, publisher and veterans' leader, Mar 1949, *Obit* Yrbk 2008

Harrison, James, American football player, Nov 2011

Harrison, James L., Oct 1962

Harrison, Jim, American poet and novelist, July 1992

Harrison, Joan, English screenwriter and producer, May 1944, *Obit* Oct 1994

Harrison, Marvin, American football player, Aug 2001

Harrison, Pat, American senator, *Obit* Aug 1941

Harrison, Rex, English actor, Jan 1947, Feb 1986, *Obit* July 1990

Harrison, Shelby M., Jan 1943

Harrison, Wallace Kirkman, architect, Mar 1947, *Obit* Jan 1982

Harrison, William B., American investment banker, Mar 2002

Harrison, William H., Feb 1949, *Obit* July 1956

Harrison, William K., American general, July 1952, *Obit* Aug 1987

Harron, Marion J., Yrbk 1949

Harron, Mary, Canadian motion picture director, Sept 2000

Harrower, David, Scottish dramatist, Jan 2007

Harry, Deborah, American singer, Nov 1981

Harryhausen, Ray, American motion picture special effects technician and animator, *Obit* Yrbk 2013

Harsanyi, Zsolt, *Obit* Apr 1944

Harsch, Joseph C., American journalist, Oct 1944, *Obit* Aug 1998

Hart, Albert Bushnell, historian, *Obit* Aug 1943

Hart, Edward J., Feb 1953, *Obit* June 1961

Hart, Gary, American senator and lawyer, May 1976

Hart, Kitty Carlisle, American singer, actress and state official, Oct 1982, *Obit* Yrbk 2007

Hart, Lorenz, American lyricist, May 1940, *Obit* Feb 1944

Hart, Merwin K., Oct 1941, *Obit* Jan 1963

Hart, Mickey, American drummer, Jan 1994

Hart, Moss, American playwright, July 1940, Nov 1960, *Obit* Feb 1962

Hart, Philip A., American senator, Sept 1959, *Obit* Feb 1977

Hart, Thomas Charles, Jan 1942, *Obit* Sept 1971

Hart, William S., American actor, *Obit* July 1946

Hartford, Huntington, American financier and patron of the arts, June 1959, *Obit* Yrbk 2008

Hartigan, Grace, American painter, Sept 1962, *Obit* Yrbk 2009

Hartke, Vance, American senator, Mar 1960, *Obit* Yrbk 2003

Hartle, Russell P., American general, June 1942, *Obit* Jan 1962

Hartley, Fred A., American congressman, June 1947, *Obit* June 1969

Hartley, Hal, American motion picture director and screenwriter, Aug 1995

Hartley, Marsden, American painter and poet, *Obit* Oct 1943

Hartman, David, actor and television personality, June 1981

Hartman, Grace, Nov 1942, *Obit* Oct 1955

Hartman, Louis F., Jan 1953, *Obit* Nov 1970

Hartman, Paul, American actor, Nov 1942, *Obit* Yrbk 1973

Hartman, Paul; and Hartman, Grace, Nov 1942

Hartmann, Heidi I., American economist and feminist, Apr 2003

Hartnell, Norman, May 1953, *Obit* Aug 1979

Hartnett, Robert C., priest, periodical editor and educator, Yrbk 1949

Hartung, Hans, French painter, July 1958, *Obit* Feb 1990

Hartwell, John A., *Obit* Jan 1941

Hartwell, Leland, American geneticist, Nov 1999

Hartwig, Walter, *Obit* Mar 1941

Harty, Hamilton, Irish composer and conductor, *Obit* Apr 1941

Hartzog, George B., American national parks director, July 1970, *Obit* Yrbk 2008

Haruka, Yoko, Japanese feminist, writer and television personality, Jan 2004

Harvard, Beverly Joyce, American police chief, Sept 1997

Harvey, David, British geographer, Aug 2008

Harvey, E. Newton, May 1952

Harvey, Laurence, British actor, May 1961, *Obit* Jan 1974

Harvey, PJ, British singer, songwriter and guitarist, May 2008

Harvey, Paul, American radio reporter, Mar 1986, *Obit* Yrbk 2009

Hasegawa, Ichiro, Japanese astronomer, Jan 2004

Hasek, Dominik, Czech hockey player, May 1998

Haseltine, William A., American molecular biologist, Nov 1998

Hashimoto, Ryutaro, Japanese prime minister, Feb 1998, *Obit* Yrbk 2006

Haskell, Molly, motion picture critic, Nov 1998

Haskell, William N., Feb 1947, *Obit* Sept 1952

Haskin, Frederic J., *Obit* June 1944

Haskins, Caryl Parker, American biophysicist, Feb 1958, *Obit* Feb 2002

Haslett, Caroline, English feminist and electrical engineer, Oct 1950, *Obit* Mar 1957

Hasluck, Paul, Australian governor-general, Oct 1946

Hass, Amira, Israeli journalist, Apr 2009

Hass, Hans, Feb 1955, *Obit* Yrbk 2013

Hass, Henry Bohn, chemist, Apr 1956, *Obit* Apr 1987

Hass, Robert, American poet, critic and translator, Feb 2001

Hassan, Sept 1964, *Obit* Oct 1999

Hassan, Mahmoud, July 1947

Hassanal Bolkiah, Oct 1989

Hassel, Kai-Uwe von, May 1963

Hassenfeld, Alan Geoffrey, American toy industry executive, July 2003

Hastert, Dennis, American congressman and Speaker of the House, Apr 1999

Hastie, William H., American lawyer, Mar 1944, *Obit* June 1976

Hastings, Reed, American computer software executive and entrepreneur, Mar 2006

Hastreiter, Kim, American magazine editor and publisher, Aug 2010

Hatch, Carl A., senator and judge, Yrbk 1944, *Obit* Nov 1963

Hatch, Orrin G., American senator, Aug 1982

Hatcher, Harlan H., literary critic, author and historian, Oct 1955, *Obit* May 1998

Hatcher, Richard G., American mayor, Feb 1972

Hatfield, Juliana, American singer and songwriter, Aug 2011

Hatfield, Mark O., American senator, Nov 1959, Mar 1984, *Obit* Yrbk 2011

Hathaway, Anne, American actress, Feb 2009

Hatoyama, Ichiro, Japanese prime minister, May 1955, *Obit* May 1959

Hatta, Mohammad, Indonesian prime minister, Yrbk 1949, *Obit* Yrbk 1991

Hatton, Ricky, British boxer, Oct 2008

Hau, Lene Vestergaard, Danish physicist, Jan 2002

Hauck, Louise Platt, *Obit* Feb 1944

Hauerwas, Stanley, American theologian, June 2003

Hauge, Gabriel, American economist, Oct 1953, *Obit* Sept 1981

Haughey, Charles, Irish prime minister, Feb 1981, *Obit* Yrbk 2006

Haughton, Daniel Jeremiah, aircraft executive, Sept 1974, *Obit* Aug 1987

Hauptmann, Gerhart, German dramatist, *Obit* July 1946

Hauser, Conrad Augustine, *Obit* Apr 1943

Hauser, Gayelord, German-American nutritionist and author, June 1955, *Obit* Feb 1985

Hauser, Philip M., demographer, July 1969, *Obit* Feb 1995

Haushofer, Karl, German geographer, Apr 1942, *Obit* Sept 1946

Havel, Vaclav, Czech dramatist and president, Mar 1985, Aug 1995, *Obit* Yrbk 2012

Havill, Edward, Yrbk 1952

Hawass, Zahi, Egyptian archaeologist, Apr 2000

Hawes, Elizabeth, American fashion designer, Oct 1940, *Obit* Yrbk 1991

Hawk, Tony, American skateboarder, June 2000

Hawke, Ethan, American actor and novelist, May 1998

Hawke, Robert J. L., Australian prime minister, Aug 1983

Hawkes, Anna L. Rose, Oct 1956

Hawkes, Herbert E., *Obit* June 1943

Hawking, Stephen W., British physicist, May 1984

Hawkins, Augustus F., American congressman, Feb 1983, *Obit* Yrbk 2008

Hawkins, Dan, British rock guitarist, Jan 2004

Hawkins, Edler G., Jan 1965

Hawkins, Erick, dancer and choreographer, Jan 1974, *Obit* Feb 1995

Hawkins, Erskine, trumpet player and band leader, Sept 1941, *Obit* Jan 1994

Hawkins, Harry C., Apr 1952

Hawkins, Jack, Nov 1959, *Obit* Oct 1973

Hawkins, Justin, British rock singer, guitarist and composer, Jan 2004

Hawkins, Lyn-Z Adams, American skateboarder, Sept 2013

Hawkins, Paula, American senator, Sept 1985, *Obit* Yrbk 2010

Hawkinson, Tim, American sculptor, Aug 2005

Hawks, Howard, American motion picture director and producer, May 1972, *Obit* Mar 1980

Hawley, Cameron, Yrbk 1957

Hawley, H. Dudley, *Obit* May 1941

Hawley, Paul R., Apr 1946, *Obit* Jan 1966

Hawley, Willis C., *Obit* Sept 1941

Hawn, Goldie, American actress, Yrbk 1971

Haworth, Leland J., Yrbk 1950, *Obit* May 1979

Hax, Carolyn, American advice columnist, Nov 2002

Hay, Charles M., *Obit* Mar 1945

Hay, Regina Deem, July 1948

Haya de la Torre, Victor Raul, Peruvian political leader, June 1942, *Obit* Sept 1979

Hayakawa, S. I., American senator and educator, Nov 1959, Jan 1977, *Obit* Apr 1992

Hayakawa, Sessue, Japanese actor, Sept 1962, *Obit* Jan 1974

Hayashi, Senjuro, *Obit* Mar 1943

Haycraft, Howard, publisher and author, Nov 1941, Feb 1954, *Obit* Jan 1992

Haydee, Marcia, Brazilian dancer, Oct 1977

Hayden, Carl Trumbull, American senator, July 1951, *Obit* Mar 1972

Hayden, Matthew, Australian cricket player, Jan 2004

Hayden, Melissa, American ballet dancer, May 1955, *Obit* Yrbk 2006

Hayden, Michael, American general and intelligence official, Nov 2006

Hayden, Sterling, actor, May 1978, *Obit* July 1986

Hayden, Tom, American state legislator and social activist, Apr 1976

Hayek, Friedrich A. von, British economist, June 1945, *Obit* May 1992

Hayes, A. J., Oct 1953

Hayes, Alfred, banker and government official, Feb 1966, *Obit* Feb 1990

Hayes, Anna Hansen, Nov 1949

Hayes, Bob, American sprinter and football player, Sept 1966, *Obit* Jan 2003

Hayes, Carlton Joseph Huntley, historian and diplomat, June 1942, *Obit* Nov 1964

Hayes, David, Apr 1966, *Obit* Yrbk 2013

Hayes, Denis, lawyer and environmentalist, Oct 1997

Hayes, Edward W., American lawyer, May 2006

Hayes, Helen, American actress, Jan 1942, Oct 1956, *Obit* May 1993

Hayes, Isaac, American singer and composer, Oct 1972, *Obit* Yrbk 2008

Hayes, Peter Lind, actor, Mar 1959, *Obit* July 1998

Hayes, Robert M., lawyer, Apr 1989

Hayes, Roland, American singer, May 1942, *Obit* Mar 1977

Hayes, Samuel P., Sept 1954

Hayes, Samuel Perkins, psychologist and teacher of the blind, Sept 1954, *Obit* Sept 1958

Hayes, Terrance, American poet, Apr 2011

Hayes, Tyrone, American biologist, May 2008

Hayes, Woody, American football coach, Feb 1975, *Obit* May 1987

Hayhoe, Katharine, Feb 2012

Haynes, George Edmund, American civil rights leader and economist, Mar 1946, *Obit* Apr 1960

Haynes, Roy Asa, *Obit* Yrbk 1940

Haynes, Todd, American film director, July 2003

Hays, Arthur Garfield, lawyer and civil rights leader, Sept 1942, *Obit* Feb 1955

Hays, Brooks, American congressman, Jan 1958, *Obit* Jan 1982

Hays, Wayne Levere, American congressman, Nov 1974, *Obit* Apr 1989

Hays, Will H., American motion picture industry censor, July 1943, *Obit* Apr 1954

Haysbert, Dennis, American actor, Nov 2006

Hayter, Stanley William, English painter and engraver, Yrbk 1945, *Obit* June 1988

Hayward, Leland, theatrical agent and producer, Feb 1949, *Obit* Apr 1971

Hayward, Susan, American actress, May 1953, *Obit* May 1975

Haywood, Allan S., American labor leader, May 1952, *Obit* Apr 1953

Haywood, Dave, American country guitarist, pianist and mandolinist, July 2011

Hayworth, Rita, American actress, May 1960, *Obit* July 1987

Hazard, Paul, Mar 1941

Hazeltine, Alan, electrical engineer and inventor, Mar 1948, *Obit* July 1964

Hazen, Charles D., *Obit* Nov 1941

Hazzard, Shirley, Australian novelist and short story writer, Jan 1991

Head, Edith, American costume designer, May 1945, *Obit* Jan 1982

Head, Henry, British neurologist, *Obit* Yrbk 1940

Head, Walter W., Apr 1945, *Obit* June 1954

Heald, Henry Townley, American civil engineer, Feb 1952, *Obit* Jan 1976

Healey, Denis, British political leader, Yrbk 1971

Healy, Bernadine P., American cardiologist and public health official, Nov 1992, *Obit* Yrbk 2011

Healy, Timothy Stafford, priest, university president and library director, Jan 1993, *Obit* Jan 1993

Heaney, Seamus, Irish poet, Jan 1982, *Obit* Yrbk 2013

Heard, Alexander, Nov 1966

Hearne, John J., July 1950, *Obit* May 1969

Hearnes, Warren Eastman, American governor, June 1968

Hearns, Thomas, American boxer, Mar 1983

Hearst, Patricia Campbell, American socialite, Aug 1982

Hearst, William Randolph, American newspaper

publisher, Oct 1955, *Obit* July 1993

Heath, Edward, British prime minister, Oct 1962, *Obit* Yrbk 2005

Heath, James R., American chemist, Oct 2003

Heath, S. Burton, Jan 1940, *Obit* Sept 1949

Heatter, Gabriel, radio commentator, Apr 1941, *Obit* May 1972

Hebert, F. Edward, American congressman, Nov 1951, *Obit* Feb 1980

Heche, Anne, American actress, Sept 1998

Hecht, Anthony, American poet, May 1986, *Obit* Yrbk 2005

Hecht, Ben, American journalist, novelist, dramatist and screenwriter, Feb 1942, *Obit* June 1964

Hecht, George Joseph, magazine publisher, Oct 1947, *Obit* June 1980

Heckart, Eileen, American actress, June 1958, *Obit* Mar 2002

Heckerling, Amy, motion picture director, July 1999

Heckler, Margaret, American Secretary of health and human services, Aug 1983

Heckscher, August, *Obit* June 1941

Heckscher, August, municipal official and journalist, Oct 1958, *Obit* June 1997

Hedden, Worth Tuttle, American novelist and short story writer, Yrbk 1957, *Obit* Jan 1986

Hedges, Chris, American foreign correspondent, June 2012

Hedin, Sven Anders, Swedish explorer, May 1940, *Obit* Jan 1953

Hedtoft, Hans, Mar 1949, *Obit* Mar 1955

Hee, Dana, American motion picture stunt performer, May 2008

Heeney, A. D. P., June 1953

Hees, George, Canadian cabinet member, Oct 1959

Heffner, Richard D., American historian and television moderator, Oct 1964

Heflin, Van, July 1943, *Obit* Sept 1971

Hefner, Christie, American magazine publisher, Oct 1986

Hefner, Hugh, American magazine publisher, Sept 1968

Heidegger, Martin, German philosopher, June 1972, *Obit* July 1976

Heiden, Eric, American speed skater and bicyclist, June 1980

Heiden, Konrad, Mar 1944, *Obit* Sept 1975

Heidenstam, Rolf von, Oct 1951, *Obit* Oct 1958

Heidenstam, Verner von, Swedish poet and novelist, *Obit* July 1940

Heifetz, Jascha, Russian-American violinist, Feb 1944, *Obit* Feb 1988

Height, Dorothy I., American civil rights activist, Sept 1972, *Obit* July 2010

Heilbroner, Robert L., American economist and writer, June 1975, *Obit* Yrbk 2005

Heilbrun, Carolyn G., American literary scholar and mystery novelist, Jan 1993, *Obit* Feb 2004

Heimlich, Henry J., American surgeon, Oct 1986

Heineman, Ben W., lawyer and machine tool executive, Jan 1962, *Obit* Yrbk 2012

Heinemann, Gustav Walter, June 1969, *Obit* Aug 1976

Heinlein, Robert A., American science fiction writer, Mar 1955, *Obit* June 1988

Heinrichs, April, American soccer player and coach, May 2000

Heintzleman, B. Frank, June 1953, *Obit* Sept 1965

Heinz, Henry John, American food industry executive, June 1947, *Obit* Apr 1987

Heinz, John, American senator, Apr 1981, *Obit* May 1991

Heisenberg, Werner, German physicist, Apr 1957, *Obit* Mar 1976

Heiser, Victor G., physician, Apr 1942, *Obit* May 1972

Heiskell, Andrew, American magazine executive, Mar 1966, *Obit* Yrbk 2003

Heiss, Carol, American figure skater, Oct 1959

Heitkamp, Heidi, state attorney general, Sept 2013

Hektoen, Ludvig, Yrbk 1947, *Obit* Sept 1951

Helburn, Theresa, theatrical producer, Sept 1944, *Obit* Nov 1959

Held, Al, American painter, Jan 1986, *Obit* Yrbk 2005

Helders, Matt, British rock drummer, Jan 2006

Helfgott, David, Australian pianist, Mar 1997

Heliker, John, painter, Jan 1969, *Obit* July 2000

Helion, Jean, French painter, Nov 1943, *Obit* Jan 1988

Hellenga, Robert, American novelist, Mar 2008

Heller, Agnes, Hungarian philosopher, Nov 2008

Heller, John Roderick, physician, Feb 1949, *Obit* July 1989

Heller, Joseph, American novelist, Jan 1973, *Obit* Mar 2000

Heller, Walter W., American economist, Sept 1961, *Obit* Aug 1987

Hellinger, Mark, columnist and motion picture producer, Sept 1947, *Obit* July 1948

Hellman, Lillian, American playwright, May 1941, June 1960, *Obit* Aug 1984

Hellyer, Paul, Sept 1969

Helms, Jesse A., American senator, July 1979, *Obit* Yrbk 2008

Helms, Richard, American intelligence official, Oct 1967, *Obit* Yrbk 2003

Helmsley, Harry B., American real estate executive, June 1985, *Obit* Mar 1997

Heloise, American advice columnist, June 1996

Helpern, Milton, May 1973, *Obit* June 1977

Helpmann, Robert, Australian dancer and actor, Feb 1950, *Obit* Nov 1986

Helprin, Mark, American short story writer and novelist, Aug 1991

Helstein, Ralph, labor leader, June 1948, *Obit* May 1985

Heming, Arthur Henry Howard, *Obit* Yrbk 1940

Hemingway, Margaux, American model and actress, Mar 1978, *Obit* Sept 1996

Hemingway, Mary, wife of American novelist Ernest Hemingway, Sept 1968, *Obit* Jan 1987

Hempleman-Adams, David, British explorer, Jan 2004

Hemsworth, Chris, Australian actor, Jan 2013

Hench, Philip Showalter, American physician, Yrbk 1950, *Obit* May 1965

Henderson, Donald A., American public health scientist and college dean, Mar 2002

Henderson, E. L., June 1950, *Obit* Oct 1953

Henderson, Fergus, British chef and restaurateur, Feb 2011

Henderson, Florence, American singer and actress, Apr 1971

Henderson, Hazel, Anglo-American environmentalist and economist, Nov 2003

Henderson, Joe, American jazz saxophonist, June 1996, *Obit* Oct 2001

Henderson, Lawrence J., American chemist, *Obit* Apr 1942

Henderson, Leon, American economist and government official, July 1940, *Obit* Jan 1987

Henderson, Loy Wesley, American diplomat, Mar 1948, *Obit* May 1986

Henderson, Nevile Meyrick, British diplomat, Apr 1940, *Obit* Feb 1943

Henderson, Rickey, American baseball player, Sept 1990

Henderson, Skitch, American conductor, July 1966, *Obit* Apr 2006

Hendl, Walter, American conductor, college president and music teacher, June 1955

Hendricks, Barbara, opera singer, Mar 1989

Hendrickson, Robert C., Nov 1952, *Obit* Feb 1965

Hendrickson, Sue, paleontologist, Oct 2001

Henie, Sonja, Norwegian-American figure

skater and actress, Sept 1940, Jan 1952, *Obit* Nov 1970

Henin, Justine, Belgian tennis player, Jan 2003

Henley, Beth, American dramatist, Feb 1983

Henner, Marilu, American actress, Feb 1999

Henning, Doug, Canadian magician, Aug 1976, *Obit* Apr 2000

Hennings, Thomas C., American senator, Oct 1954, *Obit* Nov 1960

Hennock, Frieda, lawyer and government official, Nov 1948, *Obit* Sept 1960

Henreid, Paul, Austrian actor and director, July 1943, *Obit* June 1992

Henriot, Philippe, French political leader, *Obit* Aug 1944

Henry, Brad, American governor, Jan 2005

Henry, David Dodds, college president, June 1966, *Obit* Nov 1995

Henry, E. William, Feb 1964

Henry, John, American baseball executive, May 2005

Henry, Jules, *Obit* Aug 1941

Henry, Marguerite, American children's author, Yrbk 1947, *Obit* Feb 1998

Henry, Martha, Canadian actress and theatrical director, Jan 2006

Henry, Mellinger Edward, *Obit* Mar 1946

Henry-Haye, Gaston, Nov 1940

Hensel, H. Struve, American lawyer and military official, Yrbk 1948, *Obit* July 1991

Henson, Jim, American puppeteer, Mar 1977, *Obit* July 1990

Hentoff, Nat, American journalist and young adult novelist, Aug 1986

Henze, Hans Werner, German composer, Apr 1966, *Obit* Yrbk 2013

Hepburn, Audrey, Anglo-Dutch actress, Mar 1954, *Obit* Mar 1993

Hepburn, Katharine, American actress, May 1942, Nov 1969, *Obit* Nov 2003

Hepburn, Mitchell Frederick, Canadian provincial premier, Yrbk 1941, *Obit* Feb 1953

Heppner, Ben, Canadian opera singer, Jan 1997

Hepworth, Barbara, English sculptor, Feb 1957, *Obit* Aug 1975

Herbert, Bob, American columnist, Oct 1998

Herbert, Don, American science teacher and television personality, Feb 1956, *Obit* Yrbk 2007

Herbert, Elizabeth, Feb 1954

Herbert, Gary R., American governor, May 2011

Herbert, Matthew, English record producer, composer and DJ, Nov 2012

Herbster, Ben Mohr, clergyman, July 1962, *Obit* Mar 1985

Hering, Hermann S., *Obit* July 1940

Herlihy, James Leo, American novelist, dramatist and actor, Sept 1961, *Obit* Jan 1994

Herlin, Emil, *Obit* Feb 1943

Herman, Alexis, American Secretary of labor and management consultant, Jan 1998

Herman, Jerry, American composer and lyricist, Jan 1965

Herman, Woody, American band leader, Apr 1973, *Obit* Jan 1988

Hermann Jonasson, Aug 1941

Hernandez Martinez, Maximiliano, Salvadoran general and president, June 1942, *Obit* June 1966

Hernandez, Aileen C., feminist, July 1971

Hernandez, Dave, American bassist, June 2007

Hernandez, Keith, American baseball player and sportscaster, Feb 1988

Hernandez, Livan, Cuban baseball player, Mar 1998

Hernandez, Orlando, Cuban baseball player, Apr 2000

Hernandez-Colon, Rafael, Puerto Rican governor, May 1973

Herndon, J. Marvin, American geophysicist, Nov 2003

Hern ndez, F,lix, Venezuelan baseball player, June 2012

Herod, William Rogers, mechanical engineer and

manufacturing executive, Mar 1951, *Obit* Sept 1974

Herold, J. Christopher, Yrbk 1959, *Obit* Feb 1965

Herr, Hugh, American biophysicist and mechanical engineer, Apr 2012

Herrera Campins, Luis, Venezuelan president, July 1980, *Obit* Yrbk 2008

Herrera, Carolina, Venezuelan model and daughter of fashion designer Carolina Herrera, Mar 1996

Herrera, Felipe, Mar 1968

Herrera, Paloma, Argentine ballet dancer, Apr 2000

Herrick, Elinore Morehouse, Apr 1947, *Obit* Jan 1965

Herrick, Francis Hobart, *Obit* Nov 1940

Herring, Clyde L., *Obit* Nov 1945

Herring, Pendleton, American political scientist, July 1950, *Obit* Yrbk 2004

Herriot, Edouard, French statesman, Feb 1946, *Obit* June 1957

Hersch, Fred, American jazz pianist and composer, Apr 2006

Hersey, John, American novelist and journalist, Feb 1944, *Obit* May 1993

Hersh, Seymour M., American journalist, Mar 1984

Hershey, Alfred D., American biologist, July 1970, *Obit* Aug 1997

Hershey, Barbara, American actress, Aug 1989

Hershey, Lewis Blaine, American general and government official, June 1941, June 1951, *Obit* July 1977

Hershey, Milton Snavely, American candy industry executive, *Obit* Nov 1945

Hershiser, Orel, baseball player, Feb 1990

Hershko, Avram, Israeli biochemist, Jan 2007

Hersholt, Jean, American actor, Yrbk 1944, *Obit* Sept 1956

Herskovits, Melville J., American anthropologist, Nov 1948, *Obit* Apr 1963

Herskovitz, Marshall, American film and television producer, scriptwriter and director, Sept 2000

Herter, Christian Archibald, American Secretary of state, Yrbk 1947, Mar 1958, *Obit* Feb 1967

Hertz, Alfred, *Obit* June 1942

Hertz, Emanuel, *Obit* July 1940

Hertzberg, Arthur, American rabbi and religious writer, June 1975, *Obit* Yrbk 2006

Hertzberg, Hendrik, American journalist, Mar 2011

Hertzler, Arthur E., American surgeon, *Obit* Oct 1946

Hertzog, James Barry Munnik, South African prime minister, *Obit* Jan 1943

Herzberg, Gerhard, Canadian physicist, Feb 1973, *Obit* July 1999

Herzog, Chaim, Israeli president, Apr 1988, *Obit* June 1997

Herzog, Isaac, Apr 1959

Herzog, Jacques, Swiss architect, June 2002

Herzog, Jacques and de Meuron, Pierre, June 2002

Herzog, Maurice, July 1953

Herzog, Paul M., college dean, July 1945, *Obit* Jan 1987

Herzog, Werner, German film director, Aug 1978

Hesburgh, Theodore Martin, American priest and college president, Jan 1955, July 1982

Heschel, Abraham Joshua, American rabbi and theologian, Apr 1970, *Obit* Mar 1973

Heseltine, Michael, British political leader, June 1985

Hess, Dean E., Sept 1957

Hess, Elmer, Jan 1956, *Obit* June 1961

Hess, Max, Oct 1961, *Obit* Nov 1968

Hess, Myra, English pianist, Sept 1943, *Obit* Jan 1966

Hess, Rudolf, German Nazi leader, Mar 1941, *Obit* Oct 1987

Hess, Victor Francis, American physicist, Oct 1963, *Obit* Feb 1965

Hesse, Hermann, German novelist, Oct 1962

Hesselgren, Kerstin, Swedish sociologist and member of

Parliament, Jan 1941, *Obit* Oct 1962

Hester, James M., June 1962

Heston, Charlton, American actor, May 1957, July 1986, *Obit* July 2008

Hetfield, James, American singer and guitarist, Jan 2000

Heuer, Rolf-Dieter, German physicist, Mar 2012

Heusinger, Adolf, German general, Feb 1956

Heuss, Theodor, German president, Nov 1949, *Obit* Jan 1964

Heuven Goedhart, Gerrit Jan van, Oct 1952, *Obit* Sept 1956

Hevesy, George Charles, Hungarian chemist, Apr 1959, *Obit* Sept 1966

Heward, Leslie H., *Obit* June 1943

Hewart, Gordon Hewart, *Obit* June 1943

Hewitt, Angela, Canadian pianist, Apr 2007

Hewitt, Don, American television producer, June 1988, *Obit* Yrbk 2009

Hewitt, H. Kent, American admiral, Apr 1943, *Obit* Nov 1972

Hewitt, Lleyton, Australian tennis player, Oct 2002

Hewlett, J. Monroe, *Obit* Yrbk 1941

Hewlett, Jamie, English illustrator and cartoonist, Jan 2007

Hewlett, Sylvia Ann, Welsh economist and feminist, Sept 2002

Heydrich, Reinhard, German Nazi leader, *Obit* July 1942, July 1942

Heydt, Herman A., *Obit* Oct 1941

Heyerdahl, Thor, Norwegian ethnologist and explorer, Yrbk 1947, Sept 1972, *Obit* Yrbk 2002

Heym, Stefan, German novelist, Mar 1943, *Obit* Mar 2002

Heymann, David L., American epidemiologist and international public health official, July 2004

Heymann, Lida Gustava, *Obit* Sept 1943

Heyns, Roger W., college administrator, Yrbk 1968, *Obit* Nov 1995

Heyrovsky, Jaroslav, Czech chemist, July 1961, *Obit* May 1967

Heyward, DuBose, American novelist and dramatist, *Obit* July 1940

Hiaasen, Carl, American novelist and columnist, Apr 1997

Hibbard, Edna, *Obit* Feb 1943

Hibbard, Frederick P., *Obit* Oct 1943

Hibbard, Henry D., *Obit* Yrbk 1942

Hibbs, Ben, magazine editor, July 1946, *Obit* May 1975

Hickam, Homer H., American aerospace engineer and memoirist, Oct 2000

Hickel, Walter Joseph, American Secretary of the interior and governor, May 1969, *Obit* Yrbk 2010

Hickenlooper, Bourke B., American senator and governor, May 1947, *Obit* Oct 1971

Hickerson, John Dewey, diplomat, May 1950, *Obit* Apr 1989

Hickey, Dave, American art and cultural critic, Sept 2007

Hickey, Margaret A., feminist and lawyer, Yrbk 1944, *Obit* Feb 1995

Hickey, Thomas F., *Obit* Feb 1941

Hickman, Emily, June 1945, *Obit* July 1947

Hickman, Herman, Nov 1951, *Obit* July 1958

Hicks, Beatrice Alice, mechanical engineer, Jan 1957

Hicks, Clarence J., *Obit* Feb 1945

Hicks, Granville, American literary critic and novelist, May 1942, *Obit* Aug 1982

Hicks, Henry D., Oct 1956

Hicks, Louise Day, American congresswoman and municipal official, Mar 1974, *Obit* June 2004

Hidalgo, David, American guitarist, singer and accordionist, Oct 2005

Higdon, Jennifer, Classical composer, Jan 2013

Higgins, Andrew Jackson, shipbuilding executive, May 1943, *Obit* Sept 1952

Higgins, Chester, American photojournalist, June 2002

Higgins, Daniel Paul, Yrbk 1950, *Obit* Mar 1954

Higgins, F. R., Irish poet, *Obit* Mar 1941

Higgins, Jack, American editorial cartoonist, Feb 2007

Higgins, Marguerite, journalist, June 1951, *Obit* Feb 1966

Higginson, William, *Obit* Sept 1943

Higgs, Peter, British physicist, Feb 2009

Highet, Gilbert, Scottish-American classicist, Sept 1964, *Obit* Mar 1978

Highsmith, Patricia, American mystery novelist, Jan 1990, *Obit* Apr 1995

Hightower, John B., July 1970, *Obit* Yrbk 2013

Hightower, John M., journalist, Nov 1952, *Obit* Apr 1987

Higinbotham, William A., physicist, Feb 1947, *Obit* Jan 1995

Higley, Harvey V., government official, Oct 1956, *Obit* Jan 1987

Hildebrand, Joel Henry, American chemist, Feb 1955, *Obit* July 1983

Hildegarde, American singer, Nov 1944, *Obit* Yrbk 2005

Hildred, William P., Apr 1956

Hildreth, Horace Augustus, governor, Oct 1948, *Obit* July 1988

Hilfiger, Tommy, American fashion designer, Apr 1996

Hill, Abram, theatrical director, producer and dramatist, Aug 1945, *Obit* Nov 1986

Hill, Andrew, American jazz pianist and composer, Apr 2004, *Obit* Yrbk 2007

Hill, Anita, American lawyer, Sept 1995

Hill, Arthur, Canadian actor, Mar 1977, *Obit* Yrbk 2007

Hill, Arthur M., Oct 1948, *Obit* Nov 1972

Hill, Benny, English comedian, Feb 1983, *Obit* June 1992

Hill, Billy, *Obit* Feb 1941

Hill, David G., Apr 1960

Hill, Dule, American actor, July 2003

Hill, Edwin Conger, journalist, Sept 1940, *Obit* Apr 1957

Hill, Faith, American country singer, Mar 2001

Hill, Frank Pierce, librarian, *Obit* Oct 1941

Hill, George Roy, American motion picture director, Apr 1977, *Obit* June 2003

Hill, George Washington, June 1946

Hill, Graham, English automobile racing driver, July 1973, *Obit* Jan 1976

Hill, Grant, American basketball player, Jan 2002

Hill, Harry W., American admiral, July 1950, *Obit* Sept 1971

Hill, Helen, American children's author and illustrator, *Obit* May 1942

Hill, Herbert, American civil rights leader, Sept 1970, *Obit* Yrbk 2004

Hill, Howard Copeland, *Obit* Aug 1940

Hill, J. B. P. Clayton, *Obit* July 1941

Hill, Julia, American environmentalist, Apr 2000

Hill, Justina Hamilton, Apr 1941

Hill, Lister, American senator, Oct 1943, *Obit* Feb 1985

Hill, Patty Smith, American educator, *Obit* June 1946

Hill, Robert C., American diplomat, Jan 1959, *Obit* Feb 1979

Hill, Robert Thomas, geologist, *Obit* Sept 1941

Hill, William S., Mar 1955, *Obit* Nov 1972

Hillary, Edmund, New Zealand mountaineer, Oct 1954, Jan 2002, *Obit* Yrbk 2008

Hilldring, John H., American general, Apr 1947

Hilleboe, Herman E., June 1955, *Obit* June 1974

Hillenburg, Stephen, American animator and television scriptwriter, Apr 2003

Hillenkoetter, Roscoe H., American CIA director and admiral, Jan 1950, *Obit* Aug 1982

Hiller, Stanley, American aircraft industry executive and business turnaround expert, Nov 1974, *Obit* Yrbk 2006

Hiller, Wendy, English actress, Oct 1941, *Obit* Yrbk 2003

Hillerman, Tony, American mystery novelist, Jan 1992, *Obit* Yrbk 2008

Hillings, Patrick J., congressman, Oct 1957, *Obit* Sept 1994

Hillis, Daniel, American computer scientist, Feb 1995

Hillis, Margaret, choral conductor, Feb 1956, *Obit* Apr 1998

Hillman, Sidney, American labor leader, July 1940, *Obit* July 1946

Hills, Carla Anderson, American Secretary of housing and urban development and trade representative, Nov 1975, Mar 1993

Hillyer, Robert Silliman, poet, July 1940, *Obit* Feb 1962

Hilsberg, Alexander, Oct 1953, *Obit* Nov 1961

Hilsman, Roger, American educator and government official, Mar 1964

Hilton, Conrad N., American hotel executive, Yrbk 1949, *Obit* Mar 1979

Hilton, Frank C., July 1952

Hilton, James, English novelist, Sept 1942, *Obit* Feb 1955

Himmelfarb, Gertrude, historian, May 1985

Himmler, Heinrich, German Nazi leader, June 1941, *Obit* June 1945

Hinckley, Robert C., *Obit* July 1941

Hindemith, Paul, German composer, Oct 1941, *Obit* Feb 1964

Hines, Duncan, restaurant critic and publisher, May 1946, *Obit* May 1959

Hines, Earl, pianist and band leader, Mar 1967, *Obit* June 1983

Hines, Frank T., Apr 1944, *Obit* May 1960

Hines, Gregory, American dancer and actor, July 1985, *Obit* Yrbk 2003

Hines, Jerome, American opera singer, Feb 1963, *Obit* June 2003

Hines, John Elbridge, bishop, May 1968, *Obit* Oct 1997

Hingle, Pat, American actor, Apr 1965, *Obit* Yrbk 2009

Hingson, Robert A., anesthesiologist and public health expert, June 1943, *Obit* Jan 1997

Hingson, Robert A.; Edwards, Waldo B.; and Southworth, James L., June 1943

Hinojosa, Maria, American radio reporter and memoirist, Feb 2001

Hinrichs, Gustav, German-American conductor, *Obit* May 1942

Hinshaw, Carl, American congressman, July 1951, *Obit* Oct 1956

Hinshelwood, Cyril Norman, British chemist, Apr 1957, *Obit* Yrbk 1967

Hinsley, Arthur, *Obit* Apr 1943

Hinton of Bankside, Christopher Hinton, British nuclear engineer, June 1957

Hirai, Kazuo, Japanese video game industry executive, Jan 2007

Hirohito, Jan 1942, Mar 1976, *Obit* Feb 1989

Hirsch, I. Seth, *Obit* May 1942

Hirsch, John, Canadian theatrical director, Apr 1984, *Obit* Oct 1989

Hirsch, Judd, actor, Mar 1984

Hirschfeld, Al, American caricaturist, Jan 1971, *Obit* July 2003

Hirschfelder, Joseph Oakland, physicist, Yrbk 1950, *Obit* May 1990

Hirschhorn, Thomas, Swiss installation artist, Sept 2009

Hirshfield, Morris, painter, Sept 1943

Hirshhorn, Joseph H., American stockbroker, mining executive and art collector, Nov 1966, *Obit* Oct 1981

Hirsi Ali, Ayaan, Somali-Dutch feminist and member of Parliament, Jan 2003

Hirst, Damien, English artist, Aug 2013

Hirst, Hugo, English manufacturing executive, Nov 1941, *Obit* Mar 1943

Hirt, Al, trumpet player, Feb 1967, *Obit* July 1999

Hiss, Alger, American diplomat and lawyer, Feb 1947, *Obit* Jan 1997

Hitch, Charles J., American college president, Nov 1970, *Obit* Nov 1995

Hitchcock, Alfred, Anglo-American motion picture director, Mar 1941, July 1960, *Obit* June 1980

Hitchcock, Charles B., Oct 1954, *Obit* May 1969

Hitchcock, Thomas, polo player, *Obit* June 1944

Hitchens, Christopher, British journalist, Mar 1999, *Obit* Yrbk 2012

Hite, Shere, author and feminist, Feb 1988

Hitler, Adolf, German dictator, Mar 1942, *Obit* Jan 1957

Hitti, Philip Khuri, June 1947, *Obit* Feb 1979

Hitz, Ralph, *Obit* Jan 1940

Hjejle, Iben, Danish actress, Jan 2003

Ho, Chi Minh, Vietnamese communist leader, Nov 1949, Oct 1966, *Obit* Nov 1969

Ho, David D., American physician, June 1997

Ho, Stanley, Chinese gambling casino owner, Jan 2003

Ho, Ying-Chin, Taiwanese general, Oct 1942, *Obit* Jan 1988

Hoad, Lew, Australian tennis player, Sept 1956, *Obit* Sept 1994

Hoagland, Edward, American novelist, essayist and travel writer, Sept 1982

Hoagland, Tony, American poet, May 2011

Hobbs, Leonard S., Oct 1954, *Obit* Jan 1978

Hobby, Oveta Culp, American Secretary of health, education and welfare, July 1942, Feb 1953, *Obit* Oct 1995

Hobsbawm, E. J., British historian, Jan 2003, *Obit* Yrbk 2012

Hobson Pilot, Ann, American harpist, May 2003

Hobson, John Atkinson, British economist and journalist, *Obit* Apr 1940

Hobson, Laura Keane Zametkin, author, Sept 1947, *Obit* Apr 1986

Hobson, Mellody, American investment manager, Aug 2005

Hoch, Danny, American actor, Oct 1999

Hochhuth, Rolf, German dramatist, Oct 1976

Hockenberry, John, radio and television reporter, Oct 1996

Hockfield, Susan, American neurobiologist and college president, Apr 2008

Hocking, William Ernest, American philosopher, Mar 1962, *Obit* July 1966

Hockney, David, English painter, July 1972

Hodel, Donald Paul, American organization official and Secretary of the interior, June 1987

Hodes, Henry I., American general, Feb 1959, *Obit* Apr 1962

Hodge, John R., June 1945, *Obit* Jan 1964

Hodges, Courtney H., May 1941, *Obit* Feb 1966

Hodges, Gil, American baseball player and manager, Oct 1962, *Obit* May 1972

Hodges, Luther Hartwell, American Secretary of commerce and governor, July 1956, *Obit* Nov 1974

Hodgkin, Howard, English painter, May 1991

Hodgson, James D., American aircraft industry executive and Secretary of labor, Nov 1970, *Obit* Yrbk 2013

Hodgson, Joseph V., American state attorney general and United Nations official, June 1945

Hodgson, W. R., May 1946, *Obit* Apr 1958

Hodson, William, *Obit* Mar 1943

Hodza, Milan, *Obit* Aug 1944

Hoegh, Leo A., governor and civil defense official, July 1956, *Obit* Yrbk 2000

Hoellering, Franz, Oct 1940

Hoey, Clyde R., American governor and senator, Oct 1949, *Obit* July 1954

Hoey, Jane M., American social worker and government official, Sept 1950

Hoff, Philip H., American governor, Sept 1963

Hoffa, Jimmy, American labor leader, May 1972, *Obit* Mar 1983

Hoffa, Jimmy P., American labor leader, July 1999

Hoffer, Eric, American philosopher and essayist, Mar 1965, *Obit* July 1983

Hoffman, Abbie, American political activist, Apr 1981, *Obit* June 1989

Hoffman, Alice, American novelist, Sept 1992

Hoffman, Anna Rosenberg, American public relations executive and government official, Jan 1943, Jan 1951, *Obit* July 1983

Hoffman, Clare Eugene, American congressman, Mar 1949, *Obit* Jan 1968

Hoffman, Dustin, American actor, Yrbk 1969, Jan 1996

Hoffman, Johannes, Apr 1950

Hoffman, Joseph G., May 1958, *Obit* Jan 1975

Hoffman, Malvina, American sculptor, Yrbk 1940, *Obit* Sept 1966

Hoffman, Paul G., American automobile executive, Feb 1946, *Obit* Nov 1974

Hoffman, Philip Seymour, American actor, May 2001

Hofmann, Hans, German-American painter, Oct 1958, *Obit* Mar 1966

Hofmann, Klaus Heinrich, biochemist, Apr 1961

Hofstadter, Richard, American historian, Oct 1956, *Obit* Yrbk 1970

Hofstadter, Robert, American physicist, Oct 1962, *Obit* Jan 1991

Hogan, Ben, American golfer, Oct 1948, *Obit* Oct 1997

Hogan, Frank S., American district attorney, Sept 1953, *Obit* May 1974

Hogan, Hulk, American wrestler, Nov 1998

Hogan, Paul, Australian comedian, Aug 1987

Hogben, Lancelot, English physiologist and zoologist, Yrbk 1941, *Obit* Jan 1984

Hoge, James F., American newspaper executive and magazine editor, Apr 1998

Hoggart, Richard, English social and cultural critic, Oct 1963

Hogwood, Christopher, English conductor, harpsichordist and musicologist, July 1985

Hohenlohe-Waldenburg-Schillin gsfurst, Stephanie Juliana, Austro-Hungarian princess, Jan 1940

Hoiby, Lee, American composer, Mar 1987, *Obit* Yrbk 2011

Holaday, William M., May 1958

Holaday, William Perry, *Obit* Mar 1946

Holberg, Ruth Langland, Yrbk 1949

Holbrook, Hal, American actor, May 1961

Holbrook, Sabra, author, Nov 1948

Holbrooke, Richard, American diplomat, Oct 1998, *Obit* Yrbk 2011

Holcomb, Thomas, July 1942, *Obit* July 1965

Hold Steady (Musical group), Sept 2010

Holden, Betsy, American food industry executive, July 2003

Holden, Louis Edward, *Obit* June 1942

Holden, William, actor, June 1954, *Obit* Jan 1982

Holder, Eric, American Attorney general, Mar 2009

Holder, Geoffrey, Trinidadian dancer and choreographer, Oct 1957

Holdsclaw, Chamique, American basketball player, Feb 2006

Holenstein, Thomas, May 1958, *Obit* Jan 1963

Holifield, Chet, American congressman, Oct 1955, *Obit* Apr 1995

Holl, Steven, American architect, July 2004

Holladay, Wilhelmina Cole, art collector, Oct 1987

Holland, Agnieszka, Polish film director and screenwriter, Jan 1998

Holland, Charles Thurstan, *Obit* Mar 1941

Holland, Dave, English jazz bassist, Mar 2003

Holland, Kenneth, educator, Mar 1952, *Obit* Feb 1978

Holland, Sidney, New Zealand prime minister, Jan 1950, *Obit* Nov 1961

Holland, Spessard L., American governor and senator, Feb 1950, *Obit* Yrbk 1971

Hollande, Fran‡ois, French political leader, May 2013

Hollander, Jacob Harry, *Obit* Sept 1940

Hollander, John, philologist and poet, Sept 1991, *Obit* Yrbk 2013

Hollander, Robert, American literary critic, translator and poet, Sept 2006

Hollenbeck, Don, American television newscaster, Feb 1951, *Obit* Sept 1954

Holley, Edward G., American librarian and college dean, June 1974

Holley, Robert William, American biochemist, Jan 1967, *Obit* Apr 1993

Holliday, Jennifer, American singer, June 1983

Holliday, Judy, actress, Apr 1951, *Obit* July 1965

Holliger, Heinz, Swiss oboist, Jan 1987

Hollings, Ernest F., American senator, July 1982

Hollister, John B., American lawyer, congressman and government official, Oct 1955

Hollomon, J. Herbert, college president and government official, Mar 1964, *Obit* Aug 1985

Holloway, James, American admiral, Jan 1947

Holloway, Stanley, Feb 1963, *Obit* Mar 1982

Holm, Celeste, American actress, Apr 1944, *Obit* Yrbk 2012

Holm, Georg, Icelandic bassist, Jan 2003

Holm, Hanya, German-American dancer and choreographer, July 1954, *Obit* Jan 1993

Holm, Ian, English actor, Mar 2002

Holman, Eugene, May 1948, *Obit* Oct 1962

Holmes, Burton, May 1944, *Obit* Oct 1958

Holmes, D. Brainerd, aerospace industry executive and NASA official, Mar 1963, *Obit* Yrbk 2013

Holmes, Jesse Herman, *Obit* July 1942

Holmes, John Haynes, American clergyman, theologian and social reformer, Jan 1941, *Obit* May 1964

Holmes, Julius C., Feb 1945, *Obit* Sept 1968

Holmes, Kelly, British runner, Jan 2004

Holmes, Larry, American boxer, Aug 1981

Holmes, Phillips, *Obit* Oct 1942

Holmes, Robert D., July 1958

Holmgren, Mike, American football coach, Oct 2000

Holroyd, Michael, English biographer, Mar 1989

Holsti, Rudolf, *Obit* Sept 1945

Holt, Andrew David, college president, Nov 1949, *Obit* Sept 1987

Holt, Arthur E., *Obit* Mar 1942

Holt, Cooper T., July 1957

Holt, Hamilton, periodical editor, pacifist and college president, Yrbk 1947, *Obit* May 1951

Holt, Harold, Australian prime minister, Oct 1966, *Obit* Feb 1968

Holt, Isabella, Yrbk 1956, *Obit* May 1962

Holt, John Caldwell, American educator, June 1981, *Obit* Nov 1985

Holt, Rackham, Apr 1944

Holton, A. Linwood, American lawyer and governor, Feb 1971

Holtz, Jackson J., Mar 1950

Holtz, Lou, American football coach and sportscaster, June 1989

Holtzman, Elizabeth, American congresswoman and municipal official, Nov 1973

Holyfield, Evander, American boxer, Aug 1993

Holyoake, Keith Jacka, New Zealand prime minister, Feb 1963, *Obit* Feb 1984

Holzen, Heinz von, Swiss chef and restaurateur, Jan 2002

Holzer, Jenny, American artist, June 1990

Home of the Hirsel, Alexander Frederick Douglas-Home, British prime minister, Feb 1958, *Obit* Jan 1996

Homer, Arthur B., July 1952, *Obit* Sept 1972

Honderich, Ted, Canadian philosopher, Feb 2009

Hondros, Chris, American photojournalist, Nov 2004, *Obit* Yrbk 2011

Honecker, Erich, East German communist leader, Apr 1972, *Obit* July 1994

Honegger, Arthur, Swiss composer, Apr 1941, *Obit* Feb 1956

Honeywell, Annette, July 1953

Honeywell, Harry E., *Obit* Jan 1940

Hong, Hei-Kyung, Korean opera singer, Nov 2003

Hong, Sang-Soo, Korean film director, Jan 2006

Hong, Seok Chon, Korean actor, Jan 2004

Honjo, Shigeru, *Obit* Jan 1946

Honkala, Cheri, American social activist, July 2012

Hoo, Victor, Mar 1947, *Obit* July 1972

Hood, Clifford F., Apr 1953, *Obit* Jan 1979

Hood, Gavin, South African motion picture director, Jan 2006

Hook, Peter, British bassist and singer, Jan 2006

Hook, Sidney, American philosopher, Oct 1952, Apr 1988, *Obit* Sept 1989

Hooker, John Lee, American singer and guitarist, Nov 1992, *Obit* Sept 2001

Hooks, Bell, American feminist and social critic, Apr 1995

Hooks, Benjamin L., American civil rights activist, lawyer and judge, Apr 1978, *Obit* Yrbk 2010

Hooks, Robert, Mar 1970

Hoop Scheffer, Jaap de, Dutch diplomat and NATO official, Jan 2003

Hooper, C. E., Apr 1947, *Obit* Feb 1955

Hooper, Franklin Henry, *Obit* Oct 1940

Hoopes, Darlington, socialist leader, Sept 1952, *Obit* Nov 1989

Hooton, Earnest Albert, American anthropologist, Yrbk 1940, *Obit* June 1954

Hoover, Herbert, American president, Mar 1943, *Obit* Jan 1965

Hoover, Herbert Clark, American petroleum engineer, diplomat and son of President Herbert Hoover, Oct 1954, *Obit* Sept 1969

Hoover, J. Edgar, American FBI director, Feb 1940, May 1950, *Obit* June 1972

Hoover, Lou Henry, wife of American president Herbert Hoover, *Obit* Feb 1944

Hope, Bob, American comedian and actor, June 1941, Oct 1953, *Obit* Yrbk 2003

Hope, Clifford R., American congressman, May 1953, *Obit* July 1970

Hope, Stanley C., May 1959, *Obit* Oct 1982

Hopkins, Alfred, *Obit* July 1941

Hopkins, Anthony, Welsh-American actor, Feb 1980, Mar 1997

Hopkins, Arthur M., theatrical producer and director, June 1947, *Obit* Apr 1950

Hopkins, Bernard, American boxer, Apr 2002

Hopkins, Ernest Martin, Oct 1944, *Obit* Oct 1964

Hopkins, Harry Lloyd, American diplomat, Feb 1941, *Obit* Mar 1946

Hopkins, John Jay, Mar 1954, *Obit* July 1957

Hopkins, Louis Bertram, *Obit* Sept 1940

Hopkins, Nancy, American molecular biologist, May 2002

Hopkins, Nevil Monroe, *Obit* May 1945

Hopkins, Sarah, Australian composer and cellist, Jan 2006

Hoppe, Willie, June 1947, *Obit* Apr 1959

Hoppenot, Henri, Mar 1944

Hopper, Dennis, American actor and director, Aug 1987, *Obit* Yrbk 2010

Hopper, Edward, American painter, Yrbk 1950, *Obit* July 1967

Hopper, Hedda, American gossip columnist, Nov 1942, *Obit* Mar 1966

Hoppus, Mark, American singer and bassist, Aug 2002

Horder, Thomas Jeeves Horder, English physician, July 1944, *Obit* Oct 1955

Hore-Belisha, Leslie
Hore-Belisha, British political
leader, July 1941, *Obit* May
1957
Horgan, Paul, author, Feb 1971,
Obit May 1995
Horgan, Stephen H., inventor,
Obit Oct 1941
Horlick, William, *Obit* Apr 1940
Hormel, James C., lawyer,
philanthropist and diplomat,
Oct 1999
Hormel, Jay C., July 1946, *Obit*
Oct 1954
Horn, Carl von, Swedish
general, Nov 1967
Horn, Roy, German magician
and animal trainer, Jan 1998
Hornblow, Arthur, *Obit* June
1942
Horne, Charles F., *Obit* Nov
1942
Horne, Gerald, American
historian and biographer, Sept
2011
Horne, John E., government
official, Yrbk 1952, *Obit* Apr
1985
Horne, Lena, American singer,
June 1944, Nov 1985, *Obit*
Aug 2010
Horne, Marilyn, American opera
singer, July 1967
Horner, H. M., aircraft executive,
Oct 1955, *Obit* July 1983
Horner, Henry, American
governor, *Obit* Nov 1940
Horner, James, composer, Mar
1997
Horner, John R., American
paleontologist, Sept 1992
Horner, Matina, educator, July
1973
Horney, Karen,
German-American
psychoanalyst, Aug 1941, *Obit*
Jan 1953
Hornig, Donald F., chemist,
university president and
presidential adviser, May
1964, *Obit* Yrbk 2013
Hornsby, Rogers, American
baseball player and manager,
Sept 1952, *Obit* Feb 1963
Hornung, Paul, American
football player and
sportscaster, Feb 1963
Horowitz, Vladimir,
Russian-American pianist,
Sept 1943, Mar 1966, *Obit* Jan
1990

Horrocks, Brian, British general,
Jan 1945, *Obit* Mar 1985
Horsbrugh, Florence Gertrude
Horsbrugh, British cabinet
member, Feb 1952, *Obit* Mar
1970
Horsey, David, American
political cartoonist, Sept 2008
Horsfall, Frank L., American
virologist, Mar 1941, Jan
1961, *Obit* Apr 1971
Horst, photographer, June 1992,
Obit Mar 2000
Horthy, Istvan, *Obit* Oct 1942
Horthy, Miklos, Hungarian
admiral and regent, Oct 1940,
Obit Apr 1957
Horton, Edward Everett,
American actor, Yrbk 1946,
Obit Nov 1970
Horton, Mildred McAfee, college
president and naval officer,
Sept 1942, *Obit* Jan 1995
Horwich, Frances, American
educator, Oct 1953, *Obit* Oct
2001
Horwood, William T. F., *Obit* Feb
1944
Hoshino, Naoki, Nov 1940
Hoskins, Bob, English actor,
Sept 1990
Hoskins, Lewis M., Sept 1950
Hosmer, Craig, congressman,
May 1958, *Obit* Mar 1983
Hosokawa, Morihiro, Japanese
prime minister, May 1994
Hosseini, Khaled,
Afghan-American physician
and novelist, July 2013
Hottel, Althea Kratz, Oct 1948
Hou, Hsiao-hsien, Taiwanese
film director, July 1999
Houellebecq, Michel, French
novelist and poet, Jan 2002
Hough, Henry Hughes, *Obit* Oct
1943
Houghton, Alanson Bigelow,
glass industry executive and
diplomat, *Obit* Nov 1941
Houghton, Amory, American
glass industry executive and
diplomat, Jan 1947, *Obit* Apr
1981
Houghton, Dorothy Deemer,
Sept 1950
Houghton, John Theodore,
British climatologist, Jan 2004
Houk, Ralph, American baseball
manager, July 1962, *Obit* Yrbk
2010
Houle, Cyril Orvin, May 1962

Hounsfield, Godfrey Newbold,
British electronics engineer,
Mar 1980, *Obit* Yrbk 2004
Hounsou, Djimon, Beninese
model and actor, Aug 2004
Houphouet-Boigny, Felix, Ivorian
president, Oct 1958, July
1991, *Obit* Feb 1994
Hours, Madeleine, Apr 1961
Houseman, John, theatrical
director, producer and actor,
July 1959, Apr 1984, *Obit* Jan
1989
Houser, Theodore V., Mar 1957,
Obit Feb 1964
Houssay, Bernardo Alberto,
Argentine physiologist, Jan
1948, *Obit* Nov 1971
Houston, Allan, American
basketball player, Nov 2003
Houston, Andrew Jackson, *Obit*
Aug 1941
Houston, Charles Hamilton,
American lawyer and civil
rights leader, July 1948, *Obit*
June 1950
Houston, David Franklin,
secretary of agriculture and
the treasury, *Obit* Oct 1940
Houston, Drew, American online
file hosting service executive,
May 2012
Houston, James A., Canadian
artist, novelist and children's
author, July 1987, *Obit* Yrbk
2005
Houston, Robert Griffith,
American congressman and
newspaper publisher, *Obit* Mar
1946
Houston, Whitney, American
singer and actress, Nov 1986,
Obit Yrbk 2012
Houtte, Jean van, Mar 1952
Hovde, Bryn J., Jan 1946, *Obit*
Oct 1954
Hovey, Otis Ellis, *Obit* June
1941
Hovhaness, Alan, American
composer, Apr 1965, *Obit* Oct
2000
Hoving, Thomas, American
museum director and
periodical editor, Apr 1967,
Obit Yrbk 2010
Hoving, Walter, department
store executive, Sept 1946,
Obit Feb 1990
Howar, Barbara, columnist and
television reporter, Aug 1989

Howard, Alice Sturtevant, *Obit* Nov 1945

Howard, Bart B., Jan 1940, *Obit* Apr 1941

Howard, Cordelia, actress, *Obit* Oct 1941

Howard, Elizabeth, Yrbk 1951

Howard, Elston, American baseball player and coach, Apr 1964, *Obit* Feb 1981

Howard, Frank, American baseball player, manager and coach, Jan 1972

Howard, John Winston, Australian prime minister, Mar 1999

Howard, Katherine G., American government official, July 1953

Howard, Leslie, English actor, *Obit* July 1943

Howard, Ron, American actor and film director, Jan 1979, Aug 1995

Howard, Roy Wilson, news agency and newspaper executive, Nov 1940, *Obit* Jan 1965

Howard, Ryan, American baseball player, July 2007

Howard, Terrence, American actor, June 2007

Howard, Tim, American soccer player, Sept 2005

Howard, Trevor, English actor, July 1964, *Obit* Feb 1988

Howe, C. D., American construction engineer, Sept 1945, *Obit* Feb 1961

Howe, Frederic Clemson, lawyer and reformer, *Obit* Sept 1940

Howe, Geoffrey, British cabinet member, Oct 1980

Howe, Gordie, Canadian hockey player, Mar 1962

Howe, Harold, American educator, Nov 1967, *Obit* Yrbk 2003

Howe, Harrison E., *Obit* Feb 1943

Howe, Helen Huntington, author and monologist, Yrbk 1954, *Obit* Mar 1975

Howe, Irving, American literary critic and editor, Apr 1978, *Obit* July 1993

Howe, James Wong, cinematographer, Feb 1943, *Obit* Sept 1976

Howe, Quincy, American journalist, Nov 1940, *Obit* Apr 1977

Howe, Samuel B., *Obit* Apr 1941

Howe, Tina, American dramatist, Jan 1990

Howell, Charles R., Feb 1954, *Obit* Sept 1973

Howell, Wallace E., meteorologist, July 1950, *Obit* Sept 1999

Howell, William Henry, *Obit* Mar 1945

Howland, Ben, American basketball coach, June 2007

Howlett, Liam, British DJ, Oct 2009

Howorth, Lucy Somerville, American lawyer and feminist, Oct 1951, *Obit* Nov 1997

Howrey, Edward F., July 1953

Hoxha, Enver, Albanian communist leader, Jan 1950, *Obit* June 1985

Hoxie, Charles A., *Obit* Yrbk 1941

Hoyer, Steny H., American congressman, Mar 2004

Hoyle, Fred, English astronomer and science fiction writer, Apr 1960, *Obit* Jan 2002

Hoyt, Palmer, American newspaper editor and publisher, Sept 1943, *Obit* Aug 1979

Hrawi, Elias, Lebanese president, Feb 1992, *Obit* Yrbk 2006

Hrdlicka, Ales, anthropologist and paleontologist, Nov 1941, *Obit* Oct 1943

Hrdy, Sarah Blaffer, American primatologist and anthropologist, June 2000

Hruska, Roman Lee, American senator, July 1956, *Obit* July 1999

Hsiung, S.-F, July 1942

Hu Jia, Chinese AIDS activist, Jan 2007

Hu Jintao, Chinese president, Jan 2003

Hu Yaobang, Chinese communist leader, Nov 1983, *Obit* June 1989

Hu, Shih, Chinese poet, diplomat and literary critic, Feb 1942, *Obit* Apr 1962

Hua Guofeng, Chinese prime minister, Mar 1977, *Obit* Yrbk 2008

Hubbard, Bernard, July 1943, *Obit* July 1962

Hubbard, Margaret Ann, American young adult mystery writer, Yrbk 1958

Hubeny, Maximilian J., *Obit* Sept 1942

Huberman, Bronislaw, Polish violinist, July 1941, *Obit* July 1947

Huck, Arthur, Feb 1957, *Obit* Mar 1973

Huckabee, Mike, American talk show host and former governor, Nov 2005

Huckel, Oliver, *Obit* Jan 1940

Huddleston, Trevor, South African archbishop, Oct 1963, *Obit* July 1998

Hudleston, Edmund C., May 1951

Hudlin, Reginald, American film and television director, May 1999

Hudlin, Warrington, motion picture producer, May 1999

Hudlin, Warrington; and Hudlin, Reginald, May 1999

Hudson, C. W., *Obit* June 1943

Hudson, Charles Lowell, medical association executive and physician, Apr 1967, *Obit* Nov 1992

Hudson, Harold W., *Obit* Mar 1943

Hudson, Henrietta, *Obit* May 1942

Hudson, Jennifer, American singer and actress, May 2007

Hudson, Manley O., June 1944, *Obit* June 1960

Hudson, Robert S. Hudson, Nov 1942, *Obit* Apr 1957

Hudson, Rock, American actor, Oct 1961, *Obit* Nov 1985

Huebner, Clarence R., Oct 1949, *Obit* Nov 1972

Huebner, Robert J., epidemiologist, Sept 1968, *Obit* Nov 1998

Huerta, Dolores, American labor leader, Nov 1997

Huffington, Arianna, Greek-American political adviser and commentator, July 1998

Hufstedler, Shirley M., American lawyer and Secretary of education, May 1980

Huggins, Charles B., American surgeon, Feb 1965, *Obit* Mar 1997

Hughes, Barnard, American actor, Sept 1981, *Obit* Yrbk 2006

Hughes, Cathy, American radio executive, Feb 2000

Hughes, Charles Evans, American Supreme Court justice, July 1941, *Obit* Oct 1948

Hughes, Edward Everett, *Obit* Jan 1940

Hughes, Emmet John, American journalist and presidential speechwriter and adviser, Jan 1964, *Obit* Nov 1982

Hughes, Harold E., American governor and senator, June 1963, *Obit* Jan 1997

Hughes, Hatcher, American dramatist, *Obit* Nov 1945

Hughes, Howard, American airline, aircraft and motion picture executive, Apr 1941, *Obit* May 1976

Hughes, John, American film director, producer and screenwriter, Sept 1991, *Obit* Yrbk 2009

Hughes, Karen, American diplomat and presidential adviser, Oct 2001

Hughes, Langston, American poet, novelist, short story writer and playwright, Oct 1940, *Obit* July 1967

Hughes, Paul, Yrbk 1943

Hughes, R. O., Oct 1950

Hughes, Richard J., American governor and judge, July 1962, *Obit* Feb 1993

Hughes, Robert, Australian art critic, May 1987, *Obit* Yrbk 2012

Hughes, Rowland R., American government official, Feb 1956, *Obit* June 1957

Hughes, Sarah T., American judge, Nov 1950, *Obit* July 1985

Hughes, Ted, English poet, June 1979, *Obit* Jan 1999

Hughes, Toni, May 1941

Hughley, D. L., American comedian, Mar 2000

Hugo, Chad, American record producer, singer and songwriter, May 2004

Huizenga, H. Wayne, American video chain and baseball executive, Jan 1995

Hulcy, Dechard A., Sept 1951

Hull, Bobby, Canadian hockey player, Oct 1966

Hull, Brett, Canadian hockey player, Feb 1992

Hull, Cordell, American Secretary of state, Aug 1940, *Obit* Oct 1955

Hull, Helen R., author, May 1940, *Obit* Sept 1971

Hull, Jane Dee, American governor, Feb 2002

Hull, John Adley, *Obit* June 1944

Hull, John E., Apr 1954

Hull, Josephine, Oct 1953, *Obit* May 1957

Hull, William Edgar, *Obit* July 1942

Humbard, Rex, American evangelist, Sept 1972, *Obit* Yrbk 2008

Hume, Edgar Erskine, Aug 1944, *Obit* Mar 1952

Hume, T. C., *Obit* Yrbk 1943

Humphrey, Doris, American dancer and choreographer, Apr 1942, *Obit* Mar 1959

Humphrey, Doris; and Weidman, Charles, Apr 1942

Humphrey, George Magoffin, American Secretary of the treasury, Feb 1953, *Obit* Mar 1970

Humphrey, Helen F., Nov 1952, *Obit* Oct 1963

Humphrey, Hubert Horatio, American vice-president, July 1949, Apr 1966, *Obit* Mar 1978

Humphreys, Harry E., Nov 1949, *Obit* Nov 1967

Humphry, Derek, English euthanasia advocate, Mar 1995

Hun Sen, Cambodian prime minister, Apr 1990

Hun, John Gale, *Obit* Nov 1945

Hung Huang, Chinese magazine executive, Jan 2006

Hunicke, Robin, Video game designer and producer, Mar 2012

Hunsaker, Jerome C., aeronautical engineer, Oct 1942, *Obit* Nov 1984

Hunt Lieberson, Lorraine, American opera singer, July 2004, *Obit* Yrbk 2006

Hunt, Bunker, Aug 1980

Hunt, H. L., American petroleum industry executive, Jan 1970, *Obit* Jan 1975

Hunt, Helen, Nov 1996

Hunt, Herold Christian, educator, May 1956, *Obit* Jan 1977

Hunt, James B., American governor, June 1993

Hunt, John Hunt, British army officer and mountaineer, Oct 1954, *Obit* Jan 1999

Hunt, John; Hillary, Edmund; and Tenzing, Norgay, Oct 1954

Hunt, Lester C., American senator and governor, Mar 1951, *Obit* Sept 1954

Hunt, Linda, actress, Jan 1988

Hunt, Mabel Leigh, author, Yrbk 1951

Hunt, Swanee, American international relations specialist, Mar 2006

Hunter, Aislinn, Canadian short story writer, poet and novelist, Jan 2002

Hunter, Alberta, singer and songwriter, May 1979, *Obit* Jan 1985

Hunter, Billy, American lawyer and basketball players association executive, Aug 2013

Hunter, Catfish, American baseball player, May 1975, *Obit* Nov 1999

Hunter, Charlie, American jazz guitarist, Nov 2007

Hunter, Croil, American airline executive, July 1951, *Obit* Oct 1970

Hunter, Dard, American papermaker and typographer, Sept 1960, *Obit* Mar 1966

Hunter, Evan, American novelist, short story writer and dramatist, Yrbk 1956, *Obit* Yrbk 2005

Hunter, Glenn, American actor, *Obit* Mar 1946

Hunter, Holly, American actress, July 1994

Hunter, Kermit, dramatist, May 1959, *Obit* Sept 2001

Hunter, Kim, American actress, May 1952, *Obit* Yrbk 2002

Hunter, Ross, motion picture producer, Yrbk 1967, *Obit* May 1996

Hunter-Gault, Charlayne, American television newscaster, Apr 1987

Hunthausen, Raymond G., archbishop, Aug 1987

Huntington, Anna Hyatt, American sculptor, Oct 1953, *Obit* Yrbk 1973

Huntley, Chet, American television news anchor, Oct 1956, *Obit* May 1974

Huntsman, Jr., Jon, American diplomat, May 2012

Huntziger, Charles, French general, Yrbk 1941, *Obit* Yrbk 1941

Huppert, Isabelle, French actress, Nov 1981

Hurd, Douglas, British cabinet member, Feb 1990

Hurd, Peter, American painter, Oct 1957, *Obit* Sept 1984

Hurd-Mead, Kate Campbell, *Obit* Feb 1941

Hurley, Chad, American video sharing web site founder, Jan 2007

Hurley, Charles F., American governor, *Obit* May 1946

Hurley, Laurel, American opera singer, June 1957

Hurley, Patrick J., American Secretary of war and diplomat, Nov 1944, *Obit* Sept 1963

Hurley, Roy T., American aircraft industry executive, June 1955, *Obit* Yrbk 1971

Hurok, Sol, concert manager, Sept 1941, Apr 1956, *Obit* Apr 1974

Hurston, Zora Neale, American novelist and folklorist, May 1942, *Obit* Apr 1960

Hurt, John, British actor, Jan 1982

Hurt, William, American actor, May 1986

Husain, Maqbul Fida, Indian painter, Jan 2006, *Obit* Yrbk 2011

Husain, Mishal, British television news anchor, Jan 2004

Husak, Gustav, Czech president, Oct 1971, *Obit* Jan 1992

Husayn, Taha, Egyptian educator, Oct 1953, *Obit* Yrbk 1973

Husing, Ted, sportscaster, June 1942, *Obit* Oct 1962

Hussain, Zakir, Indian percussionist and composer, Jan 2005

Hussein, July 1955, Apr 1986, *Obit* Apr 1999

Hussein, Ahmed, Egyptian diplomat, Mar 1956, *Obit* Feb 1985

Hussein, Saddam, Iraqi president, Sept 1981, Jan 2002, *Obit* Apr 2007

Husted, Marjorie Child, American home economist, June 1949, *Obit* Feb 1987

Huston, Anjelica, American actress, July 1990

Huston, John, American film director and screenwriter, Feb 1949, Mar 1981, *Obit* Oct 1987

Huston, Walter, actor, Feb 1949, *Obit* May 1950

Hutcheson, William Levi, American labor leader, Sept 1943, *Obit* Jan 1954

Hutchins, Robert Maynard, American university president, Yrbk 1940, Feb 1954, *Obit* July 1977

Hutchinson, Paul, American clergyman, magazine editor and writer, Yrbk 1949, *Obit* June 1956

Hutchinson, R. C., English novelist, Nov 1940

Hutchison, Bruce, Canadian journalist, Oct 1956

Hutchison, Kay Bailey, American senator, Sept 1997

Hutchison, Miller Reese, American electrical engineer and inventor, *Obit* Apr 1944

Hutton, Betty, American singer and actress, June 1950, *Obit* Yrbk 2007

Hutton, Lauren, American model and actress, July 1994

Hutton, Maurice, *Obit* May 1940

Hutton, Ruth Wilson, Feb 1948

Huvayda, Amir Abbas, Oct 1971, *Obit* June 1979

Huxley, Julian, British biologist, Aug 1942, Oct 1963, *Obit* Apr 1975

Huxtable, Ada Louise, American architectural critic, Mar 1973, *Obit* Yrbk 2013

Huybers, Peter, American climatologist, Apr 2011

Hvorostovsky, Dmitri, Russian opera singer, Jan 2006

Hwang, David Henry, American dramatist, May 1989

Hwang, Woo Suk, Korean veterinarian, Jan 2006

Hyde, Henry J., American congressman, Oct 1989, *Obit* Yrbk 2008

Hyde, Henry Van Zile, May 1960

Hyde, Karl, British singer, guitarist and songwriter, Nov 2011

Hylton-Foster, Harry, Jan 1961, *Obit* Nov 1965

Hymans, Paul, *Obit* Apr 1941

Hynde, Chrissie, American singer and songwriter, Apr 1993

Hynek, J. Allen, astrophysicist, Yrbk 1968, *Obit* June 1986

Hyvernat, Henri, *Obit* July 1941

H"ller, Carsten, Belgian installation artist, May 2012

I

Iacocca, Lee A., American automobile executive, Oct 1971, Oct 1988

Iakovos, July 1960, *Obit* Yrbk 2005

Ibanez del Campo, Carlos, Chilean president, Yrbk 1952, *Obit* July 1960

Ibarruri, Dolores, Spanish communist leader, June 1967, *Obit* Jan 1990

Ibn Saud, Feb 1943, *Obit* Jan 1954

Ibrahim, Hauwa, Nigerian lawyer and human rights activist, Jan 2004

Ibrahim, Mohamed, Sudanese-British telecommunications executive, Jan 2007

Ibrahim, Saad Eddin, Egyptian sociologist and political dissident, Jan 2003

Icahn, Carl C., American financier, Apr 1986

Ice Cube (Musician), American rapper and actor, Aug 1995

Ice-T, American rapper and actor, Sept 1994

Ickes, Harold L., American Secretary of the interior, July 1941, *Obit* Mar 1952

Idei, Nobuyuki, Japanese electronics industry executive, Mar 1997

Idell, Albert Edward, author, Oct 1943, *Obit* Oct 1958

Idleman, Finis Schuyler, *Obit* May 1941

Idol, Billy, British singer, songwriter and guitarist, Jan 1994

Idris, Jan 1956, *Obit* July 1983

Ifill, Gwen, American television newscaster and moderator, Sept 2005

Iginla, Jarome, Canadian hockey player, Jan 2004

Igleheart, Austin S., Oct 1950

Iglesias Pantin, Santiago, Puerto Rican labor leader, Jan 1940

Iglesias, Enrique, Spanish singer, Apr 1999

Iglesias, Julio, Spanish singer, June 1984

Iglesias, Roberto, Feb 1960

Igoe, Herbert A., *Obit* Apr 1945

Iijima, Sumio, Japanese physicist, Nov 2009

Ikeda, Hayato, Japanese prime minister, May 1961, *Obit* Oct 1965

Ilg, Frances L.; and Ames, Louise, Sept 1956

Ilg, Frances Lillian, pediatrician and educator, Sept 1956, *Obit* Sept 1981

Iliescu, Ion, Romanian president, June 1990

Ilitch, Mike, American fast food chain and baseball executive, Feb 2005

Illia, Arturo Umberto, Argentine president, Jan 1965, *Obit* Mar 1983

Illich, Ivan, American priest and philosopher, Yrbk 1969, *Obit* Yrbk 2003

Illy, Ernesto, Italian coffee company executive, Jan 2002

Ilsley, J. L., Canadian cabinet member and judge, Feb 1948

Im, Yong-Sin, Oct 1947, *Obit* Apr 1977

Imai, Chie, Japanese fur designer, Jan 2003

Imam, Adel, Egyptian actor, Jan 2002

Imamura, Shohei, Japanese motion picture director, Jan 2002, *Obit* CB Int 2006

Iman, Somali model, June 1995

Imlay, L. E., *Obit* Aug 1941

Immelman, Trevor, South African golfer, Oct 2008

Immelt, Jeffrey R., American corporation executive, Feb 2004

Impellitteri, Vincent R., American mayor, Feb 1951, *Obit* Mar 1987

Imus, Don, American radio talk show host, Feb 1996

Ince, Godfrey H., Sept 1943

India.Arie (Singer), American singer, Feb 2002

Indiana, Robert, American painter and sculptor, Mar 1973

Indigo Girls (Musical group), Aug 1998

Infeld, Leopold, May 1941, July 1963, *Obit* Mar 1968

Ingalls, Jeremy, poet, Yrbk 1954, *Obit* July 2000

Inge, William, American dramatist, June 1953, *Obit* July 1973

Ingersoll, Ralph, American journalist, July 1940, *Obit* May 1985

Ingersoll, Raymond Vail, *Obit* Mar 1940

Ingersoll, Royal E., Oct 1942, *Obit* July 1976

Ingles, Harry C., American general, Nov 1947

Inglis, John J., *Obit* Oct 1946

Ingram, Jonas H., Apr 1947, *Obit* Oct 1952

Inkster, Juli, American golfer, Sept 2002

Innaurato, Albert, dramatist, Mar 1988

Innes, Hammond, English novelist, Yrbk 1954

Innis, Roy, American civil rights leader, May 1969

Innocenti, Ferdinando, Feb 1959, *Obit* July 1966

Inonu, Ismet, Turkish president, Mar 1941, Oct 1964, *Obit* Feb 1974

Inose, Naoki, Japanese historian, Jan 2002

Inouye, Daniel K., American senator, May 1960, Sept 1987, *Obit* Yrbk 2013

Inskeep, Steve, American radio reporter, June 2009

Insulza, Jose Miguel, Chilean diplomat and international organization official, Jan 2005

International, Dana, Israeli singer, Jan 2005

Intizam, Nasr Allah, Yrbk 1950

Ionesco, Eugene, French dramatist, Oct 1959, *Obit* June 1994

Ireland, Patricia, American lawyer and feminist, June 1992

Irene, costume designer, June 1946, *Obit* Jan 1963

Irimia, Gabriela, Romanian singer, Jan 2003

Irimia, Monica, Romanian singer, Jan 2003

Irons, Ernest E., Oct 1949, *Obit* Apr 1959

Irons, Jeremy, English actor, Aug 1984

Ironside, H. A., clergyman, Feb 1945, *Obit* Feb 1951

Ironside, William Edmund Ironside, British field marshal, May 1940, *Obit* Nov 1959

Irvan, Ernie, automobile racing driver, July 1998

Irvine, Alexander, Irish-American missionary, actor and dramatist, *Obit* May 1941

Irving, Frederick A., American general, Mar 1951

Irving, John, American novelist, Oct 1979

Irving, Jules, July 1970, *Obit* Sept 1979

Irwin, Bill, American actor and mime, Oct 1987

Irwin, Elisabeth, American educator, *Obit* Yrbk 1942

Irwin, Helen G., Oct 1952

Irwin, Margaret, English author, Yrbk 1946, *Obit* Yrbk 1991

Irwin, Robert, American artist, Jan 1993

Irwin, Robert B., Mar 1948, *Obit* Jan 1952

Irwin, Steve, Australian wildlife conservationist and television personality, Aug 2000, *Obit* Yrbk 2007

Isaacs, George A., Oct 1945

Isaacs, Susan, American novelist, Oct 1993

Isaacson, Walter, American broadcasting executive, Nov 2013

Isaak, Chris, singer, May 1993

Isaias Afwerki, Eritrean president, Jan 2002

Isbin, Sharon, American classical guitarist, Aug 2003

Iselin, Columbus O'Donnell, Nov 1948, *Obit* Feb 1971

Isham, Norman Morrison, *Obit* Feb 1943

Isherwood, Christopher, Anglo-American novelist, Oct 1972, *Obit* Feb 1986

Ishibashi, Tanzan, Mar 1957, *Obit* June 1973

Ishiguro, Kazuo, Japanese-British novelist, Sept 1990

Ishii, Ken, Japanese techno musician, Jan 2002

Ishimoto, Tatsuo, Apr 1956

Ismay, Hastings Lionel Ismay, British general, Apr 1943, *Obit* Feb 1966

Isokoski, Soile, Finnish opera singer, Jan 2006

Isozaki, Arata, Japanese architect, Apr 1988

Israel, Edward L., *Obit* Yrbk 1941

Istaru, Ana, Costa Rican poet, dramatist and actress, Jan 2004

Istomin, Eugene, American pianist, Oct 1977, *Obit* Feb 2004

Italiaander, Rolf, June 1964

Itami, Juzo, Japanese actor and motion picture director, May 1990, *Obit* Mar 1998

Ittner, Martin H., Nov 1942, *Obit* May 1945

Iturbi, Jose, Spanish-American pianist and conductor, Sept 1943, *Obit* Aug 1980

Ive, Jonathan, British industrial designer, Oct 2006, May 2013

Iverson, Ethan, American jazz pianist, Oct 2011

Iverson, Kenneth R., Apr 1951

Ives, Burl, singer and actor, Jan 1946, May 1960, *Obit* June 1995

Ives, Charles Edward, American composer, June 1947, *Obit* July 1954

Ives, David, American dramatist, Feb 2013

Ives, Irving M., American senator, Feb 1948, *Obit* Apr 1962

Ives, James E., *Obit* Feb 1943

Ivey, John E., educator, July 1960, *Obit* Aug 1992

Ivey, Judith, actress, June 1993

Ivey, Susan, American tobacco industry executive, Mar 2010

Ivins, Mike, American bassist, Oct 2002

Ivins, Molly, American columnist, June 2000, *Obit* Yrbk 2007

Ivory, James, American motion picture director, July 1981

Iwata, Satoru, Japanese video game company executive, Jan 2007

Iyengar, B. K. S., Indian yogi, June 2007

Izac, Edouard V. M., American congressman, Yrbk 1945, *Obit* Mar 1990

Izetbegovic, Alija, Bosnian president, Aug 1993, *Obit* June 2004

Izzard, Eddie, British comedian and actor, Jan 2003

J

Ja Rule, American rapper, July 2002

Jaar, Alfredo, Chilean mixed-media and installation artist, Jan 2005

Jabotinsky, Vladimir, Russian Zionist leader, *Obit* Sept 1940

Jacir, Emily, Palestinian artist, Aug 2009

Jack, Homer Alexander, clergyman, pacifist and United Nations official, July 1961, *Obit* Oct 1993

Jack, William S., Mar 1944

Jackman, Hugh, Australian actor, Oct 2003

Jackson Lee, Sheila, American congresswoman, Nov 2008

Jackson, Alan, American country singer, Apr 2004

Jackson, Anne, actress, Sept 1980

Jackson, Bo, American baseball and football player, June 1991

Jackson, C. D., American publishing executive and presidential aide, Oct 1951, *Obit* Nov 1964

Jackson, Charles, novelist and short story writer, May 1944, *Obit* Nov 1968

Jackson, Chevalier, July 1940

Jackson, Daniel Dana, *Obit* Oct 1941

Jackson, Eugene B., June 1961

Jackson, Glenda, English actress and member of Parliament, Yrbk 1971

Jackson, Hal, American disc jockey and radio executive, Oct 2002, *Obit* Yrbk 2012

Jackson, Henry Martin, American senator, Oct 1953, Oct 1979, *Obit* Oct 1983

Jackson, Janet, American singer, June 1991

Jackson, Jesse L., American clergyman and civil rights activist, Yrbk 1970, Jan 1986

Jackson, Jesse L., American congressman, May 1998

Jackson, Joe, English singer and songwriter, Feb 1996

Jackson, Joe, American comedian, *Obit* July 1942

Jackson, Lauren, Australian basketball player, June 2003

Jackson, Lisa P., American government official, Mar 2010

Jackson, Mahalia, American gospel singer, Oct 1957, *Obit* Mar 1972

Jackson, Maynard H., American mayor, Sept 1976, *Obit* Yrbk 2003

Jackson, Michael, British journalist and beer expert, Aug 2005, *Obit* Yrbk 2007

Jackson, Michael, American singer and songwriter, Nov 1983, *Obit* Aug 2009

Jackson, Peter, New Zealand film director and screenwriter, Jan 2002

Jackson, Phil, American basketball coach, July 1992

Jackson, Reggie, American baseball player, Jan 1974

Jackson, Robert Houghwout, American Supreme Court justice, Mar 1940, Oct 1950, *Obit* Yrbk 1954

Jackson, Samuel L., American actor, Nov 1996

Jackson, Shirley Ann, American physicist and college president, July 1999

Jackson, Thomas Penfield, judge, June 2001, *Obit* Yrbk 2013

Jackson, William H., Mar 1951, *Obit* Nov 1971

Jackson, William K., July 1946, *Obit* Yrbk 1947

Jacob, Francois, French bacteriologist, Yrbk 1966, *Obit* Yrbk 2013

Jacob, John E., civil rights leader, Feb 1986

Jacobi, Derek, British actor, May 1981

Jacobi, Victor, European music publisher, *Obit* Nov 1942

Jacobs, Jane, American city planner, Mar 1977, *Obit* Yrbk 2006

Jacobs, Joe, *Obit* Jan 1940

Jacobs, Marc, American fashion designer, Feb 1998

Jacobs, Paul, American telecommunications executive, Feb 2007

Jacobs, Philip Peter, *Obit* Aug 1940

Jacobs, Randall, Aug 1942, *Obit* Oct 1967

Jacobs, W. W., English short story writer and novelist, *Obit* Oct 1943

Jacobson, Leon, American physician, Oct 1962, *Obit* Feb 1993

Jacobsson, Per, Swedish banker, Oct 1958, *Obit* June 1963

Jacopi, Giulio, Jan 1959

Jaffe, Harold W., epidemiologist, Sept 1992

Jaffe, Susan, dancer, Sept 1997

Jaffee, Al, American cartoonist and illustrator, July 2008

Jagan, Cheddi, Guyanese president, Apr 1963, *Obit* May 1997

Jagendorf, M. A., Yrbk 1952

Jagger, Bianca, Nicaraguan actress, Apr 1987

Jagger, Janine, American epidemiologist, Apr 2004

Jagger, Mick, British singer, Yrbk 1972

Jagr, Jaromir, Czech hockey player, Apr 1997

Jahangir, Asma, Pakistani lawyer and feminist, Jan 2003

Jahn, Helmut, German architect, Feb 1989

Jakes, John, American novelist, Sept 1988

Jakes, T. D., American clergyman, religious writer and gospel singer, June 2001

Jakobovits, Immanuel, British rabbi, June 1988, *Obit* Feb 2000

Jalal, Massouda, Afghan pediatrician, social activist and political leader, Jan 2002

Jamail, Joseph, American lawyer, Sept 2008

James, Alex, English rock bassist, Nov 2003

James, Alexander R., *Obit* Apr 1946

James, Arthur Curtiss, *Obit* July 1941

James, Arthur Horace, governor, July 1940, *Obit* June 1973

James, Bill, American baseball statistician, June 2004

James, Charles, American fashion designer, July 1956

James, Clive, Australian literary critic and journalist, Nov 1984

James, Daniel, American air force general, Mar 1976, *Obit* Apr 1978

James, E.L., June 2013

James, Edgerrin, American football player, Jan 2002

James, F. Cyril, Canadian economist and college administrator, Oct 1956

James, Harry, American band leader and trumpet player, Sept 1943, *Obit* Aug 1983

James, Jim, American rock guitarist, singer and songwriter, Nov 2008

James, LeBron, American basketball player, Nov 2005

James, P. D., English mystery novelist, Aug 1980

James, W. Frank, *Obit* Jan 1946

James, Will, American children's author and illustrator, *Obit* Nov 1942

Jameson, William James, judge, July 1954

Jamieson, J. K., June 1974

Jamieson, Leland, *Obit* Sept 1941

Jamison, Judith, American dancer, director and choreographer, Jan 1973

Jamison, Kay R., American psychologist, Feb 2009

Janas, Sigmund, Apr 1950

Janeway, Eliot, economist and investment adviser, Sept 1970, *Obit* Apr 1993

Janeway, Elizabeth, American novelist and critic, Mar 1944, *Obit* Yrbk 2005

Janis, Byron, pianist, June 1966

Janis, Sidney, American art dealer, July 1970, *Obit* Jan 1990

Janney, Russell, Mar 1947, *Obit* Sept 1963

Janov, Arthur, psychologist, May 1980

Janowitz, Tama, American novelist and short story writer, Aug 1989

Jansen, Dan, American speed skater, Sept 1994

Jansen, William, Oct 1951, *Obit* Apr 1968

Janson, Paul Emile, *Obit* Aug 1944

Janssen, Charles L., *Obit* Mar 1941

Janssen, David, American actor, Mar 1967, *Obit* Apr 1980

Janssens, Jean Baptiste, Sept 1959, *Obit* Yrbk 1964

Jarecki, Eugene, American film director, May 2006

Jarman, Sanderford, Sept 1942, *Obit* Yrbk 1955

Jarmusch, Jim, American film director, Apr 1990

Jaroussky, Philippe, French countertenor, Mar 2011

Jarreau, Al, American singer, Oct 1992

Jarrett, Keith, American jazz pianist and composer, May 1985

Jarrett, Valerie, American presidential adviser, Apr 2009

Jarring, Gunnar, Swedish diplomat, Oct 1957, *Obit* Sept 2002

Jaruzelski, Wojciech, Polish general and president, Mar 1982

Jarvi, Neeme, Estonian conductor, Nov 1993

Jarvik, Robert, American physician and inventor, July 1985

Jarvis, Erich, American neurobiologist, May 2003

Jarvis, Howard, manufacturing executive and tax reform activist, Feb 1979, *Obit* Sept 1986

Jarvis, Jeff, American journalist, Aug 2009

Jarvis, Lucy, television producer, Apr 1972

Jarvis, Robert Y., *Obit* Yrbk 1943

Jastrow, Joseph, American psychologist, *Obit* Feb 1944

Jastrow, Robert, American physicist, Jan 1973, *Obit* Yrbk 2008

Javits, Jacob K., American senator, June 1948, Oct 1958, *Obit* Apr 1986

Jaworski, Leon, American lawyer and special prosecutor, June 1974, *Obit* Feb 1983

Jay, Peter, Oct 1978

Jay, Ricky, American magician and actor, May 1994

Jay-Z, American rapper, Aug 2002

Jayewardene, Junius Richard, Sri Lankan president, Jan 1984, *Obit* Jan 1997

Jaynes, Clare, Yrbk 1954

Jazy, Michel, French runner, Apr 1967

Jealous, Benjamin T., American civil rights organization official, Feb 2009

Jean, Michaelle, Canadian broadcast journalist and governor general, June 2009

Jeanmaire, Zizi, French ballet dancer and actress, Nov 1952

Jeans, James Hopwood, British physicist and mathematician, Apr 1941, *Obit* Oct 1946

Jeffers, William M., Nov 1942, *Obit* Apr 1953

Jefferson, Margo, American literary critic, June 1999

Jefferts Schori, Katharine, American bishop, Sept 2006

Jeffords, James, American senator, Sept 2001

Jelinek, Elfriede, Austrian novelist and dramatist, Jan 2005

Jelliffe, Smith Ely, psychiatrist, *Obit* Oct 1945

Jellinek, E. M., May 1947, *Obit* Jan 1964

Jemison, Mae C., American physician and astronaut, July 1993

Jencks, Christopher, sociologist, Apr 1973

Jenike, Michael A., American psychiatrist, Jan 2010

Jenkins, Hayes Alan, American figure skater and lawyer, May 1956

Jenkins, Jerry B., American sportswriter and novelist, June 2003

Jenkins, Lew, boxer, Jan 1941, *Obit* Yrbk 1991

Jenkins, Macgregor, *Obit* Apr 1940

Jenkins, Ray H., June 1954, *Obit* Feb 1981

Jenkins, Roy, British political leader, Mar 1966, Oct 1982, *Obit* Yrbk 2003

Jenkins, Sara, Yrbk 1953

Jenks, Leon E., *Obit* Mar 1940

Jenner, Bruce, American decathlete, Aug 1977

Jenner, William E., American senator, June 1951, *Obit* May 1985

Jennings, B. Brewster, May 1951, *Obit* Yrbk 1968

Jennings, John Edward, author, Yrbk 1949

Jennings, Paul J., labor leader, Yrbk 1969, *Obit* Oct 1987

Jennings, Peter, Canadian television newscaster, Nov 1983, *Obit* Sept 2005

Jennings, Waylon, American singer and songwriter, Apr 1982, *Obit* Apr 2002

Jensen, Arthur Robert, American psychologist, Jan 1973, *Obit* Yrbk 2013

Jensen, Ben F., Feb 1960, *Obit* Apr 1970

Jensen, Jackie, baseball player, coach and manager, June 1959, *Obit* Oct 1982

Jensen, Oliver, American magazine editor and historian, May 1945, *Obit* Yrbk 2005

Jentsch, Julia, German actress, Jan 2006

Jepsen, Carly Rae, Sept 2013

Jernegan, John D., Nov 1959

Jerusalem, Siegfried, German opera singer, Sept 1992

Jessel, George, singer, dancer and comedian, Mar 1943, *Obit* July 1981

Jessup, Philip C., American judge and diplomat, Apr 1948, *Obit* Mar 1986

Jester, Beauford H., July 1948, *Obit* Sept 1949

Jet (Musical group), Jan 2005

Jett, Joan, American singer and songwriter, Sept 1993

Jeunet, Jean-Pierre, French film director, Jan 2005

Jewett, Frank B., American electrical engineer and telecommunications executive, Yrbk 1946, *Obit* Jan 1950

Jewett, James R., *Obit* May 1943

Jewison, Norman, Canadian motion picture director and producer, June 1979

Jha, Sanjay, American electronics industry executive, Jan 2010

Jhabvala, Ruth Prawer, British screenwriter and novelist, Mar 1977, *Obit* Yrbk 2013

Jiang Qing, Chinese communist leader and wife of Mao Zedong, June 1975, *Obit* Jan 1992

Jiang Zemin, Chinese president, May 1995

Jiang Zuobin, *Obit* Feb 1943

Jillette, Penn, American magician, June 2000

Jimenez, Joyce, Filipino-American actress and lingerie company founder, Jan 2003

Jimenez, Juan Ramon, Spanish poet, Feb 1957, *Obit* Sept 1958

Jimerson, Earl W., Sept 1948, *Obit* Yrbk 1958

Jin Xing, Chinese ballet dancer and choreographer, Jan 2006

Jin, Deborah, American physicist, Apr 2004

Jindal, Bobby, American governor, Jan 2008

Jinnah, Mohamed Ali, Pakistani political leader, May 1942, *Obit* Oct 1948

Jo, Sumi, Korean opera singer, Jan 2002

Jobert, Michel, French diplomat, Feb 1975, *Obit* Sept 2002

Jobim, Antonio Carlos, Brazilian singer and songwriter, July 1991, *Obit* Feb 1995

Jobs, Steven, American computer industry executive, Mar 1983, Sept 1998, *Obit* Yrbk 2011

Jodl, Alfred, German general, *Obit* Nov 1946

Jodoin, Claude, Mar 1956

Jodorowsky, Alejandro, Chilean film director and comic book writer, Jan 2005

Joel, Billy, American singer and songwriter, Sept 1979

Joesten, Joachim, June 1942

Joffrey, Robert, American ballet dancer, choreographer and director, Nov 1967, *Obit* Nov 1988

Johanna Sigurdardottir, Icelandic prime minister, July 2010

Johannesen, Grant, American pianist, June 1961, *Obit* Yrbk 2005

Johanson, Donald C., American anthropologist, Feb 1984

Johansson, Ingemar, Swedish boxer, Nov 1959, *Obit* Yrbk 2009

Johansson, Scarlett, American actress, Mar 2005

John, Feb 1959, *Obit* July 1963

John Paul, Nov 1979, Mar 2000, *Obit* June 2005

John Paul, Nov 1978, *Obit* Jan 1979

John, Augustus, English painter, Oct 1941, *Obit* Jan 1962

John, Daymond, American fashion designer, Aug 2007

John, Elton, English singer and songwriter, Mar 1975

John, Tommy, American baseball player, Oct 1981

Johns, Glynis, Sept 1973

Johns, Jasper, American painter, May 1967, May 1987

Johnson, July 1996

Johnson, Alexander, *Obit* July 1941

Johnson, Alvin Saunders, economist, author and educator, Aug 1942, *Obit* July 1971

Johnson, Amy, English aviator, *Obit* Feb 1941

Johnson, Andre, American football player, Nov 2010

Johnson, Arnold M., Oct 1955, *Obit* May 1960

Johnson, Arthur Newhall, *Obit* Sept 1940

Johnson, Avery, American basketball player and coach, Jan 2007

Johnson, Ben, Canadian runner, June 1988

Johnson, Betsey, American fashion designer, Jan 1994

Johnson, Beverly, American model, Sept 1994

Johnson, Boris, British mayor, Oct 2008

Johnson, Brian, English singer, Mar 2005

Johnson, Brian David, Futurist and author, July 2012

Johnson, C. Oscar, Feb 1948, *Obit* Jan 1966

Johnson, Charles Richard, American novelist and short story writer, Sept 1991

Johnson, Charles Spurgeon, American sociologist and university president, Nov 1946, *Obit* Jan 1957

Johnson, Chic, American comedian, Sept 1940, *Obit* Apr 1962

Johnson, Chris, American football player, Aug 2010

Johnson, Clarence Leonard, aeronautical engineer, Oct 1968, *Obit* Mar 1991

Johnson, Clifton, *Obit* Jan 1940

Johnson, Crockett, cartoonist, Yrbk 1943, *Obit* Jan 1984

Johnson, Daniel, Canadian provincial premier, Nov 1967, *Obit* Nov 1968

Johnson, Davey, American baseball manager, Sept 1999

Johnson, David M., July 1952

Johnson, Don, American actor, Apr 1986

Johnson, Douglas Wilson, American geologist, *Obit* Apr 1944

Johnson, Dwayne, American wrestler and actor, July 2000

Johnson, Earvin, American basketball player and coach, Jan 1982

Johnson, Ed, American senator and governor, Yrbk 1946, *Obit* July 1970

Johnson, Eddie Bernice, American congresswoman, July 2001

Johnson, Edward, Canadian-American opera singer and director, Mar 1943, *Obit* June 1959

Johnson, Elizabeth A., American theologian, Nov 2002

Johnson, Eric, American guitarist, keyboardist, singer and songwriter, June 2007

Johnson, F. Ross, Canadian food industry executive, May 1989

Johnson, Frank M., American judge, Aug 1978, *Obit* Oct 1999

Johnson, Hall, American composer and music arranger, Jan 1945, *Obit* June 1970

Johnson, Harold K., American general, May 1966, *Obit* Nov 1983

Johnson, Herschel, American journalist and children's author, July 1946

Johnson, Hewlett, English clergyman, May 1943, *Obit* Yrbk 1966

Johnson, Hiram, American governor and senator, Feb 1941, *Obit* Sept 1945

Johnson, Holgar J., Mar 1950

Johnson, Howard A., Apr 1964, *Obit* Sept 1974

Johnson, Howard B., Sept 1966

Johnson, Howard E., *Obit* June 1941

Johnson, Hugh S., American general and government official, Sept 1940, *Obit* June 1942

Johnson, J. Monroe, American civil engineer and government official, Feb 1945, *Obit* Sept 1964

Johnson, Jack, American boxer, *Obit* July 1946

Johnson, Jamey, American country singer and songwriter, Feb 2011

Johnson, Jimmy, American football coach and sportscaster, July 1994

Johnson, John H., American magazine publisher, Oct 1968, *Obit* Yrbk 2005

Johnson, Joseph B., July 1956

Johnson, Joseph E., American historian and foundation official, Nov 1950, *Obit* Jan 1991

Johnson, Joseph T., Feb 1952

Johnson, Keyshawn, American football player, Oct 1999

Johnson, Lady Bird, wife of American president Lyndon B. Johnson, Oct 1964, *Obit* Oct 2007

Johnson, Leroy, Sept 1949, *Obit* June 1961

Johnson, Loren, *Obit* Feb 1942

Johnson, Louis Arthur, American Secretary of defense, June 1942, Apr 1949, *Obit* May 1966

Johnson, Lyndon B., American president, Jan 1951, Mar 1964, *Obit* Mar 1973

Johnson, Malcolm, June 1949, *Obit* Aug 1976

Johnson, Mat, American novelist, Mar 2010

Johnson, Mordecai Wyatt, American college president and clergyman, Apr 1941

Johnson, Nelson Trusler, diplomat, Jan 1940, *Obit* Feb 1955

Johnson, Nicholas, Mar 1968

Johnson, Nunnally, screenwriter, Aug 1941, *Obit* May 1977

Johnson, Osa Helen Leighty, American explorer and documentary filmmaker, Apr 1940, *Obit* Feb 1953

Johnson, Pamela Hansford, English novelist and critic, Yrbk 1948, *Obit* Aug 1981

Johnson, Paul, English journalist and historian, Sept 1994

Johnson, Paul B., *Obit* Feb 1944

Johnson, Philip Cortelyou, American architect, Oct 1957, Nov 1991, *Obit* Sept 2005

Johnson, Philip G., *Obit* Nov 1944

Johnson, Rafer, American decathlete, June 1961

Johnson, Randy, American baseball player, Sept 2000

Johnson, Robert L., college president and government official, Mar 1948, *Obit* Feb 1966

Johnson, Robert Louis, American television and basketball executive, Apr 1994

Johnson, Robert Wood, American medical supply executive, Nov 1943, *Obit* Mar 1968

Johnson, Roy W., May 1958, *Obit* Oct 1965

Johnson, Sheila Crump, American broadcasting executive and philanthropist, June 2007

Johnson, Simon, American economist, Oct 2009

Johnson, Sonia, American feminist, Feb 1985

Johnson, Thomasina Walker, Mar 1947

Johnson, Thor, Oct 1949, *Obit* Mar 1975

Johnson, U. Alexis, American diplomat, Oct 1955, *Obit* June 1997

Johnson, Van, American actor, July 1945, *Obit* Yrbk 2009

Johnson, Virginia, American dancer, May 1985

Johnson, Virginia E., American psychologist, Apr 1976, *Obit* Yrbk 2013

Johnson, Walter, American historian, Apr 1957, *Obit* Sept 1985

Johnson, Wendell, American speech pathologist, Apr 1959, *Obit* Nov 1965

Johnson, William E., *Obit* Mar 1945

Johnson, Zach, American golfer, Jan 2008

Johnson-Sirleaf, Ellen, Liberian president, Jan 2006

Johnston, Alvanley, American labor leader, June 1946, *Obit* Nov 1951

Johnston, Clement D., May 1955, *Obit* Jan 1980

Johnston, Daniel, American singer, songwriter and artist, Sept 2010

Johnston, Eric, Apr 1943, Oct 1955, *Obit* Oct 1963

Johnston, Lynn, Canadian cartoonist, Feb 1998

Johnston, Olin D., American senator and governor, Nov 1951, *Obit* June 1965

Johnston, Victor A., July 1949, *Obit* May 1967

Johnston, Wayne A., American railroad executive, May 1951, *Obit* Feb 1968

Johnstone, Margaret Blair, Jan 1955

Jolie, Angelina, American actress, Oct 2000

Joliot-Curie, Frederic, French physicist, Oct 1946, *Obit* Oct 1958

Joliot-Curie, Irene, French physicist, Apr 1940, *Obit* May 1956

Jolly, Alison, American primatologist, Jan 2009

Jolson, Al, singer and actor, Nov 1940, *Obit* Yrbk 1950

Jonah, Sam, Ghanaian gold mining executive, Jan 2004

Jones, Arthur C., Jan 1948, *Obit* Jan 1965

Jones, Barry, Mar 1958

Jones, Ben, American multimedia artist, Apr 2010

Jones, Bill T., American dancer and choreographer, July 1993

Jones, Billy, *Obit* Jan 1941

Jones, Bobby, American gospel singer, June 2002

Jones, Brian, British balloonist, Jan 2004

Jones, Buck, *Obit* Jan 1943

Jones, Candy, model and talk show host, Oct 1961, *Obit* Mar 1990

Jones, Carolyn, American actress, Mar 1967, *Obit* Sept 1983

Jones, Cherry, American actress, May 1998

Jones, Chester Lloyd, *Obit* Mar 1941

Jones, Chipper, American baseball player, May 2001

Jones, Chuck, American animator, May 1996, *Obit* May 2002

Jones, Clara Stanton, librarian, July 1976

Jones, Cullen, American swimmer, Aug 2008

Jones, David, British video game creator, Jan 2006

Jones, David C., July 1982, *Obit* Yrbk 2013

Jones, E. Stanley, American missionary, May 1940, *Obit* Mar 1973

Jones, Edward P., American short story writer and novelist, Mar 2004

Jones, Elaine R., American lawyer, June 2004

Jones, George, American country singer, Feb 1995, *Obit* Yrbk 2013

Jones, George L., American bookstore chain executive, Apr 2007

Jones, Grace, American singer and actress, Sept 1987

Jones, Grover, *Obit* Nov 1940

Jones, Harold Spencer, British astronomer, Mar 1955, *Obit* Jan 1961

Jones, Howard P., American diplomat, July 1963, *Obit* Nov 1973

Jones, Idwal, author, Yrbk 1948, *Obit* Jan 1965

Jones, J. D., Welsh clergyman, *Obit* June 1942

Jones, Jack, British labor leader, May 1976

Jones, James Earl, American actor, Sept 1969, Nov 1994

Jones, James R., Oct 1981

Jones, Jennifer, American actress, May 1944, *Obit* Yrbk 2010

Jones, Jerral, American petroleum and football executive, May 1996

Jones, Jesse Holman, American Secretary of commerce, Oct 1940, *Obit* Sept 1956

Jones, Joe, American painter, Oct 1940, *Obit* June 1963

Jones, John Joseph, Nov 1940, *Obit* Jan 1942

Jones, Jon, American mixed martial artist, Mar 2013

Jones, K. C., basketball coach, Feb 1987

Jones, Lewis Webster, Oct 1958

Jones, Marion, American sprinter, long jumper and basketball player, Oct 1998

Jones, Marvin, congressman and judge, Aug 1943, *Obit* Jan 1984

Jones, Monty, Sierra Leonen plant geneticist and rice breeder, Jan 2007

Jones, Norah, American pianist and singer, May 2003

Jones, Norman L., *Obit* Jan 1941

Jones, Preston, actor and dramatist, Feb 1977, *Obit* Nov 1979

Jones, Quincy, American composer and record producer, Feb 1977

Jones, Rashida, American actress, Aug 2013

Jones, Rickie Lee, singer and songwriter, May 1990

Jones, Robert Edmond, scenic designer, Nov 1946, *Obit* Jan 1955

Jones, Roger Warren, government official, Nov 1959, *Obit* Aug 1993

Jones, Roy, American boxer, Feb 1999

Jones, Rufus Matthew, American Quaker leader, Oct 1941, *Obit* Sept 1948

Jones, Russell, Oct 1957, *Obit* Aug 1979

Jones, Sam Houston, lawyer and governor, Mar 1940, *Obit* Yrbk 1991

Jones, Sarah, American poet, playwright and performance artist, July 2005

Jones, Scott, American electronics and information technology executive, Jan 2006

Jones, Shirley, American singer and actress, Oct 1961

Jones, Tayari, American novelist and short story writer, Aug 2009

Jones, Tom, Welsh singer, Apr 1970

Jones, Tommy Lee, American actor, Oct 1995

Jones, Van, American lawyer, civil rights activist, environmentalist and presidential aide, Apr 2009

Jong, Dola de, Dutch-American mystery novelist, Yrbk 1947, *Obit* Yrbk 2004

Jong, Erica, American poet and novelist, July 1975, Apr 1997

Jonsi Thor Birgisson, Icelandic singer, Jan 2003

Jonsson, John Erik, mayor and electronics executive, Jan 1961, *Obit* Nov 1995

Jonze, Spike, American video and motion picture director, Apr 2003

Jooss, Kurt, German choreographer, dance director and teacher, July 1976, *Obit* July 1979

Jooste, Gerhardus Petrus, Apr 1951

Joplin, Janis, American singer, Mar 1970, *Obit* Mar 1970

Jordan, B. Everett, American senator, Nov 1959, *Obit* May 1974

Jordan, Barbara, American lawyer and congresswoman, Sept 1974, Apr 1993, *Obit* Apr 1996

Jordan, Frank Craig, *Obit* Apr 1941

Jordan, Hamilton, American presidential adviser and campaign consultant, Aug 1977, *Obit* Yrbk 2008

Jordan, I. King, American university president, Jan 1991

Jordan, Jim, American radio performer, Nov 1941, *Obit* May 1988

Jordan, Jim; and Jordan, Marian, Nov 1941

Jordan, Marian, radio performer, Nov 1941, *Obit* June 1961

Jordan, Michael, American basketball player, Sept 1987, Feb 1997

Jordan, Michael H., American information technology executive, Feb 1998, *Obit* Yrbk 2010

Jordan, Mildred, author, Yrbk 1951

Jordan, Neil, Irish film director, screenwriter and novelist, Aug 1993

Jordan, Philippe, Swiss opera conductor, Oct 2010

Jordan, Sara Claudia Murray, gastroenterologist, Mar 1954, *Obit* Jan 1960

Jordan, Vernon, American civil rights leader and lawyer, Feb 1972, Aug 1993

Jordan, Virgil, Oct 1947, *Obit* June 1965

Jordan, W. K., Mar 1955, *Obit* July 1980

Jordana y Souza, Francisco Gomez, Mar 1944

Jorgensen, Anker, Danish prime minister, Sept 1978

Jorgensen, Mikael, American keyboardist, Feb 2010

Jose, F. Sionil, Filipino novelist, Jan 2005

Josefowicz, Leila, American violinist, May 2007

Joseph, Ammu, Indian journalist and feminist, Jan 2004

Joseph, Keith, British cabinet member, Feb 1975, *Obit* Feb 1995

Joseph, Stephen C., physician and public health official, Jan 1989

Josephs, Devereux C., July 1953, *Obit* Mar 1977

Josephson, Walter S., *Obit* Mar 1940

Jospin, Lionel, French prime minister, June 2000

Joubert, Brian, French figure skater, Jan 2007

Jouhaux, Leon, French labor leader, Jan 1948, *Obit* July 1954

Jourdan, Louis, French actor, Jan 1967

Jouvet, Louis, French actor and theatrical director, Oct 1949, *Obit* Oct 1951

Jowitt, William Allen Jowitt, Aug 1941, *Obit* Nov 1957

Joxe, Louis, French diplomat and cabinet member, Apr 1961, *Obit* June 1991

Joy, C. Turner, American admiral, June 1951, *Obit* Sept 1956

Joya, Malalai, Afghan human rights activist and member of Parliament, Jan 2007

Joyce, James, Irish novelist, dramatist and poet, *Obit* Mar 1941

Joyce, James Avery, English lawyer, author and pacifist, Mar 1959

Joyner, Tom, American radio talk show host, Sept 2002

Joyner-Kersee, Jackie, American heptathlete and basketball player, July 1987

Juan Carlos, Oct 1964, Jan 2003

Juan Carlos, Oct 1951, *Obit* June 1993

Juanes, Colombian singer, Jan 2003

Judd, Ashley, American actress, Feb 2000

Judd, Charles Hubbard, *Obit* Sept 1946

Judd, Jackie, American television reporter, Sept 2002

Judd, Walter Henry, American congressman, Sept 1949, *Obit* Apr 1994

Judge, Mike, American motion picture director and animator, May 1997

Judson, Arthur, orchestra manager, Aug 1945, *Obit* Mar 1975

Judson, Clara Ingram, author, Yrbk 1948

Judson, Olivia P., English evolutionary biologist, Jan 2004

Juin, Alphonse, French field marshal, Aug 1943, *Obit* Mar 1967

Julia, Raul, American actor, Sept 1982, *Obit* Jan 1995

Julian, Percy L., American chemist, Sept 1947, *Obit* Jan 1975

Juliana, Sept 1944, Jan 1955, *Obit* Yrbk 2004

July, Miranda, American performance artist and filmmaker, Nov 2007

Jumblatt, Kamal, Lebanese political leader, Jan 1977, *Obit* Jan 1977

Jung, Andrea, American cosmetics industry executive, May 2000

Jung, C. G., Swiss psychologist, Apr 1943, Oct 1953, *Obit* Sept 1961

Jurgensen, Sonny, American football player and sportscaster, June 1977

Just, Ward S., American novelist, May 1989

Justo, Agustin P., Argentine general and president, *Obit* Mar 1943

K

K'naan, Somali rapper, June 2010

Kabakov, Ilya, Russian painter and illustrator, Apr 1998

Kabbah, Ahmad Tejan, Sierra Leonean president, Jan 2002

Kabila, Joseph, Congolese president, Sept 2001

Kaczynski, Lech, Polish president, Jan 2006, *Obit* Yrbk 2010

Kadar, Janos, Hungarian prime minister, May 1957, *Obit* Yrbk 1989

Kadare, Ismail, Albanian novelist, Feb 1992

Kadyrov, Ramzan, Chechen president, Jan 2007

Kael, Pauline, American film critic, Mar 1974, *Obit* Nov 2001

Kaempffert, Waldemar, Sept 1943, *Obit* Feb 1957

Kagame, Paul, Rwandan president, Jan 2002

Kagan, Elena, American Supreme Court justice, June 2007

Kagan, Frederick W., American military historian, July 2007

Kagan, Henry Enoch, Sept 1965, *Obit* Oct 1969

Kaganovich, L. M., Soviet communist leader, Apr 1942, Oct 1955, *Obit* Sept 1991

Kagawa, Toyohiko, Japanese clergyman and philosopher, Sept 1941, *Obit* June 1960

Kahal, Irving, *Obit* Apr 1942

Kahane, Meir, American-Israeli rabbi, Oct 1972, *Obit* Jan 1991

Kahane, Melanie, interior designer, July 1959, *Obit* Feb 1989

Kahf, Mohja, Syrian-American writer, Jan 2007

Kahmann, Chesley, Yrbk 1952

Kahn, Albert, American architect, *Obit* Sept 1942

Kahn, Alfred E., American economist and government official, Mar 1979, *Obit* Yrbk 2011

Kahn, Ely Jacques, American architect, Aug 1945, *Obit* Nov 1972

Kahn, Gus, American lyricist, *Obit* Yrbk 1941

Kahn, Herman, American physicist and futurist, Oct 1962, *Obit* Aug 1983

Kahn, Louis I., American architect, Oct 1964, *Obit* May 1974

Kahn, Madeline, American actress and singer, May 1977, *Obit* Mar 2000

Kahn, Oliver, German soccer player, Jan 2002

Kahn, Roger, American novelist, short story writer and sportswriter, June 2000

Kahneman, Daniel, Israeli psychologist, Jan 2007

Kaifu, Toshiki, Japanese prime minister, June 1990

Kain, Karen, Canadian ballet dancer and director, May 1980

Kainen, Jacob, American painter and printmaker, Feb 1987, *Obit* Aug 2001

Kaiser, Edgar F., chemical and metal industries executive, Sept 1964, *Obit* Feb 1982

Kaiser, Henry John, American shipbuilding executive, Oct 1942, Mar 1961, *Obit* Nov 1967

Kaiser, Jakob, German labor leader and government official, Feb 1956, *Obit* July 1961

Kaiser, John Boynton, librarian, May 1943

Kaiser, Philip M., American diplomat, Oct 1949, *Obit* Yrbk 2007

Kaka, Brazilian soccer player, May 2008

Kakfwi, Stephen, Canadian provincial government official, Jan 2003

Kalb, Marvin, television reporter and college administrator, July 1987

Kaleeba, Noerine, Ugandan AIDS activist and physiotherapist, Jan 2006

Kalikow, Peter, American real estate developer, Sept 1988

Kaline, Al, American baseball player and sportscaster, Yrbk 1970

Kaling, Mindy, American actress, playwright and television scriptwriter, Apr 2012

Kalinin, Mikhail Ivanovich, Soviet president, June 1942, *Obit* July 1946

Kallay, Nicholas, Hungarian prime minister, June 1942, *Obit* May 1967

Kallen, Horace Meyer, philosopher, Oct 1953, *Obit* Apr 1974

Kallio, Kyosti, *Obit* Feb 1941

Kalmus, Herbert T., American physicist and motion picture executive, Feb 1949, *Obit* Sept 1963

Kaltenborn, H. V., radio commentator, Aug 1940, *Obit* Sept 1965

Kaltenbrunner, Ernst, Austrian Nazi leader, Apr 1943, *Obit* Nov 1946

Kamali, Norma, American fashion designer, Nov 1998

Kamber, Michael, American photojournalist, June 2009

Kamen, Dean, American inventor and medical instrument maker, Nov 2002

Kaminska, Ida, Polish actress, Nov 1969, *Obit* July 1980

Kaminski, Janusz, Polish cinematographer, Mar 2000

Kamm, John, American chemical industry executive and human rights activist, Jan 2002

Kampelman, Max M., American diplomat, July 1986

Kampmann, Viggo, Jan 1961, *Obit* July 1976

Kamprad, Ingvar, Swedish household furnishings chain executive, June 1998

Kan, Naoto, Japanese prime minister, July 2011

Kan-In, Kotohito, *Obit* June 1945

Kander, Lizzie Black, American social worker and cookbook writer, *Obit* Sept 1940

Kandinsky, Wassily, Russian painter, *Obit* Feb 1945

Kane, Harnett T., journalist, historian and author, Yrbk 1947, *Obit* Yrbk 1984

Kane, Joseph Nathan, American historian, Nov 1985, *Obit* Nov 2002

Kane, Patrick, American hockey player, Feb 2011

Kaneko, Shu, Japanese film director, Jan 2007

Kani, John, South African actor, theatrical director and playwright, June 2001

Kania, Stanislaw, June 1981

Kanin, Garson, dramatist and director, Jan 1941, Oct 1952, *Obit* June 1999

Kann, Peter R., American publishing executive, Mar 2003

Kanter, Albert Lewis, publisher, July 1953

Kanter, Rosabeth Moss, American management consultant, teacher and writer, May 1996

Kantor, Mickey, American Secretary of commerce, Mar 1994

Kantrowitz, Adrian, American cardiac surgeon, Oct 1967, *Obit* Yrbk 2009

Kantrowitz, Arthur, American physicist, Oct 1966, *Obit* Yrbk 2009

Kanwar, Amar, Indian documentary filmmaker, Jan 2005

Kanzler, Ernest Carlton, automobile executive, Apr 1942, *Obit* Feb 1968

Kao, John J., American management consultant, Oct 2008

Kapell, William, American pianist, May 1948, *Obit* Jan 1954

Kapitsa, P. L., Russian physicist, Oct 1955, *Obit* May 1984

Kaplan, Joseph, physicist, Oct 1956, *Obit* Nov 1991

Kaplan, Justin, American biographer, July 1993

Kapoor, Anish, Indian-British video artist and sculptor, Sept 2013

Kapoor, Karisma, Indian actress, Jan 2002

Kapp, Joe, football player and management consultant, Sept 1975

Kappel, Frederick R., telephone executive, Mar 1957, *Obit* Jan 1995

Kaptur, Marcy C., American congresswoman, Jan 2003

Kapuscinski, Ryszard, Polish journalist and biographer, Sept 1992, *Obit* Yrbk 2007

Karadzic, Radovan, Bosnian Serb political leader, Oct 1995

Karajan, Herbert von, Austrian conductor, Oct 1956, Sept 1986, *Obit* Sept 1989

Karami, Rashid, Lebanese prime minister, Nov 1959, *Obit* July 1987

Karan, Donna, American fashion designer, Aug 1990

Karbo, Karen, American novelist, May 2001

Kardelj, Edvard, Yugoslav communist leader, Yrbk 1949, *Obit* Apr 1979

Karelitz, George B., *Obit* Mar 1943

Karfiol, Bernard, Nov 1947, *Obit* Oct 1952

Karim, Jawed, American video sharing web site founder, Jan 2007

Karinska, Barbara, Russian-American costume designer, Jan 1971

Karle, Isabella L., American chemist, Jan 2003

Karloff, Boris, Anglo-American actor, Mar 1941, *Obit* Mar 1969

Karmal, Babrak, Afghan president, Mar 1981, *Obit* Feb 1997

Karman, Tawakel, Mar 2013

Karmazin, Mel, American broadcasting executive, May 2000

Karnebeek, Herman Adriaan van, *Obit* May 1942

Karno, Fred, English comedian and theatrical producer, *Obit* Nov 1941

Karolyi, Bela, Romanian-American gymnastic coach, Oct 1996

Karon, Jan, American novelist, Mar 2003

Karp, David, American novelist and screenwriter, Yrbk 1957, *Obit* Feb 2000

Karpinski, Janis, American general, Apr 2006

Karpov, Anatoly, Russian chess player, Nov 1978

Karsh, Yousuf, Canadian photographer, Yrbk 1952, Feb 1980, *Obit* Nov 2002

Karsner, David, *Obit* Apr 1941

Karthikeyan, Narain, Indian automobile racing driver, Jan 2005

Karumba, Christine, Feb 2013

Karzai, Hamid, Afghan president, May 2002

Kasavubu, Joseph, Congolese president, Mar 1961, *Obit* May 1969

Kasdan, Lawrence, American film director and screenwriter, May 1992

Kase, Toshikazu, Japanese diplomat, Apr 1957, *Obit* Yrbk 2004

Kasem, Casey, disc jockey, Nov 1997

Kasich, John R., American governor, Aug 1998

Kasner, Edward, Nov 1943, *Obit* Mar 1955

Kaspar, Karel, *Obit* June 1941

Kasparov, Garry, Russian chess player, Apr 1986

Kaspersky, Eugene, Russian computer scientist, Jan 2005, June 2013

Kaspersky, Natalya, Russian information technology executive, Jan 2005

Kass, Leon, American bioethicist, Aug 2002

Kassebaum Baker, Nancy, American senator, Feb 1982

Kassovitz, Mathieu, French actor and film director, Jan 2005

Kast, Ludwig, *Obit* Oct 1941

Kasten, Robert W., senator, June 1989

Kastenmeier, Robert W., American congressman, July 1966

Kastler, Alfred, French physicist, Yrbk 1967, *Obit* Mar 1984

Kastner, Erich, German author and poet, July 1964, *Obit* Oct 1974

Katayama, Tetsu, Jan 1948

Katchor, Ben, American cartoonist, May 2000

Katina, Lena, Russian singer, Jan 2003

Katsav, Moshe, Israeli president, Feb 2001

Katsh, Abraham Isaac, Hebraist, Mar 1962, *Obit* Oct 1998

Katz, Alex, American painter, July 1975

Katz, Jackson, American anti-sexism activist, July 2004

Katz, Label A., Apr 1960, *Obit* June 1975

Katz, Milton, law professor and diplomat, Oct 1950, *Obit* Oct 1995

Katz, Sharon, South African singer, songwriter and guitarist, Jan 2007

Katz-Suchy, Juliusz, June 1951, *Obit* Yrbk 1971

Katzen, Mollie, American cookbook author, Oct 1996

Katzenbach, Nicholas deB., American Attorney general, July 1965, *Obit* Yrbk 2012

Katzenberg, Jeffrey, American motion picture executive, May 1995

Katzir, Ephraim, Israeli biophysicist and president, Jan 1975, *Obit* Yrbk 2009

Kauffmann, Henrik, Apr 1956, *Obit* July 1963

Kaufman, Charlie, American screenwriter, July 2005

Kaufman, George S., American dramatist, Aug 1941, *Obit* Sept 1961

Kaufman, Henry, American economist and financial executive, Aug 1981

Kaufman, Irving R., American judge, Apr 1953, *Obit* Apr 1992

Kaufman, Millard, American screenwriter and novelist, Jan 2008, *Obit* Yrbk 2009

Kaufman, Moises, American playwright and theatrical director, Aug 2011

Kaunda, Kenneth D., Zambian president, July 1966

Kaup, Felix F., *Obit* Apr 1940

Kaur, Rajkumari Amrit, Oct 1955, *Obit* Mar 1964

Kaurismaki, Aki, Finnish screenwriter and director, Jan 2003

Kavafian, Ani, American violinist, Oct 2006

Kavina, Lydia, Russian theremin player, Jan 2002

Kavner, Julie, American actress, Oct 1992

Kawabata, Yasunari, Japanese novelist and short story writer, Mar 1969, *Obit* June 1972

Kawaguchi, Yoriko, Japanese diplomat, Jan 2002

Kawakami, Jotaro, Mar 1963, *Obit* Jan 1966

Kawakubo, Rei, Japanese fashion designer, Aug 1999

Kay, Beatrice, Yrbk 1942

Kay, Hershy, Mar 1962, *Obit* Feb 1982

Kay-Scott, Cyril, Feb 1944

Kaye, Danny, American comedian, actor and singer, Yrbk 1941, Nov 1952, *Obit* Apr 1987

Kaye, Nora, dancer, Jan 1953, *Obit* Apr 1987

Kazan, Elia, American theatrical and film director, Jan 1948, Oct 1972, *Obit* Yrbk 2004

Kazantzakis, Nikos, Greek novelist, poet, dramatist, essayist and travel writer, July 1955, *Obit* Jan 1958

Kazin, Alfred, American literary critic, May 1966, *Obit* Aug 1998

Kcho, Cuban installation artist, Aug 2001

Keach, Stacy, American actor, Nov 1971

Kean, Thomas H., American governor and college president, July 1985

Keane, Doris, actress, *Obit* Jan 1946

Keane, Roy, Irish soccer player, Jan 2006

Keane, Sean, Irish fiddler, Mar 2004

Kearns, Carroll D., Sept 1956

Kearns, Nora Lynch, Sept 1956

Keasling, Jay, American bioengineer, Nov 2013

Keating, Kenneth Barnard, American congressman, senator and diplomat, Oct 1950, *Obit* June 1975

Keating, Paul, Australian prime minister, May 1992

Keaton, Diane, American actress and motion picture director, June 1978, May 1996

Keaton, Michael, American actor, June 1992

Keb' Mo', American blues guitarist and singer, Nov 2013

Kebede, Liya, Ethiopian model and social activist, Jan 2005

Keck, George Fred, Sept 1945

Keck, Lucile L., Mar 1954

Kee, Elizabeth, Jan 1954

Kee, John, June 1950, *Obit* June 1951

Keech, Richmond B., Mar 1950

Keegan, John, English military historian and journalist, Oct 1989, *Obit* Yrbk 2012

Keegan, Robert J., American manufacturing executive, Jan 2004

Keeler, Ruby, American dancer and actress, Yrbk 1971, *Obit* Apr 1993

Keen, Andrew, British digital media critic, July 2013

Keen, Sam, author and philosopher, Feb 1995

Keenan, Joseph B., Sept 1946, *Obit* Feb 1955

Keenan, Mike, hockey coach, Mar 1996

Keenan, Walter Francis, *Obit* Apr 1940

Keene, Christopher, conductor and opera manager, Mar 1990, *Obit* Jan 1996

Keene, Donald, American Japanologist, Jan 1988

Keener, Catherine, American actress, Oct 2002

Keeney, Barnaby C., Mar 1956, *Obit* Aug 1980

Keeny, Spurgeon Milton, United Nations official, Jan 1958, *Obit* Jan 1989

Keeshan, Bob, American television personality, May 1965, *Obit* Yrbk 2004

Keeton, Kathy, magazine executive, Sept 1993, *Obit* Jan 1998

Kefauver, Estes, American senator, Jan 1949, *Obit* Oct 1963

Keighley, William, motion picture director, Nov 1948, *Obit* Aug 1984

Keillor, Garrison, American novelist, short story writer, storyteller and radio performer, Aug 1985

Keino, Kip, Kenyan runner, June 1967

Keita, Modibo, Malian president, Apr 1960, *Obit* July 1977

Keitel, Harvey, American actor, Mar 1994

Keitel, Wilhelm, German field marshal, Sept 1940, *Obit* Nov 1946

Keith, Dora Wheeler, American painter, *Obit* Feb 1941

Keith, Harold, American children's author, Yrbk 1958

Keith, Toby, American country singer, Oct 2004

Kekilli, Sibel, Turkish-German actress, Jan 2006

Kekkonen, Urho, Finnish president, Sept 1950, *Obit* Oct 1986

Kelberine, Alexander, *Obit* Mar 1940

Keldysh, Mstislav, Russian mathematician and physicist, Feb 1962, *Obit* Aug 1978

Kellas, Eliza, *Obit* May 1943

Kelleher, Herbert David, American airline executive, Jan 2001

Kellems, Vivien, American wire and cable industry executive, Sept 1948, *Obit* Mar 1975

Keller, Bill, American newspaper editor, Oct 2003

Keller, Helen, American humanitarian, Yrbk 1942, *Obit* July 1968

Keller, James, Oct 1951, *Obit* Apr 1977

Keller, K. T., May 1947, *Obit* Feb 1966

Keller, Kasey, soccer player, Nov 1998

Keller, Marthe, Swiss actress and opera director, July 2004

Keller, Thomas, American chef and restaurateur, June 2004

Kelley, Augustine Bernard, Apr 1951, *Obit* Feb 1958

Kelley, Charles, American country singer and songwriter, July 2011

Kelley, Clarence M., American FBI director, May 1974, *Obit* Nov 1997

Kelley, David E., American television scriptwriter and producer, May 1998

Kelley, Edgar Stillman, composer, *Obit* Jan 1945

Kelley, Kitty, American biographer, Apr 1992

Kellogg, John Harvey, American physician, *Obit* Feb 1944

Kellogg, Remington, paleontologist, Nov 1949

Kellogg, Winthrop Niles, Apr 1963

Kelly, David, Irish actor, Jan 2005, *Obit* Yrbk 2012

Kelly, Edna Flannery, congresswoman, Mar 1950, *Obit* Feb 1998

Kelly, Ellsworth, American painter and sculptor, May 1970

Kelly, Emmett, American clown, July 1954, *Obit* May 1979

Kelly, Everett Lowell, psychologist, Mar 1955, *Obit* Apr 1986

Kelly, Florence Finch, journalist and author, *Obit* Jan 1940

Kelly, Gene, American dancer, singer and actor, Yrbk 1945, Feb 1977, *Obit* Apr 1996

Kelly, Howard A., American gynecologist, *Obit* Mar 1943

Kelly, Jim, American football player, Nov 1992

Kelly, Joe, June 1945, *Obit* July 1959

Kelly, John B., American rower and sports executive, June 1971, *Obit* Apr 1985

Kelly, Judith, Oct 1941, *Obit* July 1957

Kelly, Mervin J., physicist and engineer, Oct 1956, *Obit* May 1971

Kelly, Nancy, actress, June 1955, *Obit* Mar 1995

Kelly, Patrick, fashion designer, Sept 1989, *Obit* Mar 1990

Kelly, Petra, German political leader, Mar 1984, *Obit* Jan 1993

Kelly, R., American singer, songwriter and record producer, June 1999

Kelly, Raymond, American police commissioner, Sept 2008

Kelly, Regina Zimmerman, Yrbk 1956

Kelly, Sharon Pratt, American mayor, Nov 1992

Kelly, Walt, American cartoonist, Oct 1956, *Obit* Yrbk 1973

Kelman, Charles D., American ophthalmologist and saxophonist, June 1984, *Obit* Yrbk 2004

Kelsen, Hans, Austrian-American law professor, Sept 1957, *Obit* June 1973

Kelsey, Frances Oldham, American pharmacologist and regulatory agency official, Apr 1965

Kem, James P., Oct 1950, *Obit* Apr 1965

Kemeny, John G., American mathematician and college president, Feb 1971, *Obit* Feb 1993

Kemmerer, Edwin Walter, Oct 1941, *Obit* Feb 1946

Kemmis, Daniel, mayor and public policy analyst, Oct 1996

Kemp, Hal, *Obit* Feb 1941

Kemp, Jack, American football player, congressman and Secretary of housing and urban development, Mar 1980, *Obit* Yrbk 2009

Kemper, James S., American insurance executive, Apr 1941, *Obit* Nov 1981

Kempner, Robert M. W., German lawyer, May 1943, *Obit* Oct 1993

Kempthorne, Dirk, American Secretary of the interior, June 2007

Kempton, Murray, American newspaper columnist, June 1973, *Obit* July 1997

Kemsley, James Gomer Berry, British newspaper publisher, Jan 1951, *Obit* Mar 1968

Kendall, Edward Calvin, American biochemist, Yrbk 1950, *Obit* June 1972

Kendall, William Mitchell, *Obit* Oct 1941

Kendrew, John C., British biochemist, Oct 1963, *Obit* Nov 1997

Kendrick, Baynard Hardwick, author, Feb 1946, *Obit* May 1977

Keneally, Thomas, Australian novelist, June 1987

Kennan, George Frost, American historian and diplomat, Oct 1947, Jan 1959, *Obit* Yrbk 2005

Kennedy, English violinist, July 1992

Kennedy, Anthony M., American Supreme Court justice, July 1988

Kennedy, Arthur, American actor, Nov 1961

Kennedy, Claudia, general, Jan 2000

Kennedy, David Matthew, American Secretary of the treasury, June 1969, *Obit* July 1996

Kennedy, Donald, physiologist and college president, July 1984

Kennedy, Edward Moore, American senator, Sept 1963, Oct 1978, *Obit* Oct 2009

Kennedy, John B., Feb 1944, *Obit* Oct 1961

Kennedy, John F., American president, June 1950, July 1961, *Obit* Jan 1964

Kennedy, John F., American lawyer, magazine editor and son of President John F. Kennedy, Jan 1996, *Obit* Sept 1999

Kennedy, Joseph P., American financier, diplomat and father of President John F. Kennedy, Nov 1940, *Obit* Jan 1970

Kennedy, Joseph Patrick, American congressman and energy company executive, June 1988

Kennedy, Kathleen, American film producer, Feb 2009

Kennedy, Paul M., British historian, Oct 1993

Kennedy, Randall, American law professor, Aug 2002

Kennedy, Robert F., American Attorney general and senator, Feb 1958, *Obit* July 1968

Kennedy, Robert Francis, American lawyer and son of Senator Robert F. Kennedy, May 2004

Kennedy, Rose Fitzgerald, mother of President John F. Kennedy, Nov 1970, *Obit* Mar 1995

Kennedy, Stephen P., June 1956, *Obit* Jan 1979

Kennedy, Thomas, June 1960, *Obit* Feb 1963

Kennedy, William, American novelist, May 1985

Kennedy, William P., Jan 1950, *Obit* July 1968

Kennelly, Ardyth, Yrbk 1953

Kennelly, Martin H., mayor, Yrbk 1949, *Obit* Jan 1962

Kenney, George C., American general, Jan 1943, *Obit* Oct 1977

Kennon, Robert Floyd, American governor, Oct 1954, *Obit* Apr 1988

Kenny, Elizabeth, Australian nurse, Oct 1942, *Obit* Jan 1953

Kent, Allegra, American ballet dancer, Mar 1970

Kent, Corita, American artist and nun, Feb 1969, *Obit* Nov 1986

Kent, Jeff, American baseball player, May 2003

Kent, Raymond A., *Obit* Apr 1943

Kent, Rockwell, American painter and travel writer, Nov 1942, *Obit* Apr 1971

Kenton, Stan, American band leader, June 1979

Kentridge, William, South African artist, Oct 2001

Kenyatta, Jomo, Kenyan president, Oct 1953, Apr 1974, *Obit* Oct 1978

Kenyon, Cynthia, American biochemist and biotechnology executive, Jan 2005

Kenyon, Dorothy, American judge, Apr 1947, *Obit* Apr 1972

Kenyon, Helen, Oct 1948

Kepes, Gyorgy, Hungarian-American painter, graphic designer and art critic, Mar 1973, *Obit* Mar 2002

Kepler, Asher Raymond, *Obit* Oct 1942

Keppel, Francis C., American educator, May 1963, *Obit* Apr 1990

Kerensky, Aleksandr Fyodorovich, Russian socialist leader, Yrbk 1966, *Obit* Sept 1970

Kerger, Paula, American broadcasting executive, July 2013

Kerkorian, Kirk, American financier, May 1975, Mar 1996

Kerlikowske, R. Gil, American law enforcement official, Nov 2009

Kern, Jerome, American composer, June 1942, *Obit* Yrbk 1945

Kernan, W. F., Apr 1942

Kerner, Otto, American governor and judge, Oct 1961, *Obit* July 1976

Kerouac, Jack, American novelist, Nov 1959, *Obit* Yrbk 1969

Kerr, Clark, American educator, Apr 1961, *Obit* May 2004

Kerr, Deborah, British actress, Sept 1947, *Obit* Feb 2008

Kerr, James W., Oct 1959

Kerr, Jean, American humorist and dramatist, July 1958, *Obit* May 2003

Kerr, Robert Samuel, American senator and governor, May 1950, *Obit* Feb 1963

Kerr, Steve, basketball player, Oct 1998

Kerr, Walter, drama critic, Oct 1953, *Obit* Jan 1997

Kerrey, Bob, American senator and university president, Feb 1991

Kerrl, Hanns, German cabinet member, *Obit* Feb 1942

Kerry, John Forbes, American senator, June 1988, Sept 2004

Kerst, Donald William, physicist, Apr 1950, *Obit* Oct 1993

Kersten, Charles J., Sept 1952

Kertesz, Andre, American photographer, Aug 1979, *Obit* Nov 1985

Kesey, Ken, American novelist, May 1976, *Obit* Feb 2002

Kesselring, Albert, German field marshal, Nov 1942, *Obit* Oct 1960

Kessing, O. O., American admiral and football association executive, June 1949, *Obit* Mar 1963

Kessler, David A., American physician and government official, Sept 1991

Kessler, Henry H., Oct 1957

Kestnbaum, Meyer, May 1953, *Obit* Feb 1961

Ketcham, Hank, American cartoonist, Jan 1956, *Obit* Sept 2001

Kettering, Charles Franklin, American electrical engineer, May 1940, Yrbk 1951, *Obit* Feb 1959

Kevorkian, Jack, American pathologist and right to die advocate, Sept 1994, *Obit* Yrbk 2011

Key, Ben Witt, *Obit* July 1940

Key, William, July 1943, *Obit* Mar 1959

Keyhoe, Donald Edward, marine corps officer, June 1956, *Obit* Feb 1989

Keynes, John Maynard, British economist, June 1941, *Obit* May 1946

Keys, Ancel, American physiologist, Jan 1966, *Obit* Yrbk 2005

Keys, David A., Oct 1958

Keyserling, Hermann, German philosopher, *Obit* June 1946

Keyserling, Leon H., American economist, Jan 1947, *Obit* Sept 1987

Keyworth, George A., American physicist and presidential adviser, Mar 1986

Khachaturian, Aram Il'ich, Mar 1948, *Obit* June 1978

Khaleda Zia, Bangladeshi prime minister, Jan 2003

Khalid, Jan 1976, *Obit* Aug 1982

Khalilzad, Zalmay, Afghan-American diplomat, Aug 2006

Khama, Seretse, Batswana president, May 1967, *Obit* Sept 1980

Khamenei, Ali, Iranian president, Nov 1987, Jan 2005

Khan, A. Q., Pakistani nuclear scientist, Jan 2004

Khan, Aamir, Indian actor, Jan 2002

Khan, Aly, Pakistani diplomat, May 1960

Khan, Amir, British boxer, Jan 2006

Khan, Begum Liaquat Ali, July 1950

Khan, Chaka, American singer, July 1999

Khan, Daisy, American Islamic leader, June 2013

Khan, Farah, Indian film director and choreographer, Jan 2007

Khan, Imran, Pakistani cricket player and member of Parliament, Jan 2005

Khan, Irene, Bangladeshi human rights activist, Jan 2002

Khan, Liaquat Ali, June 1948, *Obit* Yrbk 1951

Khan, Muhammad Zafrulla, Yrbk 1947

Khan, Salman, American school administrator, May 2013

Khashoggi, Adnan, Saudi Arabian financier, Mar 1986

Khatami, Mohammad, Iranian Islamic leader and president, Apr 1998

Kheel, Theodore, American labor mediator, Sept 1964, *Obit* Yrbk 2011

Khodorkovsky, Mikhail, Russian energy industry executive, Jan 2003

Khomeini, Ruhollah, Iranian religious and political leader, Nov 1979, *Obit* July 1989

Khorana, Har Gobind, Indian biochemist, Yrbk 1970, *Obit* Yrbk 2012

Khorkina, Svetlana, Russian gymnast, Jan 2003

Khouri, Faris el-, Sept 1948, *Obit* Feb 1962

Khrushchev, Nikita Sergeevich, Soviet communist leader, July 1954, *Obit* Oct 1971

Ki-Zerbo, Joseph, Burkinabe historian and political scientist, Jan 2002

Kiam, Omar, Yrbk 1945, *Obit* May 1954

Kiarostami, Abbas, Iranian film director, July 1998

Kibaki, Mwai, Kenyan president, Jan 2003

Kid Rock, American rapper, Oct 2001

Kidd, Chip, American book and graphic designer, July 2005

Kidd, Isaac Campbell, *Obit* Feb 1942

Kidd, Jason, American basketball player, May 2002

Kidd, Michael, American choreographer, Mar 1960, *Obit* Yrbk 2008

Kidder, George Wallace, microbiologist, July 1949

Kidman, Nicole, Australian actress, Mar 1997

Kiefer, Anselm, German painter, June 1988

Kienholz, Edward, American painter and sculptor, Aug 1989, *Obit* Aug 1994

Kiepura, Jan, Nov 1943, *Obit* Nov 1966

Kier, Udo, German actor, Jan 2005

Kieran, John, sportswriter, Apr 1940, *Obit* Feb 1982

Kiesinger, Kurt Georg, German chancellor, Apr 1967, *Obit* Apr 1988

Kiesler, Frederick, Austrian-Ameican sculptor and architect, Jan 1944, *Obit* Feb 1966

Kieslowski, Krzysztof, Polish motion picture director, May 1995, *Obit* May 1996

Kiessling, Laura L., American biochemist, Aug 2003

Kiir, Salva, Sudanese rebel and vice-president, Jan 2005

Kilar, Jason, American Internet executive, Aug 2009

Kilbourne, Jean, American educator, May 2004

Kilday, Paul J., Oct 1958, *Obit* Yrbk 1968

Kiley, Richard, actor, Apr 1973, *Obit* May 1999

Kilgallen, Dorothy, American newspaper columnist, Feb 1952, *Obit* Jan 1966

Kilgallen, Dorothy; and Kollmar, Richard, Feb 1952

Kilgore, Harley Martin, American senator, June 1943, *Obit* May 1956

Killanin, Michael Morris, Irish sports executive and journalist, Apr 1973, *Obit* July 1999

Killebrew, Harmon, American baseball player and sportscaster, Feb 1966, *Obit* Yrbk 2011

Killian, James Rhyne, American college president and presidential adviser, Feb 1949, May 1959, *Obit* Mar 1988

Killion, George L., Nov 1952

Killy, Jean Claude, French skier, June 1968

Kilmer, Aline, *Obit* Yrbk 1941

Kilmer, Val, American actor, Jan 1996

Kilmuir, David Patrick Maxwell Fyfe, Yrbk 1951, *Obit* Mar 1967

Kilpatrick, James J., American columnist, July 1980, *Obit* Yrbk 2010

Kilpatrick, John Reed, July 1948, *Obit* July 1960

Kilpatrick, Kwame M., American mayor, Apr 2004

Kilpi, Eeva, Finnish essayist, poet, short story writer and novelist, Jan 2007

Kim, Dae Jung, South Korean president, Sept 1985, *Obit* Yrbk 2009

Kim, Il Sung, North Korean head of state, Sept 1951, *Obit* Yrbk 1994, Yrbk 1994

Kim, Jim Yong, American physician and medical anthropologist, Nov 2006

Kim, Jong Il, North Korean head of state, Jan 2002, *Obit* Yrbk 2012

Kim, Young Sam, Korean president, June 1995

Kimball, Abbott, May 1949, *Obit* Nov 1968

Kimball, Dan A., American Secretary of the navy, Sept 1951, *Obit* Oct 1970

Kimball, James Henry, *Obit* Feb 1944

Kimball, Lindsley Fiske, American social welfare leader, July 1951, *Obit* Oct 1992

Kimball, Spencer W., American clergyman and Mormon leader, Feb 1979, *Obit* Jan 1986

Kimball, Wilbur R., *Obit* Sept 1940

Kimble, George H. T., Oct 1952

Kimbrel, Monroe, June 1963

Kimbrough, Emily, lecturer and author, Mar 1944, *Obit* Apr 1989

Kimmel, Husband Edward, admiral, Jan 1942, *Obit* July 1968

Kimmel, Jimmy, American comedian, Oct 2009

Kimpton, Lawrence A., June 1951, *Obit* Jan 1978

Kincaid, Jamaica, Antiguan novelist and short story writer, Mar 1991

Kindelberger, James Howard, Mar 1951, *Obit* Oct 1962

Kinder, Katharine L., May 1957

Kindler, Hans, Sept 1946, *Obit* Oct 1949

Kiner, Ralph, American baseball player and sportscaster, May 1954

King, Alan, American comedian, June 1970, *Obit* Yrbk 2004

King, Alexander, Scottish chemist and futurist, Jan 2002

King, Angus, governor, Apr 2013

King, B. B., American blues guitarist and singer, June 1970

King, Billie Jean, American tennis player, Yrbk 1967

King, Carole, American singer and songwriter, Jan 1974

King, Cecil R., American congressman, Feb 1952, *Obit* May 1974

King, Charles Glen, biochemist and nutritionist, Yrbk 1967, *Obit* Mar 1988

King, Coretta Scott, American civil rights leader, May 1969, *Obit* Apr 2006

King, David, American jazz drummer, Oct 2011

King, Don, American boxing promoter, June 1984

King, Ernest Joseph, American admiral, Feb 1942, *Obit* Sept 1956

King, Florence, American satirist, Apr 2006

King, John, American television news anchor, Mar 2010

King, John W., governor and judge, May 1964, *Obit* Nov 1996

King, Larry, American radio and television talk show host, May 1985

King, Martin Luther, American clergyman and civil rights leader, May 1957, May 1965, *Obit* May 1968

King, Mary-Claire, American geneticist, Feb 1995

King, Muriel, Apr 1943, *Obit* May 1977

King, Samuel Wilder, Oct 1953, *Obit* June 1959

King, Stephen, American novelist and short story writer, Oct 1981

King, William Lyon Mackenzie, Canadian prime minister, Aug 1940, *Obit* Sept 1950

Kingdon, Frank, July 1944, *Obit* Apr 1972

Kingman, Dave, baseball player, Mar 1982

Kingman, Dong, American painter and illustrator, Oct 1962, *Obit* Yrbk 2000

Kings of Leon (Musical group), July 2010

Kingsbury, Tim, Canadian bassist and guitarist, Jan 2007

Kingsland, Lawrence C., Jan 1949

Kingsley, Ben, English actor, Nov 1983

Kingsley, J. Donald, Feb 1950

Kingsley, Myra, Apr 1943

Kingsley, Sidney, dramatist, June 1943, *Obit* May 1995

Kingsolver, Barbara, American novelist and short story writer, July 1994

Kingston, Maxine Hong, American novelist, Mar 1990

Kinkade, Thomas, American painter, June 2000, *Obit* Yrbk 2012

Kinkaid, Thomas Cassin, American admiral, Yrbk 1944, *Obit* Jan 1973

Kinnear, Helen Alice, Canadian judge, Apr 1957

Kinnell, Galway, American poet, Aug 1986

Kinnock, Neil, British political leader and European Commission official, Apr 1984

Kinsey, Alfred Charles, American zoologist and sex researcher, Jan 1954, *Obit* Oct 1956

Kinski, Nastassia, German actress, June 1984

Kinsley, Michael, American columnist and commentator, May 1995

Kintner, Earl W., lawyer and government official, Apr 1960, *Obit* Mar 1992

Kintner, Robert E., radio and television executive, Oct 1950, *Obit* Feb 1981

Kiphuth, Robert J. H., swimming coach, June 1957, *Obit* Mar 1967

Kipling, Caroline Starr Balestier, *Obit* Jan 1940

Kiplinger, Willard Monroe, journalist and periodical publisher, Mar 1943, Jan 1962, *Obit* Oct 1967

Kipnis, Alexander, opera singer, Yrbk 1943, *Obit* July 1978

Kipping, Norman, Yrbk 1949

Kirbo, Charles H., lawyer, Sept 1977, *Obit* Nov 1996

Kirby, George, comedian, May 1977, *Obit* Jan 1996

Kirby, Robert E., electrical generating equipment industry executive, Sept 1979, *Obit* Mar 1999

Kirby, Rollin, Yrbk 1944, *Obit* June 1952

Kirch, Leo, German broadcasting executive, Jan 2002, *Obit* Yrbk 2011

Kirchner, Cristina E. Fernandez de, Argentine president, Jan 2007

Kirchner, Leon, American composer and pianist, Yrbk 1967, *Obit* Yrbk 2009

Kirchner, Nestor, Argentine president, Jan 2004, *Obit* Yrbk 2010

Kirchwey, Freda, American magazine editor, Yrbk 1942, *Obit* Feb 1976

Kirchwey, George W., *Obit* Apr 1942

Kiriyenko, Sergei, Russian energy industry executive, Aug 1998

Kirk, Alan Goodrich, American admiral and diplomat, July 1944, *Obit* Yrbk 1963

Kirk, Alexander C., Feb 1945

Kirk, Claude R., American governor, Oct 1967, *Obit* Yrbk 2011

Kirk, Grayson Louis, American college president, May 1951, *Obit* Jan 1998

Kirk, Norman T., American surgeon and general, Feb 1944, *Obit* Nov 1960

Kirk, Paul, American senator and political party leader, Aug 1987

Kirk, Ron, American trade represenative, Apr 2010

Kirk, Russell, American political philosopher, Sept 1962, *Obit* June 1994

Kirk, William T., Feb 1960, *Obit* Mar 1974

Kirkland, Gelsey, American ballet dancer, Oct 1975

Kirkland, Lane, American labor leader, May 1980, *Obit* Oct 1999

Kirkland, Winifred Margaretta, *Obit* July 1943

Kirkpatrick, Chris, American singer, Nov 2000

Kirkpatrick, Helen, journalist, May 1941

Kirkpatrick, Ivone, June 1950, *Obit* July 1964

Kirkpatrick, Jeane J., American diplomat, July 1981, *Obit* Yrbk 2007

Kirkpatrick, Miles W., lawyer and government official, Feb 1972, *Obit* July 1998

Kirkpatrick, Ralph, harpsichordist and musicologist, Sept 1971, *Obit* Aug 1984

Kirkus, Virginia, American magazine editor and literary critic, May 1941, June 1954, *Obit* Nov 1980

Kirstein, Lincoln, American ballet manager, Yrbk 1952, Aug 1990, *Obit* Mar 1996

Kirsten, Dorothy, American opera singer, Feb 1948, *Obit* Jan 1993

Kiselyov, Yevgeny, Russian broadcast journalist and executive, Jan 2004

Kisevalter, George, *Obit* May 1941

Kish, Daniel, Echolation developer and president of World Access for the Blind, Sept 2013

Kishi, Nobusuke, Japanese prime minister, June 1957, *Obit* Sept 1987

Kiss (Musical group), Apr 1999

Kissin, Evgeny, Russian pianist, Nov 1997

Kissinger, Henry, American Secretary of state, June 1958, June 1972

Kistiakowsky, George, American chemist and presidential aide, Nov 1960, *Obit* Feb 1983

Kistler, Darci, American ballet dancer, Oct 1991

Kitaj, R. B., American painter, Apr 1982, *Obit* Yrbk 2008

Kitano, Takeshi, Japanese actor, screenwriter and director, July 1998

Kitchell, Iva, dancer, Yrbk 1951, *Obit* Jan 1984

Kitchen, Michael, British actor, Nov 2008

Kitson, Harry Dexter, Apr 1951, *Obit* Nov 1959

Kitt, Eartha, American singer and actress, Apr 1955, *Obit* Yrbk 2009

Kittredge, George Lyman, philologist, *Obit* Sept 1941

Kiviniemi, Mari, Finnish prime minister, Oct 2010

Kjartan Sveinsson, Icelandic keyboardist, Jan 2003

Klahre, Ethel S., May 1962

Klass, Perri, American pediatrician and novelist, May 1999

Klassen, Elmer Theodore, postmaster general, May 1973, *Obit* June 1990

Klaus, Josef, Austrian chancellor, Jan 1965, *Obit* Oct 2001

Klaus, Vaclav, Czech president, Nov 1997

Klawe, Maria, Canadian computer scientist, college dean and painter, June 2013

Klee, Paul, Swiss painter, *Obit* Aug 1940

Kleffens, Eelco Nicolaas van, Oct 1947

Kleiber, Carlos, German conductor, July 1991, *Obit* Yrbk 2004

Klein, Calvin, American fashion designer, July 1978

Klein, Edward E., rabbi, Sept 1966, *Obit* Sept 1985

Klein, Guillermo, Argentine jazz pianist and composer, Jan 2006

Klein, Herbert G., American newspaper executive and presidential aide, Feb 1971, *Obit* Yrbk 2009

Klein, Julius, veterans' leader and public relations consultant, July 1948, *Obit* May 1984

Klein, Naomi, Canadian journalist and social activist, Aug 2003

Klein, Robert, American comedian, Mar 1977

Klein, William, American photographer, Mar 2004

Kleindienst, Richard G., American Attorney general, Oct 1972, *Obit* June 2000

Kleinsmid, Rufus B. von, June 1958, *Obit* Sept 1964

Kleist, Ewald von, German field marshal, July 1943, *Obit* Jan 1955

Kleitman, Nathaniel, physiologist, Oct 1957, *Obit* Jan 2000

Klemperer, Otto, German conductor, Mar 1965, *Obit* Sept 1973

Klenze, Camillo von, *Obit* Apr 1943

Kleppe, Thomas S., American Secretary of the interior, Aug 1976, *Obit* Yrbk 2007

Klimecki, Tadeusz A., *Obit* Aug 1943

Kline, Allan B., American agricultural leader, Mar 1948, *Obit* Sept 1968

Kline, Clarice, May 1961

Kline, Kevin, American actor, July 1986

Kline, Nathan S., psychiatrist and educator, Oct 1965, *Obit* May 1983

Klinkenborg, Verlyn, American nonifction writer, July 2006

Klitschko, Vitali, Ukrainian boxer, Jan 2003

Klochkova, Yana, Ukrainian swimmer, Jan 2004

Klopsteg, Paul Ernest, physicist, May 1959, *Obit* July 1991

Kluckhohn, Clyde, American anthropologist, Nov 1951, *Obit* Oct 1960

Kluge, John W., American broadcasting and telecommunications executive, Sept 1993, *Obit* Yrbk 2010

Klumpp, Theodore G., Oct 1958

Knabenshue, Paul, *Obit* Mar 1942

Knappstein, Karl Heinrich, Feb 1965

Knatchbull-Hugessen, Hughe, Mar 1943, *Obit* May 1971

Knaths, Karl, painter, July 1953, *Obit* Apr 1971

Knauer, Virginia H., American government official, Apr 1970, *Obit* Yrbk 2011

Knickerbocker, Hubert Renfro, journalist, Sept 1940, *Obit* Sept 1949

Knievel, Evel, American motorcycle stunt performer, Feb 1972, *Obit* Yrbk 2008

Knievel, Robbie, American motorcycle stunt performer, Mar 2005

Knight, Bobby, American basketball coach, May 1987

Knight, Douglas M., May 1964

Knight, Eric Mowbray, Anglo-American novelist, short story writer and journalist, July 1942, *Obit* Mar 1943

Knight, Frances G., government employee, Oct 1955, *Obit* Nov 1999

Knight, Gladys, American singer, Feb 1987

Knight, Goodwin, American governor, Jan 1955, *Obit* July 1970

Knight, John Shively, American newspaper publisher, Apr 1945, *Obit* Aug 1981

Knight, O. A., June 1952

Knight, Philip H., American shoe company executive, Aug 1997

Knight, Ruth Adams, Aug 1943, Yrbk 1955

Knightley, Keira, English actress, Jan 2005

Knipfel, Jim, American memoirist, columnist and novelist, Mar 2005

Knipling, E. F., entomologist, May 1975, *Obit* Yrbk 2000

Knoblock, Edward, *Obit* Aug 1945

Knoll, Andrew H., American paleontologist, Apr 2006

Knoll, Hans G., May 1955

Knopf, Alfred, American publisher, June 1943, Nov 1966, *Obit* Oct 1984

Knopf, Blanche W., American publishing executive, July 1957, *Obit* July 1966

Knopf, Sigard Adolphus, *Obit* Sept 1940

Knopfler, Mark, British singer, songwriter and guitarist, Apr 1995

Knorr, Nathan H., Feb 1957, *Obit* Aug 1977

Knott, Sarah Gertrude, July 1947

Knowland, William Fife, American senator and newspaper publisher, Apr 1947, *Obit* Apr 1974

Knowles, John H., Yrbk 1970, *Obit* May 1979

Knowlson, James, Irish biographer, Nov 1942

Knox, Frank, American Secretary of the navy and newspaper publisher, Aug 1940, *Obit* June 1944

Knox, Louise Chambers, *Obit* Mar 1942

Knox, Ronald Arbuthnott, English priest, satirist, essayist and mystery writer, July 1950, *Obit* Nov 1957

Knox, Rose Markward, American food industry

executive, May 1949, *Obit* Nov 1950

Knox, Simmie, American painter, May 2009

Knudsen, Semon E., American automobile executive, Jan 1974, *Obit* Sept 1998

Knudsen, William S., American automobile executive, July 1940, *Obit* June 1948

Knussen, Oliver, Scottish composer and conductor, Feb 1994

Knuth-Winterfeldt, Kield Gustav, Sept 1959

Knutson, Coya, congresswoman, Mar 1956, *Obit* Jan 1997

Knutson, Harold, American congressman, Jan 1947, *Obit* Oct 1953

Kobak, Edgar, Apr 1947, *Obit* July 1962

Kobayashi, Takeru, Japanese competitive eater, Jan 2003

Kobilka, Brian, Apr 2013

Koch, Ed, American mayor, Sept 1978, *Obit* Yrbk 2013

Koch, Fred, drama teacher and theatrical director, Oct 1953, *Obit* Yrbk 2000

Koch, Frederick H., *Obit* Oct 1944

Koch, Jim, American brewing company executive, May 2012

Koch, John, American painter, May 1965, *Obit* June 1978

Koch, Kenneth, American poet, Feb 1978, *Obit* Yrbk 2002

Koch, Theodore Wesley, librarian, *Obit* May 1941

Koch, William I., American energy executive, investor and yacht racer, Mar 1999

Kock, Karin, Nov 1948

Koenig, Pierre, French general, Sept 1944, *Obit* Nov 1970

Koestler, Arthur, Hungarian-British novelist, essayist and journalist, Apr 1943, Jan 1962, *Obit* Apr 1983

Koffka, Kurt, German psychologist, *Obit* Jan 1942

Koga, Mineichi, *Obit* Oct 1943

Koh, Jennifer, American violinist, Sept 2006

Kohl, Helmut, German chancellor, Aug 1977

Kohl, Herbert, American senator, May 2008

Kohler, Foy David, American diplomat, Jan 1950, *Obit* Mar 1991

Kohler, Horst, German president, Jan 2002

Kohler, Walter Jodok, American manufacturing executive and governor, Jan 1953, *Obit* May 1976

Kohler, Walter Jodok, American manufacturing executive and governor, *Obit* May 1940

Kohout, Pavel, Czech author and dramatist, Feb 1988

Kohoutek, Lubos, June 1974

Koirala, Girija Prasad, Nepalese prime minister, Jan 2006, *Obit* Yrbk 2010

Koite, Habib, Malian guitarist, Jan 2002

Koivisto, Mauno, Finnish president, Sept 1982

Koizumi, Junichiro, Japanese prime minister, Jan 2002

Kok, Wim, Dutch prime minister, Jan 2003

Kokoschka, Oskar, Austrian painter and dramatist, Oct 1956, *Obit* Apr 1980

Kolar, Jiri, Czech poet and artist, Apr 1986, *Obit* Yrbk 2002

Kolarov, Vassil, Yrbk 1949, *Obit* Mar 1950

Kolbe, Parke Rexford, *Obit* Apr 1942

Kolff, Willem J., American physician, May 1983, *Obit* Yrbk 2009

Kollek, Teddy, Israeli mayor, Oct 1974, Mar 1993, *Obit* Yrbk 2007

Koller, Daphne, computer scientist, May 2013

Kollmar, Richard, Feb 1952, *Obit* Feb 1971

Kollontai, A., Soviet diplomat, Oct 1943, *Obit* Apr 1952

Kolodin, Irving, music critic, July 1947, *Obit* June 1988

Koltai, Lajos, Hungarian cinematographer, Jan 2003

Kolvenbach, Peter-Hans, Dutch Jesuit leader, May 1984

Koma, Japanese dancer and choreographer, May 2003

Komando, Kim, computer scientist and radio talk show host, Sept 2000

Komar, Vitali, Russian painter, Oct 1984

Komar, Vitali; and Melamid, Aleksandr, Oct 1984

Komarovsky, Mirra, American sociologist, Oct 1953, *Obit* Apr 1999

Konare, Alpha Oumar, Malian president, Oct 2001

Koner, Pauline, ballet dancer and choreographer, Oct 1964, *Obit* Apr 2001

Konev, Ivan S., Soviet field marshal, Oct 1943, Jan 1956, *Obit* July 1973

Konijnenburg, Willem Adriaan van, *Obit* Apr 1943

Konoye, Fumimaro, Japanese prime minister, Sept 1940, *Obit* Feb 1946

Konstanty, Jim, baseball player, Apr 1951, *Obit* Aug 1976

Koo, V. K. Wellington, Chinese prime minister and diplomat, July 1941, *Obit* Jan 1986

Koogle, Timothy, Internet search engine company executive, Apr 2000

Koolhaas, Rem, Dutch architect, Nov 2000

Koons, Jeff, American artist, May 1990

Koontz, Elizabeth Duncan, American labor leader and teacher, Jan 1969, *Obit* Apr 1989

Koop, C. Everett, American surgeon general, Sept 1983, *Obit* Yrbk 2013

Kopal, Zdenek, Czech astronomer, Mar 1969, *Obit* Aug 1993

Kopit, Arthur L., dramatist, Yrbk 1972

Kopp, Wendy, American teacher recruiter, Mar 2003

Koppel, Ted, American television newscaster, July 1984

Kopple, Barbara, American film and television director, July 1998

Koprowski, Hilary, Mar 1968, *Obit* Yrbk 2013

Koprulu, Mehmet Fuat, Jan 1953, *Obit* Sept 1966

Korbut, Olga, Soviet gymnast, July 1973

Korda, Alexander, British film director and producer, Sept 1946, *Obit* Mar 1956

Korda, Michael, British editor, essayist, novelist and memoirist, Aug 1985

Korine, Harmony, American filmmaker, Feb 2010

Korizis, Alexander, Mar 1941, *Obit* Mar 1941

Korman, Harvey, American actor, Oct 1979, *Obit* Yrbk 2008

Kornberg, Arthur, American biochemist, Sept 1968, *Obit* Feb 2008

Korner, Theodor, July 1951, *Obit* Mar 1957

Korngold, Erich Wolfgang, Austrian composer, Mar 1943, *Obit* Feb 1958

Korngold, Julius, *Obit* Oct 1945

Kors, Michael, American fashion designer, Jan 2000

Korth, Frederick H., secretary of the navy, July 1962, *Obit* Jan 1999

Kosaka, Zentaro, Sept 1961

Koshiba, Masatoshi, Japanese physicist, Jan 2007

Kosinski, Jerzy N., Polish-American novelist, essayist and critic, Mar 1974, *Obit* July 1991

Kossak, Zofia, June 1944, *Obit* June 1968

Kostelanetz, Andre, American conductor, July 1942, *Obit* Mar 1980

Kosteniuk, Alexandra, Russian chess player, Jan 2006

Koster, Bo, American rock keyboardist, Nov 2008

Kostunica, Vojislav, Yugoslav president, Jan 2001

Kosygin, Aleksei Nikolaevich, Soviet prime minister, Sept 1965, *Obit* Feb 1981

Kotb, Heba, Egyptian sex therapist, Jan 2007

Kotb, Hoda, American television news anchor, Apr 2011

Kotche, Glenn, American drummer and percussionist, Feb 2010

Kotelawala, John Lionel, Sri Lankan prime minister, Oct 1955

Kotschnig, Walter Maria, United Nations official and diplomat, Oct 1952, *Obit* Sept 1985

Kott, Jan, Polish literary critic, Apr 1969, *Obit* Mar 2002

Kotto, Yaphet, American actor, Mar 1995

Kouchner, Bernard, French physician and cabinet member, Aug 1993

Koufax, Sandy, American baseball player, Jan 1964

Kouka, Hone, New Zealand dramatist, Jan 2004

Kournikova, Anna, Russian tennis player, Jan 2002

Koussevitzky, Natalya, *Obit* Mar 1942

Koussevitzky, Serge, Russian conductor, Nov 1940, *Obit* July 1951

Kovacs, Ernie, American comedian, Feb 1958, *Obit* Mar 1962

Kovalchuk, Ilya, Russian hockey player, Mar 2007

Kovic, Ron, soldier and anti-war activist, Aug 1990

Kowalski, Frank, July 1960, *Obit* Yrbk 1974

Koz, Dave, American jazz saxophonist and composer, June 2013

Kozena, Magdalena, Czech opera singer, Jan 2005

Kozlenko, William, Oct 1941

Kozlov, Frol R., Nov 1959, *Obit* Mar 1965

Kozlowski, Leon, *Obit* July 1944

Kozol, Jonathan, American social critic, Jan 1986

Kozyrev, Andrei V., Russian diplomat, Sept 1992

Kozyrev, Nikolai A., Feb 1970

Kraft, Christopher C., aerospace engineer, Feb 1966

Kraft, Ole Bjorn, Feb 1953

Kraft, Robert K., American businessman and football executive, Feb 2012

Krag, Jens Otto, Danish prime minister, Oct 1962, *Obit* Aug 1978

Krainik, Ardis, opera manager, Nov 1991, *Obit* Mar 1997

Krall, Diana, Canadian singer and pianist, June 2000

Kramer, Edward Adam, *Obit* Feb 1942

Kramer, Jack, American tennis player, May 1947, *Obit* Yrbk 2009

Kramer, Joey, American rock drummer, July 2004

Kramer, Larry, American dramatist, Mar 1994

Kramer, Stanley, American motion picture producer and director, May 1951, *Obit* May 2001

Kramm, Joseph, actor and dramatist, July 1952

Kramnik, Vladimir, Russian chess player, Jan 2003

Krantz, Judith, American romance novelist, May 1982

Krasna, Norman, dramatist and screenwriter, May 1952, *Obit* Feb 1985

Krasner, Lee, American painter, Mar 1974, *Obit* Aug 1984

Kraus, Alfredo, Spanish opera singer, June 1987, *Obit* Nov 1999

Kraus, Hans Peter, American rare book dealer, July 1960, *Obit* Jan 1989

Kraus, Lili, Hungarian pianist, Oct 1975, *Obit* Jan 1987

Kraus, Rene, July 1941, *Obit* Sept 1947

Krause, Allen K., *Obit* July 1941

Krause, David W., Canadian paleontologist and anatomist, Feb 2002

Kraushaar, Otto F., college president, Nov 1949, *Obit* Nov 1989

Krauss, Alison, American fiddler and singer, May 1997

Krauss, Nicole, American novelist, Nov 2010

Krauthammer, Charles, American columnist, Jan 2008

Kravchenko, Victor, July 1946, *Obit* Mar 1966

Kravchuk, Leonid, Ukrainian president, Jan 1993

Kravis, Henry R., American financier, Mar 1989

Kravitz, Lenny, American singer and guitarist, Apr 1996

Krawcheck, Sallie, American financial executive, Mar 2006

Krebs, Hans Adolf, British biochemist, Mar 1954, *Obit* Feb 1982

Kreisky, Bruno, Austrian chancellor, Sept 1960, *Obit* Sept 1990

Kreisler, Fritz, Austrian violinist, July 1944, *Obit* Mar 1962

Krekeler, Heinz L., Yrbk 1951

Kremer, Gidon, Russian violinist, Mar 1985

Krenek, Ernst, American composer, July 1942, *Obit* Feb 1992

Krens, Thomas, American museum director, Apr 1989

Krenz, Egon, East German communist leader, Mar 1990

Kreps, Juanita Morris, American Secretary of commerce, June 1977, *Obit* Yrbk 2010

Kress, Samuel H., merchant, Oct 1955

Krick, Irving, meteorologist, July 1950, *Obit* Sept 1996

Kriebel, Hermann, *Obit* Apr 1941

Krim, Mathilde, American geneticist and virologist, Aug 1987

Kripke, Saul A., American philosopher, Oct 2004

Krips, Josef, June 1965, *Obit* Yrbk 1974

Krishna Menon, V. K., Indian lawyer and diplomat, Mar 1953, *Obit* Nov 1974

Krishnamurti, J., Indian philosopher, Oct 1974, *Obit* Apr 1986

Krishnaraja Wadiyar, *Obit* Sept 1940

Kristof, Nicholas D., American newspaper columnist, Feb 2006

Kristofferson, Kris, American actor, singer and songwriter, Nov 1974

Kristol, Irving, American political commentator, Sept 1974, *Obit* Nov 2009

Kristol, William, American political adviser, commentator and magazine editor, May 1997

Krivitsky, W. G., Soviet intelligence service agent, *Obit* Mar 1941

Kroc, Ray, American fast food restaurant chain founder and baseball team owner, Mar 1973, *Obit* Mar 1984

Krock, Arthur, American journalist, Feb 1943, *Obit* June 1974

Kroeber, A. L., American anthropologist, Oct 1958, *Obit* Yrbk 1960

Kroes, Neelie, Dutch European Commission official, Jan 2005

Kroft, Steve, American television reporter, Nov 1996

Krohg, Per, Nov 1954

Krol, John, Jan 1969, *Obit* May 1996

Kroll, Jack, American labor leader, Sept 1946, *Obit* July 1971

Kroll, Jules, American lawyer and private detective, Feb 1999

Kroll, Leon, American painter, Mar 1943, *Obit* Yrbk 1974

Krone, Julie, American jockey, Oct 1989

Kronenberger, Louis, drama critic, editor and author, Aug 1944, *Obit* July 1980

Kross, Anna M., American judge, Nov 1945, *Obit* Oct 1979

Krueger, Maynard C., May 1940

Krueger, Walter, American general, Apr 1943, *Obit* Oct 1967

Krueger, Wilhelm, *Obit* June 1943

Krug, J. A., American Secretary of the interior, Oct 1944, *Obit* May 1970

Kruger, Barbara, American artist, July 1995

Kruger-Gray, George, *Obit* June 1943

Krugman, Paul R., American economist, Aug 2001

Krupa, Gene, American drummer and band leader, Sept 1947, *Obit* Yrbk 1973

Krupp von Bohlen und Halbach, Alfried, German munitions manufacturer, May 1955, *Obit* Oct 1967

Krupp, Frederic D., American lawyer and environmentalist, Sept 2007

Krupsak, Mary Anne, July 1975

Kruspe, Richard Z., German guitarist, Jan 2007

Krutch, Joseph Wood, American critic, biographer and nature writer, Nov 1959, *Obit* July 1970

Krzyzewski, Mike, American basketball coach, Jan 1997

Kubelik, Jan, Czech violinist and composer, *Obit* Jan 1941

Kubelik, Rafael, Czech conductor, Feb 1951, *Obit* Oct 1996

Kubitschek, Juscelino, Brazilian president, Apr 1956, *Obit* Nov 1976

Kubler, Tad, American guitarist, Sept 2010

Kubler-Ross, Elisabeth, American psychiatrist, June 1980, *Obit* Yrbk 2004

Kubly, Herbert O., author and dramatist, Feb 1959, *Obit* Oct 1996

Kubrick, Stanley, American film director, Feb 1963, *Obit* May 1999

Kuchel, Thomas H., American senator, Feb 1954, *Obit* Feb 1995

Kuchler, Georg von, Sept 1943

Kuchma, Leonid, Ukrainian president, Oct 1997

Kucinich, Dennis, American congressman, Mar 1979, July 2008

Kudelka, James, Canadian ballet dancer and choreographer, Mar 1995

Kuekes, Edward D., cartoonist, Mar 1954, *Obit* Mar 1987

Kufuor, John, Ghanaian president, Jan 2002

Kuhlman, Kathryn, evangelist, July 1974, *Obit* Apr 1976

Kuhlmann, Frederick, *Obit* June 1941

Kuhn, Bowie, American lawyer and baseball commissioner, Jan 1970, *Obit* Yrbk 2007

Kuhn, Edward W., June 1966

Kuhn, Irene Corbally, journalist, Feb 1946, *Obit* Mar 1996

Kuhn, Maggie, American feminist and civil rights activist, July 1978, *Obit* July 1995

Kuiper, Gerard Peter, American astronomer, Feb 1959, *Obit* Feb 1974

Kuipers, Andre, Dutch physician and astronaut, Jan 2004

Kukoc, Toni, Croatian basketball player, July 1997

Kulik, Grigory, July 1942

Kullman, Ellen, American chemical industry executive, Nov 2011

Kullmer, Ann, Feb 1949

Kumaratunga, Chandrika Bandaranaike, Sri Lankan prime minister, Jan 1996

Kumm, Henry William, physician and foundation official, June 1955, *Obit* Mar 1991

Kummant, Alexander, American railroad executive, Jan 2007

Kundera, Milan, Czech poet, dramatist, novelist and short story writer, Mar 1983

Kung, H. H., Chinese government official, Mar 1943, *Obit* Oct 1967

Kung, Hans, Swiss theologian, July 1963

Kunin, Madeleine, American governor and diplomat, July 1987

Kunitz, Stanley, American poet, Mar 1943, Nov 1959, *Obit* Aug 2006

Kuniyoshi, Yasuo, Japanese-American painter, June 1941, *Obit* June 1953

Kunstler, William, American lawyer, Apr 1971, *Obit* Nov 1995

Kunuk, Zacharias, Canadian Inuit film director, Jan 2002

Kunz, Alfred A., Yrbk 1941

Kunz, Stanley H., *Obit* June 1946

Kuok, Robert, Malaysian financier, June 1998

Kuralt, Charles, American television newscaster, July 1981, *Obit* Sept 1997

Kurchatov, Igor Vasilevich, Russian physicist, Nov 1957, *Obit* Apr 1960

Kureishi, Hanif, English novelist, dramatist and screenwriter, Feb 1992

Kurenko, Maria, Sept 1944

Kurihara, Harumi, Japanese cook and television personality, Jan 2006

Kurosawa, Akira, Japanese motion picture director, Apr 1965, July 1991, *Obit* Nov 1998

Kurosawa, Kiyoshi, Japanese film director, Jan 2006

Kurtz, Efrem, conductor, Feb 1946, *Obit* Sept 1995

Kurtz, Howard, American journalist, Jan 2011

Kurtz, Swoosie, American actress, Oct 1987

Kurusu, Saburo, Jan 1942, *Obit* May 1954

Kurzweil, Raymond, American computer scientist and inventor, Sept 2008

Kusch, Polykarp, American physicist, Mar 1956, *Obit* May 1993

Kushner, Harold S., American rabbi and writer on religion, Apr 1997

Kushner, Jared, American newspaper publisher, June 2007

Kushner, Tony, American dramatist, July 2002

Kusner, Kathy, American equestrian, Apr 1973

Kusturica, Emir, Bosnian motion picture director and screenwriter, Nov 2005

Kutchuk, Fazil, Cypriot political leader and physician, Feb 1961, *Obit* Mar 1984

Kuter, Laurence S., American air force general, July 1948

Kuti, Femi, Nigerian singer and songwriter, Jan 2002

Kuusinen, Hertta, Finnish cabinet member, May 1949, *Obit* May 1974

Kuzmin, Iosif I., Feb 1959

Kuznets, Simon, American economist, May 1972, *Obit* Sept 1985

Kuznetsov, Nikolai G., Nov 1942, *Obit* Jan 1975

Kuznetsov, Vasilii Vasil'evich, Soviet diplomat, Jan 1956, *Obit* Aug 1990

Kuznetsova, Svetlana, Russian tennis player, Mar 2008

Kvitova, Petra, Czech tennis player, Jan 2012

Kweli, Talib, American rapper, July 2012

Kwiecie?, Mariusz, Polish opera singer, July 2012

Kydland, Finn E., Norwegian economist, Jan 2007

Kylian, Jiri, Czech dancer, choreographer and director, Sept 1982

Kyprianou, Spyros, Cypriot president, May 1979, *Obit* May 2002

Kyser, Kay, American band leader, Apr 1941, *Obit* Sept 1985

L

L'Amour, Louis, American western novelist, Feb 1980, *Obit* July 1988

L'Engle, Madeleine, American novelist and children's author, Jan 1997, *Obit* Yrbk 2007

L'Esperance, Elise Depew Strang, pathologist, Nov 1950, *Obit* Apr 1959

LL Cool J, American rapper and actor, Nov 1997

La Cava, Gregory, motion picture director, Yrbk 1941, *Obit* Apr 1952

La Farge, Oliver, American novelist and anthropologist, Jan 1953, *Obit* Oct 1963

La Follette, Charles M., Feb 1950

La Follette, Robert M., American senator, May 1944, *Obit* Apr 1953

La Gorce, John Oliver, Nov 1954, *Obit* Feb 1960

La Guardia, Fiorello Henry, American mayor, Oct 1940, *Obit* Nov 1947

La Hood, Ray, American Secretary of transportation, Mar 2009

La India, Puerto Rican salsa singer, May 2002

La Rocque, Francois de, French political leader, *Obit* June 1946

La Roe, Wilbur, Mar 1948, *Obit* July 1957

LaBelle, Patti, American singer, July 1986

LaBeouf, Shia, American actor, Aug 2009

LaChapelle, David, American photographer, June 2008

LaDuke, Winona, Native American activist, Jan 2003

LaFarge, John, American priest, Nov 1942, *Obit* Jan 1964

LaFontaine, Don, American voice-over actor, Sept 2004, *Obit* Yrbk 2008

LaHaye, Tim F., American clergyman and theologian, June 2003

LaHaye, Tim; and Jenkins, Jerry B., June 2003

LaLanne, Jack, American physical fitness expert, Oct 1994, *Obit* Yrbk 2011

LaMarsh, Judy, Apr 1968, *Obit* Jan 1981

LaMontagne, Ray, American singer, Oct 2013

LaRussa, Tony, American baseball manager, July 2003

LaValle, Victor D., American short story writer and novelist, Jan 2010

Labaki, Nadine, Lebanese actress, film director and screenwriter, July 2013

Laborde, Jean de, Feb 1943

Labouisse, Eve Curie, French biographer and daughter of Marie Curie, Mar 1940

Labouisse, Henry R., American United Nations official, Oct 1961, *Obit* May 1987

Labov, William, American sociolinguist, Mar 2006

Lacoste, Robert, French socialist leader, Nov 1957

Lacroix, Christian, French fashion designer, Apr 1988

Lacy, Dan M., publishing executive, Nov 1954, *Obit* Nov 2001

Ladd, Alan, American actor, Sept 1943, *Obit* Mar 1964

Lady Antebellum (Musical group), July 2011

Lady Gaga, American pop singer and songwriter, May 2010

Laeri, John Howard, banker, Sept 1968, *Obit* Aug 1986

Laffer, Arthur B., American economist, Feb 1982

Laffoon, Ruby, governor, *Obit* Apr 1941

Lafleur, Guy, Canadian hockey player, Mar 1980

Lafontaine, Henri Marie, Belgian judge and pacifist, *Obit* July 1943

Lafontaine, Oskar, German political leader, Sept 1990

Lafourcade, Natalia, Mexican singer and songwriter, Jan 2003

Lagarde, Christine, French interionational organization official, Jan 2007

Lagardere, Jean-Luc, French aerospace and publishing executive, Aug 1993, *Obit* Aug 2003

Lagasse, Emeril, American chef and restaurateur, May 1999

Lagat, Bernard, Kenyan-American runner, Oct 2008

Lagerfeld, Karl, German fashion designer, Jan 1982

Lagerkvist, Par, Swedish novelist, dramatist and poet, Jan 1952, *Obit* Sept 1974

Lagerlof, Selma, Swedish novelist, Apr 1940

Lagos, Ricardo, Chilean president, Jan 2005

Lahey, Frank H., American surgeon, Mar 1941, *Obit* Sept 1953

Lahlou, Mourad, Chef and restauranteur, May 2012

Lahr, Bert, actor, Jan 1952, *Obit* Feb 1968

Laich, Katherine, librarian, June 1972

Laidlaw, Patrick Playfair, *Obit* Apr 1940

Laidler, Harry Wellington, economist, Feb 1945, *Obit* Oct 1970

Laimbeer, Bill, American basketball player, coach and executive, Jan 2006

Laine, Cleo, Britlsh singer and actress, Feb 1986

Laine, Frankie, American singer, Nov 1956, *Obit* Yrbk 2007

Laing, Hugh, English dancer, Nov 1946, *Obit* June 1988

Laing, R. D., Scottish psychiatrist, Mar 1973, *Obit* Mar 1989

Laird, Donald Anderson, Sept 1946

Laird, Melvin R., American Secretary of defense, Nov 1964

Laird, Nick, Irish novelist and poet, Jan 2006

Lake, Anthony, American political scientist and presidential adviser, Oct 1994

Lake, Simon, naval architect and engineer, *Obit* July 1945

Laker, Freddie, English airline executive, June 1978, *Obit* Yrbk 2006

Lakshmi, Padma, Indian model, cookbook writer and television personality, Jan 2006

Laliberte, Guy, Canadian circus owner, Jan 2003

Lall, Arthur S., Indian diplomat, Nov 1956, *Obit* Jan 1999

Lally, Joe, American bassist, Mar 2002

Lalupu Flores, Wilmer, Peruvian painter, Jan 2005

Lamb, Brian, American television executive and moderator, Feb 1995

Lamb, Willis E., American physicist, Mar 1956, *Obit* Yrbk 2008

Lambert, Janet, Yrbk 1954

Lambert, Miranda, American country singer, Feb 2012

Lambert, Sylvester M., American physician, Oct 1941, *Obit* Feb 1947

Lambert, W. V., Nov 1955

Lamberton, Robert Eneas, American lawyer, judge and mayor, *Obit* Oct 1941

Lambsdorff, Otto von, German economist and cabinet member, May 1980, *Obit* Yrbk 2010

Lamm, Norman, Sept 1978

Lamm, Richard D., governor, May 1985

Lamond, Felix, *Obit* Apr 1940

Lamont, Ann Huntress, American venture capitalist, Feb 2007

Lamont, Corliss, American philosopher, socialist and civil rights leader, June 1946, *Obit* July 1995

Lamont, Norman, British cabinet member, Aug 1992

Lamont, Thomas William, banker, Oct 1940, *Obit* Feb 1948

Lamorisse, Albert, French screenwriter, director and producer, June 1963, *Obit* July 1970

Lampert, Edward S., American retail executive, Sept 2005

Lampley, Jim, American sportscaster, Oct 2011

Lancaster, Burt, American actor, July 1953, Apr 1986, *Obit* Jan 1995

Lancaster, Osbert, English satirist and cartoonist, Oct 1964, *Obit* Sept 1986

Lance, Bert, banker and presidential adviser, Aug 1977, *Obit* Yrbk 2013

Lanchester, Elsa, English actress, May 1950, *Obit* Feb 1987

Land, Edwin H., American inventor and photographic industry executive, Nov 1953, *Obit* May 1991

Land, Emory S., Sept 1941, *Obit* Jan 1972

Landau, Jacob, illustrator, Yrbk 1965

Landau, Lev Davidovich, Russian physicist, July 1963, *Obit* May 1968

Landers, Ann, American advice columnist, Nov 1957, *Obit* Nov 2002

Landers, Paul H., German guitarist, Jan 2007

Landes, Bertha K., mayor, *Obit* Jan 1944

Landis, James McCauley, American lawyer and regulatory agency official, Mar 1942, *Obit* Oct 1964

Landis, Kenesaw Mountain, American judge and baseball executive, May 1944, *Obit* Jan 1945

Landon, Alf, American governor, Feb 1944, *Obit* Nov 1987

Landon, Margaret, American novelist, Feb 1945, *Obit* Feb 1994

Landon, Michael, American actor, director and producer, July 1977, *Obit* Sept 1991

Landowska, Wanda, Polish harpsichordist, Nov 1945, *Obit* Nov 1959

Landrieu, Moon, American state legislator, mayor and Secretary of housing and urban development, Jan 1980

Landrum, Phil M., American congressman, May 1960, *Obit* Jan 1991

Landry, Jeff, American congressman, Jan 2012

Landry, Tom, American football coach, June 1972, *Obit* Apr 2000

Landsbergis, Vytautas, Lithuanian president, July 1990

Landsteiner, Karl, American biochemist, *Obit* Aug 1943

Landwirth, Henri, American foundation official and hotel executive, Jan 2005

Lane, Allen, British publisher, May 1954, *Obit* Sept 1970

Lane, Anthony, British film critic, Nov 2008

Lane, Arbuthnot, British surgeon, *Obit* Mar 1943

Lane, Arthur Bliss, American diplomat, Apr 1948, *Obit* Oct 1956

Lane, Burton, American composer, Mar 1967, *Obit* Mar 1997

Lane, Carl Daniel, Yrbk 1951

Lane, Gertrude Battles, magazine editor, *Obit* Nov 1941

Lane, Nathan, American actor, Aug 1996

Lane, William Preston, June 1949, *Obit* Apr 1967

Lang of Lambeth, Cosmo Gordon Lang, English archbishop, Aug 1941, *Obit* Jan 1946

Lang, David, American composer, Feb 2000

Lang, Fritz, Austrian film director, June 1943, *Obit* Sept 1976

Lang, Helmut, Austrian fashion designer, Apr 1997

Lang, Jack, French cabinet member, Aug 1983

Lang, K. D., Canadian singer, Sept 1992

Lang, Lang, Chinese pianist, Jan 2003

Lang, Pearl, American dancer and choreographer, Jan 1970, *Obit* Yrbk 2009

Lang, Robert J., American physicist and origami artist, July 2007

Langdon, Harry, American actor and comedian, *Obit* Feb 1945

Lange, David, New Zealand prime minister, Sept 1985, *Obit* Yrbk 2005

Lange, Halvard M., Norwegian diplomat, Nov 1947, *Obit* July 1970

Lange, Jessica, American actress, May 1983

Lange, Oscar Richard, Polish economist, Apr 1946, *Obit* Yrbk 1965

Langella, Frank, American actor, Sept 1980

Langer, Felicia, Israeli lawyer and human rights activist, Jan 2004

Langer, Susanne Katherina Knauth, American philosopher, Nov 1963, *Obit* Sept 1985

Langer, William, American governor and senator, Feb 1952, *Obit* Jan 1960

Langer, William Leonard, American historian, Yrbk 1968, *Obit* Feb 1978

Langevin, Jim, American congressman, Aug 2005

Langham, Michael, English theatrical director, Sept 1965, *Obit* Yrbk 2011

Langley, Adria Locke, Aug 1945

Langlie, Arthur B., Oct 1950, *Obit* Sept 1966

Langlois, Henri, French motion picture historian and collector, Jan 1973, *Obit* Mar 1977

Langmuir, Arthur Comings, *Obit* July 1941

Langmuir, Irving, American chemist, Mar 1940, Oct 1950, *Obit* Nov 1957

Langner, Lawrence, dramatist and producer, Sept 1944, *Obit* Feb 1963

Langner, Lawrence; and Helburn, Theresa, Sept 1944

Langton, Marcia, Australian anthropologist and human rights activist, Jan 2007

Laniel, Joseph, French prime minister, Feb 1954

Lanier, Cathy L., American police chief, Mar 2007

Lanier, Jaron, American computer scientist and executive, June 1997

Lanman, Charles Rockwell, *Obit* Apr 1941

Lannung, Hermod, Yrbk 1949

Lanois, Daniel, Canadian record producer, Jan 2005

Lansbury, Angela, American actress, Sept 1967

Lansbury, George, British socialist leader, *Obit* Jan 1940

Lansdowne, J. Fenwick, May 1970

Lansing, Sherry, American motion picture executive, May 1981

Lansky, Aaron, American collector and distributor of Yiddish books, Jan 1997

Lanting, Frans, Dutch-American photographer, Nov 1995

Lantos, Tom, American congressman, July 2007, *Obit* May 2008

Lanusse, Alejandro A., Argentine general and president, Apr 1973, *Obit* Nov 1996

Lanvin, Jeanne, French fashion designer, *Obit* Sept 1946

Lanzone, Jim, American Internet executive, May 2007

Lao She, Chinese novelist and short story writer, Oct 1945

Lapchick, Joe, basketball coach, June 1965, *Obit* Oct 1970

Lapham, Lewis H., American journalist and magazine editor, Mar 1989

Lapham, Roger D., July 1948, *Obit* May 1966

Lapid, Tommy, Israeli cabinet member and political leader, Jan 2003

Lapidus, Morris, American architect, Apr 1966, *Obit* Apr 2001

Lapointe, Ernest, Canadian political leader, *Obit* Jan 1942

Laporte, Genevieve, French poet and documentary filmmaker, Jan 2005

Lapp, Ralph Eugene, American physicist, Nov 1955, *Obit* Feb 2005

Lara, Brian, Trinidadian cricket player, Feb 2001

Lardner, Ring, American screenwriter, July 1987, *Obit* Feb 2001

Laredo, Jaime, violinist, Sept 1967

Laredo, Ruth, American pianist, Oct 1987, *Obit* Yrbk 2005

Largent, Steve, American congressman, June 1999

Largo Caballero, Francisco, Spanish prime minister, *Obit* May 1946

Larkin, Oliver W., art historian, July 1950, *Obit* Feb 1971

Larkin, Philip, English poet, essayist, novelist and librarian, Jan 1985, *Obit* Feb 1986

Larrick, George P., June 1965, *Obit* Oct 1968

Larrocha, Alicia de, Spanish pianist, July 1968, *Obit* Yrbk 2009

Larsen, Roy, publishing executive, Sept 1950, *Obit* Oct 1979

Larson, Arthur, Ameriacn law professor and government official, Nov 1956, *Obit* May 1993

Larson, Gary, American cartoonist, Feb 1991

Larson, Jess, American government official, June 1951

Larson, Leonard W., American medical association official and pathologist, May 1962, *Obit* Nov 1974

Lasch, Christopher, American social critic and historian, Mar 1985, *Obit* Apr 1994

Lash, Joseph P., author, Yrbk 1972, *Obit* Oct 1987

Lasker, Emanuel, chess player, *Obit* Mar 1941

Lasker, Mary, American art dealer and philanthropist, Oct 1959, *Obit* May 1994

Laski, Harold Joseph, British socialist leader and political scientist, Sept 1941, *Obit* Apr 1950

Laski, Marghanita, English author and critic, Yrbk 1951, *Obit* Apr 1988

Lasky, Jesse Louis, American film producer, Apr 1947, *Obit* Mar 1958

Lasn, Kalle, Estonian-Canadian environmentalist, Apr 2012

Lasorda, Tommy, American baseball manager, Feb 1989

Lassaw, Ibram, American sculptor, Jan 1957, *Obit* Yrbk 2004

Lasser, J. K., May 1946, *Obit* July 1954

Lasser, Louise, actress, Oct 1976

Lasseter, John, American animator, screenwriter and director, June 1997

Lasswell, Harold D., American political scientist, July 1947, *Obit* Feb 1979

Latham, Dana, Mar 1959, *Obit* Apr 1974

Latham, Harold S., Jan 1950, *Obit* Apr 1969

Latham, Jean Lee, American children's author, Yrbk 1956

Latouche, John, dramatist and lyricist, Jan 1940, *Obit* Oct 1956

Latourette, Kenneth Scott, Sinologist and church historian, Nov 1953, *Obit* Mar 1969

Lattes, C. M. G., Brazilian physicist, May 1949

Lattimore, Owen, American Sinologist, Yrbk 1945, July 1964, *Obit* July 1989

Lattre, Jean de, French field marshal, Jan 1945, *Obit* Feb 1952

Lau, Andy, Chinese singer and actor, Jan 2005

Lau, Evelyn, Canadian novelist, poet and short story writer, Jan 2005

Laubach, Frank Charles, American missionary and educator, Feb 1950, *Obit* Sept 1970

Lauda, Niki, Austrian automobile racing driver, Oct 1980

Lauder, Estee, American cosmetics executive, July 1986, *Obit* Yrbk 2004

Lauger, Paul, Oct 1945

Lauger, Paul; and Muller, Paul, Oct 1945

Laughlin, Clara Elizabeth, *Obit* Apr 1941

Laughlin, Irwin, *Obit* June 1941

Laughlin, James, American publisher and poet, May 1982, *Obit* Jan 1998

Laughton, Charles, Anglo-American actor, Nov 1948, *Obit* Jan 1963

Laugier, Henri, July 1948

Lauper, Cyndi, American singer and songwriter, Aug 1985

Laurel, Jose P., Filipino president, June 1953, *Obit* Jan 1960

Lauren, Ralph, American fashion designer, Oct 1980

Laurence, William Leonard, journalist, Oct 1945, *Obit* May 1977

Laurent, Robert, July 1942, *Obit* June 1970

Laurents, Arthur, American playwright, screenwriter and theatrical director, Nov 1984, *Obit* Yrbk 2011

Lauri, Lorenzo, *Obit* Yrbk 1941

Laurie, Hugh, English actor and television scriptwriter, Jan 2006

Lauritzen, Jonreed, Yrbk 1952

Lausche, Frank John, American governor and senator, Apr 1946, Nov 1958, *Obit* June 1990

Lautenberg, Frank, American senator, Jan 1991, *Obit* Yrbk 2013

Lauterbach, Jacob Zallel, *Obit* June 1942

Lauvergeon, Anne, French nuclear energy industry executive, Jan 2005

Laval, Pierre, French prime minister and convicted traitor, Sept 1940, *Obit* Nov 1945

Lavant, Denis, French actor, June 2013

Laver, Rod, Australian tennis player, Feb 1963

Laverty, Maura, Irish author, Yrbk 1947

Lavery, Emmet, July 1947

Lavery, John, Irish painter, *Obit* Mar 1941

Lavigne, Avril, Canadian singer and songwriter, Apr 2003

Lavin, Linda, actress, Nov 1987

Law, Tajuan, American football player, Oct 2002

Law, Vern, baseball player and coach, Apr 1961

Lawal, Kase L., Nigerian-American energy industry executive, Nov 2006

Lawe, John, labor leader, Jan 1984, *Obit* Apr 1989

Lawes, Lewis Edward, American prison warden and reformer, Oct 1941, *Obit* Mar 1947

Lawford, Ernest, *Obit* Feb 1941

Lawrence, Carol, American singer and actress, Nov 1961

Lawrence, Charles Edward, *Obit* Apr 1940

Lawrence, David, journalist and publisher, Yrbk 1943, *Obit* Apr 1973

Lawrence, David Leo, American governor, June 1959, *Obit* Jan 1967

Lawrence, Ernest Orlando, American physicist, Feb 1940, Jan 1952, *Obit* Nov 1958

Lawrence, Gertrude, English actress, Aug 1940, Sept 1952

Lawrence, Hilda, author, Yrbk 1947

Lawrence, Jacob, American painter and illustrator, July 1965, Sept 1988, *Obit* Aug 2000

Lawrence, Jennifer, American actress, May 2013

Lawrence, Marjorie, Australian opera singer, Apr 1940, *Obit* Mar 1979

Lawrence, Martin, American comedian and actor, Oct 1999

Lawrence, Mary Wells, American advertising executive, Jan 1967

Lawrence, Mildred, Yrbk 1953

Lawrence, Steve, singer, Nov 1964

Lawrence, William, *Obit* Jan 1942

Laws, Hubert, American jazz flutist, July 2007

Lawson, Edward B., Jan 1956

Lawson, Mary, *Obit* July 1941

Lawson, Nigel, British cabinet member, Mar 1987

Lawson, Nigella, English food critic and cookbook writer, Jan 2003

Lawson, Robert, Anerican children's author and illustrator, Oct 1941, *Obit* Oct 1957

Lawson, Ted W., Yrbk 1943

Lawther, William, Yrbk 1949

Lawton, Frederick J., government official, Mar 1951

Lax, Peter D., American mathematician, Oct 2005

Laxalt, Paul, American senator, Jan 1979

Laxness, Halldor, Icelandic novelist and essayist, Oct 1946, *Obit* Apr 1998

Lay, James S., intelligence official, Mar 1950, *Obit* Aug 1987

Laybourne, Geraldine, American broadcasting executive, Apr 1999

Laycock, Craven, *Obit* May 1940

Laycock, R. E., May 1944, *Obit* May 1968

Layton, Geoffrey, British admiral, Feb 1942

Layton, Jack, Canadian political leader, Nov 2009, *Obit* Yrbk 2012

Layton, Joe, theatrical director, producer and choreographer, Sept 1970, *Obit* July 1994

Layton, Olivia, Jan 1952, *Obit* Jan 1976

Lazareff, Pierre, May 1942, *Obit* June 1972

Lazarsfeld, Paul Felix, American sociologist, Nov 1964, *Obit* Oct 1976

Lazarus, Rochelle, American advertising executive, May 1997

Lazzeri, Tony, baseball player, *Obit* Sept 1946

Le Carre, John, British diplomat and novelist, Yrbk 1974

Le Clercq, Tanaquil, American ballet dancer, July 1953, *Obit* Mar 2001

Le Corbusier, Swiss-French architect, Apr 1947, *Obit* Nov 1965

Le Gallienne, Eva, American actress, director and producer, Oct 1942, Mar 1955, *Obit* Aug 1991

Le Guin, Ursula K., American science fiction and fantasy writer, Jan 1983

Le Pen, Jean-Marie, French political leader, Jan 1988

Le Roy Ladurie, Emmanuel, French historian, July 1984

Le, Duc Tho, Vietnamese communist leader, Mar 1975, *Obit* Jan 1991

Le, Tan, Australian information technology executive, Apr 2013

LeCompte, Elizabeth, American theatrical director, Aug 1997

LeDoux, Joseph E., American neuroscientist, Oct 2010

LeFrak, Samuel J., American builder, Jan 1970, *Obit* Yrbk 2003

LeMay, Curtis E., American air force general, Yrbk 1944, Nov 1954, *Obit* Nov 1990

LeMond, Greg, American cyclist, Oct 1989

LeVay, Simon, English neurobiologist, Oct 1996

LeVox, Gary, American country singer, Aug 2003

LeWitt, Sol, American sculptor, July 1986, *Obit* Yrbk 2007

Lea, Clarence F., Nov 1946, *Obit* Sept 1964

Lea, Luke, American newspaper publisher and senator, *Obit* Jan 1946

Leach, Penelope, English child psychologist, Aug 1994

Leach, Robin, British television personality and producer, Sept 1990

Leach, Ruth M., American computer industry executive, Mar 1948

Leachman, Cloris, American actress, Oct 1975

Leacock, Stephen Butler, Canadian economist, political scientist and humorist, *Obit* May 1944

Leader, George Michael, American governor, Jan 1956, *Obit* Yrbk 2013

Leahy, Frank, football coach, Yrbk 1941, *Obit* Sept 1973

Leahy, Patrick J., American senator, Sept 1990

Leahy, William D., American admiral, Jan 1941, *Obit* Oct 1959

Leake, Chauncey D., Apr 1960, *Obit* Mar 1978

Leakey, Louis Seymour Bazett, British anthropologist and archaeologist, Mar 1966, *Obit* Yrbk 1972

Leakey, Mary D., British anthropologist and paleontologist, Apr 1985, *Obit* Feb 1997

Leakey, Meave, Kenyan anthropologist and paleontologist, June 2002

Leakey, Richard E., Kenyan anthropologist and paleontologist, Nov 1976, Oct 1995

Lean, David, British film director and producer, May 1953, June 1989, *Obit* June 1991

Lear, Ben, July 1942, *Obit* Jan 1967

Lear, Evelyn, American opera singer, Apr 1973, *Obit* Yrbk 2012

Lear, Frances, magazine publisher, Apr 1991, *Obit* Jan 1997

Lear, Norman, American television scriptwriter and producer, Feb 1974

Lear, William Powell, American engineer and inventor, July 1966, *Obit* July 1978

Leary, Herbert F., Aug 1942, *Obit* Feb 1958

Leary, John Joseph, *Obit* Feb 1944

Leary, Timothy, American psychologist, Yrbk 1970, *Obit* Aug 1996

Leathers, Frederick James Leathers, June 1941, *Obit* May 1965

Leavey, Edmond H., American general and telecommunications executive, May 1951, *Obit* Apr 1980

Lebedeva, Tatyana, Russian long and triple jumper, Jan 2004

Leblanc, Georgette, French opera singer, *Obit* Yrbk 1941

Leblanc, Maurice, French author, *Obit* Jan 1942

Lebowitz, Fran, humorist, Mar 1982

Leboyer, Frederick, July 1982

Lebrun, Rico, Sept 1952, *Obit* July 1964

Lecky, Prescott, psychologist, *Obit* July 1941

Leclerc, Jacques, Oct 1944, *Obit* Yrbk 1947

Leconte, Patrice, French motion picture director, Jan 2004

Lecuona, Ernesto, Cuban composer, May 1944, *Obit* Jan 1964

Lederberg, Joshua, American geneticist, Mar 1959, *Obit* Yrbk 2008

Lederle, John W., American college president, Feb 1961, *Obit* Yrbk 2007

Lederman, Leon M., American physicist, Sept 1989

Ledger, Heath, Australian actor, June 2006, *Obit* Yrbk 2008

Ledochowski, Wlodzimierz, *Obit* Jan 1943

Ledoyen, Virginie, French actress, Jan 2002

Lee, Andrea, American novelist and short story writer, Sept 2003

Lee, Ang, Taiwanese film director, Mar 1997

Lee, Auriol, *Obit* Sept 1941

Lee, Barbara, American congresswoman, June 2004

Lee, Blair, *Obit* Feb 1945

Lee, Bum Suk, Jan 1949

Lee, Canada, American actor, Yrbk 1944, *Obit* June 1952

Lee, Christopher, English actor, Sept 1975

Lee, Clark, Yrbk 1943, *Obit* Apr 1953

Lee, Cliff, American baseball player, Aug 2009

Lee, Debra, American broadcasting executive, June 2006

Lee, Doris Emrick, American painter and illustrator, Jan 1954, *Obit* Jan 1986

Lee, Dorothy McCullough, Jan 1949

Lee, Geddy, Canadian singer, Feb 2001

Lee, Gypsy Rose, American actress and stripteaser, Yrbk 1943, *Obit* June 1970

Lee, Harper, American novelist, Nov 1961

Lee, Henry C., American forensic scientist, Aug 1996

Lee, J. Bracken, American governor and mayor, May 1949, *Obit* Jan 1997

Lee, Jeanette, American billiards player, Oct 2002

Lee, Jennie, British member of Parliament, May 1946, *Obit* Jan 1989

Lee, Jim, Artist and co-publisher of DC Comics, Apr 2012

Lee, John C. H., July 1944, *Obit* Nov 1958

Lee, John Clarence, *Obit* Nov 1940

Lee, Jong Wook, Korean physician and international public health official, Jan 2003, *Obit* CB Int 2007

Lee, Kuan Yew, Singaporean prime minister, Nov 1959, Jan 1995

Lee, Kun-hee, Korean electronics industry executive, Jan 2005

Lee, Laurence F., June 1952, *Obit* Oct 1961

Lee, Manfred, American mystery writer, July 1940

Lee, Martin, Chinese lawyer and political leader, July 1997

Lee, Ming Cho, Chinese-American set designer, June 1989

Lee, Peggy, American singer, Mar 1963, *Obit* May 2002

Lee, Percy Maxim, American civic leader, July 1950, *Obit* Jan 2003

Lee, Richard C., American mayor, Yrbk 1967, *Obit* Yrbk 2003

Lee, Robert E., American regulatory agency official, July 1967, *Obit* June 1993

Lee, Sandra, American cook, entrepreneur and television personality, Aug 2011

Lee, Sherman E., American art historian and museum director, June 1974, *Obit* Yrbk 2008

Lee, Spike, American film director, screenwriter and actor, Mar 1989

Lee, Stan, American comic book writer and editor, Aug 1993

Lee, Teng-hui, Taiwanese president, Mar 1996

Lee, Tsung Dao, American physicist, Nov 1958

Lee, Willis A., American admiral and marksman, *Obit* Sept 1945

Leech, Margaret, American historian and novelist, July 1942, Nov 1960, *Obit* Apr 1974

Leech, Paul Nicholas, *Obit* Mar 1941

Leedom, Boyd, May 1956, *Obit* Oct 1969

Leese, Oliver, British general, Yrbk 1944, *Obit* Yrbk 1991

Lefaucheux, Marie-Helene, French United Nations official, Oct 1947, *Obit* Apr 1964

Lefebvre, Marcel, French archbishop, Mar 1978, *Obit* May 1991

Lefevre, Theo, June 1962, *Obit* Nov 1973

Leffingwell, Russell Cornell, banker, Mar 1950, *Obit* Yrbk 1960

Legend, John, American singer and pianist, Feb 2007

Leger, Fernand, French painter, Jan 1943, *Obit* Oct 1955

Leger, Jules, Nov 1976, *Obit* Jan 1981

Leger, Paul-Emile, Canadian missionary, May 1953, *Obit* Jan 1992

Leggett, A. J., Anglo-American physicist, Jan 2007

Leguizamo, John, American actor and dramatist, Apr 1998

Lehane, Dennis, American mystery novelist, Oct 2005

Lehman, Herbert Henry, American governor and senator, Jan 1943, July 1955, *Obit* Jan 1964

Lehman, John F., secretary of the navy, Nov 1985

Lehmann, George, *Obit* Yrbk 1941

Lehmann, Inge, Danish geophysicist, Nov 1962

Lehmann, Lotte, German-American opera singer, May 1941, July 1970, *Obit* Oct 1976

Lehmann-Haupt, Hellmut, author and bibliographer, Apr 1942, Mar 1961, *Obit* May 1992

Lehrbas, Lloyd, June 1940, Apr 1950, *Obit* Jan 1965

Lehrer, Jim, American television newscaster, Jan 1987

Lehrer, Tom, songwriter, humorist and mathematician, July 1982

Leiber, Judith, Hungarian-American handbag designer, Sept 1996

Leibovitz, Annie, American photographer, Oct 1991

Leibowitz, Samuel Simon, American judge, Jan 1953, *Obit* Mar 1978

Leigh, Douglas, advertising executive and lighting designer, May 1940, *Obit* May 2000

Leigh, Jennifer Jason, American actress, Aug 1992

Leigh, Mike, English dramatist, motion picture director and screenwriter, June 1994

Leigh, Robert Devore, college president and dean, June 1947, *Obit* Mar 1961

Leigh, Vivien, English actress, July 1946, *Obit* Oct 1967

Leigh, William Colston, lecture agent, Jan 1942, *Obit* Sept 1992

Leigh-Mallory, Trafford, British air marshal, Mar 1944, *Obit* Mar 1945

Leighton, Margaret, English actress, Mar 1957, *Obit* Mar 1976

Leighton, Margaret Carver, author, Yrbk 1952

Leighton, Robert B., physicist, July 1966, *Obit* May 1997

Leinsdorf, Erich, conductor, May 1940, Oct 1963, *Obit* Nov 1993

Leiper, Henry Smith, Nov 1948, *Obit* Mar 1975

Leiserson, William M., Feb 1942, *Obit* Apr 1957

Leiter, Al, American baseball player, Aug 2002

Leith-Ross, Frederick, Oct 1942

Lejeune, John Archer, marine general, *Obit* Jan 1943

Lelong, Lucien, Nov 1955, *Obit* Sept 1958

Lelouch, Claude, French motion picture director and producer, Nov 1982

Lelyveld, Joseph, American newspaper editor, Nov 2005

Lem, Stanislaw, Polish science fiction novelist, short story writer and physician, Oct 1986, *Obit* Yrbk 2006

Lemass, Sean, Irish prime minister, Mar 1960, *Obit* June 1971

Lemieux, Mario, Canadian hockey player, Aug 1988

Lemkin, Raphael, American lawyer, May 1950, *Obit* Nov 1959

Lemmon, Jack, American actor, Feb 1961, Aug 1988, *Obit* Oct 2001

Lemnitzer, Lyman Louis, American general, Nov 1955, *Obit* Jan 1989

Lemon, Don, American television news anchor, May 2010

Lemon, Ralph, American dancer and choreographer, Feb 1997

Lemonnier, Andre, Nov 1952, *Obit* July 1963

Lendl, Ivan, Czech-American tennis player, Sept 1984

Lengyel, Emil, journalist and author, Feb 1942, *Obit* Apr 1985

Lennon, John, English singer and songwriter, Yrbk 1965, *Obit* Feb 1981

Lennox, Annie, Scottish singer, May 1988

Lennox-Boyd, Alan Tindal, British cabinet member and brewing industry executive, June 1956, *Obit* May 1983

Leno, Jay, American comedian and television talk show host, June 1988

Lenroot, Katherine F., American government official, May 1940, Nov 1950, *Obit* Yrbk 1991

Lentaigne, Walter D. A., July 1944, *Obit* Oct 1955

Lenya, Lotte, German singer and actress, June 1959, *Obit* Jan 1982

Leo, John, American magazine columnist, Sept 2006

Leo, Melissa, American actress, July 2009

Leon, Kenny, American theatrical director, Nov 2005

Leonard, Bill, radio and television executive, Nov 1960, *Obit* Feb 1995

Leonard, Eddie, singer and dancer, *Obit* Sept 1941

Leonard, Edward F., *Obit* Jan 1941

Leonard, Elmore, American novelist, Sept 1985, *Obit* Yrbk 2013

Leonard, Hugh, Irish playwright, Apr 1983, *Obit* Yrbk 2009

Leonard, Lucille Putnam, Feb 1953

Leonard, Sugar Ray, American boxer, Feb 1981

Leone, Giovanni, Italian president, May 1972, *Obit* Feb 2002

Leoni, Raul, Venezuelan president, Oct 1964, *Obit* Sept 1972

Leonidoff, Leon, American theatrical producer, July 1941, *Obit* Oct 1989

Leonov, Aleksei, Soviet astronaut, July 1965

Leontief, Wassily W., American economist, Jan 1967, *Obit* Apr 1999

Leopold, Yrbk 1944, *Obit* Nov 1983

Leopold, Alice, government official, Jan 1955

Lepage, Robert, Canadian theatrical director, actor and dramatist, Apr 1995

Leppard, Raymond, British conductor and harpsichordist, Mar 1980

Lequerica y Erquiza, Jose Felix de, June 1951, *Obit* July 1963

Lercaro, Giacomo, Sept 1965, *Obit* Jan 1977

Lerch, Archer L., Nov 1945, *Obit* Oct 1947

Lerche, Sondre, Norwegian singer and songwriter, Jan 2004

Lerman, Liz, American dancer and choreographer, Nov 2000

Lerner and Loewe, July 1958

Lerner, Alan Jay, American lyricist and librettist, July 1958, *Obit* Aug 1986

Lerner, Gerda, American historian, Feb 1998, *Obit* Yrbk 2013

Lerner, Max, American columnist, Oct 1942, *Obit* Aug 1992

Les Nubians (Musical group), Jan 2003

Lesage, Jean, Canadian government official, Nov 1961, *Obit* Feb 1981

Lescaze, William, American architect, Apr 1942, *Obit* Apr 1969

Lescot, Elie, Haitian president, June 1941, *Obit* Yrbk 1974

Leser, Tina, fashion designer, June 1957, *Obit* Mar 1986

Lesinski, John, July 1949, *Obit* July 1950

Lesinski, John, American congressman, June 1957

Leslie, Chris, English singer, fiddler and mandolinist, Sept 2005

Leslie, Lisa, American basketball player, Jan 1998

Lessing, Bruno, author and newspaper editor, *Obit* Jan 1940

Lessing, Doris May, English novelist and short story writer, Jan 1976, Jan 1995

Lester, Richard, British film director, Apr 1969

Lesueur, Larry, American radio newscaster, June 1943, *Obit* Yrbk 2003

Lethem, Jonathan, American novelist and short story writer, Mar 2006

Letourneau, Jean, Oct 1952

Letourneau, R. G., American inventor, Apr 1958, *Obit* July 1969

Letterman, David, American comedian and television talk show host, Nov 1980, Oct 2002

Letts, Tracy, American playwright, Oct 2008

Leung, Tony Chiu-wai, Chinese actor, Jan 2006

Leunig, Michael, Australian cartoonist and poet, Jan 2006

Lev, Ray, Jan 1949, *Obit* July 1968

Levant, Oscar, American pianist and composer, Jan 1940, Oct 1952, *Obit* Oct 1972

Levene, Phoebus Aaron Theodore, American biochemist, *Obit* Oct 1940

Levenson, Sam, American humorist, July 1959, *Obit* Nov 1980

Leverone, Nathaniel, Nov 1956, *Obit* July 1969

Levert, Gerald, American singer and songwriter, Oct 2003, *Obit* Yrbk 2007

Levertov, Denise, American poet, Aug 1991, *Obit* Mar 1998

Levesque, Rene, Canadian political leader, Jan 1975, *Obit* Jan 1988

Levi, Carlo, Italian novelist, journalist and painter, Yrbk 1952, *Obit* Feb 1975

Levi, Edward H., American Attorney general, Jan 1969, *Obit* July 2000

Levi, Julian, Apr 1943, *Obit* Apr 1982

Levi, Primo, Italian memoirist, novelist and chemist, Mar 1987, *Obit* Mar 1987

Levi-Montalcini, Rita, Italian biologist, Nov 1989, *Obit* Yrbk 2013

Levi-Strauss, Claude, French anthropologist, Mar 1972, *Obit* Jan 2010

Levi-Tanai, Sara, Israeli choreographer, May 1958

Leviero, Anthony, Sept 1952, *Obit* Nov 1956

Leviev, Lev, Israeli diamond dealer, Jan 2002

Levin, Carl, American senator, May 2004

Levin, Ira, American novelist, Aug 1991, *Obit* Feb 2008

Levin, Janna, American astrophysicist, Jan 2008

Levin, Meyer, American novelist, Apr 1940, *Obit* Sept 1981

Levin, Yehuda Leib, Sept 1969, *Obit* Jan 1972

Levine, Adam, American rock singer and guitarist, Mar 2013

Levine, David, American caricaturist, Feb 1973, *Obit* Yrbk 2010

Levine, Irving R., American television newscaster, July 1959, *Obit* Yrbk 2009

Levine, Jack, American painter, June 1956, *Obit* Yrbk 2011

Levine, James, American conductor, Apr 1975

Levine, Joseph E., American motion picture producer, Oct 1979, *Obit* Sept 1987

Levine, Melvin D., American pediatrician, Nov 2005

Levine, Philip, American poet, July 2012

Levine, Philip, American bacteriologist, May 1947, *Obit* Nov 1987

Levinson, Barry, American film director and screenwriter, July 1990

Levinson, Salmon Oliver, lawyer and pacifist, *Obit* Mar 1941

Levitt, William, American builder, Nov 1956, *Obit* Mar 1994

Levitzki, Mischa, pianist, *Obit* Feb 1941

Levy, Andrea, English novelist, Sept 2010

Levy, Bernard Henri, French philosopher, Nov 1993

Levy, Dani, Swiss actor, film director and screenwriter, Jan 2007

Levy, David, Israeli cabinet member, Mar 1998

Levy, David H., Canadian science writer and amateur astronomer, Jan 1995

Levy, Eugene, Canadian actor, film director and screenwriter, Jan 2002

Levy, Marv, football coach, Feb 1998

Lewin, Murray, *Obit* Sept 1943

Lewing, Adele, *Obit* Apr 1943

Lewis, Albert Buell, American anthropologist, *Obit* Yrbk 1940

Lewis, Ananda, American television entertainment reporter, June 2005

Lewis, Anthony, American journalist, Nov 1955, *Obit* Yrbk 2013

Lewis, C. S., English children's author, novelist and critic, Jan 1944, *Obit* Jan 1964

Lewis, Carl, American sprinter and long jumper, Nov 1984, Yrbk 1996

Lewis, Chester, librarian and archivist, May 1956, *Obit* June 1990

Lewis, Clyde A., Feb 1950

Lewis, David Levering, American historian and biographer, May 2001

Lewis, David Sloan, American aerospace industry executive, Aug 1975, *Obit* Yrbk 2004

Lewis, Dean, *Obit* Yrbk 1941

Lewis, Denise, British heptathlete, Jan 2004

Lewis, Dorothy Otnow, American psychiatrist, May 2006

Lewis, Drew, American Secretary of transportation, Feb 1982

Lewis, Ethelreda, South African author, *Obit* Sept 1946

Lewis, Flora, American columnist, Jan 1989, *Obit* Yrbk 2002

Lewis, Francis Park, *Obit* Oct 1940

Lewis, Fulton, radio commentator, Nov 1942, *Obit* Nov 1966

Lewis, Henry, American conductor, Feb 1973, *Obit* Apr 1996

Lewis, Jason, British adventurer, Jan 2007

Lewis, Jerry, American comedian, Nov 1962

Lewis, John, American congressman, Sept 1980

Lewis, John, American pianist and composer, Jan 1962, *Obit* June 2001

Lewis, John L., American labor leader, Mar 1942, *Obit* July 1969

Lewis, Juliette, American actress, Feb 1996

Lewis, Kenneth, American banker, Apr 2004

Lewis, Lawrence, *Obit* Jan 1944

Lewis, Lennox, British boxer, Jan 1999

Lewis, Loida Nicolas, American financier and wife of Reginald F. Lewis, Apr 1997

Lewis, Marvin, American football coach, Nov 2004

Lewis, Mary, retail executive, Sept 1940

Lewis, Mary, opera singer, *Obit* Feb 1942

Lewis, Michael, American investment banker and journalist, Sept 2012

Lewis, Oscar, American anthropologist, Apr 1968, *Obit* Feb 1971

Lewis, Ramsey, American jazz pianist, Oct 1996

Lewis, Ray, American football player, Jan 2007

Lewis, Richard, comedian and actor, July 1993

Lewis, Roger, aircraft executive, Yrbk 1973, *Obit* Jan 1988

Lewis, Shari, puppeteer and ventriloquist, Mar 1958, *Obit* Oct 1998

Lewis, W. S., book collector and editor, July 1973, *Obit* Jan 1980

Lewis, Willmott, May 1941, *Obit* Feb 1950

Ley, Robert, German Nazi leader, Sept 1940, *Obit* Yrbk 1945

Ley, Willy, German-American scientist and author, June 1941, Feb 1953, *Obit* Sept 1969

Leyburn, James Graham, Apr 1943

Leyland, Jim, American baseball manager, Nov 1998

Lhevinne, Josef, Russian pianist, *Obit* Jan 1945

Lhevinne, Rosina, Russian-American pianist and teacher, Nov 1961, *Obit* Jan 1977

Lhuillier, Monique, American fashion designer, June 2008

Li Dongsheng, Chinese electronics industry executive, Jan 2005

Li Gong, Chinese actress, May 1997

Li Hongzhi, Chinese religious leader, Jan 2002

Li Liejun, *Obit* Apr 1946

Li Na, Chinese tennis player, Jan 2006

Li Peng, Chinese prime minister, Nov 1988

Li Yifei, Chinese television executive, Jan 2006

Li Zongren, Chinese general, Nov 1942, *Obit* Mar 1969

Li, Choh-hao, biochemist, Apr 1963, *Obit* Jan 1988

Li, Jet, Chinese actor and martial artist, June 2001

Li, Ka-shing, Chinese real estate executive, Jan 2003

Li, Robin, Chinese Internet executive, Jan 2007

Li, Tsung-Jen; and Pai, Tsung-Hsi, Nov 1942

Libby, Frederick J., Apr 1949, *Obit* Sept 1970

Libby, Willard Frank, American chemist, Nov 1954, *Obit* Nov 1980

Liberace, American pianist, Nov 1954, Mar 1986, *Obit* Mar 1987

Liberman, Alexander, American artist and magazine executive, May 1987, *Obit* Mar 2000

Liberman, Yevsei G., June 1968, *Obit* May 1983

Libeskind, Daniel, American architect, June 2003

Licad, Cecile, Philippine pianist, Jan 2003

Lichtenberg, Bernard, *Obit* Nov 1944

Lichtenberger, Andre, *Obit* Apr 1940

Lichtenberger, Arthur, Apr 1961, *Obit* Nov 1968

Lichtenstein, Harvey, American performing arts executive, May 1987

Lichtenstein, Roy, American painter, Feb 1969, *Obit* Jan 1998

Liddel, Urner, May 1951

Liddell Hart, Basil Henry, British military historian, Jan 1940, *Obit* Mar 1970

Liddy, G. Gordon, American lawyer, actor and government official, Oct 1980

Lie, Jonas, Norwegian-American painter, Jan 1940

Lie, Trygve, Norwegian United Nations secretary-general, Mar 1946, *Obit* Feb 1969

Liebenow, Robert C., May 1956

Lieberman, Daniel, American anthropologist and biologist, May 2011

Lieberman, Joseph I., American senator, July 1994

Liebermann, Rolf, Swiss composer and opera director, Sept 1973, *Obit* Mar 1999

Lieberson, Goddard, composer, critic and record executive, Mar 1976, *Obit* July 1977

Liebes, Dorothy, American textile designer, Apr 1948, *Obit* Yrbk 1972

Liebler, Theodore A., *Obit* June 1941

Liebling, Leonard, *Obit* Yrbk 1945

Liebman, Joshua Loth, rabbi, Oct 1946, *Obit* July 1948

Liebman, Max, television producer and director, Apr 1953, *Obit* Sept 1981

Lifeson, Alex, Canadian guitarist, Feb 2001

Lifton, Robert Jay, American psychiatrist and writer, Nov 1973

Ligachev, Yegor K., Soviet communist leader, Aug 1990

Liggett, Louis Kroh, *Obit* July 1946

Lightfoot, Gordon, Canadian singer, Aug 1978

Lightner, Milton C., Nov 1958, *Obit* May 1968

Lil' Kim, American rapper, Oct 2000

Lilienthal, David E., American government official, June 1944, *Obit* Mar 1981

Lillard, George W., *Obit* Yrbk 1940

Lillehei, Clarence Walton, American surgeon, May 1969, *Obit* Nov 1999

Lillie, Beatrice, British actress, Feb 1945, Sept 1964, *Obit* Mar 1989

Lillien, Lisa, American cook, cookbook writer and entrepreneur, May 2010

Lilly, John Cunningham, American physician, Nov 1962, *Obit* Feb 2002

Lilly, Kristine, American soccer player, Apr 2004

Liman, Arthur L., lawyer, Jan 1988, *Obit* Oct 1997

Limann, Hilla, Ghanaian president, June 1981, *Obit* Apr 1998

Limb, Ben C., Jan 1951

Limbaugh, Rush, American radio and television commentator, Mar 1993

Limon, Jose, American dancer and choreographer, June 1953, Apr 1968, *Obit* Jan 1973

Lin Biao, Chinese communist leader and military official, May 1967, *Obit* Oct 1972

Lin Dan, Chinese badminton player, Jan 2007

Lin Sen, *Obit* Sept 1943

Lin Yutang, Chinese novelist, essayist and translator, May 1940, *Obit* May 1976

Lin, Jeremy, American basketball player, Feb 2013

Lin, Maya Ying, American architect and sculptor, Apr 1993

Lincecum, Tim, American baseball player, June 2010

Lincoln, Abbey, American jazz singer, Sept 2002, *Obit* Yrbk 2010

Lincoln, Blanche Lambert, American senator, Mar 2002

Lincoln, Joseph C., American short story writer, novelist and poet, *Obit* Apr 1944

Lincoln, Leroy A., June 1946, *Obit* June 1957

Lincoln, Murray D., American insurance executive, Mar 1953, *Obit* Jan 1967

Lindbergh, Anne Morrow, American memoirist, novelist, and poet, Nov 1940, June 1976, *Obit* Apr 2001

Lindbergh, Charles, American aviator, July 1941, Jan 1954, *Obit* Oct 1974

Lindemann, Till, German singer, Jan 2007

Linden, Hal, actor, Jan 1987

Lindfors, Viveca, Swedish actress, Apr 1955, *Obit* Jan 1996

Lindgren, Astrid, Swedish children's author, Oct 1996, *Obit* Apr 2002

Lindley, Ernest Hiram, *Obit* Oct 1940

Lindley, Ernest K., journalist, June 1943, *Obit* Yrbk 1991

Lindo, Delroy, American actor, Mar 2001

Lindros, Eric, Canadian hockey player, Apr 1998

Lindsay, Howard, dramatist, Apr 1942, *Obit* Apr 1968

Lindsay, Howard; and Stickney, Dorothy, Apr 1942

Lindsay, John V., American congressman and mayor, Nov 1962, *Obit* Mar 2001

Lindsay, Ronald, *Obit* Sept 1945

Lindsey, Benjamin B., judge, *Obit* May 1943

Lindsley, Thayer, Jan 1957, *Obit* July 1976

Lindt, Auguste R., Swiss diplomat and United Nations official, Nov 1959, *Obit* Yrbk 2000

Ling, James, American financier, Apr 1970, *Obit* Yrbk 2005

Lingle, Linda, American governor, June 2003

Link, Edwin A., flight simulator industry executive, Jan 1974, *Obit* Yrbk 1983

Link, O. Winston, American photographer, June 1995, *Obit* Apr 2001

Linkin Park (Musical group), Mar 2002

Linkletter, Art, American television personality, Nov 1953, *Obit* Yrbk 2010

Linlithgow, Victor Alexander John Hope, British colonial administrator, Jan 1942, *Obit* Feb 1952

Linnell, John, American singer, songwriter and accordionist, Nov 1999

Linowitz, Sol M., American lawyer and diplomat, Mar 1967, *Obit* Yrbk 2005

Linton, Frank B. A., *Obit* Jan 1944

Lionni, Leo, American children's author and illustrator, Sept 1997, *Obit* Feb 2000

Liotta, Ray, American actor, May 1994

Lipchitz, Jacques, French sculptor, Nov 1948, Apr 1962, *Obit* July 1973

Lipinski, Anne Marie, American journalist, July 2004

Lipinski, Tara, American figure skater, Apr 1998

Lipmann, Fritz, American biochemist, Mar 1954, *Obit* Sept 1986

Lippi, Marcello, Italian soccer coach, Jan 2006

Lippincott, Joseph Wharton, May 1955, *Obit* Jan 1977

Lippincott, Joshua Bertram, *Obit* Jan 1940

Lippmann, Walter, American journalist and political philosopher, Sept 1940, Nov 1962, *Obit* Jan 1975

Lippold, Richard, American sculptor, Nov 1956, *Obit* Yrbk 2002

Lipschitz, Chaim U., Yrbk 1966

Lipsky, Eleazar, author and lawyer, Yrbk 1959, *Obit* Apr 1993

Lipton, James, American television interviewer, writer and producer, July 2011

Lipton, Seymour, American sculptor, Nov 1964, *Obit* Feb 1987

Lisi, Antony Garrett, American physicist, Sept 2012

Litchfield, Edward H., Nov 1953, *Obit* May 1968

Litchfield, P. W., Yrbk 1950, *Obit* May 1959

Lithgow, John, American actor, Nov 1996

Littell, Philip, *Obit* Yrbk 1943

Little Richard, American singer, Sept 1986

Little, Clarence C., American biologist, Yrbk 1944, *Obit* Feb 1972

Little, Lou, American football coach, Nov 1945, *Obit* July 1979

Little, Philip, *Obit* May 1942

Little, Rich, Canadian impressionist, Nov 1975

Little, William Lawson, Aug 1940

Littledale, Clara Savage, Oct 1946, *Obit* Mar 1956

Littlejohn, Robert McGowan, Sept 1946, *Obit* July 1982

Littler, Gene, golfer, July 1956

Litton, Andrew, conductor, Sept 1998

Littrell, Brian, American singer, May 2000

Litvinov, Maxim Maximovich, Soviet diplomat, Yrbk 1941, *Obit* Feb 1952

Liu Binyan, Chinese journalist, Jan 2004, *Obit* CB Int 2006

Liu Bolin, Chinese painter and photographer, Nov 2013

Liu Chuanzhi, Chinese computer industry executive, Jan 2006

Liu Fang, Chinese pipa player, Jan 2006

Liu Shaoqi, Chinese communist leader, Oct 1957, *Obit* Yrbk 1974

Liu, Changle, Jan 2002

Liu, Hung, Chinese artist, Jan 2002

Liu, Lucy, American actress and artist, Oct 2003

Lively, Penelope, English novelist, short story writer and children's author, Apr 1994

Livingston, Homer J., Sept 1955, *Obit* July 1970

Livingston, John W., labor leader, July 1959, *Obit* Aug 1997

Livingston, M. Stanley, physicist, Feb 1955, *Obit* Nov 1986

Livingstone, Ken, British mayor, Jan 2003

Livni, Tzipi, Israeli lawyer and cabinet member, Jan 2006

Ljungberg, Ernst Carl, Mar 1955

Lleras Camargo, Alberto, Colombian president, Sept 1947, June 1965, *Obit* Mar 1990

Lleras Restrepo, Carlos, Colombian president, Nov 1970, *Obit* Nov 1994

Lleshanaku, Luljeta, Albanian poet, Jan 2002

Llewellyn, Richard, Welsh author, Apr 1940, *Obit* Jan 1984

Llewellyn, William, *Obit* Mar 1941

Llinas, Rodolfo R., American neurophysiologist, Sept 2009

Lloyd George, David Lloyd George, British statesman, Nov 1944, *Obit* May 1945

Lloyd Webber, Andrew, English composer, June 1982

Lloyd of Dolobran, George Ambrose Lloyd, British colonial administrator, Jan 1941, *Obit* Jan 1941

Lloyd, Alex, Australian singer and songwriter, Jan 2002

Lloyd, Charles, American saxophonist and flutist, Apr 2002

Lloyd, Harold, American actor and producer, Sept 1949, *Obit* Apr 1971

Lloyd, James T., *Obit* May 1944

Lloyd, Wesley P., educator, Jan 1952, *Obit* May 1977

Loach, Ken, British film and television director, July 1995

Lober, Georg John, Nov 1957, *Obit* Feb 1962

Lobo, Rebecca, American basketball player, Sept 1997

Lochner, Louis Paul, journalist, Aug 1942, *Obit* Feb 1975

Locke, Alain LeRoy, American philosopher and essayist, Jan 1944, *Obit* Sept 1954

Locke, Charles Edward, *Obit* Mar 1940

Locke, Edwin A., Jan 1952

Locke, Gary, American Secretary of commerce, Apr 2003

Locker, Jesse D., Mar 1955, *Obit* June 1955

Lockhart, Gene, Canadian actor, May 1950, *Obit* June 1957

Lockhart, Keith, American conductor, Aug 2008

Lockridge, Richard, American mystery novelist, Oct 1940, *Obit* Oct 1982

Lockridge, Ross, novelist, Mar 1948

Lockwood, Margaret, English actress, Sept 1948, *Obit* Sept 1990

Lockwood, Rodney M., Sept 1949

Lodge, Gonzalez, *Obit* Feb 1943

Lodge, Henry Cabot, American diplomat, Yrbk 1943, May 1954, *Obit* Apr 1985

Lodge, John Davis, governor and diplomat, Mar 1948, *Obit* Jan 1986

Lodge, Oliver Joseph, English physicist, *Obit* Oct 1940

Loeb, Abraham (Avi), July 2013

Loeb, Fritz, *Obit* Aug 1940

Loeb, James I., American diplomat and political leader, Jan 1962, *Obit* Mar 1992

Loeb, William, American newspaper publisher and journalist, Mar 1974, *Obit* Nov 1981

Loesser, Frank, American composer and lyricist, Yrbk 1945, *Obit* Oct 1969

Loewe, Frederick, American composer, July 1958, *Obit* Apr 1988

Loewe, Siegfried, American pharmacologist, Jan 1947

Loewy, Raymond Fernand, French-American industrial designer, Mar 1941, June 1953, *Obit* Sept 1986

Loftus, Cissie, Sept 1940, *Obit* Aug 1943

Loftus, Elizabeth F., American psychologist, Jan 1999

Logan, Harlan, magazine editor and publishing executive, Jan 1946, *Obit* Mar 1995

Logan, John, American screenwriter and playwright, Feb 2011

Logan, Joshua, American theatrical and motion picture director, Oct 1949, *Obit* Aug 1988

Logan, Lara, South African television reporter, July 2006

Logan, Walter, *Obit* Mar 1940

Logue, Edward J., American builder, June 1977, *Obit* June 2000

Lohan, Lindsay, American actress, Nov 2005

Lollobrigida, Gina, Italian actress, Sept 1960

Lomax, Alan, American folklorist and musicologist, Sept 1941, *Obit* Oct 2002

Lombard, Carole, American actress, *Obit* Mar 1942

Lombard, Helen, May 1943

Lombardi, Vince, American football coach, May 1963, *Obit* Nov 1970

Lombardo Toledano, Vicente, Mexican labor leader, Aug 1940, *Obit* Jan 1969

Lombardo, Guy, American band leader, Sept 1946, Feb 1975, *Obit* Jan 1978

Lomu, Jonah, New Zealand rugby player, Sept 2012

Lon Nol, Cambodian general and prime minister, Feb 1974, *Obit* Jan 1986

London, George, Canadian opera singer, Nov 1953, *Obit* June 1985

London, Julie, singer and actress, May 1960, *Obit* Feb 2001

Lonergan, Bernard J. F., Canadian priest and theologian, Jan 1972, *Obit* Feb 1985

Long, Andrew Theodore, *Obit* July 1946

Long, Breckinridge, diplomat, Nov 1943, *Obit* Yrbk 1958

Long, Earl K., American governor, Yrbk 1950, *Obit* Nov 1960

Long, Edward V., American senator, July 1964, *Obit* Jan 1973

Long, Oren E., American senator, Sept 1951, *Obit* June 1965

Long, Richard, English artist, Sept 1995

Long, Russell B., American senator, Yrbk 1951, Oct 1965, *Obit* Yrbk 2003

Long, Tania, Anglo-Russian journalist, May 1946, *Obit* June 1999

Long, William Ivey, American costume designer, Mar 2004

Longfellow, Ki, Novelist, playwright and theater producer and director, July 2012

Longman, Hubert Harry, *Obit* Apr 1940

Longo, Luigi, Feb 1966, *Obit* Jan 1981

Longo, Robert, American artist, Oct 1990

Longstreth, T. Morris, Yrbk 1950

Longworth, Alice Roosevelt, daughter of American

president Theodore Roosevelt, June 1943, Aug 1975, *Obit* Apr 1980

Loomis, Daniel P., Jan 1960

Loomis, Orland S., *Obit* Jan 1943

Loos, Anita, American novelist, dramatist and screenwriter, Feb 1974, *Obit* Oct 1981

Loosli, E. Fritz, Jan 1942

Lopez Bravo, Gregorio, Spanish diplomat, July 1971, *Obit* Apr 1985

Lopez Mateos, Adolfo, Mexican president, Mar 1959, *Obit* Nov 1969

Lopez Michelsen, Alfonso, Colombian president, Apr 1975

Lopez Obrador, Andres Manuel, Mexican mayor and political leader, Jan 2003

Lopez Portillo, Jose, Mexican president, June 1977, *Obit* Yrbk 2004

Lopez Rodo, Laureano, Feb 1972

Lopez, Al, American baseball player and manager, Feb 1960, *Obit* Yrbk 2006

Lopez, Alfonso, Colombian president, Sept 1942, *Obit* Jan 1960

Lopez, Barry Holstun, American novelist and essayist, July 1995

Lopez, George, American comedian, Mar 2010

Lopez, Nancy, American golfer, Sept 1978

Lopez, Trini, singer, Mar 1968

Lopez, Vincent, band leader and pianist, Nov 1960, Nov 1975

Loquasto, Santo, scenic designer, June 1981

Loram, Charles Templeman, *Obit* Sept 1940

Lord, F. T., *Obit* Jan 1942

Lord, John Wesley, bishop, May 1971, *Obit* Jan 1990

Lord, Mary Pillsbury, Oct 1952

Lord, Milton Edward, librarian, Feb 1950

Lord, Walter, American historian, Oct 1972, *Obit* Yrbk 2002

Lordkipanidze, David, Georgian paleontologist, Jan 2005

Loren, Sophia, Italian actress, Mar 1959

Lorentz, Pare, American motion picture director, Apr 1940, *Obit* May 1992

Lorenz, Christian, German keyboardist, Jan 2007

Lorenz, John G., Sept 1966

Lorenz, Konrad, Austrian ethologist, July 1955, Oct 1977, *Obit* Apr 1989

Lorenzo, Frank, airline executive, Feb 1987

Lorge, Irving, psychologist, July 1959, *Obit* Apr 1961

Loring, Eugene, American dancer and choreographer, Mar 1972, *Obit* Oct 1982

Lortel, Lucille, theater owner and producer, Feb 1985, *Obit* July 1999

Los Lobos (Musical group), Oct 2005

Losch, Tilly, July 1944, *Obit* Feb 1976

Losey, Joseph, American motion picture director, Yrbk 1969, *Obit* Aug 1984

Lothar, Ernst, Austrian author, Yrbk 1947

Lothian, Philip Henry Kerr, British diplomat, *Obit* Yrbk 1940

Lott, Ronnie, American investment manager and former football player, Feb 1994

Lott, Trent, American senator, Sept 1996

Lou, Liza, American bead artist, Jan 2000

Louchheim, Katie, government official, June 1956, *Obit* Apr 1991

Loud, Pat, July 1974

Loudon, Alexander, July 1942, *Obit* Mar 1953

Loudon, Dorothy, American actress and singer, June 1984, *Obit* Yrbk 2004

Louganis, Greg, American diver and actor, Oct 1984

Lougheed, Peter, Canadian political leader, Aug 1979

Loughlin, Anne, Feb 1950

Louis, Joe, American boxer, Oct 1940, *Obit* June 1981

Louis, Murray, dancer and choreographer, Oct 1968

Louis-Dreyfus, Julia, American actress, Oct 1995

Louise, *Obit* Jan 1940

Loutfi, Omar, Jan 1957, *Obit* July 1963

Louw, Eric, Mar 1962, *Obit* Sept 1968

Lovano, Joe, American jazz saxophonist, Mar 1998

Love, Courtney, American singer and actress, June 1996

Love, George Hutchinson, coal and automobile executive, Mar 1950, *Obit* Sept 1991

Love, Iris, archaeologist, Aug 1982

Love, James Spencer, textile executive, Nov 1957, *Obit* Mar 1962

Love, John A., American governor, Nov 1963, *Obit* Apr 2002

Love, Kevin, American basketball player, Jan 2013

Love, Susan M., American surgeon, Oct 1994

Loveless, Herschel Cellel, governor, July 1958, *Obit* July 1989

Lovell, Bernard, English astronomer, Oct 1959, *Obit* Yrbk 2012

Lovell, Jim, American astronaut, Mar 1969

Lovelock, James, British chemist and biophysicist, Nov 1992

Loveman, Amy, June 1943, *Obit* Feb 1956

Lovett, Lyle, American singer, Sept 1997

Lovett, Robert A., American Secretary of defense, Aug 1942, Nov 1951, *Obit* June 1986

Lovett, Robert Morss, literary critic and author, Aug 1943, *Obit* Apr 1956

Lovins, Amory B., American physicist and conservationist, June 1997

Low, David, New Zealand cartoonist, Jan 1940, *Obit* Nov 1963

Lowden, Frank O., governor, *Obit* May 1943

Lowdermilk, Walter, American soil scientist, Feb 1949, *Obit* July 1974

Lowe, Jack Warren, pianist, Jan 1954, *Obit* Aug 1996

Lowe, Rob, American actor, July 2000

Lowell, A. Lawrence, American college president and political scientist, *Obit* Feb 1943

Lowell, Mike, American baseball player, Sept 2003

Lowell, Robert, American poet, July 1947, Jan 1972, *Obit* Nov 1977

Lowensohn, Elina, Romanian actress, Jan 2005

Lowenstein, Allard K., American civil rights leader, pacifist and congressman, Sept 1971, *Obit* May 1980

Lowery, Joseph, American clergyman and civil rights leader, Nov 1982

Lowey, Nita M., American congresswoman, Sept 1997

Lownsbery, Eloise, author, Yrbk 1947

Lowrie, Jean E., June 1973

Lowry, Edward George, *Obit* Sept 1943

Loy, Myrna, American actress, Oct 1950, *Obit* Feb 1994

Loynd, Harry J., Feb 1952

Lozano, Conrad, American bassist, Oct 2005

Lozovskii, A., Nov 1941

Lozowick, Louis, American painter, Apr 1942, *Obit* Nov 1973

LuPone, Patti, American actress and singer, Apr 1989

Lubbers, Rudolphus, Dutch prime minister and United Nations official, May 1988, Jan 2003

Lubell, Samuel, journalist and public opinion analyst, Nov 1956, *Obit* Oct 1987

Lubezki, Emmanuel, Mexican cinematographer, July 2011

Lubic, Ruth Watson, American nurse and midwife, Sept 1996

Lubin, Isador, Oct 1941, Jan 1953, *Obit* Sept 1978

Lubke, Heinrich, Jan 1960, *Obit* May 1972

Lubovitch, Lar, American dancer and choreographer, Mar 1992

Lucas, Caroline, British member of European parliament, Sept 2012

Lucas, Craig, American dramatist, Sept 1991

Lucas, George, American film director, producer and screenwriter, Apr 1978, May 2002

Lucas, Jerry, American basketball player, June 1972

Lucas, John, American basketball player and coach, Oct 1995

Lucas, Scott W., American senator, Yrbk 1947, *Obit* Apr 1968

Lucci, Susan, American actress, Oct 1989

Luccock, Halford Edward, June 1960, *Obit* Jan 1961

Luce, Charles Franklin, American electric utility executive, Yrbk 1968, *Obit* Yrbk 2008

Luce, Clare Boothe, American dramatist and diplomat, Nov 1942, Apr 1953, *Obit* Nov 1987

Luce, Henry Robinson, American magazine editor and publisher, July 1941, Jan 1961, *Obit* Apr 1967

Luce, Robert, *Obit* May 1946

Lucet, Charles, Yrbk 1967

Lucia, Paco de, Spanish flamenco guitarist, Jan 2004

Lucioni, Luigi, painter, Oct 1943, *Obit* Sept 1988

Luckman, Charles, American personal care products industry executive, Oct 1947, *Obit* Apr 1999

Luckovich, Mike, American editorial cartoonist, Jan 2005

Luckstone, Isidore, *Obit* May 1941

Ludacris, American rapper, June 2004

Ludington, Flora Belle, librarian, Nov 1953

Ludlam, Charles, American actor, director and dramatist, Aug 1986, *Obit* July 1987

Ludlum, Robert, American novelist, Nov 1982, *Obit* July 2001

Ludwig, Christa, German opera singer, Mar 1971

Ludwig, Daniel Keith, shipping executive and financier, May 1979, *Obit* Oct 1992

Ludwig, Ken, American lawyer and dramatist, May 2004

Lugar, Richard G., American senator, Oct 1977

Luger, Lex (Lexus Arnel Lewis), May 2013

Luhan, Mabel Ganson Dodge, American patron of the arts

and memoirist, Jan 1940, *Obit* Oct 1962

Luhring, Oscar Raymond, *Obit* Oct 1944

Luhrmann, Baz, Australian film director, Jan 2002

Luisi, Fabio, Principal conductor of the Metropolitan Opera, Mar 2012

Lujack, Johnny, football player, Yrbk 1947

Lujan, Manuel, American Secretary of the interior, Sept 1989

Lukas, J. Anthony, American journalist, Jan 1987, *Obit* Aug 1997

Lukas, Paul, American actor, Feb 1942, *Obit* Oct 1971

Lumet, Sidney, American television and film director, Sept 1967, June 2005, *Obit* Yrbk 2011

Lumpkin, Alva M., *Obit* Sept 1941

Lumumba, Patrice, Congolese prime minister, Nov 1960, *Obit* Apr 1961

Luna, Diego, Mexican actor, Jan 2002

Lund, Wendell L., Sept 1942

Lundeberg, Harry, Nov 1952, *Obit* Mar 1957

Lundeen, Ernest, *Obit* Oct 1940

Lunden, Joan, American television personality, May 1989

Lundqvist, Henrik, Swedish hockey player, Jan 2006

Lunge-Larsen, Lise, Norwegian-American children's author, Aug 2012

Luns, Joseph M. A. H., Dutch diplomat and NATO official, Feb 1958, Apr 1982, *Obit* Yrbk 2002

Lunt, Alfred, American actor, June 1941, *Obit* Sept 1977

Lunt, Alfred; and Fontanne, Lynn, June 1941

Lunt, Storer B., Nov 1958

Lupescu, Elena, mistress of King Carol II of Romania, Oct 1940, *Obit* Aug 1977

Lupica, Mike, American sportswriter, Mar 2001

Lupino, Ida, American actress and film director, Sept 1943, *Obit* Oct 1995

Lupino, Stanley, *Obit* Aug 1942

Luquiens, Frederick Bliss, *Obit* May 1940

Lurcat, Jean, French painter and tapestry designer, Sept 1948, *Obit* Feb 1966

Luria, S. E., American biologist, Feb 1970, *Obit* Apr 1991

Lurie, Alison, American novelist, Feb 1986

Lurie, John, American saxophonist and actor, Oct 2010

Lusk, Georgia Lee, American congresswoman, Oct 1947, *Obit* Feb 1971

Lustiger, Jean Marie, Feb 1984, *Obit* Yrbk 2007

Lutes, Della T., author, *Obit* Sept 1942

Luthuli, Albert John, South African political leader, Feb 1962, *Obit* Oct 1967

Lutoslawski, Witold, Polish composer, Aug 1991, *Obit* Apr 1994

Lutyens, Edwin Landseer, British architect, June 1942, *Obit* Feb 1944

Lutz, Frank Eugene, entomologist and museum curator, *Obit* Jan 1944

Lutz, Robert A., American automobile executive, Jan 1994

Luzhkov, Yuri, Russian mayor, Nov 1999, Jan 2007

Lydenberg, Harry Miller, librarian, Sept 1941, *Obit* June 1960

Lyle, Sparky, baseball player, July 1978

Lynch, Daniel F., July 1955

Lynch, David, American film director and screenwriter, May 1987

Lynch, Jane, American actress, July 2010

Lynch, John Joseph, priest and seismologist, Oct 1946, *Obit* Aug 1987

Lynch, John Mary, Irish prime minister, May 1967, *Obit* Feb 2000

Lynch, Peg, Feb 1956

Lynch, Peter, American investment manager, Nov 1994

Lynch, William J., *Obit* Aug 1941

Lynd, Staughton, American historian and lawyer, May 1983

Lynde, Paul, Nov 1972, *Obit* Feb 1982

Lyndon, Edward, *Obit* Yrbk 1940

Lyne, Adrian, English motion picture director, Jan 1994

Lyne, Susan, American media executive, Feb 2012

Lynen, Feodor, German biochemist, June 1967, *Obit* Oct 1979

Lynes, Russell, essayist and periodical editor, Nov 1957, *Obit* Nov 1991

Lyng, Richard E., American Secretary of agriculture, Sept 1986, *Obit* Yrbk 2003

Lynn, Diana, actress, Nov 1953, *Obit* Feb 1972

Lynn, James T., American insurance executive, Yrbk 1973

Lynn, Loretta, American country singer and songwriter, Oct 1973

Lynne, Gillian, English dancer and choreographer, Jan 2002

Lynne, Shelby, American country singer and songwriter, July 2001

Lyons, Eugene, American journalist and biographer, Jan 1944, *Obit* Mar 1985

Lyons, Harry, Oct 1957

Lysenko, Trofim, Russian geneticist, Oct 1952, *Obit* Feb 1977

Lyubimov, Yuri, Russian theatrical director, Nov 1988

M

M'Bow, Amadou-Mahtar, Senegalese United Nations official, May 1987

M. I. A. (Singer), Sri Lankan-British singer and songwriter, May 2009

Ma Kai, Chinese government official, Jan 2007

Ma, G. John, July 1953

Ma, Jack, Chinese Internet service provider executive, Jan 2006

Ma, Pony, Chinese information technology executive, Jan 2005

Ma, Yo-Yo, American cellist, July 1982

Maas, Melvin Joseph, Nov 1957, *Obit* June 1964

Maathai, Wangari, Kenyan biologist and environmentalist, Sept 1993, *Obit* Yrbk 2011

Maazel, Lorin, American conductor, Yrbk 1965

Mabley, Moms, American comedienne and actress, Jan 1975, *Obit* Aug 1975

Mac, Bernie, American comedian and actor, June 2002, *Obit* Nov 2008

MacAlarney, Robert Emmet, *Obit* Jan 1946

MacArthur, Douglas, American general, Oct 1941, May 1948, *Obit* May 1964

MacArthur, Douglas, American diplomat, Nov 1954, *Obit* Jan 1998

MacBride, Sean, Irish diplomat, June 1949, *Obit* Mar 1988

MacCallum, William George, *Obit* Mar 1944

MacCormick, Austin H., May 1940, July 1951, *Obit* Jan 1980

MacCracken, Henry Noble, college president, Sept 1940, *Obit* June 1970

MacDermot, Galt, Canadian composer, July 1984

MacDonald, Betty, American memoirist and humorist, Feb 1946, *Obit* Apr 1958

MacDonald, John D., American mystery novelist, Oct 1986, *Obit* Feb 1987

MacDonald, Malcolm, British colonial administrator and diplomat, Nov 1954, *Obit* Mar 1981

MacDonald, Pirie, *Obit* June 1942

MacDonald, William J., *Obit* May 1946

MacDowell, Andie, American model and actress, Nov 1999

MacEachen, Allan Joseph, Canadian political leader, Apr 1983

MacEwen, Walter, *Obit* May 1943

MacFarlane, Seth, American animator, television scriptwriter, producer and voice-over artist, May 2010

MacGowan, Gault, Jan 1945

MacGregor, Ellen, author and librarian, Yrbk 1954

MacGregor, Joanna, British pianist, Jan 2006

MacInnes, Helen, Scottish-American novelist, Nov 1967, *Obit* Nov 1985

MacIver, Loren, American painter, Nov 1953, Nov 1987, *Obit* Aug 1998

MacKaye, Ian, American singer and guitarist, Mar 2002

MacKaye, Julia Gunther, American librarian and children's author, Yrbk 1949

MacKenzie, Warren, potter, Sept 1994

MacKinnon, Catharine A., American lawyer and feminist, June 1994

MacKintosh, Cameron, English theatrical producer, Mar 1991

MacLachlan, Kyle, American actor, Aug 1993

MacLaine, Shirley, American dancer and actress, Yrbk 1959, July 1978

MacLean, Basil C., May 1957, *Obit* Apr 1963

MacLean, Malcolm Shaw, July 1940

MacLeish, Archibald, American poet and Librarian of Congress, Oct 1940, Nov 1959, *Obit* June 1982

MacLennan, Hugh, Canadian novelist, Yrbk 1946, *Obit* Jan 1991

MacLeod, Dorothy Shaw, Apr 1949

MacMillan, Donald, American explorer, Sept 1948, *Obit* Nov 1970

MacMillan, Ernest, Canadian conductor and composer, Mar 1955, *Obit* June 1973

MacMillan, Margaret, Canadian historian, Jan 2007

MacMitchell, Leslie, American runner, Apr 1946, *Obit* Yrbk 2006

MacMurray, Fred, actor, Feb 1967, *Obit* Feb 1992

MacNeil, Cornell, American opera singer, Jan 1976, *Obit* Yrbk 2011

MacNeil, Neil, American newspaper editor, May 1940

MacNeil, Robert, Canadian television newscaster and novelist, Feb 1980

MacPhail, Larry, baseball executive, Mar 1945, *Obit* Nov 1975

MacVeagh, Lincoln, American publisher and diplomat, Nov 1941, June 1952, *Obit* Mar 1972

Macapagal, Diosdado, Filipino president, Nov 1962, *Obit* July 1997

Macapagal-Arroyo, Gloria, Filipino president, Jan 2002

Macartney, William Napier, *Obit* Aug 1940

Macauley, Jane Hamilton, Sept 1949

Macbride, Ernest William, *Obit* Jan 1941

Macdonald, Brian, Canadian ballet director and choreographer, July 1968

Macdonald, Duncan Black, American theologian, linguist and Islamist, *Obit* Oct 1943

Macdonald, Dwight, American journalist and critic, Nov 1969, *Obit* Mar 1983

Macdonald, George, classicist and archaeologist, *Obit* Sept 1940

Macdonald, Ross, American mystery novelist, Yrbk 1953, Aug 1979, *Obit* Sept 1983

Machado Hernandez, Alfredo, *Obit* Sept 1946

Machado Ventura, Jose Ramon, Cuban vice-president, Sept 2011

Machado, Bernardino, *Obit* June 1944

Machel, Graca Simbine, Mozambican social welfare leader and wife of Nelson Mandela, Oct 1997

Machel, Samora, Mozambican president, Mar 1984, *Obit* Jan 1987

Machito, Cuban band leader, Feb 1983, *Obit* June 1984

Machold, Earle J., Nov 1958

Mack, Connie, American baseball manager and executive, June 1944, *Obit* Apr 1956

Mack, Julian W., American judge, *Obit* Oct 1943

Mack, Lawrence L., Apr 1957

Mack, Nila, Yrbk 1952, *Obit* Mar 1953

Mack, Pauline Beery, chemist and college dean, Yrbk 1950

Mack, Ted, Apr 1951, *Obit* Sept 1976

Mack, Walter, beverage industry executive, Feb 1946, *Obit* May 1990

Mackay, Iven Giffard, Apr 1941, *Obit* Jan 1967

Mackay, John Alexander, American theologian and missionary, Feb 1952, *Obit* Aug 1983

Mackaye, David L., American novelist, Yrbk 1949

Mackaye, David L.; and Mackaye, Julia Gunther, Yrbk 1949

Mackenzie, Chalmers Jack, June 1952

Mackenzie, Clinton, *Obit* Mar 1940

Mackenzie, Gisele, Canadian singer, Nov 1955, *Obit* July 2004

Mackerras, Charles, Australian conductor, Feb 1985

Mackey, John, American supermarket chain executive, Nov 2008

Mackie, Bob, fashion designer, Oct 1988

Macleod, Iain Norman, British cabinet member, Apr 1956, *Obit* Oct 1970

Macmahon, Arthur W., American political scientist, Apr 1958, *Obit* Apr 1980

Macmillan, Harold, British prime minister, Mar 1943, Jan 1955, *Obit* Feb 1987

Macrae, John, *Obit* Apr 1944

Macrossie, Allan, *Obit* Mar 1940

Macy, Edith Dewing, Yrbk 1952, *Obit* Oct 1967

Macy, George, Nov 1954, *Obit* Sept 1956

Macy, John W., government official, Jan 1962, *Obit* Apr 1987

Madariaga, Salvador de, Spanish essayist, Jan 1964, *Obit* Feb 1979

Madden, John, American football coach and sportscaster, Aug 1985

Madden, Ray J., congressman, Apr 1953, *Obit* Nov 1987

Maddin, Guy, Canadian film director, Jan 2006

Maddon, Joe, American baseball manager, Sept 2012

Maddow, Rachel, American television and radio talk show host, Aug 2009

Maddox, Lester, American governor, Yrbk 1967, *Obit* Yrbk 2003

Maddox, William P., Nov 1947, *Obit* Yrbk 1972

Maddux, Greg, American baseball player, Feb 1996

Maddy, Joseph E., musician and educator, Apr 1946, *Obit* May 1966

Madeira, Jean, Oct 1963, *Obit* Sept 1972

Madeleva, Mary, American nun, poet and college president, Feb 1942, *Obit* Oct 1964

Madigan, Edward R., American Secretary of agriculture, Nov 1992, *Obit* Feb 1995

Madonna, American singer, May 1986

Madrick, Jeffrey G., American economist and journalist, Nov 2011

Madrid Hurtado, Miguel de la, Mexican president, Apr 1983, *Obit* Yrbk 2012

Madsen, Michael, American actor, Apr 2004

Maduro, Ricardo, Honduran president, Jan 2003

Maenner, T. H., Nov 1949, *Obit* Mar 1958

Magallanes, Nicholas, May 1955, *Obit* July 1977

Magaziner, Ira C., American business consultant and presidential adviser, Apr 1995

Magee, Elizabeth S., Oct 1950

Magee, James C., May 1943

Maggiolo, Walter A., labor mediator, July 1952, *Obit* Yrbk 2000

Magill, Roswell, Mar 1948, *Obit* Feb 1964

Maglie, Sal, American baseball player, June 1953, *Obit* Feb 1993

Maglione, Luigi, *Obit* Oct 1944

Magliozzi, Ray, American automobile mechanic and radio talk show host, June 2006

Magliozzi, Tom, American automobile mechanic and radio talk show host, June 2006

Magloire, Paul, Haitian president, Feb 1952, *Obit* Nov 2001

Magnani, Anna, Italian actress, Apr 1956, *Obit* Nov 1973

Magner, Thomas F., *Obit* Feb 1946

Magnuson, Paul B., June 1948, *Obit* Jan 1969

Magnuson, Warren, American senator, Oct 1945, *Obit* July 1989

Magnusson, Magnus, Icelandic-British television personality, journalist and college administrator, Jan 2006

Magoffin, Ralph Van Deman, *Obit* July 1942

Magritte, Rene, Belgian painter, Sept 1966, *Obit* Oct 1967

Magruder, William M., aeronautical engineer and airline executive, Mar 1972, *Obit* Nov 1977

Magsaysay, Ramon, Filipino president, Yrbk 1952, *Obit* May 1957

Maguire, Martie, American fiddler, July 2000

Maguire, Tobey, American actor, Sept 2002

Mahady, Henry J., July 1954

Mahan, John W., July 1959

Maharaj Ji, Indian religious leader, Yrbk 1974

Maharaj, Birju, Indian dancer, Jan 2007

Mahathir bin Mohamad, Malaysian prime minister, Aug 1988

Mahendra Bir Bikram Shaha Deva, July 1956, *Obit* Mar 1972

Maher, Ahmed, *Obit* Apr 1945

Maher, Aly, Mar 1952, *Obit* Nov 1960

Maher, Bill, American comedian and talk show host, July 1997

Mahesh Yogi, Indian yogi, Yrbk 1972, *Obit* Yrbk 2008

Mahfuz, Najib, Egyptian novelist, May 1989, *Obit* Yrbk 2007

Mahlangu, Esther, South African painter, Jan 2007

Mahon, George H., American congressman, Mar 1958, *Obit* Jan 1986

Mahoney, John, actor, Aug 1999

Mai, Mukhtar, Pakistani feminist, Jan 2006

Maier, Hermann, Austrian skier, Jan 2003

Maier, Walter Arthur, evangelist and theologian, May 1947, *Obit* Feb 1950

Maile, Boniface R., Feb 1951

Mailer, Norman, American novelist, Oct 1948, Feb 1970, *Obit* Jan 2008

Mailhouse, Max, *Obit* Yrbk 1941

Maillol, Aristide, French sculptor and illustrator, May 1942, *Obit* Nov 1944

Maimon, Shiri, Israeli pop singer, Jan 2006

Main, Charles Thomas, *Obit* Apr 1943

Main, Marjorie, actress, Oct 1951, *Obit* June 1975

Mainbocher, fashion designer, Feb 1942, *Obit* Mar 1977

Maines, Natalie, American singer, July 2000

Maiskii, I. M., Soviet diplomat, Sept 1941, *Obit* Oct 1975

Major, John, British prime minister, Oct 1990, Apr 1997

Makarios, Cypriot archbishop and president, May 1956, *Obit* Sept 1977

Makarova, Natalia, Russian ballet dancer, Feb 1972

Makeba, Miriam, South African singer, June 1965, *Obit* Yrbk 2009

Makemson, Maud Worcester, astronomer, June 1941

Makhmalbaf, Samira, Iranian motion picture director, Jan 2003

Maki, Fumihiko, Japanese architect, July 2001

Makin, Norman J. O., Mar 1946

Makiya, Kanan, Iraqi Middle Eastern studies specialist, Jan 2002

Malaby, Tony, American jazz saxophonist, Sept 2008

Malamud, Bernard, American novelist and short story writer, Yrbk 1958, July 1978, *Obit* May 1986

Malan, Daniel Francois, South African prime minister, Apr 1949, *Obit* Apr 1959

Malbin, Elaine, Feb 1959

Malcolm, Ellen, American feminist and political activist, Feb 2010

Malcolm, George A., Nov 1954

Malden, Karl, American actor, Apr 1957, *Obit* Yrbk 2009

Malenkov, Georgi M., Soviet prime minister, June 1952, *Obit* Mar 1988

Malick, Terrence, American film director, June 1999

Malik, Adam, Indonesian statesman and diplomat, Nov 1970, *Obit* Nov 1984

Malik, Charles Habib, Lebanese diplomat and United Nations official, Apr 1948, *Obit* Feb 1988

Malik, Yakov Aleksandrovich, Apr 1949, *Obit* Apr 1980

Malin, Patrick Murphy, Mar 1950, *Obit* Feb 1965

Malina, Joshua, American actor, Apr 2004

Malina, Judith, American actress and theatrical director, June 2011

Malinovskii, Rodion IAkovlevich, Soviet field marshal, Mar 1944, Nov 1960, *Obit* May 1967

Malinowski, Bronislaw, Polish anthropologist, June 1941, *Obit* July 1942

Malkin, Michelle, American journalist and political commentator, Apr 2010

Malkin, Peter Z., Israeli intelligence agent, Jan 2003

Malkovich, John, American actor, May 1988

Malle, Louis, French motion picture director, Feb 1976, *Obit* Feb 1996

Mallette, Gertrude E., Yrbk 1950

Malley, Matt, American bassist, Mar 2003

Malloch Brown, Mark, British United Nations official, Jan 2005

Mallory, C. C., Feb 1956, *Obit* Mar 1959

Mallory, F. B., *Obit* Nov 1941

Mallory, Lester D., diplomat, Sept 1960, *Obit* Sept 1994

Malloy, Dan, American governor, June 2011

Mallya, Vijay, Indian business executive, Jan 2004

Malone, George W., American senator, Yrbk 1950, *Obit* July 1961

Malone, John C., American broadcasting executive, Aug 1995

Malone, Karl, American basketball player, Jan 1993

Malone, Kyp, American guitarist and singer, Apr 2009

Malone, Moses, American basketball player, June 1986

Malone, Ross Lynn, lawyer, Mar 1959, *Obit* Oct 1974

Maloney, Carolyn B., American congresswoman, Apr 2001

Maloney, Francis T., *Obit* Mar 1945

Maloney, Walter E., American lawyer, Oct 1952, *Obit* Yrbk 2007

Malott, Deane W., college president, Mar 1951, *Obit* Nov 1996

Malraux, Andre, French novelist, essayist and art historian, Mar 1959, *Obit* Feb 1977

Maltin, Leonard, American film critic and historian, Aug 2008

Maltz, Albert, screenwriter, Jan 1940, *Obit* July 1985

Malvern, Godfrey Martin Huggins, Rhodesian prime minister, Nov 1956, *Obit* June 1971

Mam, Somaly, Cambodian social worker, June 2009

Mamdani, Mahmood, Ugandan political scientist, Jan 2010

Mamet, David, American dramatist, Aug 1978, Mar 1998

Mami, Cheb, Algerian singer, Jan 2005

Mamlok, Hans J., *Obit* Yrbk 1940

Mamoulian, Rouben, Russian-American theatrical and film director, Mar 1949, *Obit* Jan 1988

Mana (Musical group), Jan 2005

Manchester, William, American biographer and historian, Nov 1967, *Obit* Yrbk 2004

Mancini, Henry, American composer, July 1964, *Obit* Aug 1994

Mandel, Georges, French political leader, Yrbk 1940

Mandela, Nelson, South African president, Jan 1984, Nov 1995

Mandela, Winnie, South African political leader and wife of Nelson Mandela, Jan 1986

Mandelbrot, Benoit B., American mathematician, June 1987, *Obit* Yrbk 2010

Mandlikova, Hana, Czech tennis player, Jan 1986

Mandrell, Barbara, singer, Aug 1982

Manessier, Alfred, French painter, May 1957, *Obit* Oct 1993

Maney, Richard, July 1964, *Obit* Sept 1968

Manfred, Frederick Feikema, American novelist, Yrbk 1950

Mangesakara, Lata, Indian singer, Jan 2003

Mangione, Chuck, trumpet player and flugelhornist, May 1980

Mangione, Jerre, American memoirist, novelist and historian, Mar 1943, *Obit* Nov 1998

Mangrum, Lloyd, American golfer, Sept 1951, *Obit* Jan 1974

Manilow, Barry, American pop singer and songwriter, July 1978

Manji, Irshad, Canadian author and broadcasting entrepreneur, Jan 2005

Mankiewicz, Joseph L., American film director, producer and screenwriter, Sept 1949, *Obit* Apr 1993

Mankiller, Wilma, Cherokee chief, Nov 1988, *Obit* Yrbk 2010

Mankin, Helen Douglas, congresswoman and lawyer, Apr 1946

Mankoff, Robert, American cartoonist, May 2005

Mankowitz, Wolf, English author and screenwriter, Yrbk 1956, *Obit* Aug 1998

Manley, Michael, Jamaican prime minister, Jan 1976, *Obit* May 1997

Manley, Norman Washington, Jamaican prime minister, Nov 1959, *Obit* Nov 1969

Manly, John Matthews, *Obit* May 1940

Mann, Emily, American dramatist and director, June 2002

Mann, Erika, German writer, actress and daughter of Thomas Mann, Yrbk 1940, *Obit* Nov 1969

Mann, Klaus, German novelist, essayist, dramatist and son of Thomas Mann, Yrbk 1940, *Obit* July 1949

Mann, Marty, social welfare leader, June 1949, *Obit* Sept 1980

Mann, Michael, American motion picture director and television producer, Jan 1993

Mann, Thomas, German novelist, May 1942, *Obit* Oct 1955

Mann, Thomas Clifton, American diplomat, Apr 1964, *Obit* Apr 1999

Mann, Tom, English labor leader, *Obit* May 1941

Manna, Charlie, Jan 1965, *Obit* Yrbk 1971

Mannerheim, Carl Gustaf Emil, Finnish field marshal and president, Apr 1940, *Obit* Feb 1951

Mannes, Marya, author, Apr 1959

Manning, Eli, American football player, Sept 2008

Manning, Ernest, Canadian political leader, Yrbk 1959, *Obit* May 1996

Manning, Harry, May 1952, *Obit* Oct 1974

Manning, Marie, columnist, Aug 1944, *Obit* Jan 1946

Manning, Patrick A. M., Trinidadian prime minister, Jan 2006

Manning, Peyton, American football player, Sept 1998

Manning, Reg, June 1951

Manning, William Thomas, Apr 1940, *Obit* Jan 1950

Manrique, Jaime, Colombian-American novelist and poet, Jan 2005

Mansbridge, Albert, English educator, June 1942

Mansfield, Mike, American senator and diplomat, Apr 1952, Jan 1978, *Obit* Jan 2002

Mansfield, Peter, British physicist, Jan 2007

Manship, Paul, American sculptor, May 1940, *Obit* Mar 1966

Mansholt, Sicco Leendert, May 1966

Manson, John T., *Obit* Apr 1944

Manson, Marilyn, American singer, May 1999

Mansouri, Lotfi, Iranian opera director, Apr 1990, *Obit* Yrbk 2013

Manstein, Erich von, German field marshal, Oct 1942, *Obit* Sept 1973

Mantell, Marianne, American recording company executive, May 1957

Mantle, Burns, American drama critic, Nov 1944, *Obit* Mar 1948

Mantle, Mickey, American baseball player, July 1953, *Obit* Oct 1995

Manuil'skii, Dmitrii Zakhar'evich, Yrbk 1948, *Obit* May 1959

Manzu, Giacomo, Italian sculptor, Mar 1961, *Obit* Mar 1991

Mao Zedong, Chinese communist leader, Feb 1943, May 1962, *Obit* Oct 1976

Mapes, Victor, *Obit* Jan 1944

Maphai, Vincent, South African political scientist and broadcasting executive, Jan 2003

Mapplethorpe, Robert, American photographer and art collector, May 1989, *Obit* May 1989

Mara, Rooney, American actress, Oct 2012

Maradona, Diego, Argentine soccer player and coach, Nov 1990, Jan 2006

Marais, Jean, French actor, Apr 1962, *Obit* Jan 1999

Marber, Patrick, English dramatist, Jan 2007

Marble, Alice, American tennis player, Nov 1940, *Obit* Mar 1991

Marburg, Theodore, *Obit* Apr 1946

Marca-Relli, Conrad, American collage artist, Sept 1970, *Obit* Nov 2000

Marcantonio, Vito, American congressman, Feb 1949, *Obit* Oct 1954

Marceau, Marcel, French mime, Feb 1957, *Obit* Yrbk 2007

March, Charles Hoyt, *Obit* Sept 1945

March, Fredric, American actor, Mar 1943, *Obit* June 1975

March, Fredric; and Eldridge, Florence, Mar 1943

Marchais, Georges, French communist leader, June 1976, *Obit* Jan 1998

Marchal, Leon, Sept 1943, *Obit* Yrbk 1957

Marchetto, Marisa Acocella, American advertising executive and graphic novelist, Aug 2013

Marcial Dorado, Carolina, *Obit* Sept 1941

Marciano, Rocky, American boxer, Sept 1952, *Obit* Nov 1969

Marcinko, Richard, motivational speaker, Mar 2001

Marcos, Mexican revolutionary, Jan 2002

Marcos, Ferdinand E., Filipino president, Feb 1967, *Obit* Nov 1989

Marcus, Bernard, American home improvement chain executive, Aug 2007

Marcus, George E., American anthropologist, Mar 2006

Marcus, Greil, American music critic, Oct 1999

Marcus, Jacob Rader, rabbi and historian, May 1960, *Obit* Jan 1996

Marcus, Stanley, American department store executive, June 1949, *Obit* Apr 2002

Marcuse, Herbert, American political philosopher, Mar 1969, *Obit* Sept 1979

Marcy, Geoffrey W., American astrophysicist, Nov 2002

Marcy, Geoffrey W.; and Butler, R. Paul, Nov 2002

Marden, Brice, American painter and printmaker, Aug 1990

Marden, Orison Swett, author and magazine editor, July 1967, *Obit* Oct 1975

Mardikian, George M., Nov 1947

Marella, Paolo, Oct 1964

Marett, Robert R., *Obit* Apr 1943

Margai, Milton Augustus Striery, Sierra Leonean prime minister, Feb 1962, *Obit* June 1964

Margaret, Nov 1953, *Obit* May 2002

Margesson, Henry David Reginald Margesson, Feb 1941, *Obit* Feb 1966

Margoliouth, D. S., *Obit* Apr 1940

Margrethe, Nov 1972

Margueritte, Victor, *Obit* May 1942

Margulis, Lynn, American microbiologist, July 1992, *Obit* Yrbk 2012

Maria Theresa, *Obit* Apr 1944

Marias, Julian, Spanish philosopher, author and educator, Feb 1972

Marie, Andre, French political leader, Sept 1948, *Obit* Sept 1974

Marin, John, American painter, July 1949, *Obit* Yrbk 1953

Marini, Marino, Italian sculptor, Jan 1954, *Obit* Oct 1980

Marino, Dan, American football player and television sportscaster, Jan 1989

Marion, George F., *Obit* Jan 1946

Maris, Roger, American baseball player, Nov 1961, *Obit* Feb 1986

Marisol, Venezuelan sculptor, Apr 1968

Maritain, Jacques, French philosopher, May 1942, *Obit* June 1973

Marius, Emilie Alexander, *Obit* Apr 1940

Marjolin, Robert E., French economist, Yrbk 1948, *Obit* June 1986

Mark, Herman Francis, American chemist and college dean, May 1961, *Obit* June 1992

Mark, Louis, *Obit* May 1942

Mark, Mary Ellen, American photographer, Sept 1999

Mark, Rebecca, American energy industry executive, May 1999

Markel, Lester, newspaper editor, Yrbk 1952, *Obit* Jan 1978

Markell, Jack, American governor, July 2011

Marker, Laurie, American conservationist, Feb 2000

Markey, Edward J., American congressman, Nov 1997

Markham, Beryl, British aviator, Nov 1942, *Obit* Oct 1986

Markham, Edwin, poet, Mar 1940

Markova, Alicia, British ballet dancer, Sept 1943, *Obit* Yrbk 2005

Markovic, Ante, Yugoslav prime minister, Nov 1991, *Obit* Yrbk 2012

Marks of Broughton, Simon Marks, English merchant, Nov 1962, *Obit* Feb 1965

Marks, Leonard H., American lawyer and government official, June 1966, *Obit* Yrbk 2006

Marland, Sidney, American educator and government official, Apr 1972, *Obit* July 1992

Marland, William C., Apr 1956, *Obit* Jan 1966

Marlette, Doug, American editorial cartoonist, July 2002, *Obit* Yrbk 2007

Marling, Brit, American actress, film director and screenwriter, Oct 2011

Maron, Marc, American comedian, Nov 2011

Marples, Alfred Ernest Marples, May 1960

Marquand, Hilary A., Apr 1951

Marquand, John P., American novelist, Apr 1942, *Obit* Oct 1960

Marquardt, Alexandria, *Obit* June 1943

Marquis, Albert Nelson, *Obit* Feb 1944

Marriner, Neville, English conductor, Aug 1978

Marriott, Alice Lee, anthropologist and author, Yrbk 1950, *Obit* May 1992

Marriott, J. Willard, American hotel executive, June 1972, *Obit* Oct 1985

Marriott, John, *Obit* July 1945

Mars, Bruno, American singer and songwriter, May 2011

Marsalis, Branford, American jazz saxophonist, Sept 1991

Marsalis, Ellis, American jazz pianist, Aug 2000

Marsalis, Wynton, American trumpet player, Oct 1984

Marsh, Ernest Sterling, Feb 1960

Marsh, Jean, English actress, Nov 1977

Marsh, John, Mar 1960

Marsh, Reginald, American painter, Sept 1941, *Obit* Sept 1954

Marshak, Robert Eugene, American college president and physicist, July 1973, *Obit* Feb 1993

Marshall, Barry J., Australian gastroenterologist, Sept 1996

Marshall, Burke, American civil rights activist and government

official, Feb 1965, *Obit* Yrbk 2003

Marshall, C. Herbert, Oct 1949

Marshall, Catherine, American biographer and inspirational writer, Jan 1955, *Obit* May 1983

Marshall, David, Singaporean lawyer and political leader, July 1956, *Obit* Feb 1996

Marshall, E. G., actor, June 1986, *Obit* Nov 1998

Marshall, Garry, American television scriptwriter, producer and film director, Nov 1992

Marshall, George C., American general and statesmen, Oct 1940, Mar 1947, *Obit* Yrbk 1959

Marshall, Lois, Canadian singer, June 1960, *Obit* May 1997

Marshall, M. Lee, Sept 1948, *Obit* Oct 1950

Marshall, Penny, American actress and motion picture director, Mar 1980, May 1992

Marshall, Peter, Scottish-American clergyman, Apr 1948, *Obit* Feb 1949

Marshall, Ray, secretary of labor, Nov 1977

Marshall, Rob, American choreographer and film director, June 2003

Marshall, Rosamond, author, Aug 1942, *Obit* Feb 1958

Marshall, S. L. A., Nov 1953, *Obit* Mar 1978

Marshall, Susan, American choreographer, July 1999

Marshall, Thurgood, American Supreme Court justice, Nov 1954, Sept 1989, *Obit* Mar 1993

Marshall, Tully, actor, *Obit* Apr 1943

Marshall, Verne, American newspaper editor, Feb 1941, *Obit* May 1965

Marshall, Walter P., Apr 1950, *Obit* June 1969

Marta, Brazilian soccer player, Apr 2008

Martel, Giffard Le Quesne, British general, July 1943, *Obit* Nov 1958

Martel, Yann, Canadian novelist, Jan 2004

Martell, Edward, Nov 1964

Martens, Wilfried, Belgian prime minister, Feb 1987

Martin Artajo, Alberto, Nov 1949

Martin, Agnes, American painter, Sept 1989, *Obit* Apr 2005

Martin, Allie Beth, American librarian, June 1975, *Obit* June 1976

Martin, Archer, British biochemist, Nov 1953, *Obit* Yrbk 2002

Martin, Billy, American baseball manager, Oct 1976, *Obit* Feb 1990

Martin, Camilla, Danish badminton player, Jan 2004

Martin, Charles H., *Obit* Nov 1946

Martin, Chris, English singer and guitarist, May 2004

Martin, Christy, American boxer, Oct 1997

Martin, Collier Ford, *Obit* May 1941

Martin, Dean, American actor and singer, Nov 1964, *Obit* Mar 1996

Martin, Demetri, American comedian and actor, Oct 2009

Martin, Dick, American comedian, Sept 1969, *Obit* Yrbk 2008

Martin, Edgar Stanley, *Obit* Sept 1940

Martin, Edmund F., steel executive, Jan 1962, *Obit* Mar 1993

Martin, Edward, governor and senator, Oct 1945, *Obit* May 1967

Martin, Fletcher, Feb 1958, *Obit* July 1979

Martin, Frank L., American newspaper editor and college dean, *Obit* Sept 1941

Martin, George Brown, *Obit* Yrbk 1945

Martin, George R. R., American fantasy and science fiction writer, Jan 2004

Martin, Glenn L., Feb 1943, *Obit* Feb 1956

Martin, Harry, June 1948, *Obit* Mar 1959

Martin, Jackie, Apr 1943

Martin, James S., American aeronautical engineer, Mar 1977, *Obit* Yrbk 2002

Martin, Jesse L., American actor, July 2006

Martin, John Bartlow, American journalist and diplomat, Yrbk 1956, *Obit* Mar 1987

Martin, Joseph William, American congressman and Speaker of the House, Oct 1940, May 1948, *Obit* Apr 1968

Martin, Judith, American columnist and expert on etiquette, June 1986

Martin, Kenyon, American basketball player, Jan 2005

Martin, Kevin, American lawyer and regulatory official, Aug 2005

Martin, Lillien Jane, psychologist, Apr 1942, *Obit* May 1943

Martin, Lynn Morley, American Secretary of labor, Oct 1989

Martin, Mark, American automobile racing driver, Mar 2001

Martin, Mary, American actress and singer, Jan 1944, *Obit* Jan 1991

Martin, Paul, Canadian cabinet member and diplomat, Yrbk 1951, *Obit* Nov 1992

Martin, Paul, Canadian prime minister, Jan 2004

Martin, Percy Alvin, *Obit* Apr 1942

Martin, Ricky, Puerto Rican singer and actor, Sept 1999

Martin, Roland S., American journalist, June 2009

Martin, Steve, American comedian and actor, Aug 1978, Nov 2000

Martin, Thomas E., Mar 1956, *Obit* Sept 1971

Martin, Walter B., Nov 1954, *Obit* May 1966

Martin, William C., bishop, Apr 1953

Martin, William McChesney, American stockbroker and Federal Reserve chairman, May 1951, *Obit* Oct 1998

Martinelli, Giovanni, Italian opera singer, Jan 1945, *Obit* Mar 1969

Martinez Trueba, Andres, Nov 1954, *Obit* Feb 1960

Martinez, Pedro, Dominican baseball player, June 2001

Martinez, Rueben, American bookstore owner, June 2005

Martinez, Speedo, Argentine singer, Jan 2003

Martinez, Susana, American governor, Nov 2013

Martinez, Vilma, American lawyer and civil rights activist, July 2004

Martini, Helen, American zookeeper, July 1955

Martino, Gaetano, May 1956, *Obit* Oct 1967

Martins, Peter, Danish-American dancer, choreographer and director, June 1978

Martinu, Bohuslav, Czech composer and violinist, Nov 1944, *Obit* Nov 1959

Martland, Harrison Stanford, Nov 1940, *Obit* June 1954

Marton, Eva, Hungarian opera singer, Apr 1985

Marty, Martin E., American clergyman, theologian and church historian, June 1968

Martz, Judy, American governor, Mar 2005

Marvel, Elizabeth Newell, American youth leader, Apr 1962

Marvin, Charles F., American meteorologist, *Obit* July 1943

Marvin, Cloyd H., Yrbk 1949, *Obit* June 1969

Marvin, Dwight Edwards, American clergyman, *Obit* Mar 1940

Marvin, Harry, *Obit* Jan 1940

Marvin, Lee, American actor, Sept 1966, *Obit* Oct 1987

Marx Brothers, American comedians, Mar 1948

Marx, Chico, American comedian, May 1948, *Obit* Yrbk 1961

Marx, Groucho, American comedian, Mar 1948, Feb 1973, *Obit* Oct 1977

Marx, Harpo, American comedian, Mar 1948, *Obit* Nov 1964

Mary Alice, actress, Nov 1995

Mary Joseph, American nun and educator, Yrbk 1942

Marzotto, Gaetano, July 1953

Masaryk, Jan, Czech diplomat, May 1944, *Obit* Apr 1948

Mascagni, Pietro, Italian composer, *Obit* Sept 1945

Masekela, Hugh, South African trumpet player, flugelhornist and singer, Mar 1993

Mashouf, Manny, American retail executive, Feb 2009

Masina, Giulietta, Italian actress, Apr 1958, *Obit* June 1994

Masliansky, Zvi Hirsch, *Obit* Mar 1943

Mason, Bobbie Ann, American novelist and short story writer, Sept 1989

Mason, Jackie, American comedian, July 1987

Mason, James, English actor, May 1947, *Obit* Sept 1984

Mason, Joseph Warren Teets, American journalist, *Obit* July 1941

Mason, Lowell B., June 1949

Mason, Marsha, American actress, Apr 1981

Mason, Noah M., Nov 1957, *Obit* May 1965

Mason, Norman P., June 1959

Mason-MacFarlane, Noel, British general, Feb 1943

Massee, W. Wellington, *Obit* Oct 1942

Masserman, Jules H., psychiatrist, July 1980, *Obit* Jan 1995

Massevitch, Alla G., Russian astronomer, Jan 1964

Massey, Raymond, Canadian-American actor, Feb 1946, *Obit* Sept 1983

Massey, Vincent, Canadian statesman, Oct 1951, *Obit* Feb 1968

Massey, Walter E., American physicist and college president, June 1997

Massigli, Rene, May 1956

Massine, Leonide, Russian choreographer and ballet dancer, Apr 1940, *Obit* May 1979

Massive Attack (Musical group), June 2004

Masson, Andre, French painter and stage designer, Nov 1974, *Obit* Jan 1988

Masters, William H., American physician, Nov 1968, *Obit* May 2001

Mastroianni, Marcello, Italian actor, June 1963, *Obit* Feb 1997

Mastroianni, Umberto, Sept 1960

Masuku, Mario, Swazi political leader, Jan 2006

Masur, Kurt, German conductor, Sept 1990

Masursky, Harold, geologist, Aug 1986, *Obit* Oct 1990

Matalin, Mary, American publishing executive and political consultant, Sept 1996

Matare, Herbert F., German physicist, Jan 2003

Mates, Leo, Nov 1956

Mateschitz, Dietrich, Austrian beverage industry executive, Jan 2005

Mather, Kirtley F., American geologist, Jan 1951

Matheson, Samuel Pritchard, *Obit* July 1942

Mathews, David, American Secretary of health, education and welfare, Jan 1976

Mathews, Shailer, biblical scholar and college dean, *Obit* Yrbk 1941

Mathewson, Lemuel, Yrbk 1952, *Obit* Apr 1970

Mathias, Bob, American decathlete, congressman and sports executive, Sept 1952, *Obit* Yrbk 2007

Mathias, Charles, American senator, Yrbk 1972, *Obit* Yrbk 2010

Mathias, Robert, Yrbk 2007

Mathis, Johnny, American singer, July 1965, Feb 1993

Matisse, Henri, French painter, May 1943, June 1953, *Obit* Jan 1955

Matisyahu, American Hasidic reggae and rap singer, Mar 2007

Matlin, Marlee, American actress, May 1992

Matola, Sharon, American biologist and zoo director, June 1993

Matskevich, Vladimir Vladimirovich, Nov 1955

Matson, Randy, American shot putter and discus thrower, Sept 1968

Matsudaira, Koto, Japanese diplomat, Nov 1958

Matsuhisa, Nobu, Japanese chef and restaurateur, Jan 2005

Matsui, Connie L., American pharmaceutical executive and Girl Scouts leader, Aug 2002

Matsui, Hideki, Japanese baseball player, Jan 2002

Matsui, Keishiro, *Obit* July 1946

Matsui, Robert T., American congressman, Oct 1994, *Obit* Apr 2005

Matsuoka, Yosuke, Mar 1941, *Obit* July 1946

Matsuzaka, Daisuke, Japanese baseball player, Apr 2007

Matta, Chilean painter, Nov 1957, *Obit* Yrbk 2003

Mattei, Enrico, Italian energy industry executive and member of Parliament, Apr 1959, *Obit* Jan 1963

Matthau, Walter, American actor, June 1966, *Obit* Sept 2000

Matthews, Burnita Shelton, judge, Apr 1950, *Obit* June 1988

Matthews, Clay, American football player, Oct 2011

Matthews, Francis P., American Secretary of the navy, Sept 1949, *Obit* Yrbk 1952

Matthews, H. Freeman, American diplomat, Mar 1945, *Obit* Jan 1987

Matthews, Herbert L., American journalist, Nov 1943, *Obit* Sept 1977

Matthews, J. B., American senatorial aide, May 1943

Matthews, T. S., American novelist and journalist, Apr 1950, *Obit* Mar 1991

Matthews, W. Donald, Sept 1952

Matthiessen, Peter, American novelist and nature writer, Oct 1975

Mattila, Karita, Finnish opera singer, Jan 2004

Mattingly, Don, American baseball player, Oct 1988

Mattingly, Garrett, historian, Nov 1960, *Obit* Feb 1963

Mattson, Henry, Jan 1956, *Obit* Nov 1971

Mattson, Ingrid, Canadian Islamist and religious education teacher, Jan 2007

Mature, Victor, actor, Yrbk 1951, *Obit* Oct 1999

Matzinger, Polly, American immunologist, Oct 1998

Mauch, Gene, American baseball manager, Yrbk 1974, *Obit* Yrbk 2005

Maudling, Reginald, British cabinet member, May 1960, *Obit* Apr 1979

Mauer, Joe, American baseball player, Aug 2007

Maugham, W. Somerset, English novelist, short story writer and playwright, Jan 1963, *Obit* Jan 1966

Mauldin, Bill, American cartoonist, May 1945, Nov 1964, *Obit* July 2003

Maung, Cynthia, Burmese physician, Jan 2003

Maura, Carmen, Spanish actress, Apr 1992

Maurer, Ion Gheorghe, Romanian prime minister, Sept 1971, *Obit* July 2000

Mauriac, Claude, French author, Sept 1993, *Obit* June 1999

Mauroy, Pierre, French prime minister, June 1982, *Obit* Yrbk 2013

Maverick, Maury, American congressman and mayor, Mar 1944, *Obit* Sept 1954

Maw, Herbert B., governor, Oct 1948, *Obit* Jan 1991

Max, Adolphe, Belgian burgomaster, *Obit* Jan 1940

Max, Peter, American artist, May 1971

Maxim Reality (Singer), British singer and songwriter, Oct 2009

Maximos, Demetrios, Mar 1948, *Obit* Yrbk 1955

Maxon, Lou R., Aug 1943, *Obit* July 1971

Maxton, James, British member of Parliament, *Obit* Sept 1946

Maxwell, American singer, songwriter and recording producer, July 2011

Maxwell, David Farrow, lawyer and association executive, June 1957

Maxwell, Elsa, columnist and society hostess, Mar 1943, *Obit* Jan 1964

Maxwell, Robert, British publisher, Sept 1988, *Obit* Feb 1992

Maxwell, Russell L., Nov 1942, *Obit* Jan 1969

Maxwell, Vera, fashion designer, July 1977, *Obit* Mar 1995

Maxwell, William, American novelist, short story writer and

magazine editor, Yrbk 1949, *Obit* Oct 2000

May, Andrew Jackson, American congressman, Apr 1941, *Obit* Nov 1959

May, Brian, English rock guitarist, Oct 2008

May, Catherine Dean, congresswoman, Jan 1960

May, Charles H., *Obit* Jan 1944

May, Elaine, American actress, screenwriter and director, Mar 1961

May, Geraldine P., Feb 1949

May, Henry John, *Obit* Jan 1940

May, John Lawrence, archbishop, Jan 1991, *Obit* June 1994

May, Rollo, psychologist, June 1973, *Obit* Jan 1995

May, Theresa, British member of Parliament, Jan 2003

May-Treanor, Misty, American volleyball player, June 2013

Maybank, Burnet R., American senator and governor, Apr 1949, *Obit* Nov 1954

Mayer, Daniel, French socialist leader, Nov 1949

Mayer, Jane, American novelist and children's author, Yrbk 1954

Mayer, Jane, American journalist, Oct 2008

Mayer, Jean, nutritionist and college president, Sept 1970, *Obit* Feb 1993

Mayer, John, American singer and guitarist, Mar 2010

Mayer, Louis B., American motion picture executive, June 1943, *Obit* Jan 1958

Mayer, Marissa, American Internet executive, Jan 2010

Mayer, Rene, French prime minister, May 1948, *Obit* Feb 1973

Mayes, Rose Gorr, May 1950

Mayle, Peter, English humorist, Oct 1992

Maynard, John Albert, Oct 1943

Maynard, Joyce, American journalist, memoirist and novelist, Jan 1999

Maynard, Robert, American newspaper editor and publisher, June 1986, *Obit* Oct 1993

Mayne, Ethel Colburn, English author, critic and translator, *Obit* June 1941

Mayne, Thom, American architect, Oct 2005

Maynor, Dorothy, singer, Jan 1940, Yrbk 1951, *Obit* May 1996

Mayo, Charles W., Nov 1941, Nov 1954, *Obit* Oct 1968

Mayo, Katherine, American journalist and reformer, *Obit* Yrbk 1940

Mayo, Robert P., Feb 1970

Mayor, Michel, Swiss astronomer, Jan 2007

Mayor, Mireya, American primatologist and television personality, Sept 2011

Mayr, Ernst, German zoologist, Nov 1984, *Obit* May 2005

Mays, Benjamin Elijah, American civil rights leader and college president, May 1945, *Obit* May 1984

Mays, Ewing W., Jan 1952

Mays, Lowry, American broadcasting executive, Aug 2003

Mays, Willie, American baseball player, May 1955, Yrbk 1966

Mayweather, Floyd, American boxer, Oct 2004

Maza, Jose, Nov 1955, *Obit* July 1964

Mazey, Emil, labor leader, Jan 1948, *Obit* Nov 1983

Mazowiecki, Tadeusz, Polish political leader, Feb 1990

Mazumdar-Shaw, Kiran, Indian biotechnology executive, Jan 2006

Mazursky, Paul, American film director, May 1980

Mazuz, Menachem, Israeli attorney general, Jan 2007

Mazzo, Kay, July 1971

Mbeki, Thabo, South African president, Aug 1998

Mboya, Tom, Kenyan political and labor leader, June 1959, *Obit* Sept 1969

McAdams, Rachel, Canadian actress, May 2009

McAdie, Alexander, meteorologist, *Obit* Yrbk 1943

McAdoo, William G., American Secretary of the treasury and senator, *Obit* Mar 1941

McAlary, Mike, columnist, *Obit* Mar 1999

McAleese, Mary, Irish president, Jan 2006

McAliskey, Bernadette Devlin, Irish political leader, Jan 1970

McAslan, John, Scottish architect, Jan 2007

McAuliffe, Anthony C., American general, Feb 1950, *Obit* Oct 1975

McBride, Christian, American jazz bassist, Jan 2000

McBride, Katharine E., American psychologist and college president, Feb 1942, *Obit* July 1976

McBride, Lloyd, steelworkers' union leader, Feb 1978, *Obit* Jan 1984

McBride, Martina, American country singer, Mar 2004

McBride, Mary Margaret, radio talk show host, Apr 1941, Mar 1954, *Obit* June 1976

McBride, Patricia, ballet dancer, July 1966

McBurney, Simon, British actor and theatrical director, Jan 2005

McCabe, Gibson, magazine publisher, Feb 1963, *Obit* Yrbk 2000

McCabe, Thomas Bayard, American paper industry executive and Federal Reserve chairman, Sept 1948, *Obit* July 1982

McCaffrey, Barry, American general and government official, July 1997

McCaffrey, John L., Nov 1950

McCain, John S., American senator, Feb 1989, Mar 2006

McCain, John S., American admiral, June 1970, *Obit* June 1981

McCain, John Sidney, American admiral, Oct 1943, *Obit* Oct 1945

McCall Smith, Alexander, Scottish law professor, children's author and novelist, Jan 2003

McCall, Duke K., Nov 1959, *Obit* Yrbk 2013

McCall, Tom, American governor, June 1974, *Obit* Mar 1983

McCalman, Max, Maître Fromager, Mar 2012

McCambridge, Mercedes, American actress, June 1964, *Obit* Yrbk 2004

McCann, Colum, Irish novelist and short story writer, Mar 2010

McCann, Renetta, American advertising executive, May 2005

McCardell, Claire, American fashion designer, Nov 1954, Obit June 1958

McCarey, Leo, American motion picture director and producer, July 1946, Obit Sept 1969

McCarl, John Raymond, lawyer and government official, Obit Sept 1940

McCarran, Pat, American senator, July 1947, Obit Yrbk 1954

McCarrens, John S., American newspaper publisher, Obit Sept 1943

McCarthy, Carolyn, American congresswoman, Mar 1998

McCarthy, Clem, radio sportscaster, Oct 1941, Obit July 1962

McCarthy, Eugene J., American senator, Nov 1955, Obit Mar 2006

McCarthy, Frank, motion picture producer, Sept 1945, Obit Feb 1987

McCarthy, Joe, baseball manager, May 1948, Obit Mar 1978

McCarthy, Joseph, American senator, Jan 1950, Obit July 1957

McCarthy, Kenneth C., Nov 1953

McCarthy, Leighton, Oct 1942, Obit Nov 1952

McCarthy, Mary, American novelist, critic, short story writer and memoirist, Yrbk 1955, Feb 1969, Obit Jan 1990

McCarthy, Thomas, American actor and motion picture director, Jan 2012

McCartney, Paul, English singer and songwriter, Nov 1966, Jan 1986

McCarty, Dan, July 1953

McCarver, Tim, sportscaster and baseball player, May 2000

McCaw, Craig, American telecommunications executive, Sept 2001

McChrystal, Stanley, American general, Sept 2009

McClanahan, Rue, American actress, May 1989, Obit Yrbk 2010

McCleery, Albert, Feb 1955, Obit July 1972

McClellan, Harold C., Oct 1954, Obit Sept 1979

McClellan, John L., American senator, Apr 1950, Obit Feb 1978

McClintic, Guthrie, theatrical director and producer, May 1943, Obit Jan 1962

McClintock, Barbara, American geneticist, Mar 1984, Obit Nov 1992

McClintock, Robert Mills, American diplomat, Apr 1955

McClinton, Katharine Morrison, author, Mar 1958, Obit Mar 1993

McClinton, Marion, American playwright and theatrical director, Jan 2009

McCloskey, Mark A., Nov 1955, Obit Jan 1978

McCloskey, Paul N., American congressman and lawyer, Nov 1971

McCloskey, Robert, American children's author and illustrator, Sept 1942, Obit Yrbk 2003

McCloy, John Jay, American lawyer, banker and government official, Apr 1947, Nov 1961, Obit May 1989

McClurkin, Donnie, American gospel singer and clergyman, Apr 2007

McCobb, Paul, furniture designer, Nov 1958, Obit Apr 1969

McColough, C. Peter, American office equipment industry executive, Jan 1981, Obit Yrbk 2007

McComas, O. Parker, Nov 1955, Obit Feb 1958

McConachie, G. W. Grant, Nov 1958, Obit Sept 1965

McCone, John A., American steel industry executive and CIA director, Jan 1959, Obit Apr 1991

McConnell, F. B., July 1952, Obit Feb 1962

McConnell, Joseph H., radio and television executive, Nov 1950, Obit May 1997

McConnell, Mike, American intelligence official, Apr 2007

McConnell, Mitch, American senator, Feb 2008

McConnell, Page, American keyboardist, July 2003

McConnell, Samuel Kerns, Nov 1956

McCormack, Arthur Thomas, Obit Sept 1943

McCormack, Emmet J., July 1953, Obit Apr 1965

McCormack, John, Irish opera singer, Obit Oct 1945

McCormack, John William, American congressman and Speaker of the House, June 1943, Apr 1962, Obit Jan 1981

McCormick, Anne O'Hare, journalist, Mar 1940, Obit July 1954

McCormick, Edward James, surgeon, Nov 1953, Obit Feb 1975

McCormick, Edward Theodore, government official and stock exchange executive, May 1951, Obit Oct 1991

McCormick, Fowler, June 1947, Obit Feb 1973

McCormick, Jay, Apr 1943

McCormick, Lynde Dupuy, admiral, Feb 1952, Obit Oct 1956

McCormick, Myron, Jan 1954, Obit Oct 1962

McCormick, Robert Rutherford, American newspaper editor and publisher, Aug 1942, Obit May 1955

McCormick, Ruth Hanna, congresswoman, Obit Feb 1945

McCormick, William Patrick Glyn, Obit Yrbk 1940

McCourt, Frank, Irish-American memoirist, Feb 1998, Obit Yrbk 2009

McCovey, Willie, American baseball player, Nov 1970

McCowen, Alec, Oct 1969

McCoy, Charles B., American chemical executive, July 1970, Obit Mar 1995

McCoy, Frank Ross, general, Nov 1945, Obit Sept 1954

McCracken, Craig, American animator, Feb 2004

McCracken, Harold, Yrbk 1949

McCracken, James, opera singer, Nov 1963, *Obit* June 1988

McCracken, Joan, June 1945, *Obit* Jan 1962

McCracken, Paul Winston, American economist and presidential adviser, Yrbk 1969, *Obit* Yrbk 2012

McCracken, Robert James, July 1949, *Obit* Apr 1973

McCrady, Edward, Jan 1957

McCrary, Jinx Falkenburg, television performer and model, July 1953

McCrary, Tex, American journalist and talk show host, July 1953, *Obit* Yrbk 2003

McCrary, Tex; and McCrary, Jinx, July 1953

McCreery, Richard L., British general, May 1945, *Obit* Yrbk 1967

McCullers, Carson, American novelist, Sept 1940, *Obit* Yrbk 1967

McCullough, Colleen, Australian novelist, Apr 1982

McCullough, David G., American historian and biographer, Jan 1993

McCullough, Gary E., American school administrator, Nov 2009

McCune, Charles Andrew, *Obit* Yrbk 1940

McCune, Francis K., Mar 1961

McCune, George Shannon, *Obit* Feb 1942

McCurdy, William Albert, *Obit* Feb 1942

McCurry, Michael, American presidential press secretary and Internet executive, Nov 1996

McCurry, Steve, American photojournalist, Nov 2005

McCutchen, Andrew, American baseball player, Aug 2013

McDaniel, Glen, May 1952

McDaniel, Hattie, American actress, Sept 1940, *Obit* Yrbk 1952

McDaniel, James, American actor, Feb 2000

McDermott, Alice, American novelist and short story writer, Sept 1992

McDermott, Michael J., Feb 1951, *Obit* Oct 1955

McDevitt, James L., American labor leader, Mar 1959, *Obit* May 1963

McDiarmid, E. W., librarian and college dean, Yrbk 1948

McDivitt, James A., Nov 1965

McDonagh, Martin, Irish dramatist, Aug 1998

McDonald, Audra, American singer and actress, Apr 1999

McDonald, David J., June 1953, *Obit* Oct 1979

McDonald, David Lamar, admiral, Nov 1963, *Obit* Mar 1998

McDonald, Erroll, publishing executive, Oct 1999

McDonald, Eugene F., Oct 1949, *Obit* Oct 1958

McDonald, Gabrielle, judge, Oct 2001

McDonald, James Grover, diplomat, Apr 1949, *Obit* Yrbk 1964

McDonald, Trevor, British television news anchor, Sept 2010

McDonnell, Bob, American governor, Sept 2011

McDonnell, Mary, American actress, May 1997

McDonnell, William A., Feb 1959

McDonough, Roger H., state librarian, June 1968

McDonough, William, American architect, July 2006

McDormand, Frances, American actress, Sept 1997

McDowall, Roddy, actor and photographer, Apr 1961, *Obit* Jan 1999

McDowell, Malcolm, English actor, Yrbk 1973

McDuffie, Dwayne, American comic book writer, Feb 2010, *Obit* Yrbk 2011

McElroy, Neil H., American Secretary of defense, Apr 1951, *Obit* Jan 1973

McEnroe, John, American tennis player, Feb 1980

McEntee, Gerald, American labor leader, Oct 2000

McEntire, Reba, American country singer and actress, Oct 1994

McEwan, Ian, English novelist and short story writer, July 1993

McEwen, Terry A., opera director, July 1985, *Obit* Jan 1999

McFadden, Mary, American fashion designer, Apr 1983

McFarland, Ernest William, American senator, governor and state supreme court justice, Jan 1951, *Obit* Aug 1984

McFarlane, Robert C., American presidential adviser, May 1984

McFarlane, Todd, Canadian cartoonist, Feb 1999

McFate, Montgomery, American cultural anthropologist, Aug 2008

McFerrin, Bobby, American singer and conductor, Aug 1989

McGannon, Donald H., radio and television executive, Feb 1971, *Obit* July 1984

McGarry, William J., *Obit* Nov 1941

McGeachy, Mary Craig, Canadian diplomat, Apr 1944

McGee, Frank, television commentator and newscaster, June 1964, *Obit* June 1974

McGee, Gale William, American senator and diplomat, Nov 1961, *Obit* June 1992

McGhee, George Crews, American petroleum industry executive and diplomat, Sept 1950, *Obit* Yrbk 2005

McGill, Anthony, American clarinetist, Apr 2009

McGill, Ralph, American newspaper editor, June 1947, *Obit* Mar 1969

McGill, William J., college president, June 1971, *Obit* Jan 1998

McGinley, Laurence J., college president and priest, June 1949, *Obit* Oct 1992

McGinley, Phyllis, American poet and children's author, Feb 1941, Nov 1961, *Obit* Apr 1978

McGinnis, Patrick B., Nov 1955, *Obit* Apr 1973

McGinniss, Joe, American true crime writer, Jan 1984

McGonigal, Jane, American computer game designer, Apr 2013

McGovern, Francis Edward, American governor, *Obit* June 1946

McGovern, Gail, American Red Cross official, Mar 2010

McGovern, George S., American senator, Mar 1967, *Obit* Yrbk 2012

McGovern, John, American rubber company executive, Nov 1961, *Obit* June 1975

McGovern, Maureen, singer, Feb 1990

McGrady, Tracy, American basketball player, Feb 2003

McGranery, James P., American congressman, judge and Attorney general, May 1952, *Obit* Feb 1963

McGrath, Earl James, educator and government official, Apr 1949, *Obit* Apr 1993

McGrath, James Howard, American Attorney general, Jan 1948, *Obit* Nov 1966

McGrath, Judy, American broadcasting executive, Feb 2005

McGraw, Curtis W., June 1950, *Obit* Nov 1953

McGraw, Eloise Jarvis, American children's author, Yrbk 1955, *Obit* Mar 2001

McGraw, Phillip C., American psychologist and television talk show host, June 2002

McGraw, Tim, American country singer, Sept 2002

McGregor, G. R., Mar 1954, *Obit* Apr 1971

McGregor, J. Harry, Oct 1958

McGroarty, John Steven, *Obit* Sept 1944

McGruder, Aaron, American cartoonist, Sept 2001

McGuane, Thomas, American novelist and screenwriter, Nov 1987

McGuigan, James, Sept 1950, *Obit* June 1974

McGuinty, Dalton, Canadian provincial premier, Feb 2013

McGuire, Dorothy, American actress, Sept 1941, *Obit* Nov 2001

McGuire, William Anthony, *Obit* Nov 1940

McGurn, Barrett, Apr 1965

McGwire, Mark, American baseball player, July 1998

McHale, Kathryn, Jan 1947, *Obit* Yrbk 1957

McHenry, Donald F., diplomat, Sept 1980

McIlroy, Rory, Irish golfer, Nov 2011

McInerney, Jay, American novelist, Nov 1987

McIntire, Carl, American clergyman, Oct 1971, *Obit* June 2002

McIntire, Ross T., Oct 1945, *Obit* Feb 1960

McIntosh, Millicent Carey, American college dean and president, July 1947, *Obit* Mar 2001

McIntyre, James Francis Aloysius, Feb 1953, *Obit* Sept 1979

McIntyre, James T., Jan 1979

McIntyre, Marvin Hunter, American presidential aide, *Obit* Feb 1944

McIntyre, Thomas James, American senator, Nov 1963, *Obit* Oct 1992

McIver, Pearl L., nurse, Mar 1949

McKay, Christopher P., American astrophysicist, Aug 2009

McKay, David Oman, American Mormon leader, June 1951, *Obit* Mar 1970

McKay, Douglas, American Secretary of the interior and governor, May 1949, *Obit* Oct 1959

McKay, Jim, American television sportscaster, Oct 1973, *Obit* Yrbk 2008

McKayle, Donald, American dancer and choreographer, June 1971

McKeen, John E., June 1961, *Obit* Apr 1978

McKeever, Ed, Nov 1945

McKeldin, Theodore R., American governor, Oct 1952, *Obit* Oct 1974

McKellar, Kenneth Douglas, American senator, Jan 1946, *Obit* Jan 1958

McKellen, Ian, English actor, Jan 1984

McKelway, B. M., Jan 1958, *Obit* Oct 1976

McKenna, Francis Eugene, American chemist and editor, May 1966, *Obit* Feb 1979

McKenna, Reginald, British cabinet member and banker, *Obit* Oct 1943

McKenna, Siobhan, Irish actress, Nov 1956, *Obit* Jan 1987

McKenney, Ruth, author, Aug 1942, *Obit* Oct 1972

McKenzie, Bret, New Zealand comedian, Mar 2008

McKenzie, Kevin, American ballet dancer and director, Jan 2000

McKenzie, Roderick Duncan, *Obit* Jan 1940

McKenzie, Vashti, American bishop, Nov 2000

McKenzie, William P., *Obit* Oct 1942

McKeon, Jack, American baseball manager, Apr 2004

McKinley, Chuck, tennis player, Nov 1963, *Obit* Sept 1986

McKinney, Cynthia, American congresswoman, Aug 1996

McKinney, Frank Edward, banker and political leader, Jan 1952, *Obit* Mar 1974

McKinney, Robert, American newspaper editor and publisher, Jan 1957, *Obit* Yrbk 2001

McKissick, Floyd B., American lawyer and civil rights leader, Jan 1968, *Obit* June 1991

McKittrick, Thomas, July 1944, *Obit* Mar 1970

McKneally, Martin B., congressman and veterans' leader, Mar 1960, *Obit* Aug 1992

McKuen, Rod, American poet, composer and singer, Feb 1970

McLachlin, Beverley M., Canadian judge, Sept 2009

McLain, Denny, American baseball player and radio talk show host, Jan 1969

McLaren, Malcolm, English rock musician, band manager and talent agent, Aug 1997, *Obit* Yrbk 2010

McLaughlin, Ann Dore, American Secretary of labor, Nov 1988

McLaughlin, Audrey, Canadian political leader, July 1990

McLaughlin, John, American television commentator and moderator, July 1987

McLaughlin, John, British jazz guitarist, Feb 2004

McLaughlin, Leo Plowden, college president and priest, May 1970, *Obit* Nov 1996

McLean, A. J., American singer, May 2000

McLean, Alice T., July 1945, *Obit* Yrbk 1968

McLean, Don, American singer and songwriter, May 1973

McLean, Evalyn Walsh, socialite, May 1943, *Obit* May 1947

McLean, Jackie, American saxophonist, Mar 2001, *Obit* Nov 2006

McLean, Robert, American newspaper publisher, Nov 1951, *Obit* Feb 1981

McLintock, Gordon, admiral, Nov 1953, *Obit* June 1990

McLuhan, Marshall, Canadian cultural critic, June 1967, *Obit* Feb 1981

McLurkin, James, American computer scientist, Sept 2005

McMahon, Brien, American senator, Yrbk 1945, *Obit* Sept 1952

McMahon, Ed, American television personality, Apr 1977, *Obit* Yrbk 2009

McMahon, Vince, American wrestling promoter, Feb 1999

McMahon, William, Australian prime minister, Sept 1971, *Obit* May 1988

McManamy, Frank, *Obit* Nov 1944

McMath, Sidney Sanders, American governor, Mar 1949, *Obit* Jan 2004

McMeekin, Clark, American novelists, Yrbk 1957

McMeekin, Isabel McLennan, American novelist and children's author, Sept 1942, Yrbk 1957

McMein, Neysa, illustrator and painter, Feb 1941, *Obit* June 1949

McMillan, Edwin Mattison, American physicist and chemist, Feb 1952, *Obit* Nov 1991

McMillan, John L., American congressman and lawyer, Nov 1956

McMillan, Terry, American novelist, Feb 1993

McMillen, Tom, congressman, Jan 1993

McMinnies, Mary, Yrbk 1959

McMurrin, Sterling M., American educator and government official, June 1961, *Obit* June 1996

McMurtrie, Douglas Crawford, typographer, July 1944

McMurtry, Larry, American novelist, June 1984

McNabb, Donovan, American football player, Jan 2004

McNair, Arnold Duncan McNair, Feb 1955

McNair, Barbara, American singer and actress, Nov 1971, *Obit* Yrbk 2007

McNair, Lesley James, American general, Nov 1942, *Obit* Sept 1944

McNair, Steve, American football player, Jan 2005, *Obit* Yrbk 2009

McNair, Sylvia, American opera singer, Nov 1997

McNairy, Mark, American shoe designer, July 2013

McNally, Andrew, American publisher and cartographer, Nov 1956, *Obit* Feb 2002

McNally, Terrence, American dramatist, Mar 1988

McNamara, James B., American labor activist, *Obit* Apr 1941

McNamara, Patrick V., American senator, Nov 1955, *Obit* June 1966

McNamara, Robert S., American Secretary of defense and banker, Sept 1961, Mar 1987, *Obit* Yrbk 2009

McNamee, Graham, radio announcer, *Obit* July 1942

McNarney, Joseph T., American air force general and aircraft industry executive, Nov 1944, *Obit* Mar 1972

McNary, Charles Linza, American senator, Aug 1940, *Obit* Apr 1944

McNaughton, Andrew, Nov 1942, *Obit* Nov 1966

McNealy, Scott, American computer industry executive, Apr 1996

McNeely, Eugene J., Nov 1962, *Obit* Feb 1974

McNeil, Hector, Yrbk 1946, *Obit* Yrbk 1955

McNeil, John, American jazz trumpet player, June 2007

McNeil, Wilfred J., Feb 1958, *Obit* Oct 1979

McNeill, Don, radio talk show host, July 1949, *Obit* Aug 1996

McNellis, Maggi, radio and television performer, Jan 1955, *Obit* Aug 1989

McNerney, James, American aerospace industry executive, Mar 2008

McNicholas, John T., May 1949, *Obit* June 1950

McNichols, Stephen L. R., American governor, Oct 1958, *Obit* Feb 1998

McNutt, Paul V., American governor, Feb 1940, *Obit* May 1955

McPartland, Marian, American jazz pianist, June 1976, *Obit* Yrbk 2013

McPharlin, Paul, American puppeteer, Nov 1945, *Obit* Nov 1948

McPhee, John A., American journalist and nature writer, Oct 1982

McPherson, Aimee Semple, American evangelist, *Obit* Nov 1944

McPherson, James Alan, American short story writer, essayist and editor, Sept 1996

McQueen, Alexander, British fashion designer, Feb 2002, *Obit* June 2010

McQueen, Steve, American actor, Oct 1966, *Obit* Jan 1981

McRae, Carmen, American singer, Apr 1983, *Obit* Jan 1995

McReynolds, James Clark, American Supreme Court justice, *Obit* Oct 1946

McShane, Ian, English actor, July 2011

McSwigan, Marie, Yrbk 1953, *Obit* Sept 1962

McWhinney, Madeline H., July 1976

McWhirter, Norris, English sportswriter and sportscaster, Nov 1979, *Obit* Yrbk 2004

McWhorter, John H., American linguist, Feb 2003

McWilliams, Carey, American lawyer, magazine editor and

nonfiction writer, Oct 1943, *Obit* Aug 1980

Mda, Zakes, South African dramatist and novelist, Jan 2005

Meacham, Jon, American publishing executive and political commentator, June 2011

Mead, Charles Larew, *Obit* July 1941

Mead, George H., Oct 1946, *Obit* Feb 1963

Mead, James M., July 1944, *Obit* Apr 1964

Mead, Margaret, American anthropologist, Nov 1940, May 1951, *Obit* Jan 1979

Meader, George, July 1956

Meadowcroft, Enid La Monte, Yrbk 1949

Meadows, A. H., American petroleum industry executive, Apr 1960

Meadows, Audrey, actress, May 1958, *Obit* Apr 1996

Meadows, Jayne, May 1958

Means, Helen Hotchkin, Jan 1946

Means, Russell, American Indian leader, Jan 1978, *Obit* Yrbk 2013

Meany, George, American labor leader, Jan 1942, Mar 1954, *Obit* Mar 1980

Mearns, David Chambers, librarian, July 1961, *Obit* July 1981

Mearns, Hughes, Jan 1940, *Obit* Apr 1965

Mears, Helen, American Japanologist, Mar 1943

Meat Loaf (Musician), American singer and songwriter, Nov 2006

Mechau, Frank Albert, American painter, *Obit* Apr 1946

Mechem, Edwin L., American governor and senator, July 1954, *Obit* Yrbk 2003

Mechem, Merritt Cramer, *Obit* June 1946

Meciar, Vladimir, Slovak prime minister, July 1994

Medaris, John Bruce, general and clergyman, Feb 1958

Medawar, P. B., British biologist, Apr 1961, *Obit* Nov 1987

Medeiros, Humberto, Nov 1971, *Obit* Nov 1983

Medem, Julio, Spanish film director and screenwriter, Jan 2003

Medgyessy, Peter, Hungarian economist and prime minister, Jan 2003

Medici, Emilio Garrastazu, Brazilian president, Oct 1971, *Obit* Jan 1986

Medina Angarita, Isaias, Venezuelan general and president, Mar 1942, *Obit* Nov 1953

Medina, Harold R., American judge, Apr 1949, *Obit* May 1990

Medvedev, Dmitry, Russian president, June 2008

Medvedev, Roy Aleksandrovich, Russian educator and historian, Sept 1984

Medvedev, Zhores Aleksandrovich, Soviet biochemist, Nov 1973

Meehan, Thomas F., *Obit* Sept 1942

Meeker, Mary, American financial analyst, Aug 1999

Meerloo, Joost A. M., Jan 1962, *Obit* Feb 1977

Meese, Edwin, American Attorney general, Sept 1981

Mehaffey, Joseph C., Jan 1948, *Obit* Apr 1963

Mehretu, Julie, American artist, July 2010

Mehta, Deena, Indian securities broker, Jan 2005

Mehta, Deepa, Indian motion picture director, Jan 2002

Mehta, G. L., Nov 1952, *Obit* June 1974

Mehta, Hansa, July 1947

Mehta, Tyeb, Indian painter, Jan 2006

Mehta, Ved, Indian journalist, novelist and essayist, Sept 1975

Mehta, Zubin, Indian conductor, Mar 1969

Mei Lanfang, *Obit* Sept 1943

Meier, Deborah, American educational reformer and school principal, May 2006

Meier, Richard, American architect, Jan 1985

Meiling, Richard L., May 1950

Meir, Golda, Israeli prime minister, May 1950, Yrbk 1970, *Obit* Feb 1979

Meireles, Cildo, Brazilian installation artist and sculptor, Jan 2004

Meiselas, Susan, American photographer, Feb 2005

Meisner, Sanford, actor, director and teacher, Apr 1991, *Obit* Apr 1997

Meitner, Lise, Austrian physicist, Sept 1945, *Obit* Sept 1968

Melamid, Aleksandr, Russian painter, Oct 1984

Melas, George V., July 1956

Melcher, Frederic Gershom, American publisher, July 1945, *Obit* Apr 1963

Melchior, Lauritz, Danish opera singer, Jan 1941, *Obit* May 1973

Melford, Myra, American jazz pianist and composer, Apr 2010

Mellencamp, John, American singer and songwriter, Mar 1988

Mellers, Wilfrid, English musicologist and composer, Feb 1962, *Obit* Yrbk 2008

Mellett, Lowell, May 1942, *Obit* May 1960

Mello Franco, Afranio de, *Obit* Feb 1943

Mellon, Paul, American philanthropist, Apr 1966, *Obit* Apr 1999

Mellon, Richard K., May 1965, *Obit* July 1970

Mellon, William Larimer, medical missionary, June 1965, *Obit* Oct 1989

Mellor, Walter, *Obit* Jan 1940

Meloney, Marie Mattingly, *Obit* Aug 1943

Meloy, Colin, American singer and songwriter, Aug 2007

Melton, Douglas, American molecular biologist, June 2008

Melton, James, American opera singer, Sept 1945, *Obit* June 1961

Melua, Katie, British singer and songwriter, Jan 2007

Melzer, Roman F., *Obit* June 1943

Menchu, Rigoberta, Guatemalan human rights activist and memoirist, Oct 1993

Mende, Erich, July 1966

Mendelsohn, Erich, German architect, Nov 1953

Mendenhall, Harlan G., *Obit* July 1940

Mendenhall, Thomas Corwin, college president, May 1960, *Obit* Sept 1998

Menderes, Adnan, Turkish prime minister, Nov 1954, *Obit* Nov 1961

Mendes da Rocha, Paulo Archias, Brazilian architect, Jan 2006

Mendes, Sam, British theatrical and motion picture director, Oct 2002

Mendes-France, Pierre, French statesman, Oct 1954, *Obit* Jan 1983

Mendez, Kinito, Dominican singer, Jan 2004

Menem, Carlos Saul, Argentine president, Nov 1989

Meng, John J., college president, Nov 1961, *Obit* Apr 1988

Mengistu Haile-Mariam, Ethiopian head of state, July 1981

Menjou, Adolphe, actor, June 1948, *Obit* Jan 1964

Menken, Alan, American composer, Jan 2001

Mennin, Peter, composer and educator, Nov 1964, *Obit* Aug 1983

Menninger, Karl A., American psychiatrist, Oct 1948, *Obit* Sept 1990

Menninger, William Claire, Sept 1945, *Obit* Nov 1966

Menocal, Mario Garcia, Cuban president, *Obit* Oct 1941

Menon, K. P. S., Indian diplomat, Mar 1957, *Obit* Yrbk 1983

Menotti, Gian Carlo, Italian composer and librettist, Yrbk 1947, Jan 1979, *Obit* Yrbk 2007

Menshikov, Mikhail A., May 1958, *Obit* Sept 1976

Menthon, Francois, French political leader, Mar 1944

Menuhin, Yehudi, violinist, Feb 1941, May 1973, *Obit* June 1999

Menzel, Donald Howard, physicist and astronomer, Apr 1956, *Obit* Mar 1977

Menzies, Robert Gordon, Australian prime minister, Feb 1941, Jan 1950, *Obit* July 1978

Mercer, James, American guitarist and singer, June 2007

Mercer, Johnny, American lyricist, June 1948, *Obit* Aug 1976

Mercer, Mabel, singer, Feb 1973, *Obit* June 1984

Mercer, Samuel A. B., Feb 1953

Merchant, Ismail, Indian motion picture producer, Mar 1993, *Obit* Yrbk 2005

Merchant, Livingston T., American government official and diplomat, Nov 1956, *Obit* July 1976

Merchant, Natalie, American singer and songwriter, Jan 2003

Merck, George W., American pharmaceutical executive, Yrbk 1946, *Obit* Jan 1958

Mercouri, Melina, Greek actress and cabinet member, July 1965, Mar 1988, *Obit* May 1994

Meredith, Burgess, actor, July 1940, *Obit* Nov 1997

Merida, Carlos, Mexican painter, Jan 1960

Merivale, Philip, *Obit* Apr 1946

Meriwether, John W., American investment manager, Mar 1999

Meriwether, W. Delano, Jan 1978

Merkel, Angela, German chancellor, Jan 2004

Merle-Smith, Van Santvoord, *Obit* Yrbk 1943

Merman, Ethel, American actress and singer, Oct 1941, May 1955, *Obit* Apr 1984

Mernissi, Fatima, Moroccan sociologist, Jan 2005

Meron, Theodor, Polish international relations specialist, Mar 2005

Merriam, C. Hart, American mammalogist, *Obit* May 1942

Merriam, Charles Edward, American political scientist, Feb 1947, *Obit* Feb 1953

Merriam, George Ernest, *Obit* May 1941

Merriam, John C., *Obit* Yrbk 1945

Merrick, David, American theatrical producer, Jan 1961, *Obit* July 2000

Merrick, Elliott, author, Yrbk 1950, *Obit* July 1997

Merrifield, R. Bruce, American biochemist, Mar 1985, *Obit* Yrbk 2006

Merrill, Charles Edward, American stockbroker, Apr 1956

Merrill, Frank D., American general, July 1944, *Obit* Feb 1956

Merrill, James, American poet, novelist and playwright, Aug 1981, *Obit* Apr 1995

Merrill, John Douglas, *Obit* Jan 1940

Merrill, Robert, American opera singer, Mar 1952, *Obit* Feb 2005

Merritt, Matthew J., *Obit* Nov 1946

Merry del Val y Alzola, Alfonso, Nov 1965

Merton, Robert King, American sociologist, Sept 1965, *Obit* Yrbk 2003

Merwin, W. S., American poet and translator, May 1988

Merz, Charles, newspaper editor, Nov 1954, *Obit* Nov 1977

Meskill, Thomas J., American governor and judge, Mar 1974, *Obit* Yrbk 2008

Messaoud, Boubacar, Mauritanian anti-slavery activist, Jan 2006

Messer, Thomas M., museum director and art historian, Nov 1961, *Obit* Yrbk 2013

Messerschmitt, Willy, German aircraft designer, Apr 1940, *Obit* Nov 1978

Messersmith, George S., American diplomat, Oct 1942, *Obit* Apr 1960

Messi, Lionel, Argentine soccer player, Jan 2007

Messiaen, Olivier, French organist and composer, Feb 1974, *Obit* June 1992

Messick, Dale, American cartoonist, July 1961, *Obit* Yrbk 2005

Messier, Jean-Marie, French mass media industry executive, May 2002

Messier, Mark, Canadian hockey player, July 1995

Messina, Jim, American presidential adviser and political consultant, Mar 2013

Messing, Debra, American actress, Aug 2002

Messmer, Pierre, French prime minister, Nov 1963, *Obit* Yrbk 2007

Messner, Reinhold, Italian mountaineer, Mar 1980

Mesta, Perle, society leader and diplomat, Sept 1949, *Obit* May 1975

Mestrovic, Ivan, Yugoslav sculptor, Oct 1940, *Obit* Mar 1962

Meta, Ilir, Albanian prime minister, Feb 2002

Metaxas, Ioannis, Greek general and dictator, Yrbk 1940, *Obit* Mar 1941

Metcalf, Jesse H., *Obit* Yrbk 1942

Metcalf, Lee, American senator, Feb 1970, *Obit* Mar 1978

Metheny, Pat, American jazz guitarist, May 1996

Metzelthin, Pearl V., Nov 1942, *Obit* Jan 1948

Metzenbaum, Howard M., American senator, July 1980, *Obit* Yrbk 2008

Metzman, G., July 1946, *Obit* June 1960

Meuron, Pierre de, Swiss architect, June 2002

Meyer, Agnes Elizabeth Ernst, American journalist, philanthropist and newspaper publisher, Jan 1949, *Obit* Nov 1970

Meyer, Albert, Jan 1960, *Obit* May 1965

Meyer, Cord, intelligence official, Mar 1948, *Obit* Aug 2001

Meyer, Dakota, U.S. soldier and Medal of Honor recipient, Mar 2012

Meyer, Danny, American restaurateur, July 2007

Meyer, Debbie, American swimmer, May 1969

Meyer, Edgar, American bassist, June 2002

Meyer, Eugene, American investment banker, government official and newspaper publisher, Sept 1941, *Obit* Oct 1959

Meyer, Jean, Nov 1955

Meyer, Jean-Luc de, Belgian singer and lyricist, Jan 2006

Meyer, K. F., Mar 1952, *Obit* June 1974

Meyer, Ron, American motion picture executive, Mar 1997

Meyer, Stephenie, American novelist, Oct 2008

Meyerowitz, William, American etcher and painter, May 1942

Meyers, Anne Akiko, (1970-), Aug 2013

Meyers, George Julian, *Obit* Jan 1940

Meyers, Nancy, American screenwriter, director and producer, Feb 2002

Meyers, Seth, American comedian and actor, Apr 2009

Meyner, Robert Baumle, American governor, Apr 1955, *Obit* July 1990

Meyrowitz, Carol, American retail executive, Nov 2011

Mfume, Kweisi, American civil rights leader, Jan 1996

Miasha, American novelist, Oct 2009

Michael, Oct 1944

Michael, George, English pop singer, Nov 1988

Michael, Moina, *Obit* June 1944

Michaels, Anne, Canadian poet and novelist, Jan 2002

Michaels, Lorne, Canadian television scriptwriter and producer, Aug 1999

Michals, Duane, American photographer, Apr 1981

Michel, Robert H., American congressman and political leader, Sept 1981

Michel, Sia, American magazine editor, Sept 2003

Michele, Chrisette, American singer and songwriter, Apr 2011

Michelin, Edouard, French tire company executive, *Obit* Oct 1940

Michelman, Kate, American abortion rights activist, Nov 2000

Michelson, Charles, journalist, Aug 1940, *Obit* Jan 1948

Michener, Daniel Roland, Canadian government official, Jan 1968, *Obit* Nov 1991

Michener, James A., American novelist, June 1948, Aug 1975, *Obit* Jan 1998

Michie, Allan A., Nov 1942, *Obit* Jan 1974

Michnik, Adam, Polish member of Parliament and newspaper editor, July 1990

Mickelson, Phil, American golfer, Mar 2002

Middelhoff, Thomas, German publishing and recording executive, Feb 2001

Middlecoff, Cary, golfer, July 1952, *Obit* Nov 1998

Middleton, Drew, journalist and author, Sept 1943, *Obit* Mar 1990

Midgley, Thomas, American chemical engineer, *Obit* Yrbk 1944

Midler, Bette, American singer and actress, June 1973, Nov 1997

Midori, Japanese violinist, June 1990

Mielziner, Jo, Mar 1946, *Obit* May 1976

Miers, Earl Schenck, editor and publisher, Yrbk 1949, Sept 1967, *Obit* Jan 1973

Mies van der Rohe, Ludwig, German-American architect, Oct 1951, *Obit* Oct 1969

Mifune, Toshiro, Japanese actor, June 1981, *Obit* Mar 1998

Migiro, Asha-Rose Mtengeti, Tanzanian diplomat, Jan 2007

Mignone, Francisco, June 1942

Mihailovic, Draza, Yugoslav general and underground leader, Mar 1942, *Obit* Sept 1946

Mihajlov, Mihajlo, Yugoslav social and literary critic, Jan 1979, *Obit* Yrbk 2010

Miike, Takashi, Japanese motion picture director, Jan 2003

Mikell, Henry Judah, *Obit* Apr 1942

Mikhailov, Nikolai Aleksandrovich, Nov 1958

Mikhalkov, Nikita, Russian film director and actor, Oct 1995

Miki, Takeo, Japanese prime minister, Apr 1975, *Obit* Jan 1989

Mikita, Stan, American hockey player, Oct 1970

Mikolajczyk, Stanislaw, Polish political leader, Mar 1944, *Obit* Feb 1967

Mikoyan, Anastas, Soviet president, May 1955, *Obit* Jan 1979

Mikulski, Barbara A., American senator, Nov 1985

Mikva, Abner J., American judge, July 1980

Milam, Carl Hastings, American librarian, June 1945, *Obit* Oct 1963

Milanov, Zinka, Yugoslav-American opera singer, July 1944, *Obit* July 1989

Milchan, Arnon, Israeli film producer, Oct 2000

Miles, Mary, Nov 1942

Miles, Tiya, American feminist, Oct 2012

Milgram, Stanley, American social psychologist, Aug 1979, *Obit* Mar 1985

Milhaud, Darius, French composer, June 1941, May 1961, *Obit* Sept 1974

Milla, Roger, Cameroonian soccer player, Jan 2003

Millan, Cesar, American dog trainer, Jan 2009

Milland, Ray, actor, Feb 1946, *Obit* Apr 1986

Millar, Alexander Copeland, *Obit* Yrbk 1940

Millar, George, Scottish author, Yrbk 1949

Millar, Margaret, author, Yrbk 1946, *Obit* June 1994

Millard, Bailey, *Obit* May 1941

Millepied, Benjamin, French ballet dancer and choreographer, Apr 2011

Miller, Alice Duer, author, Sept 1941, *Obit* Oct 1942

Miller, Ann, American tap dancer and actress, Apr 1980, *Obit* Yrbk 2004

Miller, Arjay, Jan 1967

Miller, Arnold R., labor leader, Nov 1974, *Obit* Sept 1985

Miller, Arthur, American dramatist, Oct 1947, Feb 1973, *Obit* July 2005

Miller, Bebe, dancer and choreographer, Apr 1999

Miller, Benjamin Meek, governor and judge, *Obit* Mar 1944

Miller, Dayton C., American physicist, *Obit* Apr 1941

Miller, Douglas, Nov 1941

Miller, Edward G., June 1951, *Obit* June 1968

Miller, Frieda S., Feb 1945, *Obit* Oct 1973

Miller, G. William, American Secretary of the treasury, Federal Reserve chairman and investment banker, June 1978, *Obit* Yrbk 2007

Miller, Geoffrey F., American psychologist, July 2010

Miller, George, American congressman, Feb 1964

Miller, Gilbert, Apr 1958, *Obit* Feb 1969

Miller, Glenn, American band leader, Feb 1942, *Obit* Yrbk 1991

Miller, Harry W., Mar 1962, *Obit* Mar 1977

Miller, Henry, American novelist, Nov 1970, *Obit* July 1980

Miller, Irving, Nov 1952, *Obit* Feb 1981

Miller, J. Cloyd, Yrbk 1951

Miller, J. Irwin, American manufacturing executive and architectural patron, Nov 1961, *Obit* Yrbk 2004

Miller, James C., economist and regulatory official, May 1986

Miller, Jason, playwright and actor, Jan 1974, *Obit* Yrbk 2001

Miller, John, American FBI official, Aug 2003

Miller, Johnny, American golfer, Sept 1974

Miller, Jonathan, English physician, actor and director, Oct 1970, Nov 1986

Miller, Judith, American journalist, Jan 2006

Miller, Justin, Jan 1947, *Obit* Mar 1973

Miller, Lee P., July 1959

Miller, Leszek, Polish prime minister, Jan 2002

Miller, Marcus, American jazz bassist and composer, Feb 2006

Miller, Marshall E., Oct 1953

Miller, Marvin, American baseball players association executive, May 1973, *Obit* Yrbk 2013

Miller, Max, American journalist, May 1940, *Obit* Feb 1968

Miller, Merle, author, Yrbk 1950, *Obit* July 1986

Miller, Mildred, opera singer, June 1957

Miller, Mitch, American conductor and record producer, July 1956, *Obit* Yrbk 2010

Miller, Neal E., American professor of psychology, July 1974, *Obit* June 2002

Miller, Nicole, fashion designer, Mar 1995

Miller, Reggie, American basketball player, Mar 1996

Miller, Roger, American composer, lyricist and singer, Sept 1986, *Obit* Jan 1993

Miller, Shannon, American gymnast, July 1996

Miller, Watson B., Sept 1947, *Obit* Apr 1961

Miller, Webb, American journalist, *Obit* Jan 1940

Miller, William Edward, American congressman and lawyer, Feb 1962, *Obit* Aug 1983

Miller, William Lash, Canadian chemist, *Obit* Oct 1940

Miller, Zell, American senator, July 1996

Millerand, Alexandre, French president, *Obit* May 1943

Milles, Carl, sculptor, Yrbk 1940, Yrbk 1952, *Obit* Nov 1955

Millett, John David, American university president, Feb 1953, *Obit* Jan 1994

Millett, Kate, American feminist, artist and memoirist, Jan 1971, June 1995

Milligan, Mary Louise, May 1957

Millikan, Robert A., American physicist, Jan 1940, June 1952, *Obit* Feb 1954

Millikin, Eugene Donald, American senator, Apr 1948, *Obit* Oct 1958

Million; John Wilson, *Obit* Nov 1941

Millionaire, Tony, American cartoonist and illustrator, July 2005

Millis, Harry A., Nov 1940, *Obit* Sept 1948

Millman, Dan, American gymnast and spiritualist, Aug 2002

Millo, Aprile, American opera singer, Apr 1988

Mills, Frederick Cecil, economist, Nov 1948, *Obit* Apr 1964

Mills, Hayley, English actress, Apr 1963

Mills, John, British actor, May 1963, *Obit* Yrbk 2005

Mills, Wilbur D., American congressman, Nov 1956, *Obit* July 1992

Milner, Brenda, Canadian neuroscientist, Jan 2006

Milner, Yuri, Russian financier, Mar 2013

Milnes, Sherrill, American opera singer, Nov 1970

Milnor, John, American mathematician, July 2011

Milosevic, Slobodan, Yugoslav president, Apr 1990, *Obit* Yrbk 2006

Milosz, Czeslaw, Polish poet, Oct 1981, *Obit* Yrbk 2004

Milstein, Nathan, Russian-American violinist, Mar 1950, *Obit* Feb 1993

Minac, Matej, Czech motion picture director, Jan 2002

Minaj, Nicki, American rapper, Oct 2013

Minard, George Cann, *Obit* Aug 1940

Mindszenty, Jozsef, Jan 1957, *Obit* June 1975

Miner, Worthington C., television producer, Feb 1953, *Obit* Mar 1983

Ming, Jenny, American clothing chain executive, Jan 2011

Mingus, Charles, American jazz bassist and composer, Feb 1971, *Obit* Mar 1979

Mingus, Sue, American music director and recording executive, July 2008

Mink, Patsy T., American congresswoman, Sept 1968, *Obit* Jan 2003

Minnelli, Liza, American actress and singer, Oct 1970, July 1988

Minnelli, Vincente, American film director, May 1975, *Obit* Sept 1986

Minner, Ruth Ann, American governor, Aug 2001

Minogue, Kylie, Australian actress and singer, Jan 2003

Minor, Halsey, American media and computer software executive, Oct 1998

Minor, Robert, Apr 1941, *Obit* Jan 1953

Minow, Newton Norman, American lawyer and regulatory agency official, Oct 1961

Minsky, Marvin Lee, American computer scientist, Sept 1988

Mintoff, Dom, Maltese prime minister, Mar 1984, *Obit* Yrbk 2012

Minton, Sherman, American Supreme Court justice, Mar 1941, Yrbk 1949, *Obit* May 1965

Mirabal, Robert, Native American composer and flutist, Aug 2002

Mirabella, Grace, magazine editor, Oct 1991

Miranda, Carmen, Brazilian singer, dancer and actress, June 1941, *Obit* Oct 1955

Miranda, Lin-Manuel, American composer and lyricist, July 2013

Miranda, Mario de, Indian cartoonist and illustrator, Jan 2003

Miro Cardona, Jose, Cuban political leader, Nov 1961, *Obit* Oct 1974

Miro, Joan, Spanish painter, May 1940, Nov 1973, *Obit* Feb 1984

Mirren, Helen, English actress, July 1995

Mirvish, Edwin, Canadian theater owner and producer, Apr 1989, *Obit* Yrbk 2007

Mirvish, Robert F., Yrbk 1957

Mirza, Iskander, May 1956, *Obit* Jan 1970

Mirza, Sania, Indian tennis player, Jan 2005

Mirza, Shazia, British physics teacher and comedian, Jan 2002

Misia, Portuguese singer, Jan 2002

Mistral, Gabriela, Chilean poet and educator, Feb 1946, *Obit* Mar 1957

Mitarai, Fujio, Japanese photographic and office equipment industry executive, Jan 2002

Mitchell, Arthur, American ballet dancer and choreographer, Oct 1966

Mitchell, David, English novelist, Jan 2011

Mitchell, Dean, American painter, Aug 2002

Mitchell, Elvis, American film critic, July 2008

Mitchell, George J., American diplomat and former senator, Apr 1989

Mitchell, H. L., American farm leader, Jan 1947

Mitchell, Howard, cellist and conductor, May 1952, *Obit* Aug 1988

Mitchell, James P., American Secretary of labor, Sept 1955, *Obit* Yrbk 1964

Mitchell, Jerry, American choreographer and theatrical director, Oct 2007

Mitchell, Joan, American painter, Mar 1986, *Obit* Jan 1993

Mitchell, John Newton, American Attorney general, June 1969, *Obit* Jan 1989

Mitchell, Joni, Canadian singer and songwriter, Oct 1976

Mitchell, Patricia Edenfield, American television executive, Aug 2005

Mitchell, Stephen Arnold, American lawyer and political party leader, Oct 1952, *Obit* June 1974

Mitchell, William D., Jan 1946, *Obit* Nov 1955

Mitchell, William L., Nov 1959

Mitchum, Robert, American actor, Sept 1970, *Obit* Sept 1997

Mitford, Jessica, English journalist, memoirist and social critic, Sept 1974, *Obit* Oct 1996

Mitha, Tehreema, Pakistani dancer and choreographer, May 2004

Mitropoulos, Dimitri, Greek conductor and composer, Mar 1941, Mar 1952, *Obit* Jan 1961

Mitscher, Marc Andrew, admiral, Aug 1944, *Obit* Mar 1947

Mitsotakis, Constantine, Greek prime minister, Nov 1990

Mittal, Lakshmi, Indian steel industry executive, Jan 2006

Mittell, Philipp, *Obit* Mar 1943

Mittermeier, Russell, biologist and conservationist, Oct 1992

Mitterrand, Francois, French president, Yrbk 1968, Oct 1982, *Obit* Mar 1996

Miura, Yuichiro, Japanese mountaineer, Jan 2005

Mix, Tom, actor, *Obit* Yrbk 1940

Miyajima, Tatsuo, Japanese installation artist, Jan 2006

Miyake, Issey, Japanese fashion designer, Nov 1997

Miyamoto, Shigeru, Japanese video game creator, Jan 2002

Miyazaki, Hayao, Japanese animator, Apr 2001

Miyazawa, Kiichi, Japanese prime minister, Feb 1992, *Obit* Yrbk 2007

Mizrahi, Isaac, American fashion designer and television personality, Jan 1991

Mlambo-Ngcuka, Phumzile, South African deputy president, Jan 2005

Mlodinow, Leonard, American science writer, June 2009

Mnouchkine, Ariane, French theatrical director, Mar 1993

Mo'Nique, American comedienne and actress, Apr 2010

Moats, Alice-Leone, author and journalist, May 1943, *Obit* July 1989

Mobutu Sese Seko, Zairian president, Sept 1966, May 1997, *Obit* Nov 1997

Moby, American singer, Apr 2001

Moch, Jules, French socialist leader and cabinet member, Oct 1950, *Obit* Nov 1985

Modi, Narendra, Indian state government official, Jan 2003

Modjeski, Ralph, *Obit* Aug 1940

Moen, John, American singer and drummer, Aug 2007

Moen, Lars, May 1941

Moffat, Jay Pierrepont, diplomat, *Obit* Mar 1943

Moffatt, James, English theologian, *Obit* Aug 1944

Moffett, Mark W., American ecologist and photographer, Oct 2011

Moffo, Anna, American opera singer, May 1961, *Obit* Yrbk 2007

Mogae, Festus G., Batswana president, Jan 2004

Mohamad, Goenawan, Indonesian poet and magazine editor, Jan 2007

Mohammed Reza Pahlavi, Jan 1950, Sept 1977, *Obit* Sept 1980

Mohammed Zahir Shah, Mar 1956, *Obit* Yrbk 2007

Mohammed, Ghulam, July 1954, *Obit* Nov 1956

Mohammed, W. Deen, American Islamic leader, Jan 2004, *Obit* Yrbk 2008

Mohammed, Yanar, Iraqi feminist, Jan 2007

Mohrhardt, Foster Edward, American librarian, June 1967

Moi, Daniel Arap, Kenyan president, May 1979

Moir, Phyllis, Apr 1942

Moiseiwitsch, Tanya, English stage and costume designer, Nov 1955, *Obit* July 2003

Moiseyev, Igor, Russian ballet dancer and choreographer, Nov 1958, *Obit* Yrbk 2008

Moisseiff, Leon S., American bridge engineer, *Obit* Oct 1943

Mol, John de, Dutch television producer, Jan 2004

Moley, Raymond, American journalist and government official, July 1945, *Obit* Apr 1975

Molina, Alfred, British actor, Feb 2004

Molinari, Susan, congresswoman and television newscaster, Mar 1996

Mollenhoff, Clark R., journalist, Nov 1958, *Obit* May 1991

Mollet, Guy, French prime minister, Sept 1950, *Obit* Nov 1975

Molloy, Daniel M., *Obit* Mar 1944

Molloy, Matt, Irish flutist, Mar 2004

Molloy, Robert, author and translator, Yrbk 1948, *Obit* Mar 1977

Moloney, Paddy, Irish uillean piper, Mar 2004

Molotov, Vyacheslav, Soviet diplomat, Jan 1940, Nov 1954, *Obit* Jan 1987

Molyneux, Edward H., June 1942, *Obit* May 1974

Momaday, N. Scott, American novelist, poet and editor, Apr 1975

Momsen, C. B., American admiral and inventor, July 1946, *Obit* July 1967

Monaghan, Francis Joseph, *Obit* Jan 1943

Monaghan, Frank, Nov 1943, *Obit* Sept 1969

Monaghan, Thomas, American fast food and baseball executive, June 1990

Moncada, Salvador, Honduran pharmacologist, Jan 2003

Monckton of Brenchley, Walter Turner Monckton, British cabinet member, Yrbk 1951, *Obit* Feb 1965

Mondale, Joan, wife of American vice-president Walter F. Mondale, Jan 1980

Mondale, Walter F., American vice-president, Jan 1969, May 1978

Mondavi, Robert, American vintner, Apr 1999, *Obit* Yrbk 2008

Mondrian, Piet, Dutch painter, *Obit* Mar 1944

Moneo, Jose Rafael, Spanish architect, Jan 2004

Mongella, Gertrude, Tanzanian member of Parliament, diplomat and feminist, Jan 2004

Monheit, Jane, American jazz singer, Feb 2008

Monk, Art, American football player, Apr 1995

Monk, Meredith, American choreographer, composer and singer, Feb 1985

Monk, T. S., American drummer, Feb 2002

Monk, Thelonious, American pianist, Oct 1964, *Obit* Apr 1982

Monnet, Jean, French economist and statesman, Sept 1947, *Obit* May 1979

Monod, Jacques, French biologist, July 1971, *Obit* July 1976

Monroe, Anne Shannon, *Obit* Yrbk 1942

Monroe, Earl, American basketball player and executive, May 1978

Monroe, Lucy, singer, Aug 1942, *Obit* Nov 1987

Monroe, Marilyn, American actress, July 1959, *Obit* Oct 1962

Monroe, Vaughn, July 1942, *Obit* July 1973

Monroney, A. S. Mike, American senator, Nov 1951, *Obit* Apr 1980

Monroque, Shala, American magazine editor, Jan 2012

Monsarrat, Nicholas, English novelist, Yrbk 1950, *Obit* Oct 1979

Monseu, Stephanie, American circus performer and founder, June 2005

Monsky, Henry, Nov 1941, *Obit* June 1947

Montagne, Renee, American radio reporter, Nov 2009

Montagnier, Luc, French virologist, Aug 1988

Montagu, Ashley, Anglo-American anthropologist, Feb 1967, *Obit* Mar 2000

Montagu, Ewen, British intelligence official and lawyer, June 1956, *Obit* Sept 1985

Montague, James J., *Obit* Feb 1942

Montale, Eugenio, Italian poet and critic, Apr 1976, *Obit* Nov 1981

Montana, Claude, French fashion designer, Jan 1992

Montana, Joe, American football player, Sept 1983

Montanari, A. J., Feb 1968

Montand, Yves, French actor and singer, July 1960, Sept 1988, *Obit* Jan 1992

Monte, Elisa, American dancer and choreographer, June 2007

Montenegro, Fernanda, Brazilian actress, Oct 1999

Montero, Gabriela, Venezuelan pianist, July 2007

Montero, Mayra, Cuban novelist and short story writer, Jan 2002

Montessori, Maria, Italian educator, Nov 1940, *Obit* June 1952

Monteux, Pierre, American conductor, Apr 1946, *Obit* Sept 1964

Montgomery of Alamein, Bernard Law Montgomery, British field marshal, Yrbk 1942, *Obit* May 1976

Montgomery, Deane, mathematician, Nov 1957, *Obit* May 1992

Montgomery, Elizabeth Rider, author, Yrbk 1952

Montgomery, James Shera, Apr 1948, *Obit* Sept 1952

Montgomery, L. M., Canadian novelist, *Obit* June 1942

Montgomery, Robert, actor and director, Jan 1948, *Obit* Nov 1981

Montgomery, Ruth Shick, author and journalist, Feb 1957

Monti, Mario, Italian economist and European Commission official, Jan 2002

Montoya, Carlos, Spanish guitarist, Mar 1968, *Obit* May 1993

Montoya, Joseph M., American senator, Mar 1975, *Obit* July 1978

Montresor, Beni, Italian scenic designer, illustrator and children's author, Yrbk 1967, *Obit* Feb 2002

Mon e, Janelle, American singer, May 2013

Moody, Blair, American senator, Sept 1951, *Obit* Oct 1954

Moody, Joseph Eugene, coal association executive, Yrbk 1948, *Obit* July 1984

Moody, Ralph, Yrbk 1955

Moodysson, Lukas, Swedish screenwriter and film director, Jan 2003

Mook, Hubertus J. van, Apr 1942, *Obit* July 1965

Moon, Bucklin, American writer, Yrbk 1950

Moon, Sun Myung, Korean evangelist, Mar 1983, *Obit* Yrbk 2012

Moon, Warren, American football player, Nov 1991

Mooney, Beth, American banker, May 2012

Mooney, Edward, Apr 1946, *Obit* Jan 1959

Mooney, Thomas J., labor leader, *Obit* Apr 1942

Moore, Ann, American magazine executive, Aug 2003

Moore, Archie, American boxer, Nov 1960, *Obit* Feb 1999

Moore, Brian, Canadian novelist, Jan 1986, *Obit* Mar 1999

Moore, Bryant E., American general, Feb 1949, *Obit* Mar 1951

Moore, Demi, American actress, Sept 1993

Moore, Douglas, American composer, Nov 1947, *Obit* Oct 1969

Moore, Dudley, English actor, June 1982, *Obit* Yrbk 2002

Moore, Edward Caldwell, *Obit* May 1943

Moore, Elisabeth Luce, American philanthropist and foundation official, Oct 1960, *Obit* Yrbk 2002

Moore, Garry, American radio and television personality, Nov 1954, *Obit* Jan 1994

Moore, George E., American oncologist and surgeon, Jan 1968, *Obit* Yrbk 2008

Moore, George S., banker, May 1970, *Obit* Yrbk 2000

Moore, Gerald, English pianist, Oct 1967, *Obit* May 1987

Moore, Gordon E., American computer industry executive, Apr 2002

Moore, Grace, opera singer, Apr 1944, *Obit* Mar 1947

Moore, Henry, English sculptor, Feb 1954, Feb 1978, *Obit* Oct 1986

Moore, Henry Ruthven, Sept 1943, *Obit* May 1978

Moore, Julianne, American actress, Oct 1998

Moore, Marianne, American poet, Yrbk 1952, Apr 1968, *Obit* Mar 1972

Moore, Mary Tyler, American actress, Feb 1971

Moore, Melba, American singer and actress, Jan 1973

Moore, Michael, American documentary filmmaker, May 1997

Moore, Michael C., state attorney general, Aug 1997

Moore, Patrick, English astronomy author and television program host, Jan 2003, *Obit* Yrbk 2013

Moore, Paul, American bishop, Jan 1967, *Obit* Yrbk 2003

Moore, Preston J., Apr 1959

Moore, R. Walton, *Obit* Apr 1941

Moore, Raymond, *Obit* Mar 1940

Moore, Robert Webber, *Obit* Jan 1943

Moore, Roger, English actor, Feb 1975

Moore, Ruth, Yrbk 1954

Moore, T. Albert, *Obit* Apr 1940

Moore, Thomas W., American television executive, Sept 1967, *Obit* Yrbk 2007

Moorehead, Agnes, American actress, June 1952, *Obit* June 1974

Moorer, Thomas H., American admiral, Apr 1971, *Obit* Yrbk 2004

Moorland, Jesse Edward, American clergyman, *Obit* Jan 1940

Moos, Felix, German-American anthropologist, Jan 2005

Moos, Malcolm Charles, political scientist and college president, Nov 1968

Mora, Francis Luis, American painter, *Obit* July 1940

Mora, Jose A., Nov 1956, *Obit* Mar 1975

Moraes, F. R., Nov 1957, *Obit* July 1974

Morales, Evo, Bolivian president, Jan 2006

Moran, John, American composer, performance artist and choreographer, June 2010

Moran, Leon, *Obit* Oct 1941

Morano, Albert P., congressman, Mar 1952, *Obit* Feb 1988

Morath, Max, musician, Nov 1963

Moravia, Alberto, Italian novelist, short story writer, playwright and essayist, Apr 1970, *Obit* Nov 1990

Mordkin, Mikhail, Russian dancer, *Obit* Sept 1944

Moreau, Jeanne, French actress, Yrbk 1966

Moreell, Ben, June 1946, *Obit* Sept 1978

Morehead, Albert H., Mar 1955, *Obit* Yrbk 1966

Morehouse, John H., *Obit* July 1942

Morehouse, Daniel Walter, *Obit* Mar 1941

Morehouse, Ward, Jan 1940, *Obit* Feb 1967

Morell, Parker, *Obit* Apr 1943

Morella, Constance A., American congresswoman, Feb 2001

Moreno Ocampo, Luis, Argentine lawyer and international court prosecutor, Jan 2007

Moreno, Catalina Sandino, Colombian actress, Jan 2005

Moreno, Rita, American actress, singer and dancer, Sept 1985

Moretti, Fabrizio, Brazilian drummer, Feb 2007

Morgan, Anne Tracy, philanthropist and social worker, Jan 1946, *Obit* Mar 1952

Morgan, Arthur Ernest, American civil engineer and college president, July 1956, *Obit* Jan 1976

Morgan, Edward P., May 1951

Morgan, Edward Paddock, reporter and commentator, Apr 1964, *Obit* Mar 1993

Morgan, Frederick Edgeworth, Feb 1946, *Obit* May 1967

Morgan, Henry, American radio and television personality, Mar 1947, *Obit* July 1994

Morgan, J. P., American financier, *Obit* Apr 1943

Morgan, Joe, American baseball player and sportscaster, Sept 1984

Morgan, Joy Elmer, Jan 1946

Morgan, Lorrie, American country singer, Apr 1999

Morgan, Lucy, newspaper columnist, Mar 1959

Morgan, Piers, British talk show host, July 2012

Morgan, Thomas A., Mar 1950, *Obit* Jan 1968

Morgan, Thomas E., American congressman and physician, June 1959, *Obit* Oct 1995

Morgan, Thomas Hunt, American biologist, *Obit* Feb 1946

Morgan, Tracy, American actor and comedian, Mar 2007

Morgenstierne, Wilhelm Thorleif von Munthe af, May 1949, *Obit* Sept 1963

Morgenthau, Hans Joachim, American political scientist, Mar 1963, *Obit* Sept 1980

Morgenthau, Henry, American Secretary of the treasury, Sept 1940, *Obit* Apr 1967

Morgenthau, Robert, American district attorney, Jan 1986

Morhaime, Mike, American video game company executive, Apr 2010

Morial, Marc, American civil rights activist and former mayor, Jan 2002

Moriarty, Michael, actor, July 1976

Morimoto, Masaharu, Japanese chef and restaurateur, Jan 2004

Morin, Relman, Nov 1958, *Obit* Oct 1973

Morini, Erica, Austrian violinist, Apr 1946, *Obit* Jan 1996

Morinigo, Higinio, Paraguayan president, June 1942

Morison, Samuel Eliot, American naval historian, Oct 1951, Sept 1962, *Obit* July 1976

Morissette, Alanis, Canadian singer and songwriter, May 1997

Morita, Akio, Japanese electronics executive, Feb 1972, *Obit* Feb 2000

Morley, Malcolm, English painter, June 1984

Morley, Robert, English actor, Nov 1963, *Obit* Aug 1992

Morneau, Justin, Canadian baseball player, June 2011

Moro, Aldo, Italian prime minister, June 1964, *Obit* June 1978

Moron, Alonzo G., American college president and government official, Oct 1949, *Obit* Yrbk 1971

Morricone, Ennio, Italian composer, Oct 2000

Morrill, J. L., Feb 1951

Morris, Butch, American cornet player and composer, July 2005, *Obit* Yrbk 2013

Morris, Dave Hennen, *Obit* June 1944

Morris, Desmond, British ethologist, Nov 1974

Morris, Earl, American bar association executive, June 1968, *Obit* July 1992

Morris, Edmund, American biographer, July 1989

Morris, Errol, American documentary filmmaker, Feb 2001

Morris, James, American opera singer, July 1986

Morris, James T., American United Nations relief official, Mar 2005

Morris, Jan, English journalist and travel writer, Jan 1964, June 1986

Morris, Mark, American choreographer and dancer, Aug 1988

Morris, Newbold, American municipal official, Mar 1952, *Obit* Apr 1966

Morris, Robert, American artist, Apr 1971

Morris, Roland Sletor, lawyer and diplomat, *Obit* Jan 1946

Morris, Stephen, British drummer, Jan 2006

Morris, Willie, American writer and magazine editor, Jan 1976, *Obit* Oct 1999

Morris, Wright, American novelist, short story writer and critic, May 1982, *Obit* July 1998

Morrison of Lambeth, Herbert Stanley Morrison, British cabinet member, July 1940, Feb 1951, *Obit* Apr 1965

Morrison, Adrienne, *Obit* Jan 1941

Morrison, DeLesseps S., American mayor and diplomat, Nov 1949, *Obit* July 1964

Morrison, Denise, American food company executive, July 2012

Morrison, Frank Brenner, May 1964

Morrison, Henry Clinton, *Obit* May 1945

Morrison, Philip, American physicist, July 1981, *Obit* Aug 2005

Morrison, Toni, American novelist, May 1979

Morrison, Van, Irish singer and songwriter, Sept 1996

Morrison, William Shepherd, British statesman, Jan 1952, *Obit* Apr 1961

Morrow, Elizabeth, Apr 1943, *Obit* Mar 1955

Morrow, Honore Willsie, author, *Obit* May 1940

Morsch, Lucile M., librarian, June 1957, *Obit* Nov 1972

Morse, Clarence G., Nov 1957

Morse, David Abner, American international labor leader, Mar 1949, *Obit* Mar 1991

Morse, John Lovett, *Obit* May 1940

Morse, Marston, Mar 1957, *Obit* Aug 1977

Morse, Philip McCord, physicist, June 1948, *Obit* Nov 1985

Morse, Robert, actor, Nov 1962

Morse, True Delbert, government official, Nov 1959, *Obit* Sept 1998

Morse, Wayne Lyman, American senator, Apr 1942, Nov 1954, *Obit* Sept 1974

Mortensen, Viggo, American actor, June 2004

Mortenson, Greg, American mountaineer and humanitarian, Sept 2009

Mortier, Gerard, Belgian opera manager and director, July 1991

Mortimer, Charles G., Nov 1955, *Obit* Feb 1979

Mortimer, John, English dramatist, novelist and lawyer, Apr 1983, *Obit* Yrbk 2009

Morton, Craig, June 1978

Morton, Elizabeth Homer, Canadian librarian, July 1961

Morton, Florrinell, librarian and college dean, July 1961

Morton, Henry H., *Obit* July 1940

Morton, James, *Obit* Oct 1943

Morton, James F., *Obit* Yrbk 1941

Morton, James Madison, *Obit* Aug 1940

Morton, Joe, actor, Feb 1999

Morton, John Jamieson, Mar 1955

Morton, Rogers C. B., American Secretary of the interior and commerce, Nov 1971, *Obit* June 1979

Morton, Thruston Ballard, American senator, Nov 1957, *Obit* Oct 1982

Mos Def (Singer), American rapper, Apr 2005

Mosaddeq, Mohammad, Iranian prime minister, May 1951, *Obit* May 1967

Mosbacher, Emil, investment banker, presidential aide and yacht racer, Mar 1963, *Obit* Nov 1997

Mosbacher, Robert, American Secretary of commerce, June 1989, *Obit* Yrbk 2010

Mosca, Gaetano, Italian political philosopher, *Obit* Jan 1942

Moschen, Michael, juggler, July 2000

Moscicki, Ignacy, Polish president, *Obit* Nov 1946

Mosconi, Willie, billiards player, June 1963, *Obit* Nov 1993

Moscoso, Mireya, Panamanian president, Jan 2002

Moscoso, Teodoro, American diplomat and economist, Oct 1963, *Obit* Aug 1992

Moscovitch, Maurice, *Obit* Aug 1940

Mosel, Tad, American dramatist, Nov 1961, *Obit* Yrbk 2008

Moseley-Braun, Carol, American senator, June 1994

Moser, Fritz, June 1955

Moser-Proell, Annemarie, Austrian skier, Sept 1976

Moses, Bob, American civil rights activist and mathematics teacher, Apr 2002

Moses, Edwin, American hurdler, Nov 1986

Moses, George H., *Obit* Feb 1945

Moses, Grandma, American painter, Jan 1949, *Obit* Feb 1962

Moses, Harry M., Oct 1949, *Obit* June 1956

Moses, John, *Obit* Apr 1945

Moses, Robert, American municipal and state planning official, Nov 1940, Feb 1954, *Obit* Sept 1981

Mosher, A. R., Yrbk 1950, *Obit* Yrbk 1959

Mosher, Gouverneur Frank, *Obit* Sept 1941

Mosher, Ira, Feb 1945, *Obit* May 1968

Moskovitz, Dustin, American social networking website founder, Jan 2012

Mosley, J. Brooke, bishop, Sept 1970, *Obit* Apr 1988

Mosley, Oswald, British political leader, July 1940, *Obit* Feb 1981

Mosley, Sugar Shane, American boxer, Jan 2001

Mosley, Walter, American mystery novelist, Sept 1994

Moss, Adam, American magazine editor, Mar 2004

Moss, Cynthia, American biologist and conservationist, May 1993

Moss, Elisabeth, American actress, Nov 2013

Moss, Frank E., American senator, Yrbk 1971, *Obit* June 2003

Moss, John E., American congressman, Nov 1956, *Obit* Feb 1998

Moss, Randy, American football player, Jan 2006

Mossbauer, Rudolf L., German physicist, May 1962, *Obit* Yrbk 2012

Mostel, Zero, American actor, Apr 1943, Nov 1963, *Obit* Nov 1977

Motherwell, Hiram, *Obit* Jan 1946

Motherwell, Robert, American artist, Nov 1962, *Obit* Sept 1991

Motley, Arthur H., publisher, Jan 1961, *Obit* July 1984

Motley, Constance Baker, American judge, May 1964, *Obit* Feb 2006

Moton, Robert Russa, educator, *Obit* July 1940

Mott, Charles Stewart, American automobile executive, Sept 1969, *Obit* Apr 1973

Mott, Frank Luther, journalist and historian, Oct 1941, *Obit* Yrbk 1964

Mott, James W., *Obit* Yrbk 1945

Mott, John Raleigh, American religious and youth leader, Jan 1947, *Obit* Mar 1955

Mott, Lewis F., *Obit* Jan 1942

Mott, Stewart R., American philanthropist and political activist, Apr 1975, *Obit* Yrbk 2008

Motta, Giuseppe, *Obit* Jan 1940

Moulitsas Zuniga, Markos, American political blog writer, Mar 2007

Moulton, Forest Ray, American astronomer, Jan 1946, *Obit* Jan 1953

Moulton, Harold G., Nov 1944, *Obit* Feb 1966

Mountbatten of Burma, Louis Mountbatten, British admiral, June 1942, *Obit* Oct 1979

Mountevans, Edward Ratcliffe Garth Russell Evans, British admiral, May 1941, *Obit* Nov 1957

Mousavi, Mir Hossein, Iranian presidential candidate and former prime minister, Sept 2009

Moussa, Amr, Egyptian diplomat and international organization official, Jan 2002

Moutet, Marius, French socialist leader and cabinet member, July 1947, *Obit* Yrbk 1968

Mowat, Farley, Canadian ethnologist, historian and children's author, Feb 1986

Mowat, R. B., *Obit* Nov 1941

Mowery, Edward J., American journalist, Nov 1953, *Obit* Feb 1971

Mowinckel, Johan Ludwig, *Obit* Nov 1943

Mowrer, Edgar Ansel, journalist, Oct 1941, July 1962, *Obit* May 1977

Mowrer, Lilian Thomson, author, May 1940, *Obit* Jan 1991

Mowrey, Corma, Nov 1950

Moya, Manuel A. de, Nov 1957

Moyers, Bill, American journalist and television commentator, Jan 1966, Feb 1976

Moyet, Alison, British singer, Jan 2003

Moylan, Mary Ellen, Feb 1957

Moyne, Walter Edward Guinness, *Obit* Yrbk 1944

Moynihan, Daniel Patrick, American senator and diplomat, Feb 1968, Feb 1986, *Obit* Yrbk 2003

Moyo, Dambisa, Zambian economist, Feb 2012

Moyo, Jonathan N., Zimbabwean political leader, Jan 2007

Mr. John, milliner, Oct 1956, *Obit* Sept 1993

Mubarak, Hosni, Egyptian president, Apr 1982

Muccio, John Joseph, American diplomat, Jan 1951, *Obit* July 1989

Muck, Karl, Mar 1940

Mudd, Emily, American family and marriage counselor, Nov 1956, *Obit* July 1998

Mudd, Roger, American television newscaster, Jan 1981

Mueller, Frederick H., Yrbk 1959, *Obit* Oct 1976

Mueller, George E., aerospace industry executive and NASA official, Nov 1964

Mueller, Reuben H., bishop, Apr 1964, *Obit* Sept 1982

Mueller, Robert S., American FBI director, Aug 2010

Muench, Aloisius, Apr 1960, *Obit* Apr 1962

Mufti, Hania, Jordanian human rights activist, Jan 2005

Mugabe, Robert Gabriel, Zimbabwean president, Apr 1979, Jan 2002

Muggeridge, Malcolm, English journalist, critic and novelist, Apr 1955, July 1975, *Obit* Jan 1991

Mugler, Thierry, French fashion designer and photographer, Aug 2010

Muhammad, Jan 2002

Muhammad, Oct 1951, *Obit* Apr 1961

Muir, James, May 1950, *Obit* Jan 1960

Muir, Malcolm, Apr 1953, *Obit* Mar 1979

Muir, Percy H., English bibliographer, bookseller and collector, Apr 1963

Muir, Ramsay, *Obit* June 1941

Mujibur Rahman, Bangladeshi prime minister and president, Jan 1973, *Obit* Oct 1975

Mukasey, Michael, American Attorney general, Feb 2008

Mukherjee, Bharati, Indian-American novelist, Apr 1992

Mukherjee, Siddhartha, American oncologist, Jan 2013

Mukhtar, Aloma, Nigerian supreme court justice, Jan 2005

Mulanovich, Sofia, Peruvian surfer, Jan 2004

Mulcahy, Anne, American office equipment industry executive, Nov 2002

Mulcair, Thomas, Nov 2013

Muldoon, Robert D., New Zealand prime minister, Feb 1978, *Obit* Sept 1992

Muldowney, Shirley, American automobile racing driver, Oct 1997

Mulleavy, Kate, American fashion designer, Sept 2012

Mulleavy, Laura, American fashion designer, Sept 2012

Mullen, Mike, American admiral, Feb 2008

Mullenweg, Matt, American computer software executive, May 2013

Muller, H. J., American geneticist, Feb 1947, *Obit* June 1967

Muller, Paul Hermann, Swiss chemist, Oct 1945, *Obit* Yrbk 1965

Mulligan, Carey, British actress, Oct 2013

Mulligan, Gerry, American jazz saxophonist, Yrbk 1960, *Obit* Mar 1996

Mulliken, Robert Sanderson, American chemist, Sept 1967, *Obit* Jan 1987

Mullis, Kary B., American biochemist, Feb 1996

Mulloy, Gardnar, tennis player, Nov 1957

Mulroney, Brian, Canadian prime minister, Apr 1984

Muluzi, Bakili, Malawian president, Jan 2003

Mumford, Ethel Watts, *Obit* Jan 1940

Mumford, Lawrence Quincy, American Librarian of Congress, June 1954, *Obit* Jan 1983

Mumford, Lewis, American architectural and social critic, Nov 1940, Mar 1963, *Obit* Mar 1990

Muncey, Cameron, Australian guitarist and singer, Jan 2005

Munch, Charles, Yrbk 1947, *Obit* Yrbk 1968

Munch, Edvard, Norwegian painter, Yrbk 1940, *Obit* Mar 1944

Mundt, Karl E., American senator, July 1948, *Obit* Oct 1974

Mundy, Talbot, English novelist, *Obit* Sept 1940

Mungiu, Cristian, Romanian film director, Jan 2007

Muni, Paul, actor, Jan 1944, *Obit* Nov 1967

Muniz, Joao Carlos, Sept 1952, *Obit* Sept 1960

Munk, Kaj, Danish clergyman, poet and dramatist, *Obit* Feb 1944

Munn, Clarence L., Nov 1953

Munn, Frank, singer, May 1944, *Obit* Yrbk 1953

Munnich, Ferenc, May 1959, *Obit* Jan 1968

Munoz Marin, Luis, Puerto Rican governor, Oct 1942, Nov 1953, *Obit* June 1980

Munoz Zurita, Ricardo, Mexican chef, Jan 2003

Munro, Alice, Canadian short story writer and novelist, Sept 1990

Munro, Leslie Knox, Nov 1953, *Obit* Apr 1974

Munsel, Patrice, American opera singer, Mar 1945

Munson, Thurman, American baseball player, Nov 1977, *Obit* Sept 1979

Munyama, Gerry, Namibian broadcasting executive, Jan 2004

Murakami, Haruki, Japanese novelist, Sept 1997

Murayama, Makio, Oct 1974

Murch, Walter, American film editor, director, screenwriter and sound designer, Apr 2000

Murcutt, Glenn, Australian architect, Jan 2002

Murdoch, Iris, English novelist and philosopher, Yrbk 1958, Aug 1980, *Obit* Apr 1999

Murdoch, Rupert, Australian-American publishing, motion picture and television executive, May 1977

Murdock, George J., *Obit* Sept 1942

Murdock, George Peter, anthropologist, Mar 1957

Murdock, Victor, *Obit* Aug 1945

Muren, Dennis, American special effects technician, Mar 1997

Murguia, Janet, American civil rights activist, Jan 2010

Murkowski, Frank H., American senator and governor, July 2003

Murnane, Gerald, Australian short story writer and essayist, Jan 2007

Murphree, Eger V., Sept 1956, *Obit* Jan 1963

Murphy, Charles S., American lawyer and presidential adviser, Apr 1950, *Obit* Oct 1983

Murphy, Eddie, American comedian and actor, Nov 1983

Murphy, Frank, American Supreme Court justice, July 1940, *Obit* Sept 1949

Murphy, Franklin D., American physician, college administrator and newspaper executive, Mar 1971, *Obit* Aug 1994

Murphy, Franklin W., American farm leader, lawyer and banker, *Obit* Jan 1941

Murphy, Frederick E., American newspaper publisher, *Obit* Mar 1940

Murphy, Gardner, psychologist, May 1960, *Obit* May 1979

Murphy, George, American actor, dancer and senator, Yrbk 1965, *Obit* July 1992

Murphy, Mark, CEO fo Green Bay Packers, Oct 2012

Murphy, Mark, American jazz singer, Sept 2004

Murphy, Patricia, American restaurateur and horticulturist, Apr 1962

Murphy, Patrick V., Nov 1972, *Obit* Yrbk 2012

Murphy, Robert D., American diplomat, Feb 1943, Nov 1958, *Obit* Mar 1978

Murphy, Thomas Aquinas, American automobile executive, Oct 1979, *Obit* Yrbk 2006

Murphy, Thomas F., police commissioner and judge, Mar 1951, *Obit* Jan 1996

Murphy, William Beverly, food industry executive, Nov 1955, *Obit* Aug 1994

Murray, Albert, American novelist, essayist and music historian, May 1994, *Obit* Yrbk 2013

Murray, Anne, Canadian singer, Jan 1982

Murray, Arthur, American dance teacher, Apr 1943, *Obit* May 1991

Murray, Augustus Taber, *Obit* Mar 1940

Murray, Bill, American actor, Jan 1985, Sept 2004

Murray, Charles A., American social scientist, July 1986

Murray, Charlie, *Obit* Sept 1941

Murray, Don, actor, Sept 1959

Murray, Donald Morison, American journalist and writing instructor, July 2006

Murray, Dwight H., May 1957, *Obit* Nov 1974

Murray, Elizabeth, American painter, Apr 1995, *Obit* Yrbk 2007

Murray, J. Harold, *Obit* Feb 1941

Murray, James E., American senator, Aug 1945, *Obit* May 1961

Murray, John Courtney, American priest and theologian, May 1961, *Obit* Oct 1967

Murray, Jonathan, American television producer, May 2002

Murray, Patty, American senator, Aug 1994

Murray, Philip, American labor leader, Jan 1941, Feb 1949, *Obit* Yrbk 1952

Murray, Thomas E., Sept 1950, *Obit* Sept 1961

Murray, Tom, Nov 1956, *Obit* Jan 1972

Murray, Ty, American rodeo cowboy, May 2002

Murray, William S., *Obit* Mar 1942

Murrell, Ethel Ernest, Oct 1951

Murrow, Edward R., American radio and television newscaster, Feb 1942, Nov 1953, *Obit* June 1965

Murtaugh, Danny, baseball player and manager, Feb 1961, *Obit* Feb 1977

Museveni, Yoweri, Ugandan president, Aug 1990

Musgrave, Thea, Scottish composer, May 1978

Musharraf, Pervez, Pakistani general and president, Mar 2001, Jan 2002

Musial, Stan, American baseball player, Yrbk 1948, *Obit* Yrbk 2013

Musk, Elon, American entrepreneur, Oct 2006

Muskie, Edmund S., American senator and Secretary of state, Feb 1955, Yrbk 1968, *Obit* June 1996

Musmanno, Michael Angelo, June 1967, *Obit* Yrbk 1968

Mussert, Anton Adriaan, Dutch Nazi leader, Nov 1942

Mussolini, Benito, Italian dictator, Mar 1942, *Obit* May 1945

Mussolini, Bruno, *Obit* Oct 1941

Muste, Abraham Johannes, American clergyman and pacifist, Oct 1965, *Obit* Apr 1967

Muster, Thomas, Austrian tennis player, May 1997

Mutai, Geoffrey, Long-distance runner, June 2013

Muti, Ettore, *Obit* Oct 1943

Muti, Riccardo, Italian conductor, July 1980

Mutombo, Dikembe, Congolese basketball player, Feb 2000

Mutter, Anne-Sophie, German violinist, Jan 1990

Muzorewa, Abel Tendekai, Zimbabwean prime minister, Mar 1979, *Obit* Yrbk 2010

Mwanawasa, Levy, Zambian president, Jan 2003, *Obit* Yrbk 2008

Mwinyi, Ali Hassan, Tanzanian president, June 1995

Myasnikova, Yelena, Russian magazine editor, Jan 2002

Mydans, Carl, American photojournalist, May 1945, *Obit* Yrbk 2004

Mydans, Carl M.; and Mydans, Shelley Smith, May 1945

Mydans, Shelley Smith, American journalist and novelist, May 1945, *Obit* Aug 2002

Myer, Dillon S., government official, July 1947, *Obit* Jan 1983

Myers, B. R., American Korean studies specialist, June 2010

Myers, C. Kilmer, Feb 1960

Myers, Dee Dee, American presidential press secretary and television moderator, Aug 1994

Myers, Francis John, Apr 1949, *Obit* Sept 1956

Myers, Gustavus, journalist and historian, *Obit* Jan 1943

Myers, Jerome, *Obit* Aug 1940

Myers, Joel Norman, American meteorologist, Apr 2005

Myers, Mike, Canadian comedian, actor and screenwriter, Aug 1997

Myers, Norman, English environmentalist, May 1993

Myers, Richard B., American air force general, Apr 2002

Myhrvold, Nathan P., American physicist and computer software executive, Sept 1997

Myrdal, Alva Reimer, Swedish sociologist, Yrbk 1950, *Obit* Mar 1986

Myrdal, Gunnar, Swedish economist, Sept 1946, Mar 1975, *Obit* July 1987

N

N'Dour, Youssou, Senegalese singer, Jan 1996

Nabarro, Gerald, Nov 1963, *Obit* Jan 1974

Nabokov, Vladimir Vladimirovich, Russian-American novelist, May 1966, *Obit* Aug 1977

Nabors, Jim, American actor and singer, Nov 1969

Nabrit, James M., American lawyer, civil rights activist and university president, Jan 1961, *Obit* Mar 1998

Nabrit, Samuel Milton, American embryologist, Jan 1963, *Obit* Yrbk 2004

Nabulsi, Suleiman, Mar 1957

Nachtigall, Paul E., American marine scientist, Jan 2006

Nadal, Rafael, Spanish tennis player, Jan 2005

Nader, Ralph, American consumer rights advocate, Nov 1968, Apr 1986

Nadler, Marcus, May 1955, *Obit* June 1965

Naegle, Susan, American television executive, May 2013

Nagano, Osami, July 1942, *Obit* Feb 1947

Nagashima, Shigeo, Japanese baseball player and manager, Jan 2003

Nagin, Ray, American mayor, Jan 2006

Naguib, Mohammed, Egyptian general, Oct 1952

Nagy, Ivan, Hungarian dance director, May 1977

Naidoo, Kumi, South African human rights activist and environmentalist, Sept 2010

Naidu, Sarojini, Indian feminist, poet and government official, May 1943, *Obit* Mar 1949

Naifeh, Steven W., author, Mar 1998

Naifeh, Steven; and Smith, Gregory White, Mar 1998

Naikuni, Titus, Kenyan airline executive, Jan 2004

Naipaul, V. S., Trinidadian novelist and journalist, July 1977

Nair, Mira, Indian motion picture director, Nov 1993

Naisbitt, John, American social forecaster, Nov 1984

Naish, J. Carrol, actor, Jan 1957, *Obit* Mar 1973

Najibullah, Mohammed, Afghan president, June 1988, *Obit* Jan 1997

Najimy, Kathy, American actress and comedienne, Oct 2002

Nakamura, Shuji, Japanese electronics engineer and inventor, Jan 2006

Nakamura, Shunsuke, Japanese soccer player, Jan 2002

Nakasone, Yasuhiro, Japanese prime minister, June 1983

Nakata, Hidetoshi, Japanese soccer player, Jan 2002

Nakian, Reuben, sculptor, Feb 1985, *Obit* Feb 1987

Nam, Il, Sept 1951, *Obit* Apr 1976

Namath, Joe, American football player, Yrbk 1966

Namboodiripad, E. M. S., Indian communist leader, Nov 1976

Namegabe, Chouchou, Congolese radio reporter, Apr 2012

Namphy, Henri, Haitian general, Sept 1988

Napolitano, Giorgio, Italian president, Jan 2006

Napolitano, Janet, American Secretary of homeland security, Oct 2004, Mar 2009

Nara, Yoshitomo, Japanese installation artist, Jan 2005

Narain, Jai Prakash, Indian statesman, May 1958, *Obit* Nov 1979

Narasimha Rao, P. V., Indian prime minister, Jan 1992, *Obit* Yrbk 2005

Narathipphongpraphan, June 1954

Narayan, R. K., Indian novelist and short story writer, Sept 1987, *Obit* July 2001

Narelle, Marie, *Obit* Mar 1941

Narendra Shiromani, *Obit* Mar 1943

Nares, Owen, *Obit* Sept 1943

Nas (Musician), American rapper, Sept 2009

Nash, Ogden, American poet, Apr 1941, *Obit* July 1971

Nash, Paul, English illustrator and painter, *Obit* Sept 1946

Nash, Philleo, government official, Nov 1962, *Obit* Jan 1988

Nash, Steve, Canadian basketball player, Mar 2003

Nash, Walter, New Zealand prime minister, Oct 1942, Mar 1958, *Obit* July 1968

Nasheed, Mohamed, Maldivian president, Aug 2012

Nason, John W., American college president, July 1953, *Obit* Feb 2002

Nasrallah, Hassan, Lebanese guerrilla leader, Jan 2006

Nasrin, Taslima, Bangladeshi poet, essayist, novelist and feminist, Jan 2003

Nasser, Gamal Abdel, Egyptian president, Nov 1954, *Obit* Nov 1970

Nasser, Jacques, Lebanese-Australian automobile executive, Apr 2001

Nast, Conde, publisher, *Obit* Nov 1942

Nastase, Ilie, Romanian tennis player, Oct 1974

Nathan, George Jean, drama critic, Apr 1945, *Obit* June 1958

Nathan, Robert R., American economist, Sept 1941, *Obit* Nov 2001

Natta, Giulio, Italian chemist, Nov 1964

Nauman, Bruce, American artist, Nov 1990

Navarre, Henri, Nov 1953

Navarro Bello, Adela, Oct 2013

Navasky, Victor S., American journalist, May 1986

Navon, Yitzhak, May 1982

Navratilova, Martina, Czech-American tennis player, Sept 1977, Feb 2004

Naylor, Gloria, American novelist, Apr 1993

Nazarbayev, Nursultan, Kazakhstani president, Oct 2000

Nazimova, Alla, Russian actress, *Obit* Aug 1945

Nazimuddin, Khwaja, Mar 1949, *Obit* Yrbk 1964

Ncube, Pius Alick, Zimbabwean archbishop, Jan 2004

Ne Win, Burmese president, Apr 1971, *Obit* Yrbk 2003

Neagle, Anna, English actress, Nov 1945, *Obit* July 1986

Neagle, Anna; and Wilcox, Herbert, Nov 1945

Neal, Herbert Vincent, *Obit* Mar 1940

Neal, Patricia, American actress, Sept 1964, *Obit* Yrbk 2010

Neals, Otto, American sculptor and painter, Feb 2003

Nearing, Scott, American sociologist and homesteader, Oct 1971, *Obit* Oct 1983

Nederlander, James Morton, American theater owner, Apr 1991

Nedved, Pavel, Czech soccer player, Jan 2002

Neel, Alice, American painter, Aug 1976, *Obit* Jan 1985

Neeleman, David G., American airline executive, Sept 2003

Neely, Matthew M., Jan 1950, *Obit* Mar 1958

Neeson, Liam, Irish-American actor, Nov 1994

Negrin, Juan, Spanish physiologist and statesman, Sept 1945, *Obit* Jan 1957

Negroponte, John, American intelligence official, Apr 2003

Nehru, B. K., Indian diplomat and government official, Feb 1963, *Obit* Feb 2002

Nehru, Jawaharlal, Indian prime minister, Jan 1941, Apr 1948, *Obit* July 1964

Neier, Aryeh, German-American civil rights leader, Nov 1978

Neill, Alexander Sutherland, British child psychologist, Apr 1961, *Obit* Nov 1973

Neill, Charles Patrick, *Obit* Nov 1942

Neill, Stephen, British bishop, Mar 1960

Neilson, Frances Fullerton, Yrbk 1955

Neilson, William Allan, Scottish-American literary scholar, *Obit* Mar 1946

Neiman, LeRoy, American painter, July 1996, *Obit* Yrbk 2012

Nelles, Percy Walker, Canadian admiral, Feb 1944

Nelligan, Kate, Canadian actress, July 1983

Nelly (Musician), American rapper, Oct 2002

Nelson, Byron, American golfer, Mar 1945, *Obit* Yrbk 2007

Nelson, Don, American basketball coach, May 2007

Nelson, Donald Marr, American retail executive, Mar 1941, *Obit* Yrbk 1959

Nelson, Gaylord, American senator, governor and environmentalist, May 1960, *Obit* Yrbk 2005

Nelson, Harriet, actress and singer, May 1949, *Obit* Jan 1995

Nelson, Keith, American circus performer and founder, June 2005

Nelson, Marilyn Carlson, American hotel and restaurant industry executive, Oct 2004

Nelson, Ozzie, actor and band leader, May 1949, *Obit* Aug 1975

Nelson, Soraya Sarhaddi, Oct 2013

Nelson, Stanley, American documentary filmmaker, May 2005

Nelson, Willie, American country singer and songwriter, Feb 1979

Nemerov, Howard, American novelist, poet and critic, Oct 1964, *Obit* Sept 1991

Nemirovich-Danchenko, Vladimir Ivanovich, Russian dramatist and director, *Obit* June 1943

Nenni, Pietro, Mar 1947, *Obit* Feb 1980

Nerina, Nadia, South African ballet dancer, Nov 1957, *Obit* Yrbk 2008

Nernst, Hermann Walther, German chemist, *Obit* Jan 1942

Nero, Franco, Italian actor, Jan 2002

Neruda, Pablo, Chilean poet, Yrbk 1970, *Obit* Nov 1973

Nervi, Pier Luigi, Italian architect and structural engineer, Jan 1958, *Obit* Mar 1979

Nesbitt, Cathleen, English actress, Nov 1956, *Obit* Sept 1982

Nesbo, Jo, Norwegian novelist, singer and songwriter, Sept 2011

Neshat, Shirin, Iranian photographer and video artist, Jan 2002

Nesmeianov, A. N., Nov 1958

Nessen, Ron, American presidential press secretary and public relations executive, Jan 1976

Nestingen, Ivan A., Mar 1962, *Obit* June 1978

Netanyahu, Benjamin, Israeli prime minister, June 1996

Netherwood, Douglas B., *Obit* Oct 1943

Neto, Ernesto, Brazilian artist, Oct 2009

Netrebko, Anna, Russian opera singer, Jan 2005

Nettles, Graig, American baseball player, July 1984

Neuberger, Maurine Brown, American senator, Oct 1961, *Obit* July 2000

Neuberger, Richard L., American senator, Feb 1955, *Obit* May 1960

Neufeld, Sarah, Canadian violinist, Jan 2007

Neuharth, Allen, American newspaper publisher, Apr 1986, *Obit* Yrbk 2013

Neuhaus, Richard John, American priest, religious writer and political activist, June 1988, *Obit* Yrbk 2009

Neuman, Leo Handel, *Obit* May 1941

Neumann, Emanuel, Mar 1967, *Obit* Jan 1981

Neumann, Heinrich, *Obit* Jan 1940

Neumeier, John, American dancer and choreographer, July 1991

Neurath, Otto, Austrian sociologist and philosopher, *Obit* Feb 1946

Neustadt, Richard E., American political scientist, Nov 1968, *Obit* Yrbk 2004

Neutra, Richard Joseph, American architect, May 1947, July 1961, *Obit* June 1970

Neuwirth, Bebe, American dancer and actress, Nov 1997

Nevelson, Louise, American sculptor, Oct 1967, *Obit* May 1988

Neville, John, Jan 1959, *Obit* Yrbk 2012

Neville, Robert A. R., Nov 1953

Nevins, Allan, historian, Oct 1968, *Obit* Apr 1971

Nevinson, Christopher Richard Wynne, English painter, *Obit* Nov 1946

New Order (Musical group), Jan 2006

Newall, Cyril Louis Norton, Aug 1940

Newberry, Truman Handy, *Obit* Nov 1945

Newbolt, Francis George, *Obit* Jan 1941

Newby, P. H., English novelist and short story writer, Yrbk 1953

Newcombe, Don, American baseball player, Feb 1957

Newcombe, John, Australian tennis player, Oct 1977

Newcomer, Francis K., American general, Mar 1950, *Obit* Oct 1967

Newcomer, Mabel, Sept 1944

Newell, Edward Theodore, *Obit* Apr 1941

Newell, Homer Edward, physicist and mathematician, Nov 1954, *Obit* Sept 1983

Newell, Horatio B., *Obit* Oct 1943

Newhall, Arthur B., Oct 1942

Newhart, Bob, American comedian and actor, Mar 1962

Newhouse, Samuel I., American newspaper publisher and broadcasting executive, Mar 1961, *Obit* Oct 1979

Newkirk, Ingrid, American animal rights activist, Apr 2008

Newkirk, Kori, American mixed media and installation artist, Mar 2008

Newley, Anthony, actor, singer and songwriter, Oct 1966, *Obit* July 1999

Newlon, Jesse H., *Obit* Oct 1941

Newman, Alfred, July 1943, *Obit* Apr 1970

Newman, Arnold, American photographer, Oct 1980, *Obit* Yrbk 2006

Newman, Barnett, American painter, Sept 1969, *Obit* Sept 1970

Newman, Bernard, English author, Apr 1959, *Obit* Apr 1968

Newman, Edwin, American television reporter, commentator and moderator, Sept 1967, *Obit* Yrbk 2010

Newman, J. Wilson, American publishing executive, Apr 1955, *Obit* Yrbk 2003

Newman, Paul, American actor, Nov 1959, May 1985, *Obit* Yrbk 2008

Newman, Randy, American singer and songwriter, Oct 1982

Newmark, Craig, American software engineer and webmaster, June 2005

Newsom, Carroll Vincent, college president, Apr 1957, *Obit* Apr 1990

Newsom, Herschel D., American farmer, agricultural leader and government official, Apr 1951, *Obit* Sept 1970

Newsom, Lee A., American paleoethnobotanist, Oct 2004

Newton, A. Edward, bibliographer and book collector, *Obit* Nov 1940

Newton, Cam, American football player, Sept 2013

Newton, Christopher, Anglo-Canadian theatrical director, Feb 1995

Newton, Cleveland Alexander, *Obit* Oct 1945

Newton, Eric, British art critic, Feb 1956, *Obit* Apr 1965

Newton, Helmut, German photographer, Nov 1991, *Obit* Yrbk 2004

Newton, Huey, American revolutionary, Feb 1973, *Obit* Oct 1989

Newton, Thandie, British actress, Jan 2003

Newton, Wayne, American singer, Feb 1990

Newton-John, Olivia, Australian singer and actress, Nov 1978

Ney, Hubert, Nov 1956

Nezet-Seguin, Yannick, Canadian conductor, Nov 2011

Ngo, Dinh Diem, South Vietnamese president, Mar 1955, *Obit* Jan 1964

Nguyen, Cao Ky, South Vietnamese vice-president, Yrbk 1966, *Obit* Yrbk 2011

Nguyen, Thi Binh, Vietnamese communist leader, July 1976

Nguyen, Van Thieu, South Vietnamese president, June 1968, *Obit* Jan 2002

Niarchos, Stavros, Greek shipping executive, May 1958, *Obit* June 1996

Nice, Harry, *Obit* Apr 1941

Nichols, Dudley, screenwriter, Sept 1941, *Obit* Mar 1960

Nichols, Herbert B., American science journalist, Sept 1947

Nichols, Kenneth D., general, Nov 1948, *Obit* Sept 2000

Nichols, Mike, American theatrical and motion picture director, Mar 1961, Jan 1992

Nichols, Roy Franklin, historian, July 1949, *Obit* Mar 1973

Nichols, William I., June 1958

Nichols, William T., Oct 1953

Nicholson, Andy, British rock bassist, Jan 2006

Nicholson, Ben, English painter, Jan 1958, *Obit* Apr 1982

Nicholson, Jack, American actor, Oct 1974, Apr 1995

Nicholson, Margaret, Nov 1957

Nickerson, Albert L., petroleum executive and banking official, Nov 1959, *Obit* Nov 1994

Nicklaus, Jack, American golfer, Nov 1962

Nicol, Simon, English guitarist and singer, Sept 2005

Nicolet, Marcel, Nov 1958

Nicolson, Harold George, British diplomat, author and critic, May 1967, *Obit* June 1968

Nicolson, Marjorie Hope, literary critic and college dean, Apr 1940, *Obit* June 1981

Nidetch, Jean, American dieting organization founder, Yrbk 1973

Nie Haisheng, Chinese astronaut, Jan 2006

Niebuhr, Reinhold, American theologian, Mar 1941, Nov 1951, *Obit* July 1971

Niederland, William G., psychoanalyst, Oct 1980, *Obit* Oct 1993

Nielsen, Alice, *Obit* Apr 1943

Nielsen, Arthur C., American market research executive, Yrbk 1951, *Obit* July 1980

Niemeyer, Oscar, Brazilian architect, Feb 1960, *Obit* Yrbk 2013

Niemoller, Martin, German clergyman, Mar 1943, Mar 1965, *Obit* May 1984

Niggli, Josephina, American dramatist, poet, short story writer and novelist, Yrbk 1949

Nighy, Bill, British actor, Jan 2007

Nijinsky, Waslaw, Russian ballet dancer, Oct 1940, *Obit* May 1950

Nikolais, Alwin, American choreographer, Feb 1968, *Obit* July 1993

Nikolayev, Andrian, Soviet astronaut, Nov 1964, *Obit* Yrbk 2004

Niles, John Jacob, American singer, composer, singer and folklorist, Nov 1959, *Obit* Apr 1980

Nilsson, Birgit, Swedish opera singer, May 1960, *Obit* Sept 2006

Nimeiri, Gaafar Mohammed, Sudanese president, Nov 1977, *Obit* Yrbk 2009

Nimitz, Chester W., American admiral, Feb 1942, *Obit* Mar 1966

Nimoy, Leonard, American actor, Feb 1977

Nin, Anais, American novelist, Feb 1944, Sept 1975, *Obit* Mar 1977

Nin, Khadja, Burundian singer, Jan 2005

Ninagawa, Yukio, Japanese theatrical director, Jan 2003

Nipkow, Paul Gottlieb, German television pioneer, *Obit* Oct 1940

Nirenberg, Marshall Warren, American biochemist, Apr 1965, *Obit* Yrbk 2010

Nishi, Kazuhiko, Japanese computer services executive, Jan 2002

Nitze, Paul H., American statesman, Feb 1962, *Obit* Mar 2005

Niven, David, British actor, Mar 1957, *Obit* Sept 1983

Nixon, Agnes, American television scriptwriter, Apr 2001

Nixon, Lewis, American naval architect, *Obit* Nov 1940

Nixon, Marni, American singer, Oct 2009

Nixon, Patricia, wife of American president Richard M. Nixon, Jan 1970, *Obit* Aug 1993

Nixon, Richard M., American president, July 1948, June 1958, Yrbk 1969, *Obit* June 1994, Yrbk 1994

Niyazov, Saparmurad, Turkmen president, Jan 2003

Nizer, Louis, American lawyer, Nov 1955, *Obit* Jan 1995

Nkomo, Joshua, Zimbabwean political leader, Apr 1976, *Obit* Sept 1999

Nkontchou, Cyrille, Cameroonian securities broker, Jan 2004

Nkrumah, Kwame, Ghanaian president, July 1953, *Obit* June 1972

Noah, Yannick, French tennis player, Aug 1987

Noble, Adrian, English theatrical director, Aug 1999

Noble, Allan, May 1957

Noble, Edward J., American candy and broadcasting executive, Jan 1944, *Obit* Mar 1959

Noble, G. Kingsley, zoologist and museum curator, *Obit* Jan 1941

Noble, Ronald K., American international law enforcement official, Jan 2002

Noboa, Alvaro, Ecuadorian businessman and political leader, Jan 2007

Nobs, Ernst, Sept 1949, *Obit* June 1957

Nocera, Joseph, American journalist, Oct 2011

Nock, Albert Jay, American literary critic and essayist, May 1944, *Obit* Sept 1945

Noel Hume, Ivor, English archaeologist, Nov 1997

Noel-Baker, Philip John, British pacifist, Feb 1946, *Obit* Mar 1983

Nofziger, Lyn, American political consultant, Jan 1983, *Obit* Yrbk 2006

Noguchi, Isamu, American sculptor, Sept 1943, *Obit* Feb 1989

Nogues, Charles, Feb 1943, *Obit* June 1971

Nolan, Christopher, Irish poet and memoirist, Sept 1988, *Obit* Yrbk 2009

Nolan, Christopher, Anglo-American screenwriter and director, Jan 2005

Nolan, Jonathan, Apr 2013

Nolan, Lloyd, actor, Nov 1956, *Obit* Nov 1985

Nolan, W. I., *Obit* Sept 1943

Noland, Kenneth, American painter, Sept 1972, *Obit* Yrbk 2010

Nolde, O. Frederick, Feb 1947, *Obit* Sept 1972

Nolte, Nick, American actor, Nov 1980

Nomura, Kichisaburo, Apr 1941, *Obit* July 1964

Noon, Firoz Khan, June 1957

Noonan, Peggy, American presidential speechwriter and political writer, July 1990

Nooyi, Indra K., Indian beverage company executive, Nov 2006

Norden, Carl Lukas, American mechanical engineer and inventor, Jan 1945, *Obit* Sept 1965

Nordhoff, Heinz, German automobile executive, Nov 1956, *Obit* June 1968

Nordmann, Charles, *Obit* Yrbk 1940

Norell, Norman, fashion designer, Nov 1964, *Obit* Yrbk 1972

Noriega, Manuel Antonio, Panamanian general and head of state, Mar 1988

Norman, Christina, American broadcasting executive, Nov 2007

Norman, Greg, Australian golfer, Aug 1989

Norman, Jessye, American opera singer, Feb 1976

Norman, Marsha, American dramatist, May 1984

Norman, Montagu Collet Norman, English banker, Yrbk 1940, *Obit* Mar 1950

Norodom Sihanouk, Mar 1954, Aug 1993, *Obit* Yrbk 2012

Norquist, Grover, American economist and tax reform lobbyist, Oct 2007

Norrington, Roger, English conductor, Jan 1990

Norris, Charles Gilman, author, *Obit* Aug 1945

Norris, Chuck, American actor and martial artist, Jan 1989

Norris, George William, American senator, *Obit* Oct 1944

Norris, Henry Hutchinson, *Obit* May 1940

Norris, James F., *Obit* Sept 1940

Norris, Michele, American radio reporter, Mar 2008

Norstad, Lauris, American air force general, May 1948, Feb 1959, *Obit* Oct 1988

Norten, Enrique, Mexican architect, Jan 2005

North, John Ringling, circus owner, June 1951, *Obit* July 1985

North, Oliver L., American Marine corps officer, columnist and television personality, Mar 1992

North, Sterling, author, Nov 1943, *Obit* Feb 1975

Northrop, John H., American biochemist, June 1947, *Obit* Sept 1987

Northrop, John Knudsen, American aeronautical engineer and executive, Mar 1949, *Obit* Apr 1981

Northrop, Peggy, American magazine editor, Nov 2009

Northup, Edwin Fitch, *Obit* Jan 1940

Norton, Andre, American science fiction novelist, Jan 1957, *Obit* Yrbk 2005

Norton, Edward, American actor, June 2004

Norton, Eleanor Holmes, American civil rights leader and congresswoman, Nov 1976

Norton, Gale, American Secretary of the interior, June 2001

Norton, Graham, Irish talk show host, Jan 2004

Norton, Howard Melvin, June 1947

Norton, Mary Teresa Hopkins, congresswoman, Nov 1944, Obit Nov 1959

Norton, Thomas, Obit Jan 1942

Norton, W. W., Obit Yrbk 1945

Norville, Deborah, American television reporter and radio talk show host, Apr 1990

Notari, Aldo, Italian baseball association executive, Jan 2004, Obit CB Int 2006

Notman, J. Geoffrey, Jan 1958

Nottage, Lynn, American dramatist, Nov 2004

Noue, Jehan de, Jan 1947

Noujaim, Jehane, Egyptian-American documentary filmmaker, Jan 2005

Nour, Ayman, Egyptian member of Parliament, Jan 2005

Nourse, Edwin, American economist and presidential adviser, Oct 1946, Obit June 1974

Nouvel, Jean, French architect, Sept 2008

Novacek, Michael J., American paleontologist and museum curator, Sept 2002

Novaes, Guiomar, Brazilian pianist, June 1953, Obit May 1979

Novak, Kim, American actress, Apr 1957

Novak, Michael, American social philosopher and critic, Feb 1985

Novello, Antonia, American pediatrician and Surgeon general, May 1992

Novikov, Nikolai Vasil'evich, Feb 1947

Novogratz, Jacqueline, American investment organization official, Apr 2013

Novotna, Jarmila, Czech opera singer, Mar 1940, Obit Apr 1994

Novotny, Antonin, Czech president, May 1958, Obit Mar 1975

Nowitzki, Dirk, German basketball player, June 2002

Noyes, W. Albert, American chemist, Oct 1947

Noyes, William Albert, American chemist, Obit Yrbk 1941

Nozick, Robert, American political philosopher, June 1982, Obit Apr 2002

Nu, Burmese prime minister, Yrbk 1951, Obit Apr 1995

Nuckols, William P., May 1952

Nufer, Albert F., Mar 1955, Obit Jan 1957

Nuffield, William Richard Morris, British automobile executive, Apr 1941, Obit Oct 1963

Nugent, Elliott, July 1944, Obit Oct 1980

Nugent, Ted, American rock guitarist, Apr 2005

Nujoma, Sam, Namibian president, Feb 1990

Nunez Portuondo, Emilio, Apr 1957

Nunez, Elizabeth, Trinidadian novelist, Jan 2002

Nunn, Sam, American senator, Jan 1980

Nunn, Trevor, English theatrical director, Nov 1980

Nur el Hussein, Apr 1991

Nureyev, Rudolf, Russian ballet dancer, July 1963, Obit Feb 1993

Nuridsany, Claude, French documentary filmmaker, June 1997

Nuridsany, Claude; and Perennou, Marie, June 1997

Nutting, Anthony, British cabinet member, Feb 1955, Obit May 1999

Nutting, Wallace, American clergyman, photographer and furniture executive, Obit Sept 1941

Nwuneli, Ndidi O., Nigerian youth organization official, Jan 2007

Nyad, Diana, American swimmer and sportscaster, Aug 1979

Nyborg, Victor H., Feb 1954

Nye, Archibald E., Feb 1942, Obit Jan 1968

Nye, Bill, American comedian and television performer, July 1998

Nye, Gerald Prentice, American senator, Nov 1941, Obit Sept 1971

Nye, Russel Blaine, historian, July 1945, Obit Nov 1993

Nyerere, Julius K., Tanzanian president, Apr 1963, Obit Jan 2000

Nykvist, Sven, Swedish cinematographer, June 1989, Obit Yrbk 2007

Nylander, Olof O., Obit Sept 1943

Nyrop, Donald W., American airline executive, June 1952, Obit Yrbk 2011

Nystrom, Paul H., Mar 1951, Obit Oct 1969

N£¤ez, Francisco J., Feb 2013

O

O'Boyle, Patrick, July 1973, Obit Sept 1987

O'Brian, Hugh, actor, July 1958

O'Brian, Patrick, Irish novelist, June 1995, Obit Mar 2000

O'Brien, Bill, Aug 2013

O'Brien, Conan, American comedian and television talk show host, May 1996

O'Brien, Conor Cruise, Irish critic, historian and diplomat, Apr 1967

O'Brien, Dan, American decathlete, July 1996

O'Brien, Ed, English guitarist, June 2001

O'Brien, Edna, Irish novelist and short story writer, Sept 1980

O'Brien, Edward J., editor and critic, Obit Apr 1941

O'Brien, Lawrence F., American political party leader and basketball association executive, Nov 1961, Apr 1977, Obit Nov 1990

O'Brien, Leo W., June 1959, Obit July 1982

O'Brien, Pat, American actor, Mar 1966, Obit Jan 1984

O'Brien, Soledad, American television news anchor, Nov 2009

O'Brien, Tim, American novelist, Aug 1995

O'Byrne, Estella, Nov 1948

O'Casey, Sean, Irish dramatist, Nov 1962, Obit Nov 1964

O'Connell, Colm, Irish priest, school headmaster and track coach, Jan 2005

O'Connell, Hugh, Obit Mar 1943

O'Connell, William Henry, June 1941, *Obit* June 1944

O'Connor, Andrew, *Obit* Aug 1941

O'Connor, Basil, Sept 1944, *Obit* May 1972

O'Connor, Carroll, American actor, July 1972, *Obit* Sept 2001

O'Connor, Donald, American actor and dancer, May 1955, *Obit* Apr 2004

O'Connor, Edwin, American novelist and short story writer, Nov 1963, *Obit* May 1968

O'Connor, Flannery, American novelist and short story writer, Yrbk 1958, *Obit* Sept 1965

O'Connor, Frances, Australian actress, Jan 2002

O'Connor, James Francis, *Obit* Mar 1945

O'Connor, John Joseph, June 1984, *Obit* July 2000

O'Connor, Mark, American fiddler and composer, Sept 2013

O'Connor, Sandra Day, American Supreme Court justice, Jan 1982

O'Connor, Sinead, Irish singer, June 1991

O'Conor, Herbert R., Feb 1950, *Obit* May 1960

O'Daniel, W. Lee, American senator and governor, Oct 1947, *Obit* June 1969

O'Day, Anita, American jazz singer, June 1990, *Obit* Jan 2007

O'Day, Caroline Love Goodwin, American congresswoman, *Obit* Feb 1943

O'Donnell, E. P., *Obit* June 1943

O'Donnell, Emmett, general, July 1948, *Obit* Feb 1972

O'Donnell, Rosie, American comedienne, actress and talk show host, Aug 1995

O'Dwyer, Paul, American lawyer and municipal official, Sept 1969, *Obit* Sept 1998

O'Dwyer, William, American mayor, Sept 1941, May 1947, *Obit* Jan 1965

O'Faolain, Sean, Irish short story writer, novelist and biographer, Apr 1990, *Obit* June 1991

O'Flanagan, Michael, Irish priest and republican, *Obit* Sept 1942

O'Gorman, James A., *Obit* July 1943

O'Gorman, Juan, Mexican architect and painter, Nov 1956

O'Gorman, Patrick F., *Obit* Apr 1940

O'Hair, Madalyn Murray, American atheist, Jan 1977, *Obit* June 2001

O'Hara, John, American novelist and short story writer, Feb 1941, *Obit* June 1970

O'Hara, Kelli, American actress and singer, Oct 2008

O'Hara, Mary, author, Jan 1944, *Obit* Jan 1981

O'Hara, Maureen, Irish-American actress, Feb 1953

O'Horgan, Tom, American theatrical director and composer, Apr 1970, *Obit* Yrbk 2009

O'Keefe, Sean, American NASA official, Jan 2003

O'Keeffe, Georgia, American painter, June 1941, Feb 1964, *Obit* Apr 1986

O'Kelly, Sean T., July 1948, *Obit* Jan 1967

O'Konski, Alvin E., congressman, Nov 1955, *Obit* Aug 1987

O'Leary, Hazel R., American university president and former Secretary of energy, Jan 1994

O'Leary, James A., *Obit* May 1944

O'Mahoney, Joseph C., American senator, Oct 1945, *Obit* Jan 1963

O'Malley, Nick, British rock bassist, Jan 2006

O'Malley, Sean Patrick, Jan 2004

O'Malley, Walter Francis, American baseball executive, Mar 1954, *Obit* Oct 1979

O'Meara, Walter, author and advertising executive, Yrbk 1958, *Obit* Nov 1989

O'Melveny, Henry W., *Obit* June 1941

O'Neal, A. Daniel, June 1979

O'Neal, Edward A., banking executive, Sept 1946, *Obit* May 1958

O'Neal, Frederick, actor, Nov 1946, *Obit* Oct 1992

O'Neal, Jermaine, American basketball player, June 2004

O'Neal, Ryan, American actor, Feb 1973

O'Neal, Shaquille, American basketball player, July 1996

O'Neal, Stanley, American investment banker, May 2003

O'Neil, George, *Obit* July 1940

O'Neil, James F., Nov 1947, *Obit* Sept 1981

O'Neil, Thomas F., broadcasting executive, Nov 1955, *Obit* June 1998

O'Neill of the Maine, Terence Marne O'Neill, prime minister of Northern Ireland, Sept 1968, *Obit* Sept 1990

O'Neill, C. William, July 1958

O'Neill, Eugene F., American electronics engineer, Apr 1963

O'Neill, Francis Aloysius, labor mediator, Yrbk 1960, *Obit* Mar 1992

O'Neill, Gerard K., physicist, Feb 1979, *Obit* June 1992

O'Neill, J. E., June 1952

O'Neill, Jim, economist, Oct 2013

O'Neill, Joseph, American lawyer and novelist, June 2009

O'Neill, Paul Henry, American aluminum company executive and Secretary of the treasury, July 2001

O'Neill, Tip, American Speaker of the House, Apr 1974, *Obit* Mar 1994

O'Neill, William A., American governor, Feb 1985, *Obit* Yrbk 2008

O'Reilly, Bill, American television talk show host, Oct 2003

O'Shea, Milo, June 1982, *Obit* Yrbk 2013

O'Shea, William F., *Obit* Apr 1945

O'Sullivan, Ronnie, British snooker player, Apr 2013

O'Toole, Peter, Irish actor, Sept 1968

Oakes, Grant W., Jan 1950

Oates, Joyce Carol, American novelist, short story writer and poet, Sept 1970, June 1994

Obaid, Thoraya, Saudi Arabian United Nations official, Jan 2004

Obama, Barack, American president, July 2005, Mar 2009

Obama, Michelle, wife of American president Barack Obama, Oct 2008

Obando y Bravo, Miguel, Mar 1988

Obasanjo, Olusegun, Nigerian president, July 1999

Oberlin, Russell, opera singer, July 1960

Oberon, Merle, English actress, Nov 1941, *Obit* Jan 1980

Oberteuffer, George, *Obit* Jan 1940

Oberth, Hermann, German physicist and rocket engineer, Apr 1957, *Obit* Mar 1990

Obolensky, Serge, Oct 1959, *Obit* Nov 1978

Oboler, Arch, radio author and screenwriter, Mar 1940, *Obit* May 1987

Obote, A. Milton, Ugandan president, Apr 1981, *Obit* Yrbk 2006

Obraztsov, Sergei, Russian puppeteer, Nov 1964

Obraztsova, Elena, Russian opera singer, Feb 1983

Obst, Lynda Rosen, American motion picture producer, Oct 2000

Obuchi, Keizo, Japanese prime minister, May 1999, *Obit* Aug 2000

Occhilupo, Mark, Australian surfer, Jan 2002

Ochoa, Lorena, Mexican golfer, Jan 2007

Ochoa, Severo, Spanish-American biochemist, June 1962, *Obit* Jan 1994

Ochocinco, Chad, American football player, Aug 2009

Ochsner, Alton, surgeon, Oct 1966, *Obit* Nov 1981

Ocker, William C., *Obit* Nov 1942

Odell, George Clinton Densmore, Yrbk 1944, *Obit* Yrbk 1949

Odets, Clifford, American dramatist, Nov 1941, *Obit* Nov 1963

Odetta, American folk singer, Yrbk 1960, *Obit* Jan 2009

Odierno, Raymond, American general, Nov 2009

Odishaw, Hugh, scientific administrator, Feb 1971, *Obit* June 1984

Odlin, Reno, July 1965

Odlum, Floyd B., American financier, Nov 1941, *Obit* Aug 1976

Odom, Lamar, American basketball player, May 2009

Odria, Manuel Arturo, Peruvian president, Nov 1954, *Obit* Apr 1974

Oduber Quiros, Daniel, Costa Rican president, July 1977

Oe, Hikari, Japanese composer and son of Kenzaburo Oe, May 1999

Oe, Kenzaburo, Japanese novelist, May 1996

Oechsner, Frederick Cable, journalist and intelligence official, Mar 1943, *Obit* June 1992

Oenslager, Donald, Sept 1946, *Obit* Aug 1975

Oest, Paula van der, Dutch motion picture director, Jan 2003

Oettinger, Katherine B., government official and child welfare worker, Nov 1957, *Obit* Jan 1998

Offit, Paul A., American immunologist, Apr 2009

Ogata, Sadako, Japanese United Nations official and diplomat, Oct 1997

Ogburn, Charlton, Feb 1955, *Obit* Apr 1962

Ogburn, William Fielding, sociologist, Feb 1955, *Obit* July 1959

Ogden, C. K., English linguist, Jan 1944, *Obit* June 1957

Ogilvie, Elisabeth, American novelist, Yrbk 1951, *Obit* Yrbk 2007

Ogilvy, David, British advertising executive, July 1961, *Obit* Oct 1999

Ogilvy, Geoff, Australian golfer, Jan 2006

Oh, Sadaharu, Japanese baseball player, Jan 2002

Oh, Sandra, Canadian actress, Jan 2005

Ohga, Norio, Japanese electronics industry executive, June 1998, *Obit* Yrbk 2011

Ohira, Masayoshi, Japanese prime minister, Mar 1964, *Obit* Aug 1980

Ohlin, Lloyd E., American criminologist, Apr 1963, *Obit* Yrbk 2009

Ohlsson, Garrick, American pianist, June 1975

Ohlsson, Mikael, June 2013

Ohno, Apolo, American speed skater, Feb 2006

Oistrakh, David, Russian violinist, Mar 1956, *Obit* Yrbk 1974

Ojike, Mazi Mbonu, July 1947

Ojukwu, Chukwuemeka Odumegwu, Nigerian political leader and general, Feb 1969, *Obit* Yrbk 2012

Okayo, Margaret, Kenyan marathon runner, Jan 2004

Okereke-Onyiuke, Ndi, Nigerian stock exchange official, Jan 2005

Okolloh, Ory, Kenyan lawyer and blogger, May 2012

Okonedo, Sophie, British actress, Jan 2005

Okonjo-Iweala, Ngozi, Nigerian cabinet member, Jan 2006

Okonkwo, Festus, Nigerian general, Jan 2005

Okrent, Daniel, American newspaper editor, Nov 2004

Okun, Arthur M., American economist and presidential aide, Feb 1970, *Obit* May 1980

Olafur Eliasson, Icelandic artist, Jan 2007

Olajuwon, Hakeem, American basketball player, Nov 1993

Olav, Jan 1962, *Obit* Mar 1991

Olayan, Lubna, Saudi Arabian financial executive, Jan 2006

Olbermann, Keith, American television news anchor, Feb 2009

Oldenbroek, Jacobus H., Mar 1950

Oldenburg, Claes, Swedish-American sculptor, Feb 1970

Oldfield, Barney, American automobile racing driver, *Obit* Nov 1946

Oldman, Gary, English actor, Jan 1996

Olds, Irving S., American lawyer and steel industry executive, Oct 1948, *Obit* Apr 1963

Oleson, Lloyd F., June 1947

Olin, Lena, Swedish actress, June 2003

Oliphant, Mark, Australian physicist, Yrbk 1951, *Obit* Oct 2000

Oliphant, Patrick, Australian-American cartoonist, July 1991

Olitski, Jules, American painter, Oct 1969, *Obit* Yrbk 2007

Oliveira, Manoel de, Portuguese film director, Jan 2002

Oliver, Edna May, actress, *Obit* Jan 1943

Oliver, Garrett, American brewmaster, Nov 2008

Oliver, James A., Jan 1966, *Obit* May 1982

Oliver, Jamie, British chef and restaurateur, Jan 2005

Oliver, Lunsford E., Sept 1947

Oliver, Pam, American television sportscaster, July 2009

Olivero, Magda, Italian opera singer, Apr 1980

Olivetti, Adriano, Italian manufacturing executive, Jan 1959, *Obit* Apr 1960

Olivier, Laurence, English actor, June 1946, Jan 1979, *Obit* Sept 1989

Ollenhauer, Erich, Jan 1953, *Obit* Feb 1964

Ollila, Jorma, Finnish cellular telephone equipment industry executive, Aug 2002

Olmedo, Alex, Peruvian tennis player, Yrbk 1959

Olmert, Ehud, Israeli prime minister, Jan 2006

Olmos, Edward James, American actor, Aug 1992

Olmstead, A. T., *Obit* May 1945

Olmsted, Frederick Law, American landscape architect, June 1949, *Obit* Mar 1958

Olopade, Olufunmilayo, Nigerian-American oncologist, Sept 2006

Olsen twins, American actresses, Sept 2010

Olsen, Ashley, American actress and fashion designer, Sept 2010

Olsen, John; and Ogden, Harold, Sept 1940

Olsen, Kenneth H., American computer industry executive, *Obit* Yrbk 2011

Olsen, Mary Kate, American actress, Sept 2010

Olsen, Matthew, Director of the National Counterterrorism Center (NCTC), Aug 2012

Olsen, Ole, American comedian, Sept 1940, *Obit* Mar 1963

Olson, Harry Ferdinand, American acoustic engineer, Nov 1955, *Obit* June 1982

Olson, Theodore B., American lawyer and former Solicitor general, Nov 2010

Oltman, Florine, May 1970

Olvera, Fernando, Mexican singer and guitarist, Jan 2005

Omarion (Musician), American singer, Feb 2008

Omichinski, Linda, Canadian dietician, Jan 2004

Onassis, Aristotle Socrates, Greek-Argentine shipping executive, Mar 1963, *Obit* May 1975

Onassis, Christina, Greek shipping executive, Feb 1976, *Obit* Jan 1989

Onassis, Jacqueline Kennedy, wife of American president John F. Kennedy and Greek-Argentine shipping executive Aristotle Socrates Onassis, Oct 1961, *Obit* July 1994

Ondaatje, Michael, Canadian poet and novelist, Oct 1993

Ongania, Juan Carlos, Argentine president, Oct 1968, *Obit* Aug 1995

Ono, Yoko, Japanese artist, Nov 1972

Onsager, Lars, American chemist, Apr 1958, *Obit* Jan 1977

Onuki, Ami, Japanese pop singer, Jan 2005

Oort, Jan Hendrik, Dutch astrophysicist, June 1969, *Obit* Jan 1993

Oosterbaan, Bennie, football coach, Yrbk 1949, *Obit* Jan 1991

Opel, John R., computer executive, Mar 1986, *Obit* Yrbk 2012

Ophuls, Marcel, motion picture and television director, June 1977

Oppenheim, Chad, American architect, Sept 2006

Oppenheim, Edward Phillips, English mystery novelist, *Obit* Mar 1946

Oppenheimer, Franz, German sociologist and economist, *Obit* Nov 1943

Oppenheimer, Harry Frederick, South African diamond mining executive, Feb 1961, *Obit* Nov 2000

Oppenheimer, J. Robert, American physicist, Nov 1945, Apr 1964, *Obit* Apr 1967

Orbach, Jerry, American actor, May 1970, *Obit* Apr 2005

Orender, Donna, American basketball association executive, Sept 2010

Orff, Carl, German composer, Aug 1976, *Obit* May 1982

Origliasso, Jess, Australian singer, Jan 2006

Origliasso, Lisa, Australian singer, Jan 2006

Orlando, Vittorio Emanuele, Italian statesman, Feb 1944, *Obit* Jan 1953

Orlean, Susan, American writer, June 2003

Orlebar, Augustus H., *Obit* Sept 1943

Orlemanski, Stanislaw, Polish-American priest, June 1944

Orman, Suze, American financial adviser, May 2003

Ormandy, Eugene, conductor, Jan 1941, *Obit* May 1985

Ormond, Julia, English actress, Mar 1999

Ornish, Dean, American physician, Apr 1994

Orozco, Gabriel, Mexican conceptual artist, Jan 2004

Orozco, Jose Clemente, Mexican painter, Sept 1940, *Obit* Oct 1949

Orr, Bobby, Canadian hockey player, Nov 1969

Orr, H. Winnett, Oct 1941

Orr, Louis M., Apr 1960, *Obit* July 1961

Orri Pall Dyrason, Icelandic drummer, Jan 2003

Orsborn, Albert, Nov 1946, *Obit* Apr 1967

Ortega Gaona, Amancio, Spanish clothing retailer, Aug 2012

Ortega Saavedra, Daniel, Nicaraguan president, Oct 1984

Ortega, Kenny, American dancer, choreographer and director, Mar 2008

Ortiz Rocasolano, Letizia, Spanish television reporter and wife of Felipe, Prince of Spain, Jan 2004

Ortiz, David, Dominican-American baseball player, Aug 2005

Ortiz, Roberto M., *Obit* Sept 1942

Ortner, Sherry B., American anthropologist, Nov 2002

Orton, Helen Fuller, Jan 1941, *Obit* Apr 1955

Orville, Howard T., May 1956, *Obit* July 1960

Osama bin Laden, Saudi Arabian terrorist, *Obit* Yrbk 2012

Osato, Sono, Oct 1945

Osawa, Sandy Sunrising, American filmmaker, Jan 2001

Osborn, Fairfield, American naturalist and conservationist, Sept 1949, *Obit* Nov 1969

Osborn, Frederick Henry, railroad executive and investment banker, Nov 1941, *Obit* Mar 1981

Osborn, Robert, caricaturist, June 1959, *Obit* Feb 1995

Osborne, Barrie M., American motion picture producer, Feb 2005

Osborne, John, English dramatist, June 1959, *Obit* Feb 1995

Osborne, Oliver Thomas, *Obit* Yrbk 1940

Osborne, Tom, American university athletic director, Mar 1998

Osborne, William Hamilton, *Obit* Feb 1943

Osbourne, Ozzy, English singer, Nov 1998

Osbourne, Sharon, English musical talent agent and promoter, Jan 2001

Osgood, Charles E., psychologist, Apr 1962

Oshii, Mamoru, Japanese animator, Jan 2006

Oshiomhole, Adams, Nigerian labor leader, Jan 2005

Osman Ali, Oct 1948, *Obit* Apr 1967

Osmena, Sergio, Filipino president, Sept 1944, *Obit* Yrbk 1961

Osmond, Donny, American singer, Feb 1998

Ospina Perez, Mariano, Colombian president, Feb 1950, *Obit* June 1976

Osteen, Joel, American pastor and broadcasting executive, Jan 2006

Osumi, Mineo, *Obit* Apr 1941

Otero, Miguel Antonio, American territorial governor, *Obit* Sept 1944

Otis, Clarence, American restaurant chain executive, Oct 2009

Ott, Mel, American baseball player and manager, July 1941, *Obit* Jan 1959

Ottaviani, Alfredo, Yrbk 1966, *Obit* Sept 1979

Otter, Anne Sofie von, Swedish opera singer, Sept 1995

Ottinger, Nathan, *Obit* Jan 1941

Ottley, Roi, Oct 1943, *Obit* Yrbk 1960

Otto, Frei, German architect, Oct 1971

Otto, Miranda, Australian actress, Jan 2003

Otuken, Adnan, Turkish librarian, June 1954

Oudolf, Piet, Dutch landscape architect, Apr 2003

Ouedraogo, Idrissa, Burkinabe film director and screenwriter, May 1993

Ouma, Kassim, Ugandan boxer, June 2007

Oursler, Fulton, editor and author, Oct 1942, *Obit* July 1952

OutKast (Musical group), Apr 2004

Ovando Candia, Alfredo, Bolivian general and president, Mar 1970, *Obit* Mar 1982

Ovechkin, Alexander, Russian hockey player, June 2008

Overholser, Winfred, Nov 1953, *Obit* Yrbk 1964

Overman, Lynne, *Obit* Apr 1943

Overstreet, H. A., psychologist and philosopher, Sept 1950, *Obit* Oct 1970

Ovitz, Michael, American talent agent and motion picture executive, Oct 1995

Owen, A. David K., British economist, sociologist and United Nations official, May 1946, *Obit* Sept 1970

Owen, David, British political leader, Sept 1977

Owen, Ruth Bryan, American congresswoman, Yrbk 1944, *Obit* Oct 1954

Owen, Steve, football coach, Yrbk 1946, *Obit* July 1964

Owens, Clarence Julian, *Obit* Apr 1941

Owens, Jesse, American runner, Nov 1956, *Obit* May 1980

Owens, Robert Bowie, *Obit* Yrbk 1940

Owings, Nathaniel Alexander, architect, May 1971, *Obit* Aug 1984

Oxenham, John, English author and poet, *Obit* Mar 1941

Oxnam, G. Bromley, American bishop, Nov 1944, *Obit* Apr 1963

Oyeyemi, Helen, Nigerian-British novelist, Jan 2005

Oz, Amos, Israeli novelist, July 1983

Oz, Frank, puppeteer and motion picture director, Oct 1999

Oz, Mehmet C., American surgeon, Apr 2003

Ozal, Turgut, Turkish president, June 1985, *Obit* June 1993

Ozawa, Seiji, Japanese conductor, Feb 1968, July 1998

Ozbirn, Catharine Freeman, Jan 1962, *Obit* Mar 1974

Ozick, Cynthia, American novelist and short story writer, Aug 1983

Ozon, Francois, French film director, Jan 2003

Ozzie and Harriet, May 1949

P

Paabo, Svante, Swedish geneticist, Feb 2007

Paar, Jack, American television talk show host, Apr 1959, *Obit* Yrbk 2004

Paasikivi, Juho Kusti, Finnish president, May 1944, *Obit* Feb 1957

Pacciardi, Randolfo, Italian political leader, Mar 1944, *Obit* July 1991

Pace, Charles Ashford, *Obit* Feb 1941

Pace, Frank, American Secretary of the army, Feb 1950, *Obit* Feb 1988

Pace, Peter, American Marine corps general, June 2006

Pacelle, Wayne, American animal rights activist, Jan 2010

Pacheco de la Espriella, Abel, Costa Rican president, Jan 2002

Pacheco e Chaves, Joao, Nov 1954

Pacino, Al, American actor, July 1974

Packard, David, American computer industry executive, June 1969, *Obit* June 1996

Packard, Eleanor, Apr 1941, *Obit* June 1972

Packard, Frank Lucius, Canadian author, *Obit* Apr 1942

Packard, Vance, American journalist, Apr 1958, *Obit* Feb 1997

Packard, Winthrop, *Obit* May 1943

Packer, Fred L., July 1952, *Obit* Feb 1957

Packer, Kerry Francis Bullmore, Australian newspaper publisher, Jan 2004, *Obit* CB Int 2006

Packwood, Robert, American senator, Jan 1981

Pacquiao, Manny, Filipino boxer, Jan 2007

Paddleford, Clementine, American food writer, Feb 1958, *Obit* Jan 1968

Paddock, Charles W., sprinter, *Obit* Sept 1943

Paddon, Harry Locke, *Obit* Jan 1940

Paderewski, Ignace Jan, Polish pianist and statesman, *Obit* Aug 1941

Padilla Nervo, Luis, Yrbk 1946

Padilla, Ezequiel, Mexican diplomat, July 1942, *Obit* Oct 1971

Padover, Saul Kussiel, historian, Oct 1952, *Obit* Apr 1981

Paepcke, Walter Paul, Apr 1960

Page, Clarence, American columnist, Jan 2003

Page, Ellen, Canadian actress, May 2008

Page, Geraldine, actress, Nov 1953, *Obit* Aug 1987

Page, Greg, Australian singer and actor, Jan 2004

Page, Irvine H., physician, June 1966, *Obit* Aug 1991

Page, Joe, baseball player, Apr 1950, *Obit* June 1980

Page, Larry, American Internet search engine executive, Oct 2001

Page, Marie Danforth, *Obit* Mar 1940

Page, Patti, American singer, Sept 1965, *Obit* Yrbk 2013

Page, Robert Morris, physicist, Nov 1964, *Obit* July 1992

Page, Ruth, American ballet dancer and choreographer, June 1962, *Obit* July 1991

Pagels, Elaine H., American religion historian, Feb 1996

Paglia, Camille, American feminist writer and critic, Aug 1992

Pagnol, Marcel, French dramatist and motion picture director, Mar 1956, *Obit* June 1974

Pahlmann, William Carroll, American interior and industrial designer, Oct 1964, *Obit* Jan 1988

Pai, Chung-hsi, Nov 1942, *Obit* Feb 1967

Paige, Janis, actress and singer, Jan 1959

Paige, Rod, American Secretary of education, July 2001

Paige, Satchel, American baseball player, Sept 1952, *Obit* Aug 1982

Paik, Nam June, Korean video artist and composer, Mar 1983, *Obit* Yrbk 2006

Paine, Thomas Otten, aerospace executive and NASA official, Mar 1970, *Obit* July 1992

Painter, Nell Irvin, American historian, June 2010

Pais, Abraham, American physicist, Jan 1994, *Obit* Oct 2000

Paisley, Ian R. K., Irish clergyman and political leader, Jan 1971, June 1986

Pak, Se Ri, Korean golfer, Jan 1999

Pakula, Alan J., American film director and producer, June 1980, *Obit* Feb 1999

Palacio Gonzalez, Alfredo, Ecuadorian president, Jan 2005

Palade, George, American biologist, July 1967, *Obit* Yrbk 2008

Palance, Jack, American actor, Aug 1992, *Obit* Feb 2007

Palast, Greg, American journalist, June 2011

Palencia, Isabel de, Spanish diplomat and essayist, May 1941

Paleologue, Maurice, French diplomat, *Obit* Jan 1945

Paley, Grace, American short story writer and poet, Mar 1986, *Obit* Yrbk 2007

Paley, William S., American radio and television executive, Oct 1940, Yrbk 1951, *Obit* Jan 1991

Palin, Michael, English actor and screenwriter, Feb 2000

Palin, Sarah, American governor, Jan 2009

Pallett, Owen, Canadian singer and violinist, Jan 2007

Palme, Olof, Swedish prime minister, May 1970, *Obit* Apr 1986

Palmeiro, Rafael, Cuban-American baseball player, Aug 2001

Palmer, Albert DeForest, *Obit* Jan 1940

Palmer, Arnold, American golfer, Sept 1960

Palmer, Geoffrey, English actor, Jan 2006

Palmer, Hazel, June 1958

Palmer, James Lynwood, English painter, *Obit* Aug 1941

Palmer, Jim, American baseball player, May 1980

Palmer, John Leslie, English author and critic, *Obit* Sept 1944

Palmer, Lilli, German actress, May 1951, *Obit* Mar 1986

Palmer, Thomas Waverly, Mar 1949

Palmer, Violet, American basketball referee, Nov 2006

Palmieri, Eddie, American salsa pianist and band leader, June 1992

Paltrow, Gwyneth, American actress, Jan 2005

Pamuk, Orhan, Turkish novelist, Jan 2007

Panahi, Jafar, Iranian film director, Jan 2004

Pandit, Vijaya Lakshmi, Indian diplomat, Jan 1946, *Obit* Feb 1991

Pandit, Vikram S., American financial executive, June 2008

Panetta, Leon E., American Secretary of defense, June 1993

Panic, Milan, Yugoslav prime minister and drug industry executive, June 1993

Pannell, Anne Gary, Nov 1950

Panofsky, Wolfgang Kurt Hermann, American physicist, June 1970, *Obit* Yrbk 2007

Panov, Valery, Russian dancer, Oct 1974

Pant, Govind Ballabh, Indian cabinet member, Jan 1959, *Obit* May 1961

Pantaleoni, Helenka Adamowska, social welfare leader, Nov 1956, *Obit* Mar 1987

Pantani, Marco, Italian cyclist, Feb 1999

Panyushkin, Aleksandr S., Yrbk 1948, *Obit* Jan 1975

Papa Wemba, Congolese singer, Jan 2003

Papadopoulos, George, Greek army officer and president, Feb 1970, *Obit* Sept 1999

Papagos, Alexandros, Nov 1951, *Obit* Yrbk 1955

Papamichael, Phedon, Greek cinematographer, Sept 2012

Papandreou, Andreas, Greek prime minister, May 1970, Apr 1983, *Obit* Sept 1996

Papandreou, George, Greek political leader, Yrbk 1944, *Obit* Yrbk 1968

Papashvily, George, Georgian-American humorist and essayist, Mar 1945, *Obit* May 1978

Papashvily, George; and Papashvily, Helen, Mar 1945

Papashvily, Helen Waite, humorist and essayist, Mar 1945

Pape, Rene, German opera singer, Jan 2003

Pape, William Jamieson, American newspaper publisher, Jan 1940, *Obit* Mar 1961

Papen, Franz von, German diplomat, June 1941, *Obit* June 1969

Paper Rad (Group), Apr 2010

Papi, Gennaro, *Obit* Jan 1942

Papp, Joseph, American theatrical producer and director, May 1965, *Obit* Jan 1992

Paradis, Vanessa, French singer and actress, Jan 2004

Paradise, Nathaniel Burton, *Obit* June 1942

Parcells, Bill, American football coach, Apr 1991

Pardee, George C., *Obit* Oct 1941

Pareles, Jon, American music critic, Nov 2008

Pares, Bernard, English historian, Jan 1946, *Obit* May 1949

Paretsky, Sara, American mystery novelist, May 1992

Parizeau, Jacques, Canadian economist and political leader, July 1993

Park, Brad, Canadian hockey player, Nov 1976

Park, Chan-Wook, Korean screenwriter and film director, Jan 2004

Park, Chung Hee, Korean president, Jan 1969, *Obit* Jan 1980

Park, Geun Hye, Korean political leader, Jan 2007

Park, Ji-Sung, Korean soccer player, Apr 2010

Park, Linda Sue, American children's author, June 2002

Park, Merle, English ballet dancer, Sept 1974

Park, Rosemary, American college president, Jan 1964, *Obit* Yrbk 2004

Park, Thomas, zoologist, Jan 1963, *Obit* June 1992

Parke, William, *Obit* Sept 1941

Parkening, Christopher, American guitarist, Apr 1987

Parker, Alan, English motion picture director, Mar 1994

Parker, Barnett, *Obit* Oct 1941

Parker, Buddy, Yrbk 1955, *Obit* June 1982

Parker, Cola G., Sept 1956, *Obit* Sept 1962

Parker, Frank, tennis player, Sept 1948, *Obit* Oct 1997

Parker, Homer Cling, *Obit* July 1946

Parker, John J., American judge, Yrbk 1955, *Obit* May 1958

Parker, Karla V., Feb 1947

Parker, Louis N., English composer and dramatist, *Obit* Nov 1944

Parker, Mary-Louise, American actress, Apr 2006

Parker, Robert B., American mystery writer, Nov 1993, *Obit* Yrbk 2010

Parker, Robert M., American wine critic, May 2005

Parker, Roy H., Oct 1951

Parker, Sarah Jessica, American actress, Sept 1998

Parker, Tony, Belgian basketball player, Apr 2008

Parker, Trey, American actor, television scriptwriter, director, producer and animator, May 1998

Parker, Trey; and Stone, Matt, May 1998

Parkes, Henry Bamford, Mar 1954

Parkinson, C. Northcote, English historian, satirist, biographer and novelist, Yrbk 1960, *Obit* May 1993

Parkinson, Thomas I., Apr 1949, *Obit* Sept 1959

Parks, Bert, actor and television personality, Feb 1973, *Obit* Apr 1992

Parks, Gordon, American film director, photographer and novelist, Oct 1968, Oct 1992, *Obit* June 2006

Parks, Robert J., Feb 1968

Parks, Rosa, American civil rights activist, May 1989, *Obit* Jan 2006

Parks, Suzan-Lori, American dramatist, Apr 1999

Parma, V. Valta, *Obit* Nov 1941

Parnis, Mollie, fashion designer, May 1956, *Obit* Sept 1992

Parodi, Alexandre, French government official and diplomat, June 1946

Parr, Albert Eide, museum director and oceanographer, July 1942, *Obit* Sept 1991

Parran, Thomas J., American surgeon general, Aug 1940, *Obit* Apr 1968

Parri, Ferruccio, Nov 1945

Parrish, Maxfield, American illustrator and painter, Nov 1965, *Obit* Apr 1966

Parrish, Wayne W., American magazine and newspaper executive, Nov 1958

Parry, Albert, professor of Russian studies, Apr 1961, *Obit* July 1992

Parry, Richard Reed, Canadian instrumentalist, Jan 2007

Parseghian, Ara, football coach and sportscaster, Feb 1968

Parseval, August von, *Obit* Apr 1942

Parsons, Elsie Worthington Clews, anthropologist, *Obit* Feb 1942

Parsons, Estelle, American actress, Oct 1975

Parsons, Harriet, motion picture producer, Jan 1953, *Obit* Mar 1983

Parsons, Herbert Collins, *Obit* July 1941

Parsons, Jim, American actor, Sept 2013

Parsons, Louella, American gossip columnist, Oct 1940, *Obit* Oct 1973

Parsons, Richard D., American motion picture and broadcasting executive, Apr 2003

Parsons, Rose Peabody, feminist, Yrbk 1959, *Obit* June 1985

Parsons, Talcott, American sociologist, Jan 1961, *Obit* July 1979

Part, Arvo, Estonian composer, Feb 1995

Partch, Harry, American composer, Sept 1965, *Obit* Oct 1974

Parton, Dolly, American country singer and songwriter, Aug 1977

Partridge, Bernard, *Obit* Sept 1945

Partridge, Earle E., Apr 1955

Partridge, Eric, English lexicographer, Jan 1963, *Obit* July 1979

Partridge, Frank C., *Obit* Apr 1943

Pascal, Amy, American motion picture executive, Mar 2002

Pascal, Gabriel, Hungarian-British motion picture producer, Jan 1942, *Obit* Sept 1954

Pasolini, Pier Paolo, Italian poet, novelist, critic and film director, July 1970, *Obit* Jan 1976

Pasquel, Jorge, July 1946, *Obit* May 1955

Passman, Otto E., American congressman, Oct 1960, *Obit* Sept 1988

Passmore, George, English artist, June 2009

Pasternack, Josef, *Obit* Jan 1940

Pasternak, Boris Leonidovich, Russian poet and novelist, Feb 1959, *Obit* July 1960

Pastora Gomez, Eden, Nicaraguan political leader, July 1986

Pastore, John O., American senator, Apr 1953, *Obit* Yrbk 2000

Pastrana Borrero, Misael, Colombian president, July 1971, *Obit* Nov 1997

Pasvolsky, Leo, May 1945, *Obit* June 1953

Pataki, George, American governor, Apr 1996

Patch, Alexander McCarrell, American general, May 1943, *Obit* Jan 1946

Patchett, Ann, American novelist, Apr 2003

Pate, Martha B., college president, May 1947, *Obit* July 1983

Pate, Maurice, June 1951, *Obit* Mar 1965

Pate, Randolph McCall, general, Sept 1958, *Obit* Oct 1961

Pate, Walter L., Mar 1947, *Obit* June 1974

Patel, Vallabhbhai, Indian nationalist leader, Mar 1948, *Obit* Jan 1951

Paterno, Joe, American football coach, Feb 1984, *Obit* Yrbk 2012

Paterson, Chat, veterans' leader, Mar 1948, *Obit* May 1992

Paterson, David A., American governor, July 2008

Paterson, Katherine, American young adult author, Nov 1997

Patil, Pratibha, Indian president, Jan 2007

Patinkin, Mandy, American actor and singer, Jan 1999

Patino, Simon Iturri, Bolivian mining executive, Oct 1942, *Obit* May 1947

Patkar, Medha, Indian environmentalist, Jan 2004

Patman, Wright, American congressman, Feb 1946, *Obit* Apr 1976

Paton, Alan, South African novelist and biographer, June 1952, *Obit* May 1988

Paton, Stewart, *Obit* Mar 1942

Patri, Angelo, American school principal, Nov 1940, *Obit* Nov 1965

Patrick, Danica, American automobile racing driver, Oct 2005

Patrick, Deval L., American governor, May 2007

Patrick, Mary Mills, college president, *Obit* Mar 1940

Patrick, Mason Mathews, American general, *Obit* Mar 1942

Pattee, Alida Frances, *Obit* May 1942

Patten, Chris, British colonial governor and European Commission official, July 1993

Patterson, Alicia, American newspaper editor and publisher, Nov 1955, *Obit* Sept 1963

Patterson, Eleanor Medill, American newspaper editor and publisher, Nov 1940, *Obit* Sept 1948

Patterson, Ernest Minor, Oct 1949

Patterson, Floyd, American boxer, Oct 1960, *Obit* Yrbk 2007

Patterson, Francine, American psychologist and animal rights activist, Nov 2000

Patterson, Frederick D., American college president and veterinarian, June 1947, *Obit* June 1988

Patterson, Graham, Mar 1949, *Obit* Jan 1970

Patterson, John, American governor, Nov 1960

Patterson, Joseph Medill, American newspaper editor and publisher, Jan 1942, *Obit* June 1946

Patterson, P. J., Jamaican prime minister, Feb 1995

Patterson, Richard C., Oct 1946, *Obit* Yrbk 1966

Patterson, Robert Porter, American Secretary of war, Oct 1941, *Obit* Mar 1952

Patterson, W. A., June 1946, *Obit* Aug 1980

Patton, Frances Gray, short story writer and novelist, Yrbk 1955, *Obit* Sept 2000

Patton, George S., American general, Jan 1943, *Obit* Feb 1946

Patton, James George, American agricultural leader, Jan 1945, Feb 1966

Patton, Marguerite Courtwright, women's organization official, May 1950

Patton, Mel, June 1949

Patty, Sandi, American gospel singer, Feb 2004

Pau, Peter, Chinese cinematographer, Feb 2002

Pauker, Ana, Romanian diplomat and communist leader, Mar 1948

Paul, May 1947, *Obit* Apr 1964

Paul, Jan 1956, Nov 1963, *Obit* Sept 1978

Paul, Alice, American lawyer and feminist, Sept 1947, *Obit* Sept 1977

Paul, Chris, American basketball player, Nov 2009

Paul, Elliot, author, Feb 1940, *Obit* June 1958

Paul, Josephine Bay, American shipping executive and stockbroker, June 1957

Paul, Les, American guitarist, Aug 1987, *Obit* Yrbk 2009

Paul, Ron, American congressman, June 2008

Paul-Boncour, Joseph, French statesman, June 1945, *Obit* May 1972

Pauley, Edwin W., American petroleum executive, June 1945, *Obit* Sept 1981

Pauley, Jane, American television newscaster and talk show host, May 1980

Pauli, Wolfgang, German physicist, June 1946, *Obit* Mar 1959

Pauling, Linus C., American chemist, May 1949, Feb 1964, June 1994, *Obit* Oct 1994

Paulson, Henry M., American Secretary of the treasury, Sept 2002

Paulus, Diane, American theatrical director, May 2010

Pauly, D., Canadian fishery scientist, Jan 2003

Pausini, Laura, Italian singer, Jan 2007

Pavarotti, Luciano, Italian opera singer, June 1973, *Obit* Nov 2007

Pavelic, Ante, Croatian Nazi leader, Aug 1942, *Obit* Feb 1960

Pavle, Apr 1941, *Obit* Oct 1976

Pavolini, Paolo Emilio, *Obit* Nov 1942

Pawley, Edward, Mar 1946

Paxinou, Katina, Oct 1943, *Obit* Apr 1973

Paxman, Jeremy, British television reporter and interviewer, Jan 2007

Paxton, Robert, Mar 1959, *Obit* May 1980

Paxton, Tom, folk singer and composer, Sept 1982

Paxton, William McGregor, painter, *Obit* July 1941

Paya, Oswaldo, Cuban dissident, Jan 2003, *Obit* Yrbk 2012

Payne, Alexander, American motion picture director and screenwriter, Feb 2003

Payne, Frederick G., Yrbk 1952, *Obit* Aug 1978

Payne, Robert, English author, Yrbk 1947, *Obit* Apr 1983

Payne, Roger, marine biologist, June 1995

Payson, Joan Whitney, July 1972, *Obit* Nov 1975

Payton, John, American lawyer and civil rights activist, May 2010, *Obit* Yrbk 2012

Payton, Nicholas, American trumpet player, Sept 1999

Payton, Walter, American football player, Nov 1985, *Obit* Jan 2000

Paz Estenssoro, Victor, Bolivian president, May 1953, *Obit* Sept 2001

Paz, Hipolito J., Jan 1952

Paz, Octavio, Mexican poet and diplomat, June 1974, *Obit* July 1998

Peabody, Endicott, governor, Mar 1964, *Obit* Feb 1998

Peabody, Endicott, clergyman and school headmaster, May 1940, *Obit* Jan 1945

Peale, Mundy I., May 1956, *Obit* Jan 1973

Peale, Norman Vincent, American clergyman and inspirational writer, Jan 1946, Oct 1974, *Obit* Feb 1994

Peare, Catherine Owens, Yrbk 1959

Pearkes, George Randolph, Nov 1957

Pearl, Minnie, American comedienne, Nov 1992, *Obit* May 1996

Pearl, Raymond, American biologist, *Obit* Jan 1941

Pearlman, Edith, American short story writer and essayist, June 2011

Pearlstein, Philip, American painter, Feb 1973

Pears, Peter, English opera singer, July 1975, *Obit* May 1986

Pearson, C. C., Mar 1950

Pearson, Drew, American journalist, May 1941, *Obit* Nov 1969

Pearson, Drew; and Allen, Robert, May 1941

Pearson, Ian, British futurologist, Jan 2005

Pearson, Jay F. W., Yrbk 1953, *Obit* Oct 1965

Pearson, Lester Bowles, Canadian prime minister, Nov 1947, Nov 1963, *Obit* Feb 1973

Pearson, T. Gilbert, American ornithologist, *Obit* Oct 1943

Peart, Neil, Canadian drummer, Feb 2001

Pease, Charles G., *Obit* Yrbk 1941

Pease, Lute, political cartoonist and painter, July 1949, *Obit* Nov 1963

Peattie, Donald Culross, American naturalist, Oct 1940, *Obit* Jan 1965

Peavy, Jake, American baseball player, May 2010

Peccerelli, Fredy, Guatemalan forensic anthropologist, Jan 2004

Peck, Gregory, American actor, July 1947, Oct 1992, *Obit* Sept 2003

Peck, James L. H., Aug 1942

Peck, M. Scott, American psychiatrist and self-help writer, June 1991, *Obit* Yrbk 2005

Peck, Raoul, Haitian motion picture director and cabinet member, Jan 2002

Peckinpah, Sam, American motion picture director, May 1973, *Obit* Feb 1985

Peden, Katherine G., real estate broker and state official, May 1962

Peel, Roy V., Apr 1950

Peerce, Jan, opera singer, May 1942, *Obit* Feb 1985

Pegg, Dave, English bassist and singer, Sept 2005

Pegler, Westbrook, American columnist, Mar 1940, *Obit* Sept 1969

Pei, I. M., Chinese-American architect, May 1969, Mar 1990

Pei, Mario, linguist, Oct 1968, *Obit* May 1978

Peirce, Kimberly, American film director and screenwriter, Aug 2008

Peirce, Waldo, American painter, Yrbk 1944, *Obit* May 1970

Peiris, Malik, Sri Lankan microbiologist, Jan 2003

Peirse, R. E. C., Sept 1941, *Obit* Oct 1970

Peirsol, Aaron, American swimmer, June 2010

Peixotto, Ernest C., *Obit* Jan 1941

Pekar, Harvey, American comic book writer, Jan 2004, *Obit* Oct 2010

Peker, Recep, Sept 1947, *Obit* May 1950

Pele, Brazilian soccer player, Mar 1967

Peli, Oren, American film director and screenwriter, July 2013

Pelikan, Jaroslav Jan, American clergyman and religion historian, Sept 1987, *Obit* Yrbk 2006

Pell, Claiborne, American senator, Mar 1972, *Obit* Yrbk 2009

Pell, Edward Leigh, American clergyman and religious writer, *Obit* Aug 1943

Pella, Giuseppe, Nov 1953, *Obit* Aug 1981

Pellegrinetti, Ermenegildo, *Obit* May 1943

Pelletier, Wilfrid, Yrbk 1944, *Obit* June 1982

Pelley, John J., *Obit* Yrbk 1946

Pelley, Scott, American television news anchor, Aug 2011

Pelli, Cesar, American architect, Apr 1983

Pelosi, Nancy, American congresswoman and former Speaker of the House, Feb 2003

Pelosini, Paolo, Italian sculptor, Jan 2005

Pelt, Adrian, Feb 1948

Pelt, Jeremy, American jazz trumpet player, Feb 2009

Peltz, Mary Ellis, Apr 1954, *Obit* Jan 1982

Peltz, Nelson, American financier, Feb 2008

Pelzer, David J., American self-help writer and motivational speaker, Mar 2002

Pemberton, Brock, American theatrical producer and director, Jan 1945, *Obit* Mar 1950

Pemberton, John de J., American lawyer and civil rights activist, May 1969, *Obit* Yrbk 2010

Pena, Federico, American Secretary of transportation, Oct 1993

Pena, Pedro, *Obit* Sept 1943

Penaranda, Enrique, Bolivian president, Jan 1940

Penderecki, Krzysztof, Polish composer, June 1971

Pendergast, Tom, American political party leader, *Obit* Mar 1945

Pendleton, Clarence M., government official, Sept 1984, *Obit* July 1988

Pendleton, Moses, American dancer and choreographer, Sept 1989

Penfield, Wilder, Canadian surgeon, Nov 1955, July 1968, *Obit* June 1976

Peng Dehuai, Chinese general and communist leader, Yrbk 1951

Penn & Teller, American magicians, June 2000

Penn, Arthur, American film, theatrical and television director, Jan 1972, *Obit* Yrbk 2010

Penn, Arthur A., *Obit* Apr 1941

Penn, Irving, American photographer, Nov 1980, *Obit* Yrbk 2009

Penn, Sean, American actor and film director, June 1993

Pennario, Leonard, American pianist, Oct 1959

Pennebaker, James W., American social psychologist, Aug 2011

Pennel, John, pole vaulter, Nov 1963, *Obit* Jan 1994

Pennell, Joseph Stanley, author, Yrbk 1944

Penner, Joe, *Obit* Mar 1941

Penney, James Cash, retail executive, Yrbk 1947, *Obit* Mar 1971

Penney, William George Penney, English physicist, Feb 1953, *Obit* May 1991

Penniman, Josiah Harmer, *Obit* June 1941

Pennington, Chad, American football player, Oct 2009

Pennington, Ty, American carpenter and host of reality TV show Extreme makeover: Home edition, Feb 2006

Penrose, Roger, British mathematician, Sept 2013

Penzias, Arno Allan, American physicist, Sept 1985

Pepitone, Joe, baseball player, Jan 1973

Peppard, George, actor, Yrbk 1965, *Obit* July 1994

Pepper, Claude, American congressman, Feb 1941, Jan 1983, *Obit* July 1989

Pepperberg, Irene M., American ethologist, Sept 2008

Perahia, Murray, American pianist, Mar 1982

Percy, Charles H., American senator, Yrbk 1959, Aug 1977, *Obit* Yrbk 2011

Percy, Walker, American novelist, Sept 1976, *Obit* July 1990

Percy, William Alexander, American poet and lawyer, *Obit* Mar 1942

Perdue, Frank, American poultry industry executive, June 1979, *Obit* Oct 2005

Pereira, Irene Rice, American painter, Nov 1953, *Obit* Feb 1971

Pereira, William Leonard, architect, Jan 1979, *Obit* Jan 1986

Perelman, Grigori, Russian mathematician, Jan 2006

Perelman, Ronald Owen, American financier, Jan 1991

Perelman, S. J., humorist, Mar 1971, *Obit* Jan 1980

Perennou, Marie, French documentary filmmaker, June 1997

Perera, Frederica P., American epidemiologist, Oct 2010

Peres, Shimon, Israeli political leader, Jan 1976, Mar 1995

Peret, Raoul, *Obit* Sept 1942

Perez Esquivel, Adolfo, Argentine human rights activist, Mar 1981

Perez Jimenez, Marcos, Venezuelan president, Nov 1954, *Obit* Feb 2002

Perez de Cuellar, Javier, Peruvian diplomat and United Nations secretary-general, Aug 1982

Perez, Carlos Andres, Venezuelan president, Feb 1976, *Obit* Yrbk 2011

Perez, Louis, American drummer, Oct 2005

Perez, Rosie, American actress, dancer and choreographer, Sept 1995

Perino, Dana, American presidential press secretary, Jan 2008

Perkins, Anthony, American actor, Sept 1960, *Obit* Nov 1992

Perkins, C. H., June 1955, *Obit* Apr 1963

Perkins, Carl D., American congressman, Feb 1968, *Obit* Sept 1984

Perkins, Charles, Australian aborigine leader, Jan 1969, *Obit* Feb 2001

Perkins, Dexter, historian and educator, Jan 1958, *Obit* July 1984

Perkins, Elizabeth, American actress, Jan 2007

Perkins, Frances, American Secretary of labor, Yrbk 1940, *Obit* July 1965

Perkins, George Walbridge, Apr 1950, *Obit* Mar 1960

Perkins, James A., American college president, Apr 1964, *Obit* Nov 1998

Perkins, Marlin, zoo director and television performer, Oct 1951, *Obit* Aug 1986

Perkins, Milo, June 1942

Perla, David, Mar 1940

Perle, Richard Norman, American military official, July 2003

Perlman, Alfred E., railroad executive, Apr 1955, *Obit* July 1983

Perlman, Itzhak, American violinist, May 1975

Perlman, Philip B., American solicitor general, July 1952, *Obit* Oct 1960

Peron, Eva, wife of Argentine president Juan Domingo Peron, Mar 1949, *Obit* Sept 1952

Peron, Isabel, Argentine president, Jan 1975

Peron, Juan Domingo, Argentine president, June 1944, Feb 1974, *Obit* Feb 1974

Peroni, Carlo, *Obit* May 1944

Perot, Ross, American computer software executive and presidential candidate, July 1971, Yrbk 1996

Perret, Frank Alvord, *Obit* Mar 1943

Perrin, Francis, French physicist, July 1951

Perrin, Jacques, French actor, film producer, director and screenwriter, Jan 2004

Perrine, Valerie, actress, Oct 1975

Perry, Anne, English mystery novelist, Aug 1996

Perry, Antoinette, actress and theatrical director, *Obit* July 1946

Perry, Frank, motion picture director and producer, Oct 1972, *Obit* Nov 1995

Perry, Gaylord, American baseball player, Nov 1982

Perry, Harold, American bishop, Oct 1966, *Obit* Sept 1991

Perry, Joe, American rock guitarist, July 2004

Perry, Katy, American singer and songwriter, Jan 2012

Perry, Tyler, American playwright, screenwriter, actor and director, June 2005

Perry, William James, American Secretary of defense, Jan 1995

Persad-Bissessar, Kamla, Trinidadian prime minister, Jan 2013

Perse, Saint-John, French diplomat and poet, Apr 1961, *Obit* Nov 1975

Person, Houston, American saxophonist, June 2003

Persons, Wilton B., American general and presidential adviser, May 1953, *Obit* Nov 1977

Persson, Markus (Notch), Swedish computer programmer and game inventor, Sept 2013

Pertschuk, Michael, consumer activist and government official, Sept 1986

Perutz, Max, British biochemist, Nov 1963, *Obit* Apr 2002

Pervukhin, Mikhail G., Mar 1956, *Obit* Oct 1978

Pesci, Joe, American actor, Mar 1994

Petain, Henri Philippe, French field marshal, Aug 1940, *Obit* Sept 1951

Peter, Nov 1943, *Obit* Yrbk 1970

Peter, Luther Crouse, *Obit* Jan 1943

Peters, Bernadette, American actress and singer, Sept 1984

Peters, C. J., American epidemiologist and army officer, June 1997

Peters, Charles, periodical editor, Aug 1990

Peters, Le Roy S., *Obit* Feb 1942

Peters, Roberta, opera singer, Apr 1954

Peters, Thomas J., American management consultant and writer, Oct 1994

Petersen, Donald E., American automobile executive, Mar 1988

Petersen, Wolfgang, German motion picture director, July 2001

Peterson, Adrian, American football player, Mar 2012

Peterson, David Robert, Canadian political leader, Feb 1988

Peterson, Esther, American consumer rights advocate, Yrbk 1961, *Obit* Mar 1998

Peterson, F. Raymond, Feb 1950, *Obit* Feb 1978

Peterson, Martha Elizabeth, American college president, Feb 1969, *Obit* Yrbk 2006

Peterson, Oscar, Canadian pianist and composer, Oct 1983, *Obit* Yrbk 2008

Peterson, Peter G., American investment banker and Secretary of commerce, June 1972

Peterson, R. A., American banker, May 1964

Peterson, Reuben, *Obit* Jan 1943

Peterson, Roger Tory, American ornithologist and illustrator, Apr 1959, *Obit* Oct 1996

Peterson, Val, governor and presidential aide, June 1949, *Obit* Jan 1984

Peterson, Virgilia, Yrbk 1953, *Obit* Feb 1967

Pethick-Lawrence, Frederick William, British socialist leader, June 1946, *Obit* Nov 1961

Petit, Philippe, French aerialist, Sept 1988

Petit, Roland, French ballet dancer and choreographer, Apr 1952, *Obit* Yrbk 2011

Petitpierre, Max, Swiss president and diplomat, Yrbk 1953, *Obit* June 1994

Petraeus, David H., American general and intelligence official, Apr 2007

Petri, Egon, Dutch pianist, Nov 1942, *Obit* July 1962

Petrie, W. M. Flinders, English archaeologist, *Obit* Sept 1942

Petrillo, James C., American labor leader, Yrbk 1940, *Obit* Jan 1985

Petrini, Carlo, Italian food safety activist, Jan 2004

Petronio, Stephen, American dancer and choreographer, Mar 1998

Petrov, Evgenii, Russian humorist, *Obit* Aug 1942

Petrova, Nadia, Russian tennis player, Jan 2005

Petry, Ann Lane, American novelist, Mar 1946, *Obit* July 1997

Petry, Lucile, nursing educator and government official, Apr 1944, *Obit* June 2000

Petsche, Maurice, Nov 1949, *Obit* Nov 1951

Pettibon, Raymond, American artist, Apr 2005

Pettit, Bob, American basketball player, Oct 1961

Petty, Richard, American automobile racing driver, Aug 1980

Petty, Tom, American singer and guitarist, Nov 1991

Peurifoy, John Emil, American diplomat, Jan 1949, *Obit* Oct 1955

Pevear, Richard, American literary scholar and translator, June 2006

Pevsner, Antoine, Russian sculptor, Mar 1959, *Obit* June 1962

Pew, Joseph Newton, American petroleum industry executive and philanthropist, Sept 1941, *Obit* June 1963

Peynado, Jacinto B., *Obit* Mar 1940

Peyrouton, Marcel, Mar 1943

Peyroux, Madeleine, American singer, songwriter and guitarist, Nov 2005

Pfeiffer, Eckhard, German computer executive, June 1998

Pfeiffer, Jane, Oct 1980

Pfeiffer, Michelle, American actress, Mar 1990

Pflimlin, Pierre, French political leader, Nov 1955, *Obit* Oct 2000

Pfost, Gracie Bowers, congresswoman, May 1955, *Obit* Oct 1965

Pham, Van Dong, Vietnamese prime minister, Feb 1975, *Obit* Sept 2000

Pharrell, American record producer, singer and songwriter, May 2004

Phelan, Edward, Jan 1947

Phelan, Michael F., *Obit* Yrbk 1941

Phelps, Michael, American swimmer, Aug 2004

Phelps, William Lyon, literary scholar, Jan 1943

Philbin, Regis, American television talk show and game show host, Oct 1994

Philbrick, Herbert A., advertising executive and FBI informer, Mar 1953, *Obit* Oct 1993

Philip, Oct 1947

Philip, Andre, French economist and cabinet member, Aug 1943, *Obit* Sept 1970

Phillips, Albert, *Obit* Mar 1940

Phillips, Caryl, English novelist, dramatist and essayist, July 1994

Phillips, Frederick, *Obit* Oct 1943

Phillips, Harry Irving, American newspaper columnist and humorist, Sept 1943, *Obit* Apr 1965

Phillips, Irna, American radio and television scritpwriter and producer, Apr 1943, *Obit* Feb 1974

Phillips, John C., American governor and judge, *Obit* Aug 1943

Phillips, Kevin P., American political writer, Sept 1994

Phillips, Kyra, American television reporter, Jan 2013

Phillips, Lena Madesin, Apr 1946, *Obit* July 1955

Phillips, Morgan, British socialist leader, Sept 1949, *Obit* Feb 1963

Phillips, Ruth Schertz, Jan 1959

Phillips, Sam, American record producer, Apr 2001

Phillips, Scott, American drummer, May 2002

Phillips, Theodore Evelyn Reece, *Obit* July 1942

Phillips, Thomas Hal, Yrbk 1956

Phillips, Wendell, American explorer, archaeologist and petroleum industry executive, Nov 1958, *Obit* Feb 1976

Phillips, William, American periodical editor, Oct 1984, *Obit* Yrbk 2002

Phillips, William, American diplomat, July 1940, *Obit* Apr 1968

Phillips, Ze Barney Thorne, *Obit* July 1942

Phish (Musical group), July 2003

Phoenix (Musician), American bassist, Mar 2002

Pholien, Joseph, Feb 1951, *Obit* Mar 1968

Phoui Sananikone, Laotian prime minister, Sept 1959, *Obit* Feb 1984

Piaf, Edith, French singer, Yrbk 1950, *Obit* Nov 1963

Piaget, Jean, Swiss psychologist, Yrbk 1958, *Obit* Nov 1980

Piano, Renzo, Italian architect, Apr 2001

Piatigorsky, Gregor, Russian-American cellist, Oct 1945, *Obit* Sept 1976

Piazza, Mike, American baseball player, July 1999

Picard, Emile, *Obit* Feb 1942

Picard, Frank A., Mar 1947, *Obit* Apr 1963

Picasso, Pablo, Spanish painter, Jan 1943, Nov 1962, *Obit* May 1973

Picasso, Paloma, French jewelry and industrial designer and daughter of Pablo Picasso, Apr 1986

Piccard, Auguste, Swiss physicist, Sept 1947, *Obit* May 1962

Piccard, Auguste; and Piccard, Jean Felix, Sept 1947

Piccard, Bertrand, Swiss psychiatrist and balloonist, Jan 2004

Piccard, Jacques, Swiss oceanographer, Yrbk 1965, *Obit* Yrbk 2009

Piccard, Jean Felix, Sept 1947, *Obit* Mar 1963

Piccioni, Attilio, Oct 1967, *Obit* May 1976

Picciotto, Guy, American guitarist and songwriter, Mar 2002

Piccoli, Michel, French actor, Jan 2002

Pichot, Agustin, Argentine rugby player, Jan 2004

Pick, Behrendt, *Obit* July 1940

Pick, Lewis Andrew, American general and civil engineer, June 1946, *Obit* Feb 1957

Pick, Vernon J., Nov 1955

Picken, Mary Brooks, Yrbk 1954

Pickens, Jane, singer, Yrbk 1949, *Obit* Apr 1992

Pickens, T. Boone, American financier, July 1985

Pickerill, Elmo N., Mar 1966, *Obit* Mar 1968

Pickering, William H., American physicist, Nov 1958, *Obit* Yrbk 2004

Pickersgill, J. W., Canadian cabinet member, Mar 1968

Pickett, Clarence, June 1945, *Obit* May 1965

Pickford, Mary, American actress, Apr 1945, *Obit* July 1979

Picon, Molly, actress, June 1951, *Obit* June 1992

Pidgeon, Walter, actor, Sept 1942, *Obit* Nov 1984

Piech, Ferdinand, German automobile executive, Sept 1999

Pieck, Wilhelm, Yrbk 1949, *Obit* Nov 1960

Piel, Gerard, American magazine publisher and science writer, June 1959, *Obit* Feb 2005

Pierce, Bob, American evangelist, Yrbk 1961

Pierce, David Hyde, American actor, Apr 2001

Pierce, John Robinson, American electrical engineer, Feb 1961, *Obit* June 2002

Pierce, Lorne, Nov 1956

Pierce, Palmer Eddy, *Obit* Jan 1940

Pierce, Paul, American basketball player, Nov 2002

Pierce, Samuel R., American Secretary of housing and urban development, Nov 1982, *Obit* Feb 2001

Pierce, Wendell, American actor, Aug 2010

Piercy, Marge, American poet and novelist, Nov 1994

Pierlot, Hubert, Belgian prime minister, May 1943, *Obit* Feb 1964

Pierre, French abbot, Nov 1955

Pierson, Louise Randall, Oct 1943

Pierson, Warren Lee, June 1941, Nov 1954

Pifer, Alan J., American foundation official, Apr 1969, *Obit* Yrbk 2006

Pike, James Albert, American bishop, May 1957, *Obit* Nov 1969

Pike, Otis, American congressman, Feb 1976

Pike, Rosamund, British actress, Nov 2012

Pike, Sumner T., Mar 1947, *Obit* Apr 1976

Pilcher, Lewis F., *Obit* Aug 1941

Pile, Frederick Alfred, British general, Feb 1942, *Obit* Yrbk 1991

Pileggi, Nicholas, journalist and author, Jan 1999

Pilot, Sachin, Indian member of Parliament, Jan 2007

Pinault, Francois, French financier, Jan 2004

Pinay, Antoine, French political leader, Apr 1952, *Obit* Feb 1995

Pincay, Laffit, Panamanian jockey, Sept 2001

Pinchot, Gifford, American governor, forester and conservationist, *Obit* Nov 1946

Pincus, Gregory, American biologist, May 1966, *Obit* Oct 1967

Pincus, Mark, American computer software executive, Feb 2013

Pindling, Lynden Oscar, Bahamian prime minister, May 1968, *Obit* Yrbk 2000

Pine, David A., American judge, June 1952, *Obit* Sept 1970

Pine, William B., *Obit* Oct 1942

Pineau, Christian, French cabinet member, July 1956, *Obit* June 1995

Pinera, Sebastian, Chilean president, Nov 2010

Pinero, Jesus T., Oct 1946, *Obit* Jan 1953

Pinero, Miguel, American dramatist and actor, Nov 1983, *Obit* Aug 1988

Pingree, Chellie, American citizen advocacy organization official, Jan 2005

Piniella, Lou, American baseball player and manager, Aug 1986

Pinker, Steven, American psychologist, Sept 1998

Pinkerton, Kathrene Sutherland, American novelist, Jan 1940, *Obit* Yrbk 1967

Pinnock, Trevor, British harpsichordist and conductor, Sept 1989

Pinochet Ugarte, Augusto, Chilean general and president, Yrbk 1974, *Obit* Yrbk 2007

Pinsky, Drew, American physician and talk show host, Feb 2011

Pinsky, Robert, American poet, Feb 1999

Pinter, Harold, English dramatist, Nov 1963, *Obit* July 2009

Pintner, Rudolf, Anglo-American psychologist, *Obit* Jan 1943

Pinza, Ezio, Italian opera singer, Feb 1941, Yrbk 1953, *Obit* July 1957

Piot, Peter, Belgian public health official and epidemiologist, Jan 2004

Piotrovskii, Mikhail Borisovich, Russian museum director, Jan 2003

Piper, John, English painter, Apr 1964, *Obit* Aug 1992

Piper, W. T., American aircraft industry executive, Apr 1946, *Obit* Mar 1970

Pipher, Mary Bray, psychologist and author, Aug 1999

Pippen, Scottie, American basketball player, Mar 1994

Pippin, Horace, American painter, Aug 1945, *Obit* Yrbk 1947

Pire, Georges, Belgian priest, May 1959, *Obit* Mar 1969

Pires, Maria Joao, Portuguese pianist, Jan 2007

Pirie, John Taylor, *Obit* Mar 1940

Pisani, Elizabeth, American AIDS activist, Aug 2010

Piscator, Erwin, German theatrical director, Oct 1942, *Obit* Apr 1966

Piston, Walter, composer, June 1948, Yrbk 1961, *Obit* Jan 1977

Pitanguy, Ivo, Brazilian plastic surgeon, Jan 2004

Pitino, Rick, American basketball coach, Jan 1998

Pitkin, Walter B., author, Oct 1941, *Obit* Mar 1953

Pitt, Brad, American actor, Mar 1996

Pitt, Harvey L., American risk management consultant, Nov 2002

Pittman, Bob, American television and online computer services executive, July 2000

Pittman, Key, American senator, *Obit* Yrbk 1940

Pittman, Steuart L., American government official, Jan 1963, *Obit* Yrbk 2013

Pitts, Leonard J., American newspaper columnist, Oct 2004

Pitzer, Kenneth Sanborn, chemist, May 1950

Pius, Apr 1941, Mar 1950, *Obit* Yrbk 1958

Pivot, Bernard, French television talk show host, Oct 1990

Pla y Deniel, Enrique, Feb 1955, *Obit* Sept 1968

Plaek Phibunsongkhram, Thai prime minister, Sept 1951, *Obit* Sept 1964

Plain, Belva, American novelist, Feb 1999, *Obit* Yrbk 2010

Plaisted, Frederick William, *Obit* Apr 1943

Plant, Robert, British singer, Oct 1998

Plantinga, Alvin, Plantinga, Alvin C(arl) (1932-), Nov 2013

Plaskett, John S., Canadian astronomer, *Obit* Yrbk 1941

Plastiras, Nicholas, May 1950, *Obit* Oct 1953

Plater-Zyberk, Elizabeth, American architect and urban planner, Jan 2006

Plavsic, Biljana, Bosnian Serb political leader, Feb 1998

Player, Gary, South African golfer, Nov 1961

Player, Ian, South African conservationist, Jan 2002

Plaza Lasso, Galo, Ecuadorian president, Oct 1951, Apr 1969, *Obit* Mar 1987

Pleasence, Donald, English actor, June 1969, *Obit* Apr 1995

Plesman, Albert, Mar 1953, *Obit* Mar 1954

Pleven, Rene, French political leader, June 1950, *Obit* Mar 1993

Plimpton, George, American essayist, sportswriter and periodical editor, Feb 1969, *Obit* Jan 2004

Plimpton, Martha, American actress, Apr 2002

Plisetskaya, Maya, Russian ballet dancer, June 1963

Plotkin, Mark, American ethnobotanist, June 1997

Plouffe, David, American presidential adviser, June 2009

Plowden, David, photographer, Feb 1996

Plowden, Edwin, July 1947

Plowright, Joan, English actress, Feb 1964

Plumley, H. Ladd, Apr 1963

Plummer, Christopher, Canadian actor, July 1956, Aug 1988

Plunkett, Jim, American football player, Sept 1971, Feb 1982

Plushenko, Evgeni, Russian figure skater, Jan 2007

Poage, W. R., American congressman, Yrbk 1969, *Obit* Mar 1987

Podesta, John, American public policy organization official and former presidential adviser, Feb 2010

Podgorny, Nikolai V., Soviet president, May 1966, *Obit* Mar 1983

Podhoretz, Norman, American magazine editor and political commentator, Oct 1968

Podles, Ewa, Polish opera singer, Jan 2006

Poehler, Amy, American comedienne and actress, Aug 2008

Pogorelich, Ivo, Yugoslav pianist, Sept 1988

Pogrebin, Letty Cottin, journalist and feminist, Nov 1997

Pohamba, Hifkepunye, Namibian president, Jan 2006

Poindexter, John M., American admiral and presidential adviser, Nov 1987

Poindexter, Joseph B., Jan 1942, *Obit* Jan 1952

Poindexter, Miles, *Obit* Nov 1946

Poinso-Chapuis, Germaine, French feminist, June 1948

Poiret, Paul, French fashion designer, *Obit* June 1944

Poitier, Sidney, American actor and film director, May 1959, Sept 2000

Pol Pot, Cambodian political leader, Apr 1980, *Obit* June 1998

Polanski, Roman, Polish film director, June 1969

Polese, Kim, American computer software executive, July 1997

Poletti, Charles, American lieutenant governor and acting governor, *Obit* Yrbk 2002

Poletti, Charles E., Sept 1943

Polgar, Susan, Hungarian chess player, Feb 2008

Poliakov, Aleksandr, *Obit* Nov 1942

Poling, Daniel A., Nov 1943, *Obit* Mar 1968

Politis, Athanase G., Sept 1950, *Obit* June 1968

Politis, Nicolas, *Obit* Apr 1942

Polivka, Galen, American bassist, Sept 2010

Pollack, Jack Harrison, American journalist, Yrbk 1957, *Obit* Feb 1985

Pollack, Sydney, American motion picture director, Sept 1986, *Obit* Sept 2008

Pollain, Rene, *Obit* Yrbk 1940

Pollan, Michael, American nature writer and magazine editor, Oct 2007

Pollard, William G., Mar 1953

Polley, Sarah, Canadian actress and film director, Jan 2003

Pollini, Maurizio, Italian pianist, Nov 1980

Pollitt, Harry, British communist leader, May 1948, *Obit* Sept 1960

Pollitt, Katha, American poet and essayist, Oct 2002

Pollock, Allan, *Obit* Apr 1942

Pollock, Channing, dramatist, *Obit* Oct 1946

Pollock, Jackson, American painter, Apr 1956

Polunin, Slava, Russian clown, Jan 2004

Polyansky, Dmitry S., Soviet communist leader, Mar 1971

Pomeroy, Wardell Baxter, sex researcher, July 1974, *Obit* Yrbk 2001

Pompidou, Georges, French president, Nov 1962, *Obit* May 1974

Ponce, Enrique, Spanish bullfighter, Jan 2003

Poncins, Gontran de, French travel writer, June 1941

Ponnamperuma, Cyril, chemist, Apr 1984, *Obit* Mar 1995

Ponnelle, Jean-Pierre, French scenic designer and opera director, Mar 1983, *Obit* Sept 1988

Pons, Lily, French opera singer, Jan 1944, *Obit* Apr 1976

Pool, Joe, American congressman, Mar 1967, *Obit* Sept 1968

Poole, Dewitt C., Nov 1950, *Obit* Oct 1952

Poole, Franklin Osborne, *Obit* Mar 1943

Poole, Lynn, Yrbk 1954, *Obit* June 1969

Poon Tip, Bruce, Canadian adventure travel company founder, Jan 2006

Poor, Henry Varnum, American ceramist and painter, Apr 1942, *Obit* Jan 1971

Poore, Henry Rankin, *Obit* Oct 1940

Pop, Iggy, American singer and songwriter, Jan 1995

Popcorn, Faith, American market research executive, Feb 1993

Pope, Arthur Upham, American archaeologist and historian, July 1947, *Obit* Nov 1969

Pope, Liston, Apr 1956, *Obit* June 1974

Popeil, Ron, American kitchen utensil inventor, Mar 2001

Popenoe, Paul Bowman, American eugenicist, Yrbk 1946

Popkin, Zelda F., author, Yrbk 1951, *Obit* July 1983

Popov, Oleg, Russian clown, Mar 1964

Popovic, Koca, Yugoslav cabinet member, Jan 1957, *Obit* Jan 1993

Popovic, Vladimir, Feb 1952, *Obit* May 1972

Popper, John, singer and harpist, Jan 2012

Popper, Karl Raimund, Austrian-British philosopher, Jan 1963, *Obit* Nov 1994

Porras, Belisario, Panamanian president, *Obit* Oct 1942

Portal of Hungerford, Charles Frederick Algernon Portal, British air marshal, Mar 1941, *Obit* June 1971

Porter, Charles O., Sept 1957

Porter, Cole, American composer and lyricist, July 1940, *Obit* Yrbk 1964

Porter, Edwin S., American film director and producer, *Obit* June 1941

Porter, Eliot, American photographer, Nov 1976, *Obit* Jan 1991

Porter, Elizabeth K., Oct 1952

Porter, Katherine Anne, American short story writer, May 1940, Mar 1963, *Obit* Nov 1980

Porter, Paul A., American regulatory agency official, Jan 1945, *Obit* Jan 1976

Porter, Richard W., electrical engineer and NASA official, Nov 1958, *Obit* Jan 1997

Porter, Sylvia Field, financial columnist, Oct 1941, Apr 1980, *Obit* Aug 1991

Porter, William James, diplomat, Mar 1974, *Obit* May 1988

Porter, William N., Aug 1945, *Obit* Apr 1973

Portinari, Candido, Brazilian painter, Yrbk 1940, *Obit* Mar 1962

Portman, Eric, Mar 1957, *Obit* Feb 1970

Portuondo, Omara, Cuban singer, Jan 2005

Posen, Zac, American fashion designer, July 2006

Posey, Parker, American actress, Mar 2003

Posner, Richard A., American judge, Jan 1993

Possuelo, Sydney, Brazilian government official and human rights activist, Jan 2006

Post, Emily, American advice columnist, Mar 1941, *Obit* Nov 1960

Post, Robert P., *Obit* Sept 1943

Post, William Stone, *Obit* Sept 1940

Poston, Tom, American actor, Apr 1961, *Obit* Yrbk 2007

Potanin, Vladimir O., Russian metal industry executive and banker, Jan 2006

Pote Sarasin, Yrbk 1955

Potemkin, Vladimir P., *Obit* Apr 1946

Potente, Franka, German actress, Jan 2003

Potofsky, Jacob S., American labor leader, Oct 1946, *Obit* Sept 1979

Potok, Chaim, American novelist and historian, May 1983, *Obit* Yrbk 2002

Potro, Juan Martin del, Argentine tennis player, May 2010

Potter, Alfred Claghorn, *Obit* Yrbk 1940

Potter, Beatrix, English children's author and illustrator, *Obit* Mar 1944

Potter, Charles E., American senator, Yrbk 1954

Potter, Dan, Feb 1964

Potter, Dennis, English novelist, playwright and screenwriter, July 1994, *Obit* July 1994

Potter, Michael U., Canadian computer software executive, Jan 2005

Potter, Myrtle, American biotechnology executive, Aug 2004

Potter, William Everett, American general, Yrbk 1957, *Obit* Feb 1989

Potvin, Denis, American hockey player, Oct 1986

Poujade, Pierre, French political leader, Apr 1956, *Obit* Yrbk 2004

Poullain, Frankie, British rock bassist, Jan 2004

Poulsen, Valdemar, Danish inventor and electrical engineer, *Obit* Sept 1942

Poulton, Edward Bagnall, *Obit* Jan 1944

Pound, Dudley, Jan 1941, *Obit* Yrbk 1943

Pound, Ezra, American poet and literary critic, Nov 1942, May 1963, *Obit* Yrbk 1972

Pound, Roscoe, American law professor, May 1947, *Obit* Sept 1964

Pourtales, Guy de, *Obit* Aug 1941

Pousette-Dart, Richard, painter, Mar 1976, *Obit* Jan 1993

Poussaint, Alvin F., psychiatrist, July 1973

Powdermaker, Hortense, American anthropologist, Feb 1961, *Obit* Sept 1970

Powell, Adam Clayton, American congressman, Apr 1942, *Obit* May 1972

Powell, Anthony, English novelist, Sept 1977, *Obit* Aug 2000

Powell, Benjamin Edward, librarian, June 1959

Powell, Colin L., American Secretary of state, June 1988, Nov 2001

Powell, Dick, American actor, director and producer, Feb 1948, *Obit* Feb 1963

Powell, Enoch, British member of Parliament, Nov 1964, *Obit* June 1999

Powell, Eve Troutt, American historian, May 2004

Powell, Jane, American singer and actress, Yrbk 1974

Powell, Jody, American presidential press secretary, July 1977, *Obit* Yrbk 2009

Powell, Kevin, American journalist, poet and essayist, Jan 2004

Powell, Lawrence Clark, librarian, biographer, novelist and critic, June 1960

Powell, Lewis F., American Supreme Court justice, Feb 1965, *Obit* Nov 1998

Powell, Michael, British screenwriter, film director and producer, Aug 1987, *Obit* Apr 1990

Powell, Michael, American regulatory official and son of Secretary of state Colin L. Powell, May 2003

Powell, Mike, American long jumper, Oct 1993

Powell, Sandy, English costume designer, June 2000

Powell, William, American actor, Oct 1947, *Obit* May 1984

Power, D'Arcy, *Obit* July 1941

Power, Donald C., Mar 1960, *Obit* May 1979

Power, Samantha, American human rights activist, Aug 2008

Power, Thomas S., American air force general, Apr 1958, *Obit* Jan 1971

Power, Tyrone, American actor, Yrbk 1950, *Obit* Jan 1959

Powers, Bertram A., American labor leader, Jan 1974

Powers, J. F., short story writer and novelist, Jan 1989, *Obit* Sept 1999

Powers, James E., June 1963

Powers, James T., American actor, *Obit* Mar 1943

Powers, John Robert, June 1945, *Obit* Sept 1977

Powers, Marie, Jan 1951, *Obit* Feb 1974

Powys, Llewelyn, English author, Jan 1940

Pozner, Vladimir, Russian journalist, May 1943

Pozsgay, Imre, Hungarian communist leader, Mar 1990

Prada, Miuccia, Italian fashion designer, Feb 2006

Prado Ugarteche, Manuel, Peruvian president, June 1942, *Obit* Oct 1967

Prado, Edgar, Peruvian jockey, Sept 2007

Praeger, Frederick A., American publishing executive, Sept 1959, *Obit* Aug 1994

Prajadhipok, *Obit* July 1941

Prall, David Wight, *Obit* Yrbk 1940

Prasad, Rajendra, Apr 1950, *Obit* Apr 1963

Pratt, E. J., Canadian poet, Oct 1946, *Obit* June 1964

Pratt, Fletcher, journalist, historian and author, May 1942, *Obit* Sept 1956

Pratt, Frederic Bayley, American college president, *Obit* June 1945

Pratt, J. Gaither, Nov 1964

Pratt, Jane, American magazine editor and talk show host, June 1999

Pratt, William Veazie, June 1943, *Obit* Feb 1958

Prebisch, Raul, Argentine economist, Yrbk 1969, *Obit* July 1986

Prellwitz, Henry, *Obit* Apr 1940

Preminger, Otto, American film director, July 1959, *Obit* June 1986

Premji, Azim Hasham, Indian information technology executive, Jan 2004

Prendergast, John, American human rights activist, Jan 2012

Prentis, Henning Webb, Sept 1940, *Obit* Feb 1960

Prentiss, Henrietta, *Obit* Jan 1940

Prescott, Orville, literary critic, Mar 1957, *Obit* July 1996

Prescott, Robert W., July 1971

Presley, Elvis, American singer, Sept 1959, *Obit* Oct 1977

Presley, Priscilla Beaulieu, American actress, Sept 1990

Press, Frank, American geophysicist and presidential adviser, July 1966

Pressel, Morgan, American golfer, Nov 2007

Presser, Jackie, labor leader, Sept 1983, *Obit* Aug 1988

Pressler, Larry, senator, Oct 1983

Pressman, Edward, American film producer, Feb 2011

Pressman, Lee, American labor lawyer, May 1947, *Obit* Jan 1970

Preston, Robert, American actor, Yrbk 1958, *Obit* May 1987

Prestopino, Gregorio, painter, June 1964, *Obit* Apr 1985

Preus, Jacob A. O., clergyman and church official, May 1975, *Obit* Oct 1994

Preval, Rene, Haitian president, Jan 2006

Previn, Andre, American composer and conductor, May 1972

Previn, Dory, singer and songwriter, Sept 1975, *Obit* Yrbk 2012

Prevost, Marcel, French novelist and playwright, *Obit* June 1941

Prey, Hermann, German opera singer, Feb 1975, *Obit* Oct 1998

Prezan, Constantin, *Obit* Oct 1943

Pribichevich, Stoyan, Aug 1944, *Obit* July 1976

Price, Byron, journalist and United Nations official, Feb 1942, *Obit* Sept 1981

Price, Charles C., chemist, Yrbk 1957

Price, Don Krasher, American political scientist and college dean, Feb 1967, *Obit* Sept 1995

Price, George C., Belizean prime minister, Aug 1984, *Obit* Yrbk 2012

Price, Gwilym A., American electrical generating equipment company executive, May 1949, *Obit* Aug 1985

Price, Harrison J., American general, *Obit* Oct 1945

Price, Leontyne, American opera singer, May 1961, Oct 1978

Price, Lisa, American personal care products company founder, Feb 2011

Price, Margaret, Welsh opera singer, Aug 1986, *Obit* Yrbk 2011

Price, Nick, Zimbabwean golfer, June 1996

Price, Reynolds, American novelist and short story writer, Apr 1987, *Obit* Yrbk 2011

Price, Richard, American novelist and screenwriter, Jan 1994

Price, Vincent, American actor, Nov 1956, *Obit* Jan 1994

Pride, Alfred Melville, admiral, Nov 1954, *Obit* Feb 1989

Pride, Charley, American country singer, Apr 1975

Priebus, Reince, American political party leader, May 2012

Priest, Ivy Baker, Nov 1952, *Obit* Aug 1975

Priest, J. Percy, Sept 1950, *Obit* Yrbk 1956

Priestley, J. B., English novelist and dramatist, May 1976, *Obit* Oct 1984

Prieto, Dafnis, Cuban drummer, Oct 2012

Prieto, Rodrigo, Mexican cinematographer, Jan 2003

Prigogine, Ilya, Russian-Belgian chemist, Feb 1987, *Obit* Yrbk 2003

Primakov, Yevgeny M., Russian prime minister, Feb 1999

Primrose, William, violist, Yrbk 1946, *Obit* July 1982

Primus, Pearl, American dancer and choreographer, Apr 1944, *Obit* Jan 1995

Prince, American singer and songwriter, Feb 1986

Prince, Charles O., American financial services executive, Jan 2007

Prince, Hal, theatrical producer and director, Apr 1971

Prince, John Dyneley, *Obit* Nov 1945

Prince-Hughes, Dawn, American anthropologist, Apr 2005

Prinz, Birgit, German soccer player, Jan 2005

Prinz, Joachim, German-American rabbi and civil rights leader, Feb 1963, *Obit* Nov 1988

Prinze, Freddie, American comedian, June 1975, *Obit* Mar 1977

Prinze, Freddie, American actor, Jan 2003

Prio Socarras, Carlos, Cuban president, May 1949, *Obit* June 1977

Pritchard, Stuart, *Obit* Sept 1940

Pritchett, V. S., English short story writer, novelist and critic, Jan 1974, *Obit* June 1997

Procope, Hjalman Johan Fredrik, Apr 1940, *Obit* Apr 1954

Prodi, Romano, Italian prime minister, Jan 2006

Prodigy (Musical group), Oct 2009

Proesch, Gilbert, English artist, June 2009

Profet, Margie, biologist, Nov 1998

Profumo, John D., British cabinet member, Oct 1959, *Obit* June 2006

Prokhorov, Mikhail, Russian financier, Oct 2010

Prokofiev, Sergey, Russian composer, Nov 1941, *Obit* Apr 1953

Pronk, Johannes Pieter, Dutch United Nations official, Jan 2005

Prosper, Pierre-Richard, American lawyer and diplomat, Aug 2005

Protess, David, American journalist and social activist, Oct 1999

Proulx, Annie, American novelist and short story writer, Apr 1995

Prouty, Winston L., American senator, July 1960, *Obit* Oct 1971

Proxmire, William, American senator, June 1958, Aug 1978, *Obit* Mar 2006

Pruden, Edward Hughes, clergyman, Sept 1950

Prusiner, Stanley, American neurologist, June 1997

Pryor, Arthur, trombonist, *Obit* Aug 1942

Pryor, Richard, American comedian, Feb 1976, *Obit* Apr 2006

Pucci, Emilio, Italian fashion designer, Feb 1961, *Obit* Jan 1993

Pucheu, Pierre Firmin, French steel executive and government official, *Obit* May 1944

Puck, Wolfgang, Austrian-American restaurateur and chef, Jan 1998

Puckett, B. Earl, Sept 1950, *Obit* Apr 1976

Puente, Tito, American band leader, composer and percussionist, Nov 1977, *Obit* Aug 2000

Pueyrredon, Honorio, *Obit* Oct 1945

Puffy AmiYumi (Musical group), Jan 2005

Pugacheva, Alla, Russian singer, Jan 2004

Pugh, Herbert Lamont, Mar 1951

Pugmire, Ernest I., Apr 1945, *Obit* Sept 1953

Puig, Manuel, Argentine novelist, Jan 1988, *Obit* Sept 1990

Pujols, Albert, Dominican-American baseball player, Sept 2004

Pulitzer, Joseph, American newspaper editor and publisher, Yrbk 1954, *Obit* May 1955

Pullman, Philip, English fantasy writer, Jan 2003

Punisher (Musician), Finnish bassist, Jan 2003

Purcell, Edward M., American physicist, Sept 1954, *Obit* May 1997

Purdie, Bernard, American drummer, Jan 2010

Purtell, William A., June 1956, *Obit* July 1978

Puryear, Martin, American sculptor, Aug 1999

Pusey, Merlo J., newspaper editor and biographer, July 1952, *Obit* Jan 1986

Pusey, Nathan Marsh, American college president, Yrbk 1953, *Obit* Feb 2002

Pusey, William Allen, *Obit* Oct 1940

Putin, Vladimir, Russian prime minister, Apr 2000, Jan 2002

Putnam, Ashley, Mar 1982

Putnam, Claude Adams, Feb 1950

Putnam, James William, *Obit* Mar 1940

Putnam, Roger Lowell, Jan 1952

Putnam, Thomas M., *Obit* Nov 1942

Putt, Donald L., May 1960

Puttnam, David, English motion picture producer, Feb 1989

Puzo, Mario, American novelist and screenwriter, Mar 1975, *Obit* Sept 1999

Pyle, Ernie, American journalist, Apr 1941, *Obit* May 1945

Pyle, Howard, American governor and presidential aide, Nov 1955, *Obit* Jan 1988

Pym, Francis, British cabinet member, Sept 1982, *Obit* Yrbk 2008

Pynchon, Thomas, American novelist, Oct 1987

P,pin, Jacques, French-American chef and cookbook writer, Sept 2012

Q

Qabus bin Said, Aug 1978

Qaddafi, Muammar al-, Libyan dictator, Sept 1973, Mar 1992, *Obit* Yrbk 2011

Qassim, Abdul Karim, Iraqi general and prime minister, Nov 1959, *Obit* Mar 1963

Quadros, Janio, Brazilian mayor and president, June 1961, *Obit* Apr 1992

Quaison-Sackey, Alex, Ghanaian United Nations official and diplomat, Mar 1966, *Obit* Feb 1993

Quant, Mary, English fashion designer, Jan 1968

Quarles, Donald A., American Secretary of the air force, Nov 1955, *Obit* July 1959

Quarshie, Hugh, Ghanaian-British actor, Jan 2004

Quasimodo, Salvatore, Italian poet, Mar 1960, *Obit* Sept 1968

Quasthoff, Thomas, German classical singer, Jan 2005

Quayle, Anthony, English actor and theatrical director, Yrbk 1971, *Obit* Jan 1990

Quayle, Dan, American vice-president, June 1989

Queen Latifah, American rapper and actress, Feb 1997

Queen, Ellery, July 1940

Queler, Eve, conductor, July 1972

Queloz, Didier, Swiss astrophysicist, Feb 2002

Quennell, Peter, English biographer, poet, novelist and critic, May 1984, *Obit* Jan 1994

Query, Nate, American bassist, Aug 2007

Quesada, Elwood Richard, air force general and government official, Apr 1950, Jan 1960, *Obit* Apr 1993

Queuille, Henri, French prime minister, Oct 1948, *Obit* Sept 1970

Quezon, Manuel Luis, Filipino president, Aug 1941, *Obit* Sept 1944

Quidde, Ludwig, German historian and pacifist, *Obit* Apr 1941

Quill, Mike, American labor leader, Aug 1941, Mar 1953, *Obit* Mar 1966

Quiller-Couch, Arthur Thomas, English novelist, short story writer, essayist, poet and critic, *Obit* July 1944

Quimby, Edith Hinkley, American radiologist, July 1949, *Obit* Mar 1983

Quindlen, Anna, American novelist and columnist, Apr 1993

Quine, W. V., American philosopher, Nov 1999, *Obit* Mar 2001

Quinn, Aidan, American actor, Apr 2005

Quinn, Anthony, Mexican-American actor, Yrbk 1957, *Obit* Sept 2001

Quinn, Daniel Joseph, *Obit* Mar 1940

Quinn, Sally, American journalist, Oct 1988

Quinn, William F., American governor, Nov 1958, *Obit* Yrbk 2006

Quintanilla, Luis, Spanish painter and etcher, Nov 1940

Quintero, Jose, theatrical director, Apr 1954, *Obit* May 1999

Quirino, Elpidio, Filipino president, Sept 1948, *Obit* May 1956

Quisling, Vidkun, Norwegian traitor, Nov 1940, *Obit* Yrbk 1946

Quispe Huanca, Felipe, Bolivian Indian leader, Jan 2002

Quo, Tai-Chi, May 1946, *Obit* Apr 1952

Quwatli, Shukri al-, Syrian president, May 1956, *Obit* Oct 1967

R

Raab, Julius, Austrian chancellor, Apr 1954, *Obit* Feb 1964

Raassi, Tala, Sept 2013

Rabassa, Gregory, American translator, Jan 2005

Rabaut, Louis Charles, Jan 1952, *Obit* Jan 1962

Rabe, David, American dramatist, July 1973

Rabi, Isidor Isaac, American physicist, Apr 1948, *Obit* Mar 1988

Rabin, Yitzhak, Israeli prime minister, Sept 1974, Jan 1995, *Obit* Jan 1996

Raborn, William Francis, American admiral and intelligence official, July 1958, *Obit* June 1990

Racette, Patricia, American opera singer, Feb 2003

Rachmaninoff, Sergei, Russian composer and pianist, *Obit* May 1943

Rackmil, Milton R., motion picture and recording executive, Nov 1952, *Obit* Jan 1992

Radcliffe, Cyril John Radcliffe, British jurist and government official, June 1963, *Obit* May 1977

Radcliffe, Daniel, English actor, Nov 2010

Radcliffe, Paula, English runner, Jan 2003

Raddall, Thomas Head, Canadian author, Yrbk 1951

Radford, Arthur W., American admiral, Nov 1949, *Obit* Oct 1973

Radhakrishnan, S., Indian statesman and philosopher, June 1952, *Obit* June 1975

Radiohead (Musical group), June 2001

Radner, Gilda, American comedienne, Feb 1980, *Obit* July 1989

Radziwill, Catherine, Russian biographer, *Obit* July 1941

Radziwill, Lee, American socialite, Apr 1977

Rae, Bob, Canadian political leader, Feb 1991

Raeder, Erich, German admiral, Apr 1941, *Obit* Jan 1961

Raedler, Dorothy, opera director and choreographer, Yrbk 1954, *Obit* Feb 1994

Rael, French cult leader, Jan 2002

Raffarin, Jean-Pierre, French prime minister, Jan 2003

Rafferty, Max L., American state education official, Jan 1969, *Obit* Aug 1982

Raffi, Canadian singer, Jan 2003

Rafsanjani, Hashemi, Iranian president, Nov 1989

Rafshoon, Gerald M., American television producer and advertising executive, July 1979

Ragland, Rags, *Obit* Oct 1946

Ragon, Heartsill, *Obit* Nov 1940

Rahman, A. R., Indian composer and singer, June 2009

Rahman, Ziaur, Bangladeshi president, June 1981

Rahmani, Taqi, Iranian writer, Jan 2005

Rahmon, Emomali, Tajik president, Jan 2007

Rahmstorf, Stefan, German oceanographer and climatologist, Feb 2010

Rahner, Karl, German theologian, July 1970, *Obit* May 1984

Rai, Aishwarya, Indian actress, Jan 2003

Raimi, Sam, American film director, July 2002

Raimu, *Obit* Nov 1946

Rain (Singer), Korean pop singer, Jan 2006

Raines, Franklin D., American financial services executive, Oct 2000

Rainey, Froelich G., archaeologist and museum director, Feb 1967, *Obit* Jan 1993

Rainey, Homer Price, college president, Nov 1946, *Obit* Feb 1986

Rainier, Nov 1955, *Obit* Yrbk 2005

Rains, Albert McKinley, congressman, Sept 1959, *Obit* May 1991

Rains, Claude, Anglo-American actor, Nov 1949, *Obit* July 1967

Rainwater, Richard E., American investor, Apr 1999

Raitt, Bonnie, American singer and guitarist, Aug 1990

Rajagopalachari, C., Indian political leader, July 1942, *Obit* Feb 1973

Rajapakse, Mahinda, Sri Lankan president, Jan 2006

Raje, Vasundhara, Indian provincial government official, Jan 2007

Rajoy, Mariano, Spanish political leader, Jan 2007

Rakim, American rapper, Aug 2008

Rakoff, David, Canadian humorist, Nov 2007, *Obit* Yrbk 2012

Rakosi, Matyas, Hungarian communist leader, Mar 1949, *Obit* Mar 1971

Rakowski, Mieczyslaw F., Polish communist leader, Apr 1989, *Obit* Feb 2009

Rall, Ted, American editorial cartoonist, May 2002

Ralls, Charles C., Jan 1951

Ralston, Dennis, tennis player, Oct 1965

Ralston, Joseph W., air force general, Jan 2001

Ram, Jagjivan, Indian political leader, Oct 1978, *Obit* Aug 1986

Rama Rau, Dhanvanthi, Indian social welfare leader and

feminist, Apr 1954, *Obit* Sept 1987

Rama Rau, Santha, Indian travel writer and novelist, Aug 1945, Yrbk 1959, *Obit* Yrbk 2009

Rama, Edi, Albanian artist and mayor, Jan 2005

Ramadan, Tariq, Swiss Islamic leader, Jan 2004

Ramadier, Paul, French prime minister, June 1947, *Obit* Yrbk 1961

Raman, Chandrasekhara Venkata, Indian physicist, Nov 1948, *Obit* Jan 1971

Ramaphosa, Cyril, South African political leader and businessman, Sept 1995

Ramazzotti, Eros, Italian singer and songwriter, Jan 2004

Rambert, Marie, British ballet dancer, teacher and director, Feb 1981, *Obit* Aug 1982

Rameau, Jean, *Obit* Apr 1942

Ramey, Howard K., *Obit* May 1943

Ramey, Samuel, American opera singer, July 1981

Ramirez, Hanley, Dominican baseball player, Apr 2009

Ramirez, Manny, Dominican-American baseball player, June 2002

Ramirez, Pedro Pablo, Aug 1943, *Obit* Sept 1962

Ramirez, Tina, Venezuelan-American dancer and director, Nov 2004

Ramm, Fredrik, *Obit* Jan 1944

Rammstein (Musical group), Jan 2007

Ramo, Simon, American electronics industry executive, Apr 1958

Ramo, Simon; and Wooldridge, Dean E., Apr 1958

Ramonet, Ignacio, Spanish journalist, June 2008

Ramos, Fidel V., Filipino president, Mar 1994

Ramos, Jorge, Mexican-American television news anchor, Mar 2004

Rampal, Jean-Pierre, French flutist, Mar 1970, *Obit* Aug 2000

Rampersad, Arnold, American biographer, Sept 1998

Ramphele, Mamphela, South African college administrator and anthropologist, July 1997

Rampling, Charlotte, English actress, June 2002

Ramsay, Bertram, British admiral, Mar 1944, *Obit* Feb 1945

Ramsey, Dewitt C., Jan 1953, *Obit* Nov 1961

Ramsey, Michael, English archbishop, Apr 1960, *Obit* June 1988

Ramsey, Norman Foster, American physicist, Yrbk 1963, *Obit* Yrbk 2012

Ramspeck, Robert, June 1951, *Obit* Yrbk 1972

Rance, Hubert Elvin, Yrbk 1953, *Obit* Mar 1974

Rand, Ayn, American novelist, May 1982

Rand, Ellen G. Emmet, American painter, *Obit* Feb 1942

Rand, James Henry, *Obit* Nov 1944

Rand, William M., May 1953

Randall, Clarence B., American steel industry executive and presidential adviser, June 1952, *Obit* Oct 1967

Randall, John D., May 1960

Randall, Lisa, American physicist, May 2006

Randall, Ruth Painter, Yrbk 1957

Randall, Tony, American actor, Jan 1961, *Obit* Yrbk 2004

Randers, Gunnar, Jan 1957

Randi, James, American magician, May 1987

Randolph, Asa Philip, American labor leader, May 1940, Oct 1951, *Obit* July 1979

Randolph, Jennings, American senator, Jan 1962, *Obit* July 1998

Randolph, Willie, American baseball player, coach and manager, Sept 2005

Randolph, Woodruff, May 1948, *Obit* Jan 1967

Ranganathan, S. R., Indian librarian, Sept 1965, *Obit* Yrbk 1972

Rangel, Charles B., American congressman, Mar 1984

Rania, Feb 2001

Rank, Joseph, *Obit* Jan 1944

Rank, Joseph Arthur Rank, British motion picture executive, Nov 1945, *Obit* May 1972

Rankin, Ian, Scottish mystery novelist, Jan 2008

Rankin, J. Lee, American solicitor general, Feb 1959, *Obit* Sept 1996

Rankin, John E., American congressman, Feb 1944, *Obit* Jan 1961

Rankin, Karl Lott, American diplomat, Apr 1955, *Obit* Apr 1991

Ransom, John Crowe, American poet and literary critic, July 1964, *Obit* Sept 1974

Ransom, Victoria, American inforation technology executive, Jan 2013

Ranson, Stephen Walter, *Obit* Oct 1942

Rao, Shanta, Indian dancer, Yrbk 1957

Rapacki, Adam, July 1958, *Obit* Yrbk 1970

Rapaczynski, Wanda, Polish broadcasting executive, Jan 2004

Raphael, Spanish singer, Aug 1991

Raphael, Chaim, English author and government official, Yrbk 1963, *Obit* Jan 1995

Raphael, Sally Jessy, television talk show host, Feb 1990

Rapp, Adam, American playwright and novelist, Mar 2011

Rapp, William J., *Obit* Oct 1942

Rappard, William E., Oct 1951, *Obit* July 1958

Ras-Work, Berhane, Ethiopian human rights activist, Jan 2004

Rascal Flatts (Musical group), Aug 2003

Rashid, Ahmed, Pakistani journalist, Jan 2007

Raskin, A. H., newspaper reporter and editor, May 1978, *Obit* Feb 1994

Raskin, Judith, American opera singer, Apr 1964, *Obit* Feb 1985

Rasminsky, Louis, Yrbk 1961

Rasmussen, Gustav, Yrbk 1947, *Obit* Nov 1953

Raspberry, William J., American newspaper columnist, *Obit* Yrbk 2012

Rassweiler, Clifford F., Oct 1958

Rathbone, Basil, Anglo-American actor, Mar 1951, *Obit* Oct 1967

Rathbone, Eleanor, British feminist and member of Parliament, June 1943, *Obit* Feb 1946

Rathbone, Josephine Adams, librarian and educator, *Obit* July 1941

Rathbone, Monroe J., Mar 1957, *Obit* Sept 1976

Rather, Dan, American television newscaster, May 1975

Ratoff, Gregory, Aug 1943, *Obit* Feb 1961

Rattansi, Afshin, British journalist and novelist, Jan 2006

Rattigan, Terence, English dramatist, Yrbk 1956, *Obit* Feb 1978

Rattle, Simon, English conductor, Feb 1988

Rattner, Abraham, American painter, Mar 1948, *Obit* Apr 1978

Ratushinskaya, Irina, Russian poet, July 1988

Rau, Benegal Narsing, Yrbk 1951, *Obit* Feb 1954

Rau, Benegal Rama, Feb 1949, *Obit* Feb 1970

Rau, Johannes, German president, Mar 1987, *Obit* Yrbk 2006

Rauch, Neo, German painter, Jan 2007

Rauh, Joseph L., American lawyer and civil rights leader, Apr 1965, *Obit* Nov 1992

Rauschenberg, Robert, American artist, Oct 1965, Oct 1987, *Obit* Aug 2008

Rauschning, Hermann, German-American political philosopher, May 1941, *Obit* Apr 1983

Raut, Ujjwala, Indian model, Jan 2004

Rautenberg, Robert, Mar 1940

Rava, Enrico, Italian jazz trumpet player, Jan 2006

Ravdin, I. S., American surgeon, Apr 1968, *Obit* Oct 1972

Raven, Peter H., American botanist, Feb 1994

Raven-Symone, American actress, Sept 2008

Ravenstahl, Luke, American mayor, Aug 2008

Raveonettes (Musical group), Jan 2004

Raver, Paul J., Sept 1941

Ravitch, Diane, American educator and historian, Nov 2010

Rawalt, Marguerite, lawyer, Mar 1956

Rawl, Lawrence G., American petroleum executive, Feb 1992, *Obit* Yrbk 2005

Rawlings, Bernard, Aug 1945, *Obit* Yrbk 1962

Rawlings, Jerry J., Ghanaian head of state, June 1982

Rawlings, Marjorie Kinnan, American novelist and short story writer, July 1942, *Obit* Feb 1954

Rawls, Lou, American singer, Mar 1984, *Obit* Oct 2006

Ray, Amy, American singer and songwriter, Aug 1998

Ray, Charles, American actor, *Obit* Jan 1944

Ray, Dixy Lee, American governor, June 1973, *Obit* Mar 1994

Ray, Gordon Norton, literary critic, Mar 1968, *Obit* Feb 1987

Ray, Man, American painter and photographer, Yrbk 1965, *Obit* Jan 1977

Ray, Rachael, American cook and television personality, Aug 2005

Ray, Randolph, Apr 1945, *Obit* July 1963

Ray, Robert D., governor, Jan 1977

Ray, Satyajit, Indian motion picture director, Mar 1961, *Obit* June 1992

Ray, Ted, *Obit* Oct 1943

Rayburn, Sam, American congressman and Speaker of the House, Oct 1940, Mar 1949, *Obit* Jan 1962

Raye, Martha, American actress, singer and comedienne, July 1963, *Obit* Jan 1995

Raymond, Lee R., American energy industry executive, Nov 1999

Razmara, Hossein Ali, Iranian prime minister, Oct 1950, *Obit* Mar 1951

Rea, Gardner, May 1946, *Obit* Feb 1967

Read, Herbert Edward, English poet, essayist and art critic, Mar 1962, *Obit* Sept 1968

Reader, John, British photojournalist and writer, Jan 2007

Reading, Stella, Apr 1948, *Obit* July 1971

Reagan, Nancy, wife of American president Ronald Reagan, May 1982

Reagan, Ron, American television personality and son of President Ronald Reagan, Feb 1992

Reagan, Ronald, American president, Yrbk 1949, Feb 1967, Nov 1982, *Obit* Yrbk 2004

Reagon, Bernice Johnson, American historian and singer, Aug 1999

Reardon, John, opera singer, Nov 1974, *Obit* June 1988

Reasoner, Harry, American television newscaster, Feb 1966, *Obit* Oct 1991

Reavis, Smith Freeman, *Obit* Mar 1940

Reber, Samuel, Sept 1949, *Obit* Feb 1972

Reckord, Milton A., Mar 1945

Redd, Michael, American basketball player, Mar 2005

Redding, J. Saunders, American historian and novelist, Apr 1969, *Obit* Apr 1988

Reddy, Helen, American singer, Apr 1975

Redfield, Robert, American anthropologist, Yrbk 1953, *Obit* Jan 1959

Redford, Robert, American actor and motion picture director, Apr 1971, Mar 1982

Redgrave, Lynn, English actress, Sept 1969, *Obit* Yrbk 2010

Redgrave, Michael, English actor, Feb 1950, *Obit* May 1985

Redgrave, Steven, English rower, Jan 2000

Redgrave, Vanessa, English actress, Yrbk 1966, Sept 2003

Redlener, Irwin, American pediatrician, Nov 2007

Redman, Joshua, American jazz saxophonist, Jan 1997

Redpath, Anne, Jan 1957, *Obit* Mar 1965

Redpath, Jean, Scottish singer, Feb 1984

Redstone, Sumner, American motion picture and broadcasting executive, Jan 1996

Redway, Jacques W., *Obit* Jan 1943

Redzepi, Ren,, Danish chef and restaurateur, Apr 2012

Reece, Brazilla Carroll, American congressman, May 1946, *Obit* May 1961

Reed, Carol, British motion picture director and producer, Mar 1950, *Obit* June 1976

Reed, Daniel A., American congressman, May 1953, *Obit* Apr 1959

Reed, Edward Bliss, *Obit* Mar 1940

Reed, Herbert Calhoun, *Obit* Sept 1940

Reed, Ishmael, American novelist and poet, Oct 1986

Reed, James, naval and bridge engineer, *Obit* Sept 1941

Reed, James A., American senator, *Obit* Oct 1944

Reed, John Howard, *Obit* Mar 1940

Reed, John S., American financial executive and stock exchange official, Jan 1985

Reed, Lou, American singer, July 1989

Reed, Philip Dunham, American electronics industry executive, Jan 1949, *Obit* May 1989

Reed, Ralph, American political leader, Mar 1996

Reed, Ralph T., Apr 1951, *Obit* Mar 1968

Reed, Rex, motion picture critic, Jan 1972

Reed, Stanley Forman, American Supreme Court justice, Feb 1942, *Obit* May 1980

Reed, Willis, American basketball player, coach and executive, Jan 1973

Rees, Edward H., Jan 1958, *Obit* Yrbk 1969

Rees, Martin J., British astronomer, Jan 2007

Rees, Mina Spiegel, American mathematician and computer scientist, Nov 1957, *Obit* Jan 1998

Reese, Della, American singer and actress, Sept 1971

Reese, Everett D., Mar 1954

Reese, Pee Wee, American baseball player, June 1950, *Obit* Oct 1999

Reeve, Christopher, American actor, May 1982, *Obit* Jan 2005

Reeve, Sidney A., *Obit* Aug 1941

Reeves, Dan, football player and coach, Oct 2001

Reeves, Dianne, American jazz singer, July 2006

Reeves, Jesse S., *Obit* Aug 1942

Reeves, Keanu, Canadian actor, May 1995

Regan, Donald T., American presidential adviser, Nov 1981, *Obit* Yrbk 2003

Regan, Judith, American editor, publisher and talk show host, Sept 2000

Reggio, Godfrey, American motion picture director and foundation official, July 1995

Regine, Belgian nightclub owner, Apr 1980

Rehman, Shabana, Norwegian comedian, Jan 2004

Rehnquist, William H., American Chief Justice of the Supreme Court, Apr 1972, Nov 2003, *Obit* Yrbk 2005

Reich, Charles A., American law professor, June 1972

Reich, Nathaniel Julius, *Obit* Nov 1943

Reich, Robert B., American economist and Secretary of labor, Apr 1993

Reich, Steve, American composer, Apr 1986

Reich, Walter, American psychiatrist, Aug 2005

Reichelderfer, Francis Wilton, meteorologist, May 1949, *Obit* Mar 1983

Reichenau, Walter von, German field marshal, *Obit* Mar 1942

Reichmann, Paul, Canadian real estate developer, Jan 1991

Reichs, Kathleen J., American forensic anthropologist, Oct 2006

Reichstein, Tadeus, Swiss chemist, Feb 1951, *Obit* Oct 1996

Reid, Andy, American football coach, Nov 2012

Reid, Antonio, American recording industry producer and executive, Aug 2001

Reid, Charlotte Thompson, congresswoman and regulatory official, Jan 1975

Reid, Frank R., *Obit* Mar 1945

Reid, Harry, American senator, Mar 2003

Reid, Helen Rogers, American newspaper publisher, Feb 1941, May 1952, *Obit* Oct 1970

Reid, Ira De A., July 1946, *Obit* Oct 1968

Reid, Kate, Canadian actress, Mar 1985, *Obit* May 1993

Reid, Mont, *Obit* June 1943

Reid, Ogden R., American congressman and newspaper publisher, Feb 1956

Reid, Whitelaw, American newspaper editor and publisher, Yrbk 1954, *Obit* Yrbk 2009

Reilly, John C., American actor, Oct 2004

Reilly, Rick, American sportswriter, Feb 2005

Reilly, William K., American conservationist and government official, July 1989

Reinartz, F. Eppling, July 1953

Reiner, Carl, American producer, director, actor and screenwriter, Apr 1961

Reiner, Fritz, conductor, Apr 1941, Yrbk 1953, *Obit* Jan 1964

Reiner, Rob, American actor and film director, May 1988

Reinhard, Johan, archaeologist, Aug 1999

Reinhardt, Aurelia Henry, American college president and religious official, May 1941, *Obit* Feb 1948

Reinhardt, Max, Austrian theatrical director, *Obit* Yrbk 1943

Reinhardt, Uwe E., American economist, Mar 2004

Reinhart, Carmen, American economist, Mar 2012

Reinking, Ann, American dancer, choreographer and actress, June 2004

Reischauer, Edwin O., American historian and diplomat, May 1962, *Obit* Nov 1990

Reiser, Paul, American comedian and actor, Apr 1996

Reisner, Christian Fichthorne, *Obit* Sept 1940

Reisner, George Andrew, American Egyptologist, *Obit* July 1942

Reith, John Charles Walsham Reith, Scottish broadcasting executive, Nov 1940, *Obit* July 1971

Reitman, Ivan, Canadian film director, Mar 2001

Relander, Lauri Kristian, *Obit* Apr 1942

Rell, M. Jodi, American governor, Sept 2005

Remick, Lee, American actress, Oct 1966, *Obit* Sept 1991

Remington, John W., Feb 1960

Remnick, David, American journalist and editor, Oct 1998

Remorino, Jeronimo, Sept 1951

Ren Zhengfei, Chinese telecommunications equipment company executive, Jan 2005

Renaud, Madeleine, French actress and theatrical producer, Mar 1953, *Obit* Nov 1994

Renault, Louis, French automobile executive, *Obit* Yrbk 1944

Renault, Mary, English novelist, Jan 1959, *Obit* Feb 1984

Rendell, Ed, American governor, Apr 1998

Rendell, Ruth, English mystery writer, Apr 1994

Renne, Roland Roger, college president and agricultural economist, June 1963

Rennebohm, Oscar, July 1950, *Obit* Yrbk 1968

Renner, Karl, Austrian president, Sept 1945, *Obit* Jan 1951

Rennert, Gunther, June 1976, *Obit* Sept 1978

Reno, Janet, American Attorney general, Sept 1993

Renoir, Jean, French film director and screenwriter, Yrbk 1959, *Obit* Apr 1979

Rentzel, Delos Wilson, government official and aviation expert, Oct 1948, *Obit* Jan 1992

Reshevsky, Samuel, chess player, Feb 1955, *Obit* July 1992

Resnais, Alain, French film director, Feb 1965

Resnick, Louis, *Obit* May 1941

Resnik, Regina, opera singer, Jan 1956, *Obit* Yrbk 2013

Resor, Stanley, American advertising executive, July 1949, *Obit* Yrbk 1962

Resor, Stanley R., American Secretary of the army, Sept 1969, *Obit* Yrbk 2012

Ressler, Robert K., American criminologist, Feb 2002

Reston, James, American journalist, Mar 1943, Nov 1980, *Obit* Feb 1996

Restrepo, Laura, Colombian novelist and journalist, Jan 2006

Retton, Mary Lou, American gymnast, Feb 1986

Reubens, Paul, American comedian and actor, Jan 1988

Reuss, Henry S., American congressman and lawyer, Oct 1959, *Obit* Mar 2002

Reuter, Ernst, German mayor, Oct 1949, *Obit* Yrbk 1953

Reuter, Gabriele, German author, *Obit* Jan 1942

Reuther, Victor, American labor leader, Yrbk 1953, *Obit* Yrbk 2004

Reuther, Walter Philip, American labor leader, Apr 1941, Nov 1949, *Obit* June 1970

Revel, Jean-Francois, French philosopher, Feb 1975, *Obit* Yrbk 2006

Revelle, Roger, American oceanographer, Mar 1957, *Obit* Sept 1991

Reventlow, Ernst, *Obit* Jan 1944

Revercomb, Chapman, June 1958

Reves, Emery, British publisher and art collector, July 1946

Revueltas, Silvestre, Mexican composer, *Obit* Yrbk 1940

Rexroth, Kenneth, American poet, essayist and translator, Apr 1981, *Obit* Aug 1982

Rey, Fernando, Spanish actor, Mar 1979, *Obit* May 1994

Reybold, Eugene, June 1945, *Obit* Jan 1962

Reyes, Jose, Dominican baseball player, Aug 2008

Reyes, Silvestre, American congressman, Sept 2007

Reynaud, Paul, French prime minister, Apr 1940, May 1950, *Obit* Nov 1966

Reynolds, Albert, Irish prime minister, Sept 1994

Reynolds, Allie, American baseball player, June 1952, *Obit* Mar 1995

Reynolds, Burt, American actor, Oct 1973

Reynolds, Debbie, American actress and singer, Yrbk 1964

Reynolds, Glenn H., American law professor, Oct 2007

Reynolds, Helen Wilkinson, *Obit* Feb 1943

Reynolds, James A., *Obit* May 1940

Reynolds, John W., American judge and governor, Apr 1964, *Obit* Mar 2002

Reynolds, Quentin James, journalist, Mar 1941, *Obit* Apr 1965

Reynolds, Richard S., American manufacturing executive, May 1967, *Obit* Nov 1980

Reynolds, Richard Samuel, American aluminum industry executive, Feb 1953, *Obit* Oct 1955

Reynolds, Robert Rice, senator, Oct 1940, *Obit* Mar 1963

Reynolds, William Bradford, government official and lawyer, July 1988

Reynoso, Cruz, American lawyer and judge, Mar 2002

Reza Shah Pahlavi, *Obit* Sept 1944

Reza, Yasmina, French dramatist, Sept 1998

Rheaume, Manon, Canadian hockey player, Nov 2012

Rhee, Syngman, Korean president, Sept 1947, *Obit* Sept 1965

Rhine, J. B., American parapsychologist, Jan 1949, *Obit* Apr 1980

Rhoades, Nina, *Obit* Jan 1941

Rhoads, Cornelius P., American physician, Mar 1953, *Obit* Nov 1959

Rhodes, Edgar Nelson, *Obit* May 1942

Rhodes, James Allen, American governor and political party leader, Mar 1949, Apr 1976, *Obit* July 2001

Rhodes, John J., American congressman, Sept 1976, *Obit* Yrbk 2004

Rhodes, Randi, American radio talk show host, Feb 2005

Rhodes, Zandra, British fashion designer, Jan 2002

Rhone, Sylvia, American recording industry executive, June 1998

Rhyne, Charles S., American lawyer, May 1958, *Obit* Yrbk 2003

Rhys, Ernest, English editor, critic and poet, *Obit* Jan 1946

Rhys, Jean, English novelist and short story writer, Yrbk 1972, *Obit* July 1979

Riad, Mahmoud, Egyptian diplomat, Nov 1971, *Obit* Mar 1992

Ribadu, Nuhu, Nigerian law enforcement official, Jan 2006

Ribbentrop, Joachim von, German Nazi leader, May 1941, *Obit* Nov 1946

Ribbs, Willy T., American automobile racing driver, Nov 2000

Ribicoff, Abraham A., American senator, June 1955, *Obit* May 1998

Ricci, Nino, Canadian novelist, Jan 2007

Rice, Alice Caldwell Hegan, author, *Obit* Apr 1942

Rice, Anne, American novelist, July 1991

Rice, Condoleezza, American Secretary of state, Apr 2001

Rice, Constance L., American lawyer and civil rights activist, Apr 2011

Rice, Elmer, American dramatist, Apr 1943, *Obit* July 1967

Rice, Grantland, American sportswriter, Sept 1941, *Obit* Sept 1954

Rice, Greg, runner, Yrbk 1941, *Obit* Aug 1991

Rice, Jerry, American football player, Apr 1990

Rice, Jim, American baseball player, Sept 1979

Rice, Linda Johnson, American magazine publishing executive, July 2011

Rice, Paul North, librarian, Nov 1947, *Obit* June 1967

Rich, Adrienne, American poet, Feb 1976, *Obit* Yrbk 2012

Rich, Buddy, American drummer and band leader, June 1973, *Obit* May 1987

Rich, Daniel Catton, Yrbk 1955, *Obit* Feb 1977

Rich, Frank, American newspaper columnist, Apr 1999

Rich, Louise Dickinson, American memoirist, young adult novelist and children's author, May 1943, *Obit* July 1991

Richard 23, Belgian percussionist and singer, Jan 2006

Richard, Louis, *Obit* Sept 1940

Richard, Maurice, Canadian hockey player, Yrbk 1958, *Obit* Yrbk 2000

Richards, Alfred N., American pharmacologist, Sept 1950, *Obit* Apr 1966

Richards, Ann, American governor, Feb 1991, *Obit* Yrbk 2007

Richards, Bob, American pole vaulter and decathlete, June 1957

Richards, Cecile, American family planning advocate, May 2007

Richards, Charles Russ, *Obit* Jan 1941

Richards, Dickinson W., American physician, Mar 1957, *Obit* Apr 1973

Richards, I. A., English poet, critic and linguist, Yrbk 1972, *Obit* Oct 1979

Richards, James P., Sept 1951, *Obit* Apr 1979

Richards, John G., *Obit* Yrbk 1941

Richards, John Stewart, librarian, June 1955

Richards, Keith, British guitarist, Feb 1989

Richards, Laura Elizabeth Howe, author and poet, *Obit* May 1943

Richards, Lloyd G., American actor and theatrical director, Oct 1987, *Obit* Yrbk 2007

Richards, Michael, American actor and comedian, Nov 1997

Richards, Vincent, July 1947, *Obit* Yrbk 1959

Richards, Wayne E., July 1954

Richardson, Bill, American governor, Apr 1996

Richardson, Bobby, baseball player, May 1966

Richardson, Elliot L., American Attorney general, Mar 1971, *Obit* Mar 2000

Richardson, Henry Handel, Australian novelist, *Obit* May 1946

Richardson, Kevin, American singer, May 2000

Richardson, Miranda, English actress, Feb 1994

Richardson, Norval, *Obit* Yrbk 1940

Richardson, Ralph, English actor, Nov 1950, *Obit* Nov 1983

Richardson, Robert, American cinematographer, Jan 2010

Richardson, Seth Whitley, American government official, Feb 1948, *Obit* May 1953

Richardson, Tony, British film and theatrical director, Yrbk 1963, *Obit* Feb 1992

Richberg, Donald R., American government official, Yrbk 1949, *Obit* Jan 1961

Richie, Lionel, American singer and songwriter, July 1984

Richler, Mordecai, Canadian novelist and critic, May 1975, *Obit* Oct 2001

Richman, Charles J., *Obit* Jan 1941

Richmond, Charles Alexander, *Obit* Sept 1940

Richmond, Mitch, basketball player, June 1999

Richter, Burton, American physicist, Sept 1977

Richter, Charles F., American seismologist, May 1975, *Obit* Nov 1985

Richter, Conrad, American novelist and short story writer, June 1951, *Obit* Yrbk 1968

Richter, George Martin, *Obit* July 1942

Richter, Gerhard, German painter and printmaker, June 2002

Richter, Sviatoslav, Russian pianist, Feb 1961, *Obit* Oct 1997

Rickenbacker, Eddie, American military pilot, Nov 1940, Feb 1952, *Obit* Oct 1973

Ricketts, Louis Davidson, *Obit* Mar 1940

Rickey, Branch, American baseball manager and executive, Oct 1945, *Obit* Jan 1966

Rickey, George W., American sculptor, Feb 1980, *Obit* Yrbk 2002

Rickey, James W., *Obit* June 1943

Rickover, Hyman George, American admiral, May 1953, *Obit* Aug 1986

Ricks, Thomas E., American military writer, Nov 2007

Riddell, R. Gerald, Sept 1950, *Obit* Apr 1951

Riddleberger, James W., diplomat, May 1957, *Obit* Jan 1983

Ride, Sally K., American astronaut and astrophysicist, Oct 1983, *Obit* Yrbk 2012

Rideau, Wilbert, American convicted murderer and prison journalist, Nov 2010

Ridenour, Nina, Apr 1951

Ridge, Lola, poet, *Obit* July 1941

Ridge, Tom, American Secretary of homeland security, Feb 2001

Ridgway, Matthew B., American general, July 1947, *Obit* Sept 1993

Riebel, John P., Jan 1957

Riecken, Henry W., social psychologist, Yrbk 1961

Riedel, Oliver, German bassist, Jan 2007

Riefenstahl, Leni, German actress and motion picture director, May 1975, *Obit* Yrbk 2004

Riefler, Winfield W., May 1948, *Obit* June 1974

Riegle, Donald W., senator, Oct 1986

Riesenberg, Felix, Yrbk 1957

Riesman, David, American physician, *Obit* July 1940

Riesman, David, American sociologist, Jan 1955, *Obit* Yrbk 2002

Riess, Adam, American astrophysicist, Nov 2012

Rieve, Emil, July 1946, *Obit* Mar 1975

Rifkin, Jeremy, American social activist and foundation official, Feb 1986

Rifkind, Simon H., lawyer, May 1946, *Obit* Jan 1996

Rigg, Diana, English actress, Oct 1974

Rigg, Edgar T., June 1961

Riggio, Leonard, American book store chain executive, June 1998

Riggio, Vincent, July 1949, *Obit* Nov 1960

Riggs, Austen Fox, *Obit* Mar 1940

Riggs, Bobby, American tennis player, Sept 1949, *Obit* Jan 1996

Riggs, T. Lawrason, *Obit* June 1943

Righter, Carroll, astrologer, Oct 1972, *Obit* June 1988

Rigling, Alfred, *Obit* Jan 1941

Rihanna, Barbadian singer, Nov 2007

Riiser-Larsen, Hjalmar, Nov 1951, *Obit* July 1965

Riklis, Meshulam, financier, Yrbk 1971

Riles, Wilson, educator and state official, Yrbk 1971

Riley, Bridget, English painter, Sept 1981

Riley, Pat, American basketball coach, Aug 1988

Riley, Richard Wilson, American Secretary of education, Oct 1993

Riley, Susan B., Feb 1953

Riley, Terry, American composer and pianist, Apr 2002

Riley, William Edward, Nov 1951

Rimes, LeAnn, American country singer, May 1998

Rimm, Sylvia B., American child psychologist, Feb 2002

Rimsza, Skip, American mayor, July 2002

Rincon de Gautier, Felisa, Puerto Rican mayor, Oct 1956, *Obit* Nov 1994

Rinehart, Stanley M., Yrbk 1954, *Obit* June 1969

Rines, Robert H., American lawyer, inventor, physicist and hunter of Loch Ness monster, Jan 2003, *Obit* Yrbk 2010

Rinfret, Pierre, American economist and financial consultant, July 1972, *Obit* Yrbk 2006

Ring, Barbara T., *Obit* Nov 1941

Ringgold, Faith, American artist, children's author and illustrator, Feb 1996

Ringling, Robert E., May 1945, *Obit* Feb 1950

Ringwald, Molly, American actress, May 1987

Riopelle, Jean-Paul, Canadian painter and sculptor, Oct 1989, *Obit* Sept 2002

Riordan, Richard, American mayor and investor, May 2000

Rios Montt, Jose Efrain, Guatemalan president, May 1983

Rios, Juan Antonio, Chilean president, Apr 1942, *Obit* July 1946

Ripert, Eric, French chef and restaurateur, Mar 2013

Ripken, Cal, American baseball player, June 1992

Ripley, Alexandra, American novelist, Mar 1992, *Obit* Yrbk 2004

Ripley, Elizabeth, Yrbk 1958

Ripley, Joseph, *Obit* Nov 1940

Ripley, Robert Le Roy, cartoonist and adventurer, July 1945, *Obit* July 1949

Ripley, Sidney Dillon, American zoologist and museum director, Oct 1966, *Obit* Aug 2001

Ripley, William Z., *Obit* Oct 1941

Rirkrit Tiravanija, Thai installation artist, Jan 2005

Risen, James, American journalist, Aug 2007

Rist, Pipilotti, Swiss video artist, Jan 2005

Ritchard, Cyril, Jan 1957, *Obit* Feb 1978

Ritchie, Dennis M., American computer scientist, Mar 1999, *Obit* Yrbk 2011

Ritchie, Dennis; and Thompson, Kenneth, Mar 1999

Ritchie, Jean, American folk singer, Oct 1959

Riter, Henry G., Oct 1955, *Obit* Sept 1958

Ritner, Ann, Yrbk 1953

Ritt, Martin, motion picture director, Nov 1979, *Obit* Feb 1991

Rittenhouse, Constance, Mar 1948

Ritter, Bruce, priest and child care leader, June 1983, *Obit* Feb 2000

Ritter, John, American actor, June 1980, *Obit* Yrbk 2004

Ritter, Joseph Elmer, Yrbk 1964, *Obit* Oct 1967

Ritter, Thelma, Yrbk 1957, *Obit* Feb 1974

Rivaldo, Brazilian soccer player, Jan 2002

Rivera, Chita, American dancer, singer and actress, Oct 1984

Rivera, Diego, Mexican painter, July 1948, *Obit* Feb 1958

Rivera, Geraldo, American television reporter and talk show host, May 1975

Rivera, Mariano, Panamanian baseball player, July 2012

Rivero, Jose Ignacio, Cuban newspaper publisher, *Obit* May 1944

Rivers, Doc, American basketball coach, Nov 2008

Rivers, Joan, American comedienne and television personality, Jan 1970, Mar 1987

Rivers, L. Mendel, American congressman, Oct 1960, *Obit* Feb 1971

Rivers, Larry, American painter and sculptor, Apr 1969, *Obit* Nov 2002

Rivers, Thomas M., American virologist, July 1960, *Obit* July 1962

Rives, Amelie, American novelist, *Obit* July 1945

Rives, Hallie Erminie, American novelist, Yrbk 1956

Rivlin, Alice M., American economist and government official, Oct 1982

Rizzo, Frank Lazarro, American mayor, Mar 1973, *Obit* Sept 1991

Rizzuto, Phil, American sportscaster and baseball player, July 1950, *Obit* Yrbk 2007

Roa, Raul, Nov 1973, *Obit* Sept 1982

Roach, Mary, American writer, Jan 2011

Roach, Max, American jazz drummer, July 1986, *Obit* Nov 2007

Robaina, Alejandro, Cuban cigar manufacturer, Jan 2004, *Obit* Yrbk 2010

Robards, Jason, American actor, Oct 1959, *Obit* Mar 2001

Robarts, John P., Canadian political leader, Yrbk 1962, *Obit* Jan 1983

Robb, Charles S., American senator, Apr 1989

Robb, Hunter, *Obit* Jan 1940

Robb, Inez Callaway, American journalist, Yrbk 1958, *Obit* June 1979

Robbe-Grillet, Alain, French novelist, essayist and screenwriter, Yrbk 1974, *Obit* Yrbk 2008

Robbins, Frederick C., American bacteriologist, June 1955, *Obit* Yrbk 2003

Robbins, Harold, American novelist, May 1970, *Obit* Jan 1998

Robbins, Jerome, American dancer, choreographer and theatrical director, May 1947, May 1969, *Obit* Oct 1998

Robbins, Tim, American actor, July 1994

Robbins, Tom, American novelist, June 1993

Robbins, Tony, American motivational speaker and author, July 2001

Robbins, William J., Feb 1956

Robens of Woldingham, Alfred Robens, June 1956

Robert, Alain, French urban climber, Jan 2007

Robert, Georges, June 1943

Roberto Carlos, Brazilian soccer player, Jan 2007

Roberts, Albert H., *Obit* July 1946

Roberts, C. Wesley, American public relations executive and political party leader, Apr 1953, *Obit* June 1975

Roberts, Charles G. D., Canadian poet and short story writer, *Obit* Jan 1944

Roberts, Cokie, American television reporter and moderator, May 1994

Roberts, Dennis J., governor, Yrbk 1956, *Obit* Sept 1994

Roberts, Dorothy James, author, Yrbk 1956, *Obit* June 1990

Roberts, Elizabeth Madox, novelist, short story writer and poet, *Obit* May 1941

Roberts, Florence, *Obit* July 1940

Roberts, George Lucas, *Obit* Apr 1941

Roberts, Goodridge, Canadian painter, May 1955

Roberts, John G., American Chief Justice of the Supreme Court, Feb 2006

Roberts, Julia, American actress, May 1991

Roberts, Kate L., *Obit* Oct 1941

Roberts, Marcus, American jazz pianist, Mar 1994

Roberts, Michael, American telecommunications, real estate and publishing executive, Feb 2010

Roberts, Nora, American romance novelist, Sept 2001

Roberts, Oral, American evangelist, Nov 1960, *Obit* Feb 2010

Roberts, Owen Josephus, American Supreme Court justice, Oct 1941, *Obit* July 1955

Roberts, Robin, American baseball player, Yrbk 1953, *Obit* Yrbk 2010

Roberts, Robin, American television news anchor, Feb 2008

Roberts, Steven, American real estate, broadcasting and telecommunications executive, Feb 2010

Roberts, Tony, American actor, Oct 2006

Roberts, Walter Orr, climatologist, Yrbk 1960, *Obit* May 1990

Robertson of Oakridge, Brian Hubert Robertson, Sept 1948, *Obit* June 1974

Robertson, A. Willis, American senator, Yrbk 1949, *Obit* Yrbk 1971

Robertson, Ben, American journalist, Nov 1942

Robertson, Cliff, American actor, Yrbk 1969, *Obit* Yrbk 2011

Robertson, Constance, Yrbk 1946

Robertson, D. B., May 1950, *Obit* Yrbk 1961

Robertson, Norman A., Yrbk 1957, *Obit* Sept 1968

Robertson, Oscar, American basketball player, Jan 1966

Robertson, Pat, American evangelist and television executive, Sept 1987

Robertson, Reuben B., Yrbk 1955, *Obit* May 1960

Robertson, Robert Blackwood, May 1957

Robertson, Walter S., Yrbk 1953, *Obit* May 1970

Robeson, Eslanda Goode, American anthropologist and wife of Paul Robeson, Sept 1945, *Obit* Yrbk 1991

Robeson, Paul, American actor, civil rights activist and singer, Mar 1941, Mar 1976

Robey, Ralph W., American economist and journalist, May 1941, *Obit* Sept 1972

Robichaud, Louis J., Canadian political leader, May 1968

Robins, Edward, *Obit* July 1943

Robins, Margaret Dreier, labor leader, *Obit* Apr 1945

Robinson, Arthur Howard, American cartographer, Mar 1996, *Obit* Yrbk 2005

Robinson, Bill, American tap dancer, Feb 1941, *Obit* Jan 1950

Robinson, Boardman, Yrbk 1941, *Obit* Oct 1952

Robinson, Brooks, American baseball player, Sept 1973

Robinson, David, American basketball player, July 1993

Robinson, Eddie, American football coach, June 1988, *Obit* Yrbk 2007

Robinson, Edward G., actor, Jan 1950, *Obit* Mar 1973

Robinson, Elmer E., Nov 1955

Robinson, Frank, American baseball player and manager, June 1971

Robinson, Frederick B., *Obit* Yrbk 1941

Robinson, Henry Morton, author and poet, July 1950, *Obit* Mar 1961

Robinson, Holton D., *Obit* June 1945

Robinson, Jackie, American baseball player, Feb 1947, *Obit* Yrbk 1972

Robinson, Jancis, British wine critic, Jan 2007

Robinson, Janet L., American newspaper executive, Mar 2003

Robinson, John A. T., English bishop, Feb 1965, *Obit* Feb 1984

Robinson, Kim Stanley, American science fiction writer, Nov 1998

Robinson, Marilynne, American novelist, Oct 2005

Robinson, Mary, Irish president and United Nations official, Apr 1991

Robinson, Maurice R., Yrbk 1956, *Obit* May 1982

Robinson, Peter, English mystery novelist, Sept 2007

Robinson, Randall, American lobbyist and civil rights leader, Sept 1998

Robinson, Samuel M., Feb 1942

Robinson, Smokey, American singer and songwriter, July 1980

Robinson, Spottswood W., judge, Mar 1962, *Obit* Jan 1999

Robinson, Sugar Ray, American boxer, Mar 1951, *Obit* June 1989

Robinson, William E., American beverage industry and newspaper executive, Feb 1958, *Obit* July 1969

Robinson, William Heath, English illustrator, *Obit* Nov 1944

Robison, Emily, American banjoist and singer, July 2000

Robison, Paula, flutist, May 1982

Robitzek, Edward Heinrich, physician, Yrbk 1953, *Obit* May 1984

Robles, Marco Aurelio, Panamanian president, June 1968, *Obit* June 1990

Robsjohn-Gibbings, Terence Harold, American furniture and interior designer, Sept 1965, *Obit* Feb 1977

Robson, Flora, English actress, Jan 1951, *Obit* Sept 1984

Robson, May, actress, *Obit* Yrbk 1942

Robuchon, Joel, French chef and restaurateur, Jan 2003

Robus, Hugo, Yrbk 1962, *Obit* Feb 1964

Roca, Julio A., *Obit* Nov 1942

Rocard, Michel, French prime minister, Oct 1988

Rochberg, George, American composer, Sept 1985, *Obit* Yrbk 2005

Roche, James M., American automobile executive, Feb 1967, *Obit* Yrbk 2004

Roche, Josephine, American coal industry executive, Aug 1941, *Obit* Sept 1976

Roche, Kevin, architect, Nov 1970

Rock, John Charles, American physician, Yrbk 1964, *Obit* Jan 1985

Rock, Pete, American record producer and DJ, Aug 2009

Rockefeller, David, American banker, Mar 1959

Rockefeller, John D., American senator, Mar 1978

Rockefeller, John D., American philanthropist, June 1953, *Obit* Sept 1978

Rockefeller, John D., American philanthropist, July 1941, *Obit* July 1960

Rockefeller, Laurance S., American investor and conservationist, June 1959, *Obit* Yrbk 2004

Rockefeller, Nelson A., American vice-president, Mar 1941, Mar 1951, *Obit* Mar 1979

Rockefeller, Winthrop, American governor, philanthropist and financier, Sept 1959, *Obit* Apr 1973

Rockley, Alicia Margaret Tyssen-Amherst Cecil, *Obit* Nov 1941

Rockwell, Lew, American political commentator, June 2007

Rockwell, Norman, American painter, June 1945, *Obit* Jan 1979

Rodahl, Kare, Norwegian physiologist, Feb 1956

Roddick, Andy, American tennis player, Jan 2004

Roddick, Anita, British cosmetics industry executive, Sept 1992, *Obit* Yrbk 2007

Roderick, David M., steel executive, Apr 1987

Rodgers and Hart, May 1940

Rodgers, Aaron, American football player, Nov 2012

Rodgers, Bill, American marathon runner, Aug 1982

Rodgers, Nile, American guitarist and record producer, Jan 2012

Rodgers, Richard, American composer, May 1940, Apr 1951, *Obit* Feb 1980

Rodin, Judith, American foundation official, June 1999

Rodino, Peter W., American congressman, Oct 1954, *Obit* Yrbk 2005

Rodman, Dennis, American basketball player, Sept 1996

Rodota, Antonio, Italian aerospace engineer and European space agency official, Jan 2003

Rodriguez Veltze, Eduardo, Bolivian president, Jan 2005

Rodriguez Zapatero, Jose Luis, Spanish prime minister, Jan 2004

Rodriguez, Alex, American baseball player, Apr 2003

Rodriguez, Andres, Paraguayan general and president, Sept 1991, *Obit* June 1997

Rodriguez, Arturo, labor leader, Mar 2001

Rodriguez, Cecilia, feminist and revolutionary, May 1999

Rodriguez, Chi Chi, American golfer, Oct 1969

Rodriguez, Eloy, botanist, May 2000

Rodriguez, Ivan, Puerto Rican baseball player, June 2009

Rodriguez, Nicolas, *Obit* Sept 1940

Rodriguez, Robert, American motion picture director, Aug 1996

Rodzinski, Artur, Aug 1940, *Obit* Feb 1959

Roebling, Mary G., banker, Oct 1960, *Obit* Jan 1995

Roeg, Nicolas, British film director, Jan 1996

Roehm, Carolyne, American fashion designer, Feb 1992

Roelofs, Henrietta, *Obit* Mar 1942

Roemer, Buddy, governor, Nov 1990

Rogers, Bernard W., American general, Oct 1984

Rogers, Bruce, American typographer, Yrbk 1946, *Obit* July 1957

Rogers, Carl R., American psychologist, Yrbk 1962, *Obit* Mar 1987

Rogers, Dale Evans, American singer and actress, Sept 1956, *Obit* Apr 2001

Rogers, Desiree G., American magazine executive, June 2011

Rogers, Edith Nourse, American congresswoman, Apr 1942, *Obit* Nov 1960

Rogers, Frank Bradway, physician and librarian, June 1962

Rogers, Fred, American television performer and producer, July 1971, *Obit* July 2003

Rogers, Ginger, American actress, singer and dancer, Apr 1941, Yrbk 1967, *Obit* July 1995

Rogers, John, American investment manager, Aug 2010

Rogers, Kenny, American country singer, Jan 1981

Rogers, Lynn L., wildlife biologist, Oct 1994

Rogers, Mark Homer, *Obit* Nov 1941

Rogers, Norman McLeod, *Obit* July 1940

Rogers, Paul, Mar 1960

Rogers, Robert Emmons, *Obit* July 1941

Rogers, Roy, American cowboy singer and actor, Mar 1948, Oct 1983, *Obit* Sept 1998

Rogers, Rutherford David, June 1962

Rogers, Will, American congressman and actor, Yrbk 1953, *Obit* Sept 1993

Rogers, William Pierce, American Secretary of state, Feb 1958, Sept 1969, *Obit* Mar 2001

Rogge, Jacques, Belgian orthopedic surgeon and Olympic executive, Jan 2002

Rogge, O. John, Feb 1948, *Obit* June 1981

Roh, Moo Hyun, South Korean president, Jan 2003, *Obit* Yrbk 2009

Roh, Tae Woo, Korean president, Feb 1988

Rohatyn, Felix G., American investment banker and diplomat, May 1978

Rohmer, Eric, French film director, Apr 1977, *Obit* Yrbk 2010

Roijen, Jan Herman van, Dutch diplomat, Yrbk 1953

Rojas Pinilla, Gustavo, Colombian general and president, June 1956, *Obit* Mar 1975

Rojas, Rudy, American clothing company executive, Jan 2006

Rokossovskii, Konstantin K., Soviet field marshal, Jan 1944, *Obit* Oct 1968

Rolland, Michel, American enologist, Jan 2007

Rolland, Romain, French novelist, dramatist and biographer, *Obit* Feb 1945

Rollin, Betty, American television reporter and writer, Aug 1994

Rollins, Carl Purington, Sept 1948, *Obit* Jan 1961

Rollins, Ed, American political consultant, Mar 2001

Rollins, Henry, American performance artist, poet and singer, Sept 2001

Rollins, Sonny, American jazz saxophonist, Apr 1976

Rolvaag, Karl Fritjof, American governor, Feb 1964, *Obit* Mar 1991

Roman, Nancy Grace, astronomer, Yrbk 1960

Romano, Emanuel, painter and illustrator, Mar 1940, *Obit* Feb 1985

Romano, Umberto, Mar 1954, *Obit* Nov 1982

Romanoff, Alexis L., Yrbk 1953

Rombauer, Irma von Starkloff, American cookbook author, Yrbk 1953, *Obit* Yrbk 1962

Romberg, Sigmund, composer, Mar 1945, *Obit* Yrbk 1951

Rome, Harold, American composer and lyricist, Apr 1942, *Obit* Jan 1994

Romenesko, Jim, American journalist and webmaster, Feb 2004

Romer, John, British Egyptologist, July 2003

Romero Barcelo, Carlos, Puerto Rican governor, Oct 1977

Romero, Anthony, American lawyer and civil rights activist, July 2002

Rometty, Virginia, American marketing executive, June 2012

Rommel, Erwin, German field marshal, Aug 1942, *Obit* Yrbk 1944

Romnes, Haakon Ingolf, telecommunications executive, Feb 1968, *Obit* Jan 1974

Romney, George, American Secretary of housing and urban development, June 1958, *Obit* Oct 1995

Romney, Mitt, American governor, Sept 2006

Romulo, Carlos Pena, Filipino statesman, Mar 1943, Apr 1957, *Obit* Feb 1986

Ronaldinho, Brazilian soccer player, Jan 2005

Ronaldo, Brazilian soccer player, Aug 1998

Ronan, William J., Oct 1969

Roncagliolo, Santiago, Peruvian novelist, Jan 2006

Ronne, Finn, Norwegian-American explorer, Feb 1948, *Obit* Mar 1980

Ronson, Jon, English journalist, Apr 2012

Ronstadt, Linda, American singer, Jan 1978

Rood, Helen Martin, *Obit* Mar 1943

Roodt, Darrell, South African film director, Jan 2005

Rooks, Lowell W., Apr 1947

Rooney, Andrew A., American journalist and humorist, July 1982, *Obit* Yrbk 2012

Rooney, Joe Don, American guitarist, Aug 2003

Rooney, John J., American congressman, Yrbk 1964, *Obit* Jan 1976

Rooney, Mickey, American actor, Feb 1942, Sept 1965

Roosa, Robert V., American investment banker and government official, Yrbk 1962, *Obit* Mar 1994

Roosevelt, Anna Curtenius, American archaeologist and anthropologist, June 1997

Roosevelt, Eleanor, wife of American president Franklin D. Roosevelt and diplomat,
Nov 1940, Jan 1949, *Obit* Jan 1963

Roosevelt, Elliott, American mystery novelist, mayor and son of President Franklin D. Roosevelt, Yrbk 1946, *Obit* Jan 1991

Roosevelt, Franklin D., American president, Mar 1942, *Obit* Apr 1945

Roosevelt, Franklin D., American congressman and son of President Franklin D. Roosevelt, Jan 1950, *Obit* Sept 1988

Roosevelt, James, American congressman, business consultant and son of President Franklin D. Roosevelt, Apr 1950, *Obit* Nov 1991

Roosevelt, Kermit, army officer, steamship line executive and son of President Theodore Roosevelt, *Obit* July 1943

Roosevelt, Sara Delano, mother of American President Franklin D. Roosevelt, *Obit* Oct 1941

Roosevelt, Theodore, American government official, general and son of President Theodore Roosevelt, *Obit* Sept 1944

Root, Oren, state banking official, Aug 1940, July 1952, *Obit* Mar 1995

Root, Waverley Lewis, American journalist, May 1943, *Obit* Jan 1983

Rootes, William Edward Rootes, British automobile executive, Nov 1951, *Obit* Feb 1965

Rooth, Ivar, Yrbk 1952, *Obit* Apr 1972

Roper, Daniel C., *Obit* May 1943

Roper, Elmo, American public opinion analyst, Jan 1945, *Obit* June 1971

Rorem, Ned, American composer, July 1967

Rorimer, James J., Yrbk 1955, *Obit* June 1966

Ros-Lehtinen, Ileana, American congresswoman, Aug 2000

Rosanoff, Aaron J., *Obit* Feb 1943

Rosas, Cesar, American singer and guitarist, Oct 2005

Rose, Alex, American labor leader, Yrbk 1959, *Obit* Feb 1977

Rose, Arnold, *Obit* Oct 1946

Rose, Billy, American theatrical producer, Aug 1940, *Obit* Mar 1966

Rose, Charlie, American television newscaster and talk show host, Jan 1995

Rose, George, actor, Sept 1984, *Obit* June 1988

Rose, Jalen, American basketball player, Mar 2004

Rose, Jim, American performance artist, Mar 2003

Rose, Leonard, American cellist, Jan 1977, *Obit* Jan 1985

Rose, Mary Swartz, American chemist and nutritionist, *Obit* Mar 1941

Rose, Maurice, American general, *Obit* May 1945

Rose, Murray, swimmer, June 1962, *Obit* Yrbk 2012

Rose, Pete, American baseball player and manager, Aug 1975

Rose, William C., American biochemist, Mar 1953, *Obit* Jan 1986

Rosedale, Philip, American information technology executive, Oct 2012

Rosellini, Albert D., American governor, Yrbk 1958, *Obit* Yrbk 2012

Rosen, Al, baseball player and executive, July 1954

Rosen, Benjamin M., computer executive and financier, June 1997

Rosen, Benjamin M.; and Rosen, Harold A., June 1997

Rosen, Harold A., American electrical engineer, June 1997

Rosen, Samuel, Feb 1974, *Obit* Jan 1982

Rosenbach, A. S. W., American rare book collector and dealer, May 1946, *Obit* Sept 1952

Rosenberg, Alfred, German Nazi leader, Oct 1941, *Obit* Nov 1946

Rosenberg, Arthur, *Obit* Mar 1943

Rosenberg, Steven A., American surgeon, Feb 1991

Rosenfeld, Henry Jonas, clothing and luggage industry executive, Nov 1948

Rosenfeld, Irene, American food industry executive, July 2007

Rosenfeld, Kurt, *Obit* Nov 1943

Rosenfeld, Paul, American music, art and literary critic, *Obit* Sept 1946

Rosenfield, Harry N., lawyer, lobbyist and refugee settlement leader, Apr 1952, *Obit* Aug 1995

Rosenhaus, Drew, American sports agent, July 2011

Rosenman, Dorothy, housing advocate, Apr 1947, *Obit* Mar 1991

Rosenman, Samuel I., American state supreme court justice, Aug 1942, *Obit* Sept 1973

Rosenquist, James, American painter, Sept 1970

Rosenstock, Joseph, conductor and opera director, Jan 1954, *Obit* Jan 1986

Rosenthal, A. M., American newspaper editor, Yrbk 1960, *Obit* Sept 2006

Rosenthal, Jane, American film producer, Apr 2011

Rosenthal, Joe, American photojournalist, June 1945, *Obit* Yrbk 2007

Rosenthal, Moriz, Polish pianist, *Obit* Oct 1946

Rosenwald, Lessing J., American retail executive and book collector, Feb 1947, *Obit* Aug 1979

Rosenwinkel, Kurt, American jazz guitarist and composer, July 2011

Rosett, Joshua, *Obit* May 1940

Rosewall, Ken, Australian tennis player, Yrbk 1956

Rospars, Joe, American information technology executive, May 2010

Ross, Alex, American comic book artist, Nov 2007

Ross, C. Ben, American governor, *Obit* May 1946

Ross, Charles G., June 1945, *Obit* Jan 1951

Ross, Diana, American singer and actress, Mar 1973

Ross, Edward Denison, *Obit* Nov 1940

Ross, Gary, American screenwriter, May 2004

Ross, Harold Wallace, American periodical editor, May 1943, *Obit* Jan 1952

Ross, Herbert, American choreographer and motion picture director, Aug 1980, *Obit* Feb 2002

Ross, Jerilyn, American psychotherapist, Nov 2009, *Obit* Yrbk 2010

Ross, Malcolm, Feb 1944, *Obit* July 1965

Ross, Nancy Wilson, author, Yrbk 1952, *Obit* May 1986

Ross, Nellie Tayloe, American governor, May 1940, *Obit* Feb 1978

Ross, Rick, American rapper, June 2012

Ross, Robert, American entrepreneur, Oct 2002, *Obit* Yrbk 2011

Rossel, Agda, Yrbk 1959

Rossellini, Isabella, Italian model and actress, Aug 1988

Rossellini, Roberto, Italian film director, July 1949, *Obit* Aug 1977

Rossen, Daniel, American singer, songwriter and guitarist, Sept 2011

Rossen, Robert, American motion picture director, producer and screenwriter, Oct 1950, *Obit* Mar 1966

Rosset, Barney, American publisher and editor, Apr 1972, *Obit* Yrbk 2012

Rossi, Valentino, Italian motorcycle racer, Jan 2005

Rossi, Vasco, Italian rock singer, Jan 2005

Rossiter, Clinton Lawrence, American historian and political scientist, Apr 1967, *Obit* Yrbk 1970

Rossy, Yves, Swiss air pilot and inventor, Jan 2013

Rostand, Jean, Yrbk 1954, *Obit* Jan 1978

Rosten, Leo, American economist and humorist, Oct 1942, *Obit* Apr 1997

Rosten, Norman, poet, playwright and novelist, Apr 1944, *Obit* May 1995

Rostenkowski, Dan, American congressman, Jan 1982, *Obit* Yrbk 2010

Rostow, Eugene Victor, American lawyer and economist, Apr 1961, *Obit* Yrbk 2003

Rostow, W. W., American economist and presidential adviser, May 1961, *Obit* July 2003

Rostropovich, Mstislav, Russian cellist and conductor, May 1966, Nov 1988, *Obit* Aug 2007

Roszak, Theodore, American historian, Apr 1982, *Obit* Yrbk 2011

Roszak, Theodore J., Polish-American painter and sculptor, June 1966, *Obit* Oct 1981

Rotblat, Joseph, British physicist and pacifist, July 1997, *Obit* Feb 2006

Rote, Kyle, American football player and sportscaster, May 1965, *Obit* Yrbk 2002

Roth, Almon E., Oct 1946

Roth, Ann, costume designer, Mar 1997

Roth, Gabriel, American songwriter, bassist and recording producer, Feb 2010

Roth, Henry, American novelist and short story writer, Jan 1989, *Obit* Jan 1996

Roth, Philip, American novelist and short story writer, Mar 1970, May 1991

Roth, William V., American senator, Apr 1983, *Obit* Yrbk 2004

Rotha, Paul, English motion picture producer and director, Apr 1957, *Obit* May 1984

Rothenberg, Susan, American painter and printmaker, Mar 1985

Rothenstein, John Maurice, English art historian and museum director, Apr 1957

Rothenstein, William, English painter, *Obit* Apr 1945

Rothermere, Esmond Cecil Harmsworth, British newspaper publisher, Yrbk 1948, *Obit* Sept 1978

Rothermere, Harold Sidney Harmsworth, British newspaper publisher, *Obit* Jan 1941

Rothery, Agnes, Yrbk 1946, *Obit* Oct 1954

Rothko, Mark, American painter, May 1961, *Obit* Apr 1970

Rothschild, Guy de, French banker, Mar 1973, *Obit* Yrbk 2007

Rothschild, Louis Samuel, government official, Yrbk 1957, *Obit* Oct 1984

Rothschild, Miriam, British entomologist and botanist, Oct 1992, *Obit* Yrbk 2005

Rotten, Johnny, English singer, Nov 1996

Rouault, Georges, French painter, May 1945, *Obit* Apr 1958

Roudebush, Richard L., congressman and veterans' leader, June 1976, *Obit* Apr 1995

Roueche, Berton, American novelist and medical and travel writer, Yrbk 1959, *Obit* July 1994

Rounds, M. Michael, American governor, June 2006

Rountree, Martha, radio and television producer, Feb 1957, *Obit* Nov 1999

Rountree, William M., diplomat, June 1959, *Obit* Jan 1996

Rourke, Constance Mayfield, biographer, *Obit* May 1941

Rourke, Mickey, American actor, Oct 1991

Rous, Francis Peyton, American pathologist, Mar 1967, *Obit* Apr 1970

Rouse, James W., American real estate developer, Feb 1982, *Obit* June 1996

Rouse, Milford O., June 1968

Rousseau, Stephane, Canadian comedian and actor, Jan 2004

Rousseff, Dilma, Brazilian president, July 2012

Routley, Thomas Clarence, Jan 1956, *Obit* June 1963

Rove, Karl, American political commentator and former presidential adviser, Oct 2000

Rovere, Richard Halworth, American journalist, Apr 1977, *Obit* Jan 1980

Rowan, Andrew S., American army officer, *Obit* Mar 1943

Rowan, Carl Thomas, American newspaper columnist, Jan 1958, *Obit* Jan 2001

Rowan, Dan, American comedian, Sept 1969, *Obit* Nov 1987

Rowe, Leo Stanton, director general of the Pan American union, Aug 1945, *Obit* Jan 1947

Rowell, Chester Harvey, newspaper editor, Yrbk 1940, *Obit* May 1948

Rowland, John, American governor, Oct 1997

Rowland, Kelly, American singer, Aug 2001

Rowlands, Gena, American actress, Nov 1975

Rowley, James Joseph, secret service official, Jan 1963, *Obit* Jan 1993

Rowley, Janet D., American geneticist, Mar 2001

Rowling, J. K., English fantasy novelist, Jan 2000

Rowntree, Cecil, *Obit* Yrbk 1943

Rowntree, Dave, British drummer, Nov 2003

Rowse, A. L., English historian and biographer, July 1979, *Obit* Jan 1998

Roxas y Acuna, Manuel, May 1946, *Obit* May 1948

Roy, Maurice, Feb 1958, *Obit* Jan 1986

Roy, Patrick, Canadian hockey player, Nov 1999

Royal, Forrest B., American admiral, *Obit* July 1945

Royal, Segolene, French political leader, Jan 2007

Royall, Kenneth C., American Secretary of the army, Jan 1947, *Obit* Sept 1971

Royden, Agnes Maude, English social worker and evangelist, Apr 1942, *Obit* Oct 1956

Royko, Mike, American newspaper columnist, June 1994, *Obit* July 1997

Royle, Edwin Milton, *Obit* Apr 1942

Royster, Vermont, American journalist, Yrbk 1953, *Obit* Oct 1996

Rozelle, Pete, American football commissioner, June 1964, *Obit* Feb 1997

Rozsa, Miklos, composer, Feb 1992, *Obit* Oct 1995

Rua, Fernando de la, Argentine president, Apr 2001

Rubattel, Rodolphe, Yrbk 1954, *Obit* Yrbk 1961

Rubbia, Carlo, Italian physicist, June 1985

Rubenstein, Atoosa, American magazine editor, Oct 2004

Rubicam, Raymond, advertising executive, Yrbk 1943, *Obit* July 1978

Rubik, Erno, Hungarian professor of architecture and inventor, Feb 1987

Rubin de la Borbolla, Daniel F., Feb 1960

Rubin, Barbara Jo, Yrbk 1969

Rubin, Eddy, American geneticist, Jan 2006

Rubin, Reuven, Apr 1943, *Obit* Jan 1975

Rubin, Rick, American recording producer and executive, Sept 2007

Rubin, Robert E., American financial executive and former Secretary of the treasury, July 1997

Rubin, Theodore Isaac, Feb 1980

Rubin, William Stanley, American art historian and museum curator, Nov 1986, *Obit* Yrbk 2007

Rubinstein, Artur, Polish-American pianist, Yrbk 1945, Feb 1966, *Obit* Mar 1983

Rubinstein, Helena, American cosmetician, June 1943, *Obit* May 1965

Rubio, Ingrid, Spanish actress, Jan 2002

Rubio, Marco, American senator, Apr 2011

Rubottom, R. Richard, American diplomat, May 1959, *Obit* Yrbk 2011

Ruckelshaus, William D., American government official, July 1971

Rucker, Rudy von Bitter, American mathematician, computer programmer and science fiction writer, May 2008

Ruckstull, Frederick Wellington, sculptor, *Obit* July 1942

Rudd, Paul, American actor, Sept 1977, *Obit* Yrbk 2010

Rudd, Phil, Australian drummer, Mar 2005

Rudel, Julius, Austrian-American conductor, July 1965

Ruder, David S., American lawyer, Nov 1988

Rudkin, Margaret Fogarty, American baking executive, Sept 1959, *Obit* Oct 1967

Rudman, Warren B., senator, Nov 1989, *Obit* Yrbk 2013

Rudolph, Paul, American architect, Feb 1972, *Obit* Nov 1997

Rudolph, Wilma, American runner, Sept 1961, *Obit* Jan 1995

Rueff, Jacques, French economist, Feb 1969, *Obit* June 1978

Ruffin, William H., Feb 1951

Ruffing, Red, American baseball player, Nov 1941, *Obit* Apr 1986

Rugambwa, Laurean, Sept 1960, *Obit* Feb 1998

Rugg, Harold Ordway, American educator, May 1941, *Obit* July 1960

Ruhle, Stephanie, American investment banker, Jan 2013

Ruhmann, Heinz, Apr 1965

Ruiz Cortines, Adolfo, Mexican president, Sept 1952, *Obit* Jan 1974

Ruiz Guinazu, Enrique, Apr 1942, *Obit* Jan 1968

Ruiz Guinazu, Magdalena, Argentine journalist, Jan 2004

Ruiz Soler, Antonio, Spanish dancer, June 1968

Rukeyser, Louis, American television moderator, Feb 1983, *Obit* Nov 2006

Rukeyser, Muriel, American poet, Mar 1943, *Obit* Apr 1980

Rule, Ann, American true-crime writer, Sept 2000

Ruml, Beardsley, department store executive and banker, May 1943, *Obit* June 1960

Rummel, Joseph F., American archbishop, June 1959, *Obit* Jan 1965

Rumor, Mariano, Italian prime minister, July 1969, *Obit* Mar 1990

Rumpler, Edmund, *Obit* Oct 1940

Rumsfeld, Donald H., American Secretary of defense, Apr 1970, Mar 2002

Runbeck, Margaret Lee, Yrbk 1952, *Obit* Yrbk 1956

Runcie, Robert, English archbishop, Nov 1980, *Obit* Oct 2000

Rundstedt, Karl Rudolf Gerd von, German field marshal, Nov 1941, *Obit* Apr 1953

Runkle, Erwin W., *Obit* Apr 1941

Runyon, Damon, American journalist and short story writer, Nov 1942, *Obit* Jan 1947

Runyon, Mefford R., May 1949

Rupertus, William H., *Obit* May 1945

Ruranga, Rubaramira, Ugandan army officer and AIDs activist, Jan 2006

Rus, Daniela, Romanian computer scientist, Feb 2004

Rusby, Henry H., *Obit* Jan 1941

Ruscha, Edward, American painter, printmaker and photographer, Oct 1989

Rusesabagina, Paul, Rwandan hotel manager and humanitarian, May 2005

Rush (Musical group), Feb 2001

Rush, David Kenneth, American chemical industry executive and diplomat, May 1975, *Obit* Feb 1995

Rushdie, Salman, British novelist, Nov 1986, Jan 2003

Rushing, Matthew, American dancer, July 2000

Rushkoff, Douglas, American nonfiction writer and novelist, Nov 2013

Rushmore, David Barker, *Obit* July 1940

Rusk, Dean, American Secretary of state, June 1949, July 1961, *Obit* Feb 1995

Rusk, Howard Archibald, American physician, Mar 1946, May 1967, *Obit* Jan 1990

Russell, Anna, Canadian singer and parodist, Apr 1954, *Obit* Yrbk 2007

Russell, Bertrand, British philosopher, Apr 1940, Jan 1951, *Obit* Mar 1970

Russell, Bill, American basketball player, coach and sportscaster, July 1975

Russell, Charles Edward, American journalist, social reformer and biographer, *Obit* June 1941

Russell, Charles Hinton, American newspaper publisher and governor, Yrbk 1955, *Obit* Nov 1989

Russell, Donald J., railroad executive, May 1962, *Obit* Feb 1986

Russell, Harold, American actor and government official, Jan 1950, Jan 1966, *Obit* Apr 2002

Russell, James Earl, *Obit* Yrbk 1945

Russell, James S., admiral, Jan 1962

Russell, Karen, American short story writer and novelist, May 2011

Russell, Ken, English motion picture director, Oct 1975, *Obit* Yrbk 2012

Russell, Kurt, American actor, Nov 2004

Russell, Mark, American political satirist, Mar 1981

Russell, Pee Wee, clarinetist, Aug 1944, *Obit* Apr 1969

Russell, Richard B., American senator, Nov 1949, *Obit* Mar 1971

Russell, Rosalind, American actress, Jan 1943, *Obit* Feb 1977

Russell, William F., Apr 1947, *Obit* June 1956

Russert, Tim, American television news executive and moderator, Oct 1997, *Obit* Yrbk 2008

Russo, Pat F., American information technology executive, May 2008

Russo, Rene, American model and actress, July 1997

Rust, Bernhard, German Nazi leader, July 1942

Rustin, Bayard, American civil rights leader, June 1967, *Obit* Oct 1987

Rutan, Burt, American aeronautical engineer and executive, June 2005

Rutenberg, Pinhas, *Obit* Mar 1942

Rutenborn, Gunter, Oct 1960

Ruth, Babe, American baseball player, Aug 1944, *Obit* Oct 1948

Rutherford, J. F., religious leader, Nov 1940, *Obit* Mar 1942

Rutherford, Margaret, English actress, Jan 1964, *Obit* July 1972

Rutledge, Wiley Blount, American Supreme Court

justice, May 1943, *Obit* Oct 1949

Ryan, George H., American governor, Sept 2001

Ryan, John A., priest and theologian, *Obit* Oct 1945

Ryan, Joseph P., American longshore workers union leader, Jan 1949, *Obit* Sept 1963

Ryan, Kay, American poet, Apr 2012

Ryan, Meg, American actress, May 1999

Ryan, Nolan, American baseball player and executive, Oct 1970

Ryan, Patrick James, military chaplain, May 1955

Ryan, Paul, American congressman, Jan 2013

Ryan, Rex, American football coach, Oct 2010

Ryan, Robert, American actor, Yrbk 1963, *Obit* Sept 1973

Ryan, T. Claude, aviation pioneer, Jan 1943, *Obit* Nov 1982

Ryan, William F., American congressman, May 1967, *Obit* Yrbk 1972

Ryder, Winona, American actress, June 1994

Rykiel, Sonia, French fashion designer, May 1990

Rylance, Mark, English actor and theatrical director, Nov 2011

Ryle, Martin, British physicist and astronomer, Sept 1973, *Obit* Jan 1985

Rysanek, Leonie, Austrian opera singer, Mar 1966, *Obit* May 1998

Ryti, Risto, Feb 1941, *Obit* Jan 1957

Ryun, Jim, American runner and congressman, May 1968

S

Saab, Elie, Lebanese fashion designer, Aug 2004

Saakashvili, Mikheil, Georgian president, May 2009

Saariaho, Kaija, Finnish composer, Jan 2003

Saarinen, Aline B., American art critic and wife of architect Eero Saarinen, Yrbk 1956, *Obit* Sept 1972

Saarinen, Eero, American architect, Oct 1949, *Obit* Nov 1961

Saarinen, Eliel, Finnish-American architect, Oct 1942, *Obit* Sept 1950

Saatchi, Maurice, English advertising executive, Jan 1989

Sabath, Adolph J., American congressman, July 1946, *Obit* Yrbk 1952

Sabathia, C. C., American baseball player, Apr 2008

Sabatier, Paul, French chemist, *Obit* Oct 1941

Sabatini, Gabriela, Argentine tennis player, June 1992

Sabato, Ernesto R., Argentine novelist, physicist and human rights activist, Oct 1985, *Obit* Yrbk 2011

Sabin, Albert, American physician, Feb 1958, *Obit* Apr 1993

Sabin, Florence Rena, American anatomist, Apr 1945, *Obit* Yrbk 1953

Sabry, Hassan, *Obit* Yrbk 1940

Sacco, Joe, Maltese cartoonist and journalist, Jan 2013

Sachar, Abram Leon, historian and college president, Nov 1949, *Obit* Sept 1993

Sachs, Bernard, American neurologist, *Obit* Mar 1944

Sachs, Curt, German musicologist, Aug 1944, *Obit* Apr 1959

Sachs, Jeffrey D., American economist, Nov 1993

Sachs, Nelly, German poet, Mar 1967, *Obit* July 1970

Sackett, Frederic M., senator and diplomat, *Obit* July 1941

Sacks, Oliver W., American neurologist and medical writer, Feb 1985

Sacramone, Alicia, American gymnast, Mar 2011

Sadak, Necmeddin, Jan 1950, *Obit* Yrbk 1953

Sadat, Anwar, Egyptian president, Mar 1971, *Obit* Nov 1981

Sadat, Jehan, wife of Egyptian president Anwar Sadat, Aug 1986

Saddler, Donald, choreographer, Jan 1963

Sade, British singer, Sept 1986

Sadik, Nafis, Pakistani physician and United Nations official, Feb 1996

Sadik-Khan, Janette, American transportation official, Nov 2012

Sadler, Michael Ernest, British educator, *Obit* Yrbk 1943

Saerchinger, Cesar, Apr 1940

Saez, Emmanuel, French economist, Sept 2011

Safdie, Moshe, Canadian architect, Sept 1968

Safer, Morley, Canadian television newscaster, July 1980

Safin, Marat, Russian tennis player, Jan 2003

Safina, Carl, American marine conservationist and scientist, Apr 2005

Safire, William, American journalist, essayist and novelist, Yrbk 1973, *Obit* Yrbk 2009

Sagan, Carl, American astronomer, Apr 1970, *Obit* Feb 1997

Sagan, Francoise, French novelist and short story writer, Sept 1960, *Obit* Feb 2005

Sage, Dean, *Obit* Aug 1943

Sagendorph, Robb, American magazine editor and publisher, Yrbk 1956, *Obit* Sept 1970

Sager, Ruth, geneticist, July 1967, *Obit* June 1997

Sagnier, Ludivine, French actress, Jan 2004

Sahl, Mort, American comedian, Yrbk 1960

Said bin Taimur, Oct 1957, *Obit* Aug 1978

Said, Edward W., Palestinian-American literary and social critic, Nov 1989, *Obit* Feb 2004

Saillant, Louis, July 1948, *Obit* Jan 1975

Saint Laurent, Yves, French fashion designer, Yrbk 1964, *Obit* Oct 2008

Saint, Eva Marie, American actress, June 1955

Saint-Exupery, Antoine de, French novelist, essayist and aviator, Jan 1940, *Obit* May 1945

Saint-Gaudens, Homer Schiff, museum director, Oct 1941, *Obit* Feb 1959

Sainte-Marie, Buffy, Canadian singer and songwriter, July 1969

Saionji, Kimmochi, Japanese statesman, *Obit* Jan 1941

Sairam, Aruna, Indian singer, Jan 2006

Sajak, Pat, American television game show host, July 1989

Sakaguchi, Hironobu, Japanese video game designer, Jan 2003

Sakel, Manfred, Jan 1941, *Obit* Feb 1958

Sakharov, Andrei Dmitrievich, Russian physicist, July 1971, *Obit* Feb 1990

Saks, Elyn R., American psychiatrist and law professor, Feb 2011

Salam, Abdus, Pakistani physicist, Apr 1988, *Obit* Jan 1997

Salamun, Tomaz, Slovenian poet, Jan 2007

Salant, Richard S., television executive, Nov 1961, *Obit* Apr 1993

Salazar, Alberto, American marathon runner, May 1983

Salazar, Antonio de Oliveira, Portuguese dictator, May 1941, May 1952, *Obit* Oct 1970

Salazar, Ken, American Secretary of the interior, Mar 2009

Sale, Rhys M., Yrbk 1957

Saleh, Allah-Yar, Feb 1953

Salerno-Sonnenberg, Nadja, violinist, Nov 1987

Sales, Nykesha, basketball player, June 1999

Sales, Soupy, American comedian, Jan 1967, *Obit* Yrbk 2009

Salgado, Sebastiao, Brazilian photographer, Jan 2002

Saliers, Emily, American singer and songwriter, Aug 1998

Salih, Barham, Iraqi deputy prime minister, Jan 2007

Salinas de Gortari, Carlos, Mexican president, Mar 1989

Salinger, J. D., American novelist and short story writer, *Obit* Yrbk 2010

Salinger, Pierre, American journalist and presidential press secretary, July 1961, Mar 1987, *Obit* Feb 2005

Salisbury, Harrison Evans, American journalist, July 1955, Jan 1982, *Obit* Sept 1993

Salisbury, Robert Arthur James Gascoyne-Cecil, British member of Parliament, Nov 1941, *Obit* Apr 1972

Salit, Norman, rabbi and lawyer, Mar 1955, *Obit* Oct 1960

Salk, Jonas, American physician, May 1954, *Obit* Aug 1995

Salk, Lee, child psychologist, Sept 1979, *Obit* July 1992

Salle, David, American painter and filmmaker, Sept 1986

Salles, Walter, Brazilian motion picture director, Jan 2004

Salman, Saad, Iraqi documentary filmmaker, Jan 2004

Salomon, Henry, Yrbk 1956, *Obit* Apr 1958

Salonen, Esa-Pekka, Finnish composer and conductor, Jan 2007

Salonga, Lea, Filipino singer and actress, Jan 2007

Salote Tupou, Yrbk 1953, *Obit* Feb 1966

Salten, Felix, Austrian author, *Obit* Nov 1945

Salter, Alfred, *Obit* Sept 1945

Salter, Andrew, psychologist, May 1944, *Obit* Jan 1997

Salter, Arthur Salter, English economist and member of Parliament, May 1944

Saltonstall, Leverett, American governor and senator, June 1944, Apr 1956, *Obit* Sept 1979

Saltzman, Charles E., general, diplomat and investment banker, Oct 1947, *Obit* Aug 1994

Salvador Lavado, Joaquin, Argentine cartoonist, Jan 2004

Salvemini, Gaetano, Italian-American historian and biographer, Yrbk 1943, *Obit* Nov 1957

Salverson, Laura Goodman, Canadian author, Yrbk 1957

Salzano, Francisco M., Brazilian geneticist, Jan 2006

Samaranch, Juan Antonio, Spanish Olympics executive, Feb 1994, *Obit* Yrbk 2010

Samaras, Lucas, American sculptor, painter and photographer, Nov 1972

Samaroff, Olga, American pianist and music teacher, Mar 1946, *Obit* June 1948

Sambi, Ahmed Abdallah Mohamed, Comoran president, Jan 2006

Sambrook, Richard, British broadcasting executive, Jan 2003

Sammartino, Peter, college president, Yrbk 1958, *Obit* May 1992

Sampras, Pete, American tennis player, May 1994

Sampson, Edith S., American judge, Yrbk 1950, *Obit* Jan 1980

Samuel, Bernard, Sept 1949, *Obit* Mar 1954

Samuel, Herbert Louis Samuel, British statesman, Apr 1955, *Obit* Mar 1963

Samuelson, Joan, American marathon runner, Aug 1996

Samuelson, Paul A., American economist, May 1965, *Obit* Yrbk 2010

Sanborn, David, American saxophonist, Aug 1992

Sanborn, Pitts, music critic, author and journalist, *Obit* Apr 1941

Sanchez Junco, Eduardo, Spanish magazine publisher, Jan 2003, *Obit* Yrbk 2010

Sanchez Vicario, Arantxa, Spanish tennis player, Aug 1998

Sanchez de Lozada, Gonzalo, Bolivian president, Jan 2002

Sanchez, David, Puerto Rican jazz saxophonist, Nov 2001

Sanchez, Fernando, Mexican government official, Jan 2002

Sandage, Allan, American astronomer, Jan 1999, *Obit* Yrbk 2011

Sandberg, Ryne, American baseball player, Nov 1994

Sandberg, Sheryl, American Internet executive, June 2008

Sandburg, Carl, American poet, biographer and historian, June 1940, Yrbk 1963, *Obit* Oct 1967

Sandefer, Jefferson Davis, *Obit* Apr 1940

Sander, Jil, German fashion designer, Oct 1997

Sanders, Barry, American football player, Sept 1993

Sanders, Bernard, American senator, June 1991

Sanders, Carl E., American governor, Yrbk 1964

Sanders, Deion, American football player and sportscaster, Jan 1995

Sanders, George, British actor, June 1943, *Obit* June 1972

Sanders, Harland, American restaurateur, Apr 1973, *Obit* Feb 1981

Sanders, Jared Young, *Obit* May 1944

Sanders, Lawrence, author, Apr 1989, *Obit* May 1998

Sanders, Marlene, television newscaster, Feb 1981

Sanders, Ric, English fiddler, Sept 2005

Sanderson, Derek, Canadian hockey player and investment manager, Apr 1975

Sandford, John, American crime novelist, Mar 2002

Sandler, Adam, American comedian and actor, May 1998

Sandor, Gyorgy, American pianist, July 1947, *Obit* Yrbk 2006

Sandoval, Arturo, Cuban jazz trumpet player, Jan 2003

Sandoval, Brian, American governor, Jan 2012

Sandoval, Jesse, American drummer, June 2007

Sandstrom, Emil, Jan 1951, *Obit* Sept 1962

Sanford, Terry, American senator, Nov 1961, *Obit* July 1998

Sangare, Oumou, Malian singer, Jan 2003

Sanger, Frederick, British biochemist, July 1981

Sanger, Margaret, American family planning advocate, Aug 1944, *Obit* Nov 1966

Sanger, Stephen W., American food company executive, Mar 2004

Sanjiva Reddy, N., Indian president, Mar 1981, *Obit* Aug 1996

Sansa, Maya, Italian actress, Jan 2004

Sansone, Pat, American guitarist, percussionist and keyboardist, Feb 2010

Santa Cruz, Hernan, Yrbk 1949

Santana, Johan, Venezuelan baseball player, July 2006

Santana, Manuel, Spanish tennis player, Sept 1967

Santaolalla, Gustavo, Argentine composer and record producer, Jan 2007

Santayana, George, Spanish-American philosopher, Apr 1944, *Obit* Nov 1952

Santelli, Rick, American television reporter, July 2010

Santelmann, William F., bandmaster and marine corps officer, Apr 1953

Santmyer, Helen Hooven, author, educator and librarian, Feb 1985, *Obit* Apr 1986

Santolalla, Irene Silva de, Peruvian educator and legislator, Yrbk 1956, *Obit* Sept 1992

Santorum, Rick, American lawyer, presidential candidate and former senator, Aug 2011

Santos, Jose, Chilean jockey, Nov 2003

Santos, Jose Eduardo dos, Angolan president, May 1994

Santos, Rufino J., Yrbk 1960, *Obit* Nov 1973

Sapolsky, Robert M., American neurobiologist, Jan 2004

Saposs, David J., Nov 1940, *Obit* Jan 1969

Sapp, Warren, American football player, Sept 2003

Saracoglu, Sukru, June 1942, *Obit* Mar 1954

Saragat, Giuseppe, Italian president, Yrbk 1956, July 1965, *Obit* July 1988

Sarah, Mar 1987

Saralegui, Cristina, American television talk show host, Jan 1999

Saramago, Jose, Portuguese novelist, June 2002, *Obit* Yrbk 2010

Sarandon, Susan, American actress, Sept 1989

Sarbanes, Paul S., American senator, Jan 1997

Sardi Sr., Vincent; and Sardi Jr., Vincent, May 1957

Sardi, Vincent, American restaurateur, May 1957, *Obit* Yrbk 2008

Sardi, Vincent, American restaurateur, May 1957, *Obit* Jan 1970

Sarg, Tony, German-American puppeteer and illustrator, *Obit* Apr 1942

Sargeant, Howland Hill, diplomat, Yrbk 1952, *Obit* Apr 1984

Sargent, Francis W., governor, June 1971, *Obit* Jan 1999

Sargent, Malcolm Watts, English conductor, Yrbk 1945, *Obit* Jan 1968

Sargent, Porter, July 1941, *Obit* May 1951

Sarkis, Elias, Lebanese president, Mar 1979, *Obit* Aug 1985

Sarkozy, Nicolas, French president, Jan 2006

Sarney, Jose, Brazilian president, Mar 1986

Sarnoff, David, American radio and television executive, Nov 1940, Oct 1951, *Obit* Feb 1972

Sarnoff, Robert W., electronics executive, Yrbk 1956, *Obit* May 1997

Saroyan, William, American short story writer, novelist and dramatist, July 1940, Nov 1972, *Obit* July 1981

Sarraute, Nathalie, French novelist, June 1966, *Obit* Jan 2000

Sarris, Andrew, American film critic, Jan 2007, *Obit* Yrbk 2012

Sarton, George, American science historian, July 1942, *Obit* May 1956

Sarton, May, American poet and novelist, May 1982, *Obit* Sept 1995

Sartre, Jean Paul, French novelist and philosopher, Mar 1947, May 1971, *Obit* June 1980

Sass, Katrin, German actress, Jan 2003

Sassa, Scott Michael, American Internet executive, Jan 2000

Sasser, James R., senator and diplomat, July 1993

Sassoon, Vidal, British hairstylist and personal care products industry executive, Apr 1999, *Obit* Yrbk 2012

Sastroamidjojo, Ali, June 1950, *Obit* May 1975

Satcher, David, American surgeon general, Feb 1997

Sato, Eisaku, Japanese prime minister, Yrbk 1965, *Obit* Aug 1975

Satrapi, Marjane, Iranian graphic novelist, illustrator and memoirist, Jan 2003

Satterfield, John C., July 1962

Satyarthi, Kailash, Indian social activist, Jan 2007

Sauckel, Fritz, German Nazi leader, *Obit* Nov 1946

Saud, Apr 1954, *Obit* Apr 1969

Saud al Faisal, Jan 1948

Sauer, Emil von, German pianist, *Obit* June 1942

Sauer, George H., football coach and executive, Nov 1948, *Obit* Apr 1994

Saul, Ralph Southey, Feb 1971

Saulnier, Raymond J., American economist and presidential adviser, Yrbk 1957, *Obit* Yrbk 2009

Saund, Dalip Singh, congressman, June 1960, *Obit* June 1973

Saunders, Carl M., June 1950, *Obit* Nov 1974

Saunders, Cicely, English physician and hospice director, Jan 2004

Saunders, Hilary Aidan St. George, English author, June 1943, *Obit* Feb 1952

Saunders, John Monk, screenwriter, *Obit* Apr 1940

Saunders, Robert, Yrbk 1951, *Obit* Mar 1955

Saunders, Stuart Thomas, American railroad executive, Apr 1966, *Obit* Mar 1987

Saura, Carlos, Spanish motion picture director, Sept 1978

Sauve, Jeanne, Canadian government official, Aug 1984, *Obit* Mar 1993

Savage, Augusta Christine, American sculptor, Jan 1941, *Obit* May 1962

Savage, Dan, American advice columnist, July 2009

Savage, John Lucian, Apr 1943, *Obit* Feb 1968

Savage, Michael Joseph, *Obit* Apr 1940

Savage, Rick, English bassist and singer, Jan 2003

Savalas, Telly, actor, Feb 1976, *Obit* Mar 1994

Savery, Constance, Yrbk 1948

Saville, Curtis, long distance rower, Jan 1986

Saville, Curtis; and Saville, Kathleen, Jan 1986

Saville, Kathleen, long distance rower, Jan 1986

Saville, Peter, British graphic designer, Jan 2006

Savimbi, Jonas, Angolan rebel leader, Aug 1986, *Obit* June 2002

Savitch, Jessica, television news anchor, Jan 1983, *Obit* Mar 1984

Savitt, Dick, tennis player, June 1952

Sawhill, John C., American college president and conservationist, Apr 1979, *Obit* Yrbk 2000

Sawyer, Charles, American Secretary of commerce and diplomat, July 1948, *Obit* June 1979

Sawyer, Diane, American television news anchor, Oct 1985

Sawyer, Eddie, baseball manager, Nov 1950, *Obit* Jan 1998

Sawyer, Helen, painter, Oct 1954

Sawyer, John E., college president and foundation official, July 1961, *Obit* Apr 1995

Saxbe, William B., American Attorney general and senator, July 1974, *Obit* Yrbk 2010

Saxon, James J., Yrbk 1963, *Obit* Apr 1980

Saxon, Lyle, American novelist, *Obit* May 1946

Saxton, Alexander, American historian and novelist, Nov 1943, *Obit* Yrbk 2012

Sayao, Bidu, Brazilian opera singer, Feb 1942, *Obit* June 1999

Sayegh, Fayez A., Lebanese scholar and diplomat, July 1957

Sayles, John, American novelist, short story writer, screenwriter and film director, Feb 1984

Sayles, R. W., *Obit* Yrbk 1942

Saylor, Michael, computer software executive, Sept 2000

Sayre, Francis B., American cathedral dean, Yrbk 1956, *Obit* Yrbk 2008

Sayre, Francis Bowes, American diplomat, Jan 1940, *Obit* May 1972

Sayre, Morris, Jan 1948, *Obit* Apr 1953

Sayre, Ruth Buxton, May 1949

Scali, John A., American television newscaster and diplomat, Sept 1973, *Obit* Jan 1996

Scalia, Antonin, American Supreme Court justice, Nov 1986

Scallon, Dana Rosemary, British singer, Jan 2007

Scammon, Richard M., political scientist and public opinion analyst, Mar 1971, *Obit* Sept 2001

Scannell, Herb, American broadcasting executive, Aug 2010

Scarbrough, Roger Lumley, Jan 1958, *Obit* Sept 1969

Scardino, Marjorie, American publishing executive, Apr 2000

Scargill, Arthur, English labor leader, Jan 1985

Scaturro, Pasquale, American geophysicist, mountaineer and rafter, Oct 2005

Scavullo, Francesco, American fashion photographer, May 1985, *Obit* Yrbk 2004

Scdoris, Rachael, American sled dog racer, July 2005

Scelba, Mario, Italian prime minister, May 1953, *Obit* Feb 1992

Scelsa, Vin, American disc jockey, May 2006

Schaap, Phil, American disc jockey and jazz historian, Sept 2001

Schacht, Al, baseball entertainer and restaurateur, May 1946, *Obit* Sept 1984

Schacht, Hjalmar, German financier, Oct 1944, *Obit* Sept 1970

Schaefer, George, television director and producer, Feb 1970, *Obit* Jan 1998

Schaefer, Vincent J., American chemist and meteorologist, Jan 1948, *Obit* Sept 1993

Schaefer, William Donald, American mayor and governor, July 1988, *Obit* Yrbk 2011

Schaffer, Fritz, Mar 1953, *Obit* May 1967

Schain, Josephine, July 1945

Schakowsky, Jan, American congresswoman, July 2004

Schaller, George B., American zoologist, Aug 1985

Schama, Simon, British historian, Nov 1991

Schanberg, Sydney, journalist, Aug 1990

Schapiro, Meyer, American art historian, July 1984, *Obit* May 1996

Schapiro, Miriam, American artist, Aug 2000

Scharf, Adolf, Oct 1957, *Obit* Apr 1965

Scharf, Kenny, American painter, Feb 2012

Schary, Dore, motion picture producer, May 1948, *Obit* Sept 1980

Schaufuss, Peter, Danish ballet dancer and director, May 1982

Schechter, A. A., broadcasting executive, May 1941, *Obit* Aug 1989

Scheck, Barry, American lawyer, Mar 1998

Scheel, Walter, Feb 1971

Scheele, Leonard Andrew, surgeon general, May 1948, *Obit* Mar 1993

Scheer, Alan Austin, Jan 1964

Scheffer, Victor B., marine mammalogist, Apr 1994

Scheiberling, Edward N., Yrbk 1944, *Obit* Jan 1968

Schell, Jonathan, American journalist, July 1992

Schell, Maria, Austrian actress, June 1961, *Obit* Yrbk 2005

Schell, Maximilian, Austrian actor, Yrbk 1962

Schelling, Ernest, American composer, conductor and pianist, Jan 1940

Scherbo, Vitaly, Belarusian gymnast, July 1996

Scherer, Paul, May 1941, *Obit* May 1969

Schereschewsky, Joseph Williams, *Obit* Sept 1940

Scherman, Harry, Sept 1943, July 1963, *Obit* Jan 1970

Scherman, Thomas, American conductor, Yrbk 1954, *Obit* July 1979

Schertzinger, Victor, *Obit* Yrbk 1941

Scheuer, James H., American congressman, Apr 1968, *Obit* Apr 2006

Schiaparelli, Elsa, French fashion designer, Jan 1940, Nov 1951, *Obit* Jan 1974

Schick, Bela, pediatrician, July 1944, *Obit* Feb 1968

Schickele, Peter, American composer, May 1979

Schieffer, Bob, American television news anchor, Aug 2006

Schiff, Dorothy, American newspaper publisher, July 1945, Jan 1965, *Obit* Oct 1989

Schiffrin, Andre, American publisher, Jan 2000

Schilder, Paul, Austrian psychiatrist, *Obit* Jan 1941

Schildkraut, Joseph, Austrian actor, Apr 1956, *Obit* Mar 1964

Schillebeeckx, Edward, Belgian priest and theologian, June 1983, *Obit* May 2010

Schiller, Daniela, Israeli neuroscientist, Mar 2011

Schiller, Karl, German cabinet member, Yrbk 1971, *Obit* Mar 1995

Schiller, Vivian, American radio executive, Oct 2009

Schilling, Curt, American baseball player, Oct 2001

Schillinger, Joseph, Russian composer and music teacher, *Obit* May 1943

Schindler, Alexander M., American rabbi, Sept 1987, *Obit* Feb 2001

Schindler, John A., Mar 1956, *Obit* Jan 1958

Schiotz, Aksel, Mar 1949, *Obit* June 1975

Schiotz, Fredrik Axel, clergyman, Apr 1972, *Obit* May 1989

Schippers, Thomas, American conductor, Apr 1970, *Obit* Feb 1978

Schirra, Wally, American astronaut, June 1966, *Obit* Yrbk 2007

Schisgal, Murray, dramatist, Jan 1968

Schjeldahl, Peter, American art critic, Oct 2005

Schlafly, Phyllis, American social activist and writer, June 1978

Schlamme, Martha, singer, Feb 1964, *Obit* Jan 1986

Schlauch, Margaret, Polish professor of English, Yrbk 1942, *Obit* Sept 1986

Schleich, Michel, *Obit* June 1945

Schlein, Miriam, American children's author, Yrbk 1959, *Obit* Yrbk 2005

Schlesinger, Arthur M., American historian, Oct 1946, Jan 1979, *Obit* Aug 2007

Schlesinger, Frank, astronomer, *Obit* Aug 1943

Schlesinger, James R., American Secretary of defense and energy, Oct 1973

Schlesinger, John, British motion picture director, Nov 1970, *Obit* Yrbk 2003

Schlessinger, Laura C., American psychologist and radio talk show host, Sept 1997

Schlink, Frederick J., consumer rights advocate, Mar 1941, *Obit* Mar 1995

Schlondorff, Volker, German film director and screenwriter, Aug 1983

Schlosser, Alex L., American newspaper and magazine editor, *Obit* Mar 1943

Schmelkes, Franz C., *Obit* Feb 1943

Schmid, Carlo, Feb 1965, *Obit* Apr 1980

Schmidt, Benno C., American educator, Aug 1986

Schmidt, Eric, American information technology executive, Apr 2008

Schmidt, Fritz, *Obit* Aug 1943

Schmidt, Harald, German talk show host, Jan 2006

Schmidt, Helmut, German chancellor, Oct 1974

Schmidt, Maarten, Dutch astronomer, Sept 1966

Schmitt, Bernadotte Everly, historian, Yrbk 1942, *Obit* May 1969

Schmitt, Gladys, author, Mar 1943, *Obit* Yrbk 1972

Schmitt, Harrison H., American senator, geologist and astronaut, July 1974

Schmoke, Kurt, American college dean and mayor, Feb 1995

Schnabel, Artur, Austrian-American pianist and composer, July 1942, *Obit* Sept 1951

Schnabel, Julian, American painter and film director, Nov 1983

Schneerson, Menachem M., American rabbi, Sept 1983, *Obit* Aug 1994

Schneider, Alan, American theatrical director, Yrbk 1969, *Obit* June 1984

Schneider, Alexander, violinist, Mar 1976, *Obit* Mar 1993

Schneider, Alma K., Yrbk 1954

Schneider, Christoph, German drummer, Jan 2007

Schneider, Eugene, *Obit* Jan 1943

Schneider, Hannes, Austrian skier, Mar 1941, *Obit* June 1955

Schneider, Helge, German comedian, actor, jazz musician and composer, Jan 2007

Schneider, Romy, Austrian actress, Jan 1965, *Obit* July 1982

Schneiderman, Rose, labor leader and feminist, Feb 1946, *Obit* Oct 1972

Schneirla, T. C., Yrbk 1955, *Obit* Nov 1968

Schnittke, Alfred, Russian composer, July 1992, *Obit* Oct 1998

Schnitzler, William F., Apr 1965

Schnurer, Carolyn, Mar 1955

Schoen-Rene, Anna Eugenie, *Obit* Jan 1943

Schoenberg, Arnold, Austrian-American composer, Apr 1942, *Obit* Sept 1951

Schoenberg, Loren, American saxophonist and jazz historian, Feb 2005

Schoenbrun, David, American broadcast journalist, Jan 1960, *Obit* July 1988

Schoendienst, Red, baseball player and manager, Yrbk 1964

Schoeneman, George J., American government official, Nov 1947

Schoeppel, Andrew Frank, senator and governor, Mar 1952, *Obit* Mar 1962

Schoff, Hannah Kent, social welfare leader, *Obit* Feb 1941

Schofield, Frank H., *Obit* Apr 1942

Scholder, Fritz, American painter, Apr 1985, *Obit* Yrbk 2005

Schollander, Don, American swimmer, Sept 1965

Schomburg, August, Nov 1960

Schonborn, Christoph von, Jan 2006

Schoonmaker, Edwin Davies, *Obit* Jan 1940

Schoonmaker, Thelma, American film editor, Mar 1997

Schoonover, Lawrence L., Yrbk 1957, *Obit* Mar 1980

Schopf, J. William, American geologist, May 1995

Schorr, Daniel, American television reporter, Sept 1959, Feb 1978, *Obit* Yrbk 2010

Schorr, Friedrich, Hungarian opera singer, July 1942, *Obit* June 1954

Schott, Marge, American automobile dealer and baseball executive, Aug 1999, *Obit* Yrbk 2004

Schottland, Charles Irwin, college president and government official, Yrbk 1956, *Obit* Sept 1995

Schrader, Paul, American screenwriter and film director, Aug 1981

Schram, Emil, stock exchange official, Oct 1941, May 1953, *Obit* Nov 1987

Schranz, Karl, Austrian skier, Jan 1971

Schratt, Katharina, *Obit* May 1940

Schreiber, Georges, author and illustrator, May 1943

Schreiber, Ryan, American webmaster and rock music critic, Feb 2011

Schreiber, Walther, Feb 1954, *Obit* Sept 1958

Schrembs, Joseph, *Obit* Yrbk 1945

Schrempp, Juergen E., German automobile executive, Oct 1999

Schreyer, Edward, Canadian government official, Feb 1981

Schricker, Henry F., American governor, Sept 1950, *Obit* Feb 1967

Schriever, Bernard A., American air force general, Oct 1957, *Obit* Yrbk 2005

Schroder, Gerhard, German political leader, Yrbk 1962, *Obit* Mar 1990

Schroder, Gerhard, German chancellor, Nov 1998

Schroeder, Frederick R., American tennis player, Oct 1949, *Obit* Yrbk 2006

Schroeder, Patricia, American publishing association executive and former congresswoman, Oct 1978

Schroeder, R. W., July 1941

Schuchert, Charles, *Obit* Jan 1943

Schuck, Arthur A., Apr 1950, *Obit* Apr 1963

Schulberg, Budd, American novelist, playwright and screenwriter, June 1941, May 1951, *Obit* Yrbk 2009

Schuller, Gunther, American composer and conductor, Apr 1964

Schuller, Robert Harold, American clergyman, June 1979

Schulte, Karl Joseph, *Obit* May 1941

Schultes, Richard Evans, American botanist, Mar 1995, *Obit* Sept 2001

Schulthess, Edmund, *Obit* June 1944

Schultz, Ed, American radio talk show host, Aug 2005

Schultz, Howard, American coffee chain executive, May 1997

Schultz, Richard D., sports executive, July 1996

Schultz, Sigrid Lillian, journalist, Apr 1944

Schultze, Charles L., American economist and government official, Jan 1970

Schulz, Charles M., American cartoonist, Yrbk 1960, *Obit* Apr 2000

Schulz, Leo, *Obit* Oct 1944

Schumacher, Kurt, German socialist leader, Feb 1948, *Obit* Oct 1952

Schumacher, Michael, German automobile racing driver, Jan 2003

Schuman, Robert, French statesman, Jan 1948, *Obit* Nov 1963

Schuman, William, American composer, June 1942, Yrbk 1962, *Obit* Apr 1992

Schumann, Maurice, French cabinet member, Apr 1970, *Obit* Apr 1998

Schumer, Charles E., American senator, July 1995

Schurman, Jacob G., philosopher, college president and diplomat, *Obit* Oct 1942

Schuster, M. Lincoln, July 1941, *Obit* Feb 1971

Schwartz, Arthur, composer, Nov 1979, *Obit* Oct 1984

Schwartz, Delmore, poet and critic, June 1960, *Obit* Nov 1966

Schwartz, Felice N., management consultant, May 1993, *Obit* Apr 1996

Schwartz, Gil, American public relations executive and journalist, Aug 2007

Schwartz, Maurice, theatrical director, producer and actor, Feb 1956, *Obit* July 1960

Schwartz, Pepper, American sociologist, June 2008

Schwartz, Tony, American advertising executive and sound archivist, July 1985, *Obit* Yrbk 2008

Schwartzman, Jason, American actor, Oct 2009

Schwarz, Gerard, trumpet player and conductor, Apr 1986

Schwarzenegger, Arnold, Austrian-American actor and governor, Apr 1979, Oct 1991, Aug 2004

Schwarzhaupt, Elisabeth, German cabinet member, Jan 1967, *Obit* Jan 1987

Schwarzkopf, Elisabeth, German-British opera singer, Yrbk 1955, *Obit* Yrbk 2006

Schwarzkopf, H. Norman, American general, May 1991, *Obit* Yrbk 2013

Schwarzschild, Martin, astronomer, Feb 1967, *Obit* June 1997

Schwebel, Stephen M., American judge and international relations specialist, July 1952

Schweiker, Richard S., American Secretary of health and human services, Feb 1977

Schweitzer, Albert, German physician, missionary and theologian, Jan 1948, July 1965

Schweitzer, Pierre-Paul, French government official and IMF director, Yrbk 1963, *Obit* Mar 1994

Schwellenbach, Lewis B., American Secretary of Labor, June 1945, *Obit* July 1948

Schwidetzky, Oscar, Yrbk 1943, *Obit* Nov 1963

Schwinger, Julian, American physicist, Oct 1967, *Obit* Sept 1994

Schygulla, Hanna, German actress, July 1984

Scobie, Ronald M., Feb 1945

Scofield, Paul, English actor, Mar 1962, *Obit* Yrbk 2008

Scoggin, Margaret Clara, American librarian, July 1952, *Obit* Sept 1968

Scolari, Luiz Felipe, Brazilian soccer coach, Jan 2006

Scorsese, Martin, American film director, Feb 1979, June 2007

Scott, Arthur Carroll, *Obit* Yrbk 1940

Scott, Barbara Ann, Canadian figure skater, July 1948, *Obit* Yrbk 2012

Scott, Christian, American jazz trumpet player, Jan 2008

Scott, David R., American astronaut and engineering executive, Oct 1971

Scott, George, American gospel singer, Oct 2001, *Obit* Yrbk 2005

Scott, George C., American actor, Apr 1971, *Obit* Nov 1999

Scott, H. Lee, American retail executive, Oct 2006

Scott, Harold, Yrbk 1950

Scott, Hazel, American pianist and singer, Aug 1943, *Obit* Nov 1981

Scott, Henry L., June 1949

Scott, Hillary, American country singer, July 2011

Scott, Hugh Doggett, American senator, Sept 1948, *Obit* Sept 1994

Scott, James B., lawyer, *Obit* Aug 1943

Scott, Jill, American singer, songwriter and actress, Jan 2002

Scott, John R. K., *Obit* Feb 1946

Scott, K. Frances, Nov 1948

Scott, Michael, South African clergyman and human rights activist, Apr 1953, *Obit* Apr 1985

Scott, Peter Markham, English ornithologist and painter, May 1968, *Obit* Nov 1989

Scott, Raymond, composer and musical instrument inventor, July 1941, *Obit* May 1994

Scott, Ridley, British film director, Oct 1991

Scott, Robert Lee, American air force general, Oct 1943, *Obit* Yrbk 2006

Scott, Sheila, English aviator, Nov 1974, *Obit* Jan 1989

Scott, Stuart, American television sportscaster, Jan 2012

Scott, Tom, American composer and singer, Nov 1946

Scott, Tony, British film director, Nov 2004, *Obit* Yrbk 2012

Scott, W. Kerr, Apr 1956, *Obit* July 1958

Scott, Willard, American television weathercaster, July 1989

Scotto, Renata, Italian opera singer, Sept 1978

Scottoline, Lisa, American lawyer and novelist, July 2001

Scourby, Alexander, actor, July 1965, *Obit* Apr 1985

Scowcroft, Brent, American general and presidential adviser, July 1987

Scranton, William Warren, American governor, Jan 1964, *Obit* Yrbk 2013

Scribner, Fred C., government official, Yrbk 1958, *Obit* Apr 1994

Scrugham, James Graves, *Obit* July 1945

Scudder, Janet, painter and sculptor, *Obit* July 1940

Scull, Robert C., American taxi executive and art collector, Apr 1974, *Obit* Feb 1986

Sculley, John, American computer industry executive, Aug 1988

Scully, Vin, American television sportscaster, Oct 2001

Seaborg, Glenn, American chemist, July 1948, Yrbk 1961, *Obit* May 1999

Seabrook, William B., American occultist and travel writer, Nov 1940, *Obit* Oct 1945

Seabury, David, Sept 1941, *Obit* May 1960

Seacrest, Ryan, American television personality, Sept 2009

Seaga, Edward P. G., Jamaican prime minister, Apr 1981

Seagrave, Gordon S., American physician and missionary, Nov 1943, *Obit* May 1965

Seagren, Bob, American pole vaulter, June 1974

Seal, English singer, Feb 1997

Seamans, Robert C., American NASA official, Yrbk 1966, *Obit* Yrbk 2008

Sean Paul, Jamaican reggae singer, Jan 2007

Searing, Annie E. P., *Obit* June 1942

Sears, Martha, nurse and writer on health, Aug 2001

Sears, Paul Bigelow, botanist, July 1960

Sears, Robert Richardson, psychologist and college dean, July 1952, *Obit* Aug 1989

Sears, William, pediatrician and writer on health, Aug 2001

Sears, William Joseph, *Obit* May 1944

Sears, William; and Sears, Martha, Sears, Williamec. 9, 1939- Pediatrician; writer; educator Sears, Marthaan. 24, 1945- Nurse; writer; breastfeeding consultant, Aug 2001

Seaton, Fred A., American newspaper publisher and Secretary of the interior, Nov 1956, *Obit* Mar 1974

Seau, Junior, American football player, Sept 2001, *Obit* Yrbk 2012

Seaver, Tom, American baseball player and sportscaster, Mar 1970

Sebald, William J., naval officer, lawyer and diplomat, Oct 1951

Sebelius, Kathleen, American Secretary of health and human services, Nov 2004

Seberg, Jean, actress, Apr 1966, *Obit* Oct 1979

Seboko, Mosadi, Botswanan tribal chief, Jan 2004

Sebrell, W. H., nutritionist, May 1951, *Obit* Nov 1992

Secondari, John H., Apr 1967, *Obit* Apr 1975

Sedaka, Neil, American pop singer and songwriter, Oct 1978

Sedaris, Amy, American actress and writer, Apr 2002

Sedaris, David, American humorist, July 1997

Seddigh, Laleh, Iranian automobile racing driver, Jan 2005

Sedgman, Frank, Australian tennis player, Nov 1951

Seefried, Irmgard, German opera singer, Feb 1956, *Obit* Jan 1989

Seeger, Pete, American folk singer and songwriter, Yrbk 1963

Seferis, George, Greek poet, May 1964, *Obit* Nov 1971

Segal, Bernard G., law association official, June 1970, *Obit* Aug 1997

Segal, Erich, American novelist and classicist, Apr 1971, *Obit* Yrbk 2010

Segal, George, American sculptor, Jan 1972, *Obit* Sept 2000

Segal, George, American actor, Nov 1975

Seger, George N., *Obit* Oct 1940

Seghers, Anna, German author, Yrbk 1942, *Obit* July 1983

Segni, Antonio, Yrbk 1955, *Obit* Jan 1973

Segovia, Andres, Spanish guitarist, May 1948, June 1964, *Obit* July 1987

Segre, Emilio, American physicist, Apr 1960, *Obit* July 1989

Segura, Pancho, Ecuadorian tennis player, Sept 1951

Sehwag, Virender, Indian cricket player, Jan 2003

Seibert, Florence, American biochemist, Nov 1942, *Obit* Oct 1991

Seibold, Louis, *Obit* June 1945

Seidelman, Susan, motion picture director, May 1990

Seidman, L. William, American government official and college dean, Sept 1976, *Obit* Yrbk 2009

Seifert, Elizabeth, author, Yrbk 1951, *Obit* Oct 1983

Seifert, Shirley, Yrbk 1951

Seigner, Emmanuelle, French actress, Jan 2006

Seinfeld, Jerry, American comedian, Aug 1992

Seitz, Frederick, American physicist, Apr 1956, *Obit* Yrbk 2008

Seitz, George B., *Obit* Aug 1944

Seixas, Vic, tennis player, July 1952

Sejima, Kazuyo, Japanese architect, Apr 2012

Selden, David, teacher and labor leader, July 1974, *Obit* Aug 1998

Seldes, George, American journalist, Sept 1941, *Obit* Sept 1995

Seles, Monica, Yugoslav-American tennis player, Nov 1992

Self, Henry, Oct 1942

Selfridge, Harry Gordon, American-British merchant, Mar 1941, *Obit* June 1947

Selick, Henry, American film director, May 2009

Selig, Bud, American baseball commissioner, Jan 1999

Selinko, Annemarie, Jan 1955

Sellars, Peter, American theatrical director, Jan 1986

Selleck, Tom, American actor, Nov 1983

Sellers, Peter, English actor, Yrbk 1960, *Obit* Sept 1980

Seltzer, Louis B., Yrbk 1956, *Obit* June 1980

Selway, Phil, English drummer, June 2001

Selwyn, Edgar, *Obit* Apr 1944

Selwyn-Lloyd, John Selwyn Brooke, British cabinet member, Apr 1952, *Obit* July 1978

Selye, Hans, Canadian physician, June 1953, Jan 1981, *Obit* Jan 1983

Selzer, Richard, American surgeon, essayist and short story writer, Apr 1993

Selznick, David O., motion picture producer, June 1941, *Obit* Sept 1965

Selznick, Myron, *Obit* May 1944

Sembene, Ousmane, Senegalese novelist and film director, Apr 1994, *Obit* Yrbk 2007

Semel, Terry S., American Internet service provider executive, July 2006

Semenov, Nikolay Nikolayevich, Russian chemist, Mar 1957

Semon, Waldo Lonsbury, chemist and inventor, Yrbk 1940, *Obit* Aug 1999

Sempe, French cartoonist and illustrator, Jan 2007

Sen, Binay Ranjan, Indian diplomat, Yrbk 1952, *Obit* Aug 1993

Sen, Ivan, Australian motion picture director and screenwriter, Jan 2002

Sen, Laura, American supermarket executive, Oct 2011

Sen, Sushmita, Indian actress, Jan 2006

Senanayake, Don Stephen, Apr 1950, *Obit* May 1952

Senanayake, Dudley, Ceylonese prime minister, Yrbk 1952, *Obit* June 1973

Senarens, Luis Philip, *Obit* Jan 1940

Sendak, Maurice, American children's author and illustrator, June 1968, June 1989, *Obit* Yrbk 2012

Sender, Toni, German United Nations official, May 1950

Senderens, Alain, French chef, Jan 2005

Senghor, Leopold Sedar, Senegalese poet and president, Mar 1962, July 1994, *Obit* Mar 2002

Sengstacke, John, newspaper executive, Nov 1949, *Obit* Aug 1997

Senior, Clarence, Yrbk 1961, *Obit* Nov 1974

Senn, Milton John Edward, pediatrician and psychiatrist, June 1950, *Obit* Aug 1990

Sensenich, Roscoe L., June 1949, *Obit* Feb 1963

Sepp Blatter, Joseph, Swiss soccer association executive, Jan 2002

Serban, Andrei, Romanian theatrical director, Feb 1978

Seredy, Kate, American children's author and illustrator, May 1940, *Obit* May 1975

Sereno, Paul C., American paleontologist, June 1997

Sereny, Gitta, Hungarian-British journalist, historian and biographer, Jan 2007

Sergii, *Obit* July 1944

Sergio, Lisa, Italian radio commentator, June 1944, *Obit* Aug 1989

Serkin, Peter, pianist, June 1986

Serkin, Rudolf, Czech-American pianist, July 1940, June 1990, *Obit* July 1991

Serlin, Oscar, Mar 1943, *Obit* Apr 1971

Serling, Rod, American television scriptwriter and screenwriter, Yrbk 1959, *Obit* Aug 1975

Serov, Ivan Aleksandrovich, Soviet communist leader, Yrbk 1956

Serra, Richard, American sculptor, Jan 1985

Serrano Suner, Ramon, Spanish diplomat and political leader, Nov 1940, *Obit* Yrbk 2004

Serratosa Cibils, Joaquin, Feb 1954

Serre, Jean Pierre, French mathematician, Jan 2003

Sert, Jose Luis, Spanish-American architect, Apr 1974, *Obit* May 1983

Sert, Jose Maria, Spanish painter, *Obit* Jan 1946

Servan-Schreiber, Jean-Jacques, French political leader, Jan 1955, *Obit* Yrbk 2007

Sessions, Roger, American composer, Jan 1975, *Obit* May 1985

Sessions, William Steele, American FBI director, July 1988

Seton, Anya, author, Yrbk 1953, *Obit* Jan 1991

Seton, Ernest Thompson, Anglo-American writer, illustrator and naturalist, May 1943, *Obit* Yrbk 1946

Settle, Mary Lee, American novelist and memoirist, Yrbk 1959, *Obit* Yrbk 2006

Setzer, Philip, American violinist, July 2002

Seuss, American children's author and illustrator, Feb 1968, *Obit* Nov 1991

Sevareid, Eric, reporter and commentator, July 1942, Oct 1966, *Obit* Aug 1992

Severance, H. Craig, *Obit* Nov 1941

Severgnini, Beppe, Italian journalist, Jan 2006

Sevier, Henry Hulme, *Obit* Mar 1940

Sevigny, Chloe, American actress, Aug 2000

Sevitzky, Fabien, July 1946, *Obit* Apr 1967

Sewell, Luke, baseball manager, Nov 1944

Sewell, Winifred, American library science professor, June 1960

Sexton, W. R., *Obit* Oct 1943

Sey, Abdoulie, Gambian newspaper editor, Jan 2004

Seyferth, O. A., July 1950

Seymour, Charles, May 1941, *Obit* Nov 1963

Seymour, Flora Warren, historian and author, June 1942

Seymour, Harriet Ayer, music therapist, *Obit* Sept 1944

Seymour, Lesley Jane, magazine editor, Nov 2001

Seymour, Lynn, Canadian ballet dancer, Nov 1979

Seymour, Stephanie, American model, Oct 2002

Seymour, Whitney North, lawyer, May 1961, *Obit* July 1983

Seyss-Inquart, Artur von, Austrian Nazi leader, May 1941, *Obit* Nov 1946

Sforza, Carlo, June 1942, *Obit* Oct 1952

Sgarbi, Vittorio, Italian art critic, historian and member of Parliament, Jan 2006

Shabandar, Musa, Feb 1956

Shafer, Paul W., American congressman, July 1952, *Obit* Oct 1954

Shaffer, Peter, English dramatist, May 1967, Nov 1988

Shafik, Doria, May 1955

Shagari, Shehu, Nigerian president, Aug 1980

Shah, Idries, Indian author, June 1976, *Obit* Feb 1997

Shah, Saira, British journalist and documentary filmmaker, Jan 2003

Shahade, Jennifer, American chess player, Sept 2005

Shaham, Gil, American violinist, Apr 1997

Shaheen, Jeanne, American senator, Jan 2001

Shahn, Ben, American painter, Yrbk 1954, *Obit* May 1969

Shakespeare, Frank, Sept 1970

Shakira, Colombian singer, Jan 2002

Shalala, Donna, American Secretary of health and human services and college president, Mar 1991

Shales, Tom, American television and film critic, Jan 2009

Shalhoub, Tony, American actor, Nov 2002

Shalikashvili, John, American general, Nov 1995, *Obit* Yrbk 2011

Shambaugh, Benjamin Franklin, *Obit* May 1940

Shamir, Yitzhak, Israeli prime minister, Feb 1983, Yrbk 1996, *Obit* Yrbk 2012

Shamsie, Kamila, Pakistani novelist, Sept 2009

Shandling, Garry, American comedian, Apr 1989

Shang Zhen, July 1944

Shange, Ntozake, American poet and dramatist, Sept 1978

Shankar, Ravi, Indian sitar player, Apr 1968, *Obit* Yrbk 2013

Shanker, Albert, American labor leader and teacher, Apr 1969, *Obit* May 1997

Shannon, James A., public health official, Jan 1965, *Obit* July 1994

Shannon, Peggy, actress, *Obit* July 1941

Shannon, William V., newspaper executive, Jan 1979, *Obit* Nov 1988

Shantz, Bobby, baseball player, Apr 1953

Shapiro, Harry Lionel, anthropologist and museum curator, Yrbk 1952, *Obit* Mar 1990

Shapiro, Irving S., American lawyer and chemical company executive, Nov 1976, *Obit* Nov 2001

Shapiro, Karl Jay, American poet and critic, Oct 1944, *Obit* Aug 2000

Shapiro, Neal, American television producer and executive, May 2003

Shapley, Harlow, astronomer, Jan 1941, Yrbk 1952, Yrbk 1972

Shaposhnikov, Boris, Soviet field marshal, Mar 1942, *Obit* May 1945

Shapp, Milton Jerrold, American governor, July 1973, *Obit* Feb 1995

Sharansky, Natan, Israeli cabinet member, Feb 1987

Sharapova, Maria, Russian tennis player, Jan 2004

Sharett, Moshe, Israeli statesman, Apr 1948, *Obit* Sept 1965

Sharif, Nawaz, Pakistani prime minister, Sept 1998

Sharif, Omar, Egyptian actor, May 1970

Sharon, Ariel, Israeli prime minister, Apr 1981, Jan 2002

Sharp, Harry Clay, *Obit* Yrbk 1940

Sharp, Mitchell, Canadian political adviser, July 1966

Sharpton, Al, American clergyman and political activist, Nov 1995

Shastri, Lal Bahadur, Indian prime minister, Yrbk 1964, *Obit* Feb 1966

Shatner, William, Canadian actor, July 1987

Shaver, Dorothy, American department store executive, Jan 1946, *Obit* Sept 1959

Shaver, Erwin L., Mar 1949

Shaver, Mary, *Obit* Mar 1942

Shaw, Artie, American clarinetist and band leader, May 1941, *Obit* Apr 2005

Shaw, Bernard, Irish dramatist, June 1944, *Obit* Yrbk 1950

Shaw, Bernard, American television newscaster, Feb 1995

Shaw, Dash, American comic book artist and graphic novelist, Jan 2009

Shaw, Henry, American pediatrician, *Obit* May 1941

Shaw, Irwin, author and dramatist, Oct 1942, *Obit* July 1984

Shaw, Lloyd, Sept 1943

Shaw, Louis Agassiz, *Obit* Oct 1940

Shaw, Ralph R., American librarian, June 1956, *Obit* Yrbk 1972

Shaw, Robert, English actor and novelist, May 1968, *Obit* Oct 1978

Shaw, Robert, American conductor, Sept 1949, July 1966, *Obit* Apr 1999

Shawcross, Hartley Shawcross, British attorney general and war crimes prosecutor, Yrbk 1945, *Obit* Yrbk 2003

Shawkey, Morris Purdy, *Obit* Apr 1941

Shawn, Ted, American dancer and choreographer, Oct 1949, *Obit* Feb 1972

Shawn, Wallace, American actor and playwright, June 1986

Shay, Edith, Yrbk 1952

Shay, Edith; and Shay, Frank, Yrbk 1952

Shay, Frank, Yrbk 1952, *Obit* Mar 1954

Shazar, Zalman, Feb 1964, *Obit* Nov 1974

Shea, Andrew B., Jan 1957, *Obit* Jan 1973

Shea, William Alfred, lawyer, Oct 1965, *Obit* Nov 1991

Shear, T. Leslie, *Obit* Aug 1945

Shearer, Augustus Hunt, *Obit* July 1941

Shearer, Harry, American actor and comedian, June 2001

Shearer, Moira, Scottish ballet dancer and actress, Jan 1950, *Obit* Yrbk 2006

Shearing, George, English jazz pianist, Apr 1958, *Obit* Yrbk 2011

Shechtman, Daniel, Scientist and educator, May 2012

Sheckell, Thomas O., *Obit* Apr 1943

Sheean, Vincent, American journalist, novelist and essayist, Aug 1941, *Obit* May 1975

Sheed, F. J., American theologian and publisher, Sept 1981, *Obit* Jan 1982

Sheed, Wilfrid, American novelist, Aug 1981, *Obit* Yrbk 2011

Sheehan, Cindy, American anti-war activist, May 2007

Sheehan, Neil, American journalist, Aug 1989

Sheehan, Winfield R., *Obit* Aug 1945

Sheehy, Gail, American writer, June 1993

Sheeler, Charles, American painter and photographer, Nov 1950, *Obit* June 1965

Sheen, Fulton J., American archbishop, Nov 1941, Jan 1951, *Obit* Feb 1980

Sheen, Martin, American actor, June 1977

Shehan, Lawrence, Oct 1965, *Obit* Oct 1984

Shehu, Mehmet, Feb 1958, *Obit* Feb 1982

Sheil, Bernard J., Yrbk 1968, *Obit* Nov 1969

Sheindlin, Judith, American judge, Sept 1998

Shelby, Carroll, American automobile racing driver and manufacturer, Nov 1993, *Obit* Yrbk 2012

Sheldon, Charles M., clergyman and author, *Obit* Apr 1946

Sheldon, Edward, dramatist, *Obit* May 1946

Sheldon, Sidney, American novelist, Oct 1980, *Obit* Yrbk 2007

Shelepin, Aleksandr N., Soviet intelligence official, Feb 1971, *Obit* Jan 1995

Shellabarger, Samuel, author, May 1945, *Obit* May 1954

Shelly, Mary Jo, educator, Oct 1951, *Obit* Sept 1976

Shelly, Warner S., Feb 1952

Shelton, Hugh, American general, Aug 1998

Shelton, James E., Feb 1951

Shenouda, Egyptian patriarch, Jan 2003, *Obit* Yrbk 2013

Shepard, Alan B., American astronaut and real estate executive, Yrbk 1961, *Obit* Sept 1998

Shepard, Ernest H., English painter and illustrator, Yrbk 1963, *Obit* May 1976

Shepard, Sam, American dramatist, Apr 1979

Shepherd, Cybill, American actress, Mar 1987

Shepherd, Jean, American humorist, Apr 1984, *Obit* Jan 2000

Shepherd, Lemuel C., American Marine corps general, Feb 1952, *Obit* Oct 1990

Shepilov, Dmitrii Trofimovich, Yrbk 1955

Sheppard, Morris, *Obit* June 1941

Shera, Jesse Hauk, American librarian and dean, June 1964, *Obit* June 1982

Sherard, Robert Harborough, English author and journalist, *Obit* Mar 1943

Sherawat, Mallika, Indian actress, Jan 2007

Sherfield, Roger Mellor Makins, British diplomat, Jan 1953, *Obit* Jan 1997

Sherley, Swagar, *Obit* Apr 1941

Sherman, Allan, television performer and comedian, Sept 1966, *Obit* Jan 1974

Sherman, Cindy, American photographer, Oct 1990

Sherman, Forrest P., Mar 1948, *Obit* Sept 1951

Sherman, Frederic Fairchild, *Obit* Yrbk 1940

Sherman, Henry C., Jan 1949, *Obit* Yrbk 1955

Sherrill, Henry Knox, Mar 1947, *Obit* June 1980

Sherrod, Robert Lee, journalist, June 1944, Yrbk 1962, *Obit* May 1994

Sherwood, Robert E., American dramatist, Jan 1940, *Obit* Jan 1956

Shetty, Shilpa, Indian actress, Jan 2007

Shevardnadze, Eduard, Georgian president, Feb 1986

Shevchenko, Arkady N., Soviet diplomat and defector, Sept 1985, *Obit* May 1998

Shiber, Etta, underground leader, Yrbk 1943, *Obit* Jan 1949

Shidehara, Kijuro, Japanese diplomat and prime minister, Apr 1946, *Obit* Apr 1951

Shield, Lansing P., June 1951, *Obit* Mar 1960

Shields, Brooke, American model and actress, Oct 1982

Shields, James P., Mar 1951, *Obit* Sept 1953

Shields, Mark, American political commentator and columnist, May 2005

Shigemitsu, Mamoru, June 1943, *Obit* Mar 1957

Shikaki, Khalil, Palestinian political scientist, Jan 2004

Shikler, Aaron, painter, Yrbk 1971

Shilts, Randy, American journalist, Oct 1993, *Obit* May 1994

Shimazaki, Toson, Japanese novelist, poet and essayist, *Obit* Oct 1943

Shimkin, Leon, publisher, May 1954

Shine, F. W., *Obit* Nov 1941

Shiner, Lewis, American novelist and short story writer, July 2011

Shinn, Everett, painter, May 1951, *Obit* June 1953

Shinn, Florence Scovel, *Obit* Yrbk 1940

Shinn, Milicent Washburn, author and journalist, *Obit* Oct 1940

Shinoda, Mike, American singer, Mar 2002

Shins (Musical group), June 2007

Shinseki, Eric, American Secretary of veterans affairs, Mar 2009

Shinwell, Emanuel Shinwell, British political leader, Jan 1943, *Obit* June 1986

Shipley, Jenny, New Zealand prime minister, Mar 2000

Shipley, Ruth B., American government official, Yrbk 1947, *Obit* Jan 1967

Shippen, Katherine Binney, author, Yrbk 1954

Shiras, George, American lawyer and naturalist, *Obit* May 1942

Shirer, William L., American journalist, July 1941, May 1962, *Obit* Feb 1994

Shirley, Donna, American aerospace engineer and NASA official, Aug 1998

Shiva, Vandana, Indian physicist and environmentalist, Jan 2002

Shivers, Allan, American governor, Oct 1951, *Obit* Mar 1985

Shockley, William, American physicist, Yrbk 1953, *Obit* Oct 1989

Shoemaker, Bill, American jockey, July 1966, *Obit* Apr 2004

Shoemaker, Eugene Merle, planetary geologist, June 1967, *Obit* Oct 1997

Shoemaker, Samuel Moor, clergyman, Apr 1955, *Obit* Yrbk 1963

Sholokhov, Mikhail Aleksandrovich, Russian novelist, Jan 1942, Feb 1960, *Obit* Apr 1984

Shone, Terence Allen, Nov 1946, *Obit* Yrbk 1965

Shope, Richard E., Yrbk 1963, *Obit* Yrbk 1966

Shore, Dinah, American singer, June 1942, Yrbk 1966, *Obit* May 1994

Shoriki, Matsutaro, Japanese newspaper publisher, broadcasting executive and government official, Feb 1958

Short, Bobby, American singer and pianist, July 1972, *Obit* Nov 2005

Short, Dewey, American congressman and military official, Yrbk 1951, *Obit* Feb 1980

Short, Hassard, Nov 1948, *Obit* Yrbk 1956

Short, Joseph, American journalist and presidential press secretary, Feb 1951, *Obit* Nov 1952

Short, Martin, Canadian comedian and actor, Sept 1992

Short, Walter Campbell, general, Jan 1946, *Obit* Oct 1949

Shorter, Wayne, American jazz saxophonist, Apr 1996

Shortz, Will, American editor and puzzle maker, Apr 1996

Shostakovich, Dmitrii Dmitrievich, Russian composer, May 1941, *Obit* Oct 1975

Shotton, Burt, baseball player and manager, June 1949, *Obit* Oct 1962

Shotwell, James Thompson, Canadian-American historian, Oct 1944, *Obit* Sept 1965

Shoulders, Harrison H., Nov 1946, *Obit* Jan 1964

Shoup, Carl Sumner, American economist, Feb 1949, *Obit* Sept 2000

Shoup, David M., American Marine Corps general, Jan 1960, *Obit* Mar 1983

Shoup, Oliver Henry, *Obit* Nov 1940

Shreeve, Herbert Edward, *Obit* June 1942

Shreve, Earl Owen, Oct 1947

Shreve, Richmond Harold, Nov 1945, *Obit* Oct 1946

Shridharani, Krishnalal, Indian journalist and author, Jan 1942, *Obit* Oct 1960

Shriver, Eunice Kennedy, American social activist, July 1996, *Obit* Yrbk 2009

Shriver, Lionel, American novelist, Sept 2005

Shriver, Maria, American television newscaster and wife of Arnold Schwarzenegger, Nov 1991

Shriver, Sargent, American lawyer and government official, Yrbk 1961, *Obit* Yrbk 2011

Shubin, Neil, American biologist and paleontologist, Apr 2007

Shula, Don, American football coach, Mar 1974

Shull, Martha A., Apr 1957

Shulman, Harry, Apr 1952, *Obit* May 1955

Shulman, Irving, American novelist, Yrbk 1956, *Obit* June 1995

Shulman, Max, humorist, Oct 1959, *Obit* Oct 1988

Shultz, George P., American Secretary of state, May 1969, Apr 1988

Shuman, Charles B., American farm organization official, Feb 1956

Shumlin, Herman, Mar 1941, *Obit* Aug 1979

Shumway, Norman, American surgeon, Apr 1971, *Obit* Yrbk 2006

Shurlock, Geoffrey, Jan 1962, *Obit* June 1976

Shuster, George Nauman, college president, Jan 1941, Oct 1960, *Obit* Mar 1977

Shute, Nevil, English novelist, July 1942, *Obit* Mar 1960

Shuttleworth, Mark, South African entrepreneur, Jan 2007

Shvernik, Nikolai, Soviet communist leader, Oct 1951, *Obit* Feb 1971

Shyamalan, M. Night, American film director and screenwriter, Mar 2003

Sibley, Antoinette, English dancer, Yrbk 1970

Sickert, Walter, British painter and engraver, *Obit* Mar 1942

Siddons, Anne Rivers, American novelist, Jan 2005

Sides, John H., Jan 1961, *Obit* June 1978

Sidi Ahmed, *Obit* Aug 1942

Sidibe, Malick, Malian photographer, Jan 2004

Sidney, Sylvia, actress, Oct 1981, *Obit* Sept 1999

Siebert, Muriel, American stockbroker, Aug 1997, *Obit* Yrbk 2013

Siegel, Bernie S., surgeon, June 1993

Siegel, Robert, American radio newscaster, July 2008

Siegfried and Roy, German magicians and animal trainers, Jan 1998

Siemiller, P. L., Nov 1966

Siemionow, Maria, Polish plastic surgeon, May 2009

Siepi, Cesare, Italian opera singer, Yrbk 1955, *Obit* Yrbk 2010

Sigerist, Henry Ernest, Swiss medical historian, Sept 1940, *Obit* June 1957

Sigismondi, Floria, Canadian photographer and video and film director, July 2010

Signoret, Simone, French actress, Yrbk 1960, *Obit* Nov 1985

Sigur Ros (Musical group), Jan 2003

Sikander, Shahzia, Pakistani painter, Jan 2002

Sikorski, Wladyslaw, Polish general and statesman, Jan 1940, *Obit* Aug 1943

Sikorsky, Igor, Ukrainian-American aeronautical engineer, Oct 1940, Yrbk 1956, *Obit* Yrbk 1972

Silber, John R., American college president, Feb 1984, *Obit* Yrbk 2012

Silberman, Charles E., American journalist, July 1979, *Obit* Yrbk 2011

Siles Zuazo, Hernan, Bolivian president, Sept 1958, June 1985, *Obit* Oct 1996

Siles, Hernando, Bolivian president, *Obit* Jan 1943

Sillanpaa, Frans Eemil, Finnish novelist and short story writer, Jan 1940, *Obit* July 1964

Sillcox, Lewis Ketcham, mechanical engineer, Yrbk 1954, *Obit* May 1989

Sills, Beverly, American opera singer and manager, Nov 1969, Feb 1982, *Obit* Oct 2007

Silva Calderon, Alvaro, Venezuelan international petroleum organization official, Jan 2002

Silva, Benedita da, Brazilian governor and political leader, Jan 2002

Silva, Daniel, American television producer and novelist, Apr 2007

Silva, Luis Inacio da, Brazilian president, Jan 2003

Silver, Abba Hillel, rabbi, Yrbk 1941, May 1963, *Obit* Jan 1964

Silver, Joel, American motion picture producer, Nov 2003

Silver, Nate, American baseball statistician and pollster, Feb 2013

Silverman, Fred, television executive, Nov 1978

Silverman, Sarah, American comedienne, July 2006

Silvers, Phil, actor, Yrbk 1957, *Obit* Jan 1986

Silzer, George S., *Obit* Yrbk 1940

Simenon, Georges, Belgian novelist, Apr 1970, *Obit* Nov 1989

Simionato, Giulietta, Italian opera singer, Apr 1960, *Obit* Yrbk 2010

Simkhovitch, Mary Melinda Kingsbury, American social worker, Mar 1943, *Obit* Yrbk 1951

Simkin, William E., American labor mediator, Jan 1967, *Obit* May 1992

Simmons, Adele Smith, American college president and foundation official, May 1991

Simmons, Furnifold McLendel, American senator, *Obit* Jan 1940

Simmons, Gene, American bassist and actor, Apr 1999

Simmons, Jean, English actress, Feb 1952, *Obit* Yrbk 2010

Simmons, Richard, American fitness expert and television personality, May 1982

Simmons, Russell, American recording, motion picture and broadcasting executive, June 1998

Simmons, Ruth, American college president, Jan 1996

Simms, Hilda, actress, Nov 1944, *Obit* May 1994

Simms, John F., Sept 1956, *Obit* June 1975

Simms, Phil, American football player and sportscaster, Oct 1994

Simon, Carly, American singer and songwriter, Aug 1976

Simon, Charlie May Hogue, Yrbk 1946

Simon, Claude, French novelist, May 1992, *Obit* Yrbk 2005

Simon, David, American journalist and television scriptwriter, June 2008

Simon, Edith, Yrbk 1954

Simon, Herbert A., American social scientist, June 1979, *Obit* May 2001

Simon, John Allsebrook Simon, British statesman, July 1940, *Obit* Mar 1954

Simon, Neil, American playwright, Feb 1968, Mar 1989

Simon, Norton, American financier and art collector, Mar 1968, *Obit* Aug 1993

Simon, Paul, American singer and composer, Mar 1975

Simon, Paul, American senator, Jan 1988, *Obit* Yrbk 2004

Simon, Richard L., American publisher, July 1941, *Obit* Oct 1960

Simon, Richard L.; and Schuster, Lincoln M., July 1941

Simon, William E., American Secretary of the treasury and financier, Apr 1974, *Obit* Aug 2000

Simonds, Frederic W., *Obit* May 1941

Simonds, Guy Granville, Canadian general, Oct 1943, *Obit* July 1974

Simone, Gail, American comic book writer, Nov 2008

Simone, Nina, American singer and pianist, Apr 1968, *Obit* Yrbk 2003

Simonetta, Italian fashion designer, Yrbk 1955

Simons, David G., American physician and air force officer, Yrbk 1957, *Obit* Yrbk 2010

Simons, Elwyn L., paleontologist and primatologist, June 1994

Simons, Hans, Mar 1957, *Obit* May 1972

Simonson, Lee, Nov 1947, *Obit* Mar 1967

Simpson, Adele, fashion designer, Nov 1970, *Obit* Oct 1995

Simpson, Alan, college president, Feb 1964, *Obit* July 1998

Simpson, Alan K., American senator, Oct 1990

Simpson, Carole, American television newscaster, Nov 1999

Simpson, George Gaylord, American paleontologist, Yrbk 1964, *Obit* Jan 1985

Simpson, Helen, Australian author, *Obit* Yrbk 1940

Simpson, Howard E., railroad executive, May 1958, *Obit* Apr 1985

Simpson, J. A., English editor and lexicographer, Jan 2003

Simpson, John, British television reporter, June 2010

Simpson, Kenneth F., *Obit* Mar 1941

Simpson, Lorna, American photographer and video artist, Nov 2004

Simpson, Louis Aston Marantz, poet and educator, Yrbk 1964, *Obit* Yrbk 2012

Simpson, Milward Lee, governor and senator, Jan 1957, *Obit* Aug 1993

Simpson, Mona, American novelist, Feb 1993

Simpson, O. J., American football player and sportscaster, Apr 1969

Simpson, Richard M., Yrbk 1953, *Obit* Mar 1960

Simpson, Valerie, American singer and songwriter, Apr 1997

Simpson, William H., Feb 1945, *Obit* Oct 1980

Simpson-Miller, Portia, Jamaican prime minister, Jan 2006

Sims, Hugo S., Oct 1949

Sims, William L., Yrbk 1956

Sin, Jaime, Sept 1995, *Obit* Yrbk 2005

Sinatra, Frank, American singer and actor, June 1943, Oct 1960, *Obit* July 1998

Sinbad, American comedian and actor, Feb 1997

Sinclair, Adelaide, Canadian government official, Apr 1951, *Obit* Jan 1983

Sinclair, April, author, Sept 1999

Sinclair, Archibald, British political leader, Sept 1940, *Obit* Oct 1970

Sinclair, Cameron, British architect and housing organization official, Apr 2008

Sinclair, David, Australian molecular biologist, Sept 2008

Sinclair, Jo, author, Mar 1946, *Obit* June 1995

Sinclair, May, English novelist, *Obit* Yrbk 1946

Sinclair, Upton, American novelist and socialist leader, Yrbk 1962, *Obit* Jan 1969

Sinding, Christian, *Obit* Jan 1942

Sinegal, James D., American warehouse club executive, Aug 2007

Singer, Bryan, American motion picture director, Apr 2005

Singer, Isaac Bashevis, American novelist and short story writer, Jan 1969, *Obit* Sept 1991

Singer, Israel Joshua, Yiddish novelist and dramatist, *Obit* Mar 1944

Singer, Kurt D., American children's author and editor, Yrbk 1954

Singer, Peter, Australian bioethicist, Mar 1991

Singer, Richard, *Obit* Mar 1940

Singer, S. Fred, American physicist, Yrbk 1955

Singh, Jeev Milkha, Indian golfer, Jan 2007

Singh, Manmohan, Indian prime minister, Jan 2005

Singh, Simon, British physicist, writer and television host, Jan 2005

Singh, Swaran, Mar 1971, *Obit* Jan 1995

Singh, Talvin, British DJ, arranger and composer, Jan 2006

Singh, Vishwanath Pratap, Indian prime minister, May 1990, *Obit* Yrbk 2009

Singher, Martial, French opera singer and voice teacher, Feb 1947, *Obit* May 1990

Singletary, Mike, American football coach, Mar 1993

Singleton, John, American film director and screenwriter, Feb 1997

Sinise, Gary, American actor and director, Apr 1997

Sink, M. Virginia, Mar 1964

Sinnott, Edmund W., American botanist, Oct 1948, *Obit* Mar 1968

Sinopoli, Giuseppe, Italian conductor and composer, Mar 1991, *Obit* Sept 2001

Sinsheimer, Robert, American biologist, June 1968

Sintim-Misa, Kwaku, Ghanaian actor and comedian, Jan 2004

Sinyavsky, Andrei, Russian essayist, novelist and short story writer, July 1975, *Obit* May 1997

Siple, Paul Allman, explorer and geographer, Feb 1957, *Obit* Jan 1969

Siqueiros, David Alfaro, Mexican painter, June 1959, *Obit* Feb 1974

Sirica, John J., American judge, May 1974, *Obit* Oct 1992

Sirikit, Yrbk 1960

Siroky, Viliam, Apr 1957, *Obit* Nov 1971

Sisavang Vong, Apr 1954, *Obit* Jan 1960

Sisco, Joseph J., American diplomat, Jan 1972, *Obit* Yrbk 2005

Sissi, Brazilian soccer player, June 2001

Sitek, David Andrew, American guitarist and record producer, Apr 2009

Sitgreaves, Beverley, *Obit* Sept 1943

Sittenfeld, Curtis, American novelist and short story writer, Nov 2008

Sitterly, Charlotte Moore, American astrophysicist, Jan 1962, *Obit* June 1990

Sitwell, Osbert, English poet, short story writer and novelist, Sept 1965, *Obit* June 1969

Six, Robert F., airline executive, Oct 1970, *Obit* Nov 1986

Siza, Alvaro, Portuguese architect, Feb 2000

Sizemore, Grady, American baseball player, Apr 2010

Sizoo, Joseph R., Yrbk 1964, *Obit* Nov 1966

Skarsgard, Stellan, Swedish actor, Jan 2002

Skelton, Red, American comedian and actor, Nov 1947, *Obit* Nov 1997

Skidmore, Hubert Standish, *Obit* Mar 1946

Skidmore, Louis, architect, Yrbk 1951, *Obit* Yrbk 1962

Skillin, Edward S., magazine editor and publisher, May 1949, *Obit* Yrbk 2000

Skilton, Charles Sanford, *Obit* May 1941

Skinner, B. F., American psychologist, Jan 1964, Nov 1979, *Obit* Oct 1990

Skinner, Cornelia Otis, actress and author, Jan 1942, Yrbk 1964, *Obit* Sept 1979

Skinner, Dennis, British member of Parliament, Jan 2002

Skinner, Eleanor Oakes, May 1951

Skinner, Otis, Obit Feb 1942

Skinner, Quentin, British historian, Jan 2007

Skinner, Samuel K., American Secretary of transportation and presidential adviser, Aug 1989

Skira, Albert, Swiss art publisher, Apr 1967, Obit June 1990

Sklansky, David, American poker player, Apr 2007

Sklar, Rachel, Media blogger, author and attorney, Mar 2012

Skocpol, Theda, American political scientist, Aug 2000

Skolnick, Mark H., geneticist, June 1997

Skouras, Spyros P., American motion picture executive, June 1943, Obit Nov 1971

Skouris, Vassilios, Greek judge, Jan 2007

Skrowaczewski, Stanislaw, Yrbk 1964

Skutt, V. J., insurance executive, Yrbk 1959, Obit Apr 1993

Slade, Roy, museum director, painter and educator, June 1985

Slaney, Mary Decker, American runner, Oct 1983

Slash (Musician), British rock guitarist and songwriter, Mar 2008

Slater, John E., Nov 1951

Slater, Kelly, American surfer, July 2001

Slater, Rodney, American Secretary of transportation, Jan 1999

Slatkin, Leonard, American conductor, Feb 1986

Slaughter, Frank G., American novelist and physician, Oct 1942, Obit Yrbk 2006

Slaughter, Louise M., American congresswoman, Apr 1999

Slavenska, Mia, Croatian ballet dancer and choreographer, Feb 1954, Obit Apr 2003

Slayton, Donald Kent, astronaut and aerospace executive, Feb 1976, Obit Aug 1993

Sleeper, Ruth, nurse and educator, Oct 1952, Obit Feb 1993

Slemon, C. Roy, Yrbk 1956

Slezak, Walter, actor, Mar 1955, Obit June 1983

Slichter, Sumner H., American economist, June 1947, Obit Yrbk 1959

Slick, Grace, American singer, Apr 1982

Slifkin, Nosson, Israeli rabbi and biblical zoologist, Jan 2005

Sligh, Charles R., Apr 1953

Slim Helu, Carlos, Mexican financier, Jan 2003

Slim, Mongi, Tunisian political leader, Mar 1958, Obit Yrbk 1969

Slim, William Joseph Slim, British field marshal, June 1945, Obit Feb 1971

Slimane, Hedi, French fashion designer, Jan 2006

Sliwa, Curtis, American public safety group founder, Feb 1983

Sloan, Alfred Pritchard, American automobile executive, Nov 1940, Obit Mar 1966

Sloan, George A., Jan 1952, Obit July 1955

Sloan, Samuel, Obit May 1945

Sloane, Eric, painter and author, Sept 1972, Obit May 1985

Sloane, Everett, Jan 1957, Obit Oct 1965

Slobodkin, Louis, author and illustrator, Apr 1957, Obit Aug 1975

Slocum, Harvey, Feb 1957, Obit Jan 1962

Slonimsky, Nicolas, Russian-American musicologist, conductor and composer, Apr 1955, Feb 1991, Obit Mar 1996

Slye, Maud, American pathologist, Yrbk 1940, Obit Nov 1954

Smadel, Joseph E., May 1963

Small, John D., American admiral and government official, Feb 1946, Obit Mar 1963

Small, John Humphrey, Obit Sept 1946

Smallens, Alexander, May 1947, Obit Jan 1973

Smallpeice, Basil, English airline and shipping executive, Oct 1969

Smallwood, Joseph R., Canadian political leader, Feb 1953, Obit Mar 1992

Smallwood, Robert B., Mar 1956, Obit Sept 1974

Smart, David A., magazine publisher, June 1944

Smathers, George A., American senator, Apr 1954, Obit June 2007

Smeal, Eleanor, American feminist, Mar 1980

Smedberg, William Renwick, Yrbk 1957

Smedley, Agnes, American journalist, Jan 1944, Obit June 1950

Smedley, Constance, Obit Apr 1941

Smetona, Antanas, Lithuanian president, Obit Feb 1944

Smigel, Robert, American comedian and television scriptwriter, Nov 2011

Smiley, Jane, American novelist and short story writer, Apr 1990

Smiley, Tavis, American radio talk show host, Apr 2003

Smith, Albert W., Obit Oct 1942

Smith, Alfred Emanuel, American governor, Sept 1944

Smith, Ali, Scottish short story writer and novelist, June 2006

Smith, Amy, American mechanical engineer, June 2005

Smith, Anna Deavere, American actress and dramatist, Sept 1994

Smith, Austin E., physician and drug industry executive, Mar 1950, Obit Jan 1994

Smith, Barbara, American actress, model and restaurateur, July 1998

Smith, Ben, Oct 1945, Obit July 1964

Smith, Betty, American novelist, Nov 1943, Obit Mar 1972

Smith, Bruce, American football player, Mar 1995

Smith, Bruce, Feb 1953, Obit Nov 1955

Smith, C. Aubrey, English actor, Sept 1944, Obit Jan 1949

Smith, C. R., American airline executive, air force general and Secretary of commerce, Sept 1945, Obit June 1990

Smith, Carleton, musicologist and foundation official, Apr 1961, *Obit* July 1984

Smith, Carleton Sprague, musicologist, Yrbk 1960, *Obit* Nov 1994

Smith, Charles, American playwright, May 2011

Smith, Chesterfield H., American lawyer, Nov 1974, *Obit* Yrbk 2003

Smith, Clara E., *Obit* July 1943

Smith, Clyde Harold, *Obit* May 1940

Smith, Courtney, American college president, Yrbk 1959, *Obit* Mar 1969

Smith, Cyril Stanley, science historian, July 1948, *Obit* Oct 1992

Smith, David T., Oct 1950

Smith, Dean, American basketball coach, Apr 1994

Smith, Dick, makeup artist, Mar 1959

Smith, Eleanor, English author, *Obit* Nov 1945

Smith, Elinor, American aviator, Mar 2001, *Obit* Yrbk 2010

Smith, Ellison DuRant, American senator, *Obit* Jan 1945

Smith, Emmitt, American football player, Nov 1994

Smith, Frederick W., American air freight executive, June 2000

Smith, Gary, American sportswriter, Jan 2009

Smith, George Adam, Scottish biblical scholar, *Obit* Apr 1942

Smith, George Albert, Nov 1947, *Obit* May 1951

Smith, Gerald L. K., American clergyman, lecturer and columnist, Aug 1943, *Obit* June 1976

Smith, Gerard, American bassist and keyboardist, Apr 2009

Smith, Gerard C., American lawyer and diplomat, Oct 1970, *Obit* Sept 1994

Smith, Gregory White, lawyer and author, Mar 1998

Smith, H. Alexander, American senator, Apr 1948, *Obit* Jan 1967

Smith, Harold D., July 1943, *Obit* Mar 1947

Smith, Harrison, Yrbk 1954, *Obit* Feb 1971

Smith, Harry Allen, American humorist, May 1942, *Obit* May 1976

Smith, Hazel Brannon, American newspaper publisher, Sept 1973, *Obit* July 1994

Smith, Hedrick, American journalist, June 1991

Smith, Holland M., American Marine corps general, Apr 1945, *Obit* Mar 1967

Smith, Howard K., American television newscaster and commentator, Mar 1943, July 1976, *Obit* Aug 2002

Smith, Howard Worth, American congressman, Feb 1941, *Obit* Nov 1976

Smith, Ian Douglas, Rhodesian prime minister, May 1966, *Obit* Feb 2008

Smith, Ida B. Wise, Feb 1943, *Obit* Apr 1952

Smith, James H., government official, Jan 1958, *Obit* Feb 1983

Smith, Jeff, American cook and clergyman, Aug 1991, *Obit* Yrbk 2004

Smith, John L., June 1952, *Obit* Yrbk 1958

Smith, Josh, American basketball player, Feb 2012

Smith, Kate, singer, Yrbk 1940, Nov 1965, *Obit* Aug 1986

Smith, Kevin, American screenwriter and film director, Feb 1998

Smith, Kiki, American painter, sculptor and printmaker, Mar 2005

Smith, Lillian Eugenia, American novelist and social critic, May 1944, *Obit* Yrbk 1966

Smith, Liz, American gossip columnist, May 1987

Smith, Logan Pearsall, American lexicographer, essayist and critic, *Obit* Apr 1946

Smith, Lovie, American football coach, Sept 2007

Smith, Maggie, English actress, June 1970, July 2002

Smith, Margaret Chase, American senator, Feb 1945, Mar 1962, *Obit* Aug 1995

Smith, Martin Cruz, American novelist, Nov 1990

Smith, Mary Carter, storyteller and folklorist, Feb 1996

Smith, Mary Louise, American political party leader, Oct 1976, *Obit* Nov 1997

Smith, Merriman, journalist and author, Yrbk 1964, *Obit* Nov 1993

Smith, Mike, American football coach, Sept 2010

Smith, Oliver, American set designer, Sept 1961, *Obit* Mar 1994

Smith, Orin, American coffee retailer, Nov 2003

Smith, Ozzie, American baseball player, Feb 1997

Smith, Page, historian, Sept 1990, *Obit* Nov 1995

Smith, Patti, American rock singer, songwriter and poet, Apr 1989

Smith, Paul C., Apr 1943, *Obit* Sept 1976

Smith, Red, American sportswriter, Apr 1959, *Obit* Feb 1982

Smith, Rex, Jan 1942

Smith, Rick, British keyboardist and songwriter, Nov 2011

Smith, Robert C., American senator, Sept 2000

Smith, Robert Paul, American novelist and memoirist, Yrbk 1958

Smith, Robyn, Nov 1976

Smith, Roger B., American automobile executive, May 1986, *Obit* Yrbk 2008

Smith, Roy Burnett, *Obit* Feb 1941

Smith, Sidney, Jan 1955, *Obit* May 1959

Smith, Steve, American football player, Sept 2006

Smith, Sylvester C., July 1963

Smith, T. V., Feb 1956, *Obit* July 1964

Smith, Thomas R., *Obit* June 1942

Smith, Virginia B., American college president, June 1978, *Obit* Yrbk 2010

Smith, Walter Bedell, American general, diplomat and CIA director, Apr 1944, Yrbk 1953, *Obit* Nov 1961

Smith, Wilbur Fisk, *Obit* Sept 1940

Smith, Will, American rapper and actor, Sept 1996

Smith, William French, American Attorney general, Jan 1982, *Obit* Jan 1991

Smith, William Jay, American poet and state legislator, Mar 1974

Smith, William Ward, American admiral, Feb 1948, *Obit* July 1966

Smith, Zadie, English novelist, Aug 2000

Smithdas, Robert J., Yrbk 1966

Smits, Jimmy, American actor, May 2006

Smolyansky, Julie, American food industry executive, Nov 2013

Smoot, George, American astrophysicist, Apr 1994

Smoot, Reed, American senator, *Obit* Mar 1941

Smothers, Dick, American comedian, Yrbk 1968

Smothers, Tom, American comedian, Yrbk 1968

Smuin, Michael, American ballet dancer and choreographer, Oct 1984, *Obit* Yrbk 2007

Smuts, Jan Christiaan, South African prime minister, Aug 1941, *Obit* Oct 1950

Smylie, Robert E., American governor, Feb 1956, *Obit* Yrbk 2004

Smyslov, Vasilii, Russian chess player, July 1967, *Obit* Yrbk 2010

Smyth, Ethel Mary, English composer, *Obit* June 1944

Smyth, Henry DeWolf, physicist, Yrbk 1948, *Obit* Nov 1986

Snavely, Guy E., Apr 1951

Snead, Sam, American golfer, June 1949, *Obit* Yrbk 2002

Sneider, Vern, Yrbk 1956, *Obit* June 1981

Snell, Foster Dee, Jan 1943

Snell, George Davis, American geneticist, May 1986, *Obit* Aug 1996

Snell, Henry Bayley, *Obit* Mar 1943

Snell, Henry Snell, May 1941

Snell, Peter, New Zealand runner and physiologist, Yrbk 1962

Snider, Duke, American baseball player, May 1956, *Obit* Yrbk 2011

Snider, Stacey, American motion picture executive, Apr 2008

Snipes, Wesley, American actor, Sept 1993

Snodgrass, W. D., American poet, critic and philologist, Nov 1960, *Obit* Yrbk 2009

Snook, H. Clyde, *Obit* Nov 1942

Snow, C. P., British physicist and novelist, Yrbk 1954, Yrbk 1961, *Obit* Aug 1980

Snow, Clyde, forensic anthropologist, Apr 1997

Snow, Edgar, journalist, June 1941, *Obit* Apr 1972

Snow, Edward Rowe, Yrbk 1958

Snow, Glenn E., Nov 1947

Snow, John W., American investment manager and former Secretary of the treasury, Aug 2003

Snow, Tony, American television moderator, commentator and presidential press secretary, Sept 2006, *Obit* Yrbk 2008

Snowdon, Antony Armstrong-Jones, English photographer, Oct 1960

Snowe, Olympia J., American senator, May 1995

Snyder, Alice D., *Obit* Apr 1943

Snyder, Gary, American poet and nature writer, Nov 1978

Snyder, Howard McC., Feb 1955, *Obit* Nov 1970

Snyder, J. Buell, *Obit* Apr 1946

Snyder, John W., American Secretary of the treasury, July 1945, *Obit* Jan 1986

Snyder, Solomon H., American neuropharmacologist, Apr 1996

Snyder, Tom, American radio and television talk show host, June 1980, *Obit* Yrbk 2007

Soames, Arthur Christopher John Soames, British diplomat, Aug 1981, *Obit* Oct 1987

Soares, Jo, Brazilian television talk show host, novelist and actor, Jan 2002

Soares, Mario, Portuguese prime minister, Oct 1975

Sobchak, Anatoly, Russian mayor, July 1992, *Obit* July 2000

Sobeloff, Simon E., American Solicitor general and judge, Mar 1955, *Obit* Sept 1973

Sobers, Garfield, Barbadian cricket player, Jan 2002

Sobhuza, Mar 1982, *Obit* Mar 1982

Sobolev, Arkadii A., Apr 1955, *Obit* Jan 1965

Sockman, Ralph Washington, clergyman, June 1946, *Obit* Nov 1970

Soderberg, Alicia, American astrophysicist, Oct 2009

Soderberg, C. Richard, Feb 1958, *Obit* Jan 1980

Soderbergh, Steven, American film director and screenwriter, Oct 1998

Sodero, Cesare, conductor and composer, Mar 1943, *Obit* Jan 1948

Soderstrom, Elisabeth, Swedish opera singer, Nov 1985, *Obit* Yrbk 2010

Soeharto, Indonesian president, June 1967, Oct 1992, *Obit* Yrbk 2008

Soekarno, Indonesian president, Sept 1947, *Obit* Sept 1970

Soffer, Olga, Yusoslav-American archaeologist, July 2002

Soglow, Otto, cartoonist, Sept 1940, *Obit* May 1975

Soheily, Ali, Sept 1943, *Obit* July 1958

Sokolovsky, Vasilii D., Yrbk 1953, *Obit* July 1968

Sokolow, Anna, American dancer, choreographer and teacher, Feb 1969, *Obit* Sept 2000

Sokolsky, George E., May 1941, *Obit* Jan 1963

Solaar, MC, French rapper, Jan 2002

Solana Madariaga, Javier, Spanish European Union official, Jan 2005

Solandt, Omond M., Mar 1974

Solarz, Stephen J., American congressman, Nov 1986, *Obit* Yrbk 2011

Solberg, Thorvald A., American admiral, Yrbk 1948

Soldati, Mario, Italian film director, screenwriter, novelist and short story writer, Apr 1958, *Obit* Nov 1999

Soleri, Paolo, Italian architect, Feb 1972, *Obit* Yrbk 2013

Solex, Dutch pop singer, Jan 2005

Solh, Sami, Feb 1958, *Obit* Jan 1969

Solis, Hilda L., American Secretary of labor, Mar 2009

Solmonese, Joe, American gay rights activist, Oct 2009

Solo, Hope, American soccer player, Aug 2012

Solomon, Philip S., American film director, Oct 2007

Solomon, Susan, American atmospheric scientist, July 2005

Solti, Georg, Hungarian-British conductor, Mar 1964, *Obit* Nov 1997

Solzhenitsyn, Aleksandr, Russian novelist, Feb 1969, July 1988, *Obit* Nov 2008

Somervell, Brehon Burke, Aug 1942, *Obit* Apr 1955

Somerville, James, British admiral, Apr 1943, *Obit* Apr 1949

Somes, Michael, English dancer, Yrbk 1955, *Obit* Feb 1995

Sommerfeld, Arnold Johannes Wilhelm, German physicist, Apr 1950, *Obit* May 1951

Somoza, Anastasio, Nicaraguan dictator, June 1942, *Obit* Yrbk 1956

Somoza, Anastasio, Nicaraguan general and president, Mar 1978, *Obit* Nov 1980

Sompop Jantraka, Thai children's rights advocate, Jan 2003

Son, Masayoshi, Japanese Internet and telecommunications executive, Jan 2006

Sondheim, Stephen, American lyricist and composer, Nov 1973

Soni, Rebecca, Aug 2013

Sonnenfeld, Barry, American film director, Nov 1998

Sontag, Susan, American novelist and essayist, June 1969, Feb 1992, *Obit* May 2005

Soong, T. V., Chinese government official and financier, Mar 1941, *Obit* June 1971

Sophoulis, Themistocles, Nov 1947, *Obit* Sept 1949

Sordoni, Andrew J., July 1956, *Obit* Apr 1963

Sorel, Edward, cartoonist, Mar 1994

Sorensen, Theodore C., American presidential adviser, Yrbk 1961, *Obit* Yrbk 2011

Sorensen, Virginia Eggertsen, American children's author, Yrbk 1950

Sorenstam, Annika, Swedish golfer, Jan 2002

Sorkin, Aaron, American television scriptwriter, June 2000

Sorlie, Robert, Norwegian firefighter and sled dog racer, Jan 2005

Sorokin, Pitirim Aleksandrovich, sociologist, July 1942, *Obit* Apr 1968

Sorokin, Vladimir, Russian novelist, Jan 2005

Soros, George, American financier, Apr 1997

Sorvino, Mira, American actress, Aug 1998

Sosa, Sammy, Dominican baseball player, May 1999

Soss, Wilma Porter, publicist, Mar 1965, *Obit* Jan 1987

Soth, Lauren K., newspaper editor, Yrbk 1956, *Obit* June 1998

Sothern, Ann, American actress and singer, Yrbk 1956, *Obit* Aug 2001

Soto, Jesus Raphael, Venezuelan painter and sculptor, Jan 2004

Sotomayor, Sonia, American Supreme Court justice, Oct 2009

Soueif, Ahdaf, Egyptian-British novelist and short story writer, Jan 2003

Souers, Sidney W., American banker, insurance executive and intelligence service official, Feb 1949, *Obit* Mar 1973

Soukup, Frantisek, *Obit* Yrbk 1940

Soulages, Pierre, French painter, graphic artist and set designer, Apr 1958

Soule, George Henry, American economist, Yrbk 1945, *Obit* June 1970

Souleyman, Omar, Musician, Aug 2012

Soustelle, Jacques, French political leader, Yrbk 1958, *Obit* Oct 1990

Souter, David H., American Supreme Court justice, Jan 1991

Southworth, Billy, baseball player and manager, Nov 1944, *Obit* Jan 1970

Southworth, James L., American surgeon, June 1943

Souvanna Phouma, Nov 1962, *Obit* Mar 1984

Souzay, Gerard, French opera singer, Jan 1966, *Obit* Yrbk 2004

Sovern, Michael I., Feb 1981

Sowell, Thomas, American economist, July 1981

Soyer, Isaac, American painter, Mar 1941, *Obit* Sept 1981

Soyer, Isaac; Soyer, Moses; and Soyer, Raphael, Mar 1941

Soyer, Moses, American painter, Mar 1941, *Obit* Oct 1974

Soyer, Raphael, American painter, Mar 1941, *Obit* Jan 1988

Soyinka, Wole, Nigerian dramatist, poet and novelist, Yrbk 1974

Spaak, Paul-Henri, Belgian statesman, May 1945, Apr 1958, *Obit* Oct 1972

Spaatz, Carl, American air force general, Sept 1942, *Obit* Sept 1974

Spacek, Sissy, American actress, Jan 1978

Spacey, Kevin, American actor and director, Apr 1997

Spade, Kate, American handbag designer, Apr 2007

Spaeth, Sigmund, musicologist, July 1942, *Obit* Jan 1966

Spahn, Warren, American baseball player, May 1962, *Obit* Yrbk 2004

Spain, Frances Lander, American librarian and college administrator, June 1960

Spalding, Albert, violinist, Jan 1944, *Obit* July 1953

Spalding, Esperanza, American jazz bassist and singer, Aug 2010

Spang, J. P., June 1949, *Obit* Feb 1970

Spangler, Harrison Earl, lawyer, Aug 1943, *Obit* Oct 1965

Spanic, Gabriela, Venezuelan actress, Jan 2004

Sparano, Tony, American football coach, Jan 2010

Spark, Muriel, Scottish novelist, Nov 1975, *Obit* Yrbk 2007

Sparkman, John J., American senator, Mar 1950, *Obit* Jan 1986

Sparks, Nicholas, American novelist, Feb 2001

Sparling, Edward J., July 1948

Spassky, Boris Vasilyevich, Russian chess player, Nov 1972

Spaulding, Rolland H., *Obit* May 1942

Speakes, Larry Melvin, presidential press secretary, Mar 1985

Speaks, John Charles, *Obit* Yrbk 1945

Speare, Elizabeth George, American children's and young adult author, Yrbk 1959, *Obit* Jan 1995

Spearman, Charles E., English psychologist, *Obit* Oct 1945

Spears, Britney, American singer, Apr 2000

Specter, Arlen, American senator, Aug 1988, Aug 2009, *Obit* Yrbk 2012

Spector, Phil, American record producer, songwriter and arranger, July 1989

Spectorsky, A. C., Jan 1960, *Obit* Mar 1972

Speer, Albert, German architect and Nazi leader, Oct 1976, *Obit* Oct 1981

Speicher, Eugene Edward, American painter, Oct 1947, *Obit* July 1962

Speidel, Hans, German general, Apr 1952, *Obit* Feb 1985

Spektor, Regina, Russian-American singer, songwriter and pianist, July 2007

Spelke, Elizabeth S., American psychologist, Apr 2006

Spelling, Aaron, American television producer, May 1986, *Obit* Yrbk 2006

Spellings, Margaret, American Secretary of education, June 2005

Spellman, Francis, Apr 1940, Apr 1947, *Obit* Jan 1968

Spence, Brent, Sept 1952, *Obit* Jan 1968

Spence, Hartzell, journalist and novelist, Oct 1942, *Obit* Yrbk 2001

Spencer, John, American actor, Jan 2001, *Obit* Yrbk 2006

Spencer, P. C., July 1951, *Obit* Jan 1970

Spencer, Scott, American novelist, July 2003

Spender, John A., English newspaper editor, *Obit* Aug 1942

Spender, Percy Claude, Mar 1950

Spender, Stephen, English poet and critic, Jan 1940, Mar 1977, *Obit* Sept 1995

Spergel, David N., American astrophysicist, Jan 2005

Sperling, Gene, American economist and presidential adviser, Apr 2011

Sperry, Armstrong, American children's author and illustrator, Oct 1941

Sperry, Roger Wolcott, American psychologist, Jan 1986, *Obit* June 1994

Sperry, Willard Learoyd, theologian, May 1952, *Obit* Sept 1954

Sperti, George Speri, biophysicist, Jan 1940, *Obit* July 1991

Speyer, Jerry I., American real estate developer, May 2008

Spiegel, Clara E., novelist, Yrbk 1954

Spiegelman, Art, American cartoonist, Mar 1994

Spiegelman, Solomon, geneticist, Nov 1980, *Obit* Mar 1983

Spielberg, Steven, American film director and producer, July 1978, Feb 1996

Spilhaus, Athelstan F., American meteorologist and oceanographer, June 1965, *Obit* June 1998

Spillane, Mickey, American mystery novelist, Sept 1981, *Obit* Nov 2006

Spiller, William Gibson, *Obit* Apr 1940

Spingarn, Arthur Barnett, lawyer and civil rights leader, Jan 1965, *Obit* Jan 1972

Spinola, Antonio de, Portuguese general and president, Sept 1974, *Obit* Nov 1996

Spiropulu, Maria, Greek physicist, May 2004

Spitalny, Phil, Oct 1940, *Obit* Yrbk 1970

Spitz, Mark, American swimmer, Oct 1972

Spitzer, Eliot, American governor, Mar 2003

Spitzer, Lyman, American astrophysicist, Jan 1960, *Obit* June 1997

Spivak, Lawrence E., television moderator, May 1956, *Obit* May 1994

Spivakov, Vladimir, Russian violinist and conductor, Feb 1996

Spock, Benjamin, American pediatrician, Yrbk 1956, Nov 1969, *Obit* June 1998

Spofford, Charles Merville, lawyer and diplomat, Feb 1951, *Obit* May 1991

Sporborg, Constance Amberg, Nov 1947, *Obit* Feb 1961

Sporn, Philip, American electrical engineer, Nov 1966

Spottswood, James, *Obit* Yrbk 1940

Spottswood, Stephen Gill, American bishop and civil rights leader, Apr 1962, *Obit* Jan 1975

Sprague, Embert Hiram, *Obit* Mar 1940

Sprague, Robert Chapman, radio and television equipment executive, Jan 1951, *Obit* Nov 1991

Sprewell, Latrell, American basketball player, Feb 2001

Spring, Howard, English author, Jan 1941, *Obit* June 1965

Springer, Adele I., Apr 1947

Springer, Axel, German publishing executive, Yrbk 1968, *Obit* Nov 1985

Springsteen, Bruce, American singer and songwriter, Apr 1978, Aug 1992

Sprinkel, Beryl W., American economist and government official, July 1987, *Obit* Yrbk 2009

Sproul, Allan, banker, Yrbk 1950, *Obit* June 1978

Sproul, Robert Gordon, July 1945, *Obit* Nov 1975

Spruance, Raymond Ames, American admiral, Apr 1944, *Obit* Mar 1970

Spry, Constance, English flower arranger, May 1940, *Obit* Mar 1960

Spurgeon, Caroline F. E., *Obit* Yrbk 1942

Spurlock, Morgan, American documentary filmmaker, June 2013

Squires, Richard Anderson, *Obit* May 1940

Squyres, Steve, American planetary geologist, Nov 2006

Srichaphan, Paradorn, Thai tennis player, Jan 2004

St. Denis, Ruth, American dancer, Oct 1949, *Obit* Oct 1968

St. George, Katharine, congresswoman, Yrbk 1947, *Obit* July 1983

St. George, Thomas Richard, Jan 1944

St. John, Robert, American journalist, June 1942, *Obit* Yrbk 2003

St. Johns, Adela Rogers, author and journalist, Aug 1976, *Obit* Sept 1988

St. Laurent, Louis S., Mar 1948, *Obit* Oct 1973

St. Louis, Martin, Canadian hockey player, Feb 2007

Staats, Elmer Boyd, American government official, June 1967, *Obit* Yrbk 2011

Stabenow, Debbie, American senator, Feb 2006

Stabler, Ken, American football player, Oct 1979

Stace, W. T., Apr 1961, *Obit* Oct 1967

Stackhouse, Jerry, American basketball player, Nov 2001

Stacy, Walter P., Jan 1946, *Obit* Oct 1951

Stader, Maria, Swiss opera singer, July 1958, *Obit* Aug 1999

Stafford, Jean, American novelist and short story writer, Yrbk 1951, *Obit* May 1979

Stafford, Robert T., American senator, Sept 1960, *Obit* Yrbk 2008

Stafford, Thomas P., American astronaut and air force general, Jan 1977

Stagg, Amos Alonzo, football coach, Mar 1944, *Obit* Apr 1965

Staggers, Harley O., American congressman, Mar 1971, *Obit* Nov 1991

Stahl, Lesley, television reporter, June 1996

Stahle, Nils K., Apr 1956

Stahr, Elvis J., American Secretary of the army, Sept 1961, *Obit* Feb 1999

Stainback, Ingram Macklin, Yrbk 1947, *Obit* June 1961

Stakman, Elvin Charles, American botanist, Yrbk 1949, *Obit* Mar 1979

Staley, Dawn, American basketball player, Apr 2005

Staley, Oren Lee, farm leader, Sept 1965, *Obit* Nov 1988

Stalin, Joseph, Soviet dictator, Mar 1942, *Obit* Apr 1953

Stallone, Sylvester, American actor and screenwriter, Oct 1977, Feb 1994

Stalnaker, John Marshall, psychologist, July 1958, *Obit* Oct 1990

Stamberg, Susan, American radio newscaster, Oct 2008

Stamkos, Steven, Canadian hockey player, Apr 2013

Stamm, John S., Feb 1949, *Obit* May 1956

Stamos, Theodoros, painter, Jan 1959, *Obit* Apr 1997

Stamp, Josiah Charles, British government official, *Obit* June 1941

Standish, Burt L., American children's author, *Obit* Mar 1945

Standley, William Harrison, admiral, May 1942, *Obit* Yrbk 1963

Stanfield, Robert Lorne, Canadian political leader, Yrbk 1958, *Obit* Yrbk 2004

Stanfield, Robert Nelson, *Obit* June 1945

Stankiewicz, Richard, American sculptor, June 1967, *Obit* May 1983

Stanky, Eddie, baseball player, June 1951, *Obit* Aug 1999

Stanley, Freelan Oscar, American automotive pioneer, *Obit* Nov 1940

Stanley, Kim, American actress, May 1955, *Obit* Jan 2002

Stanley, Oliver, Apr 1943, *Obit* Jan 1951

Stanley, Paul, American guitarist, Apr 1999

Stanley, Thomas B., American governor, Yrbk 1955, *Obit* Oct 1970

Stanley, Wendell Meredith, American biochemist, Apr 1947, *Obit* Sept 1971

Stanley, Winnifred Claire, congresswoman, June 1943

Stans, Maurice H., American Secretary of commerce, Yrbk 1958, *Obit* June 1998

Stanton, Andrew, American film director, screenwriter and animator, Feb 2004

Stanton, Bill, private detective, May 2001

Stanton, Frank, American broadcasting executive, Nov 1945, Oct 1965, *Obit* Yrbk 2007

Stanton, Katie Jacobs, Internet executive and Special Adviser to the Office of Innovation at the U.S. Department of State, June 2012

Stanwyck, Barbara, American actress, July 1947, *Obit* Mar 1990

Staples, Brent, American journalist and memoirist, May 2000

Stapleton, Jean, actress, Yrbk 1972, *Obit* Yrbk 2013

Stapleton, Maureen, American actress, May 1959, *Obit* Nov 2006

Stapp, John Paul, air force officer and biophysicist, Yrbk 1959, *Obit* May 2000

Stapp, Scott, American singer and lyricist, May 2002

Starch, Daniel, psychologist and marketing analyst, Jan 1963

Stargell, Willie, American baseball player, June 1980, *Obit* Sept 2001

Stark, Harold R., admiral, May 1940, *Obit* Oct 1972

Stark, Louis, June 1945, *Obit* Sept 1954

Starker, Janos, Hungarian cellist, May 1963, *Obit* Yrbk 2013

Starkie, Walter Fitzwilliam, Anglo-Irish literary critic, May 1964, *Obit* Feb 1977

Starr, Bart, American football player and coach, Jan 1968

Starr, Cecile, American film critic, Mar 1955

Starr, Chauncey, American physicist, Apr 1954, *Obit* Yrbk 2007

Starr, Kenneth W., American law teacher and independent counsel in Whitewater Investigation, May 1998

Starr, Louis E., June 1947

Starr, Mark, labor leader, July 1946, *Obit* July 1985

Starr, Ringo, English drummer, Yrbk 1965

Starzl, Thomas E., American surgeon, Mar 1993

Stassen, Harold E., American lawyer, governor and presidential candidate, May 1940, Mar 1948, *Obit* May 2001

Statz, Hermann, Jan 1958

Staubach, Roger, American football player and real estate executive, Apr 1972

Staudinger, Hermann, German chemist, Apr 1954, *Obit* Nov 1965

Stauning, Thorvald, Danish prime minister, *Obit* June 1942

Staunton, Imelda, English actress, Jan 2005

Stauss, Emil Georg von, *Obit* Feb 1943

Stavropoulos, George, fashion designer, Mar 1985, *Obit* Feb 1991

Steacie, E. W. R., Jan 1953, *Obit* Nov 1962

Steadman, Ralph, English illustrator, May 1999

Steagall, Henry Bascom, *Obit* Jan 1944

Stearns, Harold E., journalist and critic, *Obit* Oct 1943

Stebbins, George Coles, *Obit* Nov 1945

Steber, Eleanor, American opera singer, Mar 1943, *Obit* Jan 1991

Steel, Danielle, American romance novelist, July 1989

Steel, David, British member of Parliament, July 1978

Steel, Johannes, radio commentator and columnist, June 1941, *Obit* Feb 1989

Steel, Kurt, author, *Obit* June 1946

Steele, Claude M., American social psychologist, Feb 2001

Steele, Frederic Dorr, *Obit* Aug 1944

Steele, Michael S., American political party leader, July 2004

Steele, Shelby, American writer and professor of English, Feb 1993

Steell, Willis, *Obit* Mar 1941

Steelman, John R., American presidential aide and economist, May 1941, Nov 1952, *Obit* Nov 1999

Steen, Marguerite, English author, Oct 1941, *Obit* Sept 1975

Stefan, Paul, *Obit* Jan 1944

Stefansson, Kari, Icelandic geneticist, Jan 2003

Stefansson, Vilhjalmur, American arctic explorer, Oct 1942, *Obit* Nov 1962

Stegner, Wallace Earle, American novelist and short story writer, Apr 1977, *Obit* June 1993

Steichen, Edward, American photographer, Oct 1942, Yrbk 1964, *Obit* May 1973

Steig, William, American illustrator and children's author, July 1944, *Obit* Apr 2004

Steiger, Rod, American actor, June 1965, *Obit* Yrbk 2002

Stein, Benjamin, American writer and actor, Sept 2001

Stein, Gertrude, American novelist, poet and critic, *Obit* Sept 1946

Stein, Herbert, American economist, Mar 1973, *Obit* Feb 2000

Stein, Janice Gross, Canadian international relations specialist, Aug 2006

Stein, Jules, concert and theatrical agent, May 1967, *Obit* June 1981

Steinbeck, John, American novelist, Jan 1940, May 1963, *Obit* Feb 1969

Steinberg, Milton, rabbi, Mar 1940, *Obit* Apr 1950

Steinberg, Saul, Romanian-American illustrator and cartoonist, Mar 1957, *Obit* July 1999

Steinberg, William, American conductor, Sept 1940, Mar 1958, *Obit* July 1978

Steinbrenner, George M., American baseball and shipbuilding executive, Feb 1979, *Obit* Yrbk 2010

Steincrohn, Peter Joseph, Mar 1957

Steinem, Gloria, American feminist and journalist, Mar 1972, Mar 1988

Steiner, George, American literary critic, short story writer and novelist, Oct 1983

Steiner, Max, Austrian-American composer and conductor, Sept 1943, *Obit* Feb 1972

Steiner, Walter Ralph, *Obit* Jan 1943

Steinfeld, Jesse L., Apr 1974

Steingraber, Sandra, American biologist, poet and nonfiction writer, Sept 2003

Steinhardt, Laurence Adolph, lawyer and diplomat, July 1941, *Obit* Apr 1950

Steinhaus, Edward A., Yrbk 1955

Steinkraus, Herman W., Nov 1949, *Obit* July 1974

Steinman, David Barnard, American bridge engineer, Yrbk 1957, *Obit* Nov 1960

Steinmetz, George, American photographer, July 2013

Steitz, Joan Argetsinger, American biochemist, June 2007

Stekel, Wilhelm, Austrian psychoanalyst, *Obit* Aug 1940

Stella, Antonietta, Italian opera singer, Yrbk 1959

Stella, Frank, American artist, Apr 1971, Apr 1988

Stella, Joseph, painter, *Obit* Yrbk 1946

Stelle, John, Jan 1946, *Obit* Sept 1962

Steloff, Frances, bookseller, Nov 1965, *Obit* June 1989

Stengel, Casey, American baseball manager, June 1949, *Obit* Nov 1975

Stengel, Richard, American journalist and magazine editor, Jan 2011

Stenmark, Ingemar, Swedish skier, Apr 1982

Stennis, John C., American senator, Jan 1953, *Obit* July 1995

Stephanie, Aug 1986

Stephanopoulos, George, American television news anchor, Jan 1995

Stephanopoulos, Stephanos, July 1955

Stephens, Hubert D., *Obit* Apr 1946

Stephens, John A., Yrbk 1956

Stephens, Ward, *Obit* Nov 1940

Stephens, William D., *Obit* June 1944

Stephenson, James, British actor, *Obit* Sept 1941

Stepinac, Alojzije, Feb 1953, *Obit* Apr 1960

Stepovich, Michael A., Nov 1958

Steptoe, Patrick, British surgeon, Mar 1979, *Obit* June 1988

Sterling, John Ewart Wallace, college president, Jan 1951, *Obit* Aug 1985

Stern, Arthur Cecil, sanitary engineer, Apr 1956, *Obit* July 1992

Stern, Bill, sportscaster, June 1941, *Obit* Jan 1972

Stern, David, American basketball association executive, Apr 1991

Stern, Howard, American radio personality, Jan 1996

Stern, Isaac, American violinist, Apr 1949, Feb 1989, *Obit* Jan 2002

Stern, Jessica, American terrorism expert, May 2006

Stern, Leonard, American real estate executive and newspaper publisher, Mar 1991

Stern, Martha Dodd, American novelist, translator and spy, Yrbk 1946, *Obit* Jan 1991

Stern, Nicholas Herbert, British economist and government official, Jan 2007

Stern, Richard G., American novelist and short story writer, June 1994, *Obit* Yrbk 2013

Stern, Robert A. M., American architect and college dean, June 2000

Sterne, Hedda, American painter, Mar 1957, *Obit* Yrbk 2011

Sterne, Maurice, American painter, Apr 1943, *Obit* Oct 1957

Stettinius, Edward Reilly, American Secretary of state, July 1940, *Obit* Yrbk 1949

Steuer, Max, *Obit* Oct 1940

Stevens, Edmund, American journalist, July 1950, *Obit* July 1992

Stevens, George, American film and television producer, Yrbk 1965

Stevens, George, American motion picture director, Apr 1952, *Obit* May 1975

Stevens, John Paul, American Supreme Court justice, May 1976

Stevens, Rise, American opera singer, Nov 1941, *Obit* Yrbk 2013

Stevens, Robert T., American textile industry executive and Secretary of the army, July 1953, *Obit* Mar 1983

Stevens, Roger L., real estate executive and theatrical producer, Yrbk 1955, *Obit* Apr 1998

Stevens, Ted, American senator, Oct 2001, *Obit* Yrbk 2010

Stevenson, Adlai, American senator, Apr 1974

Stevenson, Adlai E., American statesman, Jan 1949, Sept 1961, *Obit* Sept 1965

Stevenson, Bryan, lawyer and human rights activist, Mar 1996

Stevenson, E. Robert, Jan 1940

Stevenson, Elizabeth, American biographer and literary scholar, Yrbk 1956

Stevenson, George S., psychiatrist, Yrbk 1946

Stevenson, McLean, actor, June 1980, *Obit* Apr 1996

Stevenson, William E., lawyer, college president and diplomat, Nov 1943, *Obit* May 1985

Stever, H. Guyford, American aeronautical engineer, Jan 1981, *Obit* Yrbk 2010

Steves, Rick, American travel guidebook author, Jan 2009

Stew (Musician), American composer, lyricist and singer, Sept 2007

Steward, David L., American information technology executive, Nov 2004

Stewart, Alice, British epidemiologist, July 2000, *Obit* Yrbk 2002

Stewart, Anna Bird, Yrbk 1948

Stewart, Donald Ogden, screenwriter, dramatist and humorist, July 1941, *Obit* Sept 1980

Stewart, Ellen, American theatrical producer, June 1973, *Obit* Yrbk 2011

Stewart, George Craig, *Obit* Jan 1940

Stewart, George Rippey, American novelist and nonfiction writer, Jan 1942, *Obit* Nov 1980

Stewart, Harris B., oceanographer, Mar 1968

Stewart, James, American motorcycle racer, Feb 2005

Stewart, James, American actor, Apr 1941, Yrbk 1960, *Obit* Sept 1997

Stewart, Jon, American comedian and talk show host, July 2004

Stewart, Kenneth L., Yrbk 1943

Stewart, Martha, American cook, author and mass media executive, Aug 1993

Stewart, Michael, British cabinet member, Sept 1965, *Obit* June 1990

Stewart, Patrick, British actor, Aug 1994

Stewart, Potter, American Supreme Court justice, Yrbk 1959, *Obit* Feb 1986

Stewart, Rod, English singer, Aug 1979

Stewart, Rory, British diplomat and writer, Jan 2007

Stewart, Thomas, American opera singer, May 1974, *Obit* Yrbk 2007

Stewart, Tony, American automobile racing driver, Nov 2006

Stewart, William G., *Obit* Sept 1941

Stewart, William H., American surgeon general, Apr 1966, *Obit* Yrbk 2008

Stickney, Dorothy, actress, Apr 1942, *Obit* Aug 1998

Stiebeling, Hazel K., American nutritionist, Apr 1950

Stiefel, Ethan, American ballet dancer, Apr 2004

Stieglitz, Alfred, American photographer, Jan 1940, *Obit* Sept 1946

Stigler, George Joseph, American economist and educator, July 1983, *Obit* Feb 1992

Stignani, Ebe, Italian opera singer, Feb 1949, *Obit* Yrbk 1991

Stigwood, Robert, Australian film, recording and theatrical producer, Oct 1979

Stikker, Dirk U., Dutch statesman, Feb 1950, Feb 1962

Stiles, Charles Wardell, American public health official and zoologist, *Obit* Mar 1941

Still, Clyfford, American painter, Sept 1971, *Obit* Aug 1980

Still, William Grant, American composer, Jan 1941, *Obit* Feb 1979

Stiller, Ben, American actor, comedian and director, Nov 1999

Stillwell, Lewis Buckley, American electrical engineer, *Obit* Mar 1941

Stilwell, Joseph Warren, American general, May 1942, *Obit* Nov 1946

Stilwell, Richard, American opera singer, Feb 1986

Stimson, Frederic Jesup, *Obit* Jan 1944

Stimson, Henry Lewis, American statesman, Aug 1940, *Obit* Yrbk 1950

Stimson, Julia Catherine, nurse, Nov 1940, *Obit* Nov 1948

Stine, Charles Milton Altland, Jan 1940, *Obit* Sept 1954

Stine, R. L., American children's author, Sept 1999

Sting, British singer and actor, July 1985

Stipe, Michael, American singer, Apr 1997

Stirnweiss, Snuffy, baseball player, Mar 1946, *Obit* Yrbk 1958

Stirratt, John, American bassist, Feb 2010

Stock, Frederick, conductor, *Obit* Yrbk 1942

Stockberger, Warner W., government official and personnel director, Aug 1941

Stockbridge, Frank Parker, *Obit* Jan 1941

Stockhausen, Karlheinz, German composer and conductor, Yrbk 1971, *Obit* Yrbk 2008

Stockman, David Alan, American investment banker, presidential aide and manufacturing executive, Aug 1981

Stockton, John, American basketball player, June 1995

Stockwell, Dean, actor, Feb 1991

Stoddard, Alexandra, American interior designer, June 1996

Stoddard, Brandon, television executive, Feb 1989

Stoddard, Frederick Lincoln, *Obit* Mar 1940

Stoddard, George Dinsmore, American psychologist and college president, July 1946, *Obit* Feb 1982

Stoessel, Albert, *Obit* July 1943

Stoessel, Walter J., diplomat, June 1970, *Obit* Feb 1987

Stoica, Chivu, Jan 1959, *Obit* Apr 1975

Stokes, Anson Phelps, bishop, July 1962, *Obit* Jan 1987

Stokes, Carl, American mayor, judge and newscaster, Apr 1968, *Obit* June 1996

Stokes, Edward C., American governor, *Obit* Yrbk 1942

Stokes, Isaac Newton Phelps, architect and antiquarian, *Obit* Feb 1945

Stokes, Richard Rapier, British cabinet member, Sept 1951, *Obit* Oct 1957

Stokes, Thomas Lunsford, May 1947, *Obit* Sept 1958

Stokowski, Leopold, American conductor, Feb 1941, July 1953, *Obit* Nov 1977

Stolk, William C., Mar 1953

Stoller, Debbie, American magazine editor and feminist, Aug 2007

Stoltenberg, Gerhard, German cabinet member, Sept 1989, *Obit* Mar 2002

Stoltzman, Richard, clarinetist, Mar 1986

Stolz, Mary, American children's author and young adult novelist, Yrbk 1953, *Obit* Yrbk 2007

Stolz, Robert, Austrian composer, Aug 1943, *Obit* Aug 1975

Stone, Abraham, Mar 1952, *Obit* Oct 1959

Stone, Edward C., American physicist, Feb 1990

Stone, Edward Durell, American architect, June 1958, *Obit* Sept 1978

Stone, Emma, American actress, Feb 2013

Stone, Hannah M., physician and family planning advocate, *Obit* Sept 1941

Stone, Harlan Fiske, American Supreme Court justice, Aug 1941, *Obit* June 1946

Stone, I. F., American journalist, Sept 1972, *Obit* Aug 1989

Stone, Irving, biographer, Yrbk 1967, *Obit* Oct 1989

Stone, John Charles, *Obit* July 1940

Stone, Joss, British soul singer, Jan 2005

Stone, Matt, American actor, television scriptwriter, producer, director and animator, May 1998

Stone, Oliver, American film director and screenwriter, June 1987

Stone, Robert, American novelist, Jan 1987

Stone, Sharon, American actress, Apr 1996

Stone, W. Clement, American insurance executive, Feb 1972, *Obit* Yrbk 2002

Stone, William S., June 1960, *Obit* Feb 1969

Stonehaven, John Lawrence Baird, *Obit* Oct 1941

Stookey, Charley, Jan 1940

Stoopnagle, Lemuel Q., radio comedian, Oct 1947, *Obit* July 1950

Stoph, Willi, East German communist leader, Oct 1960, *Obit* Aug 1999

Stoppard, Tom, English dramatist, July 1974

Stoppelman, Jeremy, American Internet executive, June 2012

Storch, Jerry, American retail executive, June 2007

Storey, David, English dramatist and novelist, Sept 1973

Storey, Robert Gerald, Nov 1953

Storke, Thomas M., American newspaper editor and publisher, Yrbk 1963

Storms, Harrison Allen, American aeronautical engineer, Jan 1963, *Obit* Sept 1992

Storr, Anthony, English psychiatrist and psychotherapist, June 1994, *Obit* Sept 2001

Storr, Vernon Faithfull, *Obit* Yrbk 1940

Stott, John R. W., British clergyman and evangelist, May 2005, *Obit* Yrbk 2011

Stout, Rex, American mystery novelist, Mar 1946, *Obit* Jan 1976

Stout, Ruth A., Jan 1959

Stout, Wesley Winans, June 1941, *Obit* Jan 1972

Stout, William Bushnell, American aeronautical engineer and aircraft industry executive, Mar 1941, *Obit* May 1956

Stowe, Leland, journalist, July 1940, *Obit* Mar 1994

Stowell, Clarence Warner, *Obit* Jan 1941

Strachan, Paul A., Jan 1952

Strachey, Evelyn John St. Loe, British cabinet member, June 1946, *Obit* Sept 1963

Straight, Michael Whitney, American magazine editor, publisher, arts administrator and memoirist, Aug 1944, *Obit* Yrbk 2004

Strait, George, American country singer, Feb 2000

Stranahan, Frank, Sept 1951, *Obit* Yrbk 2013

Strand, Paul, American photographer, July 1965, *Obit* May 1976

Strang, Ruth, Yrbk 1960, *Obit* Feb 1971

Strasberg, Lee, American actor, director and acting teacher, Oct 1960, *Obit* Apr 1982

Strasberg, Susan, actress, May 1958, *Obit* Apr 1999

Strasser, Otto, German Nazi leader, Sept 1940, *Obit* Oct 1974

Stratas, Teresa, Canadian opera singer, Jan 1980

Stratemeyer, George E., Feb 1951, *Obit* Oct 1969

Strathmore and Kinghorne, Claud George Bowes-Lyon, *Obit* Yrbk 1944

Stratton, Dorothy C., American psychologist, college dean and Coast Guard officer, June 1943, *Obit* Yrbk 2006

Stratton, Julius Adams, American physicist and college president, May 1963, *Obit* Aug 1994

Stratton, Samuel S., congressman, Jan 1966, *Obit* Jan 1991

Stratton, William G., American governor, Apr 1953, *Obit* Aug 2001

Straub, Peter, American horror novelist, Feb 1989

Straus, Jack Isidor, department store executive, Mar 1952, *Obit* Nov 1985

Straus, Michael W., June 1952

Straus, Nathan, May 1944, *Obit* Nov 1961

Straus, Oscar, Austrian composer, Mar 1944, *Obit* Mar 1954

Straus, Percy Selden, American department store executive, *Obit* May 1944

Straus, Roger W., American metal industry executive, July 1952, *Obit* Oct 1957

Straus, Roger W., American publishing executive, Aug 1980, *Obit* Yrbk 2004

Strauss, Anna Lord, Nov 1945, *Obit* Apr 1979

Strauss, Franz Josef, German political leader, Feb 1957, Feb 1987, *Obit* Nov 1988

Strauss, J. G. N., Jan 1951

Strauss, Lewis L., American presidential aide, regulatory agency official and Secretary of commerce, Feb 1947, *Obit* Mar 1974

Strauss, Richard, German composer, July 1944, *Obit* Oct 1949

Strauss, Robert S., American political party leader and diplomat, Mar 1974, July 1992

Stravinsky, Igor, Russian composer, May 1940, Apr 1953, *Obit* May 1971

Straw, Jack, British cabinet member, Jan 2002

Strawberry, Darryl, American baseball player, June 1984

Strawbridge, Anne West, *Obit* Nov 1941

Streb, Elizabeth, American dancer and choreographer, Apr 2003

Streep, Meryl, American actress, Aug 1980, Mar 1997

Street, James, American novelist, Yrbk 1946, *Obit* Nov 1954

Street, Jessie M. G., Australian feminist, Sept 1947

Street, Picabo, American skier, Apr 1998

Streeter, Ruth Cheney, marine corps officer, July 1943, *Obit* Jan 1991

Strehler, Giorgio, Italian theatrical director, Mar 1991, *Obit* Mar 1998

Streibert, Theodore C., American government official and broadcasting executive, Feb 1955, *Obit* Mar 1987

Streicher, Julius, German Nazi leader, *Obit* Nov 1946

Streisand, Barbra, American singer and actress, June 1964, Sept 1992

Streit, Clarence K., journalist, May 1940, May 1950, *Obit* Sept 1986

Strel, Martin, Slovenian marathon swimmer, Jan 2007

Streuli, Hans, Apr 1957

Stridsberg, Gustaf, *Obit* Yrbk 1943

Strijdom, Johannes Gerhardus, May 1956, *Obit* Nov 1958

Strike, Clifford S., Nov 1949

Stringer, Howard, American electronics, film and broadcasting industry executive, Jan 2006

Stritch, Elaine, American actress, June 1988

Stritch, Samuel Alphonsus, Apr 1946, *Obit* Sept 1958

Stroessner, Alfredo, Paraguayan general and president, Yrbk 1958, Mar 1981, *Obit* Yrbk 2007

Strokes (Musical group), Feb 2007

Stroman, Susan, American choreographer and theatrical director, July 2002

Stromberg, Leonard, *Obit* Sept 1941

Strong, Anna Louise, American journalist, Mar 1949, *Obit* May 1970

Strong, Lee A., *Obit* July 1941

Strong, Maurice F., Canadian petroleum executive, environmentalist and government official, Yrbk 1973

Strong, William McCreery, *Obit* May 1941

Strossen, Nadine, American lawyer and civil rights leader, Oct 1997

Strouse, Norman H., advertising executive, May 1960, *Obit* Mar 1993

Strout, Richard Lee, journalist and columnist, Apr 1980, *Obit* Oct 1990

Struble, Arthur Dewey, admiral, Nov 1951, *Obit* July 1983

Strughold, Hubertus, July 1966

Struther, Jan, English poet, essayist and short story writer, Jan 1941, *Obit* Oct 1953

Struthers, Sally, American actress, Jan 1974

Struve, Otto, astronomer, Oct 1949, *Obit* June 1963

Struzan, Drew, American poster artist, Mar 2005

Stuart, Duane Reed, *Obit* Oct 1941

Stuart, Gloria, American actress, Apr 1998, *Obit* Yrbk 2010

Stuart, James Everett, painter, *Obit* Feb 1941

Stuart, Jesse, author, Aug 1940, *Obit* Apr 1984

Stuart, John Leighton, American missionary and diplomat, Oct 1946, *Obit* Nov 1962

Stuart, Kenneth, Feb 1944, *Obit* Yrbk 1945

Studebaker, John Ward, educator and government official, May 1942, *Obit* Oct 1989

Studebaker, Mabel, Nov 1948

Studer, Cheryl, opera singer, Apr 1992

Stuhlinger, Ernst, American rocket engineer, Nov 1957, *Obit* Yrbk 2008

Stummvoll, Josef Leopold, June 1960

Stump, Felix B., American admiral, Jan 1953, *Obit* Sept 1972

Sturdee, V. A. H., July 1942

Sturges, Preston, American screenwriter and film director, Apr 1941, *Obit* Oct 1959

Sturgis, Samuel D., Jan 1956, *Obit* Sept 1964

Sturzo, Luigi, Feb 1946, *Obit* Nov 1959

Stutz, Geraldine, American retail executive, May 1983, *Obit* Yrbk 2005

Styne, Jule, composer, May 1983, *Obit* Nov 1994

Styron, William, American novelist, July 1968, June 1986, *Obit* Yrbk 2007

Suarez, Adolfo, Spanish prime minister, May 1977

Subandrio, Indonesian cabinet member, Mar 1963, *Obit* Apr 2005

Suchocka, Hanna, Polish prime minister, Jan 1994

Sucksdorff, Arne, Swedish motion picture director, Apr 1956, *Obit* Sept 2001

Suenens, Leo Joseph, May 1965, *Obit* July 1996

Sues, Ralf, May 1944

Suesse, Dana, composer, May 1940, *Obit* Jan 1988

Sueyro, Saba H., Argentine admiral, *Obit* Sept 1943

Sugar, Bert Randolph, American sportswriter, Nov 2002, *Obit* Yrbk 2012

Suggs, Louise, American golfer, Jan 1962

Sugiyama, Hajime, Japanese field marshal, *Obit* Oct 1945

Sugrue, Thomas, journalist and author, June 1948, *Obit* Feb 1953

Suh, Ndamukong, American football player, Oct 2013

Suhr, Otto, Apr 1955, *Obit* Nov 1957

Suhrawardy, Huseyn Shaheed, Pakistani prime minister, Apr 1957, *Obit* Jan 1964

Sui, Anna, American fashion designer, July 1993

Suits, Chauncey Guy, physicist and inventor, Feb 1950, *Obit* Oct 1991

Sukarnoputri, Megawati, Indonesian president, Sept 1997

Sullavan, Margaret, actress, July 1944, *Obit* Feb 1960

Sullivan, A. M., Yrbk 1953, *Obit* Aug 1980

Sullivan, Brian, Yrbk 1957

Sullivan, Daniel, American theatrical director, Feb 2003

Sullivan, Ed, American columnist and television personality, Sept 1952, *Obit* Nov 1974

Sullivan, Francis L., June 1955, *Obit* Jan 1957

Sullivan, Gael, May 1947, *Obit* Jan 1957

Sullivan, Harry Stack, American psychiatrist, Nov 1942, *Obit* Feb 1949

Sullivan, Henry J., June 1958

Sullivan, John L., American Secretary of the navy, Sept 1948, *Obit* Oct 1982

Sullivan, Leon Howard, American clergyman and civil rights leader, Mar 1969, *Obit* Sept 2001

Sullivan, Leonor K., American congresswoman, Yrbk 1954, *Obit* Oct 1988

Sullivan, Louis W., American Secretary of health and human services, July 1989

Sullivan, Walter, American science writer, Sept 1980, *Obit* June 1996

Sullivan, William H., American diplomat, Aug 1979

Sulloway, Frank J., science historian, Sept 1997

Sulston, John, English molecular biologist, Jan 2007

Sultan, Daniel I., Jan 1945, *Obit* Feb 1947

Sulzberger, Arthur Hays, American newspaper publisher, Mar 1943, *Obit* Feb 1969

Sulzberger, Arthur O., American newspaper publisher, Jan 1997

Sulzberger, Arthur Ochs, American newspaper publisher, Nov 1966, *Obit* Yrbk 2012

Sulzberger, C. L., American journalist, May 1944, *Obit* Nov 1993

Sulzer, William, *Obit* Jan 1942

Sumac, Yma, Peruvian singer, Yrbk 1955, *Obit* Yrbk 2008

Summer, Donna, American singer, July 1979, *Obit* Yrbk 2012

Summerfield, Arthur Ellsworth, American postmaster general, Sept 1952, *Obit* June 1972

Summers, Lawrence H., American presidential adviser and former Secretary of the treasury, July 2002

Summerskill, Edith, British member of Parliament and physician, Apr 1943, July 1963, *Obit* Apr 1980

Summerville, Slim, actor, *Obit* Feb 1946

Summitt, Pat Head, American basketball coach, June 2005

Sumner, Bernard, British guitarist and singer, Jan 2006

Sumner, Cid Ricketts, American novelist and short story writer, Yrbk 1954

Sumner, James Batcheller, American biochemist, Jan 1947, *Obit* Oct 1955

Sumner, Jessie, congresswoman, Jan 1945, *Obit* Oct 1994

Sun Fo, Chinese government official, Oct 1944, *Obit* Yrbk 1973

Sun Wen, Chinese soccer player, Apr 2001

Sunay, Cevdet, Mar 1969, *Obit* Aug 1982

Sunderland, Thomas Elbert, fruit industry executive, Apr 1962, *Obit* May 1991

Sung, Ching-ling, Chinese political leader and wife of stateman Sun Yat-sen, Apr 1944, *Obit* July 1981

Sunstein, Cass R., American law professor, Oct 2008

Sununu, John, American governor and presidential adviser, May 1989

Supachai Panitchpakdi, Thai international organization official, Jan 2004

Surles, Alexander D., Nov 1945, *Obit* Yrbk 1947

Susann, Jacqueline, American novelist, May 1972, *Obit* Nov 1974

Suskind, Ron, Feb 2013

Suslov, Mikhail Andreevich, Soviet communist leader, Feb 1957, *Obit* Mar 1982

Susskind, David, American television producer, May 1960, *Obit* Apr 1987

Sutherland, Donald, Canadian actor, Feb 1981

Sutherland, George, American Supreme Court justice, *Obit* Sept 1942

Sutherland, Graham Vivian, English painter, Jan 1955, *Obit* Apr 1980

Sutherland, Joan, Australian opera singer, Yrbk 1960, *Obit* Yrbk 2010

Sutherland, Kiefer, Canadian actor, Mar 2002

Sutton, George Paul, July 1958

Sutton, Percy E., American municipal official, broadcasting executive and civil rights activist, Mar 1973, *Obit* Yrbk 2010

Suydam, E. H., *Obit* Feb 1941

Suzman, Helen, South African member of Parliament and human rights activist, Nov 1968, *Obit* Yrbk 2009

Suzman, Janet, May 1976

Suzuki, Daisetz Teitaro, Japanese philosopher, Oct 1958, *Obit* Nov 1966

Suzuki, David T., Canadian geneticist and environmentalist, July 1995

Suzuki, Ichiro, Japanese baseball player, July 2002

Suzuki, Kantaro, Japanese admiral, Aug 1945, *Obit* May 1948

Suzuki, Pat, singer and actress, Jan 1960

Suzuki, Seijun, Japanese film director, Jan 2005

Suzuki, Umetaro, *Obit* Nov 1943

Suzuki, Yu, Japanese video game developer, Jan 2003

Suzuki, Zenko, Japanese prime minister, Jan 1981, *Obit* Yrbk 2004

Svanholm, Set, Swedish opera singer, Yrbk 1956, *Obit* Yrbk 1964

Svankmajer, Jan, Czech animator and motion picture director, Jan 2006

Sveda, Michael, chemist and inventor, Yrbk 1954, *Obit* Nov 1999

Sveinn Bjornsson, Aug 1944, *Obit* Mar 1952

Svinhufvud, Pehr Evind, *Obit* Apr 1944

Swados, Elizabeth, American composer, Feb 1979

Swaggart, Jimmy Lee, evangelist, Oct 1987

Swallow, Alan, Feb 1963, *Obit* Jan 1967

Swanberg, Joe, American film director and screenwriter, Nov 2010

Swank, Hilary, American actress, Sept 2000

Swann, Donald, English pianist and composer, Jan 1970, *Obit* May 1994

Swann, William Francis Gray, Feb 1941, Yrbk 1960, *Obit* Mar 1962

Swanson, Gloria, actress, Sept 1950, *Obit* May 1983

Swart, Charles Robberts, June 1960

Swarthout, Gladys, opera singer, Mar 1944, *Obit* Sept 1969

Swartwout, Egerton, *Obit* Apr 1943

Swartz, Aaron, American electronic publisher, *Obit* Yrbk 2013

Swaythling, Jean Marcia, Sept 1942

Swayze, Patrick, American actor and dancer, Mar 1991, *Obit* Yrbk 2009

Swearingen, John E., American petroleum industry executive, Jan 1979, *Obit* Yrbk 2007

Sweeney, Anne, American television executive, June 2003

Sweeney, James Johnson, art critic, historian and museum director, Mar 1955, *Obit* July 1986

Sweeney, John J., American labor leader, June 1996

Sweet, William Ellery, *Obit* July 1942

Swenson, Alfred G., *Obit* May 1941

Swidler, Joseph C., American government official, Mar 1964, *Obit* July 1997

Swift, Ernest John, *Obit* Yrbk 1941

Swift, Gustavus Franklin, American meat packing executive, *Obit* Yrbk 1943

Swift, Harold Higgins, Feb 1950, *Obit* Sept 1962

Swift, Taylor, American singer and songwriter, Jan 2010

Swigert, Ernest Goodnough, machinery industry executive, Oct 1957, *Obit* Feb 1987

Swing, Joseph May, general and immigration official, Apr 1959, *Obit* Feb 1985

Swing, Raymond, radio commentator, Jan 1940, *Obit* Feb 1969

Swings, Pol, Belgian astronomer, Yrbk 1954

Swinton, Tilda, Scottish actress, Nov 2001

Swirbul, Leon A., Apr 1953, *Obit* Sept 1960

Swiss, Jamy Ian, American magician, Feb 2010

Switzer, George, American industrial designer and art director, *Obit* Yrbk 1940

Switzer, Mary Elizabeth, Jan 1962, *Obit* Yrbk 1971

Swoopes, Sheryl, American basketball player, July 1996

Swope, Gerard, Sept 1941, *Obit* Feb 1958

Swope, Herbert Bayard, journalist, Nov 1944, *Obit* Sept 1958

Sy, Oumou, Senegalese fashion designer, Jan 2003

Syal, Meera, English actress, novelist and screenwriter, Feb 2001

Syberberg, Hans Jurgen, German motion picture producer and director, Apr 1983

Sydow, Max von, Swedish actor, Apr 1967

Sykes, Charles H., *Obit* Feb 1943

Sykes, Eugene Octave, *Obit* July 1945

Sykes, Richard Eddy, *Obit* Nov 1942

Sykes, Wanda, American comedian, Jan 2011

Syme, John P., Mar 1957

Symes, James M., Yrbk 1955, *Obit* Sept 1976

Symington, James W., June 1968

Symington, Stuart, American senator, Sept 1945, July 1956, *Obit* Feb 1989

Symons, Arthur, English poet and critic, *Obit* Mar 1945

Synge, Richard Lawrence Millington, British biochemist, Nov 1953

Syran, Arthur George, Mar 1950

Szasz, Thomas Stephen, American psychiatrist and psychoanalyst, Jan 1975, *Obit* Yrbk 2012

Szell, George, American conductor, June 1945, *Obit* Oct 1970

Szent-Gyorgyi, Albert, Hungarian-American biochemist, Jan 1955, *Obit* Jan 1987

Szeryng, Henryk, Polish violinist, Jan 1968, *Obit* Apr 1988

Szigeti, Joseph, Hungarian violinist, May 1940, Mar 1958, *Obit* Apr 1973

Szilard, Leo, Hungarian physicist, Jan 1947, *Obit* July 1964

Szold, Henrietta, American Zionist leader, Jan 1940, *Obit* Apr 1945

Szyk, Arthur, Polish cartoonist, illustrator and miniaturist, Nov 1946, *Obit* Oct 1951

S enz Ryan, Maritza, Mar 2013

T

3D (Singer), English singer and DJ, June 2004

TV on the Radio (Musical group), Apr 2009

Taber, Gladys Bagg, editor and author, Yrbk 1952, *Obit* May 1980

Taber, John, American congressman, Feb 1948, *Obit* Jan 1966

Taber, Louis J., June 1942, *Obit* Yrbk 1960

Taboo (Musician), American singer, Oct 2006

Tabouis, Genevieve R., French journalist, Jan 1940

Tafel, Rich, American gay political activist, Feb 2000

Taft, Charles P., American lawyer, mayor and son of President William H. Taft, July 1945, *Obit* Aug 1983

Taft, Helen Herron, wife of American president William H. Taft, *Obit* July 1943

Taft, Horace D., American school administrator and brother of President William H. Taft, *Obit* Mar 1943

Taft, Robert A., American senator, May 1940, Apr 1948, *Obit* Oct 1953

Taft, Robert A., American senator, Oct 1967, *Obit* Feb 1994

Tagliabue, Paul, American football commissioner, Oct 1992

Tagliavini, Ferruccio, Italian opera singer, June 1947, *Obit* Apr 1995

Tagore, Rabindranath, Indian poet, novelist, short story writer and dramatist, *Obit* Oct 1941

Tainter, Charles Sumner, *Obit* May 1940

Taintor, Anne, American artist and entrepreneur, June 2005

Taj Mahal (Musician), American singer and songwriter, Nov 2001

Tajiri, Satoshi, Japanese video game designer, Nov 2001

Takahashi, Rumiko, Japanese cartoonist and comic book writer, Jan 2005

Takanohana, Japanese sumo wrestler, Jan 2002

Takeshita, Noboru, Japanese prime minister, May 1988, *Obit* Nov 2000

Takirambudde, Peter, Ugandan human rights activist, Jan 2005

Talabani, Jalal, Iraqi president, Jan 2005

Talal, Jan 1952, *Obit* Sept 1972

Talbert, William F., tennis player, Mar 1957, *Obit* June 1999

Talbot, A. N., *Obit* May 1942

Talbott, Harold E., American Secretary of the air force, July 1953, *Obit* May 1957

Talbott, Philip M., Apr 1958

Talbott, Strobe, American diplomat, July 2000

Taleb, Nassim, Lebanese mathematician, investment adviser and philosopher, May 2011

Talese, Gay, American journalist, July 1972

Talese, Nan A., American publishing executive, Sept 2006

Tallamy, Bertram Dalley, civil engineer and state official, Mar 1957, *Obit* Nov 1989

Tallant, Robert, author, Yrbk 1953, *Obit* June 1957

Tallchief, Maria, American ballet dancer, Nov 1951

Talley, Andre Leon, American fashion editor, July 2003

Talley, James, *Obit* Sept 1941

Talley, Truman H., *Obit* Mar 1942

Talmadge, Eugene, American governor, Sept 1941, *Obit* Feb 1947

Talmadge, Herman E., American governor and senator, Mar 1947, *Obit* June 2002

Talvela, Martti, Finnish opera singer, Oct 1983, *Obit* Sept 1989

Tamayo, Rufino, Mexican painter, Mar 1953, *Obit* Aug 1991

Tambo, Oliver, South African political leader, Apr 1987, *Obit* June 1993

Tamm, Igor Evgenievich, Russian physicist, Yrbk 1963, *Obit* June 1971

Tammet, Daniel, British autistic savant, Jan 2007

Tamura, Ryoko, Japanese judoist, Jan 2003

Tan Dun, Chinese composer, Jan 2007

Tan, Amy, American novelist, Feb 1992

Tan, Shaun, Australian illustrator, Mar 2012

Tanaka, Kakuei, Japanese prime minister, Yrbk 1972, *Obit* Feb 1994

Tanaka, Koichi, Japanese chemist, Jan 2007

Tandy, Jessica, Anglo-American actress, Mar 1956, Aug 1984, *Obit* Nov 1994

Tang, David, Chinese retail executive, Jan 2006

Tange, Kenzo, Japanese architect, Sept 1987, *Obit* Yrbk 2005

Tangerine Dream (Musical group), Jan 2005

Tani, Masayuki, May 1956

Tani, Yoshitomo, Japanese baseball player, Jan 2004

Taniguchi, Yoshio, Japanese architect, Jan 2005

Tannen, Deborah, American linguist, July 1994

Tanner, Alain, Swiss motion picture director, June 1990

Tanner, John Henry, *Obit* Mar 1940

Tanner, Vaino, Finnish statesman, Sept 1960, *Obit* May 1966

Tanning, Dorothea, American artist, *Obit* Yrbk 2012

Tanon, Olga, Puerto Rican singer, Jan 2005

Tao, Terence, Australian mathematician, Sept 2007

Tapie, Bernard, French financier, Jan 2002

Tapies, Antoni, Spanish painter and sculptor, July 1966, *Obit* Yrbk 2012

Tarantino, Quentin, American film director, screenwriter and actor, Oct 1995

Tarbell, Ida M., American journalist, biographer and historian, *Obit* Feb 1944

Tarchiani, Alberto, Jan 1950, *Obit* Jan 1965

Tardieu, Andre, French statesman, *Obit* Oct 1945

Tarkan, Turkish pop singer, Jan 2006

Tarkenton, Fran, American football player, Sept 1969

Tarkington, Booth, American novelist, *Obit* June 1946

Tarr, Curtis W., Sept 1970, *Obit* Yrbk 2013

Tarter, Jill Cornell, American astrophysicist, Feb 2001

Tartikoff, Brandon, American television and motion picture executive, Apr 1987, *Obit* Nov 1997

Tartt, Donna, American novelist, Feb 2003

Tarver, Antonio, American boxer, June 2006

Tata, J. R. D., Indian industrialist and philanthropist, Yrbk 1958, *Obit* Jan 1994

Tata, Ratan, Indian financier, Jan 2007

Tate, Allen, American poet and critic, Nov 1940, *Obit* Apr 1979

Tate, Catherine, British comedian, Oct 2012

Tatekawa, Yoshitsugu, *Obit* Oct 1945

Tati, Jacques, French actor and film director, Feb 1961, *Obit* Jan 1983

Tattersall, Ian, American anthropologist and museum curator, Aug 2007

Tatu (Musical group), Jan 2003

Tatum, Edward Lawrie, American biochemist, Mar 1959, *Obit* Jan 1976

Taubes, Frederic, Mar 1943

Taubman, A. Alfred, American real estate executive, Jan 1993

Taubman, Howard, music and drama critic, Apr 1959, *Obit* Mar 1996

Taufa'ahau Tupou, Sept 1968, *Obit* Yrbk 2007

Taurasi, Diana, American basketball player, Nov 2007

Tauscher, Ellen O., American congresswoman, Mar 2001

Taussig, Frank William, economist, *Obit* Yrbk 1940

Taussig, Helen Brooke, American pediatrician, Sept 1946, Mar 1966, *Obit* July 1986

Tautou, Audrey, French actress, Jan 2002

Tavares, Sara, Portuguese singer and songwriter, Jan 2007

Tavener, John, English composer, June 1999

Tavernier, Bertrand, French film director, June 1988

Tawes, J. Millard, Oct 1960, *Obit* Aug 1979

Tawresey, John Godwin, American admiral, *Obit* Apr 1943

Taylor, A. H., Sept 1945, *Obit* Jan 1962

Taylor, A. J. P., British historian, Nov 1983, *Obit* Nov 1990

Taylor, Billy, American jazz pianist and composer, Oct 1980, *Obit* Yrbk 2011

Taylor, Cecil, American jazz pianist, Mar 1986

Taylor, Charles, Liberian president, Sept 1992

Taylor, Charles A., *Obit* May 1942

Taylor, Chris, American bassist and singer, Sept 2011

Taylor, Deems, American composer and music critic, Mar 1940, *Obit* Nov 1966

Taylor, Edward T., *Obit* Oct 1941

Taylor, Elizabeth, Anglo-American actress, July 1952, Oct 1985, *Obit* Yrbk 2011

Taylor, Elizabeth, English novelist and short story writer, Yrbk 1948

Taylor, Francis Henry, Jan 1940, *Obit* Feb 1958

Taylor, George Braxton, clergyman, *Obit* Apr 1942

Taylor, George William, labor mediator, May 1942, *Obit* Feb 1973

Taylor, Glen Hearst, American senator, Oct 1947, *Obit* July 1984

Taylor, Harold, college president, Sept 1946, *Obit* Apr 1993

Taylor, Henry O., *Obit* June 1941

Taylor, Herman A., American cardiologist, June 2006

Taylor, James, American singer and songwriter, June 1972

Taylor, Janie, American ballet dancer, Aug 2011

Taylor, Jermain, American boxer, Apr 2006

Taylor, Jill Bolte, American neuroanatomist, Jan 2009

Taylor, John W., American college president, television executive and United Nations official, Jan 1954, *Obit* Apr 2002

Taylor, Katie, July 2013

Taylor, KoKo, American blues singer and songwriter, July 2002, *Obit* Yrbk 2009

Taylor, Laurette, American actress, July 1945, *Obit* Jan 1947

Taylor, Lawrence, American football player, July 1990

Taylor, Lili, American actress, July 2005

Taylor, M. Sayle, *Obit* Mar 1942

Taylor, Maxwell D., American general, Nov 1946, Yrbk 1961, *Obit* June 1987

Taylor, Myron C., American financier and diplomat, Feb 1940, *Obit* July 1959

Taylor, Paul, American dancer and choreographer, June 1964

Taylor, Peter Hillsman, American short story writer and novelist, Apr 1987, *Obit* Jan 1995

Taylor, Richard, June 1941, *Obit* July 1970

Taylor, Robert, American actor, May 1952, *Obit* July 1969

Taylor, Robert Lewis, biographer, Yrbk 1959, *Obit* Jan 1999

Taylor, Ron, Australian photographer and skin diver, Jan 2007, *Obit* Yrbk 2012

Taylor, Susan L., American magazine editor, Feb 1997

Taylor, Telford, lawyer and historian, Yrbk 1948, *Obit* Aug 1998

Taylor, Theodore B., American physicist, Apr 1976, *Obit* Feb 2005

Taylor, Valerie, Australian skin diver and photographer, Jan 2007

Taymor, Julie, American theatrical director and designer, Feb 1998

Tchelitchew, Pavel, Russian painter, Mar 1943, *Obit* Oct 1957

Tcherkassky, Marianna, ballet dancer, Nov 1985

Tchernichowsky, Saul, Hebrew poet and physician, *Obit* Yrbk 1943

Te Kanawa, Kiri, New Zealand opera singer, Nov 1978

Tead, Ordway, educator and management consultant, May 1942, *Obit* Jan 1974

Teagle, Walter, June 1942, *Obit* Feb 1962

Teague, Olin E., congressman, Mar 1952, *Obit* Apr 1981

Teague, Walter Dorwin, American interior designer, May 1942, *Obit* Jan 1961

Teale, Edwin Way, American naturalist and nature writer, Yrbk 1961, *Obit* Jan 1981

Tebaldi, Renata, Italian opera singer, Apr 1955, *Obit* Apr 2005

Tebbel, John William, American historian and journalist, Yrbk 1953, *Obit* Mar 2005

Tebbit, Norman, British cabinet member, Nov 1987

Tedder, Arthur William Tedder, British air marshal, Jan 1943, *Obit* Oct 1967

Tedeschi, Susan, American blues singer and guitarist, Sept 2012

Teitgen, Pierre-Henri, French political leader, Jan 1953

Teitur, Danish singer and songwriter, Jan 2004

Tejada, Miguel, Dominican baseball player, June 2003

Teleki, Pal, Hungarian statesman, *Obit* May 1941

Telkes, Maria, American chemist, Nov 1950, *Obit* Oct 1996

Teller, American magician, June 2000

Teller, Edward, American physicist, Yrbk 1954, Nov 1983, *Obit* Yrbk 2004

Teller, Juergen, German photographer, Jan 2004

Tello, Manuel, Yrbk 1959, *Obit* Jan 1972

Tempest, Marie, English actress, *Obit* Yrbk 1942

Temple, Johnny, American rock bassist and publisher, Oct 2008

Temple, William, British archbishop and theologian, Apr 1942, *Obit* Yrbk 1944

Templer, Gerald Walter Robert, British field marshal, July 1952, *Obit* Jan 1980

Templeton, Alec, Mar 1940, *Obit* May 1963

Templewood, Samuel John Gurney Hoare, British diplomat, Oct 1940, *Obit* July 1959

Tenby of Bulford, Gwilym Lloyd George, British cabinet member, Nov 1952, *Obit* Apr 1967

Tendulkar, Sachin, Indian cricket player, Jan 2002

Tener, John Kinley, baseball player, congressman and governor, *Obit* June 1946

Tenet, George J., American intelligence official, Aug 1999

Tennant, William George, British admiral, Feb 1945, *Obit* Sept 1963

Tennent, David Hilt, American biologist, *Obit* Mar 1941

Tennstedt, Klaus, German conductor, Sept 1983, *Obit* Mar 1998

Tenzing Norgay, Nepalese mountaineer, Oct 1954, *Obit* July 1986

Ter Poorten, Hein, Mar 1942

Ter-Arutunian, Rouben, Russian stage designer, June 1963, *Obit* Jan 1993

TerHorst, Jerald F., American presidential press secretary, Feb 1975, *Obit* Yrbk 2010

Terboven, Josef, German war criminal, Nov 1941, *Obit* June 1945

Teresa, Yugoslav nun and missionary, Sept 1973, *Obit* Nov 1997

Tereshkova, Valentina, Soviet astronaut, Yrbk 1963

Terhune, Albert Payson, author, *Obit* Apr 1942

Terkel, Studs, American interviewer and historian, Nov 1974, *Obit* Yrbk 2009

Terra, Daniel J., chemical executive and art collector, Nov 1987, *Obit* Sept 1996

Terra, Gabriel, Uruguayan president, *Obit* Nov 1942

Terrell, Daniel V., Apr 1954

Terrell, Mary Church, American feminist and civil rights leader, June 1942, *Obit* Oct 1954

Terrell, St. John, actor, Feb 1966, *Obit* Jan 1999

Terrett, Nicholas K., British pharmacologist and co-inventor of Viagra, Jan 2003

Terry, Luther L., American surgeon general and educator, Oct 1961, *Obit* May 1985

Terry, Randall, American anti-abortion activist, Jan 1994

Terry-Thomas, English comedian and actor, Mar 1961, *Obit* Mar 1990

Terzian, Harutyun G., *Obit* Oct 1941

Tesich, Steve, American dramatist and screenwriter, Aug 1991, *Obit* Sept 1996

Tesla, Nikola, American electrical engineer, *Obit* Feb 1943

Testino, Mario, Peruvian fashion photographer, Jan 2006

Tethong, Lhadon, Tibetan-Canadian human rights activist, Sept 2008

Tetley, Glen, American dancer and choreographer, June 1973, *Obit* Yrbk 2007

Tetrazzini, Luisa, Italian opera singer, *Obit* Jan 1940

Tewolde Berhan Gebre Egziabher, Ethiopian biologist and government official, Jan 2004

Tewson, Vincent, Feb 1952

Teyte, Maggie, English opera singer, Yrbk 1945, *Obit* July 1976

Thach, John Smith, Yrbk 1960

Thadden-Trieglaff, Reinold von, July 1959

Thain, John, American investment banker, May 2004

Thaksin Shinawatra, Thai prime minister, Jan 2002

Thaler, William J., American physicist, Feb 1960, *Obit* Yrbk 2005

Thalia, Mexican actress and singer, Jan 2004

Thanat Khoman, Mar 1958

Thanom Kittikachorn, Thai field marshal and prime minister, Yrbk 1969, *Obit* Yrbk 2004

Thant, Burmese diplomat and United Nations secretary-general, Feb 1962, *Obit* Jan 1975

Tharp, Louise Hall, American children's author, Yrbk 1955

Tharp, Twyla, American dancer and choreographer, Oct 1975

Thatcher, Margaret, British prime minister, July 1975, Nov 1989, *Obit* Yrbk 2013

Thayer, Ernest Lawrence, American journalist and poet, *Obit* Oct 1940

The Black Keys, Jan 2013

Theallet, Sophie, French fashion designer, Nov 2012

Thebom, Blanche, American opera singer, Oct 1948, *Obit* Yrbk 2010

Theiler, Max, American microbiologist, Jan 1952, *Obit* Oct 1972

Thekaekara, Matthew P., May 1974

Theodorakis, Mikis, Greek composer, July 1973

Theorell, Hugo, Swedish biochemist, Feb 1956, *Obit* Oct 1982

Thernstrom, Abigail M., American social critic, Mar 2010

Theron, Charlize, South African actress, Nov 2004

Theroux, Justin, American actor, Mar 2012

Theroux, Paul, American novelist and short story writer, Nov 1978

They Might Be Giants (Musical group), Nov 1999

Thicke, Alan, Canadian television author, producer and actor, June 1987

Thiebaud, Wayne, American painter and teacher, Mar 1987

Thielen, Gunter, German publishing executive, Jan 2005

Thimayya, Kodendera Subayya, Apr 1954, *Obit* Feb 1966

Thomas, Albert, American congressman, Oct 1950, *Obit* Mar 1966

Thomas, Augusta Read, composer, Nov 1999

Thomas, Charles Allen, Mar 1950, *Obit* May 1982

Thomas, Charles S., American airline executive and Secretary of the navy, Yrbk 1954, *Obit* Jan 1984

Thomas, Clarence, American Supreme Court justice, Apr 1992

Thomas, D. M., English novelist, poet and translator, Nov 1983

Thomas, Danny, American comedian, Feb 1959, *Obit* Apr 1991

Thomas, Dave, American fast food restaurant chain founder, Mar 1995, *Obit* Apr 2002

Thomas, Elbert Duncan, American senator, Oct 1942, *Obit* Mar 1953

Thomas, Elizabeth Marshall, American anthropologist and writer, Mar 1996

Thomas, Elmer, American senator, Yrbk 1949, *Obit* Nov 1965

Thomas, Frank, American baseball player, Aug 1994

Thomas, Franklin A., American lawyer and foundation official, Oct 1981

Thomas, Helen, American journalist, Nov 1993, *Obit* Yrbk 2013

Thomas, Isiah, American basketball player, executive and coach, Aug 1989

Thomas, Jess, American opera singer, June 1964, *Obit* Jan 1994

Thomas, John, high jumper, July 1960, *Obit* Yrbk 2013

Thomas, John Charles, May 1943, *Obit* Feb 1961

Thomas, John Parnell, American congressman, Sept 1947, *Obit* Jan 1971

Thomas, John W., *Obit* Yrbk 1945

Thomas, Lewis, American physician and biologist, July 1975, *Obit* Feb 1994

Thomas, Lowell, American radio newscaster, May 1940, Jan 1952, *Obit* Oct 1981

Thomas, Michael, American novelist, Feb 2008

Thomas, Miles Thomas, Jan 1952, *Obit* Apr 1980

Thomas, Norman, American socialist leader, Sept 1944, July 1962, *Obit* Feb 1969

Thomas, R. J., Nov 1942, *Obit* June 1967

Thomas, Richard, American actor, Nov 1975

Thomas, Sarah, American football referee, Nov 2010

Thomas, Tim, American hockey player, Oct 2012

Thomas, William H., American geriatrician, Jan 2006

Thomas, William Leroy, Mar 1958

Thomas, William Sturgis, *Obit* Feb 1942

Thomas-Graham, Pamela, American clothing industry executive and mystery novelist, July 2000

Thomason, John W., marine corps officer and author, *Obit* May 1944

Thomaz, Americo de Deus Rodrigues, Portuguese president, Yrbk 1958, *Obit* Nov 1987

Thome, Jim, American baseball player, June 2007

Thompson, Alexis, American golfer, June 2012

Thompson, Alleen, June 1965

Thompson, Daley, British decathlete, Nov 1986

Thompson, Dorothy, American columnist, July 1940, *Obit* Mar 1961

Thompson, Emma, British actress, Mar 1995

Thompson, Frank, American congressman, July 1959, *Obit* Sept 1989

Thompson, Fred, American senator, Aug 1999

Thompson, George L., *Obit* Oct 1941

Thompson, Holland, *Obit* Yrbk 1940

Thompson, Homer A., Canadian archaeologist, Apr 1948, *Obit* Yrbk 2000

Thompson, Hunter S., American journalist, Mar 1981, *Obit* Yrbk 2005

Thompson, James R., American governor and lawyer, Jan 1979

Thompson, James Westfall, *Obit* Yrbk 1941

Thompson, John, American basketball coach, Nov 2007

Thompson, John, American basketball coach, May 1989

Thompson, John Douglas, Canadian actor, Sept 2010

Thompson, John Taliaferro, American general, military engineer and inventor, *Obit* Aug 1940

Thompson, John W., American information technology executive, Mar 2005

Thompson, Kay, American singer, songwriter and children's author, Apr 1959, *Obit* Sept 1998

Thompson, Kenneth Lane, American computer scientist, Mar 1999

Thompson, Llewellyn E., American diplomat, Nov 1957, *Obit* Mar 1972

Thompson, Lonnie, American glaciologist, Jan 2004

Thompson, M. E., Mar 1947

Thompson, Mary Wolfe, Yrbk 1950

Thompson, Oscar, *Obit* Aug 1945

Thompson, Paul Williams, general and publishing executive, Nov 1942, *Obit* May 1996

Thompson, R. Campbell, *Obit* July 1941

Thompson, Roy L., Oct 1946

Thompson, Ruth, congresswoman, Nov 1951

Thompson, Sada, American actress, Mar 1973, *Obit* Yrbk 2011

Thompson, Tina, American basketball player, Jan 2011

Thompson, Tommy, American Secretary of health and human services, July 1995

Thompson, William Hale, American mayor, *Obit* May 1944

Thomson of Fleet, Roy Herbert Thomson, Canadian newspaper publisher, Jan 1960, *Obit* Sept 1976

Thomson, David, English film historian and biographer, Sept 2009

Thomson, George Paget, British physicist, Mar 1947, *Obit* Oct 1975

Thomson, J. Cameron, Yrbk 1948, *Obit* Mar 1966

Thomson, James A., American molecular biologist, Nov 2001

Thomson, Joseph John, British physicist, *Obit* Oct 1940

Thomson, Kenneth, Canadian newspaper executive, July 1989, *Obit* Yrbk 2006

Thomson, Meldrim, governor, Oct 1978, *Obit* Sept 2001

Thomson, Rupert, English novelist, Feb 2000

Thomson, Vernon Wallace, governor and congressman, July 1958, *Obit* June 1988

Thomson, Virgil, American composer and critic, Nov 1940, Oct 1966, *Obit* Nov 1989

Thorborg, Kerstin, Swedish opera singer, Mar 1940, *Obit* July 1970

Thore, Wendell Phillips, *Obit* May 1941

Thorek, Max, Jan 1951, *Obit* Mar 1960

Thorez, Maurice, French communist leader, June 1946, *Obit* Sept 1964

Thorkelson, Jacob, *Obit* Jan 1946

Thorn, James, Yrbk 1949

Thornburgh, Dick, American governor and Attorney general, Oct 1988

Thorndike, Edward L., American psychologist, Sept 1941, *Obit* Oct 1949

Thorndike, Sybil, English actress, Yrbk 1953, *Obit* Aug 1976

Thorneycroft of Dunston, Peter, British cabinet member, Yrbk 1952, *Obit* Aug 1994

Thornhill, Arthur H., Apr 1958, *Obit* Mar 1970

Thornhill, Leeroy, British keyboardist, Oct 2009

Thorning-Schmidt, Helle, Prime minister of Denmark, May 2012

Thornton, Charles Bates, defense industry executive, Feb 1970, *Obit* Jan 1982

Thornton, Dan, Feb 1954

Thorp, Willard Long, American economist and government official, July 1947, *Obit* July 1992

Thorpe, Ian, Australian swimmer, Jan 2002

Thorpe, Jeremy, British member of Parliament, Oct 1974

Thorpe, Jim, American decathlete and pentathlete, Nov 1950, *Obit* May 1953

Throckmorton, Cleon, Sept 1943, *Obit* Yrbk 1965

Thurber, James, American cartoonist and humorist, Mar 1940, Oct 1960, *Obit* Jan 1962

Thurman, Howard, American clergyman and theologian, June 1955, *Obit* June 1981

Thurman, Robert A. F., American Buddhist leader, Sept 1997

Thurman, Uma, American actress, Aug 1996

Thurmond, Strom, American senator, Sept 1948, Nov 1992, *Obit* Nov 2003

Thurow, Lester C., American economist, Nov 1990

Thye, Edward J., American governor and senator, Oct 1951, *Obit* Nov 1969

Thyssen, Fritz, German industrialist, May 1940, *Obit* Mar 1951

Thyssen-Bornemisza, Hans Heinrich, Swiss financier and art collector, Feb 1989, *Obit* Yrbk 2002

Tian Congming, Chinese broadcasting and news agency official, Jan 2005

Tian, Hao Jiang, Chinese opera singer, Feb 2009

Tiant, Luis, Cuban baseball player, June 1977

Tibbett, Lawrence, American opera singer, Feb 1945, *Obit* Oct 1960

Tice, George A., American photographer, Nov 2003

Tice, Merton B., June 1955

Tiegs, Cheryl, American model, Nov 1982

Tien, Thomas, May 1946, *Obit* Oct 1967

Tierney, John, American journalist, Aug 2005

Tietjens, Eunice Hammond, poet and author, *Obit* Nov 1944

Tiger, Lionel, anthropologist, Jan 1981

Tigerman, Stanley, American architect, Feb 2001

Tijerina, Reies Lopez, American political activist, July 1971

Tilberis, Liz, British magazine editor, Nov 1998, *Obit* July 1999

Tilghman, Shirley M., Canadian molecular biologist and university president, June 2006

Tillerson, Rex, American energy industry executive, Sept 2006

Tillich, Paul, German-American theologian, Mar 1954, *Obit* Yrbk 1965

Tillinghast, Charles C., airline executive, Feb 1962, *Obit* Oct 1998

Tillstrom, Burr, puppeteer, May 1951, *Obit* Feb 1986

Tilson Thomas, Michael, American conductor and pianist, May 1971, June 1996

Timbaland, American hip-hop musician and recording producer, Mar 2003

Timberlake, Charles B., American congressman, *Obit* July 1941

Timberlake, Clare H., Jan 1961

Timberlake, Justin, American singer, Nov 2000

Timerman, Jacobo, Argentine newspaper publisher, Nov 1981, *Obit* Jan 2000

Timmerman, George Bell, American governor and judge, Jan 1957, *Obit* Feb 1995

Timoshenko, Semen Konstantinovich, Soviet field marshal, Aug 1941, *Obit* May 1970

Tin Moe, Burmese poet and children's author, Jan 2004

Tinbergen, Niko, British zoologist and ethologist, Nov 1975, *Obit* Feb 1989

Tindemans, Leo, Belgian statesman, Mar 1978

Tinguely, Jean, Swiss artist, Jan 1966, *Obit* Oct 1991

Tinker, Clarence Leonard, American general, June 1942

Tinker, Grant, American television executive, Mar 1982

Tinkham, George H., Apr 1942, *Obit* Oct 1956

Tinney, Cal, Feb 1943

Tinney, Frank, *Obit* Jan 1941

Tippett, Michael, English composer, Sept 1974, *Obit* Mar 1998

Tipton, Jennifer, American lighting designer, July 1997

Tipton, Stuart G., Mar 1967

Tisch, Laurence A., American financier, Feb 1987, *Obit* Yrbk 2004

Tisdel, Alton P., *Obit* July 1945

Tiselius, Arne Wilhelm Kaurin, Swedish biochemist, Apr 1949, *Obit* Yrbk 1971

Tishler, Max, chemist, Mar 1952, *Obit* May 1989

Tiso, Jozef, Slovak priest and president, Mar 1943, *Obit* May 1947

Tisserant, Eugene, Apr 1963, *Obit* Apr 1972

Titchner, Mark, English installation artist, Jan 2007

Tito, Josip Broz, Yugoslav head of state, Nov 1943, Mar 1955, *Obit* June 1980

Titov, Gherman Stepanovich, Soviet astronaut, Yrbk 1962, *Obit* Jan 2001

Titterton, Lewis H., Sept 1943

Tittle, Y. A., American football player, Mar 1964

Titulescu, Nicolae, Romanian diplomat, *Obit* May 1941

Tizard, Henry Thomas, British physical chemist, Jan 1949, *Obit* Yrbk 1959

Tjarda van Starkenborgh Stachouwer, A. W. L., Feb 1942

To, Johnny, Chinese film director, Jan 2007

Tobey, Charles W., American senator and governor, June 1941, July 1951, *Obit* Oct 1953

Tobey, Mark, American painter, Mar 1957, *Obit* June 1976

Tobias, Channing H., July 1945, *Obit* Jan 1962

Tobin, Daniel J., American labor leader, Nov 1945, *Obit* Jan 1956

Tobin, Harold J., *Obit* Aug 1942

Tobin, James, American economist, Oct 1984, *Obit* May 2002

Tobin, Maurice J., American Secretary of labor, June 1946, *Obit* Oct 1953

Tobin, Richard, journalist, editor and author, Nov 1944, *Obit* Nov 1995

Toch, Maximilian, *Obit* June 1946

Todd, Alexander R., British chemist, Mar 1958, *Obit* Mar 1997

Todd, Michael, American motion picture producer, Yrbk 1955, *Obit* June 1958

Todd, Richard, American football player, May 1982

Todd, Richard, British actor, Yrbk 1955, *Obit* Yrbk 2010

Todt, Fritz, German military engineer and cabinet member, *Obit* Apr 1942

Toffler, Alvin, American futurist and writer, Apr 1975

Togliatti, Palmiro, Italian communist leader, Nov 1947, *Obit* Oct 1964

Tojo, Hideki, Japanese general and prime minister, Yrbk 1941, *Obit* Jan 1949

Tokugawa, Iyesato, *Obit* July 1940

Toland, Edmund M., *Obit* July 1942

Toland, Gregg, American cinematographer, July 1941, *Obit* Nov 1948

Tolar, Dagga, Nigerian poet, singer and social activist, Jan 2007

Tolbert, William R., Liberian president, Mar 1974, *Obit* June 1980

Tolbukhin, Fedor Ivanovich, Soviet field marshal, May 1945, *Obit* Yrbk 1949

Toledano, Ralph de, American columnist and political writer, Yrbk 1962, *Obit* Yrbk 2007

Toledo, Alejandro, Peruvian president, Nov 2001

Toles, Tom, American cartoonist, Nov 2002

Tolischus, Otto D., Jan 1940, *Obit* Apr 1967

Tolkien, Christopher, British editor and son of J.R.R. Tolkien, Jan 2007

Tolkien, J. R. R., English fantasy novelist, philologist and linguist, Yrbk 1957, Oct 1967, *Obit* Nov 1973

Tolle, Eckhart, German spiritual writer, Feb 2005

Tollefson, Thor C., Feb 1963

Tolstoy, Aleksey Nikolayevich, Russian novelist and dramatist, *Obit* Apr 1945

Tolstoy, Alexandra, Russian foundation official and daughter of novelist Leo Tolstoy, Apr 1953, *Obit* Nov 1979

Tomasi, Mari, May 1941

Tomasson, Helgi, Icelandic ballet dancer and director, Apr 1982

Tomba, Alberto, Italian skier, May 1993

Tomlin, Lily, American comedienne and actress, Sept 1973

Tomlin, Mike, American football coach, Aug 2011

Tomlinson, LaDainian, American football player, Oct 2006

Tomorrow, Tom, American political cartoonist, Apr 2000

Tonatto, Laura, Italian perfumer, Apr 2009

Tone, Franchot, actor, May 1940, *Obit* Nov 1968

Tong, Hollington K., Taiwanese diplomat, Yrbk 1956, *Obit* Feb 1971

Tonner, Robert, American doll maker, Oct 2011

Tooker, George, American painter, Mar 1958, *Obit* Yrbk 2011

Toon, Malcolm, diplomat, July 1978

Tope, John, Feb 1950

Topfer, Klaus, German environmentalist and United Nations official, Jan 2002

Topping, Norman H., physician and college president, Feb 1959, *Obit* Jan 1998

Torme, Mel, singer, Mar 1983, *Obit* Aug 1999

Torn, Rip, American actor, Apr 1977

Toro, Guillermo del, Mexican film director, Jan 2004

Torp, Oscar, Norwegian prime minister, Yrbk 1952, *Obit* July 1958

Torre, Joe, American baseball player and manager, May 1972, May 1997

Torrence, Gwen, American sprinter, July 1996

Torres Bodet, Jaime, Mexican novelist and poet, Feb 1948, *Obit* July 1974

Torrey, E. Fuller, psychiatrist, July 1998

Torrey, George Burroughs, painter, *Obit* June 1942

Torrijos Herrera, Omar, Panamanian dictator, July 1973, *Obit* Sept 1981

Tors, Ivan Lawrence, Hungarian animal trainer and motion picture producer, Feb 1969, *Obit* Aug 1983

Toscani, Oliviero, Italian photographer, Sept 1998

Toscanini, Arturo, Italian conductor, June 1942, May 1954, *Obit* Mar 1957

Totenberg, Nina, American radio and television reporter, Mar 1996

Totty, Charles H., Jan 1940

Toure, Ahmed Sekou, Guinean president, June 1959, *Obit* May 1984

Toure, Amadou Toumani, Malian president, Jan 2005

Tourel, Jennie, American opera singer, Feb 1947, *Obit* Jan 1974

Tournier, Michel, French novelist, Apr 1990

Toussaint, Jeanne, Feb 1955

Tovey, Donald Francis, English composer, pianist and musicologist, *Obit* Sept 1940

Tower, John, American senator, Yrbk 1962, *Obit* June 1991

Towers, Graham F., Canadian banker, Feb 1952

Towers, John Henry, American admiral, Oct 1941, *Obit* June 1955

Towle, Katherine A., college dean, Jan 1949, *Obit* May 1986

Towne, Robert, American screenwriter and film director, June 1989

Townes, Charles H., American physicist, Mar 1963

Townsend, Edward Waterman, American journalist and congressman, *Obit* May 1942

Townsend, Harry Everett, *Obit* Oct 1941

Townsend, Lynn A., American automobile executive, Sept 1966, *Obit* Yrbk 2000

Townsend, Robert, American car rental company executive, Nov 1970, *Obit* Mar 1998

Townsend, Robert, American actor and motion picture director, May 1994

Townsend, Willard S., American railroad porter and labor leader, Jan 1948

Townshend, Pete, British singer and guitarist, Aug 1983

Toy, Henry, May 1952

Toynbee, Arnold Joseph, British historian, July 1947, *Obit* Jan 1976

Tozzi, Giorgio, American opera singer, Oct 1961, *Obit* Yrbk 2011

Trabert, Tony, American tennis player and sportscaster, July 1954

Tracy, Spencer, American actor, Apr 1943, *Obit* Oct 1967

Train, Arthur Cheney, lawyer and author, *Obit* Feb 1946

Train, Russell E., American conservationist and government official, Oct 1970, *Obit* Yrbk 2012

Trammell, Niles, Sept 1940, *Obit* May 1973

Trampler, Walter, violist, Nov 1971, *Obit* Jan 1998

Transtr"mer, Tomas, Swedish poet, July 2012

Traphagen, Ethel, Yrbk 1948, *Obit* June 1963

Trapp, Maria von, Austrian singer, May 1968, *Obit* June 1987

Trask, James D., American pediatrician, *Obit* July 1942

Traubel, Helen, American opera singer, Jan 1940, Feb 1952, *Obit* Oct 1972

Trautman, George McNeal, baseball executive, Oct 1951, *Obit* Sept 1963

Travell, Janet, physician, Yrbk 1961, *Obit* Oct 1997

Travers, P. L., English children's author, May 1996, *Obit* June 1996

Travis, Randy, American country singer, Sept 1989

Travolta, John, American actor, Oct 1978, May 1996

Treanor, Tom, *Obit* Oct 1944

Tree, Marietta, United Nations official and city planner, Yrbk 1961, *Obit* Oct 1991

Trefflich, Henry, Jan 1953, *Obit* Sept 1978

Tregaskis, Richard, author and journalist, Aug 1943, *Obit* Oct 1973

Trehan, Naresh, Indian cardiologist, Jan 2003

Tremonti, Mark, American guitarist and composer, May 2002

Trenet, Charles, French singer and songwriter, Feb 1989, *Obit* Sept 2001

Trenkler, Freddie, American figure skater, June 1971, *Obit* Yrbk 2001

Tresca, Carlo, Italian anarchist, *Obit* Mar 1943

Trethewey, Natasha D., American poet, Aug 2007

Trevethin and Oaksey, Geoffrey Lawrence, British judge, Jan 1946, *Obit* Yrbk 1991

Trevi, Gloria, Mexican pop singer, Jan 2005

Trevino, Lee, American golfer, Nov 1971

Trevor, William, Irish novelist, short story writer and playwright, Sept 1984

Trevor-Roper, H. R., British historian, Sept 1983, *Obit* July 2003

Tribe, Laurence H., American law professor, July 1988

Trichet, Jean-Claude, French banking official, Jan 2006

Tridish, Pete, American pirate radio broadcaster and social activist, Apr 2004

Trigere, Pauline, French-American fashion designer, Feb 1960, *Obit* July 2002

Trigg, Ralph S., Nov 1950

Trillin, Calvin, American humorist, novelist and essayist, June 1990

Trilling, Diana, literary and social critic, May 1979, *Obit* Jan 1997

Trimble, David, Northern Ireland political leader, July 2000

Trimble, Vance H., Yrbk 1960

Trinidad, Felix, Puerto Rican boxer, Feb 2000

Trintignant, Jean-Louis, French actor, July 1988

Trippe, J. T., American airline executive, Aug 1942, Feb 1955, *Obit* May 1981

Tritt, Travis, American country singer, Feb 2004

Trollope, Joanna, English novelist, Jan 2006

Troost, Laurens, Jan 1953

Trotsky, Leon, Soviet communist leader, *Obit* Oct 1940

Trotta, Margarethe von, German film director, Nov 1988

Trotter, Frank Butler, *Obit* Apr 1940

Trotter, Lloyd G., American manufacturing executive, July 2005

Trottier, Bryan, Canadian hockey player, June 1985

Trout, J. D., American philosopher, July 2009

Trout, Mike, July 2013

Trout, Robert, American radio and television reporter, Oct 1965, *Obit* Jan 2001

Trowbridge, Alexander B., American Secretary of commerce, Mar 1968, *Obit* Yrbk 2006

Troyanos, Tatiana, opera singer, Aug 1979, *Obit* Oct 1993

Troyat, Henri, French novelist and biographer, Mar 1992, *Obit* Yrbk 2007

Trudeau, Arthur Gilbert, general, Apr 1958, *Obit* Aug 1991

Trudeau, G. B., American cartoonist, Aug 1975

Trudeau, Pierre Elliott, Canadian prime minister, Nov 1968, *Obit* Jan 2001

True, Rodney Howard, *Obit* May 1940

Trueblood, Elton, philosopher, Jan 1964, *Obit* Mar 1995

Truex, Ernest, Jan 1941, *Obit* Sept 1973

Truffaut, Francois, French film director, Jan 1969, *Obit* Jan 1985

Truitt, Paul T., Sept 1948

Trujillo Molina, Rafael Leonidas, Dominican general and president, July 1941, *Obit* Oct 1961

Trulock, Mussette Langford, Jan 1957

Truman, Bess Wallace, wife of American president Harry S. Truman, Feb 1947, *Obit* Jan 1983

Truman, David Bicknell, American college president and political scientist, Jan 1972, *Obit* Yrbk 2004

Truman, Harry S., American president, Jan 1942, Apr 1945, *Obit* Feb 1973

Truman, Margaret, daughter of American president Harry S. Truman and writer, June 1950, June 1987, *Obit* Yrbk 2008

Trumbo, Dalton, American screenwriter, May 1941, *Obit* Oct 1976

Trumka, Richard L., labor leader and lawyer, Apr 1986

Trump, Donald J., American real estate executive, Feb 1984

Truscott, Lucian King, American general, May 1945, *Obit* Nov 1965

Truss, Lynne, English humorist, novelist and critic, July 2006

Trussell, C. P., July 1949, *Obit* Yrbk 1968

Trussell, Ray E., municipal hospital commissioner and physician, Jan 1971, *Obit* Feb 2000

Trygger, Ernst, *Obit* Nov 1943

Tryon, George Clement Tryon, British government official, *Obit* Jan 1941

Tryon, Thomas, author and actor, Jan 1977, *Obit* Nov 1991

Tsai, Ming, American chef and restaurateur, June 2012

Tsai, Ming-Liang, Taiwanese film director, Jan 2002

Tsaldaris, Constantine, Nov 1946, *Obit* Jan 1971

Tsang, Donald, Hong Kong government official, Jan 2005

Tsarapkin, Semyon K., Soviet diplomat, June 1960, *Obit* Nov 1984

Tschirky, Oscar, Jan 1947, *Obit* Yrbk 1950

Tseng, Yani, Taiwanese golfer, Sept 2011

Tsereteli, Zurab, Russian sculptor, Jan 2007

Tshabalala-Msimang, Manto, South African public health official, Jan 2007, *Obit* Yrbk 2010

Tshombe, Moise, Congolese prime minister, Yrbk 1961, *Obit* Sept 1969

Tsiang, Tingfu F., June 1948, *Obit* Yrbk 1965

Tsongas, Paul, American senator, July 1981, *Obit* Mar 1997

Tsuchiya, Keiichi, Japanese automobile racing driver, Jan 2006

Tsui, Hark, Chinese film director, Oct 2001

Tsvangirai, Morgan, Zimbabwean prime minister, Jan 2005

Tszyu, Kostya, Russian-Australian boxer, Jan 2002

Tubb, Ernest, singer, Oct 1983, *Obit* Oct 1984

Tubman, William Vacanarat Shadrach, Liberian president, Jan 1955, *Obit* Sept 1971

Tuchman, Barbara Wertheim, American historian, Yrbk 1963, *Obit* Mar 1989

Tuck, William M., governor, Yrbk 1946, *Obit* Aug 1983

Tucker, B. Fain, Yrbk 1957

Tucker, Henry St. George, American bishop, Sept 1943, *Obit* Nov 1959

Tucker, Richard, opera singer, Mar 1956, *Obit* Feb 1975

Tucker, Sophie, singer, Apr 1945, *Obit* Mar 1966

Tuckwell, Barry, Australian horn player, July 1979

Tudjman, Franjo, Croatian president, Sept 1997, *Obit* May 2000

Tudor, Antony, English ballet dancer and choreographer, Nov 1945, *Obit* June 1987

Tufte, Edward R., American political scientist, statistician and graphic designer, Nov 2007

Tufts, James Hayden, *Obit* Sept 1942

Tugwell, Rexford G., American territorial governor, economist and political scientist, Sept 1941, Jan 1963, *Obit* Sept 1979

Tukur, Alhaji Bamanga, Nigerian business organization official, Jan 2004

Tull, Tanya, American social services organization official, Nov 2004

Tully, Alice, music patron and singer, Jan 1984, *Obit* Feb 1994

Tune, Tommy, American dancer and director, Jan 1983

Tunnard, Christopher, Canadian landscape architect, June 1959, *Obit* May 1979

Tunney, Gene, American boxer, Sept 1940, *Obit* Jan 1979

Tunney, John V., June 1971

Tunstall, KT, Scottish rock singer and songwriter, Jan 2007

Tuomioja, Sakari, Mar 1954, *Obit* Nov 1964

Tupolev, Andrei N., Jan 1957

Turbay Ayala, Julio Cesar, Colombian president, July 1979

Turcotte, Ron, Canadian jockey, Nov 1974

Ture, Kwame, American civil rights leader, Apr 1970, *Obit* Feb 1999

Tureck, Rosalyn, American pianist and harpsichordist, Sept 1959, *Obit* Yrbk 2003

Turin, Luca, British biophysicist, Aug 2008

Turkle, Sherry, American sociologist and psychologist, Aug 1997

Turnbull, Colin M., English anthropologist, Sept 1980, *Obit* Sept 1994

Turner, Alex, British rock guitarist and singer, Jan 2006

Turner, Ben, *Obit* Nov 1942

Turner, Donald Frank, American government official, lawyer

and economist, July 1967, *Obit* Sept 1994

Turner, Ewald, May 1962

Turner, John, Canadian prime minister, Nov 1984

Turner, Kathleen, American actress, June 1986

Turner, Lana, American actress, June 1943, *Obit* Sept 1995

Turner, Mark, American jazz saxophonist, Nov 2002

Turner, Richmond Kelly, admiral, Apr 1944, *Obit* Apr 1961

Turner, Stansfield, admiral and CIA director, May 1978

Turner, Ted, American television and baseball executive, May 1979, June 1998

Turner, Tina, American singer, Nov 1984

Turow, Scott, American lawyer and novelist, Aug 1991

Turpin, Ben, comedian, *Obit* Aug 1940

Turpin, Randy, British boxer, Sept 1951, *Obit* June 1966

Turre, Steve, American jazz trombonist, Apr 2001

Turrell, James, American artist, May 1999

Turturro, John, American actor, Oct 1996

Tushingham, Rita, Oct 1965

Tuttle, Charles Egbert, publisher and rare book dealer, July 1960, *Obit* Aug 1993

Tuttle, Emerson, *Obit* Apr 1946

Tuttle, Merlin D., mammalogist, June 1992

Tutu, Desmond, South African archbishop, Jan 1985, Jan 2002

Tuymans, Luc, Belgian painter, Jan 2007

Tuzun, Sibel, Turkish pop singer, Jan 2006

Tvardovskii, A., Russian poet, May 1971, *Obit* Feb 1972

Tweed, Harrison, Jan 1950, *Obit* July 1969

Tweed, Thomas Frederic, *Obit* Jan 1940

Tweedie, Ethel Brilliana, English author and traveler, *Obit* May 1940

Tweedy, Jeff, American singer and songwriter, Feb 2010

Tweet (Singer), American singer and songwriter, Nov 2002

Twiggy, English model and actress, Oct 1968

Twining, Nathan F., American air force general, Yrbk 1953, *Obit* May 1982

Two-Tone Tommy, American rock bassist, Nov 2008

Twombly, Cy, American painter, Apr 1988, *Obit* Yrbk 2011

Twomey, Paul, Australian Internet executive, Jan 2003

Tworkov, Jack, American painter, Mar 1964, *Obit* Oct 1982

Tydings, Millard E., American senator, Jan 1945, *Obit* Apr 1961

Tyler, Alice S., librarian, *Obit* June 1944

Tyler, Anne, American novelist and short story writer, June 1981

Tyler, Richard, Australian fashion designer, May 1997

Tyler, Steven, American rock singer, Aug 1996, July 2004

Tyler, the Creator (Musician), American rapper and record producer, Aug 2011

Tymoshenko, Yulia, Ukrainian economist and prime minister, Jan 2006

Tynan, Kenneth, British drama critic, Yrbk 1963, *Obit* Sept 1980

Tyner, McCoy, American jazz pianist and composer, Aug 1997

Tyson, Cicely, American actress, Aug 1975

Tyson, John H., American poultry company executive, Aug 2001

Tyson, Laura D'Andrea, American economist and presidential adviser, Sept 1996

Tyson, Mike, American boxer, Apr 1988

Tyson, Neil De Grasse, American astrophysicist, May 2000

U

Ubico, Jorge, Guatemalan president, June 1942, *Obit* July 1946

Uchida, Mitsuko, Japanese pianist, Sept 1991

Udall, Morris K., American congressman, Apr 1969, *Obit* Mar 1999

Udall, Stewart L., American Secretary of the interior, May 1961, *Obit* Yrbk 2010

Uderzo, French cartoonist, Jan 2006

Ueberroth, Peter, American entrepreneur and Olympic executive, Apr 1985

Uematsu, Nobuo, Japanese composer, Jan 2006

Uexkull, Jakob von, Swedish environmentalist, Jan 2005

Uggams, Leslie, American singer and actress, Oct 1967

Ugyen Trinley Dorje, Tibetan lama, Jan 2004

Uhlmann, Richard Frederick, grain dealer, Jan 1949, *Obit* Feb 1990

Ulanova, Galina, Russian ballet dancer, Apr 1958, *Obit* June 1998

Ulbricht, Walter, East German communist leader, July 1952, *Obit* Oct 1973

Ulianov, Dmitrii, *Obit* Sept 1943

Ulio, James Alexander, Sept 1945

Ullman, Al, congressman, Aug 1975, *Obit* Jan 1987

Ullman, James Ramsey, author, Oct 1945, *Obit* Sept 1971

Ullman, Tracey, English actress and singer, Oct 1988

Ullmann, Liv, Norwegian actress and film director, Yrbk 1973

Ullrich, Jan, German cyclist, Jan 2003

Ullstein, Herman, *Obit* Jan 1944

Ulman, Joseph N., *Obit* May 1943

Ulrich, Charles, *Obit* Aug 1941

Umanskii, Konstantin Aleksandrovich, Feb 1941, *Obit* Mar 1945

Umberto, Oct 1943, *Obit* May 1983

Unden, Osten, Feb 1947, *Obit* Apr 1974

Underhill, Charles Lee, *Obit* Mar 1946

Underhill, Ruth M., anthropologist and author, Feb 1954, *Obit* Oct 1984

Underwood, Bert E., *Obit* Feb 1944

Underwood, Carrie, American singer and contestant on

reality TV show American idol, Mar 2007

Underwood, Cecil H., American governor, May 1958, *Obit* Yrbk 2009

Underworld (Musical group), Nov 2011

Undset, Sigrid, Norwegian novelist, Sept 1940, *Obit* July 1949

Ung, Loung, Cambodian-American social activist, Jan 2006

Ungaro, Emanuel, French fashion designer, July 1980

Unitas, Johnny, American football player, Feb 1962, *Obit* Yrbk 2002

Unruh, Jesse M., American state legislator and official, Oct 1969, *Obit* Sept 1987

Untermeyer, Louis, American poet, editor and literary critic, Jan 1967, *Obit* Feb 1978

Untermyer, Samuel, American lawyer, Apr 1940

Unwin, Stanley, British publisher, Mar 1949, *Obit* Yrbk 1968

Updike, Daniel Berkeley, *Obit* Feb 1942

Updike, John, American novelist and short story writer, Feb 1966, Oct 1984, *Obit* Yrbk 2009

Upfield, Arthur W., Australian author, Yrbk 1948, *Obit* Apr 1964

Upham, Francis Bourne, *Obit* May 1941

Upshaw, Dawn, American opera singer, Feb 1990

Upshur, William P., *Obit* Sept 1943

Urey, Harold Clayton, American chemist, Feb 1941, July 1960, *Obit* Mar 1981

Uribe Velez, Alvaro, Colombian president, Jan 2002

Uris, Leon, American novelist, Yrbk 1959, Feb 1979, *Obit* Yrbk 2003

Urquhart, Brian E., British United Nations official, June 1986

Urquhart, Robert E., British general, Yrbk 1944, *Obit* Feb 1989

Urquidez, Benny, American martial artist, Nov 2001

Urrea, Luis Alberto, Mexican-American novelist

and short story writer, Nov 2005

Urrutia Lleo, Manuel, Cuban president, May 1959, *Obit* Aug 1981

Urrutia, Francisco, June 1958

Usery, W. J., American Secretary of labor, June 1976

Usher, Elizabeth Reuter, May 1967

Usmanova, Yulduz, Uzbek singer, Jan 2004

Ustinov, Peter, English actor and dramatist, Yrbk 1955, *Obit* Aug 2004

Utley, Freda, Yrbk 1958, *Obit* Mar 1978

Utley, George B., librarian, *Obit* Nov 1946

Utrillo, Maurice, French painter, Sept 1953, *Obit* Jan 1956

Utterback, Hubert, *Obit* July 1942

Utzon, Jorn, Danish architect, Jan 2003, *Obit* Yrbk 2009

Uygur, Cenk, Turkish-American radio talk show host, May 2013

V

Vadim, Roger, French motion picture director, Jan 1984, *Obit* Aug 2000

Vagnozzi, Egidio, Mar 1967, *Obit* Feb 1981

Vail, Robert W. G., librarian and bibliographer, Feb 1945, *Obit* July 1966

Vaizey, John, English economist and author, Jan 1964

Vajpayee, Atal Bihari, Indian prime minister, Aug 2000, Jan 2002

Valdes-Rodriguez, Alisa, American novelist, Jan 2006

Valensi, Nick, American guitarist, Feb 2007

Valente, Benita, opera singer, Mar 1988

Valenti, Jack, American motion picture association executive, Jan 1968, *Obit* Yrbk 2007

Valentina, fashion designer, Yrbk 1946, *Obit* Nov 1989

Valentine, Alan, American college president, Yrbk 1950, *Obit* Sept 1980

Valentine, Bobby, American baseball manager and

television sports commentator, July 2001

Valentine, Lewis J., June 1946, *Obit* Feb 1947

Valentino, Italian fashion designer, Nov 1973

Valenzuela, Fernando, Mexican baseball player, Oct 1982

Valery, Paul, French poet, *Obit* Aug 1945

Vall, Ely Ould Mohamed, Mauritanian head of state, Jan 2006

Vallee, Rudy, singer and actor, June 1947, Apr 1963, *Obit* Aug 1986

Valletta, Vittorio, Italian automobile executive, *Obit* July 1967

Valletti, Vittorio F., Italian architect, July 1967

Vallin, Sergio, Mexican guitarist and singer, Jan 2005

Valtin, Jan, German author, Apr 1941, *Obit* Jan 1951

Valuev, Nikolay, Russian boxer, Jan 2007

Van Allen, James Alfred, American astrophysicist, Jan 1959, *Obit* Yrbk 2007

Van Allsburg, Chris, American children's author and illustrator, Sept 1996

Van Arsdale, Harry, American labor leader, May 1969, *Obit* Apr 1986

Van Buren, Abigail, advice columnist, May 1960, *Obit* Yrbk 2013

Van Damme, Jean-Claude, Belgian bodybuilder, martial artist and actor, Mar 1999

Van Devanter, Willis, American Supreme Court justice, *Obit* Mar 1941

Van Doren, Harold L., May 1940, *Obit* Apr 1957

Van Doren, Irita, American newspaper editor, Sept 1941, *Obit* Feb 1967

Van Doren, Mark, American literary critic, editor and poet, Jan 1940, *Obit* Feb 1973

Van Druten, John, English dramatist, Feb 1944, *Obit* Feb 1958

Van Dusen, Henry Pitney, seminary president, Yrbk 1950, *Obit* Apr 1975

Van Duyn, Mona, American poet, Jan 1998, *Obit* Nov 2005

Van Dyke, Dick, American actor, Mar 1963

Van Dyke, W. S., American motion picture director, *Obit* Apr 1943

Van Exel, Nick, American basketball player, Mar 2002

Van Fleet, James Alward, American general, Apr 1948, *Obit* Nov 1992

Van Gundy, Jeff, American basketball coach, May 2001

Van Hamel, Martine, Dutch-American ballet dancer, Sept 1979

Van Heusen, Jimmy, American composer, June 1970, *Obit* Apr 1990

Van Horne, Harriet, radio and television critic, Yrbk 1954, *Obit* Mar 1998

Van Loen, Alfred, Feb 1961

Van Loon, Hendrik Willem, Dutch-American historian, *Obit* Apr 1944

Van Nuys, Frederick, *Obit* Mar 1944

Van Paassen, Pierre, Dutch-American clergyman, journalist and author, Oct 1942, *Obit* Mar 1968

Van Peebles, Mario, American actor and motion picture director, Nov 1993

Van Pelt, John Vredenburgh, Yrbk 1946, *Obit* Sept 1962

Van Sant, Gus, American film director, Mar 1992

Van Schmus, W. G., *Obit* Mar 1942

Van Slyke, Donald D., Jan 1943, *Obit* July 1971

Van Volkenburg, Jack Lamont, Jan 1955, *Obit* July 1963

Van Wagoner, Murray, governor, Nov 1941, *Obit* Aug 1986

Van Waters, Miriam, American penologist, Mar 1963, *Obit* Apr 1974

Van Zandt, James E., congressman, Nov 1950, *Obit* Mar 1986

Van Zandt, Steve, American guitarist and singer, Feb 2006

Van den Haag, Ernest, Dutch-American psychoanalyst, essayist and educator, Oct 1983, *Obit* July 2002

Vanbrugh, Violet, British actress, *Obit* Jan 1943

Vance, Cyrus R., American Secretary of state, Yrbk 1962, Nov 1977, *Obit* Apr 2002

Vance, Harold S., American automobile executive and government official, May 1949, *Obit* Nov 1959

Vance, John Thomas, *Obit* May 1943

Vance, Marguerite, Yrbk 1951, *Obit* July 1965

Vance, William Reynolds, *Obit* Yrbk 1940

Vandegrift, A. A., American Marine corps general, Jan 1943, *Obit* June 1973

Vanden Heuvel, Katrina, American magazine editor and publisher, May 2009

Vandenberg, Arthur H., American senator, Nov 1940, June 1948, *Obit* May 1951

Vandenberg, Hoyt Sanford, American air force general, Mar 1945, *Obit* May 1954

Vanderbilt, Amy, Feb 1954, *Obit* Feb 1975

Vanderbilt, Arthur T., judge, Feb 1947, *Obit* Oct 1957

Vanderbilt, Cornelius, American financier, *Obit* Apr 1942

Vanderbilt, Gloria, American fashion designer, July 1972

Vanderbilt, William Kissam, railroad executive and automobile racing driver, *Obit* Feb 1944

Vandercook, John W., Apr 1942, *Obit* Feb 1963

Vandervelde, Luc, Belgian retail executive, Jan 2002

Vandiver, S. Ernest, American governor, July 1962, *Obit* Yrbk 2005

Vandivert, William, Mar 1963

Vandross, Luther, American rhythm and blues singer and songwriter, Sept 1991, *Obit* Yrbk 2005

Vane, John R., British pharmacologist, May 1986, *Obit* Yrbk 2005

Vaness, Carol, American opera singer, Sept 1986

Vanessa-Mae, British violinist, Jan 2002

Vangelis, Greek composer, Jan 2003

Vangi, Giuliano, Italian sculptor, Jan 2003

Vanier, Georges, Canadian governor general, Jan 1960, *Obit* May 1967

Vann, Robert Lee, American newspaper editor and publisher, *Obit* Yrbk 1940

Vanocur, Sander, Jan 1963

Vansittart, Robert Gilbert Vansittart, British diplomat, July 1941, *Obit* Apr 1957

Varda, Agnes, French film director, July 1970

Vardaman, James Kimble, American banker and government official, Apr 1951

Vargas Llosa, Mario, Peruvian novelist, Feb 1976

Vargas, Antonio, Ecuadorian Quechua leader, Jan 2004

Vargas, Elizabeth, American television news anchor, Apr 2006

Vargas, Getulio, Brazilian president, Aug 1940, May 1951, *Obit* Oct 1954

Varian, Dorothy, Jan 1943

Varmus, Harold, American virologist and public health official, Nov 1996

Varnay, Astrid, American opera singer, May 1951, *Obit* Yrbk 2007

Varnedoe, Kirk, American museum curator and art historian, Feb 1991, *Obit* Yrbk 2003

Vasarely, Victor, Hungarian-French artist, Feb 1971, *Obit* May 1997

Vasella, Daniel, Swiss pharmaceutical executive and physician, Jan 2005

Vasilevskii, Aleksandr M., Soviet field marshal, Oct 1943, *Obit* Mar 1978

Vassa, Yossi, Ethiopian-Israeli comedian, Jan 2006

Vassallo, Ernesto, *Obit* Jan 1940

Vatutin, Nikolai Fedorovich, Soviet general, Feb 1944

Vaughan Williams, Ralph, English composer, Yrbk 1953, *Obit* Nov 1958

Vaughan, Guy W., Yrbk 1948, *Obit* Jan 1967

Vaughan, Harry H., American general, Mar 1949, *Obit* July 1981

Vaughan, Sarah, American singer, Nov 1957, Apr 1980, *Obit* May 1990

Vaughn, Jack Hood, American diplomat and government official, Apr 1966, *Obit* Yrbk 2013

Vaughn, Robert, American actor, Sept 1967

Vaughn, Vince, American actor, Sept 2006

Veeck, Bill, American baseball executive, Nov 1948, *Obit* Feb 1986

Vega, Suzanne, American singer and songwriter, Aug 1994

Veidt, Conrad, German actor, *Obit* May 1943

Veil, Simone, French judge and cabinet member, May 1980

Veiller, Bayard, dramatist, *Obit* Aug 1943

Vejjabul, Pierra, Mar 1964

Veksler, V. I., Russian physicist, Jan 1965, *Obit* Nov 1966

Velasco Alvarado, Juan, Peruvian president, June 1970, *Obit* Mar 1978

Velasco Ibarra, Jose Maria, Ecuadorian president, Nov 1952, *Obit* May 1979

Velazquez, Nydia, American congresswoman, July 1999

Velde, Harold H., American congressman, Mar 1953, *Obit* Jan 1986

Velez, Lupe, Mexican actress, *Obit* Feb 1945

Velikovsky, Immanuel, May 1957, *Obit* Jan 1980

Velloso, Pedro Leao, Sept 1946, *Obit* Mar 1947

Veloso, Caetano, Brazilian singer and songwriter, Jan 2002

Vendler, Helen Hennessy, American literary scholar, May 1986

Veneman, Ann M., American United Nations official, Sept 2009

Venizelos, Sophocles, Yrbk 1950, *Obit* Mar 1964

Venkatesh, Sudhir, American sociologist, May 2010

Venter, J. Craig, American biochemist, Feb 1995

Ventris, Michael George Francis, English architect, archaeologist and linguist, Jan 1957

Ventura, Jesse, American wrestler and governor, May 1999

Venturi, Ken, American golfer and sportscaster, Apr 1966, *Obit* Yrbk 2013

Venturi, Robert, American architect, July 1975

Venturini, Silvia, Italian handbag designer, Jan 2006

Vera-Ellen, dancer and actress, Feb 1959, *Obit* Oct 1981

Verdi-Fletcher, Mary, wheelchair dancer, Jan 1997

Verdier, Jean, *Obit* May 1940

Verdon, Gwen, American dancer, actress and choreographer, Oct 1960, *Obit* Jan 2001

Verdy, Violette, French ballet dancer and manager, Yrbk 1969, Oct 1980

Vereen, Ben, American actor, singer and dancer, Apr 1978

Vergara Madrigal, Jorge, Mexican entrepreneur, Jan 2003

Vergara, Sofia, Colombian actress, June 2013

Verges, Jacques, French lawyer, Jan 2004, *Obit* Yrbk 2013

Verghese, Abraham, American physician and novelist, Nov 2011

Verhoeven, Julie, English fashion illustrator, Apr 2012

Verity, Calvin William, American Secretary of commerce, May 1988

Verlander, Justin, American baseball player, Apr 2012

Vermeij, Geerat J., American marine biologist, June 1995

Vermilye, William M., *Obit* Oct 1944

Vernon, Grenville, *Obit* Jan 1942

Vernon, Justin, American singer and songwriter, Apr 2012

Vernon, Lillian, American mail order executive, Mar 1996

Veronese, Vittorino, June 1959

Veronicas (Musical group), Jan 2006

Verrett, Shirley, American opera singer, Apr 1967, *Obit* Yrbk 2011

Versace, Donatella, Italian fashion designer, June 1998

Versace, Gianni, Italian fashion designer, Apr 1993, *Obit* Sept 1997

Vertes, Marcel, Hungarian painter and illustrator, Apr 1961, *Obit* Jan 1962

Verveer, Melanne, Mar 2013

Verwoerd, Hendrik Frensch, South African prime minister, Mar 1959, *Obit* Nov 1966

Vezin, Charles, *Obit* May 1942

Vian, Philip, British admiral, Aug 1944, *Obit* Sept 1968

Vick, Michael, American football player, Nov 2003

Vickers, Jon, Canadian opera singer, Mar 1961

Vickery, H. L., American admiral, Yrbk 1943, *Obit* May 1946

Vickrey, Dan, American guitarist, Mar 2003

Victor Emmanuel, July 1943, *Obit* Jan 1948

Victor, Sally, Apr 1954, *Obit* July 1977

Vidal, Gore, American novelist and playwright, Feb 1965, June 1983, *Obit* Yrbk 2012

Videla, Jorge Rafael, Argentine general and president, Apr 1978, *Obit* Yrbk 2013

Vidor, King, motion picture director and producer, Feb 1957, *Obit* Jan 1983

Vieira da Silva, Maria Helena, Portuguese painter, Yrbk 1958, *Obit* May 1992

Vieira, Meredith, American television newscaster, Apr 2002

Vieira, Patrick, French soccer player, Jan 2006

Vienot, Pierre, *Obit* Oct 1944

Viereck, George Sylvester, author and poet, Nov 1940, *Obit* May 1962

Viereck, Peter, American poet and historian, Apr 1943, *Obit* Yrbk 2006

Vigidis Finnbogadottir, Icelandic president, May 1987

Viguerie, Richard A., American political fund raiser and magazine publisher, Jan 1983

Vike-Freiberga, Vaira, Latvian president, Jan 2005

Vila, George R., tire and rubber executive, Mar 1963, *Obit* Aug 1987

Vilar, Jean, French actor and director, Apr 1962, *Obit* Sept 1971

Vilas, Guillermo, Argentine tennis player and poet, Apr 1978

Villa-Komaroff, Lydia, American molecular biologist, July 2008

Villa-Lobos, Heitor, Brazilian composer, Apr 1945, *Obit* Jan 1960

Villaraigosa, Antonio R., American mayor, Aug 2007

Villard, Oswald Garrison, American journalist, Aug 1940, *Obit* Nov 1949

Villella, Edward, American ballet dancer and director, Mar 1965

Villemure, Gilles, Apr 1974

Villepin, Dominique de, French prime minister, Jan 2003

Villon, Jacques, French painter and engraver, Jan 1956, *Obit* July 1963

Vilsack, Tom, American Secretary of agriculture, Mar 2009

Vinatieri, Adam, American football player, Sept 2004

Vincent, Francis T., American motion picture executive and baseball commissioner, May 1991

Vincent, George Edgar, sociologist, college president and foundation official, *Obit* Mar 1941

Vincent, Leon H., *Obit* Apr 1941

Vining, Elizabeth Gray, American novelist, short story writer and children's author, Sept 1943

Vinson, Carl, American congressman, Apr 1942, *Obit* July 1981

Vinson, Fred M., American Supreme Court justice, Aug 1943, *Obit* Nov 1953

Vinton, Bobby, July 1977

Viola, Bill, American video artist, May 1998

Vip, cartoonist, July 1946, *Obit* Oct 1984

Virilio, Paul, French urban planner and philosopher, July 2005

Viscardi, Henry, American rehabilitation advocate, Jan 1954, Yrbk 1966, *Obit* Yrbk 2004

Visconti, Luchino, Italian film director, Jan 1965, *Obit* May 1976

Vishinski, Andrei IAnuarevich, Soviet diplomat, May 1944, *Obit* Jan 1955

Vishnevskaya, Galina, Russian opera singer, July 1966, *Obit* Yrbk 2013

Vishniac, Roman, American biologist and photographer, Feb 1967, *Obit* Mar 1990

Visser 't Hooft, Willem Adolph, Dutch clergyman and theologian, May 1949, *Obit* Aug 1985

Visser, Lesley, American television sportscaster, Apr 2007

Vitale, Dick, American basketball sportscaster, Jan 2005

Vitug, Marites, Filipino journalist, Jan 2005

Vo, Nguyen Giap, Vietnamese general, Feb 1969

Vo, Tong Xuan, Vietnamese agriculturist, Jan 2002

Vogel, Hans Jochen, German socialist leader, Jan 1984

Vogel, Herbert D., Yrbk 1954

Vogel, Paula, American dramatist, July 1998

Vogelstein, Bert, molecular biologist, Jan 1996

Vogt, William, ornithologist, Mar 1953, *Obit* Sept 1968

Voight, Jon, American actor, Apr 1974

Voigt, Deborah, American opera singer, Jan 1999

Voinovich, George, American senator, May 1997

Volcker, Paul A., American economist and Federal Reserve chairman, July 1973

Volkova, Julia, Russian singer, Jan 2003

Volkow, Nora D., American neuroscientist, Oct 2011

Vollenweider, Andreas, Swiss harpist, May 1987

Volochkova, Anastasia, Russian ballet dancer, Jan 2004

Volokhonsky, Larissa, Russian translator, June 2006

Volpe, John A., American governor and Secretary of transportation, Feb 1962, *Obit* Jan 1995

Volterra, Vito, Italian mathematician and physicist, *Obit* Yrbk 1940

Volume, Johnny, Finnish guitarist, Jan 2003

Von Arnim, Elizabeth, English novelist, *Obit* Mar 1941

Von Bekesy, Georg, Hungarian-American physicist, Yrbk 1962, *Obit* Sept 1972

Von Braun, Wernher, German-American rocket engineer, Jan 1952, *Obit* Aug 1977

Von Furstenberg, Diane, Belgian fashion designer, Sept 1976

Von Hagen, Victor Wolfgang, naturalist, biographer and explorer, Mar 1942

Von Karman, Theodore, American aeronautical engineer, May 1955, *Obit* June 1963

Von Neumann, John, American mathematician, July 1955, *Obit* Apr 1957

Von Stade, Frederica, American opera singer, Aug 1977

Von Tempski, Armine, *Obit* Jan 1944

Von Tilzer, Harry, American songwriter and music publisher, *Obit* Mar 1946

von Tobel, Alexa, American Internet executive, June 2013

Von Wicht, John, Jan 1963, *Obit* Mar 1970

Von Zell, Harry, June 1944, *Obit* Jan 1982

Von Ziegesar, Cecily, American young adult novelist, Jan 2008

Vonn, Lindsey, American skier, Feb 2010

Vonnegut, Kurt, American novelist and short story writer, July 1970, Mar 1991, *Obit* Aug 2007

Voorhees, Donald, conductor, Feb 1950, *Obit* Apr 1989

Voorhees, Tracy S., Feb 1957, *Obit* Nov 1974

Voorhis, Jerry, American congressman, Aug 1941, *Obit* Nov 1984

Voris, John Ralph, Yrbk 1948, *Obit* Mar 1968

Voronoff, Serge, Jan 1941, *Obit* Oct 1951

Voroshilov, Kliment Efremovich, Soviet field marshal and

communist leader, Mar 1941, *Obit* Jan 1970

Vorster, B. J., South African prime minister, June 1967, *Obit* Nov 1983

Vorys, John M., American congressman, Sept 1950, *Obit* Nov 1968

Vosper, Robert Gordon, librarian, July 1965

Voulkos, Peter, American sculptor and ceramist, Nov 1997, *Obit* Aug 2002

Voytek, Bradley, Neuroscientist, May 2012

Voznesenskii, Andrei, Russian poet, Mar 1967, *Obit* Yrbk 2010

Vranitzky, Franz, Austrian chancellor, Aug 1989

Vrba, Elisabeth S., South African paleontologist, June 1997

Vreeland, Diana, American magazine editor, Feb 1978, *Obit* Oct 1989

Vujanic, Milos, Serbian basketball player, Jan 2004

Vukmanovic-Tempo, Svetozar, Yrbk 1958

W

Waal, Frans de, Dutch primatologist, Mar 2006

Waart, Edo de, Dutch conductor, Mar 1990

Wachner, Linda Joy, American clothing industry executive, Nov 1998

Wachowski, Andy, American film director and screenwriter, Sept 2003

Wachowski, Andy; and Wachowski, Larry, Sept 2003

Wachowski, Larry, American film director and screenwriter, Sept 2003

Wachuku, Jaja, Apr 1963

Wada, Emi, Japanese costume designer, Jan 2007

Waddington, C. H., British embryologist, Apr 1962, *Obit* Nov 1975

Wade, Abdoulaye, Senegalese president, Jan 2006

Wade, Dwyane, American basketball player, Apr 2006

Wade, Virginia, English tennis player, May 1976

Wadhams, Robert Pelton, *Obit* Feb 1941

Wadsworth, James J., American diplomat, June 1956, *Obit* May 1984

Wadsworth, James W., July 1943, *Obit* Sept 1952

Waesche, Russell Randolph, American Coast Guard admiral, Mar 1945, *Obit* Yrbk 1946

Wagman, Frederick H., librarian, July 1963

Wagner, Aubrey J., June 1963

Wagner, J. Addington, May 1956

Wagner, Richard, Apr 1962

Wagner, Robert, American actor, June 1984

Wagner, Robert F., American senator and judge, May 1941, *Obit* June 1953

Wagner, Robert Ferdinand, American mayor, Feb 1954, *Obit* Apr 1991

Wagner, Sune Rose, Danish singer, guitarist and songwriter, Jan 2004

Wagner-Jauregg, Julius, Austrian psychiatrist, *Obit* Nov 1940

Wahlen, Friedrich T., June 1961

Wainwright, Jonathan Mayhew, American general, May 1942, *Obit* Nov 1953

Waite, Alice Vinton, *Obit* May 1943

Waite, Henry Matson, *Obit* Oct 1944

Waite, Terry, British church official, Sept 1986

Waits, Tom, American singer and songwriter, Oct 1997

Waitt, Alden H., Sept 1947

Waitz, Grete, Norwegian marathon runner, Apr 1981, *Obit* Yrbk 2011

Wajda, Andrzej, Polish motion picture and theatrical director, July 1982

Wakasugi, Kaname, *Obit* Jan 1944

Wake-Walker, William Frederick, British admiral, *Obit* Oct 1945

Wakefield, Charles Cheers Wakefield, English lubricants industry executive, *Obit* Mar 1941

Wakefield, Tim, American baseball player, Sept 2011

Wakehurst, John de Vere Loder, Yrbk 1954, *Obit* Yrbk 1970

Wakeman, Frederic, American novelist, Sept 1946

Waksman, Selman Abraham, American microbiologist, May 1946, *Obit* Oct 1973

Walcott, Derek, Saint Lucian poet and dramatist, Apr 1984

Walcott, Jersey Joe, American boxer, June 1949, *Obit* May 1994

Wald, George, American biochemist, May 1968, *Obit* June 1997

Wald, Jerry, American motion picture producer, May 1952, *Obit* Sept 1962

Wald, Lillian D., American social reformer and public health official, *Obit* Oct 1940

Wald, Patricia M., American judge, June 2000

Walden, Amelia Elizabeth, Yrbk 1956

Walden, Percy Talbot, *Obit* May 1943

Waldheim, Kurt, Austrian president and United Nations secretary-general, May 1972, Jan 1987, *Obit* Oct 2007

Waldman, Ayelet, American novelist, Sept 2009

Waldron, Hicks Benjamin, cosmetics executive, Mar 1988

Wales, George C., *Obit* May 1940

Wales, Jimmy, American Internet entrepreneur, Oct 2006

Walesa, Lech, Polish president, Apr 1981, May 1996

Walken, Christopher, American actor, Oct 1990

Walker, Alice, American novelist, poet, essayist and short story writer, Mar 1984

Walker, Daniel, governor, Aug 1976

Walker, E. Ronald, Yrbk 1956

Walker, Eric A., college president, Mar 1959, *Obit* Apr 1995

Walker, Frank Comerford, postmaster general, Oct 1940, *Obit* Nov 1959

Walker, Herschel, American football player, Mar 1985

Walker, Jay, American entrepreneur and information

technology executive, Oct 2000

Walker, John, museum director, May 1957, *Obit* Jan 1996

Walker, Kara, American silhouette artist, Mar 2000

Walker, Larry, Canadian baseball player, May 1998

Walker, Margaret, American poet and novelist, Nov 1943, *Obit* June 1999

Walker, Mildred, American novelist, Yrbk 1947, *Obit* Aug 1998

Walker, Mort, American cartoonist, Feb 2002

Walker, Nancy, actress, Feb 1965, *Obit* May 1992

Walker, Norma Ford, Canadian geneticist, Oct 1957, *Obit* Nov 1968

Walker, Olene S., American governor, Apr 2005

Walker, Paul A., May 1952, *Obit* July 1966

Walker, Ralph Thomas, Yrbk 1957, *Obit* Mar 1973

Walker, Stanley, newspaper editor, Nov 1944, *Obit* Jan 1963

Walker, Stuart, *Obit* May 1941

Walker, Walton Harris, American general, Sept 1950, *Obit* Jan 1951

Walker, Waurine, Feb 1955

Wall, Art, American golfer, Yrbk 1959, *Obit* Feb 2002

Wall, Evander Berry, *Obit* Jan 1940

Wall, Jeff, Canadian artist and photographer, Jan 2007

Walla, Kah (Edith Kabbang Walla), Aug 2013

Wallace, Ben, American basketball player, Apr 2004

Wallace, Chris, American television reporter and moderator, Feb 2011

Wallace, Clayton M., Sept 1948

Wallace, DeWitt, periodical editor and publisher, Apr 1944, May 1956, *Obit* May 1981

Wallace, Dewitt; and Wallace, Lila Acheson, May 1956

Wallace, Euan, *Obit* Apr 1941

Wallace, George Corley, American governor, Yrbk 1963, *Obit* Nov 1998

Wallace, Henry Agard, American vice-president, Aug 1940, Jan 1947, *Obit* Jan 1966

Wallace, Irving, author, Mar 1979, *Obit* Sept 1990

Wallace, Lila Acheson, American philanthropist and publisher, May 1956, *Obit* July 1984

Wallace, Lurleen, governor, Sept 1967, *Obit* July 1968

Wallace, Mike, American television newscaster, July 1957, Nov 1977, *Obit* Yrbk 2012

Wallace, Thomas W., *Obit* Sept 1943

Wallach, Eli, American actor, May 1959

Wallenstein, Alfred, American conductor, May 1940, Apr 1952, *Obit* Mar 1983

Waller, Fats, American jazz pianist and composer, Apr 1942, *Obit* Feb 1944

Waller, Fred, American inventor of Cinerama, Feb 1953, *Obit* July 1954

Waller, Robert James, author, May 1994

Wallerstein, Immanuel Maurice, American sociologist, May 2009

Wallerstein, Judith S., psychologist, Nov 1996

Wallgren, Mon C., Nov 1948, *Obit* Nov 1961

Wallin, Pamela, Canadian television newscaster and talk show host, Jan 2005

Wallis, Jim, American evangelist and writer, July 2005

Wallop, Douglass, American insurance agent and novelist, Yrbk 1956, *Obit* June 1985

Wallraff, Gunter, German journalist, Jan 2004

Waln, Nora, journalist, Jan 1940, *Obit* Nov 1964

Walpole, Hugh, English novelist, *Obit* July 1941

Walsh, Bill, American football coach, Nov 1989, *Obit* Yrbk 2007

Walsh, Chad, professor of English and author, Feb 1962, *Obit* Mar 1991

Walsh, George Ethelbert, *Obit* Apr 1941

Walsh, J. Raymond, Nov 1946

Walsh, James Joseph, *Obit* Apr 1942

Walsh, John, American victims' rights advocate and television program host, July 2001

Walsh, Joseph, *Obit* Mar 1946

Walsh, Kerri, American volleyball player, June 2013

Walsh, Lawrence E., American lawyer, Oct 1991

Walsh, William B., physician, May 1962, *Obit* Mar 1997

Walsh, William Henry, *Obit* May 1941

Walsh, William Thomas, July 1941, *Obit* Mar 1949

Waltari, Mika, Finnish novelist, Feb 1950, *Obit* Oct 1979

Walter, Bruno, conductor, Nov 1942, *Obit* Apr 1962

Walter, Eugene, American dramatist and screenwriter, *Obit* Nov 1941

Walter, Francis E., American congressman, June 1952, *Obit* July 1963

Walter, Wilmer, *Obit* Oct 1941

Walters, Barbara, American television newscaster, Feb 1971, Feb 2003

Walters, John P., American government official, May 2008

Walters, Vernon A., American general and diplomat, Feb 1988, *Obit* July 2002

Walton, Bill, American basketball player and sportscaster, Mar 1977

Walton, Ernest T. S., Irish physicist, Mar 1952, *Obit* Sept 1995

Walton, Sam, American retail executive, Mar 1992, *Obit* Mar 1992

Walton, William, English composer, Mar 1940, *Obit* May 1983

Walworth, Arthur, American biographer, Yrbk 1959, *Obit* Yrbk 2005

Wambach, Abby, American soccer player, Mar 2011

Wambaugh, Eugene, *Obit* Sept 1940

Wambaugh, Joseph, American novelist, Mar 1980

Wambaugh, Sarah, authority on plebiscites, Apr 1946, *Obit* Jan 1956

Wambugu, Florence, Kenyan plant geneticist, Jan 2004

Wampler, Cloud, Yrbk 1952

Wanamaker, Pearl A., Sept 1946

Wang Bingnan, Yrbk 1958

Wang Jingwei, Chinese political leader and collaborationist, May 1940, *Obit* Jan 1945

Wang Nan, Chinese table tennis player, Jan 2003

Wang Yongzhi, Chinese astrophysicist, Jan 2006

Wang, An, American computer industry executive, Jan 1987, *Obit* May 1990

Wang, Shih-chieh, Sept 1945, *Obit* June 1981

Wangchuk, Jigme Dorji, Oct 1956, *Obit* Sept 1972

Wanger, Walter, motion picture producer, June 1947, *Obit* Jan 1969

Wank, Roland, Yrbk 1943, *Obit* July 1970

Wapner, Joseph A., judge, Sept 1989

Warburg, James Paul, American banker, Apr 1948, *Obit* July 1969

Warburton, Herbert B., Nov 1951

Ward, Barbara, English economist and writer, Jan 1950, Jan 1977, *Obit* July 1981

Ward, Benjamin, American police commissioner, Aug 1988, *Obit* Yrbk 2002

Ward, Christopher L., *Obit* Apr 1943

Ward, Donovan F., Mar 1965

Ward, Douglas Turner, American dramatist, actor and director, Sept 1976

Ward, Lem, *Obit* Jan 1943

Ward, Maisie, English author and publisher, Jan 1966, *Obit* Mar 1975

Ward, Mary Jane, author, June 1946

Ward, Paul L., American historian and college president, Mar 1962, *Obit* Yrbk 2006

Ward, Robert, composer, July 1963, *Obit* Yrbk 2013

Ward, William E., American general, Nov 2005

Ware, David S., American jazz saxophonist, Sept 2003, *Obit* Yrbk 2013

Warhol, Andy, American artist, Feb 1968, July 1986, *Obit* Apr 1987

Waring, Fred, American band leader, Sept 1940, *Obit* Sept 1984

Waring, George J., *Obit* Apr 1943

Waring, Julius Waties, judge, Yrbk 1948, *Obit* Mar 1968

Waring, Roane, Yrbk 1943, *Obit* Yrbk 1958

Warne, Shane, Australian cricket player, Jan 2005

Warne, William Elmo, land reclamation and irrigation specialist, Nov 1952, *Obit* May 1996

Warnecke, John Carl, American architect, July 1968, *Obit* Yrbk 2010

Warner, Albert, American motion picture executive, Jan 1945, *Obit* Jan 1968

Warner, Albert; Warner, Harry M.; and Warner, Jack L., Jan 1945

Warner, Edward P., aeronautical engineer, Oct 1949, *Obit* Sept 1958

Warner, Harry M., American motion picture executive, Jan 1945, *Obit* Oct 1958

Warner, Jack L., American motion picture executive, Jan 1945, *Obit* Nov 1978

Warner, John Christian, chemist, Oct 1950, *Obit* July 1989

Warner, John W., American senator, Nov 1976

Warner, Kurt, American football player, Sept 2009

Warner, Mark R., American senator, Oct 2006

Warner, Milo J., Nov 1941

Warner, Ty, American toy industry executive, Nov 1998

Warner, W. Lloyd, American anthropologist and sociologist, Yrbk 1959, *Obit* July 1970

Warnke, Paul C., American lawyer and government official, Aug 1977, *Obit* Feb 2002

Warnock, Mary, British philosopher, Jan 2005

Warren, Althea, librarian, Feb 1942, *Obit* Feb 1960

Warren, Avra M., Feb 1955, *Obit* Mar 1957

Warren, Diane, American songwriter, June 2000

Warren, Earl, American Chief Justice of the Supreme Court, Jan 1944, Jan 1954, *Obit* Sept 1974

Warren, Edgar L., July 1947

Warren, Elizabeth, American law professor and consumer rights advocate, Feb 2012

Warren, Fletcher, diplomat, July 1960, *Obit* Mar 1992

Warren, Frank, British boxing promoter, Jan 2006

Warren, Fuller, American governor, Yrbk 1949

Warren, Harry, composer, June 1943, *Obit* Nov 1981

Warren, Harry Marsh, *Obit* Feb 1941

Warren, J. Robin, Australian pathologist, Jan 2007

Warren, Leonard, opera singer, Yrbk 1953, *Obit* Apr 1960

Warren, Lindsay C., Nov 1949

Warren, Rick, American pastor and religious writer, Oct 2006

Warren, Robert Penn, American novelist and poet, June 1970, *Obit* Nov 1989

Warren, Shields, June 1950, *Obit* Sept 1980

Warren, Whitney, *Obit* Mar 1943

Warren, William C., law school dean, Jan 1960, *Obit* Yrbk 2000

Warwick, Dionne, American singer, Feb 1969

Wash, Carlyle H., *Obit* Mar 1943

Washburn, Bradford, American photographer, explorer and museum director, June 1966, *Obit* Yrbk 2007

Washburn, Gordon Bailey, Yrbk 1955

Washington, Alonzo, American comic book artist and publisher, May 1999

Washington, Denzel, American actor, July 1992

Washington, Harold, American mayor, Feb 1984, *Obit* Jan 1988

Washington, Ron, American baseball manager, May 2011

Washington, Walter E., American mayor, July 1968, *Obit* Yrbk 2004

Wasilewska, Wanda, Polish poet and novelist, July 1944, *Obit* Oct 1964

Wason, Betty, cookbook author and journalist, Aug 1943
Wason, Edward H., *Obit* Apr 1941
Wason, Robert R., American manufacturing industry association executive, Jan 1946, *Obit* Sept 1950
Wasserburg, Gerald Joseph, American professor of geology and geophysics, Mar 1986
Wasserman, Lew R., American motion picture executive, May 1991, *Obit* Yrbk 2002
Wasserstein, Wendy, American dramatist, July 1989, *Obit* Yrbk 2006
Waste, William Harrison, *Obit* July 1940
Watanabe, Ken, Japanese actor, Jan 2004
Watanabe, Shinichiro, Japanese motion picture director, Jan 2006
Watanabe, Tsuneo, Jan 2004
Waterlow, Sydney, *Obit* Jan 1945
Waterman, Alan T., American physicist, June 1951, *Obit* Feb 1968
Waters, Alice, American chef and restaurateur, Jan 2004
Waters, Ethel, American actress and singer, Apr 1941, Mar 1951, *Obit* Oct 1977
Waters, James R., *Obit* Jan 1946
Waters, John, American film director, June 1990
Waters, Maxine, American congresswoman, Nov 1992
Waters, Muddy, American singer and guitarist, May 1981, *Obit* June 1983
Waterston, Sam, American actor, Sept 1985
Watkins, Arthur V., American senator and judge, July 1950, *Obit* Yrbk 1973
Watkins, Donald V., American lawyer and investor, Jan 2003
Watkins, James D., American admiral and Secretary of energy, Mar 1989, *Obit* Yrbk 2012
Watkins, Levi, American cardiac surgeon, Mar 2003
Watkins, Rone, Antiguan drummer, Jan 2004
Watkins, Shirley, Yrbk 1958

Watkinson, Harold Arthur Watkinson, Mar 1960
Watrous, George Dutton, *Obit* Yrbk 1940
Watrous, Harry Willson, painter, *Obit* Jan 1940
Watson, Arthur Kittredge, American computer industry executive and diplomat, Sept 1971, *Obit* Oct 1974
Watson, Bubba (Gerry Lester), American golfer, Feb 2013
Watson, Burl Stevens, petroleum executive, Apr 1957
Watson, Clarence Wayland, *Obit* July 1940
Watson, Doc, American singer and guitarist, Feb 2003, *Obit* Yrbk 2012
Watson, Edwin M., American general, *Obit* Apr 1945
Watson, Emily, British actress, May 2007
Watson, Jack H., Nov 1980
Watson, James D., American molecular biologist, Apr 1963, Oct 1990
Watson, John Broadus, American psychologist, Oct 1942, *Obit* Yrbk 1958
Watson, Lucile, actress, Yrbk 1953, *Obit* Sept 1962
Watson, Mark Skinner, journalist, Nov 1946, *Obit* Apr 1966
Watson, Samuel Newell, *Obit* May 1942
Watson, Thomas J., American computer industry executive and diplomat, Feb 1956, *Obit* Mar 1994
Watson, Thomas J., American office equipment industry executive, Nov 1940, July 1950, *Obit* Sept 1956
Watson, Tom, American golfer, July 1979
Watson-Watt, Robert Alexander, British radio engineer and physicist, Sept 1945, *Obit* Jan 1974
Watt, Donald B., Jan 1958
Watt, James G., American Secretary of the interior, Jan 1982
Watt, Robert J., Mar 1945, *Obit* Sept 1947
Wattenberg, Ben J., American political analyst and writer, June 1985

Wattleton, Faye, American nurse and birth control advocate, Jan 1990
Watts, Alan, American philosopher, Mar 1962, *Obit* Jan 1974
Watts, Andre, American pianist, May 1968
Watts, Heather, ballet dancer, May 1983
Watts, J. C., American congressman, management consultant and political commentator, Mar 1999
Watts, Jeff, American jazz drummer, Apr 2008
Watts, Lyle F., Oct 1946
Watts, Naomi, Australian actress, Mar 2007
Waugh, Auberon, English novelist and essayist, May 1990, *Obit* May 2001
Waugh, Frederick Judd, *Obit* Oct 1940
Waugh, Samuel C., Yrbk 1955, *Obit* Oct 1970
Waugh, Sidney, July 1948, *Obit* Sept 1963
Waugh, Steve, Australian cricket player, Jan 2003
Wavell, Archibald Percival Wavell, British general and colonial administrator, Mar 1941, *Obit* July 1950
Waverley, John Anderson, British statesman, July 1941, *Obit* Mar 1958
Waxman, Henry Arnold, American congressman, July 1992
Way, Niobe, psychologist, Feb 2012
Wayans, Damon, American comedian and actor, Nov 1999
Wayans, Keenen Ivory, American actor, screenwriter and director, Feb 1995
Wayans, Marlon, American comedian and actor, May 2001
Wayans, Shawn, American actor, May 2001
Wayans, Shawn; and Wayans, Marlon, May 2001
Waymack, W. W., Mar 1947, *Obit* Jan 1961
Wayne, David, actor, June 1956, *Obit* Apr 1995
Wayne, John, American actor, Feb 1951, July 1972, *Obit* Aug 1979

Weafer, Elizabeth, Jan 1958

Weagant, Roy A., *Obit* Oct 1942

Weaver, Affie, *Obit* Jan 1941

Weaver, Arthur J., *Obit* Nov 1945

Weaver, Dennis, American actor, Nov 1977, *Obit* Yrbk 2006

Weaver, Earl, American baseball manager, Feb 1983, *Obit* Yrbk 2013

Weaver, Fritz, Jan 1966

Weaver, Pat, American television executive, Jan 1955, *Obit* Sept 2002

Weaver, Robert Clifton, American Secretary of housing and urban development and educator, Apr 1961, *Obit* Oct 1997

Weaver, Sigourney, American actress, Mar 1989

Weaver, Walter Reed, *Obit* Yrbk 1944

Weaver, Warren, Apr 1952, *Obit* Feb 1979

Webb, Aileen Osborn, American art patron, Yrbk 1958, *Obit* Oct 1979

Webb, Beatrice Potter, British sociologist and reformer, *Obit* June 1943

Webb, Clifton, American actor, singer and dancer, Mar 1943, *Obit* Yrbk 1966

Webb, Jack, American actor and producer, May 1955, *Obit* Mar 1983

Webb, James E., American NASA official, Oct 1946, May 1962, *Obit* May 1992

Webb, Jim, American senator, Aug 1987, Nov 2007

Webb, Karrie, Australian golfer, Aug 2001

Webb, Maurice, May 1950, *Obit* Sept 1956

Webb, Walter Loring, *Obit* Mar 1941

Webb, Wellington E., American mayor, Aug 1999

Webb, William Flood, Yrbk 1948

Webber, Chris, American basketball player, May 2003

Webber, Mark, Australian automobile racing driver, Jan 2004

Weber, Dick, American bowler, June 1970, *Obit* Yrbk 2005

Weber, Joseph M., *Obit* July 1942

Weber, L. Lawrence, *Obit* Mar 1940

Weber, Max, American painter, June 1941, *Obit* Yrbk 1961

Webster, H. T., cartoonist, Mar 1945, *Obit* Nov 1952

Webster, Margaret, American actress and theatrical director, May 1940, Sept 1950, *Obit* Jan 1973

Webster, William, May 1950, *Obit* July 1972

Webster, William H., American FBI and CIA director, Aug 1978

Wechsberg, Joseph, American journalist, Apr 1955, *Obit* June 1983

Wecter, Dixon, historian, Nov 1944, *Obit* Sept 1950

Wedel, Cynthia C., religious leader, Mar 1970, *Obit* Oct 1986

Wedemeyer, Albert, American general, Jan 1945, *Obit* Feb 1990

Wedgwood, C. V., English historian, Jan 1957, *Obit* May 1997

Wedgwood, Josiah C., British member of Parliament, Apr 1942, *Obit* Sept 1943

Weede, Robert, Feb 1957, *Obit* Sept 1972

Weeks, Edward, editor and essayist, Yrbk 1947, *Obit* May 1989

Weeks, Sinclair, American Secretary of commerce, Mar 1953, *Obit* Mar 1972

Wegman, William, American artist, May 1992

Wegner, Nicholas H., Yrbk 1949, *Obit* May 1976

Wei Jingsheng, Chinese dissident, Sept 1997

Wei, Tao-ming, Yrbk 1942

Weicker, Lowell P., senator and governor, Jan 1974, May 1993

Weidenbaum, Murray L., economist and government official, Mar 1982

Weider, Joe, American publisher and bodybuilder, Jan 1998, *Obit* Yrbk 2013

Weidlein, Edward R., chemist and foundation official, July 1948, *Obit* Nov 1983

Weidman, Charles, American dancer and choreographer, Apr 1942, *Obit* Sept 1975

Weidman, Jerome, author and dramatist, Aug 1942, *Obit* Jan 1999

Weigle, Luther Allan, professor of religious education and dean, Mar 1946, *Obit* Oct 1976

Weil, Andrew, American physician and healer, Aug 1996

Weil, Frank L., Feb 1949, *Obit* Jan 1958

Weil, Lisl, Jan 1958

Weil, Richard, July 1951, *Obit* July 1958

Weilerstein, Alisa, American cellist, Feb 2013

Weill, Kurt, German composer, Yrbk 1941, *Obit* May 1950

Weill, Sanford I., American financial services executive, July 1999

Wein, George, Oct 1985

Weinberg, Alvin M., American physicist, Sept 1966, *Obit* Yrbk 2006

Weinberg, Robert A., American biochemist, June 1983

Weinberger, Caspar W., American Secretary of defense, June 1973, *Obit* July 2006

Weiner, Jennifer, American novelist, July 2008

Weiner, Matthew, American television producer and scriptwriter, Mar 2012

Weingartner, Felix, Austrian conductor and composer, *Obit* June 1942

Weinstein, Allen, American historian and archivist, June 2006

Weinstein, Bob, American motion picture executive, Mar 1997

Weinstein, Harvey, American motion picture executive, Mar 1997

Weinstein, Harvey; and Weinstein, Bob, Mar 1997

Weir, Ernest T., American steel industry executive, June 1941, *Obit* Oct 1957

Weir, Johnny, American figure skater, Apr 2010

Weir, Peter, Australian motion picture director, Aug 1984

Weis, Charlie, American football coach, Nov 2007

Weis, Jessica, congresswoman, Yrbk 1959, *Obit* June 1963

Weisberg, Jacob, American journalist, Oct 2007

Weisgal, Meyer W., Oct 1972, *Obit* Nov 1977

Weiskopf, Tom, American golfer, Nov 1973

Weiss, Paul, American philosopher, May 1969, *Obit* Yrbk 2002

Weiss, Paul A., American biologist, Oct 1970, *Obit* Nov 1989

Weiss, Peter, German dramatist, novelist and painter, Apr 1968, *Obit* July 1982

Weiss, Soma, *Obit* Mar 1942

Weiss, Ted, congressman, Oct 1985, *Obit* Nov 1992

Weisse, Faneuil Suydam, *Obit* Mar 1940

Weissenberg, Alexis, Bulgarian pianist, June 1978, *Obit* Yrbk 2012

Weisskopf, Victor Frederick, Austrian-American physicist, Nov 1976, *Obit* Yrbk 2002

Weitz, John, German-American fashion designer, novelist and biographer, Sept 1979, *Obit* Apr 2003

Weitzenkorn, Louis, *Obit* Mar 1943

Weizman, Ezer, Israeli president, Sept 1979, *Obit* Aug 2005

Weizmann, Chaim, Israeli president and Zionist leader, Nov 1942, Nov 1948, *Obit* Yrbk 1952

Weizsacker, Carl Friedrich von, German physicist and philosopher, Jan 1985, *Obit* Yrbk 2007

Weizsacker, Richard von, German president, Mar 1985

Wek, Alek, Sudanese model, June 2001

Welch, Florence, British singer, June 2012

Welch, John F., American corporation executive, Jan 1988

Welch, Joseph N., American lawyer, June 1954, *Obit* Yrbk 1960

Welch, Leo D., Yrbk 1963, *Obit* Jan 1979

Welch, Raquel, American actress, May 1971

Welch, Robert, American founder of John Birch Society, Nov 1976, *Obit* Mar 1985

Welch, Stanton, Australian ballet dancer, choreographer and director, July 2007

Welch, William A., *Obit* June 1941

Weld, John, motion picture stunt performer, May 1940

Weld, Tuesday, American actress, July 1974

Weld, William Floyd, American lawyer and former governor, Feb 1993

Weldon, Fay, English novelist, short story writer and dramatist, May 1990

Welensky, Roy, British colonial administrator, July 1959, *Obit* Feb 1992

Welitsch, Ljuba, Bulgarian opera singer, May 1949, *Obit* Nov 1996

Welk, Lawrence, American band leader, Feb 1957, *Obit* July 1992

Welker, Herman, American senator, Feb 1955, *Obit* Jan 1958

Welker, Wes, American football player, Nov 2012

Weller, Michael, American dramatist, May 1989

Weller, Thomas H., American virologist, June 1955, *Obit* Yrbk 2008

Welles, Orson, American actor, director and producer, May 1941, Feb 1965, *Obit* Nov 1985

Welles, Sumner, American diplomat, Mar 1940, *Obit* Nov 1961

Wellman, Manly Wade, author, Yrbk 1955

Wellman, Paul Iselin, American western writer, Yrbk 1949

Wellman, William Augustus, American motion picture director, June 1950, *Obit* Feb 1976

Wells, Agnes, Nov 1949, *Obit* Oct 1959

Wells, Carolyn, author, *Obit* May 1942

Wells, David, American baseball player, May 2004

Wells, Gabriel, bookseller, *Obit* Yrbk 1946

Wells, H. G., English science fiction novelist, *Obit* Sept 1946

Wells, H. Gideon, American pathologist, *Obit* June 1943

Wells, Herman B., American college president, Apr 1966, *Obit* Aug 2000

Wells, Peter, Aug 1942

Wells, Spencer, American geneticist, Mar 2008

Wellstone, Paul David, American senator, May 1993, *Obit* Yrbk 2003

Welman, Joseph C., May 1958

Welsh, Edward Cristy, economist, Jan 1967, *Obit* June 1990

Welsh, Herbert, *Obit* Sept 1941

Welsh, Irvine, Scottish novelist and short story writer, Nov 1997

Welsh, Matthew E., governor, June 1962, *Obit* Aug 1995

Welty, Eudora, American short story writer and novelist, Jan 1942, Oct 1975, *Obit* Nov 2001

Wen Jiabao, Chinese prime minister, Jan 2003

Wenckebach, Karel Friedrich, Dutch cardiologist, *Obit* Yrbk 1940

Wendel, Johnathan, American video game player, Apr 2007

Wenders, Wim, German film producer and director, July 1984

Wendrich, Willeke, Dutch archaeologist, Jan 2007

Wendt, Gerald Louis, scientist, Mar 1940, *Obit* Feb 1974

Weng Wenhao, Nov 1948

Wenner, Jann S., American magazine executive, Jan 1980

Wenner, Kurt, American street artist, Sept 2011

Wenner-Gren, Axel, Oct 1942, *Obit* Jan 1962

Wente, Carl F., Feb 1954

Werblin, Sonny, football executive and theatrical agent, Apr 1979, *Obit* Feb 1992

Werfel, Franz, Austrian poet, novelist and dramatist, Yrbk 1940, *Obit* Sept 1945

Werne, Isaac, *Obit* Mar 1940

Werner, Max, Yrbk 1943, *Obit* Feb 1951

Werner, Oskar, Austrian actor, June 1966, *Obit* Jan 1985

Werner, Theodor, Yrbk 1958

Werner, Wendelin, German-French mathematician, Jan 2006

Werntz, Carl N., *Obit* Yrbk 1944

Werth, Alexander, English journalist, Apr 1943, *Obit* Apr 1969

Wertham, Frederic, American psychologist, July 1949, *Obit* Jan 1982

Wertheimer, Linda, radio newscaster, Nov 1995

Wertheimer, Max, Czech psychologist, *Obit* Yrbk 1943

Wertmuller, Lina, Italian motion picture director, Sept 1976

Wesker, Arnold, English dramatist, Feb 1962

Wesley, Charles Harris, American historian and university president, Mar 1944, *Obit* Oct 1987

Wesley, Valerie Wilson, American novelist, children's author and periodical editor, July 2002

West, Annie Blythe, *Obit* May 1941

West, Claudine, *Obit* May 1943

West, Cornel, American philosopher, Oct 1993

West, Dorothy, American novelist, Feb 1997, *Obit* Oct 1998

West, Fred; and West, Rosemary, May 1944

West, Jessamyn, American novelist, short story writer, librettist, essayist, playwright and poet, Aug 1977, *Obit* Apr 1984

West, Kanye, American rapper and record producer, Aug 2006

West, Keith, Yrbk 1947

West, Levon, Feb 1948, *Obit* June 1968

West, Mae, American actress, Nov 1967, *Obit* Jan 1981

West, Morris L., Australian novelist, Jan 1966, *Obit* Feb 2000

West, Nathanael, American novelist and screenwriter, *Obit* Feb 1941

West, Rebecca, English novelist and journalist, June 1968, *Obit* May 1983

Westcott, John Howell, *Obit* July 1942

Westenra, Hayley, New Zealand singer, Jan 2006

Westergren, Tim, American information technology executive, Oct 2012

Westheimer, Ruth, American psychotherapist, Jan 1987

Westin, Av, Aug 1975

Westley, Helen, actress, *Obit* Feb 1943

Westmore, Perc, American makeup artist, Oct 1945, *Obit* Nov 1970

Westmoreland, William C., American general, June 1961, *Obit* Nov 2005

Weston, Brett, photographer, Feb 1982, *Obit* Mar 1993

Westwood, Vivienne, English fashion designer, July 1997

Wetmore, Alexander, ornithologist, Feb 1948, *Obit* Mar 1979

Wetter, Ernst, Feb 1942

Wexler, Haskell, American cinematographer, Aug 2007

Wexler, Jacqueline Grennan, college president, Mar 1970, *Obit* Yrbk 2012

Wexler, Jerry, American recording industry executive, Jan 2001, *Obit* Yrbk 2008

Wexler, Nancy S., American psychologist and neurologist, Aug 1994

Wexner, Leslie H., American fashion chain store executive and philanthropist, Feb 1994

Weyerhaeuser, Frederick E., *Obit* Nov 1945

Weyerhaeuser, George H., July 1977

Weyerhaeuser, Rudolph M., *Obit* Sept 1946

Weygand, Maxime, French general, Jan 1940, *Obit* Mar 1965

Weymouth, Frank E., *Obit* Sept 1941

Weyrich, Paul, American political activist and commentator, Feb 2005, *Obit* Yrbk 2009

Whalen, Grover A., Sept 1944, *Obit* June 1962

Wharton, Clifton R., American college president and pension plan administrator, Feb 1987

Wharton, Clifton R., American diplomat, July 1958, *Obit* June 1990

Wheat, Alfred Adams, *Obit* Apr 1943

Wheat, William Howard, *Obit* Apr 1944

Wheater, Ashley, British ballet dancer and director, May 2011

Wheaton, Anne, Jan 1958, *Obit* May 1977

Wheaton, Elizabeth, Jan 1942

Whedon, Joss, American film and television scriptwriter, July 2012

Wheeldon, Christopher, British ballet dancer and choreographer, Mar 2004

Wheeler, Burton K., American senator, Aug 1940, *Obit* Feb 1975

Wheeler, Earle G., American general, Nov 1965, *Obit* Feb 1976

Wheeler, John Archibald, American physicist, Jan 1970, *Obit* Yrbk 2008

Wheeler, Raymond A., Apr 1957, *Obit* Apr 1974

Wheeler, Robert Eric Mortimer, English archaeologist, Mar 1956, *Obit* Sept 1976

Wheeler, Tony, Australian travel writer and publisher, Jan 2005

Wheelock, Warren, Mar 1940, *Obit* Oct 1960

Wheelwright, Jere, Yrbk 1952, *Obit* Mar 1961

Wheelwright, John, poet, *Obit* Nov 1940

Whelan, Wendy, American ballet dancer, Oct 1998

Wherry, Kenneth S., American senator, Apr 1946, *Obit* Jan 1952

Whipple, Fred Lawrence, American astronomer, May 1952, *Obit* Yrbk 2005

Whipple, Maurine, American novelist, Mar 1941

Whipple, Wayne, *Obit* Yrbk 1942

Whitaker, Douglas, Nov 1951, *Obit* Yrbk 1973

Whitaker, Forest, American actor and motion picture director, Feb 1997

Whitaker, Mark, American television news executive, Aug 2003

Whitcomb, Richard T., American aeronautical engineer, Yrbk 1956, *Obit* Yrbk 2009

White Stripes (Musical group), Sept 2003

White, Alexander M., July 1951, Obit Jan 1969

White, Armond, American film critic, Oct 2006

White, Betty, American actress, June 1987

White, Byron R., American Supreme Court justice, Yrbk 1962, Obit July 2002

White, Charles M., June 1950, Obit Mar 1977

White, E. B., American humorist and poet, Oct 1960, Obit Nov 1985

White, Edmund, American novelist and biographer, Jan 1991

White, Edward Higgins, American astronaut, Nov 1965, Obit Mar 1967

White, Francis W., Jan 1954, Obit June 1957

White, Frank, Yrbk 1950, Obit Jan 1980

White, Frank, Obit May 1940

White, Gilbert Fowler, American geographer, Mar 1953, Obit Yrbk 2006

White, Harry Dexter, American economist and government official, Sept 1944, Obit Oct 1948

White, Helen Constance, literary scholar and author, July 1945

White, Herbert S., librarian, May 1968

White, Hugh Lawson, Yrbk 1955, Obit Nov 1965

White, I. D., American general, Yrbk 1958, Obit Aug 1990

White, Jack, American singer and guitarist, Sept 2003

White, John F., American television executive and college president, Nov 1967, Obit Yrbk 2005

White, John R., Jan 1956

White, Josh, guitarist and singer, Aug 1944, Obit Nov 1969

White, Katherine Elkus, diplomat and state official, Feb 1965, Obit June 1985

White, Kevin H., American mayor, Yrbk 1974, Obit Yrbk 2012

White, Marco Pierre, British chef and restaurateur, Jan 2007

White, Mark, governor, Aug 1986

White, Meg, American drummer, Sept 2003

White, Michael R., American mayor, Mar 1999

White, Nelia Gardner, author, Yrbk 1950, Obit Oct 1957

White, Patrick, Australian novelist, June 1974, Obit Nov 1990

White, Paul Dudley, American cardiologist, Yrbk 1955, Obit Yrbk 1973

White, Paul Welrose, journalist and radio executive, Mar 1940, Obit Oct 1955

White, Portia, Mar 1945

White, Randy Wayne, American mystery writer and fishing guide, Nov 2011

White, Reggie, American football player and clergyman, Nov 1995, Obit Yrbk 2005

White, Robert E., American diplomat, May 1984

White, Robert M., American newspaper editor and publisher, Mar 1960

White, Robert M., American meteorologist, Mar 1964

White, S. Harrison, Obit Feb 1946

White, Stewart Edward, author and hunter, Obit Nov 1946

White, Theodore H., American journalist, Apr 1955, Apr 1976, Obit July 1986

White, Thomas D., American air force general, Yrbk 1957, Obit Feb 1966

White, Trumbull, Obit Feb 1942

White, Vanna, American television personality, Jan 1988

White, W. Wilson, Jan 1959, Obit Jan 1965

White, Wallace H., May 1948, Obit May 1952

White, Walter Francis, American civil rights leader, Apr 1942, Obit June 1955

White, Wilbert Webster, Obit Oct 1944

White, William, Jan 1953, Obit June 1967

White, William Allen, newspaper editor, Nov 1940, Obit Apr 1944

White, William Lindsay, American journalist and writer, Jan 1943, Obit Oct 1973

White, William Smith, journalist, Yrbk 1955, Obit June 1994

Whitehead, Colson, American novelist, Nov 2001

Whitehead, Don, journalist, Yrbk 1953, Obit Mar 1981

Whitehead, Edward, British manufacturing executive, Jan 1967, Obit June 1978

Whitehill, Walter Muir, June 1960, Obit May 1978

Whitehouse, Harold Beckwith, Obit Sept 1943

Whitelaw, William Whitelaw, British cabinet member, Mar 1975, Obit Nov 1999

Whiteman, Paul, American band leader, Aug 1945, Obit Feb 1968

Whiteman, Wilberforce James, Obit Jan 1940

Whiteread, Rachel, English sculptor, Jan 2006

Whitford, Brad, American rock guitarist, July 2004

Whitford, Bradley, American actor, Apr 2003

Whitford, Harry Nichols, Obit July 1941

Whitlam, Edward Gough, Jan 1974

Whitman, Christine Todd, American government official, June 1995

Whitman, Marina von Neumann, American automobile executive and economist, Oct 1973

Whitman, Meg, American Internet auction executive, Feb 2000

Whitman, Walter G., Feb 1952, Obit June 1974

Whitmire, Kathryn J., mayor, Mar 1988

Whitmore, James, American actor, Sept 1976, Obit Yrbk 2009

Whitney, A. F., American labor leader, Feb 1946, Obit Sept 1949

Whitney, Courtney, June 1951, Obit May 1969

Whitney, Gertrude Vanderbilt, American sculptor and art patron, July 1941, Obit Yrbk 1942

Whitney, John Hay, American financier and diplomat, Yrbk 1945, Obit Apr 1982

Whitney, Phyllis A., American novelist and short story writer, Yrbk 1948, Obit Yrbk 2008

Whitson, Peggy A., American biochemist and astronaut, Sept 2003

Whittaker, Charles Evans, American Supreme Court justice, Yrbk 1957, *Obit* Jan 1974

Whittemore and Lowe, Jan 1954

Whittemore, Arthur Austin, pianist, Jan 1954, *Obit* Feb 1985

Whittle, Christopher, American publishing, broadcasting and school management company executive, Feb 1991

Whittle, Frank, British air force officer and aeronautical engineer, Jan 1945, *Obit* Oct 1996

Whittlesey, Charles F., *Obit* Feb 1941

Whitton, Charlotte Elizabeth, Canadian social worker, feminist and mayor, Apr 1953, *Obit* Mar 1975

Whitton, Rex M., May 1962

Whitty, May, English actress, Yrbk 1945, *Obit* July 1948

Whitworth, Kathy, American golfer, Apr 1976

Whyte, William H., American journalist and sociologist, Jan 1959, *Obit* Mar 1999

Wick, Charles Z., American government official, Mar 1985, *Obit* Yrbk 2008

Wick, Frances G., *Obit* Aug 1941

Wickard, Claude Raymond, American Secretary of agriculture, Oct 1940, *Obit* June 1967

Wickenden, Dan, author and editor, Yrbk 1951, *Obit* Feb 1990

Wickenheiser, Hayley, Canadian hockey player, Jan 2003

Wickens, Aryness Joy, economist and government official, Sept 1962, *Obit* Apr 1991

Wicker, Ireene, singer and storyteller, Apr 1943, *Obit* Jan 1988

Wicker, Tom, columnist, Nov 1973, *Obit* Yrbk 2012

Wickham, Madeleine, English novelist, Jan 2004

Wickware, Francis Graham, *Obit* Yrbk 1940

Wideman, John Edgar, American novelist and short story writer, Jan 1991

Widmark, Richard, American actor, Apr 1963, *Obit* Yrbk 2008

Widnall, Sheila Evans, American Secretary of the air force, Oct 1997

Wiedoeft, Rudy, *Obit* Mar 1940

Wiener, Alexander S., physician and hematologist, May 1947, *Obit* Feb 1977

Wiener, Norbert, American mathematician, Mar 1950, *Obit* May 1964

Wiesel, Elie, American novelist, journalist and human rights activist, Nov 1970, Feb 1986

Wiesenthal, Simon, Austrian Nazi hunter, Jan 1975, *Obit* Yrbk 2005

Wiesner, Jerome B., American electrical engineer and college president, Yrbk 1961, *Obit* Jan 1995

Wiest, Dianne, actress, Mar 1997

Wigand, Jeffrey, American teacher and former tobacco industry executive, Apr 2000

Wiggam, Albert Edward, July 1942, *Obit* June 1957

Wiggins, Bradley, Nov 2013

Wiggins, James Russell, American newspaper editor and diplomat, Nov 1969, *Obit* Mar 2001

Wiggles (Musical group), Jan 2004

Wigglesworth, Richard B., May 1959, *Obit* Yrbk 1960

Wigman, Mary, German dancer and choreographer, Jan 1969, *Obit* Nov 1973

Wigner, Eugene P., American physicist, Apr 1953, *Obit* Mar 1995

Wigny, Pierre, Yrbk 1960

Wiig, Kristen, American actress, July 2013

Wiigh-Masak, Susanne, Swedish ecologist, Jan 2005

Wilber, Ken, American spiritualist and author, Apr 2002

Wilbur, Bernice M., Sept 1943

Wilbur, Dwight Locke, medical association official and gastroenterologist, July 1969, *Obit* May 1997

Wilbur, Ray Lyman, Nov 1947, *Obit* Sept 1949

Wilbur, Richard, American poet, Jan 1966

Wilby, Francis B., Aug 1945, *Obit* Jan 1966

Wilco (Musical group), Feb 2010

Wilcox, Clair, Yrbk 1948

Wilcox, Francis Orlando, government official, Apr 1962, *Obit* Apr 1985

Wilcox, Herbert, Nov 1945, *Obit* July 1977

Wilcox, J. W., American admiral, *Obit* May 1942

Wild, Earl, American pianist and composer, July 1988, *Obit* Yrbk 2010

Wilde, Frazar B., insurance executive, Apr 1959, *Obit* Aug 1985

Wilde, Louise K., Apr 1954

Wilde, Patricia, Canadian ballet dancer and director, May 1968

Wilder, Alec, composer, July 1980, *Obit* Feb 1981

Wilder, Billy, Austrian-American film director and screenwriter, Feb 1951, Oct 1984, *Obit* Yrbk 2002

Wilder, Frances Farmer, July 1947

Wilder, Gene, American actor and motion picture director, Apr 1978

Wilder, L. Douglas, American governor and mayor, Apr 1990

Wilder, Laura Ingalls, American children's and young adult author, Yrbk 1948, *Obit* May 1957

Wilder, Thornton, American novelist and dramatist, Aug 1943, Nov 1971, *Obit* Feb 1976

Wildmon, Donald, clergyman, Jan 1992

Wile, Frederic William, journalist and radio commentator, *Obit* June 1941

Wile, Ira S., *Obit* Nov 1943

Wiles, Andrew, English mathematician, Mar 1996

Wiley, Alexander, American senator, Apr 1947, *Obit* Jan 1968

Wiley, Kehinde, American painter, Aug 2007

Wiley, Richard E., American lawyer, Mar 1977

Wiley, William Foust, American newspaper publisher, *Obit* Oct 1944

Wilgress, L. Dana, Jan 1954, *Obit* Oct 1969

Wilgus, Sidney Dean, *Obit* Mar 1940

Wilhelm, Hoyt, American baseball player, July 1971, *Obit* Yrbk 2002

Wilhelmina, Jan 1940, *Obit* Jan 1963

Wilkens, Lenny, American basketball player and coach, July 1996

Wilkerson, Isabel, American journalist, Oct 2011

Wilkins, Dominique, American basketball player, May 1995

Wilkins, Hubert, Australian explorer and geographer, Jan 1957, *Obit* Feb 1959

Wilkins, J. Ernest, Yrbk 1954, *Obit* Mar 1959

Wilkins, Maurice Hugh Frederick, English biochemist, June 1963, *Obit* Yrbk 2005

Wilkins, Robert W., American physician, July 1958, *Obit* Yrbk 2003

Wilkins, Roger W., American lawyer, journalist and educator, Aug 1994

Wilkins, Roy, American civil rights leader, June 1950, Jan 1964, *Obit* Oct 1981

Wilkins, T. Russell, *Obit* Feb 1941

Wilkinson, Bud, football coach, Apr 1962, *Obit* May 1994

Wilkinson, Ellen, British cabinet member, July 1941, *Obit* Mar 1947

Will, George F., American columnist and political commentator, Sept 1981

Will. i. Am (Musician), American singer, Oct 2006

Willard, John, *Obit* Nov 1942

Willes, Mark H., American newspaper publisher, Mar 1998

Willet, Anne Lee, *Obit* Mar 1943

Willet, Henry Lee, Mar 1947

William, *Obit* July 1941

Williams of Barnburgh, Thomas Williams, Apr 1946, *Obit* May 1967

Williams, Alford Joseph, Oct 1940

Williams, Andy, American singer, Feb 1960, *Obit* Yrbk 2012

Williams, Anthony, American mayor, Oct 1999

Williams, Armstrong, American newspaper columnist and radio talk show host, May 2004

Williams, Aubrey Willis, American government official, publisher and social welfare leader, May 1940, *Obit* Apr 1965

Williams, Betty, Irish pacifist, Mar 1979

Williams, Billy Dee, American actor, Apr 1984

Williams, Brian, American television news anchor, July 1998

Williams, Camilla, opera singer, June 1952, *Obit* Yrbk 2012

Williams, Cliff, English bassist, Mar 2005

Williams, Clyde E., July 1947

Williams, Dick, American baseball player and manager, Yrbk 1973, *Obit* Yrbk 2011

Williams, Doug, American football player and coach, Feb 1999

Williams, Edward Bennett, American lawyer and baseball and football executive, Jan 1965, *Obit* Sept 1988

Williams, Edwin G., May 1950

Williams, Emlyn, Welsh playwright and actor, Feb 1941, Apr 1952, *Obit* Nov 1987

Williams, Eric Eustace, Trinidadian prime minister, Feb 1966, *Obit* May 1981

Williams, Esther, American swimmer and actress, Feb 1955, *Obit* Yrbk 2013

Williams, Evan, American Internet executive, July 2009

Williams, G. Mennen, American governor and state supreme court justice, Apr 1949, June 1963, *Obit* Mar 1988

Williams, Gluyas, cartoonist, June 1946, *Obit* Apr 1982

Williams, Hank, American country singer, Mar 1998

Williams, Harrison A., American senator, Oct 1960, *Obit* Mar 2002

Williams, Jay, American novelist, Yrbk 1955, *Obit* Sept 1978

Williams, Jody, American pacifist, Mar 1998

Williams, Joe, singer, Apr 1985, *Obit* June 1999

Williams, John, Australian guitarist, July 1983

Williams, John Alfred, American novelist, Oct 1994

Williams, John Bell, American congressman and governor, Mar 1964, *Obit* May 1983

Williams, John D., *Obit* May 1941

Williams, John H., Jan 1960, *Obit* May 1966

Williams, John J., American senator, Jan 1952, *Obit* Apr 1988

Williams, John T., American composer, Oct 1980

Williams, Joseph John, *Obit* Yrbk 1940

Williams, Juan, American journalist, May 2008

Williams, Lauryn, American runner, Sept 2008

Williams, Lucinda, American singer and songwriter, Mar 1999

Williams, Mary Lou, American pianist and composer, Nov 1966, *Obit* July 1981

Williams, Michelle, American singer, Aug 2001

Williams, Paul, American singer, songwriter and actor, June 1983

Williams, Paul, American architect, Mar 1941, *Obit* Mar 1980

Williams, Preston Warren, American religious official, May 2007

Williams, Ralph E., *Obit* July 1940

Williams, Ricky, American football player, Aug 1999

Williams, Robbie, British pop singer, Jan 2004

Williams, Robert R., Sept 1951, *Obit* Yrbk 1965

Williams, Robin, American comedian and actor, June 1979, Jan 1997

Williams, Roger J., biochemist and nutritionist, July 1957, *Obit* Apr 1988

Williams, Ronald, American health insurance executive, July 2009

Williams, Rowan, British archbishop, Jan 2002

Williams, Roy, American basketball coach, Mar 2007

Williams, Saul, American rapper and poet, June 2011

Williams, Serena, American tennis player, Feb 2003

Williams, Shirley, British political leader, Oct 1976

Williams, Sunita L., American astronaut, Mar 2013

Williams, Tad, American science fiction and fantasy writer, Sept 2006

Williams, Ted, American baseball player and manager, Apr 1947, *Obit* Oct 2002

Williams, Tennessee, American dramatist, Jan 1946, Apr 1972, *Obit* Apr 1983

Williams, Thomas Sutler, *Obit* May 1940

Williams, Vanessa, American singer and actress, May 1984

Williams, Venus, American tennis player, Feb 2003

Williams, Venus; and Williams, Serena, Feb 2003

Williams, W. Walter, Nov 1948

Williams, Wendy, American talk show host, Oct 2009

Williams, William Robert, *Obit* Jan 1941

Williams, Wythe, journalist, Oct 1943, *Obit* Sept 1956

Williamson, Kevin, American screenwriter and director, Apr 2000

Williamson, Marianne, New Age preacher, Feb 1993

Williamson, Nicol, British actor, Jan 1970, *Obit* Yrbk 2012

Williamson, Ski, Finnish guitarist and singer, Jan 2003

Willimon, Beau, American playwright, June 2012

Willingdon, Freeman Freeman-Thomas, British colonial administrator, *Obit* Oct 1941

Willingham, Tyrone, American football coach, Nov 2002

Willis, Bruce, American actor, Feb 1987

Willis, Deborah, American photography historian and museum curator, Sept 2004

Willis, Dontrelle, American baseball player, Aug 2006

Willis, Frances E., Jan 1954

Willis, Kelly, singer, Oct 1999

Willis, Paul S., food and grocery trade association executive, Jan 1951, *Obit* Aug 1987

Willison, George Findlay, historian, Jan 1946

Williston, Samuel, Yrbk 1954, *Obit* Apr 1963

Willkie, Wendell Lewis, American lawyer and presidential candidate, Feb 1940, *Obit* Nov 1944

Willoughby, Charles Clark, *Obit* June 1943

Wills, Childe Harold, automobile executive, *Obit* Feb 1941

Wills, Garry, American journalist, essayist and historian, June 1982

Wills, Maury, American baseball player, June 1966

Wills, Royal Barry, Yrbk 1954, *Obit* Feb 1962

Willson, Beckles, *Obit* Nov 1942

Willson, Meredith, American composer and lyricist, June 1958, *Obit* Aug 1984

Willstatter, Richard, German chemist, *Obit* Sept 1942

Wilmore, Larry, American television scriptwriter and producer, Nov 2007

Wilmut, Ian, British embryologist, June 1997

Wilson, A. N., English novelist and biographer, Aug 1993

Wilson, Angus, English novelist and short story writer, Feb 1959, *Obit* Aug 1991

Wilson, August, American playwright, Aug 1987, *Obit* Feb 2006

Wilson, Brian, American singer and songwriter, July 1988

Wilson, Carroll Louis, energy expert and educator, May 1947, *Obit* Mar 1983

Wilson, Cassandra, American jazz singer, Mar 1998

Wilson, Charles E., American automobile executive and Secretary of defense, Aug 1941, Sept 1950, *Obit* Yrbk 1961

Wilson, Charles E., American electronics industry executive, Apr 1943, Feb 1951, *Obit* Feb 1972

Wilson, Colin, English novelist and nonfiction writer, Apr 1963

Wilson, Don, radio and television personality, Aug 1944, *Obit* Yrbk 1991

Wilson, Donald R., Jan 1952

Wilson, Donald V., Jan 1954

Wilson, Dorothy Clarke, Yrbk 1951

Wilson, Edmund, American literary critic, Apr 1945, Jan 1964, *Obit* July 1972

Wilson, Edward Foss, corporation executive and government official, Mar 1958, *Obit* May 1994

Wilson, Edward O., American myrmecologist, Oct 1979

Wilson, Eugene E., Oct 1945

Wilson, Flip, American comedian, Nov 1969, *Obit* Feb 1999

Wilson, Frank J., June 1946, *Obit* Oct 1970

Wilson, George Arthur, *Obit* Nov 1941

Wilson, Gretchen, American country singer, Apr 2011

Wilson, Halsey William, publisher, Yrbk 1941, May 1948, *Obit* Apr 1954

Wilson, Harold, British prime minister, Feb 1948, May 1963, *Obit* July 1995

Wilson, Heather, American congresswoman, July 2006

Wilson, Henry Maitland Wilson, Oct 1943, *Obit* Feb 1965

Wilson, Hugh Robert, diplomat, May 1941, *Obit* Feb 1947

Wilson, I. W., July 1952, *Obit* Jan 1978

Wilson, James Q., American political scientist, Aug 2002, *Obit* Yrbk 2012

Wilson, John Tuzo, Canadian geophysicist and educator, Apr 1973, *Obit* Aug 1993

Wilson, Joseph C., American office equipment industry executive, Oct 1966, *Obit* Jan 1972

Wilson, Kemmons, American hotel chain executive, Sept 1973, *Obit* Yrbk 2003

Wilson, Kenneth Geddes, American physicist, Sept 1983, *Obit* Yrbk 2013

Wilson, Lanford, American playwright, Mar 1979, *Obit* Yrbk 2011

Wilson, Leroy A., Apr 1948, *Obit* July 1951

Wilson, Logan, college administrator, Yrbk 1956, *Obit* Jan 1991

Wilson, Luke, American actor, Feb 2005

Wilson, Malcolm, American lawyer, banker and governor, May 1974, *Obit* Aug 2000

Wilson, Margaret Bush, American lawyer and civil rights activist, Oct 1975, *Obit* Yrbk 2009

Wilson, Margaret Stevens, *Obit* May 1943

Wilson, Marie C., American feminist, Sept 2004

Wilson, Mark, Australian bassist, Jan 2005

Wilson, Michael H., Canadian cabinet member and diplomat, Mar 1990

Wilson, O. Meredith, college president, July 1967, *Obit* Feb 1999

Wilson, O. W., Oct 1966, *Obit* Yrbk 1972

Wilson, Owen, American actor and screenwriter, Feb 2003

Wilson, Pete, governor, Apr 1991

Wilson, Peter C., English art dealer, Feb 1968, *Obit* Aug 1984

Wilson, Robert, American director, dramatist and artist, Aug 1979

Wilson, Robert R., American physicist, Aug 1989, *Obit* May 2000

Wilson, Rufus H., June 1955

Wilson, Sloan, American novelist, Sept 1959, *Obit* Yrbk 2003

Wilson, Volney C., June 1958

Wilson, William Julius, American sociologist, Feb 1996

Wilt, Fred, runner and FBI agent, Oct 1952, *Obit* Nov 1994

Wiltshire, Stephen, English artist, Jan 2007

Wiman, Dwight Deere, June 1949, *Obit* Feb 1951

Winant, John Gilbert, governor and diplomat, Feb 1941, *Obit* Yrbk 1947

Winchell, Constance Mabel, librarian, June 1967, *Obit* Sept 1984

Winchell, Walter, American columnist and radio commentator, June 1943, *Obit* Apr 1972

Winchester, Alice, magazine editor, Feb 1954

Winchester, Simon, Anglo-American journalist, Oct 2006

Windschuttle, Keith, Australian writer and historian, Jan 2006

Windsor, Edward, Sept 1944, *Obit* July 1972

Windsor, Wallis Warfield, wife of Windsor, Edward, Duke of, Sept 1944, *Obit* June 1986

Windust, Bretaigne, Mar 1943, *Obit* May 1960

Winehouse, Amy, British jazz and soul singer, Jan 2007, *Obit* Yrbk 2011

Winfield, Dave, American baseball player, Jan 1984

Winfrey, Oprah, American television talk show host, Mar 1987

Wingate, Orde Charles, British general, *Obit* May 1944

Winger, Debra, American actress, July 1984

Winiarski, Bohdan, Feb 1962

Winkler, Henry, American actor and producer, Sept 1976

Winpisinger, William W., American labor leader, Feb 1980, *Obit* Feb 1998

Winslow, Anne, Yrbk 1948

Winsor, Frederick, *Obit* Jan 1941

Winsor, Kathleen, American novelist, Yrbk 1946, *Obit* Yrbk 2003

Winster, Reginald Thomas Herbert Fletcher, Feb 1946

Winston, Harry, jeweler, Apr 1965, *Obit* Feb 1979

Winston, Stan, American special effects technician, July 2002, *Obit* Nov 2008

Winter, Ella, Yrbk 1946, *Obit* Sept 1980

Winter, Fritz, German painter, Mar 1958

Winter, George B., *Obit* May 1940

Winter, Paul, saxophonist, Oct 1987

Winters, Jonathan, American comedian, Mar 1965, *Obit* Yrbk 2013

Winters, Shelley, American actress, Apr 1952, *Obit* Apr 2006

Winthrop, Beekman, *Obit* Yrbk 1940

Wintour, Anna, British fashion editor, July 1990

Wirth, Conrad L., American national parks director, Sept 1952, *Obit* Sept 1993

Wirth, Niklaus, Swiss computer scientist, Jan 2003

Wirth, Timothy E., senator, Mar 1991

Wirtz, Willard, American Secretary of labor, Nov 1946, Feb 1963, *Obit* Yrbk 2010

Wise, James DeCamp, carpet industry executive, Apr 1954, *Obit* Apr 1984

Wise, Robert, American film director, Sept 1989, *Obit* Apr 2006

Wise, Stephen Samuel, American rabbi, July 1941, *Obit* May 1949

Wise, Tim, Jan 2013

Wiseman, Frederick, American documentary filmmaker, Yrbk 1974

Witcover, Jules, American newspaper columnist and writer, Apr 2008

Witherow, W. P., Apr 1942, *Obit* Mar 1960

Witherspoon, Reese, American actress, Jan 2004

Witos, Wincenty, *Obit* Yrbk 1945

Witt, James Lee, American emergency management official and consultant, Mar 2000

Witt, Katarina, German figure skater, July 1988

Witte, Edwin E., American eonomist and government official, July 1946, *Obit* Sept 1960

Witten, Edward, American physicist, June 1997

Wodehouse, P. G., English novelist, short story writer and dramatist, Nov 1971, *Obit* Apr 1975

Woertz, Patricia, American agribusiness executive, Mar 2007

Woese, Carl R., American microbiologist, June 2003, *Obit* Yrbk 2013

Wofford, Harris, American senator, Apr 1992

Woiwode, Larry, American novelist, Mar 1989

Wojcicki, Susan, American Internet executive, Feb 2013

Wojciechowska, Maia, Polish children's author and publisher, Sept 1976, *Obit* Yrbk 2002

Wolchok, Sam, Oct 1948, *Obit* Mar 1979

Wolcott, Jesse P., American congressman and regulatory agency official, Yrbk 1949, *Obit* Apr 1969

Wolf, Alfred, Mar 1958

Wolf, Naomi, American feminist, social critic and journalist, Nov 1993

Wolfe, Art, American photographer, June 2005

Wolfe, Deborah Cannon Partridge, American educator, Yrbk 1962

Wolfe, George C., American dramatist and director, Mar 1994

Wolfe, Hugh C., Feb 1950

Wolfe, Humbert, English poet and government official, *Obit* Jan 1940

Wolfe, Julia, American composer, Oct 2003

Wolfe, Tom, American journalist and novelist, Jan 1971

Wolfenden, John Frederick Wolfenden, English educator, social reformer and museum director, Oct 1970, *Obit* Mar 1985

Wolfensohn, James David, Australian international organization official, May 2000

Wolfert, Ira, author and journalist, Apr 1943, *Obit* Feb 1998

Wolff, Geoffrey, author, Jan 1997

Wolff, Maritta M., American novelist, July 1941, *Obit* Yrbk 2002

Wolff, Tobias, American memoirist and short story writer, Jan 1996

Wolfit, Donald, Mar 1965, *Obit* Apr 1968

Wolfowitz, Paul D., American international organization official, Feb 2003

Wolfram, Stephen, American physicist and software executive, Feb 2005

Wolfson, Evan, American lawyer and gay rights activist, July 2009

Woll, Matthew, Jan 1943, *Obit* Sept 1956

Wolman, Abel, sanitary engineer, Feb 1957, *Obit* May 1989

Wolman, Leo, Sept 1949, *Obit* Yrbk 1961

Wolper, David L., American film and television producer, Oct 1986, *Obit* Yrbk 2010

Wolpoff, Milford H., American paleoanthropologist, July 2006

Woltman, Frederick, July 1947, *Obit* Apr 1970

Womack, Lee Ann, American country singer, Apr 2010

Wonder, Stevie, American singer and songwriter, Mar 1975

Wong, Andrea, American broadcasting executive, Sept 2007

Wong, How-man, Chinese explorer and journalist, Jan 2002

Wong, Kar-Wai, Chinese film director and screenwriter, Apr 1998

Wong-Staal, Flossie, American molecular biologist, Apr 2001

Woo, John, Chinese motion picture director, Feb 1999

Wood, Charles Erskine Scott, American lawyer and satirist, *Obit* Mar 1944

Wood, Elijah, American actor, Aug 2002

Wood, Evan Rachel, American actress, June 2009

Wood, Fiona M., Australian plastic surgeon, Jan 2007

Wood, Gordon S., American historian, Oct 2011

Wood, Grant, American painter, Aug 1940, *Obit* Apr 1942

Wood, Henry Joseph, English conductor, *Obit* Oct 1944

Wood, James Madison, Feb 1947, *Obit* Yrbk 1958

Wood, John, English actor, Apr 1983, *Obit* Yrbk 2011

Wood, John S., American congressman, July 1949, *Obit* Nov 1968

Wood, Kerry, American baseball player, May 2005

Wood, Kingsley, Nov 1940

Wood, Louise Aletha, Girl Scouts leader, July 1961, *Obit* July 1988

Wood, Natalie, American actress, Apr 1962, *Obit* Jan 1982

Wood, Peggy, actress and singer, July 1942, Yrbk 1953, *Obit* May 1978

Wood, Philip, *Obit* Mar 1940

Wood, Robert D., Yrbk 1974, *Obit* July 1986

Wood, Robert Elkington, retail executive, May 1941, *Obit* Yrbk 1969

Wood, Sam, Nov 1943, *Obit* Nov 1949

Woodard, Alfre, American actress, Feb 1995

Woodard, Stacy, *Obit* Mar 1942

Woodbridge, Frederick James Eugene, American philosopher, *Obit* July 1940

Woodbury, Charles Herbert, painter, *Obit* Jan 1940

Woodcock, Charles Edward, *Obit* Mar 1940

Woodcock, George, English labor leader, Feb 1964, *Obit* Jan 1980

Woodcock, Leonard, American labor leader and diplomat, Nov 1970, *Obit* Apr 2001

Wooden, John R., American basketball coach, Jan 1976, *Obit* Yrbk 2010

Woodham Smith, Cecil Blanche Fitz Gerald, English historian, Yrbk 1955, *Obit* Mar 1977

Woodhouse, Barbara, English dog trainer and author, Feb 1985, *Obit* Aug 1988

Woodhouse, Chase Going, congresswoman, Mar 1945, *Obit* Apr 1985

Woodlock, Thomas Francis, *Obit* Sept 1945

Woodruff, Judy, American television newscaster, Sept 1986

Woods, Bill Milton, librarian, May 1966, *Obit* Sept 1974

Woods, Donald, South African newspaper editor, Feb 1982, *Obit* Nov 2001

Woods, George David, banker, July 1965, *Obit* Oct 1982

Woods, James, American actor, Nov 1989

Woods, Mark, American broadcasting executive, Mar 1946

Woods, Tiger, American golfer, Nov 1997

Woods, Tighe E., American real estate developer and government official, Oct 1948, *Obit* Sept 1974

Woodsmall, Ruth Frances, July 1949, *Obit* July 1963

Woodson, Carter Godwin, American historian, Feb 1944, *Obit* Yrbk 1984

Woodson, Rod, American football player, Oct 2004

Woodsworth, James Shaver, Canadian clergyman and political leader, *Obit* May 1942

Woodward, Arthur Smith, British paleontologist, *Obit* Oct 1944

Woodward, Bob, American journalist, Nov 1976

Woodward, C. Vann, American historian, May 1986, *Obit* June 2000

Woodward, Joanne, American actress, June 1958

Woodward, R. B., American biochemist, Feb 1952, *Obit* Sept 1979

Woodward, Robert F., diplomat, Yrbk 1962, *Obit* Yrbk 2001

Woodward, Stanley, diplomat, June 1951, *Obit* Oct 1992

Wooldridge, Dean Everett, American physicist and electronics engineer, Apr 1958, *Obit* Yrbk 2007

Woolf, Leonard, English political essayist, editor, publisher and memoirist, Yrbk 1965, *Obit* Oct 1969

Woolf, Virginia, English novelist, *Obit* May 1941

Woollcott, Alexander, journalist, June 1941, *Obit* Mar 1943

Woollen, Evans, Yrbk 1948, *Obit* Apr 1959

Woolley, Leonard, English archaeologist, Yrbk 1954, *Obit* Apr 1960

Woolley, Mary E., Mar 1942, *Obit* Nov 1947

Woolley, Monty, July 1940, *Obit* June 1963

Woolton, Frederick James Marquis, English financier, Oct 1940, Oct 1950, *Obit* Feb 1965

Wootton, Barbara, British sociologist, Feb 1964

Worcester, J. R., *Obit* June 1943

Worden, Edward Chauncey, *Obit* Nov 1940

Work, Hubert, physician and secretary of the interior, *Obit* Feb 1943

Work, Martin H., May 1951

Worner, Manfred, German cabinet member and NATO official, Oct 1988, *Obit* Oct 1994

Worsham, Lew, golfer, Jan 1954, *Obit* Jan 1991

Worsley, Frank Arthur, New Zealand ship captain and explorer, *Obit* Mar 1943

Worth, Irene, American actress, May 1968, *Obit* Aug 2002

Worthington, Leslie B., steel executive, Oct 1960, *Obit* Oct 1998

Wouk, Herman, American novelist and playwright, Yrbk 1952

Wowereit, Klaus, German mayor, Jan 2002

Wozniak, Stephen, American electronics industry executive, July 1997

Wray, John, *Obit* May 1940

Wren, P. C., English historical novelist, *Obit* Jan 1942

Wright, Anna Rose, author, Yrbk 1952

Wright, Benjamin Fletcher, professors of government and college president, July 1955, *Obit* Mar 1977

Wright, Berlin H., *Obit* Jan 1941

Wright, David, American baseball player, May 2009

Wright, Fielding, American governor, Sept 1948, *Obit* July 1956

Wright, Frank Lloyd, American architect, Jan 1941, Nov 1952, *Obit* June 1959

Wright, Harold Bell, American clergyman and novelist, *Obit* July 1944

Wright, Helen, astronomer, Mar 1956, *Obit* Feb 1998

Wright, Huntley, *Obit* Sept 1941

Wright, Irving S., professor of medicine, Oct 1968, *Obit* Mar 1998

Wright, Jane Cooke, American physician, May 1968, *Obit* Yrbk 2013

Wright, Jeffrey, American actor, May 2002

Wright, Jerauld, American admiral and diplomat, Feb 1955, *Obit* July 1995

Wright, Jim, American Speaker of the House, Apr 1979

Wright, John J., Feb 1963, *Obit* Oct 1979

Wright, Louis B., historian and librarian, Nov 1950, *Obit* June 1984

Wright, Loyd, July 1955, *Obit* Jan 1975

Wright, Martha, American singer and actress, Feb 1955

Wright, Michael, British diplomat, July 1961

Wright, Mickey, American golfer, Jan 1965

Wright, Orville, American aviation pioneer, Oct 1946, *Obit* Mar 1948

Wright, Peter, British intelligence official, Feb 1988, *Obit* July 1995

Wright, Quincy, American political scientist, Oct 1943, *Obit* Yrbk 1970

Wright, Richard, American novelist, Mar 1940, *Obit* Jan 1961

Wright, Robert Alderson Wright, July 1945, *Obit* Sept 1964

Wright, Robert Charles, American television executive, Jan 1989

Wright, Russel, American industrial designer, Sept 1940, Yrbk 1950, *Obit* Mar 1977

Wright, Steven, American comedian, May 2003

Wright, Teresa, American actress, May 1943, *Obit* Yrbk 2005

Wright, Theodore P., Nov 1945, *Obit* Nov 1970

Wright, Will, American computer game designer, Feb 2004

Wright, Winky, American boxer, July 2004

Wrigley, Philip Knight, baseball executive, Apr 1975, *Obit* June 1977

Wrinch, Dorothy, Anglo-American biochemist and mathematician, July 1947

Wriston, Henry M., May 1952, *Obit* May 1978

Wriston, Walter B., American banker, Nov 1977, *Obit* Aug 2005

Wrong, Hume, Oct 1950, *Obit* Mar 1954

Wu Chuntao, Chinese journalist, Jan 2005

Wu Man, Chinese pipa player, Jan 2007

Wu Yi, Chinese government official, Jan 2005

Wu Yifang, Chinese educator and feminist, Aug 1945, *Obit* Jan 1986

Wu, Chien Shiung, Chinese-American physicist, Oct 1959, *Obit* Apr 1997

Wu, Gordon, Chinese real estate developer, Aug 1996

Wu, Harry, Chinese-American human rights activist, Feb 1995

Wu, Kuo-Cheng, Chinese government official, Feb 1953, *Obit* Aug 1984

Wuorinen, Charles, American composer, Apr 1972

Wurf, Jerry, American labor leader, June 1979, *Obit* Feb 1982

Wurster, William Wilson, architect, Nov 1946, *Obit* Nov 1973

Wuthrich, Kurt, Swiss chemist, Jan 2007

Wyatt, Jane, American actress, May 1957, *Obit* Yrbk 2006

Wyatt, Whit, baseball player, coach and manager, Nov 1941, *Obit* Nov 1999

Wyatt, Wilson W., American government official, lawyer and civic leader, Mar 1946, *Obit* Aug 1996

Wyeth, Andrew, American painter, Apr 1955, Nov 1981, *Obit* Yrbk 2009

Wyeth, Jamie, American painter, Jan 1977

Wyeth, N. C., American painter and illustrator, *Obit* Nov 1945

Wylde, Zakk, American rock guitarist and songwriter, Oct 2004

Wyler, William, American film director, Jan 1951, *Obit* Sept 1981

Wylie, Max, Jan 1940, *Obit* Nov 1975

Wyman, Jane, American actress, Mar 1949, *Obit* Yrbk 2007

Wyman, Thomas, American radio and television executive, June 1983, *Obit* Yrbk 2003

Wynder, Ernst L., American oncologist and foundation official, Nov 1974, *Obit* Sept 1999

Wyner, Yehudi, American composer, conductor and pianist, Apr 2008

Wynette, Tammy, American country singer, June 1995, *Obit* June 1998

Wynkoop, Asa, *Obit* Yrbk 1942

Wynn, Ed, comedian, Jan 1945, *Obit* July 1966

Wynonna, American country singer, May 1996

Wyszynski, Stefan, Jan 1958, *Obit* July 1981

X

Xenakis, Iannis, Greek composer, Sept 1994, *Obit* July 2001

Xie Jin, Chinese film director, Jan 2003

Xie Xingfang, Chinese badminton player, Jan 2007

Xu Jinglei, Chinese actress and filmmaker, Jan 2007

Xu Wenli, Chinese dissident, Jan 2003

Y

Yadin, Yigael, Israeli archaeologist, general and political leader, Feb 1966, *Obit* Aug 1984

Yaffe, James, Yrbk 1957

Yagudin, Aleksei, Russian figure skater, Feb 2004

Yahya Khan, A. M., Jan 1971, *Obit* Oct 1980

Yalow, Rosalyn S., American medical physicist, July 1978, *Obit* Yrbk 2011

Yamaguchi, Kristi, American figure skater, June 1992

Yamamoto, Isoroku, Japanese admiral, Feb 1942, *Obit* July 1943

Yamamoto, Yohji, Japanese fashion designer, Nov 2000

Yamamura, Koji, Japanese animator, Jan 2003

Yamanaka, Lois-Ann, American novelist and poet, June 1999

Yamanaka, Shinya, Japanese geneticist, June 2013

Yamani, Ahmed Zaki, Saudi Arabian cabinet member, Sept 1975

Yamasaki, Minoru, American architect, Mar 1962, *Obit* Apr 1986

YamashitaYukiko, Developmental biologist, Mar 2012

Yamut, Nuri, May 1952

Yancey, Lewis Alonzo, *Obit* Jan 1940

Yang Fuxi, Chinese bow and arrow maker, Jan 2007

Yang Lan, Chinese talk show host, Jan 2003

Yang Liwei, Chinese astronaut, Jan 2004

Yang, Chen-ning, Chinese-American physicist, Nov 1958

Yang, Jerry, American Internet search engine executive, Oct 1997

Yang, You Chan, Feb 1953

Yankelovich, Daniel, American sociologist, Mar 1982

Yankovic, Al, American rock music parodist, Feb 1999

Yanni, Greek composer, Jan 2003

Yao Bin, Chinese figure skating coach, Jan 2006

Yao Ming, Chinese basketball player, Jan 2002

Yar'Adua, Umaru Musa, Nigerian president, Jan 2007, *Obit* Yrbk 2010

Yarborough, Cale, American automobile racing driver, Jan 1987

Yarborough, Ralph W., American senator, Feb 1960, *Obit* Apr 1996

Yard, Molly, American feminist and social activist, Nov 1988, *Obit* Apr 2006

Yardley, Jonathan, American literary critic and columnist, Jan 2011

Yarmolinsky, Adam, American law professor and government official, Mar 1969, *Obit* June 2000

Yaroslavski, Emel'yan Mikhailovich, Soviet

communist leader, *Obit* Jan 1944

Yarrow, William, *Obit* June 1941

Yashin, Alexei, Russian hockey player, Jan 2003

Yassin, Ahmed, Palestinian Islamic leader, July 1998, *Obit* Yrbk 2004

Yastrzemski, Carl, American baseball player, May 1968

Yates, David, British film director, Apr 2011

Yates, Donald N., air force general and meteorologist, May 1958

Yates, Elizabeth, American children's author, Yrbk 1948, *Obit* Nov 2001

Yates, Herbert J., July 1949, *Obit* Mar 1966

Yates, Sidney, American congressman, Aug 1993, *Obit* Jan 2001

Yauch, Adam, American rapper and bassist, *Obit* Yrbk 2012

Yazbek, Samar, Aug 2013

Ybarra, Thomas Russell, journalist and biographer, Jan 1940

Ydigoras Fuentes, Miguel, Nov 1958

Yeager, Chuck, American test pilot and air force general, May 1954

Yeager, Jeana, aviator, May 1987

Yeakley, Marjory Hall, Yrbk 1957

Yeang, Ken, Malaysian architect, Jan 2007

Yearwood, Trisha, American country singer, July 1998

Yeats-Brown, Francis, British army officer and author, *Obit* Feb 1945

Yegorov, Boris, Soviet astronaut and physician, Mar 1968, *Obit* Nov 1994

Yeh, George K. C., Mar 1953, *Obit* Jan 1982

Yellin, Samuel, American metalsmith, *Obit* Nov 1940

Yeltsin, Boris, Russian president, Jan 1989, *Obit* June 2007

Yen, Y. C. James, Chinese educator, July 1946, *Obit* Mar 1990

Yeoh, Michelle, Chinese actress, Jan 1998

Yepes, Narciso, Spanish guitarist, Oct 1966, *Obit* July 1997

Yerby, Frank, American novelist and short story writer, Sept 1946, *Obit* Mar 1992

Yergan, Max, American civil rights activist, Sept 1948, *Obit* June 1975

Yergin, Daniel, American energy consultant and business writer, Nov 1999

Yerushalmy, Jacob, Mar 1958

Yessa, Abdel Nasser, Mauritanian anti-slavery activist, Jan 2006

Yeutter, Clayton K., American Secretary of agriculture and political leader, July 1988

Yevtushenko, Yevgeny Aleksandrovich, Russian poet, Feb 1963, Mar 1994

Yingluck Shinawatra, Thai prime minister, Oct 2011

Yoakam, Dwight, American country singer, Nov 2000

Yoder, Albert Henry, *Obit* Nov 1940

Yokich, Stephen P., American labor leader, Nov 1998, *Obit* Yrbk 2002

Yon, Pietro A., Italian-American organist and composer, *Obit* Jan 1944

Yonai, Mitsumasa, Jan 1940, *Obit* June 1948

York, Herbert F., American physicist, Yrbk 1958, *Obit* Yrbk 2009

York, Michael, English actor, Apr 1976

Yorke, Oswald, *Obit* Mar 1943

Yorke, Thom, Scottish singer, June 2001

Yorty, Sam, American mayor, Jan 1967, *Obit* Aug 1998

Yoshida, Shigeru, Japanese statesman, Sept 1946, *Obit* Jan 1968

Yoshihara, Yoshindo, Japanese swordsmith, Jan 2005

Yoshimura, Junzo, Japanese architect, May 1956

Yoshimura, Yumi, Japanese pop singer, Jan 2005

Yoshino, Hiroyuki, Japanese automobile executive, Jan 2002

Yost, Charles Woodruff, American diplomat, Mar 1959, *Obit* July 1981

Yost, Fielding Harris, *Obit* Oct 1946

Youlou, Fulbert, Congolese political leader, Yrbk 1962, *Obit* June 1972

Youmans, Vincent, composer, Apr 1944, *Obit* May 1946

Young, Alan, Anglo-Canadian actor, June 1953

Young, Andrew, American congressman, diplomat and mayor, Apr 1977

Young, Angus, Scottish guitarist, Mar 2005

Young, Art, cartoonist, Feb 1940, *Obit* Feb 1944

Young, Charles Jac, *Obit* Apr 1940

Young, Coleman, American mayor, Sept 1977, *Obit* Feb 1998

Young, Frank E., microbiologist, educator and government official, Oct 1989

Young, Hugh, American surgeon and urologist, *Obit* Sept 1945

Young, John, American astronaut, June 1965

Young, John A., computer executive, Oct 1986

Young, Joseph Louis, American sculptor and muralist, July 1960

Young, Karl, *Obit* Jan 1944

Young, Kimberly S., American psychologist, Jan 2006

Young, Loretta, American actress, Mar 1948, *Obit* Nov 2000

Young, Malcolm, Scottish guitarist, Mar 2005

Young, Marian, June 1952, *Obit* Jan 1974

Young, Milton R., American senator, Yrbk 1954, *Obit* July 1983

Young, Neil, Canadian rock singer and guitarist, Feb 1980, Jan 1998

Young, Owen D., lawyer and manufacturing executive, Aug 1945, *Obit* Sept 1962

Young, Philip, government official and college dean, Yrbk 1951, *Obit* Mar 1987

Young, Robert, actor, July 1950, *Obit* Sept 1998

Young, Robert Ralph, railroad executive, Apr 1947, *Obit* Mar 1958

Young, Rose, *Obit* Sept 1941

Young, Sheila, American cyclist and speed skater, Jan 1977

Young, Stanley, dramatist and publishing executive, Yrbk 1951, *Obit* May 1975

Young, Stephen M., American senator, Oct 1959, *Obit* Feb 1985

Young, Steve, American football player, Oct 1993

Young, Whitney Moore, American civil rights leader, Apr 1965, *Obit* Apr 1971

Youngdahl, Luther W., Mar 1948, *Obit* Aug 1978

Younger, Kenneth Gilmour, Sept 1950

Youngerman, Jack, painter, Nov 1986

Younghusband, Francis Edward, British diplomat and explorer, *Obit* Sept 1942

Youngman, Henny, comedian, Oct 1986, *Obit* May 1998

Yount, Robin, baseball player, June 1993

Yourcenar, Marguerite, French-American novelist, poet, dramatist, essayist and translator, Nov 1982, *Obit* Feb 1988

Youskevitch, Igor, Ukrainian-American ballet dancer and master, Feb 1956, *Obit* Aug 1994

Yu, Ronny, Chinese motion picture director, Jan 2004

Yuan Longping, Chinese agriculturist, Jan 2005

Yudhoyono, Susilo Bambang, Indonesian president, Jan 2005

Yuen, Cory, Chinese actor and motion picture director, Jan 2004

Yuen, Wo-ping, Chinese martial artist and motion picture stunt choreographer, Jan 2008

Yuh Nelson, Jennifer, Korean-American animator and film director, Nov 2013

Yui, O. K., May 1955, *Obit* Sept 1960

Yukawa, Hideki, Japanese physicist, Jan 1950, *Obit* Nov 1981

Yun, Jong Yong, Korean electronics industry executive, Jan 2003

Yunus, Muhammad, Bangladeshi banker and economist, Jan 2002

Yushchenko, Viktor, Ukrainian president, Jan 2005

Yust, Walter, Apr 1943, *Obit* Apr 1960

Yusuf, Hamza, American Islamic leader, Mar 2007

Z

ZaBach, Florian, Yrbk 1955

Zabaleta, Nicanor, June 1971

Zablocki, Clement, American congressman, June 1958, June 1983, *Obit* Jan 1984

Zacharias, Ellis M., American admiral and intelligence official, Mar 1949, *Obit* Oct 1961

Zacharias, Jerrold R., physicist, Feb 1964, *Obit* Sept 1986

Zadkine, Ossip, Russian sculptor, Mar 1957, *Obit* Jan 1968

Zaentz, Saul, American recording executive and motion picture producer, Mar 1997

Zagat, Nina, American restaurant survey publisher, Mar 2008

Zagat, Tim, American restaurant survey publisher, Mar 2008

Zaharias, Babe Didrikson, American track athlete and golfer, Apr 1947, *Obit* Yrbk 1956

Zahedi, Fazlollah, Feb 1954, *Obit* Nov 1963

Zahn, Paula, American television newscaster, Feb 2002

Zail Singh, Indian president, Sept 1987, *Obit* Mar 1995

Zaillian, Steven, screenwriter and film director, Oct 2001

Zajick, Dolora, American opera singer and teacher, May 2000

Zakaria, Fareed, Indian-American political scientist and journalist, Jan 2003

Zambello, Francesca, American opera director, May 2003

Zamora, Daisy, Nicaraguan poet, Jan 2004

Zamora, Ruben, Salvadoran rebel leader, Sept 1991

Zana, Leyla, Kurdish member of Turkish parliament and political prisoner, Jan 2004

Zander, Arnold S., Oct 1947, *Obit* Sept 1975

Zandi, Mark M., American economist, May 2010

Zandonai, Riccardo, Italian composer, *Obit* Aug 1944

Zanuck, Darryl F., American motion picture producer, Aug 1941, Mar 1954, *Obit* Feb 1980

Zao, Wou-ki, French painter, *Obit* Yrbk 2013

Zapf, Hermann, German typographer and calligrapher, Jan 1965

Zapotocky, Antonin, June 1953, *Obit* Jan 1958

Zappa, Frank, American rock guitarist, Feb 1990, *Obit* Feb 1994

Zarb, Frank G., American securities exchange official, Sept 1975

Zardari, Asif Ali, Pakistani president, Jan 2009

Zarubin, Georgi N., Apr 1953, *Obit* Jan 1959

Zatopek, Emil, Czech runner, Apr 1953, *Obit* Feb 2001

Zeckendorf, William, real estate executive, Mar 1952, *Obit* Nov 1976

Zedillo Ponce de Leon, Ernesto, Mexican president, Apr 1996

Zeeland, Paul van, Mar 1950

Zeeman, Pieter, Dutch physicist, *Obit* Yrbk 1943

Zeffirelli, Franco, Italian director and set designer, Yrbk 1964

Zeidler, Carl F., July 1940, *Obit* Feb 1943

Zeineddine, Farid, Feb 1957

Zell, Samuel, American real estate investor, Jan 2009

Zellerbach, J. D., Yrbk 1948, *Obit* Nov 1963

Zellweger, Renee, American actress, Feb 2004

Zelnick, Strauss, American financier, Nov 2010

Zelomek, A. Wilbert, Yrbk 1956

Zemeckis, Robert, American motion picture director, Sept 1997

Zemlinsky, Alexander von, Austrian composer and conductor, *Obit* May 1942

Zen, Joseph, Chinese bishop, Jan 2005

Zennstrom, Niklas, Swedish computer software engineer and executive, Jan 2007

Zenos, Andrew C., *Obit* Mar 1942

Zerbe, Karl, Feb 1959, *Obit* Jan 1973

Zerhouni, Elias A., Algerian-American radiologist and public health official, Oct 2003

Zernike, Frits, Dutch physicist, Feb 1955, *Obit* Apr 1966

Zeta-Jones, Catherine, Welsh actress, Apr 2003

Zetsche, Dieter, German automobile executive, Jan 2006

Zevin, Ben David, publisher, Sept 1943, *Obit* Feb 1985

Zhang Ning, Chinese badminton player, Jan 2003

Zhang Xiaogang, Chinese painter, Jan 2005

Zhang Xin, Chinese real estate developer, Jan 2006

Zhang Yimou, Chinese film director, Aug 1992, Jan 2003

Zhang Ziyi, Chinese actress, Jan 2005

Zhao Ziyang, Chinese prime minister, June 1984, *Obit* Yrbk 2005

Zhirinovsky, Vladimir, Russian political leader, Nov 1995

Zhivkov, Todor, Bulgarian communist leader, Jan 1976, *Obit* Oct 1998

Zhou Enlai, Chinese prime minister and diplomat, Sept 1946, July 1957, *Obit* Feb 1976

Zhou Hai, Chinese photographer, Jan 2003

Zhou Xiaochuan, Chinese banker, Jan 2003

Zhu De, Chinese general, Nov 1942, *Obit* Aug 1976

Zhu Rongji, Chinese prime minister, July 2001

Zhukov, Georgii Aleksandrovich, Soviet journalist, Oct 1960

Zhukov, Georgii Konstantinovich, Soviet field marshal, Feb 1942, Apr 1955, *Obit* Sept 1974

Zia-ul-Haq, Mohammad, Pakistani general and president, June 1980, *Obit* Sept 1988

Zidane, Zinedine, Algerian-French soccer player, Jan 2002

Ziegler, Jean, Swiss sociologist, socialist leader and human rights activist, July 2010

Ziegler, Ronald L., American drug store association executive and presidential press secretary, Nov 1971, *Obit* July 2003

Ziemer, Gregor, Apr 1942

Ziff, William B., American magazine executive, Oct 1946, *Obit* Feb 1954

Zilboorg, Gregory, psychiatrist, Sept 1941, *Obit* Nov 1959

Zim, Herbert S., American educator and science writer, Sept 1956, *Obit* Feb 1995

Zimbalist, Efrem, American violinist, Mar 1949, *Obit* Apr 1985

Zimbalist, Efrem, American actor, Feb 1960

Zimmer, Carl, American science journalist, Oct 2012

Zimmer, Hans, German composer, Mar 2002

Zimmer, Heinrich Robert, German Indologist, *Obit* May 1943

Zimmerman, M. M., July 1957

Zimmermann, Arthur, German diplomat, *Obit* July 1940

Zindel, Paul, American dramatist, novelist and children's author, June 1973, *Obit* Yrbk 2007

Zinn, Howard, American historian, Aug 1999, *Obit* Yrbk 2010

Zinn, Walter H., nuclear physicist, Yrbk 1955, *Obit* Aug 2000

Zinnemann, Fred, motion picture director, Mar 1953, *Obit* June 1997

Zinni, Anthony, American Marine corps general and diplomat, May 2002

Zinsser, Hans, American bacteriologist, *Obit* Oct 1940

Zirato, Bruno, Yrbk 1959, *Obit* Jan 1973

Ziskin, Laura, American film producer, Oct 1997, *Obit* Yrbk 2011

Zito, Barry, American baseball player, July 2004

Zittel, Andrea, American installation artist, Aug 2006

Zizek, Slavoj, Slovenian philosopher, Jan 2004

Zoellick, Robert, American diplomat and international organiztation official, July 2008

Zog, Aug 1944, *Obit* June 1961

Zola, South African rapper, Jan 2004

Zoli, Adone, Mar 1958, *Obit* Apr 1960

Zollar, Jawole Willa Jo, American dancer and performance artist, July 2003

Zolotow, Maurice, author, May 1957, *Obit* May 1991

Zook, George F., Feb 1946, *Obit* Oct 1951

Zorach, William, American sculptor and painter, Feb 1943, Feb 1963, *Obit* Jan 1967

Zorbaugh, Geraldine Bone, lawyer and broadcasting executive, Yrbk 1956, *Obit* Sept 1996

Zorin, Valerian A., Soviet diplomat and United Nations official, Mar 1953, *Obit* Mar 1986

Zorina, Vera, German-American ballet dancer and actress, Jan 1941, *Obit* Yrbk 2003

Zorlu, Fatin Ruchstu, Turkish diplomat, Yrbk 1958, *Obit* Nov 1961

Zorn, John, American saxophonist, composer and conductor, Aug 1999

Zorzi, Cristian, Italian cross-country skier, Jan 2006

Zsigmond, Vilmos, Hungarian-American cinematographer, Oct 1999

Zuberbuhler, Klaus, Swiss psychologist and primatologist, July 2010

Zubiria, Alberto F., Yrbk 1956

Zubrod, Charles Gordon, oncologist, Jan 1969, *Obit* July 1999

Zucker, Jeff, American motion picture and television executive, Jan 2002

Zuckerberg, Mark, American Internet executive, Jan 2008

Zuckerman, Mortimer B., American real estate developer and magazine and newspaper publisher, Jan 1990

Zuckerman, Solly Zuckerman, English scientist, July 1972, *Obit* May 1993

Zuckert, Eugene Martin, American Secretary of the air force, Apr 1952, *Obit* Yrbk 2000

Zukerman, Eugenia, American flutist and author, Jan 2004

Zukerman, Pinchas, Israeli violinist and conductor, Nov 1978

Zukor, Adolph, American motion picture executive, Mar 1950, *Obit* Aug 1976

Zulli, Floyd, Jan 1958, *Obit* Jan 1981

Zuloaga, Ignacio, Spanish art collector and painter, *Obit* Yrbk 1945

Zuma, Jacob, South African president, Jan 2006

Zumwalt, Elmo R., American admiral, June 1971, *Obit* June 2000

Zweig, Stefan, Austrian novelist, biographer and poet, *Obit* Apr 1942

Zwicky, Fritz, Swiss astronomer, Apr 1953, *Obit* Apr 1974

Zwilich, Ellen Taaffe, American composer, Jan 1986

Zworykin, Vladimir Kosma, American physicist, Yrbk 1949, *Obit* Sept 1982

Zyuganov, Gennady, Russian communist leader, Oct 1996

Profession Index

AIDS activists

Achmat, Zackie, South African AIDS activist, Jan 2003

Hu Jia, Chinese AIDS activist, Jan 2007

Kaleeba, Noerine, Ugandan AIDS activist and physiotherapist, Jan 2006

Kramer, Larry, American dramatist, Mar 1994

Pisani, Elizabeth, American AIDS activist, Aug 2010

Ruranga, Rubaramira, Ugandan army officer and AIDs activist, Jan 2006

Abolitionists

Messaoud, Boubacar, Mauritanian anti-slavery activist, Jan 2006

Yessa, Abdel Nasser, Mauritanian anti-slavery activist, Jan 2006

Accordionists

Baker, Phil, American comedian, accordionist and radio personality, Nov 1946, *Obit* Jan 1964

Hidalgo, David, American guitarist, singer and accordionist, Oct 2005

Linnell, John, American singer, songwriter and accordionist, Nov 1999

Parry, Richard Reed, Canadian instrumentalist, Jan 2007

Accountants

Abbell, Maxwell, American accountant and lawyer, July 1951, *Obit* Sept 1957

Andrews, T. Coleman, accountant and government official, Apr 1954

Blau, Bela, American theatrical producer, *Obit* Yrbk 1940

Brundage, Percival F., American accountant and government official, Apr 1957

Coppers, George H., May 1952

Franke, William B., Sept 1959, *Obit* Aug 1979

Harrington, Russell C., Apr 1956, *Obit* Oct 1971

Lasser, J. K., May 1946, *Obit* July 1954

Marples, Alfred Ernest Marples, May 1960

Martin, Thomas E., Mar 1956, *Obit* Sept 1971

Seidman, L. William, American government official and college dean, Sept 1976, *Obit* Yrbk 2009

Stans, Maurice H., American Secretary of commerce, Yrbk 1958, *Obit* June 1998

White, Frank, Yrbk 1950, *Obit* Jan 1980

Woertz, Patricia, American agribusiness executive, Mar 2007

Acrobats

Petit, Philippe, French aerialist, Sept 1988

Activists

Abernathy, Ralph D., American clergyman and civil rights leader, July 1968, *Obit* June 1990

Abiola, Hafsat, Nigerian dissident, Jan 2007

Achmat, Zackie, South African AIDS activist, Jan 2003

Acker, Achille van, Belgian prime minister, May 1958, *Obit* Sept 1975

Al-Mubarak, Massouma, Kuwaiti cabinet member, Jan 2005

Alinsky, Saul, American social activist, Nov 1968, *Obit* July 1972

Allen, Will, American urban farmer, Sept 2013

Almada, Martin, Paraguayan educator, lawyer and human rights activist, Jan 2004

Alvarado, Elvia, Honduran human rights activist, Jan 2004

Alvarez de Toledo, Luisa Isabel, Spanish novelist and social reformer, Apr 1972

Amal'rik, Andrei, Russian essayist and historian, Apr 1974, *Obit* Jan 1981

Amato, Giuliano, Italian prime minister, Sept 1993

Ambedkar, Bhimrao Ramji, Indian statesman and reformer, Nov 1951, *Obit* Feb 1957

Ameringer, Oscar, socialist leader, *Obit* Yrbk 1943

Angell, Norman, English journalist and pacifist, May 1948, *Obit* Yrbk 1967

Aristide, Jean-Bertrand, Haitian priest and president, May 1991

Armey, Richard K., American political activist and former congressman, June 1995

Assange, Julian, Australian computer hacker and political activist, Mar 2011

Attlee, C. R., British prime minister, May 1940, Feb 1947, *Obit* Yrbk 1967

Atyam, Angelina, Ugandan peace activist and children's rights advocate, Jan 2004

Aung San Suu Kyi, Burmese human rights activist, Feb 1992

Auriol, Vincent, French president, Mar 1947, *Obit* Feb 1966

Ayers, William, American educator, Apr 2009

Baden-Powell, Olave St. Clair, British girls association founder, May 1946

Balch, Emily Greene, American economist and pacifist, Jan 1947, *Obit* Mar 1961

Baldwin, Roger Nash, American civil rights leader, Jan 1940, *Obit* Oct 1981

Baldwin, William H., American public relations executive and civil rights activist, Nov 1945

Banda, Joyce, Malawian entrepreneur, educator and social activist, Apr 2013

Banks, Dennis, American Indian leader, June 1992

Barlow, Maude, Canadian environmentalist, Feb 2009

Bauer, Gary L., political activist, Jan 1999

Beard, Mary Ritter, historian and feminist, Mar 1941, *Obit* Yrbk 1959

Bearden, Bessye J., American political activist and civic leader, *Obit* Nov 1943

Beauvoir, Simone de, French novelist and philosopher, Jan 1973, *Obit* June 1986

Begtrup, Bodil, Danish diplomat and United Nations official, Sept 1946

Benn, Tony, British member of Parliament, June 1965, Nov 1982

Benson, Allan L., American socialist leader, *Obit* Oct 1940

Beregovoy, Pierre Eugene, French prime minister, Feb 1993, *Obit* Feb 1993

Bernardino, Minerva, Dominican feminist and diplomat, Mar 1950, *Obit* Nov 1998

Bernstein, Robert L., American publishing executive and human rights activist, July 1987

Berrigan, Daniel, American priest, poet and pacifist, Sept 1970

Berrigan, Philip, American peace activist, Feb 1976, *Obit* Mar 2003

Berry, Mary Frances, American historian, civil rights leader and government official, June 1999

Besteiro, Julian, Spanish socialist leader, *Obit* Nov 1940

Bethune, Mary Jane McLeod, American educator, Jan 1942, *Obit* July 1955

Bevan, Aneurin, British cabinet member, May 1943, *Obit* Oct 1960

Beveridge, William Henry Beveridge, British economist, Jan 1943, *Obit* May 1963

Bhave, Vinoba, Indian mystic and social reformer, Sept 1953, *Obit* Jan 1983

Bird, Caroline, July 1976

Blakeslee, Francis D., American clergyman, educator and prohibitionist, *Obit* Nov 1942

Blatch, Harriot Eaton Stanton, American suffratist, *Obit* Jan 1941

Blum, Leon, French statesman, Nov 1940, *Obit* May 1950

Blum, William, American journalist, May 2007

Boesak, Allan Aubrey, South African church official and human rights activist, Nov 1986

Bond, Julian, American civil rights leader, Yrbk 1969, July 2001

Bonner, Elena, Soviet physician and human rights activist, Apr 1987, *Obit* Yrbk 2011

Boulding, Kenneth Ewart, American economist and pacifist, Mar 1965, *Obit* May 1993

Bourne, St. Clair, American documentary filmmaker, June 2000, *Obit* Mar 2008

Bove, Jose, French farmer, Jan 2002

Boyd, Malcolm, American clergyman, gay rights activist and writer, Mar 1968

Brady, James S., American presidential press secretary and gun control activist, Oct 1991

Brady, Sarah, American gun control activist and wife of James S. Brady, Oct 1996

Brandt, Willy, German chancellor, June 1958, Yrbk 1973, *Obit* Nov 1992

Bravo, Ellen, feminist, Aug 1997

Breitmeyer, Philip, *Obit* Jan 1942

Bromley, Dorothy Dunbar, journalist and feminist, Apr 1946, *Obit* Feb 1986

Brown, Rita Mae, American novelist, poet, essayist and screenwriter, Sept 1986

Brown, Robert McAfee, American theologian and human rights activist, May 1965, *Obit* Nov 2001

Brownmiller, Susan, journalist and feminist, Jan 1978

Brueggemann, Ingar, German family planning advocate, Nov 2001

Bryant, Anita, American singer, Nov 1975

Bryce, Elizabeth Marion, *Obit* Jan 1940

Buckmaster, Henrietta, Yrbk 1946, *Obit* June 1983

Budenz, Louis F., American newspaper editor, June 1951, *Obit* June 1972

Buergenthal, Thomas, American judge and human rights activist, Jan 2009

Bukovskii, Vladimir Konstantinovich, Soviet dissident, Mar 1978

Burleigh, George William, *Obit* Apr 1940

Butts, Calvin O., American clergyman and civic leader, Feb 1999

Caldicott, Helen, American pediatrician and anti-nuclear activist, Oct 1983

Callaghan, James, British prime minister, Feb 1968, *Obit* Yrbk 2005

Cannon, James, bishop, *Obit* Nov 1944

Caras, Roger A., environmentalist, journalist and animal rights activist, Apr 1988, *Obit* July 2001

Carlsson, Ingvar, Swedish prime minister, Feb 1988

Carmody, John M., American mining executive, labor mediator and government official, May 1940, *Obit* Jan 1964

Carter, Majora, American community activist and conservationist, Oct 2007, May 2013

Carter, Rubin, American boxer and victim of false imprisonment, May 2000

Castle, Barbara, British socialist leader, Jan 1967, *Obit* Yrbk 2002

Catt, Carrie Chapman, American feminist and pacifist, Oct 1940, *Obit* Apr 1947

Chase, William Sheafe, *Obit* Sept 1940

Chavis, Benjamin F., American clergyman and civil rights leader, Jan 1994

Cheney, Liz, American lawyer, political activist and daughter of Vice-president Richard B. Cheney, Aug 2010

Childs, Richard Spencer, cleaning products industry executive and civic reformer, Sept 1955, *Obit* Jan 1979

Clark, Geoff, Australian boxer, football player and government official, Jan 2004

Clark, Ramsey, American Attorney general and political activist, Oct 1967

Clay, Laura, American suffragist, *Obit* Aug 1941

Cleaver, Eldridge, American civil rights leader, Mar 1970, *Obit* July 1998

Clement, Rufus E., American college president, June 1946, *Obit* Jan 1968

Clinchy, Everett R., religious leader, Apr 1941, *Obit* Mar 1986

Cockrell, Ewing, May 1951, *Obit* Apr 1962

Coffin, William Sloane, American clergyman and pacifist, July 1968, Apr 1980, *Obit* Yrbk 2006

Cohn-Bendit, Daniel, German political activist, Jan 2003

Colvin, Mamie White, Yrbk 1944, *Obit* Jan 1956

Connerly, Ward, American business consultant and anti-affirmative action activist, Nov 2000

Corrigan, Mairead, Irish pacifist, Apr 1978

Cousins, Norman, American magazine editor, writer and anti-nuclear activist, Aug 1943, Aug 1977, *Obit* Jan 1991

Craxi, Bettino, Italian prime minister, Feb 1984, *Obit* June 2000

Cresson, Edith, French prime minister, Sept 1991

Croome, Rodney, Australian gay rights activist, Jan 2004

Crossman, R. H. S., British socialist leader, May 1947, *Obit* June 1974

Cunningham-Agee, Mary, American electronics industry executive, Nov 1984

Curtin, John, Australian prime minister, July 1941, *Obit* Aug 1945

Cyrankiewicz, Jozef, Feb 1957

Dalton, Hugh Dalton, British cabinet member, Aug 1945, *Obit* Apr 1962

Davis, Angela Yvonne, American political activist, Nov 1972

Davis, Evelyn Y., American shareholders' rights activist, Oct 2007

Day, Dorothy, American journalist and social reformer, May 1962, *Obit* Jan 1981

Dees, Morris S., American lawyer, Jan 1995

Defferre, Gaston, French cabinet member, Sept 1967, *Obit* June 1986

Delanoe, Bertrand, French mayor, Jan 2002

Dellinger, David, American peace activist, Aug 1976, *Obit* Yrbk 2004

Deutsch, Julius, Nov 1944, *Obit* Mar 1968

Devi, Mahasweta, Feb 2012

Dhebar, Uchhrangrai Navalshankar, June 1955

Dillard, James Hardy, *Obit* Sept 1940

Dirie, Waris, Somali model and social activist, Jan 2005

Dobson, James C., American psychologist and social activist, Aug 1998

Doi, Takako, Japanese socialist leader, July 1992

Dolci, Danilo, Italian social reformer and author, Sept 1961, *Obit* Mar 1998

Douglas, Emory, American illustrator, cartoonist and social activist, Feb 2010

Du Bois, W. E. B., American sociologist, historian and novelist, Jan 1940, *Obit* Oct 1963

Dumas, Roland, French cabinet member, Oct 1990

Dworkin, Andrea, American feminist and writer, Oct 1994, *Obit* Yrbk 2005

Edelman, Marian Wright, American children's rights advocate, Sept 1992

Edey, Birdsall Otis, *Obit* Aug 1940

Ehrenreich, Barbara, American feminist and social critic, Mar 1995

Eichelberger, Clark M., Jan 1947, *Obit* Mar 1980

Elijah Muhammad, American Black Muslim leader, Jan 1971, *Obit* Apr 1975

Elliott, John Lovejoy, social reformer, *Obit* June 1942

Ellis, Ruth, American gay rights activist, *Obit* Apr 2000, Sept 2000

Ellsberg, Daniel, American peace activist, Yrbk 1973

Ernst, Morris, American lawyer and civil rights activist, Aug 1940, Feb 1961, *Obit* July 1976

Evans, Anne, *Obit* Feb 1941

Evatt, Herbert Vere, Australian statesman, May 1942, *Obit* Jan 1966

Evers, Charles, American civil rights activist, mayor and brother of Medgar Evers, Apr 1969

Evers-Williams, Myrlie, civil rights leader and wife of Medgar Wiley Evers, Aug 1995

Fabius, Laurent, French political leader, Feb 1985

Faludi, Susan, American journalist and feminist, Feb 1993

Fang Lizhi, Chinese astrophysicist, Nov 1989, *Obit* Yrbk 2012

Farmer, James, American civil rights leader, Feb 1964, *Obit* Sept 1999

Farmer, Paul, American physician, Feb 2004

Farmer-Paellmann, Deadria, American activist seeking reparations for slavery, Mar 2004

Feldt, Gloria A., American birth control advocate, July 2000

Fierstein, Harvey, American dramatist and actor, Feb 1984

Figueroa, Ana, Chilean educator, diplomat and feminist, Feb 1952

Fischer, Carlos L., Feb 1959

Fleming, Amalia Koutsouri, Greek legislator, Nov 1972, *Obit* Apr 1986

Fletcher, Arthur Allen, American civil rights leader and government official, Nov 1971, *Obit* Yrbk 2005

Foot, Michael, British political leader, Yrbk 1950, May 1981, *Obit* Yrbk 2010

Fornos, Werner H., demographer and social reformer, July 1993

French, Paul Comly, May 1951, *Obit* Sept 1960

Friedan, Betty, American feminist, Nov 1970, Mar 1989, *Obit* May 2006

Friedman, Kinky, American country singer, band leader, songwriter and mystery novelist, Feb 2012

Fulani, Lenora, American psychologist and political activist, Mar 2000

Gaitskell, Hugh, British cabinet member, June 1950, *Obit* Feb 1963

Gandhi, Mahatma, Indian nationalist leader, Yrbk 1942, *Obit* Feb 1948

Gandy, Kim A., American feminist, Oct 2001

Gao Zhisheng, Chinese lawyer and dissident, Jan 2007

Garrison, Lloyd Kirkham, lawyer and reformer, June 1947, *Obit* Nov 1991

Garvey, Marcus, Jamaican-American civil rights activist, *Obit* Aug 1940

Gbowee, Leymah, Liberian peace activist, Oct 2012

Geldof, Bob, Irish rock musician and humanitarian, Mar 1986

George, Albert Bailey, *Obit* Apr 1940

Giri, V. Mohini, Indian social activist, Jan 2007

Giroud, Francoise, French journalist and cabinet member, Apr 1975, *Obit* July 2003

Glasser, Ira, American civil rights activist, Jan 1986

Goldman, Emma, American anarchist, *Obit* Jan 1940

Gonzalez, Felipe, Spanish prime minister, Jan 1978

Goodman, Paul, American poet, novelist, essayist and dramatist, June 1968, *Obit* Oct 1972

Gordon, Bruce, American civil rights organization official, Oct 2005

Graham, Frank Porter, college president and civil rights leader, May 1941, July 1951, *Obit* Apr 1972

Graham, Gwethalyn, Canadian novelist, Jan 1945, *Obit* Jan 1966

Grand, Sarah, English novelist and feminist, *Obit* July 1943

Granger, Lester Blackwell, civil rights leader, Apr 1946, *Obit* Mar 1976

Greeley, Dana McLean, clergyman, civil rights leader and pacifist, Mar 1964, *Obit* Aug 1986

Greenwood, Arthur, Oct 1940, *Obit* Sept 1954

Greer, Germaine, Australian feminist and writer, Nov 1971, Oct 1988

Gregory, Dick, American comedian, author and civil rights leader, June 1962

Guinier, Lani, American law teacher and civil rights activist, Jan 2004

Hakim, Christine, Indonesian actress and social activist, Jan 2003

Harden, Cecil Murray, congresswoman, Feb 1949, *Obit* Feb 1985

Hartmann, Heidi I., American economist and feminist, Apr 2003

Haslett, Caroline, English feminist and electrical engineer, Oct 1950, *Obit* Mar 1957

Hay, Regina Deem, July 1948

Hayden, Tom, American state legislator and social activist, Apr 1976

Haynes, George Edmund, American civil rights leader and economist, Mar 1946, *Obit* Apr 1960

Hays, Arthur Garfield, lawyer and civil rights leader, Sept 1942, *Obit* Feb 1955

Healey, Denis, British political leader, Yrbk 1971

Height, Dorothy I., American civil rights activist, Sept 1972, *Obit* July 2010

Hernandez, Aileen C., feminist, July 1971

Hewlett, Sylvia Ann, Welsh economist and feminist, Sept 2002

Heymann, Lida Gustava, *Obit* Sept 1943

Hickey, Margaret A., feminist and lawyer, Yrbk 1944, *Obit* Feb 1995

Hill, Herbert, American civil rights leader, Sept 1970, *Obit* Yrbk 2004

Hirsi Ali, Ayaan, Somali-Dutch feminist and member of Parliament, Jan 2003

Hite, Shere, author and feminist, Feb 1988

Hoffman, Abbie, American political activist, Apr 1981, *Obit* June 1989

Hollande, Fran±ois, French political leader, May 2013

Holmes, John Haynes, American clergyman, theologian and social reformer, Jan 1941, *Obit* May 1964

Holt, Hamilton, periodical editor, pacifist and college president, Yrbk 1947, *Obit* May 1951

Honkala, Cheri, American social activist, July 2012

Hooks, Benjamin L., American civil rights activist, lawyer and judge, Apr 1978, *Obit* Yrbk 2010

Hoopes, Darlington, socialist leader, Sept 1952, *Obit* Nov 1989

Houston, Charles Hamilton, American lawyer and civil rights leader, July 1948, *Obit* June 1950

Howe, Frederic Clemson, lawyer and reformer, *Obit* Sept 1940

Howorth, Lucy Somerville, American lawyer and feminist, Oct 1951, *Obit* Nov 1997

Hu Jia, Chinese AIDS activist, Jan 2007

Huerta, Dolores, American labor leader, Nov 1997

Hurd-Mead, Kate Campbell, *Obit* Feb 1941

Hyde, Henry J., American congressman, Oct 1989, *Obit* Yrbk 2008

Ibrahim, Hauwa, Nigerian lawyer and human rights activist, Jan 2004

Ibrahim, Saad Eddin, Egyptian sociologist and political dissident, Jan 2003

Innis, Roy, American civil rights leader, May 1969

Ireland, Patricia, American lawyer and feminist, June 1992

Jack, Homer Alexander, clergyman, pacifist and United Nations official, July 1961, *Obit* Oct 1993

Jackson, Jesse L., American clergyman and civil rights activist, Yrbk 1970, Jan 1986

Jacob, John E., civil rights leader, Feb 1986

Jahangir, Asma, Pakistani lawyer and feminist, Jan 2003

Jalal, Massouda, Afghan pediatrician, social activist and political leader, Jan 2002

Janeway, Elizabeth, American novelist and critic, Mar 1944, Obit Yrbk 2005

Jarvis, Howard, manufacturing executive and tax reform activist, Feb 1979, Obit Sept 1986

Jealous, Benjamin T., American civil rights organization official, Feb 2009

Johnson, Sonia, American feminist, Feb 1985

Johnson, William E., Obit Mar 1945

Jones, Elaine R., American lawyer, June 2004

Jones, Van, American lawyer, civil rights activist, environmentalist and presidential aide, Apr 2009

Jordan, Vernon, American civil rights leader and lawyer, Feb 1972, Aug 1993

Joseph, Ammu, Indian journalist and feminist, Jan 2004

Jospin, Lionel, French prime minister, June 2000

Joya, Malalai, Afghan human rights activist and member of Parliament, Jan 2007

Joyce, James Avery, English lawyer, author and pacifist, Mar 1959

Kaleeba, Noerine, Ugandan AIDS activist and physiotherapist, Jan 2006

Kamm, John, American chemical industry executive and human rights activist, Jan 2002

Karumba, Christine, Feb 2013

Katz, Jackson, American anti-sexism activist, July 2004

Katz, Label A., Apr 1960, Obit June 1975

Kebede, Liya, Ethiopian model and social activist, Jan 2005

Kerensky, Aleksandr Fyodorovich, Russian socialist leader, Yrbk 1966, Obit Sept 1970

Kevorkian, Jack, American pathologist and right to die advocate, Sept 1994, Obit Yrbk 2011

Khan, Begum Liaquat Ali, July 1950

Khan, Irene, Bangladeshi human rights activist, Jan 2002

King, Coretta Scott, American civil rights leader, May 1969, Obit Apr 2006

King, Martin Luther, American clergyman and civil rights leader, May 1957, May 1965, Obit May 1968

Kinnock, Neil, British political leader and European Commission official, Apr 1984

Klein, Naomi, Canadian journalist and social activist, Aug 2003

Kohout, Pavel, Czech author and dramatist, Feb 1988

Kollontai, A., Soviet diplomat, Oct 1943, Obit Apr 1952

Kovic, Ron, soldier and anti-war activist, Aug 1990

Kozol, Jonathan, American social critic, Jan 1986

Krag, Jens Otto, Danish prime minister, Oct 1962, Obit Aug 1978

Kramer, Larry, American dramatist, Mar 1994

Kreisky, Bruno, Austrian chancellor, Sept 1960, Obit Sept 1990

Krueger, Maynard C., May 1940

Kuhn, Maggie, American feminist and civil rights activist, July 1978, Obit July 1995

Kunstler, William, American lawyer, Apr 1971, Obit Nov 1995

La Follette, Charles M., Feb 1950

LaHaye, Tim F., American clergyman and theologian, June 2003

Lacoste, Robert, French socialist leader, Nov 1957

Lafontaine, Henri Marie, Belgian judge and pacifist, Obit July 1943

Lafontaine, Oskar, German political leader, Sept 1990

Lagos, Ricardo, Chilean president, Jan 2005

Lamont, Corliss, American philosopher, socialist and civil rights leader, June 1946, Obit July 1995

Langer, Felicia, Israeli lawyer and human rights activist, Jan 2004

Langton, Marcia, Australian anthropologist and human rights activist, Jan 2007

Lansbury, George, British socialist leader, Obit Jan 1940

Largo Caballero, Francisco, Spanish prime minister, Obit May 1946

Laski, Harold Joseph, British socialist leader and political scientist, Sept 1941, Obit Apr 1950

Lasn, Kalle, Estonian-Canadian environmentalist, Apr 2012

Lawes, Lewis Edward, American prison warden and reformer, Oct 1941, Obit Mar 1947

LeFrak, Samuel J., American builder, Jan 1970, Obit Yrbk 2003

Leary, Timothy, American psychologist, Yrbk 1970, Obit Aug 1996

Lee, Percy Maxim, American civic leader, July 1950, Obit Jan 2003

Lemkin, Raphael, American lawyer, May 1950, Obit Nov 1959

Levinson, Salmon Oliver, lawyer and pacifist, Obit Mar 1941

Lewis, John, American congressman, Sept 1980

Liu Binyan, Chinese journalist, Jan 2004, Obit CB Int 2006

Loram, Charles Templeman, Obit Sept 1940

Lowenstein, Allard K., American civil rights leader, pacifist and congressman, Sept 1971, Obit May 1980

Lowery, Joseph, American clergyman and civil rights leader, Nov 1982

Luthuli, Albert John, South African political leader, Feb 1962, Obit Oct 1967

Lynd, Staughton, American historian and lawyer, May 1983

MacKinnon, Catharine A., American lawyer and feminist, June 1994

Maddow, Rachel, American television and radio talk show host, Aug 2009

Mai, Mukhtar, Pakistani feminist, Jan 2006

Makiya, Kanan, Iraqi Middle Eastern studies specialist, Jan 2002

Malcolm, Ellen, American feminist and political activist, Feb 2010

Mam, Somaly, Cambodian social worker, June 2009

Mandela, Nelson, South African president, Jan 1984, Nov 1995

Manji, Irshad, Canadian author and broadcasting entrepreneur, Jan 2005

Marburg, Theodore, *Obit* Apr 1946

Marshall, Burke, American civil rights activist and government official, Feb 1965, *Obit* Yrbk 2003

Marshall, Thurgood, American Supreme Court justice, Nov 1954, Sept 1989, *Obit* Mar 1993

Martinez, Vilma, American lawyer and civil rights activist, July 2004

Marzotto, Gaetano, July 1953

Maung, Cynthia, Burmese physician, Jan 2003

Mauroy, Pierre, French prime minister, June 1982, *Obit* Yrbk 2013

Mayer, Daniel, French socialist leader, Nov 1949

Mayes, Rose Gorr, May 1950

Mayo, Katherine, American journalist and reformer, *Obit* Yrbk 1940

Mays, Benjamin Elijah, American civil rights leader and college president, May 1945, *Obit* May 1984

McCarthy, Carolyn, American congresswoman, Mar 1998

McKissick, Floyd B., American lawyer and civil rights leader, Jan 1968, *Obit* June 1991

Means, Russell, American Indian leader, Jan 1978, *Obit* Yrbk 2013

Mehta, Hansa, July 1947

Menchu, Rigoberta, Guatemalan human rights activist and memoirist, Oct 1993

Messaoud, Boubacar, Mauritanian anti-slavery activist, Jan 2006

Mfume, Kweisi, American civil rights leader, Jan 1996

Michelman, Kate, American abortion rights activist, Nov 2000

Mihajlov, Mihajlo, Yugoslav social and literary critic, Jan 1979, *Obit* Yrbk 2010

Miles, Tiya, American feminist, Oct 2012

Millar, Alexander Copeland, *Obit* Yrbk 1940

Millett, Kate, American feminist, artist and memoirist, Jan 1971, June 1995

Mintoff, Dom, Maltese prime minister, Mar 1984, *Obit* Yrbk 2012

Mitterrand, Francois, French president, Yrbk 1968, Oct 1982, *Obit* Mar 1996

Moch, Jules, French socialist leader and cabinet member, Oct 1950, *Obit* Nov 1985

Mohammed, Yanar, Iraqi feminist, Jan 2007

Mollet, Guy, French prime minister, Sept 1950, *Obit* Nov 1975

Mongella, Gertrude, Tanzanian member of Parliament, diplomat and feminist, Jan 2004

Moorland, Jesse Edward, American clergyman, *Obit* Jan 1940

Morial, Marc, American civil rights activist and former mayor, Jan 2002

Moses, Bob, American civil rights activist and mathematics teacher, Apr 2002

Motley, Constance Baker, American judge, May 1964, *Obit* Feb 2006

Mott, Stewart R., American philanthropist and political activist, Apr 1975, *Obit* Yrbk 2008

Moutet, Marius, French socialist leader and cabinet member, July 1947, *Obit* Yrbk 1968

Mufti, Hania, Jordanian human rights activist, Jan 2005

Murguia, Janet, American civil rights activist, Jan 2010

Muste, Abraham Johannes, American clergyman and pacifist, Oct 1965, *Obit* Apr 1967

Nabrit, James M., American lawyer, civil rights activist and university president, Jan 1961, *Obit* Mar 1998

Naidoo, Kumi, South African human rights activist and environmentalist, Sept 2010

Naidu, Sarojini, Indian feminist, poet and government official, May 1943, *Obit* Mar 1949

Namegabe, Chouchou, Congolese radio reporter, Apr 2012

Nasrin, Taslima, Bangladeshi poet, essayist, novelist and feminist, Jan 2003

Nearing, Scott, American sociologist and homesteader, Oct 1971, *Obit* Oct 1983

Neier, Aryeh, German-American civil rights leader, Nov 1978

Nenni, Pietro, Mar 1947, *Obit* Feb 1980

Neuhaus, Richard John, American priest, religious writer and political activist, June 1988, *Obit* Yrbk 2009

Newkirk, Ingrid, American animal rights activist, Apr 2008

Newton, Huey, American revolutionary, Feb 1973, *Obit* Oct 1989

Nobs, Ernst, Sept 1949, *Obit* June 1957

Noel-Baker, Philip John, British pacifist, Feb 1946, *Obit* Mar 1983

Norquist, Grover, American economist and tax reform lobbyist, Oct 2007

Norton, Eleanor Holmes, American civil rights leader and congresswoman, Nov 1976

Nour, Ayman, Egyptian member of Parliament, Jan 2005

O'Hair, Madalyn Murray, American atheist, Jan 1977, *Obit* June 2001

Okolloh, Ory, Kenyan lawyer and blogger, May 2012

Pacelle, Wayne, American animal rights activist, Jan 2010

Paglia, Camille, American feminist writer and critic, Aug 1992

Palme, Olof, Swedish prime minister, May 1970, *Obit* Apr 1986

Papandreou, Andreas, Greek prime minister, May 1970, Apr 1983, *Obit* Sept 1996

Parks, Rosa, American civil rights activist, May 1989, *Obit* Jan 2006

Parsons, Rose Peabody, feminist, Yrbk 1959, *Obit* June 1985

Patterson, Francine, American psychologist and animal rights activist, Nov 2000

Paul, Alice, American lawyer and feminist, Sept 1947, *Obit* Sept 1977

Paya, Oswaldo, Cuban dissident, Jan 2003, *Obit* Yrbk 2012

Payton, John, American lawyer and civil rights activist, May 2010, *Obit* Yrbk 2012

Pease, Charles G., *Obit* Yrbk 1941

Pemberton, John de J., American lawyer and civil rights activist, May 1969, *Obit* Yrbk 2010

Perez Esquivel, Adolfo, Argentine human rights activist, Mar 1981

Perkins, Charles, Australian aborigine leader, Jan 1969, *Obit* Feb 2001

Pethick-Lawrence, Frederick William, British socialist leader, June 1946, *Obit* Nov 1961

Phillips, Morgan, British socialist leader, Sept 1949, *Obit* Feb 1963

Piercy, Marge, American poet and novelist, Nov 1994

Pineau, Christian, French cabinet member, July 1956, *Obit* June 1995

Pirie, John Taylor, *Obit* Mar 1940

Pisani, Elizabeth, American AIDS activist, Aug 2010

Pogrebin, Letty Cottin, journalist and feminist, Nov 1997

Poinso-Chapuis, Germaine, French feminist, June 1948

Poling, Daniel A., Nov 1943, *Obit* Mar 1968

Possuelo, Sydney, Brazilian government official and human rights activist, Jan 2006

Power, Samantha, American human rights activist, Aug 2008

Pratt, Frederic Bayley, American college president, *Obit* June 1945

Prendergast, John, American human rights activist, Jan 2012

Prinz, Joachim, German-American rabbi and civil rights leader, Feb 1963, *Obit* Nov 1988

Protess, David, American journalist and social activist, Oct 1999

Quidde, Ludwig, German historian and pacifist, *Obit* Apr 1941

Rahmani, Taqi, Iranian writer, Jan 2005

Rama Rau, Dhanvanthi, Indian social welfare leader and feminist, Apr 1954, *Obit* Sept 1987

Ramadier, Paul, French prime minister, June 1947, *Obit* Yrbk 1961

Randolph, Asa Philip, American labor leader, May 1940, Oct 1951, *Obit* July 1979

Ras-Work, Berhane, Ethiopian human rights activist, Jan 2004

Rathbone, Eleanor, British feminist and member of Parliament, June 1943, *Obit* Feb 1946

Rau, Johannes, German president, Mar 1987, *Obit* Yrbk 2006

Rauh, Joseph L., American lawyer and civil rights leader, Apr 1965, *Obit* Nov 1992

Rauschning, Hermann, German-American political philosopher, May 1941, *Obit* Apr 1983

Redlener, Irwin, American pediatrician, Nov 2007

Reid, Ira De A., July 1946, *Obit* Oct 1968

Rice, Constance L., American lawyer and civil rights activist, Apr 2011

Richards, Ann, American governor, Feb 1991, *Obit* Yrbk 2007

Richards, Cecile, American family planning advocate, May 2007

Rifkin, Jeremy, American social activist and foundation official, Feb 1986

Roberts, Albert H., *Obit* July 1946

Robeson, Paul, American actor, civil rights activist and singer, Mar 1941, Mar 1976

Robinson, Randall, American lobbyist and civil rights leader, Sept 1998

Rocard, Michel, French prime minister, Oct 1988

Rockwell, Lew, American political commentator, June 2007

Rodriguez Zapatero, Jose Luis, Spanish prime minister, Jan 2004

Rodriguez, Cecilia, feminist and revolutionary, May 1999

Rodriguez, Nicolas, *Obit* Sept 1940

Roh, Moo Hyun, South Korean president, Jan 2003, *Obit* Yrbk 2009

Roosevelt, Eleanor, wife of American president Franklin D. Roosevelt and diplomat, Nov 1940, Jan 1949, *Obit* Jan 1963

Rotblat, Joseph, British physicist and pacifist, July 1997, *Obit* Feb 2006

Royal, Segolene, French political leader, Jan 2007

Ruiz Guinazu, Magdalena, Argentine journalist, Jan 2004

Rummel, Joseph F., American archbishop, June 1959, *Obit* Jan 1965

Ruranga, Rubaramira, Ugandan army officer and AIDs activist, Jan 2006

Russell, Charles Edward, American journalist, social reformer and biographer, *Obit* June 1941

Rustin, Bayard, American civil rights leader, June 1967, *Obit* Oct 1987

Sabato, Ernesto R., Argentine novelist, physicist and human rights activist, Oct 1985, *Obit* Yrbk 2011

Sadik, Nafis, Pakistani physician and United Nations official, Feb 1996

Sakharov, Andrei Dmitrievich, Russian physicist, July 1971, *Obit* Feb 1990

Sandefer, Jefferson Davis, *Obit* Apr 1940

Sanders, Bernard, American senator, June 1991

Sanger, Margaret, American family planning advocate, Aug 1944, *Obit* Nov 1966

Saragat, Giuseppe, Italian president, Yrbk 1956, July 1965, *Obit* July 1988

Satyarthi, Kailash, Indian social activist, Jan 2007

Scharf, Adolf, Oct 1957, *Obit* Apr 1965

Schiller, Karl, German cabinet member, Yrbk 1971, *Obit* Mar 1995

Schlafly, Phyllis, American social activist and writer, June 1978

Schmidt, Fritz, *Obit* Aug 1943

Schmidt, Helmut, German chancellor, Oct 1974

Schneiderman, Rose, labor leader and feminist, Feb 1946, *Obit* Oct 1972

Schroder, Gerhard, German chancellor, Nov 1998

Schumacher, Kurt, German socialist leader, Feb 1948, *Obit* Oct 1952

Scott, Michael, South African clergyman and human rights activist, Apr 1953, *Obit* Apr 1985

Searing, Annie E. P., *Obit* June 1942

Shafik, Doria, May 1955

Sharansky, Natan, Israeli cabinet member, Feb 1987

Sharpton, Al, American clergyman and political activist, Nov 1995

Sheehan, Cindy, American anti-war activist, May 2007

Shinwell, Emanuel Shinwell, British political leader, Jan 1943, *Obit* June 1986

Shiva, Vandana, Indian physicist and environmentalist, Jan 2002

Shriver, Eunice Kennedy, American social activist, July 1996, *Obit* Yrbk 2009

Sinclair, Upton, American novelist and socialist leader, Yrbk 1962, *Obit* Jan 1969

Sinyavsky, Andrei, Russian essayist, novelist and short story writer, July 1975, *Obit* May 1997

Sliwa, Curtis, American public safety group founder, Feb 1983

Smeal, Eleanor, American feminist, Mar 1980

Smith, Gerald L. K., American clergyman, lecturer and columnist, Aug 1943, *Obit* June 1976

Smith, Ida B. Wise, Feb 1943, *Obit* Apr 1952

Soares, Mario, Portuguese prime minister, Oct 1975

Solmonese, Joe, American gay rights activist, Oct 2009

Soukup, Frantisek, *Obit* Yrbk 1940

Spingarn, Arthur Barnett, lawyer and civil rights leader, Jan 1965, *Obit* Jan 1972

Spock, Benjamin, American pediatrician, Yrbk 1956, Nov 1969, *Obit* June 1998

Sporborg, Constance Amberg, Nov 1947, *Obit* Feb 1961

Spottswood, Stephen Gill, American bishop and civil rights leader, Apr 1962, *Obit* Jan 1975

Steinem, Gloria, American feminist and journalist, Mar 1972, Mar 1988

Stevenson, Bryan, lawyer and human rights activist, Mar 1996

Stoller, Debbie, American magazine editor and feminist, Aug 2007

Stone, Hannah M., physician and family planning advocate, *Obit* Sept 1941

Strachey, Evelyn John St. Loe, British cabinet member, June 1946, *Obit* Sept 1963

Straus, Jack Isidor, department store executive, Mar 1952, *Obit* Nov 1985

Strauss, Anna Lord, Nov 1945, *Obit* Apr 1979

Street, Jessie M. G., Australian feminist, Sept 1947

Strossen, Nadine, American lawyer and civil rights leader, Oct 1997

Sullivan, Leon Howard, American clergyman and civil rights leader, Mar 1969, *Obit* Sept 2001

Sung, Ching-ling, Chinese political leader and wife of stateman Sun Yat-sen, Apr 1944, *Obit* July 1981

Sutton, Percy E., American municipal official, broadcasting executive and civil rights activist, Mar 1973, *Obit* Yrbk 2010

Suzman, Helen, South African member of Parliament and human rights activist, Nov 1968, *Obit* Yrbk 2009

Tafel, Rich, American gay political activist, Feb 2000

Takirambudde, Peter, Ugandan human rights activist, Jan 2005

Taylor, Theodore B., American physicist, Apr 1976, *Obit* Feb 2005

Terrell, Mary Church, American feminist and civil rights leader, June 1942, *Obit* Oct 1954

Terry, Randall, American anti-abortion activist, Jan 1994

Tethong, Lhadon, Tibetan-Canadian human rights activist, Sept 2008

Thomas, Norman, American socialist leader, Sept 1944, July 1962, *Obit* Feb 1969

Tijerina, Reies Lopez, American political activist, July 1971

Tin Moe, Burmese poet and children's author, Jan 2004

Tobias, Channing H., July 1945, *Obit* Jan 1962

Tolar, Dagga, Nigerian poet, singer and social activist, Jan 2007

Tree, Marietta, United Nations official and city planner, Yrbk 1961, *Obit* Oct 1991

Tridish, Pete, American pirate radio broadcaster and social activist, Apr 2004

Tull, Tanya, American social services organization official, Nov 2004

Ture, Kwame, American civil rights leader, Apr 1970, *Obit* Feb 1999

Tutu, Desmond, South African archbishop, Jan 1985, Jan 2002

Ung, Loung, Cambodian-American social activist, Jan 2006

Valtin, Jan, German author, Apr 1941, *Obit* Jan 1951

Vann, Robert Lee, American newspaper editor and publisher, *Obit* Yrbk 1940

Viguerie, Richard A., American political fund raiser and magazine publisher, Jan 1983

Viscardi, Henry, American rehabilitation advocate, Jan 1954, Yrbk 1966, *Obit* Yrbk 2004

Vogel, Hans Jochen, German socialist leader, Jan 1984

Wald, Lillian D., American social reformer and public health official, *Obit* Oct 1940

Wallace, Clayton M., Sept 1948

Wallis, Jim, American evangelist and writer, July 2005

Walsh, John, American victims' rights advocate and television program host, July 2001

Wattleton, Faye, American nurse and birth control advocate, Jan 1990

Webb, Beatrice Potter, British sociologist and reformer, *Obit* June 1943

Wei Jingsheng, Chinese dissident, Sept 1997

Welsh, Herbert, *Obit* Sept 1941

Weyrich, Paul, American political activist and commentator, Feb 2005, *Obit* Yrbk 2009

Wheaton, Elizabeth, Jan 1942

Whitton, Charlotte Elizabeth, Canadian social worker, feminist and mayor, Apr 1953, *Obit* Mar 1975

Wiesel, Elie, American novelist, journalist and human rights activist, Nov 1970, Feb 1986

Wilkins, Roy, American civil rights leader, June 1950, Jan 1964, *Obit* Oct 1981

Williams, Betty, Irish pacifist, Mar 1979

Williams, Jody, American pacifist, Mar 1998

Wilson, Margaret Bush, American lawyer and civil rights activist, Oct 1975, *Obit* Yrbk 2009

Wilson, Marie C., American feminist, Sept 2004

Wise, Tim, Jan 2013

Wolf, Naomi, American feminist, social critic and journalist, Nov 1993

Wolfenden, John Frederick Wolfenden, English educator, social reformer and museum director, Oct 1970, *Obit* Mar 1985

Wolfson, Evan, American lawyer and gay rights activist, July 2009

Woods, Tighe E., American real estate developer and government official, Oct 1948, *Obit* Sept 1974

Wu Yifang, Chinese educator and feminist, Aug 1945, *Obit* Jan 1986

Wu, Harry, Chinese-American human rights activist, Feb 1995

Wyatt, Wilson W., American government official, lawyer and civic leader, Mar 1946, *Obit* Aug 1996

Xu Wenli, Chinese dissident, Jan 2003

Yard, Molly, American feminist and social activist, Nov 1988, *Obit* Apr 2006

Yergan, Max, American civil rights activist, Sept 1948, *Obit* June 1975

Yessa, Abdel Nasser, Mauritanian anti-slavery activist, Jan 2006

Young, Andrew, American congressman, diplomat and mayor, Apr 1977

Young, Rose, *Obit* Sept 1941

Young, Whitney Moore, American civil rights leader, Apr 1965, *Obit* Apr 1971

Zana, Leyla, Kurdish member of Turkish parliament and political prisoner, Jan 2004

Ziegler, Jean, Swiss sociologist, socialist leader and human rights activist, July 2010

Ziemer, Gregor, Apr 1942

Zinn, Howard, American historian, Aug 1999, *Obit* Yrbk 2010

Actors

Abbott, Bud, American comedian, Oct 1941, *Obit* June 1974

Abdul, Paula, American dancer, choreographer, singer and talent judge on television program, Sept 1991

Abraham, F. Murray, American actor, Jan 1991

Abraham, John, Indian actor, Jan 2006

Abril, Victoria, Spanish actress, Jan 2004

Abumrad, Jad, American radio producer and personality, Sept 2012

Ace, Goodman, radio and television author and actor, May 1948, *Obit* May 1982

Ace, Jane, radio performer, May 1948, *Obit* Jan 1975

Adams, Edie, American actress and singer, Feb 1954, *Obit* Yrbk 2008

Adebimpe, Tunde, American singer, songwriter, and actor, Apr 2009

Adjani, Isabelle, French actress, Jan 1990

Adler, Stella, American actress and drama teacher, Aug 1985, *Obit* Feb 1993

Affleck, Ben, American actor, Mar 1998

Aghdashloo, Shohreh, Iranian actress, Jan 2005

Aherne, Brian, English actor, Feb 1960, *Obit* Apr 1986

Aiello, Danny, American actor, June 1992

Akalaitis, JoAnne, American actress, dramatist and director, Feb 1993

Akhtar, Ayad, Aug 2013

Albert, Eddie, American actor, Jan 1954, *Obit* Yrbk 2005

Albertson, Jack, American actor, Mar 1976, *Obit* Jan 1982

Alda, Alan, American actor and film director, Jan 1977

Alexander, Jane, American actress and government official, Feb 1977

Alexander, Jason, American actor, Jan 1998

Allen, Debbie, American dancer, actress and director, Feb 1987

Allen, Fred, comedian, Feb 1941, *Obit* May 1956

Allen, Gracie, American comedienne, July 1940, Mar 1951, *Obit* Oct 1964

Allen, Robert Sharon, May 1941

Allen, Tim, American comedian and actor, May 1995

Allen, Woody, American actor, filmmaker and screenwriter, Yrbk 1966, Sept 1979

Alley, Kirstie, American actress, July 1994

Allyson, June, American actress, Jan 1952, *Obit* Yrbk 2006

Amalric, Mathieu, French actor, film director and screenwriter, Feb 2011

Ameche, Don, actor, May 1965, *Obit* Feb 1994

Anderson, Judith, English actress, Yrbk 1941, Feb 1961, *Obit* Mar 1992

Anderson, Mary, American actress, *Obit* July 1940

Andersson, Bibi, Swedish actress, Sept 1978

Andre 3000, American rapper, Apr 2004

Andrews, Anthony, English actor, June 1991

Andrews, Dana, actor, Oct 1959, *Obit* Feb 1993

Andrews, Julie, English actress and singer, July 1956, Apr 1994

Angelou, Maya, American poet and memoirist, June 1974, Feb 1994

Ann-Margret, American actress, singer and dancer, Sept 1975

Ansari, Aziz, American comedian and actor, Feb 2013

Anthony, John J., American family and marriage counselor, Jan 1942, *Obit* Oct 1970

Anu, Christine, Australian singer and actress, Jan 2003

Arau, Alfonso, Mexican motion picture director, Jan 2005

Arden, Eve, actress, Sept 1953, *Obit* Jan 1991

Argento, Asia, Italian actress, Jan 2003

Arkin, Alan, American actor, Oct 1967

Arliss, George, English actor, *Obit* Mar 1946

Armetta, Henry, American actor, *Obit* Nov 1945

Armisen, Fred, American comedian and performance artist, Oct 2013

Arnaz, Desi, Cuban-American television producer, band leader and actor, Sept 1952, *Obit* Feb 1987

Arness, James, American actor, Nov 1973, *Obit* Yrbk 2011

Arquette, Cliff, June 1961, *Obit* Nov 1974

Arquette, Patricia, American actress, Oct 1997

Arthur, Bea, American actress, Yrbk 1973, *Obit* Yrbk 2009

Arthur, Jean, actress, Mar 1945, *Obit* Aug 1991

Asano, Tadanobu, Japanese actor, Jan 2007

Ashcroft, Peggy, British actress, Sept 1963, Jan 1987, *Obit* Aug 1991

Ashley, Elizabeth, actress, Mar 1978

Asner, Edward, American actor, Aug 1978

Astaire, Fred, American dancer, singer and actor, Sept 1945, Apr 1964, *Obit* Aug 1987

Astor, Mary, American actress, Nov 1961, *Obit* Nov 1987

Atkins, Eileen, English actress, Jan 2002

Attenborough, David, British television producer and personality, Apr 1983

Attenborough, Richard, British actor and motion picture director, May 1984

Atwill, Lionel, English actor, *Obit* June 1946

Austin, Steve, American wrestler, Nov 2001

Auteuil, Daniel, French actor, Jan 2007

Autry, Gene, American cowboy singer, actor and baseball executive, Yrbk 1947, *Obit* Jan 1999

Ayckbourn, Alan, English dramatist and theatrical director, Jan 1980

Aykroyd, Dan, Canadian actor, Jan 1992

Ayres, Agnes, American actress, *Obit* Feb 1941

Azmi, Shabana, Indian actress, Jan 2002

Bacall, Lauren, American actress, Mar 1970

Bach, Reginald, British actor and theatrical director, *Obit* Feb 1941

Bacharach, Bert, American fashion critic, Yrbk 1957

Bachchan, Amitabh, Indian actor, Jan 2002

Bae, Yong Joon, Korean actor, Jan 2005

Bailey, Pearl, American singer and actress, June 1955, Oct 1969, *Obit* Oct 1990

Baker, Josephine, American actress, singer and dancer, July 1964, *Obit* June 1975

Baker, Phil, American comedian, accordionist and radio personality, Nov 1946, *Obit* Jan 1964

Baker, Tom, British actor, Jan 2004

Bakri, Mohammad, Palestinian filmmaker and actor, Jan 2005

Bakula, Scott, American actor, Feb 2002

Baldwin, Alec, American actor, July 1992

Ball, Lucille, American actress, Sept 1952, Jan 1978, *Obit* June 1989

Ballard, Kaye, American actress, singer and comedienne, Sept 1969

Baltasar Kormakur, Icelandic actor, motion picture director and screenwriter, Jan 2003

Bana, Eric, Australian comedian and actor, Jan 2003

Bancroft, Anne, American actress, June 1960, *Obit* Oct 2005

Banderas, Antonio, Spanish actor, Mar 1997

Bankhead, Tallulah, American actress, July 1941, Jan 1953, *Obit* Feb 1969

Bankole, Isaach de, Ivorian actor, Jan 2004

Banks, Tyra, American model, actress and talk show host, Apr 2007

Barber, Tiki, American football player and television personality, Oct 2003

Barbier, George W., American actor, *Obit* Aug 1945

Bardem, Javier, Spanish actor, Jan 2002

Bardot, Brigitte, French actress, Jan 1960

Barlow, Howard, Jan 1940, July 1954, *Obit* Mar 1972

Barlow, Reginald, American actor, *Obit* Aug 1943

Barnett, Etta Moten, American singer and actress, Feb 2002

Barr, Roseanne, American comedienne, May 1989

Barrault, Jean-Louis, French actor and theatrical director, Mar 1953, *Obit* Mar 1994

Barris, Chuck, American television producer and personality, Mar 2005

Barrymore, Drew, American actress, Oct 1998

Barrymore, Ethel, actress, Mar 1941, *Obit* Sept 1959

Barrymore, John, American actor, *Obit* July 1942

Barrymore, Lionel, actor, July 1943, *Obit* Jan 1955

Barsamian, David, American radio program host, Mar 2007

Baryshnikov, Mikhail, Russian-American ballet dancer, Feb 1975

Basinger, Kim, American actress, Feb 1990

Bassett, Angela, American actress, May 1996

Batali, Mario, American chef and restaurateur, Apr 2011

Bateman, Jason, American actor, Oct 2005

Bates, Alan, English actor, Mar 1969, *Obit* Yrbk 2004

Bates, Blanche, American actress, *Obit* Feb 1942

Bates, Granville, American actor, *Obit* Sept 1940

Bates, Kathy, American actress, Sept 1991

Baur, Harry, French actor, *Obit* May 1943

Baxter, Anne, actress, May 1972, *Obit* Feb 1986

Baxter, Frank C., American professor of English and television personality, Mar 1955

Bean, Orson, comedian, Feb 1967

Beart, Emmanuelle, French actress, Jan 2002

Beatty, Warren, American actor, producer and director, May 1962, May 1988

Beckett, Wendy, English nun and art critic, Jan 1998

Beckinsale, Kate, English actress, Aug 2001

Begley, Ed, American actor, Mar 1956, *Obit* June 1970

Bel Geddes, Barbara, American actress, July 1948, *Obit* Yrbk 2005

Belafonte, Harry, American singer and actor, Jan 1956

Bellamy, Ralph, actor, Nov 1951, *Obit* Jan 1992

Belle, David, French actor and roof jumper, Jan 2007

Bellucci, Monica, Italian actress, Jan 2003

Belmondo, Jean-Paul, French actor, Yrbk 1965

Belmore, Alice, British actress, *Obit* Sept 1943

Belushi, Jim, American actor, Jan 1995

Belushi, John, American comedian, Jan 1980, *Obit* Apr 1982

Benchley, Robert, humorist, Sept 1941, *Obit* Jan 1946

Bendix, William, American actor, Sept 1948, *Obit* Feb 1965

Benigni, Roberto, Italian actor and filmmaker, June 1999

Bennett, Richard, American actor, *Obit* Yrbk 1944

Benny, Jack, comedian, Aug 1941, Nov 1963, *Obit* Feb 1975

Benrimo, J. Harry, American dramatist, theatrical director and actor, *Obit* May 1942

Bentley, Irene, American actress, *Obit* July 1940

Berg, Gertrude, American actress and radio scriptwriter, July 1941, Sept 1960, *Obit* Nov 1966

Bergen, Candice, American actress, Aug 1976

Bergen, Edgar, American ventriloquist and radio performer, May 1945, *Obit* Nov 1978

Bergen, Polly, actress and singer, Sept 1958

Bergeron, Tom, American television personality, Oct 2007

Bergman, Ingrid, Swedish actress, Jan 1940, Sept 1965, *Obit* Oct 1982

Berle, Milton, American comedian, June 1949, *Obit* Yrbk 2002

Bernhard, Sandra, American comedienne and actress, Sept 1990

Bernstein, Michelle, American chef and restaurateur, Nov 2013

Berri, Claude, French actor, director and screenwriter, Mar 1989, *Obit* Yrbk 2009

Berry, Halle, American actress, May 1999

Bervoets, Gene, Dutch actor, Jan 2002

Best, Edna, English actress, July 1954, *Obit* Nov 1974

Beyonce, American singer and actress, Aug 2001

Bickel, George, American comedian and actor, *Obit* Aug 1941

Big Boi, American rapper, Apr 2004

Bikel, Theodore, American singer and actor, Mar 1960

Birkin, Jane, English actress, Jan 2002

Bishop, Joey, American comedian, Apr 1962, *Obit* Yrbk 2008

Bisset, Jacqueline, English actress, May 1977

Black, Jack, American singer and actor, Feb 2002

Black, Karen, American actress, Mar 1976, *Obit* Yrbk 2013

Black, Michael Ian, American actor, Sept 2013

Black, Shirley Temple, American actress and diplomat, Oct 1945, Apr 1970

Blades, Ruben, Panamanian salsa singer, songwriter and actor, May 1986

Blake, Robert, American actor, Oct 1975

Blanc, Mel, American animated cartoon voice specialist, June 1976, *Obit* Sept 1989

Blanchett, Cate, Australian actress, Aug 1999

Bledsoe, Jules, American opera singer, actor and composer, *Obit* Sept 1943

Bloom, Claire, English actress, May 1956

Bloom, Orlando, English actor, Jan 2003

Bogarde, Dirk, English actor and author, July 1967, *Obit* July 1999

Bogart, Humphrey, American actor, May 1942, *Obit* Mar 1957

Bogdanovich, Peter, American film director and producer, June 1972

Bogosian, Eric, American actor, playwright and monologist, Sept 1987

Bolger, Ray, American dancer, singer and actor, Aug 1942, *Obit* Mar 1987

Bon Jovi, Jon, American singer and actor, Jan 1990

Bond, Jessie, English singer and actress, *Obit* Aug 1942

Bonham Carter, Helena, English actress, Jan 1998

Boone, Richard, Feb 1964, *Obit* Mar 1981

Booth, Shirley, American actress, Nov 1942, Apr 1953, *Obit* Jan 1993

Borgnine, Ernest, American actor, Apr 1956, *Obit* Yrbk 2012

Bosworth, Hobart, American actor, *Obit* Feb 1944

Bourdain, Anthony, American chef, writer and television personality, Jan 2006

Bova, Raoul, Italian actor, Jan 2004

Bowes, Edward, radio performer, Mar 1941, *Obit* July 1946

Boyd, Stephen, Irish actor, Yrbk 1961, *Obit* Aug 1977

Boyd, William, American actor, Mar 1950, *Obit* Nov 1972

Boyer, Charles, French actor, Feb 1943, *Obit* Oct 1978

Bracken, Eddie, American actor, Oct 1944, *Obit* Feb 2003

Bradbury, James H., *Obit* Yrbk 1940

Branagh, Kenneth, Irish actor and director, Apr 1997

Brand, Russell, British comedian and actor, Jan 2011

Brandauer, Klaus Maria, Austrian actor, July 1990

Brando, Marlon, American actor, Apr 1952, Mar 1974, *Obit* Yrbk 2004

Brazzi, Rossano, Italian actor, May 1961, *Obit* Mar 1995

Brennan, Walter, actor, May 1941, *Obit* Nov 1974

Bridges, Jeff, American actor, Mar 1991

Bridges, Lloyd, actor, July 1990, *Obit* May 1998

Broderick, Matthew, American actor, May 1987

Brody, Adrien, American actor, July 2003

Brolin, Josh, American actor, Feb 2008

Bronson, Charles, American actor, Mar 1975, *Obit* Mar 2004

Brooks, Albert, American actor, director and screenwriter, Apr 1997

Brooks, Louise, American actress, Apr 1984, *Obit* Oct 1985

Brooks, Mel, American actor, writer, director and producer, Sept 1974

Brosnan, Pierce, Irish actor, Jan 1997

Brothers, Joyce, psychologist, Apr 1971, *Obit* Yrbk 2013

Brown, Jim, American football player and actor, Sept 1964

Brown, Joe E., American actor, Feb 1945, *Obit* Sept 1973

Browne, Coral, Australian actress, Yrbk 1959, *Obit* July 1991

Bruel, Patrick, French singer and actor, Jan 2007

Brynner, Yul, American actor, Sept 1956, *Obit* Nov 1985

Buchholz, Horst, German actor, Mar 1960, *Obit* Aug 2003

Bullock, Sandra, American actress, Aug 1997

Burnett, Carol, American actress, Jan 1962, Nov 1990

Burns, George, American comedian, Mar 1951, July 1976, *Obit* May 1996

Burr, Henry, *Obit* May 1941

Burr, Raymond, actor, Sept 1961, *Obit* Nov 1993

Burstyn, Ellen, American actress, June 1975

Burstyn, Mike, American actor and singer, May 2005

Burton, LeVar, American actor, Mar 2000

Burton, Richard, Welsh actor, Yrbk 1960, *Obit* Sept 1984

Buscemi, Steve, American actor and filmmaker, Apr 1999

Busch, Charles, American playwright, actor and female impersonator, June 1995

Butterworth, Charles, *Obit* July 1946

Buttons, Red, American comedian and actor, Sept 1958, *Obit* Yrbk 2006

Byington, Spring, actress, Sept 1956, *Obit* Oct 1971

Byrd, Sam, Nov 1942, *Obit* Jan 1956

Byrne, Gabriel, Irish actor, May 1999

Byron, Arthur, *Obit* Sept 1943

Caan, James, American actor, May 1976

Caesar, Sid, American comedian and actor, Apr 1951

Cage, Nicolas, American actor, Apr 1994

Cagney, James, American actor, Yrbk 1942, *Obit* May 1986

Caine, Michael, English actor, May 1968, Jan 1988

Caldwell, Zoe, Australian actress, Yrbk 1970

Calhern, Louis, July 1951, *Obit* July 1956

Cambridge, Godfrey, American actor and comedian, Mar 1969, *Obit* Feb 1977

Cameron, Hugh, *Obit* Jan 1942

Campbell, Bruce, American actor, May 2013

Campbell, Douglas, Canadian actor and theatrical director, June 1958, *Obit* Yrbk 2009

Campbell, Naomi, British model, Feb 1997

Campbell, Neve, Canadian actress, Jan 2000

Campbell, Patrick, English actress, *Obit* May 1940

Canby, Al H., *Obit* Yrbk 1940

Candy, John, Canadian actor, Feb 1990, *Obit* May 1994

Cantinflas, Mexican comedian, June 1953, *Obit* June 1993

Cantor, Eddie, singer and comedian, Nov 1941, May 1954, *Obit* Jan 1965

Carell, Steve, American comedian and actor, Feb 2007

Carey, Drew, American comedian and game show host, Mar 1998

Carle, Richard, *Obit* Aug 1941

Carlin, George, American comedian, Oct 1976, *Obit* Oct 2008

Carmichael, Hoagy, American songwriter, May 1941, *Obit* Feb 1982

Carmines, Al, American clergyman, composer, singer and actor, Sept 1972, *Obit* Yrbk 2005

Carney, Art, American actor, Apr 1958, *Obit* Yrbk 2004

Carnovsky, Morris, actor, Jan 1991

Caron, Leslie, French dancer and actress, Sept 1954

Carr, Alexander, *Obit* Yrbk 1946

Carr, Kris, American actress, photographer and documentary filmmaker, May 2012

Carradine, Keith, American actor, Aug 1991

Carrey, Jim, Canadian comedian and actor, Feb 1996

Carroll, Diahann, American singer and actress, Sept 1962

Carroll, Madeleine, actress, Apr 1949, *Obit* Nov 1987

Carroll, Pat, actress, Aug 1980

Carroll, Vinnette, American actress, dramatist and theatrical director, Sept 1983, *Obit* Feb 2003

Carson, Johnny, American television talk show host, Jan 1964, Apr 1982, *Obit* July 2005

Carvey, Dana, American comedian and actor, June 1992

Casey, Bernie, actor, screenwriter and film director, July 1999

Cassavetes, John, American actor and film director, July 1969, *Obit* Mar 1989

Cattrall, Kim, Anglo-Canadian actress, Jan 2003

Caulfield, Joan, actress, May 1954, *Obit* Aug 1991

Cavanagh, Tom, Canadian actor, June 2003

Cavett, Dick, American television talk show host, Oct 1970

Cecil, Mary, *Obit* Feb 1941

Cedric the Entertainer, American comedian, Feb 2004

Chadwick, Helene, *Obit* Oct 1940

Chaikin, Joseph, American theatrical director and actor, July 1981, *Obit* Yrbk 2003

Chamberlain, Richard, American actor, July 1963, Nov 1987

Champion, Marge, American dancer and choreographer, Sept 1953

Chan, Jackie, Chinese actor, Nov 1997

Channing, Carol, American actress, Sept 1964

Channing, Stockard, American actress, Apr 1991

Chaplin, Charlie, English actor, director and producer, Yrbk 1940, Mar 1961, *Obit* Feb 1978

Chaplin, Geraldine, actress, July 1979

Chapman, Blanche, *Obit* Aug 1941

Chapman, Duane Lee, American bounty hunter, Mar 2005

Chappelle, Dave, American comedian and actor, June 2004

Charisse, Cyd, American dancer and actress, Jan 1954, *Obit* Yrbk 2008

Charters, Spencer, *Obit* Mar 1943

Chase, Charley, actor, *Obit* Aug 1940

Chase, Chevy, American actor and comedian, Mar 1979

Chase, Ilka, May 1942, *Obit* Apr 1978

Cheadle, Don, American actor, Sept 1999

Chen Peisi, Chinese actor and comedian, Jan 2004

Chen, Joan, Chinese actress, Sept 1999

Cher, American singer and actress, Jan 1974, June 1991

Cherry, Addie, American vaudeville actress, *Obit* Yrbk 1942

Chevalier, Maurice, French singer and actor, Jan 1948, Mar 1969, *Obit* Feb 1972

Chiba, Sonny, Japanese martial artist and actor, Jan 2005

Child, Julia, American cook, Feb 1967, *Obit* Yrbk 2004

Chow, Stephen, Chinese actor, motion picture director and screenwriter, Jan 2003

Chow, Yun Fat, Chinese actor, May 1998

Christensen, Hayden, Canadian actor, Jan 2005

Christians, Mady, May 1945, *Obit* Yrbk 1951

Christie, Julie, English actress, Sept 1966

Churchill, Berton, *Obit* Yrbk 1940

Churchill, Sarah, English actress and daughter of Winston Churchill, May 1955, *Obit* Jan 1983

Claire, Ina, actress, May 1954, *Obit* Apr 1985

Clapper, Raymond, American journalist and radio commentator, Mar 1940, *Obit* Mar 1944

Clark, Bobby, May 1949, *Obit* Apr 1960

Clark, Dick, American television personality and producer, May 1959, Jan 1987, *Obit* Yrbk 2012

Clark, Marguerite, *Obit* Nov 1940

Clarkson, Kelly, American singer and contestant on reality TV show American idol, Sept 2006

Clarkson, Patricia, American actress, Aug 2005

Clash, Kevin, American muppeteer, June 2000

Clayburgh, Jill, American actress, Sept 1979, *Obit* Yrbk 2011

Cleese, John, English actor and humorist, Jan 1984

Clift, Montgomery, American actor, July 1954, *Obit* Sept 1966

Clive, E. E., *Obit* July 1940

Clooney, George, American actor, July 2008

Close, Glenn, American actress, Nov 1984

Cobb, Lee J., Feb 1960, *Obit* Apr 1976

Coburn, Charles, actor, June 1944, *Obit* Nov 1961

Coburn, James, American actor, June 1999, *Obit* Feb 2003

Coca, Imogene, American actress and comedienne, Apr 1951, *Obit* Sept 2001

Coco, James, actor, May 1974, *Obit* Apr 1987

Cohan, George M., American actor, dramatist, songwriter and producer, *Obit* Jan 1943

Colbert, Claudette, American actress, Jan 1945, May 1964, *Obit* Oct 1996

Colbert, Stephen, American comedian and actor, Nov 2006

Colicchio, Tom, American chef and restaurateur, Feb 2013

Collier, Constance, July 1954, *Obit* June 1955

Collier, William, American actor, *Obit* Mar 1944

Collins, Eddie, American actor, *Obit* Oct 1940

Collins, Joan, British actress, Jan 1984

Colman, Ronald, English actor, July 1943, *Obit* Sept 1958

Common, American rapper, Feb 2012

Connelly, Jennifer, American actress, June 2002

Conner, Nadine, American opera singer, Jan 1955, *Obit* Aug 2003

Connery, Sean, Scottish actor, Jan 1966, June 1993

Conness, Robert, *Obit* Mar 1941

Connick, Harry, American pianist and singer, Nov 1990

Connolly, Walter, actor, *Obit* July 1940

Conti, Tom, Scottish actor, June 1985

Conway, Tim, American comedian and actor, Apr 1981

Coogan, Steve, English actor and comedian, Jan 2002

Cook, Barbara, American singer, Feb 1963

Cook, Donald, July 1954, *Obit* Yrbk 1961

Cook, Murray, Australian actor and singer, Jan 2004

Cooke, Alistair, Anglo-American radio reporter and television personality, June 1952, May 1974, *Obit* Yrbk 2004

Cooper, Chris, American actor, July 2004

Cooper, Gary, American actor, Yrbk 1941, *Obit* July 1961

Cooper, Gladys, English actress, Feb 1956, *Obit* Jan 1972

Coppola, Sofia, American film director and screenwriter, Nov 2003

Cora, Cat, American chef and cookbook writer, Nov 2011

Cornelius, Don, American television program host and producer, *Obit* Yrbk 2012

Cornell, Katharine, American actress, May 1941, Mar 1952, *Obit* July 1974

Correll, Charles J., Yrbk 1947, *Obit* Nov 1972

Cosby, Bill, American actor and comedian, Apr 1967, Oct 1986

Cosell, Howard, American sportscaster, Nov 1972, *Obit* July 1995

Costello, Lou, American comedian, Oct 1941, *Obit* May 1959

Costner, Kevin, American actor and film director, June 1990

Cotten, Joseph, American actor, July 1943, *Obit* Apr 1994

Coughlin, Charles Edward, American priest and radio commentator, Sept 1940, *Obit* Jan 1980

Courtenay, Tom, English actor, May 1964

Coward, Noel, English actor, dramatist and composer, Jan 1941, Mar 1962, *Obit* May 1973

Cowell, Simon, British record producer and talent judge on television program, Jan 2004

Cox, Brian, Scottish actor, Jan 2004

Cox, Wally, Feb 1954, *Obit* Apr 1973

Craig, Daniel, British actor, Apr 2007

Crain, Jeanne, American actress, Nov 1951, *Obit* Yrbk 2004

Craven, Frank, *Obit* Oct 1945

Crawford, Broderick, actor, Apr 1950, *Obit* June 1986

Crawford, Joan, American actress, Jan 1946, Sept 1966, *Obit* July 1977

Crawford, Michael, English actor and singer, Jan 1992

Cregar, Laird, *Obit* Jan 1945

Crews, Laura Hope, actress, *Obit* Jan 1943

Cromer, David, American theatrical director and actor, Sept 2011

Cromwell, James, American actor, Aug 2005

Cronyn, Hume, Canadian actor, Mar 1956, June 1988, *Obit* Yrbk 2003

Crosby, Bing, American singer and actor, Sept 1941, June 1953, *Obit* Jan 1978

Cross, Ben, English actor, Aug 1984

Cross, Milton, Jan 1940, *Obit* Feb 1975

Crowe, Russell, Australian actor, May 2000

Cruise, Tom, American actor, Apr 1987

Crumit, Frank, *Obit* Oct 1943

Cruz, Penelope, Spanish actress, July 2001

Crystal, Billy, American comedian and actor, Feb 1987

Cummings, Robert, actor, Jan 1956, *Obit* Feb 1991

Curtin, Jane, actress, Jan 1997

Curtis, Jamie Lee, American actress, Nov 1998

Curtis, Tony, American actor, May 1959, *Obit* Nov 2010

Cusack, Joan, American actress, July 1998

Cusack, John, American actor, June 1996

D'Onofrio, Vincent, American actor, May 2004

Dafoe, Willem, American actor, Apr 1990

Dale, Clamma, Apr 1979

Dale, Jim, English actor, July 1981

Dalton, Charles, *Obit* Aug 1942

Dalton, Timothy, English actor, May 1988

Daly, James, Oct 1959, *Obit* Sept 1978

Daly, Tyne, actress, Mar 1992

Damerel, Donna, *Obit* Apr 1941

Damon, Matt, American actor, Mar 1998

Danner, Blythe, American actress, Jan 1981

Danson, Ted, American actor, Oct 1990

Darin, Bobby, American singer and actor, Mar 1963, *Obit* Feb 1974

Darin, Ricardo, Argentine actor, Jan 2002

Darwell, Jane, June 1941, *Obit* Oct 1967

Dashiell, Willard, *Obit* June 1943

Dassin, Jules, American film director, Mar 1971, *Obit* Yrbk 2008

David, Larry, American comedian, television scriptwriter and producer, Aug 1998

Davidson, John, singer and actor, Sept 1976

Davis, Bette, American actress, Oct 1941, Mar 1953, *Obit* Nov 1989

Davis, Geena, American actress, Oct 1991

Davis, Joan, comedienne and actress, June 1945, *Obit* Sept 1961

Davis, Judy, Australian actress, Nov 1993

Davis, Ossie, American actor and dramatist, Oct 1969, *Obit* Yrbk 2005

Davis, Sammy, American actor and singer, Sept 1956, July 1978, *Obit* July 1990

Day, Doris, American singer and actress, Apr 1954

Day, Laraine, American actress, Sept 1953, *Obit* Yrbk 2008

Day-Lewis, Daniel, Anglo-Irish actor, July 1990

De Havilland, Olivia, American actress, May 1944, Nov 1966

De Laurentiis, Giada, American chef and television personality, July 2013

De Lavallade, Carmen, American actress and dancer, Yrbk 1967

De Leath, Vaughn, *Obit* July 1943

De Niro, Robert, American actor, Aug 1976, May 1993

De, Shobha, Indian novelist, journalist and television personality, Jan 2005

DeGeneres, Ellen, American comedienne and talk show host, Apr 1996

DeVito, Danny, American actor and film director, Feb 1988

Dean, Jimmy, American singer, Yrbk 1965, *Obit* Aug 2010

Debbouze, Jamel, French comedian and actor, Jan 2005

Dee, Ruby, American actress, Nov 1970

Del Toro, Benicio, American actor, Sept 2001

Delaney, Frank, Irish novelist and broadcaster, Jan 2005

Delilah, American radio talk show host, Apr 2005

Delon, Alain, French actor, Apr 1964

Dench, Judi, English actress, Jan 1999

Deneuve, Catherine, French actress, Feb 1978

Dennehy, Brian, American actor, July 1991

Dennis, Sandy, actress, Jan 1969, *Obit* May 1992

Denniston, Reynolds, *Obit* Mar 1943

Denver, John, American singer and actor, Jan 1975, *Obit* Jan 1998

Depardieu, Gerard, French actor, Oct 1987

Depp, Johnny, American actor, May 1991

Dern, Bruce, American actor, Oct 1978

Dern, Laura, American actress, Oct 1992

Derwent, Clarence, Nov 1947, *Obit* Nov 1959

Deschanel, Zooey, American actress, Aug 2012

Dewhurst, Colleen, actress, July 1974, *Obit* Oct 1991

DiCaprio, Leonardo, American actor, Mar 1997

Diaz, Cameron, American actress, Apr 2005

Dickinson, Angie, American actress, Feb 1981

Diddy, American rapper, record producer and actor, Apr 1998

Dietrich, Marlene, German-American actress, June 1953, Feb 1968, *Obit* June 1992

Diggs, Taye, American actor, Aug 2011

Diller, Phyllis, American comedienne, July 1967, *Obit* Yrbk 2012

Dillman, Bradford, actor, Jan 1960

Dillon, Matt, American actor, May 1985

Dinehart, Alan, *Obit* Sept 1944

Dinklage, Peter, American actor, Apr 2013

Dixey, Henry E., *Obit* Apr 1943

Dixit, Madhuri, Indian actress, Jan 2006

Douglas, Helen Gahagan, American congresswoman, Sept 1944, *Obit* Aug 1980

Douglas, Kirk, American actor, Mar 1952

Douglas, Melvyn, actor, May 1942, *Obit* Sept 1981

Douglas, Michael, American actor and motion picture producer, Apr 1987

Douglas, Mike, American television talk show host, May 1968, *Obit* Yrbk 2007

Downey, James, American television comedy writer, June 2008

Downey, Robert, American actor, Aug 1998

Downs, Hugh, television personality, Mar 1965

Drake, Alfred, actor and singer, Apr 1944, *Obit* Sept 1992

Drescher, Fran, American actress, Apr 1998

Dreyfuss, Richard, American actor, Jan 1976

Duff, Hilary, American actress and singer, Feb 2006

Dujardin, Jean, Oct 2013

Dukakis, Olympia, American actress, July 1991

Duke, Patty, American actress, Sept 1963

Dullea, Keir, American actor, June 1970

Dunaway, Faye, American actress, Feb 1972

Duncan, Malcolm, *Obit* June 1942

Duncan, Michael Clarke, actor, Aug 2000, *Obit* Yrbk 2012

Duncan, Sandy, actress, Jan 1980

Dunne, Irene, American actress and singer, Aug 1945, *Obit* Nov 1990

Dunnock, Mildred, actress, Sept 1955, *Obit* Sept 1991

Dunst, Kirsten, American actress, Oct 2001

Durbin, Deanna, American singer and actress, June 1941, *Obit* Yrbk 2013

Durning, Charles, American actor, Sept 1997, *Obit* Yrbk 2013

Dutton, Charles S., American actor and television director, Oct 2000

Duvall, Robert, American actor and motion picture director, July 1977

Dyer, Gwynne, Canadian journalist and television documentary host, Jan 2006

Eastwood, Clint, American actor and film director, Oct 1971, Mar 1989

Ebsen, Buddy, American actor and dancer, Jan 1977, *Obit* Yrbk 2003

Eddy, Nelson, singer and actor, Feb 1943, *Obit* May 1967

Edwards, Ralph, American television producer and personality, July 1943, *Obit* Yrbk 2006

Edwards, Vince, actor, Oct 1962, *Obit* May 1996

Eggerth, Marta, Austro-Hungarian singer and actress, Nov 1943

Ejiofor, Chiwetel, British actor, Jan 2004

Eldridge, Florence, actress, Mar 1943, *Obit* Sept 1988

Elizondo, Hector, American actor, Jan 1992

Elliott, Bob, American comedian, Oct 1957

Elliott, Maxine, actress, Mar 1940

Eltinge, Julian, *Obit* Apr 1941

Emerson, Faye, American actress and television personality, Sept 1951, *Obit* May 1983

Emin, Tracey, British performance artist, Nov 2009

Eminem, American rapper, Jan 2001

Emrich, Duncan, Mar 1955

Englund, Robert, actor, Mar 1990

Enters, Angna, dancer, painter and author, Jan 1940, June 1952, *Obit* Apr 1989

Estrada, Joseph, Filipino president, Feb 2000

Evans, Bergen, Yrbk 1955, *Obit* Apr 1978

Evans, Chris, American actor, Aug 2013

Evans, Edith, English actress, June 1956, *Obit* Jan 1977

Evans, Linda, American actress, Mar 1986

Evans, Maurice, English actor, May 1940, June 1961, *Obit* May 1989

Eve (Singer), American rapper and actress, July 2003

Everett, Rupert, English actor, Jan 2005

Ewell, Tom, actor, May 1961, *Obit* Nov 1994

Fabray, Nanette, comedienne, Jan 1956

Fairbanks, Douglas, American actor, Jan 1940

Fairbanks, Douglas, American actor, Nov 1941, Feb 1956, *Obit* Aug 2000

Faith, Paloma, Aug 2013

Falco, Edie, American actress, Mar 2006

Falk, Peter, American actor, July 1972, *Obit* Yrbk 2011

Fallon, Jimmy, American comedian, actor and talk show host, July 2002

Farina, Dennis, American actor, *Obit* Yrbk 2013

Farrell, Colin, Irish actor, Jan 2004

Farrow, Mia, American actress, Apr 1970

Fatt, Jeff, Australian actor and singer, Jan 2004

Faversham, William, *Obit* May 1940

Favreau, Jon, American actor, screenwriter and film director, July 2010

Fawcett, Farrah, American actress, Feb 1978, *Obit* Aug 2009

Fay, Frank, Aug 1945, *Obit* Yrbk 1961

Ferguson, Craig, Scottish-American comedian, actor and talk show host, Jan 2005

Ferguson, Elsie, Feb 1944, *Obit* Jan 1962

Fernandel, Oct 1955, *Obit* Apr 1971

Ferrell, Will, American comedian and actor, Feb 2003

Ferrer, Jose, American actor and director, May 1944, *Obit* Mar 1992

Ferrera, America, American actress, Sept 2007

Fey, Tina, American actress and comedienne, Apr 2002

Field, Anthony, Australian actor and singer, Jan 2004

Field, Betty, Sept 1959, *Obit* Nov 1973

Field, Sally, American actress, Oct 1979

Fields, Gracie, English actress and singer, Apr 1941, *Obit* Nov 1979

Fields, Stanley, *Obit* June 1941

Fiennes, Ralph, British actor, Sept 1996

Fieri, Guy, American chef, restaurateur and television personality, Mar 2011

Fierstein, Harvey, American dramatist and actor, Feb 1984

Finch, Flora, *Obit* Jan 1940

Finch, Peter, English actor, Sept 1972, *Obit* Mar 1977

Finley, Karen, performance artist, Sept 1998

Finney, Albert, English actor, Oct 1963

Firth, Colin, English actor, Mar 2004

Fishburne, Laurence, American actor, Aug 1996

Fisher, Carrie, American actress and novelist, Feb 1991

Fisher, Sterling, Yrbk 1940

Fitzgerald, Barry, Feb 1945, *Obit* Feb 1961

Fitzgerald, Cissy, *Obit* July 1941

Fitzgerald, Geraldine, Irish actress and director, Oct 1976, *Obit* Yrbk 2005

Flagg, Fannie, American comedienne, actress and novelist, Nov 2006

Flanders, Michael, Jan 1970, *Obit* June 1975

Flay, Bobby, American chef and restaurateur, May 2008

Fleming, Maureen, American dancer and choreographer, Mar 2010

Flight of the Conchords, Mar 2008

Fo, Dario, Italian actor and dramatist, Nov 1986

Fonda, Bridget, American actress, Jan 1994

Fonda, Henry, American actor, Yrbk 1948, Nov 1974, *Obit* Sept 1982

Fonda, Jane, American actress, July 1964, June 1986

Fonda, Peter, American actor, Mar 1998

Fontaine, Joan, American actress, May 1944

Fontanne, Lynn, Anglo-American actress, June 1941, *Obit* Sept 1983

Foote, Horton, American playwright, screenwriter and novelist, Aug 1986, *Obit* Yrbk 2009

Ford, Glenn, American actor, June 1959, *Obit* Yrbk 2007

Ford, Harrison, American actor, Sept 1984, June 2008

Forrest, Alan, *Obit* Sept 1941

Forsythe, John, American actor, May 1973, *Obit* Yrbk 2010

Foster, Jodie, American actress and film director, June 1981, Aug 1992

Fox, Megan, American actress, Feb 2010

Fox, Michael J., Canadian actor, Nov 1987

Fox, Sidney, actress, *Obit* Jan 1943

Foxx, Jamie, American comedian and actor, May 2005

Foxx, Redd, American comedian, Yrbk 1972, *Obit* Jan 1992

Frakes, Jonathan, actor and motion picture director, July 1999

Franciosa, Tony, American actor, July 1961, *Obit* Yrbk 2006

Francis, Arlene, American television personality, May 1956, *Obit* Sept 2001

Francisco, Chilean television personality, Feb 2001

Franco, James, American actor, Apr 2011

Frankel, Bethenny, American chef, food service executive and participant in reality TV show Real housewives of New York City, Mar 2013

Franken, Al, American senator, June 1999

Franklin, Irene, actress, *Obit* Aug 1941

Franz, Dennis, American actor, July 1995

Fraser, Brendan, American actor, Feb 2001

Freeman, Martin, British actor, Nov 2013

Freeman, Morgan, American actor, Feb 1991

Fresnay, Pierre, Feb 1959, *Obit* Feb 1975

Fry, Stephen, English actor and novelist, Sept 1998

Fugard, Athol, South African dramatist, actor and director, June 1975

Funicello, Annette, American actress and singer, *Obit* Yrbk 2013

Funt, Allen, television producer and performer, Yrbk 1966, *Obit* Nov 1999

Furness, Betty, television commentator and consumer adviser, Feb 1968, *Obit* June 1994

Gabin, Jean, French actor, June 1941, *Obit* Jan 1977

Gable, Clark, American actor, May 1945, *Obit* Jan 1961

Gabor, Eva, Hungarian actress, July 1968, *Obit* Sept 1995

Gabor, Zsa Zsa, Hungarian-American actress, Mar 1988

Gandolfini, James, American actor, Feb 2000, *Obit* Yrbk 2013

Ganz, Bruno, Swiss actor, Jan 2006

Garbo, Greta, Swedish-American actress, Apr 1955, *Obit* June 1990

Garcia Bernal, Gael, Mexican actor, Jan 2003

Gardner, Ava, American actress, Mar 1965, *Obit* Mar 1990

Gardner, Ed, Sept 1943, *Obit* Oct 1963

Garfield, John, actor, Apr 1948, *Obit* July 1952

Garfunkel, Art, American singer and actor, June 1974

Gargan, William, Jan 1969, *Obit* Apr 1979

Garland, Judy, American singer and actress, Nov 1941, Yrbk 1952, *Obit* Sept 1969

Garner, James, American actor, Nov 1966

Garner, Jennifer, American actress, Apr 2008

Garofalo, Janeane, American comedienne and actress, Mar 2005

Garroway, Dave, American television personality, May 1952, *Obit* Sept 1982

Garson, Greer, Anglo-Irish actress, Sept 1942, *Obit* June 1996

Gassman, Vittorio, Italian actor and theatrical director, Oct 1964, *Obit* Oct 2000

Gavin, John, American actor and diplomat, Sept 1962

Gazzara, Ben, American actor, Nov 1967, *Obit* Yrbk 2012

Gere, Richard, American actor, Aug 1980

Gervais, Ricky, British comedian, Jan 2006

Gerwig, Greta, American actress, June 2010

Getty, Estelle, American actress, Mar 1990, *Obit* Yrbk 2008

Giamatti, Paul, American actor, Sept 2005

Giannini, Giancarlo, June 1979

Gibson, Mel, American actor and motion picture director, Apr 1984, Aug 2003

Gielgud, John, English actor, director and producer, Apr 1947, Feb 1984, *Obit* Aug 2000

Gifford, Kathie Lee, American singer and television personality, Nov 1994

Gillmore, Frank, *Obit* May 1943

Gingold, Hermione, English actress, Oct 1958, *Obit* July 1987

Gish, Dorothy, American actress, Aug 1944, *Obit* Sept 1968

Gish, Lillian, American actress, Aug 1944, Aug 1978, *Obit* Apr 1993

Gleason, Jackie, American actor, Oct 1955, *Obit* Aug 1987

Glover, Danny, American actor, Apr 1992

Gobel, George, comedian, Mar 1955, *Obit* Apr 1991

Goddard, Paulette, American actress, *Obit* June 1990

Godfrey, Arthur, radio and television personality, July 1948, *Obit* May 1983

Godunov, Alexander, Russian ballet dancer and actor, Feb 1983, *Obit* July 1995

Goldberg, Whoopi, American actress, Mar 1985

Goldblum, Jeff, American actor, July 1997

Googoosh, Iranian singer and actress, May 2001

Gordon, C. Henry, *Obit* Jan 1941

Gordon, Dorothy, Jan 1955, *Obit* July 1970

Gordon, Ruth, actress and screenwriter, Apr 1943, Apr 1972, *Obit* Oct 1985

Gordon-Levitt, Joseph, American actor, June 2011

Gorin, Igor, July 1942, *Obit* June 1982

Gosden, Freeman F., actor, Yrbk 1947, *Obit* Feb 1983

Gossett, Louis, American actor, Nov 1990

Gould, Elliott, American actor, Feb 1971

Goulding, Ray, American comedian, Oct 1957, *Obit* May 1990

Goulet, Robert, American singer and actor, Sept 1962, *Obit* Yrbk 2008

Gowdy, Curt, American television sportscaster, May 1967, *Obit* Yrbk 2006

Grace, Mar 1955, Oct 1977, *Obit* Nov 1982

Graham, Elinor, Yrbk 1952

Grammer, Kelsey, American actor, May 1996

Grant, Cary, Anglo-American actor, Sept 1941, Nov 1965, *Obit* Jan 1987

Grant, Hugh, English actor, Sept 1995

Grant, Lee, actress and director, Mar 1974

Graser, Earle W., *Obit* June 1941

Grauer, Ben, Feb 1941, July 1959, *Obit* July 1977

Gray, Spalding, American monologist, Sept 1986, *Obit* Yrbk 2004

Green, Martyn, June 1950, *Obit* Apr 1975

Green, Tom, Canadian comedian, Oct 2003

Greene, Brian R., American physicist, Aug 2000

Greene, Lorne, actor, Jan 1967, *Obit* Oct 1987

Greenstreet, Sydney, May 1943, *Obit* Mar 1954

Greenwood, Joan, English actress, May 1954, *Obit* Apr 1987

Grenfell, Joyce, English actress, Mar 1958, *Obit* Feb 1980

Grey, Joel, American actor and singer, Jan 1973

Grier, Pam, American actress, Feb 1998

Griffies, Ethel, Jan 1968, *Obit* Nov 1975

Griffin, Kathy, American comedienne and actress, Sept 2008

Griffith, Andy, American actor, May 1960, *Obit* Yrbk 2012

Griffith, Melanie, American actress, Oct 1990

Grimes, Tammy, actress, July 1962

Grizzard, George, American actor, June 1976, *Obit* Yrbk 2008

Grodin, Charles, American actor, Nov 1995

Gronemeyer, Herbert, German singer and actor, Jan 2003

Grylls, Bear, British adventurer and television personality, Oct 2011

Grzimek, Bernhard, German zoo director and television performer, Mar 1973, *Obit* May 1987

Guillaume, Robert, American actor, Apr 2000

Guinness, Alec, English actor, Oct 1950, Mar 1981, *Obit* Oct 2000

Gulpilil, David, Australian actor, Jan 2003

Gunn, Tim, American clothing company executive, Oct 2009

Gwenn, Edmund, Sept 1943, *Obit* Nov 1959

Hackett, Buddy, American comedian, May 1965, *Obit* Oct 2003

Hackman, Gene, American actor, July 1972

Hagen, Uta, American actress, May 1944, Oct 1963, *Obit* Yrbk 2004

Hagman, Larry, American actor, Sept 1980, *Obit* Yrbk 2013

Hakim, Christine, Indonesian actress and social activist, Jan 2003

Hall, Arsenio, American comedian and talk show host, Sept 1989

Hall, Deidre, American actress, Nov 2002

Hall, James, actor, *Obit* July 1940

Hamilton, Hale, *Obit* July 1942

Hamilton, Margaret, actress, Apr 1979, *Obit* July 1985

Hamm, Jon, American actor, Mar 2013

Hampden, Walter, American actor, May 1953, *Obit* Sept 1955

Hampshire, Susan, English actress and author, Jan 1974

Hancock, Trenton Doyle, American painter and performance artist, Apr 2006

Handler, Chelsea, American comedian and actress, Oct 2010

Hanks, Tom, American actor, Apr 1989

Hannah, Daryl, American actress, May 1990

Hansen, Liane, American radio reporter and program host, May 2003

Harden, Marcia Gay, American actress, Sept 2001

Hardwick, Chris, game show host, June 2012

Hardwicke, Cedric, English actor, Oct 1949, *Obit* Oct 1964

Harlan, Otis, *Obit* Jan 1940

Harper, Valerie, American actress, Feb 1975

Harrelson, Woody, American actor, Jan 1997

Harris, Barbara, American actress, Apr 1968

Harris, Julie, American actress, Feb 1956, Aug 1977, *Obit* Yrbk 2013

Harris, Naomie, British actress, Sept 2012

Harris, Richard, Irish actor, May 1964, *Obit* Yrbk 2003

Harris, Rolf, Australian television personality, singer and cartoonist, Jan 2002

Harris, Rosemary, British actress, Sept 1967

Harrison, Rex, English actor, Jan 1947, Feb 1986, *Obit* July 1990

Harry, Deborah, American singer, Nov 1981

Hart, Kitty Carlisle, American singer, actress and state official, Oct 1982, *Obit* Yrbk 2007

Hart, William S., American actor, *Obit* July 1946

Hartman, David, actor and television personality, June 1981

Hartman, Paul, American actor, Nov 1942, *Obit* Yrbk 1973

Haruka, Yoko, Japanese feminist, writer and television personality, Jan 2004

Harvey, Laurence, British actor, May 1961, *Obit* Jan 1974

Hathaway, Anne, American actress, Feb 2009

Hauser, Gayelord, German-American nutritionist and author, June 1955, *Obit* Feb 1985

Hawke, Ethan, American actor and novelist, May 1998

Hawkins, Jack, Nov 1959, *Obit* Oct 1973

Hawley, H. Dudley, *Obit* May 1941

Hawn, Goldie, American actress, Yrbk 1971

Hayakawa, Sessue, Japanese actor, Sept 1962, *Obit* Jan 1974

Hayden, Sterling, actor, May 1978, *Obit* July 1986

Hayes, Helen, American actress, Jan 1942, Oct 1956, *Obit* May 1993

Hayes, Peter Lind, actor, Mar 1959, *Obit* July 1998

Haysbert, Dennis, American actor, Nov 2006

Hayward, Susan, American actress, May 1953, *Obit* May 1975

Hayworth, Rita, American actress, May 1960, *Obit* July 1987

Heche, Anne, American actress, Sept 1998

Heckart, Eileen, American actress, June 1958, *Obit* Mar 2002

Hee, Dana, American motion picture stunt performer, May 2008

Heflin, Van, July 1943, *Obit* Sept 1971

Helpmann, Robert, Australian dancer and actor, Feb 1950, *Obit* Nov 1986

Hemingway, Margaux, American model and actress, Mar 1978, *Obit* Sept 1996

Hemsworth, Chris, Australian actor, Jan 2013

Henderson, Florence, American singer and actress, Apr 1971

Henderson, Skitch, American conductor, July 1966, *Obit* Apr 2006

Henie, Sonja, Norwegian-American figure skater and actress, Sept 1940, Jan 1952, *Obit* Nov 1970

Henner, Marilu, American actress, Feb 1999

Henreid, Paul, Austrian actor and director, July 1943, *Obit* June 1992

Henry, Martha, Canadian actress and theatrical director, Jan 2006

Hepburn, Audrey, Anglo-Dutch actress, Mar 1954, *Obit* Mar 1993

Hepburn, Katharine, American actress, May 1942, Nov 1969, *Obit* Nov 2003

Herbert, Don, American science teacher and television personality, Feb 1956, *Obit* Yrbk 2007

Herlihy, James Leo, American novelist, dramatist and actor, Sept 1961, *Obit* Jan 1994

Hershey, Barbara, American actress, Aug 1989

Hersholt, Jean, American actor, Yrbk 1944, *Obit* Sept 1956

Heston, Charlton, American actor, May 1957, July 1986, *Obit* July 2008

Hibbard, Edna, *Obit* Feb 1943

Hill, Arthur, Canadian actor, Mar 1977, *Obit* Yrbk 2007

Hill, Benny, English comedian, Feb 1983, *Obit* June 1992

Hill, Dule, American actor, July 2003

Hiller, Wendy, English actress, Oct 1941, *Obit* Yrbk 2003

Hines, Gregory, American dancer and actor, July 1985, *Obit* Yrbk 2003

Hingle, Pat, American actor, Apr 1965, *Obit* Yrbk 2009

Hirsch, Judd, actor, Mar 1984

Hjejle, Iben, Danish actress, Jan 2003

Hoch, Danny, American actor, Oct 1999

Hoffman, Dustin, American actor, Yrbk 1969, Jan 1996

Hoffman, Philip Seymour, American actor, May 2001

Holbrook, Hal, American actor, May 1961

Holden, William, actor, June 1954, *Obit* Jan 1982

Holliday, Judy, actress, Apr 1951, *Obit* July 1965

Holloway, Stanley, Feb 1963, *Obit* Mar 1982

Holm, Celeste, American actress, Apr 1944, *Obit* Yrbk 2012

Holm, Ian, English actor, Mar 2002

Holmes, Phillips, *Obit* Oct 1942

Hong, Seok Chon, Korean actor, Jan 2004

Hood, Gavin, South African motion picture director, Jan 2006

Hooks, Robert, Mar 1970

Hope, Bob, American comedian and actor, June 1941, Oct 1953, *Obit* Yrbk 2003

Hopkins, Anthony, Welsh-American actor, Feb 1980, Mar 1997

Hopper, Dennis, American actor and director, Aug 1987, *Obit* Yrbk 2010

Hopper, Hedda, American gossip columnist, Nov 1942, *Obit* Mar 1966

Horne, Lena, American singer, June 1944, Nov 1985, *Obit* Aug 2010

Horton, Edward Everett, American actor, Yrbk 1946, *Obit* Nov 1970

Hoskins, Bob, English actor, Sept 1990

Hounsou, Djimon, Beninese model and actor, Aug 2004

Houseman, John, theatrical director, producer and actor, July 1959, Apr 1984, *Obit* Jan 1989

Houston, Whitney, American singer and actress, Nov 1986, *Obit* Yrbk 2012

Howard, Cordelia, actress, *Obit* Oct 1941

Howard, Leslie, English actor, *Obit* July 1943

Howard, Ron, American actor and film director, Jan 1979, Aug 1995

Howard, Terrence, American actor, June 2007

Howard, Trevor, English actor, July 1964, *Obit* Feb 1988

Howe, Helen Huntington, author and monologist, Yrbk 1954, *Obit* Mar 1975

Hudson, Jennifer, American singer and actress, May 2007

Hudson, Rock, American actor, Oct 1961, *Obit* Nov 1985

Hughes, Barnard, American actor, Sept 1981, *Obit* Yrbk 2006

Hughley, D. L., American comedian, Mar 2000

Hull, Josephine, Oct 1953, *Obit* May 1957

Humbard, Rex, American evangelist, Sept 1972, *Obit* Yrbk 2008

Hunt, Helen, Nov 1996

Hunt, Linda, actress, Jan 1988

Hunter, Glenn, American actor, *Obit* Mar 1946

Hunter, Holly, American actress, July 1994

Hunter, Kim, American actress, May 1952, *Obit* Yrbk 2002

Huppert, Isabelle, French actress, Nov 1981

Hurt, John, British actor, Jan 1982

Hurt, William, American actor, May 1986

Huston, Anjelica, American actress, July 1990

Huston, Walter, actor, Feb 1949, *Obit* May 1950

Hutton, Betty, American singer and actress, June 1950, *Obit* Yrbk 2007

Hutton, Lauren, American model and actress, July 1994

Ice Cube (Musician), American rapper and actor, Aug 1995

Ice-T, American rapper and actor, Sept 1994

Imam, Adel, Egyptian actor, Jan 2002

Imus, Don, American radio talk show host, Feb 1996

Irons, Jeremy, English actor, Aug 1984

Irvine, Alexander, Irish-American missionary, actor and dramatist, *Obit* May 1941

Irving, Jules, July 1970, *Obit* Sept 1979

Irwin, Bill, American actor and mime, Oct 1987

Irwin, Steve, Australian wildlife conservationist and television personality, Aug 2000, *Obit* Yrbk 2007

Istaru, Ana, Costa Rican poet, dramatist and actress, Jan 2004

Itami, Juzo, Japanese actor and motion picture director, May 1990, *Obit* Mar 1998

Ives, Burl, singer and actor, Jan 1946, May 1960, *Obit* June 1995

Ivey, Judith, actress, June 1993

Izzard, Eddie, British comedian and actor, Jan 2003

Jacir, Emily, Palestinian artist, Aug 2009

Jackman, Hugh, Australian actor, Oct 2003

Jackson, Anne, actress, Sept 1980

Jackson, Glenda, English actress and member of Parliament, Yrbk 1971

Jackson, Jesse L., American clergyman and civil rights activist, Yrbk 1970, Jan 1986

Jackson, Joe, American comedian, *Obit* July 1942

Jackson, Samuel L., American actor, Nov 1996

Jacobi, Derek, British actor, May 1981

Jagger, Bianca, Nicaraguan actress, Apr 1987

Janssen, David, American actor, Mar 1967, *Obit* Apr 1980

Jay, Ricky, American magician and actor, May 1994

Jeanmaire, Zizi, French ballet dancer and actress, Nov 1952

Jentsch, Julia, German actress, Jan 2006

Jimenez, Joyce, Filipino-American actress and lingerie company founder, Jan 2003

Johansson, Scarlett, American actress, Mar 2005

Johns, Glynis, Sept 1973

Johnson, Don, American actor, Apr 1986

Johnson, Dwayne, American wrestler and actor, July 2000

Johnson, Van, American actor, July 1945, *Obit* Yrbk 2009

Jolie, Angelina, American actress, Oct 2000

Jolson, Al, singer and actor, Nov 1940, *Obit* Yrbk 1950

Jones, Barry, Mar 1958

Jones, Buck, *Obit* Jan 1943

Jones, Candy, model and talk show host, Oct 1961, *Obit* Mar 1990

Jones, Carolyn, American actress, Mar 1967, *Obit* Sept 1983

Jones, Cherry, American actress, May 1998

Jones, Grace, American singer and actress, Sept 1987

Jones, James Earl, American actor, Sept 1969, Nov 1994

Jones, Jennifer, American actress, May 1944, *Obit* Yrbk 2010

Jones, Preston, actor and dramatist, Feb 1977, *Obit* Nov 1979

Jones, Rashida, American actress, Aug 2013

Jones, Sarah, American poet, playwright and performance artist, July 2005

Jones, Shirley, American singer and actress, Oct 1961

Jones, Tommy Lee, American actor, Oct 1995

Jordan, Jim, American radio performer, Nov 1941, *Obit* May 1988

Jordan, Marian, radio performer, Nov 1941, *Obit* June 1961

Jourdan, Louis, French actor, Jan 1967

Jouvet, Louis, French actor and theatrical director, Oct 1949, *Obit* Oct 1951

Joyner, Tom, American radio talk show host, Sept 2002

Judd, Ashley, American actress, Feb 2000

Julia, Raul, American actor, Sept 1982, *Obit* Jan 1995

July, Miranda, American performance artist and filmmaker, Nov 2007

Kahn, Madeline, American actress and singer, May 1977, *Obit* Mar 2000

Kaling, Mindy, American actress, playwright and television scriptwriter, Apr 2012

Kaminska, Ida, Polish actress, Nov 1969, *Obit* July 1980

Kani, John, South African actor, theatrical director and playwright, June 2001

Kapoor, Karisma, Indian actress, Jan 2002

Karloff, Boris, Anglo-American actor, Mar 1941, *Obit* Mar 1969

Karno, Fred, English comedian and theatrical producer, *Obit* Nov 1941

Kassovitz, Mathieu, French actor and film director, Jan 2005

Kavner, Julie, American actress, Oct 1992

Kay, Beatrice, Yrbk 1942

Kaye, Danny, American comedian, actor and singer, Yrbk 1941, Nov 1952, *Obit* Apr 1987

Keach, Stacy, American actor, Nov 1971

Keane, Doris, actress, *Obit* Jan 1946

Keaton, Diane, American actress and motion picture director, June 1978, May 1996

Keaton, Michael, American actor, June 1992

Keeler, Ruby, American dancer and actress, Yrbk 1971, *Obit* Apr 1993

Keener, Catherine, American actress, Oct 2002

Keeshan, Bob, American television personality, May 1965, *Obit* Yrbk 2004

Keillor, Garrison, American novelist, short story writer, storyteller and radio performer, Aug 1985

Keitel, Harvey, American actor, Mar 1994

Kekilli, Sibel, Turkish-German actress, Jan 2006

Keller, Marthe, Swiss actress and opera director, July 2004

Kelly, David, Irish actor, Jan 2005, *Obit* Yrbk 2012

Kelly, Gene, American dancer, singer and actor, Yrbk 1945, Feb 1977, *Obit* Apr 1996

Kelly, Joe, June 1945, *Obit* July 1959

Kelly, Nancy, actress, June 1955, *Obit* Mar 1995

Kennedy, Arthur, American actor, Nov 1961

Kerr, Deborah, British actress, Sept 1947, *Obit* Feb 2008

Khan, Aamir, Indian actor, Jan 2002

Kidd, Michael, American choreographer, Mar 1960, *Obit* Yrbk 2008

Kidman, Nicole, Australian actress, Mar 1997

Kiepura, Jan, Nov 1943, *Obit* Nov 1966

Kier, Udo, German actor, Jan 2005

Kiley, Richard, actor, Apr 1973, *Obit* May 1999

Kilgallen, Dorothy, American newspaper columnist, Feb 1952, *Obit* Jan 1966

Kilmer, Val, American actor, Jan 1996

Kimmel, Jimmy, American comedian, Oct 2009

King, Alan, American comedian, June 1970, *Obit* Yrbk 2004

Kingsley, Ben, English actor, Nov 1983

Kinski, Nastassia, German actress, June 1984

Kitano, Takeshi, Japanese actor, screenwriter and director, July 1998

Kitchen, Michael, British actor, Nov 2008

Kitt, Eartha, American singer and actress, Apr 1955, *Obit* Yrbk 2009

Klein, Robert, American comedian, Mar 1977

Kline, Kevin, American actor, July 1986

Knightley, Keira, English actress, Jan 2005

Kollmar, Richard, Feb 1952, *Obit* Feb 1971

Korman, Harvey, American actor, Oct 1979, *Obit* Yrbk 2008

Kotto, Yaphet, American actor, Mar 1995

Kovacs, Ernie, American comedian, Feb 1958, *Obit* Mar 1962

Kramm, Joseph, actor and dramatist, July 1952

Kristofferson, Kris, American actor, singer and songwriter, Nov 1974

Kurihara, Harumi, Japanese cook and television personality, Jan 2006

Kurtz, Swoosie, American actress, Oct 1987

Kusturica, Emir, Bosnian motion picture director and screenwriter, Nov 2005

Kyser, Kay, American band leader, Apr 1941, *Obit* Sept 1985

LL Cool J, American rapper and actor, Nov 1997

LaBeouf, Shia, American actor, Aug 2009

LaFontaine, Don, American voice-over actor, Sept 2004, *Obit* Yrbk 2008

LaLanne, Jack, American physical fitness expert, Oct 1994, *Obit* Yrbk 2011

Labaki, Nadine, Lebanese actress, film director and screenwriter, July 2013

Ladd, Alan, American actor, Sept 1943, *Obit* Mar 1964

Lagasse, Emeril, American chef and restaurateur, May 1999

Lahr, Bert, actor, Jan 1952, *Obit* Feb 1968

Laine, Cleo, British singer and actress, Feb 1986

Lakshmi, Padma, Indian model, cookbook writer and television personality, Jan 2006

Lancaster, Burt, American actor, July 1953, Apr 1986, *Obit* Jan 1995

Lanchester, Elsa, English actress, May 1950, *Obit* Feb 1987

Landon, Michael, American actor, director and producer, July 1977, *Obit* Sept 1991

Lane, Nathan, American actor, Aug 1996

Langdon, Harry, American actor and comedian, *Obit* Feb 1945

Lange, Jessica, American actress, May 1983

Langella, Frank, American actor, Sept 1980

Lansbury, Angela, American actress, Sept 1967

Lasser, Louise, actress, Oct 1976

Lau, Andy, Chinese singer and actor, Jan 2005

Laughton, Charles, Anglo-American actor, Nov 1948, *Obit* Jan 1963

Laurie, Hugh, English actor and television scriptwriter, Jan 2006

Lavant, Denis, French actor, June 2013

Lavin, Linda, actress, Nov 1987

Lawford, Ernest, *Obit* Feb 1941

Lawrence, Carol, American singer and actress, Nov 1961

Lawrence, Gertrude, English actress, Aug 1940, Sept 1952

Lawrence, Jennifer, American actress, May 2013

Lawrence, Martin, American comedian and actor, Oct 1999

Lawson, Mary, *Obit* July 1941

Le Gallienne, Eva, American actress, director and producer, Oct 1942, Mar 1955, *Obit* Aug 1991

Leach, Robin, British television personality and producer, Sept 1990

Leachman, Cloris, American actress, Oct 1975

Ledger, Heath, Australian actor, June 2006, *Obit* Yrbk 2008

Ledoyen, Virginie, French actress, Jan 2002

Lee, Auriol, *Obit* Sept 1941

Lee, Canada, American actor, Yrbk 1944, *Obit* June 1952

Lee, Christopher, English actor, Sept 1975

Lee, Gypsy Rose, American actress and stripteaser, Yrbk 1943, *Obit* June 1970

Lee, Peggy, American singer, Mar 1963, *Obit* May 2002

Lee, Sandra, American cook, entrepreneur and television personality, Aug 2011

Lee, Spike, American film director, screenwriter and actor, Mar 1989

Leguizamo, John, American actor and dramatist, Apr 1998

Leigh, Jennifer Jason, American actress, Aug 1992

Leigh, Vivien, English actress, July 1946, *Obit* Oct 1967

Leighton, Margaret, English actress, Mar 1957, *Obit* Mar 1976

Lemmon, Jack, American actor, Feb 1961, Aug 1988, *Obit* Oct 2001

Lemon, Ralph, American dancer and choreographer, Feb 1997

Lenya, Lotte, German singer and actress, June 1959, *Obit* Jan 1982

Leo, Melissa, American actress, July 2009

Lepage, Robert, Canadian theatrical director, actor and dramatist, Apr 1995

Letts, Tracy, American playwright, Oct 2008

Leung, Tony Chiu-wai, Chinese actor, Jan 2006

Levant, Oscar, American pianist and composer, Jan 1940, Oct 1952, *Obit* Oct 1972

Levenson, Sam, American humorist, July 1959, *Obit* Nov 1980

Levy, Dani, Swiss actor, film director and screenwriter, Jan 2007

Levy, Eugene, Canadian actor, film director and screenwriter, Jan 2002

Lewis, Carl, American sprinter and long jumper, Nov 1984, Yrbk 1996

Lewis, Jerry, American comedian, Nov 1962

Lewis, Juliette, American actress, Feb 1996

Lewis, Richard, comedian and actor, July 1993

Lewis, Shari, puppeteer and ventriloquist, Mar 1958, *Obit* Oct 1998

Li Gong, Chinese actress, May 1997

Li, Jet, Chinese actor and martial artist, June 2001

Liddy, G. Gordon, American lawyer, actor and government official, Oct 1980

Lillie, Beatrice, British actress, Feb 1945, Sept 1964, *Obit* Mar 1989

Limbaugh, Rush, American radio and television commentator, Mar 1993

Lincoln, Abbey, American jazz singer, Sept 2002, *Obit* Yrbk 2010

Linden, Hal, actor, Jan 1987

Lindfors, Viveca, Swedish actress, Apr 1955, *Obit* Jan 1996

Lindo, Delroy, American actor, Mar 2001

Linkletter, Art, American television personality, Nov 1953, *Obit* Yrbk 2010

Liotta, Ray, American actor, May 1994

Lipton, James, American television interviewer, writer and producer, July 2011

Lithgow, John, American actor, Nov 1996

Liu, Lucy, American actress and artist, Oct 2003

Lloyd, Harold, American actor and producer, Sept 1949, *Obit* Apr 1971

Lockhart, Gene, Canadian actor, May 1950, *Obit* June 1957

Lockwood, Margaret, English actress, Sept 1948, *Obit* Sept 1990

Lodge, John Davis, governor and diplomat, Mar 1948, *Obit* Jan 1986

Loftus, Cissie, Sept 1940, *Obit* Aug 1943

Lohan, Lindsay, American actress, Nov 2005

Lollobrigida, Gina, Italian actress, Sept 1960

Lombard, Carole, American actress, *Obit* Mar 1942

London, Julie, singer and actress, May 1960, *Obit* Feb 2001

Lopez, George, American comedian, Mar 2010

Loren, Sophia, Italian actress, Mar 1959

Losch, Tilly, July 1944, *Obit* Feb 1976

Loud, Pat, July 1974

Loudon, Dorothy, American actress and singer, June 1984, *Obit* Yrbk 2004

Louganis, Greg, American diver and actor, Oct 1984

Louis-Dreyfus, Julia, American actress, Oct 1995

Love, Courtney, American singer and actress, June 1996

Lovett, Lyle, American singer, Sept 1997

Lowe, Rob, American actor, July 2000

Lowensohn, Elina, Romanian actress, Jan 2005

Loy, Myrna, American actress, Oct 1950, *Obit* Feb 1994

LuPone, Patti, American actress and singer, Apr 1989

Lucci, Susan, American actress, Oct 1989

Ludacris, American rapper, June 2004

Ludlam, Charles, American actor, director and dramatist, Aug 1986, *Obit* July 1987

Lukas, Paul, American actor, Feb 1942, *Obit* Oct 1971

Luna, Diego, Mexican actor, Jan 2002

Lunden, Joan, American television personality, May 1989

Lunt, Alfred, American actor, June 1941, *Obit* Sept 1977

Lupino, Ida, American actress and film director, Sept 1943, *Obit* Oct 1995

Lurie, John, American saxophonist and actor, Oct 2010

Lynch, Jane, American actress, July 2010

Lynch, Peg, Feb 1956

Lynde, Paul, Nov 1972, *Obit* Feb 1982

Lynn, Diana, actress, Nov 1953, *Obit* Feb 1972

Mabley, Moms, American comedienne and actress, Jan 1975, *Obit* Aug 1975

Mac, Bernie, American comedian and actor, June 2002, *Obit* Nov 2008

MacDowell, Andie, American model and actress, Nov 1999

MacFarlane, Seth, American animator, television

scriptwriter, producer and voice-over artist, May 2010

MacLachlan, Kyle, American actor, Aug 1993

MacLaine, Shirley, American dancer and actress, Yrbk 1959, July 1978

MacMurray, Fred, actor, Feb 1967, *Obit* Feb 1992

Mack, Ted, Apr 1951, *Obit* Sept 1976

Madonna, American singer, May 1986

Madsen, Michael, American actor, Apr 2004

Magliozzi, Ray, American automobile mechanic and radio talk show host, June 2006

Magliozzi, Tom, American automobile mechanic and radio talk show host, June 2006

Magnani, Anna, Italian actress, Apr 1956, *Obit* Nov 1973

Magnusson, Magnus, Icelandic-British television personality, journalist and college administrator, Jan 2006

Maguire, Tobey, American actor, Sept 2002

Mahoney, John, actor, Aug 1999

Main, Marjorie, actress, Oct 1951, *Obit* June 1975

Malden, Karl, American actor, Apr 1957, *Obit* Yrbk 2009

Malina, Joshua, American actor, Apr 2004

Malina, Judith, American actress and theatrical director, June 2011

Malkovich, John, American actor, May 1988

Mann, Erika, German writer, actress and daughter of Thomas Mann, Yrbk 1940, *Obit* Nov 1969

Manna, Charlie, Jan 1965, *Obit* Yrbk 1971

Mara, Rooney, American actress, Oct 2012

Marais, Jean, French actor, Apr 1962, *Obit* Jan 1999

Marceau, Marcel, French mime, Feb 1957, *Obit* Yrbk 2007

March, Fredric, American actor, Mar 1943, *Obit* June 1975

Marion, George F., *Obit* Jan 1946

Marling, Brit, American actress, film director and screenwriter, Oct 2011

Marsh, Jean, English actress, Nov 1977

Marshall, E. G., actor, June 1986, *Obit* Nov 1998

Marshall, Penny, American actress and motion picture director, Mar 1980, May 1992

Marshall, Tully, actor, *Obit* Apr 1943

Martin, Dean, American actor and singer, Nov 1964, *Obit* Mar 1996

Martin, Demetri, American comedian and actor, Oct 2009

Martin, Dick, American comedian, Sept 1969, *Obit* Yrbk 2008

Martin, Jesse L., American actor, July 2006

Martin, Mary, American actress and singer, Jan 1944, *Obit* Jan 1991

Martin, Ricky, Puerto Rican singer and actor, Sept 1999

Martin, Steve, American comedian and actor, Aug 1978, Nov 2000

Marvin, Lee, American actor, Sept 1966, *Obit* Oct 1987

Marx, Groucho, American comedian, Mar 1948, Feb 1973, *Obit* Oct 1977

Mary Alice, actress, Nov 1995

Masina, Giulietta, Italian actress, Apr 1958, *Obit* June 1994

Mason, James, English actor, May 1947, *Obit* Sept 1984

Mason, Marsha, American actress, Apr 1981

Massey, Raymond, Canadian-American actor, Feb 1946, *Obit* Sept 1983

Mastroianni, Marcello, Italian actor, June 1963, *Obit* Feb 1997

Matlin, Marlee, American actress, May 1992

Matthau, Walter, American actor, June 1966, *Obit* Sept 2000

Mature, Victor, actor, Yrbk 1951, *Obit* Oct 1999

Maura, Carmen, Spanish actress, Apr 1992

May, Elaine, American actress, screenwriter and director, Mar 1961

Mayor, Mireya, American primatologist and television personality, Sept 2011

McAdams, Rachel, Canadian actress, May 2009

McBurney, Simon, British actor and theatrical director, Jan 2005

McCambridge, Mercedes, American actress, June 1964, *Obit* Yrbk 2004

McCarthy, Thomas, American actor and motion picture director, Jan 2012

McClanahan, Rue, American actress, May 1989, *Obit* Yrbk 2010

McClinton, Marion, American playwright and theatrical director, Jan 2009

McCormick, Myron, Jan 1954, *Obit* Oct 1962

McCowen, Alec, Oct 1969

McCracken, Joan, June 1945, *Obit* Jan 1962

McCrary, Jinx Falkenburg, television performer and model, July 1953

McDaniel, Hattie, American actress, Sept 1940, *Obit* Yrbk 1952

McDaniel, James, American actor, Feb 2000

McDonald, Audra, American singer and actress, Apr 1999

McDonnell, Mary, American actress, May 1997

McDormand, Frances, American actress, Sept 1997

McDowall, Roddy, actor and photographer, Apr 1961, *Obit* Jan 1999

McDowell, Malcolm, English actor, Yrbk 1973

McEntire, Reba, American country singer and actress, Oct 1994

McGraw, Phillip C., American psychologist and television talk show host, June 2002

McGuire, Dorothy, American actress, Sept 1941, *Obit* Nov 2001

McKellen, Ian, English actor, Jan 1984

McKenna, Siobhan, Irish actress, Nov 1956, *Obit* Jan 1987

McMahon, Ed, American television personality, Apr 1977, *Obit* Yrbk 2009

McNair, Barbara, American singer and actress, Nov 1971, *Obit* Yrbk 2007

McNellis, Maggi, radio and television performer, Jan 1955, *Obit* Aug 1989

McQueen, Steve, American actor, Oct 1966, *Obit* Jan 1981

McShane, Ian, English actor, July 2011

Meadows, Audrey, actress, May 1958, *Obit* Apr 1996

Meadows, Jayne, May 1958

Means, Russell, American Indian leader, Jan 1978, *Obit* Yrbk 2013

Mei Lanfang, *Obit* Sept 1943

Meisner, Sanford, actor, director and teacher, Apr 1991, *Obit* Apr 1997

Melton, James, American opera singer, Sept 1945, *Obit* June 1961

Menjou, Adolphe, actor, June 1948, *Obit* Jan 1964

Mercouri, Melina, Greek actress and cabinet member, July 1965, Mar 1988, *Obit* May 1994

Meredith, Burgess, actor, July 1940, *Obit* Nov 1997

Merivale, Philip, *Obit* Apr 1946

Merman, Ethel, American actress and singer, Oct 1941, May 1955, *Obit* Apr 1984

Messing, Debra, American actress, Aug 2002

Meyer, Jean, Nov 1955

Meyers, Seth, American comedian and actor, Apr 2009

Midler, Bette, American singer and actress, June 1973, Nov 1997

Mifune, Toshiro, Japanese actor, June 1981, *Obit* Mar 1998

Mikhalkov, Nikita, Russian film director and actor, Oct 1995

Milland, Ray, actor, Feb 1946, *Obit* Apr 1986

Miller, Ann, American tap dancer and actress, Apr 1980, *Obit* Yrbk 2004

Miller, Jason, playwright and actor, Jan 1974, *Obit* Yrbk 2001

Miller, Jonathan, English physician, actor and director, Oct 1970, Nov 1986

Miller, Mitch, American conductor and record

producer, July 1956, *Obit* Yrbk 2010

Mills, Hayley, English actress, Apr 1963

Mills, John, British actor, May 1963, *Obit* Yrbk 2005

Minnelli, Liza, American actress and singer, Oct 1970, July 1988

Minogue, Kylie, Australian actress and singer, Jan 2003

Miranda, Carmen, Brazilian singer, dancer and actress, June 1941, *Obit* Oct 1955

Mirren, Helen, English actress, July 1995

Mitchum, Robert, American actor, Sept 1970, *Obit* Sept 1997

Mix, Tom, actor, *Obit* Yrbk 1940

Mizrahi, Isaac, American fashion designer and television personality, Jan 1991

Mo'Nique, American comedienne and actress, Apr 2010

Molina, Alfred, British actor, Feb 2004

Monroe, Marilyn, American actress, July 1959, *Obit* Oct 1962

Montand, Yves, French actor and singer, July 1960, Sept 1988, *Obit* Jan 1992

Montenegro, Fernanda, Brazilian actress, Oct 1999

Montgomery, Robert, actor and director, Jan 1948, *Obit* Nov 1981

Mon e, Janelle, American singer, May 2013

Moore, Demi, American actress, Sept 1993

Moore, Dudley, English actor, June 1982, *Obit* Yrbk 2002

Moore, Garry, American radio and television personality, Nov 1954, *Obit* Jan 1994

Moore, Julianne, American actress, Oct 1998

Moore, Mary Tyler, American actress, Feb 1971

Moore, Melba, American singer and actress, Jan 1973

Moore, Patrick, English astronomy author and television program host, Jan 2003, *Obit* Yrbk 2013

Moore, Roger, English actor, Feb 1975

Moorehead, Agnes, American actress, June 1952, *Obit* June 1974

Moran, John, American composer, performance artist and choreographer, June 2010

Moreau, Jeanne, French actress, Yrbk 1966

Moreno, Catalina Sandino, Colombian actress, Jan 2005

Moreno, Rita, American actress, singer and dancer, Sept 1985

Morgan, Henry, American radio and television personality, Mar 1947, *Obit* July 1994

Morgan, Piers, British talk show host, July 2012

Morgan, Tracy, American actor and comedian, Mar 2007

Moriarty, Michael, actor, July 1976

Morley, Robert, English actor, Nov 1963, *Obit* Aug 1992

Morrison, Adrienne, *Obit* Jan 1941

Morrison, Philip, American physicist, July 1981, *Obit* Aug 2005

Morse, Robert, actor, Nov 1962

Mortensen, Viggo, American actor, June 2004

Morton, Joe, actor, Feb 1999

Mos Def (Singer), American rapper, Apr 2005

Moscovitch, Maurice, *Obit* Aug 1940

Moss, Elisabeth, American actress, Nov 2013

Mostel, Zero, American actor, Apr 1943, Nov 1963, *Obit* Nov 1977

Mulligan, Carey, British actress, Oct 2013

Muni, Paul, actor, Jan 1944, *Obit* Nov 1967

Murphy, Eddie, American comedian and actor, Nov 1983

Murphy, George, American actor, dancer and senator, Yrbk 1965, *Obit* July 1992

Murray, Bill, American actor, Jan 1985, Sept 2004

Murray, Charlie, *Obit* Sept 1941

Murray, Don, actor, Sept 1959

Murray, J. Harold, *Obit* Feb 1941

Myers, Mike, Canadian comedian, actor and screenwriter, Aug 1997

Nabors, Jim, American actor and singer, Nov 1969

Naish, J. Carrol, actor, Jan 1957, *Obit* Mar 1973

Najimy, Kathy, American actress and comedienne, Oct 2002

Nares, Owen, *Obit* Sept 1943

Nazimova, Alla, Russian actress, *Obit* Aug 1945

Neagle, Anna, English actress, Nov 1945, *Obit* July 1986

Neal, Patricia, American actress, Sept 1964, *Obit* Yrbk 2010

Neeson, Liam, Irish-American actor, Nov 1994

Nelligan, Kate, Canadian actress, July 1983

Nelson, Harriet, actress and singer, May 1949, *Obit* Jan 1995

Nelson, Ozzie, actor and band leader, May 1949, *Obit* Aug 1975

Nemirovich-Danchenko, Vladimir Ivanovich, Russian dramatist and director, *Obit* June 1943

Nero, Franco, Italian actor, Jan 2002

Nesbitt, Cathleen, English actress, Nov 1956, *Obit* Sept 1982

Neuwirth, Bebe, American dancer and actress, Nov 1997

Neville, John, Jan 1959, *Obit* Yrbk 2012

Newhart, Bob, American comedian and actor, Mar 1962

Newley, Anthony, actor, singer and songwriter, Oct 1966, *Obit* July 1999

Newman, Paul, American actor, Nov 1959, May 1985, *Obit* Yrbk 2008

Newton, Thandie, British actress, Jan 2003

Newton-John, Olivia, Australian singer and actress, Nov 1978

Nicholson, Jack, American actor, Oct 1974, Apr 1995

Nighy, Bill, British actor, Jan 2007

Nimoy, Leonard, American actor, Feb 1977

Niven, David, British actor, Mar 1957, *Obit* Sept 1983

Nolan, Lloyd, actor, Nov 1956, *Obit* Nov 1985

Nolte, Nick, American actor, Nov 1980

Norris, Chuck, American actor and martial artist, Jan 1989

North, Oliver L., American Marine corps officer, columnist and television personality, Mar 1992

Norton, Edward, American actor, June 2000

Norton, Graham, Irish talk show host, Jan 2004

Norville, Deborah, American television reporter and radio talk show host, Apr 1990

Novak, Kim, American actress, Apr 1957

Nugent, Elliott, July 1944, *Obit* Oct 1980

Nye, Bill, American comedian and television performer, July 1998

O'Brian, Hugh, actor, July 1958

O'Brien, Pat, American actor, Mar 1966, *Obit* Jan 1984

O'Connell, Hugh, *Obit* Mar 1943

O'Connor, Carroll, American actor, July 1972, *Obit* Sept 2001

O'Connor, Donald, American actor and dancer, May 1955, *Obit* Apr 2004

O'Connor, Frances, Australian actress, Jan 2002

O'Donnell, Rosie, American comedienne, actress and talk show host, Aug 1995

O'Hara, Kelli, American actress and singer, Oct 2008

O'Hara, Maureen, Irish-American actress, Feb 1953

O'Neal, Frederick, actor, Nov 1946, *Obit* Oct 1992

O'Neal, Ryan, American actor, Feb 1973

O'Neal, Shaquille, American basketball player, July 1996

O'Shea, Milo, June 1982, *Obit* Yrbk 2013

O'Toole, Peter, Irish actor, Sept 1968

Oberon, Merle, English actress, Nov 1941, *Obit* Jan 1980

Oh, Sandra, Canadian actress, Jan 2005

Okonedo, Sophie, British actress, Jan 2005

Oldman, Gary, English actor, Jan 1996

Olin, Lena, Swedish actress, June 2003

Oliver, Edna May, actress, *Obit* Jan 1943

Oliver, Jamie, British chef and restaurateur, Jan 2005

Olivier, Laurence, English actor, June 1946, Jan 1979, *Obit* Sept 1989

Olmos, Edward James, American actor, Aug 1992

Olsen twins, American actresses, Sept 2010

Olsen, Ashley, American actress and fashion designer, Sept 2010

Olsen, Mary Kate, American actress, Sept 2010

Onuki, Ami, Japanese pop singer, Jan 2005

Orbach, Jerry, American actor, May 1970, *Obit* Apr 2005

Orman, Suze, American financial adviser, May 2003

Ormond, Julia, English actress, Mar 1999

Osato, Sono, Oct 1945

Osbourne, Sharon, English musical talent agent and promoter, Jan 2001

Osteen, Joel, American pastor and broadcasting executive, Jan 2006

Otto, Miranda, Australian actress, Jan 2003

Overman, Lynne, *Obit* Apr 1943

Paar, Jack, American television talk show host, Apr 1959, *Obit* Yrbk 2004

Pacino, Al, American actor, July 1974

Page, Ellen, Canadian actress, May 2008

Page, Geraldine, actress, Nov 1953, *Obit* Aug 1987

Page, Greg, Australian singer and actor, Jan 2004

Paige, Janis, actress and singer, Jan 1959

Palance, Jack, American actor, Aug 1992, *Obit* Feb 2007

Palin, Michael, English actor and screenwriter, Feb 2000

Palmer, Geoffrey, English actor, Jan 2006

Palmer, Lilli, German actress, May 1951, *Obit* Mar 1986

Paltrow, Gwyneth, American actress, Jan 2005

Paradis, Vanessa, French singer and actress, Jan 2004

Parke, William, *Obit* Sept 1941

Parker, Barnett, *Obit* Oct 1941

Parker, Mary-Louise, American actress, Apr 2006

Parker, Sarah Jessica, American actress, Sept 1998

Parker, Trey, American actor, television scriptwriter, director, producer and animator, May 1998

Parks, Bert, actor and television personality, Feb 1973, *Obit* Apr 1992

Parsons, Estelle, American actress, Oct 1975

Parsons, Jim, American actor, Sept 2013

Patinkin, Mandy, American actor and singer, Jan 1999

Pawley, Edward, Mar 1946

Paxinou, Katina, Oct 1943, *Obit* Apr 1973

Peck, Gregory, American actor, July 1947, Oct 1992, *Obit* Sept 2003

Pelletier, Wilfrid, Yrbk 1944, *Obit* June 1982

Penn, Sean, American actor and film director, June 1993

Penner, Joe, *Obit* Mar 1941

Pennington, Ty, American carpenter and host of reality TV show Extreme makeover: Home edition, Feb 2006

Peppard, George, actor, Yrbk 1965, *Obit* July 1994

Perez, Rosie, American actress, dancer and choreographer, Sept 1995

Perkins, Anthony, American actor, Sept 1960, *Obit* Nov 1992

Perkins, Elizabeth, American actress, Jan 2007

Perkins, Marlin, zoo director and television performer, Oct 1951, *Obit* Aug 1986

Perrin, Jacques, French actor, film producer, director and screenwriter, Jan 2004

Perrine, Valerie, actress, Oct 1975

Perry, Antoinette, actress and theatrical director, *Obit* July 1946

Perry, Tyler, American playwright, screenwriter, actor and director, June 2005

Pesci, Joe, American actor, Mar 1994

Peters, Bernadette, American actress and singer, Sept 1984

Pfeiffer, Michelle, American actress, Mar 1990

Phillips, Albert, *Obit* Mar 1940

Piccoli, Michel, French actor, Jan 2002

Pickerill, Elmo N., Mar 1966, *Obit* Mar 1968

Pickford, Mary, American actress, Apr 1945, *Obit* July 1979

Picon, Molly, actress, June 1951, *Obit* June 1992

Pidgeon, Walter, actor, Sept 1942, *Obit* Nov 1984

Pierce, David Hyde, American actor, Apr 2001

Pierce, Wendell, American actor, Aug 2010

Pike, Rosamund, British actress, Nov 2012

Pinero, Miguel, American dramatist and actor, Nov 1983, *Obit* Aug 1988

Pinsky, Drew, American physician and talk show host, Feb 2011

Pitt, Brad, American actor, Mar 1996

Pleasence, Donald, English actor, June 1969, *Obit* Apr 1995

Plimpton, Martha, American actress, Apr 2002

Plowright, Joan, English actress, Feb 1964

Plummer, Christopher, Canadian actor, July 1956, Aug 1988

Poehler, Amy, American comedienne and actress, Aug 2008

Poitier, Sidney, American actor and film director, May 1959, Sept 2000

Pollack, Sydney, American motion picture director, Sept 1986, *Obit* Sept 2008

Polley, Sarah, Canadian actress and film director, Jan 2003

Pollock, Allan, *Obit* Apr 1942

Portman, Eric, Mar 1957, *Obit* Feb 1970

Posey, Parker, American actress, Mar 2003

Poston, Tom, American actor, Apr 1961, *Obit* Yrbk 2007

Potente, Franka, German actress, Jan 2003

Powell, Dick, American actor, director and producer, Feb 1948, *Obit* Feb 1963

Powell, Jane, American singer and actress, Yrbk 1974

Powell, Kevin, American journalist, poet and essayist, Jan 2004

Powell, William, American actor, Oct 1947, *Obit* May 1984

Power, Tyrone, American actor, Yrbk 1950, *Obit* Jan 1959

Powers, James T., American actor, *Obit* Mar 1943

Preminger, Otto, American film director, July 1959, *Obit* June 1986

Presley, Elvis, American singer, Sept 1959, *Obit* Oct 1977

Presley, Priscilla Beaulieu, American actress, Sept 1990

Preston, Robert, American actor, Yrbk 1958, *Obit* May 1987

Price, Vincent, American actor, Nov 1956, *Obit* Jan 1994

Prinze, Freddie, American comedian, June 1975, *Obit* Mar 1977

Prinze, Freddie, American actor, Jan 2003

Pryor, Richard, American comedian, Feb 1976, *Obit* Apr 2006

P,pin, Jacques, French-American chef and cookbook writer, Sept 2012

Quarshie, Hugh, Ghanaian-British actor, Jan 2004

Quayle, Anthony, English actor and theatrical director, Yrbk 1971, *Obit* Jan 1990

Quinn, Aidan, American actor, Apr 2005

Quinn, Anthony, Mexican-American actor, Yrbk 1957, *Obit* Sept 2001

Radcliffe, Daniel, English actor, Nov 2010

Ragland, Rags, *Obit* Oct 1946

Rai, Aishwarya, Indian actress, Jan 2003

Raimu, *Obit* Nov 1946

Rain (Singer), Korean pop singer, Jan 2006

Rains, Claude, Anglo-American actor, Nov 1949, *Obit* July 1967

Rampling, Charlotte, English actress, June 2002

Randall, Tony, American actor, Jan 1961, *Obit* Yrbk 2004

Rathbone, Basil, Anglo-American actor, Mar 1951, *Obit* Oct 1967

Ratoff, Gregory, Aug 1943, *Obit* Feb 1961

Raven-Symone, American actress, Sept 2008

Ray, Charles, American actor, *Obit* Jan 1944

Ray, Rachael, American cook and television personality, Aug 2005

Raye, Martha, American actress, singer and comedienne, July 1963, *Obit* Jan 1995

Reagan, Nancy, wife of American president Ronald Reagan, May 1982

Reagan, Ron, American television personality and son of President Ronald Reagan, Feb 1992

Reagan, Ronald, American president, Yrbk 1949, Feb 1967, Nov 1982, *Obit* Yrbk 2004

Redford, Robert, American actor and motion picture director, Apr 1971, Mar 1982

Redgrave, Lynn, English actress, Sept 1969, *Obit* Yrbk 2010

Redgrave, Michael, English actor, Feb 1950, *Obit* May 1985

Redgrave, Vanessa, English actress, Yrbk 1966, Sept 2003

Reese, Della, American singer and actress, Sept 1971

Reeve, Christopher, American actor, May 1982, *Obit* Jan 2005

Reeves, Keanu, Canadian actor, May 1995

Reid, Kate, Canadian actress, Mar 1985, *Obit* May 1993

Reilly, John C., American actor, Oct 2004

Reiner, Carl, American producer, director, actor and screenwriter, Apr 1961

Reiner, Rob, American actor and film director, May 1988

Reinking, Ann, American dancer, choreographer and actress, June 2004

Reiser, Paul, American comedian and actor, Apr 1996

Remick, Lee, American actress, Oct 1966, *Obit* Sept 1991

Renaud, Madeleine, French actress and theatrical producer, Mar 1953, *Obit* Nov 1994

Reubens, Paul, American comedian and actor, Jan 1988

Rey, Fernando, Spanish actor, Mar 1979, *Obit* May 1994

Reynolds, Burt, American actor, Oct 1973

Reynolds, Debbie, American actress and singer, Yrbk 1964

Rhodes, Randi, American radio talk show host, Feb 2005

Richards, Lloyd G., American actor and theatrical director, Oct 1987, *Obit* Yrbk 2007

Richards, Michael, American actor and comedian, Nov 1997

Richardson, Miranda, English actress, Feb 1994

Richardson, Ralph, English actor, Nov 1950, *Obit* Nov 1983

Richman, Charles J., *Obit* Jan 1941

Riefenstahl, Leni, German actress and motion picture director, May 1975, *Obit* Yrbk 2004

Rigg, Diana, English actress, Oct 1974

Ringwald, Molly, American actress, May 1987

Ripert, Eric, French chef and restaurateur, Mar 2013

Ritchard, Cyril, Jan 1957, *Obit* Feb 1978

Ritter, John, American actor, June 1980, *Obit* Yrbk 2004

Ritter, Thelma, Yrbk 1957, *Obit* Feb 1974

Rivera, Chita, American dancer, singer and actress, Oct 1984

Rivers, Joan, American comedienne and television personality, Jan 1970, Mar 1987

Robards, Jason, American actor, Oct 1959, *Obit* Mar 2001

Robbins, Tim, American actor, July 1994

Roberts, Florence, *Obit* July 1940

Roberts, Julia, American actress, May 1991

Roberts, Tony, American actor, Oct 2006

Robertson, Cliff, American actor, Yrbk 1969, *Obit* Yrbk 2011

Robeson, Paul, American actor, civil rights activist and singer, Mar 1941, Mar 1976

Robinson, Bill, American tap dancer, Feb 1941, *Obit* Jan 1950

Robinson, Edward G., actor, Jan 1950, *Obit* Mar 1973

Robson, Flora, English actress, Jan 1951, *Obit* Sept 1984

Robson, May, actress, *Obit* Yrbk 1942

Rogers, Dale Evans, American singer and actress, Sept 1956, *Obit* Apr 2001

Rogers, Fred, American television performer and producer, July 1971, *Obit* July 2003

Rogers, Ginger, American actress, singer and dancer, Apr 1941, Yrbk 1967, *Obit* July 1995

Rogers, Paul, Mar 1960

Rogers, Roy, American cowboy singer and actor, Mar 1948, Oct 1983, *Obit* Sept 1998

Rogers, Will, American congressman and actor, Yrbk 1953, *Obit* Sept 1993

Rollins, Henry, American performance artist, poet and singer, Sept 2001

Rooney, Mickey, American actor, Feb 1942, Sept 1965

Rose, George, actor, Sept 1984, *Obit* June 1988

Rose, Jim, American performance artist, Mar 2003

Rossellini, Isabella, Italian model and actress, Aug 1988

Rourke, Mickey, American actor, Oct 1991

Rousseau, Stephane, Canadian comedian and actor, Jan 2004

Rowan, Dan, American comedian, Sept 1969, *Obit* Nov 1987

Rowlands, Gena, American actress, Nov 1975

Royle, Edwin Milton, *Obit* Apr 1942

Rubio, Ingrid, Spanish actress, Jan 2002

Rudd, Paul, American actor, Sept 1977, *Obit* Yrbk 2010

Ruhmann, Heinz, Apr 1965

Russell, Harold, American actor and government official, Jan 1950, Jan 1966, *Obit* Apr 2002

Russell, Kurt, American actor, Nov 2004

Russell, Mark, American political satirist, Mar 1981

Russell, Rosalind, American actress, Jan 1943, *Obit* Feb 1977

Russo, Rene, American model and actress, July 1997

Rutherford, Margaret, English actress, Jan 1964, *Obit* July 1972

Ryan, Meg, American actress, May 1999

Ryan, Robert, American actor, Yrbk 1963, *Obit* Sept 1973

Ryder, Winona, American actress, June 1994

Rylance, Mark, English actor and theatrical director, Nov 2011

Sagnier, Ludivine, French actress, Jan 2004

Saint, Eva Marie, American actress, June 1955

Sales, Soupy, American comedian, Jan 1967, *Obit* Yrbk 2009

Salonga, Lea, Filipino singer and actress, Jan 2007

Sanders, George, British actor, June 1943, *Obit* June 1972

Sandler, Adam, American comedian and actor, May 1998

Sansa, Maya, Italian actress, Jan 2004

Saralegui, Cristina, American television talk show host, Jan 1999

Sarandon, Susan, American actress, Sept 1989

Sass, Katrin, German actress, Jan 2003

Savalas, Telly, actor, Feb 1976, *Obit* Mar 1994

Schell, Maria, Austrian actress, June 1961, *Obit* Yrbk 2005

Schell, Maximilian, Austrian actor, Yrbk 1962

Schildkraut, Joseph, Austrian actor, Apr 1956, *Obit* Mar 1964

Schindler, John A., Mar 1956, *Obit* Jan 1958

Schmidt, Harald, German talk show host, Jan 2006

Schneider, Helge, German comedian, actor, jazz musician and composer, Jan 2007

Schneider, Romy, Austrian actress, Jan 1965, *Obit* July 1982

Schultz, Ed, American radio talk show host, Aug 2005

Schwartz, Maurice, theatrical director, producer and actor, Feb 1956, *Obit* July 1960

Schwartzman, Jason, American actor, Oct 2009

Schwarzenegger, Arnold, Austrian-American actor and governor, Apr 1979, Oct 1991, Aug 2004

Schygulla, Hanna, German actress, July 1984

Scofield, Paul, English actor, Mar 1962, *Obit* Yrbk 2008

Scott, George C., American actor, Apr 1971, *Obit* Nov 1999

Scott, Jill, American singer, songwriter and actress, Jan 2002

Scourby, Alexander, actor, July 1965, *Obit* Apr 1985

Seacrest, Ryan, American television personality, Sept 2009

Seberg, Jean, actress, Apr 1966, *Obit* Oct 1979

Sedaris, Amy, American actress and writer, Apr 2002

Segal, George, American actor, Nov 1975

Seigner, Emmanuelle, French actress, Jan 2006

Seinfeld, Jerry, American comedian, Aug 1992

Selleck, Tom, American actor, Nov 1983

Sellers, Peter, English actor, Yrbk 1960, *Obit* Sept 1980

Sen, Sushmita, Indian actress, Jan 2006

Sergio, Lisa, Italian radio commentator, June 1944, *Obit* Aug 1989

Sevigny, Chloe, American actress, Aug 2000

Shalhoub, Tony, American actor, Nov 2002

Shandling, Garry, American comedian, Apr 1989

Shannon, Peggy, actress, *Obit* July 1941

Sharif, Omar, Egyptian actor, May 1970

Shatner, William, Canadian actor, July 1987

Shaw, Robert, English actor and novelist, May 1968, *Obit* Oct 1978

Shawn, Wallace, American actor and playwright, June 1986

Shearer, Harry, American actor and comedian, June 2001

Shearer, Moira, Scottish ballet dancer and actress, Jan 1950, *Obit* Yrbk 2006

Sheen, Martin, American actor, June 1977

Sheindlin, Judith, American judge, Sept 1998

Shepard, Sam, American dramatist, Apr 1979

Shepherd, Cybill, American actress, Mar 1987

Shepherd, Jean, American humorist, Apr 1984, *Obit* Jan 2000

Sherawat, Mallika, Indian actress, Jan 2007

Sherman, Allan, television performer and comedian, Sept 1966, *Obit* Jan 1974

Shetty, Shilpa, Indian actress, Jan 2007

Shields, Brooke, American model and actress, Oct 1982

Short, Martin, Canadian comedian and actor, Sept 1992

Sidney, Sylvia, actress, Oct 1981, *Obit* Sept 1999

Signoret, Simone, French actress, Yrbk 1960, *Obit* Nov 1985

Silvers, Phil, actor, Yrbk 1957, *Obit* Jan 1986

Simmons, Gene, American bassist and actor, Apr 1999

Simmons, Jean, English actress, Feb 1952, *Obit* Yrbk 2010

Simmons, Richard, American fitness expert and television personality, May 1982

Simms, Hilda, actress, Nov 1944, *Obit* May 1994

Sinatra, Frank, American singer and actor, June 1943, Oct 1960, *Obit* July 1998

Sinbad, American comedian and actor, Feb 1997

Singh, Simon, British physicist, writer and television host, Jan 2005

Sinise, Gary, American actor and director, Apr 1997

Sintim-Misa, Kwaku, Ghanaian actor and comedian, Jan 2004

Sitgreaves, Beverley, *Obit* Sept 1943

Skarsgard, Stellan, Swedish actor, Jan 2002

Skelton, Red, American comedian and actor, Nov 1947, *Obit* Nov 1997

Skinner, Cornelia Otis, actress and author, Jan 1942, Yrbk 1964, *Obit* Sept 1979

Skinner, Otis, *Obit* Feb 1942

Slezak, Walter, actor, Mar 1955, *Obit* June 1983

Sliwa, Curtis, American public safety group founder, Feb 1983

Sloane, Everett, Jan 1957, *Obit* Oct 1965

Smigel, Robert, American comedian and television scriptwriter, Nov 2011

Smiley, Tavis, American radio talk show host, Apr 2003

Smith, Anna Deavere, American actress and dramatist, Sept 1994

Smith, Barbara, American actress, model and restaurateur, July 1998

Smith, C. Aubrey, English actor, Sept 1944, *Obit* Jan 1949

Smith, Jeff, American cook and clergyman, Aug 1991, *Obit* Yrbk 2004

Smith, Kevin, American screenwriter and film director, Feb 1998

Smith, Maggie, English actress, June 1970, July 2002

Smith, Will, American rapper and actor, Sept 1996

Smits, Jimmy, American actor, May 2006

Smothers, Dick, American comedian, Yrbk 1968

Smothers, Tom, American comedian, Yrbk 1968

Snipes, Wesley, American actor, Sept 1993

Snyder, Tom, American radio and television talk show host, June 1980, *Obit* Yrbk 2007

Soares, Jo, Brazilian television talk show host, novelist and actor, Jan 2002

Sorvino, Mira, American actress, Aug 1998

Sothern, Ann, American actress and singer, Yrbk 1956, *Obit* Aug 2001

Spacek, Sissy, American actress, Jan 1978

Spacey, Kevin, American actor and director, Apr 1997

Spanic, Gabriela, Venezuelan actress, Jan 2004

Spelling, Aaron, American television producer, May 1986, *Obit* Yrbk 2006

Spencer, John, American actor, Jan 2001, *Obit* Yrbk 2006

Spottswood, James, *Obit* Yrbk 1940

Stallone, Sylvester, American actor and screenwriter, Oct 1977, Feb 1994

Stanley, Kim, American actress, May 1955, *Obit* Jan 2002

Stanwyck, Barbara, American actress, July 1947, *Obit* Mar 1990

Stapleton, Jean, actress, Yrbk 1972, *Obit* Yrbk 2013

Stapleton, Maureen, American actress, May 1959, *Obit* Nov 2006

Staunton, Imelda, English actress, Jan 2005

Steiger, Rod, American actor, June 1965, *Obit* Yrbk 2002

Stein, Benjamin, American writer and actor, Sept 2001

Stephenson, James, British actor, *Obit* Sept 1941

Stern, Howard, American radio personality, Jan 1996

Stevens, Rise, American opera singer, Nov 1941, *Obit* Yrbk 2013

Stevenson, McLean, actor, June 1980, *Obit* Apr 1996

Steves, Rick, American travel guidebook author, Jan 2009

Stewart, James, American actor, Apr 1941, Yrbk 1960, *Obit* Sept 1997

Stewart, Martha, American cook, author and mass media executive, Aug 1993

Stewart, Patrick, British actor, Aug 1994

Stickney, Dorothy, actress, Apr 1942, *Obit* Aug 1998

Stiller, Ben, American actor, comedian and director, Nov 1999

Sting, British singer and actor, July 1985

Stockwell, Dean, actor, Feb 1991

Stone, Emma, American actress, Feb 2013

Stone, Matt, American actor, television scriptwriter, producer, director and animator, May 1998

Stone, Sharon, American actress, Apr 1996

Stoopnagle, Lemuel Q., radio comedian, Oct 1947, *Obit* July 1950

Stowell, Clarence Warner, *Obit* Jan 1941

Strasberg, Lee, American actor, director and acting teacher, Oct 1960, *Obit* Apr 1982

Strasberg, Susan, actress, May 1958, *Obit* Apr 1999

Streep, Meryl, American actress, Aug 1980, Mar 1997

Stritch, Elaine, American actress, June 1988

Struthers, Sally, American actress, Jan 1974

Stuart, Gloria, American actress, Apr 1998, *Obit* Yrbk 2010

Sullavan, Margaret, actress, July 1944, *Obit* Feb 1960

Sullivan, Brian, Yrbk 1957

Sullivan, Ed, American columnist and television personality, Sept 1952, *Obit* Nov 1974

Sullivan, Francis L., June 1955, *Obit* Jan 1957

Summerville, Slim, actor, *Obit* Feb 1946

Susann, Jacqueline, American novelist, May 1972, *Obit* Nov 1974

Sutherland, Donald, Canadian actor, Feb 1981

Sutherland, Kiefer, Canadian actor, Mar 2002

Suzman, Janet, May 1976

Suzuki, David T., Canadian geneticist and environmentalist, July 1995

Suzuki, Pat, singer and actress, Jan 1960

Swaggart, Jimmy Lee, evangelist, Oct 1987

Swank, Hilary, American actress, Sept 2000

Swanson, Gloria, actress, Sept 1950, *Obit* May 1983

Swayze, Patrick, American actor and dancer, Mar 1991, *Obit* Yrbk 2009

Swenson, Alfred G., *Obit* May 1941

Swinton, Tilda, Scottish actress, Nov 2001

Syal, Meera, English actress, novelist and screenwriter, Feb 2001

Sydow, Max von, Swedish actor, Apr 1967

Sykes, Wanda, American comedian, Jan 2011

Tandy, Jessica, Anglo-American actress, Mar 1956, Aug 1984, *Obit* Nov 1994

Tarantino, Quentin, American film director, screenwriter and actor, Oct 1995

Tate, Catherine, British comedian, Oct 2012

Tati, Jacques, French actor and film director, Feb 1961, *Obit* Jan 1983

Tautou, Audrey, French actress, Jan 2002

Taylor, Elizabeth, Anglo-American actress, July 1952, Oct 1985, *Obit* Yrbk 2011

Taylor, Laurette, American actress, July 1945, *Obit* Jan 1947

Taylor, Lili, American actress, July 2005

Taylor, Robert, American actor, May 1952, *Obit* July 1969

Tempest, Marie, English actress, *Obit* Yrbk 1942

Terrell, St. John, actor, Feb 1966, *Obit* Jan 1999

Terry-Thomas, English comedian and actor, Mar 1961, *Obit* Mar 1990

Thalia, Mexican actress and singer, Jan 2004

Theron, Charlize, South African actress, Nov 2004

Theroux, Justin, American actor, Mar 2012

Thicke, Alan, Canadian television author, producer and actor, June 1987

Thomas, Danny, American comedian, Feb 1959, *Obit* Apr 1991

Thomas, Dave, American fast food restaurant chain founder, Mar 1995, *Obit* Apr 2002

Thomas, Richard, American actor, Nov 1975

Thompson, Emma, British actress, Mar 1995

Thompson, Fred, American senator, Aug 1999

Thompson, John Douglas, Canadian actor, Sept 2010

Thompson, Sada, American actress, Mar 1973, *Obit* Yrbk 2011

Thorndike, Sybil, English actress, Yrbk 1953, *Obit* Aug 1976

Thurman, Uma, American actress, Aug 1996

Timberlake, Justin, American singer, Nov 2000

Tinney, Frank, *Obit* Jan 1941

Todd, Richard, British actor, Yrbk 1955, *Obit* Yrbk 2010

Tomlin, Lily, American comedienne and actress, Sept 1973

Tone, Franchot, actor, May 1940, *Obit* Nov 1968

Torn, Rip, American actor, Apr 1977

Townsend, Robert, American actor and motion picture director, May 1994

Tracy, Spencer, American actor, Apr 1943, *Obit* Oct 1967

Travolta, John, American actor, Oct 1978, May 1996

Trintignant, Jean-Louis, French actor, July 1988

Truex, Ernest, Jan 1941, *Obit* Sept 1973

Truffaut, Francois, French film director, Jan 1969, *Obit* Jan 1985

Tryon, Thomas, author and actor, Jan 1977, *Obit* Nov 1991

Tsai, Ming, American chef and restaurateur, June 2012

Tucker, Sophie, singer, Apr 1945, *Obit* Mar 1966

Turner, Kathleen, American actress, June 1986

Turner, Lana, American actress, June 1943, *Obit* Sept 1995

Turpin, Ben, comedian, *Obit* Aug 1940

Turturro, John, American actor, Oct 1996

Tushingham, Rita, Oct 1965

Twiggy, English model and actress, Oct 1968

Tyson, Cicely, American actress, Aug 1975

Uggams, Leslie, American singer and actress, Oct 1967

Ullman, Tracey, English actress and singer, Oct 1988

Ullmann, Liv, Norwegian actress and film director, Yrbk 1973

Underwood, Carrie, American singer and contestant on reality TV show American idol, Mar 2007

Ustinov, Peter, English actor and dramatist, Yrbk 1955, *Obit* Aug 2004

Vallee, Rudy, singer and actor, June 1947, Apr 1963, *Obit* Aug 1986

Van Damme, Jean-Claude, Belgian bodybuilder, martial artist and actor, Mar 1999

Van Dyke, Dick, American actor, Mar 1963

Van Peebles, Mario, American actor and motion picture director, Nov 1993

Van Zandt, Steve, American guitarist and singer, Feb 2006

Vanbrugh, Violet, British actress, *Obit* Jan 1943

Vaughn, Robert, American actor, Sept 1967

Vaughn, Vince, American actor, Sept 2006

Veidt, Conrad, German actor, *Obit* May 1943

Velez, Lupe, Mexican actress, *Obit* Feb 1945

Vera-Ellen, dancer and actress, Feb 1959, *Obit* Oct 1981

Verdon, Gwen, American dancer, actress and choreographer, Oct 1960, *Obit* Jan 2001

Vereen, Ben, American actor, singer and dancer, Apr 1978

Vergara, Sofia, Colombian actress, June 2013

Vilar, Jean, French actor and director, Apr 1962, *Obit* Sept 1971

Vinton, Bobby, July 1977

Voight, Jon, American actor, Apr 1974

Von Zell, Harry, June 1944, *Obit* Jan 1982

Wagner, Robert, American actor, June 1984

Waits, Tom, American singer and songwriter, Oct 1997

Walken, Christopher, American actor, Oct 1990

Walker, Nancy, actress, Feb 1965, *Obit* May 1992

Walker, Stuart, *Obit* May 1941

Wallach, Eli, American actor, May 1959

Walsh, John, American victims' rights advocate and television program host, July 2001

Walter, Wilmer, *Obit* Oct 1941

Ward, Douglas Turner, American dramatist, actor and director, Sept 1976

Washington, Denzel, American actor, July 1992

Watanabe, Ken, Japanese actor, Jan 2004

Waters, Ethel, American actress and singer, Apr 1941, Mar 1951, *Obit* Oct 1977

Waters, James R., *Obit* Jan 1946

Waterston, Sam, American actor, Sept 1985

Watson, Emily, British actress, May 2007

Watson, Lucile, actress, Yrbk 1953, *Obit* Sept 1962

Watts, Naomi, Australian actress, Mar 2007

Wayans, Damon, American comedian and actor, Nov 1999

Wayans, Keenen Ivory, American actor, screenwriter and director, Feb 1995

Wayans, Marlon, American comedian and actor, May 2001

Wayans, Shawn, American actor, May 2001

Wayne, David, actor, June 1956, *Obit* Apr 1995

Wayne, John, American actor, Feb 1951, July 1972, *Obit* Aug 1979

Weaver, Affie, *Obit* Jan 1941

Weaver, Dennis, American actor, Nov 1977, *Obit* Yrbk 2006

Weaver, Fritz, Jan 1966

Weaver, Sigourney, American actress, Mar 1989

Webb, Clifton, American actor, singer and dancer, Mar 1943, *Obit* Yrbk 1966

Webb, Jack, American actor and producer, May 1955, *Obit* Mar 1983

Webster, Margaret, American actress and theatrical director, May 1940, Sept 1950, *Obit* Jan 1973

Weede, Robert, Feb 1957, *Obit* Sept 1972

Welch, Raquel, American actress, May 1971

Weld, Tuesday, American actress, July 1974

Welles, Orson, American actor, director and producer, May 1941, Feb 1965, *Obit* Nov 1985

Werner, Oskar, Austrian actor, June 1966, *Obit* Jan 1985

West, Mae, American actress, Nov 1967, *Obit* Jan 1981

Westley, Helen, actress, *Obit* Feb 1943

Whitaker, Forest, American actor and motion picture director, Feb 1997

White, Betty, American actress, June 1987

White, Vanna, American television personality, Jan 1988

Whitford, Bradley, American actor, Apr 2003

Whitmore, James, American actor, Sept 1976, *Obit* Yrbk 2009

Whitty, May, English actress, Yrbk 1945, *Obit* July 1948

Widmark, Richard, American actor, Apr 1963, *Obit* Yrbk 2008

Wiest, Dianne, actress, Mar 1997

Wiig, Kristen, American actress, July 2013

Wilder, Gene, American actor and motion picture director, Apr 1978

Williams, Billy Dee, American actor, Apr 1984

Williams, Emlyn, Welsh playwright and actor, Feb 1941, Apr 1952, *Obit* Nov 1987

Williams, Esther, American swimmer and actress, Feb 1955, *Obit* Yrbk 2013

Williams, Paul, American singer, songwriter and actor, June 1983

Williams, Robin, American comedian and actor, June 1979, Jan 1997

Williams, Vanessa, American singer and actress, May 1984

Williamson, Nicol, British actor, Jan 1970, *Obit* Yrbk 2012

Willis, Bruce, American actor, Feb 1987

Wilson, Don, radio and television personality, Aug 1944, *Obit* Yrbk 1991

Wilson, Flip, American comedian, Nov 1969, *Obit* Feb 1999

Wilson, Luke, American actor, Feb 2005

Wilson, Owen, American actor and screenwriter, Feb 2003

Winchell, Walter, American columnist and radio commentator, June 1943, *Obit* Apr 1972

Windust, Bretaigne, Mar 1943, *Obit* May 1960

Winfrey, Oprah, American television talk show host, Mar 1987

Winger, Debra, American actress, July 1984

Winkler, Henry, American actor and producer, Sept 1976

Winters, Jonathan, American comedian, Mar 1965, *Obit* Yrbk 2013

Winters, Shelley, American actress, Apr 1952, *Obit* Apr 2006

Witherspoon, Reese, American actress, Jan 2004

Wolfit, Donald, Mar 1965, *Obit* Apr 1968

Wood, Elijah, American actor, Aug 2002

Wood, Evan Rachel, American actress, June 2009

Wood, John, English actor, Apr 1983, *Obit* Yrbk 2011

Wood, Natalie, American actress, Apr 1962, *Obit* Jan 1982

Wood, Peggy, actress and singer, July 1942, Yrbk 1953, *Obit* May 1978

Wood, Philip, *Obit* Mar 1940

Woodard, Alfre, American actress, Feb 1995

Woods, James, American actor, Nov 1989

Woodward, Joanne, American actress, June 1958

Woolley, Monty, July 1940, *Obit* June 1963

Worth, Irene, American actress, May 1968, *Obit* Aug 2002

Wray, John, *Obit* May 1940

Wright, Huntley, *Obit* Sept 1941

Wright, Jeffrey, American actor, May 2002

Wright, Martha, American singer and actress, Feb 1955

Wright, Teresa, American actress, May 1943, *Obit* Yrbk 2005

Wyatt, Jane, American actress, May 1957, *Obit* Yrbk 2006

Wyman, Jane, American actress, Mar 1949, *Obit* Yrbk 2007

Wynn, Ed, comedian, Jan 1945, *Obit* July 1966

Xu Jinglei, Chinese actress and filmmaker, Jan 2007

Yeoh, Michelle, Chinese actress, Jan 1998

Yoakam, Dwight, American country singer, Nov 2000

York, Michael, English actor, Apr 1976

Yorke, Oswald, *Obit* Mar 1943

Yoshimura, Yumi, Japanese pop singer, Jan 2005

Young, Alan, Anglo-Canadian actor, June 1953

Young, Loretta, American actress, Mar 1948, *Obit* Nov 2000

Young, Robert, actor, July 1950, *Obit* Sept 1998

Yuen, Cory, Chinese actor and motion picture director, Jan 2004

ZaBach, Florian, Yrbk 1955

Zaentz, Saul, American recording executive and motion picture producer, Mar 1997

Zellweger, Renee, American actress, Feb 2004

Zeta-Jones, Catherine, Welsh actress, Apr 2003

Zhang Ziyi, Chinese actress, Jan 2005

Zimbalist, Efrem, American actor, Feb 1960

Zollar, Jawole Willa Jo, American dancer and performance artist, July 2003

Zorina, Vera, German-American ballet dancer and actress, Jan 1941, *Obit* Yrbk 2003

Zulli, Floyd, Jan 1958, *Obit* Jan 1981

Administrators

Abbott, Edith, American economist, Sept 1941, *Obit* Oct 1957

Abrams, Jonathan, Canadian Internet software developer and entrepreneur, Apr 2006

Ackerman, Carl William, journalist and college dean, Oct 1945, *Obit* Yrbk 1970

Adams, Arthur S., American mechanical engineer and college president, Jan 1951

Adams, John Cranford, college president, Sept 1958, *Obit* Jan 1987

Adams, Joseph Quincy, American Shakespearean scholar, *Obit* Yrbk 1946

Adkins, Bertha S., American educator and government official, May 1953, *Obit* Mar 1983

Adler, Cyrus, college president, *Obit* May 1940

Ainsworth, William Newman, American bishop, *Obit* Aug 1942

Albion, Robert Greenhalgh, historian, May 1954, *Obit* Oct 1983

Alexander, Harold Rupert Leofric George Alexander, British field marshal, Oct 1942, *Obit* Sept 1969

Alexander, Jane, American actress and government official, Feb 1977

Allen, Raymond B., college president and physician, Mar 1952, *Obit* May 1986

Alsberg, Carl, American biochemist, *Obit* Yrbk 1940

Amedeo, Italian air force officer and colonial administrator, *Obit* Apr 1942

Ames, Joseph S., American physicist and university president, *Obit* Aug 1943

Anderson, Kenneth A. N., British general, Feb 1943, *Obit* July 1959

Andrews, Roy Chapman, American zoologist, explorer and museum director, Jan 1941, July 1953, *Obit* May 1960

Angell, James Rowland, American psychologist and university president, Yrbk 1940, *Obit* Mar 1949

Anspach, Charles L., American college president, Sept 1956

Armstrong, George E., American physician and general, Apr 1952, *Obit* Aug 1979

Bacon, George P., American physicist and college dean, *Obit* Nov 1941

Badoglio, Pietro, Italian field marshal, Oct 1940, *Obit* Jan 1957

Baehr, George, American physician and health insurance executive, May 1942

Bailey, Guy W., American university president, *Obit* Yrbk 1940

Balbo, Italo, Italian air marshal, *Obit* Aug 1940

Baltimore, David, American microbiologist, July 1983

Barr, Alfred Hamilton, American museum director, Jan 1961, *Obit* Oct 1981

Barr, John A., American lawyer and college dean, Jan 1961, *Obit* Mar 1979

Barr, Stringfellow, American college president and historian, Aug 1940, *Obit* Apr 1982

Barrett, Edward W., journalist and college dean, Feb 1947, *Obit* Feb 1990

Barringer, Paul B., American physician and college president, *Obit* Mar 1941

Barzun, Jacques, American historian, Sept 1964, *Obit* Yrbk 2013

Baur, John Ireland Howe, museum director, Yrbk 1969, *Obit* July 1987

Beadle, George W., American geneticist and college president, Apr 1956, *Obit* Aug 1989

Begg, Alexander Swanson, American physician and college dean, *Obit* Nov 1940

Belkin, Samuel, American rabbi and college president, Nov 1952, *Obit* June 1976

Belluschi, Pietro, American architect, Feb 1959, *Obit* Apr 1994

Benchley, Belle Jennings, zoo director, Oct 1940

Bender, James F., speech educator and business consultant, May 1949, *Obit* Mar 1998

Bennett, Henry Garland, American college president, Feb 1951, *Obit* Feb 1952

Bennett, John C., clergyman, ethicist and seminary president, Jan 1961, *Obit* July 1995

Berelson, Bernard, American librarian and sociologist, July 1961, *Obit* Nov 1979

Berg, Irving H., American clergyman and college dean, *Obit* Nov 1941

Berry, Edward Wilber, American paleontologist, *Obit* Oct 1945

Berry, Mary Frances, American historian, civil rights leader and government official, June 1999

Bestor, Arthur E., American educator, *Obit* Mar 1944

Betts, Rome A., American medical association official, Mar 1949

Bevis, Howard L., American university president, Jan 1940, Nov 1950, *Obit* June 1968

Bing, Rudolf, British opera manager, Feb 1950, *Obit* Nov 1997

Bissell, Claude T., May 1959

Black, Cathleen, American school superintendent and former magazine executive, Jan 1998

Blake, Francis G., American physician, Jan 1943, *Obit* Mar 1952

Blanchard, Hazel A., American school principal, June 1963

Blanding, Sarah Gibson, college president, June 1946, *Obit* Apr 1985

Bliss, A. Richard, American pharmacologist and college dean, *Obit* Oct 1941

Bliss, Anthony Addison, lawyer and opera manager, Apr 1979, *Obit* Nov 1991

Bloustein, Edward J., college president, Nov 1965, *Obit* Feb 1990

Blumenthal, George, American financier and museum and hospital administrator, *Obit* Yrbk 1941

Blumer, George Alder, American psychiatrist and hospital administrator, *Obit* Jan 1940

Boe, Lars Wilhelm, American clergyman and college president, *Obit* Feb 1943

Bok, Derek Curtis, college president, July 1971

Bollinger, Lee C., American university president, Feb 2008

Borden, Neil H., American marketing association executive and business teacher, May 1954

Boren, David L., American governor, senator and college president, Nov 1989

Botstein, Leon, college president, Aug 1996

Bowen, William G., American college president and foundation official, May 1973

Bowker, Albert H., American college administrator, Jan 1966, *Obit* Yrbk 2008

Boyer, Ernest L., American educator and foundation official, Jan 1988, *Obit* Feb 1996

Brademas, John, American congressman and university president, May 1977

Bradshaw, Lillian Moore, American library director, June 1970

Bragdon, Helen D., Feb 1951

Braly, Angela F., American health insurance executive, Aug 2011

Brandenburg, William A., *Obit* Yrbk 1940

Brewster, Kingman, American college president and diplomat, May 1964, Sept 1979, *Obit* Jan 1989

Briggs, Eugene S., Oct 1948

Briggs, James E., June 1957, *Obit* Aug 1979

Bronk, Detlev Wulf, American college president and biophysicist, Oct 1949, *Obit* Jan 1976

Brouwer, Dirk, Mar 1951, *Obit* Mar 1966

Brown, Harold, American Secretary of defense and physicist, Sept 1961, Oct 1977

Brown, J. Carter, American museum director, Apr 1976, *Obit* Yrbk 2002

Browne, Sidney Jane, *Obit* Oct 1941

Brownell, Samuel Miller, educator, Feb 1954, *Obit* Jan 1991

Bryan, James E., American library director and consultant, June 1962

Buchan, John, Scottish novelist, historian and Governor General of Canada, Jan 1940

Buchanan, Scott Milross, American college dean and educational consultant, Sept 1962, *Obit* May 1968

Buchanan, Thomas Drysdale, *Obit* Apr 1940

Buck, Paul Herman, historian, July 1955, *Obit* Apr 1989

Buechner, Thomas S., American painter and museum director, Feb 1961, *Obit* Yrbk 2010

Buford, John Lester, Apr 1956

Bugher, John C., Apr 1953

Bundesen, Herman N., Oct 1948, *Obit* Nov 1960

Bunting-Smith, Mary Ingraham, microbiologist and college president, June 1967, *Obit* Apr 1998

Burchard, John E., Apr 1958, *Obit* Mar 1976

Burdell, Edwin S., Feb 1952

Burdick, Charles K., *Obit* Aug 1940

Burns, J. A., *Obit* Oct 1940

Burrows, Millar, July 1956, *Obit* July 1980

Butler, Nicholas Murray, American educator, Nov 1940, *Obit* Yrbk 1947

Butz, Earl, American Secretary of agriculture, July 1972, *Obit* Yrbk 2008

Caldwell, Sarah, American opera director and conductor, Oct 1973, *Obit* Yrbk 2006

Caldwell, William E., *Obit* May 1943

Calfee, John Edward, *Obit* Jan 1941

Campbell, Boyd, May 1956

Campbell, Harold G., *Obit* Aug 1942

Campbell, Willis C., *Obit* June 1941

Candler, Warren A., American bishop and college president, *Obit* Nov 1941

Carlson, William S., college president, July 1952, *Obit* July 1994

Carr, Robert Kenneth, Apr 1961

Carroll, Thomas H., July 1962, *Obit* Oct 1964

Cartwright, Morse A., Sept 1947, *Obit* June 1974

Castle, Lewis G., July 1958, *Obit* Sept 1960

Caswell, Hollis L., college president, July 1956, *Obit* Sept 1989

Cates, Gilbert, American film director, producer and college dean, Mar 1997, *Obit* Yrbk 2012

Cavanaugh, John J., Mar 1947, *Obit* Feb 1980

Cavazos, Lauro Fred, American Secretary of education, Apr 1989

Chapin, Charles Value, American epidemiologist and public health official, *Obit* Mar 1941

Chapin, Schuyler, American municipal arts administrator, Feb 1974, *Obit* Yrbk 2009

Chapman, Daniel A., Apr 1959

Chase, Harry Woodburn, June 1948, *Obit* June 1955

Chisholm, Brock, Canadian psychistrist, July 1948, *Obit* Mar 1971

Churchill, Gordon, Sept 1958

Clapp, Margaret, American biographer, historian and college president, June 1948, *Obit* June 1974

Clark, Charles E., American judge, July 1959, *Obit* Mar 1964

Clark, Evans, Sept 1947, *Obit* Nov 1970

Clark, Kenneth, British art historian and museum director, Sept 1963, *Obit* July 1983

Clark, Mark W., American general, Nov 1942, *Obit* June 1984

Clement, Rufus E., American college president, June 1946, *Obit* Jan 1968

Cleveland, Harlan, American diplomat and university president, Sept 1961, *Obit* Yrbk 2008

Clyde, George D., July 1958, *Obit* May 1972

Coggeshall, Lowell T., college administrator and physician, Sept 1963, *Obit* Jan 1988

Cohen, Wilbur Joseph, American Secretary of health, education and welfare, Sept 1968, *Obit* July 1987

Cointreau, Andre, French chef and cooking school administrator, Jan 2004

Cole, Johnnetta B., American anthropologist and museum director, Aug 1994

Coleman, John R., Oct 1974

Coleman, Mary Sue, American university president, Feb 2007

Collins, Marva, American teacher, Nov 1986

Collins, Michael, American astronaut and aerospace consultant, May 1975

Compton, Wilson, Apr 1952, *Obit* May 1967

Conant, James Bryant, American college president and diplomat, Mar 1941, Feb 1951, *Obit* Apr 1978

Conway, Jill K., Australian historian and college president, June 1991

Corson, Fred Pierce, bishop, May 1961, *Obit* Apr 1985

Cox, Herald R., Apr 1961

Crawshaw, William Henry, *Obit* Aug 1940

Crosby, John O'Hea, American conductor and opera company manager, Nov 1981, *Obit* Yrbk 2003

Cunningham, Alan, British general, June 1946, *Obit* Apr 1983

Damon, Lindsay Todd, *Obit* Jan 1940

Daniel, Robert Prentiss, May 1952, *Obit* Mar 1968

Daniels, Arthur Hill, *Obit* Apr 1940

Daniels, Farrington, July 1965, *Obit* Sept 1972

Daniels, Grace B., Sept 1959

Darden, Colgate W., Sept 1948

Davenport, Eugene, *Obit* May 1941

David, Donald K., Feb 1948, *Obit* June 1979

Davis, Herbert John, Jan 1940, *Obit* May 1967

Davis, Jess H., Jan 1956

Davis, Meyer, June 1961, *Obit* June 1976

Davison, F. Trubee, Yrbk 1945

Day, Edmund, Sept 1946, *Obit* Apr 1951

De Kiewiet, C. W., college president and historian, July 1953, *Obit* Apr 1986

De Kleine, William, Apr 1941, *Obit* Yrbk 1958

De Montebello, Philippe, American museum director, Apr 1981

DeBakey, Michael E., American surgeon and inventor, Mar 1964, *Obit* Yrbk 2008

DeCoursey, Elbert, Sept 1954

Dean, H. Trendley, June 1957, *Obit* July 1962

Dickey, John Sloan, college president, Apr 1955, *Obit* Apr 1991

Dillard, James Hardy, *Obit* Sept 1940

Ditmars, Raymond Lee, herpetologist, Sept 1940, *Obit* July 1942

Dobbie, William George Shedden, British general, July 1945

Dodd, Alvin E., Nov 1947, *Obit* July 1951

Dodds, Harold W., Yrbk 1945, *Obit* Jan 1981

Dodge, Bayard, Feb 1948, *Obit* July 1972

Doherty, Robert E., Sept 1949, *Obit* Yrbk 1950

Doster, James J., *Obit* Yrbk 1942

Drinan, Robert F., American priest, lawyer and congressman, June 1971, *Obit* Yrbk 2007

DuBridge, Lee A., college president and physicist, June 1948, *Obit* Mar 1994

Duffey, Joseph D., college administrator, Mar 1971

Duggan, Laurence, May 1947, *Obit* Jan 1949

Duncan, Arne, American Secretary of education, Mar 2009

Dunham, Charles L., Mar 1966

Dunlop, John T., American economist, labor relations expert and Secretary of labor, Apr 1951, *Obit* Yrbk 2004

Dunton, Arnold Davidson, Canadian college president, Jan 1959, *Obit* Apr 1987

Durgin, C. T., Sept 1954, *Obit* May 1965

Dye, Marie, Yrbk 1948

Dykstra, Clarence A., American university president, Jan 1941, *Obit* June 1950

Early, William Ashby, Mar 1954

Eboue, Felix, French colonial governor, *Obit* July 1944

Edwards, James Burrows, American dentist, governor and Secretary of energy, Nov 1982

Egeberg, Roger Olaf, government official, physician and college dean, Jan 1970, *Obit* Nov 1997

Eghbal, Manouchehr, May 1959, *Obit* Feb 1978

Eisenhower, Dwight D., American president, Aug 1942, Feb 1948, Sept 1957, *Obit* May 1969

Eisenhower, Milton Stover, American college president, diplomat and government official, Yrbk 1946, *Obit* July 1985

Eldridge, Edward H., *Obit* June 1941

Eliot, Thomas Hopkinson, congressman, political scientist and dean, May 1942, *Obit* Jan 1992

Ellingson, Mark, college president, Sept 1957, *Obit* Apr 1993

Elliott, Harriet Wiseman, college dean, July 1940, *Obit* Sept 1947

Elliott, Osborn, American journalist and college dean, Jan 1978, *Obit* Yrbk 2008

Ellis, Elmer, college president, July 1962

Elvehjem, C. A., May 1948, *Obit* Oct 1962

Engleman, J. O., *Obit* Nov 1943

Eshelman, W. W., May 1960

Etherington, Edwin D., stock exchange official and college president, Apr 1966, *Obit* Apr 2001

Eurich, Alvin C., educator, June 1949, *Obit* Aug 1987

Evans, Daniel Jackson, American senator and governor, Aug 1975

Evans, Donald L., American Secretary of commerce, Nov 2001

Eyring, Henry, chemist, Oct 1961

Fackenthal, Frank D., Feb 1949, *Obit* Nov 1968

Fagg, Fred D., Feb 1956, *Obit* Jan 1982

Fauci, Anthony S., American immunologist, Aug 1988

Faust, Clarence H., Mar 1952, *Obit* Aug 1975

Faust, Drew Gilpin, American historian and college president, July 2007

Felix, Robert Hanna, psychiatrist, Apr 1957, *Obit* May 1990

Fellows, George Emory, American historian and university president, *Obit* Mar 1942

Fels, William C., Apr 1959, *Obit* Jan 1965

Fenimore-Cooper, Susan De Lancey, *Obit* Mar 1940

Few, William Preston, college president, *Obit* Yrbk 1940

Fine, Benjamin, Mar 1961

Finley, David E., American museum administrator and historic preservationist, Feb 1951, *Obit* Apr 1977

Fischer, John H., American college dean and president, July 1960, *Obit* Yrbk 2010

Fiske, James Porter, orthopedic surgeon and hospital administrator, *Obit* Yrbk 1941

Fitch, Robert Elliot, Apr 1962

Fleming, Robben W., American university president, Yrbk 1970, *Obit* Yrbk 2010

Flickinger, Roy Caston, *Obit* Aug 1942

Foakes-Jackson, F. J., *Obit* Jan 1942

Force, Juliana, museum director, Mar 1941, *Obit* Oct 1948

Foster, Richard C., *Obit* Jan 1942

Fox, Carol, July 1978, *Obit* Sept 1981

Fox, John McDill, *Obit* May 1940

Frank, Glenn, *Obit* Nov 1940

Franks, Oliver Shewell Franks, British diplomat, Mar 1948, *Obit* Jan 1993

Fraser, Ian Forbes, American library director, June 1954

Frazer, Spaulding, *Obit* Apr 1940

Fred, Edwin Broun, bacteriologist and college president, Yrbk 1950

French, Hollis, *Obit* Jan 1941

French, Robert W., Oct 1959

Friday, William Clyde, college president, Apr 1958, *Obit* Yrbk 2013

Froehlich, Jack E., July 1959

Frohnmayer, John E., lawyer and government official, Apr 1990

Fuller, Clara Cornelia, *Obit* Yrbk 1940

Fuller, John L., Mar 1959

Furnas, Clifford Cook, Oct 1956, *Obit* June 1969

Futter, Ellen Victoria, American college president and museum director, Oct 1985

Gale, Henry Gordon, *Obit* Jan 1943

Gallagher, Buell G., college president, May 1953, *Obit* Jan 1979

Ganfield, William Arthur, *Obit* Yrbk 1940

Garfield, Harry Augustus, American college president and son of President James A. Garfield, *Obit* Feb 1943

Garrison, Lloyd Kirkham, lawyer and reformer, June 1947, *Obit* Nov 1991

Gates, Robert M., American Secretary of defense, Apr 1992, May 2007, Mar 2009

Gauss, D. Christian, Apr 1945, *Obit* Yrbk 1951

Gentele, Goran, Sept 1972

Gerbner, George, American university dean and television critic, Aug 1983, *Obit* Yrbk 2006

Giddens, Anthony, British sociologist and college administrator, Apr 1998

Gideonse, Harry D., college president, May 1940, *Obit* May 1985

Gifford, Chloe, Mar 1959

Gildersleeve, Virginia C., Aug 1941, *Obit* Sept 1965

Ginger, Lyman V., May 1958

Ginsberg, Mitchell I., social worker and municipal official, June 1971, *Obit* May 1996

Giordani, Francesco, Sept 1957, *Obit* Mar 1961

Giral, Jose, May 1946

Givens, Willard E., Sept 1948, *Obit* July 1971

Glennan, T. Keith, American NASA official, Oct 1950, *Obit* June 1995

Glueck, Nelson, rabbi, archaeologist and college president, Oct 1948, July 1969, *Obit* Mar 1971

Goheen, Robert F., American college president, Jan 1958, *Obit* Yrbk 2008

Goldwater, S. S., American physician, hospital administrator and public health official, *Obit* Yrbk 1942

Goma y Tomas, Isidro, *Obit* Oct 1940

Good, Mary L., American chemist, Sept 2001

Goodrich, Lloyd, museum director, May 1967, *Obit* May 1987

Gort, John Standish Surtees Prendergast Vereker, British general, Oct 1940, *Obit* May 1946

Gould, Laurence McKinley, explorer and college president, Jan 1978, *Obit* Aug 1995

Gould, Samuel B., educator, Jan 1958, *Obit* Sept 1997

Grace, Alonzo G., Jan 1950, *Obit* Yrbk 1971

Graham, Frank Porter, college president and civil rights leader, May 1941, July 1951, *Obit* Apr 1972

Gray, Hanna Holborn, American historian and college president, Mar 1979

Grayson, C. Jackson, Sept 1972

Graziani, Rodolfo, Italian field marshal and colonial administrator, Apr 1941, *Obit* Mar 1955

Grebe, John J., Oct 1955

Gregg, Milton F., Oct 1955

Gregorian, Vartan, American foundation official, Oct 1985

Gregory, Menas S., *Obit* Jan 1942

Griffith, Ernest S., political scientist, Oct 1947, *Obit* Apr 1997

Griswold, A. Whitney, American college president, Apr 1950, *Obit* June 1963

Griswold, Erwin N., American solicitor general and law school dean, Oct 1956, *Obit* Jan 1995

Gross, Mason W., June 1969, *Obit* Jan 1978

Gross, Paul Magnus, chemist, May 1963, *Obit* June 1986

Grzimek, Bernhard, German zoo director and television performer, Mar 1973, *Obit* May 1987

Guillaume, Augustin, French general, Jan 1952

Gumpert, Martin, Yrbk 1951

Gunn, Tim, American clothing company executive, Oct 2009

Gupta, Mahabir P., Indian pharmacologist, Jan 2005

Haas, Francis J., bishop, Aug 1943, *Obit* Oct 1953

Haggard, William David, *Obit* Mar 1940

Halifax, Edward Frederick Lindley Wood, British statesman, Sept 1940, *Obit* Feb 1960

Halloran, Roy D., *Obit* Yrbk 1943

Hamilton, Edith, American classicist, Apr 1963

Hammon, William McDowell, physician, Sept 1957, *Obit* Nov 1989

Hancher, Virgil M., Feb 1957, *Obit* Mar 1965

Hanfmann, George Maxim Anossov, archaeologist, Oct 1967, *Obit* May 1986

Hanks, Nancy, American government official, Sept 1971, *Obit* Mar 1983

Hannah, John A., American college president, Oct 1952, *Obit* Apr 1991

Hansen, Carl F., Oct 1962

Harada, Tasuku, Japanese college teacher and president, *Obit* Mar 1940

Hardin, Clifford M., American Secretary of agriculture, May 1969, *Obit* Yrbk 2010

Harewood, George Henry Hubert Lascelles, English editor and writer on opera, Jan 1965, *Obit* Yrbk 2011

Harmon, Ernest N., American general and university president, Nov 1946, *Obit* Jan 1980

Harnwell, Gaylord Probasco, June 1956

Harrelson, Walter J., May 1959

Harris, Patricia, American cabinet member, Yrbk 1965, *Obit* May 1985

Hart, Kitty Carlisle, American singer, actress and state official, Oct 1982, *Obit* Yrbk 2007

Hartnett, Robert C., priest, periodical editor and educator, Yrbk 1949

Hartwell, John A., *Obit* Jan 1941

Hatcher, Harlan H., literary critic, author and historian, Oct 1955, *Obit* May 1998

Hatoyama, Ichiro, Japanese prime minister, May 1955, *Obit* May 1959

Hawkes, Anna L. Rose, Oct 1956

Hawkes, Herbert E., *Obit* June 1943

Haworth, Leland J., Yrbk 1950, *Obit* May 1979

Hayakawa, S. I., American senator and educator, Nov 1959, Jan 1977, *Obit* Apr 1992

Heald, Henry Townley, American civil engineer, Feb 1952, *Obit* Jan 1976

Healy, Timothy Stafford, priest, university president and library director, Jan 1993, *Obit* Jan 1993

Heard, Alexander, Nov 1966

Henderson, Donald A., American public health scientist and college dean, Mar 2002

Hendl, Walter, American conductor, college president and music teacher, June 1955

Henry, David Dodds, college president, June 1966, *Obit* Nov 1995

Herzog, Paul M., college dean, July 1945, *Obit* Jan 1987

Hesburgh, Theodore Martin, American priest and college president, Jan 1955, July 1982

Hester, James M., June 1962

Heyns, Roger W., college administrator, Yrbk 1968, *Obit* Nov 1995

Hightower, John B., July 1970, *Obit* Yrbk 2013

Hildreth, Horace Augustus, governor, Oct 1948, *Obit* July 1988

Hill, Harry W., American admiral, July 1950, *Obit* Sept 1971

Hitch, Charles J., American college president, Nov 1970, *Obit* Nov 1995

Ho, David D., American physician, June 1997

Hockfield, Susan, American neurobiologist and college president, Apr 2008

Hoffman, Joseph G., May 1958, *Obit* Jan 1975

Holaday, William M., May 1958

Holley, Edward G., American librarian and college dean, June 1974

Hollomon, J. Herbert, college president and government official, Mar 1964, *Obit* Aug 1985

Holt, Andrew David, college president, Nov 1949, *Obit* Sept 1987

Holt, Hamilton, periodical editor, pacifist and college president, Yrbk 1947, *Obit* May 1951

Hopkins, Ernest Martin, Oct 1944, *Obit* Oct 1964

Hopkins, Louis Bertram, *Obit* Sept 1940

Horner, Matina, educator, July 1973

Hornig, Donald F., chemist, university president and presidential adviser, May 1964, *Obit* Yrbk 2013

Horton, Mildred McAfee, college president and naval officer, Sept 1942, *Obit* Jan 1995

Hoskins, Lewis M., Sept 1950

Hottel, Althea Kratz, Oct 1948

Houston, Charles Hamilton, American lawyer and civil rights leader, July 1948, *Obit* June 1950

Houston, David Franklin, secretary of agriculture and the treasury, *Obit* Oct 1940

Hovde, Bryn J., Jan 1946, *Obit* Oct 1954

Hoving, Thomas, American museum director and periodical editor, Apr 1967, *Obit* Yrbk 2010

Howell, William Henry, *Obit* Mar 1945

Hunt, Herold Christian, educator, May 1956, *Obit* Jan 1977

Hurok, Sol, concert manager, Sept 1941, Apr 1956, *Obit* Apr 1974

Hutchins, Robert Maynard, American university president, Yrbk 1940, Feb 1954, *Obit* July 1977

Hutton, Maurice, *Obit* May 1940

Irving, Frederick A., American general, Mar 1951

Irwin, Steve, Australian wildlife conservationist and television

personality, Aug 2000, *Obit* Yrbk 2007

Jackson, Shirley Ann, American physicist and college president, July 1999

James, F. Cyril, Canadian economist and college administrator, Oct 1956

Jansen, William, Oct 1951, *Obit* Apr 1968

Janssens, Jean Baptiste, Sept 1959, *Obit* Yrbk 1964

Johnson, Arthur Newhall, *Obit* Sept 1940

Johnson, Charles Spurgeon, American sociologist and university president, Nov 1946, *Obit* Jan 1957

Johnson, Mordecai Wyatt, American college president and clergyman, Apr 1941

Johnson, Philip Cortelyou, American architect, Oct 1957, Nov 1991, *Obit* Sept 2005

Johnson, Robert L., college president and government official, Mar 1948, *Obit* Feb 1966

Jones, Lewis Webster, Oct 1958

Jordan, I. King, American university president, Jan 1991

Jordan, W. K., Mar 1955, *Obit* July 1980

Judson, Arthur, orchestra manager, Aug 1945, *Obit* Mar 1975

Kagan, Elena, American Supreme Court justice, June 2007

Kahn, Alfred E., American economist and government official, Mar 1979, *Obit* Yrbk 2011

Kalb, Marvin, television reporter and college administrator, July 1987

Kast, Ludwig, *Obit* Oct 1941

Kean, Thomas H., American governor and college president, July 1985

Keene, Christopher, conductor and opera manager, Mar 1990, *Obit* Jan 1996

Keeney, Barnaby C., Mar 1956, *Obit* Aug 1980

Kellas, Eliza, *Obit* May 1943

Kellogg, John Harvey, American physician, *Obit* Feb 1944

Kelly, Regina Zimmerman, Yrbk 1956

Kemeny, John G., American mathematician and college president, Feb 1971, *Obit* Feb 1993

Kemp, Hal, *Obit* Feb 1941

Kennedy, Donald, physiologist and college president, July 1984

Keppel, Francis C., American educator, May 1963, *Obit* Apr 1990

Kerr, Clark, American educator, Apr 1961, *Obit* May 2004

Kerrey, Bob, American senator and university president, Feb 1991

Kessler, David A., American physician and government official, Sept 1991

Kessler, Henry H., Oct 1957

Keys, David A., Oct 1958

Khan, Salman, American school administrator, May 2013

Killian, James Rhyne, American college president and presidential adviser, Feb 1949, May 1959, *Obit* Mar 1988

Kimpton, Lawrence A., June 1951, *Obit* Jan 1978

Kirk, Grayson Louis, American college president, May 1951, *Obit* Jan 1998

Klawe, Maria, Canadian computer scientist, college dean and painter, June 2013

Kleinsmid, Rufus B. von, June 1958, *Obit* Sept 1964

Klumpp, Theodore G., Oct 1958

Knight, Douglas M., May 1964

Knowles, John H., Yrbk 1970, *Obit* May 1979

Krainik, Ardis, opera manager, Nov 1991, *Obit* Mar 1997

Kraushaar, Otto F., college president, Nov 1949, *Obit* Nov 1989

Krens, Thomas, American museum director, Apr 1989

Kreps, Juanita Morris, American Secretary of commerce, June 1977, *Obit* Yrbk 2010

Lacoste, Robert, French socialist leader, Nov 1957

Lambert, W. V., Nov 1955

Lamm, Norman, Sept 1978

Landrum, Phil M., American congressman, May 1960, *Obit* Jan 1991

Langlois, Henri, French motion picture historian and collector, Jan 1973, *Obit* Mar 1977

Laubach, Frank Charles, American missionary and educator, Feb 1950, *Obit* Sept 1970

Laycock, Craven, *Obit* May 1940

Leake, Chauncey D., Apr 1960, *Obit* Mar 1978

Leakey, Richard E., Kenyan anthropologist and paleontologist, Nov 1976, Oct 1995

Lederle, John W., American college president, Feb 1961, *Obit* Yrbk 2007

Lee, John Clarence, *Obit* Nov 1940

Lee, Sherman E., American art historian and museum director, June 1974, *Obit* Yrbk 2008

Leigh, Robert Devore, college president and dean, June 1947, *Obit* Mar 1961

Levi, Edward H., American Attorney general, Jan 1969, *Obit* July 2000

Levine, Irving R., American television newscaster, July 1959, *Obit* Yrbk 2009

Lichtenstein, Harvey, American performing arts executive, May 1987

Liddel, Urner, May 1951

Lillard, George W., *Obit* Yrbk 1940

Lindley, Ernest Hiram, *Obit* Oct 1940

Linlithgow, Victor Alexander John Hope, British colonial administrator, Jan 1942, *Obit* Feb 1952

Lipschitz, Chaim U., Yrbk 1966

Litchfield, Edward H., Nov 1953, *Obit* May 1968

Lloyd of Dolobran, George Ambrose Lloyd, British colonial administrator, Jan 1941, *Obit* Jan 1941

Lloyd, Wesley P., educator, Jan 1952, *Obit* May 1977

Long, Oren E., American senator, Sept 1951, *Obit* June 1965

Lordkipanidze, David, Georgian paleontologist, Jan 2005

Lowell, A. Lawrence, American college president and political scientist, *Obit* Feb 1943

Lusk, Georgia Lee, American congresswoman, Oct 1947, *Obit* Feb 1971

Lyons, Harry, Oct 1957

MacCracken, Henry Noble, college president, Sept 1940, *Obit* June 1970

MacDonald, Malcolm, British colonial administrator and diplomat, Nov 1954, *Obit* Mar 1981

MacLean, Basil C., May 1957, *Obit* Apr 1963

MacLean, Malcolm Shaw, July 1940

MacMitchell, Leslie, American runner, Apr 1946, *Obit* Yrbk 2006

Mack, Pauline Beery, chemist and college dean, Yrbk 1950

Madeleva, Mary, American nun, poet and college president, Feb 1942, *Obit* Oct 1964

Magnusson, Magnus, Icelandic-British television personality, journalist and college administrator, Jan 2006

Malcolm, George A., Nov 1954

Malott, Deane W., college president, Mar 1951, *Obit* Nov 1996

Mark, Herman Francis, American chemist and college dean, May 1961, *Obit* June 1992

Marsh, John, Mar 1960

Marshak, Robert Eugene, American college president and physicist, July 1973, *Obit* Feb 1993

Martin, Collier Ford, *Obit* May 1941

Martin, Frank L., American newspaper editor and college dean, *Obit* Sept 1941

Martini, Helen, American zookeeper, July 1955

Martino, Gaetano, May 1956, *Obit* Oct 1967

Marvin, Cloyd H., Yrbk 1949, *Obit* June 1969

Mason, Noah M., Nov 1957, *Obit* May 1965

Mason, Norman P., June 1959

Massee, W. Wellington, *Obit* Oct 1942

Massey, Walter E., American physicist and college president, June 1997

Mathews, David, American Secretary of health, education and welfare, Jan 1976

Mathews, Shailer, biblical scholar and college dean, *Obit* Yrbk 1941

Matola, Sharon, American biologist and zoo director, June 1993

Mayer, Jean, nutritionist and college president, Sept 1970, *Obit* Feb 1993

Mayo, Charles W., Nov 1941, Nov 1954, *Obit* Oct 1968

Mays, Benjamin Elijah, American civil rights leader and college president, May 1945, *Obit* May 1984

McBride, Katharine E., American psychologist and college president, Feb 1942, *Obit* July 1976

McCall, Duke K., Nov 1959, *Obit* Yrbk 2013

McCormick, Lynde Dupuy, admiral, Feb 1952, *Obit* Oct 1956

McCrady, Edward, Jan 1957

McCullough, Gary E., American school administrator, Nov 2009

McDiarmid, E. W., librarian and college dean, Yrbk 1948

McGill, William J., college president, June 1971, *Obit* Jan 1998

McGinley, Laurence J., college president and priest, June 1949, *Obit* Oct 1992

McHale, Kathryn, Jan 1947, *Obit* Yrbk 1957

McIntosh, Millicent Carey, American college dean and president, July 1947, *Obit* Mar 2001

McKenzie, Roderick Duncan, *Obit* Jan 1940

McLaughlin, Leo Plowden, college president and priest, May 1970, *Obit* Nov 1996

McNutt, Paul V., American governor, Feb 1940, *Obit* May 1955

Meier, Deborah, American educational reformer and school principal, May 2006

Mendenhall, Thomas Corwin, college president, May 1960, *Obit* Sept 1998

Meng, John J., college president, Nov 1961, *Obit* Apr 1988

Menotti, Gian Carlo, Italian composer and librettist, Yrbk 1947, Jan 1979, *Obit* Yrbk 2007

Messer, Thomas M., museum director and art historian, Nov 1961, *Obit* Yrbk 2013

Messmer, Pierre, French prime minister, Nov 1963, *Obit* Yrbk 2007

Millar, Alexander Copeland, *Obit* Yrbk 1940

Miller, J. Cloyd, Yrbk 1951

Millett, John David, American university president, Feb 1953, *Obit* Jan 1994

Million; John Wilson, *Obit* Nov 1941

Mingus, Sue, American music director and recording executive, July 2008

Moore, George E., American oncologist and surgeon, Jan 1968, *Obit* Yrbk 2008

Moos, Malcolm Charles, political scientist and college president, Nov 1968

Morehouse, Daniel Walter, *Obit* Mar 1941

Morgan, Arthur Ernest, American civil engineer and college president, July 1956, *Obit* Jan 1976

Morgan, Edward P., May 1951

Moron, Alonzo G., American college president and government official, Oct 1949, *Obit* Yrbk 1971

Morrill, J. L., Feb 1951

Mortier, Gerard, Belgian opera manager and director, July 1991

Morton, Florrinell, librarian and college dean, July 1961

Morton, John Jamieson, Mar 1955

Mosley, J. Brooke, bishop, Sept 1970, *Obit* Apr 1988

Mountbatten of Burma, Louis Mountbatten, British admiral, June 1942, *Obit* Oct 1979

Muench, Aloisius, Apr 1960, *Obit* Apr 1962

Muggeridge, Malcolm, English journalist, critic and novelist, Apr 1955, July 1975, *Obit* Jan 1991

Murphree, Eger V., Sept 1956, *Obit* Jan 1963

Murphy, Franklin D., American physician, college administrator and newspaper executive, Mar 1971, *Obit* Aug 1994

Nason, John W., American college president, July 1953, *Obit* Feb 2002

Neal, Herbert Vincent, *Obit* Mar 1940

Neilson, William Allan, Scottish-American literary scholar, *Obit* Mar 1946

Nesmeianov, A. N., Nov 1958

Newlon, Jesse H., *Obit* Oct 1941

Newmark, Craig, American software engineer and webmaster, June 2005

Newsom, Carroll Vincent, college president, Apr 1957, *Obit* Apr 1990

Nicolet, Marcel, Nov 1958

Nicolson, Marjorie Hope, literary critic and college dean, Apr 1940, *Obit* June 1981

Nolde, O. Frederick, Feb 1947, *Obit* Sept 1972

Nystrom, Paul H., Mar 1951, *Obit* Oct 1969

O'Connell, Colm, Irish priest, school headmaster and track coach, Jan 2005

O'Leary, Hazel R., American university president and former Secretary of energy, Jan 1994

Obama, Michelle, wife of American president Barack Obama, Oct 2008

Obolensky, Serge, Oct 1959, *Obit* Nov 1978

Oettinger, Katherine B., government official and child welfare worker, Nov 1957, *Obit* Jan 1998

Osborne, Tom, American university athletic director, Mar 1998

Overholser, Winfred, Nov 1953, *Obit* Yrbk 1964

Paige, Rod, American Secretary of education, July 2001

Palmer, Albert DeForest, *Obit* Jan 1940

Pannell, Anne Gary, Nov 1950

Park, Rosemary, American college president, Jan 1964, *Obit* Yrbk 2004

Parr, Albert Eide, museum director and oceanographer, July 1942, *Obit* Sept 1991

Parran, Thomas J., American surgeon general, Aug 1940, *Obit* Apr 1968

Pate, Martha B., college president, May 1947, *Obit* July 1983

Patri, Angelo, American school principal, Nov 1940, *Obit* Nov 1965

Patrick, Mary Mills, college president, *Obit* Mar 1940

Patten, Chris, British colonial governor and European Commission official, July 1993

Patterson, Frederick D., American college president and veterinarian, June 1947, *Obit* June 1988

Peabody, Endicott, clergyman and school headmaster, May 1940, *Obit* Jan 1945

Pearson, Jay F. W., Yrbk 1953, *Obit* Oct 1965

Pelli, Cesar, American architect, Apr 1983

Penniman, Josiah Harmer, *Obit* June 1941

Perkins, James A., American college president, Apr 1964, *Obit* Nov 1998

Perkins, Marlin, zoo director and television performer, Oct 1951, *Obit* Aug 1986

Peterson, Martha Elizabeth, American college president, Feb 1969, *Obit* Yrbk 2006

Picken, Mary Brooks, Yrbk 1954

Piotrovskii, Mikhail Borisovich, Russian museum director, Jan 2003

Plater-Zyberk, Elizabeth, American architect and urban planner, Jan 2006

Pollard, William G., Mar 1953

Pope, Liston, Apr 1956, *Obit* June 1974

Powell, Lewis F., American Supreme Court justice, Feb 1965, *Obit* Nov 1998

Pratt, Frederic Bayley, American college president, *Obit* June 1945

Pratt, J. Gaither, Nov 1964

Price, Don Krasher, American political scientist and college dean, Feb 1967, *Obit* Sept 1995

Pusey, Nathan Marsh, American college president, Yrbk 1953, *Obit* Feb 2002

Putnam, James William, *Obit* Mar 1940

Putnam, Thomas M., *Obit* Nov 1942

Quinn, Daniel Joseph, *Obit* Mar 1940

Rafferty, Max L., American state education official, Jan 1969, *Obit* Aug 1982

Rainey, Froelich G., archaeologist and museum director, Feb 1967, *Obit* Jan 1993

Rainey, Homer Price, college president, Nov 1946, *Obit* Feb 1986

Ramphele, Mamphela, South African college administrator and anthropologist, July 1997

Rassweiler, Clifford F., Oct 1958

Rees, Mina Spiegel, American mathematician and computer scientist, Nov 1957, *Obit* Jan 1998

Reinhardt, Aurelia Henry, American college president and religious official, May 1941, *Obit* Feb 1948

Renne, Roland Roger, college president and agricultural economist, June 1963

Rice, Condoleezza, American Secretary of state, Apr 2001

Rich, Daniel Catton, Yrbk 1955, *Obit* Feb 1977

Richards, Charles Russ, *Obit* Jan 1941

Richards, Lloyd G., American actor and theatrical director, Oct 1987, *Obit* Yrbk 2007

Richmond, Charles Alexander, *Obit* Sept 1940

Ridenour, Nina, Apr 1951

Riles, Wilson, educator and state official, Yrbk 1971

Rines, Robert H., American lawyer, inventor, physicist and hunter of Loch Ness monster, Jan 2003, *Obit* Yrbk 2010

Ripley, Sidney Dillon, American zoologist and museum director, Oct 1966, *Obit* Aug 2001

Robbins, William J., Feb 1956

Roberts, George Lucas, *Obit* Apr 1941

Roberts, Oral, American evangelist, Nov 1960, *Obit* Feb 2010

Robinson, Frederick B., *Obit* Yrbk 1941

Robinson, Spottswood W., judge, Mar 1962, *Obit* Jan 1999

Rockefeller, John D., American senator, Mar 1978

Rodin, Judith, American foundation official, June 1999

Romenesko, Jim, American journalist and webmaster, Feb 2004

Roosevelt, Theodore, American government official, general and son of President Theodore Roosevelt, *Obit* Sept 1944

Rorimer, James J., Yrbk 1955, *Obit* June 1966

Rostow, Eugene Victor, American lawyer and economist, Apr 1961, *Obit* Yrbk 2003

Rothenstein, John Maurice, English art historian and museum director, Apr 1957

Rubin de la Borbolla, Daniel F., Feb 1960

Ruder, David S., American lawyer, Nov 1988

Russell, Charles Hinton, American newspaper publisher and governor, Yrbk 1955, *Obit* Nov 1989

Russell, James Earl, *Obit* Yrbk 1945

Russell, William F., Apr 1947, *Obit* June 1956

Rutledge, Wiley Blount, American Supreme Court justice, May 1943, *Obit* Oct 1949

Sachar, Abram Leon, historian and college president, Nov 1949, *Obit* Sept 1993

Sage, Dean, *Obit* Aug 1943

Saint-Gaudens, Homer Schiff, museum director, Oct 1941, *Obit* Feb 1959

Sammartino, Peter, college president, Yrbk 1958, *Obit* May 1992

Sandefer, Jefferson Davis, *Obit* Apr 1940

Sanford, Terry, American senator, Nov 1961, *Obit* July 1998

Santos, Rufino J., Yrbk 1960, *Obit* Nov 1973

Satcher, David, American surgeon general, Feb 1997

Saunders, Cicely, English physician and hospice director, Jan 2004

Sawhill, John C., American college president and conservationist, Apr 1979, *Obit* Yrbk 2000

Sawyer, John E., college president and foundation official, July 1961, *Obit* Apr 1995

Schmidt, Benno C., American educator, Aug 1986

Schmoke, Kurt, American college dean and mayor, Feb 1995

Schottland, Charles Irwin, college president and government official, Yrbk 1956, *Obit* Sept 1995

Schreiber, Ryan, American webmaster and rock music critic, Feb 2011

Schuman, William, American composer, June 1942, Yrbk 1962, *Obit* Apr 1992

Schurman, Jacob G., philosopher, college president and diplomat, *Obit* Oct 1942

Schweitzer, Albert, German physician, missionary and theologian, Jan 1948, July 1965

Scott, Arthur Carroll, *Obit* Yrbk 1940

Scott, James B., lawyer, *Obit* Aug 1943

Seaborg, Glenn, American chemist, July 1948, Yrbk 1961, *Obit* May 1999

Sears, Robert Richardson, psychologist and college dean, July 1952, *Obit* Aug 1989

Seidman, L. William, American government official and college dean, Sept 1976, *Obit* Yrbk 2009

Seitz, Frederick, American physicist, Apr 1956, *Obit* Yrbk 2008

Seymour, Charles, May 1941, *Obit* Nov 1963

Shalala, Donna, American Secretary of health and human services and college president, Mar 1991

Sharp, Harry Clay, *Obit* Yrbk 1940

Shaw, Lloyd, Sept 1943

Shawkey, Morris Purdy, *Obit* Apr 1941

Shelly, Mary Jo, educator, Oct 1951, *Obit* Sept 1976

Shera, Jesse Hauk, American librarian and dean, June 1964, *Obit* June 1982

Shuster, George Nauman, college president, Jan 1941, Oct 1960, *Obit* Mar 1977

Silber, John R., American college president, Feb 1984, *Obit* Yrbk 2012

Sills, Beverly, American opera singer and manager, Nov 1969, Feb 1982, *Obit* Oct 2007

Simmons, Adele Smith, American college president and foundation official, May 1991

Simmons, Ruth, American college president, Jan 1996

Simons, Hans, Mar 1957, *Obit* May 1972

Simpson, Alan, college president, Feb 1964, *Obit* July 1998

Sisco, Joseph J., American diplomat, Jan 1972, *Obit* Yrbk 2005

Slade, Roy, museum director, painter and educator, June 1985

Sloan, George A., Jan 1952, *Obit* July 1955

Smedberg, William Renwick, Yrbk 1957

Smith, Albert W., *Obit* Oct 1942

Smith, Courtney, American college president, Yrbk 1959, *Obit* Mar 1969

Smith, Sidney, Jan 1955, *Obit* May 1959

Smith, Virginia B., American college president, June 1978, *Obit* Yrbk 2010

Smith, Wilbur Fisk, *Obit* Sept 1940

Snavely, Guy E., Apr 1951

Snow, Glenn E., Nov 1947

Soderberg, C. Richard, Feb 1958, *Obit* Jan 1980

Solandt, Omond M., Mar 1974

Sovern, Michael I., Feb 1981

Spain, Frances Lander, American librarian and college administrator, June 1960

Sparling, Edward J., July 1948

Sperry, Willard Learoyd, theologian, May 1952, *Obit* Sept 1954

Spitalny, Phil, Oct 1940, *Obit* Yrbk 1970

Sproul, Robert Gordon, July 1945, *Obit* Nov 1975

Stahr, Elvis J., American Secretary of the army, Sept 1961, *Obit* Feb 1999

Starr, Chauncey, American physicist, Apr 1954, *Obit* Yrbk 2007

Stassen, Harold E., American lawyer, governor and presidential candidate, May 1940, Mar 1948, *Obit* May 2001

Statz, Hermann, Jan 1958

Steacie, E. W. R., Jan 1953, *Obit* Nov 1962

Stein, Jules, concert and theatrical agent, May 1967, *Obit* June 1981

Sterling, John Ewart Wallace, college president, Jan 1951, *Obit* Aug 1985

Stern, Robert A. M., American architect and college dean, June 2000

Stettinius, Edward Reilly, American Secretary of state, July 1940, *Obit* Yrbk 1949

Stevenson, William E., lawyer, college president and diplomat, Nov 1943, *Obit* May 1985

Stever, H. Guyford, American aeronautical engineer, Jan 1981, *Obit* Yrbk 2010

Stoddard, George Dinsmore, American psychologist and college president, July 1946, *Obit* Feb 1982

Stone, Abraham, Mar 1952, *Obit* Oct 1959

Stone, William S., June 1960, *Obit* Feb 1969

Storey, Robert Gerald, Nov 1953

Straight, Michael Whitney, American magazine editor, publisher, arts administrator and memoirist, Aug 1944, *Obit* Yrbk 2004

Stratton, Dorothy C., American psychologist, college dean and Coast Guard officer, June 1943, *Obit* Yrbk 2006

Stratton, Julius Adams, American physicist and college president, May 1963, *Obit* Aug 1994

Strughold, Hubertus, July 1966

Studebaker, Mabel, Nov 1948

Stuhlinger, Ernst, American rocket engineer, Nov 1957, *Obit* Yrbk 2008

Sullivan, Louis W., American Secretary of health and human services, July 1989

Summers, Lawrence H., American presidential adviser and former Secretary of the treasury, July 2002

Swann, William Francis Gray, Feb 1941, Yrbk 1960, *Obit* Mar 1962

Sweeney, James Johnson, art critic, historian and museum director, Mar 1955, *Obit* July 1986

Sykes, Richard Eddy, *Obit* Nov 1942

Taft, Horace D., American school administrator and brother of President William H. Taft, *Obit* Mar 1943

Taylor, Francis Henry, Jan 1940, *Obit* Feb 1958

Taylor, Harold, college president, Sept 1946, *Obit* Apr 1993

Taylor, John W., American college president, television executive and United Nations official, Jan 1954, *Obit* Apr 2002

Terrell, Daniel V., Apr 1954

Thomas, William H., American geriatrician, Jan 2006

Tilghman, Shirley M., Canadian molecular biologist and university president, June 2006

Topping, Norman H., physician and college president, Feb 1959, *Obit* Jan 1998

Towle, Katherine A., college dean, Jan 1949, *Obit* May 1986

Traphagen, Ethel, Yrbk 1948, *Obit* June 1963

Trotter, Frank Butler, *Obit* Apr 1940

Trulock, Mussette Langford, Jan 1957

Truman, David Bicknell, American college president

and political scientist, Jan 1972, *Obit* Yrbk 2004

Trussell, Ray E., municipal hospital commissioner and physician, Jan 1971, *Obit* Feb 2000

Tufts, James Hayden, *Obit* Sept 1942

Tyson, Neil De Grasse, American astrophysicist, May 2000

Valentine, Alan, American college president, Yrbk 1950, *Obit* Sept 1980

Van Dusen, Henry Pitney, seminary president, Yrbk 1950, *Obit* Apr 1975

Vance, William Reynolds, *Obit* Yrbk 1940

Vanier, Georges, Canadian governor general, Jan 1960, *Obit* May 1967

Vincent, George Edgar, sociologist, college president and foundation official, *Obit* Mar 1941

Waite, Alice Vinton, *Obit* May 1943

Walden, Percy Talbot, *Obit* May 1943

Walker, Eric A., college president, Mar 1959, *Obit* Apr 1995

Walker, John, museum director, May 1957, *Obit* Jan 1996

Walsh, William Henry, *Obit* May 1941

Wanamaker, Pearl A., Sept 1946

Ward, Paul L., American historian and college president, Mar 1962, *Obit* Yrbk 2006

Warner, John Christian, chemist, Oct 1950, *Obit* July 1989

Warren, Shields, June 1950, *Obit* Sept 1980

Warren, William C., law school dean, Jan 1960, *Obit* Yrbk 2000

Washburn, Bradford, American photographer, explorer and museum director, June 1966, *Obit* Yrbk 2007

Washburn, Gordon Bailey, Yrbk 1955

Wavell, Archibald Percival Wavell, British general and colonial administrator, Mar 1941, *Obit* July 1950

Weaver, Robert Clifton, American Secretary of housing and urban development and educator, Apr 1961, *Obit* Oct 1997

Webster, William, May 1950, *Obit* July 1972

Weigle, Luther Allan, professor of religious education and dean, Mar 1946, *Obit* Oct 1976

Weinstein, Allen, American historian and archivist, June 2006

Weiss, Soma, *Obit* Mar 1942

Weisse, Faneuil Suydam, *Obit* Mar 1940

Welensky, Roy, British colonial administrator, July 1959, *Obit* Feb 1992

Wells, Herman B., American college president, Apr 1966, *Obit* Aug 2000

Wesley, Charles Harris, American historian and university president, Mar 1944, *Obit* Oct 1987

Westergren, Tim, American information technology executive, Oct 2012

Wetmore, Alexander, ornithologist, Feb 1948, *Obit* Mar 1979

Wexler, Jacqueline Grennan, college president, Mar 1970, *Obit* Yrbk 2012

Wharton, Clifton R., American college president and pension plan administrator, Feb 1987

Whitaker, Douglas, Nov 1951, *Obit* Yrbk 1973

White, Alexander M., July 1951, *Obit* Jan 1969

White, Herbert S., librarian, May 1968

White, John F., American television executive and college president, Nov 1967, *Obit* Yrbk 2005

Whitman, Walter G., Feb 1952, *Obit* June 1974

Whittle, Christopher, American publishing, broadcasting and school management company executive, Feb 1991

Wiesner, Jerome B., American electrical engineer and college president, Yrbk 1961, *Obit* Jan 1995

Wilcox, Francis Orlando, government official, Apr 1962, *Obit* Apr 1985

Williams, Clyde E., July 1947

Williams, Ronald, American health insurance executive, July 2009

Willingdon, Freeman Freeman-Thomas, British colonial administrator, *Obit* Oct 1941

Willoughby, Charles Clark, *Obit* June 1943

Wilson, Logan, college administrator, Yrbk 1956, *Obit* Jan 1991

Wilson, O. Meredith, college president, July 1967, *Obit* Feb 1999

Wilson, O. W., Oct 1966, *Obit* Yrbk 1972

Wolfenden, John Frederick Wolfenden, English educator, social reformer and museum director, Oct 1970, *Obit* Mar 1985

Wood, James Madison, Feb 1947, *Obit* Yrbk 1958

Woodbridge, Frederick James Eugene, American philosopher, *Obit* July 1940

Woodward, Arthur Smith, British paleontologist, *Obit* Oct 1944

Wright, Benjamin Fletcher, professors of government and college president, July 1955, *Obit* Mar 1977

Wriston, Henry M., May 1952, *Obit* May 1978

Wu Yifang, Chinese educator and feminist, Aug 1945, *Obit* Jan 1986

Yoder, Albert Henry, *Obit* Nov 1940

Young, Philip, government official and college dean, Yrbk 1951, *Obit* Mar 1987

Young, Whitney Moore, American civil rights leader, Apr 1965, *Obit* Apr 1971

Zenos, Andrew C., *Obit* Mar 1942

Zirato, Bruno, Yrbk 1959, *Obit* Jan 1973

Admirals

Anderson, George Whelan, American admiral, Nov 1962, *Obit* May 1992

Andrewes, William, British admiral, Sept 1952, *Obit* Jan 1975

Badger, Oscar C., American admiral, May 1949, *Obit* Feb 1959

Barbey, Daniel E., admiral, Jan 1945, *Obit* June 1969

Bennett, Rawson, American admiral, Sept 1958, *Obit* Feb 1968

Bergen, John J., American financier, June 1961, *Obit* Feb 1981

Blair, Dennis, American admiral and intelligence official, May 2010

Blandy, W. H. P., American admiral, Nov 1942, *Obit* Mar 1954

Bloch, Claude Charles, American admiral, Feb 1942, *Obit* Yrbk 1967

Boone, J. T., American physician and admiral, Mar 1951, *Obit* June 1974

Brind, Patrick, British admiral, Nov 1952, *Obit* Jan 1964

Bristol, Arthur LeRoy, *Obit* June 1942

Brown, Charles R., admiral, July 1958

Burke, Arleigh A., American admiral, Sept 1955, *Obit* Mar 1996

Byrd, Richard Evelyn, American admiral and explorer, Oct 1942, May 1956, *Obit* May 1957

Callaghan, Daniel J., American admiral, *Obit* Jan 1943

Cantu, Giuseppe, *Obit* Yrbk 1940

Caperton, William B., American admiral, *Obit* Feb 1942

Carney, Robert Bostwick, admiral, Oct 1951, *Obit* Aug 1990

Castro e Silva, Jose Machado de, *Obit* Aug 1943

Clark, J. J., American admiral, Jan 1954, *Obit* Sept 1971

Crowe, William J., American admiral, July 1988, *Obit* Yrbk 2008

Cruzen, Richard H., Mar 1947, *Obit* June 1970

Cunningham of Hyndhope, Andrew Browne Cunningham, British admiral, May 1941, *Obit* Sept 1963

Darlan, Francois, French admiral, Mar 1941, *Obit* Feb 1943

Davidson, John Frederick, admiral, Nov 1960, *Obit* Apr 1989

DeLany, Walter S., admiral, Yrbk 1952

Denebrink, Francis C., admiral, Feb 1956, *Obit* June 1987

Denfeld, Louis E., American admiral, Yrbk 1947, *Obit* May 1972

Dennison, Robert L., Apr 1960, *Obit* May 1980

Denton, Jeremiah, American admiral and senator, May 1982

Donitz, Karl, German admiral, Nov 1942, *Obit* Feb 1981

Duerk, Alene, Sept 1973

Dufek, George J., Mar 1957

Durgin, C. T., Sept 1954, *Obit* May 1965

Ellsberg, Edward, admiral, salvage engineer and author, Nov 1942, *Obit* Yrbk 1991

Fallon, William J., American admiral, July 2007

Fechteler, William M., American admiral, Sept 1951, *Obit* Oct 1967

Felt, Harry D., Mar 1959

Field, Frederick Laurence, *Obit* Yrbk 1945

Fiske, Bradley A., *Obit* May 1942

Fitch, Aubrey, Oct 1945, *Obit* July 1978

Fraser, Bruce, July 1943, *Obit* Apr 1981

Gallery, Daniel V., Apr 1966, *Obit* Mar 1977

Ghormley, Robert Lee, admiral, Oct 1942, *Obit* Oct 1958

Granville, William Spencer Leveson-Gower, Sept 1950, *Obit* Sept 1953

Halsey, William Frederick, American admiral, Yrbk 1942, *Obit* Nov 1959

Hart, Thomas Charles, Jan 1942, *Obit* Sept 1971

Hewitt, H. Kent, American admiral, Apr 1943, *Obit* Nov 1972

Hill, Harry W., American admiral, July 1950, *Obit* Sept 1971

Hillenkoetter, Roscoe H., American CIA director and

admiral, Jan 1950, *Obit* Aug 1982

Holloway, James, American admiral, Jan 1947

Horthy, Miklos, Hungarian admiral and regent, Oct 1940, *Obit* Apr 1957

Hough, Henry Hughes, *Obit* Oct 1943

Ingersoll, Royal E., Oct 1942, *Obit* July 1976

Ingram, Jonas H., Apr 1947, *Obit* Oct 1952

Jacobs, Randall, Aug 1942, *Obit* Oct 1967

Joy, C. Turner, American admiral, June 1951, *Obit* Sept 1956

Kessing, O. O., American admiral and football association executive, June 1949, *Obit* Mar 1963

Kidd, Isaac Campbell, *Obit* Feb 1942

Kimmel, Husband Edward, admiral, Jan 1942, *Obit* July 1968

King, Ernest Joseph, American admiral, Feb 1942, *Obit* Sept 1956

Kinkaid, Thomas Cassin, American admiral, Yrbk 1944, *Obit* Jan 1973

Kirk, Alan Goodrich, American admiral and diplomat, July 1944, *Obit* Yrbk 1963

Koga, Mineichi, *Obit* Oct 1943

Kuznetsov, Nikolai G., Nov 1942, *Obit* Jan 1975

Laborde, Jean de, Feb 1943

Land, Emory S., Sept 1941, *Obit* Jan 1972

Layton, Geoffrey, British admiral, Feb 1942

Leahy, William D., American admiral, Jan 1941, *Obit* Oct 1959

Leary, Herbert F., Aug 1942, *Obit* Feb 1958

Lee, Willis A., American admiral and marksman, *Obit* Sept 1945

Lemonnier, Andre, Nov 1952, *Obit* July 1963

Long, Andrew Theodore, *Obit* July 1946

Ma, G. John, July 1953

McCain, John S., American admiral, June 1970, *Obit* June 1981

McCain, John Sidney, American admiral, Oct 1943, *Obit* Oct 1945

McConnell, Mike, American intelligence official, Apr 2007

McCormick, Lynde Dupuy, admiral, Feb 1952, *Obit* Oct 1956

McDonald, David Lamar, admiral, Nov 1963, *Obit* Mar 1998

McIntire, Ross T., Oct 1945, *Obit* Feb 1960

McLintock, Gordon, admiral, Nov 1953, *Obit* June 1990

Meyers, George Julian, *Obit* Jan 1940

Mitscher, Marc Andrew, admiral, Aug 1944, *Obit* Mar 1947

Momsen, C. B., American admiral and inventor, July 1946, *Obit* July 1967

Moore, Henry Ruthven, Sept 1943, *Obit* May 1978

Moorer, Thomas H., American admiral, Apr 1971, *Obit* Yrbk 2004

Moreell, Ben, June 1946, *Obit* Sept 1978

Mountbatten of Burma, Louis Mountbatten, British admiral, June 1942, *Obit* Oct 1979

Mountevans, Edward Ratcliffe Garth Russell Evans, British admiral, May 1941, *Obit* Nov 1957

Mullen, Mike, American admiral, Feb 2008

Nagano, Osami, July 1942, *Obit* Feb 1947

Nelles, Percy Walker, Canadian admiral, Feb 1944

Nimitz, Chester W., American admiral, Feb 1942, *Obit* Mar 1966

Nomura, Kichisaburo, Apr 1941, *Obit* July 1964

Osumi, Mineo, *Obit* Apr 1941

Poindexter, John M., American admiral and presidential adviser, Nov 1987

Pound, Dudley, Jan 1941, *Obit* Yrbk 1943

Pratt, William Veazie, June 1943, *Obit* Feb 1958

Pride, Alfred Melville, admiral, Nov 1954, *Obit* Feb 1989

Pugh, Herbert Lamont, Mar 1951

Raborn, William Francis, American admiral and

intelligence official, July 1958, *Obit* June 1990

Radford, Arthur W., American admiral, Nov 1949, *Obit* Oct 1973

Raeder, Erich, German admiral, Apr 1941, *Obit* Jan 1961

Ramsay, Bertram, British admiral, Mar 1944, *Obit* Feb 1945

Ramsey, Dewitt C., Jan 1953, *Obit* Nov 1961

Rawlings, Bernard, Aug 1945, *Obit* Yrbk 1962

Rickover, Hyman George, American admiral, May 1953, *Obit* Aug 1986

Robert, Georges, June 1943

Robinson, Samuel M., Feb 1942

Royal, Forrest B., American admiral, *Obit* July 1945

Russell, James S., admiral, Jan 1962

Schofield, Frank H., *Obit* Apr 1942

Sexton, W. R., *Obit* Oct 1943

Sherman, Forrest P., Mar 1948, *Obit* Sept 1951

Sides, John H., Jan 1961, *Obit* June 1978

Small, John D., American admiral and government official, Feb 1946, *Obit* Mar 1963

Smedberg, William Renwick, Yrbk 1957

Smith, William Ward, American admiral, Feb 1948, *Obit* July 1966

Solberg, Thorvald A., American admiral, Yrbk 1948

Somerville, James, British admiral, Apr 1943, *Obit* Apr 1949

Souers, Sidney W., American banker, insurance executive and intelligence service official, Feb 1949, *Obit* Mar 1973

Spruance, Raymond Ames, American admiral, Apr 1944, *Obit* Mar 1970

Standley, William Harrison, admiral, May 1942, *Obit* Yrbk 1963

Stark, Harold R., admiral, May 1940, *Obit* Oct 1972

Strauss, Lewis L., American presidential aide, regulatory agency official and Secretary

of commerce, Feb 1947, *Obit* Mar 1974

Struble, Arthur Dewey, admiral, Nov 1951, *Obit* July 1983

Stump, Felix B., American admiral, Jan 1953, *Obit* Sept 1972

Sueyro, Saba H., Argentine admiral, *Obit* Sept 1943

Suzuki, Kantaro, Japanese admiral, Aug 1945, *Obit* May 1948

Tawresey, John Godwin, American admiral, *Obit* Apr 1943

Tennant, William George, British admiral, Feb 1945, *Obit* Sept 1963

Thomaz, Americo de Deus Rodrigues, Portuguese president, Yrbk 1958, *Obit* Nov 1987

Towers, John Henry, American admiral, Oct 1941, *Obit* June 1955

Turner, Richmond Kelly, admiral, Apr 1944, *Obit* Apr 1961

Turner, Stansfield, admiral and CIA director, May 1978

Vian, Philip, British admiral, Aug 1944, *Obit* Sept 1968

Vickery, H. L., American admiral, Yrbk 1943, *Obit* May 1946

Waesche, Russell Randolph, American Coast Guard admiral, Mar 1945, *Obit* Yrbk 1946

Wake-Walker, William Frederick, British admiral, *Obit* Oct 1945

Watkins, James D., American admiral and Secretary of energy, Mar 1989, *Obit* Yrbk 2012

Wilcox, J. W., American admiral, *Obit* May 1942

Wright, Jerauld, American admiral and diplomat, Feb 1955, *Obit* July 1995

Yamamoto, Isoroku, Japanese admiral, Feb 1942, *Obit* July 1943

Zacharias, Ellis M., American admiral and intelligence official, Mar 1949, *Obit* Oct 1961

Zumwalt, Elmo R., American admiral, June 1971, *Obit* June 2000

Adventurers

Andrews, Roy Chapman, American zoologist, explorer and museum director, Jan 1941, July 1953, *Obit* May 1960

Arnesen, Liv, Norwegian teacher and cross-country skier, June 2001

Balchen, Bernt, aviator, Jan 1949, *Obit* Yrbk 1973

Bancroft, Ann, American adventurer, July 2000

Bedaux, Charles Eugene, French-American industrial engineer, *Obit* Apr 1944

Bingham, Hiram, American explorer and senator, Mar 1951, *Obit* Sept 1956

Boyd, Louise Arner, American explorer, Sept 1960, *Obit* Nov 1972

Burwash, Lachlin Taylor, *Obit* Feb 1941

Chilingarov, Artur, Russian polar explorer, Jan 2007

Chouinard, Yvon, American mail order sportswear company executive, June 1998

Clark, Leonard Frances, Jan 1956, *Obit* Sept 1957

Cook, Frederick Albert, American physician and explorer, *Obit* Sept 1940

Doyle, Adrian Conan, Sept 1954

Dunn, J. Allan, *Obit* May 1941

Dyhrenfurth, Norman G., American mountaineer, Apr 1965

Fairchild, David, American plant pathologist and explorer, July 1953, *Obit* Oct 1954

Fiennes, Ranulph, British explorer, Jan 2004

Flaherty, Robert Joseph, American film director and explorer, Mar 1949, *Obit* Sept 1951

Fossett, Steve, American stockbroker and balloonist, Apr 2005, *Obit* Yrbk 2008

Fuchs, Vivian, English explorer, Oct 1958, *Obit* Jan 2000

Gould, Laurence McKinley, explorer and college president, Jan 1978, *Obit* Aug 1995

Granger, Walter, *Obit* Oct 1941

Grylls, Bear, British adventurer and television personality, Oct 2011

Harrer, Heinrich, Austrian mountaineer, Oct 1954, *Obit* Yrbk 2006

Hass, Hans, Feb 1955, *Obit* Yrbk 2013

Hedin, Sven Anders, Swedish explorer, May 1940, *Obit* Jan 1953

Hempleman-Adams, David, British explorer, Jan 2004

Herzog, Maurice, July 1953

Heyerdahl, Thor, Norwegian ethnologist and explorer, Yrbk 1947, Sept 1972, *Obit* Yrbk 2002

Hillary, Edmund, New Zealand mountaineer, Oct 1954, Jan 2002, *Obit* Yrbk 2008

Hitchcock, Charles B., Oct 1954, *Obit* May 1969

Honeywell, Harry E., *Obit* Jan 1940

Hubbard, Bernard, July 1943, *Obit* July 1962

Hunt, John Hunt, British army officer and mountaineer, Oct 1954, *Obit* Jan 1999

Johnson, Osa Helen Leighty, American explorer and documentary filmmaker, Apr 1940, *Obit* Feb 1953

Jones, Brian, British balloonist, Jan 2004

Kay-Scott, Cyril, Feb 1944

Lewis, Jason, British adventurer, Jan 2007

MacMillan, Donald, American explorer, Sept 1948, *Obit* Nov 1970

McCrady, Edward, Jan 1957

McDonald, Eugene F., Oct 1949, *Obit* Oct 1958

Messner, Reinhold, Italian mountaineer, Mar 1980

Miura, Yuichiro, Japanese mountaineer, Jan 2005

Mortenson, Greg, American mountaineer and humanitarian, Sept 2009

Phillips, Wendell, American explorer, archaeologist and petroleum industry executive, Nov 1958, *Obit* Feb 1976

Piccard, Bertrand, Swiss psychiatrist and balloonist, Jan 2004

Riiser-Larsen, Hjalmar, Nov 1951, *Obit* July 1965

Ripley, Robert Le Roy, cartoonist and adventurer, July 1945, *Obit* July 1949

Robert, Alain, French urban climber, Jan 2007

Ronne, Finn, Norwegian-American explorer, Feb 1948, *Obit* Mar 1980

Rusby, Henry H., *Obit* Jan 1941

Scaturro, Pasquale, American geophysicist, mountaineer and rafter, Oct 2005

Siple, Paul Allman, explorer and geographer, Feb 1957, *Obit* Jan 1969

Stefansson, Vilhjalmur, American arctic explorer, Oct 1942, *Obit* Nov 1962

Tenzing Norgay, Nepalese mountaineer, Oct 1954, *Obit* July 1986

Urquhart, Brian E., British United Nations official, June 1986

Vandercook, John W., Apr 1942, *Obit* Feb 1963

Von Hagen, Victor Wolfgang, naturalist, biographer and explorer, Mar 1942

Washburn, Bradford, American photographer, explorer and museum director, June 1966, *Obit* Yrbk 2007

White, Trumbull, *Obit* Feb 1942

Wilkins, Hubert, Australian explorer and geographer, Jan 1957, *Obit* Feb 1959

Wong, How-man, Chinese explorer and journalist, Jan 2002

Worsley, Frank Arthur, New Zealand ship captain and explorer, *Obit* Mar 1943

Younghusband, Francis Edward, British diplomat and explorer, *Obit* Sept 1942

Advertising executives

Alberti, Jules, American advertising executive, July 1959

Barton, Bruce, American advertising executive, religious writer and congressman, Feb 1961, *Obit* Oct 1967

Beers, Charlotte, American advertising executive and government official, June 1998

Benson, John, American advertising executive, Apr 1940, *Obit* Nov 1962

Benton, William, American senator, publisher and diplomat, Yrbk 1945, *Obit* May 1973

Bernbach, William, American advertising executive, Mar 1967, *Obit* Nov 1982

Bowles, Chester, American government official and diplomat, Sept 1943, Jan 1957, *Obit* July 1986

Brower, Charles H., advertising executive, Feb 1965, *Obit* Nov 1984

Della Femina, Jerry, American advertising executive, restaurateur and grocery store owner, Nov 1979

Fudge, Ann M., American advertising executive, June 1998

Haldeman, H. R., American presidential adviser, Sept 1978, *Obit* Jan 1994

Harper, Marion, advertising executive, Mar 1961, *Obit* Feb 1990

Lawrence, Mary Wells, American advertising executive, Jan 1967

Lazarus, Rochelle, American advertising executive, May 1997

Leigh, Douglas, advertising executive and lighting designer, May 1940, *Obit* May 2000

Marchetto, Marisa Acocella, American advertising executive and graphic novelist, Aug 2013

McCann, Renetta, American advertising executive, May 2005

Merchant, Ismail, Indian motion picture producer, Mar 1993, *Obit* Yrbk 2005

O'Meara, Walter, author and advertising executive, Yrbk 1958, *Obit* Nov 1989

Ogilvy, David, British advertising executive, July 1961, *Obit* Oct 1999

Philbrick, Herbert A., advertising executive and FBI informer, Mar 1953, *Obit* Oct 1993

Rafshoon, Gerald M., American television producer and advertising executive, July 1979

Resor, Stanley, American advertising executive, July 1949, *Obit* Yrbk 1962

Rubicam, Raymond, advertising executive, Yrbk 1943, *Obit* July 1978

Saatchi, Maurice, English advertising executive, Jan 1989

Schwartz, Tony, American advertising executive and sound archivist, July 1985, *Obit* Yrbk 2008

Strouse, Norman H., advertising executive, May 1960, *Obit* Mar 1993

Viguerie, Richard A., American political fund raiser and magazine publisher, Jan 1983

Advice columnists

Bushnell, Candace, American advice columnist and novelist, Nov 2003

Carroll, E. Jean, American advice columnist, July 2008

Dickinson, Amy, American freelance writer and advice columnist, Apr 2004

Dix, Dorothy, American advice columnist, Jan 1940, *Obit* Feb 1952

Hax, Carolyn, American advice columnist, Nov 2002

Heloise, American advice columnist, June 1996

Landers, Ann, American advice columnist, Nov 1957, *Obit* Nov 2002

Martin, Judith, American columnist and expert on etiquette, June 1986

Post, Emily, American advice columnist, Mar 1941, *Obit* Nov 1960

Savage, Dan, American advice columnist, July 2009

Van Buren, Abigail, advice columnist, May 1960, *Obit* Yrbk 2013

Aerialists

Petit, Philippe, French aerialist, Sept 1988

Aeronautical engineers

Bell, Lawrence D., July 1942, *Obit* Jan 1957

Camm, Sydney, English aircraft designer, Apr 1942, *Obit* Apr 1966

Chidlaw, Benjamin W., Mar 1955

Coanda, Henri, July 1956, *Obit* Feb 1973

Crossfield, A. Scott, American aeronautical engineer, test pilot and consultant, Oct 1969, *Obit* Yrbk 2006

Damon, Ralph S., July 1949, *Obit* Mar 1956

Dassault, Marcel, French aircraft executive and engineer, June 1970, *Obit* June 1986

Douglas, Donald Wills, aircraft executive, Nov 1941, Yrbk 1950, *Obit* Mar 1981

Freedman, Benedict, Sept 1947, *Obit* Yrbk 2012

Froehlich, Jack E., July 1959

Goddard, Robert Hutchings, American physicist, *Obit* Sept 1945

Hobbs, Leonard S., Oct 1954, *Obit* Jan 1978

Hunsaker, Jerome C., aeronautical engineer, Oct 1942, *Obit* Nov 1984

Johnson, Clarence Leonard, aeronautical engineer, Oct 1968, *Obit* Mar 1991

Johnson, Philip G., *Obit* Nov 1944

Kimball, Wilbur R., *Obit* Sept 1940

Kisevalter, George, *Obit* May 1941

Lear, William Powell, American engineer and inventor, July 1966, *Obit* July 1978

Magruder, William M., aeronautical engineer and airline executive, Mar 1972, *Obit* Nov 1977

Martin, Glenn L., Feb 1943, *Obit* Feb 1956

Martin, James S., American aeronautical engineer, Mar 1977, *Obit* Yrbk 2002

Messerschmitt, Willy, German aircraft designer, Apr 1940, *Obit* Nov 1978

Miles, Mary, Nov 1942

Northrop, John Knudsen, American aeronautical

engineer and executive, Mar 1949, *Obit* Apr 1981

Pearson, C. C., Mar 1950

Piccard, Jean Felix, Sept 1947, *Obit* Mar 1963

Rumpler, Edmund, *Obit* Oct 1940

Rutan, Burt, American aeronautical engineer and executive, June 2005

Seamans, Robert C., American NASA official, Yrbk 1966, *Obit* Yrbk 2008

Sikorsky, Igor, Ukrainian-American aeronautical engineer, Oct 1940, Yrbk 1956, *Obit* Yrbk 1972

Stever, H. Guyford, American aeronautical engineer, Jan 1981, *Obit* Yrbk 2010

Storms, Harrison Allen, American aeronautical engineer, Jan 1963, *Obit* Sept 1992

Stout, William Bushnell, American aeronautical engineer and aircraft industry executive, Mar 1941, *Obit* May 1956

Tupolev, Andrei N., Jan 1957

Von Karman, Theodore, American aeronautical engineer, May 1955, *Obit* June 1963

Warner, Edward P., aeronautical engineer, Oct 1949, *Obit* Sept 1958

Whitcomb, Richard T., American aeronautical engineer, Yrbk 1956, *Obit* Yrbk 2009

Whittle, Frank, British air force officer and aeronautical engineer, Jan 1945, *Obit* Oct 1996

Widnall, Sheila Evans, American Secretary of the air force, Oct 1997

Wright, Theodore P., Nov 1945, *Obit* Nov 1970

Aerospace consultants

Collins, Michael, American astronaut and aerospace consultant, May 1975

Aerospace engineers

Bell, Lawrence D., July 1942, *Obit* Jan 1957

Blagonravov, A. A., Soviet rocket engineer, Feb 1958, *Obit* Apr 1975

Camm, Sydney, English aircraft designer, Apr 1942, *Obit* Apr 1966

Charyk, Joseph V., American government official and telecommunications executive, Yrbk 1970

Chidlaw, Benjamin W., Mar 1955

Coanda, Henri, July 1956, *Obit* Feb 1973

Crossfield, A. Scott, American aeronautical engineer, test pilot and consultant, Oct 1969, *Obit* Yrbk 2006

Damon, Ralph S., July 1949, *Obit* Mar 1956

Dassault, Marcel, French aircraft executive and engineer, June 1970, *Obit* June 1986

Debus, Kurt H., rocket engineer and NASA official, Nov 1973, *Obit* Nov 1983

Douglas, Donald Wills, aircraft executive, Nov 1941, Yrbk 1950, *Obit* Mar 1981

Draper, Charles Stark, aeronautic and rocket engineer, Yrbk 1965, *Obit* Sept 1987

Ehricke, Krafft A., physicist and rocket engineer, June 1958, *Obit* Feb 1985

Ericsson-Jackson, Aprille J., aerospace engineer, Mar 2001

Feoktistov, Konstantin Petrovich, Soviet astronaut and aerospace engineer, Nov 1967, *Obit* Yrbk 2010

Freedman, Benedict, Sept 1947, *Obit* Yrbk 2012

Froehlich, Jack E., July 1959

Gilruth, Robert R., American aerospace engineer and NASA official, Oct 1963, *Obit* Yrbk 2000

Goddard, Robert Hutchings, American physicist, *Obit* Sept 1945

Griffin, Michael D., American NASA official, Aug 2005

Hickam, Homer H., American aerospace engineer and memoirist, Oct 2000

Hobbs, Leonard S., Oct 1954, *Obit* Jan 1978

Hunsaker, Jerome C., aeronautical engineer, Oct 1942, *Obit* Nov 1984

Johnson, Clarence Leonard, aeronautical engineer, Oct 1968, *Obit* Mar 1991

Johnson, Philip G., *Obit* Nov 1944

Kimball, Wilbur R., *Obit* Sept 1940

Kisevalter, George, *Obit* May 1941

Kraft, Christopher C., aerospace engineer, Feb 1966

Lear, William Powell, American engineer and inventor, July 1966, *Obit* July 1978

Magruder, William M., aeronautical engineer and airline executive, Mar 1972, *Obit* Nov 1977

Martin, Glenn L., Feb 1943, *Obit* Feb 1956

Martin, James S., American aeronautical engineer, Mar 1977, *Obit* Yrbk 2002

Messerschmitt, Willy, German aircraft designer, Apr 1940, *Obit* Nov 1978

Miles, Mary, Nov 1942

Northrop, John Knudsen, American aeronautical engineer and executive, Mar 1949, *Obit* Apr 1981

Oberth, Hermann, German physicist and rocket engineer, Apr 1957, *Obit* Mar 1990

Paine, Thomas Otten, aerospace executive and NASA official, Mar 1970, *Obit* July 1992

Pearson, C. C., Mar 1950

Piccard, Jean Felix, Sept 1947, *Obit* Mar 1963

Rodota, Antonio, Italian aerospace engineer and European space agency official, Jan 2003

Rumpler, Edmund, *Obit* Oct 1940

Rutan, Burt, American aeronautical engineer and executive, June 2005

Seamans, Robert C., American NASA official, Yrbk 1966, *Obit* Yrbk 2008

Shirley, Donna, American aerospace engineer and NASA official, Aug 1998

Sikorsky, Igor, Ukrainian-American

aeronautical engineer, Oct 1940, Yrbk 1956, *Obit* Yrbk 1972

Stever, H. Guyford, American aeronautical engineer, Jan 1981, *Obit* Yrbk 2010

Storms, Harrison Allen, American aeronautical engineer, Jan 1963, *Obit* Sept 1992

Stout, William Bushnell, American aeronautical engineer and aircraft industry executive, Mar 1941, *Obit* May 1956

Stuhlinger, Ernst, American rocket engineer, Nov 1957, *Obit* Yrbk 2008

Tupolev, Andrei N., Jan 1957

Von Braun, Wernher, German-American rocket engineer, Jan 1952, *Obit* Aug 1977

Von Karman, Theodore, American aeronautical engineer, May 1955, *Obit* June 1963

Warner, Edward P., aeronautical engineer, Oct 1949, *Obit* Sept 1958

Whitcomb, Richard T., American aeronautical engineer, Yrbk 1956, *Obit* Yrbk 2009

Whittle, Frank, British air force officer and aeronautical engineer, Jan 1945, *Obit* Oct 1996

Widnall, Sheila Evans, American Secretary of the air force, Oct 1997

Wright, Theodore P., Nov 1945, *Obit* Nov 1970

Aerospace industry executives

Allen, William M., American aircraft industry executive, Mar 1953, *Obit* Jan 1986

Anders, William A., American astronaut and aerospace industry executive, Apr 1969

Anderson, Roy A., American aerospace executive, Aug 1983, *Obit* Mar 2004

Armstrong, C. Michael, American telecommunications executive, June 1999

Augustine, Norman R., aerospace executive, June 1998

Beech, Olive Ann, American aircraft executive, June 1956, *Obit* Sept 1993

Bell, James A., American aerospace industry executive, July 2006

Bendix, Vincent, American inventor and aircraft industry executive, *Obit* May 1945

Berg, Hart O., American aviation and arms expert, *Obit* Feb 1942

Bigelow, Robert T., American real estate executive and financier, Aug 2008

Boyd, Alan S., American Secretary of transportation and railroad executive, Mar 1965

Camm, Sydney, English aircraft designer, Apr 1942, *Obit* Apr 1966

Conrad, Pete, American astronaut, Yrbk 1965

Cooper, Gordon, American astronaut and aircraft industry executive, Sept 1963

Crossfield, A. Scott, American aeronautical engineer, test pilot and consultant, Oct 1969, *Obit* Yrbk 2006

Dassault, Marcel, French aircraft executive and engineer, June 1970, *Obit* June 1986

Douglas, Donald Wills, aircraft executive, Nov 1941, Yrbk 1950, *Obit* Mar 1981

Enders, Thomas, German aircraft industry executive, Mar 2011

Forgeard, Noel, French aircraft industry executive, Jan 2004

Good, Mary L., American chemist, Sept 2001

Gordon, Crawford, Canadian aircraft and steel executive, Mar 1958, *Obit* Mar 1967

Grumman, Leroy R., aircraft executive, Aug 1945, *Obit* Jan 1983

Haughton, Daniel Jeremiah, aircraft executive, Sept 1974, *Obit* Aug 1987

Hiller, Stanley, American aircraft industry executive and business turnaround expert, Nov 1974, *Obit* Yrbk 2006

Hodgson, James D., American aircraft industry executive and Secretary of labor, Nov 1970, *Obit* Yrbk 2013

Holmes, D. Brainerd, aerospace industry executive and NASA official, Mar 1963, *Obit* Yrbk 2013

Horner, H. M., aircraft executive, Oct 1955, *Obit* July 1983

Hughes, Howard, American airline, aircraft and motion picture executive, Apr 1941, *Obit* May 1976

Hurley, Roy T., American aircraft industry executive, June 1955, *Obit* Yrbk 1971

Jack, William S., Mar 1944

Lagardere, Jean-Luc, French aerospace and publishing executive, Aug 1993, *Obit* Aug 2003

Lear, William Powell, American engineer and inventor, July 1966, *Obit* July 1978

Lewis, David Sloan, American aerospace industry executive, Aug 1975, *Obit* Yrbk 2004

Lewis, Roger, aircraft executive, Yrbk 1973, *Obit* Jan 1988

McNarney, Joseph T., American air force general and aircraft industry executive, Nov 1944, *Obit* Mar 1972

McNerney, James, American aerospace industry executive, Mar 2008

Messerschmitt, Willy, German aircraft designer, Apr 1940, *Obit* Nov 1978

Mueller, George E., aerospace industry executive and NASA official, Nov 1964

Musk, Elon, American entrepreneur, Oct 2006

Northrop, John Knudsen, American aeronautical engineer and executive, Mar 1949, *Obit* Apr 1981

Paine, Thomas Otten, aerospace executive and NASA official, Mar 1970, *Obit* July 1992

Piper, W. T., American aircraft industry executive, Apr 1946, *Obit* Mar 1970

Rutan, Burt, American aeronautical engineer and executive, June 2005

Ryan, T. Claude, aviation pioneer, Jan 1943, *Obit* Nov 1982

Schrempp, Juergen E., German automobile executive, Oct 1999

Sikorsky, Igor, Ukrainian-American aeronautical engineer, Oct 1940, Yrbk 1956, *Obit* Yrbk 1972

Slayton, Donald Kent, astronaut and aerospace executive, Feb 1976, *Obit* Aug 1993

Storms, Harrison Allen, American aeronautical engineer, Jan 1963, *Obit* Sept 1992

Stout, William Bushnell, American aeronautical engineer and aircraft industry executive, Mar 1941, *Obit* May 1956

Talbott, Harold E., American Secretary of the air force, July 1953, *Obit* May 1957

Thornton, Charles Bates, defense industry executive, Feb 1970, *Obit* Jan 1982

Wright, Orville, American aviation pioneer, Oct 1946, *Obit* Mar 1948

African studies specialists

Italiaander, Rolf, June 1964

Agribusiness executives

Antinori, Piero, Italian vintner, Jan 2006

Bastianich, Joseph, American restaurateur and winemaker, June 2011

Bendetsen, Karl Robin, American paper industry executive, May 1952, *Obit* Sept 1989

Bible, Geoffrey C., American tobacco and food industry executive, Feb 2002

Black, William, coffee company executive, July 1964, *Obit* May 1983

Bowater, Eric Vansittart, English paper industry executive, Sept 1956, *Obit* Nov 1962

Butler, Hugh, American senator, Feb 1950, *Obit* Sept 1954

Deveshwar, Yogesh Chander, Indian tobacco company executive, Jan 2005

Espinoza, Alvaro, Chilean vintner, Jan 2004

Fudge, Ann M., American advertising executive, June 1998

Illy, Ernesto, Italian coffee company executive, Jan 2002

Ivey, Susan, American tobacco industry executive, Mar 2010

McCabe, Thomas Bayard, American paper industry executive and Federal Reserve chairman, Sept 1948, *Obit* July 1982

McCormick, Fowler, June 1947, *Obit* Feb 1973

Mondavi, Robert, American vintner, Apr 1999, *Obit* Yrbk 2008

Noboa, Alvaro, Ecuadorian businessman and political leader, Jan 2007

Quinn, William F., American governor, Nov 1958, *Obit* Yrbk 2006

Robaina, Alejandro, Cuban cigar manufacturer, Jan 2004, *Obit* Yrbk 2010

Rothschild, Guy de, French banker, Mar 1973, *Obit* Yrbk 2007

Smothers, Tom, American comedian, Yrbk 1968

Sunderland, Thomas Elbert, fruit industry executive, Apr 1962, *Obit* May 1991

Uhlmann, Richard Frederick, grain dealer, Jan 1949, *Obit* Feb 1990

Wigand, Jeffrey, American teacher and former tobacco industry executive, Apr 2000

Woertz, Patricia, American agribusiness executive, Mar 2007

Agricultural engineers

Pacheco e Chaves, Joao, Nov 1954

Wahlen, Friedrich T., June 1961

Agricultural laborers

Chavez, Cesar, Mexican-American labor leader, Feb 1969, *Obit* June 1993

Huerta, Dolores, American labor leader, Nov 1997

Rodriguez, Arturo, labor leader, Mar 2001

Agricultural leaders

Alvarado, Elvia, Honduran human rights activist, Jan 2004

Boyd, John W., American farmers' association executive, Feb 2001

Callander, W. F., Oct 1948

Cowden, Howard A., Mar 1952

Davenport, Eugene, *Obit* May 1941

Davis, Chester Charles, American agricultural leader, banker and government official, July 1940, *Obit* Nov 1975

Dodd, Norris E., Feb 1949, *Obit* Sept 1968

Fulmer, Hampton Pitts, *Obit* Yrbk 1944

Goss, Albert S., Mar 1945, *Obit* Yrbk 1950

Hall, Florence L., Aug 1943

Hill, William S., Mar 1955, *Obit* Nov 1972

Hudson, Robert S. Hudson, Nov 1942, *Obit* Apr 1957

Kline, Allan B., American agricultural leader, Mar 1948, *Obit* Sept 1968

Mitchell, H. L., American farm leader, Jan 1947

Murphy, Franklin W., American farm leader, lawyer and banker, *Obit* Jan 1941

Newsom, Herschel D., American farmer, agricultural leader and government official, Apr 1951, *Obit* Sept 1970

Patton, James George, American agricultural leader, Jan 1945, Feb 1966

Sayre, Ruth Buxton, May 1949

Staley, Oren Lee, farm leader, Sept 1965, *Obit* Nov 1988

Taber, Louis J., June 1942, *Obit* Yrbk 1960

Williams, Aubrey Willis, American government official, publisher and social welfare leader, May 1940, *Obit* Apr 1965

Agriculturists

Adkins, Charles, American congressman, *Obit* May 1941

Allen, Will, American urban farmer, Sept 2013

Alvarado, Elvia, Honduran human rights activist, Jan 2004

Arthur, J. C., American botanist, *Obit* June 1942

Beardsley, William S., American governor, June 1950, *Obit* Jan 1955

Bennett, Henry Garland, American college president, Feb 1951, *Obit* Feb 1952

Bennett, Hugh Hammond, American soil scientist, Yrbk 1946, *Obit* Oct 1960

Bensin, Basil M., American agriculturist, July 1948

Bergland, Bob, American Secretary of agriculture, Sept 1977

Block, John R., American Secretary of agriculture, Apr 1982

Blundell, Michael, British farmer and colonial leader, Mar 1954

Boerma, Addeke H., Dutch agronomist and United Nations official, Yrbk 1974

Borlaug, Norman, American plant pathologist and geneticist, July 1971, *Obit* Yrbk 2009

Bove, Jose, French farmer, Jan 2002

Boyd, John W., American farmers' association executive, Feb 2001

Boyd-Orr, John Boyd Orr, Scottish agriculturist, June 1946, *Obit* Sept 1971

Brenton, W. Harold, Jan 1953

Brooks, D. W., June 1951

Brossard, Edgar Bernard, July 1954

Brown, Lester Russell, American agriculturist and environmentalist, Jan 1993

Callander, W. F., Oct 1948

Cardon, P. V., May 1954, *Obit* Yrbk 1965

Cooley, Harold D., American congressman, Mar 1951, *Obit* Mar 1974

Cowden, Howard A., Mar 1952

Davenport, Eugene, *Obit* May 1941

Davis, Chester Charles, American agricultural leader, banker and government official, July 1940, *Obit* Nov 1975

Davis, Westmoreland, *Obit* Oct 1942

Dodd, Norris E., Feb 1949, *Obit* Sept 1968

Fairchild, David, American plant pathologist and explorer, July 1953, *Obit* Oct 1954

Fisher, Walter C., July 1950

Frear, J. Allen, Oct 1954

Fujimori, Alberto, Peruvian president, Nov 1990

Fulmer, Hampton Pitts, *Obit* Yrbk 1944

Gardiner, James Garfield, Canadian cabinet member, June 1956, *Obit* Mar 1962

Garst, Jonathan, Oct 1964

Garst, Roswell, agriculturist and banker, Apr 1964, *Obit* Jan 1978

Gilbert, George, *Obit* May 1943

Gilmore, John Washington, *Obit* Aug 1942

Goss, Albert S., Mar 1945, *Obit* Yrbk 1950

Grandin, Temple, American autistic animal scientist, July 1994

Hall, Florence L., Aug 1943

Harrar, J. George, Jan 1964, *Obit* June 1982

Heintzleman, B. Frank, June 1953, *Obit* Sept 1965

Hill, William S., Mar 1955, *Obit* Nov 1972

Hudson, Robert S. Hudson, Nov 1942, *Obit* Apr 1957

Jester, Beauford H., July 1948, *Obit* Sept 1949

Jones, Monty, Sierra Leonen plant geneticist and rice breeder, Jan 2007

Kline, Allan B., American agricultural leader, Mar 1948, *Obit* Sept 1968

Lowdermilk, Walter, American soil scientist, Feb 1949, *Obit* July 1974

Mansholt, Sicco Leendert, May 1966

Marzotto, Gaetano, July 1953

Matskevich, Vladimir Vladimirovich, Nov 1955

Mitchell, H. L., American farm leader, Jan 1947

Moya, Manuel A. de, Nov 1957

Murphy, Franklin W., American farm leader, lawyer and banker, *Obit* Jan 1941

Murphy, Patricia, American restaurateur and horticulturist, Apr 1962

Nearing, Scott, American sociologist and homesteader, Oct 1971, *Obit* Oct 1983

Newsom, Herschel D., American farmer, agricultural leader and government official, Apr 1951, *Obit* Sept 1970

Patton, James George, American agricultural leader, Jan 1945, Feb 1966

Pinchot, Gifford, American governor, forester and conservationist, *Obit* Nov 1946

Rolland, Michel, American enologist, Jan 2007

Sayre, Ruth Buxton, May 1949

Scott, W. Kerr, Apr 1956, *Obit* July 1958

Shuman, Charles B., American farm organization official, Feb 1956

Staley, Oren Lee, farm leader, Sept 1965, *Obit* Nov 1988

Stelle, John, Jan 1946, *Obit* Sept 1962

Stookey, Charley, Jan 1940

Taber, Louis J., June 1942, *Obit* Yrbk 1960

Thye, Edward J., American governor and senator, Oct 1951, *Obit* Nov 1969

Vo, Tong Xuan, Vietnamese agriculturist, Jan 2002

Warne, William Elmo, land reclamation and irrigation specialist, Nov 1952, *Obit* May 1996

Watts, Lyle F., Oct 1946

Weyerhaeuser, Rudolph M., *Obit* Sept 1946

Williams, Aubrey Willis, American government official, publisher and social welfare leader, May 1940, *Obit* Apr 1965

Yuan Longping, Chinese agriculturist, Jan 2005

Air force officers

Abacha, Sani, Nigerian dictator, Sept 1996, *Obit* Aug 1998

Abizaid, John P., American general, Oct 2003

Abrams, Creighton Williams, American general, Oct 1968, *Obit* Oct 1974

Al-Bashir, Omar, Sudanese head of state, Jan 2005

Aldrin, Buzz, American astronaut, Sept 1993

Allen, Frank A., American general, Mar 1945, *Obit* Jan 1980

Allen, Terry, Nov 1943, *Obit* Nov 1969

Almond, Edward M., general, Mar 1951, *Obit* Aug 1979

Amedeo, Italian air force officer and colonial administrator, *Obit* Apr 1942

Amin, Idi, Ugandan general and president, Feb 1973, *Obit* Yrbk 2003

Anders, William A., American astronaut and aerospace industry executive, Apr 1969

Anderson, Alexander E., American general, *Obit* Feb 1943

Anderson, Frederick L., American general, May 1944, *Obit* Apr 1969

Anderson, Kenneth A. N., British general, Feb 1943, *Obit* July 1959

Andreu Almazan, Juan, Mexican general and political leader, May 1940, *Obit* Yrbk 1965

Andrews, Frank M., American general, Feb 1942, *Obit* June 1943

Antonescu, Ion, Romanian dictator, Oct 1940, *Obit* July 1946

Aoun, Michel, Lebanese general and political leader, Mar 1990

Aramburu, Pedro Eugenio, Argentine president, Jan 1957, *Obit* Oct 1970

Armstrong, George E., American physician and general, Apr 1952, *Obit* Aug 1979

Armstrong, Harry G., American physician and air force general, July 1951

Arnold, Henry Harley, American air force general, Feb 1942, *Obit* Feb 1950

Arnold, William R., American military chaplain and bishop, May 1942

Assad, Hafez, Syrian president, July 1975, Apr 1992, *Obit* Aug 2000

Atkinson, Joseph Hampton, American air force general, May 1956

Babangida, Ibrahim, Nigerian general and head of state, Sept 1990

Bagramyan, Ivan K., Soviet general, Yrbk 1944, *Obit* Jan 1983

Balchen, Bernt, aviator, Jan 1949, *Obit* Yrbk 1973

Baldomir, Alfredo, Uruguayan general and president, June 1942, *Obit* Mar 1948

Banzer Suarez, Hugo, Bolivian president, Sept 1973, *Obit* Sept 2002

Barak, Ehud, Israeli political leader, Aug 1997

Barratt, Arthur Sheridan, British air marshal, Jan 1941

Batista y Zaldivar, Fulgencio, Cuban general and president, Sept 1940, Apr 1952, *Obit* Oct 1973

Beau, Lucas Victor, air force general, June 1954, *Obit* Jan 1987

Belyayev, Pavel, Soviet cosmonaut, July 1965, *Obit* Mar 1970

Bennett, Henry Gordon, Australian general, Mar 1942, *Obit* Oct 1962

Bennett, Ivan L., American military chaplain, Nov 1952, *Obit* Aug 1980

Bergquist, Kenneth P., American air force general, Mar 1961

Berry, Charles A., American flight surgeon, Apr 1969

Biddle, Anthony Joseph Drexel, American general and diplomat, Mar 1941, *Obit* Jan 1962

Bissell, Clayton L., American air force general, Feb 1943

Blamey, Thomas Albert, Australian general, June 1942, *Obit* July 1951

Blanchard, Doc, American football player and air force officer, Mar 1946, *Obit* Yrbk 2009

Bliss, Raymond W., American surgeon and general, Jan 1951, *Obit* Jan 1966

Bluford, Guion S., American astronaut, Sept 1984

Boatner, Haydon L., American general, July 1952

Bokassa, Apr 1978, *Obit* Jan 1997

Bolte, Charles Lawrence, general, Jan 1954, *Obit* May 1989

Bonesteel, Charles H., American general, June 1942, *Obit* Sept 1964

Bozize, Francois, Central African Republic general and president, Jan 2005

Bradley, Omar Nelson, American general, July 1943, *Obit* May 1981

Brereton, Lewis H., American general, Yrbk 1943, *Obit* Oct 1967

Brett, George H., American air force general, June 1942

Briggs, James E., June 1957, *Obit* Aug 1979

Brooks, Vincent, American general, June 2003

Brown, Albert Eger, Jan 1948

Brown, George S., American air force general, Oct 1975, *Obit* Feb 1979

Browning, Frederick, June 1943, *Obit* Apr 1965

Bull, Odd, Nov 1968

Burns, E. L. M., Canadian general, Feb 1955

Butler, Smedley D., American Marine corps general, *Obit* Aug 1940

Bykovskii, Valerii Fedorovich, Soviet astronaut, Jan 1965

Calles, Plutarco Elias, Mexican president, *Obit* Nov 1945

Candee, Robert C., May 1944

Carlson, Evans F., American Marine corps general, Oct 1943, *Obit* June 1947

Carmona, Antonio Oscar de Fragoso, Nov 1950, *Obit* May 1951

Carpentier, Marcel Maurice, Apr 1951

Carroll, Joseph Francis, American air force general, Apr 1962, *Obit* Mar 1991

Carton de Wiart, Adrian, May 1940, *Obit* July 1963

Casey, George W., American general, Mar 2006

Castelnau, Noel Marie Joseph Edouard de Curieres de, French general, *Obit* May 1944

Castelo Branco, Humberto de Alencar, Brazilian president, Feb 1965, *Obit* Oct 1967

Cates, Clifton B., American Marine corps officer, Nov 1950, *Obit* Sept 1970

Catroux, Georges, May 1943, *Obit* Feb 1970

Cavallero, Ugo, *Obit* Oct 1943

Cedras, Raoul, Haitian general, July 1995

Chang, Shan-tzu, *Obit* Yrbk 1940

Chapman, Leonard F., American Marine corps general, July 1968, *Obit* Sept 2000

Chase, William C., Nov 1952

Chen Cheng, Chinese general, Sept 1941, *Obit* Apr 1965

Chen Yi, Chinese general, Oct 1959, *Obit* Feb 1972

Chennault, Claire Lee, American general, Oct 1942, *Obit* Oct 1958

Cherniakhovskii, Ivan Danilovich, Oct 1944, *Obit* Apr 1945

Cheshire, Leonard, British air force officer and social welfare leader, Jan 1962, *Obit* Sept 1992

Chiang, Kai-shek, Chinese president, Jan 1940, May 1953, *Obit* May 1975

Christison, Philip, British general, Nov 1945, *Obit* Feb 1994

Chuikov, Vasilii Ivanovich, Soviet general, May 1943, *Obit* May 1982

Chun, Doo Hwan, Korean president, Mar 1981

Clark, Mark W., American general, Nov 1942, *Obit* June 1984

Clark, Wesley K., American general, July 1999

Clay, Lucius D., American general, May 1945, June 1963, *Obit* June 1978

Collins, J. Lawton, American general, Nov 1949, *Obit* Oct 1987

Collins, Seaborn P., Apr 1955

Cooper, Gordon, American astronaut and aircraft industry executive, Sept 1963

Coulter, John B., June 1954

Craig, Malin, Mar 1944, *Obit* Aug 1945

Craveiro Lopes, Francisco Higino, Mar 1956, *Obit* Nov 1964

Crerar, Henry Duncan Graham, Canadian general, Nov 1944, *Obit* May 1965

Crist, William E., Nov 1945

Cunningham, Alan, British general, June 1946, *Obit* Apr 1983

Cushman, Robert Everton, American Marine Corps general, Nov 1972, *Obit* Apr 1985

Davidson, Garrison Holt, general, June 1957, *Obit* Feb 1993

Davis, Benjamin O., American general, Yrbk 1942, *Obit* Jan 1971

Davis, Benjamin O., American air force general, Sept 1955, *Obit* Yrbk 2002

Davis, Robert C., *Obit* Oct 1944

Davison, F. Trubee, Yrbk 1945

Davison, Frederic Ellis, American general, Feb 1974

Dayan, Moshe, Israeli general, Mar 1957, *Obit* Jan 1982

De Witt, John Lesesne, American general, July 1942

DeCoursey, Elbert, Sept 1954

Dean, William F., American general, Sept 1954, *Obit* Oct 1981

Decker, George H., American general, Jan 1961

Dempsey, Miles Christopher, Oct 1944, *Obit* July 1969

Devers, Jacob Loucks, general, Sept 1942, *Obit* Jan 1980

Devine, John M., American general, Jan 1948

Devoe, Ralph G., Oct 1944, *Obit* Nov 1966

Dickerson, Debra, American journalist, Apr 2004

Dobbie, William George Shedden, British general, July 1945

Donovan, William J., American intelligence official and general, Mar 1941, Sept 1954, *Obit* Apr 1959

Doolittle, James Harold, American general, Aug 1942, Mar 1957, *Obit* Jan 1994

Dornberger, Walter, Feb 1965, *Obit* Sept 1980

Drum, Hugh A., July 1941, *Obit* Nov 1951

Dunwoody, Ann E., American general, Nov 2008

Eaker, Ira Clarence, general, Oct 1942, *Obit* Sept 1987

Eanes, Antonio dos Santos Ramalho, Portuguese president, Apr 1979

Easley, Claudius M., American general, *Obit* July 1945

Echols, Oliver P., Yrbk 1947, *Obit* July 1954

Eddy, Manton S., general, Feb 1951, *Obit* June 1962

Eichelberger, Robert L., American general, Jan 1943, *Obit* Yrbk 1961

Eikenberry, Karl W., American general and diplomat, Mar 2010

Eisenhower, Dwight D., American president, Aug 1942, Feb 1948, Sept 1957, *Obit* May 1969

Ely, Paul, Oct 1954, *Obit* Mar 1975

Emmons, Delos C., American general, Mar 1942, *Obit* Yrbk 1965

Ershad, Hussain Mohammad, Bangladeshi prime minister, Nov 1984

Erskine, G. B., American Marine corps general, July 1946, *Obit* July 1973

Erskine, George, British general, Jan 1952, *Obit* Nov 1965

Eyadema, Gnassingbe, Togolese president, Apr 2002, *Obit* Yrbk 2005

Fei Junlong, Chinese astronaut, Jan 2006

Festing, Francis, Feb 1945

Figueiredo, Joao Baptista de Oliveira, Brazilian president, Jan 1980, *Obit* May 2000

Franco, Francisco, Spanish dictator, Mar 1942, Mar 1954, *Obit* Jan 1976

Franks, Tommy, American general, Jan 2002

Freyberg, Bernard Freyberg, Oct 1940, *Obit* Sept 1963

Fuqua, Stephen Ogden, Feb 1943

Galtieri, Leopoldo Fortunato, Argentine general and president, Aug 1982, *Obit* Yrbk 2003

Gamelin, Maurice Gustave, French general, Jan 1940, *Obit* July 1958

Gaulle, Charles de, French president, Sept 1940, June

1949, Apr 1960, *Obit* Yrbk 1970

Gavin, James Maurice, American general and diplomat, Feb 1945, Sept 1961, *Obit* Apr 1990

Geiger, Roy S., American Marine general, July 1945, *Obit* Mar 1947

Geisel, Ernesto, Brazilian president, Aug 1975, *Obit* Nov 1996

George, Harold L., Yrbk 1942

Gerow, Leonard Townsend, Apr 1945, *Obit* Yrbk 1972

Giles, Barney McKinney, general, July 1944, *Obit* Aug 1984

Giraud, Henri, French general, Yrbk 1942, *Obit* Apr 1949

Gleason, John S., June 1958

Glubb, John Bagot, British general, Sept 1951, *Obit* May 1986

Golikov, Filipp Ivanovich, Soviet general, Apr 1943, *Obit* Sept 1980

Goodpaster, Andrew Jackson, American general, July 1969, *Obit* Yrbk 2005

Gort, John Standish Surtees Prendergast Vereker, British general, Oct 1940, *Obit* May 1946

Gott, William Henry Ewart, *Obit* Oct 1942

Gowon, Yakubu, Nigerian general and head of state, June 1970

Graham, Wallace Harry, physician and general, Feb 1947, *Obit* Mar 1996

Graves, William Sidney, general, *Obit* Mar 1940

Greene, Wallace M., American Marine corps general, June 1965, *Obit* Aug 2003

Gregory, Edmund B., Sept 1945, *Obit* Mar 1961

Gregory, Frederick Drew, American astronaut and NASA official, Oct 2005

Griswold, Oscar W., American general, Sept 1943, *Obit* Yrbk 1959

Grivas, Giorgios, Oct 1964, *Obit* Mar 1974

Grizodubova, Valentina S., Soviet aviator, Yrbk 1941, *Obit* July 1993

Groninger, Homer M., American general, Aug 1945

Gross, Charles P., Mar 1946, *Obit* Sept 1975

Groves, Leslie R., American general, Aug 1945, *Obit* Oct 1970

Gruenther, Alfred M., American general, Yrbk 1950, *Obit* July 1983

Guillaumat, Marie Louis Adolphe, *Obit* July 1940

Guillaume, Augustin, French general, Jan 1952

Gullion, Allen W., Feb 1943, *Obit* July 1946

Haig, Alexander Meigs, American general and Secretary of state, Jan 1973, Sept 1987, *Obit* Yrbk 2010

Hammerstein-Equord, Kurt, German general, *Obit* June 1943

Handy, Thomas T., American general, Sept 1951, *Obit* June 1982

Hansell, Haywood S., air force general, Jan 1945, *Obit* Jan 1989

Harbord, James G., American general, Mar 1945, *Obit* Sept 1947

Harington, Charles, British general, *Obit* Yrbk 1940

Harkins, Paul D., American general, Apr 1964

Harmon, Ernest N., American general and university president, Nov 1946, *Obit* Jan 1980

Harmon, Millard F., Yrbk 1942, *Obit* Apr 1945

Harris, Arthur Travers, British air marshal, Sept 1942, *Obit* May 1984

Harrison, William K., American general, July 1952, *Obit* Aug 1987

Hartle, Russell P., American general, June 1942, *Obit* Jan 1962

Hawley, Paul R., Apr 1946, *Obit* Jan 1966

Hayashi, Senjuro, *Obit* Mar 1943

Hayden, Michael, American general and intelligence official, Nov 2006

Hernandez Martinez, Maximiliano, Salvadoran general and president, June 1942, *Obit* June 1966

Hershey, Lewis Blaine, American general and government official, June 1941, June 1951, *Obit* July 1977

Hertzog, James Barry Munnik, South African prime minister, *Obit* Jan 1943

Hess, Dean E., Sept 1957

Heusinger, Adolf, German general, Feb 1956

Hilldring, John H., American general, Apr 1947

Ho, Ying-Chin, Taiwanese general, Oct 1942, *Obit* Jan 1988

Hodes, Henry I., American general, Feb 1959, *Obit* Apr 1962

Hodge, John R., June 1945, *Obit* Jan 1964

Hodges, Courtney H., May 1941, *Obit* Feb 1966

Holcomb, Thomas, July 1942, *Obit* July 1965

Holmes, Julius C., Feb 1945, *Obit* Sept 1968

Holmes, Phillips, *Obit* Oct 1942

Honjo, Shigeru, *Obit* Jan 1946

Horn, Carl von, Swedish general, Nov 1967

Horrocks, Brian, British general, Jan 1945, *Obit* Mar 1985

Horthy, Istvan, *Obit* Oct 1942

Horwood, William T. F., *Obit* Feb 1944

Hsiung, S.-F, July 1942

Hudleston, Edmund C., May 1951

Huebner, Clarence R., Oct 1949, *Obit* Nov 1972

Hull, John E., Apr 1954

Hume, Edgar Erskine, Aug 1944, *Obit* Mar 1952

Huntziger, Charles, French general, Yrbk 1941, *Obit* Yrbk 1941

Hurley, Patrick J., American Secretary of war and diplomat, Nov 1944, *Obit* Sept 1963

Ibanez del Campo, Carlos, Chilean president, Yrbk 1952, *Obit* July 1960

Ingles, Harry C., American general, Nov 1947

Irving, Frederick A., American general, Mar 1951

Ismay, Hastings Lionel Ismay, British general, Apr 1943, *Obit* Feb 1966

James, Daniel, American air force general, Mar 1976, *Obit* Apr 1978

Jarman, Sanderford, Sept 1942, *Obit* Yrbk 1955

Jaruzelski, Wojciech, Polish general and president, Mar 1982

Jodl, Alfred, German general, *Obit* Nov 1946

Johnson, Harold K., American general, May 1966, *Obit* Nov 1983

Johnson, Hugh S., American general and government official, Sept 1940, *Obit* June 1942

Jones, David C., July 1982, *Obit* Yrbk 2013

Justo, Agustin P., Argentine general and president, *Obit* Mar 1943

Karpinski, Janis, American general, Apr 2006

Kennedy, Claudia, general, Jan 2000

Kenney, George C., American general, Jan 1943, *Obit* Oct 1977

Key, William, July 1943, *Obit* Mar 1959

Kirk, Norman T., American surgeon and general, Feb 1944, *Obit* Nov 1960

Klimecki, Tadeusz A., *Obit* Aug 1943

Koenig, Pierre, French general, Sept 1944, *Obit* Nov 1970

Korner, Theodor, July 1951, *Obit* Mar 1957

Krueger, Walter, American general, Apr 1943, *Obit* Oct 1967

Kuchler, Georg von, Sept 1943

Kuter, Laurence S., American air force general, July 1948

Lanusse, Alejandro A., Argentine general and president, Apr 1973, *Obit* Nov 1996

Lawson, Ted W., Yrbk 1943

Laycock, R. E., May 1944, *Obit* May 1968

LeMay, Curtis E., American air force general, Yrbk 1944, Nov 1954, *Obit* Nov 1990

Lear, Ben, July 1942, *Obit* Jan 1967

Leavey, Edmond H., American general and telecommunications

executive, May 1951, *Obit* Apr 1980

Leclerc, Jacques, Oct 1944, *Obit* Yrbk 1947

Lee, John C. H., July 1944, *Obit* Nov 1958

Leese, Oliver, British general, Yrbk 1944, *Obit* Yrbk 1991

Leigh-Mallory, Trafford, British air marshal, Mar 1944, *Obit* Mar 1945

Lejeune, John Archer, marine general, *Obit* Jan 1943

Lemnitzer, Lyman Louis, American general, Nov 1955, *Obit* Jan 1989

Lentaigne, Walter D. A., July 1944, *Obit* Oct 1955

Leonov, Aleksei, Soviet astronaut, July 1965

Lerch, Archer L., Nov 1945, *Obit* Oct 1947

Li Zongren, Chinese general, Nov 1942, *Obit* Mar 1969

Lindbergh, Charles, American aviator, July 1941, Jan 1954, *Obit* Oct 1974

Littlejohn, Robert McGowan, Sept 1946, *Obit* July 1982

Loeb, Fritz, *Obit* Aug 1940

Lon Nol, Cambodian general and prime minister, Feb 1974, *Obit* Jan 1986

MacArthur, Douglas, American general, Oct 1941, May 1948, *Obit* May 1964

Mackay, Iven Giffard, Apr 1941, *Obit* Jan 1967

Marshall, George C., American general and statesmen, Oct 1940, Mar 1947, *Obit* Yrbk 1959

Martel, Giffard Le Quesne, British general, July 1943, *Obit* Nov 1958

Martin, Charles H., *Obit* Nov 1946

Mason-MacFarlane, Noel, British general, Feb 1943

Mathewson, Lemuel, Yrbk 1952, *Obit* Apr 1970

May, Geraldine P., Feb 1949

McAuliffe, Anthony C., American general, Feb 1950, *Obit* Oct 1975

McCaffrey, Barry, American general and government official, July 1997

McChrystal, Stanley, American general, Sept 2009

McCoy, Frank Ross, general, Nov 1945, *Obit* Sept 1954

McCreery, Richard L., British general, May 1945, *Obit* Yrbk 1967

McDivitt, James A., Nov 1965

McNair, Lesley James, American general, Nov 1942, *Obit* Sept 1944

McNarney, Joseph T., American air force general and aircraft industry executive, Nov 1944, *Obit* Mar 1972

McNaughton, Andrew, Nov 1942, *Obit* Nov 1966

Medaris, John Bruce, general and clergyman, Feb 1958

Medici, Emilio Garrastazu, Brazilian president, Oct 1971, *Obit* Jan 1986

Medina Angarita, Isaias, Venezuelan general and president, Mar 1942, *Obit* Nov 1953

Mehaffey, Joseph C., Jan 1948, *Obit* Apr 1963

Menninger, William Claire, Sept 1945, *Obit* Nov 1966

Merrill, Frank D., American general, July 1944, *Obit* Feb 1956

Metaxas, Ioannis, Greek general and dictator, Yrbk 1940, *Obit* Mar 1941

Mihailovic, Draza, Yugoslav general and underground leader, Mar 1942, *Obit* Sept 1946

Mobutu Sese Seko, Zairian president, Sept 1966, May 1997, *Obit* Nov 1997

Moore, Bryant E., American general, Feb 1949, *Obit* Mar 1951

Morgan, Frederick Edgeworth, Feb 1946, *Obit* May 1967

Moya, Manuel A. de, Nov 1957

Musharraf, Pervez, Pakistani general and president, Mar 2001, Jan 2002

Myers, Richard B., American air force general, Apr 2002

Naguib, Mohammed, Egyptian general, Oct 1952

Nam, Il, Sept 1951, *Obit* Apr 1976

Namphy, Henri, Haitian general, Sept 1988

Navarre, Henri, Nov 1953

Ne Win, Burmese president, Apr 1971, *Obit* Yrbk 2003

Newcomer, Francis K., American general, Mar 1950, *Obit* Oct 1967

Nguyen, Cao Ky, South Vietnamese vice-president, Yrbk 1966, *Obit* Yrbk 2011

Nichols, Kenneth D., general, Nov 1948, *Obit* Sept 2000

Nie Haisheng, Chinese astronaut, Jan 2006

Nikolayev, Andrian, Soviet astronaut, Nov 1964, *Obit* Yrbk 2004

Nimeiri, Gaafar Mohammed, Sudanese president, Nov 1977, *Obit* Yrbk 2009

Nogues, Charles, Feb 1943, *Obit* June 1971

Noriega, Manuel Antonio, Panamanian general and head of state, Mar 1988

Norstad, Lauris, American air force general, May 1948, Feb 1959, *Obit* Oct 1988

Nuckols, William P., May 1952

Nye, Archibald E., Feb 1942, *Obit* Jan 1968

O'Donnell, Emmett, general, July 1948, *Obit* Feb 1972

Odierno, Raymond, American general, Nov 2009

Ojukwu, Chukwuemeka Odumegwu, Nigerian political leader and general, Feb 1969, *Obit* Yrbk 2012

Okonkwo, Festus, Nigerian general, Jan 2005

Oliver, Lunsford E., Sept 1947

Ongania, Juan Carlos, Argentine president, Oct 1968, *Obit* Aug 1995

Orlebar, Augustus H., *Obit* Sept 1943

Ovando Candia, Alfredo, Bolivian general and president, Mar 1970, *Obit* Mar 1982

Pace, Peter, American Marine corps general, June 2006

Pai, Chung-hsi, Nov 1942, *Obit* Feb 1967

Papagos, Alexandros, Nov 1951, *Obit* Yrbk 1955

Park, Chung Hee, Korean president, Jan 1969, *Obit* Jan 1980

Parker, Roy H., Oct 1951

Partridge, Earle E., Apr 1955

Patch, Alexander McCarrell, American general, May 1943, *Obit* Jan 1946

Pate, Randolph McCall, general, Sept 1958, *Obit* Oct 1961

Patrick, Mason Mathews, American general, *Obit* Mar 1942

Patton, George S., American general, Jan 1943, *Obit* Feb 1946

Pearkes, George Randolph, Nov 1957

Penaranda, Enrique, Bolivian president, Jan 1940

Peng Dehuai, Chinese general and communist leader, Yrbk 1951

Peron, Juan Domingo, Argentine president, June 1944, Feb 1974, *Obit* Feb 1974

Persons, Wilton B., American general and presidential adviser, May 1953, *Obit* Nov 1977

Petraeus, David H., American general and intelligence official, Apr 2007

Pick, Lewis Andrew, American general and civil engineer, June 1946, *Obit* Feb 1957

Pierce, Palmer Eddy, *Obit* Jan 1940

Pile, Frederick Alfred, British general, Feb 1942, *Obit* Yrbk 1991

Pinochet Ugarte, Augusto, Chilean general and president, Yrbk 1974, *Obit* Yrbk 2007

Plaek Phibunsongkhram, Thai prime minister, Sept 1951, *Obit* Sept 1964

Porter, William N., Aug 1945, *Obit* Apr 1973

Potter, William Everett, American general, Yrbk 1957, *Obit* Feb 1989

Powell, Colin L., American Secretary of state, June 1988, Nov 2001

Power, Thomas S., American air force general, Apr 1958, *Obit* Jan 1971

Price, Harrison J., American general, *Obit* Oct 1945

Putt, Donald L., May 1960

Qassim, Abdul Karim, Iraqi general and prime minister, Nov 1959, *Obit* Mar 1963

Quesada, Elwood Richard, air force general and government official, Apr 1950, Jan 1960, *Obit* Apr 1993

Rahman, Ziaur, Bangladeshi president, June 1981

Ralston, Joseph W., air force general, Jan 2001

Ramey, Howard K., *Obit* May 1943

Ramirez, Pedro Pablo, Aug 1943, *Obit* Sept 1962

Ramos, Fidel V., Filipino president, Mar 1994

Rawlings, Jerry J., Ghanaian head of state, June 1982

Razmara, Hossein Ali, Iranian prime minister, Oct 1950, *Obit* Mar 1951

Reckord, Milton A., Mar 1945

Reybold, Eugene, June 1945, *Obit* Jan 1962

Ridgway, Matthew B., American general, July 1947, *Obit* Sept 1993

Riley, William Edward, Nov 1951

Rios Montt, Jose Efrain, Guatemalan president, May 1983

Robertson of Oakridge, Brian Hubert Robertson, Sept 1948, *Obit* June 1974

Rodriguez, Andres, Paraguayan general and president, Sept 1991, *Obit* June 1997

Rogers, Bernard W., American general, Oct 1984

Roh, Tae Woo, Korean president, Feb 1988

Rojas Pinilla, Gustavo, Colombian general and president, June 1956, *Obit* Mar 1975

Rooks, Lowell W., Apr 1947

Roosevelt, Elliott, American mystery novelist, mayor and son of President Franklin D. Roosevelt, Yrbk 1946, *Obit* Jan 1991

Roosevelt, Theodore, American government official, general and son of President Theodore Roosevelt, *Obit* Sept 1944

Rose, Maurice, American general, *Obit* May 1945

Rossy, Yves, Swiss air pilot and inventor, Jan 2013

Royall, Kenneth C., American Secretary of the army, Jan 1947, *Obit* Sept 1971

Rupertus, William H., *Obit* May 1945

Ryan, Patrick James, military chaplain, May 1955

Saltzman, Charles E., general, diplomat and investment banker, Oct 1947, *Obit* Aug 1994

Schomburg, August, Nov 1960

Schriever, Bernard A., American air force general, Oct 1957, *Obit* Yrbk 2005

Schroeder, R. W., July 1941

Scobie, Ronald M., Feb 1945

Scott, David R., American astronaut and engineering executive, Oct 1971

Scott, Robert Lee, American air force general, Oct 1943, *Obit* Yrbk 2006

Scowcroft, Brent, American general and presidential adviser, July 1987

Serov, Ivan Aleksandrovich, Soviet communist leader, Yrbk 1956

Shalikashvili, John, American general, Nov 1995, *Obit* Yrbk 2011

Shang Zhen, July 1944

Sharon, Ariel, Israeli prime minister, Apr 1981, Jan 2002

Shelton, Hugh, American general, Aug 1998

Shepherd, Lemuel C., American Marine corps general, Feb 1952, *Obit* Oct 1990

Shinseki, Eric, American Secretary of veterans affairs, Mar 2009

Short, Walter Campbell, general, Jan 1946, *Obit* Oct 1949

Shoup, David M., American Marine corps general, Jan 1960, *Obit* Mar 1983

Sikorski, Wladyslaw, Polish general and statesman, Jan 1940, *Obit* Aug 1943

Simonds, Guy Granville, Canadian general, Oct 1943, *Obit* July 1974

Simons, David G., American physician and air force officer, Yrbk 1957, *Obit* Yrbk 2010

Simpson, William H., Feb 1945, *Obit* Oct 1980

Slemon, C. Roy, Yrbk 1956

Smith, C. R., American airline executive, air force general and Secretary of commerce, Sept 1945, *Obit* June 1990

Smith, Holland M., American Marine corps general, Apr 1945, *Obit* Mar 1967

Smith, Walter Bedell, American general, diplomat and CIA director, Apr 1944, Yrbk 1953, *Obit* Nov 1961

Smuts, Jan Christiaan, South African prime minister, Aug 1941, *Obit* Oct 1950

Snyder, Howard McC., Feb 1955, *Obit* Nov 1970

Soeharto, Indonesian president, June 1967, Oct 1992, *Obit* Yrbk 2008

Somervell, Brehon Burke, Aug 1942, *Obit* Apr 1955

Somoza, Anastasio, Nicaraguan dictator, June 1942, *Obit* Yrbk 1956

Somoza, Anastasio, Nicaraguan general and president, Mar 1978, *Obit* Nov 1980

Spaatz, Carl, American air force general, Sept 1942, *Obit* Sept 1974

Speidel, Hans, German general, Apr 1952, *Obit* Feb 1985

Spinola, Antonio de, Portuguese general and president, Sept 1974, *Obit* Nov 1996

Spofford, Charles Merville, lawyer and diplomat, Feb 1951, *Obit* May 1991

Stafford, Thomas P., American astronaut and air force general, Jan 1977

Stapp, John Paul, air force officer and biophysicist, Yrbk 1959, *Obit* May 2000

Stilwell, Joseph Warren, American general, May 1942, *Obit* Nov 1946

Stone, William S., June 1960, *Obit* Feb 1969

Stratemeyer, George E., Feb 1951, *Obit* Oct 1969

Stroessner, Alfredo, Paraguayan general and president, Yrbk 1958, Mar 1981, *Obit* Yrbk 2007

Stuart, Kenneth, Feb 1944, *Obit* Yrbk 1945

Sturdee, V. A. H., July 1942

Sultan, Daniel I., Jan 1945, *Obit* Feb 1947

Surles, Alexander D., Nov 1945, *Obit* Yrbk 1947

Swaythling, Jean Marcia, Sept 1942

Swing, Joseph May, general and immigration official, Apr 1959, *Obit* Feb 1985

Tatekawa, Yoshitsugu, *Obit* Oct 1945

Taylor, Maxwell D., American general, Nov 1946, Yrbk 1961, *Obit* June 1987

Taylor, Telford, lawyer and historian, Yrbk 1948, *Obit* Aug 1998

Ter Poorten, Hein, Mar 1942

Thimayya, Kodendera Subayya, Apr 1954, *Obit* Feb 1966

Thompson, John Taliaferro, American general, military engineer and inventor, *Obit* Aug 1940

Thompson, Paul Williams, general and publishing executive, Nov 1942, *Obit* May 1996

Tinker, Clarence Leonard, American general, June 1942

Titov, Gherman Stepanovich, Soviet astronaut, Yrbk 1962, *Obit* Jan 2001

Tojo, Hideki, Japanese general and prime minister, Yrbk 1941, *Obit* Jan 1949

Torrijos Herrera, Omar, Panamanian dictator, July 1973, *Obit* Sept 1981

Trudeau, Arthur Gilbert, general, Apr 1958, *Obit* Aug 1991

Trujillo Molina, Rafael Leonidas, Dominican general and president, July 1941, *Obit* Oct 1961

Truscott, Lucian King, American general, May 1945, *Obit* Nov 1965

Twining, Nathan F., American air force general, Yrbk 1953, *Obit* May 1982

Ulio, James Alexander, Sept 1945

Umberto, Oct 1943, *Obit* May 1983

Upshur, William P., *Obit* Sept 1943

Urquhart, Robert E., British general, Yrbk 1944, *Obit* Feb 1989

Van Fleet, James Alward, American general, Apr 1948, *Obit* Nov 1992

Vandegrift, A. A., American Marine corps general, Jan 1943, *Obit* June 1973

Vandenberg, Hoyt Sanford, American air force general, Mar 1945, *Obit* May 1954

Vatutin, Nikolai Fedorovich, Soviet general, Feb 1944

Vaughan, Harry H., American general, Mar 1949, *Obit* July 1981

Velasco Alvarado, Juan, Peruvian president, June 1970, *Obit* Mar 1978

Videla, Jorge Rafael, Argentine general and president, Apr 1978, *Obit* Yrbk 2013

Vo, Nguyen Giap, Vietnamese general, Feb 1969

Vogel, Herbert D., Yrbk 1954

Wainwright, Jonathan Mayhew, American general, May 1942, *Obit* Nov 1953

Waitt, Alden H., Sept 1947

Walker, Walton Harris, American general, Sept 1950, *Obit* Jan 1951

Walters, Vernon A., American general and diplomat, Feb 1988, *Obit* July 2002

Ward, William E., American general, Nov 2005

Wash, Carlyle H., *Obit* Mar 1943

Watson, Edwin M., American general, *Obit* Apr 1945

Wavell, Archibald Percival Wavell, British general and colonial administrator, Mar 1941, *Obit* July 1950

Weaver, Walter Reed, *Obit* Yrbk 1944

Wedemeyer, Albert, American general, Jan 1945, *Obit* Feb 1990

Westmoreland, William C., American general, June 1961, *Obit* Nov 2005

Weygand, Maxime, French general, Jan 1940, *Obit* Mar 1965

Wheeler, Earle G., American general, Nov 1965, *Obit* Feb 1976

White, I. D., American general, Yrbk 1958, *Obit* Aug 1990

White, Thomas D., American air force general, Yrbk 1957, *Obit* Feb 1966

Whitney, Courtney, June 1951, *Obit* May 1969

Whittle, Frank, British air force officer and aeronautical engineer, Jan 1945, *Obit* Oct 1996

Wilby, Francis B., Aug 1945, *Obit* Jan 1966

Wilson, Heather, American congresswoman, July 2006

Wingate, Orde Charles, British general, *Obit* May 1944

Yadin, Yigael, Israeli archaeologist, general and political leader, Feb 1966, *Obit* Aug 1984

Yamut, Nuri, May 1952

Yang Liwei, Chinese astronaut, Jan 2004

Yates, Donald N., air force general and meteorologist, May 1958

Yeager, Chuck, American test pilot and air force general, May 1954

Yudhoyono, Susilo Bambang, Indonesian president, Jan 2005

Zahedi, Fazlollah, Feb 1954, *Obit* Nov 1963

Zhu De, Chinese general, Nov 1942, *Obit* Aug 1976

Zia-ul-Haq, Mohammad, Pakistani general and president, June 1980, *Obit* Sept 1988

Zinni, Anthony, American Marine corps general and diplomat, May 2002

Air pilots

Aldrin, Buzz, American astronaut, Sept 1993

Amedeo, Italian air force officer and colonial administrator, *Obit* Apr 1942

Anders, William A., American astronaut and aerospace industry executive, Apr 1969

Andrews, Frank M., American general, Feb 1942, *Obit* June 1943

Armstrong, Harry G., American physician and air force general, July 1951

Armstrong, Neil, American astronaut, Oct 1969, *Obit* Yrbk 2012

Arnold, Henry Harley, American air force general, Feb 1942, *Obit* Feb 1950

Atkinson, Joseph Hampton, American air force general, May 1956

Auriol, Jacqueline, French aviator, Sept 1953, *Obit* June 2000

Bach, Richard, American inspirational writer, Oct 1973

Balbo, Italo, Italian air marshal, *Obit* Aug 1940

Balchen, Bernt, aviator, Jan 1949, *Obit* Yrbk 1973

Barratt, Arthur Sheridan, British air marshal, Jan 1941

Beau, Lucas Victor, air force general, June 1954, *Obit* Jan 1987

Belyayev, Pavel, Soviet cosmonaut, July 1965, *Obit* Mar 1970

Bergquist, Kenneth P., American air force general, Mar 1961

Berkner, Lloyd, Sept 1949, *Obit* Oct 1967

Berry, Charles A., American flight surgeon, Apr 1969

Bishop, Billy, Canadian air marshal, Sept 1941

Bissell, Clayton L., American air force general, Feb 1943

Blanchard, Doc, American football player and air force officer, Mar 1946, *Obit* Yrbk 2009

Bluford, Guion S., American astronaut, Sept 1984

Bolden, Charles, American astronaut and NASA official, July 2010

Borman, Frank, American astronaut and engineering executive, Mar 1969, Apr 1980

Brabazon of Tara, John Theodore Cuthbert Moore-Brabazon, British aviator and government official, May 1941

Brereton, Lewis H., American general, Yrbk 1943, *Obit* Oct 1967

Brett, George H., American air force general, June 1942

Briggs, James E., June 1957, *Obit* Aug 1979

Brown, George S., American air force general, Oct 1975, *Obit* Feb 1979

Bull, Odd, Nov 1968

Burbank, Daniel, Astronaut, Sept 2012

Bykovskii, Valerii Fedorovich, Soviet astronaut, Jan 1965

Byrd, Richard Evelyn, American admiral and explorer, Oct 1942, May 1956, *Obit* May 1957

Carpenter, Scott, American astronaut, Sept 1962

Carroll, Joseph Francis, American air force general, Apr 1962, *Obit* Mar 1991

Cernan, Eugene A., American astronaut and business consultant, May 1973

Chang-Diaz, Franklin R., American astronaut and physicist, Aug 2011

Chennault, Claire Lee, American general, Oct 1942, *Obit* Oct 1958

Cheshire, Leonard, British air force officer and social welfare leader, Jan 1962, *Obit* Sept 1992

Chidlaw, Benjamin W., Mar 1955

Coanda, Henri, July 1956, *Obit* Feb 1973

Cobb, Geraldyn M., American aviator, Feb 1961

Cochran, Jacqueline, American aviator and cosmetics industry executive, Sept 1940, June 1963, *Obit* Oct 1980

Collins, Michael, American astronaut and aerospace consultant, May 1975

Collins, Seaborn P., Apr 1955

Conrad, Pete, American astronaut, Yrbk 1965

Cooper, Gordon, American astronaut and aircraft industry executive, Sept 1963

Craveiro Lopes, Francisco Higino, Mar 1956, *Obit* Nov 1964

Currie, Nancy, American astronaut, June 2002

Davis, Benjamin O., American air force general, Sept 1955, *Obit* Yrbk 2002

De Seversky, Alexander P., Feb 1941, *Obit* Oct 1974

Denton, Jeremiah, American admiral and senator, May 1982

Dickerson, Debra, American journalist, Apr 2004

Doolittle, James Harold, American general, Aug 1942, Mar 1957, *Obit* Jan 1994

Dougherty, Dora, Mar 1963

Dufek, George J., Mar 1957

Dwight, Edward J., American astronaut and sculptor, July 2007

Echols, Oliver P., Yrbk 1947, *Obit* July 1954

Egbert, Sherwood H., June 1963, *Obit* Oct 1969

Emmons, Delos C., American general, Mar 1942, *Obit* Yrbk 1965

Fahy, Charles, American judge and solicitor general, Jan 1942, *Obit* Nov 1979

Farnsworth, Arthur, *Obit* Oct 1943

Fei Junlong, Chinese astronaut, Jan 2006

Felt, Harry D., Mar 1959

Feoktistov, Konstantin Petrovich, Soviet astronaut and aerospace engineer, Nov 1967, *Obit* Yrbk 2010

Fitch, Aubrey, Oct 1945, *Obit* July 1978

Foss, Joe, American governor and firearms association executive, Oct 1955, *Obit* Yrbk 2003

Fossett, Steve, American stockbroker and balloonist, Apr 2005, *Obit* Yrbk 2008

Gagarin, Yuri, Soviet cosmonaut, Oct 1961, *Obit* May 1968

Gandhi, Rajiv, Indian prime minister, Apr 1985, *Obit* July 1991

Glenn, John, American astronaut and senator, June 1962, Mar 1976, Jan 1999

Gower, Pauline, English aviator, Aug 1943, *Obit* Mar 1947

Gregory, Frederick Drew, American astronaut and NASA official, Oct 2005

Grissom, Gus, American astronaut, Nov 1965, *Obit* Mar 1967

Grizodubova, Valentina S., Soviet aviator, Yrbk 1941, *Obit* July 1993

Gros, Edmund L., *Obit* Yrbk 1942

Haignere, Claudie, French astronaut and cabinet member, Jan 2003

Hailey, Arthur, Canadian novelist, Feb 1972, *Obit* Yrbk 2005

Hansell, Haywood S., air force general, Jan 1945, *Obit* Jan 1989

Harmon, Millard F., Yrbk 1942, *Obit* Apr 1945

Harris, Arthur Travers, British air marshal, Sept 1942, *Obit* May 1984

Hess, Dean E., Sept 1957

Hitchcock, Thomas, polo player, *Obit* June 1944

Holmes, Julius C., Feb 1945, *Obit* Sept 1968

Holmes, Phillips, *Obit* Oct 1942

Honeywell, Harry E., *Obit* Jan 1940

Horthy, Istvan, *Obit* Oct 1942

Hudleston, Edmund C., May 1951

James, Daniel, American air force general, Mar 1976, *Obit* Apr 1978

Jamieson, Leland, *Obit* Sept 1941

Jemison, Mae C., American physician and astronaut, July 1993

Johnson, Amy, English aviator, *Obit* Feb 1941

Jones, Brian, British balloonist, Jan 2004

Jones, David C., July 1982, *Obit* Yrbk 2013

Keyhoe, Donald Edward, marine corps officer, June 1956, *Obit* Feb 1989

Kuipers, Andre, Dutch physician and astronaut, Jan 2004

Kuter, Laurence S., American air force general, July 1948

Lawson, Ted W., Yrbk 1943

LeMay, Curtis E., American air force general, Yrbk 1944, Nov 1954, *Obit* Nov 1990

Leigh-Mallory, Trafford, British air marshal, Mar 1944, *Obit* Mar 1945

Leonov, Aleksei, Soviet astronaut, July 1965

Lindbergh, Charles, American aviator, July 1941, Jan 1954, *Obit* Oct 1974

Lovell, Jim, American astronaut, Mar 1969

Maas, Melvin Joseph, Nov 1957, *Obit* June 1964

Mahan, John W., July 1959

Markham, Beryl, British aviator, Nov 1942, *Obit* Oct 1986

Martin, Glenn L., Feb 1943, *Obit* Feb 1956

May, Geraldine P., Feb 1949

McConachie, G. W. Grant, Nov 1958, *Obit* Sept 1965

McDivitt, James A., Nov 1965

McGregor, G. R., Mar 1954, *Obit* Apr 1971

McNarney, Joseph T., American air force general and aircraft industry executive, Nov 1944, *Obit* Mar 1972

Mussolini, Bruno, *Obit* Oct 1941

Muti, Ettore, *Obit* Oct 1943

Myers, Richard B., American air force general, Apr 2002

Netherwood, Douglas B., *Obit* Oct 1943

Nguyen, Cao Ky, South Vietnamese vice-president, Yrbk 1966, *Obit* Yrbk 2011

Nie Haisheng, Chinese astronaut, Jan 2006

Nikolayev, Andrian, Soviet astronaut, Nov 1964, *Obit* Yrbk 2004

Norstad, Lauris, American air force general, May 1948, Feb 1959, *Obit* Oct 1988

Nuckols, William P., May 1952

O'Donnell, Emmett, general, July 1948, *Obit* Feb 1972

Ocker, William C., *Obit* Nov 1942

Orlebar, Augustus H., *Obit* Sept 1943

Parseval, August von, *Obit* Apr 1942

Partridge, Earle E., Apr 1955

Peck, James L. H., Aug 1942

Piccard, Bertrand, Swiss psychiatrist and balloonist, Jan 2004

Pickerill, Elmo N., Mar 1966, *Obit* Mar 1968

Power, Thomas S., American air force general, Apr 1958, *Obit* Jan 1971

Putt, Donald L., May 1960

Quesada, Elwood Richard, air force general and government official, Apr 1950, Jan 1960, *Obit* Apr 1993

Ralston, Joseph W., air force general, Jan 2001

Ramey, Howard K., *Obit* May 1943

Rawlings, Jerry J., Ghanaian head of state, June 1982

Rickenbacker, Eddie, American military pilot, Nov 1940, Feb 1952, *Obit* Oct 1973

Ride, Sally K., American astronaut and astrophysicist, Oct 1983, *Obit* Yrbk 2012

Riiser-Larsen, Hjalmar, Nov 1951, *Obit* July 1965

Rossy, Yves, Swiss air pilot and inventor, Jan 2013

Ryan, T. Claude, aviation pioneer, Jan 1943, *Obit* Nov 1982

Saint-Exupery, Antoine de, French novelist, essayist and aviator, Jan 1940, *Obit* May 1945

Schirra, Wally, American astronaut, June 1966, *Obit* Yrbk 2007

Schmitt, Harrison H., American senator, geologist and astronaut, July 1974

Schriever, Bernard A., American air force general, Oct 1957, *Obit* Yrbk 2005

Schroeder, R. W., July 1941

Scott, David R., American astronaut and engineering executive, Oct 1971

Scott, Robert Lee, American air force general, Oct 1943, *Obit* Yrbk 2006

Scott, Sheila, English aviator, Nov 1974, *Obit* Jan 1989

Scowcroft, Brent, American general and presidential adviser, July 1987

Shepard, Alan B., American astronaut and real estate executive, Yrbk 1961, *Obit* Sept 1998

Shuttleworth, Mark, South African entrepreneur, Jan 2007

Simons, David G., American physician and air force officer, Yrbk 1957, *Obit* Yrbk 2010

Slayton, Donald Kent, astronaut and aerospace executive, Feb 1976, *Obit* Aug 1993

Slemon, C. Roy, Yrbk 1956

Smith, C. R., American airline executive, air force general and Secretary of commerce, Sept 1945, *Obit* June 1990

Smith, Elinor, American aviator, Mar 2001, *Obit* Yrbk 2010

Spaatz, Carl, American air force general, Sept 1942, *Obit* Sept 1974

Stafford, Thomas P., American astronaut and air force general, Jan 1977

Stapp, John Paul, air force officer and biophysicist, Yrbk 1959, *Obit* May 2000

Stratemeyer, George E., Feb 1951, *Obit* Oct 1969

Strawbridge, Anne West, *Obit* Nov 1941

Tata, J. R. D., Indian industrialist and philanthropist, Yrbk 1958, *Obit* Jan 1994

Tereshkova, Valentina, Soviet astronaut, Yrbk 1963

Titov, Gherman Stepanovich, Soviet astronaut, Yrbk 1962, *Obit* Jan 2001

Twining, Nathan F., American air force general, Yrbk 1953, *Obit* May 1982

Vandenberg, Hoyt Sanford, American air force general, Mar 1945, *Obit* May 1954

Wash, Carlyle H., *Obit* Mar 1943

White, Edward Higgins, American astronaut, Nov 1965, *Obit* Mar 1967

White, Thomas D., American air force general, Yrbk 1957, *Obit* Feb 1966

Whitson, Peggy A., American biochemist and astronaut, Sept 2003

Williams, Alford Joseph, Oct 1940

Williams, John Bell, American congressman and governor, Mar 1964, *Obit* May 1983

Williams, Sunita L., American astronaut, Mar 2013

Wilson, Heather, American congresswoman, July 2006

Yancey, Lewis Alonzo, *Obit* Jan 1940

Yang Liwei, Chinese astronaut, Jan 2004

Yates, Donald N., air force general and meteorologist, May 1958

Yeager, Chuck, American test pilot and air force general, May 1954

Yeager, Jeana, aviator, May 1987

Yegorov, Boris, Soviet astronaut and physician, Mar 1968, *Obit* Nov 1994

Young, John, American astronaut, June 1965

Aircraft industry executives

Allen, William M., American aircraft industry executive, Mar 1953, *Obit* Jan 1986

Armstrong, C. Michael, American telecommunications executive, June 1999

Beech, Olive Ann, American aircraft executive, June 1956, *Obit* Sept 1993

Bell, James A., American aerospace industry executive, July 2006

Bendix, Vincent, American inventor and aircraft industry executive, *Obit* May 1945

Berg, Hart O., American aviation and arms expert, *Obit* Feb 1942

Boyd, Alan S., American Secretary of transportation and railroad executive, Mar 1965

Enders, Thomas, German aircraft industry executive, Mar 2011

Forgeard, Noel, French aircraft industry executive, Jan 2004

Gordon, Crawford, Canadian aircraft and steel executive, Mar 1958, *Obit* Mar 1967

Grumman, Leroy R., aircraft executive, Aug 1945, *Obit* Jan 1983

Haughton, Daniel Jeremiah, aircraft executive, Sept 1974, *Obit* Aug 1987

Hiller, Stanley, American aircraft industry executive and business turnaround expert, Nov 1974, *Obit* Yrbk 2006

Hodgson, James D., American aircraft industry executive and Secretary of labor, Nov 1970, *Obit* Yrbk 2013

Horner, H. M., aircraft executive, Oct 1955, *Obit* July 1983

Hughes, Howard, American airline, aircraft and motion picture executive, Apr 1941, *Obit* May 1976

Hurley, Roy T., American aircraft industry executive, June 1955, *Obit* Yrbk 1971

Jack, William S., Mar 1944

Lewis, Roger, aircraft executive, Yrbk 1973, *Obit* Jan 1988

Piper, W. T., American aircraft industry executive, Apr 1946, *Obit* Mar 1970

Ryan, T. Claude, aviation pioneer, Jan 1943, *Obit* Nov 1982

Talbott, Harold E., American Secretary of the air force, July 1953, *Obit* May 1957

Thornton, Charles Bates, defense industry executive, Feb 1970, *Obit* Jan 1982

Wright, Orville, American aviation pioneer, Oct 1946, *Obit* Mar 1948

Airline employees

Baker, George Theodore, American airline executive, June 1953, *Obit* Jan 1964

Beard, Charles E., American airline executive, July 1956, *Obit* Oct 1982

Bell, Lawrence D., July 1942, *Obit* Jan 1957

Bethune, Gordon M., American airline executive, June 2001

Borman, Frank, American astronaut and engineering executive, Mar 1969, Apr 1980

Boutelle, Richard S., Sept 1951

Braniff, T. E., Apr 1952, *Obit* Mar 1954

Branson, Richard, British financier, Feb 1995

Breech, Ernest, Sept 1955, *Obit* Aug 1978

Bunker, George M., Apr 1957

Burgess, Carter Lane, American airline and machinery industry executive and diplomat, Apr 1957, *Obit* Yrbk 2002

Burr, Donald C., American airline executive, Sept 1986

Chalk, O. Roy, American transportation and communications executive, Nov 1971, *Obit* Feb 1996

Cohu, La Motte T., Apr 1951, *Obit* Nov 1968

Crandall, Robert L., American airline executive, Nov 1992

Damon, Ralph S., July 1949, *Obit* Mar 1956

Ferguson, Malcolm P., May 1957

Frye, Jack, Apr 1945, *Obit* Apr 1959

Gardner, Lester Durand, Sept 1947, *Obit* Feb 1957

Gray, Harold E., Feb 1969

Gross, Robert E., Jan 1956, *Obit* Nov 1961

Grosvenor, Graham Bethune, American elevator manufacturing company and airline executive, *Obit* Yrbk 1943

Haji-Ioannou, Stelios, Greek shipping heir and entrepreneur, Jan 2007

Halaby, Najeeb E., American airline executive and regulatory agency official, Oct 1961, *Obit* Yrbk 2003

Hall, Floyd D., June 1970, *Obit* Yrbk 2012

Hildred, William P., Apr 1956

Hobbs, Leonard S., Oct 1954, *Obit* Jan 1978

Hughes, Howard, American airline, aircraft and motion picture executive, Apr 1941, *Obit* May 1976

Hunter, Croil, American airline executive, July 1951, *Obit* Oct 1970

Janas, Sigmund, Apr 1950

Johnson, Philip G., *Obit* Nov 1944

Kelleher, Herbert David, American airline executive, Jan 2001

Kindelberger, James Howard, Mar 1951, *Obit* Oct 1962

Laker, Freddie, English airline executive, June 1978, *Obit* Yrbk 2006

Lorenzo, Frank, airline executive, Feb 1987

Magruder, William M., aeronautical engineer and airline executive, Mar 1972, *Obit* Nov 1977

McConachie, G. W. Grant, Nov 1958, *Obit* Sept 1965

McGregor, G. R., Mar 1954, *Obit* Apr 1971

Naikuni, Titus, Kenyan airline executive, Jan 2004

Neeleman, David G., American airline executive, Sept 2003

Notman, J. Geoffrey, Jan 1958

Nyrop, Donald W., American airline executive, June 1952, *Obit* Yrbk 2011

Patterson, W. A., June 1946, *Obit* Aug 1980

Peale, Mundy I., May 1956, *Obit* Jan 1973

Pearson, C. C., Mar 1950

Plesman, Albert, Mar 1953, *Obit* Mar 1954

Prescott, Robert W., July 1971

Putt, Donald L., May 1960

Rentzel, Delos Wilson, government official and

aviation expert, Oct 1948, *Obit* Jan 1992

Riiser-Larsen, Hjalmar, Nov 1951, *Obit* July 1965

Schroeder, R. W., July 1941

Shea, Andrew B., Jan 1957, *Obit* Jan 1973

Six, Robert F., airline executive, Oct 1970, *Obit* Nov 1986

Smallpeice, Basil, English airline and shipping executive, Oct 1969

Smith, C. R., American airline executive, air force general and Secretary of commerce, Sept 1945, *Obit* June 1990

Smith, Frederick W., American air freight executive, June 2000

Swirbul, Leon A., Apr 1953, *Obit* Sept 1960

Thomas, Charles S., American airline executive and Secretary of the navy, Yrbk 1954, *Obit* Jan 1984

Thomas, Miles Thomas, Jan 1952, *Obit* Apr 1980

Tillinghast, Charles C., airline executive, Feb 1962, *Obit* Oct 1998

Trippe, J. T., American airline executive, Aug 1942, Feb 1955, *Obit* May 1981

Trump, Donald J., American real estate executive, Feb 1984

Vaughan, Guy W., Yrbk 1948, *Obit* Jan 1967

Wilson, Eugene E., Oct 1945

Airline executives

Baker, George Theodore, American airline executive, June 1953, *Obit* Jan 1964

Beard, Charles E., American airline executive, July 1956, *Obit* Oct 1982

Bethune, Gordon M., American airline executive, June 2001

Borman, Frank, American astronaut and engineering executive, Mar 1969, Apr 1980

Boutelle, Richard S., Sept 1951

Braniff, T. E., Apr 1952, *Obit* Mar 1954

Branson, Richard, British financier, Feb 1995

Breech, Ernest, Sept 1955, *Obit* Aug 1978

Bunker, George M., Apr 1957

Burgess, Carter Lane, American airline and machinery industry executive and diplomat, Apr 1957, *Obit* Yrbk 2002

Burr, Donald C., American airline executive, Sept 1986

Chalk, O. Roy, American transportation and communications executive, Nov 1971, *Obit* Feb 1996

Cohu, La Motte T., Apr 1951, *Obit* Nov 1968

Crandall, Robert L., American airline executive, Nov 1992

Ferguson, Malcolm P., May 1957

Frye, Jack, Apr 1945, *Obit* Apr 1959

Gardner, Lester Durand, Sept 1947, *Obit* Feb 1957

Gray, Harold E., Feb 1969

Gross, Robert E., Jan 1956, *Obit* Nov 1961

Grosvenor, Graham Bethune, American elevator manufacturing company and airline executive, *Obit* Yrbk 1943

Haji-Ioannou, Stelios, Greek shipping heir and entrepreneur, Jan 2007

Halaby, Najeeb E., American airline executive and regulatory agency official, Oct 1961, *Obit* Yrbk 2003

Hall, Floyd D., June 1970, *Obit* Yrbk 2012

Hildred, William P., Apr 1956

Hunter, Croil, American airline executive, July 1951, *Obit* Oct 1970

Janas, Sigmund, Apr 1950

Kelleher, Herbert David, American airline executive, Jan 2001

Kindelberger, James Howard, Mar 1951, *Obit* Oct 1962

Laker, Freddie, English airline executive, June 1978, *Obit* Yrbk 2006

Lorenzo, Frank, airline executive, Feb 1987

McConachie, G. W. Grant, Nov 1958, *Obit* Sept 1965

McGregor, G. R., Mar 1954, *Obit* Apr 1971

Naikuni, Titus, Kenyan airline executive, Jan 2004

Neeleman, David G., American airline executive, Sept 2003

Notman, J. Geoffrey, Jan 1958

Nyrop, Donald W., American airline executive, June 1952, *Obit* Yrbk 2011

Patterson, W. A., June 1946, *Obit* Aug 1980

Peale, Mundy I., May 1956, *Obit* Jan 1973

Plesman, Albert, Mar 1953, *Obit* Mar 1954

Prescott, Robert W., July 1971

Rentzel, Delos Wilson, government official and aviation expert, Oct 1948, *Obit* Jan 1992

Shea, Andrew B., Jan 1957, *Obit* Jan 1973

Six, Robert F., airline executive, Oct 1970, *Obit* Nov 1986

Smallpeice, Basil, English airline and shipping executive, Oct 1969

Smith, Frederick W., American air freight executive, June 2000

Swirbul, Leon A., Apr 1953, *Obit* Sept 1960

Thomas, Charles S., American airline executive and Secretary of the navy, Yrbk 1954, *Obit* Jan 1984

Thomas, Miles Thomas, Jan 1952, *Obit* Apr 1980

Tillinghast, Charles C., airline executive, Feb 1962, *Obit* Oct 1998

Trippe, J. T., American airline executive, Aug 1942, Feb 1955, *Obit* May 1981

Trump, Donald J., American real estate executive, Feb 1984

Vaughan, Guy W., Yrbk 1948, *Obit* Jan 1967

Wilson, Eugene E., Oct 1945

Alleged criminals

Khodorkovsky, Mikhail, Russian energy industry executive, Jan 2003

Simpson, O. J., American football player and sportscaster, Apr 1969

Alternative medicine practitioners

Weil, Andrew, American physician and healer, Aug 1996

Anarchists

Goldman, Emma, American anarchist, *Obit* Jan 1940

Tresca, Carlo, Italian anarchist, *Obit* Mar 1943

Anesthesiologists

Apgar, Virginia, American anesthesiologist, Feb 1968, *Obit* Oct 1974

Buchanan, Thomas Drysdale, *Obit* Apr 1940

Gwathmey, James T., *Obit* Apr 1944

Hingson, Robert A., anesthesiologist and public health expert, June 1943, *Obit* Jan 1997

Animal breeders

Bailey, Abe, South African financier and political leader, *Obit* Sept 1940

Animal rights activists

Caras, Roger A., environmentalist, journalist and animal rights activist, Apr 1988, *Obit* July 2001

Newkirk, Ingrid, American animal rights activist, Apr 2008

Pacelle, Wayne, American animal rights activist, Jan 2010

Patterson, Francine, American psychologist and animal rights activist, Nov 2000

Animal scientists

Grandin, Temple, American autistic animal scientist, July 1994

Animal trainers

Brannaman, Buck, American horse trainer and motivational speaker, Sept 2011

Fischbacher, Siegfried, German magician and animal trainer, Jan 1998

Gebel-Williams, Gunther, German animal trainer and circus owner, Yrbk 1971, *Obit* Oct 2001

Horn, Roy, German magician and animal trainer, Jan 1998

Markham, Beryl, British aviator, Nov 1942, *Obit* Oct 1986

Millan, Cesar, American dog trainer, Jan 2009

Siegfried and Roy, German magicians and animal trainers, Jan 1998

Tors, Ivan Lawrence, Hungarian animal trainer and motion picture producer, Feb 1969, *Obit* Aug 1983

Woodhouse, Barbara, English dog trainer and author, Feb 1985, *Obit* Aug 1988

Animal workers

Benchley, Belle Jennings, zoo director, Oct 1940

Brannaman, Buck, American horse trainer and motivational speaker, Sept 2011

Crane, Eva, British apiculturist, Aug 1993, *Obit* Yrbk 2007

Fischbacher, Siegfried, German magician and animal trainer, Jan 1998

Gebel-Williams, Gunther, German animal trainer and circus owner, Yrbk 1971, *Obit* Oct 2001

Gedi, Ali Mohamed, Somalian prime minister, Jan 2007

Grandin, Temple, American autistic animal scientist, July 1994

Grzimek, Bernhard, German zoo director and television performer, Mar 1973, *Obit* May 1987

Horn, Roy, German magician and animal trainer, Jan 1998

Hwang, Woo Suk, Korean veterinarian, Jan 2006

Irwin, Steve, Australian wildlife conservationist and television personality, Aug 2000, *Obit* Yrbk 2007

Markham, Beryl, British aviator, Nov 1942, *Obit* Oct 1986

Martini, Helen, American zookeeper, July 1955

Matola, Sharon, American biologist and zoo director, June 1993

Millan, Cesar, American dog trainer, Jan 2009

Murray, Ty, American rodeo cowboy, May 2002

Patterson, Frederick D., American college president

and veterinarian, June 1947, *Obit* June 1988

Rogers, Roy, American cowboy singer and actor, Mar 1948, Oct 1983, *Obit* Sept 1998

Shope, Richard E., Yrbk 1963, *Obit* Yrbk 1966

Siegfried and Roy, German magicians and animal trainers, Jan 1998

Tors, Ivan Lawrence, Hungarian animal trainer and motion picture producer, Feb 1969, *Obit* Aug 1983

Woodhouse, Barbara, English dog trainer and author, Feb 1985, *Obit* Aug 1988

Animators

Bakshi, Ralph, American animator, Mar 1979

Bosustow, Stephen, June 1958

Burton, Tim, American film director, July 1991

Disney, Walt, American animator and motion picture executive, Aug 1940, Apr 1952, *Obit* Feb 1967

Fiore, Mark, American cartoonist and animator, Apr 2011

Groening, Matt, American cartoonist and animator, Sept 1990

Hanna, William, American animator and producer, July 1983, *Obit* Sept 2001

Harryhausen, Ray, American motion picture special effects technician and animator, *Obit* Yrbk 2013

Hillenburg, Stephen, American animator and television scriptwriter, Apr 2003

Jones, Chuck, American animator, May 1996, *Obit* May 2002

Judge, Mike, American motion picture director and animator, May 1997

Lasseter, John, American animator, screenwriter and director, June 1997

MacFarlane, Seth, American animator, television scriptwriter, producer and voice-over artist, May 2010

McCracken, Craig, American animator, Feb 2004

Miyazaki, Hayao, Japanese animator, Apr 2001

Oshii, Mamoru, Japanese animator, Jan 2006

Parker, Trey, American actor, television scriptwriter, director, producer and animator, May 1998

Selick, Henry, American film director, May 2009

Stanton, Andrew, American film director, screenwriter and animator, Feb 2004

Stone, Matt, American actor, television scriptwriter, producer, director and animator, May 1998

Svankmajer, Jan, Czech animator and motion picture director, Jan 2006

Yamamura, Koji, Japanese animator, Jan 2003

Yuh Nelson, Jennifer, Korean-American animator and film director, Nov 2013

Anthropologists

Ahmed, Akbar S., Pakistani anthropologist, Jan 2005

Behar, Ruth, American anthropologist, poet and filmmaker, May 2005

Benedict, Ruth, American anthropologist, May 1941, *Obit* Nov 1948

Blakey, Michael L., biological anthropologist, Sept 2000

Boas, Franz, American anthropologist, May 1940, *Obit* Feb 1943

Cayton, Horace R., Jan 1946, *Obit* Mar 1970

Cole, Johnnetta B., American anthropologist and museum director, Aug 1994

Collier, John, American anthropologist and government official, Mar 1941, *Obit* July 1968

Coon, Carleton Stevens, American anthropologist, Sept 1955, *Obit* July 1981

Davis, Wade, Canadian ethnobotanist, Jan 2003

Dawdy, Shannon Lee, American archaeologist and anthropologist, Apr 2006

Dominy, Nathaniel J., American anthropologist, Apr 2010

Dorris, Michael, American anthropologist and memoirist, Mar 1995, *Obit* June 1997

Drake, St. Clair, anthropologist and sociologist, Jan 1946, *Obit* Aug 1990

Dubois, Eugene, Dutch anthropologist and paleontologist, *Obit* May 1941

Eiseley, Loren C., American anthropologist and science writer, June 1960, *Obit* Sept 1977

Field, Henry, anthropologist, Mar 1955, *Obit* Mar 1986

Fisher, Helen E., American anthropologist and psychologist, Oct 2010

Frazer, James George, Scottish classicist and anthropologist, *Obit* July 1941

Gheerbrant, Alain, Feb 1959

Gilmore, Melvin R., *Obit* Sept 1940

Goldenweiser, Alexander A., American anthropologist, *Obit* Sept 1940

Haddon, Alfred Cort, British anthropologist, *Obit* May 1940

Hall, Edward Twitchell, American anthropologist, Feb 1992, *Obit* Yrbk 2009

Herskovits, Melville J., American anthropologist, Nov 1948, *Obit* Apr 1963

Heyerdahl, Thor, Norwegian ethnologist and explorer, Yrbk 1947, Sept 1972, *Obit* Yrbk 2002

Hooton, Earnest Albert, American anthropologist, Yrbk 1940, *Obit* June 1954

Hrdlicka, Ales, anthropologist and paleontologist, Nov 1941, *Obit* Oct 1943

Hrdy, Sarah Blaffer, American primatologist and anthropologist, June 2000

Johanson, Donald C., American anthropologist, Feb 1984

Kim, Jim Yong, American physician and medical anthropologist, Nov 2006

Kluckhohn, Clyde, American anthropologist, Nov 1951, *Obit* Oct 1960

Kroeber, A. L., American anthropologist, Oct 1958, *Obit* Yrbk 1960

La Farge, Oliver, American novelist and anthropologist, Jan 1953, *Obit* Oct 1963

Langton, Marcia, Australian anthropologist and human rights activist, Jan 2007

Leakey, Louis Seymour Bazett, British anthropologist and archaeologist, Mar 1966, *Obit* Yrbk 1972

Leakey, Mary D., British anthropologist and paleontologist, Apr 1985, *Obit* Feb 1997

Leakey, Meave, Kenyan anthropologist and paleontologist, June 2002

Leakey, Richard E., Kenyan anthropologist and paleontologist, Nov 1976, Oct 1995

Levi-Strauss, Claude, French anthropologist, Mar 1972, *Obit* Jan 2010

Lewis, Albert Buell, American anthropologist, *Obit* Yrbk 1940

Lewis, Oscar, American anthropologist, Apr 1968, *Obit* Feb 1971

Lieberman, Daniel, American anthropologist and biologist, May 2011

Malinowski, Bronislaw, Polish anthropologist, June 1941, *Obit* July 1942

Marcus, George E., American anthropologist, Mar 2006

Marett, Robert R., *Obit* Apr 1943

Marriott, Alice Lee, anthropologist and author, Yrbk 1950, *Obit* May 1992

McFate, Montgomery, American cultural anthropologist, Aug 2008

Mead, Margaret, American anthropologist, Nov 1940, May 1951, *Obit* Jan 1979

Montagu, Ashley, Anglo-American anthropologist, Feb 1967, *Obit* Mar 2000

Moos, Felix, German-American anthropologist, Jan 2005

Mowat, Farley, Canadian ethnologist, historian and children's author, Feb 1986

Murdock, George Peter, anthropologist, Mar 1957

Nash, Philleo, government official, Nov 1962, *Obit* Jan 1988

Newsom, Lee A., American paleoethnobotanist, Oct 2004

Ortner, Sherry B., American anthropologist, Nov 2002

Parsons, Elsie Worthington Clews, anthropologist, *Obit* Feb 1942

Peccerelli, Fredy, Guatemalan forensic anthropologist, Jan 2004

Powdermaker, Hortense, American anthropologist, Feb 1961, *Obit* Sept 1970

Prince-Hughes, Dawn, American anthropologist, Apr 2005

Rainey, Froelich G., archaeologist and museum director, Feb 1967, *Obit* Jan 1993

Ramphele, Mamphela, South African college administrator and anthropologist, July 1997

Redfield, Robert, American anthropologist, Yrbk 1953, *Obit* Jan 1959

Reichs, Kathleen J., American forensic anthropologist, Oct 2006

Robeson, Eslanda Goode, American anthropologist and wife of Paul Robeson, Sept 1945, *Obit* Yrbk 1991

Roosevelt, Anna Curtenius, American archaeologist and anthropologist, June 1997

Rubin de la Borbolla, Daniel F., Feb 1960

Shapiro, Harry Lionel, anthropologist and museum curator, Yrbk 1952, *Obit* Mar 1990

Snow, Clyde, forensic anthropologist, Apr 1997

Tattersall, Ian, American anthropologist and museum curator, Aug 2007

Thomas, Elizabeth Marshall, American anthropologist and writer, Mar 1996

Tiger, Lionel, anthropologist, Jan 1981

Turnbull, Colin M., English anthropologist, Sept 1980, *Obit* Sept 1994

Underhill, Ruth M., anthropologist and author, Feb 1954, *Obit* Oct 1984

Warner, W. Lloyd, American anthropologist and sociologist, Yrbk 1959, *Obit* July 1970

Williams, Joseph John, *Obit* Yrbk 1940

Willoughby, Charles Clark, *Obit* June 1943

Wolpoff, Milford H., American paleoanthropologist, July 2006

Antiquarian booksellers

Carter, John, British bibliographer and rare book dealer, May 1959, *Obit* May 1975

Kraus, Hans Peter, American rare book dealer, July 1960, *Obit* Jan 1989

Rosenbach, A. S. W., American rare book collector and dealer, May 1946, *Obit* Sept 1952

Tuttle, Charles Egbert, publisher and rare book dealer, July 1960, *Obit* Aug 1993

Antiquarians

Brigham, Clarence Saunders, librarian, July 1959, *Obit* Oct 1963

Stokes, Isaac Newton Phelps, architect and antiquarian, *Obit* Feb 1945

Antique collectors

Nutting, Wallace, American clergyman, photographer and furniture executive, *Obit* Sept 1941

Appraisers

Fielding, Mantle, *Obit* May 1941

Toch, Maximilian, *Obit* June 1946

Archaeologists

Albright, William Foxwell, American archaeologist and biblical scholar, Sept 1955

Amsden, Charles Avery, American archaeologist, *Obit* Apr 1941

Bass, George Fletcher, American archaeologist, Mar 2000

Brier, Bob, American Egyptologist, Sept 2002

Ceram, C. W., Jan 1957, *Obit* June 1972

Cock, Guillermo A., Peruvian archaeologist, Jan 2007

Cox, Margaret, British archaeologist, Jan 2006

Davis-Kimball, Jeannine, American archaeologist, Feb 2006

Dawdy, Shannon Lee, American archaeologist and anthropologist, Apr 2006

Dorpfeld, Wilhelm, German archaeologist, *Obit* Jan 1940

Eisen, Gustavus A., *Obit* Yrbk 1940

El Mallakh, Kamal, Egyptian archaeologist, Oct 1954, *Obit* Jan 1988

Evans, Arthur John, British archaeologist, *Obit* Sept 1941

Fisher, Clarence S., *Obit* Sept 1941

Gates, William E., American archaeologist, *Obit* Jan 1940

Gilder, Robert F., American journalist and archaeologist, *Obit* Mar 1940

Glueck, Nelson, rabbi, archaeologist and college president, Oct 1948, July 1969, *Obit* Mar 1971

Goddio, Franck, French marine archaeologist, Jan 2002

Gordon, Cyrus Herzl, American biblical scholar and archaeologist, May 1963, *Obit* Aug 2001

Grant, Elihu, *Obit* Yrbk 1942

Hanfmann, George Maxim Anossov, archaeologist, Oct 1967, *Obit* May 1986

Harris, James Rendel, *Obit* Apr 1941

Hawass, Zahi, Egyptian archaeologist, Apr 2000

Jacopi, Giulio, Jan 1959

Leakey, Louis Seymour Bazett, British anthropologist and archaeologist, Mar 1966, *Obit* Yrbk 1972

Love, Iris, archaeologist, Aug 1982

Macdonald, George, classicist and archaeologist, *Obit* Sept 1940

Magoffin, Ralph Van Deman, *Obit* July 1942

Mercer, Samuel A. B., Feb 1953

Noel Hume, Ivor, English archaeologist, Nov 1997

Petrie, W. M. Flinders, English archaeologist, *Obit* Sept 1942

Phillips, Wendell, American explorer, archaeologist and petroleum industry executive, Nov 1958, *Obit* Feb 1976

Pick, Behrendt, *Obit* July 1940

Pope, Arthur Upham, American archaeologist and historian, July 1947, *Obit* Nov 1969

Rainey, Froelich G., archaeologist and museum director, Feb 1967, *Obit* Jan 1993

Reich, Nathaniel Julius, *Obit* Nov 1943

Reinhard, Johan, archaeologist, Aug 1999

Reisner, George Andrew, American Egyptologist, *Obit* July 1942

Romer, John, British Egyptologist, July 2003

Roosevelt, Anna Curtenius, American archaeologist and anthropologist, June 1997

Shear, T. Leslie, *Obit* Aug 1945

Soffer, Olga, Yusoslav-American archaeologist, July 2002

Thompson, Homer A., Canadian archaeologist, Apr 1948, *Obit* Yrbk 2000

Thompson, R. Campbell, *Obit* July 1941

Ventris, Michael George Francis, English architect, archaeologist and linguist, Jan 1957

Wendrich, Willeke, Dutch archaeologist, Jan 2007

Wheeler, Robert Eric Mortimer, English archaeologist, Mar 1956, *Obit* Sept 1976

Woolley, Leonard, English archaeologist, Yrbk 1954, *Obit* Apr 1960

Yadin, Yigael, Israeli archaeologist, general and political leader, Feb 1966, *Obit* Aug 1984

Archbishops

Akinola, Peter Jasper, Nigerian archbishop, Jan 2004

Athenagoras, Mar 1949, *Obit* Sept 1972

Camara, Helder, Brazilian archbishop, July 1971, *Obit* Jan 2000

Carey, George, British archbishop, Aug 1991

Cicognani, Amleto Giovanni, July 1951, *Obit* Feb 1974

Coggan, Frederick Donald, English archbishop, July 1974, *Obit* Sept 2000

Damaskenos, Nov 1945, *Obit* July 1949

Dolan, Timothy Michael, American archbishop, Mar 2011

Drossaerts, Arthur, *Obit* Oct 1940

Feltin, Maurice, May 1954, *Obit* Nov 1975

Fisher of Lambeth, Geoffrey Francis Fisher, British archbishop, Mar 1945, *Obit* Nov 1972

Forbes, Guillaume, *Obit* July 1940

Garbett, Cyril Forster, Feb 1951, *Obit* Mar 1956

Gauthier, Joseph Alexandre Georges, *Obit* Oct 1940

Gregory, Wilton D., American archbishop, Mar 2002

Hannan, Philip M., American archbishop, July 1968, *Obit* Yrbk 2011

Hickey, Thomas F., *Obit* Feb 1941

Hinsley, Arthur, *Obit* Apr 1943

Huddleston, Trevor, South African archbishop, Oct 1963, *Obit* July 1998

Hunthausen, Raymond G., archbishop, Aug 1987

Iakovos, July 1960, *Obit* Yrbk 2005

Kaspar, Karel, *Obit* June 1941

Lang of Lambeth, Cosmo Gordon Lang, English archbishop, Aug 1941, *Obit* Jan 1946

Lefebvre, Marcel, French archbishop, Mar 1978, *Obit* May 1991

Lercaro, Giacomo, Sept 1965, *Obit* Jan 1977

Makarios, Cypriot archbishop and president, May 1956, *Obit* Sept 1977

Matheson, Samuel Pritchard, *Obit* July 1942

May, John Lawrence, archbishop, Jan 1991, *Obit* June 1994

McGuigan, James, Sept 1950, *Obit* June 1974

McNicholas, John T., May 1949, *Obit* June 1950

Ncube, Pius Alick, Zimbabwean archbishop, Jan 2004

Pla y Deniel, Enrique, Feb 1955, *Obit* Sept 1968

Ramsey, Michael, English archbishop, Apr 1960, *Obit* June 1988

Rummel, Joseph F., American archbishop, June 1959, *Obit* Jan 1965

Runcie, Robert, English archbishop, Nov 1980, *Obit* Oct 2000

Schulte, Karl Joseph, *Obit* May 1941

Sheen, Fulton J., American archbishop, Nov 1941, Jan 1951, *Obit* Feb 1980

Spellman, Francis, Apr 1940, Apr 1947, *Obit* Jan 1968

Temple, William, British archbishop and theologian, Apr 1942, *Obit* Yrbk 1944

Tutu, Desmond, South African archbishop, Jan 1985, Jan 2002

Vagnozzi, Egidio, Mar 1967, *Obit* Feb 1981

Verdier, Jean, *Obit* May 1940

Williams, Rowan, British archbishop, Jan 2002

Architects

Aalto, Alvar, Finnish architect, Apr 1948, *Obit* July 1976

Abercrombie, Patrick, English architect, Apr 1946, *Obit* June 1957

Abrams, Charles, American city planner and lawyer, Feb 1969, *Obit* Apr 1970

Adams, Thomas, British architect and urban planner, *Obit* Apr 1940

Ai Wei Wei, Chinese artist and architect, Aug 2011

Aldrich, Chester Holmes, American architect, *Obit* Feb 1941

Alexander, Christopher, British architect, Oct 2003

Ando, Tadao, Japanese architect, Jan 2000

Arad, Michael, American architect, Oct 2013

Aronin, Jeffrey Ellis, Canadian architect, Jan 1955

Aulenti, Gae, Italian architect, Sept 1999, *Obit* Yrbk 2013

Behnisch, Stefan, German architect, Jan 2007

Belluschi, Pietro, American architect, Feb 1959, *Obit* Apr 1994

Betjeman, John, English poet and architectural historian, Mar 1973, *Obit* July 1984

Blomfield, Reginald Theodore, British architect, *Obit* Feb 1943

Botta, Mario, Swiss architect, Jan 2007

Bragdon, Claude Fayette, American architect, *Obit* Oct 1946

Breuer, Marcel, American architect and furniture designer, Sept 1941, June 1960, *Obit* Aug 1981

Brooks, Angela, American architect, Mar 1970

Brown, A. Ten Eyck, *Obit* July 1940

Bunshaft, Gordon, American architect, Mar 1989, *Obit* Oct 1990

Burchard, John E., Apr 1958, *Obit* Mar 1976

Butler, Reg, Sept 1956

Butts, Alfred, American architect and game inventor, July 1954, *Obit* June 1993

Calatrava, Santiago, Spanish architect, Aug 1997

Callender, John Hancock, architect and editor, Sept 1955, *Obit* June 1995

Candela, Felix, Spanish architect, July 1960

Casey, Edward Pearce, *Obit* Jan 1940

Chang, Gary, Chinese architect, Jan 2005

Cochrane, Edward L., Mar 1951, *Obit* Jan 1960

Cogswell, Charles N., *Obit* Feb 1942

Cooper, Edwin, English architect, *Obit* Aug 1942

Cram, Ralph Adams, American architect, Oct 1942, *Obit* Oct 1942

Cret, Paul Philippe, French-American architect, Nov 1942, *Obit* Nov 1945

Ditchy, Clair W., Mar 1954, *Obit* Oct 1967

Doxiadis, Constantinos A., Greek architect, Sept 1964, *Obit* Sept 1975

Duany, Andres, American architect and urban planner, Jan 2006

Eames, Charles, American furniture, interior and exhibit designer, Jan 1965, *Obit* Oct 1978

Eisenman, Peter, American architect, Oct 1997

Ferriss, Hugh, July 1945, *Obit* Mar 1962

Fielding, Mantle, *Obit* May 1941

Foster, Norman, British architect, Sept 2000

Fouilhoux, J. Andre, American architect, *Obit* July 1945

Freed, James Ingo, American architect, Nov 1994, *Obit* Yrbk 2006

Frisch, Max, Swiss architect, novelist and dramatist, Jan 1965, *Obit* June 1991

Fuller, R. Buckminster, American engineer and architect, Jan 1960, Feb 1976, *Obit* Aug 1983

Gang, Jeanne, American architect, Aug 2012

Gehry, Frank, American architect, June 1987

Gibbs, William Francis, naval architect, Apr 1944, *Obit* Nov 1967

Graham, John, architect, Oct 1962, *Obit* Apr 1991

Graves, Michael, American architect and designer, Jan 1989

Greenough, Carroll, *Obit* Oct 1941

Gropius, Walter, American architect, Nov 1941, Mar 1952, *Obit* Sept 1969

Gruen, Victor, American architect, Mar 1959, *Obit* Apr 1980

Gwathmey, Charles, American architect, Jan 1988, *Obit* Yrbk 2009

Hackett, Horatio B., *Obit* Nov 1941

Hadid, Zaha M., Iraqi architect, Jan 2003

Hamlin, Talbot Faulkner, Oct 1954, *Obit* Yrbk 1957

Harper, Alexander James, *Obit* Nov 1940

Harris, Harwell Hamilton, American architect, Jan 1962, *Obit* Jan 1991

Harrison, Wallace Kirkman, architect, Mar 1947, *Obit* Jan 1982

Herzog, Jacques, Swiss architect, June 2002

Hewlett, J. Monroe, *Obit* Yrbk 1941

Higgins, Daniel Paul, Yrbk 1950, *Obit* Mar 1954

Higginson, William, *Obit* Sept 1943

Holl, Steven, American architect, July 2004

Hopkins, Alfred, *Obit* July 1941

Isham, Norman Morrison, *Obit* Feb 1943

Isozaki, Arata, Japanese architect, Apr 1988

Jaar, Alfredo, Chilean mixed-media and installation artist, Jan 2005

Jacobs, Jane, American city planner, Mar 1977, *Obit* Yrbk 2006

Jahn, Helmut, German architect, Feb 1989

Johnson, Philip Cortelyou, American architect, Oct 1957, Nov 1991, *Obit* Sept 2005

Kahn, Albert, American architect, *Obit* Sept 1942

Kahn, Ely Jacques, American architect, Aug 1945, *Obit* Nov 1972

Kahn, Louis I., American architect, Oct 1964, *Obit* May 1974

Keck, George Fred, Sept 1945

Kendall, William Mitchell, *Obit* Oct 1941

Kiesler, Frederick, Austrian-Ameican sculptor and architect, Jan 1944, *Obit* Feb 1966

Koolhaas, Rem, Dutch architect, Nov 2000

Lake, Simon, naval architect and engineer, *Obit* July 1945

Lapidus, Morris, American architect, Apr 1966, *Obit* Apr 2001

Le Corbusier, Swiss-French architect, Apr 1947, *Obit* Nov 1965

Lescaze, William, American architect, Apr 1942, *Obit* Apr 1969

Libeskind, Daniel, American architect, June 2003

Lin, Maya Ying, American architect and sculptor, Apr 1993

Luckman, Charles, American personal care products industry executive, Oct 1947, *Obit* Apr 1999

Lutyens, Edwin Landseer, British architect, June 1942, *Obit* Feb 1944

Ma Kai, Chinese government official, Jan 2007

Mackenzie, Clinton, *Obit* Mar 1940

Maki, Fumihiko, Japanese architect, July 2001

Makiya, Kanan, Iraqi Middle Eastern studies specialist, Jan 2002

Mayne, Thom, American architect, Oct 2005

McAslan, John, Scottish architect, Jan 2007

McDonough, William, American architect, July 2006

Meier, Richard, American architect, Jan 1985

Mellor, Walter, *Obit* Jan 1940

Melzer, Roman F., *Obit* June 1943

Mendelsohn, Erich, German architect, Nov 1953

Mendes da Rocha, Paulo Archias, Brazilian architect, Jan 2006

Meuron, Pierre de, Swiss architect, June 2002

Mies van der Rohe, Ludwig, German-American architect, Oct 1951, *Obit* Oct 1969

Moneo, Jose Rafael, Spanish architect, Jan 2004

Moses, Robert, American municipal and state planning official, Nov 1940, Feb 1954, *Obit* Sept 1981

Mumford, Lewis, American architectural and social critic, Nov 1940, Mar 1963, *Obit* Mar 1990

Murcutt, Glenn, Australian architect, Jan 2002

Nervi, Pier Luigi, Italian architect and structural engineer, Jan 1958, *Obit* Mar 1979

Neutra, Richard Joseph, American architect, May 1947, July 1961, *Obit* June 1970

Niemeyer, Oscar, Brazilian architect, Feb 1960, *Obit* Yrbk 2013

Nixon, Lewis, American naval architect, *Obit* Nov 1940

Norten, Enrique, Mexican architect, Jan 2005

Nouvel, Jean, French architect, Sept 2008

O'Gorman, Juan, Mexican architect and painter, Nov 1956

Olmsted, Frederick Law, American landscape architect, June 1949, *Obit* Mar 1958

Oppenheim, Chad, American architect, Sept 2006

Otto, Frei, German architect, Oct 1971

Oudolf, Piet, Dutch landscape architect, Apr 2003

Owings, Nathaniel Alexander, architect, May 1971, *Obit* Aug 1984

Pei, I. M., Chinese-American architect, May 1969, Mar 1990

Pelli, Cesar, American architect, Apr 1983

Pereira, William Leonard, architect, Jan 1979, *Obit* Jan 1986

Piano, Renzo, Italian architect, Apr 2001

Pilcher, Lewis F., *Obit* Aug 1941

Plater-Zyberk, Elizabeth, American architect and urban planner, Jan 2006

Post, William Stone, *Obit* Sept 1940

Roche, Kevin, architect, Nov 1970

Rubik, Erno, Hungarian professor of architecture and inventor, Feb 1987

Rudolph, Paul, American architect, Feb 1972, *Obit* Nov 1997

Saarinen, Eero, American architect, Oct 1949, *Obit* Nov 1961

Saarinen, Eliel, Finnish-American architect, Oct 1942, *Obit* Sept 1950

Safdie, Moshe, Canadian architect, Sept 1968

Sejima, Kazuyo, Japanese architect, Apr 2012

Sert, Jose Luis, Spanish-American architect, Apr 1974, *Obit* May 1983

Severance, H. Craig, *Obit* Nov 1941

Shreve, Richmond Harold, Nov 1945, *Obit* Oct 1946

Sinclair, Cameron, British architect and housing organization official, Apr 2008

Siza, Alvaro, Portuguese architect, Feb 2000

Skidmore, Louis, architect, Yrbk 1951, *Obit* Yrbk 1962

Soleri, Paolo, Italian architect, Feb 1972, *Obit* Yrbk 2013

Speer, Albert, German architect and Nazi leader, Oct 1976, *Obit* Oct 1981

Stern, Robert A. M., American architect and college dean, June 2000

Stokes, Isaac Newton Phelps, architect and antiquarian, *Obit* Feb 1945

Stone, Edward Durell, American architect, June 1958, *Obit* Sept 1978

Streuli, Hans, Apr 1957

Swartwout, Egerton, *Obit* Apr 1943

Tange, Kenzo, Japanese architect, Sept 1987, *Obit* Yrbk 2005

Taniguchi, Yoshio, Japanese architect, Jan 2005

Tigerman, Stanley, American architect, Feb 2001

Tree, Marietta, United Nations official and city planner, Yrbk 1961, *Obit* Oct 1991

Troost, Laurens, Jan 1953

Tunnard, Christopher, Canadian landscape architect, June 1959, *Obit* May 1979

Utzon, Jorn, Danish architect, Jan 2003, *Obit* Yrbk 2009

Valletti, Vittorio F., Italian architect, July 1967

Van Pelt, John Vredenburgh, Yrbk 1946, *Obit* Sept 1962

Ventris, Michael George Francis, English architect, archaeologist and linguist, Jan 1957

Venturi, Robert, American architect, July 1975

Virilio, Paul, French urban planner and philosopher, July 2005

Walker, Ralph Thomas, Yrbk 1957, *Obit* Mar 1973

Wank, Roland, Yrbk 1943, *Obit* July 1970

Warne, William Elmo, land reclamation and irrigation specialist, Nov 1952, *Obit* May 1996

Warnecke, John Carl, American architect, July 1968, *Obit* Yrbk 2010

Warren, Whitney, *Obit* Mar 1943

Whittlesey, Charles F., *Obit* Feb 1941
Wiesenthal, Simon, Austrian Nazi hunter, Jan 1975, *Obit* Yrbk 2005
Williams, Paul, American architect, Mar 1941, *Obit* Mar 1980
Wills, Royal Barry, Yrbk 1954, *Obit* Feb 1962
Wirth, Conrad L., American national parks director, Sept 1952, *Obit* Sept 1993
Wright, Frank Lloyd, American architect, Jan 1941, Nov 1952, *Obit* June 1959
Wurster, William Wilson, architect, Nov 1946, *Obit* Nov 1973
Yamasaki, Minoru, American architect, Mar 1962, *Obit* Apr 1986
Yeang, Ken, Malaysian architect, Jan 2007
Yoshimura, Junzo, Japanese architect, May 1956

Architectural critics

Huxtable, Ada Louise, American architectural critic, Mar 1973, *Obit* Yrbk 2013
Johnson, Philip Cortelyou, American architect, Oct 1957, Nov 1991, *Obit* Sept 2005
Mumford, Lewis, American architectural and social critic, Nov 1940, Mar 1963, *Obit* Mar 1990

Architectural historians

Betjeman, John, English poet and architectural historian, Mar 1973, *Obit* July 1984

Archivists

Bettmann, Otto L., archivist, Nov 1961, *Obit* July 1998
Buck, Solon Justus, historian and archivist, May 1947, *Obit* July 1962
Emrich, Duncan, Mar 1955
Lewis, Chester, librarian and archivist, May 1956, *Obit* June 1990
Schwartz, Tony, American advertising executive and sound archivist, July 1985, *Obit* Yrbk 2008

Weinstein, Allen, American historian and archivist, June 2006

Area specialists

Abrams, Elliott, American diplomat and policy analyst, Aug 1988
Ajami, Fouad, Lebanese-American Islamic and Middle Eastern studies specialist, Feb 2007
Armstrong, Hamilton Fish, foreign policy expert and periodical editor, Jan 1948, *Obit* June 1973
Beers, Rand, American foreign policy adviser, Oct 2004
Bremmer, Ian, American international relations specialist, Aug 2013
Buell, Raymond Leslie, *Obit* Apr 1946
Bundy, William P., American international relations specialist, June 1964, *Obit* Feb 2001
Cole, Juan R. I., American Middle Eastern studies specialist, Oct 2010
Crocker, Chester A., American diplomat, July 1990
Crow, Carl, American journalist, Oct 1941, *Obit* July 1945
Dean, Vera Micheles, international relations specialist, May 1943, *Obit* Yrbk 1972
Emeny, Brooks, Nov 1947
Fairbank, John King, American Sinologist, Oct 1966, *Obit* Nov 1991
Fedorenko, Nikolai T., Yrbk 1967
Fukuyama, Francis, American international relations specialist, June 2001
Gelb, Leslie H., American journalist, government official and international relations specialist, Jan 2003
Gilchrist, Huntington, Apr 1949, *Obit* Mar 1975
Gordon, Cyrus Herzl, American biblical scholar and archaeologist, May 1963, *Obit* Aug 2001
Haass, Richard, American international relations specialist, June 2010

Hitti, Philip Khuri, June 1947, *Obit* Feb 1979
Hunt, Swanee, American international relations specialist, Mar 2006
Keene, Donald, American Japanologist, Jan 1988
Latourette, Kenneth Scott, Sinologist and church historian, Nov 1953, *Obit* Mar 1969
Lattimore, Owen, American Sinologist, Yrbk 1945, July 1964, *Obit* July 1989
Mears, Helen, American Japanologist, Mar 1943
Meron, Theodor, Polish international relations specialist, Mar 2005
Myers, B. R., American Korean studies specialist, June 2010
Olmstead, A. T., *Obit* May 1945
Parry, Albert, professor of Russian studies, Apr 1961, *Obit* July 1992
Payne, Robert, English author, Yrbk 1947, *Obit* Apr 1983
Perle, Richard Norman, American military official, July 2003
Primakov, Yevgeny M., Russian prime minister, Feb 1999
Reischauer, Edwin O., American historian and diplomat, May 1962, *Obit* Nov 1990
Schain, Josephine, July 1945
Schwebel, Stephen M., American judge and international relations specialist, July 1952
Stein, Janice Gross, Canadian international relations specialist, Aug 2006
Stern, Jessica, American terrorism expert, May 2006
White, Robert E., American diplomat, May 1984
Zimmer, Heinrich Robert, German Indologist, *Obit* May 1943

Army officers

Abacha, Sani, Nigerian dictator, Sept 1996, *Obit* Aug 1998
Abizaid, John P., American general, Oct 2003
Abrams, Creighton Williams, American general, Oct 1968, *Obit* Oct 1974

Al-Bashir, Omar, Sudanese head of state, Jan 2005

Aldrin, Buzz, American astronaut, Sept 1993

Allen, Frank A., American general, Mar 1945, *Obit* Jan 1980

Allen, Terry, Nov 1943, *Obit* Nov 1969

Almond, Edward M., general, Mar 1951, *Obit* Aug 1979

Amin, Idi, Ugandan general and president, Feb 1973, *Obit* Yrbk 2003

Anderson, Alexander E., American general, *Obit* Feb 1943

Anderson, Frederick L., American general, May 1944, *Obit* Apr 1969

Anderson, Kenneth A. N., British general, Feb 1943, *Obit* July 1959

Andreu Almazan, Juan, Mexican general and political leader, May 1940, *Obit* Yrbk 1965

Andrews, Frank M., American general, Feb 1942, *Obit* June 1943

Antonescu, Ion, Romanian dictator, Oct 1940, *Obit* July 1946

Aoun, Michel, Lebanese general and political leader, Mar 1990

Aramburu, Pedro Eugenio, Argentine president, Jan 1957, *Obit* Oct 1970

Armstrong, George E., American physician and general, Apr 1952, *Obit* Aug 1979

Armstrong, Harry G., American physician and air force general, July 1951

Arnold, Henry Harley, American air force general, Feb 1942, *Obit* Feb 1950

Arnold, William R., American military chaplain and bishop, May 1942

Arthur, George, British army officer, *Obit* Mar 1946

Assad, Hafez, Syrian president, July 1975, Apr 1992, *Obit* Aug 2000

Atherton, Warren H., American army officer, lawyer and veterans organization official, Yrbk 1943, *Obit* May 1976

Atholl, John George Stewart-Murray, British army officer and member of Parliament, *Obit* May 1942

Atkinson, Joseph Hampton, American air force general, May 1956

Babangida, Ibrahim, Nigerian general and head of state, Sept 1990

Bagramyan, Ivan K., Soviet general, Yrbk 1944, *Obit* Jan 1983

Baldomir, Alfredo, Uruguayan general and president, June 1942, *Obit* Mar 1948

Banzer Suarez, Hugo, Bolivian president, Sept 1973, *Obit* Sept 2002

Barak, Ehud, Israeli political leader, Aug 1997

Barratt, Arthur Sheridan, British air marshal, Jan 1941

Batista y Zaldivar, Fulgencio, Cuban general and president, Sept 1940, Apr 1952, *Obit* Oct 1973

Beau, Lucas Victor, air force general, June 1954, *Obit* Jan 1987

Belyayev, Pavel, Soviet cosmonaut, July 1965, *Obit* Mar 1970

Bendetsen, Karl Robin, American paper industry executive, May 1952, *Obit* Sept 1989

Bennett, Henry Gordon, Australian general, Mar 1942, *Obit* Oct 1962

Bennett, Ivan L., American military chaplain, Nov 1952, *Obit* Aug 1980

Bergquist, Kenneth P., American air force general, Mar 1961

Berry, Charles A., American flight surgeon, Apr 1969

Biddle, Anthony Joseph Drexel, American general and diplomat, Mar 1941, *Obit* Jan 1962

Bissell, Clayton L., American air force general, Feb 1943

Blaik, Earl Henry, football coach, Jan 1945, *Obit* July 1989

Blamey, Thomas Albert, Australian general, June 1942, *Obit* July 1951

Blanchard, Doc, American football player and air force officer, Mar 1946, *Obit* Yrbk 2009

Blanchfield, Florence Aby, American nurse and army officer, Sept 1943, *Obit* June 1971

Bliss, Raymond W., American surgeon and general, Jan 1951, *Obit* Jan 1966

Bluford, Guion S., American astronaut, Sept 1984

Boatner, Haydon L., American general, July 1952

Bokassa, Apr 1978, *Obit* Jan 1997

Bolte, Charles Lawrence, general, Jan 1954, *Obit* May 1989

Bonesteel, Charles H., American general, June 1942, *Obit* Sept 1964

Boumedienne, Houari, Algerian president, Jan 1971, *Obit* Feb 1979

Boyce, Westray Battle, Sept 1945, *Obit* Mar 1972

Boyle, Hal, June 1945, *Obit* May 1974

Bozize, Francois, Central African Republic general and president, Jan 2005

Bradley, Omar Nelson, American general, July 1943, *Obit* May 1981

Brannaman, Ray H., Nov 1947

Brereton, Lewis H., American general, Yrbk 1943, *Obit* Oct 1967

Brett, George H., American air force general, June 1942

Brooks, Vincent, American general, June 2003

Brown, Albert Eger, Jan 1948

Brown, George S., American air force general, Oct 1975, *Obit* Feb 1979

Brown, Scott, American senator, Aug 2010

Browning, Frederick, June 1943, *Obit* Apr 1965

Buckner, Simon Bolivar, Oct 1942, *Obit* July 1945

Bull, Odd, Nov 1968

Burns, E. L. M., Canadian general, Feb 1955

Butler, Smedley D., American Marine corps general, *Obit* Aug 1940

Bykovskii, Valerii Fedorovich, Soviet astronaut, Jan 1965

Calles, Plutarco Elias, Mexican president, *Obit* Nov 1945

Camden, Harry P., *Obit* Sept 1943

Candee, Robert C., May 1944

Carlson, Evans F., American Marine corps general, Oct 1943, *Obit* June 1947

Carmona, Antonio Oscar de Fragoso, Nov 1950, *Obit* May 1951

Carpentier, Marcel Maurice, Apr 1951

Carroll, Joseph Francis, American air force general, Apr 1962, *Obit* Mar 1991

Carton de Wiart, Adrian, May 1940, *Obit* July 1963

Casey, George W., American general, Mar 2006

Casey, Robert J., Mar 1943, *Obit* Jan 1963

Castelnau, Noel Marie Joseph Edouard de Curieres de, French general, *Obit* May 1944

Castelo Branco, Humberto de Alencar, Brazilian president, Feb 1965, *Obit* Oct 1967

Cates, Clifton B., American Marine corps officer, Nov 1950, *Obit* Sept 1970

Catroux, Georges, May 1943, *Obit* Feb 1970

Cavallero, Ugo, *Obit* Oct 1943

Cazalet, Victor Alexander, *Obit* Aug 1943

Cedras, Raoul, Haitian general, July 1995

Chandos, Oliver Lyttelton, British manufacturing executive and cabinet member, Sept 1941, Jan 1953, *Obit* Mar 1972

Chang, Shan-tzu, *Obit* Yrbk 1940

Chapman, Leonard F., American Marine corps general, July 1968, *Obit* Sept 2000

Chase, William C., Nov 1952

Chavez Frias, Hugo, Venezuelan president, May 2000

Chavez, Hugo, Venezuelan president, *Obit* Yrbk 2013

Chen Cheng, Chinese general, Sept 1941, *Obit* Apr 1965

Chen Yi, Chinese general, Oct 1959, *Obit* Feb 1972

Chennault, Claire Lee, American general, Oct 1942, *Obit* Oct 1958

Cherniakhovskii, Ivan Danilovich, Oct 1944, *Obit* Apr 1945

Cheshire, Leonard, British air force officer and social welfare leader, Jan 1962, *Obit* Sept 1992

Chiang, Kai-shek, Chinese president, Jan 1940, May 1953, *Obit* May 1975

Christison, Philip, British general, Nov 1945, *Obit* Feb 1994

Chuikov, Vasilii Ivanovich, Soviet general, May 1943, *Obit* May 1982

Chun, Doo Hwan, Korean president, Mar 1981

Clark, Leonard Frances, Jan 1956, *Obit* Sept 1957

Clark, Mark W., American general, Nov 1942, *Obit* June 1984

Clark, Wesley K., American general, July 1999

Clay, Lucius D., American general, May 1945, June 1963, *Obit* June 1978

Cocke, Erle, army officer and veterans' leader, Jan 1951, *Obit* Sept 2000

Collins, J. Lawton, American general, Nov 1949, *Obit* Oct 1987

Collins, Seaborn P., Apr 1955

Connally, Tom, American senator, Yrbk 1941, Apr 1949, *Obit* Jan 1964

Coulter, John B., June 1954

Craig, Malin, Mar 1944, *Obit* Aug 1945

Craveiro Lopes, Francisco Higino, Mar 1956, *Obit* Nov 1964

Crerar, Henry Duncan Graham, Canadian general, Nov 1944, *Obit* May 1965

Cresswell, Robert, American newspaper publisher, *Obit* Nov 1943

Crist, William E., Nov 1945

Cunningham, Alan, British general, June 1946, *Obit* Apr 1983

Currie, Nancy, American astronaut, June 2002

Cushman, Robert Everton, American Marine Corps general, Nov 1972, *Obit* Apr 1985

Darwin, Leonard, *Obit* May 1943

Davidson, Garrison Holt, general, June 1957, *Obit* Feb 1993

Davis, Benjamin O., American general, Yrbk 1942, *Obit* Jan 1971

Davis, Benjamin O., American air force general, Sept 1955, *Obit* Yrbk 2002

Davis, Herbert John, Jan 1940, *Obit* May 1967

Davis, Robert C., *Obit* Oct 1944

Davison, F. Trubee, Yrbk 1945

Davison, Frederic Ellis, American general, Feb 1974

Dayan, Moshe, Israeli general, Mar 1957, *Obit* Jan 1982

De Witt, John Lesesne, American general, July 1942

DeCoursey, Elbert, Sept 1954

Dean, William F., American general, Sept 1954, *Obit* Oct 1981

Decker, George H., American general, Jan 1961

Dempsey, Miles Christopher, Oct 1944, *Obit* July 1969

Devers, Jacob Loucks, general, Sept 1942, *Obit* Jan 1980

Devine, John M., American general, Jan 1948

Devoe, Ralph G., Oct 1944, *Obit* Nov 1966

Dickerson, Debra, American journalist, Apr 2004

Dobbie, William George Shedden, British general, July 1945

Donovan, William J., American intelligence official and general, Mar 1941, Sept 1954, *Obit* Apr 1959

Doolittle, James Harold, American general, Aug 1942, Mar 1957, *Obit* Jan 1994

Dornberger, Walter, Feb 1965, *Obit* Sept 1980

Drum, Hugh A., July 1941, *Obit* Nov 1951

Dunham, Franklin, Jan 1942, *Obit* Jan 1962

Dunwoody, Ann E., American general, Nov 2008

Dutra, Eurico Gaspar, Mar 1946, *Obit* Sept 1974

Eaker, Ira Clarence, general, Oct 1942, *Obit* Sept 1987

Eanes, Antonio dos Santos Ramalho, Portuguese president, Apr 1979

Easley, Claudius M., American general, *Obit* July 1945

Echols, Oliver P., Yrbk 1947, *Obit* July 1954

Eddy, Manton S., general, Feb 1951, *Obit* June 1962

Eichelberger, Robert L., American general, Jan 1943, *Obit* Yrbk 1961

Eikenberry, Karl W., American general and diplomat, Mar 2010

Eisenhower, Dwight D., American president, Aug 1942, Feb 1948, Sept 1957, *Obit* May 1969

Eisenhower, John S. D., army officer, diplomat and son of Dwight D. Eisenhower, July 1969

Ely, Paul, Oct 1954, *Obit* Mar 1975

Emmons, Delos C., American general, Mar 1942, *Obit* Yrbk 1965

Ershad, Hussain Mohammad, Bangladeshi prime minister, Nov 1984

Erskine, G. B., American Marine corps general, July 1946, *Obit* July 1973

Erskine, George, British general, Jan 1952, *Obit* Nov 1965

Eyadema, Gnassingbe, Togolese president, Apr 2002, *Obit* Yrbk 2005

Fei Junlong, Chinese astronaut, Jan 2006

Festing, Francis, Feb 1945

Figueiredo, Joao Baptista de Oliveira, Brazilian president, Jan 1980, *Obit* May 2000

Fitzroy, Edward Algernon, *Obit* Apr 1943

Fleming, Philip Bracken, Apr 1940, *Obit* Yrbk 1956

Flikke, Julia O., July 1942

Franco, Francisco, Spanish dictator, Mar 1942, Mar 1954, *Obit* Jan 1976

Franks, Tommy, American general, Jan 2002

Freyberg, Bernard Freyberg, Oct 1940, *Obit* Sept 1963

Fuqua, Stephen Ogden, Feb 1943

Galloway, Irene O., May 1953, *Obit* Feb 1963

Galtieri, Leopoldo Fortunato, Argentine general and

president, Aug 1982, *Obit* Yrbk 2003

Gamelin, Maurice Gustave, French general, Jan 1940, *Obit* July 1958

Gardner, Lester Durand, Sept 1947, *Obit* Feb 1957

Gaulle, Charles de, French president, Sept 1940, June 1949, Apr 1960, *Obit* Yrbk 1970

Gavin, James Maurice, American general and diplomat, Feb 1945, Sept 1961, *Obit* Apr 1990

Geiger, Roy S., American Marine general, July 1945, *Obit* Mar 1947

Geisel, Ernesto, Brazilian president, Aug 1975, *Obit* Nov 1996

George, Harold L., Yrbk 1942

Gerow, Leonard Townsend, Apr 1945, *Obit* Yrbk 1972

Giles, Barney McKinney, general, July 1944, *Obit* Aug 1984

Giraud, Henri, French general, Yrbk 1942, *Obit* Apr 1949

Gleason, John S., June 1958

Glubb, John Bagot, British general, Sept 1951, *Obit* May 1986

Golikov, Filipp Ivanovich, Soviet general, Apr 1943, *Obit* Sept 1980

Goodpaster, Andrew Jackson, American general, July 1969, *Obit* Yrbk 2005

Gort, John Standish Surtees Prendergast Vereker, British general, Oct 1940, *Obit* May 1946

Gott, William Henry Ewart, *Obit* Oct 1942

Gowon, Yakubu, Nigerian general and head of state, June 1970

Graham, Wallace Harry, physician and general, Feb 1947, *Obit* Mar 1996

Graves, William Sidney, general, *Obit* Mar 1940

Greene, Wallace M., American Marine corps general, June 1965, *Obit* Aug 2003

Gregg, Milton F., Oct 1955

Gregory, Edmund B., Sept 1945, *Obit* Mar 1961

Gregory, Frederick Drew, American astronaut and NASA official, Oct 2005

Griffith, Paul H., American management consultant and military official, Jan 1947, *Obit* Feb 1975

Griswold, Oscar W., American general, Sept 1943, *Obit* Yrbk 1959

Grivas, Giorgios, Oct 1964, *Obit* Mar 1974

Grizodubova, Valentina S., Soviet aviator, Yrbk 1941, *Obit* July 1993

Groninger, Homer M., American general, Aug 1945

Gross, Charles P., Mar 1946, *Obit* Sept 1975

Groves, Leslie R., American general, Aug 1945, *Obit* Oct 1970

Gruenther, Alfred M., American general, Yrbk 1950, *Obit* July 1983

Guillaumat, Marie Louis Adolphe, *Obit* July 1940

Guillaume, Augustin, French general, Jan 1952

Gullion, Allen W., Feb 1943, *Obit* July 1946

Hackett, Horatio B., *Obit* Nov 1941

Haig, Alexander Meigs, American general and Secretary of state, Jan 1973, Sept 1987, *Obit* Yrbk 2010

Hall, Raymond S., Oct 1953

Hallaren, Mary A., American army officer, Mar 1949, *Obit* Yrbk 2005

Hammerstein-Equord, Kurt, German general, *Obit* June 1943

Handy, Thomas T., American general, Sept 1951, *Obit* June 1982

Hansell, Haywood S., air force general, Jan 1945, *Obit* Jan 1989

Harbord, James G., American general, Mar 1945, *Obit* Sept 1947

Harington, Charles, British general, *Obit* Yrbk 1940

Harkins, Paul D., American general, Apr 1964

Harmon, Ernest N., American general and university president, Nov 1946, *Obit* Jan 1980

Harmon, Millard F., Yrbk 1942, *Obit* Apr 1945

Harris, Arthur Travers, British air marshal, Sept 1942, *Obit* May 1984

Harrison, William K., American general, July 1952, *Obit* Aug 1987

Hart, Merwin K., Oct 1941, *Obit* Jan 1963

Hartle, Russell P., American general, June 1942, *Obit* Jan 1962

Haskell, William N., Feb 1947, *Obit* Sept 1952

Hawley, Paul R., Apr 1946, *Obit* Jan 1966

Hayashi, Senjuro, *Obit* Mar 1943

Hayden, Michael, American general and intelligence official, Nov 2006

Hernandez Martinez, Maximiliano, Salvadoran general and president, June 1942, *Obit* June 1966

Hershey, Lewis Blaine, American general and government official, June 1941, June 1951, *Obit* July 1977

Hertzog, James Barry Munnik, South African prime minister, *Obit* Jan 1943

Hess, Dean E., Sept 1957

Heusinger, Adolf, German general, Feb 1956

Hill, J. B. P. Clayton, *Obit* July 1941

Hilldring, John H., American general, Apr 1947

Hilton, Frank C., July 1952

Hitchcock, Thomas, polo player, *Obit* June 1944

Ho, Ying-Chin, Taiwanese general, Oct 1942, *Obit* Jan 1988

Hobby, Oveta Culp, American Secretary of health, education and welfare, July 1942, Feb 1953, *Obit* Oct 1995

Hodes, Henry I., American general, Feb 1959, *Obit* Apr 1962

Hodge, John R., June 1945, *Obit* Jan 1964

Hodges, Courtney H., May 1941, *Obit* Feb 1966

Hodgson, W. R., May 1946, *Obit* Apr 1958

Holcomb, Thomas, July 1942, *Obit* July 1965

Holmes, Julius C., Feb 1945, *Obit* Sept 1968

Honjo, Shigeru, *Obit* Jan 1946

Hormel, Jay C., July 1946, *Obit* Oct 1954

Horn, Carl von, Swedish general, Nov 1967

Horrocks, Brian, British general, Jan 1945, *Obit* Mar 1985

Horthy, Istvan, *Obit* Oct 1942

Horwood, William T. F., *Obit* Feb 1944

Houston, Charles Hamilton, American lawyer and civil rights leader, July 1948, *Obit* June 1950

Hsiung, S.-F, July 1942

Hudleston, Edmund C., May 1951

Huebner, Clarence R., Oct 1949, *Obit* Nov 1972

Hull, John Adley, *Obit* June 1944

Hull, John E., Apr 1954

Hume, Edgar Erskine, Aug 1944, *Obit* Mar 1952

Hunt, John Hunt, British army officer and mountaineer, Oct 1954, *Obit* Jan 1999

Huntziger, Charles, French general, Yrbk 1941, *Obit* Yrbk 1941

Hurley, Patrick J., American Secretary of war and diplomat, Nov 1944, *Obit* Sept 1963

Ibanez del Campo, Carlos, Chilean president, Yrbk 1952, *Obit* July 1960

Ingles, Harry C., American general, Nov 1947

Irving, Frederick A., American general, Mar 1951

Ismay, Hastings Lionel Ismay, British general, Apr 1943, *Obit* Feb 1966

James, Daniel, American air force general, Mar 1976, *Obit* Apr 1978

Jarman, Sanderford, Sept 1942, *Obit* Yrbk 1955

Jaruzelski, Wojciech, Polish general and president, Mar 1982

Jaworski, Leon, American lawyer and special prosecutor, June 1974, *Obit* Feb 1983

Jodl, Alfred, German general, *Obit* Nov 1946

Johnson, Harold K., American general, May 1966, *Obit* Nov 1983

Johnson, Hugh S., American general and government official, Sept 1940, *Obit* June 1942

Jones, David C., July 1982, *Obit* Yrbk 2013

Jordana y Souza, Francisco Gomez, Mar 1944

Justo, Agustin P., Argentine general and president, *Obit* Mar 1943

Karpinski, Janis, American general, Apr 2006

Kennedy, Claudia, general, Jan 2000

Kenney, George C., American general, Jan 1943, *Obit* Oct 1977

Kernan, W. F., Apr 1942

Key, William, July 1943, *Obit* Mar 1959

Kirk, Norman T., American surgeon and general, Feb 1944, *Obit* Nov 1960

Klimecki, Tadeusz A., *Obit* Aug 1943

Koenig, Pierre, French general, Sept 1944, *Obit* Nov 1970

Korizis, Alexander, Mar 1941, *Obit* Mar 1941

Korner, Theodor, July 1951, *Obit* Mar 1957

Kowalski, Frank, July 1960, *Obit* Yrbk 1974

Krueger, Walter, American general, Apr 1943, *Obit* Oct 1967

Kuchler, Georg von, Sept 1943

Kuter, Laurence S., American air force general, July 1948

Lanusse, Alejandro A., Argentine general and president, Apr 1973, *Obit* Nov 1996

Lawson, Ted W., Yrbk 1943

Laycock, R. E., May 1944, *Obit* May 1968

LeMay, Curtis E., American air force general, Yrbk 1944, Nov 1954, *Obit* Nov 1990

Lear, Ben, July 1942, *Obit* Jan 1967

Leavey, Edmond H., American general and telecommunications executive, May 1951, *Obit* Apr 1980

Leclerc, Jacques, Oct 1944, *Obit* Yrbk 1947

Lee, Clark, Yrbk 1943, *Obit* Apr 1953

Lee, John C. H., July 1944, *Obit* Nov 1958

Leese, Oliver, British general, Yrbk 1944, *Obit* Yrbk 1991

Leigh-Mallory, Trafford, British air marshal, Mar 1944, *Obit* Mar 1945

Lejeune, John Archer, marine general, *Obit* Jan 1943

Lemnitzer, Lyman Louis, American general, Nov 1955, *Obit* Jan 1989

Lentaigne, Walter D. A., July 1944, *Obit* Oct 1955

Leonov, Aleksei, Soviet astronaut, July 1965

Lerch, Archer L., Nov 1945, *Obit* Oct 1947

Li Liejun, *Obit* Apr 1946

Li Zongren, Chinese general, Nov 1942, *Obit* Mar 1969

Lindbergh, Charles, American aviator, July 1941, Jan 1954, *Obit* Oct 1974

Littlejohn, Robert McGowan, Sept 1946, *Obit* July 1982

Loeb, Fritz, *Obit* Aug 1940

Lon Nol, Cambodian general and prime minister, Feb 1974, *Obit* Jan 1986

MacArthur, Douglas, American general, Oct 1941, May 1948, *Obit* May 1964

Mackay, Iven Giffard, Apr 1941, *Obit* Jan 1967

Margesson, Henry David Reginald Margesson, Feb 1941, *Obit* Feb 1966

Marshall, George C., American general and statesmen, Oct 1940, Mar 1947, *Obit* Yrbk 1959

Martel, Giffard Le Quesne, British general, July 1943, *Obit* Nov 1958

Martin, Charles H., *Obit* Nov 1946

Mason-MacFarlane, Noel, British general, Feb 1943

Mathewson, Lemuel, Yrbk 1952, *Obit* Apr 1970

Maxwell, Russell L., Nov 1942, *Obit* Jan 1969

May, Geraldine P., Feb 1949

McAuliffe, Anthony C., American general, Feb 1950, *Obit* Oct 1975

McCaffrey, Barry, American general and government official, July 1997

McChrystal, Stanley, American general, Sept 2009

McCoy, Frank Ross, general, Nov 1945, *Obit* Sept 1954

McCreery, Richard L., British general, May 1945, *Obit* Yrbk 1967

McDivitt, James A., Nov 1965

McNair, Lesley James, American general, Nov 1942, *Obit* Sept 1944

McNaughton, Andrew, Nov 1942, *Obit* Nov 1966

Medaris, John Bruce, general and clergyman, Feb 1958

Medici, Emilio Garrastazu, Brazilian president, Oct 1971, *Obit* Jan 1986

Medina Angarita, Isaias, Venezuelan general and president, Mar 1942, *Obit* Nov 1953

Mehaffey, Joseph C., Jan 1948, *Obit* Apr 1963

Mengistu Haile-Mariam, Ethiopian head of state, July 1981

Menninger, William Claire, Sept 1945, *Obit* Nov 1966

Merle-Smith, Van Santvoord, *Obit* Yrbk 1943

Merrill, Frank D., American general, July 1944, *Obit* Feb 1956

Metaxas, Ioannis, Greek general and dictator, Yrbk 1940, *Obit* Mar 1941

Mihailovic, Draza, Yugoslav general and underground leader, Mar 1942, *Obit* Sept 1946

Milligan, Mary Louise, May 1957

Mobutu Sese Seko, Zairian president, Sept 1966, May 1997, *Obit* Nov 1997

Monaghan, Frank, Nov 1943, *Obit* Sept 1969

Moore, Bryant E., American general, Feb 1949, *Obit* Mar 1951

Morgan, Frederick Edgeworth, Feb 1946, *Obit* May 1967

Moya, Manuel A. de, Nov 1957

Musharraf, Pervez, Pakistani general and president, Mar 2001, Jan 2002

Myers, Richard B., American air force general, Apr 2002

Naguib, Mohammed, Egyptian general, Oct 1952

Nam, Il, Sept 1951, *Obit* Apr 1976

Namphy, Henri, Haitian general, Sept 1988

Nastase, Ilie, Romanian tennis player, Oct 1974

Navarre, Henri, Nov 1953

Ne Win, Burmese president, Apr 1971, *Obit* Yrbk 2003

Netherwood, Douglas B., *Obit* Oct 1943

Neville, Robert A. R., Nov 1953

Newcomer, Francis K., American general, Mar 1950, *Obit* Oct 1967

Nguyen, Cao Ky, South Vietnamese vice-president, Yrbk 1966, *Obit* Yrbk 2011

Nichols, Kenneth D., general, Nov 1948, *Obit* Sept 2000

Nie Haisheng, Chinese astronaut, Jan 2006

Nikolayev, Andrian, Soviet astronaut, Nov 1964, *Obit* Yrbk 2004

Nimeiri, Gaafar Mohammed, Sudanese president, Nov 1977, *Obit* Yrbk 2009

Nogues, Charles, Feb 1943, *Obit* June 1971

Noriega, Manuel Antonio, Panamanian general and head of state, Mar 1988

Norstad, Lauris, American air force general, May 1948, Feb 1959, *Obit* Oct 1988

Noue, Jehan de, Jan 1947

Nuckols, William P., May 1952

Nye, Archibald E., Feb 1942, *Obit* Jan 1968

O'Donnell, Emmett, general, July 1948, *Obit* Feb 1972

O'Neil, James F., Nov 1947, *Obit* Sept 1981

Obolensky, Serge, Oct 1959, *Obit* Nov 1978

Ocker, William C., *Obit* Nov 1942

Odierno, Raymond, American general, Nov 2009

Ojukwu, Chukwuemeka Odumegwu, Nigerian political leader and general, Feb 1969, *Obit* Yrbk 2012

Okonkwo, Festus, Nigerian general, Jan 2005

Oliver, Lunsford E., Sept 1947

Ongania, Juan Carlos, Argentine president, Oct 1968, *Obit* Aug 1995

Orlebar, Augustus H., *Obit* Sept 1943

Ovando Candia, Alfredo, Bolivian general and president, Mar 1970, *Obit* Mar 1982

Pace, Peter, American Marine corps general, June 2006

Pai, Chung-hsi, Nov 1942, *Obit* Feb 1967

Papadopoulos, George, Greek army officer and president, Feb 1970, *Obit* Sept 1999

Papagos, Alexandros, Nov 1951, *Obit* Yrbk 1955

Park, Chung Hee, Korean president, Jan 1969, *Obit* Jan 1980

Parker, Roy H., Oct 1951

Partridge, Earle E., Apr 1955

Patch, Alexander McCarrell, American general, May 1943, *Obit* Jan 1946

Pate, Randolph McCall, general, Sept 1958, *Obit* Oct 1961

Patrick, Mason Mathews, American general, *Obit* Mar 1942

Patton, George S., American general, Jan 1943, *Obit* Feb 1946

Pearkes, George Randolph, Nov 1957

Peker, Recep, Sept 1947, *Obit* May 1950

Penaranda, Enrique, Bolivian president, Jan 1940

Peng Dehuai, Chinese general and communist leader, Yrbk 1951

Perez Jimenez, Marcos, Venezuelan president, Nov 1954, *Obit* Feb 2002

Peron, Juan Domingo, Argentine president, June 1944, Feb 1974, *Obit* Feb 1974

Persons, Wilton B., American general and presidential adviser, May 1953, *Obit* Nov 1977

Peters, C. J., American epidemiologist and army officer, June 1997

Petraeus, David H., American general and intelligence official, Apr 2007

Picard, Frank A., Mar 1947, *Obit* Apr 1963

Pick, Lewis Andrew, American general and civil engineer, June 1946, *Obit* Feb 1957

Pierce, Palmer Eddy, *Obit* Jan 1940

Pile, Frederick Alfred, British general, Feb 1942, *Obit* Yrbk 1991

Pinochet Ugarte, Augusto, Chilean general and president, Yrbk 1974, *Obit* Yrbk 2007

Plaek Phibunsongkhram, Thai prime minister, Sept 1951, *Obit* Sept 1964

Poletti, Charles, American lieutenant governor and acting governor, *Obit* Yrbk 2002

Poletti, Charles E., Sept 1943

Porter, William N., Aug 1945, *Obit* Apr 1973

Potter, William Everett, American general, Yrbk 1957, *Obit* Feb 1989

Powell, Colin L., American Secretary of state, June 1988, Nov 2001

Power, Thomas S., American air force general, Apr 1958, *Obit* Jan 1971

Price, Harrison J., American general, *Obit* Oct 1945

Qaddafi, Muammar al-, Libyan dictator, Sept 1973, Mar 1992, *Obit* Yrbk 2011

Qassim, Abdul Karim, Iraqi general and prime minister, Nov 1959, *Obit* Mar 1963

Quesada, Elwood Richard, air force general and government official, Apr 1950, Jan 1960, *Obit* Apr 1993

Rahman, Ziaur, Bangladeshi president, June 1981

Ralston, Joseph W., air force general, Jan 2001

Ramey, Howard K., *Obit* May 1943

Ramirez, Pedro Pablo, Aug 1943, *Obit* Sept 1962

Ramos, Fidel V., Filipino president, Mar 1994

Rance, Hubert Elvin, Yrbk 1953, *Obit* Mar 1974

Rawlings, Jerry J., Ghanaian head of state, June 1982

Razmara, Hossein Ali, Iranian prime minister, Oct 1950, *Obit* Mar 1951

Reckord, Milton A., Mar 1945

Reybold, Eugene, June 1945, *Obit* Jan 1962

Rickenbacker, Eddie, American military pilot, Nov 1940, Feb 1952, *Obit* Oct 1973

Ridgway, Matthew B., American general, July 1947, *Obit* Sept 1993

Riley, William Edward, Nov 1951

Rios Montt, Jose Efrain, Guatemalan president, May 1983

Robertson of Oakridge, Brian Hubert Robertson, Sept 1948, *Obit* June 1974

Robinson, Jackie, American baseball player, Feb 1947, *Obit* Yrbk 1972

Rodriguez, Andres, Paraguayan general and president, Sept 1991, *Obit* June 1997

Rogers, Bernard W., American general, Oct 1984

Roh, Tae Woo, Korean president, Feb 1988

Rojas Pinilla, Gustavo, Colombian general and president, June 1956, *Obit* Mar 1975

Rooks, Lowell W., Apr 1947

Roosevelt, Elliott, American mystery novelist, mayor and son of President Franklin D. Roosevelt, Yrbk 1946, *Obit* Jan 1991

Roosevelt, Kermit, army officer, steamship line executive and son of President Theodore Roosevelt, *Obit* July 1943

Roosevelt, Theodore, American government official, general and son of President Theodore Roosevelt, *Obit* Sept 1944

Rose, Maurice, American general, *Obit* May 1945

Ross, Malcolm, Feb 1944, *Obit* July 1965

Rossy, Yves, Swiss air pilot and inventor, Jan 2013

Rowan, Andrew S., American army officer, *Obit* Mar 1943

Royall, Kenneth C., American Secretary of the army, Jan 1947, *Obit* Sept 1971

Rupertus, William H., *Obit* May 1945

Ruranga, Rubaramira, Ugandan army officer and AIDs activist, Jan 2006

Ryan, Patrick James, military chaplain, May 1955

Saltzman, Charles E., general, diplomat and investment banker, Oct 1947, *Obit* Aug 1994

Schomburg, August, Nov 1960
Schriever, Bernard A., American air force general, Oct 1957, *Obit* Yrbk 2005
Schwarzkopf, H. Norman, American general, May 1991, *Obit* Yrbk 2013
Scobie, Ronald M., Feb 1945
Scott, David R., American astronaut and engineering executive, Oct 1971
Scott, Robert Lee, American air force general, Oct 1943, *Obit* Yrbk 2006
Scowcroft, Brent, American general and presidential adviser, July 1987
Serov, Ivan Aleksandrovich, Soviet communist leader, Yrbk 1956
Shalikashvili, John, American general, Nov 1995, *Obit* Yrbk 2011
Shang Zhen, July 1944
Sharon, Ariel, Israeli prime minister, Apr 1981, Jan 2002
Shelton, Hugh, American general, Aug 1998
Shepherd, Lemuel C., American Marine corps general, Feb 1952, *Obit* Oct 1990
Shinseki, Eric, American Secretary of veterans affairs, Mar 2009
Short, Walter Campbell, general, Jan 1946, *Obit* Oct 1949
Shoup, David M., American Marine Corps general, Jan 1960, *Obit* Mar 1983
Sikorski, Wladyslaw, Polish general and statesman, Jan 1940, *Obit* Aug 1943
Simonds, Guy Granville, Canadian general, Oct 1943, *Obit* July 1974
Simons, David G., American physician and air force officer, Yrbk 1957, *Obit* Yrbk 2010
Simpson, William H., Feb 1945, *Obit* Oct 1980
Skidmore, Hubert Standish, *Obit* Mar 1946
Slemon, C. Roy, Yrbk 1956
Smith, Holland M., American Marine corps general, Apr 1945, *Obit* Mar 1967
Smith, Rex, Jan 1942
Smith, Walter Bedell, American general, diplomat and CIA director, Apr 1944, Yrbk 1953, *Obit* Nov 1961

Smuts, Jan Christiaan, South African prime minister, Aug 1941, *Obit* Oct 1950
Snyder, Howard McC., Feb 1955, *Obit* Nov 1970
Soeharto, Indonesian president, June 1967, Oct 1992, *Obit* Yrbk 2008
Sokolovsky, Vasilii D., Yrbk 1953, *Obit* July 1968
Somervell, Brehon Burke, Aug 1942, *Obit* Apr 1955
Somoza, Anastasio, Nicaraguan dictator, June 1942, *Obit* Yrbk 1956
Somoza, Anastasio, Nicaraguan general and president, Mar 1978, *Obit* Nov 1980
Spaatz, Carl, American air force general, Sept 1942, *Obit* Sept 1974
Speidel, Hans, German general, Apr 1952, *Obit* Feb 1985
Spinola, Antonio de, Portuguese general and president, Sept 1974, *Obit* Nov 1996
Spofford, Charles Merville, lawyer and diplomat, Feb 1951, *Obit* May 1991
Stafford, Thomas P., American astronaut and air force general, Jan 1977
Stapp, John Paul, air force officer and biophysicist, Yrbk 1959, *Obit* May 2000
Starr, Louis E., June 1947
Stilwell, Joseph Warren, American general, May 1942, *Obit* Nov 1946
Stone, William S., June 1960, *Obit* Feb 1969
Stratemeyer, George E., Feb 1951, *Obit* Oct 1969
Streuli, Hans, Apr 1957
Stroessner, Alfredo, Paraguayan general and president, Yrbk 1958, Mar 1981, *Obit* Yrbk 2007
Stuart, Kenneth, Feb 1944, *Obit* Yrbk 1945
Sturdee, V. A. H., July 1942
Sturgis, Samuel D., Jan 1956, *Obit* Sept 1964
Sultan, Daniel I., Jan 1945, *Obit* Feb 1947
Surles, Alexander D., Nov 1945, *Obit* Yrbk 1947
Swaythling, Jean Marcia, Sept 1942

Swing, Joseph May, general and immigration official, Apr 1959, *Obit* Feb 1985
S enz Ryan, Maritza, Mar 2013
Tatekawa, Yoshitsugu, *Obit* Oct 1945
Taylor, Maxwell D., American general, Nov 1946, Yrbk 1961, *Obit* June 1987
Taylor, Telford, lawyer and historian, Yrbk 1948, *Obit* Aug 1998
Ter Poorten, Hein, Mar 1942
Thimayya, Kodendera Subayya, Apr 1954, *Obit* Feb 1966
Thompson, John Taliaferro, American general, military engineer and inventor, *Obit* Aug 1940
Thompson, Paul Williams, general and publishing executive, Nov 1942, *Obit* May 1996
Tice, Merton B., June 1955
Tinker, Clarence Leonard, American general, June 1942
Titov, Gherman Stepanovich, Soviet astronaut, Yrbk 1962, *Obit* Jan 2001
Tojo, Hideki, Japanese general and prime minister, Yrbk 1941, *Obit* Jan 1949
Torrijos Herrera, Omar, Panamanian dictator, July 1973, *Obit* Sept 1981
Toure, Amadou Toumani, Malian president, Jan 2005
Trammell, Niles, Sept 1940, *Obit* May 1973
Trudeau, Arthur Gilbert, general, Apr 1958, *Obit* Aug 1991
Trujillo Molina, Rafael Leonidas, Dominican general and president, July 1941, *Obit* Oct 1961
Truscott, Lucian King, American general, May 1945, *Obit* Nov 1965
Twining, Nathan F., American air force general, Yrbk 1953, *Obit* May 1982
Ulio, James Alexander, Sept 1945
Umberto, Oct 1943, *Obit* May 1983
Upshur, William P., *Obit* Sept 1943
Urquhart, Brian E., British United Nations official, June 1986

Urquhart, Robert E., British general, Yrbk 1944, *Obit* Feb 1989

Vall, Ely Ould Mohamed, Mauritanian head of state, Jan 2006

Van Fleet, James Alward, American general, Apr 1948, *Obit* Nov 1992

Vandegrift, A. A., American Marine corps general, Jan 1943, *Obit* June 1973

Vandenberg, Hoyt Sanford, American air force general, Mar 1945, *Obit* May 1954

Vatutin, Nikolai Fedorovich, Soviet general, Feb 1944

Vaughan, Harry H., American general, Mar 1949, *Obit* July 1981

Velasco Alvarado, Juan, Peruvian president, June 1970, *Obit* Mar 1978

Videla, Jorge Rafael, Argentine general and president, Apr 1978, *Obit* Yrbk 2013

Vo, Nguyen Giap, Vietnamese general, Feb 1969

Vogel, Herbert D., Yrbk 1954

Voorhees, Tracy S., Feb 1957, *Obit* Nov 1974

Wainwright, Jonathan Mayhew, American general, May 1942, *Obit* Nov 1953

Waitt, Alden H., Sept 1947

Walker, Walton Harris, American general, Sept 1950, *Obit* Jan 1951

Walters, Vernon A., American general and diplomat, Feb 1988, *Obit* July 2002

Ward, William E., American general, Nov 2005

Waring, George J., *Obit* Apr 1943

Warner, Milo J., Nov 1941

Wash, Carlyle H., *Obit* Mar 1943

Watson, Edwin M., American general, *Obit* Apr 1945

Wavell, Archibald Percival Wavell, British general and colonial administrator, Mar 1941, *Obit* July 1950

Weaver, Walter Reed, *Obit* Yrbk 1944

Wedemeyer, Albert, American general, Jan 1945, *Obit* Feb 1990

Westmoreland, William C., American general, June 1961, *Obit* Nov 2005

Weygand, Maxime, French general, Jan 1940, *Obit* Mar 1965

Wheeler, Earle G., American general, Nov 1965, *Obit* Feb 1976

Wheeler, Raymond A., Apr 1957, *Obit* Apr 1974

White, I. D., American general, Yrbk 1958, *Obit* Aug 1990

White, Thomas D., American air force general, Yrbk 1957, *Obit* Feb 1966

Whitney, Courtney, June 1951, *Obit* May 1969

Wilbur, Bernice M., Sept 1943

Wilby, Francis B., Aug 1945, *Obit* Jan 1966

Williams, John Bell, American congressman and governor, Mar 1964, *Obit* May 1983

Wilson, Heather, American congresswoman, July 2006

Wingate, Orde Charles, British general, *Obit* May 1944

Wood, Charles Erskine Scott, American lawyer and satirist, *Obit* Mar 1944

Yadin, Yigael, Israeli archaeologist, general and political leader, Feb 1966, *Obit* Aug 1984

Yamut, Nuri, May 1952

Yang Liwei, Chinese astronaut, Jan 2004

Yates, Donald N., air force general and meteorologist, May 1958

Ydigoras Fuentes, Miguel, Nov 1958

Yeager, Chuck, American test pilot and air force general, May 1954

Yeats-Brown, Francis, British army officer and author, *Obit* Feb 1945

Yudhoyono, Susilo Bambang, Indonesian president, Jan 2005

Zahedi, Fazlollah, Feb 1954, *Obit* Nov 1963

Zhu De, Chinese general, Nov 1942, *Obit* Aug 1976

Zia-ul-Haq, Mohammad, Pakistani general and president, June 1980, *Obit* Sept 1988

Zinni, Anthony, American Marine corps general and diplomat, May 2002

Art collectors

Abrams, Harry N., American publisher, June 1958, *Obit* Jan 1980

Archer, Jeffrey, English novelist, Sept 1988

Assis Chateaubriand, Brazilian newspaper and broadcasting executive, June 1957

Bache, Jules Semon, financier and art collector, *Obit* May 1944

Barnes, Albert Coombs, American chemist and pharmaceutical executive, Mar 1945, *Obit* Sept 1951

Blount, Winton Malcolm, American construction executive and postmaster general, Apr 1969, *Obit* Jan 2003

Brundage, Avery, American engineer and Olympics executive, Jan 1948, *Obit* Aug 1975

Dale, Chester, American investment banker and art collector, Sept 1958, *Obit* Jan 1963

Forbes, Malcolm Stevenson, American magazine publisher and investment adviser, Feb 1975, *Obit* Apr 1990

Guggenheim, Peggy, American patron of the arts, Oct 1962, *Obit* Feb 1980

Hammer, Armand, American petroleum executive, June 1973, *Obit* Feb 1991

Hirshhorn, Joseph H., American stockbroker, mining executive and art collector, Nov 1966, *Obit* Oct 1981

Holladay, Wilhelmina Cole, art collector, Oct 1987

Kress, Samuel H., merchant, Oct 1955

Lloyd Webber, Andrew, English composer, June 1982

Mapplethorpe, Robert, American photographer and art collector, May 1989, *Obit* May 1989

Meadows, A. H., American petroleum industry executive, Apr 1960

Mellon, Paul, American philanthropist, Apr 1966, *Obit* Apr 1999

Niarchos, Stavros, Greek shipping executive, May 1958, *Obit* June 1996

Nutting, Wallace, American clergyman, photographer and furniture executive, *Obit* Sept 1941

Otis, Clarence, American restaurant chain executive, Oct 2009

Reves, Emery, British publisher and art collector, July 1946

Rockefeller, John D., American philanthropist, June 1953, *Obit* Sept 1978

Rockefeller, Nelson A., American vice-president, Mar 1941, Mar 1951, *Obit* Mar 1979

Rubinstein, Helena, American cosmetician, June 1943, *Obit* May 1965

Scull, Robert C., American taxi executive and art collector, Apr 1974, *Obit* Feb 1986

Simon, Norton, American financier and art collector, Mar 1968, *Obit* Aug 1993

Tang, David, Chinese retail executive, Jan 2006

Terra, Daniel J., chemical executive and art collector, Nov 1987, *Obit* Sept 1996

Thyssen-Bornemisza, Hans Heinrich, Swiss financier and art collector, Feb 1989, *Obit* Yrbk 2002

Wallace, Lila Acheson, American philanthropist and publisher, May 1956, *Obit* July 1984

Zuloaga, Ignacio, Spanish art collector and painter, *Obit* Yrbk 1945

Art critics

Bawer, Bruce, American critic, poet and essayist, July 2007

Beckett, Wendy, English nun and art critic, Jan 1998

Bernard, Emile, French painter, art critic and poet, *Obit* June 1941

Bernier, Rosamond, American art critic, Feb 1988

Binyon, Laurence, English poet, dramatist and art critic, *Obit* Apr 1943

Bracco, Roberto, *Obit* June 1943

Canaday, John Edwin, art critic and author, May 1962, *Obit* Sept 1985

Craven, Thomas, American art critic, Apr 1944, *Obit* Apr 1969

Danto, Arthur Coleman, American philosopher and art critic, Apr 1995

Du Bois, Guy Pene, painter and critic, Oct 1946, *Obit* Oct 1958

Enwezor, Okwui, Nigerian art critic and exhibition curator, Jan 2002

Geldzahler, Henry, art historian, critic and curator, Sept 1978, *Obit* Oct 1994

Gillet, Louis, *Obit* Aug 1943

Goodrich, Lloyd, museum director, May 1967, *Obit* May 1987

Gopnik, Adam, American essayist and art critic, Apr 2005

Gullar, Ferreira, Brazilian poet and art critic, Jan 2004

Hickey, Dave, American art and cultural critic, Sept 2007

Hughes, Robert, Australian art critic, May 1987, *Obit* Yrbk 2012

Kepes, Gyorgy, Hungarian-American painter, graphic designer and art critic, Mar 1973, *Obit* Mar 2002

Newton, Eric, British art critic, Feb 1956, *Obit* Apr 1965

Read, Herbert Edward, English poet, essayist and art critic, Mar 1962, *Obit* Sept 1968

Rosenfeld, Paul, American music, art and literary critic, *Obit* Sept 1946

Rothenstein, William, English painter, *Obit* Apr 1945

Saarinen, Aline B., American art critic and wife of architect Eero Saarinen, Yrbk 1956, *Obit* Sept 1972

Schjeldahl, Peter, American art critic, Oct 2005

Sgarbi, Vittorio, Italian art critic, historian and member of Parliament, Jan 2006

Sherman, Frederic Fairchild, *Obit* Yrbk 1940

Simonson, Lee, Nov 1947, *Obit* Mar 1967

Sweeney, James Johnson, art critic, historian and museum director, Mar 1955, *Obit* July 1986

Art dealers

Brooks, Diana D., American art dealer and auctioneer, June 1998

Castelli, Leo, American art dealer, Aug 1984, *Obit* Jan 2000

Halpert, Edith Gregor, art dealer, July 1955, *Obit* Nov 1970

Hammer, Armand, American petroleum executive, June 1973, *Obit* Feb 1991

Janis, Sidney, American art dealer, July 1970, *Obit* Jan 1990

Lasker, Mary, American art dealer and philanthropist, Oct 1959, *Obit* May 1994

McEnroe, John, American tennis player, Feb 1980

Stieglitz, Alfred, American photographer, Jan 1940, *Obit* Sept 1946

Wilson, Peter C., English art dealer, Feb 1968, *Obit* Aug 1984

Art directors

Carson, David, American graphic designer, July 2008

Switzer, George, American industrial designer and art director, *Obit* Yrbk 1940

Art historians

Barr, Alfred Hamilton, American museum director, Jan 1961, *Obit* Oct 1981

Baur, John Ireland Howe, museum director, Yrbk 1969, *Obit* July 1987

Bazin, Germain, French art historian and museum curator, Jan 1959, *Obit* July 1990

Bernier, Rosamond, American art critic, Feb 1988

Binyon, Laurence, English poet, dramatist and art critic, *Obit* Apr 1943

Bois, Yve-Alain, French art historian, Jan 2005

Brookner, Anita, English novelist and art historian, Feb 1989

Driskell, David C., American painter and printmaker, Aug 2000

Geldzahler, Henry, art historian, critic and curator, Sept 1978, *Obit* Oct 1994

Goodrich, Lloyd, museum director, May 1967, *Obit* May 1987

Hours, Madeleine, Apr 1961

Hoving, Thomas, American museum director and periodical editor, Apr 1967, *Obit* Yrbk 2010

Krens, Thomas, American museum director, Apr 1989

Larkin, Oliver W., art historian, July 1950, *Obit* Feb 1971

Lee, Sherman E., American art historian and museum director, June 1974, *Obit* Yrbk 2008

Malraux, Andre, French novelist, essayist and art historian, Mar 1959, *Obit* Feb 1977

Messer, Thomas M., museum director and art historian, Nov 1961, *Obit* Yrbk 2013

Piotrovskii, Mikhail Borisovich, Russian museum director, Jan 2003

Richter, George Martin, *Obit* July 1942

Rothenstein, John Maurice, English art historian and museum director, Apr 1957

Rubin, William Stanley, American art historian and museum curator, Nov 1986, *Obit* Yrbk 2007

Schapiro, Meyer, American art historian, July 1984, *Obit* May 1996

Sgarbi, Vittorio, Italian art critic, historian and member of Parliament, Jan 2006

Sweeney, James Johnson, art critic, historian and museum director, Mar 1955, *Obit* July 1986

Varnedoe, Kirk, American museum curator and art historian, Feb 1991, *Obit* Yrbk 2003

Walker, John, museum director, May 1957, *Obit* Jan 1996

Art publishers

Sherman, Frederic Fairchild, *Obit* Yrbk 1940

Skira, Albert, Swiss art publisher, Apr 1967, *Obit* June 1990

Art teachers

Albers, Josef, German painter and printmaker, June 1962, *Obit* May 1976

Blanch, Arnold, American painter, May 1940, Jan 1954, *Obit* Yrbk 1968

Bolotowsky, Ilya, American painter and sculptor, Apr 1975, *Obit* Jan 1982

Chase, Joseph Cummings, May 1955

Connah, Douglas John, *Obit* Oct 1941

Curtis, George V., *Obit* Oct 1943

Driskell, David C., American painter and printmaker, Aug 2000

Ettl, John, *Obit* Feb 1941

Fingesten, Peter, painter and art teacher, Oct 1954, *Obit* Oct 1987

Freedlander, Arthur R., *Obit* Aug 1940

Gordon, John Sloan, *Obit* Yrbk 1940

Hofmann, Hans, German-American painter, Oct 1958, *Obit* Mar 1966

Kepes, Gyorgy, Hungarian-American painter, graphic designer and art critic, Mar 1973, *Obit* Mar 2002

Lie, Jonas, Norwegian-American painter, Jan 1940

Liu, Hung, Chinese artist, Jan 2002

Martin, Fletcher, Feb 1958, *Obit* July 1979

Oberteuffer, George, *Obit* Jan 1940

Robinson, Boardman, Yrbk 1941, *Obit* Oct 1952

Taubes, Frederic, Mar 1943

Thiebaud, Wayne, American painter and teacher, Mar 1987

Wegman, William, American artist, May 1992

Werntz, Carl N., *Obit* Yrbk 1944

Young, Joseph Louis, American sculptor and muralist, July 1960

Artisans

Abakanowicz, Magdalena, Polish sculptor, Jan 2001

Abel, I. W., American labor leader, Nov 1965, *Obit* Sept 1987

Behrman, Beatrice, American doll maker, Sept 1957

Dobson, William Alexander, *Obit* July 1943

Graff, Laurence, British jeweler, Sept 2011

Hunter, Dard, American papermaker and typographer, Sept 1960, *Obit* Mar 1966

McBride, Lloyd, steelworkers' union leader, Feb 1978, *Obit* Jan 1984

Mirabal, Robert, Native American composer and flutist, Aug 2002

Partch, Harry, American composer, Sept 1965, *Obit* Oct 1974

Picasso, Paloma, French jewelry and industrial designer and daughter of Pablo Picasso, Apr 1986

Scott, Raymond, composer and musical instrument inventor, July 1941, *Obit* May 1994

Tonner, Robert, American doll maker, Oct 2011

Toussaint, Jeanne, Feb 1955

Warner, Ty, American toy industry executive, Nov 1998

Winston, Harry, jeweler, Apr 1965, *Obit* Feb 1979

Yang Fuxi, Chinese bow and arrow maker, Jan 2007

Yellin, Samuel, American metalsmith, *Obit* Nov 1940

Yoshihara, Yoshindo, Japanese swordsmith, Jan 2005

Artists

Abakanowicz, Magdalena, Polish sculptor, Jan 2001

Abbott, Berenice, American photographer, July 1942, *Obit* Feb 1992

Abel, Jessica, American comic book writer and artist, Aug 2007

Abts, Tomma, British painter, Jan 2007

Adamson, Joy, Kenyan conservationist, writer and illustrator, Oct 1972, *Obit* Feb 1980

Addams, Charles, American cartoonist, Jan 1954, *Obit* Nov 1988

Afro, Nov 1958

Agam, Yaacov, Israeli artist, Apr 1981

Ai Wei Wei, Chinese artist and architect, Aug 2011

Aitken, Doug, American multimedia artist, Apr 2007

Alajalov, Constantin, American painter, illustrator and cartoonist, Jan 1942, *Obit* Jan 1988

Albers, Josef, German painter and printmaker, June 1962, *Obit* May 1976

Albright, Ivan Le Lorraine, American painter, Feb 1944, Yrbk 1969, *Obit* Jan 1984

Alechinsky, Pierre, Belgian painter and lithographer, Sept 1988

Ali, Laylah, American painter, July 2008

Allen, Joel Nott, American painter, *Obit* Mar 1940

Allen, Marion Boyd, American painter, *Obit* Feb 1942

Altenburg, Alexander, American painter, *Obit* Mar 1940

Alvarez Bravo, Manuel, Mexican photographer, Jan 1999, *Obit* Jan 2003

Amend, Bill, American cartoonist, Apr 2003

Ammann, Karl, Swiss wildlife photographer, Jan 2002

Andersen, Hendrik Christian, American sculptor, *Obit* Feb 1941

Anderson, Abraham Archibald, American painter, *Obit* Jan 1940

Anderson, Erica Kellner, Feb 1957, *Obit* Nov 1976

Anselmo, Giovanni, Italian artist, Jan 2003

Antes, Horst, German painter, etcher and sculptor, Feb 1986

Anuszkiewicz, Richard Joseph, Oct 1978

Araki, Nobuyoshi, Japanese photographer, Jan 2003

Arceneaux, Edgar, American artist, Aug 2008

Archambault, Louis, Sept 1959

Archipenko, Alexander, Russian sculptor, Sept 1953, *Obit* Apr 1964

Ardizzone, Edward, English painter, illustrator and author, May 1964, *Obit* Jan 1980

Armisen, Fred, American comedian and performance artist, Oct 2013

Armitage, Kenneth, English sculptor, Apr 1957, *Obit* May 2002

Arno, Peter, cartoonist, Aug 1942, *Obit* Apr 1968

Aronson, Naoum, Russian sculptor, *Obit* Nov 1943

Arp, Jean, French artist, poet and essayist, May 1954, *Obit* July 1966

Artschwager, Richard, painter and sculptor, July 1990, *Obit* Yrbk 2013

Artzybasheff, Boris, author and illustrator, Oct 1945, *Obit* Sept 1965

Ataman, Kutlug, Turkish video artist and film director, Jan 2006

Auerbach-Levy, William, painter and etcher, Feb 1948, *Obit* Sept 1964

Auth, Tony, American cartoonist, illustrator and children's author, Feb 2006

Avedon, Richard, American photographer, Feb 1975, *Obit* Mar 2005

Baca-Flor, Carlos, Peruvian painter, *Obit* July 1941

Bachrach, Elise Wald, American painter, *Obit* Mar 1940

Bacon, Peggy, American mystery writer and illustrator, Jan 1940, *Obit* Mar 1987

Baer, William J., American painter, *Obit* Nov 1941

Baker, George, American cartoonist, Nov 1944, *Obit* Aug 1975

Bakshi, Ralph, American animator, Mar 1979

Baldessari, John, American artist, June 1991

Balthus, French painter, Nov 1979, *Obit* May 2001

Banksy, English grafitti artist, Apr 2009

Bannister, Constance, American baby photographer, July 1955, *Obit* Yrbk 2005

Barclay, McClelland, American illustrator, Sept 1940, *Obit* Yrbk 1946

Barnard, Elinor M., American painter, *Obit* Apr 1942

Barnet, Will, American painter, June 1985, *Obit* Yrbk 2013

Barney, Matthew, American sculptor and installation and video artist, Aug 2003

Barry, Lynda, American cartoonist and novelist, Nov 1994

Barthe, Richmond, American sculptor, July 1940, *Obit* May 1989

Bartlett, Jennifer, American painter, Nov 1985

Baskin, Leonard, American sculptor and illustrator, May 1964, *Obit* Aug 2000

Bauer, Erwin A., photographer, Feb 1993

Bauer, Peggy, photographer, Feb 1993

Beard, Daniel Carter, American children's author, illustrator and Boy Scouts founder, *Obit* Aug 1941

Bearden, Romare, American artist, Jan 1972, *Obit* May 1988

Beaton, Cecil, English designer and photographer, Oct 1944, July 1962, *Obit* Mar 1980

Beaux, Cecilia, American painter, *Obit* Nov 1942

Bechdel, Alison, American cartoonist and graphic novelist, July 2009

Bell, Steve, British political cartoonist, Jan 2003

Bemelmans, Ludwig, American children's author and illustrator, Apr 1941, *Obit* Yrbk 1962

Berman, Eugene, American painter, June 1965, *Obit* Feb 1973

Bernard, Emile, French painter, art critic and poet, *Obit* June 1941

Berryman, James Thomas, cartoonist, July 1950, *Obit* Oct 1971

Beuys, Joseph, German artist, July 1980, *Obit* Mar 1986

Biddle, George, American painter and sculptor, Feb 1942, *Obit* Jan 1974

Birch, Reginald Bathurst, *Obit* Aug 1943

Bishop, Isabel, American painter, Oct 1977, *Obit* Apr 1988

Black, Alexander, American photographer, *Obit* Jan 1940

Blanch, Arnold, American painter, May 1940, Jan 1954, *Obit* Yrbk 1968

Blanche, Jacques-Emile, French painter, *Obit* Nov 1942

Blanding, Don, American poet and illustrator, Jan 1957

Block, Herbert, American editorial cartoonist, July 1954, *Obit* Jan 2002

Blume, Peter, American painter, Mar 1956, *Obit* Jan 1993

Bogert, George H., American painter, *Obit* Feb 1945

Bohrod, Aaron, painter, Feb 1955, *Obit* June 1992

Bolotowsky, Ilya, American painter and sculptor, Apr 1975, *Obit* Jan 1982

Bonney, Therese, Feb 1944

Bonomi, Maria, Brazilian artist, July 1960

Bontecou, Lee, American sculptor, assemblage artist and printmaker, Mar 2004

Borglum, Gutzon, American sculptor and painter, *Obit* Apr 1941

Borofsky, Jonathan, American artist, July 1985

Bosustow, Stephen, June 1958

Bourgeois, Louise, American sculptor, Oct 1983, *Obit* Yrbk 2010

Bourke-White, Margaret, American photographer, Jan 1940, *Obit* Oct 1971

Brackman, Robert, painter, July 1953, *Obit* Sept 1980

Brancusi, Constantin, Romanian sculptor, Sept 1955, *Obit* June 1957

Braque, Georges, French painter, Nov 1949, *Obit* Oct 1963

Brenner, Frederic, French photographer, Jan 2004

Breytenbach, Breyten, South African poet and painter, June 1986

Brinkley, Nell, *Obit* Yrbk 1944

Brook, Alexander, painter, Apr 1941, *Obit* Apr 1980

Brooks, James, painter, Feb 1959, *Obit* May 1992

Browne, George Elmer, American painter, *Obit* Sept 1946

Brush, George de Forest, American painter, *Obit* June 1941

Brustlein, Daniel, American painter, Sept 1941

Bryan, Julien, American photographer and documentary filmmaker, July 1940, *Obit* Jan 1975

Buechner, Thomas S., American painter and museum director, Feb 1961, *Obit* Yrbk 2010

Buffet, Bernard, French painter, Apr 1959, *Obit* Feb 2000

Bull, Johan, *Obit* Oct 1945

Burchfield, Charles Ephraim, American painter, May 1942, May 1961, *Obit* Mar 1967

Burliuk, David Davidovich, Russian painter and poet, Apr 1940, *Obit* Mar 1967

Burton, Tim, American film director, July 1991

Byrne, John, Anglo-Canadian comic book artist and writer, Oct 2000

Cadmus, Paul, painter and printmaker, July 1942, *Obit* Mar 2000

Calder, Alexander, American sculptor, Apr 1946, July 1966, *Obit* Jan 1977

Calder, Alexander Stirling, American sculptor, *Obit* Feb 1945

Callahan, Harry M., American photographer, Nov 1984, *Obit* July 1999

Callahan, John, American cartoonist, Sept 1998, *Obit* Yrbk 2010

Calle, Sophie, French artist, May 2001

Callery, Mary, July 1955

Camden, Harry P., *Obit* Sept 1943

Campbell, E. Simms, Jan 1941, *Obit* Mar 1971

Caniff, Milton Arthur, cartoonist, Jan 1944, *Obit* May 1988

Capogrossi, Giuseppe, Yrbk 1957

Capp, Al, cartoonist, May 1947, *Obit* Jan 1980

Carle, Eric, American illustrator and children's author, Nov 2013

Carlson, John F., *Obit* May 1945

Carone, Nicolas, American painter and draughtsman, July 2006, *Obit* Yrbk 2010

Carroll, John, painter, July 1955, *Obit* Jan 1960

Carson, David, American graphic designer, July 2008

Cartier-Bresson, Henri, French photographer, Mar 1947, May 1976, Jan 2003, *Obit* Yrbk 2004

Cartotto, Ercole, *Obit* Nov 1946

Catlett, Elizabeth, American sculptor and printmaker, May 1998, *Obit* Yrbk 2012

Cauldwell, Leslie Giffen, *Obit* July 1941

Celmins, Vija, American painter, Jan 2005

Chagall, Marc, Russian painter, Nov 1943, Nov 1960, *Obit* May 1985

Chamberlain, Samuel, American photographer and artist, Sept 1954, *Obit* Mar 1975

Chan, Paul, American video artist, Mar 2011

Chang, Shan-tzu, *Obit* Yrbk 1940

Chapin, James, American painter, Mar 1940, *Obit* Sept 1975

Charles, Michael Ray, American painter, Oct 2005

Charlot, Jean, American painter and illustrator, Sept 1945, *Obit* Yrbk 1984

Chase, Joseph Cummings, May 1955

Chast, Roz, American cartoonist, July 1997

Chastain, Madye Lee, Yrbk 1958

Cheney, Russell, American painter, *Obit* Aug 1945

Chia, Sandro, Italian painter, June 1990

Chicago, Judy, American artist, Feb 1981

Chihuly, Dale, American glass artist, Aug 1995

Chillida, Eduardo, Spanish sculptor, Sept 1985, *Obit* Yrbk 2002

Christo, Bulgarian artist, Mar 1977

Chryssa, American sculptor and painter, Nov 1978

Chukwuogo-Roy, Chinwe, Nigerian painter, Jan 2007

Chwast, Seymour, American children's author, illustrator and graphic designer, Sept 1995

Ciocci, Jacob, American multi-media artist, Apr 2010

Ciocci, Jessica, American video and installation artist, Apr 2010

Close, Chuck, American painter, July 1983

Clowes, Daniel, American comic book artist and writer, Jan 2002

Coe, Sue, Anglo-American painter and illustrator, Aug 1997

Coffin, Haskell, *Obit* July 1941

Colbert, Gregory, Canadian photographer and cinematographer, Sept 2005

Cole, Jessie Duncan Savage, *Obit* Yrbk 1940

Collins, Phil, English video artist, Jan 2007

Colville, Alex, Canadian painter, Mar 1985, *Obit* Yrbk 2013

Congdon, William, painter, May 1967, *Obit* July 1998

Connah, Douglas John, *Obit* Oct 1941

Conrad, Barnaby, author and painter, Sept 1959, *Obit* Yrbk 2013

Cook, Fannie, American novelist and painter, Yrbk 1946, *Obit* Oct 1949

Corbijn, Anton, Dutch photographer, June 2006

Corrales, Raul, Cuban photographer, Jan 2003

Covarrubias, Miguel, Mexican painter and caricaturist, July 1940, *Obit* Apr 1957

Cowles, Fleur, American painter and magazine editor, Apr 1952, *Obit* Yrbk 2009

Cox, Allyn, painter, July 1954, *Obit* Jan 1983

Crumb, R., American cartoonist, Apr 1995

Cuevas, Jose Luis, Mexican illustrator and printmaker, Jan 1968

Cunningham, Bill, American photographer, Aug 2011

Curran, Charles Courtney, American painter, *Obit* Jan 1943

Curry, John Steuart, American painter, Apr 1941, *Obit* Oct 1946

Curtis, George V., *Obit* Oct 1943

D'Aulaire, Edgar Parin, author and illustrator, Aug 1940

D'Aulaire, Ingri, author and illustrator, Aug 1940

Dallin, Cyrus Edwin, sculptor, *Obit* Jan 1945

Dardel, Nils von, Swedish painter, *Obit* July 1943

Darling, Jay Norwood, American cartoonist and conservationist, July 1942, *Obit* Mar 1962

Darrow, Whitney, cartoonist, Yrbk 1958, *Obit* Oct 1999

Daugherty, James Henry, American children's author and illustrator, July 1940, *Obit* Apr 1974

Davidson, Jo, American sculptor and engraver, Apr 1945, *Obit* Feb 1952

Davis, Gladys Rockmore, painter, Sept 1953, *Obit* Apr 1967

Davis, Stuart, American painter, engraver and illustrator, Aug 1940, July 1964

De Angeli, Marguerite Lofft, American children's author and illustrator, Yrbk 1947

De Beck, Billy, cartoonist, *Obit* Jan 1943

De Chirico, Giorgio, Italian painter, Jan 1956, June 1972, *Obit* Jan 1979

De Creeft, Jose, sculptor, Yrbk 1942, *Obit* Yrbk 1991

De Kooning, Elaine Marie Catherine, American painter, July 1982, *Obit* Mar 1989

De Kooning, Willem, American painter, June 1955, Sept 1984, *Obit* May 1997

De Paola, Tomie, American painter, illustrator and children's author, Feb 1999

DeCarava, Roy, American photographer, Aug 2008, *Obit* Yrbk 2009

DeCarlo, Dan, American comic book artist, Aug 2001, *Obit* Mar 2002

Dehn, Adolf, Apr 1941, *Obit* July 1968

Delaunay, Sonia, French painter and fashion designer, Aug 1977, *Obit* Feb 1980

Demand, Thomas C., German photographer, Mar 2010

Deming, Edwin Willard, painter and sculptor, *Obit* Yrbk 1942

Der Harootian, Koren, Jan 1955

Di Suvero, Mark, sculptor, Nov 1979

DiCorcia, Philip-Lorca, American photographer, Apr 2008

Dickinson, Edwin Walter, American painter, Sept 1963, *Obit* Feb 1979

Diebenkorn, Richard, American painter, Yrbk 1971, *Obit* May 1993

Dike, Phil, Yrbk 1942

Disney, Walt, American animator and motion picture executive, Aug 1940, Apr 1952, *Obit* Feb 1967

Djanira, Jan 1961

Dongen, Kees van, Dutch artist, Sept 1960, *Obit* July 1968

Doubilet, David, American underwater photographer, Mar 2003

Douglas, Emory, American illustrator, cartoonist and social activist, Feb 2010

Drake, James, American artist, July 2005

Driskell, David C., American painter and printmaker, Aug 2000

Drooker, Eric, American painter and graphic novelist, Feb 2011

Drouet, Bessie Clarke, *Obit* Oct 1940

Du Bois, Guy Pene, painter and critic, Oct 1946, *Obit* Oct 1958

Dubuffet, Jean, French painter and sculptor, July 1962, *Obit* July 1985

Duchamp, Marcel, French painter, June 1960, *Obit* Yrbk 1968

Duffy, Edmund, cartoonist, Jan 1940, *Obit* Nov 1962

Dufy, Raoul, French painter, Mar 1951, *Obit* May 1953

Dumas, Marlene, South African painter, Jan 2010

Dwight, Edward J., American astronaut and sculptor, July 2007

Edgerton, Harold Eugene, American electrical engineer, Nov 1966, *Obit* Mar 1990

Eggleston, Edward Mason, *Obit* Mar 1941

Eggleston, William, American photographer, Feb 2002

Eilshemius, Louis Michel, American painter, Apr 1940, *Obit* Feb 1942

Eisner, Will, American cartoonist and comic book publisher, Oct 1994, *Obit* May 2005

Elisofon, Eliot, American photographer and painter, Jan 1972, *Obit* May 1973

Emin, Tracey, British performance artist, Nov 2009

Engelbreit, Mary, American children's author, illustrator and magazine publisher, Oct 1999

Enright, Elizabeth, American children's author and illustrator, Yrbk 1947, *Obit* Sept 1968

Ensor, James, Belgian painter and engraver, *Obit* Feb 1943

Enters, Angna, dancer, painter and author, Jan 1940, June 1952, *Obit* Apr 1989

Epstein, Jacob, English sculptor and illustrator, July 1945, *Obit* Nov 1959

Ernst, Jimmy, painter, Mar 1966, *Obit* Apr 1984

Ernst, Max, German painter, Yrbk 1942, Oct 1961, *Obit* May 1976

Erte, French painter, set and costume designer, Nov 1980, *Obit* June 1990

Estern, Neil, American sculptor, Nov 2008

Estes, Eleanor, American librarian, children's author and illustrator, Yrbk 1946, *Obit* Sept 1988

Estes, Richard, American painter, Nov 1995

Ettl, John, *Obit* Feb 1941

Euclide, Gregory, May 2013

Evans, Walker, American photographer, Sept 1971, *Obit* June 1975

Evaristti, Marco, Chilean installation artist, Jan 2007

Evatt, Harriet, Yrbk 1959

Evergood, Philip, American painter, Oct 1944, Oct 1960, *Obit* Apr 1973

Everson, Kevin Jerome, American filmmaker and video artist, Nov 2011

Eves, Reginald Grenville, Sept 1940, *Obit* Aug 1941

Eyuboglu, Bedri Rahmi, Turkish artist and poet, Sept 1954

Fabre, Jan, Belgian artist, Jan 2004

Faidley, Warren, American photographer and storm chaser, Feb 2008

Farnsworth, Jerry, Oct 1954

Fasanella, Ralph, painter, June 1975, *Obit* Mar 1998

Fassett, Kaffe, American textile designer, June 1995

Feiffer, Jules, American cartoonist, children's author and dramatist, Oct 1961

Feininger, Andreas, American photographer, Oct 1957, *Obit* May 1999

Feininger, Lyonel, German painter and cartoonist, July 1955, *Obit* Mar 1956

Ferber, Herbert, American sculptor and painter, Nov 1960, *Obit* Oct 1991

Ferren, John, American painter, July 1958, *Obit* Oct 1970

Ferrer, Rafael, Puerto Rican artist, July 2001

Ferriss, Hugh, July 1945, *Obit* Mar 1962

Fiene, Ernest, American painter and printmaker, Aug 1941

Filmus, Tully, painter, Apr 1964, *Obit* June 1998

Fingesten, Peter, painter and art teacher, Oct 1954, *Obit* Oct 1987

Finley, Karen, performance artist, Sept 1998

Fiore, Mark, American cartoonist and animator, Apr 2011

Fischl, Eric, American painter and sculptor, June 1986

Fisk, Jack, American motion picture production designer, June 2011

Fitzpatrick, Daniel Robert, cartoonist, July 1941, *Obit* July 1969

Flagg, James Montgomery, painter and illustrator, Nov 1940, *Obit* Sept 1960

Flannagan, John, American sculptor, *Obit* Mar 1942

Fleming, Maureen, American dancer and choreographer, Mar 2010

Folon, Jean Michel, Belgian painter and illustrator, Feb 1981, *Obit* Yrbk 2006

Francis, Sam, American painter, Oct 1973, *Obit* Jan 1995

Frankel, Felice, American photographer, Apr 1998

Frankenthaler, Helen, American painter, Apr 1966, *Obit* Yrbk 2012

Frasconi, Antonio, Uruguayan painter and wood engraver, Mar 1972, *Obit* Yrbk 2013

Fraser, James Earle, sculptor and medalist, July 1951, *Obit* Jan 1954

Fredenthal, David, Sept 1942, *Obit* Jan 1959

Freedlander, Arthur R., *Obit* Aug 1940

Freilicher, Jane, American painter, Nov 1989

Freud, Lucian, British painter, July 1988, *Obit* Yrbk 2011

Friedman, Tom, American sculptor, Oct 2008

Frissell, Toni, photographer, June 1947, *Obit* June 1988

Funke, Cornelia Caroline, German illustrator and children's author, Jan 2007

Gabo, Naum, Russian painter and sculptor, Apr 1972, *Obit* Oct 1977

Gag, Wanda, American children's author and illustrator, *Obit* July 1946

Gallagher, Ellen, American painter, Feb 2009

Ganso, Emil, *Obit* June 1941

Garnsey, Elmer E., *Obit* Yrbk 1946

Gatch, Lee, Mar 1966, *Obit* Jan 1969

Geddes, Norman Bel, stage designer and producer, May 1940, *Obit* July 1958

Genthe, Arnold, *Obit* Oct 1942

Giacometti, Alberto, Swiss sculptor, Feb 1956, *Obit* Feb 1966

Gibbings, Robert, Irish travel writer and illustrator, Yrbk 1948, *Obit* Mar 1958

Gibson, Charles Dana, American illustrator and painter, *Obit* Feb 1945

Gibson, Lois, American forensic artist, Mar 2008

Giger, H. R., Swiss painter, sculptor and scenic designer, Jan 2002

Gilbert and George, English artists, June 2009

Gilchrist, Brad, cartoonist, Jan 1999

Gilchrist, Guy, author, illustrator and cartoonist, Jan 1999

Gilder, Robert F., American journalist and archaeologist, *Obit* Mar 1940

Gill, Eric, English sculptor, engraver and typographer, *Obit* Jan 1941

Glaser, Milton, American illustrator and designer, May 1980

Glicenstein, Enrico, *Obit* Feb 1943

Glintenkamp, H., *Obit* May 1946

Goldberg, Rube, cartoonist, Sept 1948, *Obit* Jan 1971

Goldsworthy, Andy, English photographer and sculptor, Oct 2000

Goldthwaite, Anne, American painter and printmaker, *Obit* Mar 1944

Goodman, Bertram, May 1954

Gordon, Jan, English author and illustrator, *Obit* Mar 1944

Gordon, John Sloan, *Obit* Yrbk 1940

Gordon, Leon, *Obit* Feb 1944

Gorey, Edward, American illustrator, children's author and designer, Nov 1976, *Obit* Aug 2000

Gorman, R. C., American painter and sculptor, Jan 2001

Gottlieb, Adolph, American painter, Jan 1959, *Obit* Apr 1974

Gould, Chester, American cartoonist, Sept 1971, *Obit* July 1985

Gowda, Sheela, Indian artist, Jan 2002

Grant, Gordon, June 1953, *Obit* July 1962

Graves, Morris, painter, July 1956, *Obit* Sept 2001

Graves, Nancy, American painter and sculptor, May 1981, *Obit* Jan 1996

Green, Florence Topping, *Obit* June 1945

Greene, Balcomb, painter, Nov 1965, *Obit* Jan 1991

Greene, Frank Russell, *Obit* Jan 1940

Groening, Matt, American cartoonist and animator, Sept 1990

Grooms, Red, American artist, Yrbk 1972

Groot, Adriaan M. de, *Obit* Mar 1942

Gropper, William, American cartoonist, painter and illustrator, Mar 1940, *Obit* Mar 1977

Gross, Chaim, American sculptor, Nov 1941, Feb 1966, *Obit* July 1991

Groth, John, illustrator and painter, Feb 1943, *Obit* Aug 1988

Gruber, Ruth, American journalist, photographer and humanitarian, June 2001

Gruppe, Charles Paul, *Obit* Nov 1940

Guisewite, Cathy, cartoonist, Feb 1989

Gursky, Andreas, German photographer, July 2001

Guston, Philip, American painter, Feb 1971, *Obit* July 1980

Gwathmey, Robert, American painter, Yrbk 1943, *Obit* Nov 1988

Haacke, Hans, German artist, July 1987

Halsman, Philippe, Latvian-American photographer, Mar 1960, *Obit* Aug 1979

Hammond, Aubrey, English illustrator, *Obit* Apr 1940

Hammons, David, American artist, May 2006

Hancock, Trenton Doyle, American painter and performance artist, Apr 2006

Hanna, William, American animator and producer, July 1983, *Obit* Sept 2001

Hanson, Duane, American sculptor, Oct 1983, *Obit* Mar 1996

Harding, Nelson, *Obit* Feb 1945

Haring, Keith, American artist, Aug 1986, *Obit* Apr 1990

Harris, Jonathan, American artist and web designer, Oct 2013

Harris, Rolf, Australian television personality, singer and cartoonist, Jan 2002

Harryhausen, Ray, American motion picture special effects technician and animator, *Obit* Yrbk 2013

Hartigan, Grace, American painter, Sept 1962, *Obit* Yrbk 2009

Hartley, Marsden, American painter and poet, *Obit* Oct 1943

Hartung, Hans, French painter, July 1958, *Obit* Feb 1990

Hawkinson, Tim, American sculptor, Aug 2005

Hayes, David, Apr 1966, *Obit* Yrbk 2013

Hayter, Stanley William, English painter and engraver, Yrbk 1945, *Obit* June 1988

Held, Al, American painter, Jan 1986, *Obit* Yrbk 2005

Heliker, John, painter, Jan 1969, *Obit* July 2000

Helion, Jean, French painter, Nov 1943, *Obit* Jan 1988

Heming, Arthur Henry Howard, *Obit* Yrbk 1940

Hepworth, Barbara, English sculptor, Feb 1957, *Obit* Aug 1975

Hewlett, J. Monroe, *Obit* Yrbk 1941

Hewlett, Jamie, English illustrator and cartoonist, Jan 2007

Higgins, Jack, American editorial cartoonist, Feb 2007

Hill, Helen, American children's author and illustrator, *Obit* May 1942

Hillenburg, Stephen, American animator and television scriptwriter, Apr 2003

Hinckley, Robert C., *Obit* July 1941

Hirschfeld, Al, American caricaturist, Jan 1971, *Obit* July 2003

Hirschhorn, Thomas, Swiss installation artist, Sept 2009

Hirshfield, Morris, painter, Sept 1943

Hirst, Damien, English artist, Aug 2013

Hoffman, Malvina, American sculptor, Yrbk 1940, *Obit* Sept 1966

Hofmann, Hans, German-American painter, Oct 1958, *Obit* Mar 1966

Holzer, Jenny, American artist, June 1990

Honeywell, Annette, July 1953

Hopper, Dennis, American actor and director, Aug 1987, *Obit* Yrbk 2010

Hopper, Edward, American painter, Yrbk 1950, *Obit* July 1967

Horsey, David, American political cartoonist, Sept 2008

Horst, photographer, June 1992, *Obit* Mar 2000

Houston, James A., Canadian artist, novelist and children's author, July 1987, *Obit* Yrbk 2005

Hudson, Henrietta, *Obit* May 1942

Hughes, Toni, May 1941

Hunter, Dard, American papermaker and typographer, Sept 1960, *Obit* Mar 1966

Huntington, Anna Hyatt, American sculptor, Oct 1953, *Obit* Yrbk 1973

Hurd, Peter, American painter, Oct 1957, *Obit* Sept 1984

Husain, Maqbul Fida, Indian painter, Jan 2006, *Obit* Yrbk 2011

H"ller, Carsten, Belgian installation artist, May 2012

Igoe, Herbert A., *Obit* Apr 1945

Indiana, Robert, American painter and sculptor, Mar 1973

Inglis, John J., *Obit* Oct 1946

Irwin, Robert, American artist, Jan 1993

Ishimoto, Tatsuo, Apr 1956

Jaar, Alfredo, Chilean mixed-media and installation artist, Jan 2005

Jacir, Emily, Palestinian artist, Aug 2009

Jaffee, Al, American cartoonist and illustrator, July 2008

James, Alexander R., *Obit* Apr 1946

James, Will, American children's author and illustrator, *Obit* Nov 1942

John, Augustus, English painter, Oct 1941, *Obit* Jan 1962

Johnson, Clifton, *Obit* Jan 1940

Johnson, Crockett, cartoonist, Yrbk 1943, *Obit* Jan 1984

Johnston, Daniel, American singer, songwriter and artist, Sept 2010

Johnston, Lynn, Canadian cartoonist, Feb 1998

Jones, Ben, American multimedia artist, Apr 2010

Jones, Chuck, American animator, May 1996, *Obit* May 2002

Jones, Joe, American painter, Oct 1940, *Obit* June 1963

Jones, Robert Edmond, scenic designer, Nov 1946, *Obit* Jan 1955

Jones, Sarah, American poet, playwright and performance artist, July 2005

Judge, Mike, American motion picture director and animator, May 1997

July, Miranda, American performance artist and filmmaker, Nov 2007

Kabakov, Ilya, Russian painter and illustrator, Apr 1998

Kainen, Jacob, American painter and printmaker, Feb 1987, *Obit* Aug 2001

Kandinsky, Wassily, Russian painter, *Obit* Feb 1945

Kapoor, Anish, Indian-British video artist and sculptor, Sept 2013

Karfiol, Bernard, Nov 1947, *Obit* Oct 1952

Karsh, Yousuf, Canadian photographer, Yrbk 1952, Feb 1980, *Obit* Nov 2002

Katchor, Ben, American cartoonist, May 2000

Katz, Alex, American painter, July 1975

Kay-Scott, Cyril, Feb 1944

Kcho, Cuban installation artist, Aug 2001

Keith, Dora Wheeler, American painter, *Obit* Feb 1941

Kelly, Ellsworth, American painter and sculptor, May 1970

Kelly, Walt, American cartoonist, Oct 1956, *Obit* Yrbk 1973

Kent, Corita, American artist and nun, Feb 1969, *Obit* Nov 1986

Kent, Rockwell, American painter and travel writer, Nov 1942, *Obit* Apr 1971

Kentridge, William, South African artist, Oct 2001

Kepes, Gyorgy, Hungarian-American painter, graphic designer and art critic, Mar 1973, *Obit* Mar 2002

Kertesz, Andre, American photographer, Aug 1979, *Obit* Nov 1985

Ketcham, Hank, American cartoonist, Jan 1956, *Obit* Sept 2001

Kienholz, Edward, American painter and sculptor, Aug 1989, *Obit* Aug 1994

Kiesler, Frederick, Austrian-Ameican sculptor and

architect, Jan 1944, *Obit* Feb 1966

Kingman, Dong, American painter and illustrator, Oct 1962, *Obit* Yrbk 2000

Kinkade, Thomas, American painter, June 2000, *Obit* Yrbk 2012

Kirby, Rollin, Yrbk 1944, *Obit* June 1952

Kitaj, R. B., American painter, Apr 1982, *Obit* Yrbk 2008

Klawe, Maria, Canadian computer scientist, college dean and painter, June 2013

Klee, Paul, Swiss painter, *Obit* Aug 1940

Klein, William, American photographer, Mar 2004

Knaths, Karl, painter, July 1953, *Obit* Apr 1971

Knox, Simmie, American painter, May 2009

Koch, John, American painter, May 1965, *Obit* June 1978

Kokoschka, Oskar, Austrian painter and dramatist, Oct 1956, *Obit* Apr 1980

Kolar, Jiri, Czech poet and artist, Apr 1986, *Obit* Yrbk 2002

Komar, Vitali, Russian painter, Oct 1984

Konijnenburg, Willem Adriaan van, *Obit* Apr 1943

Koons, Jeff, American artist, May 1990

Koussevitzky, Natalya, *Obit* Mar 1942

Kramer, Edward Adam, *Obit* Feb 1942

Krasner, Lee, American painter, Mar 1974, *Obit* Aug 1984

Krohg, Per, Nov 1954

Kroll, Leon, American painter, Mar 1943, *Obit* Yrbk 1974

Kruger, Barbara, American artist, July 1995

Kruger-Gray, George, *Obit* June 1943

Kuekes, Edward D., cartoonist, Mar 1954, *Obit* Mar 1987

Kuniyoshi, Yasuo, Japanese-American painter, June 1941, *Obit* June 1953

LaChapelle, David, American photographer, June 2008

Lalupu Flores, Wilmer, Peruvian painter, Jan 2005

Lancaster, Osbert, English satirist and cartoonist, Oct 1964, *Obit* Sept 1986

Landau, Jacob, illustrator, Yrbk 1965

Lang, Robert J., American physicist and origami artist, July 2007

Lansdowne, J. Fenwick, May 1970

Lanting, Frans, Dutch-American photographer, Nov 1995

Larson, Gary, American cartoonist, Feb 1991

Lassaw, Ibram, American sculptor, Jan 1957, *Obit* Yrbk 2004

Lasseter, John, American animator, screenwriter and director, June 1997

Laurent, Robert, July 1942, *Obit* June 1970

Lavery, John, Irish painter, *Obit* Mar 1941

Lawrence, Jacob, American painter and illustrator, July 1965, Sept 1988, *Obit* Aug 2000

Lawson, Robert, Anerican children's author and illustrator, Oct 1941, *Obit* Oct 1957

LeWitt, Sol, American sculptor, July 1986, *Obit* Yrbk 2007

Leboyer, Frederick, July 1982

Lebrun, Rico, Sept 1952, *Obit* July 1964

Lee, Doris Emrick, American painter and illustrator, Jan 1954, *Obit* Jan 1986

Lee, Jim, Artist and co-publisher of DC Comics, Apr 2012

Lee, Ming Cho, Chinese-American set designer, June 1989

Leibovitz, Annie, American photographer, Oct 1991

Lemon, Ralph, American dancer and choreographer, Feb 1997

Leunig, Michael, Australian cartoonist and poet, Jan 2006

Levi, Carlo, Italian novelist, journalist and painter, Yrbk 1952, *Obit* Feb 1975

Levi, Julian, Apr 1943, *Obit* Apr 1982

Levine, David, American caricaturist, Feb 1973, *Obit* Yrbk 2010

Levine, Jack, American painter, June 1956, *Obit* Yrbk 2011

Liberman, Alexander, American artist and magazine executive, May 1987, *Obit* Mar 2000

Lichtenstein, Roy, American painter, Feb 1969, *Obit* Jan 1998

Lie, Jonas, Norwegian-American painter, Jan 1940

Liebes, Dorothy, American textile designer, Apr 1948, *Obit* Yrbk 1972

Lin, Maya Ying, American architect and sculptor, Apr 1993

Link, O. Winston, American photographer, June 1995, *Obit* Apr 2001

Linton, Frank B. A., *Obit* Jan 1944

Lionni, Leo, American children's author and illustrator, Sept 1997, *Obit* Feb 2000

Lipchitz, Jacques, French sculptor, Nov 1948, Apr 1962, *Obit* July 1973

Lippold, Richard, American sculptor, Nov 1956, *Obit* Yrbk 2002

Lipton, Seymour, American sculptor, Nov 1964, *Obit* Feb 1987

Little, Philip, *Obit* May 1942

Liu Bolin, Chinese painter and photographer, Nov 2013

Liu, Hung, Chinese artist, Jan 2002

Liu, Lucy, American actress and artist, Oct 2003

Llewellyn, William, *Obit* Mar 1941

Lober, Georg John, Nov 1957, *Obit* Feb 1962

Lollobrigida, Gina, Italian actress, Sept 1960

Long, Richard, English artist, Sept 1995

Longo, Robert, American artist, Oct 1990

Loquasto, Santo, scenic designer, June 1981

Losch, Tilly, July 1944, *Obit* Feb 1976

Lou, Liza, American bead artist, Jan 2000

Low, David, New Zealand cartoonist, Jan 1940, *Obit* Nov 1963

Lozowick, Louis, American painter, Apr 1942, *Obit* Nov 1973

Lucioni, Luigi, painter, Oct 1943, *Obit* Sept 1988

Luckovich, Mike, American editorial cartoonist, Jan 2005

Lurcat, Jean, French painter and tapestry designer, Sept 1948, *Obit* Feb 1966

MacDonald, Pirie, *Obit* June 1942

MacEwen, Walter, *Obit* May 1943

MacFarlane, Seth, American animator, television scriptwriter, producer and voice-over artist, May 2010

MacIver, Loren, American painter, Nov 1953, Nov 1987, *Obit* Aug 1998

MacKenzie, Warren, potter, Sept 1994

Mahlangu, Esther, South African painter, Jan 2007

Maillol, Aristide, French sculptor and illustrator, May 1942, *Obit* Nov 1944

Malkin, Peter Z., Israeli intelligence agent, Jan 2003

Manessier, Alfred, French painter, May 1957, *Obit* Oct 1993

Mankoff, Robert, American cartoonist, May 2005

Manning, Reg, June 1951

Manship, Paul, American sculptor, May 1940, *Obit* Mar 1966

Mapplethorpe, Robert, American photographer and art collector, May 1989, *Obit* May 1989

Marca-Relli, Conrad, American collage artist, Sept 1970, *Obit* Nov 2000

Marden, Brice, American painter and printmaker, Aug 1990

Marin, John, American painter, July 1949, *Obit* Yrbk 1953

Marini, Marino, Italian sculptor, Jan 1954, *Obit* Oct 1980

Marisol, Venezuelan sculptor, Apr 1968

Mark, Louis, *Obit* May 1942

Mark, Mary Ellen, American photographer, Sept 1999

Marlette, Doug, American editorial cartoonist, July 2002, *Obit* Yrbk 2007

Marsh, Reginald, American painter, Sept 1941, *Obit* Sept 1954

Martin, Agnes, American painter, Sept 1989, *Obit* Apr 2005

Martin, Fletcher, Feb 1958, *Obit* July 1979

Martin, Jackie, Apr 1943

Masson, Andre, French painter and stage designer, Nov 1974, *Obit* Jan 1988

Mastroianni, Umberto, Sept 1960

Matisse, Henri, French painter, May 1943, June 1953, *Obit* Jan 1955

Matta, Chilean painter, Nov 1957, *Obit* Yrbk 2003

Mattson, Henry, Jan 1956, *Obit* Nov 1971

Mauldin, Bill, American cartoonist, May 1945, Nov 1964, *Obit* July 2003

Max, Peter, American artist, May 1971

McCloskey, Robert, American children's author and illustrator, Sept 1942, *Obit* Yrbk 2003

McCracken, Craig, American animator, Feb 2004

McDowall, Roddy, actor and photographer, Apr 1961, *Obit* Jan 1999

McFarlane, Todd, Canadian cartoonist, Feb 1999

McGruder, Aaron, American cartoonist, Sept 2001

McGuire, William Anthony, *Obit* Nov 1940

McMein, Neysa, illustrator and painter, Feb 1941, *Obit* June 1949

McPharlin, Paul, American puppeteer, Nov 1945, *Obit* Nov 1948

Mechau, Frank Albert, American painter, *Obit* Apr 1946

Mehretu, Julie, American artist, July 2010

Mehta, Tyeb, Indian painter, Jan 2006

Meireles, Cildo, Brazilian installation artist and sculptor, Jan 2004

Meiselas, Susan, American photographer, Feb 2005

Melamid, Aleksandr, Russian painter, Oct 1984

Messick, Dale, American cartoonist, July 1961, *Obit* Yrbk 2005

Meyerowitz, William, American etcher and painter, May 1942

Michals, Duane, American photographer, Apr 1981

Mielziner, Jo, Mar 1946, *Obit* May 1976

Milles, Carl, sculptor, Yrbk 1940, Yrbk 1952, *Obit* Nov 1955

Millett, Kate, American feminist, artist and memoirist, Jan 1971, June 1995

Millionaire, Tony, American cartoonist and illustrator, July 2005

Miranda, Mario de, Indian cartoonist and illustrator, Jan 2003

Miro, Joan, Spanish painter, May 1940, Nov 1973, *Obit* Feb 1984

Mitchell, Dean, American painter, Aug 2002

Mitchell, Joan, American painter, Mar 1986, *Obit* Jan 1993

Miyajima, Tatsuo, Japanese installation artist, Jan 2006

Miyazaki, Hayao, Japanese animator, Apr 2001

Moen, Lars, May 1941

Moffett, Mark W., American ecologist and photographer, Oct 2011

Moiseiwitsch, Tanya, English stage and costume designer, Nov 1955, *Obit* July 2003

Mondrian, Piet, Dutch painter, *Obit* Mar 1944

Montresor, Beni, Italian scenic designer, illustrator and children's author, Yrbk 1967, *Obit* Feb 2002

Moore, Henry, English sculptor, Feb 1954, Feb 1978, *Obit* Oct 1986

Mora, Francis Luis, American painter, *Obit* July 1940

Moran, John, American composer, performance artist and choreographer, June 2010

Moran, Leon, *Obit* Oct 1941

Morehouse, Ward, Jan 1940, *Obit* Feb 1967

Morris, Wright, American novelist, short story writer and critic, May 1982, *Obit* July 1998

Moses, Grandma, American painter, Jan 1949, *Obit* Feb 1962

Motherwell, Robert, American artist, Nov 1962, *Obit* Sept 1991

Mugler, Thierry, French fashion designer and photographer, Aug 2010

Munch, Edvard, Norwegian painter, Yrbk 1940, *Obit* Mar 1944

Murray, Elizabeth, American painter, Apr 1995, *Obit* Yrbk 2007

Myers, Jerome, *Obit* Aug 1940

Nakian, Reuben, sculptor, Feb 1985, *Obit* Feb 1987

Nara, Yoshitomo, Japanese installation artist, Jan 2005

Nash, Paul, English illustrator and painter, *Obit* Sept 1946

Nauman, Bruce, American artist, Nov 1990

Neals, Otto, American sculptor and painter, Feb 2003

Neel, Alice, American painter, Aug 1976, *Obit* Jan 1985

Neiman, LeRoy, American painter, July 1996, *Obit* Yrbk 2012

Neshat, Shirin, Iranian photographer and video artist, Jan 2002

Neto, Ernesto, Brazilian artist, Oct 2009

Nevelson, Louise, American sculptor, Oct 1967, *Obit* May 1988

Nevinson, Christopher Richard Wynne, English painter, *Obit* Nov 1946

Newkirk, Kori, American mixed media and installation artist, Mar 2008

Newman, Arnold, American photographer, Oct 1980, *Obit* Yrbk 2006

Newman, Barnett, American painter, Sept 1969, *Obit* Sept 1970

Newton, Helmut, German photographer, Nov 1991, *Obit* Yrbk 2004

Nicholson, Ben, English painter, Jan 1958, *Obit* Apr 1982

Noguchi, Isamu, American sculptor, Sept 1943, *Obit* Feb 1989

Noland, Kenneth, American painter, Sept 1972, *Obit* Yrbk 2010

Nutting, Wallace, American clergyman, photographer and furniture executive, *Obit* Sept 1941

O'Connor, Andrew, *Obit* Aug 1941

O'Gorman, Juan, Mexican architect and painter, Nov 1956

O'Keeffe, Georgia, American painter, June 1941, Feb 1964, *Obit* Apr 1986

O'Neil, George, *Obit* July 1940

Oberteuffer, George, *Obit* Jan 1940

Oenslager, Donald, Sept 1946, *Obit* Aug 1975

Olafur Eliasson, Icelandic artist, Jan 2007

Oliphant, Patrick, Australian-American cartoonist, July 1991

Olitski, Jules, American painter, Oct 1969, *Obit* Yrbk 2007

Ono, Yoko, Japanese artist, Nov 1972

Orozco, Gabriel, Mexican conceptual artist, Jan 2004

Osborn, Robert, caricaturist, June 1959, *Obit* Feb 1995

Oshii, Mamoru, Japanese animator, Jan 2006

Packer, Fred L., July 1952, *Obit* Feb 1957

Page, Marie Danforth, *Obit* Mar 1940

Paik, Nam June, Korean video artist and composer, Mar 1983, *Obit* Yrbk 2006

Palmer, James Lynwood, English painter, *Obit* Aug 1941

Parrish, Maxfield, American illustrator and painter, Nov 1965, *Obit* Apr 1966

Partridge, Bernard, *Obit* Sept 1945

Passmore, George, English artist, June 2009

Paxton, William McGregor, painter, *Obit* July 1941

Pearlstein, Philip, American painter, Feb 1973

Pease, Lute, political cartoonist and painter, July 1949, *Obit* Nov 1963

Peirce, Waldo, American painter, Yrbk 1944, *Obit* May 1970

Peixotto, Ernest C., *Obit* Jan 1941

Pelosini, Paolo, Italian sculptor, Jan 2005

Penn, Irving, American photographer, Nov 1980, *Obit* Yrbk 2009

Pereira, Irene Rice, American painter, Nov 1953, *Obit* Feb 1971

Perez Esquivel, Adolfo, Argentine human rights activist, Mar 1981

Peterson, Roger Tory, American ornithologist and illustrator, Apr 1959, *Obit* Oct 1996

Pettibon, Raymond, American artist, Apr 2005

Pevsner, Antoine, Russian sculptor, Mar 1959, *Obit* June 1962

Picasso, Pablo, Spanish painter, Jan 1943, Nov 1962, *Obit* May 1973

Pippin, Horace, American painter, Aug 1945, *Obit* Yrbk 1947

Plowden, David, photographer, Feb 1996

Ponnelle, Jean-Pierre, French scenic designer and opera director, Mar 1983, *Obit* Sept 1988

Poor, Henry Varnum, American ceramist and painter, Apr 1942, *Obit* Jan 1971

Poore, Henry Rankin, *Obit* Oct 1940

Porter, Eliot, American photographer, Nov 1976, *Obit* Jan 1991

Portinari, Candido, Brazilian painter, Yrbk 1940, *Obit* Mar 1962

Potter, Beatrix, English children's author and illustrator, *Obit* Mar 1944

Pousette-Dart, Richard, painter, Mar 1976, *Obit* Jan 1993

Prellwitz, Henry, *Obit* Apr 1940

Prestopino, Gregorio, painter, June 1964, *Obit* Apr 1985

Proesch, Gilbert, English artist, June 2009

Puryear, Martin, American sculptor, Aug 1999

Quintanilla, Luis, Spanish painter and etcher, Nov 1940

Rall, Ted, American editorial cartoonist, May 2002

Rama, Edi, Albanian artist and mayor, Jan 2005

Rand, Ellen G. Emmet, American painter, *Obit* Feb 1942

Rattner, Abraham, American painter, Mar 1948, *Obit* Apr 1978

Rauch, Neo, German painter, Jan 2007

Rauschenberg, Robert, American artist, Oct 1965, Oct 1987, *Obit* Aug 2008

Rautenberg, Robert, Mar 1940

Ray, Man, American painter and photographer, Yrbk 1965, *Obit* Jan 1977

Ray, Satyajit, Indian motion picture director, Mar 1961, *Obit* June 1992

Rea, Gardner, May 1946, *Obit* Feb 1967

Redpath, Anne, Jan 1957, *Obit* Mar 1965

Richard, Louis, *Obit* Sept 1940

Rickey, George W., American sculptor, Feb 1980, *Obit* Yrbk 2002

Ringgold, Faith, American artist, children's author and illustrator, Feb 1996

Riopelle, Jean-Paul, Canadian painter and sculptor, Oct 1989, *Obit* Sept 2002

Ripley, Elizabeth, Yrbk 1958

Ripley, Robert Le Roy, cartoonist and adventurer, July 1945, *Obit* July 1949

Rirkrit Tiravanija, Thai installation artist, Jan 2005

Rist, Pipilotti, Swiss video artist, Jan 2005

Roberts, Goodridge, Canadian painter, May 1955

Robinson, Boardman, Yrbk 1941, *Obit* Oct 1952

Robinson, William Heath, English illustrator, *Obit* Nov 1944

Robus, Hugo, Yrbk 1962, *Obit* Feb 1964

Rockwell, Norman, American painter, June 1945, *Obit* Jan 1979

Rollins, Henry, American performance artist, poet and singer, Sept 2001

Romano, Emanuel, painter and illustrator, Mar 1940, *Obit* Feb 1985

Romano, Umberto, Mar 1954, *Obit* Nov 1982

Rose, Jim, American performance artist, Mar 2003

Ross, Alex, American comic book artist, Nov 2007

Roszak, Theodore J., Polish-American painter and

sculptor, June 1966, *Obit* Oct 1981

Rothenberg, Susan, American painter and printmaker, Mar 1985

Rothenstein, William, English painter, *Obit* Apr 1945

Rothko, Mark, American painter, May 1961, *Obit* Apr 1970

Rouault, Georges, French painter, May 1945, *Obit* Apr 1958

Rubin, Reuven, Apr 1943, *Obit* Jan 1975

Ruckstull, Frederick Wellington, sculptor, *Obit* July 1942

Ruscha, Edward, American painter, printmaker and photographer, Oct 1989

Sacco, Joe, Maltese cartoonist and journalist, Jan 2013

Salle, David, American painter and filmmaker, Sept 1986

Salvador Lavado, Joaquin, Argentine cartoonist, Jan 2004

Samaras, Lucas, American sculptor, painter and photographer, Nov 1972

Sarg, Tony, German-American puppeteer and illustrator, *Obit* Apr 1942

Satrapi, Marjane, Iranian graphic novelist, illustrator and memoirist, Jan 2003

Savage, Augusta Christine, American sculptor, Jan 1941, *Obit* May 1962

Sawyer, Helen, painter, Oct 1954

Scavullo, Francesco, American fashion photographer, May 1985, *Obit* Yrbk 2004

Schapiro, Miriam, American artist, Aug 2000

Scharf, Kenny, American painter, Feb 2012

Schnabel, Julian, American painter and film director, Nov 1983

Scholder, Fritz, American painter, Apr 1985, *Obit* Yrbk 2005

Schreiber, Georges, author and illustrator, May 1943

Schulz, Charles M., American cartoonist, Yrbk 1960, *Obit* Apr 2000

Scott, Peter Markham, English ornithologist and painter, May 1968, *Obit* Nov 1989

Scudder, Janet, painter and sculptor, *Obit* July 1940

Segal, George, American sculptor, Jan 1972, *Obit* Sept 2000

Selick, Henry, American film director, May 2009

Sempe, French cartoonist and illustrator, Jan 2007

Sendak, Maurice, American children's author and illustrator, June 1968, June 1989, *Obit* Yrbk 2012

Seredy, Kate, American children's author and illustrator, May 1940, *Obit* May 1975

Serra, Richard, American sculptor, Jan 1985

Sert, Jose Maria, Spanish painter, *Obit* Jan 1946

Seton, Ernest Thompson, Anglo-American writer, illustrator and naturalist, May 1943, *Obit* Yrbk 1946

Seuss, American children's author and illustrator, Feb 1968, *Obit* Nov 1991

Shahn, Ben, American painter, Yrbk 1954, *Obit* May 1969

Shaw, Dash, American comic book artist and graphic novelist, Jan 2009

Sheckell, Thomas O., *Obit* Apr 1943

Sheeler, Charles, American painter and photographer, Nov 1950, *Obit* June 1965

Shepard, Ernest H., English painter and illustrator, Yrbk 1963, *Obit* May 1976

Sherman, Cindy, American photographer, Oct 1990

Shikler, Aaron, painter, Yrbk 1971

Shinn, Everett, painter, May 1951, *Obit* June 1953

Shinn, Florence Scovel, *Obit* Yrbk 1940

Sidibe, Malick, Malian photographer, Jan 2004

Sigismondi, Floria, Canadian photographer and video and film director, July 2010

Simonson, Lee, Nov 1947, *Obit* Mar 1967

Simpson, Lorna, American photographer and video artist, Nov 2004

Siqueiros, David Alfaro, Mexican painter, June 1959, *Obit* Feb 1974

Slade, Roy, museum director, painter and educator, June 1985

Sloane, Eric, painter and author, Sept 1972, *Obit* May 1985

Slobodkin, Louis, author and illustrator, Apr 1957, *Obit* Aug 1975

Smith, Kiki, American painter, sculptor and printmaker, Mar 2005

Smith, Oliver, American set designer, Sept 1961, *Obit* Mar 1994

Snell, Henry Bayley, *Obit* Mar 1943

Snowdon, Antony Armstrong-Jones, English photographer, Oct 1960

Soglow, Otto, cartoonist, Sept 1940, *Obit* May 1975

Sorel, Edward, cartoonist, Mar 1994

Soto, Jesus Raphael, Venezuelan painter and sculptor, Jan 2004

Soyer, Isaac, American painter, Mar 1941, *Obit* Sept 1981

Soyer, Moses, American painter, Mar 1941, *Obit* Oct 1974

Soyer, Raphael, American painter, Mar 1941, *Obit* Jan 1988

Speicher, Eugene Edward, American painter, Oct 1947, *Obit* July 1962

Sperry, Armstrong, American children's author and illustrator, Oct 1941

Spiegelman, Art, American cartoonist, Mar 1994

St. George, Thomas Richard, Jan 1944

Stamos, Theodoros, painter, Jan 1959, *Obit* Apr 1997

Stankiewicz, Richard, American sculptor, June 1967, *Obit* May 1983

Stanton, Andrew, American film director, screenwriter and animator, Feb 2004

Steadman, Ralph, English illustrator, May 1999

Steele, Frederic Dorr, *Obit* Aug 1944

Steichen, Edward, American photographer, Oct 1942, Yrbk 1964, *Obit* May 1973

Steig, William, American illustrator and children's author, July 1944, *Obit* Apr 2004

Steinmetz, George, American photographer, July 2013

Stella, Joseph, painter, *Obit* Yrbk 1946

Sterne, Hedda, American painter, Mar 1957, *Obit* Yrbk 2011

Sterne, Maurice, American painter, Apr 1943, *Obit* Oct 1957

Stieglitz, Alfred, American photographer, Jan 1940, *Obit* Sept 1946

Still, Clyfford, American painter, Sept 1971, *Obit* Aug 1980

Stoddard, Frederick Lincoln, *Obit* Mar 1940

Strand, Paul, American photographer, July 1965, *Obit* May 1976

Strawbridge, Anne West, *Obit* Nov 1941

Struzan, Drew, American poster artist, Mar 2005

Stuart, James Everett, painter, *Obit* Feb 1941

Sutherland, Graham Vivian, English painter, Jan 1955, *Obit* Apr 1980

Suydam, E. H., *Obit* Feb 1941

Svankmajer, Jan, Czech animator and motion picture director, Jan 2006

Switzer, George, American industrial designer and art director, *Obit* Yrbk 1940

Sykes, Charles H., *Obit* Feb 1943

Szyk, Arthur, Polish cartoonist, illustrator and miniaturist, Nov 1946, *Obit* Oct 1951

Taintor, Anne, American artist and entrepreneur, June 2005

Takahashi, Rumiko, Japanese cartoonist and comic book writer, Jan 2005

Tamayo, Rufino, Mexican painter, Mar 1953, *Obit* Aug 1991

Tan, Shaun, Australian illustrator, Mar 2012

Tanning, Dorothea, American artist, *Obit* Yrbk 2012

Taubes, Frederic, Mar 1943

Taylor, Richard, June 1941, *Obit* July 1970

Taylor, Ron, Australian photographer and skin diver, Jan 2007, *Obit* Yrbk 2012

Taylor, Valerie, Australian skin diver and photographer, Jan 2007

Taymor, Julie, American theatrical director and designer, Feb 1998

Tchelitchew, Pavel, Russian painter, Mar 1943, *Obit* Oct 1957

Teale, Edwin Way, American naturalist and nature writer, Yrbk 1961, *Obit* Jan 1981

Teller, Juergen, German photographer, Jan 2004

Ter-Arutunian, Rouben, Russian stage designer, June 1963, *Obit* Jan 1993

Testino, Mario, Peruvian fashion photographer, Jan 2006

Thiebaud, Wayne, American painter and teacher, Mar 1987

Throckmorton, Cleon, Sept 1943, *Obit* Yrbk 1965

Thurber, James, American cartoonist and humorist, Mar 1940, Oct 1960, *Obit* Jan 1962

Tice, George A., American photographer, Nov 2003

Tinguely, Jean, Swiss artist, Jan 1966, *Obit* Oct 1991

Titchner, Mark, English installation artist, Jan 2007

Tobey, Mark, American painter, Mar 1957, *Obit* June 1976

Toles, Tom, American cartoonist, Nov 2002

Tomorrow, Tom, American political cartoonist, Apr 2000

Tooker, George, American painter, Mar 1958, *Obit* Yrbk 2011

Torrey, George Burroughs, painter, *Obit* June 1942

Toscani, Oliviero, Italian photographer, Sept 1998

Townsend, Harry Everett, *Obit* Oct 1941

Trudeau, G. B., American cartoonist, Aug 1975

Tsereteli, Zurab, Russian sculptor, Jan 2007

Turrell, James, American artist, May 1999

Tuttle, Emerson, *Obit* Apr 1946

Tuymans, Luc, Belgian painter, Jan 2007

Twombly, Cy, American painter, Apr 1988, *Obit* Yrbk 2011

Tworkov, Jack, American painter, Mar 1964, *Obit* Oct 1982

Uderzo, French cartoonist, Jan 2006

Underwood, Bert E., *Obit* Feb 1944

Utrillo, Maurice, French painter, Sept 1953, *Obit* Jan 1956

Van Allsburg, Chris, American children's author and illustrator, Sept 1996

Van Doren, Harold L., May 1940, *Obit* Apr 1957

Van Loen, Alfred, Feb 1961

Van Loon, Hendrik Willem, Dutch-American historian, *Obit* Apr 1944

Vandivert, William, Mar 1963

Vangi, Giuliano, Italian sculptor, Jan 2003

Varian, Dorothy, Jan 1943

Vasarely, Victor, Hungarian-French artist, Feb 1971, *Obit* May 1997

Verhoeven, Julie, English fashion illustrator, Apr 2012

Vertes, Marcel, Hungarian painter and illustrator, Apr 1961, *Obit* Jan 1962

Vezin, Charles, *Obit* May 1942

Vieira da Silva, Maria Helena, Portuguese painter, Yrbk 1958, *Obit* May 1992

Villon, Jacques, French painter and engraver, Jan 1956, *Obit* July 1963

Viola, Bill, American video artist, May 1998

Vip, cartoonist, July 1946, *Obit* Oct 1984

Vishniac, Roman, American biologist and photographer, Feb 1967, *Obit* Mar 1990

Von Wicht, John, Jan 1963, *Obit* Mar 1970

Voulkos, Peter, American sculptor and ceramist, Nov 1997, *Obit* Aug 2002

Wales, George C., *Obit* May 1940

Walker, Kara, American silhouette artist, Mar 2000

Walker, Mort, American cartoonist, Feb 2002

Wall, Jeff, Canadian artist and photographer, Jan 2007

Warhol, Andy, American artist, Feb 1968, July 1986, *Obit* Apr 1987

Washburn, Bradford, American photographer, explorer and museum director, June 1966, *Obit* Yrbk 2007

Washington, Alonzo, American comic book artist and publisher, May 1999

Watrous, Harry Willson, painter, *Obit* Jan 1940

Waugh, Frederick Judd, *Obit* Oct 1940

Waugh, Sidney, July 1948, *Obit* Sept 1963

Webster, H. T., cartoonist, Mar 1945, *Obit* Nov 1952

Wegman, William, American artist, May 1992

Weil, Lisl, Jan 1958

Weiss, Peter, German dramatist, novelist and painter, Apr 1968, *Obit* July 1982

Wenner, Kurt, American street artist, Sept 2011

Werner, Theodor, Yrbk 1958

Werntz, Carl N., *Obit* Yrbk 1944

West, Levon, Feb 1948, *Obit* June 1968

Weston, Brett, photographer, Feb 1982, *Obit* Mar 1993

Wheelock, Warren, Mar 1940, *Obit* Oct 1960

Whitney, Gertrude Vanderbilt, American sculptor and art patron, July 1941, *Obit* Yrbk 1942

Wiley, Kehinde, American painter, Aug 2007

Willet, Anne Lee, *Obit* Mar 1943

Willet, Henry Lee, Mar 1947

Williams, Gluyas, cartoonist, June 1946, *Obit* Apr 1982

Willis, Deborah, American photography historian and museum curator, Sept 2004

Wiltshire, Stephen, English artist, Jan 2007

Winter, Fritz, German painter, Mar 1958

Wolfe, Art, American photographer, June 2005

Wood, Grant, American painter, Aug 1940, *Obit* Apr 1942

Woodard, Stacy, *Obit* Mar 1942

Woodbury, Charles Herbert, painter, *Obit* Jan 1940

Wyeth, Andrew, American painter, Apr 1955, Nov 1981, *Obit* Yrbk 2009

Wyeth, Jamie, American painter, Jan 1977

Wyeth, N. C., American painter and illustrator, *Obit* Nov 1945

Yamamura, Koji, Japanese animator, Jan 2003

Yang Fuxi, Chinese bow and arrow maker, Jan 2007

Yarrow, William, *Obit* June 1941

Yellin, Samuel, American metalsmith, *Obit* Nov 1940

Young, Art, cartoonist, Feb 1940, *Obit* Feb 1944

Young, Charles Jac, *Obit* Apr 1940

Young, Joseph Louis, American sculptor and muralist, July 1960

Youngerman, Jack, painter, Nov 1986

Yuh Nelson, Jennifer, Korean-American animator and film director, Nov 2013

Zadkine, Ossip, Russian sculptor, Mar 1957, *Obit* Jan 1968

Zao, Wou-ki, French painter, *Obit* Yrbk 2013

Zapf, Hermann, German typographer and calligrapher, Jan 1965

Zeffirelli, Franco, Italian director and set designer, Yrbk 1964

Zerbe, Karl, Feb 1959, *Obit* Jan 1973

Zhang Xiaogang, Chinese painter, Jan 2005

Zhou Hai, Chinese photographer, Jan 2003

Zittel, Andrea, American installation artist, Aug 2006

Zollar, Jawole Willa Jo, American dancer and performance artist, July 2003

Zorach, William, American sculptor and painter, Feb 1943, Feb 1963, *Obit* Jan 1967

Zuloaga, Ignacio, Spanish art collector and painter, *Obit* Yrbk 1945

Arts administrators

Alexander, Jane, American actress and government official, Feb 1977

Chapin, Schuyler, American municipal arts administrator, Feb 1974, *Obit* Yrbk 2009

Frohnmayer, John E., lawyer and government official, Apr 1990

Hanks, Nancy, American government official, Sept 1971, *Obit* Mar 1983

Hart, Kitty Carlisle, American singer, actress and state official, Oct 1982, *Obit* Yrbk 2007

Menotti, Gian Carlo, Italian composer and librettist, Yrbk 1947, Jan 1979, *Obit* Yrbk 2007

Sloan, George A., Jan 1952, *Obit* July 1955

Straight, Michael Whitney, American magazine editor, publisher, arts administrator and memoirist, Aug 1944, *Obit* Yrbk 2004

Asian studies specialists

Crow, Carl, American journalist, Oct 1941, *Obit* July 1945

Fairbank, John King, American Sinologist, Oct 1966, *Obit* Nov 1991

Fedorenko, Nikolai T., Yrbk 1967

Hitti, Philip Khuri, June 1947, *Obit* Feb 1979

Keene, Donald, American Japanologist, Jan 1988

Latourette, Kenneth Scott, Sinologist and church historian, Nov 1953, *Obit* Mar 1969

Lattimore, Owen, American Sinologist, Yrbk 1945, July 1964, *Obit* July 1989

Mears, Helen, American Japanologist, Mar 1943

Myers, B. R., American Korean studies specialist, June 2010

Olmstead, A. T., *Obit* May 1945

Payne, Robert, English author, Yrbk 1947, *Obit* Apr 1983

Reischauer, Edwin O., American historian and diplomat, May 1962, *Obit* Nov 1990

Zimmer, Heinrich Robert, German Indologist, *Obit* May 1943

Astrologers

Dixon, Jeane, American astrologer and psychic, Feb 1973, *Obit* Mar 1997

Kingsley, Myra, Apr 1943

Righter, Carroll, astrologer, Oct 1972, *Obit* June 1988

Astronauts

Armstrong, Neil, American astronaut, Oct 1969, *Obit* Yrbk 2012

Bolden, Charles, American astronaut and NASA official, July 2010

Burbank, Daniel, Astronaut, Sept 2012

Carpenter, Scott, American astronaut, Sept 1962

Cernan, Eugene A., American astronaut and business consultant, May 1973

Chang-Diaz, Franklin R., American astronaut and physicist, Aug 2011

Conrad, Pete, American astronaut, Yrbk 1965

Currie, Nancy, American astronaut, June 2002

Dwight, Edward J., American astronaut and sculptor, July 2007

Feoktistov, Konstantin Petrovich, Soviet astronaut and aerospace engineer, Nov 1967, *Obit* Yrbk 2010

Gagarin, Yuri, Soviet cosmonaut, Oct 1961, *Obit* May 1968

Glenn, John, American astronaut and senator, June 1962, Mar 1976, Jan 1999

Grissom, Gus, American astronaut, Nov 1965, *Obit* Mar 1967

Haignere, Claudie, French astronaut and cabinet member, Jan 2003

Jemison, Mae C., American physician and astronaut, July 1993

Kuipers, Andre, Dutch physician and astronaut, Jan 2004

Lovell, Jim, American astronaut, Mar 1969

Ride, Sally K., American astronaut and astrophysicist, Oct 1983, *Obit* Yrbk 2012

Schirra, Wally, American astronaut, June 1966, *Obit* Yrbk 2007

Schmitt, Harrison H., American senator, geologist and astronaut, July 1974

Shepard, Alan B., American astronaut and real estate executive, Yrbk 1961, *Obit* Sept 1998

Shuttleworth, Mark, South African entrepreneur, Jan 2007

Slayton, Donald Kent, astronaut and aerospace executive, Feb 1976, *Obit* Aug 1993

Tereshkova, Valentina, Soviet astronaut, Yrbk 1963

White, Edward Higgins, American astronaut, Nov 1965, *Obit* Mar 1967

Whitson, Peggy A., American biochemist and astronaut, Sept 2003

Williams, Sunita L., American astronaut, Mar 2013

Yegorov, Boris, Soviet astronaut and physician, Mar 1968, *Obit* Nov 1994

Young, John, American astronaut, June 1965

Astronomers

Bahcall, John N., American astrophysicist, Apr 2000, *Obit* Yrbk 2007

Barton, William H., American astronomer and planetarium curator, *Obit* Aug 1944

Bell Burnell, Jocelyn, British astronomer, May 1995

Boss, Alan P., American astrophysicist, Apr 2010

Bowen, Ira S., astrophysicist, June 1951, *Obit* Apr 1973

Brouwer, Dirk, Mar 1951, *Obit* Mar 1966

Burbidge, Eleanor Margaret, Anglo-American astronomer, Nov 2000

Butler, R. Paul, American astrophysicist, Nov 2002

Cannon, Annie Jump, American astronomer, *Obit* June 1941

Chandrasekhar, Subrahmanyan, American astrophysicist, Mar 1986, *Obit* Oct 1995

Charyk, Joseph V., American government official and telecommunications executive, Yrbk 1970

Curtis, Heber D., American astronomer, *Obit* Mar 1942

Drake, Frank Donald, American astronomer, Jan 1963

Dugan, Raymond Smith, *Obit* Oct 1940

Eddington, Arthur Stanley, British astronomer, Apr 1941, *Obit* Yrbk 1991

Ellerman, Ferdinand, *Obit* Apr 1940

Ellis, George, South African mathematician and astronomer, Jan 2006

Faber, Sandra M., American astronomer, Apr 2002

Fang Lizhi, Chinese astrophysicist, Nov 1989, *Obit* Yrbk 2012

Fowler, Alfred, English astrophysicist, *Obit* Aug 1940

Friedman, Herbert, American astrophysicist, Sept 1963, *Obit* Nov 2000

Gaposchkin, Cecilia Helena Payne, astronomer, Yrbk 1957

Geha, Marla, American astronomer, June 2010

Geller, Margaret J., American astrophysicist, June 1997

Ghez, Andrea Mia, American astronomer, Nov 2010

Gold, Thomas, American astrophysicist, June 1966, *Obit* Yrbk 2004

Gott, J. Richard, astrophysicist, Oct 1999

Greenstein, Jesse Leonard, American astrophysicist, Sept 1963, *Obit* Yrbk 2003

Haber, Heinz, Yrbk 1952

Hagen, John P., astronomer, Oct 1957, *Obit* Nov 1990

Hasegawa, Ichiro, Japanese astronomer, Jan 2004

Hoyle, Fred, English astronomer and science fiction writer, Apr 1960, *Obit* Jan 2002

Hynek, J. Allen, astrophysicist, Yrbk 1968, *Obit* June 1986

Jones, Harold Spencer, British astronomer, Mar 1955, *Obit* Jan 1961

Jordan, Frank Craig, *Obit* Apr 1941

Kohoutek, Lubos, June 1974

Kopal, Zdenek, Czech astronomer, Mar 1969, *Obit* Aug 1993

Kozyrev, Nikolai A., Feb 1970

Kuiper, Gerard Peter, American astronomer, Feb 1959, *Obit* Feb 1974

Levin, Janna, American astrophysicist, Jan 2008

Levy, David H., Canadian science writer and amateur astronomer, Jan 1995

Lovell, Bernard, English astronomer, Oct 1959, *Obit* Yrbk 2012

Makemson, Maud Worcester, astronomer, June 1941

Marcy, Geoffrey W., American astrophysicist, Nov 2002

Massevitch, Alla G., Russian astronomer, Jan 1964

Mayor, Michel, Swiss astronomer, Jan 2007

McKay, Christopher P., American astrophysicist, Aug 2009

Menzel, Donald Howard, physicist and astronomer, Apr 1956, *Obit* Mar 1977

Moore, Patrick, English astronomy author and television program host, Jan 2003, *Obit* Yrbk 2013

Morehouse, Daniel Walter, *Obit* Mar 1941

Moulton, Forest Ray, American astronomer, Jan 1946, *Obit* Jan 1953

Nicolet, Marcel, Nov 1958

Nordmann, Charles, *Obit* Yrbk 1940

Oort, Jan Hendrik, Dutch astrophysicist, June 1969, *Obit* Jan 1993

Phillips, Theodore Evelyn Reece, *Obit* July 1942

Plaskett, John S., Canadian astronomer, *Obit* Yrbk 1941

Queloz, Didier, Swiss astrophysicist, Feb 2002

Rees, Martin J., British astronomer, Jan 2007

Ride, Sally K., American astronaut and astrophysicist, Oct 1983, *Obit* Yrbk 2012

Riess, Adam, American astrophysicist, Nov 2012

Roman, Nancy Grace, astronomer, Yrbk 1960

Ryle, Martin, British physicist and astronomer, Sept 1973, *Obit* Jan 1985

Sagan, Carl, American astronomer, Apr 1970, *Obit* Feb 1997

Sandage, Allan, American astronomer, Jan 1999, *Obit* Yrbk 2011

Schlesinger, Frank, astronomer, *Obit* Aug 1943

Schmidt, Maarten, Dutch astronomer, Sept 1966

Schwarzschild, Martin, astronomer, Feb 1967, *Obit* June 1997

Shapley, Harlow, astronomer, Jan 1941, Yrbk 1952, Yrbk 1972

Sitterly, Charlotte Moore, American astrophysicist, Jan 1962, *Obit* June 1990

Smoot, George, American astrophysicist, Apr 1994

Soderberg, Alicia, American astrophysicist, Oct 2009

Spergel, David N., American astrophysicist, Jan 2005

Spitzer, Lyman, American astrophysicist, Jan 1960, *Obit* June 1997

Squyres, Steve, American planetary geologist, Nov 2006

Struve, Otto, astronomer, Oct 1949, *Obit* June 1963

Swings, Pol, Belgian astronomer, Yrbk 1954

Tarter, Jill Cornell, American astrophysicist, Feb 2001

Thekaekara, Matthew P., May 1974

Tyson, Neil De Grasse, American astrophysicist, May 2000

Van Allen, James Alfred, American astrophysicist, Jan 1959, *Obit* Yrbk 2007

Wang Yongzhi, Chinese astrophysicist, Jan 2006

Whipple, Fred Lawrence, American astronomer, May 1952, *Obit* Yrbk 2005

Wright, Berlin H., *Obit* Jan 1941

Wright, Helen, astronomer, Mar 1956, *Obit* Feb 1998

Zwicky, Fritz, Swiss astronomer, Apr 1953, *Obit* Apr 1974

Astrophysicists

Bahcall, John N., American astrophysicist, Apr 2000, *Obit* Yrbk 2007

Boss, Alan P., American astrophysicist, Apr 2010

Bowen, Ira S., astrophysicist, June 1951, *Obit* Apr 1973

Butler, R. Paul, American astrophysicist, Nov 2002

Chandrasekhar, Subrahmanyan, American astrophysicist, Mar 1986, *Obit* Oct 1995

Charyk, Joseph V., American government official and

telecommunications executive, Yrbk 1970

Fang Lizhi, Chinese astrophysicist, Nov 1989, *Obit* Yrbk 2012

Filippenko, Alex, Oct 2013

Fowler, Alfred, English astrophysicist, *Obit* Aug 1940

Friedman, Herbert, American astrophysicist, Sept 1963, *Obit* Nov 2000

Geller, Margaret J., American astrophysicist, June 1997

Gold, Thomas, American astrophysicist, June 1966, *Obit* Yrbk 2004

Gott, J. Richard, astrophysicist, Oct 1999

Greenstein, Jesse Leonard, American astrophysicist, Sept 1963, *Obit* Yrbk 2003

Haber, Heinz, Yrbk 1952

Hynek, J. Allen, astrophysicist, Yrbk 1968, *Obit* June 1986

Levin, Janna, American astrophysicist, Jan 2008

Loeb, Abraham (Avi), July 2013

Marcy, Geoffrey W., American astrophysicist, Nov 2002

McKay, Christopher P., American astrophysicist, Aug 2009

Nicolet, Marcel, Nov 1958

Oort, Jan Hendrik, Dutch astrophysicist, June 1969, *Obit* Jan 1993

Queloz, Didier, Swiss astrophysicist, Feb 2002

Sagan, Carl, American astronomer, Apr 1970, *Obit* Feb 1997

Sitterly, Charlotte Moore, American astrophysicist, Jan 1962, *Obit* June 1990

Smoot, George, American astrophysicist, Apr 1994

Soderberg, Alicia, American astrophysicist, Oct 2009

Spergel, David N., American astrophysicist, Jan 2005

Spitzer, Lyman, American astrophysicist, Jan 1960, *Obit* June 1997

Tarter, Jill Cornell, American astrophysicist, Feb 2001

Thekaekara, Matthew P., May 1974

Tyson, Neil De Grasse, American astrophysicist, May 2000

Van Allen, James Alfred, American astrophysicist, Jan 1959, *Obit* Yrbk 2007

Wang Yongzhi, Chinese astrophysicist, Jan 2006

Atheists

Dawkins, Richard, British zoologist, Aug 1997

O'Hair, Madalyn Murray, American atheist, Jan 1977, *Obit* June 2001

Athletes

Aamodt, Kjetil Andre, Norwegian skier, Jan 2002

Aaron, Hank, American baseball player, May 1958

Abbott, Jim, American baseball player, Sept 1995

Abdul-Jabbar, Kareem, American basketball player, July 1967, Feb 1997

Adriano, Leite Ribeiro, Brazilian soccer player, Jan 2004

Adu, Freddy, Ghanaian-American soccer player, Jan 2005

Agassi, Andre, American tennis player, Oct 1989

Ahn, Hyun-Soo, Korean speed skater, Jan 2006

Aikman, Troy, American football player, May 1995

Akebono, American sumo wrestler, Aug 1999

Akers, Michelle, American soccer player, Nov 2004

Albright, Tenley, American figure skater and surgeon, Sept 1956

Ali, Muhammad, American boxer, Sept 1963, Nov 1978

Allen, Dick, American baseball player, May 1973

Allen, Ethan, American baseball player and coach, Mar 1954, *Obit* Nov 1993

Allen, Marcus, American football player, Oct 1986

Allen, Ray, American basketball player, Jan 2009

Alou, Felipe, Dominican baseball player and manager, June 1999

Alou, Moises, American baseball player, Apr 1999

Amla, Hashim, South African cricket player, Jan 2006

Anderson, Sparky, American baseball manager, Apr 1977, *Obit* Yrbk 2011

Anthony, Carmelo, American basketball player, June 2005

Aouita, Said, Moroccan runner, May 1990

Arakawa, Shizuka, Japanese figure skater, Jan 2006

Arcaro, Eddie, American jockey, Sept 1958, *Obit* Jan 1998

Arenas, Gilbert, American basketball player, Feb 2009

Armstrong, Lance, American cyclist, Sept 1997

Arnesen, Liv, Norwegian teacher and cross-country skier, June 2001

Asashoryu, Mongolian sumo wrestler, Jan 2005

Ashe, Arthur, American tennis player, Nov 1966, *Obit* Mar 1993

Atwood, Donna, American figure skater, May 1954

Austin, Steve, American wrestler, Nov 2001

Austin, Tracy, American tennis player, May 1981

Azarenka, Victoria, Belarusian tennis player, Oct 2013

Bagger, Mianne, Danish golfer, Jan 2006

Baghdatis, Marcos, Cypriot tennis player, Jan 2006

Bagwell, Jeff, American baseball player, Aug 2000

Baker, Dusty, American baseball player and manager, Apr 2001

Ballesteros, Seve, Spanish golfer, Sept 1980, *Obit* Yrbk 2011

Banks, Ernie, American baseball player, May 1959

Bannister, Roger, British neurologist and runner, Apr 1956

Barber, Jerry, golfer, Apr 1962, *Obit* Nov 1994

Barber, Ronde, American football player, Oct 2003

Barber, Tiki, American football player and television personality, Oct 2003

Barbosa, Leandro, Brazilian basketball player, June 2011

Barkley, Charles, American basketball player, Oct 1991

Barry, Rick, American basketball player and sportscaster, Mar 1971

Barton, George A., American sportswriter, May 1953

Bathgate, Andy, Canadian hockey player, Feb 1964

Batistuta, Gabriel, Argentine soccer player, Jan 2002

Bauer, Hank, American baseball player and manager, Feb 1967

Bautista, Jose, Dominican baseball player, Oct 2011

Beachley, Layne, Australian surfer, Jan 2002

Beard, Frank, American golfer, May 1970

Beatty, Jim, American runner, Jan 1963

Beban, Gary J., football player and real estate executive, May 1970

Beckenbauer, Franz, German soccer player and coach, Jan 2006

Becker, Boris, German tennis player, Feb 1987

Beckett, Josh, American baseball player, July 2011

Beckham, David, British soccer player, Jan 2003

Bell, Marilyn, Canadian swimmer, Sept 1956

Bench, Johnny, American baseball player, Oct 1971

Berg, Patty, American golfer, Sept 1940, *Obit* Yrbk 2007

Berra, Yogi, American baseball player and manager, May 1952

Bettis, Jerome, American football player, Aug 2006

Billups, Chauncey, American basketball player, Feb 2011

Bird, Larry, American basketball player and coach, June 1982

Bjoerndalen, Ole Einar, Norwegian biathlete, Jan 2003

Blair, Bonnie, American speed skater, July 1992

Blake, James, American tennis player, Mar 2006

Blanda, George, American football player, Sept 1972, *Obit* Yrbk 2010

Bloom, Jeremy, American football player and skier, Sept 2013

Blue, Vida, baseball player, Mar 1972

Boggs, Wade, American baseball player, Aug 1990

Bogut, Andrew, Australian basketball player, Jan 2008

Boitano, Brian, American figure skater, Nov 1989

Bolt, Usain, Jamaican runner, July 2009

Bonaly, Surya, French figure skater, Jan 2002

Bonds, Barry, American baseball player, June 1994

Borg, Bjorn, Swedish tennis player, Yrbk 1974

Boros, Julius, American golfer, Nov 1968, *Obit* Aug 1994

Bosh, Chris, American basketball player, Mar 2010

Bossy, Mike, Canadian hockey player, June 1981

Boudreau, Lou, American baseball player and manager, Aug 1942, *Obit* Oct 2001

Bouton, Jim, American baseball player and sportscaster, Oct 1971

Bowe, Riddick, American boxer, June 1996

Boxx, Shannon, American soccer player, May 2011

Boyer, Ken, baseball player, Mar 1966, *Obit* Oct 1982

Bradley, Bill, American senator, July 1965, Sept 1982

Bradley, David, American nonfiction author, surgeon and state legislator, Apr 1949

Bradley, Pat, golfer, Feb 1994

Bradshaw, Terry, American football player, Apr 1979

Brady, Tom, American football player, Aug 2004

Brenly, Bob, American baseball player and manager, Apr 2002

Brett, George, American baseball player, July 1981

Brock, Lou, American baseball player, June 1975

Brodeur, Martin, Canadian hockey player, Nov 2002

Brosnan, Jim, American baseball player and sportswriter, Nov 1964

Brough, Louise, American tennis player, June 1948

Brown, Dustin, Jamaican tennis player, Oct 2010

Brown, Jim, American football player and actor, Sept 1964

Brown, Kwame, American basketball player, Feb 2002

Brown, Larry, American football player, Mar 1973

Brown, Troy, American football player, Oct 2007

Bruijn, Inge de, Dutch swimmer, Jan 2004

Brumel, Valerii, Russian high jumper, Apr 1963, *Obit* June 2003

Bubka, Sergei, Ukrainian pole vaulter, July 1996

Budge, Don, American tennis player, June 1941, *Obit* June 2000

Bueno, Maria, American tennis player, Apr 1965

Butcher, Susan, American sled dog racer, June 1991, *Obit* Yrbk 2006

Butterworth, Brad, New Zealand yacht racer, Jan 2007

Button, Dick, American figure skater and sportscaster, Mar 1949

Cabrera, Miguel, Venezuelan baseball player, July 2009

Camacho, Hector, boxer, *Obit* Yrbk 2013

Cambiaso, Adolfo, Argentine polo player, Jan 2007

Camby, Marcus, American basketball player, Jan 2000

Campanella, Roy, American baseball player, June 1953, *Obit* Aug 1993

Campbell, Donald, British automobile and boat racer, Feb 1964, *Obit* Feb 1967

Campbell, Earl, American football player, Apr 1983

Camplin, Alisa, Australian skier, Jan 2004

Cannavaro, Fabio, Italian soccer player, Jan 2006

Canseco, Jose, Cuban-American baseball player, Nov 1991

Capriati, Jennifer, American tennis player, Nov 2001

Carew, Rod, American baseball player, Jan 1978

Carpenter, Chris, American baseball player, Aug 2012

Carson, David, American graphic designer, July 2008

Carter, Don, American bowler, Mar 1963, *Obit* Yrbk 2012

Carter, Rubin, American boxer and victim of false imprisonment, May 2000

Carter, Vince, American basketball player, Apr 2002

Casals, Rosie, tennis player and executive, Feb 1974

Casey, Bernie, actor, screenwriter and film director, July 1999

Casper, Billy, American golfer, July 1966

Catchings, Tamika, American basketball player, Nov 2013

Cauthen, Steve, American jockey, July 1977

Cepeda, Orlando, Puerto Rican baseball player, Oct 1968

Chadwick, Florence, American swimmer and stockbroker, Oct 1950, *Obit* May 1995

Chamberlain, Wilt, American basketball player, June 1960, *Obit* Jan 2000

Chan, Jackie, Chinese actor, Nov 1997

Chance, Dean, baseball player, July 1969

Chang, Michael, American tennis player, July 1997

Chapman, Charles Frederic, American magazine editor and motorboat racer, May 1958, *Obit* Yrbk 1984

Charles, Ezzard, American boxer, June 1949, *Obit* Aug 1975

Chavez, Julio Cesar, Mexican boxer, Apr 1999

Cheeks, Maurice, American basketball player and coach, Feb 2004

Chiba, Sonny, Japanese martial artist and actor, Jan 2005

Chichester, Francis, English cartographer and boat racer, Yrbk 1967, *Obit* Oct 1972

Chouinard, Yvon, American mail order sportswear company executive, June 1998

Chrebet, Wayne, American football player, Feb 1999

Cink, Stewart, American golfer, Feb 2010

Claiborne, Loretta, American runner, July 1996

Clark, Geoff, Australian boxer, football player and government official, Jan 2004

Clarke, Ron, May 1971

Clemens, Roger, American baseball player, Nov 1988, Aug 2003

Clemente, Roberto, Puerto Rican baseball player, Feb 1972, *Obit* Feb 1973

Clijsters, Kim, Belgian tennis player, Jan 2004

Cobb, Ty, American baseball player, Sept 1951, *Obit* Oct 1961

Coe, Sebastian, British runner, Nov 1980

Cohen, Sasha, American figure skater, Feb 2006

Coleman, Georgia, diver, *Obit* Nov 1940

Coleman, Ronnie, American bodybuilder and policeman, Feb 2007

Collins, Jimmy, baseball player, *Obit* Apr 1943

Comaneci, Nadia, Romanian gymnast, Feb 1977

Cone, David, American baseball player, Feb 1998

Conerly, Charlie, football player, Apr 1960, *Obit* Apr 1996

Conigliaro, Tony, baseball player, Feb 1971, *Obit* Apr 1990

Conn, Billy, American boxer, Aug 1941, *Obit* Aug 1993

Conner, Dennis, yacht racer, Nov 1987

Connolly, Maureen, American tennis player, Nov 1951, *Obit* Sept 1969

Connors, Jimmy, American tennis player, Sept 1975

Conrad, Barnaby, author and painter, Sept 1959, *Obit* Yrbk 2013

Cooper-Dyke, Cynthia, American basketball player and coach, Aug 1998

Cordero, Angel, jockey, Oct 1975

Cordobes, Jan 1966

Costa, Albert, Spanish tennis player, Jan 2002

Costa, Ronaldo da, Brazilian marathon runner, Jan 2002

Cotto, Miguel, Puerto Rican boxer, Feb 2008

Coughlin, Natalie, American swimmer, July 2012

Counsell, Craig, American baseball player, Sept 2002

Couples, Fred, American golfer, July 1993

Court, Margaret, Australian tennis player, Sept 1973

Cousteau, Jacques Yves, French oceanographer, June 1953, Jan 1976, *Obit* Sept 1997

Cousy, Bob, American basketball player, Sept 1958

Coutts, Russell, New Zealand boat racer, Jan 2003

Cowher, Bill, American football coach, Nov 2006

Cox, Bobby, American baseball manager, Feb 1998

Cox, Lynne, American swimmer, Sept 2004

Creamer, Paula, American golfer, May 2011

Crenshaw, Ben, American golfer, Sept 1985

Cristiano Ronaldo, Portuguese soccer player, Jan 2007

Cronin, Joe, American baseball player, manager and executive, Mar 1965, *Obit* Nov 1984

Cruyff, Johan, Dutch soccer player and manager, Nov 1981

Csonka, Larry, American football player, Feb 1977

Culpepper, Daunte, American football player, Sept 2007

Cunningham, Randall, American football player, Mar 1991

Curry, John, English figure skater, July 1979, *Obit* June 1994

Curtis, Ann, swimmer, June 1945, *Obit* Yrbk 2012

D'Antoni, Mike, American basketball coach, June 2009

Dancer, Stanley, American harness racer, June 1973, *Obit* Yrbk 2005

Dark, Alvin, baseball manager, Mar 1975

Datsyuk, Pavel, Russian hockey player, Nov 2012

Davis, Glen, American basketball player, Nov 2010

Davis, Glenn W., American football player, Yrbk 1946, *Obit* Yrbk 2005

Davis, Shani, American speed skater, May 2006

Day, Pat, American jockey, Oct 1997

De La Hoya, Oscar, American boxer, Jan 1997

De Varona, Donna, American sportscaster and swimmer, Aug 2003

DeBusschere, Dave, American basketball executive and player, Oct 1973, *Obit* Yrbk 2003

Dean, Dizzy, American baseball player and sportscaster, Sept 1951, *Obit* Sept 1974

Dementieva, Elena, Russian tennis player, Jan 2005

Dempsey, Jack, American boxer, Feb 1945, *Obit* July 1983

Devers, Gail, American runner and hurdler, July 1996

DiMaggio, Joe, American baseball player, June 1941, July 1951, *Obit* May 1999

Dickey, R. A., American baseball player, Oct 2013

Ditka, Mike, American football coach, Oct 1987

Djokovic, Novak, Serbian tennis player, Apr 2012

Dodds, Gil, June 1947, *Obit* Apr 1977

Dominguin, Spanish bullfighter, Mar 1972, *Obit* July 1996

Donovan, Landon, American soccer player, June 2006

Dorsett, Tony, American football player, Apr 1980

Dressen, Chuck, baseball player and manager, July 1951, *Obit* Nov 1966

Drexler, Clyde, American basketball player and coach, Jan 1996

Drogba, Didier, Ivorian soccer player, July 2011

Drysdale, Don, American baseball player and sportscaster, Feb 1965, *Obit* Sept 1993

Du Toit, Natalie, South African swimmer, Jan 2005

Duncan, Tim, American basketball player, Nov 1999

Dungy, Tony, American football player and coach, Aug 2007

Duran, Roberto, Panamanian boxer, Sept 1980

Durant, Kevin, American basketball player, May 2010

Durocher, Leo, baseball player and manager, Sept 1940, July 1950, *Obit* Nov 1991

Duval, David, American golfer, Oct 1999

Dyhrenfurth, Norman G., American mountaineer, Apr 1965

Earle, Sylvia A., American marine botanist, May 1972, May 1992

Eastman, Howard, Guyanese-English boxer, Jan 2003

Edberg, Stefan, Swedish tennis player, Jan 1994

Edwards, Teresa, American basketball player, Mar 1998

El Juli, Spanish bullfighter, Jan 2002

El-Guerrouj, Hicham, Moroccan runner, Jan 2004

Elder, Lee, American golfer, Aug 1976

Elliott, Herb, Australian runner, July 1960

Elliott, Sean, basketball player, Apr 2001

Ellis, Monta, American basketball player, Feb 2008

Els, Ernie, South African golfer, Jan 2003

Elway, John, American football player, Nov 1990

Emerson, Roy, Australian tennis player, June 1965

Erving, Julius, American basketball player, May 1975

Esiason, Boomer, American football player, Nov 1995

Esposito, Phil, Canadian hockey player, May 1973

Eto'o, Samuel, Cameroonian soccer player, Feb 2013

Evans, Frank, British bullfighter, Jan 2005

Evans, Janet, American swimmer, July 1996

Evert, Chris, American tennis player, Apr 1973

Ewing, Patrick, American basketball player, May 1991

Exeter, David George Brownlow Cecil, British hurdler and Olympic executive, Jan 1956

Fabregas, Cesc, Spanish soccer player, Jan 2006

Fabris, Enrico, Italian speed skater, Jan 2006

Faldo, Nick, English golfer, Sept 1992

Fanning, Mick, Australian surfer, June 2013

Faulk, Marshall, American football player, Jan 2003

Favre, Brett, American football player, Nov 1996

Fawcett, Joy, American soccer player, May 2004

Federer, Roger, Swiss tennis player, Jan 2004

Feller, Bob, American baseball player, Aug 1941, *Obit* Yrbk 2011

Fidrych, Mark, American baseball player, Mar 1978, *Obit* Yrbk 2009

Fielder, Prince, American baseball player, June 2008

Figo, Luis, Portuguese soccer player, Jan 2003

Finch, Jennie, American softball player, Oct 2004

Flair, Ric, wrestler, Mar 2000

Fleck, Jack, golfer, Sept 1955

Fleming, Peggy, American figure skater, July 1968

Flowers, Vonetta, American bobsledder, May 2006

Flutie, Doug, American football player, Oct 1985

Foley, Mick, American wrestler, Sept 2001

Fonda, Jane, American actress, July 1964, June 1986

Ford, Whitey, American baseball player, Apr 1962

Foreman, George, American boxer, May 1974, Aug 1995

Forrest, Vernon, American boxer, July 2002, *Obit* Yrbk 2009

Forsberg, Peter, Swedish hockey player, Nov 2005

Fox, Nellie, American baseball player, Mar 1960, *Obit* Feb 1976

Francis, Dick, Welsh mystery novelist and jockey, Aug 1981, *Obit* May 2010

Franco, Julio, Dominican baseball player, Sept 2006

Francona, Terry, American baseball manager, July 2008

Frazier, Joe, American boxer, Apr 1971, *Obit* Yrbk 2012

Frazier, Walt, American basketball player and sportscaster, Feb 1973

Freeman, Cathy, Australian runner, Jan 2002

Fu Mingxia, Chinese diver, Jan 2002

Furuta, Atsuya, Japanese baseball player, Jan 2005

Gable, Dan, wrestler and coach, Aug 1997

Gabriel, Roman, football player, Nov 1975

Gagne, Eric, Canadian baseball player, June 2004

Garagiola, Joe, American sportscaster and baseball player, Jan 1976

Garcia, Sergio, Spanish golfer, Mar 2001

Garciaparra, Nomar, American baseball player, June 2000

Gardner, Rulon, American wrestler, Nov 2004

Garnett, Kevin, American basketball player, Sept 1998

Gasol, Pau, Spanish basketball player, Mar 2011

Gaston, Cito, American baseball player and manager, Apr 1993

Gebrselassie, Haile, Ethiopian runner, July 1999

Gehrig, Lou, American baseball player, Jan 1940, *Obit* July 1941

Gehrmann, Don, runner, Oct 1952

George, Anju Bobby, Indian long jumper, Jan 2005

Gerulaitis, Vitas, American tennis player, June 1979, *Obit* Nov 1994

Giacomin, Eddie, Canadian hockey player, Mar 1968

Gibson, Althea, American tennis player, Oct 1957, *Obit* Feb 2004

Gibson, Bob, American baseball player, Yrbk 1968

Gifford, Frank, American football player and sportscaster, May 1964, Jan 1995

Gilbert, Rod, Canadian hockey player and executive, July 1969

Ginobili, Manu, Argentine basketball player, Apr 2011

Girardi, Joe, American baseball player and manager, May 2008

Glavine, Tom, American baseball player, Oct 2006

Goldberg, wrestler, Apr 2001

Gonzales, Pancho, American tennis player, Oct 1949, *Obit* Sept 1995

Gonzalez, Tony, American football player, Jan 2011

Gooden, Dwight, American baseball player, Apr 1986

Goolagong, Evonne, Australian tennis player, Nov 1971

Gossage, Rich, American baseball player, Aug 1984

Graebner, Clark, American tennis player, Feb 1970

Graf, Steffi, German tennis player, Feb 1989

Granato, Cammi, American hockey player, Apr 1998

Green, Darrell, American football player, Jan 2001

Green, Tim, American football player, sportscaster and novelist, Aug 2000

Greenberg, Hank, American baseball player, June 1947, *Obit* Oct 1986

Greene, Nancy, Mar 1969

Greinke, Zack, American baseball player, July 2010

Gretzky, Wayne, Canadian hockey player and coach, Feb 1982

Grier, Rosey, American football player and entertainer, Mar 1975

Griffey, Ken, American baseball player, Aug 1996

Griffin, Blake, American basketball player, Jan 2012

Griffith Joyner, Florence, American sprinter, Apr 1989, *Obit* Nov 1998

Griffith, Clark, baseball player, manager and executive, June 1950, *Obit* Jan 1956

Griner, Brittney, American basketball player, Mar 2013

Groat, Dick, May 1961

Grylls, Bear, British adventurer and television personality, Oct 2011

Guerrero, Vladimir, Dominican baseball player, June 2006

Guevara, Ana, Mexican runner, Jan 2004

Guidry, Ron, American baseball player, May 1979

Guillen, Ozzie, Venezuelan baseball player and manager, May 2006

Gwynn, Tony, American baseball player, Oct 1996

Hackl, Georg, German luge racer, Jan 2003

Halladay, Roy, American baseball player, Sept 2009

Hamed, Naseem, English boxer, Oct 1998

Hamels, Cole, American baseball player, Nov 2011

Hamill, Dorothy, American figure skater, June 1976

Hamilton, Josh, American baseball player, Apr 2011

Hamilton, Laird, American surfer, Aug 2005

Hamilton, Scott, American figure skater, Apr 1985

Hamm, Mia, American soccer player, Sept 1999

Hamm, Morgan, American gymnast, Nov 2004

Hamm, Paul, American gymnast, Nov 2004

Hammon, Becky, American basketball player, Jan 2003

Haney, Fred, Jan 1967

Hannawald, Sven, German ski jumper, Jan 2002

Hansen, Fred, pole vaulter, Yrbk 1965

Hansenne, Marcel, Apr 1946

Hard, Darlene, July 1964

Hardaway, Tim, American basketball player, July 1998

Harper, Bryce, American baseball player, May 2013

Harrelson, Ken, baseball player and executive, Apr 1970

Harrer, Heinrich, Austrian mountaineer, Oct 1954, *Obit* Yrbk 2006

Harris, Bucky, baseball manager, June 1948, *Obit* Jan 1978

Harris, Franco, American football player, June 1976

Harrison, James, American football player, Nov 2011

Harrison, Marvin, American football player, Aug 2001

Hasek, Dominik, Czech hockey player, May 1998

Hatton, Ricky, British boxer, Oct 2008

Hawk, Tony, American skateboarder, June 2000

Hawkins, Lyn-Z Adams, American skateboarder, Sept 2013

Hayden, Matthew, Australian cricket player, Jan 2004

Hayes, Bob, American sprinter and football player, Sept 1966, *Obit* Jan 2003

Hearns, Thomas, American boxer, Mar 1983

Hee, Dana, American motion picture stunt performer, May 2008

Heiden, Eric, American speed skater and bicyclist, June 1980

Heinrichs, April, American soccer player and coach, May 2000

Heiss, Carol, American figure skater, Oct 1959

Henderson, Rickey, American baseball player, Sept 1990

Hendrickson, Sue, paleontologist, Oct 2001

Henie, Sonja, Norwegian-American figure skater and actress, Sept 1940, Jan 1952, *Obit* Nov 1970

Henin, Justine, Belgian tennis player, Jan 2003

Hernandez, Keith, American baseball player and sportscaster, Feb 1988

Hernandez, Livan, Cuban baseball player, Mar 1998

Hernandez, Orlando, Cuban baseball player, Apr 2000

Hern ndez, F,lix, Venezuelan baseball player, June 2012

Hershiser, Orel, baseball player, Feb 1990

Herzog, Maurice, July 1953

Hewitt, Lleyton, Australian tennis player, Oct 2002

Hickman, Herman, Nov 1951, *Obit* July 1958

Hill, Grant, American basketball player, Jan 2002

Hillary, Edmund, New Zealand mountaineer, Oct 1954, Jan 2002, *Obit* Yrbk 2008

Hitchcock, Thomas, polo player, *Obit* June 1944

Hoad, Lew, Australian tennis player, Sept 1956, *Obit* Sept 1994

Hodges, Gil, American baseball player and manager, Oct 1962, *Obit* May 1972

Hogan, Ben, American golfer, Oct 1948, *Obit* Oct 1997

Hogan, Hulk, American wrestler, Nov 1998

Holdsclaw, Chamique, American basketball player, Feb 2006

Holmes, Kelly, British runner, Jan 2004

Holmes, Larry, American boxer, Aug 1981

Holyfield, Evander, American boxer, Aug 1993

Hopkins, Bernard, American boxer, Apr 2002

Hornsby, Rogers, American baseball player and manager, Sept 1952, *Obit* Feb 1963

Hornung, Paul, American football player and sportscaster, Feb 1963

Houk, Ralph, American baseball manager, July 1962, *Obit* Yrbk 2010

Houston, Allan, American basketball player, Nov 2003

Howard, Bart B., Jan 1940, *Obit* Apr 1941

Howard, Elston, American baseball player and coach, Apr 1964, *Obit* Feb 1981

Howard, Frank, American baseball player, manager and coach, Jan 1972

Howard, Ryan, American baseball player, July 2007

Howard, Tim, American soccer player, Sept 2005

Howe, Gordie, Canadian hockey player, Mar 1962

Hull, Bobby, Canadian hockey player, Oct 1966

Hull, Brett, Canadian hockey player, Feb 1992

Hunt, John Hunt, British army officer and mountaineer, Oct 1954, *Obit* Jan 1999

Hunter, Catfish, American baseball player, May 1975, *Obit* Nov 1999

Iginla, Jarome, Canadian hockey player, Jan 2004

Immelman, Trevor, South African golfer, Oct 2008

Inkster, Juli, American golfer, Sept 2002

Jackson, Bo, American baseball and football player, June 1991

Jackson, Lauren, Australian basketball player, June 2003

Jackson, Reggie, American baseball player, Jan 1974

Jagr, Jaromir, Czech hockey player, Apr 1997

James, Edgerrin, American football player, Jan 2002

James, LeBron, American basketball player, Nov 2005

Jansen, Dan, American speed skater, Sept 1994

Jazy, Michel, French runner, Apr 1967

Jenkins, Hayes Alan, American figure skater and lawyer, May 1956

Jenkins, Lew, boxer, Jan 1941, *Obit* Yrbk 1991

Jenner, Bruce, American decathlete, Aug 1977

Jensen, Jackie, baseball player, coach and manager, June 1959, *Obit* Oct 1982

Johansson, Ingemar, Swedish boxer, Nov 1959, *Obit* Yrbk 2009

John, Tommy, American baseball player, Oct 1981

Johnson, July 1996

Johnson, Andre, American football player, Nov 2010

Johnson, Avery, American basketball player and coach, Jan 2007

Johnson, Ben, Canadian runner, June 1988

Johnson, Chris, American football player, Aug 2010

Johnson, Davey, American baseball manager, Sept 1999

Johnson, Dwayne, American wrestler and actor, July 2000

Johnson, Earvin, American basketball player and coach, Jan 1982

Johnson, Jack, American boxer, *Obit* July 1946

Johnson, Keyshawn, American football player, Oct 1999

Johnson, Rafer, American decathlete, June 1961

Johnson, Randy, American baseball player, Sept 2000

Johnson, Zach, American golfer, Jan 2008

Jones, Chipper, American baseball player, May 2001

Jones, Cullen, American swimmer, Aug 2008

Jones, Jon, American mixed martial artist, Mar 2013

Jones, K. C., basketball coach, Feb 1987

Jones, Marion, American sprinter, long jumper and basketball player, Oct 1998

Jones, Roy, American boxer, Feb 1999

Jordan, Michael, American basketball player, Sept 1987, Feb 1997

Joubert, Brian, French figure skater, Jan 2007

Joyner-Kersee, Jackie, American heptathlete and basketball player, July 1987

Jurgensen, Sonny, American football player and sportscaster, June 1977

Kahn, Oliver, German soccer player, Jan 2002

Kaka, Brazilian soccer player, May 2008

Kaline, Al, American baseball player and sportscaster, Yrbk 1970

Kane, Patrick, American hockey player, Feb 2011

Kapp, Joe, football player and management consultant, Sept 1975

Katz, Jackson, American anti-sexism activist, July 2004

Keane, Roy, Irish soccer player, Jan 2006

Keino, Kip, Kenyan runner, June 1967

Keller, Kasey, soccer player, Nov 1998

Kelly, Jim, American football player, Nov 1992

Kelly, John B., American rower and sports executive, June 1971, *Obit* Apr 1985

Kemp, Jack, American football player, congressman and Secretary of housing and urban development, Mar 1980, *Obit* Yrbk 2009

Kent, Jeff, American baseball player, May 2003

Kerr, Steve, basketball player, Oct 1998

Khan, Amir, British boxer, Jan 2006

Khan, Imran, Pakistani cricket player and member of Parliament, Jan 2005

Khorkina, Svetlana, Russian gymnast, Jan 2003

Kidd, Jason, American basketball player, May 2002

Killebrew, Harmon, American baseball player and sportscaster, Feb 1966, *Obit* Yrbk 2011

Killy, Jean Claude, French skier, June 1968

Kiner, Ralph, American baseball player and sportscaster, May 1954

King, Billie Jean, American tennis player, Yrbk 1967

Kingman, Dave, baseball player, Mar 1982

Klitschko, Vitali, Ukrainian boxer, Jan 2003

Klochkova, Yana, Ukrainian swimmer, Jan 2004

Knight, Philip H., American shoe company executive, Aug 1997

Kobayashi, Takeru, Japanese competitive eater, Jan 2003

Koch, William I., American energy executive, investor and yacht racer, Mar 1999

Konstanty, Jim, baseball player, Apr 1951, *Obit* Aug 1976

Korbut, Olga, Soviet gymnast, July 1973

Koufax, Sandy, American baseball player, Jan 1964

Kournikova, Anna, Russian tennis player, Jan 2002

Kovalchuk, Ilya, Russian hockey player, Mar 2007

Kramer, Jack, American tennis player, May 1947, *Obit* Yrbk 2009

Krone, Julie, American jockey, Oct 1989

Kukoc, Toni, Croatian basketball player, July 1997

Kusner, Kathy, American equestrian, Apr 1973

Kuznetsova, Svetlana, Russian tennis player, Mar 2008

Kvitova, Petra, Czech tennis player, Jan 2012

LaLanne, Jack, American physical fitness expert, Oct 1994, *Obit* Yrbk 2011

LaRussa, Tony, American baseball manager, July 2003

Lafleur, Guy, Canadian hockey player, Mar 1980

Lagat, Bernard, Kenyan-American runner, Oct 2008

Laimbeer, Bill, American basketball player, coach and executive, Jan 2006

Lara, Brian, Trinidadian cricket player, Feb 2001

Largent, Steve, American congressman, June 1999

Lasorda, Tommy, American baseball manager, Feb 1989

Laver, Rod, Australian tennis player, Feb 1963

Law, Tajuan, American football player, Oct 2002

Law, Vern, baseball player and coach, Apr 1961

Lazzeri, Tony, baseball player, *Obit* Sept 1946

LeMond, Greg, American cyclist, Oct 1989

Lebedeva, Tatyana, Russian long and triple jumper, Jan 2004

Lee, Cliff, American baseball player, Aug 2009

Lee, Willis A., American admiral and marksman, *Obit* Sept 1945

Leiter, Al, American baseball player, Aug 2002

Lemieux, Mario, Canadian hockey player, Aug 1988

Lendl, Ivan, Czech-American tennis player, Sept 1984

Leonard, Sugar Ray, American boxer, Feb 1981

Leslie, Lisa, American basketball player, Jan 1998

Lewin, Murray, *Obit* Sept 1943

Lewis, Carl, American sprinter and long jumper, Nov 1984, Yrbk 1996

Lewis, Denise, British heptathlete, Jan 2004

Lewis, Jason, British adventurer, Jan 2007

Lewis, Lennox, British boxer, Jan 1999

Lewis, Ray, American football player, Jan 2007

Leyland, Jim, American baseball manager, Nov 1998

Li Na, Chinese tennis player, Jan 2006

Li, Jet, Chinese actor and martial artist, June 2001

Lilly, Kristine, American soccer player, Apr 2004

Lin Dan, Chinese badminton player, Jan 2007

Lin, Jeremy, American basketball player, Feb 2013

Lincecum, Tim, American baseball player, June 2010

Lindros, Eric, Canadian hockey player, Apr 1998

Lipinski, Tara, American figure skater, Apr 1998

Lippi, Marcello, Italian soccer coach, Jan 2006

Lisi, Antony Garrett, American physicist, Sept 2012

Little, William Lawson, Aug 1940

Littler, Gene, golfer, July 1956

Lobo, Rebecca, American basketball player, Sept 1997

Lomu, Jonah, New Zealand rugby player, Sept 2012

Loosli, E. Fritz, Jan 1942

Lopez, Al, American baseball player and manager, Feb 1960, *Obit* Yrbk 2006

Lopez, Nancy, American golfer, Sept 1978

Lott, Ronnie, American investment manager and former football player, Feb 1994

Louganis, Greg, American diver and actor, Oct 1984

Louis, Joe, American boxer, Oct 1940, *Obit* June 1981

Love, Kevin, American basketball player, Jan 2013

Lowell, Mike, American baseball player, Sept 2003

Lucas, Jerry, American basketball player, June 1972

Lucas, John, American basketball player and coach, Oct 1995

Lujack, Johnny, football player, Yrbk 1947

Lundqvist, Henrik, Swedish hockey player, Jan 2006

Lyle, Sparky, baseball player, July 1978

MacMitchell, Leslie, American runner, Apr 1946, *Obit* Yrbk 2006

Mack, Connie, American baseball manager and executive, June 1944, *Obit* Apr 1956

Maddux, Greg, American baseball player, Feb 1996

Maglie, Sal, American baseball player, June 1953, *Obit* Feb 1993

Maier, Hermann, Austrian skier, Jan 2003

Malone, Karl, American basketball player, Jan 1993

Malone, Moses, American basketball player, June 1986

Mandlikova, Hana, Czech tennis player, Jan 1986

Mangrum, Lloyd, American golfer, Sept 1951, *Obit* Jan 1974

Manning, Eli, American football player, Sept 2008

Manning, Peyton, American football player, Sept 1998

Mantle, Mickey, American baseball player, July 1953, *Obit* Oct 1995

Maradona, Diego, Argentine soccer player and coach, Nov 1990, Jan 2006

Marble, Alice, American tennis player, Nov 1940, *Obit* Mar 1991

Marciano, Rocky, American boxer, Sept 1952, *Obit* Nov 1969

Marino, Dan, American football player and television sportscaster, Jan 1989

Maris, Roger, American baseball player, Nov 1961, *Obit* Feb 1986

Marta, Brazilian soccer player, Apr 2008

Martin, Billy, American baseball manager, Oct 1976, *Obit* Feb 1990

Martin, Camilla, Danish badminton player, Jan 2004

Martin, Christy, American boxer, Oct 1997

Martin, Kenyon, American basketball player, Jan 2005

Martinez, Pedro, Dominican baseball player, June 2001

Mathias, Bob, American decathlete, congressman and sports executive, Sept 1952, *Obit* Yrbk 2007

Matson, Randy, American shot putter and discus thrower, Sept 1968

Matsui, Hideki, Japanese baseball player, Jan 2002

Matsuzaka, Daisuke, Japanese baseball player, Apr 2007

Matthews, Clay, American football player, Oct 2011

Mattingly, Don, American baseball player, Oct 1988

Mauch, Gene, American baseball manager, Yrbk 1974, *Obit* Yrbk 2005

Mauer, Joe, American baseball player, Aug 2007

May-Treanor, Misty, American volleyball player, June 2013

Mays, Willie, American baseball player, May 1955, Yrbk 1966

Mayweather, Floyd, American boxer, Oct 2004

McCarver, Tim, sportscaster and baseball player, May 2000

McCovey, Willie, American baseball player, Nov 1970

McCutchen, Andrew, American baseball player, Aug 2013

McEnroe, John, American tennis player, Feb 1980

McGrady, Tracy, American basketball player, Feb 2003

McGwire, Mark, American baseball player, July 1998

McIlroy, Rory, Irish golfer, Nov 2011

McKinley, Chuck, tennis player, Nov 1963, *Obit* Sept 1986

McLain, Denny, American baseball player and radio talk show host, Jan 1969

McMillen, Tom, congressman, Jan 1993

McNabb, Donovan, American football player, Jan 2004

McNair, Steve, American football player, Jan 2005, *Obit* Yrbk 2009

Meriwether, W. Delano, Jan 1978

Messi, Lionel, Argentine soccer player, Jan 2007

Messier, Mark, Canadian hockey player, July 1995

Messner, Reinhold, Italian mountaineer, Mar 1980

Meyer, Debbie, American swimmer, May 1969

Mickelson, Phil, American golfer, Mar 2002

Middlecoff, Cary, golfer, July 1952, *Obit* Nov 1998

Mikita, Stan, American hockey player, Oct 1970

Milla, Roger, Cameroonian soccer player, Jan 2003

Miller, Johnny, American golfer, Sept 1974

Miller, Reggie, American basketball player, Mar 1996

Miller, Shannon, American gymnast, July 1996

Millman, Dan, American gymnast and spiritualist, Aug 2002

Mirza, Sania, Indian tennis player, Jan 2005

Miura, Yuichiro, Japanese mountaineer, Jan 2005

Monk, Art, American football player, Apr 1995

Monroe, Earl, American basketball player and executive, May 1978

Montana, Joe, American football player, Sept 1983

Moon, Warren, American football player, Nov 1991

Moore, Archie, American boxer, Nov 1960, *Obit* Feb 1999

Morgan, Joe, American baseball player and sportscaster, Sept 1984

Morneau, Justin, Canadian baseball player, June 2011

Mortenson, Greg, American mountaineer and humanitarian, Sept 2009

Morton, Craig, June 1978

Mosbacher, Emil, investment banker, presidential aide and yacht racer, Mar 1963, *Obit* Nov 1997

Moser-Proell, Annemarie, Austrian skier, Sept 1976

Moses, Edwin, American hurdler, Nov 1986

Mosley, Sugar Shane, American boxer, Jan 2001

Moss, Randy, American football player, Jan 2006

Mulanovich, Sofia, Peruvian surfer, Jan 2004

Mulloy, Gardnar, tennis player, Nov 1957

Munson, Thurman, American baseball player, Nov 1977, *Obit* Sept 1979

Murtaugh, Danny, baseball player and manager, Feb 1961, *Obit* Feb 1977

Musial, Stan, American baseball player, Yrbk 1948, *Obit* Yrbk 2013

Muster, Thomas, Austrian tennis player, May 1997

Mutombo, Dikembe, Congolese basketball player, Feb 2000

Nadal, Rafael, Spanish tennis player, Jan 2005

Nagashima, Shigeo, Japanese baseball player and manager, Jan 2003

Nakamura, Shunsuke, Japanese soccer player, Jan 2002

Nakata, Hidetoshi, Japanese soccer player, Jan 2002

Namath, Joe, American football player, Yrbk 1966

Nash, Steve, Canadian basketball player, Mar 2003

Nastase, Ilie, Romanian tennis player, Oct 1974

Navratilova, Martina, Czech-American tennis player, Sept 1977, Feb 2004

Nedved, Pavel, Czech soccer player, Jan 2002

Nelson, Byron, American golfer, Mar 1945, *Obit* Yrbk 2007

Nettles, Graig, American baseball player, July 1984

Newcombe, Don, American baseball player, Feb 1957

Newcombe, John, Australian tennis player, Oct 1977

Newton, Cam, American football player, Sept 2013
Nicklaus, Jack, American golfer, Nov 1962
Noah, Yannick, French tennis player, Aug 1987
Norman, Greg, Australian golfer, Aug 1989
Norris, Chuck, American actor and martial artist, Jan 1989
Nowitzki, Dirk, German basketball player, June 2002
Nyad, Diana, American swimmer and sportscaster, Aug 1979
O'Brien, Dan, American decathlete, July 1996
O'Neal, Jermaine, American basketball player, June 2004
O'Neal, Shaquille, American basketball player, July 1996
Occhilupo, Mark, Australian surfer, Jan 2002
Ochoa, Lorena, Mexican golfer, Jan 2007
Ochocinco, Chad, American football player, Aug 2009
Odom, Lamar, American basketball player, May 2009
Ogilvy, Geoff, Australian golfer, Jan 2006
Oh, Sadaharu, Japanese baseball player, Jan 2002
Ohno, Apolo, American speed skater, Feb 2006
Okayo, Margaret, Kenyan marathon runner, Jan 2004
Olajuwon, Hakeem, American basketball player, Nov 1993
Olav, Jan 1962, Obit Mar 1991
Olmedo, Alex, Peruvian tennis player, Yrbk 1959
Oosterbaan, Bennie, football coach, Yrbk 1949, Obit Jan 1991
Orender, Donna, American basketball association executive, Sept 2010
Orr, Bobby, Canadian hockey player, Nov 1969
Ortiz, David, Dominican-American baseball player, Aug 2005
Ott, Mel, American baseball player and manager, July 1941, Obit Jan 1959
Ouma, Kassim, Ugandan boxer, June 2007
Ovechkin, Alexander, Russian hockey player, June 2008
Overman, Lynne, Obit Apr 1943

Owens, Jesse, American runner, Nov 1956, Obit May 1980
Pacquiao, Manny, Filipino boxer, Jan 2007
Paddock, Charles W., sprinter, Obit Sept 1943
Page, Joe, baseball player, Apr 1950, Obit June 1980
Paige, Satchel, American baseball player, Sept 1952, Obit Aug 1982
Pak, Se Ri, Korean golfer, Jan 1999
Palmeiro, Rafael, Cuban-American baseball player, Aug 2001
Palmer, Arnold, American golfer, Sept 1960
Palmer, Jim, American baseball player, May 1980
Pantani, Marco, Italian cyclist, Feb 1999
Park, Brad, Canadian hockey player, Nov 1976
Park, Ji-Sung, Korean soccer player, Apr 2010
Parker, Buddy, Yrbk 1955, Obit June 1982
Parker, Frank, tennis player, Sept 1948, Obit Oct 1997
Parker, Tony, Belgian basketball player, Apr 2008
Pate, Walter L., Mar 1947, Obit June 1974
Patterson, Floyd, American boxer, Oct 1960, Obit Yrbk 2007
Patton, Mel, June 1949
Paul, Chris, American basketball player, Nov 2009
Payton, Walter, American football player, Nov 1985, Obit Jan 2000
Peabody, Endicott, governor, Mar 1964, Obit Feb 1998
Peavy, Jake, American baseball player, May 2010
Peirsol, Aaron, American swimmer, June 2010
Pele, Brazilian soccer player, Mar 1967
Pennel, John, pole vaulter, Nov 1963, Obit Jan 1994
Pennington, Chad, American football player, Oct 2009
Pepitone, Joe, baseball player, Jan 1973
Perry, Gaylord, American baseball player, Nov 1982
Peterson, Adrian, American football player, Mar 2012

Petrova, Nadia, Russian tennis player, Jan 2005
Pettit, Bob, American basketball player, Oct 1961
Phelps, Michael, American swimmer, Aug 2004
Piazza, Mike, American baseball player, July 1999
Pichot, Agustin, Argentine rugby player, Jan 2004
Pierce, Paul, American basketball player, Nov 2002
Pincay, Laffit, Panamanian jockey, Sept 2001
Piniella, Lou, American baseball player and manager, Aug 1986
Pippen, Scottie, American basketball player, Mar 1994
Player, Gary, South African golfer, Nov 1961
Plunkett, Jim, American football player, Sept 1971, Feb 1982
Plushenko, Evgeni, Russian figure skater, Jan 2007
Ponce, Enrique, Spanish bullfighter, Jan 2003
Potro, Juan Martin del, Argentine tennis player, May 2010
Potvin, Denis, American hockey player, Oct 1986
Powell, Mike, American long jumper, Oct 1993
Prado, Edgar, Peruvian jockey, Sept 2007
Pressel, Morgan, American golfer, Nov 2007
Price, Nick, Zimbabwean golfer, June 1996
Prinz, Birgit, German soccer player, Jan 2005
Pujols, Albert, Dominican-American baseball player, Sept 2004
Radcliffe, Paula, English runner, Jan 2003
Ralston, Dennis, tennis player, Oct 1965
Ramirez, Hanley, Dominican baseball player, Apr 2009
Ramirez, Manny, Dominican-American baseball player, June 2002
Randolph, Willie, American baseball player, coach and manager, Sept 2005
Ray, Ted, Obit Oct 1943
Redd, Michael, American basketball player, Mar 2005

Redgrave, Steven, English rower, Jan 2000

Reed, Willis, American basketball player, coach and executive, Jan 1973

Reese, Pee Wee, American baseball player, June 1950, *Obit* Oct 1999

Reeves, Dan, football player and coach, Oct 2001

Retton, Mary Lou, American gymnast, Feb 1986

Reyes, Jose, Dominican baseball player, Aug 2008

Reynolds, Allie, American baseball player, June 1952, *Obit* Mar 1995

Rheaume, Manon, Canadian hockey player, Nov 2012

Rice, Greg, runner, Yrbk 1941, *Obit* Aug 1991

Rice, Jerry, American football player, Apr 1990

Rice, Jim, American baseball player, Sept 1979

Richard, Maurice, Canadian hockey player, Yrbk 1958, *Obit* Yrbk 2000

Richards, Bob, American pole vaulter and decathlete, June 1957

Richards, Vincent, July 1947, *Obit* Yrbk 1959

Richardson, Bobby, baseball player, May 1966

Richmond, Mitch, basketball player, June 1999

Riggs, Bobby, American tennis player, Sept 1949, *Obit* Jan 1996

Riley, Pat, American basketball coach, Aug 1988

Ripken, Cal, American baseball player, June 1992

Rivaldo, Brazilian soccer player, Jan 2002

Rivera, Mariano, Panamanian baseball player, July 2012

Rivers, Doc, American basketball coach, Nov 2008

Rizzuto, Phil, American sportscaster and baseball player, July 1950, *Obit* Yrbk 2007

Robert, Alain, French urban climber, Jan 2007

Roberto Carlos, Brazilian soccer player, Jan 2007

Roberts, Robin, American baseball player, Yrbk 1953, *Obit* Yrbk 2010

Robertson, Oscar, American basketball player, Jan 1966

Robeson, Paul, American actor, civil rights activist and singer, Mar 1941, Mar 1976

Robinson, Brooks, American baseball player, Sept 1973

Robinson, David, American basketball player, July 1993

Robinson, Frank, American baseball player and manager, June 1971

Robinson, Jackie, American baseball player, Feb 1947, *Obit* Yrbk 1972

Robinson, Sugar Ray, American boxer, Mar 1951, *Obit* June 1989

Roddick, Andy, American tennis player, Jan 2004

Rodgers, Aaron, American football player, Nov 2012

Rodgers, Bill, American marathon runner, Aug 1982

Rodman, Dennis, American basketball player, Sept 1996

Rodriguez, Alex, American baseball player, Apr 2003

Rodriguez, Chi Chi, American golfer, Oct 1969

Rodriguez, Ivan, Puerto Rican baseball player, June 2009

Ronaldinho, Brazilian soccer player, Jan 2005

Ronaldo, Brazilian soccer player, Aug 1998

Rose, Jalen, American basketball player, Mar 2004

Rose, Murray, swimmer, June 1962, *Obit* Yrbk 2012

Rose, Pete, American baseball player and manager, Aug 1975

Rosen, Al, baseball player and executive, July 1954

Rosewall, Ken, Australian tennis player, Yrbk 1956

Rote, Kyle, American football player and sportscaster, May 1965, *Obit* Yrbk 2002

Roy, Patrick, Canadian hockey player, Nov 1999

Rubin, Barbara Jo, Yrbk 1969

Rudolph, Wilma, American runner, Sept 1961, *Obit* Jan 1995

Ruffing, Red, American baseball player, Nov 1941, *Obit* Apr 1986

Russell, Bill, American basketball player, coach and sportscaster, July 1975

Ruth, Babe, American baseball player, Aug 1944, *Obit* Oct 1948

Ryan, Nolan, American baseball player and executive, Oct 1970

Ryun, Jim, American runner and congressman, May 1968

Sabathia, C. C., American baseball player, Apr 2008

Sabatini, Gabriela, Argentine tennis player, June 1992

Sacramone, Alicia, American gymnast, Mar 2011

Safin, Marat, Russian tennis player, Jan 2003

Salazar, Alberto, American marathon runner, May 1983

Sales, Nykesha, basketball player, June 1999

Sampras, Pete, American tennis player, May 1994

Samuelson, Joan, American marathon runner, Aug 1996

Sanchez Vicario, Arantxa, Spanish tennis player, Aug 1998

Sandberg, Ryne, American baseball player, Nov 1994

Sanders, Barry, American football player, Sept 1993

Sanders, Deion, American football player and sportscaster, Jan 1995

Sanderson, Derek, Canadian hockey player and investment manager, Apr 1975

Santana, Johan, Venezuelan baseball player, July 2006

Santana, Manuel, Spanish tennis player, Sept 1967

Santos, Jose, Chilean jockey, Nov 2003

Sapp, Warren, American football player, Sept 2003

Sauer, George H., football coach and executive, Nov 1948, *Obit* Apr 1994

Saville, Curtis, long distance rower, Jan 1986

Saville, Kathleen, long distance rower, Jan 1986

Savitt, Dick, tennis player, June 1952

Scaturro, Pasquale, American geophysicist, mountaineer and rafter, Oct 2005

Scdoris, Rachael, American sled dog racer, July 2005

Schacht, Al, baseball entertainer and restaurateur, May 1946, *Obit* Sept 1984

Scherbo, Vitaly, Belarusian gymnast, July 1996

Schilling, Curt, American baseball player, Oct 2001

Schneider, Hannes, Austrian skier, Mar 1941, *Obit* June 1955

Schoendienst, Red, baseball player and manager, Yrbk 1964

Schollander, Don, American swimmer, Sept 1965

Schranz, Karl, Austrian skier, Jan 1971

Schroeder, Frederick R., American tennis player, Oct 1949, *Obit* Yrbk 2006

Schwarzenegger, Arnold, Austrian-American actor and governor, Apr 1979, Oct 1991, Aug 2004

Scott, Barbara Ann, Canadian figure skater, July 1948, *Obit* Yrbk 2012

Seagren, Bob, American pole vaulter, June 1974

Seau, Junior, American football player, Sept 2001, *Obit* Yrbk 2012

Seaver, Tom, American baseball player and sportscaster, Mar 1970

Sedgman, Frank, Australian tennis player, Nov 1951

Segura, Pancho, Ecuadorian tennis player, Sept 1951

Sehwag, Virender, Indian cricket player, Jan 2003

Seixas, Vic, tennis player, July 1952

Seles, Monica, Yugoslav-American tennis player, Nov 1992

Sewell, Luke, baseball manager, Nov 1944

Shantz, Bobby, baseball player, Apr 1953

Sharapova, Maria, Russian tennis player, Jan 2004

Shoemaker, Bill, American jockey, July 1966, *Obit* Apr 2004

Shotton, Burt, baseball player and manager, June 1949, *Obit* Oct 1962

Simmons, Richard, American fitness expert and television personality, May 1982

Simms, Phil, American football player and sportscaster, Oct 1994

Simpson, O. J., American football player and sportscaster, Apr 1969

Singh, Jeev Milkha, Indian golfer, Jan 2007

Singletary, Mike, American football coach, Mar 1993

Sissi, Brazilian soccer player, June 2001

Sizemore, Grady, American baseball player, Apr 2010

Slaney, Mary Decker, American runner, Oct 1983

Slater, Kelly, American surfer, July 2001

Smith, Bruce, American football player, Mar 1995

Smith, Emmitt, American football player, Nov 1994

Smith, Josh, American basketball player, Feb 2012

Smith, Ozzie, American baseball player, Feb 1997

Smith, Robyn, Nov 1976

Smith, Steve, American football player, Sept 2006

Snead, Sam, American golfer, June 1949, *Obit* Yrbk 2002

Snell, Peter, New Zealand runner and physiologist, Yrbk 1962

Snider, Duke, American baseball player, May 1956, *Obit* Yrbk 2011

Sobers, Garfield, Barbadian cricket player, Jan 2002

Solo, Hope, American soccer player, Aug 2012

Sorenstam, Annika, Swedish golfer, Jan 2002

Sorlie, Robert, Norwegian firefighter and sled dog racer, Jan 2005

Sosa, Sammy, Dominican baseball player, May 1999

Southworth, Billy, baseball player and manager, Nov 1944, *Obit* Jan 1970

Spahn, Warren, American baseball player, May 1962, *Obit* Yrbk 2004

Spitz, Mark, American swimmer, Oct 1972

Sprewell, Latrell, American basketball player, Feb 2001

Srichaphan, Paradorn, Thai tennis player, Jan 2004

St. Louis, Martin, Canadian hockey player, Feb 2007

Stabler, Ken, American football player, Oct 1979

Stackhouse, Jerry, American basketball player, Nov 2001

Staley, Dawn, American basketball player, Apr 2005

Stamkos, Steven, Canadian hockey player, Apr 2013

Stanky, Eddie, baseball player, June 1951, *Obit* Aug 1999

Stargell, Willie, American baseball player, June 1980, *Obit* Sept 2001

Starr, Bart, American football player and coach, Jan 1968

Staubach, Roger, American football player and real estate executive, Apr 1972

Stengel, Casey, American baseball manager, June 1949, *Obit* Nov 1975

Stenmark, Ingemar, Swedish skier, Apr 1982

Stevenson, William E., lawyer, college president and diplomat, Nov 1943, *Obit* May 1985

Stirnweiss, Snuffy, baseball player, Mar 1946, *Obit* Yrbk 1958

Stockton, John, American basketball player, June 1995

Stranahan, Frank, Sept 1951, *Obit* Yrbk 2013

Strawberry, Darryl, American baseball player, June 1984

Street, Picabo, American skier, Apr 1998

Strel, Martin, Slovenian marathon swimmer, Jan 2007

Suggs, Louise, American golfer, Jan 1962

Suh, Ndamukong, American football player, Oct 2013

Summitt, Pat Head, American basketball coach, June 2005

Sun Wen, Chinese soccer player, Apr 2001

Suzuki, Ichiro, Japanese baseball player, July 2002

Swoopes, Sheryl, American basketball player, July 1996

Takanohana, Japanese sumo wrestler, Jan 2002

Talbert, William F., tennis player, Mar 1957, *Obit* June 1999

Tamura, Ryoko, Japanese judoist, Jan 2003

Tani, Yoshitomo, Japanese baseball player, Jan 2004

Tarkenton, Fran, American football player, Sept 1969

Tarver, Antonio, American boxer, June 2006

Taurasi, Diana, American basketball player, Nov 2007

Taylor, Jermain, American boxer, Apr 2006

Taylor, Lawrence, American football player, July 1990

Taylor, Ron, Australian photographer and skin diver, Jan 2007, *Obit* Yrbk 2012

Taylor, Valerie, Australian skin diver and photographer, Jan 2007

Tejada, Miguel, Dominican baseball player, June 2003

Tendulkar, Sachin, Indian cricket player, Jan 2002

Tener, John Kinley, baseball player, congressman and governor, *Obit* June 1946

Tenzing Norgay, Nepalese mountaineer, Oct 1954, *Obit* July 1986

Thomas, Frank, American baseball player, Aug 1994

Thomas, Isiah, American basketball player, executive and coach, Aug 1989

Thomas, John, high jumper, July 1960, *Obit* Yrbk 2013

Thomas, Tim, American hockey player, Oct 2012

Thome, Jim, American baseball player, June 2007

Thompson, Alexis, American golfer, June 2012

Thompson, Daley, British decathlete, Nov 1986

Thompson, Tina, American basketball player, Jan 2011

Thorpe, Ian, Australian swimmer, Jan 2002

Thorpe, Jim, American decathlete and pentathlete, Nov 1950, *Obit* May 1953

Tiant, Luis, Cuban baseball player, June 1977

Tittle, Y. A., American football player, Mar 1964

Todd, Richard, American football player, May 1982

Tomba, Alberto, Italian skier, May 1993

Tomlinson, LaDainian, American football player, Oct 2006

Torre, Joe, American baseball player and manager, May 1972, May 1997

Torrence, Gwen, American sprinter, July 1996

Trabert, Tony, American tennis player and sportscaster, July 1954

Trenkler, Freddie, American figure skater, June 1971, *Obit* Yrbk 2001

Trevino, Lee, American golfer, Nov 1971

Trinidad, Felix, Puerto Rican boxer, Feb 2000

Trottier, Bryan, Canadian hockey player, June 1985

Tseng, Yani, Taiwanese golfer, Sept 2011

Tszyu, Kostya, Russian-Australian boxer, Jan 2002

Tunney, Gene, American boxer, Sept 1940, *Obit* Jan 1979

Turcotte, Ron, Canadian jockey, Nov 1974

Turner, Ted, American television and baseball executive, May 1979, June 1998

Turpin, Randy, British boxer, Sept 1951, *Obit* June 1966

Tyson, Mike, American boxer, Apr 1988

Ullrich, Jan, German cyclist, Jan 2003

Unitas, Johnny, American football player, Feb 1962, *Obit* Yrbk 2002

Urquhart, Brian E., British United Nations official, June 1986

Urquidez, Benny, American martial artist, Nov 2001

Valentine, Alan, American college president, Yrbk 1950, *Obit* Sept 1980

Valentine, Bobby, American baseball manager and television sports commentator, July 2001

Valenzuela, Fernando, Mexican baseball player, Oct 1982

Valuev, Nikolay, Russian boxer, Jan 2007

Van Damme, Jean-Claude, Belgian bodybuilder, martial artist and actor, Mar 1999

Van Exel, Nick, American basketball player, Mar 2002

Vanderbilt, Cornelius, American financier, *Obit* Apr 1942

Ventura, Jesse, American wrestler and governor, May 1999

Venturi, Ken, American golfer and sportscaster, Apr 1966, *Obit* Yrbk 2013

Verlander, Justin, American baseball player, Apr 2012

Vick, Michael, American football player, Nov 2003

Vieira, Patrick, French soccer player, Jan 2006

Vilas, Guillermo, Argentine tennis player and poet, Apr 1978

Villemure, Gilles, Apr 1974

Vinatieri, Adam, American football player, Sept 2004

Vonn, Lindsey, American skier, Feb 2010

Vujanic, Milos, Serbian basketball player, Jan 2004

Wade, Dwyane, American basketball player, Apr 2006

Wade, Virginia, English tennis player, May 1976

Waitz, Grete, Norwegian marathon runner, Apr 1981, *Obit* Yrbk 2011

Wakefield, Tim, American baseball player, Sept 2011

Walcott, Jersey Joe, American boxer, June 1949, *Obit* May 1994

Walker, Herschel, American football player, Mar 1985

Walker, Larry, Canadian baseball player, May 1998

Wall, Art, American golfer, Yrbk 1959, *Obit* Feb 2002

Wallace, Ben, American basketball player, Apr 2004

Walsh, Kerri, American volleyball player, June 2013

Walton, Bill, American basketball player and sportscaster, Mar 1977

Wambach, Abby, American soccer player, Mar 2011

Wang Nan, Chinese table tennis player, Jan 2003

Warne, Shane, Australian cricket player, Jan 2005

Warner, Kurt, American football player, Sept 2009

Washington, Ron, American baseball manager, May 2011

Watson, Bubba (Gerry Lester), American golfer, Feb 2013

Watson, Tom, American golfer, July 1979

Waugh, Steve, Australian cricket player, Jan 2003

Weaver, Earl, American baseball manager, Feb 1983, *Obit* Yrbk 2013

Webb, Karrie, Australian golfer, Aug 2001

Webber, Chris, American basketball player, May 2003

Weber, Dick, American bowler, June 1970, *Obit* Yrbk 2005

Weider, Joe, American publisher and bodybuilder, Jan 1998, *Obit* Yrbk 2013

Weir, Johnny, American figure skater, Apr 2010

Weiskopf, Tom, American golfer, Nov 1973

Welker, Wes, American football player, Nov 2012

Wells, David, American baseball player, May 2004

White, Reggie, American football player and clergyman, Nov 1995, *Obit* Yrbk 2005

Whitworth, Kathy, American golfer, Apr 1976

Wickenheiser, Hayley, Canadian hockey player, Jan 2003

Wilhelm, Hoyt, American baseball player, July 1971, *Obit* Yrbk 2002

Wilkens, Lenny, American basketball player and coach, July 1996

Wilkins, Dominique, American basketball player, May 1995

Williams, Dick, American baseball player and manager, Yrbk 1973, *Obit* Yrbk 2011

Williams, Doug, American football player and coach, Feb 1999

Williams, Esther, American swimmer and actress, Feb 1955, *Obit* Yrbk 2013

Williams, Lauryn, American runner, Sept 2008

Williams, Ricky, American football player, Aug 1999

Williams, Serena, American tennis player, Feb 2003

Williams, Ted, American baseball player and manager, Apr 1947, *Obit* Oct 2002

Williams, Venus, American tennis player, Feb 2003

Willis, Dontrelle, American baseball player, Aug 2006

Wills, Maury, American baseball player, June 1966

Wilt, Fred, runner and FBI agent, Oct 1952, *Obit* Nov 1994

Winfield, Dave, American baseball player, Jan 1984

Witt, Katarina, German figure skater, July 1988

Wolfensohn, James David, Australian international organization official, May 2000

Wood, Kerry, American baseball player, May 2005

Wooden, John R., American basketball coach, Jan 1976, *Obit* Yrbk 2010

Woods, Tiger, American golfer, Nov 1997

Woodson, Rod, American football player, Oct 2004

Worsham, Lew, golfer, Jan 1954, *Obit* Jan 1991

Wright, David, American baseball player, May 2009

Wright, Mickey, American golfer, Jan 1965

Wright, Winky, American boxer, July 2004

Wyatt, Whit, baseball player, coach and manager, Nov 1941, *Obit* Nov 1999

Xie Xingfang, Chinese badminton player, Jan 2007

Yagudin, Aleksei, Russian figure skater, Feb 2004

Yamaguchi, Kristi, American figure skater, June 1992

Yao Bin, Chinese figure skating coach, Jan 2006

Yao Ming, Chinese basketball player, Jan 2002

Yashin, Alexei, Russian hockey player, Jan 2003

Yastrzemski, Carl, American baseball player, May 1968

Young, Sheila, American cyclist and speed skater, Jan 1977

Young, Steve, American football player, Oct 1993

Yount, Robin, baseball player, June 1993

Yuen, Wo-ping, Chinese martial artist and motion picture stunt choreographer, Jan 2008

Zaharias, Babe Didrikson, American track athlete and golfer, Apr 1947, *Obit* Yrbk 1956

Zatopek, Emil, Czech runner, Apr 1953, *Obit* Feb 2001

Zhang Ning, Chinese badminton player, Jan 2003

Zidane, Zinedine, Algerian-French soccer player, Jan 2002

Zito, Barry, American baseball player, July 2004

Zorzi, Cristian, Italian cross-country skier, Jan 2006

Athletic directors

MacMitchell, Leslie, American runner, Apr 1946, *Obit* Yrbk 2006

Osborne, Tom, American university athletic director, Mar 1998

Atmospheric scientists

Solomon, Susan, American atmospheric scientist, July 2005

Attorneys general

Ashcroft, John D., American Attorney general, Sept 1999

Barr, William P., American Attorney general, June 1992

Bell, Griffin B., American Attorney general, June 1977, *Obit* Yrbk 2009

Biddle, Francis, American Attorney general, Sept 1941, *Obit* Yrbk 1968

Brownell, Herbert, American Attorney general, Aug 1944, Feb 1954, *Obit* July 1996

Civiletti, Benjamin, Feb 1980

Clark, Ramsey, American Attorney general and political activist, Oct 1967

Clark, Tom C., American Supreme Court justice, July 1945, *Obit* Aug 1977

Daugherty, Harry M., American Attorney general, *Obit* Yrbk 1941

Fulton, E. D., Jan 1959

Gonzales, Alberto R., American Attorney general, Apr 2002

Holder, Eric, American Attorney general, Mar 2009

Jackson, Robert Houghwout, American Supreme Court justice, Mar 1940, Oct 1950, *Obit* Yrbk 1954

Katzenbach, Nicholas deB., American Attorney general, July 1965, *Obit* Yrbk 2012

Kennedy, Robert F., American Attorney general and senator, Feb 1958, *Obit* July 1968

Kilmuir, David Patrick Maxwell Fyfe, Yrbk 1951, *Obit* Mar 1967

Kleindienst, Richard G., American Attorney general, Oct 1972, *Obit* June 2000

Levi, Edward H., American Attorney general, Jan 1969, *Obit* July 2000

McGranery, James P., American congressman, judge and Attorney general, May 1952, *Obit* Feb 1963

McGrath, James Howard, American Attorney general, Jan 1948, *Obit* Nov 1966

McReynolds, James Clark, American Supreme Court justice, *Obit* Oct 1946

Meese, Edwin, American Attorney general, Sept 1981

Mitchell, John Newton, American Attorney general, June 1969, *Obit* Jan 1989

Mukasey, Michael, American Attorney general, Feb 2008

Murphy, Frank, American Supreme Court justice, July 1940, *Obit* Sept 1949

Reno, Janet, American Attorney general, Sept 1993

Richardson, Elliot L., American Attorney general, Mar 1971, *Obit* Mar 2000

Rogers, William Pierce, American Secretary of state, Feb 1958, Sept 1969, *Obit* Mar 2001

Saxbe, William B., American Attorney general and senator, July 1974, *Obit* Yrbk 2010

Smith, William French, American Attorney general, Jan 1982, *Obit* Jan 1991

Stone, Harlan Fiske, American Supreme Court justice, Aug 1941, *Obit* June 1946

Thornburgh, Dick, American governor and Attorney general, Oct 1988

Auctioneers

Brooks, Diana D., American art dealer and auctioneer, June 1998

Whitman, Meg, American Internet auction executive, Feb 2000

Wilson, Peter C., English art dealer, Feb 1968, *Obit* Aug 1984

Australian aborigines

Clark, Geoff, Australian boxer, football player and government official, Jan 2004

Langton, Marcia, Australian anthropologist and human rights activist, Jan 2007

Perkins, Charles, Australian aborigine leader, Jan 1969, *Obit* Feb 2001

Authors

Abbott, George, dramatist and producer, Apr 1940, Oct 1965, *Obit* Apr 1995

Abdul-Jabbar, Kareem, American basketball player, July 1967, Feb 1997

Abdulhamid, Ammar, Syrian novelist, poet and essayist, Jan 2005

Abdullah, Achmed, British novelist and short story writer, *Obit* June 1945

Abe, Kobo, Japanese novelist, July 1989, *Obit* Mar 1993

Abel, Jessica, American comic book writer and artist, Aug 2007

Abend, Hallett, American journalist, Sept 1942, *Obit* Feb 1956

Abouet, Marguerite, French comic book writer, Nov 2012

Abrahams, Peter, South African novelist and short story writer, Yrbk 1957

Abrams, J. J., American screenwriter and film director, July 2009

Abu-Assad, Hany, Palestinian filmmaker and screenwriter, Jan 2006

Abzug, Bella, American congresswoman and feminist, July 1971, *Obit* June 1998

Ace, Goodman, radio and television author and actor, May 1948, *Obit* May 1982

Achebe, Chinua, Nigerian novelist, Jan 1992, *Obit* Yrbk 2013

Acheson, Dean, American Secretary of state, Mar 1941, Feb 1949, *Obit* Nov 1971

Ackerman, Carl William, journalist and college dean, Oct 1945, *Obit* Yrbk 1970

Ackerman, Diane, American poet, essayist, memoirist and nature writer, June 1997

Ackroyd, Peter, English novelist, biographer, poet and literary critic, May 1993

Acocella, Joan Ross, American dance critic, May 2007

Adamic, Louis, author, Yrbk 1940, *Obit* Oct 1951

Adams, Alice, American short story writer, Aug 1989, *Obit* Aug 1999

Adams, Douglas, English science fiction writer and satirist, July 1993, *Obit* Sept 2001

Adams, Franklin P., humorist, July 1941, *Obit* May 1960

Adams, Gerry, Irish political leader, Sept 1994

Adams, James Truslow, historian, Nov 1941, *Obit* July 1949

Adams, Joseph H., American inventor, philanthropist and nonfiction writer, *Obit* Apr 1941

Adams, Joseph Quincy, American Shakespearean scholar, *Obit* Yrbk 1946

Adams, Randolph Greenfield, librarian, Aug 1943

Adams, Richard, English fantasy novelist, Oct 1978

Adams, Stanley, American lyricist, Feb 1954, *Obit* Mar 1994

Adamson, Joy, Kenyan conservationist, writer and illustrator, Oct 1972, *Obit* Feb 1980

Addington, Sarah, American children's author, *Obit* Yrbk 1940

Ade, George, American humorist, *Obit* July 1944

Adler, Guido, *Obit* May 1941

Adler, Mortimer J., American philosopher and educator, Apr 1940, Sept 1952, *Obit* Sept 2001

Adler, Renata, critic, journalist, novelist and short story writer, June 1984

Adler, Stella, American actress and drama teacher, Aug 1985, *Obit* Feb 1993

Affleck, Ben, American actor, Mar 1998

Agar, Herbert, author, poet and critic, Mar 1944, *Obit* Jan 1981

Agnon, Shmuel Yosef, Israeli novelist and short story writer, Mar 1967, *Obit* Apr 1970

Ahlgren, Mildred Carlson, American newspaper columnist and organization official, July 1952

Ahmed, Leila, Egyptian Islamist, Jan 2004

Aiken, Conrad, American poet, novelist, short story writer, critic and memoirist, May 1970, *Obit* Oct 1973

Akalaitis, JoAnne, American actress, dramatist and director, Feb 1993

Akhtar, Ayad, Aug 2013

Aksenov, Vasilii Pavlovich, Russian novelist, Jan 1990, *Obit* Yrbk 2009

Al-Emam, Mahassen, Jordanian journalist, Jan 2004

Al-Mubarak, Massouma, Kuwaiti cabinet member, Jan 2005

Al-Turabi, Hassan, Sudanese political leader, Jan 1999

Albee, Edward, American dramatist, Feb 1963, Apr 1996

Albion, Robert Greenhalgh, historian, May 1954, *Obit* Oct 1983

Aldrich, Richard, theatrical producer, June 1955, *Obit* June 1986

Aldridge, James, Australian author, Mar 1943

Aldridge, John W., American literary critic, Yrbk 1958

Alegria, Ciro, Peruvian novelist, Yrbk 1941

Aleixandre, Vicente, Spanish poet, Mar 1978, *Obit* Mar 1985

Aleksievich, Svetlana, Belarusian journalist, Jan 2006

Alexander, Christopher, British architect, Oct 2003

Alexander, Holmes Moss, columnist and author, Sept 1956

Alexie, Sherman, American poet, novelist and screenwriter, Oct 1998

Alinsky, Saul, American social activist, Nov 1968, *Obit* July 1972

Allee, Marjorie Hill, author, *Obit* June 1945

Allegro, John Marco, British paleographer and philologist, Yrbk 1970, *Obit* Apr 1988

Allen, Jay, American journalist, Oct 1941, *Obit* Feb 1973

Allen, Larry, American journalist, July 1942

Allen, Ralph, Canadian periodical editor, July 1958, *Obit* Feb 1967

Allen, Robert Sharon, May 1941

Allen, Steve, American comedian and actor, July 1951, Mar 1982, *Obit* Jan 2001

Allen, Woody, American actor, filmmaker and screenwriter, Yrbk 1966, Sept 1979

Allende, Isabel, Chilean novelist, Feb 1988

Alsop, Joseph, American journalist, Oct 1952, *Obit* Oct 1989

Alsop, Stewart, American journalist, Oct 1952, *Obit* July 1974

Alterman, Eric, American journalist, Feb 2007

Altizer, Thomas J. J., American theologian, June 1967

Alvarez Quintero, Joaquin, Spanish dramatist, *Obit* Aug 1944

Alvarez de Toledo, Luisa Isabel, Spanish novelist and social reformer, Apr 1972

Alvarez, Walter C., American internist and physiologist, Sept 1953, *Obit* Aug 1978

Alvtegen, Karin, Swedish novelist, Jan 2007

Amado, Jorge, Brazilian novelist, Mar 1986, *Obit* Oct 2001

Amal'rik, Andrei, Russian essayist and historian, Apr 1974, *Obit* Jan 1981

Amalric, Mathieu, French actor, film director and screenwriter, Feb 2011

Amari, Raja, Tunisian screenwriter and motion picture director, Jan 2002

Ambler, Eric, English mystery novelist, June 1975, *Obit* Jan 1999

Ames, Jonathan, American novelist, humorist and columnist, Oct 2007

Ames, Louise Bates, child psychologist, Sept 1956, *Obit* Jan 1997

Amichai, Yehuda, Israeli poet, Feb 1998, *Obit* Jan 2001

Amis, Kingsley, English novelist, poet and critic, Yrbk 1958, Apr 1987, *Obit* Jan 1996

Amis, Martin, English novelist and short story writer, June 1990, Jan 2003

Ammondt, Jukka, Finnish literary scholar and Elvis Presley impersonator, Jan 2002

Ammons, A. R., American poet, Feb 1982, *Obit* July 2001

Anderson, Christopher, American magazine editor, Jan 2010

Anderson, George Everett, American diplomat and journalist, *Obit* Apr 1940

Anderson, Jack, American newspaper columnist, June 1972, *Obit* Yrbk 2006

Anderson, John, American drama critic and playwright, *Obit* Sept 1943

Anderson, Laurie, American performance artist and musician, July 1983

Anderson, Maxwell, American dramatist, Nov 1942, Sept 1953, *Obit* May 1959

Anderson, Robert, American dramatist and screenwriter, Sept 1954, *Obit* Yrbk 2009

Anderson, Sherwood, American novelist and short story writer, *Obit* Apr 1941

Anderson, Wes, American film director and screenwriter, May 2002

Andrews, Bert, American journalist, Sept 1948, *Obit* Oct 1953

Andrews, Roy Chapman, American zoologist, explorer and museum director, Jan 1941, July 1953, *Obit* May 1960

Andric, Ivo, Yugoslav novelist, short story writer and poet, Feb 1962, *Obit* May 1975

Angell, Marcia, American physician and medical writer, Nov 2005

Angell, Norman, English journalist and pacifist, May 1948, *Obit* Yrbk 1967

Angelopoulos, Theodoros, Greek film director and screenwriter, *Obit* Yrbk 2012

Angelou, Maya, American poet and memoirist, June 1974, Feb 1994

Angier, Natalie, American science writer, Aug 1999

Angle, Paul McClelland, historian, July 1955, *Obit* Aug 1975

Angoff, Charles, American novelist and editor, Yrbk 1955, *Obit* July 1979

Anouilh, Jean, French dramatist, Apr 1954, *Obit* Nov 1987

Appel, Karel, Dutch painter, Mar 1961, *Obit* Yrbk 2006

Apple, R. W., American journalist, Apr 1993, *Obit* Feb 2007

Applebaum, Anne, American journalist, Aug 2004

Archer, Jeffrey, English novelist, Sept 1988

Arden, John, English playwright and novelist, Sept 1988, *Obit* Yrbk 2012

Ardizzone, Edward, English painter, illustrator and author, May 1964, *Obit* Jan 1980

Ardrey, Robert, American playwright and screenwriter, July 1973, *Obit* Mar 1980

Arellano, Gustavo, American journalist, Aug 2010

Arendt, Hannah, German-American political philosopher, May 1959, *Obit* Feb 1976

Armour, Richard Willard, philologist and poet, Nov 1958, *Obit* Apr 1989

Armstrong, Charlotte, author, Yrbk 1946, *Obit* Sept 1969

Armstrong, Hamilton Fish, foreign policy expert and periodical editor, Jan 1948, *Obit* June 1973

Armstrong, Margaret Neilson, author, *Obit* Sept 1944

Arne, Sigrid, American journalist, Oct 1945

Arnold, Thurman Wesley, American lawyer and government official, Jan 1940, *Obit* Yrbk 1969

Arnow, Harriette Louisa Simpson, American novelist and historian, Yrbk 1954, *Obit* May 1986

Aron, Raymond, French political philosopher and journalist, June 1954, *Obit* Jan 1984

Aronofsky, Darren, American screenwriter and director, Feb 2009

Arp, Jean, French artist, poet and essayist, May 1954, *Obit* July 1966

Arrabal, Fernando, French-Spanish dramatist, Sept 1972

Arriaga, Guillermo, Mexican novelist, short story writer and screenwriter, Jan 2007

Arrington, Michael, American Internet executive, July 2012

Arthur, George, British army officer, *Obit* Mar 1946

Artzybasheff, Boris, author and illustrator, Oct 1945, *Obit* Sept 1965

Ascoli, Max, American political scientist and magazine editor, Feb 1954, *Obit* Mar 1978

Ashbery, John, American poet, Aug 1976

Ashe, Arthur, American tennis player, Nov 1966, *Obit* Mar 1993

Ashmun, Margaret Eliza, American children's author, *Obit* Apr 1940

Asimov, Isaac, American biochemist and science fiction writer, Yrbk 1953, Oct 1968, *Obit* May 1992

Astor, Brooke, American socialite and philanthropist, Jan 1987, *Obit* Yrbk 2007

Astor, Mary, American actress, Nov 1961, *Obit* Nov 1987

Asturias, Miguel Angel, Guatemalan novelist, Oct 1968, *Obit* July 1974

Aswell, James, American novelist, Yrbk 1951, *Obit* Apr 1955

Atherton, Gertrude Franklin Horn, American novelist, Nov 1940, *Obit* Sept 1948

Atkinson, Brooks, American drama critic, Apr 1942, Feb 1961, *Obit* Mar 1984

Atkinson, Eleanor, author, *Obit* Jan 1943

Atkinson, Kate, English novelist, Feb 2007

Atkinson, Oriana Torrey MacIlveen, author, Yrbk 1953, *Obit* Oct 1989

Attaway, William, American novelist, Yrbk 1941

Attwood, William, diplomat, publisher and author, Jan 1968, *Obit* July 1989

Atwood, Margaret, Canadian novelist and poet, May 1984

Auchincloss, Louis, American novelist, short story writer and lawyer, Yrbk 1954, Aug 1978, *Obit* Apr 2010

Auden, W. H., Anglo-American poet, Sept 1971, *Obit* Nov 1973

Auel, Jean M., American novelist, Feb 1991

Augenbraum, Harold, American literary scholar, Apr 2012

Aughinbaugh, William, American lawyer, physician and travel writer, *Obit* Feb 1941

Augstein, Rudolf, German magazine publisher, June 1966, *Obit* Jan 2003

Aung San Suu Kyi, Burmese human rights activist, Feb 1992

Auster, Paul, American novelist, poet and essayist, Mar 1996

Austin, F. Britten, English novelist, dramatist and screenwriter, *Obit* May 1941

Auth, Tony, American cartoonist, illustrator and children's author, Feb 2006

Ayckbourn, Alan, English dramatist and theatrical director, Jan 1980

Azikiwe, Nnamdi, Nigerian president, July 1957, *Obit* Aug 1996

Babson, Naomi Lane, American novelist and short story writer, Yrbk 1952

Bach, Richard, American inspirational writer, Oct 1973

Bacharach, Bert, American fashion critic, Yrbk 1957

Backman, Jules, Apr 1952, *Obit* June 1982

Bacon, Leonard, poet, critic and translator, June 1941, *Obit* Mar 1954

Bacon, Peggy, American mystery writer and illustrator, Jan 1940, *Obit* Mar 1987

Bagnold, Enid, English novelist and dramatist, June 1964, *Obit* May 1981

Bailey, Carolyn Sherwin, American children's author, Yrbk 1948

Bailey, L. H., American botanist, June 1948, *Obit* Mar 1955

Baillie, Hugh, American reporter and news agency executive, Feb 1946, *Obit* Mar 1966

Bainton, Roland Herbert, church historian, June 1962, *Obit* June 1984

Baitz, Jon Robin, American dramatist, Aug 2004

Baker, Dorothy, author, Yrbk 1943, *Obit* Sept 1968

Baker, Frank, English author, Yrbk 1948

Baker, Louise, American novelist, short story writer and memoirist, Yrbk 1954

Baker, Nicholson, American novelist, Aug 1994

Baker, Nina Brown, American young adult author, Yrbk 1947, *Obit* Nov 1957

Baker, Ray Stannard, American journalist and biographer, Jan 1940, *Obit* Sept 1946

Baker, Russell, American journalist and humorist, Mar 1980

Baker, Sara Josephine, American physician, *Obit* Apr 1945

Bakker, Robert T., American paleontologist, Aug 1995

Bakshi, Ralph, American animator, Mar 1979

Baldrige, Letitia, columnist, social secretary and public relations executive, Feb 1988, *Obit* Yrbk 2013

Baldwin, Hanson Weightman, journalist and military historian, Aug 1942, *Obit* Jan 1992

Baldwin, James, American novelist, playwright and essayist, Yrbk 1959, July 1964, *Obit* Jan 1988

Baldwin, Roger Nash, American civil rights leader, Jan 1940, *Obit* Oct 1981

Ball, Alan, American film and television screenwriter and producer, Sept 2011

Ball, George W., American diplomat, Feb 1962, *Obit* July 1994

Ball, Joseph H., American senator, Oct 1943, *Obit* Feb 1994

Ball, Zachary, Yrbk 1953

Ballard, J. G., English novelist and short story writer, May 1988, *Obit* Yrbk 2009

Baltasar Kormakur, Icelandic actor, motion picture director and screenwriter, Jan 2003

Banfield, Edward C., American political scientist, May 1972, *Obit* Feb 2000

Banks, Russell, American novelist and short story writer, Jan 1992

Banning, Kendall, American magazine editor, publisher and military writer, *Obit* Feb 1945

Banning, Margaret Culkin, author, May 1940, *Obit* Feb 1982

Banting, Frederick G., Canadian physician, *Obit* Apr 1941

Banville, John, Irish novelist, May 1992

Baraka, Imamu Amiri, American poet, playwright, essayist and short story writer, May 1970

Barber, Ronde, American football player, Oct 2003

Barber, Tiki, American football player and television personality, Oct 2003

Barbour, Ralph Henry, author, *Obit* Apr 1944

Bard, Mary, American novelist, essayist and memoirist, Yrbk 1956

Barfield, Tanya, American playwright, Mar 2011

Barmak, Siddiq, Afghan motion picture director and screenwriter, Jan 2005

Barnes, Julian, English novelist, short story writer and essayist, Mar 1988

Barnes, Margaret Campbell, English novelist, Yrbk 1953

Barnett, M. Robert, American journalist and foundation official, Jan 1950

Baron-Cohen, Sacha, British comedian, Jan 2003

Barr, Stringfellow, American college president and historian, Aug 1940, *Obit* Apr 1982

Barrett, Edward W., journalist and college dean, Feb 1947, *Obit* Feb 1990

Barry, Dave, American humorist, May 1998

Barry, Lynda, American cartoonist and novelist, Nov 1994

Barth, John, American novelist and essayist, May 1969

Barth, Karl, Swiss theologian, Nov 1962, *Obit* Feb 1969

Barthelme, Donald, American short story writer and novelist, Mar 1976, *Obit* Sept 1989

Bartlett, Bruce R., American economist and columnist, June 2006

Bartlett, Jennifer, American painter, Nov 1985

Barton, Bruce, American advertising executive, religious writer and congressman, Feb 1961, *Obit* Oct 1967

Barton, George, American journalist and mystery writer, *Obit* Apr 1940

Barton, George A., American sportswriter, May 1953

Baryshnikov, Mikhail, Russian-American ballet dancer, Feb 1975

Barzini, Luigi Giorgio, Italian journalist and author, July 1972, *Obit* May 1984

Barzun, Jacques, American historian, Sept 1964, *Obit* Yrbk 2013

Baskin, Leonard, American sculptor and illustrator, May 1964, *Obit* Aug 2000

Bass, George Fletcher, American archaeologist, Mar 2000

Bassett, Sara Ware, American novelist, Yrbk 1956

Batali, Mario, American chef and restaurateur, Apr 2011

Bates, Ernest Sutherland, biographer, historian and literary critic, Jan 1940

Bates, H. E., English short story writer and novelist, Sept 1944, *Obit* Mar 1974

Bates, Marston, zoologist, Apr 1956, *Obit* May 1974

Baudrillard, Jean, French social theorist, June 1993, *Obit* Yrbk 2007

Bauer, Erwin A., photographer, Feb 1993

Bauer, Peggy, photographer, Feb 1993

Baumbach, Noah, American film director and screenwriter, Oct 2010

Baumer, Marie, American screenwriter and novelist, Yrbk 1958

Baur, John Ireland Howe, museum director, Yrbk 1969, *Obit* July 1987

Bawer, Bruce, American critic, poet and essayist, July 2007

Beach, Edward Latimer, American naval officer, Oct 1960, *Obit* May 2003

Beals, Carleton, journalist, Yrbk 1942, *Obit* Aug 1979

Bean, Louis H., agricultural economist and public opinion analyst, Nov 1948, *Obit* Oct 1994

Beard, Charles Austin, American historian, Mar 1941, *Obit* Oct 1948

Beard, Daniel Carter, American children's author, illustrator and Boy Scouts founder, *Obit* Aug 1941

Beard, James, American chef, Yrbk 1964, *Obit* Mar 1985

Beard, Mary Ritter, historian and feminist, Mar 1941, *Obit* Yrbk 1959

Beaton, Cecil, English designer and photographer, Oct 1944, July 1962, *Obit* Mar 1980

Beattie, Ann, American novelist and short story writer, Oct 1985

Beatty, Arthur, American professor of English, *Obit* Apr 1943

Beatty, Bessie, radio commentator and journalist, Jan 1944, *Obit* Apr 1947

Beauvoir, Simone de, French novelist and philosopher, Jan 1973, *Obit* June 1986

Bebey, Francis, Cameroonian guitarist, composer and novelist, Apr 1994, *Obit* Sept 2001

Bechdel, Alison, American cartoonist and graphic novelist, July 2009

Becker, May Lamberton, author and editor, May 1941, *Obit* July 1958

Beckett, Samuel, Irish playwright and novelist, Feb 1970, *Obit* Feb 1990

Beckett, Wendy, English nun and art critic, Jan 1998

Bede, J. Adam, American congressman, *Obit* June 1942

Bedford, Sybille, English novelist, Feb 1990, *Obit* Yrbk 2006

Beebe, Lucius Morris, journalist, Sept 1940, *Obit* Mar 1966

Beebe, William, American naturalist and author, July 1941, *Obit* Sept 1962

Beecroft, John, American editor, Mar 1954, *Obit* Yrbk 1966

Beer, Thomas, author, *Obit* May 1940

Behan, Brendan, Irish dramatist, Mar 1961, *Obit* May 1964

Behar, Ruth, American anthropologist, poet and filmmaker, May 2005

Behrman, S. N., dramatist, screenwriter and author, Feb 1943, *Obit* Nov 1973

Bekmambetov, Timur, Kazakhstani film director, Jan 2006

Bell, Bernard Iddings, clergyman and educator, Apr 1953, *Obit* Yrbk 1959

Bell, Edward Price, American journalist, *Obit* Nov 1943

Bell, Elliott V., economist, editor and publisher, Mar 1953, *Obit* Mar 1983

Bell, Margaret Elizabeth, Yrbk 1952

Bell, Terrel Howard, American Secretary of education, May 1976, *Obit* Sept 1996

Bellamann, Henry, author and poet, Sept 1942, *Obit* July 1945

Bellow, Saul, American novelist, Feb 1965, Nov 1988, *Obit* Aug 2005

Belluck, Pam, New York Times science writer and journalist, June 2012

Bemelmans, Ludwig, American children's author and illustrator, Apr 1941, *Obit* Yrbk 1962

Bemis, Samuel Flagg, historian, June 1950, *Obit* Nov 1973

Benavente, Jacinto, Spanish dramatist, June 1953, *Obit* Sept 1954

Benchley, Belle Jennings, zoo director, Oct 1940

Benchley, Nathaniel, American novelist, short story writer and children's author, Sept 1953, *Obit* Feb 1982

Benchley, Peter, American novelist and journalist, July 1976, *Obit* June 2006

Benchley, Robert, humorist, Sept 1941, *Obit* Jan 1946

Benet, Stephen Vincent, American poet, novelist and short story writer, *Obit* Apr 1943

Bennett, James O'Donnell, American journalist, *Obit* Mar 1940

Bennett, John C., clergyman, ethicist and seminary president, Jan 1961, *Obit* July 1995

Bennett, Lerone, American magazine editor and historian, Jan 2001

Bennett, William John, American political commentator, Sept 1985

Benrimo, J. Harry, American dramatist, theatrical director and actor, *Obit* May 1942

Benson, E. F., English author, Mar 1940

Benson, Sally, American short story writer, dramatist and screenwriter, Aug 1941, *Obit* Sept 1972

Benyus, Janine M., American environmentalist, naturalist and science writer, Mar 2006

Berding, Andrew H., American journalist and government official, Apr 1960

Berendt, John, American writer, Apr 1998

Beresford-Kroeger, Diana, Irish botanist, Nov 2008

Berg, Elizabeth, American novelist and short story writer, Nov 1999

Berg, Gertrude, American actress and radio scriptwriter, July 1941, Sept 1960, *Obit* Nov 1966

Berger, Meyer, newspaper reporter and columnist, Jan 1943, *Obit* Apr 1959

Berger, Peter L., American sociologist, Mar 1983

Berger, Thomas, author, June 1988

Bergson, Henri, French philosopher, *Obit* Feb 1941

Berkson, Seymour, American news agency executive, Oct 1949, *Obit* Mar 1959

Berle, Adolf Augustus, American lawyer and diplomat, July 1940, June 1961, *Obit* Apr 1971

Berlin, Ellin, author and wife of Irving Berlin, Aug 1944, *Obit* Sept 1988

Berlin, Isaiah, British political philosopher, July 1964, *Obit* Jan 1998

Berlitz, Charles, American educator and writer on the paranormal, Feb 1957, *Obit* Yrbk 2004

Bernard, Emile, French painter, art critic and poet, *Obit* June 1941

Bernard, Michelle D., American journalist and political commentator, Sept 2011

Bernier, Rosamond, American art critic, Feb 1988

Bernstein, Carl, American journalist, Oct 1976

Bernstein, Michelle, American chef and restaurateur, Nov 2013

Berri, Claude, French actor, director and screenwriter, Mar 1989, *Obit* Yrbk 2009

Berrigan, Daniel, American priest, poet and pacifist, Sept 1970

Berrigan, Philip, American peace activist, Feb 1976, *Obit* Mar 2003

Berry, Mary Frances, American historian, civil rights leader and government official, June 1999

Berry, Wendell, American poet and novelist, May 1986

Berryman, James Thomas, cartoonist, July 1950, *Obit* Oct 1971

Berryman, John, American poet and critic, May 1969, *Obit* Feb 1972

Berton, Pierre, Canadian journalist and historian, Oct 1991, *Obit* Yrbk 2005

Bertrand, Louis, French novelist and historian, *Obit* Feb 1942

Bess, Demaree, American journalist, Jan 1943, *Obit* Sept 1962

Besson, Luc, French film director, Jan 2002

Bestor, Arthur, American historian, Sept 1958, *Obit* Feb 1995

Betancourt, Ingrid, Colombian political leader, Jan 2002

Betjeman, John, English poet and architectural historian, Mar 1973, *Obit* July 1984

Bettelheim, Bruno, American psychologist, July 1961, *Obit* May 1990

Bevan, Arthur Dean, American surgeon, *Obit* Aug 1943

Bialk, Elisa, author, Yrbk 1954, *Obit* May 1990

Biddle, Katherine Garrison Chapin, poet, Oct 1943, *Obit* Jan 1984

Biermann, Wolf, German poet, Jan 2003

Bigart, Homer, American journalist, June 1951, *Obit* July 1991

Bigelow, Kathryn, American film director, Mar 2010

Billingsley, Franny, American children's author, Aug 2012

Billington, James H., American historian and Librarian of Congress, May 1989

Binchy, Maeve, Irish novelist and short story writer, Nov 1995, *Obit* Yrbk 2012

Binder, Carroll, journalist, May 1951, *Obit* July 1956

Binet-Valmer, Jean, French novelist, *Obit* Sept 1940

Bingham, Millicent Todd, American geographer and conservationist, June 1961, *Obit* Jan 1969

Binyon, Laurence, English poet, dramatist and art critic, *Obit* Apr 1943

Bird, Caroline, July 1976

Bird, Will R., Canadian historian and short story writer, Sept 1954

Birmingham, Stephen, author, May 1974

Birren, Faber, industrial color consultant, May 1956, *Obit* Feb 1989

Bishop, Elizabeth, American poet, Sept 1977, *Obit* Nov 1979

Bishop, Jim, columnist and author, June 1969, *Obit* Sept 1987

Bissell, Claude T., May 1959

Bittman, Mark, American food columnist and cookbook writer, Feb 2005

Blake, Doris, Canadian journalist, Nov 1941

Blake, Tiffany, American journalist, *Obit* Nov 1943

Blakemore, Michael, Australian theatrical director, May 2001

Blaker, Richard, English author, *Obit* Mar 1940

Blalock, Alfred, American surgeon, Sept 1946, *Obit* Nov 1964

Blanding, Don, American poet and illustrator, Jan 1957

Blankenhorn, Herbert, German diplomat, Apr 1956

Blatty, William Peter, American novelist, June 1974

Blier, Bertrand, French motion picture director, Oct 1988

Blitzstein, Marc, American dramatist and composer, July 1940, *Obit* Mar 1964

Bliven, Bruce, American magazine editor, Yrbk 1941, *Obit* July 1977

Bloodworth-Thomason, Linda, American television scriptwriter and producer, Feb 1993

Bloom, Allan David, philosopher, Mar 1988, *Obit* Nov 1992

Bloom, Harold, American literary critic, Apr 1987

Bloom, Paul, June 2012

Blum, William, American journalist, May 2007

Blume, Judy, American young adult novelist, Apr 1980

Blumenthal, Heston, British chef and restaurateur, Jan 2005

Bly, Robert, American poet, critic, editor and translator, Mar 1984, Mar 1993

Boas, Franz, American anthropologist, May 1940, *Obit* Feb 1943

Bochco, Steven, American television scriptwriter and producer, May 1991

Bogarde, Dirk, English actor and author, July 1967, *Obit* July 1999

Bogosian, Eric, American actor, playwright and monologist, Sept 1987

Boileau, Ethel, English author, *Obit* Mar 1942

Bois, Jules, *Obit* Aug 1943

Bok, Sissela, philosopher, Jan 1996

Bolcom, William, American composer and pianist, Apr 1990

Boles, Paul Darcy, author, Yrbk 1956, *Obit* June 1984

Boll, Heinrich, German novelist and short story writer, July 1972, *Obit* Sept 1985

Boll, Uwe, German film director, producer and screenwriter, Sept 2010

Bolling, Richard Walker, American congressman, Mar 1960, *Obit* July 1991

Bolotowsky, Ilya, American painter and sculptor, Apr 1975, *Obit* Jan 1982

Bolt, Robert, English dramatist and screenwriter, July 1963, *Obit* Apr 1995

Bolte, Charles G., author and publishing executive, Oct 1945, *Obit* May 1994

Bombeck, Erma, American humorist, Feb 1979, *Obit* June 1996

Bond, Edward, English dramatist, June 1978

Bonner, Mary Graham, Yrbk 1950

Bonner, Paul Hyde, American novelist, Yrbk 1955, *Obit* Mar 1969

Bono, Irish singer, Mar 1993

Bonsal, Stephen, journalist, historian and biographer, Aug 1945, *Obit* July 1951

Bontemps, Arna Wendell, American novelist, poet, biographer and children's author, Yrbk 1946, *Obit* July 1973

Booker, Edna Lee, American journalist, Apr 1940

Boorstin, Daniel J., American historian and Librarian of Congress, Sept 1968, Jan 1984, *Obit* Yrbk 2004

Borges, Jorge Luis, Argentine short story writer and poet, Jan 1970, *Obit* Aug 1986

Borgese, Giuseppe Antonio, Italian-American novelist, Yrbk 1947, *Obit* Jan 1953

Borowitz, Andy, American humorist, July 2007

Borysenko, Joan, psychologist and biologist, Oct 1996

Bosch, Juan, Dominican president, June 1963, *Obit* Feb 2002

Bosselaar, Laure-Anne, Belgian poet, Sept 2006

Bothwell, Jean, Yrbk 1946

Botstein, Leon, college president, Aug 1996

Bouchard, Lucien, Canadian political leader, Apr 1999

Boucher, Anthony, American mystery and science fiction writer, June 1962, *Obit* June 1968

Boulding, Kenneth Ewart, American economist and pacifist, Mar 1965, *Obit* May 1993

Bourdain, Anthony, American chef, writer and television personality, Jan 2006

Boutell, Clarence B., July 1946

Bouton, Jim, American baseball player and sportscaster, Oct 1971

Bovet, Daniel, Swiss-Italian pharmacologist, Jan 1958, *Obit* June 1992

Bowden, Mark, American journalist, Jan 2002

Bowen, Catherine Drinker, American biographer, July 1944, *Obit* Yrbk 1973

Bower, Bertha Muzzy, American novelist, *Obit* Sept 1940

Bowers, Claude Gernade, American journalist, historian and diplomat, Sept 1941, *Obit* Mar 1958

Bowers, Faubion, critic, Sept 1959, *Obit* May 2000

Bowles, Paul, American composer, novelist, short story writer, poet and travel writer, Oct 1990, *Obit* Feb 2000

Bowron, Fletcher, American mayor, Feb 1950, *Obit* Nov 1968

Boyd, James, author, *Obit* Apr 1944

Boyd, Louise Arner, American explorer, Sept 1960, *Obit* Nov 1972

Boyd, Malcolm, American clergyman, gay rights activist and writer, Mar 1968

Boyle, Hal, June 1945, *Obit* May 1974

Boyle, Kay, American novelist, short story writer and poet, June 1942, *Obit* Feb 1993

Boyle, T. Coraghessan, American novelist and short story writer, Jan 1991

Boylston, Helen Dore, author, July 1942, *Obit* Nov 1984

Bracco, Roberto, *Obit* June 1943

Brace, Gerald Warner, author, Yrbk 1947, *Obit* Sept 1978

Brackett, Charles, American screenwriter and motion picture producer, Feb 1951, *Obit* Apr 1969

Bradbury, Ray, American science fiction writer, June 1953, July 1982, *Obit* Yrbk 2012

Bradford, Barbara Taylor, English novelist, Oct 1991

Bradlee, Benjamin C., American newspaper editor, Sept 1975

Bradley, David, American nonfiction author, surgeon and state legislator, Apr 1949

Bradley, Preston, Mar 1956

Bradshaw, John E., American philosopher, educator and writer, Apr 1993

Bragg, Rick, American journalist and memoirist, Apr 2002

Bramah, Ernest, English author, *Obit* Sept 1942

Brameld, Theodore, professor of education, June 1967, *Obit* Jan 1988

Braudel, Fernand, French historian, Apr 1985, *Obit* Jan 1986

Bravo, Ellen, feminist, Aug 1997

Brazelton, T. Berry, pediatrician, Oct 1993

Brenan, Gerald, English author, poet and critic, July 1986, *Obit* Mar 1987

Breslin, Howard, Yrbk 1958, *Obit* July 1964

Breslin, Jimmy, American author and columnist, Yrbk 1973

Breuer, Lee, dramatist and director, Oct 1999

Breytenbach, Breyten, South African poet and painter, June 1986

Brick, John, Yrbk 1953, *Obit* Yrbk 1973

Brickell, Herschel, Nov 1945, *Obit* July 1952

Brickner, Richard M., Sept 1943

Bridges, Robert, *Obit* Nov 1941

Brier, Howard M., Yrbk 1951

Briggs, Ellis Ormsbee, diplomat, Apr 1965, *Obit* Apr 1976

Brill, Steven, American lawyer, journalist and television executive, Nov 1997

Briney, Nancy, Jan 1954

Brink, Carol Ryrie, American children's author, Yrbk 1946

Brinton, Crane, American historian, June 1959, *Obit* Nov 1968

Briscoe, Connie, American romance novelist, Jan 2000

Bristow, Gwen, author, Yrbk 1940, *Obit* Yrbk 1984

Bro, Marguerite Harmon, Yrbk 1952

Brockmeier, Kevin, American novelist, short story writer and children's author, May 2010

Broder, David S., American columnist and political commentator, Sept 2010, *Obit* Yrbk 2011

Brodkey, Harold, author, Apr 1989, *Obit* Apr 1996

Brodsky, Joseph, Russian poet, July 1982, *Obit* Apr 1996

Brody, Jane E., American columnist and nutritionist, Feb 1986

Broeg, Bob, American sportswriter, May 2002

Brogan, Denis William, Scottish political scientist and historian, Yrbk 1947, *Obit* Feb 1974

Broglie, Louis de, French physicist, Sept 1955, *Obit* May 1987

Bromfield, Louis, novelist, July 1944, *Obit* May 1956

Bromley, Dorothy Dunbar, journalist and feminist, Apr 1946, *Obit* Feb 1986

Bronowski, Jacob, British mathematician, Sept 1958, *Obit* Oct 1974

Brook, Peter, English director and dramatist, May 1961

Brookner, Anita, English novelist and art historian, Feb 1989

Brooks, Albert, American actor, director and screenwriter, Apr 1997

Brooks, David, American journalist and political commentator, Apr 2004

Brooks, Geraldine, Australian journalist, Aug 2006

Brooks, Gwendolyn, American poet, June 1950, July 1977, *Obit* Feb 2001

Brooks, James L., American screenwriter, director and producer, Apr 1998

Brooks, Mel, American actor, writer, director and producer, Sept 1974

Brooks, Van Wyck, literary critic and biographer, June 1941, Sept 1960, *Obit* June 1963

Brosnan, Jim, American baseball player and sportswriter, Nov 1964

Brothers, Joyce, psychologist, Apr 1971, *Obit* Yrbk 2013

Broun, Heywood, American journalist, *Obit* Jan 1940

Browder, Earl, American communist leader, Oct 1944, *Obit* Sept 1973

Brown, Carleton, *Obit* Aug 1941

Brown, Claude, American memoirist and journalist, Nov 1967, *Obit* Apr 2002

Brown, Dan, American novelist, May 2004

Brown, Dee Alexander, American historian and novelist, Aug 1979, *Obit* Mar 2003

Brown, Harrison Scott, American geochemist, July 1955, *Obit* Feb 1987

Brown, Helen Dawes, *Obit* Nov 1941

Brown, Helen Gurley, American magazine editor, Nov 1969, *Obit* Yrbk 2012

Brown, John Franklin, *Obit* Mar 1940

Brown, John Mason, drama critic and biographer, Apr 1942, *Obit* May 1969

Brown, Lester Russell, American agriculturist and environmentalist, Jan 1993

Brown, Rita Mae, American novelist, poet, essayist and screenwriter, Sept 1986

Brown, Sterling Allen, American poet and literary critic, Aug 1982, *Obit* Apr 1989

Brown, Tina, British journalist and magazine editor, Feb 1990

Brown, Tony, American television talk show host and producer, Feb 1997

Brownlow, Kevin, English television producer and director, Mar 1992

Brownmiller, Susan, journalist and feminist, Jan 1978

Brownson, Josephine, American children's author and social worker, Mar 1940

Bruce, William Cabell, author and senator, *Obit* June 1946

Brunner, Edmund de Schweinitz, Sept 1958, *Obit* Feb 1974

Bruns, Franklin R., May 1954

Bryan, Ernest R., July 1950, *Obit* Feb 1955

Bryan, George Sands, *Obit* Feb 1944

Brynner, Rock, American historian and novelist, Mar 2005

Brzezinski, Zbigniew, American political scientist and presidential adviser, Apr 1970

Buber, Martin, Israeli philosopher, June 1953, *Obit* July 1965

Buchan, John, Scottish novelist, historian and Governor General of Canada, Jan 1940

Buchanan, Edna, American journalist and novelist, Sept 1997

Buchanan, Patrick, American political commentator, Aug 1985

Bucher, Walter Herman, geologist, Feb 1957, *Obit* Apr 1965

Buchwald, Art, American humorist, Jan 1960, *Obit* May 2007

Buck, Frank, big game hunter, June 1943, *Obit* Apr 1950

Buck, Pearl S., American novelist, July 1956, *Obit* Apr 1973

Buck, Solon Justus, historian and archivist, May 1947, *Obit* July 1962

Buckley, Christopher Taylor, American novelist, humorist and editor, Apr 1997

Buckley, Priscilla L., American magazine editor, Apr 2002, *Obit* Yrbk 2012

Buckley, William F., American magazine editor, columnist and novelist, June 1962, Oct 1982, *Obit* June 2008

Buckmaster, Henrietta, Yrbk 1946, *Obit* June 1983

Budenz, Louis F., American newspaper editor, June 1951, *Obit* June 1972

Buechner, Frederick, American novelist and clergyman, Yrbk 1959

Buell, Raymond Leslie, *Obit* Apr 1946

Buffett, Jimmy, American singer and songwriter, Mar 1999

Bukowski, Charles, American poet, novelist and short story writer, Apr 1994, *Obit* Apr 1994

Buley, R. Carlyle, historian, July 1951, *Obit* June 1968

Bulgakov, Mikhail Afanas'evich, Russian novelist and dramatist, *Obit* Mar 1940

Bullins, Ed, American dramatist, May 1977

Bullitt, William C., American diplomat, July 1940, *Obit* Apr 1967

Bulosan, Carlos, American memoirist, poet and short story writer, Yrbk 1946, *Obit* Nov 1956

Bultmann, Rudolf Karl, German theologian, Jan 1972, *Obit* Sept 1976

Bumiller, Elisabeth, American journalist, Sept 2008

Burgess, Anthony, English novelist and critic, May 1972, *Obit* Jan 1994

Burke, Thomas, English author, *Obit* Oct 1945

Burliuk, David Davidovich, Russian painter and poet, Apr 1940, *Obit* Mar 1967

Burnet, Frank Macfarlane, Australian bacteriologist, May 1954, *Obit* Oct 1985

Burnett, Charles, American film director and screenwriter, Sept 1995

Burnett, Hallie Southgate, author and editor, Yrbk 1954, *Obit* Nov 1991

Burnett, Whit, magazine editor and author, Apr 1941, *Obit* June 1973

Burnham, James, American political and social philosopher, Nov 1941, *Obit* Jan 1988

Burns, Cecil Delisle, *Obit* Mar 1942

Burns, Edward, American television scriptwriter and former police officer, May 2008

Burns, Edward McNall, Feb 1954

Burns, Eveline M., American economist and government official, Nov 1960, *Obit* Jan 1986

Burns, James MacGregor, American biographer and historian, Yrbk 1962

Burroughs, Augusten, American novelist and memoirist, Apr 2004

Burroughs, William S., American novelist, Nov 1971, *Obit* Nov 1997

Burrows, Abe, American composer, lyricist, playwright and theatrical director, Nov 1951, *Obit* July 1985

Burton, Jean, Yrbk 1948

Burton, Richard, *Obit* May 1940

Burton, Virginia Lee, American children's author, Sept 1943, *Obit* Yrbk 1968

Burtsev, Vladimir L'vovich, Russian revolutionary and journalist, *Obit* Yrbk 1942

Buscaglia, Leo F., educator and lecturer, Oct 1983, *Obit* Aug 1998

Buscemi, Steve, American actor and filmmaker, Apr 1999

Busch, Charles, American playwright, actor and female impersonator, June 1995

Bushnell, Candace, American advice columnist and novelist, Nov 2003

Busiek, Kurt, American comic book writer, Sept 2005

Butler, Reg, Sept 1956

Butler, Robert N., American gerontologist and psychiatrist, Jan 1997, *Obit* Yrbk 2010

Butterfield, Roger Place, journalist, Mar 1948, *Obit* Yrbk 1991

Byas, Hugh, Mar 1943, *Obit* Apr 1945

Byatt, A. S., English novelist, short story writer and literary critic, Sept 1991

Byrd, Richard Evelyn, American admiral and explorer, Oct 1942, May 1956, *Obit* May 1957

Byrne, John, Anglo-Canadian comic book artist and writer, Oct 2000

C. K., Louis, American comedian, Feb 2010

Caballero, Maria Cristina, Colombian journalist, Jan 2004

Cacoyannis, Michael, Greek film and theatrical director, May 1966, *Obit* Yrbk 2011

Cadell, Elizabeth, English author, Yrbk 1951

Caetano, Adrian, Argentine film director and screenwriter, Jan 2003

Cage, John, American composer, Sept 1961, *Obit* Sept 1992

Cahn, Sammy, American lyricist, Nov 1974, *Obit* Mar 1993

Cain, Herman, American restaurant chain executive, radio talk show host and political commentator, Oct 2011

Cain, James M., American novelist, Yrbk 1947, *Obit* Jan 1978

Cairns, Huntington, American lawyer, Nov 1940

Calder, Nigel, English author, June 1986

Calder, Ritchie, Scottish author and journalist, Apr 1963, *Obit* May 1986

Caldwell, Erskine, American novelist and short story writer, Oct 1940, *Obit* May 1987

Caldwell, Taylor, author, Jan 1940, *Obit* Oct 1985

Calisher, Hortense, American short story writer and novelist, Nov 1973, *Obit* Yrbk 2009

Callender, John Hancock, architect and editor, Sept 1955, *Obit* June 1995

Calve, Emma, French opera singer, *Obit* Mar 1942

Calverton, Victor Francis, American political writer, editor and literary critic, *Obit* Jan 1941

Calvino, Italo, Italian novelist and short story writer, Feb 1984, *Obit* Nov 1985

Camac, Charles Nicoll Bancker, *Obit* Nov 1940

Cameron, James, Canadian film director, producer and screenwriter, Jan 1998

Campbell, Bebe Moore, American social critic and novelist, Apr 2000, *Obit* Yrbk 2007

Campbell, Grace, Yrbk 1948, *Obit* July 1963

Campbell, Harold G., *Obit* Aug 1942

Campbell, Joseph, American mythologist, June 1984, *Obit* Jan 1988

Campbell, Patricia, Yrbk 1957

Canaday, John Edwin, art critic and author, May 1962, *Obit* Sept 1985

Canavan, Joseph J., *Obit* Yrbk 1940

Canby, Al H., *Obit* Yrbk 1940

Canby, Henry Seidel, literary critic, Sept 1942, *Obit* June 1961

Canetti, Elias, Bulgarian novelist and dramatist, Jan 1983, *Obit* Oct 1994

Canfield, Cass, publisher, Apr 1954, *Obit* May 1986

Canin, Ethan, American novelist, short story writer and physician, Aug 2001

Cannon, LeGrand, author, Mar 1943

Canseco, Jose, Cuban-American baseball player, Nov 1991

Capote, Truman, American short story writer and novelist, Sept 1951, Mar 1968, *Obit* Oct 1984

Caputo, Philip, American journalist and novelist, Apr 1996

Caras, Roger A., environmentalist, journalist and animal rights activist, Apr 1988, *Obit* July 2001

Carell, Steve, American comedian and actor, Feb 2007

Carey, Ernestine Gilbreth, American memoirist, May 1949, *Obit* Yrbk 2007

Carle, Eric, American illustrator and children's author, Nov 2013

Carlin, George, American comedian, Oct 1976, *Obit* Oct 2008

Carlino, Lewis John, dramatist and filmmaker, May 1983

Carlson, Margaret, American journalist, Nov 2003

Carnegie, Dale, American self-improvement lecturer and writer, Yrbk 1941, Sept 1955

Carnegie, Dorothy, author and corporate training executive, Sept 1955, *Obit* Jan 1999

Caro, Robert A., American biographer, Jan 1984

Carpenter, Lewis Van, *Obit* July 1940

Carr, Kris, American actress, photographer and documentary filmmaker, May 2012

Carr, Robert Kenneth, Apr 1961

Carr, William G., educator, Sept 1952, *Obit* May 1996

Carraway, Gertrude Sprague, Jan 1954

Carrel, Alexis, French surgeon and biologist, Mar 1940, *Obit* Yrbk 1944

Carrington, Elaine, Feb 1944, *Obit* July 1958

Carroll, E. Jean, American advice columnist, July 2008

Carroll, James, American novelist, May 1997

Carroll, Jim, American poet and lyricist, Oct 1995, *Obit* Yrbk 2009

Carroll, Vinnette, American actress, dramatist and theatrical director, Sept 1983, *Obit* Feb 2003

Carruth, Hayden, American poet, Apr 1992, *Obit* Yrbk 2008

Carson, Anne, Canadian classicist, poet and essayist, May 2006

Carson, Benjamin, American neurosurgeon, May 1997

Carson, Rachel, American marine biologist and environmentalist, Nov 1951, *Obit* June 1964

Carter, Hodding, American journalist and government official, Aug 1981

Carter, Hodding, American newspaper editor and publisher, July 1946, *Obit* May 1972

Carter, Huntly, *Obit* May 1942

Carter, John Franklin, journalist and author, Oct 1941, *Obit* Jan 1968

Carter, Stephen L., American law professor, July 1997

Cartland, Barbara, English romance novelist, Aug 1979, *Obit* Aug 2000

Carver, Raymond, American short story writer and poet, Feb 1984, *Obit* Sept 1988

Carville, James, American political consultant and commentator, Mar 1993

Cary, Joyce, Anglo-Irish novelist, Yrbk 1949, *Obit* June 1957

Cary, William L., American lawyer and regulatory agency official, Jan 1963, *Obit* Apr 1983

Case, Frank, *Obit* July 1946

Casey, Bernie, actor, screenwriter and film director, July 1999

Casey, Robert J., Mar 1943, *Obit* Jan 1963

Caspary, Vera, author, dramatist and screenwriter, Yrbk 1947, *Obit* Aug 1987

Cassidy, Henry Clarence, journalist, Sept 1943

Cattell, James McKeen, psychologist, *Obit* Mar 1944

Catton, Bruce, journalist and author, Yrbk 1954, *Obit* Oct 1978

Caudill, Rebecca, author, Yrbk 1950, *Obit* Jan 1986

Cavanah, Frances, author and editor, Yrbk 1954

Cavanna, Betty, American young adult novelist, Yrbk 1950, *Obit* Oct 2001

Cela, Camilo Jose, Spanish novelist, short story writer, essayist, travel writer and poet, June 1990, *Obit* Apr 2002

Ceram, C. W., Jan 1957, *Obit* June 1972

Cerf, Bennett, American publisher, Nov 1941, Sept 1958, *Obit* Oct 1971

Chabon, Michael, American novelist, Nov 2012

Chadourne, Marc, *Obit* Feb 1941

Chamberlain, John, journalist and critic, Apr 1940, *Obit* June 1995

Chamberlin, Georgia Louise, *Obit* Oct 1943

Chandler, Raymond, American mystery novelist, Yrbk 1946, *Obit* June 1959

Chaon, Dan, American novelist and short story writer, Feb 2012

Chapman, Charles Frederic, American magazine editor and motorboat racer, May 1958, *Obit* Yrbk 1984

Chapman, Frank Michler, American ornithologist, *Obit* Jan 1946

Chappell, Tom, American personal care products industry executive, May 1994

Charnwood, Godfrey Rathbone Benson, English biographer, *Obit* Mar 1945

Charques, Dorothy, Yrbk 1958

Chase, David, American television producer and scriptwriter, Mar 2001

Chase, Joseph Cummings, May 1955

Chase, Mary, dramatist, Oct 1945, *Obit* Jan 1982

Chase, Mary Ellen, author, May 1940, *Obit* Oct 1973

Chase, Stuart, economist, Oct 1940, *Obit* Jan 1986

Chastain, Madye Lee, Yrbk 1958

Chatwin, Bruce, English memoirist, travel writer and novelist, Jan 1988, *Obit* Mar 1989

Chayefsky, Paddy, American screenwriter and dramatist, Sept 1957, *Obit* Sept 1981

Cheatham, Kitty, *Obit* Feb 1946

Cheever, John, American novelist and short story writer, Sept 1975, *Obit* Aug 1982

Chen Guidi, Chinese journalist, Jan 2005

Cheney, Brainard, author, Yrbk 1959, *Obit* Mar 1990

Cheney, Lynne V., American educator, novelist and government official, Oct 1992

Chesser, Elizabeth Sloan, *Obit* Mar 1940

Chester, Edmund, Mar 1941

Chevalier, Elizabeth Pickett, Jan 1943

Child, Julia, American cook, Feb 1967, *Obit* Yrbk 2004

Childs, Marquis William, journalist and author, Jan 1943, *Obit* Sept 1990

Chin, Frank, American novelist, essayist, playwright and short story writer, Mar 1999

Chodorov, Edward, American dramatist and screenwriter, Apr 1944, *Obit* Nov 1988

Chomsky, Noam, American linguist and social critic, Oct 1970, Aug 1995

Chopra, Deepak, American physician and writer, Oct 1995

Chow, Stephen, Chinese actor, motion picture director and screenwriter, Jan 2003

Christenberry, Robert K., Mar 1952, *Obit* June 1973

Christie, Agatha, English mystery writer, Sept 1940, July 1964, *Obit* Mar 1976

Churchill, Caryl, English playwright, June 1985

Churchill, Edward D., American surgeon, Feb 1963

Churchill, Randolph S., British journalist and biographer, Oct 1947, *Obit* Sept 1968

Churchill, Winston, British statesman, July 1940, Mar 1942, July 1953, *Obit* Mar 1965

Chute, B. J., author, Yrbk 1950, *Obit* Oct 1987

Chute, Marchette Gaylord, biographer and literary historian, Yrbk 1950, *Obit* July 1994

Chwast, Seymour, American children's author, illustrator and graphic designer, Sept 1995

Ciardi, John, American poet, translator and critic, Oct 1967, *Obit* May 1986

Cimino, Michael, motion picture director, Jan 1981

Claiborne, Craig, American food critic, Sept 1969, *Obit* Apr 2000

Clampitt, Amy, American poet, Feb 1992, *Obit* Nov 1994

Clancy, Tom, American novelist, Apr 1988

Clapp, Margaret, American biographer, historian and college president, June 1948, *Obit* June 1974

Clapper, Olive Ewing, Sept 1946, *Obit* Jan 1969

Clapper, Raymond, American journalist and radio commentator, Mar 1940, *Obit* Mar 1944

Claremont, Chris, American fantasy, science fiction and comic book writer, Sept 2003

Clark, Dorothy Park, American novelist, Yrbk 1957

Clark, Eleanor, novelist, travel essayist and children's author, May 1978, *Obit* Apr 1996

Clark, Eugenie, American oceanographer, Sept 1953

Clark, Joe, Canadian prime minister, Oct 1976

Clark, Kenneth, British art historian and museum director, Sept 1963, *Obit* July 1983

Clark, Leonard Frances, Jan 1956, *Obit* Sept 1957

Clark, Mary Higgins, American mystery novelist, Jan 1994

Clark, Sydney, Sept 1956

Clarke, Arthur C., English science fiction writer, Oct 1966, *Obit* Yrbk 2008

Clavell, James, Australian-American novelist and screenwriter, Oct 1981, *Obit* Nov 1994

Cleaver, Eldridge, American civil rights leader, Mar 1970, *Obit* July 1998

Cleese, John, English actor and humorist, Jan 1984

Clendening, Logan, physician, *Obit* Mar 1945

Clooney, George, American actor, July 2008

Clowes, Daniel, American comic book artist and writer, Jan 2002

Cobb, Irvin S., American humorist, *Obit* Apr 1944

Coblentz, Stanton Arthur, American science fiction writer and poet, June 1954

Coetzee, J. M., South African novelist, Jan 1987

Cogswell, Charles N., *Obit* Feb 1942

Cohan, George M., American actor, dramatist, songwriter and producer, *Obit* Jan 1943

Cohen, Arthur, author and publisher, Sept 1960, *Obit* Jan 1987

Cohen, Roger, British journalist, May 2008

Coit, Margaret L., American biographer, June 1951

Coker, Elizabeth Boatwright, author, Yrbk 1959, *Obit* Nov 1993

Colby, Nathalie S., *Obit* July 1942

Coleman, Lonnie, Yrbk 1958, *Obit* Oct 1982

Collins, Gail, American columnist, Mar 1999

Collins, Jackie, English novelist, July 2000

Collins, James Daniel, philosopher, Yrbk 1963

Collins, Jim, American business consultant, Aug 2003

Collins, Joan, British actress, Jan 1984

Collins, Patricia Hill, American sociologist, Mar 2003

Collins, Suzanne, American young adult fantasy novelist, Sept 2012

Collison, Wilson, *Obit* July 1941

Colson, Charles W., American lawyer, presidential aide and evangelist, *Obit* Yrbk 2012

Columbus, Chris, American film director and screenwriter, Nov 2001

Comden, Betty, American lyricist, librettist and screenwriter, Mar 1945, *Obit* Yrbk 2007

Comer, James P., professor of psychiatry, Aug 1991

Cometbus, Aaron, American magazine publisher and writer, Mar 2005

Comfort, Alex, English physician, novelist and poet, Sept 1974, *Obit* Aug 2000

Companys y Jover, Luis, *Obit* Yrbk 1940

Conant, James Bryant, American college president and diplomat, Mar 1941, Feb 1951, *Obit* Apr 1978

Condon, Frank, *Obit* Feb 1941

Condon, Richard, novelist, Feb 1989, *Obit* June 1996

Connelly, Marc, dramatist, Nov 1969, *Obit* Feb 1981

Connolly, Cyril, English essayist, critic and editor, Yrbk 1947

Conrad, Barnaby, author and painter, Sept 1959, *Obit* Yrbk 2013

Conroy, Pat, American novelist, Jan 1996

Considine, Bob, columnist, Yrbk 1947, *Obit* Nov 1975

Cook, Fannie, American novelist and painter, Yrbk 1946, *Obit* Oct 1949

Cooke, Alistair, Anglo-American radio reporter and television personality, June 1952, May 1974, *Obit* Yrbk 2004

Cooke, Hope, author, Feb 1967

Coolidge, Dane, author, *Obit* Sept 1940

Coon, Carleton Stevens, American anthropologist, Sept 1955, *Obit* July 1981

Coontz, Stephanie, American historian, July 2003

Cooper, Courtney Ryley, author, *Obit* Nov 1940

Cooper, Duff, British diplomat, Aug 1940, *Obit* Mar 1954

Cooper, Kent, journalist, Oct 1944, *Obit* Mar 1965

Cooper, Louise Field, author, Yrbk 1950, *Obit* Jan 1993

Cooper-Dyke, Cynthia, American basketball player and coach, Aug 1998

Coover, Robert, American novelist, Feb 1991

Copeland, Benjamin, *Obit* Jan 1941

Coppola, Francis Ford, American film director, May 1974, July 1991

Coppola, Sofia, American film director and screenwriter, Nov 2003

Cora, Cat, American chef and cookbook writer, Nov 2011

Corbett, Jim, British game hunter, May 1946, *Obit* June 1955

Corcoran, Thomas, American lawyer, Mar 1940, *Obit* Feb 1982

Corey, Paul, American novelist, Yrbk 1940

Corman, Roger, American motion picture director,

producer and screenwriter, Feb 1983

Cornwell, Patricia Daniels, American mystery novelist, May 1997

Corsi, Jerome R., American political writer, Nov 2008

Cortazar, Julio, Argentine novelist, Feb 1974, *Obit* Apr 1984

Cortez, Jayne, American poet, *Obit* Yrbk 2013

Corwin, Norman, American radio and television scriptwriter and producer, Yrbk 1940, *Obit* Yrbk 2011

Cosby, Bill, American actor and comedian, Apr 1967, Oct 1986

Cost, March, Jan 1958, *Obit* Apr 1973

Costain, Thomas B., American novelist and editor, May 1953, *Obit* Yrbk 1965

Cottenham, Mark Everard Pepys, *Obit* Sept 1943

Cotterell, Geoffrey, Yrbk 1954

Cottrell, Dorothy, Yrbk 1955, *Obit* Sept 1957

Coudenhove-Kalergi, Richard Nicolaus, Austrian political philosopher and international organization official, Feb 1948, *Obit* Oct 1972

Coulter, Ann, American television commentator, Sept 2003

Counts, George S., author and educator, Yrbk 1941, *Obit* Jan 1975

Courant, Richard, mathematician, Sept 1966, *Obit* Mar 1972

Cousins, Margaret, author and editor, June 1954, *Obit* Oct 1996

Cousins, Norman, American magazine editor, writer and anti-nuclear activist, Aug 1943, Aug 1977, *Obit* Jan 1991

Cousteau, Jacques Yves, French oceanographer, June 1953, Jan 1976, *Obit* Sept 1997

Coutts, Frederick, English evangelist, Mar 1964

Covey, Stephen R., American business training consultant, Jan 1998, *Obit* Yrbk 2012

Coward, Noel, English actor, dramatist and composer, Jan

1941, Mar 1962, *Obit* May 1973

Cowles, Virginia, author and journalist, May 1942, *Obit* Nov 1983

Cowley, Malcolm, American literary critic, philologist and poet, June 1979, *Obit* May 1989

Coxe, Howard, *Obit* Jan 1941

Coy, Wayne, Mar 1948, *Obit* Yrbk 1958

Cozzens, James Gould, American novelist, June 1949, *Obit* Oct 1978

Craft, Robert, American conductor, Mar 1984

Craig, May, journalist, June 1949, *Obit* Sept 1975

Cram, Ralph Adams, American architect, Oct 1942, *Obit* Oct 1942

Cramer, Stuart Warren, *Obit* Aug 1940

Crane, Eva, British apiculturist, Aug 1993, *Obit* Yrbk 2007

Cranston, Alan, American senator, Feb 1950, Oct 1969, *Obit* Mar 2001

Craven, Frank, *Obit* Oct 1945

Craven, Thomas, American art critic, Apr 1944, *Obit* Apr 1969

Crawford, Phyllis, author, Nov 1940

Crawshaw, William Henry, *Obit* Aug 1940

Creasey, John, English novelist, Sept 1963, *Obit* July 1973

Creeley, Robert, American poet, novelist, short story writer and essayist, Oct 1988, *Obit* Yrbk 2005

Crichton, Michael, American novelist, screenwriter and film director, Apr 1976, Nov 1993, *Obit* Apr 2009

Crider, John H., June 1949, *Obit* Sept 1966

Crispin, Edmund, English novelist and short story writer, Yrbk 1949

Critchley, Simon, British philosopher, Apr 2010

Crittenden, Danielle, Canadian journalist, July 2003

Croce, Benedetto, Italian philosopher, historian and critic, Jan 1944, *Obit* Jan 1953

Crockett, Lucy Herndon, Yrbk 1953

Cronin, A. J., Scottish novelist and physician, July 1942, *Obit* Mar 1981

Crosby, John, journalist, novelist and television critic, June 1953

Crossman, R. H. S., British socialist leader, May 1947, *Obit* June 1974

Crouch, Stanley, American essayist and critic, Mar 1994

Crouse, Russel, dramatist, June 1941, *Obit* May 1966

Crow, Carl, American journalist, Oct 1941, *Obit* July 1945

Crowe, Cameron, American screenwriter and film director, Mar 1996

Crownfield, Gertrude, *Obit* July 1945

Crum, Bartley C., lawyer, May 1947, *Obit* Feb 1960

Crystal, Billy, American comedian and actor, Feb 1987

Cuevas, Jose Luis, Mexican illustrator and printmaker, Jan 1968

Cullen, Countee, American poet, *Obit* Mar 1946

Cummings, Robert, actor, Jan 1956, *Obit* Feb 1991

Cunningham, Michael, American novelist, July 1999

Cuomo, Mario, American governor, Aug 1983

Curry, Peggy Simson, author and poet, Yrbk 1958

Curtis, Jamie Lee, American actress, Nov 1998

Cushing, Charles C. S., *Obit* Apr 1941

Cussler, Clive, American novelist, Nov 2000

D'Aulaire, Edgar Parin, author and illustrator, Aug 1940

D'Aulaire, Ingri, author and illustrator, Aug 1940

D'Usseau, Arnaud, dramatist and screenwriter, Mar 1944, *Obit* Apr 1990

Dabney, Virginius, American newspaper editor and historian, Sept 1948, *Obit* Mar 1996

Dafoe, John Wesley, *Obit* Feb 1944

Daley, Arthur, sportswriter, Sept 1956, *Obit* Feb 1974

Dali, Salvador, Spanish painter, Sept 1940, Apr 1951, *Obit* Mar 1989

Dallapiccola, Luigi, Italian composer, Feb 1966

Daly, Cahal B., Jan 2002, *Obit* Yrbk 2010

Daly, Maureen, American young adult novelist, Jan 1946, *Obit* Yrbk 2006

Damon, Lindsay Todd, *Obit* Jan 1940

Damon, Matt, American actor, Mar 1998

Dangarembga, Tsitsi, Zimbabwean novelist and film director, Jan 2006

Dangerfield, George, American historian, Sept 1953, *Obit* Mar 1987

Daniel, Clifton, American journalist, Mar 1966, *Obit* July 2000

Daniel-Rops, Henri, Mar 1957, *Obit* Oct 1965

Daniell, Raymond, Mar 1944, *Obit* June 1969

Daniels, Jonathan, newspaper editor, Apr 1942, *Obit* Jan 1982

Daniken, Erich von, Swiss author, May 1976

Dannay, Frederic, American mystery writer, July 1940, *Obit* Oct 1982

Danto, Arthur Coleman, American philosopher and art critic, Apr 1995

Dardenne, Jean-Pierre, Belgian film director and screenwriter, May 2011

Dardenne, Luc, Belgian film director and screenwriter, May 2011

Dargan, Edwin Preston, *Obit* Feb 1941

Daringer, Helen Fern, Yrbk 1951

Darrell, R. D., music critic, Sept 1955, *Obit* June 1988

Daudet, Leon, French journalist, novelist and memoirist, *Obit* Aug 1942

Daugherty, Carroll Roop, economist, Oct 1949, *Obit* June 1988

Daugherty, James Henry, American children's author and illustrator, July 1940, *Obit* Apr 1974

Davenport, Charles B., biologist and educator, *Obit* Apr 1944

Davenport, Marcia, novelist, Jan 1944, *Obit* Mar 1996

Davenport, Russell W., Jan 1944, *Obit* June 1954

David, Larry, American comedian, television scriptwriter and producer, Aug 1998

Davidson, William L., American physicist, July 1952

Davies, Ernest, May 1951

Davies, Robertson, Canadian novelist, playwright and critic, June 1975, *Obit* Mar 1996

Davies, W. H., Welsh poet and author, *Obit* Nov 1940

Davis, Angela Yvonne, American political activist, Nov 1972

Davis, Elmer, American radio commentator and short story writer, May 1940, *Obit* Sept 1958

Davis, J. Frank, *Obit* May 1942

Davis, Ossie, American actor and dramatist, Oct 1969, *Obit* Yrbk 2005

Davis, Patti, American novelist and daughter of President Ronald Reagan, Nov 1986

Davis, Robert, Yrbk 1949

Davis, Robert H., dramatist and journalist, *Obit* Yrbk 1942

Davis, Tobe Coller, Yrbk 1959, *Obit* Feb 1963

Davis, Watson, Yrbk 1945, *Obit* Oct 1967

Dawkins, Richard, British zoologist, Aug 1997

Day Lewis, C., Anglo-Irish poet, critic and mystery writer, Jan 1940, July 1969, *Obit* July 1972

Day, Dorothy, American journalist and social reformer, May 1962, *Obit* Jan 1981

Dayan, Yael, Israeli author and daughter of Moshe Dayan, Apr 1997

De Angeli, Marguerite Lofft, American children's author and illustrator, Yrbk 1947

De Casseres, Benjamin, essayist, critic and journalist, *Obit* Feb 1946

De Chirico, Giorgio, Italian painter, Jan 1956, June 1972, *Obit* Jan 1979

De Hartog, Jan, Dutch novelist, Feb 1970, *Obit* Jan 2003

De Jong, David C., novelist, July 1944, *Obit* Nov 1967

De Kiewiet, C. W., college president and historian, July 1953, *Obit* Apr 1986

De Kruif, Paul, author and bacteriologist, May 1942, July 1963, *Obit* Apr 1971

De Lima, Sigrid, novelist, Yrbk 1958, *Obit* Feb 2000

De Long, Emma J. Wotton, *Obit* Jan 1941

De Luce, Daniel, June 1944

De Onis, Harriet, translator, Apr 1957, *Obit* May 1969

De Paola, Tomie, American painter, illustrator and children's author, Feb 1999

De Roussy de Sales, Raoul, *Obit* Jan 1943

De Selincourt, Ernest, English editor and literary critic, *Obit* July 1943

De Sherbinin, Betty, Yrbk 1948

De Voto, Bernard Augustine, American historian, literary critic and novelist, Sept 1943, *Obit* Jan 1956

De Vries, Peter, American novelist, Yrbk 1959, *Obit* Jan 1994

De Wohl, Louis, Yrbk 1955, *Obit* Oct 1961

De la Torre, Lillian, author, Yrbk 1949, *Obit* Nov 1993

De, Shobha, Indian novelist, journalist and television personality, Jan 2005

DeJong, Meindert, Dutch-American children's author, Yrbk 1952, *Obit* Sept 1991

DeLillo, Don, American novelist, Jan 1989

DeMille, Nelson, American novelist, Oct 2002

Dean, Vera Micheles, international relations specialist, May 1943, *Obit* Yrbk 1972

Dean, William F., American general, Sept 1954, *Obit* Oct 1981

Deane, Seamus, Irish literary critic and poet, Jan 2007

Deasy, Mary, Yrbk 1958

Deat, Marcel, French political leader, Jan 1942, *Obit* May 1955

Debeljak, Ales, Slovenian poet and critic, Jan 2007

Debray, Regis, French political philosopher, novelist and government official, June 1982

Decker, Karl, *Obit* Feb 1942

Decter, Midge, social critic, Apr 1982

Deen, Paula H., American cook, restaurateur and television personality, Mar 2010

Dees, Morris S., American lawyer, Jan 1995

Deford, Frank, American sportswriter and novelist, Aug 1996

Deighton, Len, English novelist, Sept 1984

Delafield, E. M., English novelist, *Obit* Jan 1944

Deland, Margaret Wade Campbell, author, *Obit* Mar 1945

Delaney, Frank, Irish novelist and broadcaster, Jan 2005

Delaney, Shelagh, English playwright and screenwriter, Apr 1962, *Obit* Yrbk 2012

Delany, Bessie, American dentist, Nov 1995, *Obit* Jan 1996

Delany, Sadie, American science teacher, Nov 1995, *Obit* Apr 1999

Dell, Robert Edward, *Obit* Sept 1940

Dellinger, David, American peace activist, Aug 1976, *Obit* Yrbk 2004

Deloria, Vine, Native American leader, historian and philosopher, Sept 1974, *Obit* Yrbk 2006

Dennis, Lawrence, American political writer and diplomat, Mar 1941, *Obit* Oct 1977

Dennis, Patrick, American novelist, May 1959, *Obit* Feb 1977

Denton, Nick, British journalist and Internet news service executive, Apr 2011

Derounian, Arthur, journalist, Oct 1943

Dershowitz, Alan M., American lawyer, Sept 1986

Desai, Kiran, Indian novelist, Jan 2007

Deuel, Wallace R., Aug 1942

Deutsch, Linda, American court reporter, Apr 2007

Devi, Mahasweta, Feb 2012

Dewey, John, American philosopher and educator, Aug 1944, *Obit* July 1952

Diamant, Gertrude, American novelist and nonfiction writer, Nov 1942

Dichter, Ernest, American psychologist and marketing research executive, Jan 1961, *Obit* Jan 1992

Dickey, James, American poet and novelist, Apr 1968, *Obit* Mar 1997

Dickinson, Amy, American freelance writer and advice columnist, Apr 2004

Dickson, Lovat, Sept 1962

Dickson, Marguerite, Yrbk 1952, *Obit* Jan 1954

Didion, Joan, American novelist, essayist and journalist, Sept 1978

Diebold, John, American management consultant, Mar 1967, *Obit* Yrbk 2006

Dietz, David, author and journalist, Oct 1940, *Obit* Apr 1985

Dietz, Howard, American lyricist, Oct 1965, *Obit* Sept 1983

Dillard, Annie, American poet, critic and nature writer, Jan 1983

Dinehart, Alan, *Obit* Sept 1944

Dionne, E. J., American columnist and political commentator, May 2006

Disney, Doris Miles, American novelist, Yrbk 1954

Ditmars, Raymond Lee, herpetologist, Sept 1940, *Obit* July 1942

Dix, Dorothy, American advice columnist, Jan 1940, *Obit* Feb 1952

Dixon, Jeane, American astrologer and psychic, Feb 1973, *Obit* Mar 1997

Dixon, Thomas, American novelist, *Obit* May 1946

Djilas, Milovan, Yugoslav communist leader, memoirist and political writer, Sept 1958, *Obit* July 1995

Dobson, James C., American psychologist and social activist, Aug 1998

Doctorow, E. L., American novelist, July 1976

Dodge, David, author, Yrbk 1956

Dodge, John V., July 1960

Doerr, Anthony, American short story writer and novelist, Oct 2011

Doig, Ivan, American western writer, Feb 2011

Dolan, Daniel Leo, Sept 1956

Dolbier, Maurice, author and literary critic, Yrbk 1956, *Obit* Jan 1994

Dolci, Danilo, Italian social reformer and author, Sept 1961, *Obit* Mar 1998

Doll, Richard, British epidemiologist, Jan 2002

Domagk, Gerhard, German bacteriologist, Mar 1958, *Obit* June 1964

Donald, David Herbert, American historian and biographer, Sept 1961, *Obit* Yrbk 2009

Donleavy, J. P., Irish novelist, dramatist and short story writer, July 1979

Donoghue, Emma, Irish novelist and dramatist, Jan 2013

Donoso, Jose, Chilean novelist, Feb 1978, *Obit* Feb 1997

Donovan, Hedley, journalist and magazine publishing executive, May 1965, *Obit* Oct 1990

Dorris, Michael, American anthropologist and memoirist, Mar 1995, *Obit* June 1997

Dos Passos, John, American novelist, Aug 1940, *Obit* Nov 1970

Douglas, Emily Taft, congresswoman, Apr 1945, *Obit* Mar 1994

Douglas, John E., American criminologist, July 2001

Douglas, Marjory Stoneman, American short story writer, novelist and conservationist, July 1953, *Obit* July 1998

Douglas, William O., American Supreme Court justice, Oct 1941, Nov 1950, *Obit* Mar 1980

Douthat, Ross Gregory, American journalist, Aug 2009

Dove, Rita, American poet and short story writer, May 1994

Dowd, Maureen, American newspaper columnist, Sept 1996

Dowling, Eddie, Feb 1946, *Obit* Apr 1976

Downey, Fairfax, author and historian, Yrbk 1949, *Obit* Aug 1990

Downey, James, American television comedy writer, June 2008

Downs, Robert B., librarian, Jan 1941, June 1952, *Obit* Apr 1991

Doyle, Adrian Conan, Sept 1954

Doyle, Roddy, Irish novelist, Oct 1997

Drabble, Margaret, English novelist and playwright, May 1981

Dreiser, Theodore, American novelist, *Obit* Feb 1946

Drew, Elizabeth, journalist, Oct 1979

Drew, George A., Canadian political leader, Yrbk 1948, *Obit* May 1984

Drooker, Eric, American painter and graphic novelist, Feb 2011

Drouet, Bessie Clarke, *Obit* Oct 1940

Drucker, Peter F., American management consultant and economist, May 1964, *Obit* Apr 2006

Drummond, Roscoe, journalist, Nov 1949, *Obit* Nov 1983

Du Bois, Guy Pene, painter and critic, Oct 1946, *Obit* Oct 1958

Du Bois, Shirley Graham, American biographer, dramatist and composer, Oct 1946, *Obit* June 1977

Du Bois, W. E. B., American sociologist, historian and novelist, Jan 1940, *Obit* Oct 1963

Du Jardin, Rosamond, Yrbk 1953

Du Maurier, Daphne, English novelist, short story writer and biographer, May 1940, *Obit* June 1989

Du Puy, William Atherton, *Obit* Oct 1941

Dublin, Louis Israel, statistician, Oct 1942, *Obit* Yrbk 1991

Dubos, Rene Jules, American bacteriologist, Oct 1952, Jan 1973, *Obit* Apr 1982

Dudley, Bide, *Obit* Feb 1944

Dugan, Alan, American poet, Nov 1990, *Obit* Yrbk 2004

Dulles, Eleanor Lansing, American memoirist and

diplomat, Sept 1962, *Obit* Jan 1997

Dunbar, Rudolph, Oct 1946

Duncan, Thomas W., Yrbk 1947

Dunn, J. Allan, *Obit* May 1941

Dunne, Dominick, American novelist, journalist and true-crime writer, May 1999, *Obit* Yrbk 2009

Dunne, John Gregory, American novelist and screenwriter, June 1983, *Obit* Yrbk 2004

Durang, Christopher, American dramatist, June 1987

Durant, William James, American historian, Sept 1964, *Obit* Jan 1982

Duranty, Walter, Anglo-American journalist, Jan 1943, *Obit* Yrbk 1958

Duras, Marguerite, French novelist, screenwriter and film director, Nov 1985, *Obit* May 1996

Durrell, Gerald M., British naturalist and conservationist, May 1985, *Obit* Apr 1995

Durrell, Lawrence, English novelist, poet and travel writer, July 1963, *Obit* Jan 1991

Durrenmatt, Friedrich, Swiss novelist and dramatist, Feb 1959, *Obit* Apr 1991

Dusser de Barenne, Joannes Gregorius, *Obit* Aug 1940

Dworkin, Andrea, American feminist and writer, Oct 1994, *Obit* Yrbk 2005

Dyer, Gwynne, Canadian journalist and television documentary host, Jan 2006

Dyson, Freeman J., American physicist, Jan 1980

Dyson, Michael Eric, American social scientist, clergyman and writer, Oct 1997

Eaker, Ira Clarence, general, Oct 1942, *Obit* Sept 1987

Early, Gerald Lyn, American essayist, editor and poet, May 1995

Early, Stephen, American presidential press secretary, July 1941, Yrbk 1949, *Obit* Sept 1951

Eastman, Max, American poet, journalist and critic, Apr 1969, *Obit* Apr 1969

Eberhart, Richard, American poet, Jan 1961, *Obit* Yrbk 2005

Eberle, Irmengarde, Yrbk 1946

Ebert, Roger, American film critic, Mar 1997, *Obit* Yrbk 2013

Eckardt, Felix von, Jan 1956

Eckstein, Gustav, physiologist, May 1942, *Obit* Nov 1981

Eco, Umberto, Italian semiotician and novelist, Apr 1985

Eddington, Arthur Stanley, British astronomer, Apr 1941, *Obit* Yrbk 1991

Edel, Leon, biographer, July 1963, *Obit* Nov 1997

Edelman, Maurice, Jan 1954, *Obit* Feb 1976

Eden, Anthony, British statesman, Yrbk 1940, Apr 1951, *Obit* Mar 1977

Edman, Irwin, philosopher, July 1953, *Obit* Oct 1954

Edmonds, Walter D., American novelist and children's author, Sept 1942, *Obit* May 1998

Edwards, Blake, American film director, producer and screenwriter, Jan 1983, *Obit* Yrbk 2011

Edwards, India, journalist and political activist, Sept 1949, *Obit* Mar 1990

Egan, Jennifer, American novelist, journalist and short story writer, Mar 2002

Eggers, Dave, American writer and publisher, July 2000

Egoyan, Atom, Canadian film director and screenwriter, May 1994

Ehrenburg, Ilya, Russian novelist, critic, memoirist and journalist, June 1966, *Obit* Nov 1967

Ehrenreich, Barbara, American feminist and social critic, Mar 1995

Ehrlich, Paul R., biologist, Sept 1970

Ehrlichman, John, American presidential adviser, Oct 1979, *Obit* Apr 1999

Ehrman, Bart D., American biblical scholar, Apr 2010

Eiseley, Loren C., American anthropologist and science writer, June 1960, *Obit* Sept 1977

Eisen, Gustavus A., *Obit* Yrbk 1940

Eisendrath, Maurice Nathan, May 1950, *Obit* Jan 1974

Eisenhower, John S. D., army officer, diplomat and son of Dwight D. Eisenhower, July 1969

Eisenschiml, Otto, Austrian-American chemist and historian, Oct 1963, *Obit* Jan 1964

Eisner, Will, American cartoonist and comic book publisher, Oct 1994, *Obit* May 2005

Ekman, Carl Gustaf, *Obit* July 1945

El Mallakh, Kamal, Egyptian archaeologist, Oct 1954, *Obit* Jan 1988

Eldridge, Edward H., *Obit* June 1941

Elgin, Suzette Haden, American linguist, science fiction writer and poet, Aug 2006

Eliade, Mircea, Romanian religion historian and novelist, Nov 1985, *Obit* June 1986

Eliot, George Fielding, American journalist, Jan 1940, *Obit* June 1971

Eliot, T. S., American poet, critic and dramatist, Oct 1962, *Obit* Feb 1965

Elkin, Stanley, American novelist and short story writer, July 1987, *Obit* Aug 1995

Ellerbee, Linda, American television newscaster, Oct 1986

Elliot, Kathleen Morrow, Mar 1940

Elliott, Osborn, American journalist and college dean, Jan 1978, *Obit* Yrbk 2008

Ellis, Bret Easton, American novelist, Nov 1994

Ellis, Carleton, *Obit* Mar 1941

Ellison, Ralph, American novelist and essayist, Oct 1968, June 1993, *Obit* June 1994

Elliston, Herbert, June 1949, *Obit* Mar 1957

Ellroy, James, American novelist, Apr 1998

Ellsberg, Daniel, American peace activist, Yrbk 1973

Ellsberg, Edward, admiral, salvage engineer and author, Nov 1942, *Obit* Yrbk 1991

Elson, Arthur, Mar 1940

Elson, Edward L. R., clergyman, Nov 1967, *Obit* Nov 1993

Elytes, Odysseus, Greek poet, Sept 1980, *Obit* June 1996

Emery, Anne, author, Yrbk 1952

Emery, DeWitt, Oct 1946, *Obit* Oct 1955

Emmerich, Roland, German film director, producer and screenwriter, Nov 2000

Emrich, Duncan, Mar 1955

Engel, Carl, musicologist and composer, *Obit* June 1944

Engelbreit, Mary, American children's author, illustrator and magazine publisher, Oct 1999

Engle, Paul, American poet and college professor, June 1942, *Obit* May 1991

English, Diane, television author and producer, June 1993

Enright, Anne, Irish novelist and short story writer, Jan 2002

Enright, Elizabeth, American children's author and illustrator, Yrbk 1947, *Obit* Sept 1968

Ensler, Eve, American dramatist, Aug 2002

Enters, Angna, dancer, painter and author, Jan 1940, June 1952, *Obit* Apr 1989

Enwezor, Okwui, Nigerian art critic and exhibition curator, Jan 2002

Ephron, Nora, American screenwriter and film director, Jan 1990, *Obit* Yrbk 2012

Epstein, Jason, American publishing executive, Aug 1990

Epstein, Joseph, American essayist, editor and critic, Mar 1990

Erdrich, Louise, American novelist and poet, Apr 1989

Erikson, Erik H., American psychoanalyst, May 1971, *Obit* July 1994

Ernst, Morris, American lawyer and civil rights activist, Aug 1940, Feb 1961, *Obit* July 1976

Estes, Eleanor, American librarian, children's author and illustrator, Yrbk 1946, *Obit* Sept 1988

Estes, Harlow, Mar 1941

Eszterhas, Joe, American screenwriter, Apr 1998

Etzioni, Amitai, American sociologist, Mar 1980

Eugenides, Jeffrey, American novelist, Oct 2003

Eustis, Helen, author, Yrbk 1955

Evanovich, Janet, American mystery novelist, Apr 2001

Evans, Bergen, Yrbk 1955, *Obit* Apr 1978

Evans, Nancy, Internet service executive and editor, Mar 2000

Evans, Walker, American photographer, Sept 1971, *Obit* June 1975

Evatt, Harriet, Yrbk 1959

Everett, Percival L., American novelist, children's author and short story writer, Sept 2004

Exley, Frederick, novelist, Oct 1989, *Obit* Aug 1992

Eyre, Katherine Wigmore, Yrbk 1949, Yrbk 1957

Eysenck, H. J., German-British psychologist, Nov 1972, *Obit* Nov 1997

Eyuboglu, Bedri Rahmi, Turkish artist and poet, Sept 1954

Fabian, Robert, Apr 1954, *Obit* Aug 1978

Fadiman, Anne, American essayist and journalist, Aug 2005

Fadiman, Clifton, literary critic, editor and television moderator, May 1941, Oct 1955, *Obit* Sept 1999

Fagles, Robert, American translator, poet and literary scholar, Apr 2006, *Obit* Yrbk 2008

Fairbank, John King, American Sinologist, Oct 1966, *Obit* Nov 1991

Fallaci, Oriana, Italian journalist and novelist, Feb 1977, *Obit* Yrbk 2007

Fallows, James M., American journalist, Nov 1996

Faludi, Susan, American journalist and feminist, Feb 1993

Falwell, Jerry, American evangelist, Jan 1981, *Obit* Aug 2007

Farley, Walter, American children's and young adult author, Yrbk 1949, *Obit* Feb 1990

Farmer, Paul, American physician, Feb 2004

Farnsworth, Jerry, Oct 1954

Farrar, John, June 1954, *Obit* Jan 1975

Farrar, Margaret, crossword puzzle editor, July 1955, *Obit* Aug 1984

Farrell, James T., American novelist and short story writer, Sept 1942, *Obit* Oct 1979

Farrelly, Bobby, American screenwriter and film director, Sept 2001

Farrelly, Peter, American screenwriter and film director, Sept 2001

Farrington, Joseph Rider, American newspaper executive and congressman, May 1948, *Obit* Sept 1954

Fassbinder, Rainer Werner, German film director and producer, May 1977, *Obit* Aug 1982

Fast, Howard, American novelist and short story writer, Apr 1943, Apr 1991, *Obit* July 2003

Fauley, Wilbur F., *Obit* Feb 1943

Faulkner, Nancy, Yrbk 1956

Faulkner, William, American novelist, Jan 1951, *Obit* Sept 1962

Faust, Frederick, American western novelist, *Obit* July 1944

Fausto-Sterling, Anne, American biologist, Sept 2005

Favreau, Jon, American actor, screenwriter and film director, July 2010

Favreau, Jonathan, American speechwriter, May 2009

Fawcett, Edward, *Obit* Nov 1942

Fedorova, Nina, Nov 1940

Feiffer, Jules, American cartoonist, children's author and dramatist, Oct 1961

Feininger, Andreas, American photographer, Oct 1957, *Obit* May 1999

Feinstein, John, American sportswriter, July 1998

Feis, Herbert, historian, Oct 1961, *Obit* May 1972

Feniger, Susan, American chef and restaurateur, Apr 2013

Ferguson, Craig, Scottish-American comedian, actor and talk show host, Jan 2005

Fergusson, Erna, Yrbk 1955

Ferlinghetti, Lawrence, American poet, novelist, dramatist and publisher, June 1991

Fermi, Laura, wife of Enrico Fermi, May 1958

Fermor, Patrick Leigh, English travel writer and novelist, Yrbk 1955, Obit Yrbk 2011

Ferrero, Guglielmo, Italian historian and author, Obit Sept 1942

Ferris, Joshua, American novelist, Oct 2010

Ferris, Timothy, American journalist and science writer, Jan 2001

Fey, Tina, American actress and comedienne, Apr 2002

Feynman, Richard Phillips, American physicist, Oct 1955, Nov 1986, Obit Apr 1988

Fiedler, Leslie A., American literary critic and novelist, Yrbk 1970, Obit Yrbk 2003

Field, Rachel, American novelist, poet and children's author, Obit May 1942

Fielding, Gabriel, English novelist, poet and physician, Feb 1962, Obit Apr 1987

Fielding, Temple Hornaday, travel book author, Apr 1969, Obit July 1983

Fields, Dorothy, American lyricist and librettist, Feb 1958, Obit May 1974

Fields, Herbert, Feb 1958

Fiennes, Ranulph, British explorer, Jan 2004

Fierstein, Harvey, American dramatist and actor, Feb 1984

Fine, Benjamin, Mar 1961

Finger, Charles Joseph, American children's author, Obit Mar 1941

Finkelstein, Louis, rabbi and educator, Nov 1940, Mar 1952, Obit Jan 1992

Finney, Gertrude E., Yrbk 1957

Fischer, John, May 1953, Obit Oct 1978

Fischer, Louis, journalist and historian, May 1940, Obit Mar 1970

Fishback, Margaret, copywriter and humorist, Apr 1941, Obit Nov 1985

Fisher, Carrie, American actress and novelist, Feb 1991

Fisher, M. F. K., American food writer, Yrbk 1948, Sept 1983, Obit Aug 1992

Fisk, Robert, British journalist, Jan 2006

Fitch, Robert Elliot, Apr 1962

FitzGerald, Frances, American journalist, June 1987

Fitzgerald, F. Scott, American novelist and short story writer, Obit Feb 1941

Fitzgerald, Robert, American poet and classicist, Sept 1976, Obit Mar 1985

Fitzmaurice, George, Obit Aug 1940

Flagg, Fannie, American comedienne, actress and novelist, Nov 2006

Flanner, Janet, American journalist and novelist, May 1943, Obit Jan 1979

Flavin, Martin, dramatist and author, Yrbk 1943, Obit Feb 1968

Fleeson, Doris, American newspaper columnist, May 1959, Obit Oct 1970

Fleming, Alexander, British bacteriologist, Apr 1944, Obit May 1955

Fleming, Berry, author, Yrbk 1953, Obit Nov 1989

Fleming, Ian, English spy novelist, Jan 1964

Fletcher, Inglis, American children's author and novelist, Yrbk 1947, Obit July 1969

Florey, Howard, Australian bacteriologist, Apr 1944, Obit Apr 1968

Floyd, William, Obit Jan 1944

Flynn, Elizabeth Gurley, American communist leader, Oct 1961, Obit Nov 1964

Flynn, Gillian, American television critic and novelist, Apr 2013

Fo, Dario, Italian actor and dramatist, Nov 1986

Foer, Jonathan Safran, American novelist, Sept 2002

Foerster, Friedrich Wilhelm, July 1962, Obit Feb 1966

Foley, Martha, author and magazine editor, Apr 1941, Obit Oct 1977

Follett, Ken, Welsh novelist, Jan 1990

Folliard, Edward T., journalist, Nov 1947, Obit Feb 1977

Fong-Torres, Ben, American music journalist, Aug 2001

Fontana, Tom, American television producer and scriptwriter, Aug 2000

Foot, Michael, British political leader, Yrbk 1950, May 1981, Obit Yrbk 2010

Foote, Horton, American playwright, screenwriter and novelist, Aug 1986, Obit Yrbk 2009

Foote, Shelby, American novelist and historian, Apr 1991, Obit Yrbk 2005

Forand, Aime J., June 1960, Obit Mar 1972

Forbes, Kathryn, Yrbk 1944, Obit June 1966

Forbes, Malcolm Stevenson, American magazine publisher and investment adviser, Feb 1975, Obit Apr 1990

Ford, Richard, American novelist and short story writer, Sept 1995

Ford, Worthington C., American historian, editor and bibliographer, Obit Apr 1941

Foreman, Richard, American theatrical director and playwright, July 1988

Forster, E. M., English novelist, short story writer and essayist, Apr 1964, Obit Sept 1970

Forster, Marc, Swiss film director, Jan 2007

Forsyth, Frederick, English journalist and novelist, May 1986

Fortey, Richard A., British paleontologist, Sept 2005

Fosdick, Harry Emerson, American clergyman, Oct 1940, Obit Nov 1969

Fossey, Dian, American primatologist, May 1985, Obit Feb 1986

Fossum, Karin, Norwegian novelist, Jan 2007

Foster, Maximilian, Obit Nov 1943

Foster, William Zebulon, American communist leader, July 1945, Obit Nov 1961

Fougner, G. Selmer, journalist and wine critic, Obit May 1941

Fowler, Gene, author, Mar 1944, Obit Sept 1960

Fowles, John, English novelist, Mar 1977, Obit Apr 2006

Fox, Genevieve, Yrbk 1949, *Obit* Yrbk 1959

Fox, Michael W., Feb 1977

Francis, Dick, Welsh mystery novelist and jockey, Aug 1981, *Obit* May 2010

Francis-Williams, Edward Francis, English author and journalist, Mar 1946, *Obit* Sept 1970

Francois-Poncet, Andre, Oct 1949, *Obit* Mar 1978

Frank, Glenn, *Obit* Nov 1940

Frank, Lawrence K., social scientist, Jan 1958, *Obit* Nov 1968

Frank, Mary Hughes, Jan 1958

Frank, Reuven, American journalist and television executive, June 1973, *Obit* Yrbk 2006

Frank, Waldo David, American novelist and essayist, Nov 1940, *Obit* Mar 1967

Frankel, Charles, philosopher and educator, Apr 1966, *Obit* July 1979

Franken, Al, American senator, June 1999

Franken, Rose, novelist and playwright, Yrbk 1941, Yrbk 1947, *Obit* Aug 1988

Franklin, John Hope, American historian, Oct 1963, *Obit* May 2009

Franzen, Jonathan, American novelist, Sept 2003

Fraser, Antonia, English biographer, historian and novelist, Oct 1974

Fraser, Brad, Canadian dramatist, July 1995

Fraser, Hugh Russell, June 1943

Frayn, Michael, English dramatist and novelist, Jan 1985

Frazier, Edward Franklin, sociologist, July 1940

Frazier, Ian, American essayist and humorist, Aug 1996

Frederick, John T., June 1941

Freed, Lynn, South African novelist, Jan 2002

Freedman, Benedict, Sept 1947, *Obit* Yrbk 2012

Freedman, Nancy, Sept 1947

Freeman, John, June 1969

Freeman, Lucy, American journalist and nonfiction writer, Oct 1953, *Obit* Yrbk 2005

Freeman, R. Austin, English physician and mystery writer, *Obit* Nov 1943

French, Marilyn, American novelist and critic, Sept 1992, *Obit* Yrbk 2009

French, Paul Comly, May 1951, *Obit* Sept 1960

Freud, Anna, British psychoanalyst, Apr 1979, *Obit* Mar 1983

Freund, Philip, Canadian novelist and short story writer, Yrbk 1948

Friedan, Betty, American feminist, Nov 1970, Mar 1989, *Obit* May 2006

Friedman, Bruce Jay, American novelist, short story writer and dramatist, June 1972

Friedman, Kinky, American country singer, band leader, songwriter and mystery novelist, Feb 2012

Friedman, Thomas L., American newspaper columnist, Oct 1995

Friel, Brian, Irish short story writer and dramatist, June 1974

Frings, Ketti, dramatist and screenwriter, Jan 1960, *Obit* Apr 1981

Frisch, Karl von, German zoologist, Feb 1974, *Obit* Yrbk 1983

Frisch, Max, Swiss architect, novelist and dramatist, Jan 1965, *Obit* June 1991

Fromm, Erich, American psychoanalyst and philosopher, Apr 1967, *Obit* May 1980

Frost, Frances, Yrbk 1950, *Obit* Apr 1959

Frost, Robert, American poet, Sept 1942, *Obit* Mar 1963

Frum, David, Canadian journalist, June 2004

Fry, Christopher, English dramatist, Feb 1951, *Obit* Yrbk 2005

Fry, Stephen, English actor and novelist, Sept 1998

Frye, David, American impressionist, Mar 1975, *Obit* Yrbk 2011

Frye, Northrop, Canadian literary critic, Aug 1983, *Obit* Mar 1991

Fuentes, Carlos, Mexican novelist, short story writer and essayist, Oct 1972, *Obit* Yrbk 2012

Fugard, Athol, South African dramatist, actor and director, June 1975

Fukuyama, Francis, American international relations specialist, June 2001

Fulghum, Robert, clergyman and essayist, July 1994

Fuller, Charles, American dramatist, June 1989

Fuller, R. Buckminster, American engineer and architect, Jan 1960, Feb 1976, *Obit* Aug 1983

Fuller, S. R., May 1941, *Obit* Mar 1966

Fuller, Samuel, American film director, Aug 1992, *Obit* Jan 1998

Funk, Wilfred, American publisher and lexicographer, Jan 1955, *Obit* July 1965

Funke, Cornelia Caroline, German illustrator and children's author, Jan 2007

Furcolo, Foster, American governor, Jan 1958, *Obit* Sept 1995

Fyfe, H. Hamilton, Yrbk 1940, *Obit* July 1951

Gaddis, William, American novelist, Nov 1987, *Obit* Mar 1999

Gaer, Joseph, author, publishing executive and foundation official, Yrbk 1951

Gag, Wanda, American children's author and illustrator, *Obit* July 1946

Gage, Nicholas, American journalist, Mar 1990

Gaines, Donna, American sociologist, June 2006

Gaines, Ernest J., American novelist and short story writer, Mar 1994

Gaither, Frances, author, Yrbk 1950, *Obit* Jan 1956

Galassi, Jonathan, American editor, poet and translator, Sept 1999

Galbraith, John Kenneth, American economist, Mar 1959, May 1975, *Obit* Yrbk 2007

Gallant, Mavis, Canadian short story writer and novelist, May 1990

Gallegos, Romulo, Venezuelan author and president, May 1948, *Obit* May 1969

Gallery, Daniel V., Apr 1966, *Obit* Mar 1977

Gallico, Paul, American novelist, short story writer and screenwriter, Apr 1946, *Obit* Sept 1976

Galloway, Joseph L., American journalist, Sept 2003

Gammons, Peter, American sportswriter, June 2011

Gamow, George, American physicist and science writer, Oct 1951, *Obit* Oct 1968

Gandhi, Mahatma, Indian nationalist leader, Yrbk 1942, *Obit* Feb 1948

Ganim, Sara, Aug 2013

Gannett, Lewis Stiles, American journalist and literary critic, Aug 1941, *Obit* Mar 1966

Garcia Marquez, Gabriel, Colombian novelist and short story writer, July 1973, Jan 2002

Garcia, Cristina, American novelist and journalist, Aug 1999

Gardner, Ed, Sept 1943, *Obit* Oct 1963

Gardner, Erle Stanley, American mystery novelist, June 1944, *Obit* Apr 1970

Gardner, Howard, American psychologist, Oct 1998

Gardner, John, American novelist, critic and translator, Oct 1978, *Obit* Nov 1982

Gardner, John William, American Secretary of health, education and welfare, Mar 1956, Mar 1976, *Obit* May 2002

Gardner, Martin, American children's author and mathematician, Sept 1999, *Obit* Yrbk 2010

Garland, Hamlin, American novelist and memoirist, Mar 1940

Garner, Helen, Australian novelist, Jan 2007

Garratt, Geoffrey Theodore, *Obit* June 1942

Garrison, Deborah, American poet and editor, Jan 2001

Garst, Shannon, Yrbk 1947

Garth, David, Yrbk 1957

Gartner, Michael G., newspaper editor, May 1990

Garvey, Marcus, Jamaican-American civil rights activist, *Obit* Aug 1940

Gaselee, Stephen, *Obit* Aug 1943

Gass, William H., American philosopher, novelist, short story writer and critic, Apr 1986

Gassner, John, Jan 1947, *Obit* June 1967

Gates, Henry Louis, American professor of African-American studies, Oct 1992

Gauss, D. Christian, Apr 1945, *Obit* Yrbk 1951

Gawande, Atul, American physician and medical writer, Mar 2005

Gay, Peter, American historian, Feb 1986

Gayda, Virginio, Sept 1940, *Obit* Sept 1943

Gelb, Leslie H., American journalist, government official and international relations specialist, Jan 2003

Geldzahler, Henry, art historian, critic and curator, Sept 1978, *Obit* Oct 1994

Gell-Mann, Murray, American physicist, Feb 1966, Oct 1998

Gellhorn, Walter, professor of law, May 1967, *Obit* Feb 1996

Genet, Jean, French dramatist, novelist and poet, Apr 1974, *Obit* June 1986

George, Elizabeth, American mystery novelist, Mar 2000

George, Manfred, German newspaper editor and writer, Oct 1965, *Obit* Feb 1966

George, Susan, American social scientist, July 2007

Geraud, Andre, Sept 1940, *Obit* Jan 1975

Gergen, David, American political commentator, Feb 1994

Germond, Jack, American columnist and political commentator, July 2005

Gershwin, Ira, American lyricist, Jan 1956, *Obit* Oct 1983

Gerson, Michael, American presidential speechwriter, Feb 2002

Gerstenmaier, Eugen, German political leader, Feb 1958, *Obit* May 1986

Gervais, Ricky, British comedian, Jan 2006

Gervasi, Frank Henry, author and journalist, June 1942, *Obit* Mar 1990

Gesell, Arnold Lucius, American psychologist, Nov 1940, *Obit* Sept 1961

Gessen, Keith, American magazine editor, novelist and critic, Sept 2008

Gessen, Masha, Russian journalist, Nov 2013

Geyer, Georgie Anne, columnist, Aug 1986

Gheerbrant, Alain, Feb 1959

Giamatti, A. Bartlett, American university president, literary scholar and baseball commissioner, Apr 1978, *Obit* Oct 1989

Gibbings, Robert, Irish travel writer and illustrator, Yrbk 1948, *Obit* Mar 1958

Gibson, Hugh, diplomat, Jan 1953, *Obit* Feb 1955

Gibson, William, American dramatist, memoirist, poet and novelist, July 1983

Gifford, Kathie Lee, American singer and television personality, Nov 1994

Gifford, Sanford R., American ophthalmologist, *Obit* Apr 1944

Gil Fortoul, Jose, *Obit* Aug 1943

Gilbert, George, *Obit* May 1943

Gilbert, Martin, English historian, Feb 1991

Gilbreth, Frank B., American journalist, memoirist and novelist, May 1949, *Obit* July 2001

Gilchrist, Brad, cartoonist, Jan 1999

Gilchrist, Guy, author, illustrator and cartoonist, Jan 1999

Gilder, Robert F., American journalist and archaeologist, *Obit* Mar 1940

Gilder, Rosamond, American drama critic, Nov 1945, *Obit* Oct 1986

Giles, Janice Holt, author, Yrbk 1958

Gillet, Louis, *Obit* Aug 1943

Gilligan, Carol, American psychologist, May 1997

Gillis, James M., priest, June 1956, *Obit* June 1957

Gilmore, Eddy, American journalist, June 1947, *Obit* Yrbk 1967

Gilroy, Frank Daniel, American playwright, screenwriter and filmmaker, Oct 1965

Gilyard, Keith, American sociolinguist, Oct 2011

Gimlette, John, English travel writer and lawyer, Apr 2012

Gingrich, Newt, American political leader and former Speaker of the House, July 1989

Ginsberg, Allen, American poet, Apr 1970, Apr 1987, *Obit* June 1997

Ginzberg, Eli, American economist and educator, Mar 1966, *Obit* Yrbk 2003

Ginzburg, Natalia, Italian novelist, July 1990, *Obit* Nov 1991

Gioia, Ted, American jazz historian, Jan 2010

Giovanni, Nikki, American poet and essayist, Apr 1973

Gipson, Frederick Benjamin, author, Yrbk 1957

Gipson, Lawrence Henry, Oct 1954, *Obit* Nov 1971

Giraudoux, Jean, French dramatist and novelist, *Obit* Mar 1944

Giroud, Francoise, French journalist and cabinet member, Apr 1975, *Obit* July 2003

Giroux, Robert, American editor and publisher, Nov 1982, *Obit* Yrbk 2008

Gladstone, Brooke, American radio reporter, Jan 2009

Gladwell, Malcolm, Canadian business writer, June 2005

Glasgow, Ellen Anderson Gholson, American novelist, *Obit* Jan 1946

Glazer, Nathan, American sociologist and educator, Yrbk 1970

Gleick, James, American science writer, July 2011

Glubb, John Bagot, British general, Sept 1951, *Obit* May 1986

Glyn, Elinor, English novelist, *Obit* Nov 1943

Godden, Rumer, English novelist and children's author, Aug 1976, *Obit* Jan 1999

Godwin, Gail, American novelist and short story writer, Oct 1995

Goertz, Arthemise, Yrbk 1953

Goetz, Delia, author and translator, Yrbk 1949, *Obit* Sept 1996

Gogarty, Oliver St. John, Irish otolaryngologist, poet and novelist, July 1941, *Obit* Yrbk 1957

Gold, Herbert, American novelist and short story writer, Yrbk 1955

Goldberg, Michelle, American journalist, Jan 2012

Golden, Harry Lewis, American newspaper publisher and essayist, Jan 1959, *Obit* Nov 1981

Golden, John, Mar 1944, *Obit* Sept 1955

Goldin, Daniel, screenwriter, June 1993

Golding, William, English novelist, Mar 1964, *Obit* Aug 1993

Goldman, Emma, American anarchist, *Obit* Jan 1940

Goldman, Eric Frederick, American historian, July 1964, *Obit* Apr 1989

Goldman, William, American novelist and screenwriter, Jan 1995

Goldsman, Akiva, American screenwriter, Sept 2004

Goldstine, Herman Heine, American mathematician and computer scientist, Nov 1952, *Obit* Yrbk 2004

Goodall, Jane, British primatologist, Nov 1967, Nov 1991

Goodman, Paul, American poet, novelist, essayist and dramatist, June 1968, *Obit* Oct 1972

Goodrich, Arthur, *Obit* Aug 1941

Goodrich, Frances, American dramatist and screenwriter, Oct 1956, *Obit* Apr 1984

Goodrich, Marcus, author, Apr 1941, *Obit* Jan 1992

Goodspeed, Edgar Johnson, biblical scholar, Nov 1946, *Obit* Mar 1962

Goodwin, Doris Kearns, American historian and television commentator, Nov 1997

Goodwin, Richard N., American speechwriter and journalist, Yrbk 1968

Gopnik, Adam, American essayist and art critic, Apr 2005

Gopnik, Alison, American psychologist, Jan 2007

Gordimer, Nadine, South African novelist, Yrbk 1959, June 1980

Gordon, Dorothy, Jan 1955, *Obit* July 1970

Gordon, Jaimy, American novelist, poet and short story writer, July 2011

Gordon, Jan, English author and illustrator, *Obit* Mar 1944

Gordon, Mary, American novelist, Nov 1981

Gordon, Ruth, actress and screenwriter, Apr 1943, Apr 1972, *Obit* Oct 1985

Gordon-Reed, Annette, American law professor, biographer and historian, May 2009

Goren, Charles Henry, bridge player, Mar 1959, *Obit* July 1991

Gorey, Edward, American illustrator, children's author and designer, Nov 1976, *Obit* Aug 2000

Gorman, Herbert Sherman, author and literary critic, Mar 1940, *Obit* Jan 1955

Gorman, Thomas Francis Xavier, mental health official, Oct 1956, *Obit* July 1989

Gorrie, Jack Osborne, Mar 1952

Gottlieb, Robert Adams, American editor and publishing executive, Sept 1987

Goudge, Elizabeth, English novelist, children's author and short story writer, Sept 1940, *Obit* Aug 1984

Gould, Bruce, magazine editor, Nov 1947, *Obit* Oct 1989

Gould, Glenn, Canadian pianist, Oct 1960, *Obit* Nov 1982

Gould, Stephen Jay, American paleontologist and science writer, Sept 1982, *Obit* Aug 2002

Gow, James Ellis, Mar 1944, *Obit* Mar 1952

Graebner, Walter, Aug 1943

Grafton, Samuel, columnist, Jan 1940, *Obit* Feb 1998

Grafton, Sue, American mystery novelist, Sept 1995

Graham, Billy, American evangelist, Apr 1951, Jan 1973

Graham, Elinor, Yrbk 1952

Graham, Evarts A., American surgeon, Feb 1952, *Obit* May 1957

Graham, Gwethalyn, Canadian novelist, Jan 1945, *Obit* Jan 1966

Graham, Jorie, American poet, May 1997

Graham, Katharine, American newspaper publisher, Jan 1971, *Obit* Oct 2001

Graham, Sheilah, American gossip columnist, Oct 1969, *Obit* Jan 1989

Graham, Winston, English novelist, Yrbk 1955, *Obit* Yrbk 2003

Grahame-Smith, Seth, American screenwriter, Nov 2012

Grand, Sarah, English novelist and feminist, *Obit* July 1943

Grandes, Almudena, Spanish novelist, Jan 2006

Grant, Gordon, June 1953, *Obit* July 1962

Grant, Kay, Yrbk 1959

Grant, Robert, author and judge, *Obit* July 1940

Grass, Gunter, German novelist, Oct 1964, July 1983

Grau, Shirley Ann, novelist and short story writer, Yrbk 1959

Graves, Florence, American journalist, May 2005

Graves, Robert, English novelist and poet, May 1978, *Obit* Feb 1986

Gray, Simon, English dramatist and novelist, June 1983, *Obit* Yrbk 2008

Greeley, Andrew M., American sociologist, priest and novelist, Yrbk 1972, *Obit* Yrbk 2013

Green, Adolph, American lyricist, librettist and screenwriter, Mar 1945, *Obit* Mar 2003

Green, Constance McLaughlin, historian, Oct 1963

Green, Julien, American novelist, essayist and memoirist, Jan 1940, *Obit* Oct 1998

Green, Mark J., American lawyer, consumer rights advocate and municipal official, Feb 1988

Green, Tim, American football player, sportscaster and novelist, Aug 2000

Greenbie, Sydney, Sept 1941, *Obit* Sept 1960

Greene, Bob, American journalist, July 1995

Greene, Brian R., American physicist, Aug 2000

Greene, Graham, English novelist, Oct 1969, *Obit* May 1991

Greer, Germaine, Australian feminist and writer, Nov 1971, Oct 1988

Gregory, Dick, American comedian, author and civil rights leader, June 1962

Grenfell, Wilfred Thomason, British medical missionary, *Obit* Yrbk 1940

Grey, Clifford, *Obit* Nov 1941

Gribble, Harry Wagstaff, Sept 1945, *Obit* Apr 1981

Grieff, Joseph Nicholas, *Obit* Aug 1941

Griffin, John Howard, American novelist and journalist, Nov 1960, *Obit* Nov 1980

Grigg, John, English journalist and biographer, Oct 1964, *Obit* Apr 2002

Grisham, John, American lawyer and novelist, Sept 1993

Griswold, A. Whitney, American college president, Apr 1950, *Obit* June 1963

Groening, Matt, American cartoonist and animator, Sept 1990

Groopman, Jerome E., American physician and medical writer, Oct 2004

Grossman, Edith, American translator and literary scholar, Mar 2006

Grossman, Lev, American literary critic and novelist, Apr 2010

Groves, Ernest R., sociologist, June 1943, *Obit* Oct 1946

Groves, Gladys Hoagland, June 1943, *Obit* Sept 1980

Gruber, Frank, American screenwriter and mystery novelist, Nov 1941, *Obit* Feb 1970

Gruber, Lilli, Italian television news anchor and member of European parliament, Jan 2007

Gruber, Ruth, American journalist, photographer and humanitarian, June 2001

Grubin, David, American documentary filmmaker, producer and screenwriter, Aug 2002

Gruenberg, Sidonie Matsner, May 1940, *Obit* May 1974

Gruening, Ernest, American territorial governor and senator, Yrbk 1946, July 1966, *Obit* Sept 1974

Guare, John, American dramatist, Aug 1982

Guedalla, Philip, English historian, *Obit* Feb 1945

Guerard, Albert J., novelist and critic, Yrbk 1946, *Obit* Mar 2001

Guest, Edgar A., American newspaper columnist, Sept 1941, *Obit* Nov 1959

Guillermoprieto, Alma, Mexican journalist, Sept 2004

Guiterman, Arthur, poet, *Obit* Mar 1943

Gullar, Ferreira, Brazilian poet and art critic, Jan 2004

Gumpert, Martin, Yrbk 1951

Gunn, Thom, English poet, Nov 1988, *Obit* Yrbk 2004

Gunther, John, journalist and author, Nov 1941, Feb 1961, *Obit* July 1970

Guptill, Arthur L., Mar 1955, *Obit* May 1956

Gurney, A. R., American dramatist, July 1986

Guterson, David, American novelist and short story writer, Nov 1996

Guthman, Edwin O., American newspaper editor, June 1950, *Obit* Yrbk 2008

Guthrie, A. B., American novelist, short story writer and poet, July 1950, *Obit* July 1991

Guthrie, Woody, American folk singer and songwriter, May 1963, *Obit* Yrbk 1967

Gwathmey, James T., *Obit* Apr 1944

Habe, Hans, German author and journalist, Feb 1943, *Obit* Nov 1977

Habermas, Jurgen, German social philosopher, Jan 2007

Hackett, Albert, American dramatist and screenwriter, Oct 1956, *Obit* May 1995

Hackett, Walter, *Obit* Mar 1944

Hadas, Moses, Mar 1960, *Obit* Nov 1966

Hagerty, James C., American journalist and presidential aide, Mar 1953, *Obit* June 1981

Haggis, Paul, Canadian screenwriter and film director, Aug 2006

Hagy, Ruth Geri, Oct 1957

Hahn, Emily, American novelist and biographer, July 1942, *Obit* Apr 1997

Hahn, Otto, German chemist, Mar 1951, *Obit* Oct 1968

Haig-Brown, Roderick Langmere, Canadian naturalist, conservationist and author, Yrbk 1950

Hailey, Arthur, Canadian novelist, Feb 1972, *Obit* Yrbk 2005

Halberstam, David, American journalist, Apr 1973, *Obit* July 2007

Haldane, J. B. S., British geneticist, Nov 1940, *Obit* Jan 1965

Hale, Richard Walden, *Obit* Apr 1943

Haley, Alex, American biographer, historian and journalist, Jan 1977, *Obit* Mar 1992

Hall, Donald, American poet, essayist, critic and children's author, May 1984

Hall, Edward Twitchell, American anthropologist, Feb 1992, *Obit* Yrbk 2009

Hall, Frank O., *Obit* Yrbk 1941

Hall, Josef Washington, journalist, historian and radio commentator, Yrbk 1944, *Obit* Jan 1961

Hall, Radclyffe, English novelist and poet, *Obit* Nov 1943

Halsey, Margaret, author, Nov 1944, *Obit* Apr 1997

Hamill, Pete, American journalist and novelist, Feb 1998

Hamilton, Alice, American physician, May 1946, *Obit* Nov 1970

Hamilton, Charles, American autograph dealer and handwriting expert, July 1976, *Obit* Feb 1997

Hamilton, Clayton Meeker, dramatist and critic, *Obit* Oct 1946

Hamilton, Cosmo, English author and dramatist, *Obit* Yrbk 1942

Hamilton, Edith, American classicist, Apr 1963

Hamlin, Talbot Faulkner, Oct 1954, *Obit* Yrbk 1957

Hammerstein, Oscar, American lyricist and librettist, Feb 1944, *Obit* Nov 1960

Hampshire, Susan, English actress and author, Jan 1974

Han, Suyin, Chinese novelist and physician, Yrbk 1957, *Obit* Yrbk 2013

Hancock, Graham, Scottish writer, Feb 2005

Handke, Peter, Austrian novelist and dramatist, Apr 1973

Handlin, Oscar, American historian, July 1952, *Obit* Yrbk 2011

Hannagan, Steve, publicist and sportswriter, Aug 1944, *Obit* Mar 1953

Hansberry, Lorraine, American dramatist, Sept 1959, *Obit* Feb 1965

Hansen, Harry, editor and critic, Yrbk 1942, *Obit* Yrbk 1991

Hansenne, Marcel, Apr 1946

Harbach, Otto, American librettist and lyricist, July 1950, *Obit* Mar 1963

Harburg, E. Y., American lyricist, July 1980, *Obit* Apr 1981

Hardin, Garrett James, American biologist, Sept 1974, *Obit* Apr 2004

Harding, Margaret S., Apr 1947

Hardwick, Chris, game show host, June 2012

Hardwick, Elizabeth, American novelist, short story writer, essayist and critic, Feb 1981, *Obit* Yrbk 2008

Hare, David, English dramatist and theatrical director, Aug 1983

Harewood, George Henry Hubert Lascelles, English editor and writer on opera, Jan 1965, *Obit* Yrbk 2011

Hargrove, Marion, American novelist and humorist, June 1946, *Obit* Yrbk 2004

Haring, Bernhard, German theologian, June 1969, *Obit* Sept 1998

Harjo, Joy, American poet, Aug 2001

Harkness, Georgia Elma, theologian, Nov 1960

Harnoncourt, Nikolaus, Austrian conductor, Jan 1991

Harper, Theodore Acland, *Obit* June 1942

Harrer, Heinrich, Austrian mountaineer, Oct 1954, *Obit* Yrbk 2006

Harrington, Michael, American social critic and political activist, Jan 1969, Oct 1988, *Obit* Sept 1989

Harris, Bernice Kelly, novelist and dramatist, Yrbk 1949

Harris, Cyril M., American acoustic engineer, Feb 1977, *Obit* Yrbk 2011

Harris, E. Lynn, American novelist, June 1996, *Obit* Yrbk 2009

Harris, Fred R., American senator, Jan 1968

Harris, Judith Rich, textbook author, Apr 1999

Harris, Mark, American novelist and memoirist, Yrbk 1959, *Obit* Yrbk 2007

Harris, Sam, American neuroscientist, Jan 2012

Harrison, Gilbert A., American magazine editor, publisher and veterans' leader, Mar 1949, *Obit* Yrbk 2008

Harrison, Jim, American poet and novelist, July 1992

Harrison, Joan, English screenwriter and producer, May 1944, *Obit* Oct 1994

Harrower, David, Scottish dramatist, Jan 2007

Harsanyi, Zsolt, *Obit* Apr 1944

Harsch, Joseph C., American journalist, Oct 1944, *Obit* Aug 1998

Hart, Albert Bushnell, historian, *Obit* Aug 1943

Hart, Lorenz, American lyricist, May 1940, *Obit* Feb 1944

Hart, Mickey, American drummer, Jan 1994

Hart, Moss, American playwright, July 1940, Nov 1960, Obit Feb 1962

Hartley, Hal, American motion picture director and screenwriter, Aug 1995

Hartley, Marsden, American painter and poet, Obit Oct 1943

Hartman, Grace, Nov 1942, Obit Oct 1955

Hartman, Louis F., Jan 1953, Obit Nov 1970

Haruka, Yoko, Japanese feminist, writer and television personality, Jan 2004

Haskell, Molly, motion picture critic, Nov 1998

Haskin, Frederic J., Obit June 1944

Hass, Amira, Israeli journalist, Apr 2009

Hass, Robert, American poet, critic and translator, Feb 2001

Hatcher, Harlan H., literary critic, author and historian, Oct 1955, Obit May 1998

Hauck, Louise Platt, Obit Feb 1944

Hauerwas, Stanley, American theologian, June 2003

Hauptmann, Gerhart, German dramatist, Obit July 1946

Hauser, Gayelord, German-American nutritionist and author, June 1955, Obit Feb 1985

Havel, Vaclav, Czech dramatist and president, Mar 1985, Aug 1995, Obit Yrbk 2012

Havill, Edward, Yrbk 1952

Hawass, Zahi, Egyptian archaeologist, Apr 2000

Hawes, Elizabeth, American fashion designer, Oct 1940, Obit Yrbk 1991

Hawke, Ethan, American actor and novelist, May 1998

Hawking, Stephen W., British physicist, May 1984

Hawley, Cameron, Yrbk 1957

Hax, Carolyn, American advice columnist, Nov 2002

Hayakawa, S. I., American senator and educator, Nov 1959, Jan 1977, Obit Apr 1992

Haycraft, Howard, publisher and author, Nov 1941, Feb 1954, Obit Jan 1992

Hayden, Sterling, actor, May 1978, Obit July 1986

Hayek, Friedrich A. von, British economist, June 1945, Obit May 1992

Hayes, Denis, lawyer and environmentalist, Oct 1997

Hayes, Terrance, American poet, Apr 2011

Hays, Arthur Garfield, lawyer and civil rights leader, Sept 1942, Obit Feb 1955

Hazard, Paul, Mar 1941

Hazzard, Shirley, Australian novelist and short story writer, Jan 1991

Head, Henry, British neurologist, Obit Yrbk 1940

Heaney, Seamus, Irish poet, Jan 1982, Obit Yrbk 2013

Heath, S. Burton, Jan 1940, Obit Sept 1949

Hebert, F. Edward, American congressman, Nov 1951, Obit Feb 1980

Hecht, Anthony, American poet, May 1986, Obit Yrbk 2005

Hecht, Ben, American journalist, novelist, dramatist and screenwriter, Feb 1942, Obit June 1964

Heckscher, August, municipal official and journalist, Oct 1958, Obit June 1997

Hedden, Worth Tuttle, American novelist and short story writer, Yrbk 1957, Obit Jan 1986

Hedges, Chris, American foreign correspondent, June 2012

Hedin, Sven Anders, Swedish explorer, May 1940, Obit Jan 1953

Heidegger, Martin, German philosopher, June 1972, Obit July 1976

Heiden, Konrad, Mar 1944, Obit Sept 1975

Heidenstam, Verner von, Swedish poet and novelist, Obit July 1940

Heilbroner, Robert L., American economist and writer, June 1975, Obit Yrbk 2005

Heilbrun, Carolyn G., American literary scholar and mystery novelist, Jan 1993, Obit Feb 2004

Heinlein, Robert A., American science fiction writer, Mar 1955, Obit June 1988

Heiser, Victor G., physician, Apr 1942, Obit May 1972

Hektoen, Ludvig, Yrbk 1947, Obit Sept 1951

Helion, Jean, French painter, Nov 1943, Obit Jan 1988

Hellenga, Robert, American novelist, Mar 2008

Heller, Joseph, American novelist, Jan 1973, Obit Mar 2000

Hellinger, Mark, columnist and motion picture producer, Sept 1947, Obit July 1948

Hellman, Lillian, American playwright, May 1941, June 1960, Obit Aug 1984

Heloise, American advice columnist, June 1996

Helprin, Mark, American short story writer and novelist, Aug 1991

Heming, Arthur Henry Howard, Obit Yrbk 1940

Hemingway, Mary, wife of American novelist Ernest Hemingway, Sept 1968, Obit Jan 1987

Hench, Philip Showalter, American physician, Yrbk 1950, Obit May 1965

Henley, Beth, American dramatist, Feb 1983

Henner, Marilu, American actress, Feb 1999

Henry, Marguerite, American children's author, Yrbk 1947, Obit Feb 1998

Henry, Mellinger Edward, Obit Mar 1946

Hentoff, Nat, American journalist and young adult novelist, Aug 1986

Herbert, Bob, American columnist, Oct 1998

Herlihy, James Leo, American novelist, dramatist and actor, Sept 1961, Obit Jan 1994

Herman, Jerry, American composer and lyricist, Jan 1965

Herold, J. Christopher, Yrbk 1959, Obit Feb 1965

Herring, Pendleton, American political scientist, July 1950, Obit Yrbk 2004

Hersey, John, American novelist and journalist, Feb 1944, Obit May 1993

Hersh, Seymour M., American journalist, Mar 1984

Herskovitz, Marshall, American film and television producer, scriptwriter and director, Sept 2000

Hertz, Emanuel, *Obit* July 1940

Hertzberg, Arthur, American rabbi and religious writer, June 1975, *Obit* Yrbk 2006

Hertzberg, Hendrik, American journalist, Mar 2011

Hertzler, Arthur E., American surgeon, *Obit* Oct 1946

Herzog, Maurice, July 1953

Heschel, Abraham Joshua, American rabbi and theologian, Apr 1970, *Obit* Mar 1973

Hesse, Hermann, German novelist, Oct 1962

Heydt, Herman A., *Obit* Oct 1941

Heyerdahl, Thor, Norwegian ethnologist and explorer, Yrbk 1947, Sept 1972, *Obit* Yrbk 2002

Heym, Stefan, German novelist, Mar 1943, *Obit* Mar 2002

Heyward, DuBose, American novelist and dramatist, *Obit* July 1940

Hiaasen, Carl, American novelist and columnist, Apr 1997

Hickam, Homer H., American aerospace engineer and memoirist, Oct 2000

Hickey, Dave, American art and cultural critic, Sept 2007

Hicks, Granville, American literary critic and novelist, May 1942, *Obit* Aug 1982

Higgins, F. R., Irish poet, *Obit* Mar 1941

Higgins, Marguerite, journalist, June 1951, *Obit* Feb 1966

Highet, Gilbert, Scottish-American classicist, Sept 1964, *Obit* Mar 1978

Highsmith, Patricia, American mystery novelist, Jan 1990, *Obit* Apr 1995

Hightower, John M., journalist, Nov 1952, *Obit* Apr 1987

Hildebrand, Joel Henry, American chemist, Feb 1955, *Obit* July 1983

Hill, Abram, theatrical director, producer and dramatist, Aug 1945, *Obit* Nov 1986

Hill, Edwin Conger, journalist, Sept 1940, *Obit* Apr 1957

Hill, Helen, American children's author and illustrator, *Obit* May 1942

Hillary, Edmund, New Zealand mountaineer, Oct 1954, Jan 2002, *Obit* Yrbk 2008

Hillenburg, Stephen, American animator and television scriptwriter, Apr 2003

Hillerman, Tony, American mystery novelist, Jan 1992, *Obit* Yrbk 2008

Hillyer, Robert Silliman, poet, July 1940, *Obit* Feb 1962

Hilton, James, English novelist, Sept 1942, *Obit* Feb 1955

Hines, Duncan, restaurant critic and publisher, May 1946, *Obit* May 1959

Hingson, Robert A., anesthesiologist and public health expert, June 1943, *Obit* Jan 1997

Hinojosa, Maria, American radio reporter and memoirist, Feb 2001

Hirsi Ali, Ayaan, Somali-Dutch feminist and member of Parliament, Jan 2003

Hitchens, Christopher, British journalist, Mar 1999, *Obit* Yrbk 2012

Hite, Shere, author and feminist, Feb 1988

Hoagland, Edward, American novelist, essayist and travel writer, Sept 1982

Hoagland, Tony, American poet, May 2011

Hobson, John Atkinson, British economist and journalist, *Obit* Apr 1940

Hobson, Laura Keane Zametkin, author, Sept 1947, *Obit* Apr 1986

Hochhuth, Rolf, German dramatist, Oct 1976

Hockenberry, John, radio and television reporter, Oct 1996

Hocking, William Ernest, American philosopher, Mar 1962, *Obit* July 1966

Hoellering, Franz, Oct 1940

Hoffer, Eric, American philosopher and essayist, Mar 1965, *Obit* July 1983

Hoffman, Abbie, American political activist, Apr 1981, *Obit* June 1989

Hoffman, Alice, American novelist, Sept 1992

Hogben, Lancelot, English physiologist and zoologist, Yrbk 1941, *Obit* Jan 1984

Hoggart, Richard, English social and cultural critic, Oct 1963

Holberg, Ruth Langland, Yrbk 1949

Holbrook, Sabra, author, Nov 1948

Holdsclaw, Chamique, American basketball player, Feb 2006

Holland, Agnieszka, Polish film director and screenwriter, Jan 1998

Hollander, John, philologist and poet, Sept 1991, *Obit* Yrbk 2013

Hollander, Robert, American literary critic, translator and poet, Sept 2006

Hollenbeck, Don, American television newscaster, Feb 1951, *Obit* Sept 1954

Hollomon, J. Herbert, college president and government official, Mar 1964, *Obit* Aug 1985

Holmes, John Haynes, American clergyman, theologian and social reformer, Jan 1941, *Obit* May 1964

Holroyd, Michael, English biographer, Mar 1989

Holt, Isabella, Yrbk 1956, *Obit* May 1962

Holt, John Caldwell, American educator, June 1981, *Obit* Nov 1985

Holt, Rackham, Apr 1944

Honderich, Ted, Canadian philosopher, Feb 2009

Hooks, Bell, American feminist and social critic, Apr 1995

Hooper, Franklin Henry, *Obit* Oct 1940

Hopkins, Alfred, *Obit* July 1941

Hopkins, Nevil Monroe, *Obit* May 1945

Hopper, Hedda, American gossip columnist, Nov 1942, *Obit* Mar 1966

Horgan, Paul, author, Feb 1971, *Obit* May 1995

Hornblow, Arthur, *Obit* June 1942

Horne, Gerald, American historian and biographer, Sept 2011

Hosseini, Khaled, Afghan-American physician and novelist, July 2013

Houellebecq, Michel, French novelist and poet, Jan 2002

Houle, Cyril Orvin, May 1962

Houssay, Bernardo Alberto, Argentine physiologist, Jan 1948, *Obit* Nov 1971

Houston, James A., Canadian artist, novelist and children's author, July 1987, *Obit* Yrbk 2005

Howar, Barbara, columnist and television reporter, Aug 1989

Howard, Bart B., Jan 1940, *Obit* Apr 1941

Howard, Elizabeth, Yrbk 1951

Howe, Frederic Clemson, lawyer and reformer, *Obit* Sept 1940

Howe, Harrison E., *Obit* Feb 1943

Howe, Helen Huntington, author and monologist, Yrbk 1954, *Obit* Mar 1975

Howe, Irving, American literary critic and editor, Apr 1978, *Obit* July 1993

Howe, Quincy, American journalist, Nov 1940, *Obit* Apr 1977

Howe, Tina, American dramatist, Jan 1990

Hoyle, Fred, English astronomer and science fiction writer, Apr 1960, *Obit* Jan 2002

Hrdy, Sarah Blaffer, American primatologist and anthropologist, June 2000

Hu, Shih, Chinese poet, diplomat and literary critic, Feb 1942, *Obit* Apr 1962

Hubbard, Bernard, July 1943, *Obit* July 1962

Hubbard, Margaret Ann, American young adult mystery writer, Yrbk 1958

Huckel, Oliver, *Obit* Jan 1940

Hudlin, Reginald, American film and television director, May 1999

Huffington, Arianna, Greek-American political adviser and commentator, July 1998

Huggins, Charles B., American surgeon, Feb 1965, *Obit* Mar 1997

Hughes, Emmet John, American journalist and presidential speechwriter and adviser, Jan 1964, *Obit* Nov 1982

Hughes, Hatcher, American dramatist, *Obit* Nov 1945

Hughes, John, American film director, producer and screenwriter, Sept 1991, *Obit* Yrbk 2009

Hughes, Langston, American poet, novelist, short story writer and playwright, Oct 1940, *Obit* July 1967

Hughes, Paul, Yrbk 1943

Hughes, Robert, Australian art critic, May 1987, *Obit* Yrbk 2012

Hughes, Ted, English poet, June 1979, *Obit* Jan 1999

Hull, Helen R., author, May 1940, *Obit* Sept 1971

Humphry, Derek, English euthanasia advocate, Mar 1995

Hung Huang, Chinese magazine executive, Jan 2006

Hunt, Mabel Leigh, author, Yrbk 1951

Hunter, Aislinn, Canadian short story writer, poet and novelist, Jan 2002

Hunter, Dard, American papermaker and typographer, Sept 1960, *Obit* Mar 1966

Hunter, Evan, American novelist, short story writer and dramatist, Yrbk 1956, *Obit* Yrbk 2005

Hunter, Kermit, dramatist, May 1959, *Obit* Sept 2001

Hunter-Gault, Charlayne, American television newscaster, Apr 1987

Hurston, Zora Neale, American novelist and folklorist, May 1942, *Obit* Apr 1960

Husayn, Taha, Egyptian educator, Oct 1953, *Obit* Yrbk 1973

Huston, John, American film director and screenwriter, Feb 1949, Mar 1981, *Obit* Oct 1987

Hutchins, Robert Maynard, American university president, Yrbk 1940, Feb 1954, *Obit* July 1977

Hutchinson, Paul, American clergyman, magazine editor and writer, Yrbk 1949, *Obit* June 1956

Hutchinson, R. C., English novelist, Nov 1940

Hutchison, Bruce, Canadian journalist, Oct 1956

Huxley, Julian, British biologist, Aug 1942, Oct 1963, *Obit* Apr 1975

Huxtable, Ada Louise, American architectural critic, Mar 1973, *Obit* Yrbk 2013

Hwang, David Henry, American dramatist, May 1989

Hynek, J. Allen, astrophysicist, Yrbk 1968, *Obit* June 1986

Iacocca, Lee A., American automobile executive, Oct 1971, Oct 1988

Ibarruri, Dolores, Spanish communist leader, June 1967, *Obit* Jan 1990

Ickes, Harold L., American Secretary of the interior, July 1941, *Obit* Mar 1952

Idell, Albert Edward, author, Oct 1943, *Obit* Oct 1958

Ifill, Gwen, American television newscaster and moderator, Sept 2005

Igoe, Herbert A., *Obit* Apr 1945

Ilg, Frances Lillian, pediatrician and educator, Sept 1956, *Obit* Sept 1981

Imus, Don, American radio talk show host, Feb 1996

Infeld, Leopold, May 1941, July 1963, *Obit* Mar 1968

Ingalls, Jeremy, poet, Yrbk 1954, *Obit* July 2000

Inge, William, American dramatist, June 1953, *Obit* July 1973

Ingersoll, Ralph, American journalist, July 1940, *Obit* May 1985

Innaurato, Albert, dramatist, Mar 1988

Innes, Hammond, English novelist, Yrbk 1954

Inose, Naoki, Japanese historian, Jan 2002

Ionesco, Eugene, French dramatist, Oct 1959, *Obit* June 1994

Irvine, Alexander, Irish-American missionary, actor and dramatist, *Obit* May 1941

Irving, John, American novelist, Oct 1979

Irwin, Margaret, English author, Yrbk 1946, *Obit* Yrbk 1991

Isaacs, Susan, American novelist, Oct 1993

Isaacson, Walter, American broadcasting executive, Nov 2013

Isherwood, Christopher, Anglo-American novelist, Oct 1972, *Obit* Feb 1986

Ishiguro, Kazuo, Japanese-British novelist, Sept 1990

Ishimoto, Tatsuo, Apr 1956

Istaru, Ana, Costa Rican poet, dramatist and actress, Jan 2004

Italiaander, Rolf, June 1964

Ives, David, American dramatist, Feb 2013

Ivey, John E., educator, July 1960, *Obit* Aug 1992

Ivins, Molly, American columnist, June 2000, *Obit* Yrbk 2007

Jackson, Charles, novelist and short story writer, May 1944, *Obit* Nov 1968

Jackson, Michael, British journalist and beer expert, Aug 2005, *Obit* Yrbk 2007

Jackson, Peter, New Zealand film director and screenwriter, Jan 2002

Jacobs, Jane, American city planner, Mar 1977, *Obit* Yrbk 2006

Jacobs, Philip Peter, *Obit* Aug 1940

Jacobs, W. W., English short story writer and novelist, *Obit* Oct 1943

Jagendorf, M. A., Yrbk 1952

Jakes, John, American novelist, Sept 1988

Jakes, T. D., American clergyman, religious writer and gospel singer, June 2001

James, Bill, American baseball statistician, June 2004

James, Clive, Australian literary critic and journalist, Nov 1984

James, E.L., June 2013

James, P. D., English mystery novelist, Aug 1980

James, Will, American children's author and illustrator, *Obit* Nov 1942

Jamieson, Leland, *Obit* Sept 1941

Janeway, Elizabeth, American novelist and critic, Mar 1944, *Obit* Yrbk 2005

Janis, Sidney, American art dealer, July 1970, *Obit* Jan 1990

Janney, Russell, Mar 1947, *Obit* Sept 1963

Janowitz, Tama, American novelist and short story writer, Aug 1989

Jarecki, Eugene, American film director, May 2006

Jarvis, Jeff, American journalist, Aug 2009

Jastrow, Joseph, American psychologist, *Obit* Feb 1944

Jastrow, Robert, American physicist, Jan 1973, *Obit* Yrbk 2008

Jay, Peter, Oct 1978

Jealous, Benjamin T., American civil rights organization official, Feb 2009

Jeans, James Hopwood, British physicist and mathematician, Apr 1941, *Obit* Oct 1946

Jefferson, Margo, American literary critic, June 1999

Jelinek, Elfriede, Austrian novelist and dramatist, Jan 2005

Jencks, Christopher, sociologist, Apr 1973

Jenkins, Jerry B., American sportswriter and novelist, June 2003

Jenkins, Macgregor, *Obit* Apr 1940

Jenkins, Roy, British political leader, Mar 1966, Oct 1982, *Obit* Yrbk 2003

Jenkins, Sara, Yrbk 1953

Jennings, John Edward, author, Yrbk 1949

Jensen, Oliver, American magazine editor and historian, May 1945, *Obit* Yrbk 2005

Jhabvala, Ruth Prawer, British screenwriter and novelist, Mar 1977, *Obit* Yrbk 2013

Jimenez, Juan Ramon, Spanish poet, Feb 1957, *Obit* Sept 1958

Jodorowsky, Alejandro, Chilean film director and comic book writer, Jan 2005

Joesten, Joachim, June 1942

Johnson, Alvin Saunders, economist, author and educator, Aug 1942, *Obit* July 1971

Johnson, Brian David, Futurist and author, July 2012

Johnson, Charles Richard, American novelist and short story writer, Sept 1991

Johnson, Clifton, *Obit* Jan 1940

Johnson, Crockett, cartoonist, Yrbk 1943, *Obit* Jan 1984

Johnson, Douglas Wilson, American geologist, *Obit* Apr 1944

Johnson, Herschel, American journalist and children's author, July 1946

Johnson, Malcolm, June 1949, *Obit* Aug 1976

Johnson, Mat, American novelist, Mar 2010

Johnson, Nunnally, screenwriter, Aug 1941, *Obit* May 1977

Johnson, Pamela Hansford, English novelist and critic, Yrbk 1948, *Obit* Aug 1981

Johnson, Paul, English journalist and historian, Sept 1994

Johnson, Simon, American economist, Oct 2009

Johnstone, Margaret Blair, Jan 1955

Jones, Candy, model and talk show host, Oct 1961, *Obit* Mar 1990

Jones, E. Stanley, American missionary, May 1940, *Obit* Mar 1973

Jones, Edward P., American short story writer and novelist, Mar 2004

Jones, Grover, *Obit* Nov 1940

Jones, Idwal, author, Yrbk 1948, *Obit* Jan 1965

Jones, Preston, actor and dramatist, Feb 1977, *Obit* Nov 1979

Jones, Rufus Matthew, American Quaker leader, Oct 1941, *Obit* Sept 1948

Jones, Russell, Oct 1957, *Obit* Aug 1979

Jones, Sarah, American poet, playwright and performance artist, July 2005

Jones, Tayari, American novelist and short story writer, Aug 2009

Jong, Dola de, Dutch-American mystery novelist, Yrbk 1947, *Obit* Yrbk 2004

Jong, Erica, American poet and novelist, July 1975, Apr 1997

Jordan, Mildred, author, Yrbk 1951

Jordan, Neil, Irish film director, screenwriter and novelist, Aug 1993

Jordan, Virgil, Oct 1947, *Obit* June 1965

Jordan, W. K., Mar 1955, *Obit* July 1980

Jose, F. Sionil, Filipino novelist, Jan 2005

Joseph, Ammu, Indian journalist and feminist, Jan 2004

Joyce, James, Irish novelist, dramatist and poet, *Obit* Mar 1941

Joyce, James Avery, English lawyer, author and pacifist, Mar 1959

Judd, Charles Hubbard, *Obit* Sept 1946

Judson, Clara Ingram, author, Yrbk 1948

Judson, Olivia P., English evolutionary biologist, Jan 2004

July, Miranda, American performance artist and filmmaker, Nov 2007

Jung, C. G., Swiss psychologist, Apr 1943, Oct 1953, *Obit* Sept 1961

Just, Ward S., American novelist, May 1989

Kadare, Ismail, Albanian novelist, Feb 1992

Kael, Pauline, American film critic, Mar 1974, *Obit* Nov 2001

Kaempffert, Waldemar, Sept 1943, *Obit* Feb 1957

Kagan, Frederick W., American military historian, July 2007

Kagan, Henry Enoch, Sept 1965, *Obit* Oct 1969

Kagawa, Toyohiko, Japanese clergyman and philosopher, Sept 1941, *Obit* June 1960

Kahf, Mohja, Syrian-American writer, Jan 2007

Kahmann, Chesley, Yrbk 1952

Kahn, Gus, American lyricist, *Obit* Yrbk 1941

Kahn, Herman, American physicist and futurist, Oct 1962, *Obit* Aug 1983

Kahn, Roger, American novelist, short story writer and sportswriter, June 2000

Kaling, Mindy, American actress, playwright and television scriptwriter, Apr 2012

Kallen, Horace Meyer, philosopher, Oct 1953, *Obit* Apr 1974

Kander, Lizzie Black, American social worker and cookbook writer, *Obit* Sept 1940

Kane, Harnett T., journalist, historian and author, Yrbk 1947, *Obit* Yrbk 1984

Kani, John, South African actor, theatrical director and playwright, June 2001

Kanin, Garson, dramatist and director, Jan 1941, Oct 1952, *Obit* June 1999

Kanter, Rosabeth Moss, American management consultant, teacher and writer, May 1996

Kao, John J., American management consultant, Oct 2008

Kaplan, Justin, American biographer, July 1993

Kapuscinski, Ryszard, Polish journalist and biographer, Sept 1992, *Obit* Yrbk 2007

Karbo, Karen, American novelist, May 2001

Karon, Jan, American novelist, Mar 2003

Karp, David, American novelist and screenwriter, Yrbk 1957, *Obit* Feb 2000

Karpinski, Janis, American general, Apr 2006

Karsner, David, *Obit* Apr 1941

Kasdan, Lawrence, American film director and screenwriter, May 1992

Kasner, Edward, Nov 1943, *Obit* Mar 1955

Kastner, Erich, German author and poet, July 1964, *Obit* Oct 1974

Katzen, Mollie, American cookbook author, Oct 1996

Kaufman, Charlie, American screenwriter, July 2005

Kaufman, George S., American dramatist, Aug 1941, *Obit* Sept 1961

Kaufman, Millard, American screenwriter and novelist, Jan 2008, *Obit* Yrbk 2009

Kaufman, Moises, American playwright and theatrical director, Aug 2011

Kaurismaki, Aki, Finnish screenwriter and director, Jan 2003

Kawabata, Yasunari, Japanese novelist and short story writer, Mar 1969, *Obit* June 1972

Kay-Scott, Cyril, Feb 1944

Kazan, Elia, American theatrical and film director, Jan 1948, Oct 1972, *Obit* Yrbk 2004

Kazantzakis, Nikos, Greek novelist, poet, dramatist, essayist and travel writer, July 1955, *Obit* Jan 1958

Kazin, Alfred, American literary critic, May 1966, *Obit* Aug 1998

Keegan, John, English military historian and journalist, Oct 1989, *Obit* Yrbk 2012

Keen, Andrew, British digital media critic, July 2013

Keen, Sam, author and philosopher, Feb 1995

Keene, Donald, American Japanologist, Jan 1988

Keeny, Spurgeon Milton, United Nations official, Jan 1958, *Obit* Jan 1989

Keeshan, Bob, American television personality, May 1965, *Obit* Yrbk 2004

Keeton, Kathy, magazine executive, Sept 1993, *Obit* Jan 1998

Keillor, Garrison, American novelist, short story writer, storyteller and radio performer, Aug 1985

Keith, Harold, American children's author, Yrbk 1958

Keller, Bill, American newspaper editor, Oct 2003

Keller, Helen, American humanitarian, Yrbk 1942, *Obit* July 1968

Keller, Thomas, American chef and restaurateur, June 2004

Kelley, David E., American television scriptwriter and producer, May 1998

Kelley, Kitty, American biographer, Apr 1992

Kellogg, John Harvey, American physician, *Obit* Feb 1944

Kelly, Florence Finch, journalist and author, *Obit* Jan 1940

Kelly, Howard A., American gynecologist, *Obit* Mar 1943

Kelly, Joe, June 1945, *Obit* July 1959

Kelly, Judith, Oct 1941, *Obit* July 1957

Kelly, Regina Zimmerman, Yrbk 1956

Kemmis, Daniel, mayor and public policy analyst, Oct 1996

Kempner, Robert M. W., German lawyer, May 1943, *Obit* Oct 1993

Kempton, Murray, American newspaper columnist, June 1973, *Obit* July 1997

Kendrick, Baynard Hardwick, author, Feb 1946, *Obit* May 1977

Keneally, Thomas, Australian novelist, June 1987

Kennan, George Frost, American historian and diplomat, Oct 1947, Jan 1959, *Obit* Yrbk 2005

Kennedy, John B., Feb 1944, *Obit* Oct 1961

Kennedy, William, American novelist, May 1985

Kennelly, Ardyth, Yrbk 1953

Kenny, Elizabeth, Australian nurse, Oct 1942, *Obit* Jan 1953

Kent, Rockwell, American painter and travel writer, Nov 1942, *Obit* Apr 1971

Kerensky, Aleksandr Fyodorovich, Russian socialist leader, Yrbk 1966, *Obit* Sept 1970

Kernan, W. F., Apr 1942

Kerouac, Jack, American novelist, Nov 1959, *Obit* Yrbk 1969

Kerr, Jean, American humorist and dramatist, July 1958, *Obit* May 2003

Kerr, Walter, drama critic, Oct 1953, *Obit* Jan 1997

Kesey, Ken, American novelist, May 1976, *Obit* Feb 2002

Keyhoe, Donald Edward, marine corps officer, June 1956, *Obit* Feb 1989

Keynes, John Maynard, British economist, June 1941, *Obit* May 1946

Ki-Zerbo, Joseph, Burkinabe historian and political scientist, Jan 2002

Kieran, John, sportswriter, Apr 1940, *Obit* Feb 1982

Kilgallen, Dorothy, American newspaper columnist, Feb 1952, *Obit* Jan 1966

Killanin, Michael Morris, Irish sports executive and journalist, Apr 1973, *Obit* July 1999

Killion, George L., Nov 1952

Kilmer, Aline, *Obit* Yrbk 1941

Kilpatrick, James J., American columnist, July 1980, *Obit* Yrbk 2010

Kilpi, Eeva, Finnish essayist, poet, short story writer and novelist, Jan 2007

Kimbrough, Emily, lecturer and author, Mar 1944, *Obit* Apr 1989

Kincaid, Jamaica, Antiguan novelist and short story writer, Mar 1991

King, Florence, American satirist, Apr 2006

King, Martin Luther, American clergyman and civil rights leader, May 1957, May 1965, *Obit* May 1968

King, Stephen, American novelist and short story writer, Oct 1981

Kingdon, Frank, July 1944, *Obit* Apr 1972

Kingsley, J. Donald, Feb 1950

Kingsley, Sidney, dramatist, June 1943, *Obit* May 1995

Kingsolver, Barbara, American novelist and short story writer, July 1994

Kingston, Maxine Hong, American novelist, Mar 1990

Kinkade, Thomas, American painter, June 2000, *Obit* Yrbk 2012

Kinnell, Galway, American poet, Aug 1986

Kinsey, Alfred Charles, American zoologist and sex researcher, Jan 1954, *Obit* Oct 1956

Kinsley, Michael, American columnist and commentator, May 1995

Kintner, Earl W., lawyer and government official, Apr 1960, *Obit* Mar 1992

Kiplinger, Willard Monroe, journalist and periodical publisher, Mar 1943, Jan 1962, *Obit* Oct 1967

Kirk, Grayson Louis, American college president, May 1951, *Obit* Jan 1998

Kirk, Russell, American political philosopher, Sept 1962, *Obit* June 1994

Kirkland, Winifred Margaretta, *Obit* July 1943

Kirkpatrick, Helen, journalist, May 1941

Kirkpatrick, Ivone, June 1950, *Obit* July 1964

Kirkpatrick, Jeane J., American diplomat, July 1981, *Obit* Yrbk 2007

Kirkpatrick, Ralph, harpsichordist and musicologist, Sept 1971, *Obit* Aug 1984

Kirkus, Virginia, American magazine editor and literary critic, May 1941, June 1954, *Obit* Nov 1980

Kirstein, Lincoln, American ballet manager, Yrbk 1952, Aug 1990, *Obit* Mar 1996

Kissinger, Henry, American Secretary of state, June 1958, June 1972

Kitano, Takeshi, Japanese actor, screenwriter and director, July 1998

Kitchell, Iva, dancer, Yrbk 1951, *Obit* Jan 1984

Kitson, Harry Dexter, Apr 1951, *Obit* Nov 1959

Kittredge, George Lyman, philologist, *Obit* Sept 1941

Klass, Perri, American pediatrician and novelist, May 1999

Klein, Herbert G., American newspaper executive and presidential aide, Feb 1971, *Obit* Yrbk 2009

Klein, Julius, veterans' leader and public relations consultant, July 1948, *Obit* May 1984

Klein, Naomi, Canadian journalist and social activist, Aug 2003

Klinkenborg, Verlyn, American nonifction writer, July 2006

Kluckhohn, Clyde, American anthropologist, Nov 1951, *Obit* Oct 1960

Knickerbocker, Hubert Renfro, journalist, Sept 1940, *Obit* Sept 1949

Knight, Eric Mowbray, Anglo-American novelist, short story writer and journalist, July 1942, *Obit* Mar 1943

Knight, Ruth Adams, Aug 1943, Yrbk 1955

Knipfel, Jim, American memoirist, columnist and novelist, Mar 2005

Knoblock, Edward, *Obit* Aug 1945

Knowlson, James, Irish biographer, Nov 1942

Knox, Ronald Arbuthnott, English priest, satirist, essayist and mystery writer, July 1950, *Obit* Nov 1957

Koch, Ed, American mayor, Sept 1978, *Obit* Yrbk 2013

Koch, Kenneth, American poet, Feb 1978, *Obit* Yrbk 2002

Koestler, Arthur, Hungarian-British novelist, essayist and journalist, Apr 1943, Jan 1962, *Obit* Apr 1983

Kohler, Foy David, American diplomat, Jan 1950, *Obit* Mar 1991

Kohout, Pavel, Czech author and dramatist, Feb 1988

Kokoschka, Oskar, Austrian painter and dramatist, Oct 1956, *Obit* Apr 1980

Kolar, Jiri, Czech poet and artist, Apr 1986, *Obit* Yrbk 2002

Kollmar, Richard, Feb 1952, *Obit* Feb 1971

Kolodin, Irving, music critic, July 1947, *Obit* June 1988

Komarovsky, Mirra, American sociologist, Oct 1953, *Obit* Apr 1999

Kopit, Arthur L., dramatist, Yrbk 1972

Koprulu, Mehmet Fuat, Jan 1953, *Obit* Sept 1966

Korda, Michael, British editor, essayist, novelist and memoirist, Aug 1985

Korine, Harmony, American filmmaker, Feb 2010

Kosinski, Jerzy N., Polish-American novelist, essayist and critic, Mar 1974, *Obit* July 1991

Kossak, Zofia, June 1944, *Obit* June 1968

Kott, Jan, Polish literary critic, Apr 1969, *Obit* Mar 2002

Kouka, Hone, New Zealand dramatist, Jan 2004

Kovic, Ron, soldier and anti-war activist, Aug 1990

Kozlenko, William, Oct 1941

Kozol, Jonathan, American social critic, Jan 1986

Kramer, Larry, American dramatist, Mar 1994

Kramm, Joseph, actor and dramatist, July 1952

Krantz, Judith, American romance novelist, May 1982

Krasna, Norman, dramatist and screenwriter, May 1952, *Obit* Feb 1985

Kraus, Rene, July 1941, *Obit* Sept 1947

Krauss, Nicole, American novelist, Nov 2010

Krauthammer, Charles, American columnist, Jan 2008

Kravchenko, Victor, July 1946, *Obit* Mar 1966

Krishnamurti, J., Indian philosopher, Oct 1974, *Obit* Apr 1986

Kristof, Nicholas D., American newspaper columnist, Feb 2006

Kristol, Irving, American political commentator, Sept 1974, *Obit* Nov 2009

Kristol, William, American political adviser, commentator and magazine editor, May 1997

Krock, Arthur, American journalist, Feb 1943, *Obit* June 1974

Kronenberger, Louis, drama critic, editor and author, Aug 1944, *Obit* July 1980

Krugman, Paul R., American economist, Aug 2001

Krutch, Joseph Wood, American critic, biographer and nature writer, Nov 1959, *Obit* July 1970

Kubler-Ross, Elisabeth, American psychiatrist, June 1980, *Obit* Yrbk 2004

Kubly, Herbert O., author and dramatist, Feb 1959, *Obit* Oct 1996

Kuhn, Irene Corbally, journalist, Feb 1946, *Obit* Mar 1996

Kundera, Milan, Czech poet, dramatist, novelist and short story writer, Mar 1983

Kung, Hans, Swiss theologian, July 1963

Kunitz, Stanley, American poet, Mar 1943, Nov 1959, *Obit* Aug 2006

Kunstler, William, American lawyer, Apr 1971, *Obit* Nov 1995

Kuralt, Charles, American television newscaster, July 1981, *Obit* Sept 1997

Kureishi, Hanif, English novelist, dramatist and screenwriter, Feb 1992

Kurihara, Harumi, Japanese cook and television personality, Jan 2006

Kurtz, Howard, American journalist, Jan 2011

Kushner, Harold S., American rabbi and writer on religion, Apr 1997

Kushner, Tony, American dramatist, July 2002

Kusturica, Emir, Bosnian motion picture director and screenwriter, Nov 2005

Kuusinen, Hertta, Finnish cabinet member, May 1949, *Obit* May 1974

L'Amour, Louis, American western novelist, Feb 1980, *Obit* July 1988

L'Engle, Madeleine, American novelist and children's author, Jan 1997, *Obit* Yrbk 2007

La Farge, Oliver, American novelist and anthropologist, Jan 1953, *Obit* Oct 1963

La Gorce, John Oliver, Nov 1954, *Obit* Feb 1960

LaDuke, Winona, Native American activist, Jan 2003

LaHaye, Tim F., American clergyman and theologian, June 2003

LaLanne, Jack, American physical fitness expert, Oct 1994, *Obit* Yrbk 2011

LaValle, Victor D., American short story writer and novelist, Jan 2010

Labaki, Nadine, Lebanese actress, film director and screenwriter, July 2013

Labouisse, Eve Curie, French biographer and daughter of Marie Curie, Mar 1940

Lagasse, Emeril, American chef and restaurateur, May 1999

Lagerkvist, Par, Swedish novelist, dramatist and poet, Jan 1952, *Obit* Sept 1974

Lagerlof, Selma, Swedish novelist, Apr 1940

Laidler, Harry Wellington, economist, Feb 1945, *Obit* Oct 1970

Laing, R. D., Scottish psychiatrist, Mar 1973, *Obit* Mar 1989

Laird, Donald Anderson, Sept 1946

Laird, Nick, Irish novelist and poet, Jan 2006

Lakshmi, Padma, Indian model, cookbook writer and television personality, Jan 2006

Lall, Arthur S., Indian diplomat, Nov 1956, *Obit* Jan 1999

Lambert, Janet, Yrbk 1954

Lamm, Norman, Sept 1978

Lamm, Richard D., governor, May 1985

Lamont, Corliss, American philosopher, socialist and civil rights leader, June 1946, *Obit* July 1995

Lamorisse, Albert, French screenwriter, director and producer, June 1963, *Obit* July 1970

Lancaster, Osbert, English satirist and cartoonist, Oct 1964, *Obit* Sept 1986

Landau, Lev Davidovich, Russian physicist, July 1963, *Obit* May 1968

Landers, Ann, American advice columnist, Nov 1957, *Obit* Nov 2002

Landon, Margaret, American novelist, Feb 1945, *Obit* Feb 1994

Lane, Arthur Bliss, American diplomat, Apr 1948, *Obit* Oct 1956

Lane, Carl Daniel, Yrbk 1951

Langer, Felicia, Israeli lawyer and human rights activist, Jan 2004

Langer, Susanne Katherina Knauth, American philosopher, Nov 1963, *Obit* Sept 1985

Langley, Adria Locke, Aug 1945

Langner, Lawrence, dramatist and producer, Sept 1944, *Obit* Feb 1963

Lanman, Charles Rockwell, *Obit* Apr 1941

Lao She, Chinese novelist and short story writer, Oct 1945

Lapham, Lewis H., American journalist and magazine editor, Mar 1989

Lapid, Tommy, Israeli cabinet member and political leader, Jan 2003

Laporte, Genevieve, French poet and documentary filmmaker, Jan 2005

Lardner, Ring, American screenwriter, July 1987, *Obit* Feb 2001

Larkin, Oliver W., art historian, July 1950, *Obit* Feb 1971

Larkin, Philip, English poet, essayist, novelist and librarian, Jan 1985, *Obit* Feb 1986

Larson, Arthur, Americacn law professor and government official, Nov 1956, *Obit* May 1993

Lash, Joseph P., author, Yrbk 1972, *Obit* Oct 1987

Laski, Harold Joseph, British socialist leader and political scientist, Sept 1941, *Obit* Apr 1950

Laski, Marghanita, English author and critic, Yrbk 1951, *Obit* Apr 1988

Lasn, Kalle, Estonian-Canadian environmentalist, Apr 2012

Lasseter, John, American animator, screenwriter and director, June 1997

Lasswell, Harold D., American political scientist, July 1947, *Obit* Feb 1979

Latham, Jean Lee, American children's author, Yrbk 1956

Latouche, John, dramatist and lyricist, Jan 1940, *Obit* Oct 1956

Latourette, Kenneth Scott, Sinologist and church historian, Nov 1953, *Obit* Mar 1969

Lattimore, Owen, American Sinologist, Yrbk 1945, July 1964, *Obit* July 1989

Lau, Evelyn, Canadian novelist, poet and short story writer, Jan 2005

Laughlin, Clara Elizabeth, *Obit* Apr 1941

Laughlin, James, American publisher and poet, May 1982, *Obit* Jan 1998

Laurence, William Leonard, journalist, Oct 1945, *Obit* May 1977

Laurents, Arthur, American playwright, screenwriter and theatrical director, Nov 1984, *Obit* Yrbk 2011

Laurie, Hugh, English actor and television scriptwriter, Jan 2006

Lauritzen, Jonreed, Yrbk 1952

Laverty, Maura, Irish author, Yrbk 1947

Lavery, Emmet, July 1947

Lawrence, Charles Edward, *Obit* Apr 1940

Lawrence, David, journalist and publisher, Yrbk 1943, *Obit* Apr 1973

Lawrence, Hilda, author, Yrbk 1947

Lawrence, Mildred, Yrbk 1953

Lawson, Nigella, English food critic and cookbook writer, Jan 2003

Lawson, Robert, Anerican children's author and illustrator, Oct 1941, *Obit* Oct 1957

Laxness, Halldor, Icelandic novelist and essayist, Oct 1946, *Obit* Apr 1998

Lazareff, Pierre, May 1942, *Obit* June 1972

Lazarsfeld, Paul Felix, American sociologist, Nov 1964, *Obit* Oct 1976

Le Carre, John, British diplomat and novelist, Yrbk 1974

Le Gallienne, Eva, American actress, director and producer, Oct 1942, Mar 1955, *Obit* Aug 1991

Le Guin, Ursula K., American science fiction and fantasy writer, Jan 1983

LeVay, Simon, English neurobiologist, Oct 1996

Leach, Penelope, English child psychologist, Aug 1994

Leach, Robin, British television personality and producer, Sept 1990

Leacock, Stephen Butler, Canadian economist, political scientist and humorist, *Obit* May 1944

Leake, Chauncey D., Apr 1960, *Obit* Mar 1978

Lear, Norman, American television scriptwriter and producer, Feb 1974

Leary, John Joseph, *Obit* Feb 1944

Leblanc, Georgette, French opera singer, *Obit* Yrbk 1941

Leblanc, Maurice, French author, *Obit* Jan 1942

Lebowitz, Fran, humorist, Mar 1982

Leboyer, Frederick, July 1982

Lederman, Leon M., American physicist, Sept 1989

Lee, Andrea, American novelist and short story writer, Sept 2003

Lee, Clark, Yrbk 1943, *Obit* Apr 1953

Lee, Gypsy Rose, American actress and stripteaser, Yrbk 1943, *Obit* June 1970

Lee, Harper, American novelist, Nov 1961

Lee, Jennie, British member of Parliament, May 1946, *Obit* Jan 1989

Lee, John Clarence, *Obit* Nov 1940

Lee, Manfred, American mystery writer, July 1940

Lee, Sandra, American cook, entrepreneur and television personality, Aug 2011

Lee, Spike, American film director, screenwriter and actor, Mar 1989

Lee, Stan, American comic book writer and editor, Aug 1993

Leech, Margaret, American historian and novelist, July 1942, Nov 1960, *Obit* Apr 1974

Leguizamo, John, American actor and dramatist, Apr 1998

Lehane, Dennis, American mystery novelist, Oct 2005

Lehmann-Haupt, Hellmut, author and bibliographer, Apr 1942, Mar 1961, *Obit* May 1992

Lehrbas, Lloyd, June 1940, Apr 1950, *Obit* Jan 1965

Lehrer, Jim, American television newscaster, Jan 1987

Lehrer, Tom, songwriter, humorist and mathematician, July 1982

Leigh, Mike, English dramatist, motion picture director and screenwriter, June 1994

Leighton, Margaret Carver, author, Yrbk 1952

Lelyveld, Joseph, American newspaper editor, Nov 2005

Lem, Stanislaw, Polish science fiction novelist, short story writer and physician, Oct 1986, *Obit* Yrbk 2006

Lengyel, Emil, journalist and author, Feb 1942, *Obit* Apr 1985

Leno, Jay, American comedian and television talk show host, June 1988

Leo, John, American magazine columnist, Sept 2006

Leonard, Elmore, American novelist, Sept 1985, *Obit* Yrbk 2013

Leonard, Hugh, Irish playwright, Apr 1983, *Obit* Yrbk 2009

Lepage, Robert, Canadian theatrical director, actor and dramatist, Apr 1995

Lerner, Alan Jay, American lyricist and librettist, July 1958, *Obit* Aug 1986

Lerner, Gerda, American historian, Feb 1998, *Obit* Yrbk 2013

Lerner, Max, American columnist, Oct 1942, *Obit* Aug 1992

Lessing, Bruno, author and newspaper editor, *Obit* Jan 1940

Lessing, Doris May, English novelist and short story writer, Jan 1976, Jan 1995

Lethem, Jonathan, American novelist and short story writer, Mar 2006

Letts, Tracy, American playwright, Oct 2008

Leunig, Michael, Australian cartoonist and poet, Jan 2006

Levant, Oscar, American pianist and composer, Jan 1940, Oct 1952, *Obit* Oct 1972

Levenson, Sam, American humorist, July 1959, *Obit* Nov 1980

Levertov, Denise, American poet, Aug 1991, *Obit* Mar 1998

Levesque, Rene, Canadian political leader, Jan 1975, *Obit* Jan 1988

Levi, Carlo, Italian novelist, journalist and painter, Yrbk 1952, *Obit* Feb 1975

Levi, Primo, Italian memoirist, novelist and chemist, Mar 1987, *Obit* Mar 1987

Levi-Strauss, Claude, French anthropologist, Mar 1972, *Obit* Jan 2010

Leviero, Anthony, Sept 1952, *Obit* Nov 1956

Levin, Ira, American novelist, Aug 1991, *Obit* Feb 2008

Levin, Meyer, American novelist, Apr 1940, *Obit* Sept 1981

Levine, Irving R., American television newscaster, July 1959, *Obit* Yrbk 2009

Levine, Philip, American poet, July 2012

Levinson, Barry, American film director and screenwriter, July 1990

Levy, Andrea, English novelist, Sept 2010

Levy, Bernard Henri, French philosopher, Nov 1993

Levy, Dani, Swiss actor, film director and screenwriter, Jan 2007

Levy, David H., Canadian science writer and amateur astronomer, Jan 1995

Levy, Eugene, Canadian actor, film director and screenwriter, Jan 2002

Lewin, Murray, *Obit* Sept 1943

Lewis, Anthony, American journalist, Nov 1955, *Obit* Yrbk 2013

Lewis, C. S., English children's author, novelist and critic, Jan 1944, *Obit* Jan 1964

Lewis, David Levering, American historian and biographer, May 2001

Lewis, Ethelreda, South African author, *Obit* Sept 1946

Lewis, Flora, American columnist, Jan 1989, *Obit* Yrbk 2002

Lewis, Loida Nicolas, American financier and wife of Reginald F. Lewis, Apr 1997

Lewis, Michael, American investment banker and journalist, Sept 2012

Lewis, Oscar, American anthropologist, Apr 1968, *Obit* Feb 1971

Lewis, W. S., book collector and editor, July 1973, *Obit* Jan 1980

Lewis, Willmott, May 1941, *Obit* Feb 1950

Ley, Willy, German-American scientist and author, June 1941, Feb 1953, *Obit* Sept 1969

Leyburn, James Graham, Apr 1943

Liberman, Yevsei G., June 1968, *Obit* May 1983

Lichtenberger, Andre, *Obit* Apr 1940

Liddell Hart, Basil Henry, British military historian, Jan 1940, *Obit* Mar 1970

Liebling, Leonard, *Obit* Yrbk 1945

Liebman, Joshua Loth, rabbi, Oct 1946, *Obit* July 1948

Lifton, Robert Jay, American psychiatrist and writer, Nov 1973

Lillien, Lisa, American cook, cookbook writer and entrepreneur, May 2010

Limbaugh, Rush, American radio and television commentator, Mar 1993

Lin Yutang, Chinese novelist, essayist and translator, May 1940, *Obit* May 1976

Lincoln, Joseph C., American short story writer, novelist and poet, *Obit* Apr 1944

Lindbergh, Anne Morrow, American memoirist, novelist, and poet, Nov 1940, June 1976, *Obit* Apr 2001

Lindgren, Astrid, Swedish children's author, Oct 1996, *Obit* Apr 2002

Lindley, Ernest K., journalist, June 1943, *Obit* Yrbk 1991

Lindsay, Howard, dramatist, Apr 1942, *Obit* Apr 1968

Lionni, Leo, American children's author and illustrator, Sept 1997, *Obit* Feb 2000

Lipinski, Anne Marie, American journalist, July 2004

Lippincott, Joseph Wharton, May 1955, *Obit* Jan 1977

Lippmann, Walter, American journalist and political philosopher, Sept 1940, Nov 1962, *Obit* Jan 1975

Lipsky, Eleazar, author and lawyer, Yrbk 1959, *Obit* Apr 1993

Lipton, James, American television interviewer, writer and producer, July 2011

Lithgow, John, American actor, Nov 1996

Littell, Philip, *Obit* Yrbk 1943

Liu Binyan, Chinese journalist, Jan 2004, *Obit* CB Int 2006

Lively, Penelope, English novelist, short story writer and children's author, Apr 1994

Livingston, M. Stanley, physicist, Feb 1955, *Obit* Nov 1986

Lleshanaku, Luljeta, Albanian poet, Jan 2002

Llewellyn, Richard, Welsh author, Apr 1940, *Obit* Jan 1984

Lochner, Louis Paul, journalist, Aug 1942, *Obit* Feb 1975

Locke, Alain LeRoy, American philosopher and essayist, Jan 1944, *Obit* Sept 1954

Lockridge, Richard, American mystery novelist, Oct 1940, *Obit* Oct 1982

Lockridge, Ross, novelist, Mar 1948

Lodge, Gonzalez, *Obit* Feb 1943

Lodge, Henry Cabot, American diplomat, Yrbk 1943, May 1954, *Obit* Apr 1985

Loeb, William, American newspaper publisher and journalist, Mar 1974, *Obit* Nov 1981

Loesser, Frank, American composer and lyricist, Yrbk 1945, *Obit* Oct 1969

Logan, John, American screenwriter and playwright, Feb 2011

Lomax, Alan, American folklorist and musicologist, Sept 1941, *Obit* Oct 2002

Lombard, Helen, May 1943

Lonergan, Bernard J. F., Canadian priest and theologian, Jan 1972, *Obit* Feb 1985

Long, Tania, Anglo-Russian journalist, May 1946, *Obit* June 1999

Longstreth, T. Morris, Yrbk 1950

Loos, Anita, American novelist, dramatist and screenwriter, Feb 1974, *Obit* Oct 1981

Lopez, Barry Holstun, American novelist and essayist, July 1995

Lord, Walter, American historian, Oct 1972, *Obit* Yrbk 2002

Lorentz, Pare, American motion picture director, Apr 1940, *Obit* May 1992

Lorenz, Konrad, Austrian ethologist, July 1955, Oct 1977, *Obit* Apr 1989

Losey, Joseph, American motion picture director, Yrbk 1969, *Obit* Aug 1984

Lothar, Ernst, Austrian author, Yrbk 1947

Lothian, Philip Henry Kerr, British diplomat, *Obit* Yrbk 1940

Louchheim, Katie, government official, June 1956, *Obit* Apr 1991

Loud, Pat, July 1974

Lovelock, James, British chemist and biophysicist, Nov 1992

Loveman, Amy, June 1943, *Obit* Feb 1956

Lovett, Robert Morss, literary critic and author, Aug 1943, *Obit* Apr 1956

Lowell, A. Lawrence, American college president and political scientist, *Obit* Feb 1943

Lowell, Robert, American poet, July 1947, Jan 1972, *Obit* Nov 1977

Lownsbery, Eloise, author, Yrbk 1947

Lowry, Edward George, *Obit* Sept 1943

Lubell, Samuel, journalist and public opinion analyst, Nov 1956, *Obit* Oct 1987

Lucas, Craig, American dramatist, Sept 1991

Lucas, George, American film director, producer and screenwriter, Apr 1978, May 2002

Luccock, Halford Edward, June 1960, *Obit* Jan 1961

Luce, Clare Boothe, American dramatist and diplomat, Nov 1942, Apr 1953, *Obit* Nov 1987

Ludlam, Charles, American actor, director and dramatist, Aug 1986, *Obit* July 1987

Ludlum, Robert, American novelist, Nov 1982, *Obit* July 2001

Ludwig, Ken, American lawyer and dramatist, May 2004

Luhan, Mabel Ganson Dodge, American patron of the arts and memoirist, Jan 1940, *Obit* Oct 1962

Luhrmann, Baz, Australian film director, Jan 2002

Lukas, J. Anthony, American journalist, Jan 1987, *Obit* Aug 1997

Lunge-Larsen, Lise, Norwegian-American children's author, Aug 2012

Lupica, Mike, American sportswriter, Mar 2001

Luquiens, Frederick Bliss, *Obit* May 1940

Lurie, Alison, American novelist, Feb 1986

Lutes, Della T., author, *Obit* Sept 1942

Lynch, David, American film director and screenwriter, May 1987

Lynch, Peg, Feb 1956

Lynch, Peter, American investment manager, Nov 1994

Lynes, Russell, essayist and periodical editor, Nov 1957, *Obit* Nov 1991

Lyons, Eugene, American journalist and biographer, Jan 1944, *Obit* Mar 1985

Lysenko, Trofim, Russian geneticist, Oct 1952, *Obit* Feb 1977

MacDonald, Betty, American memoirist and humorist, Feb 1946, *Obit* Apr 1958

MacDonald, John D., American mystery novelist, Oct 1986, *Obit* Feb 1987

MacGowan, Gault, Jan 1945

MacGregor, Ellen, author and librarian, Yrbk 1954

MacInnes, Helen, Scottish-American novelist, Nov 1967, *Obit* Nov 1985

MacKaye, Julia Gunther, American librarian and children's author, Yrbk 1949

MacKinnon, Catharine A., American lawyer and feminist, June 1994

MacLeish, Archibald, American poet and Librarian of Congress, Oct 1940, Nov 1959, *Obit* June 1982

MacLennan, Hugh, Canadian novelist, Yrbk 1946, *Obit* Jan 1991

MacNeil, Robert, Canadian television newscaster and novelist, Feb 1980

Macdonald, Dwight, American journalist and critic, Nov 1969, *Obit* Mar 1983

Macdonald, Ross, American mystery novelist, Yrbk 1953, Aug 1979, *Obit* Sept 1983

Mack, Nila, Yrbk 1952, *Obit* Mar 1953

Mackaye, David L., American novelist, Yrbk 1949

Mackey, John, American supermarket chain executive, Nov 2008

Macmahon, Arthur W., American political scientist, Apr 1958, *Obit* Apr 1980

Macy, George, Nov 1954, *Obit* Sept 1956

Madariaga, Salvador de, Spanish essayist, Jan 1964, *Obit* Feb 1979

Madeleva, Mary, American nun, poet and college president, Feb 1942, *Obit* Oct 1964

Madrick, Jeffrey G., American economist and journalist, Nov 2011

Magnusson, Magnus, Icelandic-British television personality, journalist and college administrator, Jan 2006

Maher, Bill, American comedian and talk show host, July 1997

Mahesh Yogi, Indian yogi, Yrbk 1972, *Obit* Yrbk 2008

Mahfuz, Najib, Egyptian novelist, May 1989, *Obit* Yrbk 2007

Mailer, Norman, American novelist, Oct 1948, Feb 1970, *Obit* Jan 2008

Makiya, Kanan, Iraqi Middle Eastern studies specialist, Jan 2002

Malamud, Bernard, American novelist and short story writer, Yrbk 1958, July 1978, *Obit* May 1986

Malkin, Michelle, American journalist and political commentator, Apr 2010

Mallette, Gertrude E., Yrbk 1950

Malloch Brown, Mark, British United Nations official, Jan 2005

Maloney, Francis T., *Obit* Mar 1945

Malraux, Andre, French novelist, essayist and art historian, Mar 1959, *Obit* Feb 1977

Maltz, Albert, screenwriter, Jan 1940, *Obit* July 1985

Mamet, David, American dramatist, Aug 1978, Mar 1998

Manchester, William, American biographer and historian, Nov 1967, *Obit* Yrbk 2004

Manfred, Frederick Feikema, American novelist, Yrbk 1950

Mangione, Jerre, American memoirist, novelist and historian, Mar 1943, *Obit* Nov 1998

Manji, Irshad, Canadian author and broadcasting entrepreneur, Jan 2005

Mankiewicz, Joseph L., American film director, producer and screenwriter, Sept 1949, *Obit* Apr 1993

Mankowitz, Wolf, English author and screenwriter, Yrbk 1956, *Obit* Aug 1998

Manly, John Matthews, *Obit* May 1940

Mann, Emily, American dramatist and director, June 2002

Mann, Erika, German writer, actress and daughter of Thomas Mann, Yrbk 1940, *Obit* Nov 1969

Mann, Klaus, German novelist, essayist, dramatist and son of Thomas Mann, Yrbk 1940, *Obit* July 1949

Mann, Thomas, German novelist, May 1942, *Obit* Oct 1955

Mannes, Marya, author, Apr 1959

Manning, Marie, columnist, Aug 1944, *Obit* Jan 1946

Manrique, Jaime, Colombian-American novelist and poet, Jan 2005

Mapes, Victor, *Obit* Jan 1944

Marber, Patrick, English dramatist, Jan 2007

Marble, Alice, American tennis player, Nov 1940, *Obit* Mar 1991

Marburg, Theodore, *Obit* Apr 1946

Marchal, Leon, Sept 1943, *Obit* Yrbk 1957

Marchetto, Marisa Acocella, American advertising executive and graphic novelist, Aug 2013

Marcos, Mexican revolutionary, Jan 2002

Marcus, Greil, American music critic, Oct 1999

Marcus, Jacob Rader, rabbi and historian, May 1960, *Obit* Jan 1996

Marcuse, Herbert, American political philosopher, Mar 1969, *Obit* Sept 1979

Marden, Orison Swett, author and magazine editor, July 1967, *Obit* Oct 1975

Margoliouth, D. S., *Obit* Apr 1940

Margueritte, Victor, *Obit* May 1942

Margulis, Lynn, American microbiologist, July 1992, *Obit* Yrbk 2012

Marias, Julian, Spanish philosopher, author and educator, Feb 1972

Maritain, Jacques, French philosopher, May 1942, *Obit* June 1973

Markham, Edwin, poet, Mar 1940

Marlette, Doug, American editorial cartoonist, July 2002, *Obit* Yrbk 2007

Marling, Brit, American actress, film director and screenwriter, Oct 2011

Marquand, John P., American novelist, Apr 1942, *Obit* Oct 1960

Marquis, Albert Nelson, *Obit* Feb 1944

Marriott, Alice Lee, anthropologist and author, Yrbk 1950, *Obit* May 1992

Marshall, Catherine, American biographer and inspirational writer, Jan 1955, *Obit* May 1983

Marshall, Garry, American television scriptwriter, producer and film director, Nov 1992

Marshall, Rosamond, author, Aug 1942, *Obit* Feb 1958

Marshall, S. L. A., Nov 1953, *Obit* Mar 1978

Martel, Yann, Canadian novelist, Jan 2004

Martell, Edward, Nov 1964

Martin, George R. R., American fantasy and science fiction writer, Jan 2004

Martin, Harry, June 1948, *Obit* Mar 1959

Martin, Jackie, Apr 1943

Martin, John Bartlow, American journalist and diplomat, Yrbk 1956, *Obit* Mar 1987

Martin, Judith, American columnist and expert on etiquette, June 1986

Martin, Roland S., American journalist, June 2009

Martin, Steve, American comedian and actor, Aug 1978, Nov 2000

Marty, Martin E., American clergyman, theologian and church historian, June 1968

Mason, Bobbie Ann, American novelist and short story writer, Sept 1989

Mason, Joseph Warren Teets, American journalist, *Obit* July 1941

Massee, W. Wellington, *Obit* Oct 1942

Masserman, Jules H., psychiatrist, July 1980, *Obit* Jan 1995

Matalin, Mary, American publishing executive and political consultant, Sept 1996

Matlin, Marlee, American actress, May 1992

Matthews, Herbert L., American journalist, Nov 1943, *Obit* Sept 1977

Matthews, J. B., American senatorial aide, May 1943

Matthews, T. S., American novelist and journalist, Apr 1950, *Obit* Mar 1991

Matthiessen, Peter, American novelist and nature writer, Oct 1975

Mattingly, Garrett, historian, Nov 1960, *Obit* Feb 1963

Maugham, W. Somerset, English novelist, short story writer and playwright, Jan 1963, *Obit* Jan 1966

Mauriac, Claude, French author, Sept 1993, *Obit* June 1999

Maxwell, Elsa, columnist and society hostess, Mar 1943, *Obit* Jan 1964

Maxwell, William, American novelist, short story writer and magazine editor, Yrbk 1949, *Obit* Oct 2000

May, Elaine, American actress, screenwriter and director, Mar 1961

May, Rollo, psychologist, June 1973, *Obit* Jan 1995

Mayer, Jane, American novelist and children's author, Yrbk 1954

Mayer, Jane, American journalist, Oct 2008

Mayle, Peter, English humorist, Oct 1992

Maynard, Joyce, American journalist, memoirist and novelist, Jan 1999

Mayne, Ethel Colburn, English author, critic and translator, *Obit* June 1941

Mayo, Katherine, American journalist and reformer, *Obit* Yrbk 1940

Mays, Benjamin Elijah, American civil rights leader and college president, May 1945, *Obit* May 1984

Mazursky, Paul, American film director, May 1980

McAlary, Mike, columnist, *Obit* Mar 1999

McBride, Mary Margaret, radio talk show host, Apr 1941, Mar 1954, *Obit* June 1976

McCall Smith, Alexander, Scottish law professor, children's author and novelist, Jan 2003

McCalman, Max, MaŒtre Fromager, Mar 2012

McCann, Colum, Irish novelist and short story writer, Mar 2010

McCarey, Leo, American motion picture director and producer, July 1946, *Obit* Sept 1969

McCarthy, Mary, American novelist, critic, short story writer and memoirist, Yrbk 1955, Feb 1969, *Obit* Jan 1990

McCarver, Tim, sportscaster and baseball player, May 2000

McClinton, Katharine Morrison, author, Mar 1958, *Obit* Mar 1993

McClinton, Marion, American playwright and theatrical director, Jan 2009

McCloskey, Robert, American children's author and illustrator, Sept 1942, *Obit* Yrbk 2003

McCormick, Anne O'Hare, journalist, Mar 1940, *Obit* July 1954

McCormick, Jay, Apr 1943

McCourt, Frank, Irish-American memoirist, Feb 1998, *Obit* Yrbk 2009

McCracken, Harold, Yrbk 1949

McCullers, Carson, American novelist, Sept 1940, *Obit* Yrbk 1967

McCullough, Colleen, Australian novelist, Apr 1982

McCullough, David G., American historian and biographer, Jan 1993

McDermott, Alice, American novelist and short story writer, Sept 1992

McDonagh, Martin, Irish dramatist, Aug 1998

McDonald, Erroll, publishing executive, Oct 1999

McDonald, Trevor, British television news anchor, Sept 2010

McDuffie, Dwayne, American comic book writer, Feb 2010, *Obit* Yrbk 2011

McEwan, Ian, English novelist and short story writer, July 1993

McGarry, William J., *Obit* Nov 1941

McGill, Ralph, American newspaper editor, June 1947, *Obit* Mar 1969

McGinley, Phyllis, American poet and children's author, Feb 1941, Nov 1961, *Obit* Apr 1978

McGinniss, Joe, American true crime writer, Jan 1984

McGraw, Eloise Jarvis, American children's author, Yrbk 1955, *Obit* Mar 2001

McGroarty, John Steven, *Obit* Sept 1944

McGruder, Aaron, American cartoonist, Sept 2001

McGuane, Thomas, American novelist and screenwriter, Nov 1987

McGuire, William Anthony, *Obit* Nov 1940

McGurn, Barrett, Apr 1965

McInerney, Jay, American novelist, Nov 1987

McKelway, B. M., Jan 1958, *Obit* Oct 1976

McKenna, Francis Eugene, American chemist and editor, May 1966, *Obit* Feb 1979

McKenney, Ruth, author, Aug 1942, *Obit* Oct 1972

McKenzie, William P., *Obit* Oct 1942

McKuen, Rod, American poet, composer and singer, Feb 1970

McLean, Evalyn Walsh, socialite, May 1943, *Obit* May 1947

McLuhan, Marshall, Canadian cultural critic, June 1967, *Obit* Feb 1981

McMeekin, Clark, American novelists, Yrbk 1957

McMeekin, Isabel McLennan, American novelist and children's author, Sept 1942, Yrbk 1957

McMillan, Terry, American novelist, Feb 1993

McMinnies, Mary, Yrbk 1959

McMurtry, Larry, American novelist, June 1984

McNally, Terrence, American dramatist, Mar 1988

McPhee, John A., American journalist and nature writer, Oct 1982

McPherson, James Alan, American short story writer, essayist and editor, Sept 1996

McSwigan, Marie, Yrbk 1953, *Obit* Sept 1962

McWhirter, Norris, English sportswriter and sportscaster, Nov 1979, *Obit* Yrbk 2004

McWilliams, Carey, American lawyer, magazine editor and nonfiction writer, Oct 1943, *Obit* Aug 1980

Mda, Zakes, South African dramatist and novelist, Jan 2005

Meacham, Jon, American publishing executive and political commentator, June 2011

Mead, Margaret, American anthropologist, Nov 1940, May 1951, *Obit* Jan 1979

Meadowcroft, Enid La Monte, Yrbk 1949

Mears, Helen, American Japanologist, Mar 1943

Medem, Julio, Spanish film director and screenwriter, Jan 2003

Medvedev, Zhores Aleksandrovich, Soviet biochemist, Nov 1973

Meerloo, Joost A. M., Jan 1962, *Obit* Feb 1977

Mehta, Ved, Indian journalist, novelist and essayist, Sept 1975

Mellers, Wilfrid, English musicologist and composer, Feb 1962, *Obit* Yrbk 2008

Menchu, Rigoberta, Guatemalan human rights activist and memoirist, Oct 1993

Mendelsohn, Erich, German architect, Nov 1953

Menninger, Karl A., American psychiatrist, Oct 1948, *Obit* Sept 1990

Menotti, Gian Carlo, Italian composer and librettist, Yrbk 1947, Jan 1979, *Obit* Yrbk 2007

Mercer, Samuel A. B., Feb 1953

Mernissi, Fatima, Moroccan sociologist, Jan 2005

Merriam, Charles Edward, American political scientist, Feb 1947, *Obit* Feb 1953

Merriam, George Ernest, *Obit* May 1941

Merrick, Elliott, author, Yrbk 1950, *Obit* July 1997

Merrill, James, American poet, novelist and playwright, Aug 1981, *Obit* Apr 1995

Merrill, John Douglas, *Obit* Jan 1940

Merwin, W. S., American poet and translator, May 1988

Merz, Charles, newspaper editor, Nov 1954, *Obit* Nov 1977

Meyer, Agnes Elizabeth Ernst, American journalist, philanthropist and newspaper publisher, Jan 1949, *Obit* Nov 1970

Meyer, Cord, intelligence official, Mar 1948, *Obit* Aug 2001

Meyer, Jean-Luc de, Belgian singer and lyricist, Jan 2006

Meyer, Stephenie, American novelist, Oct 2008

Meyers, Nancy, American screenwriter, director and producer, Feb 2002

Meyers, Seth, American comedian and actor, Apr 2009

Miasha, American novelist, Oct 2009

Michaels, Anne, Canadian poet and novelist, Jan 2002

Michaels, Lorne, Canadian television scriptwriter and producer, Aug 1999

Michelson, Charles, journalist, Aug 1940, *Obit* Jan 1948

Michener, James A., American novelist, June 1948, Aug 1975, *Obit* Jan 1998

Michie, Allan A., Nov 1942, *Obit* Jan 1974

Middleton, Drew, journalist and author, Sept 1943, *Obit* Mar 1990

Midler, Bette, American singer and actress, June 1973, Nov 1997

Miers, Earl Schenck, editor and publisher, Yrbk 1949, Sept 1967, *Obit* Jan 1973

Mihajlov, Mihajlo, Yugoslav social and literary critic, Jan 1979, *Obit* Yrbk 2010

Millar, Alexander Copeland, *Obit* Yrbk 1940

Millar, George, Scottish author, Yrbk 1949

Millar, Margaret, author, Yrbk 1946, *Obit* June 1994

Millard, Bailey, *Obit* May 1941

Miller, Alice Duer, author, Sept 1941, *Obit* Oct 1942

Miller, Arthur, American dramatist, Oct 1947, Feb 1973, *Obit* July 2005

Miller, Douglas, Nov 1941

Miller, Henry, American novelist, Nov 1970, *Obit* July 1980

Miller, Jason, playwright and actor, Jan 1974, *Obit* Yrbk 2001

Miller, Jonathan, English physician, actor and director, Oct 1970, Nov 1986

Miller, Judith, American journalist, Jan 2006

Miller, Max, American journalist, May 1940, *Obit* Feb 1968

Miller, Merle, author, Yrbk 1950, *Obit* July 1986

Miller, Roger, American composer, lyricist and singer, Sept 1986, *Obit* Jan 1993

Miller, Webb, American journalist, *Obit* Jan 1940

Millett, Kate, American feminist, artist and memoirist, Jan 1971, June 1995

Millman, Dan, American gymnast and spiritualist, Aug 2002

Milosz, Czeslaw, Polish poet, Oct 1981, *Obit* Yrbk 2004

Miranda, Lin-Manuel, American composer and lyricist, July 2013

Mirvish, Robert F., Yrbk 1957

Mistral, Gabriela, Chilean poet and educator, Feb 1946, *Obit* Mar 1957

Mitchell, David, English novelist, Jan 2011

Mitchell, H. L., American farm leader, Jan 1947

Mitford, Jessica, English journalist, memoirist and social critic, Sept 1974, *Obit* Oct 1996

Mlodinow, Leonard, American science writer, June 2009

Moats, Alice-Leone, author and journalist, May 1943, *Obit* July 1989

Moen, Lars, May 1941

Mohamad, Goenawan, Indonesian poet and magazine editor, Jan 2007

Moley, Raymond, American journalist and government official, July 1945, *Obit* Apr 1975

Mollenhoff, Clark R., journalist, Nov 1958, *Obit* May 1991

Molloy, Robert, author and translator, Yrbk 1948, *Obit* Mar 1977

Momaday, N. Scott, American novelist, poet and editor, Apr 1975

Monroe, Anne Shannon, *Obit* Yrbk 1942

Monroney, A. S. Mike, American senator, Nov 1951, *Obit* Apr 1980

Monsarrat, Nicholas, English novelist, Yrbk 1950, *Obit* Oct 1979

Montagu, Ashley, Anglo-American anthropologist, Feb 1967, *Obit* Mar 2000

Montague, James J., *Obit* Feb 1942

Montale, Eugenio, Italian poet and critic, Apr 1976, *Obit* Nov 1981

Montero, Mayra, Cuban novelist and short story writer, Jan 2002

Montgomery, Elizabeth Rider, author, Yrbk 1952

Montgomery, L. M., Canadian novelist, *Obit* June 1942

Montgomery, Ruth Shick, author and journalist, Feb 1957

Montresor, Beni, Italian scenic designer, illustrator and children's author, Yrbk 1967, *Obit* Feb 2002

Moody, Blair, American senator, Sept 1951, *Obit* Oct 1954

Moody, Ralph, Yrbk 1955

Moodysson, Lukas, Swedish screenwriter and film director, Jan 2003

Moon, Bucklin, American writer, Yrbk 1950

Moore, Brian, Canadian novelist, Jan 1986, *Obit* Mar 1999

Moore, Marianne, American poet, Yrbk 1952, Apr 1968, *Obit* Mar 1972

Moore, Michael, American documentary filmmaker, May 1997

Moore, Patrick, English astronomy author and television program host, Jan 2003, *Obit* Yrbk 2013

Moore, Ruth, Yrbk 1954

Moos, Malcolm Charles, political scientist and college president, Nov 1968

Moraes, F. R., Nov 1957, *Obit* July 1974

Moravia, Alberto, Italian novelist, short story writer, playwright and essayist, Apr 1970, *Obit* Nov 1990

Morehead, Albert H., Mar 1955, *Obit* Yrbk 1966

Morehouse, Ward, Jan 1940, *Obit* Feb 1967

Morell, Parker, *Obit* Apr 1943

Morgan, Edward Paddock, reporter and commentator, Apr 1964, *Obit* Mar 1993

Morgan, Lucy, newspaper columnist, Mar 1959

Morgenthau, Hans Joachim, American political scientist, Mar 1963, *Obit* Sept 1980

Morin, Relman, Nov 1958, *Obit* Oct 1973

Morison, Samuel Eliot, American naval historian, Oct 1951, Sept 1962, *Obit* July 1976

Morley, Robert, English actor, Nov 1963, *Obit* Aug 1992

Morrill, J. L., Feb 1951

Morris, Desmond, British ethologist, Nov 1974

Morris, Edmund, American biographer, July 1989

Morris, Jan, English journalist and travel writer, Jan 1964, June 1986

Morris, Willie, American writer and magazine editor, Jan 1976, *Obit* Oct 1999

Morris, Wright, American novelist, short story writer and critic, May 1982, *Obit* July 1998

Morrison, Toni, American novelist, May 1979

Morrow, Elizabeth, Apr 1943, *Obit* Mar 1955

Morrow, Honore Willsie, author, *Obit* May 1940

Morse, John Lovett, *Obit* May 1940

Morse, Philip McCord, physicist, June 1948, *Obit* Nov 1985

Mortimer, John, English dramatist, novelist and lawyer, Apr 1983, *Obit* Yrbk 2009

Morton, Henry H., *Obit* July 1940

Morton, James F., *Obit* Yrbk 1941

Mosca, Gaetano, Italian political philosopher, *Obit* Jan 1942

Mosel, Tad, American dramatist, Nov 1961, *Obit* Yrbk 2008

Moser, Fritz, June 1955

Mosley, Walter, American mystery novelist, Sept 1994

Moss, Cynthia, American biologist and conservationist, May 1993

Motherwell, Hiram, *Obit* Jan 1946

Mott, Frank Luther, journalist and historian, Oct 1941, *Obit* Yrbk 1964

Mott, Lewis F., *Obit* Jan 1942

Moulitsas Zuniga, Markos, American political blog writer, Mar 2007

Moulton, Forest Ray, American astronomer, Jan 1946, *Obit* Jan 1953

Moulton, Harold G., Nov 1944, *Obit* Feb 1966

Mowat, Farley, Canadian ethnologist, historian and children's author, Feb 1986

Mowery, Edward J., American journalist, Nov 1953, *Obit* Feb 1971

Mowrer, Edgar Ansel, journalist, Oct 1941, July 1962, *Obit* May 1977

Mowrer, Lilian Thomson, author, May 1940, *Obit* Jan 1991

Moyers, Bill, American journalist and television commentator, Jan 1966, Feb 1976

Moynihan, Daniel Patrick, American senator and diplomat, Feb 1968, Feb 1986, *Obit* Yrbk 2003

Moyo, Dambisa, Zambian economist, Feb 2012

Muggeridge, Malcolm, English journalist, critic and novelist, Apr 1955, July 1975, *Obit* Jan 1991

Mukherjee, Bharati, Indian-American novelist, Apr 1992

Mumford, Ethel Watts, *Obit* Jan 1940

Mumford, Lewis, American architectural and social critic, Nov 1940, Mar 1963, *Obit* Mar 1990

Mundy, Talbot, English novelist, *Obit* Sept 1940

Mungiu, Cristian, Romanian film director, Jan 2007

Munk, Kaj, Danish clergyman, poet and dramatist, *Obit* Feb 1944

Munoz Zurita, Ricardo, Mexican chef, Jan 2003

Munro, Alice, Canadian short story writer and novelist, Sept 1990

Murakami, Haruki, Japanese novelist, Sept 1997

Murch, Walter, American film editor, director, screenwriter and sound designer, Apr 2000

Murdoch, Iris, English novelist and philosopher, Yrbk 1958, Aug 1980, *Obit* Apr 1999

Murnane, Gerald, Australian short story writer and essayist, Jan 2007

Murphy, Gardner, psychologist, May 1960, *Obit* May 1979

Murray, Albert, American novelist, essayist and music historian, May 1994, *Obit* Yrbk 2013

Murray, Augustus Taber, *Obit* Mar 1940

Murray, Charles A., American social scientist, July 1986

Murray, Donald Morison, American journalist and writing instructor, July 2006

Musmanno, Michael Angelo, June 1967, *Obit* Yrbk 1968

Muste, Abraham Johannes, American clergyman and pacifist, Oct 1965, *Obit* Apr 1967

Mydans, Shelley Smith, American journalist and novelist, May 1945, *Obit* Aug 2002

Myers, Gustavus, journalist and historian, *Obit* Jan 1943

Myers, Mike, Canadian comedian, actor and screenwriter, Aug 1997

Myers, Norman, English environmentalist, May 1993

Myrdal, Gunnar, Swedish economist, Sept 1946, Mar 1975, *Obit* July 1987

Nabokov, Vladimir Vladimirovich, Russian-American novelist, May 1966, *Obit* Aug 1977

Nader, Ralph, American consumer rights advocate, Nov 1968, Apr 1986

Naidu, Sarojini, Indian feminist, poet and government official, May 1943, *Obit* Mar 1949

Naifeh, Steven W., author, Mar 1998

Naipaul, V. S., Trinidadian novelist and journalist, July 1977

Naisbitt, John, American social forecaster, Nov 1984

Namegabe, Chouchou, Congolese radio reporter, Apr 2012

Narayan, R. K., Indian novelist and short story writer, Sept 1987, *Obit* July 2001

Nash, Ogden, American poet, Apr 1941, *Obit* July 1971

Nasrin, Taslima, Bangladeshi poet, essayist, novelist and feminist, Jan 2003

Navasky, Victor S., American journalist, May 1986

Naylor, Gloria, American novelist, Apr 1993

Nearing, Scott, American sociologist and homesteader, Oct 1971, *Obit* Oct 1983

Nehru, Jawaharlal, Indian prime minister, Jan 1941, Apr 1948, *Obit* July 1964

Neill, Alexander Sutherland, British child psychologist, Apr 1961, *Obit* Nov 1973

Neilson, Frances Fullerton, Yrbk 1955

Neilson, William Allan, Scottish-American literary scholar, *Obit* Mar 1946

Nemerov, Howard, American novelist, poet and critic, Oct 1964, *Obit* Sept 1991

Nemirovich-Danchenko, Vladimir Ivanovich, Russian dramatist and director, *Obit* June 1943

Neruda, Pablo, Chilean poet, Yrbk 1970, *Obit* Nov 1973

Nesbo, Jo, Norwegian novelist, singer and songwriter, Sept 2011

Nessen, Ron, American presidential press secretary and public relations executive, Jan 1976

Netanyahu, Benjamin, Israeli prime minister, June 1996

Neuberger, Richard L., American senator, Feb 1955, *Obit* May 1960

Neuhaus, Richard John, American priest, religious writer and political activist, June 1988, *Obit* Yrbk 2009

Neustadt, Richard E., American political scientist, Nov 1968, *Obit* Yrbk 2004

Newby, P. H., English novelist and short story writer, Yrbk 1953

Newell, Homer Edward, physicist and mathematician, Nov 1954, *Obit* Sept 1983

Newman, Bernard, English author, Apr 1959, *Obit* Apr 1968

Newman, J. Wilson, American publishing executive, Apr 1955, *Obit* Yrbk 2003

Newton, A. Edward, bibliographer and book collector, *Obit* Nov 1940

Newton, Eric, British art critic, Feb 1956, *Obit* Apr 1965

Nichols, Dudley, screenwriter, Sept 1941, *Obit* Mar 1960

Nichols, Herbert B., American science journalist, Sept 1947

Nicholson, Margaret, Nov 1957

Nicolson, Harold George, British diplomat, author and critic, May 1967, *Obit* June 1968

Nicolson, Marjorie Hope, literary critic and college dean, Apr 1940, *Obit* June 1981

Niebuhr, Reinhold, American theologian, Mar 1941, Nov 1951, *Obit* July 1971

Niederland, William G., psychoanalyst, Oct 1980, *Obit* Oct 1993

Niemoller, Martin, German clergyman, Mar 1943, Mar 1965, *Obit* May 1984

Niggli, Josephina, American dramatist, poet, short story writer and novelist, Yrbk 1949

Nin, Anais, American novelist, Feb 1944, Sept 1975, *Obit* Mar 1977

Niven, David, British actor, Mar 1957, *Obit* Sept 1983

Nixon, Agnes, American television scriptwriter, Apr 2001

Nixon, Richard M., American president, July 1948, June 1958, Yrbk 1969, *Obit* June 1994, Yrbk 1994

Nizer, Louis, American lawyer, Nov 1955, *Obit* Jan 1995

Nocera, Joseph, American journalist, Oct 2011

Nock, Albert Jay, American literary critic and essayist, May 1944, *Obit* Sept 1945

Noel Hume, Ivor, English archaeologist, Nov 1997

Nofziger, Lyn, American political consultant, Jan 1983, *Obit* Yrbk 2006

Nolan, Christopher, Irish poet and memoirist, Sept 1988, *Obit* Yrbk 2009

Nolan, Christopher, Anglo-American screenwriter and director, Jan 2005

Nolan, Jonathan, Apr 2013

Noonan, Peggy, American presidential speechwriter and political writer, July 1990

Nordmann, Charles, *Obit* Yrbk 1940

Norman, Marsha, American dramatist, May 1984

Norris, Charles Gilman, author, *Obit* Aug 1945

Norris, Michele, American radio reporter, Mar 2008

North, Oliver L., American Marine corps officer, columnist and television personality, Mar 1992

North, Sterling, author, Nov 1943, *Obit* Feb 1975

Norton, Andre, American science fiction novelist, Jan 1957, *Obit* Yrbk 2005

Norton, Howard Melvin, June 1947

Nottage, Lynn, American dramatist, Nov 2004

Novak, Michael, American social philosopher and critic, Feb 1985

Nugent, Elliott, July 1944, *Obit* Oct 1980

Nunez, Elizabeth, Trinidadian novelist, Jan 2002

Nylander, Olof O., *Obit* Sept 1943

O'Brian, Patrick, Irish novelist, June 1995, *Obit* Mar 2000

O'Brien, Conan, American comedian and television talk show host, May 1996

O'Brien, Conor Cruise, Irish critic, historian and diplomat, Apr 1967

O'Brien, Edna, Irish novelist and short story writer, Sept 1980

O'Brien, Edward J., editor and critic, *Obit* Apr 1941

O'Brien, Leo W., June 1959, *Obit* July 1982

O'Brien, Tim, American novelist, Aug 1995

O'Casey, Sean, Irish dramatist, Nov 1962, *Obit* Nov 1964

O'Connor, Edwin, American novelist and short story writer, Nov 1963, *Obit* May 1968

O'Connor, Flannery, American novelist and short story writer, Yrbk 1958, *Obit* Sept 1965

O'Donnell, E. P., *Obit* June 1943

O'Faolain, Sean, Irish short story writer, novelist and biographer, Apr 1990, *Obit* June 1991

O'Hair, Madalyn Murray, American atheist, Jan 1977, *Obit* June 2001

O'Hara, John, American novelist and short story writer, Feb 1941, *Obit* June 1970

O'Hara, Mary, author, Jan 1944, *Obit* Jan 1981

O'Meara, Walter, author and advertising executive, Yrbk 1958, *Obit* Nov 1989

O'Neil, George, *Obit* July 1940

O'Neill, Gerard K., physicist, Feb 1979, *Obit* June 1992

O'Neill, Joseph, American lawyer and novelist, June 2009

O'Reilly, Bill, American television talk show host, Oct 2003

Oates, Joyce Carol, American novelist, short story writer and poet, Sept 1970, June 1994

Oboler, Arch, radio author and screenwriter, Mar 1940, *Obit* May 1987

Obst, Lynda Rosen, American motion picture producer, Oct 2000

Odets, Clifford, American dramatist, Nov 1941, *Obit* Nov 1963

Oe, Kenzaburo, Japanese novelist, May 1996

Oechsner, Frederick Cable, journalist and intelligence official, Mar 1943, *Obit* June 1992

Ogburn, Charlton, Feb 1955, *Obit* Apr 1962

Ogilvie, Elisabeth, American novelist, Yrbk 1951, *Obit* Yrbk 2007

Ojike, Mazi Mbonu, July 1947

Okolloh, Ory, Kenyan lawyer and blogger, May 2012

Oldenburg, Claes, Swedish-American sculptor, Feb 1970

Onassis, Jacqueline Kennedy, wife of American president John F. Kennedy and Greek-Argentine shipping executive Aristotle Socrates Onassis, Oct 1961, *Obit* July 1994

Ondaatje, Michael, Canadian poet and novelist, Oct 1993

Oppenheim, Edward Phillips, English mystery novelist, *Obit* Mar 1946

Orlean, Susan, American writer, June 2003

Ornish, Dean, American physician, Apr 1994

Orr, H. Winnett, Oct 1941

Orton, Helen Fuller, Jan 1941, *Obit* Apr 1955

Osborne, John, English dramatist, June 1959, *Obit* Feb 1995

Osborne, William Hamilton, *Obit* Feb 1943

Osteen, Joel, American pastor and broadcasting executive, Jan 2006

Otero, Miguel Antonio, American territorial governor, *Obit* Sept 1944

Ottley, Roi, Oct 1943, *Obit* Yrbk 1960

Otto, Frei, German architect, Oct 1971

Ouedraogo, Idrissa, Burkinabe film director and screenwriter, May 1993

Oursler, Fulton, editor and author, Oct 1942, *Obit* July 1952

Overstreet, H. A., psychologist and philosopher, Sept 1950, *Obit* Oct 1970

Owings, Nathaniel Alexander, architect, May 1971, *Obit* Aug 1984

Oxenham, John, English author and poet, *Obit* Mar 1941

Oyeyemi, Helen, Nigerian-British novelist, Jan 2005

Oz, Amos, Israeli novelist, July 1983

Ozick, Cynthia, American novelist and short story writer, Aug 1983

Packard, Eleanor, Apr 1941, *Obit* June 1972

Packard, Frank Lucius, Canadian author, *Obit* Apr 1942

Packard, Vance, American journalist, Apr 1958, *Obit* Feb 1997

Packard, Winthrop, *Obit* May 1943

Paddleford, Clementine, American food writer, Feb 1958, *Obit* Jan 1968

Padover, Saul Kussiel, historian, Oct 1952, *Obit* Apr 1981

Page, Clarence, American columnist, Jan 2003

Page, Irvine H., physician, June 1966, *Obit* Aug 1991

Page, Robert Morris, physicist, Nov 1964, *Obit* July 1992

Pagels, Elaine H., American religion historian, Feb 1996

Paglia, Camille, American feminist writer and critic, Aug 1992

Pagnol, Marcel, French dramatist and motion picture director, Mar 1956, *Obit* June 1974

Painter, Nell Irvin, American historian, June 2010

Pais, Abraham, American physicist, Jan 1994, *Obit* Oct 2000

Palast, Greg, American journalist, June 2011

Palencia, Isabel de, Spanish diplomat and essayist, May 1941

Paley, Grace, American short story writer and poet, Mar 1986, *Obit* Yrbk 2007

Palin, Michael, English actor and screenwriter, Feb 2000

Palmer, John Leslie, English author and critic, *Obit* Sept 1944

Palmer, Lilli, German actress, May 1951, *Obit* Mar 1986

Pamuk, Orhan, Turkish novelist, Jan 2007

Pandit, Vijaya Lakshmi, Indian diplomat, Jan 1946, *Obit* Feb 1991

Papashvily, George, Georgian-American humorist and essayist, Mar 1945, *Obit* May 1978

Papashvily, Helen Waite, humorist and essayist, Mar 1945

Paretsky, Sara, American mystery novelist, May 1992

Park, Chan-Wook, Korean screenwriter and film director, Jan 2004

Park, Linda Sue, American children's author, June 2002

Parker, Alan, English motion picture director, Mar 1994

Parker, Louis N., English composer and dramatist, *Obit* Nov 1944

Parker, Robert B., American mystery writer, Nov 1993, *Obit* Yrbk 2010

Parker, Trey, American actor, television scriptwriter, director, producer and animator, May 1998

Parkes, Henry Bamford, Mar 1954

Parkinson, C. Northcote, English historian, satirist, biographer and novelist, Yrbk 1960, *Obit* May 1993

Parks, Gordon, American film director, photographer and novelist, Oct 1968, Oct 1992, *Obit* June 2006

Parks, Suzan-Lori, American dramatist, Apr 1999

Parry, Albert, professor of Russian studies, Apr 1961, *Obit* July 1992

Parsons, Elsie Worthington Clews, anthropologist, *Obit* Feb 1942

Parsons, Louella, American gossip columnist, Oct 1940, *Obit* Oct 1973

Partridge, Eric, English lexicographer, Jan 1963, *Obit* July 1979

Pasolini, Pier Paolo, Italian poet, novelist, critic and film director, July 1970, *Obit* Jan 1976

Pasternak, Boris Leonidovich, Russian poet and novelist, Feb 1959, *Obit* July 1960

Patchett, Ann, American novelist, Apr 2003

Paterson, Katherine, American young adult author, Nov 1997

Paton, Alan, South African novelist and biographer, June 1952, *Obit* May 1988

Paton, Stewart, *Obit* Mar 1942

Patton, Frances Gray, short story writer and novelist, Yrbk 1955, *Obit* Sept 2000

Paul, Elliot, author, Feb 1940, *Obit* June 1958

Pauling, Linus C., American chemist, May 1949, Feb 1964, June 1994, *Obit* Oct 1994

Pavolini, Paolo Emilio, *Obit* Nov 1942

Paxton, Tom, folk singer and composer, Sept 1982

Payne, Alexander, American motion picture director and screenwriter, Feb 2003

Payne, Robert, English author, Yrbk 1947, *Obit* Apr 1983

Paz, Octavio, Mexican poet and diplomat, June 1974, *Obit* July 1998

Peale, Norman Vincent, American clergyman and inspirational writer, Jan 1946, Oct 1974, *Obit* Feb 1994

Peare, Catherine Owens, Yrbk 1959

Pearl, Raymond, American biologist, *Obit* Jan 1941

Pearlman, Edith, American short story writer and essayist, June 2011

Pearson, Drew, American journalist, May 1941, *Obit* Nov 1969

Pearson, T. Gilbert, American ornithologist, *Obit* Oct 1943

Peattie, Donald Culross, American naturalist, Oct 1940, *Obit* Jan 1965

Peck, M. Scott, American psychiatrist and self-help writer, June 1991, *Obit* Yrbk 2005

Peel, Roy V., Apr 1950

Pegler, Westbrook, American columnist, Mar 1940, *Obit* Sept 1969

Peirce, Kimberly, American film director and screenwriter, Aug 2008

Peixotto, Ernest C., *Obit* Jan 1941

Pekar, Harvey, American comic book writer, Jan 2004, *Obit* Oct 2010

Peli, Oren, American film director and screenwriter, July 2013

Pelikan, Jaroslav Jan, American clergyman and religion historian, Sept 1987, *Obit* Yrbk 2006

Pell, Edward Leigh, American clergyman and religious writer, *Obit* Aug 1943

Peltz, Mary Ellis, Apr 1954, *Obit* Jan 1982

Pelzer, David J., American self-help writer and motivational speaker, Mar 2002

Penfield, Wilder, Canadian surgeon, Nov 1955, July 1968, *Obit* June 1976

Pennell, Joseph Stanley, author, Yrbk 1944

Percy, Walker, American novelist, Sept 1976, *Obit* July 1990

Percy, William Alexander, American poet and lawyer, *Obit* Mar 1942

Perelman, S. J., humorist, Mar 1971, *Obit* Jan 1980

Perkins, Marlin, zoo director and television performer, Oct 1951, *Obit* Aug 1986

Perrin, Jacques, French actor, film producer, director and screenwriter, Jan 2004

Perry, Anne, English mystery novelist, Aug 1996

Perry, Frank, motion picture director and producer, Oct 1972, *Obit* Nov 1995

Perry, Tyler, American playwright, screenwriter, actor and director, June 2005

Perse, Saint-John, French diplomat and poet, Apr 1961, *Obit* Nov 1975

Peters, Thomas J., American management consultant and writer, Oct 1994

Peterson, Roger Tory, American ornithologist and illustrator, Apr 1959, *Obit* Oct 1996

Peterson, Virgilia, Yrbk 1953, *Obit* Feb 1967

Pethick-Lawrence, Frederick William, British socialist leader, June 1946, *Obit* Nov 1961

Petrie, W. M. Flinders, English archaeologist, *Obit* Sept 1942

Petrini, Carlo, Italian food safety activist, Jan 2004

Petrov, Evgenii, Russian humorist, *Obit* Aug 1942

Petry, Ann Lane, American novelist, Mar 1946, *Obit* July 1997

Pevear, Richard, American literary scholar and translator, June 2006

Phelps, William Lyon, literary scholar, Jan 1943

Philbrick, Herbert A., advertising executive and FBI informer, Mar 1953, *Obit* Oct 1993

Phillips, Caryl, English novelist, dramatist and essayist, July 1994

Phillips, Harry Irving, American newspaper columnist and humorist, Sept 1943, *Obit* Apr 1965

Phillips, Irna, American radio and television scritpwriter and producer, Apr 1943, *Obit* Feb 1974

Phillips, Kevin P., American political writer, Sept 1994

Phillips, Thomas Hal, Yrbk 1956

Piaget, Jean, Swiss psychologist, Yrbk 1958, *Obit* Nov 1980

Picken, Mary Brooks, Yrbk 1954

Piel, Gerard, American magazine publisher and science writer, June 1959, *Obit* Feb 2005

Pierce, Lorne, Nov 1956

Piercy, Marge, American poet and novelist, Nov 1994

Pierson, Louise Randall, Oct 1943

Pifer, Alan J., American foundation official, Apr 1969, *Obit* Yrbk 2006

Pileggi, Nicholas, journalist and author, Jan 1999

Pineau, Christian, French cabinet member, July 1956, *Obit* June 1995

Pinero, Miguel, American dramatist and actor, Nov 1983, *Obit* Aug 1988

Pinker, Steven, American psychologist, Sept 1998

Pinkerton, Kathrene Sutherland, American novelist, Jan 1940, *Obit* Yrbk 1967

Pinsky, Robert, American poet, Feb 1999

Pinter, Harold, English dramatist, Nov 1963, *Obit* July 2009

Piper, John, English painter, Apr 1964, *Obit* Aug 1992

Pipher, Mary Bray, psychologist and author, Aug 1999

Pisani, Elizabeth, American AIDS activist, Aug 2010

Piston, Walter, composer, June 1948, Yrbk 1961, *Obit* Jan 1977

Pitkin, Walter B., author, Oct 1941, *Obit* Mar 1953

Pitts, Leonard J., American newspaper columnist, Oct 2004

Plain, Belva, American novelist, Feb 1999, *Obit* Yrbk 2010

Plantinga, Alvin, Plantinga, Alvin C(arl) (1932-), Nov 2013

Plimpton, George, American essayist, sportswriter and periodical editor, Feb 1969, *Obit* Jan 2004

Pogrebin, Letty Cottin, journalist and feminist, Nov 1997

Poliakov, Aleksandr, *Obit* Nov 1942

Pollack, Jack Harrison, American journalist, Yrbk 1957, *Obit* Feb 1985

Pollan, Michael, American nature writer and magazine editor, Oct 2007

Polley, Sarah, Canadian actress and film director, Jan 2003

Pollitt, Katha, American poet and essayist, Oct 2002

Pollock, Channing, dramatist, *Obit* Oct 1946

Pomeroy, Wardell Baxter, sex researcher, July 1974, *Obit* Yrbk 2001

Poncins, Gontran de, French travel writer, June 1941

Poole, Lynn, Yrbk 1954, *Obit* June 1969

Poore, Henry Rankin, *Obit* Oct 1940

Popcorn, Faith, American market research executive, Feb 1993

Popenoe, Paul Bowman, American eugenicist, Yrbk 1946

Popkin, Zelda F., author, Yrbk 1951, *Obit* July 1983

Popper, Karl Raimund, Austrian-British philosopher, Jan 1963, *Obit* Nov 1994

Porter, Cole, American composer and lyricist, July 1940, *Obit* Yrbk 1964

Porter, Eliot, American photographer, Nov 1976, *Obit* Jan 1991

Porter, Katherine Anne, American short story writer, May 1940, Mar 1963, *Obit* Nov 1980

Porter, Sylvia Field, financial columnist, Oct 1941, Apr 1980, *Obit* Aug 1991

Posner, Richard A., American judge, Jan 1993

Post, Emily, American advice columnist, Mar 1941, *Obit* Nov 1960

Post, Robert P., *Obit* Sept 1943

Potok, Chaim, American novelist and historian, May 1983, *Obit* Yrbk 2002

Potter, Beatrix, English children's author and illustrator, *Obit* Mar 1944

Potter, Dennis, English novelist, playwright and screenwriter, July 1994, *Obit* July 1994

Pound, Ezra, American poet and literary critic, Nov 1942, May 1963, *Obit* Yrbk 1972

Pourtales, Guy de, *Obit* Aug 1941

Powell, Adam Clayton, American congressman, Apr 1942, *Obit* May 1972

Powell, Anthony, English novelist, Sept 1977, *Obit* Aug 2000

Powell, Enoch, British member of Parliament, Nov 1964, *Obit* June 1999

Powell, Kevin, American journalist, poet and essayist, Jan 2004

Powell, Lawrence Clark, librarian, biographer, novelist and critic, June 1960

Powell, Michael, British screenwriter, film director and producer, Aug 1987, *Obit* Apr 1990

Power, D'Arcy, *Obit* July 1941

Power, Samantha, American human rights activist, Aug 2008

Powers, J. F., short story writer and novelist, Jan 1989, *Obit* Sept 1999

Powys, Llewelyn, English author, Jan 1940

Pozner, Vladimir, Russian journalist, May 1943

Pratt, E. J., Canadian poet, Oct 1946, *Obit* June 1964

Pratt, Fletcher, journalist, historian and author, May 1942, *Obit* Sept 1956

Pratt, William Veazie, June 1943, *Obit* Feb 1958

Prescott, Orville, literary critic, Mar 1957, *Obit* July 1996

Prevost, Marcel, French novelist and playwright, *Obit* June 1941

Pribichevich, Stoyan, Aug 1944, *Obit* July 1976

Price, Byron, journalist and United Nations official, Feb 1942, *Obit* Sept 1981

Price, Don Krasher, American political scientist and college dean, Feb 1967, *Obit* Sept 1995

Price, Reynolds, American novelist and short story writer, Apr 1987, *Obit* Yrbk 2011

Price, Richard, American novelist and screenwriter, Jan 1994

Priestley, J. B., English novelist and dramatist, May 1976, *Obit* Oct 1984

Prigogine, Ilya, Russian-Belgian chemist, Feb 1987, *Obit* Yrbk 2003

Prinz, Joachim, German-American rabbi and civil rights leader, Feb 1963, *Obit* Nov 1988

Pritchett, V. S., English short story writer, novelist and critic, Jan 1974, *Obit* June 1997

Protess, David, American journalist and social activist, Oct 1999

Proulx, Annie, American novelist and short story writer, Apr 1995

Pryor, Richard, American comedian, Feb 1976, *Obit* Apr 2006

Puig, Manuel, Argentine novelist, Jan 1988, *Obit* Sept 1990

Pullman, Philip, English fantasy writer, Jan 2003

Pusey, Merlo J., newspaper editor and biographer, July 1952, *Obit* Jan 1986

Puzo, Mario, American novelist and screenwriter, Mar 1975, *Obit* Sept 1999

Pyle, Ernie, American journalist, Apr 1941, *Obit* May 1945

Pynchon, Thomas, American novelist, Oct 1987

P,pin, Jacques, French-American chef and cookbook writer, Sept 2012

Quasimodo, Salvatore, Italian poet, Mar 1960, *Obit* Sept 1968

Quennell, Peter, English biographer, poet, novelist and critic, May 1984, *Obit* Jan 1994

Quiller-Couch, Arthur Thomas, English novelist, short story writer, essayist, poet and critic, *Obit* July 1944

Quindlen, Anna, American novelist and columnist, Apr 1993

Quinn, Sally, American journalist, Oct 1988

Quintanilla, Luis, Spanish painter and etcher, Nov 1940

Rabassa, Gregory, American translator, Jan 2005

Rabe, David, American dramatist, July 1973

Raddall, Thomas Head, Canadian author, Yrbk 1951

Radhakrishnan, S., Indian statesman and philosopher, June 1952, *Obit* June 1975

Radziwill, Catherine, Russian biographer, *Obit* July 1941

Raffi, Canadian singer, Jan 2003

Rahmani, Taqi, Iranian writer, Jan 2005

Rahner, Karl, German theologian, July 1970, *Obit* May 1984

Rajagopalachari, C., Indian political leader, July 1942, *Obit* Feb 1973

Rakoff, David, Canadian humorist, Nov 2007, *Obit* Yrbk 2012

Rama Rau, Santha, Indian travel writer and novelist, Aug 1945, Yrbk 1959, *Obit* Yrbk 2009

Rameau, Jean, *Obit* Apr 1942

Ramonet, Ignacio, Spanish journalist, June 2008

Ramos, Jorge, Mexican-American television news anchor, Mar 2004

Rampersad, Arnold, American biographer, Sept 1998

Ramsey, Michael, English archbishop, Apr 1960, *Obit* June 1988

Rand, Ayn, American novelist, May 1982

Randall, Ruth Painter, Yrbk 1957

Randi, James, American magician, May 1987

Rankin, Ian, Scottish mystery novelist, Jan 2008

Ransom, John Crowe, American poet and literary critic, July 1964, *Obit* Sept 1974

Ranson, Stephen Walter, *Obit* Oct 1942

Raphael, Chaim, English author and government official, Yrbk 1963, *Obit* Jan 1995

Rapp, Adam, American playwright and novelist, Mar 2011

Rapp, William J., *Obit* Oct 1942

Rappard, William E., Oct 1951, *Obit* July 1958

Rashid, Ahmed, Pakistani journalist, Jan 2007

Raskin, A. H., newspaper reporter and editor, May 1978, *Obit* Feb 1994

Raspberry, William J., American newspaper columnist, *Obit* Yrbk 2012

Rattansi, Afshin, British journalist and novelist, Jan 2006

Rattigan, Terence, English dramatist, Yrbk 1956, *Obit* Feb 1978

Ratushinskaya, Irina, Russian poet, July 1988

Rauschning, Hermann, German-American political philosopher, May 1941, *Obit* Apr 1983

Raven, Peter H., American botanist, Feb 1994

Rawlings, Marjorie Kinnan, American novelist and short story writer, July 1942, *Obit* Feb 1954

Ray, Dixy Lee, American governor, June 1973, *Obit* Mar 1994

Ray, Gordon Norton, literary critic, Mar 1968, *Obit* Feb 1987

Ray, Rachael, American cook and television personality, Aug 2005

Read, Herbert Edward, English poet, essayist and art critic, Mar 1962, *Obit* Sept 1968

Reader, John, British photojournalist and writer, Jan 2007

Reagan, Ron, American television personality and son of President Ronald Reagan, Feb 1992

Reavis, Smith Freeman, *Obit* Mar 1940

Redding, J. Saunders, American historian and novelist, Apr 1969, *Obit* Apr 1988

Redway, Jacques W., *Obit* Jan 1943

Reed, Edward Bliss, *Obit* Mar 1940

Reed, Ishmael, American novelist and poet, Oct 1986

Reed, Rex, motion picture critic, Jan 1972

Reeve, Sidney A., *Obit* Aug 1941

Reeves, Jesse S., *Obit* Aug 1942

Regan, Judith, American editor, publisher and talk show host, Sept 2000

Reich, Robert B., American economist and Secretary of labor, Apr 1993

Reich, Walter, American psychiatrist, Aug 2005

Reichs, Kathleen J., American forensic anthropologist, Oct 2006

Reid, Ira De A., July 1946, *Obit* Oct 1968

Reid, Whitelaw, American newspaper editor and publisher, Yrbk 1954, *Obit* Yrbk 2009

Reilly, Rick, American sportswriter, Feb 2005

Reiner, Carl, American producer, director, actor and screenwriter, Apr 1961

Reiser, Paul, American comedian and actor, Apr 1996

Remnick, David, American journalist and editor, Oct 1998

Renault, Mary, English novelist, Jan 1959, *Obit* Feb 1984

Rendell, Ruth, English mystery writer, Apr 1994

Renoir, Jean, French film director and screenwriter, Yrbk 1959, *Obit* Apr 1979

Resnick, Louis, *Obit* May 1941

Ressler, Robert K., American criminologist, Feb 2002

Reston, James, American journalist, Mar 1943, Nov 1980, *Obit* Feb 1996

Restrepo, Laura, Colombian novelist and journalist, Jan 2006

Reuter, Gabriele, German author, *Obit* Jan 1942

Revel, Jean-Francois, French philosopher, Feb 1975, *Obit* Yrbk 2006

Reventlow, Ernst, *Obit* Jan 1944

Reves, Emery, British publisher and art collector, July 1946

Rexroth, Kenneth, American poet, essayist and translator, Apr 1981, *Obit* Aug 1982

Reynolds, Helen Wilkinson, *Obit* Feb 1943

Reynolds, Quentin James, journalist, Mar 1941, *Obit* Apr 1965

Reza, Yasmina, French dramatist, Sept 1998

Rhoades, Nina, *Obit* Jan 1941

Rhys, Ernest, English editor, critic and poet, *Obit* Jan 1946

Rhys, Jean, English novelist and short story writer, Yrbk 1972, *Obit* July 1979

Ricci, Nino, Canadian novelist, Jan 2007

Rice, Alice Caldwell Hegan, author, *Obit* Apr 1942

Rice, Anne, American novelist, July 1991

Rice, Elmer, American dramatist, Apr 1943, *Obit* July 1967

Rice, Grantland, American sportswriter, Sept 1941, *Obit* Sept 1954

Rich, Adrienne, American poet, Feb 1976, *Obit* Yrbk 2012

Rich, Frank, American newspaper columnist, Apr 1999

Rich, Louise Dickinson, American memoirist, young adult novelist and children's author, May 1943, *Obit* July 1991

Richards, Alfred N., American pharmacologist, Sept 1950, *Obit* Apr 1966

Richards, I. A., English poet, critic and linguist, Yrbk 1972, *Obit* Oct 1979

Richards, Laura Elizabeth Howe, author and poet, *Obit* May 1943

Richardson, Henry Handel, Australian novelist, *Obit* May 1946

Richardson, Norval, *Obit* Yrbk 1940

Richberg, Donald R., American government official, Yrbk 1949, *Obit* Jan 1961

Richler, Mordecai, Canadian novelist and critic, May 1975, *Obit* Oct 2001

Richter, Conrad, American novelist and short story writer, June 1951, *Obit* Yrbk 1968

Ricks, Thomas E., American military writer, Nov 2007

Rideau, Wilbert, American convicted murderer and prison journalist, Nov 2010

Ridge, Lola, poet, *Obit* July 1941

Ridgway, Matthew B., American general, July 1947, *Obit* Sept 1993

Riebel, John P., Jan 1957

Riesenberg, Felix, Yrbk 1957

Riesman, David, American physician, *Obit* July 1940

Riesman, David, American sociologist, Jan 1955, *Obit* Yrbk 2002

Rifkin, Jeremy, American social activist and foundation official, Feb 1986

Riggs, Austen Fox, *Obit* Mar 1940

Righter, Carroll, astrologer, Oct 1972, *Obit* June 1988

Rimes, LeAnn, American country singer, May 1998

Ring, Barbara T., *Obit* Nov 1941

Ringgold, Faith, American artist, children's author and illustrator, Feb 1996

Ripley, Alexandra, American novelist, Mar 1992, *Obit* Yrbk 2004

Ripley, Elizabeth, Yrbk 1958

Ripley, Robert Le Roy, cartoonist and adventurer, July 1945, *Obit* July 1949

Risen, James, American journalist, Aug 2007

Ritner, Ann, Yrbk 1953

Rivera, Geraldo, American television reporter and talk show host, May 1975

Rives, Amelie, American novelist, *Obit* July 1945

Rives, Hallie Erminie, American novelist, Yrbk 1956

Roa, Raul, Nov 1973, *Obit* Sept 1982

Roach, Mary, American writer, Jan 2011

Robb, Hunter, *Obit* Jan 1940

Robb, Inez Callaway, American journalist, Yrbk 1958, *Obit* June 1979

Robbe-Grillet, Alain, French novelist, essayist and screenwriter, Yrbk 1974, *Obit* Yrbk 2008

Robbins, Harold, American novelist, May 1970, *Obit* Jan 1998

Robbins, Tom, American novelist, June 1993

Robbins, Tony, American motivational speaker and author, July 2001

Roberts, Charles G. D., Canadian poet and short story writer, *Obit* Jan 1944

Roberts, Dorothy James, author, Yrbk 1956, *Obit* June 1990

Roberts, Elizabeth Madox, novelist, short story writer and poet, *Obit* May 1941

Roberts, Nora, American romance novelist, Sept 2001

Roberts, Walter Orr, climatologist, Yrbk 1960, *Obit* May 1990

Robertson, Ben, American journalist, Nov 1942

Robertson, Constance, Yrbk 1946

Robertson, Robert Blackwood, May 1957

Robeson, Eslanda Goode, American anthropologist and wife of Paul Robeson, Sept 1945, *Obit* Yrbk 1991

Robey, Ralph W., American economist and journalist, May 1941, *Obit* Sept 1972

Robins, Edward, *Obit* July 1943

Robinson, Henry Morton, author and poet, July 1950, *Obit* Mar 1961

Robinson, John A. T., English bishop, Feb 1965, *Obit* Feb 1984

Robinson, Kim Stanley, American science fiction writer, Nov 1998

Robinson, Marilynne, American novelist, Oct 2005

Robinson, Peter, English mystery novelist, Sept 2007

Rockwell, Lew, American political commentator, June 2007

Rodriguez, Alex, American baseball player, Apr 2003

Rohmer, Eric, French film director, Apr 1977, *Obit* Yrbk 2010

Rolland, Romain, French novelist, dramatist and biographer, *Obit* Feb 1945

Rollin, Betty, American television reporter and writer, Aug 1994

Rollins, Henry, American performance artist, poet and singer, Sept 2001

Rombauer, Irma von Starkloff, American cookbook author, Yrbk 1953, *Obit* Yrbk 1962

Rome, Harold, American composer and lyricist, Apr 1942, *Obit* Jan 1994

Romenesko, Jim, American journalist and webmaster, Feb 2004

Romulo, Carlos Pena, Filipino statesman, Mar 1943, Apr 1957, *Obit* Feb 1986

Roncagliolo, Santiago, Peruvian novelist, Jan 2006

Ronson, Jon, English journalist, Apr 2012

Rood, Helen Martin, *Obit* Mar 1943

Rooney, Andrew A., American journalist and humorist, July 1982, *Obit* Yrbk 2012

Roosevelt, Eleanor, wife of American president Franklin D. Roosevelt and diplomat, Nov 1940, Jan 1949, *Obit* Jan 1963

Roosevelt, Elliott, American mystery novelist, mayor and son of President Franklin D. Roosevelt, Yrbk 1946, *Obit* Jan 1991

Root, Waverley Lewis, American journalist, May 1943, *Obit* Jan 1983

Rorem, Ned, American composer, July 1967

Rose, Billy, American theatrical producer, Aug 1940, *Obit* Mar 1966

Rosenfeld, Paul, American music, art and literary critic, *Obit* Sept 1946

Rosenman, Samuel I., American state supreme court justice, Aug 1942, *Obit* Sept 1973

Ross, Alex, American comic book artist, Nov 2007

Ross, Charles G., June 1945, *Obit* Jan 1951

Ross, Edward Denison, *Obit* Nov 1940

Ross, Gary, American screenwriter, May 2004

Ross, Malcolm, Feb 1944, *Obit* July 1965

Ross, Nancy Wilson, author, Yrbk 1952, *Obit* May 1986

Rossen, Robert, American motion picture director, producer and screenwriter, Oct 1950, *Obit* Mar 1966

Rosset, Barney, American publisher and editor, Apr 1972, *Obit* Yrbk 2012

Rossiter, Clinton Lawrence, American historian and political scientist, Apr 1967, *Obit* Yrbk 1970

Rostand, Jean, Yrbk 1954, *Obit* Jan 1978

Rosten, Leo, American economist and humorist, Oct 1942, *Obit* Apr 1997

Rosten, Norman, poet, playwright and novelist, Apr 1944, *Obit* May 1995

Rostow, Eugene Victor, American lawyer and economist, Apr 1961, *Obit* Yrbk 2003

Roth, Henry, American novelist and short story writer, Jan 1989, *Obit* Jan 1996

Roth, Philip, American novelist and short story writer, Mar 1970, May 1991

Rotha, Paul, English motion picture producer and director, Apr 1957, *Obit* May 1984

Rothenstein, John Maurice, English art historian and museum director, Apr 1957

Rothenstein, William, English painter, *Obit* Apr 1945

Rothery, Agnes, Yrbk 1946, *Obit* Oct 1954

Rothschild, Miriam, British entomologist and botanist, Oct 1992, *Obit* Yrbk 2005

Roueche, Berton, American novelist and medical and travel writer, Yrbk 1959, *Obit* July 1994

Rountree, Martha, radio and television producer, Feb 1957, *Obit* Nov 1999

Rourke, Constance Mayfield, biographer, *Obit* May 1941

Rovere, Richard Halworth, American journalist, Apr 1977, *Obit* Jan 1980

Rowan, Carl Thomas, American newspaper columnist, Jan 1958, *Obit* Jan 2001

Rowling, J. K., English fantasy novelist, Jan 2000

Rowntree, Cecil, *Obit* Yrbk 1943

Rowse, A. L., English historian and biographer, July 1979, *Obit* Jan 1998

Royko, Mike, American newspaper columnist, June 1994, *Obit* July 1997

Royle, Edwin Milton, *Obit* Apr 1942

Royster, Vermont, American journalist, Yrbk 1953, *Obit* Oct 1996

Rubin, Theodore Isaac, Feb 1980

Rucker, Rudy von Bitter, American mathematician, computer programmer and science fiction writer, May 2008

Rugg, Harold Ordway, American educator, May 1941, *Obit* July 1960

Ruiz Guinazu, Magdalena, Argentine journalist, Jan 2004

Rukeyser, Louis, American television moderator, Feb 1983, *Obit* Nov 2006

Rukeyser, Muriel, American poet, Mar 1943, *Obit* Apr 1980

Rule, Ann, American true-crime writer, Sept 2000

Runbeck, Margaret Lee, Yrbk 1952, *Obit* Yrbk 1956

Runyon, Damon, American journalist and short story writer, Nov 1942, *Obit* Jan 1947

Ruscha, Edward, American painter, printmaker and photographer, Oct 1989

Rushdie, Salman, British novelist, Nov 1986, Jan 2003

Rushkoff, Douglas, American nonfiction writer and novelist, Nov 2013

Russell, Anna, Canadian singer and parodist, Apr 1954, *Obit* Yrbk 2007

Russell, Bertrand, British philosopher, Apr 1940, Jan 1951, *Obit* Mar 1970

Russell, Charles Edward, American journalist, social reformer and biographer, *Obit* June 1941

Russell, James Earl, *Obit* Yrbk 1945

Russell, Karen, American short story writer and novelist, May 2011

Russell, Ken, English motion picture director, Oct 1975, *Obit* Yrbk 2012

Russell, Mark, American political satirist, Mar 1981

Russert, Tim, American television news executive and moderator, Oct 1997, *Obit* Yrbk 2008

Rutenborn, Gunter, Oct 1960

Ryan, Kay, American poet, Apr 2012

Ryan, Paul, American congressman, Jan 2013

Rylance, Mark, English actor and theatrical director, Nov 2011

Saarinen, Aline B., American art critic and wife of architect Eero Saarinen, Yrbk 1956, *Obit* Sept 1972

Sabato, Ernesto R., Argentine novelist, physicist and human

rights activist, Oct 1985, *Obit* Yrbk 2011

Sabin, Albert, American physician, Feb 1958, *Obit* Apr 1993

Sacco, Joe, Maltese cartoonist and journalist, Jan 2013

Sachar, Abram Leon, historian and college president, Nov 1949, *Obit* Sept 1993

Sachs, Nelly, German poet, Mar 1967, *Obit* July 1970

Sacks, Oliver W., American neurologist and medical writer, Feb 1985

Saerchinger, Cesar, Apr 1940

Safire, William, American journalist, essayist and novelist, Yrbk 1973, *Obit* Yrbk 2009

Sagan, Carl, American astronomer, Apr 1970, *Obit* Feb 1997

Sagan, Francoise, French novelist and short story writer, Sept 1960, *Obit* Feb 2005

Said, Edward W., Palestinian-American literary and social critic, Nov 1989, *Obit* Feb 2004

Saint-Exupery, Antoine de, French novelist, essayist and aviator, Jan 1940, *Obit* May 1945

Salamun, Tomaz, Slovenian poet, Jan 2007

Salinger, J. D., American novelist and short story writer, *Obit* Yrbk 2010

Salinger, Pierre, American journalist and presidential press secretary, July 1961, Mar 1987, *Obit* Feb 2005

Salisbury, Harrison Evans, American journalist, July 1955, Jan 1982, *Obit* Sept 1993

Salk, Jonas, American physician, May 1954, *Obit* Aug 1995

Salk, Lee, child psychologist, Sept 1979, *Obit* July 1992

Salomon, Henry, Yrbk 1956, *Obit* Apr 1958

Salten, Felix, Austrian author, *Obit* Nov 1945

Salter, Alfred, *Obit* Sept 1945

Salter, Andrew, psychologist, May 1944, *Obit* Jan 1997

Salter, Arthur Salter, English economist and member of Parliament, May 1944

Salvemini, Gaetano, Italian-American historian and biographer, Yrbk 1943, *Obit* Nov 1957

Salverson, Laura Goodman, Canadian author, Yrbk 1957

Sammartino, Peter, college president, Yrbk 1958, *Obit* May 1992

Samuelson, Paul A., American economist, May 1965, *Obit* Yrbk 2010

Sanborn, Pitts, music critic, author and journalist, *Obit* Apr 1941

Sandburg, Carl, American poet, biographer and historian, June 1940, Yrbk 1963, *Obit* Oct 1967

Sanders, Lawrence, author, Apr 1989, *Obit* May 1998

Sandford, John, American crime novelist, Mar 2002

Sanger, Margaret, American family planning advocate, Aug 1944, *Obit* Nov 1966

Santayana, George, Spanish-American philosopher, Apr 1944, *Obit* Nov 1952

Santmyer, Helen Hooven, author, educator and librarian, Feb 1985, *Obit* Apr 1986

Santolalla, Irene Silva de, Peruvian educator and legislator, Yrbk 1956, *Obit* Sept 1992

Sarah, Mar 1987

Saramago, Jose, Portuguese novelist, June 2002, *Obit* Yrbk 2010

Sargent, Porter, July 1941, *Obit* May 1951

Saroyan, William, American short story writer, novelist and dramatist, July 1940, Nov 1972, *Obit* July 1981

Sarraute, Nathalie, French novelist, June 1966, *Obit* Jan 2000

Sarris, Andrew, American film critic, Jan 2007, *Obit* Yrbk 2012

Sarton, George, American science historian, July 1942, *Obit* May 1956

Sarton, May, American poet and novelist, May 1982, *Obit* Sept 1995

Sartre, Jean Paul, French novelist and philosopher, Mar

1947, May 1971, *Obit* June 1980

Satrapi, Marjane, Iranian graphic novelist, illustrator and memoirist, Jan 2003

Saunders, Carl M., June 1950, *Obit* Nov 1974

Saunders, Cicely, English physician and hospice director, Jan 2004

Saunders, Hilary Aidan St. George, English author, June 1943, *Obit* Feb 1952

Saunders, John Monk, screenwriter, *Obit* Apr 1940

Savage, Dan, American advice columnist, July 2009

Savery, Constance, Yrbk 1948

Saxon, Lyle, American novelist, *Obit* May 1946

Saxton, Alexander, American historian and novelist, Nov 1943, *Obit* Yrbk 2012

Sayles, John, American novelist, short story writer, screenwriter and film director, Feb 1984

Scali, John A., American television newscaster and diplomat, Sept 1973, *Obit* Jan 1996

Schaller, George B., American zoologist, Aug 1985

Schanberg, Sydney, journalist, Aug 1990

Schary, Dore, motion picture producer, May 1948, *Obit* Sept 1980

Scheffer, Victor B., marine mammalogist, Apr 1994

Schell, Jonathan, American journalist, July 1992

Scherman, Harry, Sept 1943, July 1963, *Obit* Jan 1970

Schillebeeckx, Edward, Belgian priest and theologian, June 1983, *Obit* May 2010

Schindler, John A., Mar 1956, *Obit* Jan 1958

Schisgal, Murray, dramatist, Jan 1968

Schjeldahl, Peter, American art critic, Oct 2005

Schlafly, Phyllis, American social activist and writer, June 1978

Schlein, Miriam, American children's author, Yrbk 1959, *Obit* Yrbk 2005

Schlesinger, Arthur M., American historian, Oct 1946, Jan 1979, *Obit* Aug 2007

Schlessinger, Laura C., American psychologist and radio talk show host, Sept 1997

Schlink, Frederick J., consumer rights advocate, Mar 1941, *Obit* Mar 1995

Schlondorff, Volker, German film director and screenwriter, Aug 1983

Schmitt, Gladys, author, Mar 1943, *Obit* Yrbk 1972

Schoenbrun, David, American broadcast journalist, Jan 1960, *Obit* July 1988

Schoonmaker, Edwin Davies, *Obit* Jan 1940

Schoonover, Lawrence L., Yrbk 1957, *Obit* Mar 1980

Schrader, Paul, American screenwriter and film director, Aug 1981

Schreiber, Georges, author and illustrator, May 1943

Schulberg, Budd, American novelist, playwright and screenwriter, June 1941, May 1951, *Obit* Yrbk 2009

Schuller, Gunther, American composer and conductor, Apr 1964

Schultes, Richard Evans, American botanist, Mar 1995, *Obit* Sept 2001

Schultz, Sigrid Lillian, journalist, Apr 1944

Schwartz, Delmore, poet and critic, June 1960, *Obit* Nov 1966

Schwartz, Felice N., management consultant, May 1993, *Obit* Apr 1996

Schwartz, Gil, American public relations executive and journalist, Aug 2007

Schwartz, Tony, American advertising executive and sound archivist, July 1985, *Obit* Yrbk 2008

Schweitzer, Albert, German physician, missionary and theologian, Jan 1948, July 1965

Scoggin, Margaret Clara, American librarian, July 1952, *Obit* Sept 1968

Scott, Henry L., June 1949

Scott, Peter Markham, English ornithologist and painter, May 1968, *Obit* Nov 1989

Scott, Sheila, English aviator, Nov 1974, *Obit* Jan 1989

Scottoline, Lisa, American lawyer and novelist, July 2001

Seabrook, William B., American occultist and travel writer, Nov 1940, *Obit* Oct 1945

Searing, Annie E. P., *Obit* June 1942

Sears, Martha, nurse and writer on health, Aug 2001

Sears, Paul Bigelow, botanist, July 1960

Sears, William, pediatrician and writer on health, Aug 2001

Secondari, John H., Apr 1967, *Obit* Apr 1975

Sedaris, Amy, American actress and writer, Apr 2002

Sedaris, David, American humorist, July 1997

Seferis, George, Greek poet, May 1964, *Obit* Nov 1971

Segal, Erich, American novelist and classicist, Apr 1971, *Obit* Yrbk 2010

Seghers, Anna, German author, Yrbk 1942, *Obit* July 1983

Seibold, Louis, *Obit* June 1945

Seifert, Elizabeth, author, Yrbk 1951, *Obit* Oct 1983

Seifert, Shirley, Yrbk 1951

Seldes, George, American journalist, Sept 1941, *Obit* Sept 1995

Selinko, Annemarie, Jan 1955

Selye, Hans, Canadian physician, June 1953, Jan 1981, *Obit* Jan 1983

Selzer, Richard, American surgeon, essayist and short story writer, Apr 1993

Sembene, Ousmane, Senegalese novelist and film director, Apr 1994, *Obit* Yrbk 2007

Sen, Ivan, Australian motion picture director and screenwriter, Jan 2002

Senarens, Luis Philip, *Obit* Jan 1940

Sendak, Maurice, American children's author and illustrator, June 1968, June 1989, *Obit* Yrbk 2012

Senghor, Leopold Sedar, Senegalese poet and president, Mar 1962, July 1994, *Obit* Mar 2002

Seredy, Kate, American children's author and

illustrator, May 1940, *Obit* May 1975

Sereny, Gitta, Hungarian-British journalist, historian and biographer, Jan 2007

Sergio, Lisa, Italian radio commentator, June 1944, *Obit* Aug 1989

Serling, Rod, American television scriptwriter and screenwriter, Yrbk 1959, *Obit* Aug 1975

Servan-Schreiber, Jean-Jacques, French political leader, Jan 1955, *Obit* Yrbk 2007

Seton, Anya, author, Yrbk 1953, *Obit* Jan 1991

Seton, Ernest Thompson, Anglo-American writer, illustrator and naturalist, May 1943, *Obit* Yrbk 1946

Settle, Mary Lee, American novelist and memoirist, Yrbk 1959, *Obit* Yrbk 2006

Seuss, American children's author and illustrator, Feb 1968, *Obit* Nov 1991

Sevareid, Eric, reporter and commentator, July 1942, Oct 1966, *Obit* Aug 1992

Severgnini, Beppe, Italian journalist, Jan 2006

Seymour, Flora Warren, historian and author, June 1942

Sforza, Carlo, June 1942, *Obit* Oct 1952

Sgarbi, Vittorio, Italian art critic, historian and member of Parliament, Jan 2006

Shaffer, Peter, English dramatist, May 1967, Nov 1988

Shah, Idries, Indian author, June 1976, *Obit* Feb 1997

Shah, Saira, British journalist and documentary filmmaker, Jan 2003

Shamsie, Kamila, Pakistani novelist, Sept 2009

Shange, Ntozake, American poet and dramatist, Sept 1978

Shapiro, Harry Lionel, anthropologist and museum curator, Yrbk 1952, *Obit* Mar 1990

Shapiro, Karl Jay, American poet and critic, Oct 1944, *Obit* Aug 2000

Shapley, Harlow, astronomer, Jan 1941, Yrbk 1952, Yrbk 1972

Shaw, Dash, American comic book artist and graphic novelist, Jan 2009

Shaw, Irwin, author and dramatist, Oct 1942, *Obit* July 1984

Shaw, Robert, English actor and novelist, May 1968, *Obit* Oct 1978

Shawn, Wallace, American actor and playwright, June 1986

Shay, Edith, Yrbk 1952

Shay, Frank, Yrbk 1952, *Obit* Mar 1954

Shearer, Harry, American actor and comedian, June 2001

Sheean, Vincent, American journalist, novelist and essayist, Aug 1941, *Obit* May 1975

Sheed, Wilfrid, American novelist, Aug 1981, *Obit* Yrbk 2011

Sheehan, Neil, American journalist, Aug 1989

Sheehy, Gail, American writer, June 1993

Sheldon, Charles M., clergyman and author, *Obit* Apr 1946

Sheldon, Edward, dramatist, *Obit* May 1946

Sheldon, Sidney, American novelist, Oct 1980, *Obit* Yrbk 2007

Shellabarger, Samuel, author, May 1945, *Obit* May 1954

Shepard, Sam, American dramatist, Apr 1979

Shepherd, Jean, American humorist, Apr 1984, *Obit* Jan 2000

Shera, Jesse Hauk, American librarian and dean, June 1964, *Obit* June 1982

Sherard, Robert Harborough, English author and journalist, *Obit* Mar 1943

Sherman, Frederic Fairchild, *Obit* Yrbk 1940

Sherrod, Robert Lee, journalist, June 1944, Yrbk 1962, *Obit* May 1994

Sherwood, Robert E., American dramatist, Jan 1940, *Obit* Jan 1956

Shiber, Etta, underground leader, Yrbk 1943, *Obit* Jan 1949

Shields, Mark, American political commentator and columnist, May 2005

Shilts, Randy, American journalist, Oct 1993, *Obit* May 1994

Shimazaki, Toson, Japanese novelist, poet and essayist, *Obit* Oct 1943

Shiner, Lewis, American novelist and short story writer, July 2011

Shinn, Florence Scovel, *Obit* Yrbk 1940

Shinn, Milicent Washburn, author and journalist, *Obit* Oct 1940

Shippen, Katherine Binney, author, Yrbk 1954

Shirer, William L., American journalist, July 1941, May 1962, *Obit* Feb 1994

Shiva, Vandana, Indian physicist and environmentalist, Jan 2002

Shoemaker, Samuel Moor, clergyman, Apr 1955, *Obit* Yrbk 1963

Sholokhov, Mikhail Aleksandrovich, Russian novelist, Jan 1942, Feb 1960, *Obit* Apr 1984

Short, Joseph, American journalist and presidential press secretary, Feb 1951, *Obit* Nov 1952

Shortz, Will, American editor and puzzle maker, Apr 1996

Shotwell, James Thompson, Canadian-American historian, Oct 1944, *Obit* Sept 1965

Shridharani, Krishnalal, Indian journalist and author, Jan 1942, *Obit* Oct 1960

Shriver, Lionel, American novelist, Sept 2005

Shulman, Irving, American novelist, Yrbk 1956, *Obit* June 1995

Shulman, Max, humorist, Oct 1959, *Obit* Oct 1988

Shuster, George Nauman, college president, Jan 1941, Oct 1960, *Obit* Mar 1977

Shute, Nevil, English novelist, July 1942, *Obit* Mar 1960

Shyamalan, M. Night, American film director and screenwriter, Mar 2003

Sickert, Walter, British painter and engraver, *Obit* Mar 1942

Siddons, Anne Rivers, American novelist, Jan 2005

Siegel, Bernie S., surgeon, June 1993

Sigismondi, Floria, Canadian photographer and video and film director, July 2010

Signoret, Simone, French actress, Yrbk 1960, *Obit* Nov 1985

Silberman, Charles E., American journalist, July 1979, *Obit* Yrbk 2011

Sillanpaa, Frans Eemil, Finnish novelist and short story writer, Jan 1940, *Obit* July 1964

Silva, Daniel, American television producer and novelist, Apr 2007

Silver, Abba Hillel, rabbi, Yrbk 1941, May 1963, *Obit* Jan 1964

Simenon, Georges, Belgian novelist, Apr 1970, *Obit* Nov 1989

Simkin, William E., American labor mediator, Jan 1967, *Obit* May 1992

Simon, Charlie May Hogue, Yrbk 1946

Simon, Claude, French novelist, May 1992, *Obit* Yrbk 2005

Simon, David, American journalist and television scriptwriter, June 2008

Simon, Edith, Yrbk 1954

Simon, Neil, American playwright, Feb 1968, Mar 1989

Simone, Gail, American comic book writer, Nov 2008

Simons, Elwyn L., paleontologist and primatologist, June 1994

Simonson, Lee, Nov 1947, *Obit* Mar 1967

Simpson, Alan, college president, Feb 1964, *Obit* July 1998

Simpson, George Gaylord, American paleontologist, Yrbk 1964, *Obit* Jan 1985

Simpson, Helen, Australian author, *Obit* Yrbk 1940

Simpson, J. A., English editor and lexicographer, Jan 2003

Simpson, Louis Aston Marantz, poet and educator, Yrbk 1964, *Obit* Yrbk 2012

Simpson, Mona, American novelist, Feb 1993

Sinclair, April, author, Sept 1999

Sinclair, Jo, author, Mar 1946, *Obit* June 1995

Sinclair, May, English novelist, *Obit* Yrbk 1946

Sinclair, Upton, American novelist and socialist leader, Yrbk 1962, *Obit* Jan 1969

Singer, Isaac Bashevis, American novelist and short story writer, Jan 1969, *Obit* Sept 1991

Singer, Israel Joshua, Yiddish novelist and dramatist, *Obit* Mar 1944

Singer, Kurt D., American children's author and editor, Yrbk 1954

Singer, Peter, Australian bioethicist, Mar 1991

Singh, Simon, British physicist, writer and television host, Jan 2005

Singleton, John, American film director and screenwriter, Feb 1997

Sinyavsky, Andrei, Russian essayist, novelist and short story writer, July 1975, *Obit* May 1997

Sittenfeld, Curtis, American novelist and short story writer, Nov 2008

Sitterly, Charlotte Moore, American astrophysicist, Jan 1962, *Obit* June 1990

Sitwell, Osbert, English poet, short story writer and novelist, Sept 1965, *Obit* June 1969

Skidmore, Hubert Standish, *Obit* Mar 1946

Skinner, Cornelia Otis, actress and author, Jan 1942, Yrbk 1964, *Obit* Sept 1979

Sklansky, David, American poker player, Apr 2007

Sklar, Rachel, Media blogger, author and attorney, Mar 2012

Slaughter, Frank G., American novelist and physician, Oct 1942, *Obit* Yrbk 2006

Slichter, Sumner H., American economist, June 1947, *Obit* Yrbk 1959

Slifkin, Nosson, Israeli rabbi and biblical zoologist, Jan 2005

Sloan, Samuel, *Obit* May 1945

Sloane, Eric, painter and author, Sept 1972, *Obit* May 1985

Slobodkin, Louis, author and illustrator, Apr 1957, *Obit* Aug 1975

Smedley, Agnes, American journalist, Jan 1944, *Obit* June 1950

Smedley, Constance, *Obit* Apr 1941

Smigel, Robert, American comedian and television scriptwriter, Nov 2011

Smiley, Jane, American novelist and short story writer, Apr 1990

Smith, Albert W., *Obit* Oct 1942

Smith, Ali, Scottish short story writer and novelist, June 2006

Smith, Anna Deavere, American actress and dramatist, Sept 1994

Smith, Austin E., physician and drug industry executive, Mar 1950, *Obit* Jan 1994

Smith, Betty, American novelist, Nov 1943, *Obit* Mar 1972

Smith, Bruce, Feb 1953, *Obit* Nov 1955

Smith, Charles, American playwright, May 2011

Smith, Eleanor, English author, *Obit* Nov 1945

Smith, Gary, American sportswriter, Jan 2009

Smith, Gerald L. K., American clergyman, lecturer and columnist, Aug 1943, *Obit* June 1976

Smith, Gregory White, lawyer and author, Mar 1998

Smith, Harrison, Yrbk 1954, *Obit* Feb 1971

Smith, Harry Allen, American humorist, May 1942, *Obit* May 1976

Smith, Hedrick, American journalist, June 1991

Smith, Jeff, American cook and clergyman, Aug 1991, *Obit* Yrbk 2004

Smith, Kevin, American screenwriter and film director, Feb 1998

Smith, Lillian Eugenia, American novelist and social critic, May 1944, *Obit* Yrbk 1966

Smith, Liz, American gossip columnist, May 1987

Smith, Logan Pearsall, American lexicographer, essayist and critic, *Obit* Apr 1946

Smith, Martin Cruz, American novelist, Nov 1990

Smith, Merriman, journalist and author, Yrbk 1964, *Obit* Nov 1993

Smith, Page, historian, Sept 1990, *Obit* Nov 1995

Smith, Patti, American rock singer, songwriter and poet, Apr 1989

Smith, Paul C., Apr 1943, *Obit* Sept 1976

Smith, Red, American sportswriter, Apr 1959, *Obit* Feb 1982

Smith, Robert Paul, American novelist and memoirist, Yrbk 1958

Smith, T. V., Feb 1956, *Obit* July 1964

Smith, Thomas R., *Obit* June 1942

Smith, William Jay, American poet and state legislator, Mar 1974

Smith, Zadie, English novelist, Aug 2000

Smyth, Ethel Mary, English composer, *Obit* June 1944

Sneider, Vern, Yrbk 1956, *Obit* June 1981

Snodgrass, W. D., American poet, critic and philologist, Nov 1960, *Obit* Yrbk 2009

Snow, C. P., British physicist and novelist, Yrbk 1954, Yrbk 1961, *Obit* Aug 1980

Snow, Edgar, journalist, June 1941, *Obit* Apr 1972

Snow, Edward Rowe, Yrbk 1958

Snow, Tony, American television moderator, commentator and presidential press secretary, Sept 2006, *Obit* Yrbk 2008

Snyder, Gary, American poet and nature writer, Nov 1978

Snyder, Solomon H., American neuropharmacologist, Apr 1996

Soares, Jo, Brazilian television talk show host, novelist and actor, Jan 2002

Soderbergh, Steven, American film director and screenwriter, Oct 1998

Sokolsky, George E., May 1941, *Obit* Jan 1963

Soldati, Mario, Italian film director, screenwriter, novelist and short story writer, Apr 1958, *Obit* Nov 1999

Solomon, Susan, American atmospheric scientist, July 2005

Solzhenitsyn, Aleksandr, Russian novelist, Feb 1969, July 1988, *Obit* Nov 2008

Sommerfeld, Arnold Johannes Wilhelm, German physicist, Apr 1950, *Obit* May 1951

Sontag, Susan, American novelist and essayist, June 1969, Feb 1992, *Obit* May 2005

Sorensen, Virginia Eggertsen, American children's author, Yrbk 1950

Sorkin, Aaron, American television scriptwriter, June 2000

Sorokin, Pitirim Aleksandrovich, sociologist, July 1942, *Obit* Apr 1968

Sorokin, Vladimir, Russian novelist, Jan 2005

Soros, George, American financier, Apr 1997

Soueif, Ahdaf, Egyptian-British novelist and short story writer, Jan 2003

Soustelle, Jacques, French political leader, Yrbk 1958, *Obit* Oct 1990

Sowell, Thomas, American economist, July 1981

Soyinka, Wole, Nigerian dramatist, poet and novelist, Yrbk 1974

Spacey, Kevin, American actor and director, Apr 1997

Spark, Muriel, Scottish novelist, Nov 1975, *Obit* Yrbk 2007

Sparks, Nicholas, American novelist, Feb 2001

Speare, Elizabeth George, American children's and young adult author, Yrbk 1959, *Obit* Jan 1995

Spectorsky, A. C., Jan 1960, *Obit* Mar 1972

Speer, Albert, German architect and Nazi leader, Oct 1976, *Obit* Oct 1981

Spence, Hartzell, journalist and novelist, Oct 1942, *Obit* Yrbk 2001

Spencer, Scott, American novelist, July 2003

Spender, John A., English newspaper editor, *Obit* Aug 1942

Spender, Stephen, English poet and critic, Jan 1940, Mar 1977, *Obit* Sept 1995

Sperry, Armstrong, American children's author and illustrator, Oct 1941

Spiegel, Clara E., novelist, Yrbk 1954

Spiegelman, Art, American cartoonist, Mar 1994

Spillane, Mickey, American mystery novelist, Sept 1981, *Obit* Nov 2006

Spock, Benjamin, American pediatrician, Yrbk 1956, Nov 1969, *Obit* June 1998

Sporn, Philip, American electrical engineer, Nov 1966

Spring, Howard, English author, Jan 1941, *Obit* June 1965

Spurgeon, Caroline F. E., *Obit* Yrbk 1942

St. George, Thomas Richard, Jan 1944

St. John, Robert, American journalist, June 1942, *Obit* Yrbk 2003

St. Johns, Adela Rogers, author and journalist, Aug 1976, *Obit* Sept 1988

Stace, W. T., Apr 1961, *Obit* Oct 1967

Stafford, Jean, American novelist and short story writer, Yrbk 1951, *Obit* May 1979

Stallone, Sylvester, American actor and screenwriter, Oct 1977, Feb 1994

Standish, Burt L., American children's author, *Obit* Mar 1945

Stanton, Andrew, American film director, screenwriter and animator, Feb 2004

Staples, Brent, American journalist and memoirist, May 2000

Stapp, Scott, American singer and lyricist, May 2002

Stark, Louis, June 1945, *Obit* Sept 1954

Starkie, Walter Fitzwilliam, Anglo-Irish literary critic, May 1964, *Obit* Feb 1977

Starr, Mark, labor leader, July 1946, *Obit* July 1985

Stearns, Harold E., journalist and critic, *Obit* Oct 1943

Steel, Danielle, American romance novelist, July 1989

Steel, David, British member of Parliament, July 1978

Steel, Johannes, radio commentator and columnist, June 1941, *Obit* Feb 1989

Steel, Kurt, author, *Obit* June 1946

Steele, Shelby, American writer and professor of English, Feb 1993

Steell, Willis, *Obit* Mar 1941

Steen, Marguerite, English author, Oct 1941, *Obit* Sept 1975

Stefan, Paul, *Obit* Jan 1944

Stefansson, Vilhjalmur, American arctic explorer, Oct 1942, *Obit* Nov 1962

Stegner, Wallace Earle, American novelist and short story writer, Apr 1977, *Obit* June 1993

Steig, William, American illustrator and children's author, July 1944, *Obit* Apr 2004

Stein, Benjamin, American writer and actor, Sept 2001

Stein, Gertrude, American novelist, poet and critic, *Obit* Sept 1946

Stein, Janice Gross, Canadian international relations specialist, Aug 2006

Steinbeck, John, American novelist, Jan 1940, May 1963, *Obit* Feb 1969

Steinberg, Milton, rabbi, Mar 1940, *Obit* Apr 1950

Steincrohn, Peter Joseph, Mar 1957

Steinem, Gloria, American feminist and journalist, Mar 1972, Mar 1988

Steiner, George, American literary critic, short story writer and novelist, Oct 1983

Steiner, Walter Ralph, *Obit* Jan 1943

Steingraber, Sandra, American biologist, poet and nonfiction writer, Sept 2003

Stengel, Richard, American journalist and magazine editor, Jan 2011

Steptoe, Patrick, British surgeon, Mar 1979, *Obit* June 1988

Stern, Arthur Cecil, sanitary engineer, Apr 1956, *Obit* July 1992

Stern, Martha Dodd, American novelist, translator and spy, Yrbk 1946, *Obit* Jan 1991

Stern, Richard G., American novelist and short story writer, June 1994, *Obit* Yrbk 2013

Stevens, Edmund, American journalist, July 1950, *Obit* July 1992

Stevens, George, American film and television producer, Yrbk 1965

Stevenson, Elizabeth, American biographer and literary scholar, Yrbk 1956

Steves, Rick, American travel guidebook author, Jan 2009

Stew (Musician), American composer, lyricist and singer, Sept 2007

Stewart, Anna Bird, Yrbk 1948

Stewart, Donald Ogden, screenwriter, dramatist and humorist, July 1941, *Obit* Sept 1980

Stewart, George Rippey, American novelist and nonfiction writer, Jan 1942, *Obit* Nov 1980

Stewart, Kenneth L., Yrbk 1943

Stewart, Martha, American cook, author and mass media executive, Aug 1993

Stewart, Rory, British diplomat and writer, Jan 2007

Stiller, Ben, American actor, comedian and director, Nov 1999

Stimson, Frederic Jesup, *Obit* Jan 1944

Stine, R. L., American children's author, Sept 1999

Stockhausen, Karlheinz, German composer and conductor, Yrbk 1971, *Obit* Yrbk 2008

Stokes, Thomas Lunsford, May 1947, *Obit* Sept 1958

Stoller, Debbie, American magazine editor and feminist, Aug 2007

Stolz, Mary, American children's author and young adult novelist, Yrbk 1953, *Obit* Yrbk 2007

Stone, I. F., American journalist, Sept 1972, *Obit* Aug 1989

Stone, Irving, biographer, Yrbk 1967, *Obit* Oct 1989

Stone, Matt, American actor, television scriptwriter, producer, director and animator, May 1998

Stone, Oliver, American film director and screenwriter, June 1987

Stone, Robert, American novelist, Jan 1987

Stone, W. Clement, American insurance executive, Feb 1972, *Obit* Yrbk 2002

Stoppard, Tom, English dramatist, July 1974

Storey, David, English dramatist and novelist, Sept 1973

Storr, Anthony, English psychiatrist and psychotherapist, June 1994, *Obit* Sept 2001

Stout, Rex, American mystery novelist, Mar 1946, *Obit* Jan 1976

Stowe, Leland, journalist, July 1940, *Obit* Mar 1994

Strachey, Evelyn John St. Loe, British cabinet member, June 1946, *Obit* Sept 1963

Straight, Michael Whitney, American magazine editor, publisher, arts administrator and memoirist, Aug 1944, *Obit* Yrbk 2004

Strang, Ruth, Yrbk 1960, *Obit* Feb 1971

Straub, Peter, American horror novelist, Feb 1989

Straus, Michael W., June 1952

Strawbridge, Anne West, *Obit* Nov 1941

Street, James, American novelist, Yrbk 1946, *Obit* Nov 1954

Streit, Clarence K., journalist, May 1940, May 1950, *Obit* Sept 1986

Stridsberg, Gustaf, *Obit* Yrbk 1943

Stromberg, Leonard, *Obit* Sept 1941

Strong, Anna Louise, American journalist, Mar 1949, *Obit* May 1970

Strouse, Norman H., advertising executive, May 1960, *Obit* Mar 1993

Strout, Richard Lee, journalist and columnist, Apr 1980, *Obit* Oct 1990

Struther, Jan, English poet, essayist and short story writer, Jan 1941, *Obit* Oct 1953

Stuart, Duane Reed, *Obit* Oct 1941

Stuart, Jesse, author, Aug 1940, *Obit* Apr 1984

Studebaker, John Ward, educator and government official, May 1942, *Obit* Oct 1989

Stummvoll, Josef Leopold, June 1960

Sturges, Preston, American screenwriter and film director, Apr 1941, *Obit* Oct 1959

Sturzo, Luigi, Feb 1946, *Obit* Nov 1959

Styron, William, American novelist, July 1968, June 1986, *Obit* Yrbk 2007

Suenens, Leo Joseph, May 1965, *Obit* July 1996

Sues, Ralf, May 1944

Sugar, Bert Randolph, American sportswriter, Nov 2002, *Obit* Yrbk 2012

Sugrue, Thomas, journalist and author, June 1948, *Obit* Feb 1953

Sullivan, A. M., Yrbk 1953, *Obit* Aug 1980

Sullivan, Ed, American columnist and television personality, Sept 1952, *Obit* Nov 1974

Sullivan, Harry Stack, American psychiatrist, Nov 1942, *Obit* Feb 1949

Sullivan, Walter, American science writer, Sept 1980, *Obit* June 1996

Sulloway, Frank J., science historian, Sept 1997

Sulzberger, C. L., American journalist, May 1944, *Obit* Nov 1993

Sumner, Cid Ricketts, American novelist and short story writer, Yrbk 1954

Sunstein, Cass R., American law professor, Oct 2008

Susann, Jacqueline, American novelist, May 1972, *Obit* Nov 1974

Suskind, Ron, Feb 2013

Suzuki, Daisetz Teitaro, Japanese philosopher, Oct 1958, *Obit* Nov 1966

Suzuki, David T., Canadian geneticist and environmentalist, July 1995

Swallow, Alan, Feb 1963, *Obit* Jan 1967

Swanberg, Joe, American film director and screenwriter, Nov 2010

Swann, William Francis Gray, Feb 1941, Yrbk 1960, *Obit* Mar 1962

Swing, Raymond, radio commentator, Jan 1940, *Obit* Feb 1969

Swope, Herbert Bayard, journalist, Nov 1944, *Obit* Sept 1958

Syal, Meera, English actress, novelist and screenwriter, Feb 2001

Symons, Arthur, English poet and critic, *Obit* Mar 1945

Szasz, Thomas Stephen, American psychiatrist and psychoanalyst, Jan 1975, *Obit* Yrbk 2012

Szent-Gyorgyi, Albert, Hungarian-American biochemist, Jan 1955, *Obit* Jan 1987

Taber, Gladys Bagg, editor and author, Yrbk 1952, *Obit* May 1980

Tabouis, Genevieve R., French journalist, Jan 1940

Taft, Charles P., American lawyer, mayor and son of President William H. Taft, July 1945, *Obit* Aug 1983

Tagore, Rabindranath, Indian poet, novelist, short story writer and dramatist, *Obit* Oct 1941

Takahashi, Rumiko, Japanese cartoonist and comic book writer, Jan 2005

Talbott, Strobe, American diplomat, July 2000

Talese, Gay, American journalist, July 1972

Talese, Nan A., American publishing executive, Sept 2006

Tallant, Robert, author, Yrbk 1953, *Obit* June 1957

Tan, Amy, American novelist, Feb 1992

Tan, Shaun, Australian illustrator, Mar 2012

Tange, Kenzo, Japanese architect, Sept 1987, *Obit* Yrbk 2005

Tannen, Deborah, American linguist, July 1994

Tarantino, Quentin, American film director, screenwriter and actor, Oct 1995

Tarbell, Ida M., American journalist, biographer and historian, *Obit* Feb 1944

Tarkington, Booth, American novelist, *Obit* June 1946

Tartt, Donna, American novelist, Feb 2003

Tate, Allen, American poet and critic, Nov 1940, *Obit* Apr 1979

Taubman, Howard, music and drama critic, Apr 1959, *Obit* Mar 1996

Taussig, Helen Brooke, American pediatrician, Sept 1946, Mar 1966, *Obit* July 1986

Taylor, A. J. P., British historian, Nov 1983, *Obit* Nov 1990

Taylor, Charles A., *Obit* May 1942

Taylor, Elizabeth, English novelist and short story writer, Yrbk 1948

Taylor, Henry O., *Obit* June 1941

Taylor, Maxwell D., American general, Nov 1946, Yrbk 1961, *Obit* June 1987

Taylor, Peter Hillsman, American short story writer and novelist, Apr 1987, *Obit* Jan 1995

Taylor, Robert Lewis, biographer, Yrbk 1959, *Obit* Jan 1999

Taylor, Susan L., American magazine editor, Feb 1997

Tchernichowsky, Saul, Hebrew poet and physician, *Obit* Yrbk 1943

Tead, Ordway, educator and management consultant, May 1942, *Obit* Jan 1974

Teague, Walter Dorwin, American interior designer, May 1942, *Obit* Jan 1961

Teale, Edwin Way, American naturalist and nature writer, Yrbk 1961, *Obit* Jan 1981

Tebbel, John William, American historian and journalist, Yrbk 1953, *Obit* Mar 2005

Teller, Edward, American physicist, Yrbk 1954, Nov 1983, *Obit* Yrbk 2004

TerHorst, Jerald F., American presidential press secretary, Feb 1975, *Obit* Yrbk 2010

Terhune, Albert Payson, author, *Obit* Apr 1942

Terkel, Studs, American interviewer and historian, Nov 1974, *Obit* Yrbk 2009

Terrell, Mary Church, American feminist and civil rights leader, June 1942, *Obit* Oct 1954

Tesich, Steve, American dramatist and screenwriter, Aug 1991, *Obit* Sept 1996

Tharp, Louise Hall, American children's author, Yrbk 1955

Thayer, Ernest Lawrence, American journalist and poet, *Obit* Oct 1940

Thernstrom, Abigail M., American social critic, Mar 2010

Theroux, Justin, American actor, Mar 2012

Theroux, Paul, American novelist and short story writer, Nov 1978

Thicke, Alan, Canadian television author, producer and actor, June 1987

Thomas, D. M., English novelist, poet and translator, Nov 1983

Thomas, Elizabeth Marshall, American anthropologist and writer, Mar 1996

Thomas, Helen, American journalist, Nov 1993, *Obit* Yrbk 2013

Thomas, Lewis, American physician and biologist, July 1975, *Obit* Feb 1994

Thomas, Lowell, American radio newscaster, May 1940, Jan 1952, *Obit* Oct 1981

Thomas, Michael, American novelist, Feb 2008

Thomas, Norman, American socialist leader, Sept 1944, July 1962, *Obit* Feb 1969

Thomas, William Sturgis, *Obit* Feb 1942

Thomas-Graham, Pamela, American clothing industry executive and mystery novelist, July 2000

Thomason, John W., marine corps officer and author, *Obit* May 1944

Thompson, Dorothy, American columnist, July 1940, *Obit* Mar 1961

Thompson, Holland, *Obit* Yrbk 1940

Thompson, Hunter S., American journalist, Mar 1981, *Obit* Yrbk 2005

Thompson, Kay, American singer, songwriter and children's author, Apr 1959, *Obit* Sept 1998

Thompson, Mary Wolfe, Yrbk 1950

Thompson, Oscar, *Obit* Aug 1945

Thomson, David, English film historian and biographer, Sept 2009

Thomson, Rupert, English novelist, Feb 2000

Thurber, James, American cartoonist and humorist, Mar 1940, Oct 1960, *Obit* Jan 1962

Thurman, Howard, American clergyman and theologian, June 1955, *Obit* June 1981

Thurman, Robert A. F., American Buddhist leader, Sept 1997

Thurow, Lester C., American economist, Nov 1990

Tierney, John, American journalist, Aug 2005

Tietjens, Eunice Hammond, poet and author, *Obit* Nov 1944

Tiger, Lionel, anthropologist, Jan 1981

Tillich, Paul, German-American theologian, Mar 1954, *Obit* Yrbk 1965

Timerman, Jacobo, Argentine newspaper publisher, Nov 1981, *Obit* Jan 2000

Tin Moe, Burmese poet and children's author, Jan 2004

Tinbergen, Niko, British zoologist and ethologist, Nov 1975, *Obit* Feb 1989

Tobin, Richard, journalist, editor and author, Nov 1944, *Obit* Nov 1995

Toffler, Alvin, American futurist and writer, Apr 1975

Tolar, Dagga, Nigerian poet, singer and social activist, Jan 2007

Toledano, Ralph de, American columnist and political writer, Yrbk 1962, *Obit* Yrbk 2007

Tolischus, Otto D., Jan 1940, *Obit* Apr 1967

Tolkien, Christopher, British editor and son of J.R.R. Tolkien, Jan 2007

Tolkien, J. R. R., English fantasy novelist, philologist and linguist, Yrbk 1957, Oct 1967, *Obit* Nov 1973

Tolle, Eckhart, German spiritual writer, Feb 2005

Tolstoy, Aleksey Nikolayevich, Russian novelist and dramatist, *Obit* Apr 1945

Tolstoy, Alexandra, Russian foundation official and daughter of novelist Leo Tolstoy, Apr 1953, *Obit* Nov 1979

Tomasi, Mari, May 1941

Torres Bodet, Jaime, Mexican novelist and poet, Feb 1948, *Obit* July 1974

Tournier, Michel, French novelist, Apr 1990

Towne, Robert, American screenwriter and film director, June 1989

Townsend, Edward Waterman, American journalist and congressman, *Obit* May 1942

Townsend, Robert, American car rental company executive, Nov 1970, *Obit* Mar 1998

Toynbee, Arnold Joseph, British historian, July 1947, *Obit* Jan 1976

Train, Arthur Cheney, lawyer and author, *Obit* Feb 1946

Transtr"mer, Tomas, Swedish poet, July 2012

Trapp, Maria von, Austrian singer, May 1968, *Obit* June 1987

Travers, P. L., English children's author, May 1996, *Obit* June 1996

Treanor, Tom, *Obit* Oct 1944

Tregaskis, Richard, author and journalist, Aug 1943, *Obit* Oct 1973

Trenet, Charles, French singer and songwriter, Feb 1989, *Obit* Sept 2001

Trethewey, Natasha D., American poet, Aug 2007

Trevor, William, Irish novelist, short story writer and playwright, Sept 1984

Trevor-Roper, H. R., British historian, Sept 1983, *Obit* July 2003

Trillin, Calvin, American humorist, novelist and essayist, June 1990

Trilling, Diana, literary and social critic, May 1979, *Obit* Jan 1997

Trimble, Vance H., Yrbk 1960

Trollope, Joanna, English novelist, Jan 2006

Trotsky, Leon, Soviet communist leader, *Obit* Oct 1940

Troyat, Henri, French novelist and biographer, Mar 1992, *Obit* Yrbk 2007

Trudeau, G. B., American cartoonist, Aug 1975

Trueblood, Elton, philosopher, Jan 1964, *Obit* Mar 1995

Truman, David Bicknell, American college president and political scientist, Jan 1972, *Obit* Yrbk 2004

Truman, Margaret, daughter of American president Harry S. Truman and writer, June 1950, June 1987, *Obit* Yrbk 2008

Trumbo, Dalton, American screenwriter, May 1941, *Obit* Oct 1976

Truss, Lynne, English humorist, novelist and critic, July 2006

Trussell, C. P., July 1949, *Obit* Yrbk 1968

Tryon, Thomas, author and actor, Jan 1977, *Obit* Nov 1991

Tsai, Ming, American chef and restaurateur, June 2012

Tuchman, Barbara Wertheim, American historian, Yrbk 1963, *Obit* Mar 1989

Tugwell, Rexford G., American territorial governor, economist and political scientist, Sept 1941, Jan 1963, *Obit* Sept 1979

Turkle, Sherry, American sociologist and psychologist, Aug 1997

Turnbull, Colin M., English anthropologist, Sept 1980, *Obit* Sept 1994

Turow, Scott, American lawyer and novelist, Aug 1991

Tuttle, Merlin D., mammalogist, June 1992

Tvardovskii, A., Russian poet, May 1971, *Obit* Feb 1972

Tweedie, Ethel Brilliana, English author and traveler, *Obit* May 1940

Tyler, Anne, American novelist and short story writer, June 1981

Ullman, James Ramsey, author, Oct 1945, *Obit* Sept 1971

Ulrich, Charles, *Obit* Aug 1941

Underhill, Ruth M., anthropologist and author, Feb 1954, *Obit* Oct 1984

Undset, Sigrid, Norwegian novelist, Sept 1940, *Obit* July 1949

Ung, Loung, Cambodian-American social activist, Jan 2006

Untermeyer, Louis, American poet, editor and literary critic, Jan 1967, *Obit* Feb 1978

Updike, Daniel Berkeley, *Obit* Feb 1942

Updike, John, American novelist and short story writer, Feb 1966, Oct 1984, *Obit* Yrbk 2009

Upfield, Arthur W., Australian author, Yrbk 1948, *Obit* Apr 1964

Uris, Leon, American novelist, Yrbk 1959, Feb 1979, *Obit* Yrbk 2003

Urrea, Luis Alberto, Mexican-American novelist and short story writer, Nov 2005

Ustinov, Peter, English actor and dramatist, Yrbk 1955, *Obit* Aug 2004

Vaizey, John, English economist and author, Jan 1964

Valdes-Rodriguez, Alisa, American novelist, Jan 2006

Valentine, Alan, American college president, Yrbk 1950, *Obit* Sept 1980

Valery, Paul, French poet, *Obit* Aug 1945

Vallee, Rudy, singer and actor, June 1947, Apr 1963, *Obit* Aug 1986

Valtin, Jan, German author, Apr 1941, *Obit* Jan 1951

Van Allsburg, Chris, American children's author and illustrator, Sept 1996

Van Buren, Abigail, advice columnist, May 1960, *Obit* Yrbk 2013

Van Doren, Mark, American literary critic, editor and poet, Jan 1940, *Obit* Feb 1973

Van Druten, John, English dramatist, Feb 1944, *Obit* Feb 1958

Van Duyn, Mona, American poet, Jan 1998, *Obit* Nov 2005

Van Horne, Harriet, radio and television critic, Yrbk 1954, *Obit* Mar 1998

Van Loon, Hendrik Willem, Dutch-American historian, *Obit* Apr 1944

Van Paassen, Pierre, Dutch-American clergyman, journalist and author, Oct 1942, *Obit* Mar 1968

Van den Haag, Ernest, Dutch-American psychoanalyst, essayist and educator, Oct 1983, *Obit* July 2002

Vance, Marguerite, Yrbk 1951, *Obit* July 1965

Vanderbilt, Amy, Feb 1954, *Obit* Feb 1975

Vanderbilt, Gloria, American fashion designer, July 1972

Vandercook, John W., Apr 1942, *Obit* Feb 1963

Vanocur, Sander, Jan 1963

Vansittart, Robert Gilbert Vansittart, British diplomat, July 1941, *Obit* Apr 1957

Vargas Llosa, Mario, Peruvian novelist, Feb 1976

Veiller, Bayard, dramatist, *Obit* Aug 1943

Velikovsky, Immanuel, May 1957, *Obit* Jan 1980

Vendler, Helen Hennessy, American literary scholar, May 1986

Verghese, Abraham, American physician and novelist, Nov 2011

Vernon, Grenville, *Obit* Jan 1942

Vidal, Gore, American novelist and playwright, Feb 1965, June 1983, *Obit* Yrbk 2012

Viereck, George Sylvester, author and poet, Nov 1940, *Obit* May 1962

Viereck, Peter, American poet and historian, Apr 1943, *Obit* Yrbk 2006

Vilas, Guillermo, Argentine tennis player and poet, Apr 1978

Villard, Oswald Garrison, American journalist, Aug 1940, *Obit* Nov 1949

Vincent, Leon H., *Obit* Apr 1941

Vining, Elizabeth Gray, American novelist, short story

writer and children's author,
Sept 1943

Vishnevskaya, Galina, Russian
opera singer, July 1966, *Obit*
Yrbk 2013

Vitug, Marites, Filipino journalist,
Jan 2005

Vogel, Paula, American
dramatist, July 1998

Vogt, William, ornithologist, Mar
1953, *Obit* Sept 1968

Volokhonsky, Larissa, Russian
translator, June 2006

Von Arnim, Elizabeth, English
novelist, *Obit* Mar 1941

Von Hagen, Victor Wolfgang,
naturalist, biographer and
explorer, Mar 1942

Von Tempski, Armine, *Obit* Jan
1944

Von Ziegesar, Cecily, American
young adult novelist, Jan 2008

Vonnegut, Kurt, American
novelist and short story writer,
July 1970, Mar 1991, *Obit* Aug
2007

Voznesenskii, Andrei, Russian
poet, Mar 1967, *Obit* Yrbk
2010

Wachowski, Andy, American film
director and screenwriter, Sept
2003

Wachowski, Larry, American film
director and screenwriter, Sept
2003

Waddington, C. H., British
embryologist, Apr 1962, *Obit*
Nov 1975

Wagner-Jauregg, Julius,
Austrian psychiatrist, *Obit* Nov
1940

Wakehurst, John de Vere Loder,
Yrbk 1954, *Obit* Yrbk 1970

Wakeman, Frederic, American
novelist, Sept 1946

Walcott, Derek, Saint Lucian
poet and dramatist, Apr 1984

Wald, Jerry, American motion
picture producer, May 1952,
Obit Sept 1962

Wald, Lillian D., American social
reformer and public health
official, *Obit* Oct 1940

Walden, Amelia Elizabeth, Yrbk
1956

Waldman, Ayelet, American
novelist, Sept 2009

Walker, Alice, American
novelist, poet, essayist and
short story writer, Mar 1984

Walker, John, museum director,
May 1957, *Obit* Jan 1996

Walker, Margaret, American
poet and novelist, Nov 1943,
Obit June 1999

Walker, Mildred, American
novelist, Yrbk 1947, *Obit* Aug
1998

Walker, Stuart, *Obit* May 1941

Wallace, Irving, author, Mar
1979, *Obit* Sept 1990

Waller, Robert James, author,
May 1994

Wallerstein, Judith S.,
psychologist, Nov 1996

Wallis, Jim, American evangelist
and writer, July 2005

Wallop, Douglass, American
insurance agent and novelist,
Yrbk 1956, *Obit* June 1985

Wallraff, Gunter, German
journalist, Jan 2004

Waln, Nora, journalist, Jan 1940,
Obit Nov 1964

Walpole, Hugh, English novelist,
Obit July 1941

Walsh, Chad, professor of
English and author, Feb 1962,
Obit Mar 1991

Walsh, George Ethelbert, *Obit*
Apr 1941

Walsh, J. Raymond, Nov 1946

Walsh, William Thomas, July
1941, *Obit* Mar 1949

Waltari, Mika, Finnish novelist,
Feb 1950, *Obit* Oct 1979

Walter, Eugene, American
dramatist and screenwriter,
Obit Nov 1941

Walworth, Arthur, American
biographer, Yrbk 1959, *Obit*
Yrbk 2005

Wambaugh, Joseph, American
novelist, Mar 1980

Wambaugh, Sarah, authority on
plebiscites, Apr 1946, *Obit* Jan
1956

Warburg, James Paul, American
banker, Apr 1948, *Obit* July
1969

Ward, Barbara, English
economist and writer, Jan
1950, Jan 1977, *Obit* July
1981

Ward, Christopher L., *Obit* Apr
1943

Ward, Douglas Turner,
American dramatist, actor and
director, Sept 1976

Ward, Maisie, English author
and publisher, Jan 1966, *Obit*
Mar 1975

Ward, Mary Jane, author, June
1946

Warren, Rick, American pastor
and religious writer, Oct 2006

Warren, Robert Penn, American
novelist and poet, June 1970,
Obit Nov 1989

Wasilewska, Wanda, Polish poet
and novelist, July 1944, *Obit*
Oct 1964

Wason, Betty, cookbook author
and journalist, Aug 1943

Wasserstein, Wendy, American
dramatist, July 1989, *Obit*
Yrbk 2006

Waters, John, American film
director, June 1990

Watkins, Shirley, Yrbk 1958

Watson, Mark Skinner,
journalist, Nov 1946, *Obit* Apr
1966

Wattenberg, Ben J., American
political analyst and writer,
June 1985

Watts, Alan, American
philosopher, Mar 1962, *Obit*
Jan 1974

Waugh, Auberon, English
novelist and essayist, May
1990, *Obit* May 2001

Wayans, Damon, American
comedian and actor, Nov 1999

Wayans, Keenen Ivory,
American actor, screenwriter
and director, Feb 1995

Webb, Beatrice Potter, British
sociologist and reformer, *Obit*
June 1943

Webb, Jim, American senator,
Aug 1987, Nov 2007

Weber, Max, American painter,
June 1941, *Obit* Yrbk 1961

Wechsberg, Joseph, American
journalist, Apr 1955, *Obit* June
1983

Wecter, Dixon, historian, Nov
1944, *Obit* Sept 1950

Weeks, Edward, editor and
essayist, Yrbk 1947, *Obit* May
1989

Wei Jingsheng, Chinese
dissident, Sept 1997

Weidman, Jerome, author and
dramatist, Aug 1942, *Obit* Jan
1999

Weil, Andrew, American
physician and healer, Aug
1996

Weil, Lisl, Jan 1958

Weiner, Jennifer, American novelist, July 2008

Weiner, Matthew, American television producer and scriptwriter, Mar 2012

Weisberg, Jacob, American journalist, Oct 2007

Weisgal, Meyer W., Oct 1972, *Obit* Nov 1977

Weiss, Peter, German dramatist, novelist and painter, Apr 1968, *Obit* July 1982

Weisskopf, Victor Frederick, Austrian-American physicist, Nov 1976, *Obit* Yrbk 2002

Weitz, John, German-American fashion designer, novelist and biographer, Sept 1979, *Obit* Apr 2003

Weitzenkorn, Louis, *Obit* Mar 1943

Weld, John, motion picture stunt performer, May 1940

Weldon, Fay, English novelist, short story writer and dramatist, May 1990

Weller, Michael, American dramatist, May 1989

Welles, Sumner, American diplomat, Mar 1940, *Obit* Nov 1961

Wellman, Manly Wade, author, Yrbk 1955

Wellman, Paul Iselin, American western writer, Yrbk 1949

Wells, Carolyn, author, *Obit* May 1942

Wells, H. G., English science fiction novelist, *Obit* Sept 1946

Wells, Peter, Aug 1942

Welsh, Irvine, Scottish novelist and short story writer, Nov 1997

Welty, Eudora, American short story writer and novelist, Jan 1942, Oct 1975, *Obit* Nov 2001

Wendt, Gerald Louis, scientist, Mar 1940, *Obit* Feb 1974

Werfel, Franz, Austrian poet, novelist and dramatist, Yrbk 1940, *Obit* Sept 1945

Werner, Max, Yrbk 1943, *Obit* Feb 1951

Werth, Alexander, English journalist, Apr 1943, *Obit* Apr 1969

Wertham, Frederic, American psychologist, July 1949, *Obit* Jan 1982

Wertmuller, Lina, Italian motion picture director, Sept 1976

Wesker, Arnold, English dramatist, Feb 1962

Wesley, Charles Harris, American historian and university president, Mar 1944, *Obit* Oct 1987

Wesley, Valerie Wilson, American novelist, children's author and periodical editor, July 2002

West, Claudine, *Obit* May 1943

West, Cornel, American philosopher, Oct 1993

West, Dorothy, American novelist, Feb 1997, *Obit* Oct 1998

West, Jessamyn, American novelist, short story writer, librettist, essayist, playwright and poet, Aug 1977, *Obit* Apr 1984

West, Keith, Yrbk 1947

West, Mae, American actress, Nov 1967, *Obit* Jan 1981

West, Morris L., Australian novelist, Jan 1966, *Obit* Feb 2000

West, Nathanael, American novelist and screenwriter, *Obit* Feb 1941

West, Rebecca, English novelist and journalist, June 1968, *Obit* May 1983

Westcott, John Howell, *Obit* July 1942

Westheimer, Ruth, American psychotherapist, Jan 1987

Wheaton, Anne, Jan 1958, *Obit* May 1977

Wheaton, Elizabeth, Jan 1942

Whedon, Joss, American film and television scriptwriter, July 2012

Wheeler, Robert Eric Mortimer, English archaeologist, Mar 1956, *Obit* Sept 1976

Wheeler, Tony, Australian travel writer and publisher, Jan 2005

Wheelwright, Jere, Yrbk 1952, *Obit* Mar 1961

Wheelwright, John, poet, *Obit* Nov 1940

Whipple, Fred Lawrence, American astronomer, May 1952, *Obit* Yrbk 2005

Whipple, Maurine, American novelist, Mar 1941

Whipple, Wayne, *Obit* Yrbk 1942

Whitaker, Mark, American television news executive, Aug 2003

White, E. B., American humorist and poet, Oct 1960, *Obit* Nov 1985

White, Edmund, American novelist and biographer, Jan 1991

White, Gilbert Fowler, American geographer, Mar 1953, *Obit* Yrbk 2006

White, Helen Constance, literary scholar and author, July 1945

White, Nelia Gardner, author, Yrbk 1950, *Obit* Oct 1957

White, Patrick, Australian novelist, June 1974, *Obit* Nov 1990

White, Paul Dudley, American cardiologist, Yrbk 1955, *Obit* Yrbk 1973

White, Paul Welrose, journalist and radio executive, Mar 1940, *Obit* Oct 1955

White, Randy Wayne, American mystery writer and fishing guide, Nov 2011

White, Stewart Edward, author and hunter, *Obit* Nov 1946

White, Theodore H., American journalist, Apr 1955, Apr 1976, *Obit* July 1986

White, Trumbull, *Obit* Feb 1942

White, Walter Francis, American civil rights leader, Apr 1942, *Obit* June 1955

White, William Allen, newspaper editor, Nov 1940, *Obit* Apr 1944

White, William Lindsay, American journalist and writer, Jan 1943, *Obit* Oct 1973

White, William Smith, journalist, Yrbk 1955, *Obit* June 1994

Whitehead, Colson, American novelist, Nov 2001

Whitehead, Don, journalist, Yrbk 1953, *Obit* Mar 1981

Whitehill, Walter Muir, June 1960, *Obit* May 1978

Whitford, Harry Nichols, *Obit* July 1941

Whitney, Phyllis A., American novelist and short story writer, Yrbk 1948, *Obit* Yrbk 2008

Whyte, William H., American journalist and sociologist, Jan 1959, *Obit* Mar 1999

Wickenden, Dan, author and editor, Yrbk 1951, *Obit* Feb 1990

Wicker, Tom, columnist, Nov 1973, *Obit* Yrbk 2012

Wickham, Madeleine, English novelist, Jan 2004

Wickware, Francis Graham, *Obit* Yrbk 1940

Wideman, John Edgar, American novelist and short story writer, Jan 1991

Wiener, Norbert, American mathematician, Mar 1950, *Obit* May 1964

Wiesel, Elie, American novelist, journalist and human rights activist, Nov 1970, Feb 1986

Wiesenthal, Simon, Austrian Nazi hunter, Jan 1975, *Obit* Yrbk 2005

Wiggam, Albert Edward, July 1942, *Obit* June 1957

Wiig, Kristen, American actress, July 2013

Wilber, Ken, American spiritualist and author, Apr 2002

Wilbur, Richard, American poet, Jan 1966

Wilder, Billy, Austrian-American film director and screenwriter, Feb 1951, Oct 1984, *Obit* Yrbk 2002

Wilder, Laura Ingalls, American children's and young adult author, Yrbk 1948, *Obit* May 1957

Wilder, Thornton, American novelist and dramatist, Aug 1943, Nov 1971, *Obit* Feb 1976

Wildmon, Donald, clergyman, Jan 1992

Wile, Frederic William, journalist and radio commentator, *Obit* June 1941

Wilkerson, Isabel, American journalist, Oct 2011

Wilkins, Roger W., American lawyer, journalist and educator, Aug 1994

Will, George F., American columnist and political commentator, Sept 1981

Willard, John, *Obit* Nov 1942

Williams, Armstrong, American newspaper columnist and radio talk show host, May 2004

Williams, Emlyn, Welsh playwright and actor, Feb 1941, Apr 1952, *Obit* Nov 1987

Williams, Eric Eustace, Trinidadian prime minister, Feb 1966, *Obit* May 1981

Williams, Jay, American novelist, Yrbk 1955, *Obit* Sept 1978

Williams, John Alfred, American novelist, Oct 1994

Williams, Juan, American journalist, May 2008

Williams, Rowan, British archbishop, Jan 2002

Williams, Saul, American rapper and poet, June 2011

Williams, Tad, American science fiction and fantasy writer, Sept 2006

Williams, Tennessee, American dramatist, Jan 1946, Apr 1972, *Obit* Apr 1983

Williams, Wythe, journalist, Oct 1943, *Obit* Sept 1956

Williamson, Kevin, American screenwriter and director, Apr 2000

Williamson, Marianne, New Age preacher, Feb 1993

Willimon, Beau, American playwright, June 2012

Willison, George Findlay, historian, Jan 1946

Williston, Samuel, Yrbk 1954, *Obit* Apr 1963

Wills, Garry, American journalist, essayist and historian, June 1982

Willson, Beckles, *Obit* Nov 1942

Willson, Meredith, American composer and lyricist, June 1958, *Obit* Aug 1984

Wilmore, Larry, American television scriptwriter and producer, Nov 2007

Wilson, A. N., English novelist and biographer, Aug 1993

Wilson, Angus, English novelist and short story writer, Feb 1959, *Obit* Aug 1991

Wilson, August, American playwright, Aug 1987, *Obit* Feb 2006

Wilson, Colin, English novelist and nonfiction writer, Apr 1963

Wilson, Dorothy Clarke, Yrbk 1951

Wilson, Edmund, American literary critic, Apr 1945, Jan 1964, *Obit* July 1972

Wilson, Edward O., American myrmecologist, Oct 1979

Wilson, Eugene E., Oct 1945

Wilson, James Q., American political scientist, Aug 2002, *Obit* Yrbk 2012

Wilson, John Tuzo, Canadian geophysicist and educator, Apr 1973, *Obit* Aug 1993

Wilson, Lanford, American playwright, Mar 1979, *Obit* Yrbk 2011

Wilson, Owen, American actor and screenwriter, Feb 2003

Wilson, Robert, American director, dramatist and artist, Aug 1979

Wilson, Sloan, American novelist, Sept 1959, *Obit* Yrbk 2003

Wilson, William Julius, American sociologist, Feb 1996

Winchell, Constance Mabel, librarian, June 1967, *Obit* Sept 1984

Winchell, Walter, American columnist and radio commentator, June 1943, *Obit* Apr 1972

Winchester, Alice, magazine editor, Feb 1954

Winchester, Simon, Anglo-American journalist, Oct 2006

Windschuttle, Keith, Australian writer and historian, Jan 2006

Winslow, Anne, Yrbk 1948

Winsor, Kathleen, American novelist, Yrbk 1946, *Obit* Yrbk 2003

Winster, Reginald Thomas Herbert Fletcher, Feb 1946

Winter, Ella, Yrbk 1946, *Obit* Sept 1980

Witcover, Jules, American newspaper columnist and writer, Apr 2008

Wodehouse, P. G., English novelist, short story writer and dramatist, Nov 1971, *Obit* Apr 1975

Woiwode, Larry, American novelist, Mar 1989

Wojciechowska, Maia, Polish children's author and publisher, Sept 1976, *Obit* Yrbk 2002

Wolf, Alfred, Mar 1958

Wolf, Naomi, American feminist, social critic and journalist, Nov 1993

Wolfe, George C., American dramatist and director, Mar 1994

Wolfe, Humbert, English poet and government official, *Obit* Jan 1940

Wolfe, Tom, American journalist and novelist, Jan 1971

Wolfert, Ira, author and journalist, Apr 1943, *Obit* Feb 1998

Wolff, Geoffrey, author, Jan 1997

Wolff, Maritta M., American novelist, July 1941, *Obit* Yrbk 2002

Wolff, Tobias, American memoirist and short story writer, Jan 1996

Woltman, Frederick, July 1947, *Obit* Apr 1970

Wong, How-man, Chinese explorer and journalist, Jan 2002

Wong, Kar-Wai, Chinese film director and screenwriter, Apr 1998

Wood, Charles Erskine Scott, American lawyer and satirist, *Obit* Mar 1944

Wood, Gordon S., American historian, Oct 2011

Wood, Kingsley, Nov 1940

Wood, Philip, *Obit* Mar 1940

Woodham Smith, Cecil Blanche Fitz Gerald, English historian, Yrbk 1955, *Obit* Mar 1977

Woodhouse, Barbara, English dog trainer and author, Feb 1985, *Obit* Aug 1988

Woodhouse, Chase Going, congresswoman, Mar 1945, *Obit* Apr 1985

Woodson, Carter Godwin, American historian, Feb 1944, *Obit* Yrbk 1984

Woodward, Bob, American journalist, Nov 1976

Woolf, Leonard, English political essayist, editor, publisher and memoirist, Yrbk 1965, *Obit* Oct 1969

Woolf, Virginia, English novelist, *Obit* May 1941

Woollcott, Alexander, journalist, June 1941, *Obit* Mar 1943

Woolley, Leonard, English archaeologist, Yrbk 1954, *Obit* Apr 1960

Work, Martin H., May 1951

Wouk, Herman, American novelist and playwright, Yrbk 1952

Wren, P. C., English historical novelist, *Obit* Jan 1942

Wright, Anna Rose, author, Yrbk 1952

Wright, Frank Lloyd, American architect, Jan 1941, Nov 1952, *Obit* June 1959

Wright, Harold Bell, American clergyman and novelist, *Obit* July 1944

Wright, Helen, astronomer, Mar 1956, *Obit* Feb 1998

Wright, Peter, British intelligence official, Feb 1988, *Obit* July 1995

Wright, Quincy, American political scientist, Oct 1943, *Obit* Yrbk 1970

Wright, Richard, American novelist, Mar 1940, *Obit* Jan 1961

Wrinch, Dorothy, Anglo-American biochemist and mathematician, July 1947

Wu Chuntao, Chinese journalist, Jan 2005

Wylie, Max, Jan 1940, *Obit* Nov 1975

Xu Jinglei, Chinese actress and filmmaker, Jan 2007

Yaffe, James, Yrbk 1957

Yamanaka, Lois-Ann, American novelist and poet, June 1999

Yardley, Jonathan, American literary critic and columnist, Jan 2011

Yates, Elizabeth, American children's author, Yrbk 1948, *Obit* Nov 2001

Yazbek, Samar, Aug 2013

Ybarra, Thomas Russell, journalist and biographer, Jan 1940

Yeakley, Marjory Hall, Yrbk 1957

Yeats-Brown, Francis, British army officer and author, *Obit* Feb 1945

Yerby, Frank, American novelist and short story writer, Sept 1946, *Obit* Mar 1992

Yergin, Daniel, American energy consultant and business writer, Nov 1999

Yevtushenko, Yevgeny Aleksandrovich, Russian poet, Feb 1963, Mar 1994

Yorke, Thom, Scottish singer, June 2001

Young, Art, cartoonist, Feb 1940, *Obit* Feb 1944

Young, Marian, June 1952, *Obit* Jan 1974

Young, Rose, *Obit* Sept 1941

Young, Stanley, dramatist and publishing executive, Yrbk 1951, *Obit* May 1975

Yourcenar, Marguerite, French-American novelist, poet, dramatist, essayist and translator, Nov 1982, *Obit* Feb 1988

Yust, Walter, Apr 1943, *Obit* Apr 1960

Zaillian, Steven, screenwriter and film director, Oct 2001

Zakaria, Fareed, Indian-American political scientist and journalist, Jan 2003

Zamora, Daisy, Nicaraguan poet, Jan 2004

Zhukov, Georgii Aleksandrovich, Soviet journalist, Oct 1960

Ziemer, Gregor, Apr 1942

Zim, Herbert S., American educator and science writer, Sept 1956, *Obit* Feb 1995

Zimmer, Carl, American science journalist, Oct 2012

Zimmerman, M. M., July 1957

Zindel, Paul, American dramatist, novelist and children's author, June 1973, *Obit* Yrbk 2007

Zinn, Howard, American historian, Aug 1999, *Obit* Yrbk 2010

Zinsser, Hans, American bacteriologist, *Obit* Oct 1940

Zolotow, Maurice, author, May 1957, *Obit* May 1991

Zukerman, Eugenia, American flutist and author, Jan 2004

Zweig, Stefan, Austrian novelist, biographer and poet, *Obit* Apr 1942

al-Mutawa, Naif, Kuwaiti businessman and comic book creator, May 2012

de Botton, Alain, English novelist and journalist, Sept 2013

Authors, Hebrew

Tchernichowsky, Saul, Hebrew poet and physician, *Obit* Yrbk 1943

Authors, Yiddish

Singer, Israel Joshua, Yiddish novelist and dramatist, *Obit* Mar 1944

Automobile dealers

Malone, Karl, American basketball player, Jan 1993

Schott, Marge, American automobile dealer and baseball executive, Aug 1999, *Obit* Yrbk 2004

Automobile executives

Agnelli, Giovanni, Italian automobile executive, Jan 1972, *Obit* June 2003

Austin, Herbert Austin, English automobile executive, *Obit* July 1941

Bajaj, Rahul, Indian automobile executive, Jan 2007

Bransome, Edward D., American truck company executive, Apr 1952

Breech, Ernest, Sept 1955, *Obit* Aug 1978

Budd, Edward G., July 1949, *Obit* July 1971

Bugas, John S., automobile executive, Yrbk 1947, *Obit* Feb 1983

Canaday, Ward Murphey, Mar 1951, *Obit* Apr 1976

Chevrolet, Louis, American automobile executive and engineer, *Obit* Aug 1941

Cho, Fujio, Japanese automobile executive, Jan 2006

Christopher, George T., Nov 1947, *Obit* July 1954

Chrysler, Walter Percy, American automobile executive, *Obit* Oct 1940

Colbert, Lester Lum, automobile executive, Apr 1951, *Obit* Nov 1995

Cole, Edward N., American automobile executive, July 1972, *Obit* July 1977

Crosley, Powel, American baseball and automobile executive, June 1947, *Obit* June 1961

Curtice, Harlow H., American automobile executive, Mar 1953, *Obit* Jan 1963

De Lorean, John Z., American automobile executive, Mar 1976, *Obit* Yrbk 2005

Di Montezemolo, Luca Cordero, Italian automobile executive, Jan 2006

Donner, Frederic Garrett, automobile executive, Jan 1959, *Obit* Apr 1987

Dreyfus, Pierre, French automobile executive and cabinet member, July 1958, *Obit* Mar 1995

Du Pont, Pierre S., American business executive, Sept 1940, *Obit* May 1954

Dykstra, John, American automobile executive, Apr 1963, *Obit* May 1972

Egbert, Sherwood H., June 1963, *Obit* Oct 1969

Estes, Elliott M., American automobile executive, Jan 1979, *Obit* May 1988

Ferguson, Malcolm P., May 1957

Ferrari, Enzo, Italian automobile executive, May 1967, *Obit* Sept 1988

Fields, Mark, American automobile executive, Apr 2005

Firestone, Harvey S., July 1944, *Obit* July 1973

Ford, Benson, automobile executive, Feb 1952, *Obit* Sept 1978

Ford, Edsel Bryant, American automobile executive, *Obit* July 1943

Ford, Henry, American automobile executive, Yrbk 1944, *Obit* May 1947

Ford, Henry, American automobile executive, Apr 1946, June 1978, *Obit* Nov 1987

Ghosn, Carlos, Brazilian-French automobile executive, Jan 2004

Hoffman, Paul G., American automobile executive, Feb 1946, *Obit* Nov 1974

Iacocca, Lee A., American automobile executive, Oct 1971, Oct 1988

Kanzler, Ernest Carlton, automobile executive, Apr 1942, *Obit* Feb 1968

Keller, K. T., May 1947, *Obit* Feb 1966

Kettering, Charles Franklin, American electrical engineer, May 1940, Yrbk 1951, *Obit* Feb 1959

Knudsen, Semon E., American automobile executive, Jan 1974, *Obit* Sept 1998

Knudsen, William S., American automobile executive, July 1940, *Obit* June 1948

Love, George Hutchinson, coal and automobile executive, Mar 1950, *Obit* Sept 1991

Lutz, Robert A., American automobile executive, Jan 1994

Miller, Arjay, Jan 1967

Mott, Charles Stewart, American automobile executive, Sept 1969, *Obit* Apr 1973

Murphy, Thomas Aquinas, American automobile executive, Oct 1979, *Obit* Yrbk 2006

Nasser, Jacques, Lebanese-Australian automobile executive, Apr 2001

Nordhoff, Heinz, German automobile executive, Nov 1956, *Obit* June 1968

Nuffield, William Richard Morris, British automobile executive, Apr 1941, *Obit* Oct 1963

Petersen, Donald E., American automobile executive, Mar 1988

Piech, Ferdinand, German automobile executive, Sept 1999

Renault, Louis, French automobile executive, *Obit* Yrbk 1944

Reuther, Victor, American labor leader, Yrbk 1953, *Obit* Yrbk 2004

Roche, James M., American automobile executive, Feb 1967, *Obit* Yrbk 2004

Romney, George, American Secretary of housing and urban development, June 1958, *Obit* Oct 1995

Rootes, William Edward Rootes, British automobile executive, Nov 1951, *Obit* Feb 1965

Sale, Rhys M., Yrbk 1957

Schrempp, Juergen E., German automobile executive, Oct 1999

Shelby, Carroll, American automobile racing driver and manufacturer, Nov 1993, *Obit* Yrbk 2012

Sloan, Alfred Pritchard, American automobile executive, Nov 1940, *Obit* Mar 1966

Smith, Roger B., American automobile executive, May 1986, *Obit* Yrbk 2008

Stanley, Freelan Oscar, American automotive pioneer, *Obit* Nov 1940

Stettinius, Edward Reilly, American Secretary of state, July 1940, *Obit* Yrbk 1949

Townsend, Lynn A., American automobile executive, Sept 1966, *Obit* Yrbk 2000

Valletta, Vittorio, Italian automobile executive, *Obit* July 1967

Vance, Harold S., American automobile executive and government official, May 1949, *Obit* Nov 1959

Whitman, Marina von Neumann, American automobile executive and economist, Oct 1973

Wills, Childe Harold, automobile executive, *Obit* Feb 1941

Wilson, Charles E., American automobile executive and Secretary of defense, Aug 1941, Sept 1950, *Obit* Yrbk 1961

Yoshino, Hiroyuki, Japanese automobile executive, Jan 2002

Zetsche, Dieter, German automobile executive, Jan 2006

Automobile racing drivers

Andretti, Mario, American automobile racing driver, July 1968

Arfons, Art, American automobile racing driver, Feb 1970

Breedlove, Craig, American automobile racing driver, Sept 1966

Campbell, Donald, British automobile and boat racer, Feb 1964, *Obit* Feb 1967

Campbell, Malcolm, English automobile racing driver, Sept 1947, *Obit* Feb 1949

Chevrolet, Louis, American automobile executive and engineer, *Obit* Aug 1941

Clark, Jim, Scottish automobile racing driver, Nov 1965, *Obit* June 1968

Cottenham, Mark Everard Pepys, *Obit* Sept 1943

Earnhardt, Dale, American automobile racing driver, Jan 2007

Fittipaldi, Emerson, Brazilian automobile racing driver, Apr 1992

Foyt, A. J., American automobile racing driver, Nov 1967

Gordon, Jeff, American automobile racing driver, Aug 2000

Guthrie, Janet, American automobile racing driver, Oct 1978

Hamilton, Lewis, British automobile racing driver, Jan 2007

Hill, Graham, English automobile racing driver, July 1973, *Obit* Jan 1976

Irvan, Ernie, automobile racing driver, July 1998

Karthikeyan, Narain, Indian automobile racing driver, Jan 2005

Lauda, Niki, Austrian automobile racing driver, Oct 1980

Martin, Mark, American automobile racing driver, Mar 2001

Muldowney, Shirley, American automobile racing driver, Oct 1997

Newman, Paul, American actor, Nov 1959, May 1985, *Obit* Yrbk 2008

Oldfield, Barney, American automobile racing driver, *Obit* Nov 1946

Patrick, Danica, American automobile racing driver, Oct 2005

Petty, Richard, American automobile racing driver, Aug 1980

Ribbs, Willy T., American automobile racing driver, Nov 2000

Schumacher, Michael, German automobile racing driver, Jan 2003

Seddigh, Laleh, Iranian automobile racing driver, Jan 2005

Shelby, Carroll, American automobile racing driver and manufacturer, Nov 1993, *Obit* Yrbk 2012

Stewart, Tony, American automobile racing driver, Nov 2006

Tsuchiya, Keiichi, Japanese automobile racing driver, Jan 2006

Vanderbilt, William Kissam, railroad executive and automobile racing driver, *Obit* Feb 1944

Webber, Mark, Australian automobile racing driver, Jan 2004

Yarborough, Cale, American automobile racing driver, Jan 1987

Automotive engineers

Chevrolet, Louis, American automobile executive and engineer, *Obit* Aug 1941

Cole, Edward N., American automobile executive, July 1972, *Obit* July 1977

Piech, Ferdinand, German automobile executive, Sept 1999

Stanley, Freelan Oscar, American automotive pioneer, *Obit* Nov 1940

Badminton players

Lin Dan, Chinese badminton player, Jan 2007

Martin, Camilla, Danish badminton player, Jan 2004

Xie Xingfang, Chinese badminton player, Jan 2007

Zhang Ning, Chinese badminton player, Jan 2003

Bagpipers

Moloney, Paddy, Irish uillean piper, Mar 2004

Ballet dancers

Acosta, Carlos, Cuban ballet dancer, Jan 2004

Alonso, Alicia, Cuban ballet dancer, July 1955, June 1977

Andersen, Ib, Danish ballet dancer and director, Aug 1984

Aroldingen, Karin von, German ballet dancer, Jan 1983

Arpino, Gerald, American ballet dancer and choreographer, Oct 1970, *Obit* Yrbk 2008

Ashley, Merrill, American ballet dancer, Nov 1981

Ashton, Frederick, British choreographer, May 1951, *Obit* Sept 1988

Askegard, Charles, American ballet dancer, Mar 2012

Baryshnikov, Mikhail, Russian-American ballet dancer, Feb 1975

Bejart, Maurice, French ballet dancer and choreographer, Mar 1971, *Obit* Yrbk 2008

Benesh, Joan, British ballet dancer, choreographer and teacher, July 1957

Beriosova, Svetlana, Lithuanian ballet dancer and teacher, Sept 1960, *Obit* Feb 1999

Bessmertnova, Natalia, Russian ballet dancer, Jan 1988, *Obit* Yrbk 2008

Blair, David, British ballet dancer and choreographer, Jan 1961, *Obit* May 1976

Bruhn, Erik, Danish ballet dancer and director, Apr 1959, *Obit* May 1986

Bujones, Fernando, American ballet dancer, Jan 1976, *Obit* Yrbk 2006

Chase, Lucia, American ballet dancer and manager, July 1947, Aug 1975, *Obit* Mar 1986

Clifford, John, American ballet dancer and choreographer, Nov 1972

Corella, Angel, Spanish ballet dancer, Mar 1999

Cullberg, Birgit, Swedish ballet dancer and choreographer, Nov 1982, *Obit* Nov 1999

D'Amboise, Jacques, American ballet dancer, choreographer and teacher, Sept 1964

Danilova, Alexandra, Russian ballet dancer and teacher, July 1987, *Obit* Sept 1997

De Valois, Ninette, English ballet dancer, choreographer and director, Yrbk 1949, *Obit* Aug 2001

Dowell, Anthony, English ballet dancer and manager, May 1971

Eglevsky, Andre, Feb 1953, *Obit* Feb 1978

Elo, Jorma, Finnish ballet dancer and choreographer, July 2009

Farrell, Suzanne, American ballet dancer, Sept 1967

Fokine, Michel, Russian ballet dancer and choreographer, *Obit* Oct 1942

Fonteyn, Margot, English ballet dancer, Yrbk 1949, Mar 1972, *Obit* Apr 1991

Forsythe, William, American choreographer, ballet dancer and director, Feb 2003

Fracci, Carla, Italian ballet dancer, Feb 1975

Franca, Celia, Canadian ballet director and dancer, May 1956, *Obit* Yrbk 2007

Franklin, Frederic, English ballet dancer and choreographer, Sept 1943, *Obit* Yrbk 2013

Galli, Rosina, *Obit* Jan 1940

Godunov, Alexander, Russian ballet dancer and actor, Feb 1983, *Obit* July 1995

Gomes, Marcelo, Brazilian ballet dancer, May 2007

Gregory, Cynthia, American ballet dancer, May 1977

Guillem, Sylvie, French ballet dancer and choreographer, Jan 2002

Hayden, Melissa, American ballet dancer, May 1955, *Obit* Yrbk 2006

Herrera, Paloma, Argentine ballet dancer, Apr 2000

Jeanmaire, Zizi, French ballet dancer and actress, Nov 1952

Jin Xing, Chinese ballet dancer and choreographer, Jan 2006

Joffrey, Robert, American ballet dancer, choreographer and director, Nov 1967, *Obit* Nov 1988

Kain, Karen, Canadian ballet dancer and director, May 1980

Kent, Allegra, American ballet dancer, Mar 1970

Kirkland, Gelsey, American ballet dancer, Oct 1975

Kistler, Darci, American ballet dancer, Oct 1991

Koner, Pauline, ballet dancer and choreographer, Oct 1964, *Obit* Apr 2001

Kudelka, James, Canadian ballet dancer and choreographer, Mar 1995

Le Clercq, Tanaquil, American ballet dancer, July 1953, *Obit* Mar 2001

Magallanes, Nicholas, May 1955, *Obit* July 1977

Makarova, Natalia, Russian ballet dancer, Feb 1972

Markova, Alicia, British ballet dancer, Sept 1943, *Obit* Yrbk 2005

Massine, Leonide, Russian choreographer and ballet dancer, Apr 1940, *Obit* May 1979

Mazzo, Kay, July 1971

McBride, Patricia, ballet dancer, July 1966

McKenzie, Kevin, American ballet dancer and director, Jan 2000

Millepied, Benjamin, French ballet dancer and choreographer, Apr 2011

Moiseyev, Igor, Russian ballet dancer and choreographer, Nov 1958, *Obit* Yrbk 2008

Moylan, Mary Ellen, Feb 1957

Nagy, Ivan, Hungarian dance director, May 1977

Nerina, Nadia, South African ballet dancer, Nov 1957, *Obit* Yrbk 2008

Nijinsky, Waslaw, Russian ballet dancer, Oct 1940, *Obit* May 1950

Nureyev, Rudolf, Russian ballet dancer, July 1963, *Obit* Feb 1993

Page, Ruth, American ballet dancer and choreographer, June 1962, *Obit* July 1991

Park, Merle, English ballet dancer, Sept 1974

Petit, Roland, French ballet dancer and choreographer, Apr 1952, *Obit* Yrbk 2011

Plisetskaya, Maya, Russian ballet dancer, June 1963

Rambert, Marie, British ballet dancer, teacher and director, Feb 1981, *Obit* Aug 1982

Schaufuss, Peter, Danish ballet dancer and director, May 1982

Seymour, Lynn, Canadian ballet dancer, Nov 1979

Shearer, Moira, Scottish ballet dancer and actress, Jan 1950, *Obit* Yrbk 2006

Slavenska, Mia, Croatian ballet dancer and choreographer, Feb 1954, *Obit* Apr 2003

Smuin, Michael, American ballet dancer and choreographer, Oct 1984, *Obit* Yrbk 2007

Stiefel, Ethan, American ballet dancer, Apr 2004

Tallchief, Maria, American ballet dancer, Nov 1951

Taylor, Janie, American ballet dancer, Aug 2011

Tcherkassky, Marianna, ballet dancer, Nov 1985

Tomasson, Helgi, Icelandic ballet dancer and director, Apr 1982

Tudor, Antony, English ballet dancer and choreographer, Nov 1945, *Obit* June 1987

Ulanova, Galina, Russian ballet dancer, Apr 1958, *Obit* June 1998

Van Hamel, Martine, Dutch-American ballet dancer, Sept 1979

Verdy, Violette, French ballet dancer and manager, Yrbk 1969, Oct 1980

Villella, Edward, American ballet dancer and director, Mar 1965

Volochkova, Anastasia, Russian ballet dancer, Jan 2004

Watts, Heather, ballet dancer, May 1983

Welch, Stanton, Australian ballet dancer, choreographer and director, July 2007

Wheater, Ashley, British ballet dancer and director, May 2011

Wheeldon, Christopher, British ballet dancer and choreographer, Mar 2004

Whelan, Wendy, American ballet dancer, Oct 1998

Wilde, Patricia, Canadian ballet dancer and director, May 1968

Youskevitch, Igor, Ukrainian-American ballet dancer and master, Feb 1956, *Obit* Aug 1994

Zorina, Vera, German-American ballet dancer and actress, Jan 1941, *Obit* Yrbk 2003

Balloonists

Forbes, Malcolm Stevenson, American magazine publisher and investment adviser, Feb 1975, *Obit* Apr 1990

Fossett, Steve, American stockbroker and balloonist, Apr 2005, *Obit* Yrbk 2008

Honeywell, Harry E., *Obit* Jan 1940

Jones, Brian, British balloonist, Jan 2004

Piccard, Bertrand, Swiss psychiatrist and balloonist, Jan 2004

Band leaders

Alpert, Herb, American trumpet player and composer, Jan 1967

Armstrong, Louis, American trumpet player, Sept 1944, Apr 1966, *Obit* Sept 1971

Arnaz, Desi, Cuban-American television producer, band leader and actor, Sept 1952, *Obit* Feb 1987

Barry, John, English composer, Mar 2000, *Obit* Yrbk 2011

Basie, Count, American jazz pianist and band leader, June 1942, *Obit* June 1984

Bernie, Ben, American band leader, Yrbk 1941, *Obit* Yrbk 1943

Blakey, Art, American jazz drummer and band leader, Sept 1988, *Obit* Jan 1991

Brown, Chuck, band leader and songwriter, *Obit* Yrbk 2012

Brown, James, American singer, Mar 1992, *Obit* Mar 2007

Calloway, Cab, American singer and band leader, Nov 1945, *Obit* Jan 1995

Carmichael, Hoagy, American songwriter, May 1941, *Obit* Feb 1982

Carter, Benny, American saxophonist, July 1987, *Obit* Oct 2003

Cugat, Xavier, band leader, May 1942, *Obit* Jan 1991

Davis, Meyer, June 1961, *Obit* June 1976

Davis, Miles, American jazz trumpet player and flugelhornist, June 1962, *Obit* Nov 1991

Dorsey, Jimmy, band leader, Apr 1942, *Obit* Sept 1957

Dorsey, Tommy, American band leader, Apr 1942, *Obit* Feb 1957

Duchin, Eddy, pianist and band leader, Jan 1947, *Obit* Mar 1951

Duchin, Peter, band leader, Jan 1977

Ellington, Duke, American band leader and composer, Mar 1941, Jan 1970, *Obit* July 1974

Ferguson, Maynard, Canadian jazz trumpet player, Feb 1980, *Obit* Yrbk 2006

Gillespie, Dizzy, American trumpet player, Apr 1957, Jan 1993, *Obit* Jan 1993

Goodman, Benny, American clarinetist and band leader, Jan 1942, Oct 1962, *Obit* Aug 1986

Hampton, Lionel, American band leader, Oct 1971, *Obit* Yrbk 2002

Handy, W. C., American composer and music publisher, Mar 1941, *Obit* June 1958

Hawkins, Erskine, trumpet player and band leader, Sept 1941, *Obit* Jan 1994

Henderson, Skitch, American conductor, July 1966, *Obit* Apr 2006

Herman, Woody, American band leader, Apr 1973, *Obit* Jan 1988

Hines, Earl, pianist and band leader, Mar 1967, *Obit* June 1983

James, Harry, American band leader and trumpet player, Sept 1943, *Obit* Aug 1983

Joplin, Janis, American singer, Mar 1970, *Obit* Mar 1970

Kenton, Stan, American band leader, June 1979

Kyser, Kay, American band leader, Apr 1941, *Obit* Sept 1985

Lombardo, Guy, American band leader, Sept 1946, Feb 1975, *Obit* Jan 1978

Lopez, Vincent, band leader and pianist, Nov 1960, Nov 1975
Machito, Cuban band leader, Feb 1983, *Obit* June 1984
Marsalis, Branford, American jazz saxophonist, Sept 1991
Marsalis, Wynton, American trumpet player, Oct 1984
McLaughlin, John, British jazz guitarist, Feb 2004
Metheny, Pat, American jazz guitarist, May 1996
Miller, Glenn, American band leader, Feb 1942, *Obit* Yrbk 1991
Mingus, Charles, American jazz bassist and composer, Feb 1971, *Obit* Mar 1979
Monroe, Vaughn, July 1942, *Obit* July 1973
Nelson, Ozzie, actor and band leader, May 1949, *Obit* Aug 1975
Palmieri, Eddie, American salsa pianist and band leader, June 1992
Puente, Tito, American band leader, composer and percussionist, Nov 1977, *Obit* Aug 2000
Rich, Buddy, American drummer and band leader, June 1973, *Obit* May 1987
Santelmann, William F., bandmaster and marine corps officer, Apr 1953
Schoenberg, Loren, American saxophonist and jazz historian, Feb 2005
Scott, Raymond, composer and musical instrument inventor, July 1941, *Obit* May 1994
Shaw, Artie, American clarinetist and band leader, May 1941, *Obit* Apr 2005
Stew (Musician), American composer, lyricist and singer, Sept 2007
Vinton, Bobby, July 1977
Waring, Fred, American band leader, Sept 1940, *Obit* Sept 1984
Welk, Lawrence, American band leader, Feb 1957, *Obit* July 1992
Whiteman, Paul, American band leader, Aug 1945, *Obit* Feb 1968
Winter, Paul, saxophonist, Oct 1987

Banjo players

Clark, Roy, American country singer and banjoist, June 1978
Fleck, Bela, American banjoist, Nov 1996
Robison, Emily, American banjoist and singer, July 2000

Bankers

Abs, Hermann J., German banker, Oct 1970, *Obit* May 1994
Al-Shabibi, Sinan, Iraqi banker and economist, Jan 2005
Aldrich, Winthrop Williams, American banker and diplomat, Oct 1940, Mar 1953, *Obit* Apr 1974
Alessandri Rodriguez, Jorge, Chilean president, May 1959, *Obit* Oct 1986
Alexander, Willis W., American banker and newspaper publisher, July 1969, *Obit* Jan 1986
Ames, Amyas, investment banker and music patron, Apr 1972, *Obit* June 2000
Anderson, Samuel W., American investment banker and government official, June 1954, *Obit* Jan 1963
Anderson, Victor E., American governor, Sept 1956, *Obit* Oct 1962
Araki, Eikichi, Japanese diplomat, Oct 1952, *Obit* Apr 1959
Armstrong, J. Sinclair, banker, lawyer and government official, Mar 1958, *Obit* Mar 2001
Aronson, J. Hugo, American governor, Feb 1954
Aronson, Louis V., American inventor, manufacaturing executive and banker, *Obit* Yrbk 1940
Ash, Roy, American presidential adviser and manufacturing executive, July 1968, *Obit* Yrbk 2012
Ayres, Leonard Porter, May 1940, *Obit* Yrbk 1946
Aziz, Shaukat, Pakistani prime minister, Jan 2007
Baker, John Hopkinson, American investment banker and conservationist, May 1949

Banda, Enos, South African banker, Jan 2005
Beame, Abraham D., American mayor, July 1974, *Obit* Apr 2001
Bell, Daniel W., American banker and government official, Oct 1946, *Obit* Nov 1971
Beltran, Pedro G., Peruvian newspaper publisher and statesman, Apr 1967, *Obit* Apr 1979
Bergen, John J., American financier, June 1961, *Obit* Feb 1981
Beyen, J. W., Dutch banker, economist and diplomat, Feb 1953, *Obit* June 1976
Bimson, Carl A., American banker, Mar 1961
Black, Eugene Robert, American banking official, Jan 1950, *Obit* Apr 1992
Blankfein, Lloyd C., American investment banker, Jan 2011
Blumenthal, Hugo, American investment banker and philanthropist, *Obit* Sept 1943
Boles, Ewing T., American investment banker, Apr 1953
Bond, John, British banker, Jan 2005
Botin, Ana Patricia, Spanish banker, Jan 2005
Bowles, Erskine, American presidential adviser, Aug 1998
Brady, Nicholas F., American Secretary of the treasury, Nov 1988
Brenton, W. Harold, Jan 1953
Bridges, Styles, American governor and senator, Mar 1948, *Obit* Jan 1962
Brimmer, Andrew F., American economist and financial consultant, July 1968, *Obit* Yrbk 2012
Bruce, Howard, Sept 1948, *Obit* Sept 1961
Brunsdale, Clarence Norman, governor and banker, Sept 1954
Burgess, Warren, June 1949, *Obit* Nov 1978
Burgin, William O., *Obit* May 1946
Burns, Arthur F., American economist and diplomat, Sept 1953, Aug 1976, *Obit* Aug 1987

Bush, Prescott S., American banker, senator and father of President George Bush, May 1942, Jan 1954, *Obit* Yrbk 1972

Butcher, Willard C., banker, July 1980, *Obit* Yrbk 2012

Buttenwieser, Benjamin Joseph, investment banker, Nov 1950, *Obit* Mar 1992

Carter, John Ridgely, *Obit* July 1944

Castle, Lewis G., July 1958, *Obit* Sept 1960

Catto, Thomas Sivewright Catto, English banker, Nov 1944

Champion, George, banker, Apr 1961, *Obit* Jan 1998

Chao, Elaine, American Secretary of labor, May 2001

Clark, Georgia Neese, banker and government official, Sept 1949, *Obit* Feb 1996

Clausen, A. W., banking official, Nov 1981

Cocke, Charles Francis, Mar 1952

Conable, Barber B., American congressman and banking official, July 1984, *Obit* Yrbk 2004

Corzine, Jon S., American financial executive and former governor, Aug 2006

Coyne, James E., July 1955

Cromer, George Rowland Stanley Baring, English banker and diplomat, May 1971, *Obit* May 1991

Crowley, Leo, American banker and government official, June 1943, *Obit* June 1972

Dale, Chester, American investment banker and art collector, Sept 1958, *Obit* Jan 1963

Darman, Richard, American presidential aide, May 1989, *Obit* Yrbk 2008

Davis, Archie K., May 1966

Davis, Chester Charles, American agricultural leader, banker and government official, July 1940, *Obit* Nov 1975

Davis, Norman Hezekiah, banker and diplomat, Jan 1940, *Obit* Aug 1944

Dawson, John A., investment banker, Sept 1952

Dewey, Charles Schuveldt, Jan 1949, *Obit* Feb 1981

Dillon, Douglas, American investment banker and Secretary of the treasury, Apr 1953, *Obit* May 2003

Dimon, James, American investment banker, June 2004

Dodge, Joseph Morrell, American banker and government official, Nov 1947, *Obit* Jan 1965

Douglas, James Henderson, American Secretary of the air force, Sept 1957, *Obit* Apr 1988

Draper, William Henry, banker and government official, Mar 1952, *Obit* Feb 1975

Drozniak, Edward, July 1962, *Obit* Jan 1967

Duisenberg, Willem, Dutch European banking official, Jan 2002, *Obit* CB Int 2006

Ebbott, Percy J., American banker, Oct 1954

Eberstadt, Ferdinand, investment banker, Yrbk 1942, *Obit* Jan 1970

Eccles, Marriner S., American financier and Federal Reserve chairman, Apr 1941, *Obit* Feb 1978

Emanuel, Rahm, American mayor, Apr 1998, Mar 2009

Emmerson, Louis Lincoln, *Obit* Mar 1941

Emmons, Glenn L., Oct 1954

Fleming, Donald M., Canadian cabinet member, Feb 1959, *Obit* Mar 1987

Fleming, Sam M., June 1962

Florence, Fred F., June 1956, *Obit* Feb 1961

Forrestal, James V., American Secretary of defense, Feb 1942, Jan 1948, *Obit* July 1949

Fowler, Henry H., American Secretary of the treasury, Sept 1952, *Obit* May 2000

Frank, Anthony M., postmaster general, Aug 1991

Fraser, Leon, *Obit* May 1945

Frear, J. Allen, Oct 1954

Fukui, Toshihiko, Japanese banking official, Jan 2004

Garst, Roswell, agriculturist and banker, Apr 1964, *Obit* Jan 1978

Gates, Thomas S., American Secretary of the navy, Sept 1957, *Obit* May 1983

Geithner, Timothy F., American Secretary of the treasury, Mar 2009

Giannini, Amadeo Peter, American banker, Mar 1947, *Obit* July 1949

Giannini, L. M., Nov 1950, *Obit* Oct 1952

Gidney, Ray M., Oct 1953

Gleason, John S., June 1958

Gordon, Donald, Oct 1950, *Obit* June 1969

Greenspan, Alan, American economist and Federal Reserve chairman, Yrbk 1974, Jan 1989

Griffis, Stanton, investment banker and diplomat, Oct 1944, *Obit* Oct 1974

Guinness, Arthur, June 1948

Hagel, Chuck, American senator, Aug 2004

Hancock, John M., Apr 1949, *Obit* Yrbk 1957

Harber, W. Elmer, Mar 1951

Harriman, E. Roland, Mar 1951, *Obit* Apr 1978

Harrison, William B., American investment banker, Mar 2002

Hayes, Alfred, banker and government official, Feb 1966, *Obit* Feb 1990

Herrera, Felipe, Mar 1968

Holbrooke, Richard, American diplomat, Oct 1998, *Obit* Yrbk 2011

Hughes, Rowland R., American government official, Feb 1956, *Obit* June 1957

Jackson, William H., Mar 1951, *Obit* Nov 1971

Jacobsson, Per, Swedish banker, Oct 1958, *Obit* June 1963

Johnson, Arnold M., Oct 1955, *Obit* May 1960

Johnson, Joseph T., Feb 1952

Katzenbach, Nicholas deB., American Attorney general, July 1965, *Obit* Yrbk 2012

Kennedy, David Matthew, American Secretary of the treasury, June 1969, *Obit* July 1996

Khodorkovsky, Mikhail, Russian energy industry executive, Jan 2003

Kimbrel, Monroe, June 1963

Kiriyenko, Sergei, Russian energy industry executive, Aug 1998

Kohler, Horst, German president, Jan 2002

Korth, Frederick H., secretary of the navy, July 1962, *Obit* Jan 1999

Laeri, John Howard, banker, Sept 1968, *Obit* Aug 1986

Lamont, Thomas William, banker, Oct 1940, *Obit* Feb 1948

Lance, Bert, banker and presidential adviser, Aug 1977, *Obit* Yrbk 2013

Leffingwell, Russell Cornell, banker, Mar 1950, *Obit* Yrbk 1960

Lehman, Herbert Henry, American governor and senator, Jan 1943, July 1955, *Obit* Jan 1964

Lewis, Kenneth, American banker, Apr 2004

Lewis, Michael, American investment banker and journalist, Sept 2012

Livingston, Homer J., Sept 1955, *Obit* July 1970

Locke, Edwin A., Jan 1952

Long, Edward V., American senator, July 1964, *Obit* Jan 1973

Lovett, Robert A., American Secretary of defense, Aug 1942, Nov 1951, *Obit* June 1986

Markell, Jack, American governor, July 2011

Martin, William McChesney, American stockbroker and Federal Reserve chairman, May 1951, *Obit* Oct 1998

Martinez Trueba, Andres, Nov 1954, *Obit* Feb 1960

Maximos, Demetrios, Mar 1948, *Obit* Yrbk 1955

Mayo, Robert P., Feb 1970

McCabe, Thomas Bayard, American paper industry executive and Federal Reserve chairman, Sept 1948, *Obit* July 1982

McCloy, John Jay, American lawyer, banker and government official, Apr 1947, Nov 1961, *Obit* May 1989

McConnell, Samuel Kerns, Nov 1956

McDonnell, William A., Feb 1959

McKenna, Reginald, British cabinet member and banker, *Obit* Oct 1943

McKinney, Frank Edward, banker and political leader, Jan 1952, *Obit* Mar 1974

McKittrick, Thomas, July 1944, *Obit* Mar 1970

McNamara, Robert S., American Secretary of defense and banker, Sept 1961, Mar 1987, *Obit* Yrbk 2009

McWhinney, Madeline H., July 1976

Meeker, Mary, American financial analyst, Aug 1999

Mellon, Richard K., May 1965, *Obit* July 1970

Merchant, Livingston T., American government official and diplomat, Nov 1956, *Obit* July 1976

Merle-Smith, Van Santvoord, *Obit* Yrbk 1943

Meyer, Eugene, American investment banker, government official and newspaper publisher, Sept 1941, *Obit* Oct 1959

Miller, G. William, American Secretary of the treasury, Federal Reserve chairman and investment banker, June 1978, *Obit* Yrbk 2007

Miller, Lee P., July 1959

Mooney, Beth, American banker, May 2012

Moore, George S., banker, May 1970, *Obit* Yrbk 2000

Morehead, John H., *Obit* July 1942

Morgan, J. P., American financier, *Obit* Apr 1943

Mosbacher, Emil, investment banker, presidential aide and yacht racer, Mar 1963, *Obit* Nov 1997

Muir, James, May 1950, *Obit* Jan 1960

Murphy, Franklin W., American farm leader, lawyer and banker, *Obit* Jan 1941

Nickerson, Albert L., petroleum executive and banking official, Nov 1959, *Obit* Nov 1994

Norman, Montagu Collet Norman, English banker, Yrbk 1940, *Obit* Mar 1950

O'Neal, Edward A., banking executive, Sept 1946, *Obit* May 1958

O'Neal, Stanley, American investment banker, May 2003

Odlin, Reno, July 1965

Osborn, Frederick Henry, railroad executive and investment banker, Nov 1941, *Obit* Mar 1981

Pace, Charles Ashford, *Obit* Feb 1941

Parsons, Richard D., American motion picture and broadcasting executive, Apr 2003

Pate, Maurice, June 1951, *Obit* Mar 1965

Paulson, Henry M., American Secretary of the treasury, Sept 2002

Pell, Claiborne, American senator, Mar 1972, *Obit* Yrbk 2009

Peterson, F. Raymond, Feb 1950, *Obit* Feb 1978

Peterson, Peter G., American investment banker and Secretary of commerce, June 1972

Peterson, R. A., American banker, May 1964

Pierson, Warren Lee, June 1941, Nov 1954

Potanin, Vladimir O., Russian metal industry executive and banker, Jan 2006

Price, Gwilym A., American electrical generating equipment company executive, May 1949, *Obit* Aug 1985

Rasminsky, Louis, Yrbk 1961

Reese, Everett D., Mar 1954

Remington, John W., Feb 1960

Remorino, Jeronimo, Sept 1951

Riter, Henry G., Oct 1955, *Obit* Sept 1958

Robertson, Walter S., Yrbk 1953, *Obit* May 1970

Rockefeller, David, American banker, Mar 1959

Roebling, Mary G., banker, Oct 1960, *Obit* Jan 1995

Rohatyn, Felix G., American investment banker and diplomat, May 1978

Roosa, Robert V., American investment banker and government official, Yrbk 1962, *Obit* Mar 1994

Root, Oren, state banking official, Aug 1940, July 1952, *Obit* Mar 1995

Rooth, Ivar, Yrbk 1952, *Obit* Apr 1972

Rothschild, Guy de, French banker, Mar 1973, *Obit* Yrbk 2007

Rubin, Robert E., American financial executive and former Secretary of the treasury, July 1997

Ruhle, Stephanie, American investment banker, Jan 2013

Ruml, Beardsley, department store executive and banker, May 1943, *Obit* June 1960

Ryti, Risto, Feb 1941, *Obit* Jan 1957

Saltzman, Charles E., general, diplomat and investment banker, Oct 1947, *Obit* Aug 1994

Saul, Ralph Southey, Feb 1971

Schricker, Henry F., American governor, Sept 1950, *Obit* Feb 1967

Shelton, James E., Feb 1951

Smith, Howard Worth, American congressman, Feb 1941, *Obit* Nov 1976

Souers, Sidney W., American banker, insurance executive and intelligence service official, Feb 1949, *Obit* Mar 1973

Sproul, Allan, banker, Yrbk 1950, *Obit* June 1978

Stern, Nicholas Herbert, British economist and government official, Jan 2007

Stockman, David Alan, American investment banker, presidential aide and manufacturing executive, Aug 1981

Stokes, Edward C., American governor, *Obit* Yrbk 1942

Strauss, Lewis L., American presidential aide, regulatory agency official and Secretary of commerce, Feb 1947, *Obit* Mar 1974

Sumner, Jessie, congresswoman, Jan 1945, *Obit* Oct 1994

Tauscher, Ellen O., American congresswoman, Mar 2001

Tawes, J. Millard, Oct 1960, *Obit* Aug 1979

Tener, John Kinley, baseball player, congressman and governor, *Obit* June 1946

Thain, John, American investment banker, May 2004

Thompson, Roy L., Oct 1946

Thomson, J. Cameron, Yrbk 1948, *Obit* Mar 1966

Tobey, Charles W., American senator and governor, June 1941, July 1951, *Obit* Oct 1953

Towers, Graham F., Canadian banker, Feb 1952

Trichet, Jean-Claude, French banking official, Jan 2006

Tuomioja, Sakari, Mar 1954, *Obit* Nov 1964

Vardaman, James Kimble, American banker and government official, Apr 1951

Volcker, Paul A., American economist and Federal Reserve chairman, July 1973

Vranitzky, Franz, Austrian chancellor, Aug 1989

Wampler, Cloud, Yrbk 1952

Warburg, James Paul, American banker, Apr 1948, *Obit* July 1969

Waugh, Samuel C., Yrbk 1955, *Obit* Oct 1970

Welch, Leo D., Yrbk 1963, *Obit* Jan 1979

Welman, Joseph C., May 1958

Wente, Carl F., Feb 1954

White, Alexander M., July 1951, *Obit* Jan 1969

Williams, Ralph E., *Obit* July 1940

Wilson, Malcolm, American lawyer, banker and governor, May 1974, *Obit* Aug 2000

Winthrop, Beekman, *Obit* Yrbk 1940

Wolfensohn, James David, Australian international organization official, May 2000

Woods, George David, banker, July 1965, *Obit* Oct 1982

Woollen, Evans, Yrbk 1948, *Obit* Apr 1959

Wriston, Walter B., American banker, Nov 1977, *Obit* Aug 2005

Yunus, Muhammad, Bangladeshi banker and economist, Jan 2002

Zhou Xiaochuan, Chinese banker, Jan 2003

Baseball coaches

Allen, Ethan, American baseball player and coach, Mar 1954, *Obit* Nov 1993

Berra, Yogi, American baseball player and manager, May 1952

Howard, Elston, American baseball player and coach, Apr 1964, *Obit* Feb 1981

Howard, Frank, American baseball player, manager and coach, Jan 1972

Jensen, Jackie, baseball player, coach and manager, June 1959, *Obit* Oct 1982

Law, Vern, baseball player and coach, Apr 1961

Leyland, Jim, American baseball manager, Nov 1998

Maddon, Joe, American baseball manager, Sept 2012

Randolph, Willie, American baseball player, coach and manager, Sept 2005

Richardson, Bobby, baseball player, May 1966

Stanky, Eddie, baseball player, June 1951, *Obit* Aug 1999

Tiant, Luis, Cuban baseball player, June 1977

Washington, Ron, American baseball manager, May 2011

Wyatt, Whit, baseball player, coach and manager, Nov 1941, *Obit* Nov 1999

Baseball executives

Autry, Gene, American cowboy singer, actor and baseball executive, Yrbk 1947, *Obit* Jan 1999

Beane, Billy, American baseball executive, July 2005

Busch, August Anheuser, American brewing industry and baseball executive, July 1973, *Obit* Nov 1989

Bush, George W., American president, Apr 1997, Aug 2001

Chandler, Happy, American governor, senator and baseball executive, Aug 1943, Sept 1956, *Obit* Aug 1991

Cronin, Joe, American baseball player, manager and executive, Mar 1965, *Obit* Nov 1984

Crosley, Powel, American baseball and automobile

executive, June 1947, *Obit* June 1961

Doubleday, Nelson, publisher and baseball executive, May 1987

Epstein, Theo, American baseball executive, May 2004

Finley, Charles, American baseball executive, June 1974, *Obit* Apr 1996

Frick, Ford, American baseball executive, May 1945, *Obit* June 1978

Gabriel, Roman, football player, Nov 1975

Giamatti, A. Bartlett, American university president, literary scholar and baseball commissioner, Apr 1978, *Obit* Oct 1989

Griffith, Clark, baseball player, manager and executive, June 1950, *Obit* Jan 1956

Haney, Fred, Jan 1967

Harrelson, Ken, baseball player and executive, Apr 1970

Harridge, William, baseball executive, Sept 1949, *Obit* June 1971

Henry, John, American baseball executive, May 2005

Huizenga, H. Wayne, American video chain and baseball executive, Jan 1995

Ilitch, Mike, American fast food chain and baseball executive, Feb 2005

Johnson, Arnold M., Oct 1955, *Obit* May 1960

Kroc, Ray, American fast food restaurant chain founder and baseball team owner, Mar 1973, *Obit* Mar 1984

Kuhn, Bowie, American lawyer and baseball commissioner, Jan 1970, *Obit* Yrbk 2007

Landis, Kenesaw Mountain, American judge and baseball executive, May 1944, *Obit* Jan 1945

Leverone, Nathaniel, Nov 1956, *Obit* July 1969

MacPhail, Larry, baseball executive, Mar 1945, *Obit* Nov 1975

Mack, Connie, American baseball manager and executive, June 1944, *Obit* Apr 1956

Miller, Marvin, American baseball players association

executive, May 1973, *Obit* Yrbk 2013

Monaghan, Thomas, American fast food and baseball executive, June 1990

Notari, Aldo, Italian baseball association executive, Jan 2004, *Obit* CB Int 2006

O'Malley, Walter Francis, American baseball executive, Mar 1954, *Obit* Oct 1979

Pasquel, Jorge, July 1946, *Obit* May 1955

Payson, Joan Whitney, July 1972, *Obit* Nov 1975

Rickey, Branch, American baseball manager and executive, Oct 1945, *Obit* Jan 1966

Rosen, Al, baseball player and executive, July 1954

Ryan, Nolan, American baseball player and executive, Oct 1970

Schott, Marge, American automobile dealer and baseball executive, Aug 1999, *Obit* Yrbk 2004

Selig, Bud, American baseball commissioner, Jan 1999

Steinbrenner, George M., American baseball and shipbuilding executive, Feb 1979, *Obit* Yrbk 2010

Tener, John Kinley, baseball player, congressman and governor, *Obit* June 1946

Trautman, George McNeal, baseball executive, Oct 1951, *Obit* Sept 1963

Turner, Ted, American television and baseball executive, May 1979, June 1998

Ueberroth, Peter, American entrepreneur and Olympic executive, Apr 1985

Veeck, Bill, American baseball executive, Nov 1948, *Obit* Feb 1986

Vincent, Francis T., American motion picture executive and baseball commissioner, May 1991

Williams, Edward Bennett, American lawyer and baseball and football executive, Jan 1965, *Obit* Sept 1988

Wrigley, Philip Knight, baseball executive, Apr 1975, *Obit* June 1977

Baseball managers

Alou, Felipe, Dominican baseball player and manager, June 1999

Alston, Walter, baseball manager, June 1954, *Obit* Nov 1984

Anderson, Sparky, American baseball manager, Apr 1977, *Obit* Yrbk 2011

Baker, Dusty, American baseball player and manager, Apr 2001

Bauer, Hank, American baseball player and manager, Feb 1967

Berra, Yogi, American baseball player and manager, May 1952

Boudreau, Lou, American baseball player and manager, Aug 1942, *Obit* Oct 2001

Boyer, Ken, baseball player, Mar 1966, *Obit* Oct 1982

Brenly, Bob, American baseball player and manager, Apr 2002

Cox, Bobby, American baseball manager, Feb 1998

Cronin, Joe, American baseball player, manager and executive, Mar 1965, *Obit* Nov 1984

Dark, Alvin, baseball manager, Mar 1975

Dressen, Chuck, baseball player and manager, July 1951, *Obit* Nov 1966

Durocher, Leo, baseball player and manager, Sept 1940, July 1950, *Obit* Nov 1991

Francona, Terry, American baseball manager, July 2008

Gaston, Cito, American baseball player and manager, Apr 1993

Girardi, Joe, American baseball player and manager, May 2008

Griffith, Clark, baseball player, manager and executive, June 1950, *Obit* Jan 1956

Guillen, Ozzie, Venezuelan baseball player and manager, May 2006

Haney, Fred, Jan 1967

Harris, Bucky, baseball manager, June 1948, *Obit* Jan 1978

Hodges, Gil, American baseball player and manager, Oct 1962, *Obit* May 1972

Hornsby, Rogers, American baseball player and manager, Sept 1952, *Obit* Feb 1963

Houk, Ralph, American baseball manager, July 1962, *Obit* Yrbk 2010

Howard, Frank, American baseball player, manager and coach, Jan 1972

Jensen, Jackie, baseball player, coach and manager, June 1959, *Obit* Oct 1982

Johnson, Davey, American baseball manager, Sept 1999

LaRussa, Tony, American baseball manager, July 2003

Lasorda, Tommy, American baseball manager, Feb 1989

Leyland, Jim, American baseball manager, Nov 1998

Lopez, Al, American baseball player and manager, Feb 1960, *Obit* Yrbk 2006

Mack, Connie, American baseball manager and executive, June 1944, *Obit* Apr 1956

Maddon, Joe, American baseball manager, Sept 2012

Martin, Billy, American baseball manager, Oct 1976, *Obit* Feb 1990

Mauch, Gene, American baseball manager, Yrbk 1974, *Obit* Yrbk 2005

McCarthy, Joe, baseball manager, May 1948, *Obit* Mar 1978

McKeon, Jack, American baseball manager, Apr 2004

Murtaugh, Danny, baseball player and manager, Feb 1961, *Obit* Feb 1977

Nagashima, Shigeo, Japanese baseball player and manager, Jan 2003

Oh, Sadaharu, Japanese baseball player, Jan 2002

Ott, Mel, American baseball player and manager, July 1941, *Obit* Jan 1959

Piniella, Lou, American baseball player and manager, Aug 1986

Randolph, Willie, American baseball player, coach and manager, Sept 2005

Rickey, Branch, American baseball manager and executive, Oct 1945, *Obit* Jan 1966

Robinson, Frank, American baseball player and manager, June 1971

Rose, Pete, American baseball player and manager, Aug 1975

Sawyer, Eddie, baseball manager, Nov 1950, *Obit* Jan 1998

Schoendienst, Red, baseball player and manager, Yrbk 1964

Sewell, Luke, baseball manager, Nov 1944

Shotton, Burt, baseball player and manager, June 1949, *Obit* Oct 1962

Southworth, Billy, baseball player and manager, Nov 1944, *Obit* Jan 1970

Stanky, Eddie, baseball player, June 1951, *Obit* Aug 1999

Stengel, Casey, American baseball manager, June 1949, *Obit* Nov 1975

Torre, Joe, American baseball player and manager, May 1972, May 1997

Valentine, Bobby, American baseball manager and television sports commentator, July 2001

Washington, Ron, American baseball manager, May 2011

Weaver, Earl, American baseball manager, Feb 1983, *Obit* Yrbk 2013

Williams, Dick, American baseball player and manager, Yrbk 1973, *Obit* Yrbk 2011

Williams, Ted, American baseball player and manager, Apr 1947, *Obit* Oct 2002

Wills, Maury, American baseball player, June 1966

Wyatt, Whit, baseball player, coach and manager, Nov 1941, *Obit* Nov 1999

Baseball players

Aaron, Hank, American baseball player, May 1958

Abbott, Jim, American baseball player, Sept 1995

Allen, Dick, American baseball player, May 1973

Allen, Ethan, American baseball player and coach, Mar 1954, *Obit* Nov 1993

Alou, Felipe, Dominican baseball player and manager, June 1999

Alou, Moises, American baseball player, Apr 1999

Anderson, Sparky, American baseball manager, Apr 1977, *Obit* Yrbk 2011

Bagwell, Jeff, American baseball player, Aug 2000

Baker, Dusty, American baseball player and manager, Apr 2001

Banks, Ernie, American baseball player, May 1959

Bauer, Hank, American baseball player and manager, Feb 1967

Bautista, Jose, Dominican baseball player, Oct 2011

Beckett, Josh, American baseball player, July 2011

Bench, Johnny, American baseball player, Oct 1971

Blue, Vida, baseball player, Mar 1972

Boggs, Wade, American baseball player, Aug 1990

Bonds, Barry, American baseball player, June 1994

Boudreau, Lou, American baseball player and manager, Aug 1942, *Obit* Oct 2001

Bouton, Jim, American baseball player and sportscaster, Oct 1971

Boyer, Ken, baseball player, Mar 1966, *Obit* Oct 1982

Brenly, Bob, American baseball player and manager, Apr 2002

Brett, George, American baseball player, July 1981

Brock, Lou, American baseball player, June 1975

Brosnan, Jim, American baseball player and sportswriter, Nov 1964

Cabrera, Miguel, Venezuelan baseball player, July 2009

Campanella, Roy, American baseball player, June 1953, *Obit* Aug 1993

Canseco, Jose, Cuban-American baseball player, Nov 1991

Carew, Rod, American baseball player, Jan 1978

Carpenter, Chris, American baseball player, Aug 2012

Cepeda, Orlando, Puerto Rican baseball player, Oct 1968

Chance, Dean, baseball player, July 1969

Clemens, Roger, American baseball player, Nov 1988, Aug 2003

Clemente, Roberto, Puerto Rican baseball player, Feb 1972, *Obit* Feb 1973

Cobb, Ty, American baseball player, Sept 1951, *Obit* Oct 1961

Collins, Jimmy, baseball player, *Obit* Apr 1943

Cone, David, American baseball player, Feb 1998

Conigliaro, Tony, baseball player, Feb 1971, *Obit* Apr 1990

Counsell, Craig, American baseball player, Sept 2002

Cox, Bobby, American baseball manager, Feb 1998

Dark, Alvin, baseball manager, Mar 1975

Dean, Dizzy, American baseball player and sportscaster, Sept 1951, *Obit* Sept 1974

DiMaggio, Joe, American baseball player, June 1941, July 1951, *Obit* May 1999

Dickey, R. A., American baseball player, Oct 2013

Dressen, Chuck, baseball player and manager, July 1951, *Obit* Nov 1966

Drysdale, Don, American baseball player and sportscaster, Feb 1965, *Obit* Sept 1993

Durocher, Leo, baseball player and manager, Sept 1940, July 1950, *Obit* Nov 1991

Feller, Bob, American baseball player, Aug 1941, *Obit* Yrbk 2011

Fidrych, Mark, American baseball player, Mar 1978, *Obit* Yrbk 2009

Fielder, Prince, American baseball player, June 2008

Ford, Whitey, American baseball player, Apr 1962

Fox, Nellie, American baseball player, Mar 1960, *Obit* Feb 1976

Franco, Julio, Dominican baseball player, Sept 2006

Francona, Terry, American baseball manager, July 2008

Furuta, Atsuya, Japanese baseball player, Jan 2005

Gagne, Eric, Canadian baseball player, June 2004

Garagiola, Joe, American sportscaster and baseball player, Jan 1976

Garciaparra, Nomar, American baseball player, June 2000

Gaston, Cito, American baseball player and manager, Apr 1993

Gehrig, Lou, American baseball player, Jan 1940, *Obit* July 1941

Gibson, Bob, American baseball player, Yrbk 1968

Girardi, Joe, American baseball player and manager, May 2008

Glavine, Tom, American baseball player, Oct 2006

Gooden, Dwight, American baseball player, Apr 1986

Gossage, Rich, American baseball player, Aug 1984

Greenberg, Hank, American baseball player, June 1947, *Obit* Oct 1986

Greinke, Zack, American baseball player, July 2010

Griffey, Ken, American baseball player, Aug 1996

Groat, Dick, May 1961

Guerrero, Vladimir, Dominican baseball player, June 2006

Guidry, Ron, American baseball player, May 1979

Guillen, Ozzie, Venezuelan baseball player and manager, May 2006

Gwynn, Tony, American baseball player, Oct 1996

Halladay, Roy, American baseball player, Sept 2009

Hamels, Cole, American baseball player, Nov 2011

Hamilton, Josh, American baseball player, Apr 2011

Harper, Bryce, American baseball player, May 2013

Harrelson, Ken, baseball player and executive, Apr 1970

Harris, Bucky, baseball manager, June 1948, *Obit* Jan 1978

Henderson, Rickey, American baseball player, Sept 1990

Hernandez, Keith, American baseball player and sportscaster, Feb 1988

Hernandez, Livan, Cuban baseball player, Mar 1998

Hernandez, Orlando, Cuban baseball player, Apr 2000

Hern ndez, F,lix, Venezuelan baseball player, June 2012

Hershiser, Orel, baseball player, Feb 1990

Hodges, Gil, American baseball player and manager, Oct 1962, *Obit* May 1972

Hornsby, Rogers, American baseball player and manager, Sept 1952, *Obit* Feb 1963

Houk, Ralph, American baseball manager, July 1962, *Obit* Yrbk 2010

Howard, Bart B., Jan 1940, *Obit* Apr 1941

Howard, Elston, American baseball player and coach, Apr 1964, *Obit* Feb 1981

Howard, Ryan, American baseball player, July 2007

Hunter, Catfish, American baseball player, May 1975, *Obit* Nov 1999

Jackson, Bo, American baseball and football player, June 1991

Jackson, Reggie, American baseball player, Jan 1974

John, Tommy, American baseball player, Oct 1981

Johnson, Davey, American baseball manager, Sept 1999

Johnson, Randy, American baseball player, Sept 2000

Jones, Chipper, American baseball player, May 2001

Jordan, Michael, American basketball player, Sept 1987, Feb 1997

Kaline, Al, American baseball player and sportscaster, Yrbk 1970

Kent, Jeff, American baseball player, May 2003

Killebrew, Harmon, American baseball player and sportscaster, Feb 1966, *Obit* Yrbk 2011

Kiner, Ralph, American baseball player and sportscaster, May 1954

Kingman, Dave, baseball player, Mar 1982

Konstanty, Jim, baseball player, Apr 1951, *Obit* Aug 1976

Koufax, Sandy, American baseball player, Jan 1964

LaRussa, Tony, American baseball manager, July 2003

Lasorda, Tommy, American baseball manager, Feb 1989

Law, Vern, baseball player and coach, Apr 1961

Lazzeri, Tony, baseball player, *Obit* Sept 1946

Lee, Cliff, American baseball player, Aug 2009

Leiter, Al, American baseball player, Aug 2002

Lincecum, Tim, American baseball player, June 2010

Lopez, Al, American baseball player and manager, Feb 1960, *Obit* Yrbk 2006

Lowell, Mike, American baseball player, Sept 2003

Lyle, Sparky, baseball player, July 1978

Maddux, Greg, American baseball player, Feb 1996

Maglie, Sal, American baseball player, June 1953, *Obit* Feb 1993

Mantle, Mickey, American baseball player, July 1953, *Obit* Oct 1995

Maris, Roger, American baseball player, Nov 1961, *Obit* Feb 1986

Martin, Billy, American baseball manager, Oct 1976, *Obit* Feb 1990

Martinez, Pedro, Dominican baseball player, June 2001

Matsui, Hideki, Japanese baseball player, Jan 2002

Matsuzaka, Daisuke, Japanese baseball player, Apr 2007

Mattingly, Don, American baseball player, Oct 1988

Mauch, Gene, American baseball manager, Yrbk 1974, *Obit* Yrbk 2005

Mauer, Joe, American baseball player, Aug 2007

Mays, Willie, American baseball player, May 1955, Yrbk 1966

McCarver, Tim, sportscaster and baseball player, May 2000

McCovey, Willie, American baseball player, Nov 1970

McCutchen, Andrew, American baseball player, Aug 2013

McGwire, Mark, American baseball player, July 1998

McLain, Denny, American baseball player and radio talk show host, Jan 1969

Morgan, Joe, American baseball player and sportscaster, Sept 1984

Morneau, Justin, Canadian baseball player, June 2011

Munson, Thurman, American baseball player, Nov 1977, *Obit* Sept 1979

Murtaugh, Danny, baseball player and manager, Feb 1961, *Obit* Feb 1977

Musial, Stan, American baseball player, Yrbk 1948, *Obit* Yrbk 2013

Nagashima, Shigeo, Japanese baseball player and manager, Jan 2003

Nettles, Graig, American baseball player, July 1984

Newcombe, Don, American baseball player, Feb 1957

Oh, Sadaharu, Japanese baseball player, Jan 2002

Ortiz, David, Dominican-American baseball player, Aug 2005

Ott, Mel, American baseball player and manager, July 1941, *Obit* Jan 1959

Page, Joe, baseball player, Apr 1950, *Obit* June 1980

Paige, Satchel, American baseball player, Sept 1952, *Obit* Aug 1982

Palmeiro, Rafael, Cuban-American baseball player, Aug 2001

Palmer, Jim, American baseball player, May 1980

Peavy, Jake, American baseball player, May 2010

Pepitone, Joe, baseball player, Jan 1973

Perry, Gaylord, American baseball player, Nov 1982

Piazza, Mike, American baseball player, July 1999

Piniella, Lou, American baseball player and manager, Aug 1986

Pujols, Albert, Dominican-American baseball player, Sept 2004

Ramirez, Hanley, Dominican baseball player, Apr 2009

Ramirez, Manny, Dominican-American baseball player, June 2002

Reese, Pee Wee, American baseball player, June 1950, *Obit* Oct 1999

Reyes, Jose, Dominican baseball player, Aug 2008

Reynolds, Allie, American baseball player, June 1952, *Obit* Mar 1995

Rice, Jim, American baseball player, Sept 1979

Richardson, Bobby, baseball player, May 1966

Ripken, Cal, American baseball player, June 1992

Rivera, Mariano, Panamanian baseball player, July 2012

Rizzuto, Phil, American sportscaster and baseball player, July 1950, *Obit* Yrbk 2007

Roberts, Robin, American baseball player, Yrbk 1953, *Obit* Yrbk 2010

Robinson, Brooks, American baseball player, Sept 1973

Robinson, Frank, American baseball player and manager, June 1971

Robinson, Jackie, American baseball player, Feb 1947, *Obit* Yrbk 1972

Rodriguez, Alex, American baseball player, Apr 2003

Rodriguez, Ivan, Puerto Rican baseball player, June 2009

Rose, Pete, American baseball player and manager, Aug 1975

Rosen, Al, baseball player and executive, July 1954

Ruffing, Red, American baseball player, Nov 1941, *Obit* Apr 1986

Ruth, Babe, American baseball player, Aug 1944, *Obit* Oct 1948

Ryan, Nolan, American baseball player and executive, Oct 1970

Sabathia, C. C., American baseball player, Apr 2008

Sandberg, Ryne, American baseball player, Nov 1994

Sanders, Deion, American football player and sportscaster, Jan 1995

Santana, Johan, Venezuelan baseball player, July 2006

Schacht, Al, baseball entertainer and restaurateur, May 1946, *Obit* Sept 1984

Schilling, Curt, American baseball player, Oct 2001

Schoendienst, Red, baseball player and manager, Yrbk 1964

Seaver, Tom, American baseball player and sportscaster, Mar 1970

Sewell, Luke, baseball manager, Nov 1944

Shantz, Bobby, baseball player, Apr 1953

Shotton, Burt, baseball player and manager, June 1949, *Obit* Oct 1962

Sizemore, Grady, American baseball player, Apr 2010

Smith, Ozzie, American baseball player, Feb 1997

Snider, Duke, American baseball player, May 1956, *Obit* Yrbk 2011

Sosa, Sammy, Dominican baseball player, May 1999

Southworth, Billy, baseball player and manager, Nov 1944, *Obit* Jan 1970

Spahn, Warren, American baseball player, May 1962, *Obit* Yrbk 2004

Stargell, Willie, American baseball player, June 1980, *Obit* Sept 2001

Stengel, Casey, American baseball manager, June 1949, *Obit* Nov 1975

Stirnweiss, Snuffy, baseball player, Mar 1946, *Obit* Yrbk 1958

Strawberry, Darryl, American baseball player, June 1984

Suzuki, Ichiro, Japanese baseball player, July 2002

Tani, Yoshitomo, Japanese baseball player, Jan 2004

Tejada, Miguel, Dominican baseball player, June 2003

Thomas, Frank, American baseball player, Aug 1994

Thome, Jim, American baseball player, June 2007

Tiant, Luis, Cuban baseball player, June 1977

Torre, Joe, American baseball player and manager, May 1972, May 1997

Trout, Mike, July 2013

Valentine, Bobby, American baseball manager and television sports commentator, July 2001

Valenzuela, Fernando, Mexican baseball player, Oct 1982

Verlander, Justin, American baseball player, Apr 2012

Wakefield, Tim, American baseball player, Sept 2011

Walker, Larry, Canadian baseball player, May 1998

Weaver, Earl, American baseball manager, Feb 1983, *Obit* Yrbk 2013

Wells, David, American baseball player, May 2004

Wilhelm, Hoyt, American baseball player, July 1971, *Obit* Yrbk 2002

Williams, Dick, American baseball player and manager, Yrbk 1973, *Obit* Yrbk 2011

Williams, Ted, American baseball player and manager, Apr 1947, *Obit* Oct 2002

Willis, Dontrelle, American baseball player, Aug 2006

Wills, Maury, American baseball player, June 1966

Winfield, Dave, American baseball player, Jan 1984

Wood, Kerry, American baseball player, May 2005

Wright, David, American baseball player, May 2009

Yastrzemski, Carl, American baseball player, May 1968

Yount, Robin, baseball player, June 1993

Zito, Barry, American baseball player, July 2004

Basketball coaches

Auerbach, Red, American basketball executive, Feb 1969, *Obit* Yrbk 2007

Bird, Larry, American basketball player and coach, June 1982

Brown, Larry, American basketball coach, Apr 1996

Calhoun, Jim, American basketball coach, May 2011

Chaney, John, American basketball coach, Mar 1999

Cheeks, Maurice, American basketball player and coach, Feb 2004

Cooper-Dyke, Cynthia, American basketball player and coach, Aug 1998

D'Antoni, Mike, American basketball coach, June 2009

Daly, Chuck, American basketball coach, Apr 1991, *Obit* Yrbk 2009

Donovan, Billy, American basketball coach, Feb 2007

Drexler, Clyde, American basketball player and coach, Jan 1996

Ewing, Patrick, American basketball player, May 1991

Howland, Ben, American basketball coach, June 2007

Jackson, Phil, American basketball coach, July 1992

Johnson, Avery, American basketball player and coach, Jan 2007

Johnson, Earvin, American basketball player and coach, Jan 1982

Jones, K. C., basketball coach, Feb 1987

Knight, Bobby, American basketball coach, May 1987

Krzyzewski, Mike, American basketball coach, Jan 1997

Laimbeer, Bill, American basketball player, coach and executive, Jan 2006

Lapchick, Joe, basketball coach, June 1965, *Obit* Oct 1970

Lucas, John, American basketball player and coach, Oct 1995

Nelson, Don, American basketball coach, May 2007

Pitino, Rick, American basketball coach, Jan 1998

Reed, Willis, American basketball player, coach and executive, Jan 1973

Riley, Pat, American basketball coach, Aug 1988

Rivers, Doc, American basketball coach, Nov 2008

Russell, Bill, American basketball player, coach and sportscaster, July 1975

Smith, Dean, American basketball coach, Apr 1994

Summitt, Pat Head, American basketball coach, June 2005

Thomas, Isiah, American basketball player, executive and coach, Aug 1989

Thompson, John, American basketball coach, Nov 2007

Thompson, John, American basketball coach, May 1989

Van Gundy, Jeff, American basketball coach, May 2001

Vitale, Dick, American basketball sportscaster, Jan 2005

Wilkens, Lenny, American basketball player and coach, July 1996

Williams, Roy, American basketball coach, Mar 2007

Wooden, John R., American basketball coach, Jan 1976, *Obit* Yrbk 2010

Basketball executives

Allen, Paul, American computer software executive and investor, July 1998

Auerbach, Red, American basketball executive, Feb 1969, *Obit* Yrbk 2007

Bettman, Gary, American lawyer and hockey commissioner, Mar 1999

Cuban, Mark, American broadcasting and basketball executive, Mar 2001

DeBusschere, Dave, American basketball executive and player, Oct 1973, *Obit* Yrbk 2003

Drexler, Clyde, American basketball player and coach, Jan 1996

Hunter, Billy, American lawyer and basketball players association executive, Aug 2013

Johnson, Robert Louis, American television and basketball executive, Apr 1994

Johnson, Sheila Crump, American broadcasting executive and philanthropist, June 2007

Kohl, Herbert, American senator, May 2008

Laimbeer, Bill, American basketball player, coach and executive, Jan 2006

Monroe, Earl, American basketball player and executive, May 1978

O'Brien, Lawrence F., American political party leader and basketball association executive, Nov 1961, Apr 1977, *Obit* Nov 1990

Orender, Donna, American basketball association executive, Sept 2010

Prokhorov, Mikhail, Russian financier, Oct 2010

Reed, Willis, American basketball player, coach and executive, Jan 1973

Stern, David, American basketball association executive, Apr 1991

Thomas, Isiah, American basketball player, executive and coach, Aug 1989

Basketball players

Abdul-Jabbar, Kareem, American basketball player, July 1967, Feb 1997

Allen, Ray, American basketball player, Jan 2009

Allen, Will, American urban farmer, Sept 2013

Anthony, Carmelo, American basketball player, June 2005

Arenas, Gilbert, American basketball player, Feb 2009

Barbosa, Leandro, Brazilian basketball player, June 2011

Barkley, Charles, American basketball player, Oct 1991

Barry, Rick, American basketball player and sportscaster, Mar 1971

Billups, Chauncey, American basketball player, Feb 2011

Bird, Larry, American basketball player and coach, June 1982

Bogut, Andrew, Australian basketball player, Jan 2008

Bosh, Chris, American basketball player, Mar 2010

Bradley, Bill, American senator, July 1965, Sept 1982

Brown, Kwame, American basketball player, Feb 2002

Camby, Marcus, American basketball player, Jan 2000

Carter, Vince, American basketball player, Apr 2002

Catchings, Tamika, American basketball player, Nov 2013

Chamberlain, Wilt, American basketball player, June 1960, *Obit* Jan 2000

Cheeks, Maurice, American basketball player and coach, Feb 2004

Cousy, Bob, American basketball player, Sept 1958

D'Antoni, Mike, American basketball coach, June 2009

Davis, Glen, American basketball player, Nov 2010

DeBusschere, Dave, American basketball executive and player, Oct 1973, *Obit* Yrbk 2003

Duncan, Tim, American basketball player, Nov 1999

Durant, Kevin, American basketball player, May 2010

Edwards, Teresa, American basketball player, Mar 1998

Elliott, Sean, basketball player, Apr 2001

Ellis, Monta, American basketball player, Feb 2008

Erving, Julius, American basketball player, May 1975

Ewing, Patrick, American basketball player, May 1991

Frazier, Walt, American basketball player and sportscaster, Feb 1973

Garnett, Kevin, American basketball player, Sept 1998

Gasol, Pau, Spanish basketball player, Mar 2011

Ginobili, Manu, Argentine basketball player, Apr 2011

Griffin, Blake, American basketball player, Jan 2012

Griner, Brittney, American basketball player, Mar 2013

Hammon, Becky, American basketball player, Jan 2003

Hardaway, Tim, American basketball player, July 1998

Hill, Grant, American basketball player, Jan 2002

Holdsclaw, Chamique, American basketball player, Feb 2006

Houston, Allan, American basketball player, Nov 2003

Jackson, Lauren, Australian basketball player, June 2003

James, LeBron, American basketball player, Nov 2005

Johnson, Avery, American basketball player and coach, Jan 2007

Johnson, Earvin, American basketball player and coach, Jan 1982

Jones, K. C., basketball coach, Feb 1987

Jones, Marion, American sprinter, long jumper and basketball player, Oct 1998

Jordan, Michael, American basketball player, Sept 1987, Feb 1997

Joyner-Kersee, Jackie,
  American heptathlete and
  basketball player, July 1987
Kerr, Steve, basketball player,
  Oct 1998
Kidd, Jason, American
  basketball player, May 2002
Kukoc, Toni, Croatian basketball
  player, July 1997
Leslie, Lisa, American
  basketball player, Jan 1998
Lin, Jeremy, American
  basketball player, Feb 2013
Lobo, Rebecca, American
  basketball player, Sept 1997
Love, Kevin, American
  basketball player, Jan 2013
Lucas, Jerry, American
  basketball player, June 1972
Lucas, John, American
  basketball player and coach,
  Oct 1995
Malone, Karl, American
  basketball player, Jan 1993
Malone, Moses, American
  basketball player, June 1986
Martin, Kenyon, American
  basketball player, Jan 2005
McGrady, Tracy, American
  basketball player, Feb 2003
McMillen, Tom, congressman,
  Jan 1993
Miller, Reggie, American
  basketball player, Mar 1996
Monroe, Earl, American
  basketball player and
  executive, May 1978
Mutombo, Dikembe, Congolese
  basketball player, Feb 2000
Nash, Steve, Canadian
  basketball player, Mar 2003
Nowitzki, Dirk, German
  basketball player, June 2002
O'Neal, Jermaine, American
  basketball player, June 2004
O'Neal, Shaquille, American
  basketball player, July 1996
Odom, Lamar, American
  basketball player, May 2009
Olajuwon, Hakeem, American
  basketball player, Nov 1993
Orender, Donna, American
  basketball association
  executive, Sept 2010
Parker, Tony, Belgian basketball
  player, Apr 2008
Paul, Chris, American basketball
  player, Nov 2009
Pettit, Bob, American basketball
  player, Oct 1961

Pierce, Paul, American
  basketball player, Nov 2002
Pippen, Scottie, American
  basketball player, Mar 1994
Redd, Michael, American
  basketball player, Mar 2005
Richmond, Mitch, basketball
  player, June 1999
Riley, Pat, American basketball
  coach, Aug 1988
Rivers, Doc, American
  basketball coach, Nov 2008
Robertson, Oscar, American
  basketball player, Jan 1966
Robinson, David, American
  basketball player, July 1993
Rodman, Dennis, American
  basketball player, Sept 1996
Rose, Jalen, American
  basketball player, Mar 2004
Russell, Bill, American
  basketball player, coach and
  sportscaster, July 1975
Sales, Nykesha, basketball
  player, June 1999
Smith, Josh, American
  basketball player, Feb 2012
Sprewell, Latrell, American
  basketball player, Feb 2001
Stackhouse, Jerry, American
  basketball player, Nov 2001
Staley, Dawn, American
  basketball player, Apr 2005
Stockton, John, American
  basketball player, June 1995
Summitt, Pat Head, American
  basketball coach, June 2005
Swoopes, Sheryl, American
  basketball player, July 1996
Taurasi, Diana, American
  basketball player, Nov 2007
Thompson, Tina, American
  basketball player, Jan 2011
Van Exel, Nick, American
  basketball player, Mar 2002
Vujanic, Milos, Serbian
  basketball player, Jan 2004
Wade, Dwyane, American
  basketball player, Apr 2006
Wallace, Ben, American
  basketball player, Apr 2004
Walton, Bill, American
  basketball player and
  sportscaster, Mar 1977
Webber, Chris, American
  basketball player, May 2003
Wilkens, Lenny, American
  basketball player and coach,
  July 1996
Wilkins, Dominique, American
  basketball player, May 1995

Wooden, John R., American
  basketball coach, Jan 1976,
  Obit Yrbk 2010
Yao Ming, Chinese basketball
  player, Jan 2002

Basketball referees

Palmer, Violet, American
  basketball referee, Nov 2006

Bassists

Anderson, Reid, American jazz
  bassist, Oct 2011
Berryman, Guy, Scottish bassist,
  May 2004
Butler, Will, American bassist,
  guitarist and percussionist,
  Jan 2007
Calleros, Juan, Mexican bassist,
  Jan 2005
Dirnt, Mike, American bassist
  and singer, Aug 2005
Edwards, David, Antiguan
  bassist, Jan 2004
Followill, Jared, American
  bassist, July 2010
Foo, Sharin, Danish singer and
  bassist, Jan 2004
Fraiture, Nikolai, American
  bassist, Feb 2007
Gordon, Mike, American bassist,
  July 2003
Greenwood, Colin, English
  bassist, June 2001
Hamilton, Tom, American rock
  bassist, July 2004
Hernandez, Dave, American
  bassist, June 2007
Holland, Dave, English jazz
  bassist, Mar 2003
Holm, Georg, Icelandic bassist,
  Jan 2003
Hook, Peter, British bassist and
  singer, Jan 2006
Hoppus, Mark, American singer
  and bassist, Aug 2002
Ivins, Mike, American bassist,
  Oct 2002
James, Alex, English rock
  bassist, Nov 2003
Kingsbury, Tim, Canadian
  bassist and guitarist, Jan 2007
Lally, Joe, American bassist,
  Mar 2002
Lozano, Conrad, American
  bassist, Oct 2005
Malley, Matt, American bassist,
  Mar 2003
McBride, Christian, American
  jazz bassist, Jan 2000

Meyer, Edgar, American bassist, June 2002

Miller, Marcus, American jazz bassist and composer, Feb 2006

Mingus, Charles, American jazz bassist and composer, Feb 1971, *Obit* Mar 1979

Nicholson, Andy, British rock bassist, Jan 2006

O'Malley, Nick, British rock bassist, Jan 2006

Pegg, Dave, English bassist and singer, Sept 2005

Phoenix (Musician), American bassist, Mar 2002

Polivka, Galen, American bassist, Sept 2010

Poullain, Frankie, British rock bassist, Jan 2004

Punisher (Musician), Finnish bassist, Jan 2003

Query, Nate, American bassist, Aug 2007

Riedel, Oliver, German bassist, Jan 2007

Roth, Gabriel, American songwriter, bassist and recording producer, Feb 2010

Savage, Rick, English bassist and singer, Jan 2003

Sevitzky, Fabien, July 1946, *Obit* Apr 1967

Simmons, Gene, American bassist and actor, Apr 1999

Smith, Gerard, American bassist and keyboardist, Apr 2009

Spalding, Esperanza, American jazz bassist and singer, Aug 2010

Stirratt, John, American bassist, Feb 2010

Taylor, Chris, American bassist and singer, Sept 2011

Temple, Johnny, American rock bassist and publisher, Oct 2008

Two-Tone Tommy, American rock bassist, Nov 2008

Williams, Cliff, English bassist, Mar 2005

Wilson, Mark, Australian bassist, Jan 2005

Yauch, Adam, American rapper and bassist, *Obit* Yrbk 2012

Bassoonists

Gaubatz, Lynn, bassoonist, Feb 2001

Beauty contest winners

Williams, Vanessa, American singer and actress, May 1984

Beekeepers

Crane, Eva, British apiculturist, Aug 1993, *Obit* Yrbk 2007

Beverage industry executives

Antinori, Piero, Italian vintner, Jan 2006

Aramburuzabala, Maria Asuncion, Mexican brewing executive, Jan 2002

Barnes, Brenda, American food industry executive, May 2006

Bastianich, Joseph, American restaurateur and winemaker, June 2011

Bronfman, Edgar M., American liquor industry executive, July 1974

Bronfman, Edgar M., American recording industry executive, Oct 1995

Busch, August Anheuser, American brewing industry and baseball executive, July 1973, *Obit* Nov 1989

Calagione, Sam, American brewing company executive, Jan 2013

Charoen Sirivadhanabhakdi, Chinese-Thai liquor industry executive, Jan 2005

Collier, Sophia, American television and Internet service executive, July 2002

Daft, Doug, Australian beverage industry executive, May 2001

Espinoza, Alvaro, Chilean vintner, Jan 2004

Gass, Michelle, American coffee chain executive, Apr 2012

Goizueta, Roberto C., American beverage industry executive, Aug 1996, *Obit* Jan 1998

Jacob, John E., civil rights leader, Feb 1986

Jordan, Michael H., American information technology executive, Feb 1998, *Obit* Yrbk 2010

Koch, Jim, American brewing company executive, May 2012

Lennox-Boyd, Alan Tindal, British cabinet member and

brewing industry executive, June 1956, *Obit* May 1983

Mack, Walter, beverage industry executive, Feb 1946, *Obit* May 1990

Mallya, Vijay, Indian business executive, Jan 2004

Mateschitz, Dietrich, Austrian beverage industry executive, Jan 2005

Mondavi, Robert, American vintner, Apr 1999, *Obit* Yrbk 2008

Nooyi, Indra K., Indian beverage company executive, Nov 2006

Patrick, Deval L., American governor, May 2007

Robinson, William E., American beverage industry and newspaper executive, Feb 1958, *Obit* July 1969

Rothschild, Guy de, French banker, Mar 1973, *Obit* Yrbk 2007

Sculley, John, American computer industry executive, Aug 1988

Smothers, Tom, American comedian, Yrbk 1968

Biathletes

Bjoerndalen, Ole Einar, Norwegian biathlete, Jan 2003

Biblical scholars

Albright, William Foxwell, American archaeologist and biblical scholar, Sept 1955

Coggan, Frederick Donald, English archbishop, July 1974, *Obit* Sept 2000

Ehrman, Bart D., American biblical scholar, Apr 2010

Glueck, Nelson, rabbi, archaeologist and college president, Oct 1948, July 1969, *Obit* Mar 1971

Goodspeed, Edgar Johnson, biblical scholar, Nov 1946, *Obit* Mar 1962

Gordon, Cyrus Herzl, American biblical scholar and archaeologist, May 1963, *Obit* Aug 2001

Hartman, Louis F., Jan 1953, *Obit* Nov 1970

Luccock, Halford Edward, June 1960, *Obit* Jan 1961

Mathews, Shailer, biblical scholar and college dean, *Obit* Yrbk 1941

Slifkin, Nosson, Israeli rabbi and biblical zoologist, Jan 2005

Smith, George Adam, Scottish biblical scholar, *Obit* Apr 1942

Bibliographers

Brigham, Clarence Saunders, librarian, July 1959, *Obit* Oct 1963

Carter, John, British bibliographer and rare book dealer, May 1959, *Obit* May 1975

Ford, Worthington C., American historian, editor and bibliographer, *Obit* Apr 1941

Forsythe, Robert S., *Obit* Aug 1941

Harrelson, Walter J., May 1959

Lehmann-Haupt, Hellmut, author and bibliographer, Apr 1942, Mar 1961, *Obit* May 1992

Muir, Percy H., English bibliographer, bookseller and collector, Apr 1963

Newton, A. Edward, bibliographer and book collector, *Obit* Nov 1940

Sheppard, Morris, *Obit* June 1941

Vail, Robert W. G., librarian and bibliographer, Feb 1945, *Obit* July 1966

Winchell, Constance Mabel, librarian, June 1967, *Obit* Sept 1984

Biochemists

Alsberg, Carl, American biochemist, *Obit* Yrbk 1940

Ames, Bruce N., American biochemist, Oct 1993

Asimov, Isaac, American biochemist and science fiction writer, Yrbk 1953, Oct 1968, *Obit* May 1992

Baulieu, Etienne-Emile, French biochemist, Nov 1995

Behe, Michael J., American biochemist and intelligent design advocate, Feb 2006

Belcher, Angela, American chemical engineer, July 2006

Blumberg, Baruch S., American physician and biochemist, Nov 1977, *Obit* Yrbk 2011

Bodansky, Meyer, American biochemist and pathologist, *Obit* Aug 1941

Calvin, Melvin, American biochemist, Apr 1962, *Obit* Mar 1997

Chain, Ernst Boris, British biochemist, Nov 1965, *Obit* Oct 1979

Ciechanover, Aaron J., Israeli biochemist, Jan 2007

Coleman, Mary Sue, American university president, Feb 2007

Cori, Carl F., American biochemist, Yrbk 1947, *Obit* Feb 1985

Cori, Gerty Theresa, American biochemist, Yrbk 1947, *Obit* Jan 1958

Crick, Francis, British biochemist, Mar 1983, *Obit* Yrbk 2004

Cullen, Glenn Ernest, *Obit* May 1940

Dam, Henrik, Danish biochemist, Sept 1949, *Obit* June 1976

Doisy, Edward Adelbert, American biochemist, Mar 1949, *Obit* Jan 1987

Doudna, Jennifer A., American biochemist, Feb 2005

Du Vigneaud, Vincent, American biochemist, Jan 1956, *Obit* Feb 1979

Edelman, Gerald M., American biochemist, Apr 1995

Elion, Gertrude B., American biochemist, Mar 1995, *Obit* May 1999

Elvehjem, C. A., May 1948, *Obit* Oct 1962

Funk, Casimir, biochemist, May 1945, *Obit* Jan 1968

Gallo, Robert C., biochemist, Oct 1986

Goulian, Mehran, July 1968

Handler, Philip, biochemist, Feb 1964, *Obit* Feb 1982

Harden, Arthur, British biochemist, *Obit* Aug 1940

Hershko, Avram, Israeli biochemist, Jan 2007

Hofmann, Klaus Heinrich, biochemist, Apr 1961

Holley, Robert William, American biochemist, Jan 1967, *Obit* Apr 1993

Kendall, Edward Calvin, American biochemist, Yrbk 1950, *Obit* June 1972

Kendrew, John C., British biochemist, Oct 1963, *Obit* Nov 1997

Kenyon, Cynthia, American biochemist and biotechnology executive, Jan 2005

Khorana, Har Gobind, Indian biochemist, Yrbk 1970, *Obit* Yrbk 2012

Kiessling, Laura L., American biochemist, Aug 2003

King, Charles Glen, biochemist and nutritionist, Yrbk 1967, *Obit* Mar 1988

Kornberg, Arthur, American biochemist, Sept 1968, *Obit* Feb 2008

Krebs, Hans Adolf, British biochemist, Mar 1954, *Obit* Feb 1982

Landsteiner, Karl, American biochemist, *Obit* Aug 1943

Levene, Phoebus Aaron Theodore, American biochemist, *Obit* Oct 1940

Li, Choh-hao, biochemist, Apr 1963, *Obit* Jan 1988

Lipmann, Fritz, American biochemist, Mar 1954, *Obit* Sept 1986

Lynen, Feodor, German biochemist, June 1967, *Obit* Oct 1979

Martin, Archer, British biochemist, Nov 1953, *Obit* Yrbk 2002

Medvedev, Zhores Aleksandrovich, Soviet biochemist, Nov 1973

Merrifield, R. Bruce, American biochemist, Mar 1985, *Obit* Yrbk 2006

Mullis, Kary B., American biochemist, Feb 1996

Murayama, Makio, Oct 1974

Nirenberg, Marshall Warren, American biochemist, Apr 1965, *Obit* Yrbk 2010

Northrop, John H., American biochemist, June 1947, *Obit* Sept 1987

Ochoa, Severo, Spanish-American biochemist, June 1962, *Obit* Jan 1994

Perutz, Max, British biochemist, Nov 1963, *Obit* Apr 2002

Rose, William C., American biochemist, Mar 1953, *Obit* Jan 1986

Sanger, Frederick, British biochemist, July 1981

Seibert, Florence, American biochemist, Nov 1942, *Obit* Oct 1991

Sherman, Henry C., Jan 1949, *Obit* Yrbk 1955

Stanley, Wendell Meredith, American biochemist, Apr 1947, *Obit* Sept 1971

Steitz, Joan Argetsinger, American biochemist, June 2007

Sumner, James Batcheller, American biochemist, Jan 1947, *Obit* Oct 1955

Synge, Richard Lawrence Millington, British biochemist, Nov 1953

Szent-Gyorgyi, Albert, Hungarian-American biochemist, Jan 1955, *Obit* Jan 1987

Tatum, Edward Lawrie, American biochemist, Mar 1959, *Obit* Jan 1976

Theorell, Hugo, Swedish biochemist, Feb 1956, *Obit* Oct 1982

Tiselius, Arne Wilhelm Kaurin, Swedish biochemist, Apr 1949, *Obit* Yrbk 1971

Venter, J. Craig, American biochemist, Feb 1995

Wald, George, American biochemist, May 1968, *Obit* June 1997

Weinberg, Robert A., American biochemist, June 1983

Whitson, Peggy A., American biochemist and astronaut, Sept 2003

Wilkins, Maurice Hugh Frederick, English biochemist, June 1963, *Obit* Yrbk 2005

Williams, Roger J., biochemist and nutritionist, July 1957, *Obit* Apr 1988

Woodward, R. B., American biochemist, Feb 1952, *Obit* Sept 1979

Wrinch, Dorothy, Anglo-American biochemist and mathematician, July 1947

Bioengineers

Keasling, Jay, American bioengineer, Nov 2013

Bioethicists

Kass, Leon, American bioethicist, Aug 2002

Singer, Peter, Australian bioethicist, Mar 1991

Biographers

Abzug, Bella, American congresswoman and feminist, July 1971, *Obit* June 1998

Ackerman, Diane, American poet, essayist, memoirist and nature writer, June 1997

Ackroyd, Peter, English novelist, biographer, poet and literary critic, May 1993

Acocella, Joan Ross, American dance critic, May 2007

Aiken, Conrad, American poet, novelist, short story writer, critic and memoirist, May 1970, *Obit* Oct 1973

Alexander, Holmes Moss, columnist and author, Sept 1956

Amal'rik, Andrei, Russian essayist and historian, Apr 1974, *Obit* Jan 1981

Angelou, Maya, American poet and memoirist, June 1974, Feb 1994

Angle, Paul McClelland, historian, July 1955, *Obit* Aug 1975

Armstrong, Margaret Neilson, author, *Obit* Sept 1944

Arthur, George, British army officer, *Obit* Mar 1946

Astor, Mary, American actress, Nov 1961, *Obit* Nov 1987

Atkinson, Oriana Torrey MacIlveen, author, Yrbk 1953, *Obit* Oct 1989

Auchincloss, Louis, American novelist, short story writer and lawyer, Yrbk 1954, Aug 1978, *Obit* Apr 2010

Bagnold, Enid, English novelist and dramatist, June 1964, *Obit* May 1981

Bainton, Roland Herbert, church historian, June 1962, *Obit* June 1984

Baker, Louise, American novelist, short story writer and memoirist, Yrbk 1954

Baker, Nina Brown, American young adult author, Yrbk 1947, *Obit* Nov 1957

Baker, Ray Stannard, American journalist and biographer, Jan 1940, *Obit* Sept 1946

Baker, Russell, American journalist and humorist, Mar 1980

Bard, Mary, American novelist, essayist and memoirist, Yrbk 1956

Barr, Stringfellow, American college president and historian, Aug 1940, *Obit* Apr 1982

Bates, Ernest Sutherland, biographer, historian and literary critic, Jan 1940

Beauvoir, Simone de, French novelist and philosopher, Jan 1973, *Obit* June 1986

Bedford, Sybille, English novelist, Feb 1990, *Obit* Yrbk 2006

Beebe, William, American naturalist and author, July 1941, *Obit* Sept 1962

Beer, Thomas, author, *Obit* May 1940

Behan, Brendan, Irish dramatist, Mar 1961, *Obit* May 1964

Behrman, S. N., dramatist, screenwriter and author, Feb 1943, *Obit* Nov 1973

Benson, E. F., English author, Mar 1940

Betancourt, Ingrid, Colombian political leader, Jan 2002

Birmingham, Stephen, author, May 1974

Bliven, Bruce, American magazine editor, Yrbk 1941, *Obit* July 1977

Bloom, Harold, American literary critic, Apr 1987

Bogarde, Dirk, English actor and author, July 1967, *Obit* July 1999

Bonsal, Stephen, journalist, historian and biographer, Aug 1945, *Obit* July 1951

Bontemps, Arna Wendell, American novelist, poet, biographer and children's author, Yrbk 1946, *Obit* July 1973

Bourdain, Anthony, American chef, writer and television personality, Jan 2006

Bowen, Catherine Drinker, American biographer, July 1944, *Obit* Yrbk 1973

Boylston, Helen Dore, author, July 1942, *Obit* Nov 1984

Bragg, Rick, American journalist and memoirist, Apr 2002

Brenan, Gerald, English author, poet and critic, July 1986, *Obit* Mar 1987

Briggs, Ellis Ormsbee, diplomat, Apr 1965, *Obit* Apr 1976

Broeg, Bob, American sportswriter, May 2002

Brooks, Gwendolyn, American poet, June 1950, July 1977, *Obit* Feb 2001

Brooks, Van Wyck, literary critic and biographer, June 1941, Sept 1960, *Obit* June 1963

Brown, Claude, American memoirist and journalist, Nov 1967, *Obit* Apr 2002

Brown, John Mason, drama critic and biographer, Apr 1942, *Obit* May 1969

Brown, Tina, British journalist and magazine editor, Feb 1990

Bruce, William Cabell, author and senator, *Obit* June 1946

Bryan, George Sands, *Obit* Feb 1944

Brynner, Rock, American historian and novelist, Mar 2005

Buchan, John, Scottish novelist, historian and Governor General of Canada, Jan 1940

Buck, Pearl S., American novelist, July 1956, *Obit* Apr 1973

Budenz, Louis F., American newspaper editor, June 1951, *Obit* June 1972

Bullitt, William C., American diplomat, July 1940, *Obit* Apr 1967

Bulosan, Carlos, American memoirist, poet and short story writer, Yrbk 1946, *Obit* Nov 1956

Burgess, Anthony, English novelist and critic, May 1972, *Obit* Jan 1994

Burns, James MacGregor, American biographer and historian, Yrbk 1962

Burroughs, Augusten, American novelist and memoirist, Apr 2004

Burton, Jean, Yrbk 1948

Calisher, Hortense, American short story writer and novelist, Nov 1973, *Obit* Yrbk 2009

Calve, Emma, French opera singer, *Obit* Mar 1942

Canetti, Elias, Bulgarian novelist and dramatist, Jan 1983, *Obit* Oct 1994

Canfield, Cass, publisher, Apr 1954, *Obit* May 1986

Caputo, Philip, American journalist and novelist, Apr 1996

Carey, Ernestine Gilbreth, American memoirist, May 1949, *Obit* Yrbk 2007

Caro, Robert A., American biographer, Jan 1984

Carroll, James, American novelist, May 1997

Carroll, Jim, American poet and lyricist, Oct 1995, *Obit* Yrbk 2009

Cavanah, Frances, author and editor, Yrbk 1954

Charnwood, Godfrey Rathbone Benson, English biographer, *Obit* Mar 1945

Chatwin, Bruce, English memoirist, travel writer and novelist, Jan 1988, *Obit* Mar 1989

Chute, Marchette Gaylord, biographer and literary historian, Yrbk 1950, *Obit* July 1994

Clapp, Margaret, American biographer, historian and college president, June 1948, *Obit* June 1974

Clark, Eleanor, novelist, travel essayist and children's author, May 1978, *Obit* Apr 1996

Cleaver, Eldridge, American civil rights leader, Mar 1970, *Obit* July 1998

Coit, Margaret L., American biographer, June 1951

Colson, Charles W., American lawyer, presidential aide and evangelist, *Obit* Yrbk 2012

Cooper, Duff, British diplomat, Aug 1940, *Obit* Mar 1954

Corsi, Jerome R., American political writer, Nov 2008

Cowley, Malcolm, American literary critic, philologist and poet, June 1979, *Obit* May 1989

Craft, Robert, American conductor, Mar 1984

Daniel-Rops, Henri, Mar 1957, *Obit* Oct 1965

Daudet, Leon, French journalist, novelist and memoirist, *Obit* Aug 1942

Davenport, Marcia, novelist, Jan 1944, *Obit* Mar 1996

Davies, W. H., Welsh poet and author, *Obit* Nov 1940

Davis, Angela Yvonne, American political activist, Nov 1972

Davis, Ossie, American actor and dramatist, Oct 1969, *Obit* Yrbk 2005

Davis, Patti, American novelist and daughter of President Ronald Reagan, Nov 1986

Dayan, Yael, Israeli author and daughter of Moshe Dayan, Apr 1997

De Selincourt, Ernest, English editor and literary critic, *Obit* July 1943

Dees, Morris S., American lawyer, Jan 1995

Dickson, Lovat, Sept 1962

Djilas, Milovan, Yugoslav communist leader, memoirist and political writer, Sept 1958, *Obit* July 1995

Donald, David Herbert, American historian and biographer, Sept 1961, *Obit* Yrbk 2009

Dorris, Michael, American anthropologist and memoirist, Mar 1995, *Obit* June 1997

Downey, Fairfax, author and historian, Yrbk 1949, *Obit* Aug 1990

Du Bois, Shirley Graham, American biographer, dramatist and composer, Oct 1946, *Obit* June 1977

Du Maurier, Daphne, English novelist, short story writer and biographer, May 1940, *Obit* June 1989

Dulles, Eleanor Lansing, American memoirist and diplomat, Sept 1962, *Obit* Jan 1997

Durrell, Lawrence, English novelist, poet and travel writer, July 1963, *Obit* Jan 1991

Eastman, Max, American poet, journalist and critic, Apr 1969, *Obit* Apr 1969

Edel, Leon, biographer, July 1963, *Obit* Nov 1997

Eden, Anthony, British statesman, Yrbk 1940, Apr 1951, *Obit* Mar 1977

Eggers, Dave, American writer and publisher, July 2000

Fast, Howard, American novelist and short story writer, Apr 1943, Apr 1991, *Obit* July 2003

Fermi, Laura, wife of Enrico Fermi, May 1958

Fisher, Carrie, American actress and novelist, Feb 1991

Flynn, Elizabeth Gurley, American communist leader, Oct 1961, *Obit* Nov 1964

Fowler, Gene, author, Mar 1944, *Obit* Sept 1960

Franklin, John Hope, American historian, Oct 1963, *Obit* May 2009

Fraser, Antonia, English biographer, historian and novelist, Oct 1974

Freeman, Lucy, American journalist and nonfiction writer, Oct 1953, *Obit* Yrbk 2005

Fry, Stephen, English actor and novelist, Sept 1998

Gandhi, Mahatma, Indian nationalist leader, Yrbk 1942, *Obit* Feb 1948

Gardner, John, American novelist, critic and translator, Oct 1978, *Obit* Nov 1982

Garland, Hamlin, American novelist and memoirist, Mar 1940

Garst, Shannon, Yrbk 1947

George, Manfred, German newspaper editor and writer, Oct 1965, *Obit* Feb 1966

Gibson, William, American dramatist, memoirist, poet and novelist, July 1983

Gilbert, Martin, English historian, Feb 1991

Gilbreth, Frank B., American journalist, memoirist and novelist, May 1949, *Obit* July 2001

Ginzburg, Natalia, Italian novelist, July 1990, *Obit* Nov 1991

Giovanni, Nikki, American poet and essayist, Apr 1973

Godden, Rumer, English novelist and children's author, Aug 1976, *Obit* Jan 1999

Goodwin, Doris Kearns, American historian and television commentator, Nov 1997

Gordon-Reed, Annette, American law professor, biographer and historian, May 2009

Gorman, Herbert Sherman, author and literary critic, Mar 1940, *Obit* Jan 1955

Graham, Elinor, Yrbk 1952

Graham, Katharine, American newspaper publisher, Jan 1971, *Obit* Oct 2001

Grass, Gunter, German novelist, Oct 1964, July 1983

Graves, Robert, English novelist and poet, May 1978, *Obit* Feb 1986

Green, Julien, American novelist, essayist and memoirist, Jan 1940, *Obit* Oct 1998

Grigg, John, English journalist and biographer, Oct 1964, *Obit* Apr 2002

Guedalla, Philip, English historian, *Obit* Feb 1945

Gumpert, Martin, Yrbk 1951

Guthrie, Woody, American folk singer and songwriter, May 1963, *Obit* Yrbk 1967

Hahn, Emily, American novelist and biographer, July 1942, *Obit* Apr 1997

Haley, Alex, American biographer, historian and journalist, Jan 1977, *Obit* Mar 1992

Hall, Donald, American poet, essayist, critic and children's author, May 1984

Hamill, Pete, American journalist and novelist, Feb 1998

Han, Suyin, Chinese novelist and physician, Yrbk 1957, *Obit* Yrbk 2013

Harris, Mark, American novelist and memoirist, Yrbk 1959, *Obit* Yrbk 2007

Harrison, Gilbert A., American magazine editor, publisher and veterans' leader, Mar 1949, *Obit* Yrbk 2008

Haskell, Molly, motion picture critic, Nov 1998

Hellman, Lillian, American playwright, May 1941, June 1960, *Obit* Aug 1984

Henry, Marguerite, American children's author, Yrbk 1947, *Obit* Feb 1998

Hersh, Seymour M., American journalist, Mar 1984

Hickam, Homer H., American aerospace engineer and memoirist, Oct 2000

Hinojosa, Maria, American radio reporter and memoirist, Feb 2001

Hirsi Ali, Ayaan, Somali-Dutch feminist and member of Parliament, Jan 2003

Holroyd, Michael, English biographer, Mar 1989

Holt, Rackham, Apr 1944

Horgan, Paul, author, Feb 1971, *Obit* May 1995

Horne, Gerald, American historian and biographer, Sept 2011

Hung Huang, Chinese magazine executive, Jan 2006

Hunter-Gault, Charlayne, American television newscaster, Apr 1987

Hurston, Zora Neale, American novelist and folklorist, May 1942, *Obit* Apr 1960

Hutchison, Bruce, Canadian journalist, Oct 1956

Iacocca, Lee A., American automobile executive, Oct 1971, Oct 1988

Ibarruri, Dolores, Spanish communist leader, June 1967, *Obit* Jan 1990

Isherwood, Christopher, Anglo-American novelist, Oct 1972, *Obit* Feb 1986

James, Clive, Australian literary critic and journalist, Nov 1984

Jenkins, Roy, British political leader, Mar 1966, Oct 1982, *Obit* Yrbk 2003

Jong, Erica, American poet and novelist, July 1975, Apr 1997

Kaplan, Justin, American biographer, July 1993

Kapuscinski, Ryszard, Polish journalist and biographer, Sept 1992, *Obit* Yrbk 2007

Karsner, David, *Obit* Apr 1941

Kazan, Elia, American theatrical and film director, Jan 1948, Oct 1972, *Obit* Yrbk 2004

Kazin, Alfred, American literary critic, May 1966, *Obit* Aug 1998

Keller, Helen, American humanitarian, Yrbk 1942, *Obit* July 1968

Kelley, Kitty, American biographer, Apr 1992

Kelly, Florence Finch, journalist and author, *Obit* Jan 1940

Kendrick, Baynard Hardwick, author, Feb 1946, *Obit* May 1977

Keyhoe, Donald Edward, marine corps officer, June 1956, *Obit* Feb 1989

Kincaid, Jamaica, Antiguan novelist and short story writer, Mar 1991

Kingston, Maxine Hong, American novelist, Mar 1990

Kirkpatrick, Ralph, harpsichordist and musicologist, Sept 1971, *Obit* Aug 1984

Knipfel, Jim, American memoirist, columnist and novelist, Mar 2005

Korda, Michael, British editor, essayist, novelist and memoirist, Aug 1985

Kraus, Rene, July 1941, *Obit* Sept 1947

Krutch, Joseph Wood, American critic, biographer and nature writer, Nov 1959, *Obit* July 1970

La Farge, Oliver, American novelist and anthropologist, Jan 1953, *Obit* Oct 1963

Labouisse, Eve Curie, French biographer and daughter of Marie Curie, Mar 1940

Lagerlof, Selma, Swedish novelist, Apr 1940

Lash, Joseph P., author, Yrbk 1972, *Obit* Oct 1987

Lau, Evelyn, Canadian novelist, poet and short story writer, Jan 2005

Le Gallienne, Eva, American actress, director and producer, Oct 1942, Mar 1955, *Obit* Aug 1991

Leblanc, Georgette, French opera singer, *Obit* Yrbk 1941

Leech, Margaret, American historian and novelist, July 1942, Nov 1960, *Obit* Apr 1974

Leonard, Hugh, Irish playwright, Apr 1983, *Obit* Yrbk 2009

Levi, Carlo, Italian novelist, journalist and painter, Yrbk 1952, *Obit* Feb 1975

Levi, Primo, Italian memoirist, novelist and chemist, Mar 1987, *Obit* Mar 1987

Lewis, David Levering, American historian and biographer, May 2001

Lewis, W. S., book collector and editor, July 1973, *Obit* Jan 1980

Lindbergh, Anne Morrow, American memoirist, novelist, and poet, Nov 1940, June 1976, *Obit* Apr 2001

Lionni, Leo, American children's author and illustrator, Sept 1997, *Obit* Feb 2000

Longstreth, T. Morris, Yrbk 1950

Lopez, Barry Holstun, American novelist and essayist, July 1995

Loud, Pat, July 1974

Luhan, Mabel Ganson Dodge, American patron of the arts and memoirist, Jan 1940, *Obit* Oct 1962

Lyons, Eugene, American journalist and biographer, Jan 1944, *Obit* Mar 1985

MacDonald, Betty, American memoirist and humorist, Feb 1946, *Obit* Apr 1958

Macdonald, Dwight, American journalist and critic, Nov 1969, *Obit* Mar 1983

Madariaga, Salvador de, Spanish essayist, Jan 1964, *Obit* Feb 1979

Malraux, Andre, French novelist, essayist and art historian, Mar 1959, *Obit* Feb 1977

Manchester, William, American biographer and historian, Nov 1967, *Obit* Yrbk 2004

Mann, Erika, German writer, actress and daughter of Thomas Mann, Yrbk 1940, *Obit* Nov 1969

Marshall, Catherine, American biographer and inspirational writer, Jan 1955, *Obit* May 1983

Martin, John Bartlow, American journalist and diplomat, Yrbk 1956, *Obit* Mar 1987

Martin, Steve, American comedian and actor, Aug 1978, Nov 2000

Mason, Bobbie Ann, American novelist and short story writer, Sept 1989

Maynard, Joyce, American journalist, memoirist and novelist, Jan 1999

Mayne, Ethel Colburn, English author, critic and translator, *Obit* June 1941

McBride, Mary Margaret, radio talk show host, Apr 1941, Mar 1954, *Obit* June 1976

McCarthy, Mary, American novelist, critic, short story writer and memoirist, Yrbk 1955, Feb 1969, *Obit* Jan 1990

McCourt, Frank, Irish-American memoirist, Feb 1998, *Obit* Yrbk 2009

McCullough, David G., American historian and biographer, Jan 1993

McDonald, Trevor, British television news anchor, Sept 2010

Mehta, Ved, Indian journalist, novelist and essayist, Sept 1975

Menchu, Rigoberta, Guatemalan human rights activist and memoirist, Oct 1993

Merriam, George Ernest, *Obit* May 1941

Merrick, Elliott, author, Yrbk 1950, *Obit* July 1997

Miers, Earl Schenck, editor and publisher, Yrbk 1949, Sept 1967, *Obit* Jan 1973

Miller, Merle, author, Yrbk 1950, *Obit* July 1986

Mitford, Jessica, English journalist, memoirist and social critic, Sept 1974, *Obit* Oct 1996

Moley, Raymond, American journalist and government official, July 1945, *Obit* Apr 1975

Momaday, N. Scott, American novelist, poet and editor, Apr 1975

Monsarrat, Nicholas, English novelist, Yrbk 1950, *Obit* Oct 1979

Morris, Edmund, American biographer, July 1989

Morris, Willie, American writer and magazine editor, Jan 1976, *Obit* Oct 1999

Morrow, Honore Willsie, author, *Obit* May 1940

Mott, Lewis F., *Obit* Jan 1942

Mowrer, Lilian Thomson, author, May 1940, *Obit* Jan 1991

Muggeridge, Malcolm, English journalist, critic and novelist,

Apr 1955, July 1975, *Obit* Jan 1991

Nabokov, Vladimir Vladimirovich, Russian-American novelist, May 1966, *Obit* Aug 1977

Nicolson, Harold George, British diplomat, author and critic, May 1967, *Obit* June 1968

Niemoller, Martin, German clergyman, Mar 1943, Mar 1965, *Obit* May 1984

Niven, David, British actor, Mar 1957, *Obit* Sept 1983

Nolan, Christopher, Irish poet and memoirist, Sept 1988, *Obit* Yrbk 2009

O'Brian, Patrick, Irish novelist, June 1995, *Obit* Mar 2000

O'Brien, Tim, American novelist, Aug 1995

O'Casey, Sean, Irish dramatist, Nov 1962, *Obit* Nov 1964

O'Faolain, Sean, Irish short story writer, novelist and biographer, Apr 1990, *Obit* June 1991

O'Neil, George, *Obit* July 1940

Orlean, Susan, American writer, June 2003

Otero, Miguel Antonio, American territorial governor, *Obit* Sept 1944

Padover, Saul Kussiel, historian, Oct 1952, *Obit* Apr 1981

Parkinson, C. Northcote, English historian, satirist, biographer and novelist, Yrbk 1960, *Obit* May 1993

Parks, Gordon, American film director, photographer and novelist, Oct 1968, Oct 1992, *Obit* June 2006

Patchett, Ann, American novelist, Apr 2003

Paton, Alan, South African novelist and biographer, June 1952, *Obit* May 1988

Peare, Catherine Owens, Yrbk 1959

Pelzer, David J., American self-help writer and motivational speaker, Mar 2002

Peterson, Virgilia, Yrbk 1953, *Obit* Feb 1967

Philbrick, Herbert A., advertising executive and FBI informer, Mar 1953, *Obit* Oct 1993

Pourtales, Guy de, *Obit* Aug 1941

Powell, Adam Clayton, American congressman, Apr 1942, *Obit* May 1972

Powell, Anthony, English novelist, Sept 1977, *Obit* Aug 2000

Pratt, Fletcher, journalist, historian and author, May 1942, *Obit* Sept 1956

Pusey, Merlo J., newspaper editor and biographer, July 1952, *Obit* Jan 1986

Quennell, Peter, English biographer, poet, novelist and critic, May 1984, *Obit* Jan 1994

Ramos, Jorge, Mexican-American television news anchor, Mar 2004

Rampersad, Arnold, American biographer, Sept 1998

Randall, Ruth Painter, Yrbk 1957

Raphael, Chaim, English author and government official, Yrbk 1963, *Obit* Jan 1995

Ratushinskaya, Irina, Russian poet, July 1988

Ray, Gordon Norton, literary critic, Mar 1968, *Obit* Feb 1987

Rich, Louise Dickinson, American memoirist, young adult novelist and children's author, May 1943, *Obit* July 1991

Ripley, Elizabeth, Yrbk 1958

Rivera, Geraldo, American television reporter and talk show host, May 1975

Rives, Hallie Erminie, American novelist, Yrbk 1956

Robeson, Eslanda Goode, American anthropologist and wife of Paul Robeson, Sept 1945, *Obit* Yrbk 1991

Rolland, Romain, French novelist, dramatist and biographer, *Obit* Feb 1945

Rourke, Constance Mayfield, biographer, *Obit* May 1941

Rovere, Richard Halworth, American journalist, Apr 1977, *Obit* Jan 1980

Rowan, Carl Thomas, American newspaper columnist, Jan 1958, *Obit* Jan 2001

Rowse, A. L., English historian and biographer, July 1979, *Obit* Jan 1998

Royko, Mike, American newspaper columnist, June 1994, *Obit* July 1997

Russell, Charles Edward, American journalist, social reformer and biographer, *Obit* June 1941

Salvemini, Gaetano, Italian-American historian and biographer, Yrbk 1943, *Obit* Nov 1957

Sandburg, Carl, American poet, biographer and historian, June 1940, Yrbk 1963, *Obit* Oct 1967

Sanger, Margaret, American family planning advocate, Aug 1944, *Obit* Nov 1966

Satrapi, Marjane, Iranian graphic novelist, illustrator and memoirist, Jan 2003

Schlesinger, Arthur M., American historian, Oct 1946, Jan 1979, *Obit* Aug 2007

Scott, Sheila, English aviator, Nov 1974, *Obit* Jan 1989

Selzer, Richard, American surgeon, essayist and short story writer, Apr 1993

Sereny, Gitta, Hungarian-British journalist, historian and biographer, Jan 2007

Sergio, Lisa, Italian radio commentator, June 1944, *Obit* Aug 1989

Settle, Mary Lee, American novelist and memoirist, Yrbk 1959, *Obit* Yrbk 2006

Sevareid, Eric, reporter and commentator, July 1942, Oct 1966, *Obit* Aug 1992

Sheehy, Gail, American writer, June 1993

Shellabarger, Samuel, author, May 1945, *Obit* May 1954

Shippen, Katherine Binney, author, Yrbk 1954

Sillanpaa, Frans Eemil, Finnish novelist and short story writer, Jan 1940, *Obit* July 1964

Sinclair, Jo, author, Mar 1946, *Obit* June 1995

Sinclair, Upton, American novelist and socialist leader, Yrbk 1962, *Obit* Jan 1969

Singer, Kurt D., American children's author and editor, Yrbk 1954

Sitwell, Osbert, English poet, short story writer and novelist, Sept 1965, *Obit* June 1969

Smith, Page, historian, Sept 1990, *Obit* Nov 1995

Smith, Robert Paul, American novelist and memoirist, Yrbk 1958

Soyinka, Wole, Nigerian dramatist, poet and novelist, Yrbk 1974

Spark, Muriel, Scottish novelist, Nov 1975, *Obit* Yrbk 2007

Speer, Albert, German architect and Nazi leader, Oct 1976, *Obit* Oct 1981

Spender, Stephen, English poet and critic, Jan 1940, Mar 1977, *Obit* Sept 1995

Staples, Brent, American journalist and memoirist, May 2000

Starkie, Walter Fitzwilliam, Anglo-Irish literary critic, May 1964, *Obit* Feb 1977

Steele, Shelby, American writer and professor of English, Feb 1993

Stefan, Paul, *Obit* Jan 1944

Stegner, Wallace Earle, American novelist and short story writer, Apr 1977, *Obit* June 1993

Stein, Gertrude, American novelist, poet and critic, *Obit* Sept 1946

Steinem, Gloria, American feminist and journalist, Mar 1972, Mar 1988

Stern, Martha Dodd, American novelist, translator and spy, Yrbk 1946, *Obit* Jan 1991

Stevenson, Elizabeth, American biographer and literary scholar, Yrbk 1956

Stewart, George Rippey, American novelist and nonfiction writer, Jan 1942, *Obit* Nov 1980

Stone, Irving, biographer, Yrbk 1967, *Obit* Oct 1989

Sugrue, Thomas, journalist and author, June 1948, *Obit* Feb 1953

Tarbell, Ida M., American journalist, biographer and historian, *Obit* Feb 1944

Tate, Allen, American poet and critic, Nov 1940, *Obit* Apr 1979

Taubman, Howard, music and drama critic, Apr 1959, *Obit* Mar 1996

Taylor, Robert Lewis, biographer, Yrbk 1959, *Obit* Jan 1999

Terrell, Mary Church, American feminist and civil rights leader, June 1942, *Obit* Oct 1954

Tharp, Louise Hall, American children's author, Yrbk 1955

Thomson, David, English film historian and biographer, Sept 2009

Tolstoy, Alexandra, Russian foundation official and daughter of novelist Leo Tolstoy, Apr 1953, *Obit* Nov 1979

Torres Bodet, Jaime, Mexican novelist and poet, Feb 1948, *Obit* July 1974

Trapp, Maria von, Austrian singer, May 1968, *Obit* June 1987

Troyat, Henri, French novelist and biographer, Mar 1992, *Obit* Yrbk 2007

Truman, Margaret, daughter of American president Harry S. Truman and writer, June 1950, June 1987, *Obit* Yrbk 2008

Tuchman, Barbara Wertheim, American historian, Yrbk 1963, *Obit* Mar 1989

Ung, Loung, Cambodian-American social activist, Jan 2006

Untermeyer, Louis, American poet, editor and literary critic, Jan 1967, *Obit* Feb 1978

Vallee, Rudy, singer and actor, June 1947, Apr 1963, *Obit* Aug 1986

Van Doren, Mark, American literary critic, editor and poet, Jan 1940, *Obit* Feb 1973

Vance, Marguerite, Yrbk 1951, *Obit* July 1965

Vishnevskaya, Galina, Russian opera singer, July 1966, *Obit* Yrbk 2013

Von Hagen, Victor Wolfgang, naturalist, biographer and explorer, Mar 1942

Vonnegut, Kurt, American novelist and short story writer, July 1970, Mar 1991, *Obit* Aug 2007

Wald, Lillian D., American social reformer and public health official, *Obit* Oct 1940

Wallace, Irving, author, Mar 1979, *Obit* Sept 1990

Walworth, Arthur, American biographer, Yrbk 1959, *Obit* Yrbk 2005

Wechsberg, Joseph, American journalist, Apr 1955, *Obit* June 1983

Weisskopf, Victor Frederick, Austrian-American physicist, Nov 1976, *Obit* Yrbk 2002

Weitz, John, German-American fashion designer, novelist and biographer, Sept 1979, *Obit* Apr 2003

Wellman, Manly Wade, author, Yrbk 1955

West, Dorothy, American novelist, Feb 1997, *Obit* Oct 1998

West, Jessamyn, American novelist, short story writer, librettist, essayist, playwright and poet, Aug 1977, *Obit* Apr 1984

West, Mae, American actress, Nov 1967, *Obit* Jan 1981

White, Edmund, American novelist and biographer, Jan 1991

White, William Allen, newspaper editor, Nov 1940, *Obit* Apr 1944

White, William Smith, journalist, Yrbk 1955, *Obit* June 1994

Wideman, John Edgar, American novelist and short story writer, Jan 1991

Wiesenthal, Simon, Austrian Nazi hunter, Jan 1975, *Obit* Yrbk 2005

Willson, Beckles, *Obit* Nov 1942

Wilson, A. N., English novelist and biographer, Aug 1993

Wilson, Angus, English novelist and short story writer, Feb 1959, *Obit* Aug 1991

Wolff, Geoffrey, author, Jan 1997

Wolff, Tobias, American memoirist and short story writer, Jan 1996

Woodham Smith, Cecil Blanche Fitz Gerald, English historian, Yrbk 1955, *Obit* Mar 1977

Woodward, Bob, American journalist, Nov 1976

Woolf, Leonard, English political essayist, editor, publisher and memoirist, Yrbk 1965, *Obit* Oct 1969

Wright, Helen, astronomer, Mar 1956, *Obit* Feb 1998

Ybarra, Thomas Russell, journalist and biographer, Jan 1940

Zolotow, Maurice, author, May 1957, *Obit* May 1991

Zukerman, Eugenia, American flutist and author, Jan 2004

Biologists

Adrian, Edgar Douglas Adrian, British physiologist, Feb 1955, *Obit* Oct 1977

Alibek, Ken, Kazakh biological weapons expert, June 2002

Allen, Edgar, American anatomist, *Obit* Mar 1943

Alvarez, Walter C., American internist and physiologist, Sept 1953, *Obit* Aug 1978

Anderson, William French, American geneticist, Oct 1994

Anderson, Winston A., American biologist, Mar 2007

Armour, Allison V., American botanist, *Obit* Apr 1941

Arsonval, Jacques Arsene d', French physiologist, *Obit* Feb 1941

Arthur, J. C., American botanist, *Obit* June 1942

Atwell, Wayne J., American anatomist, *Obit* May 1941

Ayala, Francisco, American geneticist, Oct 2012

Bailey, L. H., American botanist, June 1948, *Obit* Mar 1955

Baltimore, David, American microbiologist, July 1983

Bassler, Bonnie L., American molecular biologist, Apr 2003

Bates, Marston, zoologist, Apr 1956, *Obit* May 1974

Beadle, George W., American geneticist and college president, Apr 1956, *Obit* Aug 1989

Bedford, Herbrand Arthur Russell, English zoologist, *Obit* Oct 1940

Bennett, H. S., anatomist, Apr 1966, *Obit* Oct 1992

Beresford-Kroeger, Diana, Irish botanist, Nov 2008

Best, Charles Herbert, Canadian physiologist, June 1957, *Obit* May 1978

Blackburn, Elizabeth H., Australian molecular biologist, July 2001

Blakeslee, Albert Francis, American botanist, Oct 1941, *Obit* Jan 1955

Borysenko, Joan, psychologist and biologist, Oct 1996

Braun, Werner, German microbiologist, June 1957, *Obit* Jan 1973

Brenner, Sydney, British geneticist, Jan 2007

Brooks, Matilda Moldenhauer, physiologist, Nov 1941

Bunting-Smith, Mary Ingraham, microbiologist and college president, June 1967, *Obit* Apr 1998

Burnet, Frank Macfarlane, Australian bacteriologist, May 1954, *Obit* Oct 1985

Burton, Alan C., Sept 1956

Calderone, Mary Steichen, sexologist, Nov 1967, *Obit* Jan 1999

Cannon, Walter Bradford, American physiologist, *Obit* Nov 1945

Carlson, Anton Julius, physiologist, Jan 1948, *Obit* Nov 1956

Carrel, Alexis, French surgeon and biologist, Mar 1940, *Obit* Yrbk 1944

Carson, Rachel, American marine biologist and environmentalist, Nov 1951, *Obit* June 1964

Carver, George Washington, American botanist, Nov 1940, *Obit* Feb 1943

Cavalli-Sforza, Luigi Luca, Italian geneticist, Aug 1997

Cavazos, Lauro Fred, American Secretary of education, Apr 1989

Colwell, Rita R., American microbiologist, May 1999

Commoner, Barry, American biologist and environmentalist, Sept 1970, *Obit* Yrbk 2012

Coons, Albert H., June 1960

Coulter, Calvin Brewster, *Obit* Jan 1940

Cowdry, E. V., anatomist and gerontologist, Jan 1948

Cox, Herald R., Apr 1961

Cullis, Winifred C., Nov 1943, *Obit* Jan 1957

Damasio, Antonio R., American neurobiologist, Oct 2007

Dart, Raymond A., South African anatomist, Sept 1966, *Obit* Jan 1989

Davenport, Charles B., biologist and educator, *Obit* Apr 1944

Davis, Wade, Canadian ethnobotanist, Jan 2003

Dawkins, Richard, British zoologist, Aug 1997

Day, Albert M., biologist, Yrbk 1948

De Kruif, Paul, author and bacteriologist, May 1942, July 1963, *Obit* Apr 1971

Delgado, Jose Manuel R., Spanish neurobiologist, Feb 1976

Dobzhansky, Theodosius Grigorievich, American geneticist, Sept 1962, *Obit* Feb 1976

Domagk, Gerhard, German bacteriologist, Mar 1958, *Obit* June 1964

Driesch, Hans, German biologist and philosopher, *Obit* June 1941

Dubos, Rene Jules, American bacteriologist, Oct 1952, Jan 1973, *Obit* Apr 1982

Duesberg, Peter H., German molecular biologist, June 2004

Duggar, Benjamin Minge, botanist, Nov 1952, *Obit* Nov 1956

Dusser de Barenne, Joannes Gregorius, *Obit* Aug 1940

Earle, Sylvia A., American marine botanist, May 1972, May 1992

Eccles, John C., Australian physiologist, Oct 1972, *Obit* July 1997

Eckstein, Gustav, physiologist, May 1942, *Obit* Nov 1981

Ehrlich, Paul R., biologist, Sept 1970

Eisen, Gustavus A., *Obit* Yrbk 1940

Ellis, Albert, American psychologist, July 1994, *Obit* Yrbk 2007

Enders, John F., American virologist, June 1955, *Obit* Jan 1986

Espinoza Fuentes, Fernando, Ecuadorian biologist, Jan 2004

Evans, Alice Catherine, American bacteriologist, Oct 1943, *Obit* Oct 1975

Evans, Herbert McLean, endocrinologist and anatomist, July 1959, *Obit* Apr 1971

Fausto-Sterling, Anne, American biologist, Sept 2005

Fawcett, Edward, *Obit* Nov 1942

Fay, Michael, American biologist and conservationist, Sept 2001

Ferris, Harry Burr, *Obit* Yrbk 1940

Finch, Caleb Ellicott, American neurobiologist, Sept 2004

Fleming, Alexander, British bacteriologist, Apr 1944, *Obit* May 1955

Flexner, Simon, American physician, *Obit* June 1946

Florey, Howard, Australian bacteriologist, Apr 1944, *Obit* Apr 1968

Ford, W. W., *Obit* Aug 1941

Fred, Edwin Broun, bacteriologist and college president, Yrbk 1950

Frisch, Karl von, German zoologist, Feb 1974, *Obit* Yrbk 1983

Fuchs, Elaine V., American cytologist, Jan 2011

Fuller, John L., Mar 1959

Gajdusek, Daniel Carleton, American virologist, June 1981, *Obit* Yrbk 2009

Gasser, Herbert Spencer, American physiologist, Oct 1945, *Obit* July 1963

Gerard, Ralph W., May 1965, *Obit* Apr 1974

Gilbert, Walter, American molecular biologist and genetic engineering executive, Nov 1992

Gillespie, Louis J., *Obit* Mar 1941

Glass, Bentley, American biologist, Apr 1966, *Obit* Yrbk 2005

Greider, Carol W., American molecular biologist, Feb 2008

Gruber, Samuel H., American marine biologist, Aug 2004

Guarente, Leonard, American biologist, May 2007

Gurdon, John Bertrand, British microbiologist, Jan 2007

Hagens, Gunther von, German anatomist, Jan 2005

Hair, Jay D., American zoologist and conservationist, Nov 1993, *Obit* Jan 2003

Haldane, J. B. S., British geneticist, Nov 1940, *Obit* Jan 1965

Hamer, Dean H., geneticist, June 1997

Hammond, E. Cuyler, biologist and statistician, June 1957, *Obit* Jan 1987

Hardin, Garrett James, American biologist, Sept 1974, *Obit* Apr 2004

Harrar, J. George, Jan 1964, *Obit* June 1982

Harris, Eva, American geneticist, Mar 2004

Hartwell, Leland, American geneticist, Nov 1999

Harvey, E. Newton, May 1952

Haseltine, William A., American molecular biologist, Nov 1998

Hass, Hans, Feb 1955, *Obit* Yrbk 2013

Hayes, Tyrone, American biologist, May 2008

Herrick, Francis Hobart, *Obit* Nov 1940

Hershey, Alfred D., American biologist, July 1970, *Obit* Aug 1997

Hill, Justina Hamilton, Apr 1941

Hogben, Lancelot, English physiologist and zoologist, Yrbk 1941, *Obit* Jan 1984

Hopkins, Nancy, American molecular biologist, May 2002

Horsfall, Frank L., American virologist, Mar 1941, Jan 1961, *Obit* Apr 1971

Houssay, Bernardo Alberto, Argentine physiologist, Jan 1948, *Obit* Nov 1971

Howell, William Henry, *Obit* Mar 1945

Huxley, Julian, British biologist, Aug 1942, Oct 1963, *Obit* Apr 1975

Jacob, Francois, French bacteriologist, Yrbk 1966, *Obit* Yrbk 2013

Jarvis, Erich, American neurobiologist, May 2003

Jellinek, E. M., May 1947, *Obit* Jan 1964

Johnson, Virginia E., American psychologist, Apr 1976, *Obit* Yrbk 2013

Judson, Olivia P., English evolutionary biologist, Jan 2004

Keasling, Jay, American bioengineer, Nov 2013

Kennedy, Donald, physiologist and college president, July 1984

Kenyon, Cynthia, American biochemist and biotechnology executive, Jan 2005

Keys, Ancel, American physiologist, Jan 1966, *Obit* Yrbk 2005

Kidder, George Wallace, microbiologist, July 1949

King, Mary-Claire, American geneticist, Feb 1995

Kinsey, Alfred Charles, American zoologist and sex researcher, Jan 1954, *Obit* Oct 1956

Kleitman, Nathaniel, physiologist, Oct 1957, *Obit* Jan 2000

Koprowski, Hilary, Mar 1968, *Obit* Yrbk 2013

Krause, David W., Canadian paleontologist and anatomist, Feb 2002

Krim, Mathilde, American geneticist and virologist, Aug 1987

Laidlaw, Patrick Playfair, *Obit* Apr 1940

Lambert, W. V., Nov 1955

LeVay, Simon, English neurobiologist, Oct 1996

Lederberg, Joshua, American geneticist, Mar 1959, *Obit* Yrbk 2008

Levi-Montalcini, Rita, Italian biologist, Nov 1989, *Obit* Yrbk 2013

Levine, Philip, American bacteriologist, May 1947, *Obit* Nov 1987

Lieberman, Daniel, American anthropologist and biologist, May 2011

Little, Clarence C., American biologist, Yrbk 1944, *Obit* Feb 1972

Llinas, Rodolfo R., American neurophysiologist, Sept 2009

Luria, S. E., American biologist, Feb 1970, *Obit* Apr 1991

Lynch, William J., *Obit* Aug 1941

Lysenko, Trofim, Russian geneticist, Oct 1952, *Obit* Feb 1977

Maathai, Wangari, Kenyan biologist and environmentalist, Sept 1993, *Obit* Yrbk 2011

Macbride, Ernest William, *Obit* Jan 1941

Margulis, Lynn, American microbiologist, July 1992, *Obit* Yrbk 2012

Masters, William H., American physician, Nov 1968, *Obit* May 2001

Matola, Sharon, American biologist and zoo director, June 1993

Mayr, Ernst, German zoologist, Nov 1984, *Obit* May 2005

McClintock, Barbara, American geneticist, Mar 1984, *Obit* Nov 1992

McCrady, Edward, Jan 1957

Medawar, P. B., British biologist, Apr 1961, *Obit* Nov 1987

Melton, Douglas, American molecular biologist, June 2008

Mittermeier, Russell, biologist and conservationist, Oct 1992

Monod, Jacques, French biologist, July 1971, *Obit* July 1976

Montagnier, Luc, French virologist, Aug 1988

Morgan, Thomas Hunt, American biologist, *Obit* Feb 1946

Moss, Cynthia, American biologist and conservationist, May 1993

Muller, H. J., American geneticist, Feb 1947, *Obit* June 1967

Nabrit, Samuel Milton, American embryologist, Jan 1963, *Obit* Yrbk 2004

Nachtigall, Paul E., American marine scientist, Jan 2006

Neal, Herbert Vincent, *Obit* Mar 1940

Negrin, Juan, Spanish physiologist and statesman, Sept 1945, *Obit* Jan 1957

Newsom, Lee A., American paleoethnobotanist, Oct 2004

Noble, G. Kingsley, zoologist and museum curator, *Obit* Jan 1941

Paabo, Svante, Swedish geneticist, Feb 2007

Palade, George, American biologist, July 1967, *Obit* Yrbk 2008

Park, Thomas, zoologist, Jan 1963, *Obit* June 1992

Payne, Roger, marine biologist, June 1995

Pearl, Raymond, American biologist, *Obit* Jan 1941

Pearson, Jay F. W., Yrbk 1953, *Obit* Oct 1965

Peiris, Malik, Sri Lankan microbiologist, Jan 2003

Pincus, Gregory, American biologist, May 1966, *Obit* Oct 1967

Plotkin, Mark, American ethnobotanist, June 1997

Pomeroy, Wardell Baxter, sex researcher, July 1974, *Obit* Yrbk 2001

Popenoe, Paul Bowman, American eugenicist, Yrbk 1946

Profet, Margie, biologist, Nov 1998

Raven, Peter H., American botanist, Feb 1994

Ray, Dixy Lee, American governor, June 1973, *Obit* Mar 1994

Richards, Dickinson W., American physician, Mar 1957, *Obit* Apr 1973

Ripley, Sidney Dillon, American zoologist and museum director, Oct 1966, *Obit* Aug 2001

Rivers, Thomas M., American virologist, July 1960, *Obit* July 1962

Robbins, Frederick C., American bacteriologist, June 1955, *Obit* Yrbk 2003

Robbins, William J., Feb 1956

Rodahl, Kare, Norwegian physiologist, Feb 1956

Rodriguez, Eloy, botanist, May 2000

Rogers, Lynn L., wildlife biologist, Oct 1994

Romanoff, Alexis L., Yrbk 1953

Rosett, Joshua, *Obit* May 1940

Rostand, Jean, Yrbk 1954, *Obit* Jan 1978

Rothschild, Miriam, British entomologist and botanist, Oct 1992, *Obit* Yrbk 2005

Rubin, Eddy, American geneticist, Jan 2006

Rusby, Henry H., *Obit* Jan 1941

Sabin, Florence Rena, American anatomist, Apr 1945, *Obit* Yrbk 1953

Safina, Carl, American marine conservationist and scientist, Apr 2005

Sager, Ruth, geneticist, July 1967, *Obit* June 1997

Salk, Jonas, American physician, May 1954, *Obit* Aug 1995

Salzano, Francisco M., Brazilian geneticist, Jan 2006

Schaller, George B., American zoologist, Aug 1985

Schlessinger, Laura C., American psychologist and radio talk show host, Sept 1997

Schneirla, T. C., Yrbk 1955, *Obit* Nov 1968

Schultes, Richard Evans, American botanist, Mar 1995, *Obit* Sept 2001

Schwartz, Pepper, American sociologist, June 2008

Sears, Paul Bigelow, botanist, July 1960

Shannon, James A., public health official, Jan 1965, *Obit* July 1994

Shope, Richard E., Yrbk 1963, *Obit* Yrbk 1966

Shubin, Neil, American biologist and paleontologist, Apr 2007

Sinclair, David, Australian molecular biologist, Sept 2008

Sinnott, Edmund W., American botanist, Oct 1948, *Obit* Mar 1968

Sinsheimer, Robert, American biologist, June 1968

Skolnick, Mark H., geneticist, June 1997

Snell, George Davis, American geneticist, May 1986, *Obit* Aug 1996

Snell, Peter, New Zealand runner and physiologist, Yrbk 1962

Spiegelman, Solomon, geneticist, Nov 1980, *Obit* Mar 1983

Stakman, Elvin Charles, American botanist, Yrbk 1949, *Obit* Mar 1979

Stefansson, Kari, Icelandic geneticist, Jan 2003

Steingraber, Sandra, American biologist, poet and nonfiction writer, Sept 2003

Steinhaus, Edward A., Yrbk 1955

Steitz, Joan Argetsinger, American biochemist, June 2007

Stiles, Charles Wardell, American public health official and zoologist, *Obit* Mar 1941

Strughold, Hubertus, July 1966
Sulston, John, English molecular biologist, Jan 2007
Suzuki, David T., Canadian geneticist and environmentalist, July 1995
Tatum, Edward Lawrie, American biochemist, Mar 1959, *Obit* Jan 1976
Tennent, David Hilt, American biologist, *Obit* Mar 1941
Tewolde Berhan Gebre Egziabher, Ethiopian biologist and government official, Jan 2004
Theiler, Max, American microbiologist, Jan 1952, *Obit* Oct 1972
Thomas, Lewis, American physician and biologist, July 1975, *Obit* Feb 1994
Thomson, James A., American molecular biologist, Nov 2001
Tilghman, Shirley M., Canadian molecular biologist and university president, June 2006
Tinbergen, Niko, British zoologist and ethologist, Nov 1975, *Obit* Feb 1989
True, Rodney Howard, *Obit* May 1940
Varmus, Harold, American virologist and public health official, Nov 1996
Vermeij, Geerat J., American marine biologist, June 1995
Villa-Komaroff, Lydia, American molecular biologist, July 2008
Vishniac, Roman, American biologist and photographer, Feb 1967, *Obit* Mar 1990
Vogelstein, Bert, molecular biologist, Jan 1996
Waddington, C. H., British embryologist, Apr 1962, *Obit* Nov 1975
Waksman, Selman Abraham, American microbiologist, May 1946, *Obit* Oct 1973
Walker, Norma Ford, Canadian geneticist, Oct 1957, *Obit* Nov 1968
Watson, James D., American molecular biologist, Apr 1963, Oct 1990
Weiss, Paul A., American biologist, Oct 1970, *Obit* Nov 1989

Weller, Thomas H., American virologist, June 1955, *Obit* Yrbk 2008
Wells, Spencer, American geneticist, Mar 2008
Whitaker, Douglas, Nov 1951, *Obit* Yrbk 1973
Wiener, Alexander S., physician and hematologist, May 1947, *Obit* Feb 1977
Williams, Edwin G., May 1950
Wilmut, Ian, British embryologist, June 1997
Wilson, Edward O., American myrmecologist, Oct 1979
Woese, Carl R., American microbiologist, June 2003, *Obit* Yrbk 2013
Wong-Staal, Flossie, American molecular biologist, Apr 2001
Yamanaka, Shinya, Japanese geneticist, June 2013
Yamashita Yukiko, Developmental biologist, Mar 2012
Young, Frank E., microbiologist, educator and government official, Oct 1989
Zinsser, Hans, American bacteriologist, *Obit* Oct 1940

Biomedical engineers

Greatbatch, Wilson, American biomedical engineer and inventor of pacemaker, *Obit* Yrbk 2012
Jarvik, Robert, American physician and inventor, July 1985

Biophysicists

Benzer, Seymour, American biophysicist, May 2001, *Obit* Yrbk 2008
Bronk, Detlev Wulf, American college president and biophysicist, Oct 1949, *Obit* Jan 1976
Burton, Alan C., Sept 1956
Haskins, Caryl Parker, American biophysicist, Feb 1958, *Obit* Feb 2002
Herr, Hugh, American biophysicist and mechanical engineer, Apr 2012
Hoffman, Joseph G., May 1958, *Obit* Jan 1975
Katzir, Ephraim, Israeli biophysicist and president, Jan 1975, *Obit* Yrbk 2009

Lovelock, James, British chemist and biophysicist, Nov 1992
Sperti, George Speri, biophysicist, Jan 1940, *Obit* July 1991
Turin, Luca, British biophysicist, Aug 2008
Wilkins, Maurice Hugh Frederick, English biochemist, June 1963, *Obit* Yrbk 2005
Woese, Carl R., American microbiologist, June 2003, *Obit* Yrbk 2013

Biotechnology executives

Desmond-Hellman, Susan, American oncologist and biotechnology executive, Nov 2012
Gilbert, Walter, American molecular biologist and genetic engineering executive, Nov 1992
Haseltine, William A., American molecular biologist, Nov 1998
Kenyon, Cynthia, American biochemist and biotechnology executive, Jan 2005
Mazumdar-Shaw, Kiran, Indian biotechnology executive, Jan 2006
Potter, Myrtle, American biotechnology executive, Aug 2004
Wong-Staal, Flossie, American molecular biologist, Apr 2001

Bishops

Ainsworth, William Newman, American bishop, *Obit* Aug 1942
Akinola, Peter Jasper, Nigerian archbishop, Jan 2004
Aleksii, Mar 1953, *Obit* June 1970
Aleksii, Jan 2003, *Obit* Yrbk 2009
Arnold, William R., American military chaplain and bishop, May 1942
Athenagoras, Mar 1949, *Obit* Sept 1972
Barry, Patrick, Irish-American bishop, *Obit* Sept 1940
Bartholomeos, Jan 2004
Bayne, Stephen F., Jan 1964, *Obit* Mar 1974

Berggrav, Eivind, Norwegian bishop, Oct 1950, *Obit* Mar 1959

Blackie, Ernest Morell, British bishop, *Obit* Apr 1943

Blake, Edgar, American bishop, *Obit* July 1943

Brewster, Benjamin, American bishop, *Obit* Mar 1941

Brewster, Chauncey B., American bishop, *Obit* June 1941

Burton, Lewis William, *Obit* Yrbk 1940

Camara, Helder, Brazilian archbishop, July 1971, *Obit* Jan 2000

Candler, Warren A., American bishop and college president, *Obit* Nov 1941

Cannon, James, bishop, *Obit* Nov 1944

Carey, George, British archbishop, Aug 1991

Cicognani, Amleto Giovanni, July 1951, *Obit* Feb 1974

Coggan, Frederick Donald, English archbishop, July 1974, *Obit* Sept 2000

Corrigan, Joseph M., *Obit* Aug 1942

Corson, Fred Pierce, bishop, May 1961, *Obit* Apr 1985

Damaskenos, Nov 1945, *Obit* July 1949

De Wolfe, James P., Aug 1942, *Obit* Mar 1966

Denny, Collins, *Obit* July 1943

Dibelius, Friedrich Karl Otto, German bishop, May 1953, *Obit* Mar 1967

Dolan, Timothy Michael, American archbishop, Mar 2011

Donegan, Horace William Baden, bishop, July 1954, *Obit* Jan 1992

Drossaerts, Arthur, *Obit* Oct 1940

Du Bose, Horace M., *Obit* Mar 1941

Feltin, Maurice, May 1954, *Obit* Nov 1975

Fisher of Lambeth, Geoffrey Francis Fisher, British archbishop, Mar 1945, *Obit* Nov 1972

Fiske, Charles, *Obit* Mar 1942

Forbes, Guillaume, *Obit* July 1940

Freeman, James Edward, American bishop, *Obit* July 1943

Garbett, Cyril Forster, Feb 1951, *Obit* Mar 1956

Gauthier, Joseph Alexandre Georges, *Obit* Oct 1940

Graves, Frederick Rogers, *Obit* July 1940

Gregory, Wilton D., American archbishop, Mar 2002

Haas, Francis J., bishop, Aug 1943, *Obit* Oct 1953

Hanna, Edward Joseph, *Obit* Aug 1944

Hannan, Philip M., American archbishop, July 1968, *Obit* Yrbk 2011

Harris, Barbara C., American bishop, June 1989

Hickey, Thomas F., *Obit* Feb 1941

Hines, John Elbridge, bishop, May 1968, *Obit* Oct 1997

Hinsley, Arthur, *Obit* Apr 1943

Huddleston, Trevor, South African archbishop, Oct 1963, *Obit* July 1998

Hunthausen, Raymond G., archbishop, Aug 1987

Iakovos, July 1960, *Obit* Yrbk 2005

Jefferts Schori, Katharine, American bishop, Sept 2006

Kaspar, Karel, *Obit* June 1941

Lang of Lambeth, Cosmo Gordon Lang, English archbishop, Aug 1941, *Obit* Jan 1946

Lawrence, William, *Obit* Jan 1942

Lefebvre, Marcel, French archbishop, Mar 1978, *Obit* May 1991

Lercaro, Giacomo, Sept 1965, *Obit* Jan 1977

Lichtenberger, Arthur, Apr 1961, *Obit* Nov 1968

Locke, Charles Edward, *Obit* Mar 1940

Lord, John Wesley, bishop, May 1971, *Obit* Jan 1990

Makarios, Cypriot archbishop and president, May 1956, *Obit* Sept 1977

Manning, William Thomas, Apr 1940, *Obit* Jan 1950

Martin, William C., bishop, Apr 1953

Matheson, Samuel Pritchard, *Obit* July 1942

May, John Lawrence, archbishop, Jan 1991, *Obit* June 1994

McGuigan, James, Sept 1950, *Obit* June 1974

McKenzie, Vashti, American bishop, Nov 2000

McNicholas, John T., May 1949, *Obit* June 1950

Mead, Charles Larew, *Obit* July 1941

Mikell, Henry Judah, *Obit* Apr 1942

Monaghan, Francis Joseph, *Obit* Jan 1943

Moore, Paul, American bishop, Jan 1967, *Obit* Yrbk 2003

Mosher, Gouverneur Frank, *Obit* Sept 1941

Mosley, J. Brooke, bishop, Sept 1970, *Obit* Apr 1988

Mueller, Reuben H., bishop, Apr 1964, *Obit* Sept 1982

Muzorewa, Abel Tendekai, Zimbabwean prime minister, Mar 1979, *Obit* Yrbk 2010

Ncube, Pius Alick, Zimbabwean archbishop, Jan 2004

Neill, Stephen, British bishop, Mar 1960

O'Shea, William F., *Obit* Apr 1945

Oxnam, G. Bromley, American bishop, Nov 1944, *Obit* Apr 1963

Perry, Harold, American bishop, Oct 1966, *Obit* Sept 1991

Pike, James Albert, American bishop, May 1957, *Obit* Nov 1969

Pla y Deniel, Enrique, Feb 1955, *Obit* Sept 1968

Ramsey, Michael, English archbishop, Apr 1960, *Obit* June 1988

Robinson, John A. T., English bishop, Feb 1965, *Obit* Feb 1984

Rummel, Joseph F., American archbishop, June 1959, *Obit* Jan 1965

Runcie, Robert, English archbishop, Nov 1980, *Obit* Oct 2000

Schrembs, Joseph, *Obit* Yrbk 1945

Schulte, Karl Joseph, *Obit* May 1941

Sheen, Fulton J., American archbishop, Nov 1941, Jan 1951, *Obit* Feb 1980

Sheil, Bernard J., Yrbk 1968, *Obit* Nov 1969

Shenouda, Egyptian patriarch, Jan 2003, *Obit* Yrbk 2013

Sherrill, Henry Knox, Mar 1947, *Obit* June 1980

Spellman, Francis, Apr 1940, Apr 1947, *Obit* Jan 1968

Spottswood, Stephen Gill, American bishop and civil rights leader, Apr 1962, *Obit* Jan 1975

Stamm, John S., Feb 1949, *Obit* May 1956

Stewart, George Craig, *Obit* Jan 1940

Stokes, Anson Phelps, bishop, July 1962, *Obit* Jan 1987

Temple, William, British archbishop and theologian, Apr 1942, *Obit* Yrbk 1944

Tucker, Henry St. George, American bishop, Sept 1943, *Obit* Nov 1959

Tutu, Desmond, South African archbishop, Jan 1985, Jan 2002

Vagnozzi, Egidio, Mar 1967, *Obit* Feb 1981

Verdier, Jean, *Obit* May 1940

Williams, Preston Warren, American religious official, May 2007

Williams, Rowan, British archbishop, Jan 2002

Woodcock, Charles Edward, *Obit* Mar 1940

Zen, Joseph, Chinese bishop, Jan 2005

Black Muslim leaders

Elijah Muhammad, American Black Muslim leader, Jan 1971, *Obit* Apr 1975

Farrakhan, Louis, American Black Muslim leader, Apr 1992

Blind

Bagayoko, Amadou, Malian singer and guitarist, Jan 2006

Barnett, M. Robert, American journalist and foundation official, Jan 1950

Bocelli, Andrea, Italian singer, Jan 2002

Charles, Ray, American singer and pianist, Apr 1965, June 1992, *Obit* Yrbk 2004

Doumbia, Mariam, Malian singer, Jan 2006

Feliciano, Jose, singer and guitarist, July 1969

Hayes, Samuel Perkins, psychologist and teacher of the blind, Sept 1954, *Obit* Sept 1958

Husayn, Taha, Egyptian educator, Oct 1953, *Obit* Yrbk 1973

Keller, Helen, American humanitarian, Yrbk 1942, *Obit* July 1968

Kish, Daniel, Echolation developer and president of World Access for the Blind, Sept 2013

Mehta, Ved, Indian journalist, novelist and essayist, Sept 1975

Paterson, David A., American governor, July 2008

Shearing, George, English jazz pianist, Apr 1958, *Obit* Yrbk 2011

Watson, Doc, American singer and guitarist, Feb 2003, *Obit* Yrbk 2012

Bloggers

Arrington, Michael, American Internet executive, July 2012

Denton, Nick, British journalist and Internet news service executive, Apr 2011

Huffington, Arianna, Greek-American political adviser and commentator, July 1998

Jarvis, Jeff, American journalist, Aug 2009

Johnson, Simon, American economist, Oct 2009

Keen, Andrew, British digital media critic, July 2013

Moulitsas Zuniga, Markos, American political blog writer, Mar 2007

Okolloh, Ory, Kenyan lawyer and blogger, May 2012

Simone, Gail, American comic book writer, Nov 2008

Sklar, Rachel, Media blogger, author and attorney, Mar 2012

Xu Jinglei, Chinese actress and filmmaker, Jan 2007

Bluegrass musicians

Douglas, Jerry, American dobro guitar player, Aug 2004

Krauss, Alison, American fiddler and singer, May 1997

Watson, Doc, American singer and guitarist, Feb 2003, *Obit* Yrbk 2012

Blues musicians

Auerbach, Dan, American singer and guitarist, Jan 2013

Bland, Bobby Blue, singer, *Obit* Yrbk 2013

Bonamassa, Joe, Apr 2013

Carney, Patrick, American drummer, Jan 2013

Dixon, Willie, American blues singer, May 1989, *Obit* Apr 1992

Guy, Buddy, American blues guitarist, Feb 2000

Hooker, John Lee, American singer and guitarist, Nov 1992, *Obit* Sept 2001

Hunter, Alberta, singer and songwriter, May 1979, *Obit* Jan 1985

Keb' Mo', American blues guitarist and singer, Nov 2013

King, B. B., American blues guitarist and singer, June 1970

Mayer, John, American singer and guitarist, Mar 2010

Popper, John, singer and harpist, Jan 2012

Raitt, Bonnie, American singer and guitarist, Aug 1990

Taj Mahal (Musician), American singer and songwriter, Nov 2001

Taylor, KoKo, American blues singer and songwriter, July 2002, *Obit* Yrbk 2009

Tedeschi, Susan, American blues singer and guitarist, Sept 2012

The Black Keys, Jan 2013

Waits, Tom, American singer and songwriter, Oct 1997

Waters, Muddy, American singer and guitarist, May 1981, *Obit* June 1983

Boat racers

Armour, Allison V., American botanist, *Obit* Apr 1941

Butterworth, Brad, New Zealand yacht racer, Jan 2007

Campbell, Donald, British automobile and boat racer, Feb 1964, *Obit* Feb 1967

Chapman, Charles Frederic, American magazine editor and motorboat racer, May 1958, *Obit* Yrbk 1984

Chichester, Francis, English cartographer and boat racer, Yrbk 1967, *Obit* Oct 1972

Conner, Dennis, yacht racer, Nov 1987

Coutts, Russell, New Zealand boat racer, Jan 2003

Koch, William I., American energy executive, investor and yacht racer, Mar 1999

Mosbacher, Emil, investment banker, presidential aide and yacht racer, Mar 1963, *Obit* Nov 1997

Olav, Jan 1962, *Obit* Mar 1991

Turner, Ted, American television and baseball executive, May 1979, June 1998

Vanderbilt, Cornelius, American financier, *Obit* Apr 1942

Boatbuilders

Dobson, William Alexander, *Obit* July 1943

Boaters

Armour, Allison V., American botanist, *Obit* Apr 1941

Bobsled racers

Flowers, Vonetta, American bobsledder, May 2006

Bodybuilders

Coleman, Ronnie, American bodybuilder and policeman, Feb 2007

Schwarzenegger, Arnold, Austrian-American actor and governor, Apr 1979, Oct 1991, Aug 2004

Van Damme, Jean-Claude, Belgian bodybuilder, martial artist and actor, Mar 1999

Weider, Joe, American publisher and bodybuilder, Jan 1998, *Obit* Yrbk 2013

Book collectors

Barrett, Clifton Waller, American shipping executive and book collector, Mar 1965

Benjamin, William Evarts, American publisher, *Obit* Mar 1940

Bonner, Paul Hyde, American novelist, Yrbk 1955, *Obit* Mar 1969

Evans, Herbert McLean, endocrinologist and anatomist, July 1959, *Obit* Apr 1971

Gingrich, Arnold, magazine editor and book collector, Feb 1961, *Obit* Sept 1976

Lansky, Aaron, American collector and distributor of Yiddish books, Jan 1997

Lewis, W. S., book collector and editor, July 1973, *Obit* Jan 1980

Muir, Percy H., English bibliographer, bookseller and collector, Apr 1963

Newton, A. Edward, bibliographer and book collector, *Obit* Nov 1940

Rosenbach, A. S. W., American rare book collector and dealer, May 1946, *Obit* Sept 1952

Rosenwald, Lessing J., American retail executive and book collector, Feb 1947, *Obit* Aug 1979

Book designers

Kidd, Chip, American book and graphic designer, July 2005

Rollins, Carl Purington, Sept 1948, *Obit* Jan 1961

Booksellers

Barnes, William R., American publisher and bookseller, *Obit* Mar 1945

Carter, John, British bibliographer and rare book dealer, May 1959, *Obit* May 1975

Foyle, Gilbert, June 1954, *Obit* Jan 1972

Foyle, William Alfred, English bookseller, June 1954, *Obit* July 1963

Kraus, Hans Peter, American rare book dealer, July 1960, *Obit* Jan 1989

Martinez, Rueben, American bookstore owner, June 2005

Muir, Percy H., English bibliographer, bookseller and collector, Apr 1963

Riggio, Leonard, American book store chain executive, June 1998

Rosenbach, A. S. W., American rare book collector and dealer, May 1946, *Obit* Sept 1952

Scherman, Harry, Sept 1943, July 1963, *Obit* Jan 1970

Steloff, Frances, bookseller, Nov 1965, *Obit* June 1989

Tuttle, Charles Egbert, publisher and rare book dealer, July 1960, *Obit* Aug 1993

Wells, Gabriel, bookseller, *Obit* Yrbk 1946

Botanists

Arnon, Daniel I., American plant physiologist, June 1955, *Obit* Mar 1995

Arthur, J. C., American botanist, *Obit* June 1942

Bailey, L. H., American botanist, June 1948, *Obit* Mar 1955

Bennett, Henry Garland, American college president, Feb 1951, *Obit* Feb 1952

Bennett, Hugh Hammond, American soil scientist, Yrbk 1946, *Obit* Oct 1960

Bensin, Basil M., American agriculturist, July 1948

Beresford-Kroeger, Diana, Irish botanist, Nov 2008

Blakeslee, Albert Francis, American botanist, Oct 1941, *Obit* Jan 1955

Boerma, Addeke H., Dutch agronomist and United Nations official, Yrbk 1974

Borlaug, Norman, American plant pathologist and geneticist, July 1971, *Obit* Yrbk 2009

Boyd-Orr, John Boyd Orr, Scottish agriculturist, June 1946, *Obit* Sept 1971

Brooks, D. W., June 1951

Brossard, Edgar Bernard, July 1954

Brown, Lester Russell, American agriculturist and environmentalist, Jan 1993

Cardon, P. V., May 1954, *Obit* Yrbk 1965

Carver, George Washington, American botanist, Nov 1940, *Obit* Feb 1943

Davis, Wade, Canadian ethnobotanist, Jan 2003

Duggar, Benjamin Minge, botanist, Nov 1952, *Obit* Nov 1956

Earle, Sylvia A., American marine botanist, May 1972, May 1992

Fairchild, David, American plant pathologist and explorer, July 1953, *Obit* Oct 1954

Fujimori, Alberto, Peruvian president, Nov 1990

Gardiner, James Garfield, Canadian cabinet member, June 1956, *Obit* Mar 1962

Garst, Jonathan, Oct 1964

Garst, Roswell, agriculturist and banker, Apr 1964, *Obit* Jan 1978

Gilmore, John Washington, *Obit* Aug 1942

Harrar, J. George, Jan 1964, *Obit* June 1982

Heintzleman, B. Frank, June 1953, *Obit* Sept 1965

Jones, Monty, Sierra Leonen plant geneticist and rice breeder, Jan 2007

Lowdermilk, Walter, American soil scientist, Feb 1949, *Obit* July 1974

Mansholt, Sicco Leendert, May 1966

Matskevich, Vladimir Vladimirovich, Nov 1955

Murphy, Patricia, American restaurateur and horticulturist, Apr 1962

Newsom, Lee A., American paleoethnobotanist, Oct 2004

Pinchot, Gifford, American governor, forester and conservationist, *Obit* Nov 1946

Plotkin, Mark, American ethnobotanist, June 1997

Raven, Peter H., American botanist, Feb 1994

Robbins, William J., Feb 1956

Rodriguez, Eloy, botanist, May 2000

Rothschild, Miriam, British entomologist and botanist, Oct 1992, *Obit* Yrbk 2005

Rusby, Henry H., *Obit* Jan 1941

Schultes, Richard Evans, American botanist, Mar 1995, *Obit* Sept 2001

Sears, Paul Bigelow, botanist, July 1960

Sinnott, Edmund W., American botanist, Oct 1948, *Obit* Mar 1968

Stakman, Elvin Charles, American botanist, Yrbk 1949, *Obit* Mar 1979

True, Rodney Howard, *Obit* May 1940

Vo, Tong Xuan, Vietnamese agriculturist, Jan 2002

Wambugu, Florence, Kenyan plant geneticist, Jan 2004

Warne, William Elmo, land reclamation and irrigation specialist, Nov 1952, *Obit* May 1996

Watts, Lyle F., Oct 1946

Weyerhaeuser, Rudolph M., *Obit* Sept 1946

Yuan Longping, Chinese agriculturist, Jan 2005

Bounty hunters

Chapman, Duane Lee, American bounty hunter, Mar 2005

Bowlers

Carter, Don, American bowler, Mar 1963, *Obit* Yrbk 2012

Weber, Dick, American bowler, June 1970, *Obit* Yrbk 2005

Boxers (Persons)

Ali, Muhammad, American boxer, Sept 1963, Nov 1978

Barton, George A., American sportswriter, May 1953

Bowe, Riddick, American boxer, June 1996

Camacho, Hector, boxer, *Obit* Yrbk 2013

Carter, Rubin, American boxer and victim of false imprisonment, May 2000

Charles, Ezzard, American boxer, June 1949, *Obit* Aug 1975

Chavez, Julio Cesar, Mexican boxer, Apr 1999

Conn, Billy, American boxer, Aug 1941, *Obit* Aug 1993

Cotto, Miguel, Puerto Rican boxer, Feb 2008

De La Hoya, Oscar, American boxer, Jan 1997

Dempsey, Jack, American boxer, Feb 1945, *Obit* July 1983

Duran, Roberto, Panamanian boxer, Sept 1980

Eastman, Howard, Guyanese-English boxer, Jan 2003

Foreman, George, American boxer, May 1974, Aug 1995

Forrest, Vernon, American boxer, July 2002, *Obit* Yrbk 2009

Frazier, Joe, American boxer, Apr 1971, *Obit* Yrbk 2012

Hamed, Naseem, English boxer, Oct 1998

Hatton, Ricky, British boxer, Oct 2008

Hearns, Thomas, American boxer, Mar 1983

Holmes, Larry, American boxer, Aug 1981

Holyfield, Evander, American boxer, Aug 1993

Hopkins, Bernard, American boxer, Apr 2002

Jenkins, Lew, boxer, Jan 1941, *Obit* Yrbk 1991

Johansson, Ingemar, Swedish boxer, Nov 1959, *Obit* Yrbk 2009

Johnson, Jack, American boxer, *Obit* July 1946

Jones, Roy, American boxer, Feb 1999

Khan, Amir, British boxer, Jan 2006

Klitschko, Vitali, Ukrainian boxer, Jan 2003

Leonard, Sugar Ray, American boxer, Feb 1981

Lewin, Murray, *Obit* Sept 1943

Lewis, Lennox, British boxer, Jan 1999

Louis, Joe, American boxer, Oct 1940, *Obit* June 1981

Marciano, Rocky, American boxer, Sept 1952, *Obit* Nov 1969

Martin, Christy, American boxer, Oct 1997

Mayweather, Floyd, American boxer, Oct 2004

Moore, Archie, American boxer, Nov 1960, *Obit* Feb 1999

Mosley, Sugar Shane, American boxer, Jan 2001

Ouma, Kassim, Ugandan boxer, June 2007

Pacquiao, Manny, Filipino boxer, Jan 2007

Patterson, Floyd, American boxer, Oct 1960, *Obit* Yrbk 2007

Robinson, Sugar Ray, American boxer, Mar 1951, *Obit* June 1989

Tarver, Antonio, American boxer, June 2006

Taylor, Jermain, American boxer, Apr 2006

Taylor, Katie, July 2013

Trinidad, Felix, Puerto Rican boxer, Feb 2000

Tszyu, Kostya, Russian-Australian boxer, Jan 2002

Tunney, Gene, American boxer, Sept 1940, *Obit* Jan 1979

Turpin, Randy, British boxer, Sept 1951, *Obit* June 1966

Tyson, Mike, American boxer, Apr 1988

Valuev, Nikolay, Russian boxer, Jan 2007

Walcott, Jersey Joe, American boxer, June 1949, *Obit* May 1994

Wright, Winky, American boxer, July 2004

Boxing managers

Duva, Lou, American boxing manager and promoter, Nov 1999

Bridge engineers

Moisseiff, Leon S., American bridge engineer, *Obit* Oct 1943

Reed, James, naval and bridge engineer, *Obit* Sept 1941

Steinman, David Barnard, American bridge engineer, Yrbk 1957, *Obit* Nov 1960

Broadcasters

Abrams, J. J., American screenwriter and film director, July 2009

Abumrad, Jad, American radio producer and personality, Sept 2012

Aikman, Troy, American football player, May 1995

Allen, Debbie, American dancer, actress and director, Feb 1987

Allen, Marcus, American football player, Oct 1986

Allen, Mel, sportscaster, Oct 1950, *Obit* Aug 1996

Allen, Steve, American comedian and actor, July 1951, Mar 1982, *Obit* Jan 2001

Altman, Robert, American motion picture director and producer, Feb 1974, *Obit* Yrbk 2007

Amanpour, Christiane, British television reporter and moderator, Apr 1996

Andrews, Erin, American television sportscaster, Sept 2013

Arledge, Roone, American television executive, Feb 1977, *Obit* Apr 2003

Arnaz, Desi, Cuban-American television producer, band leader and actor, Sept 1952, *Obit* Feb 1987

Arnett, Peter, New Zealand television reporter, Nov 1991

Arraras, Maria Celeste, Puerto Rican television news anchor, Aug 2002

Attenborough, David, British television producer and personality, Apr 1983

Baitz, Jon Robin, American dramatist, Aug 2004

Ball, Alan, American film and television screenwriter and producer, Sept 2011

Banfield, Ashleigh, Canadian television newscaster, July 2002

Banks, Tyra, American model, actress and talk show host, Apr 2007

Barber, Red, sportscaster, July 1943, *Obit* Jan 1993

Barker, Bob, American game show host, Nov 1999

Barkley, Charles, American basketball player, Oct 1991

Barr, Roseanne, American comedienne, May 1989

Barris, Chuck, American television producer and personality, Mar 2005

Barry, Rick, American basketball player and sportscaster, Mar 1971

Barsamian, David, American radio program host, Mar 2007

Bartiromo, Maria, American television reporter, Nov 2003

Bates, Kathy, American actress, Sept 1991

Beatty, Bessie, radio commentator and journalist, Jan 1944, *Obit* Apr 1947

Bell, Art, American radio talk show host, Apr 2000

Bergeron, Tom, American television personality, Oct 2007

Berman, Chris, American television sportscaster, Aug 1998

Bernard, Michelle D., American journalist and political commentator, Sept 2011

Berton, Pierre, Canadian journalist and historian, Oct 1991, *Obit* Yrbk 2005

Bettis, Jerome, American football player, Aug 2006

Bishop, Joey, American comedian, Apr 1962, *Obit* Yrbk 2008

Blanc, Mel, American animated cartoon voice specialist, June 1976, *Obit* Sept 1989

Blitzer, Wolf, American television news anchor, Feb 2007

Bloodworth-Thomason, Linda, American television scriptwriter and producer, Feb 1993

Bochco, Steven, American television scriptwriter and producer, May 1991

Boone, Richard, Feb 1964, *Obit* Mar 1981

Borowitz, Andy, American humorist, July 2007

Bradley, Ed, American television reporter, May 1988, *Obit* Yrbk 2007

Bradley, Preston, Mar 1956

Brinkley, David, American television newscaster and moderator, Mar 1960, Sept 1987, *Obit* Sept 2003

Brinkley, John Richard, American physician and swindler, *Obit* July 1942

Broder, David S., American columnist and political commentator, Sept 2010, *Obit* Yrbk 2011

Brokaw, Tom, American television news anchor, May 1981, Nov 2002

Brokenshire, Norman, May 1950, *Obit* June 1965

Brooks, David, American journalist and political commentator, Apr 2004

Brooks, James L., American screenwriter, director and producer, Apr 1998

Brown, Aaron, American television news anchor, Mar 2003

Brown, Campbell, American television news anchor, Nov 2008

Brown, Cecil, radio newscaster, Mar 1942, *Obit* Jan 1988

Brown, Tony, American television talk show host and producer, Feb 1997

Brownlow, Kevin, English television producer and director, Mar 1992

Brzezinski, Mika, American television news anchor, July 2010

Bunim, Mary-Ellis, American television producer, May 2002, *Obit* Yrbk 2004

Burdett, Winston, radio reporters, Oct 1943, *Obit* July 1993

Burke, James, British science historian, Jan 2005

Burnett, Charles, American film director and screenwriter, Sept 1995

Burnett, Erin, American television news anchor, Sept 2012

Burnett, Mark, British television producer, May 2001

Burns, Ken, American documentary filmmaker, May 1992

Burnside, Iain, Scottish pianist, Jan 2004

Burrows, James, American television director, Oct 2006

Button, Dick, American figure skater and sportscaster, Mar 1949

Cafferty, Jack, American television newscaster, Oct 2008

Cain, Herman, American restaurant chain executive, radio talk show host and political commentator, Oct 2011

Carey, Drew, American comedian and game show host, Mar 1998

Carlson, Margaret, American journalist, Nov 2003

Carsey, Marcy, American television producer, Jan 1997

Carson, Johnny, American television talk show host, Jan 1964, Apr 1982, *Obit* July 2005

Carter, Boake, radio commentator, Jan 1942, *Obit* Yrbk 1947

Carville, James, American political consultant and commentator, Mar 1993

Cates, Gilbert, American film director, producer and college dean, Mar 1997, *Obit* Yrbk 2012

Cavett, Dick, American television talk show host, Oct 1970

Chancellor, John, American television news anchor and commentator, Jan 1962, Nov 1988, *Obit* Sept 1996

Chang, Juju, television reporter, Aug 2013

Chase, Chevy, American actor and comedian, Mar 1979

Chase, David, American television producer and scriptwriter, Mar 2001

Chavez, Linda, American policy scientist and commentator, Nov 1999

Chen, Steve S., American video sharing web site founder, Jan 2007

Cheney, Liz, American lawyer, political activist and daughter of Vice-president Richard B. Cheney, Aug 2010

Cherry, Don, Canadian hockey coach and sportscaster, Jan 2004

Chung, Connie, American television newscaster, July 1989

Clapper, Raymond, American journalist and radio commentator, Mar 1940, *Obit* Mar 1944

Clark, Dick, American television personality and producer, May 1959, Jan 1987, *Obit* Yrbk 2012

Clash, Kevin, American muppeteer, June 2000

Coe, Fred, television producer, Jan 1959, *Obit* June 1979

Cohn, Linda, American television sportscaster, Aug 2002

Collingwood, Charles, American radio and television reporter, June 1943, *Obit* Nov 1985

Collins, Gail, American columnist, Mar 1999

Cooke, Alistair, Anglo-American radio reporter and television personality, June 1952, May 1974, *Obit* Yrbk 2004

Cooney, Joan Ganz, American television executive, July 1970

Cooper, Anderson, American television news anchor and talk show host, June 2006

Cornelius, Don, American television program host and producer, *Obit* Yrbk 2012

Corwin, Norman, American radio and television scriptwriter and producer, Yrbk 1940, *Obit* Yrbk 2011

Cosell, Howard, American sportscaster, Nov 1972, *Obit* July 1995

Costas, Bob, American sportscaster, Jan 1993

Coughlin, Charles Edward, American priest and radio commentator, Sept 1940, *Obit* Jan 1980

Coulter, Ann, American television commentator, Sept 2003

Couric, Katie, American television news anchor, Mar 1993, Apr 2008

Craig, May, journalist, June 1949, *Obit* Sept 1975

Crittenden, Danielle, Canadian journalist, July 2003

Cronkite, Walter, American television news anchor, Jan 1956, Nov 1975, *Obit* Sept 2009

Crowley, Candy, American television reporter, Jan 2011

Crystal, Billy, American comedian and actor, Feb 1987

Cullen, Bill, television game show host, Jan 1960, *Obit* Sept 1990

Curry, Ann, American television newscaster, June 2004

Daly, Carson, American video jockey and talk show host, Nov 2009

Daly, John Charles, radio reporter and television moderator, May 1948, *Obit* May 1991

David, Larry, American comedian, television scriptwriter and producer, Aug 1998

Davidson, John, singer and actor, Sept 1976

Davis, Elmer, American radio commentator and short story writer, May 1940, *Obit* Sept 1958

Davis, Peter, American film and television producer and director, Feb 1983

De Varona, Donna, American sportscaster and swimmer, Aug 2003

DeGeneres, Ellen, American comedienne and talk show host, Apr 1996

Dean, Dizzy, American baseball player and sportscaster, Sept 1951, *Obit* Sept 1974

Delaney, Frank, Irish novelist and broadcaster, Jan 2005

Delilah, American radio talk show host, Apr 2005

Denny, George V., Sept 1940, Sept 1950, *Obit* Jan 1960

Dhaliwal, Daljit, English television newscaster, Nov 2000

Dickerson, Nancy, American television reporter, Sept 1962, *Obit* Jan 1998

Dionne, E. J., American columnist and political commentator, May 2006

Dobbs, Lou, American television newscaster, Nov 2006

Dobson, James C., American psychologist and social activist, Aug 1998

Donahue, Phil, American television talk show host, May 1980

Donaldson, Sam, American television newscaster, Sept 1987

Douglas, Mike, American television talk show host, May 1968, *Obit* Yrbk 2007

Drysdale, Don, American baseball player and sportscaster, Feb 1965, *Obit* Sept 1993

Dutton, Charles S., American actor and television director, Oct 2000

Edwards, Bob, American radio newscaster, Sept 2001

Edwards, Douglas, radio and television newscaster, Aug 1988, *Obit* Jan 1991

Edwards, Ralph, American television producer and personality, July 1943, *Obit* Yrbk 2006

Ellerbee, Linda, American television newscaster, Oct 1986

English, Diane, television author and producer, June 1993

Enright, Anne, Irish novelist and short story writer, Jan 2002

Ezarik, Justine, American webcaster, Mar 2013

Fadiman, Clifton, literary critic, editor and television moderator, May 1941, Oct 1955, *Obit* Sept 1999

Fager, Jeff, American television producer, Jan 2012

Fallon, Jimmy, American comedian, actor and talk show host, July 2002

Falwell, Jerry, American evangelist, Jan 1981, *Obit* Aug 2007

Ferguson, Craig, Scottish-American comedian, actor and talk show host, Jan 2005

Ferraro, Geraldine A., American lawyer, congresswoman, political commentator and vice-presidential candidate, Sept 1984, *Obit* Yrbk 2011

Fisher, Sterling, Yrbk 1940

Fitzgerald, Edward, radio talk show host, Apr 1947, *Obit* June 1982

Fitzgerald, Pegeen, radio talk show host, Apr 1947, *Obit* Apr 1989

Flannery, Harry W., Oct 1943

Fontana, Tom, American television producer and scriptwriter, Aug 2000

Ford, Harold, American financial executive and political commentator, Nov 1999

Frakes, Jonathan, actor and motion picture director, July 1999

Frank, Reuven, American journalist and television executive, June 1973, *Obit* Yrbk 2006

Frazier, Walt, American basketball player and sportscaster, Feb 1973

Frederick, John T., June 1941

Frederick, Pauline, American television reporter and commentator, Oct 1954, *Obit* July 1990

Friendly, Fred W., American broadcast news executive, Sept 1957, Aug 1987, *Obit* May 1998

Frost, David, English talk show host, July 1969, *Obit* Yrbk 2013

Funt, Allen, television producer and performer, Yrbk 1966, *Obit* Nov 1999

Gambling, John B., radio announcer, Mar 1950, *Obit* Jan 1975

Gammons, Peter, American sportswriter, June 2011

Garagiola, Joe, American sportscaster and baseball player, Jan 1976

Garofalo, Janeane, American comedienne and actress, Mar 2005

Garrels, Anne, American television and radio reporter, Mar 2004

Germond, Jack, American columnist and political commentator, July 2005

Gibson, Charles, American television news anchor, Sept 2002

Gibson, Mel, American actor and motion picture director, Apr 1984, Aug 2003

Gifford, Frank, American football player and sportscaster, May 1964, Jan 1995

Gifford, Kathie Lee, American singer and television personality, Nov 1994

Gladstone, Brooke, American radio reporter, Jan 2009

Goldberg, Whoopi, American actress, Mar 1985

Gondry, Michel, French film director, May 2007

Goodman, Julian, Feb 1967, *Obit* Yrbk 2012

Goodson, Mark, television producer, May 1978, *Obit* Feb 1993

Goodwin, Doris Kearns, American historian and television commentator, Nov 1997

Gordon, Dorothy, Jan 1955, *Obit* July 1970

Gordon, Ed, American television newscaster, July 2005

Gowdy, Curt, American television sportscaster, May 1967, *Obit* Yrbk 2006

Grade, Lew, British film and television producer, Aug 1979, *Obit* Mar 1999

Graham, Virginia, radio and television talk show host, Oct 1956, *Obit* Mar 1999

Granik, Samuel Theodore, Yrbk 1952, *Obit* Nov 1970

Grauer, Ben, Feb 1941, July 1959, *Obit* July 1977

Gray, Jim, American sportscaster, Jan 2011

Green, Tim, American football player, sportscaster and novelist, Aug 2000

Gregory, David, American television reporter and moderator, Oct 2010

Griffin, Merv, American talk show host and television producer, Sept 1967, *Obit* Yrbk 2007

Griffith, Andy, American actor, May 1960, *Obit* Yrbk 2012

Grodin, Charles, American actor, Nov 1995

Gumbel, Bryant, American television newscaster, July 1986

Gumbel, Greg, American television sportscaster, Sept 1996

Gupta, Sanjay, American neurosurgeon and television reporter, Aug 2006

Gurney, Chan, Oct 1950

Gwynn, Tony, American baseball player, Oct 1996

Haggis, Paul, Canadian screenwriter and film director, Aug 2006

Hagy, Ruth Geri, Oct 1957

Hall, Arsenio, American comedian and talk show host, Sept 1989

Hall, Josef Washington, journalist, historian and radio commentator, Yrbk 1944, *Obit* Jan 1961

Hanna, William, American animator and producer, July 1983, *Obit* Sept 2001

Hannity, Sean, American television moderator, Apr 2005

Hansen, Chris, American television reporter, June 2010

Hansen, Liane, American radio reporter and program host, May 2003

Harcourt, Nic, American disc jockey, Oct 2005

Harsch, Joseph C., American journalist, Oct 1944, *Obit* Aug 1998

Harvey, Paul, American radio reporter, Mar 1986, *Obit* Yrbk 2009

Heatter, Gabriel, radio commentator, Apr 1941, *Obit* May 1972

Heffner, Richard D., American historian and television moderator, Oct 1964

Helms, Jesse A., American senator, July 1979, *Obit* Yrbk 2008

Henner, Marilu, American actress, Feb 1999

Henreid, Paul, Austrian actor and director, July 1943, *Obit* June 1992

Hernandez, Keith, American baseball player and sportscaster, Feb 1988

Herskovitz, Marshall, American film and television producer, scriptwriter and director, Sept 2000

Hewitt, Don, American television producer, June 1988, *Obit* Yrbk 2009

Hill, Edwin Conger, journalist, Sept 1940, *Obit* Apr 1957

Hinojosa, Maria, American radio reporter and memoirist, Feb 2001

Hockenberry, John, radio and television reporter, Oct 1996

Hollenbeck, Don, American television newscaster, Feb 1951, *Obit* Sept 1954

Holtz, Lou, American football coach and sportscaster, June 1989

Hornung, Paul, American football player and sportscaster, Feb 1963

Horrocks, Brian, British general, Jan 1945, *Obit* Mar 1985

Howar, Barbara, columnist and television reporter, Aug 1989

Howe, Quincy, American journalist, Nov 1940, *Obit* Apr 1977

Huckabee, Mike, American talk show host and former governor, Nov 2005

Hudlin, Reginald, American film and television director, May 1999

Huffington, Arianna, Greek-American political adviser and commentator, July 1998

Hughes, Cathy, American radio executive, Feb 2000

Hughes, Paul, Yrbk 1943

Hunter-Gault, Charlayne, American television newscaster, Apr 1987

Huntley, Chet, American television news anchor, Oct 1956, *Obit* May 1974

Hurley, Chad, American video sharing web site founder, Jan 2007

Husain, Mishal, British television news anchor, Jan 2004

Husing, Ted, sportscaster, June 1942, *Obit* Oct 1962

Ifill, Gwen, American television newscaster and moderator, Sept 2005

Imus, Don, American radio talk show host, Feb 1996

Inskeep, Steve, American radio reporter, June 2009

Jackson, Hal, American disc jockey and radio executive, Oct 2002, *Obit* Yrbk 2012

Jarvis, Lucy, television producer, Apr 1972

Jean, Michaelle, Canadian broadcast journalist and governor general, June 2009

Jennings, Peter, Canadian television newscaster, Nov 1983, *Obit* Sept 2005

Johnson, Jimmy, American football coach and sportscaster, July 1994

Jones, Candy, model and talk show host, Oct 1961, *Obit* Mar 1990

Joyner, Tom, American radio talk show host, Sept 2002

Judd, Jackie, American television reporter, Sept 2002

Jurgensen, Sonny, American football player and sportscaster, June 1977

Kalb, Marvin, television reporter and college administrator, July 1987

Kaline, Al, American baseball player and sportscaster, Yrbk 1970

Kaltenborn, H. V., radio commentator, Aug 1940, *Obit* Sept 1965

Karim, Jawed, American video sharing web site founder, Jan 2007

Kasem, Casey, disc jockey, Nov 1997

Kasich, John R., American governor, Aug 1998

Keen, Andrew, British digital media critic, July 2013

Kelley, David E., American television scriptwriter and producer, May 1998

Kennedy, John B., Feb 1944, *Obit* Oct 1961

Khan, Daisy, American Islamic leader, June 2013

Killebrew, Harmon, American baseball player and sportscaster, Feb 1966, *Obit* Yrbk 2011

Kilpatrick, James J., American columnist, July 1980, *Obit* Yrbk 2010

Kimbrough, Emily, lecturer and author, Mar 1944, *Obit* Apr 1989

Kiner, Ralph, American baseball player and sportscaster, May 1954

King, Billie Jean, American tennis player, Yrbk 1967

King, John, American television news anchor, Mar 2010

King, Larry, American radio and television talk show host, May 1985

Kingdon, Frank, July 1944, *Obit* Apr 1972

Kinsley, Michael, American columnist and commentator, May 1995

Kiselyov, Yevgeny, Russian broadcast journalist and executive, Jan 2004

Komando, Kim, computer scientist and radio talk show host, Sept 2000

Koppel, Ted, American television newscaster, July 1984

Kopple, Barbara, American film and television director, July 1998

Kotb, Hoda, American television news anchor, Apr 2011

Krauthammer, Charles, American columnist, Jan 2008

Kristol, Irving, American political commentator, Sept 1974, *Obit* Nov 2009

Kristol, William, American political adviser, commentator and magazine editor, May 1997

Kroft, Steve, American television reporter, Nov 1996

Kuralt, Charles, American television newscaster, July 1981, *Obit* Sept 1997

Kurtz, Howard, American journalist, Jan 2011

LaFontaine, Don, American voice-over actor, Sept 2004, *Obit* Yrbk 2008

Lamb, Brian, American television executive and moderator, Feb 1995

Lampley, Jim, American sportscaster, Oct 2011

Landon, Michael, American actor, director and producer, July 1977, *Obit* Sept 1991

Leach, Robin, British television personality and producer, Sept 1990

Lear, Norman, American television scriptwriter and producer, Feb 1974

Lehrbas, Lloyd, June 1940, Apr 1950, *Obit* Jan 1965

Lehrer, Jim, American television newscaster, Jan 1987

Lemon, Don, American television news anchor, May 2010

Leno, Jay, American comedian and television talk show host, June 1988

Leonard, Bill, radio and television executive, Nov 1960, *Obit* Feb 1995

Lesueur, Larry, American radio newscaster, June 1943, *Obit* Yrbk 2003

Letterman, David, American comedian and television talk show host, Nov 1980, Oct 2002

Levesque, Rene, Canadian political leader, Jan 1975, *Obit* Jan 1988

Levine, Irving R., American television newscaster, July 1959, *Obit* Yrbk 2009

Lewis, Ananda, American television entertainment reporter, June 2005

Lewis, Fulton, radio commentator, Nov 1942, *Obit* Nov 1966

Liebman, Max, television producer and director, Apr 1953, *Obit* Sept 1981

Limbaugh, Rush, American radio and television commentator, Mar 1993

Lipton, James, American television interviewer, writer and producer, July 2011

Loach, Ken, British film and television director, July 1995

Logan, Lara, South African television reporter, July 2006

Lopez, George, American comedian, Mar 2010

Lumet, Sidney, American television and film director, Sept 1967, June 2005, *Obit* Yrbk 2011

Lynch, David, American film director and screenwriter, May 1987

MacNeil, Robert, Canadian television newscaster and novelist, Feb 1980

Mack, Nila, Yrbk 1952, *Obit* Mar 1953

Mack, Ted, Apr 1951, *Obit* Sept 1976

Madden, John, American football coach and sportscaster, Aug 1985

Maddow, Rachel, American television and radio talk show host, Aug 2009

Magliozzi, Ray, American automobile mechanic and radio talk show host, June 2006

Magliozzi, Tom, American automobile mechanic and radio talk show host, June 2006

Maher, Bill, American comedian and talk show host, July 1997

Malkin, Michelle, American journalist and political commentator, Apr 2010

Mann, Michael, American motion picture director and television producer, Jan 1993

Marino, Dan, American football player and television sportscaster, Jan 1989

Marshall, Garry, American television scriptwriter, producer and film director, Nov 1992

Marx, Groucho, American comedian, Mar 1948, Feb 1973, *Obit* Oct 1977

McBride, Mary Margaret, radio talk show host, Apr 1941, Mar 1954, *Obit* June 1976

McCarthy, Clem, radio sportscaster, Oct 1941, *Obit* July 1962

McCleery, Albert, Feb 1955, *Obit* July 1972

McCormick, William Patrick Glyn, *Obit* Yrbk 1940

McCrary, Tex, American journalist and talk show host, July 1953, *Obit* Yrbk 2003

McDonald, Trevor, British television news anchor, Sept 2010

McGee, Frank, television commentator and newscaster, June 1964, *Obit* June 1974

McGraw, Phillip C., American psychologist and television talk show host, June 2002

McKay, Jim, American television sportscaster, Oct 1973, *Obit* Yrbk 2008

McLain, Denny, American baseball player and radio talk show host, Jan 1969

McLaughlin, John, American television commentator and moderator, July 1987

McNamee, Graham, radio announcer, *Obit* July 1942

McNeill, Don, radio talk show host, July 1949, *Obit* Aug 1996

McWhirter, Norris, English sportswriter and sportscaster, Nov 1979, *Obit* Yrbk 2004

Meacham, Jon, American publishing executive and political commentator, June 2011

Merrill, John Douglas, *Obit* Jan 1940

Michaels, Lorne, Canadian television scriptwriter and producer, Aug 1999

Miller, John, American FBI official, Aug 2003

Miner, Worthington C., television producer, Feb 1953, *Obit* Mar 1983

Mizrahi, Isaac, American fashion designer and television personality, Jan 1991

Mol, John de, Dutch television producer, Jan 2004

Molinari, Susan, congresswoman and television newscaster, Mar 1996

Montagne, Renee, American radio reporter, Nov 2009

Montague, James J., *Obit* Feb 1942

Montgomery, Robert, actor and director, Jan 1948, *Obit* Nov 1981

Moore, Thomas W., American television executive, Sept 1967, *Obit* Yrbk 2007

Morgan, Edward Paddock, reporter and commentator, Apr 1964, *Obit* Mar 1993

Morgan, Joe, American baseball player and sportscaster, Sept 1984

Morgan, Piers, British talk show host, July 2012

Mudd, Roger, American television newscaster, Jan 1981

Murray, Jonathan, American television producer, May 2002

Murrow, Edward R., American radio and television newscaster, Feb 1942, Nov 1953, *Obit* June 1965

Myers, Dee Dee, American presidential press secretary and television moderator, Aug 1994

Myers, Joel Norman, American meteorologist, Apr 2005

Naipaul, V. S., Trinidadian novelist and journalist, July 1977

Namegabe, Chouchou, Congolese radio reporter, Apr 2012

Newby, P. H., English novelist and short story writer, Yrbk 1953

Newman, Edwin, American television reporter, commentator and moderator, Sept 1967, *Obit* Yrbk 2010

Noonan, Peggy, American presidential speechwriter and political writer, July 1990

Norris, Michele, American radio reporter, Mar 2008

Norton, Graham, Irish talk show host, Jan 2004

Norville, Deborah, American television reporter and radio talk show host, Apr 1990

Nyad, Diana, American swimmer and sportscaster, Aug 1979

O'Brien, Conan, American comedian and television talk show host, May 1996

O'Brien, Leo W., June 1959, *Obit* July 1982

O'Brien, Soledad, American television news anchor, Nov 2009

O'Donnell, Rosie, American comedienne, actress and talk show host, Aug 1995

O'Reilly, Bill, American television talk show host, Oct 2003

Olbermann, Keith, American television news anchor, Feb 2009

Oliver, Pam, American television sportscaster, July 2009

Olmos, Edward James, American actor, Aug 1992

Ophuls, Marcel, motion picture and television director, June 1977

Ortega, Kenny, American dancer, choreographer and director, Mar 2008

Ortiz Rocasolano, Letizia, Spanish television reporter and wife of Felipe, Prince of Spain, Jan 2004

Osbourne, Sharon, English musical talent agent and promoter, Jan 2001

Osteen, Joel, American pastor and broadcasting executive, Jan 2006

Paar, Jack, American television talk show host, Apr 1959, *Obit* Yrbk 2004

Page, Clarence, American columnist, Jan 2003

Parseghian, Ara, football coach and sportscaster, Feb 1968

Pauley, Jane, American television newscaster and talk show host, May 1980

Paxman, Jeremy, British television reporter and interviewer, Jan 2007

Pelley, Scott, American television news anchor, Aug 2011

Penn, Arthur, American film, theatrical and television director, Jan 1972, *Obit* Yrbk 2010

Perry, Tyler, American playwright, screenwriter, actor and director, June 2005

Philbin, Regis, American television talk show and game show host, Oct 1994

Phillips, Irna, American radio and television scriptwriter and producer, Apr 1943, *Obit* Feb 1974

Phillips, Kevin P., American political writer, Sept 1994

Phillips, Kyra, American television reporter, Jan 2013

Pinsky, Drew, American physician and talk show host, Feb 2011

Pippen, Scottie, American basketball player, Mar 1994

Pivot, Bernard, French television talk show host, Oct 1990

Podhoretz, Norman, American magazine editor and political commentator, Oct 1968

Poole, Lynn, Yrbk 1954, *Obit* June 1969

Powell, Dick, American actor, director and producer, Feb 1948, *Obit* Feb 1963

Pozner, Vladimir, Russian journalist, May 1943

Pratt, Jane, American magazine editor and talk show host, June 1999

Rafshoon, Gerald M., American television producer and advertising executive, July 1979

Ramos, Jorge, Mexican-American television news anchor, Mar 2004

Raphael, Sally Jessy, television talk show host, Feb 1990

Rather, Dan, American television newscaster, May 1975

Rattansi, Afshin, British journalist and novelist, Jan 2006

Ray, Rachael, American cook and television personality, Aug 2005

Reagan, Ron, American television personality and son of President Ronald Reagan, Feb 1992

Reasoner, Harry, American television newscaster, Feb 1966, *Obit* Oct 1991

Regan, Judith, American editor, publisher and talk show host, Sept 2000

Reiner, Carl, American producer, director, actor and screenwriter, Apr 1961

Rhodes, Randi, American radio talk show host, Feb 2005

Rich, Frank, American newspaper columnist, Apr 1999

Rivera, Geraldo, American television reporter and talk show host, May 1975

Rivers, Joan, American comedienne and television personality, Jan 1970, Mar 1987

Rizzuto, Phil, American sportscaster and baseball player, July 1950, *Obit* Yrbk 2007

Roberts, Cokie, American television reporter and moderator, May 1994

Roberts, Robin, American television news anchor, Feb 2008

Robertson, Pat, American evangelist and television executive, Sept 1987

Rockwell, Lew, American political commentator, June 2007

Rogers, Fred, American television performer and producer, July 1971, *Obit* July 2003

Rollin, Betty, American television reporter and writer, Aug 1994

Rose, Charlie, American television newscaster and talk show host, Jan 1995

Rote, Kyle, American football player and sportscaster, May 1965, *Obit* Yrbk 2002

Rountree, Martha, radio and television producer, Feb 1957, *Obit* Nov 1999

Rove, Karl, American political commentator and former presidential adviser, Oct 2000

Rowan, Carl Thomas, American newspaper columnist, Jan 1958, *Obit* Jan 2001

Rukeyser, Louis, American television moderator, Feb 1983, *Obit* Nov 2006

Russell, Ken, English motion picture director, Oct 1975, *Obit* Yrbk 2012

Russell, Mark, American political satirist, Mar 1981

Russert, Tim, American television news executive and moderator, Oct 1997, *Obit* Yrbk 2008

Saerchinger, Cesar, Apr 1940

Safer, Morley, Canadian television newscaster, July 1980

Sajak, Pat, American television game show host, July 1989

Salinger, Pierre, American journalist and presidential press secretary, July 1961, Mar 1987, *Obit* Feb 2005

Salomon, Henry, Yrbk 1956, *Obit* Apr 1958

Sanders, Deion, American football player and sportscaster, Jan 1995

Sanders, Marlene, television newscaster, Feb 1981

Santelli, Rick, American television reporter, July 2010

Saralegui, Cristina, American television talk show host, Jan 1999

Savitch, Jessica, television news anchor, Jan 1983, *Obit* Mar 1984

Sawyer, Diane, American television news anchor, Oct 1985

Scali, John A., American television newscaster and diplomat, Sept 1973, *Obit* Jan 1996

Scelsa, Vin, American disc jockey, May 2006

Schaap, Phil, American disc jockey and jazz historian, Sept 2001

Schaefer, George, television director and producer, Feb 1970, *Obit* Jan 1998

Scherer, Paul, May 1941, *Obit* May 1969

Schieffer, Bob, American television news anchor, Aug 2006

Schmidt, Harald, German talk show host, Jan 2006

Schoenbrun, David, American broadcast journalist, Jan 1960, *Obit* July 1988

Schorr, Daniel, American television reporter, Sept 1959, Feb 1978, *Obit* Yrbk 2010

Schuller, Robert Harold, American clergyman, June 1979

Schultz, Ed, American radio talk show host, Aug 2005

Scott, Stuart, American television sportscaster, Jan 2012

Scott, Willard, American television weathercaster, July 1989

Scully, Vin, American television sportscaster, Oct 2001

Seaver, Tom, American baseball player and sportscaster, Mar 1970

Secondari, John H., Apr 1967, *Obit* Apr 1975

Sevareid, Eric, reporter and commentator, July 1942, Oct 1966, *Obit* Aug 1992

Shapiro, Neal, American television producer and executive, May 2003

Shaw, Bernard, American television newscaster, Feb 1995

Sherman, Allan, television performer and comedian, Sept 1966, *Obit* Jan 1974

Shields, Mark, American political commentator and columnist, May 2005

Shirer, William L., American journalist, July 1941, May 1962, *Obit* Feb 1994

Short, Martin, Canadian comedian and actor, Sept 1992

Shriver, Maria, American television newscaster and wife of Arnold Schwarzenegger, Nov 1991

Siegel, Robert, American radio newscaster, July 2008

Silva, Daniel, American television producer and novelist, Apr 2007

Silverman, Fred, television executive, Nov 1978

Simms, Phil, American football player and sportscaster, Oct 1994

Simon, David, American journalist and television scriptwriter, June 2008

Simpson, Carole, American television newscaster, Nov 1999

Simpson, John, British television reporter, June 2010

Simpson, O. J., American football player and sportscaster, Apr 1969

Singer, Bryan, American motion picture director, Apr 2005

Smiley, Tavis, American radio talk show host, Apr 2003

Smith, Howard K., American television newscaster and commentator, Mar 1943, July 1976, *Obit* Aug 2002

Smith, Ozzie, American baseball player, Feb 1997

Snow, Tony, American television moderator, commentator and presidential press secretary, Sept 2006, *Obit* Yrbk 2008

Snyder, Tom, American radio and television talk show host, June 1980, *Obit* Yrbk 2007

Soares, Jo, Brazilian television talk show host, novelist and actor, Jan 2002

Spelling, Aaron, American television producer, May 1986, *Obit* Yrbk 2006

Spivak, Lawrence E., television moderator, May 1956, *Obit* May 1994

Stahl, Lesley, television reporter, June 1996

Stamberg, Susan, American radio newscaster, Oct 2008

Steel, Johannes, radio commentator and columnist, June 1941, *Obit* Feb 1989

Stein, Benjamin, American writer and actor, Sept 2001

Stephanopoulos, George, American television news anchor, Jan 1995

Stern, Bill, sportscaster, June 1941, *Obit* Jan 1972

Stevens, George, American film and television producer, Yrbk 1965

Stewart, Jon, American comedian and talk show host, July 2004

Stokes, Carl, American mayor, judge and newscaster, Apr 1968, *Obit* June 1996

Stokes, Thomas Lunsford, May 1947, *Obit* Sept 1958

Stookey, Charley, Jan 1940

Stowe, Leland, journalist, July 1940, *Obit* Mar 1994

Stringer, Howard, American electronics, film and broadcasting industry executive, Jan 2006

Sununu, John, American governor and presidential adviser, May 1989

Susskind, David, American television producer, May 1960, *Obit* Apr 1987

Swing, Raymond, radio commentator, Jan 1940, *Obit* Feb 1969

Taylor, M. Sayle, *Obit* Mar 1942

TerHorst, Jerald F., American presidential press secretary, Feb 1975, *Obit* Yrbk 2010

Terkel, Studs, American interviewer and historian, Nov 1974, *Obit* Yrbk 2009

Thicke, Alan, Canadian television author, producer and actor, June 1987

Thomas, Danny, American comedian, Feb 1959, *Obit* Apr 1991

Thomas, Lowell, American radio newscaster, May 1940, Jan 1952, *Obit* Oct 1981

Tinker, Grant, American television executive, Mar 1982

Tinney, Cal, Feb 1943

Tors, Ivan Lawrence, Hungarian animal trainer and motion picture producer, Feb 1969, *Obit* Aug 1983

Totenberg, Nina, American radio and television reporter, Mar 1996

Trabert, Tony, American tennis player and sportscaster, July 1954

Tridish, Pete, American pirate radio broadcaster and social activist, Apr 2004

Trout, Robert, American radio and television reporter, Oct 1965, *Obit* Jan 2001

Uygur, Cenk, Turkish-American radio talk show host, May 2013

Vandercook, John W., Apr 1942, *Obit* Feb 1963

Vanocur, Sander, Jan 1963

Vargas, Elizabeth, American television news anchor, Apr 2006

Ventura, Jesse, American wrestler and governor, May 1999

Venturi, Ken, American golfer and sportscaster, Apr 1966, *Obit* Yrbk 2013

Vieira, Meredith, American television newscaster, Apr 2002

Visser, Lesley, American television sportscaster, Apr 2007

Vitale, Dick, American basketball sportscaster, Jan 2005

Wallace, Chris, American television reporter and moderator, Feb 2011

Wallace, Mike, American television newscaster, July 1957, Nov 1977, *Obit* Yrbk 2012

Wallin, Pamela, Canadian television newscaster and talk show host, Jan 2005

Walsh, J. Raymond, Nov 1946

Walters, Barbara, American television newscaster, Feb 1971, Feb 2003

Walton, Bill, American basketball player and sportscaster, Mar 1977

Wattenberg, Ben J., American political analyst and writer, June 1985

Watts, J. C., American congressman, management consultant and political commentator, Mar 1999

Wayans, Keenen Ivory, American actor, screenwriter and director, Feb 1995

Webb, Jack, American actor and producer, May 1955, *Obit* Mar 1983

Webb, Maurice, May 1950, *Obit* Sept 1956

Wertheimer, Linda, radio newscaster, Nov 1995

Westheimer, Ruth, American psychotherapist, Jan 1987

Westin, Av, Aug 1975

Weyrich, Paul, American political activist and commentator, Feb 2005, *Obit* Yrbk 2009

Wile, Frederic William, journalist and radio commentator, *Obit* June 1941

Will, George F., American columnist and political commentator, Sept 1981

Williams, Armstrong, American newspaper columnist and radio talk show host, May 2004

Williams, Brian, American television news anchor, July 1998

Williams, Juan, American journalist, May 2008

Williams, Wendy, American talk show host, Oct 2009

Wilmore, Larry, American television scriptwriter and producer, Nov 2007

Winchell, Walter, American columnist and radio commentator, June 1943, *Obit* Apr 1972

Winfrey, Oprah, American television talk show host, Mar 1987

Winkler, Henry, American actor and producer, Sept 1976

Wolper, David L., American film and television producer, Oct 1986, *Obit* Yrbk 2010

Woodruff, Judy, American television newscaster, Sept 1986

Yang Lan, Chinese talk show host, Jan 2003

Yates, David, British film director, Apr 2011

Young, Marian, June 1952, *Obit* Jan 1974

Zahn, Paula, American television newscaster, Feb 2002

Zakaria, Fareed, Indian-American political scientist and journalist, Jan 2003

Zucker, Jeff, American motion picture and television executive, Jan 2002

Broadcasting engineers

Arco, Georg, German radio engineer, *Obit* Jan 1940

Armstrong, Edwin Howard, American radio engineer and inventor, Apr 1940, *Obit* Mar 1954

Ballantine, Stuart, American radio engineer, *Obit* June 1944

Breazeal, Cynthia, American electronics engineer and inventor, June 2011

De Forest, Lee, American radio engineer, May 1941, *Obit* Oct 1961

Dubilier, William, Sept 1957, *Obit* Oct 1969

Engstrom, Elmer W., electronics engineer and executive, Yrbk 1951, *Obit* Feb 1985

Goldmark, Peter Carl, American physicist and television engineer, Nov 1940, Yrbk 1950, *Obit* Feb 1978

Guy, Raymond F., May 1950

Hounsfield, Godfrey Newbold, British electronics engineer, Mar 1980, *Obit* Yrbk 2004

Kaspersky, Natalya, Russian information technology executive, Jan 2005

Liu Chuanzhi, Chinese computer industry executive, Jan 2006

McNeely, Eugene J., Nov 1962, *Obit* Feb 1974

Nakamura, Shuji, Japanese electronics engineer and inventor, Jan 2006

Nipkow, Paul Gottlieb, German television pioneer, *Obit* Oct 1940

O'Neill, Eugene F., American electronics engineer, Apr 1963

Ramo, Simon, American electronics industry executive, Apr 1958

Watson-Watt, Robert Alexander, British radio engineer and physicist, Sept 1945, *Obit* Jan 1974

Wirth, Niklaus, Swiss computer scientist, Jan 2003

Wooldridge, Dean Everett, American physicist and electronics engineer, Apr 1958, *Obit* Yrbk 2007

Wozniak, Stephen, American electronics industry executive, July 1997

Zworykin, Vladimir Kosma, American physicist, Yrbk 1949, *Obit* Sept 1982

Broadcasting executives

Ailes, Roger, American political campaign consultant and television news executive, Jan 1989

Arledge, Roone, American television executive, Feb 1977, *Obit* Apr 2003

Assis Chateaubriand, Brazilian newspaper and broadcasting executive, June 1957

Aubrey, James T., American television and motion picture executive, Mar 1972, *Obit* Nov 1994

Autry, Gene, American cowboy singer, actor and baseball executive, Yrbk 1947, *Obit* Jan 1999

Backe, John David, Apr 1978

Barsamian, David, American radio program host, Mar 2007

Berlusconi, Silvio, Italian prime minister, Aug 1994

Bewkes, Jeffrey L., American mass media executive, Nov 2010

Bloomberg, Michael, American mayor, June 1996, Mar 2002

Brill, Steven, American lawyer, journalist and television executive, Nov 1997

Buckley, James L., American senator and judge, Oct 1971

Cadogan, Alexander, British diplomat, Oct 1944, *Obit* Sept 1968

Case, Steve, American mass media executive, Oct 1996

Chalk, O. Roy, American transportation and communications executive, Nov 1971, *Obit* Feb 1996

Chasins, Abram, American pianist and composer, Feb 1960, *Obit* Aug 1987

Chester, Edmund, Mar 1941

Cisneros, Henry, American urban development organization official, broadcasting executive and former Secretary of housing and urban development, Aug 1987

Collier, Sophia, American television and Internet service executive, July 2002

Cooney, Joan Ganz, American television executive, July 1970

Cowles, Gardner, American publisher, June 1943, *Obit* Aug 1985

Cuban, Mark, American broadcasting and basketball executive, Mar 2001

Cuthbert, Margaret, May 1947, *Obit* Oct 1968

Davis, Martin S., motion picture, television and publishing executive, Nov 1989, *Obit* Jan 2000

Denny, Charles R., May 1947

Depinet, Ned E., June 1950

Diller, Barry, American motion picture and television executive, Apr 1986

Dubuc, Nancy, American television executive, May 2012

Duggan, Ervin S., public broadcasting executive, Oct 1998

Dyke, Greg, British broadcasting executive, Jan 2002

Ebersol, Dick, American television executive, July 1996

Erikson, Leonard F., Oct 1953

Fellows, Harold E., Feb 1952, *Obit* May 1960

Fili-Krushel, Patricia, television executive, Nov 1999

Folsom, Frank M., Feb 1949, *Obit* Mar 1970

Ford, Frederick W., government official, Nov 1960, *Obit* Sept 1986

Fowler, Mark S., government official, Mar 1986

Frank, Reuven, American journalist and television executive, June 1973, *Obit* Yrbk 2006

Fraser, Robert, British television executive, Oct 1956

Freston, Tom, American television executive, Aug 2003

Friendly, Fred W., American broadcast news executive, Sept 1957, Aug 1987, *Obit* May 1998

Fry, Kenneth D., Apr 1947

Fuchs, Michael Joseph, cable television executive, Feb 1996

Gartner, Michael G., newspaper editor, May 1990

Gary, Willie, American lawyer, Apr 2001

Goldenson, Leonard H., radio and television executive, Sept 1957, *Obit* May 2000

Greene, Hugh, English radio and television executive, Sept 1963, *Obit* Apr 1987

Griffin, R. Allen, American newspaper publisher, Feb 1951

Gurney, Chan, Oct 1950

Hagerty, James C., American journalist and presidential aide, Mar 1953, *Obit* June 1981

Haley, William, English newspaper editor and broadcasting executive, Apr 1948, *Obit* Oct 1987

Hammer, Bonnie, American television executive, Apr 2006

Harlech, William David Ormsby Gore, British statesman and diplomat, Mar 1961, *Obit* Mar 1985

Hughes, Cathy, American radio executive, Feb 2000

Ingles, Harry C., American general, Nov 1947

Isaacson, Walter, American broadcasting executive, Nov 2013

Jackson, Hal, American disc jockey and radio executive, Oct 2002, *Obit* Yrbk 2012

Johnson, Robert Louis, American television and basketball executive, Apr 1994

Johnson, Sheila Crump, American broadcasting executive and philanthropist, June 2007

Jordan, Michael H., American information technology executive, Feb 1998, *Obit* Yrbk 2010

Judson, Arthur, orchestra manager, Aug 1945, *Obit* Mar 1975

Karmazin, Mel, American broadcasting executive, May 2000

Kerger, Paula, American broadcasting executive, July 2013

Kintner, Robert E., radio and television executive, Oct 1950, *Obit* Feb 1981

Kirch, Leo, German broadcasting executive, Jan 2002, *Obit* Yrbk 2011

Kirkpatrick, Ivone, June 1950, *Obit* July 1964

Kiselyov, Yevgeny, Russian broadcast journalist and executive, Jan 2004

Kluge, John W., American broadcasting and telecommunications executive, Sept 1993, *Obit* Yrbk 2010

Kobak, Edgar, Apr 1947, *Obit* July 1962

Lamb, Brian, American television executive and moderator, Feb 1995

Laybourne, Geraldine, American broadcasting executive, Apr 1999

Lee, Debra, American broadcasting executive, June 2006

Leonard, Bill, radio and television executive, Nov 1960, *Obit* Feb 1995

Li Yifei, Chinese television executive, Jan 2006

Liu, Changle, Jan 2002

Lyne, Susan, American media executive, Feb 2012

Malone, John C., American broadcasting executive, Aug 1995

Manji, Irshad, Canadian author and broadcasting entrepreneur, Jan 2005

Maphai, Vincent, South African political scientist and broadcasting executive, Jan 2003

Markell, Jack, American governor, July 2011

Mays, Lowry, American broadcasting executive, Aug 2003

McConnell, Joseph H., radio and television executive, Nov 1950, *Obit* May 1997

McDonald, Eugene F., Oct 1949, *Obit* Oct 1958

McGannon, Donald H., radio and television executive, Feb 1971, *Obit* July 1984

McGrath, Judy, American broadcasting executive, Feb 2005

Messier, Jean-Marie, French mass media industry executive, May 2002

Miller, Justin, Jan 1947, *Obit* Mar 1973

Minor, Halsey, American media and computer software executive, Oct 1998

Mitchell, Patricia Edenfield, American television executive, Aug 2005

Moore, Thomas W., American television executive, Sept 1967, *Obit* Yrbk 2007

Munyama, Gerry, Namibian broadcasting executive, Jan 2004

Murdoch, Rupert, Australian-American publishing, motion picture and television executive, May 1977

Naegle, Susan, American television executive, May 2013

Nagin, Ray, American mayor, Jan 2006

Nessen, Ron, American presidential press secretary and public relations executive, Jan 1976

Newhouse, Samuel I., American newspaper publisher and broadcasting executive, Mar 1961, *Obit* Oct 1979

Newsom, Carroll Vincent, college president, Apr 1957, *Obit* Apr 1990

Noble, Edward J., American candy and broadcasting executive, Jan 1944, *Obit* Mar 1959

Norman, Christina, American broadcasting executive, Nov 2007

O'Konski, Alvin E., congressman, Nov 1955, *Obit* Aug 1987

O'Neil, Thomas F., broadcasting executive, Nov 1955, *Obit* June 1998

Pace, Frank, American Secretary of the army, Feb 1950, *Obit* Feb 1988

Packer, Kerry Francis Bullmore, Australian newspaper publisher, Jan 2004, *Obit* CB Int 2006

Paley, William S., American radio and television executive, Oct 1940, Yrbk 1951, *Obit* Jan 1991

Parsons, Richard D., American motion picture and broadcasting executive, Apr 2003

Pittman, Bob, American television and online computer services executive, July 2000

Rapaczynski, Wanda, Polish broadcasting executive, Jan 2004

Redstone, Sumner, American motion picture and broadcasting executive, Jan 1996

Reith, John Charles Walsham Reith, Scottish broadcasting executive, Nov 1940, *Obit* July 1971

Roberts, Michael, American telecommunications, real estate and publishing executive, Feb 2010

Roberts, Steven, American real estate, broadcasting and telecommunications executive, Feb 2010

Robertson, Pat, American evangelist and television executive, Sept 1987

Russert, Tim, American television news executive and moderator, Oct 1997, *Obit* Yrbk 2008

Salant, Richard S., television executive, Nov 1961, *Obit* Apr 1993

Sambrook, Richard, British broadcasting executive, Jan 2003

Sarnoff, David, American radio and television executive, Nov 1940, Oct 1951, *Obit* Feb 1972

Sassa, Scott Michael, American Internet executive, Jan 2000

Scannell, Herb, American broadcasting executive, Aug 2010

Schechter, A. A., broadcasting executive, May 1941, *Obit* Aug 1989

Schiller, Vivian, American radio executive, Oct 2009

Seaton, Fred A., American newspaper publisher and Secretary of the interior, Nov 1956, *Obit* Mar 1974

Shakespeare, Frank, Sept 1970

Shapiro, Neal, American television producer and executive, May 2003

Shoriki, Matsutaro, Japanese newspaper publisher, broadcasting executive and government official, Feb 1958

Silverman, Fred, television executive, Nov 1978

Simmons, Russell, American recording, motion picture and broadcasting executive, June 1998

Stanton, Frank, American broadcasting executive, Nov 1945, Oct 1965, *Obit* Yrbk 2007

Stewart, Martha, American cook, author and mass media executive, Aug 1993

Stoddard, Brandon, television executive, Feb 1989

Straus, Nathan, May 1944, *Obit* Nov 1961

Streibert, Theodore C., American government official and broadcasting executive, Feb 1955, *Obit* Mar 1987

Stringer, Howard, American electronics, film and broadcasting industry executive, Jan 2006

Sutton, Percy E., American municipal official, broadcasting executive and civil rights activist, Mar 1973, *Obit* Yrbk 2010

Sweeney, Anne, American television executive, June 2003

Tartikoff, Brandon, American television and motion picture executive, Apr 1987, *Obit* Nov 1997

Taylor, John W., American college president, television executive and United Nations official, Jan 1954, *Obit* Apr 2002

Thomas-Graham, Pamela, American clothing industry executive and mystery novelist, July 2000

Tian Congming, Chinese broadcasting and news agency official, Jan 2005

Tinker, Grant, American television executive, Mar 1982

Tisch, Laurence A., American financier, Feb 1987, *Obit* Yrbk 2004

Titterton, Lewis H., Sept 1943

Trammell, Niles, Sept 1940, *Obit* May 1973

Van Schmus, W. G., *Obit* Mar 1942

Van Volkenburg, Jack Lamont, Jan 1955, *Obit* July 1963

Weaver, Pat, American television executive, Jan 1955, *Obit* Sept 2002

Whitaker, Mark, American television news executive, Aug 2003

White, Frank, Yrbk 1950, *Obit* Jan 1980

White, John F., American television executive and college president, Nov 1967, *Obit* Yrbk 2005

White, Paul Welrose, journalist and radio executive, Mar 1940, *Obit* Oct 1955

Whittle, Christopher, American publishing, broadcasting and school management company executive, Feb 1991

Wilder, Frances Farmer, July 1947

Wong, Andrea, American broadcasting executive, Sept 2007

Wood, Robert D., Yrbk 1974, *Obit* July 1986

Woods, Mark, American broadcasting executive, Mar 1946

Wright, Robert Charles, American television executive, Jan 1989

Wyman, Thomas, American radio and television executive, June 1983, *Obit* Yrbk 2003

Zorbaugh, Geraldine Bone, lawyer and broadcasting executive, Yrbk 1956, *Obit* Sept 1996

Zucker, Jeff, American motion picture and television executive, Jan 2002

Buddhist leaders

Dalai Lama, Tibetan religious and political leader (deposed 1959), July 1951, June 1982

Thurman, Robert A. F., American Buddhist leader, Sept 1997

Ugyen Trinley Dorje, Tibetan lama, Jan 2004

Buddhist monks

Ugyen Trinley Dorje, Tibetan lama, Jan 2004

Bullfighters

Cordobes, Jan 1966

Dominguin, Spanish bullfighter, Mar 1972, *Obit* July 1996

El Juli, Spanish bullfighter, Jan 2002

Evans, Frank, British bullfighter, Jan 2005

Ponce, Enrique, Spanish bullfighter, Jan 2003

Business organization officials

Bannow, Rudolph F., American manufacturing executive, Yrbk 1960, *Obit* Sept 1962

Bennett, Wallace F., American senator, Feb 1949, *Obit* Feb 1994

Benson, John, American advertising executive, Apr 1940, *Obit* Nov 1962

Bimson, Carl A., American banker, Mar 1961

Borden, Neil H., American marketing association executive and business teacher, May 1954

Breen, Joseph Ignatius, American motion picture censor and association executive, July 1950, *Obit* Jan 1966

Bunting, Earl, American manufacturing association official, Feb 1947

Dodd, Christopher J., American motion picture association executive and former senator, Oct 1989

Fuller, Walter Deane, American publishing executive, Mar 1941, *Obit* Jan 1965

Kohler, Horst, German president, Jan 2002

Rometty, Virginia, American marketing executive, June 2012

Schroeder, Patricia, American publishing association executive and former congresswoman, Oct 1978

Trowbridge, Alexander B., American Secretary of commerce, Mar 1968, *Obit* Yrbk 2006

Tukur, Alhaji Bamanga, Nigerian business organization official, Jan 2004

Wason, Robert R., American manufacturing industry association executive, Jan 1946, *Obit* Sept 1950

Ziegler, Ronald L., American drug store association executive and presidential press secretary, Nov 1971, *Obit* July 2003

Business teachers

Borden, Neil H., American marketing association executive and business teacher, May 1954

Kanter, Rosabeth Moss, American management consultant, teacher and writer, May 1996

Kao, John J., American management consultant, Oct 2008

McGovern, Gail, American Red Cross official, Mar 2010

Businesspeople

Abbott, Robert S., American newspaper publisher, *Obit* Mar 1940

Abelson, Nat, American clothing industry executive, Nov 1957

Abramovich, Roman, Russian energy industry executive and provincial governor, Jan 2004

Abrams, Harry N., American publisher, June 1958, *Obit* Jan 1980

Abrams, Jonathan, Canadian Internet software developer and entrepreneur, Apr 2006

Abramson, Jill, American newspaper executive, Sept 2011

Achatz, Grant, American chef and restaurateur, Jan 2011

Adams, Ernie, American football executive, Jan 2009

Adelson, Jay, American information technology executive, June 2012

Adler, Harry Clay, American newspaper executive, *Obit* Apr 1940

Adler, Julius Ochs, American newspaper executive, June 1948, *Obit* Yrbk 1956

Adria, Ferran, Spanish chef and restaurateur, Jan 2006

Aga Khan, Swiss Islamic leader and financier, Mar 1960, Jan 2004

Agassi, Shai, Israeli entrepreneur, Sept 2010

Agnelli, Giovanni, Italian automobile executive, Jan 1972, *Obit* June 2003

Ahrents, Angela, American clothing industry executive, May 2012

Aigner-Clark, Julie, American child development products company founder, Jan 2002

Ailes, Roger, American political campaign consultant and television news executive, Jan 1989

Akers, John F., computer industry executive, May 1988

Al-Rajhi, Sulaiman Abdel-Aziz, Saudi Arabian financier, Jan 2006

Alberti, Jules, American advertising executive, July 1959

Alexander, Willis W., American banker and newspaper publisher, July 1969, *Obit* Jan 1986

Allen, Paul, American computer software executive and investor, July 1998

Allen, William M., American aircraft industry executive, Mar 1953, *Obit* Jan 1986

Allyn, Stanley C., American cash register company executive, Mar 1956, *Obit* Yrbk 1970

Alpert, George, railroad executive and lawyer, Sept 1961, *Obit* Oct 1988

Alwaleed bin Talal al Saud, Saudi Arabian entrepreneur and financier, Jan 2006

Ambani, Anil, Indian telecommunications, textile and chemical conglomerate executive, Feb 2009

Ambani, Mukesh, Indian telecommunications, textile and chemical conglomerate executive, June 2009

Amdahl, Gene M., American electrical engineer and computer executive, Aug 1982

Amory, Derick Heathcoat Amory, British textile industry executive and cabinet member, Apr 1958

Amos, Wally, American baking industry executive, July 1995

Anderson, Frederick L., American general, May 1944, *Obit* Apr 1969

Anderson, Ray C., American carpet industry executive, May 2005, *Obit* Yrbk 2012

Anderson, Robert Orville, American petroleum industry executive, Sept 1982, *Obit* Yrbk 2008

Anderson, Roy A., American aerospace executive, Aug 1983, *Obit* Mar 2004

Anderson, Tom, American Internet executive, July 2007

Andreas, Dwayne O., food industry executive, Mar 1992

Andreessen, Marc, American computer programmer and software executive, June 1997

Andr,s, Jos,, Spanish chef and restaurateur, June 2013

Annenberg, Walter H., American magazine and newspaper publisher, diplomat and philanthropist, Jan 1970, *Obit* Jan 2003

Ansari, Anousheh, Iranian-American information technology executive, Jan 2005

Antinori, Piero, Italian vintner, Jan 2006

Aoki, Rocky, American restaurant chain executive, June 2005, *Obit* Yrbk 2008

Appleton, Edward Dale, American publishing executive, *Obit* Mar 1942

Appleton, Robert, American publishing executive, *Obit* Mar 1945

Aramburuzabala, Maria Asuncion, Mexican brewing executive, Jan 2002

Araskog, Rand V., telecommunications executive, Nov 1991

Arden, Elizabeth, American cosmetician, July 1957, *Obit* Yrbk 1966

Arledge, Roone, American television executive, Feb 1977, *Obit* Apr 2003

Armand, Louis, French railroad executive, Sept 1957, *Obit* Oct 1971

Armstrong, C. Michael, American telecommunications executive, June 1999

Arnault, Bernard, French manufacturing executive, June 1998

Arnstein, Daniel, American taxi executive, Mar 1942

Aronson, Louis V., American inventor, manufacaturing executive and banker, *Obit* Yrbk 1940

Arrington, Michael, American Internet executive, July 2012

Arzak, Juan Mari, Spanish chef and restaurateur, Jan 2007

Ascoli, Max, American political scientist and magazine editor, Feb 1954, *Obit* Mar 1978

Ash, Mary Kay, American cosmetics executive, May 1995, *Obit* Feb 2002

Ash, Roy, American presidential adviser and manufacturing executive, July 1968, *Obit* Yrbk 2012

Ashbrook, John M., American congressman, Oct 1973, *Obit* June 1982

Ashwell, Rachel, British interior designer and home furnishings retailer, Oct 2004

Assis Chateaubriand, Brazilian newspaper and broadcasting executive, June 1957

Astor of Hever, John Jacob Astor, British newspaper publisher, May 1954, *Obit* Sept 1971

Atkins, Chet, American guitarist and record industry executive, Jan 1975, *Obit* Sept 2001

Attwood, William, diplomat, publisher and author, Jan 1968, *Obit* July 1989

Aubrey, James T., American television and motion picture executive, Mar 1972, *Obit* Nov 1994

Auerbach, Red, American basketball executive, Feb 1969, *Obit* Yrbk 2007

Augstein, Rudolf, German magazine publisher, June 1966, *Obit* Jan 2003

Augustine, Norman R., aerospace executive, June 1998

Austin, Herbert Austin, English automobile executive, *Obit* July 1941

Avery, Sewell, American manufacturing and retail executive, June 1944, *Obit* Jan 1961

Ba, Amadou Mahtar, Senegalese multi-media content service provider executive, Jan 2004

Bache, Jules Semon, financier and art collector, *Obit* May 1944

Backe, John David, Apr 1978

Backstrand, C. J., American manufacturing executive, Feb 1954, *Obit* Yrbk 1968

Baehr, George, American physician and health insurance executive, May 1942

Bailar, Benjamin F., American chemical industry executive and Postmaster general, July 1976

Bailey, Abe, South African financier and political leader, *Obit* Sept 1940

Baillie, Hugh, American reporter and news agency executive, Feb 1946, *Obit* Mar 1966

Bajaj, Rahul, Indian automobile executive, Jan 2007

Baker, Asa George, American publishing executive, *Obit* Oct 1940

Baker, George Theodore, American airline executive, June 1953, *Obit* Jan 1964

Baker, Melvin H., American constructon materials industry executive, Feb 1960

Baker, Mitchell, American Internet executive, Apr 2009

Balaban, Barney, American motion picture executive, Oct 1946, *Obit* Apr 1971

Baldauf, Sari, Finnish cellular telephone equipment industry executive, Jan 2004

Balderston, William, radio equipment industry executive, Sept 1949, *Obit* Oct 1983

Baldrige, Malcolm, American Secretary of commerce, Aug 1982, *Obit* Sept 1987

Ball, Stuart S., American retail executive, July 1952

Ballantine, Ian, publisher, May 1954, *Obit* May 1995

Banda, Joyce, Malawian entrepreneur, educator and social activist, Apr 2013

Banning, Kendall, American magazine editor, publisher and military writer, *Obit* Feb 1945

Bannow, Rudolph F., American manufacturing executive, Yrbk 1960, *Obit* Sept 1962

Barad, Jill E., American toy industry executive, Sept 1995

Barnard, Chester Irving, American telephone executive and foundation official, Mar 1945, *Obit* Sept 1961

Barnes, Albert Coombs, American chemist and pharmaceutical executive, Mar 1945, *Obit* Sept 1951

Barnes, Brenda, American food industry executive, May 2006

Barnes, William R., American publisher and bookseller, *Obit* Mar 1945

Barr, John A., American lawyer and college dean, Jan 1961, *Obit* Mar 1979

Barrett, Clifton Waller, American shipping executive and book collector, Mar 1965

Barrett, Craig, American semiconductor industry executive, Mar 1999

Barton, Bruce, American advertising executive, religious writer and congressman, Feb 1961, *Obit* Oct 1967

Barton, Robert B. M., games industry executive, Apr 1959, *Obit* Apr 1995

Bartz, Carol A., American computer software executive, July 1999

Baruch, Bernard Mannes, American financier and presidential adviser, Aug 1941, July 1950, *Obit* Sept 1965

Bass, Robert M., investor, July 1989

Bastianich, Joseph, American restaurateur and winemaker, June 2011

Batali, Mario, American chef and restaurateur, Apr 2011

Batcheller, Hiland Garfield, American steel industry executive, Apr 1949, *Obit* July 1961

Batt, William L., American manufacturing executive, Feb 1942, *Obit* Mar 1965

Bausch, Edward, American optical equipment company executive, *Obit* Sept 1944

Bausch, William, *Obit* Yrbk 1944

Beane, Billy, American baseball executive, July 2005

Beard, Charles E., American airline executive, July 1956, *Obit* Oct 1982

Beaverbrook, Max Aitken, British newspaper publisher, July 1940, *Obit* Sept 1964

Bechtel, Stephen Davison, builder, Apr 1957, *Obit* May 1989

Beckman, Arnold O., American chemist, inventor and instrument industry executive, Jan 2002, *Obit* Yrbk 2004

Beech, Olive Ann, American aircraft executive, June 1956, *Obit* Sept 1993

Beeching, Richard, British physicist, government official and chemical industry executive, Sept 1963

Beers, Charlotte, American advertising executive and government official, June 1998

Behn, Sosthenes, American telephone executive, Jan 1947, *Obit* Sept 1957

Behrman, Beatrice, American doll maker, Sept 1957

Beitz, Berthold, German steel executive, Feb 1973, *Obit* Yrbk 2013

Bell, Bert, American football commissioner, Sept 1950, *Obit* Yrbk 1959

Bell, Elliott V., economist, editor and publisher, Mar 1953, *Obit* Mar 1983

Bell, James A., American aerospace industry executive, July 2006

Bendetsen, Karl Robin, American paper industry executive, May 1952, *Obit* Sept 1989

Bendix, Vincent, American inventor and aircraft industry executive, *Obit* May 1945

Benjamin, William Evarts, American publisher, *Obit* Mar 1940

Bennett, Wallace F., American senator, Feb 1949, *Obit* Feb 1994

Bennett, William John, Canadian government official and energy industry executive, June 1954

Benson, John, American advertising executive, Apr 1940, *Obit* Nov 1962

Benton, William, American senator, publisher and diplomat, Yrbk 1945, *Obit* May 1973

Berezovsky, Boris A., Russian financier and government official, Jan 2002, *Obit* Yrbk 2013

Berg, Hart O., American aviation and arms expert, *Obit* Feb 1942

Berge, Pierre, French clothing industry executive, Jan 1990

Bergen, John J., American financier, June 1961, *Obit* Feb 1981

Berkson, Seymour, American news agency executive, Oct 1949, *Obit* Mar 1959

Berlusconi, Silvio, Italian prime minister, Aug 1994

Bernbach, William, American advertising executive, Mar 1967, *Obit* Nov 1982

Bernstein, Michelle, American chef and restaurateur, Nov 2013

Bernstein, Robert L., American publishing executive and human rights activist, July 1987

Bertozzi, Carolyn R., American chemist, July 2003

Bethune, Gordon M., American airline executive, June 2001

Bettman, Gary, American lawyer and hockey commissioner, Mar 1999

Bewkes, Jeffrey L., American mass media executive, Nov 2010

Bezos, Jeffrey, American Internet and retail executive, June 1998

Bianchini, Gina, American Internet executive, Oct 2013

Bible, Geoffrey C., American tobacco and food industry executive, Feb 2002

Bigelow, Robert T., American real estate executive and financier, Aug 2008

Biggers, John D., American manufacturing executive, Sept 1941, *Obit* Feb 1974

Billingsley, Sherman, American nightclub owner, Feb 1946, *Obit* Yrbk 1966

Bingham, Barry, American newspaper publisher, Sept 1949, *Obit* Sept 1988

Birdseye, Clarence, American inventor and frozen food industry executive, Mar 1946, *Obit* Yrbk 1957

Bishop, Hazel, American chemist and cosmetics executive, Sept 1957, *Obit* Feb 1999

Black, Cathleen, American school superintendent and former magazine executive, Jan 1998

Black, Conrad M., Canadian financier and newspaper publisher, Aug 1992

Black, William, coffee company executive, July 1964, *Obit* May 1983

Blackall, Frederick S., American manufacturing executive, Jan 1953

Blakely, Sara, American hosiery company executive, Jan 2013

Blancke, Harold, American chemical industry executive, June 1957

Blanco, Kathleen, American governor, June 2004

Blattenberger, Raymond, American printing industry executive and government official, Mar 1958, *Obit* June 1971

Blaustein, Jacob, American petroleum industry executive and Jewish leader, Apr 1949, *Obit* Jan 1971

Bliss, Ray C., American political party leader, Jan 1966, *Obit* Oct 1981

Bloch, Charles Edward, American publishing executive, *Obit* Oct 1940

Block, Joseph L., steel executive, June 1961, *Obit* Feb 1993

Block, Paul, American newspaper publisher, *Obit* Aug 1941

Bloom, Sol, American congressman, May 1943, *Obit* Mar 1949

Bloomberg, Michael, American mayor, June 1996, Mar 2002

Blough, Roger M., American steel industry executive, July 1955, *Obit* Jan 1986

Blount, Winton Malcolm, American construction executive and postmaster general, Apr 1969, *Obit* Jan 2003

Blumenthal, George, American financier and museum and

hospital administrator, *Obit* Yrbk 1941

Blumenthal, Heston, British chef and restaurateur, Jan 2005

Blumenthal, W. Michael, American Secretary of the treasury, July 1977

Bobst, Elmer Holmes, American pharmaceutical executive, Yrbk 1973, *Obit* Sept 1978

Bocuse, Paul, French chef and restaurateur, Jan 1988

Boeschenstein, Harold, American manufacturing executive, Feb 1961, *Obit* Yrbk 1972

Boggs, Charles Reid, American chemist and manufacturing executive, *Obit* Apr 1940

Bolles, Stephen, American newspaper editor and congressman, *Obit* Sept 1941

Bolte, Charles G., author and publishing executive, Oct 1945, *Obit* May 1994

Bonner, Paul Hyde, American novelist, Yrbk 1955, *Obit* Mar 1969

Borch, Fred J., manufacturing executive, Oct 1971

Bosch, Robert, German manufacturing executive, *Obit* Apr 1942

Boulud, Daniel, French chef and restaurateur, Jan 2005

Bourguiba, Habib, Tunisian president, Sept 1955, *Obit* Aug 2000

Boutelle, Richard S., Sept 1951

Bowater, Eric Vansittart, English paper industry executive, Sept 1956, *Obit* Nov 1962

Bowditch, Richard L., July 1953, *Obit* Nov 1959

Bowles, Chester, American government official and diplomat, Sept 1943, Jan 1957, *Obit* July 1986

Boyd, Alan S., American Secretary of transportation and railroad executive, Mar 1965

Brabeck-Letmathe, Peter, Austrian-Swiss food industry executive, Jan 2005

Bracken, Brendan Bracken, British cabinet member, Yrbk 1941

Bradshaw, Thornton F., petroleum and electronics

executive, June 1982, *Obit* Feb 1989

Brady, William Thomas, food industry executive, Jan 1961, *Obit* July 1984

Braly, Angela F., American health insurance executive, Aug 2011

Braniff, T. E., Apr 1952, *Obit* Mar 1954

Bransome, Edward D., American truck company executive, Apr 1952

Branson, Richard, British financier, Feb 1995

Bravo, Rose Marie, American clothing industry executive, June 2004

Breathitt, Edward T., American governor, July 1964, *Obit* Yrbk 2004

Breen, Edward D., American electronics industry executive, July 2004

Breen, Joseph Ignatius, American motion picture censor and association executive, July 1950, *Obit* Jan 1966

Breitmeyer, Philip, *Obit* Jan 1942

Brennan, Edward A., American retail executive, Nov 1990, *Obit* Yrbk 2008

Brett, George Platt, publisher, Yrbk 1948, *Obit* May 1984

Brill, Steven, American lawyer, journalist and television executive, Nov 1997

Brin, Sergey, American Internet search engine executive, Oct 2001

Briney, Nancy, Jan 1954

Bristol, Lee H., Sept 1962

Bronfman, Edgar M., American liquor industry executive, July 1974

Bronfman, Edgar M., American recording industry executive, Oct 1995

Brooks, Diana D., American art dealer and auctioneer, June 1998

Brophy, Thomas D'Arcy, Sept 1952, *Obit* Oct 1967

Browdy, Benjamin G., July 1951

Brower, Charles H., advertising executive, Feb 1965, *Obit* Nov 1984

Brown, Charles L., American telephone executive, Sept 1981, *Obit* Yrbk 2004

Brown, Clarence J., American congressman, Feb 1947, *Obit* Nov 1965

Brown, David M., American coal executive and veterans' leader, June 1950

Brown, George Hay, marketing executive and consultant, Jan 1971

Browne, E. John P., British petroleum industry executive, Jan 2002

Brule, Tyler, Canadian magazine publisher, Mar 2011

Bryant, Gyude, Liberian businessman and interim leader, Jan 2005

Buchanan, Patrick, American political commentator, Aug 1985

Buckley, George W., British manufacturing executive, Sept 2011

Buckley, James L., American senator and judge, Oct 1971

Budd, Edward G., July 1949, *Obit* July 1971

Budd, Ralph, July 1940, *Obit* Mar 1962

Buetow, Herbert P., Mar 1960, *Obit* Mar 1972

Buffett, Warren E., American financier, Nov 1987

Bugas, John S., automobile executive, Yrbk 1947, *Obit* Feb 1983

Buitoni, Giovanni, June 1962, *Obit* Mar 1979

Bullis, Harry A., Oct 1946, *Obit* Jan 1964

Bunge, Alejandro E., *Obit* July 1943

Bunker, George M., Apr 1957

Bunting, Earl, American manufacturing association official, Feb 1947

Burgess, Carter Lane, American airline and machinery industry executive and diplomat, Apr 1957, *Obit* Yrbk 2002

Burke, Brian, American hockey executive, Mar 2013

Burke, Michael, sports executive, Apr 1972, *Obit* Mar 1987

Burnett, Mark, British television producer, May 2001

Burns, H. S. M., May 1954, *Obit* Yrbk 1971

Burns, Ursula, American office equipment industry executive, Oct 2007

Burr, Donald C., American airline executive, Sept 1986

Busch, August Anheuser, American brewing industry and baseball executive, July 1973, *Obit* Nov 1989

Bush, George W., American president, Apr 1997, Aug 2001

Bushnell, Asa S., July 1952, *Obit* May 1975

Butler, Hugh, American senator, Feb 1950, *Obit* Sept 1954

Cabot, Thomas D., chemical executive and philanthropist, June 1951, *Obit* Aug 1995

Cadogan, Alexander, British diplomat, Oct 1944, *Obit* Sept 1968

Cahill, Michael Harrison, *Obit* Apr 1940

Cain, Herman, American restaurant chain executive, radio talk show host and political commentator, Oct 2011

Calagione, Sam, American brewing company executive, Jan 2013

Campeau, Robert, Canadian real estate and retail executive, Mar 1989

Camrose, William Ewert Berry, British newspaper publisher, Oct 1941, *Obit* Sept 1954

Canaday, Ward Murphey, Mar 1951, *Obit* Apr 1976

Canfield, Cass, publisher, Apr 1954, *Obit* May 1986

Capehart, H. E., American senator, Apr 1947, *Obit* Oct 1979

Capper, Arthur, American senator and governor, Sept 1946, *Obit* Feb 1952

Carey, Walter F., Feb 1965

Carmack, John, American software engineer and video game company executive, Mar 2000

Carmody, John M., American mining executive, labor mediator and government official, May 1940, *Obit* Jan 1964

Carnegie, Dorothy, author and corporate training executive, Sept 1955, *Obit* Jan 1999

Carroll, Cynthia, American mining executive, May 2011

Carroll, E. Jean, American advice columnist, July 2008

Carter, Hodding, American journalist and government official, Aug 1981

Carter, Hodding, American newspaper editor and publisher, July 1946, *Obit* May 1972

Carvel, Elbert N., June 1963

Cary, Frank Taylor, American computer industry executive, Jan 1980, *Obit* May 2006

Casals, Rosie, tennis player and executive, Feb 1974

Case, Francis H., American senator and congressman, May 1946, *Obit* Sept 1962

Case, Frank, *Obit* July 1946

Case, Steve, American mass media executive, Oct 1996

Castelli, Leo, American art dealer, Aug 1984, *Obit* Jan 2000

Catz, Safra, American computer software executive, Jan 2008

Cerf, Bennett, American publisher, Nov 1941, Sept 1958, *Obit* Oct 1971

Chamorro, Violeta Barrios de, Nicaraguan president, June 1990

Chandler, Dorothy Buffum, American newspaper publisher and patron of the arts, July 1957, *Obit* Sept 1997

Chandler, Happy, American governor, senator and baseball executive, Aug 1943, Sept 1956, *Obit* Aug 1991

Chandler, Norman, American newspaper publisher, July 1957, *Obit* Yrbk 1973

Chandler, Otis, American newspaper publisher, Nov 1968, *Obit* Yrbk 2006

Chandos, Oliver Lyttelton, British manufacturing executive and cabinet member, Sept 1941, Jan 1953, *Obit* Mar 1972

Chanel, Coco, French fashion designer and perfumer, Sept 1954, *Obit* Feb 1971

Chang, David, American chef and restaurateur, Aug 2010

Chapman, Albert Kinkade, photographic industry executive, Sept 1952, *Obit* Yrbk 1984

Chapman, Gilbert W., June 1957, *Obit* Feb 1980

Chappell, Tom, American personal care products industry executive, May 1994

Charney, Dov, American t-shirt manufacturer, Sept 2009

Charoen Sirivadhanabhakdi, Chinese-Thai liquor industry executive, Jan 2005

Charriol, Philippe, French watch, jewelry and accessories manufacturer, Jan 2004

Chasins, Abram, American pianist and composer, Feb 1960, *Obit* Aug 1987

Chauncey, Henry, American educational testing service executive, July 1951, *Obit* Mar 2003

Chen, Eugene, Chinese newspaper executive and diplomat, *Obit* July 1944

Chen, Steve S., American video sharing web site founder, Jan 2007

Chenault, Kenneth I., American financial services executive, June 1998

Cheney, Richard B., American vice-president, Aug 1989, Jan 2002

Chester, Edmund, Mar 1941

Childs, Richard Spencer, cleaning products industry executive and civic reformer, Sept 1955, *Obit* Jan 1979

Chinery-Hesse, Hermann, Ghanaian computer software executive, Jan 2003

Cho, Fujio, Japanese automobile executive, Jan 2006

Chouinard, Yvon, American mail order sportswear company executive, June 1998

Christenberry, Robert K., Mar 1952, *Obit* June 1973

Christopher, George T., Nov 1947, *Obit* July 1954

Chrysler, Walter Percy, American automobile executive, *Obit* Oct 1940

Church, Samuel Harden, American railroad executive

and foundation official, *Obit* Nov 1943

Cico, Carla, Italian telecommunications executive, Jan 2005

Cisler, Walker Lee, electric utility executive, Sept 1955, *Obit* Jan 1995

Cisneros, Henry, American urban development organization official, broadcasting executive and former Secretary of housing and urban development, Aug 1987

Citrine, Walter McLennan Citrine, English electric utility executive, Feb 1941, *Obit* Apr 1983

Clark, James H., American computer software executive, June 1997

Clayton, William Lockhart, American cotton executive and government official, Apr 1944, *Obit* Mar 1966

Claytor, W. Graham, railroad executive, May 1979, *Obit* July 1994

Clement, Martin W., Nov 1946, *Obit* Nov 1966

Cochran, Jacqueline, American aviator and cosmetics industry executive, Sept 1940, June 1963, *Obit* Oct 1980

Cohen, Arthur, author and publisher, Sept 1960, *Obit* Jan 1987

Cohen, Barbara, American poetry recorder, May 1957

Cohen, Ben, American ice cream company executive, Apr 1994

Cohen, Lyor, American recording industry executive, Aug 2012

Cohu, La Motte T., Apr 1951, *Obit* Nov 1968

Colbert, Lester Lum, automobile executive, Apr 1951, *Obit* Nov 1995

Cole, Edward N., American automobile executive, July 1972, *Obit* July 1977

Coleman, John S., American manufacturing executive, Apr 1953, *Obit* July 1958

Colicchio, Tom, American chef and restaurateur, Feb 2013

Collier, Sophia, American television and Internet service executive, July 2002

Cometbus, Aaron, American magazine publisher and writer, Mar 2005

Conde, Cristobal, Chilean-American computer software executive, Sept 2010

Cone, Fairfax, July 1966, *Obit* Aug 1977

Connor, John T., American Secretary of commerce, Apr 1961, *Obit* Feb 2001

Cook, Richard, American motion picture executive, July 2003

Cook, Tim, American computer industry executive, Sept 2012

Cooney, Joan Ganz, American television executive, July 1970

Cooper, Kent, journalist, Oct 1944, *Obit* Mar 1965

Cooper, R. Conrad, Jan 1960

Copeland, Lammot Du Pont, chemical executive, May 1963

Coppers, George H., May 1952

Cordiner, Ralph, Jan 1951, *Obit* Jan 1974

Cornelius, John C., June 1960

Cortelyou, George Bruce, postmaster general and secretary of the treasury, *Obit* Yrbk 1940

Covey, Stephen R., American business training consultant, Jan 1998, *Obit* Yrbk 2012

Cowen, Joshua Lionel, American inventor and toy train manufacturer, Sept 1954, *Obit* Nov 1965

Cowles, Gardner, American publisher, June 1943, *Obit* Aug 1985

Cowles, John, American newspaper publisher, June 1954, *Obit* Apr 1983

Craig, Cleo F., Sept 1951, *Obit* June 1978

Cramer, Stuart Warren, *Obit* Aug 1940

Crandall, Robert L., American airline executive, Nov 1992

Crawford, Frederick C., defense industries executive, Feb 1943, *Obit* Feb 1995

Cresswell, Robert, American newspaper publisher, *Obit* Nov 1943

Crockett, Lucy Herndon, Yrbk 1953

Crompton, Rookes Evelyn Bell, English electrical equipment industry executive, *Obit* Mar 1940

Cromwell, James H. R., American financial executive, diplomat and developer, Mar 1940, *Obit* May 1990

Crosley, Powel, American baseball and automobile executive, June 1947, *Obit* June 1961

Crowell, T. Irving, *Obit* Mar 1942

Crown, Henry, financier, Jan 1972, *Obit* Oct 1990

Crump, N. R., Sept 1957

Cuban, Mark, American broadcasting and basketball executive, Mar 2001

Cullen, Hugh Roy, petroleum executive, July 1955, *Obit* Sept 1957

Cullman, Howard S., June 1951, *Obit* Sept 1972

Cunningham-Agee, Mary, American electronics industry executive, Nov 1984

Curtice, Harlow H., American automobile executive, Mar 1953, *Obit* Jan 1963

Custin, Mildred, retail executive, Nov 1967, *Obit* June 1997

Cuthbert, Margaret, May 1947, *Obit* Oct 1968

Daft, Doug, Australian beverage industry executive, May 2001

Dallas, C. Donald, Apr 1949, *Obit* June 1959

Dalmia, Ramkrishna, Yrbk 1948

Daniels, Josephus, American Secretary of the navy and diplomat, Oct 1944, *Obit* Feb 1948

Dart, Justin Whitlock, drug industry executive, Nov 1946, *Obit* Mar 1984

David, Edward E., physicist and engineer, May 1974

Davis, Al, American football executive, July 1985, *Obit* Yrbk 2011

Davis, Clive, American recording executive, July 2000

Davis, Evelyn Y., American shareholders' rights activist, Oct 2007

Davis, Martin S., motion picture, television and publishing executive, Nov 1989, *Obit* Jan 2000

Davis, Nathanael V., American aluminum industry executive, Jan 1959, *Obit* Yrbk 2005

Davis, Roy H., Feb 1955, *Obit* Sept 1956

Davis, Westmoreland, *Obit* Oct 1942

Davis, William Rhodes, Mar 1941, *Obit* Mar 1941

Dawes, Rufus Cutler, *Obit* Jan 1940

Day, James Edward, American postmaster general, May 1962, *Obit* Jan 1997

De Benedetti, Carlo, Italian computer and telecommunications executive, May 1990

De Graff, Robert F., May 1943

De Lorean, John Z., American automobile executive, Mar 1976, *Obit* Yrbk 2005

De Seversky, Alexander P., Feb 1941, *Obit* Oct 1974

De Vry, Herman A., *Obit* May 1941

DeMott, Richard H., Feb 1951, *Obit* Nov 1968

DeWolfe, Chris, American Internet executive, July 2007

Dean, Jimmy, American singer, Yrbk 1965, *Obit* Aug 2010

Debutts, Harry A., Apr 1953

Deen, Paula H., American cook, restaurateur and television personality, Mar 2010

Delacorte, George T., American publisher and philanthropist, Nov 1965, *Obit* July 1991

Della Femina, Jerry, American advertising executive, restaurateur and grocery store owner, Nov 1979

Dennis, Felix, British magazine publisher, Apr 2000

Denny, Charles R., May 1947

Dent, Frederick B., American Secretary of commerce, Apr 1974

Denton, Nick, British journalist and Internet news service executive, Apr 2011

Depinet, Ned E., June 1950

Deripaska, Oleg, Russian aluminum industry executive, Jan 2006

Desmond-Hellman, Susan, American oncologist and biotechnology executive, Nov 2012

Deveshwar, Yogesh Chander, Indian tobacco company executive, Jan 2005

Dewart, William T., American newspaper publisher, *Obit* Mar 1944

Di Montezemolo, Luca Cordero, Italian automobile executive, Jan 2006

DiSpirito, Rocco, American chef and restaurateur, Feb 2012

Dial, Morse G., chemical executive, Mar 1956, *Obit* Jan 1983

Dichter, Ernest, American psychologist and marketing research executive, Jan 1961, *Obit* Jan 1992

Dickson, Lovat, Sept 1962

Diddy, American rapper, record producer and actor, Apr 1998

Diller, Barry, American motion picture and television executive, Apr 1986

Dimon, James, American investment banker, June 2004

Diniz, Abilio, Brazilian supermarket and department store executive, Jan 2006

Disney, Anthea, English publishing executive, June 1998

Disney, Walt, American animator and motion picture executive, Aug 1940, Apr 1952, *Obit* Feb 1967

Doan, Leland I., American chemical industry executive, Oct 1952, *Obit* May 1974

Dodd, Christopher J., American motion picture association executive and former senator, Oct 1989

Doerr, John, American financier, May 2009

Doherty, Henry Latham, American gas and electric utility executive, *Obit* Jan 1940

Donald, Arnold, American food industry executive, Nov 2005

Donaldson, William, American regulatory agency official, June 2003

Donner, Frederic Garrett, automobile executive, Jan 1959, *Obit* Apr 1987

Donovan, Hedley, journalist and magazine publishing executive, May 1965, *Obit* Oct 1990

Doubleday, Nelson, publisher and baseball executive, May 1987

Drexler, Millard S., American clothing chain executive, Jan 1993

Dreyfus, Camille, May 1955, *Obit* Yrbk 1957

Dreyfus, Pierre, French automobile executive and cabinet member, July 1958, *Obit* Mar 1995

Driscoll, Alfred E., American governor, Jan 1949, *Obit* May 1975

Dryfoos, Orvil Eugene, American newspaper publisher, Jan 1962, *Obit* July 1963

Du Pont, Pierre S., American business executive, Sept 1940, *Obit* May 1954

Dubuc, Nancy, American television executive, May 2012

Dudley, Robert, American petroleum industry executive, June 2011

Duffy, Bernard C., July 1952, *Obit* Nov 1972

Duggan, Ervin S., public broadcasting executive, Oct 1998

Duncan, Charles W., American Secretary of energy, Apr 1980

Dworshak, Henry C., American senator, congressman and newspaper publisher, Jan 1950, *Obit* Oct 1962

Dyke, Greg, British broadcasting executive, Jan 2002

Dykstra, John, American automobile executive, Apr 1963, *Obit* May 1972

Eaton, Cyrus, American financier, July 1948, *Obit* July 1979

Ebbers, Bernard, American telecommunications executive, Feb 1998

Ebersol, Dick, American television executive, July 1996

Eccles, Marriner S., American financier and Federal Reserve chairman, Apr 1941, *Obit* Feb 1978

Eckert, Robert, American toy industry executive, Mar 2003

Egbert, Sherwood H., June 1963, *Obit* Oct 1969

Eisenschiml, Otto, Austrian-American chemist

and historian, Oct 1963, *Obit* Jan 1964

Eisner, Michael, American motion picture executive, Nov 1987

Eisner, Will, American cartoonist and comic book publisher, Oct 1994, *Obit* May 2005

Ek, Daniel, Swedish computer software executive, Mar 2012

Ellena, Jean-Claude, French perfumer, Jan 2005

Ellison, Lawrence J., American computer software executive, Jan 1998

Ells, Steve, American restaurant chain executive, May 2012

Elsenhans, Lynn Laverty, American petroleum company executive, July 2011

Elway, John, American football player, Nov 1990

Emanuel, Victor, American manufacturing executive, May 1951, *Obit* Jan 1961

Emery, DeWitt, Oct 1946, *Obit* Oct 1955

Enders, Thomas, German aircraft industry executive, Mar 2011

Engelbreit, Mary, American children's author, illustrator and magazine publisher, Oct 1999

Engibous, Thomas J., American semiconductor industry executive, Oct 2003

English, Todd, American chef and restaurateur, Jan 2012

Engstrom, Elmer W., electronics engineer and executive, Yrbk 1951, *Obit* Feb 1985

Epstein, Jason, American publishing executive, Aug 1990

Epstein, Theo, American baseball executive, May 2004

Erikson, Leonard F., Oct 1953

Espinoza, Alvaro, Chilean vintner, Jan 2004

Estes, Elliott M., American automobile executive, Jan 1979, *Obit* May 1988

Ethridge, Mark Foster, American newspaper publisher and diplomat, Jan 1946, *Obit* June 1981

Ettinger, Richard P., Yrbk 1951, *Obit* Apr 1971

Evans, Donald L., American Secretary of commerce, Nov 2001

Evans, Harold, British publishing executive, Apr 1985

Evans, Nancy, Internet service executive and editor, Mar 2000

Eyler, John, American toy store chain executive, Aug 2000

Fairchild, John, American magazine publisher, June 1971

Fairless, Benjamin F., American steel industry executive, June 1942, May 1957, *Obit* Feb 1962

Farber, Sid, builder, Sept 1967, *Obit* May 1973

Faricy, William T., June 1948

Farrington, Elizabeth Pruett, American newspaper publisher, June 1955, *Obit* Sept 1984

Feld, Irvin, circus owner, Feb 1979, *Obit* Nov 1984

Felker, Clay, American magazine founder and editor, Feb 1975, *Obit* Yrbk 2008

Fellows, Harold E., Feb 1952, *Obit* May 1960

Feniger, Susan, American chef and restaurateur, Apr 2013

Ferguson, Harry, Irish inventor, Mar 1956, *Obit* Jan 1961

Ferguson, Howard, *Obit* Apr 1946

Ferlinghetti, Lawrence, American poet, novelist, dramatist and publisher, June 1991

Ferrari, Enzo, Italian automobile executive, May 1967, *Obit* Sept 1988

Ferre, Luis A., Puerto Rican governor, Mar 1970, *Obit* Mar 2004

Field, Marshall, American department store executives and newspaper publisher, Apr 1941, Mar 1952, *Obit* Jan 1957

Fields, Mark, American automobile executive, Apr 2005

Fieri, Guy, American chef, restaurateur and television personality, Mar 2011

Fili-Krushel, Patricia, television executive, Nov 1999

Filo, David, American Internet search engine executive, Oct 1997

Finley, Charles, American baseball executive, June 1974, *Obit* Apr 1996

Fiorina, Carly, American computer industry executive, Jan 2000

Fireman, Paul, American shoe company executive, Mar 1992

Firestone, Harvey S., July 1944, *Obit* July 1973

Flay, Bobby, American chef and restaurateur, May 2008

Fleck, Alexander Fleck, Scottish chemical executive, Apr 1956, *Obit* Oct 1968

Fleming, Arthur Henry, *Obit* Sept 1940

Flynt, Larry, American magazine publisher, Sept 1999

Folsom, Frank M., Feb 1949, *Obit* Mar 1970

Forbes, Bertie Charles, publisher, Mar 1950, *Obit* July 1954

Forbes, Malcolm S., American magazine publisher, May 1996

Ford, Benson, automobile executive, Feb 1952, *Obit* Sept 1978

Ford, Edsel Bryant, American automobile executive, *Obit* July 1943

Ford, Frederick W., government official, Nov 1960, *Obit* Sept 1986

Ford, Harold, American financial executive and political commentator, Nov 1999

Ford, Henry, American automobile executive, Yrbk 1944, *Obit* May 1947

Ford, Henry, American automobile executive, Apr 1946, June 1978, *Obit* Nov 1987

Forgeard, Noel, French aircraft industry executive, Jan 2004

Forsee, Gary, American telecommunications executive, Oct 2005

Foss, Joe, American governor and firearms association executive, Oct 1955, *Obit* Yrbk 2003

Foster, William C., American government official, Nov 1950

Fowler, Mark S., government official, Mar 1986

Foyle, Gilbert, June 1954, *Obit* Jan 1972

Foyle, William Alfred, English bookseller, June 1954, *Obit* July 1963

Francis, Clarence, food industry executive, Feb 1948, *Obit* Mar 1986

Frankel, Bethenny, American chef, food service executive and participant in reality TV show Real housewives of New York City, Mar 2013

Franklin, John M., Sept 1949, *Obit* Aug 1975

Franklin, Walter S., Feb 1950, *Obit* Oct 1972

Fraser, Robert, British television executive, Oct 1956

Freeman, Orville L., American governor, Secretary of agriculture and magazine publishing executive, June 1956, *Obit* Yrbk 2003

Frere, Albert, Belgian financier, Jan 2002

Freston, Tom, American television executive, Aug 2003

Frick, Ford, American baseball executive, May 1945, *Obit* June 1978

Friedman, Jane, American publisher, Mar 2001

Friendly, Edwin S., American newspaper executive, July 1949, *Obit* Sept 1970

Friendly, Fred W., American broadcast news executive, Sept 1957, Aug 1987, *Obit* May 1998

Friis, Janus, Danish computer software engineer and executive, Jan 2007

Frische, Carl A., Oct 1962

Fruehauf, Roy, Feb 1953, *Obit* Jan 1966

Fry, Kenneth D., Apr 1947

Frye, Jack, Apr 1945, *Obit* Apr 1959

Fu Chengyu, Chinese petroleum company executive, Jan 2005

Fu, Ping, Chinese computer software executive, Oct 2006

Fuchs, Michael Joseph, cable television executive, Feb 1996

Fudge, Ann M., American advertising executive, June 1998

Fuller, Alfred C., brush industry executive, Oct 1950, *Obit* Jan 1974

Fuller, Millard, American lawyer and humanitarian, Apr 1995, *Obit* Yrbk 2009

Fuller, S. R., May 1941, *Obit* Mar 1966

Fuller, Walter Deane, American publishing executive, Mar 1941, *Obit* Jan 1965

Funk, Walther, German financier and cabinet member, Oct 1940, *Obit* Sept 1960

Funk, Wilfred, American publisher and lexicographer, Jan 1955, *Obit* July 1965

Funston, Keith, American stock exchange official, July 1951, *Obit* July 1992

Gabriel, Roman, football player, Nov 1975

Gaer, Joseph, author, publishing executive and foundation official, Yrbk 1951

Gainza Paz, Alberto, Argentine newspaper publisher, Apr 1951, *Obit* Feb 1978

Galvin, Robert W., American electronics industry executive, Mar 1960, *Obit* Yrbk 2011

Gannett, Frank Ernest, American newspaper publisher, Mar 1945, *Obit* Feb 1958

Gardner, Arthur, Jan 1956, *Obit* June 1967

Gartner, Michael G., newspaper editor, May 1990

Garvin, Clifton Canter, petroleum executive, Nov 1980

Gary, Willie, American lawyer, Apr 2001

Gass, Michelle, American coffee chain executive, Apr 2012

Gates, Bill, American computer software executive, May 1991

Gates, Melinda French, American philanthropist and wife of Bill Gates, Feb 2004

Gaumont, Leon, *Obit* Sept 1946

Gaylord, Robert M., Mar 1944

Gebel-Williams, Gunther, German animal trainer and circus owner, Yrbk 1971, *Obit* Oct 2001

Geffen, David, American recording and motion picture executive, Jan 1992

Geis, Bernard, American publisher, Sept 1960, *Obit* Mar 2001

Geneen, Harold S., American financier, Feb 1974, *Obit* Jan 1998

Gerstacker, Carl A., American chemical executive, Oct 1961, *Obit* July 1995

Gerstner, Louis V., American computer industry executive, June 1991

Getty, Gordon P., American petroleum executive and composer, Feb 1985

Ghosn, Carlos, Brazilian-French automobile executive, Jan 2004

Giamatti, A. Bartlett, American university president, literary scholar and baseball commissioner, Apr 1978, *Obit* Oct 1989

Giannulli, Mossimo, American fashion designer and clothing executive, Feb 2003

Gifford, Walter Sherman, telephone executive, Jan 1945, *Obit* June 1966

Gilbert, Rod, Canadian hockey player and executive, July 1969

Gilbert, Walter, American molecular biologist and genetic engineering executive, Nov 1992

Gimbel, Bernard F., Mar 1950, *Obit* Yrbk 1966

Girdler, Tom M., American steel executive, Apr 1944, *Obit* Mar 1965

Giroux, Robert, American editor and publisher, Nov 1982, *Obit* Yrbk 2008

Goizueta, Roberto C., American beverage industry executive, Aug 1996, *Obit* Jan 1998

Golden, Harry Lewis, American newspaper publisher and essayist, Jan 1959, *Obit* Nov 1981

Goldenson, Leonard H., radio and television executive, Sept 1957, *Obit* May 2000

Goldsmith, James, English financier, Feb 1988, *Obit* Oct 1997

Gollancz, Victor, British publisher, Oct 1963, *Obit* Apr 1967

Gomez, Laureano, Colombian president, May 1950, *Obit* Sept 1965

Good, Mary L., American chemist, Sept 2001

Goodman, Andrew, American department store executive, Apr 1975, *Obit* June 1993

Gopinath, Suhas, Indian information technology executive, July 2008

Gordon, Bruce, American civil rights organization official, Oct 2005

Gordon, Crawford, Canadian aircraft and steel executive, Mar 1958, *Obit* Mar 1967

Gordon, Donald, Oct 1950, *Obit* June 1969

Gordy, Berry, American recording executive, July 1975

Gorman, James P., Australian financial executive, June 2010

Goshorn, Clarence B., Mar 1950, *Obit* Jan 1951

Gottlieb, Robert Adams, American editor and publishing executive, Sept 1987

Goussinsky, Vladimir, Russian financier, Jan 2002

Grace, Eugene G., American steel company executive, Apr 1941, *Obit* Oct 1960

Grace, J. Peter, chemical industry executive, Mar 1960, *Obit* June 1995

Grady, Henry Francis, American diplomat and trade expert, July 1947, *Obit* Nov 1957

Graham, Donald E., American newspaper publisher, May 1998

Graham, Katharine, American newspaper publisher, Jan 1971, *Obit* Oct 2001

Graham, Philip Leslie, American newspaper publisher, Feb 1948, *Obit* Oct 1963

Graves, Earl G., American magazine publishing executive, Aug 1997

Graves, Florence, American journalist, May 2005

Gray, Carl R., Mar 1948, *Obit* Feb 1956

Gray, Gordon, American broadcasting executive and military official, Sept 1949, *Obit* Feb 1983

Gray, Harold E., Feb 1969

Grede, William J., iron and steel executive, Feb 1952, *Obit* Aug 1989

Greenberg, Jack, fast food industry executive, Nov 2001

Greenberg, Maurice R., American insurance executive, Nov 2000

Greene, Hugh, English radio and television executive, Sept 1963, *Obit* Apr 1987

Greenebaum, Leon C., Jan 1962, *Obit* May 1968

Greenewalt, Crawford H., American chemical industry executive, Jan 1949

Greenfield, Jerry, American ice cream company executive, Apr 1994

Greenwald, Julie, American recording industry executive, Nov 2009

Gregg, Hugh, Jan 1954

Griffin, R. Allen, American newspaper publisher, Feb 1951

Griswold, Augustus H., *Obit* Mar 1940

Gross, Robert E., Jan 1956, *Obit* Nov 1961

Grosvenor, Graham Bethune, American elevator manufacturing company and airline executive, *Obit* Yrbk 1943

Grove, Andrew S., American semiconductor industry executive, Mar 1998

Groves, Leslie R., American general, Aug 1945, *Obit* Oct 1970

Grumman, Leroy R., aircraft executive, Aug 1945, *Obit* Jan 1983

Guccione, Bob, American magazine publisher, Aug 1994, *Obit* Yrbk 2010

Guerlain, Jean-Paul, French perfumer, Jan 2006

Guggenheim, Harry Frank, American mining executive, Oct 1956, *Obit* Mar 1971

Guinzburg, Harold K., July 1957, *Obit* Jan 1962

Gullander, W. P., Oct 1963

Gunn, Tim, American clothing company executive, Oct 2009

Guptill, Arthur L., Mar 1955, *Obit* May 1956

Gurney, Chan, Oct 1950

Gutt, Camille, Apr 1948

Hagel, Chuck, American senator, Aug 2004

Hagerty, James C., American journalist and presidential aide, Mar 1953, *Obit* June 1981

Haji-Ioannou, Stelios, Greek shipping heir and entrepreneur, Jan 2007

Halaby, Najeeb E., American airline executive and regulatory agency official, Oct 1961, *Obit* Yrbk 2003

Haldeman, H. R., American presidential adviser, Sept 1978, *Obit* Jan 1994

Haley, William, English newspaper editor and broadcasting executive, Apr 1948, *Obit* Oct 1987

Hall, Floyd D., June 1970, *Obit* Yrbk 2012

Hall, Joyce Clyde, greeting card executive, May 1953, *Obit* Jan 1983

Halligan, William J., Oct 1957

Halpert, Edith Gregor, art dealer, July 1955, *Obit* Nov 1970

Hamied, Yusuf K., Indian pharmaceutical executive, Jan 2004

Hamilton, Charles, American autograph dealer and handwriting expert, July 1976, *Obit* Feb 1997

Hamilton, Gabrielle, American chef and restaurateur, May 2013

Hamlin, Clarence Clark, American lawyer and newspaper executive, *Obit* Yrbk 1940

Hammer, Armand, American petroleum executive, June 1973, *Obit* Feb 1991

Hammer, Bonnie, American television executive, Apr 2006

Hammond, Caleb D., American map publisher and cartographer, Apr 1956, *Obit* Yrbk 2006

Hammond, Godfrey, Oct 1953, *Obit* Oct 1969

Hammond, John, American recording industry executive, July 1979, *Obit* Aug 1987

Harbord, James G., American general, Mar 1945, *Obit* Sept 1947

Hardenbrook, Donald J., July 1962, *Obit* Aug 1976

Hardie, S. J. L., July 1951

Harding, Margaret S., Apr 1947

Hargrave, Thomas J., Apr 1949, *Obit* Apr 1962

Hariri, Saad, Lebanese telecommunications executive and political leader, Jan 2005

Harkness, Edward Stephen, Jan 1940

Harlech, William David Ormsby Gore, British statesman and diplomat, Mar 1961, *Obit* Mar 1985

Harper, Marion, advertising executive, Mar 1961, *Obit* Feb 1990

Harridge, William, baseball executive, Sept 1949, *Obit* June 1971

Harriman, E. Roland, Mar 1951, *Obit* Apr 1978

Harrison, Gilbert A., American magazine editor, publisher and veterans' leader, Mar 1949, *Obit* Yrbk 2008

Harrison, William H., Feb 1949, *Obit* July 1956

Hartford, Huntington, American financier and patron of the arts, June 1959, *Obit* Yrbk 2008

Haseltine, William A., American molecular biologist, Nov 1998

Hassenfeld, Alan Geoffrey, American toy industry executive, July 2003

Hastings, Reed, American computer software executive and entrepreneur, Mar 2006

Hastreiter, Kim, American magazine editor and publisher, Aug 2010

Haughton, Daniel Jeremiah, aircraft executive, Sept 1974, *Obit* Aug 1987

Haycraft, Howard, publisher and author, Nov 1941, Feb 1954, *Obit* Jan 1992

Hays, Will H., American motion picture industry censor, July 1943, *Obit* Apr 1954

Hearst, William Randolph, American newspaper publisher, Oct 1955, *Obit* July 1993

Hecht, George Joseph, magazine publisher, Oct 1947, *Obit* June 1980

Heckscher, August, *Obit* June 1941

Hefner, Christie, American magazine publisher, Oct 1986

Hefner, Hugh, American magazine publisher, Sept 1968

Heidenstam, Rolf von, Oct 1951, *Obit* Oct 1958

Heineman, Ben W., lawyer and machine tool executive, Jan 1962, *Obit* Yrbk 2012

Heinz, Henry John, American food industry executive, June 1947, *Obit* Apr 1987

Heiskell, Andrew, American magazine executive, Mar 1966, *Obit* Yrbk 2003

Henderson, Fergus, British chef and restaurateur, Feb 2011

Henry, John, American baseball executive, May 2005

Herod, William Rogers, mechanical engineer and manufacturing executive, Mar 1951, *Obit* Sept 1974

Hershey, Milton Snavely, American candy industry executive, *Obit* Nov 1945

Hess, Max, Oct 1961, *Obit* Nov 1968

Hickel, Walter Joseph, American Secretary of the interior and governor, May 1969, *Obit* Yrbk 2010

Hicks, Clarence J., *Obit* Feb 1945

Higgins, Andrew Jackson, shipbuilding executive, May 1943, *Obit* Sept 1952

Higley, Harvey V., government official, Oct 1956, *Obit* Jan 1987

Hildred, William P., Apr 1956

Hill, Arthur M., Oct 1948, *Obit* Nov 1972

Hill, David G., Apr 1960

Hill, George Washington, June 1946

Hill, William S., Mar 1955, *Obit* Nov 1972

Hiller, Stanley, American aircraft industry executive and business turnaround expert, Nov 1974, *Obit* Yrbk 2006

Hines, Duncan, restaurant critic and publisher, May 1946, *Obit* May 1959

Hirai, Kazuo, Japanese video game industry executive, Jan 2007

Hirshhorn, Joseph H., American stockbroker, mining executive and art collector, Nov 1966, *Obit* Oct 1981

Hirst, Hugo, English manufacturing executive, Nov 1941, *Obit* Mar 1943

Hitz, Ralph, *Obit* Jan 1940

Ho, Stanley, Chinese gambling casino owner, Jan 2003

Hobby, Oveta Culp, American Secretary of health, education and welfare, July 1942, Feb 1953, *Obit* Oct 1995

Hodgson, James D., American aircraft industry executive and Secretary of labor, Nov 1970, *Obit* Yrbk 2013

Hoffa, Jimmy, American labor leader, May 1972, *Obit* Mar 1983

Hoffman, Paul G., American automobile executive, Feb 1946, *Obit* Nov 1974

Hoge, James F., American newspaper executive and magazine editor, Apr 1998

Holden, Betsy, American food industry executive, July 2003

Holmes, D. Brainerd, aerospace industry executive and NASA official, Mar 1963, *Obit* Yrbk 2013

Holt, Cooper T., July 1957

Holzen, Heinz von, Swiss chef and restaurateur, Jan 2002

Homer, Arthur B., July 1952, *Obit* Sept 1972

Hood, Clifford F., Apr 1953, *Obit* Jan 1979

Hooper, C. E., Apr 1947, *Obit* Feb 1955

Hope, Stanley C., May 1959, *Obit* Oct 1982

Hopkins, John Jay, Mar 1954, *Obit* July 1957

Hormel, Jay C., July 1946, *Obit* Oct 1954

Horner, H. M., aircraft executive, Oct 1955, *Obit* July 1983

Houghton, Alanson Bigelow, glass industry executive and diplomat, *Obit* Nov 1941

Houghton, Amory, American glass industry executive and diplomat, Jan 1947, *Obit* Apr 1981

Houser, Theodore V., Mar 1957, *Obit* Feb 1964

Houston, Drew, American online file hosting service executive, May 2012

Houston, Robert Griffith, American congressman and

newspaper publisher, *Obit* Mar 1946

Hoving, Walter, department store executive, Sept 1946, *Obit* Feb 1990

Howard, Roy Wilson, news agency and newspaper executive, Nov 1940, *Obit* Jan 1965

Howe, Gordie, Canadian hockey player, Mar 1962

Howe, Samuel B., *Obit* Apr 1941

Hoyt, Palmer, American newspaper editor and publisher, Sept 1943, *Obit* Aug 1979

Hughes, Cathy, American radio executive, Feb 2000

Hughes, Edward Everett, *Obit* Jan 1940

Huizenga, H. Wayne, American video chain and baseball executive, Jan 1995

Humphrey, George Magoffin, American Secretary of the treasury, Feb 1953, *Obit* Mar 1970

Hung Huang, Chinese magazine executive, Jan 2006

Hunt, H. L., American petroleum industry executive, Jan 1970, *Obit* Jan 1975

Hunter, Billy, American lawyer and basketball players association executive, Aug 2013

Hunter, Croil, American airline executive, July 1951, *Obit* Oct 1970

Huntsman, Jr., Jon, American diplomat, May 2012

Hurley, Chad, American video sharing web site founder, Jan 2007

Hurley, Roy T., American aircraft industry executive, June 1955, *Obit* Yrbk 1971

Ibrahim, Mohamed, Sudanese-British telecommunications executive, Jan 2007

Icahn, Carl C., American financier, Apr 1986

Idei, Nobuyuki, Japanese electronics industry executive, Mar 1997

Igleheart, Austin S., Oct 1950

Ilitch, Mike, American fast food chain and baseball executive, Feb 2005

Illy, Ernesto, Italian coffee company executive, Jan 2002

Immelt, Jeffrey R., American corporation executive, Feb 2004

Ingersoll, Ralph, American journalist, July 1940, *Obit* May 1985

Ingram, Jonas H., Apr 1947, *Obit* Oct 1952

Innocenti, Ferdinando, Feb 1959, *Obit* July 1966

Isaacson, Walter, American broadcasting executive, Nov 2013

Ishimoto, Tatsuo, Apr 1956

Ive, Jonathan, British industrial designer, Oct 2006, May 2013

Ivey, Susan, American tobacco industry executive, Mar 2010

Iwata, Satoru, Japanese video game company executive, Jan 2007

Jack, William S., Mar 1944

Jackson, C. D., American publishing executive and presidential aide, Oct 1951, *Obit* Nov 1964

Jackson, Hal, American disc jockey and radio executive, Oct 2002, *Obit* Yrbk 2012

Jacob, John E., civil rights leader, Feb 1986

Jacobs, Paul, American telecommunications executive, Feb 2007

James, Arthur Curtiss, *Obit* July 1941

Janas, Sigmund, Apr 1950

Janis, Sidney, American art dealer, July 1970, *Obit* Jan 1990

Jarvis, Howard, manufacturing executive and tax reform activist, Feb 1979, *Obit* Sept 1986

Jay-Z, American rapper, Aug 2002

Jeffers, William M., Nov 1942, *Obit* Apr 1953

Jenkins, Macgregor, *Obit* Apr 1940

Jensen, Ben F., Feb 1960, *Obit* Apr 1970

Jewett, Frank B., American electrical engineer and telecommunications executive, Yrbk 1946, *Obit* Jan 1950

Jha, Sanjay, American electronics industry executive, Jan 2010

Jimenez, Joyce, Filipino-American actress and lingerie company founder, Jan 2003

Jobs, Steven, American computer industry executive, Mar 1983, Sept 1998, *Obit* Yrbk 2011

John, Daymond, American fashion designer, Aug 2007

Johnson, Arnold M., Oct 1955, *Obit* May 1960

Johnson, F. Ross, Canadian food industry executive, May 1989

Johnson, Howard B., Sept 1966

Johnson, John H., American magazine publisher, Oct 1968, *Obit* Yrbk 2005

Johnson, Robert Louis, American television and basketball executive, Apr 1994

Johnson, Robert Wood, American medical supply executive, Nov 1943, *Obit* Mar 1968

Johnson, Sheila Crump, American broadcasting executive and philanthropist, June 2007

Johnston, Clement D., May 1955, *Obit* Jan 1980

Johnston, Wayne A., American railroad executive, May 1951, *Obit* Feb 1968

Jonah, Sam, Ghanaian gold mining executive, Jan 2004

Jones, David, British video game creator, Jan 2006

Jones, George L., American bookstore chain executive, Apr 2007

Jones, Jerral, American petroleum and football executive, May 1996

Jones, Scott, American electronics and information technology executive, Jan 2006

Jonsson, John Erik, mayor and electronics executive, Jan 1961, *Obit* Nov 1995

Jordan, B. Everett, American senator, Nov 1959, *Obit* May 1974

Jordan, Michael H., American information technology

executive, Feb 1998, *Obit* Yrbk 2010

Josephson, Walter S., *Obit* Mar 1940

Judson, Arthur, orchestra manager, Aug 1945, *Obit* Mar 1975

Julian, Percy L., American chemist, Sept 1947, *Obit* Jan 1975

Jung, Andrea, American cosmetics industry executive, May 2000

Kaiser, Edgar F., chemical and metal industries executive, Sept 1964, *Obit* Feb 1982

Kaiser, Henry John, American shipbuilding executive, Oct 1942, Mar 1961, *Obit* Nov 1967

Kalikow, Peter, American real estate developer, Sept 1988

Kalmus, Herbert T., American physicist and motion picture executive, Feb 1949, *Obit* Sept 1963

Kamm, John, American chemical industry executive and human rights activist, Jan 2002

Kamprad, Ingvar, Swedish household furnishings chain executive, June 1998

Kann, Peter R., American publishing executive, Mar 2003

Kanter, Albert Lewis, publisher, July 1953

Kanzler, Ernest Carlton, automobile executive, Apr 1942, *Obit* Feb 1968

Kappel, Frederick R., telephone executive, Mar 1957, *Obit* Jan 1995

Karim, Jawed, American video sharing web site founder, Jan 2007

Karmazin, Mel, American broadcasting executive, May 2000

Kaspersky, Natalya, Russian information technology executive, Jan 2005

Katzenberg, Jeffrey, American motion picture executive, May 1995

Kaufman, Henry, American economist and financial executive, Aug 1981

Keegan, Robert J., American manufacturing executive, Jan 2004

Keeton, Kathy, magazine executive, Sept 1993, *Obit* Jan 1998

Kelleher, Herbert David, American airline executive, Jan 2001

Kellems, Vivien, American wire and cable industry executive, Sept 1948, *Obit* Mar 1975

Keller, K. T., May 1947, *Obit* Feb 1966

Keller, Thomas, American chef and restaurateur, June 2004

Kelley, Augustine Bernard, Apr 1951, *Obit* Feb 1958

Kelly, John B., American rower and sports executive, June 1971, *Obit* Apr 1985

Kelly, Sharon Pratt, American mayor, Nov 1992

Kemper, James S., American insurance executive, Apr 1941, *Obit* Nov 1981

Kemsley, James Gomer Berry, British newspaper publisher, Jan 1951, *Obit* Mar 1968

Kennedy, Joseph P., American financier, diplomat and father of President John F. Kennedy, Nov 1940, *Obit* Jan 1970

Kennedy, Joseph Patrick, American congressman and energy company executive, June 1988

Kerger, Paula, American broadcasting executive, July 2013

Kerkorian, Kirk, American financier, May 1975, Mar 1996

Kerr, Robert Samuel, American senator and governor, May 1950, *Obit* Feb 1963

Kessing, O. O., American admiral and football association executive, June 1949, *Obit* Mar 1963

Kestnbaum, Meyer, May 1953, *Obit* Feb 1961

Kettering, Charles Franklin, American electrical engineer, May 1940, Yrbk 1951, *Obit* Feb 1959

Khashoggi, Adnan, Saudi Arabian financier, Mar 1986

Khodorkovsky, Mikhail, Russian energy industry executive, Jan 2003

Kilar, Jason, American Internet executive, Aug 2009

Killanin, Michael Morris, Irish sports executive and journalist, Apr 1973, *Obit* July 1999

Killion, George L., Nov 1952

Kilpatrick, John Reed, July 1948, *Obit* July 1960

Kimball, Abbott, May 1949, *Obit* Nov 1968

Kimball, Dan A., American Secretary of the navy, Sept 1951, *Obit* Oct 1970

Kindelberger, James Howard, Mar 1951, *Obit* Oct 1962

Kintner, Robert E., radio and television executive, Oct 1950, *Obit* Feb 1981

Kiplinger, Willard Monroe, journalist and periodical publisher, Mar 1943, Jan 1962, *Obit* Oct 1967

Kirby, Robert E., electrical generating equipment industry executive, Sept 1979, *Obit* Mar 1999

Kirch, Leo, German broadcasting executive, Jan 2002, *Obit* Yrbk 2011

Kiriyenko, Sergei, Russian energy industry executive, Aug 1998

Kirk, Claude R., American governor, Oct 1967, *Obit* Yrbk 2011

Kirkpatrick, Ivone, June 1950, *Obit* July 1964

Kirkus, Virginia, American magazine editor and literary critic, May 1941, June 1954, *Obit* Nov 1980

Kiselyov, Yevgeny, Russian broadcast journalist and executive, Jan 2004

Klassen, Elmer Theodore, postmaster general, May 1973, *Obit* June 1990

Klein, Herbert G., American newspaper executive and presidential aide, Feb 1971, *Obit* Yrbk 2009

Kleppe, Thomas S., American Secretary of the interior, Aug 1976, *Obit* Yrbk 2007

Kluge, John W., American broadcasting and telecommunications executive, Sept 1993, *Obit* Yrbk 2010

Klumpp, Theodore G., Oct 1958

Knight, John Shively, American newspaper publisher, Apr 1945, *Obit* Aug 1981

Knight, Philip H., American shoe company executive, Aug 1997

Knoll, Hans G., May 1955

Knopf, Alfred, American publisher, June 1943, Nov 1966, *Obit* Oct 1984

Knopf, Blanche W., American publishing executive, July 1957, *Obit* July 1966

Knowland, William Fife, American senator and newspaper publisher, Apr 1947, *Obit* Apr 1974

Knox, Frank, American Secretary of the navy and newspaper publisher, Aug 1940, *Obit* June 1944

Knox, Rose Markward, American food industry executive, May 1949, *Obit* Nov 1950

Knudsen, Semon E., American automobile executive, Jan 1974, *Obit* Sept 1998

Knudsen, William S., American automobile executive, July 1940, *Obit* June 1948

Knutson, Harold, American congressman, Jan 1947, *Obit* Oct 1953

Kobak, Edgar, Apr 1947, *Obit* July 1962

Koch, Jim, American brewing company executive, May 2012

Koch, William I., American energy executive, investor and yacht racer, Mar 1999

Kohl, Herbert, American senator, May 2008

Kohler, Walter Jodok, American manufacturing executive and governor, Jan 1953, *Obit* May 1976

Kohler, Walter Jodok, American manufacturing executive and governor, *Obit* May 1940

Koogle, Timothy, Internet search engine company executive, Apr 2000

Kraft, Robert K., American businessman and football executive, Feb 2012

Kravis, Henry R., American financier, Mar 1989

Krawcheck, Sallie, American financial executive, Mar 2006

Kress, Samuel H., merchant, Oct 1955

Kroc, Ray, American fast food restaurant chain founder and baseball team owner, Mar 1973, *Obit* Mar 1984

Krupp von Bohlen und Halbach, Alfried, German munitions manufacturer, May 1955, *Obit* Oct 1967

Kuhn, Bowie, American lawyer and baseball commissioner, Jan 1970, *Obit* Yrbk 2007

Kullman, Ellen, American chemical industry executive, Nov 2011

Kummant, Alexander, American railroad executive, Jan 2007

Kuok, Robert, Malaysian financier, June 1998

Kurzweil, Raymond, American computer scientist and inventor, Sept 2008

Kushner, Jared, American newspaper publisher, June 2007

Lacy, Dan M., publishing executive, Nov 1954, *Obit* Nov 2001

Lagardere, Jean-Luc, French aerospace and publishing executive, Aug 1993, *Obit* Aug 2003

Lagasse, Emeril, American chef and restaurateur, May 1999

Lahlou, Mourad, Chef and restauranteur, May 2012

Laker, Freddie, English airline executive, June 1978, *Obit* Yrbk 2006

Laliberte, Guy, Canadian circus owner, Jan 2003

Lamb, Brian, American television executive and moderator, Feb 1995

Lamont, Ann Huntress, American venture capitalist, Feb 2007

Lampert, Edward S., American retail executive, Sept 2005

Land, Edwin H., American inventor and photographic industry executive, Nov 1953, *Obit* May 1991

Landis, Kenesaw Mountain, American judge and baseball executive, May 1944, *Obit* Jan 1945

Lane, Allen, British publisher, May 1954, *Obit* Sept 1970

Lanier, Jaron, American computer scientist and executive, June 1997

Lansing, Sherry, American motion picture executive, May 1981

Lansky, Aaron, American collector and distributor of Yiddish books, Jan 1997

Lanzone, Jim, American Internet executive, May 2007

Larsen, Roy, publishing executive, Sept 1950, *Obit* Oct 1979

Lasker, Mary, American art dealer and philanthropist, Oct 1959, *Obit* May 1994

Lasky, Jesse Louis, American film producer, Apr 1947, *Obit* Mar 1958

Latham, Harold S., Jan 1950, *Obit* Apr 1969

Lauder, Estee, American cosmetics executive, July 1986, *Obit* Yrbk 2004

Laughlin, James, American publisher and poet, May 1982, *Obit* Jan 1998

Lautenberg, Frank, American senator, Jan 1991, *Obit* Yrbk 2013

Lauvergeon, Anne, French nuclear energy industry executive, Jan 2005

Lawal, Kase L., Nigerian-American energy industry executive, Nov 2006

Lawrence, David, journalist and publisher, Yrbk 1943, *Obit* Apr 1973

Lawrence, Mary Wells, American advertising executive, Jan 1967

Laybourne, Geraldine, American broadcasting executive, Apr 1999

Lazarus, Rochelle, American advertising executive, May 1997

Le, Tan, Australian information technology executive, Apr 2013

LeFrak, Samuel J., American builder, Jan 1970, *Obit* Yrbk 2003

Lea, Luke, American newspaper publisher and senator, *Obit* Jan 1946

Leach, Ruth M., American computer industry executive, Mar 1948

Lear, Frances, magazine publisher, Apr 1991, *Obit* Jan 1997

Leavey, Edmond H., American general and telecommunications executive, May 1951, *Obit* Apr 1980

Lee, Debra, American broadcasting executive, June 2006

Lee, Jim, Artist and co-publisher of DC Comics, Apr 2012

Lee, Kun-hee, Korean electronics industry executive, Jan 2005

Lee, Sandra, American cook, entrepreneur and television personality, Aug 2011

Leigh, Douglas, advertising executive and lighting designer, May 1940, *Obit* May 2000

Lelong, Lucien, Nov 1955, *Obit* Sept 1958

Lennox-Boyd, Alan Tindal, British cabinet member and brewing industry executive, June 1956, *Obit* May 1983

Leonard, Bill, radio and television executive, Nov 1960, *Obit* Feb 1995

Lesinski, John, American congressman, June 1957

Letourneau, R. G., American inventor, Apr 1958, *Obit* July 1969

Leverone, Nathaniel, Nov 1956, *Obit* July 1969

Levitt, William, American builder, Nov 1956, *Obit* Mar 1994

Lewis, Chester, librarian and archivist, May 1956, *Obit* June 1990

Lewis, David Sloan, American aerospace industry executive, Aug 1975, *Obit* Yrbk 2004

Lewis, Loida Nicolas, American financier and wife of Reginald F. Lewis, Apr 1997

Lewis, Mary, retail executive, Sept 1940

Lewis, Roger, aircraft executive, Yrbk 1973, *Obit* Jan 1988

Li Dongsheng, Chinese electronics industry executive, Jan 2005

Li Yifei, Chinese television executive, Jan 2006

Li, Ka-shing, Chinese real estate executive, Jan 2003

Li, Robin, Chinese Internet executive, Jan 2007

Liberman, Alexander, American artist and magazine executive, May 1987, *Obit* Mar 2000

Lichtenberg, Bernard, *Obit* Nov 1944

Lieberson, Goddard, composer, critic and record executive, Mar 1976, *Obit* July 1977

Liggett, Louis Kroh, *Obit* July 1946

Lightner, Milton C., Nov 1958, *Obit* May 1968

Lilienthal, David E., American government official, June 1944, *Obit* Mar 1981

Lillien, Lisa, American cook, cookbook writer and entrepreneur, May 2010

Lincoln, Murray D., American insurance executive, Mar 1953, *Obit* Jan 1967

Ling, James, American financier, Apr 1970, *Obit* Yrbk 2005

Link, Edwin A., flight simulator industry executive, Jan 1974, *Obit* Yrbk 1983

Lippincott, Joseph Wharton, May 1955, *Obit* Jan 1977

Lippincott, Joshua Bertram, *Obit* Jan 1940

Litchfield, P. W., Yrbk 1950, *Obit* May 1959

Liu Chuanzhi, Chinese computer industry executive, Jan 2006

Liu, Changle, Jan 2002

Loeb, William, American newspaper publisher and journalist, Mar 1974, *Obit* Nov 1981

Logan, Harlan, magazine editor and publishing executive, Jan 1946, *Obit* Mar 1995

Logue, Edward J., American builder, June 1977, *Obit* June 2000

Longman, Hubert Harry, *Obit* Apr 1940

Loomis, Daniel P., Jan 1960

Lorenzo, Frank, airline executive, Feb 1987

Love, George Hutchinson, coal and automobile executive, Mar 1950, *Obit* Sept 1991

Love, James Spencer, textile executive, Nov 1957, *Obit* Mar 1962

Lovell, Jim, American astronaut, Mar 1969

Loynd, Harry J., Feb 1952

Luce, Charles Franklin, American electric utility executive, Yrbk 1968, *Obit* Yrbk 2008

Luce, Henry Robinson, American magazine editor and publisher, July 1941, Jan 1961, *Obit* Apr 1967

Luckman, Charles, American personal care products industry executive, Oct 1947, *Obit* Apr 1999

Ludwig, Daniel Keith, shipping executive and financier, May 1979, *Obit* Oct 1992

Lunt, Storer B., Nov 1958

Lutz, Robert A., American automobile executive, Jan 1994

Lyne, Susan, American media executive, Feb 2012

Lynn, James T., American insurance executive, Yrbk 1973

Ma, Jack, Chinese Internet service provider executive, Jan 2006

Ma, Pony, Chinese information technology executive, Jan 2005

MacPhail, Larry, baseball executive, Mar 1945, *Obit* Nov 1975

MacVeagh, Lincoln, American publisher and diplomat, Nov 1941, June 1952, *Obit* Mar 1972

Mack, Lawrence L., Apr 1957

Mack, Walter, beverage industry executive, Feb 1946, *Obit* May 1990

Mackey, John, American supermarket chain executive, Nov 2008

Macmillan, Harold, British prime minister, Mar 1943, Jan 1955, *Obit* Feb 1987

Macrae, John, *Obit* Apr 1944

Macy, George, Nov 1954, *Obit* Sept 1956

Maddox, Lester, American governor, Yrbk 1967, *Obit* Yrbk 2003

Mallory, C. C., Feb 1956, *Obit* Mar 1959

Mallya, Vijay, Indian business executive, Jan 2004

Malone, John C., American broadcasting executive, Aug 1995

Mantell, Marianne, American recording company executive, May 1957

Maphai, Vincent, South African political scientist and broadcasting executive, Jan 2003

Marchetto, Marisa Acocella, American advertising executive and graphic novelist, Aug 2013

Marcus, Bernard, American home improvement chain executive, Aug 2007

Marcus, Stanley, American department store executive, June 1949, *Obit* Apr 2002

Mardikian, George M., Nov 1947

Mark, Rebecca, American energy industry executive, May 1999

Markell, Jack, American governor, July 2011

Marks of Broughton, Simon Marks, English merchant, Nov 1962, *Obit* Feb 1965

Marquis, Albert Nelson, *Obit* Feb 1944

Marriott, J. Willard, American hotel executive, June 1972, *Obit* Oct 1985

Marsh, Ernest Sterling, Feb 1960

Marshall, Walter P., Apr 1950, *Obit* June 1969

Martin, Edmund F., steel executive, Jan 1962, *Obit* Mar 1993

Martinez, Rueben, American bookstore owner, June 2005

Marzotto, Gaetano, July 1953

Mashouf, Manny, American retail executive, Feb 2009

Mason, Norman P., June 1959

Mateschitz, Dietrich, Austrian beverage industry executive, Jan 2005

Mathias, Bob, American decathlete, congressman and sports executive, Sept 1952, *Obit* Yrbk 2007

Matsuhisa, Nobu, Japanese chef and restaurateur, Jan 2005

Matsui, Connie L., American pharmaceutical executive and Girl Scouts leader, Aug 2002

Mattei, Enrico, Italian energy industry executive and member of Parliament, Apr 1959, *Obit* Jan 1963

Maxon, Lou R., Aug 1943, *Obit* July 1971

Maxwell, Robert, British publisher, Sept 1988, *Obit* Feb 1992

Mayer, Louis B., American motion picture executive, June 1943, *Obit* Jan 1958

Mayer, Marissa, American Internet executive, Jan 2010

Maynard, Robert, American newspaper editor and publisher, June 1986, *Obit* Oct 1993

Mays, Lowry, American broadcasting executive, Aug 2003

Mazumdar-Shaw, Kiran, Indian biotechnology executive, Jan 2006

McCabe, Gibson, magazine publisher, Feb 1963, *Obit* Yrbk 2000

McCabe, Thomas Bayard, American paper industry executive and Federal Reserve chairman, Sept 1948, *Obit* July 1982

McCaffrey, John L., Nov 1950

McCann, Renetta, American advertising executive, May 2005

McCarrens, John S., American newspaper publisher, *Obit* Sept 1943

McCaw, Craig, American telecommunications executive, Sept 2001

McClellan, Harold C., Oct 1954, *Obit* Sept 1979

McColough, C. Peter, American office equipment industry executive, Jan 1981, *Obit* Yrbk 2007

McCone, John A., American steel industry executive and CIA director, Jan 1959, *Obit* Apr 1991

McConnell, F. B., July 1952, *Obit* Feb 1962

McConnell, Joseph H., radio and television executive, Nov 1950, *Obit* May 1997

McCormack, Emmet J., July 1953, *Obit* Apr 1965

McCormick, Fowler, June 1947, *Obit* Feb 1973

McCormick, Robert Rutherford, American newspaper editor and publisher, Aug 1942, *Obit* May 1955

McCoy, Charles B., American chemical executive, July 1970, *Obit* Mar 1995

McCullough, Gary E., American school administrator, Nov 2009

McCurry, Michael, American presidential press secretary and Internet executive, Nov 1996

McDonald, Erroll, publishing executive, Oct 1999

McDonald, Eugene F., Oct 1949, *Obit* Oct 1958

McElroy, Neil H., American Secretary of defense, Apr 1951, *Obit* Jan 1973

McEnroe, John, American tennis player, Feb 1980

McGannon, Donald H., radio and television executive, Feb 1971, *Obit* July 1984

McGhee, George Crews, American petroleum industry executive and diplomat, Sept 1950, *Obit* Yrbk 2005

McGill, Ralph, American newspaper editor, June 1947, *Obit* Mar 1969

McGinnis, Patrick B., Nov 1955, *Obit* Apr 1973

McGovern, Gail, American Red Cross official, Mar 2010

McGovern, John, American rubber company executive, Nov 1961, *Obit* June 1975

McGrath, Judy, American broadcasting executive, Feb 2005

McGraw, Curtis W., June 1950, *Obit* Nov 1953

McKeen, John E., June 1961, *Obit* Apr 1978

McKinney, Robert, American newspaper editor and publisher, Jan 1957, *Obit* Yrbk 2001

McLean, Robert, American newspaper publisher, Nov 1951, *Obit* Feb 1981

McNally, Andrew, American publisher and cartographer, Nov 1956, *Obit* Feb 2002

McNamara, Patrick V., American senator, Nov 1955, *Obit* June 1966

McNealy, Scott, American computer industry executive, Apr 1996

McNeely, Eugene J., Nov 1962, *Obit* Feb 1974

McNerney, James, American aerospace industry executive, Mar 2008

Meacham, Jon, American publishing executive and political commentator, June 2011

Meadows, A. H., American petroleum industry executive, Apr 1960

Medvedev, Dmitry, Russian president, June 2008

Melcher, Frederic Gershom, American publisher, July 1945, *Obit* Apr 1963

Mellon, Richard K., May 1965, *Obit* July 1970

Merchant, Ismail, Indian motion picture producer, Mar 1993, *Obit* Yrbk 2005

Merck, George W., American pharmaceutical executive, Yrbk 1946, *Obit* Jan 1958

Messier, Jean-Marie, French mass media industry executive, May 2002

Metzman, G., July 1946, *Obit* June 1960

Meyer, Agnes Elizabeth Ernst, American journalist, philanthropist and newspaper publisher, Jan 1949, *Obit* Nov 1970

Meyer, Danny, American restaurateur, July 2007

Meyer, Eugene, American investment banker, government official and newspaper publisher, Sept 1941, *Obit* Oct 1959

Meyer, Ron, American motion picture executive, Mar 1997

Meyrowitz, Carol, American retail executive, Nov 2011

Michelin, Edouard, French tire company executive, *Obit* Oct 1940

Middelhoff, Thomas, German publishing and recording executive, Feb 2001

Miers, Earl Schenck, editor and publisher, Yrbk 1949, Sept 1967, *Obit* Jan 1973

Miller, Arjay, Jan 1967

Miller, J. Irwin, American manufacturing executive and architectural patron, Nov 1961, *Obit* Yrbk 2004

Miller, Justin, Jan 1947, *Obit* Mar 1973

Miller, Marvin, American baseball players association executive, May 1973, *Obit* Yrbk 2013

Milner, Yuri, Russian financier, Mar 2013

Ming, Jenny, American clothing chain executive, Jan 2011

Mingus, Sue, American music director and recording executive, July 2008

Minor, Halsey, American media and computer software executive, Oct 1998

Mirvish, Edwin, Canadian theater owner and producer, Apr 1989, *Obit* Yrbk 2007

Mitarai, Fujio, Japanese photographic and office equipment industry executive, Jan 2002

Mitchell, George J., American diplomat and former senator, Apr 1989

Mitchell, Patricia Edenfield, American television executive, Aug 2005

Mittal, Lakshmi, Indian steel industry executive, Jan 2006

Monaghan, Thomas, American fast food and baseball executive, June 1990

Mondavi, Robert, American vintner, Apr 1999, *Obit* Yrbk 2008

Monroney, A. S. Mike, American senator, Nov 1951, *Obit* Apr 1980

Monseu, Stephanie, American circus performer and founder, June 2005

Moody, Joseph Eugene, coal association executive, Yrbk 1948, *Obit* July 1984

Moore, Ann, American magazine executive, Aug 2003

Moore, Gordon E., American computer industry executive, Apr 2002

Moore, Thomas W., American television executive, Sept 1967, *Obit* Yrbk 2007

Morgan, Arthur Ernest, American civil engineer and college president, July 1956, *Obit* Jan 1976

Morgan, J. P., American financier, *Obit* Apr 1943

Morgan, Thomas A., Mar 1950, *Obit* Jan 1968

Morhaime, Mike, American video game company executive, Apr 2010

Morimoto, Masaharu, Japanese chef and restaurateur, Jan 2004

Morita, Akio, Japanese electronics executive, Feb 1972, *Obit* Feb 2000

Morrison, Denise, American food company executive, July 2012

Mortimer, Charles G., Nov 1955, *Obit* Feb 1979

Morton, James, *Obit* Oct 1943

Morton, Rogers C. B., American Secretary of the interior and commerce, Nov 1971, *Obit* June 1979

Mosbacher, Robert, American Secretary of commerce, June 1989, *Obit* Yrbk 2010

Mosher, Ira, Feb 1945, *Obit* May 1968

Moskovitz, Dustin, American social networking website founder, Jan 2012

Motley, Arthur H., publisher, Jan 1961, *Obit* July 1984

Mott, Charles Stewart, American automobile executive, Sept 1969, *Obit* Apr 1973

Mott, Stewart R., American philanthropist and political activist, Apr 1975, *Obit* Yrbk 2008

Moyers, Bill, American journalist and television commentator, Jan 1966, Feb 1976

Mueller, Frederick H., Yrbk 1959, *Obit* Oct 1976

Mueller, George E., aerospace industry executive and NASA official, Nov 1964

Muir, Malcolm, Apr 1953, *Obit* Mar 1979

Mulcahy, Anne, American office equipment industry executive, Nov 2002

Mullenweg, Matt, American computer software executive, May 2013

Munyama, Gerry, Namibian broadcasting executive, Jan 2004

Murdoch, Rupert, Australian-American publishing, motion picture and television executive, May 1977

Murphy, Franklin D., American physician, college

administrator and newspaper executive, Mar 1971, *Obit* Aug 1994

Murphy, Frederick E., American newspaper publisher, *Obit* Mar 1940

Murphy, Patricia, American restaurateur and horticulturist, Apr 1962

Murphy, Thomas Aquinas, American automobile executive, Oct 1979, *Obit* Yrbk 2006

Murphy, William Beverly, food industry executive, Nov 1955, *Obit* Aug 1994

Murray, Thomas E., Sept 1950, *Obit* Sept 1961

Musk, Elon, American entrepreneur, Oct 2006

Myhrvold, Nathan P., American physicist and computer software executive, Sept 1997

Naegle, Susan, American television executive, May 2013

Nagin, Ray, American mayor, Jan 2006

Naikuni, Titus, Kenyan airline executive, Jan 2004

Nasser, Jacques, Lebanese-Australian automobile executive, Apr 2001

Nast, Conde, publisher, *Obit* Nov 1942

Neeleman, David G., American airline executive, Sept 2003

Nelson, Donald Marr, American retail executive, Mar 1941, *Obit* Yrbk 1959

Nelson, Keith, American circus performer and founder, June 2005

Nelson, Marilyn Carlson, American hotel and restaurant industry executive, Oct 2004

Nessen, Ron, American presidential press secretary and public relations executive, Jan 1976

Neuharth, Allen, American newspaper publisher, Apr 1986, *Obit* Yrbk 2013

Newhouse, Samuel I., American newspaper publisher and broadcasting executive, Mar 1961, *Obit* Oct 1979

Newman, J. Wilson, American publishing executive, Apr 1955, *Obit* Yrbk 2003

Newsom, Carroll Vincent, college president, Apr 1957, *Obit* Apr 1990

Niarchos, Stavros, Greek shipping executive, May 1958, *Obit* June 1996

Nichols, William I., June 1958

Nickerson, Albert L., petroleum executive and banking official, Nov 1959, *Obit* Nov 1994

Nidetch, Jean, American dieting organization founder, Yrbk 1973

Nielsen, Arthur C., American market research executive, Yrbk 1951, *Obit* July 1980

Nishi, Kazuhiko, Japanese computer services executive, Jan 2002

Nixon, Lewis, American naval architect, *Obit* Nov 1940

Noble, Edward J., American candy and broadcasting executive, Jan 1944, *Obit* Mar 1959

Noboa, Alvaro, Ecuadorian businessman and political leader, Jan 2007

Nooyi, Indra K., Indian beverage company executive, Nov 2006

Nordhoff, Heinz, German automobile executive, Nov 1956, *Obit* June 1968

Norman, Christina, American broadcasting executive, Nov 2007

North, John Ringling, circus owner, June 1951, *Obit* July 1985

Norton, W. W., *Obit* Yrbk 1945

Notari, Aldo, Italian baseball association executive, Jan 2004, *Obit* CB Int 2006

Notman, J. Geoffrey, Jan 1958

Novogratz, Jacqueline, American investment organization official, Apr 2013

Nuffield, William Richard Morris, British automobile executive, Apr 1941, *Obit* Oct 1963

Nyrop, Donald W., American airline executive, June 1952, *Obit* Yrbk 2011

O'Brien, Lawrence F., American political party leader and basketball association executive, Nov 1961, Apr 1977, *Obit* Nov 1990

O'Konski, Alvin E., congressman, Nov 1955, *Obit* Aug 1987

O'Leary, Hazel R., American university president and former Secretary of energy, Jan 1994

O'Malley, Walter Francis, American baseball executive, Mar 1954, *Obit* Oct 1979

O'Meara, Walter, author and advertising executive, Yrbk 1958, *Obit* Nov 1989

O'Neil, Thomas F., broadcasting executive, Nov 1955, *Obit* June 1998

O'Neill, Paul Henry, American aluminum company executive and Secretary of the treasury, July 2001

Odlum, Floyd B., American financier, Nov 1941, *Obit* Aug 1976

Ogilvy, David, British advertising executive, July 1961, *Obit* Oct 1999

Ohga, Norio, Japanese electronics industry executive, June 1998, *Obit* Yrbk 2011

Okrent, Daniel, American newspaper editor, Nov 2004

Olayan, Lubna, Saudi Arabian financial executive, Jan 2006

Olds, Irving S., American lawyer and steel industry executive, Oct 1948, *Obit* Apr 1963

Oliver, Jamie, British chef and restaurateur, Jan 2005

Olivetti, Adriano, Italian manufacturing executive, Jan 1959, *Obit* Apr 1960

Ollila, Jorma, Finnish cellular telephone equipment industry executive, Aug 2002

Olsen, Kenneth H., American computer industry executive, *Obit* Yrbk 2011

Onassis, Aristotle Socrates, Greek-Argentine shipping executive, Mar 1963, *Obit* May 1975

Onassis, Christina, Greek shipping executive, Feb 1976, *Obit* Jan 1989

Opel, John R., computer executive, Mar 1986, *Obit* Yrbk 2012

Oppenheimer, Harry Frederick, South African diamond mining executive, Feb 1961, *Obit* Nov 2000

Ortega Gaona, Amancio, Spanish clothing retailer, Aug 2012

Osborn, Frederick Henry, railroad executive and investment banker, Nov 1941, *Obit* Mar 1981

Otis, Clarence, American restaurant chain executive, Oct 2009

Ovitz, Michael, American talent agent and motion picture executive, Oct 1995

Pace, Frank, American Secretary of the army, Feb 1950, *Obit* Feb 1988

Packard, David, American computer industry executive, June 1969, *Obit* June 1996

Packer, Kerry Francis Bullmore, Australian newspaper publisher, Jan 2004, *Obit* CB Int 2006

Paepcke, Walter Paul, Apr 1960

Page, Larry, American Internet search engine executive, Oct 2001

Paine, Thomas Otten, aerospace executive and NASA official, Mar 1970, *Obit* July 1992

Paley, William S., American radio and television executive, Oct 1940, Yrbk 1951, *Obit* Jan 1991

Pandit, Vikram S., American financial executive, June 2008

Panic, Milan, Yugoslav prime minister and drug industry executive, June 1993

Pape, William Jamieson, American newspaper publisher, Jan 1940, *Obit* Mar 1961

Parker, Cola G., Sept 1956, *Obit* Sept 1962

Parrish, Wayne W., American magazine and newspaper executive, Nov 1958

Parsons, Richard D., American motion picture and broadcasting executive, Apr 2003

Partridge, Eric, English lexicographer, Jan 1963, *Obit* July 1979

Pascal, Amy, American motion picture executive, Mar 2002

Pasquel, Jorge, July 1946, *Obit* May 1955

Patino, Simon Iturri, Bolivian mining executive, Oct 1942, *Obit* May 1947

Patrick, Deval L., American governor, May 2007

Patrick, Mason Mathews, American general, *Obit* Mar 1942

Patterson, Alicia, American newspaper editor and publisher, Nov 1955, *Obit* Sept 1963

Patterson, Eleanor Medill, American newspaper editor and publisher, Nov 1940, *Obit* Sept 1948

Patterson, Graham, Mar 1949, *Obit* Jan 1970

Patterson, Joseph Medill, American newspaper editor and publisher, Jan 1942, *Obit* June 1946

Patterson, W. A., June 1946, *Obit* Aug 1980

Paul, Josephine Bay, American shipping executive and stockbroker, June 1957

Pauley, Edwin W., American petroleum executive, June 1945, *Obit* Sept 1981

Payson, Joan Whitney, July 1972, *Obit* Nov 1975

Peale, Mundy I., May 1956, *Obit* Jan 1973

Pelley, John J., *Obit* Yrbk 1946

Peltz, Nelson, American financier, Feb 2008

Penney, James Cash, retail executive, Yrbk 1947, *Obit* Mar 1971

Percy, Charles H., American senator, Yrbk 1959, Aug 1977, *Obit* Yrbk 2011

Perdue, Frank, American poultry industry executive, June 1979, *Obit* Oct 2005

Perelman, Ronald Owen, American financier, Jan 1991

Perkins, C. H., June 1955, *Obit* Apr 1963

Perkins, George Walbridge, Apr 1950, *Obit* Mar 1960

Perkins, Milo, June 1942

Perlman, Alfred E., railroad executive, Apr 1955, *Obit* July 1983

Perot, Ross, American computer software executive and presidential candidate, July 1971, Yrbk 1996

Petersen, Donald E., American automobile executive, Mar 1988

Peterson, Peter G., American investment banker and Secretary of commerce, June 1972

Pew, Joseph Newton, American petroleum industry executive and philanthropist, Sept 1941, *Obit* June 1963

Pfeiffer, Eckhard, German computer executive, June 1998

Pfeiffer, Jane, Oct 1980

Phillips, Sam, American record producer, Apr 2001

Phillips, Wendell, American explorer, archaeologist and petroleum industry executive, Nov 1958, *Obit* Feb 1976

Pick, Vernon J., Nov 1955

Pickens, T. Boone, American financier, July 1985

Piech, Ferdinand, German automobile executive, Sept 1999

Piel, Gerard, American magazine publisher and science writer, June 1959, *Obit* Feb 2005

Pike, Sumner T., Mar 1947, *Obit* Apr 1976

Pinault, Francois, French financier, Jan 2004

Pincus, Mark, American computer software executive, Feb 2013

Pinera, Sebastian, Chilean president, Nov 2010

Piper, W. T., American aircraft industry executive, Apr 1946, *Obit* Mar 1970

Pittman, Bob, American television and online computer services executive, July 2000

Plesman, Albert, Mar 1953, *Obit* Mar 1954

Polese, Kim, American computer software executive, July 1997

Poon Tip, Bruce, Canadian adventure travel company founder, Jan 2006

Popcorn, Faith, American market research executive, Feb 1993

Popeil, Ron, American kitchen utensil inventor, Mar 2001

Potanin, Vladimir O., Russian metal industry executive and banker, Jan 2006

Potter, Michael U., Canadian computer software executive, Jan 2005

Potter, Myrtle, American biotechnology executive, Aug 2004

Power, Donald C., Mar 1960, *Obit* May 1979

Praeger, Frederick A., American publishing executive, Sept 1959, *Obit* Aug 1994

Premji, Azim Hasham, Indian information technology executive, Jan 2004

Prentis, Henning Webb, Sept 1940, *Obit* Feb 1960

Prescott, Robert W., July 1971

Price, Gwilym A., American electrical generating equipment company executive, May 1949, *Obit* Aug 1985

Price, Lisa, American personal care products company founder, Feb 2011

Prince, Charles O., American financial services executive, Jan 2007

Prokhorov, Mikhail, Russian financier, Oct 2010

Pucheu, Pierre Firmin, French steel executive and government official, *Obit* May 1944

Puck, Wolfgang, Austrian-American restaurateur and chef, Jan 1998

Puckett, B. Earl, Sept 1950, *Obit* Apr 1976

Pulitzer, Joseph, American newspaper editor and publisher, Yrbk 1954, *Obit* May 1955

Purtell, William A., June 1956, *Obit* July 1978

Putnam, Claude Adams, Feb 1950

Putnam, Roger Lowell, Jan 1952

Puttnam, David, English motion picture producer, Feb 1989

Quinn, William F., American governor, Nov 1958, *Obit* Yrbk 2006

Rackmil, Milton R., motion picture and recording executive, Nov 1952, *Obit* Jan 1992

Rafshoon, Gerald M., American television producer and advertising executive, July 1979

Raines, Franklin D., American financial services executive, Oct 2000

Rainwater, Richard E., American investor, Apr 1999

Rakoff, David, Canadian humorist, Nov 2007, *Obit* Yrbk 2012

Ramaphosa, Cyril, South African political leader and businessman, Sept 1995

Ramo, Simon, American electronics industry executive, Apr 1958

Rand, James Henry, *Obit* Nov 1944

Rand, William M., May 1953

Randall, Clarence B., American steel industry executive and presidential adviser, June 1952, *Obit* Oct 1967

Rank, Joseph Arthur Rank, British motion picture executive, Nov 1945, *Obit* May 1972

Ransom, Victoria, American inforation technology executive, Jan 2013

Rapaczynski, Wanda, Polish broadcasting executive, Jan 2004

Rawl, Lawrence G., American petroleum executive, Feb 1992, *Obit* Yrbk 2005

Raymond, Lee R., American energy industry executive, Nov 1999

Redstone, Sumner, American motion picture and broadcasting executive, Jan 1996

Redzepi, Ren,, Danish chef and restaurateur, Apr 2012

Reed, John S., American financial executive and stock exchange official, Jan 1985

Reed, Philip Dunham, American electronics industry executive, Jan 1949, *Obit* May 1989

Regan, Judith, American editor, publisher and talk show host, Sept 2000

Regine, Belgian nightclub owner, Apr 1980

Reid, Antonio, American recording industry producer and executive, Aug 2001

Reid, Helen Rogers, American newspaper publisher, Feb 1941, May 1952, *Obit* Oct 1970

Reid, Whitelaw, American newspaper editor and publisher, Yrbk 1954, *Obit* Yrbk 2009

Reith, John Charles Walsham Reith, Scottish broadcasting executive, Nov 1940, *Obit* July 1971

Ren Zhengfei, Chinese telecommunications equipment company executive, Jan 2005

Renault, Louis, French automobile executive, *Obit* Yrbk 1944

Rennebohm, Oscar, July 1950, *Obit* Yrbk 1968

Rentzel, Delos Wilson, government official and aviation expert, Oct 1948, *Obit* Jan 1992

Resor, Stanley, American advertising executive, July 1949, *Obit* Yrbk 1962

Reuther, Victor, American labor leader, Yrbk 1953, *Obit* Yrbk 2004

Reves, Emery, British publisher and art collector, July 1946

Reynolds, Richard S., American manufacturing executive, May 1967, *Obit* Nov 1980

Reynolds, Richard Samuel, American aluminum industry executive, Feb 1953, *Obit* Oct 1955

Rhone, Sylvia, American recording industry executive, June 1998

Rice, Linda Johnson, American magazine publishing executive, July 2011

Richards, Vincent, July 1947, *Obit* Yrbk 1959

Richards, Wayne E., July 1954

Rickey, Branch, American baseball manager and executive, Oct 1945, *Obit* Jan 1966

Rigg, Edgar T., June 1961

Riggio, Leonard, American book store chain executive, June 1998

Riklis, Meshulam, financier, Yrbk 1971

Rinehart, Stanley M., Yrbk 1954, *Obit* June 1969

Riordan, Richard, American mayor and investor, May 2000

Ripert, Eric, French chef and restaurateur, Mar 2013

Riter, Henry G., Oct 1955, *Obit* Sept 1958

Rivero, Jose Ignacio, Cuban newspaper publisher, *Obit* May 1944

Robaina, Alejandro, Cuban cigar manufacturer, Jan 2004, *Obit* Yrbk 2010

Roberts, C. Wesley, American public relations executive and political party leader, Apr 1953, *Obit* June 1975

Roberts, Michael, American telecommunications, real estate and publishing executive, Feb 2010

Roberts, Steven, American real estate, broadcasting and telecommunications executive, Feb 2010

Robertson, Pat, American evangelist and television executive, Sept 1987

Robertson, Reuben B., Yrbk 1955, *Obit* May 1960

Robinson, Janet L., American newspaper executive, Mar 2003

Robinson, Maurice R., Yrbk 1956, *Obit* May 1982

Robinson, William E., American beverage industry and newspaper executive, Feb 1958, *Obit* July 1969

Robuchon, Joel, French chef and restaurateur, Jan 2003

Roche, James M., American automobile executive, Feb 1967, *Obit* Yrbk 2004

Roche, Josephine, American coal industry executive, Aug 1941, *Obit* Sept 1976

Rockefeller, Laurance S., American investor and conservationist, June 1959, *Obit* Yrbk 2004

Rockefeller, Winthrop, American governor, philanthropist and financier, Sept 1959, *Obit* Apr 1973

Roddick, Anita, British cosmetics industry executive, Sept 1992, *Obit* Yrbk 2007

Roderick, David M., steel executive, Apr 1987

Rogers, Desiree G., American magazine executive, June 2011

Rogers, Roy, American cowboy singer and actor, Mar 1948, Oct 1983, *Obit* Sept 1998

Rojas, Rudy, American clothing company executive, Jan 2006

Romnes, Haakon Ingolf, telecommunications executive, Feb 1968, *Obit* Jan 1974

Romney, George, American Secretary of housing and urban development, June 1958, *Obit* Oct 1995

Romney, Mitt, American governor, Sept 2006

Roosevelt, James, American congressman, business consultant and son of President Franklin D. Roosevelt, Apr 1950, *Obit* Nov 1991

Roosevelt, Kermit, army officer, steamship line executive and son of President Theodore Roosevelt, *Obit* July 1943

Rootes, William Edward Rootes, British automobile executive, Nov 1951, *Obit* Feb 1965

Roper, Elmo, American public opinion analyst, Jan 1945, *Obit* June 1971

Rose, Billy, American theatrical producer, Aug 1940, *Obit* Mar 1966

Rosedale, Philip, American information technology executive, Oct 2012

Rosen, Benjamin M., computer executive and financier, June 1997

Rosenfeld, Henry Jonas, clothing and luggage industry executive, Nov 1948

Rosenfeld, Irene, American food industry executive, July 2007

Rosenwald, Lessing J., American retail executive and book collector, Feb 1947, *Obit* Aug 1979

Rospars, Joe, American information technology executive, May 2010

Ross, Robert, American entrepreneur, Oct 2002, *Obit* Yrbk 2011

Rosset, Barney, American publisher and editor, Apr 1972, *Obit* Yrbk 2012

Rothermere, Esmond Cecil Harmsworth, British

newspaper publisher, Yrbk 1948, *Obit* Sept 1978

Rothermere, Harold Sidney Harmsworth, British newspaper publisher, *Obit* Jan 1941

Rozelle, Pete, American football commissioner, June 1964, *Obit* Feb 1997

Rubicam, Raymond, advertising executive, Yrbk 1943, *Obit* July 1978

Rubin, Rick, American recording producer and executive, Sept 2007

Rubin, Robert E., American financial executive and former Secretary of the treasury, July 1997

Rubinstein, Helena, American cosmetician, June 1943, *Obit* May 1965

Rudkin, Margaret Fogarty, American baking executive, Sept 1959, *Obit* Oct 1967

Ruffin, William H., Feb 1951

Ruml, Beardsley, department store executive and banker, May 1943, *Obit* June 1960

Rumsfeld, Donald H., American Secretary of defense, Apr 1970, Mar 2002

Rush, David Kenneth, American chemical industry executive and diplomat, May 1975, *Obit* Feb 1995

Russell, Charles Hinton, American newspaper publisher and governor, Yrbk 1955, *Obit* Nov 1989

Russell, Donald J., railroad executive, May 1962, *Obit* Feb 1986

Russo, Pat F., American information technology executive, May 2008

Saatchi, Maurice, English advertising executive, Jan 1989

Sagendorph, Robb, American magazine editor and publisher, Yrbk 1956, *Obit* Sept 1970

Salant, Richard S., television executive, Nov 1961, *Obit* Apr 1993

Sale, Rhys M., Yrbk 1957

Sambi, Ahmed Abdallah Mohamed, Comoran president, Jan 2006

Sambrook, Richard, British broadcasting executive, Jan 2003

Sanchez Junco, Eduardo, Spanish magazine publisher, Jan 2003, *Obit* Yrbk 2010

Sandberg, Sheryl, American Internet executive, June 2008

Sanders, Harland, American restaurateur, Apr 1973, *Obit* Feb 1981

Sanger, Stephen W., American food company executive, Mar 2004

Sardi, Vincent, American restaurateur, May 1957, *Obit* Yrbk 2008

Sardi, Vincent, American restaurateur, May 1957, *Obit* Jan 1970

Sargent, Porter, July 1941, *Obit* May 1951

Sarnoff, David, American radio and television executive, Nov 1940, Oct 1951, *Obit* Feb 1972

Sarnoff, Robert W., electronics executive, Yrbk 1956, *Obit* May 1997

Sassa, Scott Michael, American Internet executive, Jan 2000

Sassoon, Vidal, British hairstylist and personal care products industry executive, Apr 1999, *Obit* Yrbk 2012

Sauer, George H., football coach and executive, Nov 1948, *Obit* Apr 1994

Saunders, Stuart Thomas, American railroad executive, Apr 1966, *Obit* Mar 1987

Sawhill, John C., American college president and conservationist, Apr 1979, *Obit* Yrbk 2000

Saylor, Michael, computer software executive, Sept 2000

Sayre, Morris, Jan 1948, *Obit* Apr 1953

Scannell, Herb, American broadcasting executive, Aug 2010

Scardino, Marjorie, American publishing executive, Apr 2000

Schacht, Al, baseball entertainer and restaurateur, May 1946, *Obit* Sept 1984

Schacht, Hjalmar, German financier, Oct 1944, *Obit* Sept 1970

Schechter, A. A., broadcasting executive, May 1941, *Obit* Aug 1989

Scherman, Harry, Sept 1943, July 1963, *Obit* Jan 1970

Schiff, Dorothy, American newspaper publisher, July 1945, Jan 1965, *Obit* Oct 1989

Schiffrin, Andre, American publisher, Jan 2000

Schiller, Vivian, American radio executive, Oct 2009

Schmidt, Eric, American information technology executive, Apr 2008

Schneider, Eugene, *Obit* Jan 1943

Schott, Marge, American automobile dealer and baseball executive, Aug 1999, *Obit* Yrbk 2004

Schrempp, Juergen E., German automobile executive, Oct 1999

Schroeder, Patricia, American publishing association executive and former congresswoman, Oct 1978

Schultz, Howard, American coffee chain executive, May 1997

Schultz, Richard D., sports executive, July 1996

Schuster, M. Lincoln, July 1941, *Obit* Feb 1971

Scott, H. Lee, American retail executive, Oct 2006

Scull, Robert C., American taxi executive and art collector, Apr 1974, *Obit* Feb 1986

Sculley, John, American computer industry executive, Aug 1988

Seaton, Fred A., American newspaper publisher and Secretary of the interior, Nov 1956, *Obit* Mar 1974

Selfridge, Harry Gordon, American-British merchant, Mar 1941, *Obit* June 1947

Selig, Bud, American baseball commissioner, Jan 1999

Semel, Terry S., American Internet service provider executive, July 2006

Sen, Laura, American supermarket executive, Oct 2011

Sengstacke, John, newspaper executive, Nov 1949, *Obit* Aug 1997

Sepp Blatter, Joseph, Swiss soccer association executive, Jan 2002

Seyferth, O. A., July 1950

Shafik, Doria, May 1955

Shakespeare, Frank, Sept 1970

Shannon, William V., newspaper executive, Jan 1979, *Obit* Nov 1988

Shapiro, Irving S., American lawyer and chemical company executive, Nov 1976, *Obit* Nov 2001

Shapiro, Neal, American television producer and executive, May 2003

Shapp, Milton Jerrold, American governor, July 1973, *Obit* Feb 1995

Shaver, Dorothy, American department store executive, Jan 1946, *Obit* Sept 1959

Shea, Andrew B., Jan 1957, *Obit* Jan 1973

Sheed, F. J., American theologian and publisher, Sept 1981, *Obit* Jan 1982

Shelby, Carroll, American automobile racing driver and manufacturer, Nov 1993, *Obit* Yrbk 2012

Shelly, Warner S., Feb 1952

Shield, Lansing P., June 1951, *Obit* Mar 1960

Shimkin, Leon, publisher, May 1954

Shoriki, Matsutaro, Japanese newspaper publisher, broadcasting executive and government official, Feb 1958

Shultz, George P., American Secretary of state, May 1969, Apr 1988

Shurlock, Geoffrey, Jan 1962, *Obit* June 1976

Shuttleworth, Mark, South African entrepreneur, Jan 2007

Silverman, Fred, television executive, Nov 1978

Simmons, Russell, American recording, motion picture and broadcasting executive, June 1998

Simon, Norton, American financier and art collector, Mar 1968, *Obit* Aug 1993

Simon, Richard L., American publisher, July 1941, *Obit* Oct 1960

Simon, William E., American Secretary of the treasury and financier, Apr 1974, *Obit* Aug 2000

Simpson, Howard E., railroad executive, May 1958, *Obit* Apr 1985

Sims, William L., Yrbk 1956

Sinegal, James D., American warehouse club executive, Aug 2007

Six, Robert F., airline executive, Oct 1970, *Obit* Nov 1986

Skillin, Edward S., magazine editor and publisher, May 1949, *Obit* Yrbk 2000

Skouras, Spyros P., American motion picture executive, June 1943, *Obit* Nov 1971

Skutt, V. J., insurance executive, Yrbk 1959, *Obit* Apr 1993

Slater, John E., Nov 1951

Sligh, Charles R., Apr 1953

Slim Helu, Carlos, Mexican financier, Jan 2003

Sloan, Alfred Pritchard, American automobile executive, Nov 1940, *Obit* Mar 1966

Sloan, Samuel, *Obit* May 1945

Smallpeice, Basil, English airline and shipping executive, Oct 1969

Smart, David A., magazine publisher, June 1944

Smith, Austin E., physician and drug industry executive, Mar 1950, *Obit* Jan 1994

Smith, Barbara, American actress, model and restaurateur, July 1998

Smith, Frederick W., American air freight executive, June 2000

Smith, Harrison, Yrbk 1954, *Obit* Feb 1971

Smith, Hazel Brannon, American newspaper publisher, Sept 1973, *Obit* July 1994

Smith, Orin, American coffee retailer, Nov 2003

Smith, Roger B., American automobile executive, May 1986, *Obit* Yrbk 2008

Smolyansky, Julie, American food industry executive, Nov 2013

Snider, Stacey, American motion picture executive, Apr 2008

Snow, John W., American investment manager and former Secretary of the treasury, Aug 2003

Snyder, John W., American Secretary of the treasury, July 1945, *Obit* Jan 1986

Solandt, Omond M., Mar 1974

Son, Masayoshi, Japanese Internet and telecommunications executive, Jan 2006

Soong, T. V., Chinese government official and financier, Mar 1941, *Obit* June 1971

Soros, George, American financier, Apr 1997

Souers, Sidney W., American banker, insurance executive and intelligence service official, Feb 1949, *Obit* Mar 1973

Spectorsky, A. C., Jan 1960, *Obit* Mar 1972

Spivak, Lawrence E., television moderator, May 1956, *Obit* May 1994

Sporn, Philip, American electrical engineer, Nov 1966

Sprague, Robert Chapman, radio and television equipment executive, Jan 1951, *Obit* Nov 1991

Springer, Axel, German publishing executive, Yrbk 1968, *Obit* Nov 1985

Stamp, Josiah Charles, British government official, *Obit* June 1941

Stanley, Freelan Oscar, American automotive pioneer, *Obit* Nov 1940

Stanley, Thomas B., American governor, Yrbk 1955, *Obit* Oct 1970

Stanton, Frank, American broadcasting executive, Nov 1945, Oct 1965, *Obit* Yrbk 2007

Stanton, Katie Jacobs, Internet executive and Special Adviser to the Office of Innovation at the U.S. Department of State, June 2012

Starch, Daniel, psychologist and marketing analyst, Jan 1963

Statz, Hermann, Jan 1958

Steinbrenner, George M., American baseball and

shipbuilding executive, Feb 1979, *Obit* Yrbk 2010

Steloff, Frances, bookseller, Nov 1965, *Obit* June 1989

Stern, David, American basketball association executive, Apr 1991

Stern, Leonard, American real estate executive and newspaper publisher, Mar 1991

Stettinius, Edward Reilly, American Secretary of state, July 1940, *Obit* Yrbk 1949

Stevens, Robert T., American textile industry executive and Secretary of the army, July 1953, *Obit* Mar 1983

Steward, David L., American information technology executive, Nov 2004

Stieglitz, Alfred, American photographer, Jan 1940, *Obit* Sept 1946

Stoddard, Brandon, television executive, Feb 1989

Stolk, William C., Mar 1953

Stone, W. Clement, American insurance executive, Feb 1972, *Obit* Yrbk 2002

Stoppelman, Jeremy, American Internet executive, June 2012

Storch, Jerry, American retail executive, June 2007

Storke, Thomas M., American newspaper editor and publisher, Yrbk 1963

Straus, Jack Isidor, department store executive, Mar 1952, *Obit* Nov 1985

Straus, Nathan, May 1944, *Obit* Nov 1961

Straus, Percy Selden, American department store executive, *Obit* May 1944

Straus, Roger W., American metal industry executive, July 1952, *Obit* Oct 1957

Straus, Roger W., American publishing executive, Aug 1980, *Obit* Yrbk 2004

Streibert, Theodore C., American government official and broadcasting executive, Feb 1955, *Obit* Mar 1987

Stringer, Howard, American electronics, film and broadcasting industry executive, Jan 2006

Strong, Maurice F., Canadian petroleum executive,

environmentalist and government official, Yrbk 1973

Strong, William McCreery, *Obit* May 1941

Strouse, Norman H., advertising executive, May 1960, *Obit* Mar 1993

Stutz, Geraldine, American retail executive, May 1983, *Obit* Yrbk 2005

Sullivan, A. M., Yrbk 1953, *Obit* Aug 1980

Sulzberger, Arthur Hays, American newspaper publisher, Mar 1943, *Obit* Feb 1969

Sulzberger, Arthur O., American newspaper publisher, Jan 1997

Sulzberger, Arthur Ochs, American newspaper publisher, Nov 1966, *Obit* Yrbk 2012

Sunderland, Thomas Elbert, fruit industry executive, Apr 1962, *Obit* May 1991

Sutton, Percy E., American municipal official, broadcasting executive and civil rights activist, Mar 1973, *Obit* Yrbk 2010

Swallow, Alan, Feb 1963, *Obit* Jan 1967

Swartz, Aaron, American electronic publisher, *Obit* Yrbk 2013

Swearingen, John E., American petroleum industry executive, Jan 1979, *Obit* Yrbk 2007

Sweeney, Anne, American television executive, June 2003

Swidler, Joseph C., American government official, Mar 1964, *Obit* July 1997

Swift, Gustavus Franklin, American meat packing executive, *Obit* Yrbk 1943

Swift, Harold Higgins, Feb 1950, *Obit* Sept 1962

Swigert, Ernest Goodnough, machinery industry executive, Oct 1957, *Obit* Feb 1987

Swirbul, Leon A., Apr 1953, *Obit* Sept 1960

Syme, John P., Mar 1957

Symes, James M., Yrbk 1955, *Obit* Sept 1976

Tagliabue, Paul, American football commissioner, Oct 1992

Taintor, Anne, American artist and entrepreneur, June 2005

Talbott, Harold E., American Secretary of the air force, July 1953, *Obit* May 1957

Talbott, Philip M., Apr 1958

Talese, Nan A., American publishing executive, Sept 2006

Tang, David, Chinese retail executive, Jan 2006

Tapie, Bernard, French financier, Jan 2002

Tarkenton, Fran, American football player, Sept 1969

Tartikoff, Brandon, American television and motion picture executive, Apr 1987, *Obit* Nov 1997

Tata, J. R. D., Indian industrialist and philanthropist, Yrbk 1958, *Obit* Jan 1994

Tata, Ratan, Indian financier, Jan 2007

Taylor, John W., American college president, television executive and United Nations official, Jan 1954, *Obit* Apr 2002

Taylor, Myron C., American financier and diplomat, Feb 1940, *Obit* July 1959

Taylor, Susan L., American magazine editor, Feb 1997

Temple, Johnny, American rock bassist and publisher, Oct 2008

Terra, Daniel J., chemical executive and art collector, Nov 1987, *Obit* Sept 1996

Thaksin Shinawatra, Thai prime minister, Jan 2002

Thielen, Gunter, German publishing executive, Jan 2005

Thomas, Charles Allen, Mar 1950, *Obit* May 1982

Thomas, Charles S., American airline executive and Secretary of the navy, Yrbk 1954, *Obit* Jan 1984

Thomas, Dave, American fast food restaurant chain founder, Mar 1995, *Obit* Apr 2002

Thomas, Helen, American journalist, Nov 1993, *Obit* Yrbk 2013

Thomas, John Parnell, American congressman, Sept 1947, *Obit* Jan 1971

Thomas, Miles Thomas, Jan 1952, *Obit* Apr 1980

Thomas-Graham, Pamela, American clothing industry executive and mystery novelist, July 2000

Thompson, John W., American information technology executive, Mar 2005

Thompson, Paul Williams, general and publishing executive, Nov 1942, *Obit* May 1996

Thomson of Fleet, Roy Herbert Thomson, Canadian newspaper publisher, Jan 1960, *Obit* Sept 1976

Thomson, Kenneth, Canadian newspaper executive, July 1989, *Obit* Yrbk 2006

Thornhill, Arthur H., Apr 1958, *Obit* Mar 1970

Thornton, Charles Bates, defense industry executive, Feb 1970, *Obit* Jan 1982

Thyssen, Fritz, German industrialist, May 1940, *Obit* Mar 1951

Thyssen-Bornemisza, Hans Heinrich, Swiss financier and art collector, Feb 1989, *Obit* Yrbk 2002

Tian Congming, Chinese broadcasting and news agency official, Jan 2005

Tillerson, Rex, American energy industry executive, Sept 2006

Tillinghast, Charles C., airline executive, Feb 1962, *Obit* Oct 1998

Timerman, Jacobo, Argentine newspaper publisher, Nov 1981, *Obit* Jan 2000

Tinker, Grant, American television executive, Mar 1982

Tisch, Laurence A., American financier, Feb 1987, *Obit* Yrbk 2004

Titterton, Lewis H., Sept 1943

Tong, Hollington K., Taiwanese diplomat, Yrbk 1956, *Obit* Feb 1971

Tonner, Robert, American doll maker, Oct 2011

Townsend, Lynn A., American automobile executive, Sept 1966, *Obit* Yrbk 2000

Townsend, Robert, American car rental company executive, Nov 1970, *Obit* Mar 1998

Trammell, Niles, Sept 1940, *Obit* May 1973

Trautman, George McNeal, baseball executive, Oct 1951, *Obit* Sept 1963

Trefflich, Henry, Jan 1953, *Obit* Sept 1978

Trippe, J. T., American airline executive, Aug 1942, Feb 1955, *Obit* May 1981

Trotter, Lloyd G., American manufacturing executive, July 2005

Truitt, Paul T., Sept 1948

Trump, Donald J., American real estate executive, Feb 1984

Tsai, Ming, American chef and restaurateur, June 2012

Tukur, Alhaji Bamanga, Nigerian business organization official, Jan 2004

Tuttle, Charles Egbert, publisher and rare book dealer, July 1960, *Obit* Aug 1993

Twomey, Paul, Australian Internet executive, Jan 2003

Tyson, John H., American poultry company executive, Aug 2001

Ueberroth, Peter, American entrepreneur and Olympic executive, Apr 1985

Uhlmann, Richard Frederick, grain dealer, Jan 1949, *Obit* Feb 1990

Ullstein, Herman, *Obit* Jan 1944

Unwin, Stanley, British publisher, Mar 1949, *Obit* Yrbk 1968

Valenti, Jack, American motion picture association executive, Jan 1968, *Obit* Yrbk 2007

Valletta, Vittorio, Italian automobile executive, *Obit* July 1967

Van Schmus, W. G., *Obit* Mar 1942

Van Volkenburg, Jack Lamont, Jan 1955, *Obit* July 1963

Vance, Harold S., American automobile executive and government official, May 1949, *Obit* Nov 1959

Vanden Heuvel, Katrina, American magazine editor and publisher, May 2009

Vanderbilt, Cornelius, American financier, *Obit* Apr 1942

Vanderbilt, William Kissam, railroad executive and

automobile racing driver, *Obit* Feb 1944

Vandervelde, Luc, Belgian retail executive, Jan 2002

Vann, Robert Lee, American newspaper editor and publisher, *Obit* Yrbk 1940

Vasella, Daniel, Swiss pharmaceutical executive and physician, Jan 2005

Vaughan, Guy W., Yrbk 1948, *Obit* Jan 1967

Veeck, Bill, American baseball executive, Nov 1948, *Obit* Feb 1986

Vergara Madrigal, Jorge, Mexican entrepreneur, Jan 2003

Verity, Calvin William, American Secretary of commerce, May 1988

Vernon, Lillian, American mail order executive, Mar 1996

Viguerie, Richard A., American political fund raiser and magazine publisher, Jan 1983

Vila, George R., tire and rubber executive, Mar 1963, *Obit* Aug 1987

Villard, Oswald Garrison, American journalist, Aug 1940, *Obit* Nov 1949

Vincent, Francis T., American motion picture executive and baseball commissioner, May 1991

Wachner, Linda Joy, American clothing industry executive, Nov 1998

Wagner, Richard, Apr 1962

Wakefield, Charles Cheers Wakefield, English lubricants industry executive, *Obit* Mar 1941

Waldron, Hicks Benjamin, cosmetics executive, Mar 1988

Wales, Jimmy, American Internet entrepreneur, Oct 2006

Walker, Jay, American entrepreneur and information technology executive, Oct 2000

Walker, Olene S., American governor, Apr 2005

Wallace, DeWitt, periodical editor and publisher, Apr 1944, May 1956, *Obit* May 1981

Wallace, Lila Acheson, American philanthropist and publisher, May 1956, *Obit* July 1984

Walton, Sam, American retail executive, Mar 1992, *Obit* Mar 1992

Wampler, Cloud, Yrbk 1952

Wang, An, American computer industry executive, Jan 1987, *Obit* May 1990

Warburg, James Paul, American banker, Apr 1948, *Obit* July 1969

Ward, Maisie, English author and publisher, Jan 1966, *Obit* Mar 1975

Warner, Albert, American motion picture executive, Jan 1945, *Obit* Jan 1968

Warner, Harry M., American motion picture executive, Jan 1945, *Obit* Oct 1958

Warner, Jack L., American motion picture executive, Jan 1945, *Obit* Nov 1978

Warner, Mark R., American senator, Oct 2006

Warner, Ty, American toy industry executive, Nov 1998

Washington, Alonzo, American comic book artist and publisher, May 1999

Wason, Robert R., American manufacturing industry association executive, Jan 1946, *Obit* Sept 1950

Wasserman, Lew R., American motion picture executive, May 1991, *Obit* Yrbk 2002

Waters, Alice, American chef and restaurateur, Jan 2004

Watkins, Donald V., American lawyer and investor, Jan 2003

Watson, Arthur Kittredge, American computer industry executive and diplomat, Sept 1971, *Obit* Oct 1974

Watson, Burl Stevens, petroleum executive, Apr 1957

Watson, Thomas J., American computer industry executive and diplomat, Feb 1956, *Obit* Mar 1994

Watson, Thomas J., American office equipment industry executive, Nov 1940, July 1950, *Obit* Sept 1956

Weaver, Pat, American television executive, Jan 1955, *Obit* Sept 2002

Weeks, Sinclair, American Secretary of commerce, Mar 1953, *Obit* Mar 1972

Weider, Joe, American publisher and bodybuilder, Jan 1998, *Obit* Yrbk 2013

Weil, Richard, July 1951, *Obit* July 1958

Weill, Sanford I., American financial services executive, July 1999

Weinstein, Bob, American motion picture executive, Mar 1997

Weinstein, Harvey, American motion picture executive, Mar 1997

Weir, Ernest T., American steel industry executive, June 1941, *Obit* Oct 1957

Welch, John F., American corporation executive, Jan 1988

Welch, Leo D., Yrbk 1963, *Obit* Jan 1979

Welch, Robert, American founder of John Birch Society, Nov 1976, *Obit* Mar 1985

Wells, Gabriel, bookseller, *Obit* Yrbk 1946

Wenner, Jann S., American magazine executive, Jan 1980

Werblin, Sonny, football executive and theatrical agent, Apr 1979, *Obit* Feb 1992

Westergren, Tim, American information technology executive, Oct 2012

Wexler, Jerry, American recording industry executive, Jan 2001, *Obit* Yrbk 2008

Wexner, Leslie H., American fashion chain store executive and philanthropist, Feb 1994

Weyerhaeuser, Frederick E., *Obit* Nov 1945

Weyerhaeuser, George H., July 1977

Whalen, Grover A., Sept 1944, *Obit* June 1962

Wheeler, Tony, Australian travel writer and publisher, Jan 2005

Whitaker, Mark, American television news executive, Aug 2003

White, Charles M., June 1950, *Obit* Mar 1977

White, Francis W., Jan 1954, *Obit* June 1957

White, Frank, Yrbk 1950, *Obit* Jan 1980

White, John F., American television executive and college president, Nov 1967, *Obit* Yrbk 2005

White, Marco Pierre, British chef and restaurateur, Jan 2007

White, Paul Welrose, journalist and radio executive, Mar 1940, *Obit* Oct 1955

White, Robert M., American newspaper editor and publisher, Mar 1960

White, William, Jan 1953, *Obit* June 1967

White, William Lindsay, American journalist and writer, Jan 1943, *Obit* Oct 1973

Whitehead, Edward, British manufacturing executive, Jan 1967, *Obit* June 1978

Whitman, Marina von Neumann, American automobile executive and economist, Oct 1973

Whitman, Meg, American Internet auction executive, Feb 2000

Whitney, John Hay, American financier and diplomat, Yrbk 1945, *Obit* Apr 1982

Whittle, Christopher, American publishing, broadcasting and school management company executive, Feb 1991

Wigand, Jeffrey, American teacher and former tobacco industry executive, Apr 2000

Wilde, Frazar B., insurance executive, Apr 1959, *Obit* Aug 1985

Wilder, Frances Farmer, July 1947

Wiley, William Foust, American newspaper publisher, *Obit* Oct 1944

Willes, Mark H., American newspaper publisher, Mar 1998

Williams, Aubrey Willis, American government official, publisher and social welfare leader, May 1940, *Obit* Apr 1965

Williams, Edward Bennett, American lawyer and baseball and football executive, Jan 1965, *Obit* Sept 1988

Williams, Evan, American Internet executive, July 2009

Williams, John J., American senator, Jan 1952, *Obit* Apr 1988

Williams, Ronald, American health insurance executive, July 2009

Willis, Paul S., food and grocery trade association executive, Jan 1951, *Obit* Aug 1987

Willkie, Wendell Lewis, American lawyer and presidential candidate, Feb 1940, *Obit* Nov 1944

Wills, Childe Harold, automobile executive, *Obit* Feb 1941

Wilson, Charles E., American automobile executive and Secretary of defense, Aug 1941, Sept 1950, *Obit* Yrbk 1961

Wilson, Charles E., American electronics industry executive, Apr 1943, Feb 1951, *Obit* Feb 1972

Wilson, Edward Foss, corporation executive and government official, Mar 1958, *Obit* May 1994

Wilson, Halsey William, publisher, Yrbk 1941, May 1948, *Obit* Apr 1954

Wilson, I. W., July 1952, *Obit* Jan 1978

Wilson, Joseph C., American office equipment industry executive, Oct 1966, *Obit* Jan 1972

Wilson, Leroy A., Apr 1948, *Obit* July 1951

Wilson, Peter C., English art dealer, Feb 1968, *Obit* Aug 1984

Wise, James DeCamp, carpet industry executive, Apr 1954, *Obit* Apr 1984

Witherow, W. P., Apr 1942, *Obit* Mar 1960

Woertz, Patricia, American agribusiness executive, Mar 2007

Wojcicki, Susan, American Internet executive, Feb 2013

Wojciechowska, Maia, Polish children's author and publisher, Sept 1976, *Obit* Yrbk 2002

Wolfram, Stephen, American physicist and software executive, Feb 2005

Wong, Andrea, American broadcasting executive, Sept 2007

Wong-Staal, Flossie, American molecular biologist, Apr 2001

Wood, Robert D., Yrbk 1974, *Obit* July 1986

Wood, Robert Elkington, retail executive, May 1941, *Obit* Yrbk 1969

Woods, Mark, American broadcasting executive, Mar 1946

Woolf, Leonard, English political essayist, editor, publisher and memoirist, Yrbk 1965, *Obit* Oct 1969

Woolton, Frederick James Marquis, English financier, Oct 1940, Oct 1950, *Obit* Feb 1965

Worthington, Leslie B., steel executive, Oct 1960, *Obit* Oct 1998

Wozniak, Stephen, American electronics industry executive, July 1997

Wright, Orville, American aviation pioneer, Oct 1946, *Obit* Mar 1948

Wright, Robert Charles, American television executive, Jan 1989

Wrigley, Philip Knight, baseball executive, Apr 1975, *Obit* June 1977

Wyman, Thomas, American radio and television executive, June 1983, *Obit* Yrbk 2003

Yang, Jerry, American Internet search engine executive, Oct 1997

Yankelovich, Daniel, American sociologist, Mar 1982

Yates, Herbert J., July 1949, *Obit* Mar 1966

Yessa, Abdel Nasser, Mauritanian anti-slavery activist, Jan 2006

Yoshino, Hiroyuki, Japanese automobile executive, Jan 2002

Young, John A., computer executive, Oct 1986

Young, Owen D., lawyer and manufacturing executive, Aug 1945, *Obit* Sept 1962

Young, Robert Ralph, railroad executive, Apr 1947, *Obit* Mar 1958

Young, Stanley, dramatist and publishing executive, Yrbk 1951, *Obit* May 1975

Yun, Jong Yong, Korean electronics industry executive, Jan 2003

Zaentz, Saul, American recording executive and motion picture producer, Mar 1997

Zagat, Nina, American restaurant survey publisher, Mar 2008

Zagat, Tim, American restaurant survey publisher, Mar 2008

Zanuck, Darryl F., American motion picture producer, Aug 1941, Mar 1954, *Obit* Feb 1980

Zarb, Frank G., American securities exchange official, Sept 1975

Zell, Samuel, American real estate investor, Jan 2009

Zellerbach, J. D., Yrbk 1948, *Obit* Nov 1963

Zelnick, Strauss, American financier, Nov 2010

Zennstrom, Niklas, Swedish computer software engineer and executive, Jan 2007

Zetsche, Dieter, German automobile executive, Jan 2006

Zevin, Ben David, publisher, Sept 1943, *Obit* Feb 1985

Ziegler, Ronald L., American drug store association executive and presidential press secretary, Nov 1971, *Obit* July 2003

Ziff, William B., American magazine executive, Oct 1946, *Obit* Feb 1954

Zimmerman, M. M., July 1957

Zorbaugh, Geraldine Bone, lawyer and broadcasting executive, Yrbk 1956, *Obit* Sept 1996

Zucker, Jeff, American motion picture and television executive, Jan 2002

Zuckerberg, Mark, American Internet executive, Jan 2008

Zuckerman, Mortimer B., American real estate developer and magazine and newspaper publisher, Jan 1990

Zukor, Adolph, American motion picture executive, Mar 1950, *Obit* Aug 1976

al-Mutawa, Naif, Kuwaiti businessman and comic book creator, May 2012

von Tobel, Alexa, American Internet executive, June 2013

Cabinet members

Abbott, Douglas, Canadian supreme court justice, June 1949

Abe, Shinzo, Japanese prime minister, Jan 2006

Abraham, Spencer, American Secretary of energy, May 2001

Acheson, Dean, American Secretary of state, Mar 1941, Feb 1949, *Obit* Nov 1971

Adams, Brock, American Secretary of transportation and senator, July 1977, *Obit* Yrbk 2004

Adoula, Cyrille, Congolese prime minister, Mar 1962

Aguirre Cerda, Pedro, Chilean president, Jan 1941, *Obit* Jan 1941

Aichi, Kiichi, Japanese statesman, July 1971, *Obit* Jan 1974

Al-Maktoum, Mohammed bin Rashid, United Arab Emirates prime minister, Apr 2008

Al-Mubarak, Massouma, Kuwaiti cabinet member, Jan 2005

Ala, Hussein, Iranian prime minister, May 1951, *Obit* Sept 1964

Albright, Madeleine Korbel, American Secretary of state, May 1995, Apr 2000

Alexander, Harold Rupert Leofric George Alexander, British field marshal, Oct 1942, *Obit* Sept 1969

Alexander, Lamar, American senator, July 1991

Alliot-Marie, Michele, French cabinet member, Jan 2003

Allon, Yigal, Israeli political leader, Sept 1975, *Obit* Apr 1980

Amery, Leopold Charles Maurice Stennett, British cabinet member, July 1942, *Obit* Yrbk 1956

Amory, Derick Heathcoat Amory, British textile industry

executive and cabinet member, Apr 1958

Anderson, Clinton P., American Secretary of agriculture and senator, June 1945, *Obit* Jan 1976

Anderson, Robert Bernerd, American Secretary of the treasury, June 1953, *Obit* Oct 1989

Andreotti, Giulio, Italian prime minister, Feb 1977, *Obit* Yrbk 2013

Andrus, Cecil D., governor, Aug 1977

Aranha, Oswaldo, Brazilian diplomat, Mar 1942, *Obit* Apr 1960

Areilza, Jose Maria de, Spanish diplomat and political leader, Apr 1955, *Obit* May 1998

Arens, Moshe, Israeli cabinet member, July 1989

Arias Sanchez, Oscar, Costa Rican president, Aug 1987

Ashcroft, John D., American Attorney general, Sept 1999

Aspin, Les, American Secretary of defense, Feb 1986, *Obit* July 1995

Averoff-Tossizza, Evangelos, Greek political leader, May 1957, *Obit* Mar 1990

Azimi, Abdul Salam, Afghan supreme court justice, Jan 2006

Aziz, Shaukat, Pakistani prime minister, Jan 2007

Aziz, Tariq, Iraqi cabinet member, May 1991

Babbitt, Bruce E., American Secretary of the interior, Apr 1987

Bachelet, Michelle, Chilean president, Jan 2006

Bailar, Benjamin F., American chemical industry executive and Postmaster general, July 1976

Baker, James A., American Secretary of state, Feb 1982, Mar 2007

Bakoyianni, Dora, Greek mayor, Jan 2003

Balbo, Italo, Italian air marshal, *Obit* Aug 1940

Baldrige, Malcolm, American Secretary of commerce, Aug 1982, *Obit* Sept 1987

Balladur, Edouard, French prime minister, Feb 1994

Ban, Ki Moon, Korean diplomat and United Nations secretary-general, Jan 2007

Barak, Ehud, Israeli political leader, Aug 1997

Barr, Joseph W., American Secretary of the treasury, Jan 1968, *Obit* May 1996

Barr, William P., American Attorney general, June 1992

Beale, Howard, Australian cabinet member and diplomat, Mar 1959

Bech, Joseph, Luxembourgian statesman, Feb 1950, *Obit* May 1975

Beck, Jozef, Polish diplomat, *Obit* July 1944

Bell, Griffin B., American Attorney general, June 1977, *Obit* Yrbk 2009

Bell, Terrel Howard, American Secretary of education, May 1976, *Obit* Sept 1996

Beltran, Pedro G., Peruvian newspaper publisher and statesman, Apr 1967, *Obit* Apr 1979

Benn, Tony, British member of Parliament, June 1965, Nov 1982

Benson, Ezra Taft, American Secretary of agriculture and Mormon leader, Feb 1953, *Obit* Aug 1994

Bentsen, Lloyd, American Secretary of the treasury, Sept 1973, Apr 1993, *Obit* Oct 2006

Beregovoy, Pierre Eugene, French prime minister, Feb 1993, *Obit* Feb 1993

Bergland, Bob, American Secretary of agriculture, Sept 1977

Bessmertnykh, Aleksandr A., Soviet diplomat, June 1991

Besteiro, Julian, Spanish socialist leader, *Obit* Nov 1940

Bevan, Aneurin, British cabinet member, May 1943, *Obit* Oct 1960

Bevin, Ernest, British statesman, Sept 1940, June 1949, *Obit* May 1951

Beyen, J. W., Dutch banker, economist and diplomat, Feb 1953, *Obit* June 1976

Bidault, Georges, French statesman, May 1945, *Obit* Mar 1983

Biddle, Francis, American Attorney general, Sept 1941, *Obit* Yrbk 1968

Blanco Galindo, Carlos, Bolivian president, *Obit* Nov 1943

Blix, Hans, Swedish diplomat and United Nations official, Jan 2003

Block, John R., American Secretary of agriculture, Apr 1982

Blount, Winton Malcolm, American construction executive and postmaster general, Apr 1969, *Obit* Jan 2003

Blucher, Franz, German cabinet member, Jan 1956, *Obit* June 1959

Blumenthal, W. Michael, American Secretary of the treasury, July 1977

Boateng, Paul, British cabinet member, Jan 2002

Bolger, William F., postmaster general, Oct 1979, *Obit* Oct 1989

Bolz, Lothar, East German diplomat, Sept 1959, *Obit* Apr 1987

Bonino, Emma, Italian trade official, Jan 2006

Botha, Pieter W., South African president, Sept 1979, *Obit* Yrbk 2007

Botha, R. F., South African diplomat, May 1984

Bouchard, Lucien, Canadian political leader, Apr 1999

Boumedienne, Houari, Algerian president, Jan 1971, *Obit* Feb 1979

Bourges-Maunoury, Maurice, French political leader, July 1957

Boutros-Ghali, Boutros, Egyptian diplomat and United Nations secretary-general, Apr 1992

Bowen, Otis R., American governor and Secretary of health and human services, Nov 1986, *Obit* Yrbk 2013

Bracken, Brendan Bracken, British cabinet member, Yrbk 1941

Brady, Nicholas F., American Secretary of the treasury, Nov 1988

Bramuglia, Juan Atilio, Argentine cabinet member, May 1949, *Obit* Nov 1962

Brannan, Charles F., American Secretary of agriculture, Sept 1948

Brennan, Peter J., American Secretary of labor, Apr 1973, *Obit* Jan 1997

Brittan, Leon, British cabinet member and European Commission official, Aug 1994

Brock, William Emerson, American senator and Secretary of labor, May 1971

Brown, Gordon, British prime minister, Jan 2002

Brown, Harold, American Secretary of defense and physicist, Sept 1961, Oct 1977

Brown, Jesse, American Secretary of veterans affairs, Nov 1993, *Obit* Yrbk 2002

Brown, Ron, American Secretary of commerce, July 1989, *Obit* June 1996

Brownell, Herbert, American Attorney general, Aug 1944, Feb 1954, *Obit* July 1996

Butler of Saffron Walden, Richard Austen Butler, British cabinet member, May 1944, Sept 1964, *Obit* May 1982

Butz, Earl, American Secretary of agriculture, July 1972, *Obit* Yrbk 2008

Byrnes, James Francis, American senator, Supreme Court justice and Secretary of state, June 1941, Oct 1951, *Obit* June 1972

Cai Yuanpei, Chinese educator, *Obit* Mar 1940

Calderon Hinojosa, Felipe, Mexican president, Jan 2006

Califano, Joseph A., American Secretary of health, education and welfare, June 1977

Calmy-Rey, Micheline, Swiss president, Jan 2007

Calvo-Sotelo y Bustelo, Leopoldo, Spanish prime minister, Aug 1981

Card, Andrew H., American presidential adviser, Nov 2003

Carlucci, Frank Charles, American Secretary of defense, Oct 1981

Carrington, Peter Alexander Rupert Carington, British statesman, June 1971

Castle, Barbara, British socialist leader, Jan 1967, *Obit* Yrbk 2002

Cavazos, Lauro Fred, American Secretary of education, Apr 1989

Celebrezze, Anthony J., American Secretary of health, education and welfare, Jan 1963, *Obit* Jan 1999

Chambas, Mohamed Ibn, Ghanaian diplomat and international organization official, Jan 2003

Chamberlain, Neville, British prime minister, *Obit* Yrbk 1940

Chandos, Oliver Lyttelton, British manufacturing executive and cabinet member, Sept 1941, Jan 1953, *Obit* Mar 1972

Chao, Elaine, American Secretary of labor, May 2001

Chapman, Oscar L., American Secretary of the interior, Feb 1949, *Obit* Apr 1978

Cheney, Richard B., American vice-president, Aug 1989, Jan 2002

Chertoff, Michael, American Secretary of homeland security, Oct 2005

Chissano, Joaquim Alberto, Mozambican president, Nov 1990

Chretien, Jean, Canadian prime minister, Apr 1990

Christopher, Warren, American Secretary of state, June 1981, Nov 1995, *Obit* Yrbk 2011

Chu, Steven, American physicist and Secretary of energy, Mar 2009

Churchill, Winston, British statesman, July 1940, Mar 1942, July 1953, *Obit* Mar 1965

Ciano, Galeazzo, Italian diplomat, July 1940, *Obit* Feb 1944

Cisneros, Henry, American urban development organization official, broadcasting executive and former Secretary of housing and urban development, Aug 1987

Civiletti, Benjamin, Feb 1980

Clark, Joe, Canadian prime minister, Oct 1976

Clark, Ramsey, American Attorney general and political activist, Oct 1967

Clark, Tom C., American Supreme Court justice, July 1945, *Obit* Aug 1977

Clark, William Patrick, American Secretary of the interior, July 1982, *Obit* Yrbk 2013

Clarke, Kenneth H., British political leader, Jan 2002

Clifford, Clark M., American presidential adviser, lawyer and Secretary of defense, Mar 1947, Sept 1968, *Obit* Jan 1999

Clinton, Hillary Rodham, American Secretary of state, Nov 1993, Jan 2002, Mar 2009

Cohen, Wilbur Joseph, American Secretary of health, education and welfare, Sept 1968, *Obit* July 1987

Cohen, William S., American Secretary of defense, Apr 1982, Jan 1998

Coleman, William T., American Secretary of transportation, Mar 1976

Colijn, Hendrikus, Dutch prime minister, *Obit* Jan 1945

Connally, John B., American governor, presidential adviser and Secretary of the treasury, July 1961, *Obit* Aug 1993

Connor, John T., American Secretary of commerce, Apr 1961, *Obit* Feb 2001

Cooper, Duff, British diplomat, Aug 1940, *Obit* Mar 1954

Correa, Rafael, Ecuadorian president, Jan 2007

Cortelyou, George Bruce, postmaster general and secretary of the treasury, *Obit* Yrbk 1940

Cossiga, Francesco, Italian president, Jan 1981, *Obit* Yrbk 2010

Cot, Pierre, French political leader, June 1944, *Obit* Oct 1977

Cotler, Irwin, Canadian member of Parliament, Jan 2006

Couve de Murville, Maurice, French diplomat and prime minister, Apr 1955, *Obit* June 2000

Cresson, Edith, French prime minister, Sept 1991

Cripps, Richard Stafford, British statesman, July 1940, Apr 1948, *Obit* June 1952

Crosbie, John Carnell, Canadian political leader, Jan 1990

Crosland, Anthony, British cabinet member, Sept 1963, *Obit* Apr 1977

Crossman, R. H. S., British socialist leader, May 1947, *Obit* June 1974

Cuomo, Andrew, American governor, Oct 1998

Daladier, Edouard, French statesman, Apr 1940, *Obit* Yrbk 1970

Daley, William, American presidential adviser, Mar 1998

Dalton, Hugh Dalton, British cabinet member, Aug 1945, *Obit* Apr 1962

Darre, R. Walther, German Nazi leader, Nov 1941, *Obit* Jan 1957

Dati, Rachida, French lawyer and cabinet member, Apr 2009

Daugherty, Harry M., American Attorney general, *Obit* Yrbk 1941

Day, James Edward, American postmaster general, May 1962, *Obit* Jan 1997

Dayan, Moshe, Israeli general, Mar 1957, *Obit* Jan 1982

Defferre, Gaston, French cabinet member, Sept 1967, *Obit* June 1986

Dent, Frederick B., American Secretary of commerce, Apr 1974

Derwinski, Edward J., American Secretary of veterans affairs, Aug 1991, *Obit* Yrbk 2012

Deuba, Sher Bahadur, Nepalese prime minister, Jan 2002

Devold, Kristin Krohn, Norwegian military official, Jan 2003

Diaz Ordaz, Gustavo, Mexican president, May 1965, *Obit* Sept 1979

Dillon, Douglas, American investment banker and Secretary of the treasury, Apr 1953, *Obit* May 2003

Diogo, Luisa, Mozambican prime minister, Jan 2004

Dion, Stephane, Canadian political leader, Jan 2007

Dole, Elizabeth Hanford, American senator, June 1983, Jan 1997

Donaldson, Jesse M., American postmaster general, Jan 1948, *Obit* May 1970

Donovan, Raymond James, American Secretary of labor, Jan 1982

Donovan, Shaun, American Secretary of housing and urban development, Mar 2009

Dreyfus, Pierre, French automobile executive and cabinet member, July 1958, *Obit* Mar 1995

Duarte Frutos, Nicanor, Paraguayan president, Jan 2004

Dulles, John Foster, American Secretary of state, Aug 1944, Sept 1953, *Obit* July 1959

Dumas, Roland, French cabinet member, Oct 1990

Duncan, Arne, American Secretary of education, Mar 2009

Duncan, Charles W., American Secretary of energy, Apr 1980

Duncan-Sandys, Duncan Edwin Duncan-Sandys, British cabinet member, May 1952

Durkin, Martin Patrick, American Secretary of labor, Feb 1953, *Obit* Jan 1956

Eagleburger, Lawrence S., American diplomat, Nov 1992, *Obit* Yrbk 2011

Eccles, David, British cabinet member, Jan 1952, *Obit* May 1999

Echeverria Alvarez, Luis, Mexican president, Nov 1972

Edwards, James Burrows, American dentist, governor and Secretary of energy, Nov 1982

Erhard, Ludwig, German chancellor, Jan 1950, June 1964, *Obit* July 1977

Espy, Mike, American Secretary of agriculture, Oct 1993

Etzel, Franz, German economist and cabinet member, Sept 1957

Evans, Donald L., American Secretary of commerce, Nov 2001

Evatt, Herbert Vere, Australian statesman, May 1942, *Obit* Jan 1966

Eytan, Walter, Israeli diplomat, Oct 1958, *Obit* Oct 2001

Fabius, Laurent, French political leader, Feb 1985

Fairclough, Ellen Louks, Canadian cabinet member, Oct 1957, *Obit* Yrbk 2005

Fall, Albert B., American Secretary of the interior, *Obit* Jan 1945

Farley, James Aloysius, American political leader, Sept 1944, *Obit* Aug 1976

Faure, Edgar, French statesman, Feb 1952, *Obit* May 1988

Fernandez de la Vega, Maria Teresa, Spanish vice-president, Jan 2007

Finch, Robert H., American secretary of health, education and welfare, Mar 1969, *Obit* Jan 1996

Fischer, Joschka, German political leader and diplomat, Jan 2002

Flandin, Pierre Etienne, French political leader, Jan 1941, *Obit* Oct 1958

Fleming, Donald M., Canadian cabinet member, Feb 1959, *Obit* Mar 1987

Flemming, Arthur S., American Secretary of health, education and welfare, June 1951, Apr 1960, *Obit* Nov 1996

Folsom, Marion Bayard, American Secretary of health, education and welfare, Jan 1950, *Obit* Nov 1976

Forrestal, James V., American Secretary of defense, Feb 1942, Jan 1948, *Obit* July 1949

Fowler, Henry H., American Secretary of the treasury, Sept 1952, *Obit* May 2000

Fraga Iribarne, Manuel, Spanish political leader, May 1965, *Obit* Yrbk 2012

Frank, Anthony M., postmaster general, Aug 1991

Fraser, Malcolm, Australian prime minister, Mar 1976

Frick, Wilhelm, German Nazi leader, Aug 1942, *Obit* Nov 1946

Fujiyama, Aiichiro, Japanese cabinet member, Apr 1958, *Obit* May 1985

Fulton, E. D., Jan 1959

Funk, Walther, German financier and cabinet member, Oct 1940, *Obit* Sept 1960

Gaitskell, Hugh, British cabinet member, June 1950, *Obit* Feb 1963

Gardiner, James Garfield, Canadian cabinet member, June 1956, *Obit* Mar 1962

Gardner, John William, American Secretary of health, education and welfare, Mar 1956, Mar 1976, *Obit* May 2002

Gates, Robert M., American Secretary of defense, Apr 1992, May 2007, Mar 2009

Geithner, Timothy F., American Secretary of the treasury, Mar 2009

Genscher, Hans Dietrich, German diplomat and political leader, June 1975

Geoffrey-Lloyd, Geoffrey William, British cabinet member, Feb 1956

George-Brown, George Alfred George-Brown, British cabinet member, Yrbk 1963, *Obit* July 1985

Gilani, Yusuf Raza, Pakistani prime minister, Nov 2008

Gilmour, John, British cabinet member, *Obit* Apr 1940

Giroud, Francoise, French journalist and cabinet member, Apr 1975, *Obit* July 2003

Giscard d'Estaing, Valery, French president, July 1967, Oct 1974

Glass, Carter, American senator, Oct 1941, *Obit* June 1946

Goldberg, Arthur J., American diplomat and Supreme Court justice, July 1949, July 1961, *Obit* Mar 1990

Goldschmidt, Neil E., American Secretary of transportation and governor, Aug 1980

Gonzales, Alberto R., American Attorney general, Apr 2002

Gorbachev, Mikhail, Soviet president, Aug 1985

Gordon-Walker, Patrick Chrestien Gordon Walker, Jan 1966

Gorton, John Grey, Australian prime minister, July 1968, *Obit* Sept 2002

Grechko, Andrei Antonovich, Soviet field marshal, Nov 1968, *Obit* June 1976

Grigg, James, Apr 1942, *Obit* July 1964

Gromyko, Andrei Andreevich, Soviet diplomat, Oct 1943, Oct 1958, *Obit* Aug 1989

Gronouski, John A., American postmaster general, Jan 1966, *Obit* Mar 1996

Gruber, Karl, Austrian diplomat, Feb 1947

Gujral, Inder K., Indian prime minister, *Obit* Yrbk 2013

Gunter, Ray, July 1967, *Obit* June 1977

Gurtner, Franz, German cabinet member, *Obit* Mar 1941

Habibie, Bacharuddin Jusuf, Indonesian president, Oct 1998

Haig, Alexander Meigs, American general and Secretary of state, Jan 1973, Sept 1987, *Obit* Yrbk 2010

Haignere, Claudie, French astronaut and cabinet member, Jan 2003

Hailsham of St. Marylebone, Quintin Hogg, British cabinet member, Sept 1957, *Obit* Feb 2002

Halifax, Edward Frederick Lindley Wood, British statesman, Sept 1940, *Obit* Feb 1960

Hallstein, Walter, German diplomat, Oct 1953, *Obit* May 1982

Halonen, Tarja, Finnish president, Jan 2006

Han, Seung-Soo, Korean economist and diplomat, Jan 2002

Hannegan, Robert Emmet, American postmaster general, June 1944, *Obit* Nov 1949

Hardin, Clifford M., American Secretary of agriculture, May 1969, *Obit* Yrbk 2010

Harrington, Francis Clark, *Obit* Mar 1940

Hasluck, Paul, Australian governor-general, Oct 1946

Hassel, Kai-Uwe von, May 1963

Hatoyama, Ichiro, Japanese prime minister, May 1955, *Obit* May 1959

Hays, Will H., American motion picture industry censor, July 1943, *Obit* Apr 1954

Healey, Denis, British political leader, Yrbk 1971

Heath, Edward, British prime minister, Oct 1962, *Obit* Yrbk 2005

Heckler, Margaret, American Secretary of health and human services, Aug 1983

Hees, George, Canadian cabinet member, Oct 1959

Herman, Alexis, American Secretary of labor and management consultant, Jan 1998

Herter, Christian Archibald, American Secretary of state, Yrbk 1947, Mar 1958, *Obit* Feb 1967

Heseltine, Michael, British political leader, June 1985

Hickel, Walter Joseph, American Secretary of the interior and governor, May 1969, *Obit* Yrbk 2010

Hills, Carla Anderson, American Secretary of housing and urban development and trade representative, Nov 1975, Mar 1993

Hobby, Oveta Culp, American Secretary of health, education and welfare, July 1942, Feb 1953, *Obit* Oct 1995

Hodel, Donald Paul, American organization official and Secretary of the interior, June 1987

Holder, Eric, American Attorney general, Mar 2009

Holt, Harold, Australian prime minister, Oct 1966, *Obit* Feb 1968

Home of the Hirsel, Alexander Frederick Douglas-Home, British prime minister, Feb 1958, *Obit* Jan 1996

Hoop Scheffer, Jaap de, Dutch diplomat and NATO official, Jan 2003

Hoover, Herbert, American president, Mar 1943, *Obit* Jan 1965

Hopkins, Harry Lloyd, American diplomat, Feb 1941, *Obit* Mar 1946

Hore-Belisha, Leslie Hore-Belisha, British political

leader, July 1941, *Obit* May 1957

Horsbrugh, Florence Gertrude Horsbrugh, British cabinet member, Feb 1952, *Obit* Mar 1970

Houston, David Franklin, secretary of agriculture and the treasury, *Obit* Oct 1940

Howe, Geoffrey, British cabinet member, Oct 1980

Hufstedler, Shirley M., American lawyer and Secretary of education, May 1980

Hughes, Charles Evans, American Supreme Court justice, July 1941, *Obit* Oct 1948

Hull, Cordell, American Secretary of state, Aug 1940, *Obit* Oct 1955

Humphrey, George Magoffin, American Secretary of the treasury, Feb 1953, *Obit* Mar 1970

Hun Sen, Cambodian prime minister, Apr 1990

Hurd, Douglas, British cabinet member, Feb 1990

Ickes, Harold L., American Secretary of the interior, July 1941, *Obit* Mar 1952

Ilsley, J. L., Canadian cabinet member and judge, Feb 1948

Insulza, Jose Miguel, Chilean diplomat and international organization official, Jan 2005

Jackson, Robert Houghwout, American Supreme Court justice, Mar 1940, Oct 1950, *Obit* Yrbk 1954

Jobert, Michel, French diplomat, Feb 1975, *Obit* Sept 2002

Johanna Sigurdardottir, Icelandic prime minister, July 2010

Johnson, Louis Arthur, American Secretary of defense, June 1942, Apr 1949, *Obit* May 1966

Johnson-Sirleaf, Ellen, Liberian president, Jan 2006

Jones, Jesse Holman, American Secretary of commerce, Oct 1940, *Obit* Sept 1956

Joseph, Keith, British cabinet member, Feb 1975, *Obit* Feb 1995

Jospin, Lionel, French prime minister, June 2000

Joxe, Louis, French diplomat and cabinet member, Apr 1961, *Obit* June 1991

Kaczynski, Lech, Polish president, Jan 2006, *Obit* Yrbk 2010

Kan, Naoto, Japanese prime minister, July 2011

Kantor, Mickey, American Secretary of commerce, Mar 1994

Katsav, Moshe, Israeli president, Feb 2001

Katzenbach, Nicholas deB., American Attorney general, July 1965, *Obit* Yrbk 2012

Kawaguchi, Yoriko, Japanese diplomat, Jan 2002

Keating, Paul, Australian prime minister, May 1992

Kempthorne, Dirk, American Secretary of the interior, June 2007

Kennedy, David Matthew, American Secretary of the treasury, June 1969, *Obit* July 1996

Kennedy, Robert F., American Attorney general and senator, Feb 1958, *Obit* July 1968

Kerrl, Hanns, German cabinet member, *Obit* Feb 1942

Kilmuir, David Patrick Maxwell Fyfe, Yrbk 1951, *Obit* Mar 1967

Kiriyenko, Sergei, Russian energy industry executive, Aug 1998

Kiviniemi, Mari, Finnish prime minister, Oct 2010

Klassen, Elmer Theodore, postmaster general, May 1973, *Obit* June 1990

Klaus, Vaclav, Czech president, Nov 1997

Kleindienst, Richard G., American Attorney general, Oct 1972, *Obit* June 2000

Kleppe, Thomas S., American Secretary of the interior, Aug 1976, *Obit* Yrbk 2007

Koizumi, Junichiro, Japanese prime minister, Jan 2002

Koo, V. K. Wellington, Chinese prime minister and diplomat, July 1941, *Obit* Jan 1986

Koprulu, Mehmet Fuat, Jan 1953, *Obit* Sept 1966

Kouchner, Bernard, French physician and cabinet member, Aug 1993

Kozyrev, Andrei V., Russian diplomat, Sept 1992

Kraft, Ole Bjorn, Feb 1953

Kreps, Juanita Morris, American Secretary of commerce, June 1977, *Obit* Yrbk 2010

Kroes, Neelie, Dutch European Commission official, Jan 2005

Krug, J. A., American Secretary of the interior, Oct 1944, *Obit* May 1970

Kuusinen, Hertta, Finnish cabinet member, May 1949, *Obit* May 1974

La Hood, Ray, American Secretary of transportation, Mar 2009

Lafontaine, Oskar, German political leader, Sept 1990

Lagarde, Christine, French interionational organization official, Jan 2007

Laird, Melvin R., American Secretary of defense, Nov 1964

Lambsdorff, Otto von, German economist and cabinet member, May 1980, *Obit* Yrbk 2010

Lamont, Norman, British cabinet member, Aug 1992

Landrieu, Moon, American state legislator, mayor and Secretary of housing and urban development, Jan 1980

Lang, Jack, French cabinet member, Aug 1983

Lange, Halvard M., Norwegian diplomat, Nov 1947, *Obit* July 1970

Laniel, Joseph, French prime minister, Feb 1954

Lapid, Tommy, Israeli cabinet member and political leader, Jan 2003

Lapointe, Ernest, Canadian political leader, *Obit* Jan 1942

Laval, Pierre, French prime minister and convicted traitor, Sept 1940, *Obit* Nov 1945

Lawson, Nigel, British cabinet member, Mar 1987

Lennox-Boyd, Alan Tindal, British cabinet member and brewing industry executive, June 1956, *Obit* May 1983

Letourneau, Jean, Oct 1952

Levi, Edward H., American Attorney general, Jan 1969, *Obit* July 2000

Levy, David, Israeli cabinet member, Mar 1998

Lewis, Drew, American Secretary of transportation, Feb 1982

Lie, Trygve, Norwegian United Nations secretary-general, Mar 1946, *Obit* Feb 1969

Lin Biao, Chinese communist leader and military official, May 1967, *Obit* Oct 1972

Livni, Tzipi, Israeli lawyer and cabinet member, Jan 2006

Lleras Restrepo, Carlos, Colombian president, Nov 1970, *Obit* Nov 1994

Locke, Gary, American Secretary of commerce, Apr 2003

Lon Nol, Cambodian general and prime minister, Feb 1974, *Obit* Jan 1986

Lovett, Robert A., American Secretary of defense, Aug 1942, Nov 1951, *Obit* June 1986

Lujan, Manuel, American Secretary of the interior, Sept 1989

Luns, Joseph M. A. H., Dutch diplomat and NATO official, Feb 1958, Apr 1982, *Obit* Yrbk 2002

Lyng, Richard E., American Secretary of agriculture, Sept 1986, *Obit* Yrbk 2003

MacBride, Sean, Irish diplomat, June 1949, *Obit* Mar 1988

MacEachen, Allan Joseph, Canadian political leader, Apr 1983

Machel, Graca Simbine, Mozambican social welfare leader and wife of Nelson Mandela, Oct 1997

Macleod, Iain Norman, British cabinet member, Apr 1956, *Obit* Oct 1970

Macmillan, Harold, British prime minister, Mar 1943, Jan 1955, *Obit* Feb 1987

Madigan, Edward R., American Secretary of agriculture, Nov 1992, *Obit* Feb 1995

Major, John, British prime minister, Oct 1990, Apr 1997

Malinovskii, Rodion IAkovlevich, Soviet field marshal, Mar 1944, Nov 1960, *Obit* May 1967

Mandel, Georges, French political leader, Yrbk 1940

Marie, Andre, French political leader, Sept 1948, *Obit* Sept 1974

Marquand, Hilary A., Apr 1951

Marshall, George C., American general and statesmen, Oct 1940, Mar 1947, *Obit* Yrbk 1959

Marshall, Ray, secretary of labor, Nov 1977

Martens, Wilfried, Belgian prime minister, Feb 1987

Martin, Lynn Morley, American Secretary of labor, Oct 1989

Martin, Paul, Canadian cabinet member and diplomat, Yrbk 1951, *Obit* Nov 1992

Martin, Paul, Canadian prime minister, Jan 2004

Masaryk, Jan, Czech diplomat, May 1944, *Obit* Apr 1948

Massey, Vincent, Canadian statesman, Oct 1951, *Obit* Feb 1968

Mathews, David, American Secretary of health, education and welfare, Jan 1976

Maudling, Reginald, British cabinet member, May 1960, *Obit* Apr 1979

Mayer, Rene, French prime minister, May 1948, *Obit* Feb 1973

Mazuz, Menachem, Israeli attorney general, Jan 2007

McAdoo, William G., American Secretary of the treasury and senator, *Obit* Mar 1941

McElroy, Neil H., American Secretary of defense, Apr 1951, *Obit* Jan 1973

McGranery, James P., American congressman, judge and Attorney general, May 1952, *Obit* Feb 1963

McGrath, James Howard, American Attorney general, Jan 1948, *Obit* Nov 1966

McKay, Douglas, American Secretary of the interior and governor, May 1949, *Obit* Oct 1959

McKenna, Reginald, British cabinet member and banker, *Obit* Oct 1943

McLaughlin, Ann Dore, American Secretary of labor, Nov 1988

McNamara, Robert S., American Secretary of defense and banker, Sept 1961, Mar 1987, *Obit* Yrbk 2009

McReynolds, James Clark, American Supreme Court justice, *Obit* Oct 1946

Medgyessy, Peter, Hungarian economist and prime minister, Jan 2003

Meese, Edwin, American Attorney general, Sept 1981

Meir, Golda, Israeli prime minister, May 1950, Yrbk 1970, *Obit* Feb 1979

Menthon, Francois, French political leader, Mar 1944

Mercouri, Melina, Greek actress and cabinet member, July 1965, Mar 1988, *Obit* May 1994

Messmer, Pierre, French prime minister, Nov 1963, *Obit* Yrbk 2007

Migiro, Asha-Rose Mtengeti, Tanzanian diplomat, Jan 2007

Mitchell, James P., American Secretary of labor, Sept 1955, *Obit* Yrbk 1964

Mitchell, John Newton, American Attorney general, June 1969, *Obit* Jan 1989

Miyazawa, Kiichi, Japanese prime minister, Feb 1992, *Obit* Yrbk 2007

Moch, Jules, French socialist leader and cabinet member, Oct 1950, *Obit* Nov 1985

Molotov, Vyacheslav, Soviet diplomat, Jan 1940, Nov 1954, *Obit* Jan 1987

Monckton of Brenchley, Walter Turner Monckton, British cabinet member, Yrbk 1951, *Obit* Feb 1965

Morgenthau, Henry, American Secretary of the treasury, Sept 1940, *Obit* Apr 1967

Morrison of Lambeth, Herbert Stanley Morrison, British cabinet member, July 1940, Feb 1951, *Obit* Apr 1965

Morrison, William Shepherd, British statesman, Jan 1952, *Obit* Apr 1961

Morse, David Abner, American international labor leader, Mar 1949, *Obit* Mar 1991

Mosbacher, Robert, American Secretary of commerce, June 1989, *Obit* Yrbk 2010

Moussa, Amr, Egyptian diplomat and international organization official, Jan 2002

Moutet, Marius, French socialist leader and cabinet member, July 1947, *Obit* Yrbk 1968

Moyo, Jonathan N., Zimbabwean political leader, Jan 2007

Mueller, Frederick H., Yrbk 1959, *Obit* Oct 1976

Mukasey, Michael, American Attorney general, Feb 2008

Murphy, Frank, American Supreme Court justice, July 1940, *Obit* Sept 1949

Muskie, Edmund S., American senator and Secretary of state, Feb 1955, Yrbk 1968, *Obit* June 1996

Myrdal, Gunnar, Swedish economist, Sept 1946, Mar 1975, *Obit* July 1987

Napolitano, Giorgio, Italian president, Jan 2006

Napolitano, Janet, American Secretary of homeland security, Oct 2004, Mar 2009

Narasimha Rao, P. V., Indian prime minister, Jan 1992, *Obit* Yrbk 2005

Narathipphongpraphan, June 1954

Nash, Walter, New Zealand prime minister, Oct 1942, Mar 1958, *Obit* July 1968

Nestingen, Ivan A., Mar 1962, *Obit* June 1978

Noel-Baker, Philip John, British pacifist, Feb 1946, *Obit* Mar 1983

Norton, Gale, American Secretary of the interior, June 2001

Nutting, Anthony, British cabinet member, Feb 1955, *Obit* May 1999

O'Leary, Hazel R., American university president and former Secretary of energy, Jan 1994

O'Neill, Paul Henry, American aluminum company executive and Secretary of the treasury, July 2001

Obuchi, Keizo, Japanese prime minister, May 1999, *Obit* Aug 2000

Okonjo-Iweala, Ngozi, Nigerian cabinet member, Jan 2006

Olmert, Ehud, Israeli prime minister, Jan 2006

Owen, David, British political leader, Sept 1977

Ozal, Turgut, Turkish president, June 1985, *Obit* June 1993

Pacciardi, Randolfo, Italian political leader, Mar 1944, *Obit* July 1991

Padilla, Ezequiel, Mexican diplomat, July 1942, *Obit* Oct 1971

Paige, Rod, American Secretary of education, July 2001

Palacio Gonzalez, Alfredo, Ecuadorian president, Jan 2005

Paleologue, Maurice, French diplomat, *Obit* Jan 1945

Panetta, Leon E., American Secretary of defense, June 1993

Pant, Govind Ballabh, Indian cabinet member, Jan 1959, *Obit* May 1961

Patterson, Robert Porter, American Secretary of war, Oct 1941, *Obit* Mar 1952

Pauker, Ana, Romanian diplomat and communist leader, Mar 1948

Paul-Boncour, Joseph, French statesman, June 1945, *Obit* May 1972

Paulson, Henry M., American Secretary of the treasury, Sept 2002

Paz, Hipolito J., Jan 1952

Peck, Raoul, Haitian motion picture director and cabinet member, Jan 2002

Pena, Federico, American Secretary of transportation, Oct 1993

Perkins, Frances, American Secretary of labor, Yrbk 1940, *Obit* July 1965

Perry, William James, American Secretary of defense, Jan 1995

Persad-Bissessar, Kamla, Trinidadian prime minister, Jan 2013

Peterson, Peter G., American investment banker and Secretary of commerce, June 1972

Pethick-Lawrence, Frederick William, British socialist leader, June 1946, *Obit* Nov 1961

Petitpierre, Max, Swiss president and diplomat, Yrbk 1953, *Obit* June 1994

Pflimlin, Pierre, French political leader, Nov 1955, *Obit* Oct 2000

Philip, Andre, French economist and cabinet member, Aug 1943, *Obit* Sept 1970

Piccioni, Attilio, Oct 1967, *Obit* May 1976

Pickersgill, J. W., Canadian cabinet member, Mar 1968

Pierce, Samuel R., American Secretary of housing and urban development, Nov 1982, *Obit* Feb 2001

Pinay, Antoine, French political leader, Apr 1952, *Obit* Feb 1995

Pineau, Christian, French cabinet member, July 1956, *Obit* June 1995

Pleven, Rene, French political leader, June 1950, *Obit* Mar 1993

Poinso-Chapuis, Germaine, French feminist, June 1948

Popovic, Koca, Yugoslav cabinet member, Jan 1957, *Obit* Jan 1993

Powell, Colin L., American Secretary of state, June 1988, Nov 2001

Powell, Enoch, British member of Parliament, Nov 1964, *Obit* June 1999

Priest, Ivy Baker, Nov 1952, *Obit* Aug 1975

Primakov, Yevgeny M., Russian prime minister, Feb 1999

Prodi, Romano, Italian prime minister, Jan 2006

Profumo, John D., British cabinet member, Oct 1959, *Obit* June 2006

Pronk, Johannes Pieter, Dutch United Nations official, Jan 2005

Pym, Francis, British cabinet member, Sept 1982, *Obit* Yrbk 2008

Queuille, Henri, French prime minister, Oct 1948, *Obit* Sept 1970

Rabin, Yitzhak, Israeli prime minister, Sept 1974, Jan 1995, *Obit* Jan 1996

Rajapakse, Mahinda, Sri Lankan president, Jan 2006

Ram, Jagjivan, Indian political leader, Oct 1978, *Obit* Aug 1986

Ramadier, Paul, French prime minister, June 1947, *Obit* Yrbk 1961

Regan, Donald T., American presidential adviser, Nov 1981, *Obit* Yrbk 2003

Reich, Robert B., American economist and Secretary of labor, Apr 1993

Remorino, Jeronimo, Sept 1951

Reno, Janet, American Attorney general, Sept 1993

Reynaud, Paul, French prime minister, Apr 1940, May 1950, *Obit* Nov 1966

Riad, Mahmoud, Egyptian diplomat, Nov 1971, *Obit* Mar 1992

Ribicoff, Abraham A., American senator, June 1955, *Obit* May 1998

Rice, Condoleezza, American Secretary of state, Apr 2001

Richardson, Elliot L., American Attorney general, Mar 1971, *Obit* Mar 2000

Ridge, Tom, American Secretary of homeland security, Feb 2001

Riley, Richard Wilson, American Secretary of education, Oct 1993

Rogers, William Pierce, American Secretary of state, Feb 1958, Sept 1969, *Obit* Mar 2001

Romney, George, American Secretary of housing and urban development, June 1958, *Obit* Oct 1995

Romulo, Carlos Pena, Filipino statesman, Mar 1943, Apr 1957, *Obit* Feb 1986

Rousseff, Dilma, Brazilian president, July 2012

Royall, Kenneth C., American Secretary of the army, Jan 1947, *Obit* Sept 1971

Rubattel, Rodolphe, Yrbk 1954, *Obit* Yrbk 1961

Rubin, Robert E., American financial executive and former Secretary of the treasury, July 1997

Rusk, Dean, American Secretary of state, June 1949, July 1961, *Obit* Feb 1995

Rust, Bernhard, German Nazi leader, July 1942

Sadak, Necmeddin, Jan 1950, *Obit* Yrbk 1953

Salazar, Antonio de Oliveira, Portuguese dictator, May 1941, May 1952, *Obit* Oct 1970

Salazar, Ken, American Secretary of the interior, Mar 2009

Samuel, Herbert Louis Samuel, British statesman, Apr 1955, *Obit* Mar 1963

Sarkozy, Nicolas, French president, Jan 2006

Saud al Faisal, Jan 1948

Sawyer, Charles, American Secretary of commerce and diplomat, July 1948, *Obit* June 1979

Saxbe, William B., American Attorney general and senator, July 1974, *Obit* Yrbk 2010

Scelba, Mario, Italian prime minister, May 1953, *Obit* Feb 1992

Schacht, Hjalmar, German financier, Oct 1944, *Obit* Sept 1970

Schaffer, Fritz, Mar 1953, *Obit* May 1967

Schiller, Karl, German cabinet member, Yrbk 1971, *Obit* Mar 1995

Schlesinger, James R., American Secretary of defense and energy, Oct 1973

Schroder, Gerhard, German political leader, Yrbk 1962, *Obit* Mar 1990

Schuman, Robert, French statesman, Jan 1948, *Obit* Nov 1963

Schumann, Maurice, French cabinet member, Apr 1970, *Obit* Apr 1998

Schwarzhaupt, Elisabeth, German cabinet member, Jan 1967, *Obit* Jan 1987

Schweiker, Richard S., American Secretary of health and human services, Feb 1977

Schwellenbach, Lewis B., American Secretary of Labor, June 1945, *Obit* July 1948

Seaton, Fred A., American newspaper publisher and Secretary of the interior, Nov 1956, *Obit* Mar 1974

Sebelius, Kathleen, American Secretary of health and human services, Nov 2004

Selwyn-Lloyd, John Selwyn Brooke, British cabinet member, Apr 1952, *Obit* July 1978

Serrano Suner, Ramon, Spanish diplomat and political leader, Nov 1940, *Obit* Yrbk 2004

Shalala, Donna, American Secretary of health and human services and college president, Mar 1991

Shamir, Yitzhak, Israeli prime minister, Feb 1983, Yrbk 1996, *Obit* Yrbk 2012

Sharansky, Natan, Israeli cabinet member, Feb 1987

Sharett, Moshe, Israeli statesman, Apr 1948, *Obit* Sept 1965

Sharon, Ariel, Israeli prime minister, Apr 1981, Jan 2002

Shastri, Lal Bahadur, Indian prime minister, Yrbk 1964, *Obit* Feb 1966

Shawcross, Hartley Shawcross, British attorney general and war crimes prosecutor, Yrbk 1945, *Obit* Yrbk 2003

Shidehara, Kijuro, Japanese diplomat and prime minister, Apr 1946, *Obit* Apr 1951

Shinseki, Eric, American Secretary of veterans affairs, Mar 2009

Shinwell, Emanuel Shinwell, British political leader, Jan 1943, *Obit* June 1986

Simon, William E., American Secretary of the treasury and financier, Apr 1974, *Obit* Aug 2000

Simpson-Miller, Portia, Jamaican prime minister, Jan 2006

Singh, Manmohan, Indian prime minister, Jan 2005

Singh, Vishwanath Pratap, Indian prime minister, May 1990, *Obit* Yrbk 2009

Skinner, Samuel K., American Secretary of transportation and presidential adviser, Aug 1989

Slater, Rodney, American Secretary of transportation, Jan 1999

Smith, William French, American Attorney general, Jan 1982, *Obit* Jan 1991

Snow, John W., American investment manager and former Secretary of the treasury, Aug 2003

Snyder, John W., American Secretary of the treasury, July 1945, *Obit* Jan 1986

Soames, Arthur Christopher John Soames, British diplomat, Aug 1981, *Obit* Oct 1987

Solana Madariaga, Javier, Spanish European Union official, Jan 2005

Solis, Hilda L., American Secretary of labor, Mar 2009

Soustelle, Jacques, French political leader, Yrbk 1958, *Obit* Oct 1990

Spaak, Paul-Henri, Belgian statesman, May 1945, Apr 1958, *Obit* Oct 1972

Spellings, Margaret, American Secretary of education, June 2005

Stans, Maurice H., American Secretary of commerce, Yrbk 1958, *Obit* June 1998

Stauning, Thorvald, Danish prime minister, *Obit* June 1942

Stewart, Michael, British cabinet member, Sept 1965, *Obit* June 1990

Stikker, Dirk U., Dutch statesman, Feb 1950, Feb 1962

Stimson, Henry Lewis, American statesman, Aug 1940, *Obit* Yrbk 1950

Stokes, Richard Rapier, British cabinet member, Sept 1951, *Obit* Oct 1957

Stoltenberg, Gerhard, German cabinet member, Sept 1989, *Obit* Mar 2002

Stone, Harlan Fiske, American Supreme Court justice, Aug 1941, *Obit* June 1946

Strachey, Evelyn John St. Loe, British cabinet member, June 1946, *Obit* Sept 1963

Strauss, Franz Josef, German political leader, Feb 1957, Feb 1987, *Obit* Nov 1988

Strauss, J. G. N., Jan 1951

Straw, Jack, British cabinet member, Jan 2002

Subandrio, Indonesian cabinet member, Mar 1963, *Obit* Apr 2005

Sullivan, Louis W., American Secretary of health and human services, July 1989

Summerfield, Arthur Ellsworth, American postmaster general, Sept 1952, *Obit* June 1972

Suzuki, Zenko, Japanese prime minister, Jan 1981, *Obit* Yrbk 2004

Takeshita, Noboru, Japanese prime minister, May 1988, *Obit* Nov 2000

Tanner, Vaino, Finnish statesman, Sept 1960, *Obit* May 1966

Tardieu, Andre, French statesman, *Obit* Oct 1945

Tebbit, Norman, British cabinet member, Nov 1987

Teleki, Pal, Hungarian statesman, *Obit* May 1941

Templewood, Samuel John Gurney Hoare, British diplomat, Oct 1940, *Obit* July 1959

Tenby of Bulford, Gwilym Lloyd George, British cabinet member, Nov 1952, *Obit* Apr 1967

Thompson, Tommy, American Secretary of health and human services, July 1995

Thorez, Maurice, French communist leader, June 1946, *Obit* Sept 1964

Thornburgh, Dick, American governor and Attorney general, Oct 1988

Thorneycroft of Dunston, Peter, British cabinet member, Yrbk 1952, *Obit* Aug 1994

Tobin, Maurice J., American Secretary of labor, June 1946, *Obit* Oct 1953

Todt, Fritz, German military engineer and cabinet member, *Obit* Apr 1942

Topfer, Klaus, German environmentalist and United Nations official, Jan 2002

Torp, Oscar, Norwegian prime minister, Yrbk 1952, *Obit* July 1958

Trowbridge, Alexander B., American Secretary of commerce, Mar 1968, *Obit* Yrbk 2006

Tshabalala-Msimang, Manto, South African public health official, Jan 2007, *Obit* Yrbk 2010

Turner, John, Canadian prime minister, Nov 1984

Udall, Stewart L., American Secretary of the interior, May 1961, *Obit* Yrbk 2010

Usery, W. J., American Secretary of labor, June 1976

Vance, Cyrus R., American Secretary of state, Yrbk 1962, Nov 1977, *Obit* Apr 2002

Vasilevskii, Aleksandr M., Soviet field marshal, Oct 1943, *Obit* Mar 1978

Veil, Simone, French judge and cabinet member, May 1980

Veneman, Ann M., American United Nations official, Sept 2009

Verity, Calvin William, American Secretary of commerce, May 1988

Villepin, Dominique de, French prime minister, Jan 2003

Vilsack, Tom, American Secretary of agriculture, Mar 2009

Vinson, Fred M., American Supreme Court justice, Aug 1943, *Obit* Nov 1953

Vogel, Hans Jochen, German socialist leader, Jan 1984

Volpe, John A., American governor and Secretary of transportation, Feb 1962, *Obit* Jan 1995

Wachuku, Jaja, Apr 1963

Walker, Frank Comerford, postmaster general, Oct 1940, *Obit* Nov 1959

Wallace, Henry Agard, American vice-president, Aug 1940, Jan 1947, *Obit* Jan 1966

Watkins, James D., American admiral and Secretary of energy, Mar 1989, *Obit* Yrbk 2012

Watt, James G., American Secretary of the interior, Jan 1982

Webb, Maurice, May 1950, *Obit* Sept 1956

Weeks, Sinclair, American Secretary of commerce, Mar 1953, *Obit* Mar 1972

Weinberger, Caspar W., American Secretary of

defense, June 1973, *Obit* July 2006

Weizman, Ezer, Israeli president, Sept 1979, *Obit* Aug 2005

White, Frank, *Obit* May 1940

Whitelaw, William Whitelaw, British cabinet member, Mar 1975, *Obit* Nov 1999

Wickard, Claude Raymond, American Secretary of agriculture, Oct 1940, *Obit* June 1967

Wilkinson, Ellen, British cabinet member, July 1941, *Obit* Mar 1947

Williams, Shirley, British political leader, Oct 1976

Wilson, Charles E., American automobile executive and Secretary of defense, Aug 1941, Sept 1950, *Obit* Yrbk 1961

Wilson, Michael H., Canadian cabinet member and diplomat, Mar 1990

Wirtz, Willard, American Secretary of labor, Nov 1946, Feb 1963, *Obit* Yrbk 2010

Woolton, Frederick James Marquis, English financier, Oct 1940, Oct 1950, *Obit* Feb 1965

Work, Hubert, physician and secretary of the interior, *Obit* Feb 1943

Worner, Manfred, German cabinet member and NATO official, Oct 1988, *Obit* Oct 1994

Wu Yi, Chinese government official, Jan 2005

Yamani, Ahmed Zaki, Saudi Arabian cabinet member, Sept 1975

Yeh, George K. C., Mar 1953, *Obit* Jan 1982

Yeutter, Clayton K., American Secretary of agriculture and political leader, July 1988

Yoshida, Shigeru, Japanese statesman, Sept 1946, *Obit* Jan 1968

Yudhoyono, Susilo Bambang, Indonesian president, Jan 2005

Zedillo Ponce de Leon, Ernesto, Mexican president, Apr 1996

Zeeland, Paul van, Mar 1950

Zhao Ziyang, Chinese prime minister, June 1984, *Obit* Yrbk 2005

Zimmermann, Arthur, German diplomat, *Obit* July 1940

Zorlu, Fatin Ruchstu, Turkish diplomat, Yrbk 1958, *Obit* Nov 1961

Calligraphers

Zapf, Hermann, German typographer and calligrapher, Jan 1965

Cancer patients

Carr, Kris, American actress, photographer and documentary filmmaker, May 2012

Rowley, Janet D., American geneticist, Mar 2001

Woese, Carl R., American microbiologist, June 2003, *Obit* Yrbk 2013

Canon lawyers

Elliott, William Thompson, English theologian and canonist, *Obit* Aug 1940

Janssens, Jean Baptiste, Sept 1959, *Obit* Yrbk 1964

Card players

Bruel, Patrick, French singer and actor, Jan 2007

Brunson, Doyle, American poker player, Sept 2007

Culbertson, Ely, bridge player, May 1940, *Obit* Mar 1956

Duke, Annie, American poker player, Aug 2006

Goren, Charles Henry, bridge player, Mar 1959, *Obit* July 1991

Pennario, Leonard, American pianist, Oct 1959

Sklansky, David, American poker player, Apr 2007

Cardinals

Alfrink, Bernard, May 1966, *Obit* Feb 1988

Baudrillart, Alfred, *Obit* July 1942

Baum, William W., Oct 1976

Bea, Augustin, Sept 1964, *Obit* Jan 1969

Benelli, Giovanni Cardinal, Sept 1977, *Obit* Jan 1983

Bernardin, Joseph L., Oct 1982, *Obit* Jan 1997

Bertram, Adolf, *Obit* Aug 1945

Boggiani, Tommaso Pio, *Obit* Apr 1942

Brennan, Francis, Oct 1967, *Obit* Sept 1968

Cattani-Amadori, Federico, *Obit* May 1943

Cody, John Patrick, Nov 1965, *Obit* June 1982

Cooke, Terence James, Sept 1968, *Obit* Nov 1983

Cushing, Richard James, June 1952, *Obit* Yrbk 1970

Daly, Cahal B., Jan 2002, *Obit* Yrbk 2010

Dearden, John, July 1969, *Obit* Sept 1988

Egan, Edward M., July 2001

Enrique y Tarancon, Vicente, Oct 1972, *Obit* Feb 1995

Feltin, Maurice, May 1954, *Obit* Nov 1975

Francis, July 2013

Galen, Clemens August von, *Obit* Apr 1946

Glemp, Jozef, Sept 1982, *Obit* Yrbk 2013

Glennon, John Joseph, *Obit* Apr 1946

Griffin, Bernard, Oct 1946, *Obit* Oct 1956

Hinsley, Arthur, *Obit* Apr 1943

Krol, John, Jan 1969, *Obit* May 1996

Lauri, Lorenzo, *Obit* Yrbk 1941

Leger, Paul-Emile, Canadian missionary, May 1953, *Obit* Jan 1992

Lercaro, Giacomo, Sept 1965, *Obit* Jan 1977

Lustiger, Jean Marie, Feb 1984, *Obit* Yrbk 2007

Maglione, Luigi, *Obit* Oct 1944

Marella, Paolo, Oct 1964

McIntyre, James Francis Aloysius, Feb 1953, *Obit* Sept 1979

Medeiros, Humberto, Nov 1971, *Obit* Nov 1983

Mindszenty, Jozsef, Jan 1957, *Obit* June 1975

Mooney, Edward, Apr 1946, *Obit* Jan 1959

O'Boyle, Patrick, July 1973, *Obit* Sept 1987

O'Connell, William Henry, June 1941, *Obit* June 1944

O'Connor, John Joseph, June 1984, *Obit* July 2000

O'Malley, Sean Patrick, Jan 2004

Obando y Bravo, Miguel, Mar 1988

Ottaviani, Alfredo, Yrbk 1966, *Obit* Sept 1979

Pellegrinetti, Ermenegildo, *Obit* May 1943

Ritter, Joseph Elmer, Yrbk 1964, *Obit* Oct 1967

Roy, Maurice, Feb 1958, *Obit* Jan 1986

Rugambwa, Laurean, Sept 1960, *Obit* Feb 1998

Schonborn, Christoph von, Jan 2006

Schulte, Karl Joseph, *Obit* May 1941

Shehan, Lawrence, Oct 1965, *Obit* Oct 1984

Sin, Jaime, Sept 1995, *Obit* Yrbk 2005

Spellman, Francis, Apr 1940, Apr 1947, *Obit* Jan 1968

Stepinac, Alojzije, Feb 1953, *Obit* Apr 1960

Stritch, Samuel Alphonsus, Apr 1946, *Obit* Sept 1958

Suenens, Leo Joseph, May 1965, *Obit* July 1996

Tien, Thomas, May 1946, *Obit* Oct 1967

Tisserant, Eugene, Apr 1963, *Obit* Apr 1972

Vagnozzi, Egidio, Mar 1967, *Obit* Feb 1981

Wright, John J., Feb 1963, *Obit* Oct 1979

Wyszynski, Stefan, Jan 1958, *Obit* July 1981

Cardiologists

Agatston, Arthur, American cardiologist, Mar 2007

Barnard, Christiaan, South African heart surgeon, May 1968, *Obit* Nov 2001

Bauer, Louis Hopewell, American cardiologist, Oct 1948, *Obit* Mar 1964

Healy, Bernadine P., American cardiologist and public health official, Nov 1992, *Obit* Yrbk 2011

Kantrowitz, Adrian, American cardiac surgeon, Oct 1967, *Obit* Yrbk 2009

Neuman, Leo Handel, *Obit* May 1941

Palacio Gonzalez, Alfredo, Ecuadorian president, Jan 2005

Steincrohn, Peter Joseph, Mar 1957

Talley, James, *Obit* Sept 1941

Taylor, Herman A., American cardiologist, June 2006

Trehan, Naresh, Indian cardiologist, Jan 2003

Watkins, Levi, American cardiac surgeon, Mar 2003

Wenckebach, Karel Friedrich, Dutch cardiologist, *Obit* Yrbk 1940

White, Paul Dudley, American cardiologist, Yrbk 1955, *Obit* Yrbk 1973

Carpenters

Boland, Patrick J., American congressman, *Obit* July 1942

Hutcheson, William Levi, American labor leader, Sept 1943, *Obit* Jan 1954

Pennington, Ty, American carpenter and host of reality TV show Extreme makeover: Home edition, Feb 2006

Cartographers

Chichester, Francis, English cartographer and boat racer, Yrbk 1967, *Obit* Oct 1972

Hammond, Caleb D., American map publisher and cartographer, Apr 1956, *Obit* Yrbk 2006

McNally, Andrew, American publisher and cartographer, Nov 1956, *Obit* Feb 2002

Robinson, Arthur Howard, American cartographer, Mar 1996, *Obit* Yrbk 2005

Cartoonists

Abel, Jessica, American comic book writer and artist, Aug 2007

Addams, Charles, American cartoonist, Jan 1954, *Obit* Nov 1988

Alajalov, Constantin, American painter, illustrator and cartoonist, Jan 1942, *Obit* Jan 1988

Amend, Bill, American cartoonist, Apr 2003

Arno, Peter, cartoonist, Aug 1942, *Obit* Apr 1968

Auth, Tony, American cartoonist, illustrator and children's author, Feb 2006

Baker, George, American cartoonist, Nov 1944, *Obit* Aug 1975

Barry, Lynda, American cartoonist and novelist, Nov 1994

Bechdel, Alison, American cartoonist and graphic novelist, July 2009

Bell, Steve, British political cartoonist, Jan 2003

Berryman, James Thomas, cartoonist, July 1950, *Obit* Oct 1971

Block, Herbert, American editorial cartoonist, July 1954, *Obit* Jan 2002

Bosustow, Stephen, June 1958

Brustlein, Daniel, American painter, Sept 1941

Bull, Johan, *Obit* Oct 1945

Burton, Tim, American film director, July 1991

Byrne, John, Anglo-Canadian comic book artist and writer, Oct 2000

Callahan, John, American cartoonist, Sept 1998, *Obit* Yrbk 2010

Campbell, E. Simms, Jan 1941, *Obit* Mar 1971

Caniff, Milton Arthur, cartoonist, Jan 1944, *Obit* May 1988

Capp, Al, cartoonist, May 1947, *Obit* Jan 1980

Chast, Roz, American cartoonist, July 1997

Clowes, Daniel, American comic book artist and writer, Jan 2002

Covarrubias, Miguel, Mexican painter and caricaturist, July 1940, *Obit* Apr 1957

Crumb, R., American cartoonist, Apr 1995

Darling, Jay Norwood, American cartoonist and conservationist, July 1942, *Obit* Mar 1962

Darrow, Whitney, cartoonist, Yrbk 1958, *Obit* Oct 1999

De Beck, Billy, cartoonist, *Obit* Jan 1943

DeCarlo, Dan, American comic book artist, Aug 2001, *Obit* Mar 2002

Douglas, Emory, American illustrator, cartoonist and social activist, Feb 2010

Duffy, Edmund, cartoonist, Jan 1940, *Obit* Nov 1962

Feiffer, Jules, American cartoonist, children's author and dramatist, Oct 1961

Feininger, Lyonel, German painter and cartoonist, July 1955, *Obit* Mar 1956

Fiore, Mark, American cartoonist and animator, Apr 2011

Fitzpatrick, Daniel Robert, cartoonist, July 1941, *Obit* July 1969

Flagg, James Montgomery, painter and illustrator, Nov 1940, *Obit* Sept 1960

Gilchrist, Brad, cartoonist, Jan 1999

Gilchrist, Guy, author, illustrator and cartoonist, Jan 1999

Glintenkamp, H., *Obit* May 1946

Goldberg, Rube, cartoonist, Sept 1948, *Obit* Jan 1971

Gould, Chester, American cartoonist, Sept 1971, *Obit* July 1985

Gropper, William, American cartoonist, painter and illustrator, Mar 1940, *Obit* Mar 1977

Grosz, George, American painter and cartoonist, Apr 1942, *Obit* Oct 1959

Guisewite, Cathy, cartoonist, Feb 1989

Harding, Nelson, *Obit* Feb 1945

Harris, Rolf, Australian television personality, singer and cartoonist, Jan 2002

Harryhausen, Ray, American motion picture special effects technician and animator, *Obit* Yrbk 2013

Hewlett, Jamie, English illustrator and cartoonist, Jan 2007

Higgins, Jack, American editorial cartoonist, Feb 2007

Hirschfeld, Al, American caricaturist, Jan 1971, *Obit* July 2003

Horsey, David, American political cartoonist, Sept 2008

Igoe, Herbert A., *Obit* Apr 1945

Jaffee, Al, American cartoonist and illustrator, July 2008

Johnson, Crockett, cartoonist, Yrbk 1943, *Obit* Jan 1984

Johnston, Lynn, Canadian cartoonist, Feb 1998

Jones, Chuck, American animator, May 1996, *Obit* May 2002

Judge, Mike, American motion picture director and animator, May 1997

Katchor, Ben, American cartoonist, May 2000

Kelly, Walt, American cartoonist, Oct 1956, *Obit* Yrbk 1973

Ketcham, Hank, American cartoonist, Jan 1956, *Obit* Sept 2001

Kirby, Rollin, Yrbk 1944, *Obit* June 1952

Kuekes, Edward D., cartoonist, Mar 1954, *Obit* Mar 1987

Lancaster, Osbert, English satirist and cartoonist, Oct 1964, *Obit* Sept 1986

Larson, Gary, American cartoonist, Feb 1991

Leunig, Michael, Australian cartoonist and poet, Jan 2006

Levine, David, American caricaturist, Feb 1973, *Obit* Yrbk 2010

Low, David, New Zealand cartoonist, Jan 1940, *Obit* Nov 1963

Luckovich, Mike, American editorial cartoonist, Jan 2005

Mankoff, Robert, American cartoonist, May 2005

Manning, Reg, June 1951

Marlette, Doug, American editorial cartoonist, July 2002, *Obit* Yrbk 2007

Mauldin, Bill, American cartoonist, May 1945, Nov 1964, *Obit* July 2003

McCracken, Craig, American animator, Feb 2004

McFarlane, Todd, Canadian cartoonist, Feb 1999

McGruder, Aaron, American cartoonist, Sept 2001

Messick, Dale, American cartoonist, July 1961, *Obit* Yrbk 2005

Millionaire, Tony, American cartoonist and illustrator, July 2005

Miranda, Mario de, Indian cartoonist and illustrator, Jan 2003

Miyazaki, Hayao, Japanese animator, Apr 2001

Oliphant, Patrick, Australian-American cartoonist, July 1991

Osborn, Robert, caricaturist, June 1959, *Obit* Feb 1995

Oshii, Mamoru, Japanese animator, Jan 2006

Packer, Fred L., July 1952, *Obit* Feb 1957

Partridge, Bernard, *Obit* Sept 1945

Pease, Lute, political cartoonist and painter, July 1949, *Obit* Nov 1963

Rall, Ted, American editorial cartoonist, May 2002

Rea, Gardner, May 1946, *Obit* Feb 1967

Ross, Alex, American comic book artist, Nov 2007

Sacco, Joe, Maltese cartoonist and journalist, Jan 2013

Salvador Lavado, Joaquin, Argentine cartoonist, Jan 2004

Schulz, Charles M., American cartoonist, Yrbk 1960, *Obit* Apr 2000

Selick, Henry, American film director, May 2009

Sempe, French cartoonist and illustrator, Jan 2007

Soglow, Otto, cartoonist, Sept 1940, *Obit* May 1975

Sorel, Edward, cartoonist, Mar 1994

Spiegelman, Art, American cartoonist, Mar 1994

St. George, Thomas Richard, Jan 1944

Steadman, Ralph, English illustrator, May 1999

Steig, William, American illustrator and children's author, July 1944, *Obit* Apr 2004

Steinberg, Saul, Romanian-American illustrator and cartoonist, Mar 1957, *Obit* July 1999

Svankmajer, Jan, Czech animator and motion picture director, Jan 2006

Sykes, Charles H., *Obit* Feb 1943

Szyk, Arthur, Polish cartoonist, illustrator and miniaturist, Nov 1946, *Obit* Oct 1951

Takahashi, Rumiko, Japanese cartoonist and comic book writer, Jan 2005

Taylor, Richard, June 1941, *Obit* July 1970

Thurber, James, American cartoonist and humorist, Mar 1940, Oct 1960, *Obit* Jan 1962

Toles, Tom, American cartoonist, Nov 2002

Tomorrow, Tom, American political cartoonist, Apr 2000

Trudeau, G. B., American cartoonist, Aug 1975

Uderzo, French cartoonist, Jan 2006

Vip, cartoonist, July 1946, *Obit* Oct 1984

Walker, Mort, American cartoonist, Feb 2002

Washington, Alonzo, American comic book artist and publisher, May 1999

Webster, H. T., cartoonist, Mar 1945, *Obit* Nov 1952

Williams, Gluyas, cartoonist, June 1946, *Obit* Apr 1982

Yamamura, Koji, Japanese animator, Jan 2003

Young, Art, cartoonist, Feb 1940, *Obit* Feb 1944

Yuh Nelson, Jennifer, Korean-American animator and film director, Nov 2013

Caterers

De Laurentiis, Giada, American chef and television personality, July 2013

Cellists

Beiser, Maya, American cellist, May 2009

Casals, Pablo, Spanish cellist, Nov 1950, Nov 1964, *Obit* Yrbk 1973

Daniels, Grace B., Sept 1959

Du Pre, Jacqueline, British cellist, May 1970, *Obit* Nov 1987

Feuermann, Emanuel, *Obit* July 1942

Finckel, David, American cellist and recording producer, July 2002

Hannikainen, Tauno, July 1955, *Obit* Yrbk 1968

Harnoncourt, Nikolaus, Austrian conductor, Jan 1991

Harrell, Lynn, cellist, Feb 1983

Hopkins, Sarah, Australian composer and cellist, Jan 2006

Kindler, Hans, Sept 1946, *Obit* Oct 1949

Ma, Yo-Yo, American cellist, July 1982

Mitchell, Howard, cellist and conductor, May 1952, *Obit* Aug 1988

Piatigorsky, Gregor, Russian-American cellist, Oct 1945, *Obit* Sept 1976

Rose, Leonard, American cellist, Jan 1977, *Obit* Jan 1985

Rostropovich, Mstislav, Russian cellist and conductor, May 1966, Nov 1988, *Obit* Aug 2007

Schulz, Leo, *Obit* Oct 1944

Starker, Janos, Hungarian cellist, May 1963, *Obit* Yrbk 2013

Swann, William Francis Gray, Feb 1941, Yrbk 1960, *Obit* Mar 1962

Villa-Lobos, Heitor, Brazilian composer, Apr 1945, *Obit* Jan 1960

Wallenstein, Alfred, American conductor, May 1940, Apr 1952, *Obit* Mar 1983

Weilerstein, Alisa, American cellist, Feb 2013

Censors

Breen, Joseph Ignatius, American motion picture censor and association executive, July 1950, *Obit* Jan 1966

Hays, Will H., American motion picture industry censor, July 1943, *Obit* Apr 1954

Centenarians

Abbott, George, dramatist and producer, Apr 1940, Oct 1965, *Obit* Apr 1995

Alvarez Bravo, Manuel, Mexican photographer, Jan 1999, *Obit* Jan 2003

Anderson, Constance, youth leader, May 1948, *Obit* Apr 2001

Astor, Brooke, American socialite and philanthropist, Jan 1987, *Obit* Yrbk 2007

Barnet, Will, American painter, June 1985, *Obit* Yrbk 2013

Barnett, Etta Moten, American singer and actress, Feb 2002

Barzun, Jacques, American historian, Sept 1964, *Obit* Yrbk 2013

Bayar, Celal, Turkish president, July 1950, *Obit* Oct 1986

Beckman, Arnold O., American chemist, inventor and instrument industry executive, Jan 2002, *Obit* Yrbk 2004

Bernays, Edward L., American public relations consultant, Feb 1942, Sept 1960, *Obit* May 1995

Burns, George, American comedian, Mar 1951, July 1976, *Obit* May 1996

Carter, Elliott, American composer, Nov 1960, *Obit* Yrbk 2013

Christison, Philip, British general, Nov 1945, *Obit* Feb 1994

Coolidge, William David, American physical chemist and inventor, June 1947, *Obit* Mar 1975

Corwin, Norman, American radio and television scriptwriter and producer, Yrbk 1940, *Obit* Yrbk 2011

Cowles, Fleur, American painter and magazine editor, Apr 1952, *Obit* Yrbk 2009

Crawford, Frederick C., defense industries executive, Feb 1943, *Obit* Feb 1995

Delany, Bessie, American dentist, Nov 1995, *Obit* Jan 1996

Delany, Sadie, American science teacher, Nov 1995, *Obit* Apr 1999

Denning, Alfred Thompson Denning, British judge, July 1965, *Obit* June 1999

Douglas, Marjory Stoneman, American short story writer, novelist and conservationist, July 1953, *Obit* July 1998

Drees, Willem, Dutch prime minister, Jan 1949, *Obit* July 1988

Dulles, Eleanor Lansing, American memoirist and

diplomat, Sept 1962, *Obit* Jan 1997

Eberhart, Richard, American poet, Jan 1961, *Obit* Yrbk 2005

Elizabeth, Aug 1981, *Obit* June 2002

Ellis, Ruth, American gay rights activist, *Obit* Apr 2000, Sept 2000

Fish, Hamilton, American congressman, Jan 1941, *Obit* Mar 1991

Fisher, Welthy Honsinger, educator, Yrbk 1969, *Obit* Feb 1981

Griffith, Ernest S., political scientist, Oct 1947, *Obit* Apr 1997

Gulick, Luther Halsey, American municipal official, June 1945, *Obit* Mar 1993

Hamilton, Alice, American physician, May 1946, *Obit* Nov 1970

Hawkins, Augustus F., American congressman, Feb 1983, *Obit* Yrbk 2008

Hildebrand, Joel Henry, American chemist, Feb 1955, *Obit* July 1983

Howorth, Lucy Somerville, American lawyer and feminist, Oct 1951, *Obit* Nov 1997

Kane, Joseph Nathan, American historian, Nov 1985, *Obit* Nov 2002

Kase, Toshikazu, Japanese diplomat, Apr 1957, *Obit* Yrbk 2004

Kennan, George Frost, American historian and diplomat, Oct 1947, Jan 1959, *Obit* Yrbk 2005.

Kennedy, Rose Fitzgerald, mother of President John F. Kennedy, Nov 1970, *Obit* Mar 1995

Keys, Ancel, American physiologist, Jan 1966, *Obit* Yrbk 2005

Kleitman, Nathaniel, physiologist, Oct 1957, *Obit* Jan 2000

Klopsteg, Paul Ernest, physicist, May 1959, *Obit* July 1991

Labouisse, Eve Curie, French biographer and daughter of Marie Curie, Mar 1940

Landon, Alf, American governor, Feb 1944, *Obit* Nov 1987

Lehmann, Inge, Danish geophysicist, Nov 1962

Levi-Strauss, Claude, French anthropologist, Mar 1972, *Obit* Jan 2010

McIntosh, Millicent Carey, American college dean and president, July 1947, *Obit* Mar 2001

Medina, Harold R., American judge, Apr 1949, *Obit* May 1990

Moiseyev, Igor, Russian ballet dancer and choreographer, Nov 1958, *Obit* Yrbk 2008

Morse, True Delbert, government official, Nov 1959, *Obit* Sept 1998

Moses, Grandma, American painter, Jan 1949, *Obit* Feb 1962

Mowrer, Lilian Thomson, author, May 1940, *Obit* Jan 1991

Pinay, Antoine, French political leader, Apr 1952, *Obit* Feb 1995

Riefenstahl, Leni, German actress and motion picture director, May 1975, *Obit* Yrbk 2004

Rosellini, Albert D., American governor, Yrbk 1958, *Obit* Yrbk 2012

Saulnier, Raymond J., American economist and presidential adviser, Yrbk 1957, *Obit* Yrbk 2009

Schlink, Frederick J., consumer rights advocate, Mar 1941, *Obit* Mar 1995

Seldes, George, American journalist, Sept 1941, *Obit* Sept 1995

Semon, Waldo Lonsbury, chemist and inventor, Yrbk 1940, *Obit* Aug 1999

Serrano Suner, Ramon, Spanish diplomat and political leader, Nov 1940, *Obit* Yrbk 2004

Shinwell, Emanuel Shinwell, British political leader, Jan 1943, *Obit* June 1986

Sillcox, Lewis Ketcham, mechanical engineer, Yrbk 1954, *Obit* May 1989

Slonimsky, Nicolas, Russian-American musicologist, conductor and composer, Apr 1955, Feb 1991, *Obit* Mar 1996

Stagg, Amos Alonzo, football coach, Mar 1944, *Obit* Apr 1965

Steloff, Frances, bookseller, Nov 1965, *Obit* June 1989

Sterne, Hedda, American painter, Mar 1957, *Obit* Yrbk 2011

Stickney, Dorothy, actress, Apr 1942, *Obit* Aug 1998

Stone, W. Clement, American insurance executive, Feb 1972, *Obit* Yrbk 2002

Stratton, Dorothy C., American psychologist, college dean and Coast Guard officer, June 1943, *Obit* Yrbk 2006

Stuart, Gloria, American actress, Apr 1998, *Obit* Yrbk 2010

Studebaker, John Ward, educator and government official, May 1942, *Obit* Oct 1989

Van Fleet, James Alward, American general, Apr 1948, *Obit* Nov 1992

Whitney, Phyllis A., American novelist and short story writer, Yrbk 1948, *Obit* Yrbk 2008

Zukor, Adolph, American motion picture executive, Mar 1950, *Obit* Aug 1976

Ceramists

MacKenzie, Warren, potter, Sept 1994

Poor, Henry Varnum, American ceramist and painter, Apr 1942, *Obit* Jan 1971

Voulkos, Peter, American sculptor and ceramist, Nov 1997, *Obit* Aug 2002

Chaplains

Bennett, Ivan L., American military chaplain, Nov 1952, *Obit* Aug 1980

Berg, Irving H., American clergyman and college dean, *Obit* Nov 1941

Marshall, Peter, Scottish-American clergyman, Apr 1948, *Obit* Feb 1949

Ryan, Patrick James, military chaplain, May 1955

Chemical engineers

Alexander, Harry Held, American metallurgist, *Obit* Feb 1941

Belcher, Angela, American chemical engineer, July 2006

Boyer, Marion W., chemical engineer, Jan 1951, *Obit* Jan 1983

Callow, John Michael, *Obit* Sept 1940

Carpenter, Henry Cort Harold, *Obit* Nov 1940

Furnas, Clifford Cook, Oct 1956, *Obit* June 1969

Hadfield, Robert Abbott, *Obit* Nov 1940

Jackson, Daniel Dana, *Obit* Oct 1941

Khan, A. Q., Pakistani nuclear scientist, Jan 2004

McKeen, John E., June 1961, *Obit* Apr 1978

Midgley, Thomas, American chemical engineer, *Obit* Yrbk 1944

Murphree, Eger V., Sept 1956, *Obit* Jan 1963

Nichols, William T., Oct 1953

Rassweiler, Clifford F., Oct 1958

Rathbone, Monroe J., Mar 1957, *Obit* Sept 1976

Ricketts, Louis Davidson, *Obit* Mar 1940

Vila, George R., tire and rubber executive, Mar 1963, *Obit* Aug 1987

Welch, John F., American corporation executive, Jan 1988

Whitman, Walter G., Feb 1952, *Obit* June 1974

Williams, Clyde E., July 1947

Chemical industry executives

Ambani, Anil, Indian telecommunications, textile and chemical conglomerate executive, Feb 2009

Ambani, Mukesh, Indian telecommunications, textile and chemical conglomerate executive, June 2009

Arden, Elizabeth, American cosmetician, July 1957, *Obit* Yrbk 1966

Ash, Mary Kay, American cosmetics executive, May 1995, *Obit* Feb 2002

Bailar, Benjamin F., American chemical industry executive and Postmaster general, July 1976

Barnes, Albert Coombs, American chemist and pharmaceutical executive, Mar 1945, *Obit* Sept 1951

Beeching, Richard, British physicist, government official and chemical industry executive, Sept 1963

Bennett, Wallace F., American senator, Feb 1949, *Obit* Feb 1994

Bertozzi, Carolyn R., American chemist, July 2003

Bishop, Hazel, American chemist and cosmetics executive, Sept 1957, *Obit* Feb 1999

Blancke, Harold, American chemical industry executive, June 1957

Bobst, Elmer Holmes, American pharmaceutical executive, Yrbk 1973, *Obit* Sept 1978

Bristol, Lee H., Sept 1962

Cabot, Thomas D., chemical executive and philanthropist, June 1951, *Obit* Aug 1995

Chanel, Coco, French fashion designer and perfumer, Sept 1954, *Obit* Feb 1971

Chappell, Tom, American personal care products industry executive, May 1994

Childs, Richard Spencer, cleaning products industry executive and civic reformer, Sept 1955, *Obit* Jan 1979

Cochran, Jacqueline, American aviator and cosmetics industry executive, Sept 1940, June 1963, *Obit* Oct 1980

Connor, John T., American Secretary of commerce, Apr 1961, *Obit* Feb 2001

Copeland, Lammot Du Pont, chemical executive, May 1963

Dart, Justin Whitlock, drug industry executive, Nov 1946, *Obit* Mar 1984

Dial, Morse G., chemical executive, Mar 1956, *Obit* Jan 1983

Doan, Leland I., American chemical industry executive, Oct 1952, *Obit* May 1974

Driscoll, Alfred E., American governor, Jan 1949, *Obit* May 1975

Du Pont, Pierre S., American business executive, Sept 1940, *Obit* May 1954

Ellena, Jean-Claude, French perfumer, Jan 2005

Fleck, Alexander Fleck, Scottish chemical executive, Apr 1956, *Obit* Oct 1968

Foster, William C., American government official, Nov 1950

Gerstacker, Carl A., American chemical executive, Oct 1961, *Obit* July 1995

Grace, J. Peter, chemical industry executive, Mar 1960, *Obit* June 1995

Greenewalt, Crawford H., American chemical industry executive, Jan 1949

Guerlain, Jean-Paul, French perfumer, Jan 2006

Hamied, Yusuf K., Indian pharmaceutical executive, Jan 2004

Higley, Harvey V., government official, Oct 1956, *Obit* Jan 1987

Huntsman, Jr., Jon, American diplomat, May 2012

Julian, Percy L., American chemist, Sept 1947, *Obit* Jan 1975

Jung, Andrea, American cosmetics industry executive, May 2000

Kaiser, Edgar F., chemical and metal industries executive, Sept 1964, *Obit* Feb 1982

Kamm, John, American chemical industry executive and human rights activist, Jan 2002

Klumpp, Theodore G., Oct 1958

Kullman, Ellen, American chemical industry executive, Nov 2011

Lauder, Estee, American cosmetics executive, July 1986, *Obit* Yrbk 2004

Li, Ka-shing, Chinese real estate executive, Jan 2003

Loynd, Harry J., Feb 1952

Luckman, Charles, American personal care products industry executive, Oct 1947, *Obit* Apr 1999

Matsui, Connie L., American pharmaceutical executive and Girl Scouts leader, Aug 2002

McConnell, Joseph H., radio and television executive, Nov 1950, *Obit* May 1997

McCoy, Charles B., American chemical executive, July 1970, *Obit* Mar 1995

McCullough, Gary E., American school administrator, Nov 2009

McKeen, John E., June 1961, *Obit* Apr 1978

Merck, George W., American pharmaceutical executive, Yrbk 1946, *Obit* Jan 1958

Messier, Jean-Marie, French mass media industry executive, May 2002

Panic, Milan, Yugoslav prime minister and drug industry executive, June 1993

Perkins, George Walbridge, Apr 1950, *Obit* Mar 1960

Potter, Myrtle, American biotechnology executive, Aug 2004

Price, Lisa, American personal care products company founder, Feb 2011

Rennebohm, Oscar, July 1950, *Obit* Yrbk 1968

Roddick, Anita, British cosmetics industry executive, Sept 1992, *Obit* Yrbk 2007

Rubinstein, Helena, American cosmetician, June 1943, *Obit* May 1965

Rumsfeld, Donald H., American Secretary of defense, Apr 1970, Mar 2002

Rush, David Kenneth, American chemical industry executive and diplomat, May 1975, *Obit* Feb 1995

Sassoon, Vidal, British hairstylist and personal care products industry executive, Apr 1999, *Obit* Yrbk 2012

Shapiro, Irving S., American lawyer and chemical company executive, Nov 1976, *Obit* Nov 2001

Smith, Austin E., physician and drug industry executive, Mar 1950, *Obit* Jan 1994

Stamp, Josiah Charles, British government official, *Obit* June 1941

Taylor, Susan L., American magazine editor, Feb 1997

Terra, Daniel J., chemical executive and art collector, Nov 1987, *Obit* Sept 1996

Vasella, Daniel, Swiss pharmaceutical executive and physician, Jan 2005

Wakefield, Charles Cheers Wakefield, English lubricants industry executive, *Obit* Mar 1941

Waldron, Hicks Benjamin, cosmetics executive, Mar 1988

Wilson, Edward Foss, corporation executive and government official, Mar 1958, *Obit* May 1994

Ziegler, Ronald L., American drug store association executive and presidential press secretary, Nov 1971, *Obit* July 2003

Chemists

Adams, Roger, American chemist, June 1947, *Obit* Sept 1971

Alberto, Alvaro, Brazilian chemist and United Nations official, Mar 1947

Allyn, Lewis B., American food chemist, *Obit* Jan 1940

Alsberg, Carl, American biochemist, *Obit* Yrbk 1940

Ames, Bruce N., American biochemist, Oct 1993

Asimov, Isaac, American biochemist and science fiction writer, Yrbk 1953, Oct 1968, *Obit* May 1992

Aston, Francis William, British chemist, *Obit* Jan 1946

Baekeland, Leo Hendrik, Belgian-American chemist, *Obit* Apr 1944

Bailar, John Christian, American chemist, July 1959

Barbour, Henry Gray, American pharmacologist, *Obit* Nov 1943

Barton, Jacqueline K., American chemist, Sept 2006

Baulieu, Etienne-Emile, French biochemist, Nov 1995

Beardsley, William S., American governor, June 1950, *Obit* Jan 1955

Beckman, Arnold O., American chemist, inventor and instrument industry executive, Jan 2002, *Obit* Yrbk 2004

Behe, Michael J., American biochemist and intelligent design advocate, Feb 2006

Belcher, Angela, American chemical engineer, July 2006

Bertozzi, Carolyn R., American chemist, July 2003

Bishop, Hazel, American chemist and cosmetics executive, Sept 1957, *Obit* Feb 1999

Bliss, A. Richard, American pharmacologist and college dean, *Obit* Oct 1941

Blumberg, Baruch S., American physician and biochemist, Nov 1977, *Obit* Yrbk 2011

Bodansky, Meyer, American biochemist and pathologist, *Obit* Aug 1941

Boggs, Charles Reid, American chemist and manufacturing executive, *Obit* Apr 1940

Bosch, Carl, German chemist, *Obit* Jan 1940

Bovet, Daniel, Swiss-Italian pharmacologist, Jan 1958, *Obit* June 1992

Boyer, Marion W., chemical engineer, Jan 1951, *Obit* Jan 1983

Britton, Edgar C., Apr 1952, *Obit* Oct 1962

Brode, Wallace R., June 1958, *Obit* Oct 1974

Brodie, Bernard B., American pharmacologist, Sept 1969, *Obit* May 1989

Brown, Harrison Scott, American geochemist, July 1955, *Obit* Feb 1987

Calvin, Melvin, American biochemist, Apr 1962, *Obit* Mar 1997

Carr, Emma Perry, American chemist, Apr 1959

Catlin, Don H., American pharmacologist, Mar 2010

Chain, Ernst Boris, British biochemist, Nov 1965, *Obit* Oct 1979

Chauvin, Yves, French chemist, Jan 2007

Chizmadzhev, IUrii Aleksandrovich, Russian physical chemist, Jan 2005

Ciechanover, Aaron J., Israeli biochemist, Jan 2007

Clemensen, Erik Christian, *Obit* July 1941

Coleman, Mary Sue, American university president, Feb 2007

Conant, James Bryant, American college president and diplomat, Mar 1941, Feb 1951, *Obit* Apr 1978

Coolidge, William David, American physical chemist and inventor, June 1947, *Obit* Mar 1975

Cori, Carl F., American biochemist, Yrbk 1947, *Obit* Feb 1985

Cori, Gerty Theresa, American biochemist, Yrbk 1947, *Obit* Jan 1958

Craig, Lyman C., Apr 1964, *Obit* Sept 1974

Crick, Francis, British biochemist, Mar 1983, *Obit* Yrbk 2004

Cullen, Glenn Ernest, *Obit* May 1940

Dam, Henrik, Danish biochemist, Sept 1949, *Obit* June 1976

Daniels, Farrington, July 1965, *Obit* Sept 1972

Debye, Peter J. W., Dutch physical chemist, July 1963, *Obit* Jan 1967

Djerassi, Carl, American chemist, Oct 2001

Doisy, Edward Adelbert, American biochemist, Mar 1949, *Obit* Jan 1987

Doudna, Jennifer A., American biochemist, Feb 2005

Dow, Willard H., Feb 1944, *Obit* May 1949

Dreyfus, Camille, May 1955, *Obit* Yrbk 1957

Du Pont, Francis Irenee, *Obit* May 1942

Du Vigneaud, Vincent, American biochemist, Jan 1956, *Obit* Feb 1979

Dunbar, P. B., July 1949, *Obit* Nov 1968

Durham, Carl, American congressman, July 1957, *Obit* June 1974

Edelman, Gerald M., American biochemist, Apr 1995

Egloff, Gustav, Sept 1940

Eisenschiml, Otto, Austrian-American chemist

and historian, Oct 1963, *Obit* Jan 1964

El-Sayed, Karimat, Egyptian crystallographer, Jan 2004

Elder, Albert L., Sept 1960

Elion, Gertrude B., American biochemist, Mar 1995, *Obit* May 1999

Ellis, Carleton, *Obit* Mar 1941

Elvehjem, C. A., May 1948, *Obit* Oct 1962

Eyde, Samuel, *Obit* Aug 1940

Eyring, Henry, chemist, Oct 1961

Fischer, Hans, German chemist, *Obit* May 1945

Fisher, Harry L., Oct 1954

Flory, Paul J., American chemist, Mar 1975, *Obit* Nov 1985

Folkers, Karl August, American chemist, Oct 1962

Foote, H. W., *Obit* Mar 1942

Franck, James, German-American physicist, May 1957, *Obit* July 1964

Freundlich, Herbert, German chemist, *Obit* May 1941

Funk, Casimir, biochemist, May 1945, *Obit* Jan 1968

Furman, N. Howell, Yrbk 1951, *Obit* Oct 1965

Furnas, Clifford Cook, Oct 1956, *Obit* June 1969

Gallo, Robert C., biochemist, Oct 1986

Getman, Frederick H., *Obit* Jan 1942

Giauque, William Francis, American chemist, Jan 1950, *Obit* May 1982

Gillespie, Louis J., *Obit* Mar 1941

Giordani, Francesco, Sept 1957, *Obit* Mar 1961

Goulian, Mehran, July 1968

Grebe, John J., Oct 1955

Gross, Paul Magnus, chemist, May 1963, *Obit* June 1986

Gupta, Mahabir P., Indian pharmacologist, Jan 2005

Haagen-Smit, A. J., chemist, Mar 1966, *Obit* May 1977

Hahn, Otto, German chemist, Mar 1951, *Obit* Oct 1968

Handler, Philip, biochemist, Feb 1964, *Obit* Feb 1982

Harden, Arthur, British biochemist, *Obit* Aug 1940

Hass, Henry Bohn, chemist, Apr 1956, *Obit* Apr 1987

Heath, James R., American chemist, Oct 2003

Henderson, Lawrence J., American chemist, *Obit* Apr 1942

Hershko, Avram, Israeli biochemist, Jan 2007

Hevesy, George Charles, Hungarian chemist, Apr 1959, *Obit* Sept 1966

Heyrovsky, Jaroslav, Czech chemist, July 1961, *Obit* May 1967

Hildebrand, Joel Henry, American chemist, Feb 1955, *Obit* July 1983

Hinshelwood, Cyril Norman, British chemist, Apr 1957, *Obit* Yrbk 1967

Hofmann, Klaus Heinrich, biochemist, Apr 1961

Holley, Robert William, American biochemist, Jan 1967, *Obit* Apr 1993

Hornig, Donald F., chemist, university president and presidential adviser, May 1964, *Obit* Yrbk 2013

Howe, Harrison E., *Obit* Feb 1943

Ittner, Martin H., Nov 1942, *Obit* May 1945

Jackson, Daniel Dana, *Obit* Oct 1941

Jenks, Leon E., *Obit* Mar 1940

Julian, Percy L., American chemist, Sept 1947, *Obit* Jan 1975

Karle, Isabella L., American chemist, Jan 2003

Kelsey, Frances Oldham, American pharmacologist and regulatory agency official, Apr 1965

Kendall, Edward Calvin, American biochemist, Yrbk 1950, *Obit* June 1972

Kendrew, John C., British biochemist, Oct 1963, *Obit* Nov 1997

Khorana, Har Gobind, Indian biochemist, Yrbk 1970, *Obit* Yrbk 2012

Kiessling, Laura L., American biochemist, Aug 2003

King, Alexander, Scottish chemist and futurist, Jan 2002

King, Charles Glen, biochemist and nutritionist, Yrbk 1967, *Obit* Mar 1988

Kistiakowsky, George, American chemist and presidential aide, Nov 1960, *Obit* Feb 1983

Kobilka, Brian, Apr 2013

Kornberg, Arthur, American biochemist, Sept 1968, *Obit* Feb 2008

Krebs, Hans Adolf, British biochemist, Mar 1954, *Obit* Feb 1982

Landsteiner, Karl, American biochemist, *Obit* Aug 1943

Langmuir, Arthur Comings, *Obit* July 1941

Langmuir, Irving, American chemist, Mar 1940, Oct 1950, *Obit* Nov 1957

Lauger, Paul, Oct 1945

Leake, Chauncey D., Apr 1960, *Obit* Mar 1978

Leech, Paul Nicholas, *Obit* Mar 1941

Levene, Phoebus Aaron Theodore, American biochemist, *Obit* Oct 1940

Levi, Primo, Italian memoirist, novelist and chemist, Mar 1987, *Obit* Mar 1987

Li, Choh-hao, biochemist, Apr 1963, *Obit* Jan 1988

Libby, Willard Frank, American chemist, Nov 1954, *Obit* Nov 1980

Lipmann, Fritz, American biochemist, Mar 1954, *Obit* Sept 1986

Loewe, Siegfried, American pharmacologist, Jan 1947

Lovelock, James, British chemist and biophysicist, Nov 1992

Lynen, Feodor, German biochemist, June 1967, *Obit* Oct 1979

Mack, Pauline Beery, chemist and college dean, Yrbk 1950

Mark, Herman Francis, American chemist and college dean, May 1961, *Obit* June 1992

Marsh, John, Mar 1960

Martin, Archer, British biochemist, Nov 1953, *Obit* Yrbk 2002

McKenna, Francis Eugene, American chemist and editor, May 1966, *Obit* Feb 1979

McMillan, Edwin Mattison, American physicist and chemist, Feb 1952, *Obit* Nov 1991

Medvedev, Zhores Aleksandrovich, Soviet biochemist, Nov 1973

Merrifield, R. Bruce, American biochemist, Mar 1985, *Obit* Yrbk 2006

Midgley, Thomas, American chemical engineer, *Obit* Yrbk 1944

Miller, William Lash, Canadian chemist, *Obit* Oct 1940

Moncada, Salvador, Honduran pharmacologist, Jan 2003

Moore, Gordon E., American computer industry executive, Apr 2002

Moscicki, Ignacy, Polish president, *Obit* Nov 1946

Muller, Paul Hermann, Swiss chemist, Oct 1945, *Obit* Yrbk 1965

Mulliken, Robert Sanderson, American chemist, Sept 1967, *Obit* Jan 1987

Mullis, Kary B., American biochemist, Feb 1996

Murayama, Makio, Oct 1974

Murphree, Eger V., Sept 1956, *Obit* Jan 1963

Natta, Giulio, Italian chemist, Nov 1964

Nernst, Hermann Walther, German chemist, *Obit* Jan 1942

Nesmeianov, A. N., Nov 1958

Nichols, William T., Oct 1953

Nirenberg, Marshall Warren, American biochemist, Apr 1965, *Obit* Yrbk 2010

Norris, James F., *Obit* Sept 1940

Northrop, John H., American biochemist, June 1947, *Obit* Sept 1987

Norton, Thomas, *Obit* Jan 1942

Noyes, W. Albert, American chemist, Oct 1947

Noyes, William Albert, American chemist, *Obit* Yrbk 1941

Ochoa, Severo, Spanish-American biochemist, June 1962, *Obit* Jan 1994

Onsager, Lars, American chemist, Apr 1958, *Obit* Jan 1977

Pauling, Linus C., American chemist, May 1949, Feb 1964, June 1994, *Obit* Oct 1994

Perutz, Max, British biochemist, Nov 1963, *Obit* Apr 2002

Piccard, Jean Felix, Sept 1947, *Obit* Mar 1963

Pitzer, Kenneth Sanborn, chemist, May 1950

Ponnamperuma, Cyril, chemist, Apr 1984, *Obit* Mar 1995

Price, Charles C., chemist, Yrbk 1957

Prigogine, Ilya, Russian-Belgian chemist, Feb 1987, *Obit* Yrbk 2003

Rassweiler, Clifford F., Oct 1958

Rathbone, Monroe J., Mar 1957, *Obit* Sept 1976

Reed, Herbert Calhoun, *Obit* Sept 1940

Reichstein, Tadeus, Swiss chemist, Feb 1951, *Obit* Oct 1996

Richards, Alfred N., American pharmacologist, Sept 1950, *Obit* Apr 1966

Rose, Mary Swartz, American chemist and nutritionist, *Obit* Mar 1941

Rose, William C., American biochemist, Mar 1953, *Obit* Jan 1986

Sabatier, Paul, French chemist, *Obit* Oct 1941

Sanger, Frederick, British biochemist, July 1981

Schaefer, Vincent J., American chemist and meteorologist, Jan 1948, *Obit* Sept 1993

Schmelkes, Franz C., *Obit* Feb 1943

Seaborg, Glenn, American chemist, July 1948, Yrbk 1961, *Obit* May 1999

Seibert, Florence, American biochemist, Nov 1942, *Obit* Oct 1991

Semenov, Nikolay Nikolayevich, Russian chemist, Mar 1957

Semon, Waldo Lonsbury, chemist and inventor, Yrbk 1940, *Obit* Aug 1999

Sherman, Henry C., Jan 1949, *Obit* Yrbk 1955

Smith, Roy Burnett, *Obit* Feb 1941

Snell, Foster Dee, Jan 1943

Snyder, Solomon H., American neuropharmacologist, Apr 1996

Stanley, Wendell Meredith, American biochemist, Apr 1947, *Obit* Sept 1971

Staudinger, Hermann, German chemist, Apr 1954, *Obit* Nov 1965

Steacie, E. W. R., Jan 1953, *Obit* Nov 1962

Steitz, Joan Argetsinger, American biochemist, June 2007

Stern, Jessica, American terrorism expert, May 2006

Stine, Charles Milton Altland, Jan 1940, *Obit* Sept 1954

Sumner, James Batcheller, American biochemist, Jan 1947, *Obit* Oct 1955

Sveda, Michael, chemist and inventor, Yrbk 1954, *Obit* Nov 1999

Synge, Richard Lawrence Millington, British biochemist, Nov 1953

Szent-Gyorgyi, Albert, Hungarian-American biochemist, Jan 1955, *Obit* Jan 1987

Tanaka, Koichi, Japanese chemist, Jan 2007

Tatum, Edward Lawrie, American biochemist, Mar 1959, *Obit* Jan 1976

Telkes, Maria, American chemist, Nov 1950, *Obit* Oct 1996

Terrett, Nicholas K., British pharmacologist and co-inventor of Viagra, Jan 2003

Theorell, Hugo, Swedish biochemist, Feb 1956, *Obit* Oct 1982

Thomas, Charles Allen, Mar 1950, *Obit* May 1982

Tiselius, Arne Wilhelm Kaurin, Swedish biochemist, Apr 1949, *Obit* Yrbk 1971

Tishler, Max, chemist, Mar 1952, *Obit* May 1989

Tizard, Henry Thomas, British physical chemist, Jan 1949, *Obit* Yrbk 1959

Toch, Maximilian, *Obit* June 1946

Todd, Alexander R., British chemist, Mar 1958, *Obit* Mar 1997

Urey, Harold Clayton, American chemist, Feb 1941, July 1960, *Obit* Mar 1981

Van Slyke, Donald D., Jan 1943, *Obit* July 1971

Vane, John R., British pharmacologist, May 1986, *Obit* Yrbk 2005

Venter, J. Craig, American biochemist, Feb 1995

Vila, George R., tire and rubber executive, Mar 1963, *Obit* Aug 1987

Wald, George, American biochemist, May 1968, *Obit* June 1997

Walden, Percy Talbot, *Obit* May 1943

Warner, John Christian, chemist, Oct 1950, *Obit* July 1989

Weidlein, Edward R., chemist and foundation official, July 1948, *Obit* Nov 1983

Weinberg, Robert A., American biochemist, June 1983

Weizmann, Chaim, Israeli president and Zionist leader, Nov 1942, Nov 1948, *Obit* Yrbk 1952

Welch, John F., American corporation executive, Jan 1988

Whitman, Walter G., Feb 1952, *Obit* June 1974

Wilkins, Maurice Hugh Frederick, English biochemist, June 1963, *Obit* Yrbk 2005

Williams, Robert R., Sept 1951, *Obit* Yrbk 1965

Williams, Roger J., biochemist and nutritionist, July 1957, *Obit* Apr 1988

Willstatter, Richard, German chemist, *Obit* Sept 1942

Wilson, I. W., July 1952, *Obit* Jan 1978

Woodward, R. B., American biochemist, Feb 1952, *Obit* Sept 1979

Worden, Edward Chauncey, *Obit* Nov 1940

Wrinch, Dorothy, Anglo-American biochemist and mathematician, July 1947

Wuthrich, Kurt, Swiss chemist, Jan 2007

Yar'Adua, Umaru Musa, Nigerian president, Jan 2007, *Obit* Yrbk 2010

Chess players

Alekhine, Alexander, Russian chess player, *Obit* May 1946

Ashley, Maurice, Jamaican-American chess player, Sept 1999

Botvinnik, M. M., Russian chess player, June 1965, *Obit* July 1995

Carlsen, Magnus, Norwegian chess player, July 2013

Fischer, Bobby, American chess player, Oct 1963, May 1994, *Obit* Yrbk 2008

Karpov, Anatoly, Russian chess player, Nov 1978

Kasparov, Garry, Russian chess player, Apr 1986

Kosteniuk, Alexandra, Russian chess player, Jan 2006

Kramnik, Vladimir, Russian chess player, Jan 2003

Lasker, Emanuel, chess player, *Obit* Mar 1941

Polgar, Susan, Hungarian chess player, Feb 2008

Reshevsky, Samuel, chess player, Feb 1955, *Obit* July 1992

Shahade, Jennifer, American chess player, Sept 2005

Smyslov, Vasilii, Russian chess player, July 1967, *Obit* Yrbk 2010

Spassky, Boris Vasilyevich, Russian chess player, Nov 1972

Child benefactors

Aronson, Jane, American pediatrician, Feb 2011

Flanagan, Edward Joseph, American priest and youth leader, Sept 1941, *Obit* June 1948

Gmeiner, Hermann, Austrian social worker, May 1963, *Obit* June 1986

Hale, Clara, American child benefactor, July 1985, *Obit* Feb 1993

Joyner-Kersee, Jackie, American heptathlete and basketball player, July 1987

Landwirth, Henri, American foundation official and hotel executive, Jan 2005

Oettinger, Katherine B., government official and child welfare worker, Nov 1957, *Obit* Jan 1998

Ritter, Bruce, priest and child care leader, June 1983, *Obit* Feb 2000

Child psychologists

Ames, Louise Bates, child psychologist, Sept 1956, *Obit* Jan 1997

Leach, Penelope, English child psychologist, Aug 1994

Minard, George Cann, *Obit* Aug 1940

Neill, Alexander Sutherland, British child psychologist, Apr 1961, *Obit* Nov 1973

Rimm, Sylvia B., American child psychologist, Feb 2002

Salk, Lee, child psychologist, Sept 1979, *Obit* July 1992

Children

Allilueva, Svetlana, daughter of Joseph Stalin, Oct 1968, *Obit* Yrbk 2012

Churchill, Randolph S., British journalist and biographer, Oct 1947, *Obit* Sept 1968

Churchill, Sarah, English actress and daughter of Winston Churchill, May 1955, *Obit* Jan 1983

Dayan, Yael, Israeli author and daughter of Moshe Dayan, Apr 1997

Graham, Franklin, American evangelist and son of Billy Graham, May 2002

Herrera, Carolina, Venezuelan model and daughter of fashion designer Carolina Herrera, Mar 1996

Hoffa, Jimmy P., American labor leader, July 1999

Kennedy, Joseph Patrick, American congressman and energy company executive, June 1988

Kennedy, Robert Francis, American lawyer and son of Senator Robert F. Kennedy, May 2004

Mann, Klaus, German novelist, essayist, dramatist and son of Thomas Mann, Yrbk 1940, *Obit* July 1949

Oe, Hikari, Japanese composer and son of Kenzaburo Oe, May 1999

Picasso, Paloma, French jewelry and industrial designer and daughter of Pablo Picasso, Apr 1986

Powell, Michael, American regulatory official and son of Secretary of state Colin L. Powell, May 2003

Rogers, Will, American congressman and actor, Yrbk 1953, *Obit* Sept 1993

Rossellini, Isabella, Italian model and actress, Aug 1988

Thompson, John, American basketball coach, Nov 2007

Tolkien, Christopher, British editor and son of J.R.R. Tolkien, Jan 2007

Children of presidents

Bush, George W., American president, Apr 1997, Aug 2001

Bush, Jeb, American governor, Feb 1999

Davis, Patti, American novelist and daughter of President Ronald Reagan, Nov 1986

Eisenhower, John S. D., army officer, diplomat and son of Dwight D. Eisenhower, July 1969

Garfield, Harry Augustus, American college president and son of President James A. Garfield, *Obit* Feb 1943

Hoover, Herbert Clark, American petroleum engineer, diplomat and son of President Herbert Hoover, Oct 1954, *Obit* Sept 1969

Kennedy, John F., American lawyer, magazine editor and son of President John F. Kennedy, Jan 1996, *Obit* Sept 1999

Longworth, Alice Roosevelt, daughter of American president Theodore Roosevelt, June 1943, Aug 1975, *Obit* Apr 1980

Park, Geun Hye, Korean political leader, Jan 2007

Roosevelt, Franklin D., American congressman and son of President Franklin D. Roosevelt, Jan 1950, *Obit* Sept 1988

Roosevelt, James, American congressman, business consultant and son of President Franklin D. Roosevelt, Apr 1950, *Obit* Nov 1991

Roosevelt, Kermit, army officer, steamship line executive and son of President Theodore Roosevelt, *Obit* July 1943

Sukarnoputri, Megawati, Indonesian president, Sept 1997

Taft, Charles P., American lawyer, mayor and son of President William H. Taft, July 1945, *Obit* Aug 1983

Truman, Margaret, daughter of American president Harry S. Truman and writer, June 1950, June 1987, *Obit* Yrbk 2008

Children of prominent persons

Allilueva, Svetlana, daughter of Joseph Stalin, Oct 1968, *Obit* Yrbk 2012

Bush, Jeb, American governor, Feb 1999

Cheney, Liz, American lawyer, political activist and daughter of Vice-president Richard B. Cheney, Aug 2010

Churchill, Randolph S., British journalist and biographer, Oct 1947, *Obit* Sept 1968

Churchill, Sarah, English actress and daughter of Winston Churchill, May 1955, *Obit* Jan 1983

Garfield, Harry Augustus, American college president and son of President James A. Garfield, *Obit* Feb 1943

Graham, Franklin, American evangelist and son of Billy Graham, May 2002

Herrera, Carolina, Venezuelan model and daughter of fashion designer Carolina Herrera, Mar 1996

Hoffa, Jimmy P., American labor leader, July 1999

Hoover, Herbert Clark, American petroleum engineer, diplomat and son of President Herbert Hoover, Oct 1954, *Obit* Sept 1969

Kennedy, John F., American lawyer, magazine editor and son of President John F. Kennedy, Jan 1996, *Obit* Sept 1999

Kennedy, Joseph Patrick, American congressman and energy company executive, June 1988

Kennedy, Robert Francis, American lawyer and son of Senator Robert F. Kennedy, May 2004

Longworth, Alice Roosevelt, daughter of American president Theodore Roosevelt, June 1943, Aug 1975, *Obit* Apr 1980

Mann, Klaus, German novelist, essayist, dramatist and son of Thomas Mann, Yrbk 1940, *Obit* July 1949

Oe, Hikari, Japanese composer and son of Kenzaburo Oe, May 1999

Park, Geun Hye, Korean political leader, Jan 2007

Picasso, Paloma, French jewelry and industrial designer and daughter of Pablo Picasso, Apr 1986

Powell, Michael, American regulatory official and son of Secretary of state Colin L. Powell, May 2003

Rogers, Will, American congressman and actor, Yrbk 1953, *Obit* Sept 1993

Roosevelt, Franklin D., American congressman and son of President Franklin D. Roosevelt, Jan 1950, *Obit* Sept 1988

Roosevelt, James, American congressman, business consultant and son of President Franklin D. Roosevelt, Apr 1950, *Obit* Nov 1991

Rossellini, Isabella, Italian model and actress, Aug 1988

Sukarnoputri, Megawati, Indonesian president, Sept 1997

Taft, Charles P., American lawyer, mayor and son of President William H. Taft, July 1945, *Obit* Aug 1983

Thompson, John, American basketball coach, Nov 2007

Tolkien, Christopher, British editor and son of J.R.R. Tolkien, Jan 2007

Children's authors

Adamson, Joy, Kenyan conservationist, writer and illustrator, Oct 1972, *Obit* Feb 1980

Addington, Sarah, American children's author, *Obit* Yrbk 1940

Allee, Marjorie Hill, author, *Obit* June 1945

Allende, Isabel, Chilean novelist, Feb 1988

Ardizzone, Edward, English painter, illustrator and author, May 1964, *Obit* Jan 1980

Armour, Richard Willard, philologist and poet, Nov 1958, *Obit* Apr 1989

Artzybasheff, Boris, author and illustrator, Oct 1945, *Obit* Sept 1965

Ashmun, Margaret Eliza, American children's author, *Obit* Apr 1940

Atwood, Margaret, Canadian novelist and poet, May 1984

Bacon, Peggy, American mystery writer and illustrator, Jan 1940, *Obit* Mar 1987

Bagnold, Enid, English novelist and dramatist, June 1964, *Obit* May 1981

Bailey, Carolyn Sherwin, American children's author, Yrbk 1948

Ball, Zachary, Yrbk 1953

Barber, Ronde, American football player, Oct 2003

Barbour, Ralph Henry, author, *Obit* Apr 1944

Baskin, Leonard, American sculptor and illustrator, May 1964, *Obit* Aug 2000

Beard, Daniel Carter, American children's author, illustrator and Boy Scouts founder, *Obit* Aug 1941

Bell, Margaret Elizabeth, Yrbk 1952

Bemelmans, Ludwig, American children's author and illustrator, Apr 1941, *Obit* Yrbk 1962

Benchley, Nathaniel, American novelist, short story writer and children's author, Sept 1953, *Obit* Feb 1982

Benchley, Peter, American novelist and journalist, July 1976, *Obit* June 2006

Besson, Luc, French film director, Jan 2002

Bialk, Elisa, author, Yrbk 1954, *Obit* May 1990

Billingsley, Franny, American children's author, Aug 2012

Blume, Judy, American young adult novelist, Apr 1980

Bonner, Mary Graham, Yrbk 1950

Bontemps, Arna Wendell, American novelist, poet, biographer and children's author, Yrbk 1946, *Obit* July 1973

Bothwell, Jean, Yrbk 1946

Boylston, Helen Dore, author, July 1942, *Obit* Nov 1984

Bradbury, Ray, American science fiction writer, June 1953, July 1982, *Obit* Yrbk 2012

Brier, Howard M., Yrbk 1951

Brink, Carol Ryrie, American children's author, Yrbk 1946

Bro, Marguerite Harmon, Yrbk 1952

Brockmeier, Kevin, American novelist, short story writer and children's author, May 2010

Brownson, Josephine, American children's author and social worker, Mar 1940

Buckmaster, Henrietta, Yrbk 1946, *Obit* June 1983

Burton, Virginia Lee, American children's author, Sept 1943, *Obit* Yrbk 1968

Campbell, Bebe Moore, American social critic and novelist, Apr 2000, *Obit* Yrbk 2007

Carle, Eric, American illustrator and children's author, Nov 2013

Caudill, Rebecca, author, Yrbk 1950, *Obit* Jan 1986

Cavanah, Frances, author and editor, Yrbk 1954

Cavanna, Betty, American young adult novelist, Yrbk 1950, *Obit* Oct 2001

Chase, Mary Ellen, author, May 1940, *Obit* Oct 1973

Chastain, Madye Lee, Yrbk 1958

Cheatham, Kitty, *Obit* Feb 1946

Chute, B. J., author, Yrbk 1950, *Obit* Oct 1987

Chute, Marchette Gaylord, biographer and literary

historian, Yrbk 1950, *Obit* July 1994

Chwast, Seymour, American children's author, illustrator and graphic designer, Sept 1995

Ciardi, John, American poet, translator and critic, Oct 1967, *Obit* May 1986

Cousins, Margaret, author and editor, June 1954, *Obit* Oct 1996

Crawford, Phyllis, author, Nov 1940

Crockett, Lucy Herndon, Yrbk 1953

Crownfield, Gertrude, *Obit* July 1945

Cullen, Countee, American poet, *Obit* Mar 1946

Curtis, Jamie Lee, American actress, Nov 1998

D'Aulaire, Edgar Parin, author and illustrator, Aug 1940

Daniel-Rops, Henri, Mar 1957, *Obit* Oct 1965

Daringer, Helen Fern, Yrbk 1951

Daugherty, James Henry, American children's author and illustrator, July 1940, *Obit* Apr 1974

Davis, Robert, Yrbk 1949

De Angeli, Marguerite Lofft, American children's author and illustrator, Yrbk 1947

De Paola, Tomie, American painter, illustrator and children's author, Feb 1999

DeJong, Meindert, Dutch-American children's author, Yrbk 1952, *Obit* Sept 1991

Dickson, Marguerite, Yrbk 1952, *Obit* Jan 1954

Ditmars, Raymond Lee, herpetologist, Sept 1940, *Obit* July 1942

Dolbier, Maurice, author and literary critic, Yrbk 1956, *Obit* Jan 1994

Donoso, Jose, Chilean novelist, Feb 1978, *Obit* Feb 1997

Du Jardin, Rosamond, Yrbk 1953

Durrell, Gerald M., British naturalist and conservationist, May 1985, *Obit* Apr 1995

Eberle, Irmengarde, Yrbk 1946

Edmonds, Walter D., American novelist and children's author, Sept 1942, *Obit* May 1998

Elliot, Kathleen Morrow, Mar 1940

Ellsberg, Edward, admiral, salvage engineer and author, Nov 1942, *Obit* Yrbk 1991

Emery, Anne, author, Yrbk 1952

Enright, Elizabeth, American children's author and illustrator, Yrbk 1947, *Obit* Sept 1968

Erdrich, Louise, American novelist and poet, Apr 1989

Estes, Eleanor, American librarian, children's author and illustrator, Yrbk 1946, *Obit* Sept 1988

Evatt, Harriet, Yrbk 1959

Everett, Percival L., American novelist, children's author and short story writer, Sept 2004

Eyre, Katherine Wigmore, Yrbk 1949, Yrbk 1957

Farley, Walter, American children's and young adult author, Yrbk 1949, *Obit* Feb 1990

Faulkner, Nancy, Yrbk 1956

Field, Rachel, American novelist, poet and children's author, *Obit* May 1942

Finger, Charles Joseph, American children's author, *Obit* Mar 1941

Fleming, Ian, English spy novelist, Jan 1964

Fletcher, Inglis, American children's author and novelist, Yrbk 1947, *Obit* July 1969

Fox, Michael W., Feb 1977

Frost, Frances, Yrbk 1950, *Obit* Apr 1959

Funke, Cornelia Caroline, German illustrator and children's author, Jan 2007

Gaer, Joseph, author, publishing executive and foundation official, Yrbk 1951

Gag, Wanda, American children's author and illustrator, *Obit* July 1946

Gaines, Ernest J., American novelist and short story writer, Mar 1994

Gallico, Paul, American novelist, short story writer and screenwriter, Apr 1946, *Obit* Sept 1976

Gardner, John, American novelist, critic and translator, Oct 1978, *Obit* Nov 1982

Gardner, Martin, American children's author and mathematician, Sept 1999, *Obit* Yrbk 2010

Giovanni, Nikki, American poet and essayist, Apr 1973

Gipson, Frederick Benjamin, author, Yrbk 1957

Godden, Rumer, English novelist and children's author, Aug 1976, *Obit* Jan 1999

Goetz, Delia, author and translator, Yrbk 1949, *Obit* Sept 1996

Gorey, Edward, American illustrator, children's author and designer, Nov 1976, *Obit* Aug 2000

Goudge, Elizabeth, English novelist, children's author and short story writer, Sept 1940, *Obit* Aug 1984

Hall, Donald, American poet, essayist, critic and children's author, May 1984

Harper, Theodore Acland, *Obit* June 1942

Heinlein, Robert A., American science fiction writer, Mar 1955, *Obit* June 1988

Henry, Marguerite, American children's author, Yrbk 1947, *Obit* Feb 1998

Hentoff, Nat, American journalist and young adult novelist, Aug 1986

Hill, Helen, American children's author and illustrator, *Obit* May 1942

Hoffman, Alice, American novelist, Sept 1992

Holberg, Ruth Langland, Yrbk 1949

Hooks, Bell, American feminist and social critic, Apr 1995

Houston, James A., Canadian artist, novelist and children's author, July 1987, *Obit* Yrbk 2005

Howard, Elizabeth, Yrbk 1951

Hunt, Mabel Leigh, author, Yrbk 1951

Ives, David, American dramatist, Feb 2013

Jagendorf, M. A., Yrbk 1952

James, Will, American children's author and illustrator, *Obit* Nov 1942

Jimenez, Juan Ramon, Spanish poet, Feb 1957, *Obit* Sept 1958

Johnson, Herschel, American journalist and children's author, July 1946

Jong, Dola de, Dutch-American mystery novelist, Yrbk 1947, *Obit* Yrbk 2004

Jordan, Mildred, author, Yrbk 1951

Judson, Clara Ingram, author, Yrbk 1948

Kastner, Erich, German author and poet, July 1964, *Obit* Oct 1974

Keeshan, Bob, American television personality, May 1965, *Obit* Yrbk 2004

Keith, Harold, American children's author, Yrbk 1958

Kelly, Regina Zimmerman, Yrbk 1956

Knight, Ruth Adams, Aug 1943, Yrbk 1955

L'Engle, Madeleine, American novelist and children's author, Jan 1997, *Obit* Yrbk 2007

Lambert, Janet, Yrbk 1954

Lamorisse, Albert, French screenwriter, director and producer, June 1963, *Obit* July 1970

Lane, Carl Daniel, Yrbk 1951

Latham, Jean Lee, American children's author, Yrbk 1956

Lawrence, Mildred, Yrbk 1953

Lawson, Robert, Anerican children's author and illustrator, Oct 1941, *Obit* Oct 1957

Le Guin, Ursula K., American science fiction and fantasy writer, Jan 1983

Leighton, Margaret Carver, author, Yrbk 1952

Leno, Jay, American comedian and television talk show host, June 1988

Leonard, Elmore, American novelist, Sept 1985, *Obit* Yrbk 2013

Lewis, C. S., English children's author, novelist and critic, Jan 1944, *Obit* Jan 1964

Ley, Willy, German-American scientist and author, June 1941, Feb 1953, *Obit* Sept 1969

Lichtenberger, Andre, *Obit* Apr 1940

Lindgren, Astrid, Swedish children's author, Oct 1996, *Obit* Apr 2002

Lippincott, Joseph Wharton, May 1955, *Obit* Jan 1977

Lithgow, John, American actor, Nov 1996

Lively, Penelope, English novelist, short story writer and children's author, Apr 1994

Longstreth, T. Morris, Yrbk 1950

Lownsbery, Eloise, author, Yrbk 1947

Lunge-Larsen, Lise, Norwegian-American children's author, Aug 2012

Lurie, Alison, American novelist, Feb 1986

MacDonald, Betty, American memoirist and humorist, Feb 1946, *Obit* Apr 1958

MacGregor, Ellen, author and librarian, Yrbk 1954

MacKaye, Julia Gunther, American librarian and children's author, Yrbk 1949

Mallette, Gertrude E., Yrbk 1950

Mankowitz, Wolf, English author and screenwriter, Yrbk 1956, *Obit* Aug 1998

Marcos, Mexican revolutionary, Jan 2002

Marshall, Rosamond, author, Aug 1942, *Obit* Feb 1958

Martin, George R. R., American fantasy and science fiction writer, Jan 2004

Matlin, Marlee, American actress, May 1992

Mayer, Jane, American novelist and children's author, Yrbk 1954

Mayle, Peter, English humorist, Oct 1992

McCall Smith, Alexander, Scottish law professor, children's author and novelist, Jan 2003

McCloskey, Robert, American children's author and illustrator, Sept 1942, *Obit* Yrbk 2003

McCracken, Harold, Yrbk 1949

McGinley, Phyllis, American poet and children's author, Feb 1941, Nov 1961, *Obit* Apr 1978

McGraw, Eloise Jarvis, American children's author, Yrbk 1955, *Obit* Mar 2001

McMeekin, Isabel McLennan, American novelist and children's author, Sept 1942, Yrbk 1957

McSwigan, Marie, Yrbk 1953, *Obit* Sept 1962

Meadowcroft, Enid La Monte, Yrbk 1949

Midler, Bette, American singer and actress, June 1973, Nov 1997

Montgomery, Elizabeth Rider, author, Yrbk 1952

Montresor, Beni, Italian scenic designer, illustrator and children's author, Yrbk 1967, *Obit* Feb 2002

Mowat, Farley, Canadian ethnologist, historian and children's author, Feb 1986

Nash, Ogden, American poet, Apr 1941, *Obit* July 1971

Neilson, Frances Fullerton, Yrbk 1955

Nesbo, Jo, Norwegian novelist, singer and songwriter, Sept 2011

North, Sterling, author, Nov 1943, *Obit* Feb 1975

Norton, Andre, American science fiction novelist, Jan 1957, *Obit* Yrbk 2005

O'Hara, Mary, author, Jan 1944, *Obit* Jan 1981

Oates, Joyce Carol, American novelist, short story writer and poet, Sept 1970, June 1994

Orton, Helen Fuller, Jan 1941, *Obit* Apr 1955

Park, Linda Sue, American children's author, June 2002

Paxton, Tom, folk singer and composer, Sept 1982

Peare, Catherine Owens, Yrbk 1959

Peattie, Donald Culross, American naturalist, Oct 1940, *Obit* Jan 1965

Petry, Ann Lane, American novelist, Mar 1946, *Obit* July 1997

Poole, Lynn, Yrbk 1954, *Obit* June 1969

Potter, Beatrix, English children's author and illustrator, *Obit* Mar 1944

Raffi, Canadian singer, Jan 2003

Rawlings, Marjorie Kinnan, American novelist and short story writer, July 1942, *Obit* Feb 1954

Rhoades, Nina, *Obit* Jan 1941

Rich, Louise Dickinson, American memoirist, young

adult novelist and children's author, May 1943, *Obit* July 1991

Richards, Laura Elizabeth Howe, author and poet, *Obit* May 1943

Riesenberg, Felix, Yrbk 1957

Rimes, LeAnn, American country singer, May 1998

Ringgold, Faith, American artist, children's author and illustrator, Feb 1996

Rood, Helen Martin, *Obit* Mar 1943

Rourke, Constance Mayfield, biographer, *Obit* May 1941

Rowling, J. K., English fantasy novelist, Jan 2000

Rushdie, Salman, British novelist, Nov 1986, Jan 2003

Saint-Exupery, Antoine de, French novelist, essayist and aviator, Jan 1940, *Obit* May 1945

Salten, Felix, Austrian author, *Obit* Nov 1945

Sarah, Mar 1987

Sarton, May, American poet and novelist, May 1982, *Obit* Sept 1995

Savery, Constance, Yrbk 1948

Schlein, Miriam, American children's author, Yrbk 1959, *Obit* Yrbk 2005

Schlessinger, Laura C., American psychologist and radio talk show host, Sept 1997

Sendak, Maurice, American children's author and illustrator, June 1968, June 1989, *Obit* Yrbk 2012

Seredy, Kate, American children's author and illustrator, May 1940, *Obit* May 1975

Seton, Ernest Thompson, Anglo-American writer, illustrator and naturalist, May 1943, *Obit* Yrbk 1946

Seuss, American children's author and illustrator, Feb 1968, *Obit* Nov 1991

Shippen, Katherine Binney, author, Yrbk 1954

Simon, Charlie May Hogue, Yrbk 1946

Singer, Isaac Bashevis, American novelist and short story writer, Jan 1969, *Obit* Sept 1991

Singer, Kurt D., American children's author and editor, Yrbk 1954

Slobodkin, Louis, author and illustrator, Apr 1957, *Obit* Aug 1975

Smith, Robert Paul, American novelist and memoirist, Yrbk 1958

Smith, William Jay, American poet and state legislator, Mar 1974

Sorensen, Virginia Eggertsen, American children's author, Yrbk 1950

Speare, Elizabeth George, American children's and young adult author, Yrbk 1959, *Obit* Jan 1995

Sperry, Armstrong, American children's author and illustrator, Oct 1941

Spillane, Mickey, American mystery novelist, Sept 1981, *Obit* Nov 2006

Standish, Burt L., American children's author, *Obit* Mar 1945

Stewart, Anna Bird, Yrbk 1948

Stine, R. L., American children's author, Sept 1999

Stolz, Mary, American children's author and young adult novelist, Yrbk 1953, *Obit* Yrbk 2007

Taber, Gladys Bagg, editor and author, Yrbk 1952, *Obit* May 1980

Tan, Amy, American novelist, Feb 1992

Teale, Edwin Way, American naturalist and nature writer, Yrbk 1961, *Obit* Jan 1981

Tharp, Louise Hall, American children's author, Yrbk 1955

Thompson, Kay, American singer, songwriter and children's author, Apr 1959, *Obit* Sept 1998

Thompson, Mary Wolfe, Yrbk 1950

Tin Moe, Burmese poet and children's author, Jan 2004

Tolkien, J. R. R., English fantasy novelist, philologist and linguist, Yrbk 1957, Oct 1967, *Obit* Nov 1973

Travers, P. L., English children's author, May 1996, *Obit* June 1996

Tyler, Anne, American novelist and short story writer, June 1981

Ullman, James Ramsey, author, Oct 1945, *Obit* Sept 1971

Van Allsburg, Chris, American children's author and illustrator, Sept 1996

Van Loon, Hendrik Willem, Dutch-American historian, *Obit* Apr 1944

Vance, Marguerite, Yrbk 1951, *Obit* July 1965

Vining, Elizabeth Gray, American novelist, short story writer and children's author, Sept 1943

Walden, Amelia Elizabeth, Yrbk 1956

Walsh, Chad, professor of English and author, Feb 1962, *Obit* Mar 1991

Weil, Lisl, Jan 1958

Wellman, Manly Wade, author, Yrbk 1955

Wellman, Paul Iselin, American western writer, Yrbk 1949

Wells, Carolyn, author, *Obit* May 1942

Wells, Peter, Aug 1942

Wesley, Valerie Wilson, American novelist, children's author and periodical editor, July 2002

White, E. B., American humorist and poet, Oct 1960, *Obit* Nov 1985

White, Nelia Gardner, author, Yrbk 1950, *Obit* Oct 1957

Whitney, Phyllis A., American novelist and short story writer, Yrbk 1948, *Obit* Yrbk 2008

Wickenden, Dan, author and editor, Yrbk 1951, *Obit* Feb 1990

Wilder, Laura Ingalls, American children's and young adult author, Yrbk 1948, *Obit* May 1957

Wilson, A. N., English novelist and biographer, Aug 1993

Wojciechowska, Maia, Polish children's author and publisher, Sept 1976, *Obit* Yrbk 2002

Yates, Elizabeth, American children's author, Yrbk 1948, *Obit* Nov 2001

Zim, Herbert S., American educator and science writer, Sept 1956, *Obit* Feb 1995

Zindel, Paul, American dramatist, novelist and children's author, June 1973, *Obit* Yrbk 2007

Children's rights advocates

Atyam, Angelina, Ugandan peace activist and children's rights advocate, Jan 2004
Edelman, Marian Wright, American children's rights advocate, Sept 1992
Redlener, Irwin, American pediatrician, Nov 2007
Ziemer, Gregor, Apr 1942

Chiropractors

Dhalla, Ruby, Canadian member of Parliament, Jan 2006

Choral conductors

Davies, Walford, *Obit* May 1941
Finn, William J., July 1940
Hillis, Margaret, choral conductor, Feb 1956, *Obit* Apr 1998
Lamond, Felix, *Obit* Apr 1940
N£¤ez, Francisco J., Feb 2013

Choreographers

Abdul, Paula, American dancer, choreographer, singer and talent judge on television program, Sept 1991
Ailey, Alvin, American dancer and choreographer, Mar 1968, *Obit* Jan 1990
Allen, Debbie, American dancer, actress and director, Feb 1987
Alonso, Alicia, Cuban ballet dancer, July 1955, June 1977
Argentinita, Spanish dancer and choreographer, June 1942, *Obit* Oct 1945
Arpino, Gerald, American ballet dancer and choreographer, Oct 1970, *Obit* Yrbk 2008
Ashton, Frederick, British choreographer, May 1951, *Obit* Sept 1988
Balanchine, George, Russian-American choreographer, Nov 1942, June 1954, *Obit* June 1983
Bausch, Pina, German dancer, choreographer and director, Sept 1986, *Obit* Yrbk 2009

Bejart, Maurice, French ballet dancer and choreographer, Mar 1971, *Obit* Yrbk 2008
Benesh, Joan, British ballet dancer, choreographer and teacher, July 1957
Bennett, Michael, American choreographer, Mar 1981, *Obit* Aug 1987
Berkeley, Busby, American choreographer and film director, Apr 1971, *Obit* May 1976
Bettis, Valerie, dancer and choreographer, May 1953, *Obit* Nov 1982
Blair, David, British ballet dancer and choreographer, Jan 1961, *Obit* May 1976
Blankenbuehler, Andy, American choreographer and dancer, Apr 2009
Bourne, Matthew, English dancer and choreographer, Jan 2005
Brown, Ronald K., American choreographer, May 2002
Brown, Trisha, American dancer and choreographer, Apr 1997
Bruhn, Erik, Danish ballet dancer and director, Apr 1959, *Obit* May 1986
Butler, John, American dancer and choreographer, June 1955, *Obit* Nov 1993
Champion, Gower, American dancer, choreographer and theatrical director, Sept 1953, *Obit* Oct 1980
Champion, Marge, American dancer and choreographer, Sept 1953
Chase, Alison Becker, American choreographer, Nov 2006
Childs, Lucinda, American dancer and choreographer, Apr 1984
Clarke, Martha, American dancer and choreographer, Jan 1989
Clifford, John, American ballet dancer and choreographer, Nov 1972
Cranko, John, South African dancer and choreographer, July 1970, *Obit* Sept 1973
Cullberg, Birgit, Swedish ballet dancer and choreographer, Nov 1982, *Obit* Nov 1999

Cunningham, Merce, American dancer and choreographer, May 1966, *Obit* Yrbk 2009
D'Amboise, Jacques, American ballet dancer, choreographer and teacher, Sept 1964
De Mille, Agnes, American choreographer, Oct 1943, Jan 1985, *Obit* Jan 1994
De Valois, Ninette, English ballet dancer, choreographer and director, Yrbk 1949, *Obit* Aug 2001
Dean, Laura, dancer and choreographer, Oct 1988
Dolin, Anton, English dancer and choreographer, Jan 1946, *Obit* Jan 1984
Dunham, Katherine, American dancer and choreographer, Mar 1941, *Obit* Yrbk 2006
Eiko, Japanese dancer and choreographer, May 2003
Elo, Jorma, Finnish ballet dancer and choreographer, July 2009
Erdman, Jean, dancer, choreographer and teacher, Sept 1971
Fagan, Garth, American dancer, director and choreographer, Aug 1998
Feld, Eliot, American choreographer and dance teacher, Oct 1971
Fleming, Maureen, American dancer and choreographer, Mar 2010
Fokine, Michel, Russian ballet dancer and choreographer, *Obit* Oct 1942
Forsythe, William, American choreographer, ballet dancer and director, Feb 2003
Fortier, Paul-Andre, Canadian choreographer and dancer, Nov 2010
Fosse, Bob, American director and choreographer, June 1972, *Obit* Nov 1987
Franca, Celia, Canadian ballet director and dancer, May 1956, *Obit* Yrbk 2007
Franklin, Frederic, English ballet dancer and choreographer, Sept 1943, *Obit* Yrbk 2013
Gades, Antonio, Spanish flamenco dancer and choreographer, Feb 1973, *Obit* Yrbk 2004

Gennaro, Peter, American dancer and choreographer, June 1964, *Obit* Feb 2001

Glover, Savion, American tap dancer, Mar 1996

Gordon, David, American choreographer, June 1994

Graham, Martha, American dancer and choreographer, Feb 1944, June 1961, *Obit* May 1991

Greco, Jose, American dancer and choreographer, Mar 1952, *Obit* Mar 2001

Grigorovich, Yuri, Russian choreographer and dance director, Sept 1975

Guillem, Sylvie, French ballet dancer and choreographer, Jan 2002

Hawkins, Erick, dancer and choreographer, Jan 1974, *Obit* Feb 1995

Helpmann, Robert, Australian dancer and actor, Feb 1950, *Obit* Nov 1986

Holder, Geoffrey, Trinidadian dancer and choreographer, Oct 1957

Holm, Hanya, German-American dancer and choreographer, July 1954, *Obit* Jan 1993

Humphrey, Doris, American dancer and choreographer, Apr 1942, *Obit* Mar 1959

Iglesias, Roberto, Feb 1960

Jamison, Judith, American dancer, director and choreographer, Jan 1973

Jin Xing, Chinese ballet dancer and choreographer, Jan 2006

Joffrey, Robert, American ballet dancer, choreographer and director, Nov 1967, *Obit* Nov 1988

Jones, Bill T., American dancer and choreographer, July 1993

Jooss, Kurt, German choreographer, dance director and teacher, July 1976, *Obit* July 1979

Khan, Farah, Indian film director and choreographer, Jan 2007

Kidd, Michael, American choreographer, Mar 1960, *Obit* Yrbk 2008

Koma, Japanese dancer and choreographer, May 2003

Koner, Pauline, ballet dancer and choreographer, Oct 1964, *Obit* Apr 2001

Kudelka, James, Canadian ballet dancer and choreographer, Mar 1995

Kylian, Jiri, Czech dancer, choreographer and director, Sept 1982

Lang, Pearl, American dancer and choreographer, Jan 1970, *Obit* Yrbk 2009

Layton, Joe, theatrical director, producer and choreographer, Sept 1970, *Obit* July 1994

Lemon, Ralph, American dancer and choreographer, Feb 1997

Lerman, Liz, American dancer and choreographer, Nov 2000

Levi-Tanai, Sara, Israeli choreographer, May 1958

Limon, Jose, American dancer and choreographer, June 1953, Apr 1968, *Obit* Jan 1973

Loring, Eugene, American dancer and choreographer, Mar 1972, *Obit* Oct 1982

Louis, Murray, dancer and choreographer, Oct 1968

Lubovitch, Lar, American dancer and choreographer, Mar 1992

Lynne, Gillian, English dancer and choreographer, Jan 2002

Macdonald, Brian, Canadian ballet director and choreographer, July 1968

Marshall, Rob, American choreographer and film director, June 2003

Marshall, Susan, American choreographer, July 1999

Martins, Peter, Danish-American dancer, choreographer and director, June 1978

Massine, Leonide, Russian choreographer and ballet dancer, Apr 1940, *Obit* May 1979

McKayle, Donald, American dancer and choreographer, June 1971

Millepied, Benjamin, French ballet dancer and choreographer, Apr 2011

Miller, Bebe, dancer and choreographer, Apr 1999

Mitchell, Arthur, American ballet dancer and choreographer, Oct 1966

Mitchell, Jerry, American choreographer and theatrical director, Oct 2007

Mitha, Tehreema, Pakistani dancer and choreographer, May 2004

Moiseyev, Igor, Russian ballet dancer and choreographer, Nov 1958, *Obit* Yrbk 2008

Monk, Meredith, American choreographer, composer and singer, Feb 1985

Monte, Elisa, American dancer and choreographer, June 2007

Moran, John, American composer, performance artist and choreographer, June 2010

Morris, Mark, American choreographer and dancer, Aug 1988

Neumeier, John, American dancer and choreographer, July 1991

Nikolais, Alwin, American choreographer, Feb 1968, *Obit* July 1993

Ortega, Kenny, American dancer, choreographer and director, Mar 2008

Page, Ruth, American ballet dancer and choreographer, June 1962, *Obit* July 1991

Pendleton, Moses, American dancer and choreographer, Sept 1989

Perez, Rosie, American actress, dancer and choreographer, Sept 1995

Petit, Roland, French ballet dancer and choreographer, Apr 1952, *Obit* Yrbk 2011

Petronio, Stephen, American dancer and choreographer, Mar 1998

Plisetskaya, Maya, Russian ballet dancer, June 1963

Primus, Pearl, American dancer and choreographer, Apr 1944, *Obit* Jan 1995

Raedler, Dorothy, opera director and choreographer, Yrbk 1954, *Obit* Feb 1994

Reinking, Ann, American dancer, choreographer and actress, June 2004

Robbins, Jerome, American dancer, choreographer and theatrical director, May 1947, May 1969, *Obit* Oct 1998

Ross, Herbert, American choreographer and motion

picture director, Aug 1980, *Obit* Feb 2002

Saddler, Donald, choreographer, Jan 1963

Shawn, Ted, American dancer and choreographer, Oct 1949, *Obit* Feb 1972

Slavenska, Mia, Croatian ballet dancer and choreographer, Feb 1954, *Obit* Apr 2003

Smuin, Michael, American ballet dancer and choreographer, Oct 1984, *Obit* Yrbk 2007

Sokolow, Anna, American dancer, choreographer and teacher, Feb 1969, *Obit* Sept 2000

Streb, Elizabeth, American dancer and choreographer, Apr 2003

Stroman, Susan, American choreographer and theatrical director, July 2002

Taylor, Paul, American dancer and choreographer, June 1964

Tetley, Glen, American dancer and choreographer, June 1973, *Obit* Yrbk 2007

Tharp, Twyla, American dancer and choreographer, Oct 1975

Tomasson, Helgi, Icelandic ballet dancer and director, Apr 1982

Tudor, Antony, English ballet dancer and choreographer, Nov 1945, *Obit* June 1987

Tune, Tommy, American dancer and director, Jan 1983

Verdon, Gwen, American dancer, actress and choreographer, Oct 1960, *Obit* Jan 2001

Weidman, Charles, American dancer and choreographer, Apr 1942, *Obit* Sept 1975

Welch, Stanton, Australian ballet dancer, choreographer and director, July 2007

Wheeldon, Christopher, British ballet dancer and choreographer, Mar 2004

Wigman, Mary, German dancer and choreographer, Jan 1969, *Obit* Nov 1973

Yuen, Wo-ping, Chinese martial artist and motion picture stunt choreographer, Jan 2008

Christian Science leaders

Canham, Erwin Dain, newspaper editor, July 1945, Jan 1960, *Obit* Feb 1982

Hering, Hermann S., *Obit* July 1940

McKenzie, William P., *Obit* Oct 1942

Church historians

Bainton, Roland Herbert, church historian, June 1962, *Obit* June 1984

Ellis, John Tracy, American priest and church historian, Mar 1990, *Obit* Jan 1993

Johnson, Howard A., Apr 1964, *Obit* Sept 1974

Marty, Martin E., American clergyman, theologian and church historian, June 1968

Nolde, O. Frederick, Feb 1947, *Obit* Sept 1972

Zenos, Andrew C., *Obit* Mar 1942

Cinematographers

Almendros, Nestor, Cuban cinematographer and director, Nov 1989, *Obit* May 1992

Bryan, Julien, American photographer and documentary filmmaker, July 1940, *Obit* Jan 1975

Colbert, Gregory, Canadian photographer and cinematographer, Sept 2005

Deakins, Roger, British cinematographer, May 2001

Demarbre, Lee Gordon, Canadian film director, Jan 2003

Deschanel, Caleb, American cinematographer and film director, Feb 2008

Dickerson, Ernest, American cinematographer and film director, July 2000

Doyle, Christopher, Australian cinematographer, Jan 2006

Hall, Conrad L., American cinematographer, Aug 2000, *Obit* May 2003

Howe, James Wong, cinematographer, Feb 1943, *Obit* Sept 1976

Kaminski, Janusz, Polish cinematographer, Mar 2000

Koltai, Lajos, Hungarian cinematographer, Jan 2003

Lubezki, Emmanuel, Mexican cinematographer, July 2011

Nykvist, Sven, Swedish cinematographer, June 1989, *Obit* Yrbk 2007

Papamichael, Phedon, Greek cinematographer, Sept 2012

Pau, Peter, Chinese cinematographer, Feb 2002

Prieto, Rodrigo, Mexican cinematographer, Jan 2003

Richardson, Robert, American cinematographer, Jan 2010

Sonnenfeld, Barry, American film director, Nov 1998

Toland, Gregg, American cinematographer, July 1941, *Obit* Nov 1948

Waller, Fred, American inventor of Cinerama, Feb 1953, *Obit* July 1954

Wexler, Haskell, American cinematographer, Aug 2007

Zsigmond, Vilmos, Hungarian-American cinematographer, Oct 1999

Circus executives

Feld, Irvin, circus owner, Feb 1979, *Obit* Nov 1984

Laliberte, Guy, Canadian circus owner, Jan 2003

Monseu, Stephanie, American circus performer and founder, June 2005

Nelson, Keith, American circus performer and founder, June 2005

North, John Ringling, circus owner, June 1951, *Obit* July 1985

Circus performers

Clark, Bobby, May 1949, *Obit* Apr 1960

Fratellini, Paul, *Obit* Yrbk 1940

Kelly, Emmett, American clown, July 1954, *Obit* May 1979

Monseu, Stephanie, American circus performer and founder, June 2005

Nelson, Keith, American circus performer and founder, June 2005

Petit, Philippe, French aerialist, Sept 1988

Polunin, Slava, Russian clown, Jan 2004

Popov, Oleg, Russian clown, Mar 1964

Rose, Jim, American performance artist, Mar 2003

City managers

Goode, W. Wilson, American mayor, Oct 1985

Civic leaders

Bearden, Bessye J., American political activist and civic leader, *Obit* Nov 1943

Breitmeyer, Philip, *Obit* Jan 1942

Burleigh, George William, *Obit* Apr 1940

Butts, Calvin O., American clergyman and civic leader, Feb 1999

Carmody, John M., American mining executive, labor mediator and government official, May 1940, *Obit* Jan 1964

Carter, Majora, American community activist and conservationist, Oct 2007, May 2013

Evans, Anne, *Obit* Feb 1941

Hay, Regina Deem, July 1948

LeFrak, Samuel J., American builder, Jan 1970, *Obit* Yrbk 2003

Lee, Percy Maxim, American civic leader, July 1950, *Obit* Jan 2003

Moorland, Jesse Edward, American clergyman, *Obit* Jan 1940

Murguia, Janet, American civil rights activist, Jan 2010

Pirie, John Taylor, *Obit* Mar 1940

Pratt, Frederic Bayley, American college president, *Obit* June 1945

Sliwa, Curtis, American public safety group founder, Feb 1983

Sporborg, Constance Amberg, Nov 1947, *Obit* Feb 1961

Straus, Jack Isidor, department store executive, Mar 1952, *Obit* Nov 1985

Strauss, Anna Lord, Nov 1945, *Obit* Apr 1979

Tobias, Channing H., July 1945, *Obit* Jan 1962

Tree, Marietta, United Nations official and city planner, Yrbk 1961, *Obit* Oct 1991

Woods, Tighe E., American real estate developer and government official, Oct 1948, *Obit* Sept 1974

Wyatt, Wilson W., American government official, lawyer and civic leader, Mar 1946, *Obit* Aug 1996

Civil engineers

Abrams, Charles, American city planner and lawyer, Feb 1969, *Obit* Apr 1970

Adams, Thomas, British architect and urban planner, *Obit* Apr 1940

Alessandri Rodriguez, Jorge, Chilean president, May 1959, *Obit* Oct 1986

Ammann, Othmar Hermann, American civil engineer, Jan 1963, *Obit* Nov 1965

Bailey, Donald Coleman, English civil engineer and inventor, Oct 1945, *Obit* July 1985

Baker, Charles Whiting, American civil engineer, *Obit* Aug 1941

Barnes, Henry A., American traffic engineer, June 1955, *Obit* Nov 1968

Barney, Samuel E., American civil engineer, *Obit* Mar 1940

Beard, James T., American mining engineer, *Obit* Yrbk 1942

Bennett, John W. F., American civil engineer, *Obit* Oct 1943

Birdseye, Claude Hale, American topographer, *Obit* July 1941

Brundage, Avery, American engineer and Olympics executive, Jan 1948, *Obit* Aug 1975

Bunau-Varilla, Philippe, *Obit* July 1940

Calvo-Sotelo y Bustelo, Leopoldo, Spanish prime minister, Aug 1981

Dennis, Olive Wetzel, civil engineer, June 1941

Douglas, Walter Jules, American civil engineer, *Obit* Sept 1941

Duany, Andres, American architect and urban planner, Jan 2006

Fairless, Benjamin F., American steel industry executive, June 1942, May 1957, *Obit* Feb 1962

Goldmark, Henry, *Obit* Mar 1941

Goldsborough, John Byron, *Obit* May 1943

Heald, Henry Townley, American civil engineer, Feb 1952, *Obit* Jan 1976

Hoover, Herbert Clark, American petroleum engineer, diplomat and son of President Herbert Hoover, Oct 1954, *Obit* Sept 1969

Hovey, Otis Ellis, *Obit* June 1941

Howe, C. D., American construction engineer, Sept 1945, *Obit* Feb 1961

Jacobs, Jane, American city planner, Mar 1977, *Obit* Yrbk 2006

Johnson, J. Monroe, American civil engineer and government official, Feb 1945, *Obit* Sept 1964

Ma Kai, Chinese government official, Jan 2007

Mackenzie, Chalmers Jack, June 1952

Malone, George W., American senator, Yrbk 1950, *Obit* July 1961

Marples, Alfred Ernest Marples, May 1960

Moisseiff, Leon S., American bridge engineer, *Obit* Oct 1943

Morgan, Arthur Ernest, American civil engineer and college president, July 1956, *Obit* Jan 1976

Moses, Robert, American municipal and state planning official, Nov 1940, Feb 1954, *Obit* Sept 1981

Neutra, Richard Joseph, American architect, May 1947, July 1961, *Obit* June 1970

Newcomer, Francis K., American general, Mar 1950, *Obit* Oct 1967

Owings, Nathaniel Alexander, architect, May 1971, *Obit* Aug 1984

Pacheco e Chaves, Joao, Nov 1954

Pick, Lewis Andrew, American general and civil engineer, June 1946, *Obit* Feb 1957

Plater-Zyberk, Elizabeth, American architect and urban planner, Jan 2006

Reed, James, naval and bridge engineer, *Obit* Sept 1941

Rickey, James W., *Obit* June 1943

Ripley, Joseph, *Obit* Nov 1940

Robinson, Holton D., *Obit* June 1945

Savage, John Lucian, Apr 1943, *Obit* Feb 1968

Sprague, Embert Hiram, *Obit* Mar 1940

Steinman, David Barnard, American bridge engineer, Yrbk 1957, *Obit* Nov 1960

Stern, Arthur Cecil, sanitary engineer, Apr 1956, *Obit* July 1992

Tallamy, Bertram Dalley, civil engineer and state official, Mar 1957, *Obit* Nov 1989

Terrell, Daniel V., Apr 1954

Virilio, Paul, French urban planner and philosopher, July 2005

Vogel, Herbert D., Yrbk 1954

Wagner, Aubrey J., June 1963

Wahlen, Friedrich T., June 1961

Webb, Walter Loring, *Obit* Mar 1941

Welch, William A., *Obit* June 1941

Whitton, Rex M., May 1962

Wolman, Abel, sanitary engineer, Feb 1957, *Obit* May 1989

Worcester, J. R., *Obit* June 1943

Zander, Arnold S., Oct 1947, *Obit* Sept 1975

Civil rights activists

Abernathy, Ralph D., American clergyman and civil rights leader, July 1968, *Obit* June 1990

Alinsky, Saul, American social activist, Nov 1968, *Obit* July 1972

Baldwin, Roger Nash, American civil rights leader, Jan 1940, *Obit* Oct 1981

Baldwin, William H., American public relations executive and civil rights activist, Nov 1945

Bethune, Mary Jane McLeod, American educator, Jan 1942, *Obit* July 1955

Bond, Julian, American civil rights leader, Yrbk 1969, July 2001

Boyd, Malcolm, American clergyman, gay rights activist and writer, Mar 1968

Chavis, Benjamin F., American clergyman and civil rights leader, Jan 1994

Clement, Rufus E., American college president, June 1946, *Obit* Jan 1968

Croome, Rodney, Australian gay rights activist, Jan 2004

Du Bois, W. E. B., American sociologist, historian and novelist, Jan 1940, *Obit* Oct 1963

Elijah Muhammad, American Black Muslim leader, Jan 1971, *Obit* Apr 1975

Ellis, Ruth, American gay rights activist, *Obit* Apr 2000, Sept 2000

Ernst, Morris, American lawyer and civil rights activist, Aug 1940, Feb 1961, *Obit* July 1976

Evers, Charles, American civil rights activist, mayor and brother of Medgar Evers, Apr 1969

Evers-Williams, Myrlie, civil rights leader and wife of Medgar Wiley Evers, Aug 1995

Farmer, James, American civil rights leader, Feb 1964, *Obit* Sept 1999

Farmer-Paellmann, Deadria, American activist seeking reparations for slavery, Mar 2004

Fletcher, Arthur Allen, American civil rights leader and government official, Nov 1971, *Obit* Yrbk 2005

Garvey, Marcus, Jamaican-American civil rights activist, *Obit* Aug 1940

George, Albert Bailey, *Obit* Apr 1940

Glasser, Ira, American civil rights activist, Jan 1986

Gordon, Bruce, American civil rights organization official, Oct 2005

Graham, Frank Porter, college president and civil rights leader, May 1941, July 1951, *Obit* Apr 1972

Granger, Lester Blackwell, civil rights leader, Apr 1946, *Obit* Mar 1976

Greeley, Dana McLean, clergyman, civil rights leader and pacifist, Mar 1964, *Obit* Aug 1986

Gregory, Dick, American comedian, author and civil rights leader, June 1962

Guinier, Lani, American law teacher and civil rights activist, Jan 2004

Haynes, George Edmund, American civil rights leader and economist, Mar 1946, *Obit* Apr 1960

Hays, Arthur Garfield, lawyer and civil rights leader, Sept 1942, *Obit* Feb 1955

Height, Dorothy I., American civil rights activist, Sept 1972, *Obit* July 2010

Hill, Herbert, American civil rights leader, Sept 1970, *Obit* Yrbk 2004

Hooks, Benjamin L., American civil rights activist, lawyer and judge, Apr 1978, *Obit* Yrbk 2010

Innis, Roy, American civil rights leader, May 1969

Jackson, Jesse L., American clergyman and civil rights activist, Yrbk 1970, Jan 1986

Jealous, Benjamin T., American civil rights organization official, Feb 2009

Jones, Elaine R., American lawyer, June 2004

Jones, Van, American lawyer, civil rights activist, environmentalist and presidential aide, Apr 2009

Jordan, Vernon, American civil rights leader and lawyer, Feb 1972, Aug 1993

Katz, Label A., Apr 1960, *Obit* June 1975

King, Coretta Scott, American civil rights leader, May 1969, *Obit* Apr 2006

King, Martin Luther, American clergyman and civil rights leader, May 1957, May 1965, *Obit* May 1968

Kuhn, Maggie, American feminist and civil rights activist, July 1978, *Obit* July 1995

Kunstler, William, American lawyer, Apr 1971, *Obit* Nov 1995

Lamont, Corliss, American philosopher, socialist and civil rights leader, June 1946, *Obit* July 1995

Lewis, John, American congressman, Sept 1980

Loram, Charles Templeman, *Obit* Sept 1940

Lowenstein, Allard K., American civil rights leader, pacifist and congressman, Sept 1971, *Obit* May 1980

Lowery, Joseph, American clergyman and civil rights leader, Nov 1982

Marshall, Burke, American civil rights activist and government official, Feb 1965, *Obit* Yrbk 2003

Marshall, Thurgood, American Supreme Court justice, Nov 1954, Sept 1989, *Obit* Mar 1993

Martinez, Vilma, American lawyer and civil rights activist, July 2004

McKissick, Floyd B., American lawyer and civil rights leader, Jan 1968, *Obit* June 1991

Messaoud, Boubacar, Mauritanian anti-slavery activist, Jan 2006

Mfume, Kweisi, American civil rights leader, Jan 1996

Morial, Marc, American civil rights activist and former mayor, Jan 2002

Moses, Bob, American civil rights activist and mathematics teacher, Apr 2002

Motley, Constance Baker, American judge, May 1964, *Obit* Feb 2006

Murguia, Janet, American civil rights activist, Jan 2010

Nabrit, James M., American lawyer, civil rights activist and university president, Jan 1961, *Obit* Mar 1998

Neier, Aryeh, German-American civil rights leader, Nov 1978

Newton, Huey, American revolutionary, Feb 1973, *Obit* Oct 1989

Norton, Eleanor Holmes, American civil rights leader and congresswoman, Nov 1976

Parks, Rosa, American civil rights activist, May 1989, *Obit* Jan 2006

Payton, John, American lawyer and civil rights activist, May 2010, *Obit* Yrbk 2012

Pemberton, John de J., American lawyer and civil rights activist, May 1969, *Obit* Yrbk 2010

Prinz, Joachim, German-American rabbi and civil rights leader, Feb 1963, *Obit* Nov 1988

Randolph, Asa Philip, American labor leader, May 1940, Oct 1951, *Obit* July 1979

Rauh, Joseph L., American lawyer and civil rights leader, Apr 1965, *Obit* Nov 1992

Reid, Ira De A., July 1946, *Obit* Oct 1968

Rice, Constance L., American lawyer and civil rights activist, Apr 2011

Robinson, Randall, American lobbyist and civil rights leader, Sept 1998

Romero, Anthony, American lawyer and civil rights activist, July 2002

Rustin, Bayard, American civil rights leader, June 1967, *Obit* Oct 1987

Sharpton, Al, American clergyman and political activist, Nov 1995

Solmonese, Joe, American gay rights activist, Oct 2009

Spingarn, Arthur Barnett, lawyer and civil rights leader, Jan 1965, *Obit* Jan 1972

Spottswood, Stephen Gill, American bishop and civil rights leader, Apr 1962, *Obit* Jan 1975

Strossen, Nadine, American lawyer and civil rights leader, Oct 1997

Sullivan, Leon Howard, American clergyman and civil rights leader, Mar 1969, *Obit* Sept 2001

Tafel, Rich, American gay political activist, Feb 2000

Ture, Kwame, American civil rights leader, Apr 1970, *Obit* Feb 1999

Vann, Robert Lee, American newspaper editor and publisher, *Obit* Yrbk 1940

White, Walter Francis, American civil rights leader, Apr 1942, *Obit* June 1955

Wilkins, Roy, American civil rights leader, June 1950, Jan 1964, *Obit* Oct 1981

Wilson, Margaret Bush, American lawyer and civil rights activist, Oct 1975, *Obit* Yrbk 2009

Wolfson, Evan, American lawyer and gay rights activist, July 2009

Yergan, Max, American civil rights activist, Sept 1948, *Obit* June 1975

Young, Andrew, American congressman, diplomat and mayor, Apr 1977

Young, Whitney Moore, American civil rights leader, Apr 1965, *Obit* Apr 1971

Clarinetists

Byron, Don, American jazz clarinetist, Sept 2000

Dorsey, Jimmy, band leader, Apr 1942, *Obit* Sept 1957

Goodman, Benny, American clarinetist and band leader, Jan 1942, Oct 1962, *Obit* Aug 1986

McGill, Anthony, American clarinetist, Apr 2009

Russell, Pee Wee, clarinetist, Aug 1944, *Obit* Apr 1969

Shaw, Artie, American clarinetist and band leader, May 1941, *Obit* Apr 2005

Stoltzman, Richard, clarinetist, Mar 1986

Classical musicians

Adamowski, Timothee, Polish violinist, *Obit* May 1943

Barrere, Georges, *Obit* Aug 1944

Beach, Amy Marcy Cheney, American composer and pianist, *Obit* Feb 1945

Beinum, Eduard van, Apr 1955, *Obit* June 1959

Beiser, Maya, American cellist, May 2009

Bodanzky, Artur, *Obit* Jan 1940

Boguslawski, Moissaye, American pianist, composer and teacher, *Obit* Oct 1944

Bostridge, Ian, British classical singer, Jan 2006

Bronfman, Yefim, American pianist, Jan 2007

Browning, John, American pianist, May 1969, *Obit* June 2003

Castagnetta, Grace, Feb 1954

Chung, Kyung-Wha, Korean violinist, Feb 2007

Cliburn, Van, American pianist, Sept 1958, *Obit* Yrbk 2013

Curzon, Clifford, English pianist, May 1950, *Obit* Oct 1982

Defauw, Desire, Jan 1940, *Obit* Oct 1960

Drucker, Eugene, American violinist, July 2002

Du Pre, Jacqueline, British cellist, May 1970, *Obit* Nov 1987

Dutton, Lawrence, American violist, July 2002

Eddins, William Frederick, American conductor and pianist, Feb 2002

Entremont, Philippe, French pianist and conductor, Mar 1977

Eschenbach, Christoph, German pianist and conductor, Aug 1989

Feuermann, Emanuel, *Obit* July 1942

Finckel, David, American cellist and recording producer, July 2002

Fodor, Eugene, American violinist, Apr 1976, *Obit* Yrbk 2011

Fou Ts'ong, Chinese pianist, Jan 2003

Fox, Virgil, Jan 1964, *Obit* Jan 1981

Francescatti, Zino, French violinist, Oct 1947, *Obit* Nov 1991

Galbraith, Paul, British guitarist, Jan 2007

Golschmann, Vladimir, Apr 1951, *Obit* May 1972

Goode, Richard, American pianist, Nov 1988

Goossens, Eugene, English conductor and composer, May 1945, *Obit* Sept 1962

Gorin, Igor, July 1942, *Obit* June 1982

Grimaud, Helene, French pianist, Jan 2007

Hahn, Hilary, American violinist, Sept 2002

Hannikainen, Tauno, July 1955, *Obit* Yrbk 1968

Hertz, Alfred, *Obit* June 1942

Hess, Myra, English pianist, Sept 1943, *Obit* Jan 1966

Higdon, Jennifer, Classical composer, Jan 2013

Hilsberg, Alexander, Oct 1953, *Obit* Nov 1961

Hobson Pilot, Ann, American harpist, May 2003

Horowitz, Vladimir, Russian-American pianist, Sept 1943, Mar 1966, *Obit* Jan 1990

Isbin, Sharon, American classical guitarist, Aug 2003

Istomin, Eugene, American pianist, Oct 1977, *Obit* Feb 2004

Josefowicz, Leila, American violinist, May 2007

Kavafian, Ani, American violinist, Oct 2006

Kindler, Hans, Sept 1946, *Obit* Oct 1949

Koh, Jennifer, American violinist, Sept 2006

Kremer, Gidon, Russian violinist, Mar 1985

Krips, Josef, June 1965, *Obit* Yrbk 1974

Lang, Lang, Chinese pianist, Jan 2003

Laredo, Ruth, American pianist, Oct 1987, *Obit* Yrbk 2005

Larrocha, Alicia de, Spanish pianist, July 1968, *Obit* Yrbk 2009

Lev, Ray, Jan 1949, *Obit* July 1968

Licad, Cecile, Philippine pianist, Jan 2003

MacGregor, Joanna, British pianist, Jan 2006

Martinu, Bohuslav, Czech composer and violinist, Nov 1944, *Obit* Nov 1959

McGill, Anthony, American clarinetist, Apr 2009

Menuhin, Yehudi, violinist, Feb 1941, May 1973, *Obit* June 1999

Meyer, Edgar, American bassist, June 2002

Mignone, Francisco, June 1942

Montero, Gabriela, Venezuelan pianist, July 2007

Muck, Karl, Mar 1940

Ohlsson, Garrick, American pianist, June 1975

Pennario, Leonard, American pianist, Oct 1959

Perlman, Itzhak, American violinist, May 1975

Piatigorsky, Gregor, Russian-American cellist, Oct 1945, *Obit* Sept 1976

Pires, Maria Joao, Portuguese pianist, Jan 2007

Quasthoff, Thomas, German classical singer, Jan 2005

Revueltas, Silvestre, Mexican composer, *Obit* Yrbk 1940

Richter, Sviatoslav, Russian pianist, Feb 1961, *Obit* Oct 1997

Rose, Leonard, American cellist, Jan 1977, *Obit* Jan 1985

Rostropovich, Mstislav, Russian cellist and conductor, May 1966, Nov 1988, *Obit* Aug 2007

Rubinstein, Artur, Polish-American pianist, Yrbk 1945, Feb 1966, *Obit* Mar 1983

Salerno-Sonnenberg, Nadja, violinist, Nov 1987

Schnabel, Artur, Austrian-American pianist and composer, July 1942, *Obit* Sept 1951

Serkin, Rudolf, Czech-American pianist, July 1940, June 1990, *Obit* July 1991

Setzer, Philip, American violinist, July 2002

Sevitzky, Fabien, July 1946, *Obit* Apr 1967

Shaham, Gil, American violinist, Apr 1997

Sinding, Christian, *Obit* Jan 1942

Skilton, Charles Sanford, *Obit* May 1941

Skrowaczewski, Stanislaw, Yrbk 1964

Smallens, Alexander, May 1947, *Obit* Jan 1973

Stern, Isaac, American violinist, Apr 1949, Feb 1989, *Obit* Jan 2002

Stoessel, Albert, *Obit* July 1943

Vanessa-Mae, British violinist, Jan 2002

Weilerstein, Alisa, American cellist, Feb 2013

Weissenberg, Alexis, Bulgarian pianist, June 1978, *Obit* Yrbk 2012

Wild, Earl, American pianist and composer, July 1988, *Obit* Yrbk 2010

Zabaleta, Nicanor, June 1971

Zukerman, Eugenia, American flutist and author, Jan 2004

Classicists

Carson, Anne, Canadian classicist, poet and essayist, May 2006

Fitzgerald, Robert, American poet and classicist, Sept 1976, *Obit* Mar 1985

Frazer, James George, Scottish classicist and anthropologist, *Obit* July 1941

Gleason, Clarence Willard, American classicist, *Obit* Yrbk 1942

Goheen, Robert F., American college president, Jan 1958, *Obit* Yrbk 2008

Hamilton, Edith, American classicist, Apr 1963

Highet, Gilbert, Scottish-American classicist, Sept 1964, *Obit* Mar 1978

Macdonald, George, classicist and archaeologist, *Obit* Sept 1940

Segal, Erich, American novelist and classicist, Apr 1971, *Obit* Yrbk 2010

Clergy

Aberhart, William, Canadian evangelist and political leader, *Obit* July 1943

Abernathy, Ralph D., American clergyman and civil rights leader, July 1968, *Obit* June 1990

Ainsworth, William Newman, American bishop, *Obit* Aug 1942

Aked, Charles F., American clergyman, *Obit* Oct 1941

Akinola, Peter Jasper, Nigerian archbishop, Jan 2004

Al-Sadr, Muqtada, Iraqi Islamic cleric, Jan 2007

Aleksii, Mar 1953, *Obit* June 1970

Aleksii, Jan 2003, *Obit* Yrbk 2009

Alfrink, Bernard, May 1966, *Obit* Feb 1988

Allan, John J., American Salvation Army leader, Jan 1950, *Obit* Jan 1961

Aristide, Jean-Bertrand, Haitian priest and president, May 1991

Arrupe, Pedro, Spanish priest, Feb 1970, *Obit* Apr 1991

Athenagoras, Mar 1949, *Obit* Sept 1972

Barnes, Clifford Webster, American clergyman and sociologist, *Obit* Nov 1944

Barr, Norman B., American clergyman, *Obit* May 1943

Barry, Patrick, Irish-American bishop, *Obit* Sept 1940

Bartholomeos, Jan 2004

Baudrillart, Alfred, *Obit* July 1942

Baum, William W., Oct 1976

Bayne, Stephen F., Jan 1964, *Obit* Mar 1974

Bea, Augustin, Sept 1964, *Obit* Jan 1969

Belkin, Samuel, American rabbi and college president, Nov 1952, *Obit* June 1976

Bell, Bernard Iddings, clergyman and educator, Apr 1953, *Obit* Yrbk 1959

Bell, Rob, American pastor, Mar 2013

Benelli, Giovanni Cardinal, Sept 1977, *Obit* Jan 1983

Bennett, John C., clergyman, ethicist and seminary president, Jan 1961, *Obit* July 1995

Berg, Irving H., American clergyman and college dean, *Obit* Nov 1941

Berggrav, Eivind, Norwegian bishop, Oct 1950, *Obit* Mar 1959

Bernardin, Joseph L., Oct 1982, *Obit* Jan 1997

Bernstein, Philip S., American rabbi, Nov 1951, *Obit* Feb 1986

Berrigan, Daniel, American priest, poet and pacifist, Sept 1970

Berrigan, Philip, American peace activist, Feb 1976, *Obit* Mar 2003

Bertram, Adolf, *Obit* Aug 1945

Binder, Theodor, German physician and missionary, Sept 1964

Blackie, Ernest Morell, British bishop, *Obit* Apr 1943

Blake, Edgar, American bishop, *Obit* July 1943

Blake, Eugene Carson, American clergyman and church leader, Sept 1955, *Obit* Oct 1985

Blakeslee, Francis D., American clergyman, educator and prohibitionist, *Obit* Nov 1942

Boe, Lars Wilhelm, American clergyman and college president, *Obit* Feb 1943

Boesak, Allan Aubrey, South African church official and human rights activist, Nov 1986

Boff, Leonardo, Brazilian theologian, Jan 1988

Boggiani, Tommaso Pio, *Obit* Apr 1942

Bonnell, John Sutherland, clergyman, June 1945, *Obit* Apr 1992

Booth, Ballington, American evangelist and social reformer, *Obit* Nov 1940

Booth, Evangeline C., English evangelist and Salvation Army leader, Feb 1941, *Obit* Sept 1950

Bradley, Preston, Mar 1956

Brennan, Francis, Oct 1967, *Obit* Sept 1968

Brewster, Benjamin, American bishop, *Obit* Mar 1941

Brewster, Chauncey B., American bishop, *Obit* June 1941

Brookes, George S., Aug 1940

Browning, Webster E., *Obit* June 1942

Buchman, Frank Nathan Daniel, missionary, Oct 1940, *Obit* Nov 1961

Buechner, Frederick, American novelist and clergyman, Yrbk 1959

Burns, J. A., *Obit* Oct 1940

Burrows, Millar, July 1956, *Obit* July 1980

Burton, Charles Emerson, *Obit* Oct 1940

Burton, Lewis William, *Obit* Yrbk 1940

Butts, Calvin O., American clergyman and civic leader, Feb 1999

Cadle, E. Howard, *Obit* Feb 1943

Camara, Helder, Brazilian archbishop, July 1971, *Obit* Jan 2000

Candler, Warren A., American bishop and college president, *Obit* Nov 1941

Cannon, James, bishop, *Obit* Nov 1944

Carey, George, British archbishop, Aug 1991

Carmines, Al, American clergyman, composer, singer and actor, Sept 1972, *Obit* Yrbk 2005

Carpenter, George L., Jan 1943, *Obit* May 1948

Carpenter, J. Henry, Feb 1943, *Obit* Sept 1954

Carroll, James, American novelist, May 1997

Carroll-Abbing, J. Patrick, priest and social worker, July 1967, *Obit* Nov 2001

Cattani-Amadori, Federico, *Obit* May 1943

Cavanaugh, John J., Mar 1947, *Obit* Feb 1980

Cavert, Samuel McCrea, Jan 1951, *Obit* Mar 1977

Chase, William Sheafe, *Obit* Sept 1940

Chavis, Benjamin F., American clergyman and civil rights leader, Jan 1994

Cicognani, Amleto Giovanni, July 1951, *Obit* Feb 1974

Clayton, P. B., May 1955, *Obit* Mar 1973

Cody, John Patrick, Nov 1965, *Obit* June 1982

Coffin, Henry S., clergyman and educator, Apr 1944, *Obit* Jan 1955

Coffin, William Sloane, American clergyman and pacifist, July 1968, Apr 1980, *Obit* Yrbk 2006

Colson, Charles W., American lawyer, presidential aide and evangelist, *Obit* Yrbk 2012

Cooke, Leslie E., June 1962, *Obit* Apr 1967

Cooke, Terence James, Sept 1968, *Obit* Nov 1983

Copeland, Benjamin, *Obit* Jan 1941

Corrigan, Joseph M., *Obit* Aug 1942

Corson, Fred Pierce, bishop, May 1961, *Obit* Apr 1985

Coughlin, Charles Edward, American priest and radio commentator, Sept 1940, *Obit* Jan 1980

Coutts, Frederick, English evangelist, Mar 1964

Crossan, John Dominic, Irish theologian, May 2011

Crowley, John J., priest, *Obit* Apr 1940

Curran, Charles E., American priest and theologian, Jan 1987

Cushing, Richard James, June 1952, *Obit* Yrbk 1970

D'Arcy, Martin Cyril, British priest and philosopher, Jan 1960, *Obit* Mar 1977

Dahlberg, Edwin T., clergyman, May 1958, *Obit* Oct 1986

Daly, Cahal B., Jan 2002, *Obit* Yrbk 2010

Daly, Thomas A., *Obit* Mar 1941

Damaskenos, Nov 1945, *Obit* July 1949

Danforth, John C., American senator, Jan 1992

Danner, Louise Rutledge, *Obit* Nov 1943

Davis, William Ellsworth, Apr 1940

De Pauw, Gommar A., May 1974

De Wolfe, James P., Aug 1942, *Obit* Mar 1966

Dearden, John, July 1969, *Obit* Sept 1988

Denny, Collins, *Obit* July 1943

Dibelius, Friedrich Karl Otto, German bishop, May 1953, *Obit* Mar 1967

Divine, Frank H., *Obit* May 1941

Dodds, Gil, June 1947, *Obit* Apr 1977

Dolan, Timothy Michael, American archbishop, Mar 2011

Donegan, Horace William Baden, bishop, July 1954, *Obit* Jan 1992

Dooley, Tom, American physician and missionary, July 1957, *Obit* Mar 1961

Douglas, T. C., Canadian political leader, July 1957, *Obit* Apr 1986

Drossaerts, Arthur, *Obit* Oct 1940

Du Bose, Horace M., *Obit* Mar 1941

Dyson, Michael Eric, American social scientist, clergyman and writer, Oct 1997

Eaton, Charles A., American congressman, May 1945, *Obit* Mar 1953

Egan, Edward M., July 2001

Eisendrath, Maurice Nathan, May 1950, *Obit* Jan 1974

Ellis, John Tracy, American priest and church historian, Mar 1990, *Obit* Jan 1993

Elson, Edward L. R., clergyman, Nov 1967, *Obit* Nov 1993

Empie, Paul C., Oct 1958

Enrique y Tarancon, Vicente, Oct 1972, *Obit* Feb 1995

Evans, Hugh Ivan, Nov 1950, *Obit* July 1958

Falwell, Jerry, American evangelist, Jan 1981, *Obit* Aug 2007

Fauntroy, Walter E., American congressman, Feb 1979

Faust, Clarence H., Mar 1952, *Obit* Aug 1975

Finkelstein, Louis, rabbi and educator, Nov 1940, Mar 1952, *Obit* Jan 1992

Finn, William J., July 1940

Fisher of Lambeth, Geoffrey Francis Fisher, British archbishop, Mar 1945, *Obit* Nov 1972

Fiske, Charles, *Obit* Mar 1942

Fitzpatrick, George L., *Obit* June 1941

Flanagan, Edward Joseph, American priest and youth leader, Sept 1941, *Obit* June 1948

Forbes, Guillaume, *Obit* July 1940

Foreman, George, American boxer, May 1974, Aug 1995

Fosdick, Harry Emerson, American clergyman, Oct 1940, *Obit* Nov 1969

Fox, Robert John, priest and social welfare leader, May 1970, *Obit* June 1984

Francis, July 2013

Fredman, Samuel, *Obit* June 1941

Freeman, James Edward, American bishop, *Obit* July 1943

Fry, Franklin, June 1946, *Obit* Sept 1968

Fulghum, Robert, clergyman and essayist, July 1994

Fuller, Charles E., evangelist, Yrbk 1951, *Obit* May 1968

Fuller, George Washington, *Obit* Yrbk 1940

Galen, Clemens August von, *Obit* Apr 1946

Gallagher, Buell G., college president, May 1953, *Obit* Jan 1979

Ganfield, William Arthur, *Obit* Yrbk 1940

Gannon, Robert I., Mar 1945, *Obit* May 1978

Garbett, Cyril Forster, Feb 1951, *Obit* Mar 1956

Gauthier, Joseph Alexandre Georges, *Obit* Oct 1940

Gillis, James M., priest, June 1956, *Obit* June 1957

Glemp, Jozef, Sept 1982, *Obit* Yrbk 2013

Glennon, John Joseph, *Obit* Apr 1946

Goldstein, Israel, Zionist leader and rabbi, July 1946, *Obit* June 1986

Goma y Tomas, Isidro, *Obit* Oct 1940

Graham, Billy, American evangelist, Apr 1951, Jan 1973

Graham, Franklin, American evangelist and son of Billy Graham, May 2002

Graham, Harry Chrysostom, Apr 1950

Grant, Elihu, *Obit* Yrbk 1942

Graves, Frederick Rogers, *Obit* July 1940

Gray, William H., American congressman and college fund administrator, Feb 1988, *Obit* Yrbk 2013

Greeley, Andrew M., American sociologist, priest and novelist, Yrbk 1972, *Obit* Yrbk 2013

Greeley, Dana McLean, clergyman, civil rights leader and pacifist, Mar 1964, *Obit* Aug 1986

Greenway, Walter Burton, *Obit* Feb 1941

Gregory, Wilton D., American archbishop, Mar 2002

Grenfell, Wilfred Thomason, British medical missionary, *Obit* Yrbk 1940

Grey, J. D., clergyman, Sept 1952, *Obit* Sept 1985

Grieff, Joseph Nicholas, *Obit* Aug 1941

Grier, Rosey, American football player and entertainer, Mar 1975

Griffin, Bernard, Oct 1946, *Obit* Oct 1956

Guthrie, Charles Ellsworth, *Obit* Sept 1940

Gutierrez, Gustavo, Peruvian priest and theologian, Jan 2004

Haas, Francis J., bishop, Aug 1943, *Obit* Oct 1953

Hale, Arthur, *Obit* Mar 1940

Hall, Frank O., *Obit* Yrbk 1941

Hall, Raymond S., Oct 1953

Hanna, Edward Joseph, *Obit* Aug 1944

Hannan, Philip M., American archbishop, July 1968, *Obit* Yrbk 2011

Hargis, Billy James, American clergyman, Mar 1972, *Obit* Yrbk 2005

Harp, Edward B., Oct 1953

Harrelson, Walter J., May 1959

Harris, Barbara C., American bishop, June 1989

Hartman, Louis F., Jan 1953, *Obit* Nov 1970

Hartnett, Robert C., priest, periodical editor and educator, Yrbk 1949

Hawkins, Edler G., Jan 1965

Healy, Timothy Stafford, priest, university president and library director, Jan 1993, *Obit* Jan 1993

Herbster, Ben Mohr, clergyman, July 1962, *Obit* Mar 1985

Hertzberg, Arthur, American rabbi and religious writer, June 1975, *Obit* Yrbk 2006

Herzog, Isaac, Apr 1959

Hesburgh, Theodore Martin, American priest and college president, Jan 1955, July 1982

Heschel, Abraham Joshua, American rabbi and theologian, Apr 1970, *Obit* Mar 1973

Hickey, Thomas F., *Obit* Feb 1941

Hines, John Elbridge, bishop, May 1968, *Obit* Oct 1997

Holmes, John Haynes, American clergyman, theologian and social reformer, Jan 1941, *Obit* May 1964

Hooks, Benjamin L., American civil rights activist, lawyer and judge, Apr 1978, *Obit* Yrbk 2010

Hubbard, Bernard, July 1943, *Obit* July 1962

Huckabee, Mike, American talk show host and former governor, Nov 2005

Huddleston, Trevor, South African archbishop, Oct 1963, *Obit* July 1998

Humbard, Rex, American evangelist, Sept 1972, *Obit* Yrbk 2008

Hume, T. C., *Obit* Yrbk 1943

Hunthausen, Raymond G., archbishop, Aug 1987

Hutchinson, Paul, American clergyman, magazine editor and writer, Yrbk 1949, *Obit* June 1956

Iakovos, July 1960, *Obit* Yrbk 2005

Idleman, Finis Schuyler, *Obit* May 1941

Illich, Ivan, American priest and philosopher, Yrbk 1969, *Obit* Yrbk 2003

Ironside, H. A., clergyman, Feb 1945, *Obit* Feb 1951

Irvine, Alexander, Irish-American missionary, actor and dramatist, *Obit* May 1941

Israel, Edward L., *Obit* Yrbk 1941

Jack, Homer Alexander, clergyman, pacifist and United Nations official, July 1961, *Obit* Oct 1993

Jakes, T. D., American clergyman, religious writer and gospel singer, June 2001

Jakobovits, Immanuel, British rabbi, June 1988, *Obit* Feb 2000

Janssens, Jean Baptiste, Sept 1959, *Obit* Yrbk 1964

Jefferts Schori, Katharine, American bishop, Sept 2006

Johnson, C. Oscar, Feb 1948, *Obit* Jan 1966

Johnson, Hewlett, English clergyman, May 1943, *Obit* Yrbk 1966

Johnson, Howard A., Apr 1964, *Obit* Sept 1974

Johnson, Mordecai Wyatt, American college president and clergyman, Apr 1941

Johnstone, Margaret Blair, Jan 1955

Jones, E. Stanley, American missionary, May 1940, *Obit* Mar 1973

Jones, J. D., Welsh clergyman, *Obit* June 1942

Judd, Walter Henry, American congressman, Sept 1949, *Obit* Apr 1994

Kagan, Henry Enoch, Sept 1965, *Obit* Oct 1969

Kagawa, Toyohiko, Japanese clergyman and philosopher, Sept 1941, *Obit* June 1960

Kahane, Meir, American-Israeli rabbi, Oct 1972, *Obit* Jan 1991

Kaspar, Karel, *Obit* June 1941

Kaup, Felix F., *Obit* Apr 1940

Keller, James, Oct 1951, *Obit* Apr 1977

Kenyon, Helen, Oct 1948

Kepler, Asher Raymond, *Obit* Oct 1942

Kimball, Spencer W., American clergyman and Mormon leader, Feb 1979, *Obit* Jan 1986

Kingdon, Frank, July 1944, *Obit* Apr 1972

Klein, Edward E., rabbi, Sept 1966, *Obit* Sept 1985

Knorr, Nathan H., Feb 1957, *Obit* Aug 1977

Knox, Ronald Arbuthnott, English priest, satirist, essayist and mystery writer, July 1950, *Obit* Nov 1957

Kolvenbach, Peter-Hans, Dutch Jesuit leader, May 1984

Krol, John, Jan 1969, *Obit* May 1996

Kuhlman, Kathryn, evangelist, July 1974, *Obit* Apr 1976

Kung, Hans, Swiss theologian, July 1963

Kushner, Harold S., American rabbi and writer on religion, Apr 1997

La Roe, Wilbur, Mar 1948, *Obit* July 1957

LaFarge, John, American priest, Nov 1942, *Obit* Jan 1964

LaHaye, Tim F., American clergyman and theologian, June 2003

Lamm, Norman, Sept 1978

Lang of Lambeth, Cosmo Gordon Lang, English archbishop, Aug 1941, *Obit* Jan 1946

Laubach, Frank Charles, American missionary and educator, Feb 1950, *Obit* Sept 1970

Lauri, Lorenzo, *Obit* Yrbk 1941

Lawrence, William, *Obit* Jan 1942

Lee, John Clarence, *Obit* Nov 1940

Lefebvre, Marcel, French archbishop, Mar 1978, *Obit* May 1991

Leger, Paul-Emile, Canadian missionary, May 1953, *Obit* Jan 1992

Leiper, Henry Smith, Nov 1948, *Obit* Mar 1975

Leonard, Edward F., *Obit* Jan 1941

Levin, Yehuda Leib, Sept 1969, *Obit* Jan 1972

Libby, Frederick J., Apr 1949, *Obit* Sept 1970

Lichtenberger, Arthur, Apr 1961, *Obit* Nov 1968

Liebman, Joshua Loth, rabbi, Oct 1946, *Obit* July 1948

Lipschitz, Chaim U., Yrbk 1966

Locke, Charles Edward, *Obit* Mar 1940

Lonergan, Bernard J. F., Canadian priest and theologian, Jan 1972, *Obit* Feb 1985

Lord, John Wesley, bishop, May 1971, *Obit* Jan 1990

Lowery, Joseph, American clergyman and civil rights leader, Nov 1982

Luccock, Halford Edward, June 1960, *Obit* Jan 1961

Lustiger, Jean Marie, Feb 1984, *Obit* Yrbk 2007

Lynch, John Joseph, priest and seismologist, Oct 1946, *Obit* Aug 1987

Mackay, John Alexander, American theologian and missionary, Feb 1952, *Obit* Aug 1983

Macrossie, Allan, *Obit* Mar 1940

Maglione, Luigi, *Obit* Oct 1944

Maier, Walter Arthur, evangelist and theologian, May 1947, *Obit* Feb 1950

Makarios, Cypriot archbishop and president, May 1956, *Obit* Sept 1977

Manning, William Thomas, Apr 1940, *Obit* Jan 1950

Marcus, Jacob Rader, rabbi and historian, May 1960, *Obit* Jan 1996

Marella, Paolo, Oct 1964

Marsh, John, Mar 1960

Marshall, Peter, Scottish-American clergyman, Apr 1948, *Obit* Feb 1949

Martin, William C., bishop, Apr 1953

Marty, Martin E., American clergyman, theologian and church historian, June 1968

Marvin, Dwight Edwards, American clergyman, *Obit* Mar 1940

Matheson, Samuel Pritchard, *Obit* July 1942

May, John Lawrence, archbishop, Jan 1991, *Obit* June 1994

McCall, Duke K., Nov 1959, *Obit* Yrbk 2013

McClurkin, Donnie, American gospel singer and clergyman, Apr 2007

McCracken, Robert James, July 1949, *Obit* Apr 1973

McCune, George Shannon, *Obit* Feb 1942

McCurdy, William Albert, *Obit* Feb 1942

McGinley, Laurence J., college president and priest, June 1949, *Obit* Oct 1992

McGuigan, James, Sept 1950, *Obit* June 1974

McIntire, Carl, American clergyman, Oct 1971, *Obit* June 2002

McIntyre, James Francis Aloysius, Feb 1953, *Obit* Sept 1979

McKenzie, Vashti, American bishop, Nov 2000

McLaughlin, John, American television commentator and moderator, July 1987

McLaughlin, Leo Plowden, college president and priest, May 1970, *Obit* Nov 1996

McNicholas, John T., May 1949, *Obit* June 1950

McPherson, Aimee Semple, American evangelist, *Obit* Nov 1944

Mead, Charles Larew, *Obit* July 1941

Medaris, John Bruce, general and clergyman, Feb 1958

Medeiros, Humberto, Nov 1971, *Obit* Nov 1983

Mellon, William Larimer, medical missionary, June 1965, *Obit* Oct 1989

Mendenhall, Harlan G., *Obit* July 1940

Mercer, Samuel A. B., Feb 1953

Merriam, George Ernest, *Obit* May 1941

Mikell, Henry Judah, *Obit* Apr 1942

Miller, Harry W., Mar 1962, *Obit* Mar 1977

Miller, Irving, Nov 1952, *Obit* Feb 1981

Mindszenty, Jozsef, Jan 1957, *Obit* June 1975

Monaghan, Francis Joseph, *Obit* Jan 1943

Montgomery, James Shera, Apr 1948, *Obit* Sept 1952

Moon, Sun Myung, Korean evangelist, Mar 1983, *Obit* Yrbk 2012

Mooney, Edward, Apr 1946, *Obit* Jan 1959

Moore, Paul, American bishop, Jan 1967, *Obit* Yrbk 2003

Moorland, Jesse Edward, American clergyman, *Obit* Jan 1940

Mosher, Gouverneur Frank, *Obit* Sept 1941

Mosley, J. Brooke, bishop, Sept 1970, *Obit* Apr 1988

Mueller, Reuben H., bishop, Apr 1964, *Obit* Sept 1982

Munk, Kaj, Danish clergyman, poet and dramatist, *Obit* Feb 1944

Murray, John Courtney, American priest and theologian, May 1961, *Obit* Oct 1967

Muste, Abraham Johannes, American clergyman and pacifist, Oct 1965, *Obit* Apr 1967

Muzorewa, Abel Tendekai, Zimbabwean prime minister, Mar 1979, *Obit* Yrbk 2010

Myers, C. Kilmer, Feb 1960

Ncube, Pius Alick, Zimbabwean archbishop, Jan 2004

Neill, Stephen, British bishop, Mar 1960

Neuhaus, Richard John, American priest, religious writer and political activist, June 1988, *Obit* Yrbk 2009

Newell, Horatio B., *Obit* Oct 1943

Niebuhr, Reinhold, American theologian, Mar 1941, Nov 1951, *Obit* July 1971

Niemoller, Martin, German clergyman, Mar 1943, Mar 1965, *Obit* May 1984

Nolde, O. Frederick, Feb 1947, *Obit* Sept 1972

O'Boyle, Patrick, July 1973, *Obit* Sept 1987

O'Connell, Colm, Irish priest, school headmaster and track coach, Jan 2005

O'Connell, William Henry, June 1941, *Obit* June 1944

O'Connor, John Joseph, June 1984, *Obit* July 2000

O'Flanagan, Michael, Irish priest and republican, *Obit* Sept 1942

O'Gorman, Patrick F., *Obit* Apr 1940

O'Malley, Sean Patrick, Jan 2004

O'Shea, William F., *Obit* Apr 1945

Obando y Bravo, Miguel, Mar 1988

Orlemanski, Stanislaw, Polish-American priest, June 1944

Ottaviani, Alfredo, Yrbk 1966, *Obit* Sept 1979

Oxnam, G. Bromley, American bishop, Nov 1944, *Obit* Apr 1963

Paisley, Ian R. K., Irish clergyman and political leader, Jan 1971, June 1986

Parker, Roy H., Oct 1951

Peabody, Endicott, clergyman and school headmaster, May 1940, *Obit* Jan 1945

Peale, Norman Vincent, American clergyman and inspirational writer, Jan 1946, Oct 1974, *Obit* Feb 1994

Pelikan, Jaroslav Jan, American clergyman and religion historian, Sept 1987, *Obit* Yrbk 2006

Pell, Edward Leigh, American clergyman and religious writer, *Obit* Aug 1943

Pellegrinetti, Ermenegildo, *Obit* May 1943

Perry, Harold, American bishop, Oct 1966, *Obit* Sept 1991

Phillips, Theodore Evelyn Reece, *Obit* July 1942

Phillips, Ze Barney Thorne, *Obit* July 1942

Pierce, Bob, American evangelist, Yrbk 1961

Pike, James Albert, American bishop, May 1957, *Obit* Nov 1969

Pire, Georges, Belgian priest, May 1959, *Obit* Mar 1969

Pla y Deniel, Enrique, Feb 1955, *Obit* Sept 1968

Pollard, William G., Mar 1953

Pope, Liston, Apr 1956, *Obit* June 1974

Potter, Dan, Feb 1964

Powell, Adam Clayton, American congressman, Apr 1942, *Obit* May 1972

Preus, Jacob A. O., clergyman and church official, May 1975, *Obit* Oct 1994

Pruden, Edward Hughes, clergyman, Sept 1950

Quinn, Daniel Joseph, *Obit* Mar 1940

Ray, Randolph, Apr 1945, *Obit* July 1963

Reinartz, F. Eppling, July 1953

Reisner, Christian Fichthorne, *Obit* Sept 1940

Richmond, Charles Alexander, *Obit* Sept 1940

Riggs, T. Lawrason, *Obit* June 1943

Ritter, Bruce, priest and child care leader, June 1983, *Obit* Feb 2000

Ritter, Joseph Elmer, Yrbk 1964, *Obit* Oct 1967

Roberts, Oral, American evangelist, Nov 1960, *Obit* Feb 2010

Robinson, John A. T., English bishop, Feb 1965, *Obit* Feb 1984

Roy, Maurice, Feb 1958, *Obit* Jan 1986

Royden, Agnes Maude, English social worker and evangelist, Apr 1942, *Obit* Oct 1956

Rugambwa, Laurean, Sept 1960, *Obit* Feb 1998

Runcie, Robert, English archbishop, Nov 1980, *Obit* Oct 2000

Rutenborn, Gunter, Oct 1960

Ryan, John A., priest and theologian, *Obit* Oct 1945

Salit, Norman, rabbi and lawyer, Mar 1955, *Obit* Oct 1960

Sandefer, Jefferson Davis, *Obit* Apr 1940

Sayre, Francis B., American cathedral dean, Yrbk 1956, *Obit* Yrbk 2008

Scherer, Paul, May 1941, *Obit* May 1969

Schillebeeckx, Edward, Belgian priest and theologian, June 1983, *Obit* May 2010

Schindler, Alexander M., American rabbi, Sept 1987, *Obit* Feb 2001

Schiotz, Fredrik Axel, clergyman, Apr 1972, *Obit* May 1989

Schleich, Michel, *Obit* June 1945

Schneerson, Menachem M., American rabbi, Sept 1983, *Obit* Aug 1994

Schonborn, Christoph von, Jan 2006

Schrembs, Joseph, *Obit* Yrbk 1945

Schuller, Robert Harold, American clergyman, June 1979

Scott, Michael, South African clergyman and human rights activist, Apr 1953, *Obit* Apr 1985

Seagrave, Gordon S., American physician and missionary, Nov 1943, *Obit* May 1965

Sergii, *Obit* July 1944

Sharpton, Al, American clergyman and political activist, Nov 1995

Sheen, Fulton J., American archbishop, Nov 1941, Jan 1951, *Obit* Feb 1980

Shehan, Lawrence, Oct 1965, *Obit* Oct 1984

Sheil, Bernard J., Yrbk 1968, *Obit* Nov 1969

Sheldon, Charles M., clergyman and author, *Obit* Apr 1946

Shenouda, Egyptian patriarch, Jan 2003, *Obit* Yrbk 2013

Sherrill, Henry Knox, Mar 1947, *Obit* June 1980

Shoemaker, Samuel Moor, clergyman, Apr 1955, *Obit* Yrbk 1963

Short, Dewey, American congressman and military official, Yrbk 1951, *Obit* Feb 1980

Silver, Abba Hillel, rabbi, Yrbk 1941, May 1963, *Obit* Jan 1964

Sin, Jaime, Sept 1995, *Obit* Yrbk 2005

Sizoo, Joseph R., Yrbk 1964, *Obit* Nov 1966

Slifkin, Nosson, Israeli rabbi and biblical zoologist, Jan 2005

Smith, Gerald L. K., American clergyman, lecturer and columnist, Aug 1943, *Obit* June 1976

Smith, Jeff, American cook and clergyman, Aug 1991, *Obit* Yrbk 2004

Sockman, Ralph Washington, clergyman, June 1946, *Obit* Nov 1970

Sperry, Willard Learoyd, theologian, May 1952, *Obit* Sept 1954

Stamm, John S., Feb 1949, *Obit* May 1956

Steinberg, Milton, rabbi, Mar 1940, *Obit* Apr 1950

Stepinac, Alojzije, Feb 1953, *Obit* Apr 1960

Stewart, George Craig, *Obit* Jan 1940

Stokes, Anson Phelps, bishop, July 1962, *Obit* Jan 1987

Stott, John R. W., British clergyman and evangelist, May 2005, *Obit* Yrbk 2011

Stritch, Samuel Alphonsus, Apr 1946, *Obit* Sept 1958

Stromberg, Leonard, *Obit* Sept 1941

Stuart, John Leighton, American missionary and diplomat, Oct 1946, *Obit* Nov 1962

Suenens, Leo Joseph, May 1965, *Obit* July 1996

Sullivan, Leon Howard, American clergyman and civil rights leader, Mar 1969, *Obit* Sept 2001

Swaggart, Jimmy Lee, evangelist, Oct 1987

Sykes, Richard Eddy, *Obit* Nov 1942

Taylor, George Braxton, clergyman, *Obit* Apr 1942

Temple, William, British archbishop and theologian, Apr 1942, *Obit* Yrbk 1944

Teresa, Yugoslav nun and missionary, Sept 1973, *Obit* Nov 1997

Terry, Randall, American anti-abortion activist, Jan 1994

Thekaekara, Matthew P., May 1974

Thomas, Elbert Duncan, American senator, Oct 1942, *Obit* Mar 1953

Thurman, Howard, American clergyman and theologian, June 1955, *Obit* June 1981

Tien, Thomas, May 1946, *Obit* Oct 1967

Tiso, Jozef, Slovak priest and president, Mar 1943, *Obit* May 1947

Tisserant, Eugene, Apr 1963, *Obit* Apr 1972

Tucker, Henry St. George, American bishop, Sept 1943, *Obit* Nov 1959

Ugyen Trinley Dorje, Tibetan lama, Jan 2004

Upham, Francis Bourne, *Obit* May 1941

Van Dusen, Henry Pitney, seminary president, Yrbk 1950, *Obit* Apr 1975

Van Paassen, Pierre, Dutch-American clergyman, journalist and author, Oct 1942, *Obit* Mar 1968

Verdier, Jean, *Obit* May 1940

Visser 't Hooft, Willem Adolph, Dutch clergyman and theologian, May 1949, *Obit* Aug 1985

Voris, John Ralph, Yrbk 1948, *Obit* Mar 1968

Wallis, Jim, American evangelist and writer, July 2005

Walsh, Chad, professor of English and author, Feb 1962, *Obit* Mar 1991

Waring, George J., *Obit* Apr 1943

Warren, Harry Marsh, *Obit* Feb 1941

Warren, Rick, American pastor and religious writer, Oct 2006

Watson, Samuel Newell, *Obit* May 1942

Watts, Alan, American philosopher, Mar 1962, *Obit* Jan 1974

Wegner, Nicholas H., Yrbk 1949, *Obit* May 1976

Weigle, Luther Allan, professor of religious education and dean, Mar 1946, *Obit* Oct 1976

Werne, Isaac, *Obit* Mar 1940

West, Annie Blythe, *Obit* May 1941

White, Reggie, American football player and clergyman, Nov 1995, *Obit* Yrbk 2005

White, Wilbert Webster, *Obit* Oct 1944

Wildmon, Donald, clergyman, Jan 1992

Williams, Joseph John, *Obit* Yrbk 1940

Williams, Preston Warren, American religious official, May 2007

Williamson, Marianne, New Age preacher, Feb 1993

Wise, Stephen Samuel, American rabbi, July 1941, *Obit* May 1949

Wolf, Alfred, Mar 1958

Woodcock, Charles Edward, *Obit* Mar 1940

Woodsworth, James Shaver, Canadian clergyman and political leader, *Obit* May 1942

Wright, Harold Bell, American clergyman and novelist, *Obit* July 1944

Wright, John J., Feb 1963, *Obit* Oct 1979

Wyszynski, Stefan, Jan 1958, *Obit* July 1981

Young, Andrew, American congressman, diplomat and mayor, Apr 1977

Zen, Joseph, Chinese bishop, Jan 2005

Zenos, Andrew C., *Obit* Mar 1942

Climatologists

Bradley, Raymond S., July 2012

Hayhoe, Katharine, Feb 2012

Houghton, John Theodore, British climatologist, Jan 2004

Huybers, Peter, American climatologist, Apr 2011

Rahmstorf, Stefan, German oceanographer and climatologist, Feb 2010

Roberts, Walter Orr, climatologist, Yrbk 1960, *Obit* May 1990

Clothing industry executives

Abelson, Nat, American clothing industry executive, Nov 1957

Aberra, Amsale, Ethiopian fashion designer, Jan 2005

Adolfo, fashion designer, Nov 1972

Adrian, American costume and fashion designer, Feb 1941, *Obit* Nov 1959

Ahrents, Angela, American clothing industry executive, May 2012

Alphadi, Malian fashion designer, Jan 2004

Ambani, Anil, Indian telecommunications, textile and chemical conglomerate executive, Feb 2009

Ambani, Mukesh, Indian telecommunications, textile and chemical conglomerate executive, June 2009

Amies, Hardy, English fashion designer, Mar 1962, *Obit* Aug 2003

Amoruso, Sophia, Sept 2013

Amory, Derick Heathcoat Amory, British textile industry executive and cabinet member, Apr 1958

Anderson, Ray C., American carpet industry executive, May 2005, *Obit* Yrbk 2012

Armani, Giorgio, Italian fashion designer, Jan 1983

Balenciaga, Spanish fashion designer, May 1954, *Obit* May 1972

Beaton, Cecil, English designer and photographer, Oct 1944, July 1962, *Obit* Mar 1980

Beene, Geoffrey, American fashion designer, Apr 1978, *Obit* Mar 2005

Berge, Pierre, French clothing industry executive, Jan 1990

Blakely, Sara, American hosiery company executive, Jan 2013

Blancke, Harold, American chemical industry executive, June 1957

Blass, Bill, American fashion designer, Sept 1966, *Obit* Nov 2002

Boateng, Ozwald, British fashion designer, Jan 2006

Bohan, Marc, French fashion designer, Apr 1965

Bravo, Rose Marie, American clothing industry executive, June 2004

Brooks, Donald, American fashion and costume designer, Mar 1972, *Obit* Yrbk 2005

Burch, Tory, American fashion designer and philanthropist, Sept 2010

Burrows, Stephen, American fashion designer, Nov 2003

Byers, Margaretta, Sept 1941

Carnegie, Hattie, fashion designer, Oct 1942, *Obit* May 1956

Cashin, Bonnie, American fashion designer, May 1970, *Obit* June 2000

Cassini, Oleg, French-American fashion designer, July 1961, *Obit* Yrbk 2006

Chanel, Coco, French fashion designer and perfumer, Sept 1954, *Obit* Feb 1971

Charney, Dov, American t-shirt manufacturer, Sept 2009

Claiborne, Liz, American fashion designer, June 1989, *Obit* Yrbk 2007

Clayton, William Lockhart, American cotton executive and government official, Apr 1944, *Obit* Mar 1966

Courreges, Andre, French fashion designer, Jan 1970

Dache, Lilly, French milliner, July 1941, *Obit* Mar 1990

Davis, Tobe Coller, Yrbk 1959, *Obit* Feb 1963

Delaunay, Sonia, French painter and fashion designer, Aug 1977, *Obit* Feb 1980

Dent, Frederick B., American Secretary of commerce, Apr 1974

Desses, Jean, Jan 1956, *Obit* Oct 1970

Diddy, American rapper, record producer and actor, Apr 1998

Dior, Christian, French fashion designer, Oct 1948, *Obit* Jan 1958

Dolce, Domenico, Italian fashion designer, Jan 2005

Drexler, Millard S., American clothing chain executive, Jan 1993

Farhi, Nicole, French fashion designer, Nov 2001

Fath, Jacques, French fashion designer, Apr 1951, *Obit* Jan 1955

Ferre, Gianfranco, Italian fashion designer, July 1991, *Obit* Yrbk 2007

Field, Patricia, American fashion and costume designer, Nov 2010

Fireman, Paul, American shoe company executive, Mar 1992

Fogarty, Anne, fashion designer, Oct 1958, *Obit* Mar 1980

Ford, Tom, American fashion designer, May 1998

Gabbana, Stefano, Italian fashion designer, Jan 2005

Gernreich, Rudi, American fashion designer, Yrbk 1968, *Obit* June 1985

Ghesquiere, Nicolas, French fashion designer, Jan 2011

Giannulli, Mossimo, American fashion designer and clothing executive, Feb 2003

Gigli, Romeo, Italian fashion designer, Aug 1998

Givenchy, Hubert de, French fashion designer, May 1955

Gres, Alix, French fashion designer, June 1980, *Obit* Feb 1995

Griffith Joyner, Florence, American sprinter, Apr 1989, *Obit* Nov 1998

Halston, American fashion designer, Yrbk 1972, *Obit* May 1990

Hartnell, Norman, May 1953, *Obit* Aug 1979

Hawes, Elizabeth, American fashion designer, Oct 1940, *Obit* Yrbk 1991

Hilfiger, Tommy, American fashion designer, Apr 1996

Jacobs, Marc, American fashion designer, Feb 1998

James, Charles, American fashion designer, July 1956

Jimenez, Joyce, Filipino-American actress and lingerie company founder, Jan 2003

John, Daymond, American fashion designer, Aug 2007

Jordan, B. Everett, American senator, Nov 1959, *Obit* May 1974

Kamali, Norma, American fashion designer, Nov 1998

Karan, Donna, American fashion designer, Aug 1990

Kawakubo, Rei, Japanese fashion designer, Aug 1999

Kelly, Patrick, fashion designer, Sept 1989, *Obit* Mar 1990

Kiam, Omar, Yrbk 1945, *Obit* May 1954

King, Muriel, Apr 1943, *Obit* May 1977

Knight, Philip H., American shoe company executive, Aug 1997

Kors, Michael, American fashion designer, Jan 2000

Lang, Helmut, Austrian fashion designer, Apr 1997

Lanvin, Jeanne, French fashion designer, *Obit* Sept 1946

Leiber, Judith, Hungarian-American handbag designer, Sept 1996

Lelong, Lucien, Nov 1955, *Obit* Sept 1958

Leser, Tina, fashion designer, June 1957, *Obit* Mar 1986

Lhuillier, Monique, American fashion designer, June 2008

Love, James Spencer, textile executive, Nov 1957, *Obit* Mar 1962

Mackie, Bob, fashion designer, Oct 1988

Mainbocher, fashion designer, Feb 1942, *Obit* Mar 1977

Mashouf, Manny, American retail executive, Feb 2009

Maxwell, Vera, fashion designer, July 1977, *Obit* Mar 1995

McCardell, Claire, American fashion designer, Nov 1954, *Obit* June 1958

McFadden, Mary, American fashion designer, Apr 1983

McQueen, Alexander, British fashion designer, Feb 2002, *Obit* June 2010

Miller, Nicole, fashion designer, Mar 1995

Ming, Jenny, American clothing chain executive, Jan 2011

Mizrahi, Isaac, American fashion designer and television personality, Jan 1991

Molyneux, Edward H., June 1942, *Obit* May 1974

Montana, Claude, French fashion designer, Jan 1992

Mugler, Thierry, French fashion designer and photographer, Aug 2010

Mulleavy, Kate, American fashion designer, Sept 2012

Mulleavy, Laura, American fashion designer, Sept 2012

Norell, Norman, fashion designer, Nov 1964, *Obit* Yrbk 1972

Olsen, Ashley, American actress and fashion designer, Sept 2010

Parnis, Mollie, fashion designer, May 1956, *Obit* Sept 1992

Poiret, Paul, French fashion designer, *Obit* June 1944

Posen, Zac, American fashion designer, July 2006

Prada, Miuccia, Italian fashion designer, Feb 2006

Pucci, Emilio, Italian fashion designer, Feb 1961, *Obit* Jan 1993

Roehm, Carolyne, American fashion designer, Feb 1992

Rojas, Rudy, American clothing company executive, Jan 2006

Rosenfeld, Henry Jonas, clothing and luggage industry executive, Nov 1948

Rykiel, Sonia, French fashion designer, May 1990

Saab, Elie, Lebanese fashion designer, Aug 2004

Saint Laurent, Yves, French fashion designer, Yrbk 1964, *Obit* Oct 2008

Sander, Jil, German fashion designer, Oct 1997

Schiaparelli, Elsa, French fashion designer, Jan 1940, Nov 1951, *Obit* Jan 1974

Schnurer, Carolyn, Mar 1955

Simonetta, Italian fashion designer, Yrbk 1955

Simpson, Adele, fashion designer, Nov 1970, *Obit* Oct 1995

Slimane, Hedi, French fashion designer, Jan 2006

Spade, Kate, American handbag designer, Apr 2007

Stavropoulos, George, fashion designer, Mar 1985, *Obit* Feb 1991

Stevens, Robert T., American textile industry executive and Secretary of the army, July 1953, *Obit* Mar 1983

Sy, Oumou, Senegalese fashion designer, Jan 2003

Theallet, Sophie, French fashion designer, Nov 2012

Tonner, Robert, American doll maker, Oct 2011

Traphagen, Ethel, Yrbk 1948, *Obit* June 1963

Trigere, Pauline, French-American fashion designer, Feb 1960, *Obit* July 2002

Tyler, Richard, Australian fashion designer, May 1997

Ungaro, Emanuel, French fashion designer, July 1980

Valentina, fashion designer, Yrbk 1946, *Obit* Nov 1989

Valentino, Italian fashion designer, Nov 1973

Vanderbilt, Gloria, American fashion designer, July 1972

Venturini, Silvia, Italian handbag designer, Jan 2006

Verhoeven, Julie, English fashion illustrator, Apr 2012

Versace, Donatella, Italian fashion designer, June 1998

Versace, Gianni, Italian fashion designer, Apr 1993, *Obit* Sept 1997

Wachner, Linda Joy, American clothing industry executive, Nov 1998

Weitz, John, German-American fashion designer, novelist and biographer, Sept 1979, *Obit* Apr 2003

Wise, James DeCamp, carpet industry executive, Apr 1954, *Obit* Apr 1984

Clowns

Abbott and Costello, comedians, Oct 1941

Abbott, Bud, American comedian, Oct 1941, *Obit* June 1974

Allen, Fred, comedian, Feb 1941, *Obit* May 1956

Allen, Gracie, American comedienne, July 1940, Mar 1951, *Obit* Oct 1964

Allen, Steve, American comedian and actor, July 1951, Mar 1982, *Obit* Jan 2001

Allen, Tim, American comedian and actor, May 1995

Armisen, Fred, American comedian and performance artist, Oct 2013

Arquette, Cliff, June 1961, *Obit* Nov 1974

Baker, Phil, American comedian, accordionist and radio personality, Nov 1946, *Obit* Jan 1964

Ballard, Kaye, American actress, singer and comedienne, Sept 1969

Bamford, Maria, comedian, Jan 2012

Bana, Eric, Australian comedian and actor, Jan 2003

Baron-Cohen, Sacha, British comedian, Jan 2003

Barr, Roseanne, American comedienne, May 1989

Bean, Orson, comedian, Feb 1967

Belushi, John, American comedian, Jan 1980, *Obit* Apr 1982

Benny, Jack, comedian, Aug 1941, Nov 1963, *Obit* Feb 1975

Berle, Milton, American comedian, June 1949, *Obit* Yrbk 2002

Bernhard, Sandra, American comedienne and actress, Sept 1990

Bickel, George, American comedian and actor, *Obit* Aug 1941

Bishop, Joey, American comedian, Apr 1962, *Obit* Yrbk 2008

Black, Jack, American singer and actor, Feb 2002

Bob and Ray, American comedians, Oct 1957

Boosler, Elayne, comedienne, May 1993

Borge, Victor, American pianist and comedian, Mar 1946, May 1993, *Obit* Mar 2001

Borowitz, Andy, American humorist, July 2007

Bradbury, James H., *Obit* Yrbk 1940

Brand, Russell, British comedian and actor, Jan 2011

Brenner, David, American comedian, Mar 1987

Brice, Fanny, American singer and comedian, June 1946, *Obit* July 1951

Burns, George, American comedian, Mar 1951, July 1976, *Obit* May 1996

Butterworth, Charles, *Obit* July 1946

Buttons, Red, American comedian and actor, Sept 1958, *Obit* Yrbk 2006

C. K., Louis, American comedian, Feb 2010

Caesar, Sid, American comedian and actor, Apr 1951

Cambridge, Godfrey, American actor and comedian, Mar 1969, *Obit* Feb 1977

Cantinflas, Mexican comedian, June 1953, *Obit* June 1993

Carell, Steve, American comedian and actor, Feb 2007

Carey, Drew, American comedian and game show host, Mar 1998

Carlin, George, American comedian, Oct 1976, *Obit* Oct 2008

Carr, Alexander, *Obit* Yrbk 1946

Carrey, Jim, Canadian comedian and actor, Feb 1996

Carson, Johnny, American television talk show host, Jan 1964, Apr 1982, *Obit* July 2005

Carvey, Dana, American comedian and actor, June 1992

Cedric the Entertainer, American comedian, Feb 2004

Chappelle, Dave, American comedian and actor, June 2004

Chase, Chevy, American actor and comedian, Mar 1979

Chen Peisi, Chinese actor and comedian, Jan 2004

Cho, Margaret, American comedienne, Oct 2000

Clark, Bobby, May 1949, *Obit* Apr 1960

Clement, Jemaine, New Zealand comedian, Mar 2008

Coca, Imogene, American actress and comedienne, Apr 1951, *Obit* Sept 2001

Colbert, Stephen, American comedian and actor, Nov 2006

Conway, Tim, American comedian and actor, Apr 1981

Coogan, Steve, English actor and comedian, Jan 2002

Correll, Charles J., Yrbk 1947, *Obit* Nov 1972

Cosby, Bill, American actor and comedian, Apr 1967, Oct 1986

Costello, Lou, American comedian, Oct 1941, *Obit* May 1959

Dale, Jim, English actor, July 1981

Dangerfield, Rodney, American comedian, *Obit* Feb 2005

Davis, Joan, comedienne and actress, June 1945, *Obit* Sept 1961

DeGeneres, Ellen, American comedienne and talk show host, Apr 1996

Debbouze, Jamel, French comedian and actor, Jan 2005

Durante, Jimmy, comedian, Sept 1946, *Obit* Mar 1980

Elliott, Bob, American comedian, Oct 1957

Fabray, Nanette, comedienne, Jan 1956

Fallon, Jimmy, American comedian, actor and talk show host, July 2002

Fay, Frank, Aug 1945, *Obit* Yrbk 1961

Ferrell, Will, American comedian and actor, Feb 2003

Fey, Tina, American actress and comedienne, Apr 2002

Fields, Lew, comedian, *Obit* Sept 1941

Finch, Flora, *Obit* Jan 1940

Flagg, Fannie, American comedienne, actress and novelist, Nov 2006

Flanders, Michael, Jan 1970, *Obit* June 1975

Foxx, Jamie, American comedian and actor, May 2005

Foxx, Redd, American comedian, Yrbk 1972, *Obit* Jan 1992

Fratellini, Paul, *Obit* Yrbk 1940

Frye, David, American impressionist, Mar 1975, *Obit* Yrbk 2011

Garofalo, Janeane, American comedienne and actress, Mar 2005

Gervais, Ricky, British comedian, Jan 2006

Gleason, Jackie, American actor, Oct 1955, *Obit* Aug 1987

Gobel, George, comedian, Mar 1955, *Obit* Apr 1991

Goldthwait, Bobcat, American comedian, Sept 2010

Goodwin, Harry, *Obit* Yrbk 1942

Goulding, Ray, American comedian, Oct 1957, *Obit* May 1990

Green, Tom, Canadian comedian, Oct 2003

Griffin, Kathy, American comedienne and actress, Sept 2008

Hackett, Buddy, American comedian, May 1965, *Obit* Oct 2003

Hall, Arsenio, American comedian and talk show host, Sept 1989

Handler, Chelsea, American comedian and actress, Oct 2010

Hardwick, Chris, game show host, June 2012

Hibbard, Edna, *Obit* Feb 1943

Hill, Benny, English comedian, Feb 1983, *Obit* June 1992

Hogan, Paul, Australian comedian, Aug 1987

Hope, Bob, American comedian and actor, June 1941, Oct 1953, *Obit* Yrbk 2003

Hughley, D. L., American comedian, Mar 2000

Izzard, Eddie, British comedian and actor, Jan 2003

Jackson, Joe, American comedian, *Obit* July 1942

Jessel, George, singer, dancer and comedian, Mar 1943, *Obit* July 1981

Johnson, Chic, American comedian, Sept 1940, *Obit* Apr 1962

Jones, Billy, *Obit* Jan 1941

Jordan, Jim, American radio performer, Nov 1941, *Obit* May 1988

Karno, Fred, English comedian and theatrical producer, *Obit* Nov 1941

Kay, Beatrice, Yrbk 1942

Kaye, Danny, American comedian, actor and singer, Yrbk 1941, Nov 1952, *Obit* Apr 1987

Kelly, Emmett, American clown, July 1954, *Obit* May 1979

Kimmel, Jimmy, American comedian, Oct 2009

King, Alan, American comedian, June 1970, *Obit* Yrbk 2004

Kirby, George, comedian, May 1977, *Obit* Jan 1996

Klein, Robert, American comedian, Mar 1977

Korman, Harvey, American actor, Oct 1979, *Obit* Yrbk 2008

Kovacs, Ernie, American comedian, Feb 1958, *Obit* Mar 1962

Langdon, Harry, American actor and comedian, *Obit* Feb 1945

Lawrence, Martin, American comedian and actor, Oct 1999

Letterman, David, American comedian and television talk show host, Nov 1980, Oct 2002

Lewis, Jerry, American comedian, Nov 1962

Lewis, Richard, comedian and actor, July 1993

Little, Rich, Canadian impressionist, Nov 1975

Loftus, Cissie, Sept 1940, *Obit* Aug 1943

Lopez, George, American comedian, Mar 2010

Lupino, Stanley, *Obit* Aug 1942

Lynde, Paul, Nov 1972, *Obit* Feb 1982

Mabley, Moms, American comedienne and actress, Jan 1975, *Obit* Aug 1975

Mac, Bernie, American comedian and actor, June 2002, *Obit* Nov 2008

Maher, Bill, American comedian and talk show host, July 1997

Manna, Charlie, Jan 1965, *Obit* Yrbk 1971

Maron, Marc, American comedian, Nov 2011

Martin, Demetri, American comedian and actor, Oct 2009

Martin, Dick, American comedian, Sept 1969, *Obit* Yrbk 2008

Marx Brothers, American comedians, Mar 1948

Marx, Chico, American comedian, May 1948, *Obit* Yrbk 1961

Marx, Groucho, American comedian, Mar 1948, Feb 1973, *Obit* Oct 1977

Marx, Harpo, American comedian, Mar 1948, *Obit* Nov 1964

Mason, Jackie, American comedian, July 1987

McKenzie, Bret, New Zealand comedian, Mar 2008

Meyers, Seth, American comedian and actor, Apr 2009

Mirza, Shazia, British physics teacher and comedian, Jan 2002

Mo'Nique, American comedienne and actress, Apr 2010

Morgan, Tracy, American actor and comedian, Mar 2007

Murphy, Eddie, American comedian and actor, Nov 1983

Murray, Charlie, Obit Sept 1941

Myers, Mike, Canadian comedian, actor and screenwriter, Aug 1997

Najimy, Kathy, American actress and comedienne, Oct 2002

Newhart, Bob, American comedian and actor, Mar 1962

Nye, Bill, American comedian and television performer, July 1998

O'Brien, Conan, American comedian and television talk show host, May 1996

O'Donnell, Rosie, American comedienne, actress and talk show host, Aug 1995

Olsen, Ole, American comedian, Sept 1940, Obit Mar 1963

Parker, Barnett, Obit Oct 1941

Pearl, Minnie, American comedienne, Nov 1992, Obit May 1996

Penner, Joe, Obit Mar 1941

Polunin, Slava, Russian clown, Jan 2004

Popov, Oleg, Russian clown, Mar 1964

Prinze, Freddie, American comedian, June 1975, Obit Mar 1977

Pryor, Richard, American comedian, Feb 1976, Obit Apr 2006

Radner, Gilda, American comedienne, Feb 1980, Obit July 1989

Ragland, Rags, Obit Oct 1946

Raimu, Obit Nov 1946

Raye, Martha, American actress, singer and comedienne, July 1963, Obit Jan 1995

Rehman, Shabana, Norwegian comedian, Jan 2004

Reiser, Paul, American comedian and actor, Apr 1996

Reubens, Paul, American comedian and actor, Jan 1988

Richards, Michael, American actor and comedian, Nov 1997

Rivers, Joan, American comedienne and television personality, Jan 1970, Mar 1987

Rousseau, Stephane, Canadian comedian and actor, Jan 2004

Rowan, Dan, American comedian, Sept 1969, Obit Nov 1987

Sahl, Mort, American comedian, Yrbk 1960

Sales, Soupy, American comedian, Jan 1967, Obit Yrbk 2009

Sandler, Adam, American comedian and actor, May 1998

Schmidt, Harald, German talk show host, Jan 2006

Schneider, Helge, German comedian, actor, jazz musician and composer, Jan 2007

Seinfeld, Jerry, American comedian, Aug 1992

Shandling, Garry, American comedian, Apr 1989

Shearer, Harry, American actor and comedian, June 2001

Sherman, Allan, television performer and comedian, Sept 1966, Obit Jan 1974

Short, Martin, Canadian comedian and actor, Sept 1992

Silverman, Sarah, American comedienne, July 2006

Sinbad, American comedian and actor, Feb 1997

Sintim-Misa, Kwaku, Ghanaian actor and comedian, Jan 2004

Skelton, Red, American comedian and actor, Nov 1947, Obit Nov 1997

Smigel, Robert, American comedian and television scriptwriter, Nov 2011

Smothers, Dick, American comedian, Yrbk 1968

Stewart, Jon, American comedian and talk show host, July 2004

Stewart, William G., Obit Sept 1941

Stiller, Ben, American actor, comedian and director, Nov 1999

Stoopnagle, Lemuel Q., radio comedian, Oct 1947, Obit July 1950

Sykes, Wanda, American comedian, Jan 2011

Terry-Thomas, English comedian and actor, Mar 1961, Obit Mar 1990

Thomas, Danny, American comedian, Feb 1959, Obit Apr 1991

Tinney, Frank, Obit Jan 1941

Tomlin, Lily, American comedienne and actress, Sept 1973

Turpin, Ben, comedian, Obit Aug 1940

Vassa, Yossi, Ethiopian-Israeli comedian, Jan 2006

Waters, James R., Obit Jan 1946

Wayans, Damon, American comedian and actor, Nov 1999

Wayans, Marlon, American comedian and actor, May 2001

Weber, Joseph M., Obit July 1942

Williams, Robin, American comedian and actor, June 1979, Jan 1997

Wilmore, Larry, American television scriptwriter and producer, Nov 2007

Wilson, Flip, American comedian, Nov 1969, Obit Feb 1999

Winters, Jonathan, American comedian, Mar 1965, Obit Yrbk 2013

Wright, Huntley, Obit Sept 1941

Wright, Steven, American comedian, May 2003

Wynn, Ed, comedian, Jan 1945, Obit July 1966

Youngman, Henny, comedian, Oct 1986, Obit May 1998

Coaches (Athletics)

Allen, George, American football coach, Jan 1975, Obit Mar 1991

Alston, Walter, baseball manager, June 1954, Obit Nov 1984

Arena, Bruce, American soccer coach, Sept 2010

Beckenbauer, Franz, German soccer player and coach, Jan 2006

Belichick, Bill, American football coach, Sept 2002

Blaik, Earl Henry, football coach, Jan 1945, Obit July 1989

Bowden, Bobby, American football coach, Nov 1996

Bowman, Scotty, Canadian hockey coach, Jan 1999

Bradley, Bob, American soccer coach, Aug 2010

Brown, Larry, American basketball coach, Apr 1996

Bryant, Bear, American football coach, June 1980, *Obit* Mar 1983

Calhoun, Jim, American basketball coach, May 2011

Chaney, John, American basketball coach, Mar 1999

Cherry, Don, Canadian hockey coach and sportscaster, Jan 2004

Coughlin, Tom, American football coach, Aug 2008

Cowher, Bill, American football coach, Nov 2006

Crisler, Herbert Orin, football coach, Feb 1948, *Obit* Oct 1982

Cruyff, Johan, Dutch soccer player and manager, Nov 1981

Daly, Chuck, American basketball coach, Apr 1991, *Obit* Yrbk 2009

Ditka, Mike, American football coach, Oct 1987

Donovan, Billy, American basketball coach, Feb 2007

Dungy, Tony, American football player and coach, Aug 2007

Duva, Lou, American boxing manager and promoter, Nov 1999

Ewbank, Weeb, football coach, June 1969, *Obit* Feb 1999

Ferguson, Alex, Scottish soccer manager, June 2010

Francis, Emile, Apr 1968

Gable, Dan, wrestler and coach, Aug 1997

Gagliardi, John, American football coach, Jan 2008

Giacomin, Eddie, Canadian hockey player, Mar 1968

Gibbs, Joe, American football coach, Apr 1992

Gretzky, Wayne, Canadian hockey player and coach, Feb 1982

Hayes, Woody, American football coach, Feb 1975, *Obit* May 1987

Heinrichs, April, American soccer player and coach, May 2000

Hickman, Herman, Nov 1951, *Obit* July 1958

Holmgren, Mike, American football coach, Oct 2000

Holtz, Lou, American football coach and sportscaster, June 1989

Howland, Ben, American basketball coach, June 2007

Jackson, Phil, American basketball coach, July 1992

Jansen, Dan, American speed skater, Sept 1994

Johnson, Jimmy, American football coach and sportscaster, July 1994

Karolyi, Bela, Romanian-American gymnastic coach, Oct 1996

Keenan, Mike, hockey coach, Mar 1996

Kiphuth, Robert J. H., swimming coach, June 1957, *Obit* Mar 1967

Knight, Bobby, American basketball coach, May 1987

Krzyzewski, Mike, American basketball coach, Jan 1997

Landry, Tom, American football coach, June 1972, *Obit* Apr 2000

Lapchick, Joe, basketball coach, June 1965, *Obit* Oct 1970

Leahy, Frank, football coach, Yrbk 1941, *Obit* Sept 1973

Levy, Marv, football coach, Feb 1998

Lewis, Marvin, American football coach, Nov 2004

Lippi, Marcello, Italian soccer coach, Jan 2006

Little, Lou, American football coach, Nov 1945, *Obit* July 1979

Lombardi, Vince, American football coach, May 1963, *Obit* Nov 1970

Loosli, E. Fritz, Jan 1942

Madden, John, American football coach and sportscaster, Aug 1985

Maddon, Joe, American baseball manager, Sept 2012

Maradona, Diego, Argentine soccer player and coach, Nov 1990, Jan 2006

McCarthy, Joe, baseball manager, May 1948, *Obit* Mar 1978

McKeever, Ed, Nov 1945

McKeon, Jack, American baseball manager, Apr 2004

Munn, Clarence L., Nov 1953

Nelson, Don, American basketball coach, May 2007

O'Connell, Colm, Irish priest, school headmaster and track coach, Jan 2005

Oosterbaan, Bennie, football coach, Yrbk 1949, *Obit* Jan 1991

Osborne, Tom, American university athletic director, Mar 1998

Owen, Steve, football coach, Yrbk 1946, *Obit* July 1964

Parcells, Bill, American football coach, Apr 1991

Parker, Buddy, Yrbk 1955, *Obit* June 1982

Parseghian, Ara, football coach and sportscaster, Feb 1968

Paterno, Joe, American football coach, Feb 1984, *Obit* Yrbk 2012

Pitino, Rick, American basketball coach, Jan 1998

Reeves, Dan, football player and coach, Oct 2001

Reid, Andy, American football coach, Nov 2012

Robinson, Eddie, American football coach, June 1988, *Obit* Yrbk 2007

Ryan, Rex, American football coach, Oct 2010

Sauer, George H., football coach and executive, Nov 1948, *Obit* Apr 1994

Sawyer, Eddie, baseball manager, Nov 1950, *Obit* Jan 1998

Scolari, Luiz Felipe, Brazilian soccer coach, Jan 2006

Shula, Don, American football coach, Mar 1974

Singletary, Mike, American football coach, Mar 1993

Smith, Dean, American basketball coach, Apr 1994

Smith, Lovie, American football coach, Sept 2007

Smith, Mike, American football coach, Sept 2010

Sparano, Tony, American football coach, Jan 2010

Stagg, Amos Alonzo, football coach, Mar 1944, *Obit* Apr 1965

Starr, Bart, American football player and coach, Jan 1968

Thompson, John, American basketball coach, May 1989

Tomlin, Mike, American football coach, Aug 2011

Van Gundy, Jeff, American basketball coach, May 2001

Vitale, Dick, American basketball sportscaster, Jan 2005

Walsh, Bill, American football coach, Nov 1989, *Obit* Yrbk 2007

Weis, Charlie, American football coach, Nov 2007

Wilkinson, Bud, football coach, Apr 1962, *Obit* May 1994

Williams, Doug, American football player and coach, Feb 1999

Williams, Roy, American basketball coach, Mar 2007

Willingham, Tyrone, American football coach, Nov 2002

Yao Bin, Chinese figure skating coach, Jan 2006

Yost, Fielding Harris, *Obit* Oct 1946

Coast Guard officers

Pell, Claiborne, American senator, Mar 1972, *Obit* Yrbk 2009

Stratton, Dorothy C., American psychologist, college dean and Coast Guard officer, June 1943, *Obit* Yrbk 2006

Waesche, Russell Randolph, American Coast Guard admiral, Mar 1945, *Obit* Yrbk 1946

Collaborationists

Doriot, Jacques, French political leader and wartime collaborationist, Nov 1940

Laval, Pierre, French prime minister and convicted traitor, Sept 1940, *Obit* Nov 1945

Quisling, Vidkun, Norwegian traitor, Nov 1940, *Obit* Yrbk 1946

Wang Jingwei, Chinese political leader and collaborationist, May 1940, *Obit* Jan 1945

Collectibles dealers

Hamilton, Charles, American autograph dealer and handwriting expert, July 1976, *Obit* Feb 1997

Collectors

Abrams, Harry N., American publisher, June 1958, *Obit* Jan 1980

Archer, Jeffrey, English novelist, Sept 1988

Bache, Jules Semon, financier and art collector, *Obit* May 1944

Barrett, Clifton Waller, American shipping executive and book collector, Mar 1965

Benjamin, William Evarts, American publisher, *Obit* Mar 1940

Brundage, Avery, American engineer and Olympics executive, Jan 1948, *Obit* Aug 1975

Bruns, Franklin R., May 1954

Chamberlain, Paul M., *Obit* July 1940

Dale, Chester, American investment banker and art collector, Sept 1958, *Obit* Jan 1963

Evans, Herbert McLean, endocrinologist and anatomist, July 1959, *Obit* Apr 1971

Gingrich, Arnold, magazine editor and book collector, Feb 1961, *Obit* Sept 1976

Guggenheim, Peggy, American patron of the arts, Oct 1962, *Obit* Feb 1980

Hirshhorn, Joseph H., American stockbroker, mining executive and art collector, Nov 1966, *Obit* Oct 1981

Hodgkin, Howard, English painter, May 1991

Holladay, Wilhelmina Cole, art collector, Oct 1987

Horner, Henry, American governor, *Obit* Nov 1940

Kress, Samuel H., merchant, Oct 1955

Langlois, Henri, French motion picture historian and collector, Jan 1973, *Obit* Mar 1977

Lansky, Aaron, American collector and distributor of Yiddish books, Jan 1997

Lloyd Webber, Andrew, English composer, June 1982

Mapplethorpe, Robert, American photographer and art collector, May 1989, *Obit* May 1989

Meadows, A. H., American petroleum industry executive, Apr 1960

Mellon, Paul, American philanthropist, Apr 1966, *Obit* Apr 1999

Morton, James F., *Obit* Yrbk 1941

Newell, Edward Theodore, *Obit* Apr 1941

Niarchos, Stavros, Greek shipping executive, May 1958, *Obit* June 1996

Niles, John Jacob, American singer, composer, singer and folklorist, Nov 1959, *Obit* Apr 1980

Otis, Clarence, American restaurant chain executive, Oct 2009

Pick, Behrendt, *Obit* July 1940

Rockefeller, John D., American philanthropist, June 1953, *Obit* Sept 1978

Rockefeller, Nelson A., American vice-president, Mar 1941, Mar 1951, *Obit* Mar 1979

Roosevelt, Franklin D., American president, Mar 1942, *Obit* Apr 1945

Rosenwald, Lessing J., American retail executive and book collector, Feb 1947, *Obit* Aug 1979

Scull, Robert C., American taxi executive and art collector, Apr 1974, *Obit* Feb 1986

Simon, Norton, American financier and art collector, Mar 1968, *Obit* Aug 1993

Tang, David, Chinese retail executive, Jan 2006

Thyssen-Bornemisza, Hans Heinrich, Swiss financier and art collector, Feb 1989, *Obit* Yrbk 2002

Wallace, Lila Acheson, American philanthropist and publisher, May 1956, *Obit* July 1984

Zuloaga, Ignacio, Spanish art collector and painter, *Obit* Yrbk 1945

College administrators

Abbott, Edith, American economist, Sept 1941, *Obit* Oct 1957

Ackerman, Carl William, journalist and college dean, Oct 1945, *Obit* Yrbk 1970

Adams, Arthur S., American mechanical engineer and college president, Jan 1951

Adams, John Cranford, college president, Sept 1958, *Obit* Jan 1987

Adkins, Bertha S., American educator and government official, May 1953, *Obit* Mar 1983

Adler, Cyrus, college president, *Obit* May 1940

Albion, Robert Greenhalgh, historian, May 1954, *Obit* Oct 1983

Allen, Raymond B., college president and physician, Mar 1952, *Obit* May 1986

Ames, Joseph S., American physicist and university president, *Obit* Aug 1943

Angell, James Rowland, American psychologist and university president, Yrbk 1940, *Obit* Mar 1949

Anspach, Charles L., American college president, Sept 1956

Bacon, George P., American physicist and college dean, *Obit* Nov 1941

Bailey, Guy W., American university president, *Obit* Yrbk 1940

Baltimore, David, American microbiologist, July 1983

Barr, John A., American lawyer and college dean, Jan 1961, *Obit* Mar 1979

Barrett, Edward W., journalist and college dean, Feb 1947, *Obit* Feb 1990

Barringer, Paul B., American physician and college president, *Obit* Mar 1941

Beadle, George W., American geneticist and college president, Apr 1956, *Obit* Aug 1989

Begg, Alexander Swanson, American physician and college dean, *Obit* Nov 1940

Belkin, Samuel, American rabbi and college president, Nov 1952, *Obit* June 1976

Belluschi, Pietro, American architect, Feb 1959, *Obit* Apr 1994

Bender, James F., speech educator and business consultant, May 1949, *Obit* Mar 1998

Berelson, Bernard, American librarian and sociologist, July 1961, *Obit* Nov 1979

Berry, Edward Wilber, American paleontologist, *Obit* Oct 1945

Bevis, Howard L., American university president, Jan 1940, Nov 1950, *Obit* June 1968

Bissell, Claude T., May 1959

Blake, Francis G., American physician, Jan 1943, *Obit* Mar 1952

Blanding, Sarah Gibson, college president, June 1946, *Obit* Apr 1985

Bliss, A. Richard, American pharmacologist and college dean, *Obit* Oct 1941

Bloustein, Edward J., college president, Nov 1965, *Obit* Feb 1990

Boe, Lars Wilhelm, American clergyman and college president, *Obit* Feb 1943

Bok, Derek Curtis, college president, July 1971

Bollinger, Lee C., American university president, Feb 2008

Boren, David L., American governor, senator and college president, Nov 1989

Botstein, Leon, college president, Aug 1996

Bowen, William G., American college president and foundation official, May 1973

Bowker, Albert H., American college administrator, Jan 1966, *Obit* Yrbk 2008

Boyer, Ernest L., American educator and foundation official, Jan 1988, *Obit* Feb 1996

Brademas, John, American congressman and university president, May 1977

Bragdon, Helen D., Feb 1951

Brandenburg, William A., *Obit* Yrbk 1940

Brewster, Kingman, American college president and diplomat, May 1964, Sept 1979, *Obit* Jan 1989

Briggs, Eugene S., Oct 1948

Bronk, Detlev Wulf, American college president and biophysicist, Oct 1949, *Obit* Jan 1976

Brown, Harold, American Secretary of defense and physicist, Sept 1961, Oct 1977

Browne, Sidney Jane, *Obit* Oct 1941

Buchanan, Scott Milross, American college dean and educational consultant, Sept 1962, *Obit* May 1968

Buck, Paul Herman, historian, July 1955, *Obit* Apr 1989

Bunting-Smith, Mary Ingraham, microbiologist and college president, June 1967, *Obit* Apr 1998

Burchard, John E., Apr 1958, *Obit* Mar 1976

Burdell, Edwin S., Feb 1952

Burdick, Charles K., *Obit* Aug 1940

Burns, J. A., *Obit* Oct 1940

Butler, Nicholas Murray, American educator, Nov 1940, *Obit* Yrbk 1947

Butz, Earl, American Secretary of agriculture, July 1972, *Obit* Yrbk 2008

Calfee, John Edward, *Obit* Jan 1941

Carlson, William S., college president, July 1952, *Obit* July 1994

Carr, Robert Kenneth, Apr 1961

Carroll, Thomas H., July 1962, *Obit* Oct 1964

Carson, Benjamin, American neurosurgeon, May 1997

Caswell, Hollis L., college president, July 1956, *Obit* Sept 1989

Cates, Gilbert, American film director, producer and college dean, Mar 1997, *Obit* Yrbk 2012

Cavanaugh, John J., Mar 1947, *Obit* Feb 1980

Chapin, Schuyler, American municipal arts administrator, Feb 1974, *Obit* Yrbk 2009

Chase, Harry Woodburn, June 1948, *Obit* June 1955

Clark, Charles E., American judge, July 1959, *Obit* Mar 1964

Cleveland, Harlan, American diplomat and university president, Sept 1961, *Obit* Yrbk 2008

Clyde, George D., July 1958, *Obit* May 1972

Coggeshall, Lowell T., college administrator and physician, Sept 1963, *Obit* Jan 1988

Cohen, Wilbur Joseph, American Secretary of health, education and welfare, Sept 1968, *Obit* July 1987

Cole, Johnnetta B., American anthropologist and museum director, Aug 1994

Coleman, John R., Oct 1974

Compton, Wilson, Apr 1952, *Obit* May 1967

Conway, Jill K., Australian historian and college president, June 1991

Crawshaw, William Henry, *Obit* Aug 1940

Damon, Lindsay Todd, *Obit* Jan 1940

Daniel, Robert Prentiss, May 1952, *Obit* Mar 1968

Daniels, Arthur Hill, *Obit* Apr 1940

Darden, Colgate W., Sept 1948

David, Donald K., Feb 1948, *Obit* June 1979

Davis, Herbert John, Jan 1940, *Obit* May 1967

Davis, Jess H., Jan 1956

Day, Edmund, Sept 1946, *Obit* Apr 1951

De Kiewiet, C. W., college president and historian, July 1953, *Obit* Apr 1986

DeBakey, Michael E., American surgeon and inventor, Mar 1964, *Obit* Yrbk 2008

Dickey, John Sloan, college president, Apr 1955, *Obit* Apr 1991

Dillard, James Hardy, *Obit* Sept 1940

Dodds, Harold W., Yrbk 1945, *Obit* Jan 1981

Dodge, Bayard, Feb 1948, *Obit* July 1972

Doherty, Robert E., Sept 1949, *Obit* Yrbk 1950

Doster, James J., *Obit* Yrbk 1942

Drinan, Robert F., American priest, lawyer and congressman, June 1971, *Obit* Yrbk 2007

DuBridge, Lee A., college president and physicist, June 1948, *Obit* Mar 1994

Duffey, Joseph D., college administrator, Mar 1971

Dunlop, John T., American economist, labor relations expert and Secretary of labor, Apr 1951, *Obit* Yrbk 2004

Dunton, Arnold Davidson, Canadian college president, Jan 1959, *Obit* Apr 1987

Durgin, C. T., Sept 1954, *Obit* May 1965

Dye, Marie, Yrbk 1948

Dykstra, Clarence A., American university president, Jan 1941, *Obit* June 1950

Edwards, James Burrows, American dentist, governor and Secretary of energy, Nov 1982

Egeberg, Roger Olaf, government official, physician and college dean, Jan 1970, *Obit* Nov 1997

Eisenhower, Milton Stover, American college president, diplomat and government official, Yrbk 1946, *Obit* July 1985

Eldridge, Edward H., *Obit* June 1941

Eliot, Thomas Hopkinson, congressman, political scientist and dean, May 1942, *Obit* Jan 1992

Ellingson, Mark, college president, Sept 1957, *Obit* Apr 1993

Elliott, Harriet Wiseman, college dean, July 1940, *Obit* Sept 1947

Elliott, Osborn, American journalist and college dean, Jan 1978, *Obit* Yrbk 2008

Ellis, Elmer, college president, July 1962

Engleman, J. O., *Obit* Nov 1943

Etherington, Edwin D., stock exchange official and college president, Apr 1966, *Obit* Apr 2001

Eurich, Alvin C., educator, June 1949, *Obit* Aug 1987

Evans, Daniel Jackson, American senator and governor, Aug 1975

Eyring, Henry, chemist, Oct 1961

Fackenthal, Frank D., Feb 1949, *Obit* Nov 1968

Fagg, Fred D., Feb 1956, *Obit* Jan 1982

Faust, Clarence H., Mar 1952, *Obit* Aug 1975

Faust, Drew Gilpin, American historian and college president, July 2007

Felix, Robert Hanna, psychiatrist, Apr 1957, *Obit* May 1990

Fellows, George Emory, American historian and university president, *Obit* Mar 1942

Fels, William C., Apr 1959, *Obit* Jan 1965

Few, William Preston, college president, *Obit* Yrbk 1940

Fine, Benjamin, Mar 1961

Fischer, John H., American college dean and president, July 1960, *Obit* Yrbk 2010

Fitch, Robert Elliot, Apr 1962

Fleming, Robben W., American university president, Yrbk 1970, *Obit* Yrbk 2010

Flickinger, Roy Caston, *Obit* Aug 1942

Foakes-Jackson, F. J., *Obit* Jan 1942

Foster, Richard C., *Obit* Jan 1942

Fox, John McDill, *Obit* May 1940

Frank, Glenn, *Obit* Nov 1940

Franks, Oliver Shewell Franks, British diplomat, Mar 1948, *Obit* Jan 1993

Frazer, Spaulding, *Obit* Apr 1940

Fred, Edwin Broun, bacteriologist and college president, Yrbk 1950

French, Robert W., Oct 1959

Friday, William Clyde, college president, Apr 1958, *Obit* Yrbk 2013

Futter, Ellen Victoria, American college president and museum director, Oct 1985

Gale, Henry Gordon, *Obit* Jan 1943

Gallagher, Buell G., college president, May 1953, *Obit* Jan 1979

Ganfield, William Arthur, *Obit* Yrbk 1940

Garrison, Lloyd Kirkham, lawyer and reformer, June 1947, *Obit* Nov 1991

Gates, Robert M., American Secretary of defense, Apr 1992, May 2007, Mar 2009

Gauss, D. Christian, Apr 1945, *Obit* Yrbk 1951

Gerbner, George, American university dean and television critic, Aug 1983, *Obit* Yrbk 2006

Giddens, Anthony, British sociologist and college administrator, Apr 1998

Gideonse, Harry D., college president, May 1940, *Obit* May 1985

Gifford, Chloe, Mar 1959

Gildersleeve, Virginia C., Aug 1941, *Obit* Sept 1965

Ginger, Lyman V., May 1958

Ginsberg, Mitchell I., social worker and municipal official, June 1971, *Obit* May 1996

Giral, Jose, May 1946

Glennan, T. Keith, American NASA official, Oct 1950, *Obit* June 1995

Goheen, Robert F., American college president, Jan 1958, *Obit* Yrbk 2008

Goma y Tomas, Isidro, *Obit* Oct 1940

Gould, Laurence McKinley, explorer and college president, Jan 1978, *Obit* Aug 1995

Gould, Samuel B., educator, Jan 1958, *Obit* Sept 1997

Gray, Hanna Holborn, American historian and college president, Mar 1979

Grayson, C. Jackson, Sept 1972

Gregg, Milton F., Oct 1955

Gregorian, Vartan, American foundation official, Oct 1985

Griffith, Ernest S., political scientist, Oct 1947, *Obit* Apr 1997

Griswold, A. Whitney, American college president, Apr 1950, *Obit* June 1963

Griswold, Erwin N., American solicitor general and law school dean, Oct 1956, *Obit* Jan 1995

Gross, Mason W., June 1969, *Obit* Jan 1978

Gross, Paul Magnus, chemist, May 1963, *Obit* June 1986

Gupta, Mahabir P., Indian pharmacologist, Jan 2005

Haggard, William David, *Obit* Mar 1940

Hammon, William McDowell, physician, Sept 1957, *Obit* Nov 1989

Hancher, Virgil M., Feb 1957, *Obit* Mar 1965

Hannah, John A., American college president, Oct 1952, *Obit* Apr 1991

Harada, Tasuku, Japanese college teacher and president, *Obit* Mar 1940

Hardin, Clifford M., American Secretary of agriculture, May 1969, *Obit* Yrbk 2010

Harnwell, Gaylord Probasco, June 1956

Harris, Patricia, American cabinet member, Yrbk 1965, *Obit* May 1985

Hartnett, Robert C., priest, periodical editor and educator, Yrbk 1949

Hatcher, Harlan H., literary critic, author and historian, Oct 1955, *Obit* May 1998

Hatoyama, Ichiro, Japanese prime minister, May 1955, *Obit* May 1959

Hawkes, Anna L. Rose, Oct 1956

Hawkes, Herbert E., *Obit* June 1943

Hayakawa, S. I., American senator and educator, Nov 1959, Jan 1977, *Obit* Apr 1992

Heald, Henry Townley, American civil engineer, Feb 1952, *Obit* Jan 1976

Healy, Timothy Stafford, priest, university president and library director, Jan 1993, *Obit* Jan 1993

Henderson, Donald A., American public health scientist and college dean, Mar 2002

Hendl, Walter, American conductor, college president and music teacher, June 1955

Henry, David Dodds, college president, June 1966, *Obit* Nov 1995

Herzog, Paul M., college dean, July 1945, *Obit* Jan 1987

Hesburgh, Theodore Martin, American priest and college president, Jan 1955, July 1982

Hester, James M., June 1962

Heyns, Roger W., college administrator, Yrbk 1968, *Obit* Nov 1995

Hildreth, Horace Augustus, governor, Oct 1948, *Obit* July 1988

Hill, Harry W., American admiral, July 1950, *Obit* Sept 1971

Hitch, Charles J., American college president, Nov 1970, *Obit* Nov 1995

Hockfield, Susan, American neurobiologist and college president, Apr 2008

Holley, Edward G., American librarian and college dean, June 1974

Hollomon, J. Herbert, college president and government official, Mar 1964, *Obit* Aug 1985

Holt, Andrew David, college president, Nov 1949, *Obit* Sept 1987

Holt, Hamilton, periodical editor, pacifist and college president, Yrbk 1947, *Obit* May 1951

Hopkins, Ernest Martin, Oct 1944, *Obit* Oct 1964

Hopkins, Louis Bertram, *Obit* Sept 1940

Horner, Matina, educator, July 1973

Hornig, Donald F., chemist, university president and presidential adviser, May 1964, *Obit* Yrbk 2013

Horton, Mildred McAfee, college president and naval officer, Sept 1942, *Obit* Jan 1995

Hoskins, Lewis M., Sept 1950

Hottel, Althea Kratz, Oct 1948

Houston, David Franklin, secretary of agriculture and the treasury, *Obit* Oct 1940

Hovde, Bryn J., Jan 1946, *Obit* Oct 1954

Howell, William Henry, *Obit* Mar 1945

Hutchins, Robert Maynard, American university president, Yrbk 1940, Feb 1954, *Obit* July 1977

Hutton, Maurice, *Obit* May 1940

Jackson, Shirley Ann, American physicist and college president, July 1999

James, F. Cyril, Canadian economist and college administrator, Oct 1956

Johnson, Arthur Newhall, *Obit* Sept 1940

Johnson, Charles Spurgeon, American sociologist and university president, Nov 1946, *Obit* Jan 1957

Johnson, Mordecai Wyatt, American college president and clergyman, Apr 1941

Johnson, Robert L., college president and government official, Mar 1948, *Obit* Feb 1966

Jones, Lewis Webster, Oct 1958

Jordan, I. King, American university president, Jan 1991

Jordan, W. K., Mar 1955, *Obit* July 1980

Kahn, Alfred E., American economist and government official, Mar 1979, *Obit* Yrbk 2011

Kalb, Marvin, television reporter and college administrator, July 1987

Kean, Thomas H., American governor and college president, July 1985

Keeney, Barnaby C., Mar 1956, *Obit* Aug 1980

Kemeny, John G., American mathematician and college president, Feb 1971, *Obit* Feb 1993

Kennedy, Donald, physiologist and college president, July 1984

Keppel, Francis C., American educator, May 1963, *Obit* Apr 1990

Kerr, Clark, American educator, Apr 1961, *Obit* May 2004

Kerrey, Bob, American senator and university president, Feb 1991

Killian, James Rhyne, American college president and presidential adviser, Feb 1949, May 1959, *Obit* Mar 1988

Kirk, Grayson Louis, American college president, May 1951, *Obit* Jan 1998

Klawe, Maria, Canadian computer scientist, college dean and painter, June 2013

Kleinsmid, Rufus B. von, June 1958, *Obit* Sept 1964

Knight, Douglas M., May 1964

Kraushaar, Otto F., college president, Nov 1949, *Obit* Nov 1989

Kreps, Juanita Morris, American Secretary of commerce, June 1977, *Obit* Yrbk 2010

Lambert, W. V., Nov 1955

Laubach, Frank Charles, American missionary and educator, Feb 1950, *Obit* Sept 1970

Laycock, Craven, *Obit* May 1940

Lederle, John W., American college president, Feb 1961, *Obit* Yrbk 2007

Leigh, Robert Devore, college president and dean, June 1947, *Obit* Mar 1961

Lillard, George W., *Obit* Yrbk 1940

Lindley, Ernest Hiram, *Obit* Oct 1940

Litchfield, Edward H., Nov 1953, *Obit* May 1968

Lloyd, Wesley P., educator, Jan 1952, *Obit* May 1977

Lowell, A. Lawrence, American college president and political scientist, *Obit* Feb 1943

Lyons, Harry, Oct 1957

MacCracken, Henry Noble, college president, Sept 1940, *Obit* June 1970

MacLean, Malcolm Shaw, July 1940

Mack, Pauline Beery, chemist and college dean, Yrbk 1950

Madeleva, Mary, American nun, poet and college president, Feb 1942, *Obit* Oct 1964

Malcolm, George A., Nov 1954

Malott, Deane W., college president, Mar 1951, *Obit* Nov 1996

Mark, Herman Francis, American chemist and college dean, May 1961, *Obit* June 1992

Marshak, Robert Eugene, American college president and physicist, July 1973, *Obit* Feb 1993

Martin, Collier Ford, *Obit* May 1941

Martin, Frank L., American newspaper editor and college dean, *Obit* Sept 1941

Martino, Gaetano, May 1956, *Obit* Oct 1967

Marvin, Cloyd H., Yrbk 1949, *Obit* June 1969

Massey, Walter E., American physicist and college president, June 1997

Mathews, David, American Secretary of health, education and welfare, Jan 1976

Mathews, Shailer, biblical scholar and college dean, *Obit* Yrbk 1941

Mayer, Jean, nutritionist and college president, Sept 1970, *Obit* Feb 1993

McBride, Katharine E., American psychologist and college president, Feb 1942, *Obit* July 1976

McCormick, Lynde Dupuy, admiral, Feb 1952, *Obit* Oct 1956

McDiarmid, E. W., librarian and college dean, Yrbk 1948

McGill, William J., college president, June 1971, *Obit* Jan 1998

McGinley, Laurence J., college president and priest, June 1949, *Obit* Oct 1992

McHale, Kathryn, Jan 1947, *Obit* Yrbk 1957

McIntosh, Millicent Carey, American college dean and president, July 1947, *Obit* Mar 2001

McKenzie, Roderick Duncan, *Obit* Jan 1940

McLaughlin, Leo Plowden, college president and priest, May 1970, *Obit* Nov 1996

McNutt, Paul V., American governor, Feb 1940, *Obit* May 1955

Mendenhall, Thomas Corwin, college president, May 1960, *Obit* Sept 1998

Meng, John J., college president, Nov 1961, *Obit* Apr 1988

Millett, John David, American university president, Feb 1953, *Obit* Jan 1994

Million; John Wilson, *Obit* Nov 1941

Moos, Malcolm Charles, political scientist and college president, Nov 1968

Morehouse, Daniel Walter, *Obit* Mar 1941

Moron, Alonzo G., American college president and government official, Oct 1949, *Obit* Yrbk 1971

Morrill, J. L., Feb 1951

Morton, Florrinell, librarian and college dean, July 1961

Muench, Aloisius, Apr 1960, *Obit* Apr 1962

Murphy, Franklin D., American physician, college administrator and newspaper executive, Mar 1971, *Obit* Aug 1994

Napolitano, Janet, American Secretary of homeland security, Oct 2004, Mar 2009

Nason, John W., American college president, July 1953, *Obit* Feb 2002

Neal, Herbert Vincent, *Obit* Mar 1940

Neilson, William Allan, Scottish-American literary scholar, *Obit* Mar 1946

Nicolson, Marjorie Hope, literary critic and college dean, Apr 1940, *Obit* June 1981

Oettinger, Katherine B., government official and child welfare worker, Nov 1957, *Obit* Jan 1998

Paige, Rod, American Secretary of education, July 2001

Palmer, Albert DeForest, *Obit* Jan 1940

Pannell, Anne Gary, Nov 1950

Park, Rosemary, American college president, Jan 1964, *Obit* Yrbk 2004

Parran, Thomas J., American surgeon general, Aug 1940, *Obit* Apr 1968

Pate, Martha B., college president, May 1947, *Obit* July 1983

Patrick, Mary Mills, college president, *Obit* Mar 1940

Patterson, Frederick D., American college president and veterinarian, June 1947, *Obit* June 1988

Pearson, Jay F. W., Yrbk 1953, *Obit* Oct 1965

Pelli, Cesar, American architect, Apr 1983

Penniman, Josiah Harmer, *Obit* June 1941

Perkins, James A., American college president, Apr 1964, *Obit* Nov 1998

Peterson, Martha Elizabeth, American college president, Feb 1969, *Obit* Yrbk 2006

Pope, Liston, Apr 1956, *Obit* June 1974

Price, Don Krasher, American political scientist and college dean, Feb 1967, *Obit* Sept 1995

Pusey, Nathan Marsh, American college president, Yrbk 1953, *Obit* Feb 2002

Putnam, James William, *Obit* Mar 1940

Putnam, Thomas M., *Obit* Nov 1942

Quinn, Daniel Joseph, *Obit* Mar 1940

Rainey, Homer Price, college president, Nov 1946, *Obit* Feb 1986

Ramphele, Mamphela, South African college administrator and anthropologist, July 1997

Rees, Mina Spiegel, American mathematician and computer scientist, Nov 1957, *Obit* Jan 1998

Reinhardt, Aurelia Henry, American college president and religious official, May 1941, *Obit* Feb 1948

Renne, Roland Roger, college president and agricultural economist, June 1963

Rice, Condoleezza, American Secretary of state, Apr 2001

Richards, Charles Russ, *Obit* Jan 1941

Richards, Lloyd G., American actor and theatrical director, Oct 1987, *Obit* Yrbk 2007

Richmond, Charles Alexander, *Obit* Sept 1940

Rines, Robert H., American lawyer, inventor, physicist and hunter of Loch Ness monster, Jan 2003, *Obit* Yrbk 2010

Roberts, George Lucas, *Obit* Apr 1941

Roberts, Oral, American evangelist, Nov 1960, *Obit* Feb 2010

Robinson, Frederick B., *Obit* Yrbk 1941

Robinson, Spottswood W., judge, Mar 1962, *Obit* Jan 1999

Rockefeller, John D., American senator, Mar 1978

Rodin, Judith, American foundation official, June 1999

Rostow, Eugene Victor, American lawyer and

economist, Apr 1961, *Obit* Yrbk 2003

Ruder, David S., American lawyer, Nov 1988

Russell, Charles Hinton, American newspaper publisher and governor, Yrbk 1955, *Obit* Nov 1989

Russell, James Earl, *Obit* Yrbk 1945

Russell, William F., Apr 1947, *Obit* June 1956

Rutledge, Wiley Blount, American Supreme Court justice, May 1943, *Obit* Oct 1949

Sachar, Abram Leon, historian and college president, Nov 1949, *Obit* Sept 1993

Sammartino, Peter, college president, Yrbk 1958, *Obit* May 1992

Sanford, Terry, American senator, Nov 1961, *Obit* July 1998

Satcher, David, American surgeon general, Feb 1997

Sawhill, John C., American college president and conservationist, Apr 1979, *Obit* Yrbk 2000

Sawyer, John E., college president and foundation official, July 1961, *Obit* Apr 1995

Schmidt, Benno C., American educator, Aug 1986

Schmoke, Kurt, American college dean and mayor, Feb 1995

Schottland, Charles Irwin, college president and government official, Yrbk 1956, *Obit* Sept 1995

Schurman, Jacob G., philosopher, college president and diplomat, *Obit* Oct 1942

Scott, James B., lawyer, *Obit* Aug 1943

Seaborg, Glenn, American chemist, July 1948, Yrbk 1961, *Obit* May 1999

Sears, Robert Richardson, psychologist and college dean, July 1952, *Obit* Aug 1989

Seidman, L. William, American government official and college dean, Sept 1976, *Obit* Yrbk 2009

Seitz, Frederick, American physicist, Apr 1956, *Obit* Yrbk 2008

Seymour, Charles, May 1941, *Obit* Nov 1963

Shalala, Donna, American Secretary of health and human services and college president, Mar 1991

Shawkey, Morris Purdy, *Obit* Apr 1941

Shelly, Mary Jo, educator, Oct 1951, *Obit* Sept 1976

Shera, Jesse Hauk, American librarian and dean, June 1964, *Obit* June 1982

Shuster, George Nauman, college president, Jan 1941, Oct 1960, *Obit* Mar 1977

Silber, John R., American college president, Feb 1984, *Obit* Yrbk 2012

Simmons, Adele Smith, American college president and foundation official, May 1991

Simmons, Ruth, American college president, Jan 1996

Simpson, Alan, college president, Feb 1964, *Obit* July 1998

Sisco, Joseph J., American diplomat, Jan 1972, *Obit* Yrbk 2005

Smith, Albert W., *Obit* Oct 1942

Smith, Courtney, American college president, Yrbk 1959, *Obit* Mar 1969

Smith, Sidney, Jan 1955, *Obit* May 1959

Smith, Virginia B., American college president, June 1978, *Obit* Yrbk 2010

Smith, Wilbur Fisk, *Obit* Sept 1940

Snavely, Guy E., Apr 1951

Soderberg, C. Richard, Feb 1958, *Obit* Jan 1980

Sovern, Michael I., Feb 1981

Spain, Frances Lander, American librarian and college administrator, June 1960

Sparling, Edward J., July 1948

Sperry, Willard Learoyd, theologian, May 1952, *Obit* Sept 1954

Sproul, Robert Gordon, July 1945, *Obit* Nov 1975

Stahr, Elvis J., American Secretary of the army, Sept 1961, *Obit* Feb 1999

Starr, Chauncey, American physicist, Apr 1954, *Obit* Yrbk 2007

Stassen, Harold E., American lawyer, governor and presidential candidate, May 1940, Mar 1948, *Obit* May 2001

Sterling, John Ewart Wallace, college president, Jan 1951, *Obit* Aug 1985

Stern, Robert A. M., American architect and college dean, June 2000

Stevenson, William E., lawyer, college president and diplomat, Nov 1943, *Obit* May 1985

Stoddard, George Dinsmore, American psychologist and college president, July 1946, *Obit* Feb 1982

Stone, Abraham, Mar 1952, *Obit* Oct 1959

Storey, Robert Gerald, Nov 1953

Stratton, Julius Adams, American physicist and college president, May 1963, *Obit* Aug 1994

Sullivan, Louis W., American Secretary of health and human services, July 1989

Summers, Lawrence H., American presidential adviser and former Secretary of the treasury, July 2002

Sykes, Richard Eddy, *Obit* Nov 1942

Taylor, Harold, college president, Sept 1946, *Obit* Apr 1993

Terrell, Daniel V., Apr 1954

Tilghman, Shirley M., Canadian molecular biologist and university president, June 2006

Topping, Norman H., physician and college president, Feb 1959, *Obit* Jan 1998

Towle, Katherine A., college dean, Jan 1949, *Obit* May 1986

Trotter, Frank Butler, *Obit* Apr 1940

Truman, David Bicknell, American college president and political scientist, Jan 1972, *Obit* Yrbk 2004

Trussell, Ray E., municipal hospital commissioner and physician, Jan 1971, *Obit* Feb 2000

Tufts, James Hayden, *Obit* Sept 1942

Van Dusen, Henry Pitney, seminary president, Yrbk 1950, *Obit* Apr 1975

Vance, William Reynolds, *Obit* Yrbk 1940

Vincent, George Edgar, sociologist, college president and foundation official, *Obit* Mar 1941

Waite, Alice Vinton, *Obit* May 1943

Walden, Percy Talbot, *Obit* May 1943

Walker, Eric A., college president, Mar 1959, *Obit* Apr 1995

Ward, Paul L., American historian and college president, Mar 1962, *Obit* Yrbk 2006

Warner, John Christian, chemist, Oct 1950, *Obit* July 1989

Warren, William C., law school dean, Jan 1960, *Obit* Yrbk 2000

Weaver, Robert Clifton, American Secretary of housing and urban development and educator, Apr 1961, *Obit* Oct 1997

Weigle, Luther Allan, professor of religious education and dean, Mar 1946, *Obit* Oct 1976

Weinstein, Allen, American historian and archivist, June 2006

Wells, Herman B., American college president, Apr 1966, *Obit* Aug 2000

Wesley, Charles Harris, American historian and university president, Mar 1944, *Obit* Oct 1987

Wexler, Jacqueline Grennan, college president, Mar 1970, *Obit* Yrbk 2012

Wharton, Clifton R., American college president and pension plan administrator, Feb 1987

Whitaker, Douglas, Nov 1951, *Obit* Yrbk 1973

White, Herbert S., librarian, May 1968

Wiesner, Jerome B., American electrical engineer and college president, Yrbk 1961, *Obit* Jan 1995

Wilcox, Francis Orlando, government official, Apr 1962, *Obit* Apr 1985

Wilson, Logan, college administrator, Yrbk 1956, *Obit* Jan 1991

Wilson, O. Meredith, college president, July 1967, *Obit* Feb 1999

Wilson, O. W., Oct 1966, *Obit* Yrbk 1972

Wood, James Madison, Feb 1947, *Obit* Yrbk 1958

Woodbridge, Frederick James Eugene, American philosopher, *Obit* July 1940

Wright, Benjamin Fletcher, professors of government and college president, July 1955, *Obit* Mar 1977

Wriston, Henry M., May 1952, *Obit* May 1978

Wu Yifang, Chinese educator and feminist, Aug 1945, *Obit* Jan 1986

Yoder, Albert Henry, *Obit* Nov 1940

Young, Philip, government official and college dean, Yrbk 1951, *Obit* Mar 1987

College deans

Abbott, Edith, American economist, Sept 1941, *Obit* Oct 1957

Adkins, Bertha S., American educator and government official, May 1953, *Obit* Mar 1983

Bacon, George P., American physicist and college dean, *Obit* Nov 1941

Begg, Alexander Swanson, American physician and college dean, *Obit* Nov 1940

Bender, James F., speech educator and business consultant, May 1949, *Obit* Mar 1998

Berelson, Bernard, American librarian and sociologist, July 1961, *Obit* Nov 1979

Berry, Edward Wilber, American paleontologist, *Obit* Oct 1945

Blake, Francis G., American physician, Jan 1943, *Obit* Mar 1952

Blanding, Sarah Gibson, college president, June 1946, *Obit* Apr 1985

Bollinger, Lee C., American university president, Feb 2008

Bowker, Albert H., American college administrator, Jan 1966, *Obit* Yrbk 2008

Bragdon, Helen D., Feb 1951

Buchanan, Scott Milross, American college dean and educational consultant, Sept 1962, *Obit* May 1968

Buck, Paul Herman, historian, July 1955, *Obit* Apr 1989

Buergenthal, Thomas, American judge and human rights activist, Jan 2009

Burdell, Edwin S., Feb 1952

Burdick, Charles K., *Obit* Aug 1940

Clark, Charles E., American judge, July 1959, *Obit* Mar 1964

Clyde, George D., July 1958, *Obit* May 1972

David, Donald K., Feb 1948, *Obit* June 1979

Doster, James J., *Obit* Yrbk 1942

Drinan, Robert F., American priest, lawyer and congressman, June 1971, *Obit* Yrbk 2007

Dunlop, John T., American economist, labor relations expert and Secretary of labor, Apr 1951, *Obit* Yrbk 2004

Dye, Marie, Yrbk 1948

Egeberg, Roger Olaf, government official, physician and college dean, Jan 1970, *Obit* Nov 1997

Eliot, Thomas Hopkinson, congressman, political scientist and dean, May 1942, *Obit* Jan 1992

Elliott, Harriet Wiseman, college dean, July 1940, *Obit* Sept 1947

Fagg, Fred D., Feb 1956, *Obit* Jan 1982

Faust, Drew Gilpin, American historian and college president, July 2007

Felix, Robert Hanna, psychiatrist, Apr 1957, *Obit* May 1990

Fischer, John H., American college dean and president, July 1960, *Obit* Yrbk 2010

Flickinger, Roy Caston, *Obit* Aug 1942

Foakes-Jackson, F. J., *Obit* Jan 1942

Fox, John McDill, *Obit* May 1940

Frazer, Spaulding, *Obit* Apr 1940

French, Robert W., Oct 1959

Gale, Henry Gordon, *Obit* Jan 1943

Gerbner, George, American university dean and television critic, Aug 1983, *Obit* Yrbk 2006

Gildersleeve, Virginia C., Aug 1941, *Obit* Sept 1965

Ginger, Lyman V., May 1958

Ginsberg, Mitchell I., social worker and municipal official, June 1971, *Obit* May 1996

Grayson, C. Jackson, Sept 1972

Griswold, Erwin N., American solicitor general and law school dean, Oct 1956, *Obit* Jan 1995

Hammon, William McDowell, physician, Sept 1957, *Obit* Nov 1989

Harris, Patricia, American cabinet member, Yrbk 1965, *Obit* May 1985

Hawkes, Anna L. Rose, Oct 1956

Hawkes, Herbert E., *Obit* June 1943

Henderson, Donald A., American public health scientist and college dean, Mar 2002

Herzog, Paul M., college dean, July 1945, *Obit* Jan 1987

Hester, James M., June 1962

Holley, Edward G., American librarian and college dean, June 1974

Horner, Matina, educator, July 1973

Hoskins, Lewis M., Sept 1950

Hottel, Althea Kratz, Oct 1948

Johnson, Arthur Newhall, *Obit* Sept 1940

Kagan, Elena, American Supreme Court justice, June 2007

Kahn, Alfred E., American economist and government official, Mar 1979, *Obit* Yrbk 2011

Keeney, Barnaby C., Mar 1956, *Obit* Aug 1980

Keppel, Francis C., American educator, May 1963, *Obit* Apr 1990

Laycock, Craven, *Obit* May 1940

Leigh, Robert Devore, college president and dean, June 1947, *Obit* Mar 1961

Litchfield, Edward H., Nov 1953, *Obit* May 1968

Lloyd, Wesley P., educator, Jan 1952, *Obit* May 1977

Lyons, Harry, Oct 1957

Malcolm, George A., Nov 1954

Martin, Collier Ford, *Obit* May 1941

Martin, Frank L., American newspaper editor and college dean, *Obit* Sept 1941

McDiarmid, E. W., librarian and college dean, Yrbk 1948

McNutt, Paul V., American governor, Feb 1940, *Obit* May 1955

Morton, Florrinell, librarian and college dean, July 1961

Muench, Aloisius, Apr 1960, *Obit* Apr 1962

Pannell, Anne Gary, Nov 1950

Parran, Thomas J., American surgeon general, Aug 1940, *Obit* Apr 1968

Pate, Martha B., college president, May 1947, *Obit* July 1983

Peterson, Martha Elizabeth, American college president, Feb 1969, *Obit* Yrbk 2006

Putnam, Thomas M., *Obit* Nov 1942

Roberts, George Lucas, *Obit* Apr 1941

Robinson, Spottswood W., judge, Mar 1962, *Obit* Jan 1999

Ruder, David S., American lawyer, Nov 1988

Russell, William F., Apr 1947, *Obit* June 1956

Rutledge, Wiley Blount, American Supreme Court justice, May 1943, *Obit* Oct 1949

Schmidt, Benno C., American educator, Aug 1986

Schmoke, Kurt, American college dean and mayor, Feb 1995

Scott, James B., lawyer, *Obit* Aug 1943

Sears, Robert Richardson, psychologist and college dean, July 1952, *Obit* Aug 1989

Smith, Sidney, Jan 1955, *Obit* May 1959

Soderberg, C. Richard, Feb 1958, *Obit* Jan 1980

Starr, Chauncey, American physicist, Apr 1954, *Obit* Yrbk 2007

Stone, Abraham, Mar 1952, *Obit* Oct 1959

Storey, Robert Gerald, Nov 1953

Towle, Katherine A., college dean, Jan 1949, *Obit* May 1986

Trussell, Ray E., municipal hospital commissioner and physician, Jan 1971, *Obit* Feb 2000

Vance, William Reynolds, *Obit* Yrbk 1940

Vincent, George Edgar, sociologist, college president and foundation official, *Obit* Mar 1941

Waite, Alice Vinton, *Obit* May 1943

Warren, William C., law school dean, Jan 1960, *Obit* Yrbk 2000

White, Herbert S., librarian, May 1968

Wilcox, Francis Orlando, government official, Apr 1962, *Obit* Apr 1985

Wilson, O. W., Oct 1966, *Obit* Yrbk 1972

Woodbridge, Frederick James Eugene, American philosopher, *Obit* July 1940

Young, Philip, government official and college dean, Yrbk 1951, *Obit* Mar 1987

College presidents

Adams, Arthur S., American mechanical engineer and college president, Jan 1951

Adams, John Cranford, college president, Sept 1958, *Obit* Jan 1987

Adler, Cyrus, college president, *Obit* May 1940

Allen, Raymond B., college president and physician, Mar 1952, *Obit* May 1986

Ames, Joseph S., American physicist and university president, *Obit* Aug 1943

Angell, James Rowland, American psychologist and university president, Yrbk 1940, *Obit* Mar 1949

Anspach, Charles L., American college president, Sept 1956

Bailey, Guy W., American university president, *Obit* Yrbk 1940

Barringer, Paul B., American physician and college president, *Obit* Mar 1941

Bevis, Howard L., American university president, Jan 1940, Nov 1950, *Obit* June 1968

Bloustein, Edward J., college president, Nov 1965, *Obit* Feb 1990

Bok, Derek Curtis, college president, July 1971

Boren, David L., American governor, senator and college president, Nov 1989

Bowen, William G., American college president and foundation official, May 1973

Boyer, Ernest L., American educator and foundation official, Jan 1988, *Obit* Feb 1996

Brademas, John, American congressman and university president, May 1977

Brandenburg, William A., *Obit* Yrbk 1940

Brewster, Kingman, American college president and diplomat, May 1964, Sept 1979, *Obit* Jan 1989

Briggs, Eugene S., Oct 1948

Browne, Sidney Jane, *Obit* Oct 1941

Butler, Nicholas Murray, American educator, Nov 1940, *Obit* Yrbk 1947

Calfee, John Edward, *Obit* Jan 1941

Carlson, William S., college president, July 1952, *Obit* July 1994

Carroll, Thomas H., July 1962, *Obit* Oct 1964

Caswell, Hollis L., college president, July 1956, *Obit* Sept 1989

Chase, Harry Woodburn, June 1948, *Obit* June 1955

Cleveland, Harlan, American diplomat and university president, Sept 1961, *Obit* Yrbk 2008

Coleman, John R., Oct 1974

Compton, Wilson, Apr 1952, *Obit* May 1967

Conway, Jill K., Australian historian and college president, June 1991

Daniel, Robert Prentiss, May 1952, *Obit* Mar 1968

Daniels, Arthur Hill, *Obit* Apr 1940

Darden, Colgate W., Sept 1948

Davis, Jess H., Jan 1956

Day, Edmund, Sept 1946, *Obit* Apr 1951

DeBakey, Michael E., American surgeon and inventor, Mar 1964, *Obit* Yrbk 2008

Dickey, John Sloan, college president, Apr 1955, *Obit* Apr 1991

Dodds, Harold W., Yrbk 1945, *Obit* Jan 1981

Dodge, Bayard, Feb 1948, *Obit* July 1972

Doherty, Robert E., Sept 1949, *Obit* Yrbk 1950

DuBridge, Lee A., college president and physicist, June 1948, *Obit* Mar 1994

Dunton, Arnold Davidson, Canadian college president, Jan 1959, *Obit* Apr 1987

Dykstra, Clarence A., American university president, Jan 1941, *Obit* June 1950

Eisenhower, Milton Stover, American college president, diplomat and government official, Yrbk 1946, *Obit* July 1985

Ellingson, Mark, college president, Sept 1957, *Obit* Apr 1993

Ellis, Elmer, college president, July 1962

Engleman, J. O., *Obit* Nov 1943

Etherington, Edwin D., stock exchange official and college president, Apr 1966, *Obit* Apr 2001

Eurich, Alvin C., educator, June 1949, *Obit* Aug 1987

Evans, Daniel Jackson, American senator and governor, Aug 1975

Fellows, George Emory, American historian and university president, *Obit* Mar 1942

Fels, William C., Apr 1959, *Obit* Jan 1965

Few, William Preston, college president, *Obit* Yrbk 1940

Fleming, Robben W., American university president, Yrbk 1970, *Obit* Yrbk 2010

Foster, Richard C., *Obit* Jan 1942

Friday, William Clyde, college president, Apr 1958, *Obit* Yrbk 2013

Futter, Ellen Victoria, American college president and museum director, Oct 1985

Gideonse, Harry D., college president, May 1940, *Obit* May 1985

Giral, Jose, May 1946

Glennan, T. Keith, American NASA official, Oct 1950, *Obit* June 1995

Gould, Samuel B., educator, Jan 1958, *Obit* Sept 1997

Gray, Hanna Holborn, American historian and college president, Mar 1979

Gregorian, Vartan, American foundation official, Oct 1985

Gross, Mason W., June 1969, *Obit* Jan 1978

Haggard, William David, *Obit* Mar 1940

Hancher, Virgil M., Feb 1957, *Obit* Mar 1965

Hannah, John A., American college president, Oct 1952, *Obit* Apr 1991

Harada, Tasuku, Japanese college teacher and president, *Obit* Mar 1940

Harnwell, Gaylord Probasco, June 1956

Hendl, Walter, American conductor, college president and music teacher, June 1955

Henry, David Dodds, college president, June 1966, *Obit* Nov 1995

Hildreth, Horace Augustus, governor, Oct 1948, *Obit* July 1988

Hitch, Charles J., American college president, Nov 1970, *Obit* Nov 1995

Hockfield, Susan, American neurobiologist and college president, Apr 2008

Holt, Andrew David, college president, Nov 1949, *Obit* Sept 1987

Hopkins, Ernest Martin, Oct 1944, *Obit* Oct 1964

Hopkins, Louis Bertram, *Obit* Sept 1940

Horton, Mildred McAfee, college president and naval officer, Sept 1942, *Obit* Jan 1995

Hovde, Bryn J., Jan 1946, *Obit* Oct 1954

Hutton, Maurice, *Obit* May 1940

Jackson, Shirley Ann, American physicist and college president, July 1999

Johnson, Charles Spurgeon, American sociologist and university president, Nov 1946, *Obit* Jan 1957

Johnson, Robert L., college president and government official, Mar 1948, *Obit* Feb 1966

Jones, Lewis Webster, Oct 1958

Jordan, I. King, American university president, Jan 1991

Kean, Thomas H., American governor and college president, July 1985

Kemeny, John G., American mathematician and college president, Feb 1971, *Obit* Feb 1993

Kerr, Clark, American educator, Apr 1961, *Obit* May 2004

Kerrey, Bob, American senator and university president, Feb 1991

Killian, James Rhyne, American college president and presidential adviser, Feb 1949, May 1959, *Obit* Mar 1988

Kleinsmid, Rufus B. von, June 1958, *Obit* Sept 1964

Knight, Douglas M., May 1964

Kraushaar, Otto F., college president, Nov 1949, *Obit* Nov 1989

Lederle, John W., American college president, Feb 1961, *Obit* Yrbk 2007

Lindley, Ernest Hiram, *Obit* Oct 1940

MacCracken, Henry Noble, college president, Sept 1940, *Obit* June 1970

MacLean, Malcolm Shaw, July 1940

Malott, Deane W., college president, Mar 1951, *Obit* Nov 1996

Marshak, Robert Eugene, American college president

and physicist, July 1973, *Obit* Feb 1993

Marvin, Cloyd H., Yrbk 1949, *Obit* June 1969

Massey, Walter E., American physicist and college president, June 1997

Mayer, Jean, nutritionist and college president, Sept 1970, *Obit* Feb 1993

McBride, Katharine E., American psychologist and college president, Feb 1942, *Obit* July 1976

McGill, William J., college president, June 1971, *Obit* Jan 1998

Mendenhall, Thomas Corwin, college president, May 1960, *Obit* Sept 1998

Meng, John J., college president, Nov 1961, *Obit* Apr 1988

Millett, John David, American university president, Feb 1953, *Obit* Jan 1994

Million; John Wilson, *Obit* Nov 1941

Moron, Alonzo G., American college president and government official, Oct 1949, *Obit* Yrbk 1971

Nabrit, James M., American lawyer, civil rights activist and university president, Jan 1961, *Obit* Mar 1998

Nason, John W., American college president, July 1953, *Obit* Feb 2002

Park, Rosemary, American college president, Jan 1964, *Obit* Yrbk 2004

Patrick, Mary Mills, college president, *Obit* Mar 1940

Penniman, Josiah Harmer, *Obit* June 1941

Perkins, James A., American college president, Apr 1964, *Obit* Nov 1998

Pusey, Nathan Marsh, American college president, Yrbk 1953, *Obit* Feb 2002

Putnam, James William, *Obit* Mar 1940

Rainey, Homer Price, college president, Nov 1946, *Obit* Feb 1986

Reinhardt, Aurelia Henry, American college president and religious official, May 1941, *Obit* Feb 1948

Renne, Roland Roger, college president and agricultural economist, June 1963

Richards, Charles Russ, *Obit* Jan 1941

Rines, Robert H., American lawyer, inventor, physicist and hunter of Loch Ness monster, Jan 2003, *Obit* Yrbk 2010

Robinson, Frederick B., *Obit* Yrbk 1941

Rockefeller, John D., American senator, Mar 1978

Rodin, Judith, American foundation official, June 1999

Sanford, Terry, American senator, Nov 1961, *Obit* July 1998

Satcher, David, American surgeon general, Feb 1997

Sawyer, John E., college president and foundation official, July 1961, *Obit* Apr 1995

Schottland, Charles Irwin, college president and government official, Yrbk 1956, *Obit* Sept 1995

Schurman, Jacob G., philosopher, college president and diplomat, *Obit* Oct 1942

Seitz, Frederick, American physicist, Apr 1956, *Obit* Yrbk 2008

Seymour, Charles, May 1941, *Obit* Nov 1963

Shawkey, Morris Purdy, *Obit* Apr 1941

Silber, John R., American college president, Feb 1984, *Obit* Yrbk 2012

Simmons, Adele Smith, American college president and foundation official, May 1991

Simmons, Ruth, American college president, Jan 1996

Sisco, Joseph J., American diplomat, Jan 1972, *Obit* Yrbk 2005

Smith, Courtney, American college president, Yrbk 1959, *Obit* Mar 1969

Smith, Virginia B., American college president, June 1978, *Obit* Yrbk 2010

Smith, Wilbur Fisk, *Obit* Sept 1940

Snavely, Guy E., Apr 1951

Sovern, Michael I., Feb 1981

Sparling, Edward J., July 1948

Sproul, Robert Gordon, July 1945, *Obit* Nov 1975

Stahr, Elvis J., American Secretary of the army, Sept 1961, *Obit* Feb 1999

Stassen, Harold E., American lawyer, governor and presidential candidate, May 1940, Mar 1948, *Obit* May 2001

Sterling, John Ewart Wallace, college president, Jan 1951, *Obit* Aug 1985

Stoddard, George Dinsmore, American psychologist and college president, July 1946, *Obit* Feb 1982

Stratton, Julius Adams, American physicist and college president, May 1963, *Obit* Aug 1994

Summers, Lawrence H., American presidential adviser and former Secretary of the treasury, July 2002

Taylor, Harold, college president, Sept 1946, *Obit* Apr 1993

Topping, Norman H., physician and college president, Feb 1959, *Obit* Jan 1998

Trotter, Frank Butler, *Obit* Apr 1940

Tufts, James Hayden, *Obit* Sept 1942

Walker, Eric A., college president, Mar 1959, *Obit* Apr 1995

Ward, Paul L., American historian and college president, Mar 1962, *Obit* Yrbk 2006

Weaver, Robert Clifton, American Secretary of housing and urban development and educator, Apr 1961, *Obit* Oct 1997

Wells, Herman B., American college president, Apr 1966, *Obit* Aug 2000

Wexler, Jacqueline Grennan, college president, Mar 1970, *Obit* Yrbk 2012

Wharton, Clifton R., American college president and pension plan administrator, Feb 1987

Wiesner, Jerome B., American electrical engineer and college president, Yrbk 1961, *Obit* Jan 1995

Wilson, O. Meredith, college president, July 1967, *Obit* Feb 1999

Wood, James Madison, Feb 1947, *Obit* Yrbk 1958

Wright, Benjamin Fletcher, professors of government and college president, July 1955, *Obit* Mar 1977

Wriston, Henry M., May 1952, *Obit* May 1978

Yoder, Albert Henry, *Obit* Nov 1940

College teachers

Abrams, Charles, American city planner and lawyer, Feb 1969, *Obit* Apr 1970

Acheson, Albert R., American mechanical and electrical engineer, *Obit* Apr 1941

Ackley, H. Gardner, American economist, diplomat and presidential adviser, Apr 1968, *Obit* May 1998

Adams, Joseph Quincy, American Shakespearean scholar, *Obit* Yrbk 1946

Adams, Roger, American chemist, June 1947, *Obit* Sept 1971

Adler, Guido, *Obit* May 1941

Agar, William, American geologist, May 1949, *Obit* July 1972

Ahmed, Leila, Egyptian Islamist, Jan 2004

Ajami, Fouad, Lebanese-American Islamic and Middle Eastern studies specialist, Feb 2007

Al-Hilali, Ahmad Najib, July 1952, *Obit* Mar 1959

Alberto, Alvaro, Brazilian chemist and United Nations official, Mar 1947

Albright, Madeleine Korbel, American Secretary of state, May 1995, Apr 2000

Aldridge, John W., American literary critic, Yrbk 1958

Alessandri Rodriguez, Jorge, Chilean president, May 1959, *Obit* Oct 1986

Alexander, Christopher, British architect, Oct 2003

Alger, Ellice M., American ophthalmologist, *Obit* Apr 1945

Allen, Arthur Augustus, American ornithologist, Jan 1961, *Obit* Mar 1964

Allen, Edgar, American anatomist, *Obit* Mar 1943

Alliot-Marie, Michele, French cabinet member, Jan 2003

Allyn, Lewis B., American food chemist, *Obit* Jan 1940

Altizer, Thomas J. J., American theologian, June 1967

Alvarez, Walter C., American internist and physiologist, Sept 1953, *Obit* Aug 1978

Ames, Bruce N., American biochemist, Oct 1993

Ammondt, Jukka, Finnish literary scholar and Elvis Presley impersonator, Jan 2002

Ammons, A. R., American poet, Feb 1982, *Obit* July 2001

Anderson, Don L., American geophysicist, Oct 2002

Anderson, Gaylord W., American physician, Feb 1953

Anderson, Winston A., American biologist, Mar 2007

Appiah, Anthony, American professor of African-American studies, June 2002

Archer, Glenn L., May 1949

Arciniegas, German, Colombian historian, May 1954, *Obit* June 2000

Armour, Richard Willard, philologist and poet, Nov 1958, *Obit* Apr 1989

Arnett, Jeffrey Jensen, American psychologist, Feb 2011

Arsuaga, Juan Luis, Spanish paleontologist, Jan 2006

Ashbery, John, American poet, Aug 1976

Athey, Susan, American economist, Sept 2007

Auden, W. H., Anglo-American poet, Sept 1971, *Obit* Nov 1973

Augenbraum, Harold, American literary scholar, Apr 2012

Aumann, Robert J., Israeli economist, Jan 2007

Ayala, Francisco, American geneticist, Oct 2012

Ayer, A. J., British philosopher, May 1964, *Obit* Aug 1989

Azimi, Abdul Salam, Afghan supreme court justice, Jan 2006

Backman, Jules, Apr 1952, *Obit* June 1982

Bacon, Selden Daskam, sociologist, May 1952, *Obit* Feb 1993

Badinter, Elisabeth, French philosopher, Nov 2011

Bahcall, John N., American astrophysicist, Apr 2000, *Obit* Yrbk 2007

Bailar, John Christian, American chemist, July 1959

Bakke, E. Wight, Sept 1953, *Obit* Jan 1972

Banfield, Edward C., American political scientist, May 1972, *Obit* Feb 2000

Banfield, Jillian Fiona, Australian geologist, Feb 2000

Banzhaf, John F., law professor, Yrbk 1973

Barbour, Henry Gray, American pharmacologist, *Obit* Nov 1943

Bardeen, John, American physicist and electrical engineer, Sept 1957, *Obit* Apr 1991

Barker, Lewellys Franklin, American physician, *Obit* Sept 1943

Barnard, James Lynn, American political scientist, *Obit* Oct 1941

Barnes, Clifford Webster, American clergyman and sociologist, *Obit* Nov 1944

Barney, Samuel E., American civil engineer, *Obit* Mar 1940

Barnouw, Erik, American sociologist, Nov 1940, *Obit* Oct 2001

Barrett, William, professor of philosophy, Aug 1982, *Obit* Nov 1992

Bartol, William Cyrus, American mathematician, *Obit* Yrbk 1940

Barton, Jacqueline K., American chemist, Sept 2006

Bass, George Fletcher, American archaeologist, Mar 2000

Bassler, Bonnie L., American molecular biologist, Apr 2003

Bates, Marston, zoologist, Apr 1956, *Obit* May 1974

Baumgartner, Leona, American physician and public health official, Jan 1950, *Obit* Mar 1991

Bawer, Bruce, American critic, poet and essayist, July 2007

Baxter, Frank C., American professor of English and television personality, Mar 1955

Baxter, James Phinney, American historian, July 1947, *Obit* Aug 1975

Beard, Charles Austin, American historian, Mar 1941, *Obit* Oct 1948

Beatty, Arthur, American professor of English, *Obit* Apr 1943

Becker, Gary Stanley, American economist, Sept 1993

Behe, Michael J., American biochemist and intelligent design advocate, Feb 2006

Bell, Daniel, American sociologist, Yrbk 1973, *Obit* Yrbk 2011

Bell, David E., American economist and government official, June 1961, *Obit* Yrbk 2000

Bell, Derrick A., American law professor, Feb 1993, *Obit* Yrbk 2011

Bennett, H. S., anatomist, Apr 1966, *Obit* Oct 1992

Bensin, Basil M., American agriculturist, July 1948

Benzer, Seymour, American biophysicist, May 2001, *Obit* Yrbk 2008

Berger, Peter L., American sociologist, Mar 1983

Berle, Adolf Augustus, American lawyer and diplomat, July 1940, June 1961, *Obit* Apr 1971

Berlin, Isaiah, British political philosopher, July 1964, *Obit* Jan 1998

Berry, Wendell, American poet and novelist, May 1986

Berryman, John, American poet and critic, May 1969, *Obit* Feb 1972

Besteiro, Julian, Spanish socialist leader, *Obit* Nov 1940

Bestor, Arthur, American historian, Sept 1958, *Obit* Feb 1995

Bevan, Arthur Dean, American surgeon, *Obit* Aug 1943

Bevier, Isabel, home economist, *Obit* May 1942

Bigelow, William P., American music teacher, *Obit* May 1941

Billington, James H., American historian and Librarian of Congress, May 1989

Bingham, Millicent Todd, American geographer and conservationist, June 1961, *Obit* Jan 1969

Binkley, Robert Cedric, American historian, *Obit* May 1940

Birge, Raymond T., American physicist, Mar 1940

Blackburn, Elizabeth H., Australian molecular biologist, July 2001

Blackfan, K. D., American pediatrician, *Obit* Jan 1942

Blaisdell, Thomas Charles, economist and government official, July 1949, *Obit* Feb 1989

Blalock, Alfred, American surgeon, Sept 1946, *Obit* Nov 1964

Bloom, Allan David, philosopher, Mar 1988, *Obit* Nov 1992

Bloom, Harold, American literary critic, Apr 1987

Bloom, Paul, June 2012

Blough, Roy, economist, July 1950, *Obit* Sept 2000

Blunt, Katharine, home economist and nutritionist, Yrbk 1946, *Obit* Oct 1954

Bodansky, Meyer, American biochemist and pathologist, *Obit* Aug 1941

Bois, Yve-Alain, French art historian, Jan 2005

Bok, Sissela, philosopher, Jan 1996

Bonham, Milledge Louis, American historian, *Obit* Mar 1941

Borcherds, Richard, English mathematician, Feb 1999

Boring, E. G., American psychologist, Mar 1962, *Obit* Sept 1968

Borst, Lyle B., American nuclear physicist, July 1954, *Obit* Yrbk 2002

Boskin, Michael J., American economist and government official, Sept 1989

Bosselaar, Laure-Anne, Belgian poet, Sept 2006

Boulding, Kenneth Ewart, American economist and pacifist, Mar 1965, *Obit* May 1993

Boyd, Julian P., historian and librarian, June 1976, *Obit* Aug 1980

Bradbury, Norris Edwin, physicist, Apr 1949, *Obit* Nov 1997

Brameld, Theodore, professor of education, June 1967, *Obit* Jan 1988

Braun, Werner, German microbiologist, June 1957, *Obit* Jan 1973

Brazelton, T. Berry, pediatrician, Oct 1993

Breckenridge, L. P., American mechanical engineer, *Obit* Oct 1940

Bridgman, P. W., American physicist, Apr 1955, *Obit* Nov 1961

Brier, Bob, American Egyptologist, Sept 2002

Brigham, Carl C., *Obit* Mar 1943

Brinton, Crane, American historian, June 1959, *Obit* Nov 1968

Brode, Wallace R., June 1958, *Obit* Oct 1974

Brooks, Gwendolyn, American poet, June 1950, July 1977, *Obit* Feb 2001

Brooks, Matilda Moldenhauer, physiologist, Nov 1941

Brouwer, Dirk, Mar 1951, *Obit* Mar 1966

Brown, George Hay, marketing executive and consultant, Jan 1971

Brown, Robert McAfee, American theologian and human rights activist, May 1965, *Obit* Nov 2001

Brown, Sterling Allen, American poet and literary critic, Aug 1982, *Obit* Apr 1989

Brunner, Edmund de Schweinitz, Sept 1958, *Obit* Feb 1974

Brustein, Robert, American theatrical director and critic, Aug 1975

Brzezinski, Zbigniew, American political scientist and presidential adviser, Apr 1970

Bucher, Walter Herman, geologist, Feb 1957, *Obit* Apr 1965

Buergenthal, Thomas, American judge and human rights activist, Jan 2009

Buley, R. Carlyle, historian, July 1951, *Obit* June 1968

Bultmann, Rudolf Karl, German theologian, Jan 1972, *Obit* Sept 1976

Bunge, Alejandro E., *Obit* July 1943

Burbidge, Eleanor Margaret, Anglo-American astronomer, Nov 2000

Burgess, Robert Wilbur, July 1960, *Obit* July 1969

Burnham, James, American political and social philosopher, Nov 1941, *Obit* Jan 1988

Burns, Edward McNall, Feb 1954

Burns, Eveline M., American economist and government official, Nov 1960, *Obit* Jan 1986

Burns, James MacGregor, American biographer and historian, Yrbk 1962

Burrows, Millar, July 1956, *Obit* July 1980

Burton, Alan C., Sept 1956

Burton, Richard, *Obit* May 1940

Bush, Wendell T., *Obit* Mar 1941

Cam, Helen Maud, English medievalist, Sept 1948, *Obit* Apr 1968

Camden, Harry P., *Obit* Sept 1943

Campbell, Joseph, American mythologist, June 1984, *Obit* Jan 1988

Campbell, Willis C., *Obit* June 1941

Cannon, Clarence, American congressman, Nov 1949, *Obit* July 1964

Caplin, Mortimer Maxwell, American lawyer, Sept 1961

Cardon, P. V., May 1954, *Obit* Yrbk 1965

Carlson, Anton Julius, physiologist, Jan 1948, *Obit* Nov 1956

Carmona, Richard, American Surgeon general, Jan 2003

Carpenter, Henry Cort Harold, *Obit* Nov 1940

Carpenter, Lewis Van, *Obit* July 1940

Carr, Emma Perry, American chemist, Apr 1959

Carson, Anne, Canadian classicist, poet and essayist, May 2006

Carson, Benjamin, American neurosurgeon, May 1997

Carson, Rachel, American marine biologist and environmentalist, Nov 1951, *Obit* June 1964

Carter, Stephen L., American law professor, July 1997

Cary, William L., American lawyer and regulatory agency official, Jan 1963, *Obit* Apr 1983

Castiella, Fernando Maria, May 1958, *Obit* Feb 1977

Catlin, Don H., American pharmacologist, Mar 2010

Cattell, James McKeen, psychologist, *Obit* Mar 1944

Cayton, Horace R., Jan 1946, *Obit* Mar 1970

Chaddock, Robert Emmet, *Obit* Yrbk 1940

Chafee, Zechariah, American law professor, Aug 1942, *Obit* Apr 1957

Chapman, Sydney, English geophysicist, July 1957, *Obit* Sept 1970

Charlesworth, James Clyde, Sept 1954, *Obit* Mar 1974

Cherwell, Frederick Alexander Lindemann, British physicist, Mar 1952, *Obit* Sept 1957

Chin, Frank, American novelist, essayist, playwright and short story writer, Mar 1999

Chomsky, Noam, American linguist and social critic, Oct 1970, Aug 1995

Chu, Steven, American physicist and Secretary of energy, Mar 2009

Churchill, Edward D., American surgeon, Feb 1963

Churchland, Patricia Smith, Canadian philosopher, May 2003

Clague, Ewan, statistician and government official, July 1947, *Obit* June 1987

Clark, Kenneth B., American psychologist, Sept 1964, *Obit* Sept 2005

Clarke, Walter, American physician, May 1947, *Obit* Jan 1965

Clement, Paul D., American law professor, Oct 2012

Coetzee, J. M., South African novelist, Jan 1987

Cole, Juan R. I., American Middle Eastern studies specialist, Oct 2010

Coleman, James Samuel, American sociologist, Oct 1970, *Obit* June 1995

Coles, Robert, American psychiatrist, Nov 1969

Collins, James Daniel, philosopher, Yrbk 1963

Collins, Patricia Hill, American sociologist, Mar 2003

Colwell, Rita R., American microbiologist, May 1999

Comer, James P., professor of psychiatry, Aug 1991

Compton, Arthur Holly, American physicist, Aug 1940, Sept 1958, *Obit* May 1962

Condon, Edward Uhler, American physicist and government official, Apr 1946, *Obit* May 1974

Conway, John Horton, British mathematician, Sept 2003

Cook, W. W., *Obit* Yrbk 1943

Coon, Carleton Stevens, American anthropologist, Sept 1955, *Obit* July 1981

Coons, Albert H., June 1960

Coontz, Stephanie, American historian, July 2003

Cori, Carl F., American biochemist, Yrbk 1947, *Obit* Feb 1985

Cori, Gerty Theresa, American biochemist, Yrbk 1947, *Obit* Jan 1958

Cotler, Irwin, Canadian member of Parliament, Jan 2006

Coulter, Calvin Brewster, *Obit* Jan 1940

Cournand, Andre F., American physician, Mar 1957, *Obit* Apr 1988

Cox, Harvey Gallagher, American theologian, Nov 1968

Craig, Lyman C., Apr 1964, *Obit* Sept 1974

Crawford, Morris Barker, *Obit* Yrbk 1940

Crenshaw, Kimberle Williams, American law professor, May 2011

Crewe, Albert, American physicist, Feb 1964, *Obit* Yrbk 2010

Critchley, Simon, British philosopher, Apr 2010

Crocker, Chester A., American diplomat, July 1990

Crossan, John Dominic, Irish theologian, May 2011

Crosser, Robert, Mar 1953, *Obit* Sept 1957

Crumb, George, American composer, Yrbk 1979

Cubberley, Ellwood Patterson, educator, *Obit* Nov 1941

Cullen, Glenn Ernest, *Obit* May 1940

Curran, Charles E., American priest and theologian, Jan 1987

Dale, Benjamin James, *Obit* Sept 1943

Dallek, Robert, American historian, Sept 2007

Damasio, Antonio R., American neurobiologist, Oct 2007

Dangerfield, George, American historian, Sept 1953, *Obit* Mar 1987

Daniels, Farrington, July 1965, *Obit* Sept 1972

Danto, Arthur Coleman, American philosopher and art critic, Apr 1995

Dargan, Edwin Preston, *Obit* Feb 1941

Darman, Richard, American presidential aide, May 1989, *Obit* Yrbk 2008

Daugherty, Carroll Roop, economist, Oct 1949, *Obit* June 1988

Davidson, Richard J., American neuroscientist, Aug 2004

Davies, P. C. W., English physicist, Jan 2002

Davies, Robertson, Canadian novelist, playwright and critic, June 1975, *Obit* Mar 1996

Davis, Edward W., Sept 1955, *Obit* Feb 1974

Davis, Harvey N., July 1947, *Obit* Jan 1953

Dawdy, Shannon Lee, American archaeologist and anthropologist, Apr 2006

De Branges, Louis, American mathematician, Nov 2005

De Geer, Gerard, *Obit* Sept 1943

De Selincourt, Ernest, English editor and literary critic, *Obit* July 1943

Deane, Seamus, Irish literary critic and poet, Jan 2007

Deane, Sidney N., *Obit* June 1943

Debeljak, Ales, Slovenian poet and critic, Jan 2007

Debye, Peter J. W., Dutch physical chemist, July 1963, *Obit* Jan 1967

Delgado, Jose Manuel R., Spanish neurobiologist, Feb 1976

Deloria, Vine, Native American leader, historian and philosopher, Sept 1974, *Obit* Yrbk 2006

Denenberg, Herbert S., Yrbk 1972

Derrida, Jacques, French philosopher, July 1993, *Obit* Mar 2005

Dershowitz, Alan M., American lawyer, Sept 1986

Desmond-Hellman, Susan, American oncologist and biotechnology executive, Nov 2012

Diamond, Peter, American economist, Nov 2012

Dickey, James, American poet and novelist, Apr 1968, *Obit* Mar 1997

Dinsmore, Charles Allen, *Obit* Oct 1941

Djerassi, Carl, American chemist, Oct 2001

Dobie, J. Frank, American folklorist, Yrbk 1945, *Obit* Nov 1964

Dodge, Raymond, *Obit* May 1942

Doisy, Edward Adelbert, American biochemist, Mar 1949, *Obit* Jan 1987

Dominy, Nathaniel J., American anthropologist, Apr 2010

Donald, David Herbert, American historian and biographer, Sept 1961, *Obit* Yrbk 2009

Donaldson, Simon K., English mathematician, Jan 2005

Dooyeweerd, Herman, Dutch philosopher, Sept 1958

Doten, Carroll W., *Obit* Aug 1942

Doudna, Jennifer A., American biochemist, Feb 2005

Douglas, Paul H., American senator and economist, Apr 1949, *Obit* Nov 1976

Dove, Rita, American poet and short story writer, May 1994

Drake, Frank Donald, American astronomer, Jan 1963

Drake, St. Clair, anthropologist and sociologist, Jan 1946, *Obit* Aug 1990

Drew, Charles Richard, American surgeon, May 1944, *Obit* May 1950

Du Vigneaud, Vincent, American biochemist, Jan 1956, *Obit* Feb 1979

Duarte Frutos, Nicanor, Paraguayan president, Jan 2004

Dubos, Rene Jules, American bacteriologist, Oct 1952, Jan 1973, *Obit* Apr 1982

Duesberg, Peter H., German molecular biologist, June 2004

Duflo, Esther, French economist, Aug 2011

Dugan, Raymond Smith, *Obit* Oct 1940

Duggar, Benjamin Minge, botanist, Nov 1952, *Obit* Nov 1956

Duncan, Thomas W., Yrbk 1947

Dunning, John R., May 1948, *Obit* Oct 1975

Dusser de Barenne, Joannes Gregorius, *Obit* Aug 1940

Dutton, Denis, American philosopher, Aug 2009, *Obit* Yrbk 2011

Dworkin, Ronald Myles, American law professor, *Obit* Yrbk 2013

Dyke, Cornelius G., *Obit* June 1943

Dyson, Freeman J., American physicist, Jan 1980

Dyson, Michael Eric, American social scientist, clergyman and writer, Oct 1997

Eagleman, David, American neuroscientist, Jan 2012

Early, Gerald Lyn, American essayist, editor and poet, May 1995

Eckstein, Gustav, physiologist, May 1942, *Obit* Nov 1981

Eco, Umberto, Italian semiotician and novelist, Apr 1985

Edel, Leon, biographer, July 1963, *Obit* Nov 1997

Edelman, Gerald M., American biochemist, Apr 1995

Edgerton, Harold Eugene, American electrical engineer, Nov 1966, *Obit* Mar 1990

Edman, Irwin, philosopher, July 1953, *Obit* Oct 1954

Ehrlich, Paul R., biologist, Sept 1970

Ehrman, Bart D., American biblical scholar, Apr 2010

Eidmann, Frank Lewis, *Obit* Nov 1941

Eiseley, Loren C., American anthropologist and science writer, June 1960, *Obit* Sept 1977

Eisner, Thomas, American entomologist, Mar 1993, *Obit* Yrbk 2011

El-Sayed, Karimat, Egyptian crystallographer, Jan 2004

Elder, Albert L., Sept 1960

Elgin, Suzette Haden, American linguist, science fiction writer and poet, Aug 2006

Elliott, William Thompson, English theologian and canonist, *Obit* Aug 1940

Ellis, Albert, American psychologist, July 1994, *Obit* Yrbk 2007

Ellis, George, South African mathematician and astronomer, Jan 2006

Ellis, John Tracy, American priest and church historian, Mar 1990, *Obit* Jan 1993

Ely, Richard Theodore, American economist, *Obit* Nov 1943

Emeny, Brooks, Nov 1947

Engle, Paul, American poet and college professor, June 1942, *Obit* May 1991

Epstein, Samuel S., Anglo-American physician, Aug 2001

Ettinger, Richard P., Yrbk 1951, *Obit* Apr 1971

Etzioni, Amitai, American sociologist, Mar 1980

Evans, Bergen, Yrbk 1955, *Obit* Apr 1978

Evans, Luther Harris, American Librarian of Congress and United Nations official, Aug 1945, *Obit* Feb 1982

Ewing, Maurice, American geophysicist, Jan 1953, *Obit* June 1974

Faber, Sandra M., American astronomer, Apr 2002

Fagles, Robert, American translator, poet and literary scholar, Apr 2006, *Obit* Yrbk 2008

Fagnani, Charles P., *Obit* Mar 1941

Fairchild, Henry Pratt, sociologist and economist, Yrbk 1942, *Obit* Yrbk 1957

Fausto-Sterling, Anne, American biologist, Sept 2005

Feinsinger, Nathan P., professor of law and labor mediator, May 1952, *Obit* Jan 1984

Feldstein, Martin S., American economist and presidential adviser, May 1983

Felton, Ralph A., Sept 1957

Ferguson, Niall, Scottish historian, July 2012

Fermi, Enrico, Italian-American physicist, Oct 1945, *Obit* Jan 1955

Ferris, Harry Burr, *Obit* Yrbk 1940

Fiedler, Leslie A., American literary critic and novelist, Yrbk 1970, *Obit* Yrbk 2003

Fielding, Gabriel, English novelist, poet and physician, Feb 1962, *Obit* Apr 1987

Filippenko, Alex, Oct 2013

Finch, Caleb Ellicott, American neurobiologist, Sept 2004

Fisher, Harry L., Oct 1954

Fitzgerald, Robert, American poet and classicist, Sept 1976, *Obit* Mar 1985

Flory, Paul J., American chemist, Mar 1975, *Obit* Nov 1985

Foerster, Friedrich Wilhelm, July 1962, *Obit* Feb 1966

Folkers, Karl August, American chemist, Oct 1962

Foner, Eric, American historian, Aug 2004

Ford, W. W., *Obit* Aug 1941

Fowler, William A., American physicist, Sept 1974, *Obit* May 1995

Fowler-Billings, Katharine Stevens, geologist, Jan 1940

Fox, Michael W., Feb 1977

Frank, Louis, *Obit* May 1941

Franklin, John Hope, American historian, Oct 1963, *Obit* May 2009

Frazier, Edward Franklin, sociologist, July 1940

Friedman, Milton, American economist, Oct 1969, *Obit* Yrbk 2007

Fryer, Jr., Roland G., American economist, May 2012

Fuchs, Elaine V., American cytologist, Jan 2011

Fukuyama, Francis, American international relations specialist, June 2001

Fuller, John L., Mar 1959

Funston, Keith, American stock exchange official, July 1951, *Obit* July 1992

Furey, Warren W., May 1950, *Obit* Jan 1959

Furman, N. Howell, Yrbk 1951, *Obit* Oct 1965

Gajdusek, Daniel Carleton, American virologist, June 1981, *Obit* Yrbk 2009

Galbraith, James K., American economist, Feb 2006

Galbraith, John Kenneth, American economist, Mar 1959, May 1975, *Obit* Yrbk 2007

Gamow, George, American physicist and science writer, Oct 1951, *Obit* Oct 1968

Gannon, Robert I., Mar 1945, *Obit* May 1978

Gaposchkin, Cecilia Helena Payne, astronomer, Yrbk 1957

Gardiner, Robert, July 1975

Gardner, Howard, American psychologist, Oct 1998

Gardner, John William, American Secretary of health, education and welfare, Mar 1956, Mar 1976, *Obit* May 2002

Garreton Merino, Manuel A., Chilean sociologist, Jan 2006

Gass, William H., American philosopher, novelist, short story writer and critic, Apr 1986

Gasser, Herbert Spencer, American physiologist, Oct 1945, *Obit* July 1963

Gates, Henry Louis, American professor of African-American studies, Oct 1992

Gates, William E., American archaeologist, *Obit* Jan 1940

Gay, Peter, American historian, Feb 1986

Geha, Marla, American astronomer, June 2010

Gell-Mann, Murray, American physicist, Feb 1966, Oct 1998

Geller, Margaret J., American astrophysicist, June 1997

Gellhorn, Walter, professor of law, May 1967, *Obit* Feb 1996

Gerard, Ralph W., May 1965, *Obit* Apr 1974

Gergen, David, American political commentator, Feb 1994

Ghez, Andrea Mia, American astronomer, Nov 2010

Giauque, William Francis, American chemist, Jan 1950, *Obit* May 1982

Giddens, Anthony, British sociologist and college administrator, Apr 1998

Gilbreth, Lillian Moller, American industrial engineer, May 1940, Sept 1951, *Obit* Feb 1972

Gillespie, Louis J., *Obit* Mar 1941

Gilligan, Carol, American psychologist, May 1997

Gilmore, John Washington, *Obit* Aug 1942

Gilyard, Keith, American sociolinguist, Oct 2011

Giordani, Francesco, Sept 1957, *Obit* Mar 1961

Gipson, Lawrence Henry, Oct 1954, *Obit* Nov 1971

Glaser, Donald Arthur, American physicist, Mar 1961, *Obit* Yrbk 2013

Glass, Bentley, American biologist, Apr 1966, *Obit* Yrbk 2005

Glasser, Ira, American civil rights activist, Jan 1986

Glazer, Nathan, American sociologist and educator, Yrbk 1970

Goeppert-Mayer, Maria, American physicist, June 1964, *Obit* Apr 1972

Gold, Thomas, American astrophysicist, June 1966, *Obit* Yrbk 2004

Goldman, Eric Frederick, American historian, July 1964, *Obit* Apr 1989

Good, Robert A., American physician, Mar 1972, *Obit* Yrbk 2003

Goodhart, Arthur L., American lawyer, July 1964, *Obit* Feb 1979

Gordon, Edmund W., American psychologist, June 2003

Gordon, Kermit, economist, July 1963, *Obit* Aug 1976

Gordon, Lincoln, American diplomat, Feb 1962, *Obit* Yrbk 2010

Gordon-Reed, Annette, American law professor, biographer and historian, May 2009

Gott, J. Richard, astrophysicist, Oct 1999

Goudsmit, Samuel Abraham, American physicist, Oct 1954, *Obit* Feb 1979

Gould, Stephen Jay, American paleontologist and science writer, Sept 1982, *Obit* Aug 2002

Gowers, Tim, English mathematician, Jan 2001

Grady, Henry Francis, American diplomat and trade expert, July 1947, *Obit* Nov 1957

Graham, Evarts A., American surgeon, Feb 1952, *Obit* May 1957

Graham, Harry Chrysostom, Apr 1950

Graham, Jorie, American poet, May 1997

Gramm, Phil, American senator and economist, May 1986

Granger, Clive W. J., British economist, Jan 2007, *Obit* Yrbk 2009

Graves, Alvin C., American physicist, Yrbk 1952, *Obit* Oct 1965

Greeley, Andrew M., American sociologist, priest and novelist, Yrbk 1972, *Obit* Yrbk 2013

Greene, Brian R., American physicist, Aug 2000

Greenfield, Abraham Lincoln, *Obit* Sept 1941

Greenstein, Jesse Leonard, American astrophysicist, Sept 1963, *Obit* Yrbk 2003

Greenway, Walter Burton, *Obit* Feb 1941

Greenwood, Allen, *Obit* Yrbk 1942

Greiner, Markus, Physicist and educator, June 2012

Grewe, Wilhelm, Oct 1958

Grossman, Edith, American translator and literary scholar, Mar 2006

Grotzinger, John, Apr 2013

Grove, Andrew S., American semiconductor industry executive, Mar 1998

Groves, Ernest R., sociologist, June 1943, *Obit* Oct 1946

Groves, Gladys Hoagland, June 1943, *Obit* Sept 1980

Gruber, Samuel H., American marine biologist, Aug 2004

Guarente, Leonard, American biologist, May 2007

Guion, Connie M., Feb 1962

Gulick, Luther Halsey, American municipal official, June 1945, *Obit* Mar 1993

Gupta, Sanjay, American neurosurgeon and television reporter, Aug 2006

Guth, Alan H., physicist, Sept 1987

Guthrie, William Buck, *Obit* Yrbk 1940

Haagen-Smit, A. J., chemist, Mar 1966, *Obit* May 1977

Haas, Arthur E., *Obit* Apr 1941

Haber, Heinz, Yrbk 1952

Hadas, Moses, Mar 1960, *Obit* Nov 1966

Hagen, John P., astronomer, Oct 1957, *Obit* Nov 1990

Hall, Edward Twitchell, American anthropologist, Feb 1992, *Obit* Yrbk 2009

Hall, Frank O., *Obit* Yrbk 1941

Hamilton, George Livingston, *Obit* Nov 1940

Hamlin, Talbot Faulkner, Oct 1954, *Obit* Yrbk 1957

Handlin, Oscar, American historian, July 1952, *Obit* Yrbk 2011

Hanfmann, George Maxim Anossov, archaeologist, Oct 1967, *Obit* May 1986

Hansen, Alvin Harvey, American economist, Sept 1945, *Obit* Aug 1975

Hanus, Paul H., *Obit* Feb 1942

Hardin, Garrett James, American biologist, Sept 1974, *Obit* Apr 2004

Hardwick, Elizabeth, American novelist, short story writer, essayist and critic, Feb 1981, *Obit* Yrbk 2008

Haring, Bernhard, German theologian, June 1969, *Obit* Sept 1998

Harjo, Joy, American poet, Aug 2001

Harkness, Georgia Elma, theologian, Nov 1960

Harper, Samuel Northrup, *Obit* Mar 1943

Harrington, Michael, American social critic and political activist, Jan 1969, Oct 1988, *Obit* Sept 1989

Harris, Harwell Hamilton, American architect, Jan 1962, *Obit* Jan 1991

Hart, Albert Bushnell, historian, *Obit* Aug 1943

Hartmann, Heidi I., American economist and feminist, Apr 2003

Hartwell, John A., *Obit* Jan 1941

Harvey, David, British geographer, Aug 2008

Harvey, E. Newton, May 1952

Hass, Henry Bohn, chemist, Apr 1956, *Obit* Apr 1987

Hass, Robert, American poet, critic and translator, Feb 2001

Hau, Lene Vestergaard, Danish physicist, Jan 2002

Hauerwas, Stanley, American theologian, June 2003

Hauser, Philip M., demographer, July 1969, *Obit* Feb 1995

Hawking, Stephen W., British physicist, May 1984

Hawkins, Harry C., Apr 1952

Hayes, Samuel P., Sept 1954

Hayes, Terrance, American poet, Apr 2011

Hayes, Tyrone, American biologist, May 2008

Hazard, Paul, Mar 1941

Hazen, Charles D., *Obit* Nov 1941

Heard, Alexander, Nov 1966

Heath, James R., American chemist, Oct 2003

Heffner, Richard D., American historian and television moderator, Oct 1964

Heilbroner, Robert L., American economist and writer, June 1975, *Obit* Yrbk 2005

Heilbrun, Carolyn G., American literary scholar and mystery novelist, Jan 1993, *Obit* Feb 2004

Hellenga, Robert, American novelist, Mar 2008

Heller, Agnes, Hungarian philosopher, Nov 2008

Heller, Walter W., American economist, Sept 1961, *Obit* Aug 1987

Henderson, Lawrence J., American chemist, *Obit* Apr 1942

Herr, Hugh, American biophysicist and mechanical engineer, Apr 2012

Herrick, Francis Hobart, *Obit* Nov 1940

Herring, Pendleton, American political scientist, July 1950, *Obit* Yrbk 2004

Hershey, Alfred D., American biologist, July 1970, *Obit* Aug 1997

Hershko, Avram, Israeli biochemist, Jan 2007

Herskovits, Melville J., American anthropologist, Nov 1948, *Obit* Apr 1963

Hickey, Dave, American art and cultural critic, Sept 2007

Hickman, Emily, June 1945, *Obit* July 1947

Highet, Gilbert, Scottish-American classicist, Sept 1964, *Obit* Mar 1978

Hill, Anita, American lawyer, Sept 1995

Hill, Herbert, American civil rights leader, Sept 1970, *Obit* Yrbk 2004

Hill, Howard Copeland, *Obit* Aug 1940

Hill, Robert Thomas, geologist, *Obit* Sept 1941

Himmelfarb, Gertrude, historian, May 1985

Hingson, Robert A., anesthesiologist and public health expert, June 1943, *Obit* Jan 1997

Hirsch, I. Seth, *Obit* May 1942

Hirschfelder, Joseph Oakland, physicist, Yrbk 1950, *Obit* May 1990

Hitti, Philip Khuri, June 1947, *Obit* Feb 1979

Hobsbawm, E. J., British historian, Jan 2003, *Obit* Yrbk 2012

Hoffman, Joseph G., May 1958, *Obit* Jan 1975

Hofmann, Klaus Heinrich, biochemist, Apr 1961

Hofstadter, Richard, American historian, Oct 1956, *Obit* Yrbk 1970

Hogben, Lancelot, English physiologist and zoologist, Yrbk 1941, *Obit* Jan 1984

Hoggart, Richard, English social and cultural critic, Oct 1963

Holden, Louis Edward, *Obit* June 1942

Hollander, Jacob Harry, *Obit* Sept 1940

Hollander, John, philologist and poet, Sept 1991, *Obit* Yrbk 2013

Hollander, Robert, American literary critic, translator and poet, Sept 2006

Holley, Robert William, American biochemist, Jan 1967, *Obit* Apr 1993

Holmes, Jesse Herman, *Obit* July 1942

Holt, Arthur E., *Obit* Mar 1942

Honderich, Ted, Canadian philosopher, Feb 2009

Hook, Sidney, American philosopher, Oct 1952, Apr 1988, *Obit* Sept 1989

Hooks, Bell, American feminist and social critic, Apr 1995

Hooton, Earnest Albert, American anthropologist, Yrbk 1940, *Obit* June 1954

Hopkins, Nancy, American molecular biologist, May 2002

Horne, Charles F., *Obit* Nov 1942

Horne, Gerald, American historian and biographer, Sept 2011

Horner, John R., American paleontologist, Sept 1992

Horney, Karen, German-American psychoanalyst, Aug 1941, *Obit* Jan 1953

Houle, Cyril Orvin, May 1962

Houtte, Jean van, Mar 1952

Hrdy, Sarah Blaffer, American primatologist and anthropologist, June 2000

Hudson, Charles Lowell, medical association executive and physician, Apr 1967, *Obit* Nov 1992

Hudson, Manley O., June 1944, *Obit* June 1960

Hun, John Gale, *Obit* Nov 1945

Huybers, Peter, American climatologist, Apr 2011

Hwang, Woo Suk, Korean veterinarian, Jan 2006

Hymans, Paul, *Obit* Apr 1941

Hyvernat, Henri, *Obit* July 1941

Ingalls, Jeremy, poet, Yrbk 1954, *Obit* July 2000

Isham, Norman Morrison, *Obit* Feb 1943

Italiaander, Rolf, June 1964

Jackson, Daniel Dana, *Obit* Oct 1941

Jacopi, Giulio, Jan 1959

Jagger, Janine, American epidemiologist, Apr 2004

James, F. Cyril, Canadian economist and college administrator, Oct 1956

Jamison, Kay R., American psychologist, Feb 2009

Janssen, Charles L., *Obit* Mar 1941

Jarvis, Erich, American neurobiologist, May 2003

Jastrow, Joseph, American psychologist, *Obit* Feb 1944

Jencks, Christopher, sociologist, Apr 1973

Jenike, Michael A., American psychiatrist, Jan 2010

Jenks, Leon E., *Obit* Mar 1940

Jensen, Arthur Robert, American psychologist, Jan 1973, *Obit* Yrbk 2013

Jewett, James R., *Obit* May 1943

Jin, Deborah, American physicist, Apr 2004

Johnson, Charles Richard, American novelist and short story writer, Sept 1991

Johnson, Douglas Wilson, American geologist, *Obit* Apr 1944

Johnson, Elizabeth A., American theologian, Nov 2002

Johnson, Joseph E., American historian and foundation official, Nov 1950, *Obit* Jan 1991

Johnson, Loren, *Obit* Feb 1942

Johnson, Nicholas, Mar 1968

Johnson, Simon, American economist, Oct 2009

Johnson, Thor, Oct 1949, *Obit* Mar 1975

Johnson, Walter, American historian, Apr 1957, *Obit* Sept 1985

Johnson, Wendell, American speech pathologist, Apr 1959, *Obit* Nov 1965

Joliot-Curie, Irene, French physicist, Apr 1940, *Obit* May 1956

Jones, Chester Lloyd, *Obit* Mar 1941

Jones, Tayari, American novelist and short story writer, Aug 2009

Judd, Charles Hubbard, *Obit* Sept 1946

Judson, Olivia P., English evolutionary biologist, Jan 2004

Kagan, Elena, American Supreme Court justice, June 2007

Kahf, Mohja, Syrian-American writer, Jan 2007

Kahneman, Daniel, Israeli psychologist, Jan 2007

Kantrowitz, Adrian, American cardiac surgeon, Oct 1967, *Obit* Yrbk 2009

Kantrowitz, Arthur, American physicist, Oct 1966, *Obit* Yrbk 2009

Kao, John J., American management consultant, Oct 2008

Kaplan, Joseph, physicist, Oct 1956, *Obit* Nov 1991

Karelitz, George B., *Obit* Mar 1943

Kasner, Edward, Nov 1943, *Obit* Mar 1955

Kass, Leon, American bioethicist, Aug 2002

Katsh, Abraham Isaac, Hebraist, Mar 1962, *Obit* Oct 1998

Katz, Milton, law professor and diplomat, Oct 1950, *Obit* Oct 1995

Kellas, Eliza, *Obit* May 1943

Kelly, Everett Lowell, psychologist, Mar 1955, *Obit* Apr 1986

Kelly, Howard A., American gynecologist, *Obit* Mar 1943

Kelsen, Hans, Austrian-American law professor, Sept 1957, *Obit* June 1973

Kennedy, Paul M., British historian, Oct 1993

Kennedy, Randall, American law professor, Aug 2002

Kennedy, William, American novelist, May 1985

Kent, Raymond A., *Obit* Apr 1943

Kerst, Donald William, physicist, Apr 1950, *Obit* Oct 1993

Kessler, Henry H., Oct 1957

Keys, Ancel, American physiologist, Jan 1966, *Obit* Yrbk 2005

Khorana, Har Gobind, Indian biochemist, Yrbk 1970, *Obit* Yrbk 2012

Ki-Zerbo, Joseph, Burkinabe historian and political scientist, Jan 2002

Kidder, George Wallace, microbiologist, July 1949

Kiessling, Laura L., American biochemist, Aug 2003

Kim, Jim Yong, American physician and medical anthropologist, Nov 2006

Kimble, George H. T., Oct 1952

King, Mary-Claire, American geneticist, Feb 1995

Kingsley, J. Donald, Feb 1950

Kingston, Maxine Hong, American novelist, Mar 1990

Kirchner, Leon, American composer and pianist, Yrbk 1967, *Obit* Yrbk 2009

Kirkpatrick, Jeane J., American diplomat, July 1981, *Obit* Yrbk 2007

Kissinger, Henry, American Secretary of state, June 1958, June 1972

Kistiakowsky, George, American chemist and presidential aide, Nov 1960, *Obit* Feb 1983

Kitson, Harry Dexter, Apr 1951, *Obit* Nov 1959

Kittredge, George Lyman, philologist, *Obit* Sept 1941

Kleitman, Nathaniel, physiologist, Oct 1957, *Obit* Jan 2000

Klenze, Camillo von, *Obit* Apr 1943

Klopsteg, Paul Ernest, physicist, May 1959, *Obit* July 1991

Kluckhohn, Clyde, American anthropologist, Nov 1951, *Obit* Oct 1960

Knoll, Andrew H., American paleontologist, Apr 2006

Knopf, Sigard Adolphus, *Obit* Sept 1940

Kobilka, Brian, Apr 2013

Koch, Frederick H., *Obit* Oct 1944

Kock, Karin, Nov 1948

Kolbe, Parke Rexford, *Obit* Apr 1942

Komarovsky, Mirra, American sociologist, Oct 1953, *Obit* Apr 1999

Kopal, Zdenek, Czech astronomer, Mar 1969, *Obit* Aug 1993

Koprulu, Mehmet Fuat, Jan 1953, *Obit* Sept 1966

Kornberg, Arthur, American biochemist, Sept 1968, *Obit* Feb 2008

Koshiba, Masatoshi, Japanese physicist, Jan 2007

Krause, David W., Canadian paleontologist and anatomist, Feb 2002

Krebs, Hans Adolf, British biochemist, Mar 1954, *Obit* Feb 1982

Kripke, Saul A., American philosopher, Oct 2004

Krohg, Per, Nov 1954

Krueger, Maynard C., May 1940

Krugman, Paul R., American economist, Aug 2001

Kubler-Ross, Elisabeth, American psychiatrist, June 1980, *Obit* Yrbk 2004

Kuiper, Gerard Peter, American astronomer, Feb 1959, *Obit* Feb 1974

Kusch, Polykarp, American physicist, Mar 1956, *Obit* May 1993

Kydland, Finn E., Norwegian economist, Jan 2007

L'Esperance, Elise Depew Strang, pathologist, Nov 1950, *Obit* Apr 1959

Labov, William, American sociolinguist, Mar 2006

Lake, Anthony, American political scientist and presidential adviser, Oct 1994

Lange, Oscar Richard, Polish economist, Apr 1946, *Obit* Yrbk 1965

Langer, William Leonard, American historian, Yrbk 1968, *Obit* Feb 1978

Langmuir, Irving, American chemist, Mar 1940, Oct 1950, *Obit* Nov 1957

Lanman, Charles Rockwell, *Obit* Apr 1941

Larkin, Oliver W., art historian, July 1950, *Obit* Feb 1971

Larson, Arthur, Ameriacn law professor and government official, Nov 1956, *Obit* May 1993

Lasch, Christopher, American social critic and historian, Mar 1985, *Obit* Apr 1994

Laski, Harold Joseph, British socialist leader and political scientist, Sept 1941, *Obit* Apr 1950

Lasswell, Harold D., American political scientist, July 1947, *Obit* Feb 1979

Laugier, Henri, July 1948

Lauterbach, Jacob Zallel, *Obit* June 1942

Lawrence, Ernest Orlando, American physicist, Feb 1940, Jan 1952, *Obit* Nov 1958

Lax, Peter D., American mathematician, Oct 2005

Lazarsfeld, Paul Felix, American sociologist, Nov 1964, *Obit* Oct 1976

Le Guin, Ursula K., American science fiction and fantasy writer, Jan 1983

LeDoux, Joseph E., American neuroscientist, Oct 2010

LeVay, Simon, English neurobiologist, Oct 1996

Leacock, Stephen Butler, Canadian economist, political scientist and humorist, *Obit* May 1944

Leary, Timothy, American psychologist, Yrbk 1970, *Obit* Aug 1996

Lecky, Prescott, psychologist, *Obit* July 1941

Lederberg, Joshua, American geneticist, Mar 1959, *Obit* Yrbk 2008

Lederman, Leon M., American physicist, Sept 1989

Lee, Tsung Dao, American physicist, Nov 1958

Leggett, A. J., Anglo-American physicist, Jan 2007

Leighton, Robert B., physicist, July 1966, *Obit* May 1997

Lemkin, Raphael, American lawyer, May 1950, *Obit* Nov 1959

Lerner, Gerda, American historian, Feb 1998, *Obit* Yrbk 2013

Lerner, Max, American columnist, Oct 1942, *Obit* Aug 1992

Levertov, Denise, American poet, Aug 1991, *Obit* Mar 1998

Levin, Janna, American astrophysicist, Jan 2008

Levine, Philip, American poet, July 2012

Lewis, David Levering, American historian and biographer, May 2001

Lewis, Dean, *Obit* Yrbk 1941

Lewis, Dorothy Otnow, American psychiatrist, May 2006

Lewis, Michael, American investment banker and journalist, Sept 2012

Liberman, Yevsei G., June 1968, *Obit* May 1983

Libeskind, Daniel, American architect, June 2003

Lieberman, Daniel, American anthropologist and biologist, May 2011

Lifton, Robert Jay, American psychiatrist and writer, Nov 1973

Lillehei, Clarence Walton, American surgeon, May 1969, *Obit* Nov 1999

Lipmann, Fritz, American biochemist, Mar 1954, *Obit* Sept 1986

Llinas, Rodolfo R., American neurophysiologist, Sept 2009

Locke, Alain LeRoy, American philosopher and essayist, Jan 1944, *Obit* Sept 1954

Lodge, Gonzalez, *Obit* Feb 1943

Loeb, Abraham (Avi), July 2013

Loftus, Elizabeth F., American psychologist, Jan 1999

Lopez Rodo, Laureano, Feb 1972

Loram, Charles Templeman, *Obit* Sept 1940

Lord, F. T., *Obit* Jan 1942

Love, John A., American governor, Nov 1963, *Obit* Apr 2002

Love, Susan M., American surgeon, Oct 1994

Lowrie, Jean E., June 1973

Lubin, Isador, Oct 1941, Jan 1953, *Obit* Sept 1978

Lunge-Larsen, Lise, Norwegian-American children's author, Aug 2012

Luquiens, Frederick Bliss, *Obit* May 1940

Luria, S. E., American biologist, Feb 1970, *Obit* Apr 1991

Lynch, Daniel F., July 1955

Lynd, Staughton, American historian and lawyer, May 1983

MacAlarney, Robert Emmet, *Obit* Jan 1946

MacCallum, William George, *Obit* Mar 1944

MacKinnon, Catharine A., American lawyer and feminist, June 1994

MacLean, Basil C., May 1957, *Obit* Apr 1963
MacMillan, Margaret, Canadian historian, Jan 2007
Macbride, Ernest William, *Obit* Jan 1941
Macdonald, Duncan Black, American theologian, linguist and Islamist, *Obit* Oct 1943
Mackay, John Alexander, American theologian and missionary, Feb 1952, *Obit* Aug 1983
Mackenzie, Chalmers Jack, June 1952
Macmahon, Arthur W., American political scientist, Apr 1958, *Obit* Apr 1980
Madrick, Jeffrey G., American economist and journalist, Nov 2011
Magoffin, Ralph Van Deman, *Obit* July 1942
Mailhouse, Max, *Obit* Yrbk 1941
Makemson, Maud Worcester, astronomer, June 1941
Malin, Patrick Murphy, Mar 1950, *Obit* Feb 1965
Malinowski, Bronislaw, Polish anthropologist, June 1941, *Obit* July 1942
Mallory, F. B., *Obit* Nov 1941
Mamdani, Mahmood, Ugandan political scientist, Jan 2010
Mamlok, Hans J., *Obit* Yrbk 1940
Mandelbrot, Benoit B., American mathematician, June 1987, *Obit* Yrbk 2010
Manly, John Matthews, *Obit* May 1940
Manrique, Jaime, Colombian-American novelist and poet, Jan 2005
Mansfield, Peter, British physicist, Jan 2007
Maphai, Vincent, South African political scientist and broadcasting executive, Jan 2003
Marcial Dorado, Carolina, *Obit* Sept 1941
Marcus, George E., American anthropologist, Mar 2006
Marcy, Geoffrey W., American astrophysicist, Nov 2002
Margoliouth, D. S., *Obit* Apr 1940
Marias, Julian, Spanish philosopher, author and educator, Feb 1972

Marks, Leonard H., American lawyer and government official, June 1966, *Obit* Yrbk 2006
Marshall, Barry J., Australian gastroenterologist, Sept 1996
Marshall, Ray, secretary of labor, Nov 1977
Martel, Yann, Canadian novelist, Jan 2004
Martin, Percy Alvin, *Obit* Apr 1942
Martino, Gaetano, May 1956, *Obit* Oct 1967
Mather, Kirtley F., American geologist, Jan 1951
Mattson, Ingrid, Canadian Islamist and religious education teacher, Jan 2007
Mayr, Ernst, German zoologist, Nov 1984, *Obit* May 2005
McAleese, Mary, Irish president, Jan 2006
McCall Smith, Alexander, Scottish law professor, children's author and novelist, Jan 2003
McCracken, Paul Winston, American economist and presidential adviser, Yrbk 1969, *Obit* Yrbk 2012
McCracken, Robert James, July 1949, *Obit* Apr 1973
McGarry, William J., *Obit* Nov 1941
McGee, Gale William, American senator and diplomat, Nov 1961, *Obit* June 1992
McGovern, Gail, American Red Cross official, Mar 2010
McMillan, Edwin Mattison, American physicist and chemist, Feb 1952, *Obit* Nov 1991
McPhee, John A., American journalist and nature writer, Oct 1982
Mearns, Hughes, Jan 1940, *Obit* Apr 1965
Meiling, Richard L., May 1950
Mellers, Wilfrid, English musicologist and composer, Feb 1962, *Obit* Yrbk 2008
Mernissi, Fatima, Moroccan sociologist, Jan 2005
Merriam, Charles Edward, American political scientist, Feb 1947, *Obit* Feb 1953
Merrifield, R. Bruce, American biochemist, Mar 1985, *Obit* Yrbk 2006

Merton, Robert King, American sociologist, Sept 1965, *Obit* Yrbk 2003
Merwin, W. S., American poet and translator, May 1988
Meyer, Albert, Jan 1960, *Obit* May 1965
Meyer, K. F., Mar 1952, *Obit* June 1974
Miles, Tiya, American feminist, Oct 2012
Milgram, Stanley, American social psychologist, Aug 1979, *Obit* Mar 1985
Miller, Geoffrey F., American psychologist, July 2010
Miller, Neal E., American professor of psychology, July 1974, *Obit* June 2002
Millikan, Robert A., American physicist, Jan 1940, June 1952, *Obit* Feb 1954
Milnor, John, American mathematician, July 2011
Minard, George Cann, *Obit* Aug 1940
Miro Cardona, Jose, Cuban political leader, Nov 1961, *Obit* Oct 1974
Monaghan, Frank, Nov 1943, *Obit* Sept 1969
Montagu, Ashley, Anglo-American anthropologist, Feb 1967, *Obit* Mar 2000
Montgomery, Deane, mathematician, Nov 1957, *Obit* May 1992
Mooney, Edward, Apr 1946, *Obit* Jan 1959
Moore, Edward Caldwell, *Obit* May 1943
Moore, Robert Webber, *Obit* Jan 1943
Moos, Felix, German-American anthropologist, Jan 2005
Morgan, Thomas Hunt, American biologist, *Obit* Feb 1946
Morgenthau, Hans Joachim, American political scientist, Mar 1963, *Obit* Sept 1980
Morrison, Philip, American physicist, July 1981, *Obit* Aug 2005
Morrison, Toni, American novelist, May 1979
Morse, Marston, Mar 1957, *Obit* Aug 1977

Morse, Wayne Lyman, American senator, Apr 1942, Nov 1954, *Obit* Sept 1974

Morton, John Jamieson, Mar 1955

Mott, Lewis F., *Obit* Jan 1942

Mowat, R. B., *Obit* Nov 1941

Mukherjee, Bharati, Indian-American novelist, Apr 1992

Mukherjee, Siddhartha, American oncologist, Jan 2013

Muller, H. J., American geneticist, Feb 1947, *Obit* June 1967

Mulliken, Robert Sanderson, American chemist, Sept 1967, *Obit* Jan 1987

Murphy, Gardner, psychologist, May 1960, *Obit* May 1979

Murray, Augustus Taber, *Obit* Mar 1940

Murray, Donald Morison, American journalist and writing instructor, July 2006

Murray, John Courtney, American priest and theologian, May 1961, *Obit* Oct 1967

Myers, B. R., American Korean studies specialist, June 2010

Nabokov, Vladimir Vladimirovich, Russian-American novelist, May 1966, *Obit* Aug 1977

Nabrit, Samuel Milton, American embryologist, Jan 1963, *Obit* Yrbk 2004

Nadler, Marcus, May 1955, *Obit* June 1965

Nakamura, Shuji, Japanese electronics engineer and inventor, Jan 2006

Nesmeianov, A. N., Nov 1958

Neustadt, Richard E., American political scientist, Nov 1968, *Obit* Yrbk 2004

Nevins, Allan, historian, Oct 1968, *Obit* Apr 1971

Newbolt, Francis George, *Obit* Jan 1941

Newcomer, Mabel, Sept 1944

Niederland, William G., psychoanalyst, Oct 1980, *Obit* Oct 1993

Niggli, Josephina, American dramatist, poet, short story writer and novelist, Yrbk 1949

Noble, Ronald K., American international law enforcement official, Jan 2002

Norris, James F., *Obit* Sept 1940

Northrop, John H., American biochemist, June 1947, *Obit* Sept 1987

Northup, Edwin Fitch, *Obit* Jan 1940

Noyes, W. Albert, American chemist, Oct 1947

Noyes, William Albert, American chemist, *Obit* Yrbk 1941

Nozick, Robert, American political philosopher, June 1982, *Obit* Apr 2002

Nunez, Elizabeth, Trinidadian novelist, Jan 2002

Nye, Russel Blaine, historian, July 1945, *Obit* Nov 1993

Nystrom, Paul H., Mar 1951, *Obit* Oct 1969

Ochoa, Severo, Spanish-American biochemist, June 1962, *Obit* Jan 1994

Odell, George Clinton Densmore, Yrbk 1944, *Obit* Yrbk 1949

Ogburn, William Fielding, sociologist, Feb 1955, *Obit* July 1959

Ohlin, Lloyd E., American criminologist, Apr 1963, *Obit* Yrbk 2009

Okun, Arthur M., American economist and presidential aide, Feb 1970, *Obit* May 1980

Oliphant, Mark, Australian physicist, Yrbk 1951, *Obit* Oct 2000

Oliver, James A., Jan 1966, *Obit* May 1982

Olmstead, A. T., *Obit* May 1945

Olopade, Olufunmilayo, Nigerian-American oncologist, Sept 2006

Ondaatje, Michael, Canadian poet and novelist, Oct 1993

Onsager, Lars, American chemist, Apr 1958, *Obit* Jan 1977

Oppenheimer, J. Robert, American physicist, Nov 1945, Apr 1964, *Obit* Apr 1967

Orr, H. Winnett, Oct 1941

Ortner, Sherry B., American anthropologist, Nov 2002

Osborne, Oliver Thomas, *Obit* Yrbk 1940

Overholser, Winfred, Nov 1953, *Obit* Yrbk 1964

Overstreet, H. A., psychologist and philosopher, Sept 1950, *Obit* Oct 1970

Oz, Mehmet C., American surgeon, Apr 2003

Padover, Saul Kussiel, historian, Oct 1952, *Obit* Apr 1981

Pagels, Elaine H., American religion historian, Feb 1996

Paglia, Camille, American feminist writer and critic, Aug 1992

Painter, Nell Irvin, American historian, June 2010

Pais, Abraham, American physicist, Jan 1994, *Obit* Oct 2000

Palade, George, American biologist, July 1967, *Obit* Yrbk 2008

Palmer, Albert DeForest, *Obit* Jan 1940

Park, Thomas, zoologist, Jan 1963, *Obit* June 1992

Parker, Robert B., American mystery writer, Nov 1993, *Obit* Yrbk 2010

Parkes, Henry Bamford, Mar 1954

Parr, Albert Eide, museum director and oceanographer, July 1942, *Obit* Sept 1991

Parry, Albert, professor of Russian studies, Apr 1961, *Obit* July 1992

Parsons, Talcott, American sociologist, Jan 1961, *Obit* July 1979

Patterson, Ernest Minor, Oct 1949

Pauling, Linus C., American chemist, May 1949, Feb 1964, June 1994, *Obit* Oct 1994

Pauly, D., Canadian fishery scientist, Jan 2003

Pavolini, Paolo Emilio, *Obit* Nov 1942

Paz, Hipolito J., Jan 1952

Pearson, T. Gilbert, American ornithologist, *Obit* Oct 1943

Peel, Roy V., Apr 1950

Pei, Mario, linguist, Oct 1968, *Obit* May 1978

Pelikan, Jaroslav Jan, American clergyman and religion historian, Sept 1987, *Obit* Yrbk 2006

Pemberton, John de J., American lawyer and civil

rights activist, May 1969, *Obit* Yrbk 2010

Penfield, Wilder, Canadian surgeon, Nov 1955, July 1968, *Obit* June 1976

Pennebaker, James W., American social psychologist, Aug 2011

Penrose, Roger, British mathematician, Sept 2013

Pepperberg, Irene M., American ethologist, Sept 2008

Perera, Frederica P., American epidemiologist, Oct 2010

Perkins, Frances, American Secretary of labor, Yrbk 1940, *Obit* July 1965

Perry, William James, American Secretary of defense, Jan 1995

Peter, Luther Crouse, *Obit* Jan 1943

Peterson, Reuben, *Obit* Jan 1943

Pevear, Richard, American literary scholar and translator, June 2006

Phelps, William Lyon, literary scholar, Jan 1943

Picard, Emile, *Obit* Feb 1942

Pierce, John Robinson, American electrical engineer, Feb 1961, *Obit* June 2002

Pinker, Steven, American psychologist, Sept 1998

Pinsky, Robert, American poet, Feb 1999

Pintner, Rudolf, Anglo-American psychologist, *Obit* Jan 1943

Piston, Walter, composer, June 1948, Yrbk 1961, *Obit* Jan 1977

Pitzer, Kenneth Sanborn, chemist, May 1950

Pollard, William G., Mar 1953

Ponnamperuma, Cyril, chemist, Apr 1984, *Obit* Mar 1995

Pope, Arthur Upham, American archaeologist and historian, July 1947, *Obit* Nov 1969

Porter, Elizabeth K., Oct 1952

Poulton, Edward Bagnall, *Obit* Jan 1944

Pound, Roscoe, American law professor, May 1947, *Obit* Sept 1964

Poussaint, Alvin F., psychiatrist, July 1973

Powell, Eve Troutt, American historian, May 2004

Prall, David Wight, *Obit* Yrbk 1940

Prasad, Rajendra, Apr 1950, *Obit* Apr 1963

Prentiss, Henrietta, *Obit* Jan 1940

Price, Charles C., chemist, Yrbk 1957

Price, Reynolds, American novelist and short story writer, Apr 1987, *Obit* Yrbk 2011

Primus, Pearl, American dancer and choreographer, Apr 1944, *Obit* Jan 1995

Prince, John Dyneley, *Obit* Nov 1945

Prince-Hughes, Dawn, American anthropologist, Apr 2005

Protess, David, American journalist and social activist, Oct 1999

Quimby, Edith Hinkley, American radiologist, July 1949, *Obit* Mar 1983

Quine, W. V., American philosopher, Nov 1999, *Obit* Mar 2001

Rabassa, Gregory, American translator, Jan 2005

Rabi, Isidor Isaac, American physicist, Apr 1948, *Obit* Mar 1988

Rahmstorf, Stefan, German oceanographer and climatologist, Feb 2010

Rampersad, Arnold, American biographer, Sept 1998

Ramsey, Norman Foster, American physicist, Yrbk 1963, *Obit* Yrbk 2012

Randall, Lisa, American physicist, May 2006

Ranson, Stephen Walter, *Obit* Oct 1942

Rappard, William E., Oct 1951, *Obit* July 1958

Ravdin, I. S., American surgeon, Apr 1968, *Obit* Oct 1972

Ray, Gordon Norton, literary critic, Mar 1968, *Obit* Feb 1987

Redding, J. Saunders, American historian and novelist, Apr 1969, *Obit* Apr 1988

Redfield, Robert, American anthropologist, Yrbk 1953, *Obit* Jan 1959

Reed, Edward Bliss, *Obit* Mar 1940

Rees, Martin J., British astronomer, Jan 2007

Rees, Mina Spiegel, American mathematician and computer scientist, Nov 1957, *Obit* Jan 1998

Reich, Charles A., American law professor, June 1972

Reich, Robert B., American economist and Secretary of labor, Apr 1993

Reich, Walter, American psychiatrist, Aug 2005

Reichs, Kathleen J., American forensic anthropologist, Oct 2006

Reinhardt, Uwe E., American economist, Mar 2004

Reinhart, Carmen, American economist, Mar 2012

Reynolds, Glenn H., American law professor, Oct 2007

Reynolds, James A., *Obit* May 1940

Rich, Adrienne, American poet, Feb 1976, *Obit* Yrbk 2012

Richards, Alfred N., American pharmacologist, Sept 1950, *Obit* Apr 1966

Richter, Charles F., American seismologist, May 1975, *Obit* Nov 1985

Riddell, R. Gerald, Sept 1950, *Obit* Apr 1951

Riecken, Henry W., social psychologist, Yrbk 1961

Riesman, David, American sociologist, Jan 1955, *Obit* Yrbk 2002

Riess, Adam, American astrophysicist, Nov 2012

Riley, Susan B., Feb 1953

Ripley, Sidney Dillon, American zoologist and museum director, Oct 1966, *Obit* Aug 2001

Ripley, William Z., *Obit* Oct 1941

Rivlin, Alice M., American economist and government official, Oct 1982

Robey, Ralph W., American economist and journalist, May 1941, *Obit* Sept 1972

Robinson, Arthur Howard, American cartographer, Mar 1996, *Obit* Yrbk 2005

Rodriguez, Eloy, botanist, May 2000

Rogers, Mark Homer, *Obit* Nov 1941

Rogers, Robert Emmons, *Obit* July 1941

Romanoff, Alexis L., Yrbk 1953

Ronan, William J., Oct 1969

Rose, Mary Swartz, American chemist and nutritionist, *Obit* Mar 1941

Rose, William C., American biochemist, Mar 1953, *Obit* Jan 1986

Rosenberg, Arthur, *Obit* Mar 1943

Rosett, Joshua, *Obit* May 1940

Rossiter, Clinton Lawrence, American historian and political scientist, Apr 1967, *Obit* Yrbk 1970

Rostow, W. W., American economist and presidential adviser, May 1961, *Obit* July 2003

Roszak, Theodore, American historian, Apr 1982, *Obit* Yrbk 2011

Rowley, Janet D., American geneticist, Mar 2001

Royster, Vermont, American journalist, Yrbk 1953, *Obit* Oct 1996

Rubbia, Carlo, Italian physicist, June 1985

Rubik, Erno, Hungarian professor of architecture and inventor, Feb 1987

Rubin de la Borbolla, Daniel F., Feb 1960

Rubin, William Stanley, American art historian and museum curator, Nov 1986, *Obit* Yrbk 2007

Rucker, Rudy von Bitter, American mathematician, computer programmer and science fiction writer, May 2008

Runkle, Erwin W., *Obit* Apr 1941

Rus, Daniela, Romanian computer scientist, Feb 2004

Rusk, Dean, American Secretary of state, June 1949, July 1961, *Obit* Feb 1995

Sabin, Florence Rena, American anatomist, Apr 1945, *Obit* Yrbk 1953

Sachs, Curt, German musicologist, Aug 1944, *Obit* Apr 1959

Saez, Emmanuel, French economist, Sept 2011

Saks, Elyn R., American psychiatrist and law professor, Feb 2011

Salam, Abdus, Pakistani physicist, Apr 1988, *Obit* Jan 1997

Salvemini, Gaetano, Italian-American historian and biographer, Yrbk 1943, *Obit* Nov 1957

Samuelson, Paul A., American economist, May 1965, *Obit* Yrbk 2010

Sapolsky, Robert M., American neurobiologist, Jan 2004

Sarton, George, American science historian, July 1942, *Obit* May 1956

Saulnier, Raymond J., American economist and presidential adviser, Yrbk 1957, *Obit* Yrbk 2009

Saxton, Alexander, American historian and novelist, Nov 1943, *Obit* Yrbk 2012

Schama, Simon, British historian, Nov 1991

Schapiro, Meyer, American art historian, July 1984, *Obit* May 1996

Schilder, Paul, Austrian psychiatrist, *Obit* Jan 1941

Schlauch, Margaret, Polish professor of English, Yrbk 1942, *Obit* Sept 1986

Schmid, Carlo, Feb 1965, *Obit* Apr 1980

Schmitt, Bernadotte Everly, historian, Yrbk 1942, *Obit* May 1969

Schneirla, T. C., Yrbk 1955, *Obit* Nov 1968

Schoen-Rene, Anna Eugenie, *Obit* Jan 1943

Schopf, J. William, American geologist, May 1995

Schultze, Charles L., American economist and government official, Jan 1970

Schulz, Leo, *Obit* Oct 1944

Schwartz, Pepper, American sociologist, June 2008

Schwinger, Julian, American physicist, Oct 1967, *Obit* Sept 1994

Scott, K. Frances, Nov 1948

Sears, William, pediatrician and writer on health, Aug 2001

Segal, Erich, American novelist and classicist, Apr 1971, *Obit* Yrbk 2010

Segni, Antonio, Yrbk 1955, *Obit* Jan 1973

Segre, Emilio, American physicist, Apr 1960, *Obit* July 1989

Seibert, Florence, American biochemist, Nov 1942, *Obit* Oct 1991

Selzer, Richard, American surgeon, essayist and short story writer, Apr 1993

Senior, Clarence, Yrbk 1961, *Obit* Nov 1974

Sereno, Paul C., American paleontologist, June 1997

Serre, Jean Pierre, French mathematician, Jan 2003

Sessions, Roger, American composer, Jan 1975, *Obit* May 1985

Sewell, Winifred, American library science professor, June 1960

Shambaugh, Benjamin Franklin, *Obit* May 1940

Shange, Ntozake, American poet and dramatist, Sept 1978

Shannon, James A., public health official, Jan 1965, *Obit* July 1994

Shapiro, Karl Jay, American poet and critic, Oct 1944, *Obit* Aug 2000

Shechtman, Daniel, Scientist and educator, May 2012

Sherman, Henry C., Jan 1949, *Obit* Yrbk 1955

Shockley, William, American physicist, Yrbk 1953, *Obit* Oct 1989

Short, Dewey, American congressman and military official, Yrbk 1951, *Obit* Feb 1980

Shotwell, James Thompson, Canadian-American historian, Oct 1944, *Obit* Sept 1965

Shoup, Carl Sumner, American economist, Feb 1949, *Obit* Sept 2000

Shubin, Neil, American biologist and paleontologist, Apr 2007

Shulman, Harry, Apr 1952, *Obit* May 1955

Shultz, George P., American Secretary of state, May 1969, Apr 1988

Shumway, Norman, American surgeon, Apr 1971, *Obit* Yrbk 2006

Silva Calderon, Alvaro, Venezuelan international

petroleum organization official, Jan 2002

Simkin, William E., American labor mediator, Jan 1967, *Obit* May 1992

Simon, Herbert A., American social scientist, June 1979, *Obit* May 2001

Simonds, Frederic W., *Obit* May 1941

Simons, Elwyn L., paleontologist and primatologist, June 1994

Simons, Hans, Mar 1957, *Obit* May 1972

Singer, Peter, Australian bioethicist, Mar 1991

Singer, S. Fred, American physicist, Yrbk 1955

Sinnott, Edmund W., American botanist, Oct 1948, *Obit* Mar 1968

Sinsheimer, Robert, American biologist, June 1968

Sizoo, Joseph R., Yrbk 1964, *Obit* Nov 1966

Skilton, Charles Sanford, *Obit* May 1941

Skocpol, Theda, American political scientist, Aug 2000

Slichter, Sumner H., American economist, June 1947, *Obit* Yrbk 1959

Smith, Amy, American mechanical engineer, June 2005

Smith, Anna Deavere, American actress and dramatist, Sept 1994

Smith, Clara E., *Obit* July 1943

Smith, Cyril Stanley, science historian, July 1948, *Obit* Oct 1992

Smith, David T., Oct 1950

Smith, Page, historian, Sept 1990, *Obit* Nov 1995

Smith, Roy Burnett, *Obit* Feb 1941

Smith, T. V., Feb 1956, *Obit* July 1964

Smith, William Jay, American poet and state legislator, Mar 1974

Smoot, George, American astrophysicist, Apr 1994

Snell, George Davis, American geneticist, May 1986, *Obit* Aug 1996

Snodgrass, W. D., American poet, critic and philologist, Nov 1960, *Obit* Yrbk 2009

Snyder, Alice D., *Obit* Apr 1943

Soderberg, Alicia, American astrophysicist, Oct 2009

Soffer, Olga, Yusoslav-American archaeologist, July 2002

Sowell, Thomas, American economist, July 1981

Spain, Frances Lander, American librarian and college administrator, June 1960

Spelke, Elizabeth S., American psychologist, Apr 2006

Spergel, David N., American astrophysicist, Jan 2005

Sperry, Roger Wolcott, American psychologist, Jan 1986, *Obit* June 1994

Spiegelman, Solomon, geneticist, Nov 1980, *Obit* Mar 1983

Spiller, William Gibson, *Obit* Apr 1940

Spitzer, Lyman, American astrophysicist, Jan 1960, *Obit* June 1997

Sprague, Embert Hiram, *Obit* Mar 1940

Spurgeon, Caroline F. E., *Obit* Yrbk 1942

Squyres, Steve, American planetary geologist, Nov 2006

Stakman, Elvin Charles, American botanist, Yrbk 1949, *Obit* Mar 1979

Stanley, Wendell Meredith, American biochemist, Apr 1947, *Obit* Sept 1971

Starkie, Walter Fitzwilliam, Anglo-Irish literary critic, May 1964, *Obit* Feb 1977

Steele, Claude M., American social psychologist, Feb 2001

Steele, Shelby, American writer and professor of English, Feb 1993

Stein, Herbert, American economist, Mar 1973, *Obit* Feb 2000

Stein, Janice Gross, Canadian international relations specialist, Aug 2006

Stern, Jessica, American terrorism expert, May 2006

Stern, Richard G., American novelist and short story writer, June 1994, *Obit* Yrbk 2013

Stiebeling, Hazel K., American nutritionist, Apr 1950

Stiles, Charles Wardell, American public health official and zoologist, *Obit* Mar 1941

Stoessel, Albert, *Obit* July 1943

Stone, John Charles, *Obit* July 1940

Stowe, Leland, journalist, July 1940, *Obit* Mar 1994

Strang, Ruth, Yrbk 1960, *Obit* Feb 1971

Stuart, Duane Reed, *Obit* Oct 1941

Stuhlinger, Ernst, American rocket engineer, Nov 1957, *Obit* Yrbk 2008

Sumner, James Batcheller, American biochemist, Jan 1947, *Obit* Oct 1955

Sunstein, Cass R., American law professor, Oct 2008

Suzuki, Umetaro, *Obit* Nov 1943

Swallow, Alan, Feb 1963, *Obit* Jan 1967

Szasz, Thomas Stephen, American psychiatrist and psychoanalyst, Jan 1975, *Obit* Yrbk 2012

S enz Ryan, Maritza, Mar 2013

Talbot, A. N., *Obit* May 1942

Talley, James, *Obit* Sept 1941

Tannen, Deborah, American linguist, July 1994

Tanner, John Henry, *Obit* Mar 1940

Tao, Terence, Australian mathematician, Sept 2007

Tarr, Curtis W., Sept 1970, *Obit* Yrbk 2013

Taussig, Helen Brooke, American pediatrician, Sept 1946, Mar 1966, *Obit* July 1986

Taylor, George William, labor mediator, May 1942, *Obit* Feb 1973

Taylor, Herman A., American cardiologist, June 2006

Taylor, Jill Bolte, American neuroanatomist, Jan 2009

Teleki, Pal, Hungarian statesman, *Obit* May 1941

Tennent, David Hilt, American biologist, *Obit* Mar 1941

Thernstrom, Abigail M., American social critic, Mar 2010

Thomas, Michael, American novelist, Feb 2008

Thompson, Holland, *Obit* Yrbk 1940

Thompson, Homer A., Canadian archaeologist, Apr 1948, *Obit* Yrbk 2000

Thompson, James Westfall, *Obit* Yrbk 1941

Thomson, James A., American molecular biologist, Nov 2001

Thorek, Max, Jan 1951, *Obit* Mar 1960

Thurman, Howard, American clergyman and theologian, June 1955, *Obit* June 1981

Thurow, Lester C., American economist, Nov 1990

Tiger, Lionel, anthropologist, Jan 1981

Tillich, Paul, German-American theologian, Mar 1954, *Obit* Yrbk 1965

Titulescu, Nicolae, Romanian diplomat, *Obit* May 1941

Tobin, Harold J., *Obit* Aug 1942

Tobin, James, American economist, Oct 1984, *Obit* May 2002

Toledo, Alejandro, Peruvian president, Nov 2001

Tower, John, American senator, Yrbk 1962, *Obit* June 1991

Townes, Charles H., American physicist, Mar 1963

Trask, James D., American pediatrician, *Obit* July 1942

Trethewey, Natasha D., American poet, Aug 2007

Trevor-Roper, H. R., British historian, Sept 1983, *Obit* July 2003

Tribe, Laurence H., American law professor, July 1988

Troost, Laurens, Jan 1953

Trout, J. D., American philosopher, July 2009

True, Rodney Howard, *Obit* May 1940

Trueblood, Elton, philosopher, Jan 1964, *Obit* Mar 1995

Tufte, Edward R., American political scientist, statistician and graphic designer, Nov 2007

Tugwell, Rexford G., American territorial governor, economist and political scientist, Sept 1941, Jan 1963, *Obit* Sept 1979

Tunnard, Christopher, Canadian landscape architect, June 1959, *Obit* May 1979

Turin, Luca, British biophysicist, Aug 2008

Turkle, Sherry, American sociologist and psychologist, Aug 1997

Turnbull, Colin M., English anthropologist, Sept 1980, *Obit* Sept 1994

Tyson, Laura D'Andrea, American economist and presidential adviser, Sept 1996

Unden, Osten, Feb 1947, *Obit* Apr 1974

Urey, Harold Clayton, American chemist, Feb 1941, July 1960, *Obit* Mar 1981

Van Allen, James Alfred, American astrophysicist, Jan 1959, *Obit* Yrbk 2007

Varmus, Harold, American virologist and public health official, Nov 1996

Vendler, Helen Hennessy, American literary scholar, May 1986

Venkatesh, Sudhir, American sociologist, May 2010

Vermeij, Geerat J., American marine biologist, June 1995

Villa-Komaroff, Lydia, American molecular biologist, July 2008

Von Neumann, John, American mathematician, July 1955, *Obit* Apr 1957

Vrba, Elisabeth S., South African paleontologist, June 1997

Waal, Frans de, Dutch primatologist, Mar 2006

Waddington, C. H., British embryologist, Apr 1962, *Obit* Nov 1975

Wadhams, Robert Pelton, *Obit* Feb 1941

Wald, George, American biochemist, May 1968, *Obit* June 1997

Walker, Alice, American novelist, poet, essayist and short story writer, Mar 1984

Walker, Margaret, American poet and novelist, Nov 1943, *Obit* June 1999

Walker, Mildred, American novelist, Yrbk 1947, *Obit* Aug 1998

Walker, Norma Ford, Canadian geneticist, Oct 1957, *Obit* Nov 1968

Waller, Robert James, author, May 1994

Wallerstein, Immanuel Maurice, American sociologist, May 2009

Walsh, William Thomas, July 1941, *Obit* Mar 1949

Wambaugh, Eugene, *Obit* Sept 1940

Warnock, Mary, British philosopher, Jan 2005

Warren, Shields, June 1950, *Obit* Sept 1980

Wasserburg, Gerald Joseph, American professor of geology and geophysics, Mar 1986

Watrous, George Dutton, *Obit* Yrbk 1940

Watson, James D., American molecular biologist, Apr 1963, Oct 1990

Way, Niobe, psychologist, Feb 2012

Weaver, Warren, Apr 1952, *Obit* Feb 1979

Webb, Walter Loring, *Obit* Mar 1941

Wecter, Dixon, historian, Nov 1944, *Obit* Sept 1950

Weiss, Paul, American philosopher, May 1969, *Obit* Yrbk 2002

Weiss, Paul A., American biologist, Oct 1970, *Obit* Nov 1989

Weiss, Soma, *Obit* Mar 1942

Weisskopf, Victor Frederick, Austrian-American physicist, Nov 1976, *Obit* Yrbk 2002

Wells, Agnes, Nov 1949, *Obit* Oct 1959

Wells, H. Gideon, American pathologist, *Obit* June 1943

Wellstone, Paul David, American senator, May 1993, *Obit* Yrbk 2003

Welsh, Edward Cristy, economist, Jan 1967, *Obit* June 1990

Wendrich, Willeke, Dutch archaeologist, Jan 2007

Werner, Wendelin, German-French mathematician, Jan 2006

West, Cornel, American philosopher, Oct 1993

Westcott, John Howell, *Obit* July 1942

Wexler, Nancy S., American psychologist and neurologist, Aug 1994

Wheeler, John Archibald, American physicist, Jan 1970, *Obit* Yrbk 2008

Whipple, Fred Lawrence, American astronomer, May 1952, *Obit* Yrbk 2005

White, Gilbert Fowler, American geographer, Mar 1953, *Obit* Yrbk 2006

White, Helen Constance, literary scholar and author, July 1945

White, Robert E., American diplomat, May 1984

Wick, Frances G., *Obit* Aug 1941

Wideman, John Edgar, American novelist and short story writer, Jan 1991

Widnall, Sheila Evans, American Secretary of the air force, Oct 1997

Wigner, Eugene P., American physicist, Apr 1953, *Obit* Mar 1995

Wilbur, Ray Lyman, Nov 1947, *Obit* Sept 1949

Wilcox, Clair, Yrbk 1948

Wiles, Andrew, English mathematician, Mar 1996

Wilkins, Robert W., American physician, July 1958, *Obit* Yrbk 2003

Wilkins, T. Russell, *Obit* Feb 1941

Williams, John Alfred, American novelist, Oct 1994

Williams, John H., Jan 1960, *Obit* May 1966

Williams, Joseph John, *Obit* Yrbk 1940

Williams, William Robert, *Obit* Jan 1941

Williston, Samuel, Yrbk 1954, *Obit* Apr 1963

Wills, Garry, American journalist, essayist and historian, June 1982

Wilson, Carroll Louis, energy expert and educator, May 1947, *Obit* Mar 1983

Wilson, George Arthur, *Obit* Nov 1941

Wilson, James Q., American political scientist, Aug 2002, *Obit* Yrbk 2012

Wilson, Kenneth Geddes, American physicist, Sept 1983, *Obit* Yrbk 2013

Wilson, Sloan, American novelist, Sept 1959, *Obit* Yrbk 2003

Wilson, William Julius, American sociologist, Feb 1996

Windschuttle, Keith, Australian writer and historian, Jan 2006

Winter, George B., *Obit* May 1940

Wirth, Niklaus, Swiss computer scientist, Jan 2003

Wirtz, Willard, American Secretary of labor, Nov 1946, Feb 1963, *Obit* Yrbk 2010

Witte, Edwin E., American eonomist and government official, July 1946, *Obit* Sept 1960

Witten, Edward, American physicist, June 1997

Wolfe, Hugh C., Feb 1950

Wolff, Tobias, American memoirist and short story writer, Jan 1996

Wolman, Leo, Sept 1949, *Obit* Yrbk 1961

Wolpoff, Milford H., American paleoanthropologist, July 2006

Wood, Gordon S., American historian, Oct 2011

Woodward, R. B., American biochemist, Feb 1952, *Obit* Sept 1979

Woolley, Mary E., Mar 1942, *Obit* Nov 1947

Wright, Irving S., professor of medicine, Oct 1968, *Obit* Mar 1998

Wright, Jane Cooke, American physician, May 1968, *Obit* Yrbk 2013

Wright, Quincy, American political scientist, Oct 1943, *Obit* Yrbk 1970

Wu, Chien Shiung, Chinese-American physicist, Oct 1959, *Obit* Apr 1997

Yarmolinsky, Adam, American law professor and government official, Mar 1969, *Obit* June 2000

Yeh, George K. C., Mar 1953, *Obit* Jan 1982

Yerushalmy, Jacob, Mar 1958

Yeutter, Clayton K., American Secretary of agriculture and political leader, July 1988

Young, Hugh, American surgeon and urologist, *Obit* Sept 1945

Young, Karl, *Obit* Jan 1944

Young, Kimberly S., American psychologist, Jan 2006

Yunus, Muhammad, Bangladeshi banker and economist, Jan 2002

Zacharias, Jerrold R., physicist, Feb 1964, *Obit* Sept 1986

Ziegler, Jean, Swiss sociologist, socialist leader and human rights activist, July 2010

Zinn, Howard, American historian, Aug 1999, *Obit* Yrbk 2010

Zinsser, Hans, American bacteriologist, *Obit* Oct 1940

Zuberbuhler, Klaus, Swiss psychologist and primatologist, July 2010

Zulli, Floyd, Jan 1958, *Obit* Jan 1981

Colonial administrators

Alexander, Harold Rupert Leofric George Alexander, British field marshal, Oct 1942, *Obit* Sept 1969

Badoglio, Pietro, Italian field marshal, Oct 1940, *Obit* Jan 1957

Eboue, Felix, French colonial governor, *Obit* July 1944

Graziani, Rodolfo, Italian field marshal and colonial administrator, Apr 1941, *Obit* Mar 1955

Halifax, Edward Frederick Lindley Wood, British statesman, Sept 1940, *Obit* Feb 1960

Lacoste, Robert, French socialist leader, Nov 1957

Linlithgow, Victor Alexander John Hope, British colonial administrator, Jan 1942, *Obit* Feb 1952

Lloyd of Dolobran, George Ambrose Lloyd, British colonial administrator, Jan 1941, *Obit* Jan 1941

MacDonald, Malcolm, British colonial administrator and diplomat, Nov 1954, *Obit* Mar 1981

Messmer, Pierre, French prime minister, Nov 1963, *Obit* Yrbk 2007

Mountbatten of Burma, Louis Mountbatten, British admiral, June 1942, *Obit* Oct 1979

Patten, Chris, British colonial governor and European Commission official, July 1993

Vanier, Georges, Canadian governor general, Jan 1960, *Obit* May 1967

Welensky, Roy, British colonial administrator, July 1959, *Obit* Feb 1992

Willingdon, Freeman Freeman-Thomas, British colonial administrator, *Obit* Oct 1941

Colonial leaders

Blundell, Michael, British farmer and colonial leader, Mar 1954

Color consultants

Birren, Faber, industrial color consultant, May 1956, *Obit* Feb 1989

Columnists

Adams, Franklin P., humorist, July 1941, *Obit* May 1960

Ahlgren, Mildred Carlson, American newspaper columnist and organization official, July 1952

Alexander, Holmes Moss, columnist and author, Sept 1956

Allen, Robert Sharon, May 1941

Alsop, Joseph, American journalist, Oct 1952, *Obit* Oct 1989

Alsop, Stewart, American journalist, Oct 1952, *Obit* July 1974

Ames, Jonathan, American novelist, humorist and columnist, Oct 2007

Anderson, Jack, American newspaper columnist, June 1972, *Obit* Yrbk 2006

Bacharach, Bert, American fashion critic, Yrbk 1957

Baldrige, Letitia, columnist, social secretary and public relations executive, Feb 1988, *Obit* Yrbk 2013

Barry, Dave, American humorist, May 1998

Bartlett, Bruce R., American economist and columnist, June 2006

Berendt, John, American writer, Apr 1998

Berger, Meyer, newspaper reporter and columnist, Jan 1943, *Obit* Apr 1959

Binchy, Maeve, Irish novelist and short story writer, Nov 1995, *Obit* Yrbk 2012

Bishop, Jim, columnist and author, June 1969, *Obit* Sept 1987

Bittman, Mark, American food columnist and cookbook writer, Feb 2005

Bombeck, Erma, American humorist, Feb 1979, *Obit* June 1996

Boutell, Clarence B., July 1946

Bradford, Barbara Taylor, English novelist, Oct 1991

Breslin, Jimmy, American author and columnist, Yrbk 1973

Broder, David S., American columnist and political commentator, Sept 2010, *Obit* Yrbk 2011

Brody, Jane E., American columnist and nutritionist, Feb 1986

Brooks, David, American journalist and political commentator, Apr 2004

Brothers, Joyce, psychologist, Apr 1971, *Obit* Yrbk 2013

Broun, Heywood, American journalist, *Obit* Jan 1940

Brown, Helen Gurley, American magazine editor, Nov 1969, *Obit* Yrbk 2012

Brown, Tony, American television talk show host and producer, Feb 1997

Bruns, Franklin R., May 1954

Buchanan, Patrick, American political commentator, Aug 1985

Buchwald, Art, American humorist, Jan 1960, *Obit* May 2007

Buckley, William F., American magazine editor, columnist and novelist, June 1962, Oct 1982, *Obit* June 2008

Bushnell, Candace, American advice columnist and novelist, Nov 2003

Carlson, Margaret, American journalist, Nov 2003

Carter, John Franklin, journalist and author, Oct 1941, *Obit* Jan 1968

Chamberlain, John, journalist and critic, Apr 1940, *Obit* June 1995

Childs, Marquis William, journalist and author, Jan 1943, *Obit* Sept 1990

Claiborne, Craig, American food critic, Sept 1969, *Obit* Apr 2000

Cohen, Roger, British journalist, May 2008

Collins, Gail, American columnist, Mar 1999

Considine, Bob, columnist, Yrbk 1947, *Obit* Nov 1975

Crittenden, Danielle, Canadian journalist, July 2003

Crouch, Stanley, American essayist and critic, Mar 1994

Daly, Maureen, American young adult novelist, Jan 1946, *Obit* Yrbk 2006

Davis, Tobe Coller, Yrbk 1959, *Obit* Feb 1963

Dickinson, Amy, American freelance writer and advice columnist, Apr 2004

Dionne, E. J., American columnist and political commentator, May 2006

Dix, Dorothy, American advice columnist, Jan 1940, *Obit* Feb 1952

Douthat, Ross Gregory, American journalist, Aug 2009

Dowd, Maureen, American newspaper columnist, Sept 1996

Fleeson, Doris, American newspaper columnist, May 1959, *Obit* Oct 1970

Frayn, Michael, English dramatist and novelist, Jan 1985

Friedman, Thomas L., American newspaper columnist, Oct 1995

Fulghum, Robert, clergyman and essayist, July 1994

Germond, Jack, American columnist and political commentator, July 2005

Geyer, Georgie Anne, columnist, Aug 1986

Gilbreth, Frank B., American journalist, memoirist and novelist, May 1949, *Obit* July 2001

Gleick, James, American science writer, July 2011

Grafton, Samuel, columnist, Jan 1940, *Obit* Feb 1998

Graham, Sheilah, American gossip columnist, Oct 1969, *Obit* Jan 1989

Granderson, LZ, Journalist and online columnist, Oct 2012

Greene, Bob, American journalist, July 1995

Guest, Edgar A., American newspaper columnist, Sept 1941, *Obit* Nov 1959

Hagy, Ruth Geri, Oct 1957

Haskin, Frederic J., *Obit* June 1944

Hauser, Gayelord, German-American nutritionist and author, June 1955, *Obit* Feb 1985

Hax, Carolyn, American advice columnist, Nov 2002

Hebert, F. Edward, American congressman, Nov 1951, *Obit* Feb 1980

Hellinger, Mark, columnist and motion picture producer, Sept 1947, *Obit* July 1948

Heloise, American advice columnist, June 1996

Helprin, Mark, American short story writer and novelist, Aug 1991

Hentoff, Nat, American journalist and young adult novelist, Aug 1986

Herbert, Bob, American columnist, Oct 1998

Hiaasen, Carl, American novelist and columnist, Apr 1997

Hopper, Hedda, American gossip columnist, Nov 1942, *Obit* Mar 1966

Howar, Barbara, columnist and television reporter, Aug 1989

Ivins, Molly, American columnist, June 2000, *Obit* Yrbk 2007

Karbo, Karen, American novelist, May 2001

Kempton, Murray, American newspaper columnist, June 1973, *Obit* July 1997

Kilgallen, Dorothy, American newspaper columnist, Feb 1952, *Obit* Jan 1966

Kilpatrick, James J., American columnist, July 1980, *Obit* Yrbk 2010

King, Florence, American satirist, Apr 2006

Kinsley, Michael, American columnist and commentator, May 1995

Klein, Naomi, Canadian journalist and social activist, Aug 2003

Knight, Ruth Adams, Aug 1943, Yrbk 1955

Knipfel, Jim, American memoirist, columnist and novelist, Mar 2005

Kollmar, Richard, Feb 1952, *Obit* Feb 1971

Krauthammer, Charles, American columnist, Jan 2008

Kristof, Nicholas D., American newspaper columnist, Feb 2006

Krugman, Paul R., American economist, Aug 2001

Kurtz, Howard, American journalist, Jan 2011

La Gorce, John Oliver, Nov 1954, *Obit* Feb 1960

Landers, Ann, American advice columnist, Nov 1957, *Obit* Nov 2002

Leo, John, American magazine columnist, Sept 2006

Leonard, Hugh, Irish playwright, Apr 1983, *Obit* Yrbk 2009

Lerner, Max, American columnist, Oct 1942, *Obit* Aug 1992

Lewis, Anthony, American journalist, Nov 1955, *Obit* Yrbk 2013

Lewis, Flora, American columnist, Jan 1989, *Obit* Yrbk 2002

Lindley, Ernest K., journalist, June 1943, *Obit* Yrbk 1991

Littell, Philip, *Obit* Yrbk 1943

Lupica, Mike, American sportswriter, Mar 2001

Manning, Marie, columnist, Aug 1944, *Obit* Jan 1946

Martin, Judith, American columnist and expert on etiquette, June 1986

Martin, Roland S., American journalist, June 2009

Maxwell, Elsa, columnist and society hostess, Mar 1943, *Obit* Jan 1964

Maynard, Joyce, American journalist, memoirist and novelist, Jan 1999

McAlary, Mike, columnist, *Obit* Mar 1999

McCormick, Anne O'Hare, journalist, Mar 1940, *Obit* July 1954

McGill, Ralph, American newspaper editor, June 1947, *Obit* Mar 1969

Moley, Raymond, American journalist and government

official, July 1945, *Obit* Apr 1975

Mollenhoff, Clark R., journalist, Nov 1958, *Obit* May 1991

Montgomery, Ruth Shick, author and journalist, Feb 1957

Morehead, Albert H., Mar 1955, *Obit* Yrbk 1966

Morehouse, Ward, Jan 1940, *Obit* Feb 1967

Morgan, Lucy, newspaper columnist, Mar 1959

Morin, Relman, Nov 1958, *Obit* Oct 1973

Mowrer, Edgar Ansel, journalist, Oct 1941, July 1962, *Obit* May 1977

Nocera, Joseph, American journalist, Oct 2011

North, Oliver L., American Marine corps officer, columnist and television personality, Mar 1992

Paddleford, Clementine, American food writer, Feb 1958, *Obit* Jan 1968

Page, Clarence, American columnist, Jan 2003

Parsons, Louella, American gossip columnist, Oct 1940, *Obit* Oct 1973

Pearson, Drew, American journalist, May 1941, *Obit* Nov 1969

Pegler, Westbrook, American columnist, Mar 1940, *Obit* Sept 1969

Petrini, Carlo, Italian food safety activist, Jan 2004

Phillips, Harry Irving, American newspaper columnist and humorist, Sept 1943, *Obit* Apr 1965

Phillips, Kevin P., American political writer, Sept 1994

Pitts, Leonard J., American newspaper columnist, Oct 2004

Porter, Sylvia Field, financial columnist, Oct 1941, Apr 1980, *Obit* Aug 1991

Post, Emily, American advice columnist, Mar 1941, *Obit* Nov 1960

Pratt, William Veazie, June 1943, *Obit* Feb 1958

Quindlen, Anna, American novelist and columnist, Apr 1993

Raspberry, William J., American newspaper columnist, *Obit* Yrbk 2012

Reston, James, American journalist, Mar 1943, Nov 1980, *Obit* Feb 1996

Rich, Frank, American newspaper columnist, Apr 1999

Righter, Carroll, astrologer, Oct 1972, *Obit* June 1988

Robb, Inez Callaway, American journalist, Yrbk 1958, *Obit* June 1979

Roosevelt, Eleanor, wife of American president Franklin D. Roosevelt and diplomat, Nov 1940, Jan 1949, *Obit* Jan 1963

Rose, Billy, American theatrical producer, Aug 1940, *Obit* Mar 1966

Royko, Mike, American newspaper columnist, June 1994, *Obit* July 1997

Rubin, Theodore Isaac, Feb 1980

Rukeyser, Louis, American television moderator, Feb 1983, *Obit* Nov 2006

Runbeck, Margaret Lee, Yrbk 1952, *Obit* Yrbk 1956

Runyon, Damon, American journalist and short story writer, Nov 1942, *Obit* Jan 1947

Safire, William, American journalist, essayist and novelist, Yrbk 1973, *Obit* Yrbk 2009

Savage, Dan, American advice columnist, July 2009

Schlafly, Phyllis, American social activist and writer, June 1978

Shields, Mark, American political commentator and columnist, May 2005

Smith, Liz, American gossip columnist, May 1987

Smith, Red, American sportswriter, Apr 1959, *Obit* Feb 1982

Snow, Tony, American television moderator, commentator and presidential press secretary, Sept 2006, *Obit* Yrbk 2008

Sokolsky, George E., May 1941, *Obit* Jan 1963

Sowell, Thomas, American economist, July 1981

Steel, Johannes, radio commentator and columnist, June 1941, *Obit* Feb 1989

Strout, Richard Lee, journalist and columnist, Apr 1980, *Obit* Oct 1990

Sullivan, Ed, American columnist and television personality, Sept 1952, *Obit* Nov 1974

Sulzberger, C. L., American journalist, May 1944, *Obit* Nov 1993

TerHorst, Jerald F., American presidential press secretary, Feb 1975, *Obit* Yrbk 2010

Thompson, Dorothy, American columnist, July 1940, *Obit* Mar 1961

Thompson, Hunter S., American journalist, Mar 1981, *Obit* Yrbk 2005

Tierney, John, American journalist, Aug 2005

Toledano, Ralph de, American columnist and political writer, Yrbk 1962, *Obit* Yrbk 2007

Van Buren, Abigail, advice columnist, May 1960, *Obit* Yrbk 2013

Van Horne, Harriet, radio and television critic, Yrbk 1954, *Obit* Mar 1998

Wicker, Tom, columnist, Nov 1973, *Obit* Yrbk 2012

Will, George F., American columnist and political commentator, Sept 1981

Williams, Armstrong, American newspaper columnist and radio talk show host, May 2004

Witcover, Jules, American newspaper columnist and writer, Apr 2008

Wood, Kingsley, Nov 1940

Yardley, Jonathan, American literary critic and columnist, Jan 2011

Yeakley, Marjory Hall, Yrbk 1957

Zakaria, Fareed, Indian-American political scientist and journalist, Jan 2003

Comedians

Abbott and Costello, comedians, Oct 1941

Abbott, Bud, American comedian, Oct 1941, *Obit* June 1974

Allen, Fred, comedian, Feb 1941, *Obit* May 1956

Allen, Gracie, American comedienne, July 1940, Mar 1951, *Obit* Oct 1964

Allen, Tim, American comedian and actor, May 1995

Ansari, Aziz, American comedian and actor, Feb 2013

Arquette, Cliff, June 1961, *Obit* Nov 1974

Ballard, Kaye, American actress, singer and comedienne, Sept 1969

Bamford, Maria, comedian, Jan 2012

Bana, Eric, Australian comedian and actor, Jan 2003

Baron-Cohen, Sacha, British comedian, Jan 2003

Bean, Orson, comedian, Feb 1967

Belushi, John, American comedian, Jan 1980, *Obit* Apr 1982

Benny, Jack, comedian, Aug 1941, Nov 1963, *Obit* Feb 1975

Berle, Milton, American comedian, June 1949, *Obit* Yrbk 2002

Bernhard, Sandra, American comedienne and actress, Sept 1990

Bickel, George, American comedian and actor, *Obit* Aug 1941

Black, Jack, American singer and actor, Feb 2002

Black, Michael Ian, American actor, Sept 2013

Bob and Ray, American comedians, Oct 1957

Boosler, Elayne, comedienne, May 1993

Borge, Victor, American pianist and comedian, Mar 1946, May 1993, *Obit* Mar 2001

Bradbury, James H., *Obit* Yrbk 1940

Brand, Russell, British comedian and actor, Jan 2011

Brenner, David, American comedian, Mar 1987

Brice, Fanny, American singer and comedian, June 1946, *Obit* July 1951

Buress, Hannibal, American comedian, Aug 2012

Butterworth, Charles, *Obit* July 1946

Buttons, Red, American comedian and actor, Sept 1958, *Obit* Yrbk 2006

C. K., Louis, American comedian, Feb 2010

Caesar, Sid, American comedian and actor, Apr 1951

Cambridge, Godfrey, American actor and comedian, Mar 1969, *Obit* Feb 1977

Cantinflas, Mexican comedian, June 1953, *Obit* June 1993

Carr, Alexander, *Obit* Yrbk 1946

Carrey, Jim, Canadian comedian and actor, Feb 1996

Carvey, Dana, American comedian and actor, June 1992

Cedric the Entertainer, American comedian, Feb 2004

Chappelle, Dave, American comedian and actor, June 2004

Chen Peisi, Chinese actor and comedian, Jan 2004

Cho, Margaret, American comedienne, Oct 2000

Clement, Jemaine, New Zealand comedian, Mar 2008

Coca, Imogene, American actress and comedienne, Apr 1951, *Obit* Sept 2001

Colbert, Stephen, American comedian and actor, Nov 2006

Conway, Tim, American comedian and actor, Apr 1981

Coogan, Steve, English actor and comedian, Jan 2002

Correll, Charles J., Yrbk 1947, *Obit* Nov 1972

Costello, Lou, American comedian, Oct 1941, *Obit* May 1959

Dale, Jim, English actor, July 1981

Dangerfield, Rodney, American comedian, *Obit* Feb 2005

Davis, Joan, comedienne and actress, June 1945, *Obit* Sept 1961

Debbouze, Jamel, French comedian and actor, Jan 2005

Diller, Phyllis, American comedienne, July 1967, *Obit* Yrbk 2012

Dujardin, Jean, Oct 2013

Durante, Jimmy, comedian, Sept 1946, *Obit* Mar 1980

Elliott, Bob, American comedian, Oct 1957

Fabray, Nanette, comedienne, Jan 1956

Fay, Frank, Aug 1945, *Obit* Yrbk 1961

Ferrell, Will, American comedian and actor, Feb 2003

Fields, Lew, comedian, *Obit* Sept 1941

Finch, Flora, *Obit* Jan 1940

Flanders, Michael, Jan 1970, *Obit* June 1975

Flight of the Conchords, Mar 2008

Foxx, Jamie, American comedian and actor, May 2005

Foxx, Redd, American comedian, Yrbk 1972, *Obit* Jan 1992

Franken, Al, American senator, June 1999

Frye, David, American impressionist, Mar 1975, *Obit* Yrbk 2011

Gleason, Jackie, American actor, Oct 1955, *Obit* Aug 1987

Gobel, George, comedian, Mar 1955, *Obit* Apr 1991

Goldthwait, Bobcat, American comedian, Sept 2010

Goodwin, Harry, *Obit* Yrbk 1942

Goulding, Ray, American comedian, Oct 1957, *Obit* May 1990

Green, Tom, Canadian comedian, Oct 2003

Griffin, Kathy, American comedienne and actress, Sept 2008

Hackett, Buddy, American comedian, May 1965, *Obit* Oct 2003

Handler, Chelsea, American comedian and actress, Oct 2010

Hibbard, Edna, *Obit* Feb 1943

Hill, Benny, English comedian, Feb 1983, *Obit* June 1992

Hogan, Paul, Australian comedian, Aug 1987

Hope, Bob, American comedian and actor, June 1941, Oct 1953, *Obit* Yrbk 2003

Hughley, D. L., American comedian, Mar 2000

Izzard, Eddie, British comedian and actor, Jan 2003

Jackson, Joe, American comedian, *Obit* July 1942

Jessel, George, singer, dancer and comedian, Mar 1943, *Obit* July 1981

Johnson, Chic, American comedian, Sept 1940, *Obit* Apr 1962

Jones, Billy, *Obit* Jan 1941

Jordan, Jim, American radio performer, Nov 1941, *Obit* May 1988

Karno, Fred, English comedian and theatrical producer, *Obit* Nov 1941

Kay, Beatrice, Yrbk 1942

Kaye, Danny, American comedian, actor and singer, Yrbk 1941, Nov 1952, *Obit* Apr 1987

Kimmel, Jimmy, American comedian, Oct 2009

King, Alan, American comedian, June 1970, *Obit* Yrbk 2004

Kirby, George, comedian, May 1977, *Obit* Jan 1996

Klein, Robert, American comedian, Mar 1977

Korman, Harvey, American actor, Oct 1979, *Obit* Yrbk 2008

Kovacs, Ernie, American comedian, Feb 1958, *Obit* Mar 1962

Langdon, Harry, American actor and comedian, *Obit* Feb 1945

Lawrence, Martin, American comedian and actor, Oct 1999

Letterman, David, American comedian and television talk show host, Nov 1980, Oct 2002

Lewis, Jerry, American comedian, Nov 1962

Lewis, Richard, comedian and actor, July 1993

Little, Rich, Canadian impressionist, Nov 1975

Loftus, Cissie, Sept 1940, *Obit* Aug 1943

Lupino, Stanley, *Obit* Aug 1942

Lynde, Paul, Nov 1972, *Obit* Feb 1982

Mabley, Moms, American comedienne and actress, Jan 1975, *Obit* Aug 1975

Mac, Bernie, American comedian and actor, June 2002, *Obit* Nov 2008

Manna, Charlie, Jan 1965, *Obit* Yrbk 1971

Maron, Marc, American comedian, Nov 2011

Martin, Demetri, American comedian and actor, Oct 2009

Martin, Dick, American comedian, Sept 1969, *Obit* Yrbk 2008

Marx Brothers, American comedians, Mar 1948

Marx, Chico, American comedian, May 1948, *Obit* Yrbk 1961

Marx, Harpo, American comedian, Mar 1948, *Obit* Nov 1964

Mason, Jackie, American comedian, July 1987

McKenzie, Bret, New Zealand comedian, Mar 2008

Mirza, Shazia, British physics teacher and comedian, Jan 2002

Mo'Nique, American comedienne and actress, Apr 2010

Morgan, Tracy, American actor and comedian, Mar 2007

Murphy, Eddie, American comedian and actor, Nov 1983

Murray, Charlie, *Obit* Sept 1941

Najimy, Kathy, American actress and comedienne, Oct 2002

Newhart, Bob, American comedian and actor, Mar 1962

Nye, Bill, American comedian and television performer, July 1998

Olsen, Ole, American comedian, Sept 1940, *Obit* Mar 1963

Parker, Barnett, *Obit* Oct 1941

Pearl, Minnie, American comedienne, Nov 1992, *Obit* May 1996

Penner, Joe, *Obit* Mar 1941

Poehler, Amy, American comedienne and actress, Aug 2008

Prinze, Freddie, American comedian, June 1975, *Obit* Mar 1977

Radner, Gilda, American comedienne, Feb 1980, *Obit* July 1989

Ragland, Rags, *Obit* Oct 1946

Raimu, *Obit* Nov 1946

Raye, Martha, American actress, singer and comedienne, July 1963, *Obit* Jan 1995

Rehman, Shabana, Norwegian comedian, Jan 2004

Reubens, Paul, American comedian and actor, Jan 1988

Richards, Michael, American actor and comedian, Nov 1997

Rousseau, Stephane, Canadian comedian and actor, Jan 2004

Rowan, Dan, American comedian, Sept 1969, *Obit* Nov 1987

Sahl, Mort, American comedian, Yrbk 1960

Sales, Soupy, American comedian, Jan 1967, *Obit* Yrbk 2009

Sandler, Adam, American comedian and actor, May 1998

Schneider, Helge, German comedian, actor, jazz musician and composer, Jan 2007

Sedaris, Amy, American actress and writer, Apr 2002

Seinfeld, Jerry, American comedian, Aug 1992

Shandling, Garry, American comedian, Apr 1989

Silverman, Sarah, American comedienne, July 2006

Sinbad, American comedian and actor, Feb 1997

Sintim-Misa, Kwaku, Ghanaian actor and comedian, Jan 2004

Skelton, Red, American comedian and actor, Nov 1947, *Obit* Nov 1997

Smothers, Dick, American comedian, Yrbk 1968

Stewart, Jon, American comedian and talk show host, July 2004

Stewart, William G., *Obit* Sept 1941

Stoopnagle, Lemuel Q., radio comedian, Oct 1947, *Obit* July 1950

Syal, Meera, English actress, novelist and screenwriter, Feb 2001

Sykes, Wanda, American comedian, Jan 2011

Tate, Catherine, British comedian, Oct 2012

Terry-Thomas, English comedian and actor, Mar 1961, *Obit* Mar 1990

Tinney, Frank, *Obit* Jan 1941

Tomlin, Lily, American comedienne and actress, Sept 1973

Turpin, Ben, comedian, *Obit* Aug 1940

Vassa, Yossi, Ethiopian-Israeli comedian, Jan 2006

Waters, James R., *Obit* Jan 1946

Wayans, Marlon, American comedian and actor, May 2001

Weber, Joseph M., *Obit* July 1942

Williams, Robin, American comedian and actor, June 1979, Jan 1997

Wilson, Flip, American comedian, Nov 1969, *Obit* Feb 1999

Winters, Jonathan, American comedian, Mar 1965, *Obit* Yrbk 2013

Wright, Huntley, *Obit* Sept 1941

Wright, Steven, American comedian, May 2003

Wynn, Ed, comedian, Jan 1945, *Obit* July 1966

Youngman, Henny, comedian, Oct 1986, *Obit* May 1998

Comic book writers

Abouet, Marguerite, French comic book writer, Nov 2012

Busiek, Kurt, American comic book writer, Sept 2005

Claremont, Chris, American fantasy, science fiction and comic book writer, Sept 2003

Drooker, Eric, American painter and graphic novelist, Feb 2011

Jodorowsky, Alejandro, Chilean film director and comic book writer, Jan 2005

Lee, Stan, American comic book writer and editor, Aug 1993

McDuffie, Dwayne, American comic book writer, Feb 2010, *Obit* Yrbk 2011

Pekar, Harvey, American comic book writer, Jan 2004, *Obit* Oct 2010

Shaw, Dash, American comic book artist and graphic novelist, Jan 2009

Simone, Gail, American comic book writer, Nov 2008

al-Mutawa, Naif, Kuwaiti businessman and comic book creator, May 2012

Commercial agents

Abbell, Maxwell, American accountant and lawyer, July 1951, *Obit* Sept 1957

Boras, Scott, American baseball agent, May 2009

Conover, Harry, Feb 1949, *Obit* Oct 1965

Dewart, William T., American newspaper publisher, *Obit* Mar 1944

Emanuel, Ariel, American talent agent, July 2009

Ford, Eileen, American model agent, Oct 1971

Hayward, Leland, theatrical agent and producer, Feb 1949, *Obit* Apr 1971

Herbert, Gary R., American governor, May 2011

Janney, Russell, Mar 1947, *Obit* Sept 1963

Kopp, Wendy, American teacher recruiter, Mar 2003

Leigh, William Colston, lecture agent, Jan 1942, *Obit* Sept 1992

Leviev, Lev, Israeli diamond dealer, Jan 2002

Mallory, C. C., Feb 1956, *Obit* Mar 1959

McLaren, Malcolm, English rock musician, band manager and talent agent, Aug 1997, *Obit* Yrbk 2010

Meyer, Ron, American motion picture executive, Mar 1997

Morrison, Adrienne, *Obit* Jan 1941

Naegle, Susan, American television executive, May 2013

Osbourne, Sharon, English musical talent agent and promoter, Jan 2001

Ovitz, Michael, American talent agent and motion picture executive, Oct 1995

Peden, Katherine G., real estate broker and state official, May 1962

Pierson, Warren Lee, June 1941, Nov 1954

Powers, John Robert, June 1945, *Obit* Sept 1977

Rosenhaus, Drew, American sports agent, July 2011

Ross, Robert, American entrepreneur, Oct 2002, *Obit* Yrbk 2011

Smith, Robert C., American senator, Sept 2000

Stein, Jules, concert and theatrical agent, May 1967, *Obit* June 1981

Wallop, Douglass, American insurance agent and novelist, Yrbk 1956, *Obit* June 1985

Wasserman, Lew R., American motion picture executive, May 1991, *Obit* Yrbk 2002

Werblin, Sonny, football executive and theatrical agent, Apr 1979, *Obit* Feb 1992

Whitman, Meg, American Internet auction executive, Feb 2000

Communist leaders

Alia, Ramiz, Albanian president, Jan 1991, *Obit* Yrbk 2011

Aliyev, Heydar, Azerbaijani president, Sept 1999, *Obit* July 2004

Andropov, Yuri, Soviet communist leader, May 1983, *Obit* Apr 1984

Beria, Lavrenti, Soviet intelligence official, Yrbk 1942, *Obit* Sept 1954

Berlinguer, Enrico, Italian communist leader, July 1976, *Obit* Aug 1984

Bierut, Boleslaw, Polish president, Sept 1949, *Obit* May 1956

Bolz, Lothar, East German diplomat, Sept 1959, *Obit* Apr 1987

Brazauskas, Algirdas, Lithuanian president and prime minister, Jan 2002, *Obit* Yrbk 2010

Brezhnev, Leonid Il'ich, Soviet communist leader, Jan 1963, Nov 1978, *Obit* Jan 1983

Browder, Earl, American communist leader, Oct 1944, *Obit* Sept 1973

Bulganin, Nikolai Aleksandrovich, Soviet communist leader, Feb 1955, *Obit* Apr 1975

Castro, Fidel, Cuban president, July 1958, July 1970, June 2001

Castro, Raul, Cuban president, Feb 1977

Ceausescu, Nicolae, Romanian dictator, Nov 1967, *Obit* Feb 1990

Chernenko, Konstantin Ustinovich, Soviet communist leader, Aug 1984, *Obit* May 1985

Cunhal, Alvaro, Portuguese communist leader, Sept 1975, *Obit* Yrbk 2005

Deng Xiaoping, Chinese communist leader, May 1976, June 1994, *Obit* Apr 1997

Dennis, Eugene, American communist leader, May 1949, *Obit* Mar 1961

Dimitrov, Georgi, Bulgarian prime minister, May 1949

Djilas, Milovan, Yugoslav communist leader, memoirist and political writer, Sept 1958, *Obit* July 1995

Dubcek, Alexander, Czech communist leader, Nov 1968

Duclos, Jacques, French communist leader, Feb 1946, *Obit* June 1975

Flynn, Elizabeth Gurley, American communist leader, Oct 1961, *Obit* Nov 1964

Foster, William Zebulon, American communist leader, July 1945, *Obit* Nov 1961

Furtseva, Ekaterina A., Soviet communist leader, June 1956, *Obit* Yrbk 1974

Gheorghiu-Dej, Gheorghe, Romanian prime minister, Oct 1958, *Obit* May 1965

Gierek, Edward, Polish communist leader, May 1971, *Obit* Oct 2001

Gomulka, Wladyslaw, Polish communist leader, Jan 1957, *Obit* Oct 1982

Gorbachev, Mikhail, Soviet president, Aug 1985

Gottwald, Klement, Czech president, Apr 1948, *Obit* Apr 1953

Grechko, Andrei Antonovich, Soviet field marshal, Nov 1968, *Obit* June 1976

Gromyko, Andrei Andreevich, Soviet diplomat, Oct 1943, Oct 1958, *Obit* Aug 1989

Grosz, Karoly, Hungarian prime minister, Sept 1988, *Obit* Mar 1996

Hall, Gus, American communist leader, May 1973, *Obit* Jan 2001

Ho, Chi Minh, Vietnamese communist leader, Nov 1949, Oct 1966, *Obit* Nov 1969

Honecker, Erich, East German communist leader, Apr 1972, *Obit* July 1994

Hoxha, Enver, Albanian communist leader, Jan 1950, *Obit* June 1985

Hu Jintao, Chinese president, Jan 2003

Hu Yaobang, Chinese communist leader, Nov 1983, *Obit* June 1989

Hua Guofeng, Chinese prime minister, Mar 1977, *Obit* Yrbk 2008

Husak, Gustav, Czech president, Oct 1971, *Obit* Jan 1992

Ibarruri, Dolores, Spanish communist leader, June 1967, *Obit* Jan 1990

Jaruzelski, Wojciech, Polish general and president, Mar 1982

Jiang Qing, Chinese communist leader and wife of Mao Zedong, June 1975, *Obit* Jan 1992

Jiang Zemin, Chinese president, May 1995

Kadar, Janos, Hungarian prime minister, May 1957, *Obit* Yrbk 1989

Kaganovich, L. M., Soviet communist leader, Apr 1942, Oct 1955, *Obit* Sept 1991

Kalinin, Mikhail Ivanovich, Soviet president, June 1942, *Obit* July 1946

Kania, Stanislaw, June 1981

Kardelj, Edvard, Yugoslav communist leader, Yrbk 1949, *Obit* Apr 1979

Karmal, Babrak, Afghan president, Mar 1981, *Obit* Feb 1997

Keldysh, Mstislav, Russian mathematician and physicist, Feb 1962, *Obit* Aug 1978

Khrushchev, Nikita Sergeevich, Soviet communist leader, July 1954, *Obit* Oct 1971

Kim, Il Sung, North Korean head of state, Sept 1951, *Obit* Yrbk 1994, Yrbk 1994

Kim, Jong Il, North Korean head of state, Jan 2002, *Obit* Yrbk 2012

Kosygin, Aleksei Nikolaevich, Soviet prime minister, Sept 1965, *Obit* Feb 1981

Kozlov, Frol R., Nov 1959, *Obit* Mar 1965

Krenz, Egon, East German communist leader, Mar 1990

Kuusinen, Hertta, Finnish cabinet member, May 1949, *Obit* May 1974

Kuzmin, Iosif I., Feb 1959

Kuznetsov, Nikolai G., Nov 1942, *Obit* Jan 1975

Kuznetsov, Vasilii Vasil'evich, Soviet diplomat, Jan 1956, *Obit* Aug 1990

Le, Duc Tho, Vietnamese communist leader, Mar 1975, *Obit* Jan 1991

Li Peng, Chinese prime minister, Nov 1988

Ligachev, Yegor K., Soviet communist leader, Aug 1990

Lin Biao, Chinese communist leader and military official, May 1967, *Obit* Oct 1972

Liu Shaoqi, Chinese communist leader, Oct 1957, *Obit* Yrbk 1974

Longo, Luigi, Feb 1966, *Obit* Jan 1981

Machado Ventura, Jose Ramon, Cuban vice-president, Sept 2011

Malenkov, Georgi M., Soviet prime minister, June 1952, *Obit* Mar 1988

Malinovskii, Rodion IAkovlevich, Soviet field marshal, Mar 1944, Nov 1960, *Obit* May 1967

Mao Zedong, Chinese communist leader, Feb 1943, May 1962, *Obit* Oct 1976

Marchais, Georges, French communist leader, June 1976, *Obit* Jan 1998

Maurer, Ion Gheorghe, Romanian prime minister, Sept 1971, *Obit* July 2000

Mikhailov, Nikolai Aleksandrovich, Nov 1958

Mikoyan, Anastas, Soviet president, May 1955, *Obit* Jan 1979

Milosevic, Slobodan, Yugoslav president, Apr 1990, *Obit* Yrbk 2006

Minor, Robert, Apr 1941, *Obit* Jan 1953

Molotov, Vyacheslav, Soviet diplomat, Jan 1940, Nov 1954, *Obit* Jan 1987

Munnich, Ferenc, May 1959, *Obit* Jan 1968

Najibullah, Mohammed, Afghan president, June 1988, *Obit* Jan 1997

Namboodiripad, E. M. S., Indian communist leader, Nov 1976

Nazarbayev, Nursultan, Kazakhstani president, Oct 2000

Nguyen, Thi Binh, Vietnamese communist leader, July 1976

Novotny, Antonin, Czech president, May 1958, *Obit* Mar 1975

Pauker, Ana, Romanian diplomat and communist leader, Mar 1948

Peng Dehuai, Chinese general and communist leader, Yrbk 1951

Pervukhin, Mikhail G., Mar 1956, *Obit* Oct 1978

Pham, Van Dong, Vietnamese prime minister, Feb 1975, *Obit* Sept 2000

Podgorny, Nikolai V., Soviet president, May 1966, *Obit* Mar 1983

Pol Pot, Cambodian political leader, Apr 1980, *Obit* June 1998

Pollitt, Harry, British communist leader, May 1948, *Obit* Sept 1960

Polyansky, Dmitry S., Soviet communist leader, Mar 1971

Popovic, Koca, Yugoslav cabinet member, Jan 1957, *Obit* Jan 1993

Pozsgay, Imre, Hungarian communist leader, Mar 1990

Rakosi, Matyas, Hungarian communist leader, Mar 1949, *Obit* Mar 1971

Rakowski, Mieczyslaw F., Polish communist leader, Apr 1989, *Obit* Feb 2009

Serov, Ivan Aleksandrovich, Soviet communist leader, Yrbk 1956

Shehu, Mehmet, Feb 1958, *Obit* Feb 1982

Shelepin, Aleksandr N., Soviet intelligence official, Feb 1971, *Obit* Jan 1995

Shepilov, Dmitrii Trofimovich, Yrbk 1955

Shevardnadze, Eduard, Georgian president, Feb 1986

Shvernik, Nikolai, Soviet communist leader, Oct 1951, *Obit* Feb 1971

Siroky, Viliam, Apr 1957, *Obit* Nov 1971

Stalin, Joseph, Soviet dictator, Mar 1942, *Obit* Apr 1953

Stoica, Chivu, Jan 1959, *Obit* Apr 1975

Stoph, Willi, East German communist leader, Oct 1960, *Obit* Aug 1999

Suslov, Mikhail Andreevich, Soviet communist leader, Feb 1957, *Obit* Mar 1982

Thorez, Maurice, French communist leader, June 1946, *Obit* Sept 1964

Tito, Josip Broz, Yugoslav head of state, Nov 1943, Mar 1955, *Obit* June 1980

Togliatti, Palmiro, Italian communist leader, Nov 1947, *Obit* Oct 1964

Trotsky, Leon, Soviet communist leader, *Obit* Oct 1940

Ulbricht, Walter, East German communist leader, July 1952, *Obit* Oct 1973

Vo, Nguyen Giap, Vietnamese general, Feb 1969

Voroshilov, Kliment Efremovich, Soviet field marshal and communist leader, Mar 1941, *Obit* Jan 1970

Vukmanovic-Tempo, Svetozar, Yrbk 1958

Wang Bingnan, Yrbk 1958

Wasilewska, Wanda, Polish poet and novelist, July 1944, *Obit* Oct 1964

Wu Yi, Chinese government official, Jan 2005

Yaroslavski, Emel'yan Mikhailovich, Soviet communist leader, *Obit* Jan 1944

Zhao Ziyang, Chinese prime minister, June 1984, *Obit* Yrbk 2005

Zhivkov, Todor, Bulgarian communist leader, Jan 1976, *Obit* Oct 1998

Zhou Enlai, Chinese prime minister and diplomat, Sept 1946, July 1957, *Obit* Feb 1976

Zhu Rongji, Chinese prime minister, July 2001

Zhukov, Georgii Aleksandrovich, Soviet journalist, Oct 1960

Zhukov, Georgii Konstantinovich, Soviet field marshal, Feb 1942, Apr 1955, *Obit* Sept 1974

Zyuganov, Gennady, Russian communist leader, Oct 1996

Composers

Adams, John, American composer, May 1988

Adebimpe, Tunde, American singer, songwriter, and actor, Apr 2009

Adele, British singer, July 2009

Al-Madfai, Ilham, Iraqi guitarist and songwriter, Jan 2004

Al-Sahir, Kazem, Iraqi singer, Jan 2003

Albarn, Damon, British singer, songwriter and keyboardist, Nov 2003

Alexie, Sherman, American poet, novelist and screenwriter, Oct 1998

Allen, Lily, British pop singer and songwriter, Jan 2007

Allen, Peter, Australian singer and songwriter, Mar 1983, *Obit* Aug 1992

Alpert, Herb, American trumpet player and composer, Jan 1967

Amos, Tori, American singer and songwriter, Sept 1998

Amram, David, American composer, conductor and French horn player, Nov 1969

Anastasio, Trey, American guitarist and songwriter, July 2003

Anderson, Ian, British singer, flutist and songwriter, Feb 1998

Anderson, Leroy, American composer, Sept 1952, *Obit* Aug 1975

Anderson, Reid, American jazz bassist, Oct 2011

Anka, Paul, Canadian singer and songwriter, Feb 1964

Antheil, George, American composer, July 1954, *Obit* Apr 1959

Apple, Fiona, American singer and songwriter, Nov 2006

Argento, Dominick, composer, May 1977

Arlen, Harold, American composer, July 1955, *Obit* June 1986

Armstrong, Billie Joe, American singer and songwriter, Aug 2005

Ascher, Leo, Austrian composer, *Obit* Apr 1942

Ashford, Nickolas, American singer and songwriter, Apr 1997, *Obit* Yrbk 2011

Babbitt, Milton, American composer, Sept 1962, *Obit* Yrbk 2011

Babyface, American singer, songwriter and producer, July 1998

Bacharach, Burt, American composer, Oct 1970

Badu, Erykah, American singer and songwriter, Apr 1998

Baez, Joan, American folk singer and songwriter, Nov 1963

Bantock, Granville, English composer, *Obit* Yrbk 1946

Barber, Samuel, American composer, Sept 1944, Sept 1963, *Obit* Mar 1981

Barry, John, English composer, Mar 2000, *Obit* Yrbk 2011

Bartok, Bela, Hungarian composer, Sept 1940, *Obit* Oct 1945

Bax, Arnold, English composer, Sept 1943, *Obit* Jan 1954

Beach, Amy Marcy Cheney, American composer and pianist, *Obit* Feb 1945

Beam, Sam (Iron and Wine), American folk singer and songwriter, Mar 2013

Bebey, Francis, Cameroonian guitarist, composer and novelist, Apr 1994, *Obit* Sept 2001

Bennett, Richard Rodney, English composer, Mar 1992, *Obit* Yrbk 2013

Bennett, Robert Russell, American composer, arranger and conductor, Apr 1962, May 1962, *Obit* Oct 1981

Berio, Luciano, Italian composer, Mar 1971, *Obit* Yrbk 2003

Berlin, Irving, American composer and lyricist, May

1942, May 1963, *Obit* Nov 1989

Bernie, Ben, American band leader, Yrbk 1941, *Obit* Yrbk 1943

Bernstein, Elmer, American composer, June 2003

Bernstein, Leonard, American conductor and composer, Feb 1944, Feb 1960, *Obit* Nov 1990

Black, Clint, American country singer and songwriter, Aug 1994

Blake, Eubie, American pianist and composer, Apr 1974, *Obit* Apr 1983

Bledsoe, Jules, American opera singer, actor and composer, *Obit* Sept 1943

Blitzstein, Marc, American dramatist and composer, July 1940, *Obit* Mar 1964

Bloch, Ernest, American composer, Sept 1953, *Obit* Oct 1959

Boguslawski, Moissaye, American pianist, composer and teacher, *Obit* Oct 1944

Bohlen, Dieter, German pop singer, songwriter and producer, Jan 2006

Bolcom, William, American composer and pianist, Apr 1990

Bolton, Michael, American singer and songwriter, Aug 1993

Bono, Irish singer, Mar 1993

Boulanger, Nadia, French conductor and teacher, May 1962, *Obit* Jan 1980

Boulez, Pierre, French composer and conductor, Mar 1969

Bowles, Paul, American composer, novelist, short story writer, poet and travel writer, Oct 1990, *Obit* Feb 2000

Boy George, British pop singer and songwriter, Oct 1985

Boyer, Lucien, *Obit* Aug 1942

Branch, Michelle, American singer and songwriter, May 2005

Bregovic, Goran, Bosnian composer, Jan 2006

Brel, Jacques, French singer and songwriter, Mar 1971, *Obit* Nov 1978

Britten, Benjamin, English composer, Oct 1942, Apr 1961, *Obit* Feb 1977

Brooks, Kix, American country singer and songwriter, Sept 2004

Brown, Chuck, band leader and songwriter, *Obit* Yrbk 2012

Brown, James, American singer, Mar 1992, *Obit* Mar 2007

Browne, Jackson, American singer and songwriter, Oct 1989

Brubeck, Dave, American jazz pianist and composer, Mar 1956, Apr 1993, *Obit* Yrbk 2013

Buck, Gene, Feb 1941, *Obit* May 1957

Buffett, Jimmy, American singer and songwriter, Mar 1999

Burgess, Anthony, English novelist and critic, May 1972, *Obit* Jan 1994

Burleigh, Harry T., American singer and composer, Aug 1941, *Obit* Oct 1949

Burrows, Abe, American composer, lyricist, playwright and theatrical director, Nov 1951, *Obit* July 1985

Busch, Carl, *Obit* Feb 1944

Butler, Win, American singer and songwriter, Jan 2007

Buzzi-Peccia, Arturo, *Obit* Oct 1943

Byrne, David, Scottish-American rock singer and songwriter, June 1985

Cage, John, American composer, Sept 1961, *Obit* Sept 1992

Carlos, Wendy, American composer, Sept 2008

Carmines, Al, American clergyman, composer, singer and actor, Sept 1972, *Obit* Yrbk 2005

Carpenter, John Alden, composer, May 1947, *Obit* May 1951

Carpenter, Mary Chapin, American singer and songwriter, Feb 1994

Carter, Benny, American saxophonist, July 1987, *Obit* Oct 2003

Carter, Elliott, American composer, Nov 1960, *Obit* Yrbk 2013

Casablancas, Julian, American singer and songwriter, Feb 2007

Casadesus, Robert, French pianist and composer, Jan 1945, *Obit* Nov 1972

Case, Neko, American singer and songwriter, June 2013

Cash, Johnny, American country singer and songwriter, Sept 1969, *Obit* Jan 2004

Cash, Rosanne, American country singer and songwriter, Oct 1991

Castagnetta, Grace, Feb 1954

Cat Power (Singer), American singer and songwriter, Oct 2007

Cave, Nick, Australian singer and songwriter, June 2005

Chaminade, Cecile, French composer, *Obit* June 1944

Chapman, Steven Curtis, American Christian rock singer and songwriter, Oct 2004

Chapman, Tracy, American singer and songwriter, Aug 1989

Chasins, Abram, American pianist and composer, Feb 1960, *Obit* Aug 1987

Chavez, Carlos, Mexican composer and conductor, May 1949, *Obit* Sept 1978

Cheatham, Kitty, *Obit* Feb 1946

Clegg, Johnny, South African singer and songwriter, Jan 2005

Cleveland, James, American clergyman and gospel singer, Aug 1985, *Obit* Apr 1991

Clinton, George, American singer and songwriter, July 1993

Cockburn, Bruce, Canadian singer and songwriter, Jan 2005

Cocker, Jarvis, English rock singer, Nov 1998

Cohan, George M., American actor, dramatist, songwriter and producer, *Obit* Jan 1943

Coleman, Cy, American composer, Aug 1990, *Obit* Feb 2005

Coleman, Ornette, American jazz saxophonist, June 1961

Collins, Phil, British singer, songwriter and drummer, Nov 1986

Comden, Betty, American lyricist, librettist and screenwriter, Mar 1945, *Obit* Yrbk 2007

Converse, Frederick Shepherd, composer, *Obit* Aug 1940

Copland, Aaron, American composer, Sept 1940, Mar 1951, *Obit* Yrbk 1991

Corea, Chick, American jazz pianist, Oct 1988

Coward, Noel, English actor, dramatist and composer, Jan 1941, Mar 1962, *Obit* May 1973

Coyne, Wayne, American guitarist, singer and songwriter, Oct 2002

Crow, Sheryl, American singer and songwriter, May 1998

Crumb, George, American composer, Yrbk 1979

Crumit, Frank, *Obit* Oct 1943

Cugat, Xavier, band leader, May 1942, *Obit* Jan 1991

Curran, Pearl G., *Obit* June 1941

Dale, Benjamin James, *Obit* Sept 1943

Dallapiccola, Luigi, Italian composer, Feb 1966

Damrosch, Walter, American conductor and composer, Mar 1944, *Obit* Jan 1951

Daniels, Charles N., composer, *Obit* Mar 1943

Darin, Bobby, American singer and actor, Mar 1963, *Obit* Feb 1974

David, Hal, songwriter, Sept 1980, *Obit* Yrbk 2012

Davies, Peter Maxwell, English composer, Mar 1980

Davies, Walford, *Obit* May 1941

Davis, Anthony, American composer and pianist, May 1990

Davis, Mac, American country singer and songwriter, Aug 1980

De Sylva, Buddy, songwriter and motion picture producer, Sept 1943, *Obit* Sept 1950

Del Tredici, David, American composer, Mar 1983

Dello Joio, Norman, American composer, Sept 1957, *Obit* Yrbk 2008

Desplat, Alexandre, French composer, June 2011

Dett, Robert Nathaniel, composer, *Obit* Nov 1943

DiFranco, Ani, American singer and songwriter, Aug 1997

Diamond, David, American composer, Nov 1966, *Obit* Yrbk 2005

Diamond, Neil, American singer and songwriter, May 1981

Diddley, Bo, American guitarist, singer and songwriter, June 1989, *Obit* Sept 2008

Dietz, Howard, American lyricist, Oct 1965, *Obit* Sept 1983

Dodge, Charles, American composer, Aug 2007

Dorati, Antal, Hungarian conductor and composer, July 1948, *Obit* Jan 1989

Douglas, Dave, American jazz trumpet player and composer, Mar 2006

Drexler, Jorge, Uruguayan singer and songwriter, Jan 2005

Druckman, Jacob, composer, May 1981, *Obit* Aug 1996

Du Bois, Shirley Graham, American biographer, dramatist and composer, Oct 1946, *Obit* June 1977

Duke, Vernon, American composer, June 1941, *Obit* Mar 1969

Dunbar, Rudolph, Oct 1946

Dunn, Ronnie Gene, American country singer and songwriter, Sept 2004

Duritz, Adam, American singer and songwriter, Mar 2003

Dusapin, Pascal, French composer, Jan 2007

Edwards, Gus, songwriter, *Obit* Yrbk 1945

Edwards, Joan, singer and composer, Oct 1953, *Obit* Oct 1981

Edwards, Kathleen, Canadian singer and songwriter, Oct 2012

Eichheim, Henry, American violinist, conductor and composer, *Obit* Oct 1942

Einem, Gottfried von, Austrian composer, July 1953, *Obit* Sept 1996

Eisler, Hanns, German composer, May 1942, *Obit* Nov 1962

Elfman, Danny, American composer, Jan 2007

Ellington, Duke, American band leader and composer, Mar 1941, Jan 1970, *Obit* July 1974

Eminem, American rapper, Jan 2001

Engel, Carl, musicologist and composer, *Obit* June 1944

Escoffery, Wayne, American jazz saxophonist and composer, Jan 2011

Estefan, Gloria, Cuban-American singer and songwriter, Oct 1995

Etheridge, Melissa, American singer and guitarist, May 1995

Evans, Faith, American singer and songwriter, Feb 1999

Falla, Manuel de, Spanish composer, *Obit* Yrbk 1946

Fals, Iwan, Indonesian singer and songwriter, Jan 2002

Feist (Musician), Canadian singer and songwriter, June 2008

Fenton, George, English composer, July 2010

Fields, Dorothy, American lyricist and librettist, Feb 1958, *Obit* May 1974

Fields, Herbert, Feb 1958

Finn, Craig, American singer and songwriter, Sept 2010

Fisher, Fred, songwriter and composer, *Obit* Mar 1942

Floyd, Carlisle, American composer, July 1960

Formell, Juan-Carlos, Cuban singer, songwriter and guitarist, Jan 2005

Forsyth, Cecil, *Obit* Feb 1942

Foss, Lukas, American composer, conductor and pianist, June 1966, *Obit* Yrbk 2009

Furtado, Nelly, Canadian singer, songwriter and guitarist, Jan 2007

Gabriel, Peter, English singer and songwriter, Jan 1990

Garner, Erroll, American jazz pianist, Sept 1959, *Obit* Mar 1977

Gary, John, singer and songwriter, July 1967, *Obit* Mar 1998

Getty, Gordon P., American petroleum executive and composer, Feb 1985

Gibb, Barry, English singer and songwriter, Sept 1981

Gil, Gilberto, Brazilian singer and songwriter, Jan 2003

Ginastera, Alberto, Argentine composer, Jan 1971

Gioia, Ted, American jazz historian, Jan 2010

Glass, Philip, American composer, Mar 1981

Golden, John, Mar 1944, *Obit* Sept 1955

Goldsmith, Jerry, American composer, May 2001, *Obit* Yrbk 2004

Golijov, Osvaldo, Argentine composer, Jan 2006

Goossens, Eugene, English conductor and composer, May 1945, *Obit* Sept 1962

Gorecki, Henryk, Polish composer, May 1994, *Obit* Yrbk 2011

Gorin, Igor, July 1942, *Obit* June 1982

Gould, Glenn, Canadian pianist, Oct 1960, *Obit* Nov 1982

Gould, Morton, pianist and composer, Sept 1945, Jan 1968, *Obit* May 1996

Goulding, Ellie, British guitarist, singer and songwriter, Apr 2013

Grandjany, Marcel, May 1943, *Obit* Apr 1975

Gray, David, British singer and songwriter, Jan 2004

Gray, Macy, American singer and songwriter, May 2000

Green, Adolph, American lyricist, librettist and screenwriter, Mar 1945, *Obit* Mar 2003

Grey, Clifford, *Obit* Nov 1941

Griffith, Nanci, American folk and country singer and songwriter, Feb 1998

Grofe, Ferde, July 1940, *Obit* May 1972

Grohl, Dave, American singer and guitarist, May 2002

Gubaidulina, Sofia Asgatovna, Russian composer, Oct 1999

Guthrie, Arlo, American folk singer and songwriter, Feb 1982

Guthrie, Woody, American folk singer and songwriter, May 1963, *Obit* Yrbk 1967

Hamlisch, Marvin, American composer and pianist, May 1976, *Obit* Yrbk 2012

Hammerstein, Oscar, American lyricist and librettist, Feb 1944, *Obit* Nov 1960

Hancock, Herbie, American jazz keyboardist and composer, Apr 1988

Handy, W. C., American composer and music publisher, Mar 1941, *Obit* June 1958

Hanley, James Frederick, songwriter, *Obit* Apr 1942

Hanson, Howard, American composer, Oct 1941, Sept 1966, *Obit* Apr 1981

Harbach, Otto, American librettist and lyricist, July 1950, *Obit* Mar 1963

Harbison, John, composer, Feb 1993

Harkness, Rebekah West, American composer, ballet manager and dance patron, Apr 1974, *Obit* Sept 1982

Harris, Roy, composer, Aug 1940, *Obit* Nov 1979

Harrison, George, British singer and guitarist, Nov 1966, Jan 1989, *Obit* Mar 2002

Harty, Hamilton, Irish composer and conductor, *Obit* Apr 1941

Harvey, PJ, British singer, songwriter and guitarist, May 2008

Hatfield, Juliana, American singer and songwriter, Aug 2011

Hawkins, Justin, British rock singer, guitarist and composer, Jan 2004

Hayes, Isaac, American singer and composer, Oct 1972, *Obit* Yrbk 2008

Henderson, Joe, American jazz saxophonist, June 1996, *Obit* Oct 2001

Henze, Hans Werner, German composer, Apr 1966, *Obit* Yrbk 2013

Herbert, Matthew, English record producer, composer and DJ, Nov 2012

Herman, Jerry, American composer and lyricist, Jan 1965

Hersch, Fred, American jazz pianist and composer, Apr 2006

Hertz, Alfred, *Obit* June 1942

Heward, Leslie H., *Obit* June 1943

Higdon, Jennifer, Classical composer, Jan 2013

Hill, Andrew, American jazz pianist and composer, Apr 2004, *Obit* Yrbk 2007

Hill, Billy, *Obit* Feb 1941

Hill, Patty Smith, American educator, *Obit* June 1946

Hindemith, Paul, German composer, Oct 1941, *Obit* Feb 1964

Hoiby, Lee, American composer, Mar 1987, *Obit* Yrbk 2011

Holliger, Heinz, Swiss oboist, Jan 1987

Honegger, Arthur, Swiss composer, Apr 1941, *Obit* Feb 1956

Hopkins, Sarah, Australian composer and cellist, Jan 2006

Horner, James, composer, Mar 1997

Hovhaness, Alan, American composer, Apr 1965, *Obit* Oct 2000

Hugo, Chad, American record producer, singer and songwriter, May 2004

Hunter, Alberta, singer and songwriter, May 1979, *Obit* Jan 1985

Hussain, Zakir, Indian percussionist and composer, Jan 2005

Hyde, Karl, British singer, guitarist and songwriter, Nov 2011

Hynde, Chrissie, American singer and songwriter, Apr 1993

Idol, Billy, British singer, songwriter and guitarist, Jan 1994

Ishii, Ken, Japanese techno musician, Jan 2002

Iverson, Ethan, American jazz pianist, Oct 2011

Ives, Charles Edward, American composer, June 1947, *Obit* July 1954

Jackson, Joe, English singer and songwriter, Feb 1996

James, Alex, English rock bassist, Nov 2003

James, Harry, American band leader and trumpet player, Sept 1943, *Obit* Aug 1983

James, Jim, American rock guitarist, singer and songwriter, Nov 2008

Jarrett, Keith, American jazz pianist and composer, May 1985

Jett, Joan, American singer and songwriter, Sept 1993

Jobim, Antonio Carlos, Brazilian singer and songwriter, July 1991, *Obit* Feb 1995

John, Elton, English singer and songwriter, Mar 1975

Johnson, Eric, American guitarist, keyboardist, singer and songwriter, June 2007

Johnson, Hall, American composer and music arranger, Jan 1945, *Obit* June 1970

Johnson, Howard E., *Obit* June 1941

Johnson, Jamey, American country singer and songwriter, Feb 2011

Johnston, Daniel, American singer, songwriter and artist, Sept 2010

Jones, Quincy, American composer and record producer, Feb 1977

Jones, Rickie Lee, singer and songwriter, May 1990

Kahal, Irving, *Obit* Apr 1942

Katz, Sharon, South African singer, songwriter and guitarist, Jan 2007

Kay, Hershy, Mar 1962, *Obit* Feb 1982

Keith, Toby, American country singer, Oct 2004

Kelley, Charles, American country singer and songwriter, July 2011

Kelley, Edgar Stillman, composer, *Obit* Jan 1945

Kelly, R., American singer, songwriter and record producer, June 1999

Kern, Jerome, American composer, June 1942, *Obit* Yrbk 1945

Khachaturian, Aram Il'ich, Mar 1948, *Obit* June 1978

King, Carole, American singer and songwriter, Jan 1974

King, David, American jazz drummer, Oct 2011

Kirchner, Leon, American composer and pianist, Yrbk 1967, *Obit* Yrbk 2009

Klein, Guillermo, Argentine jazz pianist and composer, Jan 2006

Knopfler, Mark, British singer, songwriter and guitarist, Apr 1995

Knussen, Oliver, Scottish composer and conductor, Feb 1994

Korngold, Erich Wolfgang, Austrian composer, Mar 1943, *Obit* Feb 1958

Koz, Dave, American jazz saxophonist and composer, June 2013

Kreisler, Fritz, Austrian violinist, July 1944, *Obit* Mar 1962

Krenek, Ernst, American composer, July 1942, *Obit* Feb 1992

Kristofferson, Kris, American actor, singer and songwriter, Nov 1974

Kubelik, Jan, Czech violinist and composer, *Obit* Jan 1941

Kuti, Femi, Nigerian singer and songwriter, Jan 2002

Lady Gaga, American pop singer and songwriter, May 2010

Lafourcade, Natalia, Mexican singer and songwriter, Jan 2003

Lambert, Miranda, American country singer, Feb 2012

Lane, Burton, American composer, Mar 1967, *Obit* Mar 1997

Lang, David, American composer, Feb 2000

Lauper, Cyndi, American singer and songwriter, Aug 1985

Laurents, Arthur, American playwright, screenwriter and theatrical director, Nov 1984, *Obit* Yrbk 2011

Lavigne, Avril, Canadian singer and songwriter, Apr 2003

Lecuona, Ernesto, Cuban composer, May 1944, *Obit* Jan 1964

Legend, John, American singer and pianist, Feb 2007

Lehmann, George, *Obit* Yrbk 1941

Lehrer, Tom, songwriter, humorist and mathematician, July 1982

Leppard, Raymond, British conductor and harpsichordist, Mar 1980

Lerche, Sondre, Norwegian singer and songwriter, Jan 2004

Lerner, Alan Jay, American lyricist and librettist, July 1958, *Obit* Aug 1986

Levant, Oscar, American pianist and composer, Jan 1940, Oct 1952, *Obit* Oct 1972

Levert, Gerald, American singer and songwriter, Oct 2003, *Obit* Yrbk 2007

Lewing, Adele, *Obit* Apr 1943

Lewis, John, American pianist and composer, Jan 1962, *Obit* June 2001

Liebermann, Rolf, Swiss composer and opera director, Sept 1973, *Obit* Mar 1999

Lieberson, Goddard, composer, critic and record executive, Mar 1976, *Obit* July 1977

Liebling, Leonard, *Obit* Yrbk 1945

Lincoln, Abbey, American jazz singer, Sept 2002, *Obit* Yrbk 2010

Linnell, John, American singer, songwriter and accordionist, Nov 1999

Lloyd Webber, Andrew, English composer, June 1982

Lloyd, Alex, Australian singer and songwriter, Jan 2002

Loesser, Frank, American composer and lyricist, Yrbk 1945, *Obit* Oct 1969

Loewe, Frederick, American composer, July 1958, *Obit* Apr 1988

Logan, Walter, *Obit* Mar 1940

Lutoslawski, Witold, Polish composer, Aug 1991, *Obit* Apr 1994

Lynne, Shelby, American country singer and songwriter, July 2001

M. I. A. (Singer), Sri Lankan-British singer and songwriter, May 2009

Maazel, Lorin, American conductor, Yrbk 1965

MacDermot, Galt, Canadian composer, July 1984

MacMillan, Ernest, Canadian conductor and composer, Mar 1955, *Obit* June 1973

Mancini, Henry, American composer, July 1964, *Obit* Aug 1994

Mars, Bruno, American singer and songwriter, May 2011

Marsalis, Wynton, American trumpet player, Oct 1984

Martinu, Bohuslav, Czech composer and violinist, Nov 1944, *Obit* Nov 1959

Mascagni, Pietro, Italian composer, *Obit* Sept 1945

Masekela, Hugh, South African trumpet player, flugelhornist and singer, Mar 1993

Maxim Reality (Singer), British singer and songwriter, Oct 2009

Maxwell, American singer, songwriter and recording producer, July 2011

McCartney, Paul, English singer and songwriter, Nov 1966, Jan 1986

McKuen, Rod, American poet, composer and singer, Feb 1970

McLaughlin, John, British jazz guitarist, Feb 2004

McLean, Don, American singer and songwriter, May 1973

McPartland, Marian, American jazz pianist, June 1976, *Obit* Yrbk 2013

Melford, Myra, American jazz pianist and composer, Apr 2010

Mellencamp, John, American singer and songwriter, Mar 1988

Mellers, Wilfrid, English musicologist and composer, Feb 1962, *Obit* Yrbk 2008

Meloy, Colin, American singer and songwriter, Aug 2007

Melua, Katie, British singer and songwriter, Jan 2007

Menken, Alan, American composer, Jan 2001

Mennin, Peter, composer and educator, Nov 1964, *Obit* Aug 1983

Mercer, Johnny, American lyricist, June 1948, *Obit* Aug 1976

Merchant, Natalie, American singer and songwriter, Jan 2003

Messiaen, Olivier, French organist and composer, Feb 1974, *Obit* June 1992

Metheny, Pat, American jazz guitarist, May 1996

Meyer, Edgar, American bassist, June 2002

Michele, Chrisette, American singer and songwriter, Apr 2011

Mignone, Francisco, June 1942

Milhaud, Darius, French composer, June 1941, May 1961, *Obit* Sept 1974

Miller, Marcus, American jazz bassist and composer, Feb 2006

Miller, Roger, American composer, lyricist and singer, Sept 1986, *Obit* Jan 1993

Mingus, Charles, American jazz bassist and composer, Feb 1971, *Obit* Mar 1979

Mirabal, Robert, Native American composer and flutist, Aug 2002

Miranda, Lin-Manuel, American composer and lyricist, July 2013

Mitchell, Joni, Canadian singer and songwriter, Oct 1976

Mitropoulos, Dimitri, Greek conductor and composer, Mar 1941, Mar 1952, *Obit* Jan 1961

Moby, American singer, Apr 2001

Monk, Meredith, American choreographer, composer and singer, Feb 1985

Monk, Thelonious, American pianist, Oct 1964, *Obit* Apr 1982

Mon e, Janelle, American singer, May 2013

Moore, Douglas, American composer, Nov 1947, *Obit* Oct 1969

Morissette, Alanis, Canadian singer and songwriter, May 1997

Morricone, Ennio, Italian composer, Oct 2000

Morris, Butch, American cornet player and composer, July 2005, *Obit* Yrbk 2013

Musgrave, Thea, Scottish composer, May 1978

Newley, Anthony, actor, singer and songwriter, Oct 1966, *Obit* July 1999

Newman, Alfred, July 1943, *Obit* Apr 1970

Newman, Randy, American singer and songwriter, Oct 1982

Niles, John Jacob, American singer, composer, singer and folklorist, Nov 1959, *Obit* Apr 1980

N£¤ez, Francisco J., Feb 2013

O'Connor, Mark, American fiddler and composer, Sept 2013

O'Horgan, Tom, American theatrical director and composer, Apr 1970, *Obit* Yrbk 2009

Oe, Hikari, Japanese composer and son of Kenzaburo Oe, May 1999

Ono, Yoko, Japanese artist, Nov 1972

Orff, Carl, German composer, Aug 1976, *Obit* May 1982

Paderewski, Ignace Jan, Polish pianist and statesman, *Obit* Aug 1941

Paik, Nam June, Korean video artist and composer, Mar 1983, *Obit* Yrbk 2006

Palmieri, Eddie, American salsa pianist and band leader, June 1992

Parker, Louis N., English composer and dramatist, *Obit* Nov 1944

Parks, Gordon, American film director, photographer and novelist, Oct 1968, Oct 1992, *Obit* June 2006

Part, Arvo, Estonian composer, Feb 1995

Partch, Harry, American composer, Sept 1965, *Obit* Oct 1974

Paxton, Tom, folk singer and composer, Sept 1982

Penderecki, Krzysztof, Polish composer, June 1971

Penn, Arthur A., *Obit* Apr 1941

Perry, Katy, American singer and songwriter, Jan 2012

Peterson, Oscar, Canadian pianist and composer, Oct 1983, *Obit* Yrbk 2008

Petty, Tom, American singer and guitarist, Nov 1991

Peyroux, Madeleine, American singer, songwriter and guitarist, Nov 2005

Pharrell, American record producer, singer and songwriter, May 2004

Picciotto, Guy, American guitarist and songwriter, Mar 2002

Piston, Walter, composer, June 1948, Yrbk 1961, *Obit* Jan 1977

Porter, Cole, American composer and lyricist, July 1940, *Obit* Yrbk 1964

Previn, Andre, American composer and conductor, May 1972

Previn, Dory, singer and songwriter, Sept 1975, *Obit* Yrbk 2012

Prokofiev, Sergey, Russian composer, Nov 1941, *Obit* Apr 1953

Puente, Tito, American band leader, composer and percussionist, Nov 1977, *Obit* Aug 2000

Rachmaninoff, Sergei, Russian composer and pianist, *Obit* May 1943

Rahman, A. R., Indian composer and singer, June 2009

Raitt, Bonnie, American singer and guitarist, Aug 1990

Ramazzotti, Eros, Italian singer and songwriter, Jan 2004

Ray, Amy, American singer and songwriter, Aug 1998

Reddy, Helen, American singer, Apr 1975

Reich, Steve, American composer, Apr 1986

Reid, Antonio, American recording industry producer and executive, Aug 2001

Revueltas, Silvestre, Mexican composer, *Obit* Yrbk 1940

Riley, Terry, American composer and pianist, Apr 2002

Ritchie, Jean, American folk singer, Oct 1959

Roach, Max, American jazz drummer, July 1986, *Obit* Nov 2007

Rochberg, George, American composer, Sept 1985, *Obit* Yrbk 2005

Rodgers, Nile, American guitarist and record producer, Jan 2012

Rodgers, Richard, American composer, May 1940, Apr 1951, *Obit* Feb 1980

Rodriguez, Robert, American motion picture director, Aug 1996

Rogers, Dale Evans, American singer and actress, Sept 1956, *Obit* Apr 2001

Romberg, Sigmund, composer, Mar 1945, *Obit* Yrbk 1951

Rome, Harold, American composer and lyricist, Apr 1942, *Obit* Jan 1994

Rorem, Ned, American composer, July 1967

Rosenwinkel, Kurt, American jazz guitarist and composer, July 2011

Rossen, Daniel, American singer, songwriter and guitarist, Sept 2011

Roth, Gabriel, American songwriter, bassist and recording producer, Feb 2010

Rozsa, Miklos, composer, Feb 1992, *Obit* Oct 1995

Saariaho, Kaija, Finnish composer, Jan 2003

Sainte-Marie, Buffy, Canadian singer and songwriter, July 1969

Saliers, Emily, American singer and songwriter, Aug 1998

Salonen, Esa-Pekka, Finnish composer and conductor, Jan 2007

Santaolalla, Gustavo, Argentine composer and record producer, Jan 2007

Scallon, Dana Rosemary, British singer, Jan 2007

Schelling, Ernest, American composer, conductor and pianist, Jan 1940

Schertzinger, Victor, *Obit* Yrbk 1941

Schickele, Peter, American composer, May 1979

Schillinger, Joseph, Russian composer and music teacher, *Obit* May 1943

Schnabel, Artur, Austrian-American pianist and composer, July 1942, *Obit* Sept 1951

Schnittke, Alfred, Russian composer, July 1992, *Obit* Oct 1998

Schoenberg, Arnold, Austrian-American composer, Apr 1942, *Obit* Sept 1951

Schuller, Gunther, American composer and conductor, Apr 1964

Schuman, William, American composer, June 1942, Yrbk 1962, *Obit* Apr 1992

Schwartz, Arthur, composer, Nov 1979, *Obit* Oct 1984

Scott, Jill, American singer, songwriter and actress, Jan 2002

Scott, Raymond, composer and musical instrument inventor, July 1941, *Obit* May 1994

Scott, Tom, American composer and singer, Nov 1946

Sedaka, Neil, American pop singer and songwriter, Oct 1978

Seeger, Pete, American folk singer and songwriter, Yrbk 1963

Sessions, Roger, American composer, Jan 1975, *Obit* May 1985

Sevitzky, Fabien, July 1946, *Obit* Apr 1967

Shankar, Ravi, Indian sitar player, Apr 1968, *Obit* Yrbk 2013

Shearing, George, English jazz pianist, Apr 1958, *Obit* Yrbk 2011

Sheldon, Sidney, American novelist, Oct 1980, *Obit* Yrbk 2007

Shorter, Wayne, American jazz saxophonist, Apr 1996

Shostakovich, Dmitrii Dmitrievich, Russian composer, May 1941, *Obit* Oct 1975

Simon, Carly, American singer and songwriter, Aug 1976

Simon, Paul, American singer and composer, Mar 1975

Simone, Nina, American singer and pianist, Apr 1968, *Obit* Yrbk 2003

Simpson, Valerie, American singer and songwriter, Apr 1997

Sinding, Christian, *Obit* Jan 1942

Singh, Talvin, British DJ, arranger and composer, Jan 2006

Sinopoli, Giuseppe, Italian conductor and composer, Mar 1991, *Obit* Sept 2001

Skilton, Charles Sanford, *Obit* May 1941

Skrowaczewski, Stanislaw, Yrbk 1964

Slash (Musician), British rock guitarist and songwriter, Mar 2008

Slonimsky, Nicolas, Russian-American

musicologist, conductor and composer, Apr 1955, Feb 1991, *Obit* Mar 1996

Smith, Rick, British keyboardist and songwriter, Nov 2011

Smyth, Ethel Mary, English composer, *Obit* June 1944

Sodero, Cesare, conductor and composer, Mar 1943, *Obit* Jan 1948

Sondheim, Stephen, American lyricist and composer, Nov 1973

Spector, Phil, American record producer, songwriter and arranger, July 1989

Spektor, Regina, Russian-American singer, songwriter and pianist, July 2007

Stebbins, George Coles, *Obit* Nov 1945

Steiner, Max, Austrian-American composer and conductor, Sept 1943, *Obit* Feb 1972

Stephens, Ward, *Obit* Nov 1940

Stew (Musician), American composer, lyricist and singer, Sept 2007

Stewart, Rod, English singer, Aug 1979

Still, William Grant, American composer, Jan 1941, *Obit* Feb 1979

Sting, British singer and actor, July 1985

Stockhausen, Karlheinz, German composer and conductor, Yrbk 1971, *Obit* Yrbk 2008

Stolz, Robert, Austrian composer, Aug 1943, *Obit* Aug 1975

Straus, Oscar, Austrian composer, Mar 1944, *Obit* Mar 1954

Strauss, Richard, German composer, July 1944, *Obit* Oct 1949

Stravinsky, Igor, Russian composer, May 1940, Apr 1953, *Obit* May 1971

Struther, Jan, English poet, essayist and short story writer, Jan 1941, *Obit* Oct 1953

Styne, Jule, composer, May 1983, *Obit* Nov 1994

Suesse, Dana, composer, May 1940, *Obit* Jan 1988

Swados, Elizabeth, American composer, Feb 1979

Swann, Donald, English pianist and composer, Jan 1970, *Obit* May 1994

Taj Mahal (Musician), American singer and songwriter, Nov 2001

Tan Dun, Chinese composer, Jan 2007

Tavares, Sara, Portuguese singer and songwriter, Jan 2007

Tavener, John, English composer, June 1999

Taylor, Billy, American jazz pianist and composer, Oct 1980, *Obit* Yrbk 2011

Taylor, Cecil, American jazz pianist, Mar 1986

Taylor, Deems, American composer and music critic, Mar 1940, *Obit* Nov 1966

Taylor, James, American singer and songwriter, June 1972

Taylor, KoKo, American blues singer and songwriter, July 2002, *Obit* Yrbk 2009

Teitur, Danish singer and songwriter, Jan 2004

Templeton, Alec, Mar 1940, *Obit* May 1963

Theodorakis, Mikis, Greek composer, July 1973

Thomas, Augusta Read, composer, Nov 1999

Thompson, Kay, American singer, songwriter and children's author, Apr 1959, *Obit* Sept 1998

Thomson, Virgil, American composer and critic, Nov 1940, Oct 1966, *Obit* Nov 1989

Tilson Thomas, Michael, American conductor and pianist, May 1971, June 1996

Tippett, Michael, English composer, Sept 1974, *Obit* Mar 1998

Tovey, Donald Francis, English composer, pianist and musicologist, *Obit* Sept 1940

Tremonti, Mark, American guitarist and composer, May 2002

Trenet, Charles, French singer and songwriter, Feb 1989, *Obit* Sept 2001

Tunstall, KT, Scottish rock singer and songwriter, Jan 2007

Tweedy, Jeff, American singer and songwriter, Feb 2010

Tweet (Singer), American singer and songwriter, Nov 2002

Tyner, McCoy, American jazz pianist and composer, Aug 1997

Uematsu, Nobuo, Japanese composer, Jan 2006

Van Heusen, Jimmy, American composer, June 1970, *Obit* Apr 1990

Vandross, Luther, American rhythm and blues singer and songwriter, Sept 1991, *Obit* Yrbk 2005

Vangelis, Greek composer, Jan 2003

Vaughan Williams, Ralph, English composer, Yrbk 1953, *Obit* Nov 1958

Vega, Suzanne, American singer and songwriter, Aug 1994

Veloso, Caetano, Brazilian singer and songwriter, Jan 2002

Vernon, Justin, American singer and songwriter, Apr 2012

Villa-Lobos, Heitor, Brazilian composer, Apr 1945, *Obit* Jan 1960

Von Tilzer, Harry, American songwriter and music publisher, *Obit* Mar 1946

Wagner, Sune Rose, Danish singer, guitarist and songwriter, Jan 2004

Waits, Tom, American singer and songwriter, Oct 1997

Waller, Fats, American jazz pianist and composer, Apr 1942, *Obit* Feb 1944

Walter, Bruno, conductor, Nov 1942, *Obit* Apr 1962

Walton, William, English composer, Mar 1940, *Obit* May 1983

Ward, Robert, composer, July 1963, *Obit* Yrbk 2013

Warren, Diane, American songwriter, June 2000

Weill, Kurt, German composer, Yrbk 1941, *Obit* May 1950

Weingartner, Felix, Austrian conductor and composer, *Obit* June 1942

Welch, Florence, British singer, June 2012

Wild, Earl, American pianist and composer, July 1988, *Obit* Yrbk 2010

Wilder, Alec, composer, July 1980, *Obit* Feb 1981

Williams, John T., American composer, Oct 1980

Williams, Lucinda, American singer and songwriter, Mar 1999

Williams, Mary Lou, American pianist and composer, Nov 1966, *Obit* July 1981

Williams, Paul, American singer, songwriter and actor, June 1983

Willson, Meredith, American composer and lyricist, June 1958, *Obit* Aug 1984

Wilson, Brian, American singer and songwriter, July 1988

Wilson, Gretchen, American country singer, Apr 2011

Winehouse, Amy, British jazz and soul singer, Jan 2007, *Obit* Yrbk 2011

Winter, Paul, saxophonist, Oct 1987

Wolfe, Julia, American composer, Oct 2003

Wuorinen, Charles, American composer, Apr 1972

Wylde, Zakk, American rock guitarist and songwriter, Oct 2004

Wyner, Yehudi, American composer, conductor and pianist, Apr 2008

Xenakis, Iannis, Greek composer, Sept 1994, *Obit* July 2001

Yanni, Greek composer, Jan 2003

Yon, Pietro A., Italian-American organist and composer, *Obit* Jan 1944

Youmans, Vincent, composer, Apr 1944, *Obit* May 1946

Zandonai, Riccardo, Italian composer, *Obit* Aug 1944

Zappa, Frank, American rock guitarist, Feb 1990, *Obit* Feb 1994

Zemlinsky, Alexander von, Austrian composer and conductor, *Obit* May 1942

Zimbalist, Efrem, American violinist, Mar 1949, *Obit* Apr 1985

Zimmer, Hans, German composer, Mar 2002

Zorn, John, American saxophonist, composer and conductor, Aug 1999

Zwilich, Ellen Taaffe, American composer, Jan 1986

Computer consultants

Rospars, Joe, American information technology executive, May 2010

Twomey, Paul, Australian Internet executive, Jan 2003

Computer hackers

Assange, Julian, Australian computer hacker and political activist, Mar 2011

Computer industry executives

Agassi, Shai, Israeli entrepreneur, Sept 2010

Akers, John F., computer industry executive, May 1988

Allen, Paul, American computer software executive and investor, July 1998

Amdahl, Gene M., American electrical engineer and computer executive, Aug 1982

Andreessen, Marc, American computer programmer and software executive, June 1997

Ansari, Anousheh, Iranian-American information technology executive, Jan 2005

Bartz, Carol A., American computer software executive, July 1999

Blumenthal, W. Michael, American Secretary of the treasury, July 1977

Cary, Frank Taylor, American computer industry executive, Jan 1980, *Obit* May 2006

Catz, Safra, American computer software executive, Jan 2008

Chinery-Hesse, Hermann, Ghanaian computer software executive, Jan 2003

Clark, James H., American computer software executive, June 1997

Conde, Cristobal, Chilean-American computer software executive, Sept 2010

Cook, Tim, American computer industry executive, Sept 2012

De Benedetti, Carlo, Italian computer and telecommunications executive, May 1990

Ek, Daniel, Swedish computer software executive, Mar 2012

Ellison, Lawrence J., American computer software executive, Jan 1998

Fiorina, Carly, American computer industry executive, Jan 2000

Friis, Janus, Danish computer software engineer and executive, Jan 2007

Fu, Ping, Chinese computer software executive, Oct 2006

Gates, Bill, American computer software executive, May 1991

Gates, Melinda French, American philanthropist and wife of Bill Gates, Feb 2004

Gerstner, Louis V., American computer industry executive, June 1991

Hastings, Reed, American computer software executive and entrepreneur, Mar 2006

Hirai, Kazuo, Japanese video game industry executive, Jan 2007

Houston, Drew, American online file hosting service executive, May 2012

Ive, Jonathan, British industrial designer, Oct 2006, May 2013

Iwata, Satoru, Japanese video game company executive, Jan 2007

Jobs, Steven, American computer industry executive, Mar 1983, Sept 1998, *Obit* Yrbk 2011

Jones, David, British video game creator, Jan 2006

Lanier, Jaron, American computer scientist and executive, June 1997

Lautenberg, Frank, American senator, Jan 1991, *Obit* Yrbk 2013

Leach, Ruth M., American computer industry executive, Mar 1948

Liu Chuanzhi, Chinese computer industry executive, Jan 2006

Mallya, Vijay, Indian business executive, Jan 2004

McNealy, Scott, American computer industry executive, Apr 1996

Minor, Halsey, American media and computer software executive, Oct 1998

Moore, Gordon E., American computer industry executive, Apr 2002

Morhaime, Mike, American video game company executive, Apr 2010

Moskovitz, Dustin, American social networking website founder, Jan 2012

Mullenweg, Matt, American computer software executive, May 2013

Myhrvold, Nathan P., American physicist and computer software executive, Sept 1997

Nishi, Kazuhiko, Japanese computer services executive, Jan 2002

Olsen, Kenneth H., American computer industry executive, *Obit* Yrbk 2011

Opel, John R., computer executive, Mar 1986, *Obit* Yrbk 2012

Packard, David, American computer industry executive, June 1969, *Obit* June 1996

Perot, Ross, American computer software executive and presidential candidate, July 1971, Yrbk 1996

Pfeiffer, Eckhard, German computer executive, June 1998

Pfeiffer, Jane, Oct 1980

Pincus, Mark, American computer software executive, Feb 2013

Pittman, Bob, American television and online computer services executive, July 2000

Polese, Kim, American computer software executive, July 1997

Potter, Michael U., Canadian computer software executive, Jan 2005

Rosedale, Philip, American information technology executive, Oct 2012

Rosen, Benjamin M., computer executive and financier, June 1997

Saylor, Michael, computer software executive, Sept 2000

Schmidt, Eric, American information technology executive, Apr 2008

Sculley, John, American computer industry executive, Aug 1988

Tagliabue, Paul, American football commissioner, Oct 1992

Thompson, John W., American information technology executive, Mar 2005

Wang, An, American computer industry executive, Jan 1987, *Obit* May 1990

Watson, Arthur Kittredge, American computer industry executive and diplomat, Sept 1971, *Obit* Oct 1974

Watson, Thomas J., American computer industry executive and diplomat, Feb 1956, *Obit* Mar 1994

Williams, Evan, American Internet executive, July 2009

Wolfram, Stephen, American physicist and software executive, Feb 2005

Wozniak, Stephen, American electronics industry executive, July 1997

Young, John A., computer executive, Oct 1986

Zelnick, Strauss, American financier, Nov 2010

Zennstrom, Niklas, Swedish computer software engineer and executive, Jan 2007

Computer personnel

Abrams, Jonathan, Canadian Internet software developer and entrepreneur, Apr 2006

Agassi, Shai, Israeli entrepreneur, Sept 2010

Aiken, Howard Hathaway, American mathematician and computer scientist, Mar 1947, *Obit* May 1973

Akers, John F., computer industry executive, May 1988

Amdahl, Gene M., American electrical engineer and computer executive, Aug 1982

Anderson, Tom, American Internet executive, July 2007

Andreessen, Marc, American computer programmer and software executive, June 1997

Ansari, Anousheh, Iranian-American information technology executive, Jan 2005

Assange, Julian, Australian computer hacker and political activist, Mar 2011

Ba, Amadou Mahtar, Senegalese multi-media content service provider executive, Jan 2004

Baker, Mitchell, American Internet executive, Apr 2009

Bartz, Carol A., American computer software executive, July 1999

Beck, Kent, American computer programmer, Jan 2007

Bezos, Jeffrey, American Internet and retail executive, June 1998

Bianchini, Gina, American Internet executive, Oct 2013

Brin, Sergey, American Internet search engine executive, Oct 2001

Carmack, John, American software engineer and video game company executive, Mar 2000

Cary, Frank Taylor, American computer industry executive, Jan 1980, *Obit* May 2006

Case, Steve, American mass media executive, Oct 1996

Catz, Safra, American computer software executive, Jan 2008

Cerf, Vinton G., American computer scientist, Sept 1998

Chen, Steve S., American video sharing web site founder, Jan 2007

Chinery-Hesse, Hermann, Ghanaian computer software executive, Jan 2003

Clark, James H., American computer software executive, June 1997

Conde, Cristobal, Chilean-American computer software executive, Sept 2010

Cook, Tim, American computer industry executive, Sept 2012

De Benedetti, Carlo, Italian computer and telecommunications executive, May 1990

DeWolfe, Chris, American Internet executive, July 2007

Ellison, Lawrence J., American computer software executive, Jan 1998

Evans, Nancy, Internet service executive and editor, Mar 2000

Ezarik, Justine, American webcaster, Mar 2013

Filo, David, American Internet search engine executive, Oct 1997

Fiorina, Carly, American computer industry executive, Jan 2000

Friis, Janus, Danish computer software engineer and executive, Jan 2007

Fu, Ping, Chinese computer software executive, Oct 2006

Gates, Bill, American computer software executive, May 1991

Gates, Melinda French, American philanthropist and wife of Bill Gates, Feb 2004

Gerstner, Louis V., American computer industry executive, June 1991

Goldstine, Herman Heine, American mathematician and computer scientist, Nov 1952, *Obit* Yrbk 2004

Gould, Wayne, New Zealand judge, Jan 2006

Harper, Stephen, Canadian prime minister, Jan 2006

Harris, Jonathan, American artist and web designer, Oct 2013

Hastings, Reed, American computer software executive and entrepreneur, Mar 2006

Hillis, Daniel, American computer scientist, Feb 1995

Hirai, Kazuo, Japanese video game industry executive, Jan 2007

Hurley, Chad, American video sharing web site founder, Jan 2007

Ive, Jonathan, British industrial designer, Oct 2006, May 2013

Iwata, Satoru, Japanese video game company executive, Jan 2007

Jobs, Steven, American computer industry executive, Mar 1983, Sept 1998, *Obit* Yrbk 2011

Jones, David, British video game creator, Jan 2006

Karim, Jawed, American video sharing web site founder, Jan 2007

Kaspersky, Eugene, Russian computer scientist, Jan 2005, June 2013

Kilar, Jason, American Internet executive, Aug 2009

Koller, Daphne, computer scientist, May 2013

Komando, Kim, computer scientist and radio talk show host, Sept 2000

Koogle, Timothy, Internet search engine company executive, Apr 2000

Kurzweil, Raymond, American computer scientist and inventor, Sept 2008

Lanier, Jaron, American computer scientist and executive, June 1997

Lanzone, Jim, American Internet executive, May 2007

Lautenberg, Frank, American senator, Jan 1991, *Obit* Yrbk 2013

Leach, Ruth M., American computer industry executive, Mar 1948

Li, Robin, Chinese Internet executive, Jan 2007

Ma, Jack, Chinese Internet service provider executive, Jan 2006

Mayer, Marissa, American Internet executive, Jan 2010

McCurry, Michael, American presidential press secretary and Internet executive, Nov 1996

McGonigal, Jane, American computer game designer, Apr 2013

McLurkin, James, American computer scientist, Sept 2005

McNealy, Scott, American computer industry executive, Apr 1996

Minsky, Marvin Lee, American computer scientist, Sept 1988

Miyamoto, Shigeru, Japanese video game creator, Jan 2002

Morhaime, Mike, American video game company executive, Apr 2010

Moskovitz, Dustin, American social networking website founder, Jan 2012

Mullenweg, Matt, American computer software executive, May 2013

Myhrvold, Nathan P., American physicist and computer software executive, Sept 1997

Newmark, Craig, American software engineer and webmaster, June 2005

Nishi, Kazuhiko, Japanese computer services executive, Jan 2002

Olsen, Kenneth H., American computer industry executive, *Obit* Yrbk 2011

Opel, John R., computer executive, Mar 1986, *Obit* Yrbk 2012

Packard, David, American computer industry executive, June 1969, *Obit* June 1996

Page, Larry, American Internet search engine executive, Oct 2001

Perot, Ross, American computer software executive and presidential candidate, July 1971, Yrbk 1996

Persson, Markus (Notch), Swedish computer programmer and game inventor, Sept 2013

Pfeiffer, Eckhard, German computer executive, June 1998

Pfeiffer, Jane, Oct 1980

Pincus, Mark, American computer software executive, Feb 2013

Polese, Kim, American computer software executive, July 1997

Potter, Michael U., Canadian computer software executive, Jan 2005

Ritchie, Dennis M., American computer scientist, Mar 1999, *Obit* Yrbk 2011

Romenesko, Jim, American journalist and webmaster, Feb 2004

Rosedale, Philip, American information technology executive, Oct 2012

Rosen, Benjamin M., computer executive and financier, June 1997

Rospars, Joe, American information technology executive, May 2010

Rucker, Rudy von Bitter, American mathematician, computer programmer and science fiction writer, May 2008

Rus, Daniela, Romanian computer scientist, Feb 2004

Sakaguchi, Hironobu, Japanese video game designer, Jan 2003

Sandberg, Sheryl, American Internet executive, June 2008

Sassa, Scott Michael, American Internet executive, Jan 2000

Saylor, Michael, computer software executive, Sept 2000

Schmidt, Eric, American information technology executive, Apr 2008

Schreiber, Ryan, American webmaster and rock music critic, Feb 2011

Semel, Terry S., American Internet service provider executive, July 2006

Sharansky, Natan, Israeli cabinet member, Feb 1987

Son, Masayoshi, Japanese Internet and telecommunications executive, Jan 2006

Suzuki, Yu, Japanese video game developer, Jan 2003

Tagliabue, Paul, American football commissioner, Oct 1992

Tajiri, Satoshi, Japanese video game designer, Nov 2001

Thompson, John W., American information technology executive, Mar 2005

Thompson, Kenneth Lane, American computer scientist, Mar 1999

Twomey, Paul, Australian Internet executive, Jan 2003

Wales, Jimmy, American Internet entrepreneur, Oct 2006

Walker, Jay, American entrepreneur and information technology executive, Oct 2000

Wang, An, American computer industry executive, Jan 1987, *Obit* May 1990

Watson, Arthur Kittredge, American computer industry executive and diplomat, Sept 1971, *Obit* Oct 1974

Watson, Thomas J., American computer industry executive and diplomat, Feb 1956, *Obit* Mar 1994

Westergren, Tim, American information technology executive, Oct 2012

Williams, Evan, American Internet executive, July 2009

Wirth, Niklaus, Swiss computer scientist, Jan 2003

Wojcicki, Susan, American Internet executive, Feb 2013

Wolfram, Stephen, American physicist and software executive, Feb 2005

Wright, Will, American computer game designer, Feb 2004

Yang, Jerry, American Internet search engine executive, Oct 1997

Young, John A., computer executive, Oct 1986

Zelnick, Strauss, American financier, Nov 2010

Zennstrom, Niklas, Swedish computer software engineer and executive, Jan 2007

Zuckerberg, Mark, American Internet executive, Jan 2008

von Tobel, Alexa, American Internet executive, June 2013

Computer programmers

Beck, Kent, American computer programmer, Jan 2007

Gould, Wayne, New Zealand judge, Jan 2006

Harper, Stephen, Canadian prime minister, Jan 2006

McGonigal, Jane, American computer game designer, Apr 2013

Persson, Markus (Notch), Swedish computer programmer and game inventor, Sept 2013

Ritchie, Dennis M., American computer scientist, Mar 1999, *Obit* Yrbk 2011

Sakaguchi, Hironobu, Japanese video game designer, Jan 2003

Suzuki, Yu, Japanese video game developer, Jan 2003

Tajiri, Satoshi, Japanese video game designer, Nov 2001

Wright, Will, American computer game designer, Feb 2004

Computer scientists

Aiken, Howard Hathaway, American mathematician and computer scientist, Mar 1947, *Obit* May 1973

Brin, Sergey, American Internet search engine executive, Oct 2001

Cerf, Vinton G., American computer scientist, Sept 1998

Goldstine, Herman Heine, American mathematician and computer scientist, Nov 1952, *Obit* Yrbk 2004

Hillis, Daniel, American computer scientist, Feb 1995

Kaspersky, Eugene, Russian computer scientist, Jan 2005, June 2013

Koller, Daphne, computer scientist, May 2013

Komando, Kim, computer scientist and radio talk show host, Sept 2000

Kurzweil, Raymond, American computer scientist and inventor, Sept 2008

McLurkin, James, American computer scientist, Sept 2005

Minsky, Marvin Lee, American computer scientist, Sept 1988

Page, Larry, American Internet search engine executive, Oct 2001

Ritchie, Dennis M., American computer scientist, Mar 1999, *Obit* Yrbk 2011

Rus, Daniela, Romanian computer scientist, Feb 2004

Thompson, Kenneth Lane, American computer scientist, Mar 1999

Computer software executives

Adelson, Jay, American information technology executive, June 2012

Anderson, Tom, American Internet executive, July 2007

Ba, Amadou Mahtar, Senegalese multi-media content service provider executive, Jan 2004

Baker, Mitchell, American Internet executive, Apr 2009

Bezos, Jeffrey, American Internet and retail executive, June 1998

Bianchini, Gina, American Internet executive, Oct 2013

Carmack, John, American software engineer and video game company executive, Mar 2000

DeWolfe, Chris, American Internet executive, July 2007

Ek, Daniel, Swedish computer software executive, Mar 2012

Filo, David, American Internet search engine executive, Oct 1997

Fong, Dennis, American computer game player and executive, Aug 2012

Houston, Drew, American online file hosting service executive, May 2012

Kilar, Jason, American Internet executive, Aug 2009

Koogle, Timothy, Internet search engine company executive, Apr 2000

Lanzone, Jim, American Internet executive, May 2007

Li, Robin, Chinese Internet executive, Jan 2007

Ma, Jack, Chinese Internet service provider executive, Jan 2006

Mayer, Marissa, American Internet executive, Jan 2010

McCurry, Michael, American presidential press secretary and Internet executive, Nov 1996

Miyamoto, Shigeru, Japanese video game creator, Jan 2002

Newmark, Craig, American software engineer and webmaster, June 2005

Sandberg, Sheryl, American Internet executive, June 2008

Semel, Terry S., American Internet service provider executive, July 2006

Son, Masayoshi, Japanese Internet and telecommunications executive, Jan 2006

Stanton, Katie Jacobs, Internet executive and Special Adviser to the Office of Innovation at the U.S. Department of State, June 2012

Stoppelman, Jeremy, American Internet executive, June 2012

Wales, Jimmy, American Internet entrepreneur, Oct 2006

Walker, Jay, American entrepreneur and information technology executive, Oct 2000

Wojcicki, Susan, American Internet executive, Feb 2013

Yang, Jerry, American Internet search engine executive, Oct 1997

Zuckerberg, Mark, American Internet executive, Jan 2008

von Tobel, Alexa, American Internet executive, June 2013

Concert promoters

Guggenheimer, Minnie, Oct 1962, *Obit* June 1966

Wein, George, Oct 1985

Conductors (Music)

Abbado, Claudio, Italian conductor, May 1973

Adams, John, American composer, May 1988

Adler, Kurt Herbert, opera director and conductor, Mar 1979, *Obit* Apr 1988

Alpert, Herb, American trumpet player and composer, Jan 1967

Amram, David, American composer, conductor and French horn player, Nov 1969

Ansermet, Ernest, Swiss conductor, July 1949, *Obit* Apr 1969

Ashkenazy, Vladimir, Russian pianist and conductor, July 1967

Barbirolli, John, British conductor, Yrbk 1940, *Obit* Oct 1970

Barenboim, Daniel, Israeli pianist and conductor, Apr 1969

Barlow, Howard, Jan 1940, July 1954, *Obit* Mar 1972

Barrere, Georges, *Obit* Aug 1944

Barry, John, English composer, Mar 2000, *Obit* Yrbk 2011

Barzin, Leon, conductor, May 1951, *Obit* Aug 1999

Basie, Count, American jazz pianist and band leader, June 1942, *Obit* June 1984

Beecham, Thomas, English conductor, Yrbk 1941, Jan 1951, *Obit* May 1961

Beinum, Eduard van, Apr 1955, *Obit* June 1959

Bennett, Robert Russell, American composer, arranger and conductor, Apr 1942, May 1962, *Obit* Oct 1981

Berio, Luciano, Italian composer, Mar 1971, *Obit* Yrbk 2003

Bernie, Ben, American band leader, Yrbk 1941, *Obit* Yrbk 1943

Bernstein, Leonard, American conductor and composer, Feb 1944, Feb 1960, *Obit* Nov 1990

Blakey, Art, American jazz drummer and band leader, Sept 1988, *Obit* Jan 1991

Bodanzky, Artur, *Obit* Jan 1940

Bohm, Karl, Austrian conductor, June 1968, *Obit* Oct 1981

Bonynge, Richard, Australian conductor, Feb 1981

Boulanger, Nadia, French conductor and teacher, May 1962, *Obit* Jan 1980

Boulez, Pierre, French composer and conductor, Mar 1969

Boult, Adrian Cedric, English conductor, Mar 1946, *Obit* Apr 1983

Brico, Antonia, conductor, Sept 1948, *Obit* Oct 1989

Brown, Chuck, band leader and songwriter, *Obit* Yrbk 2012

Busch, Carl, *Obit* Feb 1944

Busch, Fritz, German conductor, Jan 1946, *Obit* Oct 1951

Caldwell, Sarah, American opera director and conductor, Oct 1973, *Obit* Yrbk 2006

Calloway, Cab, American singer and band leader, Nov 1945, *Obit* Jan 1995

Cameron, Basil, English conductor, Apr 1943

Chailly, Riccardo, Italian conductor, June 1991

Chavez, Carlos, Mexican composer and conductor, May 1949, *Obit* Sept 1978

Christie, William, American harpsichordist and conductor, Jan 1992

Chung, Myung-Whun, Korean pianist and conductor, Aug 1990

Craft, Robert, American conductor, Mar 1984

Crosby, John O'Hea, American conductor and opera company manager, Nov 1981, *Obit* Yrbk 2003

Cugat, Xavier, band leader, May 1942, *Obit* Jan 1991

Damrosch, Walter, American conductor and composer, Mar 1944, *Obit* Jan 1951

Davies, Dennis Russell, conductor, May 1993

Davies, Walford, *Obit* May 1941

Davis, Andrew, British conductor, May 1983

Davis, Colin, British conductor, Nov 1968, *Obit* Yrbk 2013

Davis, Meyer, June 1961, *Obit* June 1976

Davis, Miles, American jazz trumpet player and flugelhornist, June 1962, *Obit* Nov 1991

DePreist, James, conductor, Oct 1990

Defauw, Desire, Jan 1940, *Obit* Oct 1960

Dixon, Dean, conductor, Apr 1943, *Obit* Jan 1977

Dohnanyi, Christoph von, German conductor, Oct 1985

Dorati, Antal, Hungarian conductor and composer, July 1948, *Obit* Jan 1989

Dorsey, Jimmy, band leader, Apr 1942, *Obit* Sept 1957

Dorsey, Tommy, American band leader, Apr 1942, *Obit* Feb 1957

Duchin, Eddy, pianist and band leader, Jan 1947, *Obit* Mar 1951

Duchin, Peter, band leader, Jan 1977

Dudamel, Gustavo, Venezuelan conductor, Apr 2010

Dunbar, Rudolph, Oct 1946

Dutoit, Charles, Swiss conductor, Feb 1987

Eddins, William Frederick, American conductor and pianist, Feb 2002

Eichheim, Henry, American violinist, conductor and composer, *Obit* Oct 1942

Ellington, Duke, American band leader and composer, Mar 1941, Jan 1970, *Obit* July 1974

Entremont, Philippe, French pianist and conductor, Mar 1977

Eschenbach, Christoph, German pianist and conductor, Aug 1989

Ferguson, Maynard, Canadian jazz trumpet player, Feb 1980, *Obit* Yrbk 2006

Fiedler, Arthur, American conductor, Sept 1945, May 1977, *Obit* Sept 1979

Finn, William J., July 1940

Fleisher, Leon, American pianist and conductor, Jan 1971

Foss, Lukas, American composer, conductor and pianist, June 1966, *Obit* Yrbk 2009

Gardiner, John Eliot, English conductor, Aug 1991

Gergiev, Valery, Russian conductor and opera director, Jan 1998

Gillespie, Dizzy, American trumpet player, Apr 1957, Jan 1993, *Obit* Jan 1993

Giulini, Carlo Maria, Italian conductor, Mar 1978, *Obit* Yrbk 2005

Goldman, Edwin Franko, Sept 1942, *Obit* May 1956

Goldovsky, Boris, Russian-American pianist, conductor and opera director, Yrbk 1966, *Obit* Aug 2001

Golschmann, Vladimir, Apr 1951, *Obit* May 1972

Goodman, Benny, American clarinetist and band leader, Jan 1942, Oct 1962, *Obit* Aug 1986

Goossens, Eugene, English conductor and composer, May 1945, *Obit* Sept 1962

Greenberg, Noah, conductor and musicologist, May 1964, *Obit* Feb 1966

Haitink, Bernard, Dutch conductor, Nov 1977

Halasz, Laszlo, Hungarian-American conductor and pianist, Jan 1949, *Obit* Feb 2002

Hampton, Lionel, American band leader, Oct 1971, *Obit* Yrbk 2002

Hannikainen, Tauno, July 1955, *Obit* Yrbk 1968

Hanson, Howard, American composer, Oct 1941, Sept 1966, *Obit* Apr 1981

Harnoncourt, Nikolaus, Austrian conductor, Jan 1991

Harty, Hamilton, Irish composer and conductor, *Obit* Apr 1941

Hawkins, Erskine, trumpet player and band leader, Sept 1941, *Obit* Jan 1994

Henderson, Skitch, American conductor, July 1966, *Obit* Apr 2006

Herman, Woody, American band leader, Apr 1973, *Obit* Jan 1988

Hertz, Alfred, *Obit* June 1942

Heward, Leslie H., *Obit* June 1943

Hillis, Margaret, choral conductor, Feb 1956, *Obit* Apr 1998

Hilsberg, Alexander, Oct 1953, *Obit* Nov 1961

Hinrichs, Gustav, German-American conductor, *Obit* May 1942

Hogwood, Christopher, English conductor, harpsichordist and musicologist, July 1985

Holliger, Heinz, Swiss oboist, Jan 1987

Iturbi, Jose, Spanish-American pianist and conductor, Sept 1943, *Obit* Aug 1980

Iverson, Ethan, American jazz pianist, Oct 2011

James, Harry, American band leader and trumpet player, Sept 1943, *Obit* Aug 1983

Jarvi, Neeme, Estonian conductor, Nov 1993

Johnson, Hall, American composer and music arranger, Jan 1945, *Obit* June 1970

Johnson, Thor, Oct 1949, *Obit* Mar 1975

Jordan, Philippe, Swiss opera conductor, Oct 2010

Karajan, Herbert von, Austrian conductor, Oct 1956, Sept 1986, *Obit* Sept 1989

Kearns, Carroll D., Sept 1956

Keene, Christopher, conductor and opera manager, Mar 1990, *Obit* Jan 1996

Kemp, Hal, *Obit* Feb 1941

Kenton, Stan, American band leader, June 1979

Kindler, Hans, Sept 1946, *Obit* Oct 1949

Kirchner, Leon, American composer and pianist, Yrbk 1967, *Obit* Yrbk 2009

Kleiber, Carlos, German conductor, July 1991, *Obit* Yrbk 2004

Klemperer, Otto, German conductor, Mar 1965, *Obit* Sept 1973

Knussen, Oliver, Scottish composer and conductor, Feb 1994

Kostelanetz, Andre, American conductor, July 1942, *Obit* Mar 1980

Koussevitzky, Serge, Russian conductor, Nov 1940, *Obit* July 1951

Krips, Josef, June 1965, *Obit* Yrbk 1974

Kubelik, Rafael, Czech conductor, Feb 1951, *Obit* Oct 1996

Kullmer, Ann, Feb 1949

Kurtz, Efrem, conductor, Feb 1946, *Obit* Sept 1995

Kyser, Kay, American band leader, Apr 1941, *Obit* Sept 1985

Lamond, Felix, *Obit* Apr 1940

Lehmann, George, *Obit* Yrbk 1941

Leinsdorf, Erich, conductor, May 1940, Oct 1963, *Obit* Nov 1993

Leppard, Raymond, British conductor and harpsichordist, Mar 1980

Levine, James, American conductor, Apr 1975

Lewis, Henry, American conductor, Feb 1973, *Obit* Apr 1996

Litton, Andrew, conductor, Sept 1998

Lockhart, Keith, American conductor, Aug 2008

Logan, Walter, *Obit* Mar 1940

Lombardo, Guy, American band leader, Sept 1946, Feb 1975, *Obit* Jan 1978

Lopez, Vincent, band leader and pianist, Nov 1960, Nov 1975

Luckstone, Isidore, *Obit* May 1941

Luisi, Fabio, Principal conductor of the Metropolitan Opera, Mar 2012

Maazel, Lorin, American conductor, Yrbk 1965

MacMillan, Ernest, Canadian conductor and composer, Mar 1955, *Obit* June 1973

Machito, Cuban band leader, Feb 1983, *Obit* June 1984

Mackerras, Charles, Australian conductor, Feb 1985

Mancini, Henry, American composer, July 1964, *Obit* Aug 1994

Marriner, Neville, English conductor, Aug 1978

Marsalis, Branford, American jazz saxophonist, Sept 1991

Masur, Kurt, German conductor, Sept 1990

McFerrin, Bobby, American singer and conductor, Aug 1989

Mehta, Zubin, Indian conductor, Mar 1969

Miller, Glenn, American band leader, Feb 1942, *Obit* Yrbk 1991

Miller, Mitch, American conductor and record producer, July 1956, *Obit* Yrbk 2010

Mitchell, Howard, cellist and conductor, May 1952, *Obit* Aug 1988

Mitropoulos, Dimitri, Greek conductor and composer, Mar 1941, Mar 1952, *Obit* Jan 1961

Monroe, Vaughn, July 1942, *Obit* July 1973

Monteux, Pierre, American conductor, Apr 1946, *Obit* Sept 1964

Muck, Karl, Mar 1940

Munch, Charles, Yrbk 1947, *Obit* Yrbk 1968

Muti, Riccardo, Italian conductor, July 1980

Nelson, Ozzie, actor and band leader, May 1949, *Obit* Aug 1975

Newman, Alfred, July 1943, *Obit* Apr 1970

Nezet-Seguin, Yannick, Canadian conductor, Nov 2011

Norrington, Roger, English conductor, Jan 1990

N£¤ez, Francisco J., Feb 2013

Ormandy, Eugene, conductor, Jan 1941, *Obit* May 1985

Ozawa, Seiji, Japanese conductor, Feb 1968, July 1998

Papi, Gennaro, *Obit* Jan 1942

Pasternack, Josef, *Obit* Jan 1940

Pelletier, Wilfrid, Yrbk 1944, *Obit* June 1982

Penderecki, Krzysztof, Polish composer, June 1971

Peroni, Carlo, *Obit* May 1944

Pinnock, Trevor, British harpsichordist and conductor, Sept 1989

Pollain, Rene, *Obit* Yrbk 1940

Previn, Andre, American composer and conductor, May 1972

Puente, Tito, American band leader, composer and percussionist, Nov 1977, *Obit* Aug 2000

Queler, Eve, conductor, July 1972

Rachmaninoff, Sergei, Russian composer and pianist, *Obit* May 1943

Rattle, Simon, English conductor, Feb 1988

Reiner, Fritz, conductor, Apr 1941, Yrbk 1953, *Obit* Jan 1964

Revueltas, Silvestre, Mexican composer, *Obit* Yrbk 1940

Rich, Buddy, American drummer and band leader, June 1973, *Obit* May 1987

Rodzinski, Artur, Aug 1940, *Obit* Feb 1959

Rosenstock, Joseph, conductor and opera director, Jan 1954, *Obit* Jan 1986

Rostropovich, Mstislav, Russian cellist and conductor, May 1966, Nov 1988, *Obit* Aug 2007

Rudel, Julius, Austrian-American conductor, July 1965

Salonen, Esa-Pekka, Finnish composer and conductor, Jan 2007

Santelmann, William F., bandmaster and marine corps officer, Apr 1953

Sargent, Malcolm Watts, English conductor, Yrbk 1945, *Obit* Jan 1968

Schelling, Ernest, American composer, conductor and pianist, Jan 1940

Scherman, Thomas, American conductor, Yrbk 1954, *Obit* July 1979

Schertzinger, Victor, *Obit* Yrbk 1941

Schippers, Thomas, American conductor, Apr 1970, *Obit* Feb 1978

Schoenberg, Loren, American saxophonist and jazz historian, Feb 2005

Schuller, Gunther, American composer and conductor, Apr 1964

Schwarz, Gerard, trumpet player and conductor, Apr 1986

Shaw, Artie, American clarinetist and band leader, May 1941, *Obit* Apr 2005

Shaw, Robert, American conductor, Sept 1949, July 1966, *Obit* Apr 1999

Sinopoli, Giuseppe, Italian conductor and composer, Mar 1991, *Obit* Sept 2001

Skrowaczewski, Stanislaw, Yrbk 1964

Slatkin, Leonard, American conductor, Feb 1986

Slonimsky, Nicolas, Russian-American musicologist, conductor and composer, Apr 1955, Feb 1991, *Obit* Mar 1996

Smallens, Alexander, May 1947, *Obit* Jan 1973

Sodero, Cesare, conductor and composer, Mar 1943, *Obit* Jan 1948

Solti, Georg, Hungarian-British conductor, Mar 1964, *Obit* Nov 1997

Spitalny, Phil, Oct 1940, *Obit* Yrbk 1970

Spivakov, Vladimir, Russian violinist and conductor, Feb 1996

Steinberg, William, American conductor, Sept 1940, Mar 1958, *Obit* July 1978

Steiner, Max, Austrian-American composer and conductor, Sept 1943, *Obit* Feb 1972

Stephens, Ward, *Obit* Nov 1940

Stock, Frederick, conductor, *Obit* Yrbk 1942

Stockhausen, Karlheinz, German composer and conductor, Yrbk 1971, *Obit* Yrbk 2008

Stoessel, Albert, *Obit* July 1943

Stokowski, Leopold, American conductor, Feb 1941, July 1953, *Obit* Nov 1977

Stolz, Robert, Austrian composer, Aug 1943, *Obit* Aug 1975

Strauss, Richard, German composer, July 1944, *Obit* Oct 1949

Szell, George, American conductor, June 1945, *Obit* Oct 1970

Tennstedt, Klaus, German conductor, Sept 1983, *Obit* Mar 1998

Tilson Thomas, Michael, American conductor and pianist, May 1971, June 1996

Toscanini, Arturo, Italian conductor, June 1942, May 1954, *Obit* Mar 1957

Tovey, Donald Francis, English composer, pianist and musicologist, *Obit* Sept 1940

Vinton, Bobby, July 1977

Voorhees, Donald, conductor, Feb 1950, *Obit* Apr 1989

Waart, Edo de, Dutch conductor, Mar 1990

Wallenstein, Alfred, American conductor, May 1940, Apr 1952, *Obit* Mar 1983

Walter, Bruno, conductor, Nov 1942, *Obit* Apr 1962

Waring, Fred, American band leader, Sept 1940, *Obit* Sept 1984

Weingartner, Felix, Austrian conductor and composer, *Obit* June 1942

Welk, Lawrence, American band leader, Feb 1957, *Obit* July 1992

Whiteman, Paul, American band leader, Aug 1945, *Obit* Feb 1968

Williams, John T., American composer, Oct 1980

Willson, Meredith, American composer and lyricist, June 1958, *Obit* Aug 1984

Wood, Henry Joseph, English conductor, *Obit* Oct 1944

Wyner, Yehudi, American composer, conductor and pianist, Apr 2008

Zemlinsky, Alexander von, Austrian composer and conductor, *Obit* May 1942

Conservationists

Anderson, Ray C., American carpet industry executive, May 2005, *Obit* Yrbk 2012

Baker, John Hopkinson, American investment banker and conservationist, May 1949

Barlow, Maude, Canadian environmentalist, Feb 2009

Beehler, Bruce McP., American ornithologist and conservationist, Aug 2006

Benyus, Janine M., American environmentalist, naturalist and science writer, Mar 2006

Berry, Wendell, American poet and novelist, May 1986

Bingham, Millicent Todd, American geographer and conservationist, June 1961, *Obit* Jan 1969

Brower, David, American conservationist, June 1973, *Obit* Feb 2001

Browner, Carol M., American environmentalist and government official, May 1994

Carter, Majora, American community activist and conservationist, Oct 2007, May 2013

Commoner, Barry, American biologist and environmentalist, Sept 1970, *Obit* Yrbk 2012

Corbett, Jim, British game hunter, May 1946, *Obit* June 1955

Darling, Jay Norwood, American cartoonist and conservationist, July 1942, *Obit* Mar 1962

Douglas, Marjory Stoneman, American short story writer, novelist and conservationist, July 1953, *Obit* July 1998

Durrell, Gerald M., British naturalist and conservationist, May 1985, *Obit* Apr 1995

Fay, Michael, American biologist and conservationist, Sept 2001

Finley, David E., American museum administrator and historic preservationist, Feb 1951, *Obit* Apr 1977

Fuller, Kathryn, conservationist and lawyer, Jan 1994

Gibbs, Lois, American environmentalist, Sept 1999

Gore, Al, American vice-president, June 1987

Haig-Brown, Roderick Langmere, Canadian naturalist, conservationist and author, Yrbk 1950

Hair, Jay D., American zoologist and conservationist, Nov 1993, *Obit* Jan 2003

Hawass, Zahi, Egyptian archaeologist, Apr 2000

Hayes, Denis, lawyer and environmentalist, Oct 1997

Henderson, Hazel, Anglo-American environmentalist and economist, Nov 2003

Hill, Julia, American environmentalist, Apr 2000

Jones, Van, American lawyer, civil rights activist, environmentalist and presidential aide, Apr 2009

Kennedy, Robert Francis, American lawyer and son of Senator Robert F. Kennedy, May 2004

Krupp, Frederic D., American lawyer and environmentalist, Sept 2007

LaDuke, Winona, Native American activist, Jan 2003

Lovins, Amory B., American physicist and conservationist, June 1997

Lowdermilk, Walter, American soil scientist, Feb 1949, *Obit* July 1974

Maathai, Wangari, Kenyan biologist and environmentalist, Sept 1993, *Obit* Yrbk 2011

Marker, Laurie, American conservationist, Feb 2000

Mittermeier, Russell, biologist and conservationist, Oct 1992

Moss, Cynthia, American biologist and conservationist, May 1993

Myers, Norman, English environmentalist, May 1993

Naidoo, Kumi, South African human rights activist and environmentalist, Sept 2010

Nelson, Gaylord, American senator, governor and environmentalist, May 1960, *Obit* Yrbk 2005

Osborn, Fairfield, American naturalist and conservationist, Sept 1949, *Obit* Nov 1969

Patkar, Medha, Indian environmentalist, Jan 2004

Payne, Roger, marine biologist, June 1995

Pearson, T. Gilbert, American ornithologist, *Obit* Oct 1943

Petrini, Carlo, Italian food safety activist, Jan 2004

Pinchot, Gifford, American governor, forester and conservationist, *Obit* Nov 1946

Player, Ian, South African conservationist, Jan 2002

Podesta, John, American public policy organization official and former presidential adviser, Feb 2010

Reilly, William K., American conservationist and government official, July 1989

Rockefeller, Laurance S., American investor and conservationist, June 1959, *Obit* Yrbk 2004

Ruckelshaus, William D., American government official, July 1971

Safina, Carl, American marine conservationist and scientist, Apr 2005

Shiva, Vandana, Indian physicist and environmentalist, Jan 2002

Steingraber, Sandra, American biologist, poet and nonfiction writer, Sept 2003

Strong, Maurice F., Canadian petroleum executive, environmentalist and government official, Yrbk 1973

Topfer, Klaus, German environmentalist and United Nations official, Jan 2002

Train, Russell E., American conservationist and government official, Oct 1970, *Obit* Yrbk 2012

Uexkull, Jakob von, Swedish environmentalist, Jan 2005

Ward, Barbara, English economist and writer, Jan 1950, Jan 1977, *Obit* July 1981

Construction industry executives

Avery, Sewell, American manufacturing and retail executive, June 1944, *Obit* Jan 1961

Baker, Melvin H., American constructon materials industry executive, Feb 1960

Bechtel, Stephen Davison, builder, Apr 1957, *Obit* May 1989

Bloom, Sol, American congressman, May 1943, *Obit* Mar 1949

Farber, Sid, builder, Sept 1967, *Obit* May 1973

Ferre, Luis A., Puerto Rican governor, Mar 1970, *Obit* Mar 2004

Fuller, Millard, American lawyer and humanitarian, Apr 1995, *Obit* Yrbk 2009

Lesinski, John, American congressman, June 1957

Levitt, William, American builder, Nov 1956, *Obit* Mar 1994

Logue, Edward J., American builder, June 1977, *Obit* June 2000

McNamara, Patrick V., American senator, Nov 1955, *Obit* June 1966

Noboa, Alvaro, Ecuadorian businessman and political leader, Jan 2007

Shultz, George P., American Secretary of state, May 1969, Apr 1988

Weyerhaeuser, Frederick E., *Obit* Nov 1945

Weyerhaeuser, George H., July 1977

Construction materials industry executives

Avery, Sewell, American manufacturing and retail executive, June 1944, *Obit* Jan 1961

Baker, Melvin H., American constructon materials industry executive, Feb 1960

Ferre, Luis A., Puerto Rican governor, Mar 1970, *Obit* Mar 2004

Lesinski, John, American congressman, June 1957

Weyerhaeuser, Frederick E., *Obit* Nov 1945

Weyerhaeuser, George H., July 1977

Construction workers

Bechtel, Stephen Davison, builder, Apr 1957, *Obit* May 1989

Bloom, Sol, American congressman, May 1943, *Obit* Mar 1949

Boland, Patrick J., American congressman, *Obit* July 1942

Dobson, William Alexander, *Obit* July 1943

Farber, Sid, builder, Sept 1967, *Obit* May 1973

Fuller, Millard, American lawyer and humanitarian, Apr 1995, *Obit* Yrbk 2009

Hudson, Harold W., *Obit* Mar 1943

Hutcheson, William Levi, American labor leader, Sept 1943, *Obit* Jan 1954

Levitt, William, American builder, Nov 1956, *Obit* Mar 1994

Lockwood, Rodney M., Sept 1949

Logue, Edward J., American builder, June 1977, *Obit* June 2000

Marples, Alfred Ernest Marples, May 1960

McNamara, Patrick V., American senator, Nov 1955, *Obit* June 1966

Pennington, Ty, American carpenter and host of reality TV show Extreme makeover: Home edition, Feb 2006

Slocum, Harvey, Feb 1957, *Obit* Jan 1962

Consultants

Abagnale, Frank, American security consultant and former con artist, Apr 2011

Adelman, Kenneth L., diplomat and management consultant, July 1985

Ailes, Roger, American political campaign consultant and television news executive, Jan 1989

Appley, Lawrence A., business consultant, July 1950, *Obit* June 1997

Arnold, Bion J., American electrical engineer, *Obit* Mar 1942

Arnold, Edwin G., American economic development consultant and foundation official, Sept 1947, *Obit* Jan 1961

Arnstein, Daniel, American taxi executive, Mar 1942

Atwater, Lee, American presidential adviser, June 1989, *Obit* May 1991

Avenol, Joseph, Jan 1940, *Obit* Oct 1952

Axelrod, David, American presidential adviser, Apr 2009

Ayres, Leonard Porter, May 1940, *Obit* Yrbk 1946

Bailar, John Christian, American chemist, July 1959

Baker, Charles Whiting, American civil engineer, *Obit* Aug 1941

Bakke, E. Wight, Sept 1953, *Obit* Jan 1972

Baldwin, William H., American public relations executive and civil rights activist, Nov 1945

Bedaux, Charles Eugene, French-American industrial engineer, *Obit* Apr 1944

Beers, Rand, American foreign policy adviser, Oct 2004

Bernays, Edward L., American public relations consultant, Feb 1942, Sept 1960, *Obit* May 1995

Bernstein, William, American investment adviser and neurologist, Nov 2009

Birdwell, Russell, July 1946, *Obit* Mar 1978

Birren, Faber, industrial color consultant, May 1956, *Obit* Feb 1989

Bolten, Josh, American presidential adviser, July 2006

Bradshaw, John E., American philosopher, educator and writer, Apr 1993

Brazile, Donna, American political consultant, Mar 2006

Brimmer, Andrew F., American economist and financial consultant, July 1968, *Obit* Yrbk 2012

Bryan, James E., American library director and consultant, June 1962

Buckingham, Marcus, American management consultant, Aug 2006

Burke, William R., July 1961

Carville, James, American political consultant and commentator, Mar 1993

Cassel, Karl Gustav, *Obit* Mar 1945

Cernan, Eugene A., American astronaut and business consultant, May 1973

Clarke, Richard A., American presidential aide and security consultant, May 2006

Cohen, Abby Joseph, American investment adviser, June 1998

Collins, Jim, American business consultant, Aug 2003

Connerly, Ward, American business consultant and anti-affirmative action activist, Nov 2000

Courant, Richard, mathematician, Sept 1966, *Obit* Mar 1972

Covey, Stephen R., American business training consultant, Jan 1998, *Obit* Yrbk 2012

Croft, Arthur C., June 1952

Dalrymple, Jean, theatrical producer, Sept 1953, *Obit* Feb 1999

Deming, W. Edwards, American statistician and business consultant, Sept 1993, *Obit* Mar 1994

Diebold, John, American management consultant, Mar 1967, *Obit* Yrbk 2006

Donald, W. H., July 1946

Douglas, Walter Jules, American civil engineer, *Obit* Sept 1941

Drucker, Peter F., American management consultant and economist, May 1964, *Obit* Apr 2006

Duffy, James J., *Obit* Feb 1942

Farny, George W., *Obit* Oct 1941

Finkelstein, Arthur, American political consultant, Nov 1999

Fraser, Leon, *Obit* May 1945

French, Hollis, *Obit* Jan 1941

Furman, N. Howell, Yrbk 1951, *Obit* Oct 1965

Garth, Dave, political consultant, Jan 1981

Garzarelli, Elaine, American investment adviser, Sept 1995

Griffith, Paul H., American management consultant and military official, Jan 1947, *Obit* Feb 1975

Grimshaw, Robert, *Obit* June 1941

Hafstad, Lawrence R., physicist, Oct 1956, *Obit* Jan 1994

Hannagan, Steve, publicist and sportswriter, Aug 1944, *Obit* Mar 1953

Herman, Alexis, American Secretary of labor and management consultant, Jan 1998

Herrick, Elinore Morehouse, Apr 1947, *Obit* Jan 1965

Hibbard, Henry D., *Obit* Yrbk 1942

Hills, Carla Anderson, American Secretary of housing and urban development and trade representative, Nov 1975, Mar 1993

Hodges, Luther Hartwell, American Secretary of commerce and governor, July 1956, *Obit* Nov 1974

Hoffman, Anna Rosenberg, American public relations executive and government official, Jan 1943, Jan 1951, *Obit* July 1983

Houle, Cyril Orvin, May 1962

Hudson, C. W., *Obit* June 1943

Janeway, Eliot, economist and investment adviser, Sept 1970, *Obit* Apr 1993

Jordan, Hamilton, American presidential adviser and campaign consultant, Aug 1977, *Obit* Yrbk 2008

Kanter, Rosabeth Moss, American management consultant, teacher and writer, May 1996

Kapp, Joe, football player and management consultant, Sept 1975

Kendrew, John C., British biochemist, Oct 1963, *Obit* Nov 1997

Keys, David A., Oct 1958

Kheel, Theodore, American labor mediator, Sept 1964, *Obit* Yrbk 2011

Klein, Julius, veterans' leader and public relations consultant, July 1948, *Obit* May 1984

Kopp, Wendy, American teacher recruiter, Mar 2003

Kristol, William, American political adviser, commentator and magazine editor, May 1997

Lapp, Ralph Eugene, American physicist, Nov 1955, *Obit* Feb 2005

Lasser, J. K., May 1946, *Obit* July 1954

Lichtenberg, Bernard, *Obit* Nov 1944

Magaziner, Ira C., American business consultant and presidential adviser, Apr 1995

Magill, Roswell, Mar 1948, *Obit* Feb 1964

Main, Charles Thomas, *Obit* Apr 1943

Malloch Brown, Mark, British United Nations official, Jan 2005

Malone, George W., American senator, Yrbk 1950, *Obit* July 1961

Maney, Richard, July 1964, *Obit* Sept 1968

Mather, Kirtley F., American geologist, Jan 1951

McConnell, Mike, American intelligence official, Apr 2007

McGraw, Phillip C., American psychologist and television talk show host, June 2002

Messina, Jim, American presidential adviser and political consultant, Mar 2013

Michelson, Charles, journalist, Aug 1940, *Obit* Jan 1948

Millis, Harry A., Nov 1940, *Obit* Sept 1948

Moisseiff, Leon S., American bridge engineer, *Obit* Oct 1943

Nadler, Marcus, May 1955, *Obit* June 1965

Nobs, Ernst, Sept 1949, *Obit* June 1957

Nofziger, Lyn, American political consultant, Jan 1983, *Obit* Yrbk 2006

Orman, Suze, American financial adviser, May 2003

Peters, Thomas J., American management consultant and writer, Oct 1994

Phillips, Frederick, *Obit* Oct 1943

Pilcher, Lewis F., *Obit* Aug 1941

Pirie, John Taylor, *Obit* Mar 1940

Pitt, Harvey L., American risk management consultant, Nov 2002

Plouffe, David, American presidential adviser, June 2009

Ramsey, Norman Foster, American physicist, Yrbk 1963, *Obit* Yrbk 2012

Rappard, William E., Oct 1951, *Obit* July 1958

Reed, Ralph, American political leader, Mar 1996

Reeve, Sidney A., *Obit* Aug 1941

Riebel, John P., Jan 1957

Rinfret, Pierre, American economist and financial

consultant, July 1972, *Obit* Yrbk 2006

Rodahl, Kare, Norwegian physiologist, Feb 1956

Rollins, Ed, American political consultant, Mar 2001

Saposs, David J., Nov 1940, *Obit* Jan 1969

Schwartz, Felice N., management consultant, May 1993, *Obit* Apr 1996

Sharp, Mitchell, Canadian political adviser, July 1966

Sherley, Swagar, *Obit* Apr 1941

Shockley, William, American physicist, Yrbk 1953, *Obit* Oct 1989

Shulman, Harry, Apr 1952, *Obit* May 1955

Siple, Paul Allman, explorer and geographer, Feb 1957, *Obit* Jan 1969

Slocum, Harvey, Feb 1957, *Obit* Jan 1962

Smith, Bruce, Feb 1953, *Obit* Nov 1955

Sokolsky, George E., May 1941, *Obit* Jan 1963

Solandt, Omond M., Mar 1974

Soss, Wilma Porter, publicist, Mar 1965, *Obit* Jan 1987

Starch, Daniel, psychologist and marketing analyst, Jan 1963

Stephanopoulos, George, American television news anchor, Jan 1995

Stummvoll, Josef Leopold, June 1960

Swings, Pol, Belgian astronomer, Yrbk 1954

Taleb, Nassim, Lebanese mathematician, investment adviser and philosopher, May 2011

Tead, Ordway, educator and management consultant, May 1942, *Obit* Jan 1974

Tweed, Thomas Frederic, *Obit* Jan 1940

Vanderbilt, Amy, Feb 1954, *Obit* Feb 1975

Walsh, William Henry, *Obit* May 1941

Watts, J. C., American congressman, management consultant and political commentator, Mar 1999

Weld, William Floyd, American lawyer and former governor, Feb 1993

Wheaton, Anne, Jan 1958, *Obit* May 1977

Wheeler, Raymond A., Apr 1957, *Obit* Apr 1974

Wheelwright, Jere, Yrbk 1952, *Obit* Mar 1961

Wick, Charles Z., American government official, Mar 1985, *Obit* Yrbk 2008

Wilder, Frances Farmer, July 1947

Witt, James Lee, American emergency management official and consultant, Mar 2000

Yergin, Daniel, American energy consultant and business writer, Nov 1999

Zelomek, A. Wilbert, Yrbk 1956

Consumer rights advocates

Furness, Betty, television commentator and consumer adviser, Feb 1968, *Obit* June 1994

Green, Mark J., American lawyer, consumer rights advocate and municipal official, Feb 1988

Hawkins, Paula, American senator, Sept 1985, *Obit* Yrbk 2010

Nader, Ralph, American consumer rights advocate, Nov 1968, Apr 1986

Pertschuk, Michael, consumer activist and government official, Sept 1986

Peterson, Esther, American consumer rights advocate, Yrbk 1961, *Obit* Mar 1998

Schlink, Frederick J., consumer rights advocate, Mar 1941, *Obit* Mar 1995

Warren, Elizabeth, American law professor and consumer rights advocate, Feb 2012

Container industry executives

Klassen, Elmer Theodore, postmaster general, May 1973, *Obit* June 1990

Contractors

Boland, Patrick J., American congressman, *Obit* July 1942

Lockwood, Rodney M., Sept 1949

Cookbook writers

Beard, James, American chef, Yrbk 1964, *Obit* Mar 1985

Bittman, Mark, American food columnist and cookbook writer, Feb 2005

Blumenthal, Heston, British chef and restaurateur, Jan 2005

Case, Frank, *Obit* July 1946

Child, Julia, American cook, Feb 1967, *Obit* Yrbk 2004

Claiborne, Craig, American food critic, Sept 1969, *Obit* Apr 2000

Cora, Cat, American chef and cookbook writer, Nov 2011

Deen, Paula H., American cook, restaurateur and television personality, Mar 2010

Feniger, Susan, American chef and restaurateur, Apr 2013

Fisher, M. F. K., American food writer, Yrbk 1948, Sept 1983, *Obit* Aug 1992

Kander, Lizzie Black, American social worker and cookbook writer, *Obit* Sept 1940

Katzen, Mollie, American cookbook author, Oct 1996

Keller, Thomas, American chef and restaurateur, June 2004

Kurihara, Harumi, Japanese cook and television personality, Jan 2006

Lakshmi, Padma, Indian model, cookbook writer and television personality, Jan 2006

Laverty, Maura, Irish author, Yrbk 1947

Lawson, Nigella, English food critic and cookbook writer, Jan 2003

Lillien, Lisa, American cook, cookbook writer and entrepreneur, May 2010

McMeekin, Isabel McLennan, American novelist and children's author, Sept 1942, Yrbk 1957

Munoz Zurita, Ricardo, Mexican chef, Jan 2003

P,pin, Jacques, French-American chef and cookbook writer, Sept 2012

Rombauer, Irma von Starkloff, American cookbook author, Yrbk 1953, *Obit* Yrbk 1962

Root, Waverley Lewis, American journalist, May 1943, *Obit* Jan 1983

Wason, Betty, cookbook author and journalist, Aug 1943

Cooking teachers

Cointreau, Andre, French chef and cooking school administrator, Jan 2004

Cooks

Achatz, Grant, American chef and restaurateur, Jan 2011

Adria, Ferran, Spanish chef and restaurateur, Jan 2006

Andr,s, Jos,, Spanish chef and restaurateur, June 2013

Arzak, Juan Mari, Spanish chef and restaurateur, Jan 2007

Beard, James, American chef, Yrbk 1964, *Obit* Mar 1985

Bocuse, Paul, French chef and restaurateur, Jan 1988

Boulud, Daniel, French chef and restaurateur, Jan 2005

Chang, David, American chef and restaurateur, Aug 2010

Cointreau, Andre, French chef and cooking school administrator, Jan 2004

Colicchio, Tom, American chef and restaurateur, Feb 2013

De Laurentiis, Giada, American chef and television personality, July 2013

DiSpirito, Rocco, American chef and restaurateur, Feb 2012

English, Todd, American chef and restaurateur, Jan 2012

Fieri, Guy, American chef, restaurateur and television personality, Mar 2011

Fisher, M. F. K., American food writer, Yrbk 1948, Sept 1983, *Obit* Aug 1992

Flay, Bobby, American chef and restaurateur, May 2008

Florence, Tyler, American chef, Aug 2012

Frankel, Bethenny, American chef, food service executive and participant in reality TV show Real housewives of New York City, Mar 2013

Hamilton, Gabrielle, American chef and restaurateur, May 2013

Henderson, Fergus, British chef and restaurateur, Feb 2011

Holzen, Heinz von, Swiss chef and restaurateur, Jan 2002
Kander, Lizzie Black, American social worker and cookbook writer, *Obit* Sept 1940
Katzen, Mollie, American cookbook author, Oct 1996
Lahlou, Mourad, Chef and restauranteur, May 2012
Laverty, Maura, Irish author, Yrbk 1947
Lawson, Nigella, English food critic and cookbook writer, Jan 2003
Matsuhisa, Nobu, Japanese chef and restaurateur, Jan 2005
Morimoto, Masaharu, Japanese chef and restaurateur, Jan 2004
Munoz Zurita, Ricardo, Mexican chef, Jan 2003
Oliver, Jamie, British chef and restaurateur, Jan 2005
Puck, Wolfgang, Austrian-American restaurateur and chef, Jan 1998
Redzepi, Ren,, Danish chef and restaurateur, Apr 2012
Ripert, Eric, French chef and restaurateur, Mar 2013
Robuchon, Joel, French chef and restaurateur, Jan 2003
Rombauer, Irma von Starkloff, American cookbook author, Yrbk 1953, *Obit* Yrbk 1962
Root, Waverley Lewis, American journalist, May 1943, *Obit* Jan 1983
Senderens, Alain, French chef, Jan 2005
Wason, Betty, cookbook author and journalist, Aug 1943
Waters, Alice, American chef and restaurateur, Jan 2004
White, Marco Pierre, British chef and restaurateur, Jan 2007

Copywriters

Fishback, Margaret, copywriter and humorist, Apr 1941, *Obit* Nov 1985
Johnson, Mat, American novelist, Mar 2010

Cornet players

Morris, Butch, American cornet player and composer, July 2005, *Obit* Yrbk 2013

Correctional personnel

Additon, Henrietta Silvis, American social worker, prison superintendent and police official, Sept 1940
Bennett, James V., American penologist and prison official, Apr 1949, *Obit* Feb 1979
Canavan, Joseph J., *Obit* Yrbk 1940
Lawes, Lewis Edward, American prison warden and reformer, Oct 1941, *Obit* Mar 1947
Ross, Rick, American rapper, June 2012
Van Waters, Miriam, American penologist, Mar 1963, *Obit* Apr 1974

Cosmeticians

Arden, Elizabeth, American cosmetician, July 1957, *Obit* Yrbk 1966
Baker, Rick, American makeup artist, Mar 1997
Smith, Dick, makeup artist, Mar 1959
Westmore, Perc, American makeup artist, Oct 1945, *Obit* Nov 1970
Winston, Stan, American special effects technician, July 2002, *Obit* Nov 2008

Cosmetics industry executives

Ash, Mary Kay, American cosmetics executive, May 1995, *Obit* Feb 2002
Ellena, Jean-Claude, French perfumer, Jan 2005
Guerlain, Jean-Paul, French perfumer, Jan 2006
Jung, Andrea, American cosmetics industry executive, May 2000
Lauder, Estee, American cosmetics executive, July 1986, *Obit* Yrbk 2004
Roddick, Anita, British cosmetics industry executive, Sept 1992, *Obit* Yrbk 2007
Waldron, Hicks Benjamin, cosmetics executive, Mar 1988

Costume designers

Adrian, American costume and fashion designer, Feb 1941, *Obit* Nov 1959
Aldredge, Theoni, American costume designer, Feb 1994, *Obit* Yrbk 2011
Atwood, Colleen, American costume designer, Oct 2010
Bonomi, Maria, Brazilian artist, July 1960
Brooks, Donald, American fashion and costume designer, Mar 1972, *Obit* Yrbk 2005
Cuevas, Manuel, Mexican-American costume designer, Jan 2005
Czettel, Ladislas, Mar 1941, *Obit* Apr 1949
Erte, French painter, set and costume designer, Nov 1980, *Obit* June 1990
Field, Patricia, American fashion and costume designer, Nov 2010
Head, Edith, American costume designer, May 1945, *Obit* Jan 1982
Irene, costume designer, June 1946, *Obit* Jan 1963
Karinska, Barbara, Russian-American costume designer, Jan 1971
Long, William Ivey, American costume designer, Mar 2004
Mackie, Bob, fashion designer, Oct 1988
Moiseiwitsch, Tanya, English stage and costume designer, Nov 1955, *Obit* July 2003
Powell, Sandy, English costume designer, June 2000
Roth, Ann, costume designer, Mar 1997
Wada, Emi, Japanese costume designer, Jan 2007

Counselors

Anthony, John J., American family and marriage counselor, Jan 1942, *Obit* Oct 1970
Johnstone, Margaret Blair, Jan 1955
Mudd, Emily, American family and marriage counselor, Nov 1956, *Obit* July 1998
Popenoe, Paul Bowman, American eugenicist, Yrbk 1946

Schwartz, Felice N., management consultant, May 1993, *Obit* Apr 1996

Country musicians

Acuff, Roy, singer, June 1976, *Obit* Jan 1993

Arnold, Eddy, American country singer, Mar 1970, *Obit* Yrbk 2008

Atkins, Chet, American guitarist and record industry executive, Jan 1975, *Obit* Sept 2001

Black, Clint, American country singer and songwriter, Aug 1994

Brooks, Garth, American country singer, Mar 1992

Brooks, Kix, American country singer and songwriter, Sept 2004

Brown, Junior, American country singer and guitarist, Nov 2004

Campbell, Glen, American singer and guitarist, July 1969

Carpenter, Mary Chapin, American singer and songwriter, Feb 1994

Case, Neko, American singer and songwriter, June 2013

Cash, Johnny, American country singer and songwriter, Sept 1969, *Obit* Jan 2004

Cash, Rosanne, American country singer and songwriter, Oct 1991

Chesney, Kenny, American country singer, May 2004

Clark, Roy, American country singer and banjoist, June 1978

Davis, Mac, American country singer and songwriter, Aug 1980

DeMarcus, Jay, American keyboardist and singer, Aug 2003

Dean, Jimmy, American singer, Yrbk 1965, *Obit* Aug 2010

Denver, John, American singer and actor, Jan 1975, *Obit* Jan 1998

Douglas, Jerry, American dobro guitar player, Aug 2004

Dunn, Ronnie Gene, American country singer and songwriter, Sept 2004

Earle, Steve, American country singer and guitarist, Oct 1998

Ford, Tennessee Ernie, singer, Mar 1958, *Obit* Jan 1992

Gayle, Crystal, singer, Mar 1986

Griffith, Nanci, American folk and country singer and songwriter, Feb 1998

Haggard, Merle, American country singer, Jan 1977

Harris, Emmylou, American singer, Oct 1994

Haywood, Dave, American country guitarist, pianist and mandolinist, July 2011

Hill, Faith, American country singer, Mar 2001

Jackson, Alan, American country singer, Apr 2004

Jennings, Waylon, American singer and songwriter, Apr 1982, *Obit* Apr 2002

Johnson, Jamey, American country singer and songwriter, Feb 2011

Jones, George, American country singer, Feb 1995, *Obit* Yrbk 2013

Keith, Toby, American country singer, Oct 2004

Kelley, Charles, American country singer and songwriter, July 2011

Krauss, Alison, American fiddler and singer, May 1997

Lambert, Miranda, American country singer, Feb 2012

LeVox, Gary, American country singer, Aug 2003

Lovett, Lyle, American singer, Sept 1997

Lynn, Loretta, American country singer and songwriter, Oct 1973

Lynne, Shelby, American country singer and songwriter, July 2001

Maguire, Martie, American fiddler, July 2000

Maines, Natalie, American singer, July 2000

Mandrell, Barbara, singer, Aug 1982

McBride, Martina, American country singer, Mar 2004

McEntire, Reba, American country singer and actress, Oct 1994

McGraw, Tim, American country singer, Sept 2002

Morgan, Lorrie, American country singer, Apr 1999

Nelson, Willie, American country singer and songwriter, Feb 1979

Parton, Dolly, American country singer and songwriter, Aug 1977

Pearl, Minnie, American comedienne, Nov 1992, *Obit* May 1996

Pride, Charley, American country singer, Apr 1975

Rimes, LeAnn, American country singer, May 1998

Robison, Emily, American banjoist and singer, July 2000

Rogers, Dale Evans, American singer and actress, Sept 1956, *Obit* Apr 2001

Rogers, Kenny, American country singer, Jan 1981

Rooney, Joe Don, American guitarist, Aug 2003

Scott, Hillary, American country singer, July 2011

Strait, George, American country singer, Feb 2000

Travis, Randy, American country singer, Sept 1989

Tritt, Travis, American country singer, Feb 2004

Tubb, Ernest, singer, Oct 1983, *Obit* Oct 1984

Watson, Doc, American singer and guitarist, Feb 2003, *Obit* Yrbk 2012

Williams, Hank, American country singer, Mar 1998

Willis, Kelly, singer, Oct 1999

Wilson, Gretchen, American country singer, Apr 2011

Womack, Lee Ann, American country singer, Apr 2010

Wynette, Tammy, American country singer, June 1995, *Obit* June 1998

Wynonna, American country singer, May 1996

Yearwood, Trisha, American country singer, July 1998

Yoakam, Dwight, American country singer, Nov 2000

County government employees

McEntee, Gerald, American labor leader, Oct 2000

County government officials

Beall, J. Glenn, American senator, Apr 1955, *Obit* Mar 1971

Daley, Richard M., American mayor, Aug 1992

Herbert, Gary R., American governor, May 2011

Hruska, Roman Lee, American senator, July 1956, *Obit* July 1999

Locke, Gary, American Secretary of commerce, Apr 2003

Moseley-Braun, Carol, American senator, June 1994

Pendergast, Tom, American political party leader, *Obit* Mar 1945

Richards, Ann, American governor, Feb 1991, *Obit* Yrbk 2007

Robertson, A. Willis, American senator, Yrbk 1949, *Obit* Yrbk 1971

Stabenow, Debbie, American senator, Feb 2006

Courtiers

Lupescu, Elena, mistress of King Carol II of Romania, Oct 1940, *Obit* Aug 1977

Cowboys

Brannaman, Buck, American horse trainer and motivational speaker, Sept 2011

Murray, Ty, American rodeo cowboy, May 2002

Cricket players

Amla, Hashim, South African cricket player, Jan 2006

Hayden, Matthew, Australian cricket player, Jan 2004

Khan, Imran, Pakistani cricket player and member of Parliament, Jan 2005

Lara, Brian, Trinidadian cricket player, Feb 2001

Sehwag, Virender, Indian cricket player, Jan 2003

Sobers, Garfield, Barbadian cricket player, Jan 2002

Tendulkar, Sachin, Indian cricket player, Jan 2002

Warne, Shane, Australian cricket player, Jan 2005

Waugh, Steve, Australian cricket player, Jan 2003

Criminals

Abagnale, Frank, American security consultant and former con artist, Apr 2011

Brinkley, John Richard, American physician and swindler, *Obit* July 1942

Chapman, Duane Lee, American bounty hunter, Mar 2005

Frank, Hans, German jurist and Nazi leader, Mar 1941, *Obit* Nov 1946

Goring, Hermann, German Nazi leader, Aug 1941, *Obit* Nov 1946

Habash, George, Palestinian nationalist leader, Mar 1988, *Obit* Yrbk 2008

Hess, Rudolf, German Nazi leader, Mar 1941, *Obit* Oct 1987

Jodl, Alfred, German general, *Obit* Nov 1946

Krupp von Bohlen und Halbach, Alfried, German munitions manufacturer, May 1955, *Obit* Oct 1967

Osama bin Laden, Saudi Arabian terrorist, *Obit* Yrbk 2012

Perry, Anne, English mystery novelist, Aug 1996

Ribbentrop, Joachim von, German Nazi leader, May 1941, *Obit* Nov 1946

Rideau, Wilbert, American convicted murderer and prison journalist, Nov 2010

Streicher, Julius, German Nazi leader, *Obit* Nov 1946

Terboven, Josef, German war criminal, Nov 1941, *Obit* June 1945

Criminologists

Bates, Sanford, American penologist, Jan 1961, *Obit* Nov 1972

Bennett, James V., American penologist and prison official, Apr 1949, *Obit* Feb 1979

Douglas, John E., American criminologist, July 2001

Faurot, Joseph A., *Obit* Jan 1943

Glueck, Eleanor Touroff, Oct 1957, *Obit* Nov 1972

Glueck, Sheldon, Oct 1957, *Obit* May 1980

Kirchwey, George W., *Obit* Apr 1942

Lawes, Lewis Edward, American prison warden and reformer, Oct 1941, *Obit* Mar 1947

MacCormick, Austin H., May 1940, July 1951, *Obit* Jan 1980

Morehead, Albert H., Mar 1955, *Obit* Yrbk 1966

Ohlin, Lloyd E., American criminologist, Apr 1963, *Obit* Yrbk 2009

Ressler, Robert K., American criminologist, Feb 2002

Ulman, Joseph N., *Obit* May 1943

Van Waters, Miriam, American penologist, Mar 1963, *Obit* Apr 1974

Critics

Abdulhamid, Ammar, Syrian novelist, poet and essayist, Jan 2005

Ackroyd, Peter, English novelist, biographer, poet and literary critic, May 1993

Acocella, Joan Ross, American dance critic, May 2007

Adler, Renata, critic, journalist, novelist and short story writer, June 1984

Agar, Herbert, author, poet and critic, Mar 1944, *Obit* Jan 1981

Aiken, Conrad, American poet, novelist, short story writer, critic and memoirist, May 1970, *Obit* Oct 1973

Aldridge, John W., American literary critic, Yrbk 1958

Amis, Kingsley, English novelist, poet and critic, Yrbk 1958, Apr 1987, *Obit* Jan 1996

Amis, Martin, English novelist and short story writer, June 1990, Jan 2003

Ammondt, Jukka, Finnish literary scholar and Elvis Presley impersonator, Jan 2002

Anderson, John, American drama critic and playwright, *Obit* Sept 1943

Apple, R. W., American journalist, Apr 1993, *Obit* Feb 2007

Ashbery, John, American poet, Aug 1976

Atkinson, Brooks, American drama critic, Apr 1942, Feb 1961, *Obit* Mar 1984

Augenbraum, Harold, American literary scholar, Apr 2012

Bacon, Leonard, poet, critic and translator, June 1941, *Obit* Mar 1954

Barnes, Clive, British dance and drama critic, Mar 1972, *Obit* Feb 2009

Barnes, Julian, English novelist, short story writer and essayist, Mar 1988

Barrett, Wilton Agnew, American film critic, *Obit* Mar 1940

Barthes, Roland, French literary critic, Feb 1979, *Obit* May 1980

Bates, Ernest Sutherland, biographer, historian and literary critic, Jan 1940

Baudrillard, Jean, French social theorist, June 1993, *Obit* Yrbk 2007

Beatty, Arthur, American professor of English, *Obit* Apr 1943

Berryman, John, American poet and critic, May 1969, *Obit* Feb 1972

Bly, Robert, American poet, critic, editor and translator, Mar 1984, Mar 1993

Borges, Jorge Luis, Argentine short story writer and poet, Jan 1970, *Obit* Aug 1986

Bowers, Faubion, critic, Sept 1959, *Obit* May 2000

Bracco, Roberto, *Obit* June 1943

Brantley, Ben, American drama critic, Aug 2011

Brenan, Gerald, English author, poet and critic, July 1986, *Obit* Mar 1987

Brooks, Van Wyck, literary critic and biographer, June 1941, Sept 1960, *Obit* June 1963

Brown, Carleton, *Obit* Aug 1941

Brown, John Mason, drama critic and biographer, Apr 1942, *Obit* May 1969

Brown, Sterling Allen, American poet and literary critic, Aug 1982, *Obit* Apr 1989

Brustein, Robert, American theatrical director and critic, Aug 1975

Burton, Richard, *Obit* May 1940

Byatt, A. S., English novelist, short story writer and literary critic, Sept 1991

Cairns, Huntington, American lawyer, Nov 1940

Calverton, Victor Francis, American political writer, editor and literary critic, *Obit* Jan 1941

Campbell, Bebe Moore, American social critic and novelist, Apr 2000, *Obit* Yrbk 2007

Canaday, John Edwin, art critic and author, May 1962, *Obit* Sept 1985

Canby, Henry Seidel, literary critic, Sept 1942, *Obit* June 1961

Cassidy, Claudia, drama and music critic, Sept 1955, *Obit* Oct 1996

Ceram, C. W., Jan 1957, *Obit* June 1972

Chamberlain, John, journalist and critic, Apr 1940, *Obit* June 1995

Chambers, R. W., *Obit* June 1942

Champion, Pierre, *Obit* Aug 1942

Chomsky, Noam, American linguist and social critic, Oct 1970, Aug 1995

Ciardi, John, American poet, translator and critic, Oct 1967, *Obit* May 1986

Clark, Kenneth, British art historian and museum director, Sept 1963, *Obit* July 1983

Clurman, Harold, theatrical director and critic, Feb 1959, *Obit* Nov 1980

Coddington, Grace, British fashion editor, Apr 2005

Coetzee, J. M., South African novelist, Jan 1987

Colles, H. C., *Obit* Apr 1943

Connolly, Cyril, English essayist, critic and editor, Yrbk 1947

Craven, Thomas, American art critic, Apr 1944, *Obit* Apr 1969

Croce, Benedetto, Italian philosopher, historian and critic, Jan 1944, *Obit* Jan 1953

Crosby, John, journalist, novelist and television critic, June 1953

Crouch, Stanley, American essayist and critic, Mar 1994

Crowther, Bosley, motion picture critic, July 1957, *Obit* Apr 1981

D'Arcy, Martin Cyril, British priest and philosopher, Jan 1960, *Obit* Mar 1977

Dargan, Edwin Preston, *Obit* Feb 1941

Darrell, R. D., music critic, Sept 1955, *Obit* June 1988

Davies, Robertson, Canadian novelist, playwright and critic, June 1975, *Obit* Mar 1996

Day Lewis, C., Anglo-Irish poet, critic and mystery writer, Jan 1940, July 1969, *Obit* July 1972

De Casseres, Benjamin, essayist, critic and journalist, *Obit* Feb 1946

De Voto, Bernard Augustine, American historian, literary critic and novelist, Sept 1943, *Obit* Jan 1956

Deane, Seamus, Irish literary critic and poet, Jan 2007

Debeljak, Ales, Slovenian poet and critic, Jan 2007

Decter, Midge, social critic, Apr 1982

Dillard, Annie, American poet, critic and nature writer, Jan 1983

Dolbier, Maurice, author and literary critic, Yrbk 1956, *Obit* Jan 1994

Donovan, Carrie, American fashion editor, Sept 1999, *Obit* Feb 2002

Downes, Olin, music critic and historian, Mar 1943, *Obit* Oct 1955

Dudley, Bide, *Obit* Feb 1944

Eastman, Max, American poet, journalist and critic, Apr 1969, *Obit* Apr 1969

Ebert, Roger, American film critic, Mar 1997, *Obit* Yrbk 2013

Eco, Umberto, Italian semiotician and novelist, Apr 1985

Ehrenreich, Barbara, American feminist and social critic, Mar 1995

Ellison, Ralph, American novelist and essayist, Oct 1968, June 1993, *Obit* June 1994

Elson, Arthur, Mar 1940

Enwezor, Okwui, Nigerian art critic and exhibition curator, Jan 2002

Epstein, Joseph, American essayist, editor and critic, Mar 1990

Fadiman, Clifton, literary critic, editor and television moderator, May 1941, Oct 1955, *Obit* Sept 1999

Fagles, Robert, American translator, poet and literary scholar, Apr 2006, *Obit* Yrbk 2008

Farrar, John, June 1954, *Obit* Jan 1975

Fiedler, Leslie A., American literary critic and novelist, Yrbk 1970, *Obit* Yrbk 2003

Flynn, Gillian, American television critic and novelist, Apr 2013

Forster, E. M., English novelist, short story writer and essayist, Apr 1964, *Obit* Sept 1970

Fougner, G. Selmer, journalist and wine critic, *Obit* May 1941

Frederick, John T., June 1941

Freedley, George, American theater historian and librarian, Sept 1947, *Obit* Nov 1967

French, Marilyn, American novelist and critic, Sept 1992, *Obit* Yrbk 2009

Frye, Northrop, Canadian literary critic, Aug 1983, *Obit* Mar 1991

Gannett, Lewis Stiles, American journalist and literary critic, Aug 1941, *Obit* Mar 1966

Gaselee, Stephen, *Obit* Aug 1943

Gass, William H., American philosopher, novelist, short story writer and critic, Apr 1986

Gassner, John, Jan 1947, *Obit* June 1967

Gates, Henry Louis, American professor of African-American studies, Oct 1992

Gessen, Keith, American magazine editor, novelist and critic, Sept 2008

Gilder, Rosamond, American drama critic, Nov 1945, *Obit* Oct 1986

Gillet, Louis, *Obit* Aug 1943

Gioia, Ted, American jazz historian, Jan 2010

Gopnik, Adam, American essayist and art critic, Apr 2005

Gorman, Herbert Sherman, author and literary critic, Mar 1940, *Obit* Jan 1955

Greene, Graham, English novelist, Oct 1969, *Obit* May 1991

Greer, Germaine, Australian feminist and writer, Nov 1971, Oct 1988

Grossman, Edith, American translator and literary scholar, Mar 2006

Grossman, Lev, American literary critic and novelist, Apr 2010

Guerard, Albert J., novelist and critic, Yrbk 1946, *Obit* Mar 2001

Gullar, Ferreira, Brazilian poet and art critic, Jan 2004

Hadas, Moses, Mar 1960, *Obit* Nov 1966

Hamilton, Clayton Meeker, dramatist and critic, *Obit* Oct 1946

Hammond, John, American recording industry executive, July 1979, *Obit* Aug 1987

Hansen, Harry, editor and critic, Yrbk 1942, *Obit* Yrbk 1991

Hardwick, Elizabeth, American novelist, short story writer, essayist and critic, Feb 1981, *Obit* Yrbk 2008

Harrington, Michael, American social critic and political activist, Jan 1969, Oct 1988, *Obit* Sept 1989

Haskell, Molly, motion picture critic, Nov 1998

Hass, Robert, American poet, critic and translator, Feb 2001

Haycraft, Howard, publisher and author, Nov 1941, Feb 1954, *Obit* Jan 1992

Hazard, Paul, Mar 1941

Heilbrun, Carolyn G., American literary scholar and mystery novelist, Jan 1993, *Obit* Feb 2004

Hicks, Granville, American literary critic and novelist, May 1942, *Obit* Aug 1982

Hines, Duncan, restaurant critic and publisher, May 1946, *Obit* May 1959

Hobson, John Atkinson, British economist and journalist, *Obit* Apr 1940

Hoggart, Richard, English social and cultural critic, Oct 1963

Hollander, Robert, American literary critic, translator and poet, Sept 2006

Howe, Irving, American literary critic and editor, Apr 1978, *Obit* July 1993

Hu, Shih, Chinese poet, diplomat and literary critic, Feb 1942, *Obit* Apr 1962

Hughes, Robert, Australian art critic, May 1987, *Obit* Yrbk 2012

Huxtable, Ada Louise, American architectural critic, Mar 1973, *Obit* Yrbk 2013

Jackson, Michael, British journalist and beer expert, Aug 2005, *Obit* Yrbk 2007

James, Clive, Australian literary critic and journalist, Nov 1984

Janeway, Elizabeth, American novelist and critic, Mar 1944, *Obit* Yrbk 2005

Jefferson, Margo, American literary critic, June 1999

Johnson, Pamela Hansford, English novelist and critic, Yrbk 1948, *Obit* Aug 1981

Kael, Pauline, American film critic, Mar 1974, *Obit* Nov 2001

Kazin, Alfred, American literary critic, May 1966, *Obit* Aug 1998

Kerr, Walter, drama critic, Oct 1953, *Obit* Jan 1997

Kirkus, Virginia, American magazine editor and literary critic, May 1941, June 1954, *Obit* Nov 1980

Kolodin, Irving, music critic, July 1947, *Obit* June 1988

Korngold, Julius, *Obit* Oct 1945

Kosinski, Jerzy N., Polish-American novelist, essayist and critic, Mar 1974, *Obit* July 1991

Kott, Jan, Polish literary critic, Apr 1969, *Obit* Mar 2002

Kozol, Jonathan, American social critic, Jan 1986

Kronenberger, Louis, drama critic, editor and author, Aug 1944, *Obit* July 1980

Krutch, Joseph Wood, American critic, biographer and nature

writer, Nov 1959, *Obit* July 1970

Kundera, Milan, Czech poet, dramatist, novelist and short story writer, Mar 1983

Lane, Anthony, British film critic, Nov 2008

Lanman, Charles Rockwell, *Obit* Apr 1941

Lasch, Christopher, American social critic and historian, Mar 1985, *Obit* Apr 1994

Laski, Marghanita, English author and critic, Yrbk 1951, *Obit* Apr 1988

Lewis, C. S., English children's author, novelist and critic, Jan 1944, *Obit* Jan 1964

Lieberson, Goddard, composer, critic and record executive, Mar 1976, *Obit* July 1977

Liebling, Leonard, *Obit* Yrbk 1945

Lodge, Gonzalez, *Obit* Feb 1943

Lorentz, Pare, American motion picture director, Apr 1940, *Obit* May 1992

Lovett, Robert Morss, literary critic and author, Aug 1943, *Obit* Apr 1956

Luquiens, Frederick Bliss, *Obit* May 1940

Macdonald, Dwight, American journalist and critic, Nov 1969, *Obit* Mar 1983

Maltin, Leonard, American film critic and historian, Aug 2008

Manly, John Matthews, *Obit* May 1940

Mantle, Burns, American drama critic, Nov 1944, *Obit* Mar 1948

Mapes, Victor, *Obit* Jan 1944

Marcus, Greil, American music critic, Oct 1999

Mason, Bobbie Ann, American novelist and short story writer, Sept 1989

Mayne, Ethel Colburn, English author, critic and translator, *Obit* June 1941

McCarthy, Mary, American novelist, critic, short story writer and memoirist, Yrbk 1955, Feb 1969, *Obit* Jan 1990

McLuhan, Marshall, Canadian cultural critic, June 1967, *Obit* Feb 1981

Mihajlov, Mihajlo, Yugoslav social and literary critic, Jan 1979, *Obit* Yrbk 2010

Milosz, Czeslaw, Polish poet, Oct 1981, *Obit* Yrbk 2004

Mitchell, Elvis, American film critic, July 2008

Mitford, Jessica, English journalist, memoirist and social critic, Sept 1974, *Obit* Oct 1996

Moore, Michael, American documentary filmmaker, May 1997

Moravia, Alberto, Italian novelist, short story writer, playwright and essayist, Apr 1970, *Obit* Nov 1990

Morris, Wright, American novelist, short story writer and critic, May 1982, *Obit* July 1998

Murray, Augustus Taber, *Obit* Mar 1940

Nathan, George Jean, drama critic, Apr 1945, *Obit* June 1958

Nemerov, Howard, American novelist, poet and critic, Oct 1964, *Obit* Sept 1991

Newton, Eric, British art critic, Feb 1956, *Obit* Apr 1965

Nicolson, Harold George, British diplomat, author and critic, May 1967, *Obit* June 1968

Nock, Albert Jay, American literary critic and essayist, May 1944, *Obit* Sept 1945

Novak, Michael, American social philosopher and critic, Feb 1985

O'Brien, Conor Cruise, Irish critic, historian and diplomat, Apr 1967

O'Brien, Edward J., editor and critic, *Obit* Apr 1941

Oliver, Garrett, American brewmaster, Nov 2008

Ondaatje, Michael, Canadian poet and novelist, Oct 1993

Packard, Vance, American journalist, Apr 1958, *Obit* Feb 1997

Paddleford, Clementine, American food writer, Feb 1958, *Obit* Jan 1968

Palmer, John Leslie, English author and critic, *Obit* Sept 1944

Pareles, Jon, American music critic, Nov 2008

Parker, Robert M., American wine critic, May 2005

Pasolini, Pier Paolo, Italian poet, novelist, critic and film director, July 1970, *Obit* Jan 1976

Phelps, William Lyon, literary scholar, Jan 1943

Picken, Mary Brooks, Yrbk 1954

Pound, Ezra, American poet and literary critic, Nov 1942, May 1963, *Obit* Yrbk 1972

Powell, Lawrence Clark, librarian, biographer, novelist and critic, June 1960

Prescott, Orville, literary critic, Mar 1957, *Obit* July 1996

Pritchett, V. S., English short story writer, novelist and critic, Jan 1974, *Obit* June 1997

Quennell, Peter, English biographer, poet, novelist and critic, May 1984, *Obit* Jan 1994

Quiller-Couch, Arthur Thomas, English novelist, short story writer, essayist, poet and critic, *Obit* July 1944

Ransom, John Crowe, American poet and literary critic, July 1964, *Obit* Sept 1974

Read, Herbert Edward, English poet, essayist and art critic, Mar 1962, *Obit* Sept 1968

Redding, J. Saunders, American historian and novelist, Apr 1969, *Obit* Apr 1988

Reed, Rex, motion picture critic, Jan 1972

Rhys, Ernest, English editor, critic and poet, *Obit* Jan 1946

Richards, I. A., English poet, critic and linguist, Yrbk 1972, *Obit* Oct 1979

Richler, Mordecai, Canadian novelist and critic, May 1975, *Obit* Oct 2001

Robinson, Jancis, British wine critic, Jan 2007

Rohmer, Eric, French film director, Apr 1977, *Obit* Yrbk 2010

Rosenfeld, Paul, American music, art and literary critic, *Obit* Sept 1946

Saarinen, Aline B., American art critic and wife of architect Eero Saarinen, Yrbk 1956, *Obit* Sept 1972

Said, Edward W., Palestinian-American literary

and social critic, Nov 1989, *Obit* Feb 2004

Sanborn, Pitts, music critic, author and journalist, *Obit* Apr 1941

Sarris, Andrew, American film critic, Jan 2007, *Obit* Yrbk 2012

Schaap, Phil, American disc jockey and jazz historian, Sept 2001

Schjeldahl, Peter, American art critic, Oct 2005

Schreiber, Ryan, American webmaster and rock music critic, Feb 2011

Schwartz, Delmore, poet and critic, June 1960, *Obit* Nov 1966

Shales, Tom, American television and film critic, Jan 2009

Shapiro, Karl Jay, American poet and critic, Oct 1944, *Obit* Aug 2000

Shaw, Bernard, Irish dramatist, June 1944, *Obit* Yrbk 1950

Sheed, Wilfrid, American novelist, Aug 1981, *Obit* Yrbk 2011

Smith, Harrison, Yrbk 1954, *Obit* Feb 1971

Smith, Lillian Eugenia, American novelist and social critic, May 1944, *Obit* Yrbk 1966

Smith, Logan Pearsall, American lexicographer, essayist and critic, *Obit* Apr 1946

Snodgrass, W. D., American poet, critic and philologist, Nov 1960, *Obit* Yrbk 2009

Sontag, Susan, American novelist and essayist, June 1969, Feb 1992, *Obit* May 2005

Spender, Stephen, English poet and critic, Jan 1940, Mar 1977, *Obit* Sept 1995

Spurgeon, Caroline F. E., *Obit* Yrbk 1942

Starr, Cecile, American film critic, Mar 1955

Stearns, Harold E., journalist and critic, *Obit* Oct 1943

Stefan, Paul, *Obit* Jan 1944

Stein, Gertrude, American novelist, poet and critic, *Obit* Sept 1946

Steiner, George, American literary critic, short story writer and novelist, Oct 1983

Stern, Richard G., American novelist and short story writer, June 1994, *Obit* Yrbk 2013

Stevenson, Elizabeth, American biographer and literary scholar, Yrbk 1956

Stuart, Duane Reed, *Obit* Oct 1941

Symons, Arthur, English poet and critic, *Obit* Mar 1945

Talley, Andre Leon, American fashion editor, July 2003

Tate, Allen, American poet and critic, Nov 1940, *Obit* Apr 1979

Taubman, Howard, music and drama critic, Apr 1959, *Obit* Mar 1996

Taylor, Deems, American composer and music critic, Mar 1940, *Obit* Nov 1966

Thernstrom, Abigail M., American social critic, Mar 2010

Thompson, Oscar, *Obit* Aug 1945

Thomson, Virgil, American composer and critic, Nov 1940, Oct 1966, *Obit* Nov 1989

Trilling, Diana, literary and social critic, May 1979, *Obit* Jan 1997

Truss, Lynne, English humorist, novelist and critic, July 2006

Tynan, Kenneth, British drama critic, Yrbk 1963, *Obit* Sept 1980

Untermeyer, Louis, American poet, editor and literary critic, Jan 1967, *Obit* Feb 1978

Van Doren, Mark, American literary critic, editor and poet, Jan 1940, *Obit* Feb 1973

Van Horne, Harriet, radio and television critic, Yrbk 1954, *Obit* Mar 1998

Vendler, Helen Hennessy, American literary scholar, May 1986

Vernon, Grenville, *Obit* Jan 1942

Warren, Robert Penn, American novelist and poet, June 1970, *Obit* Nov 1989

Waugh, Auberon, English novelist and essayist, May 1990, *Obit* May 2001

West, Cornel, American philosopher, Oct 1993

Westcott, John Howell, *Obit* July 1942

White, Armond, American film critic, Oct 2006

White, Helen Constance, literary scholar and author, July 1945

Wills, Garry, American journalist, essayist and historian, June 1982

Wilson, Edmund, American literary critic, Apr 1945, Jan 1964, *Obit* July 1972

Wolf, Naomi, American feminist, social critic and journalist, Nov 1993

Woollcott, Alexander, journalist, June 1941, *Obit* Mar 1943

Yaffe, James, Yrbk 1957

Yardley, Jonathan, American literary critic and columnist, Jan 2011

Zagat, Nina, American restaurant survey publisher, Mar 2008

Zagat, Tim, American restaurant survey publisher, Mar 2008

de Botton, Alain, English novelist and journalist, Sept 2013

Cult leaders

Asahara, Shoko, Japanese cult leader, Jan 2003

Rael, French cult leader, Jan 2002

Curators

Amsden, Charles Avery, American archaeologist, *Obit* Apr 1941

Barton, William H., American astronomer and planetarium curator, *Obit* Aug 1944

Bazin, Germain, French art historian and museum curator, Jan 1959, *Obit* July 1990

Cannon, Annie Jump, American astronomer, *Obit* June 1941

D'Harnoncourt, Rene, Sept 1952, *Obit* Oct 1968

Gilmore, Melvin R., *Obit* Sept 1940

Golden, Thelma, American museum curator, Sept 2001

Horner, John R., American paleontologist, Sept 1992

Kellogg, Remington, paleontologist, Nov 1949

Knoll, Andrew H., American paleontologist, Apr 2006

Lewis, Albert Buell, American anthropologist, *Obit* Yrbk 1940

Lutz, Frank Eugene, entomologist and museum curator, *Obit* Jan 1944

Mead, Margaret, American anthropologist, Nov 1940, May 1951, *Obit* Jan 1979

Morton, James F., *Obit* Yrbk 1941

Noble, G. Kingsley, zoologist and museum curator, *Obit* Jan 1941

Novacek, Michael J., American paleontologist and museum curator, Sept 2002

Oliver, James A., Jan 1966, *Obit* May 1982

Paradise, Nathaniel Burton, *Obit* June 1942

Parma, V. Valta, *Obit* Nov 1941

Reagon, Bernice Johnson, American historian and singer, Aug 1999

Reisner, George Andrew, American Egyptologist, *Obit* July 1942

Rubin, William Stanley, American art historian and museum curator, Nov 1986, *Obit* Yrbk 2007

Sayles, R. W., *Obit* Yrbk 1942

Schneirla, T. C., Yrbk 1955, *Obit* Nov 1968

Schuchert, Charles, *Obit* Jan 1943

Shapiro, Harry Lionel, anthropologist and museum curator, Yrbk 1952, *Obit* Mar 1990

Tattersall, Ian, American anthropologist and museum curator, Aug 2007

Tolstoy, Alexandra, Russian foundation official and daughter of novelist Leo Tolstoy, Apr 1953, *Obit* Nov 1979

Tuttle, Emerson, *Obit* Apr 1946

Varnedoe, Kirk, American museum curator and art historian, Feb 1991, *Obit* Yrbk 2003

Willis, Deborah, American photography historian and museum curator, Sept 2004

Cyclists

Armstrong, Lance, American cyclist, Sept 1997

Heiden, Eric, American speed skater and bicyclist, June 1980

LeMond, Greg, American cyclist, Oct 1989

Lewis, Jason, British adventurer, Jan 2007

Pantani, Marco, Italian cyclist, Feb 1999

Rossi, Valentino, Italian motorcycle racer, Jan 2005

Stewart, James, American motorcycle racer, Feb 2005

Ullrich, Jan, German cyclist, Jan 2003

Wiggins, Bradley, Nov 2013

Young, Sheila, American cyclist and speed skater, Jan 1977

Cytologists

Fuchs, Elaine V., American cytologist, Jan 2011

Dance critics

Barnes, Clive, British dance and drama critic, Mar 1972, *Obit* Feb 2009

Bowers, Faubion, critic, Sept 1959, *Obit* May 2000

Dance directors

Alonso, Alicia, Cuban ballet dancer, July 1955, June 1977

Andersen, Ib, Danish ballet dancer and director, Aug 1984

Bausch, Pina, German dancer, choreographer and director, Sept 1986, *Obit* Yrbk 2009

Bourne, Matthew, English dancer and choreographer, Jan 2005

Bruhn, Erik, Danish ballet dancer and director, Apr 1959, *Obit* May 1986

Chase, Alison Becker, American choreographer, Nov 2006

Clifford, John, American ballet dancer and choreographer, Nov 1972

Cullberg, Birgit, Swedish ballet dancer and choreographer, Nov 1982, *Obit* Nov 1999

De Valois, Ninette, English ballet dancer, choreographer and director, Yrbk 1949, *Obit* Aug 2001

Fagan, Garth, American dancer, director and choreographer, Aug 1998

Forsythe, William, American choreographer, ballet dancer and director, Feb 2003

Franca, Celia, Canadian ballet director and dancer, May 1956, *Obit* Yrbk 2007

Grigorovich, Yuri, Russian choreographer and dance director, Sept 1975

Jamison, Judith, American dancer, director and choreographer, Jan 1973

Joffrey, Robert, American ballet dancer, choreographer and director, Nov 1967, *Obit* Nov 1988

Jooss, Kurt, German choreographer, dance director and teacher, July 1976, *Obit* July 1979

Kain, Karen, Canadian ballet dancer and director, May 1980

Kirstein, Lincoln, American ballet manager, Yrbk 1952, Aug 1990, *Obit* Mar 1996

Kylian, Jiri, Czech dancer, choreographer and director, Sept 1982

Macdonald, Brian, Canadian ballet director and choreographer, July 1968

Martins, Peter, Danish-American dancer, choreographer and director, June 1978

McKenzie, Kevin, American ballet dancer and director, Jan 2000

Mitchell, Arthur, American ballet dancer and choreographer, Oct 1966

Nagy, Ivan, Hungarian dance director, May 1977

Neumeier, John, American dancer and choreographer, July 1991

Rambert, Marie, British ballet dancer, teacher and director, Feb 1981, *Obit* Aug 1982

Ramirez, Tina, Venezuelan-American dancer and director, Nov 2004

Schaufuss, Peter, Danish ballet dancer and director, May 1982

Tomasson, Helgi, Icelandic ballet dancer and director, Apr 1982

Villella, Edward, American ballet dancer and director, Mar 1965

Welch, Stanton, Australian ballet dancer, choreographer and director, July 2007

Wilde, Patricia, Canadian ballet dancer and director, May 1968

Dance managers

Chase, Lucia, American ballet dancer and manager, July 1947, Aug 1975, *Obit* Mar 1986

Dowell, Anthony, English ballet dancer and manager, May 1971

Harkness, Rebekah West, American composer, ballet manager and dance patron, Apr 1974, *Obit* Sept 1982

Kirstein, Lincoln, American ballet manager, Yrbk 1952, Aug 1990, *Obit* Mar 1996

Lichtenstein, Harvey, American performing arts executive, May 1987

Verdy, Violette, French ballet dancer and manager, Yrbk 1969, Oct 1980

Wheater, Ashley, British ballet dancer and director, May 2011

Dance teachers

Adams, Diana, dancer and teacher, Apr 1954, *Obit* Mar 1993

Andersen, Ib, Danish ballet dancer and director, Aug 1984

Benesh, Joan, British ballet dancer, choreographer and teacher, July 1957

Beriosova, Svetlana, Lithuanian ballet dancer and teacher, Sept 1960, *Obit* Feb 1999

Blankenbuehler, Andy, American choreographer and dancer, Apr 2009

Chase, Alison Becker, American choreographer, Nov 2006

D'Amboise, Jacques, American ballet dancer, choreographer and teacher, Sept 1964

Danilova, Alexandra, Russian ballet dancer and teacher, July 1987, *Obit* Sept 1997

Erdman, Jean, dancer, choreographer and teacher, Sept 1971

Farrell, Suzanne, American ballet dancer, Sept 1967

Feld, Eliot, American choreographer and dance teacher, Oct 1971

Graham, Martha, American dancer and choreographer,

Feb 1944, June 1961, *Obit* May 1991

Hayden, Melissa, American ballet dancer, May 1955, *Obit* Yrbk 2006

Holm, Hanya, German-American dancer and choreographer, July 1954, *Obit* Jan 1993

Jooss, Kurt, German choreographer, dance director and teacher, July 1976, *Obit* July 1979

Kirkland, Gelsey, American ballet dancer, Oct 1975

Koner, Pauline, ballet dancer and choreographer, Oct 1964, *Obit* Apr 2001

Lang, Pearl, American dancer and choreographer, Jan 1970, *Obit* Yrbk 2009

Limon, Jose, American dancer and choreographer, June 1953, Apr 1968, *Obit* Jan 1973

Murray, Arthur, American dance teacher, Apr 1943, *Obit* May 1991

Rambert, Marie, British ballet dancer, teacher and director, Feb 1981, *Obit* Aug 1982

Sokolow, Anna, American dancer, choreographer and teacher, Feb 1969, *Obit* Sept 2000

St. Denis, Ruth, American dancer, Oct 1949, *Obit* Oct 1968

Tallchief, Maria, American ballet dancer, Nov 1951

Villella, Edward, American ballet dancer and director, Mar 1965

Wigman, Mary, German dancer and choreographer, Jan 1969, *Obit* Nov 1973

Youskevitch, Igor, Ukrainian-American ballet dancer and master, Feb 1956, *Obit* Aug 1994

Dancers

Abdul, Paula, American dancer, choreographer, singer and talent judge on television program, Sept 1991

Acosta, Carlos, Cuban ballet dancer, Jan 2004

Adams, Diana, dancer and teacher, Apr 1954, *Obit* Mar 1993

Ailey, Alvin, American dancer and choreographer, Mar 1968, *Obit* Jan 1990

Ann-Margret, American actress, singer and dancer, Sept 1975

Argentinita, Spanish dancer and choreographer, June 1942, *Obit* Oct 1945

Aroldingen, Karin von, German ballet dancer, Jan 1983

Arpino, Gerald, American ballet dancer and choreographer, Oct 1970, *Obit* Yrbk 2008

Ashley, Merrill, American ballet dancer, Nov 1981

Ashton, Frederick, British choreographer, May 1951, *Obit* Sept 1988

Askegard, Charles, American ballet dancer, Mar 2012

Astaire, Fred, American dancer, singer and actor, Sept 1945, Apr 1964, *Obit* Aug 1987

Azuma, Tokuho, Japanese dancer, Apr 1954

Baker, Josephine, American actress, singer and dancer, July 1964, *Obit* June 1975

Balanchine, George, Russian-American choreographer, Nov 1942, June 1954, *Obit* June 1983

Bausch, Pina, German dancer, choreographer and director, Sept 1986, *Obit* Yrbk 2009

Bejart, Maurice, French ballet dancer and choreographer, Mar 1971, *Obit* Yrbk 2008

Bennett, Michael, American choreographer, Mar 1981, *Obit* Aug 1987

Beriosova, Svetlana, Lithuanian ballet dancer and teacher, Sept 1960, *Obit* Feb 1999

Berkeley, Busby, American choreographer and film director, Apr 1971, *Obit* May 1976

Bessmertnova, Natalia, Russian ballet dancer, Jan 1988, *Obit* Yrbk 2008

Bettis, Valerie, dancer and choreographer, May 1953, *Obit* Nov 1982

Blair, David, British ballet dancer and choreographer, Jan 1961, *Obit* May 1976

Blankenbuehler, Andy, American choreographer and dancer, Apr 2009

Bolger, Ray, American dancer, singer and actor, Aug 1942, *Obit* Mar 1987

Bourne, Matthew, English dancer and choreographer, Jan 2005

Brown, Ronald K., American choreographer, May 2002

Brown, Trisha, American dancer and choreographer, Apr 1997

Bujones, Fernando, American ballet dancer, Jan 1976, *Obit* Yrbk 2006

Butler, John, American dancer and choreographer, June 1955, *Obit* Nov 1993

Caron, Leslie, French dancer and actress, Sept 1954

Champion, Gower, American dancer, choreographer and theatrical director, Sept 1953, *Obit* Oct 1980

Champion, Marge, American dancer and choreographer, Sept 1953

Charisse, Cyd, American dancer and actress, Jan 1954, *Obit* Yrbk 2008

Chase, Lucia, American ballet dancer and manager, July 1947, Aug 1975, *Obit* Mar 1986

Childs, Lucinda, American dancer and choreographer, Apr 1984

Clarke, Martha, American dancer and choreographer, Jan 1989

Corella, Angel, Spanish ballet dancer, Mar 1999

Cranko, John, South African dancer and choreographer, July 1970, *Obit* Sept 1973

Cunningham, Merce, American dancer and choreographer, May 1966, *Obit* Yrbk 2009

Danilova, Alexandra, Russian ballet dancer and teacher, July 1987, *Obit* Sept 1997

Daratista, Inul, Indonesian singer and dancer, Jan 2003

De Lavallade, Carmen, American actress and dancer, Yrbk 1967

De Mille, Agnes, American choreographer, Oct 1943, Jan 1985, *Obit* Jan 1994

Dean, Laura, dancer and choreographer, Oct 1988

Dolin, Anton, English dancer and choreographer, Jan 1946, *Obit* Jan 1984

Dolly, Jenny, *Obit* July 1941

Dowell, Anthony, English ballet dancer and manager, May 1971

Draper, Paul, dancer, Feb 1944, *Obit* Jan 1997

Dunham, Katherine, American dancer and choreographer, Mar 1941, *Obit* Yrbk 2006

Ebsen, Buddy, American actor and dancer, Jan 1977, *Obit* Yrbk 2003

Eglevsky, Andre, Feb 1953, *Obit* Feb 1978

Eiko, Japanese dancer and choreographer, May 2003

Elo, Jorma, Finnish ballet dancer and choreographer, July 2009

Erdman, Jean, dancer, choreographer and teacher, Sept 1971

Fagan, Garth, American dancer, director and choreographer, Aug 1998

Farrell, Suzanne, American ballet dancer, Sept 1967

Feld, Eliot, American choreographer and dance teacher, Oct 1971

Flint, Keith, British singer and dancer, Oct 2009

Fokine, Michel, Russian ballet dancer and choreographer, *Obit* Oct 1942

Fonteyn, Margot, English ballet dancer, Yrbk 1949, Mar 1972, *Obit* Apr 1991

Fortier, Paul-Andre, Canadian choreographer and dancer, Nov 2010

Fosse, Bob, American director and choreographer, June 1972, *Obit* Nov 1987

Fracci, Carla, Italian ballet dancer, Feb 1975

Franklin, Frederic, English ballet dancer and choreographer, Sept 1943, *Obit* Yrbk 2013

Gades, Antonio, Spanish flamenco dancer and choreographer, Feb 1973, *Obit* Yrbk 2004

Galli, Rosina, *Obit* Jan 1940

Gennaro, Peter, American dancer and choreographer, June 1964, *Obit* Feb 2001

Glover, Savion, American tap dancer, Mar 1996

Godunov, Alexander, Russian ballet dancer and actor, Feb 1983, *Obit* July 1995

Gomes, Marcelo, Brazilian ballet dancer, May 2007

Gordon, David, American choreographer, June 1994

Graham, Martha, American dancer and choreographer, Feb 1944, June 1961, *Obit* May 1991

Greco, Jose, American dancer and choreographer, Mar 1952, *Obit* Mar 2001

Gregory, Cynthia, American ballet dancer, May 1977

Grigorovich, Yuri, Russian choreographer and dance director, Sept 1975

Guillem, Sylvie, French ballet dancer and choreographer, Jan 2002

Harkness, Rebekah West, American composer, ballet manager and dance patron, Apr 1974, *Obit* Sept 1982

Hartman, Grace, Nov 1942, *Obit* Oct 1955

Hawkins, Erick, dancer and choreographer, Jan 1974, *Obit* Feb 1995

Haydee, Marcia, Brazilian dancer, Oct 1977

Hayden, Melissa, American ballet dancer, May 1955, *Obit* Yrbk 2006

Helpmann, Robert, Australian dancer and actor, Feb 1950, *Obit* Nov 1986

Herrera, Paloma, Argentine ballet dancer, Apr 2000

Hines, Gregory, American dancer and actor, July 1985, *Obit* Yrbk 2003

Holder, Geoffrey, Trinidadian dancer and choreographer, Oct 1957

Holm, Hanya, German-American dancer and choreographer, July 1954, *Obit* Jan 1993

Humphrey, Doris, American dancer and choreographer, Apr 1942, *Obit* Mar 1959

Iglesias, Roberto, Feb 1960

Jaffe, Susan, dancer, Sept 1997

Jamison, Judith, American dancer, director and choreographer, Jan 1973

Jeanmaire, Zizi, French ballet dancer and actress, Nov 1952

Jessel, George, singer, dancer and comedian, Mar 1943, *Obit* July 1981

Jin Xing, Chinese ballet dancer and choreographer, Jan 2006

Johnson, Virginia, American dancer, May 1985

Jones, Bill T., American dancer and choreographer, July 1993

Kain, Karen, Canadian ballet dancer and director, May 1980

Kaye, Nora, dancer, Jan 1953, *Obit* Apr 1987

Keeler, Ruby, American dancer and actress, Yrbk 1971, *Obit* Apr 1993

Kelly, Gene, American dancer, singer and actor, Yrbk 1945, Feb 1977, *Obit* Apr 1996

Kent, Allegra, American ballet dancer, Mar 1970

Khan, Farah, Indian film director and choreographer, Jan 2007

Kidd, Michael, American choreographer, Mar 1960, *Obit* Yrbk 2008

Kirkland, Gelsey, American ballet dancer, Oct 1975

Kistler, Darci, American ballet dancer, Oct 1991

Kitchell, Iva, dancer, Yrbk 1951, *Obit* Jan 1984

Koma, Japanese dancer and choreographer, May 2003

Kudelka, James, Canadian ballet dancer and choreographer, Mar 1995

Kylian, Jiri, Czech dancer, choreographer and director, Sept 1982

Laing, Hugh, English dancer, Nov 1946, *Obit* June 1988

Lang, Pearl, American dancer and choreographer, Jan 1970, *Obit* Yrbk 2009

Layton, Joe, theatrical director, producer and choreographer, Sept 1970, *Obit* July 1994

Le Clercq, Tanaquil, American ballet dancer, July 1953, *Obit* Mar 2001

Leonard, Eddie, singer and dancer, *Obit* Sept 1941

Lerman, Liz, American dancer and choreographer, Nov 2000

Levi-Tanai, Sara, Israeli choreographer, May 1958

Lichtenstein, Harvey, American performing arts executive, May 1987

Limon, Jose, American dancer and choreographer, June 1953, Apr 1968, *Obit* Jan 1973

Loring, Eugene, American dancer and choreographer, Mar 1972, *Obit* Oct 1982

Losch, Tilly, July 1944, *Obit* Feb 1976

Louganis, Greg, American diver and actor, Oct 1984

Louis, Murray, dancer and choreographer, Oct 1968

Lubovitch, Lar, American dancer and choreographer, Mar 1992

Lynne, Gillian, English dancer and choreographer, Jan 2002

MacLaine, Shirley, American dancer and actress, Yrbk 1959, July 1978

Macdonald, Brian, Canadian ballet director and choreographer, July 1968

Magallanes, Nicholas, May 1955, *Obit* July 1977

Maharaj, Birju, Indian dancer, Jan 2007

Makarova, Natalia, Russian ballet dancer, Feb 1972

Markova, Alicia, British ballet dancer, Sept 1943, *Obit* Yrbk 2005

Marshall, Rob, American choreographer and film director, June 2003

Marshall, Susan, American choreographer, July 1999

Martin, Mary, American actress and singer, Jan 1944, *Obit* Jan 1991

Martins, Peter, Danish-American dancer, choreographer and director, June 1978

Massine, Leonide, Russian choreographer and ballet dancer, Apr 1940, *Obit* May 1979

Mazzo, Kay, July 1971

McBride, Patricia, ballet dancer, July 1966

McCracken, Joan, June 1945, *Obit* Jan 1962

McKayle, Donald, American dancer and choreographer, June 1971

McKenzie, Kevin, American ballet dancer and director, Jan 2000

Millepied, Benjamin, French ballet dancer and choreographer, Apr 2011

Miller, Ann, American tap dancer and actress, Apr 1980, *Obit* Yrbk 2004

Miller, Bebe, dancer and choreographer, Apr 1999

Minnelli, Liza, American actress and singer, Oct 1970, July 1988

Miranda, Carmen, Brazilian singer, dancer and actress, June 1941, *Obit* Oct 1955

Mitchell, Arthur, American ballet dancer and choreographer, Oct 1966

Mitchell, Jerry, American choreographer and theatrical director, Oct 2007

Mitha, Tehreema, Pakistani dancer and choreographer, May 2004

Monk, Meredith, American choreographer, composer and singer, Feb 1985

Monte, Elisa, American dancer and choreographer, June 2007

Mordkin, Mikhail, Russian dancer, *Obit* Sept 1944

Moreno, Rita, American actress, singer and dancer, Sept 1985

Morris, Mark, American choreographer and dancer, Aug 1988

Moylan, Mary Ellen, Feb 1957

Murphy, George, American actor, dancer and senator, Yrbk 1965, *Obit* July 1992

Nagy, Ivan, Hungarian dance director, May 1977

Nerina, Nadia, South African ballet dancer, Nov 1957, *Obit* Yrbk 2008

Neumeier, John, American dancer and choreographer, July 1991

Neuwirth, Bebe, American dancer and actress, Nov 1997

Nijinsky, Waslaw, Russian ballet dancer, Oct 1940, *Obit* May 1950

Nikolais, Alwin, American choreographer, Feb 1968, *Obit* July 1993

Nureyev, Rudolf, Russian ballet dancer, July 1963, *Obit* Feb 1993

O'Connor, Donald, American actor and dancer, May 1955, *Obit* Apr 2004

Ortega, Kenny, American dancer, choreographer and director, Mar 2008

Osato, Sono, Oct 1945

Page, Ruth, American ballet dancer and choreographer, June 1962, *Obit* July 1991

Panov, Valery, Russian dancer, Oct 1974

Park, Merle, English ballet dancer, Sept 1974

Pendleton, Moses, American dancer and choreographer, Sept 1989

Perez, Rosie, American actress, dancer and choreographer, Sept 1995

Petit, Roland, French ballet dancer and choreographer, Apr 1952, *Obit* Yrbk 2011

Petronio, Stephen, American dancer and choreographer, Mar 1998

Plisetskaya, Maya, Russian ballet dancer, June 1963

Primus, Pearl, American dancer and choreographer, Apr 1944, *Obit* Jan 1995

Raedler, Dorothy, opera director and choreographer, Yrbk 1954, *Obit* Feb 1994

Ramirez, Tina, Venezuelan-American dancer and director, Nov 2004

Rao, Shanta, Indian dancer, Yrbk 1957

Reinking, Ann, American dancer, choreographer and actress, June 2004

Rivera, Chita, American dancer, singer and actress, Oct 1984

Robbins, Jerome, American dancer, choreographer and theatrical director, May 1947, May 1969, *Obit* Oct 1998

Robinson, Bill, American tap dancer, Feb 1941, *Obit* Jan 1950

Rogers, Ginger, American actress, singer and dancer, Apr 1941, Yrbk 1967, *Obit* July 1995

Ross, Herbert, American choreographer and motion picture director, Aug 1980, *Obit* Feb 2002

Ruiz Soler, Antonio, Spanish dancer, June 1968

Rushing, Matthew, American dancer, July 2000

Saddler, Donald, choreographer, Jan 1963

Schaufuss, Peter, Danish ballet dancer and director, May 1982

Seymour, Lynn, Canadian ballet dancer, Nov 1979

Shawn, Ted, American dancer and choreographer, Oct 1949, *Obit* Feb 1972

Shearer, Moira, Scottish ballet dancer and actress, Jan 1950, *Obit* Yrbk 2006

Sibley, Antoinette, English dancer, Yrbk 1970

Slavenska, Mia, Croatian ballet dancer and choreographer, Feb 1954, *Obit* Apr 2003

Smuin, Michael, American ballet dancer and choreographer, Oct 1984, *Obit* Yrbk 2007

Sokolow, Anna, American dancer, choreographer and teacher, Feb 1969, *Obit* Sept 2000

Somes, Michael, English dancer, Yrbk 1955, *Obit* Feb 1995

St. Denis, Ruth, American dancer, Oct 1949, *Obit* Oct 1968

Stiefel, Ethan, American ballet dancer, Apr 2004

Streb, Elizabeth, American dancer and choreographer, Apr 2003

Stroman, Susan, American choreographer and theatrical director, July 2002

Swayze, Patrick, American actor and dancer, Mar 1991, *Obit* Yrbk 2009

Tallchief, Maria, American ballet dancer, Nov 1951

Taylor, Janie, American ballet dancer, Aug 2011

Taylor, Paul, American dancer and choreographer, June 1964

Tcherkassky, Marianna, ballet dancer, Nov 1985

Tetley, Glen, American dancer and choreographer, June 1973, *Obit* Yrbk 2007

Tharp, Twyla, American dancer and choreographer, Oct 1975

Thornhill, Leeroy, British keyboardist, Oct 2009

Tudor, Antony, English ballet dancer and choreographer, Nov 1945, *Obit* June 1987

Tune, Tommy, American dancer and director, Jan 1983

Ulanova, Galina, Russian ballet dancer, Apr 1958, *Obit* June 1998

Van Hamel, Martine, Dutch-American ballet dancer, Sept 1979

Vera-Ellen, dancer and actress, Feb 1959, *Obit* Oct 1981

Verdi-Fletcher, Mary, wheelchair dancer, Jan 1997

Verdon, Gwen, American dancer, actress and choreographer, Oct 1960, *Obit* Jan 2001

Verdy, Violette, French ballet dancer and manager, Yrbk 1969, Oct 1980

Vereen, Ben, American actor, singer and dancer, Apr 1978

Volochkova, Anastasia, Russian ballet dancer, Jan 2004

Watts, Heather, ballet dancer, May 1983

Webb, Clifton, American actor, singer and dancer, Mar 1943, *Obit* Yrbk 1966

Weidman, Charles, American dancer and choreographer, Apr 1942, *Obit* Sept 1975

Wheater, Ashley, British ballet dancer and director, May 2011

Wheeldon, Christopher, British ballet dancer and choreographer, Mar 2004

Whelan, Wendy, American ballet dancer, Oct 1998

Wigman, Mary, German dancer and choreographer, Jan 1969, *Obit* Nov 1973

Wilde, Patricia, Canadian ballet dancer and director, May 1968

Youskevitch, Igor, Ukrainian-American ballet dancer and master, Feb 1956, *Obit* Aug 1994

Yuen, Wo-ping, Chinese martial artist and motion picture stunt choreographer, Jan 2008

Zollar, Jawole Willa Jo, American dancer and performance artist, July 2003

Zorina, Vera, German-American ballet dancer and actress, Jan 1941, *Obit* Yrbk 2003

Deaf

Benedict, Ruth, American anthropologist, May 1941, *Obit* Nov 1948

Cannon, Annie Jump, American astronomer, *Obit* June 1941

Catchings, Tamika, American basketball player, Nov 2013

Fleming, John Ambrose, English electrical engineer, *Obit* May 1945

Glennie, Evelyn, Scottish percussionist, July 1997

Wells, Carolyn, author, *Obit* May 1942

Decathletes

Jenner, Bruce, American decathlete, Aug 1977

Johnson, Rafer, American decathlete, June 1961

Mathias, Bob, American decathlete, congressman and sports executive, Sept 1952, *Obit* Yrbk 2007

O'Brien, Dan, American decathlete, July 1996

Richards, Bob, American pole vaulter and decathlete, June 1957

Thompson, Daley, British decathlete, Nov 1986

Thorpe, Jim, American decathlete and pentathlete, Nov 1950, *Obit* May 1953

Defectors

Hernandez, Livan, Cuban baseball player, Mar 1998

Hernandez, Orlando, Cuban baseball player, Apr 2000

Krivitsky, W. G., Soviet intelligence service agent, *Obit* Mar 1941

Shevchenko, Arkady N., Soviet diplomat and defector, Sept 1985, *Obit* May 1998

Defense industry executives

Anderson, Roy A., American aerospace executive, Aug 1983, *Obit* Mar 2004

Augustine, Norman R., aerospace executive, June 1998

Bigelow, Robert T., American real estate executive and financier, Aug 2008

Crawford, Frederick C., defense industries executive, Feb 1943, *Obit* Feb 1995

Holmes, D. Brainerd, aerospace industry executive and NASA official, Mar 1963, *Obit* Yrbk 2013

Krupp von Bohlen und Halbach, Alfried, German munitions manufacturer, May 1955, *Obit* Oct 1967

Lagardere, Jean-Luc, French aerospace and publishing executive, Aug 1993, *Obit* Aug 2003

Lewis, David Sloan, American aerospace industry executive, Aug 1975, *Obit* Yrbk 2004

McNerney, James, American aerospace industry executive, Mar 2008

Mueller, George E., aerospace industry executive and NASA official, Nov 1964

Musk, Elon, American entrepreneur, Oct 2006

Delivery personnel

Biller, Moe, American labor leader, June 1987, *Obit* Yrbk 2004

Hoffa, Jimmy, American labor leader, May 1972, *Obit* Mar 1983

Kappel, Frederick R., telephone executive, Mar 1957, *Obit* Jan 1995

Ludwig, Daniel Keith, shipping executive and financier, May 1979, *Obit* Oct 1992

Murray, Tom, Nov 1956, *Obit* Jan 1972

Onassis, Aristotle Socrates, Greek-Argentine shipping executive, Mar 1963, *Obit* May 1975

Onassis, Christina, Greek shipping executive, Feb 1976, *Obit* Jan 1989

Paul, Josephine Bay, American shipping executive and stockbroker, June 1957

Stans, Maurice H., American Secretary of commerce, Yrbk 1958, *Obit* June 1998

Tryon, George Clement Tryon, British government official, *Obit* Jan 1941

Demographers

Chandrasekhar, S., Indian economist and demographer, Oct 1969, *Obit* Sept 2001

Fornos, Werner H., demographer and social reformer, July 1993

Hauser, Philip M., demographer, July 1969, *Obit* Feb 1995

Dentists

Alstadt, W. R., American dentist, July 1958

Dean, H. Trendley, June 1957, *Obit* July 1962

Delany, Bessie, American dentist, Nov 1995, *Obit* Jan 1996

Fitz Gerald, Leslie M., Sept 1954

Hansen, Fred, pole vaulter, Yrbk 1965

Hunt, Lester C., American senator and governor, Mar 1951, *Obit* Sept 1954

Lynch, Daniel F., July 1955

Mamlok, Hans J., *Obit* Yrbk 1940

Middlecoff, Cary, golfer, July 1952, *Obit* Nov 1998

Pease, Charles G., *Obit* Yrbk 1941

Reed, John Howard, *Obit* Mar 1940

Winter, George B., *Obit* May 1940

Dermatologists

Exner, Max J., *Obit* Nov 1943

Pusey, William Allen, *Obit* Oct 1940

Designers

Aalto, Alvar, Finnish architect, Apr 1948, *Obit* July 1976

Abercrombie, Patrick, English architect, Apr 1946, *Obit* June 1957

Aberra, Amsale, Ethiopian fashion designer, Jan 2005

Adams, Thomas, British architect and urban planner, *Obit* Apr 1940

Adolfo, fashion designer, Nov 1972

Adrian, American costume and fashion designer, Feb 1941, *Obit* Nov 1959

Ai Wei Wei, Chinese artist and architect, Aug 2011

Aldredge, Theoni, American costume designer, Feb 1994, *Obit* Yrbk 2011

Aldrich, Chester Holmes, American architect, *Obit* Feb 1941

Alphadi, Malian fashion designer, Jan 2004

Amies, Hardy, English fashion designer, Mar 1962, *Obit* Aug 2003

Appel, Karel, Dutch painter, Mar 1961, *Obit* Yrbk 2006

Arad, Michael, American architect, Oct 2013

Armani, Giorgio, Italian fashion designer, Jan 1983

Aronin, Jeffrey Ellis, Canadian architect, Jan 1955

Ashwell, Rachel, British interior designer and home furnishings retailer, Oct 2004

Atwood, Colleen, American costume designer, Oct 2010

Aulenti, Gae, Italian architect, Sept 1999, *Obit* Yrbk 2013

Balenciaga, Spanish fashion designer, May 1954, *Obit* May 1972

Beall, Lester, American graphic designer, Nov 1949, *Obit* Sept 1969

Beene, Geoffrey, American fashion designer, Apr 1978, *Obit* Mar 2005

Behnisch, Stefan, German architect, Jan 2007

Blahnik, Manolo, Spanish shoe designer, Jan 2004

Blass, Bill, American fashion designer, Sept 1966, *Obit* Nov 2002

Blomfield, Reginald Theodore, British architect, *Obit* Feb 1943

Boateng, Ozwald, British fashion designer, Jan 2006

Bohan, Marc, French fashion designer, Apr 1965

Bonomi, Maria, Brazilian artist, July 1960

Borne, Mortimer, Apr 1954

Bragdon, Claude Fayette, American architect, *Obit* Oct 1946

Breuer, Marcel, American architect and furniture designer, Sept 1941, June 1960, *Obit* Aug 1981

Brooks, Angela, American architect, Mar 1970

Brooks, Donald, American fashion and costume designer, Mar 1972, *Obit* Yrbk 2005

Brown, A. Ten Eyck, *Obit* July 1940

Buatta, Mario, American interior designer, May 1991

Bunshaft, Gordon, American architect, Mar 1989, *Obit* Oct 1990

Burch, Tory, American fashion designer and philanthropist, Sept 2010

Burtt, Ben, American motion picture sound designer, editor and documentary filmmaker, May 2003

Butts, Alfred, American architect and game inventor, July 1954, *Obit* June 1993

Byers, Margaretta, Sept 1941

Calatrava, Santiago, Spanish architect, Aug 1997

Callender, John Hancock, architect and editor, Sept 1955, *Obit* June 1995

Candela, Felix, Spanish architect, July 1960

Cardin, Pierre, French fashion designer, Mar 1965

Carnegie, Hattie, fashion designer, Oct 1942, *Obit* May 1956

Casey, Edward Pearce, *Obit* Jan 1940

Cassini, Oleg, French-American fashion designer, July 1961, *Obit* Yrbk 2006

Cauldwell, Leslie Giffen, *Obit* July 1941

Chang, Gary, Chinese architect, Jan 2005

Chicago, Judy, American artist, Feb 1981

Claiborne, Liz, American fashion designer, June 1989, *Obit* Yrbk 2007

Cochrane, Edward L., Mar 1951, *Obit* Jan 1960

Cogswell, Charles N., *Obit* Feb 1942

Cooper, Edwin, English architect, *Obit* Aug 1942

Cooper, Kyle, American graphic designer, Nov 2009

Courreges, Andre, French fashion designer, Jan 1970

Cram, Ralph Adams, American architect, Oct 1942, *Obit* Oct 1942

Cret, Paul Philippe, French-American architect, Nov 1942, *Obit* Nov 1945

Cuevas, Manuel, Mexican-American costume designer, Jan 2005

Czettel, Ladislas, Mar 1941, *Obit* Apr 1949

Dache, Lilly, French milliner, July 1941, *Obit* Mar 1990

Delaunay, Sonia, French painter and fashion designer, Aug 1977, *Obit* Feb 1980

Desses, Jean, Jan 1956, *Obit* Oct 1970

Dior, Christian, French fashion designer, Oct 1948, *Obit* Jan 1958

Ditchy, Clair W., Mar 1954, *Obit* Oct 1967

Dolce, Domenico, Italian fashion designer, Jan 2005

Doxiadis, Constantinos A., Greek architect, Sept 1964, *Obit* Sept 1975

Draper, Dorothy, American interior designer, May 1941, *Obit* Apr 1969

Dreyfuss, Henry, American industrial designer, May 1948, Oct 1959, *Obit* Yrbk 1972

Duany, Andres, American architect and urban planner, Jan 2006

Eames, Charles, American furniture, interior and exhibit designer, Jan 1965, *Obit* Oct 1978

Eisenman, Peter, American architect, Oct 1997

Erte, French painter, set and costume designer, Nov 1980, *Obit* June 1990

Eyuboglu, Bedri Rahmi, Turkish artist and poet, Sept 1954

Fahmy, Azza, Egyptian jewelry designer, Jan 2004

Farhi, Nicole, French fashion designer, Nov 2001

Fassett, Kaffe, American textile designer, June 1995

Fath, Jacques, French fashion designer, Apr 1951, *Obit* Jan 1955

Ferre, Gianfranco, Italian fashion designer, July 1991, *Obit* Yrbk 2007

Ferriss, Hugh, July 1945, *Obit* Mar 1962

Field, Patricia, American fashion and costume designer, Nov 2010

Fielding, Mantle, *Obit* May 1941

Fisk, Jack, American motion picture production designer, June 2011

Fogarty, Anne, fashion designer, Oct 1958, *Obit* Mar 1980

Ford, Tom, American fashion designer, May 1998

Fouilhoux, J. Andre, American architect, *Obit* July 1945

Freed, James Ingo, American architect, Nov 1994, *Obit* Yrbk 2006

Frisch, Max, Swiss architect, novelist and dramatist, Jan 1965, *Obit* June 1991

Fuller, R. Buckminster, American engineer and architect, Jan 1960, Feb 1976, *Obit* Aug 1983

Gabbana, Stefano, Italian fashion designer, Jan 2005

Gang, Jeanne, American architect, Aug 2012

Geddes, Norman Bel, stage designer and producer, May 1940, *Obit* July 1958

Gernreich, Rudi, American fashion designer, Yrbk 1968, *Obit* June 1985

Ghesquiere, Nicolas, French fashion designer, Jan 2011

Giannulli, Mossimo, American fashion designer and clothing executive, Feb 2003

Gibbs, William Francis, naval architect, Apr 1944, *Obit* Nov 1967

Giger, H. R., Swiss painter, sculptor and scenic designer, Jan 2002

Gigli, Romeo, Italian fashion designer, Aug 1998

Glaser, Milton, American illustrator and designer, May 1980

Graham, John, architect, Oct 1962, *Obit* Apr 1991

Graves, Michael, American architect and designer, Jan 1989

Greenough, Carroll, *Obit* Oct 1941

Gres, Alix, French fashion designer, June 1980, *Obit* Feb 1995

Griffith Joyner, Florence, American sprinter, Apr 1989, *Obit* Nov 1998

Gropius, Walter, American architect, Nov 1941, Mar 1952, *Obit* Sept 1969

Gruen, Victor, American architect, Mar 1959, *Obit* Apr 1980

Gwathmey, Charles, American architect, Jan 1988, *Obit* Yrbk 2009

Hackett, Horatio B., *Obit* Nov 1941

Hadid, Zaha M., Iraqi architect, Jan 2003

Halston, American fashion designer, Yrbk 1972, *Obit* May 1990

Harper, Alexander James, *Obit* Nov 1940

Harris, Harwell Hamilton, American architect, Jan 1962, *Obit* Jan 1991

Harris, Jonathan, American artist and web designer, Oct 2013

Harrison, Wallace Kirkman, architect, Mar 1947, *Obit* Jan 1982

Hartnell, Norman, May 1953, *Obit* Aug 1979

Hawes, Elizabeth, American fashion designer, Oct 1940, *Obit* Yrbk 1991

Head, Edith, American costume designer, May 1945, *Obit* Jan 1982

Herzog, Jacques, Swiss architect, June 2002

Hewlett, J. Monroe, *Obit* Yrbk 1941

Higgins, Daniel Paul, Yrbk 1950, *Obit* Mar 1954

Higginson, William, *Obit* Sept 1943

Hilfiger, Tommy, American fashion designer, Apr 1996

Holl, Steven, American architect, July 2004

Honeywell, Annette, July 1953

Hopkins, Alfred, *Obit* July 1941

Husain, Maqbul Fida, Indian painter, Jan 2006, *Obit* Yrbk 2011

Irene, costume designer, June 1946, *Obit* Jan 1963

Isham, Norman Morrison, *Obit* Feb 1943

Isozaki, Arata, Japanese architect, Apr 1988

Jacobs, Marc, American fashion designer, Feb 1998

Jahn, Helmut, German architect, Feb 1989

James, Charles, American fashion designer, July 1956

John, Daymond, American fashion designer, Aug 2007

Jones, Robert Edmond, scenic designer, Nov 1946, *Obit* Jan 1955

Kahane, Melanie, interior designer, July 1959, *Obit* Feb 1989

Kahn, Albert, American architect, *Obit* Sept 1942

Kahn, Ely Jacques, American architect, Aug 1945, *Obit* Nov 1972

Kahn, Louis I., American architect, Oct 1964, *Obit* May 1974

Kamali, Norma, American fashion designer, Nov 1998

Karan, Donna, American fashion designer, Aug 1990

Karinska, Barbara, Russian-American costume designer, Jan 1971

Kawakubo, Rei, Japanese fashion designer, Aug 1999

Keck, George Fred, Sept 1945

Kelly, Patrick, fashion designer, Sept 1989, *Obit* Mar 1990

Kendall, William Mitchell, *Obit* Oct 1941

Kiam, Omar, Yrbk 1945, *Obit* May 1954

Kidd, Chip, American book and graphic designer, July 2005

Kiesler, Frederick, Austrian-Ameican sculptor and architect, Jan 1944, *Obit* Feb 1966

King, Muriel, Apr 1943, *Obit* May 1977

Koolhaas, Rem, Dutch architect, Nov 2000

Kors, Michael, American fashion designer, Jan 2000

Lake, Simon, naval architect and engineer, *Obit* July 1945

Lang, Helmut, Austrian fashion designer, Apr 1997

Lanvin, Jeanne, French fashion designer, *Obit* Sept 1946

Lapidus, Morris, American architect, Apr 1966, *Obit* Apr 2001

Le Corbusier, Swiss-French architect, Apr 1947, *Obit* Nov 1965

Lee, Ming Cho, Chinese-American set designer, June 1989

Leiber, Judith, Hungarian-American handbag designer, Sept 1996

Leigh, Douglas, advertising executive and lighting designer, May 1940, *Obit* May 2000

Lelong, Lucien, Nov 1955, *Obit* Sept 1958

Leser, Tina, fashion designer, June 1957, *Obit* Mar 1986

Lhuillier, Monique, American fashion designer, June 2008

Libeskind, Daniel, American architect, June 2003

Liebes, Dorothy, American textile designer, Apr 1948, *Obit* Yrbk 1972

Lin, Maya Ying, American architect and sculptor, Apr 1993

Loewy, Raymond Fernand, French-American industrial designer, Mar 1941, June 1953, *Obit* Sept 1986

Long, William Ivey, American costume designer, Mar 2004

Loquasto, Santo, scenic designer, June 1981

Lurcat, Jean, French painter and tapestry designer, Sept 1948, *Obit* Feb 1966

Lutyens, Edwin Landseer, British architect, June 1942, *Obit* Feb 1944

Ma Kai, Chinese government official, Jan 2007

Mackenzie, Clinton, *Obit* Mar 1940

Mackie, Bob, fashion designer, Oct 1988

Mainbocher, fashion designer, Feb 1942, *Obit* Mar 1977

Maki, Fumihiko, Japanese architect, July 2001

Maxwell, Vera, fashion designer, July 1977, *Obit* Mar 1995

Mayne, Thom, American architect, Oct 2005

McAslan, John, Scottish architect, Jan 2007

McCardell, Claire, American fashion designer, Nov 1954, *Obit* June 1958

McCobb, Paul, furniture designer, Nov 1958, *Obit* Apr 1969

McDonough, William, American architect, July 2006

McFadden, Mary, American fashion designer, Apr 1983

McGuire, William Anthony, *Obit* Nov 1940

McNairy, Mark, American shoe designer, July 2013

McPharlin, Paul, American puppeteer, Nov 1945, *Obit* Nov 1948

McQueen, Alexander, British fashion designer, Feb 2002, *Obit* June 2010

Meier, Richard, American architect, Jan 1985

Mellor, Walter, *Obit* Jan 1940

Melzer, Roman F., *Obit* June 1943

Mendelsohn, Erich, German architect, Nov 1953

Mendes da Rocha, Paulo Archias, Brazilian architect, Jan 2006

Meuron, Pierre de, Swiss architect, June 2002

Mielziner, Jo, Mar 1946, *Obit* May 1976

Mies van der Rohe, Ludwig, German-American architect, Oct 1951, *Obit* Oct 1969

Miller, Nicole, fashion designer, Mar 1995

Moiseiwitsch, Tanya, English stage and costume designer, Nov 1955, *Obit* July 2003

Molyneux, Edward H., June 1942, *Obit* May 1974

Moneo, Jose Rafael, Spanish architect, Jan 2004

Montana, Claude, French fashion designer, Jan 1992

Moses, Robert, American municipal and state planning official, Nov 1940, Feb 1954, *Obit* Sept 1981

Mugler, Thierry, French fashion designer and photographer, Aug 2010

Mulleavy, Kate, American fashion designer, Sept 2012

Mulleavy, Laura, American fashion designer, Sept 2012

Murcutt, Glenn, Australian architect, Jan 2002

Nervi, Pier Luigi, Italian architect and structural engineer, Jan 1958, *Obit* Mar 1979

Neurath, Otto, Austrian sociologist and philosopher, *Obit* Feb 1946

Neutra, Richard Joseph, American architect, May 1947, July 1961, *Obit* June 1970

Niemeyer, Oscar, Brazilian architect, Feb 1960, *Obit* Yrbk 2013

Nixon, Lewis, American naval architect, *Obit* Nov 1940

Noguchi, Isamu, American sculptor, Sept 1943, *Obit* Feb 1989

Norell, Norman, fashion designer, Nov 1964, *Obit* Yrbk 1972

Norten, Enrique, Mexican architect, Jan 2005

Nouvel, Jean, French architect, Sept 2008

O'Gorman, Juan, Mexican architect and painter, Nov 1956

Oenslager, Donald, Sept 1946, *Obit* Aug 1975

Olmsted, Frederick Law, American landscape architect, June 1949, *Obit* Mar 1958

Olsen, Ashley, American actress and fashion designer, Sept 2010

Oppenheim, Chad, American architect, Sept 2006

Oudolf, Piet, Dutch landscape architect, Apr 2003

Pahlmann, William Carroll, American interior and industrial designer, Oct 1964, *Obit* Jan 1988

Parnis, Mollie, fashion designer, May 1956, *Obit* Sept 1992

Pereira, William Leonard, architect, Jan 1979, *Obit* Jan 1986

Piano, Renzo, Italian architect, Apr 2001

Pilcher, Lewis F., *Obit* Aug 1941

Poiret, Paul, French fashion designer, *Obit* June 1944

Ponnelle, Jean-Pierre, French scenic designer and opera director, Mar 1983, *Obit* Sept 1988

Popeil, Ron, American kitchen utensil inventor, Mar 2001

Posen, Zac, American fashion designer, July 2006

Post, William Stone, *Obit* Sept 1940

Powell, Sandy, English costume designer, June 2000

Prada, Miuccia, Italian fashion designer, Feb 2006

Pucci, Emilio, Italian fashion designer, Feb 1961, *Obit* Jan 1993

Robsjohn-Gibbings, Terence Harold, American furniture and interior designer, Sept 1965, *Obit* Feb 1977

Roehm, Carolyne, American fashion designer, Feb 1992

Rollins, Carl Purington, Sept 1948, *Obit* Jan 1961

Roth, Ann, costume designer, Mar 1997

Rubik, Erno, Hungarian professor of architecture and inventor, Feb 1987

Rykiel, Sonia, French fashion designer, May 1990

Saab, Elie, Lebanese fashion designer, Aug 2004

Saarinen, Eero, American architect, Oct 1949, *Obit* Nov 1961

Saarinen, Eliel, Finnish-American architect, Oct 1942, *Obit* Sept 1950

Saint Laurent, Yves, French fashion designer, Yrbk 1964, *Obit* Oct 2008

Sander, Jil, German fashion designer, Oct 1997

Saville, Peter, British graphic designer, Jan 2006

Schiaparelli, Elsa, French fashion designer, Jan 1940, Nov 1951, *Obit* Jan 1974

Schnurer, Carolyn, Mar 1955

Sejima, Kazuyo, Japanese architect, Apr 2012

Severance, H. Craig, *Obit* Nov 1941

Simonetta, Italian fashion designer, Yrbk 1955

Simpson, Adele, fashion designer, Nov 1970, *Obit* Oct 1995

Sinclair, Cameron, British architect and housing organization official, Apr 2008

Siza, Alvaro, Portuguese architect, Feb 2000

Skidmore, Louis, architect, Yrbk 1951, *Obit* Yrbk 1962

Slimane, Hedi, French fashion designer, Jan 2006

Smith, Oliver, American set designer, Sept 1961, *Obit* Mar 1994

Soleri, Paolo, Italian architect, Feb 1972, *Obit* Yrbk 2013

Spade, Kate, American handbag designer, Apr 2007

Spry, Constance, English flower arranger, May 1940, *Obit* Mar 1960

Stavropoulos, George, fashion designer, Mar 1985, *Obit* Feb 1991

Stoddard, Alexandra, American interior designer, June 1996

Stokes, Isaac Newton Phelps, architect and antiquarian, *Obit* Feb 1945

Stone, Edward Durell, American architect, June 1958, *Obit* Sept 1978

Streuli, Hans, Apr 1957

Swartwout, Egerton, *Obit* Apr 1943

Switzer, George, American industrial designer and art director, *Obit* Yrbk 1940

Sy, Oumou, Senegalese fashion designer, Jan 2003

Taniguchi, Yoshio, Japanese architect, Jan 2005

Taymor, Julie, American theatrical director and designer, Feb 1998

Teague, Walter Dorwin, American interior designer, May 1942, *Obit* Jan 1961

Ter-Arutunian, Rouben, Russian stage designer, June 1963, *Obit* Jan 1993

Theallet, Sophie, French fashion designer, Nov 2012

Throckmorton, Cleon, Sept 1943, *Obit* Yrbk 1965

Tigerman, Stanley, American architect, Feb 2001

Tipton, Jennifer, American lighting designer, July 1997

Traphagen, Ethel, Yrbk 1948, *Obit* June 1963

Trigere, Pauline, French-American fashion designer, Feb 1960, *Obit* July 2002

Troost, Laurens, Jan 1953

Tufte, Edward R., American political scientist, statistician and graphic designer, Nov 2007

Tunnard, Christopher, Canadian landscape architect, June 1959, *Obit* May 1979

Turrell, James, American artist, May 1999

Tyler, Richard, Australian fashion designer, May 1997

Ungaro, Emanuel, French fashion designer, July 1980

Valentina, fashion designer, Yrbk 1946, *Obit* Nov 1989

Valentino, Italian fashion designer, Nov 1973

Valletti, Vittorio F., Italian architect, July 1967

Van Pelt, John Vredenburgh, Yrbk 1946, *Obit* Sept 1962

Vanderbilt, Gloria, American fashion designer, July 1972

Vasarely, Victor, Hungarian-French artist, Feb 1971, *Obit* May 1997

Ventris, Michael George Francis, English architect, archaeologist and linguist, Jan 1957

Venturini, Silvia, Italian handbag designer, Jan 2006

Verhoeven, Julie, English fashion illustrator, Apr 2012

Versace, Donatella, Italian fashion designer, June 1998

Versace, Gianni, Italian fashion designer, Apr 1993, *Obit* Sept 1997

Virilio, Paul, French urban planner and philosopher, July 2005

Wada, Emi, Japanese costume designer, Jan 2007

Walker, Ralph Thomas, Yrbk 1957, *Obit* Mar 1973

Wank, Roland, Yrbk 1943, *Obit* July 1970

Warnecke, John Carl, American architect, July 1968, *Obit* Yrbk 2010

Warren, Whitney, *Obit* Mar 1943

Whittlesey, Charles F., *Obit* Feb 1941

Williams, Paul, American architect, Mar 1941, *Obit* Mar 1980

Wills, Royal Barry, Yrbk 1954, *Obit* Feb 1962

Wirth, Conrad L., American national parks director, Sept 1952, *Obit* Sept 1993

Wright, Frank Lloyd, American architect, Jan 1941, Nov 1952, *Obit* June 1959

Wright, Russel, American industrial designer, Sept 1940, Yrbk 1950, *Obit* Mar 1977

Wurster, William Wilson, architect, Nov 1946, *Obit* Nov 1973

Yamasaki, Minoru, American architect, Mar 1962, *Obit* Apr 1986

Yeang, Ken, Malaysian architect, Jan 2007

Yoshimura, Junzo, Japanese architect, May 1956

Zeffirelli, Franco, Italian director and set designer, Yrbk 1964

Detectives

Burns, Edward, American television scriptwriter and former police officer, May 2008

Fabian, Robert, Apr 1954, *Obit* Aug 1978

Kroll, Jules, American lawyer and private detective, Feb 1999

Stanton, Bill, private detective, May 2001

Diarists

Lindbergh, Anne Morrow, American memoirist, novelist, and poet, Nov 1940, June 1976, *Obit* Apr 2001

Nin, Anais, American novelist, Feb 1944, Sept 1975, *Obit* Mar 1977

Rajagopalachari, C., Indian political leader, July 1942, *Obit* Feb 1973

Robertson, Robert Blackwood, May 1957

Sarton, May, American poet and novelist, May 1982, *Obit* Sept 1995

Diplomats

Abetz, Otto, German diplomat, Feb 1941

Abrams, Elliott, American diplomat and policy analyst, Aug 1988

Acheson, Dean, American Secretary of state, Mar 1941, Feb 1949, *Obit* Nov 1971

Ackley, H. Gardner, American economist, diplomat and presidential adviser, Apr 1968, *Obit* May 1998

Adelman, Kenneth L., diplomat and management consultant, July 1985

Adoula, Cyrille, Congolese prime minister, Mar 1962

Agar, William, American geologist, May 1949, *Obit* July 1972

Aichi, Kiichi, Japanese statesman, July 1971, *Obit* Jan 1974

Al-Hassan, Seif al-Islam, Feb 1957

Ala, Hussein, Iranian prime minister, May 1951, *Obit* Sept 1964

Alberto, Alvaro, Brazilian chemist and United Nations official, Mar 1947

Albright, Madeleine Korbel, American Secretary of state, May 1995, Apr 2000

Aldrich, Winthrop Williams, American banker and diplomat, Oct 1940, Mar 1953, *Obit* Apr 1974

Ali, Asaf, June 1947, *Obit* May 1953

Ali, Mohammed, Pakistani prime minister and diplomat, Oct 1952, *Obit* Mar 1963

Allen, George Venable, American diplomat, Nov 1948, *Obit* Oct 1970

Allison, John Moore, American diplomat, Mar 1956, *Obit* Feb 1979

Alphand, Herve, French diplomat, Nov 1951, *Obit* Mar 1994

Amerasinghe, Hamilton Shirley, Sri Lankan diplomat, Mar 1977, *Obit* Feb 1981

Anderson, Eugenie M., American diplomat, Jan 1950

Anderson, George Everett, American diplomat and journalist, *Obit* Apr 1940

Anderson, George Whelan, American admiral, Nov 1962, *Obit* May 1992

Andrade, Victor, Bolivian diplomat, Feb 1953

Andrewes, William, British admiral, Sept 1952, *Obit* Jan 1975

Andric, Ivo, Yugoslav novelist, short story writer and poet, Feb 1962, *Obit* May 1975

Annan, Kofi, Ghanaian United Nations secretary-general, Mar 2000

Annenberg, Walter H., American magazine and newspaper publisher, diplomat and philanthropist, Jan 1970, *Obit* Jan 2003

Araki, Eikichi, Japanese diplomat, Oct 1952, *Obit* Apr 1959

Aranha, Oswaldo, Brazilian diplomat, Mar 1942, *Obit* Apr 1960

Aras, Tevfik Rustu, Turkish diplomat, June 1942

Arce, Jose, Nov 1947, *Obit* Oct 1968

Ardalan, Ali Gholi, Iranian diplomat, Apr 1954

Areilza, Jose Maria de, Spanish diplomat and political leader, Apr 1955, *Obit* May 1998

Arens, Moshe, Israeli cabinet member, July 1989

Arias, Arnulfo, May 1941, *Obit* Sept 1988

Armitage, Richard L., American government official, Oct 2003

Armour, Norman, American diplomat, Apr 1945, *Obit* Nov 1982

Armstrong, Anne, American presidential adviser and diplomat, May 1976, *Obit* Yrbk 2008

Asakai, Koichiro, Japanese diplomat, Sept 1957

Ashida, Hitoshi, Japanese prime minister, June 1948, *Obit* Sept 1959

Atcheson, George, American diplomat, Sept 1946, *Obit* Oct 1947

Attwood, William, diplomat, publisher and author, Jan 1968, *Obit* July 1989

Austin, Margretta, American diplomat, Feb 1954

Austin, Warren Robinson, American senator and diplomat, Jan 1944, *Obit* Feb 1963

Avenol, Joseph, Jan 1940, *Obit* Oct 1952

Aziz, Tariq, Iraqi cabinet member, May 1991

Azzam, Abd al-Rahman, Egyptian diplomat, Apr 1947

Baker, Howard H., American senator and presidential adviser, Mar 1974, Aug 1987

Baker, James A., American Secretary of state, Feb 1982, Mar 2007

Ball, George W., American diplomat, Feb 1962, *Obit* July 1994

Ban, Ki Moon, Korean diplomat and United Nations secretary-general, Jan 2007

Barrere, Camille, French diplomat, *Obit* Yrbk 1940

Barrette, Antonio, Canadian provincial premier, July 1960, *Obit* Feb 1969

Barros Hurtado, Cesar, Argentine lawyer, sociologist and diplomat, Jan 1959

Barshefsky, Charlene, American trade representative, Feb 2000

Basdevant, Jules, French lawyer, diplomat and judge, Feb 1950, *Obit* Mar 1968

Beale, Howard, Australian cabinet member and diplomat, Mar 1959

Beam, Jacob Dyneley, American diplomat, July 1959, *Obit* Oct 1993

Beaulac, Willard Leon, diplomat, Sept 1958, *Obit* Oct 1990

Bebler, Ales, Yugoslav diplomat, Apr 1950

Bech, Joseph, Luxembourgian statesman, Feb 1950, *Obit* May 1975

Beck, Jozef, Polish diplomat, *Obit* July 1944

Becker, Ralph E., lawyer and diplomat, Nov 1948, *Obit* Oct 1994

Begtrup, Bodil, Danish diplomat and United Nations official, Sept 1946

Belaunde, Victor Andres, Peruvian diplomat, Feb 1960, *Obit* Feb 1967

Bellamy, Carol, American United Nations official, Oct 1999

Belt, Guillermo, Cuban diplomat, Nov 1947, *Obit* Sept 1989

Beltran, Pedro G., Peruvian newspaper publisher and statesman, Apr 1967, *Obit* Apr 1979

Benavides, Oscar R., Peruvian president, *Obit* Aug 1945

Benoit-Levy, Jean, Oct 1947, *Obit* Nov 1959

Bensouda, Fatou, Gambian lawyer and international court prosecutor, Jan 2007

Benton, William, American senator, publisher and diplomat, Yrbk 1945, *Obit* May 1973

Berendsen, Carl August, New Zealand diplomat, Oct 1948, *Obit* Yrbk 1973

Berle, Adolf Augustus, American lawyer and diplomat, July 1940, June 1961, *Obit* Apr 1971

Berlin, Isaiah, British political philosopher, July 1964, *Obit* Jan 1998

Bernadotte, Folke, Swedish diplomat, May 1945, *Obit* Nov 1948

Bernardino, Minerva, Dominican feminist and diplomat, Mar 1950, *Obit* Nov 1998

Bessmertnykh, Aleksandr A., Soviet diplomat, June 1991

Bevin, Ernest, British statesman, Sept 1940, June 1949, *Obit* May 1951

Beyen, J. W., Dutch banker, economist and diplomat, Feb 1953, *Obit* June 1976

Bidault, Georges, French statesman, May 1945, *Obit* Mar 1983

Biddle, Anthony Joseph Drexel, American general and diplomat, Mar 1941, *Obit* Jan 1962

Binder, Carroll, journalist, May 1951, *Obit* July 1956

Bitar, Salah al-Din, Syrian political leader, Feb 1958, *Obit* Sept 1980

Black, Eugene Robert, American banking official, Jan 1950, *Obit* Apr 1992

Black, Shirley Temple, American actress and diplomat, Oct 1945, Apr 1970

Blankenhorn, Herbert, German diplomat, Apr 1956

Blix, Hans, Swedish diplomat and United Nations official, Jan 2003

Blough, Roy, economist, July 1950, *Obit* Sept 2000

Boerma, Addeke H., Dutch agronomist and United Nations official, Yrbk 1974

Boheman, Erik, Swedish diplomat, Mar 1951

Bohlen, Charles E., American diplomat, June 1948, May 1960, *Obit* Feb 1974

Boland, Frederick H., Irish United Nations official and diplomat, Feb 1961, *Obit* Feb 1986

Bolton, John R., American diplomat, Feb 2006

Bolz, Lothar, East German diplomat, Sept 1959, *Obit* Apr 1987

Bonino, Emma, Italian trade official, Jan 2006

Bonnet, Henri, French diplomat, Feb 1945, *Obit* Feb 1979

Bonsal, Philip Wilson, diplomat, June 1959, *Obit* Sept 1995

Borberg, William, Nov 1952, *Obit* Sept 1958

Botha, R. F., South African diplomat, May 1984

Bouchard, Lucien, Canadian political leader, Apr 1999

Bouteflika, Abdelaziz, Algerian president, Feb 1976

Boutros-Ghali, Boutros, Egyptian diplomat and United Nations secretary-general, Apr 1992

Bowers, Claude Gernade, American journalist, historian and diplomat, Sept 1941, *Obit* Mar 1958

Bowles, Chester, American government official and diplomat, Sept 1943, Jan 1957, *Obit* July 1986

Braden, Spruille, American diplomat, Sept 1945, *Obit* Mar 1978

Bramuglia, Juan Atilio, Argentine cabinet member, May 1949, *Obit* Nov 1962

Brandt, Willy, German chancellor, June 1958, Yrbk 1973, *Obit* Nov 1992

Brentano, Heinrich von, Feb 1955, *Obit* Jan 1965

Briggs, Ellis Ormsbee, diplomat, Apr 1965, *Obit* Apr 1976

Brind, Patrick, British admiral, Nov 1952, *Obit* Jan 1964

Brittan, Leon, British cabinet member and European Commission official, Aug 1994

Brosio, Manlio, Italian diplomat, Sept 1955, *Obit* May 1980

Brown, Charles R., admiral, July 1958

Bruce, David K. E., American diplomat, June 1949, Sept 1961, *Obit* Feb 1978

Bruce, James, diplomat, Jan 1949, *Obit* Sept 1980

Bruce, Robert Randolph, *Obit* Apr 1942

Brunauer, Esther Caukin, American diplomat, Nov 1947, *Obit* Sept 1959

Brundtland, Gro Harlem, Norwegian prime minister and international health official, Nov 1981

Buchanan, Wiley T., diplomat, Nov 1957, *Obit* Mar 1986

Bullitt, William C., American diplomat, July 1940, *Obit* Apr 1967

Bunche, Ralph J., American diplomat, Feb 1948, *Obit* Jan 1972

Bundy, William P., American international relations specialist, June 1964, *Obit* Feb 2001

Bunker, Ellsworth, American diplomat, Apr 1954, Mar 1978, *Obit* Nov 1984

Burns, Alan, Sept 1953

Burns, Arthur F., American economist and diplomat, Sept 1953, Aug 1976, *Obit* Aug 1987

Burns, E. L. M., Canadian general, Feb 1955

Bush, George, American president, Jan 1972, Sept 1983

Butler, Nevile Montagu, Apr 1941

Byrnes, James Francis, American senator, Supreme Court justice and Secretary of state, June 1941, Oct 1951, *Obit* June 1972

Byroade, Henry Alfred, diplomat, Feb 1952, *Obit* Mar 1994

Cabot, John M., American diplomat, Sept 1953, *Obit* Apr 1981

Caccia, Harold Anthony, British diplomat, Feb 1957, *Obit* Jan 1991

Cadogan, Alexander, British diplomat, Oct 1944, *Obit* Sept 1968

Caffery, Jefferson, diplomat, Nov 1943, *Obit* June 1974

Calderone, Frank A., physician and public health official, July 1952, *Obit* Apr 1987

Calmy-Rey, Micheline, Swiss president, Jan 2007

Campa, Miguel Angel, Sept 1957, *Obit* Nov 1965

Campbell, Gerald, Mar 1941, *Obit* Sept 1964

Candau, Marcolino G., Brazilian physican and public health official, Sept 1954

Cannon, Cavendish Welles, diplomat, July 1957, *Obit* Yrbk 1962

Caradon, Hugh Foot, British diplomat, Oct 1953, *Obit* Nov 1990

Carlucci, Frank Charles, American Secretary of defense, Oct 1981

Carney, Robert Bostwick, admiral, Oct 1951, *Obit* Aug 1990

Carpentier, Marcel Maurice, Apr 1951

Carr, Wilbur J., diplomat, *Obit* Aug 1942

Carrington, Peter Alexander Rupert Carington, British statesman, June 1971

Carter, John Ridgely, *Obit* July 1944

Cartier de Marchienne, Emile de, *Obit* July 1946

Castiella, Fernando Maria, May 1958, *Obit* Feb 1977

Chagla, Mahomed Ali Currim, Indian diplomat, June 1959, *Obit* Jan 1984

Chalmers, Philip O., *Obit* Mar 1946

Chambas, Mohamed Ibn, Ghanaian diplomat and international organization official, Jan 2003

Chan, Margaret F. C., Chinese physician and public health official, Jan 2007

Chang, John M., June 1949, *Obit* July 1966

Chapman, Daniel A., Apr 1959

Charles-Roux, Francois, Jan 1952, *Obit* Sept 1961

Chauvel, Jean, French diplomat, Oct 1950, *Obit* July 1979

Chen, Eugene, Chinese newspaper executive and diplomat, *Obit* July 1944

Chisholm, Brock, Canadian psychistrist, July 1948, *Obit* Mar 1971

Chissano, Joaquim Alberto, Mozambican president, Nov 1990

Christopher, Warren, American Secretary of state, June 1981, Nov 1995, *Obit* Yrbk 2011

Ciano, Galeazzo, Italian diplomat, July 1940, *Obit* Feb 1944

Clark Kerr, Archibald John Kerr, Yrbk 1942, *Obit* Sept 1951

Clark, Wesley K., American general, July 1999

Clausen, A. W., banking official, Nov 1981

Clinton, Hillary Rodham, American Secretary of state, Nov 1993, Jan 2002, Mar 2009

Cochran, H. Merle, Feb 1950, *Obit* Nov 1973

Cohen, Benjamin, Chilean diplomat and United Nations official, May 1948, *Obit* May 1960

Cohen, Benjamin V., American government official and lawyer, Apr 1941, *Obit* Oct 1983

Cohn-Bendit, Daniel, German political activist, Jan 2003

Colina, Rafael de la, Jan 1951

Conable, Barber B., American congressman and banking official, July 1984, *Obit* Yrbk 2004

Concheso, Aurelio Fernandez, May 1942, *Obit* Jan 1956

Cooper, John Sherman, American senator and diplomat, June 1950, *Obit* Apr 1991

Cordier, Constant, *Obit* Mar 1940

Corea, Claude, Mar 1961, *Obit* Nov 1962

Corell, Hans, Swedish diplomat, lawyer and United Nations official, Jan 2003

Coudenhove-Kalergi, Richard Nicolaus, Austrian political philosopher and international organization official, Feb 1948, *Obit* Oct 1972

Coulter, John B., June 1954

Couve de Murville, Maurice, French diplomat and prime

minister, Apr 1955, *Obit* June 2000

Craigie, Robert, British diplomat, July 1942, *Obit* July 1959

Cripps, C. A., *Obit* Aug 1941

Cripps, Richard Stafford, British statesman, July 1940, Apr 1948, *Obit* June 1952

Crocker, Chester A., American diplomat, July 1990

Crocker, Ryan, American diplomat, Oct 2007

Cromer, George Rowland Stanley Baring, English banker and diplomat, May 1971, *Obit* May 1991

Cromwell, James H. R., American financial executive, diplomat and developer, Mar 1940, *Obit* May 1990

Cross, Ronald H., June 1941

Crowe, William J., American admiral, July 1988, *Obit* Yrbk 2008

Csaky, Stephen, *Obit* Mar 1941

Cudahy, John, diplomat, *Obit* Oct 1943

Danforth, John C., American senator, Jan 1992

Daniels, Josephus, American Secretary of the navy and diplomat, Oct 1944, *Obit* Feb 1948

Daud Khan, Sardar Mohammed, Mar 1957

Davies, Ernest, May 1951

Davies, Joseph Edward, American lawyer and diplomat, Apr 1942, *Obit* July 1958

Davis, John William, American lawyer, congressman and diplomat, Mar 1953, *Obit* May 1955

Davis, Norman Hezekiah, banker and diplomat, Jan 1940, *Obit* Aug 1944

Dawson, William, diplomat, Apr 1941, *Obit* Sept 1972

Dayal, Rajeshwar, Feb 1961

De Silva, Desmond, British barrister and United Nations war crimes prosecutor, Jan 2006

DeLany, Walter S., admiral, Yrbk 1952

Dean, Arthur Hobson, American lawyer and diplomat, Mar 1954, *Obit* Jan 1988

Dean, Patrick, British diplomat, May 1961, *Obit* Jan 1995

Delors, Jacques, French economist and government official, June 1989

Dendramis, Vassili, June 1947, *Obit* July 1956

Dennis, Lawrence, American political writer and diplomat, Mar 1941, *Obit* Oct 1977

Des Graz, Charles Louis, *Obit* Yrbk 1940

Des Portes, Fay Allen, *Obit* Nov 1944

Dillon, Douglas, American investment banker and Secretary of the treasury, Apr 1953, *Obit* May 2003

Dimechkie, Nadim, Feb 1960

Dixon, Owen, Australian judge and diplomat, Aug 1942

Dixon, Pierson, British diplomat, Sept 1954, *Obit* June 1965

Dobrynin, Anatoly F., Soviet diplomat, Sept 1962, *Obit* Yrbk 2010

Dodd, Norris E., Feb 1949, *Obit* Sept 1968

Dodd, William Edward, historian and diplomat, *Obit* Mar 1940

Donnelly, Walter Joseph, diplomat, Sept 1952, *Obit* Jan 1971

Donovan, William J., American intelligence official and general, Mar 1941, Sept 1954, *Obit* Apr 1959

Douglas, Lewis W., American government official, Mar 1947, *Obit* May 1974

Dowling, Walter, American diplomat, Mar 1963, *Obit* Sept 1977

Drozniak, Edward, July 1962, *Obit* Jan 1967

Duisenberg, Willem, Dutch European banking official, Jan 2002, *Obit* CB Int 2006

Duke, Angier Biddle, diplomat, Feb 1962, *Obit* July 1995

Dulles, Allen Welsh, American diplomat and intelligence official, Mar 1949, *Obit* Mar 1969

Dulles, John Foster, American Secretary of state, Aug 1944, Sept 1953, *Obit* July 1959

Dumas, Roland, French cabinet member, Oct 1990

Duncan-Sandys, Duncan Edwin Duncan-Sandys, British cabinet member, May 1952

Dunn, James Clement, May 1943, *Obit* June 1979

Eagleburger, Lawrence S., American diplomat, Nov 1992, *Obit* Yrbk 2011

Eban, Abba, Israeli diplomat, Oct 1948, May 1957, *Obit* Mar 2003

Eckardt, Felix von, Jan 1956

Eden, Anthony, British statesman, Yrbk 1940, Apr 1951, *Obit* Mar 1977

Edge, Walter Evans, senator and governor, June 1945, *Obit* Jan 1957

Eichelberger, Clark M., Jan 1947, *Obit* Mar 1980

Eikenberry, Karl W., American general and diplomat, Mar 2010

Eklund, Sigvard, July 1962

El Baradei, Mohamed, Egyptian diplomat and international organization official, Jan 2003

Elath, Eliahu, Israeli Zionist leader, Yrbk 1948, *Obit* Aug 1990

Eliasson, Jan, Swedish diplomat, Jan 2005

Elizalde, Joaquin M., Feb 1948, *Obit* Mar 1965

Emmet of Amberley, Evelyn, Mar 1953

Enckell, Carl J. A., Apr 1950, *Obit* June 1959

Erkin, Feridun C., Jan 1952

Ertegun, Mehmet Munir, *Obit* Jan 1945

Ethridge, Mark Foster, American newspaper publisher and diplomat, Jan 1946, *Obit* June 1981

Evans, Luther Harris, American Librarian of Congress and United Nations official, Aug 1945, *Obit* Feb 1982

Evatt, Herbert Vere, Australian statesman, May 1942, *Obit* Jan 1966

Eytan, Walter, Israeli diplomat, Oct 1958, *Obit* Oct 2001

Fawzi, Mahmoud, Yrbk 1951

Fedorenko, Nikolai T., Yrbk 1967

Feller, Abraham H., Nov 1946, *Obit* Jan 1953

Ferguson, Homer, American diplomat and senator, May 1943, *Obit* Mar 1983

Fernandes, L. Esteves, Oct 1950

Figueroa, Ana, Chilean educator, diplomat and feminist, Feb 1952

Finletter, Thomas K., American diplomat and government official, Jan 1948, *Obit* June 1980

Fischer, Joschka, German political leader and diplomat, Jan 2002

Fish, Bert, *Obit* Sept 1943

Flynn, Raymond, American mayor and diplomat, Oct 1993

Foley, Thomas S., American Speaker of the House, Sept 1989

Forsyth, W. D., Apr 1952

Foster, William C., American government official, Nov 1950

Fraga Iribarne, Manuel, Spanish political leader, May 1965, *Obit* Yrbk 2012

Francois-Poncet, Andre, Oct 1949, *Obit* Mar 1978

Franks, Oliver Shewell Franks, British diplomat, Mar 1948, *Obit* Jan 1993

Freeman, John, June 1969

Gaffney, T. St. John, *Obit* Mar 1945

Galbraith, John Kenneth, American economist, Mar 1959, May 1975, *Obit* Yrbk 2007

Gardiner, Robert, July 1975

Gardner, Arthur, Jan 1956, *Obit* June 1967

Gardner, O. Max, Jan 1947

Garreau, Roger, Apr 1950

Garrels, Arthur, *Obit* Aug 1943

Gauss, Clarence Edward, diplomat, Jan 1941, *Obit* June 1960

Gavin, James Maurice, American general and diplomat, Feb 1945, Sept 1961, *Obit* Apr 1990

Gavin, John, American actor and diplomat, Sept 1962

Genscher, Hans Dietrich, German diplomat and political leader, June 1975

Gibson, Hugh, diplomat, Jan 1953, *Obit* Feb 1955

Gifford, Walter Sherman, telephone executive, Jan 1945, *Obit* June 1966

Gil Fortoul, Jose, *Obit* Aug 1943

Gladwyn, Hubert Miles Gladwyn Jebb, British diplomat, Yrbk 1948

Goldberg, Arthur J., American diplomat and Supreme Court justice, July 1949, July 1961, *Obit* Mar 1990

Goldman, Olive Mortimer Remington, Sept 1950

Gomes, Manuel Teixeira, *Obit* Yrbk 1941

Gonzalez, Cesar, Oct 1954

Goodpaster, Andrew Jackson, American general, July 1969, *Obit* Yrbk 2005

Gordon, Lincoln, American diplomat, Feb 1962, *Obit* Yrbk 2010

Gork, Haydar, Oct 1956

Gossett, William T., lawyer and diplomat, July 1969, *Obit* Oct 1998

Grady, Henry Francis, American diplomat and trade expert, July 1947, *Obit* Nov 1957

Grew, Joseph C., American diplomat, Feb 1941, *Obit* July 1965

Grewe, Wilhelm, Oct 1958

Griffis, Stanton, investment banker and diplomat, Oct 1944, *Obit* Oct 1974

Griswold, Dwight P., American senator, governor and diplomat, Yrbk 1947, *Obit* June 1954

Groenman, Frans Eyso Henricus, *Obit* Aug 1943

Gromyko, Andrei Andreevich, Soviet diplomat, Oct 1943, Oct 1958, *Obit* Aug 1989

Gronouski, John A., American postmaster general, Jan 1966, *Obit* Mar 1996

Gross, Ernest A., diplomat and lawyer, Feb 1951, *Obit* July 1999

Gruber, Karl, Austrian diplomat, Feb 1947

Gruber, Lilli, Italian television news anchor and member of European parliament, Jan 2007

Guerrero, Jose Gustavo, Jan 1947, *Obit* Jan 1959

Guggenheim, Harry Frank, American mining executive, Oct 1956, *Obit* Mar 1971

Guinness, Arthur, June 1948

Gujral, Inder K., Indian prime minister, *Obit* Yrbk 2013

Gunther, Franklin Mott, *Obit* Feb 1942

Habib, Philip Charles, American diplomat, Sept 1981, *Obit* July 1992

Habsburg, Otto, German member of European Parliament, June 1941, *Obit* Yrbk 2011

Hallstein, Walter, German diplomat, Oct 1953, *Obit* May 1982

Hammarskjold, Dag, Swedish United Nations secretary-general, May 1953, *Obit* Nov 1961

Han, Seung-Soo, Korean economist and diplomat, Jan 2002

Hansen, H. C., Mar 1956, *Obit* Apr 1960

Hare, Raymond Arthur, American diplomat, July 1957, *Obit* May 1994

Harlech, William David Ormsby Gore, British statesman and diplomat, Mar 1961, *Obit* Mar 1985

Harriman, Averell, American statesman, Apr 1941, Nov 1946, *Obit* Sept 1986

Harriman, Florence Jaffray Hurst, social welfare leader, Mar 1940, *Obit* Nov 1967

Hasluck, Paul, Australian governor-general, Oct 1946

Hassan, Mahmoud, July 1947

Hawkins, Harry C., Apr 1952

Hayes, Carlton Joseph Huntley, historian and diplomat, June 1942, *Obit* Nov 1964

Hearne, John J., July 1950, *Obit* May 1969

Heckler, Margaret, American Secretary of health and human services, Aug 1983

Heeney, A. D. P., June 1953

Helms, Richard, American intelligence official, Oct 1967, *Obit* Yrbk 2003

Henderson, Loy Wesley, American diplomat, Mar 1948, *Obit* May 1986

Henderson, Nevile Meyrick, British diplomat, Apr 1940, *Obit* Feb 1943

Henry, Jules, *Obit* Aug 1941

Henry-Haye, Gaston, Nov 1940

Herter, Christian Archibald, American Secretary of state, Yrbk 1947, Mar 1958, *Obit* Feb 1967

Herzog, Chaim, Israeli president, Apr 1988, *Obit* June 1997

Heuven Goedhart, Gerrit Jan van, Oct 1952, *Obit* Sept 1956

Heymann, David L., American epidemiologist and international public health official, July 2004

Hibbard, Frederick P., *Obit* Oct 1943

Hickerson, John Dewey, diplomat, May 1950, *Obit* Apr 1989

Hill, Robert C., American diplomat, Jan 1959, *Obit* Feb 1979

Hilldring, John H., American general, Apr 1947

Hills, Carla Anderson, American Secretary of housing and urban development and trade representative, Nov 1975, Mar 1993

Hiss, Alger, American diplomat and lawyer, Feb 1947, *Obit* Jan 1997

Hodgson, Joseph V., American state attorney general and United Nations official, June 1945

Hodgson, W. R., May 1946, *Obit* Apr 1958

Hoffman, Paul G., American automobile executive, Feb 1946, *Obit* Nov 1974

Holbrooke, Richard, American diplomat, Oct 1998, *Obit* Yrbk 2011

Holsti, Rudolf, *Obit* Sept 1945

Hoo, Victor, Mar 1947, *Obit* July 1972

Hoop Scheffer, Jaap de, Dutch diplomat and NATO official, Jan 2003

Hopkins, Harry Lloyd, American diplomat, Feb 1941, *Obit* Mar 1946

Hoppenot, Henri, Mar 1944

Hormel, James C., lawyer, philanthropist and diplomat, Oct 1999

Houghton, Alanson Bigelow, glass industry executive and diplomat, *Obit* Nov 1941

Houghton, Amory, American glass industry executive and diplomat, Jan 1947, *Obit* Apr 1981

Hsiung, S.-F, July 1942

Hu, Shih, Chinese poet, diplomat and literary critic, Feb 1942, *Obit* Apr 1962

Hughes, Charles Evans, American Supreme Court justice, July 1941, *Obit* Oct 1948

Hughes, Karen, American diplomat and presidential adviser, Oct 2001

Hull, Cordell, American Secretary of state, Aug 1940, *Obit* Oct 1955

Hun Sen, Cambodian prime minister, Apr 1990

Hunt, Swanee, American international relations specialist, Mar 2006

Huntsman, Jr., Jon, American diplomat, May 2012

Hurd, Douglas, British cabinet member, Feb 1990

Hurley, Patrick J., American Secretary of war and diplomat, Nov 1944, *Obit* Sept 1963

Hussein, Ahmed, Egyptian diplomat, Mar 1956, *Obit* Feb 1985

Huxley, Julian, British biologist, Aug 1942, Oct 1963, *Obit* Apr 1975

Hyde, Henry Van Zile, May 1960

Hymans, Paul, *Obit* Apr 1941

Im, Yong-Sin, Oct 1947, *Obit* Apr 1977

Insulza, Jose Miguel, Chilean diplomat and international organization official, Jan 2005

Intizam, Nasr Allah, Yrbk 1950

Jack, Homer Alexander, clergyman, pacifist and United Nations official, July 1961, *Obit* Oct 1993

Jarring, Gunnar, Swedish diplomat, Oct 1957, *Obit* Sept 2002

Jarvis, Robert Y., *Obit* Yrbk 1943

Jay, Peter, Oct 1978

Jernegan, John D., Nov 1959

Jessup, Philip C., American judge and diplomat, Apr 1948, *Obit* Mar 1986

Jiang Zuobin, *Obit* Feb 1943

Jobert, Michel, French diplomat, Feb 1975, *Obit* Sept 2002

Johnson, David M., July 1952

Johnson, Joseph E., American historian and foundation official, Nov 1950, *Obit* Jan 1991

Johnson, Louis Arthur, American Secretary of defense, June 1942, Apr 1949, *Obit* May 1966

Johnson, Nelson Trusler, diplomat, Jan 1940, *Obit* Feb 1955

Johnson, U. Alexis, American diplomat, Oct 1955, *Obit* June 1997

Johnston, Eric, Apr 1943, Oct 1955, *Obit* Oct 1963

Jones, Howard P., American diplomat, July 1963, *Obit* Nov 1973

Jooste, Gerhardus Petrus, Apr 1951

Jordana y Souza, Francisco Gomez, Mar 1944

Joxe, Louis, French diplomat and cabinet member, Apr 1961, *Obit* June 1991

Kaiser, Philip M., American diplomat, Oct 1949, *Obit* Yrbk 2007

Kampelman, Max M., American diplomat, July 1986

Kantor, Mickey, American Secretary of commerce, Mar 1994

Karnebeek, Herman Adriaan van, *Obit* May 1942

Kase, Toshikazu, Japanese diplomat, Apr 1957, *Obit* Yrbk 2004

Katz, Milton, law professor and diplomat, Oct 1950, *Obit* Oct 1995

Katz-Suchy, Juliusz, June 1951, *Obit* Yrbk 1971

Kauffmann, Henrik, Apr 1956, *Obit* July 1963

Kawaguchi, Yoriko, Japanese diplomat, Jan 2002

Keating, Kenneth Barnard, American congressman, senator and diplomat, Oct 1950, *Obit* June 1975

Keeny, Spurgeon Milton, United Nations official, Jan 1958, *Obit* Jan 1989

Kennan, George Frost, American historian and diplomat, Oct 1947, Jan 1959, *Obit* Yrbk 2005

Kennedy, David Matthew, American Secretary of the treasury, June 1969, *Obit* July 1996

Kennedy, Joseph P., American financier, diplomat and father

of President John F. Kennedy, Nov 1940, *Obit* Jan 1970

Khalilzad, Zalmay, Afghan-American diplomat, Aug 2006

Khan, Aly, Pakistani diplomat, May 1960

Khan, Muhammad Zafrulla, Yrbk 1947

Khouri, Faris el-, Sept 1948, *Obit* Feb 1962

Kingsley, J. Donald, Feb 1950

Kinnock, Neil, British political leader and European Commission official, Apr 1984

Kirk, Alan Goodrich, American admiral and diplomat, July 1944, *Obit* Yrbk 1963

Kirk, Alexander C., Feb 1945

Kirk, Ron, American trade represenative, Apr 2010

Kirkpatrick, Jeane J., American diplomat, July 1981, *Obit* Yrbk 2007

Kleffens, Eelco Nicolaas van, Oct 1947

Knabenshue, Paul, *Obit* Mar 1942

Knappstein, Karl Heinrich, Feb 1965

Knatchbull-Hugessen, Hughe, Mar 1943, *Obit* May 1971

Knuth-Winterfeldt, Kield Gustav, Sept 1959

Kohler, Foy David, American diplomat, Jan 1950, *Obit* Mar 1991

Kollontai, A., Soviet diplomat, Oct 1943, *Obit* Apr 1952

Koo, V. K. Wellington, Chinese prime minister and diplomat, July 1941, *Obit* Jan 1986

Kotschnig, Walter Maria, United Nations official and diplomat, Oct 1952, *Obit* Sept 1985

Kouchner, Bernard, French physician and cabinet member, Aug 1993

Kozyrev, Andrei V., Russian diplomat, Sept 1992

Krekeler, Heinz L., Yrbk 1951

Krishna Menon, V. K., Indian lawyer and diplomat, Mar 1953, *Obit* Nov 1974

Kroes, Neelie, Dutch European Commission official, Jan 2005

Kunin, Madeleine, American governor and diplomat, July 1987

Kurusu, Saburo, Jan 1942, *Obit* May 1954

Kuznetsov, Vasilii Vasil'evich, Soviet diplomat, Jan 1956, *Obit* Aug 1990

La Guardia, Fiorello Henry, American mayor, Oct 1940, *Obit* Nov 1947

Labouisse, Henry R., American United Nations official, Oct 1961, *Obit* May 1987

Lagarde, Christine, French interionational organization official, Jan 2007

Lall, Arthur S., Indian diplomat, Nov 1956, *Obit* Jan 1999

Lane, Arthur Bliss, American diplomat, Apr 1948, *Obit* Oct 1956

Lange, Halvard M., Norwegian diplomat, Nov 1947, *Obit* July 1970

Lange, Oscar Richard, Polish economist, Apr 1946, *Obit* Yrbk 1965

Lannung, Hermod, Yrbk 1949

Laughlin, Irwin, *Obit* June 1941

Laugier, Henri, July 1948

Lawson, Edward B., Jan 1956

Le Carre, John, British diplomat and novelist, Yrbk 1974

Leahy, William D., American admiral, Jan 1941, *Obit* Oct 1959

Lee, Jong Wook, Korean physician and international public health official, Jan 2003, *Obit* CB Int 2007

Lefaucheux, Marie-Helene, French United Nations official, Oct 1947, *Obit* Apr 1964

Leger, Jules, Nov 1976, *Obit* Jan 1981

Leith-Ross, Frederick, Oct 1942

Lequerica y Erquiza, Jose Felix de, June 1951, *Obit* July 1963

Letourneau, Jean, Oct 1952

Lie, Trygve, Norwegian United Nations secretary-general, Mar 1946, *Obit* Feb 1969

Limb, Ben C., Jan 1951

Lindsay, Ronald, *Obit* Sept 1945

Lindt, Auguste R., Swiss diplomat and United Nations official, Nov 1959, *Obit* Yrbk 2000

Linowitz, Sol M., American lawyer and diplomat, Mar 1967, *Obit* Yrbk 2005

Litvinov, Maxim Maximovich, Soviet diplomat, Yrbk 1941, *Obit* Feb 1952

Livni, Tzipi, Israeli lawyer and cabinet member, Jan 2006

Lleras Camargo, Alberto, Colombian president, Sept 1947, June 1965, *Obit* Mar 1990

Locker, Jesse D., Mar 1955, *Obit* June 1955

Lodge, Henry Cabot, American diplomat, Yrbk 1943, May 1954, *Obit* Apr 1985

Lodge, John Davis, governor and diplomat, Mar 1948, *Obit* Jan 1986

Loeb, James I., American diplomat and political leader, Jan 1962, *Obit* Mar 1992

Long, Breckinridge, diplomat, Nov 1943, *Obit* Yrbk 1958

Lopez Bravo, Gregorio, Spanish diplomat, July 1971, *Obit* Apr 1985

Lopez, Alfonso, Colombian president, Sept 1942, *Obit* Jan 1960

Lothian, Philip Henry Kerr, British diplomat, *Obit* Yrbk 1940

Loudon, Alexander, July 1942, *Obit* Mar 1953

Loutfi, Omar, Jan 1957, *Obit* July 1963

Louw, Eric, Mar 1962, *Obit* Sept 1968

Lozovskii, A., Nov 1941

Lubbers, Rudolphus, Dutch prime minister and United Nations official, May 1988, Jan 2003

Lucas, Caroline, British member of European parliament, Sept 2012

Luce, Clare Boothe, American dramatist and diplomat, Nov 1942, Apr 1953, *Obit* Nov 1987

Lucet, Charles, Yrbk 1967

Luns, Joseph M. A. H., Dutch diplomat and NATO official, Feb 1958, Apr 1982, *Obit* Yrbk 2002

M'Bow, Amadou-Mahtar, Senegalese United Nations official, May 1987

MacArthur, Douglas, American diplomat, Nov 1954, *Obit* Jan 1998

MacBride, Sean, Irish diplomat, June 1949, *Obit* Mar 1988

MacDonald, Malcolm, British colonial administrator and

diplomat, Nov 1954, *Obit* Mar 1981

MacVeagh, Lincoln, American publisher and diplomat, Nov 1941, June 1952, *Obit* Mar 1972

Machado Hernandez, Alfredo, *Obit* Sept 1946

Madariaga, Salvador de, Spanish essayist, Jan 1964, *Obit* Feb 1979

Maddox, William P., Nov 1947, *Obit* Yrbk 1972

Maiskii, I. M., Soviet diplomat, Sept 1941, *Obit* Oct 1975

Makin, Norman J. O., Mar 1946

Malik, Adam, Indonesian statesman and diplomat, Nov 1970, *Obit* Nov 1984

Malik, Charles Habib, Lebanese diplomat and United Nations official, Apr 1948, *Obit* Feb 1988

Malik, Yakov Aleksandrovich, Apr 1949, *Obit* Apr 1980

Malloch Brown, Mark, British United Nations official, Jan 2005

Mallory, Lester D., diplomat, Sept 1960, *Obit* Sept 1994

Mann, Thomas Clifton, American diplomat, Apr 1964, *Obit* Apr 1999

Mansfield, Mike, American senator and diplomat, Apr 1952, Jan 1978, *Obit* Jan 2002

Mansholt, Sicco Leendert, May 1966

Manuil'skii, Dmitrii Zakhar'evich, Yrbk 1948, *Obit* May 1959

Marchal, Leon, Sept 1943, *Obit* Yrbk 1957

Marshall, M. Lee, Sept 1948, *Obit* Oct 1950

Martin Artajo, Alberto, Nov 1949

Martin, John Bartlow, American journalist and diplomat, Yrbk 1956, *Obit* Mar 1987

Martin, Paul, Canadian cabinet member and diplomat, Yrbk 1951, *Obit* Nov 1992

Masaryk, Jan, Czech diplomat, May 1944, *Obit* Apr 1948

Massey, Vincent, Canadian statesman, Oct 1951, *Obit* Feb 1968

Massigli, Rene, May 1956

Mates, Leo, Nov 1956

Matsudaira, Koto, Japanese diplomat, Nov 1958

Matsui, Keishiro, *Obit* July 1946

Matsuoka, Yosuke, Mar 1941, *Obit* July 1946

Matthews, Francis P., American Secretary of the navy, Sept 1949, *Obit* Yrbk 1952

Matthews, H. Freeman, American diplomat, Mar 1945, *Obit* Jan 1987

Matthews, W. Donald, Sept 1952

Mayo, Charles W., Nov 1941, Nov 1954, *Obit* Oct 1968

Maza, Jose, Nov 1955, *Obit* July 1964

Mazowiecki, Tadeusz, Polish political leader, Feb 1990

McCarthy, Leighton, Oct 1942, *Obit* Nov 1952

McClintock, Robert Mills, American diplomat, Apr 1955

McCloy, John Jay, American lawyer, banker and government official, Apr 1947, Nov 1961, *Obit* May 1989

McDonald, James Grover, diplomat, Apr 1949, *Obit* Yrbk 1964

McGeachy, Mary Craig, Canadian diplomat, Apr 1944

McGee, Gale William, American senator and diplomat, Nov 1961, *Obit* June 1992

McGhee, George Crews, American petroleum industry executive and diplomat, Sept 1950, *Obit* Yrbk 2005

McHenry, Donald F., diplomat, Sept 1980

McNamara, Robert S., American Secretary of defense and banker, Sept 1961, Mar 1987, *Obit* Yrbk 2009

Mehta, G. L., Nov 1952, *Obit* June 1974

Mehta, Hansa, July 1947

Meir, Golda, Israeli prime minister, May 1950, Yrbk 1970, *Obit* Feb 1979

Melas, George V., July 1956

Mello Franco, Afranio de, *Obit* Feb 1943

Menon, K. P. S., Indian diplomat, Mar 1957, *Obit* Yrbk 1983

Menshikov, Mikhail A., May 1958, *Obit* Sept 1976

Merchant, Livingston T., American government official and diplomat, Nov 1956, *Obit* July 1976

Merry del Val y Alzola, Alfonso, Nov 1965

Messersmith, George S., American diplomat, Oct 1942, *Obit* Apr 1960

Mesta, Perle, society leader and diplomat, Sept 1949, *Obit* May 1975

Migiro, Asha-Rose Mtengeti, Tanzanian diplomat, Jan 2007

Miller, Douglas, Nov 1941

Miro Cardona, Jose, Cuban political leader, Nov 1961, *Obit* Oct 1974

Mitchell, George J., American diplomat and former senator, Apr 1989

Mitchell, William L., Nov 1959

Moffat, Jay Pierrepont, diplomat, *Obit* Mar 1943

Molotov, Vyacheslav, Soviet diplomat, Jan 1940, Nov 1954, *Obit* Jan 1987

Mondale, Walter F., American vice-president, Jan 1969, May 1978

Mongella, Gertrude, Tanzanian member of Parliament, diplomat and feminist, Jan 2004

Monnet, Jean, French economist and statesman, Sept 1947, *Obit* May 1979

Monti, Mario, Italian economist and European Commission official, Jan 2002

Mora, Jose A., Nov 1956, *Obit* Mar 1975

Moreno Ocampo, Luis, Argentine lawyer and international court prosecutor, Jan 2007

Morgenstierne, Wilhelm Thorleif von Munthe af, May 1949, *Obit* Sept 1963

Morris, Dave Hennen, *Obit* June 1944

Morris, James T., American United Nations relief official, Mar 2005

Morris, Roland Sletor, lawyer and diplomat, *Obit* Jan 1946

Morrison, DeLesseps S., American mayor and diplomat, Nov 1949, *Obit* July 1964

Morse, David Abner, American international labor leader, Mar 1949, *Obit* Mar 1991

Moscoso, Teodoro, American diplomat and economist, Oct 1963, *Obit* Aug 1992

Moussa, Amr, Egyptian diplomat and international organization official, Jan 2002

Moyne, Walter Edward Guinness, *Obit* Yrbk 1944

Moynihan, Daniel Patrick, American senator and diplomat, Feb 1968, Feb 1986, *Obit* Yrbk 2003

Muccio, John Joseph, American diplomat, Jan 1951, *Obit* July 1989

Muniz, Joao Carlos, Sept 1952, *Obit* Sept 1960

Munnich, Ferenc, May 1959, *Obit* Jan 1968

Munro, Leslie Knox, Nov 1953, *Obit* Apr 1974

Munyama, Gerry, Namibian broadcasting executive, Jan 2004

Murphy, Robert D., American diplomat, Feb 1943, Nov 1958, *Obit* Mar 1978

Muskie, Edmund S., American senator and Secretary of state, Feb 1955, Yrbk 1968, *Obit* June 1996

Myrdal, Alva Reimer, Swedish sociologist, Yrbk 1950, *Obit* Mar 1986

Nabulsi, Suleiman, Mar 1957

Naidoo, Kumi, South African human rights activist and environmentalist, Sept 2010

Narathipphongpraphan, June 1954

Nash, Walter, New Zealand prime minister, Oct 1942, Mar 1958, *Obit* July 1968

Negroponte, John, American intelligence official, Apr 2003

Nehru, B. K., Indian diplomat and government official, Feb 1963, *Obit* Feb 2002

Neruda, Pablo, Chilean poet, Yrbk 1970, *Obit* Nov 1973

Netanyahu, Benjamin, Israeli prime minister, June 1996

Nitze, Paul H., American statesman, Feb 1962, *Obit* Mar 2005

Noble, Allan, May 1957

Noble, Ronald K., American international law enforcement official, Jan 2002

Noel-Baker, Philip John, British pacifist, Feb 1946, *Obit* Mar 1983

Nomura, Kichisaburo, Apr 1941, *Obit* July 1964

Noon, Firoz Khan, June 1957

Noue, Jehan de, Jan 1947

Novello, Antonia, American pediatrician and Surgeon general, May 1992

Novikov, Nikolai Vasil'evich, Feb 1947

Nufer, Albert F., Mar 1955, *Obit* Jan 1957

Nunez Portuondo, Emilio, Apr 1957

O'Brien, Conor Cruise, Irish critic, historian and diplomat, Apr 1967

O'Dwyer, William, American mayor, Sept 1941, May 1947, *Obit* Jan 1965

Obaid, Thoraya, Saudi Arabian United Nations official, Jan 2004

Ogata, Sadako, Japanese United Nations official and diplomat, Oct 1997

Owen, A. David K., British economist, sociologist and United Nations official, May 1946, *Obit* Sept 1970

Owen, David, British political leader, Sept 1977

Padilla Nervo, Luis, Yrbk 1946

Padilla, Ezequiel, Mexican diplomat, July 1942, *Obit* Oct 1971

Palencia, Isabel de, Spanish diplomat and essayist, May 1941

Paleologue, Maurice, French diplomat, *Obit* Jan 1945

Palmer, Thomas Waverly, Mar 1949

Pandit, Vijaya Lakshmi, Indian diplomat, Jan 1946, *Obit* Feb 1991

Panyushkin, Aleksandr S., Yrbk 1948, *Obit* Jan 1975

Papen, Franz von, German diplomat, June 1941, *Obit* June 1969

Parodi, Alexandre, French government official and diplomat, June 1946

Partridge, Frank C., *Obit* Apr 1943

Pate, Maurice, June 1951, *Obit* Mar 1965

Patten, Chris, British colonial governor and European Commission official, July 1993

Patterson, Richard C., Oct 1946, *Obit* Yrbk 1966

Pauker, Ana, Romanian diplomat and communist leader, Mar 1948

Paul-Boncour, Joseph, French statesman, June 1945, *Obit* May 1972

Paz, Hipolito J., Jan 1952

Paz, Octavio, Mexican poet and diplomat, June 1974, *Obit* July 1998

Pearson, Lester Bowles, Canadian prime minister, Nov 1947, Nov 1963, *Obit* Feb 1973

Pell, Claiborne, American senator, Mar 1972, *Obit* Yrbk 2009

Pelt, Adrian, Feb 1948

Pena, Pedro, *Obit* Sept 1943

Peres, Shimon, Israeli political leader, Jan 1976, Mar 1995

Perez de Cuellar, Javier, Peruvian diplomat and United Nations secretary-general, Aug 1982

Perse, Saint-John, French diplomat and poet, Apr 1961, *Obit* Nov 1975

Peterson, R. A., American banker, May 1964

Petitpierre, Max, Swiss president and diplomat, Yrbk 1953, *Obit* June 1994

Peurifoy, John Emil, American diplomat, Jan 1949, *Obit* Oct 1955

Phillips, William, American diplomat, July 1940, *Obit* Apr 1968

Pierson, Warren Lee, June 1941, Nov 1954

Pinay, Antoine, French political leader, Apr 1952, *Obit* Feb 1995

Piot, Peter, Belgian public health official and epidemiologist, Jan 2004

Plaza Lasso, Galo, Ecuadorian president, Oct 1951, Apr 1969, *Obit* Mar 1987

Poindexter, Miles, *Obit* Nov 1946

Politis, Athanase G., Sept 1950, *Obit* June 1968

Politis, Nicolas, *Obit* Apr 1942

Polyansky, Dmitry S., Soviet communist leader, Mar 1971

Poole, Dewitt C., Nov 1950, *Obit* Oct 1952

Popovic, Vladimir, Feb 1952, *Obit* May 1972

Porter, William James, diplomat, Mar 1974, *Obit* May 1988

Pote Sarasin, Yrbk 1955

Potemkin, Vladimir P., *Obit* Apr 1946

Prebisch, Raul, Argentine economist, Yrbk 1969, *Obit* July 1986

Price, Byron, journalist and United Nations official, Feb 1942, *Obit* Sept 1981

Primakov, Yevgeny M., Russian prime minister, Feb 1999

Prince, John Dyneley, *Obit* Nov 1945

Procope, Hjalman Johan Fredrik, Apr 1940, *Obit* Apr 1954

Prodi, Romano, Italian prime minister, Jan 2006

Pronk, Johannes Pieter, Dutch United Nations official, Jan 2005

Prosper, Pierre-Richard, American lawyer and diplomat, Aug 2005

Pueyrredon, Honorio, *Obit* Oct 1945

Quaison-Sackey, Alex, Ghanaian United Nations official and diplomat, Mar 1966, *Obit* Feb 1993

Quo, Tai-Chi, May 1946, *Obit* Apr 1952

Rankin, Karl Lott, American diplomat, Apr 1955, *Obit* Apr 1991

Rapacki, Adam, July 1958, *Obit* Yrbk 1970

Rasmussen, Gustav, Yrbk 1947, *Obit* Nov 1953

Rau, Benegal Narsing, Yrbk 1951, *Obit* Feb 1954

Rau, Benegal Rama, Feb 1949, *Obit* Feb 1970

Reber, Samuel, Sept 1949, *Obit* Feb 1972

Reid, Ogden R., American congressman and newspaper publisher, Feb 1956

Reischauer, Edwin O., American historian and diplomat, May 1962, *Obit* Nov 1990

Riad, Mahmoud, Egyptian diplomat, Nov 1971, *Obit* Mar 1992

Ribbentrop, Joachim von, German Nazi leader, May 1941, *Obit* Nov 1946

Richardson, Bill, American governor, Apr 1996

Richardson, Norval, *Obit* Yrbk 1940

Riddell, R. Gerald, Sept 1950, *Obit* Apr 1951

Riddleberger, James W., diplomat, May 1957, *Obit* Jan 1983

Riefler, Winfield W., May 1948, *Obit* June 1974

Riley, William Edward, Nov 1951

Robertson, Norman A., Yrbk 1957, *Obit* Sept 1968

Robertson, Walter S., Yrbk 1953, *Obit* May 1970

Robinson, Mary, Irish president and United Nations official, Apr 1991

Roca, Julio A., *Obit* Nov 1942

Rodota, Antonio, Italian aerospace engineer and European space agency official, Jan 2003

Rogers, Bernard W., American general, Oct 1984

Rogers, William Pierce, American Secretary of state, Feb 1958, Sept 1969, *Obit* Mar 2001

Rohatyn, Felix G., American investment banker and diplomat, May 1978

Roijen, Jan Herman van, Dutch diplomat, Yrbk 1953

Rolvaag, Karl Fritjof, American governor, Feb 1964, *Obit* Mar 1991

Romulo, Carlos Pena, Filipino statesman, Mar 1943, Apr 1957, *Obit* Feb 1986

Rooks, Lowell W., Apr 1947

Rossel, Agda, Yrbk 1959

Rountree, William M., diplomat, June 1959, *Obit* Jan 1996

Rowe, Leo Stanton, director general of the Pan American union, Aug 1945, *Obit* Jan 1947

Rubottom, R. Richard, American diplomat, May 1959, *Obit* Yrbk 2011

Ruiz Guinazu, Enrique, Apr 1942, *Obit* Jan 1968

Rumsfeld, Donald H., American Secretary of defense, Apr 1970, Mar 2002

Rush, David Kenneth, American chemical industry executive and diplomat, May 1975, *Obit* Feb 1995

Rusk, Dean, American Secretary of state, June 1949, July 1961, *Obit* Feb 1995

Russell, James S., admiral, Jan 1962

Sackett, Frederic M., senator and diplomat, *Obit* July 1941

Sadak, Necmeddin, Jan 1950, *Obit* Yrbk 1953

Sadik, Nafis, Pakistani physician and United Nations official, Feb 1996

Saionji, Kimmochi, Japanese statesman, *Obit* Jan 1941

Saleh, Allah-Yar, Feb 1953

Sampson, Edith S., American judge, Yrbk 1950, *Obit* Jan 1980

Sandstrom, Emil, Jan 1951, *Obit* Sept 1962

Santa Cruz, Hernan, Yrbk 1949

Sargeant, Howland Hill, diplomat, Yrbk 1952, *Obit* Apr 1984

Sasser, James R., senator and diplomat, July 1993

Sastroamidjojo, Ali, June 1950, *Obit* May 1975

Saud al Faisal, Jan 1948

Sawyer, Charles, American Secretary of commerce and diplomat, July 1948, *Obit* June 1979

Saxbe, William B., American Attorney general and senator, July 1974, *Obit* Yrbk 2010

Sayegh, Fayez A., Lebanese scholar and diplomat, July 1957

Sayre, Francis Bowes, American diplomat, Jan 1940, *Obit* May 1972

Scali, John A., American television newscaster and diplomat, Sept 1973, *Obit* Jan 1996

Schmid, Carlo, Feb 1965, *Obit* Apr 1980

Schoonmaker, Edwin Davies, *Obit* Jan 1940

Schuman, Robert, French statesman, Jan 1948, *Obit* Nov 1963

Schumann, Maurice, French cabinet member, Apr 1970, *Obit* Apr 1998

Schwebel, Stephen M., American judge and international relations specialist, July 1952

Schweitzer, Pierre-Paul, French government official and IMF director, Yrbk 1963, *Obit* Mar 1994

Scranton, William Warren, American governor, Jan 1964, *Obit* Yrbk 2013

Sebald, William J., naval officer, lawyer and diplomat, Oct 1951

Seferis, George, Greek poet, May 1964, *Obit* Nov 1971

Self, Henry, Oct 1942

Selwyn-Lloyd, John Selwyn Brooke, British cabinet member, Apr 1952, *Obit* July 1978

Sen, Binay Ranjan, Indian diplomat, Yrbk 1952, *Obit* Aug 1993

Sender, Toni, German United Nations official, May 1950

Serrano Suner, Ramon, Spanish diplomat and political leader, Nov 1940, *Obit* Yrbk 2004

Sevier, Henry Hulme, *Obit* Mar 1940

Sforza, Carlo, June 1942, *Obit* Oct 1952

Shabandar, Musa, Feb 1956

Shalikashvili, John, American general, Nov 1995, *Obit* Yrbk 2011

Sharett, Moshe, Israeli statesman, Apr 1948, *Obit* Sept 1965

Sherfield, Roger Mellor Makins, British diplomat, Jan 1953, *Obit* Jan 1997

Shevardnadze, Eduard, Georgian president, Feb 1986

Shevchenko, Arkady N., Soviet diplomat and defector, Sept 1985, *Obit* May 1998

Shidehara, Kijuro, Japanese diplomat and prime minister, Apr 1946, *Obit* Apr 1951

Shigemitsu, Mamoru, June 1943, *Obit* Mar 1957

Shone, Terence Allen, Nov 1946, *Obit* Yrbk 1965

Shriver, Sargent, American lawyer and government official, Yrbk 1961, *Obit* Yrbk 2011

Silva Calderon, Alvaro, Venezuelan international petroleum organization official, Jan 2002

Sinclair, Adelaide, Canadian government official, Apr 1951, *Obit* Jan 1983

Skouris, Vassilios, Greek judge, Jan 2007

Smith, Gerard C., American lawyer and diplomat, Oct 1970, *Obit* Sept 1994

Smith, Walter Bedell, American general, diplomat and CIA director, Apr 1944, Yrbk 1953, *Obit* Nov 1961

Soames, Arthur Christopher John Soames, British diplomat, Aug 1981, *Obit* Oct 1987

Sobolev, Arkadii A., Apr 1955, *Obit* Jan 1965

Soheily, Ali, Sept 1943, *Obit* July 1958

Solana Madariaga, Javier, Spanish European Union official, Jan 2005

Spaak, Paul-Henri, Belgian statesman, May 1945, Apr 1958, *Obit* Oct 1972

Spender, Percy Claude, Mar 1950

Spofford, Charles Merville, lawyer and diplomat, Feb 1951, *Obit* May 1991

Stahle, Nils K., Apr 1956

Standley, William Harrison, admiral, May 1942, *Obit* Yrbk 1963

Steinhardt, Laurence Adolph, lawyer and diplomat, July 1941, *Obit* Apr 1950

Stephanopoulos, Stephanos, July 1955

Stevenson, Adlai E., American statesman, Jan 1949, Sept 1961, *Obit* Sept 1965

Stewart, Rory, British diplomat and writer, Jan 2007

Stikker, Dirk U., Dutch statesman, Feb 1950, Feb 1962

Stimson, Frederic Jesup, *Obit* Jan 1944

Stimson, Henry Lewis, American statesman, Aug 1940, *Obit* Yrbk 1950

Stoessel, Walter J., diplomat, June 1970, *Obit* Feb 1987

Stokes, Carl, American mayor, judge and newscaster, Apr 1968, *Obit* June 1996

Strauss, Robert S., American political party leader and diplomat, Mar 1974, July 1992

Straw, Jack, British cabinet member, Jan 2002

Strong, Maurice F., Canadian petroleum executive, environmentalist and government official, Yrbk 1973

Stuart, John Leighton, American missionary and diplomat, Oct 1946, *Obit* Nov 1962

Subandrio, Indonesian cabinet member, Mar 1963, *Obit* Apr 2005

Sullivan, William H., American diplomat, Aug 1979

Supachai Panitchpakdi, Thai international organization official, Jan 2004

Talbott, Strobe, American diplomat, July 2000

Tani, Masayuki, May 1956

Tanner, Vaino, Finnish statesman, Sept 1960, *Obit* May 1966

Tarchiani, Alberto, Jan 1950, *Obit* Jan 1965

Tardieu, Andre, French statesman, *Obit* Oct 1945

Tatekawa, Yoshitsugu, *Obit* Oct 1945

Taylor, Myron C., American financier and diplomat, Feb 1940, *Obit* July 1959

Teleki, Pal, Hungarian statesman, *Obit* May 1941

Tello, Manuel, Yrbk 1959, *Obit* Jan 1972

Templewood, Samuel John Gurney Hoare, British diplomat, Oct 1940, *Obit* July 1959

Thanat Khoman, Mar 1958

Thant, Burmese diplomat and United Nations secretary-general, Feb 1962, *Obit* Jan 1975

Thomas, Elbert Duncan, American senator, Oct 1942, *Obit* Mar 1953

Thompson, Llewellyn E., American diplomat, Nov 1957, *Obit* Mar 1972

Thorn, James, Yrbk 1949

Thornburgh, Dick, American governor and Attorney general, Oct 1988

Timberlake, Clare H., Jan 1961

Tindemans, Leo, Belgian statesman, Mar 1978

Titulescu, Nicolae, Romanian diplomat, *Obit* May 1941

Tong, Hollington K., Taiwanese diplomat, Yrbk 1956, *Obit* Feb 1971

Toon, Malcolm, diplomat, July 1978

Topfer, Klaus, German environmentalist and United Nations official, Jan 2002

Trichet, Jean-Claude, French banking official, Jan 2006

Trygger, Ernst, *Obit* Nov 1943

Tsarapkin, Semyon K., Soviet diplomat, June 1960, *Obit* Nov 1984

Tsiang, Tingfu F., June 1948, *Obit* Yrbk 1965

Uexkull, Jakob von, Swedish environmentalist, Jan 2005

Umanskii, Konstantin Aleksandrovich, Feb 1941, *Obit* Mar 1945

Unden, Osten, Feb 1947, *Obit* Apr 1974

Urrutia, Francisco, June 1958

Vance, Cyrus R., American Secretary of state, Yrbk 1962, Nov 1977, *Obit* Apr 2002

Vanier, Georges, Canadian governor general, Jan 1960, *Obit* May 1967

Vansittart, Robert Gilbert Vansittart, British diplomat, July 1941, *Obit* Apr 1957

Vassallo, Ernesto, *Obit* Jan 1940

Vaughn, Jack Hood, American diplomat and government official, Apr 1966, *Obit* Yrbk 2013

Velloso, Pedro Leao, Sept 1946, *Obit* Mar 1947

Veneman, Ann M., American United Nations official, Sept 2009

Villepin, Dominique de, French prime minister, Jan 2003

Vishinski, Andrei IAnuarevich, Soviet diplomat, May 1944, *Obit* Jan 1955

Volpe, John A., American governor and Secretary of transportation, Feb 1962, *Obit* Jan 1995

Wachuku, Jaja, Apr 1963

Wadsworth, James J., American diplomat, June 1956, *Obit* May 1984

Wagner, Robert Ferdinand, American mayor, Feb 1954, *Obit* Apr 1991

Wakasugi, Kaname, *Obit* Jan 1944

Waldheim, Kurt, Austrian president and United Nations secretary-general, May 1972, Jan 1987, *Obit* Oct 2007

Walker, E. Ronald, Yrbk 1956

Walters, Vernon A., American general and diplomat, Feb 1988, *Obit* July 2002

Wang Bingnan, Yrbk 1958

Wang, Shih-chieh, Sept 1945, *Obit* June 1981

Warren, Avra M., Feb 1955, *Obit* Mar 1957

Warren, Fletcher, diplomat, July 1960, *Obit* Mar 1992

Waterlow, Sydney, *Obit* Jan 1945

Webb, James E., American NASA official, Oct 1946, May 1962, *Obit* May 1992

Wei, Tao-ming, Yrbk 1942

Welles, Sumner, American diplomat, Mar 1940, *Obit* Nov 1961

Wharton, Clifton R., American diplomat, July 1958, *Obit* June 1990

White, Katherine Elkus, diplomat and state official, Feb 1965, *Obit* June 1985

White, Robert E., American diplomat, May 1984

Whitney, John Hay, American financier and diplomat, Yrbk 1945, *Obit* Apr 1982

Wiggins, James Russell, American newspaper editor and diplomat, Nov 1969, *Obit* Mar 2001

Wigglesworth, Richard B., May 1959, *Obit* Yrbk 1960

Wilgress, L. Dana, Jan 1954, *Obit* Oct 1969

Williams, G. Mennen, American governor and state supreme court justice, Apr 1949, June 1963, *Obit* Mar 1988

Willis, Frances E., Jan 1954

Wilson, Hugh Robert, diplomat, May 1941, *Obit* Feb 1947

Wilson, Michael H., Canadian cabinet member and diplomat, Mar 1990

Winant, John Gilbert, governor and diplomat, Feb 1941, *Obit* Yrbk 1947

Winiarski, Bohdan, Feb 1962

Wolfensohn, James David, Australian international organization official, May 2000

Wolfowitz, Paul D., American international organization official, Feb 2003

Woodcock, Leonard, American labor leader and diplomat, Nov 1970, *Obit* Apr 2001

Woods, George David, banker, July 1965, *Obit* Oct 1982

Woodward, Robert F., diplomat, Yrbk 1962, *Obit* Yrbk 2001

Woodward, Stanley, diplomat, June 1951, *Obit* Oct 1992

Worner, Manfred, German cabinet member and NATO official, Oct 1988, *Obit* Oct 1994

Wright, Jerauld, American admiral and diplomat, Feb 1955, *Obit* July 1995

Wright, Michael, British diplomat, July 1961

Wright, Robert Alderson Wright, July 1945, *Obit* Sept 1964

Wrong, Hume, Oct 1950, *Obit* Mar 1954

Yang, You Chan, Feb 1953

Ydigoras Fuentes, Miguel, Nov 1958

Yoshida, Shigeru, Japanese statesman, Sept 1946, *Obit* Jan 1968

Yost, Charles Woodruff, American diplomat, Mar 1959, *Obit* July 1981

Younghusband, Francis Edward, British diplomat and explorer, *Obit* Sept 1942

Zarubin, Georgi N., Apr 1953, *Obit* Jan 1959

Zeineddine, Farid, Feb 1957

Zhou Enlai, Chinese prime minister and diplomat, Sept 1946, July 1957, *Obit* Feb 1976

Zimmermann, Arthur, German diplomat, *Obit* July 1940

Zinni, Anthony, American Marine corps general and diplomat, May 2002

Zoellick, Robert, American diplomat and international organiztation official, July 2008

Zorin, Valerian A., Soviet diplomat and United Nations official, Mar 1953, *Obit* Mar 1986

Zorlu, Fatin Ruchstu, Turkish diplomat, Yrbk 1958, *Obit* Nov 1961

Disc jockeys

Brokenshire, Norman, May 1950, *Obit* June 1965
Burnside, Iain, Scottish pianist, Jan 2004
Daly, Carson, American video jockey and talk show host, Nov 2009
Harcourt, Nic, American disc jockey, Oct 2005
Joyner, Tom, American radio talk show host, Sept 2002
Kasem, Casey, disc jockey, Nov 1997
Rhodes, Randi, American radio talk show host, Feb 2005
Scelsa, Vin, American disc jockey, May 2006
Schaap, Phil, American disc jockey and jazz historian, Sept 2001

Disc jockeys (Club)

3D (Singer), English singer and DJ, June 2004
Conte, Nicola, Italian DJ and record producer, Jan 2005
Daddy G (Singer), English singer and DJ, June 2004
Hahn, Joseph, American DJ, Mar 2002
Herbert, Matthew, English record producer, composer and DJ, Nov 2012
Howlett, Liam, British DJ, Oct 2009
Ishii, Ken, Japanese techno musician, Jan 2002
Rock, Pete, American record producer and DJ, Aug 2009
Singh, Talvin, British DJ, arranger and composer, Jan 2006

Discus throwers

Matson, Randy, American shot putter and discus thrower, Sept 1968

Dissenters

Abiola, Hafsat, Nigerian dissident, Jan 2007
Almada, Martin, Paraguayan educator, lawyer and human rights activist, Jan 2004
Aung San Suu Kyi, Burmese human rights activist, Feb 1992

Bernstein, Robert L., American publishing executive and human rights activist, July 1987
Bethune, Mary Jane McLeod, American educator, Jan 1942, *Obit* July 1955
Blum, William, American journalist, May 2007
Boesak, Allan Aubrey, South African church official and human rights activist, Nov 1986
Bond, Julian, American civil rights leader, Yrbk 1969, July 2001
Bonner, Elena, Soviet physician and human rights activist, Apr 1987, *Obit* Yrbk 2011
Bove, Jose, French farmer, Jan 2002
Brown, Robert McAfee, American theologian and human rights activist, May 1965, *Obit* Nov 2001
Bukovskii, Vladimir Konstantinovich, Soviet dissident, Mar 1978
Companys y Jover, Luis, *Obit* Yrbk 1940
Ellsberg, Daniel, American peace activist, Yrbk 1973
Evers, Charles, American civil rights activist, mayor and brother of Medgar Evers, Apr 1969
Evers-Williams, Myrlie, civil rights leader and wife of Medgar Wiley Evers, Aug 1995
Farmer, James, American civil rights leader, Feb 1964, *Obit* Sept 1999
Farmer-Paellmann, Deadria, American activist seeking reparations for slavery, Mar 2004
Fletcher, Arthur Allen, American civil rights leader and government official, Nov 1971, *Obit* Yrbk 2005
French, Paul Comly, May 1951, *Obit* Sept 1960
Fulani, Lenora, American psychologist and political activist, Mar 2000
Gao Zhisheng, Chinese lawyer and dissident, Jan 2007
George, Albert Bailey, *Obit* Apr 1940

Goodman, Paul, American poet, novelist, essayist and dramatist, June 1968, *Obit* Oct 1972
Granger, Lester Blackwell, civil rights leader, Apr 1946, *Obit* Mar 1976
Guinier, Lani, American law teacher and civil rights activist, Jan 2004
Havel, Vaclav, Czech dramatist and president, Mar 1985, Aug 1995, *Obit* Yrbk 2012
Haynes, George Edmund, American civil rights leader and economist, Mar 1946, *Obit* Apr 1960
Height, Dorothy I., American civil rights activist, Sept 1972, *Obit* July 2010
Hoffman, Abbie, American political activist, Apr 1981, *Obit* June 1989
Hu Jia, Chinese AIDS activist, Jan 2007
Ibrahim, Hauwa, Nigerian lawyer and human rights activist, Jan 2004
Ibrahim, Saad Eddin, Egyptian sociologist and political dissident, Jan 2003
Innis, Roy, American civil rights leader, May 1969
Jones, Elaine R., American lawyer, June 2004
Jordan, Vernon, American civil rights leader and lawyer, Feb 1972, Aug 1993
Joya, Malalai, Afghan human rights activist and member of Parliament, Jan 2007
Katz, Label A., Apr 1960, *Obit* June 1975
Khan, Irene, Bangladeshi human rights activist, Jan 2002
King, Coretta Scott, American civil rights leader, May 1969, *Obit* Apr 2006
Kohout, Pavel, Czech author and dramatist, Feb 1988
Kuhn, Maggie, American feminist and civil rights activist, July 1978, *Obit* July 1995
Langer, Felicia, Israeli lawyer and human rights activist, Jan 2004
Lemkin, Raphael, American lawyer, May 1950, *Obit* Nov 1959

Lewis, John, American congressman, Sept 1980

Liu Binyan, Chinese journalist, Jan 2004, *Obit* CB Int 2006

Lowenstein, Allard K., American civil rights leader, pacifist and congressman, Sept 1971, *Obit* May 1980

Luthuli, Albert John, South African political leader, Feb 1962, *Obit* Oct 1967

Mam, Somaly, Cambodian social worker, June 2009

Mandela, Nelson, South African president, Jan 1984, Nov 1995

Marshall, Burke, American civil rights activist and government official, Feb 1965, *Obit* Yrbk 2003

Marshall, Thurgood, American Supreme Court justice, Nov 1954, Sept 1989, *Obit* Mar 1993

Martinez, Vilma, American lawyer and civil rights activist, July 2004

McKissick, Floyd B., American lawyer and civil rights leader, Jan 1968, *Obit* June 1991

Mfume, Kweisi, American civil rights leader, Jan 1996

Michnik, Adam, Polish member of Parliament and newspaper editor, July 1990

Mohammed, Yanar, Iraqi feminist, Jan 2007

Morial, Marc, American civil rights activist and former mayor, Jan 2002

Moses, Bob, American civil rights activist and mathematics teacher, Apr 2002

Motley, Constance Baker, American judge, May 1964, *Obit* Feb 2006

Mufti, Hania, Jordanian human rights activist, Jan 2005

Neier, Aryeh, German-American civil rights leader, Nov 1978

Newton, Huey, American revolutionary, Feb 1973, *Obit* Oct 1989

Norton, Eleanor Holmes, American civil rights leader and congresswoman, Nov 1976

Nour, Ayman, Egyptian member of Parliament, Jan 2005

Parks, Rosa, American civil rights activist, May 1989, *Obit* Jan 2006

Paya, Oswaldo, Cuban dissident, Jan 2003, *Obit* Yrbk 2012

Payton, John, American lawyer and civil rights activist, May 2010, *Obit* Yrbk 2012

Perez Esquivel, Adolfo, Argentine human rights activist, Mar 1981

Perkins, Charles, Australian aborigine leader, Jan 1969, *Obit* Feb 2001

Possuelo, Sydney, Brazilian government official and human rights activist, Jan 2006

Power, Samantha, American human rights activist, Aug 2008

Prendergast, John, American human rights activist, Jan 2012

Rahmani, Taqi, Iranian writer, Jan 2005

Randolph, Asa Philip, American labor leader, May 1940, Oct 1951, *Obit* July 1979

Ras-Work, Berhane, Ethiopian human rights activist, Jan 2004

Rauh, Joseph L., American lawyer and civil rights leader, Apr 1965, *Obit* Nov 1992

Rauschning, Hermann, German-American political philosopher, May 1941, *Obit* Apr 1983

Rice, Constance L., American lawyer and civil rights activist, Apr 2011

Robinson, Randall, American lobbyist and civil rights leader, Sept 1998

Rodriguez, Nicolas, *Obit* Sept 1940

Roh, Moo Hyun, South Korean president, Jan 2003, *Obit* Yrbk 2009

Romero, Anthony, American lawyer and civil rights activist, July 2002

Ruiz Guinazu, Magdalena, Argentine journalist, Jan 2004

Rustin, Bayard, American civil rights leader, June 1967, *Obit* Oct 1987

Sabato, Ernesto R., Argentine novelist, physicist and human

rights activist, Oct 1985, *Obit* Yrbk 2011

Sakharov, Andrei Dmitrievich, Russian physicist, July 1971, *Obit* Feb 1990

Scott, Michael, South African clergyman and human rights activist, Apr 1953, *Obit* Apr 1985

Sinyavsky, Andrei, Russian essayist, novelist and short story writer, July 1975, *Obit* May 1997

Spingarn, Arthur Barnett, lawyer and civil rights leader, Jan 1965, *Obit* Jan 1972

Stevenson, Bryan, lawyer and human rights activist, Mar 1996

Strossen, Nadine, American lawyer and civil rights leader, Oct 1997

Suzman, Helen, South African member of Parliament and human rights activist, Nov 1968, *Obit* Yrbk 2009

Takirambudde, Peter, Ugandan human rights activist, Jan 2005

Tethong, Lhadon, Tibetan-Canadian human rights activist, Sept 2008

Ture, Kwame, American civil rights leader, Apr 1970, *Obit* Feb 1999

Valtin, Jan, German author, Apr 1941, *Obit* Jan 1951

Wei Jingsheng, Chinese dissident, Sept 1997

Welsh, Herbert, *Obit* Sept 1941

White, Walter Francis, American civil rights leader, Apr 1942, *Obit* June 1955

Wiesel, Elie, American novelist, journalist and human rights activist, Nov 1970, Feb 1986

Wilkins, Roy, American civil rights leader, June 1950, Jan 1964, *Obit* Oct 1981

Wilson, Margaret Bush, American lawyer and civil rights activist, Oct 1975, *Obit* Yrbk 2009

Wise, Tim, Jan 2013

Wu, Harry, Chinese-American human rights activist, Feb 1995

Xu Wenli, Chinese dissident, Jan 2003

Yergan, Max, American civil rights activist, Sept 1948, *Obit* June 1975

Zana, Leyla, Kurdish member of Turkish parliament and political prisoner, Jan 2004

Ziegler, Jean, Swiss sociologist, socialist leader and human rights activist, July 2010

District attorneys

Anderson, John Bayard, American congressman, Sept 1979

Barry, William Bernard, American congressman, *Obit* Yrbk 1946

Biddle, Francis, American Attorney general, Sept 1941, *Obit* Yrbk 1968

Bok, Curtis, American state supreme court justice, May 1954, *Obit* July 1962

Brown, Edmund G., American governor, Mar 1960, *Obit* Apr 1996

Chertoff, Michael, American Secretary of homeland security, Oct 2005

Darden, Christopher, district attorney, Feb 1997

Dewey, Thomas E., American governor, July 1940, Sept 1944, *Obit* Apr 1971

Fitzgerald, Patrick, American district attorney, Jan 2006

Giuliani, Rudolph W., American mayor and lawyer, Apr 1988, Jan 2008

Harrison, Pat, American senator, *Obit* Aug 1941

Hogan, Frank S., American district attorney, Sept 1953, *Obit* May 1974

Holder, Eric, American Attorney general, Mar 2009

Holtzman, Elizabeth, American congresswoman and municipal official, Nov 1973

Inouye, Daniel K., American senator, May 1960, Sept 1987, *Obit* Yrbk 2013

Johnson, Hiram, American governor and senator, Feb 1941, *Obit* Sept 1945

Laxalt, Paul, American senator, Jan 1979

Lipsky, Eleazar, author and lawyer, Yrbk 1959, *Obit* Apr 1993

Mahon, George H., American congressman, Mar 1958, *Obit* Jan 1986

Malloy, Dan, American governor, June 2011

Marcantonio, Vito, American congressman, Feb 1949, *Obit* Oct 1954

Martinez, Susana, American governor, Nov 2013

Morgenthau, Robert, American district attorney, Jan 1986

Mueller, Robert S., American FBI director, Aug 2010

Napolitano, Janet, American Secretary of homeland security, Oct 2004, Mar 2009

Patman, Wright, American congressman, Feb 1946, *Obit* Apr 1976

Prosper, Pierre-Richard, American lawyer and diplomat, Aug 2005

Rankin, John E., American congressman, Feb 1944, *Obit* Jan 1961

Rendell, Ed, American governor, Apr 1998

Reno, Janet, American Attorney general, Sept 1993

Reynolds, Robert Rice, senator, Oct 1940, *Obit* Mar 1963

Richardson, Seth Whitley, American government official, Feb 1948, *Obit* May 1953

Roberts, Owen Josephus, American Supreme Court justice, Oct 1941, *Obit* July 1955

Ryan, William F., American congressman, May 1967, *Obit* Yrbk 1972

Scott, Hugh Doggett, American senator, Sept 1948, *Obit* Sept 1994

Skinner, Samuel K., American Secretary of transportation and presidential adviser, Aug 1989

Sotomayor, Sonia, American Supreme Court justice, Oct 2009

Stanley, Winnifred Claire, congresswoman, June 1943

Stennis, John C., American senator, Jan 1953, *Obit* July 1995

Stimson, Henry Lewis, American statesman, Aug 1940, *Obit* Yrbk 1950

Udall, Morris K., American congressman, Apr 1969, *Obit* Mar 1999

Weld, William Floyd, American lawyer and former governor, Feb 1993

Wheeler, Burton K., American senator, Aug 1940, *Obit* Feb 1975

Williams, John Bell, American congressman and governor, Mar 1964, *Obit* May 1983

Divers

Coleman, Georgia, diver, *Obit* Nov 1940

Cousteau, Jacques Yves, French oceanographer, June 1953, Jan 1976, *Obit* Sept 1997

Fu Mingxia, Chinese diver, Jan 2002

Hendrickson, Sue, paleontologist, Oct 2001

Taylor, Ron, Australian photographer and skin diver, Jan 2007, *Obit* Yrbk 2012

Taylor, Valerie, Australian skin diver and photographer, Jan 2007

Drafters

Anderson, Laurie, American performance artist and musician, July 1983

Butler, Reg, Sept 1956

Canovas del Castillo, Antonio, Sept 1962

Carone, Nicolas, American painter and draughtsman, July 2006, *Obit* Yrbk 2010

Chamberlain, Samuel, American photographer and artist, Sept 1954, *Obit* Mar 1975

Chicago, Judy, American artist, Feb 1981

Dali, Salvador, Spanish painter, Sept 1940, Apr 1951, *Obit* Mar 1989

Dean, Tacita, English installation artist, May 2010

Epstein, Jacob, English sculptor and illustrator, July 1945, *Obit* Nov 1959

Gibson, Lois, American forensic artist, Mar 2008

Gross, Chaim, American sculptor, Nov 1941, Feb 1966, *Obit* July 1991

Grosz, George, American painter and cartoonist, Apr 1942, *Obit* Oct 1959

Hartung, Hans, French painter, July 1958, *Obit* Feb 1990

Hockney, David, English painter, July 1972

Lassaw, Ibram, American sculptor, Jan 1957, *Obit* Yrbk 2004

LeWitt, Sol, American sculptor, July 1986, *Obit* Yrbk 2007

Leger, Fernand, French painter, Jan 1943, *Obit* Oct 1955

Lozowick, Louis, American painter, Apr 1942, *Obit* Nov 1973

Magritte, Rene, Belgian painter, Sept 1966, *Obit* Oct 1967

Manzu, Giacomo, Italian sculptor, Mar 1961, *Obit* Mar 1991

Masson, Andre, French painter and stage designer, Nov 1974, *Obit* Jan 1988

Moore, Henry, English sculptor, Feb 1954, Feb 1978, *Obit* Oct 1986

O'Keeffe, Georgia, American painter, June 1941, Feb 1964, *Obit* Apr 1986

Oldenburg, Claes, Swedish-American sculptor, Feb 1970

Orozco, Jose Clemente, Mexican painter, Sept 1940, *Obit* Oct 1949

Pearlstein, Philip, American painter, Feb 1973

Rattner, Abraham, American painter, Mar 1948, *Obit* Apr 1978

Rivera, Diego, Mexican painter, July 1948, *Obit* Feb 1958

Serra, Richard, American sculptor, Jan 1985

Steinberg, Saul, Romanian-American illustrator and cartoonist, Mar 1957, *Obit* July 1999

Tapies, Antoni, Spanish painter and sculptor, July 1966, *Obit* Yrbk 2012

Whiteread, Rachel, English sculptor, Jan 2006

Wilson, Robert, American director, dramatist and artist, Aug 1979

Drama critics

Adler, Renata, critic, journalist, novelist and short story writer, June 1984

Anderson, John, American drama critic and playwright, *Obit* Sept 1943

Atkinson, Brooks, American drama critic, Apr 1942, Feb 1961, *Obit* Mar 1984

Barnes, Clive, British dance and drama critic, Mar 1972, *Obit* Feb 2009

Barnes, Julian, English novelist, short story writer and essayist, Mar 1988

Barrett, Wilton Agnew, American film critic, *Obit* Mar 1940

Brantley, Ben, American drama critic, Aug 2011

Brustein, Robert, American theatrical director and critic, Aug 1975

Cassidy, Claudia, drama and music critic, Sept 1955, *Obit* Oct 1996

Clurman, Harold, theatrical director and critic, Feb 1959, *Obit* Nov 1980

Crosby, John, journalist, novelist and television critic, June 1953

Crowther, Bosley, motion picture critic, July 1957, *Obit* Apr 1981

De Casseres, Benjamin, essayist, critic and journalist, *Obit* Feb 1946

Dudley, Bide, *Obit* Feb 1944

Ebert, Roger, American film critic, Mar 1997, *Obit* Yrbk 2013

Flynn, Gillian, American television critic and novelist, Apr 2013

Freedley, George, American theater historian and librarian, Sept 1947, *Obit* Nov 1967

Gassner, John, Jan 1947, *Obit* June 1967

Gilder, Rosamond, American drama critic, Nov 1945, *Obit* Oct 1986

Greene, Graham, English novelist, Oct 1969, *Obit* May 1991

Hamilton, Clayton Meeker, dramatist and critic, *Obit* Oct 1946

Kael, Pauline, American film critic, Mar 1974, *Obit* Nov 2001

Kerr, Walter, drama critic, Oct 1953, *Obit* Jan 1997

Kronenberger, Louis, drama critic, editor and author, Aug 1944, *Obit* July 1980

Lane, Anthony, British film critic, Nov 2008

Lorentz, Pare, American motion picture director, Apr 1940, *Obit* May 1992

Maltin, Leonard, American film critic and historian, Aug 2008

Mantle, Burns, American drama critic, Nov 1944, *Obit* Mar 1948

Mapes, Victor, *Obit* Jan 1944

McLuhan, Marshall, Canadian cultural critic, June 1967, *Obit* Feb 1981

Mitchell, Elvis, American film critic, July 2008

Moravia, Alberto, Italian novelist, short story writer, playwright and essayist, Apr 1970, *Obit* Nov 1990

Nathan, George Jean, drama critic, Apr 1945, *Obit* June 1958

Palmer, John Leslie, English author and critic, *Obit* Sept 1944

Reed, Rex, motion picture critic, Jan 1972

Rohmer, Eric, French film director, Apr 1977, *Obit* Yrbk 2010

Sarris, Andrew, American film critic, Jan 2007, *Obit* Yrbk 2012

Shales, Tom, American television and film critic, Jan 2009

Starr, Cecile, American film critic, Mar 1955

Tynan, Kenneth, British drama critic, Yrbk 1963, *Obit* Sept 1980

White, Armond, American film critic, Oct 2006

Woollcott, Alexander, journalist, June 1941, *Obit* Mar 1943

de Botton, Alain, English novelist and journalist, Sept 2013

Drama teachers

Adler, Stella, American actress and drama teacher, Aug 1985, *Obit* Feb 1993

Bullins, Ed, American dramatist, May 1977

Corsaro, Frank, American theatrical director and drama teacher, Aug 1975

Eustis, Oskar, American theatrical director and drama teacher, Oct 2002

Howe, Tina, American dramatist, Jan 1990

Koch, Fred, drama teacher and theatrical director, Oct 1953, *Obit* Yrbk 2000

Lasser, Louise, actress, Oct 1976

Meisner, Sanford, actor, director and teacher, Apr 1991, *Obit* Apr 1997

Parks, Suzan-Lori, American dramatist, Apr 1999

Strasberg, Lee, American actor, director and acting teacher, Oct 1960, *Obit* Apr 1982

Vogel, Paula, American dramatist, July 1998

Dramatists

Abbott, George, dramatist and producer, Apr 1940, Oct 1965, *Obit* Apr 1995

Abrams, J. J., American screenwriter and film director, July 2009

Abu-Assad, Hany, Palestinian filmmaker and screenwriter, Jan 2006

Ace, Goodman, radio and television author and actor, May 1948, *Obit* May 1982

Ade, George, American humorist, *Obit* July 1944

Affleck, Ben, American actor, Mar 1998

Akalaitis, JoAnne, American actress, dramatist and director, Feb 1993

Albee, Edward, American dramatist, Feb 1963, Apr 1996

Alexie, Sherman, American poet, novelist and screenwriter, Oct 1998

Allen, Woody, American actor, filmmaker and screenwriter, Yrbk 1966, Sept 1979

Allende, Isabel, Chilean novelist, Feb 1988

Alvarez Quintero, Joaquin, Spanish dramatist, *Obit* Aug 1944

Amado, Jorge, Brazilian novelist, Mar 1986, *Obit* Oct 2001

Amalric, Mathieu, French actor, film director and screenwriter, Feb 2011

Amari, Raja, Tunisian screenwriter and motion picture director, Jan 2002

Amichai, Yehuda, Israeli poet, Feb 1998, *Obit* Jan 2001

Anderson, Maxwell, American dramatist, Nov 1942, Sept 1953, *Obit* May 1959

Anderson, Robert, American dramatist and screenwriter, Sept 1954, *Obit* Yrbk 2009

Anderson, Wes, American film director and screenwriter, May 2002

Angelopoulos, Theodoros, Greek film director and screenwriter, *Obit* Yrbk 2012

Anouilh, Jean, French dramatist, Apr 1954, *Obit* Nov 1987

Arden, John, English playwright and novelist, Sept 1988, *Obit* Yrbk 2012

Ardrey, Robert, American playwright and screenwriter, July 1973, *Obit* Mar 1980

Aronofsky, Darren, American screenwriter and director, Feb 2009

Arrabal, Fernando, French-Spanish dramatist, Sept 1972

Arriaga, Guillermo, Mexican novelist, short story writer and screenwriter, Jan 2007

Atkinson, Kate, English novelist, Feb 2007

Attaway, William, American novelist, Yrbk 1941

Auster, Paul, American novelist, poet and essayist, Mar 1996

Austin, F. Britten, English novelist, dramatist and screenwriter, *Obit* May 1941

Ayckbourn, Alan, English dramatist and theatrical director, Jan 1980

Baitz, Jon Robin, American dramatist, Aug 2004

Baker, Frank, English author, Yrbk 1948

Baldwin, James, American novelist, playwright and

essayist, Yrbk 1959, July 1964, *Obit* Jan 1988

Ball, Alan, American film and television screenwriter and producer, Sept 2011

Baltasar Kormakur, Icelandic actor, motion picture director and screenwriter, Jan 2003

Baraka, Imamu Amiri, American poet, playwright, essayist and short story writer, May 1970

Barfield, Tanya, American playwright, Mar 2011

Barmak, Siddiq, Afghan motion picture director and screenwriter, Jan 2005

Baumbach, Noah, American film director and screenwriter, Oct 2010

Baumer, Marie, American screenwriter and novelist, Yrbk 1958

Beckett, Samuel, Irish playwright and novelist, Feb 1970, *Obit* Feb 1990

Behan, Brendan, Irish dramatist, Mar 1961, *Obit* May 1964

Behrman, S. N., dramatist, screenwriter and author, Feb 1943, *Obit* Nov 1973

Bekmambetov, Timur, Kazakhstani film director, Jan 2006

Bellow, Saul, American novelist, Feb 1965, Nov 1988, *Obit* Aug 2005

Benavente, Jacinto, Spanish dramatist, June 1953, *Obit* Sept 1954

Benrimo, J. Harry, American dramatist, theatrical director and actor, *Obit* May 1942

Benson, Sally, American short story writer, dramatist and screenwriter, Aug 1941, *Obit* Sept 1972

Berg, Gertrude, American actress and radio scriptwriter, July 1941, Sept 1960, *Obit* Nov 1966

Berri, Claude, French actor, director and screenwriter, Mar 1989, *Obit* Yrbk 2009

Bigelow, Kathryn, American film director, Mar 2010

Blatty, William Peter, American novelist, June 1974

Blitzstein, Marc, American dramatist and composer, July 1940, *Obit* Mar 1964

Bloodworth-Thomason, Linda, American television scriptwriter and producer, Feb 1993

Blum, Leon, French statesman, Nov 1940, *Obit* May 1950

Bochco, Steven, American television scriptwriter and producer, May 1991

Bogosian, Eric, American actor, playwright and monologist, Sept 1987

Bois, Jules, *Obit* Aug 1943

Boll, Uwe, German film director, producer and screenwriter, Sept 2010

Bolt, Robert, English dramatist and screenwriter, July 1963, *Obit* Apr 1995

Bond, Edward, English dramatist, June 1978

Brackett, Charles, American screenwriter and motion picture producer, Feb 1951, *Obit* Apr 1969

Bradbury, Ray, American science fiction writer, June 1953, July 1982, *Obit* Yrbk 2012

Breuer, Lee, dramatist and director, Oct 1999

Brodsky, Joseph, Russian poet, July 1982, *Obit* Apr 1996

Brook, Peter, English director and dramatist, May 1961

Brooks, Albert, American actor, director and screenwriter, Apr 1997

Brooks, James L., American screenwriter, director and producer, Apr 1998

Brooks, Mel, American actor, writer, director and producer, Sept 1974

Brown, Rita Mae, American novelist, poet, essayist and screenwriter, Sept 1986

Bulgakov, Mikhail Afanas'evich, Russian novelist and dramatist, *Obit* Mar 1940

Bullins, Ed, American dramatist, May 1977

Burnett, Charles, American film director and screenwriter, Sept 1995

Burns, Edward, American television scriptwriter and former police officer, May 2008

Burrows, Abe, American composer, lyricist, playwright

and theatrical director, Nov 1951, *Obit* July 1985

Buscemi, Steve, American actor and filmmaker, Apr 1999

Busch, Charles, American playwright, actor and female impersonator, June 1995

Cacoyannis, Michael, Greek film and theatrical director, May 1966, *Obit* Yrbk 2011

Caetano, Adrian, Argentine film director and screenwriter, Jan 2003

Caldwell, Erskine, American novelist and short story writer, Oct 1940, *Obit* May 1987

Cameron, James, Canadian film director, producer and screenwriter, Jan 1998

Canetti, Elias, Bulgarian novelist and dramatist, Jan 1983, *Obit* Oct 1994

Carlino, Lewis John, dramatist and filmmaker, May 1983

Carrington, Elaine, Feb 1944, *Obit* July 1958

Carroll, Vinnette, American actress, dramatist and theatrical director, Sept 1983, *Obit* Feb 2003

Caspary, Vera, author, dramatist and screenwriter, Yrbk 1947, *Obit* Aug 1987

Chandler, Raymond, American mystery novelist, Yrbk 1946, *Obit* June 1959

Chase, David, American television producer and scriptwriter, Mar 2001

Chase, Mary, dramatist, Oct 1945, *Obit* Jan 1982

Chayefsky, Paddy, American screenwriter and dramatist, Sept 1957, *Obit* Sept 1981

Chin, Frank, American novelist, essayist, playwright and short story writer, Mar 1999

Chodorov, Edward, American dramatist and screenwriter, Apr 1944, *Obit* Nov 1988

Chow, Stephen, Chinese actor, motion picture director and screenwriter, Jan 2003

Christie, Agatha, English mystery writer, Sept 1940, July 1964, *Obit* Mar 1976

Churchill, Caryl, English playwright, June 1985

Cimino, Michael, motion picture director, Jan 1981

Clavell, James, Australian-American novelist and screenwriter, Oct 1981, *Obit* Nov 1994

Cleese, John, English actor and humorist, Jan 1984

Clooney, George, American actor, July 2008

Collison, Wilson, *Obit* July 1941

Columbus, Chris, American film director and screenwriter, Nov 2001

Comden, Betty, American lyricist, librettist and screenwriter, Mar 1945, *Obit* Yrbk 2007

Comfort, Alex, English physician, novelist and poet, Sept 1974, *Obit* Aug 2000

Connelly, Marc, dramatist, Nov 1969, *Obit* Feb 1981

Coppola, Francis Ford, American film director, May 1974, July 1991

Coppola, Sofia, American film director and screenwriter, Nov 2003

Corman, Roger, American motion picture director, producer and screenwriter, Feb 1983

Craven, Frank, *Obit* Oct 1945

Crichton, Michael, American novelist, screenwriter and film director, Apr 1976, Nov 1993, *Obit* Apr 2009

Crouse, Russel, dramatist, June 1941, *Obit* May 1966

Crowe, Cameron, American screenwriter and film director, Mar 1996

Cushing, Charles C. S., *Obit* Apr 1941

D'Usseau, Arnaud, dramatist and screenwriter, Mar 1944, *Obit* Apr 1990

Damon, Matt, American actor, Mar 1998

Dangarembga, Tsitsi, Zimbabwean novelist and film director, Jan 2006

Dardenne, Jean-Pierre, Belgian film director and screenwriter, May 2011

Dardenne, Luc, Belgian film director and screenwriter, May 2011

Davis, J. Frank, *Obit* May 1942

Davis, Robert H., dramatist and journalist, *Obit* Yrbk 1942

Delaney, Shelagh, English playwright and screenwriter, Apr 1962, *Obit* Yrbk 2012

Didion, Joan, American novelist, essayist and journalist, Sept 1978

Dietz, Howard, American lyricist, Oct 1965, *Obit* Sept 1983

Dinehart, Alan, *Obit* Sept 1944

Donleavy, J. P., Irish novelist, dramatist and short story writer, July 1979

Donoghue, Emma, Irish novelist and dramatist, Jan 2013

Dove, Rita, American poet and short story writer, May 1994

Dowling, Eddie, Feb 1946, *Obit* Apr 1976

Downey, James, American television comedy writer, June 2008

Drabble, Margaret, English novelist and playwright, May 1981

Dunne, John Gregory, American novelist and screenwriter, June 1983, *Obit* Yrbk 2004

Durang, Christopher, American dramatist, June 1987

Duras, Marguerite, French novelist, screenwriter and film director, Nov 1985, *Obit* May 1996

Durrenmatt, Friedrich, Swiss novelist and dramatist, Feb 1959, *Obit* Apr 1991

Dyer, Gwynne, Canadian journalist and television documentary host, Jan 2006

Eckardt, Felix von, Jan 1956

Edwards, Blake, American film director, producer and screenwriter, Jan 1983, *Obit* Yrbk 2011

Eggers, Dave, American writer and publisher, July 2000

Egoyan, Atom, Canadian film director and screenwriter, May 1994

Eliot, T. S., American poet, critic and dramatist, Oct 1962, *Obit* Feb 1965

Emmerich, Roland, German film director, producer and screenwriter, Nov 2000

English, Diane, television author and producer, June 1993

Ensler, Eve, American dramatist, Aug 2002

Ephron, Nora, American screenwriter and film director, Jan 1990, *Obit* Yrbk 2012

Eszterhas, Joe, American screenwriter, Apr 1998

Farrar, John, June 1954, *Obit* Jan 1975

Farrelly, Bobby, American screenwriter and film director, Sept 2001

Farrelly, Peter, American screenwriter and film director, Sept 2001

Fassbinder, Rainer Werner, German film director and producer, May 1977, *Obit* Aug 1982

Faulkner, William, American novelist, Jan 1951, *Obit* Sept 1962

Favreau, Jon, American actor, screenwriter and film director, July 2010

Ferlinghetti, Lawrence, American poet, novelist, dramatist and publisher, June 1991

Fields, Dorothy, American lyricist and librettist, Feb 1958, *Obit* May 1974

Fields, Herbert, Feb 1958

Fitzgerald, F. Scott, American novelist and short story writer, *Obit* Feb 1941

Fitzmaurice, George, *Obit* Aug 1940

Flavin, Martin, dramatist and author, Yrbk 1943, *Obit* Feb 1968

Fo, Dario, Italian actor and dramatist, Nov 1986

Fontana, Tom, American television producer and scriptwriter, Aug 2000

Foote, Horton, American playwright, screenwriter and novelist, Aug 1986, *Obit* Yrbk 2009

Foreman, Richard, American theatrical director and playwright, July 1988

Forster, Marc, Swiss film director, Jan 2007

Fowler, Gene, author, Mar 1944, *Obit* Sept 1960

Franken, Rose, novelist and playwright, Yrbk 1941, Yrbk 1947, *Obit* Aug 1988

Fraser, Brad, Canadian dramatist, July 1995

Frayn, Michael, English dramatist and novelist, Jan 1985

Freund, Philip, Canadian novelist and short story writer, Yrbk 1948

Friedman, Bruce Jay, American novelist, short story writer and dramatist, June 1972

Friel, Brian, Irish short story writer and dramatist, June 1974

Frings, Ketti, dramatist and screenwriter, Jan 1960, *Obit* Apr 1981

Fry, Christopher, English dramatist, Feb 1951, *Obit* Yrbk 2005

Fuentes, Carlos, Mexican novelist, short story writer and essayist, Oct 1972, *Obit* Yrbk 2012

Fugard, Athol, South African dramatist, actor and director, June 1975

Fuller, Charles, American dramatist, June 1989

Fuller, Samuel, American film director, Aug 1992, *Obit* Jan 1998

Gallico, Paul, American novelist, short story writer and screenwriter, Apr 1946, *Obit* Sept 1976

Gardner, Ed, Sept 1943, *Obit* Oct 1963

Genet, Jean, French dramatist, novelist and poet, Apr 1974, *Obit* June 1986

Gibson, William, American dramatist, memoirist, poet and novelist, July 1983

Gilroy, Frank Daniel, American playwright, screenwriter and filmmaker, Oct 1965

Giraudoux, Jean, French dramatist and novelist, *Obit* Mar 1944

Golden, John, Mar 1944, *Obit* Sept 1955

Goldin, Daniel, screenwriter, June 1993

Goldman, William, American novelist and screenwriter, Jan 1995

Goldsman, Akiva, American screenwriter, Sept 2004

Goodrich, Arthur, *Obit* Aug 1941

Goodrich, Frances, American dramatist and screenwriter, Oct 1956, *Obit* Apr 1984

Goodrich, Marcus, author, Apr 1941, *Obit* Jan 1992

Gordimer, Nadine, South African novelist, Yrbk 1959, June 1980

Gordon, Ruth, actress and screenwriter, Apr 1943, Apr 1972, *Obit* Oct 1985

Gow, James Ellis, Mar 1944, *Obit* Mar 1952

Grahame-Smith, Seth, American screenwriter, Nov 2012

Grass, Gunter, German novelist, Oct 1964, July 1983

Gray, Simon, English dramatist and novelist, June 1983, *Obit* Yrbk 2008

Green, Adolph, American lyricist, librettist and screenwriter, Mar 1945, *Obit* Mar 2003

Grey, Clifford, *Obit* Nov 1941

Gribble, Harry Wagstaff, Sept 1945, *Obit* Apr 1981

Grieff, Joseph Nicholas, *Obit* Aug 1941

Gruber, Frank, American screenwriter and mystery novelist, Nov 1941, *Obit* Feb 1970

Grubin, David, American documentary filmmaker, producer and screenwriter, Aug 2002

Guare, John, American dramatist, Aug 1982

Gurney, A. R., American dramatist, July 1986

Hackett, Albert, American dramatist and screenwriter, Oct 1956, *Obit* May 1995

Hackett, Walter, *Obit* Mar 1944

Haggis, Paul, Canadian screenwriter and film director, Aug 2006

Hamilton, Cosmo, English author and dramatist, *Obit* Yrbk 1942

Hammerstein, Oscar, American lyricist and librettist, Feb 1944, *Obit* Nov 1960

Handke, Peter, Austrian novelist and dramatist, Apr 1973

Hansberry, Lorraine, American dramatist, Sept 1959, *Obit* Feb 1965

Harbach, Otto, American librettist and lyricist, July 1950, *Obit* Mar 1963

Hare, David, English dramatist and theatrical director, Aug 1983

Harjo, Joy, American poet, Aug 2001

Harris, Bernice Kelly, novelist and dramatist, Yrbk 1949

Harrison, Joan, English screenwriter and producer, May 1944, *Obit* Oct 1994

Harrower, David, Scottish dramatist, Jan 2007

Hart, Moss, American playwright, July 1940, Nov 1960, *Obit* Feb 1962

Hartley, Hal, American motion picture director and screenwriter, Aug 1995

Hauptmann, Gerhart, German dramatist, *Obit* July 1946

Havel, Vaclav, Czech dramatist and president, Mar 1985, Aug 1995, *Obit* Yrbk 2012

Hecht, Ben, American journalist, novelist, dramatist and screenwriter, Feb 1942, *Obit* June 1964

Hellman, Lillian, American playwright, May 1941, June 1960, *Obit* Aug 1984

Henley, Beth, American dramatist, Feb 1983

Herlihy, James Leo, American novelist, dramatist and actor, Sept 1961, *Obit* Jan 1994

Herskovitz, Marshall, American film and television producer, scriptwriter and director, Sept 2000

Heyward, DuBose, American novelist and dramatist, *Obit* July 1940

Hill, Abram, theatrical director, producer and dramatist, Aug 1945, *Obit* Nov 1986

Hilton, James, English novelist, Sept 1942, *Obit* Feb 1955

Hochhuth, Rolf, German dramatist, Oct 1976

Holland, Agnieszka, Polish film director and screenwriter, Jan 1998

Howe, Tina, American dramatist, Jan 1990

Hudlin, Reginald, American film and television director, May 1999

Hughes, Hatcher, American dramatist, *Obit* Nov 1945

Hughes, John, American film director, producer and

screenwriter, Sept 1991, *Obit* Yrbk 2009

Hughes, Langston, American poet, novelist, short story writer and playwright, Oct 1940, *Obit* July 1967

Hunter, Evan, American novelist, short story writer and dramatist, Yrbk 1956, *Obit* Yrbk 2005

Hunter, Kermit, dramatist, May 1959, *Obit* Sept 2001

Hurston, Zora Neale, American novelist and folklorist, May 1942, *Obit* Apr 1960

Huston, John, American film director and screenwriter, Feb 1949, Mar 1981, *Obit* Oct 1987

Hwang, David Henry, American dramatist, May 1989

Inge, William, American dramatist, June 1953, *Obit* July 1973

Innaurato, Albert, dramatist, Mar 1988

Ionesco, Eugene, French dramatist, Oct 1959, *Obit* June 1994

Istaru, Ana, Costa Rican poet, dramatist and actress, Jan 2004

Ives, David, American dramatist, Feb 2013

Jackson, Peter, New Zealand film director and screenwriter, Jan 2002

Janney, Russell, Mar 1947, *Obit* Sept 1963

Jarecki, Eugene, American film director, May 2006

Jelinek, Elfriede, Austrian novelist and dramatist, Jan 2005

Jhabvala, Ruth Prawer, British screenwriter and novelist, Mar 1977, *Obit* Yrbk 2013

Johnson, Nunnally, screenwriter, Aug 1941, *Obit* May 1977

Jones, Grover, *Obit* Nov 1940

Jones, Preston, actor and dramatist, Feb 1977, *Obit* Nov 1979

Jordan, Neil, Irish film director, screenwriter and novelist, Aug 1993

Joyce, James, Irish novelist, dramatist and poet, *Obit* Mar 1941

Kaling, Mindy, American actress, playwright and

television scriptwriter, Apr 2012

Kani, John, South African actor, theatrical director and playwright, June 2001

Kanin, Garson, dramatist and director, Jan 1941, Oct 1952, *Obit* June 1999

Karp, David, American novelist and screenwriter, Yrbk 1957, *Obit* Feb 2000

Kasdan, Lawrence, American film director and screenwriter, May 1992

Kaufman, Charlie, American screenwriter, July 2005

Kaufman, George S., American dramatist, Aug 1941, *Obit* Sept 1961

Kaufman, Millard, American screenwriter and novelist, Jan 2008, *Obit* Yrbk 2009

Kaufman, Moises, American playwright and theatrical director, Aug 2011

Kaurismaki, Aki, Finnish screenwriter and director, Jan 2003

Kazantzakis, Nikos, Greek novelist, poet, dramatist, essayist and travel writer, July 1955, *Obit* Jan 1958

Kelley, David E., American television scriptwriter and producer, May 1998

Kelly, Joe, June 1945, *Obit* July 1959

Keneally, Thomas, Australian novelist, June 1987

Kerr, Jean, American humorist and dramatist, July 1958, *Obit* May 2003

Kingsley, Sidney, dramatist, June 1943, *Obit* May 1995

Kitano, Takeshi, Japanese actor, screenwriter and director, July 1998

Knoblock, Edward, *Obit* Aug 1945

Kokoschka, Oskar, Austrian painter and dramatist, Oct 1956, *Obit* Apr 1980

Kopit, Arthur L., dramatist, Yrbk 1972

Korine, Harmony, American filmmaker, Feb 2010

Kouka, Hone, New Zealand dramatist, Jan 2004

Kozlenko, William, Oct 1941

Kramm, Joseph, actor and dramatist, July 1952

Krasna, Norman, dramatist and screenwriter, May 1952, *Obit* Feb 1985

Kubly, Herbert O., author and dramatist, Feb 1959, *Obit* Oct 1996

Kundera, Milan, Czech poet, dramatist, novelist and short story writer, Mar 1983

Kureishi, Hanif, English novelist, dramatist and screenwriter, Feb 1992

Kushner, Tony, American dramatist, July 2002

Kusturica, Emir, Bosnian motion picture director and screenwriter, Nov 2005

Labaki, Nadine, Lebanese actress, film director and screenwriter, July 2013

Lagerkvist, Par, Swedish novelist, dramatist and poet, Jan 1952, *Obit* Sept 1974

Lagerlof, Selma, Swedish novelist, Apr 1940

Lamorisse, Albert, French screenwriter, director and producer, June 1963, *Obit* July 1970

Langner, Lawrence, dramatist and producer, Sept 1944, *Obit* Feb 1963

Lao She, Chinese novelist and short story writer, Oct 1945

Lardner, Ring, American screenwriter, July 1987, *Obit* Feb 2001

Latouche, John, dramatist and lyricist, Jan 1940, *Obit* Oct 1956

Laurents, Arthur, American playwright, screenwriter and theatrical director, Nov 1984, *Obit* Yrbk 2011

Laurie, Hugh, English actor and television scriptwriter, Jan 2006

Lavery, Emmet, July 1947

Lawrence, Charles Edward, *Obit* Apr 1940

Lear, Norman, American television scriptwriter and producer, Feb 1974

Lee, Spike, American film director, screenwriter and actor, Mar 1989

Leguizamo, John, American actor and dramatist, Apr 1998

Lehrer, Jim, American television newscaster, Jan 1987

Leigh, Mike, English dramatist, motion picture director and screenwriter, June 1994

Lem, Stanislaw, Polish science fiction novelist, short story writer and physician, Oct 1986, *Obit* Yrbk 2006

Leonard, Elmore, American novelist, Sept 1985, *Obit* Yrbk 2013

Lepage, Robert, Canadian theatrical director, actor and dramatist, Apr 1995

Lerner, Alan Jay, American lyricist and librettist, July 1958, *Obit* Aug 1986

Lessing, Doris May, English novelist and short story writer, Jan 1976, Jan 1995

Letts, Tracy, American playwright, Oct 2008

Levin, Ira, American novelist, Aug 1991, *Obit* Feb 2008

Levinson, Barry, American film director and screenwriter, July 1990

Levy, Dani, Swiss actor, film director and screenwriter, Jan 2007

Levy, Eugene, Canadian actor, film director and screenwriter, Jan 2002

Lindsay, Howard, dramatist, Apr 1942, *Obit* Apr 1968

Littell, Philip, *Obit* Yrbk 1943

Logan, John, American screenwriter and playwright, Feb 2011

Longfellow, Ki, Novelist, playwright and theater producer and director, July 2012

Loos, Anita, American novelist, dramatist and screenwriter, Feb 1974, *Obit* Oct 1981

Losey, Joseph, American motion picture director, Yrbk 1969, *Obit* Aug 1984

Lucas, Craig, American dramatist, Sept 1991

Lucas, George, American film director, producer and screenwriter, Apr 1978, May 2002

Luce, Clare Boothe, American dramatist and diplomat, Nov 1942, Apr 1953, *Obit* Nov 1987

Ludlam, Charles, American actor, director and dramatist, Aug 1986, *Obit* July 1987

Ludwig, Ken, American lawyer and dramatist, May 2004

Luhrmann, Baz, Australian film director, Jan 2002

Lynch, David, American film director and screenwriter, May 1987

Lynch, Peg, Feb 1956

Mack, Nila, Yrbk 1952, *Obit* Mar 1953

Maltz, Albert, screenwriter, Jan 1940, *Obit* July 1985

Mamet, David, American dramatist, Aug 1978, Mar 1998

Mankiewicz, Joseph L., American film director, producer and screenwriter, Sept 1949, *Obit* Apr 1993

Mankowitz, Wolf, English author and screenwriter, Yrbk 1956, *Obit* Aug 1998

Mann, Emily, American dramatist and director, June 2002

Marber, Patrick, English dramatist, Jan 2007

Marling, Brit, American actress, film director and screenwriter, Oct 2011

Marshall, Garry, American television scriptwriter, producer and film director, Nov 1992

Martin, George R. R., American fantasy and science fiction writer, Jan 2004

Massee, W. Wellington, *Obit* Oct 1942

Maugham, W. Somerset, English novelist, short story writer and playwright, Jan 1963, *Obit* Jan 1966

May, Elaine, American actress, screenwriter and director, Mar 1961

Mazursky, Paul, American film director, May 1980

McCarey, Leo, American motion picture director and producer, July 1946, *Obit* Sept 1969

McClinton, Marion, American playwright and theatrical director, Jan 2009

McCullers, Carson, American novelist, Sept 1940, *Obit* Yrbk 1967

McDonagh, Martin, Irish dramatist, Aug 1998

McDuffie, Dwayne, American comic book writer, Feb 2010, *Obit* Yrbk 2011

McEwan, Ian, English novelist and short story writer, July 1993

McGroarty, John Steven, *Obit* Sept 1944

McGuane, Thomas, American novelist and screenwriter, Nov 1987

McMillan, Terry, American novelist, Feb 1993

McNally, Terrence, American dramatist, Mar 1988

Mda, Zakes, South African dramatist and novelist, Jan 2005

Medem, Julio, Spanish film director and screenwriter, Jan 2003

Merrill, James, American poet, novelist and playwright, Aug 1981, *Obit* Apr 1995

Meyers, Nancy, American screenwriter, director and producer, Feb 2002

Michaels, Lorne, Canadian television scriptwriter and producer, Aug 1999

Miller, Arthur, American dramatist, Oct 1947, Feb 1973, *Obit* July 2005

Miller, Jason, playwright and actor, Jan 1974, *Obit* Yrbk 2001

Mlodinow, Leonard, American science writer, June 2009

Montale, Eugenio, Italian poet and critic, Apr 1976, *Obit* Nov 1981

Moodysson, Lukas, Swedish screenwriter and film director, Jan 2003

Moore, Michael, American documentary filmmaker, May 1997

Morell, Parker, *Obit* Apr 1943

Morrison, Toni, American novelist, May 1979

Mortimer, John, English dramatist, novelist and lawyer, Apr 1983, *Obit* Yrbk 2009

Mosel, Tad, American dramatist, Nov 1961, *Obit* Yrbk 2008

Mumford, Ethel Watts, *Obit* Jan 1940

Mungiu, Cristian, Romanian film director, Jan 2007

Munk, Kaj, Danish clergyman, poet and dramatist, *Obit* Feb 1944

Murch, Walter, American film editor, director, screenwriter and sound designer, Apr 2000

Naylor, Gloria, American novelist, Apr 1993

Nemirovich-Danchenko, Vladimir Ivanovich, Russian dramatist and director, *Obit* June 1943

Nichols, Dudley, screenwriter, Sept 1941, *Obit* Mar 1960

Niggli, Josephina, American dramatist, poet, short story writer and novelist, Yrbk 1949

Nixon, Agnes, American television scriptwriter, Apr 2001

Nolan, Christopher, Anglo-American screenwriter and director, Jan 2005

Norman, Marsha, American dramatist, May 1984

Nottage, Lynn, American dramatist, Nov 2004

Nugent, Elliott, July 1944, *Obit* Oct 1980

O'Casey, Sean, Irish dramatist, Nov 1962, *Obit* Nov 1964

O'Donnell, E. P., *Obit* June 1943

O'Hara, Mary, author, Jan 1944, *Obit* Jan 1981

Oboler, Arch, radio author and screenwriter, Mar 1940, *Obit* May 1987

Odets, Clifford, American dramatist, Nov 1941, *Obit* Nov 1963

Osborne, John, English dramatist, June 1959, *Obit* Feb 1995

Ouedraogo, Idrissa, Burkinabe film director and screenwriter, May 1993

Pagnol, Marcel, French dramatist and motion picture director, Mar 1956, *Obit* June 1974

Palin, Michael, English actor and screenwriter, Feb 2000

Park, Chan-Wook, Korean screenwriter and film director, Jan 2004

Parker, Louis N., English composer and dramatist, *Obit* Nov 1944

Parks, Suzan-Lori, American dramatist, Apr 1999

Payne, Alexander, American motion picture director and screenwriter, Feb 2003

Peirce, Kimberly, American film director and screenwriter, Aug 2008

Peli, Oren, American film director and screenwriter, July 2013

Perelman, S. J., humorist, Mar 1971, *Obit* Jan 1980

Perrin, Jacques, French actor, film producer, director and screenwriter, Jan 2004

Perry, Frank, motion picture director and producer, Oct 1972, *Obit* Nov 1995

Phillips, Caryl, English novelist, dramatist and essayist, July 1994

Phillips, Irna, American radio and television scritpwriter and producer, Apr 1943, *Obit* Feb 1974

Pinero, Miguel, American dramatist and actor, Nov 1983, *Obit* Aug 1988

Pinter, Harold, English dramatist, Nov 1963, *Obit* July 2009

Polley, Sarah, Canadian actress and film director, Jan 2003

Pollock, Channing, dramatist, *Obit* Oct 1946

Potter, Dennis, English novelist, playwright and screenwriter, July 1994, *Obit* July 1994

Powell, Michael, British screenwriter, film director and producer, Aug 1987, *Obit* Apr 1990

Prevost, Marcel, French novelist and playwright, *Obit* June 1941

Price, Richard, American novelist and screenwriter, Jan 1994

Priestley, J. B., English novelist and dramatist, May 1976, *Obit* Oct 1984

Puzo, Mario, American novelist and screenwriter, Mar 1975, *Obit* Sept 1999

Rabe, David, American dramatist, July 1973

Rapp, Adam, American playwright and novelist, Mar 2011

Rapp, William J., *Obit* Oct 1942

Rattigan, Terence, English dramatist, Yrbk 1956, *Obit* Feb 1978

Reed, Ishmael, American novelist and poet, Oct 1986

Renoir, Jean, French film director and screenwriter, Yrbk 1959, *Obit* Apr 1979

Reza, Yasmina, French dramatist, Sept 1998

Rice, Elmer, American dramatist, Apr 1943, *Obit* July 1967

Ring, Barbara T., *Obit* Nov 1941

Robbe-Grillet, Alain, French novelist, essayist and screenwriter, Yrbk 1974, *Obit* Yrbk 2008

Rolland, Romain, French novelist, dramatist and biographer, *Obit* Feb 1945

Ross, Gary, American screenwriter, May 2004

Rossen, Robert, American motion picture director, producer and screenwriter, Oct 1950, *Obit* Mar 1966

Rosten, Norman, poet, playwright and novelist, Apr 1944, *Obit* May 1995

Royle, Edwin Milton, *Obit* Apr 1942

Russell, Ken, English motion picture director, Oct 1975, *Obit* Yrbk 2012

Rutenborn, Gunter, Oct 1960

Rylance, Mark, English actor and theatrical director, Nov 2011

Sachs, Nelly, German poet, Mar 1967, *Obit* July 1970

Salomon, Henry, Yrbk 1956, *Obit* Apr 1958

Saroyan, William, American short story writer, novelist and dramatist, July 1940, Nov 1972, *Obit* July 1981

Sarraute, Nathalie, French novelist, June 1966, *Obit* Jan 2000

Sartre, Jean Paul, French novelist and philosopher, Mar 1947, May 1971, *Obit* June 1980

Saunders, John Monk, screenwriter, *Obit* Apr 1940

Sayles, John, American novelist, short story writer, screenwriter and film director, Feb 1984

Schary, Dore, motion picture producer, May 1948, *Obit* Sept 1980

Schisgal, Murray, dramatist, Jan 1968

Schlondorff, Volker, German film director and screenwriter, Aug 1983

Schrader, Paul, American screenwriter and film director, Aug 1981

Schulberg, Budd, American novelist, playwright and screenwriter, June 1941, May 1951, *Obit* Yrbk 2009

Secondari, John H., Apr 1967, *Obit* Apr 1975

Sen, Ivan, Australian motion picture director and screenwriter, Jan 2002

Serling, Rod, American television scriptwriter and screenwriter, Yrbk 1959, *Obit* Aug 1975

Shaffer, Peter, English dramatist, May 1967, Nov 1988

Shange, Ntozake, American poet and dramatist, Sept 1978

Shaw, Bernard, Irish dramatist, June 1944, *Obit* Yrbk 1950

Shaw, Irwin, author and dramatist, Oct 1942, *Obit* July 1984

Shawn, Wallace, American actor and playwright, June 1986

Sheldon, Edward, dramatist, *Obit* May 1946

Sheldon, Sidney, American novelist, Oct 1980, *Obit* Yrbk 2007

Shepard, Sam, American dramatist, Apr 1979

Sherwood, Robert E., American dramatist, Jan 1940, *Obit* Jan 1956

Shulman, Irving, American novelist, Yrbk 1956, *Obit* June 1995

Shyamalan, M. Night, American film director and screenwriter, Mar 2003

Sigismondi, Floria, Canadian photographer and video and film director, July 2010

Simon, David, American journalist and television scriptwriter, June 2008

Simon, Neil, American playwright, Feb 1968, Mar 1989

Singer, Israel Joshua, Yiddish novelist and dramatist, *Obit* Mar 1944

Singleton, John, American film director and screenwriter, Feb 1997

Sitwell, Osbert, English poet, short story writer and novelist, Sept 1965, *Obit* June 1969

Smedley, Constance, *Obit* Apr 1941

Smith, Ali, Scottish short story writer and novelist, June 2006

Smith, Charles, American playwright, May 2011

Smith, Kevin, American screenwriter and film director, Feb 1998

Smyth, Ethel Mary, English composer, *Obit* June 1944

Soderbergh, Steven, American film director and screenwriter, Oct 1998

Soldati, Mario, Italian film director, screenwriter, novelist and short story writer, Apr 1958, *Obit* Nov 1999

Sorkin, Aaron, American television scriptwriter, June 2000

Sorokin, Vladimir, Russian novelist, Jan 2005

Soyinka, Wole, Nigerian dramatist, poet and novelist, Yrbk 1974

Spacey, Kevin, American actor and director, Apr 1997

Stallone, Sylvester, American actor and screenwriter, Oct 1977, Feb 1994

Steell, Willis, *Obit* Mar 1941

Steinbeck, John, American novelist, Jan 1940, May 1963, *Obit* Feb 1969

Stevens, George, American film and television producer, Yrbk 1965

Stewart, Donald Ogden, screenwriter, dramatist and humorist, July 1941, *Obit* Sept 1980

Stone, Oliver, American film director and screenwriter, June 1987

Stone, Robert, American novelist, Jan 1987

Stoppard, Tom, English dramatist, July 1974

Storey, David, English dramatist and novelist, Sept 1973

Sturges, Preston, American screenwriter and film director, Apr 1941, *Obit* Oct 1959

Swanberg, Joe, American film director and screenwriter, Nov 2010

Tagore, Rabindranath, Indian poet, novelist, short story writer and dramatist, *Obit* Oct 1941

Tarantino, Quentin, American film director, screenwriter and actor, Oct 1995

Taylor, Charles A., *Obit* May 1942

Tesich, Steve, American dramatist and screenwriter, Aug 1991, *Obit* Sept 1996

Theroux, Justin, American actor, Mar 2012

Tolstoy, Aleksey Nikolayevich, Russian novelist and dramatist, *Obit* Apr 1945

Towne, Robert, American screenwriter and film director, June 1989

Trevor, William, Irish novelist, short story writer and playwright, Sept 1984

Trumbo, Dalton, American screenwriter, May 1941, *Obit* Oct 1976

Ulrich, Charles, *Obit* Aug 1941

Ustinov, Peter, English actor and dramatist, Yrbk 1955, *Obit* Aug 2004

Van Druten, John, English dramatist, Feb 1944, *Obit* Feb 1958

Veiller, Bayard, dramatist, *Obit* Aug 1943

Vidal, Gore, American novelist and playwright, Feb 1965, June 1983, *Obit* Yrbk 2012

Vogel, Paula, American dramatist, July 1998

Wachowski, Andy, American film director and screenwriter, Sept 2003

Wachowski, Larry, American film director and screenwriter, Sept 2003

Walcott, Derek, Saint Lucian poet and dramatist, Apr 1984

Wald, Jerry, American motion picture producer, May 1952, *Obit* Sept 1962

Walker, Stuart, *Obit* May 1941

Walter, Eugene, American dramatist and screenwriter, *Obit* Nov 1941

Ward, Douglas Turner, American dramatist, actor and director, Sept 1976

Wasserstein, Wendy, American dramatist, July 1989, *Obit* Yrbk 2006

Waters, John, American film director, June 1990

Weidman, Jerome, author and dramatist, Aug 1942, *Obit* Jan 1999

Weiner, Matthew, American television producer and scriptwriter, Mar 2012

Weiss, Peter, German dramatist, novelist and painter, Apr 1968, *Obit* July 1982

Weitzenkorn, Louis, *Obit* Mar 1943

Weldon, Fay, English novelist, short story writer and dramatist, May 1990

Weller, Michael, American dramatist, May 1989

Wellman, Paul Iselin, American western writer, Yrbk 1949

Werfel, Franz, Austrian poet, novelist and dramatist, Yrbk 1940, *Obit* Sept 1945

Wertmuller, Lina, Italian motion picture director, Sept 1976

Wesker, Arnold, English dramatist, Feb 1962

West, Claudine, *Obit* May 1943

West, Jessamyn, American novelist, short story writer, librettist, essayist, playwright and poet, Aug 1977, *Obit* Apr 1984

West, Nathanael, American novelist and screenwriter, *Obit* Feb 1941

Whedon, Joss, American film and television scriptwriter, July 2012

White, Patrick, Australian novelist, June 1974, *Obit* Nov 1990

Wiig, Kristen, American actress, July 2013

Wilder, Billy, Austrian-American film director and screenwriter, Feb 1951, Oct 1984, *Obit* Yrbk 2002

Wilder, Thornton, American novelist and dramatist, Aug 1943, Nov 1971, *Obit* Feb 1976

Willard, John, *Obit* Nov 1942

Williams, Emlyn, Welsh playwright and actor, Feb

1941, Apr 1952, *Obit* Nov 1987

Williams, Tennessee, American dramatist, Jan 1946, Apr 1972, *Obit* Apr 1983

Williamson, Kevin, American screenwriter and director, Apr 2000

Willimon, Beau, American playwright, June 2012

Wilson, August, American playwright, Aug 1987, *Obit* Feb 2006

Wilson, Lanford, American playwright, Mar 1979, *Obit* Yrbk 2011

Wilson, Owen, American actor and screenwriter, Feb 2003

Wodehouse, P. G., English novelist, short story writer and dramatist, Nov 1971, *Obit* Apr 1975

Wolfe, George C., American dramatist and director, Mar 1994

Wong, Kar-Wai, Chinese film director and screenwriter, Apr 1998

Wood, Philip, *Obit* Mar 1940

Work, Martin H., May 1951

Wouk, Herman, American novelist and playwright, Yrbk 1952

Wright, Richard, American novelist, Mar 1940, *Obit* Jan 1961

Wylie, Max, Jan 1940, *Obit* Nov 1975

Yaffe, James, Yrbk 1957

Young, Stanley, dramatist and publishing executive, Yrbk 1951, *Obit* May 1975

Yourcenar, Marguerite, French-American novelist, poet, dramatist, essayist and translator, Nov 1982, *Obit* Feb 1988

Zaillian, Steven, screenwriter and film director, Oct 2001

Zindel, Paul, American dramatist, novelist and children's author, June 1973, *Obit* Yrbk 2007

Drummers

Allen, Rick, English drummer, Jan 2003

Barker, Travis, American drummer, Aug 2002

Bear, Christopher, American drummer, Sept 2011

Blackman, Cindy, American drummer, Oct 2010

Blakey, Art, American jazz drummer and band leader, Sept 1988, *Obit* Jan 1991

Bourdon, Rob, American drummer, Mar 2002

Bunton, Jaleel, American drummer, Apr 2009

Burnside, Jay, Finnish drummer, Jan 2003

Canty, Brendan, American drummer, Mar 2002

Carney, Patrick, American drummer, Jan 2013

Cester, Chris, Australian drummer and singer, Jan 2005

Champion, Will, English drummer, May 2004

Collins, Phil, British singer, songwriter and drummer, Nov 1986

Conneff, Kevin, Irish bodhran player and singer, Mar 2004

Conway, Gerry, English drummer, Sept 2005

Cool, Tre, American drummer, Aug 2005

Criss, Peter, American drummer, Apr 1999

Drake, Bobby, American drummer, Sept 2010

Drozd, Steven, American drummer, guitarist and keyboardist, Oct 2002

Fishman, Jon, American drummer, July 2003

Followill, Nathan, American drummer, July 2010

Gara, Jeremy, Canadian drummer, Jan 2007

Gonzalez, Alex, Mexican drummer, Jan 2005

Graham, Ed, British drummer, Jan 2004

Grohl, Dave, American singer and guitarist, May 2002

Hallahan, Patrick, American rock drummer, Nov 2008

Hampton, Lionel, American band leader, Oct 1971, *Obit* Yrbk 2002

Hart, Mickey, American drummer, Jan 1994

Helders, Matt, British rock drummer, Jan 2006

King, David, American jazz drummer, Oct 2011

Kotche, Glenn, American drummer and percussionist, Feb 2010

Kramer, Joey, American rock drummer, July 2004

Krupa, Gene, American drummer and band leader, Sept 1947, *Obit* Yrbk 1973

Moen, John, American singer and drummer, Aug 2007

Monk, T. S., American drummer, Feb 2002

Moretti, Fabrizio, Brazilian drummer, Feb 2007

Morris, Stephen, British drummer, Jan 2006

Orri Pall Dyrason, Icelandic drummer, Jan 2003

Peart, Neil, Canadian drummer, Feb 2001

Peck, James L. H., Aug 1942

Perez, Louis, American drummer, Oct 2005

Phillips, Scott, American drummer, May 2002

Prieto, Dafnis, Cuban drummer, Oct 2012

Purdie, Bernard, American drummer, Jan 2010

Rich, Buddy, American drummer and band leader, June 1973, *Obit* May 1987

Roach, Max, American jazz drummer, July 1986, *Obit* Nov 2007

Rowntree, Dave, British drummer, Nov 2003

Rudd, Phil, Australian drummer, Mar 2005

Sandoval, Jesse, American drummer, June 2007

Schneider, Christoph, German drummer, Jan 2007

Selway, Phil, English drummer, June 2001

Starr, Ringo, English drummer, Yrbk 1965

Watkins, Rone, Antiguan drummer, Jan 2004

Watts, Jeff, American jazz drummer, Apr 2008

White, Meg, American drummer, Sept 2003

Wonder, Stevie, American singer and songwriter, Mar 1975

Ecologists

Burpee, David, Mar 1955, *Obit* Aug 1980

Moffett, Mark W., American ecologist and photographer, Oct 2011

Perkins, C. H., June 1955, *Obit* Apr 1963

Rockley, Alicia Margaret Tyssen-Amherst Cecil, *Obit* Nov 1941

Strong, Lee A., *Obit* July 1941

Totty, Charles H., Jan 1940

Wiigh-Masak, Susanne, Swedish ecologist, Jan 2005

Wilson, Edward O., American myrmecologist, Oct 1979

Economic development consultants

Arnold, Edwin G., American economic development consultant and foundation official, Sept 1947, *Obit* Jan 1961

Economics teachers

Duflo, Esther, French economist, Aug 2011

Reinhart, Carmen, American economist, Mar 2012

Saez, Emmanuel, French economist, Sept 2011

Economists

Ackley, H. Gardner, American economist, diplomat and presidential adviser, Apr 1968, *Obit* May 1998

Al-Shabibi, Sinan, Iraqi banker and economist, Jan 2005

Alexander, Ruth, American economist and lecturer, Mar 1943

Alliot-Marie, Michele, French cabinet member, Jan 2003

Amin, Samir, Egyptian economist, Aug 2012

Anderson, H. Dewey, American economist, Jan 1950

Andrews, John Bertram, economist, *Obit* Feb 1943

Armey, Richard K., American political activist and former congressman, June 1995

Athey, Susan, American economist, Sept 2007

Aumann, Robert J., Israeli economist, Jan 2007

Ayres, Leonard Porter, May 1940, *Obit* Yrbk 1946

Babson, Roger W., statistician, Feb 1945, *Obit* May 1967

Backman, Jules, Apr 1952, *Obit* June 1982

Balch, Emily Greene, American economist and pacifist, Jan 1947, *Obit* Mar 1961

Barber, Mary I., American dietician and home economist, July 1941, *Obit* Apr 1963

Bartlett, Bruce R., American economist and columnist, June 2006

Bean, Louis H., agricultural economist and public opinion analyst, Nov 1948, *Obit* Oct 1994

Becker, Gary Stanley, American economist, Sept 1993

Bell, David E., American economist and government official, June 1961, *Obit* Yrbk 2000

Bell, Elliott V., economist, editor and publisher, Mar 1953, *Obit* Mar 1983

Bernanke, Ben, American economist and Federal Reserve chairman, Mar 2006

Beveridge, William Henry Beveridge, British economist, Jan 1943, *Obit* May 1963

Bevier, Isabel, home economist, *Obit* May 1942

Bigelow, Karl W., economist and educator, Feb 1949, *Obit* June 1980

Blaisdell, Thomas Charles, economist and government official, July 1949, *Obit* Feb 1989

Blough, Roy, economist, July 1950, *Obit* Sept 2000

Blunt, Katharine, home economist and nutritionist, Yrbk 1946, *Obit* Oct 1954

Boskin, Michael J., American economist and government official, Sept 1989

Bourassa, Robert, Canadian economist and political leader, Sept 1976, *Obit* Jan 1997

Brimmer, Andrew F., American economist and financial consultant, July 1968, *Obit* Yrbk 2012

Bunge, Alejandro E., *Obit* July 1943

Burns, Arthur F., American economist and diplomat, Sept

1953, Aug 1976, *Obit* Aug 1987

Burns, Eveline M., American economist and government official, Nov 1960, *Obit* Jan 1986

Calkins, Robert DeBlois, economist and foundation official, Oct 1952, *Obit* Sept 1992

Callander, W. F., Oct 1948

Cassel, Karl Gustav, *Obit* Mar 1945

Chandrasekhar, S., Indian economist and demographer, Oct 1969, *Obit* Sept 2001

Chase, Stuart, economist, Oct 1940, *Obit* Jan 1986

Cherne, Leo, economist and humanitarian, Yrbk 1940, *Obit* Mar 1999

Ciller, Tansu, Turkish political leader, Sept 1994

Clark, John Davidson, Jan 1947

Cohen, Abby Joseph, American investment adviser, June 1998

Correa, Rafael, Ecuadorian president, Jan 2007

Cortney, Philip, Jan 1958, *Obit* July 1971

Currie, Lauchlin Bernard, American economist, May 1941, *Obit* Mar 1994

Dalton, Hugh Dalton, British cabinet member, Aug 1945, *Obit* Apr 1962

Daugherty, Carroll Roop, economist, Oct 1949, *Obit* June 1988

Davis, Joseph S., July 1947, *Obit* June 1975

Delors, Jacques, French economist and government official, June 1989

Dewhurst, J. Frederic, Jan 1948, *Obit* July 1967

Diamond, Peter, American economist, Nov 2012

Djuanda, Apr 1958, *Obit* Jan 1964

Donald, W. H., July 1946

Doten, Carroll W., *Obit* Aug 1942

Douglas, Paul H., American senator and economist, Apr 1949, *Obit* Nov 1976

Drucker, Peter F., American management consultant and economist, May 1964, *Obit* Apr 2006

Duflo, Esther, French economist, Aug 2011

Eckstein, Otto, American economist, Feb 1967, *Obit* May 1984

Einaudi, Luigi, July 1948, *Obit* Jan 1962

Ely, Richard Theodore, American economist, *Obit* Nov 1943

Eyskens, Gaston, Belgian prime minister, Nov 1949, *Obit* Feb 1988

Fairchild, Henry Pratt, sociologist and economist, Yrbk 1942, *Obit* Yrbk 1957

Falkner, Roland Post, *Obit* Jan 1941

Feis, Herbert, historian, Oct 1961, *Obit* May 1972

Feldstein, Martin S., American economist and presidential adviser, May 1983

Friedman, Milton, American economist, Oct 1969, *Obit* Yrbk 2007

Fryer, Jr., Roland G., American economist, May 2012

Galbraith, James K., American economist, Feb 2006

Gardiner, Robert, July 1975

Gilder, George F., American economist and forecaster, Oct 1981

Ginzberg, Eli, American economist and educator, Mar 1966, *Obit* Yrbk 2003

Gordon, Kermit, economist, July 1963, *Obit* Aug 1976

Gordon, Lincoln, American diplomat, Feb 1962, *Obit* Yrbk 2010

Gramm, Phil, American senator and economist, May 1986

Granger, Clive W. J., British economist, Jan 2007, *Obit* Yrbk 2009

Greenspan, Alan, American economist and Federal Reserve chairman, Yrbk 1974, Jan 1989

Gronouski, John A., American postmaster general, Jan 1966, *Obit* Mar 1996

Hainisch, Michael, *Obit* Mar 1940

Hammarskjold, Dag, Swedish United Nations secretary-general, May 1953, *Obit* Nov 1961

Han, Seung-Soo, Korean economist and diplomat, Jan 2002

Hansen, Alvin Harvey, American economist, Sept 1945, *Obit* Aug 1975

Harper, Stephen, Canadian prime minister, Jan 2006

Harris, Seymour Edwin, American economist, Feb 1965, *Obit* Yrbk 1974

Hartmann, Heidi I., American economist and feminist, Apr 2003

Hauge, Gabriel, American economist, Oct 1953, *Obit* Sept 1981

Hayek, Friedrich A. von, British economist, June 1945, *Obit* May 1992

Hayes, Samuel P., Sept 1954

Heilbroner, Robert L., American economist and writer, June 1975, *Obit* Yrbk 2005

Heller, Walter W., American economist, Sept 1961, *Obit* Aug 1987

Henderson, Hazel, Anglo-American environmentalist and economist, Nov 2003

Henderson, Leon, American economist and government official, July 1940, *Obit* Jan 1987

Herrera, Felipe, Mar 1968

Hewlett, Sylvia Ann, Welsh economist and feminist, Sept 2002

Hobson, John Atkinson, British economist and journalist, *Obit* Apr 1940

Hollander, Jacob Harry, *Obit* Sept 1940

Husted, Marjorie Child, American home economist, June 1949, *Obit* Feb 1987

Ikeda, Hayato, Japanese prime minister, May 1961, *Obit* Oct 1965

Ishibashi, Tanzan, Mar 1957, *Obit* June 1973

Janeway, Eliot, economist and investment adviser, Sept 1970, *Obit* Apr 1993

Johnson, Alvin Saunders, economist, author and educator, Aug 1942, *Obit* July 1971

Johnson-Sirleaf, Ellen, Liberian president, Jan 2006

Jones, Chester Lloyd, *Obit* Mar 1941

Jordan, Virgil, Oct 1947, *Obit* June 1965

Kaiser, Philip M., American diplomat, Oct 1949, *Obit* Yrbk 2007

Katsav, Moshe, Israeli president, Feb 2001

Kaufman, Henry, American economist and financial executive, Aug 1981

Kemmerer, Edwin Walter, Oct 1941, *Obit* Feb 1946

Keynes, John Maynard, British economist, June 1941, *Obit* May 1946

Keyserling, Leon H., American economist, Jan 1947, *Obit* Sept 1987

Klaus, Vaclav, Czech president, Nov 1997

Kock, Karin, Nov 1948

Krueger, Maynard C., May 1940

Kuznets, Simon, American economist, May 1972, *Obit* Sept 1985

Kydland, Finn E., Norwegian economist, Jan 2007

Laffer, Arthur B., American economist, Feb 1982

Laidler, Harry Wellington, economist, Feb 1945, *Obit* Oct 1970

Lambsdorff, Otto von, German economist and cabinet member, May 1980, *Obit* Yrbk 2010

Lange, Oscar Richard, Polish economist, Apr 1946, *Obit* Yrbk 1965

Leacock, Stephen Butler, Canadian economist, political scientist and humorist, *Obit* May 1944

Leary, John Joseph, *Obit* Feb 1944

Leiserson, William M., Feb 1942, *Obit* Apr 1957

Leith-Ross, Frederick, Oct 1942

Leontief, Wassily W., American economist, Jan 1967, *Obit* Apr 1999

Liberman, Yevsei G., June 1968, *Obit* May 1983

Lleras Restrepo, Carlos, Colombian president, Nov 1970, *Obit* Nov 1994

Lubin, Isador, Oct 1941, Jan 1953, *Obit* Sept 1978

Madrick, Jeffrey G., American economist and journalist, Nov 2011

Magill, Roswell, Mar 1948, *Obit* Feb 1964

Marjolin, Robert E., French economist, Yrbk 1948, *Obit* June 1986

Marshall, Ray, secretary of labor, Nov 1977

Mayo, Robert P., Feb 1970

McCracken, Paul Winston, American economist and presidential adviser, Yrbk 1969, *Obit* Yrbk 2012

McWhinney, Madeline H., July 1976

Medgyessy, Peter, Hungarian economist and prime minister, Jan 2003

Mendes-France, Pierre, French statesman, Oct 1954, *Obit* Jan 1983

Menthon, Francois, French political leader, Mar 1944

Miller, Douglas, Nov 1941

Miller, James C., economist and regulatory official, May 1986

Miller, Marvin, American baseball players association executive, May 1973, *Obit* Yrbk 2013

Mills, Frederick Cecil, economist, Nov 1948, *Obit* Apr 1964

Mohammed, Ghulam, July 1954, *Obit* Nov 1956

Monnet, Jean, French economist and statesman, Sept 1947, *Obit* May 1979

Monti, Mario, Italian economist and European Commission official, Jan 2002

Moscoso, Teodoro, American diplomat and economist, Oct 1963, *Obit* Aug 1992

Moulton, Harold G., Nov 1944, *Obit* Feb 1966

Moyo, Dambisa, Zambian economist, Feb 2012

Myrdal, Gunnar, Swedish economist, Sept 1946, Mar 1975, *Obit* July 1987

Nadler, Marcus, May 1955, *Obit* June 1965

Nathan, Robert R., American economist, Sept 1941, *Obit* Nov 2001

Newcomer, Mabel, Sept 1944

Norquist, Grover, American economist and tax reform lobbyist, Oct 2007

Nourse, Edwin, American economist and presidential adviser, Oct 1946, *Obit* June 1974

Nystrom, Paul H., Mar 1951, *Obit* Oct 1969

O'Neill, Jim, economist, Oct 2013

Okun, Arthur M., American economist and presidential aide, Feb 1970, *Obit* May 1980

Oppenheimer, Franz, German sociologist and economist, *Obit* Nov 1943

Owen, A. David K., British economist, sociologist and United Nations official, May 1946, *Obit* Sept 1970

Parizeau, Jacques, Canadian economist and political leader, July 1993

Pasvolsky, Leo, May 1945, *Obit* June 1953

Pella, Giuseppe, Nov 1953, *Obit* Aug 1981

Philip, Andre, French economist and cabinet member, Aug 1943, *Obit* Sept 1970

Porter, Sylvia Field, financial columnist, Oct 1941, Apr 1980, *Obit* Aug 1991

Prebisch, Raul, Argentine economist, Yrbk 1969, *Obit* July 1986

Prentis, Henning Webb, Sept 1940, *Obit* Feb 1960

Prodi, Romano, Italian prime minister, Jan 2006

Reinhardt, Uwe E., American economist, Mar 2004

Reinhart, Carmen, American economist, Mar 2012

Riefler, Winfield W., May 1948, *Obit* June 1974

Rinfret, Pierre, American economist and financial consultant, July 1972, *Obit* Yrbk 2006

Rivlin, Alice M., American economist and government official, Oct 1982

Robey, Ralph W., American economist and journalist, May 1941, *Obit* Sept 1972

Roosa, Robert V., American investment banker and

government official, Yrbk 1962, *Obit* Mar 1994

Rosten, Leo, American economist and humorist, Oct 1942, *Obit* Apr 1997

Rostow, W. W., American economist and presidential adviser, May 1961, *Obit* July 2003

Rousseff, Dilma, Brazilian president, July 2012

Rueff, Jacques, French economist, Feb 1969, *Obit* June 1978

Sachs, Jeffrey D., American economist, Nov 1993

Saez, Emmanuel, French economist, Sept 2011

Salter, Arthur Salter, English economist and member of Parliament, May 1944

Samuelson, Paul A., American economist, May 1965, *Obit* Yrbk 2010

Saposs, David J., Nov 1940, *Obit* Jan 1969

Saulnier, Raymond J., American economist and presidential adviser, Yrbk 1957, *Obit* Yrbk 2009

Schiller, Karl, German cabinet member, Yrbk 1971, *Obit* Mar 1995

Schmidt, Helmut, German chancellor, Oct 1974

Schultze, Charles L., American economist and government official, Jan 1970

Shoup, Carl Sumner, American economist, Feb 1949, *Obit* Sept 2000

Simon, Herbert A., American social scientist, June 1979, *Obit* May 2001

Slichter, Sumner H., American economist, June 1947, *Obit* Yrbk 1959

Soule, George Henry, American economist, Yrbk 1945, *Obit* June 1970

Sperling, Gene, American economist and presidential adviser, Apr 2011

Sprinkel, Beryl W., American economist and government official, July 1987, *Obit* Yrbk 2009

Steelman, John R., American presidential aide and economist, May 1941, Nov 1952, *Obit* Nov 1999

Stein, Herbert, American economist, Mar 1973, *Obit* Feb 2000

Stephanopoulos, Stephanos, July 1955

Stern, Nicholas Herbert, British economist and government official, Jan 2007

Stigler, George Joseph, American economist and educator, July 1983, *Obit* Feb 1992

Suhr, Otto, Apr 1955, *Obit* Nov 1957

Switzer, Mary Elizabeth, Jan 1962, *Obit* Yrbk 1971

Taussig, Frank William, economist, *Obit* Yrbk 1940

Thorp, Willard Long, American economist and government official, July 1947, *Obit* July 1992

Thurow, Lester C., American economist, Nov 1990

Tobin, James, American economist, Oct 1984, *Obit* May 2002

Toledo, Alejandro, Peruvian president, Nov 2001

Tugwell, Rexford G., American territorial governor, economist and political scientist, Sept 1941, Jan 1963, *Obit* Sept 1979

Turner, Donald Frank, American government official, lawyer and economist, July 1967, *Obit* Sept 1994

Tymoshenko, Yulia, Ukrainian economist and prime minister, Jan 2006

Tyson, Laura D'Andrea, American economist and presidential adviser, Sept 1996

Vaizey, John, English economist and author, Jan 1964

Volcker, Paul A., American economist and Federal Reserve chairman, July 1973

Walker, E. Ronald, Yrbk 1956

Walsh, J. Raymond, Nov 1946

Ward, Barbara, English economist and writer, Jan 1950, Jan 1977, *Obit* July 1981

Weidenbaum, Murray L., economist and government official, Mar 1982

Welsh, Edward Cristy, economist, Jan 1967, *Obit* June 1990

White, Harry Dexter, American economist and government official, Sept 1944, *Obit* Oct 1948

Whitman, Marina von Neumann, American automobile executive and economist, Oct 1973

Wickens, Aryness Joy, economist and government official, Sept 1962, *Obit* Apr 1991

Wilcox, Clair, Yrbk 1948

Witte, Edwin E., American eonomist and government official, July 1946, *Obit* Sept 1960

Wolman, Leo, Sept 1949, *Obit* Yrbk 1961

Yunus, Muhammad, Bangladeshi banker and economist, Jan 2002

Zandi, Mark M., American economist, May 2010

Zedillo Ponce de Leon, Ernesto, Mexican president, Apr 1996

Zelomek, A. Wilbert, Yrbk 1956

Zimmerman, M. M., July 1957

Zoellick, Robert, American diplomat and international organiztation official, July 2008

Editors

Abelson, Philip H., American physicist and periodical editor, Oct 1965, *Obit* Yrbk 2004

Abramson, Jill, American newspaper executive, Sept 2011

Adler, Guido, *Obit* May 1941

Adzhubei, Aleksei I., Russian newspaper editor and son-in-law of Nikita Sergeevich Khrushchev, Sept 1964, *Obit* May 1993

Agar, Herbert, author, poet and critic, Mar 1944, *Obit* Jan 1981

Allen, Ralph, Canadian periodical editor, July 1958, *Obit* Feb 1967

Anderson, Christopher, American magazine editor, Jan 2010

Angell, Marcia, American physician and medical writer, Nov 2005

Angoff, Charles, American novelist and editor, Yrbk 1955, *Obit* July 1979

Armstrong, Hamilton Fish, foreign policy expert and periodical editor, Jan 1948, *Obit* June 1973

Ascoli, Max, American political scientist and magazine editor, Feb 1954, *Obit* Mar 1978

Ashmore, Harry S., American newspaper editor and foundation official, Sept 1958, *Obit* Apr 1998

Astor, Brooke, American socialite and philanthropist, Jan 1987, *Obit* Yrbk 2007

Bach, Richard, American inspirational writer, Oct 1973

Bacon, Charles Reade, American newspaper editor and state librarian, *Obit* June 1943

Bailey, Glenda, American magazine editor, Oct 2001

Bailey, Josiah W., American senator, Apr 1945, *Obit* Jan 1947

Baker, Charles Whiting, American civil engineer, *Obit* Aug 1941

Banning, Kendall, American magazine editor, publisher and military writer, *Obit* Feb 1945

Becker, May Lamberton, author and editor, May 1941, *Obit* July 1958

Beecroft, John, American editor, Mar 1954, *Obit* Yrbk 1966

Bennett, Lerone, American magazine editor and historian, Jan 2001

Berendt, John, American writer, Apr 1998

Binder, Carroll, journalist, May 1951, *Obit* July 1956

Bird, Caroline, July 1976

Birnie, William A. H., American magazine editor, Sept 1952, *Obit* Oct 1979

Blackwell, Betsy Talbot, American magazine editor, June 1954, *Obit* Apr 1985

Bliven, Bruce, American magazine editor, Yrbk 1941, *Obit* July 1977

Bly, Robert, American poet, critic, editor and translator, Mar 1984, Mar 1993

Bolles, Stephen, American newspaper editor and congressman, *Obit* Sept 1941

Bradlee, Benjamin C., American newspaper editor, Sept 1975

Brick, John, Yrbk 1953, *Obit* Yrbk 1973

Brickell, Herschel, Nov 1945, *Obit* July 1952

Bridges, Robert, *Obit* Nov 1941

Briney, Nancy, Jan 1954

Bromley, Dorothy Dunbar, journalist and feminist, Apr 1946, *Obit* Feb 1986

Brown, Helen Gurley, American magazine editor, Nov 1969, *Obit* Yrbk 2012

Brown, John Franklin, *Obit* Mar 1940

Brown, Tina, British journalist and magazine editor, Feb 1990

Brule, Tyler, Canadian magazine publisher, Mar 2011

Brunner, Edmund de Schweinitz, Sept 1958, *Obit* Feb 1974

Bryan, Ernest R., July 1950, *Obit* Feb 1955

Bryan, George Sands, *Obit* Feb 1944

Buckley, Christopher Taylor, American novelist, humorist and editor, Apr 1997

Buckley, Priscilla L., American magazine editor, Apr 2002, *Obit* Yrbk 2012

Buckley, William F., American magazine editor, columnist and novelist, June 1962, Oct 1982, *Obit* June 2008

Buell, Raymond Leslie, *Obit* Apr 1946

Bundy, William P., American international relations specialist, June 1964, *Obit* Feb 2001

Burnett, Hallie Southgate, author and editor, Yrbk 1954, *Obit* Nov 1991

Burnett, Whit, magazine editor and author, Apr 1941, *Obit* June 1973

Burtt, Ben, American motion picture sound designer, editor and documentary filmmaker, May 2003

Calverton, Victor Francis, American political writer, editor and literary critic, *Obit* Jan 1941

Canby, Henry Seidel, literary critic, Sept 1942, *Obit* June 1961

Canham, Erwin Dain, newspaper editor, July 1945, Jan 1960, *Obit* Feb 1982

Carraway, Gertrude Sprague, Jan 1954

Carruth, Hayden, American poet, Apr 1992, *Obit* Yrbk 2008

Carter, Hodding, American journalist and government official, Aug 1981

Carter, Hodding, American newspaper editor and publisher, July 1946, *Obit* May 1972

Case, Francis H., American senator and congressman, May 1946, *Obit* Sept 1962

Catledge, Turner, American newspaper editor, July 1975, *Obit* July 1983

Chase, Edna Woolman, magazine editor, Nov 1940, *Obit* June 1957

Chen, Eugene, Chinese newspaper executive and diplomat, *Obit* July 1944

Clarke, Arthur C., English science fiction writer, Oct 1966, *Obit* Yrbk 2008

Coblentz, Stanton Arthur, American science fiction writer and poet, June 1954

Coddington, Grace, British fashion editor, Apr 2005

Coleman, Lonnie, Yrbk 1958, *Obit* Oct 1982

Cometbus, Aaron, American magazine publisher and writer, Mar 2005

Connolly, Cyril, English essayist, critic and editor, Yrbk 1947

Costain, Thomas B., American novelist and editor, May 1953, *Obit* Yrbk 1965

Cousins, Margaret, author and editor, June 1954, *Obit* Oct 1996

Cousins, Norman, American magazine editor, writer and anti-nuclear activist, Aug 1943, Aug 1977, *Obit* Jan 1991

Cowles, Fleur, American painter and magazine editor, Apr 1952, *Obit* Yrbk 2009

Cowley, Malcolm, American literary critic, philologist and

poet, June 1979, *Obit* May 1989

Creel, George, American newspaper editor and government official, June 1944, *Obit* Jan 1954

Crider, John H., June 1949, *Obit* Sept 1966

Dabney, Virginius, American newspaper editor and historian, Sept 1948, *Obit* Mar 1996

Daniels, Jonathan, newspaper editor, Apr 1942, *Obit* Jan 1982

Daniels, Josephus, American Secretary of the navy and diplomat, Oct 1944, *Obit* Feb 1948

Davis, Watson, Yrbk 1945, *Obit* Oct 1967

Day, Dorothy, American journalist and social reformer, May 1962, *Obit* Jan 1981

Decter, Midge, social critic, Apr 1982

Dennis, Charles H., newspaper editor, *Obit* Nov 1943

Disney, Anthea, English publishing executive, June 1998

Dodge, John V., July 1960

Donovan, Carrie, American fashion editor, Sept 1999, *Obit* Feb 2002

Early, Gerald Lyn, American essayist, editor and poet, May 1995

Eliot, T. S., American poet, critic and dramatist, Oct 1962, *Obit* Feb 1965

Elliston, Herbert, June 1949, *Obit* Mar 1957

Engel, Carl, musicologist and composer, *Obit* June 1944

Epstein, Jason, American publishing executive, Aug 1990

Epstein, Joseph, American essayist, editor and critic, Mar 1990

Evans, Harold, British publishing executive, Apr 1985

Fadiman, Anne, American essayist and journalist, Aug 2005

Fallows, James M., American journalist, Nov 1996

Farrar, Margaret, crossword puzzle editor, July 1955, *Obit* Aug 1984

Fauley, Wilbur F., *Obit* Feb 1943
Faulkner, Nancy, Yrbk 1956
Feldmann, Markus, June 1956, *Obit* Jan 1959
Felker, Clay, American magazine founder and editor, Feb 1975, *Obit* Yrbk 2008
Finley, John Huston, Mar 1940
Fischer, John, May 1953, *Obit* Oct 1978
Fishbein, Morris, American periodical editor and physician, May 1940, *Obit* Nov 1976
Foley, Martha, author and magazine editor, Apr 1941, *Obit* Oct 1977
Ford, Worthington C., American historian, editor and bibliographer, *Obit* Apr 1941
Forrest, Wilbur S., May 1948, *Obit* May 1977
Frankel, Max, newspaper editor, Apr 1987
Fuller, Bonnie, American magazine editor, May 2000
Fuoss, Robert M., Feb 1959, *Obit* Mar 1980
Gainza Paz, Alberto, Argentine newspaper publisher, Apr 1951, *Obit* Feb 1978
Galassi, Jonathan, American editor, poet and translator, Sept 1999
Garrison, Deborah, American poet and editor, Jan 2001
Gayda, Virginio, Sept 1940, *Obit* Sept 1943
George, Manfred, German newspaper editor and writer, Oct 1965, *Obit* Feb 1966
Gessen, Keith, American magazine editor, novelist and critic, Sept 2008
Ghezali, Salima, Algerian newspaper editor, May 1998
Gillis, James M., priest, June 1956, *Obit* June 1957
Gingrich, Arnold, magazine editor and book collector, Feb 1961, *Obit* Sept 1976
Giroux, Robert, American editor and publisher, Nov 1982, *Obit* Yrbk 2008
Golden, Harry Lewis, American newspaper publisher and essayist, Jan 1959, *Obit* Nov 1981
Gottlieb, Robert Adams, American editor and

publishing executive, Sept 1987
Gould, Beatrice Blackmar, magazine editor, Nov 1947, *Obit* Apr 1989
Gould, Bruce, magazine editor, Nov 1947, *Obit* Oct 1989
Griffin, Marvin, American governor, June 1956, *Obit* Aug 1982
Grimes, W. H., June 1947, *Obit* Mar 1972
Grosvenor, Gilbert Hovey, magazine editor, Yrbk 1946, *Obit* Mar 1966
Grosvenor, Melville Bell, periodical editor, Apr 1960, *Obit* June 1982
Gumbel, Bryant, American television newscaster, July 1986
Guptill, Arthur L., Mar 1955, *Obit* May 1956
Guthman, Edwin O., American newspaper editor, June 1950, *Obit* Yrbk 2008
Haffajee, Ferial, South African newspaper editor, Jan 2004
Haley, William, English newspaper editor and broadcasting executive, Apr 1948, *Obit* Oct 1987
Hamill, Pete, American journalist and novelist, Feb 1998
Hamlin, Clarence Clark, American lawyer and newspaper executive, *Obit* Yrbk 1940
Hansberry, Lorraine, American dramatist, Sept 1959, *Obit* Feb 1965
Hansen, Harry, editor and critic, Yrbk 1942, *Obit* Yrbk 1991
Harding, Margaret S., Apr 1947
Harewood, George Henry Hubert Lascelles, English editor and writer on opera, Jan 1965, *Obit* Yrbk 2011
Harris, E. Lynn, American novelist, June 1996, *Obit* Yrbk 2009
Hastreiter, Kim, American magazine editor and publisher, Aug 2010
Hebert, F. Edward, American congressman, Nov 1951, *Obit* Feb 1980
Hektoen, Ludvig, Yrbk 1947, *Obit* Sept 1951
Henry, Mellinger Edward, *Obit* Mar 1946

Herbert, Bob, American columnist, Oct 1998
Herbert, Elizabeth, Feb 1954
Heuven Goedhart, Gerrit Jan van, Oct 1952, *Obit* Sept 1956
Hibbs, Ben, magazine editor, July 1946, *Obit* May 1975
Hickey, Margaret A., feminist and lawyer, Yrbk 1944, *Obit* Feb 1995
Higgins, F. R., Irish poet, *Obit* Mar 1941
Hoge, James F., American newspaper executive and magazine editor, Apr 1998
Hooper, Franklin Henry, *Obit* Oct 1940
Hornblow, Arthur, *Obit* June 1942
Houston, Robert Griffith, American congressman and newspaper publisher, *Obit* Mar 1946
Hoving, Thomas, American museum director and periodical editor, Apr 1967, *Obit* Yrbk 2010
Howe, Harrison E., *Obit* Feb 1943
Howe, Irving, American literary critic and editor, Apr 1978, *Obit* July 1993
Howe, Quincy, American journalist, Nov 1940, *Obit* Apr 1977
Hoyt, Palmer, American newspaper editor and publisher, Sept 1943, *Obit* Aug 1979
Hutchinson, Paul, American clergyman, magazine editor and writer, Yrbk 1949, *Obit* June 1956
Ingersoll, Ralph, American journalist, July 1940, *Obit* May 1985
Jagendorf, M. A., Yrbk 1952
Jay, Peter, Oct 1978
Jensen, Oliver, American magazine editor and historian, May 1945, *Obit* Yrbk 2005
Joesten, Joachim, June 1942
Johnson, Boris, British mayor, Oct 2008
Johnson, Clifton, *Obit* Jan 1940
Jones, Howard P., American diplomat, July 1963, *Obit* Nov 1973
Jones, Russell, Oct 1957, *Obit* Aug 1979

Jose, F. Sionil, Filipino novelist, Jan 2005

Just, Ward S., American novelist, May 1989

Kaempffert, Waldemar, Sept 1943, *Obit* Feb 1957

Karsner, David, *Obit* Apr 1941

Keller, Bill, American newspaper editor, Oct 2003

Kennedy, John F., American lawyer, magazine editor and son of President John F. Kennedy, Jan 1996, *Obit* Sept 1999

Kirchwey, Freda, American magazine editor, Yrbk 1942, *Obit* Feb 1976

Klein, Herbert G., American newspaper executive and presidential aide, Feb 1971, *Obit* Yrbk 2009

Knappstein, Karl Heinrich, Feb 1965

Korda, Michael, British editor, essayist, novelist and memoirist, Aug 1985

Kristol, Irving, American political commentator, Sept 1974, *Obit* Nov 2009

Krock, Arthur, American journalist, Feb 1943, *Obit* June 1974

Kunitz, Stanley, American poet, Mar 1943, Nov 1959, *Obit* Aug 2006

La Gorce, John Oliver, Nov 1954, *Obit* Feb 1960

LaFarge, John, American priest, Nov 1942, *Obit* Jan 1964

Lane, Gertrude Battles, magazine editor, *Obit* Nov 1941

Lapham, Lewis H., American journalist and magazine editor, Mar 1989

Laughlin, James, American publisher and poet, May 1982, *Obit* Jan 1998

Lawrence, Charles Edward, *Obit* Apr 1940

Lee, Stan, American comic book writer and editor, Aug 1993

Lelyveld, Joseph, American newspaper editor, Nov 2005

Lessing, Bruno, author and newspaper editor, *Obit* Jan 1940

Lipinski, Anne Marie, American journalist, July 2004

Lipschitz, Chaim U., Yrbk 1966

Littledale, Clara Savage, Oct 1946, *Obit* Mar 1956

Loveman, Amy, June 1943, *Obit* Feb 1956

Lowry, Edward George, *Obit* Sept 1943

Luce, Henry Robinson, American magazine editor and publisher, July 1941, Jan 1961, *Obit* Apr 1967

Lynes, Russell, essayist and periodical editor, Nov 1957, *Obit* Nov 1991

Lyons, Eugene, American journalist and biographer, Jan 1944, *Obit* Mar 1985

MacAlarney, Robert Emmet, *Obit* Jan 1946

MacNeil, Neil, American newspaper editor, May 1940

Macy, George, Nov 1954, *Obit* Sept 1956

Mankoff, Robert, American cartoonist, May 2005

Marden, Orison Swett, author and magazine editor, July 1967, *Obit* Oct 1975

Markel, Lester, newspaper editor, Yrbk 1952, *Obit* Jan 1978

Marquis, Albert Nelson, *Obit* Feb 1944

Marshall, Verne, American newspaper editor, Feb 1941, *Obit* May 1965

Martell, Edward, Nov 1964

Martin, Joseph William, American congressman and Speaker of the House, Oct 1940, May 1948, *Obit* Apr 1968

Matalin, Mary, American publishing executive and political consultant, Sept 1996

Maxwell, William, American novelist, short story writer and magazine editor, Yrbk 1949, *Obit* Oct 2000

Maynard, Robert, American newspaper editor and publisher, June 1986, *Obit* Oct 1993

Mayo, Charles W., Nov 1941, Nov 1954, *Obit* Oct 1968

McCormick, Robert Rutherford, American newspaper editor and publisher, Aug 1942, *Obit* May 1955

McCullough, David G., American historian and biographer, Jan 1993

McDonald, Erroll, publishing executive, Oct 1999

McGarry, William J., *Obit* Nov 1941

McKelway, B. M., Jan 1958, *Obit* Oct 1976

McKenna, Francis Eugene, American chemist and editor, May 1966, *Obit* Feb 1979

McKinney, Robert, American newspaper editor and publisher, Jan 1957, *Obit* Yrbk 2001

McLaughlin, John, American television commentator and moderator, July 1987

McMillan, Terry, American novelist, Feb 1993

McPherson, James Alan, American short story writer, essayist and editor, Sept 1996

McWilliams, Carey, American lawyer, magazine editor and nonfiction writer, Oct 1943, *Obit* Aug 1980

Meloney, Marie Mattingly, *Obit* Aug 1943

Merrill, John Douglas, *Obit* Jan 1940

Merz, Charles, newspaper editor, Nov 1954, *Obit* Nov 1977

Michel, Sia, American magazine editor, Sept 2003

Michnik, Adam, Polish member of Parliament and newspaper editor, July 1990

Millard, Bailey, *Obit* May 1941

Mirabella, Grace, magazine editor, Oct 1991

Mohamad, Goenawan, Indonesian poet and magazine editor, Jan 2007

Moir, Phyllis, Apr 1942

Momaday, N. Scott, American novelist, poet and editor, Apr 1975

Monroque, Shala, American magazine editor, Jan 2012

Moraes, F. R., Nov 1957, *Obit* July 1974

Morgan, Joy Elmer, Jan 1946

Morgan, Piers, British talk show host, July 2012

Morris, Willie, American writer and magazine editor, Jan 1976, *Obit* Oct 1999

Moser, Fritz, June 1955

Moss, Adam, American magazine editor, Mar 2004

Motherwell, Hiram, *Obit* Jan 1946

Mowery, Edward J., American journalist, Nov 1953, *Obit* Feb 1971

Muir, Malcolm, Apr 1953, *Obit* Mar 1979

Munoz Marin, Luis, Puerto Rican governor, Oct 1942, Nov 1953, *Obit* June 1980

Munro, Leslie Knox, Nov 1953, *Obit* Apr 1974

Murch, Walter, American film editor, director, screenwriter and sound designer, Apr 2000

Murray, John Courtney, American priest and theologian, May 1961, *Obit* Oct 1967

Myasnikova, Yelena, Russian magazine editor, Jan 2002

Navasky, Victor S., American journalist, May 1986

Nichols, Herbert B., American science journalist, Sept 1947

Nichols, William I., June 1958

Nock, Albert Jay, American literary critic and essayist, May 1944, *Obit* Sept 1945

Northrop, Peggy, American magazine editor, Nov 2009

Nye, Gerald Prentice, American senator, Nov 1941, *Obit* Sept 1971

O'Brien, Edward J., editor and critic, *Obit* Apr 1941

Okrent, Daniel, American newspaper editor, Nov 2004

Onassis, Jacqueline Kennedy, wife of American president John F. Kennedy and Greek-Argentine shipping executive Aristotle Socrates Onassis, Oct 1961, *Obit* July 1994

Oursler, Fulton, editor and author, Oct 1942, *Obit* July 1952

Parker, Robert B., American mystery writer, Nov 1993, *Obit* Yrbk 2010

Patterson, Alicia, American newspaper editor and publisher, Nov 1955, *Obit* Sept 1963

Patterson, Eleanor Medill, American newspaper editor and publisher, Nov 1940, *Obit* Sept 1948

Patterson, Joseph Medill, American newspaper editor and publisher, Jan 1942, *Obit* June 1946

Peltz, Mary Ellis, Apr 1954, *Obit* Jan 1982

Perlman, Philip B., American solicitor general, July 1952, *Obit* Oct 1960

Peters, Charles, periodical editor, Aug 1990

Phillips, Harry Irving, American newspaper columnist and humorist, Sept 1943, *Obit* Apr 1965

Phillips, Lena Madesin, Apr 1946, *Obit* July 1955

Phillips, William, American periodical editor, Oct 1984, *Obit* Yrbk 2002

Pierce, Lorne, Nov 1956

Piercy, Marge, American poet and novelist, Nov 1994

Plimpton, George, American essayist, sportswriter and periodical editor, Feb 1969, *Obit* Jan 2004

Podhoretz, Norman, American magazine editor and political commentator, Oct 1968

Pogrebin, Letty Cottin, journalist and feminist, Nov 1997

Pollan, Michael, American nature writer and magazine editor, Oct 2007

Pratt, Jane, American magazine editor and talk show host, June 1999

Priest, J. Percy, Sept 1950, *Obit* Yrbk 1956

Proulx, Annie, American novelist and short story writer, Apr 1995

Pulitzer, Joseph, American newspaper editor and publisher, Yrbk 1954, *Obit* May 1955

Pusey, Merlo J., newspaper editor and biographer, July 1952, *Obit* Jan 1986

Quiller-Couch, Arthur Thomas, English novelist, short story writer, essayist, poet and critic, *Obit* July 1944

Ramm, Fredrik, *Obit* Jan 1944

Rapp, William J., *Obit* Oct 1942

Raskin, A. H., newspaper reporter and editor, May 1978, *Obit* Feb 1994

Reavis, Smith Freeman, *Obit* Mar 1940

Reed, Ishmael, American novelist and poet, Oct 1986

Reeves, Jesse S., *Obit* Aug 1942

Reid, Ogden R., American congressman and newspaper publisher, Feb 1956

Reid, Whitelaw, American newspaper editor and publisher, Yrbk 1954, *Obit* Yrbk 2009

Remnick, David, American journalist and editor, Oct 1998

Rhys, Ernest, English editor, critic and poet, *Obit* Jan 1946

Roach, Mary, American writer, Jan 2011

Robinson, Maurice R., Yrbk 1956, *Obit* May 1982

Rosenthal, A. M., American newspaper editor, Yrbk 1960, *Obit* Sept 2006

Ross, Harold Wallace, American periodical editor, May 1943, *Obit* Jan 1952

Rosset, Barney, American publisher and editor, Apr 1972, *Obit* Yrbk 2012

Rowell, Chester Harvey, newspaper editor, Yrbk 1940, *Obit* May 1948

Royster, Vermont, American journalist, Yrbk 1953, *Obit* Oct 1996

Rubenstein, Atoosa, American magazine editor, Oct 2004

Rushkoff, Douglas, American nonfiction writer and novelist, Nov 2013

Sagendorph, Robb, American magazine editor and publisher, Yrbk 1956, *Obit* Sept 1970

Salisbury, Harrison Evans, American journalist, July 1955, Jan 1982, *Obit* Sept 1993

Saralegui, Cristina, American television talk show host, Jan 1999

Saunders, Carl M., June 1950, *Obit* Nov 1974

Schanberg, Sydney, journalist, Aug 1990

Schlosser, Alex L., American newspaper and magazine editor, *Obit* Mar 1943

Schoonmaker, Thelma, American film editor, Mar 1997

Schricker, Henry F., American governor, Sept 1950, *Obit* Feb 1967

Scoggin, Margaret Clara, American librarian, July 1952, *Obit* Sept 1968

Seltzer, Louis B., Yrbk 1956, *Obit* June 1980

Sey, Abdoulie, Gambian newspaper editor, Jan 2004

Seymour, Lesley Jane, magazine editor, Nov 2001

Shafer, Paul W., American congressman, July 1952, *Obit* Oct 1954

Shafik, Doria, May 1955

Shepilov, Dmitrii Trofimovich, Yrbk 1955

Shortz, Will, American editor and puzzle maker, Apr 1996

Simpson, J. A., English editor and lexicographer, Jan 2003

Skillin, Edward S., magazine editor and publisher, May 1949, *Obit* Yrbk 2000

Sloan, Samuel, *Obit* May 1945

Smith, Rex, Jan 1942

Smith, Thomas R., *Obit* June 1942

Soth, Lauren K., newspaper editor, Yrbk 1956, *Obit* June 1998

Spectorsky, A. C., Jan 1960, *Obit* Mar 1972

Spender, John A., English newspaper editor, *Obit* Aug 1942

Staples, Brent, American journalist and memoirist, May 2000

Steiner, George, American literary critic, short story writer and novelist, Oct 1983

Stengel, Richard, American journalist and magazine editor, Jan 2011

Stevenson, E. Robert, Jan 1940

Stine, R. L., American children's author, Sept 1999

Stockbridge, Frank Parker, *Obit* Jan 1941

Stoller, Debbie, American magazine editor and feminist, Aug 2007

Stone, I. F., American journalist, Sept 1972, *Obit* Aug 1989

Storke, Thomas M., American newspaper editor and publisher, Yrbk 1963

Stout, Wesley Winans, June 1941, *Obit* Jan 1972

Straus, Michael W., June 1952

Stummvoll, Josef Leopold, June 1960

Sullivan, A. M., Yrbk 1953, *Obit* Aug 1980

Sullivan, Walter, American science writer, Sept 1980, *Obit* June 1996

Swope, Herbert Bayard, journalist, Nov 1944, *Obit* Sept 1958

Taber, Gladys Bagg, editor and author, Yrbk 1952, *Obit* May 1980

Talese, Nan A., American publishing executive, Sept 2006

Talley, Andre Leon, American fashion editor, July 2003

Tarchiani, Alberto, Jan 1950, *Obit* Jan 1965

Thompson, Holland, *Obit* Yrbk 1940

Thompson, Oscar, *Obit* Aug 1945

Tilberis, Liz, British magazine editor, Nov 1998, *Obit* July 1999

Tobin, Richard, journalist, editor and author, Nov 1944, *Obit* Nov 1995

Tong, Hollington K., Taiwanese diplomat, Yrbk 1956, *Obit* Feb 1971

Trimble, Vance H., Yrbk 1960

Truss, Lynne, English humorist, novelist and critic, July 2006

Tvardovskii, A., Russian poet, May 1971, *Obit* Feb 1972

Van Doren, Irita, American newspaper editor, Sept 1941, *Obit* Feb 1967

Vanden Heuvel, Katrina, American magazine editor and publisher, May 2009

Vandenberg, Arthur H., American senator, Nov 1940, June 1948, *Obit* May 1951

Vanderbilt, Amy, Feb 1954, *Obit* Feb 1975

Vitug, Marites, Filipino journalist, Jan 2005

Vreeland, Diana, American magazine editor, Feb 1978, *Obit* Oct 1989

Walker, Alice, American novelist, poet, essayist and short story writer, Mar 1984

Walker, Stanley, newspaper editor, Nov 1944, *Obit* Jan 1963

Wallace, DeWitt, periodical editor and publisher, Apr

1944, May 1956, *Obit* May 1981

Waymack, W. W., Mar 1947, *Obit* Jan 1961

Weeks, Edward, editor and essayist, Yrbk 1947, *Obit* May 1989

Weisberg, Jacob, American journalist, Oct 2007

Weisgal, Meyer W., Oct 1972, *Obit* Nov 1977

Wesley, Valerie Wilson, American novelist, children's author and periodical editor, July 2002

White, Robert M., American newspaper editor and publisher, Mar 1960

White, Trumbull, *Obit* Feb 1942

White, William Allen, newspaper editor, Nov 1940, *Obit* Apr 1944

Whitehill, Walter Muir, June 1960, *Obit* May 1978

Wickenden, Dan, author and editor, Yrbk 1951, *Obit* Feb 1990

Wickware, Francis Graham, *Obit* Yrbk 1940

Wiggins, James Russell, American newspaper editor and diplomat, Nov 1969, *Obit* Mar 2001

Williams, John Alfred, American novelist, Oct 1994

Winchester, Alice, magazine editor, Feb 1954

Wintour, Anna, British fashion editor, July 1990

Wise, Robert, American film director, Sept 1989, *Obit* Apr 2006

Woodlock, Thomas Francis, *Obit* Sept 1945

Woods, Donald, South African newspaper editor, Feb 1982, *Obit* Nov 2001

Woodson, Carter Godwin, American historian, Feb 1944, *Obit* Yrbk 1984

Woodward, Bob, American journalist, Nov 1976

Young, Marian, June 1952, *Obit* Jan 1974

Yust, Walter, Apr 1943, *Obit* Apr 1960

Zim, Herbert S., American educator and science writer, Sept 1956, *Obit* Feb 1995

Educational consultants

Brock, William Emerson, American senator and Secretary of labor, May 1971

Educational reformers

Flesch, Rudolf Franz, American educational reformer, Apr 1948, *Obit* Nov 1986

Meier, Deborah, American educational reformer and school principal, May 2006

Educational services executives

Chauncey, Henry, American educational testing service executive, July 1951, *Obit* Mar 2003

Educators

Acheson, Albert R., American mechanical and electrical engineer, *Obit* Apr 1941

Adams, Diana, dancer and teacher, Apr 1954, *Obit* Mar 1993

Adams, Roger, American chemist, June 1947, *Obit* Sept 1971

Adler, Mortimer J., American philosopher and educator, Apr 1940, Sept 1952, *Obit* Sept 2001

Afro, Nov 1958

Agacinski, Sylviane, Feb 2012

Agar, William, American geologist, May 1949, *Obit* July 1972

Aguirre Cerda, Pedro, Chilean president, Jan 1941, *Obit* Jan 1941

Ahmed, Leila, Egyptian Islamist, Jan 2004

Ajami, Fouad, Lebanese-American Islamic and Middle Eastern studies specialist, Feb 2007

Al-Hilali, Ahmad Najib, July 1952, *Obit* Mar 1959

Albers, Josef, German painter and printmaker, June 1962, *Obit* May 1976

Alexander, Lamar, American senator, July 1991

Alger, Ellice M., American ophthalmologist, *Obit* Apr 1945

Allen, Arthur Augustus, American ornithologist, Jan 1961, *Obit* Mar 1964

Allen, Betty, American opera singer, Nov 1990, *Obit* Yrbk 2009

Allen, Edgar, American anatomist, *Obit* Mar 1943

Allen, James Edward, American government official and educator, June 1969, *Obit* Yrbk 1971

Allen, Martha F., American social worker and youth leader, Oct 1959

Allyn, Lewis B., American food chemist, *Obit* Jan 1940

Almada, Martin, Paraguayan educator, lawyer and human rights activist, Jan 2004

Altizer, Thomas J. J., American theologian, June 1967

Ammons, A. R., American poet, Feb 1982, *Obit* July 2001

Anderson, Don L., American geophysicist, Oct 2002

Anderson, Gaylord W., American physician, Feb 1953

Anderson, Howard R., American educator, Jan 1955

Anderson, Winston A., American biologist, Mar 2007

Antoine, Josephine, American opera singer, Aug 1944

Appiah, Anthony, American professor of African-American studies, June 2002

Archer, Glenn L., May 1949

Arciniegas, German, Colombian historian, May 1954, *Obit* June 2000

Arnesen, Liv, Norwegian teacher and cross-country skier, June 2001

Arnett, Jeffrey Jensen, American psychologist, Feb 2011

Arsuaga, Juan Luis, Spanish paleontologist, Jan 2006

Athey, Susan, American economist, Sept 2007

Auden, W. H., Anglo-American poet, Sept 1971, *Obit* Nov 1973

Aumann, Robert J., Israeli economist, Jan 2007

Ayala, Francisco, American geneticist, Oct 2012

Aydelotte, Frank, educator, Oct 1941, Apr 1952, *Obit* Feb 1957

Ayer, A. J., British philosopher, May 1964, *Obit* Aug 1989

Ayers, William, American educator, Apr 2009

Azimi, Abdul Salam, Afghan supreme court justice, Jan 2006

Bacon, Selden Daskam, sociologist, May 1952, *Obit* Feb 1993

Badinter, Elisabeth, French philosopher, Nov 2011

Bagley, William Chandler, American educator, *Obit* July 1946

Bakke, E. Wight, Sept 1953, *Obit* Jan 1972

Banda, Joyce, Malawian entrepreneur, educator and social activist, Apr 2013

Banfield, Edward C., American political scientist, May 1972, *Obit* Feb 2000

Banfield, Jillian Fiona, Australian geologist, Feb 2000

Banzhaf, John F., law professor, Yrbk 1973

Barbour, Henry Gray, American pharmacologist, *Obit* Nov 1943

Bardeen, John, American physicist and electrical engineer, Sept 1957, *Obit* Apr 1991

Barker, Lewellys Franklin, American physician, *Obit* Sept 1943

Barnard, James Lynn, American political scientist, *Obit* Oct 1941

Barnes, Clifford Webster, American clergyman and sociologist, *Obit* Nov 1944

Barney, Samuel E., American civil engineer, *Obit* Mar 1940

Barnouw, Erik, American sociologist, Nov 1940, *Obit* Oct 2001

Barrett, William, professor of philosophy, Aug 1982, *Obit* Nov 1992

Bartol, William Cyrus, American mathematician, *Obit* Yrbk 1940

Barton, Jacqueline K., American chemist, Sept 2006

Bassler, Bonnie L., American molecular biologist, Apr 2003

Baumgartner, Leona, American physician and public health

official, Jan 1950, *Obit* Mar 1991

Baur, Bertha, American music teacher, *Obit* Nov 1940

Baxter, Frank C., American professor of English and television personality, Mar 1955

Baxter, James Phinney, American historian, July 1947, *Obit* Aug 1975

Beard, Charles Austin, American historian, Mar 1941, *Obit* Oct 1948

Becker, Gary Stanley, American economist, Sept 1993

Bell, Bernard Iddings, clergyman and educator, Apr 1953, *Obit* Yrbk 1959

Bell, Daniel, American sociologist, Yrbk 1973, *Obit* Yrbk 2011

Bell, David E., American economist and government official, June 1961, *Obit* Yrbk 2000

Bell, Derrick A., American law professor, Feb 1993, *Obit* Yrbk 2011

Bell, Terrel Howard, American Secretary of education, May 1976, *Obit* Sept 1996

Bell, Thomas M., *Obit* May 1941

Bennett, H. S., anatomist, Apr 1966, *Obit* Oct 1992

Bennett, William John, American political commentator, Sept 1985

Benzer, Seymour, American biophysicist, May 2001, *Obit* Yrbk 2008

Berger, Peter L., American sociologist, Mar 1983

Berio, Luciano, Italian composer, Mar 1971, *Obit* Yrbk 2003

Berlitz, Charles, American educator and writer on the paranormal, Feb 1957, *Obit* Yrbk 2004

Berry, Martha, Apr 1940, *Obit* Apr 1942

Bestor, Arthur, American historian, Sept 1958, *Obit* Feb 1995

Bestor, Arthur E., American educator, *Obit* Mar 1944

Bevan, Arthur Dean, American surgeon, *Obit* Aug 1943

Bevier, Isabel, home economist, *Obit* May 1942

Bigelow, Karl W., economist and educator, Feb 1949, *Obit* June 1980

Bigelow, William P., American music teacher, *Obit* May 1941

Billington, James H., American historian and Librarian of Congress, May 1989

Binkley, Robert Cedric, American historian, *Obit* May 1940

Birge, Raymond T., American physicist, Mar 1940

Black, Cathleen, American school superintendent and former magazine executive, Jan 1998

Blackburn, Elizabeth H., Australian molecular biologist, July 2001

Blackfan, K. D., American pediatrician, *Obit* Jan 1942

Blaisdell, Thomas Charles, economist and government official, July 1949, *Obit* Feb 1989

Blakeslee, Francis D., American clergyman, educator and prohibitionist, *Obit* Nov 1942

Blalock, Alfred, American surgeon, Sept 1946, *Obit* Nov 1964

Blanch, Arnold, American painter, May 1940, Jan 1954, *Obit* Yrbk 1968

Blanchard, Hazel A., American school principal, June 1963

Bloom, Allan David, philosopher, Mar 1988, *Obit* Nov 1992

Bloom, Paul, June 2012

Blunt, Katharine, home economist and nutritionist, Yrbk 1946, *Obit* Oct 1954

Boguslawski, Moissaye, American pianist, composer and teacher, *Obit* Oct 1944

Bois, Yve-Alain, French art historian, Jan 2005

Bok, Sissela, philosopher, Jan 1996

Bond, Horace Mann, educator, Mar 1954

Bonham, Milledge Louis, American historian, *Obit* Mar 1941

Borcherds, Richard, English mathematician, Feb 1999

Boring, E. G., American psychologist, Mar 1962, *Obit* Sept 1968

Borne, Mortimer, Apr 1954

Borst, Lyle B., American nuclear physicist, July 1954, *Obit* Yrbk 2002

Boskin, Michael J., American economist and government official, Sept 1989

Bosselaar, Laure-Anne, Belgian poet, Sept 2006

Boulanger, Nadia, French conductor and teacher, May 1962, *Obit* Jan 1980

Boyd, Julian P., historian and librarian, June 1976, *Obit* Aug 1980

Bradbury, Norris Edwin, physicist, Apr 1949, *Obit* Nov 1997

Bradshaw, John E., American philosopher, educator and writer, Apr 1993

Bragg, William Henry, British physicist, *Obit* Apr 1942

Brameld, Theodore, professor of education, June 1967, *Obit* Jan 1988

Braun, Werner, German microbiologist, June 1957, *Obit* Jan 1973

Brazelton, T. Berry, pediatrician, Oct 1993

Breckenridge, L. P., American mechanical engineer, *Obit* Oct 1940

Bridgman, P. W., American physicist, Apr 1955, *Obit* Nov 1961

Brier, Bob, American Egyptologist, Sept 2002

Brigham, Carl C., *Obit* Mar 1943

Brinton, Crane, American historian, June 1959, *Obit* Nov 1968

Brinton, Howard H., American educator, July 1949, *Obit* Yrbk 1984

Britton, Edgar C., Apr 1952, *Obit* Oct 1962

Brode, Wallace R., June 1958, *Obit* Oct 1974

Brooks, Matilda Moldenhauer, physiologist, Nov 1941

Brooks, Robert C., *Obit* Apr 1941

Brown, Carleton, *Obit* Aug 1941

Brown, George Hay, marketing executive and consultant, Jan 1971

Brown, Helen Dawes, *Obit* Nov 1941

Brown, John Franklin, *Obit* Mar 1940

Brownell, Samuel Miller, educator, Feb 1954, *Obit* Jan 1991

Bruner, Jerome Seymour, American psychologist and law professor, Oct 1984

Bryson, Lyman, educator, Sept 1940, Sept 1951, *Obit* Feb 1960

Brzezinski, Zbigniew, American political scientist and presidential adviser, Apr 1970

Bucher, Walter Herman, geologist, Feb 1957, *Obit* Apr 1965

Buffum, Charles A., *Obit* Sept 1941

Buford, John Lester, Apr 1956

Buley, R. Carlyle, historian, July 1951, *Obit* June 1968

Bultmann, Rudolf Karl, German theologian, Jan 1972, *Obit* Sept 1976

Bundy, McGeorge, American presidential adviser, Mar 1962, *Obit* Jan 1997

Burbidge, Eleanor Margaret, Anglo-American astronomer, Nov 2000

Burgess, Robert Wilbur, July 1960, *Obit* July 1969

Burke, Edmund J., *Obit* Feb 1941

Burnham, James, American political and social philosopher, Nov 1941, *Obit* Jan 1988

Burns, Cecil Delisle, *Obit* Mar 1942

Burns, Edward McNall, Feb 1954

Burnside, Iain, Scottish pianist, Jan 2004

Buscaglia, Leo F., educator and lecturer, Oct 1983, *Obit* Aug 1998

Bush, Laura, wife of American president George W. Bush, June 2001

Bush, Wendell T., *Obit* Mar 1941

Butler, Marie Joseph, American nun and educator, *Obit* Jan 1940

Buzzi-Peccia, Arturo, *Obit* Oct 1943

Cai Yuanpei, Chinese educator, *Obit* Mar 1940

Caldwell, Sarah C., Jan 1953

Calkins, Robert DeBlois, economist and foundation

official, Oct 1952, *Obit* Sept 1992

Cam, Helen Maud, English medievalist, Sept 1948, *Obit* Apr 1968

Camac, Charles Nicoll Bancker, *Obit* Nov 1940

Campbell, Boyd, May 1956

Campbell, Harold G., *Obit* Aug 1942

Campbell, Joseph, American mythologist, June 1984, *Obit* Jan 1988

Campbell, Willis C., *Obit* June 1941

Cannon, Clarence, American congressman, Nov 1949, *Obit* July 1964

Caplin, Mortimer Maxwell, American lawyer, Sept 1961

Carlson, Anton Julius, physiologist, Jan 1948, *Obit* Nov 1956

Carmichael, Oliver C., Jan 1946, *Obit* Yrbk 1966

Carmona, Richard, American Surgeon general, Jan 2003

Carnegie, Dorothy, author and corporate training executive, Sept 1955, *Obit* Jan 1999

Carpenter, Henry Cort Harold, *Obit* Nov 1940

Carpenter, Lewis Van, *Obit* July 1940

Carr, Emma Perry, American chemist, Apr 1959

Carr, William G., educator, Sept 1952, *Obit* May 1996

Carter, Stephen L., American law professor, July 1997

Cartwright, Morse A., Sept 1947, *Obit* June 1974

Cary, William L., American lawyer and regulatory agency official, Jan 1963, *Obit* Apr 1983

Castagnetta, Grace, Feb 1954

Castiella, Fernando Maria, May 1958, *Obit* Feb 1977

Catlin, Don H., American pharmacologist, Mar 2010

Cattell, James McKeen, psychologist, *Obit* Mar 1944

Cayton, Horace R., Jan 1946, *Obit* Mar 1970

Chaddock, Robert Emmet, *Obit* Yrbk 1940

Chafee, Zechariah, American law professor, Aug 1942, *Obit* Apr 1957

Chang, John M., June 1949, *Obit* July 1966

Chapman, Helen B., Apr 1955

Chapman, Sydney, English geophysicist, July 1957, *Obit* Sept 1970

Charlesworth, James Clyde, Sept 1954, *Obit* Mar 1974

Cheney, Lynne V., American educator, novelist and government official, Oct 1992

Chu, Steven, American physicist and Secretary of energy, Mar 2009

Churchill, Edward D., American surgeon, Feb 1963

Churchill, Gordon, Sept 1958

Churchland, Patricia Smith, Canadian philosopher, May 2003

Clague, Ewan, statistician and government official, July 1947, *Obit* June 1987

Clark, Evans, Sept 1947, *Obit* Nov 1970

Clark, Kenneth B., American psychologist, Sept 1964, *Obit* Sept 2005

Clarke, Walter, American physician, May 1947, *Obit* Jan 1965

Clement, Paul D., American law professor, Oct 2012

Coffin, Henry S., clergyman and educator, Apr 1944, *Obit* Jan 1955

Cole, Juan R. I., American Middle Eastern studies specialist, Oct 2010

Coleman, James Samuel, American sociologist, Oct 1970, *Obit* June 1995

Coles, Robert, American psychiatrist, Nov 1969

Collins, James Daniel, philosopher, Yrbk 1963

Collins, Marva, American teacher, Nov 1986

Collins, Patricia Hill, American sociologist, Mar 2003

Colwell, Rita R., American microbiologist, May 1999

Comer, James P., professor of psychiatry, Aug 1991

Compton, Arthur Holly, American physicist, Aug 1940, Sept 1958, *Obit* May 1962

Condon, Edward Uhler, American physicist and government official, Apr 1946, *Obit* May 1974

Conley, William Gustavus, *Obit* Yrbk 1940

Connah, Douglas John, *Obit* Oct 1941

Conway, John Horton, British mathematician, Sept 2003

Cook, W. W., *Obit* Yrbk 1943

Coons, Albert H., June 1960

Coontz, Stephanie, American historian, July 2003

Corsaro, Frank, American theatrical director and drama teacher, Aug 1975

Cotler, Irwin, Canadian member of Parliament, Jan 2006

Coulter, Calvin Brewster, *Obit* Jan 1940

Counts, George S., author and educator, Yrbk 1941, *Obit* Jan 1975

Cournand, Andre F., American physician, Mar 1957, *Obit* Apr 1988

Cox, Archibald, American lawyer and special counsel in Watergate investigation, July 1961, *Obit* Yrbk 2004

Cox, Harvey Gallagher, American theologian, Nov 1968

Crabtree, James W., *Obit* July 1945

Craig, Lyman C., Apr 1964, *Obit* Sept 1974

Crawford, Morris Barker, *Obit* Yrbk 1940

Crenshaw, Kimberle Williams, American law professor, May 2011

Crewe, Albert, American physicist, Feb 1964, *Obit* Yrbk 2010

Critchley, Simon, British philosopher, Apr 2010

Crossan, John Dominic, Irish theologian, May 2011

Crosser, Robert, Mar 1953, *Obit* Sept 1957

Crumb, George, American composer, Yrbk 1979

Cruz, Ted, American state solicitor general, May 2013

Cubberley, Ellwood Patterson, educator, *Obit* Nov 1941

Cullis, Winifred C., Nov 1943, *Obit* Jan 1957

Curran, Charles E., American priest and theologian, Jan 1987

Curtin, Phyllis, American opera singer and teacher, Sept 1964

Curtis, George V., *Obit* Oct 1943

D'Arcy, Martin Cyril, British priest and philosopher, Jan 1960, *Obit* Mar 1977

Dahanayake, Wijeyananda, Apr 1960

Dale, Benjamin James, *Obit* Sept 1943

Dallek, Robert, American historian, Sept 2007

Damasio, Antonio R., American neurobiologist, Oct 2007

Dangerfield, George, American historian, Sept 1953, *Obit* Mar 1987

Daniels, Grace B., Sept 1959

Darling, Sharon, American literacy advocate, May 2003

Darman, Richard, American presidential aide, May 1989, *Obit* Yrbk 2008

Davenport, Charles B., biologist and educator, *Obit* Apr 1944

Davidson, Richard J., American neuroscientist, Aug 2004

Davies, P. C. W., English physicist, Jan 2002

Davis, Edward W., Sept 1955, *Obit* Feb 1974

Davis, Harvey N., July 1947, *Obit* Jan 1953

De Branges, Louis, American mathematician, Nov 2005

De Geer, Gerard, *Obit* Sept 1943

Dean, Gordon E., American government official, Sept 1950, *Obit* Nov 1958

Deane, Sidney N., *Obit* June 1943

Dearborn, Ned Harland, Jan 1947, *Obit* Oct 1962

Debye, Peter J. W., Dutch physical chemist, July 1963, *Obit* Jan 1967

Delany, Sadie, American science teacher, Nov 1995, *Obit* Apr 1999

Delgado, Jose Manuel R., Spanish neurobiologist, Feb 1976

Deming, Dorothy, nurse and educator, May 1943

Denenberg, Herbert S., Yrbk 1972

Denny, George V., Sept 1940, Sept 1950, *Obit* Jan 1960

Derrida, Jacques, French philosopher, July 1993, *Obit* Mar 2005

Dershowitz, Alan M., American lawyer, Sept 1986

Derthick, Lawrence Gridley, educator and government official, Apr 1957, *Obit* Mar 1993

Dewey, John, American philosopher and educator, Aug 1944, *Obit* July 1952

Diamond, Peter, American economist, Nov 2012

Dickey, James, American poet and novelist, Apr 1968, *Obit* Mar 1997

Dimechkie, Nadim, Feb 1960

Dinsmore, Charles Allen, *Obit* Oct 1941

Djerassi, Carl, American chemist, Oct 2001

Dobie, J. Frank, American folklorist, Yrbk 1945, *Obit* Nov 1964

Dodd, Alvin E., Nov 1947, *Obit* July 1951

Dodge, Raymond, *Obit* May 1942

Dollard, Charles, Yrbk 1948, *Obit* Apr 1977

Dominy, Nathaniel J., American anthropologist, Apr 2010

Donaldson, Simon K., English mathematician, Jan 2005

Dooyeweerd, Herman, Dutch philosopher, Sept 1958

Dornay, Louis, *Obit* Sept 1940

Doten, Carroll W., *Obit* Aug 1942

Dougherty, Dora, Mar 1963

Douglas, Paul H., American senator and economist, Apr 1949, *Obit* Nov 1976

Drake, Frank Donald, American astronomer, Jan 1963

Drake, St. Clair, anthropologist and sociologist, Jan 1946, *Obit* Aug 1990

Drew, Charles Richard, American surgeon, May 1944, *Obit* May 1950

Drucker, Eugene, American violinist, July 2002

Duarte Frutos, Nicanor, Paraguayan president, Jan 2004

Dudamel, Gustavo, Venezuelan conductor, Apr 2010

Duerk, Alene, Sept 1973

Duesberg, Peter H., German molecular biologist, June 2004

Dugan, Raymond Smith, *Obit* Oct 1940

Duggan, Laurence, May 1947, *Obit* Jan 1949

Duncan, Arne, American Secretary of education, Mar 2009

Duncan, Thomas W., Yrbk 1947

Duncan, Todd, singer and voice teacher, July 1942, *Obit* May 1998

Dunning, John R., May 1948, *Obit* Oct 1975

Dutton, Denis, American philosopher, Aug 2009, *Obit* Yrbk 2011

Dutton, Lawrence, American violist, July 2002

Dworkin, Ronald Myles, American law professor, *Obit* Yrbk 2013

Dyke, Cornelius G., *Obit* June 1943

Dyson, Freeman J., American physicist, Jan 1980

Eagleman, David, American neuroscientist, Jan 2012

Early, William Ashby, Mar 1954

Edgerton, Harold Eugene, American electrical engineer, Nov 1966, *Obit* Mar 1990

Edman, Irwin, philosopher, July 1953, *Obit* Oct 1954

Eidmann, Frank Lewis, *Obit* Nov 1941

Eisner, Thomas, American entomologist, Mar 1993, *Obit* Yrbk 2011

Eklund, John M., labor leader and teacher, Yrbk 1949, *Obit* Mar 1997

El-Sayed, Karimat, Egyptian crystallographer, Jan 2004

Elder, Albert L., Sept 1960

Elgin, Suzette Haden, American linguist, science fiction writer and poet, Aug 2006

Elion, Gertrude B., American biochemist, Mar 1995, *Obit* May 1999

Elliott, William Thompson, English theologian and canonist, *Obit* Aug 1940

Ellis, Albert, American psychologist, July 1994, *Obit* Yrbk 2007

Ellis, George, South African mathematician and astronomer, Jan 2006

Ely, Richard Theodore, American economist, *Obit* Nov 1943

Emeny, Brooks, Nov 1947

Engle, Paul, American poet and college professor, June 1942, *Obit* May 1991

Epstein, Samuel S., Anglo-American physician, Aug 2001

Erhard, Werner, self-actualization educator, Apr 1977

Eshelman, W. W., May 1960

Ettinger, Richard P., Yrbk 1951, *Obit* Apr 1971

Ettl, John, *Obit* Feb 1941

Etzioni, Amitai, American sociologist, Mar 1980

Eustis, Oskar, American theatrical director and drama teacher, Oct 2002

Evans, Luther Harris, American Librarian of Congress and United Nations official, Aug 1945, *Obit* Feb 1982

Ewing, Maurice, American geophysicist, Jan 1953, *Obit* June 1974

Faber, Sandra M., American astronomer, Apr 2002

Fagnani, Charles P., *Obit* Mar 1941

Fairchild, Henry Pratt, sociologist and economist, Yrbk 1942, *Obit* Yrbk 1957

Falkner, Roland Post, *Obit* Jan 1941

Farnsworth, Jerry, Oct 1954

Fawcett, Sherwood L., Yrbk 1972

Feinsinger, Nathan P., professor of law and labor mediator, May 1952, *Obit* Jan 1984

Feldstein, Martin S., American economist and presidential adviser, May 1983

Felton, Ralph A., Sept 1957

Fenimore-Cooper, Susan De Lancey, *Obit* Mar 1940

Ferguson, Niall, Scottish historian, July 2012

Fermi, Enrico, Italian-American physicist, Oct 1945, *Obit* Jan 1955

Ferris, Harry Burr, *Obit* Yrbk 1940

Fielding, Gabriel, English novelist, poet and physician, Feb 1962, *Obit* Apr 1987

Figueroa, Ana, Chilean educator, diplomat and feminist, Feb 1952

Finch, Caleb Ellicott, American neurobiologist, Sept 2004

Fingesten, Peter, painter and art teacher, Oct 1954, *Obit* Oct 1987

Finkelstein, Louis, rabbi and educator, Nov 1940, Mar 1952, *Obit* Jan 1992

Fisher, Harry L., Oct 1954

Fisher, Sterling, Yrbk 1940

Fisher, Welthy Honsinger, educator, Yrbk 1969, *Obit* Feb 1981

Flemming, Arthur S., American Secretary of health, education and welfare, June 1951, Apr 1960, *Obit* Nov 1996

Flesch, Carl, Hungarian violinist, *Obit* Jan 1945

Flesch, Rudolf Franz, American educational reformer, Apr 1948, *Obit* Nov 1986

Flexner, Abraham, American educator, June 1941, *Obit* Nov 1959

Flory, Paul J., American chemist, Mar 1975, *Obit* Nov 1985

Foerster, Friedrich Wilhelm, July 1962, *Obit* Feb 1966

Folkers, Karl August, American chemist, Oct 1962

Foner, Eric, American historian, Aug 2004

Ford, W. W., *Obit* Aug 1941

Fowler, William A., American physicist, Sept 1974, *Obit* May 1995

Fowler-Billings, Katharine Stevens, geologist, Jan 1940

Frank, Louis, *Obit* May 1941

Frank, Mary Hughes, Jan 1958

Frankel, Charles, philosopher and educator, Apr 1966, *Obit* July 1979

Fraser, Hugh Russell, June 1943

Fraser, Ian Forbes, American library director, June 1954

Frazier, Edward Franklin, sociologist, July 1940

Freedlander, Arthur R., *Obit* Aug 1940

Friedman, Milton, American economist, Oct 1969, *Obit* Yrbk 2007

Frye, Northrop, Canadian literary critic, Aug 1983, *Obit* Mar 1991

Fryer, Jr., Roland G., American economist, May 2012

Fuller, Clara Cornelia, *Obit* Yrbk 1940

Funston, Keith, American stock exchange official, July 1951, *Obit* July 1992

Furey, Warren W., May 1950, *Obit* Jan 1959

Gajdusek, Daniel Carleton, American virologist, June 1981, *Obit* Yrbk 2009

Galbraith, James K., American economist, Feb 2006

Galinsky, Ellen, American educator and organization official, Oct 2003

Gamow, George, American physicist and science writer, Oct 1951, *Obit* Oct 1968

Gannon, Robert I., Mar 1945, *Obit* May 1978

Gaposchkin, Cecilia Helena Payne, astronomer, Yrbk 1957

Gardner, Howard, American psychologist, Oct 1998

Garreton Merino, Manuel A., Chilean sociologist, Jan 2006

Garst, Jonathan, Oct 1964

Gasser, Herbert Spencer, American physiologist, Oct 1945, *Obit* July 1963

Gates, William E., American archaeologist, *Obit* Jan 1940

Gaubatz, Lynn, bassoonist, Feb 2001

Gay, Peter, American historian, Feb 1986

Geha, Marla, American astronomer, June 2010

Gell-Mann, Murray, American physicist, Feb 1966, Oct 1998

Gellhorn, Walter, professor of law, May 1967, *Obit* Feb 1996

Gerard, Ralph W., May 1965, *Obit* Apr 1974

Gergen, David, American political commentator, Feb 1994

Ghez, Andrea Mia, American astronomer, Nov 2010

Giauque, William Francis, American chemist, Jan 1950, *Obit* May 1982

Gifford, Chloe, Mar 1959

Gilbreth, Lillian Moller, American industrial engineer, May 1940, Sept 1951, *Obit* Feb 1972

Gilligan, Carol, American psychologist, May 1997

Gilyard, Keith, American sociolinguist, Oct 2011

Ginsburg, Ruth Bader, American Supreme Court justice, Feb 1994

Ginzberg, Eli, American economist and educator, Mar 1966, *Obit* Yrbk 2003

Gipson, Lawrence Henry, Oct 1954, *Obit* Nov 1971

Givens, Willard E., Sept 1948, *Obit* July 1971

Glaser, Donald Arthur, American physicist, Mar 1961, *Obit* Yrbk 2013

Glass, Bentley, American biologist, Apr 1966, *Obit* Yrbk 2005

Glazer, Nathan, American sociologist and educator, Yrbk 1970

Gleason, Clarence Willard, American classicist, *Obit* Yrbk 1942

Goeppert-Mayer, Maria, American physicist, June 1964, *Obit* Apr 1972

Goldman, Eric Frederick, American historian, July 1964, *Obit* Apr 1989

Goldstein, Israel, Zionist leader and rabbi, July 1946, *Obit* June 1986

Good, Robert A., American physician, Mar 1972, *Obit* Yrbk 2003

Goodhart, Arthur L., American lawyer, July 1964, *Obit* Feb 1979

Gordon, Edmund W., American psychologist, June 2003

Gordon, John Sloan, *Obit* Yrbk 1940

Gordon, Kermit, economist, July 1963, *Obit* Aug 1976

Goudsmit, Samuel Abraham, American physicist, Oct 1954, *Obit* Feb 1979

Gould, Ronald, English labor leader and teacher, Nov 1952

Gould, Stephen Jay, American paleontologist and science writer, Sept 1982, *Obit* Aug 2002

Gowers, Tim, English mathematician, Jan 2001

Grace, Alonzo G., Jan 1950, *Obit* Yrbk 1971

Graham, Evarts A., American surgeon, Feb 1952, *Obit* May 1957

Graham, Harry Chrysostom, Apr 1950

Graham, Jorie, American poet, May 1997

Grandjany, Marcel, May 1943, *Obit* Apr 1975

Granger, Clive W. J., British economist, Jan 2007, *Obit* Yrbk 2009

Graves, Alvin C., American physicist, Yrbk 1952, *Obit* Oct 1965

Greenfield, Abraham Lincoln, *Obit* Sept 1941

Greenway, Walter Burton, *Obit* Feb 1941

Greenwood, Allen, *Obit* Yrbk 1942

Greiner, Markus, Physicist and educator, June 2012

Grewe, Wilhelm, Oct 1958

Grotzinger, John, Apr 2013

Grove, Andrew S., American semiconductor industry executive, Mar 1998

Groves, Ernest R., sociologist, June 1943, *Obit* Oct 1946

Groves, Gladys Hoagland, June 1943, *Obit* Sept 1980

Gruber, Samuel H., American marine biologist, Aug 2004

Gruenberg, Sidonie Matsner, May 1940, *Obit* May 1974

Guarente, Leonard, American biologist, May 2007

Guion, Connie M., Feb 1962

Gulick, Luther Halsey, American municipal official, June 1945, *Obit* Mar 1993

Gupta, Sanjay, American neurosurgeon and television reporter, Aug 2006

Guth, Alan H., physicist, Sept 1987

Guthrie, William Buck, *Obit* Yrbk 1940

Haagen-Smit, A. J., chemist, Mar 1966, *Obit* May 1977

Haas, Arthur E., *Obit* Apr 1941

Haas, Jonathan, American timpanist, June 2003

Hagen, John P., astronomer, Oct 1957, *Obit* Nov 1990

Hamilton, George Livingston, *Obit* Nov 1940

Handlin, Oscar, American historian, July 1952, *Obit* Yrbk 2011

Hansen, Alvin Harvey, American economist, Sept 1945, *Obit* Aug 1975

Hansen, Carl F., Oct 1962

Hanson, Howard, American composer, Oct 1941, Sept 1966, *Obit* Apr 1981

Hanus, Paul H., *Obit* Feb 1942

Hardy, Ashley Kingsley, *Obit* Sept 1940

Haring, Bernhard, German theologian, June 1969, *Obit* Sept 1998

Harkness, Georgia Elma, theologian, Nov 1960

Harper, Samuel Northrup, *Obit* Mar 1943

Harrell, Lynn, cellist, Feb 1983

Hart, Albert Bushnell, historian, *Obit* Aug 1943

Hartwell, John A., *Obit* Jan 1941

Harvey, David, British geographer, Aug 2008

Harvey, E. Newton, May 1952

Hass, Henry Bohn, chemist, Apr 1956, *Obit* Apr 1987

Hau, Lene Vestergaard, Danish physicist, Jan 2002

Hauerwas, Stanley, American theologian, June 2003

Hauser, Philip M., demographer, July 1969, *Obit* Feb 1995

Hawking, Stephen W., British physicist, May 1984

Hawkins, Harry C., Apr 1952

Hayek, Friedrich A. von, British economist, June 1945, *Obit* May 1992

Hayes, Samuel P., Sept 1954

Hayes, Samuel Perkins, psychologist and teacher of the blind, Sept 1954, *Obit* Sept 1958

Hayes, Terrance, American poet, Apr 2011

Hayes, Tyrone, American biologist, May 2008

Hazen, Charles D., *Obit* Nov 1941

Heard, Alexander, Nov 1966

Heath, James R., American chemist, Oct 2003

Heffner, Richard D., American historian and television moderator, Oct 1964

Hellenga, Robert, American novelist, Mar 2008

Heller, Agnes, Hungarian philosopher, Nov 2008

Heller, Walter W., American economist, Sept 1961, *Obit* Aug 1987

Henderson, Lawrence J., American chemist, *Obit* Apr 1942

Henry, Mellinger Edward, *Obit* Mar 1946

Herbert, Don, American science teacher and television personality, Feb 1956, *Obit* Yrbk 2007

Herbert, Elizabeth, Feb 1954

Herr, Hugh, American biophysicist and mechanical engineer, Apr 2012

Herrick, Francis Hobart, *Obit* Nov 1940

Herring, Pendleton, American political scientist, July 1950, *Obit* Yrbk 2004

Hershey, Alfred D., American biologist, July 1970, *Obit* Aug 1997

Herskovits, Melville J., American anthropologist, Nov 1948, *Obit* Apr 1963

Heydt, Herman A., *Obit* Oct 1941

Hickman, Emily, June 1945, *Obit* July 1947

Hill, Anita, American lawyer, Sept 1995

Hill, Howard Copeland, *Obit* Aug 1940

Hill, Patty Smith, American educator, *Obit* June 1946

Hill, Robert Thomas, geologist, *Obit* Sept 1941

Hilsberg, Alexander, Oct 1953, *Obit* Nov 1961

Hilsman, Roger, American educator and government official, Mar 1964

Himmelfarb, Gertrude, historian, May 1985

Hirsch, I. Seth, *Obit* May 1942

Hirschfelder, Joseph Oakland, physicist, Yrbk 1950, *Obit* May 1990

Hobsbawm, E. J., British historian, Jan 2003, *Obit* Yrbk 2012

Hofmann, Hans, German-American painter, Oct 1958, *Obit* Mar 1966

Hofstadter, Richard, American historian, Oct 1956, *Obit* Yrbk 1970

Holden, Louis Edward, *Obit* June 1942

Holland, Kenneth, educator, Mar 1952, *Obit* Feb 1978

Hollander, Jacob Harry, *Obit* Sept 1940

Hollander, John, philologist and poet, Sept 1991, *Obit* Yrbk 2013

Holmes, Jesse Herman, *Obit* July 1942

Holt, Arthur E., *Obit* Mar 1942

Holt, John Caldwell, American educator, June 1981, *Obit* Nov 1985

Honderich, Ted, Canadian philosopher, Feb 2009

Hook, Sidney, American philosopher, Oct 1952, Apr 1988, *Obit* Sept 1989

Hooks, Robert, Mar 1970

Hooton, Earnest Albert, American anthropologist, Yrbk 1940, *Obit* June 1954

Hopkins, Nancy, American molecular biologist, May 2002

Horne, Charles F., *Obit* Nov 1942

Horner, John R., American paleontologist, Sept 1992

Horney, Karen, German-American psychoanalyst, Aug 1941, *Obit* Jan 1953

Horwich, Frances, American educator, Oct 1953, *Obit* Oct 2001

Houtte, Jean van, Mar 1952

Howe, Harold, American educator, Nov 1967, *Obit* Yrbk 2003

Howe, Samuel B., *Obit* Apr 1941

Hudson, Charles Lowell, medical association executive and physician, Apr 1967, *Obit* Nov 1992

Hudson, Manley O., June 1944, *Obit* June 1960

Hufstedler, Shirley M., American lawyer and Secretary of education, May 1980

Hughes, Charles Evans, American Supreme Court justice, July 1941, *Obit* Oct 1948

Hun, John Gale, *Obit* Nov 1945

Hunt, Herold Christian, educator, May 1956, *Obit* Jan 1977

Husayn, Taha, Egyptian educator, Oct 1953, *Obit* Yrbk 1973

Huybers, Peter, American climatologist, Apr 2011

Hwang, Woo Suk, Korean veterinarian, Jan 2006

Hymans, Paul, *Obit* Apr 1941

Hyvernat, Henri, *Obit* July 1941

Ilg, Frances Lillian, pediatrician and educator, Sept 1956, *Obit* Sept 1981

Ingalls, Jeremy, poet, Yrbk 1954, *Obit* July 2000

Irwin, Elisabeth, American educator, *Obit* Yrbk 1942

Irwin, Robert B., Mar 1948, *Obit* Jan 1952

Iselin, Columbus O'Donnell, Nov 1948, *Obit* Feb 1971

Ivey, John E., educator, July 1960, *Obit* Aug 1992

Jacopi, Giulio, Jan 1959

Jagger, Janine, American epidemiologist, Apr 2004

Jamison, Kay R., American psychologist, Feb 2009

Jansen, William, Oct 1951, *Obit* Apr 1968

Janssen, Charles L., *Obit* Mar 1941

Jarvis, Erich, American neurobiologist, May 2003

Jastrow, Joseph, American psychologist, *Obit* Feb 1944

Jencks, Christopher, sociologist, Apr 1973

Jenike, Michael A., American psychiatrist, Jan 2010

Jenks, Leon E., *Obit* Mar 1940

Jensen, Arthur Robert, American psychologist, Jan 1973, *Obit* Yrbk 2013

Jewett, James R., *Obit* May 1943

Jin, Deborah, American physicist, Apr 2004

Johnson, Alvin Saunders, economist, author and educator, Aug 1942, *Obit* July 1971

Johnson, Charles Richard, American novelist and short story writer, Sept 1991

Johnson, Douglas Wilson, American geologist, *Obit* Apr 1944

Johnson, Elizabeth A., American theologian, Nov 2002

Johnson, Loren, *Obit* Feb 1942

Johnson, Nicholas, Mar 1968

Johnson, Thor, Oct 1949, *Obit* Mar 1975

Johnson, Walter, American historian, Apr 1957, *Obit* Sept 1985

Johnson, Wendell, American speech pathologist, Apr 1959, *Obit* Nov 1965

Joliot-Curie, Irene, French physicist, Apr 1940, *Obit* May 1956

Jones, Chester Lloyd, *Obit* Mar 1941

Jones, Tayari, American novelist and short story writer, Aug 2009

Judd, Charles Hubbard, *Obit* Sept 1946

Kagan, Frederick W., American military historian, July 2007

Kahf, Mohja, Syrian-American writer, Jan 2007

Kahneman, Daniel, Israeli psychologist, Jan 2007

Kantrowitz, Adrian, American cardiac surgeon, Oct 1967, *Obit* Yrbk 2009

Kantrowitz, Arthur, American physicist, Oct 1966, *Obit* Yrbk 2009

Kaplan, Joseph, physicist, Oct 1956, *Obit* Nov 1991

Karelitz, George B., *Obit* Mar 1943

Kasner, Edward, Nov 1943, *Obit* Mar 1955

Kass, Leon, American bioethicist, Aug 2002

Katsh, Abraham Isaac, Hebraist, Mar 1962, *Obit* Oct 1998

Katz, Milton, law professor and diplomat, Oct 1950, *Obit* Oct 1995

Kearns, Nora Lynch, Sept 1956

Kellas, Eliza, *Obit* May 1943

Kellogg, John Harvey, American physician, *Obit* Feb 1944

Kelly, Everett Lowell, psychologist, Mar 1955, *Obit* Apr 1986

Kelly, Howard A., American gynecologist, *Obit* Mar 1943

Kelsen, Hans, Austrian-American law professor, Sept 1957, *Obit* June 1973

Kennedy, Anthony M., American Supreme Court justice, July 1988

Kennedy, Paul M., British historian, Oct 1993

Kennedy, Randall, American law professor, Aug 2002

Kennedy, William, American novelist, May 1985

Kent, Raymond A., *Obit* Apr 1943

Kerst, Donald William, physicist, Apr 1950, *Obit* Oct 1993

Kessler, Henry H., Oct 1957

Khan, Salman, American school administrator, May 2013

Ki-Zerbo, Joseph, Burkinabe historian and political scientist, Jan 2002

Kidder, George Wallace, microbiologist, July 1949

Kilbourne, Jean, American educator, May 2004

Kim, Jim Yong, American physician and medical anthropologist, Nov 2006

Kimble, George H. T., Oct 1952

Kimpton, Lawrence A., June 1951, *Obit* Jan 1978

King, Mary-Claire, American geneticist, Feb 1995

Kirkland, Winifred Margaretta, *Obit* July 1943

Kistiakowsky, George, American chemist and presidential aide, Nov 1960, *Obit* Feb 1983

Kitson, Harry Dexter, Apr 1951, *Obit* Nov 1959

Kittredge, George Lyman, philologist, *Obit* Sept 1941

Klenze, Camillo von, *Obit* Apr 1943

Kline, Clarice, May 1961

Kline, Nathan S., psychiatrist and educator, Oct 1965, *Obit* May 1983

Klopsteg, Paul Ernest, physicist, May 1959, *Obit* July 1991

Knoll, Andrew H., American paleontologist, Apr 2006

Knopf, Sigard Adolphus, *Obit* Sept 1940

Koch, Fred, drama teacher and theatrical director, Oct 1953, *Obit* Yrbk 2000

Koch, Frederick H., *Obit* Oct 1944

Kock, Karin, Nov 1948

Kolbe, Parke Rexford, *Obit* Apr 1942

Komarovsky, Mirra, American sociologist, Oct 1953, *Obit* Apr 1999

Koontz, Elizabeth Duncan, American labor leader and teacher, Jan 1969, *Obit* Apr 1989

Kopal, Zdenek, Czech astronomer, Mar 1969, *Obit* Aug 1993

Koshiba, Masatoshi, Japanese physicist, Jan 2007

Krause, David W., Canadian paleontologist and anatomist, Feb 2002

Kripke, Saul A., American philosopher, Oct 2004

Krohg, Per, Nov 1954

Kubler-Ross, Elisabeth, American psychiatrist, June 1980, *Obit* Yrbk 2004

Kuiper, Gerard Peter, American astronomer, Feb 1959, *Obit* Feb 1974

Kusch, Polykarp, American physicist, Mar 1956, *Obit* May 1993

Kydland, Finn E., Norwegian economist, Jan 2007

L'Esperance, Elise Depew Strang, pathologist, Nov 1950, *Obit* Apr 1959

Labov, William, American sociolinguist, Mar 2006

Lake, Anthony, American political scientist and presidential adviser, Oct 1994

Lamond, Felix, *Obit* Apr 1940

Landrum, Phil M., American congressman, May 1960, *Obit* Jan 1991

Langer, William Leonard, American historian, Yrbk 1968, *Obit* Feb 1978

Langmuir, Irving, American chemist, Mar 1940, Oct 1950, *Obit* Nov 1957

Larson, Arthur, Ameriacn law professor and government official, Nov 1956, *Obit* May 1993

Lasch, Christopher, American social critic and historian, Mar 1985, *Obit* Apr 1994

Lasser, Louise, actress, Oct 1976

Lasswell, Harold D., American political scientist, July 1947, *Obit* Feb 1979

Laugier, Henri, July 1948

Lauterbach, Jacob Zallel, *Obit* June 1942

Lawrence, Ernest Orlando, American physicist, Feb 1940, Jan 1952, *Obit* Nov 1958

Lax, Peter D., American mathematician, Oct 2005

Lazarsfeld, Paul Felix, American sociologist, Nov 1964, *Obit* Oct 1976

LeDoux, Joseph E., American neuroscientist, Oct 2010

Leary, Timothy, American psychologist, Yrbk 1970, *Obit* Aug 1996

Lecky, Prescott, psychologist, *Obit* July 1941

Lederberg, Joshua, American geneticist, Mar 1959, *Obit* Yrbk 2008

Lederman, Leon M., American physicist, Sept 1989

Lee, Tsung Dao, American physicist, Nov 1958

Leggett, A. J., Anglo-American physicist, Jan 2007

Lehmann, George, *Obit* Yrbk 1941

Leighton, Robert B., physicist, July 1966, *Obit* May 1997

Leonard, Lucille Putnam, Feb 1953

Lerner, Gerda, American historian, Feb 1998, *Obit* Yrbk 2013

Levertov, Denise, American poet, Aug 1991, *Obit* Mar 1998

Levine, Philip, American poet, July 2012

Lewing, Adele, *Obit* Apr 1943

Lewis, Dean, *Obit* Yrbk 1941

Lewis, Dorothy Otnow, American psychiatrist, May 2006

Lhevinne, Rosina, Russian-American pianist and teacher, Nov 1961, *Obit* Jan 1977

Lie, Jonas, Norwegian-American painter, Jan 1940

Lifton, Robert Jay, American psychiatrist and writer, Nov 1973

Lillehei, Clarence Walton, American surgeon, May 1969, *Obit* Nov 1999

Liu, Hung, Chinese artist, Jan 2002

Llinas, Rodolfo R., American neurophysiologist, Sept 2009

Locke, Alain LeRoy, American philosopher and essayist, Jan 1944, *Obit* Sept 1954

Loeb, Abraham (Avi), July 2013

Loftus, Elizabeth F., American psychologist, Jan 1999

Lonergan, Bernard J. F., Canadian priest and theologian, Jan 1972, *Obit* Feb 1985

Long, Oren E., American senator, Sept 1951, *Obit* June 1965

Lopez Rodo, Laureano, Feb 1972

Lord, F. T., *Obit* Jan 1942

Love, John A., American governor, Nov 1963, *Obit* Apr 2002

Love, Susan M., American surgeon, Oct 1994

Lowrie, Jean E., June 1973

Lubin, Isador, Oct 1941, Jan 1953, *Obit* Sept 1978

Luckstone, Isidore, *Obit* May 1941

Luria, S. E., American biologist, Feb 1970, *Obit* Apr 1991

Lusk, Georgia Lee, American congresswoman, Oct 1947, *Obit* Feb 1971

Lynch, Daniel F., July 1955

Lynd, Staughton, American historian and lawyer, May 1983

MacAlarney, Robert Emmet, *Obit* Jan 1946

MacCallum, William George, *Obit* Mar 1944

MacCormick, Austin H., May 1940, July 1951, *Obit* Jan 1980

MacGregor, Joanna, British pianist, Jan 2006

MacLean, Basil C., May 1957, *Obit* Apr 1963

MacMillan, Margaret, Canadian historian, Jan 2007

Macbride, Ernest William, *Obit* Jan 1941

Macdonald, Duncan Black, American theologian, linguist and Islamist, *Obit* Oct 1943

Machel, Graca Simbine, Mozambican social welfare leader and wife of Nelson Mandela, Oct 1997

Mackay, John Alexander, American theologian and missionary, Feb 1952, *Obit* Aug 1983

Mackenzie, Chalmers Jack, June 1952

Macmahon, Arthur W., American political scientist, Apr 1958, *Obit* Apr 1980

Macrossie, Allan, *Obit* Mar 1940

Maddy, Joseph E., musician and educator, Apr 1946, *Obit* May 1966

Magee, Elizabeth S., Oct 1950

Magoffin, Ralph Van Deman, *Obit* July 1942

Mailhouse, Max, *Obit* Yrbk 1941

Makemson, Maud Worcester, astronomer, June 1941

Malin, Patrick Murphy, Mar 1950, *Obit* Feb 1965

Malinowski, Bronislaw, Polish anthropologist, June 1941, *Obit* July 1942

Mallory, F. B., *Obit* Nov 1941

Mamdani, Mahmood, Ugandan political scientist, Jan 2010

Mamlok, Hans J., *Obit* Yrbk 1940

Mandelbrot, Benoit B., American mathematician, June 1987, *Obit* Yrbk 2010

Manrique, Jaime, Colombian-American novelist and poet, Jan 2005

Mansbridge, Albert, English educator, June 1942

Mansfield, Peter, British physicist, Jan 2007

Marcial Dorado, Carolina, *Obit* Sept 1941

Marcus, George E., American anthropologist, Mar 2006

Margoliouth, D. S., *Obit* Apr 1940

Marias, Julian, Spanish philosopher, author and educator, Feb 1972

Marius, Emilie Alexander, *Obit* Apr 1940

Marks, Leonard H., American lawyer and government official, June 1966, *Obit* Yrbk 2006

Marland, Sidney, American educator and government official, Apr 1972, *Obit* July 1992

Marshall, Barry J., Australian gastroenterologist, Sept 1996

Martel, Yann, Canadian novelist, Jan 2004

Martin, Edgar Stanley, *Obit* Sept 1940

Martin, Fletcher, Feb 1958, *Obit* July 1979

Martin, Percy Alvin, *Obit* Apr 1942

Mary Joseph, American nun and educator, Yrbk 1942

Mason, Noah M., Nov 1957, *Obit* May 1965

Mather, Kirtley F., American geologist, Jan 1951

Mattson, Ingrid, Canadian Islamist and religious education teacher, Jan 2007

Maynard, John Albert, Oct 1943

Mayr, Ernst, German zoologist, Nov 1984, *Obit* May 2005

McAleese, Mary, Irish president, Jan 2006

McCall, Duke K., Nov 1959, *Obit* Yrbk 2013

McCloskey, Mark A., Nov 1955, *Obit* Jan 1978

McCourt, Frank, Irish-American memoirist, Feb 1998, *Obit* Yrbk 2009

McCracken, Paul Winston, American economist and presidential adviser, Yrbk 1969, *Obit* Yrbk 2012

McCracken, Robert James, July 1949, *Obit* Apr 1973

McGee, Gale William, American senator and diplomat, Nov 1961, *Obit* June 1992

McGrath, Earl James, educator and government official, Apr 1949, *Obit* Apr 1993

McMillan, Edwin Mattison, American physicist and chemist, Feb 1952, *Obit* Nov 1991

McMurrin, Sterling M., American educator and government official, June 1961, *Obit* June 1996

McPhee, John A., American journalist and nature writer, Oct 1982

McReynolds, James Clark, American Supreme Court justice, *Obit* Oct 1946

Mearns, Hughes, Jan 1940, *Obit* Apr 1965

Medvedev, Roy Aleksandrovich, Russian educator and historian, Sept 1984

Meier, Deborah, American educational reformer and school principal, May 2006

Meiling, Richard L., May 1950

Meisner, Sanford, actor, director and teacher, Apr 1991, *Obit* Apr 1997

Mennin, Peter, composer and educator, Nov 1964, *Obit* Aug 1983

Mernissi, Fatima, Moroccan sociologist, Jan 2005

Meron, Theodor, Polish international relations specialist, Mar 2005

Merriam, Charles Edward, American political scientist, Feb 1947, *Obit* Feb 1953

Merton, Robert King, American sociologist, Sept 1965, *Obit* Yrbk 2003

Merwin, W. S., American poet and translator, May 1988

Meyer, Albert, Jan 1960, *Obit* May 1965

Meyer, K. F., Mar 1952, *Obit* June 1974

Miles, Tiya, American feminist, Oct 2012

Milgram, Stanley, American social psychologist, Aug 1979, *Obit* Mar 1985

Miller, Geoffrey F., American psychologist, July 2010

Miller, J. Cloyd, Yrbk 1951

Miller, Neal E., American professor of psychology, July 1974, *Obit* June 2002

Millikan, Robert A., American physicist, Jan 1940, June 1952, *Obit* Feb 1954

Milnor, John, American mathematician, July 2011

Minard, George Cann, *Obit* Aug 1940

Miro Cardona, Jose, Cuban political leader, Nov 1961, *Obit* Oct 1974

Mirza, Shazia, British physics teacher and comedian, Jan 2002

Mistral, Gabriela, Chilean poet and educator, Feb 1946, *Obit* Mar 1957

Mittell, Philipp, *Obit* Mar 1943

Monaghan, Frank, Nov 1943, *Obit* Sept 1969

Montanari, A. J., Feb 1968

Montessori, Maria, Italian educator, Nov 1940, *Obit* June 1952

Montgomery, Deane, mathematician, Nov 1957, *Obit* May 1992

Moore, Edward Caldwell, *Obit* May 1943

Moore, Robert Webber, *Obit* Jan 1943

Moos, Felix, German-American anthropologist, Jan 2005

Morgan, Edward P., May 1951

Morgan, Joy Elmer, Jan 1946

Morgan, Thomas Hunt, American biologist, *Obit* Feb 1946

Morgenthau, Hans Joachim, American political scientist, Mar 1963, *Obit* Sept 1980

Morrison, Henry Clinton, *Obit* May 1945

Morrison, Philip, American physicist, July 1981, *Obit* Aug 2005

Morrow, Elizabeth, Apr 1943, *Obit* Mar 1955

Morse, Marston, Mar 1957, *Obit* Aug 1977

Morse, Wayne Lyman, American senator, Apr 1942, Nov 1954, *Obit* Sept 1974

Morton, John Jamieson, Mar 1955

Moton, Robert Russa, educator, *Obit* July 1940

Mowat, R. B., *Obit* Nov 1941

Mowrey, Corma, Nov 1950

Mukherjee, Bharati, Indian-American novelist, Apr 1992

Mukherjee, Siddhartha, American oncologist, Jan 2013

Muller, H. J., American geneticist, Feb 1947, *Obit* June 1967

Mulliken, Robert Sanderson, American chemist, Sept 1967, *Obit* Jan 1987

Murphy, Gardner, psychologist, May 1960, *Obit* May 1979

Murray, Arthur, American dance teacher, Apr 1943, *Obit* May 1991

Murray, Donald Morison, American journalist and writing instructor, July 2006

Nabrit, Samuel Milton, American embryologist, Jan 1963, *Obit* Yrbk 2004

Nakamura, Shuji, Japanese electronics engineer and inventor, Jan 2006

Neustadt, Richard E., American political scientist, Nov 1968, *Obit* Yrbk 2004

Nevins, Allan, historian, Oct 1968, *Obit* Apr 1971

Newbolt, Francis George, *Obit* Jan 1941

Newcomer, Mabel, Sept 1944

Newlon, Jesse H., *Obit* Oct 1941

Niederland, William G., psychoanalyst, Oct 1980, *Obit* Oct 1993

Noble, Ronald K., American international law enforcement official, Jan 2002

Norris, James F., *Obit* Sept 1940

Northup, Edwin Fitch, *Obit* Jan 1940

Noyes, W. Albert, American chemist, Oct 1947

Noyes, William Albert, American chemist, *Obit* Yrbk 1941

Nozick, Robert, American political philosopher, June 1982, *Obit* Apr 2002

Nunez, Elizabeth, Trinidadian novelist, Jan 2002

Nye, Russel Blaine, historian, July 1945, *Obit* Nov 1993

O'Gorman, Patrick F., *Obit* Apr 1940

Oberteuffer, George, *Obit* Jan 1940

Odell, George Clinton Densmore, Yrbk 1944, *Obit* Yrbk 1949

Odishaw, Hugh, scientific administrator, Feb 1971, *Obit* June 1984

Oenslager, Donald, Sept 1946, *Obit* Aug 1975

Ogburn, William Fielding, sociologist, Feb 1955, *Obit* July 1959

Ohlin, Lloyd E., American criminologist, Apr 1963, *Obit* Yrbk 2009

Okun, Arthur M., American economist and presidential aide, Feb 1970, *Obit* May 1980

Oliphant, Mark, Australian physicist, Yrbk 1951, *Obit* Oct 2000

Oliver, James A., Jan 1966, *Obit* May 1982

Olopade, Olufunmilayo, Nigerian-American oncologist, Sept 2006

Onsager, Lars, American chemist, Apr 1958, *Obit* Jan 1977

Oppenheimer, J. Robert, American physicist, Nov 1945, Apr 1964, *Obit* Apr 1967

Orr, H. Winnett, Oct 1941

Ortner, Sherry B., American anthropologist, Nov 2002

Osborne, Oliver Thomas, *Obit* Yrbk 1940

Overholser, Winfred, Nov 1953, *Obit* Yrbk 1964

Overstreet, H. A., psychologist and philosopher, Sept 1950, *Obit* Oct 1970

Oz, Mehmet C., American surgeon, Apr 2003

Pace, Charles Ashford, *Obit* Feb 1941

Pagels, Elaine H., American religion historian, Feb 1996

Painter, Nell Irvin, American historian, June 2010

Pais, Abraham, American physicist, Jan 1994, *Obit* Oct 2000

Palade, George, American biologist, July 1967, *Obit* Yrbk 2008

Park, Thomas, zoologist, Jan 1963, *Obit* June 1992

Parkes, Henry Bamford, Mar 1954

Parr, Albert Eide, museum director and oceanographer, July 1942, *Obit* Sept 1991

Parsons, Talcott, American sociologist, Jan 1961, *Obit* July 1979

Patri, Angelo, American school principal, Nov 1940, *Obit* Nov 1965

Patterson, Ernest Minor, Oct 1949

Pauly, D., Canadian fishery scientist, Jan 2003

Pavolini, Paolo Emilio, *Obit* Nov 1942

Peabody, Endicott, clergyman and school headmaster, May 1940, *Obit* Jan 1945

Peel, Roy V., Apr 1950

Pei, Mario, linguist, Oct 1968, *Obit* May 1978

Penfield, Wilder, Canadian surgeon, Nov 1955, July 1968, *Obit* June 1976

Pennebaker, James W., American social psychologist, Aug 2011

Penrose, Roger, British mathematician, Sept 2013

Pepperberg, Irene M., American ethologist, Sept 2008

Perera, Frederica P., American epidemiologist, Oct 2010

Perkins, Dexter, historian and educator, Jan 1958, *Obit* July 1984

Perkins, Frances, American Secretary of labor, Yrbk 1940, *Obit* July 1965

Perry, William James, American Secretary of defense, Jan 1995

Peter, Luther Crouse, *Obit* Jan 1943

Peterson, Reuben, Obit Jan 1943

Petry, Lucile, nursing educator and government official, Apr 1944, Obit June 2000

Pevear, Richard, American literary scholar and translator, June 2006

Picard, Emile, Obit Feb 1942

Pierce, John Robinson, American electrical engineer, Feb 1961, Obit June 2002

Pifer, Alan J., American foundation official, Apr 1969, Obit Yrbk 2006

Pinker, Steven, American psychologist, Sept 1998

Pinsky, Robert, American poet, Feb 1999

Pintner, Rudolf, Anglo-American psychologist, Obit Jan 1943

Pitzer, Kenneth Sanborn, chemist, May 1950

Ponnamperuma, Cyril, chemist, Apr 1984, Obit Mar 1995

Pope, Arthur Upham, American archaeologist and historian, July 1947, Obit Nov 1969

Porter, Elizabeth K., Oct 1952

Posner, Richard A., American judge, Jan 1993

Poulton, Edward Bagnall, Obit Jan 1944

Pound, Roscoe, American law professor, May 1947, Obit Sept 1964

Poussaint, Alvin F., psychiatrist, July 1973

Powell, Eve Troutt, American historian, May 2004

Prall, David Wight, Obit Yrbk 1940

Prasad, Rajendra, Apr 1950, Obit Apr 1963

Pratt, J. Gaither, Nov 1964

Prentiss, Henrietta, Obit Jan 1940

Price, Charles C., chemist, Yrbk 1957

Price, Reynolds, American novelist and short story writer, Apr 1987, Obit Yrbk 2011

Priest, J. Percy, Sept 1950, Obit Yrbk 1956

Prince, John Dyneley, Obit Nov 1945

Prince-Hughes, Dawn, American anthropologist, Apr 2005

Quimby, Edith Hinkley, American radiologist, July 1949, Obit Mar 1983

Quine, W. V., American philosopher, Nov 1999, Obit Mar 2001

Rabassa, Gregory, American translator, Jan 2005

Rabi, Isidor Isaac, American physicist, Apr 1948, Obit Mar 1988

Rafferty, Max L., American state education official, Jan 1969, Obit Aug 1982

Rahmstorf, Stefan, German oceanographer and climatologist, Feb 2010

Ramsey, Norman Foster, American physicist, Yrbk 1963, Obit Yrbk 2012

Randall, Lisa, American physicist, May 2006

Ranson, Stephen Walter, Obit Oct 1942

Rathbone, Josephine Adams, librarian and educator, Obit July 1941

Ravdin, I. S., American surgeon, Apr 1968, Obit Oct 1972

Ravitch, Diane, American educator and historian, Nov 2010

Redfield, Robert, American anthropologist, Yrbk 1953, Obit Jan 1959

Reed, Edward Bliss, Obit Mar 1940

Rees, Martin J., British astronomer, Jan 2007

Reich, Charles A., American law professor, June 1972

Reich, Walter, American psychiatrist, Aug 2005

Reinhardt, Uwe E., American economist, Mar 2004

Reynolds, Glenn H., American law professor, Oct 2007

Reynolds, James A., Obit May 1940

Rich, Adrienne, American poet, Feb 1976, Obit Yrbk 2012

Richter, Charles F., American seismologist, May 1975, Obit Nov 1985

Riddell, R. Gerald, Sept 1950, Obit Apr 1951

Riebel, John P., Jan 1957

Riecken, Henry W., social psychologist, Yrbk 1961

Riesman, David, American sociologist, Jan 1955, Obit Yrbk 2002

Riess, Adam, American astrophysicist, Nov 2012

Riles, Wilson, educator and state official, Yrbk 1971

Riley, Richard Wilson, American Secretary of education, Oct 1993

Riley, Susan B., Feb 1953

Ripley, William Z., Obit Oct 1941

Rivlin, Alice M., American economist and government official, Oct 1982

Robinson, Arthur Howard, American cartographer, Mar 1996, Obit Yrbk 2005

Robinson, Boardman, Yrbk 1941, Obit Oct 1952

Rochberg, George, American composer, Sept 1985, Obit Yrbk 2005

Rogers, Mark Homer, Obit Nov 1941

Rogers, Robert Emmons, Obit July 1941

Romano, Umberto, Mar 1954, Obit Nov 1982

Romanoff, Alexis L., Yrbk 1953

Ronan, William J., Oct 1969

Rose, Mary Swartz, American chemist and nutritionist, Obit Mar 1941

Rosen, Samuel, Feb 1974, Obit Jan 1982

Rosenberg, Arthur, Obit Mar 1943

Rosett, Joshua, Obit May 1940

Rossiter, Clinton Lawrence, American historian and political scientist, Apr 1967, Obit Yrbk 1970

Rostow, W. W., American economist and presidential adviser, May 1961, Obit July 2003

Roszak, Theodore, American historian, Apr 1982, Obit Yrbk 2011

Rubbia, Carlo, Italian physicist, June 1985

Rugg, Harold Ordway, American educator, May 1941, Obit July 1960

Runkle, Erwin W., Obit Apr 1941

Ryan, Kay, American poet, Apr 2012

Sabin, Florence Rena, American anatomist, Apr 1945, Obit Yrbk 1953

Sachs, Curt, German musicologist, Aug 1944, Obit Apr 1959

Sadler, Michael Ernest, British educator, Obit Yrbk 1943

Saks, Elyn R., American psychiatrist and law professor, Feb 2011

Salam, Abdus, Pakistani physicist, Apr 1988, *Obit* Jan 1997

Samaroff, Olga, American pianist and music teacher, Mar 1946, *Obit* June 1948

Santmyer, Helen Hooven, author, educator and librarian, Feb 1985, *Obit* Apr 1986

Santolalla, Irene Silva de, Peruvian educator and legislator, Yrbk 1956, *Obit* Sept 1992

Santos, Rufino J., Yrbk 1960, *Obit* Nov 1973

Sapolsky, Robert M., American neurobiologist, Jan 2004

Sarton, George, American science historian, July 1942, *Obit* May 1956

Saxton, Alexander, American historian and novelist, Nov 1943, *Obit* Yrbk 2012

Schama, Simon, British historian, Nov 1991

Schapiro, Meyer, American art historian, July 1984, *Obit* May 1996

Schilder, Paul, Austrian psychiatrist, *Obit* Jan 1941

Schillinger, Joseph, Russian composer and music teacher, *Obit* May 1943

Schlauch, Margaret, Polish professor of English, Yrbk 1942, *Obit* Sept 1986

Schmid, Carlo, Feb 1965, *Obit* Apr 1980

Schmitt, Bernadotte Everly, historian, Yrbk 1942, *Obit* May 1969

Schoen-Rene, Anna Eugenie, *Obit* Jan 1943

Schopf, J. William, American geologist, May 1995

Schultze, Charles L., American economist and government official, Jan 1970

Schulz, Leo, *Obit* Oct 1944

Schwartz, Pepper, American sociologist, June 2008

Schwinger, Julian, American physicist, Oct 1967, *Obit* Sept 1994

Scott, K. Frances, Nov 1948

Sears, William, pediatrician and writer on health, Aug 2001

Segni, Antonio, Yrbk 1955, *Obit* Jan 1973

Segre, Emilio, American physicist, Apr 1960, *Obit* July 1989

Selden, David, teacher and labor leader, July 1974, *Obit* Aug 1998

Senior, Clarence, Yrbk 1961, *Obit* Nov 1974

Sereno, Paul C., American paleontologist, June 1997

Serre, Jean Pierre, French mathematician, Jan 2003

Sessions, Roger, American composer, Jan 1975, *Obit* May 1985

Setzer, Philip, American violinist, July 2002

Sewell, Winifred, American library science professor, June 1960

Shambaugh, Benjamin Franklin, *Obit* May 1940

Shanker, Albert, American labor leader and teacher, Apr 1969, *Obit* May 1997

Shannon, James A., public health official, Jan 1965, *Obit* July 1994

Shaw, Lloyd, Sept 1943

Shechtman, Daniel, Scientist and educator, May 2012

Shelly, Mary Jo, educator, Oct 1951, *Obit* Sept 1976

Shockley, William, American physicist, Yrbk 1953, *Obit* Oct 1989

Shotwell, James Thompson, Canadian-American historian, Oct 1944, *Obit* Sept 1965

Shoup, Carl Sumner, American economist, Feb 1949, *Obit* Sept 2000

Shubin, Neil, American biologist and paleontologist, Apr 2007

Shull, Martha A., Apr 1957

Shulman, Harry, Apr 1952, *Obit* May 1955

Shumway, Norman, American surgeon, Apr 1971, *Obit* Yrbk 2006

Silva Calderon, Alvaro, Venezuelan international petroleum organization official, Jan 2002

Simkin, William E., American labor mediator, Jan 1967, *Obit* May 1992

Simon, Herbert A., American social scientist, June 1979, *Obit* May 2001

Simonds, Frederic W., *Obit* May 1941

Simons, Elwyn L., paleontologist and primatologist, June 1994

Simons, Hans, Mar 1957, *Obit* May 1972

Simpson, Louis Aston Marantz, poet and educator, Yrbk 1964, *Obit* Yrbk 2012

Sinding, Christian, *Obit* Jan 1942

Singer, S. Fred, American physicist, Yrbk 1955

Singher, Martial, French opera singer and voice teacher, Feb 1947, *Obit* May 1990

Sinsheimer, Robert, American biologist, June 1968

Sizoo, Joseph R., Yrbk 1964, *Obit* Nov 1966

Skocpol, Theda, American political scientist, Aug 2000

Skouris, Vassilios, Greek judge, Jan 2007

Slade, Roy, museum director, painter and educator, June 1985

Sleeper, Ruth, nurse and educator, Oct 1952, *Obit* Feb 1993

Smedberg, William Renwick, Yrbk 1957

Smith, Amy, American mechanical engineer, June 2005

Smith, Clara E., *Obit* July 1943

Smith, Cyril Stanley, science historian, July 1948, *Obit* Oct 1992

Smith, David T., Oct 1950

Smith, H. Alexander, American senator, Apr 1948, *Obit* Jan 1967

Smith, Roy Burnett, *Obit* Feb 1941

Snell, George Davis, American geneticist, May 1986, *Obit* Aug 1996

Snow, Glenn E., Nov 1947

Snyder, Alice D., *Obit* Apr 1943

Snyder, J. Buell, *Obit* Apr 1946

Soffer, Olga, Yusoslav-American archaeologist, July 2002

Spalding, Esperanza, American jazz bassist and singer, Aug 2010

Spelke, Elizabeth S., American psychologist, Apr 2006

Spellings, Margaret, American Secretary of education, June 2005

Sperry, Roger Wolcott, American psychologist, Jan 1986, *Obit* June 1994

Spiegelman, Solomon, geneticist, Nov 1980, *Obit* Mar 1983

Spiller, William Gibson, *Obit* Apr 1940

Sprague, Embert Hiram, *Obit* Mar 1940

Squyres, Steve, American planetary geologist, Nov 2006

St. Denis, Ruth, American dancer, Oct 1949, *Obit* Oct 1968

Staggers, Harley O., American congressman, Mar 1971, *Obit* Nov 1991

Stalnaker, John Marshall, psychologist, July 1958, *Obit* Oct 1990

Starr, Kenneth W., American law teacher and independent counsel in Whitewater Investigation, May 1998

Starr, Mark, labor leader, July 1946, *Obit* July 1985

Steele, Claude M., American social psychologist, Feb 2001

Stein, Herbert, American economist, Mar 1973, *Obit* Feb 2000

Stiebeling, Hazel K., American nutritionist, Apr 1950

Stigler, George Joseph, American economist and educator, July 1983, *Obit* Feb 1992

Stiles, Charles Wardell, American public health official and zoologist, *Obit* Mar 1941

Stone, John Charles, *Obit* July 1940

Stout, Ruth A., Jan 1959

Stowell, Clarence Warner, *Obit* Jan 1941

Strang, Ruth, Yrbk 1960, *Obit* Feb 1971

Strasberg, Lee, American actor, director and acting teacher, Oct 1960, *Obit* Apr 1982

Studebaker, John Ward, educator and government official, May 1942, *Obit* Oct 1989

Studebaker, Mabel, Nov 1948

Sunstein, Cass R., American law professor, Oct 2008

Suzuki, Umetaro, *Obit* Nov 1943

Szasz, Thomas Stephen, American psychiatrist and psychoanalyst, Jan 1975, *Obit* Yrbk 2012

Taft, Horace D., American school administrator and brother of President William H. Taft, *Obit* Mar 1943

Talbot, A. N., *Obit* May 1942

Talley, James, *Obit* Sept 1941

Tannen, Deborah, American linguist, July 1994

Tanner, John Henry, *Obit* Mar 1940

Tao, Terence, Australian mathematician, Sept 2007

Tarr, Curtis W., Sept 1970, *Obit* Yrbk 2013

Taubes, Frederic, Mar 1943

Taussig, Helen Brooke, American pediatrician, Sept 1946, Mar 1966, *Obit* July 1986

Taylor, Billy, American jazz pianist and composer, Oct 1980, *Obit* Yrbk 2011

Taylor, George William, labor mediator, May 1942, *Obit* Feb 1973

Taylor, Herman A., American cardiologist, June 2006

Taylor, Jill Bolte, American neuroanatomist, Jan 2009

Tead, Ordway, educator and management consultant, May 1942, *Obit* Jan 1974

Tennent, David Hilt, American biologist, *Obit* Mar 1941

Terry, Luther L., American surgeon general and educator, Oct 1961, *Obit* May 1985

Thiebaud, Wayne, American painter and teacher, Mar 1987

Thomas, Michael, American novelist, Feb 2008

Thompson, Homer A., Canadian archaeologist, Apr 1948, *Obit* Yrbk 2000

Thompson, James Westfall, *Obit* Yrbk 1941

Thomson, James A., American molecular biologist, Nov 2001

Thorek, Max, Jan 1951, *Obit* Mar 1960

Tillich, Paul, German-American theologian, Mar 1954, *Obit* Yrbk 1965

Titulescu, Nicolae, Romanian diplomat, *Obit* May 1941

Tobin, Harold J., *Obit* Aug 1942

Tobin, James, American economist, Oct 1984, *Obit* May 2002

Toledo, Alejandro, Peruvian president, Nov 2001

Tower, John, American senator, Yrbk 1962, *Obit* June 1991

Townes, Charles H., American physicist, Mar 1963

Trask, James D., American pediatrician, *Obit* July 1942

Trethewey, Natasha D., American poet, Aug 2007

Trevor-Roper, H. R., British historian, Sept 1983, *Obit* July 2003

Tribe, Laurence H., American law professor, July 1988

Trout, J. D., American philosopher, July 2009

Trueblood, Elton, philosopher, Jan 1964, *Obit* Mar 1995

Tufte, Edward R., American political scientist, statistician and graphic designer, Nov 2007

Turin, Luca, British biophysicist, Aug 2008

Turkle, Sherry, American sociologist and psychologist, Aug 1997

Turner, Ewald, May 1962

Tuttle, Emerson, *Obit* Apr 1946

Tyson, Laura D'Andrea, American economist and presidential adviser, Sept 1996

Unden, Osten, Feb 1947, *Obit* Apr 1974

Urey, Harold Clayton, American chemist, Feb 1941, July 1960, *Obit* Mar 1981

Vaizey, John, English economist and author, Jan 1964

Van Loen, Alfred, Feb 1961

Van den Haag, Ernest, Dutch-American psychoanalyst, essayist and educator, Oct 1983, *Obit* July 2002

Varmus, Harold, American virologist and public health official, Nov 1996

Venkatesh, Sudhir, American sociologist, May 2010

Vermeij, Geerat J., American marine biologist, June 1995

Villa-Komaroff, Lydia, American molecular biologist, July 2008

Von Neumann, John, American mathematician, July 1955, *Obit* Apr 1957

Vrba, Elisabeth S., South African paleontologist, June 1997

Waal, Frans de, Dutch primatologist, Mar 2006

Wadhams, Robert Pelton, *Obit* Feb 1941

Walker, Margaret, American poet and novelist, Nov 1943, *Obit* June 1999

Walker, Mildred, American novelist, Yrbk 1947, *Obit* Aug 1998

Walker, Norma Ford, Canadian geneticist, Oct 1957, *Obit* Nov 1968

Walker, Waurine, Feb 1955

Waller, Robert James, author, May 1994

Wallerstein, Immanuel Maurice, American sociologist, May 2009

Walsh, William Thomas, July 1941, *Obit* Mar 1949

Wambaugh, Eugene, *Obit* Sept 1940

Wanamaker, Pearl A., Sept 1946

Warnock, Mary, British philosopher, Jan 2005

Warren, Shields, June 1950, *Obit* Sept 1980

Wasserburg, Gerald Joseph, American professor of geology and geophysics, Mar 1986

Watrous, George Dutton, *Obit* Yrbk 1940

Watson, James D., American molecular biologist, Apr 1963, Oct 1990

Way, Niobe, psychologist, Feb 2012

Weaver, Warren, Apr 1952, *Obit* Feb 1979

Webb, Walter Loring, *Obit* Mar 1941

Wecter, Dixon, historian, Nov 1944, *Obit* Sept 1950

Wegman, William, American artist, May 1992

Weiss, Paul, American philosopher, May 1969, *Obit* Yrbk 2002

Weiss, Paul A., American biologist, Oct 1970, *Obit* Nov 1989

Weiss, Soma, *Obit* Mar 1942

Wells, Agnes, Nov 1949, *Obit* Oct 1959

Wells, H. Gideon, American pathologist, *Obit* June 1943

Wellstone, Paul David, American senator, May 1993, *Obit* Yrbk 2003

Welsh, Edward Cristy, economist, Jan 1967, *Obit* June 1990

Wendrich, Willeke, Dutch archaeologist, Jan 2007

Werner, Wendelin, German-French mathematician, Jan 2006

Werntz, Carl N., *Obit* Yrbk 1944

Wexler, Nancy S., American psychologist and neurologist, Aug 1994

Wheeler, John Archibald, American physicist, Jan 1970, *Obit* Yrbk 2008

Wheeler, Raymond A., Apr 1957, *Obit* Apr 1974

White, Gilbert Fowler, American geographer, Mar 1953, *Obit* Yrbk 2006

Whiteman, Wilberforce James, *Obit* Jan 1940

Wick, Frances G., *Obit* Aug 1941

Wigand, Jeffrey, American teacher and former tobacco industry executive, Apr 2000

Wigner, Eugene P., American physicist, Apr 1953, *Obit* Mar 1995

Wilbur, Ray Lyman, Nov 1947, *Obit* Sept 1949

Wilcox, Clair, Yrbk 1948

Wile, Ira S., *Obit* Nov 1943

Wiles, Andrew, English mathematician, Mar 1996

Wilkins, Robert W., American physician, July 1958, *Obit* Yrbk 2003

Wilkins, Roger W., American lawyer, journalist and educator, Aug 1994

Wilkins, T. Russell, *Obit* Feb 1941

Williams, John H., Jan 1960, *Obit* May 1966

Williams, William Robert, *Obit* Jan 1941

Willis, Frances E., Jan 1954

Williston, Samuel, Yrbk 1954, *Obit* Apr 1963

Wilson, Carroll Louis, energy expert and educator, May 1947, *Obit* Mar 1983

Wilson, George Arthur, *Obit* Nov 1941

Wilson, James Q., American political scientist, Aug 2002, *Obit* Yrbk 2012

Wilson, John Tuzo, Canadian geophysicist and educator, Apr 1973, *Obit* Aug 1993

Wilson, Kenneth Geddes, American physicist, Sept 1983, *Obit* Yrbk 2013

Wilson, Sloan, American novelist, Sept 1959, *Obit* Yrbk 2003

Wilson, William Julius, American sociologist, Feb 1996

Windschuttle, Keith, Australian writer and historian, Jan 2006

Winsor, Frederick, *Obit* Jan 1941

Winter, George B., *Obit* May 1940

Wirtz, Willard, American Secretary of labor, Nov 1946, Feb 1963, *Obit* Yrbk 2010

Wise, Tim, Jan 2013

Witte, Edwin E., American eonomist and government official, July 1946, *Obit* Sept 1960

Witten, Edward, American physicist, June 1997

Wolfe, Deborah Cannon Partridge, American educator, Yrbk 1962

Wolfe, Hugh C., Feb 1950

Wolfenden, John Frederick Wolfenden, English educator, social reformer and museum director, Oct 1970, *Obit* Mar 1985

Wolman, Leo, Sept 1949, *Obit* Yrbk 1961

Wolpoff, Milford H., American paleoanthropologist, July 2006

Wood, Gordon S., American historian, Oct 2011

Woolley, Mary E., Mar 1942, *Obit* Nov 1947

Work, Martin H., May 1951

Wright, Irving S., professor of medicine, Oct 1968, *Obit* Mar 1998

Wright, Jane Cooke, American physician, May 1968, *Obit* Yrbk 2013

Wright, Quincy, American political scientist, Oct 1943, *Obit* Yrbk 1970

Wu, Chien Shiung, Chinese-American physicist, Oct 1959, *Obit* Apr 1997

Wyner, Yehudi, American composer, conductor and pianist, Apr 2008

Yarmolinsky, Adam, American law professor and government official, Mar 1969, *Obit* June 2000

Yeh, George K. C., Mar 1953, *Obit* Jan 1982

Yen, Y. C. James, Chinese educator, July 1946, *Obit* Mar 1990

Yerushalmy, Jacob, Mar 1958

Yeutter, Clayton K., American Secretary of agriculture and political leader, July 1988

Young, Frank E., microbiologist, educator and government official, Oct 1989

Young, Hugh, American surgeon and urologist, *Obit* Sept 1945

Young, Joseph Louis, American sculptor and muralist, July 1960

Young, Karl, *Obit* Jan 1944

Young, Kimberly S., American psychologist, Jan 2006

Zacharias, Jerrold R., physicist, Feb 1964, *Obit* Sept 1986

Zajick, Dolora, American opera singer and teacher, May 2000

Zook, George F., Feb 1946, *Obit* Oct 1951

Zuberbuhler, Klaus, Swiss psychologist and primatologist, July 2010

Zulli, Floyd, Jan 1958, *Obit* Jan 1981

Electrical engineers

Acheson, Albert R., American mechanical and electrical engineer, *Obit* Apr 1941

Alexanderson, Ernst Fredrik Werner, Swedish electrical engineer and inventor, Sept 1955, *Obit* Aug 1975

Anderson, William Robert, American naval officer and congressman, Apr 1959, *Obit* Yrbk 2007

Appleyard, Rollo, British electrical engineer and inventor, *Obit* Apr 1943

Arco, Georg, German radio engineer, *Obit* Jan 1940

Armstrong, Edwin Howard, American radio engineer and inventor, Apr 1940, *Obit* Mar 1954

Arnold, Bion J., American electrical engineer, *Obit* Mar 1942

Ballantine, Stuart, American radio engineer, *Obit* June 1944

Bardeen, John, American physicist and electrical engineer, Sept 1957, *Obit* Apr 1991

Bennett, Rawson, American admiral, Sept 1958, *Obit* Feb 1968

Berg, Ernst Julius, Swedish electrical engineer, *Obit* Nov 1941

Breazeal, Cynthia, American electronics engineer and inventor, June 2011

Bush, Vannevar, American electrical engineer and inventor, Sept 1940, May 1947, *Obit* Sept 1974

Canton, Allen A., *Obit* Apr 1940

Carson, John Renshaw, *Obit* Yrbk 1940

Chubb, L. Warrington, Feb 1947, *Obit* May 1952

David, Edward E., physicist and engineer, May 1974

De Forest, Lee, American radio engineer, May 1941, *Obit* Oct 1961

Du Mont, Allen B., American electrical engineer and inventor, June 1946, *Obit* Jan 1966

Dubilier, William, Sept 1957, *Obit* Oct 1969

Emmet, William L., *Obit* Nov 1941

Engstrom, Elmer W., electronics engineer and executive, Yrbk 1951, *Obit* Feb 1985

Fleming, John Ambrose, English electrical engineer, *Obit* May 1945

Goldmark, Peter Carl, American physicist and television engineer, Nov 1940, Yrbk 1950, *Obit* Feb 1978

Guy, Raymond F., May 1950

Haslett, Caroline, English feminist and electrical engineer, Oct 1950, *Obit* Mar 1957

Hazeltine, Alan, electrical engineer and inventor, Mar 1948, *Obit* July 1964

Hounsfield, Godfrey Newbold, British electronics engineer, Mar 1980, *Obit* Yrbk 2004

Hutchison, Miller Reese, American electrical engineer and inventor, *Obit* Apr 1944

Imlay, L. E., *Obit* Aug 1941

Jacobs, Paul, American telecommunications executive, Feb 2007

Jewett, Frank B., American electrical engineer and telecommunications executive, Yrbk 1946, *Obit* Jan 1950

Kaspersky, Natalya, Russian information technology executive, Jan 2005

Kerr, James W., Oct 1959

Kettering, Charles Franklin, American electrical engineer, May 1940, Yrbk 1951, *Obit* Feb 1959

Lyndon, Edward, *Obit* Yrbk 1940

McCune, Francis K., Mar 1961

McNeely, Eugene J., Nov 1962, *Obit* Feb 1974

Nipkow, Paul Gottlieb, German television pioneer, *Obit* Oct 1940

Norris, Henry Hutchinson, *Obit* May 1940

O'Neill, Eugene F., American electronics engineer, Apr 1963

Owens, Robert Bowie, *Obit* Yrbk 1940

Pervukhin, Mikhail G., Mar 1956, *Obit* Oct 1978

Pickering, William H., American physicist, Nov 1958, *Obit* Yrbk 2004

Pierce, John Robinson, American electrical engineer, Feb 1961, *Obit* June 2002

Porter, Richard W., electrical engineer and NASA official, Nov 1958, *Obit* Jan 1997

Poulsen, Valdemar, Danish inventor and electrical engineer, *Obit* Sept 1942

Quarles, Donald A., American Secretary of the air force, Nov 1955, *Obit* July 1959

Ramo, Simon, American electronics industry executive, Apr 1958

Reed, Philip Dunham, American electronics industry executive, Jan 1949, *Obit* May 1989

Reynolds, James A., *Obit* May 1940

Romnes, Haakon Ingolf, telecommunications executive, Feb 1968, *Obit* Jan 1974

Rosen, Harold A., American electrical engineer, June 1997

Rushmore, David Barker, *Obit* July 1940

Sobolev, Arkadii A., Apr 1955, *Obit* Jan 1965

Sporn, Philip, American electrical engineer, Nov 1966

Stillwell, Lewis Buckley, American electrical engineer, *Obit* Mar 1941

Taylor, A. H., Sept 1945, *Obit* Jan 1962

Tesla, Nikola, American electrical engineer, *Obit* Feb 1943

Watson-Watt, Robert Alexander, British radio engineer and physicist, Sept 1945, *Obit* Jan 1974

Weagant, Roy A., *Obit* Oct 1942

Wooldridge, Dean Everett, American physicist and electronics engineer, Apr 1958, *Obit* Yrbk 2007

Zworykin, Vladimir Kosma, American physicist, Yrbk 1949, *Obit* Sept 1982

Electronic musicians

Akita, Masami, Japanese electronic musician, Jan 2006

Flint, Keith, British singer and dancer, Oct 2009

Froese, Edgar, German electronic musician, Jan 2005

Froese, Jerome, German keyboardist, Jan 2005

Howlett, Liam, British DJ, Oct 2009

Hyde, Karl, British singer, guitarist and songwriter, Nov 2011

Maxim Reality (Singer), British singer and songwriter, Oct 2009

Smith, Rick, British keyboardist and songwriter, Nov 2011

Thornhill, Leeroy, British keyboardist, Oct 2009

Vangelis, Greek composer, Jan 2003

Electronic publishers

Swartz, Aaron, American electronic publisher, *Obit* Yrbk 2013

Electronics engineers

Beranek, Leo Leroy, American acoustic engineer, Mar 1963

Bolt, Richard H., American sound engineer, June 1954

Breazeal, Cynthia, American electronics engineer and inventor, June 2011

Dubilier, William, Sept 1957, *Obit* Oct 1969

Guy, Raymond F., May 1950

Harris, Cyril M., American acoustic engineer, Feb 1977, *Obit* Yrbk 2011

Hounsfield, Godfrey Newbold, British electronics engineer, Mar 1980, *Obit* Yrbk 2004

O'Neill, Eugene F., American electronics engineer, Apr 1963

Olson, Harry Ferdinand, American acoustic engineer, Nov 1955, *Obit* June 1982

Wooldridge, Dean Everett, American physicist and electronics engineer, Apr 1958, *Obit* Yrbk 2007

Electronics industry executives

Baldauf, Sari, Finnish cellular telephone equipment industry executive, Jan 2004

Balderston, William, radio equipment industry executive, Sept 1949, *Obit* Oct 1983

Barrett, Craig, American semiconductor industry executive, Mar 1999

Bradshaw, Thornton F., petroleum and electronics executive, June 1982, *Obit* Feb 1989

Breen, Edward D., American electronics industry executive, July 2004

Cunningham-Agee, Mary, American electronics industry executive, Nov 1984

Engibous, Thomas J., American semiconductor industry executive, Oct 2003

Galvin, Robert W., American electronics industry executive, Mar 1960, *Obit* Yrbk 2011

Geneen, Harold S., American financier, Feb 1974, *Obit* Jan 1998

Idei, Nobuyuki, Japanese electronics industry executive, Mar 1997

Immelt, Jeffrey R., American corporation executive, Feb 2004

Jha, Sanjay, American electronics industry executive, Jan 2010

Jones, Scott, American electronics and information technology executive, Jan 2006

Jonsson, John Erik, mayor and electronics executive, Jan 1961, *Obit* Nov 1995

Lee, Kun-hee, Korean electronics industry executive, Jan 2005

Li Dongsheng, Chinese electronics industry executive, Jan 2005

Ling, James, American financier, Apr 1970, *Obit* Yrbk 2005

Morita, Akio, Japanese electronics executive, Feb 1972, *Obit* Feb 2000

Ohga, Norio, Japanese electronics industry executive, June 1998, *Obit* Yrbk 2011

Ollila, Jorma, Finnish cellular telephone equipment industry executive, Aug 2002

Pace, Frank, American Secretary of the army, Feb 1950, *Obit* Feb 1988

Reed, Philip Dunham, American electronics industry executive, Jan 1949, *Obit* May 1989

Ren Zhengfei, Chinese telecommunications equipment company executive, Jan 2005

Sarnoff, Robert W., electronics executive, Yrbk 1956, *Obit* May 1997

Shapp, Milton Jerrold, American governor, July 1973, *Obit* Feb 1995

Sprague, Robert Chapman, radio and television equipment executive, Jan 1951, *Obit* Nov 1991

Wilson, Charles E., American electronics industry executive,

Apr 1943, Feb 1951, *Obit* Feb 1972

Yun, Jong Yong, Korean electronics industry executive, Jan 2003

Elementary school teachers

Blanchard, Hazel A., American school principal, June 1963

Emperors

Akihito, Apr 1959, Aug 1991

Bokassa, Apr 1978, *Obit* Jan 1997

Haile Selassie, Apr 1941, Oct 1954, *Obit* Oct 1975

Hirohito, Jan 1942, Mar 1976, *Obit* Feb 1989

William, *Obit* July 1941

Employment agents

Kopp, Wendy, American teacher recruiter, Mar 2003

Empresses

Farah, Mar 1976

Endocrinologists

Lynch, William J., *Obit* Aug 1941

Energy consultants

Yergin, Daniel, American energy consultant and business writer, Nov 1999

Energy industry executives

Abramovich, Roman, Russian energy industry executive and provincial governor, Jan 2004

Anderson, Robert Orville, American petroleum industry executive, Sept 1982, *Obit* Yrbk 2008

Behn, Sosthenes, American telephone executive, Jan 1947, *Obit* Sept 1957

Beitz, Berthold, German steel executive, Feb 1973, *Obit* Yrbk 2013

Bennett, William John, Canadian government official and energy industry executive, June 1954

Blaustein, Jacob, American petroleum industry executive

and Jewish leader, Apr 1949, *Obit* Jan 1971

Bradshaw, Thornton F., petroleum and electronics executive, June 1982, *Obit* Feb 1989

Browne, E. John P., British petroleum industry executive, Jan 2002

Cheney, Richard B., American vice-president, Aug 1989, Jan 2002

Cisler, Walker Lee, electric utility executive, Sept 1955, *Obit* Jan 1995

Citrine, Walter McLennan Citrine, English electric utility executive, Feb 1941, *Obit* Apr 1983

Cortelyou, George Bruce, postmaster general and secretary of the treasury, *Obit* Yrbk 1940

Cullen, Hugh Roy, petroleum executive, July 1955, *Obit* Sept 1957

David, Edward E., physicist and engineer, May 1974

Davis, William Rhodes, Mar 1941, *Obit* Mar 1941

Doherty, Henry Latham, American gas and electric utility executive, *Obit* Jan 1940

Dudley, Robert, American petroleum industry executive, June 2011

Elsenhans, Lynn Laverty, American petroleum company executive, July 2011

Fu Chengyu, Chinese petroleum company executive, Jan 2005

Garvin, Clifton Canter, petroleum executive, Nov 1980

Getty, Gordon P., American petroleum executive and composer, Feb 1985

Hickel, Walter Joseph, American Secretary of the interior and governor, May 1969, *Obit* Yrbk 2010

Hicks, Clarence J., *Obit* Feb 1945

Hunt, H. L., American petroleum industry executive, Jan 1970, *Obit* Jan 1975

Jones, Jerral, American petroleum and football executive, May 1996

Kelly, Sharon Pratt, American mayor, Nov 1992

Kerr, Robert Samuel, American senator and governor, May 1950, *Obit* Feb 1963

Lauvergeon, Anne, French nuclear energy industry executive, Jan 2005

Lawal, Kase L., Nigerian-American energy industry executive, Nov 2006

Lilienthal, David E., American government official, June 1944, *Obit* Mar 1981

Love, George Hutchinson, coal and automobile executive, Mar 1950, *Obit* Sept 1991

Luce, Charles Franklin, American electric utility executive, Yrbk 1968, *Obit* Yrbk 2008

Mark, Rebecca, American energy industry executive, May 1999

Mattei, Enrico, Italian energy industry executive and member of Parliament, Apr 1959, *Obit* Jan 1963

McGhee, George Crews, American petroleum industry executive and diplomat, Sept 1950, *Obit* Yrbk 2005

Medvedev, Dmitry, Russian president, June 2008

Moody, Joseph Eugene, coal association executive, Yrbk 1948, *Obit* July 1984

Mosbacher, Robert, American Secretary of commerce, June 1989, *Obit* Yrbk 2010

Nickerson, Albert L., petroleum executive and banking official, Nov 1959, *Obit* Nov 1994

Pauley, Edwin W., American petroleum executive, June 1945, *Obit* Sept 1981

Pew, Joseph Newton, American petroleum industry executive and philanthropist, Sept 1941, *Obit* June 1963

Pickens, T. Boone, American financier, July 1985

Rawl, Lawrence G., American petroleum executive, Feb 1992, *Obit* Yrbk 2005

Raymond, Lee R., American energy industry executive, Nov 1999

Roche, Josephine, American coal industry executive, Aug 1941, *Obit* Sept 1976

Rogers, Desiree G., American magazine executive, June 2011

Swearingen, John E., American petroleum industry executive, Jan 1979, *Obit* Yrbk 2007

Swidler, Joseph C., American government official, Mar 1964, *Obit* July 1997

Tillerson, Rex, American energy industry executive, Sept 2006

Watson, Burl Stevens, petroleum executive, Apr 1957

Willkie, Wendell Lewis, American lawyer and presidential candidate, Feb 1940, *Obit* Nov 1944

Engineering consultants

Arnold, Bion J., American electrical engineer, *Obit* Mar 1942

Douglas, Walter Jules, American civil engineer, *Obit* Sept 1941

French, Hollis, *Obit* Jan 1941

Grimshaw, Robert, *Obit* June 1941

Hibbard, Henry D., *Obit* Yrbk 1942

Malone, George W., American senator, Yrbk 1950, *Obit* July 1961

Reeve, Sidney A., *Obit* Aug 1941

Slocum, Harvey, Feb 1957, *Obit* Jan 1962

Engineering executives

Agnelli, Giovanni, Italian automobile executive, Jan 1972, *Obit* June 2003

Austin, Herbert Austin, English automobile executive, *Obit* July 1941

Bajaj, Rahul, Indian automobile executive, Jan 2007

Bausch, Edward, American optical equipment company executive, *Obit* Sept 1944

Bransome, Edward D., American truck company executive, Apr 1952

Budd, Edward G., July 1949, *Obit* July 1971

Bugas, John S., automobile executive, Yrbk 1947, *Obit* Feb 1983

Canaday, Ward Murphey, Mar 1951, *Obit* Apr 1976

Cho, Fujio, Japanese automobile executive, Jan 2006

Christopher, George T., Nov 1947, *Obit* July 1954

Chrysler, Walter Percy, American automobile executive, *Obit* Oct 1940

Colbert, Lester Lum, automobile executive, Apr 1951, *Obit* Nov 1995

Curtice, Harlow H., American automobile executive, Mar 1953, *Obit* Jan 1963

De Lorean, John Z., American automobile executive, Mar 1976, *Obit* Yrbk 2005

Di Montezemolo, Luca Cordero, Italian automobile executive, Jan 2006

Donner, Frederic Garrett, automobile executive, Jan 1959, *Obit* Apr 1987

Dykstra, John, American automobile executive, Apr 1963, *Obit* May 1972

Estes, Elliott M., American automobile executive, Jan 1979, *Obit* May 1988

Ferrari, Enzo, Italian automobile executive, May 1967, *Obit* Sept 1988

Fields, Mark, American automobile executive, Apr 2005

Firestone, Harvey S., July 1944, *Obit* July 1973

Ford, Benson, automobile executive, Feb 1952, *Obit* Sept 1978

Ford, Edsel Bryant, American automobile executive, *Obit* July 1943

Ford, Henry, American automobile executive, Yrbk 1944, *Obit* May 1947

Ford, Henry, American automobile executive, Apr 1946, June 1978, *Obit* Nov 1987

Ghosn, Carlos, Brazilian-French automobile executive, Jan 2004

Higgins, Andrew Jackson, shipbuilding executive, May 1943, *Obit* Sept 1952

Kaiser, Henry John, American shipbuilding executive, Oct 1942, Mar 1961, *Obit* Nov 1967

Kanzler, Ernest Carlton, automobile executive, Apr 1942, *Obit* Feb 1968

Keller, K. T., May 1947, *Obit* Feb 1966

Knudsen, Semon E., American automobile executive, Jan 1974, *Obit* Sept 1998

Knudsen, William S., American automobile executive, July 1940, *Obit* June 1948

Lutz, Robert A., American automobile executive, Jan 1994

Miller, Arjay, Jan 1967

Miller, J. Irwin, American manufacturing executive and architectural patron, Nov 1961, *Obit* Yrbk 2004

Mott, Charles Stewart, American automobile executive, Sept 1969, *Obit* Apr 1973

Murphy, Thomas Aquinas, American automobile executive, Oct 1979, *Obit* Yrbk 2006

Nasser, Jacques, Lebanese-Australian automobile executive, Apr 2001

Nordhoff, Heinz, German automobile executive, Nov 1956, *Obit* June 1968

Nuffield, William Richard Morris, British automobile executive, Apr 1941, *Obit* Oct 1963

Petersen, Donald E., American automobile executive, Mar 1988

Renault, Louis, French automobile executive, *Obit* Yrbk 1944

Reuther, Victor, American labor leader, Yrbk 1953, *Obit* Yrbk 2004

Roche, James M., American automobile executive, Feb 1967, *Obit* Yrbk 2004

Rootes, William Edward Rootes, British automobile executive, Nov 1951, *Obit* Feb 1965

Sale, Rhys M., Yrbk 1957

Sloan, Alfred Pritchard, American automobile executive, Nov 1940, *Obit* Mar 1966

Smith, Roger B., American automobile executive, May 1986, *Obit* Yrbk 2008

Steinbrenner, George M., American baseball and

shipbuilding executive, Feb 1979, *Obit* Yrbk 2010

Townsend, Lynn A., American automobile executive, Sept 1966, *Obit* Yrbk 2000

Trotter, Lloyd G., American manufacturing executive, July 2005

Valletta, Vittorio, Italian automobile executive, *Obit* July 1967

Vance, Harold S., American automobile executive and government official, May 1949, *Obit* Nov 1959

Wills, Childe Harold, automobile executive, *Obit* Feb 1941

Yoshino, Hiroyuki, Japanese automobile executive, Jan 2002

Zetsche, Dieter, German automobile executive, Jan 2006

Engineers

Alexander, Archie Alphonse, American engineer and territorial governor, June 1955, *Obit* Mar 1958

Alexander, Harry Held, American metallurgist, *Obit* Feb 1941

Alexanderson, Ernst Fredrik Werner, Swedish electrical engineer and inventor, Sept 1955, *Obit* Aug 1975

Ammann, Othmar Hermann, American civil engineer, Jan 1963, *Obit* Nov 1965

Anderson, William Robert, American naval officer and congressman, Apr 1959, *Obit* Yrbk 2007

Appleyard, Rollo, British electrical engineer and inventor, *Obit* Apr 1943

Arco, Georg, German radio engineer, *Obit* Jan 1940

Armstrong, Edwin Howard, American radio engineer and inventor, Apr 1940, *Obit* Mar 1954

Bailey, Donald Coleman, English civil engineer and inventor, Oct 1945, *Obit* July 1985

Ballantine, Stuart, American radio engineer, *Obit* June 1944

Barnes, Henry A., American traffic engineer, June 1955, *Obit* Nov 1968

Beard, James T., American mining engineer, *Obit* Yrbk 1942

Bedaux, Charles Eugene, French-American industrial engineer, *Obit* Apr 1944

Bennett, John W. F., American civil engineer, *Obit* Oct 1943

Bennett, Rawson, American admiral, Sept 1958, *Obit* Feb 1968

Beranek, Leo Leroy, American acoustic engineer, Mar 1963

Berg, Ernst Julius, Swedish electrical engineer, *Obit* Nov 1941

Birdseye, Claude Hale, American topographer, *Obit* July 1941

Blagonravov, A. A., Soviet rocket engineer, Feb 1958, *Obit* Apr 1975

Bolt, Richard H., American sound engineer, June 1954

Boyer, Harold Raymond, Feb 1952

Boyer, Marion W., chemical engineer, Jan 1951, *Obit* Jan 1983

Breckenridge, L. P., American mechanical engineer, *Obit* Oct 1940

Bunau-Varilla, Philippe, *Obit* July 1940

Burns, Ursula, American office equipment industry executive, Oct 2007

Bush, Vannevar, American electrical engineer and inventor, Sept 1940, May 1947, *Obit* Sept 1974

Callow, John Michael, *Obit* Sept 1940

Calvo-Sotelo y Bustelo, Leopoldo, Spanish prime minister, Aug 1981

Canton, Allen A., *Obit* Apr 1940

Carson, John Renshaw, *Obit* Yrbk 1940

Chamberlain, Paul M., *Obit* July 1940

Christie, J. Walter, *Obit* Feb 1944

Christofilos, Nicholas C., Nov 1965, *Obit* Nov 1972

Chubb, L. Warrington, Feb 1947, *Obit* May 1952

Cisler, Walker Lee, electric utility executive, Sept 1955, *Obit* Jan 1995

Collyer, John L., Mar 1947

Cooke, Morris Llewellyn, American industrial engineer and government official, May 1950, *Obit* May 1960

Cooper, R. Conrad, Jan 1960

Crump, N. R., Sept 1957

Davidson, Roy E., Sept 1963, *Obit* Sept 1964

Davis, Edward W., Sept 1955, *Obit* Feb 1974

Davis, Harvey N., July 1947, *Obit* Jan 1953

De Forest, Lee, American radio engineer, May 1941, *Obit* Oct 1961

DeMott, Richard H., Feb 1951, *Obit* Nov 1968

Debus, Kurt H., rocket engineer and NASA official, Nov 1973, *Obit* Nov 1983

Dennis, Olive Wetzel, civil engineer, June 1941

Dexheimer, W. A., Feb 1955

Djuanda, Apr 1958, *Obit* Jan 1964

Draper, Charles Stark, aeronautic and rocket engineer, Yrbk 1965, *Obit* Sept 1987

Du Mont, Allen B., American electrical engineer and inventor, June 1946, *Obit* Jan 1966

Eger, Ernst, Oct 1942

Ehricke, Krafft A., physicist and rocket engineer, June 1958, *Obit* Feb 1985

Eidmann, Frank Lewis, *Obit* Nov 1941

Emerson, Victor Lee, *Obit* July 1941

Emmet, William L., *Obit* Nov 1941

Enckell, Carl J. A., Apr 1950, *Obit* June 1959

Englebright, Harry L., *Obit* July 1943

Ericsson-Jackson, Aprille J., aerospace engineer, Mar 2001

Eyde, Samuel, *Obit* Aug 1940

Fairless, Benjamin F., American steel industry executive, June 1942, May 1957, *Obit* Feb 1962

Farny, George W., *Obit* Oct 1941

Flanders, Ralph E., American senator, Jan 1948, *Obit* Apr 1970

Fleming, John Ambrose, English electrical engineer, *Obit* May 1945

Forbes, John J., Apr 1952

Frische, Carl A., Oct 1962

Garand, John C., American design engineer and inventor, Aug 1945, *Obit* Apr 1974

Gibbs, George, *Obit* July 1940

Gilbreth, Lillian Moller, American industrial engineer, May 1940, Sept 1951, *Obit* Feb 1972

Gilruth, Robert R., American aerospace engineer and NASA official, Oct 1963, *Obit* Yrbk 2000

Goddard, Robert Hutchings, American physicist, *Obit* Sept 1945

Goldmark, Henry, *Obit* Mar 1941

Goldmark, Peter Carl, American physicist and television engineer, Nov 1940, Yrbk 1950, *Obit* Feb 1978

Goldsborough, John Byron, *Obit* May 1943

Goldsmith, Lester Morris, Apr 1940

Greatbatch, Wilson, American biomedical engineer and inventor of pacemaker, *Obit* Yrbk 2012

Gresley, Nigel, *Obit* May 1941

Griffin, Michael D., American NASA official, Aug 2005

Grimshaw, Robert, *Obit* June 1941

Habibie, Bacharuddin Jusuf, Indonesian president, Oct 1998

Hadfield, Robert Abbott, *Obit* Nov 1940

Harris, Cyril M., American acoustic engineer, Feb 1977, *Obit* Yrbk 2011

Haslett, Caroline, English feminist and electrical engineer, Oct 1950, *Obit* Mar 1957

Hazeltine, Alan, electrical engineer and inventor, Mar 1948, *Obit* July 1964

Herod, William Rogers, mechanical engineer and manufacturing executive, Mar 1951, *Obit* Sept 1974

Hibbard, Henry D., *Obit* Yrbk 1942

Hicks, Beatrice Alice, mechanical engineer, Jan 1957

Higginson, William, *Obit* Sept 1943

Hinton of Bankside, Christopher Hinton, British nuclear engineer, June 1957

Holaday, William M., May 1958

Hopkins, Nevil Monroe, *Obit* May 1945

Hovey, Otis Ellis, *Obit* June 1941

Howe, C. D., American construction engineer, Sept 1945, *Obit* Feb 1961

Hudson, C. W., *Obit* June 1943

Hudson, Harold W., *Obit* Mar 1943

Hunsaker, Jerome C., aeronautical engineer, Oct 1942, *Obit* Nov 1984

Hutchison, Miller Reese, American electrical engineer and inventor, *Obit* Apr 1944

Imlay, L. E., *Obit* Aug 1941

Jacobs, Paul, American telecommunications executive, Feb 2007

Jarvik, Robert, American physician and inventor, July 1985

Jewett, Frank B., American electrical engineer and telecommunications executive, Yrbk 1946, *Obit* Jan 1950

Johnson, Clarence Leonard, aeronautical engineer, Oct 1968, *Obit* Mar 1991

Johnson, J. Monroe, American civil engineer and government official, Feb 1945, *Obit* Sept 1964

Johnson, Joseph B., July 1956

Karelitz, George B., *Obit* Mar 1943

Keasling, Jay, American bioengineer, Nov 2013

Keenan, Walter Francis, *Obit* Apr 1940

Kelly, Mervin J., physicist and engineer, Oct 1956, *Obit* May 1971

Kerr, James W., Oct 1959

Khan, A. Q., Pakistani nuclear scientist, Jan 2004

Kimball, Wilbur R., *Obit* Sept 1940

Kisevalter, George, *Obit* May 1941

Kraft, Christopher C., aerospace engineer, Feb 1966

Kravchenko, Victor, July 1946, *Obit* Mar 1966

Kuzmin, Iosif I., Feb 1959

Lake, Simon, naval architect and engineer, *Obit* July 1945

Lindsley, Thayer, Jan 1957, *Obit* July 1976

Ljungberg, Ernst Carl, Mar 1955

Lyndon, Edward, *Obit* Yrbk 1940

Main, Charles Thomas, *Obit* Apr 1943

Martin, James S., American aeronautical engineer, Mar 1977, *Obit* Yrbk 2002

McCune, Charles Andrew, *Obit* Yrbk 1940

McCune, Francis K., Mar 1961

Mehaffey, Joseph C., Jan 1948, *Obit* Apr 1963

Midgley, Thomas, American chemical engineer, *Obit* Yrbk 1944

Miles, Mary, Nov 1942

Miyamoto, Shigeru, Japanese video game creator, Jan 2002

Modjeski, Ralph, *Obit* Aug 1940

Moreell, Ben, June 1946, *Obit* Sept 1978

Morton, James, *Obit* Oct 1943

Murdock, George J., *Obit* Sept 1942

Murray, Thomas E., Sept 1950, *Obit* Sept 1961

Murray, William S., *Obit* Mar 1942

Nervi, Pier Luigi, Italian architect and structural engineer, Jan 1958, *Obit* Mar 1979

Newhall, Arthur B., Oct 1942

Nichols, Kenneth D., general, Nov 1948, *Obit* Sept 2000

Nichols, William T., Oct 1953

Nipkow, Paul Gottlieb, German television pioneer, *Obit* Oct 1940

Norden, Carl Lukas, American mechanical engineer and inventor, Jan 1945, *Obit* Sept 1965

Norris, Henry Hutchinson, *Obit* May 1940

Northup, Edwin Fitch, *Obit* Jan 1940

Oberth, Hermann, German physicist and rocket engineer, Apr 1957, *Obit* Mar 1990

Olson, Harry Ferdinand, American acoustic engineer, Nov 1955, *Obit* June 1982

Owens, Robert Bowie, *Obit* Yrbk 1940

Pacheco e Chaves, Joao, Nov 1954

Parks, Robert J., Feb 1968

Parseval, August von, *Obit* Apr 1942

Paxton, Robert, Mar 1959, *Obit* May 1980

Pervukhin, Mikhail G., Mar 1956, *Obit* Oct 1978

Pickering, William H., American physicist, Nov 1958, *Obit* Yrbk 2004

Porter, Richard W., electrical engineer and NASA official, Nov 1958, *Obit* Jan 1997

Potter, William Everett, American general, Yrbk 1957, *Obit* Feb 1989

Poulsen, Valdemar, Danish inventor and electrical engineer, *Obit* Sept 1942

Quarles, Donald A., American Secretary of the air force, Nov 1955, *Obit* July 1959

Rathbone, Monroe J., Mar 1957, *Obit* Sept 1976

Raver, Paul J., Sept 1941

Reed, James, naval and bridge engineer, *Obit* Sept 1941

Reybold, Eugene, June 1945, *Obit* Jan 1962

Ricketts, Louis Davidson, *Obit* Mar 1940

Rickey, James W., *Obit* June 1943

Ripley, Joseph, *Obit* Nov 1940

Robinson, Holton D., *Obit* June 1945

Rodota, Antonio, Italian aerospace engineer and European space agency official, Jan 2003

Romnes, Haakon Ingolf, telecommunications executive, Feb 1968, *Obit* Jan 1974

Rosen, Harold A., American electrical engineer, June 1997

Rumpler, Edmund, *Obit* Oct 1940

Rushmore, David Barker, *Obit* July 1940

Rutenberg, Pinhas, *Obit* Mar 1942

Savage, John Lucian, Apr 1943, *Obit* Feb 1968

Seamans, Robert C., American NASA official, Yrbk 1966, *Obit* Yrbk 2008

Shirley, Donna, American aerospace engineer and NASA official, Aug 1998

Shreeve, Herbert Edward, *Obit* June 1942

Sillcox, Lewis Ketcham, mechanical engineer, Yrbk 1954, *Obit* May 1989

Sink, M. Virginia, Mar 1964

Smith, Amy, American mechanical engineer, June 2005

Sobolev, Arkadii A., Apr 1955, *Obit* Jan 1965

Somervell, Brehon Burke, Aug 1942, *Obit* Apr 1955

Steinman, David Barnard, American bridge engineer, Yrbk 1957, *Obit* Nov 1960

Stern, Arthur Cecil, sanitary engineer, Apr 1956, *Obit* July 1992

Stillwell, Lewis Buckley, American electrical engineer, *Obit* Mar 1941

Stoppelman, Jeremy, American Internet executive, June 2012

Strike, Clifford S., Nov 1949

Sturgis, Samuel D., Jan 1956, *Obit* Sept 1964

Sutton, George Paul, July 1958

Syme, John P., Mar 1957

Talbot, A. N., *Obit* May 1942

Tallamy, Bertram Dalley, civil engineer and state official, Mar 1957, *Obit* Nov 1989

Taylor, A. H., Sept 1945, *Obit* Jan 1962

Terzian, Harutyun G., *Obit* Oct 1941

Tesla, Nikola, American electrical engineer, *Obit* Feb 1943

Thompson, John Taliaferro, American general, military engineer and inventor, *Obit* Aug 1940

Todt, Fritz, German military engineer and cabinet member, *Obit* Apr 1942

Tupolev, Andrei N., Jan 1957

Van Schmus, W. G., *Obit* Mar 1942

Von Braun, Wernher, German-American rocket engineer, Jan 1952, *Obit* Aug 1977

Von Karman, Theodore, American aeronautical engineer, May 1955, *Obit* June 1963

Wagner, Aubrey J., June 1963

Wahlen, Friedrich T., June 1961

Waite, Henry Matson, *Obit* Oct 1944

Warner, Edward P., aeronautical engineer, Oct 1949, *Obit* Sept 1958

Watson-Watt, Robert Alexander, British radio engineer and physicist, Sept 1945, *Obit* Jan 1974

Weagant, Roy A., *Obit* Oct 1942

Welch, William A., *Obit* June 1941

Weymouth, Frank E., *Obit* Sept 1941

Whitcomb, Richard T., American aeronautical engineer, Yrbk 1956, *Obit* Yrbk 2009

White, John R., Jan 1956

Whitton, Rex M., May 1962

Williams, Clyde E., July 1947

Wilson, Carroll Louis, energy expert and educator, May 1947, *Obit* Mar 1983

Wolman, Abel, sanitary engineer, Feb 1957, *Obit* May 1989

Worcester, J. R., *Obit* June 1943

Wright, Theodore P., Nov 1945, *Obit* Nov 1970

Ydigoras Fuentes, Miguel, Nov 1958

Zander, Arnold S., Oct 1947, *Obit* Sept 1975

Zworykin, Vladimir Kosma, American physicist, Yrbk 1949, *Obit* Sept 1982

Engravers

Antes, Horst, German painter, etcher and sculptor, Feb 1986

Auerbach-Levy, William, painter and etcher, Feb 1948, *Obit* Sept 1964

Davidson, Jo, American sculptor and engraver, Apr 1945, *Obit* Feb 1952

Davis, Stuart, American painter, engraver and illustrator, Aug 1940, July 1964

Ensor, James, Belgian painter and engraver, *Obit* Feb 1943

Frasconi, Antonio, Uruguayan painter and wood engraver, Mar 1972, *Obit* Yrbk 2013

Gibbings, Robert, Irish travel writer and illustrator, Yrbk 1948, *Obit* Mar 1958

Gill, Eric, English sculptor, engraver and typographer, *Obit* Jan 1941

Hayter, Stanley William, English painter and engraver, Yrbk 1945, *Obit* June 1988

Lozowick, Louis, American painter, Apr 1942, *Obit* Nov 1973

Meyerowitz, William, American etcher and painter, May 1942

Olitski, Jules, American painter, Oct 1969, *Obit* Yrbk 2007

Quintanilla, Luis, Spanish painter and etcher, Nov 1940

Villon, Jacques, French painter and engraver, Jan 1956, *Obit* July 1963

Enologists

Rolland, Michel, American enologist, Jan 2007

Entertainers

3D (Singer), English singer and DJ, June 2004

A-mei, Taiwanese pop singer, Jan 2002

Abbott and Costello, comedians, Oct 1941

Abraham, F. Murray, American actor, Jan 1991

Abraham, John, Indian actor, Jan 2006

Abril, Victoria, Spanish actress, Jan 2004

Abumrad, Jad, American radio producer and personality, Sept 2012

Ace, Jane, radio performer, May 1948, *Obit* Jan 1975

Acosta, Carlos, Cuban ballet dancer, Jan 2004

Acuff, Roy, singer, June 1976, *Obit* Jan 1993

Adamowski, Timothee, Polish violinist, *Obit* May 1943

Adams, Edie, American actress and singer, Feb 1954, *Obit* Yrbk 2008

Adams, Yolanda, American gospel singer, Mar 2002

Adderley, Cannonball, American jazz saxophonist, July 1961, *Obit* Oct 1975

Adebimpe, Tunde, American singer, songwriter, and actor, Apr 2009

Adele, British singer, July 2009

Adjani, Isabelle, French actress, Jan 1990

Adler, Kurt Herbert, opera director and conductor, Mar 1979, *Obit* Apr 1988

Adler, Larry, American harmonica player, Feb 1944, *Obit* Oct 2001

Aghdashloo, Shohreh, Iranian actress, Jan 2005

Aguilera, Christina, American singer, Aug 2000

Aherne, Brian, English actor, Feb 1960, *Obit* Apr 1986

Aiello, Danny, American actor, June 1992

Ailey, Alvin, American dancer and choreographer, Mar 1968, *Obit* Jan 1990

Akita, Masami, Japanese electronic musician, Jan 2006

Akon, Senegalese-American rap and rhythm and blues singer, Jan 2008

Al-Jazairia, Warda, Algerian singer, Jan 2006

Al-Madfai, Ilham, Iraqi guitarist and songwriter, Jan 2004

Al-Sahir, Kazem, Iraqi singer, Jan 2003

Alagna, Roberto, French opera singer, July 1997

Albanese, Licia, Italian opera singer, Mar 1946

Albarn, Damon, British singer, songwriter and keyboardist, Nov 2003

Alberghetti, Anna Maria, Italian singer, Jan 1955

Albert, Eddie, American actor, Jan 1954, *Obit* Yrbk 2005

Albertson, Jack, American actor, Mar 1976, *Obit* Jan 1982

Alda, Alan, American actor and film director, Jan 1977

Alexander, Jason, American actor, Jan 1998

Allen, Betty, American opera singer, Nov 1990, *Obit* Yrbk 2009

Allen, J. D., American jazz saxophonist, Nov 2010

Allen, Lily, British pop singer and songwriter, Jan 2007

Allen, Peter, Australian singer and songwriter, Mar 1983, *Obit* Aug 1992

Allen, Rick, English drummer, Jan 2003

Alley, Kirstie, American actress, July 1994

Allyson, June, American actress, Jan 1952, *Obit* Yrbk 2006

Amato, Pasquale, Italian opera singer, *Obit* Oct 1942

Ameche, Don, actor, May 1965, *Obit* Feb 1994

Ameling, Elly, Dutch singer, Oct 1982

Amos, Tori, American singer and songwriter, Sept 1998

Amram, David, American composer, conductor and French horn player, Nov 1969

Anastasio, Trey, American guitarist and songwriter, July 2003

Anderson, Ian, British singer, flutist and songwriter, Feb 1998

Anderson, Judith, English actress, Yrbk 1941, Feb 1961, *Obit* Mar 1992

Anderson, June, opera singer, May 1991

Anderson, Leroy, American composer, Sept 1952, *Obit* Aug 1975

Anderson, Marian, American opera singer, May 1940, Apr 1950, *Obit* June 1993

Anderson, Mary, American actress, *Obit* July 1940

Anderson, Reid, American jazz bassist, Oct 2011

Andersson, Bibi, Swedish actress, Sept 1978

Andre 3000, American rapper, Apr 2004

Andrews, Anthony, English actor, June 1991

Andrews, Dana, actor, Oct 1959, *Obit* Feb 1993

Angeles, Victoria de los, Spanish opera singer, Feb 1955, *Obit* Aug 2005

Anka, Paul, Canadian singer and songwriter, Feb 1964

Ann-Margret, American actress, singer and dancer, Sept 1975

Ansari, Aziz, American comedian and actor, Feb 2013

Ansermet, Ernest, Swiss conductor, July 1949, *Obit* Apr 1969

Antheil, George, American composer, July 1954, *Obit* Apr 1959

Anthony, John J., American family and marriage counselor, Jan 1942, *Obit* Oct 1970

Antoine, Josephine, American opera singer, Aug 1944

Anu, Christine, Australian singer and actress, Jan 2003

Apl. de. Ap (Musician), American singer, Oct 2006

Apple, Fiona, American singer and songwriter, Nov 2006

Arau, Alfonso, Mexican motion picture director, Jan 2005

Arden, Eve, actress, Sept 1953, *Obit* Jan 1991

Argentinita, Spanish dancer and choreographer, June 1942, *Obit* Oct 1945

Argento, Asia, Italian actress, Jan 2003

Argerich, Martha, Argentine pianist, Sept 1999

Arkin, Alan, American actor, Oct 1967

Arliss, George, English actor, *Obit* Mar 1946

Armetta, Henry, American actor, *Obit* Nov 1945

Armstrong, Billie Joe, American singer and songwriter, Aug 2005

Armstrong, Vic, British motion picture stunt coordinator, Aug 2003

Arness, James, American actor, Nov 1973, *Obit* Yrbk 2011

Arnold, Eddy, American country singer, Mar 1970, *Obit* Yrbk 2008

Aroldingen, Karin von, German ballet dancer, Jan 1983

Arquette, Patricia, American actress, Oct 1997

Arrau, Claudio, Chilean pianist, Jan 1942, Nov 1986, *Obit* Aug 1991

Arroyo, Martina, American opera singer, Feb 1971

Arthur, Bea, American actress, Yrbk 1973, *Obit* Yrbk 2009

Arthur, Jean, actress, Mar 1945, *Obit* Aug 1991

Asano, Tadanobu, Japanese actor, Jan 2007

Ascher, Leo, Austrian composer, *Obit* Apr 1942

Ashanti (Singer), American rhythm and blues singer, Jan 2003

Ashcroft, Peggy, British actress, Sept 1963, Jan 1987, *Obit* Aug 1991

Ashford, Nickolas, American singer and songwriter, Apr 1997, *Obit* Yrbk 2011

Ashkenazy, Vladimir, Russian pianist and conductor, July 1967

Ashley, Elizabeth, actress, Mar 1978

Ashley, Merrill, American ballet dancer, Nov 1981

Asner, Edward, American actor, Aug 1978

Astaire, Fred, American dancer, singer and actor, Sept 1945, Apr 1964, *Obit* Aug 1987

Atkins, Chet, American guitarist and record industry executive, Jan 1975, *Obit* Sept 2001

Atkins, Eileen, English actress, Jan 2002

Attenborough, David, British television producer and personality, Apr 1983

Attenborough, Richard, British actor and motion picture director, May 1984

Atwill, Lionel, English actor, *Obit* June 1946

Auerbach, Dan, American singer and guitarist, Jan 2013

Auger, Arleen, American opera singer, Feb 1989, *Obit* Aug 1993

Austin, Steve, American wrestler, Nov 2001

Auteuil, Daniel, French actor, Jan 2007

Aykroyd, Dan, Canadian actor, Jan 1992

Ayres, Agnes, American actress, *Obit* Feb 1941

Azmi, Shabana, Indian actress, Jan 2002

Azuma, Tokuho, Japanese dancer, Apr 1954

Babbitt, Milton, American composer, Sept 1962, *Obit* Yrbk 2011

Babyface, American singer, songwriter and producer, July 1998

Bacall, Lauren, American actress, Mar 1970

Baccaloni, Salvatore, Oct 1944, *Obit* Feb 1970

Bach, Reginald, British actor and theatrical director, *Obit* Feb 1941

Bacharach, Burt, American composer, Oct 1970

Bachauer, Gina, Greek pianist, June 1954, *Obit* Sept 1977

Bachchan, Amitabh, Indian actor, Jan 2002

Bada, Angelo, Italian opera singer, *Obit* May 1941

Badu, Erykah, American singer and songwriter, Apr 1998

Bae, Yong Joon, Korean actor, Jan 2005

Baez, Joan, American folk singer and songwriter, Nov 1963

Bagayoko, Amadou, Malian singer and guitarist, Jan 2006

Bailey, Pearl, American singer and actress, June 1955, Oct 1969, *Obit* Oct 1990

Baird, Bil, puppeteer, Mar 1954, *Obit* May 1987

Baird, Cora, American puppeteer, Mar 1954, *Obit* Feb 1968

Baker, Anita, American singer, Apr 1989

Baker, Tom, British actor, Jan 2004

Bakri, Mohammad, Palestinian filmmaker and actor, Jan 2005

Bakula, Scott, American actor, Feb 2002

Balanchine, George, Russian-American choreographer, Nov 1942, June 1954, *Obit* June 1983

Baldwin, Alec, American actor, July 1992

Ball, Lucille, American actress, Sept 1952, Jan 1978, *Obit* June 1989

Bamford, Maria, comedian, Jan 2012

Bampton, Rose, American opera singer, Mar 1940, *Obit* Yrbk 2007

Bancroft, Anne, American actress, June 1960, *Obit* Oct 2005

Banderas, Antonio, Spanish actor, Mar 1997

Bankhead, Tallulah, American actress, July 1941, Jan 1953, *Obit* Feb 1969

Bankole, Isaach de, Ivorian actor, Jan 2004

Banks, Tyra, American model, actress and talk show host, Apr 2007

Bantock, Granville, English composer, *Obit* Yrbk 1946

Barber, Patricia, American jazz singer and pianist, Sept 2007

Barber, Samuel, American composer, Sept 1944, Sept 1963, *Obit* Mar 1981

Barbier, George W., American actor, *Obit* Aug 1945

Barbieri, Fedora, Italian opera singer, Feb 1957, *Obit* Aug 2003

Barbirolli, John, British conductor, Yrbk 1940, *Obit* Oct 1970

Bardem, Javier, Spanish actor, Jan 2002

Bardot, Brigitte, French actress, Jan 1960

Barker, Bob, American game show host, Nov 1999

Barker, Travis, American drummer, Aug 2002

Barlow, Howard, Jan 1940, July 1954, *Obit* Mar 1972

Barlow, Reginald, American actor, *Obit* Aug 1943

Barnett, Etta Moten, American singer and actress, Feb 2002

Barrault, Jean-Louis, French actor and theatrical director, Mar 1953, *Obit* Mar 1994

Barrere, Georges, *Obit* Aug 1944

Barris, Chuck, American television producer and personality, Mar 2005

Barrymore, Drew, American actress, Oct 1998

Barrymore, Ethel, actress, Mar 1941, *Obit* Sept 1959

Barrymore, John, American actor, *Obit* July 1942

Barrymore, Lionel, actor, July 1943, *Obit* Jan 1955

Bartok, Bela, Hungarian composer, Sept 1940, *Obit* Oct 1945

Barzin, Leon, conductor, May 1951, *Obit* Aug 1999

Basie, Count, American jazz pianist and band leader, June 1942, *Obit* June 1984

Basinger, Kim, American actress, Feb 1990

Bass, Lance, American singer, Nov 2000

Bassett, Angela, American actress, May 1996

Bateman, Jason, American actor, Oct 2005

Bates, Alan, English actor, Mar 1969, *Obit* Yrbk 2004

Bates, Blanche, American actress, *Obit* Feb 1942

Bates, Granville, American actor, *Obit* Sept 1940

Bates, Kathy, American actress, Sept 1991

Baum, Kurt, opera singer, Sept 1956, *Obit* Feb 1990

Baur, Harry, French actor, *Obit* May 1943

Bax, Arnold, English composer, Sept 1943, *Obit* Jan 1954

Baxter, Anne, actress, May 1972, *Obit* Feb 1986

Beach, Amy Marcy Cheney, American composer and pianist, *Obit* Feb 1945

Beam, Sam (Iron and Wine), American folk singer and songwriter, Mar 2013

Bear, Christopher, American drummer, Sept 2011

Beart, Emmanuelle, French actress, Jan 2002

Beatty, Warren, American actor, producer and director, May 1962, May 1988

Bebey, Francis, Cameroonian guitarist, composer and novelist, Apr 1994, *Obit* Sept 2001

Beckinsale, Kate, English actress, Aug 2001

Beecham, Thomas, English conductor, Yrbk 1941, Jan 1951, *Obit* May 1961

Begley, Ed, American actor, Mar 1956, *Obit* June 1970

Behrens, Hildegard, German opera singer, Jan 1985, *Obit* Yrbk 2009

Beinum, Eduard van, Apr 1955, *Obit* June 1959

Beiser, Maya, American cellist, May 2009

Bel Geddes, Barbara, American actress, July 1948, *Obit* Yrbk 2005

Bell, Art, American radio talk show host, Apr 2000

Bellamy, Ralph, actor, Nov 1951, *Obit* Jan 1992

Belle, David, French actor and roof jumper, Jan 2007

Bellucci, Monica, Italian actress, Jan 2003

Belmondo, Jean-Paul, French actor, Yrbk 1965

Belmore, Alice, British actress, *Obit* Sept 1943

Belushi, Jim, American actor, Jan 1995

Benchley, Robert, humorist, Sept 1941, *Obit* Jan 1946

Bendix, William, American actor, Sept 1948, *Obit* Feb 1965

Benigni, Roberto, Italian actor and filmmaker, June 1999

Bennett, Michael, American choreographer, Mar 1981, *Obit* Aug 1987

Bennett, Richard, American actor, *Obit* Yrbk 1944

Bennett, Richard Rodney, English composer, Mar 1992, *Obit* Yrbk 2013

Bennett, Robert Russell, American composer, arranger and conductor, Apr 1942, May 1962, *Obit* Oct 1981

Bennett, Tony, American singer, Mar 1965, June 1995

Bennington, Chester, American singer, Mar 2002

Bentley, Irene, American actress, *Obit* July 1940

Berganza, Teresa, Spanish opera singer, Jan 1979

Bergen, Candice, American actress, Aug 1976

Bergen, Edgar, American ventriloquist and radio performer, May 1945, *Obit* Nov 1978

Bergen, Polly, actress and singer, Sept 1958

Bergeron, Tom, American television personality, Oct 2007

Bergman, Ingrid, Swedish actress, Jan 1940, Sept 1965, *Obit* Oct 1982

Bergonzi, Carlo, Italian opera singer, Nov 1992

Berigan, Bunny, American jazz trumpet player, *Obit* July 1942

Berkeley, Busby, American choreographer and film director, Apr 1971, *Obit* May 1976

Berlin, Steve, American keyboardist and saxophonist, Oct 2005

Berman, Lazar, Russian pianist, Sept 1977, *Obit* Yrbk 2005

Bernstein, Elmer, American composer, June 2003

Berry, Halle, American actress, May 1999

Berryman, Guy, Scottish bassist, May 2004

Berton, Pierre, Canadian journalist and historian, Oct 1991, *Obit* Yrbk 2005

Bervoets, Gene, Dutch actor, Jan 2002

Bessmertnova, Natalia, Russian ballet dancer, Jan 1988, *Obit* Yrbk 2008

Best, Edna, English actress, July 1954, *Obit* Nov 1974

Bettis, Valerie, dancer and choreographer, May 1953, *Obit* Nov 1982

Beyonce, American singer and actress, Aug 2001

Bhosle, Asha, Indian singer, Jan 2006

Big Boi, American rapper, Apr 2004

Biggs, E. Power, organist, Nov 1950, *Obit* May 1977

Bikel, Theodore, American singer and actor, Mar 1960

Birkin, Jane, English actress, Jan 2002

Bisset, Jacqueline, English actress, May 1977

Bjork, Icelandic singer, July 2001

Bjorling, Jussi, Swedish opera singer, Sept 1947, *Obit* Nov 1960

Black, Clint, American country singer and songwriter, Aug 1994

Black, Karen, American actress, Mar 1976, *Obit* Yrbk 2013

Black, Michael Ian, American actor, Sept 2013

Black, Shirley Temple, American actress and diplomat, Oct 1945, Apr 1970

Blackman, Cindy, American drummer, Oct 2010

Blades, Ruben, Panamanian salsa singer, songwriter and actor, May 1986

Blaine, David, American magician, Apr 2001

Blake, Robert, American actor, Oct 1975

Blanc, Mel, American animated cartoon voice specialist, June 1976, *Obit* Sept 1989

Blanchett, Cate, Australian actress, Aug 1999

Bland, Bobby Blue, singer, *Obit* Yrbk 2013

Bledsoe, Jules, American opera singer, actor and composer, *Obit* Sept 1943

Blegen, Judith, American opera singer, June 1977

Bloom, Claire, English actress, May 1956

Bloom, Orlando, English actor, Jan 2003

Blythe, Stephanie, American opera singer, Aug 2004

Bob and Ray, American comedians, Oct 1957

Bocelli, Andrea, Italian singer, Jan 2002

Bodanzky, Artur, *Obit* Jan 1940

Bogart, Humphrey, American actor, May 1942, *Obit* Mar 1957

Bogdanovich, Peter, American film director and producer, June 1972

Bohlen, Dieter, German pop singer, songwriter and producer, Jan 2006

Bohm, Karl, Austrian conductor, June 1968, *Obit* Oct 1981

Bolger, Ray, American dancer, singer and actor, Aug 1942, *Obit* Mar 1987

Bolton, Michael, American singer and songwriter, Aug 1993

Bon Jovi, Jon, American singer and actor, Jan 1990

Bonci, Alessandro, Italian opera singer, *Obit* Sept 1940

Bond, Jessie, English singer and actress, *Obit* Aug 1942

Bonham Carter, Helena, English actress, Jan 1998

Bono, Irish singer, Mar 1993

Bono, Sonny, American singer, songwriter and congressman, Feb 1974, *Obit* Mar 1998

Bonynge, Richard, Australian conductor, Feb 1981

Boone, Richard, Feb 1964, *Obit* Mar 1981

Boosler, Elayne, comedienne, May 1993

Booth, Shirley, American actress, Nov 1942, Apr 1953, *Obit* Jan 1993

Borge, Victor, American pianist and comedian, Mar 1946, May 1993, *Obit* Mar 2001

Borgnine, Ernest, American actor, Apr 1956, *Obit* Yrbk 2012

Borodina, Olga, Russian opera singer, Feb 2002

Bostic, Onika, Trinidadian singer, Jan 2004

Bostridge, Ian, British classical singer, Jan 2006

Bosworth, Hobart, American actor, *Obit* Feb 1944

Boult, Adrian Cedric, English conductor, Mar 1946, *Obit* Apr 1983

Bourdon, Rob, American drummer, Mar 2002

Bova, Raoul, Italian actor, Jan 2004

Bowes, Edward, radio performer, Mar 1941, *Obit* July 1946

Boy George, British pop singer and songwriter, Oct 1985

Boyd, Stephen, Irish actor, Yrbk 1961, *Obit* Aug 1977

Boyd, William, American actor, Mar 1950, *Obit* Nov 1972

Boyer, Charles, French actor, Feb 1943, *Obit* Oct 1978

Boyer, Lucien, *Obit* Aug 1942

Bracken, Eddie, American actor, Oct 1944, *Obit* Feb 2003

Brailowsky, Alexander, French pianist, June 1956, *Obit* June 1976

Branagh, Kenneth, Irish actor and director, Apr 1997

Branch, Michelle, American singer and songwriter, May 2005

Brandauer, Klaus Maria, Austrian actor, July 1990

Brando, Marlon, American actor, Apr 1952, Mar 1974, *Obit* Yrbk 2004

Branzell, Karin, Swedish opera singer, Feb 1946, *Obit* Feb 1975

Braxton, Toni, American singer, Sept 2000

Brazzi, Rossano, Italian actor, May 1961, *Obit* Mar 1995

Bregovic, Goran, Bosnian composer, Jan 2006

Brel, Jacques, French singer and songwriter, Mar 1971, *Obit* Nov 1978

Brennan, Walter, actor, May 1941, *Obit* Nov 1974

Brenner, David, American comedian, Mar 1987

Bressanutti, Daniel, Belgian rock musician, Jan 2006

Brice, Fanny, American singer and comedian, June 1946, *Obit* July 1951

Brico, Antonia, conductor, Sept 1948, *Obit* Oct 1989

Bridge, Frank, English composer and conductor, *Obit* Mar 1941

Bridges, Jeff, American actor, Mar 1991

Bridges, Lloyd, actor, July 1990, *Obit* May 1998

Bridgewater, Dee Dee, American jazz singer, Oct 2008

Britten, Benjamin, English composer, Oct 1942, Apr 1961, *Obit* Feb 1977

Broderick, Matthew, American actor, May 1987

Brody, Adrien, American actor, July 2003

Broemel, Carl, American rock guitarist and singer, Nov 2008

Brokenshire, Norman, May 1950, *Obit* June 1965

Brolin, Josh, American actor, Feb 2008

Bronfman, Yefim, American pianist, Jan 2007

Bronson, Charles, American actor, Mar 1975, *Obit* Mar 2004

Brooks, Garth, American country singer, Mar 1992

Brooks, Kix, American country singer and songwriter, Sept 2004

Brooks, Louise, American actress, Apr 1984, *Obit* Oct 1985

Brosnan, Pierce, Irish actor, Jan 1997

Brown, Bobby, American singer, Apr 1991

Brown, James, American singer, Mar 1992, *Obit* Mar 2007

Brown, Jim, American football player and actor, Sept 1964

Brown, Joe E., American actor, Feb 1945, *Obit* Sept 1973

Brown, Junior, American country singer and guitarist, Nov 2004

Brown, Ronald K., American choreographer, May 2002

Brown, Trisha, American dancer and choreographer, Apr 1997

Browne, Coral, Australian actress, Yrbk 1959, *Obit* July 1991

Browne, Jackson, American singer and songwriter, Oct 1989

Browning, John, American pianist, May 1969, *Obit* June 2003

Brubeck, Dave, American jazz pianist and composer, Mar 1956, Apr 1993, *Obit* Yrbk 2013

Bruel, Patrick, French singer and actor, Jan 2007

Bruni-Sarkozy, Carla, Italian model, singer and wife of French president Nicolas Sarkozy, Jan 2007

Bryant, Anita, American singer, Nov 1975

Brynner, Yul, American actor, Sept 1956, *Obit* Nov 1985

Bryson, David, American guitarist, Mar 2003

Buble, Michael, Canadian singer, May 2009

Buchholz, Horst, German actor, Mar 1960, *Obit* Aug 2003

Buckland, Jon, English guitarist, May 2004

Buffett, Jimmy, American singer and songwriter, Mar 1999

Bujones, Fernando, American ballet dancer, Jan 1976, *Obit* Yrbk 2006

Bullock, Sandra, American actress, Aug 1997

Bumbry, Grace, American opera singer, Mar 1964

Bunton, Jaleel, American drummer, Apr 2009

Burleigh, Harry T., American singer and composer, Aug 1941, *Obit* Oct 1949

Burnett, Carol, American actress, Jan 1962, Nov 1990

Burnside, Jay, Finnish drummer, Jan 2003

Burr, Henry, *Obit* May 1941

Burr, Raymond, actor, Sept 1961, *Obit* Nov 1993

Burstyn, Ellen, American actress, June 1975

Burstyn, Mike, American actor and singer, May 2005

Burton, LeVar, American actor, Mar 2000

Burton, Richard, Welsh actor, Yrbk 1960, *Obit* Sept 1984

Busch, Carl, *Obit* Feb 1944

Busch, Fritz, German conductor, Jan 1946, *Obit* Oct 1951

Butler, John, American dancer and choreographer, June 1955, *Obit* Nov 1993

Butler, Will, American bassist, guitarist and percussionist, Jan 2007

Butler, Win, American singer and songwriter, Jan 2007

Buzzi-Peccia, Arturo, *Obit* Oct 1943

Byington, Spring, actress, Sept 1956, *Obit* Oct 1971

Byrd, Charlie, American jazz guitarist, Oct 1967, *Obit* Mar 2000

Byrd, Sam, Nov 1942, *Obit* Jan 1956

Byrne, David, Scottish-American rock singer and songwriter, June 1985

Byrne, Gabriel, Irish actor, May 1999

Byron, Arthur, *Obit* Sept 1943

Byron, Don, American jazz clarinetist, Sept 2000

Caan, James, American actor, May 1976

Caballe, Montserrat, Spanish opera singer, June 1967

Cage, John, American composer, Sept 1961, *Obit* Sept 1992

Cage, Nicolas, American actor, Apr 1994

Cagney, James, American actor, Yrbk 1942, *Obit* May 1986

Caine, Michael, English actor, May 1968, Jan 1988

Caldwell, Sarah, American opera director and conductor, Oct 1973, *Obit* Yrbk 2006

Caldwell, Zoe, Australian actress, Yrbk 1970

Calhern, Louis, July 1951, *Obit* July 1956

Callas, Maria, American opera singer, Sept 1956, *Obit* Nov 1977

Calleros, Juan, Mexican bassist, Jan 2005

Calloway, Cab, American singer and band leader, Nov 1945, *Obit* Jan 1995

Calve, Emma, French opera singer, *Obit* Mar 1942

Cam'Ron (Musician), American rapper, Feb 2011

Cameron, Basil, English conductor, Apr 1943

Cameron, Hugh, *Obit* Jan 1942

Campbell, Bruce, American actor, May 2013

Campbell, Douglas, Canadian actor and theatrical director, June 1958, *Obit* Yrbk 2009

Campbell, Glen, American singer and guitarist, July 1969

Campbell, Naomi, British model, Feb 1997

Campbell, Neve, Canadian actress, Jan 2000

Campbell, Patrick, English actress, *Obit* May 1940

Campbell, Vivian, English guitarist and singer, Jan 2003

Campora, Giuseppe, Italian opera singer, July 1957

Canby, Al H., *Obit* Yrbk 1940

Candy, John, Canadian actor, Feb 1990, *Obit* May 1994

Cantor, Eddie, singer and comedian, Nov 1941, May 1954, *Obit* Jan 1965

Canty, Brendan, American drummer, Mar 2002

Carey, Mariah, American singer, July 1992

Carle, Richard, *Obit* Aug 1941

Carlos, Wendy, American composer, Sept 2008

Carney, Art, American actor, Apr 1958, *Obit* Yrbk 2004

Carney, Patrick, American drummer, Jan 2013

Carnovsky, Morris, actor, Jan 1991

Caron, Leslie, French dancer and actress, Sept 1954

Carpenter, John Alden, composer, May 1947, *Obit* May 1951

Carpenter, Mary Chapin, American singer and songwriter, Feb 1994

Carradine, Keith, American actor, Aug 1991

Carroll, Diahann, American singer and actress, Sept 1962

Carroll, Jim, American poet and lyricist, Oct 1995, *Obit* Yrbk 2009

Carroll, Madeleine, actress, Apr 1949, *Obit* Nov 1987

Carroll, Pat, actress, Aug 1980

Carter, Betty, American jazz singer, Mar 1982, *Obit* Jan 1999

Carter, Elliott, American composer, Nov 1960, *Obit* Yrbk 2013

Carter, James, American jazz saxophonist, Feb 1997

Carter, Jimmy, American gospel singer, Oct 2001

Carter, Nick, American singer, May 2000

Carter, Regina, American jazz violinist, Oct 2003

Casablancas, Julian, American singer and songwriter, Feb 2007

Casadesus, Robert, French pianist and composer, Jan 1945, *Obit* Nov 1972

Casals, Pablo, Spanish cellist, Nov 1950, Nov 1964, *Obit* Yrbk 1973

Case, Neko, American singer and songwriter, June 2013

Cash, Johnny, American country singer and songwriter, Sept 1969, *Obit* Jan 2004

Cash, Rosanne, American country singer and songwriter, Oct 1991

Cassavetes, John, American actor and film director, July 1969, *Obit* Mar 1989

Cat Power (Singer), American singer and songwriter, Oct 2007

Cattrall, Kim, Anglo-Canadian actress, Jan 2003

Caulfield, Joan, actress, May 1954, *Obit* Aug 1991

Cavanagh, Tom, Canadian actor, June 2003

Cave, Nick, Australian singer and songwriter, June 2005

Cavett, Dick, American television talk show host, Oct 1970

Cecil, Mary, *Obit* Feb 1941

Cester, Chris, Australian drummer and singer, Jan 2005

Cester, Nic, Australian guitarist and singer, Jan 2005

Chadwick, Helene, *Obit* Oct 1940

Chaikin, Joseph, American theatrical director and actor, July 1981, *Obit* Yrbk 2003

Chailly, Riccardo, Italian conductor, June 1991

Chamberlain, Richard, American actor, July 1963, Nov 1987

Chaminade, Cecile, French composer, *Obit* June 1944

Champion, Gower, American dancer, choreographer and theatrical director, Sept 1953, *Obit* Oct 1980

Champion, Will, English drummer, May 2004

Chan, Jackie, Chinese actor, Nov 1997

Channing, Carol, American actress, Sept 1964

Channing, Stockard, American actress, Apr 1991

Chao, Manu, French singer, Jan 2002

Chaplin, Charlie, English actor, director and producer, Yrbk 1940, Mar 1961, *Obit* Feb 1978

Chaplin, Geraldine, actress, July 1979

Chapman, Blanche, *Obit* Aug 1941

Chapman, Steven Curtis, American Christian rock singer and songwriter, Oct 2004

Chapman, Tracy, American singer and songwriter, Aug 1989

Charisse, Cyd, American dancer and actress, Jan 1954, *Obit* Yrbk 2008

Charters, Spencer, *Obit* Mar 1943

Chase, Charley, actor, *Obit* Aug 1940

Chase, Ilka, May 1942, *Obit* Apr 1978

Chasez, JC, American singer, Nov 2000

Chassagne, Regine, Canadian singer and instrumentalist, Jan 2007

Chavchavadze, George, Mar 1943, *Obit* Apr 1962

Chavez, Carlos, Mexican composer and conductor, May 1949, *Obit* Sept 1978

Cheadle, Don, American actor, Sept 1999

Chen, Joan, Chinese actress, Sept 1999

Cher, American singer and actress, Jan 1974, June 1991

Cherkassky, Shura, American pianist, Oct 1990, *Obit* Mar 1996

Cherry, Addie, American vaudeville actress, *Obit* Yrbk 1942

Chesney, Kenny, American country singer, May 2004

Chestnut, Cyrus, American jazz pianist, July 2009

Chevalier, Maurice, French singer and actor, Jan 1948, Mar 1969, *Obit* Feb 1972

Chiba, Sonny, Japanese martial artist and actor, Jan 2005

Chicherina, Julia, Russian pop singer, Jan 2006

Childs, Lucinda, American dancer and choreographer, Apr 1984

Cho, Margaret, American comedienne, Oct 2000

Chotzinoff, Samuel, pianist, Apr 1940, *Obit* Apr 1964

Chow, Yun Fat, Chinese actor, May 1998

Christensen, Hayden, Canadian actor, Jan 2005

Christians, Mady, May 1945, *Obit* Yrbk 1951

Christie, Julie, English actress, Sept 1966

Christie, William, American harpsichordist and conductor, Jan 1992

Chung, Kyung-Wha, Korean violinist, Feb 2007

Chung, Myung-Whun, Korean pianist and conductor, Aug 1990

Churchill, Berton, *Obit* Yrbk 1940

Claire, Ina, actress, May 1954, *Obit* Apr 1985

Clark, Dick, American television personality and producer, May 1959, Jan 1987, *Obit* Yrbk 2012

Clark, Marguerite, *Obit* Nov 1940

Clark, Petula, English singer, Feb 1970

Clark, Roy, American country singer and banjoist, June 1978

Clarke, Martha, American dancer and choreographer, Jan 1989

Clarkson, Kelly, American singer and contestant on reality TV show American idol, Sept 2006

Clarkson, Patricia, American actress, Aug 2005

Clash, Kevin, American muppeteer, June 2000

Claussen, Julia, *Obit* June 1941

Clayburgh, Jill, American actress, Sept 1979, *Obit* Yrbk 2011

Clegg, Johnny, South African singer and songwriter, Jan 2005

Clement, Jemaine, New Zealand comedian, Mar 2008

Cliburn, Van, American pianist, Sept 1958, *Obit* Yrbk 2013

Clift, Montgomery, American actor, July 1954, *Obit* Sept 1966

Cline, Nels, American guitarist, Feb 2010

Clinton, George, American singer and songwriter, July 1993

Clive, E. E., *Obit* July 1940

Clooney, Rosemary, American singer, Feb 1957, *Obit* Nov 2002

Close, Glenn, American actress, Nov 1984

Coates, John, *Obit* Oct 1941

Cobb, Lee J., Feb 1960, *Obit* Apr 1976

Coburn, Charles, actor, June 1944, *Obit* Nov 1961

Coburn, James, American actor, June 1999, *Obit* Feb 2003

Cockburn, Bruce, Canadian singer and songwriter, Jan 2005

Cocker, Jarvis, English rock singer, Nov 1998

Coco, James, actor, May 1974, *Obit* Apr 1987

Codenys, Patrick, Belgian rock musician, Jan 2006

Colbert, Claudette, American actress, Jan 1945, May 1964, *Obit* Oct 1996

Cole, Nat King, American singer and pianist, Feb 1956, *Obit* Mar 1965

Cole, Natalie, American singer, Nov 1991

Coleman, Cy, American composer, Aug 1990, *Obit* Feb 2005

Coleman, Steve, American jazz saxophonist, July 2004

Collen, Phil, English guitarist and singer, Jan 2003

Collier, Constance, July 1954, *Obit* June 1955

Collier, William, American actor, *Obit* Mar 1944

Collins, Eddie, American actor, *Obit* Oct 1940

Collins, Joan, British actress, Jan 1984

Collins, Judy, American singer and songwriter, Apr 1969

Colman, Ronald, English actor, July 1943, *Obit* Sept 1958

Colvin, Shawn, singer, Mar 1999

Common, American rapper, Feb 2012

Como, Perry, American singer, Apr 1947, *Obit* July 2001

Condon, Eddie, American jazz guitarist, Oct 1944, *Obit* Oct 1973

Conlee, Jenny, American keyboardist, Aug 2007

Conley, Eugene, July 1954, *Obit* Feb 1982

Conneff, Kevin, Irish bodhran player and singer, Mar 2004

Connelly, Jennifer, American actress, June 2002

Conner, Nadine, American opera singer, Jan 1955, *Obit* Aug 2003

Connery, Sean, Scottish actor, Jan 1966, June 1993

Conness, Robert, *Obit* Mar 1941

Connick, Harry, American pianist and singer, Nov 1990

Connolly, Walter, actor, *Obit* July 1940

Conte, Nicola, Italian DJ and record producer, Jan 2005

Conti, Tom, Scottish actor, June 1985

Converse, Frederick Shepherd, composer, *Obit* Aug 1940

Conway, Gerry, English drummer, Sept 2005

Cook, Donald, July 1954, *Obit* Yrbk 1961

Cook, Jamie, British rock singer, Jan 2006

Cook, Murray, Australian actor and singer, Jan 2004

Cool, Tre, American drummer, Aug 2005

Coolio, American rapper, Aug 1998

Cooper, Anderson, American television news anchor and talk show host, June 2006

Cooper, Chris, American actor, July 2004

Cooper, Gary, American actor, Yrbk 1941, *Obit* July 1961

Cooper, Gladys, English actress, Feb 1956, *Obit* Jan 1972

Copland, Aaron, American composer, Sept 1940, Mar 1951, *Obit* Yrbk 1991

Copperfield, David, American magician, July 1992

Corea, Chick, American jazz pianist, Oct 1988

Corella, Angel, Spanish ballet dancer, Mar 1999

Corelli, Franco, Italian opera singer, Feb 1964, *Obit* Mar 2004

Cornelius, Don, American television program host and producer, *Obit* Yrbk 2012

Cornell, Katharine, American actress, May 1941, Mar 1952, *Obit* July 1974

Cortez, Jayne, American poet, *Obit* Yrbk 2013

Cosell, Howard, American sportscaster, Nov 1972, *Obit* July 1995

Costner, Kevin, American actor and film director, June 1990

Cotrubas, Ileana, Oct 1981

Cotten, Joseph, American actor, July 1943, *Obit* Apr 1994

Courtenay, Tom, English actor, May 1964

Cowell, Simon, British record producer and talent judge on television program, Jan 2004

Cox, Brian, Scottish actor, Jan 2004

Cox, Wally, Feb 1954, *Obit* Apr 1973

Coyne, Wayne, American guitarist, singer and songwriter, Oct 2002

Craig, Daniel, British actor, Apr 2007

Crain, Jeanne, American actress, Nov 1951, *Obit* Yrbk 2004

Crandall, Martin, American keyboardist, June 2007

Cranko, John, South African dancer and choreographer, July 1970, *Obit* Sept 1973

Crawford, Broderick, actor, Apr 1950, *Obit* June 1986

Crawford, Joan, American actress, Jan 1946, Sept 1966, *Obit* July 1977

Crawford, Michael, English actor and singer, Jan 1992

Cregar, Laird, *Obit* Jan 1945

Crespin, Regine, French opera singer, Sept 1979, *Obit* Yrbk 2007

Crews, Laura Hope, actress, *Obit* Jan 1943

Criss, Peter, American drummer, Apr 1999

Cromer, David, American theatrical director and actor, Sept 2011

Cromwell, James, American actor, Aug 2005

Cronyn, Hume, Canadian actor, Mar 1956, June 1988, *Obit* Yrbk 2003

Crosby, Bing, American singer and actor, Sept 1941, June 1953, *Obit* Jan 1978

Crosby, John O'Hea, American conductor and opera company manager, Nov 1981, *Obit* Yrbk 2003

Cross, Ben, English actor, Aug 1984

Cross, Milton, Jan 1940, *Obit* Feb 1975

Crow, Sheryl, American singer and songwriter, May 1998

Crowe, Russell, Australian actor, May 2000

Cruise, Tom, American actor, Apr 1987

Crumit, Frank, *Obit* Oct 1943

Cruz, Celia, Cuban-American singer, July 1983, *Obit* Nov 2003

Cruz, Penelope, Spanish actress, July 2001

Cui Jian, Chinese rock musician, Jan 2002

Cullen, Bill, television game show host, Jan 1960, *Obit* Sept 1990

Cummings, Robert, actor, Jan 1956, *Obit* Feb 1991

Cunningham, Merce, American dancer and choreographer, May 1966, *Obit* Yrbk 2009

Cunningham, Phil, British guitarist and keyboardist, Jan 2006

Curtin, Jane, actress, Jan 1997

Curtin, Phyllis, American opera singer and teacher, Sept 1964

Curtis, Tony, American actor, May 1959, *Obit* Nov 2010

Curzon, Clifford, English pianist, May 1950, *Obit* Oct 1982

Cusack, Joan, American actress, July 1998

Cusack, John, American actor, June 1996

D'Angelo, American singer, May 2001

D'Onofrio, Vincent, American actor, May 2004

DMX, American rapper, Aug 2003

Daddy G (Singer), English singer and DJ, June 2004

Dafoe, Willem, American actor, Apr 1990

Dale, Clamma, Apr 1979

Dalton, Charles, *Obit* Aug 1942

Dalton, Timothy, English actor, May 1988

Daly, Carson, American video jockey and talk show host, Nov 2009

Daly, James, Oct 1959, *Obit* Sept 1978

Daly, Tyne, actress, Mar 1992

Damerel, Donna, *Obit* Apr 1941

Damrosch, Walter, American conductor and composer, Mar 1944, *Obit* Jan 1951

Danforth, William, *Obit* June 1941

Dangerfield, Rodney, American comedian, *Obit* Feb 2005

Daniels, Charles N., composer, *Obit* Mar 1943

Danner, Blythe, American actress, Jan 1981

Danson, Ted, American actor, Oct 1990

Daratista, Inul, Indonesian singer and dancer, Jan 2003

Darin, Bobby, American singer and actor, Mar 1963, *Obit* Feb 1974

Darin, Ricardo, Argentine actor, Jan 2002

Darwell, Jane, June 1941, *Obit* Oct 1967

Dashiell, Willard, *Obit* June 1943

Dassin, Jules, American film director, Mar 1971, *Obit* Yrbk 2008

Davidovich, Bella, Russian pianist, May 1989

Davidson, John, singer and actor, Sept 1976

Davies, Dennis Russell, conductor, May 1993

Davis, Andrew, British conductor, May 1983

Davis, Anthony, American composer and pianist, May 1990

Davis, Bette, American actress, Oct 1941, Mar 1953, *Obit* Nov 1989

Davis, Colin, British conductor, Nov 1968, *Obit* Yrbk 2013

Davis, Geena, American actress, Oct 1991

Davis, Judy, Australian actress, Nov 1993

Davis, Mac, American country singer and songwriter, Aug 1980

Davis, Miles, American jazz trumpet player and

flugelhornist, June 1962, *Obit* Nov 1991

Davis, Sammy, American actor and singer, Sept 1956, July 1978, *Obit* July 1990

Day, Doris, American singer and actress, Apr 1954

Day, Laraine, American actress, Sept 1953, *Obit* Yrbk 2008

Day-Lewis, Daniel, Anglo-Irish actor, July 1990

De Havilland, Olivia, American actress, May 1944, Nov 1966

De La Hoya, Oscar, American boxer, Jan 1997

De Lavallade, Carmen, American actress and dancer, Yrbk 1967

De Leath, Vaughn, *Obit* July 1943

De Luca, Giuseppe, Italian opera singer, Mar 1947, *Obit* Oct 1950

De Mille, Agnes, American choreographer, Oct 1943, Jan 1985, *Obit* Jan 1994

De Niro, Robert, American actor, Aug 1976, May 1993

De, Shobha, Indian novelist, journalist and television personality, Jan 2005

DeBarge, El, American singer, June 2011

DeGaetani, Jan, opera singer, Oct 1977

DeLonge, Tom, American guitarist, Aug 2002

DeMarcus, Jay, American keyboardist and singer, Aug 2003

DePreist, James, conductor, Oct 1990

DeVito, Danny, American actor and film director, Feb 1988

Dean, Laura, dancer and choreographer, Oct 1988

Dearie, Blossom, American singer, Feb 1989, *Obit* Yrbk 2009

Deasy, Mary, Yrbk 1958

Dee, Ruby, American actress, Nov 1970

Defauw, Desire, Jan 1940, *Obit* Oct 1960

Del Monaco, Mario, Feb 1957, *Obit* Jan 1983

Del Toro, Benicio, American actor, Sept 2001

Delilah, American radio talk show host, Apr 2005

Della Casa, Lisa, Swiss opera singer, July 1956, *Obit* Yrbk 2013

Della Chiesa, Vivian, American opera singer, Nov 1943

Dello Joio, Norman, American composer, Sept 1957, *Obit* Yrbk 2008

Delon, Alain, French actor, Apr 1964

Delson, Brad, American guitarist, Mar 2002

Dench, Judi, English actress, Jan 1999

Deneuve, Catherine, French actress, Feb 1978

Dennehy, Brian, American actor, July 1991

Dennis, Sandy, actress, Jan 1969, *Obit* May 1992

Denniston, Reynolds, *Obit* Mar 1943

Denver, John, American singer and actor, Jan 1975, *Obit* Jan 1998

Depardieu, Gerard, French actor, Oct 1987

Depp, Johnny, American actor, May 1991

Dern, Bruce, American actor, Oct 1978

Dern, Laura, American actress, Oct 1992

Derwent, Clarence, Nov 1947, *Obit* Nov 1959

Deschanel, Zooey, American actress, Aug 2012

Desplat, Alexandre, French composer, June 2011

Dett, Robert Nathaniel, composer, *Obit* Nov 1943

Dewhurst, Colleen, actress, July 1974, *Obit* Oct 1991

DiCaprio, Leonardo, American actor, Mar 1997

DiFranco, Ani, American singer and songwriter, Aug 1997

Diamond, David, American composer, Nov 1966, *Obit* Yrbk 2005

Diamond, Neil, American singer and songwriter, May 1981

Diaz, Cameron, American actress, Apr 2005

Dickinson, Angie, American actress, Feb 1981

Diddley, Bo, American guitarist, singer and songwriter, June 1989, *Obit* Sept 2008

Dietrich, Marlene, German-American actress, June 1953, Feb 1968, *Obit* June 1992

Diggs, Taye, American actor, Aug 2011

Diller, Phyllis, American comedienne, July 1967, *Obit* Yrbk 2012

Dillman, Bradford, actor, Jan 1960

Dillon, Matt, American actor, May 1985

Dinklage, Peter, American actor, Apr 2013

Dirnt, Mike, American bassist and singer, Aug 2005

Dixey, Henry E., *Obit* Apr 1943

Dixit, Madhuri, Indian actress, Jan 2006

Dixon, Dean, conductor, Apr 1943, *Obit* Jan 1977

Dixon, Willie, American blues singer, May 1989, *Obit* Apr 1992

Dobbs, Mattiwilda, American opera singer, Sept 1955

Dodge, Charles, American composer, Aug 2007

Dohnanyi, Christoph von, German conductor, Oct 1985

Dolin, Anton, English dancer and choreographer, Jan 1946, *Obit* Jan 1984

Dolly, Jenny, *Obit* July 1941

Donahue, Phil, American television talk show host, May 1980

Dorati, Antal, Hungarian conductor and composer, July 1948, *Obit* Jan 1989

Dornay, Louis, *Obit* Sept 1940

Dorough, Howie, American singer, May 2000

Dorsey, Tommy, American band leader, Apr 1942, *Obit* Feb 1957

Douglas, Dave, American jazz trumpet player and composer, Mar 2006

Douglas, Helen Gahagan, American congresswoman, Sept 1944, *Obit* Aug 1980

Douglas, Jerry, American dobro guitar player, Aug 2004

Douglas, Kirk, American actor, Mar 1952

Douglas, Melvyn, actor, May 1942, *Obit* Sept 1981

Douglas, Michael, American actor and motion picture producer, Apr 1987

Douglas, Mike, American television talk show host, May 1968, *Obit* Yrbk 2007

Doumbia, Mariam, Malian singer, Jan 2006

Downey, Morton, American singer, July 1949, *Obit* Jan 1986

Downey, Robert, American actor, Aug 1998

Downs, Hugh, television personality, Mar 1965

Drake, Alfred, actor and singer, Apr 1944, *Obit* Sept 1992

Drake, Bobby, American drummer, Sept 2010

Draper, Paul, dancer, Feb 1944, *Obit* Jan 1997

Drescher, Fran, American actress, Apr 1998

Drexler, Jorge, Uruguayan singer and songwriter, Jan 2005

Dreyfuss, Richard, American actor, Jan 1976

Droste, Ed, American guitarist and singer, Sept 2011

Drozd, Steven, American drummer, guitarist and keyboardist, Oct 2002

Drucker, Eugene, American violinist, July 2002

Druckman, Jacob, composer, May 1981, *Obit* Aug 1996

Du Pre, Jacqueline, British cellist, May 1970, *Obit* Nov 1987

Duchin, Eddy, pianist and band leader, Jan 1947, *Obit* Mar 1951

Duchin, Peter, band leader, Jan 1977

Dudamel, Gustavo, Venezuelan conductor, Apr 2010

Duff, Hilary, American actress and singer, Feb 2006

Dujardin, Jean, Oct 2013

Dukakis, Olympia, American actress, July 1991

Duke, Patty, American actress, Sept 1963

Duke, Vernon, American composer, June 1941, *Obit* Mar 1969

Dullea, Keir, American actor, June 1970

Dunaway, Faye, American actress, Feb 1972

Duncan, Malcolm, *Obit* June 1942

Duncan, Michael Clarke, actor, Aug 2000, *Obit* Yrbk 2012

Duncan, Sandy, actress, Jan 1980

Duncan, Todd, singer and voice teacher, July 1942, *Obit* May 1998

Dunham, Katherine, American dancer and choreographer, Mar 1941, *Obit* Yrbk 2006

Dunmall, Paul, British jazz saxophonist, May 2011

Dunn, Ronnie Gene, American country singer and songwriter, Sept 2004

Dunne, Irene, American actress and singer, Aug 1945, *Obit* Nov 1990

Dunninger, Joseph, magician and mind reader, Sept 1944, *Obit* May 1975

Dunnock, Mildred, actress, Sept 1955, *Obit* Sept 1991

Dunst, Kirsten, American actress, Oct 2001

Durante, Jimmy, comedian, Sept 1946, *Obit* Mar 1980

Durbin, Deanna, American singer and actress, June 1941, *Obit* Yrbk 2013

Duritz, Adam, American singer and songwriter, Mar 2003

Durning, Charles, American actor, Sept 1997, *Obit* Yrbk 2013

Dutton, Charles S., American actor and television director, Oct 2000

Dutton, Lawrence, American violist, July 2002

Duvall, Robert, American actor and motion picture director, July 1977

Dyer-Bennet, Richard, singer, June 1944, *Obit* Feb 1992

Earle, Steve, American country singer and guitarist, Oct 1998

Eastwood, Clint, American actor and film director, Oct 1971, Mar 1989

Ebsen, Buddy, American actor and dancer, Jan 1977, *Obit* Yrbk 2003

Eckstine, Billy, American jazz singer, July 1952, *Obit* Apr 1993

Eddins, William Frederick, American conductor and pianist, Feb 2002

Eddy, Nelson, singer and actor, Feb 1943, *Obit* May 1967

Edwards, Clarence, Antiguan keyboardist and singer, Jan 2004

Edwards, David, Antiguan bassist, Jan 2004

Edwards, Joan, singer and composer, Oct 1953, *Obit* Oct 1981

Edwards, Kathleen, Canadian singer and songwriter, Oct 2012

Edwards, Ralph, American television producer and personality, July 1943, *Obit* Yrbk 2006

Edwards, Toriano, Antiguan guitarist and singer, Jan 2004

Edwards, Vince, actor, Oct 1962, *Obit* May 1996

Eggerth, Marta, Austro-Hungarian singer and actress, Nov 1943

Eglevsky, Andre, Feb 1953, *Obit* Feb 1978

Eichheim, Henry, American violinist, conductor and composer, *Obit* Oct 1942

Eiko, Japanese dancer and choreographer, May 2003

Einem, Gottfried von, Austrian composer, July 1953, *Obit* Sept 1996

Eisler, Hanns, German composer, May 1942, *Obit* Nov 1962

Ejiofor, Chiwetel, British actor, Jan 2004

Eldridge, Florence, actress, Mar 1943, *Obit* Sept 1988

Eldridge, Roy, American trumpet player, Mar 1987, *Obit* Apr 1989

Elias, Rosalind, Jan 1967

Elizondo, Hector, American actor, Jan 1992

Elling, Kurt, American jazz singer, Jan 2005

Elliott, Joe, English singer, Jan 2003

Elliott, Maxine, actress, Mar 1940

Elman, Mischa, American violinist, Oct 1945, *Obit* June 1967

Eltinge, Julian, *Obit* Apr 1941

Elzy, Ruby, *Obit* Aug 1943

Emerson, Faye, American actress and television personality, Sept 1951, *Obit* May 1983

Eminem, American rapper, Jan 2001

Engel, Kurt, *Obit* Mar 1942

Englund, Robert, actor, Mar 1990

Entremont, Philippe, French pianist and conductor, Mar 1977

Escoffery, Wayne, American jazz saxophonist and composer, Jan 2011

Estefan, Gloria, Cuban-American singer and songwriter, Oct 1995

Estes, Simon, American opera singer, Aug 1986

Estrada, Joseph, Filipino president, Feb 2000

Etheridge, Melissa, American singer and guitarist, May 1995

Evans, Chris, American actor, Aug 2013

Evans, Edith, English actress, June 1956, *Obit* Jan 1977

Evans, Faith, American singer and songwriter, Feb 1999

Evans, Linda, American actress, Mar 1986

Evans, Maurice, English actor, May 1940, June 1961, *Obit* May 1989

Eve (Singer), American rapper and actress, July 2003

Everett, Rupert, English actor, Jan 2005

Ewell, Tom, actor, May 1961, *Obit* Nov 1994

Ewing, Maria, American opera singer, Apr 1990

Fairbanks, Douglas, American actor, Jan 1940

Fairbanks, Douglas, American actor, Nov 1941, Feb 1956, *Obit* Aug 2000

Falco, Edie, American actress, Mar 2006

Falk, Peter, American actor, July 1972, *Obit* Yrbk 2011

Falla, Manuel de, Spanish composer, *Obit* Yrbk 1946

Fals, Iwan, Indonesian singer and songwriter, Jan 2002

Farina, Dennis, American actor, *Obit* Yrbk 2013

Farrell, Colin, Irish actor, Jan 2004

Farrell, Eileen, American singer, Feb 1961, *Obit* June 2002

Farrow, Mia, American actress, Apr 1970

Fassbaender, Brigitte, German opera singer, June 1994

Fatone, Joey, American singer, Nov 2000

Fatt, Jeff, Australian actor and singer, Jan 2004

Faussart, Celia, French singer, Jan 2003

Faussart, Helene, French singer, Jan 2003

Faversham, William, *Obit* May 1940

Fawcett, Farrah, American actress, Feb 1978, *Obit* Aug 2009

Fay, Martin, Irish fiddler, Mar 2004, *Obit* Yrbk 2013

Feinstein, Michael, American pianist and singer, Apr 1988

Feist (Musician), Canadian singer and songwriter, June 2008

Feliciano, Jose, singer and guitarist, July 1969

Feltsman, Vladimir, Russian pianist, Apr 1988

Fenton, George, English composer, July 2010

Fergie, American singer, Oct 2006

Ferguson, Elsie, Feb 1944, *Obit* Jan 1962

Ferguson, Maynard, Canadian jazz trumpet player, Feb 1980, *Obit* Yrbk 2006

Fernandel, Oct 1955, *Obit* Apr 1971

Fernandez, Alejandro, Mexican singer, Jan 2005

Ferrer, Jose, American actor and director, May 1944, *Obit* Mar 1992

Ferrera, America, American actress, Sept 2007

Ferrier, Kathleen, British opera singer, Oct 1951, *Obit* Yrbk 1953

Feuermann, Emanuel, *Obit* July 1942

Fiedler, Arthur, American conductor, Sept 1945, May 1977, *Obit* Sept 1979

Field, Anthony, Australian actor and singer, Jan 2004

Field, Betty, Sept 1959, *Obit* Nov 1973

Field, Sally, American actress, Oct 1979

Fields, Gracie, English actress and singer, Apr 1941, *Obit* Nov 1979

Fields, Lew, comedian, *Obit* Sept 1941

Fields, Stanley, *Obit* June 1941

Fiennes, Ralph, British actor, Sept 1996

Finch, Peter, English actor, Sept 1972, *Obit* Mar 1977

Finckel, David, American cellist and recording producer, July 2002

Finn, Craig, American singer and songwriter, Sept 2010

Finney, Albert, English actor, Oct 1963

Firkusny, Rudolf, Czech pianist, Oct 1979, *Obit* Sept 1994

Firth, Colin, English actor, Mar 2004

Fischbacher, Siegfried, German magician and animal trainer, Jan 1998

Fischer-Dieskau, Dietrich, German opera singer, Feb 1967, *Obit* Yrbk 2012

Fishburne, Laurence, American actor, Aug 1996

Fisher, Eddie, American singer, Oct 1954, *Obit* Yrbk 2010

Fisher, Fred, songwriter and composer, *Obit* Mar 1942

Fishman, Jon, American drummer, July 2003

Fitzgerald, Barry, Feb 1945, *Obit* Feb 1961

Fitzgerald, Cissy, *Obit* July 1941

Fitzgerald, Edward, radio talk show host, Apr 1947, *Obit* June 1982

Fitzgerald, Ella, American singer, Oct 1956, July 1990, *Obit* Aug 1996

Fitzgerald, Geraldine, Irish actress and director, Oct 1976, *Obit* Yrbk 2005

Fitzgerald, Pegeen, radio talk show host, Apr 1947, *Obit* Apr 1989

Flack, Roberta, American singer, Nov 1973

Flagstad, Kirsten, Norwegian opera singer, May 1947, *Obit* Jan 1963

Flanagan, Tommy, American pianist, Apr 1995, *Obit* Mar 2002

Flansburgh, John, guitarist, Nov 1999

Fleck, Bela, American banjoist, Nov 1996

Fleisher, Leon, American pianist and conductor, Jan 1971

Fleming, Renee, American opera singer, May 1997

Flesch, Carl, Hungarian violinist, *Obit* Jan 1945

Flint, Keith, British singer and dancer, Oct 2009

Florez, Juan Diego, Peruvian opera singer, Jan 2007

Fodor, Eugene, American violinist, Apr 1976, *Obit* Yrbk 2011

Followill, Caleb, American singer and guitarist, July 2010

Followill, Jared, American bassist, July 2010

Followill, Matthew, American guitarist, July 2010

Followill, Nathan, American drummer, July 2010

Fonda, Bridget, American actress, Jan 1994

Fonda, Henry, American actor, Yrbk 1948, Nov 1974, *Obit* Sept 1982

Fonda, Jane, American actress, July 1964, June 1986

Fonda, Peter, American actor, Mar 1998

Fontaine, Joan, American actress, May 1944

Fontanne, Lynn, Anglo-American actress, June 1941, *Obit* Sept 1983

Fonteyn, Margot, English ballet dancer, Yrbk 1949, Mar 1972, *Obit* Apr 1991

Foo, Sharin, Danish singer and bassist, Jan 2004

Ford, Glenn, American actor, June 1959, *Obit* Yrbk 2007

Ford, Harrison, American actor, Sept 1984, June 2008

Ford, Tennessee Ernie, singer, Mar 1958, *Obit* Jan 1992

Formell, Juan-Carlos, Cuban singer, songwriter and guitarist, Jan 2005

Forrest, Alan, *Obit* Sept 1941

Forrester, Maureen, Canadian opera singer, July 1962, *Obit* Yrbk 2010

Forsyth, Cecil, *Obit* Feb 1942

Forsythe, John, American actor, May 1973, *Obit* Yrbk 2010

Fortier, Paul-Andre, Canadian choreographer and dancer, Nov 2010

Foss, Lukas, American composer, conductor and pianist, June 1966, *Obit* Yrbk 2009

Fosse, Bob, American director and choreographer, June 1972, *Obit* Nov 1987

Foster, Jodie, American actress and film director, June 1981, Aug 1992

Fou Ts'ong, Chinese pianist, Jan 2003

Fountain, Clarence, American gospel singer, Oct 2001

Fox, Megan, American actress, Feb 2010

Fox, Michael J., Canadian actor, Nov 1987

Fox, Sidney, actress, *Obit* Jan 1943

Fox, Virgil, Jan 1964, *Obit* Jan 1981

Fracci, Carla, Italian ballet dancer, Feb 1975

Frager, Malcolm, pianist, Apr 1967, *Obit* Aug 1991

Fraiture, Nikolai, American bassist, Feb 2007

Frakes, Jonathan, actor and motion picture director, July 1999

Frampton, Peter, English guitarist and singer, May 1978

Francescatti, Zino, French violinist, Oct 1947, *Obit* Nov 1991

Franciosa, Tony, American actor, July 1961, *Obit* Yrbk 2006

Francis, Arlene, American television personality, May 1956, *Obit* Sept 2001

Francis, Connie, singer, July 1962

Francisco, Chilean television personality, Feb 2001

Franco, James, American actor, Apr 2011

Franklin, Irene, actress, *Obit* Aug 1941

Franklin, Kirk, American gospel rap singer, Mar 2000

Franz, Dennis, American actor, July 1995

Fraser, Brendan, American actor, Feb 2001

Fratellini, Paul, *Obit* Yrbk 1940

Freeman, Martin, British actor, Nov 2013

Freeman, Morgan, American actor, Feb 1991

Frehley, Ace, American guitarist, Apr 1999

Fresnay, Pierre, Feb 1959, *Obit* Feb 1975

Friedman, Kinky, American country singer, band leader, songwriter and mystery novelist, Feb 2012

Froese, Edgar, German electronic musician, Jan 2005

Froese, Jerome, German keyboardist, Jan 2005

Frost, David, English talk show host, July 1969, *Obit* Yrbk 2013

Fuchs, Joseph, violinist, Oct 1962, *Obit* May 1997

Fujii, Satoko, Japanese jazz pianist, June 2010

Funicello, Annette, American actress and singer, *Obit* Yrbk 2013

Funk, Chris, American guitarist and thereminist, Aug 2007

Funt, Allen, television producer and performer, Yrbk 1966, *Obit* Nov 1999

Furness, Betty, television commentator and consumer adviser, Feb 1968, *Obit* June 1994

Furtado, Nelly, Canadian singer, songwriter and guitarist, Jan 2007

G, Kenny, American saxophonist, Nov 1995

Gabin, Jean, French actor, June 1941, *Obit* Jan 1977

Gable, Clark, American actor, May 1945, *Obit* Jan 1961

Gabor, Eva, Hungarian actress, July 1968, *Obit* Sept 1995

Gabor, Zsa Zsa, Hungarian-American actress, Mar 1988

Gabriel, Peter, English singer and songwriter, Jan 1990

Gades, Antonio, Spanish flamenco dancer and choreographer, Feb 1973, *Obit* Yrbk 2004

Galbraith, Paul, British guitarist, Jan 2007

Galli, Rosina, *Obit* Jan 1940

Gandolfini, James, American actor, Feb 2000, *Obit* Yrbk 2013

Ganz, Bruno, Swiss actor, Jan 2006

Gara, Jeremy, Canadian drummer, Jan 2007

Garbo, Greta, Swedish-American actress, Apr 1955, *Obit* June 1990

Garcia Bernal, Gael, Mexican actor, Jan 2003

Garcia, Jerry, American guitarist and singer, May 1990, *Obit* Oct 1995

Gardner, Ava, American actress, Mar 1965, *Obit* Mar 1990

Garfield, John, actor, Apr 1948, *Obit* July 1952

Garfunkel, Art, American singer and actor, June 1974

Gargan, William, Jan 1969, *Obit* Apr 1979

Garland, Judy, American singer and actress, Nov 1941, Yrbk 1952, *Obit* Sept 1969

Garner, Erroll, American jazz pianist, Sept 1959, *Obit* Mar 1977

Garner, James, American actor, Nov 1966

Garner, Jennifer, American actress, Apr 2008

Garroway, Dave, American television personality, May 1952, *Obit* Sept 1982

Garson, Greer, Anglo-Irish actress, Sept 1942, *Obit* June 1996

Gary, John, singer and songwriter, July 1967, *Obit* Mar 1998

Gassman, Vittorio, Italian actor and theatrical director, Oct 1964, *Obit* Oct 2000

Gaubatz, Lynn, bassoonist, Feb 2001

Gavin, John, American actor and diplomat, Sept 1962

Gavrilov, Andrei, Russian pianist, Oct 2000

Gayle, Crystal, singer, Mar 1986

Gazzara, Ben, American actor, Nov 1967, *Obit* Yrbk 2012

Gedda, Nicolai, Swedish opera singer, Nov 1965

Geldof, Bob, Irish rock musician and humanitarian, Mar 1986

Gennaro, Peter, American dancer and choreographer, June 1964, *Obit* Feb 2001

George, Zelma Watson, sociologist and opera singer, Oct 1961, *Obit* Sept 1994

Gere, Richard, American actor, Aug 1980

Gergiev, Valery, Russian conductor and opera director, Jan 1998

Gerwig, Greta, American actress, June 2010

Getty, Estelle, American actress, Mar 1990, *Obit* Yrbk 2008

Getz, Stan, American jazz saxophonist, Apr 1971, *Obit* Aug 1991

Ghostface Killah, American rapper, June 2008

Giamatti, Paul, American actor, Sept 2005

Giannini, Giancarlo, June 1979

Gibb, Barry, English singer and songwriter, Sept 1981

Gibson, Mel, American actor and motion picture director, Apr 1984, Aug 2003

Gielgud, John, English actor, director and producer, Apr 1947, Feb 1984, *Obit* Aug 2000

Gieseking, Walter, German pianist, Oct 1956, *Obit* Jan 1957

Gilbert, Gillian, British guitarist, keyboardist and singer, Jan 2006

Gilels, Emil, Russian pianist, Oct 1956, *Obit* Jan 1986

Gillespie, Dizzy, American trumpet player, Apr 1957, Jan 1993, *Obit* Jan 1993

Gillingham, Charlie, American keyboardist, Mar 2003

Gillmore, Frank, *Obit* May 1943

Gingold, Hermione, English actress, Oct 1958, *Obit* July 1987

Giordani, Marcello, Italian opera singer, May 2008

Gish, Dorothy, American actress, Aug 1944, *Obit* Sept 1968

Gish, Lillian, American actress, Aug 1944, Aug 1978, *Obit* Apr 1993

Giulini, Carlo Maria, Italian conductor, Mar 1978, *Obit* Yrbk 2005

Glasper, Robert, American jazz pianist, Mar 2011

Glennie, Evelyn, Scottish percussionist, July 1997

Glover, Danny, American actor, Apr 1992

Glover, Savion, American tap dancer, Mar 1996

Gobbi, Tito, Italian opera singer, Jan 1957, *Obit* May 1984

Goddard, Paulette, American actress, *Obit* June 1990

Godfrey, Arthur, radio and television personality, July 1948, *Obit* May 1983

Goerne, Matthias, German opera singer, Jan 2006

Goldberg, Whoopi, American actress, Mar 1985

Goldblum, Jeff, American actor, July 1997

Goldman, Edwin Franko, Sept 1942, *Obit* May 1956

Goldovsky, Boris, Russian-American pianist, conductor and opera director, Yrbk 1966, *Obit* Aug 2001

Goldsmith, Jerry, American composer, May 2001, *Obit* Yrbk 2004

Goldthwait, Bobcat, American comedian, Sept 2010

Golijov, Osvaldo, Argentine composer, Jan 2006

Golschmann, Vladimir, Apr 1951, *Obit* May 1972

Gomes, Marcelo, Brazilian ballet dancer, May 2007

Gonzalez, Alex, Mexican drummer, Jan 2005

Goode, Richard, American pianist, Nov 1988

Goodwin, Harry, *Obit* Yrbk 1942

Googoosh, Iranian singer and actress, May 2001

Gordon, C. Henry, *Obit* Jan 1941

Gordon, David, American choreographer, June 1994

Gordon, Ed, American television newscaster, July 2005

Gordon, Mike, American bassist, July 2003

Gordon, Wycliffe, American jazz trombonist, Sept 2009

Gordon-Levitt, Joseph, American actor, June 2011

Gorecki, Henryk, Polish composer, May 1994, *Obit* Yrbk 2011

Gorme, Eydie, singer, Feb 1965, *Obit* Yrbk 2013

Gosden, Freeman F., actor, Yrbk 1947, *Obit* Feb 1983

Gossett, Louis, American actor, Nov 1990

Gould, Elliott, American actor, Feb 1971

Gould, Glenn, Canadian pianist, Oct 1960, *Obit* Nov 1982

Gould, Morton, pianist and composer, Sept 1945, Jan 1968, *Obit* May 1996

Goulding, Ellie, British guitarist, singer and songwriter, Apr 2013

Goulet, Robert, American singer and actor, Sept 1962, *Obit* Yrbk 2008

Gowdy, Curt, American television sportscaster, May 1967, *Obit* Yrbk 2006

Grace, Mar 1955, Oct 1977, *Obit* Nov 1982

Graffman, Gary, pianist, July 1970

Graham, Ed, British drummer, Jan 2004

Graham, Susan, American opera singer, Oct 2005

Graham, Virginia, radio and television talk show host, Oct 1956, *Obit* Mar 1999

Gramm, Donald, opera singer, Nov 1975, *Obit* July 1983

Grammer, Kelsey, American actor, May 1996

Grandjany, Marcel, May 1943, *Obit* Apr 1975

Grant, Cary, Anglo-American actor, Sept 1941, Nov 1965, *Obit* Jan 1987

Grant, Hugh, English actor, Sept 1995

Grant, Lee, actress and director, Mar 1974

Grappelli, Stephane, French jazz violinist, Aug 1988, *Obit* Feb 1998

Graser, Earle W., *Obit* June 1941

Grauer, Ben, Feb 1941, July 1959, *Obit* July 1977

Gray, David, British singer and songwriter, Jan 2004

Gray, Macy, American singer and songwriter, May 2000

Gray, Spalding, American monologist, Sept 1986, *Obit* Yrbk 2004

Grebenshikov, Boris, Russian singer, Jan 2002

Greco, Jose, American dancer and choreographer, Mar 1952, *Obit* Mar 2001

Greco, Juliette, French singer, Jan 1992

Green, Martyn, June 1950, *Obit* Apr 1975

Greenberg, Noah, conductor and musicologist, May 1964, *Obit* Feb 1966

Greene, Lorne, actor, Jan 1967, *Obit* Oct 1987

Greenstreet, Sydney, May 1943, *Obit* Mar 1954

Greenwood, Colin, English bassist, June 2001

Greenwood, Joan, English actress, May 1954, *Obit* Apr 1987

Greenwood, Jonny, English guitarist, June 2001

Gregory, Cynthia, American ballet dancer, May 1977

Grenfell, Joyce, English actress, Mar 1958, *Obit* Feb 1980

Grey, Joel, American actor and singer, Jan 1973

Grier, Pam, American actress, Feb 1998

Grier, Rosey, American football player and entertainer, Mar 1975

Griffies, Ethel, Jan 1968, *Obit* Nov 1975

Griffin, Merv, American talk show host and television producer, Sept 1967, *Obit* Yrbk 2007

Griffith, Andy, American actor, May 1960, *Obit* Yrbk 2012

Griffith, Melanie, American actress, Oct 1990

Griffith, Nanci, American folk and country singer and songwriter, Feb 1998

Grimaud, Helene, French pianist, Jan 2007

Grimes, Tammy, actress, July 1962

Grizzard, George, American actor, June 1976, *Obit* Yrbk 2008

Groban, Josh, American pop singer, Aug 2009

Grodin, Charles, American actor, Nov 1995

Grofe, Ferde, July 1940, *Obit* May 1972

Grohl, Dave, American singer and guitarist, May 2002

Gronemeyer, Herbert, German singer and actor, Jan 2003

Gubaidulina, Sofia Asgatovna, Russian composer, Oct 1999

Gueden, Hilde, Apr 1955

Guillaume, Robert, American actor, Apr 2000

Guinness, Alec, English actor, Oct 1950, Mar 1981, *Obit* Oct 2000

Gulpilil, David, Australian actor, Jan 2003

Guthrie, Arlo, American folk singer and songwriter, Feb 1982

Guy, Buddy, American blues guitarist, Feb 2000

Gwenn, Edmund, Sept 1943, *Obit* Nov 1959

Haas, Jonathan, American timpanist, June 2003

Hackett, Charles, American opera singer, *Obit* Feb 1942

Hackman, Gene, American actor, July 1972

Hadley, Jerry, American opera singer, Nov 1991, *Obit* Yrbk 2007

Hagegard, Hakan, Swedish opera singer, May 1985

Hagen, Uta, American actress, May 1944, Oct 1963, *Obit* Yrbk 2004

Haggard, Merle, American country singer, Jan 1977

Hagman, Larry, American actor, Sept 1980, *Obit* Yrbk 2013

Hahn, Hilary, American violinist, Sept 2002

Hahn, Joseph, American DJ, Mar 2002

Haitink, Bernard, Dutch conductor, Nov 1977

Hakim, Christine, Indonesian actress and social activist, Jan 2003

Halasz, Laszlo, Hungarian-American conductor and pianist, Jan 1949, *Obit* Feb 2002

Hall, Deidre, American actress, Nov 2002

Hall, James, actor, *Obit* July 1940

Hallahan, Patrick, American rock drummer, Nov 2008

Hallyday, Johnny, French singer, Jan 2003

Hamilton, Hale, *Obit* July 1942

Hamilton, Margaret, actress, Apr 1979, *Obit* July 1985

Hamilton, Tom, American rock bassist, July 2004

Hamlisch, Marvin, American composer and pianist, May 1976, *Obit* Yrbk 2012

Hamm, Jon, American actor, Mar 2013

Hammer (Musician), American rapper, Apr 1991

Hammond, Albert, American guitarist, Feb 2007

Hampden, Walter, American actor, May 1953, *Obit* Sept 1955

Hampshire, Susan, English actress and author, Jan 1974

Hampson, Thomas, American opera singer, Mar 1991

Handy, W. C., American composer and music publisher, Mar 1941, *Obit* June 1958

Hanks, Tom, American actor, Apr 1989

Hannah, Daryl, American actress, May 1990

Hannity, Sean, American television moderator, Apr 2005

Hansen, Liane, American radio reporter and program host, May 2003

Harbison, John, composer, Feb 1993

Harcourt, Nic, American disc jockey, Oct 2005

Harden, Marcia Gay, American actress, Sept 2001

Hardwicke, Cedric, English actor, Oct 1949, *Obit* Oct 1964

Hardy, Francoise, French singer, Jan 2005

Hargrove, Roy, American jazz trumpet player, Apr 2000

Harlan, Otis, *Obit* Jan 1940

Harper, Ben, American singer and guitarist, Jan 2004

Harper, Valerie, American actress, Feb 1975

Harrell, Lynn, cellist, Feb 1983

Harrelson, Woody, American actor, Jan 1997

Harrington, David, violinist, Nov 1998

Harris, Barbara, American actress, Apr 1968

Harris, Emmylou, American singer, Oct 1994

Harris, Julie, American actress, Feb 1956, Aug 1977, *Obit* Yrbk 2013

Harris, Naomie, British actress, Sept 2012

Harris, Richard, Irish actor, May 1964, *Obit* Yrbk 2003

Harris, Rosemary, British actress, Sept 1967

Harris, Roy, composer, Aug 1940, *Obit* Nov 1979

Harrison, George, British singer and guitarist, Nov 1966, Jan 1989, *Obit* Mar 2002

Harrison, Rex, English actor, Jan 1947, Feb 1986, *Obit* July 1990

Harry, Deborah, American singer, Nov 1981

Hart, Mickey, American drummer, Jan 1994

Hart, William S., American actor, *Obit* July 1946

Hartman, David, actor and television personality, June 1981

Hartman, Grace, Nov 1942, *Obit* Oct 1955

Hartman, Paul, American actor, Nov 1942, *Obit* Yrbk 1973

Harty, Hamilton, Irish composer and conductor, *Obit* Apr 1941

Haruka, Yoko, Japanese feminist, writer and television personality, Jan 2004

Harvey, Laurence, British actor, May 1961, *Obit* Jan 1974

Harvey, PJ, British singer, songwriter and guitarist, May 2008

Hatfield, Juliana, American singer and songwriter, Aug 2011

Hathaway, Anne, American actress, Feb 2009

Hawke, Ethan, American actor and novelist, May 1998

Hawkins, Dan, British rock guitarist, Jan 2004

Hawkins, Erick, dancer and choreographer, Jan 1974, *Obit* Feb 1995

Hawkins, Erskine, trumpet player and band leader, Sept 1941, *Obit* Jan 1994

Hawkins, Jack, Nov 1959, *Obit* Oct 1973

Hawkins, Justin, British rock singer, guitarist and composer, Jan 2004

Hawley, H. Dudley, *Obit* May 1941

Hawn, Goldie, American actress, Yrbk 1971

Hayakawa, Sessue, Japanese actor, Sept 1962, *Obit* Jan 1974

Haydee, Marcia, Brazilian dancer, Oct 1977

Hayden, Sterling, actor, May 1978, *Obit* July 1986

Hayes, Helen, American actress, Jan 1942, Oct 1956, *Obit* May 1993

Hayes, Isaac, American singer and composer, Oct 1972, *Obit* Yrbk 2008

Hayes, Peter Lind, actor, Mar 1959, *Obit* July 1998

Hayes, Roland, American singer, May 1942, *Obit* Mar 1977

Haysbert, Dennis, American actor, Nov 2006

Hayward, Susan, American actress, May 1953, *Obit* May 1975

Haywood, Dave, American country guitarist, pianist and mandolinist, July 2011

Hayworth, Rita, American actress, May 1960, *Obit* July 1987

Heche, Anne, American actress, Sept 1998

Heckart, Eileen, American actress, June 1958, *Obit* Mar 2002

Hee, Dana, American motion picture stunt performer, May 2008

Heflin, Van, July 1943, *Obit* Sept 1971

Heifetz, Jascha, Russian-American violinist, Feb 1944, *Obit* Feb 1988

Helders, Matt, British rock drummer, Jan 2006

Helfgott, David, Australian pianist, Mar 1997

Hemingway, Margaux, American model and actress, Mar 1978, *Obit* Sept 1996

Hemsworth, Chris, Australian actor, Jan 2013

Henderson, Florence, American singer and actress, Apr 1971

Henderson, Joe, American jazz saxophonist, June 1996, *Obit* Oct 2001

Hendricks, Barbara, opera singer, Mar 1989

Henie, Sonja, Norwegian-American figure skater and actress, Sept 1940, Jan 1952, *Obit* Nov 1970

Henning, Doug, Canadian magician, Aug 1976, *Obit* Apr 2000

Henreid, Paul, Austrian actor and director, July 1943, *Obit* June 1992

Henry, Martha, Canadian actress and theatrical director, Jan 2006

Henson, Jim, American puppeteer, Mar 1977, *Obit* July 1990

Hepburn, Audrey, Anglo-Dutch actress, Mar 1954, *Obit* Mar 1993

Hepburn, Katharine, American actress, May 1942, Nov 1969, *Obit* Nov 2003

Heppner, Ben, Canadian opera singer, Jan 1997

Herbert, Don, American science teacher and television personality, Feb 1956, *Obit* Yrbk 2007

Herbert, Matthew, English record producer, composer and DJ, Nov 2012

Herman, Jerry, American composer and lyricist, Jan 1965

Herman, Woody, American band leader, Apr 1973, *Obit* Jan 1988

Hernandez, Dave, American bassist, June 2007

Herrera, Paloma, Argentine ballet dancer, Apr 2000

Hersch, Fred, American jazz pianist and composer, Apr 2006

Hershey, Barbara, American actress, Aug 1989

Hersholt, Jean, American actor, Yrbk 1944, *Obit* Sept 1956

Hess, Myra, English pianist, Sept 1943, *Obit* Jan 1966

Heston, Charlton, American actor, May 1957, July 1986, *Obit* July 2008

Hetfield, James, American singer and guitarist, Jan 2000

Heward, Leslie H., *Obit* June 1943

Hewitt, Angela, Canadian pianist, Apr 2007

Heydt, Herman A., *Obit* Oct 1941

Hidalgo, David, American guitarist, singer and accordionist, Oct 2005

Hildegarde, American singer, Nov 1944, *Obit* Yrbk 2005

Hill, Andrew, American jazz pianist and composer, Apr 2004, *Obit* Yrbk 2007

Hill, Arthur, Canadian actor, Mar 1977, *Obit* Yrbk 2007

Hill, Billy, *Obit* Feb 1941

Hill, Dule, American actor, July 2003

Hill, Faith, American country singer, Mar 2001

Hiller, Wendy, English actress, Oct 1941, *Obit* Yrbk 2003

Hillis, Margaret, choral conductor, Feb 1956, *Obit* Apr 1998

Hindemith, Paul, German composer, Oct 1941, *Obit* Feb 1964

Hines, Gregory, American dancer and actor, July 1985, *Obit* Yrbk 2003

Hines, Jerome, American opera singer, Feb 1963, *Obit* June 2003

Hingle, Pat, American actor, Apr 1965, *Obit* Yrbk 2009

Hinrichs, Gustav, German-American conductor, *Obit* May 1942

Hirsch, Judd, actor, Mar 1984

Hirt, Al, trumpet player, Feb 1967, *Obit* July 1999

Hjejle, Iben, Danish actress, Jan 2003

Hobson Pilot, Ann, American harpist, May 2003

Hoch, Danny, American actor, Oct 1999

Hoffman, Dustin, American actor, Yrbk 1969, Jan 1996

Hoffman, Philip Seymour, American actor, May 2001

Hogan, Paul, Australian comedian, Aug 1987

Hogwood, Christopher, English conductor, harpsichordist and musicologist, July 1985

Hoiby, Lee, American composer, Mar 1987, *Obit* Yrbk 2011

Holbrook, Hal, American actor, May 1961

Holden, William, actor, June 1954, *Obit* Jan 1982

Holder, Geoffrey, Trinidadian dancer and choreographer, Oct 1957

Holland, Dave, English jazz bassist, Mar 2003

Holliday, Jennifer, American singer, June 1983

Holliday, Judy, actress, Apr 1951, *Obit* July 1965

Holloway, Stanley, Feb 1963, *Obit* Mar 1982

Holm, Celeste, American actress, Apr 1944, *Obit* Yrbk 2012

Holm, Georg, Icelandic bassist, Jan 2003

Holm, Ian, English actor, Mar 2002

Honegger, Arthur, Swiss composer, Apr 1941, *Obit* Feb 1956

Hong, Hei-Kyung, Korean opera singer, Nov 2003

Hong, Seok Chon, Korean actor, Jan 2004

Hood, Gavin, South African motion picture director, Jan 2006

Hook, Peter, British bassist and singer, Jan 2006

Hooker, John Lee, American singer and guitarist, Nov 1992, *Obit* Sept 2001

Hooks, Robert, Mar 1970

Hopkins, Anthony, Welsh-American actor, Feb 1980, Mar 1997

Hopkins, Sarah, Australian composer and cellist, Jan 2006

Hopper, Dennis, American actor and director, Aug 1987, *Obit* Yrbk 2010

Hoppus, Mark, American singer and bassist, Aug 2002

Horn, Roy, German magician and animal trainer, Jan 1998

Horne, Lena, American singer, June 1944, Nov 1985, *Obit* Aug 2010

Horne, Marilyn, American opera singer, July 1967

Horner, James, composer, Mar 1997

Horowitz, Vladimir, Russian-American pianist, Sept 1943, Mar 1966, *Obit* Jan 1990

Horton, Edward Everett, American actor, Yrbk 1946, *Obit* Nov 1970

Hoskins, Bob, English actor, Sept 1990

Hounsou, Djimon, Beninese model and actor, Aug 2004

Houseman, John, theatrical director, producer and actor, July 1959, Apr 1984, *Obit* Jan 1989

Houston, Whitney, American singer and actress, Nov 1986, *Obit* Yrbk 2012

Hovhaness, Alan, American composer, Apr 1965, *Obit* Oct 2000

Howard, Cordelia, actress, *Obit* Oct 1941

Howard, Leslie, English actor, *Obit* July 1943

Howard, Ron, American actor and film director, Jan 1979, Aug 1995

Howard, Terrence, American actor, June 2007

Howard, Trevor, English actor, July 1964, *Obit* Feb 1988

Howe, Helen Huntington, author and monologist, Yrbk 1954, *Obit* Mar 1975

Howlett, Liam, British DJ, Oct 2009

Huberman, Bronislaw, Polish violinist, July 1941, *Obit* July 1947

Huckabee, Mike, American talk show host and former governor, Nov 2005

Hudson, Jennifer, American singer and actress, May 2007

Hudson, Rock, American actor, Oct 1961, *Obit* Nov 1985

Hughes, Barnard, American actor, Sept 1981, *Obit* Yrbk 2006

Hugo, Chad, American record producer, singer and songwriter, May 2004

Hull, Josephine, Oct 1953, *Obit* May 1957

Humbard, Rex, American evangelist, Sept 1972, *Obit* Yrbk 2008

Humphrey, Doris, American dancer and choreographer, Apr 1942, *Obit* Mar 1959

Hunt Lieberson, Lorraine, American opera singer, July 2004, *Obit* Yrbk 2006

Hunt, Helen, Nov 1996

Hunt, Linda, actress, Jan 1988

Hunter, Alberta, singer and songwriter, May 1979, *Obit* Jan 1985

Hunter, Charlie, American jazz guitarist, Nov 2007

Hunter, Glenn, American actor, *Obit* Mar 1946

Hunter, Holly, American actress, July 1994

Hunter, Kim, American actress, May 1952, *Obit* Yrbk 2002

Huppert, Isabelle, French actress, Nov 1981

Hurley, Laurel, American opera singer, June 1957

Hurt, John, British actor, Jan 1982

Hurt, William, American actor, May 1986

Hussain, Zakir, Indian percussionist and composer, Jan 2005

Huston, Anjelica, American actress, July 1990

Huston, Walter, actor, Feb 1949, *Obit* May 1950

Hutton, Betty, American singer and actress, June 1950, *Obit* Yrbk 2007

Hutton, Lauren, American model and actress, July 1994

Hvorostovsky, Dmitri, Russian opera singer, Jan 2006

Hyde, Karl, British singer, guitarist and songwriter, Nov 2011

Hynde, Chrissie, American singer and songwriter, Apr 1993

Ice Cube (Musician), American rapper and actor, Aug 1995

Ice-T, American rapper and actor, Sept 1994

Idol, Billy, British singer, songwriter and guitarist, Jan 1994

Iglesias, Enrique, Spanish singer, Apr 1999

Iglesias, Julio, Spanish singer, June 1984

Iglesias, Roberto, Feb 1960

Imam, Adel, Egyptian actor, Jan 2002

India.Arie (Singer), American singer, Feb 2002

International, Dana, Israeli singer, Jan 2005

Irimia, Gabriela, Romanian singer, Jan 2003

Irimia, Monica, Romanian singer, Jan 2003

Irons, Jeremy, English actor, Aug 1984

Irving, Jules, July 1970, *Obit* Sept 1979

Irwin, Bill, American actor and mime, Oct 1987

Isaak, Chris, singer, May 1993

Isbin, Sharon, American classical guitarist, Aug 2003

Ishii, Ken, Japanese techno musician, Jan 2002

Isokoski, Soile, Finnish opera singer, Jan 2006

Istomin, Eugene, American pianist, Oct 1977, *Obit* Feb 2004

Itami, Juzo, Japanese actor and motion picture director, May 1990, *Obit* Mar 1998

Iturbi, Jose, Spanish-American pianist and conductor, Sept 1943, *Obit* Aug 1980

Iverson, Ethan, American jazz pianist, Oct 2011

Ives, Burl, singer and actor, Jan 1946, May 1960, *Obit* June 1995

Ives, Charles Edward, American composer, June 1947, *Obit* July 1954

Ivey, Judith, actress, June 1993

Ivins, Mike, American bassist, Oct 2002

Ja Rule, American rapper, July 2002

Jackman, Hugh, Australian actor, Oct 2003

Jackson, Alan, American country singer, Apr 2004

Jackson, Anne, actress, Sept 1980

Jackson, Glenda, English actress and member of Parliament, Yrbk 1971

Jackson, Janet, American singer, June 1991

Jackson, Joe, English singer and songwriter, Feb 1996

Jackson, Mahalia, American gospel singer, Oct 1957, *Obit* Mar 1972

Jackson, Michael, American singer and songwriter, Nov 1983, *Obit* Aug 2009

Jackson, Samuel L., American actor, Nov 1996

Jacobi, Derek, British actor, May 1981

Jaffe, Susan, dancer, Sept 1997

Jagger, Bianca, Nicaraguan actress, Apr 1987

Jagger, Mick, British singer, Yrbk 1972

Jakes, T. D., American clergyman, religious writer and gospel singer, June 2001

James, Alex, English rock bassist, Nov 2003

James, Jim, American rock guitarist, singer and songwriter, Nov 2008

Janis, Byron, pianist, June 1966

Janssen, David, American actor, Mar 1967, *Obit* Apr 1980

Jaroussky, Philippe, French countertenor, Mar 2011

Jarreau, Al, American singer, Oct 1992

Jay, Ricky, American magician and actor, May 1994

Jay-Z, American rapper, Aug 2002

Jentsch, Julia, German actress, Jan 2006

Jerusalem, Siegfried, German opera singer, Sept 1992

Jett, Joan, American singer and songwriter, Sept 1993

Jillette, Penn, American magician, June 2000

Jo, Sumi, Korean opera singer, Jan 2002

Johannesen, Grant, American pianist, June 1961, *Obit* Yrbk 2005

Johansson, Scarlett, American actress, Mar 2005

Johns, Glynis, Sept 1973

Johnson, Brian, English singer, Mar 2005

Johnson, Chic, American comedian, Sept 1940, *Obit* Apr 1962

Johnson, Don, American actor, Apr 1986

Johnson, Dwayne, American wrestler and actor, July 2000

Johnson, Edward, Canadian-American opera singer and director, Mar 1943, *Obit* June 1959

Johnson, Eric, American guitarist, keyboardist, singer and songwriter, June 2007

Johnson, Hall, American composer and music arranger, Jan 1945, *Obit* June 1970

Johnson, Howard E., *Obit* June 1941

Johnson, Jamey, American country singer and songwriter, Feb 2011

Johnson, Van, American actor, July 1945, *Obit* Yrbk 2009

Johnson, Virginia, American dancer, May 1985

Johnston, Daniel, American singer, songwriter and artist, Sept 2010

Jolie, Angelina, American actress, Oct 2000

Jolson, Al, singer and actor, Nov 1940, *Obit* Yrbk 1950

Jones, Barry, Mar 1958

Jones, Bill T., American dancer and choreographer, July 1993

Jones, Billy, *Obit* Jan 1941

Jones, Bobby, American gospel singer, June 2002

Jones, Buck, *Obit* Jan 1943

Jones, Carolyn, American actress, Mar 1967, *Obit* Sept 1983

Jones, Cherry, American actress, May 1998

Jones, George, American country singer, Feb 1995, *Obit* Yrbk 2013

Jones, Grace, American singer and actress, Sept 1987

Jones, James Earl, American actor, Sept 1969, Nov 1994

Jones, Jennifer, American actress, May 1944, *Obit* Yrbk 2010

Jones, Norah, American pianist and singer, May 2003

Jones, Rashida, American actress, Aug 2013

Jones, Rickie Lee, singer and songwriter, May 1990

Jones, Tommy Lee, American actor, Oct 1995

Jonsi Thor Birgisson, Icelandic singer, Jan 2003

Jordan, Marian, radio performer, Nov 1941, *Obit* June 1961

Jordan, Philippe, Swiss opera conductor, Oct 2010

Jorgensen, Mikael, American keyboardist, Feb 2010

Josefowicz, Leila, American violinist, May 2007

Jourdan, Louis, French actor, Jan 1967

Jouvet, Louis, French actor and theatrical director, Oct 1949, *Obit* Oct 1951

Juanes, Colombian singer, Jan 2003

Judd, Ashley, American actress, Feb 2000

Julia, Raul, American actor, Sept 1982, *Obit* Jan 1995

K'naan, Somali rapper, June 2010

Kahn, Madeline, American actress and singer, May 1977, *Obit* Mar 2000

Kaminska, Ida, Polish actress, Nov 1969, *Obit* July 1980

Kapell, William, American pianist, May 1948, *Obit* Jan 1954

Kapoor, Karisma, Indian actress, Jan 2002

Karajan, Herbert von, Austrian conductor, Oct 1956, Sept 1986, *Obit* Sept 1989

Karloff, Boris, Anglo-American actor, Mar 1941, *Obit* Mar 1969

Kasem, Casey, disc jockey, Nov 1997

Kassovitz, Mathieu, French actor and film director, Jan 2005

Katz, Sharon, South African singer, songwriter and guitarist, Jan 2007

Kavafian, Ani, American violinist, Oct 2006

Kavina, Lydia, Russian theremin player, Jan 2002

Kavner, Julie, American actress, Oct 1992

Kaye, Nora, dancer, Jan 1953, *Obit* Apr 1987

Keach, Stacy, American actor, Nov 1971

Keane, Doris, actress, *Obit* Jan 1946

Keane, Sean, Irish fiddler, Mar 2004

Kearns, Carroll D., Sept 1956

Keaton, Diane, American actress and motion picture director, June 1978, May 1996

Keaton, Michael, American actor, June 1992

Keb' Mo', American blues guitarist and singer, Nov 2013

Keeler, Ruby, American dancer and actress, Yrbk 1971, *Obit* Apr 1993

Keene, Christopher, conductor and opera manager, Mar 1990, *Obit* Jan 1996

Keener, Catherine, American actress, Oct 2002

Keillor, Garrison, American novelist, short story writer, storyteller and radio performer, Aug 1985

Keitel, Harvey, American actor, Mar 1994

Keith, Toby, American country singer, Oct 2004

Kekilli, Sibel, Turkish-German actress, Jan 2006

Kelberine, Alexander, *Obit* Mar 1940

Keller, Marthe, Swiss actress and opera director, July 2004

Kelley, Charles, American country singer and songwriter, July 2011

Kelley, Edgar Stillman, composer, *Obit* Jan 1945

Kelly, David, Irish actor, Jan 2005, *Obit* Yrbk 2012

Kelly, Emmett, American clown, July 1954, *Obit* May 1979

Kelly, Gene, American dancer, singer and actor, Yrbk 1945, Feb 1977, *Obit* Apr 1996

Kelly, Nancy, actress, June 1955, *Obit* Mar 1995

Kelly, R., American singer, songwriter and record producer, June 1999

Kelman, Charles D., American ophthalmologist and saxophonist, June 1984, *Obit* Yrbk 2004

Kemp, Hal, *Obit* Feb 1941

Kennedy, English violinist, July 1992

Kennedy, Arthur, American actor, Nov 1961

Kent, Allegra, American ballet dancer, Mar 1970

Kenton, Stan, American band leader, June 1979

Kern, Jerome, American composer, June 1942, *Obit* Yrbk 1945

Kerr, Deborah, British actress, Sept 1947, *Obit* Feb 2008

Khachaturian, Aram Il'ich, Mar 1948, *Obit* June 1978

Khan, Aamir, Indian actor, Jan 2002

Khan, Chaka, American singer, July 1999

Khan, Farah, Indian film director and choreographer, Jan 2007

Kid Rock, American rapper, Oct 2001

Kidman, Nicole, Australian actress, Mar 1997

Kiepura, Jan, Nov 1943, *Obit* Nov 1966

Kier, Udo, German actor, Jan 2005

Kiley, Richard, actor, Apr 1973, *Obit* May 1999

Kilmer, Val, American actor, Jan 1996

King, Carole, American singer and songwriter, Jan 1974

King, David, American jazz drummer, Oct 2011

King, Larry, American radio and television talk show host, May 1985

Kingsbury, Tim, Canadian bassist and guitarist, Jan 2007

Kingsley, Ben, English actor, Nov 1983

Kinski, Nastassia, German actress, June 1984

Kipnis, Alexander, opera singer, Yrbk 1943, *Obit* July 1978

Kirby, George, comedian, May 1977, *Obit* Jan 1996

Kirkpatrick, Chris, American singer, Nov 2000

Kirkpatrick, Ralph, harpsichordist and musicologist, Sept 1971, *Obit* Aug 1984

Kirsten, Dorothy, American opera singer, Feb 1948, *Obit* Jan 1993

Kissin, Evgeny, Russian pianist, Nov 1997

Kistler, Darci, American ballet dancer, Oct 1991

Kitchell, Iva, dancer, Yrbk 1951, *Obit* Jan 1984

Kitchen, Michael, British actor, Nov 2008

Kitt, Eartha, American singer and actress, Apr 1955, *Obit* Yrbk 2009

Kjartan Sveinsson, Icelandic keyboardist, Jan 2003

Kleiber, Carlos, German conductor, July 1991, *Obit* Yrbk 2004

Klein, Guillermo, Argentine jazz pianist and composer, Jan 2006

Klemperer, Otto, German conductor, Mar 1965, *Obit* Sept 1973

Kline, Kevin, American actor, July 1986

Knievel, Evel, American motorcycle stunt performer, Feb 1972, *Obit* Yrbk 2008

Knievel, Robbie, American motorcycle stunt performer, Mar 2005

Knight, Gladys, American singer, Feb 1987

Knightley, Keira, English actress, Jan 2005

Knopfler, Mark, British singer, songwriter and guitarist, Apr 1995

Koh, Jennifer, American violinist, Sept 2006

Koite, Habib, Malian guitarist, Jan 2002

Koma, Japanese dancer and choreographer, May 2003

Korngold, Erich Wolfgang, Austrian composer, Mar 1943, *Obit* Feb 1958

Kostelanetz, Andre, American conductor, July 1942, *Obit* Mar 1980

Koster, Bo, American rock keyboardist, Nov 2008

Kotche, Glenn, American drummer and percussionist, Feb 2010

Kotto, Yaphet, American actor, Mar 1995

Koussevitzky, Serge, Russian conductor, Nov 1940, *Obit* July 1951

Koz, Dave, American jazz saxophonist and composer, June 2013

Kozena, Magdalena, Czech opera singer, Jan 2005

Krall, Diana, Canadian singer and pianist, June 2000

Kramer, Joey, American rock drummer, July 2004

Kraus, Alfredo, Spanish opera singer, June 1987, *Obit* Nov 1999

Kraus, Lili, Hungarian pianist, Oct 1975, *Obit* Jan 1987

Krauss, Alison, American fiddler and singer, May 1997

Kravitz, Lenny, American singer and guitarist, Apr 1996

Kremer, Gidon, Russian violinist, Mar 1985

Krenek, Ernst, American composer, July 1942, *Obit* Feb 1992

Krips, Josef, June 1965, *Obit* Yrbk 1974

Kristofferson, Kris, American actor, singer and songwriter, Nov 1974

Kruspe, Richard Z., German guitarist, Jan 2007

Kubelik, Jan, Czech violinist and composer, *Obit* Jan 1941

Kubelik, Rafael, Czech conductor, Feb 1951, *Obit* Oct 1996

Kubler, Tad, American guitarist, Sept 2010

Kullmer, Ann, Feb 1949

Kurenko, Maria, Sept 1944

Kurtz, Efrem, conductor, Feb 1946, *Obit* Sept 1995

Kurtz, Swoosie, American actress, Oct 1987

Kuti, Femi, Nigerian singer and songwriter, Jan 2002

Kweli, Talib, American rapper, July 2012

Kwiecie?, Mariusz, Polish opera singer, July 2012

LL Cool J, American rapper and actor, Nov 1997

La India, Puerto Rican salsa singer, May 2002

LaBelle, Patti, American singer, July 1986

LaBeouf, Shia, American actor, Aug 2009

LaFontaine, Don, American voice-over actor, Sept 2004, *Obit* Yrbk 2008

LaMontagne, Ray, American singer, Oct 2013

Ladd, Alan, American actor, Sept 1943, *Obit* Mar 1964

Lady Gaga, American pop singer and songwriter, May 2010

Lafourcade, Natalia, Mexican singer and songwriter, Jan 2003

Lahr, Bert, actor, Jan 1952, *Obit* Feb 1968

Laine, Cleo, Britlsh singer and actress, Feb 1986

Laine, Frankie, American singer, Nov 1956, *Obit* Yrbk 2007

Laing, Hugh, English dancer, Nov 1946, *Obit* June 1988

Lally, Joe, American bassist, Mar 2002

Lambert, Miranda, American country singer, Feb 2012

Lancaster, Burt, American actor, July 1953, Apr 1986, *Obit* Jan 1995

Lanchester, Elsa, English actress, May 1950, *Obit* Feb 1987

Landers, Paul H., German guitarist, Jan 2007

Landon, Michael, American actor, director and producer, July 1977, *Obit* Sept 1991

Landowska, Wanda, Polish harpsichordist, Nov 1945, *Obit* Nov 1959

Lane, Burton, American composer, Mar 1967, *Obit* Mar 1997

Lane, Nathan, American actor, Aug 1996

Lang, David, American composer, Feb 2000

Lang, Lang, Chinese pianist, Jan 2003

Lange, Jessica, American actress, May 1983

Langella, Frank, American actor, Sept 1980

Lansbury, Angela, American actress, Sept 1967

Laredo, Jaime, violinist, Sept 1967

Laredo, Ruth, American pianist, Oct 1987, *Obit* Yrbk 2005

Larrocha, Alicia de, Spanish pianist, July 1968, *Obit* Yrbk 2009

Lau, Andy, Chinese singer and actor, Jan 2005

Laughton, Charles, Anglo-American actor, Nov 1948, *Obit* Jan 1963

Lauper, Cyndi, American singer and songwriter, Aug 1985

Lavant, Denis, French actor, June 2013

Lavigne, Avril, Canadian singer and songwriter, Apr 2003

Lavin, Linda, actress, Nov 1987

Lawford, Ernest, *Obit* Feb 1941

Lawrence, Carol, American singer and actress, Nov 1961

Lawrence, Gertrude, English actress, Aug 1940, Sept 1952

Lawrence, Jennifer, American actress, May 2013

Lawrence, Marjorie, Australian opera singer, Apr 1940, *Obit* Mar 1979

Lawrence, Steve, singer, Nov 1964

Laws, Hubert, American jazz flutist, July 2007

Lawson, Mary, *Obit* July 1941

Layton, Joe, theatrical director, producer and choreographer, Sept 1970, *Obit* July 1994

Le Clercq, Tanaquil, American ballet dancer, July 1953, *Obit* Mar 2001

LeVox, Gary, American country singer, Aug 2003

Leachman, Cloris, American actress, Oct 1975

Lear, Evelyn, American opera singer, Apr 1973, *Obit* Yrbk 2012

Leblanc, Georgette, French opera singer, *Obit* Yrbk 1941

Lecuona, Ernesto, Cuban composer, May 1944, *Obit* Jan 1964

Ledger, Heath, Australian actor, June 2006, *Obit* Yrbk 2008

Ledoyen, Virginie, French actress, Jan 2002

Lee, Auriol, *Obit* Sept 1941

Lee, Canada, American actor, Yrbk 1944, *Obit* June 1952

Lee, Christopher, English actor, Sept 1975

Lee, Geddy, Canadian singer, Feb 2001

Lee, Gypsy Rose, American actress and stripteaser, Yrbk 1943, *Obit* June 1970

Lee, Peggy, American singer, Mar 1963, *Obit* May 2002

Legend, John, American singer and pianist, Feb 2007

Lehmann, Lotte, German-American opera singer, May 1941, July 1970, *Obit* Oct 1976

Leigh, Jennifer Jason, American actress, Aug 1992

Leigh, Vivien, English actress, July 1946, *Obit* Oct 1967

Leighton, Margaret, English actress, Mar 1957, *Obit* Mar 1976

Leinsdorf, Erich, conductor, May 1940, Oct 1963, *Obit* Nov 1993

Lemmon, Jack, American actor, Feb 1961, Aug 1988, *Obit* Oct 2001

Lennox, Annie, Scottish singer, May 1988

Lenya, Lotte, German singer and actress, June 1959, *Obit* Jan 1982

Leo, Melissa, American actress, July 2009

Leonard, Eddie, singer and dancer, *Obit* Sept 1941

Leppard, Raymond, British conductor and harpsichordist, Mar 1980

Lerche, Sondre, Norwegian singer and songwriter, Jan 2004

Lerman, Liz, American dancer and choreographer, Nov 2000

Leslie, Chris, English singer, fiddler and mandolinist, Sept 2005

Leung, Tony Chiu-wai, Chinese actor, Jan 2006

Lev, Ray, Jan 1949, *Obit* July 1968

Levenson, Sam, American humorist, July 1959, *Obit* Nov 1980

Levert, Gerald, American singer and songwriter, Oct 2003, *Obit* Yrbk 2007

Levi-Tanai, Sara, Israeli choreographer, May 1958

Levine, Adam, American rock singer and guitarist, Mar 2013

Levine, James, American conductor, Apr 1975

Levitzki, Mischa, pianist, *Obit* Feb 1941

Lewing, Adele, *Obit* Apr 1943

Lewis, Ananda, American television entertainment reporter, June 2005

Lewis, Carl, American sprinter and long jumper, Nov 1984, Yrbk 1996

Lewis, Henry, American conductor, Feb 1973, *Obit* Apr 1996

Lewis, John, American pianist and composer, Jan 1962, *Obit* June 2001

Lewis, Juliette, American actress, Feb 1996

Lewis, Mary, opera singer, *Obit* Feb 1942

Lewis, Ramsey, American jazz pianist, Oct 1996

Lewis, Shari, puppeteer and ventriloquist, Mar 1958, *Obit* Oct 1998

Lhevinne, Josef, Russian pianist, *Obit* Jan 1945

Lhevinne, Rosina, Russian-American pianist and teacher, Nov 1961, *Obit* Jan 1977

Li Gong, Chinese actress, May 1997

Li, Jet, Chinese actor and martial artist, June 2001

Liberace, American pianist, Nov 1954, Mar 1986, *Obit* Mar 1987

Licad, Cecile, Philippine pianist, Jan 2003

Liddy, G. Gordon, American lawyer, actor and government official, Oct 1980

Liebermann, Rolf, Swiss composer and opera director, Sept 1973, *Obit* Mar 1999

Lifeson, Alex, Canadian guitarist, Feb 2001

Lightfoot, Gordon, Canadian singer, Aug 1978

Lil' Kim, American rapper, Oct 2000

Lillie, Beatrice, British actress, Feb 1945, Sept 1964, *Obit* Mar 1989

Lincoln, Abbey, American jazz singer, Sept 2002, *Obit* Yrbk 2010

Lindemann, Till, German singer, Jan 2007

Linden, Hal, actor, Jan 1987

Lindfors, Viveca, Swedish actress, Apr 1955, *Obit* Jan 1996

Lindo, Delroy, American actor, Mar 2001

Linkletter, Art, American television personality, Nov 1953, *Obit* Yrbk 2010

Linnell, John, American singer, songwriter and accordionist, Nov 1999

Liotta, Ray, American actor, May 1994

Little Richard, American singer, Sept 1986

Little, Rich, Canadian impressionist, Nov 1975

Litton, Andrew, conductor, Sept 1998

Littrell, Brian, American singer, May 2000

Liu Fang, Chinese pipa player, Jan 2006

Liu, Lucy, American actress and artist, Oct 2003

Lloyd, Alex, Australian singer and songwriter, Jan 2002

Lloyd, Charles, American saxophonist and flutist, Apr 2002

Lloyd, Harold, American actor and producer, Sept 1949, *Obit* Apr 1971

Lockhart, Gene, Canadian actor, May 1950, *Obit* June 1957

Lockhart, Keith, American conductor, Aug 2008

Lockwood, Margaret, English actress, Sept 1948, *Obit* Sept 1990

Lodge, John Davis, governor and diplomat, Mar 1948, *Obit* Jan 1986

Loesser, Frank, American composer and lyricist, Yrbk 1945, *Obit* Oct 1969

Loewe, Frederick, American composer, July 1958, *Obit* Apr 1988

Logan, Walter, *Obit* Mar 1940

Lohan, Lindsay, American actress, Nov 2005

Lollobrigida, Gina, Italian actress, Sept 1960

Lombard, Carole, American actress, *Obit* Mar 1942

Lombardo, Guy, American band leader, Sept 1946, Feb 1975, *Obit* Jan 1978

London, George, Canadian opera singer, Nov 1953, *Obit* June 1985

London, Julie, singer and actress, May 1960, *Obit* Feb 2001

Lopez, Trini, singer, Mar 1968

Lopez, Vincent, band leader and pianist, Nov 1960, Nov 1975

Loren, Sophia, Italian actress, Mar 1959

Lorenz, Christian, German keyboardist, Jan 2007

Loring, Eugene, American dancer and choreographer, Mar 1972, *Obit* Oct 1982

Loudon, Dorothy, American actress and singer, June 1984, *Obit* Yrbk 2004

Louis, Murray, dancer and choreographer, Oct 1968

Louis-Dreyfus, Julia, American actress, Oct 1995

Lovano, Joe, American jazz saxophonist, Mar 1998

Love, Courtney, American singer and actress, June 1996

Lovett, Lyle, American singer, Sept 1997

Lowe, Jack Warren, pianist, Jan 1954, *Obit* Aug 1996

Lowe, Rob, American actor, July 2000

Lowensohn, Elina, Romanian actress, Jan 2005

Loy, Myrna, American actress, Oct 1950, *Obit* Feb 1994

Lozano, Conrad, American bassist, Oct 2005

LuPone, Patti, American actress and singer, Apr 1989

Lubovitch, Lar, American dancer and choreographer, Mar 1992

Lucci, Susan, American actress, Oct 1989

Lucia, Paco de, Spanish flamenco guitarist, Jan 2004

Luckstone, Isidore, *Obit* May 1941

Ludacris, American rapper, June 2004

Ludwig, Christa, German opera singer, Mar 1971

Lukas, Paul, American actor, Feb 1942, *Obit* Oct 1971

Luna, Diego, Mexican actor, Jan 2002

Lunden, Joan, American television personality, May 1989

Lunt, Alfred, American actor, June 1941, *Obit* Sept 1977

Lupino, Ida, American actress and film director, Sept 1943, *Obit* Oct 1995

Lupino, Stanley, *Obit* Aug 1942

Lurie, John, American saxophonist and actor, Oct 2010

Lynch, Jane, American actress, July 2010

Lynn, Diana, actress, Nov 1953, *Obit* Feb 1972

Lynne, Gillian, English dancer and choreographer, Jan 2002

Lynne, Shelby, American country singer and songwriter, July 2001

M. I. A. (Singer), Sri Lankan-British singer and songwriter, May 2009

MacDermot, Galt, Canadian composer, July 1984

MacDowell, Andie, American model and actress, Nov 1999

MacGregor, Joanna, British pianist, Jan 2006

MacKaye, Ian, American singer and guitarist, Mar 2002

MacLachlan, Kyle, American actor, Aug 1993

MacLaine, Shirley, American dancer and actress, Yrbk 1959, July 1978

MacMillan, Ernest, Canadian conductor and composer, Mar 1955, *Obit* June 1973

MacMurray, Fred, actor, Feb 1967, *Obit* Feb 1992

MacNeil, Cornell, American opera singer, Jan 1976, *Obit* Yrbk 2011

Machito, Cuban band leader, Feb 1983, *Obit* June 1984

Mack, Ted, Apr 1951, *Obit* Sept 1976

Mackenzie, Gisele, Canadian singer, Nov 1955, *Obit* July 2004

Mackerras, Charles, Australian conductor, Feb 1985

Maddow, Rachel, American television and radio talk show host, Aug 2009

Maddy, Joseph E., musician and educator, Apr 1946, *Obit* May 1966

Madeira, Jean, Oct 1963, *Obit* Sept 1972

Madsen, Michael, American actor, Apr 2004

Magallanes, Nicholas, May 1955, *Obit* July 1977

Magliozzi, Ray, American automobile mechanic and radio talk show host, June 2006

Magliozzi, Tom, American automobile mechanic and radio talk show host, June 2006

Magnani, Anna, Italian actress, Apr 1956, *Obit* Nov 1973

Maguire, Martie, American fiddler, July 2000

Maguire, Tobey, American actor, Sept 2002

Maharaj, Birju, Indian dancer, Jan 2007

Mahoney, John, actor, Aug 1999

Maimon, Shiri, Israeli pop singer, Jan 2006

Main, Marjorie, actress, Oct 1951, *Obit* June 1975

Maines, Natalie, American singer, July 2000

Makarova, Natalia, Russian ballet dancer, Feb 1972

Makeba, Miriam, South African singer, June 1965, *Obit* Yrbk 2009

Malaby, Tony, American jazz saxophonist, Sept 2008

Malbin, Elaine, Feb 1959

Malden, Karl, American actor, Apr 1957, *Obit* Yrbk 2009

Malina, Joshua, American actor, Apr 2004

Malina, Judith, American actress and theatrical director, June 2011

Malkovich, John, American actor, May 1988

Malley, Matt, American bassist, Mar 2003

Malone, Kyp, American guitarist and singer, Apr 2009

Mami, Cheb, Algerian singer, Jan 2005

Mandrell, Barbara, singer, Aug 1982

Mangesakara, Lata, Indian singer, Jan 2003

Mangione, Chuck, trumpet player and flugelhornist, May 1980

Manson, Marilyn, American singer, May 1999

Mara, Rooney, American actress, Oct 2012

Marais, Jean, French actor, Apr 1962, *Obit* Jan 1999

Marceau, Marcel, French mime, Feb 1957, *Obit* Yrbk 2007

March, Fredric, American actor, Mar 1943, *Obit* June 1975

Marion, George F., *Obit* Jan 1946

Marius, Emilie Alexander, *Obit* Apr 1940

Markova, Alicia, British ballet dancer, Sept 1943, *Obit* Yrbk 2005

Maron, Marc, American comedian, Nov 2011

Marquardt, Alexandria, *Obit* June 1943

Marriner, Neville, English conductor, Aug 1978

Mars, Bruno, American singer and songwriter, May 2011

Marsalis, Branford, American jazz saxophonist, Sept 1991

Marsalis, Ellis, American jazz pianist, Aug 2000

Marsalis, Wynton, American trumpet player, Oct 1984

Marsh, Jean, English actress, Nov 1977

Marshall, E. G., actor, June 1986, *Obit* Nov 1998

Marshall, Lois, Canadian singer, June 1960, *Obit* May 1997

Marshall, Penny, American actress and motion picture director, Mar 1980, May 1992

Marshall, Rob, American choreographer and film director, June 2003

Marshall, Susan, American choreographer, July 1999

Marshall, Tully, actor, *Obit* Apr 1943

Martin, Chris, English singer and guitarist, May 2004

Martin, Dean, American actor and singer, Nov 1964, *Obit* Mar 1996

Martin, Jesse L., American actor, July 2006

Martin, Ricky, Puerto Rican singer and actor, Sept 1999

Martinelli, Giovanni, Italian opera singer, Jan 1945, *Obit* Mar 1969

Martinez, Speedo, Argentine singer, Jan 2003

Martinu, Bohuslav, Czech composer and violinist, Nov 1944, *Obit* Nov 1959

Marton, Eva, Hungarian opera singer, Apr 1985

Marvin, Lee, American actor, Sept 1966, *Obit* Oct 1987

Marx Brothers, American comedians, Mar 1948

Marx, Chico, American comedian, May 1948, *Obit* Yrbk 1961

Marx, Harpo, American comedian, Mar 1948, *Obit* Nov 1964

Mary Alice, actress, Nov 1995

Mascagni, Pietro, Italian composer, *Obit* Sept 1945

Masekela, Hugh, South African trumpet player, flugelhornist and singer, Mar 1993

Masina, Giulietta, Italian actress, Apr 1958, *Obit* June 1994

Mason, Jackie, American comedian, July 1987

Mason, James, English actor, May 1947, *Obit* Sept 1984

Mason, Marsha, American actress, Apr 1981

Massey, Raymond, Canadian-American actor, Feb 1946, *Obit* Sept 1983

Mastroianni, Marcello, Italian actor, June 1963, *Obit* Feb 1997

Mathis, Johnny, American singer, July 1965, Feb 1993

Matisyahu, American Hasidic reggae and rap singer, Mar 2007

Matthau, Walter, American actor, June 1966, *Obit* Sept 2000

Mattila, Karita, Finnish opera singer, Jan 2004

Mature, Victor, actor, Yrbk 1951, *Obit* Oct 1999

Maura, Carmen, Spanish actress, Apr 1992

Maxim Reality (Singer), British singer and songwriter, Oct 2009

Maxwell, American singer, songwriter and recording producer, July 2011

May, Brian, English rock guitarist, Oct 2008

Mayer, John, American singer and guitarist, Mar 2010

Maynor, Dorothy, singer, Jan 1940, Yrbk 1951, *Obit* May 1996

Mayor, Mireya, American primatologist and television personality, Sept 2011

Mazzo, Kay, July 1971

McAdams, Rachel, Canadian actress, May 2009

McBride, Christian, American jazz bassist, Jan 2000

McBride, Martina, American country singer, Mar 2004

McBride, Patricia, ballet dancer, July 1966

McBurney, Simon, British actor and theatrical director, Jan 2005

McCambridge, Mercedes, American actress, June 1964, *Obit* Yrbk 2004

McCarthy, Thomas, American actor and motion picture director, Jan 2012

McClanahan, Rue, American actress, May 1989, *Obit* Yrbk 2010

McClurkin, Donnie, American gospel singer and clergyman, Apr 2007

McConnell, Page, American keyboardist, July 2003

McCormick, Myron, Jan 1954, *Obit* Oct 1962

McCowen, Alec, Oct 1969

McCracken, James, opera singer, Nov 1963, *Obit* June 1988

McCracken, Joan, June 1945, *Obit* Jan 1962

McCrary, Jinx Falkenburg, television performer and model, July 1953

McDaniel, Hattie, American actress, Sept 1940, *Obit* Yrbk 1952

McDaniel, James, American actor, Feb 2000

McDonald, Audra, American singer and actress, Apr 1999

McDonnell, Mary, American actress, May 1997

McDormand, Frances, American actress, Sept 1997

McDowall, Roddy, actor and photographer, Apr 1961, *Obit* Jan 1999

McDowell, Malcolm, English actor, Yrbk 1973

McEntire, Reba, American country singer and actress, Oct 1994

McFerrin, Bobby, American singer and conductor, Aug 1989

McGill, Anthony, American clarinetist, Apr 2009

McGovern, Maureen, singer, Feb 1990

McGraw, Tim, American country singer, Sept 2002

McGuire, Dorothy, American actress, Sept 1941, *Obit* Nov 2001

McKayle, Donald, American dancer and choreographer, June 1971

McKellen, Ian, English actor, Jan 1984

McKenna, Siobhan, Irish actress, Nov 1956, *Obit* Jan 1987

McKenzie, Bret, New Zealand comedian, Mar 2008

McKuen, Rod, American poet, composer and singer, Feb 1970

McLean, A. J., American singer, May 2000

McLean, Don, American singer and songwriter, May 1973

McLean, Jackie, American saxophonist, Mar 2001, *Obit* Nov 2006

McMahon, Ed, American television personality, Apr 1977, *Obit* Yrbk 2009

McNair, Barbara, American singer and actress, Nov 1971, *Obit* Yrbk 2007

McNair, Sylvia, American opera singer, Nov 1997

McNeil, John, American jazz trumpet player, June 2007

McNeill, Don, radio talk show host, July 1949, *Obit* Aug 1996

McNellis, Maggi, radio and television performer, Jan 1955, *Obit* Aug 1989

McPartland, Marian, American jazz pianist, June 1976, *Obit* Yrbk 2013

McPharlin, Paul, American puppeteer, Nov 1945, *Obit* Nov 1948

McQueen, Steve, American actor, Oct 1966, *Obit* Jan 1981

McRae, Carmen, American singer, Apr 1983, *Obit* Jan 1995

McShane, Ian, English actor, July 2011

Meadows, Audrey, actress, May 1958, *Obit* Apr 1996

Meadows, Jayne, May 1958

Means, Russell, American Indian leader, Jan 1978, *Obit* Yrbk 2013

Mei Lanfang, *Obit* Sept 1943

Melchior, Lauritz, Danish opera singer, Jan 1941, *Obit* May 1973

Melford, Myra, American jazz pianist and composer, Apr 2010

Mellencamp, John, American singer and songwriter, Mar 1988

Meloy, Colin, American singer and songwriter, Aug 2007

Melton, James, American opera singer, Sept 1945, *Obit* June 1961

Melua, Katie, British singer and songwriter, Jan 2007

Mendez, Kinito, Dominican singer, Jan 2004

Menjou, Adolphe, actor, June 1948, *Obit* Jan 1964

Menken, Alan, American composer, Jan 2001

Mennin, Peter, composer and educator, Nov 1964, *Obit* Aug 1983

Menuhin, Yehudi, violinist, Feb 1941, May 1973, *Obit* June 1999

Mercer, James, American guitarist and singer, June 2007

Mercer, Mabel, singer, Feb 1973, *Obit* June 1984

Merchant, Natalie, American singer and songwriter, Jan 2003

Mercouri, Melina, Greek actress and cabinet member, July 1965, Mar 1988, *Obit* May 1994

Meredith, Burgess, actor, July 1940, *Obit* Nov 1997

Merivale, Philip, *Obit* Apr 1946

Merrill, Robert, American opera singer, Mar 1952, *Obit* Feb 2005

Messing, Debra, American actress, Aug 2002

Meyer, Jean, Nov 1955

Meyer, Jean-Luc de, Belgian singer and lyricist, Jan 2006

Michael, George, English pop singer, Nov 1988

Michele, Chrisette, American singer and songwriter, Apr 2011

Midori, Japanese violinist, June 1990

Mifune, Toshiro, Japanese actor, June 1981, *Obit* Mar 1998

Mignone, Francisco, June 1942

Mikhalkov, Nikita, Russian film director and actor, Oct 1995

Milanov, Zinka, Yugoslav-American opera singer, July 1944, *Obit* July 1989

Milhaud, Darius, French composer, June 1941, May 1961, *Obit* Sept 1974

Milland, Ray, actor, Feb 1946, *Obit* Apr 1986

Miller, Ann, American tap dancer and actress, Apr 1980, *Obit* Yrbk 2004

Miller, Bebe, dancer and choreographer, Apr 1999

Miller, Glenn, American band leader, Feb 1942, *Obit* Yrbk 1991

Miller, Jonathan, English physician, actor and director, Oct 1970, Nov 1986

Miller, Marcus, American jazz bassist and composer, Feb 2006

Miller, Mildred, opera singer, June 1957

Miller, Mitch, American conductor and record producer, July 1956, *Obit* Yrbk 2010

Miller, Roger, American composer, lyricist and singer, Sept 1986, *Obit* Jan 1993

Millo, Aprile, American opera singer, Apr 1988

Mills, Hayley, English actress, Apr 1963

Mills, John, British actor, May 1963, *Obit* Yrbk 2005

Milnes, Sherrill, American opera singer, Nov 1970

Milstein, Nathan, Russian-American violinist, Mar 1950, *Obit* Feb 1993

Minaj, Nicki, American rapper, Oct 2013

Minnelli, Liza, American actress and singer, Oct 1970, July 1988

Minogue, Kylie, Australian actress and singer, Jan 2003

Mirabal, Robert, Native American composer and flutist, Aug 2002

Miranda, Carmen, Brazilian singer, dancer and actress, June 1941, *Obit* Oct 1955

Miranda, Lin-Manuel, American composer and lyricist, July 2013

Mirren, Helen, English actress, July 1995

Misia, Portuguese singer, Jan 2002

Mitchell, Howard, cellist and conductor, May 1952, *Obit* Aug 1988

Mitchell, Jerry, American choreographer and theatrical director, Oct 2007

Mitchell, Joni, Canadian singer and songwriter, Oct 1976

Mitchum, Robert, American actor, Sept 1970, *Obit* Sept 1997

Mitha, Tehreema, Pakistani dancer and choreographer, May 2004

Mitropoulos, Dimitri, Greek conductor and composer, Mar 1941, Mar 1952, *Obit* Jan 1961

Mittell, Philipp, *Obit* Mar 1943

Mix, Tom, actor, *Obit* Yrbk 1940

Moby, American singer, Apr 2001

Moen, John, American singer and drummer, Aug 2007

Moffo, Anna, American opera singer, May 1961, *Obit* Yrbk 2007

Molina, Alfred, British actor, Feb 2004

Molloy, Matt, Irish flutist, Mar 2004

Moloney, Paddy, Irish uillean piper, Mar 2004

Monheit, Jane, American jazz singer, Feb 2008

Monk, T. S., American drummer, Feb 2002

Monk, Thelonious, American pianist, Oct 1964, *Obit* Apr 1982

Monroe, Lucy, singer, Aug 1942, *Obit* Nov 1987

Monroe, Marilyn, American actress, July 1959, *Obit* Oct 1962

Monroe, Vaughn, July 1942, *Obit* July 1973

Montand, Yves, French actor and singer, July 1960, Sept 1988, *Obit* Jan 1992

Monte, Elisa, American dancer and choreographer, June 2007

Montenegro, Fernanda, Brazilian actress, Oct 1999

Montero, Gabriela, Venezuelan pianist, July 2007

Monteux, Pierre, American conductor, Apr 1946, *Obit* Sept 1964

Montgomery, Robert, actor and director, Jan 1948, *Obit* Nov 1981

Montoya, Carlos, Spanish guitarist, Mar 1968, *Obit* May 1993

Mon e, Janelle, American singer, May 2013

Moore, Demi, American actress, Sept 1993

Moore, Douglas, American composer, Nov 1947, *Obit* Oct 1969

Moore, Dudley, English actor, June 1982, *Obit* Yrbk 2002

Moore, Garry, American radio and television personality, Nov 1954, *Obit* Jan 1994

Moore, Gerald, English pianist, Oct 1967, *Obit* May 1987

Moore, Grace, opera singer, Apr 1944, *Obit* Mar 1947

Moore, Julianne, American actress, Oct 1998

Moore, Mary Tyler, American actress, Feb 1971

Moore, Melba, American singer and actress, Jan 1973

Moore, Roger, English actor, Feb 1975

Moorehead, Agnes, American actress, June 1952, *Obit* June 1974

Morath, Max, musician, Nov 1963

Mordkin, Mikhail, Russian dancer, *Obit* Sept 1944

Moreau, Jeanne, French actress, Yrbk 1966

Moreno, Catalina Sandino, Colombian actress, Jan 2005

Moreno, Rita, American actress, singer and dancer, Sept 1985

Moretti, Fabrizio, Brazilian drummer, Feb 2007

Morgan, Henry, American radio and television personality, Mar 1947, *Obit* July 1994

Morgan, Lorrie, American country singer, Apr 1999

Moriarty, Michael, actor, July 1976

Morini, Erica, Austrian violinist, Apr 1946, *Obit* Jan 1996

Morissette, Alanis, Canadian singer and songwriter, May 1997

Morley, Robert, English actor, Nov 1963, *Obit* Aug 1992

Morris, Butch, American cornet player and composer, July 2005, *Obit* Yrbk 2013

Morris, James, American opera singer, July 1986

Morris, Mark, American choreographer and dancer, Aug 1988

Morris, Stephen, British drummer, Jan 2006

Morrison, Adrienne, *Obit* Jan 1941

Morse, Robert, actor, Nov 1962

Mortensen, Viggo, American actor, June 2004

Morton, Joe, actor, Feb 1999

Mos Def (Singer), American rapper, Apr 2005

Moschen, Michael, juggler, July 2000

Moscovitch, Maurice, *Obit* Aug 1940

Moss, Elisabeth, American actress, Nov 2013

Mostel, Zero, American actor, Apr 1943, Nov 1963, *Obit* Nov 1977

Moyet, Alison, British singer, Jan 2003

Moylan, Mary Ellen, Feb 1957

Muck, Karl, Mar 1940

Mulligan, Carey, British actress, Oct 2013

Mulligan, Gerry, American jazz saxophonist, Yrbk 1960, *Obit* Mar 1996

Muncey, Cameron, Australian guitarist and singer, Jan 2005

Munch, Charles, Yrbk 1947, *Obit* Yrbk 1968

Muni, Paul, actor, Jan 1944, *Obit* Nov 1967

Munn, Frank, singer, May 1944, *Obit* Yrbk 1953

Munsel, Patrice, American opera singer, Mar 1945

Murphy, George, American actor, dancer and senator, Yrbk 1965, *Obit* July 1992

Murphy, Mark, American jazz singer, Sept 2004

Murray, Anne, Canadian singer, Jan 1982

Murray, Bill, American actor, Jan 1985, Sept 2004

Murray, Don, actor, Sept 1959

Murray, J. Harold, *Obit* Feb 1941

Murray, Ty, American rodeo cowboy, May 2002

N'Dour, Youssou, Senegalese singer, Jan 1996

Nabors, Jim, American actor and singer, Nov 1969

Naish, J. Carrol, actor, Jan 1957, *Obit* Mar 1973

Narelle, Marie, *Obit* Mar 1941

Nares, Owen, *Obit* Sept 1943

Nas (Musician), American rapper, Sept 2009

Nazimova, Alla, Russian actress, *Obit* Aug 1945

Neagle, Anna, English actress, Nov 1945, *Obit* July 1986

Neal, Patricia, American actress, Sept 1964, *Obit* Yrbk 2010

Neeson, Liam, Irish-American actor, Nov 1994

Nelligan, Kate, Canadian actress, July 1983

Nelly (Musician), American rapper, Oct 2002

Nelson, Harriet, actress and singer, May 1949, *Obit* Jan 1995

Nerina, Nadia, South African ballet dancer, Nov 1957, *Obit* Yrbk 2008

Nero, Franco, Italian actor, Jan 2002

Nesbitt, Cathleen, English actress, Nov 1956, *Obit* Sept 1982

Nesbo, Jo, Norwegian novelist, singer and songwriter, Sept 2011

Netrebko, Anna, Russian opera singer, Jan 2005

Neufeld, Sarah, Canadian violinist, Jan 2007

Neuwirth, Bebe, American dancer and actress, Nov 1997

Neville, John, Jan 1959, *Obit* Yrbk 2012

Newley, Anthony, actor, singer and songwriter, Oct 1966, *Obit* July 1999

Newman, Alfred, July 1943, *Obit* Apr 1970

Newman, Paul, American actor, Nov 1959, May 1985, *Obit* Yrbk 2008

Newman, Randy, American singer and songwriter, Oct 1982

Newton, Thandie, British actress, Jan 2003

Newton, Wayne, American singer, Feb 1990

Newton-John, Olivia, Australian singer and actress, Nov 1978

Nezet-Seguin, Yannick, Canadian conductor, Nov 2011

Nicholson, Andy, British rock bassist, Jan 2006

Nicholson, Jack, American actor, Oct 1974, Apr 1995

Nicol, Simon, English guitarist and singer, Sept 2005

Nielsen, Alice, *Obit* Apr 1943

Nighy, Bill, British actor, Jan 2007

Nijinsky, Waslaw, Russian ballet dancer, Oct 1940, *Obit* May 1950

Nikolais, Alwin, American choreographer, Feb 1968, *Obit* July 1993

Niles, John Jacob, American singer, composer, singer and folklorist, Nov 1959, *Obit* Apr 1980

Nilsson, Birgit, Swedish opera singer, May 1960, *Obit* Sept 2006

Nimoy, Leonard, American actor, Feb 1977

Nin, Khadja, Burundian singer, Jan 2005

Nixon, Marni, American singer, Oct 2009

Nolan, Lloyd, actor, Nov 1956, *Obit* Nov 1985

Nolte, Nick, American actor, Nov 1980

Norman, Jessye, American opera singer, Feb 1976

Norrington, Roger, English conductor, Jan 1990

Norris, Chuck, American actor and martial artist, Jan 1989

Norton, Edward, American actor, June 2000

Norton, Graham, Irish talk show host, Jan 2004

Norville, Deborah, American television reporter and radio talk show host, Apr 1990

Novaes, Guiomar, Brazilian pianist, June 1953, *Obit* May 1979

Novak, Kim, American actress, Apr 1957

Novotna, Jarmila, Czech opera singer, Mar 1940, *Obit* Apr 1994

Nugent, Ted, American rock guitarist, Apr 2005

Nureyev, Rudolf, Russian ballet dancer, July 1963, *Obit* Feb 1993

O'Brian, Hugh, actor, July 1958

O'Brien, Ed, English guitarist, June 2001

O'Brien, Pat, American actor, Mar 1966, *Obit* Jan 1984

O'Connell, Hugh, *Obit* Mar 1943

O'Connor, Carroll, American actor, July 1972, *Obit* Sept 2001

O'Connor, Donald, American actor and dancer, May 1955, *Obit* Apr 2004

O'Connor, Frances, Australian actress, Jan 2002

O'Connor, Mark, American fiddler and composer, Sept 2013

O'Connor, Sinead, Irish singer, June 1991

O'Day, Anita, American jazz singer, June 1990, *Obit* Jan 2007

O'Hara, Kelli, American actress and singer, Oct 2008

O'Hara, Maureen, Irish-American actress, Feb 1953

O'Horgan, Tom, American theatrical director and composer, Apr 1970, *Obit* Yrbk 2009

O'Malley, Nick, British rock bassist, Jan 2006

O'Neal, Frederick, actor, Nov 1946, *Obit* Oct 1992

O'Neal, Ryan, American actor, Feb 1973

O'Reilly, Bill, American television talk show host, Oct 2003

O'Shea, Milo, June 1982, *Obit* Yrbk 2013

O'Toole, Peter, Irish actor, Sept 1968

Oberlin, Russell, opera singer, July 1960

Oberon, Merle, English actress, Nov 1941, *Obit* Jan 1980

Obraztsov, Sergei, Russian puppeteer, Nov 1964

Obraztsova, Elena, Russian opera singer, Feb 1983

Odetta, American folk singer, Yrbk 1960, *Obit* Jan 2009

Oh, Sandra, Canadian actress, Jan 2005

Ohga, Norio, Japanese electronics industry executive, June 1998, *Obit* Yrbk 2011

Ohlsson, Garrick, American pianist, June 1975

Oistrakh, David, Russian violinist, Mar 1956, *Obit* Yrbk 1974

Okonedo, Sophie, British actress, Jan 2005

Olbermann, Keith, American television news anchor, Feb 2009

Oldman, Gary, English actor, Jan 1996

Olin, Lena, Swedish actress, June 2003

Oliver, Edna May, actress, *Obit* Jan 1943

Olivero, Magda, Italian opera singer, Apr 1980

Olivier, Laurence, English actor, June 1946, Jan 1979, *Obit* Sept 1989

Olmos, Edward James, American actor, Aug 1992

Olsen twins, American actresses, Sept 2010

Olsen, Mary Kate, American actress, Sept 2010

Olsen, Ole, American comedian, Sept 1940, *Obit* Mar 1963

Olvera, Fernando, Mexican singer and guitarist, Jan 2005

Omarion (Musician), American singer, Feb 2008

Onuki, Ami, Japanese pop singer, Jan 2005

Orbach, Jerry, American actor, May 1970, *Obit* Apr 2005

Orff, Carl, German composer, Aug 1976, *Obit* May 1982

Origliasso, Jess, Australian singer, Jan 2006

Origliasso, Lisa, Australian singer, Jan 2006

Orman, Suze, American financial adviser, May 2003

Ormandy, Eugene, conductor, Jan 1941, *Obit* May 1985

Ormond, Julia, English actress, Mar 1999

Orri Pall Dyrason, Icelandic drummer, Jan 2003

Osato, Sono, Oct 1945

Osbourne, Ozzy, English singer, Nov 1998

Osmond, Donny, American singer, Feb 1998

Otter, Anne Sofie von, Swedish opera singer, Sept 1995

Otto, Miranda, Australian actress, Jan 2003

Overman, Lynne, *Obit* Apr 1943

Oz, Frank, puppeteer and motion picture director, Oct 1999

Oz, Mehmet C., American surgeon, Apr 2003

Paar, Jack, American television talk show host, Apr 1959, *Obit* Yrbk 2004

Pacino, Al, American actor, July 1974

Page, Ellen, Canadian actress, May 2008

Page, Geraldine, actress, Nov 1953, *Obit* Aug 1987

Page, Greg, Australian singer and actor, Jan 2004

Page, Patti, American singer, Sept 1965, *Obit* Yrbk 2013

Paige, Janis, actress and singer, Jan 1959

Paik, Nam June, Korean video artist and composer, Mar 1983, *Obit* Yrbk 2006

Palance, Jack, American actor, Aug 1992, *Obit* Feb 2007

Pallett, Owen, Canadian singer and violinist, Jan 2007

Palmer, Geoffrey, English actor, Jan 2006

Palmer, Lilli, German actress, May 1951, *Obit* Mar 1986

Paltrow, Gwyneth, American actress, Jan 2005

Panov, Valery, Russian dancer, Oct 1974

Papa Wemba, Congolese singer, Jan 2003

Pape, Rene, German opera singer, Jan 2003

Papi, Gennaro, *Obit* Jan 1942

Paradis, Vanessa, French singer and actress, Jan 2004

Park, Merle, English ballet dancer, Sept 1974

Parke, William, *Obit* Sept 1941

Parker, Mary-Louise, American actress, Apr 2006

Parker, Sarah Jessica, American actress, Sept 1998

Parks, Bert, actor and television personality, Feb 1973, *Obit* Apr 1992

Parry, Richard Reed, Canadian instrumentalist, Jan 2007

Parsons, Estelle, American actress, Oct 1975

Parsons, Jim, American actor, Sept 2013

Part, Arvo, Estonian composer, Feb 1995

Partch, Harry, American composer, Sept 1965, *Obit* Oct 1974

Pasternack, Josef, *Obit* Jan 1940

Patinkin, Mandy, American actor and singer, Jan 1999

Patty, Sandi, American gospel singer, Feb 2004

Paul, Les, American guitarist, Aug 1987, *Obit* Yrbk 2009

Pauley, Jane, American television newscaster and talk show host, May 1980

Pausini, Laura, Italian singer, Jan 2007

Pavarotti, Luciano, Italian opera singer, June 1973, *Obit* Nov 2007

Pawley, Edward, Mar 1946

Paxinou, Katina, Oct 1943, *Obit* Apr 1973

Paxman, Jeremy, British television reporter and interviewer, Jan 2007

Payton, Nicholas, American trumpet player, Sept 1999

Peart, Neil, Canadian drummer, Feb 2001

Peck, Gregory, American actor, July 1947, Oct 1992, *Obit* Sept 2003

Peck, James L. H., Aug 1942

Peerce, Jan, opera singer, May 1942, *Obit* Feb 1985

Pegg, Dave, English bassist and singer, Sept 2005

Pelletier, Wilfrid, Yrbk 1944, *Obit* June 1982

Pelt, Jeremy, American jazz trumpet player, Feb 2009

Pendleton, Moses, American dancer and choreographer, Sept 1989

Penn & Teller, American magicians, June 2000

Penn, Arthur A., *Obit* Apr 1941

Penn, Sean, American actor and film director, June 1993

Pennario, Leonard, American pianist, Oct 1959

Peppard, George, actor, Yrbk 1965, *Obit* July 1994

Perahia, Murray, American pianist, Mar 1982

Perez, Louis, American drummer, Oct 2005

Perkins, Anthony, American actor, Sept 1960, *Obit* Nov 1992

Perkins, Elizabeth, American actress, Jan 2007

Perlman, Itzhak, American violinist, May 1975

Peroni, Carlo, *Obit* May 1944

Perrine, Valerie, actress, Oct 1975

Perry, Antoinette, actress and theatrical director, *Obit* July 1946

Perry, Joe, American rock guitarist, July 2004

Perry, Katy, American singer and songwriter, Jan 2012

Person, Houston, American saxophonist, June 2003

Pesci, Joe, American actor, Mar 1994

Peters, Bernadette, American actress and singer, Sept 1984

Peters, Roberta, opera singer, Apr 1954

Peterson, Oscar, Canadian pianist and composer, Oct 1983, *Obit* Yrbk 2008

Petri, Egon, Dutch pianist, Nov 1942, *Obit* July 1962

Petrillo, James C., American labor leader, Yrbk 1940, *Obit* Jan 1985

Petronio, Stephen, American dancer and choreographer, Mar 1998

Peyroux, Madeleine, American singer, songwriter and guitarist, Nov 2005

Pfeiffer, Michelle, American actress, Mar 1990

Pharrell, American record producer, singer and songwriter, May 2004

Philbin, Regis, American television talk show and game show host, Oct 1994

Phillips, Albert, *Obit* Mar 1940

Phillips, Scott, American drummer, May 2002

Phoenix (Musician), American bassist, Mar 2002

Piaf, Edith, French singer, Yrbk 1950, *Obit* Nov 1963

Piatigorsky, Gregor, Russian-American cellist, Oct 1945, *Obit* Sept 1976

Picciotto, Guy, American guitarist and songwriter, Mar 2002

Piccoli, Michel, French actor, Jan 2002

Pickens, Jane, singer, Yrbk 1949, *Obit* Apr 1992

Pickerill, Elmo N., Mar 1966, *Obit* Mar 1968

Pickford, Mary, American actress, Apr 1945, *Obit* July 1979

Picon, Molly, actress, June 1951, *Obit* June 1992

Pidgeon, Walter, actor, Sept 1942, *Obit* Nov 1984

Pierce, David Hyde, American actor, Apr 2001

Pierce, Wendell, American actor, Aug 2010

Pike, Rosamund, British actress, Nov 2012

Pinnock, Trevor, British harpsichordist and conductor, Sept 1989

Pinsky, Drew, American physician and talk show host, Feb 2011

Pinza, Ezio, Italian opera singer, Feb 1941, Yrbk 1953, *Obit* July 1957

Pires, Maria Joao, Portuguese pianist, Jan 2007

Pitt, Brad, American actor, Mar 1996

Pivot, Bernard, French television talk show host, Oct 1990

Plant, Robert, British singer, Oct 1998

Pleasence, Donald, English actor, June 1969, *Obit* Apr 1995

Plimpton, Martha, American actress, Apr 2002

Plowright, Joan, English actress, Feb 1964

Plummer, Christopher, Canadian actor, July 1956, Aug 1988

Podles, Ewa, Polish opera singer, Jan 2006

Poehler, Amy, American comedienne and actress, Aug 2008

Pogorelich, Ivo, Yugoslav pianist, Sept 1988

Poitier, Sidney, American actor and film director, May 1959, Sept 2000

Polivka, Galen, American bassist, Sept 2010

Pollack, Sydney, American motion picture director, Sept 1986, *Obit* Sept 2008

Pollain, Rene, *Obit* Yrbk 1940

Pollini, Maurizio, Italian pianist, Nov 1980

Pollock, Allan, *Obit* Apr 1942

Polunin, Slava, Russian clown, Jan 2004

Pons, Lily, French opera singer, Jan 1944, *Obit* Apr 1976

Popov, Oleg, Russian clown, Mar 1964

Popper, John, singer and harpist, Jan 2012

Porter, Cole, American composer and lyricist, July 1940, *Obit* Yrbk 1964

Portman, Eric, Mar 1957, *Obit* Feb 1970

Portuondo, Omara, Cuban singer, Jan 2005

Posey, Parker, American actress, Mar 2003

Poston, Tom, American actor, Apr 1961, *Obit* Yrbk 2007

Potente, Franka, German actress, Jan 2003

Poullain, Frankie, British rock bassist, Jan 2004

Powell, Dick, American actor, director and producer, Feb 1948, *Obit* Feb 1963

Powell, Jane, American singer and actress, Yrbk 1974

Powell, Kevin, American journalist, poet and essayist, Jan 2004

Powell, William, American actor, Oct 1947, *Obit* May 1984

Power, Tyrone, American actor, Yrbk 1950, *Obit* Jan 1959

Powers, James T., American actor, *Obit* Mar 1943

Powers, Marie, Jan 1951, *Obit* Feb 1974

Pratt, Jane, American magazine editor and talk show host, June 1999

Preminger, Otto, American film director, July 1959, *Obit* June 1986

Presley, Elvis, American singer, Sept 1959, *Obit* Oct 1977

Presley, Priscilla Beaulieu, American actress, Sept 1990

Preston, Robert, American actor, Yrbk 1958, *Obit* May 1987

Previn, Andre, American composer and conductor, May 1972

Previn, Dory, singer and songwriter, Sept 1975, *Obit* Yrbk 2012

Prey, Hermann, German opera singer, Feb 1975, *Obit* Oct 1998

Price, Leontyne, American opera singer, May 1961, Oct 1978

Price, Margaret, Welsh opera singer, Aug 1986, *Obit* Yrbk 2011

Price, Vincent, American actor, Nov 1956, *Obit* Jan 1994

Pride, Charley, American country singer, Apr 1975

Prieto, Dafnis, Cuban drummer, Oct 2012

Primrose, William, violist, Yrbk 1946, *Obit* July 1982

Prinze, Freddie, American actor, Jan 2003

Prokofiev, Sergey, Russian composer, Nov 1941, *Obit* Apr 1953

Pryor, Arthur, trombonist, *Obit* Aug 1942

Pugacheva, Alla, Russian singer, Jan 2004

Punisher (Musician), Finnish bassist, Jan 2003

Purdie, Bernard, American drummer, Jan 2010

Putnam, Ashley, Mar 1982

Quarshie, Hugh, Ghanaian-British actor, Jan 2004

Quasthoff, Thomas, German classical singer, Jan 2005

Quayle, Anthony, English actor and theatrical director, Yrbk 1971, *Obit* Jan 1990

Queler, Eve, conductor, July 1972

Query, Nate, American bassist, Aug 2007

Quinn, Aidan, American actor, Apr 2005

Quinn, Anthony, Mexican-American actor, Yrbk 1957, *Obit* Sept 2001

Racette, Patricia, American opera singer, Feb 2003

Radcliffe, Daniel, English actor, Nov 2010

Radner, Gilda, American comedienne, Feb 1980, *Obit* July 1989

Raedler, Dorothy, opera director and choreographer, Yrbk 1954, *Obit* Feb 1994

Raffi, Canadian singer, Jan 2003

Rahman, A. R., Indian composer and singer, June 2009

Rai, Aishwarya, Indian actress, Jan 2003

Rain (Singer), Korean pop singer, Jan 2006

Rains, Claude, Anglo-American actor, Nov 1949, *Obit* July 1967

Raitt, Bonnie, American singer and guitarist, Aug 1990

Rakim, American rapper, Aug 2008

Ramazzotti, Eros, Italian singer and songwriter, Jan 2004

Ramey, Samuel, American opera singer, July 1981

Ramirez, Tina, Venezuelan-American dancer and director, Nov 2004

Rampal, Jean-Pierre, French flutist, Mar 1970, *Obit* Aug 2000

Rampling, Charlotte, English actress, June 2002

Randall, Tony, American actor, Jan 1961, *Obit* Yrbk 2004

Randi, James, American magician, May 1987

Rao, Shanta, Indian dancer, Yrbk 1957

Raphael, Spanish singer, Aug 1991

Raphael, Sally Jessy, television talk show host, Feb 1990

Raskin, Judith, American opera singer, Apr 1964, *Obit* Feb 1985

Rathbone, Basil, Anglo-American actor, Mar 1951, *Obit* Oct 1967

Ratoff, Gregory, Aug 1943, *Obit* Feb 1961

Rava, Enrico, Italian jazz trumpet player, Jan 2006

Raven-Symone, American actress, Sept 2008

Rawls, Lou, American singer, Mar 1984, *Obit* Oct 2006

Ray, Amy, American singer and songwriter, Aug 1998

Ray, Charles, American actor, *Obit* Jan 1944

Reagan, Nancy, wife of American president Ronald Reagan, May 1982

Reagan, Ronald, American president, Yrbk 1949, Feb 1967, Nov 1982, *Obit* Yrbk 2004

Reagon, Bernice Johnson, American historian and singer, Aug 1999

Reardon, John, opera singer, Nov 1974, *Obit* June 1988

Reddy, Helen, American singer, Apr 1975

Redford, Robert, American actor and motion picture director, Apr 1971, Mar 1982

Redgrave, Lynn, English actress, Sept 1969, *Obit* Yrbk 2010

Redgrave, Michael, English actor, Feb 1950, *Obit* May 1985

Redgrave, Vanessa, English actress, Yrbk 1966, Sept 2003

Redman, Joshua, American jazz saxophonist, Jan 1997

Redpath, Jean, Scottish singer, Feb 1984

Reed, Lou, American singer, July 1989

Reese, Della, American singer and actress, Sept 1971

Reeve, Christopher, American actor, May 1982, *Obit* Jan 2005

Reeves, Dianne, American jazz singer, July 2006

Reeves, Keanu, Canadian actor, May 1995

Rehman, Shabana, Norwegian comedian, Jan 2004

Reid, Charlotte Thompson, congresswoman and regulatory official, Jan 1975

Reid, Kate, Canadian actress, Mar 1985, *Obit* May 1993

Reilly, John C., American actor, Oct 2004

Reiner, Fritz, conductor, Apr 1941, Yrbk 1953, *Obit* Jan 1964

Reiner, Rob, American actor and film director, May 1988

Remick, Lee, American actress, Oct 1966, *Obit* Sept 1991

Renaud, Madeleine, French actress and theatrical producer, Mar 1953, *Obit* Nov 1994

Resnik, Regina, opera singer, Jan 1956, *Obit* Yrbk 2013

Rey, Fernando, Spanish actor, Mar 1979, *Obit* May 1994

Reynolds, Burt, American actor, Oct 1973

Reynolds, Debbie, American actress and singer, Yrbk 1964

Richard 23, Belgian percussionist and singer, Jan 2006

Richards, Keith, British guitarist, Feb 1989

Richardson, Kevin, American singer, May 2000

Richardson, Miranda, English actress, Feb 1994

Richardson, Ralph, English actor, Nov 1950, *Obit* Nov 1983

Richman, Charles J., *Obit* Jan 1941

Richter, Sviatoslav, Russian pianist, Feb 1961, *Obit* Oct 1997

Riedel, Oliver, German bassist, Jan 2007

Riefenstahl, Leni, German actress and motion picture director, May 1975, *Obit* Yrbk 2004

Rigg, Diana, English actress, Oct 1974

Rihanna, Barbadian singer, Nov 2007

Riley, Terry, American composer and pianist, Apr 2002

Ringling, Robert E., May 1945, *Obit* Feb 1950

Ringwald, Molly, American actress, May 1987

Ritchard, Cyril, Jan 1957, *Obit* Feb 1978

Ritchie, Jean, American folk singer, Oct 1959

Ritter, John, American actor, June 1980, *Obit* Yrbk 2004

Ritter, Thelma, Yrbk 1957, *Obit* Feb 1974

Rivera, Chita, American dancer, singer and actress, Oct 1984

Roach, Max, American jazz drummer, July 1986, *Obit* Nov 2007

Robards, Jason, American actor, Oct 1959, *Obit* Mar 2001

Robbins, Jerome, American dancer, choreographer and theatrical director, May 1947, May 1969, *Obit* Oct 1998

Robbins, Tim, American actor, July 1994

Robert, Alain, French urban climber, Jan 2007

Roberts, Florence, *Obit* July 1940

Roberts, Julia, American actress, May 1991

Roberts, Tony, American actor, Oct 2006

Robertson, Cliff, American actor, Yrbk 1969, *Obit* Yrbk 2011

Robinson, Bill, American tap dancer, Feb 1941, *Obit* Jan 1950

Robinson, Edward G., actor, Jan 1950, *Obit* Mar 1973

Robison, Emily, American banjoist and singer, July 2000

Robison, Paula, flutist, May 1982

Robson, Flora, English actress, Jan 1951, *Obit* Sept 1984

Robson, May, actress, *Obit* Yrbk 1942

Rochberg, George, American composer, Sept 1985, *Obit* Yrbk 2005

Rock, Pete, American record producer and DJ, Aug 2009

Rodgers, Nile, American guitarist and record producer, Jan 2012

Rodgers, Richard, American composer, May 1940, Apr 1951, *Obit* Feb 1980

Rodzinski, Artur, Aug 1940, *Obit* Feb 1959

Rogers, Fred, American television performer and producer, July 1971, *Obit* July 2003

Rogers, Ginger, American actress, singer and dancer, Apr 1941, Yrbk 1967, *Obit* July 1995

Rogers, Kenny, American country singer, Jan 1981

Rogers, Paul, Mar 1960

Romberg, Sigmund, composer, Mar 1945, *Obit* Yrbk 1951

Rome, Harold, American composer and lyricist, Apr 1942, *Obit* Jan 1994

Rooney, Joe Don, American guitarist, Aug 2003

Rooney, Mickey, American actor, Feb 1942, Sept 1965

Rosas, Cesar, American singer and guitarist, Oct 2005

Rose, Arnold, *Obit* Oct 1946

Rose, Charlie, American television newscaster and talk show host, Jan 1995

Rose, George, actor, Sept 1984, *Obit* June 1988

Rose, Leonard, American cellist, Jan 1977, *Obit* Jan 1985

Rosenstock, Joseph, conductor and opera director, Jan 1954, *Obit* Jan 1986

Rosenthal, Moriz, Polish pianist, *Obit* Oct 1946

Rosenwinkel, Kurt, American jazz guitarist and composer, July 2011

Ross, Herbert, American choreographer and motion picture director, Aug 1980, *Obit* Feb 2002

Rossen, Daniel, American singer, songwriter and guitarist, Sept 2011

Rossi, Vasco, Italian rock singer, Jan 2005

Roth, Gabriel, American songwriter, bassist and recording producer, Feb 2010

Rotten, Johnny, English singer, Nov 1996

Rourke, Mickey, American actor, Oct 1991

Rowland, Kelly, American singer, Aug 2001

Rowlands, Gena, American actress, Nov 1975

Rowntree, Dave, British drummer, Nov 2003

Rubinstein, Artur, Polish-American pianist, Yrbk 1945, Feb 1966, *Obit* Mar 1983

Rubio, Ingrid, Spanish actress, Jan 2002

Rudd, Paul, American actor, Sept 1977, *Obit* Yrbk 2010

Rudd, Phil, Australian drummer, Mar 2005

Rudel, Julius, Austrian-American conductor, July 1965

Ruhmann, Heinz, Apr 1965

Ruiz Soler, Antonio, Spanish dancer, June 1968

Rushing, Matthew, American dancer, July 2000

Russell, Anna, Canadian singer and parodist, Apr 1954, *Obit* Yrbk 2007

Russell, Harold, American actor and government official, Jan 1950, Jan 1966, *Obit* Apr 2002

Russell, Kurt, American actor, Nov 2004

Russell, Pee Wee, clarinetist, Aug 1944, *Obit* Apr 1969

Russell, Rosalind, American actress, Jan 1943, *Obit* Feb 1977

Russo, Rene, American model and actress, July 1997

Rutherford, Margaret, English actress, Jan 1964, *Obit* July 1972

Ryan, Meg, American actress, May 1999

Ryan, Robert, American actor, Yrbk 1963, *Obit* Sept 1973

Ryder, Winona, American actress, June 1994

Rysanek, Leonie, Austrian opera singer, Mar 1966, *Obit* May 1998

Saddler, Donald, choreographer, Jan 1963

Sade, British singer, Sept 1986

Sagnier, Ludivine, French actress, Jan 2004

Sahl, Mort, American comedian, Yrbk 1960

Saint, Eva Marie, American actress, June 1955

Sainte-Marie, Buffy, Canadian singer and songwriter, July 1969

Sairam, Aruna, Indian singer, Jan 2006

Sajak, Pat, American television game show host, July 1989

Salerno-Sonnenberg, Nadja, violinist, Nov 1987

Saliers, Emily, American singer and songwriter, Aug 1998

Salonen, Esa-Pekka, Finnish composer and conductor, Jan 2007

Salonga, Lea, Filipino singer and actress, Jan 2007

Samaroff, Olga, American pianist and music teacher, Mar 1946, *Obit* June 1948

Sanchez, David, Puerto Rican jazz saxophonist, Nov 2001

Sanders, George, British actor, June 1943, *Obit* June 1972

Sanders, Ric, English fiddler, Sept 2005

Sandor, Gyorgy, American pianist, July 1947, *Obit* Yrbk 2006

Sandoval, Arturo, Cuban jazz trumpet player, Jan 2003

Sandoval, Jesse, American drummer, June 2007

Sangare, Oumou, Malian singer, Jan 2003

Sansa, Maya, Italian actress, Jan 2004

Sansone, Pat, American guitarist, percussionist and keyboardist, Feb 2010

Santaolalla, Gustavo, Argentine composer and record producer, Jan 2007

Santelmann, William F., bandmaster and marine corps officer, Apr 1953

Sarandon, Susan, American actress, Sept 1989

Sarg, Tony, German-American puppeteer and illustrator, *Obit* Apr 1942

Sargent, Malcolm Watts, English conductor, Yrbk 1945, *Obit* Jan 1968

Sass, Katrin, German actress, Jan 2003

Sauer, Emil von, German pianist, *Obit* June 1942

Savage, Rick, English bassist and singer, Jan 2003, *Obit* Mar 1994

Savalas, Telly, actor, Feb 1976

Sayao, Bidu, Brazilian opera singer, Feb 1942, *Obit* June 1999

Scallon, Dana Rosemary, British singer, Jan 2007

Scelsa, Vin, American disc jockey, May 2006

Schell, Maria, Austrian actress, June 1961, *Obit* Yrbk 2005

Schell, Maximilian, Austrian actor, Yrbk 1962

Schelling, Ernest, American composer, conductor and pianist, Jan 1940

Scherman, Thomas, American conductor, Yrbk 1954, *Obit* July 1979

Schertzinger, Victor, *Obit* Yrbk 1941

Schildkraut, Joseph, Austrian actor, Apr 1956, *Obit* Mar 1964

Schillinger, Joseph, Russian composer and music teacher, *Obit* May 1943

Schindler, John A., Mar 1956, *Obit* Jan 1958

Schiotz, Aksel, Mar 1949, *Obit* June 1975

Schippers, Thomas, American conductor, Apr 1970, *Obit* Feb 1978

Schlamme, Martha, singer, Feb 1964, *Obit* Jan 1986

Schnabel, Artur, Austrian-American pianist and composer, July 1942, *Obit* Sept 1951

Schneider, Alexander, violinist, Mar 1976, *Obit* Mar 1993

Schneider, Christoph, German drummer, Jan 2007

Schneider, Romy, Austrian actress, Jan 1965, *Obit* July 1982

Schnittke, Alfred, Russian composer, July 1992, *Obit* Oct 1998

Schoenberg, Arnold, Austrian-American composer, Apr 1942, *Obit* Sept 1951

Schoenberg, Loren, American saxophonist and jazz historian, Feb 2005

Schorr, Friedrich, Hungarian opera singer, July 1942, *Obit* June 1954

Schultz, Ed, American radio talk show host, Aug 2005

Schuman, William, American composer, June 1942, Yrbk 1962, *Obit* Apr 1992

Schwartz, Arthur, composer, Nov 1979, *Obit* Oct 1984

Schwartz, Maurice, theatrical director, producer and actor, Feb 1956, *Obit* July 1960

Schwartzman, Jason, American actor, Oct 2009

Schwarz, Gerard, trumpet player and conductor, Apr 1986

Schwarzkopf, Elisabeth, German-British opera singer, Yrbk 1955, *Obit* Yrbk 2006

Schygulla, Hanna, German actress, July 1984

Scofield, Paul, English actor, Mar 1962, *Obit* Yrbk 2008

Scott, Christian, American jazz trumpet player, Jan 2008

Scott, George, American gospel singer, Oct 2001, *Obit* Yrbk 2005

Scott, George C., American actor, Apr 1971, *Obit* Nov 1999

Scott, Hazel, American pianist and singer, Aug 1943, *Obit* Nov 1981

Scott, Henry L., June 1949

Scott, Hillary, American country singer, July 2011

Scott, Jill, American singer, songwriter and actress, Jan 2002

Scott, Tom, American composer and singer, Nov 1946

Scotto, Renata, Italian opera singer, Sept 1978

Scourby, Alexander, actor, July 1965, *Obit* Apr 1985

Seacrest, Ryan, American television personality, Sept 2009

Seal, English singer, Feb 1997

Sean Paul, Jamaican reggae singer, Jan 2007

Seberg, Jean, actress, Apr 1966, *Obit* Oct 1979

Sedaka, Neil, American pop singer and songwriter, Oct 1978

Seefried, Irmgard, German opera singer, Feb 1956, *Obit* Jan 1989

Seeger, Pete, American folk singer and songwriter, Yrbk 1963

Segal, George, American actor, Nov 1975

Segovia, Andres, Spanish guitarist, May 1948, June 1964, *Obit* July 1987

Seigner, Emmanuelle, French actress, Jan 2006

Selleck, Tom, American actor, Nov 1983

Sellers, Peter, English actor, Yrbk 1960, *Obit* Sept 1980

Selway, Phil, English drummer, June 2001

Sen, Sushmita, Indian actress, Jan 2006

Serkin, Peter, pianist, June 1986

Serkin, Rudolf, Czech-American pianist, July 1940, June 1990, *Obit* July 1991

Setzer, Philip, American violinist, July 2002

Sevigny, Chloe, American actress, Aug 2000

Seymour, Lynn, Canadian ballet dancer, Nov 1979

Shaham, Gil, American violinist, Apr 1997

Shakira, Colombian singer, Jan 2002

Shalhoub, Tony, American actor, Nov 2002

Shannon, Peggy, actress, *Obit* July 1941

Sharif, Omar, Egyptian actor, May 1970

Shatner, William, Canadian actor, July 1987

Shaw, Robert, English actor and novelist, May 1968, *Obit* Oct 1978

Shawn, Ted, American dancer and choreographer, Oct 1949, *Obit* Feb 1972

Shearing, George, English jazz pianist, Apr 1958, *Obit* Yrbk 2011

Sheen, Martin, American actor, June 1977

Sheindlin, Judith, American judge, Sept 1998

Shepherd, Cybill, American actress, Mar 1987

Shepherd, Jean, American humorist, Apr 1984, *Obit* Jan 2000

Sherawat, Mallika, Indian actress, Jan 2007

Shetty, Shilpa, Indian actress, Jan 2007

Shields, Brooke, American model and actress, Oct 1982

Shinoda, Mike, American singer, Mar 2002

Shore, Dinah, American singer, June 1942, Yrbk 1966, *Obit* May 1994

Sibley, Antoinette, English dancer, Yrbk 1970

Sidney, Sylvia, actress, Oct 1981, *Obit* Sept 1999

Siegfried and Roy, German magicians and animal trainers, Jan 1998

Siepi, Cesare, Italian opera singer, Yrbk 1955, *Obit* Yrbk 2010

Signoret, Simone, French actress, Yrbk 1960, *Obit* Nov 1985

Sills, Beverly, American opera singer and manager, Nov 1969, Feb 1982, *Obit* Oct 2007

Silverman, Sarah, American comedienne, July 2006

Silvers, Phil, actor, Yrbk 1957, *Obit* Jan 1986

Simionato, Giulietta, Italian opera singer, Apr 1960, *Obit* Yrbk 2010

Simmons, Gene, American bassist and actor, Apr 1999

Simmons, Jean, English actress, Feb 1952, *Obit* Yrbk 2010

Simmons, Richard, American fitness expert and television personality, May 1982

Simms, Hilda, actress, Nov 1944, *Obit* May 1994

Simon, Carly, American singer and songwriter, Aug 1976

Simon, Paul, American singer and composer, Mar 1975

Simone, Nina, American singer and pianist, Apr 1968, *Obit* Yrbk 2003

Simpson, Valerie, American singer and songwriter, Apr 1997

Sinatra, Frank, American singer and actor, June 1943, Oct 1960, *Obit* July 1998

Singer, Richard, *Obit* Mar 1940

Singh, Simon, British physicist, writer and television host, Jan 2005

Singh, Talvin, British DJ, arranger and composer, Jan 2006

Singher, Martial, French opera singer and voice teacher, Feb 1947, *Obit* May 1990

Sinise, Gary, American actor and director, Apr 1997

Sinopoli, Giuseppe, Italian conductor and composer, Mar 1991, *Obit* Sept 2001

Sitek, David Andrew, American guitarist and record producer, Apr 2009

Sitgreaves, Beverley, *Obit* Sept 1943

Skarsgard, Stellan, Swedish actor, Jan 2002

Skinner, Cornelia Otis, actress and author, Jan 1942, Yrbk 1964, *Obit* Sept 1979

Skinner, Otis, *Obit* Feb 1942

Slash (Musician), British rock guitarist and songwriter, Mar 2008

Slezak, Walter, actor, Mar 1955, *Obit* June 1983

Slick, Grace, American singer, Apr 1982

Sloane, Everett, Jan 1957, *Obit* Oct 1965

Smallens, Alexander, May 1947, *Obit* Jan 1973

Smiley, Tavis, American radio talk show host, Apr 2003

Smith, Barbara, American actress, model and restaurateur, July 1998

Smith, C. Aubrey, English actor, Sept 1944, *Obit* Jan 1949

Smith, Gerard, American bassist and keyboardist, Apr 2009

Smith, Kate, singer, Yrbk 1940, Nov 1965, *Obit* Aug 1986

Smith, Maggie, English actress, June 1970, July 2002

Smith, Mary Carter, storyteller and folklorist, Feb 1996

Smith, Rick, British keyboardist and songwriter, Nov 2011

Smith, Will, American rapper and actor, Sept 1996

Smits, Jimmy, American actor, May 2006

Snipes, Wesley, American actor, Sept 1993

Snyder, Tom, American radio and television talk show host, June 1980, *Obit* Yrbk 2007

Sodero, Cesare, conductor and composer, Mar 1943, *Obit* Jan 1948

Soderstrom, Elisabeth, Swedish opera singer, Nov 1985, *Obit* Yrbk 2010

Solaar, MC, French rapper, Jan 2002

Solex, Dutch pop singer, Jan 2005

Solti, Georg, Hungarian-British conductor, Mar 1964, *Obit* Nov 1997

Somes, Michael, English dancer, Yrbk 1955, *Obit* Feb 1995

Sorvino, Mira, American actress, Aug 1998

Sothern, Ann, American actress and singer, Yrbk 1956, *Obit* Aug 2001

Souzay, Gerard, French opera singer, Jan 1966, *Obit* Yrbk 2004

Spacek, Sissy, American actress, Jan 1978

Spalding, Albert, violinist, Jan 1944, *Obit* July 1953

Spalding, Esperanza, American jazz bassist and singer, Aug 2010

Spanic, Gabriela, Venezuelan actress, Jan 2004

Spears, Britney, American singer, Apr 2000

Spektor, Regina, Russian-American singer, songwriter and pianist, July 2007

Spelling, Aaron, American television producer, May 1986, *Obit* Yrbk 2006

Spencer, John, American actor, Jan 2001, *Obit* Yrbk 2006

Spitalny, Phil, Oct 1940, *Obit* Yrbk 1970

Spivakov, Vladimir, Russian violinist and conductor, Feb 1996

Spottswood, James, *Obit* Yrbk 1940

Stader, Maria, Swiss opera singer, July 1958, *Obit* Aug 1999

Stanley, Kim, American actress, May 1955, *Obit* Jan 2002

Stanley, Paul, American guitarist, Apr 1999

Stanwyck, Barbara, American actress, July 1947, *Obit* Mar 1990

Stapleton, Jean, actress, Yrbk 1972, *Obit* Yrbk 2013

Stapleton, Maureen, American actress, May 1959, *Obit* Nov 2006

Stapp, Scott, American singer and lyricist, May 2002

Starker, Janos, Hungarian cellist, May 1963, *Obit* Yrbk 2013

Starr, Ringo, English drummer, Yrbk 1965

Staunton, Imelda, English actress, Jan 2005

Stebbins, George Coles, *Obit* Nov 1945

Steber, Eleanor, American opera singer, Mar 1943, *Obit* Jan 1991

Steiger, Rod, American actor, June 1965, *Obit* Yrbk 2002

Steinberg, William, American conductor, Sept 1940, Mar 1958, *Obit* July 1978

Steiner, Max, Austrian-American composer and conductor, Sept 1943, *Obit* Feb 1972

Stella, Antonietta, Italian opera singer, Yrbk 1959

Stephens, Ward, *Obit* Nov 1940

Stephenson, James, British actor, *Obit* Sept 1941

Stern, Howard, American radio personality, Jan 1996

Stern, Isaac, American violinist, Apr 1949, Feb 1989, *Obit* Jan 2002

Stevens, Rise, American opera singer, Nov 1941, *Obit* Yrbk 2013

Stevenson, McLean, actor, June 1980, *Obit* Apr 1996

Steves, Rick, American travel guidebook author, Jan 2009

Stewart, James, American actor, Apr 1941, Yrbk 1960, *Obit* Sept 1997

Stewart, Patrick, British actor, Aug 1994

Stewart, Rod, English singer, Aug 1979

Stewart, Thomas, American opera singer, May 1974, *Obit* Yrbk 2007

Stewart, William G., *Obit* Sept 1941

Stickney, Dorothy, actress, Apr 1942, *Obit* Aug 1998

Stiefel, Ethan, American ballet dancer, Apr 2004

Stignani, Ebe, Italian opera singer, Feb 1949, *Obit* Yrbk 1991

Still, William Grant, American composer, Jan 1941, *Obit* Feb 1979

Stilwell, Richard, American opera singer, Feb 1986

Sting, British singer and actor, July 1985

Stipe, Michael, American singer, Apr 1997

Stirratt, John, American bassist, Feb 2010

Stock, Frederick, conductor, *Obit* Yrbk 1942

Stockwell, Dean, actor, Feb 1991

Stokowski, Leopold, American conductor, Feb 1941, July 1953, *Obit* Nov 1977

Stoltzman, Richard, clarinetist, Mar 1986

Stolz, Robert, Austrian composer, Aug 1943, *Obit* Aug 1975

Stone, Emma, American actress, Feb 2013

Stone, Joss, British soul singer, Jan 2005

Stone, Sharon, American actress, Apr 1996

Stowell, Clarence Warner, *Obit* Jan 1941

Strait, George, American country singer, Feb 2000

Strasberg, Susan, actress, May 1958, *Obit* Apr 1999

Stratas, Teresa, Canadian opera singer, Jan 1980

Straus, Oscar, Austrian composer, Mar 1944, *Obit* Mar 1954

Stravinsky, Igor, Russian composer, May 1940, Apr 1953, *Obit* May 1971

Streb, Elizabeth, American dancer and choreographer, Apr 2003

Streep, Meryl, American actress, Aug 1980, Mar 1997

Stritch, Elaine, American actress, June 1988

Stroman, Susan, American choreographer and theatrical director, July 2002

Struthers, Sally, American actress, Jan 1974

Stuart, Gloria, American actress, Apr 1998, *Obit* Yrbk 2010

Studer, Cheryl, opera singer, Apr 1992

Styne, Jule, composer, May 1983, *Obit* Nov 1994

Suesse, Dana, composer, May 1940, *Obit* Jan 1988

Sullavan, Margaret, actress, July 1944, *Obit* Feb 1960

Sullivan, Brian, Yrbk 1957

Sullivan, Francis L., June 1955, *Obit* Jan 1957

Sumac, Yma, Peruvian singer, Yrbk 1955, *Obit* Yrbk 2008

Summer, Donna, American singer, July 1979, *Obit* Yrbk 2012

Summerville, Slim, actor, *Obit* Feb 1946

Sumner, Bernard, British guitarist and singer, Jan 2006

Susann, Jacqueline, American novelist, May 1972, *Obit* Nov 1974

Sutherland, Donald, Canadian actor, Feb 1981

Sutherland, Joan, Australian opera singer, Yrbk 1960, *Obit* Yrbk 2010

Sutherland, Kiefer, Canadian actor, Mar 2002

Suzman, Janet, May 1976

Suzuki, Pat, singer and actress, Jan 1960

Svanholm, Set, Swedish opera singer, Yrbk 1956, *Obit* Yrbk 1964

Swados, Elizabeth, American composer, Feb 1979

Swaggart, Jimmy Lee, evangelist, Oct 1987

Swank, Hilary, American actress, Sept 2000

Swann, Donald, English pianist and composer, Jan 1970, *Obit* May 1994

Swanson, Gloria, actress, Sept 1950, *Obit* May 1983

Swarthout, Gladys, opera singer, Mar 1944, *Obit* Sept 1969

Swayze, Patrick, American actor and dancer, Mar 1991, *Obit* Yrbk 2009

Swenson, Alfred G., *Obit* May 1941

Swinton, Tilda, Scottish actress, Nov 2001

Swiss, Jamy Ian, American magician, Feb 2010

Sydow, Max von, Swedish actor, Apr 1967

Szell, George, American conductor, June 1945, *Obit* Oct 1970

Szeryng, Henryk, Polish violinist, Jan 1968, *Obit* Apr 1988

Szigeti, Joseph, Hungarian violinist, May 1940, Mar 1958, *Obit* Apr 1973

Taboo (Musician), American singer, Oct 2006

Tagliavini, Ferruccio, Italian opera singer, June 1947, *Obit* Apr 1995

Taj Mahal (Musician), American singer and songwriter, Nov 2001

Talvela, Martti, Finnish opera singer, Oct 1983, *Obit* Sept 1989

Tan Dun, Chinese composer, Jan 2007

Tandy, Jessica, Anglo-American actress, Mar 1956, Aug 1984, *Obit* Nov 1994

Tanon, Olga, Puerto Rican singer, Jan 2005

Tarkan, Turkish pop singer, Jan 2006

Tate, Catherine, British comedian, Oct 2012

Tati, Jacques, French actor and film director, Feb 1961, *Obit* Jan 1983

Tautou, Audrey, French actress, Jan 2002

Tavares, Sara, Portuguese singer and songwriter, Jan 2007

Tavener, John, English composer, June 1999

Taylor, Billy, American jazz pianist and composer, Oct 1980, *Obit* Yrbk 2011

Taylor, Cecil, American jazz pianist, Mar 1986

Taylor, Chris, American bassist and singer, Sept 2011

Taylor, Deems, American composer and music critic, Mar 1940, *Obit* Nov 1966

Taylor, Elizabeth, Anglo-American actress, July 1952, Oct 1985, *Obit* Yrbk 2011

Taylor, James, American singer and songwriter, June 1972

Taylor, Janie, American ballet dancer, Aug 2011

Taylor, KoKo, American blues singer and songwriter, July 2002, *Obit* Yrbk 2009

Taylor, Laurette, American actress, July 1945, *Obit* Jan 1947

Taylor, Lili, American actress, July 2005

Taylor, Paul, American dancer and choreographer, June 1964

Taylor, Robert, American actor, May 1952, *Obit* July 1969

Tcherkassky, Marianna, ballet dancer, Nov 1985

Te Kanawa, Kiri, New Zealand opera singer, Nov 1978

Tebaldi, Renata, Italian opera singer, Apr 1955, *Obit* Apr 2005

Tedeschi, Susan, American blues singer and guitarist, Sept 2012

Teitur, Danish singer and songwriter, Jan 2004

Teller, American magician, June 2000

Tempest, Marie, English actress, *Obit* Yrbk 1942

Temple, Johnny, American rock bassist and publisher, Oct 2008

Templeton, Alec, Mar 1940, *Obit* May 1963

Tennstedt, Klaus, German conductor, Sept 1983, *Obit* Mar 1998

Terkel, Studs, American interviewer and historian, Nov 1974, *Obit* Yrbk 2009

Terrell, St. John, actor, Feb 1966, *Obit* Jan 1999

Tetley, Glen, American dancer and choreographer, June 1973, *Obit* Yrbk 2007

Tetrazzini, Luisa, Italian opera singer, *Obit* Jan 1940

Teyte, Maggie, English opera singer, Yrbk 1945, *Obit* July 1976

Thalia, Mexican actress and singer, Jan 2004

Tharp, Twyla, American dancer and choreographer, Oct 1975

The Black Keys, Jan 2013

Thebom, Blanche, American opera singer, Oct 1948, *Obit* Yrbk 2010

Theodorakis, Mikis, Greek composer, July 1973

Theron, Charlize, South African actress, Nov 2004

Thomas, Augusta Read, composer, Nov 1999

Thomas, Dave, American fast food restaurant chain founder, Mar 1995, *Obit* Apr 2002

Thomas, Jess, American opera singer, June 1964, *Obit* Jan 1994

Thomas, John Charles, May 1943, *Obit* Feb 1961

Thomas, Richard, American actor, Nov 1975

Thompson, Emma, British actress, Mar 1995

Thompson, Fred, American senator, Aug 1999

Thompson, John Douglas, Canadian actor, Sept 2010

Thompson, Sada, American actress, Mar 1973, *Obit* Yrbk 2011

Thomson, Virgil, American composer and critic, Nov 1940, Oct 1966, *Obit* Nov 1989

Thorborg, Kerstin, Swedish opera singer, Mar 1940, *Obit* July 1970

Thorndike, Sybil, English actress, Yrbk 1953, *Obit* Aug 1976

Thornhill, Leeroy, British keyboardist, Oct 2009

Thurman, Uma, American actress, Aug 1996

Tian, Hao Jiang, Chinese opera singer, Feb 2009

Tibbett, Lawrence, American opera singer, Feb 1945, *Obit* Oct 1960

Tillstrom, Burr, puppeteer, May 1951, *Obit* Feb 1986

Timbaland, American hip-hop musician and recording producer, Mar 2003

Timberlake, Justin, American singer, Nov 2000

Tippett, Michael, English composer, Sept 1974, *Obit* Mar 1998

Todd, Richard, British actor, Yrbk 1955, *Obit* Yrbk 2010

Tolar, Dagga, Nigerian poet, singer and social activist, Jan 2007

Tone, Franchot, actor, May 1940, *Obit* Nov 1968

Torme, Mel, singer, Mar 1983, *Obit* Aug 1999

Torn, Rip, American actor, Apr 1977

Toscanini, Arturo, Italian conductor, June 1942, May 1954, *Obit* Mar 1957

Tourel, Jennie, American opera singer, Feb 1947, *Obit* Jan 1974

Tovey, Donald Francis, English composer, pianist and musicologist, *Obit* Sept 1940

Townsend, Robert, American actor and motion picture director, May 1994

Townshend, Pete, British singer and guitarist, Aug 1983

Tozzi, Giorgio, American opera singer, Oct 1961, *Obit* Yrbk 2011

Tracy, Spencer, American actor, Apr 1943, *Obit* Oct 1967

Trampler, Walter, violist, Nov 1971, *Obit* Jan 1998

Trapp, Maria von, Austrian singer, May 1968, *Obit* June 1987

Traubel, Helen, American opera singer, Jan 1940, Feb 1952, *Obit* Oct 1972

Travis, Randy, American country singer, Sept 1989

Travolta, John, American actor, Oct 1978, May 1996

Tremonti, Mark, American guitarist and composer, May 2002

Trenet, Charles, French singer and songwriter, Feb 1989, *Obit* Sept 2001

Trevi, Gloria, Mexican pop singer, Jan 2005

Trintignant, Jean-Louis, French actor, July 1988

Tritt, Travis, American country singer, Feb 2004

Troyanos, Tatiana, opera singer, Aug 1979, *Obit* Oct 1993

Truex, Ernest, Jan 1941, *Obit* Sept 1973

Truffaut, Francois, French film director, Jan 1969, *Obit* Jan 1985

Trulock, Mussette Langford, Jan 1957

Tryon, Thomas, author and actor, Jan 1977, *Obit* Nov 1991

Tubb, Ernest, singer, Oct 1983, *Obit* Oct 1984

Tucker, Richard, opera singer, Mar 1956, *Obit* Feb 1975

Tucker, Sophie, singer, Apr 1945, *Obit* Mar 1966

Tuckwell, Barry, Australian horn player, July 1979

Tully, Alice, music patron and singer, Jan 1984, *Obit* Feb 1994

Tune, Tommy, American dancer and director, Jan 1983

Tunstall, KT, Scottish rock singer and songwriter, Jan 2007

Tureck, Rosalyn, American pianist and harpsichordist, Sept 1959, *Obit* Yrbk 2003

Turner, Alex, British rock guitarist and singer, Jan 2006

Turner, Kathleen, American actress, June 1986

Turner, Lana, American actress, June 1943, *Obit* Sept 1995

Turner, Mark, American jazz saxophonist, Nov 2002

Turre, Steve, American jazz trombonist, Apr 2001

Turturro, John, American actor, Oct 1996

Tushingham, Rita, Oct 1965

Tuzun, Sibel, Turkish pop singer, Jan 2006

Tweedy, Jeff, American singer and songwriter, Feb 2010

Tweet (Singer), American singer and songwriter, Nov 2002

Twiggy, English model and actress, Oct 1968

Two-Tone Tommy, American rock bassist, Nov 2008

Tyler, Steven, American rock singer, Aug 1996, July 2004

Tyler, the Creator (Musician), American rapper and record producer, Aug 2011

Tyner, McCoy, American jazz pianist and composer, Aug 1997

Tyson, Cicely, American actress, Aug 1975

Uchida, Mitsuko, Japanese pianist, Sept 1991

Uematsu, Nobuo, Japanese composer, Jan 2006

Uggams, Leslie, American singer and actress, Oct 1967

Ulanova, Galina, Russian ballet dancer, Apr 1958, *Obit* June 1998

Ullman, Tracey, English actress and singer, Oct 1988

Ullmann, Liv, Norwegian actress and film director, Yrbk 1973

Underwood, Carrie, American singer and contestant on reality TV show American idol, Mar 2007

Upshaw, Dawn, American opera singer, Feb 1990

Usmanova, Yulduz, Uzbek singer, Jan 2004

Uygur, Cenk, Turkish-American radio talk show host, May 2013

Valensi, Nick, American guitarist, Feb 2007

Valente, Benita, opera singer, Mar 1988

Vallin, Sergio, Mexican guitarist and singer, Jan 2005

Van Dyke, Dick, American actor, Mar 1963

Van Hamel, Martine, Dutch-American ballet dancer, Sept 1979

Van Heusen, Jimmy, American composer, June 1970, *Obit* Apr 1990

Van Peebles, Mario, American actor and motion picture director, Nov 1993

Van Zandt, Steve, American guitarist and singer, Feb 2006

Vanbrugh, Violet, British actress, *Obit* Jan 1943

Vandross, Luther, American rhythm and blues singer and songwriter, Sept 1991, *Obit* Yrbk 2005

Vaness, Carol, American opera singer, Sept 1986

Vanessa-Mae, British violinist, Jan 2002

Vangelis, Greek composer, Jan 2003

Varnay, Astrid, American opera singer, May 1951, *Obit* Yrbk 2007

Vassa, Yossi, Ethiopian-Israeli comedian, Jan 2006

Vaughan Williams, Ralph, English composer, Yrbk 1953, *Obit* Nov 1958

Vaughn, Robert, American actor, Sept 1967

Vaughn, Vince, American actor, Sept 2006

Vega, Suzanne, American singer and songwriter, Aug 1994

Veidt, Conrad, German actor, *Obit* May 1943

Velez, Lupe, Mexican actress, *Obit* Feb 1945

Veloso, Caetano, Brazilian singer and songwriter, Jan 2002

Vera-Ellen, dancer and actress, Feb 1959, *Obit* Oct 1981

Verdi-Fletcher, Mary, wheelchair dancer, Jan 1997

Vereen, Ben, American actor, singer and dancer, Apr 1978

Vergara, Sofia, Colombian actress, June 2013

Vernon, Justin, American singer and songwriter, Apr 2012

Verrett, Shirley, American opera singer, Apr 1967, *Obit* Yrbk 2011

Vickers, Jon, Canadian opera singer, Mar 1961

Vickrey, Dan, American guitarist, Mar 2003

Vieira, Meredith, American television newscaster, Apr 2002

Vilar, Jean, French actor and director, Apr 1962, *Obit* Sept 1971

Villa-Lobos, Heitor, Brazilian composer, Apr 1945, *Obit* Jan 1960

Vishnevskaya, Galina, Russian opera singer, July 1966, *Obit* Yrbk 2013

Voight, Jon, American actor, Apr 1974

Voigt, Deborah, American opera singer, Jan 1999

Volkova, Julia, Russian singer, Jan 2003

Vollenweider, Andreas, Swiss harpist, May 1987

Volochkova, Anastasia, Russian ballet dancer, Jan 2004

Volume, Johnny, Finnish guitarist, Jan 2003

Von Stade, Frederica, American opera singer, Aug 1977

Von Tilzer, Harry, American songwriter and music publisher, *Obit* Mar 1946

Von Zell, Harry, June 1944, *Obit* Jan 1982

Voorhees, Donald, conductor, Feb 1950, *Obit* Apr 1989

Waart, Edo de, Dutch conductor, Mar 1990

Wagner, Robert, American actor, June 1984

Wagner, Sune Rose, Danish singer, guitarist and songwriter, Jan 2004

Walken, Christopher, American actor, Oct 1990

Walker, Nancy, actress, Feb 1965, *Obit* May 1992

Wallach, Eli, American actor, May 1959

Wallenstein, Alfred, American conductor, May 1940, Apr 1952, *Obit* Mar 1983

Waller, Fats, American jazz pianist and composer, Apr 1942, *Obit* Feb 1944

Wallin, Pamela, Canadian television newscaster and talk show host, Jan 2005

Walsh, John, American victims' rights advocate and television program host, July 2001

Walter, Wilmer, *Obit* Oct 1941

Walters, Barbara, American television newscaster, Feb 1971, Feb 2003

Walton, William, English composer, Mar 1940, *Obit* May 1983

Ward, Robert, composer, July 1963, *Obit* Yrbk 2013

Ware, David S., American jazz saxophonist, Sept 2003, *Obit* Yrbk 2013

Waring, Fred, American band leader, Sept 1940, *Obit* Sept 1984

Warren, Leonard, opera singer, Yrbk 1953, *Obit* Apr 1960

Washington, Denzel, American actor, July 1992

Watanabe, Ken, Japanese actor, Jan 2004

Waters, Ethel, American actress and singer, Apr 1941, Mar 1951, *Obit* Oct 1977

Waters, Muddy, American singer and guitarist, May 1981, *Obit* June 1983

Waterston, Sam, American actor, Sept 1985

Watkins, Rone, Antiguan drummer, Jan 2004

Watson, Emily, British actress, May 2007

Watson, Lucile, actress, Yrbk 1953, *Obit* Sept 1962

Watts, Andre, American pianist, May 1968

Watts, Heather, ballet dancer, May 1983

Watts, Jeff, American jazz drummer, Apr 2008

Watts, Naomi, Australian actress, Mar 2007

Wayans, Shawn, American actor, May 2001

Wayne, David, actor, June 1956, *Obit* Apr 1995

Wayne, John, American actor, Feb 1951, July 1972, *Obit* Aug 1979

Weaver, Affie, *Obit* Jan 1941

Weaver, Dennis, American actor, Nov 1977, *Obit* Yrbk 2006

Weaver, Fritz, Jan 1966

Weaver, Sigourney, American actress, Mar 1989

Webb, Clifton, American actor, singer and dancer, Mar 1943, *Obit* Yrbk 1966

Webb, Jack, American actor and producer, May 1955, *Obit* Mar 1983

Weber, Joseph M., *Obit* July 1942

Webster, Margaret, American actress and theatrical director, May 1940, Sept 1950, *Obit* Jan 1973

Weede, Robert, Feb 1957, *Obit* Sept 1972

Weidman, Charles, American dancer and choreographer, Apr 1942, *Obit* Sept 1975

Weilerstein, Alisa, American cellist, Feb 2013

Weill, Kurt, German composer, Yrbk 1941, *Obit* May 1950

Wein, George, Oct 1985

Weingartner, Felix, Austrian conductor and composer, *Obit* June 1942

Weissenberg, Alexis, Bulgarian pianist, June 1978, *Obit* Yrbk 2012

Welch, Florence, British singer, June 2012

Welch, Raquel, American actress, May 1971

Weld, John, motion picture stunt performer, May 1940

Weld, Tuesday, American actress, July 1974

Welitsch, Ljuba, Bulgarian opera singer, May 1949, *Obit* Nov 1996

Welk, Lawrence, American band leader, Feb 1957, *Obit* July 1992

Welles, Orson, American actor, director and producer, May 1941, Feb 1965, *Obit* Nov 1985

Werner, Oskar, Austrian actor, June 1966, *Obit* Jan 1985

West, Kanye, American rapper and record producer, Aug 2006

Westenra, Hayley, New Zealand singer, Jan 2006

Westheimer, Ruth, American psychotherapist, Jan 1987

Westley, Helen, actress, *Obit* Feb 1943

Whelan, Wendy, American ballet dancer, Oct 1998

Whitaker, Forest, American actor and motion picture director, Feb 1997

White, Betty, American actress, June 1987

White, Jack, American singer and guitarist, Sept 2003

White, Josh, guitarist and singer, Aug 1944, *Obit* Nov 1969

White, Meg, American drummer, Sept 2003

White, Portia, Mar 1945

White, Vanna, American television personality, Jan 1988

Whiteman, Paul, American band leader, Aug 1945, *Obit* Feb 1968

Whitford, Brad, American rock guitarist, July 2004

Whitford, Bradley, American actor, Apr 2003

Whitmore, James, American actor, Sept 1976, *Obit* Yrbk 2009

Whittemore, Arthur Austin, pianist, Jan 1954, *Obit* Feb 1985

Whitty, May, English actress, Yrbk 1945, *Obit* July 1948

Wicker, Ireene, singer and storyteller, Apr 1943, *Obit* Jan 1988

Widmark, Richard, American actor, Apr 1963, *Obit* Yrbk 2008

Wiedoeft, Rudy, *Obit* Mar 1940

Wiest, Dianne, actress, Mar 1997

Wild, Earl, American pianist and composer, July 1988, *Obit* Yrbk 2010

Wilder, Alec, composer, July 1980, *Obit* Feb 1981

Wilder, Gene, American actor and motion picture director, Apr 1978

Will. i. Am (Musician), American singer, Oct 2006

Williams of Barnburgh, Thomas Williams, Apr 1946, *Obit* May 1967

Williams, Andy, American singer, Feb 1960, *Obit* Yrbk 2012

Williams, Billy Dee, American actor, Apr 1984

Williams, Camilla, opera singer, June 1952, *Obit* Yrbk 2012

Williams, Cliff, English bassist, Mar 2005

Williams, Esther, American swimmer and actress, Feb 1955, *Obit* Yrbk 2013

Williams, Hank, American country singer, Mar 1998

Williams, Joe, singer, Apr 1985, *Obit* June 1999

Williams, John, Australian guitarist, July 1983

Williams, Lucinda, American singer and songwriter, Mar 1999

Williams, Mary Lou, American pianist and composer, Nov 1966, *Obit* July 1981

Williams, Michelle, American singer, Aug 2001

Williams, Paul, American singer, songwriter and actor, June 1983

Williams, Robbie, British pop singer, Jan 2004

Williams, Saul, American rapper and poet, June 2011

Williams, Vanessa, American singer and actress, May 1984

Williams, Wendy, American talk show host, Oct 2009

Williamson, Nicol, British actor, Jan 1970, *Obit* Yrbk 2012

Williamson, Ski, Finnish guitarist and singer, Jan 2003

Willis, Bruce, American actor, Feb 1987

Willis, Kelly, singer, Oct 1999

Wilson, Brian, American singer and songwriter, July 1988

Wilson, Cassandra, American jazz singer, Mar 1998

Wilson, Don, radio and television personality, Aug 1944, *Obit* Yrbk 1991

Wilson, Gretchen, American country singer, Apr 2011

Wilson, Luke, American actor, Feb 2005

Wilson, Mark, Australian bassist, Jan 2005

Windust, Bretaigne, Mar 1943, *Obit* May 1960

Winehouse, Amy, British jazz and soul singer, Jan 2007, *Obit* Yrbk 2011

Winfrey, Oprah, American television talk show host, Mar 1987

Winger, Debra, American actress, July 1984

Winkler, Henry, American actor and producer, Sept 1976

Winters, Shelley, American actress, Apr 1952, *Obit* Apr 2006

Witherspoon, Reese, American actress, Jan 2004

Wolfe, Julia, American composer, Oct 2003

Wolfit, Donald, Mar 1965, *Obit* Apr 1968

Womack, Lee Ann, American country singer, Apr 2010

Wood, Elijah, American actor, Aug 2002

Wood, Evan Rachel, American actress, June 2009

Wood, John, English actor, Apr 1983, *Obit* Yrbk 2011

Wood, Natalie, American actress, Apr 1962, *Obit* Jan 1982

Wood, Peggy, actress and singer, July 1942, Yrbk 1953, *Obit* May 1978

Woodard, Alfre, American actress, Feb 1995

Woods, James, American actor, Nov 1989

Woodward, Joanne, American actress, June 1958

Woolley, Monty, July 1940, *Obit* June 1963

Worth, Irene, American actress, May 1968, *Obit* Aug 2002

Wray, John, *Obit* May 1940

Wright, Jeffrey, American actor, May 2002

Wright, Martha, American singer and actress, Feb 1955

Wright, Steven, American comedian, May 2003

Wright, Teresa, American actress, May 1943, *Obit* Yrbk 2005

Wu Man, Chinese pipa player, Jan 2007

Wyatt, Jane, American actress, May 1957, *Obit* Yrbk 2006

Wylde, Zakk, American rock guitarist and songwriter, Oct 2004

Wyman, Jane, American actress, Mar 1949, *Obit* Yrbk 2007

Wynette, Tammy, American country singer, June 1995, *Obit* June 1998

Wynonna, American country singer, May 1996

Xenakis, Iannis, Greek composer, Sept 1994, *Obit* July 2001

Yang Lan, Chinese talk show host, Jan 2003

Yankovic, Al, American rock music parodist, Feb 1999

Yanni, Greek composer, Jan 2003

Yauch, Adam, American rapper and bassist, *Obit* Yrbk 2012

Yearwood, Trisha, American country singer, July 1998

Yeoh, Michelle, Chinese actress, Jan 1998

Yepes, Narciso, Spanish guitarist, Oct 1966, *Obit* July 1997

Yoakam, Dwight, American country singer, Nov 2000

Yon, Pietro A., Italian-American organist and composer, *Obit* Jan 1944

York, Michael, English actor, Apr 1976

Yorke, Oswald, *Obit* Mar 1943

Yorke, Thom, Scottish singer, June 2001

Yoshimura, Yumi, Japanese pop singer, Jan 2005

Youmans, Vincent, composer, Apr 1944, *Obit* May 1946

Young, Alan, Anglo-Canadian actor, June 1953

Young, Angus, Scottish guitarist, Mar 2005

Young, Loretta, American actress, Mar 1948, *Obit* Nov 2000

Young, Malcolm, Scottish guitarist, Mar 2005

Young, Robert, actor, July 1950, *Obit* Sept 1998

Youngman, Henny, comedian, Oct 1986, *Obit* May 1998

Yuen, Cory, Chinese actor and motion picture director, Jan 2004

ZaBach, Florian, Yrbk 1955

Zabaleta, Nicanor, June 1971

Zajick, Dolora, American opera singer and teacher, May 2000

Zandonai, Riccardo, Italian composer, *Obit* Aug 1944

Zappa, Frank, American rock guitarist, Feb 1990, *Obit* Feb 1994

Zellweger, Renee, American actress, Feb 2004

Zemlinsky, Alexander von, Austrian composer and conductor, *Obit* May 1942

Zeta-Jones, Catherine, Welsh actress, Apr 2003

Zhang Ziyi, Chinese actress, Jan 2005

Zimbalist, Efrem, American actor, Feb 1960

Zimmer, Hans, German composer, Mar 2002

Zola, South African rapper, Jan 2004

Entomologists

Blatchley, W. S., American entomologist and geologist, *Obit* July 1940

Eisner, Thomas, American entomologist, Mar 1993, *Obit* Yrbk 2011

Goff, M. Lee, forensic entomologist, June 2001

Knipling, E. F., entomologist, May 1975, *Obit* Yrbk 2000

Lutz, Frank Eugene, entomologist and museum curator, *Obit* Jan 1944

Poulton, Edward Bagnall, *Obit* Jan 1944

Strong, Lee A., *Obit* July 1941

Entrepreneurs

Adelson, Jay, American information technology executive, June 2012

Aigner-Clark, Julie, American child development products company founder, Jan 2002

Alwaleed bin Talal al Saud, Saudi Arabian entrepreneur and financier, Jan 2006

Amoruso, Sophia, Sept 2013

Ashwell, Rachel, British interior designer and home furnishings retailer, Oct 2004

Bloom, Jeremy, American football player and skier, Sept 2013

Burnett, Mark, British television producer, May 2001

Charriol, Philippe, French watch, jewelry and accessories manufacturer, Jan 2004

Gopinath, Suhas, Indian information technology executive, July 2008

Jones, Quincy, American composer and record producer, Feb 1977

Le, Tan, Australian information technology executive, Apr 2013

Ma, Pony, Chinese information technology executive, Jan 2005

Mack, Lawrence L., Apr 1957

Novogratz, Jacqueline, American investment organization official, Apr 2013

Poon Tip, Bruce, Canadian adventure travel company founder, Jan 2006

Price, Lisa, American personal care products company founder, Feb 2011

Ransom, Victoria, American inforation technology executive, Jan 2013

Ross, Robert, American entrepreneur, Oct 2002, *Obit* Yrbk 2011

Swartz, Aaron, American electronic publisher, *Obit* Yrbk 2013

Taintor, Anne, American artist and entrepreneur, June 2005

Tapie, Bernard, French financier, Jan 2002

Tarkenton, Fran, American football player, Sept 1969

Ueberroth, Peter, American entrepreneur and Olympic executive, Apr 1985

Vergara Madrigal, Jorge, Mexican entrepreneur, Jan 2003

Epidemiologists

Chapin, Charles Value, American epidemiologist and public health official, *Obit* Mar 1941

Dean, H. Trendley, June 1957, *Obit* July 1962

Doll, Richard, British epidemiologist, Jan 2002

Gayle, Helene D., American epidemiologist, Jan 2002

Heymann, David L., American epidemiologist and international public health official, July 2004

Huebner, Robert J., epidemiologist, Sept 1968, *Obit* Nov 1998

Jaffe, Harold W., epidemiologist, Sept 1992

Jagger, Janine, American epidemiologist, Apr 2004

Perera, Frederica P., American epidemiologist, Oct 2010

Peters, C. J., American epidemiologist and army officer, June 1997

Piot, Peter, Belgian public health official and epidemiologist, Jan 2004

Stewart, Alice, British epidemiologist, July 2000, *Obit* Yrbk 2002

Equestrians

Arcaro, Eddie, American jockey, Sept 1958, *Obit* Jan 1998

Cauthen, Steve, American jockey, July 1977

Cordero, Angel, jockey, Oct 1975

Dancer, Stanley, American harness racer, June 1973, *Obit* Yrbk 2005

Day, Pat, American jockey, Oct 1997

Francis, Dick, Welsh mystery novelist and jockey, Aug 1981, *Obit* May 2010

Krone, Julie, American jockey, Oct 1989

Kusner, Kathy, American equestrian, Apr 1973

Pincay, Laffit, Panamanian jockey, Sept 2001

Prado, Edgar, Peruvian jockey, Sept 2007

Rubin, Barbara Jo, Yrbk 1969

Santos, Jose, Chilean jockey, Nov 2003

Shoemaker, Bill, American jockey, July 1966, *Obit* Apr 2004

Smith, Robyn, Nov 1976

Turcotte, Ron, Canadian jockey, Nov 1974

Essayists

Abdulhamid, Ammar, Syrian novelist, poet and essayist, Jan 2005

Abrahams, Peter, South African novelist and short story writer, Yrbk 1957

Achebe, Chinua, Nigerian novelist, Jan 1992, *Obit* Yrbk 2013

Ackerman, Diane, American poet, essayist, memoirist and nature writer, June 1997

Ames, Louise Bates, child psychologist, Sept 1956, *Obit* Jan 1997

Amis, Kingsley, English novelist, poet and critic, Yrbk 1958, Apr 1987, *Obit* Jan 1996

Andric, Ivo, Yugoslav novelist, short story writer and poet, Feb 1962, *Obit* May 1975

Angle, Paul McClelland, historian, July 1955, *Obit* Aug 1975

Arp, Jean, French artist, poet and essayist, May 1954, *Obit* July 1966

Atwood, Margaret, Canadian novelist and poet, May 1984

Auster, Paul, American novelist, poet and essayist, Mar 1996

Baker, Ray Stannard, American journalist and biographer, Jan 1940, *Obit* Sept 1946

Baker, Russell, American journalist and humorist, Mar 1980

Baldwin, James, American novelist, playwright and essayist, Yrbk 1959, July 1964, *Obit* Jan 1988

Banning, Margaret Culkin, author, May 1940, *Obit* Feb 1982

Baraka, Imamu Amiri, American poet, playwright, essayist and short story writer, May 1970

Bard, Mary, American novelist, essayist and memoirist, Yrbk 1956

Barth, John, American novelist and essayist, May 1969

Bartlett, Jennifer, American painter, Nov 1985

Barzini, Luigi Giorgio, Italian journalist and author, July 1972, *Obit* May 1984

Benson, E. F., English author, Mar 1940

Bergson, Henri, French philosopher, *Obit* Feb 1941

Binet-Valmer, Jean, French novelist, *Obit* Sept 1940

Bird, Will R., Canadian historian and short story writer, Sept 1954

Blum, Leon, French statesman, Nov 1940, *Obit* May 1950

Boll, Heinrich, German novelist and short story writer, July 1972, *Obit* Sept 1985

Borges, Jorge Luis, Argentine short story writer and poet, Jan 1970, *Obit* Aug 1986

Bosch, Juan, Dominican president, June 1963, *Obit* Feb 2002

Boyle, Kay, American novelist, short story writer and poet, June 1942, *Obit* Feb 1993

Breytenbach, Breyten, South African poet and painter, June 1986

Brodkey, Harold, author, Apr 1989, *Obit* Apr 1996

Brodsky, Joseph, Russian poet, July 1982, *Obit* Apr 1996

Broun, Heywood, American journalist, *Obit* Jan 1940

Brown, Claude, American memoirist and journalist, Nov 1967, *Obit* Apr 2002

Buber, Martin, Israeli philosopher, June 1953, *Obit* July 1965

Buck, Pearl S., American novelist, July 1956, *Obit* Apr 1973

Bulosan, Carlos, American memoirist, poet and short story writer, Yrbk 1946, *Obit* Nov 1956

Burke, Thomas, English author, *Obit* Oct 1945

Byatt, A. S., English novelist, short story writer and literary critic, Sept 1991

Cela, Camilo Jose, Spanish novelist, short story writer, essayist, travel writer and poet, June 1990, *Obit* Apr 2002

Chadourne, Marc, *Obit* Feb 1941

Clampitt, Amy, American poet, Feb 1992, *Obit* Nov 1994

Clark, Eleanor, novelist, travel essayist and children's author, May 1978, *Obit* Apr 1996

Clarke, Arthur C., English science fiction writer, Oct 1966, *Obit* Yrbk 2008

Cohen, Arthur, author and publisher, Sept 1960, *Obit* Jan 1987

Coker, Elizabeth Boatwright, author, Yrbk 1959, *Obit* Nov 1993

Colby, Nathalie S., *Obit* July 1942

Cortazar, Julio, Argentine novelist, Feb 1974, *Obit* Apr 1984

Creeley, Robert, American poet, novelist, short story writer and essayist, Oct 1988, *Obit* Yrbk 2005

Cuevas, Jose Luis, Mexican illustrator and printmaker, Jan 1968

Dellinger, David, American peace activist, Aug 1976, *Obit* Yrbk 2004

Didion, Joan, American novelist, essayist and journalist, Sept 1978

Dillard, Annie, American poet, critic and nature writer, Jan 1983

Durant, William James, American historian, Sept 1964, *Obit* Jan 1982

Durrenmatt, Friedrich, Swiss novelist and dramatist, Feb 1959, *Obit* Apr 1991

Ehrenburg, Ilya, Russian novelist, critic, memoirist and journalist, June 1966, *Obit* Nov 1967

Eliade, Mircea, Romanian religion historian and novelist, Nov 1985, *Obit* June 1986

Ellis, Bret Easton, American novelist, Nov 1994

Ellison, Ralph, American novelist and essayist, Oct 1968, June 1993, *Obit* June 1994

Elytes, Odysseus, Greek poet, Sept 1980, *Obit* June 1996

Ephron, Nora, American screenwriter and film director, Jan 1990, *Obit* Yrbk 2012

Erdrich, Louise, American novelist and poet, Apr 1989

Erikson, Erik H., American psychoanalyst, May 1971, *Obit* July 1994

Fadiman, Anne, American essayist and journalist, Aug 2005

Fallaci, Oriana, Italian journalist and novelist, Feb 1977, *Obit* Yrbk 2007

Flanner, Janet, American journalist and novelist, May 1943, *Obit* Jan 1979

Forster, E. M., English novelist, short story writer and essayist, Apr 1964, *Obit* Sept 1970

Frank, Waldo David, American novelist and essayist, Nov 1940, *Obit* Mar 1967

Frazier, Ian, American essayist and humorist, Aug 1996

French, Marilyn, American novelist and critic, Sept 1992, *Obit* Yrbk 2009

Fuentes, Carlos, Mexican novelist, short story writer and essayist, Oct 1972, *Obit* Yrbk 2012

Furcolo, Foster, American governor, Jan 1958, *Obit* Sept 1995

Ginzburg, Natalia, Italian novelist, July 1990, *Obit* Nov 1991

Giraudoux, Jean, French dramatist and novelist, *Obit* Mar 1944

Golding, William, English novelist, Mar 1964, *Obit* Aug 1993

Gordimer, Nadine, South African novelist, Yrbk 1959, June 1980

Gordon, Jaimy, American novelist, poet and short story writer, July 2011

Gorman, Thomas Francis Xavier, mental health official, Oct 1956, *Obit* July 1989

Grant, Robert, author and judge, *Obit* July 1940

Graves, Robert, English novelist and poet, May 1978, *Obit* Feb 1986

Green, Julien, American novelist, essayist and memoirist, Jan 1940, *Obit* Oct 1998

Guedalla, Philip, English historian, *Obit* Feb 1945

Guthrie, A. B., American novelist, short story writer and poet, July 1950, *Obit* July 1991

Handke, Peter, Austrian novelist and dramatist, Apr 1973

Harrison, Jim, American poet and novelist, July 1992

Hartley, Marsden, American painter and poet, *Obit* Oct 1943

Hauptmann, Gerhart, German dramatist, *Obit* July 1946

Heaney, Seamus, Irish poet, Jan 1982, *Obit* Yrbk 2013

Hersey, John, American novelist and journalist, Feb 1944, *Obit* May 1993

Hersh, Seymour M., American journalist, Mar 1984

Hitchens, Christopher, British journalist, Mar 1999, *Obit* Yrbk 2012

Hoagland, Edward, American novelist, essayist and travel writer, Sept 1982

Hoffer, Eric, American philosopher and essayist, Mar 1965, *Obit* July 1983

Holroyd, Michael, English biographer, Mar 1989

Irving, John, American novelist, Oct 1979

Ivins, Molly, American columnist, June 2000, *Obit* Yrbk 2007

Jones, Idwal, author, Yrbk 1948, *Obit* Jan 1965

Jong, Erica, American poet and novelist, July 1975, Apr 1997

Kastner, Erich, German author and poet, July 1964, *Obit* Oct 1974

Kazantzakis, Nikos, Greek novelist, poet, dramatist, essayist and travel writer, July 1955, *Obit* Jan 1958

Kilmer, Aline, *Obit* Yrbk 1941

Kilpi, Eeva, Finnish essayist, poet, short story writer and novelist, Jan 2007

Kincaid, Jamaica, Antiguan novelist and short story writer, Mar 1991

King, Florence, American satirist, Apr 2006

Kirk, Russell, American political philosopher, Sept 1962, *Obit* June 1994

Knox, Ronald Arbuthnott, English priest, satirist, essayist and mystery writer, July 1950, *Obit* Nov 1957

Koestler, Arthur, Hungarian-British novelist, essayist and journalist, Apr 1943, Jan 1962, *Obit* Apr 1983

Kosinski, Jerzy N., Polish-American novelist, essayist and critic, Mar 1974, *Obit* July 1991

L'Engle, Madeleine, American novelist and children's author, Jan 1997, *Obit* Yrbk 2007

LaDuke, Winona, Native American activist, Jan 2003

Lagerkvist, Par, Swedish novelist, dramatist and poet, Jan 1952, *Obit* Sept 1974

Langer, Susanne Katherina Knauth, American philosopher, Nov 1963, *Obit* Sept 1985

Larkin, Philip, English poet, essayist, novelist and librarian, Jan 1985, *Obit* Feb 1986

Lau, Evelyn, Canadian novelist, poet and short story writer, Jan 2005

Laxness, Halldor, Icelandic novelist and essayist, Oct 1946, *Obit* Apr 1998

Lee, Harper, American novelist, Nov 1961

Lessing, Doris May, English novelist and short story writer, Jan 1976, Jan 1995

Lin Yutang, Chinese novelist, essayist and translator, May 1940, *Obit* May 1976

Lopez, Barry Holstun, American novelist and essayist, July 1995

Lubell, Samuel, journalist and public opinion analyst, Nov 1956, *Obit* Oct 1987

Lynes, Russell, essayist and periodical editor, Nov 1957, *Obit* Nov 1991

MacLeish, Archibald, American poet and Librarian of Congress, Oct 1940, Nov 1959, *Obit* June 1982

MacLennan, Hugh, Canadian novelist, Yrbk 1946, *Obit* Jan 1991

Mailer, Norman, American novelist, Oct 1948, Feb 1970, *Obit* Jan 2008

Mann, Thomas, German novelist, May 1942, *Obit* Oct 1955

Mannes, Marya, author, Apr 1959

Matthiessen, Peter, American novelist and nature writer, Oct 1975

McGinley, Phyllis, American poet and children's author, Feb 1941, Nov 1961, *Obit* Apr 1978

McMurtry, Larry, American novelist, June 1984

McPherson, James Alan, American short story writer, essayist and editor, Sept 1996

Miller, Henry, American novelist, Nov 1970, *Obit* July 1980

Milosz, Czeslaw, Polish poet, Oct 1981, *Obit* Yrbk 2004

Mistral, Gabriela, Chilean poet and educator, Feb 1946, *Obit* Mar 1957

Monroe, Anne Shannon, *Obit* Yrbk 1942

Montale, Eugenio, Italian poet and critic, Apr 1976, *Obit* Nov 1981

Moore, Marianne, American poet, Yrbk 1952, Apr 1968, *Obit* Mar 1972

Munro, Alice, Canadian short story writer and novelist, Sept 1990

Murdoch, Iris, English novelist and philosopher, Yrbk 1958, Aug 1980, *Obit* Apr 1999

Murnane, Gerald, Australian short story writer and essayist, Jan 2007

Murray, Albert, American novelist, essayist and music historian, May 1994, *Obit* Yrbk 2013

Naipaul, V. S., Trinidadian novelist and journalist, July 1977

Narayan, R. K., Indian novelist and short story writer, Sept 1987, *Obit* July 2001

Nasrin, Taslima, Bangladeshi poet, essayist, novelist and feminist, Jan 2003

Naylor, Gloria, American novelist, Apr 1993

Nemerov, Howard, American novelist, poet and critic, Oct 1964, *Obit* Sept 1991

Novak, Michael, American social philosopher and critic, Feb 1985

O'Brien, Tim, American novelist, Aug 1995

O'Faolain, Sean, Irish short story writer, novelist and biographer, Apr 1990, *Obit* June 1991

Oates, Joyce Carol, American novelist, short story writer and poet, Sept 1970, June 1994

Oe, Kenzaburo, Japanese novelist, May 1996

Oz, Amos, Israeli novelist, July 1983

Ozick, Cynthia, American novelist and short story writer, Aug 1983

Pagnol, Marcel, French dramatist and motion picture director, Mar 1956, *Obit* June 1974

Palencia, Isabel de, Spanish diplomat and essayist, May 1941

Papashvily, George, Georgian-American humorist and essayist, Mar 1945, *Obit* May 1978

Papashvily, Helen Waite, humorist and essayist, Mar 1945

Parkinson, C. Northcote, English historian, satirist, biographer and novelist, Yrbk 1960, *Obit* May 1993

Pasolini, Pier Paolo, Italian poet, novelist, critic and film director, July 1970, *Obit* Jan 1976

Paton, Alan, South African novelist and biographer, June 1952, *Obit* May 1988

Paz, Octavio, Mexican poet and diplomat, June 1974, *Obit* July 1998

Peale, Norman Vincent, American clergyman and inspirational writer, Jan 1946, Oct 1974, *Obit* Feb 1994

Pearlman, Edith, American short story writer and essayist, June 2011

Percy, Walker, American novelist, Sept 1976, *Obit* July 1990

Phillips, Caryl, English novelist, dramatist and essayist, July 1994

Plimpton, George, American essayist, sportswriter and periodical editor, Feb 1969, *Obit* Jan 2004

Pollan, Michael, American nature writer and magazine editor, Oct 2007

Pollitt, Katha, American poet and essayist, Oct 2002

Pollock, Channing, dramatist, *Obit* Oct 1946

Powell, Lawrence Clark, librarian, biographer, novelist and critic, June 1960

Powys, Llewelyn, English author, Jan 1940

Puzo, Mario, American novelist and screenwriter, Mar 1975, *Obit* Sept 1999

Pynchon, Thomas, American novelist, Oct 1987

Quasimodo, Salvatore, Italian poet, Mar 1960, *Obit* Sept 1968

Quindlen, Anna, American novelist and columnist, Apr 1993

Rakoff, David, Canadian humorist, Nov 2007, *Obit* Yrbk 2012

Remnick, David, American journalist and editor, Oct 1998

Revel, Jean-Francois, French philosopher, Feb 1975, *Obit* Yrbk 2006

Rexroth, Kenneth, American poet, essayist and translator, Apr 1981, *Obit* Aug 1982

Richler, Mordecai, Canadian novelist and critic, May 1975, *Obit* Oct 2001

Roa, Raul, Nov 1973, *Obit* Sept 1982

Robbe-Grillet, Alain, French novelist, essayist and screenwriter, Yrbk 1974, *Obit* Yrbk 2008

Robinson, Marilynne, American novelist, Oct 2005

Ross, Nancy Wilson, author, Yrbk 1952, *Obit* May 1986

Rostand, Jean, Yrbk 1954, *Obit* Jan 1978

Roth, Henry, American novelist and short story writer, Jan 1989, *Obit* Jan 1996

Rushdie, Salman, British novelist, Nov 1986, Jan 2003

Russell, Bertrand, British philosopher, Apr 1940, Jan 1951, *Obit* Mar 1970

Safire, William, American journalist, essayist and novelist, Yrbk 1973, *Obit* Yrbk 2009

Said, Edward W., Palestinian-American literary and social critic, Nov 1989, *Obit* Feb 2004

Salten, Felix, Austrian author, *Obit* Nov 1945

Santmyer, Helen Hooven, author, educator and librarian, Feb 1985, *Obit* Apr 1986

Sarraute, Nathalie, French novelist, June 1966, *Obit* Jan 2000

Sartre, Jean Paul, French novelist and philosopher, Mar 1947, May 1971, *Obit* June 1980

Sayles, John, American novelist, short story writer, screenwriter and film director, Feb 1984

Schell, Jonathan, American journalist, July 1992

Sedaris, David, American humorist, July 1997

Seferis, George, Greek poet, May 1964, *Obit* Nov 1971

Seghers, Anna, German author, Yrbk 1942, *Obit* July 1983

Senghor, Leopold Sedar, Senegalese poet and president, Mar 1962, July 1994, *Obit* Mar 2002

Sheean, Vincent, American journalist, novelist and essayist, Aug 1941, *Obit* May 1975

Sheed, Wilfrid, American novelist, Aug 1981, *Obit* Yrbk 2011

Shimazaki, Toson, Japanese novelist, poet and essayist, *Obit* Oct 1943

Siddons, Anne Rivers, American novelist, Jan 2005

Sillanpaa, Frans Eemil, Finnish novelist and short story writer, Jan 1940, *Obit* July 1964

Singer, Isaac Bashevis, American novelist and short story writer, Jan 1969, *Obit* Sept 1991

Smith, Harry Allen, American humorist, May 1942, *Obit* May 1976

Smith, Logan Pearsall, American lexicographer, essayist and critic, *Obit* Apr 1946

Snyder, Gary, American poet and nature writer, Nov 1978

Sontag, Susan, American novelist and essayist, June 1969, Feb 1992, *Obit* May 2005

Soueif, Ahdaf, Egyptian-British novelist and short story writer, Jan 2003

Stegner, Wallace Earle, American novelist and short story writer, Apr 1977, *Obit* June 1993

Storr, Anthony, English psychiatrist and psychotherapist, June 1994, *Obit* Sept 2001

Struther, Jan, English poet, essayist and short story writer, Jan 1941, *Obit* Oct 1953

Styron, William, American novelist, July 1968, June 1986, *Obit* Yrbk 2007

Tagore, Rabindranath, Indian poet, novelist, short story writer and dramatist, *Obit* Oct 1941

Tan, Amy, American novelist, Feb 1992

Tolstoy, Aleksey Nikolayevich, Russian novelist and dramatist, *Obit* Apr 1945

Torres Bodet, Jaime, Mexican novelist and poet, Feb 1948, *Obit* July 1974

Tournier, Michel, French novelist, Apr 1990

Trillin, Calvin, American humorist, novelist and essayist, June 1990

Trilling, Diana, literary and social critic, May 1979, *Obit* Jan 1997

Ullman, James Ramsey, author, Oct 1945, *Obit* Sept 1971

Undset, Sigrid, Norwegian novelist, Sept 1940, *Obit* July 1949

Van den Haag, Ernest, Dutch-American psychoanalyst, essayist and educator, Oct 1983, *Obit* July 2002

Vargas Llosa, Mario, Peruvian novelist, Feb 1976

Vidal, Gore, American novelist and playwright, Feb 1965, June 1983, *Obit* Yrbk 2012

Walcott, Derek, Saint Lucian poet and dramatist, Apr 1984

Warren, Robert Penn, American novelist and poet, June 1970, *Obit* Nov 1989

Wasserstein, Wendy, American dramatist, July 1989, *Obit* Yrbk 2006

Waugh, Auberon, English novelist and essayist, May 1990, *Obit* May 2001

Weeks, Edward, editor and essayist, Yrbk 1947, *Obit* May 1989

Werfel, Franz, Austrian poet, novelist and dramatist, Yrbk 1940, *Obit* Sept 1945

White, E. B., American humorist and poet, Oct 1960, *Obit* Nov 1985

Wilson, August, American playwright, Aug 1987, *Obit* Feb 2006

Wilson, Edmund, American literary critic, Apr 1945, Jan 1964, *Obit* July 1972

Wolfe, Humbert, English poet and government official, *Obit* Jan 1940

Wolff, Geoffrey, author, Jan 1997

Wood, Charles Erskine Scott, American lawyer and satirist, *Obit* Mar 1944

Woolf, Virginia, English novelist, *Obit* May 1941

Wright, Richard, American novelist, Mar 1940, *Obit* Jan 1961

Yourcenar, Marguerite, French-American novelist, poet, dramatist, essayist and translator, Nov 1982, *Obit* Feb 1988

Etchers

Chamberlain, Samuel, American photographer and artist, Sept 1954, *Obit* Mar 1975

Ethnobiologists

Plotkin, Mark, American ethnobotanist, June 1997

Ethnologists

Ahmed, Akbar S., Pakistani anthropologist, Jan 2005

Behar, Ruth, American anthropologist, poet and filmmaker, May 2005

Benedict, Ruth, American anthropologist, May 1941, *Obit* Nov 1948

Blakey, Michael L., biological anthropologist, Sept 2000

Boas, Franz, American anthropologist, May 1940, *Obit* Feb 1943

Brand, Oscar, folklorist, June 1962

Collier, John, American anthropologist and government official, Mar 1941, *Obit* July 1968

Dobie, J. Frank, American folklorist, Yrbk 1945, *Obit* Nov 1964

Dubois, Eugene, Dutch anthropologist and paleontologist, *Obit* May 1941

Field, Henry, anthropologist, Mar 1955, *Obit* Mar 1986

Fisher, Helen E., American anthropologist and psychologist, Oct 2010

Frazer, James George, Scottish classicist and anthropologist, *Obit* July 1941

Gheerbrant, Alain, Feb 1959

Gilmore, Melvin R., *Obit* Sept 1940

Goldenweiser, Alexander A., American anthropologist, *Obit* Sept 1940

Haddon, Alfred Cort, British anthropologist, *Obit* May 1940

Hrdlicka, Ales, anthropologist and paleontologist, Nov 1941, *Obit* Oct 1943

Johanson, Donald C., American anthropologist, Feb 1984

Kroeber, A. L., American anthropologist, Oct 1958, *Obit* Yrbk 1960

Leakey, Louis Seymour Bazett, British anthropologist and archaeologist, Mar 1966, *Obit* Yrbk 1972

Leakey, Mary D., British anthropologist and paleontologist, Apr 1985, *Obit* Feb 1997

Leakey, Meave, Kenyan anthropologist and paleontologist, June 2002

Leakey, Richard E., Kenyan anthropologist and paleontologist, Nov 1976, Oct 1995

Lewis, Albert Buell, American anthropologist, *Obit* Yrbk 1940

Lewis, Oscar, American anthropologist, Apr 1968, *Obit* Feb 1971

Lomax, Alan, American folklorist and musicologist, Sept 1941, *Obit* Oct 2002

Marett, Robert R., *Obit* Apr 1943

Marriott, Alice Lee, anthropologist and author, Yrbk 1950, *Obit* May 1992

McFate, Montgomery, American cultural anthropologist, Aug 2008

Murdock, George Peter, anthropologist, Mar 1957

Nash, Philleo, government official, Nov 1962, *Obit* Jan 1988

Parsons, Elsie Worthington Clews, anthropologist, *Obit* Feb 1942

Peccerelli, Fredy, Guatemalan forensic anthropologist, Jan 2004

Powdermaker, Hortense, American anthropologist, Feb 1961, *Obit* Sept 1970

Roosevelt, Anna Curtenius, American archaeologist and anthropologist, June 1997

Smith, Mary Carter, storyteller and folklorist, Feb 1996

Snow, Clyde, forensic anthropologist, Apr 1997

Tattersall, Ian, American anthropologist and museum curator, Aug 2007

Thomas, Elizabeth Marshall, American anthropologist and writer, Mar 1996

Underhill, Ruth M., anthropologist and author, Feb 1954, *Obit* Oct 1984

Warner, W. Lloyd, American anthropologist and sociologist, Yrbk 1959, *Obit* July 1970

Willoughby, Charles Clark, *Obit* June 1943

Ethologists

Lorenz, Konrad, Austrian ethologist, July 1955, Oct 1977, *Obit* Apr 1989

Morris, Desmond, British ethologist, Nov 1974

Pepperberg, Irene M., American ethologist, Sept 2008

Tinbergen, Niko, British zoologist and ethologist, Nov 1975, *Obit* Feb 1989

European Commission officials

Brittan, Leon, British cabinet member and European Commission official, Aug 1994

Cohn-Bendit, Daniel, German political activist, Jan 2003

Duisenberg, Willem, Dutch European banking official, Jan 2002, *Obit* CB Int 2006

Gruber, Lilli, Italian television news anchor and member of European parliament, Jan 2007

Habsburg, Otto, German member of European Parliament, June 1941, *Obit* Yrbk 2011

Kinnock, Neil, British political leader and European Commission official, Apr 1984

Kroes, Neelie, Dutch European Commission official, Jan 2005

Lucas, Caroline, British member of European parliament, Sept 2012

Monti, Mario, Italian economist and European Commission official, Jan 2002

Skouris, Vassilios, Greek judge, Jan 2007

Solana Madariaga, Javier, Spanish European Union official, Jan 2005

Trichet, Jean-Claude, French banking official, Jan 2006

Uexkull, Jakob von, Swedish environmentalist, Jan 2005

Evangelists

Aberhart, William, Canadian evangelist and political leader, *Obit* July 1943

Allan, John J., American Salvation Army leader, Jan 1950, *Obit* Jan 1961

Booth, Ballington, American evangelist and social reformer, *Obit* Nov 1940

Booth, Evangeline C., English evangelist and Salvation Army leader, Feb 1941, *Obit* Sept 1950

Cadle, E. Howard, *Obit* Feb 1943

Coutts, Frederick, English evangelist, Mar 1964

Divine, Frank H., *Obit* May 1941

Fuller, Charles E., evangelist, Yrbk 1951, *Obit* May 1968

Graham, Billy, American evangelist, Apr 1951, Jan 1973

Hargis, Billy James, American clergyman, Mar 1972, *Obit* Yrbk 2005

Ironside, H. A., clergyman, Feb 1945, *Obit* Feb 1951

Jones, E. Stanley, American missionary, May 1940, *Obit* Mar 1973

Kuhlman, Kathryn, evangelist, July 1974, *Obit* Apr 1976

Maier, Walter Arthur, evangelist and theologian, May 1947, *Obit* Feb 1950

McPherson, Aimee Semple, American evangelist, *Obit* Nov 1944

Moon, Sun Myung, Korean evangelist, Mar 1983, *Obit* Yrbk 2012

Pierce, Bob, American evangelist, Yrbk 1961

Royden, Agnes Maude, English social worker and evangelist, Apr 1942, *Obit* Oct 1956

Schuller, Robert Harold, American clergyman, June 1979

Stott, John R. W., British clergyman and evangelist, May 2005, *Obit* Yrbk 2011

Terry, Randall, American anti-abortion activist, Jan 1994

West, Annie Blythe, *Obit* May 1941

Executives

Abbott, Robert S., American newspaper publisher, *Obit* Mar 1940

Abelson, Nat, American clothing industry executive, Nov 1957

Abramovich, Roman, Russian energy industry executive and provincial governor, Jan 2004

Abramson, Jill, American newspaper executive, Sept 2011

Abs, Hermann J., German banker, Oct 1970, *Obit* May 1994

Adams, Ernie, American football executive, Jan 2009

Adler, Harry Clay, American newspaper executive, *Obit* Apr 1940

Adler, Julius Ochs, American newspaper executive, June 1948, *Obit* Yrbk 1956

Ahrents, Angela, American clothing industry executive, May 2012

Aigner-Clark, Julie, American child development products company founder, Jan 2002

Al-Shabibi, Sinan, Iraqi banker and economist, Jan 2005

Alberti, Jules, American advertising executive, July 1959

Aldrich, Winthrop Williams, American banker and diplomat, Oct 1940, Mar 1953, *Obit* Apr 1974

Alexander, Willis W., American banker and newspaper publisher, July 1969, *Obit* Jan 1986

Allyn, Stanley C., American cash register company executive, Mar 1956, *Obit* Yrbk 1970

Alpert, George, railroad executive and lawyer, Sept 1961, *Obit* Oct 1988

Amos, Wally, American baking industry executive, July 1995

Anderson, Robert Orville, American petroleum industry executive, Sept 1982, *Obit* Yrbk 2008

Anderson, Victor E., American governor, Sept 1956, *Obit* Oct 1962

Andreas, Dwayne O., food industry executive, Mar 1992

Angelopoulos-Daskalaki, Gianna, Greek Olympic executive, Jan 2004

Annenberg, Walter H., American magazine and newspaper publisher, diplomat and philanthropist, Jan 1970, *Obit* Jan 2003

Aoki, Rocky, American restaurant chain executive, June 2005, *Obit* Yrbk 2008

Appleton, Edward Dale, American publishing executive, *Obit* Mar 1942

Appleton, Robert, American publishing executive, *Obit* Mar 1945

Araki, Eikichi, Japanese diplomat, Oct 1952, *Obit* Apr 1959

Aramburuzabala, Maria Asuncion, Mexican brewing executive, Jan 2002

Araskog, Rand V., telecommunications executive, Nov 1991

Armand, Louis, French railroad executive, Sept 1957, *Obit* Oct 1971

Armstrong, J. Sinclair, banker, lawyer and government official, Mar 1958, *Obit* Mar 2001

Arnault, Bernard, French manufacturing executive, June 1998

Arnstein, Daniel, American taxi executive, Mar 1942

Aronson, J. Hugo, American governor, Feb 1954

Aronson, Louis V., American inventor, manufacaturing executive and banker, *Obit* Yrbk 1940

Ash, Roy, American presidential adviser and manufacturing executive, July 1968, *Obit* Yrbk 2012

Ashbrook, John M., American congressman, Oct 1973, *Obit* June 1982

Astor of Hever, John Jacob Astor, British newspaper publisher, May 1954, *Obit* Sept 1971

Aubrey, James T., American television and motion picture executive, Mar 1972, *Obit* Nov 1994

Augstein, Rudolf, German magazine publisher, June 1966, *Obit* Jan 2003

Backe, John David, Apr 1978

Backstrand, C. J., American manufacturing executive, Feb 1954, *Obit* Yrbk 1968

Baehr, George, American physician and health insurance executive, May 1942

Baillie, Hugh, American reporter and news agency executive, Feb 1946, *Obit* Mar 1966

Baker, Asa George, American publishing executive, *Obit* Oct 1940

Balaban, Barney, American motion picture executive, Oct 1946, *Obit* Apr 1971

Baldauf, Sari, Finnish cellular telephone equipment industry executive, Jan 2004

Balderston, William, radio equipment industry executive, Sept 1949, *Obit* Oct 1983

Baldrige, Malcolm, American Secretary of commerce, Aug 1982, *Obit* Sept 1987

Ball, Stuart S., American retail executive, July 1952

Ballantine, Ian, publisher, May 1954, *Obit* May 1995

Banda, Enos, South African banker, Jan 2005

Bannow, Rudolph F., American manufacturing executive, Yrbk 1960, *Obit* Sept 1962

Barad, Jill E., American toy industry executive, Sept 1995

Barnard, Chester Irving, American telephone executive and foundation official, Mar 1945, *Obit* Sept 1961

Barnes, Brenda, American food industry executive, May 2006

Barnes, William R., American publisher and bookseller, *Obit* Mar 1945

Barrett, Craig, American semiconductor industry executive, Mar 1999

Barton, Robert B. M., games industry executive, Apr 1959, *Obit* Apr 1995

Batcheller, Hiland Garfield, American steel industry executive, Apr 1949, *Obit* July 1961

Batt, William L., American manufacturing executive, Feb 1942, *Obit* Mar 1965

Bausch, Edward, American optical equipment company executive, *Obit* Sept 1944

Bausch, William, *Obit* Yrbk 1944

Beame, Abraham D., American mayor, July 1974, *Obit* Apr 2001

Beane, Billy, American baseball executive, July 2005

Beaverbrook, Max Aitken, British newspaper publisher, July 1940, *Obit* Sept 1964

Beck, Martin, American theater owner, *Obit* Jan 1941

Beeching, Richard, British physicist, government official and chemical industry executive, Sept 1963

Beers, Charlotte, American advertising executive and government official, June 1998

Behn, Sosthenes, American telephone executive, Jan 1947, *Obit* Sept 1957

Behrman, Beatrice, American doll maker, Sept 1957

Beitz, Berthold, German steel executive, Feb 1973, *Obit* Yrbk 2013

Bell, Bert, American football commissioner, Sept 1950, *Obit* Yrbk 1959

Bell, Daniel W., American banker and government official, Oct 1946, *Obit* Nov 1971

Bennett, William John, Canadian government official and energy industry executive, June 1954

Berge, Pierre, French clothing industry executive, Jan 1990

Berkson, Seymour, American news agency executive, Oct 1949, *Obit* Mar 1959

Berlusconi, Silvio, Italian prime minister, Aug 1994

Bernbach, William, American advertising executive, Mar 1967, *Obit* Nov 1982

Bettman, Gary, American lawyer and hockey commissioner, Mar 1999

Betts, Rome A., American medical association official, Mar 1949

Bewkes, Jeffrey L., American mass media executive, Nov 2010

Bible, Geoffrey C., American tobacco and food industry executive, Feb 2002

Biggers, John D., American manufacturing executive, Sept 1941, *Obit* Feb 1974

Bimson, Carl A., American banker, Mar 1961

Bingham, Barry, American newspaper publisher, Sept 1949, *Obit* Sept 1988

Binns, Joseph Patterson, American hotel executive, June 1954, *Obit* Mar 1981

Birdseye, Clarence, American inventor and frozen food industry executive, Mar 1946, *Obit* Yrbk 1957

Black, Conrad M., Canadian financier and newspaper publisher, Aug 1992

Black, Eugene Robert, American banking official, Jan 1950, *Obit* Apr 1992

Black, William, coffee company executive, July 1964, *Obit* May 1983

Blackall, Frederick S., American manufacturing executive, Jan 1953

Blakely, Sara, American hosiery company executive, Jan 2013

Blattenberger, Raymond, American printing industry executive and government official, Mar 1958, *Obit* June 1971

Blaustein, Jacob, American petroleum industry executive and Jewish leader, Apr 1949, *Obit* Jan 1971

Bliss, Ray C., American political party leader, Jan 1966, *Obit* Oct 1981

Bloch, Charles Edward, American publishing executive, *Obit* Oct 1940

Block, Joseph L., steel executive, June 1961, *Obit* Feb 1993

Block, Paul, American newspaper publisher, *Obit* Aug 1941

Bloomberg, Michael, American mayor, June 1996, Mar 2002

Blough, Roger M., American steel industry executive, July 1955, *Obit* Jan 1986

Blumenthal, George, American financier and museum and hospital administrator, *Obit* Yrbk 1941

Blumer, George Alder, American psychiatrist and hospital administrator, *Obit* Jan 1940

Bobst, Elmer Holmes, American pharmaceutical executive, Yrbk 1973, *Obit* Sept 1978

Boeschenstein, Harold, American manufacturing executive, Feb 1961, *Obit* Yrbk 1972

Boggs, Charles Reid, American chemist and manufacturing executive, *Obit* Apr 1940

Bolles, Stephen, American newspaper editor and congressman, *Obit* Sept 1941

Bolte, Charles G., author and publishing executive, Oct 1945, *Obit* May 1994

Bond, John, British banker, Jan 2005

Borch, Fred J., manufacturing executive, Oct 1971

Bosch, Robert, German manufacturing executive, *Obit* Apr 1942

Botin, Ana Patricia, Spanish banker, Jan 2005

Bourguiba, Habib, Tunisian president, Sept 1955, *Obit* Aug 2000

Bowater, Eric Vansittart, English paper industry executive, Sept 1956, *Obit* Nov 1962

Bowditch, Richard L., July 1953, *Obit* Nov 1959

Brabeck-Letmathe, Peter, Austrian-Swiss food industry executive, Jan 2005

Bracken, Brendan Bracken, British cabinet member, Yrbk 1941

Brady, William Thomas, food industry executive, Jan 1961, *Obit* July 1984

Braly, Angela F., American health insurance executive, Aug 2011

Bravo, Rose Marie, American clothing industry executive, June 2004

Breathitt, Edward T., American governor, July 1964, *Obit* Yrbk 2004

Breen, Edward D., American electronics industry executive, July 2004

Brennan, Edward A., American retail executive, Nov 1990, *Obit* Yrbk 2008

Brentano, Arthur, *Obit* Mar 1944

Brenton, W. Harold, Jan 1953

Brett, George Platt, publisher, Yrbk 1948, *Obit* May 1984

Bristol, Lee H., Sept 1962

Bronfman, Edgar M., American liquor industry executive, July 1974

Bronfman, Edgar M., American recording industry executive, Oct 1995

Brophy, Thomas D'Arcy, Sept 1952, *Obit* Oct 1967

Browdy, Benjamin G., July 1951

Brower, Charles H., advertising executive, Feb 1965, *Obit* Nov 1984

Brown, Charles L., American telephone executive, Sept 1981, *Obit* Yrbk 2004

Brown, Clarence J., American congressman, Feb 1947, *Obit* Nov 1965

Brown, David M., American coal executive and veterans' leader, June 1950

Brown, Lewis H, Oct 1947, *Obit* Mar 1951

Browne, E. John P., British petroleum industry executive, Jan 2002

Brownson, Charles B., July 1955

Bruce, Howard, Sept 1948, *Obit* Sept 1961

Brule, Tyler, Canadian magazine publisher, Mar 2011

Brunsdale, Clarence Norman, governor and banker, Sept 1954

Buchanan, Thomas Drysdale, *Obit* Apr 1940

Buckley, George W., British manufacturing executive, Sept 2011

Buckley, James L., American senator and judge, Oct 1971

Budd, Ralph, July 1940, *Obit* Mar 1962

Buetow, Herbert P., Mar 1960, *Obit* Mar 1972

Buitoni, Giovanni, June 1962, *Obit* Mar 1979

Bullis, Harry A., Oct 1946, *Obit* Jan 1964

Bundesen, Herman N., Oct 1948, *Obit* Nov 1960

Bunting, Earl, American manufacturing association official, Feb 1947

Burgess, Warren, June 1949, *Obit* Nov 1978

Burgin, William O., *Obit* May 1946

Burke, Brian, American hockey executive, Mar 2013

Burke, Michael, sports executive, Apr 1972, *Obit* Mar 1987

Burnham, Donald C., Nov 1968

Burns, H. S. M., May 1954, *Obit* Yrbk 1971

Burns, Ursula, American office equipment industry executive, Oct 2007

Burpee, David, Mar 1955, *Obit* Aug 1980

Bush, Prescott S., American banker, senator and father of President George Bush, May 1942, Jan 1954, *Obit* Yrbk 1972

Bushnell, Asa S., July 1952, *Obit* May 1975

Butcher, Willard C., banker, July 1980, *Obit* Yrbk 2012

Butler, Hugh, American senator, Feb 1950, *Obit* Sept 1954

Cabot, Thomas D., chemical executive and philanthropist, June 1951, *Obit* Aug 1995

Cahill, Michael Harrison, *Obit* Apr 1940

Calagione, Sam, American brewing company executive, Jan 2013

Caldwell, William E., *Obit* May 1943

Campbell, Boyd, May 1956

Campeau, Robert, Canadian real estate and retail executive, Mar 1989

Camrose, William Ewert Berry, British newspaper publisher, Oct 1941, *Obit* Sept 1954

Capehart, H. E., American senator, Apr 1947, *Obit* Oct 1979

Capper, Arthur, American senator and governor, Sept 1946, *Obit* Feb 1952

Carey, Walter F., Feb 1965

Carroll, Cynthia, American mining executive, May 2011

Carter, John Ridgely, *Obit* July 1944

Carvel, Elbert N., June 1963

Casals, Rosie, tennis player and executive, Feb 1974

Case, Francis H., American senator and congressman, May 1946, *Obit* Sept 1962

Castle, Lewis G., July 1958, *Obit* Sept 1960

Catto, Thomas Sivewright Catto, English banker, Nov 1944

Cerf, Bennett, American publisher, Nov 1941, Sept 1958, *Obit* Oct 1971

Chamorro, Violeta Barrios de, Nicaraguan president, June 1990

Champion, George, banker, Apr 1961, *Obit* Jan 1998

Chandler, Dorothy Buffum, American newspaper publisher and patron of the arts, July 1957, *Obit* Sept 1997

Chandler, Happy, American governor, senator and baseball executive, Aug 1943, Sept 1956, *Obit* Aug 1991

Chandler, Norman, American newspaper publisher, July 1957, *Obit* Yrbk 1973

Chandler, Otis, American newspaper publisher, Nov 1968, *Obit* Yrbk 2006

Chao, Elaine, American Secretary of labor, May 2001

Chapin, Charles Value, American epidemiologist and public health official, *Obit* Mar 1941

Chapman, Albert Kinkade, photographic industry executive, Sept 1952, *Obit* Yrbk 1984

Chapman, Gilbert W., June 1957, *Obit* Feb 1980

Charles-Roux, Francois, Jan 1952, *Obit* Sept 1961

Charney, Dov, American t-shirt manufacturer, Sept 2009

Charoen Sirivadhanabhakdi, Chinese-Thai liquor industry executive, Jan 2005

Charriol, Philippe, French watch, jewelry and accessories manufacturer, Jan 2004

Chauncey, Henry, American educational testing service executive, July 1951, *Obit* Mar 2003

Chenault, Kenneth I., American financial services executive, June 1998

Chisholm, Brock, Canadian psychistrist, July 1948, *Obit* Mar 1971

Christenberry, Robert K., Mar 1952, *Obit* June 1973

Church, Samuel Harden, American railroad executive and foundation official, *Obit* Nov 1943

Cico, Carla, Italian telecommunications executive, Jan 2005

Citrine, Walter McLennan Citrine, English electric utility executive, Feb 1941, *Obit* Apr 1983

Clark, Fred G., Oct 1949

Clark, Georgia Neese, banker and government official, Sept 1949, *Obit* Feb 1996

Clark, Paul F., Apr 1955, *Obit* Mar 1973

Clausen, A. W., banking official, Nov 1981

Clayton, William Lockhart, American cotton executive and government official, Apr 1944, *Obit* Mar 1966

Claytor, W. Graham, railroad executive, May 1979, *Obit* July 1994

Clement, Martin W., Nov 1946, *Obit* Nov 1966

Cocke, Charles Francis, Mar 1952

Cohen, Barbara, American poetry recorder, May 1957

Cohen, Ben, American ice cream company executive, Apr 1994

Cohen, Lyor, American recording industry executive, Aug 2012

Coleman, John S., American manufacturing executive, Apr 1953, *Obit* July 1958

Collyer, John L., Mar 1947

Conable, Barber B., American congressman and banking official, July 1984, *Obit* Yrbk 2004

Cone, Fairfax, July 1966, *Obit* Aug 1977

Connell, Arthur J., Feb 1954

Cook, Richard, American motion picture executive, July 2003

Cooper, Kent, journalist, Oct 1944, *Obit* Mar 1965

Cooper, R. Conrad, Jan 1960

Copeland, Lammot Du Pont, chemical executive, May 1963

Coppers, George H., May 1952

Cordiner, Ralph, Jan 1951, *Obit* Jan 1974

Cornelius, John C., June 1960

Cowen, Joshua Lionel, American inventor and toy train manufacturer, Sept 1954, *Obit* Nov 1965

Cowles, Gardner, American publisher, June 1943, *Obit* Aug 1985

Cowles, John, American newspaper publisher, June 1954, *Obit* Apr 1983

Coyne, James E., July 1955

Craig, Cleo F., Sept 1951, *Obit* June 1978

Cramer, Stuart Warren, *Obit* Aug 1940

Cresap, Mark W., Oct 1959, *Obit* Sept 1963

Cresswell, Robert, American newspaper publisher, *Obit* Nov 1943

Cromer, George Rowland Stanley Baring, English banker and diplomat, May 1971, *Obit* May 1991

Crompton, Rookes Evelyn Bell, English electrical equipment industry executive, *Obit* Mar 1940

Cromwell, James H. R., American financial executive, diplomat and developer, Mar 1940, *Obit* May 1990

Crowell, T. Irving, *Obit* Mar 1942

Crowley, Leo, American banker and government official, June 1943, *Obit* June 1972

Crump, N. R., Sept 1957

Cullen, Hugh Roy, petroleum executive, July 1955, *Obit* Sept 1957

Cuneo, John F., June 1950

Custin, Mildred, retail executive, Nov 1967, *Obit* June 1997

Cuthbert, Margaret, May 1947, *Obit* Oct 1968

D'Oyly Carte, Rupert, Feb 1948

Daft, Doug, Australian beverage industry executive, May 2001

Dallas, C. Donald, Apr 1949, *Obit* June 1959

Dalmia, Ramkrishna, Yrbk 1948

Dart, Justin Whitlock, drug industry executive, Nov 1946, *Obit* Mar 1984

Davis, Al, American football executive, July 1985, *Obit* Yrbk 2011

Davis, Archie K., May 1966

Davis, Clive, American recording executive, July 2000

Davis, Martin S., motion picture, television and publishing executive, Nov 1989, *Obit* Jan 2000

Davis, Nathanael V., American aluminum industry executive, Jan 1959, *Obit* Yrbk 2005

Davis, Norman Hezekiah, banker and diplomat, Jan 1940, *Obit* Aug 1944

Davis, Roy H., Feb 1955, *Obit* Sept 1956

Davis, Westmoreland, *Obit* Oct 1942

Davis, William Rhodes, Mar 1941, *Obit* Mar 1941

Day, James Edward, American postmaster general, May 1962, *Obit* Jan 1997

De Graff, Robert F., May 1943

De Kleine, William, Apr 1941, *Obit* Yrbk 1958

De Seversky, Alexander P., Feb 1941, *Obit* Oct 1974

De Vry, Herman A., *Obit* May 1941

DeMott, Richard H., Feb 1951, *Obit* Nov 1968

Dearborn, Ned Harland, Jan 1947, *Obit* Oct 1962

Debutts, Harry A., Apr 1953

Delacorte, George T., American publisher and philanthropist, Nov 1965, *Obit* July 1991

Della Femina, Jerry, American advertising executive, restaurateur and grocery store owner, Nov 1979

Dennis, Felix, British magazine publisher, Apr 2000

Denny, Charles R., May 1947

Depinet, Ned E., June 1950

Deripaska, Oleg, Russian aluminum industry executive, Jan 2006

Deupree, Richard R., Apr 1946, *Obit* May 1974

Deveshwar, Yogesh Chander, Indian tobacco company executive, Jan 2005

Dewart, William T., American newspaper publisher, *Obit* Mar 1944

Dewey, Charles Schuveldt, Jan 1949, *Obit* Feb 1981

Dial, Morse G., chemical executive, Mar 1956, *Obit* Jan 1983

Dichter, Ernest, American psychologist and marketing research executive, Jan 1961, *Obit* Jan 1992

Diller, Barry, American motion picture and television executive, Apr 1986

Dimon, James, American investment banker, June 2004

Diniz, Abilio, Brazilian supermarket and department store executive, Jan 2006

Disney, Anthea, English publishing executive, June 1998

Doan, Leland I., American chemical industry executive, Oct 1952, *Obit* May 1974

Dodd, Christopher J., American motion picture association executive and former senator, Oct 1989

Dodge, Joseph Morrell, American banker and government official, Nov 1947, *Obit* Jan 1965

Doherty, Henry Latham, American gas and electric utility executive, *Obit* Jan 1940

Dollard, Charles, Yrbk 1948, *Obit* Apr 1977

Donahey, Vic, *Obit* May 1946

Donald, Arnold, American food industry executive, Nov 2005

Donaldson, William, American regulatory agency official, June 2003

Donovan, Hedley, journalist and magazine publishing executive, May 1965, *Obit* Oct 1990

Doubleday, Nelson, publisher and baseball executive, May 1987

Douglas, Arthur F., Nov 1950, *Obit* May 1956

Dowling, Robert W., Oct 1952, *Obit* Nov 1973

Drabinsky, Garth, Canadian theatrical producer, Oct 1997

Draper, William Henry, banker and government official, Mar 1952, *Obit* Feb 1975

Drexler, Millard S., American clothing chain executive, Jan 1993

Dreyfus, Camille, May 1955, *Obit* Yrbk 1957

Driscoll, Alfred E., American governor, Jan 1949, *Obit* May 1975

Drozniak, Edward, July 1962, *Obit* Jan 1967

Dryfoos, Orvil Eugene, American newspaper publisher, Jan 1962, *Obit* July 1963

Dubuc, Nancy, American television executive, May 2012

Dudley, Robert, American petroleum industry executive, June 2011

Duffy, Bernard C., July 1952, *Obit* Nov 1972

Duggan, Ervin S., public broadcasting executive, Oct 1998

Duncan, Charles W., American Secretary of energy, Apr 1980

Dworshak, Henry C., American senator, congressman and newspaper publisher, Jan 1950, *Obit* Oct 1962

Dyke, Greg, British broadcasting executive, Jan 2002

Ebbers, Bernard, American telecommunications executive, Feb 1998

Ebbott, Percy J., American banker, Oct 1954

Ebersol, Dick, American television executive, July 1996

Eccles, Marriner S., American financier and Federal Reserve chairman, Apr 1941, *Obit* Feb 1978

Ecker, Frederick H., June 1948, *Obit* May 1964

Eckert, Robert, American toy industry executive, Mar 2003

Eghbal, Manouchehr, May 1959, *Obit* Feb 1978

Eisner, Michael, American motion picture executive, Nov 1987

Ells, Steve, American restaurant chain executive, May 2012

Elsenhans, Lynn Laverty, American petroleum company executive, July 2011

Elway, John, American football player, Nov 1990

Emanuel, Victor, American manufacturing executive, May 1951, *Obit* Jan 1961

Emmerson, Louis Lincoln, *Obit* Mar 1941

Emmons, Glenn L., Oct 1954

Engibous, Thomas J., American semiconductor industry executive, Oct 2003

Epstein, Theo, American baseball executive, May 2004

Erikson, Leonard F., Oct 1953

Ethridge, Mark Foster, American newspaper publisher and diplomat, Jan 1946, *Obit* June 1981

Evans, Harold, British publishing executive, Apr 1985

Exeter, David George Brownlow Cecil, British hurdler and Olympic executive, Jan 1956

Eyde, Samuel, *Obit* Aug 1940

Eyler, John, American toy store chain executive, Aug 2000

Fairchild, John, American magazine publisher, June 1971

Faricy, William T., June 1948

Farish, William Stamps, *Obit* Jan 1943

Farrington, Elizabeth Pruett, American newspaper publisher, June 1955, *Obit* Sept 1984

Fauci, Anthony S., American immunologist, Aug 1988

Feld, Irvin, circus owner, Feb 1979, *Obit* Nov 1984

Felker, Clay, American magazine founder and editor, Feb 1975, *Obit* Yrbk 2008

Fellows, Harold E., Feb 1952, *Obit* May 1960

Ferguson, Harry, Irish inventor, Mar 1956, *Obit* Jan 1961

Field, Marshall, American department store executives and newspaper publisher, Apr 1941, Mar 1952, *Obit* Jan 1957

Figgis, D. W., Nov 1948, *Obit* Jan 1965

Fili-Krushel, Patricia, television executive, Nov 1999

Finley, Charles, American baseball executive, June 1974, *Obit* Apr 1996

Fireman, Paul, American shoe company executive, Mar 1992

Fiske, James Porter, orthopedic surgeon and hospital administrator, *Obit* Yrbk 1941

Fleck, Alexander Fleck, Scottish chemical executive, Apr 1956, *Obit* Oct 1968

Fleming, Arthur Henry, *Obit* Sept 1940

Fleming, Donald M., Canadian cabinet member, Feb 1959, *Obit* Mar 1987

Fleming, Sam M., June 1962

Fletcher, C. Scott, Feb 1953

Florence, Fred F., June 1956, *Obit* Feb 1961

Flynt, Larry, American magazine publisher, Sept 1999

Folsom, Frank M., Feb 1949, *Obit* Mar 1970

Forbes, Bertie Charles, publisher, Mar 1950, *Obit* July 1954

Forbes, Malcolm S., American magazine publisher, May 1996

Ford, Frederick W., government official, Nov 1960, *Obit* Sept 1986

Ford, Harold, American financial executive and political commentator, Nov 1999

Forsee, Gary, American telecommunications executive, Oct 2005

Foss, Joe, American governor and firearms association executive, Oct 1955, *Obit* Yrbk 2003

Fowler, Mark S., government official, Mar 1986

Francis, Clarence, food industry executive, Feb 1948, *Obit* Mar 1986

Frank, Anthony M., postmaster general, Aug 1991

Franklin, John M., Sept 1949, *Obit* Aug 1975

Franklin, Walter S., Feb 1950, *Obit* Oct 1972

Fraser, Leon, *Obit* May 1945

Fraser, Robert, British television executive, Oct 1956

Frazer, Joseph W., Mar 1946, *Obit* Sept 1971

Frear, J. Allen, Oct 1954

Freeman, Orville L., American governor, Secretary of agriculture and magazine publishing executive, June 1956, *Obit* Yrbk 2003

Freston, Tom, American television executive, Aug 2003

Frick, Ford, American baseball executive, May 1945, *Obit* June 1978

Friedman, Jane, American publisher, Mar 2001

Friendly, Edwin S., American newspaper executive, July 1949, *Obit* Sept 1970

Frische, Carl A., Oct 1962

Frohman, Daniel, *Obit* Feb 1941

Fruehauf, Roy, Feb 1953, *Obit* Jan 1966

Fry, Kenneth D., Apr 1947

Fu Chengyu, Chinese petroleum company executive, Jan 2005

Fuchs, Michael Joseph, cable television executive, Feb 1996

Fukui, Toshihiko, Japanese banking official, Jan 2004

Fuller, Alfred C., brush industry executive, Oct 1950, *Obit* Jan 1974

Fuller, S. R., May 1941, *Obit* Mar 1966

Fuller, Walter Deane, American publishing executive, Mar 1941, *Obit* Jan 1965

Funk, Wilfred, American publisher and lexicographer, Jan 1955, *Obit* July 1965

Gainza Paz, Alberto, Argentine newspaper publisher, Apr 1951, *Obit* Feb 1978

Galvin, Robert W., American electronics industry executive, Mar 1960, *Obit* Yrbk 2011

Gannett, Frank Ernest, American newspaper publisher, Mar 1945, *Obit* Feb 1958

Gardner, Arthur, Jan 1956, *Obit* June 1967

Garvin, Clifton Canter, petroleum executive, Nov 1980

Gary, Willie, American lawyer, Apr 2001

Gass, Michelle, American coffee chain executive, Apr 2012

Gates, Thomas S., American Secretary of the navy, Sept 1957, *Obit* May 1983

Gaumont, Leon, *Obit* Sept 1946

Gaylord, Robert M., Mar 1944

Geffen, David, American recording and motion picture executive, Jan 1992

Geis, Bernard, American publisher, Sept 1960, *Obit* Mar 2001

Geithner, Timothy F., American Secretary of the treasury, Mar 2009

Geneen, Harold S., American financier, Feb 1974, *Obit* Jan 1998

Gerstacker, Carl A., American chemical executive, Oct 1961, *Obit* July 1995

Giannini, Amadeo Peter, American banker, Mar 1947, *Obit* July 1949

Giannini, L. M., Nov 1950, *Obit* Oct 1952

Gidney, Ray M., Oct 1953

Gifford, Walter Sherman, telephone executive, Jan 1945, *Obit* June 1966

Gilbert, Rod, Canadian hockey player and executive, July 1969

Gilchrist, Huntington, Apr 1949, *Obit* Mar 1975

Gilmore, Voit, Feb 1962

Gimbel, Bernard F., Mar 1950, *Obit* Yrbk 1966

Girdler, Tom M., American steel executive, Apr 1944, *Obit* Mar 1965

Goizueta, Roberto C., American beverage industry executive, Aug 1996, *Obit* Jan 1998

Goldenson, Leonard H., radio and television executive, Sept 1957, *Obit* May 2000

Goldwater, S. S., American physician, hospital administrator and public health official, *Obit* Yrbk 1942

Gollancz, Victor, British publisher, Oct 1963, *Obit* Apr 1967

Gomez, Laureano, Colombian president, May 1950, *Obit* Sept 1965

Goodman, Andrew, American department store executive, Apr 1975, *Obit* June 1993

Gopinath, Suhas, Indian information technology executive, July 2008

Gordon, Donald, Oct 1950, *Obit* June 1969

Gordy, Berry, American recording executive, July 1975

Gorman, James P., Australian financial executive, June 2010

Goshorn, Clarence B., Mar 1950, *Obit* Jan 1951

Grace, Eugene G., American steel company executive, Apr 1941, *Obit* Oct 1960

Grace, J. Peter, chemical industry executive, Mar 1960, *Obit* June 1995

Graham, Donald E., American newspaper publisher, May 1998

Graham, Philip Leslie, American newspaper publisher, Feb 1948, *Obit* Oct 1963

Graves, Earl G., American magazine publishing executive, Aug 1997

Graves, Florence, American journalist, May 2005

Gray, Carl R., Mar 1948, *Obit* Feb 1956

Gray, Gordon, American broadcasting executive and military official, Sept 1949, *Obit* Feb 1983

Grede, William J., iron and steel executive, Feb 1952, *Obit* Aug 1989

Greenberg, Jack, fast food industry executive, Nov 2001

Greenberg, Maurice R., American insurance executive, Nov 2000

Greene, Hugh, English radio and television executive, Sept 1963, *Obit* Apr 1987

Greenebaum, Leon C., Jan 1962, *Obit* May 1968

Greenewalt, Crawford H., American chemical industry executive, Jan 1949

Greenfield, Jerry, American ice cream company executive, Apr 1994

Greenspan, Alan, American economist and Federal Reserve chairman, Yrbk 1974, Jan 1989

Greenwald, Julie, American recording industry executive, Nov 2009

Gregg, Hugh, Jan 1954

Gregory, Menas S., *Obit* Jan 1942

Griffin, Merv, American talk show host and television producer, Sept 1967, *Obit* Yrbk 2007

Griffin, R. Allen, American newspaper publisher, Feb 1951

Griswold, Augustus H., *Obit* Mar 1940

Grossinger, Jennie, American resort owner, Oct 1956, *Obit* Jan 1973

Guccione, Bob, American magazine publisher, Aug 1994, *Obit* Yrbk 2010

Guggenheim, Harry Frank, American mining executive, Oct 1956, *Obit* Mar 1971

Guinness, Arthur, June 1948

Guinzburg, Harold K., July 1957, *Obit* Jan 1962

Gullander, W. P., Oct 1963

Hagel, Chuck, American senator, Aug 2004

Haldeman, H. R., American presidential adviser, Sept 1978, *Obit* Jan 1994

Hall, Joyce Clyde, greeting card executive, May 1953, *Obit* Jan 1983

Halligan, William J., Oct 1957

Halloran, Roy D., *Obit* Yrbk 1943

Hamied, Yusuf K., Indian pharmaceutical executive, Jan 2004

Hamlin, Clarence Clark, American lawyer and newspaper executive, *Obit* Yrbk 1940

Hammer, Bonnie, American television executive, Apr 2006

Hammond, Caleb D., American map publisher and cartographer, Apr 1956, *Obit* Yrbk 2006

Hammond, Godfrey, Oct 1953, *Obit* Oct 1969

Hammond, John, American recording industry executive, July 1979, *Obit* Aug 1987

Hancock, John M., Apr 1949, *Obit* Yrbk 1957

Harber, W. Elmer, Mar 1951

Hardenbrook, Donald J., July 1962, *Obit* Aug 1976

Hardie, S. J. L., July 1951

Hargrave, Thomas J., Apr 1949, *Obit* Apr 1962

Hariri, Saad, Lebanese telecommunications executive and political leader, Jan 2005

Harper, Marion, advertising executive, Mar 1961, *Obit* Feb 1990

Harridge, William, baseball executive, Sept 1949, *Obit* June 1971

Harriman, E. Roland, Mar 1951, *Obit* Apr 1978

Harrison, William H., Feb 1949, *Obit* July 1956

Hassenfeld, Alan Geoffrey, American toy industry executive, July 2003

Hastreiter, Kim, American magazine editor and publisher, Aug 2010

Hayes, Alfred, banker and government official, Feb 1966, *Obit* Feb 1990

Head, Walter W., Apr 1945, *Obit* June 1954

Hearst, William Randolph, American newspaper publisher, Oct 1955, *Obit* July 1993

Hecht, George Joseph, magazine publisher, Oct 1947, *Obit* June 1980

Hefner, Christie, American magazine publisher, Oct 1986

Hefner, Hugh, American magazine publisher, Sept 1968

Heidenstam, Rolf von, Oct 1951, *Obit* Oct 1958

Heineman, Ben W., lawyer and machine tool executive, Jan 1962, *Obit* Yrbk 2012

Heinz, Henry John, American food industry executive, June 1947, *Obit* Apr 1987

Heiskell, Andrew, American magazine executive, Mar 1966, *Obit* Yrbk 2003

Henry, John, American baseball executive, May 2005

Herod, William Rogers, mechanical engineer and manufacturing executive, Mar 1951, *Obit* Sept 1974

Herrera, Felipe, Mar 1968

Hershey, Milton Snavely, American candy industry executive, *Obit* Nov 1945

Hess, Max, Oct 1961, *Obit* Nov 1968

Hicks, Clarence J., *Obit* Feb 1945

Higgins, Andrew Jackson, shipbuilding executive, May 1943, *Obit* Sept 1952

Higley, Harvey V., government official, Oct 1956, *Obit* Jan 1987

Hill, Arthur M., Oct 1948, *Obit* Nov 1972

Hill, David G., Apr 1960

Hill, George Washington, June 1946

Hilton, Conrad N., American hotel executive, Yrbk 1949, *Obit* Mar 1979

Hilton, Frank C., July 1952

Hirst, Hugo, English manufacturing executive, Nov 1941, *Obit* Mar 1943

Hitz, Ralph, *Obit* Jan 1940

Ho, David D., American physician, June 1997

Ho, Stanley, Chinese gambling casino owner, Jan 2003

Hoffa, Jimmy, American labor leader, May 1972, *Obit* Mar 1983

Hoge, James F., American newspaper executive and magazine editor, Apr 1998

Holden, Betsy, American food industry executive, July 2003

Holman, Eugene, May 1948, *Obit* Oct 1962

Holt, Cooper T., July 1957

Homer, Arthur B., July 1952, *Obit* Sept 1972

Hood, Clifford F., Apr 1953, *Obit* Jan 1979

Hope, Stanley C., May 1959, *Obit* Oct 1982

Hopkins, John Jay, Mar 1954, *Obit* July 1957

Hormel, Jay C., July 1946, *Obit* Oct 1954

Houghton, Alanson Bigelow, glass industry executive and diplomat, *Obit* Nov 1941

Houghton, Amory, American glass industry executive and diplomat, Jan 1947, *Obit* Apr 1981

Houser, Theodore V., Mar 1957, *Obit* Feb 1964

Hoving, Walter, department store executive, Sept 1946, *Obit* Feb 1990

Howard, Roy Wilson, news agency and newspaper executive, Nov 1940, *Obit* Jan 1965

Howe, Gordie, Canadian hockey player, Mar 1962

Howe, Samuel B., *Obit* Apr 1941

Hoyt, Palmer, American newspaper editor and publisher, Sept 1943, *Obit* Aug 1979

Hughes, Edward Everett, *Obit* Jan 1940

Hughes, Rowland R., American government official, Feb 1956, *Obit* June 1957

Huizenga, H. Wayne, American video chain and baseball executive, Jan 1995

Hulcy, Dechard A., Sept 1951

Humphrey, George Magoffin, American Secretary of the treasury, Feb 1953, *Obit* Mar 1970

Humphreys, Harry E., Nov 1949, *Obit* Nov 1967

Hunt, Bunker, Aug 1980

Hunt, H. L., American petroleum industry executive, Jan 1970, *Obit* Jan 1975

Hunter, Billy, American lawyer and basketball players association executive, Aug 2013

Ibrahim, Mohamed, Sudanese-British telecommunications executive, Jan 2007

Idei, Nobuyuki, Japanese electronics industry executive, Mar 1997

Igleheart, Austin S., Oct 1950

Ilitch, Mike, American fast food chain and baseball executive, Feb 2005

Illy, Ernesto, Italian coffee company executive, Jan 2002

Immelt, Jeffrey R., American corporation executive, Feb 2004

Ingram, Jonas H., Apr 1947, *Obit* Oct 1952

Innocenti, Ferdinando, Feb 1959, *Obit* July 1966

Ivey, Susan, American tobacco industry executive, Mar 2010

Jackson, C. D., American publishing executive and presidential aide, Oct 1951, *Obit* Nov 1964

Jackson, William K., July 1946, *Obit* Yrbk 1947

Jacobsson, Per, Swedish banker, Oct 1958, *Obit* June 1963

Jamieson, J. K., June 1974

Jarvis, Howard, manufacturing executive and tax reform activist, Feb 1979, *Obit* Sept 1986

Jay-Z, American rapper, Aug 2002

Jeffers, William M., Nov 1942, *Obit* Apr 1953

Jenkins, Macgregor, *Obit* Apr 1940

Jennings, B. Brewster, May 1951, *Obit* Yrbk 1968

Jensen, Ben F., Feb 1960, *Obit* Apr 1970

Jha, Sanjay, American electronics industry executive, Jan 2010

Johnson, F. Ross, Canadian food industry executive, May 1989

Johnson, Holgar J., Mar 1950

Johnson, Howard B., Sept 1966

Johnson, John H., American magazine publisher, Oct 1968, *Obit* Yrbk 2005

Johnson, Robert Wood, American medical supply executive, Nov 1943, *Obit* Mar 1968

Johnson, Roy W., May 1958, *Obit* Oct 1965

Johnston, Clement D., May 1955, *Obit* Jan 1980

Johnston, Wayne A., American railroad executive, May 1951, *Obit* Feb 1968

Jonah, Sam, Ghanaian gold mining executive, Jan 2004

Jones, George L., American bookstore chain executive, Apr 2007

Jones, Jerral, American petroleum and football executive, May 1996

Jones, Scott, American electronics and information technology executive, Jan 2006

Jonsson, John Erik, mayor and electronics executive, Jan 1961, *Obit* Nov 1995

Jordan, B. Everett, American senator, Nov 1959, *Obit* May 1974

Josephs, Devereux C., July 1953, *Obit* Mar 1977

Kaiser, Edgar F., chemical and metal industries executive, Sept 1964, *Obit* Feb 1982

Kaiser, Henry John, American shipbuilding executive, Oct 1942, Mar 1961, *Obit* Nov 1967

Kalikow, Peter, American real estate developer, Sept 1988

Kalmus, Herbert T., American physicist and motion picture executive, Feb 1949, *Obit* Sept 1963

Kamprad, Ingvar, Swedish household furnishings chain executive, June 1998

Kann, Peter R., American publishing executive, Mar 2003

Kanter, Albert Lewis, publisher, July 1953

Kappel, Frederick R., telephone executive, Mar 1957, *Obit* Jan 1995

Karmazin, Mel, American broadcasting executive, May 2000

Kast, Ludwig, *Obit* Oct 1941

Katzenberg, Jeffrey, American motion picture executive, May 1995

Kaufman, Henry, American economist and financial executive, Aug 1981

Keegan, Robert J., American manufacturing executive, Jan 2004

Keenan, Walter Francis, *Obit* Apr 1940

Keeton, Kathy, magazine executive, Sept 1993, *Obit* Jan 1998

Kellems, Vivien, American wire and cable industry executive, Sept 1948, *Obit* Mar 1975

Kelley, Augustine Bernard, Apr 1951, *Obit* Feb 1958

Kelly, John B., American rower and sports executive, June 1971, *Obit* Apr 1985

Kelly, Sharon Pratt, American mayor, Nov 1992

Kemper, James S., American insurance executive, Apr 1941, *Obit* Nov 1981

Kemsley, James Gomer Berry, British newspaper publisher, Jan 1951, *Obit* Mar 1968

Kerger, Paula, American broadcasting executive, July 2013

Kerkorian, Kirk, American financier, May 1975, Mar 1996

Kerr, James W., Oct 1959

Kerr, Robert Samuel, American senator and governor, May 1950, *Obit* Feb 1963

Kessing, O. O., American admiral and football association executive, June 1949, *Obit* Mar 1963

Kessler, David A., American physician and government official, Sept 1991

Kestnbaum, Meyer, May 1953, *Obit* Feb 1961

Killanin, Michael Morris, Irish sports executive and journalist, Apr 1973, *Obit* July 1999

Killion, George L., Nov 1952

Kilpatrick, John Reed, July 1948, *Obit* July 1960

Kimball, Abbott, May 1949, *Obit* Nov 1968

Kimball, Dan A., American Secretary of the navy, Sept 1951, *Obit* Oct 1970

Kimbrel, Monroe, June 1963

Kintner, Robert E., radio and television executive, Oct 1950, *Obit* Feb 1981

Kiplinger, Willard Monroe, journalist and periodical publisher, Mar 1943, Jan 1962, *Obit* Oct 1967

Kipping, Norman, Yrbk 1949

Kirby, Robert E., electrical generating equipment industry executive, Sept 1979, *Obit* Mar 1999

Kirch, Leo, German broadcasting executive, Jan 2002, *Obit* Yrbk 2011

Kirk, Claude R., American governor, Oct 1967, *Obit* Yrbk 2011

Kleppe, Thomas S., American Secretary of the interior, Aug 1976, *Obit* Yrbk 2007

Kluge, John W., American broadcasting and telecommunications executive, Sept 1993, *Obit* Yrbk 2010

Knight, John Shively, American newspaper publisher, Apr 1945, *Obit* Aug 1981

Knoll, Hans G., May 1955

Knopf, Alfred, American publisher, June 1943, Nov 1966, *Obit* Oct 1984

Knopf, Blanche W., American publishing executive, July 1957, *Obit* July 1966

Knowland, William Fife, American senator and newspaper publisher, Apr 1947, *Obit* Apr 1974

Knowles, John H., Yrbk 1970, *Obit* May 1979

Knox, Frank, American Secretary of the navy and newspaper publisher, Aug 1940, *Obit* June 1944

Knox, Rose Markward, American food industry executive, May 1949, *Obit* Nov 1950

Knutson, Harold, American congressman, Jan 1947, *Obit* Oct 1953

Kobak, Edgar, Apr 1947, *Obit* July 1962

Koch, Jim, American brewing company executive, May 2012

Kohl, Herbert, American senator, May 2008

Kohler, Horst, German president, Jan 2002

Kohler, Walter Jodok, American manufacturing executive and governor, Jan 1953, *Obit* May 1976

Kohler, Walter Jodok, American manufacturing executive and governor, *Obit* May 1940

Korth, Frederick H., secretary of the navy, July 1962, *Obit* Jan 1999

Kraft, Robert K., American businessman and football executive, Feb 2012

Krawcheck, Sallie, American financial executive, Mar 2006

Kroc, Ray, American fast food restaurant chain founder and baseball team owner, Mar 1973, *Obit* Mar 1984

Kuhn, Bowie, American lawyer and baseball commissioner, Jan 1970, *Obit* Yrbk 2007

Kullman, Ellen, American chemical industry executive, Nov 2011

Kummant, Alexander, American railroad executive, Jan 2007

Kushner, Jared, American newspaper publisher, June 2007

Lacy, Dan M., publishing executive, Nov 1954, *Obit* Nov 2001

Laeri, John Howard, banker, Sept 1968, *Obit* Aug 1986

Laliberte, Guy, Canadian circus owner, Jan 2003

Lamont, Thomas William, banker, Oct 1940, *Obit* Feb 1948

Lampert, Edward S., American retail executive, Sept 2005

Lance, Bert, banker and presidential adviser, Aug 1977, *Obit* Yrbk 2013

Land, Edwin H., American inventor and photographic industry executive, Nov 1953, *Obit* May 1991

Landis, Kenesaw Mountain, American judge and baseball executive, May 1944, *Obit* Jan 1945

Landwirth, Henri, American foundation official and hotel executive, Jan 2005

Lane, Allen, British publisher, May 1954, *Obit* Sept 1970

Lansing, Sherry, American motion picture executive, May 1981

Larsen, Roy, publishing executive, Sept 1950, *Obit* Oct 1979

Lasky, Jesse Louis, American film producer, Apr 1947, *Obit* Mar 1958

Latham, Dana, Mar 1959, *Obit* Apr 1974

Latham, Harold S., Jan 1950, *Obit* Apr 1969

Lauvergeon, Anne, French nuclear energy industry executive, Jan 2005

Lawal, Kase L., Nigerian-American energy industry executive, Nov 2006

Lawrence, David, journalist and publisher, Yrbk 1943, *Obit* Apr 1973

Lawrence, Mary Wells, American advertising executive, Jan 1967

Laybourne, Geraldine, American broadcasting executive, Apr 1999

Lazarus, Rochelle, American advertising executive, May 1997

Le, Tan, Australian information technology executive, Apr 2013

Lea, Luke, American newspaper publisher and senator, *Obit* Jan 1946

Lear, Frances, magazine publisher, Apr 1991, *Obit* Jan 1997

Lee, Debra, American broadcasting executive, June 2006

Lee, Jim, Artist and co-publisher of DC Comics, Apr 2012

Lee, Kun-hee, Korean electronics industry executive, Jan 2005

Lee, Laurence F., June 1952, *Obit* Oct 1961

Leffingwell, Russell Cornell, banker, Mar 1950, *Obit* Yrbk 1960

Letourneau, R. G., American inventor, Apr 1958, *Obit* July 1969

Leverone, Nathaniel, Nov 1956, *Obit* July 1969

Lewis, Chester, librarian and archivist, May 1956, *Obit* June 1990

Lewis, Kenneth, American banker, Apr 2004

Lewis, Mary, retail executive, Sept 1940

Li Dongsheng, Chinese electronics industry executive, Jan 2005

Li Yifei, Chinese television executive, Jan 2006

Li, Ka-shing, Chinese real estate executive, Jan 2003

Liberman, Alexander, American artist and magazine executive, May 1987, *Obit* Mar 2000

Lichtenberg, Bernard, *Obit* Nov 1944

Lightner, Milton C., Nov 1958, *Obit* May 1968

Lilienthal, David E., American government official, June 1944, *Obit* Mar 1981

Lincoln, Leroy A., June 1946, *Obit* June 1957

Lincoln, Murray D., American insurance executive, Mar 1953, *Obit* Jan 1967

Lindsley, Thayer, Jan 1957, *Obit* July 1976

Ling, James, American financier, Apr 1970, *Obit* Yrbk 2005

Link, Edwin A., flight simulator industry executive, Jan 1974, *Obit* Yrbk 1983

Lippincott, Joshua Bertram, *Obit* Jan 1940

Litchfield, P. W., Yrbk 1950, *Obit* May 1959

Liu, Changle, Jan 2002

Livingston, Homer J., Sept 1955, *Obit* July 1970

Locke, Edwin A., Jan 1952

Loeb, William, American newspaper publisher and journalist, Mar 1974, *Obit* Nov 1981

Logan, Harlan, magazine editor and publishing executive, Jan 1946, *Obit* Mar 1995

Long, Edward V., American senator, July 1964, *Obit* Jan 1973

Longman, Hubert Harry, *Obit* Apr 1940

Loomis, Daniel P., Jan 1960

Lortel, Lucille, theater owner and producer, Feb 1985, *Obit* July 1999

Love, James Spencer, textile executive, Nov 1957, *Obit* Mar 1962

Loynd, Harry J., Feb 1952

Luce, Charles Franklin, American electric utility executive, Yrbk 1968, *Obit* Yrbk 2008

Luce, Henry Robinson, American magazine editor and publisher, July 1941, Jan 1961, *Obit* Apr 1967

Ludwig, Daniel Keith, shipping executive and financier, May 1979, *Obit* Oct 1992

Lunt, Storer B., Nov 1958

Lyne, Susan, American media executive, Feb 2012

Lynn, James T., American insurance executive, Yrbk 1973

Ma, Pony, Chinese information technology executive, Jan 2005

MacPhail, Larry, baseball executive, Mar 1945, *Obit* Nov 1975

MacVeagh, Lincoln, American publisher and diplomat, Nov 1941, June 1952, *Obit* Mar 1972

Machold, Earle J., Nov 1958

Mack, Lawrence L., Apr 1957

Mack, Walter, beverage industry executive, Feb 1946, *Obit* May 1990

Macmillan, Harold, British prime minister, Mar 1943, Jan 1955, *Obit* Feb 1987

Macrae, John, *Obit* Apr 1944

Maenner, T. H., Nov 1949, *Obit* Mar 1958

Mallory, C. C., Feb 1956, *Obit* Mar 1959

Malone, John C., American broadcasting executive, Aug 1995

Mantell, Marianne, American recording company executive, May 1957

Marcus, Bernard, American home improvement chain executive, Aug 2007

Marcus, Stanley, American department store executive, June 1949, *Obit* Apr 2002

Mark, Rebecca, American energy industry executive, May 1999

Marriott, J. Willard, American hotel executive, June 1972, *Obit* Oct 1985

Marsh, Ernest Sterling, Feb 1960

Marshall, M. Lee, Sept 1948, *Obit* Oct 1950

Marshall, Walter P., Apr 1950, *Obit* June 1969

Martin, Edmund F., steel executive, Jan 1962, *Obit* Mar 1993

Martin, William McChesney, American stockbroker and Federal Reserve chairman, May 1951, *Obit* Oct 1998

Martinez Trueba, Andres, Nov 1954, *Obit* Feb 1960

Mashouf, Manny, American retail executive, Feb 2009

Mason, Norman P., June 1959

Mateschitz, Dietrich, Austrian beverage industry executive, Jan 2005

Matsui, Connie L., American pharmaceutical executive and Girl Scouts leader, Aug 2002

Mattei, Enrico, Italian energy industry executive and member of Parliament, Apr 1959, *Obit* Jan 1963

Maximos, Demetrios, Mar 1948, *Obit* Yrbk 1955

Maxwell, Robert, British publisher, Sept 1988, *Obit* Feb 1992

Mayer, Louis B., American motion picture executive, June 1943, *Obit* Jan 1958

Maynard, Robert, American newspaper editor and publisher, June 1986, *Obit* Oct 1993

Mayo, Robert P., Feb 1970

Mays, Lowry, American broadcasting executive, Aug 2003

Mazumdar-Shaw, Kiran, Indian biotechnology executive, Jan 2006

McCabe, Gibson, magazine publisher, Feb 1963, *Obit* Yrbk 2000

McCaffrey, John L., Nov 1950

McCann, Renetta, American advertising executive, May 2005

McCarrens, John S., American newspaper publisher, *Obit* Sept 1943

McCaw, Craig, American telecommunications executive, Sept 2001

McClellan, Harold C., Oct 1954, *Obit* Sept 1979

McCloy, John Jay, American lawyer, banker and government official, Apr 1947, Nov 1961, *Obit* May 1989

McColough, C. Peter, American office equipment industry executive, Jan 1981, *Obit* Yrbk 2007

McComas, O. Parker, Nov 1955, *Obit* Feb 1958

McCone, John A., American steel industry executive and CIA director, Jan 1959, *Obit* Apr 1991

McConnell, F. B., July 1952, *Obit* Feb 1962

McCormack, Emmet J., July 1953, *Obit* Apr 1965

McCormick, Fowler, June 1947, *Obit* Feb 1973

McCormick, Robert Rutherford, American newspaper editor and publisher, Aug 1942, *Obit* May 1955

McCoy, Charles B., American chemical executive, July 1970, *Obit* Mar 1995

McCune, Francis K., Mar 1961

McDonnell, William A., Feb 1959

McElroy, Neil H., American Secretary of defense, Apr 1951, *Obit* Jan 1973

McGannon, Donald H., radio and television executive, Feb 1971, *Obit* July 1984

McGinnis, Patrick B., Nov 1955, *Obit* Apr 1973

McGovern, John, American rubber company executive, Nov 1961, *Obit* June 1975

McGrath, Judy, American broadcasting executive, Feb 2005

McGraw, Curtis W., June 1950, *Obit* Nov 1953

McKenna, Reginald, British cabinet member and banker, *Obit* Oct 1943

McKinney, Frank Edward, banker and political leader, Jan 1952, *Obit* Mar 1974

McKinney, Robert, American newspaper editor and publisher, Jan 1957, *Obit* Yrbk 2001

McKittrick, Thomas, July 1944, *Obit* Mar 1970

McLean, Robert, American newspaper publisher, Nov 1951, *Obit* Feb 1981

McNally, Andrew, American publisher and cartographer, Nov 1956, *Obit* Feb 2002

McWhinney, Madeline H., July 1976

Mead, George H., Oct 1946, *Obit* Feb 1963

Medvedev, Dmitry, Russian president, June 2008

Melcher, Frederic Gershom, American publisher, July 1945, *Obit* Apr 1963

Mellon, Richard K., May 1965, *Obit* July 1970

Merchant, Ismail, Indian motion picture producer, Mar 1993, *Obit* Yrbk 2005

Merchant, Livingston T., American government official and diplomat, Nov 1956, *Obit* July 1976

Merck, George W., American pharmaceutical executive, Yrbk 1946, *Obit* Jan 1958

Merle-Smith, Van Santvoord, *Obit* Yrbk 1943

Metzman, G., July 1946, *Obit* June 1960

Meyer, Agnes Elizabeth Ernst, American journalist, philanthropist and newspaper publisher, Jan 1949, *Obit* Nov 1970

Meyer, Eugene, American investment banker, government official and newspaper publisher, Sept 1941, *Obit* Oct 1959

Meyer, Ron, American motion picture executive, Mar 1997

Meyrowitz, Carol, American retail executive, Nov 2011

Michelin, Edouard, French tire company executive, *Obit* Oct 1940

Middelhoff, Thomas, German publishing and recording executive, Feb 2001

Miller, G. William, American Secretary of the treasury, Federal Reserve chairman and investment banker, June 1978, *Obit* Yrbk 2007

Miller, J. Irwin, American manufacturing executive and architectural patron, Nov 1961, *Obit* Yrbk 2004

Miller, Justin, Jan 1947, *Obit* Mar 1973

Miller, Lee P., July 1959

Ming, Jenny, American clothing chain executive, Jan 2011

Mingus, Sue, American music director and recording executive, July 2008

Mirvish, Edwin, Canadian theater owner and producer, Apr 1989, *Obit* Yrbk 2007

Mitarai, Fujio, Japanese photographic and office equipment industry executive, Jan 2002

Mitchell, George J., American diplomat and former senator, Apr 1989

Mitchell, Patricia Edenfield, American television executive, Aug 2005

Mittal, Lakshmi, Indian steel industry executive, Jan 2006

Monaghan, Thomas, American fast food and baseball executive, June 1990

Moody, Joseph Eugene, coal association executive, Yrbk 1948, *Obit* July 1984

Moody, Ralph, Yrbk 1955

Mooney, Beth, American banker, May 2012

Moore, Ann, American magazine executive, Aug 2003

Moore, George E., American oncologist and surgeon, Jan 1968, *Obit* Yrbk 2008

Moore, George S., banker, May 1970, *Obit* Yrbk 2000

Morehead, John H., *Obit* July 1942

Morgan, J. P., American financier, *Obit* Apr 1943

Morgan, Thomas A., Mar 1950, *Obit* Jan 1968

Morin, Relman, Nov 1958, *Obit* Oct 1973

Morita, Akio, Japanese electronics executive, Feb 1972, *Obit* Feb 2000

Morrison, Denise, American food company executive, July 2012

Mortimer, Charles G., Nov 1955, *Obit* Feb 1979

Morton, James, *Obit* Oct 1943

Morton, Rogers C. B., American Secretary of the interior and commerce, Nov 1971, *Obit* June 1979

Moses, Harry M., Oct 1949, *Obit* June 1956

Mosher, Ira, Feb 1945, *Obit* May 1968

Motley, Arthur H., publisher, Jan 1961, *Obit* July 1984

Moyers, Bill, American journalist and television commentator, Jan 1966, Feb 1976

Mueller, Frederick H., Yrbk 1959, *Obit* Oct 1976

Muir, James, May 1950, *Obit* Jan 1960

Muir, Malcolm, Apr 1953, *Obit* Mar 1979

Mulcahy, Anne, American office equipment industry executive, Nov 2002

Murdoch, Rupert, Australian-American publishing, motion picture and television executive, May 1977

Murphy, Frederick E., American newspaper publisher, *Obit* Mar 1940

Murphy, William Beverly, food industry executive, Nov 1955, *Obit* Aug 1994

Murray, Thomas E., Sept 1950, *Obit* Sept 1961

Nagin, Ray, American mayor, Jan 2006

Nast, Conde, publisher, *Obit* Nov 1942

Nederlander, James Morton, American theater owner, Apr 1991

Nelson, Donald Marr, American retail executive, Mar 1941, *Obit* Yrbk 1959

Nelson, Marilyn Carlson, American hotel and restaurant industry executive, Oct 2004

Neuharth, Allen, American newspaper publisher, Apr 1986, *Obit* Yrbk 2013

Newhouse, Samuel I., American newspaper publisher and broadcasting executive, Mar 1961, *Obit* Oct 1979

Newman, J. Wilson, American publishing executive, Apr 1955, *Obit* Yrbk 2003

Nichols, William I., June 1958

Nidetch, Jean, American dieting organization founder, Yrbk 1973

Nielsen, Arthur C., American market research executive, Yrbk 1951, *Obit* July 1980

Noble, Edward J., American candy and broadcasting executive, Jan 1944, *Obit* Mar 1959

Nooyi, Indra K., Indian beverage company executive, Nov 2006

Norman, Christina, American broadcasting executive, Nov 2007

Norman, Montagu Collet Norman, English banker, Yrbk 1940, *Obit* Mar 1950

North, John Ringling, circus owner, June 1951, *Obit* July 1985

Norton, W. W., *Obit* Yrbk 1945

Notari, Aldo, Italian baseball association executive, Jan 2004, *Obit* CB Int 2006

O'Brien, Lawrence F., American political party leader and basketball association executive, Nov 1961, Apr 1977, *Obit* Nov 1990

O'Konski, Alvin E., congressman, Nov 1955, *Obit* Aug 1987

O'Malley, Walter Francis, American baseball executive, Mar 1954, *Obit* Oct 1979

O'Neal, Edward A., banking executive, Sept 1946, *Obit* May 1958

O'Neil, Thomas F., broadcasting executive, Nov 1955, *Obit* June 1998

O'Neill, J. E., June 1952

O'Neill, Paul Henry, American aluminum company executive and Secretary of the treasury, July 2001

Obama, Michelle, wife of American president Barack Obama, Oct 2008

Obolensky, Serge, Oct 1959, *Obit* Nov 1978

Odlin, Reno, July 1965

Ogilvy, David, British advertising executive, July 1961, *Obit* Oct 1999

Okrent, Daniel, American newspaper editor, Nov 2004

Olayan, Lubna, Saudi Arabian financial executive, Jan 2006

Olds, Irving S., American lawyer and steel industry executive, Oct 1948, *Obit* Apr 1963

Olivetti, Adriano, Italian manufacturing executive, Jan 1959, *Obit* Apr 1960

Ollila, Jorma, Finnish cellular telephone equipment industry executive, Aug 2002

Onassis, Aristotle Socrates, Greek-Argentine shipping executive, Mar 1963, *Obit* May 1975

Onassis, Christina, Greek shipping executive, Feb 1976, *Obit* Jan 1989

Oppenheimer, Harry Frederick, South African diamond mining executive, Feb 1961, *Obit* Nov 2000

Osborn, Frederick Henry, railroad executive and investment banker, Nov 1941, *Obit* Mar 1981

Ovitz, Michael, American talent agent and motion picture executive, Oct 1995

Pace, Charles Ashford, *Obit* Feb 1941

Packer, Kerry Francis Bullmore, Australian newspaper publisher, Jan 2004, *Obit* CB Int 2006

Paepcke, Walter Paul, Apr 1960

Paley, William S., American radio and television executive, Oct 1940, Yrbk 1951, *Obit* Jan 1991

Pandit, Vikram S., American financial executive, June 2008

Panic, Milan, Yugoslav prime minister and drug industry executive, June 1993

Pape, William Jamieson, American newspaper publisher, Jan 1940, *Obit* Mar 1961

Parker, Cola G., Sept 1956, *Obit* Sept 1962

Parkinson, Thomas I., Apr 1949, *Obit* Sept 1959

Parrish, Wayne W., American magazine and newspaper executive, Nov 1958

Partridge, Eric, English lexicographer, Jan 1963, *Obit* July 1979

Pascal, Amy, American motion picture executive, Mar 2002

Pasquel, Jorge, July 1946, *Obit* May 1955

Pate, Maurice, June 1951, *Obit* Mar 1965

Patino, Simon Iturri, Bolivian mining executive, Oct 1942, *Obit* May 1947

Patrick, Deval L., American governor, May 2007

Patterson, Alicia, American newspaper editor and publisher, Nov 1955, *Obit* Sept 1963

Patterson, Eleanor Medill, American newspaper editor and publisher, Nov 1940, *Obit* Sept 1948

Patterson, Graham, Mar 1949, *Obit* Jan 1970

Patterson, Joseph Medill, American newspaper editor and publisher, Jan 1942, *Obit* June 1946

Patterson, Richard C., Oct 1946, *Obit* Yrbk 1966

Paul, Josephine Bay, American shipping executive and stockbroker, June 1957

Pauley, Edwin W., American petroleum executive, June 1945, *Obit* Sept 1981

Paxton, Robert, Mar 1959, *Obit* May 1980

Payne, Frederick G., Yrbk 1952, *Obit* Aug 1978

Payson, Joan Whitney, July 1972, *Obit* Nov 1975

Pelley, John J., *Obit* Yrbk 1946

Penney, James Cash, retail executive, Yrbk 1947, *Obit* Mar 1971

Percy, Charles H., American senator, Yrbk 1959, Aug 1977, *Obit* Yrbk 2011

Perdue, Frank, American poultry industry executive, June 1979, *Obit* Oct 2005

Perkins, George Walbridge, Apr 1950, *Obit* Mar 1960

Perlman, Alfred E., railroad executive, Apr 1955, *Obit* July 1983

Peterson, F. Raymond, Feb 1950, *Obit* Feb 1978

Peterson, R. A., American banker, May 1964

Pew, Joseph Newton, American petroleum industry executive and philanthropist, Sept 1941, *Obit* June 1963

Phillips, Sam, American record producer, Apr 2001

Pickens, T. Boone, American financier, July 1985

Piel, Gerard, American magazine publisher and science writer, June 1959, *Obit* Feb 2005

Pierce, Palmer Eddy, *Obit* Jan 1940

Pine, William B., *Obit* Oct 1942

Pitt, Harvey L., American risk management consultant, Nov 2002

Plumley, H. Ladd, Apr 1963

Poon Tip, Bruce, Canadian adventure travel company founder, Jan 2006

Popcorn, Faith, American market research executive, Feb 1993

Popeil, Ron, American kitchen utensil inventor, Mar 2001

Potanin, Vladimir O., Russian metal industry executive and banker, Jan 2006

Power, Donald C., Mar 1960, *Obit* May 1979

Praeger, Frederick A., American publishing executive, Sept 1959, *Obit* Aug 1994

Premji, Azim Hasham, Indian information technology executive, Jan 2004

Prentis, Henning Webb, Sept 1940, *Obit* Feb 1960

Price, Gwilym A., American electrical generating equipment company executive, May 1949, *Obit* Aug 1985

Prince, Charles O., American financial services executive, Jan 2007

Prokhorov, Mikhail, Russian financier, Oct 2010

Pucheu, Pierre Firmin, French steel executive and government official, *Obit* May 1944

Puckett, B. Earl, Sept 1950, *Obit* Apr 1976

Pulitzer, Joseph, American newspaper editor and publisher, Yrbk 1954, *Obit* May 1955

Purtell, William A., June 1956, *Obit* July 1978

Putnam, Claude Adams, Feb 1950

Putnam, Roger Lowell, Jan 1952

Puttnam, David, English motion picture producer, Feb 1989

Quinn, William F., American governor, Nov 1958, *Obit* Yrbk 2006

Rackmil, Milton R., motion picture and recording executive, Nov 1952, *Obit* Jan 1992

Raines, Franklin D., American financial services executive, Oct 2000

Rand, James Henry, *Obit* Nov 1944

Rand, William M., May 1953

Randall, Clarence B., American steel industry executive and presidential adviser, June 1952, *Obit* Oct 1967

Rank, Joseph Arthur Rank, British motion picture executive, Nov 1945, *Obit* May 1972

Ransom, Victoria, American inforation technology executive, Jan 2013

Rapaczynski, Wanda, Polish broadcasting executive, Jan 2004

Rasminsky, Louis, Yrbk 1961

Rawl, Lawrence G., American petroleum executive, Feb 1992, *Obit* Yrbk 2005

Raymond, Lee R., American energy industry executive, Nov 1999

Redstone, Sumner, American motion picture and broadcasting executive, Jan 1996

Reed, John S., American financial executive and stock exchange official, Jan 1985

Reed, Ralph T., Apr 1951, *Obit* Mar 1968

Reese, Everett D., Mar 1954

Reid, Antonio, American recording industry producer and executive, Aug 2001

Reid, Helen Rogers, American newspaper publisher, Feb 1941, May 1952, *Obit* Oct 1970

Reith, John Charles Walsham Reith, Scottish broadcasting

executive, Nov 1940, *Obit* July 1971

Remington, John W., Feb 1960

Remorino, Jeronimo, Sept 1951

Ren Zhengfei, Chinese telecommunications equipment company executive, Jan 2005

Rennebohm, Oscar, July 1950, *Obit* Yrbk 1968

Resor, Stanley, American advertising executive, July 1949, *Obit* Yrbk 1962

Reynolds, Richard S., American manufacturing executive, May 1967, *Obit* Nov 1980

Reynolds, Richard Samuel, American aluminum industry executive, Feb 1953, *Obit* Oct 1955

Rhone, Sylvia, American recording industry executive, June 1998

Rice, Linda Johnson, American magazine publishing executive, July 2011

Richards, Vincent, July 1947, *Obit* Yrbk 1959

Richards, Wayne E., July 1954

Ricketts, Louis Davidson, *Obit* Mar 1940

Rigg, Edgar T., June 1961

Riggio, Leonard, American book store chain executive, June 1998

Riggio, Vincent, July 1949, *Obit* Nov 1960

Rinehart, Stanley M., Yrbk 1954, *Obit* June 1969

Ringling, Robert E., May 1945, *Obit* Feb 1950

Riter, Henry G., Oct 1955, *Obit* Sept 1958

Rivero, Jose Ignacio, Cuban newspaper publisher, *Obit* May 1944

Robaina, Alejandro, Cuban cigar manufacturer, Jan 2004, *Obit* Yrbk 2010

Roberts, C. Wesley, American public relations executive and political party leader, Apr 1953, *Obit* June 1975

Roberts, Michael, American telecommunications, real estate and publishing executive, Feb 2010

Roberts, Steven, American real estate, broadcasting and telecommunications executive, Feb 2010

Robertson, Reuben B., Yrbk 1955, *Obit* May 1960

Robinson, Janet L., American newspaper executive, Mar 2003

Robinson, Maurice R., Yrbk 1956, *Obit* May 1982

Robinson, William E., American beverage industry and newspaper executive, Feb 1958, *Obit* July 1969

Roche, Josephine, American coal industry executive, Aug 1941, *Obit* Sept 1976

Rockefeller, David, American banker, Mar 1959

Roderick, David M., steel executive, Apr 1987

Roebling, Mary G., banker, Oct 1960, *Obit* Jan 1995

Rogers, Desiree G., American magazine executive, June 2011

Rogge, Jacques, Belgian orthopedic surgeon and Olympic executive, Jan 2002

Rojas, Rudy, American clothing company executive, Jan 2006

Rometty, Virginia, American marketing executive, June 2012

Root, Oren, state banking official, Aug 1940, July 1952, *Obit* Mar 1995

Rooth, Ivar, Yrbk 1952, *Obit* Apr 1972

Roper, Elmo, American public opinion analyst, Jan 1945, *Obit* June 1971

Rosenfeld, Henry Jonas, clothing and luggage industry executive, Nov 1948

Rosenfeld, Irene, American food industry executive, July 2007

Rothermere, Esmond Cecil Harmsworth, British newspaper publisher, Yrbk 1948, *Obit* Sept 1978

Rothermere, Harold Sidney Harmsworth, British newspaper publisher, *Obit* Jan 1941

Rozelle, Pete, American football commissioner, June 1964, *Obit* Feb 1997

Rubicam, Raymond, advertising executive, Yrbk 1943, *Obit* July 1978

Rubin, Rick, American recording producer and executive, Sept 2007

Rudkin, Margaret Fogarty, American baking executive, Sept 1959, *Obit* Oct 1967

Ruffin, William H., Feb 1951

Ruml, Beardsley, department store executive and banker, May 1943, *Obit* June 1960

Rushmore, David Barker, *Obit* July 1940

Russell, Donald J., railroad executive, May 1962, *Obit* Feb 1986

Russo, Pat F., American information technology executive, May 2008

Ryti, Risto, Feb 1941, *Obit* Jan 1957

Saatchi, Maurice, English advertising executive, Jan 1989

Sage, Dean, *Obit* Aug 1943

Sagendorph, Robb, American magazine editor and publisher, Yrbk 1956, *Obit* Sept 1970

Salant, Richard S., television executive, Nov 1961, *Obit* Apr 1993

Samaranch, Juan Antonio, Spanish Olympics executive, Feb 1994, *Obit* Yrbk 2010

Sambi, Ahmed Abdallah Mohamed, Comoran president, Jan 2006

Sambrook, Richard, British broadcasting executive, Jan 2003

Sanchez Junco, Eduardo, Spanish magazine publisher, Jan 2003, *Obit* Yrbk 2010

Sanger, Stephen W., American food company executive, Mar 2004

Sargent, Porter, July 1941, *Obit* May 1951

Sarnoff, David, American radio and television executive, Nov 1940, Oct 1951, *Obit* Feb 1972

Sarnoff, Robert W., electronics executive, Yrbk 1956, *Obit* May 1997

Sassoon, Vidal, British hairstylist and personal care products industry executive, Apr 1999, *Obit* Yrbk 2012

Saul, Ralph Southey, Feb 1971

Saunders, Cicely, English physician and hospice director, Jan 2004

Saunders, Robert, Yrbk 1951, *Obit* Mar 1955

Saunders, Stuart Thomas, American railroad executive, Apr 1966, *Obit* Mar 1987

Sayre, Morris, Jan 1948, *Obit* Apr 1953

Scannell, Herb, American broadcasting executive, Aug 2010

Scardino, Marjorie, American publishing executive, Apr 2000

Schechter, A. A., broadcasting executive, May 1941, *Obit* Aug 1989

Schiff, Dorothy, American newspaper publisher, July 1945, Jan 1965, *Obit* Oct 1989

Schiffrin, Andre, American publisher, Jan 2000

Schiller, Vivian, American radio executive, Oct 2009

Schneider, Eugene, *Obit* Jan 1943

Schricker, Henry F., American governor, Sept 1950, *Obit* Feb 1967

Schroeder, Patricia, American publishing association executive and former congresswoman, Oct 1978

Schultz, Howard, American coffee chain executive, May 1997

Schultz, Richard D., sports executive, July 1996

Schuster, M. Lincoln, July 1941, *Obit* Feb 1971

Scott, Arthur Carroll, *Obit* Yrbk 1940

Scott, H. Lee, American retail executive, Oct 2006

Selfridge, Harry Gordon, American-British merchant, Mar 1941, *Obit* June 1947

Selig, Bud, American baseball commissioner, Jan 1999

Sen, Laura, American supermarket executive, Oct 2011

Sengstacke, John, newspaper executive, Nov 1949, *Obit* Aug 1997

Sepp Blatter, Joseph, Swiss soccer association executive, Jan 2002

Serratosa Cibils, Joaquin, Feb 1954

Seyferth, O. A., July 1950

Shakespeare, Frank, Sept 1970

Shannon, William V., newspaper executive, Jan 1979, *Obit* Nov 1988

Shapiro, Irving S., American lawyer and chemical company executive, Nov 1976, *Obit* Nov 2001

Shapp, Milton Jerrold, American governor, July 1973, *Obit* Feb 1995

Sharp, Harry Clay, *Obit* Yrbk 1940

Shaver, Dorothy, American department store executive, Jan 1946, *Obit* Sept 1959

Sheed, F. J., American theologian and publisher, Sept 1981, *Obit* Jan 1982

Shelly, Warner S., Feb 1952

Shelton, James E., Feb 1951

Shield, Lansing P., June 1951, *Obit* Mar 1960

Shimkin, Leon, publisher, May 1954

Shoriki, Matsutaro, Japanese newspaper publisher, broadcasting executive and government official, Feb 1958

Shreve, Earl Owen, Oct 1947

Shurlock, Geoffrey, Jan 1962, *Obit* June 1976

Simmons, Russell, American recording, motion picture and broadcasting executive, June 1998

Simon, Richard L., American publisher, July 1941, *Obit* Oct 1960

Simpson, Howard E., railroad executive, May 1958, *Obit* Apr 1985

Sims, William L., Yrbk 1956

Sinegal, James D., American warehouse club executive, Aug 2007

Skillin, Edward S., magazine editor and publisher, May 1949, *Obit* Yrbk 2000

Skouras, Spyros P., American motion picture executive, June 1943, *Obit* Nov 1971

Skutt, V. J., insurance executive, Yrbk 1959, *Obit* Apr 1993

Slater, John E., Nov 1951

Sligh, Charles R., Apr 1953

Smallwood, Robert B., Mar 1956, *Obit* Sept 1974

Smart, David A., magazine publisher, June 1944

Smith, Hazel Brannon, American newspaper publisher, Sept 1973, *Obit* July 1994

Smith, Howard Worth, American congressman, Feb 1941, *Obit* Nov 1976

Smith, Orin, American coffee retailer, Nov 2003

Smolyansky, Julie, American food industry executive, Nov 2013

Snider, Stacey, American motion picture executive, Apr 2008

Snow, John W., American investment manager and former Secretary of the treasury, Aug 2003

Spang, J. P., June 1949, *Obit* Feb 1970

Spencer, P. C., July 1951, *Obit* Jan 1970

Spivak, Lawrence E., television moderator, May 1956, *Obit* May 1994

Sprague, Robert Chapman, radio and television equipment executive, Jan 1951, *Obit* Nov 1991

Springer, Axel, German publishing executive, Yrbk 1968, *Obit* Nov 1985

Sproul, Allan, banker, Yrbk 1950, *Obit* June 1978

Stamp, Josiah Charles, British government official, *Obit* June 1941

Stanley, Thomas B., American governor, Yrbk 1955, *Obit* Oct 1970

Stanton, Frank, American broadcasting executive, Nov 1945, Oct 1965, *Obit* Yrbk 2007

Stanton, Katie Jacobs, Internet executive and Special Adviser to the Office of Innovation at the U.S. Department of State, June 2012

Statz, Hermann, Jan 1958

Steinkraus, Herman W., Nov 1949, *Obit* July 1974

Stern, David, American basketball association executive, Apr 1991

Stern, Leonard, American real estate executive and newspaper publisher, Mar 1991

Stern, Nicholas Herbert, British economist and government official, Jan 2007

Stevens, Robert T., American textile industry executive and Secretary of the army, July 1953, *Obit* Mar 1983

Steward, David L., American information technology executive, Nov 2004

Stockberger, Warner W., government official and personnel director, Aug 1941

Stoddard, Brandon, television executive, Feb 1989

Stokes, Edward C., American governor, *Obit* Yrbk 1942

Stolk, William C., Mar 1953

Storch, Jerry, American retail executive, June 2007

Storke, Thomas M., American newspaper editor and publisher, Yrbk 1963

Straus, Nathan, May 1944, *Obit* Nov 1961

Straus, Percy Selden, American department store executive, *Obit* May 1944

Straus, Roger W., American metal industry executive, July 1952, *Obit* Oct 1957

Straus, Roger W., American publishing executive, Aug 1980, *Obit* Yrbk 2004

Streibert, Theodore C., American government official and broadcasting executive, Feb 1955, *Obit* Mar 1987

Strike, Clifford S., Nov 1949

Strong, William McCreery, *Obit* May 1941

Stutz, Geraldine, American retail executive, May 1983, *Obit* Yrbk 2005

Sullivan, Henry J., June 1958

Sulzberger, Arthur Hays, American newspaper publisher, Mar 1943, *Obit* Feb 1969

Sulzberger, Arthur O., American newspaper publisher, Jan 1997

Sulzberger, Arthur Ochs, American newspaper publisher, Nov 1966, *Obit* Yrbk 2012

Sumner, Jessie, congresswoman, Jan 1945, *Obit* Oct 1994

Sunderland, Thomas Elbert, fruit industry executive, Apr 1962, *Obit* May 1991

Swearingen, John E., American petroleum industry executive, Jan 1979, *Obit* Yrbk 2007

Sweeney, Anne, American television executive, June 2003

Swidler, Joseph C., American government official, Mar 1964, *Obit* July 1997

Swift, Gustavus Franklin, American meat packing executive, *Obit* Yrbk 1943

Swift, Harold Higgins, Feb 1950, *Obit* Sept 1962

Swigert, Ernest Goodnough, machinery industry executive, Oct 1957, *Obit* Feb 1987

Swope, Gerard, Sept 1941, *Obit* Feb 1958

Syme, John P., Mar 1957

Symes, James M., Yrbk 1955, *Obit* Sept 1976

Talbott, Philip M., Apr 1958

Tartikoff, Brandon, American television and motion picture executive, Apr 1987, *Obit* Nov 1997

Tata, J. R. D., Indian industrialist and philanthropist, Yrbk 1958, *Obit* Jan 1994

Tawes, J. Millard, Oct 1960, *Obit* Aug 1979

Taylor, Myron C., American financier and diplomat, Feb 1940, *Obit* July 1959

Teagle, Walter, June 1942, *Obit* Feb 1962

Thaksin Shinawatra, Thai prime minister, Jan 2002

Thielen, Gunter, German publishing executive, Jan 2005

Thomas, Charles Allen, Mar 1950, *Obit* May 1982

Thomas, Helen, American journalist, Nov 1993, *Obit* Yrbk 2013

Thomas, William H., American geriatrician, Jan 2006

Thompson, Roy L., Oct 1946

Thomson of Fleet, Roy Herbert Thomson, Canadian newspaper publisher, Jan 1960, *Obit* Sept 1976

Thomson, J. Cameron, Yrbk 1948, *Obit* Mar 1966

Thomson, Kenneth, Canadian newspaper executive, July 1989, *Obit* Yrbk 2006

Thornhill, Arthur H., Apr 1958, *Obit* Mar 1970

Thyssen, Fritz, German industrialist, May 1940, *Obit* Mar 1951

Tian Congming, Chinese broadcasting and news agency official, Jan 2005

Tillerson, Rex, American energy industry executive, Sept 2006

Timerman, Jacobo, Argentine newspaper publisher, Nov 1981, *Obit* Jan 2000

Tisch, Laurence A., American financier, Feb 1987, *Obit* Yrbk 2004

Titterton, Lewis H., Sept 1943

Tobey, Charles W., American senator and governor, June 1941, July 1951, *Obit* Oct 1953

Towers, Graham F., Canadian banker, Feb 1952

Townsend, Robert, American car rental company executive, Nov 1970, *Obit* Mar 1998

Trautman, George McNeal, baseball executive, Oct 1951, *Obit* Sept 1963

Trefflich, Henry, Jan 1953, *Obit* Sept 1978

Trotter, Lloyd G., American manufacturing executive, July 2005

Truitt, Paul T., Sept 1948

Tschirky, Oscar, Jan 1947, *Obit* Yrbk 1950

Tuomioja, Sakari, Mar 1954, *Obit* Nov 1964

Tyson, John H., American poultry company executive, Aug 2001

Uhlmann, Richard Frederick, grain dealer, Jan 1949, *Obit* Feb 1990

Ullstein, Herman, *Obit* Jan 1944

Unwin, Stanley, British publisher, Mar 1949, *Obit* Yrbk 1968

Valenti, Jack, American motion picture association executive, Jan 1968, *Obit* Yrbk 2007

Van Volkenburg, Jack Lamont, Jan 1955, *Obit* July 1963

Vanden Heuvel, Katrina, American magazine editor and publisher, May 2009

Vanderbilt, William Kissam, railroad executive and automobile racing driver, *Obit* Feb 1944

Vandervelde, Luc, Belgian retail executive, Jan 2002

Vardaman, James Kimble, American banker and government official, Apr 1951

Vasella, Daniel, Swiss pharmaceutical executive and physician, Jan 2005

Veeck, Bill, American baseball executive, Nov 1948, *Obit* Feb 1986

Verity, Calvin William, American Secretary of commerce, May 1988

Vermilye, William M., *Obit* Oct 1944

Vernon, Lillian, American mail order executive, Mar 1996

Villard, Oswald Garrison, American journalist, Aug 1940, *Obit* Nov 1949

Vincent, Francis T., American motion picture executive and baseball commissioner, May 1991

Volcker, Paul A., American economist and Federal Reserve chairman, July 1973

Vranitzky, Franz, Austrian chancellor, Aug 1989

Wachner, Linda Joy, American clothing industry executive, Nov 1998

Wagner, Richard, Apr 1962

Wakefield, Charles Cheers Wakefield, English lubricants industry executive, *Obit* Mar 1941

Walker, Olene S., American governor, Apr 2005

Walker, Ralph Thomas, Yrbk 1957, *Obit* Mar 1973

Wallace, DeWitt, periodical editor and publisher, Apr 1944, May 1956, *Obit* May 1981

Walsh, William Henry, *Obit* May 1941

Walton, Sam, American retail executive, Mar 1992, *Obit* Mar 1992

Wampler, Cloud, Yrbk 1952

Ward, Maisie, English author and publisher, Jan 1966, *Obit* Mar 1975

Warner, Albert, American motion picture executive, Jan 1945, *Obit* Jan 1968

Warner, Harry M., American motion picture executive, Jan 1945, *Obit* Oct 1958

Warner, Jack L., American motion picture executive, Jan 1945, *Obit* Nov 1978

Warner, Mark R., American senator, Oct 2006

Warner, Ty, American toy industry executive, Nov 1998

Wason, Robert R., American manufacturing industry association executive, Jan 1946, *Obit* Sept 1950

Wasserman, Lew R., American motion picture executive, May 1991, *Obit* Yrbk 2002

Watson, Burl Stevens, petroleum executive, Apr 1957

Watson, Clarence Wayland, *Obit* July 1940

Watson, Thomas J., American office equipment industry executive, Nov 1940, July 1950, *Obit* Sept 1956

Waugh, Samuel C., Yrbk 1955, *Obit* Oct 1970

Weaver, Pat, American television executive, Jan 1955, *Obit* Sept 2002

Webster, William, May 1950, *Obit* July 1972

Weeks, Sinclair, American Secretary of commerce, Mar 1953, *Obit* Mar 1972

Weil, Richard, July 1951, *Obit* July 1958

Weill, Sanford I., American financial services executive, July 1999

Weinstein, Bob, American motion picture executive, Mar 1997

Weinstein, Harvey, American motion picture executive, Mar 1997

Weir, Ernest T., American steel industry executive, June 1941, *Obit* Oct 1957

Weisse, Faneuil Suydam, *Obit* Mar 1940

Welch, Leo D., Yrbk 1963, *Obit* Jan 1979

Welch, Robert, American founder of John Birch Society, Nov 1976, *Obit* Mar 1985

Welman, Joseph C., May 1958

Wenner, Jann S., American magazine executive, Jan 1980

Wente, Carl F., Feb 1954

Werblin, Sonny, football executive and theatrical agent, Apr 1979, *Obit* Feb 1992

Wexler, Jerry, American recording industry executive, Jan 2001, *Obit* Yrbk 2008

Wexner, Leslie H., American fashion chain store executive and philanthropist, Feb 1994

Weyerhaeuser, Rudolph M., *Obit* Sept 1946

Wheeler, Tony, Australian travel writer and publisher, Jan 2005

White, Charles M., June 1950, *Obit* Mar 1977

White, Francis W., Jan 1954, *Obit* June 1957

White, Hugh Lawson, Yrbk 1955, *Obit* Nov 1965

White, Robert M., American newspaper editor and publisher, Mar 1960

White, William, Jan 1953, *Obit* June 1967

White, William Lindsay, American journalist and writer, Jan 1943, *Obit* Oct 1973

Whitehead, Edward, British manufacturing executive, Jan 1967, *Obit* June 1978

Wilde, Frazar B., insurance executive, Apr 1959, *Obit* Aug 1985

Wiley, William Foust, American newspaper publisher, *Obit* Oct 1944

Willes, Mark H., American newspaper publisher, Mar 1998

Williams, Edward Bennett, American lawyer and baseball and football executive, Jan 1965, *Obit* Sept 1988

Williams, John J., American senator, Jan 1952, *Obit* Apr 1988

Williams, Ralph E., *Obit* July 1940

Williams, Ronald, American health insurance executive, July 2009

Williams, W. Walter, Nov 1948

Willis, Paul S., food and grocery trade association executive, Jan 1951, *Obit* Aug 1987

Willkie, Wendell Lewis, American lawyer and

presidential candidate, Feb 1940, *Obit* Nov 1944

Wilson, Charles E., American electronics industry executive, Apr 1943, Feb 1951, *Obit* Feb 1972

Wilson, Edward Foss, corporation executive and government official, Mar 1958, *Obit* May 1994

Wilson, Halsey William, publisher, Yrbk 1941, May 1948, *Obit* Apr 1954

Wilson, I. W., July 1952, *Obit* Jan 1978

Wilson, Joseph C., American office equipment industry executive, Oct 1966, *Obit* Jan 1972

Wilson, Kemmons, American hotel chain executive, Sept 1973, *Obit* Yrbk 2003

Wilson, Leroy A., Apr 1948, *Obit* July 1951

Wilson, Malcolm, American lawyer, banker and governor, May 1974, *Obit* Aug 2000

Winthrop, Beekman, *Obit* Yrbk 1940

Wise, James DeCamp, carpet industry executive, Apr 1954, *Obit* Apr 1984

Witherow, W. P., Apr 1942, *Obit* Mar 1960

Wong, Andrea, American broadcasting executive, Sept 2007

Wood, Robert D., Yrbk 1974, *Obit* July 1986

Wood, Robert Elkington, retail executive, May 1941, *Obit* Yrbk 1969

Woods, George David, banker, July 1965, *Obit* Oct 1982

Woods, Mark, American broadcasting executive, Mar 1946

Woollen, Evans, Yrbk 1948, *Obit* Apr 1959

Worthington, Leslie B., steel executive, Oct 1960, *Obit* Oct 1998

Wright, Loyd, July 1955, *Obit* Jan 1975

Wright, Robert Charles, American television executive, Jan 1989

Wrigley, Philip Knight, baseball executive, Apr 1975, *Obit* June 1977

Wriston, Walter B., American banker, Nov 1977, *Obit* Aug 2005

Wyman, Thomas, American radio and television executive, June 1983, *Obit* Yrbk 2003

Yates, Herbert J., July 1949, *Obit* Mar 1966

Young, Owen D., lawyer and manufacturing executive, Aug 1945, *Obit* Sept 1962

Young, Robert Ralph, railroad executive, Apr 1947, *Obit* Mar 1958

Yun, Jong Yong, Korean electronics industry executive, Jan 2003

Zaentz, Saul, American recording executive and motion picture producer, Mar 1997

Zagat, Nina, American restaurant survey publisher, Mar 2008

Zagat, Tim, American restaurant survey publisher, Mar 2008

Zanuck, Darryl F., American motion picture producer, Aug 1941, Mar 1954, *Obit* Feb 1980

Zarb, Frank G., American securities exchange official, Sept 1975

Zellerbach, J. D., Yrbk 1948, *Obit* Nov 1963

Zevin, Ben David, publisher, Sept 1943, *Obit* Feb 1985

Zhou Xiaochuan, Chinese banker, Jan 2003

Ziff, William B., American magazine executive, Oct 1946, *Obit* Feb 1954

Zorbaugh, Geraldine Bone, lawyer and broadcasting executive, Yrbk 1956, *Obit* Sept 1996

Zuckerman, Mortimer B., American real estate developer and magazine and newspaper publisher, Jan 1990

Zukor, Adolph, American motion picture executive, Mar 1950, *Obit* Aug 1976

Exhibit designers

Eames, Charles, American furniture, interior and exhibit designer, Jan 1965, *Obit* Oct 1978

Gehry, Frank, American architect, June 1987

Exiles

Nguyen, Van Thieu, South Vietnamese president, June 1968, *Obit* Jan 2002

Explorers

Bingham, Hiram, American explorer and senator, Mar 1951, *Obit* Sept 1956

Boyd, Louise Arner, American explorer, Sept 1960, *Obit* Nov 1972

Burwash, Lachlin Taylor, *Obit* Feb 1941

Chilingarov, Artur, Russian polar explorer, Jan 2007

Cook, Frederick Albert, American physician and explorer, *Obit* Sept 1940

Doyle, Adrian Conan, Sept 1954

Dunn, J. Allan, *Obit* May 1941

Dyhrenfurth, Norman G., American mountaineer, Apr 1965

Fiennes, Ranulph, British explorer, Jan 2004

Flaherty, Robert Joseph, American film director and explorer, Mar 1949, *Obit* Sept 1951

Fuchs, Vivian, English explorer, Oct 1958, *Obit* Jan 2000

Granger, Walter, *Obit* Oct 1941

Hass, Hans, Feb 1955, *Obit* Yrbk 2013

Hedin, Sven Anders, Swedish explorer, May 1940, *Obit* Jan 1953

Hempleman-Adams, David, British explorer, Jan 2004

Hitchcock, Charles B., Oct 1954, *Obit* May 1969

Johnson, Osa Helen Leighty, American explorer and documentary filmmaker, Apr 1940, *Obit* Feb 1953

MacMillan, Donald, American explorer, Sept 1948, *Obit* Nov 1970

Ronne, Finn, Norwegian-American explorer, Feb 1948, *Obit* Mar 1980

Siple, Paul Allman, explorer and geographer, Feb 1957, *Obit* Jan 1969

Stefansson, Vilhjalmur, American arctic explorer, Oct 1942, *Obit* Nov 1962

Wilkins, Hubert, Australian explorer and geographer, Jan 1957, *Obit* Feb 1959

Wong, How-man, Chinese explorer and journalist, Jan 2002

Worsley, Frank Arthur, New Zealand ship captain and explorer, *Obit* Mar 1943

Younghusband, Francis Edward, British diplomat and explorer, *Obit* Sept 1942

FBI agents

Clement, Frank Goad, American governor, July 1955, *Obit* Yrbk 1969

Douglas, John E., American criminologist, July 2001

Fleming, Ian, English spy novelist, Jan 1964

Krivitsky, W. G., Soviet intelligence service agent, *Obit* Mar 1941

Langer, William Leonard, American historian, Yrbk 1968, *Obit* Feb 1978

Liddy, G. Gordon, American lawyer, actor and government official, Oct 1980

Malkin, Peter Z., Israeli intelligence agent, Jan 2003

Montagu, Ewen, British intelligence official and lawyer, June 1956, *Obit* Sept 1985

Morgan, Edward P., May 1951

Wilt, Fred, runner and FBI agent, Oct 1952, *Obit* Nov 1994

FBI officials

Felt, W. Mark, American FBI official and Watergate informant Deep Throat, Sept 2005, *Obit* Yrbk 2009

Freeh, Louis J., American FBI director, May 1996

Gray, L. Patrick, American FBI director, Sept 1972, *Obit* Yrbk 2005

Hoover, J. Edgar, American FBI director, Feb 1940, May 1950, *Obit* June 1972

Kelley, Clarence M., American FBI director, May 1974, *Obit* Nov 1997

Lillard, George W., *Obit* Yrbk 1940

Miller, John, American FBI official, Aug 2003

Mueller, Robert S., American FBI director, Aug 2010

Sessions, William Steele, American FBI director, July 1988

Webster, William H., American FBI and CIA director, Aug 1978

Factory workers

Bieber, Owen, labor leader, Apr 1986

Fraser, Douglas Andrew, American labor leader, Oct 1977, *Obit* Yrbk 2008

Hillman, Sidney, American labor leader, July 1940, *Obit* July 1946

Livingston, John W., labor leader, July 1959, *Obit* Aug 1997

Reuther, Walter Philip, American labor leader, Apr 1941, Nov 1949, *Obit* June 1970

Woodcock, Leonard, American labor leader and diplomat, Nov 1970, *Obit* Apr 2001

Yokich, Stephen P., American labor leader, Nov 1998, *Obit* Yrbk 2002

Faith healers

Kuhlman, Kathryn, evangelist, July 1974, *Obit* Apr 1976

Family counselors

Mudd, Emily, American family and marriage counselor, Nov 1956, *Obit* July 1998

Family planning advocates

Brueggemann, Ingar, German family planning advocate, Nov 2001

Feldt, Gloria A., American birth control advocate, July 2000

Michelman, Kate, American abortion rights activist, Nov 2000

Richards, Cecile, American family planning advocate, May 2007

Sadik, Nafis, Pakistani physician and United Nations official, Feb 1996

Stone, Hannah M., physician and family planning advocate, *Obit* Sept 1941

Wattleton, Faye, American nurse and birth control advocate, Jan 1990

Fantasy writers

Adams, Richard, English fantasy novelist, Oct 1978

Billingsley, Franny, American children's author, Aug 2012

Claremont, Chris, American fantasy, science fiction and comic book writer, Sept 2003

Collins, Suzanne, American young adult fantasy novelist, Sept 2012

Norton, Andre, American science fiction novelist, Jan 1957, *Obit* Yrbk 2005

Pullman, Philip, English fantasy writer, Jan 2003

Rowling, J. K., English fantasy novelist, Jan 2000

Tolkien, J. R. R., English fantasy novelist, philologist and linguist, Yrbk 1957, Oct 1967, *Obit* Nov 1973

Williams, Tad, American science fiction and fantasy writer, Sept 2006

Farmers

Adkins, Charles, American congressman, *Obit* May 1941

Barrett, Frank A., American senator and governor, July 1956, *Obit* July 1962

Beardsley, William S., American governor, June 1950, *Obit* Jan 1955

Bergland, Bob, American Secretary of agriculture, Sept 1977

Block, John R., American Secretary of agriculture, Apr 1982

Blundell, Michael, British farmer and colonial leader, Mar 1954

Boyd, John W., American farmers' association executive, Feb 2001

Chavez, Cesar, Mexican-American labor leader, Feb 1969, *Obit* June 1993

Cooley, Harold D., American congressman, Mar 1951, *Obit* Mar 1974

Fisher, Walter C., July 1950

Gilbert, George, *Obit* May 1943

Huerta, Dolores, American labor leader, Nov 1997

Jester, Beauford H., July 1948, *Obit* Sept 1949

McCarty, Dan, July 1953

Morehead, John H., *Obit* July 1942

Newsom, Herschel D., American farmer, agricultural leader and government official, Apr 1951, *Obit* Sept 1970

O'Neill, J. E., June 1952

Rodriguez, Arturo, labor leader, Mar 2001

Scott, W. Kerr, Apr 1956, *Obit* July 1958

Shuman, Charles B., American farm organization official, Feb 1956

Stelle, John, Jan 1946, *Obit* Sept 1962

Stookey, Charley, Jan 1940

Thornton, Dan, Feb 1954

Thye, Edward J., American governor and senator, Oct 1951, *Obit* Nov 1969

Fashion critics

Coddington, Grace, British fashion editor, Apr 2005

Donovan, Carrie, American fashion editor, Sept 1999, *Obit* Feb 2002

Talley, Andre Leon, American fashion editor, July 2003

Fashion designers

Aberra, Amsale, Ethiopian fashion designer, Jan 2005

Adolfo, fashion designer, Nov 1972

Alaia, Azzedine, Tunisian fashion designer, Oct 1992

Aldredge, Theoni, American costume designer, Feb 1994, *Obit* Yrbk 2011

Alphadi, Malian fashion designer, Jan 2004

Amies, Hardy, English fashion designer, Mar 1962, *Obit* Aug 2003

Armani, Giorgio, Italian fashion designer, Jan 1983

Atwood, Colleen, American costume designer, Oct 2010

Balenciaga, Spanish fashion designer, May 1954, *Obit* May 1972

Balmain, Pierre, French fashion designer, July 1954, *Obit* Aug 1982

Beene, Geoffrey, American fashion designer, Apr 1978, *Obit* Mar 2005

Blass, Bill, American fashion designer, Sept 1966, *Obit* Nov 2002

Boateng, Ozwald, British fashion designer, Jan 2006

Bohan, Marc, French fashion designer, Apr 1965

Burch, Tory, American fashion designer and philanthropist, Sept 2010

Burrows, Stephen, American fashion designer, Nov 2003

Byers, Margaretta, Sept 1941

Carnegie, Hattie, fashion designer, Oct 1942, *Obit* May 1956

Cashin, Bonnie, American fashion designer, May 1970, *Obit* June 2000

Cassini, Oleg, French-American fashion designer, July 1961, *Obit* Yrbk 2006

Claiborne, Liz, American fashion designer, June 1989, *Obit* Yrbk 2007

Courreges, Andre, French fashion designer, Jan 1970

Cuevas, Manuel, Mexican-American costume designer, Jan 2005

Czettel, Ladislas, Mar 1941, *Obit* Apr 1949

Dache, Lilly, French milliner, July 1941, *Obit* Mar 1990

De la Renta, Oscar, Dominican fashion designer, Mar 1970

Desses, Jean, Jan 1956, *Obit* Oct 1970

Dior, Christian, French fashion designer, Oct 1948, *Obit* Jan 1958

Dolce, Domenico, Italian fashion designer, Jan 2005

Ellis, Perry, fashion designer, Jan 1986, *Obit* Jan 1986

Farhi, Nicole, French fashion designer, Nov 2001

Fath, Jacques, French fashion designer, Apr 1951, *Obit* Jan 1955

Ferre, Gianfranco, Italian fashion designer, July 1991, *Obit* Yrbk 2007

Fogarty, Anne, fashion designer, Oct 1958, *Obit* Mar 1980

Ford, Tom, American fashion designer, May 1998

Gabbana, Stefano, Italian fashion designer, Jan 2005

Galanos, James, American fashion designer, Sept 1970

Galliano, John, British fashion designer, Oct 1996

Gaultier, Jean-Paul, French fashion designer, Jan 1999

Gernreich, Rudi, American fashion designer, Yrbk 1968, *Obit* June 1985

Ghesquiere, Nicolas, French fashion designer, Jan 2011

Gigli, Romeo, Italian fashion designer, Aug 1998

Givenchy, Hubert de, French fashion designer, May 1955

Gres, Alix, French fashion designer, June 1980, *Obit* Feb 1995

Halston, American fashion designer, Yrbk 1972, *Obit* May 1990

Hartnell, Norman, May 1953, *Obit* Aug 1979

Head, Edith, American costume designer, May 1945, *Obit* Jan 1982

Hilfiger, Tommy, American fashion designer, Apr 1996

Irene, costume designer, June 1946, *Obit* Jan 1963

Jacobs, Marc, American fashion designer, Feb 1998

James, Charles, American fashion designer, July 1956

Johnson, Betsey, American fashion designer, Jan 1994

Kamali, Norma, American fashion designer, Nov 1998

Karan, Donna, American fashion designer, Aug 1990

Karinska, Barbara, Russian-American costume designer, Jan 1971

Kawakubo, Rei, Japanese fashion designer, Aug 1999

Kelly, Patrick, fashion designer, Sept 1989, *Obit* Mar 1990

Kiam, Omar, Yrbk 1945, *Obit* May 1954

King, Muriel, Apr 1943, *Obit* May 1977

Klein, Calvin, American fashion designer, July 1978

Kors, Michael, American fashion designer, Jan 2000

Lacroix, Christian, French fashion designer, Apr 1988

Lagerfeld, Karl, German fashion designer, Jan 1982

Lang, Helmut, Austrian fashion designer, Apr 1997

Lanvin, Jeanne, French fashion designer, *Obit* Sept 1946

Lauren, Ralph, American fashion designer, Oct 1980

Leiber, Judith, Hungarian-American handbag designer, Sept 1996

Leser, Tina, fashion designer, June 1957, *Obit* Mar 1986

Lhuillier, Monique, American fashion designer, June 2008

Long, William Ivey, American costume designer, Mar 2004

Mainbocher, fashion designer, Feb 1942, *Obit* Mar 1977

Maxwell, Vera, fashion designer, July 1977, *Obit* Mar 1995

McCardell, Claire, American fashion designer, Nov 1954, *Obit* June 1958

McFadden, Mary, American fashion designer, Apr 1983

McQueen, Alexander, British fashion designer, Feb 2002, *Obit* June 2010

Miller, Nicole, fashion designer, Mar 1995

Miyake, Issey, Japanese fashion designer, Nov 1997

Molyneux, Edward H., June 1942, *Obit* May 1974

Montana, Claude, French fashion designer, Jan 1992

Mulleavy, Kate, American fashion designer, Sept 2012

Mulleavy, Laura, American fashion designer, Sept 2012

Norell, Norman, fashion designer, Nov 1964, *Obit* Yrbk 1972

Parnis, Mollie, fashion designer, May 1956, *Obit* Sept 1992

Poiret, Paul, French fashion designer, *Obit* June 1944

Posen, Zac, American fashion designer, July 2006

Powell, Sandy, English costume designer, June 2000

Prada, Miuccia, Italian fashion designer, Feb 2006

Pucci, Emilio, Italian fashion designer, Feb 1961, *Obit* Jan 1993

Quant, Mary, English fashion designer, Jan 1968

Raassi, Tala, Sept 2013

Rhodes, Zandra, British fashion designer, Jan 2002

Roehm, Carolyne, American fashion designer, Feb 1992

Roth, Ann, costume designer, Mar 1997

Rykiel, Sonia, French fashion designer, May 1990

Saab, Elie, Lebanese fashion designer, Aug 2004

Saint Laurent, Yves, French fashion designer, Yrbk 1964, *Obit* Oct 2008

Sander, Jil, German fashion designer, Oct 1997

Schiaparelli, Elsa, French fashion designer, Jan 1940, Nov 1951, *Obit* Jan 1974

Schnurer, Carolyn, Mar 1955

Simonetta, Italian fashion designer, Yrbk 1955

Simpson, Adele, fashion designer, Nov 1970, *Obit* Oct 1995

Slimane, Hedi, French fashion designer, Jan 2006

Spade, Kate, American handbag designer, Apr 2007

Stavropoulos, George, fashion designer, Mar 1985, *Obit* Feb 1991

Sui, Anna, American fashion designer, July 1993

Sy, Oumou, Senegalese fashion designer, Jan 2003

Theallet, Sophie, French fashion designer, Nov 2012

Trigere, Pauline, French-American fashion designer, Feb 1960, *Obit* July 2002

Tyler, Richard, Australian fashion designer, May 1997

Ungaro, Emanuel, French fashion designer, July 1980

Valentina, fashion designer, Yrbk 1946, *Obit* Nov 1989

Valentino, Italian fashion designer, Nov 1973

Venturini, Silvia, Italian handbag designer, Jan 2006

Versace, Donatella, Italian fashion designer, June 1998

Versace, Gianni, Italian fashion designer, Apr 1993, *Obit* Sept 1997

Von Furstenberg, Diane, Belgian fashion designer, Sept 1976

Wada, Emi, Japanese costume designer, Jan 2007

Westwood, Vivienne, English fashion designer, July 1997

Yamamoto, Yohji, Japanese fashion designer, Nov 2000

Feminists

Abzug, Bella, American congresswoman and feminist, July 1971, *Obit* June 1998

Beard, Mary Ritter, historian and feminist, Mar 1941, *Obit* Yrbk 1959

Begtrup, Bodil, Danish diplomat and United Nations official, Sept 1946

Bernardino, Minerva, Dominican feminist and diplomat, Mar 1950, *Obit* Nov 1998

Blatch, Harriot Eaton Stanton, American suffratist, *Obit* Jan 1941

Bravo, Ellen, feminist, Aug 1997

Brownmiller, Susan, journalist and feminist, Jan 1978

Bryce, Elizabeth Marion, *Obit* Jan 1940

Catt, Carrie Chapman, American feminist and pacifist, Oct 1940, *Obit* Apr 1947

Clay, Laura, American suffragist, *Obit* Aug 1941

Dworkin, Andrea, American feminist and writer, Oct 1994, *Obit* Yrbk 2005

Edey, Birdsall Otis, *Obit* Aug 1940

Faludi, Susan, American journalist and feminist, Feb 1993

Friedan, Betty, American feminist, Nov 1970, Mar 1989, *Obit* May 2006

Gandy, Kim A., American feminist, Oct 2001

Grand, Sarah, English novelist and feminist, *Obit* July 1943

Harden, Cecil Murray, congresswoman, Feb 1949, *Obit* Feb 1985

Hernandez, Aileen C., feminist, July 1971

Hewlett, Sylvia Ann, Welsh economist and feminist, Sept 2002

Heymann, Lida Gustava, *Obit* Sept 1943

Hickey, Margaret A., feminist and lawyer, Yrbk 1944, *Obit* Feb 1995

Hite, Shere, author and feminist, Feb 1988

Howorth, Lucy Somerville, American lawyer and feminist, Oct 1951, *Obit* Nov 1997

Hurd-Mead, Kate Campbell, *Obit* Feb 1941

Ireland, Patricia, American lawyer and feminist, June 1992

Jahangir, Asma, Pakistani lawyer and feminist, Jan 2003

Johnson, Sonia, American feminist, Feb 1985

Joseph, Ammu, Indian journalist and feminist, Jan 2004

Katz, Jackson, American anti-sexism activist, July 2004

Khan, Begum Liaquat Ali, July 1950

Kollontai, A., Soviet diplomat, Oct 1943, *Obit* Apr 1952

Mai, Mukhtar, Pakistani feminist, Jan 2006

Malcolm, Ellen, American feminist and political activist, Feb 2010

Mehta, Hansa, July 1947

Mohammed, Yanar, Iraqi feminist, Jan 2007

Mongella, Gertrude, Tanzanian member of Parliament, diplomat and feminist, Jan 2004

Naidu, Sarojini, Indian feminist, poet and government official, May 1943, *Obit* Mar 1949

Parsons, Rose Peabody, feminist, Yrbk 1959, *Obit* June 1985

Paul, Alice, American lawyer and feminist, Sept 1947, *Obit* Sept 1977

Poinso-Chapuis, Germaine, French feminist, June 1948

Rama Rau, Dhanvanthi, Indian social welfare leader and feminist, Apr 1954, *Obit* Sept 1987

Ras-Work, Berhane, Ethiopian human rights activist, Jan 2004

Rathbone, Eleanor, British feminist and member of Parliament, June 1943, *Obit* Feb 1946

Richards, Ann, American governor, Feb 1991, *Obit* Yrbk 2007

Roberts, Albert H., *Obit* July 1946

Rodriguez, Cecilia, feminist and revolutionary, May 1999

Schneiderman, Rose, labor leader and feminist, Feb 1946, *Obit* Oct 1972

Searing, Annie E. P., *Obit* June 1942

Smeal, Eleanor, American feminist, Mar 1980

Street, Jessie M. G., Australian feminist, Sept 1947

Sung, Ching-ling, Chinese political leader and wife of stateman Sun Yat-sen, Apr 1944, *Obit* July 1981

Wheaton, Elizabeth, Jan 1942

Whitton, Charlotte Elizabeth, Canadian social worker, feminist and mayor, Apr 1953, *Obit* Mar 1975

Wilson, Marie C., American feminist, Sept 2004

Yard, Molly, American feminist and social activist, Nov 1988, *Obit* Apr 2006

Young, Rose, *Obit* Sept 1941

Fiddlers

Fay, Martin, Irish fiddler, Mar 2004, *Obit* Yrbk 2013

Keane, Sean, Irish fiddler, Mar 2004

Leslie, Chris, English singer, fiddler and mandolinist, Sept 2005

Maguire, Martie, American fiddler, July 2000

O'Connor, Mark, American fiddler and composer, Sept 2013

Sanders, Ric, English fiddler, Sept 2005

Field hockey players

Aymar, Luciana, Feb 2013

Film historians

Langlois, Henri, French motion picture historian and collector, Jan 1973, *Obit* Mar 1977

Maltin, Leonard, American film critic and historian, Aug 2008

Thomson, David, English film historian and biographer, Sept 2009

Financial analysts

Babson, Roger W., statistician, Feb 1945, *Obit* May 1967

Dyson, Esther, American computer industry analyst, Aug 1997

Krawcheck, Sallie, American financial executive, Mar 2006

Meeker, Mary, American financial analyst, Aug 1999

Financial consultants

Avenol, Joseph, Jan 1940, *Obit* Oct 1952

Bernstein, William, American investment adviser and neurologist, Nov 2009

Cassel, Karl Gustav, *Obit* Mar 1945

Cohen, Abby Joseph, American investment adviser, June 1998

Garzarelli, Elaine, American investment adviser, Sept 1995

Janeway, Eliot, economist and investment adviser, Sept 1970, *Obit* Apr 1993

Lasser, J. K., May 1946, *Obit* July 1954

Magill, Roswell, Mar 1948, *Obit* Feb 1964

Nobs, Ernst, Sept 1949, *Obit* June 1957

Phillips, Frederick, *Obit* Oct 1943

Rinfret, Pierre, American economist and financial consultant, July 1972, *Obit* Yrbk 2006

Sherley, Swagar, *Obit* Apr 1941

Taleb, Nassim, Lebanese mathematician, investment adviser and philosopher, May 2011

Weld, William Floyd, American lawyer and former governor, Feb 1993

Financial executives

Abbell, Maxwell, American accountant and lawyer, July 1951, *Obit* Sept 1957

Abs, Hermann J., German banker, Oct 1970, *Obit* May 1994

Aga Khan, Swiss Islamic leader and financier, Mar 1960, Jan 2004

Al-Rajhi, Sulaiman Abdel-Aziz, Saudi Arabian financier, Jan 2006

Alwaleed bin Talal al Saud, Saudi Arabian entrepreneur and financier, Jan 2006

Ames, Amyas, investment banker and music patron, Apr 1972, *Obit* June 2000

Anderson, Samuel W., American investment banker and government official, June 1954, *Obit* Jan 1963

Anderson, Victor E., American governor, Sept 1956, *Obit* Oct 1962

Andrews, T. Coleman, accountant and government official, Apr 1954

Armstrong, J. Sinclair, banker, lawyer and government official, Mar 1958, *Obit* Mar 2001

Aronson, J. Hugo, American governor, Feb 1954

Aziz, Shaukat, Pakistani prime minister, Jan 2007

Bailey, Abe, South African financier and political leader, *Obit* Sept 1940

Baker, John Hopkinson, American investment banker and conservationist, May 1949

Banda, Enos, South African banker, Jan 2005

Baruch, Bernard Mannes, American financier and presidential adviser, Aug 1941, July 1950, *Obit* Sept 1965

Bass, Robert M., investor, July 1989

Beame, Abraham D., American mayor, July 1974, *Obit* Apr 2001

Bell, Daniel W., American banker and government official, Oct 1946, *Obit* Nov 1971

Berezovsky, Boris A., Russian financier and government official, Jan 2002, *Obit* Yrbk 2013

Bernstein, William, American investment adviser and neurologist, Nov 2009

Black, Conrad M., Canadian financier and newspaper publisher, Aug 1992

Blankfein, Lloyd C., American investment banker, Jan 2011

Blau, Bela, American theatrical producer, *Obit* Yrbk 1940

Blumenthal, Hugo, American investment banker and philanthropist, *Obit* Sept 1943

Boles, Ewing T., American investment banker, Apr 1953

Bond, John, British banker, Jan 2005

Botin, Ana Patricia, Spanish banker, Jan 2005

Bowles, Erskine, American presidential adviser, Aug 1998

Brady, Nicholas F., American Secretary of the treasury, Nov 1988

Bridges, Styles, American governor and senator, Mar 1948, *Obit* Jan 1962

Bruce, Howard, Sept 1948, *Obit* Sept 1961

Brundage, Percival F., American accountant and government official, Apr 1957

Brunsdale, Clarence Norman, governor and banker, Sept 1954

Buffett, Warren E., American financier, Nov 1987

Burgess, Warren, June 1949, *Obit* Nov 1978

Burgin, William O., *Obit* May 1946

Bush, Prescott S., American banker, senator and father of President George Bush, May 1942, Jan 1954, *Obit* Yrbk 1972

Butcher, Willard C., banker, July 1980, *Obit* Yrbk 2012

Buttenwieser, Benjamin Joseph, investment banker, Nov 1950, *Obit* Mar 1992

Catto, Thomas Sivewright Catto, English banker, Nov 1944

Champion, George, banker, Apr 1961, *Obit* Jan 1998

Chenault, Kenneth I., American financial services executive, June 1998

Clark, Georgia Neese, banker and government official, Sept 1949, *Obit* Feb 1996

Cocke, Charles Francis, Mar 1952

Corzine, Jon S., American financial executive and former governor, Aug 2006

Coyne, James E., July 1955

Crowley, Leo, American banker and government official, June 1943, *Obit* June 1972

Crown, Henry, financier, Jan 1972, *Obit* Oct 1990

Cullman, Howard S., June 1951, *Obit* Sept 1972

Davis, Archie K., May 1966

Davis, Evelyn Y., American shareholders' rights activist, Oct 2007

Dawes, Rufus Cutler, *Obit* Jan 1940

Dawson, John A., investment banker, Sept 1952

Dewey, Charles Schuveldt, Jan 1949, *Obit* Feb 1981

Dodge, Joseph Morrell, American banker and government official, Nov 1947, *Obit* Jan 1965

Doerr, John, American financier, May 2009

Domini, Amy L., American investment manager, Nov 2005

Douglas, James Henderson, American Secretary of the air force, Sept 1957, *Obit* Apr 1988

Draper, William Henry, banker and government official, Mar 1952, *Obit* Feb 1975

Eaton, Cyrus, American financier, July 1948, *Obit* July 1979

Ebbott, Percy J., American banker, Oct 1954

Eberstadt, Ferdinand, investment banker, Yrbk 1942, *Obit* Jan 1970

Emmerson, Louis Lincoln, *Obit* Mar 1941

Emmons, Glenn L., Oct 1954

Faber, Joachim, German investment manager, Jan 2002

Fleming, Sam M., June 1962

Florence, Fred F., June 1956, *Obit* Feb 1961

Forrestal, James V., American Secretary of defense, Feb 1942, Jan 1948, *Obit* July 1949

Fowler, Henry H., American Secretary of the treasury, Sept 1952, *Obit* May 2000

Franke, William B., Sept 1959, *Obit* Aug 1979

Frere, Albert, Belgian financier, Jan 2002

Fukui, Toshihiko, Japanese banking official, Jan 2004

Funk, Walther, German financier and cabinet member, Oct 1940, *Obit* Sept 1960

Garzarelli, Elaine, American investment adviser, Sept 1995

Gates, Thomas S., American Secretary of the navy, Sept 1957, *Obit* May 1983

Giannini, Amadeo Peter, American banker, Mar 1947, *Obit* July 1949

Giannini, L. M., Nov 1950, *Obit* Oct 1952

Gidney, Ray M., Oct 1953

Goldsmith, James, English financier, Feb 1988, *Obit* Oct 1997

Gorman, James P., Australian financial executive, June 2010

Goussinsky, Vladimir, Russian financier, Jan 2002

Griffis, Stanton, investment banker and diplomat, Oct 1944, *Obit* Oct 1974

Gross, William H., American investment manager, July 2010

Gutt, Camille, Apr 1948

Hancock, John M., Apr 1949, *Obit* Yrbk 1957

Harber, W. Elmer, Mar 1951

Harkness, Edward Stephen, Jan 1940

Harrington, Russell C., Apr 1956, *Obit* Oct 1971

Harrison, William B., American investment banker, Mar 2002

Hartford, Huntington, American financier and patron of the arts, June 1959, *Obit* Yrbk 2008

Hayes, Alfred, banker and government official, Feb 1966, *Obit* Feb 1990

Heckscher, August, *Obit* June 1941

Hobson, Mellody, American investment manager, Aug 2005

Holbrooke, Richard, American diplomat, Oct 1998, *Obit* Yrbk 2011

Hughes, Rowland R., American government official, Feb 1956, *Obit* June 1957

Icahn, Carl C., American financier, Apr 1986

Jackson, William H., Mar 1951, *Obit* Nov 1971

Jacobsson, Per, Swedish banker, Oct 1958, *Obit* June 1963

James, Arthur Curtiss, *Obit* July 1941

Johnson, Joseph T., Feb 1952

Kennedy, Joseph P., American financier, diplomat and father of President John F. Kennedy, Nov 1940, *Obit* Jan 1970

Kerkorian, Kirk, American financier, May 1975, Mar 1996

Khan, Salman, American school administrator, May 2013

Khashoggi, Adnan, Saudi Arabian financier, Mar 1986

Kimbrel, Monroe, June 1963

Korth, Frederick H., secretary of the navy, July 1962, *Obit* Jan 1999

Kravis, Henry R., American financier, Mar 1989

Kuok, Robert, Malaysian financier, June 1998

Laeri, John Howard, banker, Sept 1968, *Obit* Aug 1986

Lamont, Ann Huntress, American venture capitalist, Feb 2007

Lamont, Thomas William, banker, Oct 1940, *Obit* Feb 1948

Lampert, Edward S., American retail executive, Sept 2005

Lance, Bert, banker and presidential adviser, Aug 1977, *Obit* Yrbk 2013

Leffingwell, Russell Cornell, banker, Mar 1950, *Obit* Yrbk 1960

Lehman, Herbert Henry, American governor and senator, Jan 1943, July 1955, *Obit* Jan 1964

Lewis, Kenneth, American banker, Apr 2004

Lewis, Loida Nicolas, American financier and wife of Reginald F. Lewis, Apr 1997

Livingston, Homer J., Sept 1955, *Obit* July 1970

Locke, Edwin A., Jan 1952

Long, Edward V., American senator, July 1964, *Obit* Jan 1973

Lott, Ronnie, American investment manager and former football player, Feb 1994

Lovett, Robert A., American Secretary of defense, Aug 1942, Nov 1951, *Obit* June 1986

Lynch, Peter, American investment manager, Nov 1994

Martin, Thomas E., Mar 1956, *Obit* Sept 1971

Martin, William McChesney, American stockbroker and Federal Reserve chairman, May 1951, *Obit* Oct 1998

Martinez Trueba, Andres, Nov 1954, *Obit* Feb 1960

Maximos, Demetrios, Mar 1948, *Obit* Yrbk 1955

McConnell, Samuel Kerns, Nov 1956

McDonnell, William A., Feb 1959

McKinney, Frank Edward, banker and political leader, Jan 1952, *Obit* Mar 1974

McKittrick, Thomas, July 1944, *Obit* Mar 1970

Meeker, Mary, American financial analyst, Aug 1999

Meriwether, John W., American investment manager, Mar 1999

Miller, G. William, American Secretary of the treasury, Federal Reserve chairman and investment banker, June 1978, *Obit* Yrbk 2007

Miller, Lee P., July 1959

Milner, Yuri, Russian financier, Mar 2013

Mooney, Beth, American banker, May 2012

Moore, George S., banker, May 1970, *Obit* Yrbk 2000

Mott, Stewart R., American philanthropist and political activist, Apr 1975, *Obit* Yrbk 2008

Muir, James, May 1950, *Obit* Jan 1960

Norman, Montagu Collet Norman, English banker, Yrbk 1940, *Obit* Mar 1950

Novogratz, Jacqueline, American investment organization official, Apr 2013

O'Neal, Edward A., banking executive, Sept 1946, *Obit* May 1958

O'Neal, Stanley, American investment banker, May 2003

Odlin, Reno, July 1965

Odlum, Floyd B., American financier, Nov 1941, *Obit* Aug 1976

Olayan, Lubna, Saudi Arabian financial executive, Jan 2006

Pandit, Vikram S., American financial executive, June 2008

Paulson, Henry M., American Secretary of the treasury, Sept 2002

Peltz, Nelson, American financier, Feb 2008

Perelman, Ronald Owen, American financier, Jan 1991

Peterson, F. Raymond, Feb 1950, *Obit* Feb 1978

Phillips, Frederick, *Obit* Oct 1943

Pike, Sumner T., Mar 1947, *Obit* Apr 1976

Pinault, Francois, French financier, Jan 2004

Pinera, Sebastian, Chilean president, Nov 2010

Prince, Charles O., American financial services executive, Jan 2007

Raines, Franklin D., American financial services executive, Oct 2000

Rainwater, Richard E., American investor, Apr 1999

Rasminsky, Louis, Yrbk 1961

Reed, John S., American financial executive and stock exchange official, Jan 1985

Reese, Everett D., Mar 1954

Remington, John W., Feb 1960

Riklis, Meshulam, financier, Yrbk 1971

Riordan, Richard, American mayor and investor, May 2000

Robertson, Walter S., Yrbk 1953, *Obit* May 1970

Rockefeller, David, American banker, Mar 1959

Rockefeller, Laurance S., American investor and conservationist, June 1959, *Obit* Yrbk 2004

Rockefeller, Winthrop, American governor, philanthropist and financier, Sept 1959, *Obit* Apr 1973

Roebling, Mary G., banker, Oct 1960, *Obit* Jan 1995

Rogers, John, American investment manager, Aug 2010

Rohatyn, Felix G., American investment banker and diplomat, May 1978

Romney, Mitt, American governor, Sept 2006

Roosa, Robert V., American investment banker and government official, Yrbk 1962, *Obit* Mar 1994

Root, Oren, state banking official, Aug 1940, July 1952, *Obit* Mar 1995

Rooth, Ivar, Yrbk 1952, *Obit* Apr 1972

Ruhle, Stephanie, American investment banker, Jan 2013

Ryti, Risto, Feb 1941, *Obit* Jan 1957

Sanderson, Derek, Canadian hockey player and investment manager, Apr 1975

Saul, Ralph Southey, Feb 1971

Schacht, Hjalmar, German financier, Oct 1944, *Obit* Sept 1970

Shelton, James E., Feb 1951

Sherley, Swagar, *Obit* Apr 1941

Simon, William E., American Secretary of the treasury and financier, Apr 1974, *Obit* Aug 2000

Slim Helu, Carlos, Mexican financier, Jan 2003

Smith, Howard Worth, American congressman, Feb 1941, *Obit* Nov 1976

Soong, T. V., Chinese government official and financier, Mar 1941, *Obit* June 1971

Soros, George, American financier, Apr 1997

Sproul, Allan, banker, Yrbk 1950, *Obit* June 1978

Stockman, David Alan, American investment banker, presidential aide and manufacturing executive, Aug 1981

Stokes, Edward C., American governor, *Obit* Yrbk 1942

Strauss, Lewis L., American presidential aide, regulatory agency official and Secretary of commerce, Feb 1947, *Obit* Mar 1974

Sumner, Jessie, congresswoman, Jan 1945, *Obit* Oct 1994

Taleb, Nassim, Lebanese mathematician, investment adviser and philosopher, May 2011

Tapie, Bernard, French financier, Jan 2002

Tata, Ratan, Indian financier, Jan 2007

Tauscher, Ellen O., American congresswoman, Mar 2001

Tawes, J. Millard, Oct 1960, *Obit* Aug 1979

Thain, John, American investment banker, May 2004

Thompson, Roy L., Oct 1946

Thomson, J. Cameron, Yrbk 1948, *Obit* Mar 1966

Tobey, Charles W., American senator and governor, June 1941, July 1951, *Obit* Oct 1953

Towers, Graham F., Canadian banker, Feb 1952

Tuomioja, Sakari, Mar 1954, *Obit* Nov 1964

Vardaman, James Kimble, American banker and government official, Apr 1951

Vergara Madrigal, Jorge, Mexican entrepreneur, Jan 2003

Vranitzky, Franz, Austrian chancellor, Aug 1989

Watkins, Donald V., American lawyer and investor, Jan 2003

Waugh, Samuel C., Yrbk 1955, *Obit* Oct 1970

Weill, Sanford I., American financial services executive, July 1999

Welman, Joseph C., May 1958

Wente, Carl F., Feb 1954

White, Alexander M., July 1951, *Obit* Jan 1969

Whitney, John Hay, American financier and diplomat, Yrbk 1945, *Obit* Apr 1982

Williams, Ralph E., *Obit* July 1940

Wilson, Malcolm, American lawyer, banker and governor, May 1974, *Obit* Aug 2000

Winthrop, Beekman, *Obit* Yrbk 1940

Woollen, Evans, Yrbk 1948, *Obit* Apr 1959

Woolton, Frederick James Marquis, English financier, Oct

1940, Oct 1950, *Obit* Feb 1965

Wriston, Walter B., American banker, Nov 1977, *Obit* Aug 2005

Zarb, Frank G., American securities exchange official, Sept 1975

Zell, Samuel, American real estate investor, Jan 2009

Zhou Xiaochuan, Chinese banker, Jan 2003

Financiers

Aga Khan, Swiss Islamic leader and financier, Mar 1960, Jan 2004

Al-Rajhi, Sulaiman Abdel-Aziz, Saudi Arabian financier, Jan 2006

Bache, Harold L., American securities broker, May 1959

Baruch, Bernard Mannes, American financier and presidential adviser, Aug 1941, July 1950, *Obit* Sept 1965

Bass, Robert M., investor, July 1989

Berezovsky, Boris A., Russian financier and government official, Jan 2002, *Obit* Yrbk 2013

Boylan, Robert P., Apr 1950

Buffett, Warren E., American financier, Nov 1987

Chadwick, Florence, American swimmer and stockbroker, Oct 1950, *Obit* May 1995

Crown, Henry, financier, Jan 1972, *Obit* Oct 1990

Cullman, Howard S., June 1951, *Obit* Sept 1972

Dawes, Rufus Cutler, *Obit* Jan 1940

Doerr, John, American financier, May 2009

Eaton, Cyrus, American financier, July 1948, *Obit* July 1979

Frere, Albert, Belgian financier, Jan 2002

Goldsmith, James, English financier, Feb 1988, *Obit* Oct 1997

Goussinsky, Vladimir, Russian financier, Jan 2002

Gutt, Camille, Apr 1948

Harkness, Edward Stephen, Jan 1940

Hartford, Huntington, American financier and patron of the arts, June 1959, *Obit* Yrbk 2008

Heckscher, August, *Obit* June 1941

Icahn, Carl C., American financier, Apr 1986

James, Arthur Curtiss, *Obit* July 1941

Khashoggi, Adnan, Saudi Arabian financier, Mar 1986

Kravis, Henry R., American financier, Mar 1989

Kuok, Robert, Malaysian financier, June 1998

Lamont, Ann Huntress, American venture capitalist, Feb 2007

Mehta, Deena, Indian securities broker, Jan 2005

Merrill, Charles Edward, American stockbroker, Apr 1956

Milner, Yuri, Russian financier, Mar 2013

Nkontchou, Cyrille, Cameroonian securities broker, Jan 2004

Odlum, Floyd B., American financier, Nov 1941, *Obit* Aug 1976

Peltz, Nelson, American financier, Feb 2008

Perelman, Ronald Owen, American financier, Jan 1991

Pike, Sumner T., Mar 1947, *Obit* Apr 1976

Pinault, Francois, French financier, Jan 2004

Pinera, Sebastian, Chilean president, Nov 2010

Rainwater, Richard E., American investor, Apr 1999

Regan, Donald T., American presidential adviser, Nov 1981, *Obit* Yrbk 2003

Riklis, Meshulam, financier, Yrbk 1971

Riordan, Richard, American mayor and investor, May 2000

Rockefeller, Winthrop, American governor, philanthropist and financier, Sept 1959, *Obit* Apr 1973

Romney, Mitt, American governor, Sept 2006

Siebert, Muriel, American stockbroker, Aug 1997, *Obit* Yrbk 2013

Slim Helu, Carlos, Mexican financier, Jan 2003

Soong, T. V., Chinese government official and financier, Mar 1941, *Obit* June 1971

Tata, Ratan, Indian financier, Jan 2007

Watkins, Donald V., American lawyer and investor, Jan 2003

Zell, Samuel, American real estate investor, Jan 2009

Firefighters

Sorlie, Robert, Norwegian firefighter and sled dog racer, Jan 2005

Flight crews

Auriol, Jacqueline, French aviator, Sept 1953, *Obit* June 2000

Berkner, Lloyd, Sept 1949, *Obit* Oct 1967

Bishop, Billy, Canadian air marshal, Sept 1941

Brabazon of Tara, John Theodore Cuthbert Moore-Brabazon, British aviator and government official, May 1941

Cobb, Geraldyn M., American aviator, Feb 1961

Denton, Jeremiah, American admiral and senator, May 1982

Dougherty, Dora, Mar 1963

Dufek, George J., Mar 1957

Fahy, Charles, American judge and solicitor general, Jan 1942, *Obit* Nov 1979

Farnsworth, Arthur, *Obit* Oct 1943

Felt, Harry D., Mar 1959

Fitch, Aubrey, Oct 1945, *Obit* July 1978

Gandhi, Rajiv, Indian prime minister, Apr 1985, *Obit* July 1991

Gower, Pauline, English aviator, Aug 1943, *Obit* Mar 1947

Gros, Edmund L., *Obit* Yrbk 1942

Hailey, Arthur, Canadian novelist, Feb 1972, *Obit* Yrbk 2005

Jamieson, Leland, *Obit* Sept 1941

Johnson, Amy, English aviator, *Obit* Feb 1941

Maas, Melvin Joseph, Nov 1957, *Obit* June 1964
Mahan, John W., July 1959
Mussolini, Bruno, *Obit* Oct 1941
Muti, Ettore, *Obit* Oct 1943
Netherwood, Douglas B., *Obit* Oct 1943
Ocker, William C., *Obit* Nov 1942
Parseval, August von, *Obit* Apr 1942
Rickenbacker, Eddie, American military pilot, Nov 1940, Feb 1952, *Obit* Oct 1973
Smith, Elinor, American aviator, Mar 2001, *Obit* Yrbk 2010
Williams, Alford Joseph, Oct 1940
Yancey, Lewis Alonzo, *Obit* Jan 1940
Yeager, Jeana, aviator, May 1987

Flower arrangers

Spry, Constance, English flower arranger, May 1940, *Obit* Mar 1960

Flugelhornists

Mangione, Chuck, trumpet player and flugelhornist, May 1980
Masekela, Hugh, South African trumpet player, flugelhornist and singer, Mar 1993

Flutists

Anderson, Ian, British singer, flutist and songwriter, Feb 1998
Galway, James, Irish flutist, June 1980
Laws, Hubert, American jazz flutist, July 2007
Lloyd, Charles, American saxophonist and flutist, Apr 2002
Molloy, Matt, Irish flutist, Mar 2004
Rampal, Jean-Pierre, French flutist, Mar 1970, *Obit* Aug 2000
Robison, Paula, flutist, May 1982

Folk musicians

Amos, Tori, American singer and songwriter, Sept 1998

Baez, Joan, American folk singer and songwriter, Nov 1963
Beam, Sam (Iron and Wine), American folk singer and songwriter, Mar 2013
Bikel, Theodore, American singer and actor, Mar 1960
Conneff, Kevin, Irish bodhran player and singer, Mar 2004
Conway, Gerry, English drummer, Sept 2005
DiFranco, Ani, American singer and songwriter, Aug 1997
Dyer-Bennet, Richard, singer, June 1944, *Obit* Feb 1992
Fay, Martin, Irish fiddler, Mar 2004, *Obit* Yrbk 2013
Flight of the Conchords, Mar 2008
Guthrie, Arlo, American folk singer and songwriter, Feb 1982
Ives, Burl, singer and actor, Jan 1946, May 1960, *Obit* June 1995
Keane, Sean, Irish fiddler, Mar 2004
Leslie, Chris, English singer, fiddler and mandolinist, Sept 2005
Lightfoot, Gordon, Canadian singer, Aug 1978
Mitchell, Joni, Canadian singer and songwriter, Oct 1976
Molloy, Matt, Irish flutist, Mar 2004
Moloney, Paddy, Irish uillean piper, Mar 2004
Nicol, Simon, English guitarist and singer, Sept 2005
Odetta, American folk singer, Yrbk 1960, *Obit* Jan 2009
Pegg, Dave, English bassist and singer, Sept 2005
Ray, Amy, American singer and songwriter, Aug 1998
Reagon, Bernice Johnson, American historian and singer, Aug 1999
Redpath, Jean, Scottish singer, Feb 1984
Ritchie, Jean, American folk singer, Oct 1959
Sainte-Marie, Buffy, Canadian singer and songwriter, July 1969
Saliers, Emily, American singer and songwriter, Aug 1998
Sanders, Ric, English fiddler, Sept 2005

Schlamme, Martha, singer, Feb 1964, *Obit* Jan 1986
Seeger, Pete, American folk singer and songwriter, Yrbk 1963
Vega, Suzanne, American singer and songwriter, Aug 1994
Vernon, Justin, American singer and songwriter, Apr 2012
White, Josh, guitarist and singer, Aug 1944, *Obit* Nov 1969

Folklorists

Brand, Oscar, folklorist, June 1962
Lomax, Alan, American folklorist and musicologist, Sept 1941, *Obit* Oct 2002
Smith, Mary Carter, storyteller and folklorist, Feb 1996

Food critics

Apple, R. W., American journalist, Apr 1993, *Obit* Feb 2007
Fougner, G. Selmer, journalist and wine critic, *Obit* May 1941
Jackson, Michael, British journalist and beer expert, Aug 2005, *Obit* Yrbk 2007
Oliver, Garrett, American brewmaster, Nov 2008
Parker, Robert M., American wine critic, May 2005
Robinson, Jancis, British wine critic, Jan 2007

Food industry employees

Amos, Wally, American baking industry executive, July 1995
Andreas, Dwayne O., food industry executive, Mar 1992
Birdseye, Clarence, American inventor and frozen food industry executive, Mar 1946, *Obit* Yrbk 1957
Brabeck-Letmathe, Peter, Austrian-Swiss food industry executive, Jan 2005
Brady, William Thomas, food industry executive, Jan 1961, *Obit* July 1984
Cohen, Ben, American ice cream company executive, Apr 1994

Diniz, Abilio, Brazilian supermarket and department store executive, Jan 2006

Donald, Arnold, American food industry executive, Nov 2005

Eckert, Robert, American toy industry executive, Mar 2003

Francis, Clarence, food industry executive, Feb 1948, *Obit* Mar 1986

Greenfield, Jerry, American ice cream company executive, Apr 1994

Heinz, Henry John, American food industry executive, June 1947, *Obit* Apr 1987

Hershey, Milton Snavely, American candy industry executive, *Obit* Nov 1945

Holden, Betsy, American food industry executive, July 2003

Johnson, F. Ross, Canadian food industry executive, May 1989

Knox, Rose Markward, American food industry executive, May 1949, *Obit* Nov 1950

Mackey, John, American supermarket chain executive, Nov 2008

Morrison, Denise, American food company executive, July 2012

Morton, Rogers C. B., American Secretary of the interior and commerce, Nov 1971, *Obit* June 1979

Murphy, William Beverly, food industry executive, Nov 1955, *Obit* Aug 1994

Perdue, Frank, American poultry industry executive, June 1979, *Obit* Oct 2005

Rosenfeld, Irene, American food industry executive, July 2007

Rudkin, Margaret Fogarty, American baking executive, Sept 1959, *Obit* Oct 1967

Sanger, Stephen W., American food company executive, Mar 2004

Sen, Laura, American supermarket executive, Oct 2011

Smolyansky, Julie, American food industry executive, Nov 2013

Swift, Gustavus Franklin, American meat packing executive, *Obit* Yrbk 1943

Tyson, John H., American poultry company executive, Aug 2001

Walker, Olene S., American governor, Apr 2005

Welch, Robert, American founder of John Birch Society, Nov 1976, *Obit* Mar 1985

Willes, Mark H., American newspaper publisher, Mar 1998

Williams, John J., American senator, Jan 1952, *Obit* Apr 1988

Willis, Paul S., food and grocery trade association executive, Jan 1951, *Obit* Aug 1987

Food technicians

Davis, Joseph S., July 1947, *Obit* June 1975

Football coaches

Allen, George, American football coach, Jan 1975, *Obit* Mar 1991

Belichick, Bill, American football coach, Sept 2002

Blaik, Earl Henry, football coach, Jan 1945, *Obit* July 1989

Bowden, Bobby, American football coach, Nov 1996

Bryant, Bear, American football coach, June 1980, *Obit* Mar 1983

Coughlin, Tom, American football coach, Aug 2008

Cowher, Bill, American football coach, Nov 2006

Crisler, Herbert Orin, football coach, Feb 1948, *Obit* Oct 1982

Ditka, Mike, American football coach, Oct 1987

Dungy, Tony, American football player and coach, Aug 2007

Ewbank, Weeb, football coach, June 1969, *Obit* Feb 1999

Gagliardi, John, American football coach, Jan 2008

Gibbs, Joe, American football coach, Apr 1992

Hayes, Woody, American football coach, Feb 1975, *Obit* May 1987

Hickman, Herman, Nov 1951, *Obit* July 1958

Holmgren, Mike, American football coach, Oct 2000

Holtz, Lou, American football coach and sportscaster, June 1989

Johnson, Jimmy, American football coach and sportscaster, July 1994

Landry, Tom, American football coach, June 1972, *Obit* Apr 2000

Leahy, Frank, football coach, Yrbk 1941, *Obit* Sept 1973

Levy, Marv, football coach, Feb 1998

Lewis, Marvin, American football coach, Nov 2004

Little, Lou, American football coach, Nov 1945, *Obit* July 1979

Lombardi, Vince, American football coach, May 1963, *Obit* Nov 1970

Madden, John, American football coach and sportscaster, Aug 1985

McKeever, Ed, Nov 1945

Munn, Clarence L., Nov 1953

Murphy, Mark, CEO fo Green Bay Packers, Oct 2012

O'Brien, Bill, Aug 2013

Oosterbaan, Bennie, football coach, Yrbk 1949, *Obit* Jan 1991

Owen, Steve, football coach, Yrbk 1946, *Obit* July 1964

Parcells, Bill, American football coach, Apr 1991

Parker, Buddy, Yrbk 1955, *Obit* June 1982

Parseghian, Ara, football coach and sportscaster, Feb 1968

Paterno, Joe, American football coach, Feb 1984, *Obit* Yrbk 2012

Reeves, Dan, football player and coach, Oct 2001

Reid, Andy, American football coach, Nov 2012

Robinson, Eddie, American football coach, June 1988, *Obit* Yrbk 2007

Ryan, Rex, American football coach, Oct 2010

Shula, Don, American football coach, Mar 1974

Singletary, Mike, American football coach, Mar 1993

Smith, Lovie, American football coach, Sept 2007

Smith, Mike, American football coach, Sept 2010

Sparano, Tony, American football coach, Jan 2010

Stagg, Amos Alonzo, football coach, Mar 1944, *Obit* Apr 1965

Starr, Bart, American football player and coach, Jan 1968

Tomlin, Mike, American football coach, Aug 2011

Walsh, Bill, American football coach, Nov 1989, *Obit* Yrbk 2007

Weis, Charlie, American football coach, Nov 2007

Wilkinson, Bud, football coach, Apr 1962, *Obit* May 1994

Williams, Doug, American football player and coach, Feb 1999

Willingham, Tyrone, American football coach, Nov 2002

Yost, Fielding Harris, *Obit* Oct 1946

Football executives

Adams, Ernie, American football executive, Jan 2009

Bell, Bert, American football commissioner, Sept 1950, *Obit* Yrbk 1959

Davis, Al, American football executive, July 1985, *Obit* Yrbk 2011

Kraft, Robert K., American businessman and football executive, Feb 2012

Rozelle, Pete, American football commissioner, June 1964, *Obit* Feb 1997

Football players

Aikman, Troy, American football player, May 1995

Allen, Marcus, American football player, Oct 1986

Beban, Gary J., football player and real estate executive, May 1970

Bettis, Jerome, American football player, Aug 2006

Blanda, George, American football player, Sept 1972, *Obit* Yrbk 2010

Bloom, Jeremy, American football player and skier, Sept 2013

Bradshaw, Terry, American football player, Apr 1979

Brady, Tom, American football player, Aug 2004

Brown, Larry, American football player, Mar 1973

Brown, Troy, American football player, Oct 2007

Campbell, Earl, American football player, Apr 1983

Chrebet, Wayne, American football player, Feb 1999

Conerly, Charlie, football player, Apr 1960, *Obit* Apr 1996

Csonka, Larry, American football player, Feb 1977

Culpepper, Daunte, American football player, Sept 2007

Cunningham, Randall, American football player, Mar 1991

Davis, Glenn W., American football player, Yrbk 1946, *Obit* Yrbk 2005

Dorsett, Tony, American football player, Apr 1980

Esiason, Boomer, American football player, Nov 1995

Faulk, Marshall, American football player, Jan 2003

Favre, Brett, American football player, Nov 1996

Flutie, Doug, American football player, Oct 1985

Gifford, Frank, American football player and sportscaster, May 1964, Jan 1995

Gonzalez, Tony, American football player, Jan 2011

Green, Darrell, American football player, Jan 2001

Harris, Franco, American football player, June 1976

Harrison, James, American football player, Nov 2011

Harrison, Marvin, American football player, Aug 2001

Hayes, Bob, American sprinter and football player, Sept 1966, *Obit* Jan 2003

Hornung, Paul, American football player and sportscaster, Feb 1963

Jackson, Bo, American baseball and football player, June 1991

James, Edgerrin, American football player, Jan 2002

Johnson, Andre, American football player, Nov 2010

Johnson, Chris, American football player, Aug 2010

Johnson, Keyshawn, American football player, Oct 1999

Jurgensen, Sonny, American football player and sportscaster, June 1977

Kapp, Joe, football player and management consultant, Sept 1975

Kelly, Jim, American football player, Nov 1992

Kemp, Jack, American football player, congressman and Secretary of housing and urban development, Mar 1980, *Obit* Yrbk 2009

Largent, Steve, American congressman, June 1999

Law, Tajuan, American football player, Oct 2002

Lewis, Ray, American football player, Jan 2007

Lott, Ronnie, American investment manager and former football player, Feb 1994

Lujack, Johnny, football player, Yrbk 1947

Manning, Eli, American football player, Sept 2008

Manning, Peyton, American football player, Sept 1998

Marino, Dan, American football player and television sportscaster, Jan 1989

Matthews, Clay, American football player, Oct 2011

McNabb, Donovan, American football player, Jan 2004

McNair, Steve, American football player, Jan 2005, *Obit* Yrbk 2009

Monk, Art, American football player, Apr 1995

Montana, Joe, American football player, Sept 1983

Moon, Warren, American football player, Nov 1991

Morton, Craig, June 1978

Moss, Randy, American football player, Jan 2006

Namath, Joe, American football player, Yrbk 1966

Newton, Cam, American football player, Sept 2013

Ochocinco, Chad, American football player, Aug 2009

Payton, Walter, American football player, Nov 1985, *Obit* Jan 2000

Peabody, Endicott, governor, Mar 1964, *Obit* Feb 1998

Pennington, Chad, American football player, Oct 2009

Peterson, Adrian, American football player, Mar 2012

Plunkett, Jim, American football player, Sept 1971, Feb 1982
Rice, Jerry, American football player, Apr 1990
Rodgers, Aaron, American football player, Nov 2012
Rote, Kyle, American football player and sportscaster, May 1965, *Obit* Yrbk 2002
Sanders, Barry, American football player, Sept 1993
Sapp, Warren, American football player, Sept 2003
Seau, Junior, American football player, Sept 2001, *Obit* Yrbk 2012
Simms, Phil, American football player and sportscaster, Oct 1994
Smith, Bruce, American football player, Mar 1995
Smith, Emmitt, American football player, Nov 1994
Smith, Steve, American football player, Sept 2006
Stabler, Ken, American football player, Oct 1979
Staubach, Roger, American football player and real estate executive, Apr 1972
Suh, Ndamukong, American football player, Oct 2013
Taylor, Lawrence, American football player, July 1990
Tittle, Y. A., American football player, Mar 1964
Todd, Richard, American football player, May 1982
Tomlinson, LaDainian, American football player, Oct 2006
Unitas, Johnny, American football player, Feb 1962, *Obit* Yrbk 2002
Vick, Michael, American football player, Nov 2003
Vinatieri, Adam, American football player, Sept 2004
Walker, Herschel, American football player, Mar 1985
Warner, Kurt, American football player, Sept 2009
Welker, Wes, American football player, Nov 2012
White, Reggie, American football player and clergyman, Nov 1995, *Obit* Yrbk 2005
Williams, Ricky, American football player, Aug 1999
Woodson, Rod, American football player, Oct 2004

Young, Steve, American football player, Oct 1993

Football referees

Thomas, Sarah, American football referee, Nov 2010

Forensic scientists

Cox, Margaret, British archaeologist, Jan 2006
Goff, M. Lee, forensic entomologist, June 2001
Lee, Henry C., American forensic scientist, Aug 1996
Peccerelli, Fredy, Guatemalan forensic anthropologist, Jan 2004

Foresters

Heintzleman, B. Frank, June 1953, *Obit* Sept 1965
Watts, Lyle F., Oct 1946

Foundation officials

Arnold, Edwin G., American economic development consultant and foundation official, Sept 1947, *Obit* Jan 1961
Ashmore, Harry S., American newspaper editor and foundation official, Sept 1958, *Obit* Apr 1998
Barnard, Chester Irving, American telephone executive and foundation official, Mar 1945, *Obit* Sept 1961
Barnett, M. Robert, American journalist and foundation official, Jan 1950
Bevis, Palmer, American public relations executive, Apr 1953
Bundy, McGeorge, American presidential adviser, Mar 1962, *Obit* Jan 1997
Calkins, Robert DeBlois, economist and foundation official, Oct 1952, *Obit* Sept 1992
Carmichael, Oliver C., Jan 1946, *Obit* Yrbk 1966
Church, Samuel Harden, American railroad executive and foundation official, *Obit* Nov 1943
Cornelius, John C., June 1960
Dodge, Cleveland E., Mar 1954, *Obit* Feb 1983

Embree, Edwin R., Yrbk 1948, *Obit* Mar 1950
Erhard, Werner, self-actualization educator, Apr 1977
Espinoza Fuentes, Fernando, Ecuadorian biologist, Jan 2004
Faulk, Marshall, American football player, Jan 2003
Fosdick, Raymond Blaine, Feb 1945, *Obit* Sept 1972
Frank, Lawrence K., social scientist, Jan 1958, *Obit* Nov 1968
Gaither, H. Rowan, American foundation official, May 1953, *Obit* June 1961
Gorman, Thomas Francis Xavier, mental health official, Oct 1956, *Obit* July 1989
Gray, William H., American congressman and college fund administrator, Feb 1988, *Obit* Yrbk 2013
Harrison, Shelby M., Jan 1943
Haskins, Caryl Parker, American biophysicist, Feb 1958, *Obit* Feb 2002
Howe, Harold, American educator, Nov 1967, *Obit* Yrbk 2003
Johnson, Joseph E., American historian and foundation official, Nov 1950, *Obit* Jan 1991
Kimball, Lindsley Fiske, American social welfare leader, July 1951, *Obit* Oct 1992
Kirk, Paul, American senator and political party leader, Aug 1987
Kumm, Henry William, physician and foundation official, June 1955, *Obit* Mar 1991
Landwirth, Henri, American foundation official and hotel executive, Jan 2005
Mellon, Paul, American philanthropist, Apr 1966, *Obit* Apr 1999
Meyer, K. F., Mar 1952, *Obit* June 1974
Moore, Elisabeth Luce, American philanthropist and foundation official, Oct 1960, *Obit* Yrbk 2002
Morris, James T., American United Nations relief official, Mar 2005

Pifer, Alan J., American foundation official, Apr 1969, *Obit* Yrbk 2006

Reggio, Godfrey, American motion picture director and foundation official, July 1995

Reilly, William K., American conservationist and government official, July 1989

Rifkin, Jeremy, American social activist and foundation official, Feb 1986

Robins, Edward, *Obit* July 1943

Shriver, Eunice Kennedy, American social activist, July 1996, *Obit* Yrbk 2009

Sloan, George A., Jan 1952, *Obit* July 1955

Smith, Carleton, musicologist and foundation official, Apr 1961, *Obit* July 1984

Staats, Elmer Boyd, American government official, June 1967, *Obit* Yrbk 2011

Stahle, Nils K., Apr 1956

Stalnaker, John Marshall, psychologist, July 1958, *Obit* Oct 1990

Thomas, Franklin A., American lawyer and foundation official, Oct 1981

Vejjabul, Pierra, Mar 1964

Viscardi, Henry, American rehabilitation advocate, Jan 1954, Yrbk 1966, *Obit* Yrbk 2004

Wambugu, Florence, Kenyan plant geneticist, Jan 2004

Weaver, Warren, Apr 1952, *Obit* Feb 1979

Weidlein, Edward R., chemist and foundation official, July 1948, *Obit* Nov 1983

Wilkins, Roger W., American lawyer, journalist and educator, Aug 1994

Wilson, Marie C., American feminist, Sept 2004

Wynder, Ernst L., American oncologist and foundation official, Nov 1974, *Obit* Sept 1999

French horn players

Tuckwell, Barry, Australian horn player, July 1979

Fund raisers (Persons)

Emanuel, Rahm, American mayor, Apr 1998, Mar 2009

Kimball, Lindsley Fiske, American social welfare leader, July 1951, *Obit* Oct 1992

Funk musicians

Blackman, Cindy, American drummer, Oct 2010

Clinton, George, American singer and songwriter, July 1993

Furniture designers

Aalto, Alvar, Finnish architect, Apr 1948, *Obit* July 1976

Breuer, Marcel, American architect and furniture designer, Sept 1941, June 1960, *Obit* Aug 1981

Gehry, Frank, American architect, June 1987

Glaser, Milton, American illustrator and designer, May 1980

Le Corbusier, Swiss-French architect, Apr 1947, *Obit* Nov 1965

McCobb, Paul, furniture designer, Nov 1958, *Obit* Apr 1969

Mies van der Rohe, Ludwig, German-American architect, Oct 1951, *Obit* Oct 1969

Robsjohn-Gibbings, Terence Harold, American furniture and interior designer, Sept 1965, *Obit* Feb 1977

Saarinen, Eero, American architect, Oct 1949, *Obit* Nov 1961

Furniture industry executives

Ohlsson, Mikael, June 2013

Stanley, Thomas B., American governor, Yrbk 1955, *Obit* Oct 1970

Futurists

Gilder, George F., American economist and forecaster, Oct 1981

Johnson, Brian David, Futurist and author, July 2012

Kahn, Herman, American physicist and futurist, Oct 1962, *Obit* Aug 1983

King, Alexander, Scottish chemist and futurist, Jan 2002

Naisbitt, John, American social forecaster, Nov 1984

Toffler, Alvin, American futurist and writer, Apr 1975

Futurologists

Pearson, Ian, British futurologist, Jan 2005

Gamblers

Duke, Annie, American poker player, Aug 2006

Game inventors

Butts, Alfred, American architect and game inventor, July 1954, *Obit* June 1993

Gygax, Gary, American game inventor, Mar 2007, *Obit* Yrbk 2008

McGonigal, Jane, American computer game designer, Apr 2013

Persson, Markus (Notch), Swedish computer programmer and game inventor, Sept 2013

Sakaguchi, Hironobu, Japanese video game designer, Jan 2003

Suzuki, Yu, Japanese video game developer, Jan 2003

Tajiri, Satoshi, Japanese video game designer, Nov 2001

Wright, Will, American computer game designer, Feb 2004

Game players

Alekhine, Alexander, Russian chess player, *Obit* May 1946

Ashley, Maurice, Jamaican-American chess player, Sept 1999

Botvinnik, M. M., Russian chess player, June 1965, *Obit* July 1995

Brunson, Doyle, American poker player, Sept 2007

Carlsen, Magnus, Norwegian chess player, July 2013

Culbertson, Ely, bridge player, May 1940, *Obit* Mar 1956

Duke, Annie, American poker player, Aug 2006

Fischer, Bobby, American chess player, Oct 1963, May 1994, *Obit* Yrbk 2008

Fong, Dennis, American computer game player and executive, Aug 2012

Goren, Charles Henry, bridge player, Mar 1959, *Obit* July 1991

Hoppe, Willie, June 1947, *Obit* Apr 1959

Karpov, Anatoly, Russian chess player, Nov 1978

Kasparov, Garry, Russian chess player, Apr 1986

Kosteniuk, Alexandra, Russian chess player, Jan 2006

Kramnik, Vladimir, Russian chess player, Jan 2003

Lasker, Emanuel, chess player, *Obit* Mar 1941

Lee, Jeanette, American billiards player, Oct 2002

Mosconi, Willie, billiards player, June 1963, *Obit* Nov 1993

O'Sullivan, Ronnie, British snooker player, Apr 2013

Polgar, Susan, Hungarian chess player, Feb 2008

Reshevsky, Samuel, chess player, Feb 1955, *Obit* July 1992

Shahade, Jennifer, American chess player, Sept 2005

Sklansky, David, American poker player, Apr 2007

Smyslov, Vasilii, Russian chess player, July 1967, *Obit* Yrbk 2010

Spassky, Boris Vasilyevich, Russian chess player, Nov 1972

Wendel, Johnathan, American video game player, Apr 2007

Game show hosts

Barker, Bob, American game show host, Nov 1999

Cooper, Anderson, American television news anchor and talk show host, June 2006

Cullen, Bill, television game show host, Jan 1960, *Obit* Sept 1990

Philbin, Regis, American television talk show and game show host, Oct 1994

Sajak, Pat, American television game show host, July 1989

Vieira, Meredith, American television newscaster, Apr 2002

Gay rights activists

Croome, Rodney, Australian gay rights activist, Jan 2004

Solmonese, Joe, American gay rights activist, Oct 2009

Tafel, Rich, American gay political activist, Feb 2000

Wolfson, Evan, American lawyer and gay rights activist, July 2009

Generals

Abacha, Sani, Nigerian dictator, Sept 1996, *Obit* Aug 1998

Abizaid, John P., American general, Oct 2003

Abrams, Creighton Williams, American general, Oct 1968, *Obit* Oct 1974

Al-Bashir, Omar, Sudanese head of state, Jan 2005

Alanbrooke, Alan Francis Brooke, British field marshal, Jan 1941, *Obit* Sept 1963

Allen, Frank A., American general, Mar 1945, *Obit* Jan 1980

Allen, Terry, Nov 1943, *Obit* Nov 1969

Almond, Edward M., general, Mar 1951, *Obit* Aug 1979

Amin, Idi, Ugandan general and president, Feb 1973, *Obit* Yrbk 2003

Anderson, Alexander E., American general, *Obit* Feb 1943

Andreu Almazan, Juan, Mexican general and political leader, May 1940, *Obit* Yrbk 1965

Antonescu, Ion, Romanian dictator, Oct 1940, *Obit* July 1946

Aoun, Michel, Lebanese general and political leader, Mar 1990

Aramburu, Pedro Eugenio, Argentine president, Jan 1957, *Obit* Oct 1970

Assad, Hafez, Syrian president, July 1975, Apr 1992, *Obit* Aug 2000

Auchinleck, Claude John Eyre, British field marshal, Feb 1942, *Obit* May 1981

Babangida, Ibrahim, Nigerian general and head of state, Sept 1990

Badoglio, Pietro, Italian field marshal, Oct 1940, *Obit* Jan 1957

Bagramyan, Ivan K., Soviet general, Yrbk 1944, *Obit* Jan 1983

Baldomir, Alfredo, Uruguayan general and president, June 1942, *Obit* Mar 1948

Banzer Suarez, Hugo, Bolivian president, Sept 1973, *Obit* Sept 2002

Batista y Zaldivar, Fulgencio, Cuban general and president, Sept 1940, Apr 1952, *Obit* Oct 1973

Benavides, Oscar R., Peruvian president, *Obit* Aug 1945

Bennett, Henry Gordon, Australian general, Mar 1942, *Obit* Oct 1962

Bishop, Billy, Canadian air marshal, Sept 1941

Blamey, Thomas Albert, Australian general, June 1942, *Obit* July 1951

Bliss, Raymond W., American surgeon and general, Jan 1951, *Obit* Jan 1966

Boatner, Haydon L., American general, July 1952

Bock, Fedor von, German field marshal, Oct 1942, *Obit* June 1945

Bolte, Charles Lawrence, general, Jan 1954, *Obit* May 1989

Bonesteel, Charles H., American general, June 1942, *Obit* Sept 1964

Bozize, Francois, Central African Republic general and president, Jan 2005

Bradley, Omar Nelson, American general, July 1943, *Obit* May 1981

Brauchitsch, Walther von, German field marshal, Mar 1940, *Obit* Yrbk 1948

Broadhurst, Harry, May 1943

Brooke-Popham, Robert, Oct 1941, *Obit* Jan 1954

Brooks, Vincent, American general, June 2003

Brown, Albert Eger, Jan 1948

Browning, Frederick, June 1943, *Obit* Apr 1965

Budennyi, Semen M., Soviet field marshal, Sept 1941, *Obit* Yrbk 1973

Butler, Smedley D., American Marine corps general, *Obit* Aug 1940

Calles, Plutarco Elias, Mexican president, *Obit* Nov 1945

Candee, Robert C., May 1944

Carlson, Evans F., American Marine corps general, Oct 1943, *Obit* June 1947

Carmona, Antonio Oscar de Fragoso, Nov 1950, *Obit* May 1951

Carton de Wiart, Adrian, May 1940, *Obit* July 1963

Casey, George W., American general, Mar 2006

Castelnau, Noel Marie Joseph Edouard de Curieres de, French general, *Obit* May 1944

Castelo Branco, Humberto de Alencar, Brazilian president, Feb 1965, *Obit* Oct 1967

Cates, Clifton B., American Marine corps officer, Nov 1950, *Obit* Sept 1970

Catroux, Georges, May 1943, *Obit* Feb 1970

Cavallero, Ugo, *Obit* Oct 1943

Cedras, Raoul, Haitian general, July 1995

Chapman, Leonard F., American Marine corps general, July 1968, *Obit* Sept 2000

Chase, William C., Nov 1952

Chen Cheng, Chinese general, Sept 1941, *Obit* Apr 1965

Chen Yi, Chinese general, Oct 1959, *Obit* Feb 1972

Cherniakhovskii, Ivan Danilovich, Oct 1944, *Obit* Apr 1945

Chiang, Kai-shek, Chinese president, Jan 1940, May 1953, *Obit* May 1975

Chuikov, Vasilii Ivanovich, Soviet general, May 1943, *Obit* May 1982

Chun, Doo Hwan, Korean president, Mar 1981

Clay, Lucius D., American general, May 1945, June 1963, *Obit* June 1978

Cole-Hamilton, J. B., *Obit* Sept 1945

Collins, J. Lawton, American general, Nov 1949, *Obit* Oct 1987

Coningham, Arthur, British air marshal, Nov 1944, *Obit* Feb 1948

Costa e Silva, Arthur da, Sept 1967, *Obit* Feb 1970

Craig, Malin, Mar 1944, *Obit* Aug 1945

Crerar, Henry Duncan Graham, Canadian general, Nov 1944, *Obit* May 1965

Crist, William E., Nov 1945

Cushman, Robert Everton, American Marine Corps general, Nov 1972, *Obit* Apr 1985

Davidson, Garrison Holt, general, June 1957, *Obit* Feb 1993

Davis, Benjamin O., American general, Yrbk 1942, *Obit* Jan 1971

Davis, Robert C., *Obit* Oct 1944

Davison, Frederic Ellis, American general, Feb 1974

De Bono, Emilio, Italian field marshal, *Obit* Feb 1944

De Witt, John Lesesne, American general, July 1942

Decker, George H., American general, Jan 1961

Dempsey, Miles Christopher, Oct 1944, *Obit* July 1969

Devers, Jacob Loucks, general, Sept 1942, *Obit* Jan 1980

Devine, John M., American general, Jan 1948

Devoe, Ralph G., Oct 1944, *Obit* Nov 1966

Dill, John Greer, British field marshal, Feb 1941, *Obit* Yrbk 1944

Doihara, Kenji, Mar 1942, *Obit* Feb 1949

Dornberger, Walter, Feb 1965, *Obit* Sept 1980

Douglas of Kirtleside, William Sholto Douglas, British air marshal, June 1943, *Obit* Yrbk 1969

Dowding, Hugh Caswall Tremenheere Dowding, British air marshal, Nov 1940, *Obit* Apr 1970

Drum, Hugh A., July 1941, *Obit* Nov 1951

Dunwoody, Ann E., American general, Nov 2008

Eanes, Antonio dos Santos Ramalho, Portuguese president, Apr 1979

Easley, Claudius M., American general, *Obit* July 1945

Eddy, Manton S., general, Feb 1951, *Obit* June 1962

Eichelberger, Robert L., American general, Jan 1943, *Obit* Yrbk 1961

Ely, Paul, Oct 1954, *Obit* Mar 1975

Ershad, Hussain Mohammad, Bangladeshi prime minister, Nov 1984

Erskine, G. B., American Marine corps general, July 1946, *Obit* July 1973

Erskine, George, British general, Jan 1952, *Obit* Nov 1965

Estigarribia, Jose Felix, Paraguayan field marshal and president, Mar 1940, *Obit* Mar 1940

Eyadema, Gnassingbe, Togolese president, Apr 2002, *Obit* Yrbk 2005

Festing, Francis, Feb 1945

Figueiredo, Joao Baptista de Oliveira, Brazilian president, Jan 1980, *Obit* May 2000

Franchet d'Esperey, Louis Felix Marie Francois, French field marshal, *Obit* Sept 1942

Franco, Francisco, Spanish dictator, Mar 1942, Mar 1954, *Obit* Jan 1976

Franks, Tommy, American general, Jan 2002

Freyberg, Bernard Freyberg, Oct 1940, *Obit* Sept 1963

Fuqua, Stephen Ogden, Feb 1943

Galtieri, Leopoldo Fortunato, Argentine general and president, Aug 1982, *Obit* Yrbk 2003

Gamelin, Maurice Gustave, French general, Jan 1940, *Obit* July 1958

Gaulle, Charles de, French president, Sept 1940, June 1949, Apr 1960, *Obit* Yrbk 1970

Geiger, Roy S., American Marine general, July 1945, *Obit* Mar 1947

Geisel, Ernesto, Brazilian president, Aug 1975, *Obit* Nov 1996

George, Harold L., Yrbk 1942

Gerow, Leonard Townsend, Apr 1945, *Obit* Yrbk 1972

Giles, Barney McKinney, general, July 1944, *Obit* Aug 1984

Giraud, Henri, French general, Yrbk 1942, *Obit* Apr 1949

Golikov, Filipp Ivanovich, Soviet general, Apr 1943, *Obit* Sept 1980

Goring, Hermann, German Nazi leader, Aug 1941, *Obit* Nov 1946

Gott, William Henry Ewart, *Obit* Oct 1942

Gowon, Yakubu, Nigerian general and head of state, June 1970

Graham, Wallace Harry, physician and general, Feb 1947, *Obit* Mar 1996

Graves, William Sidney, general, *Obit* Mar 1940

Graziani, Rodolfo, Italian field marshal and colonial administrator, Apr 1941, *Obit* Mar 1955

Grechko, Andrei Antonovich, Soviet field marshal, Nov 1968, *Obit* June 1976

Greene, Wallace M., American Marine corps general, June 1965, *Obit* Aug 2003

Gregory, Edmund B., Sept 1945, *Obit* Mar 1961

Griswold, Oscar W., American general, Sept 1943, *Obit* Yrbk 1959

Grivas, Giorgios, Oct 1964, *Obit* Mar 1974

Groninger, Homer M., American general, Aug 1945

Gross, Charles P., Mar 1946, *Obit* Sept 1975

Gruenther, Alfred M., American general, Yrbk 1950, *Obit* July 1983

Guillaumat, Marie Louis Adolphe, *Obit* July 1940

Gullion, Allen W., Feb 1943, *Obit* July 1946

Hammerstein-Equord, Kurt, German general, *Obit* June 1943

Handy, Thomas T., American general, Sept 1951, *Obit* June 1982

Harding of Petherton, John Harding, British field marshal, Oct 1952

Harington, Charles, British general, *Obit* Yrbk 1940

Harkins, Paul D., American general, Apr 1964

Harrison, William K., American general, July 1952, *Obit* Aug 1987

Hartle, Russell P., American general, June 1942, *Obit* Jan 1962

Hawley, Paul R., Apr 1946, *Obit* Jan 1966

Hayashi, Senjuro, *Obit* Mar 1943

Hayden, Michael, American general and intelligence official, Nov 2006

Hernandez Martinez, Maximiliano, Salvadoran general and president, June 1942, *Obit* June 1966

Hershey, Lewis Blaine, American general and government official, June 1941, June 1951, *Obit* July 1977

Hertzog, James Barry Munnik, South African prime minister, *Obit* Jan 1943

Heusinger, Adolf, German general, Feb 1956

Ho, Ying-Chin, Taiwanese general, Oct 1942, *Obit* Jan 1988

Hodes, Henry I., American general, Feb 1959, *Obit* Apr 1962

Hodge, John R., June 1945, *Obit* Jan 1964

Hodges, Courtney H., May 1941, *Obit* Feb 1966

Holcomb, Thomas, July 1942, *Obit* July 1965

Honjo, Shigeru, *Obit* Jan 1946

Horn, Carl von, Swedish general, Nov 1967

Horwood, William T. F., *Obit* Feb 1944

Huebner, Clarence R., Oct 1949, *Obit* Nov 1972

Hull, John E., Apr 1954

Hume, Edgar Erskine, Aug 1944, *Obit* Mar 1952

Huntziger, Charles, French general, Yrbk 1941, *Obit* Yrbk 1941

Ibanez del Campo, Carlos, Chilean president, Yrbk 1952, *Obit* July 1960

Ironside, William Edmund Ironside, British field marshal, May 1940, *Obit* Nov 1959

Ismay, Hastings Lionel Ismay, British general, Apr 1943, *Obit* Feb 1966

Jarman, Sanderford, Sept 1942, *Obit* Yrbk 1955

Johnson, Harold K., American general, May 1966, *Obit* Nov 1983

Johnson, Hugh S., American general and government official, Sept 1940, *Obit* June 1942

Juin, Alphonse, French field marshal, Aug 1943, *Obit* Mar 1967

Justo, Agustin P., Argentine general and president, *Obit* Mar 1943

Kan-In, Kotohito, *Obit* June 1945

Keitel, Wilhelm, German field marshal, Sept 1940, *Obit* Nov 1946

Kennedy, Claudia, general, Jan 2000

Kenney, George C., American general, Jan 1943, *Obit* Oct 1977

Kesselring, Albert, German field marshal, Nov 1942, *Obit* Oct 1960

Key, William, July 1943, *Obit* Mar 1959

Kirk, Norman T., American surgeon and general, Feb 1944, *Obit* Nov 1960

Kleist, Ewald von, German field marshal, July 1943, *Obit* Jan 1955

Klimecki, Tadeusz A., *Obit* Aug 1943

Koenig, Pierre, French general, Sept 1944, *Obit* Nov 1970

Konev, Ivan S., Soviet field marshal, Oct 1943, Jan 1956, *Obit* July 1973

Korner, Theodor, July 1951, *Obit* Mar 1957

Krueger, Walter, American general, Apr 1943, *Obit* Oct 1967

Kuchler, Georg von, Sept 1943

Kulik, Grigory, July 1942

Lanusse, Alejandro A., Argentine general and president, Apr 1973, *Obit* Nov 1996

Lattre, Jean de, French field marshal, Jan 1945, *Obit* Feb 1952

Laycock, R. E., May 1944, *Obit* May 1968

Lear, Ben, July 1942, *Obit* Jan 1967

Leclerc, Jacques, Oct 1944, *Obit* Yrbk 1947

Lee, John C. H., July 1944, *Obit* Nov 1958

Leese, Oliver, British general, Yrbk 1944, *Obit* Yrbk 1991

Lejeune, John Archer, marine general, *Obit* Jan 1943

Lemnitzer, Lyman Louis, American general, Nov 1955, *Obit* Jan 1989

Lentaigne, Walter D. A., July 1944, *Obit* Oct 1955

Lerch, Archer L., Nov 1945, *Obit* Oct 1947

Li Zongren, Chinese general, Nov 1942, *Obit* Mar 1969

Littlejohn, Robert McGowan, Sept 1946, *Obit* July 1982

Loeb, Fritz, *Obit* Aug 1940

MacArthur, Douglas, American general, Oct 1941, May 1948, *Obit* May 1964

Mackay, Iven Giffard, Apr 1941, *Obit* Jan 1967

Malinovskii, Rodion IAkovlevich, Soviet field marshal, Mar 1944, Nov 1960, *Obit* May 1967

Mannerheim, Carl Gustaf Emil, Finnish field marshal and president, Apr 1940, *Obit* Feb 1951

Manstein, Erich von, German field marshal, Oct 1942, *Obit* Sept 1973

Martel, Giffard Le Quesne, British general, July 1943, *Obit* Nov 1958

Martin, Charles H., *Obit* Nov 1946

Mason-MacFarlane, Noel, British general, Feb 1943

Mathewson, Lemuel, Yrbk 1952, *Obit* Apr 1970

McAuliffe, Anthony C., American general, Feb 1950, *Obit* Oct 1975

McCaffrey, Barry, American general and government official, July 1997

McChrystal, Stanley, American general, Sept 2009

McCoy, Frank Ross, general, Nov 1945, *Obit* Sept 1954

McCreery, Richard L., British general, May 1945, *Obit* Yrbk 1967

McNair, Lesley James, American general, Nov 1942, *Obit* Sept 1944

McNaughton, Andrew, Nov 1942, *Obit* Nov 1966

Medici, Emilio Garrastazu, Brazilian president, Oct 1971, *Obit* Jan 1986

Medina Angarita, Isaias, Venezuelan general and president, Mar 1942, *Obit* Nov 1953

Menninger, William Claire, Sept 1945, *Obit* Nov 1966

Merrill, Frank D., American general, July 1944, *Obit* Feb 1956

Metaxas, Ioannis, Greek general and dictator, Yrbk 1940, *Obit* Mar 1941

Mihailovic, Draza, Yugoslav general and underground leader, Mar 1942, *Obit* Sept 1946

Mobutu Sese Seko, Zairian president, Sept 1966, May 1997, *Obit* Nov 1997

Montgomery of Alamein, Bernard Law Montgomery, British field marshal, Yrbk 1942, *Obit* May 1976

Moore, Bryant E., American general, Feb 1949, *Obit* Mar 1951

Morgan, Frederick Edgeworth, Feb 1946, *Obit* May 1967

Musharraf, Pervez, Pakistani general and president, Mar 2001, Jan 2002

Naguib, Mohammed, Egyptian general, Oct 1952

Nam, Il, Sept 1951, *Obit* Apr 1976

Namphy, Henri, Haitian general, Sept 1988

Navarre, Henri, Nov 1953

Ne Win, Burmese president, Apr 1971, *Obit* Yrbk 2003

Newall, Cyril Louis Norton, Aug 1940

Nimeiri, Gaafar Mohammed, Sudanese president, Nov 1977, *Obit* Yrbk 2009

Nogues, Charles, Feb 1943, *Obit* June 1971

Noriega, Manuel Antonio, Panamanian general and head of state, Mar 1988

Nye, Archibald E., Feb 1942, *Obit* Jan 1968

Obasanjo, Olusegun, Nigerian president, July 1999

Odierno, Raymond, American general, Nov 2009

Ojukwu, Chukwuemeka Odumegwu, Nigerian political

leader and general, Feb 1969, *Obit* Yrbk 2012

Okonkwo, Festus, Nigerian general, Jan 2005

Oliver, Lunsford E., Sept 1947

Ongania, Juan Carlos, Argentine president, Oct 1968, *Obit* Aug 1995

Ovando Candia, Alfredo, Bolivian general and president, Mar 1970, *Obit* Mar 1982

Pace, Peter, American Marine corps general, June 2006

Pai, Chung-hsi, Nov 1942, *Obit* Feb 1967

Papagos, Alexandros, Nov 1951, *Obit* Yrbk 1955

Park, Chung Hee, Korean president, Jan 1969, *Obit* Jan 1980

Patch, Alexander McCarrell, American general, May 1943, *Obit* Jan 1946

Pate, Randolph McCall, general, Sept 1958, *Obit* Oct 1961

Patton, George S., American general, Jan 1943, *Obit* Feb 1946

Pearkes, George Randolph, Nov 1957

Peirse, R. E. C., Sept 1941, *Obit* Oct 1970

Penaranda, Enrique, Bolivian president, Jan 1940

Peron, Juan Domingo, Argentine president, June 1944, Feb 1974, *Obit* Feb 1974

Persons, Wilton B., American general and presidential adviser, May 1953, *Obit* Nov 1977

Petain, Henri Philippe, French field marshal, Aug 1940, *Obit* Sept 1951

Petraeus, David H., American general and intelligence official, Apr 2007

Pile, Frederick Alfred, British general, Feb 1942, *Obit* Yrbk 1991

Pinochet Ugarte, Augusto, Chilean general and president, Yrbk 1974, *Obit* Yrbk 2007

Plaek Phibunsongkhram, Thai prime minister, Sept 1951, *Obit* Sept 1964

Portal of Hungerford, Charles Frederick Algernon Portal, British air marshal, Mar 1941, *Obit* June 1971

Porter, William N., Aug 1945, *Obit* Apr 1973

Prezan, Constantin, *Obit* Oct 1943

Price, Harrison J., American general, *Obit* Oct 1945

Qassim, Abdul Karim, Iraqi general and prime minister, Nov 1959, *Obit* Mar 1963

Rahman, Ziaur, Bangladeshi president, June 1981

Ramirez, Pedro Pablo, Aug 1943, *Obit* Sept 1962

Ramos, Fidel V., Filipino president, Mar 1994

Razmara, Hossein Ali, Iranian prime minister, Oct 1950, *Obit* Mar 1951

Reckord, Milton A., Mar 1945

Reichenau, Walter von, German field marshal, *Obit* Mar 1942

Rios Montt, Jose Efrain, Guatemalan president, May 1983

Robertson of Oakridge, Brian Hubert Robertson, Sept 1948, *Obit* June 1974

Rodriguez, Andres, Paraguayan general and president, Sept 1991, *Obit* June 1997

Roh, Tae Woo, Korean president, Feb 1988

Rojas Pinilla, Gustavo, Colombian general and president, June 1956, *Obit* Mar 1975

Rokossovskii, Konstantin K., Soviet field marshal, Jan 1944, *Obit* Oct 1968

Rommel, Erwin, German field marshal, Aug 1942, *Obit* Yrbk 1944

Rose, Maurice, American general, *Obit* May 1945

Rundstedt, Karl Rudolf Gerd von, German field marshal, Nov 1941, *Obit* Apr 1953

Rupertus, William H., *Obit* May 1945

Schomburg, August, Nov 1960

Schwarzkopf, H. Norman, American general, May 1991, *Obit* Yrbk 2013

Scobie, Ronald M., Feb 1945

Shang Zhen, July 1944

Shaposhnikov, Boris, Soviet field marshal, Mar 1942, *Obit* May 1945

Shelton, Hugh, American general, Aug 1998

Shepherd, Lemuel C., American Marine corps general, Feb 1952, *Obit* Oct 1990

Short, Walter Campbell, general, Jan 1946, *Obit* Oct 1949

Shoup, David M., American Marine Corps general, Jan 1960, *Obit* Mar 1983

Sikorski, Wladyslaw, Polish general and statesman, Jan 1940, *Obit* Aug 1943

Simonds, Guy Granville, Canadian general, Oct 1943, *Obit* July 1974

Simpson, William H., Feb 1945, *Obit* Oct 1980

Slim, William Joseph Slim, British field marshal, June 1945, *Obit* Feb 1971

Smith, Holland M., American Marine corps general, Apr 1945, *Obit* Mar 1967

Smuts, Jan Christiaan, South African prime minister, Aug 1941, *Obit* Oct 1950

Snyder, Howard McC., Feb 1955, *Obit* Nov 1970

Soeharto, Indonesian president, June 1967, Oct 1992, *Obit* Yrbk 2008

Somoza, Anastasio, Nicaraguan dictator, June 1942, *Obit* Yrbk 1956

Somoza, Anastasio, Nicaraguan general and president, Mar 1978, *Obit* Nov 1980

Speidel, Hans, German general, Apr 1952, *Obit* Feb 1985

Spinola, Antonio de, Portuguese general and president, Sept 1974, *Obit* Nov 1996

Stilwell, Joseph Warren, American general, May 1942, *Obit* Nov 1946

Stroessner, Alfredo, Paraguayan general and president, Yrbk 1958, Mar 1981, *Obit* Yrbk 2007

Stuart, Kenneth, Feb 1944, *Obit* Yrbk 1945

Sturdee, V. A. H., July 1942

Sugiyama, Hajime, Japanese field marshal, *Obit* Oct 1945

Sultan, Daniel I., Jan 1945, *Obit* Feb 1947

Surles, Alexander D., Nov 1945, *Obit* Yrbk 1947

Swaythling, Jean Marcia, Sept 1942

Swing, Joseph May, general and immigration official, Apr 1959, *Obit* Feb 1985

Taylor, Telford, lawyer and historian, Yrbk 1948, *Obit* Aug 1998

Tedder, Arthur William Tedder, British air marshal, Jan 1943, *Obit* Oct 1967

Templer, Gerald Walter Robert, British field marshal, July 1952, *Obit* Jan 1980

Ter Poorten, Hein, Mar 1942

Thanom Kittikachorn, Thai field marshal and prime minister, Yrbk 1969, *Obit* Yrbk 2004

Thimayya, Kodendera Subayya, Apr 1954, *Obit* Feb 1966

Timoshenko, Semen Konstantinovich, Soviet field marshal, Aug 1941, *Obit* May 1970

Tinker, Clarence Leonard, American general, June 1942

Tojo, Hideki, Japanese general and prime minister, Yrbk 1941, *Obit* Jan 1949

Tolbukhin, Fedor Ivanovich, Soviet field marshal, May 1945, *Obit* Yrbk 1949

Torrijos Herrera, Omar, Panamanian dictator, July 1973, *Obit* Sept 1981

Trudeau, Arthur Gilbert, general, Apr 1958, *Obit* Aug 1991

Trujillo Molina, Rafael Leonidas, Dominican general and president, July 1941, *Obit* Oct 1961

Truscott, Lucian King, American general, May 1945, *Obit* Nov 1965

Ulio, James Alexander, Sept 1945

Umberto, Oct 1943, *Obit* May 1983

Upshur, William P., *Obit* Sept 1943

Urquhart, Robert E., British general, Yrbk 1944, *Obit* Feb 1989

Vandegrift, A. A., American Marine corps general, Jan 1943, *Obit* June 1973

Vasilevskii, Aleksandr M., Soviet field marshal, Oct 1943, *Obit* Mar 1978

Vatutin, Nikolai Fedorovich, Soviet general, Feb 1944

Vaughan, Harry H., American general, Mar 1949, *Obit* July 1981

Velasco Alvarado, Juan, Peruvian president, June 1970, *Obit* Mar 1978

Videla, Jorge Rafael, Argentine general and president, Apr 1978, *Obit* Yrbk 2013

Voroshilov, Kliment Efremovich, Soviet field marshal and communist leader, Mar 1941, *Obit* Jan 1970

Wainwright, Jonathan Mayhew, American general, May 1942, *Obit* Nov 1953

Waitt, Alden H., Sept 1947

Walker, Walton Harris, American general, Sept 1950, *Obit* Jan 1951

Ward, William E., American general, Nov 2005

Watson, Edwin M., American general, *Obit* Apr 1945

Weaver, Walter Reed, *Obit* Yrbk 1944

Wedemeyer, Albert, American general, Jan 1945, *Obit* Feb 1990

Westmoreland, William C., American general, June 1961, *Obit* Nov 2005

Weygand, Maxime, French general, Jan 1940, *Obit* Mar 1965

Wheeler, Earle G., American general, Nov 1965, *Obit* Feb 1976

White, I. D., American general, Yrbk 1958, *Obit* Aug 1990

Whitney, Courtney, June 1951, *Obit* May 1969

Wilby, Francis B., Aug 1945, *Obit* Jan 1966

Wilson, Henry Maitland Wilson, Oct 1943, *Obit* Feb 1965

Wingate, Orde Charles, British general, *Obit* May 1944

Yamut, Nuri, May 1952

Zahedi, Fazlollah, Feb 1954, *Obit* Nov 1963

Zhu De, Chinese general, Nov 1942, *Obit* Aug 1976

Zhukov, Georgii Konstantinovich, Soviet field marshal, Feb 1942, Apr 1955, *Obit* Sept 1974

Zia-ul-Haq, Mohammad, Pakistani general and president, June 1980, *Obit* Sept 1988

Geneticists

Anderson, William French, American geneticist, Oct 1994

Borlaug, Norman, American plant pathologist and geneticist, July 1971, *Obit* Yrbk 2009

Brenner, Sydney, British geneticist, Jan 2007

Cavalli-Sforza, Luigi Luca, Italian geneticist, Aug 1997

Dobzhansky, Theodosius Grigorievich, American geneticist, Sept 1962, *Obit* Feb 1976

Haldane, J. B. S., British geneticist, Nov 1940, *Obit* Jan 1965

Hamer, Dean H., geneticist, June 1997

Harris, Eva, American geneticist, Mar 2004

Hartwell, Leland, American geneticist, Nov 1999

Jacob, Francois, French bacteriologist, Yrbk 1966, *Obit* Yrbk 2013

Jones, Monty, Sierra Leonen plant geneticist and rice breeder, Jan 2007

Krim, Mathilde, American geneticist and virologist, Aug 1987

Lysenko, Trofim, Russian geneticist, Oct 1952, *Obit* Feb 1977

Margulis, Lynn, American microbiologist, July 1992, *Obit* Yrbk 2012

McClintock, Barbara, American geneticist, Mar 1984, *Obit* Nov 1992

Paabo, Svante, Swedish geneticist, Feb 2007

Rowley, Janet D., American geneticist, Mar 2001

Rubin, Eddy, American geneticist, Jan 2006

Sager, Ruth, geneticist, July 1967, *Obit* June 1997

Salzano, Francisco M., Brazilian geneticist, Jan 2006

Skolnick, Mark H., geneticist, June 1997

Stefansson, Kari, Icelandic geneticist, Jan 2003

Wambugu, Florence, Kenyan plant geneticist, Jan 2004

Wells, Spencer, American geneticist, Mar 2008

Yamanaka, Shinya, Japanese geneticist, June 2013

Geochemists

Brown, Harrison Scott, American geochemist, July 1955, *Obit* Feb 1987

Geographers

Adkinson, Burton W., American geographer and librarian, June 1959

Bingham, Hiram, American explorer and senator, Mar 1951, *Obit* Sept 1956

Birdseye, Claude Hale, American topographer, *Obit* July 1941

Bowman, Isaiah, American geographer, Jan 1945, *Obit* Feb 1950

Burwash, Lachlin Taylor, *Obit* Feb 1941

Chapman, Daniel A., Apr 1959

Chilingarov, Artur, Russian polar explorer, Jan 2007

Cook, Frederick Albert, American physician and explorer, *Obit* Sept 1940

Flaherty, Robert Joseph, American film director and explorer, Mar 1949, *Obit* Sept 1951

Fuchs, Vivian, English explorer, Oct 1958, *Obit* Jan 2000

Granger, Walter, *Obit* Oct 1941

Harvey, David, British geographer, Aug 2008

Haushofer, Karl, German geographer, Apr 1942, *Obit* Sept 1946

Hayhoe, Katharine, Feb 2012

Hempleman-Adams, David, British explorer, Jan 2004

Herlin, Emil, *Obit* Feb 1943

Hitchcock, Charles B., Oct 1954, *Obit* May 1969

Houghton, John Theodore, British climatologist, Jan 2004

Johnson, Osa Helen Leighty, American explorer and documentary filmmaker, Apr 1940, *Obit* Feb 1953

Kimble, George H. T., Oct 1952

MacMillan, Donald, American explorer, Sept 1948, *Obit* Nov 1970

Redway, Jacques W., *Obit* Jan 1943

Roberts, Walter Orr, climatologist, Yrbk 1960, *Obit* May 1990

Ronne, Finn, Norwegian-American explorer, Feb 1948, *Obit* Mar 1980

Thomas, William Leroy, Mar 1958

Wilkins, Hubert, Australian explorer and geographer, Jan 1957, *Obit* Feb 1959

Worsley, Frank Arthur, New Zealand ship captain and explorer, *Obit* Mar 1943

Geologists

Anderson, Don L., American geophysicist, Oct 2002

Arsuaga, Juan Luis, Spanish paleontologist, Jan 2006

Bakker, Robert T., American paleontologist, Aug 1995

Ballard, Robert D., American oceanographer, June 1986

Banfield, Jillian Fiona, Australian geologist, Feb 2000

Bennett, Hugh Hammond, American soil scientist, Yrbk 1946, *Obit* Oct 1960

Blatchley, W. S., American entomologist and geologist, *Obit* July 1940

Bullard, Edward Crisp, English geophysicist, Sept 1954, *Obit* May 1980

Burns, H. S. M., May 1954, *Obit* Yrbk 1971

Casey, Richard Gardiner Casey, Australian governor-general, Jan 1940, *Obit* Aug 1976

Chapman, Sydney, English geophysicist, July 1957, *Obit* Sept 1970

Clark, Eugenie, American oceanographer, Sept 1953

Colbert, Edwin Harris, American paleontologist, Sept 1965, *Obit* Feb 2002

Cousteau, Fabien, Aquatic filmmaker and oceanographer, June 2012

De Geer, Gerard, *Obit* Sept 1943

Dubois, Eugene, Dutch anthropologist and paleontologist, *Obit* May 1941

Egloff, Gustav, Sept 1940

Ewing, Maurice, American geophysicist, Jan 1953, *Obit* June 1974

Fish, Marie Poland, oceanographer, Oct 1941, *Obit* Apr 1989

Fleming, John A., May 1940, *Obit* Oct 1956

Fortey, Richard A., British paleontologist, Sept 2005

Fowler-Billings, Katharine Stevens, geologist, Jan 1940

Grotzinger, John, Apr 2013

Hendrickson, Sue, paleontologist, Oct 2001

Herndon, J. Marvin, American geophysicist, Nov 2003

Hill, Robert Thomas, geologist, *Obit* Sept 1941

Holman, Eugene, May 1948, *Obit* Oct 1962

Hrdlicka, Ales, anthropologist and paleontologist, Nov 1941, *Obit* Oct 1943

Iselin, Columbus O'Donnell, Nov 1948, *Obit* Feb 1971

Jefferts Schori, Katharine, American bishop, Sept 2006

Kellogg, Remington, paleontologist, Nov 1949

Keys, David A., Oct 1958

Leakey, Mary D., British anthropologist and paleontologist, Apr 1985, *Obit* Feb 1997

Leakey, Meave, Kenyan anthropologist and paleontologist, June 2002

Lehmann, Inge, Danish geophysicist, Nov 1962

Lindsley, Thayer, Jan 1957, *Obit* July 1976

Lordkipanidze, David, Georgian paleontologist, Jan 2005

Lynch, John Joseph, priest and seismologist, Oct 1946, *Obit* Aug 1987

Masursky, Harold, geologist, Aug 1986, *Obit* Oct 1990

Merriam, John C., *Obit* Yrbk 1945

Novacek, Michael J., American paleontologist and museum curator, Sept 2002

Nylander, Olof O., *Obit* Sept 1943

Odishaw, Hugh, scientific administrator, Feb 1971, *Obit* June 1984

Perret, Frank Alvord, *Obit* Mar 1943

Piccard, Jacques, Swiss oceanographer, Yrbk 1965, *Obit* Yrbk 2009

Press, Frank, American geophysicist and presidential adviser, July 1966

Revelle, Roger, American oceanographer, Mar 1957, *Obit* Sept 1991

Richter, Charles F., American seismologist, May 1975, *Obit* Nov 1985

Sayles, R. W., *Obit* Yrbk 1942

Scaturro, Pasquale, American geophysicist, mountaineer and rafter, Oct 2005

Schmitt, Harrison H., American senator, geologist and astronaut, July 1974

Schopf, J. William, American geologist, May 1995

Schuchert, Charles, *Obit* Jan 1943

Sereno, Paul C., American paleontologist, June 1997

Shoemaker, Eugene Merle, planetary geologist, June 1967, *Obit* Oct 1997

Simonds, Frederic W., *Obit* May 1941

Simpson, George Gaylord, American paleontologist, Yrbk 1964, *Obit* Jan 1985

Spilhaus, Athelstan F., American meteorologist and oceanographer, June 1965, *Obit* June 1998

Stewart, Harris B., oceanographer, Mar 1968

Thompson, Alleen, June 1965

Thompson, Lonnie, American glaciologist, Jan 2004

Vrba, Elisabeth S., South African paleontologist, June 1997

Wasserburg, Gerald Joseph, American professor of geology and geophysics, Mar 1986

Weng Wenhao, Nov 1948

Wilson, John Tuzo, Canadian geophysicist and educator, Apr 1973, *Obit* Aug 1993

Woodward, Arthur Smith, British paleontologist, *Obit* Oct 1944

Wright, Berlin H., *Obit* Jan 1941

Geophysicists

Bullard, Edward Crisp, English geophysicist, Sept 1954, *Obit* May 1980

Fleming, John A., May 1940, *Obit* Oct 1956

Herndon, J. Marvin, American geophysicist, Nov 2003

Lehmann, Inge, Danish geophysicist, Nov 1962

Lynch, John Joseph, priest and seismologist, Oct 1946, *Obit* Aug 1987

Odishaw, Hugh, scientific administrator, Feb 1971, *Obit* June 1984

Press, Frank, American geophysicist and presidential adviser, July 1966

Geriatricians

Thomas, William H., American geriatrician, Jan 2006

Gerontologists

Butler, Robert N., American gerontologist and psychiatrist, Jan 1997, *Obit* Yrbk 2010

Comfort, Alex, English physician, novelist and poet, Sept 1974, *Obit* Aug 2000

Cowdry, E. V., anatomist and gerontologist, Jan 1948

Glass artists

Chihuly, Dale, American glass artist, Aug 1995

Golfers

Bagger, Mianne, Danish golfer, Jan 2006

Ballesteros, Seve, Spanish golfer, Sept 1980, *Obit* Yrbk 2011

Barber, Jerry, golfer, Apr 1962, *Obit* Nov 1994

Beard, Frank, American golfer, May 1970

Berg, Patty, American golfer, Sept 1940, *Obit* Yrbk 2007

Boros, Julius, American golfer, Nov 1968, *Obit* Aug 1994

Bradley, Pat, golfer, Feb 1994

Casper, Billy, American golfer, July 1966

Cink, Stewart, American golfer, Feb 2010

Couples, Fred, American golfer, July 1993

Creamer, Paula, American golfer, May 2011

Crenshaw, Ben, American golfer, Sept 1985

Duval, David, American golfer, Oct 1999

Elder, Lee, American golfer, Aug 1976

Els, Ernie, South African golfer, Jan 2003

Faldo, Nick, English golfer, Sept 1992

Fleck, Jack, golfer, Sept 1955

Garcia, Sergio, Spanish golfer, Mar 2001

Hogan, Ben, American golfer, Oct 1948, *Obit* Oct 1997

Immelman, Trevor, South African golfer, Oct 2008

Inkster, Juli, American golfer, Sept 2002

Johnson, Zach, American golfer, Jan 2008

Little, William Lawson, Aug 1940

Littler, Gene, golfer, July 1956

Lopez, Nancy, American golfer, Sept 1978

Mangrum, Lloyd, American golfer, Sept 1951, *Obit* Jan 1974

McIlroy, Rory, Irish golfer, Nov 2011

Mickelson, Phil, American golfer, Mar 2002

Middlecoff, Cary, golfer, July 1952, *Obit* Nov 1998

Miller, Johnny, American golfer, Sept 1974

Nelson, Byron, American golfer, Mar 1945, *Obit* Yrbk 2007

Nicklaus, Jack, American golfer, Nov 1962

Norman, Greg, Australian golfer, Aug 1989

Ochoa, Lorena, Mexican golfer, Jan 2007

Ogilvy, Geoff, Australian golfer, Jan 2006

Pak, Se Ri, Korean golfer, Jan 1999

Palmer, Arnold, American golfer, Sept 1960

Player, Gary, South African golfer, Nov 1961

Pressel, Morgan, American golfer, Nov 2007

Price, Nick, Zimbabwean golfer, June 1996

Ray, Ted, *Obit* Oct 1943

Rodriguez, Chi Chi, American golfer, Oct 1969

Singh, Jeev Milkha, Indian golfer, Jan 2007

Snead, Sam, American golfer, June 1949, *Obit* Yrbk 2002

Sorenstam, Annika, Swedish golfer, Jan 2002

Stranahan, Frank, Sept 1951, *Obit* Yrbk 2013

Suggs, Louise, American golfer, Jan 1962

Thompson, Alexis, American golfer, June 2012

Trevino, Lee, American golfer, Nov 1971

Tseng, Yani, Taiwanese golfer, Sept 2011

Venturi, Ken, American golfer and sportscaster, Apr 1966, *Obit* Yrbk 2013

Wall, Art, American golfer, Yrbk 1959, *Obit* Feb 2002

Watson, Bubba (Gerry Lester), American golfer, Feb 2013

Watson, Tom, American golfer, July 1979

Webb, Karrie, Australian golfer, Aug 2001

Weiskopf, Tom, American golfer, Nov 1973

Whitworth, Kathy, American golfer, Apr 1976

Woods, Tiger, American golfer, Nov 1997

Worsham, Lew, golfer, Jan 1954, *Obit* Jan 1991

Wright, Mickey, American golfer, Jan 1965

Zaharias, Babe Didrikson, American track athlete and golfer, Apr 1947, *Obit* Yrbk 1956

Gospel musicians

Adams, Yolanda, American gospel singer, Mar 2002

Carter, Jimmy, American gospel singer, Oct 2001

Cleveland, James, American clergyman and gospel singer, Aug 1985, *Obit* Apr 1991

Fountain, Clarence, American gospel singer, Oct 2001

Franklin, Kirk, American gospel rap singer, Mar 2000

Jackson, Mahalia, American gospel singer, Oct 1957, *Obit* Mar 1972

Jones, Bobby, American gospel singer, June 2002

McClurkin, Donnie, American gospel singer and clergyman, Apr 2007

Patty, Sandi, American gospel singer, Feb 2004

Scott, George, American gospel singer, Oct 2001, *Obit* Yrbk 2005

Gossip columnists

Graham, Sheilah, American gossip columnist, Oct 1969, *Obit* Jan 1989

Parsons, Louella, American gossip columnist, Oct 1940, *Obit* Oct 1973

Smith, Liz, American gossip columnist, May 1987

Government employees

Baldrige, Letitia, columnist, social secretary and public relations executive, Feb 1988, *Obit* Yrbk 2013

Biaggi, Mario, congressman, Jan 1986

Biller, Moe, American labor leader, June 1987, *Obit* Yrbk 2004

Bradley, Tom, American lawyer and mayor, Nov 1973, Oct 1992, *Obit* Jan 1999

Clement, Frank Goad, American governor, July 1955, *Obit* Yrbk 1969

Coleman, Ronnie, American bodybuilder and policeman, Feb 2007

Farina, Dennis, American actor, *Obit* Yrbk 2013

Knight, Frances G., government employee, Oct 1955, *Obit* Nov 1999

Krivitsky, W. G., Soviet intelligence service agent, *Obit* Mar 1941

Malkin, Peter Z., Israeli intelligence agent, Jan 2003

McEntee, Gerald, American labor leader, Oct 2000

Montagu, Ewen, British intelligence official and lawyer, June 1956, *Obit* Sept 1985

Reyes, Silvestre, American congressman, Sept 2007

Rizzo, Frank Lazarro, American mayor, Mar 1973, *Obit* Sept 1991

Rowley, James Joseph, secret service official, Jan 1963, *Obit* Jan 1993

Sorlie, Robert, Norwegian firefighter and sled dog racer, Jan 2005

Wilt, Fred, runner and FBI agent, Oct 1952, *Obit* Nov 1994

Government officials

Aandahl, Fred G., American governor, Sept 1958, *Obit* May 1966

Abbott, Douglas, Canadian supreme court justice, June 1949

Abbott, Edwin Milton, American lawyer, *Obit* Jan 1941

Abdul Rahman, Malaysian prime minister, Yrbk 1957, *Obit* Mar 1991

Abdul-Razaq, Alhaji, Nigerian lawyer and government official, Jan 2005

Abe, Shinzo, Japanese prime minister, Jan 2006

Abetz, Otto, German diplomat, Feb 1941

Abraham, Spencer, American Secretary of energy, May 2001

Abrams, Elliott, American diplomat and policy analyst, Aug 1988

Acker, Achille van, Belgian prime minister, May 1958, *Obit* Sept 1975

Acland, Richard, British member of Parliament, Aug 1944

Adams, Alva B., American senator, *Obit* Jan 1942

Adams, Brock, American Secretary of transportation and senator, July 1977, *Obit* Yrbk 2004

Adams, Eva Bertrand, government official, Sept 1962, *Obit* Oct 1991

Adams, Grantley Herbert, Barbadian prime minister, Sept 1958, *Obit* Jan 1972

Adams, Sherman, American presidential adviser, Nov 1952, *Obit* Jan 1987

Addington, David, American lawyer and vice-presidential aide, Jan 2007

Additon, Henrietta Silvis, American social worker, prison superintendent and police official, Sept 1940

Adebari, Rotimi, Nigerian-Irish mayor, Jan 2007

Adelman, Kenneth L., diplomat and management consultant, July 1985

Adenauer, Konrad, German statesman, July 1949, Apr 1958, *Obit* June 1967

Adkins, Charles, American congressman, *Obit* May 1941

Adoula, Cyrille, Congolese prime minister, Mar 1962

Agnew, Spiro, American vice-president, Yrbk 1968, *Obit* Nov 1996

Aguirre Cerda, Pedro, Chilean president, Jan 1941, *Obit* Jan 1941

Ahern, Bertie, Irish prime minister, July 1998

Ahmadinejad, Mahmoud, Iranian president, Jan 2005

Aichi, Kiichi, Japanese statesman, July 1971, *Obit* Jan 1974

Aiken, George D., American senator, June 1947, *Obit* Feb 1985

Ailes, Stephen, lawyer and secretary of the army, Jan 1965, *Obit* Oct 2001

Al-Hassan, Seif al-Islam, Feb 1957

Al-Hilali, Ahmad Najib, July 1952, *Obit* Mar 1959

Al-Jaafari, Ibrahim, Iraqi prime minister and physician, Jan 2006

Al-Jamali, Mohammed Fadhel, Iraqi prime minister, Jan 1954, *Obit* Aug 1997

Al-Maktoum, Mohammed bin Rashid, United Arab Emirates prime minister, Apr 2008

Al-Maliki, Nuri Kamal, Iraqi prime minister, Jan 2006

Al-Said, Nuri, Iraqi prime minister, June 1955, *Obit* Oct 1958

Al-Yafi, Abdullah Aref, June 1956

Ala, Hussein, Iranian prime minister, May 1951, *Obit* Sept 1964

Albert, Carl, American congressman and Speaker of the House, June 1957, *Obit* June 2000

Aldrich, Richard S., American congressman, *Obit* Feb 1942

Alegria, Ciro, Peruvian novelist, Yrbk 1941

Aleman Valdez, Miguel, Mexican president, Sept 1946, *Obit* July 1983

Alexander, Albert, Yrbk 1940, *Obit* Feb 1965

Alexander, Archie Alphonse, American engineer and territorial governor, June 1955, *Obit* Mar 1958

Alexander, Clifford, American Secretary of the army, Sept 1977

Alexander, Donald C., American lawyer and tax official, Yrbk 1974, *Obit* Yrbk 2009

Alexander, Lamar, American senator, July 1991

Alfonsin, Raul, Argentine president, July 1984, *Obit* Yrbk 2009

Ali, Asaf, June 1947, *Obit* May 1953

Ali, Chaudhri Muhammad, Pakistani prime minister, Feb 1956

Ali, Mohammed, Pakistani prime minister and diplomat, Oct 1952, *Obit* Mar 1963

Alia, Ramiz, Albanian president, Jan 1991, *Obit* Yrbk 2011

Alioto, Joseph L., mayor, Sept 1969, *Obit* Apr 1998

Aliyev, Heydar, Azerbaijani president, Sept 1999, *Obit* July 2004

Alkatiri, Mari, East Timorese prime minister, Jan 2006

Allawi, Iyad, Iraqi interim prime minister and neurologist, Jan 2004

Allen, George E., American lawyer and government official, Mar 1946, *Obit* June 1973

Allen, George Venable, American diplomat, Nov 1948, *Obit* Oct 1970

Allen, James Edward, American government official and educator, June 1969, *Obit* Yrbk 1971

Allen, Leo E., American congressman, June 1948, *Obit* Mar 1973

Allende Gossens, Salvador, Chilean president, Sept 1971, *Obit* Nov 1973

Allison, John Moore, American diplomat, Mar 1956, *Obit* Feb 1979

Allon, Yigal, Israeli political leader, Sept 1975, *Obit* Apr 1980

Allott, Gordon, American senator, May 1955, *Obit* Apr 1989

Almirante, Giorgio, Italian political leader, Jan 1974, *Obit* July 1988

Almond, J. Lindsay, American governor, Mar 1958, *Obit* June 1986

Alphand, Herve, French diplomat, Nov 1951, *Obit* Mar 1994

Alter, George Elias, American lawyer and state attorney general, *Obit* Oct 1940

Altmeyer, Arthur Joseph, American government official, Nov 1946, *Obit* Yrbk 1972

Alvear, Marcelo Torcuato de, *Obit* May 1942

Amato, Giuliano, Italian prime minister, Sept 1993

Amerasinghe, Hamilton Shirley, Sri Lankan diplomat, Mar 1977, *Obit* Feb 1981

Amery, Leopold Charles Maurice Stennett, British cabinet member, July 1942, *Obit* Yrbk 1956

Amini, Ali, Iranian prime minister, Jan 1962

Amulree, William Warrender Mackenzie, British government official, *Obit* June 1942

Anderson, Clinton P., American Secretary of agriculture and senator, June 1945, *Obit* Jan 1976

Anderson, Eugenie M., American diplomat, Jan 1950

Anderson, George Everett, American diplomat and journalist, *Obit* Apr 1940

Anderson, George Whelan, American admiral, Nov 1962, *Obit* May 1992

Anderson, H. Dewey, American economist, Jan 1950

Anderson, John Bayard, American congressman, Sept 1979

Anderson, Mary, American labor leader and government official, Sept 1940, *Obit* Mar 1964

Anderson, Robert Bernerd, American Secretary of the treasury, June 1953, *Obit* Oct 1989

Anderson, Samuel W., American investment banker and government official, June 1954, *Obit* Jan 1963

Anderson, Sigurd, governor, Sept 1953, *Obit* Mar 1991

Anderson, William Robert, American naval officer and congressman, Apr 1959, *Obit* Yrbk 2007

Andrade, Victor, Bolivian diplomat, Feb 1953

Andreotti, Giulio, Italian prime minister, Feb 1977, *Obit* Yrbk 2013

Andresen, August H., American congressman, Feb 1956, *Obit* Mar 1958

Andrews, Charles O., American senator, *Obit* Nov 1946

Andrews, T. Coleman, accountant and government official, Apr 1954

Andropov, Yuri, Soviet communist leader, May 1983, *Obit* Apr 1984

Andrus, Cecil D., governor, Aug 1977

Angelopoulos-Daskalaki, Gianna, Greek Olympic executive, Jan 2004

Annan, Kofi, Ghanaian United Nations secretary-general, Mar 2000

Anslinger, Harry Jacob, government official, May 1948, *Obit* Jan 1976

Antall, Jozsef, Hungarian prime minister, Sept 1990, *Obit* Feb 1994

Apgar, Virginia, American anesthesiologist, Feb 1968, *Obit* Oct 1974

Aquino, Corazon, Filipino president, Aug 1986, *Obit* Yrbk 2009

Aranha, Oswaldo, Brazilian diplomat, Mar 1942, *Obit* Apr 1960

Aras, Tevfik Rustu, Turkish diplomat, June 1942

Arbenz Guzman, Jacobo, Guatemalan president, Sept 1953, *Obit* Mar 1971

Arce, Jose, Nov 1947, *Obit* Oct 1968

Archer, Dennis, American mayor, Feb 1997

Ardalan, Ali Gholi, Iranian diplomat, Apr 1954

Areilza, Jose Maria de, Spanish diplomat and political leader, Apr 1955, *Obit* May 1998

Arends, Leslie Cornelius, American congressman, Feb 1948, *Obit* Sept 1985

Arens, Moshe, Israeli cabinet member, July 1989

Argeseanu, George, Romanian prime minister, *Obit* Jan 1941

Arias Navarro, Carlos, Spanish prime minister, Oct 1974, *Obit* Jan 1990

Arias Sanchez, Oscar, Costa Rican president, Aug 1987

Arias, Arnulfo, May 1941, *Obit* Sept 1988

Aristide, Jean-Bertrand, Haitian priest and president, May 1991

Ariyoshi, George R., governor, Jan 1985

Armey, Richard K., American political activist and former congressman, June 1995

Armitage, Richard L., American government official, Oct 2003

Armour, Norman, American diplomat, Apr 1945, *Obit* Nov 1982

Armstrong, Anne, American presidential adviser and diplomat, May 1976, *Obit* Yrbk 2008

Arnall, Ellis Gibbs, governor, Aug 1945, *Obit* Feb 1993

Arnold, George Stanleigh, American lawyer, *Obit* Mar 1942

Arnold, Thurman Wesley, American lawyer and government official, Jan 1940, *Obit* Yrbk 1969

Arroyo del Rio, Carlos Alberto, Ecuadorian president, June 1942

Asakai, Koichiro, Japanese diplomat, Sept 1957

Asgeir Asgeirsson, Icelandic president, Sept 1952

Ashbrook, John M., American congressman, Oct 1973, *Obit* June 1982

Ashcroft, John D., American Attorney general, Sept 1999

Ashdown, Paddy, British political leader, Oct 1992

Ashida, Hitoshi, Japanese prime minister, June 1948, *Obit* Sept 1959

Ashley, Thomas L., American lobbyist and congressman, May 1979, *Obit* Yrbk 2010

Askew, Reubin, governor, Apr 1973

Askwith, George Ranken Askwith, British labor mediator and government official, *Obit* July 1942

Aspin, Les, American Secretary of defense, Feb 1986, *Obit* July 1995

Aspinall, Wayne N., American congressman, Apr 1968, *Obit* Nov 1983

Astin, Allen Varley, physicist, May 1956, *Obit* Apr 1984

Astor, Nancy Witcher Langhorne, British member of Parliament, Nov 1940, *Obit* July 1964

Atcheson, George, American diplomat, Sept 1946, *Obit* Oct 1947

Atholl, John George Stewart-Murray, British army officer and member of Parliament, *Obit* May 1942

Attlee, C. R., British prime minister, May 1940, Feb 1947, *Obit* Yrbk 1967

Atwater, Lee, American presidential adviser, June 1989, *Obit* May 1991

Auriol, Vincent, French president, Mar 1947, *Obit* Feb 1966

Austin, Margretta, American diplomat, Feb 1954

Austin, Warren Robinson, American senator and diplomat, Jan 1944, *Obit* Feb 1963

Austin, William Lane, American statistician, Apr 1940

Averoff-Tossizza, Evangelos, Greek political leader, May 1957, *Obit* Mar 1990

Avila Camacho, Manuel, Mexican president, Sept 1940, *Obit* Yrbk 1956

Awolowo, Obafemi, Nigerian prime minister, July 1957, *Obit* July 1987

Axelrod, David, American presidential adviser, Apr 2009

Ayala, Eusebio, Paraguayan president, *Obit* July 1942

Aylwin, Patricio, Chilean president, Aug 1990

Ayub Khan, Mohammad, Pakistani president, Apr 1959, *Obit* June 1974

Azana, Manuel, Spanish president, *Obit* Yrbk 1940

Azcona Hoyo, Jose, Honduran president, Feb 1988, *Obit* Yrbk 2006

Azikiwe, Nnamdi, Nigerian president, July 1957, *Obit* Aug 1996

Aziz, Tariq, Iraqi cabinet member, May 1991

Aznar, Jose Maria, Spanish prime minister, Jan 2002

Azzam, Abd al-Rahman, Egyptian diplomat, Apr 1947

Babbitt, Bruce E., American Secretary of the interior, Apr 1987

Bachelet, Michelle, Chilean president, Jan 2006

Bacher, Robert F., American physicist, Feb 1947, *Obit* Yrbk 2005

Bacon, Charles Reade, American newspaper editor and state librarian, *Obit* June 1943

Badillo, Herman, American municipal official and congressman, May 1971

Bailey, Consuelo Northrop, American lawyer and state legislator, June 1954

Bailey, John Moran, American lawyer and political leader, June 1962, *Obit* June 1975

Bailey, Josiah W., American senator, Apr 1945, *Obit* Jan 1947

Bailey, Thomas L., American governor, *Obit* Yrbk 1946

Bair, Sheila C., American regulatory agency official, Feb 2010

Baker, Howard H., American senator and presidential adviser, Mar 1974, Aug 1987

Baker, James A., American Secretary of state, Feb 1982, Mar 2007

Baker, Sara Josephine, American physician, *Obit* Apr 1945

Bakiyev, Kurmanbek, Kirghiz president, Jan 2007

Bakoyianni, Dora, Greek mayor, Jan 2003

Bakshi, Ghulam Mohammad, June 1956, *Obit* Sept 1972

Balaguer, Joaquin, Dominican president, Nov 1966, *Obit* Yrbk 2002

Baldwin, C. B., American political leader, Nov 1943

Baldwin, Raymond Earl, American governor and senator, July 1946, *Obit* Nov 1986

Baldwin, Tammy, American congresswoman, June 2005

Balewa, Abubakar Tafawa, Nigerian prime minister, Sept 1961, *Obit* Feb 1966

Ball, George W., American diplomat, Feb 1962, *Obit* July 1994

Ball, Joseph H., American senator, Oct 1943, *Obit* Feb 1994

Ball, Robert M., American government official, Jan 1968, *Obit* Yrbk 2008

Balladur, Edouard, French prime minister, Feb 1994

Ban, Ki Moon, Korean diplomat and United Nations secretary-general, Jan 2007

Banda, Hastings Kamuzu, Malawian president, Jan 1963, *Obit* Feb 1998

Bandaranaike, S. W. R. D., Sri Lankan prime minister, Sept 1956, *Obit* Nov 1959

Bandaranaike, Sirimavo, Sri Lankan prime minister, May 1961, *Obit* Jan 2001

Bani-Sadr, Abu al-Hasan, Iranian president, Feb 1981

Bankhead, John Hollis, American senator, May 1943, *Obit* July 1946

Bankhead, William Brockman, American Speaker of the House, Oct 1940, *Obit* Oct 1940

Barber, Anthony, Jan 1971

Barbour, Haley, American governor, Nov 1996

Barbour, W. Warren, American senator, *Obit* Jan 1944

Barco Vargas, Virgilio, Colombian president, Feb 1990, *Obit* Aug 1997

Barden, Graham Arthur, American congressman, Sept 1949, *Obit* Mar 1967

Barkley, Alben William, American vice-president, May 1941, Jan 1949, *Obit* July 1956

Barnes, Henry A., American traffic engineer, June 1955, *Obit* Nov 1968

Barnes, Roy E., American governor, Jan 2000

Barnes, Wendell B., government official and congressman, June 1957, *Obit* Aug 1985

Barnett, Ross Robert, American governor, Sept 1961, *Obit* Jan 1988

Barr, Joseph W., American Secretary of the treasury, Jan 1968, *Obit* May 1996

Barr, William P., American Attorney general, June 1992

Barre, Raymond, French prime minister, July 1977, *Obit* Yrbk 2007

Barrere, Camille, French diplomat, *Obit* Yrbk 1940

Barrett, Frank A., American senator and governor, July 1956, *Obit* July 1962

Barrette, Antonio, Canadian provincial premier, July 1960, *Obit* Feb 1969

Barros Hurtado, Cesar, Argentine lawyer, sociologist and diplomat, Jan 1959

Barrow, Errol W., Barbadian prime minister, Sept 1968, *Obit* July 1987

Barry, Marion, American mayor, May 1987

Barry, William Bernard, American congressman, *Obit* Yrbk 1946

Barshefsky, Charlene, American trade representative, Feb 2000

Bartlett, Edward Lewis, American senator, June 1951, *Obit* Mar 1969

Barzel, Rainer, German political leader, May 1967, *Obit* Yrbk 2006

Barzini, Luigi Giorgio, Italian journalist and author, July 1972, *Obit* May 1984

Basdevant, Jules, French lawyer, diplomat and judge, Feb 1950, *Obit* Mar 1968

Bates, Sanford, American penologist, Jan 1961, *Obit* Nov 1972

Batt, William L., American government official, Sept 1962

Battle, John S., American lawyer and governor, Nov 1950, *Obit* June 1972

Bauer, Gary L., political activist, Jan 1999

Baumgartner, Leona, American physician and public health official, Jan 1950, *Obit* Mar 1991

Bayar, Celal, Turkish president, July 1950, *Obit* Oct 1986

Bayard, Thomas Francis, American senator, *Obit* Sept 1942

Bayh, Birch, American senator and governor, June 1965

Bayh, Evan, American senator, Nov 1998

Beale, Howard, Australian cabinet member and diplomat, Mar 1959

Beall, J. Glenn, American senator, Apr 1955, *Obit* Mar 1971

Beam, Jacob Dyneley, American diplomat, July 1959, *Obit* Oct 1993

Bean, Louis H., agricultural economist and public opinion analyst, Nov 1948, *Obit* Oct 1994

Beaulac, Willard Leon, diplomat, Sept 1958, *Obit* Oct 1990

Bebler, Ales, Yugoslav diplomat, Apr 1950

Bech, Joseph, Luxembourgian statesman, Feb 1950, *Obit* May 1975

Beck, Jozef, Polish diplomat, *Obit* July 1944

Becker, Ralph E., lawyer and diplomat, Nov 1948, *Obit* Oct 1994

Becker, William Dee, American judge and mayor, *Obit* Sept 1943

Bede, J. Adam, American congressman, *Obit* June 1942

Beers, Rand, American foreign policy adviser, Oct 2004

Begin, Menachem, Israeli prime minister, Oct 1977, *Obit* Apr 1992

Belaunde Terry, Fernando, Peruvian president, July 1965, *Obit* Sept 2002

Belaunde, Victor Andres, Peruvian diplomat, Feb 1960, *Obit* Feb 1967

Bell, Griffin B., American Attorney general, June 1977, *Obit* Yrbk 2009

Bell, Thomas M., *Obit* May 1941

Bellamy, Carol, American United Nations official, Oct 1999

Bellmon, Henry, American governor and senator, July 1963, *Obit* Yrbk 2009

Belt, Guillermo, Cuban diplomat, Nov 1947, *Obit* Sept 1989

Belton, Sharon Sayles, American mayor, Jan 2001

Ben Bella, Ahmed, Algerian president, Feb 1963, *Obit* Yrbk 2012

Ben-Gurion, David, Israeli prime minister, Oct 1947, Jan 1957, *Obit* Jan 1974

Ben-Zvi, Itzhak, Israeli president, Apr 1953, *Obit* June 1963

Benavides, Oscar R., Peruvian president, *Obit* Aug 1945

Bender, George H., American congressman and senator, Jan 1952, *Obit* Sept 1961

Benes, Edvard, Czech statesman, Jan 1942, *Obit* Oct 1948

Benjamin, Regina, American Surgeon general, Jan 2010

Benn, Tony, British member of Parliament, June 1965, Nov 1982

Bennett, James V., American penologist and prison official, Apr 1949, *Obit* Feb 1979

Bennett, Robert LaFollette, American lawyer and government official, Sept 1967

Bennett, William John, American political commentator, Sept 1985

Benson, Ezra Taft, American Secretary of agriculture and Mormon leader, Feb 1953, *Obit* Aug 1994

Bensouda, Fatou, Gambian lawyer and international court prosecutor, Jan 2007

Bentley, Helen Delich, American congresswoman, Yrbk 1971

Bentsen, Lloyd, American Secretary of the treasury, Sept 1973, Apr 1993, *Obit* Oct 2006

Berding, Andrew H., American journalist and government official, Apr 1960

Beregovoy, Pierre Eugene, French prime minister, Feb 1993, *Obit* Feb 1993

Berendsen, Carl August, New Zealand diplomat, Oct 1948, *Obit* Yrbk 1973

Berge, Wendell, American lawyer and government official, Feb 1946, *Obit* Yrbk 1956

Berger Perdomo, Oscar, Guatemalan president, Jan 2004

Berger, Sandy, American presidential adviser, Feb 1998

Bergson, Herbert A., American lawyer, Sept 1950

Beria, Lavrenti, Soviet intelligence official, Yrbk 1942, *Obit* Sept 1954

Berkner, Lloyd, Sept 1949, *Obit* Oct 1967

Bernadotte, Folke, Swedish diplomat, May 1945, *Obit* Nov 1948

Bernanke, Ben, American economist and Federal Reserve chairman, Mar 2006

Berry, George L., American labor leader, Jan 1948, *Obit* Jan 1949

Bessmertnykh, Aleksandr A., Soviet diplomat, June 1991

Betancourt, Ingrid, Colombian political leader, Jan 2002

Betancourt, Romulo, Venezuelan president, May 1960, *Obit* Nov 1981

Betancur, Belisario, Colombian president, Apr 1985

Bevan, Aneurin, British cabinet member, May 1943, *Obit* Oct 1960

Beveridge, William Henry Beveridge, British economist, Jan 1943, *Obit* May 1963

Bevin, Ernest, British statesman, Sept 1940, June 1949, *Obit* May 1951

Bhutto, Benazir, Pakistani prime minister, July 1986, *Obit* Apr 2008

Bhutto, Zulfikar Ali, Pakistani president, Apr 1972, *Obit* May 1979

Biaggi, Mario, congressman, Jan 1986

Bible, Alan, American senator, Feb 1957, *Obit* Oct 1988

Bidault, Georges, French statesman, May 1945, *Obit* Mar 1983

Biden, Joseph R., American vice-president, Jan 1987, Mar 2009

Bierut, Boleslaw, Polish president, Sept 1949, *Obit* May 1956

Biffle, Leslie L., American presidential aide, Sept 1946, *Obit* May 1966

Bilandic, Michael A., American mayor, Feb 1979, *Obit* Apr 2002

Bilbo, Theodore G., American senator, Apr 1943, *Obit* Oct 1947

Bildt, Carl, Swedish prime minister, Jan 1993

Bingham, Jonathan B., congressman, July 1954, *Obit* Aug 1986

Bitar, Salah al-Din, Syrian political leader, Feb 1958, *Obit* Sept 1980

Black, Hugo LaFayette, American Supreme Court justice, Sept 1941, May 1964, *Obit* Nov 1971

Blades, Ruben, Panamanian salsa singer, songwriter and actor, May 1986

Blair, David H., American tax official and lawyer, *Obit* Nov 1944

Blair, Dennis, American admiral and intelligence official, May 2010

Blair, James T., American governor, Apr 1958, *Obit* Sept 1962

Blair, Tony, British prime minister, Aug 1996, Jan 2005

Blanco Galindo, Carlos, Bolivian president, *Obit* Nov 1943

Blanco, Kathleen, American governor, June 2004

Blandford, John B., American government official, May 1942, *Obit* Mar 1972

Blank, Theodor, Sept 1952, *Obit* July 1972

Blankenhorn, Herbert, German diplomat, Apr 1956

Blatchford, Joseph H., Mar 1971

Blatnik, John A., American congressman, Feb 1958, *Obit* Feb 1992

Blattenberger, Raymond, American printing industry executive and government official, Mar 1958, *Obit* June 1971

Blease, Coleman Livingston, American senator and governor, *Obit* Mar 1942

Blitch, Iris Faircloth, congresswoman, Apr 1956, *Obit* Oct 1993

Blix, Hans, Swedish diplomat and United Nations official, Jan 2003

Blucher, Franz, German cabinet member, Jan 1956, *Obit* June 1959

Blue, Robert Donald, American governor, Yrbk 1948, *Obit* Feb 1990

Blunt, Roy, American senator, Mar 2008

Boateng, Paul, British cabinet member, Jan 2002

Boehner, John, American congressman and Speaker of the House, Apr 2006

Boggs, Hale, American congressman and political leader, Apr 1958, *Obit* Mar 1973

Boggs, J. Caleb, American governor and senator, July 1956

Boheman, Erik, Swedish diplomat, Mar 1951

Bohlen, Charles E., American diplomat, June 1948, May 1960, *Obit* Feb 1974

Boissieu, Pierre de, Feb 1943, *Obit* Sept 1948

Bok, Curtis, American state supreme court justice, May 1954, *Obit* July 1962

Boland, Edward P., American congressman, Oct 1987, *Obit* Feb 2002

Boland, Frederick H., Irish United Nations official and diplomat, Feb 1961, *Obit* Feb 1986

Bolden, Charles, American astronaut and NASA official, July 2010

Bolger, William F., postmaster general, Oct 1979, *Obit* Oct 1989

Bolling, Richard Walker, American congressman, Mar 1960, *Obit* July 1991

Bolten, Josh, American presidential adviser, July 2006

Bolton, Frances Payne Bingham, American congresswoman, Mar 1940, Apr 1954, *Obit* May 1977

Bolton, John R., American diplomat, Feb 2006

Bonino, Emma, Italian trade official, Jan 2006

Bonner, Herbert C., American congressman, July 1956, *Obit* Jan 1966

Bonnet, Henri, French diplomat, Feb 1945, *Obit* Feb 1979

Bono, Sonny, American singer, songwriter and congressman, Feb 1974, *Obit* Mar 1998

Bonomi, Ivanhoe, Aug 1944, *Obit* May 1951

Bonsal, Philip Wilson, diplomat, June 1959, *Obit* Sept 1995

Booker, Cory, American mayor, Feb 2007

Boorstin, Daniel J., American historian and Librarian of Congress, Sept 1968, Jan 1984, *Obit* Yrbk 2004

Borah, William Edgar, American senator, Jan 1940

Bordaberry, Juan Maria, Uruguayan president, Apr 1975, *Obit* Yrbk 2011

Bordes, Pierre-Louis, *Obit* Sept 1943

Borno, Louis, *Obit* Sept 1942

Bosch, Juan, Dominican president, June 1963, *Obit* Feb 2002

Bosone, Reva Zilpha Beck, congresswoman and judge, Jan 1949

Botha, Pieter W., South African president, Sept 1979, *Obit* Yrbk 2007

Botha, R. F., South African diplomat, May 1984

Boumedienne, Houari, Algerian president, Jan 1971, *Obit* Feb 1979

Bourges-Maunoury, Maurice, French political leader, July 1957

Bourguiba, Habib, Tunisian president, Sept 1955, *Obit* Aug 2000

Bourne, Jonathan, American senator, *Obit* Oct 1940

Bouteflika, Abdelaziz, Algerian president, Feb 1976

Boutros-Ghali, Boutros, Egyptian diplomat and United Nations secretary-general, Apr 1992

Bowen, Otis R., American governor and Secretary of health and human services, Nov 1986, *Obit* Yrbk 2013

Bowers, Claude Gernade, American journalist, historian and diplomat, Sept 1941, *Obit* Mar 1958

Bowles, Erskine, American presidential adviser, Aug 1998

Bowron, Fletcher, American mayor, Feb 1950, *Obit* Nov 1968

Boxer, Barbara, American senator, Apr 1994

Boyer, Harold Raymond, Feb 1952

Brabazon of Tara, John Theodore Cuthbert Moore-Brabazon, British aviator and government official, May 1941

Braddock, E. M., British labor leader and member of Parliament, July 1957, *Obit* Jan 1971

Braden, Spruille, American diplomat, Sept 1945, *Obit* Mar 1978

Bradford, Robert F., governor, Yrbk 1948, *Obit* May 1983

Bradley, Bill, American senator, July 1965, Sept 1982

Bradley, David, American nonfiction author, surgeon and state legislator, Apr 1949

Bradley, Tom, American lawyer and mayor, Nov 1973, Oct 1992, *Obit* Jan 1999

Brady, James S., American presidential press secretary and gun control activist, Oct 1991

Bramuglia, Juan Atilio, Argentine cabinet member, May 1949, *Obit* Nov 1962

Brandt, Willy, German chancellor, June 1958, Yrbk 1973, *Obit* Nov 1992

Brannan, Charles F., American Secretary of agriculture, Sept 1948

Bray, Robert S., Feb 1966, *Obit* Feb 1975

Brazauskas, Algirdas, Lithuanian president and prime minister, Jan 2002, *Obit* Yrbk 2010

Breathitt, Edward T., American governor, July 1964, *Obit* Yrbk 2004

Brennan, Peter J., American Secretary of labor, Apr 1973, *Obit* Jan 1997

Brentano, Heinrich von, Feb 1955, *Obit* Jan 1965

Brewer, Jan, American governor, Jan 2011

Brewster, Owen, American senator, May 1947, *Obit* Feb 1962

Brickell, Herschel, Nov 1945, *Obit* July 1952

Bricker, John William, American senator and governor, Apr 1943, July 1956, *Obit* May 1986

Bridges, Styles, American governor and senator, Mar 1948, *Obit* Jan 1962

Briscoe, Robert, Irish member of Parliament and mayor, May 1957, *Obit* July 1969

Bristow, Joseph Little, *Obit* Sept 1944

Broadbent, Edward, Canadian political leader, May 1988

Brock, William Emerson, American senator and Secretary of labor, May 1971

Broder, Samuel, physician and government official, Aug 1992

Brooke, Edward, American senator, Apr 1967

Brookhart, Smith W., American senator, *Obit* Jan 1945

Brooks, C. Wayland, Sept 1947, *Obit* Mar 1957

Brooks, Jack, congressman, June 1992, *Obit* Yrbk 2013

Brooks, Overton, June 1957, *Obit* Yrbk 1961

Brosio, Manlio, Italian diplomat, Sept 1955, *Obit* May 1980

Brossard, Edgar Bernard, July 1954

Brown, Clarence J., American congressman, Feb 1947, *Obit* Nov 1965

Brown, Edmund G., American governor, Mar 1960, *Obit* Apr 1996

Brown, Francis Shunk, *Obit* Jan 1940

Brown, Gordon, British prime minister, Jan 2002

Brown, Jerry, American governor, Apr 1975

Brown, Jesse, American Secretary of veterans affairs, Nov 1993, *Obit* Yrbk 2002

Brown, Lee Patrick, American mayor, Sept 2002

Brown, Lewis H, Oct 1947, *Obit* Mar 1951

Brown, Newell, government official, Sept 1959, *Obit* Sept 2000

Brown, Prentiss M., American senator, Jan 1943, *Obit* Feb 1974

Brown, Ron, American Secretary of commerce, July 1989, *Obit* June 1996

Brown, Scott, American senator, Aug 2010

Brown, Virginia Mae, lawyer and government official, July 1970, *Obit* May 1991

Brown, Willie Lewis, American mayor and political leader, Apr 1997

Brownback, Sam, American senator, Apr 2008

Browne, Edward E., *Obit* Jan 1946

Brownell, Herbert, American Attorney general, Aug 1944, Feb 1954, *Obit* July 1996

Brownell, Samuel Miller, educator, Feb 1954, *Obit* Jan 1991

Browner, Carol M., American environmentalist and government official, May 1994

Brownson, Charles B., July 1955

Broyhill, Joel T., American congressman, May 1974, *Obit* Feb 2007

Bruce, David K. E., American diplomat, June 1949, Sept 1961, *Obit* Feb 1978

Bruce, James, diplomat, Jan 1949, *Obit* Sept 1980

Bruce, Louis Rooks, American government official, May 1972, *Obit* July 1989

Bruce, Robert Randolph, *Obit* Apr 1942

Bruce, William Cabell, author and senator, *Obit* June 1946

Brucker, Wilber M., American Secretary of the army, Sept 1955, *Obit* Yrbk 1968

Bruckner, Henry, *Obit* June 1942

Brunauer, Esther Caukin, American diplomat, Nov 1947, *Obit* Sept 1959

Brundage, Percival F., American accountant and government official, Apr 1957

Brundtland, Gro Harlem, Norwegian prime minister and international health official, Nov 1981

Bruton, John, Irish prime minister, Nov 1996

Bryan, Charles W., governor, *Obit* Apr 1945

Bryan, Ernest R., July 1950, *Obit* Feb 1955

Bryant, C. Farris, American governor, Sept 1961, *Obit* Yrbk 2002

Bryce, Quentin, Australian governor general, Feb 2010

Buchanan, Frank, Feb 1951

Buchanan, Wiley T., diplomat, Nov 1957, *Obit* Mar 1986

Budd, Ralph, July 1940, *Obit* Mar 1962

Budge, Hamer H., American congressman and regulatory agency official, Yrbk 1970, *Obit* Yrbk 2003

Bugher, John C., Apr 1953

Bulganin, Nikolai Aleksandrovich, Soviet communist leader, Feb 1955, *Obit* Apr 1975

Bumpers, Dale, American senator, Aug 1979

Bunche, Ralph J., American diplomat, Feb 1948, *Obit* Jan 1972

Bundy, McGeorge, American presidential adviser, Mar 1962, *Obit* Jan 1997

Bunker, Ellsworth, American diplomat, Apr 1954, Mar 1978, *Obit* Nov 1984

Burdick, Quentin, American senator, May 1963, *Obit* Nov 1992

Burdick, Usher L., American congressman, Apr 1952, *Obit* Nov 1960

Burford, Anne McGill, American regulatory agency official, Sept 1982, *Obit* Yrbk 2004

Burger, Warren E., American Chief Justice of the Supreme Court, Nov 1969, *Obit* Aug 1995

Burgess, Robert Wilbur, July 1960, *Obit* July 1969

Burke, Charles H., *Obit* May 1944

Burke, Edward Raymond, Sept 1940, *Obit* Yrbk 1968

Burke, Thomas A., July 1954, *Obit* Jan 1972

Burke, Yvonne Brathwaite, American lawyer and congresswoman, Oct 1975

Burney, Leroy E., surgeon general, July 1957, *Obit* Oct 1998

Burnham, Forbes, Guyanese president, Nov 1966, *Obit* Oct 1985

Burns, Alan, Sept 1953

Burns, John A., American governor, Feb 1972, *Obit* June 1975

Burris, Roland W., American senator, June 2009

Burton, Dan, American congressman, Sept 1998

Burton, Harold Hitz, American senator and Supreme Court justice, Apr 1945, *Obit* Jan 1965

Bush, George, American president, Jan 1972, Sept 1983

Bush, Jeb, American governor, Feb 1999

Bush, Vannevar, American electrical engineer and inventor, Sept 1940, May 1947, *Obit* Sept 1974

Bustamante, Alexander, Jamaican prime minister, May 1965, *Obit* Sept 1977

Butler of Saffron Walden, Richard Austen Butler, British cabinet member, May 1944, Sept 1964, *Obit* May 1982

Butler, John Marshall, American senator, May 1954, *Obit* May 1978

Butler, Nevile Montagu, Apr 1941

Buttenwieser, Benjamin Joseph, investment banker, Nov 1950, *Obit* Mar 1992

Byrd, Harry Flood, American senator, Apr 1942, Sept 1955, *Obit* Yrbk 1966

Byrd, Robert C., American senator, Mar 1960, Feb 1978, *Obit* Sept 2010

Byrne, Brendan T., May 1974

Byrne, Jane, American mayor, Jan 1980

Byrnes, James Francis, American senator, Supreme Court justice and Secretary of state, June 1941, Oct 1951, *Obit* June 1972

Byrnes, John W., American congressman, Oct 1960, *Obit* Mar 1985

Byroade, Henry Alfred, diplomat, Feb 1952, *Obit* Mar 1994

Byron, William D., *Obit* Apr 1941

Cabot, John M., American diplomat, Sept 1953, *Obit* Apr 1981

Caccia, Harold Anthony, British diplomat, Feb 1957, *Obit* Jan 1991

Caddell, Patrick, public opinion analyst and presidential adviser, Nov 1979

Caetano, Marcello, Portuguese prime minister, Mar 1970, *Obit* Jan 1981

Cafe Filho, Joao, Jan 1955, *Obit* Apr 1970

Caffery, Jefferson, diplomat, Nov 1943, *Obit* June 1974

Caffrey, James J., June 1947, *Obit* May 1961

Cahill, William Thomas, governor, June 1970, *Obit* Sept 1996

Cai Yuanpei, Chinese educator, *Obit* Mar 1940

Caillaux, Joseph, French statesman, *Obit* Jan 1945

Cain, Harry P., American senator, Apr 1949, *Obit* May 1979

Calder, William M., *Obit* Apr 1945

Caldera, Rafael, Venezuelan president, July 1969, *Obit* Yrbk 2010

Calderon Guardia, Rafael Angel, Costa Rican president, June 1942, *Obit* Sept 1970

Calderon Hinojosa, Felipe, Mexican president, Jan 2006

Calderon, Sila M., Puerto Rican governor, Nov 2001

Calderone, Frank A., physician and public health official, July 1952, *Obit* Apr 1987

Caldwell, Millard Fillmore, American governor, Nov 1948, *Obit* Feb 1985

Califano, Joseph A., American Secretary of health, education and welfare, June 1977

Callaghan, James, British prime minister, Feb 1968, *Obit* Yrbk 2005

Calmy-Rey, Micheline, Swiss president, Jan 2007

Calwell, A. A., Oct 1947

Cameron, David, British prime minister, Aug 2010

Cammerer, Arno B., *Obit* June 1941

Campa, Miguel Angel, Sept 1957, *Obit* Nov 1965

Campbell, Ben Nighthorse, American senator, Oct 1994

Campbell, Bill, American mayor, July 1996

Campbell, Gerald, Mar 1941, *Obit* Sept 1964

Campbell, Philip P., Speaker of the House, *Obit* July 1941

Campney, Ralph Osborne, Sept 1955, *Obit* Yrbk 1967

Campora, Hector Jose, Argentine political leader, Oct 1973, *Obit* Feb 1981

Candau, Marcolino G., Brazilian physican and public health official, Sept 1954

Cannon, Cavendish Welles, diplomat, July 1957, *Obit* Yrbk 1962

Cannon, Clarence, American congressman, Nov 1949, *Obit* July 1964

Cannon, Howard W., American senator, Feb 1960, *Obit* Sept 2002

Cantwell, Maria, American senator, Feb 2005

Cao, Joseph, American congressman, June 2009

Capehart, H. E., American senator, Apr 1947, *Obit* Oct 1979

Caplin, Mortimer Maxwell, American lawyer, Sept 1961

Capper, Arthur, American senator and governor, Sept 1946, *Obit* Feb 1952

Capps, Lois, American congresswoman, Mar 2008

Caradon, Hugh Foot, British diplomat, Oct 1953, *Obit* Nov 1990

Caramanlis, Constantinos, Greek president, May 1956, Apr 1976, *Obit* July 1998

Caramanlis, Constantinos, Greek prime minister, Jan 2004

Caraway, Hattie Wyatt, American senator, Mar 1945, *Obit* Jan 1951

Card, Andrew H., American presidential adviser, Nov 2003

Cardoso, Fernando Henrique, Brazilian president, Oct 1996

Carey, Hugh L., American governor, Sept 1965, *Obit* Yrbk 2011

Carias Andino, Tiburcio, Honduran president, June 1942, *Obit* Feb 1970

Carlson, Frank, American governor and senator, Apr 1949, *Obit* July 1987

Carlsson, Ingvar, Swedish prime minister, Feb 1988

Carlucci, Frank Charles, American Secretary of defense, Oct 1981

Carmona, Richard, American Surgeon general, Jan 2003

Carr, Robert, Jan 1973

Carr, Wilbur J., diplomat, *Obit* Aug 1942

Carrero Blanco, Luis, Oct 1973, *Obit* Feb 1974

Carrington, Peter Alexander Rupert Carington, British statesman, June 1971

Carroll, John A., American senator, May 1958, *Obit* Oct 1983

Carstens, Karl, German president, Apr 1980, *Obit* Aug 1992

Carter, Jimmy, American president, Sept 1971, Nov 1977

Cartier de Marchienne, Emile de, *Obit* July 1946

Carusi, Ugo, government official, Oct 1948, *Obit* Sept 1994

Carvel, Elbert N., June 1963

Case, Clifford Philip, American senator, Mar 1955, *Obit* Apr 1982

Casey, Ralph E., Feb 1966

Casey, Richard Gardiner Casey, Australian governor-general, Jan 1940, *Obit* Aug 1976

Casey, William J., American intelligence official, Mar 1972, *Obit* June 1987

Castillo Armas, Carlos, Guatemalan president, Jan 1955, *Obit* Sept 1957

Castillo Najera, Francisco, May 1946, *Obit* Feb 1955

Castillo, Ramon S., July 1941, *Obit* Yrbk 1944

Castle, Barbara, British socialist leader, Jan 1967, *Obit* Yrbk 2002

Castro, Fidel, Cuban president, July 1958, July 1970, June 2001

Castro, Julian, American mayor, June 2013

Castro, Raul, Cuban president, Feb 1977

Cavaco Silva, Anibal, Portuguese prime minister, Mar 1991

Cavanagh, Jerome P., Apr 1968, *Obit* Jan 1980

Cavero, Salvador, Peruvian vice-president, *Obit* Mar 1940

Ceausescu, Nicolae, Romanian dictator, Nov 1967, *Obit* Feb 1990

Celebrezze, Anthony J., American Secretary of health, education and welfare, Jan 1963, *Obit* Jan 1999

Celler, Emanuel, American congressman, Oct 1949, Nov 1966, *Obit* Mar 1981

Cerezo Arevalo, Vinicio, Guatemalan president, Mar 1987

Chaban-Delmas, Jacques, French prime minister, July 1958, *Obit* Feb 2001

Chadli, Bendjedid, Algerian president, Apr 1991, *Obit* Yrbk 2012

Chafee, John, American senator and governor, Nov 1969, *Obit* Jan 2000

Chafee, Lincoln, American senator, Jan 2004

Chagla, Mahomed Ali Currim, Indian diplomat, June 1959, *Obit* Jan 1984

Chalmers, Philip O., *Obit* Mar 1946

Chambas, Mohamed Ibn, Ghanaian diplomat and international organization official, Jan 2003

Chamberlain, Neville, British prime minister, *Obit* Yrbk 1940

Chamorro, Violeta Barrios de, Nicaraguan president, June 1990

Chamoun, Camille Nimer, Lebanese president, July 1956, *Obit* Sept 1987

Chan, Margaret F. C., Chinese physician and public health official, Jan 2007

Chang, John M., June 1949, *Obit* July 1966

Chapman, Oscar L., American Secretary of the interior, Feb 1949, *Obit* Apr 1978

Chappedelaine, Louis de, *Obit* Jan 1940

Charles, Eugenia, Dominica prime minister, Oct 1986, *Obit* Yrbk 2006

Charles-Roux, Francois, Jan 1952, *Obit* Sept 1961

Charnwood, Godfrey Rathbone Benson, English biographer, *Obit* Mar 1945

Chatel, Yves, *Obit* Yrbk 1944

Chauvel, Jean, French diplomat, Oct 1950, *Obit* July 1979

Chavan, Yashwantrao Balwantrao, Apr 1963

Chavez Frias, Hugo, Venezuelan president, May 2000

Chavez, Dennis, American senator, Mar 1946, *Obit* Jan 1963

Chavez, Hugo, Venezuelan president, *Obit* Yrbk 2013

Chavez, Linda, American policy scientist and commentator, Nov 1999

Chelf, Frank L., June 1952

Chen, Shui-bian, Taiwanese president, Sept 2000

Cheney, Lynne V., American educator, novelist and government official, Oct 1992

Chernomyrdin, Viktor, Russian prime minister, Aug 1998, *Obit* Yrbk 2011

Cherry, Francis Adams, American governor, July 1954, *Obit* Sept 1965

Chertoff, Michael, American Secretary of homeland security, Oct 2005

Chevrier, Lionel, June 1952

Chiang, Ching-kuo, Taiwanese president, Sept 1954, *Obit* Mar 1988

Chiappe, Jean, French government official, *Obit* Jan 1941

Chiari, Roberto F., Panamanian president, Feb 1961

Chifley, Joseph B., Aug 1945, *Obit* July 1951

Chiles, Lawton, senator and governor, Sept 1971, *Obit* Mar 1999

Chiluba, Frederick, Zambian president, May 1992, *Obit* Yrbk 2011

Ching, Cyrus S., labor mediator, Jan 1948, *Obit* Feb 1968

Chiperfield, Robert B., Sept 1956, *Obit* May 1971

Chirac, Jacques, French president, June 1975, Apr 1993

Chisholm, Shirley, American congresswoman, Oct 1969, *Obit* Apr 2005

Chissano, Joaquim Alberto, Mozambican president, Nov 1990

Chretien, Jean, Canadian prime minister, Apr 1990

Christopher, George, mayor, Feb 1958, *Obit* Yrbk 2000

Christopher, Warren, American Secretary of state, June 1981, Nov 1995, *Obit* Yrbk 2011

Chu, Shen, *Obit* Aug 1943

Chuan Leekpai, Thai prime minister, Nov 1998

Church, Frank, American senator, Mar 1958, Mar 1978, *Obit* May 1984

Church, Marguerite Stitt, congresswoman, Feb 1951, *Obit* July 1990

Churchill, Gordon, Sept 1958

Churchill, Winston, British statesman, July 1940, Mar 1942, July 1953, *Obit* Mar 1965

Ciano, Galeazzo, Italian diplomat, July 1940, *Obit* Feb 1944

Ciller, Tansu, Turkish political leader, Sept 1994

Civiletti, Benjamin, Feb 1980

Clague, Ewan, statistician and government official, July 1947, *Obit* June 1987

Clapp, Gordon R., Feb 1947, *Obit* June 1963

Clark Kerr, Archibald John Kerr, Yrbk 1942, *Obit* Sept 1951

Clark, Bennett Champ, Nov 1941, *Obit* Sept 1954

Clark, Helen, New Zealand prime minister, Nov 2000

Clark, Joe, Canadian prime minister, Oct 1976

Clark, John Davidson, Jan 1947

Clark, Joseph S., American senator, June 1952, *Obit* Mar 1990

Clark, Robert L., Nov 1952

Clark, Tom C., American Supreme Court justice, July 1945, *Obit* Aug 1977

Clark, William Patrick, American Secretary of the interior, July 1982, *Obit* Yrbk 2013

Clarke, Kenneth H., British political leader, Jan 2002

Clarke, Richard A., American presidential aide and security consultant, May 2006

Claxton, Brooke, Yrbk 1947, *Obit* Sept 1960

Clayton, Eva, American congresswoman, June 2000

Claytor, W. Graham, railroad executive, May 1979, *Obit* July 1994

Cleland, Max, American senator, Feb 1978

Clement, Frank Goad, American governor, July 1955, *Obit* Yrbk 1969

Clement, Paul D., American law professor, Oct 2012

Clements, Earle C., senator and governor, Sept 1955, *Obit* May 1985

Clifford, Clark M., American presidential adviser, lawyer and Secretary of defense, Mar 1947, Sept 1968, *Obit* Jan 1999

Clinton, Bill, American president, Apr 1988, Nov 1994

Clinton, Hillary Rodham, American Secretary of state, Nov 1993, Jan 2002, Mar 2009

Clyburn, James E., American congressman, Oct 2001

Coates, Gordon, *Obit* July 1943

Cobham, Charles John Lyttelton, Apr 1962

Cobo, Albert E., Nov 1951, *Obit* Yrbk 1958

Cochran, H. Merle, Feb 1950, *Obit* Nov 1973

Cochran, Thad, American senator, Apr 2002

Cochrane, Edward L., Mar 1951, *Obit* Jan 1960

Coe, Sebastian, British runner, Nov 1980

Coffee, John M., Oct 1946

Coffin, Frank M., American judge, Apr 1959, *Obit* Yrbk 2010

Cohen, Benjamin, Chilean diplomat and United Nations official, May 1948, *Obit* May 1960

Cohen, Benjamin V., American government official and lawyer, Apr 1941, *Obit* Oct 1983

Cohen, Manuel F., Apr 1967, *Obit* Aug 1977

Cohen, William S., American Secretary of defense, Apr 1982, Jan 1998

Colby, William E., American intelligence official, Jan 1975, *Obit* July 1996

Coldwell, M. J., Canadian member of Parliament, Sept 1943, *Obit* Oct 1974

Cole, Albert M., Jan 1954

Cole, William Sterling, congressman, Mar 1954, *Obit* May 1987

Coleman, J. P., American governor and judge, Sept 1956, *Obit* Nov 1991

Coleman, Norman, American senator, Sept 2004

Coleman, William T., American Secretary of transportation, Mar 1976

Coleraine, Richard Kidston Law, Feb 1944

Colijn, Hendrikus, Dutch prime minister, *Obit* Jan 1945

Colina, Rafael de la, Jan 1951

Collier, John, American anthropologist and government official, Mar 1941, *Obit* July 1968

Collins, Cardiss, American congresswoman, Feb 1997, *Obit* Yrbk 2013

Collins, George Lewis, *Obit* Aug 1940

Collins, John F., American mayor, Jan 1965, *Obit* Feb 1996

Collins, LeRoy, American governor, June 1956, Apr 1965, *Obit* May 1991

Collins, Lorin Cone, *Obit* Yrbk 1940

Collins, Martha Layne, governor, Jan 1986

Collins, Susan, American senator, May 2000

Collor de Mello, Fernando, Brazilian president, Mar 1990

Colombo, Emilio, Apr 1971, *Obit* Yrbk 2013

Colquitt, Oscar Branch, *Obit* Mar 1940

Combs, Bert Thomas, governor and lawyer, June 1960, *Obit* Feb 1992

Companys y Jover, Luis, *Obit* Yrbk 1940

Concheso, Aurelio Fernandez, May 1942, *Obit* Jan 1956

Condon, Edward Uhler, American physicist and government official, Apr 1946, *Obit* May 1974

Conley, William Gustavus, *Obit* Yrbk 1940

Connally, John B., American governor, presidential adviser and Secretary of the treasury, July 1961, *Obit* Aug 1993

Connally, Tom, American senator, Yrbk 1941, Apr 1949, *Obit* Jan 1964

Connerly, Ward, American business consultant and anti-affirmative action activist, Nov 2000

Connery, Lawrence J., *Obit* Yrbk 1941

Conroy, Patrick Dominic, July 1954

Conyers, John, American congressman, Sept 1970

Cook, Donald C., May 1952, *Obit* Feb 1982

Cook, Marlow W., Jan 1972

Cooke, Morris Llewellyn, American industrial engineer and government official, May 1950, *Obit* May 1960

Cooley, Harold D., American congressman, Mar 1951, *Obit* Mar 1974

Cooper, Jere, American congressman, Mar 1955, *Obit* Feb 1958

Cooper, John Sherman, American senator and diplomat, June 1950, *Obit* Apr 1991

Cooper, Joseph David, Feb 1952

Corcoran, Thomas, American lawyer, Mar 1940, *Obit* Feb 1982

Cordier, Constant, *Obit* Mar 1940

Cordon, Guy, American senator, Apr 1952, *Obit* July 1969

Corea, Claude, Mar 1961, *Obit* Nov 1962

Corell, Hans, Swedish diplomat, lawyer and United Nations official, Jan 2003

Correa, Rafael, Ecuadorian president, Jan 2007

Corzine, Jon S., American financial executive and former governor, Aug 2006

Cosgrave, Liam, Irish prime minister, June 1977

Cossiga, Francesco, Italian president, Jan 1981, *Obit* Yrbk 2010

Costa e Silva, Arthur da, Sept 1967, *Obit* Feb 1970

Costanza, Midge, American presidential aide, June 1978, *Obit* Yrbk 2010

Costello, John A., Apr 1948, *Obit* Feb 1976

Costle, Douglas M., June 1980

Cot, Pierre, French political leader, June 1944, *Obit* Oct 1977

Cotton, Joseph Bell, *Obit* Sept 1940

Cotton, Norris, American senator, Feb 1956, *Obit* May 1989

Coty, Rene, French president, Apr 1954, *Obit* Jan 1963

Coudert, Frederic Rene, American congressman, June 1941, *Obit* July 1972

Cousins, Frank, English labor leader, Feb 1960, *Obit* July 1986

Couve de Murville, Maurice, French diplomat and prime minister, Apr 1955, *Obit* June 2000

Cox, Archibald, American lawyer and special counsel in Watergate investigation, July 1961, *Obit* Yrbk 2004

Cox, Christopher, American regulatory agency official, July 1999

Cox, E. Eugene, American congressman, Apr 1943, *Obit* Feb 1953

Coy, Wayne, Mar 1948, *Obit* Yrbk 1958

Craig, George North, governor, Feb 1950, *Obit* Feb 1993

Craigie, Robert, British diplomat, July 1942, *Obit* July 1959

Crane, Philip M., American congressman, May 1980

Cranston, Alan, American senator, Feb 1950, Oct 1969, *Obit* Mar 2001

Craxi, Bettino, Italian prime minister, Feb 1984, *Obit* June 2000

Creel, George, American newspaper editor and government official, June 1944, *Obit* Jan 1954

Cresson, Edith, French prime minister, Sept 1991

Crewe, Robert Offley Ashburton Crew-Milnes, *Obit* July 1945

Cripps, C. A., *Obit* Aug 1941

Cripps, Richard Stafford, British statesman, July 1940, Apr 1948, *Obit* June 1952

Cristiani, Alfredo, Salvadoran president, Jan 1990

Crocker, Ryan, American diplomat, Oct 2007

Crosbie, John Carnell, Canadian political leader, Jan 1990

Crosby, Robert, June 1954

Crosland, Anthony, British cabinet member, Sept 1963, *Obit* Apr 1977

Cross, Burton Melvin, governor, Apr 1954, *Obit* Jan 1999

Cross, Ronald H., June 1941

Crosser, Robert, Mar 1953, *Obit* Sept 1957

Crow, John O., Mar 1969

Crowe, William J., American admiral, July 1988, *Obit* Yrbk 2008

Cruz, Ted, American state solicitor general, May 2013

Csaky, Stephen, *Obit* Mar 1941

Cudahy, John, diplomat, *Obit* Oct 1943

Culkin, Francis D., *Obit* Sept 1943

Cullen, Thomas H., *Obit* Apr 1944

Culver, John C., Nov 1979

Cummings, Elijah E., American congressman, Feb 2004

Cuomo, Andrew, American governor, Oct 1998

Cuomo, Mario, American governor, Aug 1983

Currie, Lauchlin Bernard, American economist, May 1941, *Obit* Mar 1994

Curtin, John, Australian prime minister, July 1941, *Obit* Aug 1945

Curtis, Carl T., American senator, Sept 1954, *Obit* June 2000

Curtis, Thomas B., American congressman, Mar 1965, *Obit* Mar 1993

Cyrankiewicz, Jozef, Feb 1957

D'Amato, Alfonse, American senator, Sept 1983

Dahanayake, Wijeyananda, Apr 1960

Daladier, Edouard, French statesman, Apr 1940, *Obit* Yrbk 1970

Daley, Richard J., American mayor, Sept 1955, June 1976

Daley, Richard M., American mayor, Aug 1992

Daley, William, American presidential adviser, Mar 1998

Dandurand, Raoul, *Obit* Apr 1942

Danforth, John C., American senator, Jan 1992

Daniel, Dan, congressman, June 1957

Daniel, Price, American senator and governor, Jan 1956, *Obit* Oct 1988

Darden, Christopher, district attorney, Feb 1997

Darre, R. Walther, German Nazi leader, Nov 1941, *Obit* Jan 1957

Darwin, Leonard, *Obit* May 1943

Daschle, Thomas, American senator, Oct 1995

Dati, Rachida, French lawyer and cabinet member, Apr 2009

Daud Khan, Sardar Mohammed, Mar 1957

Daugherty, Harry M., American Attorney general, *Obit* Yrbk 1941

Davey, Martin L., American governor, congressman and mayor, *Obit* May 1946

Davidovitch, Ljuba, *Obit* Mar 1940

Davidson, Irwin D., American congressman, Jan 1956

Davidson, William L., American physicist, July 1952

Davies, Clement, Oct 1950, *Obit* May 1962

Davies, Ernest, May 1951

Davies, Joseph Edward, American lawyer and diplomat, Apr 1942, *Obit* July 1958

Davis, Artur, American congressman, Feb 2009

Davis, Gray, American governor, June 1999

Davis, James C., Apr 1957, *Obit* Feb 1982

Davis, John William, American lawyer, congressman and diplomat, Mar 1953, *Obit* May 1955

Davis, Jonathan M., governor, *Obit* Aug 1943

Dawson, William, diplomat, Apr 1941, *Obit* Sept 1972

Dawson, William Levi, American congressman, Apr 1945, *Obit* Yrbk 1970

Day, Albert M., biologist, Yrbk 1948

De Castro, Morris F., May 1950

De Klerk, Frederik Willem, South African president, Feb 1990

De Lille, Patricia, South African political leader, Jan 2004

De Quay, Jan Eduard, Dutch prime minister, May 1963, *Obit* Aug 1985

De Sapio, Carmine G., American political leader, Sept 1955, *Obit* Yrbk 2004

De Valera, Eamon, Irish statesman, Nov 1940, Sept 1951, *Obit* Oct 1975

DeConcini, Dennis, American senator, Feb 1992

DeLauro, Rosa, American congresswoman, Mar 2000

DeLay, Tom, American congressman, May 1999

Dean, Arthur Hobson, American lawyer and diplomat, Mar 1954, *Obit* Jan 1988

Dean, Gordon E., American government official, Sept 1950, *Obit* Nov 1958

Dean, Howard, American governor and political party leader, Oct 2002

Dean, Patrick, British diplomat, May 1961, *Obit* Jan 1995

Debray, Regis, French political philosopher, novelist and government official, June 1982

Debre, Michel, French prime minister, May 1959, *Obit* Oct 1996

Debus, Kurt H., rocket engineer and NASA official, Nov 1973, *Obit* Nov 1983

Deer, Ada, Native American leader and government official, Sept 1994

Defferre, Gaston, French cabinet member, Sept 1967, *Obit* June 1986

Delanoe, Bertrand, French mayor, Jan 2002

Dellums, Ronald V., American congressman, Sept 1972, Sept 1993

Delors, Jacques, French economist and government official, June 1989

Demirel, Suleyman, Turkish prime minister, Feb 1980

Dempsey, John Noel, governor, June 1961, *Obit* Sept 1989

Denebrink, Francis C., admiral, Feb 1956, *Obit* June 1987

Denenberg, Herbert S., Yrbk 1972

Denham, R. N., American regulatory agency official, Oct 1947, *Obit* Sept 1954

Dennis, Lawrence, American political writer and diplomat, Mar 1941, *Obit* Oct 1977

Derthick, Lawrence Gridley, educator and government official, Apr 1957, *Obit* Mar 1993

Derwinski, Edward J., American Secretary of veterans affairs, Aug 1991, *Obit* Yrbk 2012

Des Graz, Charles Louis, *Obit* Yrbk 1940

Des Portes, Fay Allen, *Obit* Nov 1944

Desai, Morarji, Indian prime minister, Sept 1958, Jan 1978, *Obit* June 1995

Deuba, Sher Bahadur, Nepalese prime minister, Jan 2002

Deukmejian, George, governor, June 1983

Deupree, Richard R., Apr 1946, *Obit* May 1974

Dever, Paul A., American governor, May 1949, *Obit* July 1958

Deviny, John J., Sept 1948, *Obit* Apr 1955

Devold, Kristin Krohn, Norwegian military official, Jan 2003

Dewey, Thomas E., American governor, July 1940, Sept 1944, *Obit* Apr 1971

Dexheimer, W. A., Feb 1955

Dhalla, Ruby, Canadian member of Parliament, Jan 2006

Dhebar, Uchhrangrai Navalshankar, June 1955

DiSalle, Michael V., American governor, Jan 1951, *Obit* Nov 1981

Diaz Ordaz, Gustavo, Mexican president, May 1965, *Obit* Sept 1979

Dick, Charles, *Obit* May 1945

Dickerson, Roy E., *Obit* Apr 1944

Dickinson, Luren D., *Obit* June 1943

Dickinson, Willoughby Hyett Dickinson, British member of Parliament, *Obit* July 1943

Diefenbaker, John George, Canadian prime minister, May 1957, *Obit* Oct 1979

Dies, Martin, American lawyer and congressman, Apr 1940, *Obit* Jan 1973

Dieterich, William H., *Obit* Yrbk 1940

Diggs, Charles, American congressman, July 1957, *Obit* Nov 1998

Dimechkie, Nadim, Feb 1960

Dimitrov, Georgi, Bulgarian prime minister, May 1949

Dingell, John D., American congressman, Mar 1949, *Obit* Yrbk 1956

Dingell, John D., American congressman, Aug 1983

Dinkins, David, American mayor, Mar 1990

Diogo, Luisa, Mozambican prime minister, Jan 2004

Dion, Stephane, Canadian political leader, Jan 2007

Dirksen, Everett McKinley, American senator, Apr 1941, Sept 1957, *Obit* Nov 1969

Ditter, J. William, *Obit* Jan 1944

Dixon, Owen, Australian judge and diplomat, Aug 1942

Dixon, Paul Rand, American regulatory agency official, Jan 1968

Dixon, Pierson, British diplomat, Sept 1954, *Obit* June 1965

Djuanda, Apr 1958, *Obit* Jan 1964

Djukanovic, Milo, Montenegrin president, Aug 2001

Dobrynin, Anatoly F., Soviet diplomat, Sept 1962, *Obit* Yrbk 2010

Docking, George, governor, June 1958, *Obit* Mar 1964

Dodd, Thomas, American senator, Sept 1959, *Obit* July 1971

Dodd, William Edward, historian and diplomat, *Obit* Mar 1940

Doe, Samuel Kanyon, Liberian president, May 1981, *Obit* Nov 1990

Doi, Takako, Japanese socialist leader, July 1992

Dolan, Daniel Leo, Sept 1956

Dole, Elizabeth Hanford, American senator, June 1983, Jan 1997

Dole, Robert J., American senator, Apr 1972, Oct 1987

Domenici, Pete, American senator, June 1982

Donahey, Vic, *Obit* May 1946

Donaldson, Jesse M., American postmaster general, Jan 1948, *Obit* May 1970

Donaldson, William, American regulatory agency official, June 2003

Donlon, Mary H., July 1949, *Obit* May 1977

Donnell, Forrest C., American governor and senator, Sept 1949

Donnelly, Phil M., June 1956, *Obit* Nov 1961

Donnelly, Walter Joseph, diplomat, Sept 1952, *Obit* Jan 1971

Donovan, James B., American lawyer, June 1961, *Obit* Mar 1970

Donovan, Raymond James, American Secretary of labor, Jan 1982

Donovan, Shaun, American Secretary of housing and urban development, Mar 2009

Dorticos Torrado, Osvaldo, Cuban president, Feb 1963, *Obit* Aug 1983

Doughton, Robert L., American congressman, July 1942, *Obit* Yrbk 1955

Douglas, Denzil, Saint Kitts-Nevis prime minister, Jan 2007

Douglas, Emily Taft, congresswoman, Apr 1945, *Obit* Mar 1994

Douglas, Helen Gahagan, American congresswoman, Sept 1944, *Obit* Aug 1980

Douglas, James Henderson, American Secretary of the air force, Sept 1957, *Obit* Apr 1988

Douglas, Lewis W., American government official, Mar 1947, *Obit* May 1974

Douglas, T. C., Canadian political leader, July 1957, *Obit* Apr 1986

Douglas, William O., American Supreme Court justice, Oct 1941, Nov 1950, *Obit* Mar 1980

Dover, Elmer, *Obit* Nov 1940

Dowling, Walter, American diplomat, Mar 1963, *Obit* Sept 1977

Downey, Sheridan, Oct 1949, *Obit* Jan 1962

Drapeau, Jean, Canadian mayor, Yrbk 1967, *Obit* Oct 1999

Drees, Willem, Dutch prime minister, Jan 1949, *Obit* July 1988

Dryden, Hugh L., American physicist and NASA official, Apr 1959, *Obit* Jan 1966

Duarte, Jose Napoleon, Salvadoran president, Sept 1981, *Obit* Apr 1990

Duff, James Henderson, senator and governor, Apr 1948, *Obit* Feb 1970

Dukakis, Michael, American governor, Feb 1978

Duke, Angier Biddle, diplomat, Feb 1962, *Obit* July 1995

Dulles, Allen Welsh, American diplomat and intelligence official, Mar 1949, *Obit* Mar 1969

Dulles, John Foster, American Secretary of state, Aug 1944, Sept 1953, *Obit* July 1959

Dunbar, P. B., July 1949, *Obit* Nov 1968

Duncan Smith, Iain, British political leader, Jan 2002

Duncan, Andrew Rae, July 1941, *Obit* May 1952

Duncan, Patrick, South African governor-general, *Obit* Sept 1943

Duncan-Sandys, Duncan Edwin Duncan-Sandys, British cabinet member, May 1952

Dunlap, John B., Yrbk 1951, *Obit* Feb 1965

Dunn, James Clement, May 1943, *Obit* June 1979

Dunn, Jennifer, American congresswoman, Mar 1999, *Obit* Nov 2007

Durbin, Richard J., American senator, Aug 2006

Durenberger, David, American senator, Oct 1988

Durham, Carl, American congressman, July 1957, *Obit* June 1974

Durkin, Martin Patrick, American Secretary of labor, Feb 1953, *Obit* Jan 1956

Dutra, Eurico Gaspar, Mar 1946, *Obit* Sept 1974

Duvalier, Francois, Haitian president, Sept 1958, *Obit* June 1971

Duvalier, Jean-Claude, Haitian president, June 1972

Dwinell, Lane, governor, June 1956, *Obit* June 1997

Dworshak, Henry C., American senator, congressman and newspaper publisher, Jan 1950, *Obit* Oct 1962

Eady, Wilfrid, Oct 1947, *Obit* Feb 1962

Eagleburger, Lawrence S., American diplomat, Nov 1992, *Obit* Yrbk 2011

Eagleton, Thomas F., American senator, Nov 1973, *Obit* Yrbk 2007

Early, Stephen, American presidential press secretary, July 1941, Yrbk 1949, *Obit* Sept 1951

Eastland, James O., American senator, Jan 1949, *Obit* Apr 1986

Eastman, Joseph B., July 1942, *Obit* May 1944

Eastwood, Clint, American actor and film director, Oct 1971, Mar 1989

Eaton, Charles A., American congressman, May 1945, *Obit* Mar 1953

Eban, Abba, Israeli diplomat, Oct 1948, May 1957, *Obit* Mar 2003

Eboue, Felix, French colonial governor, *Obit* July 1944

Eccles, David, British cabinet member, Jan 1952, *Obit* May 1999

Ecevit, Bulent, Turkish prime minister, Jan 1975, *Obit* Yrbk 2007

Echeverria Alvarez, Luis, Mexican president, Nov 1972

Eckstein, Otto, American economist, Feb 1967, *Obit* May 1984

Ede, James Chuter, May 1946, *Obit* Jan 1966

Edelman, Maurice, Jan 1954, *Obit* Feb 1976

Edge, Walter Evans, senator and governor, June 1945, *Obit* Jan 1957

Edison, Charles, July 1940, *Obit* Oct 1969

Edwards, Charles C., American surgeon and regulatory official, Oct 1973, *Obit* Yrbk 2011

Edwards, Don, American congressman, Mar 1983

Edwards, John, American senator and lawyer, Oct 2004

Edwards, John H., American congressman and government official, *Obit* Yrbk 1945

Egan, William Allen, American governor, Sept 1959, *Obit* July 1984

Eghbal, Manouchehr, May 1959, *Obit* Feb 1978

Ehlers, Vernon J., American congressman, Jan 2005

Ehrlichman, John, American presidential adviser, Oct 1979, *Obit* Apr 1999

Ekman, Carl Gustaf, *Obit* July 1945

El Baradei, Mohamed, Egyptian diplomat and international organization official, Jan 2003

El-Khoury, Beshira, Yrbk 1951, *Obit* Feb 1964

El-Nahas, Mustafa, July 1951, *Obit* Nov 1965

Elath, Eliahu, Israeli Zionist leader, Yrbk 1948, *Obit* Aug 1990

Elders, Joycelyn, American surgeon general, Mar 1994

Eliasson, Jan, Swedish diplomat, Jan 2005

Elizalde, Joaquin M., Feb 1948, *Obit* Mar 1965

Ellender, Allen J., American senator, July 1946, *Obit* Oct 1972

Ellington, Buford, governor, Sept 1960, *Obit* May 1972

Ellison, Keith, American congressman, Apr 2007

Emanuel, Rahm, American mayor, Apr 1998, Mar 2009

Emerson, Lee E., Oct 1953

Emmet of Amberley, Evelyn, Mar 1953

Enckell, Carl J. A., Apr 1950, *Obit* June 1959

Endara, Guillermo, Panamanian president, Feb 1991, *Obit* Yrbk 2009

Endeley, E. M. L., July 1959

Engle, Clair, American senator, Mar 1957, *Obit* Oct 1964

Englebright, Harry L., *Obit* July 1943

Enkhbayar, Nambaryn, Mongolian president, Jan 2007

Erdogan, Recep Tayyip, Turkish prime minister, Jan 2003

Erhard, Ludwig, German chancellor, Jan 1950, June 1964, *Obit* July 1977

Erickson, John Edward, *Obit* June 1946

Erkin, Feridun C., Jan 1952

Erlander, Tage F., Swedish prime minister, Oct 1947, *Obit* Aug 1985

Ertegun, Mehmet Munir, *Obit* Jan 1945

Ervin, Sam J., American senator, Jan 1955, Oct 1973, *Obit* June 1985

Esch, John J., *Obit* June 1941

Eshkol, Levi, Israeli prime minister, Oct 1963, *Obit* Apr 1969

Espy, Mike, American Secretary of agriculture, Oct 1993

Estigarribia, Jose Felix, Paraguayan field marshal and president, Mar 1940, *Obit* Mar 1940

Estrada, Joseph, Filipino president, Feb 2000

Etzel, Franz, German economist and cabinet member, Sept 1957

Evren, Kenan, Turkish president, Apr 1984

Ewing, Oscar R., American government official, July 1948, *Obit* Mar 1980

Exeter, David George Brownlow Cecil, British hurdler and Olympic executive, Jan 1956

Exon, J. James, American senator, Nov 1996, *Obit* Yrbk 2005

Eyskens, Gaston, Belgian prime minister, Nov 1949, *Obit* Feb 1988

Eytan, Walter, Israeli diplomat, Oct 1958, *Obit* Oct 2001

Fabian, Robert, Apr 1954, *Obit* Aug 1978

Fabius, Laurent, French political leader, Feb 1985

Fagerholm, Karl August, Finnish prime minister, Oct 1948, *Obit* July 1984

Fahy, Charles, American judge and solicitor general, Jan 1942, *Obit* Nov 1979

Fairchild, Benjamin Lewis, *Obit* Yrbk 1946

Fairclough, Ellen Louks, Canadian cabinet member, Oct 1957, *Obit* Yrbk 2005

Fall, Albert B., American Secretary of the interior, *Obit* Jan 1945

Falldin, Thorbjorn, Swedish prime minister, May 1978

Fallin, Mary, American congresswoman, Mar 2011

Fanfani, Amintore, Italian prime minister, Oct 1958, *Obit* Mar 2000

Farley, James Aloysius, American political leader, Sept 1944, *Obit* Aug 1976

Farmer, Guy, Feb 1955

Farrington, Joseph Rider, American newspaper executive and congressman, May 1948, *Obit* Sept 1954

Fascell, Dante B., congressman, Apr 1960, *Obit* Feb 1999

Fattah, Chaka, American congressman, Sept 2003

Faubus, Orval, American governor, Oct 1956, *Obit* Feb 1995

Fauntroy, Walter E., American congressman, Feb 1979

Faure, Edgar, French statesman, Feb 1952, *Obit* May 1988

Faurot, Joseph A., *Obit* Jan 1943

Favreau, Jonathan, American speechwriter, May 2009

Fawzi, Mahmoud, Yrbk 1951

Feingold, Russ, American senator, July 1998

Feinsinger, Nathan P., professor of law and labor mediator, May 1952, *Obit* Jan 1984

Feinstein, Dianne, American senator, June 1979, Aug 1995

Feith, Douglas J., American military official, July 2008

Feldmann, Markus, June 1956, *Obit* Jan 1959

Felt, W. Mark, American FBI official and Watergate informant Deep Throat, Sept 2005, *Obit* Yrbk 2009

Fenty, Adrian, American mayor, Mar 2007

Fenwick, Millicent, American congresswoman, Apr 1977, *Obit* Nov 1992

Ferguson, Garland S., July 1949, *Obit* June 1963

Ferguson, Homer, American diplomat and senator, May 1943, *Obit* Mar 1983

Ferguson, Howard, *Obit* Apr 1946

Ferguson, James Edward, governor, *Obit* Nov 1944

Fernandes, L. Esteves, Oct 1950

Fernandez de la Vega, Maria Teresa, Spanish vice-president, Jan 2007

Ferraro, Geraldine A., American lawyer, congresswoman, political commentator and vice-presidential candidate, Sept 1984, *Obit* Yrbk 2011

Ferris, Scott, *Obit* July 1945

Figueres Ferrer, Jose, Costa Rican president, Oct 1953, *Obit* Aug 1990

Filov, Bogdan, Apr 1941

Finch, Robert H., American secretary of health, education and welfare, Mar 1969, *Obit* Jan 1996

Fine, John Sydney, governor, Sept 1951, *Obit* July 1978

Fini, Gianfranco, Italian political leader, Jan 2003

Finletter, Thomas K., American diplomat and government official, Jan 1948, *Obit* June 1980

Finley, John Huston, Mar 1940

Finnegan, Joseph F., Apr 1959, *Obit* Apr 1964

Fischer, Carlos L., Feb 1959

Fischer, Israel Frederick, judge and congressman, *Obit* Apr 1940

Fischer, Joschka, German political leader and diplomat, Jan 2002

Fish, Bert, *Obit* Sept 1943

Fish, Hamilton, American congressman, Jan 1941, *Obit* Mar 1991

Fisher, John Stuchell, governor, *Obit* Aug 1940

FitzGerald, Garret, Irish prime minister, Aug 1984, *Obit* Yrbk 2011

Fitzgerald, Patrick, American district attorney, Jan 2006

Fitzgibbons, John, *Obit* Oct 1941

Fitzroy, Edward Algernon, *Obit* Apr 1943

Fitzwater, Marlin, American presidential press secretary, May 1988

Flanders, Ralph E., American senator, Jan 1948, *Obit* Apr 1970

Flandin, Pierre Etienne, French political leader, Jan 1941, *Obit* Oct 1958

Fleischmann, Manly, lawyer, July 1951

Fleming, Amalia Koutsouri, Greek legislator, Nov 1972, *Obit* Apr 1986

Fleming, Philip Bracken, Apr 1940, *Obit* Yrbk 1956

Flemming, Arthur S., American Secretary of health, education and welfare, June 1951, Apr 1960, *Obit* Nov 1996

Fletcher, Angus, Sept 1946, *Obit* Nov 1960

Fletcher, James C., American physicist and NASA official, May 1972, *Obit* Feb 1992

Flood, Daniel J., American congressman, Aug 1978, *Obit* Aug 1994

Flore, Edward F., *Obit* Oct 1945

Flores Nano, Lourdes, Peruvian political leader, Jan 2006

Florio, James J., governor, May 1990

Fly, James L., lawyer, Sept 1940, *Obit* Feb 1966

Flynn, Raymond, American mayor and diplomat, Oct 1993

Fogarty, John Edward, congressman, Apr 1964, *Obit* Mar 1967

Fogh Rasmussen, Anders, Danish prime minister, Jan 2004

Foley, Raymond M., Oct 1949, *Obit* Apr 1975

Foley, Thomas S., American Speaker of the House, Sept 1989

Folger, A. D., *Obit* June 1941

Folks, Homer, Yrbk 1940

Folsom, James Elisha, American governor, Sept 1949, *Obit* Jan 1988

Folsom, Marion Bayard, American Secretary of health, education and welfare, Jan 1950, *Obit* Nov 1976

Fong, Hiram, American senator, Feb 1960, *Obit* Yrbk 2004

Foot, Michael, British political leader, Yrbk 1950, May 1981, *Obit* Yrbk 2010

Forand, Aime J., June 1960, *Obit* Mar 1972

Forbes, John J., Apr 1952

Ford, Gerald R., American president, Mar 1961, Nov 1975, *Obit* Feb 2007

Forster, Rudolph, *Obit* Aug 1943

Fortas, Abe, American Supreme Court justice, Feb 1966, *Obit* May 1982

Foster, John S., Yrbk 1971

Fowler, R. M., Oct 1954

Fox Quesada, Vicente, Mexican president, May 2001

Fraga Iribarne, Manuel, Spanish political leader, May 1965, *Obit* Yrbk 2012

Francois-Poncet, Andre, Oct 1949, *Obit* Mar 1978

Frank, Barney, American congressman, Apr 1995

Frank, Jerome N., American judge, Apr 1941, *Obit* Mar 1957

Franke, William B., Sept 1959, *Obit* Aug 1979

Frankfurter, Felix, American Supreme Court justice, June 1941, July 1957, *Obit* Apr 1965

Franklin, Shirley, American mayor, Aug 2002

Fraser, I., Yrbk 1947

Fraser, Malcolm, Australian prime minister, Mar 1976

Fraser, Peter, May 1942, *Obit* Jan 1951

Freeh, Louis J., American FBI director, May 1996

Freeman, John, June 1969

Freeman, Orville L., American governor, Secretary of agriculture and magazine publishing executive, June 1956, *Obit* Yrbk 2003

Frei Montalva, Eduardo, Chilean president, Apr 1965, *Obit* Mar 1982

Fremantle, Francis Edward, *Obit* Oct 1943

Frick, Wilhelm, German Nazi leader, Aug 1942, *Obit* Nov 1946

Frist, Bill, American surgeon and senator, Nov 2002

Frohnmayer, John E., lawyer and government official, Apr 1990

Frondizi, Arturo, Argentine president, Oct 1958, *Obit* June 1995

Frost, Leslie M., Canadian political leader, Oct 1953, *Obit* July 1973

Fujimori, Alberto, Peruvian president, Nov 1990

Fujiyama, Aiichiro, Japanese cabinet member, Apr 1958, *Obit* May 1985

Fukuda, Takeo, Japanese prime minister, June 1974, *Obit* Sept 1995

Fulbright, J. William, American senator, Nov 1943, Oct 1955, *Obit* Apr 1995

Fulmer, Hampton Pitts, *Obit* Yrbk 1944

Fulton, E. D., Jan 1959

Furcolo, Foster, American governor, Jan 1958, *Obit* Sept 1995

Furtseva, Ekaterina A., Soviet communist leader, June 1956, *Obit* Yrbk 1974

Fyan, Loleta Dawson, librarian, Yrbk 1951

Gabrielson, Guy George, American lawyer, Oct 1949, *Obit* June 1976

Gaffney, T. St. John, *Obit* Mar 1945

Gaillard, Felix, French prime minister, Feb 1958, *Obit* Oct 1970

Gaitskell, Hugh, British cabinet member, June 1950, *Obit* Feb 1963

Gallagher, William J., *Obit* Oct 1946

Gallegos, Romulo, Venezuelan author and president, May 1948, *Obit* May 1969

Galloway, George, British member of Parliament, Jan 2005

Gamble, Ralph A., Jan 1953, *Obit* May 1959

Gandhi, Indira, Indian prime minister, Oct 1959, June 1966, *Obit* Jan 1985

Gandhi, Rajiv, Indian prime minister, Apr 1985, *Obit* July 1991

Garcia Medina, Amalia, Mexican provincial governor, Jan 2004

Garcia Perez, Alan, Peruvian president, Nov 1985

Garcia, Carlos P., Filipino president, June 1957, *Obit* July 1971

Gardner, O. Max, Jan 1947

Garn, Jake, senator, Aug 1985

Garrels, Arthur, *Obit* Aug 1943

Garvey, Jane F., government official, Sept 2000

Gary, Raymond, governor, Oct 1955, *Obit* Feb 1994

Garza, Ed, American mayor, June 2002

Gaspard, Patrick, American presidential aide, July 2010

Gasperi, Alcide de, Italian statesman, Yrbk 1946, *Obit* Oct 1954

Gates, Ralph F., Sept 1947

Gatov, Elizabeth Rudel, Yrbk 1961

Gaud, William S., Jan 1969, *Obit* Feb 1978

Gauss, Clarence Edward, diplomat, Jan 1941, *Obit* June 1960

Gavrilovic, Stoyan, May 1946, *Obit* Mar 1965

Gayatri Devi, Mar 1968, *Obit* Yrbk 2009

Gbagbo, Laurent, Ivorian president, Jan 2004

Gedi, Ali Mohamed, Somalian prime minister, Jan 2007

Geijer, Arne, Swedish labor leader and member of Parliament, July 1964

Gelb, Leslie H., American journalist, government official and international relations specialist, Jan 2003

Gemayel, Amin, Lebanese president, Mar 1983

Genscher, Hans Dietrich, German diplomat and political leader, June 1975

Geoffrey-Lloyd, Geoffrey William, British cabinet member, Feb 1956

George, Walter F., American senator, June 1943, June 1955, *Obit* Oct 1957

George-Brown, George Alfred
George-Brown, British cabinet
member, Yrbk 1963, *Obit* July
1985
Gephardt, Richard A., American
congressman, Oct 1987
Gerberding, Julie, American
physician and public health
official, Sept 2004
Gerhardsen, Einar, Norwegian
prime minister, Mar 1949, *Obit*
Nov 1987
Gerson, Michael, American
presidential speechwriter, Feb
2002
Gerstenmaier, Eugen, German
political leader, Feb 1958, *Obit*
May 1986
Gheorghiu-Dej, Gheorghe,
Romanian prime minister, Oct
1958, *Obit* May 1965
Gibbs, Robert, American
presidential press secretary,
Apr 2009
Gibson, Ernest W., American
governor and judge, July
1949, *Obit* Yrbk 1969
Gibson, Ernest Willard,
American senator, *Obit* Aug
1940
Gibson, Hugh, diplomat, Jan
1953, *Obit* Feb 1955
Gibson, John W., Oct 1947
Gibson, Kenneth A., American
mayor, May 1971
Giegengack, A. E., Nov 1944,
Obit Sept 1974
Giffords, Gabrielle, American
congresswoman, Mar 2012
Gil Fortoul, Jose, *Obit* Aug 1943
Gilani, Yusuf Raza, Pakistani
prime minister, Nov 2008
Gillette, Guy M., Sept 1946, *Obit*
Apr 1973
Gillibrand, Kirsten, American
senator, Oct 2013
Gilligan, John J., American
governor and congressman,
May 1972, *Obit* Yrbk 2013
Gilmore, James S., governor,
June 2001
Gilmore, Voit, Feb 1962
Gilmour, John, British cabinet
member, *Obit* Apr 1940
Gilpatric, Roswell L., American
lawyer and government
official, Mar 1964, *Obit* May
1996
Gilruth, Robert R., American
aerospace engineer and

NASA official, Oct 1963, *Obit*
Yrbk 2000
Gingrich, Newt, American
political leader and former
Speaker of the House, July
1989
Giri, V. V., Jan 1970, *Obit* Aug
1980
Giscard d'Estaing, Valery,
French president, July 1967,
Oct 1974
Giuliani, Rudolph W., American
mayor and lawyer, Apr 1988,
Jan 2008
Gladwyn, Hubert Miles Gladwyn
Jebb, British diplomat, Yrbk
1948
Glass, Carter, American
senator, Oct 1941, *Obit* June
1946
Glenn, John, American
astronaut and senator, June
1962, Mar 1976, Jan 1999
Gnassingbe, Faure, Togolese
president, Jan 2005
Goddard, James L., American
regulatory agency official, Oct
1968, *Obit* Yrbk 2010
Goldberg, Arthur J., American
diplomat and Supreme Court
justice, July 1949, July 1961,
Obit Mar 1990
Golden, Clinton S., Apr 1948,
Obit Sept 1961
Golding, Bruce, Jamaican prime
minister, Mar 2008
Goldman, Olive Mortimer
Remington, Sept 1950
Goldsborough, Phillips Lee, *Obit*
Yrbk 1946
Goldschmidt, Neil E., American
Secretary of transportation
and governor, Aug 1980
Goldwater, Barry M., American
senator, May 1955, June
1978, *Obit* Aug 1998
Goldwater, S. S., American
physician, hospital
administrator and public health
official, *Obit* Yrbk 1942
Gomes, Francisco da Costa,
Portuguese president, May
1976
Gomes, Manuel Teixeira, *Obit*
Yrbk 1941
Gomez, Laureano, Colombian
president, May 1950, *Obit*
Sept 1965
Gonzales, Alberto R., American
Attorney general, Apr 2002

Gonzalez Videla, Gabriel,
Cuban president, June 1950
Gonzalez, Cesar, Oct 1954
Gonzalez, Felipe, Spanish prime
minister, Jan 1978
Gonzalez, Henry B., American
congressman, June 1964, Feb
1993, *Obit* Feb 2001
Goode, W. Wilson, American
mayor, Oct 1985
Goodell, Charles E., American
senator, Yrbk 1968, *Obit* Mar
1987
Goodloe, John D., Apr 1947
Goodrich, James P., *Obit* Oct
1940
Goodwin, Richard N., American
speechwriter and journalist,
Yrbk 1968
Goodwin, Robert C., May 1951
Gorbach, Alfons, Oct 1961, *Obit*
Oct 1972
Gorbachev, Mikhail, Soviet
president, Aug 1985
Gordon, Thomas S., American
congressman, Apr 1957, *Obit*
Apr 1959
Gordon-Walker, Patrick
Chrestien Gordon Walker, Jan
1966
Gore, Al, American
vice-president, June 1987
Gore, Albert A., American
senator and father of
Vice-President Albert Gore,
Jr., Jan 1952, *Obit* Feb 1999
Gork, Haydar, Oct 1956
Gorrie, Jack Osborne, Mar 1952
Gorton, John Grey, Australian
prime minister, July 1968, *Obit*
Sept 2002
Gorton, Slade, senator, Aug
1993
Gossett, William T., lawyer and
diplomat, July 1969, *Obit* Oct
1998
Gottwald, Klement, Czech
president, Apr 1948, *Obit* Apr
1953
Gough, Lewis K., Jan 1953, *Obit*
Jan 1968
Gouin, Felix, French statesman,
Mar 1946, *Obit* Oct 1979
Goulart, Joao Belchior Marques,
Brazilian president, Sept 1962,
Obit Feb 1977
Gould, Arthur R., *Obit* Sept 1946
Grace, Alonzo G., Jan 1950,
Obit Yrbk 1971
Graham, Bob, American
senator, July 1986

Graham, Horace F., *Obit* Jan 1942

Gramm, Phil, American senator and economist, May 1986

Granahan, Kathryn Elizabeth, congresswoman, Oct 1959, *Obit* Sept 1979

Granholm, Jennifer M., American governor, Oct 2003

Grantham, Alexander, May 1954

Grantley, John Richard Brinsley Norton, *Obit* Sept 1943

Granville, William Spencer Leveson-Gower, Sept 1950, *Obit* Sept 1953

Grasso, Ella, American governor, May 1975, *Obit* Mar 1981

Grau San Martin, Ramon, Cuban president, Oct 1944, *Obit* Oct 1969

Gravel, Mike, American senator, Jan 1972

Graves, Bibb, governor, *Obit* May 1942

Graves, Earl G., American magazine publishing executive, Aug 1997

Gray, C. Boyden, American lawyer and presidential adviser, Aug 1989

Gray, Carl R., Mar 1948, *Obit* Feb 1956

Gray, Gordon, American broadcasting executive and military official, Sept 1949, *Obit* Feb 1983

Gray, L. Patrick, American FBI director, Sept 1972, *Obit* Yrbk 2005

Gray, William H., American congressman and college fund administrator, Feb 1988, *Obit* Yrbk 2013

Green, Dwight H., American governor, Apr 1948, *Obit* Apr 1958

Green, Edith, American congresswoman, May 1956, *Obit* June 1987

Green, Howard, Jan 1960

Green, Mark J., American lawyer, consumer rights advocate and municipal official, Feb 1988

Green, Theodore Francis, American senator and governor, Feb 1950, *Obit* June 1966

Gregg, Hugh, Jan 1954

Grew, Joseph C., American diplomat, Feb 1941, *Obit* July 1965

Griffin, Marvin, American governor, June 1956, *Obit* Aug 1982

Griffin, Michael D., American NASA official, Aug 2005

Griffin, Robert P., American senator, May 1960

Griffith, Paul H., American management consultant and military official, Jan 1947, *Obit* Feb 1975

Griffiths, Martha Wright, American congresswoman and state official, Oct 1955, *Obit* Yrbk 2003

Grigg, James, Apr 1942, *Obit* July 1964

Grimond, Jo, British political leader, Oct 1963, *Obit* Jan 1994

Griswold, Dwight P., American senator, governor and diplomat, Yrbk 1947, *Obit* June 1954

Groenman, Frans Eyso Henricus, *Obit* Aug 1943

Gronchi, Giovanni, Oct 1955, *Obit* Jan 1979

Gross, Ernest A., diplomat and lawyer, Feb 1951, *Obit* July 1999

Gross, H. R., American congressman, Jan 1964, *Obit* Oct 1987

Grosz, Karoly, Hungarian prime minister, Sept 1988, *Obit* Mar 1996

Grotewohl, Otto, July 1950, *Obit* Nov 1964

Gruber, Karl, Austrian diplomat, Feb 1947

Gruber, Ruth, American journalist, photographer and humanitarian, June 2001

Gruening, Ernest, American territorial governor and senator, Yrbk 1946, July 1966, *Obit* Sept 1974

Guardia, Ernesto de la, Panamanian president, Jan 1957

Guardia, Ricardo Adolfo de la, Panamanian president, May 1942, *Obit* Feb 1970

Guffey, Joseph F., Mar 1944, *Obit* May 1959

Gujral, Inder K., Indian prime minister, *Obit* Yrbk 2013

Gul, Abdullah, Turkish prime minister, Jan 2007

Gunn, Selskar M., *Obit* Sept 1944

Gunter, Julius Caldeen, *Obit* Yrbk 1940

Gunter, Ray, July 1967, *Obit* June 1977

Gunther, Franklin Mott, *Obit* Feb 1942

Gurtner, Franz, German cabinet member, *Obit* Mar 1941

Gusmao, Xanana, East Timorese president, Jan 2002

Guthman, Edwin O., American newspaper editor, June 1950, *Obit* Yrbk 2008

Guyer, Ulysses Samuel, *Obit* July 1943

Haass, Richard, American international relations specialist, June 2010

Habib, Philip Charles, American diplomat, Sept 1981, *Obit* July 1992

Habibie, Bacharuddin Jusuf, Indonesian president, Oct 1998

Habre, Hissene, Chadian president, Aug 1987

Habsburg, Otto, German member of European Parliament, June 1941, *Obit* Yrbk 2011

Hacha, Emil, Yrbk 1942, *Obit* Sept 1945

Hackworth, Green H., Jan 1958, *Obit* Sept 1973

Haddon, William, government official and physician, Feb 1969, *Obit* Apr 1985

Hadley, Stephen J., American national security adviser, Nov 2006

Hailsham of St. Marylebone, Quintin Hogg, British cabinet member, Sept 1957, *Obit* Feb 2002

Hainisch, Michael, *Obit* Mar 1940

Haley, Nikki, American governor, Feb 2011

Halim, Mustafa ben, Libyan prime minister, Sept 1956

Hall, Frederick Lee, American judge and governor, Oct 1955, *Obit* May 1970

Hall, Leonard Wood, American congressman, July 1953, *Obit* July 1979

Hallaren, Mary A., American army officer, Mar 1949, *Obit* Yrbk 2005

Halleck, Charles A., American congressman and political leader, Mar 1947, *Obit* Apr 1986

Halley, Rudolph, June 1953, *Obit* Jan 1957

Hallstein, Walter, German diplomat, Oct 1953, *Obit* May 1982

Halonen, Tarja, Finnish president, Jan 2006

Halsey, Edwin A., *Obit* Mar 1945

Hambro, Carl Joachim, May 1940, *Obit* Feb 1965

Hamilton, Lee H., American congressman, Mar 1988

Hammarskjold, Dag, Swedish United Nations secretary-general, May 1953, *Obit* Nov 1961

Han, Myeong Sook, Korean prime minister, Jan 2006

Handley, Harold W., July 1960, *Obit* Nov 1972

Haniyeh, Ismail, Palestinian prime minister, Jan 2006

Hanks, Nancy, American government official, Sept 1971, *Obit* Mar 1983

Hannegan, Robert Emmet, American postmaster general, June 1944, *Obit* Nov 1949

Hansen, H. C., Mar 1956, *Obit* Apr 1960

Hansen, James E., American physicist, meteorologist and government official, May 1996

Hanson, Ole, *Obit* Sept 1940

Hansson, Per Albin, Oct 1942, *Obit* Nov 1946

Harden, Cecil Murray, congresswoman, Feb 1949, *Obit* Feb 1985

Hardie, S. J. L., July 1951

Hardy, Porter, congressman, May 1957, *Obit* June 1995

Hare, Raymond Arthur, American diplomat, July 1957, *Obit* May 1994

Hargrave, Thomas J., Apr 1949, *Obit* Apr 1962

Harkin, Tom, American senator, Jan 1992

Harkness, Douglas S., Oct 1961

Harriman, Averell, American statesman, Apr 1941, Nov 1946, *Obit* Sept 1986

Harriman, Florence Jaffray Hurst, social welfare leader, Mar 1940, *Obit* Nov 1967

Harrington, Francis Clark, *Obit* Mar 1940

Harrington, Russell C., Apr 1956, *Obit* Oct 1971

Harris, Fred R., American senator, Jan 1968

Harris, Oren, American congressman and judge, May 1956

Harris, Walter, June 1955

Harrison, Earl G., Aug 1943, *Obit* Oct 1955

Harrison, James L., Oct 1962

Harrison, Pat, American senator, *Obit* Aug 1941

Harron, Marion J., Yrbk 1949

Hart, Edward J., Feb 1953, *Obit* June 1961

Hart, Gary, American senator and lawyer, May 1976

Hart, Merwin K., Oct 1941, *Obit* Jan 1963

Hart, Philip A., American senator, Sept 1959, *Obit* Feb 1977

Hartke, Vance, American senator, Mar 1960, *Obit* Yrbk 2003

Hartley, Fred A., American congressman, June 1947, *Obit* June 1969

Hartzog, George B., American national parks director, July 1970, *Obit* Yrbk 2008

Harvard, Beverly Joyce, American police chief, Sept 1997

Hashimoto, Ryutaro, Japanese prime minister, Feb 1998, *Obit* Yrbk 2006

Hasluck, Paul, Australian governor-general, Oct 1946

Hassan, Mahmoud, July 1947

Hassel, Kai-Uwe von, May 1963

Hastert, Dennis, American congressman and Speaker of the House, Apr 1999

Hatch, Carl A., senator and judge, Yrbk 1944, *Obit* Nov 1963

Hatch, Orrin G., American senator, Aug 1982

Hatcher, Richard G., American mayor, Feb 1972

Hatfield, Mark O., American senator, Nov 1959, Mar 1984, *Obit* Yrbk 2011

Hatta, Mohammad, Indonesian prime minister, Yrbk 1949, *Obit* Yrbk 1991

Hauge, Gabriel, American economist, Oct 1953, *Obit* Sept 1981

Haughey, Charles, Irish prime minister, Feb 1981, *Obit* Yrbk 2006

Hawke, Robert J. L., Australian prime minister, Aug 1983

Hawkins, Augustus F., American congressman, Feb 1983, *Obit* Yrbk 2008

Hawkins, Paula, American senator, Sept 1985, *Obit* Yrbk 2010

Hawley, Willis C., *Obit* Sept 1941

Hay, Charles M., *Obit* Mar 1945

Hayden, Carl Trumbull, American senator, July 1951, *Obit* Mar 1972

Hayden, Tom, American state legislator and social activist, Apr 1976

Hayes, Carlton Joseph Huntley, historian and diplomat, June 1942, *Obit* Nov 1964

Haynes, Roy Asa, *Obit* Yrbk 1940

Hays, Brooks, American congressman, Jan 1958, *Obit* Jan 1982

Hays, Wayne Levere, American congressman, Nov 1974, *Obit* Apr 1989

Healey, Denis, British political leader, Yrbk 1971

Healy, Bernadine P., American cardiologist and public health official, Nov 1992, *Obit* Yrbk 2011

Hearne, John J., July 1950, *Obit* May 1969

Hearnes, Warren Eastman, American governor, June 1968

Heath, Edward, British prime minister, Oct 1962, *Obit* Yrbk 2005

Heckler, Margaret, American Secretary of health and human services, Aug 1983

Heckscher, August, municipal official and journalist, Oct 1958, *Obit* June 1997

Hedtoft, Hans, Mar 1949, *Obit* Mar 1955

Heeney, A. D. P., June 1953

Hees, George, Canadian cabinet member, Oct 1959

Heinemann, Gustav Walter, June 1969, *Obit* Aug 1976

Heinz, John, American senator, Apr 1981, *Obit* May 1991

Heitkamp, Heidi, state attorney general, Sept 2013

Heller, John Roderick, physician, Feb 1949, *Obit* July 1989

Hellyer, Paul, Sept 1969

Helms, Jesse A., American senator, July 1979, *Obit* Yrbk 2008

Helms, Richard, American intelligence official, Oct 1967, *Obit* Yrbk 2003

Helpern, Milton, May 1973, *Obit* June 1977

Henderson, Leon, American economist and government official, July 1940, *Obit* Jan 1987

Henderson, Loy Wesley, American diplomat, Mar 1948, *Obit* May 1986

Henderson, Nevile Meyrick, British diplomat, Apr 1940, *Obit* Feb 1943

Hendrickson, Robert C., Nov 1952, *Obit* Feb 1965

Hennings, Thomas C., American senator, Oct 1954, *Obit* Nov 1960

Hennock, Frieda, lawyer and government official, Nov 1948, *Obit* Sept 1960

Henry, Brad, American governor, Jan 2005

Henry, E. William, Feb 1964

Henry, Jules, *Obit* Aug 1941

Henry-Haye, Gaston, Nov 1940

Hensel, H. Struve, American lawyer and military official, Yrbk 1948, *Obit* July 1991

Hepburn, Mitchell Frederick, Canadian provincial premier, Yrbk 1941, *Obit* Feb 1953

Herbert, Gary R., American governor, May 2011

Herman, Alexis, American Secretary of labor and management consultant, Jan 1998

Hermann Jonasson, Aug 1941

Hernandez-Colon, Rafael, Puerto Rican governor, May 1973

Herrera Campins, Luis, Venezuelan president, July 1980, *Obit* Yrbk 2008

Herring, Clyde L., *Obit* Nov 1945

Herriot, Edouard, French statesman, Feb 1946, *Obit* June 1957

Herter, Christian Archibald, American Secretary of state, Yrbk 1947, Mar 1958, *Obit* Feb 1967

Herzog, Chaim, Israeli president, Apr 1988, *Obit* June 1997

Heseltine, Michael, British political leader, June 1985

Hesselgren, Kerstin, Swedish sociologist and member of Parliament, Jan 1941, *Obit* Oct 1962

Heuss, Theodor, German president, Nov 1949, *Obit* Jan 1964

Heuven Goedhart, Gerrit Jan van, Oct 1952, *Obit* Sept 1956

Heymann, David L., American epidemiologist and international public health official, July 2004

Hibbard, Frederick P., *Obit* Oct 1943

Hickenlooper, Bourke B., American senator and governor, May 1947, *Obit* Oct 1971

Hickerson, John Dewey, diplomat, May 1950, *Obit* Apr 1989

Hicks, Henry D., Oct 1956

Hicks, Louise Day, American congresswoman and municipal official, Mar 1974, *Obit* June 2004

Hill, J. B. P. Clayton, *Obit* July 1941

Hill, Lister, American senator, Oct 1943, *Obit* Feb 1985

Hill, Robert C., American diplomat, Jan 1959, *Obit* Feb 1979

Hilleboe, Herman E., June 1955, *Obit* June 1974

Hillenkoetter, Roscoe H., American CIA director and admiral, Jan 1950, *Obit* Aug 1982

Hillings, Patrick J., congressman, Oct 1957, *Obit* Sept 1994

Hilsman, Roger, American educator and government official, Mar 1964

Hines, Frank T., Apr 1944, *Obit* May 1960

Hinshaw, Carl, American congressman, July 1951, *Obit* Oct 1956

Hiss, Alger, American diplomat and lawyer, Feb 1947, *Obit* Jan 1997

Hodel, Donald Paul, American organization official and Secretary of the interior, June 1987

Hodges, Luther Hartwell, American Secretary of commerce and governor, July 1956, *Obit* Nov 1974

Hodgson, Joseph V., American state attorney general and United Nations official, June 1945

Hodgson, W. R., May 1946, *Obit* Apr 1958

Hodson, William, *Obit* Mar 1943

Hodza, Milan, *Obit* Aug 1944

Hoegh, Leo A., governor and civil defense official, July 1956, *Obit* Yrbk 2000

Hoey, Clyde R., American governor and senator, Oct 1949, *Obit* July 1954

Hoey, Jane M., American social worker and government official, Sept 1950

Hoff, Philip H., American governor, Sept 1963

Hoffman, Anna Rosenberg, American public relations executive and government official, Jan 1943, Jan 1951, *Obit* July 1983

Hoffman, Clare Eugene, American congressman, Mar 1949, *Obit* Jan 1968

Hoffman, Johannes, Apr 1950

Hogan, Frank S., American district attorney, Sept 1953, *Obit* May 1974

Holaday, William M., May 1958

Holaday, William Perry, *Obit* Mar 1946

Holenstein, Thomas, May 1958, *Obit* Jan 1963

Holifield, Chet, American congressman, Oct 1955, *Obit* Apr 1995

Holland, Sidney, New Zealand prime minister, Jan 1950, *Obit* Nov 1961

Holland, Spessard L., American governor and senator, Feb 1950, *Obit* Yrbk 1971

Hollande, Fran‡ois, French political leader, May 2013

Hollings, Ernest F., American senator, July 1982

Hollister, John B., American lawyer, congressman and government official, Oct 1955

Holmes, Robert D., July 1958

Holsti, Rudolf, *Obit* Sept 1945

Holt, Harold, Australian prime minister, Oct 1966, *Obit* Feb 1968

Holton, A. Linwood, American lawyer and governor, Feb 1971

Holtz, Jackson J., Mar 1950

Holtzman, Elizabeth, American congresswoman and municipal official, Nov 1973

Holyoake, Keith Jacka, New Zealand prime minister, Feb 1963, *Obit* Feb 1984

Home of the Hirsel, Alexander Frederick Douglas-Home, British prime minister, Feb 1958, *Obit* Jan 1996

Hoop Scheffer, Jaap de, Dutch diplomat and NATO official, Jan 2003

Hoopes, Darlington, socialist leader, Sept 1952, *Obit* Nov 1989

Hoover, Herbert, American president, Mar 1943, *Obit* Jan 1965

Hoover, J. Edgar, American FBI director, Feb 1940, May 1950, *Obit* June 1972

Hope, Clifford R., American congressman, May 1953, *Obit* July 1970

Hopkins, Harry Lloyd, American diplomat, Feb 1941, *Obit* Mar 1946

Hoppenot, Henri, Mar 1944

Hore-Belisha, Leslie Hore-Belisha, British political leader, July 1941, *Obit* May 1957

Hormel, James C., lawyer, philanthropist and diplomat, Oct 1999

Horne, John E., government official, Yrbk 1952, *Obit* Apr 1985

Horner, Henry, American governor, *Obit* Nov 1940

Horsbrugh, Florence Gertrude Horsbrugh, British cabinet member, Feb 1952, *Obit* Mar 1970

Hoshino, Naoki, Nov 1940

Hosmer, Craig, congressman, May 1958, *Obit* Mar 1983

Hosokawa, Morihiro, Japanese prime minister, May 1994

Houghton, Dorothy Deemer, Sept 1950

Houphouet-Boigny, Felix, Ivorian president, Oct 1958, July 1991, *Obit* Feb 1994

Houston, Andrew Jackson, *Obit* Aug 1941

Houston, Robert Griffith, American congressman and newspaper publisher, *Obit* Mar 1946

Houtte, Jean van, Mar 1952

Howard, John Winston, Australian prime minister, Mar 1999

Howard, Katherine G., American government official, July 1953

Howe, C. D., American construction engineer, Sept 1945, *Obit* Feb 1961

Howe, Frederic Clemson, lawyer and reformer, *Obit* Sept 1940

Howe, Geoffrey, British cabinet member, Oct 1980

Howe, Harold, American educator, Nov 1967, *Obit* Yrbk 2003

Howell, Charles R., Feb 1954, *Obit* Sept 1973

Howrey, Edward F., July 1953

Hoyer, Steny H., American congressman, Mar 2004

Hrawi, Elias, Lebanese president, Feb 1992, *Obit* Yrbk 2006

Hruska, Roman Lee, American senator, July 1956, *Obit* July 1999

Hu Jintao, Chinese president, Jan 2003

Hua Guofeng, Chinese prime minister, Mar 1977, *Obit* Yrbk 2008

Hudson, Robert S. Hudson, Nov 1942, *Obit* Apr 1957

Hufstedler, Shirley M., American lawyer and Secretary of education, May 1980

Hughes, Emmet John, American journalist and presidential speechwriter and adviser, Jan 1964, *Obit* Nov 1982

Hughes, Harold E., American governor and senator, June 1963, *Obit* Jan 1997

Hughes, Karen, American diplomat and presidential adviser, Oct 2001

Hughes, Richard J., American governor and judge, July 1962, *Obit* Feb 1993

Hughes, Sarah T., American judge, Nov 1950, *Obit* July 1985

Hull, Cordell, American Secretary of state, Aug 1940, *Obit* Oct 1955

Hull, Jane Dee, American governor, Feb 2002

Hull, William Edgar, *Obit* July 1942

Humphrey, Helen F., Nov 1952, *Obit* Oct 1963

Humphrey, Hubert Horatio, American vice-president, July 1949, Apr 1966, *Obit* Mar 1978

Hun Sen, Cambodian prime minister, Apr 1990

Hunt, Herold Christian, educator, May 1956, *Obit* Jan 1977

Hunt, James B., American governor, June 1993

Hunt, Lester C., American senator and governor, Mar 1951, *Obit* Sept 1954

Hunt, Swanee, American international relations specialist, Mar 2006

Hurd, Douglas, British cabinet member, Feb 1990

Hurley, Charles F., American governor, *Obit* May 1946

Husak, Gustav, Czech president, Oct 1971, *Obit* Jan 1992

Hussein, Ahmed, Egyptian diplomat, Mar 1956, *Obit* Feb 1985

Hussein, Saddam, Iraqi president, Sept 1981, Jan 2002, *Obit* Apr 2007

Hutchison, Kay Bailey, American senator, Sept 1997

Huvayda, Amir Abbas, Oct 1971, *Obit* June 1979

Hyde, Henry J., American congressman, Oct 1989, *Obit* Yrbk 2008

Hyde, Henry Van Zile, May 1960

Hylton-Foster, Harry, Jan 1961, *Obit* Nov 1965

Ickes, Harold L., American Secretary of the interior, July 1941, *Obit* Mar 1952

Ikeda, Hayato, Japanese prime minister, May 1961, *Obit* Oct 1965

Iliescu, Ion, Romanian president, June 1990

Illia, Arturo Umberto, Argentine president, Jan 1965, *Obit* Mar 1983

Ilsley, J. L., Canadian cabinet member and judge, Feb 1948

Impellitteri, Vincent R., American mayor, Feb 1951, *Obit* Mar 1987

Ince, Godfrey H., Sept 1943

Ingersoll, Raymond Vail, *Obit* Mar 1940

Inonu, Ismet, Turkish president, Mar 1941, Oct 1964, *Obit* Feb 1974

Inouye, Daniel K., American senator, May 1960, Sept 1987, *Obit* Yrbk 2013

Insulza, Jose Miguel, Chilean diplomat and international organization official, Jan 2005

Intizam, Nasr Allah, Yrbk 1950

Isaacs, George A., Oct 1945

Isaias Afwerki, Eritrean president, Jan 2002

Ishibashi, Tanzan, Mar 1957, *Obit* June 1973

Iverson, Kenneth R., Apr 1951

Ives, Irving M., American senator, Feb 1948, *Obit* Apr 1962

Ives, James E., *Obit* Feb 1943

Izac, Edouard V. M., American congressman, Yrbk 1945, *Obit* Mar 1990

Izetbegovic, Alija, Bosnian president, Aug 1993, *Obit* June 2004

Jackson Lee, Sheila, American congresswoman, Nov 2008

Jackson, C. D., American publishing executive and presidential aide, Oct 1951, *Obit* Nov 1964

Jackson, Glenda, English actress and member of Parliament, Yrbk 1971

Jackson, Henry Martin, American senator, Oct 1953, Oct 1979, *Obit* Oct 1983

Jackson, Jesse L., American congressman, May 1998

Jackson, Lisa P., American government official, Mar 2010

Jackson, Maynard H., American mayor, Sept 1976, *Obit* Yrbk 2003

Jackson, Robert Houghwout, American Supreme Court justice, Mar 1940, Oct 1950, *Obit* Yrbk 1954

Jackson, William H., Mar 1951, *Obit* Nov 1971

Jackson, William K., July 1946, *Obit* Yrbk 1947

Jagan, Cheddi, Guyanese president, Apr 1963, *Obit* May 1997

James, Arthur Horace, governor, July 1940, *Obit* June 1973

James, W. Frank, *Obit* Jan 1946

Janson, Paul Emile, *Obit* Aug 1944

Jarrett, Valerie, American presidential adviser, Apr 2009

Jarring, Gunnar, Swedish diplomat, Oct 1957, *Obit* Sept 2002

Jarvis, Robert Y., *Obit* Yrbk 1943

Jastrow, Robert, American physicist, Jan 1973, *Obit* Yrbk 2008

Javits, Jacob K., American senator, June 1948, Oct 1958, *Obit* Apr 1986

Jaworski, Leon, American lawyer and special prosecutor, June 1974, *Obit* Feb 1983

Jayewardene, Junius Richard, Sri Lankan president, Jan 1984, *Obit* Jan 1997

Jean, Michaelle, Canadian broadcast journalist and governor general, June 2009

Jeffords, James, American senator, Sept 2001

Jenner, William E., American senator, June 1951, *Obit* May 1985

Jensen, Ben F., Feb 1960, *Obit* Apr 1970

Jernegan, John D., Nov 1959

Jessup, Philip C., American judge and diplomat, Apr 1948, *Obit* Mar 1986

Jester, Beauford H., July 1948, *Obit* Sept 1949

Jiang Zemin, Chinese president, May 1995

Jiang Zuobin, *Obit* Feb 1943

Jindal, Bobby, American governor, Jan 2008

Jobert, Michel, French diplomat, Feb 1975, *Obit* Sept 2002

Jodoin, Claude, Mar 1956

Johanna Sigurdardottir, Icelandic prime minister, July 2010

Johnson, Boris, British mayor, Oct 2008

Johnson, Daniel, Canadian provincial premier, Nov 1967, *Obit* Nov 1968

Johnson, Ed, American senator and governor, Yrbk 1946, *Obit* July 1970

Johnson, Eddie Bernice, American congresswoman, July 2001

Johnson, Hiram, American governor and senator, Feb 1941, *Obit* Sept 1945

Johnson, J. Monroe, American civil engineer and government official, Feb 1945, *Obit* Sept 1964

Johnson, Joseph B., July 1956

Johnson, Leroy, Sept 1949, *Obit* June 1961

Johnson, Louis Arthur, American Secretary of defense, June 1942, Apr 1949, *Obit* May 1966

Johnson, Lyndon B., American president, Jan 1951, Mar 1964, *Obit* Mar 1973

Johnson, Nelson Trusler, diplomat, Jan 1940, *Obit* Feb 1955

Johnson, Nicholas, Mar 1968

Johnson, Paul B., *Obit* Feb 1944

Johnson, Roy W., May 1958, *Obit* Oct 1965

Johnson, Thomasina Walker, Mar 1947

Johnson, U. Alexis, American diplomat, Oct 1955, *Obit* June 1997

Johnson-Sirleaf, Ellen, Liberian president, Jan 2006

Johnston, Eric, Apr 1943, Oct 1955, *Obit* Oct 1963

Johnston, Olin D., American senator and governor, Nov 1951, *Obit* June 1965

Jones, Arthur C., Jan 1948, *Obit* Jan 1965

Jones, Howard P., American diplomat, July 1963, *Obit* Nov 1973

Jones, James R., Oct 1981

Jones, Jesse Holman, American Secretary of commerce, Oct 1940, *Obit* Sept 1956

Jones, John Joseph, Nov 1940, *Obit* Jan 1942

Jones, Marvin, congressman and judge, Aug 1943, *Obit* Jan 1984

Jones, Roger Warren, government official, Nov 1959, *Obit* Aug 1993

Jones, Sam Houston, lawyer and governor, Mar 1940, *Obit* Yrbk 1991

Jooste, Gerhardus Petrus, Apr 1951

Jordan, Barbara, American lawyer and congresswoman, Sept 1974, Apr 1993, *Obit* Apr 1996

Jordan, Hamilton, American presidential adviser and campaign consultant, Aug 1977, *Obit* Yrbk 2008

Jordana y Souza, Francisco Gomez, Mar 1944

Jorgensen, Anker, Danish prime minister, Sept 1978

Joseph, Keith, British cabinet member, Feb 1975, *Obit* Feb 1995

Joseph, Stephen C., physician and public health official, Jan 1989

Jospin, Lionel, French prime minister, June 2000

Jowitt, William Allen Jowitt, Aug 1941, *Obit* Nov 1957

Joxe, Louis, French diplomat and cabinet member, Apr 1961, *Obit* June 1991

Joya, Malalai, Afghan human rights activist and member of Parliament, Jan 2007

Judd, Walter Henry, American congressman, Sept 1949, *Obit* Apr 1994

Kabbah, Ahmad Tejan, Sierra Leonean president, Jan 2002

Kabila, Joseph, Congolese president, Sept 2001

Kaczynski, Lech, Polish president, Jan 2006, *Obit* Yrbk 2010

Kadar, Janos, Hungarian prime minister, May 1957, *Obit* Yrbk 1989

Kadyrov, Ramzan, Chechen president, Jan 2007

Kagame, Paul, Rwandan president, Jan 2002

Kahane, Meir, American-Israeli rabbi, Oct 1972, *Obit* Jan 1991

Kaifu, Toshiki, Japanese prime minister, June 1990

Kaiser, Jakob, German labor leader and government official, Feb 1956, *Obit* July 1961

Kaiser, Philip M., American diplomat, Oct 1949, *Obit* Yrbk 2007

Kakfwi, Stephen, Canadian provincial government official, Jan 2003

Kalinin, Mikhail Ivanovich, Soviet president, June 1942, *Obit* July 1946

Kallay, Nicholas, Hungarian prime minister, June 1942, *Obit* May 1967

Kallio, Kyosti, *Obit* Feb 1941

Kampelman, Max M., American diplomat, July 1986

Kampmann, Viggo, Jan 1961, *Obit* July 1976

Kan, Naoto, Japanese prime minister, July 2011

Kania, Stanislaw, June 1981

Kantor, Mickey, American Secretary of commerce, Mar 1994

Kaptur, Marcy C., American congresswoman, Jan 2003

Karami, Rashid, Lebanese prime minister, Nov 1959, *Obit* July 1987

Karmal, Babrak, Afghan president, Mar 1981, *Obit* Feb 1997

Karnebeek, Herman Adriaan van, *Obit* May 1942

Karzai, Hamid, Afghan president, May 2002

Kasavubu, Joseph, Congolese president, Mar 1961, *Obit* May 1969

Kase, Toshikazu, Japanese diplomat, Apr 1957, *Obit* Yrbk 2004

Kasich, John R., American governor, Aug 1998

Kassebaum Baker, Nancy, American senator, Feb 1982

Kasten, Robert W., senator, June 1989

Kastenmeier, Robert W., American congressman, July 1966

Katayama, Tetsu, Jan 1948

Katsav, Moshe, Israeli president, Feb 2001

Katzir, Ephraim, Israeli biophysicist and president, Jan 1975, *Obit* Yrbk 2009

Kauffmann, Henrik, Apr 1956, *Obit* July 1963

Kaunda, Kenneth D., Zambian president, July 1966

Kaur, Rajkumari Amrit, Oct 1955, *Obit* Mar 1964

Kawaguchi, Yoriko, Japanese diplomat, Jan 2002

Kearns, Carroll D., Sept 1956

Keating, Kenneth Barnard, American congressman, senator and diplomat, Oct 1950, *Obit* June 1975

Keating, Paul, Australian prime minister, May 1992

Kee, Elizabeth, Jan 1954

Kee, John, June 1950, *Obit* June 1951

Keech, Richmond B., Mar 1950

Keenan, Joseph B., Sept 1946, *Obit* Feb 1955

Kefauver, Estes, American senator, Jan 1949, *Obit* Oct 1963

Keita, Modibo, Malian president, Apr 1960, *Obit* July 1977

Kekkonen, Urho, Finnish president, Sept 1950, *Obit* Oct 1986

Keldysh, Mstislav, Russian mathematician and physicist, Feb 1962, *Obit* Aug 1978

Kelley, Augustine Bernard, Apr 1951, *Obit* Feb 1958

Kelley, Clarence M., American FBI director, May 1974, *Obit* Nov 1997

Kelly, Edna Flannery, congresswoman, Mar 1950, *Obit* Feb 1998

Kelly, Raymond, American police commissioner, Sept 2008

Kelsey, Frances Oldham, American pharmacologist and regulatory agency official, Apr 1965

Kem, James P., Oct 1950, *Obit* Apr 1965

Kemmis, Daniel, mayor and public policy analyst, Oct 1996

Kemp, Jack, American football player, congressman and Secretary of housing and urban development, Mar 1980, *Obit* Yrbk 2009

Kempthorne, Dirk, American Secretary of the interior, June 2007

Kennedy, Edward Moore, American senator, Sept 1963, Oct 1978, *Obit* Oct 2009

Kennedy, John F., American president, June 1950, July 1961, *Obit* Jan 1964

Kennedy, Robert F., American Attorney general and senator, Feb 1958, *Obit* July 1968

Kennedy, Stephen P., June 1956, *Obit* Jan 1979

Kennelly, Martin H., mayor, Yrbk 1949, *Obit* Jan 1962

Kennon, Robert Floyd, American governor, Oct 1954, *Obit* Apr 1988

Kent, Raymond A., *Obit* Apr 1943

Kenyatta, Jomo, Kenyan president, Oct 1953, Apr 1974, *Obit* Oct 1978

Kerlikowske, R. Gil, American law enforcement official, Nov 2009

Kerner, Otto, American governor and judge, Oct 1961, *Obit* July 1976

Kerrl, Hanns, German cabinet member, *Obit* Feb 1942

Kerry, John Forbes, American senator, June 1988, Sept 2004

Kersten, Charles J., Sept 1952

Kessler, David A., American physician and government official, Sept 1991

Keyserling, Leon H., American economist, Jan 1947, *Obit* Sept 1987

Keyworth, George A., American physicist and presidential adviser, Mar 1986

Khaleda Zia, Bangladeshi prime minister, Jan 2003

Khalilzad, Zalmay, Afghan-American diplomat, Aug 2006

Khama, Seretse, Batswana president, May 1967, *Obit* Sept 1980

Khamenei, Ali, Iranian president, Nov 1987, Jan 2005

Khan, Aly, Pakistani diplomat, May 1960

Khan, Imran, Pakistani cricket player and member of Parliament, Jan 2005

Khan, Liaquat Ali, June 1948, *Obit* Yrbk 1951

Khatami, Mohammad, Iranian Islamic leader and president, Apr 1998

Khouri, Faris el-, Sept 1948, *Obit* Feb 1962

Kibaki, Mwai, Kenyan president, Jan 2003

Kiesinger, Kurt Georg, German chancellor, Apr 1967, *Obit* Apr 1988

Kilday, Paul J., Oct 1958, *Obit* Yrbk 1968

Kilgore, Harley Martin, American senator, June 1943, *Obit* May 1956

Kilmuir, David Patrick Maxwell Fyfe, Yrbk 1951, *Obit* Mar 1967

Kilpatrick, Kwame M., American mayor, Apr 2004

Kim, Dae Jung, South Korean president, Sept 1985, *Obit* Yrbk 2009

Kim, Young Sam, Korean president, June 1995

Kimball, Dan A., American Secretary of the navy, Sept 1951, *Obit* Oct 1970

King, Angus, governor, Apr 2013

King, Cecil R., American congressman, Feb 1952, *Obit* May 1974

King, John W., governor and judge, May 1964, *Obit* Nov 1996

King, Samuel Wilder, Oct 1953, *Obit* June 1959

King, William Lyon Mackenzie, Canadian prime minister, Aug 1940, *Obit* Sept 1950

Kingsland, Lawrence C., Jan 1949

Kintner, Earl W., lawyer and government official, Apr 1960, *Obit* Mar 1992

Kirbo, Charles H., lawyer, Sept 1977, *Obit* Nov 1996

Kirchner, Cristina E. Fernandez de, Argentine president, Jan 2007

Kirchner, Nestor, Argentine president, Jan 2004, *Obit* Yrbk 2010

Kirk, Alan Goodrich, American admiral and diplomat, July 1944, *Obit* Yrbk 1963

Kirk, Alexander C., Feb 1945

Kirk, Claude R., American governor, Oct 1967, *Obit* Yrbk 2011

Kirk, Paul, American senator and political party leader, Aug 1987

Kirk, Ron, American trade represenative, Apr 2010

Kirkland, Lane, American labor leader, May 1980, *Obit* Oct 1999

Kirkpatrick, Miles W., lawyer and government official, Feb 1972, *Obit* July 1998

Kishi, Nobusuke, Japanese prime minister, June 1957, *Obit* Sept 1987

Kissinger, Henry, American Secretary of state, June 1958, June 1972

Kiviniemi, Mari, Finnish prime minister, Oct 2010

Klaus, Josef, Austrian chancellor, Jan 1965, *Obit* Oct 2001

Klaus, Vaclav, Czech president, Nov 1997

Kleffens, Eelco Nicolaas van, Oct 1947

Kleindienst, Richard G., American Attorney general, Oct 1972, *Obit* June 2000

Knabenshue, Paul, *Obit* Mar 1942

Knappstein, Karl Heinrich, Feb 1965

Knatchbull-Hugessen, Hughe, Mar 1943, *Obit* May 1971

Knauer, Virginia H., American government official, Apr 1970, *Obit* Yrbk 2011

Knight, Goodwin, American governor, Jan 1955, *Obit* July 1970

Knowland, William Fife, American senator and newspaper publisher, Apr 1947, *Obit* Apr 1974

Knox, Frank, American Secretary of the navy and newspaper publisher, Aug 1940, *Obit* June 1944

Knuth-Winterfeldt, Kield Gustav, Sept 1959

Knutson, Coya, congresswoman, Mar 1956, *Obit* Jan 1997

Knutson, Harold, American congressman, Jan 1947, *Obit* Oct 1953

Koch, Ed, American mayor, Sept 1978, *Obit* Yrbk 2013

Kohl, Helmut, German chancellor, Aug 1977

Kohler, Foy David, American diplomat, Jan 1950, *Obit* Mar 1991

Kohler, Walter Jodok, American manufacturing executive and governor, Jan 1953, *Obit* May 1976

Kohler, Walter Jodok, American manufacturing executive and governor, *Obit* May 1940

Koirala, Girija Prasad, Nepalese prime minister, Jan 2006, *Obit* Yrbk 2010

Koivisto, Mauno, Finnish president, Sept 1982

Koizumi, Junichiro, Japanese prime minister, Jan 2002

Kok, Wim, Dutch prime minister, Jan 2003

Kolarov, Vassil, Yrbk 1949, *Obit* Mar 1950

Kollek, Teddy, Israeli mayor, Oct 1974, Mar 1993, *Obit* Yrbk 2007

Konare, Alpha Oumar, Malian president, Oct 2001

Konoye, Fumimaro, Japanese prime minister, Sept 1940, *Obit* Feb 1946

Koo, V. K. Wellington, Chinese prime minister and diplomat, July 1941, *Obit* Jan 1986

Koontz, Elizabeth Duncan, American labor leader and teacher, Jan 1969, *Obit* Apr 1989

Koop, C. Everett, American surgeon general, Sept 1983, *Obit* Yrbk 2013

Korizis, Alexander, Mar 1941, *Obit* Mar 1941

Kosaka, Zentaro, Sept 1961

Kostunica, Vojislav, Yugoslav president, Jan 2001

Kosygin, Aleksei Nikolaevich, Soviet prime minister, Sept 1965, *Obit* Feb 1981

Kotelawala, John Lionel, Sri Lankan prime minister, Oct 1955

Kotschnig, Walter Maria, United Nations official and diplomat, Oct 1952, *Obit* Sept 1985

Kouchner, Bernard, French physician and cabinet member, Aug 1993

Kowalski, Frank, July 1960, *Obit* Yrbk 1974

Kozlov, Frol R., Nov 1959, *Obit* Mar 1965

Kozlowski, Leon, *Obit* July 1944

Kozyrev, Andrei V., Russian diplomat, Sept 1992

Kraft, Christopher C., aerospace engineer, Feb 1966

Kraft, Ole Bjorn, Feb 1953

Krag, Jens Otto, Danish prime minister, Oct 1962, *Obit* Aug 1978

Kravchuk, Leonid, Ukrainian president, Jan 1993

Kreisky, Bruno, Austrian chancellor, Sept 1960, *Obit* Sept 1990

Krekeler, Heinz L., Yrbk 1951

Kriebel, Hermann, *Obit* Apr 1941

Krishna Menon, V. K., Indian lawyer and diplomat, Mar 1953, *Obit* Nov 1974

Krueger, Wilhelm, *Obit* June 1943

Krug, J. A., American Secretary of the interior, Oct 1944, *Obit* May 1970

Krupsak, Mary Anne, July 1975

Kubitschek, Juscelino, Brazilian president, Apr 1956, *Obit* Nov 1976

Kuchel, Thomas H., American senator, Feb 1954, *Obit* Feb 1995

Kuchma, Leonid, Ukrainian president, Oct 1997

Kucinich, Dennis, American congressman, Mar 1979, July 2008

Kufuor, John, Ghanaian president, Jan 2002

Kumaratunga, Chandrika Bandaranaike, Sri Lankan prime minister, Jan 1996

Kung, H. H., Chinese government official, Mar 1943, *Obit* Oct 1967

Kunin, Madeleine, American governor and diplomat, July 1987

Kunz, Stanley H., *Obit* June 1946

Kurusu, Saburo, Jan 1942, *Obit* May 1954

Kuzmin, Iosif I., Feb 1959

Kuznetsov, Nikolai G., Nov 1942, *Obit* Jan 1975

Kuznetsov, Vasilii Vasil'evich, Soviet diplomat, Jan 1956, *Obit* Aug 1990

Kyprianou, Spyros, Cypriot president, May 1979, *Obit* May 2002

La Follette, Charles M., Feb 1950

La Follette, Robert M., American senator, May 1944, *Obit* Apr 1953

La Guardia, Fiorello Henry, American mayor, Oct 1940, *Obit* Nov 1947

La Hood, Ray, American Secretary of transportation, Mar 2009

LaMarsh, Judy, Apr 1968, *Obit* Jan 1981

Labouisse, Henry R., American United Nations official, Oct 1961, *Obit* May 1987

Laffoon, Ruby, governor, *Obit* Apr 1941

Lafontaine, Oskar, German political leader, Sept 1990

Lagarde, Christine, French interionational organization official, Jan 2007

Lagos, Ricardo, Chilean president, Jan 2005

Laird, Melvin R., American Secretary of defense, Nov 1964

Lake, Anthony, American political scientist and presidential adviser, Oct 1994

Lall, Arthur S., Indian diplomat, Nov 1956, *Obit* Jan 1999

Lamberton, Robert Eneas, American lawyer, judge and mayor, *Obit* Oct 1941

Lambsdorff, Otto von, German economist and cabinet member, May 1980, *Obit* Yrbk 2010

Lamm, Richard D., governor, May 1985

Lamont, Norman, British cabinet member, Aug 1992

Land, Emory S., Sept 1941, *Obit* Jan 1972

Landes, Bertha K., mayor, *Obit* Jan 1944

Landis, James McCauley, American lawyer and regulatory agency official, Mar 1942, *Obit* Oct 1964

Landon, Alf, American governor, Feb 1944, *Obit* Nov 1987

Landrieu, Moon, American state legislator, mayor and Secretary of housing and urban development, Jan 1980

Landrum, Phil M., American congressman, May 1960, *Obit* Jan 1991

Landry, Jeff, American congressman, Jan 2012

Lane, Arthur Bliss, American diplomat, Apr 1948, *Obit* Oct 1956

Lane, William Preston, June 1949, *Obit* Apr 1967

Lang, Jack, French cabinet member, Aug 1983

Lange, David, New Zealand prime minister, Sept 1985, *Obit* Yrbk 2005

Lange, Halvard M., Norwegian diplomat, Nov 1947, *Obit* July 1970

Langer, William, American governor and senator, Feb 1952, *Obit* Jan 1960

Langevin, Jim, American congressman, Aug 2005

Langlie, Arthur B., Oct 1950, *Obit* Sept 1966

Laniel, Joseph, French prime minister, Feb 1954

Lanier, Cathy L., American police chief, Mar 2007

Lansbury, George, British socialist leader, *Obit* Jan 1940

Lantos, Tom, American congressman, July 2007, *Obit* May 2008

Lapham, Roger D., July 1948, *Obit* May 1966

Lapid, Tommy, Israeli cabinet member and political leader, Jan 2003

Lapointe, Ernest, Canadian political leader, *Obit* Jan 1942

Largent, Steve, American congressman, June 1999

Largo Caballero, Francisco, Spanish prime minister, *Obit* May 1946

Larrick, George P., June 1965, *Obit* Oct 1968

Larson, Jess, American government official, June 1951

Latham, Dana, Mar 1959, *Obit* Apr 1974

Laughlin, Irwin, *Obit* June 1941

Laurel, Jose P., Filipino president, June 1953, *Obit* Jan 1960

Lausche, Frank John, American governor and senator, Apr 1946, Nov 1958, *Obit* June 1990

Laval, Pierre, French prime minister and convicted traitor, Sept 1940, *Obit* Nov 1945

Lawrence, David Leo, American governor, June 1959, *Obit* Jan 1967

Lawson, Edward B., Jan 1956

Lawson, Nigel, British cabinet member, Mar 1987

Lawton, Frederick J., government official, Mar 1951

Laxalt, Paul, American senator, Jan 1979

Lay, James S., intelligence official, Mar 1950, *Obit* Aug 1987

Layton, Jack, Canadian political leader, Nov 2009, *Obit* Yrbk 2012

Le Carre, John, British diplomat and novelist, Yrbk 1974

Lea, Clarence F., Nov 1946, *Obit* Sept 1964

Lea, Luke, American newspaper publisher and senator, *Obit* Jan 1946

Leader, George Michael, American governor, Jan 1956, *Obit* Yrbk 2013

Leahy, Patrick J., American senator, Sept 1990

Leahy, William D., American admiral, Jan 1941, *Obit* Oct 1959

Leathers, Frederick James Leathers, June 1941, *Obit* May 1965

Lee, Barbara, American congresswoman, June 2004

Lee, Blair, *Obit* Feb 1945

Lee, Bum Suk, Jan 1949

Lee, Dorothy McCullough, Jan 1949

Lee, J. Bracken, American governor and mayor, May 1949, *Obit* Jan 1997

Lee, Jennie, British member of Parliament, May 1946, *Obit* Jan 1989

Lee, Jong Wook, Korean physician and international public health official, Jan 2003, *Obit* CB Int 2007

Lee, Kuan Yew, Singaporean prime minister, Nov 1959, Jan 1995

Lee, Richard C., American mayor, Yrbk 1967, *Obit* Yrbk 2003

Lee, Robert E., American regulatory agency official, July 1967, *Obit* June 1993

Lee, Teng-hui, Taiwanese president, Mar 1996

Leedom, Boyd, May 1956, *Obit* Oct 1969

Lefevre, Theo, June 1962, *Obit* Nov 1973

Leger, Jules, Nov 1976, *Obit* Jan 1981

Lehman, Herbert Henry, American governor and senator, Jan 1943, July 1955, *Obit* Jan 1964

Lehman, John F., secretary of the navy, Nov 1985

Lehrbas, Lloyd, June 1940, Apr 1950, *Obit* Jan 1965

Leith-Ross, Frederick, Oct 1942

Lemass, Sean, Irish prime minister, Mar 1960, *Obit* June 1971

Lenroot, Katherine F., American government official, May 1940, Nov 1950, *Obit* Yrbk 1991

Leone, Giovanni, Italian president, May 1972, *Obit* Feb 2002

Leoni, Raul, Venezuelan president, Oct 1964, *Obit* Sept 1972

Leopold, Alice, government official, Jan 1955

Lequerica y Erquiza, Jose Felix de, June 1951, *Obit* July 1963

Lesage, Jean, Canadian government official, Nov 1961, *Obit* Feb 1981

Lescot, Elie, Haitian president, June 1941, *Obit* Yrbk 1974

Lesinski, John, July 1949, *Obit* July 1950

Letourneau, Jean, Oct 1952

Levesque, Rene, Canadian political leader, Jan 1975, *Obit* Jan 1988

Levin, Carl, American senator, May 2004

Levy, David, Israeli cabinet member, Mar 1998

Lewis, Drew, American Secretary of transportation, Feb 1982

Lewis, Lawrence, *Obit* Jan 1944

Li Peng, Chinese prime minister, Nov 1988

Liddel, Urner, May 1951

Lie, Trygve, Norwegian United Nations secretary-general, Mar 1946, *Obit* Feb 1969

Lieberman, Joseph I., American senator, July 1994

Limann, Hilla, Ghanaian president, June 1981, *Obit* Apr 1998

Limb, Ben C., Jan 1951

Lin Biao, Chinese communist leader and military official, May 1967, *Obit* Oct 1972

Lin Sen, *Obit* Sept 1943

Lincoln, Blanche Lambert, American senator, Mar 2002

Lindsay, John V., American congressman and mayor, Nov 1962, *Obit* Mar 2001

Lindsay, Ronald, *Obit* Sept 1945

Lindt, Auguste R., Swiss diplomat and United Nations official, Nov 1959, *Obit* Yrbk 2000

Lingle, Linda, American governor, June 2003

Linlithgow, Victor Alexander John Hope, British colonial administrator, Jan 1942, *Obit* Feb 1952

Linowitz, Sol M., American lawyer and diplomat, Mar 1967, *Obit* Yrbk 2005

Lipsky, Eleazar, author and lawyer, Yrbk 1959, *Obit* Apr 1993

Litvinov, Maxim Maximovich, Soviet diplomat, Yrbk 1941, *Obit* Feb 1952

Livingstone, Ken, British mayor, Jan 2003

Livni, Tzipi, Israeli lawyer and cabinet member, Jan 2006

Lleras Camargo, Alberto, Colombian president, Sept 1947, June 1965, *Obit* Mar 1990

Lleras Restrepo, Carlos, Colombian president, Nov 1970, *Obit* Nov 1994

Lloyd George, David Lloyd George, British statesman, Nov 1944, *Obit* May 1945

Lloyd of Dolobran, George Ambrose Lloyd, British colonial administrator, Jan 1941, *Obit* Jan 1941

Lloyd, James T., *Obit* May 1944

Locke, Gary, American Secretary of commerce, Apr 2003

Locker, Jesse D., Mar 1955, *Obit* June 1955

Lodge, Henry Cabot, American diplomat, Yrbk 1943, May 1954, *Obit* Apr 1985

Loeb, James I., American diplomat and political leader, Jan 1962, *Obit* Mar 1992

Logan, Harlan, magazine editor and publishing executive, Jan 1946, *Obit* Mar 1995

Long, Breckinridge, diplomat, Nov 1943, *Obit* Yrbk 1958

Long, Earl K., American governor, Yrbk 1950, *Obit* Nov 1960

Long, Oren E., American senator, Sept 1951, *Obit* June 1965

Long, Russell B., American senator, Yrbk 1951, Oct 1965, *Obit* Yrbk 2003

Loomis, Orland S., *Obit* Jan 1943

Lopez Bravo, Gregorio, Spanish diplomat, July 1971, *Obit* Apr 1985

Lopez Mateos, Adolfo, Mexican president, Mar 1959, *Obit* Nov 1969

Lopez Michelsen, Alfonso, Colombian president, Apr 1975

Lopez Obrador, Andres Manuel, Mexican mayor and political leader, Jan 2003

Lopez Portillo, Jose, Mexican president, June 1977, *Obit* Yrbk 2004

Lopez Rodo, Laureano, Feb 1972

Lopez, Alfonso, Colombian president, Sept 1942, *Obit* Jan 1960

Lord, Mary Pillsbury, Oct 1952

Lothian, Philip Henry Kerr, British diplomat, *Obit* Yrbk 1940

Lott, Trent, American senator, Sept 1996

Louchheim, Katie, government official, June 1956, *Obit* Apr 1991

Loudon, Alexander, July 1942, *Obit* Mar 1953

Lougheed, Peter, Canadian political leader, Aug 1979

Loutfi, Omar, Jan 1957, *Obit* July 1963

Louw, Eric, Mar 1962, *Obit* Sept 1968

Love, John A., American governor, Nov 1963, *Obit* Apr 2002

Loveless, Herschel Cellel, governor, July 1958, *Obit* July 1989

Lowden, Frank O., governor, *Obit* May 1943

Lowey, Nita M., American congresswoman, Sept 1997

Lozovskii, A., Nov 1941

Lubbers, Rudolphus, Dutch prime minister and United Nations official, May 1988, Jan 2003

Lubke, Heinrich, Jan 1960, *Obit* May 1972

Lucas, Scott W., American senator, Yrbk 1947, *Obit* Apr 1968

Luce, Robert, *Obit* May 1946

Lucet, Charles, Yrbk 1967

Lugar, Richard G., American senator, Oct 1977

Luhring, Oscar Raymond, *Obit* Oct 1944

Lujan, Manuel, American Secretary of the interior, Sept 1989

Lumpkin, Alva M., *Obit* Sept 1941

Lumumba, Patrice, Congolese prime minister, Nov 1960, *Obit* Apr 1961

Lund, Wendell L., Sept 1942

Lundeen, Ernest, *Obit* Oct 1940

Luns, Joseph M. A. H., Dutch diplomat and NATO official, Feb 1958, Apr 1982, *Obit* Yrbk 2002

Lusk, Georgia Lee, American congresswoman, Oct 1947, *Obit* Feb 1971

Luzhkov, Yuri, Russian mayor, Nov 1999, Jan 2007

Lynch, John Mary, Irish prime minister, May 1967, *Obit* Feb 2000

Lyng, Richard E., American Secretary of agriculture, Sept 1986, *Obit* Yrbk 2003

Lynn, James T., American insurance executive, Yrbk 1973

M'Bow, Amadou-Mahtar, Senegalese United Nations official, May 1987

Maas, Melvin Joseph, Nov 1957, *Obit* June 1964

MacArthur, Douglas, American diplomat, Nov 1954, *Obit* Jan 1998

MacBride, Sean, Irish diplomat, June 1949, *Obit* Mar 1988

MacCormick, Austin H., May 1940, July 1951, *Obit* Jan 1980

MacDonald, William J., *Obit* May 1946

MacEachen, Allan Joseph, Canadian political leader, Apr 1983

MacLeish, Archibald, American poet and Librarian of Congress, Oct 1940, Nov 1959, *Obit* June 1982

Macapagal, Diosdado, Filipino president, Nov 1962, *Obit* July 1997

Macapagal-Arroyo, Gloria, Filipino president, Jan 2002

Machado Hernandez, Alfredo, *Obit* Sept 1946

Machado Ventura, Jose Ramon, Cuban vice-president, Sept 2011

Machado, Bernardino, *Obit* June 1944

Machel, Graca Simbine, Mozambican social welfare leader and wife of Nelson Mandela, Oct 1997

Machel, Samora, Mozambican president, Mar 1984, *Obit* Jan 1987

Macleod, Iain Norman, British cabinet member, Apr 1956, *Obit* Oct 1970

Macy, John W., government official, Jan 1962, *Obit* Apr 1987

Madden, Ray J., congressman, Apr 1953, *Obit* Nov 1987

Maddox, Lester, American governor, Yrbk 1967, *Obit* Yrbk 2003

Maddox, William P., Nov 1947, *Obit* Yrbk 1972

Madigan, Edward R., American Secretary of agriculture, Nov 1992, *Obit* Feb 1995

Madrid Hurtado, Miguel de la, Mexican president, Apr 1983, *Obit* Yrbk 2012

Magaziner, Ira C., American business consultant and presidential adviser, Apr 1995

Magee, James C., May 1943

Maggiolo, Walter A., labor mediator, July 1952, *Obit* Yrbk 2000

Magloire, Paul, Haitian president, Feb 1952, *Obit* Nov 2001

Magner, Thomas F., *Obit* Feb 1946

Magnuson, Warren, American senator, Oct 1945, *Obit* July 1989

Magsaysay, Ramon, Filipino president, Yrbk 1952, *Obit* May 1957

Mahathir bin Mohamad, Malaysian prime minister, Aug 1988

Maher, Ahmed, *Obit* Apr 1945

Maher, Aly, Mar 1952, *Obit* Nov 1960

Mahon, George H., American congressman, Mar 1958, *Obit* Jan 1986

Maiskii, I. M., Soviet diplomat, Sept 1941, *Obit* Oct 1975

Major, John, British prime minister, Oct 1990, Apr 1997

Makin, Norman J. O., Mar 1946

Malan, Daniel Francois, South African prime minister, Apr 1949, *Obit* Apr 1959

Malenkov, Georgi M., Soviet prime minister, June 1952, *Obit* Mar 1988

Malik, Adam, Indonesian statesman and diplomat, Nov 1970, *Obit* Nov 1984

Malik, Charles Habib, Lebanese diplomat and United Nations official, Apr 1948, *Obit* Feb 1988

Malik, Yakov Aleksandrovich, Apr 1949, *Obit* Apr 1980

Mallory, Lester D., diplomat, Sept 1960, *Obit* Sept 1994

Malloy, Dan, American governor, June 2011

Maloney, Carolyn B., American congresswoman, Apr 2001

Maloney, Francis T., *Obit* Mar 1945

Malvern, Godfrey Martin Huggins, Rhodesian prime minister, Nov 1956, *Obit* June 1971

Mandel, Georges, French political leader, Yrbk 1940

Mandela, Nelson, South African president, Jan 1984, Nov 1995

Mankin, Helen Douglas, congresswoman and lawyer, Apr 1946

Manley, Michael, Jamaican prime minister, Jan 1976, *Obit* May 1997

Manley, Norman Washington, Jamaican prime minister, Nov 1959, *Obit* Nov 1969

Mann, Thomas Clifton, American diplomat, Apr 1964, *Obit* Apr 1999

Mannerheim, Carl Gustaf Emil, Finnish field marshal and president, Apr 1940, *Obit* Feb 1951

Manning, Ernest, Canadian political leader, Yrbk 1959, *Obit* May 1996

Manning, Patrick A. M., Trinidadian prime minister, Jan 2006

Mansfield, Mike, American senator and diplomat, Apr 1952, Jan 1978, *Obit* Jan 2002

Manuil'skii, Dmitrii Zakhar'evich, Yrbk 1948, *Obit* May 1959

Marcantonio, Vito, American congressman, Feb 1949, *Obit* Oct 1954

March, Charles Hoyt, *Obit* Sept 1945

Marchal, Leon, Sept 1943, *Obit* Yrbk 1957

Marcos, Ferdinand E., Filipino president, Feb 1967, *Obit* Nov 1989

Margai, Milton Augustus Striery, Sierra Leonean prime minister, Feb 1962, *Obit* June 1964

Margesson, Henry David Reginald Margesson, Feb 1941, *Obit* Feb 1966

Marie, Andre, French political leader, Sept 1948, *Obit* Sept 1974

Markey, Edward J., American congressman, Nov 1997

Markovic, Ante, Yugoslav prime minister, Nov 1991, *Obit* Yrbk 2012

Marks, Leonard H., American lawyer and government official, June 1966, *Obit* Yrbk 2006

Marland, Sidney, American educator and government official, Apr 1972, *Obit* July 1992

Marland, William C., Apr 1956, *Obit* Jan 1966

Marquand, Hilary A., Apr 1951

Martens, Wilfried, Belgian prime minister, Feb 1987

Martin Artajo, Alberto, Nov 1949

Martin, Edward, governor and senator, Oct 1945, *Obit* May 1967

Martin, George Brown, *Obit* Yrbk 1945

Martin, Joseph William, American congressman and Speaker of the House, Oct 1940, May 1948, *Obit* Apr 1968

Martin, Kevin, American lawyer and regulatory official, Aug 2005

Martin, Lynn Morley, American Secretary of labor, Oct 1989

Martin, Paul, Canadian cabinet member and diplomat, Yrbk 1951, *Obit* Nov 1992

Martin, Paul, Canadian prime minister, Jan 2004

Martin, Thomas E., Mar 1956, *Obit* Sept 1971

Martinez, Susana, American governor, Nov 2013

Martz, Judy, American governor, Mar 2005

Masaryk, Jan, Czech diplomat, May 1944, *Obit* Apr 1948

Mason, Lowell B., June 1949

Mason, Noah M., Nov 1957, *Obit* May 1965

Massey, Vincent, Canadian statesman, Oct 1951, *Obit* Feb 1968

Massigli, Rene, May 1956

Matalin, Mary, American publishing executive and political consultant, Sept 1996

Mates, Leo, Nov 1956

Mathias, Charles, American senator, Yrbk 1972, *Obit* Yrbk 2010

Matskevich, Vladimir Vladimirovich, Nov 1955

Matsudaira, Koto, Japanese diplomat, Nov 1958

Matsui, Keishiro, *Obit* July 1946

Matsui, Robert T., American congressman, Oct 1994, *Obit* Apr 2005

Matsuoka, Yosuke, Mar 1941, *Obit* July 1946

Matthews, Francis P., American Secretary of the navy, Sept 1949, *Obit* Yrbk 1952

Matthews, H. Freeman, American diplomat, Mar 1945, *Obit* Jan 1987

Matthews, J. B., American senatorial aide, May 1943

Matthews, W. Donald, Sept 1952

Maudling, Reginald, British cabinet member, May 1960, *Obit* Apr 1979

Maurer, Ion Gheorghe, Romanian prime minister, Sept 1971, *Obit* July 2000

Mauroy, Pierre, French prime minister, June 1982, *Obit* Yrbk 2013

Maverick, Maury, American congressman and mayor, Mar 1944, *Obit* Sept 1954

Maw, Herbert B., governor, Oct 1948, *Obit* Jan 1991

Max, Adolphe, Belgian burgomaster, *Obit* Jan 1940

Maxton, James, British member of Parliament, *Obit* Sept 1946

Maxwell, Robert, British publisher, Sept 1988, *Obit* Feb 1992

May, Andrew Jackson, American congressman, Apr 1941, *Obit* Nov 1959

May, Catherine Dean, congresswoman, Jan 1960

May, Theresa, British member of Parliament, Jan 2003

Maybank, Burnet R., American senator and governor, Apr 1949, *Obit* Nov 1954

Mayer, Rene, French prime minister, May 1948, *Obit* Feb 1973

Mays, Ewing W., Jan 1952

Maza, Jose, Nov 1955, *Obit* July 1964

Mazowiecki, Tadeusz, Polish political leader, Feb 1990

Mazuz, Menachem, Israeli attorney general, Jan 2007

Mbeki, Thabo, South African president, Aug 1998

McAdoo, William G., American Secretary of the treasury and senator, *Obit* Mar 1941

McAleese, Mary, Irish president, Jan 2006

McAliskey, Bernadette Devlin, Irish political leader, Jan 1970

McCain, John S., American senator, Feb 1989, Mar 2006

McCall, Tom, American governor, June 1974, *Obit* Mar 1983

McCarl, John Raymond, lawyer and government official, *Obit* Sept 1940

McCarran, Pat, American senator, July 1947, *Obit* Yrbk 1954

McCarthy, Carolyn, American congresswoman, Mar 1998

McCarthy, Eugene J., American senator, Nov 1955, *Obit* Mar 2006

McCarthy, Joseph, American senator, Jan 1950, *Obit* July 1957

McCarthy, Leighton, Oct 1942, *Obit* Nov 1952

McCarty, Dan, July 1953

McClellan, John L., American senator, Apr 1950, *Obit* Feb 1978

McClintock, Robert Mills, American diplomat, Apr 1955

McCloskey, Paul N., American congressman and lawyer, Nov 1971

McCone, John A., American steel industry executive and CIA director, Jan 1959, *Obit* Apr 1991

McConnell, Mike, American intelligence official, Apr 2007

McConnell, Mitch, American senator, Feb 2008

McConnell, Samuel Kerns, Nov 1956

McCormack, Arthur Thomas, *Obit* Sept 1943

McCormack, John William, American congressman and Speaker of the House, June 1943, Apr 1962, *Obit* Jan 1981

McCormick, Edward Theodore, government official and stock exchange executive, May 1951, *Obit* Oct 1991

McCormick, Ruth Hanna, congresswoman, *Obit* Feb 1945

McDermott, Michael J., Feb 1951, *Obit* Oct 1955

McDonald, James Grover, diplomat, Apr 1949, *Obit* Yrbk 1964

McDonnell, Bob, American governor, Sept 2011

McDonough, Roger H., state librarian, June 1968

McFarland, Ernest William, American senator, governor and state supreme court justice, Jan 1951, *Obit* Aug 1984

McFarlane, Robert C., American presidential adviser, May 1984

McGeachy, Mary Craig, Canadian diplomat, Apr 1944

McGovern, Francis Edward, American governor, *Obit* June 1946

McGovern, George S., American senator, Mar 1967, *Obit* Yrbk 2012

McGranery, James P., American congressman, judge and Attorney general, May 1952, *Obit* Feb 1963

McGrath, Earl James, educator and government official, Apr 1949, *Obit* Apr 1993

McGrath, James Howard, American Attorney general, Jan 1948, *Obit* Nov 1966

McGregor, J. Harry, Oct 1958

McGroarty, John Steven, *Obit* Sept 1944

McGuinty, Dalton, Canadian provincial premier, Feb 2013

McHenry, Donald F., diplomat, Sept 1980

McIntyre, James T., Jan 1979

McIntyre, Marvin Hunter, American presidential aide, *Obit* Feb 1944

McIntyre, Thomas James, American senator, Nov 1963, *Obit* Oct 1992

McKay, Douglas, American Secretary of the interior and governor, May 1949, *Obit* Oct 1959

McKeldin, Theodore R., American governor, Oct 1952, *Obit* Oct 1974

McKellar, Kenneth Douglas, American senator, Jan 1946, *Obit* Jan 1958

McKinney, Cynthia, American congresswoman, Aug 1996

McKneally, Martin B., congressman and veterans' leader, Mar 1960, *Obit* Aug 1992

McLaughlin, Ann Dore, American Secretary of labor, Nov 1988

McLaughlin, Audrey, Canadian political leader, July 1990

McMahon, Brien, American senator, Yrbk 1945, *Obit* Sept 1952

McMahon, William, Australian prime minister, Sept 1971, *Obit* May 1988

McManamy, Frank, *Obit* Nov 1944

McMath, Sidney Sanders, American governor, Mar 1949, *Obit* Jan 2004

McMillan, John L., American congressman and lawyer, Nov 1956

McMillen, Tom, congressman, Jan 1993

McMurrin, Sterling M., American educator and government official, June 1961, *Obit* June 1996

McNary, Charles Linza, American senator, Aug 1940, *Obit* Apr 1944

McNeil, Hector, Yrbk 1946, *Obit* Yrbk 1955

McNeil, Wilfred J., Feb 1958, *Obit* Oct 1979

McNichols, Stephen L. R., American governor, Oct 1958, *Obit* Feb 1998

Mead, George H., Oct 1946, *Obit* Feb 1963

Mead, James M., July 1944, *Obit* Apr 1964

Meader, George, July 1956

Mechem, Edwin L., American governor and senator, July 1954, *Obit* Yrbk 2003

Mechem, Merritt Cramer, *Obit* June 1946

Meciar, Vladimir, Slovak prime minister, July 1994

Medgyessy, Peter, Hungarian economist and prime minister, Jan 2003

Meese, Edwin, American Attorney general, Sept 1981

Mehta, G. L., Nov 1952, *Obit* June 1974

Meiling, Richard L., May 1950

Meir, Golda, Israeli prime minister, May 1950, Yrbk 1970, *Obit* Feb 1979

Melas, George V., July 1956

Mellett, Lowell, May 1942, *Obit* May 1960

Mello Franco, Afranio de, *Obit* Feb 1943

Mende, Erich, July 1966

Menderes, Adnan, Turkish prime minister, Nov 1954, *Obit* Nov 1961

Mendes-France, Pierre, French statesman, Oct 1954, *Obit* Jan 1983

Menem, Carlos Saul, Argentine president, Nov 1989

Menocal, Mario Garcia, Cuban president, *Obit* Oct 1941

Menon, K. P. S., Indian diplomat, Mar 1957, *Obit* Yrbk 1983

Menshikov, Mikhail A., May 1958, *Obit* Sept 1976

Menthon, Francois, French political leader, Mar 1944

Menzies, Robert Gordon, Australian prime minister, Feb 1941, Jan 1950, *Obit* July 1978

Meriwether, W. Delano, Jan 1978

Merkel, Angela, German chancellor, Jan 2004

Merriam, C. Hart, American mammalogist, *Obit* May 1942

Merritt, Matthew J., *Obit* Nov 1946

Merry del Val y Alzola, Alfonso, Nov 1965

Meskill, Thomas J., American governor and judge, Mar 1974, *Obit* Yrbk 2008

Messersmith, George S., American diplomat, Oct 1942, *Obit* Apr 1960

Messina, Jim, American presidential adviser and political consultant, Mar 2013

Mesta, Perle, society leader and diplomat, Sept 1949, *Obit* May 1975

Meta, Ilir, Albanian prime minister, Feb 2002

Metcalf, Jesse H., *Obit* Yrbk 1942

Metcalf, Lee, American senator, Feb 1970, *Obit* Mar 1978

Metzenbaum, Howard M., American senator, July 1980, *Obit* Yrbk 2008

Meyer, Cord, intelligence official, Mar 1948, *Obit* Aug 2001

Meyner, Robert Baumle, American governor, Apr 1955, *Obit* July 1990

Michel, Robert H., American congressman and political leader, Sept 1981

Michener, Daniel Roland, Canadian government official, Jan 1968, *Obit* Nov 1991

Michnik, Adam, Polish member of Parliament and newspaper editor, July 1990

Migiro, Asha-Rose Mtengeti, Tanzanian diplomat, Jan 2007

Mikhailov, Nikolai Aleksandrovich, Nov 1958

Miki, Takeo, Japanese prime minister, Apr 1975, *Obit* Jan 1989

Mikolajczyk, Stanislaw, Polish political leader, Mar 1944, *Obit* Feb 1967

Mikoyan, Anastas, Soviet president, May 1955, *Obit* Jan 1979

Mikulski, Barbara A., American senator, Nov 1985

Mikva, Abner J., American judge, July 1980

Miller, Benjamin Meek, governor and judge, *Obit* Mar 1944

Miller, Edward G., June 1951, *Obit* June 1968

Miller, Frieda S., Feb 1945, *Obit* Oct 1973

Miller, George, American congressman, Feb 1964

Miller, James C., economist and regulatory official, May 1986

Miller, John, American FBI official, Aug 2003

Miller, Leszek, Polish prime minister, Jan 2002

Miller, Watson B., Sept 1947, *Obit* Apr 1961

Miller, William Edward, American congressman and lawyer, Feb 1962, *Obit* Aug 1983

Miller, Zell, American senator, July 1996

Millerand, Alexandre, French president, *Obit* May 1943

Millikin, Eugene Donald, American senator, Apr 1948, *Obit* Oct 1958

Millis, Harry A., Nov 1940, *Obit* Sept 1948

Mills, Wilbur D., American congressman, Nov 1956, *Obit* July 1992

Milosevic, Slobodan, Yugoslav president, Apr 1990, *Obit* Yrbk 2006

Mink, Patsy T., American congresswoman, Sept 1968, *Obit* Jan 2003

Minner, Ruth Ann, American governor, Aug 2001

Minow, Newton Norman, American lawyer and regulatory agency official, Oct 1961

Mintoff, Dom, Maltese prime minister, Mar 1984, *Obit* Yrbk 2012

Minton, Sherman, American Supreme Court justice, Mar 1941, Yrbk 1949, *Obit* May 1965

Mirza, Iskander, May 1956, *Obit* Jan 1970

Mitchell, James P., American Secretary of labor, Sept 1955, *Obit* Yrbk 1964

Mitchell, John Newton, American Attorney general, June 1969, *Obit* Jan 1989

Mitchell, William L., Nov 1959

Mitsotakis, Constantine, Greek prime minister, Nov 1990

Mitterrand, Francois, French president, Yrbk 1968, Oct 1982, *Obit* Mar 1996

Miyazawa, Kiichi, Japanese prime minister, Feb 1992, *Obit* Yrbk 2007

Mlambo-Ngcuka, Phumzile, South African deputy president, Jan 2005

Moch, Jules, French socialist leader and cabinet member, Oct 1950, *Obit* Nov 1985

Modi, Narendra, Indian state government official, Jan 2003

Moffat, Jay Pierrepont, diplomat, *Obit* Mar 1943

Mogae, Festus G., Batswana president, Jan 2004

Mohammed, Ghulam, July 1954, *Obit* Nov 1956

Moi, Daniel Arap, Kenyan president, May 1979

Molinari, Susan, congresswoman and television newscaster, Mar 1996

Mollenhoff, Clark R., journalist, Nov 1958, *Obit* May 1991

Mollet, Guy, French prime minister, Sept 1950, *Obit* Nov 1975

Molloy, Daniel M., *Obit* Mar 1944

Monckton of Brenchley, Walter Turner Monckton, British cabinet member, Yrbk 1951, *Obit* Feb 1965

Mondale, Walter F., American vice-president, Jan 1969, May 1978

Monnet, Jean, French economist and statesman, Sept 1947, *Obit* May 1979

Monroney, A. S. Mike, American senator, Nov 1951, *Obit* Apr 1980

Montgomery, James Shera, Apr 1948, *Obit* Sept 1952

Montoya, Joseph M., American senator, Mar 1975, *Obit* July 1978

Moody, Blair, American senator, Sept 1951, *Obit* Oct 1954

Mook, Hubertus J. van, Apr 1942, *Obit* July 1965

Moore, Michael C., state attorney general, Aug 1997

Moore, R. Walton, *Obit* Apr 1941

Moorer, Thomas H., American admiral, Apr 1971, *Obit* Yrbk 2004

Mora, Jose A., Nov 1956, *Obit* Mar 1975

Morales, Evo, Bolivian president, Jan 2006

Morano, Albert P., congressman, Mar 1952, *Obit* Feb 1988

Morella, Constance A., American congresswoman, Feb 2001

Moreno Ocampo, Luis, Argentine lawyer and international court prosecutor, Jan 2007

Morgan, Thomas E., American congressman and physician, June 1959, *Obit* Oct 1995

Morgenstierne, Wilhelm Thorleif von Munthe af, May 1949, *Obit* Sept 1963

Morgenthau, Henry, American Secretary of the treasury, Sept 1940, *Obit* Apr 1967

Morgenthau, Robert, American district attorney, Jan 1986

Morinigo, Higinio, Paraguayan president, June 1942

Moro, Aldo, Italian prime minister, June 1964, *Obit* June 1978

Morris, Dave Hennen, *Obit* June 1944

Morris, Newbold, American municipal official, Mar 1952, *Obit* Apr 1966

Morris, Roland Sletor, lawyer and diplomat, *Obit* Jan 1946

Morrison of Lambeth, Herbert Stanley Morrison, British cabinet member, July 1940, Feb 1951, *Obit* Apr 1965

Morrison, DeLesseps S., American mayor and diplomat, Nov 1949, *Obit* July 1964

Morrison, Frank Brenner, May 1964

Morrison, William Shepherd, British statesman, Jan 1952, *Obit* Apr 1961

Morse, Clarence G., Nov 1957

Morse, David Abner, American international labor leader, Mar 1949, *Obit* Mar 1991

Morse, True Delbert, government official, Nov 1959, *Obit* Sept 1998

Morse, Wayne Lyman, American senator, Apr 1942, Nov 1954, *Obit* Sept 1974

Morton, James Madison, *Obit* Aug 1940

Morton, Thruston Ballard, American senator, Nov 1957, *Obit* Oct 1982

Mosaddeq, Mohammad, Iranian prime minister, May 1951, *Obit* May 1967

Moscicki, Ignacy, Polish president, *Obit* Nov 1946

Moscoso, Mireya, Panamanian president, Jan 2002

Moscoso, Teodoro, American diplomat and economist, Oct 1963, *Obit* Aug 1992

Moseley-Braun, Carol, American senator, June 1994

Moses, George H., *Obit* Feb 1945

Moses, John, *Obit* Apr 1945

Mosley, Oswald, British political leader, July 1940, *Obit* Feb 1981

Moss, Frank E., American senator, Yrbk 1971, *Obit* June 2003

Moss, John E., American congressman, Nov 1956, *Obit* Feb 1998

Mott, James W., *Obit* Yrbk 1945

Motta, Giuseppe, *Obit* Jan 1940

Mousavi, Mir Hossein, Iranian presidential candidate and former prime minister, Sept 2009

Moussa, Amr, Egyptian diplomat and international organization official, Jan 2002

Moutet, Marius, French socialist leader and cabinet member, July 1947, *Obit* Yrbk 1968

Mowinckel, Johan Ludwig, *Obit* Nov 1943

Moyne, Walter Edward Guinness, *Obit* Yrbk 1944

Moynihan, Daniel Patrick, American senator and diplomat, Feb 1968, Feb 1986, *Obit* Yrbk 2003

Moyo, Jonathan N., Zimbabwean political leader, Jan 2007

Mubarak, Hosni, Egyptian president, Apr 1982

Muccio, John Joseph, American diplomat, Jan 1951, *Obit* July 1989

Mueller, Robert S., American FBI director, Aug 2010

Mugabe, Robert Gabriel, Zimbabwean president, Apr 1979, Jan 2002

Muir, Ramsay, *Obit* June 1941

Mujibur Rahman, Bangladeshi prime minister and president, Jan 1973, *Obit* Oct 1975

Mukasey, Michael, American Attorney general, Feb 2008

Muldoon, Robert D., New Zealand prime minister, Feb 1978, *Obit* Sept 1992

Mulroney, Brian, Canadian prime minister, Apr 1984

Muluzi, Bakili, Malawian president, Jan 2003

Mumford, Lawrence Quincy, American Librarian of Congress, June 1954, *Obit* Jan 1983

Mundt, Karl E., American senator, July 1948, *Obit* Oct 1974

Munnich, Ferenc, May 1959, *Obit* Jan 1968

Munoz Marin, Luis, Puerto Rican governor, Oct 1942, Nov 1953, *Obit* June 1980

Munro, Leslie Knox, Nov 1953, *Obit* Apr 1974

Murdock, Victor, *Obit* Aug 1945

Murkowski, Frank H., American senator and governor, July 2003

Murphy, Charles S., American lawyer and presidential adviser, Apr 1950, *Obit* Oct 1983

Murphy, Frank, American Supreme Court justice, July 1940, *Obit* Sept 1949

Murphy, Patrick V., Nov 1972, *Obit* Yrbk 2012

Murphy, Robert D., American diplomat, Feb 1943, Nov 1958, *Obit* Mar 1978

Murphy, Thomas F., police commissioner and judge, Mar 1951, *Obit* Jan 1996

Murray, James E., American senator, Aug 1945, *Obit* May 1961

Murray, Patty, American senator, Aug 1994

Murray, Tom, Nov 1956, *Obit* Jan 1972

Murrow, Edward R., American radio and television newscaster, Feb 1942, Nov 1953, *Obit* June 1965

Museveni, Yoweri, Ugandan president, Aug 1990

Muskie, Edmund S., American senator and Secretary of state, Feb 1955, Yrbk 1968, *Obit* June 1996

Muzorewa, Abel Tendekai, Zimbabwean prime minister, Mar 1979, *Obit* Yrbk 2010

Mwanawasa, Levy, Zambian president, Jan 2003, *Obit* Yrbk 2008

Mwinyi, Ali Hassan, Tanzanian president, June 1995

Myer, Dillon S., government official, July 1947, *Obit* Jan 1983

Myers, Dee Dee, American presidential press secretary and television moderator, Aug 1994

Myers, Francis John, Apr 1949, *Obit* Sept 1956

Myrdal, Alva Reimer, Swedish sociologist, Yrbk 1950, *Obit* Mar 1986

Nabarro, Gerald, Nov 1963, *Obit* Jan 1974

Nabulsi, Suleiman, Mar 1957

Najibullah, Mohammed, Afghan president, June 1988, *Obit* Jan 1997

Nakasone, Yasuhiro, Japanese prime minister, June 1983

Namboodiripad, E. M. S., Indian communist leader, Nov 1976

Napolitano, Giorgio, Italian president, Jan 2006

Narasimha Rao, P. V., Indian prime minister, Jan 1992, *Obit* Yrbk 2005

Narathipphongpraphan, June 1954

Nash, Philleo, government official, Nov 1962, *Obit* Jan 1988

Nash, Walter, New Zealand prime minister, Oct 1942, Mar 1958, *Obit* July 1968

Nasser, Gamal Abdel, Egyptian president, Nov 1954, *Obit* Nov 1970

Nathan, Robert R., American economist, Sept 1941, *Obit* Nov 2001

Navon, Yitzhak, May 1982

Nazarbayev, Nursultan, Kazakhstani president, Oct 2000

Nazimuddin, Khwaja, Mar 1949, *Obit* Yrbk 1964

Neely, Matthew M., Jan 1950, *Obit* Mar 1958

Negrin, Juan, Spanish physiologist and statesman, Sept 1945, *Obit* Jan 1957

Negroponte, John, American intelligence official, Apr 2003

Nehru, B. K., Indian diplomat and government official, Feb 1963, *Obit* Feb 2002

Nehru, Jawaharlal, Indian prime minister, Jan 1941, Apr 1948, *Obit* July 1964

Neill, Charles Patrick, *Obit* Nov 1942

Nelson, Donald Marr, American retail executive, Mar 1941, *Obit* Yrbk 1959

Nelson, Gaylord, American senator, governor and environmentalist, May 1960, *Obit* Yrbk 2005

Neruda, Pablo, Chilean poet, Yrbk 1970, *Obit* Nov 1973

Nestingen, Ivan A., Mar 1962, *Obit* June 1978

Netanyahu, Benjamin, Israeli prime minister, June 1996

Neuberger, Maurine Brown, American senator, Oct 1961, *Obit* July 2000

Neuberger, Richard L., American senator, Feb 1955, *Obit* May 1960

Neville, Robert A. R., Nov 1953

Newall, Cyril Louis Norton, Aug 1940

Newberry, Truman Handy, *Obit* Nov 1945

Newhall, Arthur B., Oct 1942

Newton, Cleveland Alexander, *Obit* Oct 1945

Ney, Hubert, Nov 1956

Ngo, Dinh Diem, South Vietnamese president, Mar 1955, *Obit* Jan 1964

Nguyen, Van Thieu, South Vietnamese president, June 1968, *Obit* Jan 2002

Nice, Harry, *Obit* Apr 1941

Nitze, Paul H., American statesman, Feb 1962, *Obit* Mar 2005

Nixon, Richard M., American president, July 1948, June 1958, Yrbk 1969, *Obit* June 1994, Yrbk 1994

Niyazov, Saparmurad, Turkmen president, Jan 2003

Nkrumah, Kwame, Ghanaian president, July 1953, *Obit* June 1972

Noble, Allan, May 1957

Nofziger, Lyn, American political consultant, Jan 1983, *Obit* Yrbk 2006

Nolan, W. I., *Obit* Sept 1943

Nomura, Kichisaburo, Apr 1941, *Obit* July 1964

Noon, Firoz Khan, June 1957

Noonan, Peggy, American presidential speechwriter and political writer, July 1990

Norris, George William, American senator, *Obit* Oct 1944

Norton, Gale, American Secretary of the interior, June 2001

Norton, Mary Teresa Hopkins, congresswoman, Nov 1944, *Obit* Nov 1959

Nour, Ayman, Egyptian member of Parliament, Jan 2005

Nourse, Edwin, American economist and presidential adviser, Oct 1946, *Obit* June 1974

Novello, Antonia, American pediatrician and Surgeon general, May 1992

Novikov, Nikolai Vasil'evich, Feb 1947

Novotny, Antonin, Czech president, May 1958, *Obit* Mar 1975

Nu, Burmese prime minister, Yrbk 1951, *Obit* Apr 1995

Nufer, Albert F., Mar 1955, *Obit* Jan 1957

Nujoma, Sam, Namibian president, Feb 1990

Nunez Portuondo, Emilio, Apr 1957

Nunn, Sam, American senator, Jan 1980

Nutting, Anthony, British cabinet member, Feb 1955, *Obit* May 1999

Nye, Gerald Prentice, American senator, Nov 1941, *Obit* Sept 1971

Nyerere, Julius K., Tanzanian president, Apr 1963, *Obit* Jan 2000

O'Brien, Leo W., June 1959, *Obit* July 1982

O'Connor, James Francis, *Obit* Mar 1945

O'Conor, Herbert R., Feb 1950, *Obit* May 1960

O'Daniel, W. Lee, American senator and governor, Oct 1947, *Obit* June 1969

O'Day, Caroline Love Goodwin, American congresswoman, *Obit* Feb 1943

O'Dwyer, Paul, American lawyer and municipal official, Sept 1969, *Obit* Sept 1998

O'Dwyer, William, American mayor, Sept 1941, May 1947, *Obit* Jan 1965

O'Gorman, James A., *Obit* July 1943

O'Keefe, Sean, American NASA official, Jan 2003

O'Kelly, Sean T., July 1948, *Obit* Jan 1967

O'Leary, James A., *Obit* May 1944

O'Mahoney, Joseph C., American senator, Oct 1945, *Obit* Jan 1963

O'Neal, A. Daniel, June 1979

O'Neill of the Maine, Terence Marne O'Neill, prime minister of Northern Ireland, Sept 1968, *Obit* Sept 1990

O'Neill, C. William, July 1958

O'Neill, Tip, American Speaker of the House, Apr 1974, *Obit* Mar 1994

O'Neill, William A., American governor, Feb 1985, *Obit* Yrbk 2008

Obama, Barack, American president, July 2005, Mar 2009

Obasanjo, Olusegun, Nigerian president, July 1999

Obote, A. Milton, Ugandan president, Apr 1981, *Obit* Yrbk 2006

Obuchi, Keizo, Japanese prime minister, May 1999, *Obit* Aug 2000

Odria, Manuel Arturo, Peruvian president, Nov 1954, *Obit* Apr 1974

Oduber Quiros, Daniel, Costa Rican president, July 1977

Oechsner, Frederick Cable, journalist and intelligence official, Mar 1943, *Obit* June 1992

Ogata, Sadako, Japanese United Nations official and diplomat, Oct 1997

Ohira, Masayoshi, Japanese prime minister, Mar 1964, *Obit* Aug 1980

Okonjo-Iweala, Ngozi, Nigerian cabinet member, Jan 2006

Olivetti, Adriano, Italian manufacturing executive, Jan 1959, *Obit* Apr 1960

Olmert, Ehud, Israeli prime minister, Jan 2006

Olson, Theodore B., American lawyer and former Solicitor general, Nov 2010

Oppenheimer, J. Robert, American physicist, Nov 1945, Apr 1964, *Obit* Apr 1967

Orlando, Vittorio Emanuele, Italian statesman, Feb 1944, *Obit* Jan 1953

Ortega Saavedra, Daniel, Nicaraguan president, Oct 1984

Ortiz, Roberto M., *Obit* Sept 1942

Osmena, Sergio, Filipino president, Sept 1944, *Obit* Yrbk 1961

Ospina Perez, Mariano, Colombian president, Feb 1950, *Obit* June 1976

Otero, Miguel Antonio, American territorial governor, *Obit* Sept 1944

Owen, David, British political leader, Sept 1977

Owen, Ruth Bryan, American congresswoman, Yrbk 1944, *Obit* Oct 1954

Owens, Clarence Julian, *Obit* Apr 1941

Ozal, Turgut, Turkish president, June 1985, *Obit* June 1993

Paasikivi, Juho Kusti, Finnish president, May 1944, *Obit* Feb 1957

Pacciardi, Randolfo, Italian political leader, Mar 1944, *Obit* July 1991

Pacheco de la Espriella, Abel, Costa Rican president, Jan 2002

Packwood, Robert, American senator, Jan 1981

Padilla, Ezequiel, Mexican diplomat, July 1942, *Obit* Oct 1971

Palacio Gonzalez, Alfredo, Ecuadorian president, Jan 2005

Paleologue, Maurice, French diplomat, *Obit* Jan 1945

Palin, Sarah, American governor, Jan 2009

Palme, Olof, Swedish prime minister, May 1970, *Obit* Apr 1986

Pandit, Vijaya Lakshmi, Indian diplomat, Jan 1946, *Obit* Feb 1991

Panetta, Leon E., American Secretary of defense, June 1993

Pant, Govind Ballabh, Indian cabinet member, Jan 1959, *Obit* May 1961

Panyushkin, Aleksandr S., Yrbk 1948, *Obit* Jan 1975

Papadopoulos, George, Greek army officer and president, Feb 1970, *Obit* Sept 1999

Papandreou, Andreas, Greek prime minister, May 1970, Apr 1983, *Obit* Sept 1996

Papandreou, George, Greek political leader, Yrbk 1944, *Obit* Yrbk 1968

Papen, Franz von, German diplomat, June 1941, *Obit* June 1969

Pardee, George C., *Obit* Oct 1941

Park, Geun Hye, Korean political leader, Jan 2007

Parker, Homer Cling, *Obit* July 1946

Parodi, Alexandre, French government official and diplomat, June 1946

Parri, Ferruccio, Nov 1945

Parsons, Herbert Collins, *Obit* July 1941

Partridge, Frank C., *Obit* Apr 1943

Passman, Otto E., American congressman, Oct 1960, *Obit* Sept 1988

Pastore, John O., American senator, Apr 1953, *Obit* Yrbk 2000

Pastrana Borrero, Misael, Colombian president, July 1971, *Obit* Nov 1997

Pasvolsky, Leo, May 1945, *Obit* June 1953

Pataki, George, American governor, Apr 1996

Paterson, David A., American governor, July 2008

Patil, Pratibha, Indian president, Jan 2007

Patman, Wright, American congressman, Feb 1946, *Obit* Apr 1976

Patterson, John, American governor, Nov 1960

Patterson, P. J., Jamaican prime minister, Feb 1995

Patterson, Richard C., Oct 1946, *Obit* Yrbk 1966

Patterson, Robert Porter, American Secretary of war, Oct 1941, *Obit* Mar 1952

Paul, Ron, American congressman, June 2008

Paul-Boncour, Joseph, French statesman, June 1945, *Obit* May 1972

Pauly, D., Canadian fishery scientist, Jan 2003

Payne, Frederick G., Yrbk 1952, *Obit* Aug 1978

Paz Estenssoro, Victor, Bolivian president, May 1953, *Obit* Sept 2001

Peabody, Endicott, governor, Mar 1964, *Obit* Feb 1998

Pearson, Lester Bowles, Canadian prime minister, Nov 1947, Nov 1963, *Obit* Feb 1973

Peck, Raoul, Haitian motion picture director and cabinet member, Jan 2002

Peden, Katherine G., real estate broker and state official, May 1962

Peker, Recep, Sept 1947, *Obit* May 1950

Pella, Giuseppe, Nov 1953, *Obit* Aug 1981

Pelosi, Nancy, American congresswoman and former

Speaker of the House, Feb 2003

Pena, Federico, American Secretary of transportation, Oct 1993

Pena, Pedro, *Obit* Sept 1943

Pendergast, Tom, American political party leader, *Obit* Mar 1945

Pendleton, Clarence M., government official, Sept 1984, *Obit* July 1988

Pepper, Claude, American congressman, Feb 1941, Jan 1983, *Obit* July 1989

Percy, Charles H., American senator, Yrbk 1959, Aug 1977, *Obit* Yrbk 2011

Peres, Shimon, Israeli political leader, Jan 1976, Mar 1995

Peret, Raoul, *Obit* Sept 1942

Perez Jimenez, Marcos, Venezuelan president, Nov 1954, *Obit* Feb 2002

Perez de Cuellar, Javier, Peruvian diplomat and United Nations secretary-general, Aug 1982

Perez, Carlos Andres, Venezuelan president, Feb 1976, *Obit* Yrbk 2011

Perino, Dana, American presidential press secretary, Jan 2008

Perkins, Carl D., American congressman, Feb 1968, *Obit* Sept 1984

Perkins, Milo, June 1942

Perle, Richard Norman, American military official, July 2003

Perlman, Philip B., American solicitor general, July 1952, *Obit* Oct 1960

Peron, Isabel, Argentine president, Jan 1975

Perrin, Francis, French physicist, July 1951

Persad-Bissessar, Kamla, Trinidadian prime minister, Jan 2013

Perse, Saint-John, French diplomat and poet, Apr 1961, *Obit* Nov 1975

Pertschuk, Michael, consumer activist and government official, Sept 1986

Petain, Henri Philippe, French field marshal, Aug 1940, *Obit* Sept 1951

Peterson, David Robert, Canadian political leader, Feb 1988

Peterson, Esther, American consumer rights advocate, Yrbk 1961, *Obit* Mar 1998

Peterson, Val, governor and presidential aide, June 1949, *Obit* Jan 1984

Petitpierre, Max, Swiss president and diplomat, Yrbk 1953, *Obit* June 1994

Petry, Lucile, nursing educator and government official, Apr 1944, *Obit* June 2000

Petsche, Maurice, Nov 1949, *Obit* Nov 1951

Peurifoy, John Emil, American diplomat, Jan 1949, *Obit* Oct 1955

Peynado, Jacinto B., *Obit* Mar 1940

Peyrouton, Marcel, Mar 1943

Pflimlin, Pierre, French political leader, Nov 1955, *Obit* Oct 2000

Pfost, Gracie Bowers, congresswoman, May 1955, *Obit* Oct 1965

Pham, Van Dong, Vietnamese prime minister, Feb 1975, *Obit* Sept 2000

Phelan, Michael F., *Obit* Yrbk 1941

Philip, Andre, French economist and cabinet member, Aug 1943, *Obit* Sept 1970

Phillips, John C., American governor and judge, *Obit* Aug 1943

Phillips, William, American diplomat, July 1940, *Obit* Apr 1968

Pholien, Joseph, Feb 1951, *Obit* Mar 1968

Phoui Sananikone, Laotian prime minister, Sept 1959, *Obit* Feb 1984

Piccioni, Attilio, Oct 1967, *Obit* May 1976

Pickersgill, J. W., Canadian cabinet member, Mar 1968

Pieck, Wilhelm, Yrbk 1949, *Obit* Nov 1960

Pierce, Samuel R., American Secretary of housing and urban development, Nov 1982, *Obit* Feb 2001

Pierlot, Hubert, Belgian prime minister, May 1943, *Obit* Feb 1964

Pike, Otis, American congressman, Feb 1976

Pilot, Sachin, Indian member of Parliament, Jan 2007

Pindling, Lynden Oscar, Bahamian prime minister, May 1968, *Obit* Yrbk 2000

Pine, David A., American judge, June 1952, *Obit* Sept 1970

Pine, William B., *Obit* Oct 1942

Pinero, Jesus T., Oct 1946, *Obit* Jan 1953

Pingree, Chellie, American citizen advocacy organization official, Jan 2005

Piot, Peter, Belgian public health official and epidemiologist, Jan 2004

Pitt, Harvey L., American risk management consultant, Nov 2002

Pittman, Key, American senator, *Obit* Yrbk 1940

Pittman, Steuart L., American government official, Jan 1963, *Obit* Yrbk 2013

Plaisted, Frederick William, *Obit* Apr 1943

Plastiras, Nicholas, May 1950, *Obit* Oct 1953

Plaza Lasso, Galo, Ecuadorian president, Oct 1951, Apr 1969, *Obit* Mar 1987

Pleven, Rene, French political leader, June 1950, *Obit* Mar 1993

Plouffe, David, American presidential adviser, June 2009

Plowden, Edwin, July 1947

Poage, W. R., American congressman, Yrbk 1969, *Obit* Mar 1987

Podesta, John, American public policy organization official and former presidential adviser, Feb 2010

Podgorny, Nikolai V., Soviet president, May 1966, *Obit* Mar 1983

Pohamba, Hifkepunye, Namibian president, Jan 2006

Poindexter, John M., American admiral and presidential adviser, Nov 1987

Poindexter, Joseph B., Jan 1942, *Obit* Jan 1952

Poindexter, Miles, *Obit* Nov 1946

Poletti, Charles, American lieutenant governor and acting governor, *Obit* Yrbk 2002

Poletti, Charles E., Sept 1943

Politis, Athanase G., Sept 1950, *Obit* June 1968

Politis, Nicolas, *Obit* Apr 1942

Polyansky, Dmitry S., Soviet communist leader, Mar 1971

Pompidou, Georges, French president, Nov 1962, *Obit* May 1974

Pool, Joe, American congressman, Mar 1967, *Obit* Sept 1968

Poole, Dewitt C., Nov 1950, *Obit* Oct 1952

Popovic, Koca, Yugoslav cabinet member, Jan 1957, *Obit* Jan 1993

Popovic, Vladimir, Feb 1952, *Obit* May 1972

Porras, Belisario, Panamanian president, *Obit* Oct 1942

Porter, Charles O., Sept 1957

Porter, Paul A., American regulatory agency official, Jan 1945, *Obit* Jan 1976

Porter, Richard W., electrical engineer and NASA official, Nov 1958, *Obit* Jan 1997

Porter, William James, diplomat, Mar 1974, *Obit* May 1988

Possuelo, Sydney, Brazilian government official and human rights activist, Jan 2006

Pote Sarasin, Yrbk 1955

Potemkin, Vladimir P., *Obit* Apr 1946

Potter, Charles E., American senator, Yrbk 1954

Powell, Enoch, British member of Parliament, Nov 1964, *Obit* June 1999

Powell, Jody, American presidential press secretary, July 1977, *Obit* Yrbk 2009

Powell, Michael, American regulatory official and son of Secretary of state Colin L. Powell, May 2003

Prado Ugarteche, Manuel, Peruvian president, June 1942, *Obit* Oct 1967

Prasad, Rajendra, Apr 1950, *Obit* Apr 1963

Press, Frank, American geophysicist and presidential adviser, July 1966

Pressler, Larry, senator, Oct 1983

Preval, Rene, Haitian president, Jan 2006

Price, George C., Belizean prime minister, Aug 1984, *Obit* Yrbk 2012

Priest, Ivy Baker, Nov 1952, *Obit* Aug 1975

Priest, J. Percy, Sept 1950, *Obit* Yrbk 1958

Prio Socarras, Carlos, Cuban president, May 1949, *Obit* June 1977

Procope, Hjalman Johan Fredrik, Apr 1940, *Obit* Apr 1954

Profumo, John D., British cabinet member, Oct 1959, *Obit* June 2006

Pronk, Johannes Pieter, Dutch United Nations official, Jan 2005

Prosper, Pierre-Richard, American lawyer and diplomat, Aug 2005

Prouty, Winston L., American senator, July 1960, *Obit* Oct 1971

Proxmire, William, American senator, June 1958, Aug 1978, *Obit* Mar 2006

Pucheu, Pierre Firmin, French steel executive and government official, *Obit* May 1944

Pueyrredon, Honorio, *Obit* Oct 1945

Purtell, William A., June 1956, *Obit* July 1978

Putin, Vladimir, Russian prime minister, Apr 2000, Jan 2002

Putnam, Roger Lowell, Jan 1952

Pyle, Howard, American governor and presidential aide, Nov 1955, *Obit* Jan 1988

Pym, Francis, British cabinet member, Sept 1982, *Obit* Yrbk 2008

Quadros, Janio, Brazilian mayor and president, June 1961, *Obit* Apr 1992

Quaison-Sackey, Alex, Ghanaian United Nations official and diplomat, Mar 1966, *Obit* Feb 1993

Quarles, Donald A., American Secretary of the air force, Nov 1955, *Obit* July 1959

Quayle, Dan, American vice-president, June 1989

Queuille, Henri, French prime minister, Oct 1948, *Obit* Sept 1970

Quezon, Manuel Luis, Filipino president, Aug 1941, *Obit* Sept 1944

Quirino, Elpidio, Filipino president, Sept 1948, *Obit* May 1956

Quo, Tai-Chi, May 1946, *Obit* Apr 1952

Quwatli, Shukri al-, Syrian president, May 1956, *Obit* Oct 1967

Raab, Julius, Austrian chancellor, Apr 1954, *Obit* Feb 1964

Rabaut, Louis Charles, Jan 1952, *Obit* Jan 1962

Rabin, Yitzhak, Israeli prime minister, Sept 1974, Jan 1995, *Obit* Jan 1996

Raborn, William Francis, American admiral and intelligence official, July 1958, *Obit* June 1990

Radcliffe, Cyril John Radcliffe, British jurist and government official, June 1963, *Obit* May 1977

Rae, Bob, Canadian political leader, Feb 1991

Raffarin, Jean-Pierre, French prime minister, Jan 2003

Rafferty, Max L., American state education official, Jan 1969, *Obit* Aug 1982

Rafsanjani, Hashemi, Iranian president, Nov 1989

Ragon, Heartsill, *Obit* Nov 1940

Rahmon, Emomali, Tajik president, Jan 2007

Rains, Albert McKinley, congressman, Sept 1959, *Obit* May 1991

Rajapakse, Mahinda, Sri Lankan president, Jan 2006

Raje, Vasundhara, Indian provincial government official, Jan 2007

Rajoy, Mariano, Spanish political leader, Jan 2007

Rakosi, Matyas, Hungarian communist leader, Mar 1949, *Obit* Mar 1971

Rakowski, Mieczyslaw F., Polish communist leader, Apr 1989, *Obit* Feb 2009

Ram, Jagjivan, Indian political leader, Oct 1978, *Obit* Aug 1986

Rama, Edi, Albanian artist and mayor, Jan 2005

Ramadier, Paul, French prime minister, June 1947, *Obit* Yrbk 1961

Ramsey, Dewitt C., Jan 1953, *Obit* Nov 1961

Ramspeck, Robert, June 1951, *Obit* Yrbk 1972

Rance, Hubert Elvin, Yrbk 1953, *Obit* Mar 1974

Rand, William M., May 1953

Randall, Clarence B., American steel industry executive and presidential adviser, June 1952, *Obit* Oct 1967

Randers, Gunnar, Jan 1957

Randolph, Jennings, American senator, Jan 1962, *Obit* July 1998

Rangel, Charles B., American congressman, Mar 1984

Rankin, J. Lee, American solicitor general, Feb 1959, *Obit* Sept 1996

Rankin, John E., American congressman, Feb 1944, *Obit* Jan 1961

Rankin, Karl Lott, American diplomat, Apr 1955, *Obit* Apr 1991

Rapacki, Adam, July 1958, *Obit* Yrbk 1970

Raphael, Chaim, English author and government official, Yrbk 1963, *Obit* Jan 1995

Rasmussen, Gustav, Yrbk 1947, *Obit* Nov 1953

Rathbone, Eleanor, British feminist and member of Parliament, June 1943, *Obit* Feb 1946

Rau, Benegal Narsing, Yrbk 1951, *Obit* Feb 1954

Rau, Benegal Rama, Feb 1949, *Obit* Feb 1970

Rau, Johannes, German president, Mar 1987, *Obit* Yrbk 2006

Ravenstahl, Luke, American mayor, Aug 2008

Raver, Paul J., Sept 1941

Ravitch, Diane, American educator and historian, Nov 2010

Ray, Dixy Lee, American governor, June 1973, *Obit* Mar 1994

Ray, Robert D., governor, Jan 1977

Rayburn, Sam, American congressman and Speaker of the House, Oct 1940, Mar 1949, *Obit* Jan 1962

Reagan, Ronald, American president, Yrbk 1949, Feb 1967, Nov 1982, *Obit* Yrbk 2004

Reber, Samuel, Sept 1949, *Obit* Feb 1972

Reece, Brazilla Carroll, American congressman, May 1946, *Obit* May 1961

Reed, Daniel A., American congressman, May 1953, *Obit* Apr 1959

Reed, Herbert Calhoun, *Obit* Sept 1940

Reed, James A., American senator, *Obit* Oct 1944

Reed, Stanley Forman, American Supreme Court justice, Feb 1942, *Obit* May 1980

Rees, Edward H., Jan 1958, *Obit* Yrbk 1969

Regan, Donald T., American presidential adviser, Nov 1981, *Obit* Yrbk 2003

Rehnquist, William H., American Chief Justice of the Supreme Court, Apr 1972, Nov 2003, *Obit* Yrbk 2005

Reichelderfer, Francis Wilton, meteorologist, May 1949, *Obit* Mar 1983

Reid, Charlotte Thompson, congresswoman and regulatory official, Jan 1975

Reid, Frank R., *Obit* Mar 1945

Reid, Harry, American senator, Mar 2003

Reid, Ogden R., American congressman and newspaper publisher, Feb 1956

Reilly, William K., American conservationist and government official, July 1989

Relander, Lauri Kristian, *Obit* Apr 1942

Rell, M. Jodi, American governor, Sept 2005

Rendell, Ed, American governor, Apr 1998

Renner, Karl, Austrian president, Sept 1945, *Obit* Jan 1951

Resor, Stanley R., American Secretary of the army, Sept 1969, *Obit* Yrbk 2012

Reuss, Henry S., American congressman and lawyer, Oct 1959, *Obit* Mar 2002

Reuter, Ernst, German mayor, Oct 1949, *Obit* Yrbk 1953

Revercomb, Chapman, June 1958

Reyes, Silvestre, American congressman, Sept 2007

Reynaud, Paul, French prime minister, Apr 1940, May 1950, *Obit* Nov 1966

Reynolds, Albert, Irish prime minister, Sept 1994

Reynolds, John W., American judge and governor, Apr 1964, *Obit* Mar 2002

Reynolds, Robert Rice, senator, Oct 1940, *Obit* Mar 1963

Reynolds, William Bradford, government official and lawyer, July 1988

Rhee, Syngman, Korean president, Sept 1947, *Obit* Sept 1965

Rhodes, Edgar Nelson, *Obit* May 1942

Rhodes, James Allen, American governor and political party leader, Mar 1949, Apr 1976, *Obit* July 2001

Rhodes, John J., American congressman, Sept 1976, *Obit* Yrbk 2004

Riad, Mahmoud, Egyptian diplomat, Nov 1971, *Obit* Mar 1992

Ribadu, Nuhu, Nigerian law enforcement official, Jan 2006

Ribbentrop, Joachim von, German Nazi leader, May 1941, *Obit* Nov 1946

Ribicoff, Abraham A., American senator, June 1955, *Obit* May 1998

Richards, James P., Sept 1951, *Obit* Apr 1979

Richards, John G., *Obit* Yrbk 1941

Richardson, Bill, American governor, Apr 1996

Richardson, Elliot L., American Attorney general, Mar 1971, *Obit* Mar 2000

Richardson, Norval, *Obit* Yrbk 1940

Richardson, Seth Whitley, American government official, Feb 1948, *Obit* May 1953

Richberg, Donald R., American government official, Yrbk 1949, *Obit* Jan 1961

Riddleberger, James W., diplomat, May 1957, *Obit* Jan 1983

Ridge, Tom, American Secretary of homeland security, Feb 2001

Riegle, Donald W., senator, Oct 1986

Riles, Wilson, educator and state official, Yrbk 1971

Riley, Richard Wilson, American Secretary of education, Oct 1993

Rimsza, Skip, American mayor, July 2002

Rincon de Gautier, Felisa, Puerto Rican mayor, Oct 1956, *Obit* Nov 1994

Rios, Juan Antonio, Chilean president, Apr 1942, *Obit* July 1946

Rivers, L. Mendel, American congressman, Oct 1960, *Obit* Feb 1971

Rizzo, Frank Lazarro, American mayor, Mar 1973, *Obit* Sept 1991

Roa, Raul, Nov 1973, *Obit* Sept 1982

Robb, Charles S., American senator, Apr 1989

Robens of Woldingham, Alfred Robens, June 1956

Robert, Georges, June 1943

Roberts, Albert H., *Obit* July 1946

Roberts, Dennis J., governor, Yrbk 1956, *Obit* Sept 1994

Roberts, Owen Josephus, American Supreme Court justice, Oct 1941, *Obit* July 1955

Robertson, A. Willis, American senator, Yrbk 1949, *Obit* Yrbk 1971

Robertson, Norman A., Yrbk 1957, *Obit* Sept 1968

Robertson, Reuben B., Yrbk 1955, *Obit* May 1960

Robichaud, Louis J., Canadian political leader, May 1968

Robinson, Elmer E., Nov 1955

Robinson, Mary, Irish president and United Nations official, Apr 1991

Robles, Marco Aurelio, Panamanian president, June 1968, *Obit* June 1990

Roca, Julio A., *Obit* Nov 1942

Rocard, Michel, French prime minister, Oct 1988

Rockefeller, Nelson A., American vice-president, Mar 1941, Mar 1951, *Obit* Mar 1979

Rodino, Peter W., American congressman, Oct 1954, *Obit* Yrbk 2005

Rodriguez Veltze, Eduardo, Bolivian president, Jan 2005

Rodriguez Zapatero, Jose Luis, Spanish prime minister, Jan 2004

Roemer, Buddy, governor, Nov 1990

Rogers, Edith Nourse, American congresswoman, Apr 1942, *Obit* Nov 1960

Rogers, Norman McLeod, *Obit* July 1940

Roh, Moo Hyun, South Korean president, Jan 2003, *Obit* Yrbk 2009

Roijen, Jan Herman van, Dutch diplomat, Yrbk 1953

Rokossovskii, Konstantin K., Soviet field marshal, Jan 1944, *Obit* Oct 1968

Rollins, Ed, American political consultant, Mar 2001

Rolvaag, Karl Fritjof, American governor, Feb 1964, *Obit* Mar 1991

Romero Barcelo, Carlos, Puerto Rican governor, Oct 1977

Ronan, William J., Oct 1969

Rooney, John J., American congressman, Yrbk 1964, *Obit* Jan 1976

Roosevelt, Franklin D., American president, Mar 1942, *Obit* Apr 1945

Roosevelt, Franklin D., American congressman and son of President Franklin D. Roosevelt, Jan 1950, *Obit* Sept 1988

Roper, Daniel C., *Obit* May 1943

Ros-Lehtinen, Ileana, American congresswoman, Aug 2000

Rosanoff, Aaron J., *Obit* Feb 1943

Rosellini, Albert D., American governor, Yrbk 1958, *Obit* Yrbk 2012

Rosenman, Samuel I., American state supreme court justice, Aug 1942, *Obit* Sept 1973

Ross, C. Ben, American governor, *Obit* May 1946

Ross, Charles G., June 1945, *Obit* Jan 1951

Ross, Edward Denison, *Obit* Nov 1940

Ross, Malcolm, Feb 1944, *Obit* July 1965

Ross, Nellie Tayloe, American governor, May 1940, *Obit* Feb 1978

Rossel, Agda, Yrbk 1959

Rostenkowski, Dan, American congressman, Jan 1982, *Obit* Yrbk 2010

Roth, William V., American senator, Apr 1983, *Obit* Yrbk 2004

Rothermere, Esmond Cecil Harmsworth, British newspaper publisher, Yrbk 1948, *Obit* Sept 1978

Rothschild, Louis Samuel, government official, Yrbk 1957, *Obit* Oct 1984

Roudebush, Richard L., congressman and veterans' leader, June 1976, *Obit* Apr 1995

Rounds, M. Michael, American governor, June 2006

Rountree, William M., diplomat, June 1959, *Obit* Jan 1996

Rousseff, Dilma, Brazilian president, July 2012

Rove, Karl, American political commentator and former presidential adviser, Oct 2000

Rowland, John, American governor, Oct 1997

Rowley, James Joseph, secret service official, Jan 1963, *Obit* Jan 1993

Roxas y Acuna, Manuel, May 1946, *Obit* May 1948

Royal, Segolene, French political leader, Jan 2007

Rua, Fernando de la, Argentine president, Apr 2001

Rubattel, Rodolphe, Yrbk 1954, *Obit* Yrbk 1961

Rubio, Marco, American senator, Apr 2011

Rubottom, R. Richard, American diplomat, May 1959, *Obit* Yrbk 2011

Ruckelshaus, William D., American government official, July 1971

Rudman, Warren B., senator, Nov 1989, *Obit* Yrbk 2013

Ruiz Cortines, Adolfo, Mexican president, Sept 1952, *Obit* Jan 1974

Ruiz Guinazu, Enrique, Apr 1942, *Obit* Jan 1968

Rumor, Mariano, Italian prime minister, July 1969, *Obit* Mar 1990

Russell, Harold, American actor and government official, Jan 1950, Jan 1966, *Obit* Apr 2002

Russell, Richard B., American senator, Nov 1949, *Obit* Mar 1971

Rust, Bernhard, German Nazi leader, July 1942

Ryan, George H., American governor, Sept 2001

Ryan, Paul, American congressman, Jan 2013

Ryan, William F., American congressman, May 1967, *Obit* Yrbk 1972

Ryun, Jim, American runner and congressman, May 1968

Saakashvili, Mikheil, Georgian president, May 2009

Sabath, Adolph J., American congressman, July 1946, *Obit* Yrbk 1952

Sabry, Hassan, *Obit* Yrbk 1940

Sackett, Frederic M., senator and diplomat, *Obit* July 1941

Sadak, Necmeddin, Jan 1950, *Obit* Yrbk 1953

Sadat, Anwar, Egyptian president, Mar 1971, *Obit* Nov 1981

Sadik-Khan, Janette, American transportation official, Nov 2012

Saionji, Kimmochi, Japanese statesman, *Obit* Jan 1941

Salazar, Antonio de Oliveira, Portuguese dictator, May 1941, May 1952, *Obit* Oct 1970

Salazar, Ken, American Secretary of the interior, Mar 2009

Saleh, Allah-Yar, Feb 1953

Salih, Barham, Iraqi deputy prime minister, Jan 2007

Salinas de Gortari, Carlos, Mexican president, Mar 1989

Salinger, Pierre, American journalist and presidential press secretary, July 1961, Mar 1987, *Obit* Feb 2005

Salisbury, Robert Arthur James Gascoyne-Cecil, British

member of Parliament, Nov 1941, *Obit* Apr 1972

Salter, Alfred, *Obit* Sept 1945

Salter, Arthur Salter, English economist and member of Parliament, May 1944

Saltonstall, Leverett, American governor and senator, June 1944, Apr 1956, *Obit* Sept 1979

Sambi, Ahmed Abdallah Mohamed, Comoran president, Jan 2006

Sampson, Edith S., American judge, Yrbk 1950, *Obit* Jan 1980

Samuel, Bernard, Sept 1949, *Obit* Mar 1954

Samuel, Herbert Louis Samuel, British statesman, Apr 1955, *Obit* Mar 1963

Sanchez de Lozada, Gonzalo, Bolivian president, Jan 2002

Sanchez, Fernando, Mexican government official, Jan 2002

Sanders, Bernard, American senator, June 1991

Sanders, Carl E., American governor, Yrbk 1964

Sanders, Jared Young, *Obit* May 1944

Sandoval, Brian, American governor, Jan 2012

Sanjiva Reddy, N., Indian president, Mar 1981, *Obit* Aug 1996

Santolalla, Irene Silva de, Peruvian educator and legislator, Yrbk 1956, *Obit* Sept 1992

Santorum, Rick, American lawyer, presidential candidate and former senator, Aug 2011

Santos, Jose Eduardo dos, Angolan president, May 1994

Saracoglu, Sukru, June 1942, *Obit* Mar 1954

Saragat, Giuseppe, Italian president, Yrbk 1956, July 1965, *Obit* July 1988

Sarbanes, Paul S., American senator, Jan 1997

Sargeant, Howland Hill, diplomat, Yrbk 1952, *Obit* Apr 1984

Sargent, Francis W., governor, June 1971, *Obit* Jan 1999

Sarkis, Elias, Lebanese president, Mar 1979, *Obit* Aug 1985

Sarkozy, Nicolas, French president, Jan 2006

Sarney, Jose, Brazilian president, Mar 1986

Sasser, James R., senator and diplomat, July 1993

Sastroamidjojo, Ali, June 1950, *Obit* May 1975

Sato, Eisaku, Japanese prime minister, Yrbk 1965, *Obit* Aug 1975

Satterfield, John C., July 1962

Saud al Faisal, Jan 1948

Saund, Dalip Singh, congressman, June 1960, *Obit* June 1973

Saunders, Robert, Yrbk 1951, *Obit* Mar 1955

Sauve, Jeanne, Canadian government official, Aug 1984, *Obit* Mar 1993

Savage, Michael Joseph, *Obit* Apr 1940

Sawyer, Charles, American Secretary of commerce and diplomat, July 1948, *Obit* June 1979

Sawyer, Diane, American television news anchor, Oct 1985

Saxon, James J., Yrbk 1963, *Obit* Apr 1980

Sayegh, Fayez A., Lebanese scholar and diplomat, July 1957

Sayre, Francis Bowes, American diplomat, Jan 1940, *Obit* May 1972

Scarbrough, Roger Lumley, Jan 1958, *Obit* Sept 1969

Scelba, Mario, Italian prime minister, May 1953, *Obit* Feb 1992

Schaefer, William Donald, American mayor and governor, July 1988, *Obit* Yrbk 2011

Schaffer, Fritz, Mar 1953, *Obit* May 1967

Schakowsky, Jan, American congresswoman, July 2004

Scharf, Adolf, Oct 1957, *Obit* Apr 1965

Scheel, Walter, Feb 1971

Scheele, Leonard Andrew, surgeon general, May 1948, *Obit* Mar 1993

Scheuer, James H., American congressman, Apr 1968, *Obit* Apr 2006

Schlesinger, Arthur M., American historian, Oct 1946, Jan 1979, *Obit* Aug 2007

Schlesinger, James R., American Secretary of defense and energy, Oct 1973

Schmidt, Helmut, German chancellor, Oct 1974

Schneider, Alma K., Yrbk 1954

Schoeneman, George J., American government official, Nov 1947

Schoeppel, Andrew Frank, senator and governor, Mar 1952, *Obit* Mar 1962

Schoonmaker, Edwin Davies, *Obit* Jan 1940

Schram, Emil, stock exchange official, Oct 1941, May 1953, *Obit* Nov 1987

Schreiber, Walther, Feb 1954, *Obit* Sept 1958

Schreyer, Edward, Canadian government official, Feb 1981

Schroder, Gerhard, German political leader, Yrbk 1962, *Obit* Mar 1990

Schroder, Gerhard, German chancellor, Nov 1998

Schuman, Robert, French statesman, Jan 1948, *Obit* Nov 1963

Schumann, Maurice, French cabinet member, Apr 1970, *Obit* Apr 1998

Schumer, Charles E., American senator, July 1995

Schwarzhaupt, Elisabeth, German cabinet member, Jan 1967, *Obit* Jan 1987

Schweiker, Richard S., American Secretary of health and human services, Feb 1977

Schweitzer, Pierre-Paul, French government official and IMF director, Yrbk 1963, *Obit* Mar 1994

Schwellenbach, Lewis B., American Secretary of Labor, June 1945, *Obit* July 1948

Scott, Harold, Yrbk 1950

Scott, Hugh Doggett, American senator, Sept 1948, *Obit* Sept 1994

Scott, John R. K., *Obit* Feb 1946

Scott, W. Kerr, Apr 1956, *Obit* July 1958

Scranton, William Warren, American governor, Jan 1964, *Obit* Yrbk 2013

Scribner, Fred C., government official, Yrbk 1958, *Obit* Apr 1994

Scrugham, James Graves, *Obit* July 1945

Seaga, Edward P. G., Jamaican prime minister, Apr 1981

Sears, William Joseph, *Obit* May 1944

Sebald, William J., naval officer, lawyer and diplomat, Oct 1951

Sebelius, Kathleen, American Secretary of health and human services, Nov 2004

Seger, George N., *Obit* Oct 1940

Segni, Antonio, Yrbk 1955, *Obit* Jan 1973

Self, Henry, Oct 1942

Selwyn-Lloyd, John Selwyn Brooke, British cabinet member, Apr 1952, *Obit* July 1978

Sen, Binay Ranjan, Indian diplomat, Yrbk 1952, *Obit* Aug 1993

Senanayake, Don Stephen, Apr 1950, *Obit* May 1952

Senanayake, Dudley, Ceylonese prime minister, Yrbk 1952, *Obit* June 1973

Sender, Toni, German United Nations official, May 1950

Senghor, Leopold Sedar, Senegalese poet and president, Mar 1962, July 1994, *Obit* Mar 2002

Senior, Clarence, Yrbk 1961, *Obit* Nov 1974

Servan-Schreiber, Jean-Jacques, French political leader, Jan 1955, *Obit* Yrbk 2007

Sessions, William Steele, American FBI director, July 1988

Sevier, Henry Hulme, *Obit* Mar 1940

Sforza, Carlo, June 1942, *Obit* Oct 1952

Shabandar, Musa, Feb 1956

Shafer, Paul W., American congressman, July 1952, *Obit* Oct 1954

Shagari, Shehu, Nigerian president, Aug 1980

Shaheen, Jeanne, American senator, Jan 2001

Shamir, Yitzhak, Israeli prime minister, Feb 1983, Yrbk 1996, *Obit* Yrbk 2012

Sharett, Moshe, Israeli statesman, Apr 1948, *Obit* Sept 1965

Sharif, Nawaz, Pakistani prime minister, Sept 1998

Sharp, Harry Clay, *Obit* Yrbk 1940

Shastri, Lal Bahadur, Indian prime minister, Yrbk 1964, *Obit* Feb 1966

Shawcross, Hartley Shawcross, British attorney general and war crimes prosecutor, Yrbk 1945, *Obit* Yrbk 2003

Shazar, Zalman, Feb 1964, *Obit* Nov 1974

Shehu, Mehmet, Feb 1958, *Obit* Feb 1982

Shelepin, Aleksandr N., Soviet intelligence official, Feb 1971, *Obit* Jan 1995

Shepilov, Dmitrii Trofimovich, Yrbk 1955

Sheppard, Morris, *Obit* June 1941

Sherfield, Roger Mellor Makins, British diplomat, Jan 1953, *Obit* Jan 1997

Shevardnadze, Eduard, Georgian president, Feb 1986

Shevchenko, Arkady N., Soviet diplomat and defector, Sept 1985, *Obit* May 1998

Shidehara, Kijuro, Japanese diplomat and prime minister, Apr 1946, *Obit* Apr 1951

Shigemitsu, Mamoru, June 1943, *Obit* Mar 1957

Shipley, Jenny, New Zealand prime minister, Mar 2000

Shipley, Ruth B., American government official, Yrbk 1947, *Obit* Jan 1967

Shirley, Donna, American aerospace engineer and NASA official, Aug 1998

Shivers, Allan, American governor, Oct 1951, *Obit* Mar 1985

Shone, Terence Allen, Nov 1946, *Obit* Yrbk 1965

Short, Dewey, American congressman and military official, Yrbk 1951, *Obit* Feb 1980

Short, Joseph, American journalist and presidential press secretary, Feb 1951, *Obit* Nov 1952

Shoup, Oliver Henry, *Obit* Nov 1940

Shreve, Earl Owen, Oct 1947

Shriver, Sargent, American lawyer and government official, Yrbk 1961, *Obit* Yrbk 2011

Siebert, Muriel, American stockbroker, Aug 1997, *Obit* Yrbk 2013

Siles Zuazo, Hernan, Bolivian president, Sept 1958, June 1985, *Obit* Oct 1996

Siles, Hernando, Bolivian president, *Obit* Jan 1943

Silva, Benedita da, Brazilian governor and political leader, Jan 2002

Silva, Luis Inacio da, Brazilian president, Jan 2003

Silzer, George S., *Obit* Yrbk 1940

Simmons, Furnifold McLendel, American senator, *Obit* Jan 1940

Simms, John F., Sept 1956, *Obit* June 1975

Simon, John Allsebrook Simon, British statesman, July 1940, *Obit* Mar 1954

Simon, Paul, American senator, Jan 1988, *Obit* Yrbk 2004

Simpson, Alan K., American senator, Oct 1990

Simpson, Kenneth F., *Obit* Mar 1941

Simpson, Milward Lee, governor and senator, Jan 1957, *Obit* Aug 1993

Simpson, Richard M., Yrbk 1953, *Obit* Mar 1960

Simpson-Miller, Portia, Jamaican prime minister, Jan 2006

Sims, Hugo S., Oct 1949

Sinclair, Adelaide, Canadian government official, Apr 1951, *Obit* Jan 1983

Sinclair, Archibald, British political leader, Sept 1940, *Obit* Oct 1970

Singh, Manmohan, Indian prime minister, Jan 2005

Singh, Swaran, Mar 1971, *Obit* Jan 1995

Singh, Vishwanath Pratap, Indian prime minister, May 1990, *Obit* Yrbk 2009

Siroky, Viliam, Apr 1957, *Obit* Nov 1971

Skinner, Dennis, British member of Parliament, Jan 2002

Skinner, Samuel K., American Secretary of transportation and presidential adviser, Aug 1989

Slater, Rodney, American Secretary of transportation, Jan 1999

Slaughter, Louise M., American congresswoman, Apr 1999

Smadel, Joseph E., May 1963

Small, John D., American admiral and government official, Feb 1946, *Obit* Mar 1963

Small, John Humphrey, *Obit* Sept 1946

Smathers, George A., American senator, Apr 1954, *Obit* June 2007

Smetona, Antanas, Lithuanian president, *Obit* Feb 1944

Smith, Alfred Emanuel, American governor, Sept 1944

Smith, Ben, Oct 1945, *Obit* July 1964

Smith, Clyde Harold, *Obit* May 1940

Smith, Ellison DuRant, American senator, *Obit* Jan 1945

Smith, Gerard C., American lawyer and diplomat, Oct 1970, *Obit* Sept 1994

Smith, H. Alexander, American senator, Apr 1948, *Obit* Jan 1967

Smith, Harold D., July 1943, *Obit* Mar 1947

Smith, Ian Douglas, Rhodesian prime minister, May 1966, *Obit* Feb 2008

Smith, James H., government official, Jan 1958, *Obit* Feb 1983

Smith, John L., June 1952, *Obit* Yrbk 1958

Smith, Margaret Chase, American senator, Feb 1945, Mar 1962, *Obit* Aug 1995

Smith, Robert C., American senator, Sept 2000

Smith, T. V., Feb 1956, *Obit* July 1964

Smith, William French, American Attorney general, Jan 1982, *Obit* Jan 1991

Smoot, Reed, American senator, *Obit* Mar 1941

Smylie, Robert E., American governor, Feb 1956, *Obit* Yrbk 2004

Snell, Henry Snell, May 1941

Snow, C. P., British physicist and novelist, Yrbk 1954, Yrbk 1961, *Obit* Aug 1980

Snowe, Olympia J., American senator, May 1995

Snyder, J. Buell, *Obit* Apr 1946

Snyder, John W., American Secretary of the treasury, July 1945, *Obit* Jan 1986

Soames, Arthur Christopher John Soames, British diplomat, Aug 1981, *Obit* Oct 1987

Soares, Mario, Portuguese prime minister, Oct 1975

Sobchak, Anatoly, Russian mayor, July 1992, *Obit* July 2000

Sobeloff, Simon E., American Solicitor general and judge, Mar 1955, *Obit* Sept 1973

Soekarno, Indonesian president, Sept 1947, *Obit* Sept 1970

Soheily, Ali, Sept 1943, *Obit* July 1958

Solarz, Stephen J., American congressman, Nov 1986, *Obit* Yrbk 2011

Solh, Sami, Feb 1958, *Obit* Jan 1969

Solis, Hilda L., American Secretary of labor, Mar 2009

Sophoulis, Themistocles, Nov 1947, *Obit* Sept 1949

Sordoni, Andrew J., July 1956, *Obit* Apr 1963

Sorensen, Theodore C., American presidential adviser, Yrbk 1961, *Obit* Yrbk 2011

Sotomayor, Sonia, American Supreme Court justice, Oct 2009

Soukup, Frantisek, *Obit* Yrbk 1940

Soustelle, Jacques, French political leader, Yrbk 1958, *Obit* Oct 1990

Souvanna Phouma, Nov 1962, *Obit* Mar 1984

Spaak, Paul-Henri, Belgian statesman, May 1945, Apr 1958, *Obit* Oct 1972

Sparkman, John J., American senator, Mar 1950, *Obit* Jan 1986

Spaulding, Rolland H., *Obit* May 1942

Speakes, Larry Melvin, presidential press secretary, Mar 1985

Speaks, John Charles, *Obit* Yrbk 1945

Specter, Arlen, American senator, Aug 1988, Aug 2009, *Obit* Yrbk 2012

Spellings, Margaret, American Secretary of education, June 2005

Spence, Brent, Sept 1952, *Obit* Jan 1968

Spender, Percy Claude, Mar 1950

Sperling, Gene, American economist and presidential adviser, Apr 2011

Spitzer, Eliot, American governor, Mar 2003

Sprinkel, Beryl W., American economist and government official, July 1987, *Obit* Yrbk 2009

Squires, Richard Anderson, *Obit* May 1940

St. George, Katharine, congresswoman, Yrbk 1947, *Obit* July 1983

St. Laurent, Louis S., Mar 1948, *Obit* Oct 1973

Staats, Elmer Boyd, American government official, June 1967, *Obit* Yrbk 2011

Stabenow, Debbie, American senator, Feb 2006

Stace, W. T., Apr 1961, *Obit* Oct 1967

Stafford, Robert T., American senator, Sept 1960, *Obit* Yrbk 2008

Staggers, Harley O., American congressman, Mar 1971, *Obit* Nov 1991

Stahle, Nils K., Apr 1956

Stainback, Ingram Macklin, Yrbk 1947, *Obit* June 1961

Standley, William Harrison, admiral, May 1942, *Obit* Yrbk 1963

Stanfield, Robert Lorne, Canadian political leader, Yrbk 1958, *Obit* Yrbk 2004

Stanfield, Robert Nelson, *Obit* June 1945

Stanley, Oliver, Apr 1943, *Obit* Jan 1951

Stanley, Winnifred Claire, congresswoman, June 1943

Starr, Kenneth W., American law teacher and independent counsel in Whitewater Investigation, May 1998

Stauning, Thorvald, Danish prime minister, *Obit* June 1942

Stauss, Emil Georg von, *Obit* Feb 1943

Steacie, E. W. R., Jan 1953, *Obit* Nov 1962

Steagall, Henry Bascom, *Obit* Jan 1944

Steel, David, British member of Parliament, July 1978

Steele, Michael S., American political party leader, July 2004

Steelman, John R., American presidential aide and economist, May 1941, Nov 1952, *Obit* Nov 1999

Steinfeld, Jesse L., Apr 1974

Steinhardt, Laurence Adolph, lawyer and diplomat, July 1941, *Obit* Apr 1950

Stennis, John C., American senator, Jan 1953, *Obit* July 1995

Stephanopoulos, George, American television news anchor, Jan 1995

Stephanopoulos, Stephanos, July 1955

Stephens, Hubert D., *Obit* Apr 1946

Stephens, William D., *Obit* June 1944

Stepovich, Michael A., Nov 1958

Stevens, Ted, American senator, Oct 2001, *Obit* Yrbk 2010

Stevenson, Adlai, American senator, Apr 1974

Stevenson, Adlai E., American statesman, Jan 1949, Sept 1961, *Obit* Sept 1965

Stewart, Michael, British cabinet member, Sept 1965, *Obit* June 1990

Stewart, Rory, British diplomat and writer, Jan 2007

Stewart, William H., American surgeon general, Apr 1966, *Obit* Yrbk 2008

Stikker, Dirk U., Dutch statesman, Feb 1950, Feb 1962

Stimson, Frederic Jesup, *Obit* Jan 1944

Stockberger, Warner W., government official and personnel director, Aug 1941

Stockman, David Alan, American investment banker, presidential aide and

manufacturing executive, Aug 1981

Stoessel, Walter J., diplomat, June 1970, *Obit* Feb 1987

Stoica, Chivu, Jan 1959, *Obit* Apr 1975

Stokes, Carl, American mayor, judge and newscaster, Apr 1968, *Obit* June 1996

Stokes, Richard Rapier, British cabinet member, Sept 1951, *Obit* Oct 1957

Stoltenberg, Gerhard, German cabinet member, Sept 1989, *Obit* Mar 2002

Stone, Harlan Fiske, American Supreme Court justice, Aug 1941, *Obit* June 1946

Stonehaven, John Lawrence Baird, *Obit* Oct 1941

Stratton, Samuel S., congressman, Jan 1966, *Obit* Jan 1991

Stratton, William G., American governor, Apr 1953, *Obit* Aug 2001

Straus, Michael W., June 1952

Strauss, Franz Josef, German political leader, Feb 1957, Feb 1987, *Obit* Nov 1988

Strauss, J. G. N., Jan 1951

Strauss, Robert S., American political party leader and diplomat, Mar 1974, July 1992

Straw, Jack, British cabinet member, Jan 2002

Strijdom, Johannes Gerhardus, May 1956, *Obit* Nov 1958

Strughold, Hubertus, July 1966

Stuart, John Leighton, American missionary and diplomat, Oct 1946, *Obit* Nov 1962

Suarez, Adolfo, Spanish prime minister, May 1977

Subandrio, Indonesian cabinet member, Mar 1963, *Obit* Apr 2005

Suchocka, Hanna, Polish prime minister, Jan 1994

Sueyro, Saba H., Argentine admiral, *Obit* Sept 1943

Suhr, Otto, Apr 1955, *Obit* Nov 1957

Suhrawardy, Huseyn Shaheed, Pakistani prime minister, Apr 1957, *Obit* Jan 1964

Sukarnoputri, Megawati, Indonesian president, Sept 1997

Sullivan, John L., American Secretary of the navy, Sept 1948, *Obit* Oct 1982

Sullivan, Leonor K., American congresswoman, Yrbk 1954, *Obit* Oct 1988

Sullivan, William H., American diplomat, Aug 1979

Sulzer, William, *Obit* Jan 1942

Summerfield, Arthur Ellsworth, American postmaster general, Sept 1952, *Obit* June 1972

Summerskill, Edith, British member of Parliament and physician, Apr 1943, July 1963, *Obit* Apr 1980

Sun Fo, Chinese government official, Oct 1944, *Obit* Yrbk 1973

Sunay, Cevdet, Mar 1969, *Obit* Aug 1982

Sununu, John, American governor and presidential adviser, May 1989

Supachai Panitchpakdi, Thai international organization official, Jan 2004

Sutherland, George, American Supreme Court justice, *Obit* Sept 1942

Suzman, Helen, South African member of Parliament and human rights activist, Nov 1968, *Obit* Yrbk 2009

Suzuki, Kantaro, Japanese admiral, Aug 1945, *Obit* May 1948

Suzuki, Zenko, Japanese prime minister, Jan 1981, *Obit* Yrbk 2004

Sveinn Bjornsson, Aug 1944, *Obit* Mar 1952

Svinhufvud, Pehr Evind, *Obit* Apr 1944

Swart, Charles Robberts, June 1960

Sweet, William Ellery, *Obit* July 1942

Switzer, Mary Elizabeth, Jan 1962, *Obit* Yrbk 1971

Swope, Gerard, Sept 1941, *Obit* Feb 1958

Symington, James W., June 1968

Symington, Stuart, American senator, Sept 1945, July 1956, *Obit* Feb 1989

Syran, Arthur George, Mar 1950

Taber, John, American congressman, Feb 1948, *Obit* Jan 1966

Taber, Louis J., June 1942, *Obit* Yrbk 1960

Taft, Robert A., American senator, May 1940, Apr 1948, *Obit* Oct 1953

Taft, Robert A., American senator, Oct 1967, *Obit* Feb 1994

Takeshita, Noboru, Japanese prime minister, May 1988, *Obit* Nov 2000

Talabani, Jalal, Iraqi president, Jan 2005

Talbott, Strobe, American diplomat, July 2000

Tallamy, Bertram Dalley, civil engineer and state official, Mar 1957, *Obit* Nov 1989

Talmadge, Eugene, American governor, Sept 1941, *Obit* Feb 1947

Talmadge, Herman E., American governor and senator, Mar 1947, *Obit* June 2002

Tanaka, Kakuei, Japanese prime minister, Yrbk 1972, *Obit* Feb 1994

Tani, Masayuki, May 1956

Tanner, Vaino, Finnish statesman, Sept 1960, *Obit* May 1966

Tarchiani, Alberto, Jan 1950, *Obit* Jan 1965

Tardieu, Andre, French statesman, *Obit* Oct 1945

Tarr, Curtis W., Sept 1970, *Obit* Yrbk 2013

Tauscher, Ellen O., American congresswoman, Mar 2001

Taylor, Charles, Liberian president, Sept 1992

Taylor, Edward T., *Obit* Oct 1941

Taylor, Glen Hearst, American senator, Oct 1947, *Obit* July 1984

Teague, Olin E., congressman, Mar 1952, *Obit* Apr 1981

Tebbit, Norman, British cabinet member, Nov 1987

Teitgen, Pierre-Henri, French political leader, Jan 1953

Tello, Manuel, Yrbk 1959, *Obit* Jan 1972

Templewood, Samuel John Gurney Hoare, British diplomat, Oct 1940, *Obit* July 1959

Tenby of Bulford, Gwilym Lloyd George, British cabinet

member, Nov 1952, *Obit* Apr 1967

Tenet, George J., American intelligence official, Aug 1999

Terra, Gabriel, Uruguayan president, *Obit* Nov 1942

Terry, Luther L., American surgeon general and educator, Oct 1961, *Obit* May 1985

Tewolde Berhan Gebre Egziabher, Ethiopian biologist and government official, Jan 2004

Thaksin Shinawatra, Thai prime minister, Jan 2002

Thanat Khoman, Mar 1958

Thanom Kittikachorn, Thai field marshal and prime minister, Yrbk 1969, *Obit* Yrbk 2004

Thant, Burmese diplomat and United Nations secretary-general, Feb 1962, *Obit* Jan 1975

Thatcher, Margaret, British prime minister, July 1975, Nov 1989, *Obit* Yrbk 2013

Thomas, Albert, American congressman, Oct 1950, *Obit* Mar 1966

Thomas, Clarence, American Supreme Court justice, Apr 1992

Thomas, Elbert Duncan, American senator, Oct 1942, *Obit* Mar 1953

Thomas, Elmer, American senator, Yrbk 1949, *Obit* Nov 1965

Thomas, John Parnell, American congressman, Sept 1947, *Obit* Jan 1971

Thomas, John W., *Obit* Yrbk 1945

Thomaz, Americo de Deus Rodrigues, Portuguese president, Yrbk 1958, *Obit* Nov 1987

Thompson, Frank, American congressman, July 1959, *Obit* Sept 1989

Thompson, Fred, American senator, Aug 1999

Thompson, George L., *Obit* Oct 1941

Thompson, James R., American governor and lawyer, Jan 1979

Thompson, Llewellyn E., American diplomat, Nov 1957, *Obit* Mar 1972

Thompson, M. E., Mar 1947

Thompson, Ruth, congresswoman, Nov 1951

Thompson, Tommy, American Secretary of health and human services, July 1995

Thompson, William Hale, American mayor, *Obit* May 1944

Thomson, Meldrim, governor, Oct 1978, *Obit* Sept 2001

Thomson, Vernon Wallace, governor and congressman, July 1958, *Obit* June 1988

Thorez, Maurice, French communist leader, June 1946, *Obit* Sept 1964

Thorkelson, Jacob, *Obit* Jan 1946

Thorn, James, Yrbk 1949

Thorneycroft of Dunston, Peter, British cabinet member, Yrbk 1952, *Obit* Aug 1994

Thorning-Schmidt, Helle, Prime minister of Denmark, May 2012

Thornton, Dan, Feb 1954

Thorp, Willard Long, American economist and government official, July 1947, *Obit* July 1992

Thorpe, Jeremy, British member of Parliament, Oct 1974

Thurmond, Strom, American senator, Sept 1948, Nov 1992, *Obit* Nov 2003

Thye, Edward J., American governor and senator, Oct 1951, *Obit* Nov 1969

Timberlake, Charles B., American congressman, *Obit* July 1941

Timberlake, Clare H., Jan 1961

Timmerman, George Bell, American governor and judge, Jan 1957, *Obit* Feb 1995

Tindemans, Leo, Belgian statesman, Mar 1978

Tinkham, George H., Apr 1942, *Obit* Oct 1956

Tisdel, Alton P., *Obit* July 1945

Tiso, Jozef, Slovak priest and president, Mar 1943, *Obit* May 1947

Tjarda van Starkenborgh Stachouwer, A. W. L., Feb 1942

Tobin, Maurice J., American Secretary of labor, June 1946, *Obit* Oct 1953

Todt, Fritz, German military engineer and cabinet member, *Obit* Apr 1942

Tokugawa, Iyesato, *Obit* July 1940

Toland, Edmund M., *Obit* July 1942

Tolbert, William R., Liberian president, Mar 1974, *Obit* June 1980

Toon, Malcolm, diplomat, July 1978

Torp, Oscar, Norwegian prime minister, Yrbk 1952, *Obit* July 1958

Toure, Ahmed Sekou, Guinean president, June 1959, *Obit* May 1984

Toure, Amadou Toumani, Malian president, Jan 2005

Tower, John, American senator, Yrbk 1962, *Obit* June 1991

Townsend, Edward Waterman, American journalist and congressman, *Obit* May 1942

Train, Russell E., American conservationist and government official, Oct 1970, *Obit* Yrbk 2012

Trigg, Ralph S., Nov 1950

Trimble, David, Northern Ireland political leader, July 2000

Trowbridge, Alexander B., American Secretary of commerce, Mar 1968, *Obit* Yrbk 2006

Trudeau, Pierre Elliott, Canadian prime minister, Nov 1968, *Obit* Jan 2001

Truman, Harry S., American president, Jan 1942, Apr 1945, *Obit* Feb 1973

Trygger, Ernst, *Obit* Nov 1943

Tryon, George Clement Tryon, British government official, *Obit* Jan 1941

Tsaldaris, Constantine, Nov 1946, *Obit* Jan 1971

Tsang, Donald, Hong Kong government official, Jan 2005

Tsarapkin, Semyon K., Soviet diplomat, June 1960, *Obit* Nov 1984

Tshabalala-Msimang, Manto, South African public health official, Jan 2007, *Obit* Yrbk 2010

Tshombe, Moise, Congolese prime minister, Yrbk 1961, *Obit* Sept 1969

Tsiang, Tingfu F., June 1948, *Obit* Yrbk 1965

Tsongas, Paul, American senator, July 1981, *Obit* Mar 1997

Tsvangirai, Morgan, Zimbabwean prime minister, Jan 2005

Tubman, William Vacanarat Shadrach, Liberian president, Jan 1955, *Obit* Sept 1971

Tuck, William M., governor, Yrbk 1946, *Obit* Aug 1983

Tudjman, Franjo, Croatian president, Sept 1997, *Obit* May 2000

Tukur, Alhaji Bamanga, Nigerian business organization official, Jan 2004

Tunney, John V., June 1971

Turbay Ayala, Julio Cesar, Colombian president, July 1979

Turner, Ben, *Obit* Nov 1942

Turner, Donald Frank, American government official, lawyer and economist, July 1967, *Obit* Sept 1994

Turner, John, Canadian prime minister, Nov 1984

Turner, Stansfield, admiral and CIA director, May 1978

Tydings, Millard E., American senator, Jan 1945, *Obit* Apr 1961

Tymoshenko, Yulia, Ukrainian economist and prime minister, Jan 2006

Ubico, Jorge, Guatemalan president, June 1942, *Obit* July 1946

Udall, Morris K., American congressman, Apr 1969, *Obit* Mar 1999

Udall, Stewart L., American Secretary of the interior, May 1961, *Obit* Yrbk 2010

Ullman, Al, congressman, Aug 1975, *Obit* Jan 1987

Umanskii, Konstantin Aleksandrovich, Feb 1941, *Obit* Mar 1945

Underhill, Charles Lee, *Obit* Mar 1946

Underwood, Cecil H., American governor, May 1958, *Obit* Yrbk 2009

Unruh, Jesse M., American state legislator and official, Oct 1969, *Obit* Sept 1987

Uribe Velez, Alvaro, Colombian president, Jan 2002

Urrutia Lleo, Manuel, Cuban president, May 1959, *Obit* Aug 1981

Urrutia, Francisco, June 1958

Usery, W. J., American Secretary of labor, June 1976

Utterback, Hubert, *Obit* July 1942

Vajpayee, Atal Bihari, Indian prime minister, Aug 2000, Jan 2002

Valenti, Jack, American motion picture association executive, Jan 1968, *Obit* Yrbk 2007

Valentine, Lewis J., June 1946, *Obit* Feb 1947

Van Nuys, Frederick, *Obit* Mar 1944

Van Wagoner, Murray, governor, Nov 1941, *Obit* Aug 1986

Van Zandt, James E., congressman, Nov 1950, *Obit* Mar 1986

Vance, Cyrus R., American Secretary of state, Yrbk 1962, Nov 1977, *Obit* Apr 2002

Vandenberg, Arthur H., American senator, Nov 1940, June 1948, *Obit* May 1951

Vandiver, S. Ernest, American governor, July 1962, *Obit* Yrbk 2005

Vansittart, Robert Gilbert Vansittart, British diplomat, July 1941, *Obit* Apr 1957

Vargas, Getulio, Brazilian president, Aug 1940, May 1951, *Obit* Oct 1954

Vasilevskii, Aleksandr M., Soviet field marshal, Oct 1943, *Obit* Mar 1978

Vassallo, Ernesto, *Obit* Jan 1940

Vaughn, Jack Hood, American diplomat and government official, Apr 1966, *Obit* Yrbk 2013

Veil, Simone, French judge and cabinet member, May 1980

Vejjabul, Pierra, Mar 1964

Velasco Ibarra, Jose Maria, Ecuadorian president, Nov 1952, *Obit* May 1979

Velazquez, Nydia, American congresswoman, July 1999

Velde, Harold H., American congressman, Mar 1953, *Obit* Jan 1986

Velloso, Pedro Leao, Sept 1946, *Obit* Mar 1947

Veneman, Ann M., American United Nations official, Sept 2009

Venizelos, Sophocles, Yrbk 1950, *Obit* Mar 1964

Ventura, Jesse, American wrestler and governor, May 1999

Verwoerd, Hendrik Frensch, South African prime minister, Mar 1959, *Obit* Nov 1966

Vigidis Finnbogadottir, Icelandic president, May 1987

Vike-Freiberga, Vaira, Latvian president, Jan 2005

Villaraigosa, Antonio R., American mayor, Aug 2007

Villepin, Dominique de, French prime minister, Jan 2003

Vilsack, Tom, American Secretary of agriculture, Mar 2009

Vinson, Carl, American congressman, Apr 1942, *Obit* July 1981

Vinson, Fred M., American Supreme Court justice, Aug 1943, *Obit* Nov 1953

Vishinski, Andrei IAnuarevich, Soviet diplomat, May 1944, *Obit* Jan 1955

Vogel, Hans Jochen, German socialist leader, Jan 1984

Voinovich, George, American senator, May 1997

Volpe, John A., American governor and Secretary of transportation, Feb 1962, *Obit* Jan 1995

Von Braun, Wernher, German-American rocket engineer, Jan 1952, *Obit* Aug 1977

Voorhees, Tracy S., Feb 1957, *Obit* Nov 1974

Voorhis, Jerry, American congressman, Aug 1941, *Obit* Nov 1984

Vorster, B. J., South African prime minister, June 1967, *Obit* Nov 1983

Vorys, John M., American congressman, Sept 1950, *Obit* Nov 1968

Vukmanovic-Tempo, Svetozar, Yrbk 1958

Wachuku, Jaja, Apr 1963

Wade, Abdoulaye, Senegalese president, Jan 2006

Wadsworth, James J., American diplomat, June 1956, *Obit* May 1984

Wadsworth, James W., July 1943, *Obit* Sept 1952

Wagner, Aubrey J., June 1963

Wagner, Robert F., American senator and judge, May 1941, *Obit* June 1953

Wagner, Robert Ferdinand, American mayor, Feb 1954, *Obit* Apr 1991

Waite, Henry Matson, *Obit* Oct 1944

Wakasugi, Kaname, *Obit* Jan 1944

Wakehurst, John de Vere Loder, Yrbk 1954, *Obit* Yrbk 1970

Waldheim, Kurt, Austrian president and United Nations secretary-general, May 1972, Jan 1987, *Obit* Oct 2007

Walesa, Lech, Polish president, Apr 1981, May 1996

Walker, Daniel, governor, Aug 1976

Walker, E. Ronald, Yrbk 1956

Walker, Frank Comerford, postmaster general, Oct 1940, *Obit* Nov 1959

Walker, Paul A., May 1952, *Obit* July 1966

Wallace, Euan, *Obit* Apr 1941

Wallace, George Corley, American governor, Yrbk 1963, *Obit* Nov 1998

Wallace, Henry Agard, American vice-president, Aug 1940, Jan 1947, *Obit* Jan 1966

Wallace, Lurleen, governor, Sept 1967, *Obit* July 1968

Wallace, Thomas W., *Obit* Sept 1943

Wallgren, Mon C., Nov 1948, *Obit* Nov 1961

Walsh, Joseph, *Obit* Mar 1946

Walsh, Lawrence E., American lawyer, Oct 1991

Walter, Francis E., American congressman, June 1952, *Obit* July 1963

Walters, John P., American government official, May 2008

Wang Bingnan, Yrbk 1958

Wang, Shih-chieh, Sept 1945, *Obit* June 1981

Ward, Benjamin, American police commissioner, Aug 1988, *Obit* Yrbk 2002

Warner, John W., American senator, Nov 1976

Warner, Mark R., American senator, Oct 2006

Warnke, Paul C., American lawyer and government official, Aug 1977, *Obit* Feb 2002

Warren, Avra M., Feb 1955, *Obit* Mar 1957

Warren, Earl, American Chief Justice of the Supreme Court, Jan 1944, Jan 1954, *Obit* Sept 1974

Warren, Edgar L., July 1947

Warren, Elizabeth, American law professor and consumer rights advocate, Feb 2012

Warren, Fletcher, diplomat, July 1960, *Obit* Mar 1992

Warren, Fuller, American governor, Yrbk 1949

Warren, Lindsay C., Nov 1949

Washington, Harold, American mayor, Feb 1984, *Obit* Jan 1988

Washington, Walter E., American mayor, July 1968, *Obit* Yrbk 2004

Wason, Edward H., *Obit* Apr 1941

Waterlow, Sydney, *Obit* Jan 1945

Waters, Maxine, American congresswoman, Nov 1992

Watkins, Arthur V., American senator and judge, July 1950, *Obit* Yrbk 1973

Watkins, James D., American admiral and Secretary of energy, Mar 1989, *Obit* Yrbk 2012

Watkinson, Harold Arthur Watkinson, Mar 1960

Watson, Clarence Wayland, *Obit* July 1940

Watson, Jack H., Nov 1980

Watt, James G., American Secretary of the interior, Jan 1982

Watt, Robert J., Mar 1945, *Obit* Sept 1947

Watts, J. C., American congressman, management consultant and political commentator, Mar 1999

Waverley, John Anderson, British statesman, July 1941, *Obit* Mar 1958

Waxman, Henry Arnold, American congressman, July 1992

Waymack, W. W., Mar 1947, *Obit* Jan 1961

Weaver, Arthur J., *Obit* Nov 1945

Webb, James E., American NASA official, Oct 1946, May 1962, *Obit* May 1992

Webb, Jim, American senator, Aug 1987, Nov 2007

Webb, Maurice, May 1950, *Obit* Sept 1956

Webb, Wellington E., American mayor, Aug 1999

Webster, William, May 1950, *Obit* July 1972

Webster, William H., American FBI and CIA director, Aug 1978

Wedgwood, Josiah C., British member of Parliament, Apr 1942, *Obit* Sept 1943

Wei, Tao-ming, Yrbk 1942

Weicker, Lowell P., senator and governor, Jan 1974, May 1993

Weidenbaum, Murray L., economist and government official, Mar 1982

Weinberger, Caspar W., American Secretary of defense, June 1973, *Obit* July 2006

Weis, Jessica, congresswoman, Yrbk 1959, *Obit* June 1963

Weiss, Ted, congressman, Oct 1985, *Obit* Nov 1992

Weizman, Ezer, Israeli president, Sept 1979, *Obit* Aug 2005

Weizmann, Chaim, Israeli president and Zionist leader, Nov 1942, Nov 1948, *Obit* Yrbk 1952

Weizsacker, Richard von, German president, Mar 1985

Welensky, Roy, British colonial administrator, July 1959, *Obit* Feb 1992

Welker, Herman, American senator, Feb 1955, *Obit* Jan 1958

Welles, Sumner, American diplomat, Mar 1940, *Obit* Nov 1961

Wellstone, Paul David, American senator, May 1993, *Obit* Yrbk 2003

Welsh, Matthew E., governor, June 1962, *Obit* Aug 1995

Wen Jiabao, Chinese prime minister, Jan 2003

Weng Wenhao, Nov 1948

Wetter, Ernst, Feb 1942

Whalen, Grover A., Sept 1944, *Obit* June 1962

Wharton, Clifton R., American diplomat, July 1958, *Obit* June 1990

Wheat, William Howard, *Obit* Apr 1944

Wheeler, Burton K., American senator, Aug 1940, *Obit* Feb 1975

Wherry, Kenneth S., American senator, Apr 1946, *Obit* Jan 1952

White, Byron R., American Supreme Court justice, Yrbk 1962, *Obit* July 2002

White, Frank, *Obit* May 1940

White, Harry Dexter, American economist and government official, Sept 1944, *Obit* Oct 1948

White, Hugh Lawson, Yrbk 1955, *Obit* Nov 1965

White, Katherine Elkus, diplomat and state official, Feb 1965, *Obit* June 1985

White, Kevin H., American mayor, Yrbk 1974, *Obit* Yrbk 2012

White, Mark, governor, Aug 1986

White, Michael R., American mayor, Mar 1999

White, Robert M., American meteorologist, Mar 1964

White, S. Harrison, *Obit* Feb 1946

White, W. Wilson, Jan 1959, *Obit* Jan 1965

White, Wallace H., May 1948, *Obit* May 1952

Whitelaw, William Whitelaw, British cabinet member, Mar 1975, *Obit* Nov 1999

Whitlam, Edward Gough, Jan 1974

Whitman, Christine Todd, American government official, June 1995

Whitmire, Kathryn J., mayor, Mar 1988

Whitton, Charlotte Elizabeth, Canadian social worker, feminist and mayor, Apr 1953, *Obit* Mar 1975

Whitton, Rex M., May 1962

Wick, Charles Z., American government official, Mar 1985, *Obit* Yrbk 2008

Wickard, Claude Raymond, American Secretary of agriculture, Oct 1940, *Obit* June 1967

Wickens, Aryness Joy, economist and government official, Sept 1962, *Obit* Apr 1991

Wiggins, James Russell, American newspaper editor and diplomat, Nov 1969, *Obit* Mar 2001

Wigglesworth, Richard B., May 1959, *Obit* Yrbk 1960

Wigny, Pierre, Yrbk 1960

Wilder, L. Douglas, American governor and mayor, Apr 1990

Wiley, Alexander, American senator, Apr 1947, *Obit* Jan 1968

Wiley, Richard E., American lawyer, Mar 1977

Wilgress, L. Dana, Jan 1954, *Obit* Oct 1969

Wilkins, J. Ernest, Yrbk 1954, *Obit* Mar 1959

Wilkinson, Ellen, British cabinet member, July 1941, *Obit* Mar 1947

Williams of Barnburgh, Thomas Williams, Apr 1946, *Obit* May 1967

Williams, Anthony, American mayor, Oct 1999

Williams, Edwin G., May 1950

Williams, Eric Eustace, Trinidadian prime minister, Feb 1966, *Obit* May 1981

Williams, G. Mennen, American governor and state supreme court justice, Apr 1949, June 1963, *Obit* Mar 1988

Williams, Harrison A., American senator, Oct 1960, *Obit* Mar 2002

Williams, Shirley, British political leader, Oct 1976

Williams, Thomas Sutler, *Obit* May 1940

Willingdon, Freeman Freeman-Thomas, British colonial administrator, *Obit* Oct 1941

Willis, Frances E., Jan 1954

Wilson, Donald V., Jan 1954

Wilson, Frank J., June 1946, *Obit* Oct 1970

Wilson, Harold, British prime minister, Feb 1948, May 1963, *Obit* July 1995

Wilson, Hugh Robert, diplomat, May 1941, *Obit* Feb 1947

Wilson, Michael H., Canadian cabinet member and diplomat, Mar 1990

Wilson, Pete, governor, Apr 1991

Winant, John Gilbert, governor and diplomat, Feb 1941, *Obit* Yrbk 1947

Winster, Reginald Thomas Herbert Fletcher, Feb 1946

Wirth, Conrad L., American national parks director, Sept 1952, *Obit* Sept 1993

Wirth, Timothy E., senator, Mar 1991

Witos, Wincenty, *Obit* Yrbk 1945

Witt, James Lee, American emergency management official and consultant, Mar 2000

Wofford, Harris, American senator, Apr 1992

Wolcott, Jesse P., American congressman and regulatory agency official, Yrbk 1949, *Obit* Apr 1969

Wolfe, Humbert, English poet and government official, *Obit* Jan 1940

Wolfowitz, Paul D., American international organization official, Feb 2003

Wood, John S., American congressman, July 1949, *Obit* Nov 1968

Wood, Kingsley, Nov 1940

Woodcock, Leonard, American labor leader and diplomat, Nov 1970, *Obit* Apr 2001

Woodhouse, Chase Going, congresswoman, Mar 1945, *Obit* Apr 1985

Woodlock, Thomas Francis, *Obit* Sept 1945

Woods, Tighe E., American real estate developer and government official, Oct 1948, *Obit* Sept 1974

Woodsmall, Ruth Frances, July 1949, *Obit* July 1963

Woodsworth, James Shaver, Canadian clergyman and political leader, *Obit* May 1942

Woodward, Robert F., diplomat, Yrbk 1962, *Obit* Yrbk 2001

Woodward, Stanley, diplomat, June 1951, *Obit* Oct 1992

Work, Hubert, physician and secretary of the interior, *Obit* Feb 1943

Worner, Manfred, German cabinet member and NATO official, Oct 1988, *Obit* Oct 1994

Wowereit, Klaus, German mayor, Jan 2002

Wright, Fielding, American governor, Sept 1948, *Obit* July 1956

Wright, Jerauld, American admiral and diplomat, Feb 1955, *Obit* July 1995

Wright, Jim, American Speaker of the House, Apr 1979

Wright, Michael, British diplomat, July 1961

Wright, Peter, British intelligence official, Feb 1988, *Obit* July 1995

Wrong, Hume, Oct 1950, *Obit* Mar 1954

Wu Yi, Chinese government official, Jan 2005

Wu, Kuo-Cheng, Chinese government official, Feb 1953, *Obit* Aug 1984

Wyatt, Wilson W., American government official, lawyer and civic leader, Mar 1946, *Obit* Aug 1996

Yahya Khan, A. M., Jan 1971, *Obit* Oct 1980

Yamani, Ahmed Zaki, Saudi Arabian cabinet member, Sept 1975

Yang, You Chan, Feb 1953

Yar'Adua, Umaru Musa, Nigerian president, Jan 2007, *Obit* Yrbk 2010

Yarborough, Ralph W., American senator, Feb 1960, *Obit* Apr 1996

Yarmolinsky, Adam, American law professor and government official, Mar 1969, *Obit* June 2000

Yates, Sidney, American congressman, Aug 1993, *Obit* Jan 2001

Yeltsin, Boris, Russian president, Jan 1989, *Obit* June 2007

Yerushalmy, Jacob, Mar 1958

Yingluck Shinawatra, Thai prime minister, Oct 2011

Yonai, Mitsumasa, Jan 1940, *Obit* June 1948

Yorty, Sam, American mayor, Jan 1967, *Obit* Aug 1998

Yoshida, Shigeru, Japanese statesman, Sept 1946, *Obit* Jan 1968

Yost, Charles Woodruff, American diplomat, Mar 1959, *Obit* July 1981

Young, Coleman, American mayor, Sept 1977, *Obit* Feb 1998

Young, Frank E., microbiologist, educator and government official, Oct 1989

Young, Milton R., American senator, Yrbk 1954, *Obit* July 1983

Young, Stephen M., American senator, Oct 1959, *Obit* Feb 1985

Youngdahl, Luther W., Mar 1948, *Obit* Aug 1978

Younger, Kenneth Gilmour, Sept 1950

Yui, O. K., May 1955, *Obit* Sept 1960

Yushchenko, Viktor, Ukrainian president, Jan 2005

Zablocki, Clement, American congressman, June 1958, June 1983, *Obit* Jan 1984

Zacharias, Ellis M., American admiral and intelligence official, Mar 1949, *Obit* Oct 1961

Zail Singh, Indian president, Sept 1987, *Obit* Mar 1995

Zana, Leyla, Kurdish member of Turkish parliament and political prisoner, Jan 2004

Zapotocky, Antonin, June 1953, *Obit* Jan 1958

Zardari, Asif Ali, Pakistani president, Jan 2009

Zarubin, Georgi N., Apr 1953, *Obit* Jan 1959

Zedillo Ponce de Leon, Ernesto, Mexican president, Apr 1996

Zeeland, Paul van, Mar 1950

Zeidler, Carl F., July 1940, *Obit* Feb 1943

Zeineddine, Farid, Feb 1957

Zellerbach, J. D., Yrbk 1948, *Obit* Nov 1963

Zerhouni, Elias A., Algerian-American radiologist and public health official, Oct 2003

Zhao Ziyang, Chinese prime minister, June 1984, *Obit* Yrbk 2005

Zhou Enlai, Chinese prime minister and diplomat, Sept 1946, July 1957, *Obit* Feb 1976

Zhu Rongji, Chinese prime minister, July 2001

Zimmermann, Arthur, German diplomat, *Obit* July 1940

Zoellick, Robert, American diplomat and international organiztation official, July 2008

Zoli, Adone, Mar 1958, *Obit* Apr 1960

Zorin, Valerian A., Soviet diplomat and United Nations official, Mar 1953, *Obit* Mar 1986

Zorlu, Fatin Ruchstu, Turkish diplomat, Yrbk 1958, *Obit* Nov 1961

Zubiria, Alberto F., Yrbk 1956

Zuckerman, Solly Zuckerman, English scientist, July 1972, *Obit* May 1993

Zuckert, Eugene Martin, American Secretary of the air force, Apr 1952, *Obit* Yrbk 2000

Zuma, Jacob, South African president, Jan 2006

Governors

Aandahl, Fred G., American governor, Sept 1958, *Obit* May 1966

Adams, Sherman, American presidential adviser, Nov 1952, *Obit* Jan 1987

Agnew, Spiro, American vice-president, Yrbk 1968, *Obit* Nov 1996

Aiken, George D., American senator, June 1947, *Obit* Feb 1985

Alexander, Archie Alphonse, American engineer and territorial governor, June 1955, *Obit* Mar 1958

Almond, J. Lindsay, American governor, Mar 1958, *Obit* June 1986

Anderson, Sigurd, governor, Sept 1953, *Obit* Mar 1991

Andrus, Cecil D., governor, Aug 1977

Ariyoshi, George R., governor, Jan 1985

Arnall, Ellis Gibbs, governor, Aug 1945, *Obit* Feb 1993

Askew, Reubin, governor, Apr 1973

Babbitt, Bruce E., American Secretary of the interior, Apr 1987

Bailey, Thomas L., American governor, *Obit* Yrbk 1946

Baldwin, Raymond Earl, American governor and senator, July 1946, *Obit* Nov 1986

Barbour, Haley, American governor, Nov 1996

Barnes, Roy E., American governor, Jan 2000

Barnett, Ross Robert, American governor, Sept 1961, *Obit* Jan 1988

Barrett, Frank A., American senator and governor, July 1956, *Obit* July 1962

Battle, John S., American lawyer and governor, Nov 1950, *Obit* June 1972

Bayh, Birch, American senator and governor, June 1965

Bayh, Evan, American senator, Nov 1998

Bellmon, Henry, American governor and senator, July 1963, *Obit* Yrbk 2009

Blair, James T., American governor, Apr 1958, *Obit* Sept 1962

Blanco, Kathleen, American governor, June 2004

Blease, Coleman Livingston, American senator and governor, *Obit* Mar 1942

Blue, Robert Donald, American governor, Yrbk 1948, *Obit* Feb 1990

Boggs, J. Caleb, American governor and senator, July 1956

Bordes, Pierre-Louis, *Obit* Sept 1943

Bowen, Otis R., American governor and Secretary of health and human services, Nov 1986, *Obit* Yrbk 2013

Bradford, Robert F., governor, Yrbk 1948, *Obit* May 1983

Brewer, Jan, American governor, Jan 2011

Bricker, John William, American senator and governor, Apr 1943, July 1956, *Obit* May 1986

Brown, Edmund G., American governor, Mar 1960, *Obit* Apr 1996

Brown, Jerry, American governor, Apr 1975

Bruce, Robert Randolph, *Obit* Apr 1942

Brucker, Wilber M., American Secretary of the army, Sept 1955, *Obit* Yrbk 1968

Bryan, Charles W., governor, *Obit* Apr 1945

Bryant, C. Farris, American governor, Sept 1961, *Obit* Yrbk 2002

Bumpers, Dale, American senator, Aug 1979

Burns, John A., American governor, Feb 1972, *Obit* June 1975

Byrd, Harry Flood, American senator, Apr 1942, Sept 1955, *Obit* Yrbk 1966

Byrne, Brendan T., May 1974

Cahill, William Thomas, governor, June 1970, *Obit* Sept 1996

Calderon, Sila M., Puerto Rican governor, Nov 2001

Caldwell, Millard Fillmore, American governor, Nov 1948, *Obit* Feb 1985

Carey, Hugh L., American governor, Sept 1965, *Obit* Yrbk 2011

Carlson, Frank, American governor and senator, Apr 1949, *Obit* July 1987

Carter, Jimmy, American president, Sept 1971, Nov 1977

Chafee, John, American senator and governor, Nov 1969, *Obit* Jan 2000

Cherry, Francis Adams, American governor, July 1954, *Obit* Sept 1965

Chiles, Lawton, senator and governor, Sept 1971, *Obit* Mar 1999

Clements, Earle C., senator and governor, Sept 1955, *Obit* May 1985

Clinton, Bill, American president, Apr 1988, Nov 1994

Cobham, Charles John Lyttelton, Apr 1962

Coleman, J. P., American governor and judge, Sept 1956, *Obit* Nov 1991

Collins, LeRoy, American governor, June 1956, Apr 1965, *Obit* May 1991

Collins, Martha Layne, governor, Jan 1986

Colquitt, Oscar Branch, *Obit* Mar 1940

Combs, Bert Thomas, governor and lawyer, June 1960, *Obit* Feb 1992

Conley, William Gustavus, *Obit* Yrbk 1940

Connally, John B., American governor, presidential adviser and Secretary of the treasury, July 1961, *Obit* Aug 1993

Craig, George North, governor, Feb 1950, *Obit* Feb 1993

Crosby, Robert, June 1954

Cross, Burton Melvin, governor, Apr 1954, *Obit* Jan 1999

Cuomo, Andrew, American governor, Oct 1998

Cuomo, Mario, American governor, Aug 1983

Daniel, Price, American senator and governor, Jan 1956, *Obit* Oct 1988

Davey, Martin L., American governor, congressman and mayor, *Obit* May 1946

Davis, Gray, American governor, June 1999

Davis, Jonathan M., governor, *Obit* Aug 1943

De Castro, Morris F., May 1950

Dean, Howard, American governor and political party leader, Oct 2002

Dempsey, John Noel, governor, June 1961, *Obit* Sept 1989

Deukmejian, George, governor, June 1983

Dever, Paul A., American governor, May 1949, *Obit* July 1958

Dewey, Thomas E., American governor, July 1940, Sept 1944, *Obit* Apr 1971

DiSalle, Michael V., American governor, Jan 1951, *Obit* Nov 1981

Dickinson, Luren D., *Obit* June 1943

Docking, George, governor, June 1958, *Obit* Mar 1964

Donahey, Vic, *Obit* May 1946

Donnell, Forrest C., American governor and senator, Sept 1949

Donnelly, Phil M., June 1956, *Obit* Nov 1961

Duff, James Henderson, senator and governor, Apr 1948, *Obit* Feb 1970

Dukakis, Michael, American governor, Feb 1978

Dwinell, Lane, governor, June 1956, *Obit* June 1997

Edge, Walter Evans, senator and governor, June 1945, *Obit* Jan 1957

Edison, Charles, July 1940, *Obit* Oct 1969

Egan, William Allen, American governor, Sept 1959, *Obit* July 1984

Ellington, Buford, governor, Sept 1960, *Obit* May 1972

Emerson, Lee E., Oct 1953

Erickson, John Edward, *Obit* June 1946

Faubus, Orval, American governor, Oct 1956, *Obit* Feb 1995

Ferguson, James Edward, governor, *Obit* Nov 1944

Fine, John Sydney, governor, Sept 1951, *Obit* July 1978

Fisher, John Stuchell, governor, *Obit* Aug 1940

Florio, James J., governor, May 1990

Folsom, James Elisha, American governor, Sept 1949, *Obit* Jan 1988

Gary, Raymond, governor, Oct 1955, *Obit* Feb 1994

Gates, Ralph F., Sept 1947

Gibson, Ernest W., American governor and judge, July 1949, *Obit* Yrbk 1969

Gilligan, John J., American governor and congressman, May 1972, *Obit* Yrbk 2013

Gilmore, James S., governor, June 2001

Giri, V. V., Jan 1970, *Obit* Aug 1980

Goldsborough, Phillips Lee, *Obit* Yrbk 1946

Goldschmidt, Neil E., American Secretary of transportation and governor, Aug 1980

Goodrich, James P., *Obit* Oct 1940

Graham, Bob, American senator, July 1986

Graham, Horace F., *Obit* Jan 1942

Granholm, Jennifer M., American governor, Oct 2003

Grantham, Alexander, May 1954

Grasso, Ella, American governor, May 1975, *Obit* Mar 1981

Graves, Bibb, governor, *Obit* May 1942

Green, Dwight H., American governor, Apr 1948, *Obit* Apr 1958

Green, Theodore Francis, American senator and governor, Feb 1950, *Obit* June 1966

Griffin, Marvin, American governor, June 1956, *Obit* Aug 1982

Gruening, Ernest, American territorial governor and senator, Yrbk 1946, July 1966, *Obit* Sept 1974

Gunter, Julius Caldeen, *Obit* Yrbk 1940

Haley, Nikki, American governor, Feb 2011

Hall, Frederick Lee, American judge and governor, Oct 1955, *Obit* May 1970

Handley, Harold W., July 1960, *Obit* Nov 1972

Harriman, Averell, American statesman, Apr 1941, Nov 1946, *Obit* Sept 1986

Hatfield, Mark O., American senator, Nov 1959, Mar 1984, *Obit* Yrbk 2011

Hearnes, Warren Eastman, American governor, June 1968

Henry, Brad, American governor, Jan 2005

Hernandez-Colon, Rafael, Puerto Rican governor, May 1973

Hickenlooper, Bourke B., American senator and governor, May 1947, *Obit* Oct 1971

Hodges, Luther Hartwell, American Secretary of commerce and governor, July 1956, *Obit* Nov 1974

Hoegh, Leo A., governor and civil defense official, July 1956, *Obit* Yrbk 2000

Hoey, Clyde R., American governor and senator, Oct 1949, *Obit* July 1954

Hoff, Philip H., American governor, Sept 1963

Holland, Spessard L., American governor and senator, Feb 1950, *Obit* Yrbk 1971

Hollings, Ernest F., American senator, July 1982

Holmes, Robert D., July 1958

Holton, A. Linwood, American lawyer and governor, Feb 1971

Horner, Henry, American governor, *Obit* Nov 1940

Hughes, Harold E., American governor and senator, June 1963, *Obit* Jan 1997

Hughes, Richard J., American governor and judge, July 1962, *Obit* Feb 1993

Hull, Jane Dee, American governor, Feb 2002

Hunt, James B., American governor, June 1993

Hunt, Lester C., American senator and governor, Mar 1951, *Obit* Sept 1954

Hurley, Charles F., American governor, *Obit* May 1946

Inose, Naoki, Japanese historian, Jan 2002

James, Arthur Horace, governor, July 1940, *Obit* June 1973

Jindal, Bobby, American governor, Jan 2008

Johnson, Ed, American senator and governor, Yrbk 1946, *Obit* July 1970

Johnson, Hiram, American governor and senator, Feb 1941, *Obit* Sept 1945

Johnson, Joseph B., July 1956

Johnson, Paul B., *Obit* Feb 1944

Johnston, Olin D., American senator and governor, Nov 1951, *Obit* June 1965

Jones, Sam Houston, lawyer and governor, Mar 1940, *Obit* Yrbk 1991

Kasich, John R., American governor, Aug 1998

Kempthorne, Dirk, American Secretary of the interior, June 2007

Kennon, Robert Floyd, American governor, Oct 1954, *Obit* Apr 1988

Kerner, Otto, American governor and judge, Oct 1961, *Obit* July 1976

King, Angus, governor, Apr 2013

King, John W., governor and judge, May 1964, *Obit* Nov 1996

King, Samuel Wilder, Oct 1953, *Obit* June 1959

Knight, Goodwin, American governor, Jan 1955, *Obit* July 1970

Kunin, Madeleine, American governor and diplomat, July 1987

Laffoon, Ruby, governor, *Obit* Apr 1941

Lamm, Richard D., governor, May 1985

Landon, Alf, American governor, Feb 1944, *Obit* Nov 1987

Lane, William Preston, June 1949, *Obit* Apr 1967

Langer, William, American governor and senator, Feb 1952, *Obit* Jan 1960

Langlie, Arthur B., Oct 1950, *Obit* Sept 1966

Lausche, Frank John, American governor and senator, Apr 1946, Nov 1958, *Obit* June 1990

Lawrence, David Leo, American governor, June 1959, *Obit* Jan 1967

Laxalt, Paul, American senator, Jan 1979

Leader, George Michael, American governor, Jan 1956, *Obit* Yrbk 2013

Lee, J. Bracken, American governor and mayor, May 1949, *Obit* Jan 1997

Lingle, Linda, American governor, June 2003

Long, Earl K., American governor, Yrbk 1950, *Obit* Nov 1960

Loomis, Orland S., *Obit* Jan 1943

Loveless, Herschel Cellel, governor, July 1958, *Obit* July 1989

Lowden, Frank O., governor, *Obit* May 1943

Maddox, Lester, American governor, Yrbk 1967, *Obit* Yrbk 2003

Malloy, Dan, American governor, June 2011

Marland, William C., Apr 1956, *Obit* Jan 1966

Martin, Edward, governor and senator, Oct 1945, *Obit* May 1967

Martinez, Susana, American governor, Nov 2013

Martz, Judy, American governor, Mar 2005

Maw, Herbert B., governor, Oct 1948, *Obit* Jan 1991

Maybank, Burnet R., American senator and governor, Apr 1949, *Obit* Nov 1954

McCall, Tom, American governor, June 1974, *Obit* Mar 1983

McCarty, Dan, July 1953

McDonnell, Bob, American governor, Sept 2011

McFarland, Ernest William, American senator, governor and state supreme court justice, Jan 1951, *Obit* Aug 1984

McGovern, Francis Edward, American governor, *Obit* June 1946

McKay, Douglas, American Secretary of the interior and governor, May 1949, *Obit* Oct 1959

McKeldin, Theodore R., American governor, Oct 1952, *Obit* Oct 1974

McMath, Sidney Sanders, American governor, Mar 1949, *Obit* Jan 2004

McNichols, Stephen L. R., American governor, Oct 1958, *Obit* Feb 1998

Mechem, Edwin L., American governor and senator, July 1954, *Obit* Yrbk 2003

Mechem, Merritt Cramer, *Obit* June 1946

Meskill, Thomas J., American governor and judge, Mar 1974, *Obit* Yrbk 2008

Meyner, Robert Baumle, American governor, Apr 1955, *Obit* July 1990

Miller, Benjamin Meek, governor and judge, *Obit* Mar 1944

Miller, Zell, American senator, July 1996

Minner, Ruth Ann, American governor, Aug 2001

Mohammed, Ghulam, July 1954, *Obit* Nov 1956

Mook, Hubertus J. van, Apr 1942, *Obit* July 1965

Morrison, Frank Brenner, May 1964

Moses, John, *Obit* Apr 1945

Munoz Marin, Luis, Puerto Rican governor, Oct 1942, Nov 1953, *Obit* June 1980

Murkowski, Frank H., American senator and governor, July 2003

Nazimuddin, Khwaja, Mar 1949, *Obit* Yrbk 1964

Nelson, Gaylord, American senator, governor and environmentalist, May 1960, *Obit* Yrbk 2005

Neville, Robert A. R., Nov 1953

Nice, Harry, *Obit* Apr 1941

O'Conor, Herbert R., Feb 1950, *Obit* May 1960

O'Daniel, W. Lee, American senator and governor, Oct 1947, *Obit* June 1969

O'Neill, C. William, July 1958

O'Neill, William A., American governor, Feb 1985, *Obit* Yrbk 2008

Palin, Sarah, American governor, Jan 2009

Pardee, George C., *Obit* Oct 1941

Pastore, John O., American senator, Apr 1953, *Obit* Yrbk 2000

Pataki, George, American governor, Apr 1996

Paterson, David A., American governor, July 2008

Patterson, John, American governor, Nov 1960

Payne, Frederick G., Yrbk 1952, *Obit* Aug 1978

Peterson, Val, governor and presidential aide, June 1949, *Obit* Jan 1984

Phillips, John C., American governor and judge, *Obit* Aug 1943

Pinero, Jesus T., Oct 1946, *Obit* Jan 1953

Plaisted, Frederick William, *Obit* Apr 1943

Poindexter, Joseph B., Jan 1942, *Obit* Jan 1952

Poletti, Charles, American lieutenant governor and acting governor, *Obit* Yrbk 2002

Poletti, Charles E., Sept 1943

Pyle, Howard, American governor and presidential aide, Nov 1955, *Obit* Jan 1988

Rance, Hubert Elvin, Yrbk 1953, *Obit* Mar 1974

Ray, Robert D., governor, Jan 1977

Rell, M. Jodi, American governor, Sept 2005

Rendell, Ed, American governor, Apr 1998

Reynolds, John W., American judge and governor, Apr 1964, *Obit* Mar 2002

Rhodes, James Allen, American governor and political party leader, Mar 1949, Apr 1976, *Obit* July 2001

Ribicoff, Abraham A., American senator, June 1955, *Obit* May 1998

Richards, John G., *Obit* Yrbk 1941

Richardson, Bill, American governor, Apr 1996

Ridge, Tom, American Secretary of homeland security, Feb 2001

Robb, Charles S., American senator, Apr 1989

Roberts, Dennis J., governor, Yrbk 1956, *Obit* Sept 1994

Roemer, Buddy, governor, Nov 1990

Rolvaag, Karl Fritjof, American governor, Feb 1964, *Obit* Mar 1991

Romero Barcelo, Carlos, Puerto Rican governor, Oct 1977

Roosevelt, Franklin D., American president, Mar 1942, *Obit* Apr 1945

Rosellini, Albert D., American governor, Yrbk 1958, *Obit* Yrbk 2012

Ross, C. Ben, American governor, *Obit* May 1946

Ross, Nellie Tayloe, American governor, May 1940, *Obit* Feb 1978

Rounds, M. Michael, American governor, June 2006

Rowland, John, American governor, Oct 1997

Russell, Richard B., American senator, Nov 1949, *Obit* Mar 1971

Ryan, George H., American governor, Sept 2001

Saltonstall, Leverett, American governor and senator, June 1944, Apr 1956, *Obit* Sept 1979

Sanders, Carl E., American governor, Yrbk 1964

Sanders, Jared Young, *Obit* May 1944

Sandoval, Brian, American governor, Jan 2012

Sargent, Francis W., governor, June 1971, *Obit* Jan 1999

Schaefer, William Donald, American mayor and governor, July 1988, *Obit* Yrbk 2011

Schoeppel, Andrew Frank, senator and governor, Mar 1952, *Obit* Mar 1962

Scranton, William Warren, American governor, Jan 1964, *Obit* Yrbk 2013

Scrugham, James Graves, *Obit* July 1945

Sebelius, Kathleen, American Secretary of health and human services, Nov 2004

Shaheen, Jeanne, American senator, Jan 2001

Shivers, Allan, American governor, Oct 1951, *Obit* Mar 1985

Shoup, Oliver Henry, *Obit* Nov 1940

Silzer, George S., *Obit* Yrbk 1940

Simms, John F., Sept 1956, *Obit* June 1975

Simpson, Milward Lee, governor and senator, Jan 1957, *Obit* Aug 1993

Smith, Alfred Emanuel, American governor, Sept 1944

Smylie, Robert E., American governor, Feb 1956, *Obit* Yrbk 2004

Spaulding, Rolland H., *Obit* May 1942

Spitzer, Eliot, American governor, Mar 2003

Stafford, Robert T., American senator, Sept 1960, *Obit* Yrbk 2008

Stainback, Ingram Macklin, Yrbk 1947, *Obit* June 1961

Stephens, William D., *Obit* June 1944

Stepovich, Michael A., Nov 1958

Stevenson, Adlai E., American statesman, Jan 1949, Sept 1961, *Obit* Sept 1965

Stonehaven, John Lawrence Baird, *Obit* Oct 1941

Stratton, William G., American governor, Apr 1953, *Obit* Aug 2001

Sulzer, William, *Obit* Jan 1942

Sununu, John, American governor and presidential adviser, May 1989

Sweet, William Ellery, *Obit* July 1942

Talmadge, Eugene, American governor, Sept 1941, *Obit* Feb 1947

Talmadge, Herman E., American governor and senator, Mar 1947, *Obit* June 2002

Thompson, James R., American governor and lawyer, Jan 1979

Thompson, M. E., Mar 1947

Thompson, Tommy, American Secretary of health and human services, July 1995

Thomson, Meldrim, governor, Oct 1978, *Obit* Sept 2001

Thomson, Vernon Wallace, governor and congressman, July 1958, *Obit* June 1988

Thornton, Dan, Feb 1954

Thurmond, Strom, American senator, Sept 1948, Nov 1992, *Obit* Nov 2003

Timmerman, George Bell, American governor and judge, Jan 1957, *Obit* Feb 1995

Tjarda van Starkenborgh Stachouwer, A. W. L., Feb 1942

Tobin, Maurice J., American Secretary of labor, June 1946, *Obit* Oct 1953

Tuck, William M., governor, Yrbk 1946, *Obit* Aug 1983

Underwood, Cecil H., American governor, May 1958, *Obit* Yrbk 2009

Van Wagoner, Murray, governor, Nov 1941, *Obit* Aug 1986

Vandiver, S. Ernest, American governor, July 1962, *Obit* Yrbk 2005

Vilsack, Tom, American Secretary of agriculture, Mar 2009

Voinovich, George, American senator, May 1997

Wakehurst, John de Vere Loder, Yrbk 1954, *Obit* Yrbk 1970

Walker, Daniel, governor, Aug 1976

Wallace, George Corley, American governor, Yrbk 1963, *Obit* Nov 1998

Wallace, Lurleen, governor, Sept 1967, *Obit* July 1968

Wallace, Thomas W., *Obit* Sept 1943

Wallgren, Mon C., Nov 1948, *Obit* Nov 1961

Warren, Earl, American Chief Justice of the Supreme Court, Jan 1944, Jan 1954, *Obit* Sept 1974

Warren, Fuller, American governor, Yrbk 1949

Weaver, Arthur J., *Obit* Nov 1945

Weicker, Lowell P., senator and governor, Jan 1974, May 1993

Welsh, Matthew E., governor, June 1962, *Obit* Aug 1995

White, Frank, *Obit* May 1940

White, Hugh Lawson, Yrbk 1955, *Obit* Nov 1965

White, Mark, governor, Aug 1986

Whitman, Christine Todd, American government official, June 1995

Wilder, L. Douglas, American governor and mayor, Apr 1990

Williams, G. Mennen, American governor and state supreme court justice, Apr 1949, June 1963, *Obit* Mar 1988

Wilson, Pete, governor, Apr 1991

Winant, John Gilbert, governor and diplomat, Feb 1941, *Obit* Yrbk 1947

Wright, Fielding, American governor, Sept 1948, *Obit* July 1956

Youngdahl, Luther W., Mar 1948, *Obit* Aug 1978

Graphic designers

Beall, Lester, American graphic designer, Nov 1949, *Obit* Sept 1969

Borne, Mortimer, Apr 1954

Cooper, Kyle, American graphic designer, Nov 2009

Honeywell, Annette, July 1953

Kidd, Chip, American book and graphic designer, July 2005

Saville, Peter, British graphic designer, Jan 2006

Vasarely, Victor, Hungarian-French artist, Feb 1971, *Obit* May 1997

Guerrillas

Kagame, Paul, Rwandan president, Jan 2002

Nasrallah, Hassan, Lebanese guerrilla leader, Jan 2006

Guides (Persons)

White, Randy Wayne, American mystery writer and fishing guide, Nov 2011

Guitarists

Al-Madfai, Ilham, Iraqi guitarist and songwriter, Jan 2004

Anastasio, Trey, American guitarist and songwriter, July 2003

Auerbach, Dan, American singer and guitarist, Jan 2013

Bagayoko, Amadou, Malian singer and guitarist, Jan 2006

Berry, Chuck, American singer and guitarist, Apr 1977

Bonamassa, Joe, Apr 2013

Bream, Julian, English guitarist, Mar 1968

Broemel, Carl, American rock guitarist and singer, Nov 2008

Brown, Junior, American country singer and guitarist, Nov 2004

Bryson, David, American guitarist, Mar 2003

Buckland, Jon, English guitarist, May 2004

Butler, Will, American bassist, guitarist and percussionist, Jan 2007

Byrd, Charlie, American jazz guitarist, Oct 1967, *Obit* Mar 2000

Campbell, Glen, American singer and guitarist, July 1969

Campbell, Vivian, English guitarist and singer, Jan 2003

Cat Power (Singer), American singer and songwriter, Oct 2007

Cester, Nic, Australian guitarist and singer, Jan 2005

Clapton, Eric, British guitarist and singer, June 1987

Cline, Nels, American guitarist, Feb 2010

Collen, Phil, English guitarist and singer, Jan 2003

Condon, Eddie, American jazz guitarist, Oct 1944, *Obit* Oct 1973

Coyne, Wayne, American guitarist, singer and songwriter, Oct 2002

Cunningham, Phil, British guitarist and keyboardist, Jan 2006

DeLonge, Tom, American guitarist, Aug 2002

Delson, Brad, American guitarist, Mar 2002

Diddley, Bo, American guitarist, singer and songwriter, June 1989, *Obit* Sept 2008

Droste, Ed, American guitarist and singer, Sept 2011

Drozd, Steven, American drummer, guitarist and keyboardist, Oct 2002

Earle, Steve, American country singer and guitarist, Oct 1998

Edwards, Toriano, Antiguan guitarist and singer, Jan 2004

Elfman, Danny, American composer, Jan 2007

Etheridge, Melissa, American singer and guitarist, May 1995

Feliciano, Jose, singer and guitarist, July 1969

Flansburgh, John, guitarist, Nov 1999

Followill, Caleb, American singer and guitarist, July 2010

Followill, Matthew, American guitarist, July 2010

Formell, Juan-Carlos, Cuban singer, songwriter and guitarist, Jan 2005

Frampton, Peter, English guitarist and singer, May 1978

Frehley, Ace, American guitarist, Apr 1999

Funk, Chris, American guitarist and thereminist, Aug 2007

Furtado, Nelly, Canadian singer, songwriter and guitarist, Jan 2007

Galbraith, Paul, British guitarist, Jan 2007

Garcia, Jerry, American guitarist and singer, May 1990, *Obit* Oct 1995

Gilbert, Gillian, British guitarist, keyboardist and singer, Jan 2006

Goulding, Ellie, British guitarist, singer and songwriter, Apr 2013

Greenwood, Jonny, English guitarist, June 2001

Guy, Buddy, American blues guitarist, Feb 2000

Hammond, Albert, American guitarist, Feb 2007

Harper, Ben, American singer and guitarist, Jan 2004

Harrison, George, British singer and guitarist, Nov 1966, Jan 1989, *Obit* Mar 2002

Harvey, PJ, British singer, songwriter and guitarist, May 2008

Hawkins, Dan, British rock guitarist, Jan 2004

Hawkins, Justin, British rock singer, guitarist and composer, Jan 2004

Haywood, Dave, American country guitarist, pianist and mandolinist, July 2011

Hetfield, James, American singer and guitarist, Jan 2000

Hidalgo, David, American guitarist, singer and accordionist, Oct 2005

Hooker, John Lee, American singer and guitarist, Nov 1992, *Obit* Sept 2001

Hunter, Charlie, American jazz guitarist, Nov 2007

Idol, Billy, British singer, songwriter and guitarist, Jan 1994

Isbin, Sharon, American classical guitarist, Aug 2003

James, Jim, American rock guitarist, singer and songwriter, Nov 2008

Jobim, Antonio Carlos, Brazilian singer and songwriter, July 1991, *Obit* Feb 1995

Johnson, Eric, American guitarist, keyboardist, singer and songwriter, June 2007

Katz, Sharon, South African singer, songwriter and guitarist, Jan 2007

Keb' Mo', American blues guitarist and singer, Nov 2013

King, B. B., American blues guitarist and singer, June 1970

Kingsbury, Tim, Canadian bassist and guitarist, Jan 2007

Knopfler, Mark, British singer, songwriter and guitarist, Apr 1995

Koite, Habib, Malian guitarist, Jan 2002

Kravitz, Lenny, American singer and guitarist, Apr 1996

Kruspe, Richard Z., German guitarist, Jan 2007

Kubler, Tad, American guitarist, Sept 2010

Landers, Paul H., German guitarist, Jan 2007

LeVox, Gary, American country singer, Aug 2003

Lennon, John, English singer and songwriter, Yrbk 1965, *Obit* Feb 1981

Levine, Adam, American rock singer and guitarist, Mar 2013

Lifeson, Alex, Canadian guitarist, Feb 2001

Lucia, Paco de, Spanish flamenco guitarist, Jan 2004

MacKaye, Ian, American singer and guitarist, Mar 2002

Malone, Kyp, American guitarist and singer, Apr 2009

Martin, Chris, English singer and guitarist, May 2004

May, Brian, English rock guitarist, Oct 2008

Mayer, John, American singer and guitarist, Mar 2010

McLaughlin, John, British jazz guitarist, Feb 2004

Mercer, James, American guitarist and singer, June 2007

Metheny, Pat, American jazz guitarist, May 1996

Montoya, Carlos, Spanish guitarist, Mar 1968, *Obit* May 1993

Muncey, Cameron, Australian guitarist and singer, Jan 2005

Nicol, Simon, English guitarist and singer, Sept 2005

Nugent, Ted, American rock guitarist, Apr 2005

O'Brien, Ed, English guitarist, June 2001

Olvera, Fernando, Mexican singer and guitarist, Jan 2005

Parkening, Christopher, American guitarist, Apr 1987

Parry, Richard Reed, Canadian instrumentalist, Jan 2007

Paul, Les, American guitarist, Aug 1987, *Obit* Yrbk 2009

Perry, Joe, American rock guitarist, July 2004

Petty, Tom, American singer and guitarist, Nov 1991

Peyroux, Madeleine, American singer, songwriter and guitarist, Nov 2005

Picciotto, Guy, American guitarist and songwriter, Mar 2002

Richards, Keith, British guitarist, Feb 1989

Rodgers, Nile, American guitarist and record producer, Jan 2012

Rooney, Joe Don, American guitarist, Aug 2003

Rosas, Cesar, American singer and guitarist, Oct 2005

Rosenwinkel, Kurt, American jazz guitarist and composer, July 2011

Rossen, Daniel, American singer, songwriter and guitarist, Sept 2011

Sansone, Pat, American guitarist, percussionist and keyboardist, Feb 2010

Segovia, Andres, Spanish guitarist, May 1948, June 1964, *Obit* July 1987

Simon, Paul, American singer and composer, Mar 1975

Sitek, David Andrew, American guitarist and record producer, Apr 2009

Slash (Musician), British rock guitarist and songwriter, Mar 2008

Stanley, Paul, American guitarist, Apr 1999

Sumner, Bernard, British guitarist and singer, Jan 2006

Swift, Taylor, American singer and songwriter, Jan 2010

Tedeschi, Susan, American blues singer and guitarist, Sept 2012

Townshend, Pete, British singer and guitarist, Aug 1983

Tremonti, Mark, American guitarist and composer, May 2002

Turner, Alex, British rock guitarist and singer, Jan 2006

Valensi, Nick, American guitarist, Feb 2007

Vallin, Sergio, Mexican guitarist and singer, Jan 2005

Van Zandt, Steve, American guitarist and singer, Feb 2006

Vickrey, Dan, American guitarist, Mar 2003

Volume, Johnny, Finnish guitarist, Jan 2003

Wagner, Sune Rose, Danish singer, guitarist and songwriter, Jan 2004

Waters, Muddy, American singer and guitarist, May 1981, *Obit* June 1983

White, Jack, American singer and guitarist, Sept 2003

White, Josh, guitarist and singer, Aug 1944, *Obit* Nov 1969

Whitford, Brad, American rock guitarist, July 2004

Williams, John, Australian guitarist, July 1983

Williamson, Ski, Finnish guitarist and singer, Jan 2003

Wylde, Zakk, American rock guitarist and songwriter, Oct 2004

Yepes, Narciso, Spanish guitarist, Oct 1966, *Obit* July 1997

Young, Angus, Scottish guitarist, Mar 2005

Young, Malcolm, Scottish guitarist, Mar 2005

Young, Neil, Canadian rock singer and guitarist, Feb 1980, Jan 1998

Zappa, Frank, American rock guitarist, Feb 1990, *Obit* Feb 1994

Gun control activists

Brady, James S., American presidential press secretary and gun control activist, Oct 1991

Brady, Sarah, American gun control activist and wife of James S. Brady, Oct 1996

McCarthy, Carolyn, American congresswoman, Mar 1998

Gurus

Chinmoy, Sri, Indian guru, Apr 1976, *Obit* Yrbk 2008

Gymnastic coaches

Karolyi, Bela, Romanian-American gymnastic coach, Oct 1996

Gymnasts

Comaneci, Nadia, Romanian gymnast, Feb 1977

Hamm, Morgan, American gymnast, Nov 2004

Hamm, Paul, American gymnast, Nov 2004

Khorkina, Svetlana, Russian gymnast, Jan 2003

Korbut, Olga, Soviet gymnast, July 1973

Miller, Shannon, American gymnast, July 1996

Millman, Dan, American gymnast and spiritualist, Aug 2002

Retton, Mary Lou, American gymnast, Feb 1986
Sacramone, Alicia, American gymnast, Mar 2011
Scherbo, Vitaly, Belarusian gymnast, July 1996

Gynecologists

Bang, Rani, Indian gynecologist and public health scientist, Jan 2007
Dickinson, Robert Latou, American gynecologist and obstetrician, Mar 1950, *Obit* Jan 1951
Robb, Hunter, *Obit* Jan 1940

Hairstylists

Antoine, Polish hairstylist, June 1955, *Obit* Sept 1976

Handicapped

Abbott, Jim, American baseball player, Sept 1995
Baker, Louise, American novelist, short story writer and memoirist, Yrbk 1954
Bocelli, Andrea, Italian singer, Jan 2002
Callahan, John, American cartoonist, Sept 1998, *Obit* Yrbk 2010
Capp, Al, cartoonist, May 1947, *Obit* Jan 1980
Claiborne, Loretta, American runner, July 1996
Doumbia, Mariam, Malian singer, Jan 2006
Du Toit, Natalie, South African swimmer, Jan 2005
Glennie, Evelyn, Scottish percussionist, July 1997
Hockenberry, John, radio and television reporter, Oct 1996
Kovic, Ron, soldier and anti-war activist, Aug 1990
Nolan, Christopher, Irish poet and memoirist, Sept 1988, *Obit* Yrbk 2009
Reeve, Christopher, American actor, May 1982, *Obit* Jan 2005
Scdoris, Rachael, American sled dog racer, July 2005
Turcotte, Ron, Canadian jockey, Nov 1974
Verdi-Fletcher, Mary, wheelchair dancer, Jan 1997

Viscardi, Henry, American rehabilitation advocate, Jan 1954, Yrbk 1966, *Obit* Yrbk 2004

Harmonica players

Adler, Larry, American harmonica player, Feb 1944, *Obit* Oct 2001
Wonder, Stevie, American singer and songwriter, Mar 1975

Harpists

Hobson Pilot, Ann, American harpist, May 2003
Marquardt, Alexandria, *Obit* June 1943
Popper, John, singer and harpist, Jan 2012
Vollenweider, Andreas, Swiss harpist, May 1987
Zabaleta, Nicanor, June 1971

Harpsichordists

Christie, William, American harpsichordist and conductor, Jan 1992
Hogwood, Christopher, English conductor, harpsichordist and musicologist, July 1985
Landowska, Wanda, Polish harpsichordist, Nov 1945, *Obit* Nov 1959
Pinnock, Trevor, British harpsichordist and conductor, Sept 1989
Tureck, Rosalyn, American pianist and harpsichordist, Sept 1959, *Obit* Yrbk 2003

Heads of state

Abdul Rahman, Malaysian head of state, Yrbk 1957, *Obit* May 1960
Abdullah, Jan 2002
Abdullah, June 1948, *Obit* Sept 1951
Abdullah, Jan 2000
Ahmad, Mar 1956, *Obit* Nov 1962
Ahmadinejad, Mahmoud, Iranian president, Jan 2005
Akihito, Apr 1959, Aug 1991
Al Thani, Hamad ibn Khalifa, July 2009
Al-Sabah, Abdullah al-Salem, Kuwaiti ruler, July 1957, *Obit* Jan 1966

Al-Sabah, Jaber al-Ahmad al-Jaber, Aug 1988, *Obit* Yrbk 2006
Aleman Valdez, Miguel, Mexican president, Sept 1946, *Obit* July 1983
Alfonsin, Raul, Argentine president, July 1984, *Obit* Yrbk 2009
Alfonso, *Obit* Apr 1941
Alia, Ramiz, Albanian president, Jan 1991, *Obit* Yrbk 2011
Aliyev, Heydar, Azerbaijani president, Sept 1999, *Obit* July 2004
Allende Gossens, Salvador, Chilean president, Sept 1971, *Obit* Nov 1973
Alvear, Marcelo Torcuato de, *Obit* May 1942
Ananda Mahidol, *Obit* July 1946
Andropov, Yuri, Soviet communist leader, May 1983, *Obit* Apr 1984
Aquino, Corazon, Filipino president, Aug 1986, *Obit* Yrbk 2009
Arbenz Guzman, Jacobo, Guatemalan president, Sept 1953, *Obit* Mar 1971
Arias Sanchez, Oscar, Costa Rican president, Aug 1987
Arias, Arnulfo, May 1941, *Obit* Sept 1988
Arroyo del Rio, Carlos Alberto, Ecuadorian president, June 1942
Asgeir Asgeirsson, Icelandic president, Sept 1952
Auriol, Vincent, French president, Mar 1947, *Obit* Feb 1966
Avila Camacho, Manuel, Mexican president, Sept 1940, *Obit* Yrbk 1956
Ayala, Eusebio, Paraguayan president, *Obit* July 1942
Aylwin, Patricio, Chilean president, Aug 1990
Ayub Khan, Mohammad, Pakistani president, Apr 1959, *Obit* June 1974
Azana, Manuel, Spanish president, *Obit* Yrbk 1940
Azcona Hoyo, Jose, Honduran president, Feb 1988, *Obit* Yrbk 2006
Azikiwe, Nnamdi, Nigerian president, July 1957, *Obit* Aug 1996

Bachelet, Michelle, Chilean president, Jan 2006

Bakiyev, Kurmanbek, Kirghiz president, Jan 2007

Balaguer, Joaquin, Dominican president, Nov 1966, *Obit* Yrbk 2002

Banda, Hastings Kamuzu, Malawian president, Jan 1963, *Obit* Feb 1998

Bani-Sadr, Abu al-Hasan, Iranian president, Feb 1981

Bao Dai, Nov 1949, *Obit* Oct 1997

Barco Vargas, Virgilio, Colombian president, Feb 1990, *Obit* Aug 1997

Baudouin, Sept 1950, *Obit* Oct 1993

Bayar, Celal, Turkish president, July 1950, *Obit* Oct 1986

Beatrix, May 1981

Belaunde Terry, Fernando, Peruvian president, July 1965, *Obit* Sept 2002

Ben Bella, Ahmed, Algerian president, Feb 1963, *Obit* Yrbk 2012

Ben-Zvi, Itzhak, Israeli president, Apr 1953, *Obit* June 1963

Benes, Edvard, Czech statesman, Jan 1942, *Obit* Oct 1948

Berger Perdomo, Oscar, Guatemalan president, Jan 2004

Betancourt, Romulo, Venezuelan president, May 1960, *Obit* Nov 1981

Betancur, Belisario, Colombian president, Apr 1985

Bhumibol Adulyadej, July 1950

Bhutto, Zulfikar Ali, Pakistani president, Apr 1972, *Obit* May 1979

Bierut, Boleslaw, Polish president, Sept 1949, *Obit* May 1956

Birendra Bir Bikram Shah Deva, Aug 1975, *Obit* Sept 2001

Blanco Galindo, Carlos, Bolivian president, *Obit* Nov 1943

Bordaberry, Juan Maria, Uruguayan president, Apr 1975, *Obit* Yrbk 2011

Boris, Feb 1941, *Obit* Yrbk 1991

Borno, Louis, *Obit* Sept 1942

Botha, Pieter W., South African president, Sept 1979, *Obit* Yrbk 2007

Bouteflika, Abdelaziz, Algerian president, Feb 1976

Brazauskas, Algirdas, Lithuanian president and prime minister, Jan 2002, *Obit* Yrbk 2010

Brezhnev, Leonid Il'ich, Soviet communist leader, Jan 1963, Nov 1978, *Obit* Jan 1983

Burnham, Forbes, Guyanese president, Nov 1966, *Obit* Oct 1985

Bush, George, American president, Jan 1972, Sept 1983

Cafe Filho, Joao, Jan 1955, *Obit* Apr 1970

Caldera, Rafael, Venezuelan president, July 1969, *Obit* Yrbk 2010

Calderon Guardia, Rafael Angel, Costa Rican president, June 1942, *Obit* Sept 1970

Calderon Hinojosa, Felipe, Mexican president, Jan 2006

Campora, Hector Jose, Argentine political leader, Oct 1973, *Obit* Feb 1981

Caramanlis, Constantinos, Greek president, May 1956, Apr 1976, *Obit* July 1998

Cardoso, Fernando Henrique, Brazilian president, Oct 1996

Carias Andino, Tiburcio, Honduran president, June 1942, *Obit* Feb 1970

Carl, Feb 1974

Carol, Aug 1940, *Obit* May 1953

Carstens, Karl, German president, Apr 1980, *Obit* Aug 1992

Carter, Jimmy, American president, Sept 1971, Nov 1977

Castillo Armas, Carlos, Guatemalan president, Jan 1955, *Obit* Sept 1957

Castillo, Ramon S., July 1941, *Obit* Yrbk 1944

Castro, Fidel, Cuban president, July 1958, July 1970, June 2001

Castro, Raul, Cuban president, Feb 1977

Ceausescu, Nicolae, Romanian dictator, Nov 1967, *Obit* Feb 1990

Cerezo Arevalo, Vinicio, Guatemalan president, Mar 1987

Chadli, Bendjedid, Algerian president, Apr 1991, *Obit* Yrbk 2012

Chamoun, Camille Nimer, Lebanese president, July 1956, *Obit* Sept 1987

Charles, May 1946, *Obit* July 1983

Chavez Frias, Hugo, Venezuelan president, May 2000

Chavez, Hugo, Venezuelan president, *Obit* Yrbk 2013

Chen, Shui-bian, Taiwanese president, Sept 2000

Chernenko, Konstantin Ustinovich, Soviet communist leader, Aug 1984, *Obit* May 1985

Chiang, Ching-kuo, Taiwanese president, Sept 1954, *Obit* Mar 1988

Chiari, Roberto F., Panamanian president, Feb 1961

Chiluba, Frederick, Zambian president, May 1992, *Obit* Yrbk 2011

Chirac, Jacques, French president, June 1975, Apr 1993

Christian, Nov 1943, *Obit* May 1947

Clinton, Bill, American president, Apr 1988, Nov 1994

Collor de Mello, Fernando, Brazilian president, Mar 1990

Constantine, Apr 1967

Cossiga, Francesco, Italian president, Jan 1981, *Obit* Yrbk 2010

Costa e Silva, Arthur da, Sept 1967, *Obit* Feb 1970

Coty, Rene, French president, Apr 1954, *Obit* Jan 1963

Cristiani, Alfredo, Salvadoran president, Jan 1990

Daud Khan, Sardar Mohammed, Mar 1957

De Klerk, Frederik Willem, South African president, Feb 1990

De Valera, Eamon, Irish statesman, Nov 1940, Sept 1951, *Obit* Oct 1975

Diaz Ordaz, Gustavo, Mexican president, May 1965, *Obit* Sept 1979

Djukanovic, Milo, Montenegrin president, Aug 2001

Doe, Samuel Kanyon, Liberian president, May 1981, *Obit* Nov 1990

Donitz, Karl, German admiral, Nov 1942, *Obit* Feb 1981

Dorticos Torrado, Osvaldo, Cuban president, Feb 1963, *Obit* Aug 1983

Duarte, Jose Napoleon, Salvadoran president, Sept 1981, *Obit* Apr 1990

Dubcek, Alexander, Czech communist leader, Nov 1968

Duvalier, Francois, Haitian president, Sept 1958, *Obit* June 1971

Duvalier, Jean-Claude, Haitian president, June 1972

Duvieusart, Jean, Sept 1950

Echeverria Alvarez, Luis, Mexican president, Nov 1972

El-Khoury, Beshira, Yrbk 1951, *Obit* Feb 1964

Elizabeth, June 1944, June 1955, Jan 2002

Elizabeth, Aug 1981, *Obit* June 2002

Endara, Guillermo, Panamanian president, Feb 1991, *Obit* Yrbk 2009

Enkhbayar, Nambaryn, Mongolian president, Jan 2007

Estigarribia, Jose Felix, Paraguayan field marshal and president, Mar 1940, *Obit* Mar 1940

Evren, Kenan, Turkish president, Apr 1984

Fahd, May 1979, *Obit* Yrbk 2005

Faisal, July 1955, *Obit* Oct 1958

Faisal, May 1966, *Obit* May 1975

Farah, Mar 1976

Farouk, Oct 1942, *Obit* May 1965

Feldmann, Markus, June 1956, *Obit* Jan 1959

Figl, Leopold, Apr 1948, *Obit* June 1965

Figueres Ferrer, Jose, Costa Rican president, Oct 1953, *Obit* Aug 1990

Ford, Gerald R., American president, Mar 1961, Nov 1975, *Obit* Feb 2007

Fox Quesada, Vicente, Mexican president, May 2001

Frederick, Nov 1947, *Obit* Mar 1972

Frederika, Queen, consort of Paul I, King Of The Hellenes, Jan 1955, *Obit* Apr 1981

Frei Montalva, Eduardo, Chilean president, Apr 1965, *Obit* Mar 1982

Frondizi, Arturo, Argentine president, Oct 1958, *Obit* June 1995

Gallegos, Romulo, Venezuelan author and president, May 1948, *Obit* May 1969

Garcia Perez, Alan, Peruvian president, Nov 1985

Garcia, Carlos P., Filipino president, June 1957, *Obit* July 1971

Gbagbo, Laurent, Ivorian president, Jan 2004

Gemayel, Amin, Lebanese president, Mar 1983

George, Yrbk 1943, *Obit* Apr 1947

George, Mar 1942, *Obit* Mar 1952

Gierek, Edward, Polish communist leader, May 1971, *Obit* Oct 2001

Giri, V. V., Jan 1970, *Obit* Aug 1980

Giscard d'Estaing, Valery, French president, July 1967, Oct 1974

Gnassingbe, Faure, Togolese president, Jan 2005

Gomes, Francisco da Costa, Portuguese president, May 1976

Gomes, Manuel Teixeira, *Obit* Yrbk 1941

Gomulka, Wladyslaw, Polish communist leader, Jan 1957, *Obit* Oct 1982

Gonzalez Videla, Gabriel, Cuban president, June 1950

Gorbach, Alfons, Oct 1961, *Obit* Oct 1972

Gottwald, Klement, Czech president, Apr 1948, *Obit* Apr 1953

Goulart, Joao Belchior Marques, Brazilian president, Sept 1962, *Obit* Feb 1977

Grau San Martin, Ramon, Cuban president, Oct 1944, *Obit* Oct 1969

Gronchi, Giovanni, Oct 1955, *Obit* Jan 1979

Guardia, Ernesto de la, Panamanian president, Jan 1957

Guardia, Ricardo Adolfo de la, Panamanian president, May 1942, *Obit* Feb 1970

Gusmao, Xanana, East Timorese president, Jan 2002

Gustaf, Sept 1942, *Obit* Yrbk 1950

Gustaf, Yrbk 1950, *Obit* Nov 1973

Gyanendra Bir Bikram Shah, Jan 2005

Haakon, May 1940, *Obit* Yrbk 1957

Habre, Hissene, Chadian president, Aug 1987

Hacha, Emil, Yrbk 1942, *Obit* Sept 1945

Haile Selassie, Apr 1941, Oct 1954, *Obit* Oct 1975

Hainisch, Michael, *Obit* Mar 1940

Halonen, Tarja, Finnish president, Jan 2006

Hassan, Sept 1964, *Obit* Oct 1999

Heinemann, Gustav Walter, June 1969, *Obit* Aug 1976

Herrera Campins, Luis, Venezuelan president, July 1980, *Obit* Yrbk 2008

Herzog, Chaim, Israeli president, Apr 1988, *Obit* June 1997

Heuss, Theodor, German president, Nov 1949, *Obit* Jan 1964

Hirohito, Jan 1942, Mar 1976, *Obit* Feb 1989

Hitler, Adolf, German dictator, Mar 1942, *Obit* Jan 1957

Ho, Chi Minh, Vietnamese communist leader, Nov 1949, Oct 1966, *Obit* Nov 1969

Holenstein, Thomas, May 1958, *Obit* Jan 1963

Honecker, Erich, East German communist leader, Apr 1972, *Obit* July 1994

Hoover, Herbert, American president, Mar 1943, *Obit* Jan 1965

Horthy, Miklos, Hungarian admiral and regent, Oct 1940, *Obit* Apr 1957

Houphouet-Boigny, Felix, Ivorian president, Oct 1958, July 1991, *Obit* Feb 1994

Hoxha, Enver, Albanian communist leader, Jan 1950, *Obit* June 1985

Hrawi, Elias, Lebanese president, Feb 1992, *Obit* Yrbk 2006

Hu Jintao, Chinese president, Jan 2003

Husak, Gustav, Czech president, Oct 1971, *Obit* Jan 1992

Hussein, July 1955, Apr 1986, *Obit* Apr 1999

Hussein, Saddam, Iraqi president, Sept 1981, Jan 2002, *Obit* Apr 2007

Ibn Saud, Feb 1943, *Obit* Jan 1954

Idris, Jan 1956, *Obit* July 1983

Iliescu, Ion, Romanian president, June 1990

Illia, Arturo Umberto, Argentine president, Jan 1965, *Obit* Mar 1983

Inonu, Ismet, Turkish president, Mar 1941, Oct 1964, *Obit* Feb 1974

Isaias Afwerki, Eritrean president, Jan 2002

Izetbegovic, Alija, Bosnian president, Aug 1993, *Obit* June 2004

Jagan, Cheddi, Guyanese president, Apr 1963, *Obit* May 1997

Jayewardene, Junius Richard, Sri Lankan president, Jan 1984, *Obit* Jan 1997

Jiang Zemin, Chinese president, May 1995

Johnson, Lyndon B., American president, Jan 1951, Mar 1964, *Obit* Mar 1973

Juan Carlos, Oct 1964, Jan 2003

Juliana, Sept 1944, Jan 1955, *Obit* Yrbk 2004

Kabbah, Ahmad Tejan, Sierra Leonean president, Jan 2002

Kabila, Joseph, Congolese president, Sept 2001

Kaczynski, Lech, Polish president, Jan 2006, *Obit* Yrbk 2010

Kagame, Paul, Rwandan president, Jan 2002

Kalinin, Mikhail Ivanovich, Soviet president, June 1942, *Obit* July 1946

Kallio, Kyosti, *Obit* Feb 1941

Karmal, Babrak, Afghan president, Mar 1981, *Obit* Feb 1997

Karzai, Hamid, Afghan president, May 2002

Kasavubu, Joseph, Congolese president, Mar 1961, *Obit* May 1969

Katzir, Ephraim, Israeli biophysicist and president, Jan 1975, *Obit* Yrbk 2009

Kaunda, Kenneth D., Zambian president, July 1966

Keita, Modibo, Malian president, Apr 1960, *Obit* July 1977

Kekkonen, Urho, Finnish president, Sept 1950, *Obit* Oct 1986

Kennedy, John F., American president, June 1950, July 1961, *Obit* Jan 1964

Kenyatta, Jomo, Kenyan president, Oct 1953, Apr 1974, *Obit* Oct 1978

Khalid, Jan 1976, *Obit* Aug 1982

Khama, Seretse, Batswana president, May 1967, *Obit* Sept 1980

Khamenei, Ali, Iranian president, Nov 1987, Jan 2005

Khatami, Mohammad, Iranian Islamic leader and president, Apr 1998

Khrushchev, Nikita Sergeevich, Soviet communist leader, July 1954, *Obit* Oct 1971

Kibaki, Mwai, Kenyan president, Jan 2003

Kim, Dae Jung, South Korean president, Sept 1985, *Obit* Yrbk 2009

Kim, Il Sung, North Korean head of state, Sept 1951, *Obit* Yrbk 1994, Yrbk 1994

Kim, Jong Il, North Korean head of state, Jan 2002, *Obit* Yrbk 2012

Kim, Young Sam, Korean president, June 1995

Kirchner, Cristina E. Fernandez de, Argentine president, Jan 2007

Kirchner, Nestor, Argentine president, Jan 2004, *Obit* Yrbk 2010

Koivisto, Mauno, Finnish president, Sept 1982

Konare, Alpha Oumar, Malian president, Oct 2001

Kostunica, Vojislav, Yugoslav president, Jan 2001

Kravchuk, Leonid, Ukrainian president, Jan 1993

Krenz, Egon, East German communist leader, Mar 1990

Krishnaraja Wadiyar, *Obit* Sept 1940

Kubitschek, Juscelino, Brazilian president, Apr 1956, *Obit* Nov 1976

Kuchma, Leonid, Ukrainian president, Oct 1997

Kufuor, John, Ghanaian president, Jan 2002

Kyprianou, Spyros, Cypriot president, May 1979, *Obit* May 2002

Lagos, Ricardo, Chilean president, Jan 2005

Laurel, Jose P., Filipino president, June 1953, *Obit* Jan 1960

Lee, Teng-hui, Taiwanese president, Mar 1996

Leone, Giovanni, Italian president, May 1972, *Obit* Feb 2002

Leoni, Raul, Venezuelan president, Oct 1964, *Obit* Sept 1972

Leopold, Yrbk 1944, *Obit* Nov 1983

Lescot, Elie, Haitian president, June 1941, *Obit* Yrbk 1974

Limann, Hilla, Ghanaian president, June 1981, *Obit* Apr 1998

Lleras Camargo, Alberto, Colombian president, Sept 1947, June 1965, *Obit* Mar 1990

Lopez Mateos, Adolfo, Mexican president, Mar 1959, *Obit* Nov 1969

Lopez Michelsen, Alfonso, Colombian president, Apr 1975

Lopez Portillo, Jose, Mexican president, June 1977, *Obit* Yrbk 2004

Lopez, Alfonso, Colombian president, Sept 1942, *Obit* Jan 1960

Lubke, Heinrich, Jan 1960, *Obit* May 1972

Macapagal, Diosdado, Filipino president, Nov 1962, *Obit* July 1997

Macapagal-Arroyo, Gloria, Filipino president, Jan 2002

Machado, Bernardino, *Obit* June 1944

Machel, Samora, Mozambican president, Mar 1984, *Obit* Jan 1987

Madrid Hurtado, Miguel de la, Mexican president, Apr 1983, *Obit* Yrbk 2012

Magloire, Paul, Haitian president, Feb 1952, *Obit* Nov 2001

Magsaysay, Ramon, Filipino president, Yrbk 1952, *Obit* May 1957

Mahendra Bir Bikram Shaha Deva, July 1956, *Obit* Mar 1972

Mannerheim, Carl Gustaf Emil, Finnish field marshal and president, Apr 1940, *Obit* Feb 1951

Mao Zedong, Chinese communist leader, Feb 1943, May 1962, *Obit* Oct 1976

Marcos, Ferdinand E., Filipino president, Feb 1967, *Obit* Nov 1989

Margrethe, Nov 1972

Mbeki, Thabo, South African president, Aug 1998

Menem, Carlos Saul, Argentine president, Nov 1989

Mengistu Haile-Mariam, Ethiopian head of state, July 1981

Menocal, Mario Garcia, Cuban president, *Obit* Oct 1941

Michael, Oct 1944

Mikoyan, Anastas, Soviet president, May 1955, *Obit* Jan 1979

Millerand, Alexandre, French president, *Obit* May 1943

Milosevic, Slobodan, Yugoslav president, Apr 1990, *Obit* Yrbk 2006

Mirza, Iskander, May 1956, *Obit* Jan 1970

Mitterrand, Francois, French president, Yrbk 1968, Oct 1982, *Obit* Mar 1996

Mogae, Festus G., Batswana president, Jan 2004

Mohammed Reza Pahlavi, Jan 1950, Sept 1977, *Obit* Sept 1980

Mohammed Zahir Shah, Mar 1956, *Obit* Yrbk 2007

Moi, Daniel Arap, Kenyan president, May 1979

Morales, Evo, Bolivian president, Jan 2006

Morinigo, Higinio, Paraguayan president, June 1942

Moscicki, Ignacy, Polish president, *Obit* Nov 1946

Moscoso, Mireya, Panamanian president, Jan 2002

Motta, Giuseppe, *Obit* Jan 1940

Mubarak, Hosni, Egyptian president, Apr 1982

Mugabe, Robert Gabriel, Zimbabwean president, Apr 1979, Jan 2002

Muhammad, Jan 2002

Muhammad, Oct 1951, *Obit* Apr 1961

Mujibur Rahman, Bangladeshi prime minister and president, Jan 1973, *Obit* Oct 1975

Muluzi, Bakili, Malawian president, Jan 2003

Museveni, Yoweri, Ugandan president, Aug 1990

Mussolini, Benito, Italian dictator, Mar 1942, *Obit* May 1945

Mwanawasa, Levy, Zambian president, Jan 2003, *Obit* Yrbk 2008

Mwinyi, Ali Hassan, Tanzanian president, June 1995

Najibullah, Mohammed, Afghan president, June 1988, *Obit* Jan 1997

Napolitano, Giorgio, Italian president, Jan 2006

Nasheed, Mohamed, Maldivian president, Aug 2012

Nasser, Gamal Abdel, Egyptian president, Nov 1954, *Obit* Nov 1970

Navon, Yitzhak, May 1982

Nazarbayev, Nursultan, Kazakhstani president, Oct 2000

Ngo, Dinh Diem, South Vietnamese president, Mar 1955, *Obit* Jan 1964

Nguyen, Van Thieu, South Vietnamese president, June 1968, *Obit* Jan 2002

Nixon, Richard M., American president, July 1948, June 1958, Yrbk 1969, *Obit* June 1994, Yrbk 1994

Niyazov, Saparmurad, Turkmen president, Jan 2003

Nkrumah, Kwame, Ghanaian president, July 1953, *Obit* June 1972

Norodom Sihanouk, Mar 1954, Aug 1993, *Obit* Yrbk 2012

Novotny, Antonin, Czech president, May 1958, *Obit* Mar 1975

Nujoma, Sam, Namibian president, Feb 1990

Nur el Hussein, Apr 1991

Nyerere, Julius K., Tanzanian president, Apr 1963, *Obit* Jan 2000

O'Kelly, Sean T., July 1948, *Obit* Jan 1967

Obama, Barack, American president, July 2005, Mar 2009

Obasanjo, Olusegun, Nigerian president, July 1999

Obote, A. Milton, Ugandan president, Apr 1981, *Obit* Yrbk 2006

Odria, Manuel Arturo, Peruvian president, Nov 1954, *Obit* Apr 1974

Oduber Quiros, Daniel, Costa Rican president, July 1977

Olav, Jan 1962, *Obit* Mar 1991

Ortega Saavedra, Daniel, Nicaraguan president, Oct 1984

Ortiz, Roberto M., *Obit* Sept 1942

Osmena, Sergio, Filipino president, Sept 1944, *Obit* Yrbk 1961

Ospina Perez, Mariano, Colombian president, Feb 1950, *Obit* June 1976

Ozal, Turgut, Turkish president, June 1985, *Obit* June 1993

Paasikivi, Juho Kusti, Finnish president, May 1944, *Obit* Feb 1957

Pacheco de la Espriella, Abel, Costa Rican president, Jan 2002

Papadopoulos, George, Greek army officer and president, Feb 1970, *Obit* Sept 1999

Pastrana Borrero, Misael, Colombian president, July 1971, *Obit* Nov 1997

Patil, Pratibha, Indian president, Jan 2007

Paul, May 1947, *Obit* Apr 1964

Paz Estenssoro, Victor, Bolivian president, May 1953, *Obit* Sept 2001

Pena, Pedro, *Obit* Sept 1943

Perez Jimenez, Marcos, Venezuelan president, Nov 1954, *Obit* Feb 2002

Perez, Carlos Andres, Venezuelan president, Feb 1976, *Obit* Yrbk 2011

Peron, Isabel, Argentine president, Jan 1975

Petain, Henri Philippe, French field marshal, Aug 1940, *Obit* Sept 1951

Peter, Nov 1943, *Obit* Yrbk 1970

Peynado, Jacinto B., *Obit* Mar 1940

Pieck, Wilhelm, Yrbk 1949, *Obit* Nov 1960

Plaza Lasso, Galo, Ecuadorian president, Oct 1951, Apr 1969, *Obit* Mar 1987

Podgorny, Nikolai V., Soviet president, May 1966, *Obit* Mar 1983

Pohamba, Hifkepunye, Namibian president, Jan 2006

Pol Pot, Cambodian political leader, Apr 1980, *Obit* June 1998

Pompidou, Georges, French president, Nov 1962, *Obit* May 1974

Porras, Belisario, Panamanian president, *Obit* Oct 1942

Prado Ugarteche, Manuel, Peruvian president, June 1942, *Obit* Oct 1967

Prajadhipok, *Obit* July 1941

Preval, Rene, Haitian president, Jan 2006

Prio Socarras, Carlos, Cuban president, May 1949, *Obit* June 1977

Putin, Vladimir, Russian prime minister, Apr 2000, Jan 2002

Qaddafi, Muammar al-, Libyan dictator, Sept 1973, Mar 1992, *Obit* Yrbk 2011

Quadros, Janio, Brazilian mayor and president, June 1961, *Obit* Apr 1992

Quezon, Manuel Luis, Filipino president, Aug 1941, *Obit* Sept 1944

Quirino, Elpidio, Filipino president, Sept 1948, *Obit* May 1956

Quwatli, Shukri al-, Syrian president, May 1956, *Obit* Oct 1967

Rafsanjani, Hashemi, Iranian president, Nov 1989

Rahmon, Emomali, Tajik president, Jan 2007

Rajapakse, Mahinda, Sri Lankan president, Jan 2006

Rania, Feb 2001

Rau, Johannes, German president, Mar 1987, *Obit* Yrbk 2006

Relander, Lauri Kristian, *Obit* Apr 1942

Renner, Karl, Austrian president, Sept 1945, *Obit* Jan 1951

Reza Shah Pahlavi, *Obit* Sept 1944

Rhee, Syngman, Korean president, Sept 1947, *Obit* Sept 1965

Rios, Juan Antonio, Chilean president, Apr 1942, *Obit* July 1946

Robinson, Mary, Irish president and United Nations official, Apr 1991

Robles, Marco Aurelio, Panamanian president, June 1968, *Obit* June 1990

Rodriguez Veltze, Eduardo, Bolivian president, Jan 2005

Roxas y Acuna, Manuel, May 1946, *Obit* May 1948

Rua, Fernando de la, Argentine president, Apr 2001

Rubattel, Rodolphe, Yrbk 1954, *Obit* Yrbk 1961

Ruiz Cortines, Adolfo, Mexican president, Sept 1952, *Obit* Jan 1974

Saakashvili, Mikheil, Georgian president, May 2009

Sadat, Anwar, Egyptian president, Mar 1971, *Obit* Nov 1981

Salazar, Antonio de Oliveira, Portuguese dictator, May 1941, May 1952, *Obit* Oct 1970

Salinas de Gortari, Carlos, Mexican president, Mar 1989

Salote Tupou, Yrbk 1953, *Obit* Feb 1966

Sanchez de Lozada, Gonzalo, Bolivian president, Jan 2002

Sanjiva Reddy, N., Indian president, Mar 1981, *Obit* Aug 1996

Santos, Jose Eduardo dos, Angolan president, May 1994

Saragat, Giuseppe, Italian president, Yrbk 1956, July 1965, *Obit* July 1988

Sarkis, Elias, Lebanese president, Mar 1979, *Obit* Aug 1985

Sarkozy, Nicolas, French president, Jan 2006

Sarney, Jose, Brazilian president, Mar 1986

Saud, Apr 1954, *Obit* Apr 1969

Scharf, Adolf, Oct 1957, *Obit* Apr 1965

Shagari, Shehu, Nigerian president, Aug 1980

Shazar, Zalman, Feb 1964, *Obit* Nov 1974

Shvernik, Nikolai, Soviet communist leader, Oct 1951, *Obit* Feb 1971

Sidi Ahmed, *Obit* Aug 1942

Siles Zuazo, Hernan, Bolivian president, Sept 1958, June 1985, *Obit* Oct 1996

Siles, Hernando, Bolivian president, *Obit* Jan 1943

Silva, Luis Inacio da, Brazilian president, Jan 2003

Sirikit, Yrbk 1960

Sisavang Vong, Apr 1954, *Obit* Jan 1960

Smetona, Antanas, Lithuanian president, *Obit* Feb 1944

Sobhuza, Mar 1982, *Obit* Mar 1982

Soekarno, Indonesian president, Sept 1947, *Obit* Sept 1970

Stalin, Joseph, Soviet dictator, Mar 1942, *Obit* Apr 1953

Sunay, Cevdet, Mar 1969, *Obit* Aug 1982

Sveinn Bjornsson, Aug 1944, *Obit* Mar 1952

Svinhufvud, Pehr Evind, *Obit* Apr 1944

Talabani, Jalal, Iraqi president, Jan 2005

Talal, Jan 1952, *Obit* Sept 1972

Taufa'ahau Tupou, Sept 1968, *Obit* Yrbk 2007

Taylor, Charles, Liberian president, Sept 1992

Terra, Gabriel, Uruguayan president, *Obit* Nov 1942

Thomaz, Americo de Deus Rodrigues, Portuguese president, Yrbk 1958, *Obit* Nov 1987

Tiso, Jozef, Slovak priest and president, Mar 1943, *Obit* May 1947

Tito, Josip Broz, Yugoslav head of state, Nov 1943, Mar 1955, *Obit* June 1980

Tolbert, William R., Liberian president, Mar 1974, *Obit* June 1980

Toure, Ahmed Sekou, Guinean president, June 1959, *Obit* May 1984

Toure, Amadou Toumani, Malian president, Jan 2005

Truman, Harry S., American president, Jan 1942, Apr 1945, *Obit* Feb 1973

Tubman, William Vacanarat Shadrach, Liberian president, Jan 1955, *Obit* Sept 1971

Tudjman, Franjo, Croatian president, Sept 1997, *Obit* May 2000

Turbay Ayala, Julio Cesar, Colombian president, July 1979

Ubico, Jorge, Guatemalan president, June 1942, *Obit* July 1946

Ulbricht, Walter, East German communist leader, July 1952, *Obit* Oct 1973

Uribe Velez, Alvaro, Colombian president, Jan 2002

Urrutia Lleo, Manuel, Cuban president, May 1959, *Obit* Aug 1981

Vall, Ely Ould Mohamed, Mauritanian head of state, Jan 2006

Vargas, Getulio, Brazilian president, Aug 1940, May 1951, *Obit* Oct 1954

Velasco Ibarra, Jose Maria, Ecuadorian president, Nov 1952, *Obit* May 1979

Victor Emmanuel, July 1943, *Obit* Jan 1948

Vigidis Finnbogadottir, Icelandic president, May 1987

Vike-Freiberga, Vaira, Latvian president, Jan 2005

Wade, Abdoulaye, Senegalese president, Jan 2006

Waldheim, Kurt, Austrian president and United Nations secretary-general, May 1972, Jan 1987, *Obit* Oct 2007

Walesa, Lech, Polish president, Apr 1981, May 1996

Wangchuk, Jigme Dorji, Oct 1956, *Obit* Sept 1972

Weizman, Ezer, Israeli president, Sept 1979, *Obit* Aug 2005

Weizmann, Chaim, Israeli president and Zionist leader, Nov 1942, Nov 1948, *Obit* Yrbk 1952

Weizsacker, Richard von, German president, Mar 1985

Wetter, Ernst, Feb 1942

Wilhelmina, Jan 1940, *Obit* Jan 1963

William, *Obit* July 1941

Windsor, Edward, Sept 1944, *Obit* July 1972

Yahya Khan, A. M., Jan 1971, *Obit* Oct 1980

Yar'Adua, Umaru Musa, Nigerian president, Jan 2007, *Obit* Yrbk 2010

Yeltsin, Boris, Russian president, Jan 1989, *Obit* June 2007

Yushchenko, Viktor, Ukrainian president, Jan 2005

Zail Singh, Indian president, Sept 1987, *Obit* Mar 1995

Zapotocky, Antonin, June 1953, *Obit* Jan 1958

Zardari, Asif Ali, Pakistani president, Jan 2009

Zhivkov, Todor, Bulgarian communist leader, Jan 1976, *Obit* Oct 1998

Zog, Aug 1944, *Obit* June 1961

Zubiria, Alberto F., Yrbk 1956

Zuma, Jacob, South African president, Jan 2006

Health care administrators

Betts, Rome A., American medical association official, Mar 1949

Blumer, George Alder, American psychiatrist and hospital administrator, *Obit* Jan 1940

Bundesen, Herman N., Oct 1948, *Obit* Nov 1960

Caldwell, William E., *Obit* May 1943

De Kleine, William, Apr 1941, *Obit* Yrbk 1958

Fauci, Anthony S., American immunologist, Aug 1988

Fiske, James Porter, orthopedic surgeon and hospital administrator, *Obit* Yrbk 1941

Gregory, Menas S., *Obit* Jan 1942

Halloran, Roy D., *Obit* Yrbk 1943

Ho, David D., American physician, June 1997

Kast, Ludwig, *Obit* Oct 1941

Knowles, John H., Yrbk 1970, *Obit* May 1979

Moore, George E., American oncologist and surgeon, Jan 1968, *Obit* Yrbk 2008

Obama, Michelle, wife of American president Barack Obama, Oct 2008

Sage, Dean, *Obit* Aug 1943

Scott, Arthur Carroll, *Obit* Yrbk 1940

Weisse, Faneuil Suydam, *Obit* Mar 1940

Health care personnel

Adair, Frank E., American surgeon, May 1946, *Obit* Feb 1982

Adrian, Edgar Douglas Adrian, British physiologist, Feb 1955, *Obit* Oct 1977

Agatston, Arthur, American cardiologist, Mar 2007

Al-Jaafari, Ibrahim, Iraqi prime minister and physician, Jan 2006

Albee, Fred H., May 1943, *Obit* Apr 1945

Albright, Tenley, American figure skater and surgeon, Sept 1956

Alexander, Franz, Austrian psychiatrist, Aug 1942, Sept 1960, *Obit* Apr 1964

Alger, Ellice M., American ophthalmologist, *Obit* Apr 1945

Allawi, Iyad, Iraqi interim prime minister and neurologist, Jan 2004

Allende Gossens, Salvador, Chilean president, Sept 1971, *Obit* Nov 1973

Allman, David B., American surgeon and medical association official, Feb 1958, *Obit* May 1971

Alstadt, W. R., American dentist, July 1958

Anderson, Gaylord W., American physician, Feb 1953

Angell, Marcia, American physician and medical writer, Nov 2005

Annis, Edward R., Apr 1964

Antinori, Severino, Italian physician, Jan 2002

Apgar, Virginia, American anesthesiologist, Feb 1968, *Obit* Oct 1974

Appel, James Z., American physician and medical

association official, Mar 1966, *Obit* Oct 1981

Aras, Tevfik Rustu, Turkish diplomat, June 1942

Arce, Jose, Nov 1947, *Obit* Oct 1968

Aronson, Jane, American pediatrician, Feb 2011

Arsonval, Jacques Arsene d', French physiologist, *Obit* Feb 1941

Askey, E. Vincent, American surgeon, Feb 1961, *Obit* Feb 1975

Aughinbaugh, William, American lawyer, physician and travel writer, *Obit* Feb 1941

Baker, Sara Josephine, American physician, *Obit* Apr 1945

Banda, Hastings Kamuzu, Malawian president, Jan 1963, *Obit* Feb 1998

Bang, Abhay, Indian physician and public health scientist, Jan 2007

Bang, Rani, Indian gynecologist and public health scientist, Jan 2007

Bannister, Roger, British neurologist and runner, Apr 1956

Banting, Frederick G., Canadian physician, *Obit* Apr 1941

Barker, Lewellys Franklin, American physician, *Obit* Sept 1943

Barnard, Christiaan, South African heart surgeon, May 1968, *Obit* Nov 2001

Barringer, Emily Dunning, physician, Mar 1940, *Obit* June 1961

Bauer, Louis Hopewell, American cardiologist, Oct 1948, *Obit* Mar 1964

Beers, Clifford Whittingham, American mental hygienist, *Obit* Aug 1943

Begg, Colin Luke, American physician, *Obit* Mar 1941

Benjamin, Regina, American Surgeon general, Jan 2010

Benson, Francis Colgate, American surgeon and radiologist, *Obit* Apr 1941

Bernheim, Bertram M., American surgeon, Sept 1943

Best, Charles Herbert, Canadian physiologist, June 1957, *Obit* May 1978

Binder, Theodor, German physician and missionary, Sept 1964

Blackfan, K. D., American pediatrician, *Obit* Jan 1942

Blaese, R. Michael, physician, Mar 2000

Blain, Daniel, American psychiatrist, Sept 1947

Blanchfield, Florence Aby, American nurse and army officer, Sept 1943, *Obit* June 1971

Blanton, Smiley, June 1956, *Obit* Jan 1967

Blumberg, Baruch S., American physician and biochemist, Nov 1977, *Obit* Yrbk 2011

Bonine, Frederick N., American ophthalmologist, *Obit* Oct 1941

Bonner, Elena, Soviet physician and human rights activist, Apr 1987, *Obit* Yrbk 2011

Boone, J. T., American physician and admiral, Mar 1951, *Obit* June 1974

Bortz, Edward Leroy, physician, Sept 1947, *Obit* Apr 1970

Brickner, Richard M., Sept 1943

Brinkley, John Richard, American physician and swindler, *Obit* July 1942

Broder, Samuel, physician and government official, Aug 1992

Brundtland, Gro Harlem, Norwegian prime minister and international health official, Nov 1981

Bugher, John C., Apr 1953

Burney, Leroy E., surgeon general, July 1957, *Obit* Oct 1998

Butler, Robert N., American gerontologist and psychiatrist, Jan 1997, *Obit* Yrbk 2010

Calderon Guardia, Rafael Angel, Costa Rican president, June 1942, *Obit* Sept 1970

Calderone, Frank A., physician and public health official, July 1952, *Obit* Apr 1987

Caldicott, Helen, American pediatrician and anti-nuclear activist, Oct 1983

Califano, Joseph A., American Secretary of health, education and welfare, June 1977

Camac, Charles Nicoll Bancker, *Obit* Nov 1940

Cameron, Charles S., Sept 1954

Canady, Alexa, neurosurgeon, Aug 2000

Candau, Marcolino G., Brazilian physican and public health official, Sept 1954

Canin, Ethan, American novelist, short story writer and physician, Aug 2001

Cannon, Walter Bradford, American physiologist, *Obit* Nov 1945

Capps, Lois, American congresswoman, Mar 2008

Carrel, Alexis, French surgeon and biologist, Mar 1940, *Obit* Yrbk 1944

Caturani, Michele Gaetano, *Obit* Mar 1940

Celebrezze, Anthony J., American Secretary of health, education and welfare, Jan 1963, *Obit* Jan 1999

Chamberlain, Francis L., July 1959

Chan, Margaret F. C., Chinese physician and public health official, Jan 2007

Chesser, Elizabeth Sloan, *Obit* Mar 1940

Chopra, Deepak, American physician and writer, Oct 1995

Clarke, Walter, American physician, May 1947, *Obit* Jan 1965

Clendening, Logan, physician, *Obit* Mar 1945

Cline, John Wesley, June 1951, *Obit* Sept 1974

Coggeshall, Lowell T., college administrator and physician, Sept 1963, *Obit* Jan 1988

Colby, Charles De Witt, *Obit* Nov 1941

Coles, Robert, American psychiatrist, Nov 1969

Collins, George Lewis, *Obit* Aug 1940

Connell, Karl, *Obit* Yrbk 1941

Cooley, Denton A., American cardiac surgeon, Jan 1976

Cooper, Irving S., neurosurgeon, Apr 1974, *Obit* Jan 1986

Cournand, Andre F., American physician, Mar 1957, *Obit* Apr 1988

Crile, George Washington, American surgeon, *Obit* Feb 1943

Cronin, A. J., Scottish novelist and physician, July 1942, *Obit* Mar 1981

Cullis, Winifred C., Nov 1943, *Obit* Jan 1957

Cunningham, William Francis, *Obit* Jan 1941

Dafoe, Allan Roy, *Obit* July 1943

Damadian, Raymond, American physician and inventor, Jan 2000

Dandy, Walter E., American neurosurgeon, *Obit* May 1946

Dauser, Sue S., Aug 1944

Dausset, Jean, French immunologist, May 1981, *Obit* Yrbk 2009

Davis, William Ellsworth, Apr 1940

Dawson of Penn, Bertrand Edward Dawson, English physician, *Obit* Apr 1945

DeVries, William C., surgeon, Jan 1985

Dean, Howard, American governor and political party leader, Oct 2002

Demikhov, Vladimir P., Russian surgeon, June 1960, *Obit* Feb 1999

Deming, Dorothy, nurse and educator, May 1943

Densen-Gerber, Judianne, American lawyer and psychiatrist, Nov 1983, *Obit* July 2003

Densford, Katharine J., Feb 1947

Dhalla, Ruby, Canadian member of Parliament, Jan 2006

Dickinson, Robert Latou, American gynecologist and obstetrician, Mar 1950, *Obit* Jan 1951

Diefendorf, Allen Ross, *Obit* Sept 1943

Dodge, Raymond, *Obit* May 1942

Doll, Richard, British epidemiologist, Jan 2002

Dooley, Tom, American physician and missionary, July 1957, *Obit* Mar 1961

Dorman, Gerald D., June 1970

Drew, Charles Richard, American surgeon, May 1944, *Obit* May 1950

Due-Gundersen, Gunnar, Feb 1959, *Obit* Aug 1979

Duffy, James J., *Obit* Feb 1942

Dunham, Charles L., Mar 1966

Durham, Carl, American congressman, July 1957, *Obit* June 1974

Duvalier, Francois, Haitian president, Sept 1958, *Obit* June 1971

Dyke, Cornelius G., *Obit* June 1943

Eccles, John C., Australian physiologist, Oct 1972, *Obit* July 1997

Edwards, Charles C., American surgeon and regulatory official, Oct 1973, *Obit* Yrbk 2011

Edwards, Waldo B., American obstetrician, June 1943

Elders, Joycelyn, American surgeon general, Mar 1994

Eliot, Martha May, American pediatrician, Oct 1948, *Obit* Apr 1978

Epstein, Samuel S., Anglo-American physician, Aug 2001

Erikson, Erik H., American psychoanalyst, May 1971, *Obit* July 1994

Ewing, James, *Obit* July 1943

Exner, Max J., *Obit* Nov 1943

Farmer, Paul, American physician, Feb 2004

Finch, Robert H., American secretary of health, education and welfare, Mar 1969, *Obit* Jan 1996

Fishbein, Morris, American periodical editor and physician, May 1940, *Obit* Nov 1976

Fister, George M., June 1963, *Obit* July 1976

Fitz Gerald, Leslie M., Sept 1954

Flexner, Simon, American physician, *Obit* June 1946

Flikke, Julia O., July 1942

Folkman, Judah, American surgeon, May 1998, *Obit* Yrbk 2008

Folks, Homer, Yrbk 1940

Folsom, Marion Bayard, American Secretary of health, education and welfare, Jan 1950, *Obit* Nov 1976

Forssmann, Werner, German physician, Mar 1957, *Obit* Aug 1979

Frank, Louis, *Obit* May 1941

Frankl, Viktor E., Austrian psychiatrist, July 1997, *Obit* Nov 1997

Freeman, R. Austin, English physician and mystery writer, *Obit* Nov 1943

Freud, Anna, British psychoanalyst, Apr 1979, *Obit* Mar 1983

Frist, Bill, American surgeon and senator, Nov 2002

Fromm, Erich, American psychoanalyst and philosopher, Apr 1967, *Obit* May 1980

Frothingham, Channing, Mar 1948, *Obit* Nov 1959

Furey, Warren W., May 1950, *Obit* Jan 1959

Galard Terraube, Genevieve de, Oct 1954

Gale, Robert Peter, physician, Jan 1987

Gaskin, Ina May, midwife, May 2001

Gawande, Atul, American physician and medical writer, Mar 2005

Gayle, Helene D., American epidemiologist, Jan 2002

Gedi, Ali Mohamed, Somalian prime minister, Jan 2007

Gerberding, Julie, American physician and public health official, Sept 2004

Gifford, Sanford R., American ophthalmologist, *Obit* Apr 1944

Goddard, James L., American regulatory agency official, Oct 1968, *Obit* Yrbk 2010

Gogarty, Oliver St. John, Irish otolaryngologist, poet and novelist, July 1941, *Obit* Yrbk 1957

Goldstein, Joseph Leonard, American physician, July 1987

Goler, George Washington, American physician, *Obit* Nov 1940

Good, Robert A., American physician, Mar 1972, *Obit* Yrbk 2003

Goulian, Mehran, July 1968

Greatbatch, Wilson, American biomedical engineer and inventor of pacemaker, *Obit* Yrbk 2012

Greenfield, Abraham Lincoln, *Obit* Sept 1941

Greenwood, Allen, *Obit* Yrbk 1942

Grenfell, Wilfred Thomason, British medical missionary, *Obit* Yrbk 1940

Griffin, John Douglas Morecroft, May 1957

Griffith, J. P. Crozer, *Obit* Sept 1941

Groopman, Jerome E., American physician and medical writer, Oct 2004

Gros, Edmund L., *Obit* Yrbk 1942

Guevara, Ernesto, Argentine-Cuban revolutionary, June 1963, *Obit* Yrbk 1967

Guion, Connie M., Feb 1962

Gunn, Selskar M., *Obit* Sept 1944

Guttmacher, Alan Frank, physician, Oct 1965, *Obit* May 1974

Gwathmey, James T., *Obit* Apr 1944

Haddon, William, government official and physician, Feb 1969, *Obit* Apr 1985

Hall, George W., *Obit* Yrbk 1941

Hamilton, Alice, American physician, May 1946, *Obit* Nov 1970

Hammond, Graeme M., *Obit* Yrbk 1944

Han, Suyin, Chinese novelist and physician, Yrbk 1957, *Obit* Yrbk 2013

Hansen, Fred, pole vaulter, Yrbk 1965

Head, Henry, British neurologist, *Obit* Yrbk 1940

Healy, Bernadine P., American cardiologist and public health official, Nov 1992, *Obit* Yrbk 2011

Heimlich, Henry J., American surgeon, Oct 1986

Heiser, Victor G., physician, Apr 1942, *Obit* May 1972

Hektoen, Ludvig, Yrbk 1947, *Obit* Sept 1951

Heller, John Roderick, physician, Feb 1949, *Obit* July 1989

Helpern, Milton, May 1973, *Obit* June 1977

Hench, Philip Showalter, American physician, Yrbk 1950, *Obit* May 1965

Henderson, E. L., June 1950, *Obit* Oct 1953

Hertzler, Arthur E., American surgeon, *Obit* Oct 1946

Hess, Elmer, Jan 1956, *Obit* June 1961

Hilleboe, Herman E., June 1955, *Obit* June 1974

Hirsch, I. Seth, *Obit* May 1942

Holland, Charles Thurstan, *Obit* Mar 1941

Horder, Thomas Jeeves Horder, English physician, July 1944, *Obit* Oct 1955

Horney, Karen, German-American psychoanalyst, Aug 1941, *Obit* Jan 1953

Houphouet-Boigny, Felix, Ivorian president, Oct 1958, July 1991, *Obit* Feb 1994

Houssay, Bernardo Alberto, Argentine physiologist, Jan 1948, *Obit* Nov 1971

Hubeny, Maximilian J., *Obit* Sept 1942

Hudson, Charles Lowell, medical association executive and physician, Apr 1967, *Obit* Nov 1992

Huebner, Robert J., epidemiologist, Sept 1968, *Obit* Nov 1998

Huggins, Charles B., American surgeon, Feb 1965, *Obit* Mar 1997

Hurd-Mead, Kate Campbell, *Obit* Feb 1941

Hyde, Henry Van Zile, May 1960

Ilg, Frances Lillian, pediatrician and educator, Sept 1956, *Obit* Sept 1981

Illia, Arturo Umberto, Argentine president, Jan 1965, *Obit* Mar 1983

Irons, Ernest E., Oct 1949, *Obit* Apr 1959

Ives, James E., *Obit* Feb 1943

Jackson, Chevalier, July 1940

Jacobson, Leon, American physician, Oct 1962, *Obit* Feb 1993

Jaffe, Harold W., epidemiologist, Sept 1992

Jalal, Massouda, Afghan pediatrician, social activist and political leader, Jan 2002

Janssen, Charles L., *Obit* Mar 1941

Jarvik, Robert, American physician and inventor, July 1985

Jelliffe, Smith Ely, psychiatrist, *Obit* Oct 1945

Jellinek, E. M., May 1947, *Obit* Jan 1964

Jemison, Mae C., American physician and astronaut, July 1993

Jenike, Michael A., American psychiatrist, Jan 2010

Jindal, Bobby, American governor, Jan 2008

Johnson, Loren, *Obit* Feb 1942

Johnson, Robert Wood, American medical supply executive, Nov 1943, *Obit* Mar 1968

Jordan, Sara Claudia Murray, gastroenterologist, Mar 1954, *Obit* Jan 1960

Joseph, Stephen C., physician and public health official, Jan 1989

Judd, Walter Henry, American congressman, Sept 1949, *Obit* Apr 1994

Jung, C. G., Swiss psychologist, Apr 1943, Oct 1953, *Obit* Sept 1961

Kaleeba, Noerine, Ugandan AIDS activist and physiotherapist, Jan 2006

Kamen, Dean, American inventor and medical instrument maker, Nov 2002

Karadzic, Radovan, Bosnian Serb political leader, Oct 1995

Kelman, Charles D., American ophthalmologist and saxophonist, June 1984, *Obit* Yrbk 2004

Kelsey, Frances Oldham, American pharmacologist and regulatory agency official, Apr 1965

Kenny, Elizabeth, Australian nurse, Oct 1942, *Obit* Jan 1953

Kevorkian, Jack, American pathologist and right to die advocate, Sept 1994, *Obit* Yrbk 2011

Key, Ben Witt, *Obit* July 1940

Klass, Perri, American pediatrician and novelist, May 1999

Kline, Nathan S., psychiatrist and educator, Oct 1965, *Obit* May 1983

Knopf, Sigard Adolphus, *Obit* Sept 1940

Kolff, Willem J., American physician, May 1983, *Obit* Yrbk 2009

Koop, C. Everett, American surgeon general, Sept 1983, *Obit* Yrbk 2013

Kotb, Heba, Egyptian sex therapist, Jan 2007

Krause, Allen K., *Obit* July 1941

Kuhlmann, Frederick, *Obit* June 1941

Kuipers, Andre, Dutch physician and astronaut, Jan 2004

Kumm, Henry William, physician and foundation official, June 1955, *Obit* Mar 1991

Kutchuk, Fazil, Cypriot political leader and physician, Feb 1961, *Obit* Mar 1984

L'Esperance, Elise Depew Strang, pathologist, Nov 1950, *Obit* Apr 1959

Lahey, Frank H., American surgeon, Mar 1941, *Obit* Sept 1953

Laidlaw, Patrick Playfair, *Obit* Apr 1940

Laing, R. D., Scottish psychiatrist, Mar 1973, *Obit* Mar 1989

Lambert, Sylvester M., American physician, Oct 1941, *Obit* Feb 1947

Landsteiner, Karl, American biochemist, *Obit* Aug 1943

Lane, Arbuthnot, British surgeon, *Obit* Mar 1943

Larson, Leonard W., American medical association official and pathologist, May 1962, *Obit* Nov 1974

Leboyer, Frederick, July 1982

Lee, Jong Wook, Korean physician and international public health official, Jan 2003, *Obit* CB Int 2007

Lem, Stanislaw, Polish science fiction novelist, short story writer and physician, Oct 1986, *Obit* Yrbk 2006

Levine, Melvin D., American pediatrician, Nov 2005

Lewis, Dean, *Obit* Yrbk 1941

Lewis, Dorothy Otnow, American psychiatrist, May 2006

Lillehei, Clarence Walton, American surgeon, May 1969, *Obit* Nov 1999

Lilly, John Cunningham, American physician, Nov 1962, *Obit* Feb 2002

Lord, F. T., *Obit* Jan 1942

Lord, Mary Pillsbury, Oct 1952

Love, Susan M., American surgeon, Oct 1994

Lubic, Ruth Watson, American nurse and midwife, Sept 1996

Lynch, William J., *Obit* Aug 1941

MacCallum, William George, *Obit* Mar 1944

Macartney, William Napier, *Obit* Aug 1940

Magee, James C., May 1943

Magnuson, Paul B., June 1948, *Obit* Jan 1969

Mailhouse, Max, *Obit* Yrbk 1941

Mallory, F. B., *Obit* Nov 1941

Marshall, Barry J., Australian gastroenterologist, Sept 1996

Marshall, C. Herbert, Oct 1949

Martin, Walter B., Nov 1954, *Obit* May 1966

Martland, Harrison Stanford, Nov 1940, *Obit* June 1954

Masserman, Jules H., psychiatrist, July 1980, *Obit* Jan 1995

Masters, William H., American physician, Nov 1968, *Obit* May 2001

Maung, Cynthia, Burmese physician, Jan 2003

May, Charles H., *Obit* Jan 1944

McCarthy, Kenneth C., Nov 1953

McCormack, Arthur Thomas, *Obit* Sept 1943

McCormick, Edward James, surgeon, Nov 1953, *Obit* Feb 1975

McIntire, Ross T., Oct 1945, *Obit* Feb 1960

McIver, Pearl L., nurse, Mar 1949

Meerloo, Joost A. M., Jan 1962, *Obit* Feb 1977

Mellon, William Larimer, medical missionary, June 1965, *Obit* Oct 1989

Menninger, Karl A., American psychiatrist, Oct 1948, *Obit* Sept 1990

Meriwether, W. Delano, Jan 1978

Miller, Harry W., Mar 1962, *Obit* Mar 1977

Molloy, Daniel M., *Obit* Mar 1944

Montessori, Maria, Italian educator, Nov 1940, *Obit* June 1952

Morgan, Thomas E., American congressman and physician, June 1959, *Obit* Oct 1995

Morse, John Lovett, *Obit* May 1940

Morton, Henry H., *Obit* July 1940

Mukherjee, Siddhartha, American oncologist, Jan 2013

Murray, Dwight H., May 1957, *Obit* Nov 1974

Negrin, Juan, Spanish physiologist and statesman, Sept 1945, *Obit* Jan 1957

Nestingen, Ivan A., Mar 1962, *Obit* June 1978

Neuman, Leo Handel, *Obit* May 1941

Neumann, Heinrich, *Obit* Jan 1940

Novello, Antonia, American pediatrician and Surgeon general, May 1992

Ochsner, Alton, surgeon, Oct 1966, *Obit* Nov 1981

Offit, Paul A., American immunologist, Apr 2009

Olopade, Olufunmilayo, Nigerian-American oncologist, Sept 2006

Ornish, Dean, American physician, Apr 1994

Orr, Louis M., Apr 1960, *Obit* July 1961

Osborne, Oliver Thomas, *Obit* Yrbk 1940

Owens, Robert Bowie, *Obit* Yrbk 1940

Pacheco de la Espriella, Abel, Costa Rican president, Jan 2002

Paddon, Harry Locke, *Obit* Jan 1940

Page, Irvine H., physician, June 1966, *Obit* Aug 1991

Paton, Stewart, *Obit* Mar 1942

Paul, Ron, American congressman, June 2008

Pease, Charles G., *Obit* Yrbk 1941

Peck, M. Scott, American psychiatrist and self-help writer, June 1991, *Obit* Yrbk 2005

Perla, David, Mar 1940

Peter, Luther Crouse, *Obit* Jan 1943

Peters, C. J., American epidemiologist and army officer, June 1997

Peterson, Reuben, *Obit* Jan 1943

Petry, Lucile, nursing educator and government official, Apr 1944, *Obit* June 2000

Pitanguy, Ivo, Brazilian plastic surgeon, Jan 2004

Porter, Elizabeth K., Oct 1952

Poussaint, Alvin F., psychiatrist, July 1973

Power, D'Arcy, *Obit* July 1941

Pritchard, Stuart, *Obit* Sept 1940

Prusiner, Stanley, American neurologist, June 1997

Pusey, William Allen, *Obit* Oct 1940

Quimby, Edith Hinkley, American radiologist, July 1949, *Obit* Mar 1983

Ravdin, I. S., American surgeon, Apr 1968, *Obit* Oct 1972

Redlener, Irwin, American pediatrician, Nov 2007

Reed, John Howard, *Obit* Mar 1940

Reid, Mont, *Obit* June 1943

Rhoads, Cornelius P., American physician, Mar 1953, *Obit* Nov 1959

Richards, Dickinson W., American physician, Mar 1957, *Obit* Apr 1973

Riesman, David, American physician, *Obit* July 1940

Riggs, Austen Fox, *Obit* Mar 1940

Ring, Barbara T., *Obit* Nov 1941

Robb, Hunter, *Obit* Jan 1940

Robbins, Frederick C., American bacteriologist, June 1955, *Obit* Yrbk 2003

Robertson, Robert Blackwood, May 1957

Robitzek, Edward Heinrich, physician, Yrbk 1953, *Obit* May 1984

Rock, John Charles, American physician, Yrbk 1964, *Obit* Jan 1985

Rodahl, Kare, Norwegian physiologist, Feb 1956

Rogers, Frank Bradway, physician and librarian, June 1962

Rogers, Mark Homer, *Obit* Nov 1941

Rogge, Jacques, Belgian orthopedic surgeon and Olympic executive, Jan 2002

Rosanoff, Aaron J., *Obit* Feb 1943

Rosen, Samuel, Feb 1974, *Obit* Jan 1982

Rosenberg, Steven A., American surgeon, Feb 1991

Ross, Jerilyn, American psychotherapist, Nov 2009, *Obit* Yrbk 2010

Rous, Francis Peyton, American pathologist, Mar 1967, *Obit* Apr 1970

Rouse, Milford O., June 1968

Routley, Thomas Clarence, Jan 1956, *Obit* June 1963

Rowntree, Cecil, *Obit* Yrbk 1943

Rubin, Theodore Isaac, Feb 1980

Rusk, Howard Archibald, American physician, Mar 1946, May 1967, *Obit* Jan 1990

Sabin, Albert, American physician, Feb 1958, *Obit* Apr 1993

Sachs, Bernard, American neurologist, *Obit* Mar 1944

Sacks, Oliver W., American neurologist and medical writer, Feb 1985

Sakel, Manfred, Jan 1941, *Obit* Feb 1958

Saks, Elyn R., American psychiatrist and law professor, Feb 2011

Salk, Jonas, American physician, May 1954, *Obit* Aug 1995

Salter, Alfred, *Obit* Sept 1945

Scheele, Leonard Andrew, surgeon general, May 1948, *Obit* Mar 1993

Scheer, Alan Austin, Jan 1964

Schereschewsky, Joseph Williams, *Obit* Sept 1940

Schick, Bela, pediatrician, July 1944, *Obit* Feb 1968

Schilder, Paul, Austrian psychiatrist, *Obit* Jan 1941

Schwarzhaupt, Elisabeth, German cabinet member, Jan 1967, *Obit* Jan 1987

Schweiker, Richard S., American Secretary of health and human services, Feb 1977

Scott, K. Frances, Nov 1948

Seagrave, Gordon S., American physician and missionary, Nov 1943, *Obit* May 1965

Sears, Martha, nurse and writer on health, Aug 2001

Selye, Hans, Canadian physician, June 1953, Jan 1981, *Obit* Jan 1983

Senn, Milton John Edward, pediatrician and psychiatrist, June 1950, *Obit* Aug 1990

Shaw, Henry, American pediatrician, *Obit* May 1941

Shine, F. W., *Obit* Nov 1941

Shope, Richard E., Yrbk 1963, *Obit* Yrbk 1966

Shoulders, Harrison H., Nov 1946, *Obit* Jan 1964

Shumway, Norman, American surgeon, Apr 1971, *Obit* Yrbk 2006

Siegel, Bernie S., surgeon, June 1993

Siemionow, Maria, Polish plastic surgeon, May 2009

Slaughter, Frank G., American novelist and physician, Oct 1942, *Obit* Yrbk 2006

Sleeper, Ruth, nurse and educator, Oct 1952, *Obit* Feb 1993

Slye, Maud, American pathologist, Yrbk 1940, *Obit* Nov 1954

Smith, David T., Oct 1950

Snell, Peter, New Zealand runner and physiologist, Yrbk 1962

Snyder, Solomon H., American neuropharmacologist, Apr 1996

Southworth, James L., American surgeon, June 1943

Spiller, William Gibson, *Obit* Apr 1940

Spock, Benjamin, American pediatrician, Yrbk 1956, Nov 1969, *Obit* June 1998

Starzl, Thomas E., American surgeon, Mar 1993

Steincrohn, Peter Joseph, Mar 1957

Steiner, Walter Ralph, *Obit* Jan 1943

Steinfeld, Jesse L., Apr 1974

Steinhaus, Edward A., Yrbk 1955

Stekel, Wilhelm, Austrian psychoanalyst, *Obit* Aug 1940

Steptoe, Patrick, British surgeon, Mar 1979, *Obit* June 1988

Stevenson, George S., psychiatrist, Yrbk 1946

Stewart, Alice, British epidemiologist, July 2000, *Obit* Yrbk 2002

Stewart, William H., American surgeon general, Apr 1966, *Obit* Yrbk 2008

Stimson, Julia Catherine, nurse, Nov 1940, *Obit* Nov 1948

Stone, Hannah M., physician and family planning advocate, *Obit* Sept 1941

Storr, Anthony, English psychiatrist and psychotherapist, June 1994, *Obit* Sept 2001

Sullivan, Harry Stack, American psychiatrist, Nov 1942, *Obit* Feb 1949

Summerskill, Edith, British member of Parliament and physician, Apr 1943, July 1963, *Obit* Apr 1980

Switzer, Mary Elizabeth, Jan 1962, *Obit* Yrbk 1971

Tchernichowsky, Saul, Hebrew poet and physician, *Obit* Yrbk 1943

Terry, Luther L., American surgeon general and educator, Oct 1961, *Obit* May 1985

Thomas, Lewis, American physician and biologist, July 1975, *Obit* Feb 1994

Thomas, William Sturgis, *Obit* Feb 1942

Thorek, Max, Jan 1951, *Obit* Mar 1960

Thorkelson, Jacob, *Obit* Jan 1946

Torrey, E. Fuller, psychiatrist, July 1998

Trask, James D., American pediatrician, *Obit* July 1942

Travell, Janet, physician, Yrbk 1961, *Obit* Oct 1997

Trehan, Naresh, Indian cardiologist, Jan 2003

Tshabalala-Msimang, Manto, South African public health official, Jan 2007, *Obit* Yrbk 2010

Ulianov, Dmitrii, *Obit* Sept 1943

Veil, Simone, French judge and cabinet member, May 1980

Vejjabul, Pierra, Mar 1964

Velikovsky, Immanuel, May 1957, *Obit* Jan 1980

Verghese, Abraham, American physician and novelist, Nov 2011

Volkow, Nora D., American neuroscientist, Oct 2011

Voronoff, Serge, Jan 1941, *Obit* Oct 1951

Wadhams, Robert Pelton, *Obit* Feb 1941

Wagner-Jauregg, Julius, Austrian psychiatrist, *Obit* Nov 1940

Walsh, James Joseph, *Obit* Apr 1942

Walsh, William B., physician, May 1962, *Obit* Mar 1997

Ward, Donovan F., Mar 1965

Warren, J. Robin, Australian pathologist, Jan 2007

Watkins, Levi, American cardiac surgeon, Mar 2003

Wattleton, Faye, American nurse and birth control advocate, Jan 1990

Weil, Andrew, American physician and healer, Aug 1996

Weinberger, Caspar W., American Secretary of defense, June 1973, *Obit* July 2006

Wells, H. Gideon, American pathologist, *Obit* June 1943

Wenckebach, Karel Friedrich, Dutch cardiologist, *Obit* Yrbk 1940

Wexler, Nancy S., American psychologist and neurologist, Aug 1994

White, Paul Dudley, American cardiologist, Yrbk 1955, *Obit* Yrbk 1973

Whitehouse, Harold Beckwith, *Obit* Sept 1943

Wick, Frances G., *Obit* Aug 1941

Wiener, Alexander S., physician and hematologist, May 1947, *Obit* Feb 1977

Wilbur, Bernice M., Sept 1943

Wilbur, Dwight Locke, medical association official and gastroenterologist, July 1969, *Obit* May 1997

Wilbur, Ray Lyman, Nov 1947, *Obit* Sept 1949

Wile, Ira S., *Obit* Nov 1943

Wilgus, Sidney Dean, *Obit* Mar 1940

Wilkins, Robert W., American physician, July 1958, *Obit* Yrbk 2003

Williams, Edwin G., May 1950

Williams, William Robert, *Obit* Jan 1941

Wood, Fiona M., Australian plastic surgeon, Jan 2007

Work, Hubert, physician and secretary of the interior, *Obit* Feb 1943

Wright, Irving S., professor of medicine, Oct 1968, *Obit* Mar 1998

Wright, Jane Cooke, American physician, May 1968, *Obit* Yrbk 2013

Wynder, Ernst L., American oncologist and foundation official, Nov 1974, *Obit* Sept 1999

Yang, You Chan, Feb 1953

Yegorov, Boris, Soviet astronaut and physician, Mar 1968, *Obit* Nov 1994

Young, Hugh, American surgeon and urologist, *Obit* Sept 1945

Zerhouni, Elias A., Algerian-American radiologist and public health official, Oct 2003

Zilboorg, Gregory, psychiatrist, Sept 1941, *Obit* Nov 1959

Zubrod, Charles Gordon, oncologist, Jan 1969, *Obit* July 1999

Health teachers

Frank, Mary Hughes, Jan 1958

Heavy metal musicians

Allen, Rick, English drummer, Jan 2003

Campbell, Vivian, English guitarist and singer, Jan 2003

Collen, Phil, English guitarist and singer, Jan 2003

Elliott, Joe, English singer, Jan 2003

Johnson, Brian, English singer, Mar 2005

Kruspe, Richard Z., German guitarist, Jan 2007

Landers, Paul H., German guitarist, Jan 2007

Lindemann, Till, German singer, Jan 2007

Lorenz, Christian, German keyboardist, Jan 2007

Riedel, Oliver, German bassist, Jan 2007

Rudd, Phil, Australian drummer, Mar 2005

Savage, Rick, English bassist and singer, Jan 2003
Schneider, Christoph, German drummer, Jan 2007
Williams, Cliff, English bassist, Mar 2005
Young, Angus, Scottish guitarist, Mar 2005
Young, Malcolm, Scottish guitarist, Mar 2005

Hebraists

Katsh, Abraham Isaac, Hebraist, Mar 1962, *Obit* Oct 1998

Hematologists

Wiener, Alexander S., physician and hematologist, May 1947, *Obit* Feb 1977

Heptathletes

Lewis, Denise, British heptathlete, Jan 2004

High jumpers

Brumel, Valerii, Russian high jumper, Apr 1963, *Obit* June 2003
Thomas, John, high jumper, July 1960, *Obit* Yrbk 2013
Zaharias, Babe Didrikson, American track athlete and golfer, Apr 1947, *Obit* Yrbk 1956

High school teachers

Gleason, Clarence Willard, American classicist, *Obit* Yrbk 1942

Hindu leaders

Ammachi, Indian Hindu mystic, Jan 2003
Chinmoy, Sri, Indian guru, Apr 1976, *Obit* Yrbk 2008
Choudhury, Bikram, Indian yogi, Jan 2004
Iyengar, B. K. S., Indian yogi, June 2007
Mahesh Yogi, Indian yogi, Yrbk 1972, *Obit* Yrbk 2008

Historians

Adams, James Truslow, historian, Nov 1941, *Obit* July 1949

Albright, William Foxwell, American archaeologist and biblical scholar, Sept 1955
Allegro, John Marco, British paleographer and philologist, Yrbk 1970, *Obit* Apr 1988
Amsden, Charles Avery, American archaeologist, *Obit* Apr 1941
Andrews, Charles McLean, American historian, *Obit* Oct 1943
Antall, Jozsef, Hungarian prime minister, Sept 1990, *Obit* Feb 1994
Arciniegas, German, Colombian historian, May 1954, *Obit* June 2000
Arnow, Harriette Louisa Simpson, American novelist and historian, Yrbk 1954, *Obit* May 1986
Baldwin, Hanson Weightman, journalist and military historian, Aug 1942, *Obit* Jan 1992
Barr, Alfred Hamilton, American museum director, Jan 1961, *Obit* Oct 1981
Baxter, James Phinney, American historian, July 1947, *Obit* Aug 1975
Bazin, Germain, French art historian and museum curator, Jan 1959, *Obit* July 1990
Bemis, Samuel Flagg, historian, June 1950, *Obit* Nov 1973
Bennett, Lerone, American magazine editor and historian, Jan 2001
Bertrand, Louis, French novelist and historian, *Obit* Feb 1942
Binkley, Robert Cedric, American historian, *Obit* May 1940
Bird, Will R., Canadian historian and short story writer, Sept 1954
Bonham, Milledge Louis, American historian, *Obit* Mar 1941
Bonsal, Stephen, journalist, historian and biographer, Aug 1945, *Obit* July 1951
Boorstin, Daniel J., American historian and Librarian of Congress, Sept 1968, Jan 1984, *Obit* Yrbk 2004
Bowman, George Ernest, American historian, *Obit* Nov 1941

Boyd, Julian P., historian and librarian, June 1976, *Obit* Aug 1980
Braudel, Fernand, French historian, Apr 1985, *Obit* Jan 1986
Breslin, Howard, Yrbk 1958, *Obit* July 1964
Brigham, Clarence Saunders, librarian, July 1959, *Obit* Oct 1963
Brogan, Denis William, Scottish political scientist and historian, Yrbk 1947, *Obit* Feb 1974
Brookner, Anita, English novelist and art historian, Feb 1989
Brown, Dee Alexander, American historian and novelist, Aug 1979, *Obit* Mar 2003
Brynner, Rock, American historian and novelist, Mar 2005
Buck, Solon Justus, historian and archivist, May 1947, *Obit* July 1962
Burdick, Usher L., American congressman, Apr 1952, *Obit* Nov 1960
Burke, James, British science historian, Jan 2005
Cam, Helen Maud, English medievalist, Sept 1948, *Obit* Apr 1968
Catton, Bruce, journalist and author, Yrbk 1954, *Obit* Oct 1978
Champion, Pierre, *Obit* Aug 1942
Charques, Dorothy, Yrbk 1958
Cock, Guillermo A., Peruvian archaeologist, Jan 2007
Collingwood, R. G., British philosopher and historian, *Obit* Mar 1943
Commager, Henry Steele, historian, Jan 1946, *Obit* May 1998
Cox, Margaret, British archaeologist, Jan 2006
Croce, Benedetto, Italian philosopher, historian and critic, Jan 1944, *Obit* Jan 1953
Crownfield, Gertrude, *Obit* July 1945
Dabney, Virginius, American newspaper editor and historian, Sept 1948, *Obit* Mar 1996
Dallek, Robert, American historian, Sept 2007

Davis-Kimball, Jeannine, American archaeologist, Feb 2006

De Branges, Louis, American mathematician, Nov 2005

De Voto, Bernard Augustine, American historian, literary critic and novelist, Sept 1943, *Obit* Jan 1956

Deloria, Vine, Native American leader, historian and philosopher, Sept 1974, *Obit* Yrbk 2006

Dickson, Marguerite, Yrbk 1952, *Obit* Jan 1954

Dodd, William Edward, historian and diplomat, *Obit* Mar 1940

Dorpfeld, Wilhelm, German archaeologist, *Obit* Jan 1940

Downes, Olin, music critic and historian, Mar 1943, *Obit* Oct 1955

Downey, Fairfax, author and historian, Yrbk 1949, *Obit* Aug 1990

Durant, William James, American historian, Sept 1964, *Obit* Jan 1982

El Mallakh, Kamal, Egyptian archaeologist, Oct 1954, *Obit* Jan 1988

Eliade, Mircea, Romanian religion historian and novelist, Nov 1985, *Obit* June 1986

Evans, Arthur John, British archaeologist, *Obit* Sept 1941

Feis, Herbert, historian, Oct 1961, *Obit* May 1972

Ferguson, Niall, Scottish historian, July 2012

Ferrero, Guglielmo, Italian historian and author, *Obit* Sept 1942

Finley, David E., American museum administrator and historic preservationist, Feb 1951, *Obit* Apr 1977

Fischer, Louis, journalist and historian, May 1940, *Obit* Mar 1970

Fisher, Clarence S., *Obit* Sept 1941

Florinsky, Michael T., Russian historian, Oct 1941, *Obit* Jan 1982

Foner, Eric, American historian, Aug 2004

Foote, Shelby, American novelist and historian, Apr 1991, *Obit* Yrbk 2005

Forsyth, W. D., Apr 1952

Fraser, Antonia, English biographer, historian and novelist, Oct 1974

Fraser, Hugh Russell, June 1943

Freedley, George, American theater historian and librarian, Sept 1947, *Obit* Nov 1967

Fuller, George Washington, *Obit* Yrbk 1940

Gilbert, Martin, English historian, Feb 1991

Goddio, Franck, French marine archaeologist, Jan 2002

Grant, Elihu, *Obit* Yrbk 1942

Green, Constance McLaughlin, historian, Oct 1963

Halberstam, David, American journalist, Apr 1973, *Obit* July 2007

Haley, Alex, American biographer, historian and journalist, Jan 1977, *Obit* Mar 1992

Hall, Josef Washington, journalist, historian and radio commentator, Yrbk 1944, *Obit* Jan 1961

Harris, James Rendel, *Obit* Apr 1941

Hayes, Carlton Joseph Huntley, historian and diplomat, June 1942, *Obit* Nov 1964

Hazen, Charles D., *Obit* Nov 1941

Hertz, Emanuel, *Obit* July 1940

Himmelfarb, Gertrude, historian, May 1985

Hobsbawm, E. J., British historian, Jan 2003, *Obit* Yrbk 2012

Hofstadter, Richard, American historian, Oct 1956, *Obit* Yrbk 1970

Holmes, Jesse Herman, *Obit* July 1942

Horne, Charles F., *Obit* Nov 1942

Hours, Madeleine, Apr 1961

Inose, Naoki, Japanese historian, Jan 2002

Jensen, Oliver, American magazine editor and historian, May 1945, *Obit* Yrbk 2005

Johnson, Howard A., Apr 1964, *Obit* Sept 1974

Johnson, Paul, English journalist and historian, Sept 1994

Johnson, Walter, American historian, Apr 1957, *Obit* Sept 1985

Jones, Rufus Matthew, American Quaker leader, Oct 1941, *Obit* Sept 1948

Kagan, Frederick W., American military historian, July 2007

Kane, Harnett T., journalist, historian and author, Yrbk 1947, *Obit* Yrbk 1984

Kane, Joseph Nathan, American historian, Nov 1985, *Obit* Nov 2002

Keegan, John, English military historian and journalist, Oct 1989, *Obit* Yrbk 2012

Keith, Harold, American children's author, Yrbk 1958

Kennedy, Paul M., British historian, Oct 1993

Kolodin, Irving, music critic, July 1947, *Obit* June 1988

Krens, Thomas, American museum director, Apr 1989

Le Roy Ladurie, Emmanuel, French historian, July 1984

Lee, Sherman E., American art historian and museum director, June 1974, *Obit* Yrbk 2008

Liddell Hart, Basil Henry, British military historian, Jan 1940, *Obit* Mar 1970

Lord, Walter, American historian, Oct 1972, *Obit* Yrbk 2002

Love, Iris, archaeologist, Aug 1982

MacMillan, Margaret, Canadian historian, Jan 2007

Macdonald, George, classicist and archaeologist, *Obit* Sept 1940

Mangione, Jerre, American memoirist, novelist and historian, Mar 1943, *Obit* Nov 1998

Marcus, Jacob Rader, rabbi and historian, May 1960, *Obit* Jan 1996

Marshall, S. L. A., Nov 1953, *Obit* Mar 1978

Mattingly, Garrett, historian, Nov 1960, *Obit* Feb 1963

Meadowcroft, Enid La Monte, Yrbk 1949

Medvedev, Roy Aleksandrovich, Russian educator and historian, Sept 1984

Messer, Thomas M., museum director and art historian, Nov 1961, *Obit* Yrbk 2013

Morison, Samuel Eliot, American naval historian, Oct 1951, Sept 1962, *Obit* July 1976

Mott, Frank Luther, journalist and historian, Oct 1941, *Obit* Yrbk 1964

Mowat, R. B., *Obit* Nov 1941

Murray, Albert, American novelist, essayist and music historian, May 1994, *Obit* Yrbk 2013

Myers, Gustavus, journalist and historian, *Obit* Jan 1943

Nevins, Allan, historian, Oct 1968, *Obit* Apr 1971

Nichols, Roy Franklin, historian, July 1949, *Obit* Mar 1973

Noel Hume, Ivor, English archaeologist, Nov 1997

Nye, Russel Blaine, historian, July 1945, *Obit* Nov 1993

Odell, George Clinton Densmore, Yrbk 1944, *Obit* Yrbk 1949

Orton, Helen Fuller, Jan 1941, *Obit* Apr 1955

Pares, Bernard, English historian, Jan 1946, *Obit* May 1949

Perkins, Dexter, historian and educator, Jan 1958, *Obit* July 1984

Petrie, W. M. Flinders, English archaeologist, *Obit* Sept 1942

Pick, Behrendt, *Obit* July 1940

Piotrovskii, Mikhail Borisovich, Russian museum director, Jan 2003

Potok, Chaim, American novelist and historian, May 1983, *Obit* Yrbk 2002

Powell, Eve Troutt, American historian, May 2004

Pratt, Fletcher, journalist, historian and author, May 1942, *Obit* Sept 1956

Quidde, Ludwig, German historian and pacifist, *Obit* Apr 1941

Ravitch, Diane, American educator and historian, Nov 2010

Redway, Jacques W., *Obit* Jan 1943

Reich, Nathaniel Julius, *Obit* Nov 1943

Reinhard, Johan, archaeologist, Aug 1999

Reisner, George Andrew, American Egyptologist, *Obit* July 1942

Richter, George Martin, *Obit* July 1942

Robins, Edward, *Obit* July 1943

Romer, John, British Egyptologist, July 2003

Rosenberg, Arthur, *Obit* Mar 1943

Roszak, Theodore, American historian, Apr 1982, *Obit* Yrbk 2011

Rowse, A. L., English historian and biographer, July 1979, *Obit* Jan 1998

Sandburg, Carl, American poet, biographer and historian, June 1940, Yrbk 1963, *Obit* Oct 1967

Schama, Simon, British historian, Nov 1991

Schmitt, Bernadotte Everly, historian, Yrbk 1942, *Obit* May 1969

Schoonover, Lawrence L., Yrbk 1957, *Obit* Mar 1980

Sereny, Gitta, Hungarian-British journalist, historian and biographer, Jan 2007

Seymour, Flora Warren, historian and author, June 1942

Shambaugh, Benjamin Franklin, *Obit* May 1940

Shear, T. Leslie, *Obit* Aug 1945

Sherrod, Robert Lee, journalist, June 1944, Yrbk 1962, *Obit* May 1994

Sigerist, Henry Ernest, Swiss medical historian, Sept 1940, *Obit* June 1957

Simon, Edith, Yrbk 1954

Skinner, Quentin, British historian, Jan 2007

Smith, Cyril Stanley, science historian, July 1948, *Obit* Oct 1992

Soares, Mario, Portuguese prime minister, Oct 1975

Sulloway, Frank J., science historian, Sept 1997

Tarbell, Ida M., American journalist, biographer and historian, *Obit* Feb 1944

Taylor, A. J. P., British historian, Nov 1983, *Obit* Nov 1990

Taylor, Henry O., *Obit* June 1941

Tebbel, John William, American historian and journalist, Yrbk 1953, *Obit* Mar 2005

Thompson, James Westfall, *Obit* Yrbk 1941

Thompson, R. Campbell, *Obit* July 1941

Toynbee, Arnold Joseph, British historian, July 1947, *Obit* Jan 1976

Tuchman, Barbara Wertheim, American historian, Yrbk 1963, *Obit* Mar 1989

Tudjman, Franjo, Croatian president, Sept 1997, *Obit* May 2000

Utley, Freda, Yrbk 1958, *Obit* Mar 1978

Varnedoe, Kirk, American museum curator and art historian, Feb 1991, *Obit* Yrbk 2003

Viereck, Peter, American poet and historian, Apr 1943, *Obit* Yrbk 2006

Walsh, James Joseph, *Obit* Apr 1942

Ward, Christopher L., *Obit* Apr 1943

Watkins, Shirley, Yrbk 1958

Wedgwood, C. V., English historian, Jan 1957, *Obit* May 1997

Wells, H. G., English science fiction novelist, *Obit* Sept 1946

Wheeler, Robert Eric Mortimer, English archaeologist, Mar 1956, *Obit* Sept 1976

White, Theodore H., American journalist, Apr 1955, Apr 1976, *Obit* July 1986

Whitehill, Walter Muir, June 1960, *Obit* May 1978

Williams, Eric Eustace, Trinidadian prime minister, Feb 1966, *Obit* May 1981

Willis, Deborah, American photography historian and museum curator, Sept 2004

Willison, George Findlay, historian, Jan 1946

Woodham Smith, Cecil Blanche Fitz Gerald, English historian, Yrbk 1955, *Obit* Mar 1977

Woodson, Carter Godwin, American historian, Feb 1944, *Obit* Yrbk 1984

Woodward, C. Vann, American historian, May 1986, *Obit* June 2000

Woolley, Leonard, English archaeologist, Yrbk 1954, *Obit* Apr 1960

Wright, Louis B., historian and librarian, Nov 1950, *Obit* June 1984

Hobbyists

Chamberlain, Paul M., *Obit* July 1940

Hockey coaches

Bowman, Scotty, Canadian hockey coach, Jan 1999

Cherry, Don, Canadian hockey coach and sportscaster, Jan 2004

Francis, Emile, Apr 1968

Giacomin, Eddie, Canadian hockey player, Mar 1968

Gretzky, Wayne, Canadian hockey player and coach, Feb 1982

Keenan, Mike, hockey coach, Mar 1996

Hockey executives

Burke, Brian, American hockey executive, Mar 2013

Hockey players

Bathgate, Andy, Canadian hockey player, Feb 1964

Bossy, Mike, Canadian hockey player, June 1981

Brodeur, Martin, Canadian hockey player, Nov 2002

Datsyuk, Pavel, Russian hockey player, Nov 2012

Esposito, Phil, Canadian hockey player, May 1973

Forsberg, Peter, Swedish hockey player, Nov 2005

Granato, Cammi, American hockey player, Apr 1998

Hasek, Dominik, Czech hockey player, May 1998

Hull, Bobby, Canadian hockey player, Oct 1966

Hull, Brett, Canadian hockey player, Feb 1992

Iginla, Jarome, Canadian hockey player, Jan 2004

Jagr, Jaromir, Czech hockey player, Apr 1997

Kane, Patrick, American hockey player, Feb 2011

Kovalchuk, Ilya, Russian hockey player, Mar 2007

Lafleur, Guy, Canadian hockey player, Mar 1980

Lemieux, Mario, Canadian hockey player, Aug 1988

Lindros, Eric, Canadian hockey player, Apr 1998

Lundqvist, Henrik, Swedish hockey player, Jan 2006

Messier, Mark, Canadian hockey player, July 1995

Mikita, Stan, American hockey player, Oct 1970

Orr, Bobby, Canadian hockey player, Nov 1969

Ovechkin, Alexander, Russian hockey player, June 2008

Park, Brad, Canadian hockey player, Nov 1976

Potvin, Denis, American hockey player, Oct 1986

Rheaume, Manon, Canadian hockey player, Nov 2012

Richard, Maurice, Canadian hockey player, Yrbk 1958, *Obit* Yrbk 2000

Roy, Patrick, Canadian hockey player, Nov 1999

Sanderson, Derek, Canadian hockey player and investment manager, Apr 1975

St. Louis, Martin, Canadian hockey player, Feb 2007

Stamkos, Steven, Canadian hockey player, Apr 2013

Thomas, Tim, American hockey player, Oct 2012

Trottier, Bryan, Canadian hockey player, June 1985

Villemure, Gilles, Apr 1974

Wickenheiser, Hayley, Canadian hockey player, Jan 2003

Yashin, Alexei, Russian hockey player, Jan 2003

Holocaust survivors

Lantos, Tom, American congressman, July 2007, *Obit* May 2008

Home economists

Barber, Mary I., American dietician and home economist, July 1941, *Obit* Apr 1963

Boyd-Orr, John Boyd Orr, Scottish agriculturist, June 1946, *Obit* Sept 1971

Brody, Jane E., American columnist and nutritionist, Feb 1986

Davis, Adelle, nutritionist, Jan 1973, *Obit* July 1974

Husted, Marjorie Child, American home economist, June 1949, *Obit* Feb 1987

King, Charles Glen, biochemist and nutritionist, Yrbk 1967, *Obit* Mar 1988

Metzelthin, Pearl V., Nov 1942, *Obit* Jan 1948

Omichinski, Linda, Canadian dietician, Jan 2004

Pattee, Alida Frances, *Obit* May 1942

Sebrell, W. H., nutritionist, May 1951, *Obit* Nov 1992

Stiebeling, Hazel K., American nutritionist, Apr 1950

Williams, Roger J., biochemist and nutritionist, July 1957, *Obit* Apr 1988

Hospital administrators

Schweitzer, Albert, German physician, missionary and theologian, Jan 1948, July 1965

Hotel employees

Rusesabagina, Paul, Rwandan hotel manager and humanitarian, May 2005

Townsend, Willard S., American railroad porter and labor leader, Jan 1948

Hotel executives

Binns, Joseph Patterson, American hotel executive, June 1954, *Obit* Mar 1981

Grossinger, Jennie, American resort owner, Oct 1956, *Obit* Jan 1973

Hilton, Conrad N., American hotel executive, Yrbk 1949, *Obit* Mar 1979

Ho, Stanley, Chinese gambling casino owner, Jan 2003

Marriott, J. Willard, American hotel executive, June 1972, *Obit* Oct 1985

Nelson, Marilyn Carlson, American hotel and restaurant industry executive, Oct 2004

Wilson, Kemmons, American hotel chain executive, Sept 1973, *Obit* Yrbk 2003

Household products industry executives

Hirst, Hugo, English manufacturing executive, Nov 1941, *Obit* Mar 1943

Human resource managers

Stockberger, Warner W., government official and personnel director, Aug 1941

Human rights activists

Ibrahim, Hauwa, Nigerian lawyer and human rights activist, Jan 2004

Karman, Tawakel, Mar 2013

Khan, Irene, Bangladeshi human rights activist, Jan 2002

Mam, Somaly, Cambodian social worker, June 2009

Mufti, Hania, Jordanian human rights activist, Jan 2005

Prendergast, John, American human rights activist, Jan 2012

Romero, Anthony, American lawyer and civil rights activist, July 2002

Stevenson, Bryan, lawyer and human rights activist, Mar 1996

Takirambudde, Peter, Ugandan human rights activist, Jan 2005

Tethong, Lhadon, Tibetan-Canadian human rights activist, Sept 2008

Verveer, Melanne, Mar 2013

Welsh, Herbert, *Obit* Sept 1941

Wu, Harry, Chinese-American human rights activist, Feb 1995

Humanitarians

Aronson, Jane, American pediatrician, Feb 2011

Boardman, Mabel Thorp, Red Cross official, Aug 1944, *Obit* Apr 1946

Bronowski, Jacob, British mathematician, Sept 1958, *Obit* Oct 1974

Bryce, Elizabeth Marion, *Obit* Jan 1940

Cherne, Leo, economist and humanitarian, Yrbk 1940, *Obit* Mar 1999

Dole, Elizabeth Hanford, American senator, June 1983, Jan 1997

Flanagan, Edward Joseph, American priest and youth leader, Sept 1941, *Obit* June 1948

Geldof, Bob, Irish rock musician and humanitarian, Mar 1986

Gmeiner, Hermann, Austrian social worker, May 1963, *Obit* June 1986

Hale, Clara, American child benefactor, July 1985, *Obit* Feb 1993

Mortenson, Greg, American mountaineer and humanitarian, Sept 2009

Pierre, French abbot, Nov 1955

Ritter, Bruce, priest and child care leader, June 1983, *Obit* Feb 2000

Rusesabagina, Paul, Rwandan hotel manager and humanitarian, May 2005

Shriver, Eunice Kennedy, American social activist, July 1996, *Obit* Yrbk 2009

Sinclair, Cameron, British architect and housing organization official, Apr 2008

Humorists

Adams, Douglas, English science fiction writer and satirist, July 1993, *Obit* Sept 2001

Adams, Franklin P., humorist, July 1941, *Obit* May 1960

Addams, Charles, American cartoonist, Jan 1954, *Obit* Nov 1988

Ade, George, American humorist, *Obit* July 1944

Alajalov, Constantin, American painter, illustrator and cartoonist, Jan 1942, *Obit* Jan 1988

Amend, Bill, American cartoonist, Apr 2003

Ames, Jonathan, American novelist, humorist and columnist, Oct 2007

Arellano, Gustavo, American journalist, Aug 2010

Arno, Peter, cartoonist, Aug 1942, *Obit* Apr 1968

Baker, George, American cartoonist, Nov 1944, *Obit* Aug 1975

Barry, Dave, American humorist, May 1998

Bell, Steve, British political cartoonist, Jan 2003

Block, Herbert, American editorial cartoonist, July 1954, *Obit* Jan 2002

Bombeck, Erma, American humorist, Feb 1979, *Obit* June 1996

Brustlein, Daniel, American painter, Sept 1941

Buchwald, Art, American humorist, Jan 1960, *Obit* May 2007

Buckley, Christopher Taylor, American novelist, humorist and editor, Apr 1997

Bulgakov, Mikhail Afanas'evich, Russian novelist and dramatist, *Obit* Mar 1940

Bull, Johan, *Obit* Oct 1945

Campbell, E. Simms, Jan 1941, *Obit* Mar 1971

Caniff, Milton Arthur, cartoonist, Jan 1944, *Obit* May 1988

Chast, Roz, American cartoonist, July 1997

Cobb, Irvin S., American humorist, *Obit* Apr 1944

Condon, Frank, *Obit* Feb 1941

Covarrubias, Miguel, Mexican painter and caricaturist, July 1940, *Obit* Apr 1957

Crumb, R., American cartoonist, Apr 1995

Darrow, Whitney, cartoonist, Yrbk 1958, *Obit* Oct 1999

De Beck, Billy, cartoonist, *Obit* Jan 1943

De Vries, Peter, American novelist, Yrbk 1959, *Obit* Jan 1994

DeCarlo, Dan, American comic book artist, Aug 2001, *Obit* Mar 2002

Dennis, Patrick, American novelist, May 1959, *Obit* Feb 1977

Duffy, Edmund, cartoonist, Jan 1940, *Obit* Nov 1962

Feininger, Lyonel, German painter and cartoonist, July 1955, *Obit* Mar 1956

Fishback, Margaret, copywriter and humorist, Apr 1941, *Obit* Nov 1985

Fitzpatrick, Daniel Robert, cartoonist, July 1941, *Obit* July 1969

Flagg, James Montgomery, painter and illustrator, Nov 1940, *Obit* Sept 1960

Frazier, Ian, American essayist and humorist, Aug 1996

Glintenkamp, H., *Obit* May 1946

Goldberg, Rube, cartoonist, Sept 1948, *Obit* Jan 1971

Gould, Chester, American cartoonist, Sept 1971, *Obit* July 1985

Gropper, William, American cartoonist, painter and illustrator, Mar 1940, *Obit* Mar 1977

Grosz, George, American painter and cartoonist, Apr 1942, *Obit* Oct 1959

Guest, Edgar A., American newspaper columnist, Sept 1941, *Obit* Nov 1959

Guisewite, Cathy, cartoonist, Feb 1989

Halsey, Margaret, author, Nov 1944, *Obit* Apr 1997

Harding, Nelson, *Obit* Feb 1945

Hargrove, Marion, American novelist and humorist, June 1946, *Obit* Yrbk 2004

Hewlett, Jamie, English illustrator and cartoonist, Jan 2007

Higgins, Jack, American editorial cartoonist, Feb 2007

Hirschfeld, Al, American caricaturist, Jan 1971, *Obit* July 2003

Horsey, David, American political cartoonist, Sept 2008

Jaffee, Al, American cartoonist and illustrator, July 2008

Johnston, Lynn, Canadian cartoonist, Feb 1998

Katchor, Ben, American cartoonist, May 2000

Kelly, Walt, American cartoonist, Oct 1956, *Obit* Yrbk 1973

Kerr, Jean, American humorist and dramatist, July 1958, *Obit* May 2003

Ketcham, Hank, American cartoonist, Jan 1956, *Obit* Sept 2001

Kirby, Rollin, Yrbk 1944, *Obit* June 1952

Kuekes, Edward D., cartoonist, Mar 1954, *Obit* Mar 1987

Lao She, Chinese novelist and short story writer, Oct 1945

Larson, Gary, American cartoonist, Feb 1991

Laski, Marghanita, English author and critic, Yrbk 1951, *Obit* Apr 1988

Lebowitz, Fran, humorist, Mar 1982

Lehrer, Tom, songwriter, humorist and mathematician, July 1982

Levine, David, American caricaturist, Feb 1973, *Obit* Yrbk 2010

Lincoln, Joseph C., American short story writer, novelist and poet, *Obit* Apr 1944

Low, David, New Zealand cartoonist, Jan 1940, *Obit* Nov 1963

Luckovich, Mike, American editorial cartoonist, Jan 2005

Mannes, Marya, author, Apr 1959

Manning, Reg, June 1951

Matthews, T. S., American novelist and journalist, Apr 1950, *Obit* Mar 1991

Mauldin, Bill, American cartoonist, May 1945, Nov 1964, *Obit* July 2003

Mayle, Peter, English humorist, Oct 1992

McFarlane, Todd, Canadian cartoonist, Feb 1999

McInerney, Jay, American novelist, Nov 1987

McKenney, Ruth, author, Aug 1942, *Obit* Oct 1972

Messick, Dale, American cartoonist, July 1961, *Obit* Yrbk 2005

Millionaire, Tony, American cartoonist and illustrator, July 2005

Miranda, Mario de, Indian cartoonist and illustrator, Jan 2003

Nash, Ogden, American poet, Apr 1941, *Obit* July 1971

Oliphant, Patrick, Australian-American cartoonist, July 1991

Osborn, Robert, caricaturist, June 1959, *Obit* Feb 1995

Packer, Fred L., July 1952, *Obit* Feb 1957

Papashvily, George, Georgian-American humorist and essayist, Mar 1945, *Obit* May 1978

Papashvily, Helen Waite, humorist and essayist, Mar 1945

Partridge, Bernard, *Obit* Sept 1945

Pease, Lute, political cartoonist and painter, July 1949, *Obit* Nov 1963

Perelman, S. J., humorist, Mar 1971, *Obit* Jan 1980

Petrov, Evgenii, Russian humorist, *Obit* Aug 1942

Rall, Ted, American editorial cartoonist, May 2002

Rea, Gardner, May 1946, *Obit* Feb 1967

Rooney, Andrew A., American journalist and humorist, July 1982, *Obit* Yrbk 2012

Rosten, Leo, American economist and humorist, Oct 1942, *Obit* Apr 1997

Runyon, Damon, American journalist and short story writer, Nov 1942, *Obit* Jan 1947

Russell, Anna, Canadian singer and parodist, Apr 1954, *Obit* Yrbk 2007

Salvador Lavado, Joaquin, Argentine cartoonist, Jan 2004

Schickele, Peter, American composer, May 1979

Schulz, Charles M., American cartoonist, Yrbk 1960, *Obit* Apr 2000

Scott, Henry L., June 1949

Sedaris, David, American humorist, July 1997

Sempe, French cartoonist and illustrator, Jan 2007

Shulman, Max, humorist, Oct 1959, *Obit* Oct 1988

Smith, Harry Allen, American humorist, May 1942, *Obit* May 1976

Soglow, Otto, cartoonist, Sept 1940, *Obit* May 1975

Sorel, Edward, cartoonist, Mar 1994

Steadman, Ralph, English illustrator, May 1999

Steinberg, Saul, Romanian-American illustrator and cartoonist, Mar 1957, *Obit* July 1999

Stewart, Donald Ogden, screenwriter, dramatist and humorist, July 1941, *Obit* Sept 1980

Sykes, Charles H., *Obit* Feb 1943

Szyk, Arthur, Polish cartoonist, illustrator and miniaturist, Nov 1946, *Obit* Oct 1951

Taylor, Richard, June 1941, *Obit* July 1970

Thompson, Hunter S., American journalist, Mar 1981, *Obit* Yrbk 2005

Toles, Tom, American cartoonist, Nov 2002

Tomorrow, Tom, American political cartoonist, Apr 2000

Trillin, Calvin, American humorist, novelist and essayist, June 1990

Uderzo, French cartoonist, Jan 2006

Vip, cartoonist, July 1946, *Obit* Oct 1984

Walker, Mort, American cartoonist, Feb 2002

Webster, H. T., cartoonist, Mar 1945, *Obit* Nov 1952

Williams, Gluyas, cartoonist, June 1946, *Obit* Apr 1982

Wodehouse, P. G., English novelist, short story writer and dramatist, Nov 1971, *Obit* Apr 1975

Hunters

Buck, Frank, big game hunter, June 1943, *Obit* Apr 1950

Corbett, Jim, British game hunter, May 1946, *Obit* June 1955

Nugent, Ted, American rock guitarist, Apr 2005

White, Stewart Edward, author and hunter, *Obit* Nov 1946

Hurdlers

Devers, Gail, American runner and hurdler, July 1996

Moses, Edwin, American hurdler, Nov 1986

Ice skaters

Ahn, Hyun-Soo, Korean speed skater, Jan 2006

Albright, Tenley, American figure skater and surgeon, Sept 1956

Arakawa, Shizuka, Japanese figure skater, Jan 2006

Atwood, Donna, American figure skater, May 1954

Blair, Bonnie, American speed skater, July 1992

Boitano, Brian, American figure skater, Nov 1989

Bonaly, Surya, French figure skater, Jan 2002

Button, Dick, American figure skater and sportscaster, Mar 1949

Cohen, Sasha, American figure skater, Feb 2006

Curry, John, English figure skater, July 1979, *Obit* June 1994

Davis, Shani, American speed skater, May 2006

Fabris, Enrico, Italian speed skater, Jan 2006

Fleming, Peggy, American figure skater, July 1968

Hamill, Dorothy, American figure skater, June 1976

Hamilton, Scott, American figure skater, Apr 1985

Heiden, Eric, American speed skater and bicyclist, June 1980

Heiss, Carol, American figure skater, Oct 1959

Jansen, Dan, American speed skater, Sept 1994

Jenkins, Hayes Alan, American figure skater and lawyer, May 1956

Joubert, Brian, French figure skater, Jan 2007

Lipinski, Tara, American figure skater, Apr 1998

Ohno, Apolo, American speed skater, Feb 2006

Plushenko, Evgeni, Russian figure skater, Jan 2007

Scott, Barbara Ann, Canadian figure skater, July 1948, *Obit* Yrbk 2012

Trenkler, Freddie, American figure skater, June 1971, *Obit* Yrbk 2001

Weir, Johnny, American figure skater, Apr 2010

Witt, Katarina, German figure skater, July 1988

Yagudin, Aleksei, Russian figure skater, Feb 2004

Yamaguchi, Kristi, American figure skater, June 1992

Yao Bin, Chinese figure skating coach, Jan 2006

Young, Sheila, American cyclist and speed skater, Jan 1977

Illustrators

Barclay, McClelland, American illustrator, Sept 1940, *Obit* Yrbk 1946

Benton, Thomas Hart, American painter, Oct 1940, *Obit* Mar 1975

Blanding, Don, American poet and illustrator, Jan 1957

Chapin, James, American painter, Mar 1940, *Obit* Sept 1975

Charlot, Jean, American painter and illustrator, Sept 1945, *Obit* Yrbk 1984

Coe, Sue, Anglo-American painter and illustrator, Aug 1997

D'Aulaire, Ingri, author and illustrator, Aug 1940

Dali, Salvador, Spanish painter, Sept 1940, Apr 1951, *Obit* Mar 1989

Davis, Stuart, American painter, engraver and illustrator, Aug 1940, July 1964

Dine, Jim, American painter, June 1969

Epstein, Jacob, English sculptor and illustrator, July 1945, *Obit* Nov 1959

Ernst, Jimmy, painter, Mar 1966, *Obit* Apr 1984

Folon, Jean Michel, Belgian painter and illustrator, Feb 1981, *Obit* Yrbk 2006

Frasconi, Antonio, Uruguayan painter and wood engraver, Mar 1972, *Obit* Yrbk 2013

Gibson, Charles Dana, American illustrator and painter, *Obit* Feb 1945

Gordon, Jan, English author and illustrator, *Obit* Mar 1944

Groth, John, illustrator and painter, Feb 1943, *Obit* Aug 1988

Hammond, Aubrey, English illustrator, *Obit* Apr 1940

Hurd, Peter, American painter, Oct 1957, *Obit* Sept 1984

Kabakov, Ilya, Russian painter and illustrator, Apr 1998

Kent, Rockwell, American painter and travel writer, Nov 1942, *Obit* Apr 1971

Kingman, Dong, American painter and illustrator, Oct 1962, *Obit* Yrbk 2000

Landau, Jacob, illustrator, Yrbk 1965

Lawrence, Jacob, American painter and illustrator, July 1965, Sept 1988, *Obit* Aug 2000

Lee, Doris Emrick, American painter and illustrator, Jan 1954, *Obit* Jan 1986

Leger, Fernand, French painter, Jan 1943, *Obit* Oct 1955

Maillol, Aristide, French sculptor and illustrator, May 1942, *Obit* Nov 1944

Marsh, Reginald, American painter, Sept 1941, *Obit* Sept 1954

McMein, Neysa, illustrator and painter, Feb 1941, *Obit* June 1949

Nash, Paul, English illustrator and painter, *Obit* Sept 1946

Parrish, Maxfield, American illustrator and painter, Nov 1965, *Obit* Apr 1966

Peirce, Waldo, American painter, Yrbk 1944, *Obit* May 1970

Peterson, Roger Tory, American ornithologist and illustrator, Apr 1959, *Obit* Oct 1996

Ray, Satyajit, Indian motion picture director, Mar 1961, *Obit* June 1992

Robinson, William Heath, English illustrator, *Obit* Nov 1944

Rockwell, Norman, American painter, June 1945, *Obit* Jan 1979

Romano, Emanuel, painter and illustrator, Mar 1940, *Obit* Feb 1985

Sarg, Tony, German-American puppeteer and illustrator, *Obit* Apr 1942

Schreiber, Georges, author and illustrator, May 1943

Shahn, Ben, American painter, Yrbk 1954, *Obit* May 1969

Shepard, Ernest H., English painter and illustrator, Yrbk 1963, *Obit* May 1976

Struzan, Drew, American poster artist, Mar 2005

Tan, Shaun, Australian illustrator, Mar 2012

Vertes, Marcel, Hungarian painter and illustrator, Apr 1961, *Obit* Jan 1962

Wyeth, N. C., American painter and illustrator, *Obit* Nov 1945

Immunologists

Dausset, Jean, French immunologist, May 1981, *Obit* Yrbk 2009

Koprowski, Hilary, Mar 1968, *Obit* Yrbk 2013

Matzinger, Polly, American immunologist, Oct 1998

Offit, Paul A., American immunologist, Apr 2009

Perla, David, Mar 1940

Rosenberg, Steven A., American surgeon, Feb 1991

In-line skaters

Rheaume, Manon, Canadian hockey player, Nov 2012

Indexers

Sheppard, Morris, *Obit* June 1941

Indian chiefs

Al-Dari, Harith, Iraqi Islamic cleric and tribal leader, Jan 2007

Al-Glawi, Thami al-Mezouari, Sept 1954, *Obit* Mar 1956

Mankiller, Wilma, Cherokee chief, Nov 1988, *Obit* Yrbk 2010

Seboko, Mosadi, Botswanan tribal chief, Jan 2004

Indian leaders

Banks, Dennis, American Indian leader, June 1992

Begaye, Kelsey, Navajo leader, Jan 2000

Bennett, Robert LaFollette, American lawyer and government official, Sept 1967

Bruce, Louis Rooks, American government official, May 1972, *Obit* July 1989

Deer, Ada, Native American leader and government official, Sept 1994

Hall, Tex G., Native American leader, May 2005

Mankiller, Wilma, Cherokee chief, Nov 1988, *Obit* Yrbk 2010

Quispe Huanca, Felipe, Bolivian Indian leader, Jan 2002

Vargas, Antonio, Ecuadorian Quechua leader, Jan 2004

Industrial designers

Dreyfuss, Henry, American industrial designer, May 1948, Oct 1959, *Obit* Yrbk 1972

Loewy, Raymond Fernand, French-American industrial designer, Mar 1941, June 1953, *Obit* Sept 1986

Noguchi, Isamu, American sculptor, Sept 1943, *Obit* Feb 1989

Pahlmann, William Carroll, American interior and industrial designer, Oct 1964, *Obit* Jan 1988

Teague, Walter Dorwin, American interior designer, May 1942, *Obit* Jan 1961

Wright, Russel, American industrial designer, Sept 1940, Yrbk 1950, *Obit* Mar 1977

Industrial engineers

Cooke, Morris Llewellyn, American industrial engineer and government official, May 1950, *Obit* May 1960

Eger, Ernst, Oct 1942

Garand, John C., American design engineer and inventor, Aug 1945, *Obit* Apr 1974

Kravchenko, Victor, July 1946, *Obit* Mar 1966

Information brokers

Blackwell, Earl, society leader and celebrity information service executive, Nov 1960, *Obit* May 1995

Information professionals

Adams, Randolph Greenfield, librarian, Aug 1943

Adkinson, Burton W., American geographer and librarian, June 1959

Babb, James Tinkham, American librarian, July 1955, *Obit* Oct 1968

Beals, Ralph Albert, librarian, Feb 1947, *Obit* Yrbk 1954

Bettmann, Otto L., archivist, Nov 1961, *Obit* July 1998

Blackwell, Earl, society leader and celebrity information service executive, Nov 1960, *Obit* May 1995

Bliss, Henry Evelyn, librarian, Sept 1953, *Obit* Oct 1955

Bostwick, Arthur Elmore, American librarian, *Obit* Apr 1942

Bradshaw, Lillian Moore, American library director, June 1970

Bray, Robert S., Feb 1966, *Obit* Feb 1975

Brode, Mildred H., Sept 1963

Brown, Alberta L., May 1958

Brown, Charles Harvey, librarian, Aug 1941, *Obit* Mar 1960

Bryan, James E., American library director and consultant, June 1962

Budington, William S., June 1964

Bush, Laura, wife of American president George W. Bush, June 2001

Carlton, W. N. C., *Obit* Mar 1943

Castagna, Edwin, librarian, June 1964

Clapp, Verner W., librarian, Mar 1959, *Obit* Sept 1972

Clift, David Horace, librarian, June 1952, *Obit* Yrbk 1973

Colwell, Eileen, British librarian, July 1963

Cory, John Mackenzie, librarian, Sept 1949, *Obit* May 1988

Culver, Essae Martha, American librarian, Sept 1940

Deane, Sidney N., *Obit* June 1943

Dix, William S., librarian, June 1969, *Obit* Apr 1978

Doms, Keith, June 1971

Downs, Robert B., librarian, Jan 1941, June 1952, *Obit* Apr 1991

Fletcher, Angus, Sept 1946, *Obit* Nov 1960

Flexner, Jennie Maas, librarian, *Obit* Jan 1945

Forsythe, Robert S., *Obit* Aug 1941

Francis, Frank Chalton, British librarian, July 1959, *Obit* Apr 1989

Fraser, Ian Forbes, American library director, June 1954

Freehafer, Edward G., librarian, June 1955, *Obit* Feb 1986

Fuller, George Washington, *Obit* Yrbk 1940

Fuller, Margaret H., American librarian, June 1959

Fyan, Loleta Dawson, librarian, Yrbk 1951

Gaselee, Stephen, *Obit* Aug 1943

Gaver, Mary Virginia, American librarian, June 1966, *Obit* Mar 1992

Gibson, Robert William, May 1969

Gonzalez, Efren W., Jan 1971

Graham, Clarence R., librarian, Nov 1950

Greenaway, Emerson, librarian, July 1958, *Obit* June 1990

Hill, Frank Pierce, librarian, *Obit* Oct 1941

Holt, Rackham, Apr 1944

Howard, Alice Sturtevant, *Obit* Nov 1945

Jackson, Eugene B., June 1961

Jones, Clara Stanton, librarian, July 1976

Kaiser, John Boynton, librarian, May 1943

Keck, Lucile L., Mar 1954

Kinder, Katharine L., May 1957

Klahre, Ethel S., May 1962

Koch, Theodore Wesley, librarian, *Obit* May 1941

Laich, Katherine, librarian, June 1972

Larkin, Philip, English poet, essayist, novelist and librarian, Jan 1985, *Obit* Feb 1986

Lehmann-Haupt, Hellmut, author and bibliographer, Apr 1942, Mar 1961, *Obit* May 1992

Lord, Milton Edward, librarian, Feb 1950

Lorenz, John G., Sept 1966

Lowrie, Jean E., June 1973

Ludington, Flora Belle, librarian, Nov 1953

Lydenberg, Harry Miller, librarian, Sept 1941, *Obit* June 1960

MacGregor, Ellen, author and librarian, Yrbk 1954

MacKaye, Julia Gunther, American librarian and children's author, Yrbk 1949

Martin, Allie Beth, American librarian, June 1975, *Obit* June 1976

McDonough, Roger H., state librarian, June 1968

Mearns, David Chambers, librarian, July 1961, *Obit* July 1981

Milam, Carl Hastings, American librarian, June 1945, *Obit* Oct 1963

Mohrhardt, Foster Edward, American librarian, June 1967

Morsch, Lucile M., librarian, June 1957, *Obit* Nov 1972

Morton, Elizabeth Homer, Canadian librarian, July 1961

Moser, Fritz, June 1955

Mumford, Lawrence Quincy, American Librarian of Congress, June 1954, *Obit* Jan 1983

Oltman, Florine, May 1970

Otuken, Adnan, Turkish librarian, June 1954

Paradise, Nathaniel Burton, *Obit* June 1942

Parma, V. Valta, *Obit* Nov 1941

Poole, Franklin Osborne, *Obit* Mar 1943

Potter, Alfred Claghorn, *Obit* Yrbk 1940

Powell, Benjamin Edward, librarian, June 1959

Ranganathan, S. R., Indian librarian, Sept 1965, *Obit* Yrbk 1972

Rathbone, Josephine Adams, librarian and educator, *Obit* July 1941

Rice, Paul North, librarian, Nov 1947, *Obit* June 1967

Richards, John Stewart, librarian, June 1955

Rigling, Alfred, *Obit* Jan 1941

Roberts, Kate L., *Obit* Oct 1941

Rogers, Frank Bradway, physician and librarian, June 1962

Rogers, Rutherford David, June 1962

Runkle, Erwin W., *Obit* Apr 1941

Scoggin, Margaret Clara, American librarian, July 1952, *Obit* Sept 1968

Sewell, Winifred, American library science professor, June 1960

Shaver, Mary, *Obit* Mar 1942

Shaw, Ralph R., American librarian, June 1956, *Obit* Yrbk 1972

Shearer, Augustus Hunt, *Obit* July 1941

Smith, Carleton Sprague, musicologist, Yrbk 1960, *Obit* Nov 1994

Thompson, Alleen, June 1965

Tyler, Alice S., librarian, *Obit* June 1944

Usher, Elizabeth Reuter, May 1967

Utley, George B., librarian, *Obit* Nov 1946

Vail, Robert W. G., librarian and bibliographer, Feb 1945, *Obit* July 1966

Vance, John Thomas, *Obit* May 1943

Vosper, Robert Gordon, librarian, July 1965

Wagman, Frederick H., librarian, July 1963

Warren, Althea, librarian, Feb 1942, *Obit* Feb 1960

Wilson, Margaret Stevens, *Obit* May 1943

Winchell, Constance Mabel, librarian, June 1967, *Obit* Sept 1984

Woods, Bill Milton, librarian, May 1966, *Obit* Sept 1974

Wright, Louis B., historian and librarian, Nov 1950, *Obit* June 1984

Wynkoop, Asa, *Obit* Yrbk 1942

Information technology executives

Premji, Azim Hasham, Indian information technology executive, Jan 2004

Russo, Pat F., American information technology executive, May 2008

Steward, David L., American information technology executive, Nov 2004

Inspirational writers

Borysenko, Joan, psychologist and biologist, Oct 1996

Chopra, Deepak, American physician and writer, Oct 1995

Krishnamurti, J., Indian philosopher, Oct 1974, *Obit* Apr 1986

Kushner, Harold S., American rabbi and writer on religion, Apr 1997

Mahesh Yogi, Indian yogi, Yrbk 1972, *Obit* Yrbk 2008

Marshall, Catherine, American biographer and inspirational writer, Jan 1955, *Obit* May 1983

Monroe, Anne Shannon, *Obit* Yrbk 1942

Robbins, Tony, American motivational speaker and author, July 2001

Tolle, Eckhart, German spiritual writer, Feb 2005

Instrumentalists

Chassagne, Regine, Canadian singer and instrumentalist, Jan 2007

Gil, Gilberto, Brazilian singer and songwriter, Jan 2003

Lewis, Henry, American conductor, Feb 1973, *Obit* Apr 1996

Wu Man, Chinese pipa player, Jan 2007

Insurance agents

Wallop, Douglass, American insurance agent and novelist, Yrbk 1956, *Obit* June 1985

Insurance executives

Bliss, Ray C., American political party leader, Jan 1966, *Obit* Oct 1981

Greenberg, Maurice R., American insurance executive, Nov 2000

Kemper, James S., American insurance executive, Apr 1941, *Obit* Nov 1981

Lincoln, Murray D., American insurance executive, Mar 1953, *Obit* Jan 1967

Skutt, V. J., insurance executive, Yrbk 1959, *Obit* Apr 1993

Thomas, John Parnell, American congressman, Sept 1947, *Obit* Jan 1971

Wilde, Frazar B., insurance executive, Apr 1959, *Obit* Aug 1985

Intelligence service agents

Montagu, Ewen, British intelligence official and lawyer, June 1956, *Obit* Sept 1985

Stern, Martha Dodd, American novelist, translator and spy, Yrbk 1946, *Obit* Jan 1991

Intelligence service officials

Beria, Lavrenti, Soviet intelligence official, Yrbk 1942, *Obit* Sept 1954

Blair, Dennis, American admiral and intelligence official, May 2010

Bulganin, Nikolai Aleksandrovich, Soviet communist leader, Feb 1955, *Obit* Apr 1975

Casey, William J., American intelligence official, Mar 1972, *Obit* June 1987

Colby, William E., American intelligence official, Jan 1975, *Obit* July 1996

Dulles, Allen Welsh, American diplomat and intelligence official, Mar 1949, *Obit* Mar 1969

Helms, Richard, American intelligence official, Oct 1967, *Obit* Yrbk 2003

Hillenkoetter, Roscoe H., American CIA director and admiral, Jan 1950, *Obit* Aug 1982

Lay, James S., intelligence official, Mar 1950, *Obit* Aug 1987

Meyer, Cord, intelligence official, Mar 1948, *Obit* Aug 2001

Negroponte, John, American intelligence official, Apr 2003

Oechsner, Frederick Cable, journalist and intelligence official, Mar 1943, *Obit* June 1992

Olsen, Matthew, Director of the National Counterterrorism Center (NCTC), Aug 2012

Panetta, Leon E., American Secretary of defense, June 1993

Raborn, William Francis, American admiral and intelligence official, July 1958, *Obit* June 1990

Schlesinger, James R., American Secretary of defense and energy, Oct 1973

Shelepin, Aleksandr N., Soviet intelligence official, Feb 1971, *Obit* Jan 1995

Tenet, George J., American intelligence official, Aug 1999

Turner, Stansfield, admiral and CIA director, May 1978

Webster, William H., American FBI and CIA director, Aug 1978

Wilson, Frank J., June 1946, *Obit* Oct 1970

Wright, Peter, British intelligence official, Feb 1988, *Obit* July 1995

Zacharias, Ellis M., American admiral and intelligence official, Mar 1949, *Obit* Oct 1961

Interior designers

Buatta, Mario, American interior designer, May 1991

Cauldwell, Leslie Giffen, *Obit* July 1941

Draper, Dorothy, American interior designer, May 1941, *Obit* Apr 1969

Kahane, Melanie, interior designer, July 1959, *Obit* Feb 1989

Pahlmann, William Carroll, American interior and industrial designer, Oct 1964, *Obit* Jan 1988

Robsjohn-Gibbings, Terence Harold, American furniture and interior designer, Sept 1965, *Obit* Feb 1977

Stoddard, Alexandra, American interior designer, June 1996

International organization officials

Amerasinghe, Hamilton Shirley, Sri Lankan diplomat, Mar 1977, *Obit* Feb 1981

Andrewes, William, British admiral, Sept 1952, *Obit* Jan 1975

Annan, Kofi, Ghanaian United Nations secretary-general, Mar 2000

Ardalan, Ali Gholi, Iranian diplomat, Apr 1954

Austin, Warren Robinson, American senator and diplomat, Jan 1944, *Obit* Feb 1963

Azzam, Abd al-Rahman, Egyptian diplomat, Apr 1947

Basdevant, Jules, French lawyer, diplomat and judge, Feb 1950, *Obit* Mar 1968

Belaunde, Victor Andres, Peruvian diplomat, Feb 1960, *Obit* Feb 1967

Bellamy, Carol, American United Nations official, Oct 1999

Benoit-Levy, Jean, Oct 1947, *Obit* Nov 1959

Bensouda, Fatou, Gambian lawyer and international court prosecutor, Jan 2007

Boland, Frederick H., Irish United Nations official and diplomat, Feb 1961, *Obit* Feb 1986

Bolton, John R., American diplomat, Feb 2006

Borberg, William, Nov 1952, *Obit* Sept 1958

Brind, Patrick, British admiral, Nov 1952, *Obit* Jan 1964

Brosio, Manlio, Italian diplomat, Sept 1955, *Obit* May 1980

Brown, Charles R., admiral, July 1958

Bunche, Ralph J., American diplomat, Feb 1948, *Obit* Jan 1972

Burns, Alan, Sept 1953

Caradon, Hugh Foot, British diplomat, Oct 1953, *Obit* Nov 1990

Carney, Robert Bostwick, admiral, Oct 1951, *Obit* Aug 1990

Cohen, Benjamin, Chilean diplomat and United Nations official, May 1948, *Obit* May 1960

Cohen, Benjamin V., American government official and lawyer, Apr 1941, *Obit* Oct 1983

Corell, Hans, Swedish diplomat, lawyer and United Nations official, Jan 2003

Coudenhove-Kalergi, Richard Nicolaus, Austrian political philosopher and international organization official, Feb 1948, *Obit* Oct 1972

Dayal, Rajeshwar, Feb 1961

De Silva, Desmond, British barrister and United Nations war crimes prosecutor, Jan 2006

DeLany, Walter S., admiral, Yrbk 1952

Dean, Patrick, British diplomat, May 1961, *Obit* Jan 1995

Dendramis, Vassili, June 1947, *Obit* July 1956

Dixon, Pierson, British diplomat, Sept 1954, *Obit* June 1965

Eichelberger, Clark M., Jan 1947, *Obit* Mar 1980

Eklund, Sigvard, July 1962

El Baradei, Mohamed, Egyptian diplomat and international organization official, Jan 2003

Eliasson, Jan, Swedish diplomat, Jan 2005

Emmet of Amberley, Evelyn, Mar 1953

Feller, Abraham H., Nov 1946, *Obit* Jan 1953

Finletter, Thomas K., American diplomat and government official, Jan 1948, *Obit* June 1980

Forsyth, W. D., Apr 1952

Garreau, Roger, Apr 1950

Goldman, Olive Mortimer Remington, Sept 1950

Gross, Ernest A., diplomat and lawyer, Feb 1951, *Obit* July 1999

Guerrero, Jose Gustavo, Jan 1947, *Obit* Jan 1959

Hassan, Mahmoud, July 1947

Hodgson, Joseph V., American state attorney general and United Nations official, June 1945

Hoo, Victor, Mar 1947, *Obit* July 1972

Im, Yong-Sin, Oct 1947, *Obit* Apr 1977

Intizam, Nasr Allah, Yrbk 1950

Jessup, Philip C., American judge and diplomat, Apr 1948, *Obit* Mar 1986

Johnson, David M., July 1952

Karumba, Christine, Feb 2013

Katz-Suchy, Juliusz, June 1951, *Obit* Yrbk 1971

Keeny, Spurgeon Milton, United Nations official, Jan 1958, *Obit* Jan 1989

Khan, Muhammad Zafrulla, Yrbk 1947

Khouri, Faris el-, Sept 1948, *Obit* Feb 1962

Kotschnig, Walter Maria, United Nations official and diplomat, Oct 1952, *Obit* Sept 1985

La Guardia, Fiorello Henry, American mayor, Oct 1940, *Obit* Nov 1947

Labouisse, Henry R., American United Nations official, Oct 1961, *Obit* May 1987

Lannung, Hermod, Yrbk 1949

Lefaucheux, Marie-Helene, French United Nations official, Oct 1947, *Obit* Apr 1964

Limb, Ben C., Jan 1951

Lindt, Auguste R., Swiss diplomat and United Nations official, Nov 1959, *Obit* Yrbk 2000

Loutfi, Omar, Jan 1957, *Obit* July 1963

Lubbers, Rudolphus, Dutch prime minister and United Nations official, May 1988, Jan 2003

Lucas, Caroline, British member of European parliament, Sept 2012

M'Bow, Amadou-Mahtar, Senegalese United Nations official, May 1987

Malik, Charles Habib, Lebanese diplomat and United Nations official, Apr 1948, *Obit* Feb 1988

Malik, Yakov Aleksandrovich, Apr 1949, *Obit* Apr 1980

Manuil'skii, Dmitrii Zakhar'evich, Yrbk 1948, *Obit* May 1959

Marshall, M. Lee, Sept 1948, *Obit* Oct 1950

Mates, Leo, Nov 1956

Matsudaira, Koto, Japanese diplomat, Nov 1958

Maza, Jose, Nov 1955, *Obit* July 1964

Mazowiecki, Tadeusz, Polish political leader, Feb 1990

McGeachy, Mary Craig, Canadian diplomat, Apr 1944

McHenry, Donald F., diplomat, Sept 1980

Melas, George V., July 1956

Mora, Jose A., Nov 1956, *Obit* Mar 1975

Moreno Ocampo, Luis, Argentine lawyer and international court prosecutor, Jan 2007

Morris, James T., American United Nations relief official, Mar 2005

Muniz, Joao Carlos, Sept 1952, *Obit* Sept 1960

Myrdal, Alva Reimer, Swedish sociologist, Yrbk 1950, *Obit* Mar 1986

Noble, Allan, May 1957

Noue, Jehan de, Jan 1947

Nunez Portuondo, Emilio, Apr 1957

Obaid, Thoraya, Saudi Arabian United Nations official, Jan 2004

Ogata, Sadako, Japanese United Nations official and diplomat, Oct 1997

Owen, A. David K., British economist, sociologist and United Nations official, May 1946, *Obit* Sept 1970

Padilla Nervo, Luis, Yrbk 1946

Palmer, Thomas Waverly, Mar 1949

Pelt, Adrian, Feb 1948

Perez de Cuellar, Javier, Peruvian diplomat and United Nations secretary-general, Aug 1982

Pote Sarasin, Yrbk 1955

Prebisch, Raul, Argentine economist, Yrbk 1969, *Obit* July 1986

Price, Byron, journalist and United Nations official, Feb 1942, *Obit* Sept 1981

Quaison-Sackey, Alex, Ghanaian United Nations official and diplomat, Mar 1966, *Obit* Feb 1993

Rau, Benegal Narsing, Yrbk 1951, *Obit* Feb 1954

Riefler, Winfield W., May 1948, *Obit* June 1974

Rossel, Agda, Yrbk 1959

Rowe, Leo Stanton, director general of the Pan American union, Aug 1945, *Obit* Jan 1947

Russell, James S., admiral, Jan 1962

Sandstrom, Emil, Jan 1951, *Obit* Sept 1962

Santa Cruz, Hernan, Yrbk 1949

Sayegh, Fayez A., Lebanese scholar and diplomat, July 1957

Schwebel, Stephen M., American judge and international relations specialist, July 1952

Schweitzer, Pierre-Paul, French government official and IMF director, Yrbk 1963, *Obit* Mar 1994

Sen, Binay Ranjan, Indian diplomat, Yrbk 1952, *Obit* Aug 1993

Sender, Toni, German United Nations official, May 1950

Supachai Panitchpakdi, Thai international organization official, Jan 2004

Thanat Khoman, Mar 1958

Thant, Burmese diplomat and United Nations secretary-general, Feb 1962, *Obit* Jan 1975

Thorn, James, Yrbk 1949

Tsiang, Tingfu F., June 1948, *Obit* Yrbk 1965

Urrutia, Francisco, June 1958

Velloso, Pedro Leao, Sept 1946, *Obit* Mar 1947

Winiarski, Bohdan, Feb 1962

Wolfowitz, Paul D., American international organization official, Feb 2003

Wright, Robert Alderson Wright, July 1945, *Obit* Sept 1964

Yost, Charles Woodruff, American diplomat, Mar 1959, *Obit* July 1981

Zeineddine, Farid, Feb 1957

Zorin, Valerian A., Soviet diplomat and United Nations official, Mar 1953, *Obit* Mar 1986

International relations specialists

Bremmer, Ian, American international relations specialist, Aug 2013

Dean, Vera Micheles, international relations specialist, May 1943, *Obit* Yrbk 1972

Gilchrist, Huntington, Apr 1949, *Obit* Mar 1975

Haass, Richard, American international relations specialist, June 2010

Meron, Theodor, Polish international relations specialist, Mar 2005

Perle, Richard Norman, American military official, July 2003

Schain, Josephine, July 1945

Internet games players

Wendel, Johnathan, American video game player, Apr 2007

Internists

Jordan, Sara Claudia Murray, gastroenterologist, Mar 1954, *Obit* Jan 1960

Wilbur, Dwight Locke, medical association official and gastroenterologist, July 1969, *Obit* May 1997

Inventors

Adams, Joseph H., American inventor, philanthropist and nonfiction writer, *Obit* Apr 1941

Alexanderson, Ernst Fredrik Werner, Swedish electrical engineer and inventor, Sept 1955, *Obit* Aug 1975

Appleyard, Rollo, British electrical engineer and inventor, *Obit* Apr 1943

Baekeland, Leo Hendrik, Belgian-American chemist, *Obit* Apr 1944

Bailey, Donald Coleman, English civil engineer and inventor, Oct 1945, *Obit* July 1985

Benesh, Rudolf, British mathematician, July 1957

Branly, Edouard, French physicist and inventor, *Obit* Apr 1940

Callow, John Michael, *Obit* Sept 1940

Canton, Allen A., *Obit* Apr 1940

Christie, J. Walter, *Obit* Feb 1944

Connell, Karl, *Obit* Yrbk 1941

Coolidge, William David, American physical chemist and inventor, June 1947, *Obit* Mar 1975

Cowen, Joshua Lionel, American inventor and toy train manufacturer, Sept 1954, *Obit* Nov 1965

Damadian, Raymond, American physician and inventor, Jan 2000

De Vry, Herman A., *Obit* May 1941

Du Mont, Allen B., American electrical engineer and inventor, June 1946, *Obit* Jan 1966

Ellis, Carleton, *Obit* Mar 1941

Emerson, Victor Lee, *Obit* July 1941

Emmet, William L., *Obit* Nov 1941

Ferguson, Harry, Irish inventor, Mar 1956, *Obit* Jan 1961

Fiske, Bradley A., *Obit* May 1942

Garand, John C., American design engineer and inventor, Aug 1945, *Obit* Apr 1974

Gaumont, Leon, *Obit* Sept 1946

Grebe, John J., Oct 1955

Gygax, Gary, American game inventor, Mar 2007, *Obit* Yrbk 2008

Hadfield, Robert Abbott, *Obit* Nov 1940

Hammond, John Hays, July 1962, *Obit* Apr 1965

Hazeltine, Alan, electrical engineer and inventor, Mar 1948, *Obit* July 1964

Heimlich, Henry J., American surgeon, Oct 1986

Hopkins, Nevil Monroe, *Obit* May 1945

Horgan, Stephen H., inventor, *Obit* Oct 1941

Hoxie, Charles A., *Obit* Yrbk 1941

Hutchison, Miller Reese, American electrical engineer and inventor, *Obit* Apr 1944

Kamen, Dean, American inventor and medical instrument maker, Nov 2002

Kolff, Willem J., American physician, May 1983, *Obit* Yrbk 2009

Land, Edwin H., American inventor and photographic industry executive, Nov 1953, *Obit* May 1991

Letourneau, R. G., American inventor, Apr 1958, *Obit* July 1969

Lyndon, Edward, *Obit* Yrbk 1940

Marvin, Harry, *Obit* Jan 1940

Michelin, Edouard, French tire company executive, *Obit* Oct 1940

Momsen, C. B., American admiral and inventor, July 1946, *Obit* July 1967

Murdock, George J., *Obit* Sept 1942

Norden, Carl Lukas, American mechanical engineer and inventor, Jan 1945, *Obit* Sept 1965

Olson, Harry Ferdinand, American acoustic engineer, Nov 1955, *Obit* June 1982

Poulsen, Valdemar, Danish inventor and electrical engineer, *Obit* Sept 1942

Rosen, Harold A., American electrical engineer, June 1997

Schwidetzky, Oscar, Yrbk 1943, *Obit* Nov 1963

Semon, Waldo Lonsbury, chemist and inventor, Yrbk 1940, *Obit* Aug 1999

Shaw, Louis Agassiz, *Obit* Oct 1940

Shreeve, Herbert Edward, *Obit* June 1942

Snook, H. Clyde, *Obit* Nov 1942

Suits, Chauncey Guy, physicist and inventor, Feb 1950, *Obit* Oct 1991

Sveda, Michael, chemist and inventor, Yrbk 1954, *Obit* Nov 1999

Tainter, Charles Sumner, *Obit* May 1940

Terrett, Nicholas K., British pharmacologist and co-inventor of Viagra, Jan 2003

Tesla, Nikola, American electrical engineer, *Obit* Feb 1943

Tizard, Henry Thomas, British physical chemist, Jan 1949, *Obit* Yrbk 1959

Waller, Fred, American inventor of Cinerama, Feb 1953, *Obit* July 1954

Weagant, Roy A., *Obit* Oct 1942

Williams, Robert R., Sept 1951, *Obit* Yrbk 1965

Investment bankers

Ames, Amyas, investment banker and music patron, Apr 1972, *Obit* June 2000

Blankfein, Lloyd C., American investment banker, Jan 2011

Blumenthal, Hugo, American investment banker and philanthropist, *Obit* Sept 1943

Boles, Ewing T., American investment banker, Apr 1953

Dawson, John A., investment banker, Sept 1952

Eberstadt, Ferdinand, investment banker, Yrbk 1942, *Obit* Jan 1970

Harrison, William B., American investment banker, Mar 2002

Johnson, Joseph T., Feb 1952

O'Neal, Stanley, American investment banker, May 2003

Ruhle, Stephanie, American investment banker, Jan 2013

Thain, John, American investment banker, May 2004

Investment managers

Domini, Amy L., American investment manager, Nov 2005

Faber, Joachim, German investment manager, Jan 2002

Gross, William H., American investment manager, July 2010

Hobson, Mellody, American investment manager, Aug 2005

Lynch, Peter, American investment manager, Nov 1994

Meriwether, John W., American investment manager, Mar 1999

Rogers, John, American investment manager, Aug 2010

Islamic leaders

Aga Khan, Indian Islamic leader, May 1946, *Obit* Sept 1957

Al-Dari, Harith, Iraqi Islamic cleric and tribal leader, Jan 2007

Al-Sadr, Muqtada, Iraqi Islamic cleric, Jan 2007

Al-Sistani, Ali, Iraqi Islamic leader, Jan 2004

Al-Turabi, Hassan, Sudanese political leader, Jan 1999

Azad, Abulkalam, Indian political leader, July 1942, *Obit* May 1958

Farooq, Umar, Kashmiri Islamic leader, Jan 2002

Farrakhan, Louis, American Black Muslim leader, Apr 1992

Hadi Awang, Malaysian Islamic leader, Jan 2004

Jinnah, Mohamed Ali, Pakistani political leader, May 1942, *Obit* Oct 1948

Khamenei, Ali, Iranian president, Nov 1987, Jan 2005

Khan, Daisy, American Islamic leader, June 2013

Khatami, Mohammad, Iranian Islamic leader and president, Apr 1998

Khomeini, Ruhollah, Iranian religious and political leader, Nov 1979, *Obit* July 1989

Mohammed, W. Deen, American Islamic leader, Jan 2004, *Obit* Yrbk 2008

Osman Ali, Oct 1948, *Obit* Apr 1967

Ramadan, Tariq, Swiss Islamic leader, Jan 2004

Yassin, Ahmed, Palestinian Islamic leader, July 1998, *Obit* Yrbk 2004

Yusuf, Hamza, American Islamic leader, Mar 2007

Islamists

Macdonald, Duncan Black, American theologian, linguist and Islamist, *Obit* Oct 1943

Mattson, Ingrid, Canadian Islamist and religious education teacher, Jan 2007

Jazz musicians

Adderley, Cannonball, American jazz saxophonist, July 1961, *Obit* Oct 1975

Allen, J. D., American jazz saxophonist, Nov 2010

Armstrong, Louis, American trumpet player, Sept 1944, Apr 1966, *Obit* Sept 1971

Barber, Patricia, American jazz singer and pianist, Sept 2007

Berigan, Bunny, American jazz trumpet player, *Obit* July 1942

Bridgewater, Dee Dee, American jazz singer, Oct 2008

Brubeck, Dave, American jazz pianist and composer, Mar 1956, Apr 1993, *Obit* Yrbk 2013

Byrd, Charlie, American jazz guitarist, Oct 1967, *Obit* Mar 2000

Byron, Don, American jazz clarinetist, Sept 2000

Carter, Benny, American saxophonist, July 1987, *Obit* Oct 2003

Carter, Betty, American jazz singer, Mar 1982, *Obit* Jan 1999

Carter, James, American jazz saxophonist, Feb 1997

Carter, Regina, American jazz violinist, Oct 2003

Chestnut, Cyrus, American jazz pianist, July 2009

Coleman, Steve, American jazz saxophonist, July 2004

Condon, Eddie, American jazz guitarist, Oct 1944, *Obit* Oct 1973

Connick, Harry, American pianist and singer, Nov 1990

Conte, Nicola, Italian DJ and record producer, Jan 2005

Cortez, Jayne, American poet, *Obit* Yrbk 2013

Davis, Anthony, American composer and pianist, May 1990

Douglas, Dave, American jazz trumpet player and composer, Mar 2006

Dunmall, Paul, British jazz saxophonist, May 2011

Eckstine, Billy, American jazz singer, July 1952, *Obit* Apr 1993

Eldridge, Roy, American trumpet player, Mar 1987, *Obit* Apr 1989

Elling, Kurt, American jazz singer, Jan 2005

Escoffery, Wayne, American jazz saxophonist and composer, Jan 2011

Flanagan, Tommy, American pianist, Apr 1995, *Obit* Mar 2002

Fujii, Satoko, Japanese jazz pianist, June 2010

Garner, Erroll, American jazz pianist, Sept 1959, *Obit* Mar 1977

Getz, Stan, American jazz saxophonist, Apr 1971, *Obit* Aug 1991

Glasper, Robert, American jazz pianist, Mar 2011

Gordon, Wycliffe, American jazz trombonist, Sept 2009

Grappelli, Stephane, French jazz violinist, Aug 1988, *Obit* Feb 1998

Hargrove, Roy, American jazz trumpet player, Apr 2000

Henderson, Joe, American jazz saxophonist, June 1996, *Obit* Oct 2001

Hersch, Fred, American jazz pianist and composer, Apr 2006

Hill, Andrew, American jazz pianist and composer, Apr 2004, *Obit* Yrbk 2007

Hill, Billy, *Obit* Feb 1941

Hines, Earl, pianist and band leader, Mar 1967, *Obit* June 1983

Hirt, Al, trumpet player, Feb 1967, *Obit* July 1999

Holland, Dave, English jazz bassist, Mar 2003

Hunter, Charlie, American jazz guitarist, Nov 2007

Jarrett, Keith, American jazz pianist and composer, May 1985

Jones, Norah, American pianist and singer, May 2003

Klein, Guillermo, Argentine jazz pianist and composer, Jan 2006

Koz, Dave, American jazz saxophonist and composer, June 2013

Krall, Diana, Canadian singer and pianist, June 2000

Laws, Hubert, American jazz flutist, July 2007

Lewis, John, American pianist and composer, Jan 1962, *Obit* June 2001

Lewis, Ramsey, American jazz pianist, Oct 1996

Lloyd, Charles, American saxophonist and flutist, Apr 2002

Lovano, Joe, American jazz saxophonist, Mar 1998

Malaby, Tony, American jazz saxophonist, Sept 2008

Mangione, Chuck, trumpet player and flugelhornist, May 1980

Marsalis, Ellis, American jazz pianist, Aug 2000

McBride, Christian, American jazz bassist, Jan 2000

McLean, Jackie, American saxophonist, Mar 2001, *Obit* Nov 2006

McNeil, John, American jazz trumpet player, June 2007

McPartland, Marian, American jazz pianist, June 1976, *Obit* Yrbk 2013

McRae, Carmen, American singer, Apr 1983, *Obit* Jan 1995

Melford, Myra, American jazz pianist and composer, Apr 2010

Monheit, Jane, American jazz singer, Feb 2008

Monk, T. S., American drummer, Feb 2002

Monk, Thelonious, American pianist, Oct 1964, *Obit* Apr 1982

Mulligan, Gerry, American jazz saxophonist, Yrbk 1960, *Obit* Mar 1996

Murphy, Mark, American jazz singer, Sept 2004

O'Day, Anita, American jazz singer, June 1990, *Obit* Jan 2007

Payton, Nicholas, American trumpet player, Sept 1999

Pelt, Jeremy, American jazz trumpet player, Feb 2009

Person, Houston, American saxophonist, June 2003

Peterson, Oscar, Canadian pianist and composer, Oct 1983, *Obit* Yrbk 2008

Prieto, Dafnis, Cuban drummer, Oct 2012

Purdie, Bernard, American drummer, Jan 2010

Rava, Enrico, Italian jazz trumpet player, Jan 2006

Redman, Joshua, American jazz saxophonist, Jan 1997

Reeves, Dianne, American jazz singer, July 2006

Roberts, Marcus, American jazz pianist, Mar 1994

Rollins, Sonny, American jazz saxophonist, Apr 1976

Russell, Pee Wee, clarinetist, Aug 1944, *Obit* Apr 1969

Sanborn, David, American saxophonist, Aug 1992

Sanchez, David, Puerto Rican jazz saxophonist, Nov 2001

Sandoval, Arturo, Cuban jazz trumpet player, Jan 2003

Scott, Christian, American jazz trumpet player, Jan 2008

Shorter, Wayne, American jazz saxophonist, Apr 1996

Simone, Nina, American singer and pianist, Apr 1968, *Obit* Yrbk 2003

Taylor, Cecil, American jazz pianist, Mar 1986

Turner, Mark, American jazz saxophonist, Nov 2002

Turre, Steve, American jazz trombonist, Apr 2001

Tyner, McCoy, American jazz pianist and composer, Aug 1997

Waller, Fats, American jazz pianist and composer, Apr 1942, *Obit* Feb 1944

Ware, David S., American jazz saxophonist, Sept 2003, *Obit* Yrbk 2013

Watts, Jeff, American jazz drummer, Apr 2008

Wein, George, Oct 1985

Williams, Joe, singer, Apr 1985, *Obit* June 1999

Williams, Mary Lou, American pianist and composer, Nov 1966, *Obit* July 1981

Wilson, Cassandra, American jazz singer, Mar 1998

Winehouse, Amy, British jazz and soul singer, Jan 2007, *Obit* Yrbk 2011

Jewelers

Graff, Laurence, British jeweler, Sept 2011

Toussaint, Jeanne, Feb 1955

Winston, Harry, jeweler, Apr 1965, *Obit* Feb 1979

Jewelry designers

Fahmy, Azza, Egyptian jewelry designer, Jan 2004

Husain, Maqbul Fida, Indian painter, Jan 2006, *Obit* Yrbk 2011

Jewish leaders

Ben-Gurion, David, Israeli prime minister, Oct 1947, Jan 1957, *Obit* Jan 1974

Ben-Zvi, Itzhak, Israeli president, Apr 1953, *Obit* June 1963

Bernstein, Philip S., American rabbi, Nov 1951, *Obit* Feb 1986

Bloch, Charles Edward, American publishing executive, *Obit* Oct 1940

Eisendrath, Maurice Nathan, May 1950, *Obit* Jan 1974

Elath, Eliahu, Israeli Zionist leader, Yrbk 1948, *Obit* Aug 1990

Fredman, Samuel, *Obit* June 1941

Goldmann, Nahum, Israeli Zionist leader, May 1957, *Obit* Oct 1982

Goldstein, Israel, Zionist leader and rabbi, July 1946, *Obit* June 1986

Hertzberg, Arthur, American rabbi and religious writer, June 1975, *Obit* Yrbk 2006

Herzog, Isaac, Apr 1959

Heschel, Abraham Joshua, American rabbi and theologian, Apr 1970, *Obit* Mar 1973

Israel, Edward L., *Obit* Yrbk 1941

Jabotinsky, Vladimir, Russian Zionist leader, *Obit* Sept 1940

Jakobovits, Immanuel, British rabbi, June 1988, *Obit* Feb 2000

Kagan, Henry Enoch, Sept 1965, *Obit* Oct 1969

Kahane, Meir, American-Israeli rabbi, Oct 1972, *Obit* Jan 1991

Klein, Edward E., rabbi, Sept 1966, *Obit* Sept 1985

Kollek, Teddy, Israeli mayor, Oct 1974, Mar 1993, *Obit* Yrbk 2007

Levin, Yehuda Leib, Sept 1969, *Obit* Jan 1972

Liebman, Joshua Loth, rabbi, Oct 1946, *Obit* July 1948

Mack, Julian W., American judge, *Obit* Oct 1943

Miller, Irving, Nov 1952, *Obit* Feb 1981

Salit, Norman, rabbi and lawyer, Mar 1955, *Obit* Oct 1960

Schindler, Alexander M., American rabbi, Sept 1987, *Obit* Feb 2001

Schneerson, Menachem M., American rabbi, Sept 1983, *Obit* Aug 1994

Silver, Abba Hillel, rabbi, Yrbk 1941, May 1963, *Obit* Jan 1964

Steinberg, Milton, rabbi, Mar 1940, *Obit* Apr 1950

Szold, Henrietta, American Zionist leader, Jan 1940, *Obit* Apr 1945

Werne, Isaac, *Obit* Mar 1940

Wise, Stephen Samuel, American rabbi, July 1941, *Obit* May 1949

Wolf, Alfred, Mar 1958

Jockeys

Arcaro, Eddie, American jockey, Sept 1958, *Obit* Jan 1998

Cauthen, Steve, American jockey, July 1977

Cordero, Angel, jockey, Oct 1975

Dancer, Stanley, American harness racer, June 1973, *Obit* Yrbk 2005

Day, Pat, American jockey, Oct 1997

Krone, Julie, American jockey, Oct 1989

Pincay, Laffit, Panamanian jockey, Sept 2001

Prado, Edgar, Peruvian jockey, Sept 2007

Rubin, Barbara Jo, Yrbk 1969

Santos, Jose, Chilean jockey, Nov 2003

Shoemaker, Bill, American jockey, July 1966, *Obit* Apr 2004

Smith, Robyn, Nov 1976

Journalists

Abelson, Philip H., American physicist and periodical editor, Oct 1965, *Obit* Yrbk 2004

Abend, Hallett, American journalist, Sept 1942, *Obit* Feb 1956

Abrahams, Peter, South African novelist and short story writer, Yrbk 1957

Addario, Lynsey, American photojournalist, Apr 2013

Adzhubei, Aleksei I., Russian newspaper editor and son-in-law of Nikita Sergeevich Khrushchev, Sept 1964, *Obit* May 1993

Ahlgren, Mildred Carlson, American newspaper columnist and organization official, July 1952

Al-Emam, Mahassen, Jordanian journalist, Jan 2004

Aleksievich, Svetlana, Belarusian journalist, Jan 2006

Allen, Jay, American journalist, Oct 1941, *Obit* Feb 1973

Allen, Larry, American journalist, July 1942

Allen, Ralph, Canadian periodical editor, July 1958, *Obit* Feb 1967

Alsop, Joseph, American journalist, Oct 1952, *Obit* Oct 1989

Alsop, Stewart, American journalist, Oct 1952, *Obit* July 1974

Alterman, Eric, American journalist, Feb 2007

Amanpour, Christiane, British television reporter and moderator, Apr 1996

Anderson, Christopher, American magazine editor, Jan 2010

Anderson, Jack, American newspaper columnist, June 1972, *Obit* Yrbk 2006

Andrews, Bert, American journalist, Sept 1948, *Obit* Oct 1953

Andrews, Erin, American television sportscaster, Sept 2013

Angell, Norman, English journalist and pacifist, May 1948, *Obit* Yrbk 1967

Angier, Natalie, American science writer, Aug 1999

Applebaum, Anne, American journalist, Aug 2004

Arellano, Gustavo, American journalist, Aug 2010

Arne, Sigrid, American journalist, Oct 1945

Arnett, Peter, New Zealand television reporter, Nov 1991

Arnold, Eve, American photojournalist, Oct 2005, *Obit* Yrbk 2012

Aron, Raymond, French political philosopher and journalist, June 1954, *Obit* Jan 1984

Arraras, Maria Celeste, Puerto Rican television news anchor, Aug 2002

Ashmore, Harry S., American newspaper editor and foundation official, Sept 1958, *Obit* Apr 1998

Aswell, James, American novelist, Yrbk 1951, *Obit* Apr 1955

Bacon, Charles Reade, American newspaper editor and state librarian, *Obit* June 1943

Bailey, Glenda, American magazine editor, Oct 2001

Bailey, Josiah W., American senator, Apr 1945, *Obit* Jan 1947

Baldwin, Hanson Weightman, journalist and military historian, Aug 1942, *Obit* Jan 1992

Ball, Joseph H., American senator, Oct 1943, *Obit* Feb 1994

Banfield, Ashleigh, Canadian television newscaster, July 2002

Bartiromo, Maria, American television reporter, Nov 2003

Barton, George, American journalist and mystery writer, *Obit* Apr 1940

Beals, Carleton, journalist, Yrbk 1942, *Obit* Aug 1979

Beatty, Bessie, radio commentator and journalist, Jan 1944, *Obit* Apr 1947

Bede, J. Adam, American congressman, *Obit* June 1942

Beebe, Lucius Morris, journalist, Sept 1940, *Obit* Mar 1966

Bell, Edward Price, American journalist, *Obit* Nov 1943

Belluck, Pam, New York Times science writer and journalist, June 2012

Benchley, Peter, American novelist and journalist, July 1976, *Obit* June 2006

Bennett, James O'Donnell, American journalist, *Obit* Mar 1940

Berding, Andrew H., American journalist and government official, Apr 1960

Bergen, Candice, American actress, Aug 1976

Berger, Meyer, newspaper reporter and columnist, Jan 1943, *Obit* Apr 1959

Bernard, Michelle D., American journalist and political commentator, Sept 2011

Bernstein, Carl, American journalist, Oct 1976

Bess, Demaree, American journalist, Jan 1943, *Obit* Sept 1962

Bigart, Homer, American journalist, June 1951, *Obit* July 1991

Binchy, Maeve, Irish novelist and short story writer, Nov 1995, *Obit* Yrbk 2012

Birnie, William A. H., American magazine editor, Sept 1952, *Obit* Oct 1979

Bishop, Jim, columnist and author, June 1969, *Obit* Sept 1987

Blackwell, Betsy Talbot, American magazine editor, June 1954, *Obit* Apr 1985

Blake, Doris, Canadian journalist, Nov 1941

Blake, Tiffany, American journalist, *Obit* Nov 1943

Blitzer, Wolf, American television news anchor, Feb 2007

Booker, Edna Lee, American journalist, Apr 1940

Bourke-White, Margaret, American photographer, Jan 1940, *Obit* Oct 1971

Boutell, Clarence B., July 1946

Bowden, Mark, American journalist, Jan 2002

Bowron, Fletcher, American mayor, Feb 1950, *Obit* Nov 1968

Boyle, Hal, June 1945, *Obit* May 1974

Bradford, Barbara Taylor, English novelist, Oct 1991

Bradlee, Benjamin C., American newspaper editor, Sept 1975

Bradley, Ed, American television reporter, May 1988, *Obit* Yrbk 2007

Bragg, Rick, American journalist and memoirist, Apr 2002

Breslin, Jimmy, American author and columnist, Yrbk 1973

Brick, John, Yrbk 1953, *Obit* Yrbk 1973

Bridges, Robert, *Obit* Nov 1941

Brier, Howard M., Yrbk 1951

Brinkley, David, American television newscaster and moderator, Mar 1960, Sept 1987, *Obit* Sept 2003

Broeg, Bob, American sportswriter, May 2002

Brokaw, Tom, American television news anchor, May 1981, Nov 2002

Brooks, Geraldine, Australian journalist, Aug 2006

Brown, Aaron, American television news anchor, Mar 2003

Brown, Campbell, American television news anchor, Nov 2008

Brown, Cecil, radio newscaster, Mar 1942, *Obit* Jan 1988

Brzezinski, Mika, American television news anchor, July 2010

Buchanan, Edna, American journalist and novelist, Sept 1997

Buckley, Priscilla L., American magazine editor, Apr 2002, *Obit* Yrbk 2012

Bumiller, Elisabeth, American journalist, Sept 2008

Burdett, Winston, radio reporters, Oct 1943, *Obit* July 1993

Burnett, Erin, American television news anchor, Sept 2012

Burnett, Whit, magazine editor and author, Apr 1941, *Obit* June 1973

Burri, Rene, Swiss photojournalist, Jan 2007

Burtsev, Vladimir L'vovich, Russian revolutionary and journalist, *Obit* Yrbk 1942

Butterfield, Roger Place, journalist, Mar 1948, *Obit* Yrbk 1991

Byas, Hugh, Mar 1943, *Obit* Apr 1945

Caballero, Maria Cristina, Colombian journalist, Jan 2004

Cafferty, Jack, American television newscaster, Oct 2008

Calder, Ritchie, Scottish author and journalist, Apr 1963, *Obit* May 1986

Caldwell, Erskine, American novelist and short story writer, Oct 1940, *Obit* May 1987

Calvino, Italo, Italian novelist and short story writer, Feb 1984, *Obit* Nov 1985

Canavan, Joseph J., *Obit* Yrbk 1940

Canham, Erwin Dain, newspaper editor, July 1945, Jan 1960, *Obit* Feb 1982

Capa, Cornell, American photojournalist, July 2005, *Obit* Yrbk 2008

Caputo, Philip, American journalist and novelist, Apr 1996

Caro, Robert A., American biographer, Jan 1984

Carraway, Gertrude Sprague, Jan 1954

Carter, Boake, radio commentator, Jan 1942, *Obit* Yrbk 1947

Carter, John Franklin, journalist and author, Oct 1941, *Obit* Jan 1968

Casey, Robert J., Mar 1943, *Obit* Jan 1963

Cassidy, Henry Clarence, journalist, Sept 1943

Catledge, Turner, American newspaper editor, July 1975, *Obit* July 1983

Catton, Bruce, journalist and author, Yrbk 1954, *Obit* Oct 1978

Chancellor, John, American television news anchor and commentator, Jan 1962, Nov 1988, *Obit* Sept 1996

Chang, Juju, television reporter, Aug 2013

Chase, Edna Woolman, magazine editor, Nov 1940, *Obit* June 1957

Chavez, Linda, American policy scientist and commentator, Nov 1999

Chen Guidi, Chinese journalist, Jan 2005

Childs, Marquis William, journalist and author, Jan 1943, *Obit* Sept 1990

Chung, Connie, American television newscaster, July 1989

Coblentz, Stanton Arthur, American science fiction writer and poet, June 1954

Cohen, Roger, British journalist, May 2008

Coleman, Lonnie, Yrbk 1958, *Obit* Oct 1982

Collingwood, Charles, American radio and television reporter, June 1943, *Obit* Nov 1985

Considine, Bob, columnist, Yrbk 1947, *Obit* Nov 1975

Coulter, Ann, American television commentator, Sept 2003

Couric, Katie, American television news anchor, Mar 1993, Apr 2008

Cowles, Virginia, author and journalist, May 1942, *Obit* Nov 1983

Coxe, Howard, *Obit* Jan 1941

Coy, Wayne, Mar 1948, *Obit* Yrbk 1958

Craig, May, journalist, June 1949, *Obit* Sept 1975

Creel, George, American newspaper editor and government official, June 1944, *Obit* Jan 1954

Crider, John H., June 1949, *Obit* Sept 1966

Cronkite, Walter, American television news anchor, Jan

1956, Nov 1975, *Obit* Sept 2009

Crowley, Candy, American television reporter, Jan 2011

Curry, Ann, American television newscaster, June 2004

Dafoe, John Wesley, *Obit* Feb 1944

Daley, Arthur, sportswriter, Sept 1956, *Obit* Feb 1974

Daly, John Charles, radio reporter and television moderator, May 1948, *Obit* May 1991

Daly, Maureen, American young adult novelist, Jan 1946, *Obit* Yrbk 2006

Daniel, Clifton, American journalist, Mar 1966, *Obit* July 2000

Daniell, Raymond, Mar 1944, *Obit* June 1969

Daniels, Jonathan, newspaper editor, Apr 1942, *Obit* Jan 1982

Daudet, Leon, French journalist, novelist and memoirist, *Obit* Aug 1942

Davis, Elmer, American radio commentator and short story writer, May 1940, *Obit* Sept 1958

Davis, J. Frank, *Obit* May 1942

Davis, Robert, Yrbk 1949

Davis, Robert H., dramatist and journalist, *Obit* Yrbk 1942

De Luce, Daniel, June 1944

De Roussy de Sales, Raoul, *Obit* Jan 1943

Decker, Karl, *Obit* Feb 1942

Deford, Frank, American sportswriter and novelist, Aug 1996

Dennis, Charles H., newspaper editor, *Obit* Nov 1943

Derounian, Arthur, journalist, Oct 1943

Deuel, Wallace R., Aug 1942

Deutsch, Linda, American court reporter, Apr 2007

Dhaliwal, Daljit, English television newscaster, Nov 2000

Dickerson, Nancy, American television reporter, Sept 1962, *Obit* Jan 1998

Dietz, David, author and journalist, Oct 1940, *Obit* Apr 1985

Dith, Pran, Cambodian photojournalist, Oct 1996, *Obit* Yrbk 2008

Dobbs, Lou, American television newscaster, Nov 2006

Dolan, Daniel Leo, Sept 1956

Donaldson, Sam, American television newscaster, Sept 1987

Douthat, Ross Gregory, American journalist, Aug 2009

Dowd, Maureen, American newspaper columnist, Sept 1996

Drew, Elizabeth, journalist, Oct 1979

Drummond, Roscoe, journalist, Nov 1949, *Obit* Nov 1983

Du Puy, William Atherton, *Obit* Oct 1941

Duncan, David Douglas, American photojournalist, Nov 1968

Dunne, Dominick, American novelist, journalist and true-crime writer, May 1999, *Obit* Yrbk 2009

Duranty, Walter, Anglo-American journalist, Jan 1943, *Obit* Yrbk 1958

Early, Stephen, American presidential press secretary, July 1941, Yrbk 1949, *Obit* Sept 1951

Eberle, Irmengarde, Yrbk 1946

Edwards, Bob, American radio newscaster, Sept 2001

Edwards, Douglas, radio and television newscaster, Aug 1988, *Obit* Jan 1991

Edwards, India, journalist and political activist, Sept 1949, *Obit* Mar 1990

Egan, Jennifer, American novelist, journalist and short story writer, Mar 2002

Ehrenburg, Ilya, Russian novelist, critic, memoirist and journalist, June 1966, *Obit* Nov 1967

Eisenstaedt, Alfred, American photojournalist, Jan 1975, *Obit* Oct 1995

Ekman, Carl Gustaf, *Obit* July 1945

Eliot, George Fielding, American journalist, Jan 1940, *Obit* June 1971

Ellerbee, Linda, American television newscaster, Oct 1986

Elliston, Herbert, June 1949, *Obit* Mar 1957

Fallaci, Oriana, Italian journalist and novelist, Feb 1977, *Obit* Yrbk 2007

Fallows, James M., American journalist, Nov 1996

Farrington, Joseph Rider, American newspaper executive and congressman, May 1948, *Obit* Sept 1954

Fauley, Wilbur F., *Obit* Feb 1943

Feinstein, John, American sportswriter, July 1998

Ferraro, Geraldine A., American lawyer, congresswoman, political commentator and vice-presidential candidate, Sept 1984, *Obit* Yrbk 2011

Ferris, Timothy, American journalist and science writer, Jan 2001

Finley, John Huston, Mar 1940

Fischer, John, May 1953, *Obit* Oct 1978

Fischer, Louis, journalist and historian, May 1940, *Obit* Mar 1970

Fishbein, Morris, American periodical editor and physician, May 1940, *Obit* Nov 1976

Fisk, Robert, British journalist, Jan 2006

FitzGerald, Frances, American journalist, June 1987

Flanner, Janet, American journalist and novelist, May 1943, *Obit* Jan 1979

Flannery, Harry W., Oct 1943

Fleeson, Doris, American newspaper columnist, May 1959, *Obit* Oct 1970

Floyd, William, *Obit* Jan 1944

Foley, Martha, author and magazine editor, Apr 1941, *Obit* Oct 1977

Folliard, Edward T., journalist, Nov 1947, *Obit* Feb 1977

Fong-Torres, Ben, American music journalist, Aug 2001

Forand, Aime J., June 1960, *Obit* Mar 1972

Forrest, Wilbur S., May 1948, *Obit* May 1977

Forsyth, Frederick, English journalist and novelist, May 1986

Foster, Maximilian, *Obit* Nov 1943

Francis-Williams, Edward Francis, English author and journalist, Mar 1946, *Obit* Sept 1970

Frankel, Max, newspaper editor, Apr 1987

Frederick, Pauline, American television reporter and commentator, Oct 1954, *Obit* July 1990

Freeman, Lucy, American journalist and nonfiction writer, Oct 1953, *Obit* Yrbk 2005

Friedman, Thomas L., American newspaper columnist, Oct 1995

Frum, David, Canadian journalist, June 2004

Fuller, Bonnie, American magazine editor, May 2000

Fuoss, Robert M., Feb 1959, *Obit* Mar 1980

Fyfe, H. Hamilton, Yrbk 1940, *Obit* July 1951

Gage, Nicholas, American journalist, Mar 1990

Gallagher, William M., Oct 1953, *Obit* Nov 1975

Galloway, Joseph L., American journalist, Sept 2003

Gammons, Peter, American sportswriter, June 2011

Ganim, Sara, Aug 2013

Gannett, Lewis Stiles, American journalist and literary critic, Aug 1941, *Obit* Mar 1966

Garcia Marquez, Gabriel, Colombian novelist and short story writer, July 1973, Jan 2002

Garcia, Cristina, American novelist and journalist, Aug 1999

Garrels, Anne, American television and radio reporter, Mar 2004

Garrison, Deborah, American poet and editor, Jan 2001

Gayda, Virginio, Sept 1940, *Obit* Sept 1943

Geraud, Andre, Sept 1940, *Obit* Jan 1975

Gervasi, Frank Henry, author and journalist, June 1942, *Obit* Mar 1990

Gessen, Masha, Russian journalist, Nov 2013

Geyer, Georgie Anne, columnist, Aug 1986

Ghezali, Salima, Algerian newspaper editor, May 1998

Gibson, Charles, American television news anchor, Sept 2002

Gilmore, Eddy, American journalist, June 1947, *Obit* Yrbk 1967

Gladstone, Brooke, American radio reporter, Jan 2009

Gladwell, Malcolm, Canadian business writer, June 2005

Gleick, James, American science writer, July 2011

Goldberg, Michelle, American journalist, Jan 2012

Goodwin, Richard N., American speechwriter and journalist, Yrbk 1968

Gordon, Ed, American television newscaster, July 2005

Gorrie, Jack Osborne, Mar 1952

Gould, Beatrice Blackmar, magazine editor, Nov 1947, *Obit* Apr 1989

Gould, Bruce, magazine editor, Nov 1947, *Obit* Oct 1989

Graebner, Walter, Aug 1943

Grafton, Samuel, columnist, Jan 1940, *Obit* Feb 1998

Granderson, LZ, Journalist and online columnist, Oct 2012

Greene, Bob, American journalist, July 1995

Gregory, David, American television reporter and moderator, Oct 2010

Griffin, John Howard, American novelist and journalist, Nov 1960, *Obit* Nov 1980

Grigg, John, English journalist and biographer, Oct 1964, *Obit* Apr 2002

Grimes, W. H., June 1947, *Obit* Mar 1972

Grosvenor, Gilbert Hovey, magazine editor, Yrbk 1946, *Obit* Mar 1966

Grosvenor, Melville Bell, periodical editor, Apr 1960, *Obit* June 1982

Guillermoprieto, Alma, Mexican journalist, Sept 2004

Gumbel, Bryant, American television newscaster, July 1986

Gunther, John, journalist and author, Nov 1941, Feb 1961, *Obit* July 1970

Guzy, Carol, American photojournalist, Feb 2000

Habe, Hans, German author and journalist, Feb 1943, *Obit* Nov 1977

Hafezi, Parisa, Journalist and bureau chief for Reuters in Iran, Sept 2012

Haffajee, Ferial, South African newspaper editor, Jan 2004

Halberstam, David, American journalist, Apr 1973, *Obit* July 2007

Hannagan, Steve, publicist and sportswriter, Aug 1944, *Obit* Mar 1953

Hannity, Sean, American television moderator, Apr 2005

Hansen, Chris, American television reporter, June 2010

Hansenne, Marcel, Apr 1946

Harsanyi, Zsolt, *Obit* Apr 1944

Harsch, Joseph C., American journalist, Oct 1944, *Obit* Aug 1998

Harvey, Paul, American radio reporter, Mar 1986, *Obit* Yrbk 2009

Haskin, Frederic J., *Obit* June 1944

Hass, Amira, Israeli journalist, Apr 2009

Heath, S. Burton, Jan 1940, *Obit* Sept 1949

Heatter, Gabriel, radio commentator, Apr 1941, *Obit* May 1972

Hecht, Ben, American journalist, novelist, dramatist and screenwriter, Feb 1942, *Obit* June 1964

Heckscher, August, municipal official and journalist, Oct 1958, *Obit* June 1997

Hedges, Chris, American foreign correspondent, June 2012

Heiden, Konrad, Mar 1944, *Obit* Sept 1975

Hellinger, Mark, columnist and motion picture producer, Sept 1947, *Obit* July 1948

Helms, Jesse A., American senator, July 1979, *Obit* Yrbk 2008

Helprin, Mark, American short story writer and novelist, Aug 1991

Hemingway, Mary, wife of American novelist Ernest Hemingway, Sept 1968, *Obit* Jan 1987

Herbert, Elizabeth, Feb 1954

Hersey, John, American novelist and journalist, Feb 1944, *Obit* May 1993

Hertzberg, Hendrik, American journalist, Mar 2011

Hiaasen, Carl, American novelist and columnist, Apr 1997

Hibbs, Ben, magazine editor, July 1946, *Obit* May 1975

Higgins, Chester, American photojournalist, June 2002

Higgins, F. R., Irish poet, *Obit* Mar 1941

Higgins, Marguerite, journalist, June 1951, *Obit* Feb 1966

Hightower, John M., journalist, Nov 1952, *Obit* Apr 1987

Hill, Edwin Conger, journalist, Sept 1940, *Obit* Apr 1957

Hillerman, Tony, American mystery novelist, Jan 1992, *Obit* Yrbk 2008

Hitchens, Christopher, British journalist, Mar 1999, *Obit* Yrbk 2012

Hoellering, Franz, Oct 1940

Hollenbeck, Don, American television newscaster, Feb 1951, *Obit* Sept 1954

Hondros, Chris, American photojournalist, Nov 2004, *Obit* Yrbk 2011

Hughes, Emmet John, American journalist and presidential speechwriter and adviser, Jan 1964, *Obit* Nov 1982

Hughes, Paul, Yrbk 1943

Huntley, Chet, American television news anchor, Oct 1956, *Obit* May 1974

Husain, Mishal, British television news anchor, Jan 2004

Hutchison, Bruce, Canadian journalist, Oct 1956

Ifill, Gwen, American television newscaster and moderator, Sept 2005

Inskeep, Steve, American radio reporter, June 2009

James, Bill, American baseball statistician, June 2004

Jarvis, Jeff, American journalist, Aug 2009

Jean, Michaelle, Canadian broadcast journalist and governor general, June 2009

Jefferson, Margo, American literary critic, June 1999

Jenkins, Jerry B., American sportswriter and novelist, June 2003

Jennings, Peter, Canadian television newscaster, Nov 1983, *Obit* Sept 2005

Joesten, Joachim, June 1942

Johnson, Boris, British mayor, Oct 2008

Johnson, Herschel, American journalist and children's author, July 1946

Johnson, Malcolm, June 1949, *Obit* Aug 1976

Johnson, Paul, English journalist and historian, Sept 1994

Jones, Russell, Oct 1957, *Obit* Aug 1979

Jose, F. Sionil, Filipino novelist, Jan 2005

Judd, Jackie, American television reporter, Sept 2002

Just, Ward S., American novelist, May 1989

Kaempffert, Waldemar, Sept 1943, *Obit* Feb 1957

Kahn, Roger, American novelist, short story writer and sportswriter, June 2000

Kaltenborn, H. V., radio commentator, Aug 1940, *Obit* Sept 1965

Kamber, Michael, American photojournalist, June 2009

Kane, Harnett T., journalist, historian and author, Yrbk 1947, *Obit* Yrbk 1984

Kapuscinski, Ryszard, Polish journalist and biographer, Sept 1992, *Obit* Yrbk 2007

Karbo, Karen, American novelist, May 2001

Karman, Tawakel, Mar 2013

Keegan, John, English military historian and journalist, Oct 1989, *Obit* Yrbk 2012

Keller, Bill, American newspaper editor, Oct 2003

Kelley, Kitty, American biographer, Apr 1992

Kelly, Florence Finch, journalist and author, *Obit* Jan 1940

Kempton, Murray, American newspaper columnist, June 1973, *Obit* July 1997

Kennedy, John B., Feb 1944, *Obit* Oct 1961

Khan, Daisy, American Islamic leader, June 2013

Kieran, John, sportswriter, Apr 1940, *Obit* Feb 1982

Kimbrough, Emily, lecturer and author, Mar 1944, *Obit* Apr 1989

King, John, American television news anchor, Mar 2010

Kirchwey, Freda, American magazine editor, Yrbk 1942, *Obit* Feb 1976

Kirkpatrick, Helen, journalist, May 1941

Klein, Julius, veterans' leader and public relations consultant, July 1948, *Obit* May 1984

Knickerbocker, Hubert Renfro, journalist, Sept 1940, *Obit* Sept 1949

Knight, Eric Mowbray, Anglo-American novelist, short story writer and journalist, July 1942, *Obit* Mar 1943

Koestler, Arthur, Hungarian-British novelist, essayist and journalist, Apr 1943, Jan 1962, *Obit* Apr 1983

Koppel, Ted, American television newscaster, July 1984

Kotb, Hoda, American television news anchor, Apr 2011

Kraus, Rene, July 1941, *Obit* Sept 1947

Kristof, Nicholas D., American newspaper columnist, Feb 2006

Krock, Arthur, American journalist, Feb 1943, *Obit* June 1974

Kroft, Steve, American television reporter, Nov 1996

Kuhn, Irene Corbally, journalist, Feb 1946, *Obit* Mar 1996

Kuralt, Charles, American television newscaster, July 1981, *Obit* Sept 1997

LaFarge, John, American priest, Nov 1942, *Obit* Jan 1964

Lane, Gertrude Battles, magazine editor, *Obit* Nov 1941

Lapham, Lewis H., American journalist and magazine editor, Mar 1989

Laurence, William Leonard, journalist, Oct 1945, *Obit* May 1977

Lawrence, Mildred, Yrbk 1953

Lazareff, Pierre, May 1942, *Obit* June 1972

Leary, John Joseph, *Obit* Feb 1944

Lee, Clark, Yrbk 1943, *Obit* Apr 1953

Lelyveld, Joseph, American newspaper editor, Nov 2005

Lemon, Don, American television news anchor, May 2010

Lengyel, Emil, journalist and author, Feb 1942, *Obit* Apr 1985

Leo, John, American magazine columnist, Sept 2006

Lessing, Bruno, author and newspaper editor, *Obit* Jan 1940

Lesueur, Larry, American radio newscaster, June 1943, *Obit* Yrbk 2003

Leviero, Anthony, Sept 1952, *Obit* Nov 1956

Lewis, Ananda, American television entertainment reporter, June 2005

Lewis, Anthony, American journalist, Nov 1955, *Obit* Yrbk 2013

Lewis, Flora, American columnist, Jan 1989, *Obit* Yrbk 2002

Lewis, Fulton, radio commentator, Nov 1942, *Obit* Nov 1966

Lewis, Willmott, May 1941, *Obit* Feb 1950

Lindley, Ernest K., journalist, June 1943, *Obit* Yrbk 1991

Lipinski, Anne Marie, American journalist, July 2004

Lippmann, Walter, American journalist and political philosopher, Sept 1940, Nov 1962, *Obit* Jan 1975

Littledale, Clara Savage, Oct 1946, *Obit* Mar 1956

Lochner, Louis Paul, journalist, Aug 1942, *Obit* Feb 1975

Logan, Lara, South African television reporter, July 2006

Lombard, Helen, May 1943

Long, Tania, Anglo-Russian journalist, May 1946, *Obit* June 1999

Lowry, Edward George, *Obit* Sept 1943

Lubell, Samuel, journalist and public opinion analyst, Nov 1956, *Obit* Oct 1987

Lukas, J. Anthony, American journalist, Jan 1987, *Obit* Aug 1997

Lupica, Mike, American sportswriter, Mar 2001

MacGowan, Gault, Jan 1945

MacNeil, Neil, American newspaper editor, May 1940

MacNeil, Robert, Canadian television newscaster and novelist, Feb 1980

Malkin, Michelle, American journalist and political commentator, Apr 2010

Maloney, Francis T., *Obit* Mar 1945

Manchester, William, American biographer and historian, Nov 1967, *Obit* Yrbk 2004

Manning, Marie, columnist, Aug 1944, *Obit* Jan 1946

Marden, Orison Swett, author and magazine editor, July 1967, *Obit* Oct 1975

Mark, Mary Ellen, American photographer, Sept 1999

Markel, Lester, newspaper editor, Yrbk 1952, *Obit* Jan 1978

Marshall, Verne, American newspaper editor, Feb 1941, *Obit* May 1965

Martin, Harry, June 1948, *Obit* Mar 1959

Martin, Jackie, Apr 1943

Martin, Joseph William, American congressman and Speaker of the House, Oct 1940, May 1948, *Obit* Apr 1968

Martin, Roland S., American journalist, June 2009

Mason, Joseph Warren Teets, American journalist, *Obit* July 1941

Matthews, Herbert L., American journalist, Nov 1943, *Obit* Sept 1977

Matthews, T. S., American novelist and journalist, Apr 1950, *Obit* Mar 1991

Maxwell, Elsa, columnist and society hostess, Mar 1943, *Obit* Jan 1964

Maxwell, William, American novelist, short story writer and magazine editor, Yrbk 1949, *Obit* Oct 2000

Mayer, Jane, American journalist, Oct 2008

Mayo, Katherine, American journalist and reformer, *Obit* Yrbk 1940

McAlary, Mike, columnist, *Obit* Mar 1999

McCann, Colum, Irish novelist and short story writer, Mar 2010

McCormick, Anne O'Hare, journalist, Mar 1940, *Obit* July 1954

McCrary, Tex, American journalist and talk show host, July 1953, *Obit* Yrbk 2003

McCurry, Steve, American photojournalist, Nov 2005

McGee, Frank, television commentator and newscaster, June 1964, *Obit* June 1974

McGinniss, Joe, American true crime writer, Jan 1984

McGurn, Barrett, Apr 1965

McKelway, B. M., Jan 1958, *Obit* Oct 1976

McSwigan, Marie, Yrbk 1953, *Obit* Sept 1962

McWhirter, Norris, English sportswriter and sportscaster, Nov 1979, *Obit* Yrbk 2004

McWilliams, Carey, American lawyer, magazine editor and nonfiction writer, Oct 1943, *Obit* Aug 1980

Meloney, Marie Mattingly, *Obit* Aug 1943

Merz, Charles, newspaper editor, Nov 1954, *Obit* Nov 1977

Michel, Sia, American magazine editor, Sept 2003

Michelson, Charles, journalist, Aug 1940, *Obit* Jan 1948

Michie, Allan A., Nov 1942, *Obit* Jan 1974

Middleton, Drew, journalist and author, Sept 1943, *Obit* Mar 1990

Millard, Bailey, *Obit* May 1941

Miller, Judith, American journalist, Jan 2006

Miller, Max, American journalist, May 1940, *Obit* Feb 1968

Miller, Webb, American journalist, *Obit* Jan 1940

Mirabella, Grace, magazine editor, Oct 1991

Moats, Alice-Leone, author and journalist, May 1943, *Obit* July 1989

Mohamad, Goenawan, Indonesian poet and magazine editor, Jan 2007

Moir, Phyllis, Apr 1942

Molinari, Susan, congresswoman and television newscaster, Mar 1996

Monroque, Shala, American magazine editor, Jan 2012

Montagne, Renee, American radio reporter, Nov 2009

Montague, James J., *Obit* Feb 1942

Montgomery, Ruth Shick, author and journalist, Feb 1957

Moody, Blair, American senator, Sept 1951, *Obit* Oct 1954

Moraes, F. R., Nov 1957, *Obit* July 1974

Morell, Parker, *Obit* Apr 1943

Morgan, Edward Paddock, reporter and commentator, Apr 1964, *Obit* Mar 1993

Morgan, Joy Elmer, Jan 1946

Morgan, Lucy, newspaper columnist, Mar 1959

Morris, Jan, English journalist and travel writer, Jan 1964, June 1986

Moss, Adam, American magazine editor, Mar 2004

Motherwell, Hiram, *Obit* Jan 1946

Mott, Frank Luther, journalist and historian, Oct 1941, *Obit* Yrbk 1964

Moulitsas Zuniga, Markos, American political blog writer, Mar 2007

Mowery, Edward J., American journalist, Nov 1953, *Obit* Feb 1971

Mowrer, Edgar Ansel, journalist, Oct 1941, July 1962, *Obit* May 1977

Mudd, Roger, American television newscaster, Jan 1981

Murrow, Edward R., American radio and television newscaster, Feb 1942, Nov 1953, *Obit* June 1965

Myasnikova, Yelena, Russian magazine editor, Jan 2002

Mydans, Carl, American photojournalist, May 1945, *Obit* Yrbk 2004

Mydans, Shelley Smith, American journalist and novelist, May 1945, *Obit* Aug 2002

Myers, Gustavus, journalist and historian, *Obit* Jan 1943

Navarro Bello, Adela, Oct 2013

Navasky, Victor S., American journalist, May 1986

Neuberger, Richard L., American senator, Feb 1955, *Obit* May 1960

Newman, Edwin, American television reporter, commentator and moderator, Sept 1967, *Obit* Yrbk 2010

Nichols, Herbert B., American science journalist, Sept 1947

Nocera, Joseph, American journalist, Oct 2011

Norris, Michele, American radio reporter, Mar 2008

Northrop, Peggy, American magazine editor, Nov 2009

Norton, Howard Melvin, June 1947

Nye, Gerald Prentice, American senator, Nov 1941, *Obit* Sept 1971

O'Brien, Soledad, American television news anchor, Nov 2009

Olbermann, Keith, American television news anchor, Feb 2009

Orlean, Susan, American writer, June 2003

Ortiz Rocasolano, Letizia, Spanish television reporter and wife of Felipe, Prince of Spain, Jan 2004

Ottley, Roi, Oct 1943, *Obit* Yrbk 1960

Packard, Eleanor, Apr 1941, *Obit* June 1972

Packard, Vance, American journalist, Apr 1958, *Obit* Feb 1997

Palast, Greg, American journalist, June 2011

Pauley, Jane, American television newscaster and talk show host, May 1980

Paxman, Jeremy, British television reporter and interviewer, Jan 2007

Pearson, Drew, American journalist, May 1941, *Obit* Nov 1969

Pegler, Westbrook, American columnist, Mar 1940, *Obit* Sept 1969

Pelley, Scott, American television news anchor, Aug 2011

Peltz, Mary Ellis, Apr 1954, *Obit* Jan 1982

Perlman, Philip B., American solicitor general, July 1952, *Obit* Oct 1960

Peters, Charles, periodical editor, Aug 1990

Peters, Thomas J., American management consultant and writer, Oct 1994

Phillips, Kyra, American television reporter, Jan 2013

Phillips, Lena Madesin, Apr 1946, *Obit* July 1955

Phillips, William, American periodical editor, Oct 1984, *Obit* Yrbk 2002

Pileggi, Nicholas, journalist and author, Jan 1999

Pitkin, Walter B., author, Oct 1941, *Obit* Mar 1953

Pitts, Leonard J., American newspaper columnist, Oct 2004

Podhoretz, Norman, American magazine editor and political commentator, Oct 1968

Poliakov, Aleksandr, *Obit* Nov 1942

Pollack, Jack Harrison, American journalist, Yrbk 1957, *Obit* Feb 1985

Post, Robert P., *Obit* Sept 1943

Pozner, Vladimir, Russian journalist, May 1943

Pribichevich, Stoyan, Aug 1944, *Obit* July 1976

Proulx, Annie, American novelist and short story writer, Apr 1995

Pyle, Ernie, American journalist, Apr 1941, *Obit* May 1945

Quinn, Sally, American journalist, Oct 1988

Ramm, Fredrik, *Obit* Jan 1944

Ramonet, Ignacio, Spanish journalist, June 2008

Rashid, Ahmed, Pakistani journalist, Jan 2007

Raskin, A. H., newspaper reporter and editor, May 1978, *Obit* Feb 1994

Raspberry, William J., American newspaper columnist, *Obit* Yrbk 2012

Rather, Dan, American television newscaster, May 1975

Rattansi, Afshin, British journalist and novelist, Jan 2006

Reader, John, British photojournalist and writer, Jan 2007

Reasoner, Harry, American television newscaster, Feb 1966, *Obit* Oct 1991

Reavis, Smith Freeman, *Obit* Mar 1940

Reilly, Rick, American sportswriter, Feb 2005

Resnick, Louis, *Obit* May 1941

Reston, James, American journalist, Mar 1943, Nov 1980, *Obit* Feb 1996

Restrepo, Laura, Colombian novelist and journalist, Jan 2006

Reventlow, Ernst, *Obit* Jan 1944

Reynolds, Quentin James, journalist, Mar 1941, *Obit* Apr 1965

Rice, Grantland, American sportswriter, Sept 1941, *Obit* Sept 1954

Ricks, Thomas E., American military writer, Nov 2007

Rideau, Wilbert, American convicted murderer and prison journalist, Nov 2010

Risen, James, American journalist, Aug 2007

Roach, Mary, American writer, Jan 2011

Robb, Inez Callaway, American journalist, Yrbk 1958, *Obit* June 1979

Roberts, Cokie, American television reporter and moderator, May 1994

Roberts, Robin, American television news anchor, Feb 2008

Robertson, Ben, American journalist, Nov 1942

Rollin, Betty, American television reporter and writer, Aug 1994

Ronson, Jon, English journalist, Apr 2012

Rooney, Andrew A., American journalist and humorist, July 1982, *Obit* Yrbk 2012

Rose, Charlie, American television newscaster and talk show host, Jan 1995

Rosenthal, A. M., American newspaper editor, Yrbk 1960, *Obit* Sept 2006

Rosenthal, Joe, American photojournalist, June 1945, *Obit* Yrbk 2007

Ross, Charles G., June 1945, *Obit* Jan 1951

Ross, Harold Wallace, American periodical editor, May 1943, *Obit* Jan 1952

Roueche, Berton, American novelist and medical and travel writer, Yrbk 1959, *Obit* July 1994

Rountree, Martha, radio and television producer, Feb 1957, *Obit* Nov 1999

Rove, Karl, American political commentator and former presidential adviser, Oct 2000

Rovere, Richard Halworth, American journalist, Apr 1977, *Obit* Jan 1980

Rowell, Chester Harvey, newspaper editor, Yrbk 1940, *Obit* May 1948

Rubenstein, Atoosa, American magazine editor, Oct 2004

Runbeck, Margaret Lee, Yrbk 1952, *Obit* Yrbk 1956

Saerchinger, Cesar, Apr 1940

Safer, Morley, Canadian television newscaster, July 1980

Salisbury, Harrison Evans, American journalist, July 1955, Jan 1982, *Obit* Sept 1993

Sanborn, Pitts, music critic, author and journalist, *Obit* Apr 1941

Sanders, Marlene, television newscaster, Feb 1981

Sandford, John, American crime novelist, Mar 2002

Santelli, Rick, American television reporter, July 2010

Saunders, Carl M., June 1950, *Obit* Nov 1974

Savitch, Jessica, television news anchor, Jan 1983, *Obit* Mar 1984

Sawyer, Diane, American television news anchor, Oct 1985

Schanberg, Sydney, journalist, Aug 1990

Schell, Jonathan, American journalist, July 1992

Schieffer, Bob, American television news anchor, Aug 2006

Schlosser, Alex L., American newspaper and magazine editor, *Obit* Mar 1943

Schoenbrun, David, American broadcast journalist, Jan 1960, *Obit* July 1988

Schorr, Daniel, American television reporter, Sept 1959, Feb 1978, *Obit* Yrbk 2010

Schultz, Sigrid Lillian, journalist, Apr 1944

Schwartz, Gil, American public relations executive and journalist, Aug 2007

Seibold, Louis, *Obit* June 1945

Seldes, George, American journalist, Sept 1941, *Obit* Sept 1995

Seltzer, Louis B., Yrbk 1956, *Obit* June 1980

Servan-Schreiber, Jean-Jacques, French political leader, Jan 1955, *Obit* Yrbk 2007

Severgnini, Beppe, Italian journalist, Jan 2006

Sey, Abdoulie, Gambian newspaper editor, Jan 2004

Seymour, Lesley Jane, magazine editor, Nov 2001

Shafer, Paul W., American congressman, July 1952, *Obit* Oct 1954

Shah, Saira, British journalist and documentary filmmaker, Jan 2003

Shamsie, Kamila, Pakistani novelist, Sept 2009

Shaw, Bernard, American television newscaster, Feb 1995

Sheean, Vincent, American journalist, novelist and essayist, Aug 1941, *Obit* May 1975

Sheehan, Neil, American journalist, Aug 1989

Sheehy, Gail, American writer, June 1993

Sherard, Robert Harborough, English author and journalist, *Obit* Mar 1943

Sherrod, Robert Lee, journalist, June 1944, Yrbk 1962, *Obit* May 1994

Shilts, Randy, American journalist, Oct 1993, *Obit* May 1994

Shinn, Milicent Washburn, author and journalist, *Obit* Oct 1940

Shirer, William L., American journalist, July 1941, May 1962, *Obit* Feb 1994

Short, Joseph, American journalist and presidential press secretary, Feb 1951, *Obit* Nov 1952

Shridharani, Krishnalal, Indian journalist and author, Jan 1942, *Obit* Oct 1960

Shriver, Maria, American television newscaster and wife of Arnold Schwarzenegger, Nov 1991

Siegel, Robert, American radio newscaster, July 2008

Silberman, Charles E., American journalist, July 1979, *Obit* Yrbk 2011

Simpson, Carole, American television newscaster, Nov 1999

Simpson, John, British television reporter, June 2010

Smedley, Agnes, American journalist, Jan 1944, *Obit* June 1950

Smith, Gary, American sportswriter, Jan 2009

Smith, Hedrick, American journalist, June 1991

Smith, Howard K., American television newscaster and commentator, Mar 1943, July 1976, *Obit* Aug 2002

Smith, Merriman, journalist and author, Yrbk 1964, *Obit* Nov 1993

Smith, Paul C., Apr 1943, *Obit* Sept 1976

Smith, Red, American sportswriter, Apr 1959, *Obit* Feb 1982

Smith, Rex, Jan 1942

Snow, Edgar, journalist, June 1941, *Obit* Apr 1972

Soth, Lauren K., newspaper editor, Yrbk 1956, *Obit* June 1998

Spence, Hartzell, journalist and novelist, Oct 1942, *Obit* Yrbk 2001

Spender, John A., English newspaper editor, *Obit* Aug 1942

St. John, Robert, American journalist, June 1942, *Obit* Yrbk 2003

St. Johns, Adela Rogers, author and journalist, Aug 1976, *Obit* Sept 1988

Stahl, Lesley, television reporter, June 1996

Stamberg, Susan, American radio newscaster, Oct 2008

Stark, Louis, June 1945, *Obit* Sept 1954

Stearns, Harold E., journalist and critic, *Obit* Oct 1943

Steel, David, British member of Parliament, July 1978

Steell, Willis, *Obit* Mar 1941

Stengel, Richard, American journalist and magazine editor, Jan 2011

Stevens, Edmund, American journalist, July 1950, *Obit* July 1992

Stevenson, E. Robert, Jan 1940

Stewart, Kenneth L., Yrbk 1943

Stockbridge, Frank Parker, *Obit* Jan 1941

Stokes, Thomas Lunsford, May 1947, *Obit* Sept 1958

Stone, I. F., American journalist, Sept 1972, *Obit* Aug 1989

Stout, Wesley Winans, June 1941, *Obit* Jan 1972

Streit, Clarence K., journalist, May 1940, May 1950, *Obit* Sept 1986

Strong, Anna Louise, American journalist, Mar 1949, *Obit* May 1970

Strout, Richard Lee, journalist and columnist, Apr 1980, *Obit* Oct 1990

Sugar, Bert Randolph, American sportswriter, Nov 2002, *Obit* Yrbk 2012

Sugrue, Thomas, journalist and author, June 1948, *Obit* Feb 1953

Sullivan, Walter, American science writer, Sept 1980, *Obit* June 1996

Sulzberger, C. L., American journalist, May 1944, *Obit* Nov 1993

Suskind, Ron, Feb 2013

Swing, Raymond, radio commentator, Jan 1940, *Obit* Feb 1969

Swope, Herbert Bayard, journalist, Nov 1944, *Obit* Sept 1958

Tabouis, Genevieve R., French journalist, Jan 1940

Talese, Gay, American journalist, July 1972

Taylor, M. Sayle, *Obit* Mar 1942

Tebbel, John William, American historian and journalist, Yrbk 1953, *Obit* Mar 2005

Terhune, Albert Payson, author, *Obit* Apr 1942

Thayer, Ernest Lawrence, American journalist and poet, *Obit* Oct 1940

Thomas, Lowell, American radio newscaster, May 1940, Jan 1952, *Obit* Oct 1981

Thompson, Dorothy, American columnist, July 1940, *Obit* Mar 1961

Tierney, John, American journalist, Aug 2005

Tilberis, Liz, British magazine editor, Nov 1998, *Obit* July 1999

Tinney, Cal, Feb 1943

Tobin, Richard, journalist, editor and author, Nov 1944, *Obit* Nov 1995

Toledano, Ralph de, American columnist and political writer, Yrbk 1962, *Obit* Yrbk 2007

Tolischus, Otto D., Jan 1940, *Obit* Apr 1967

Totenberg, Nina, American radio and television reporter, Mar 1996

Townsend, Edward Waterman, American journalist and congressman, *Obit* May 1942

Treanor, Tom, *Obit* Oct 1944

Tregaskis, Richard, author and journalist, Aug 1943, *Obit* Oct 1973

Trimble, Vance H., Yrbk 1960

Trout, Robert, American radio and television reporter, Oct 1965, *Obit* Jan 2001

Trussell, C. P., July 1949, *Obit* Yrbk 1968

Ulrich, Charles, *Obit* Aug 1941

Uygur, Cenk, Turkish-American radio talk show host, May 2013

Valdes-Rodriguez, Alisa, American novelist, Jan 2006

Van Doren, Irita, American newspaper editor, Sept 1941, *Obit* Feb 1967

Van Paassen, Pierre, Dutch-American clergyman, journalist and author, Oct 1942, *Obit* Mar 1968

Vandenberg, Arthur H., American senator, Nov 1940, June 1948, *Obit* May 1951

Vanocur, Sander, Jan 1963

Vargas, Elizabeth, American television news anchor, Apr 2006

Vernon, Grenville, *Obit* Jan 1942

Vitug, Marites, Filipino journalist, Jan 2005

Vonnegut, Kurt, American novelist and short story writer, July 1970, Mar 1991, *Obit* Aug 2007

Vreeland, Diana, American magazine editor, Feb 1978, *Obit* Oct 1989

Walker, Stanley, newspaper editor, Nov 1944, *Obit* Jan 1963

Wallace, Chris, American television reporter and moderator, Feb 2011

Wallace, Mike, American television newscaster, July 1957, Nov 1977, *Obit* Yrbk 2012

Wallin, Pamela, Canadian television newscaster and talk show host, Jan 2005

Wallraff, Gunter, German journalist, Jan 2004

Waln, Nora, journalist, Jan 1940, *Obit* Nov 1964

Walsh, George Ethelbert, *Obit* Apr 1941

Walter, Eugene, American dramatist and screenwriter, *Obit* Nov 1941

Walters, Barbara, American television newscaster, Feb 1971, Feb 2003

Watson, Mark Skinner, journalist, Nov 1946, *Obit* Apr 1966

Wattenberg, Ben J., American political analyst and writer, June 1985

Waymack, W. W., Mar 1947, *Obit* Jan 1961

Wechsberg, Joseph, American journalist, Apr 1955, *Obit* June 1983

Weisberg, Jacob, American journalist, Oct 2007

Weisgal, Meyer W., Oct 1972, *Obit* Nov 1977

Werth, Alexander, English journalist, Apr 1943, *Obit* Apr 1969

Wertheimer, Linda, radio newscaster, Nov 1995

West, Dorothy, American novelist, Feb 1997, *Obit* Oct 1998

West, Rebecca, English novelist and journalist, June 1968, *Obit* May 1983

Weyrich, Paul, American political activist and commentator, Feb 2005, *Obit* Yrbk 2009

Wheaton, Anne, Jan 1958, *Obit* May 1977

White, Theodore H., American journalist, Apr 1955, Apr 1976, *Obit* July 1986

White, William Smith, journalist, Yrbk 1955, *Obit* June 1994

Whitehead, Don, journalist, Yrbk 1953, *Obit* Mar 1981

Whyte, William H., American journalist and sociologist, Jan 1959, *Obit* Mar 1999

Wicker, Tom, columnist, Nov 1973, *Obit* Yrbk 2012

Wile, Frederic William, journalist and radio commentator, *Obit* June 1941

Wilkerson, Isabel, American journalist, Oct 2011

Williams, Brian, American television news anchor, July 1998

Williams, Juan, American journalist, May 2008

Williams, Wythe, journalist, Oct 1943, *Obit* Sept 1956

Willson, Beckles, *Obit* Nov 1942

Winchester, Alice, magazine editor, Feb 1954

Winchester, Simon, Anglo-American journalist, Oct 2006

Winster, Reginald Thomas Herbert Fletcher, Feb 1946

Winter, Ella, Yrbk 1946, *Obit* Sept 1980

Wintour, Anna, British fashion editor, July 1990

Witcover, Jules, American newspaper columnist and writer, Apr 2008

Wolfe, Tom, American journalist and novelist, Jan 1971

Wolfert, Ira, author and journalist, Apr 1943, *Obit* Feb 1998

Woltman, Frederick, July 1947, *Obit* Apr 1970

Woodlock, Thomas Francis, *Obit* Sept 1945

Woodruff, Judy, American television newscaster, Sept 1986

Woods, Donald, South African newspaper editor, Feb 1982, *Obit* Nov 2001

Wu Chuntao, Chinese journalist, Jan 2005

Yazbek, Samar, Aug 2013

Ybarra, Thomas Russell, journalist and biographer, Jan 1940

Yeakley, Marjory Hall, Yrbk 1957

Zahn, Paula, American television newscaster, Feb 2002

Zhukov, Georgii Aleksandrovich, Soviet journalist, Oct 1960

Zimmer, Carl, American science journalist, Oct 2012

Judges

Abbott, Douglas, Canadian supreme court justice, June 1949

Alito, Samuel A., American Supreme Court justice, Apr 2006

Allen, Florence Ellinwood, American judge, Feb 1941, July 1963, Obit Nov 1966

Almond, J. Lindsay, American governor, Mar 1958, Obit June 1986

Amsterdam, Birdie, judge, Mar 1940, Obit Sept 1996

Anderson, John Crawford, American state supreme court justice, Obit Jan 1940

Andrews, Charles O., American senator, Obit Nov 1946

Archer, Dennis, American mayor, Feb 1997

Arnold, Thurman Wesley, American lawyer and government official, Jan 1940, Obit Yrbk 1969

Baldwin, Raymond Earl, American governor and senator, July 1946, Obit Nov 1986

Barnes, Stanley N., American judge, Sept 1953

Bazelon, David L., American judge, Jan 1971, Obit Apr 1993

Becker, William Dee, American judge and mayor, Obit Sept 1943

Bird, Rose Elizabeth, judge, May 1984, Obit May 2000

Black, Hugo LaFayette, American Supreme Court justice, Sept 1941, May 1964, Obit Nov 1971

Blackmun, Harry A., American Supreme Court justice, Oct 1970, Obit May 1999

Bok, Curtis, American state supreme court justice, May 1954, Obit July 1962

Bosone, Reva Zilpha Beck, congresswoman and judge, Jan 1949

Brandeis, Louis Dembitz, American Supreme Court justice, Obit Nov 1941

Brennan, William J., American Supreme Court justice, June 1957, Obit Oct 1997

Breyer, Stephen G., American Supreme Court justice, June 1996

Burger, Warren E., American Chief Justice of the Supreme Court, Nov 1969, Obit Aug 1995

Burton, Harold Hitz, American senator and Supreme Court justice, Apr 1945, Obit Jan 1965

Byrne, Brendan T., May 1974

Chandy, Anna, Apr 1960

Chaudhry, Iftikhar Mohammad, Pakistani supreme court justice, Jan 2007

Cherry, Francis Adams, American governor, July 1954, Obit Sept 1965

Clark, William Patrick, American Secretary of the interior, July 1982, Obit Yrbk 2013

Clarke, John Hessin, Supreme Court justice, Obit May 1945

Clements, Earle C., senator and governor, Sept 1955, Obit May 1985

Coffin, Frank M., American judge, Apr 1959, Obit Yrbk 2010

Coleman, J. P., American governor and judge, Sept 1956, Obit Nov 1991

Collet, John C., Feb 1946, Obit Feb 1956

Collins, Lorin Cone, Obit Yrbk 1940

Cox, E. Eugene, American congressman, Apr 1943, Obit Feb 1953

Craig, Walter Early, judge, June 1964, Obit Sept 1986

Daniel, Price, American senator and governor, Jan 1956, Obit Oct 1988

Davidson, Irwin D., American congressman, Jan 1956

Davies, Ronald N., American judge, Sept 1958, Obit June 1996

Davis, James C., Apr 1957, Obit Feb 1982

Deasy, Luere B., Obit Apr 1940

Dehler, Thomas, July 1955, Obit Oct 1967

Denning, Alfred Thompson Denning, British judge, July 1965, Obit June 1999

Devaney, John Patrick, Obit Nov 1941

Dixon, Owen, Australian judge and diplomat, Aug 1942

Douglas, William O., American Supreme Court justice, Oct 1941, Nov 1950, Obit Mar 1980

Eicher, Edward C., May 1941, Obit Jan 1945

Erlanger, Mitchell Louis, Obit Oct 1940

Ervin, Sam J., American senator, Jan 1955, Oct 1973, Obit June 1985

Fischer, Israel Frederick, judge and congressman, Obit Apr 1940

Fortas, Abe, American Supreme Court justice, Feb 1966, Obit May 1982

Frank, Jerome N., American judge, Apr 1941, Obit Mar 1957

Frankfurter, Felix, American Supreme Court justice, June 1941, July 1957, Obit Apr 1965

Freeh, Louis J., American FBI director, May 1996

Garzon, Baltasar, Spanish judge, Mar 2001

George, Walter F., American senator, June 1943, June 1955, Obit Oct 1957

Gibson, Ernest W., American governor and judge, July 1949, Obit Yrbk 1969

Ginsburg, Ruth Bader, American Supreme Court justice, Feb 1994

Goldsborough, T. Alan, June 1948, Obit July 1951

Gomez, Jean-Jacques, French judge, Jan 2002

Gould, Wayne, New Zealand judge, Jan 2006

Grant, Robert, author and judge, *Obit* July 1940

Greene, Harold H., American judge, Aug 1985, *Obit* May 2000

Griffiths, Martha Wright, American congresswoman and state official, Oct 1955, *Obit* Yrbk 2003

Guerrero, Jose Gustavo, Jan 1947, *Obit* Jan 1959

Hackworth, Green H., Jan 1958, *Obit* Sept 1973

Hall, Frederick Lee, American judge and governor, Oct 1955, *Obit* May 1970

Hand, Learned, American judge, Apr 1950, *Obit* Nov 1961

Harlan, John Marshall, American Supreme Court justice, May 1955, *Obit* Feb 1972

Harris, Oren, American congressman and judge, May 1956

Harron, Marion J., Yrbk 1949

Hatch, Carl A., senator and judge, Yrbk 1944, *Obit* Nov 1963

Hewart, Gordon Hewart, *Obit* June 1943

Holland, Spessard L., American governor and senator, Feb 1950, *Obit* Yrbk 1971

Hudson, Manley O., June 1944, *Obit* June 1960

Hughes, Richard J., American governor and judge, July 1962, *Obit* Feb 1993

Hughes, Sarah T., American judge, Nov 1950, *Obit* July 1985

Hull, John Adley, *Obit* June 1944

Ilsley, J. L., Canadian cabinet member and judge, Feb 1948

Impellitteri, Vincent R., American mayor, Feb 1951, *Obit* Mar 1987

Jackson Lee, Sheila, American congresswoman, Nov 2008

Jackson, Thomas Penfield, judge, June 2001, *Obit* Yrbk 2013

Jameson, William James, judge, July 1954

Johnson, Frank M., American judge, Aug 1978, *Obit* Oct 1999

Jones, Marvin, congressman and judge, Aug 1943, *Obit* Jan 1984

Jones, Norman L., *Obit* Jan 1941

Kaufman, Irving R., American judge, Apr 1953, *Obit* Apr 1992

Keech, Richmond B., Mar 1950

Kennedy, Anthony M., American Supreme Court justice, July 1988

Kennon, Robert Floyd, American governor, Oct 1954, *Obit* Apr 1988

Kenyon, Dorothy, American judge, Apr 1947, *Obit* Apr 1972

Kerner, Otto, American governor and judge, Oct 1961, *Obit* July 1976

Kilgore, Harley Martin, American senator, June 1943, *Obit* May 1956

King, John W., governor and judge, May 1964, *Obit* Nov 1996

Kinnear, Helen Alice, Canadian judge, Apr 1957

Knight, Goodwin, American governor, Jan 1955, *Obit* July 1970

Kross, Anna M., American judge, Nov 1945, *Obit* Oct 1979

Lafontaine, Henri Marie, Belgian judge and pacifist, *Obit* July 1943

Lamberton, Robert Eneas, American lawyer, judge and mayor, *Obit* Oct 1941

Leibowitz, Samuel Simon, American judge, Jan 1953, *Obit* Mar 1978

Lindsey, Benjamin B., judge, *Obit* May 1943

Mack, Julian W., American judge, *Obit* Oct 1943

Martin, George Brown, *Obit* Yrbk 1945

Matthews, Burnita Shelton, judge, Apr 1950, *Obit* June 1988

McConnell, Mitch, American senator, Feb 2008

McDonald, Gabrielle, judge, Oct 2001

McFarland, Ernest William, American senator, governor and state supreme court justice, Jan 1951, *Obit* Aug 1984

McLachlin, Beverley M., Canadian judge, Sept 2009

McNair, Arnold Duncan McNair, Feb 1955

McNary, Charles Linza, American senator, Aug 1940, *Obit* Apr 1944

Mechem, Edwin L., American governor and senator, July 1954, *Obit* Yrbk 2003

Medina, Harold R., American judge, Apr 1949, *Obit* May 1990

Meskill, Thomas J., American governor and judge, Mar 1974, *Obit* Yrbk 2008

Metcalf, Lee, American senator, Feb 1970, *Obit* Mar 1978

Mikva, Abner J., American judge, July 1980

Miller, Benjamin Meek, governor and judge, *Obit* Mar 1944

Mills, Wilbur D., American congressman, Nov 1956, *Obit* July 1992

Minton, Sherman, American Supreme Court justice, Mar 1941, Yrbk 1949, *Obit* May 1965

Morton, James Madison, *Obit* Aug 1940

Moss, Frank E., American senator, Yrbk 1971, *Obit* June 2003

Mukhtar, Aloma, Nigerian supreme court justice, Jan 2005

Murphy, Thomas F., police commissioner and judge, Mar 1951, *Obit* Jan 1996

Musmanno, Michael Angelo, June 1967, *Obit* Yrbk 1968

Norris, George William, American senator, *Obit* Oct 1944

O'Connor, Sandra Day, American Supreme Court justice, Jan 1982

Ottinger, Nathan, *Obit* Jan 1941

Parker, John J., American judge, Yrbk 1955, *Obit* May 1958

Phillips, John C., American governor and judge, *Obit* Aug 1943

Picard, Frank A., Mar 1947, *Obit* Apr 1963

Pierce, Samuel R., American Secretary of housing and urban development, Nov 1982, *Obit* Feb 2001

Pine, David A., American judge, June 1952, *Obit* Sept 1970

Poindexter, Miles, *Obit* Nov 1946

Posner, Richard A., American judge, Jan 1993

Powell, Lewis F., American Supreme Court justice, Feb 1965, *Obit* Nov 1998

Radcliffe, Cyril John Radcliffe, British jurist and government official, June 1963, *Obit* May 1977

Ragon, Heartsill, *Obit* Nov 1940

Reed, Stanley Forman, American Supreme Court justice, Feb 1942, *Obit* May 1980

Rehnquist, William H., American Chief Justice of the Supreme Court, Apr 1972, Nov 2003, *Obit* Yrbk 2005

Reynolds, John W., American judge and governor, Apr 1964, *Obit* Mar 2002

Reynoso, Cruz, American lawyer and judge, Mar 2002

Richards, James P., Sept 1951, *Obit* Apr 1979

Rifkind, Simon H., lawyer, May 1946, *Obit* Jan 1996

Roberts, John G., American Chief Justice of the Supreme Court, Feb 2006

Roberts, Owen Josephus, American Supreme Court justice, Oct 1941, *Obit* July 1955

Robinson, Elmer E., Nov 1955

Rodriguez Veltze, Eduardo, Bolivian president, Jan 2005

Rosenfeld, Kurt, *Obit* Nov 1943

Rosenman, Samuel I., American state supreme court justice, Aug 1942, *Obit* Sept 1973

Sabath, Adolph J., American congressman, July 1946, *Obit* Yrbk 1952

Sampson, Edith S., American judge, Yrbk 1950, *Obit* Jan 1980

Sandoval, Brian, American governor, Jan 2012

Sandstrom, Emil, Jan 1951, *Obit* Sept 1962

Saund, Dalip Singh, congressman, June 1960, *Obit* June 1973

Scalia, Antonin, American Supreme Court justice, Nov 1986

Sessions, William Steele, American FBI director, July 1988

Sheindlin, Judith, American judge, Sept 1998

Silzer, George S., *Obit* Yrbk 1940

Sirica, John J., American judge, May 1974, *Obit* Oct 1992

Sobeloff, Simon E., American Solicitor general and judge, Mar 1955, *Obit* Sept 1973

Sotomayor, Sonia, American Supreme Court justice, Oct 2009

Souter, David H., American Supreme Court justice, Jan 1991

Squires, Richard Anderson, *Obit* May 1940

Stacy, Walter P., Jan 1946, *Obit* Oct 1951

Starr, Kenneth W., American law teacher and independent counsel in Whitewater Investigation, May 1998

Stennis, John C., American senator, Jan 1953, *Obit* July 1995

Stevens, John Paul, American Supreme Court justice, May 1976

Stewart, Potter, American Supreme Court justice, Yrbk 1959, *Obit* Feb 1986

Sutherland, George, American Supreme Court justice, *Obit* Sept 1942

Sykes, Eugene Octave, *Obit* July 1945

Thomas, Clarence, American Supreme Court justice, Apr 1992

Tice, Merton B., June 1955

Timmerman, George Bell, American governor and judge, Jan 1957, *Obit* Feb 1995

Trevethin and Oaksey, Geoffrey Lawrence, British judge, Jan 1946, *Obit* Yrbk 1991

Tucker, B. Fain, Yrbk 1957

Ulman, Joseph N., *Obit* May 1943

Utterback, Hubert, *Obit* July 1942

Van Devanter, Willis, American Supreme Court justice, *Obit* Mar 1941

Vanderbilt, Arthur T., judge, Feb 1947, *Obit* Oct 1957

Vinson, Fred M., American Supreme Court justice, Aug 1943, *Obit* Nov 1953

Wagner, Robert F., American senator and judge, May 1941, *Obit* June 1953

Wald, Patricia M., American judge, June 2000

Walsh, Joseph, *Obit* Mar 1946

Walsh, Lawrence E., American lawyer, Oct 1991

Wapner, Joseph A., judge, Sept 1989

Waring, Julius Waties, judge, Yrbk 1948, *Obit* Mar 1968

Warren, Earl, American Chief Justice of the Supreme Court, Jan 1944, Jan 1954, *Obit* Sept 1974

Waste, William Harrison, *Obit* July 1940

Watkins, Arthur V., American senator and judge, July 1950, *Obit* Yrbk 1973

Webb, William Flood, Yrbk 1948

Wheat, Alfred Adams, *Obit* Apr 1943

White, Byron R., American Supreme Court justice, Yrbk 1962, *Obit* July 2002

White, S. Harrison, *Obit* Feb 1946

Whittaker, Charles Evans, American Supreme Court justice, Yrbk 1957, *Obit* Jan 1974

Winiarski, Bohdan, Feb 1962

Wood, John S., American congressman, July 1949, *Obit* Nov 1968

Wright, Loyd, July 1955, *Obit* Jan 1975

Wright, Robert Alderson Wright, July 1945, *Obit* Sept 1964

Yarborough, Ralph W., American senator, Feb 1960, *Obit* Apr 1996

Jugglers

Moschen, Michael, juggler, July 2000

Keyboardists

Albarn, Damon, British singer, songwriter and keyboardist, Nov 2003

Berlin, Steve, American keyboardist and saxophonist, Oct 2005

Codenys, Patrick, Belgian rock musician, Jan 2006

Conlee, Jenny, American keyboardist, Aug 2007

Corea, Chick, American jazz pianist, Oct 1988

Crandall, Martin, American keyboardist, June 2007

Cunningham, Phil, British guitarist and keyboardist, Jan 2006

DeMarcus, Jay, American keyboardist and singer, Aug 2003

Edwards, Clarence, Antiguan keyboardist and singer, Jan 2004

Froese, Jerome, German keyboardist, Jan 2005

Gilbert, Gillian, British guitarist, keyboardist and singer, Jan 2006

Gillingham, Charlie, American keyboardist, Mar 2003

Hancock, Herbie, American jazz keyboardist and composer, Apr 1988

Jorgensen, Mikael, American keyboardist, Feb 2010

Kjartan Sveinsson, Icelandic keyboardist, Jan 2003

Koster, Bo, American rock keyboardist, Nov 2008

Lorenz, Christian, German keyboardist, Jan 2007

McConnell, Page, American keyboardist, July 2003

Sansone, Pat, American guitarist, percussionist and keyboardist, Feb 2010

Smith, Gerard, American bassist and keyboardist, Apr 2009

Wonder, Stevie, American singer and songwriter, Mar 1975

Kidnap victims

Hearst, Patricia Campbell, American socialite, Aug 1982

Waite, Terry, British church official, Sept 1986

Kings

Abdullah, Jan 2002

Abdullah, June 1948, *Obit* Sept 1951

Abdullah, Jan 2000

Ahmad, Mar 1956, *Obit* Nov 1962

Akihito, Apr 1959, Aug 1991

Al Thani, Hamad ibn Khalifa, July 2009

Al-Sabah, Abdullah al-Salem, Kuwaiti ruler, July 1957, *Obit* Jan 1966

Al-Sabah, Jaber al-Ahmad al-Jaber, Aug 1988, *Obit* Yrbk 2006

Alfonso, *Obit* Apr 1941

Ananda Mahidol, *Obit* July 1946

Bao Dai, Nov 1949, *Obit* Oct 1997

Baudouin, Sept 1950, *Obit* Oct 1993

Bhumibol Adulyadej, July 1950

Birendra Bir Bikram Shah Deva, Aug 1975, *Obit* Sept 2001

Boris, Feb 1941, *Obit* Yrbk 1991

Carl, Feb 1974

Carol, Aug 1940, *Obit* May 1953

Christian, Nov 1943, *Obit* May 1947

Constantine, Apr 1967

Fahd, May 1979, *Obit* Yrbk 2005

Faisal, July 1955, *Obit* Oct 1958

Faisal, May 1966, *Obit* May 1975

Farouk, Oct 1942, *Obit* May 1965

Frederick, Nov 1947, *Obit* Mar 1972

George, Yrbk 1943, *Obit* Apr 1947

George, Mar 1942, *Obit* Mar 1952

Gustaf, Sept 1942, *Obit* Yrbk 1950

Gustaf, Yrbk 1950, *Obit* Nov 1973

Gyanendra Bir Bikram Shah, Jan 2005

Haakon, May 1940, *Obit* Yrbk 1957

Haile Selassie, Apr 1941, Oct 1954, *Obit* Oct 1975

Hassan, Sept 1964, *Obit* Oct 1999

Hassanal Bolkiah, Oct 1989

Hirohito, Jan 1942, Mar 1976, *Obit* Feb 1989

Hussein, July 1955, Apr 1986, *Obit* Apr 1999

Ibn Saud, Feb 1943, *Obit* Jan 1954

Idris, Jan 1956, *Obit* July 1983

Juan Carlos, Oct 1964, Jan 2003

Juan Carlos, Oct 1951, *Obit* June 1993

Khalid, Jan 1976, *Obit* Aug 1982

Leopold, Yrbk 1944, *Obit* Nov 1983

Mahendra Bir Bikram Shaha Deva, July 1956, *Obit* Mar 1972

Michael, Oct 1944

Mohammed Reza Pahlavi, Jan 1950, Sept 1977, *Obit* Sept 1980

Mohammed Zahir Shah, Mar 1956, *Obit* Yrbk 2007

Muhammad, Jan 2002

Muhammad, Oct 1951, *Obit* Apr 1961

Norodom Sihanouk, Mar 1954, Aug 1993, *Obit* Yrbk 2012

Paul, May 1947, *Obit* Apr 1964

Peter, Nov 1943, *Obit* Yrbk 1970

Prajadhipok, *Obit* July 1941

Qabus bin Said, Aug 1978

Reza Shah Pahlavi, *Obit* Sept 1944

Said bin Taimur, Oct 1957, *Obit* Aug 1978

Saud, Apr 1954, *Obit* Apr 1969

Sidi Ahmed, *Obit* Aug 1942

Sisavang Vong, Apr 1954, *Obit* Jan 1960

Sobhuza, Mar 1982, *Obit* Mar 1982

Talal, Jan 1952, *Obit* Sept 1972

Taufa'ahau Tupou, Sept 1968, *Obit* Yrbk 2007

Victor Emmanuel, July 1943, *Obit* Jan 1948

Wangchuk, Jigme Dorji, Oct 1956, *Obit* Sept 1972

William, *Obit* July 1941

Windsor, Edward, Sept 1944, *Obit* July 1972

Zog, Aug 1944, *Obit* June 1961

Labor leaders

Abel, I. W., American labor leader, Nov 1965, *Obit* Sept 1987

Allen, William L., Canadian labor leader, Sept 1953

Amulree, William Warrender Mackenzie, British government official, *Obit* June 1942

Anderson, Mary, American labor leader and government official, Sept 1940, *Obit* Mar 1964

Askwith, George Ranken Askwith, British labor mediator and government official, *Obit* July 1942

Beck, Dave, American labor leader, May 1949, *Obit* Feb 1994

Beirne, Joseph A., American labor leader, Mar 1946, *Obit* Oct 1974

Bengough, Percy R., Canadian labor leader, Apr 1951

Berry, George L., American labor leader, Jan 1948, *Obit* Jan 1949

Bieber, Owen, labor leader, Apr 1986

Biller, Moe, American labor leader, June 1987, *Obit* Yrbk 2004

Bittner, Van A., American labor leader, Mar 1947, *Obit* Sept 1949

Blank, Theodor, Sept 1952, *Obit* July 1972

Boyle, Tony, American labor leader, July 1970, *Obit* July 1985

Braddock, E. M., British labor leader and member of Parliament, July 1957, *Obit* Jan 1971

Brennan, Peter J., American Secretary of labor, Apr 1973, *Obit* Jan 1997

Brewer, Roy M., American labor leader, Sept 1953, *Obit* Yrbk 2006

Bridges, Harry, American labor leader, Nov 1940, May 1950, *Obit* May 1990

Brown, Irving, American labor leader, July 1951, *Obit* May 1989

Caldwell, Sarah C., Jan 1953

Carey, James B., American labor leader, Nov 1941, July 1951, *Obit* Nov 1973

Carey, Ron, American labor leader, May 1992, *Obit* Yrbk 2009

Cenerazzo, Walter W., Sept 1955

Chaikin, Sol C., garment workers' union leader, Apr 1979, *Obit* June 1991

Chavez, Cesar, Mexican-American labor leader, Feb 1969, *Obit* June 1993

Chavez-Thompson, Linda, American labor leader, Mar 2000

Chiluba, Frederick, Zambian president, May 1992, *Obit* Yrbk 2011

Ching, Cyrus S., labor mediator, Jan 1948, *Obit* Feb 1968

Church, Sam, American labor leader, Oct 1981, *Obit* Yrbk 2009

Clark, John, American labor leader, Apr 1952

Cole, David L., Jan 1949, *Obit* Mar 1978

Cousins, Frank, English labor leader, Feb 1960, *Obit* July 1986

Craxi, Bettino, Italian prime minister, Feb 1984, *Obit* June 2000

Croft, Arthur C., June 1952

Curran, Joseph E., American labor leader, Apr 1945, *Obit* Oct 1981

Davidson, Roy E., Sept 1963, *Obit* Sept 1964

Davis, William H., June 1941, *Obit* Oct 1964

De Lille, Patricia, South African political leader, Jan 2004

Deakin, Arthur, English labor leader, Jan 1948, *Obit* June 1955

Dennis, Eugene, American communist leader, May 1949, *Obit* Mar 1961

Derwent, Clarence, Nov 1947, *Obit* Nov 1959

Donovan, Raymond James, American Secretary of labor, Jan 1982

Dubinsky, David, American labor leader, Yrbk 1942, June 1957, *Obit* Jan 1983

Durkin, Martin Patrick, American Secretary of labor, Feb 1953, *Obit* Jan 1956

Eklund, John M., labor leader and teacher, Yrbk 1949, *Obit* Mar 1997

Farmer, Guy, Feb 1955

Feather, Vic, Mar 1973, *Obit* Sept 1976

Finet, Paul, Belgian labor leader, Sept 1951

Fitzgerald, Albert J., American labor leader, Oct 1948, *Obit* July 1982

Fitzgibbons, John, *Obit* Oct 1941

Fitzsimmons, Frank Edward, American labor leader, May 1971, *Obit* July 1981

Flore, Edward F., *Obit* Oct 1945

Frankensteen, Richard T., Yrbk 1945

Fraser, Douglas Andrew, American labor leader, Oct 1977, *Obit* Yrbk 2008

Freitag, Walter, Jan 1954, *Obit* Oct 1958

Gaspard, Patrick, American presidential aide, July 2010

Geijer, Arne, Swedish labor leader and member of Parliament, July 1964

Gibson, John W., Oct 1947

Gleason, Thomas W., American labor leader, Oct 1965, *Obit* Mar 1993

Golden, Clinton S., Apr 1948, *Obit* Sept 1961

Googe, George L., July 1947, *Obit* Yrbk 1961

Gould, Ronald, English labor leader and teacher, Nov 1952

Green, William, American labor leader, Mar 1942, *Obit* Jan 1953

Greenwood, Arthur, Oct 1940, *Obit* Sept 1954

Grogan, John J., Yrbk 1951

Guinan, Matthew, labor leader, Sept 1974, *Obit* May 1995

Hall, Paul, Feb 1966, *Obit* Aug 1980

Hancock, Florence, Nov 1948

Harrison, George M., Jan 1949, *Obit* Jan 1969

Hawke, Robert J. L., Australian prime minister, Aug 1983

Hayes, A. J., Oct 1953

Haywood, Allan S., American labor leader, May 1952, *Obit* Apr 1953

Helstein, Ralph, labor leader, June 1948, *Obit* May 1985

Herrick, Elinore Morehouse, Apr 1947, *Obit* Jan 1965

Hillman, Sidney, American labor leader, July 1940, *Obit* July 1946

Hoffa, Jimmy P., American labor leader, July 1999

Hughes, R. O., Oct 1950

Hutcheson, William Levi, American labor leader, Sept 1943, *Obit* Jan 1954

Iglesias Pantin, Santiago, Puerto Rican labor leader, Jan 1940

Isaacs, George A., Oct 1945

Jennings, Paul J., labor leader, Yrbk 1969, *Obit* Oct 1987

Jimerson, Earl W., Sept 1948, *Obit* Yrbk 1958

Jodoin, Claude, Mar 1956

Johnston, Alvanley, American labor leader, June 1946, *Obit* Nov 1951

Jones, Jack, British labor leader, May 1976

Jones, John Joseph, Nov 1940, *Obit* Jan 1942

Jorgensen, Anker, Danish prime minister, Sept 1978

Jouhaux, Leon, French labor leader, Jan 1948, *Obit* July 1954

Kaiser, Jakob, German labor leader and government official, Feb 1956, *Obit* July 1961

Kennedy, Thomas, June 1960, *Obit* Feb 1963

Kennedy, William P., Jan 1950, *Obit* July 1968

Kheel, Theodore, American labor mediator, Sept 1964, *Obit* Yrbk 2011

Kirkland, Lane, American labor leader, May 1980, *Obit* Oct 1999

Kline, Clarice, May 1961

Knight, O. A., June 1952

Kok, Wim, Dutch prime minister, Jan 2003

Koontz, Elizabeth Duncan, American labor leader and teacher, Jan 1969, *Obit* Apr 1989

Kroll, Jack, American labor leader, Sept 1946, *Obit* July 1971

Lawe, John, labor leader, Jan 1984, *Obit* Apr 1989

Lawther, William, Yrbk 1949

Leedom, Boyd, May 1956, *Obit* Oct 1969

Leiserson, William M., Feb 1942, *Obit* Apr 1957

Lewis, John L., American labor leader, Mar 1942, *Obit* July 1969

Livingston, John W., labor leader, July 1959, *Obit* Aug 1997

Lombardo Toledano, Vicente, Mexican labor leader, Aug 1940, *Obit* Jan 1969

Loughlin, Anne, Feb 1950

Lund, Wendell L., Sept 1942

Lundeberg, Harry, Nov 1952, *Obit* Mar 1957

Magee, Elizabeth S., Oct 1950

Maggiolo, Walter A., labor mediator, July 1952, *Obit* Yrbk 2000

Mann, Tom, English labor leader, *Obit* May 1941

Martin, Harry, June 1948, *Obit* Mar 1959

Martin, Lynn Morley, American Secretary of labor, Oct 1989

Mazey, Emil, labor leader, Jan 1948, *Obit* Nov 1983

Mboya, Tom, Kenyan political and labor leader, June 1959, *Obit* Sept 1969

McBride, Lloyd, steelworkers' union leader, Feb 1978, *Obit* Jan 1984

McDevitt, James L., American labor leader, Mar 1959, *Obit* May 1963

McDonald, David J., June 1953, *Obit* Oct 1979

McEntee, Gerald, American labor leader, Oct 2000

McLaughlin, Ann Dore, American Secretary of labor, Nov 1988

McNamara, James B., American labor activist, *Obit* Apr 1941

Meany, George, American labor leader, Jan 1942, Mar 1954, *Obit* Mar 1980

Miller, Arnold R., labor leader, Nov 1974, *Obit* Sept 1985

Miller, Frieda S., Feb 1945, *Obit* Oct 1973

Millis, Harry A., Nov 1940, *Obit* Sept 1948

Mitchell, James P., American Secretary of labor, Sept 1955, *Obit* Yrbk 1964

Mooney, Thomas J., labor leader, *Obit* Apr 1942

Moses, Harry M., Oct 1949, *Obit* June 1956

Mosher, A. R., Yrbk 1950, *Obit* Yrbk 1959

Mowrey, Corma, Nov 1950

Murray, Philip, American labor leader, Jan 1941, Feb 1949, *Obit* Yrbk 1952

Neill, Charles Patrick, *Obit* Nov 1942

O'Neill, Francis Aloysius, labor mediator, Yrbk 1960, *Obit* Mar 1992

Oakes, Grant W., Jan 1950

Oldenbroek, Jacobus H., Mar 1950

Oshiomhole, Adams, Nigerian labor leader, Jan 2005

Patton, James George, American agricultural leader, Jan 1945, Feb 1966

Peterson, Esther, American consumer rights advocate, Yrbk 1961, *Obit* Mar 1998

Petrillo, James C., American labor leader, Yrbk 1940, *Obit* Jan 1985

Phelan, Edward, Jan 1947

Phillips, Morgan, British socialist leader, Sept 1949, *Obit* Feb 1963

Potofsky, Jacob S., American labor leader, Oct 1946, *Obit* Sept 1979

Powers, Bertram A., American labor leader, Jan 1974

Presser, Jackie, labor leader, Sept 1983, *Obit* Aug 1988

Pressman, Lee, American labor lawyer, May 1947, *Obit* Jan 1970

Quill, Mike, American labor leader, Aug 1941, Mar 1953, *Obit* Mar 1966

Ramaphosa, Cyril, South African political leader and businessman, Sept 1995

Randolph, Woodruff, May 1948, *Obit* Jan 1967

Reuther, Walter Philip, American labor leader, Apr 1941, Nov 1949, *Obit* June 1970

Rieve, Emil, July 1946, *Obit* Mar 1975

Robertson, D. B., May 1950, *Obit* Yrbk 1961

Robins, Margaret Dreier, labor leader, *Obit* Apr 1945

Rodriguez, Arturo, labor leader, Mar 2001

Rose, Alex, American labor leader, Yrbk 1959, *Obit* Feb 1977

Roth, Almon E., Oct 1946

Ryan, Joseph P., American longshore workers union leader, Jan 1949, *Obit* Sept 1963

Saillant, Louis, July 1948, *Obit* Jan 1975

Saposs, David J., Nov 1940, *Obit* Jan 1969

Savage, Michael Joseph, *Obit* Apr 1940

Scargill, Arthur, English labor leader, Jan 1985

Schneiderman, Rose, labor leader and feminist, Feb 1946, *Obit* Oct 1972

Schnitzler, William F., Apr 1965

Schwellenbach, Lewis B., American Secretary of Labor, June 1945, *Obit* July 1948

Selden, David, teacher and labor leader, July 1974, *Obit* Aug 1998

Seyferth, O. A., July 1950

Shanker, Albert, American labor leader and teacher, Apr 1969, *Obit* May 1997

Shields, James P., Mar 1951, *Obit* Sept 1953

Siemiller, P. L., Nov 1966

Silva, Luis Inacio da, Brazilian president, Jan 2003

Smith, Ben, Oct 1945, *Obit* July 1964

Solis, Hilda L., American Secretary of labor, Mar 2009

Stacy, Walter P., Jan 1946, *Obit* Oct 1951

Stark, Louis, June 1945, *Obit* Sept 1954

Starr, Mark, labor leader, July 1946, *Obit* July 1985

Stauning, Thorvald, Danish prime minister, *Obit* June 1942

Stephens, John A., Yrbk 1956

Sweeney, John J., American labor leader, June 1996

Taylor, George William, labor mediator, May 1942, *Obit* Feb 1973

Tewson, Vincent, Feb 1952

Thomas, R. J., Nov 1942, *Obit* June 1967

Tobin, Daniel J., American labor leader, Nov 1945, *Obit* Jan 1956

Townsend, Willard S., American railroad porter and labor leader, Jan 1948

Trumka, Richard L., labor leader and lawyer, Apr 1986

Tsvangirai, Morgan, Zimbabwean prime minister, Jan 2005

Turner, Ben, *Obit* Nov 1942

Turner, Ewald, May 1962

Usery, W. J., American Secretary of labor, June 1976

Van Arsdale, Harry, American labor leader, May 1969, *Obit* Apr 1986

Walesa, Lech, Polish president, Apr 1981, May 1996

Warren, Edgar L., July 1947

Watt, Robert J., Mar 1945, *Obit* Sept 1947

Wedgwood, Josiah C., British member of Parliament, Apr 1942, *Obit* Sept 1943

Whitney, A. F., American labor leader, Feb 1946, *Obit* Sept 1949

Winpisinger, William W., American labor leader, Feb 1980, *Obit* Feb 1998

Wolchok, Sam, Oct 1948, *Obit* Mar 1979

Woll, Matthew, Jan 1943, *Obit* Sept 1956

Woodcock, George, English labor leader, Feb 1964, *Obit* Jan 1980

Wurf, Jerry, American labor leader, June 1979, *Obit* Feb 1982

Yokich, Stephen P., American labor leader, Nov 1998, *Obit* Yrbk 2002

Zander, Arnold S., Oct 1947, *Obit* Sept 1975

Labor negotiators

Amulree, William Warrender Mackenzie, British government official, *Obit* June 1942

Askwith, George Ranken Askwith, British labor mediator and government official, *Obit* July 1942

Ching, Cyrus S., labor mediator, Jan 1948, *Obit* Feb 1968

Cole, David L., Jan 1949, *Obit* Mar 1978

Davis, William H., June 1941, *Obit* Oct 1964

Kheel, Theodore, American labor mediator, Sept 1964, *Obit* Yrbk 2011

Leiserson, William M., Feb 1942, *Obit* Apr 1957

Maggiolo, Walter A., labor mediator, July 1952, *Obit* Yrbk 2000

Moses, Harry M., Oct 1949, *Obit* June 1956

O'Neill, Francis Aloysius, labor mediator, Yrbk 1960, *Obit* Mar 1992

Stacy, Walter P., Jan 1946, *Obit* Oct 1951

Warren, Edgar L., July 1947

Labor relations consultants

Croft, Arthur C., June 1952

Herrick, Elinore Morehouse, Apr 1947, *Obit* Jan 1965

Landscape architects

Olmsted, Frederick Law, American landscape architect, June 1949, *Obit* Mar 1958

Oudolf, Piet, Dutch landscape architect, Apr 2003

Law enforcement officials

Alter, George Elias, American lawyer and state attorney general, *Obit* Oct 1940

Bergson, Herbert A., American lawyer, Sept 1950

Brown, Jerry, American governor, Apr 1975

Burris, Roland W., American senator, June 2009

Costle, Douglas M., June 1980

Dever, Paul A., American governor, May 1949, *Obit* July 1958

Kerlikowske, R. Gil, American law enforcement official, Nov 2009

Mazuz, Menachem, Israeli attorney general, Jan 2007

McDonnell, Bob, American governor, Sept 2011

Ribadu, Nuhu, Nigerian law enforcement official, Jan 2006

Richardson, Seth Whitley, American government official, Feb 1948, *Obit* May 1953

Salazar, Ken, American Secretary of the interior, Mar 2009

Shawcross, Hartley Shawcross, British attorney general and war crimes prosecutor, Yrbk 1945, *Obit* Yrbk 2003

Sobeloff, Simon E., American Solicitor general and judge, Mar 1955, *Obit* Sept 1973

Spitzer, Eliot, American governor, Mar 2003

Law teachers

Bell, Derrick A., American law professor, Feb 1993, *Obit* Yrbk 2011

Bruner, Jerome Seymour, American psychologist and law professor, Oct 1984

Chafee, Zechariah, American law professor, Aug 1942, *Obit* Apr 1957

Cox, Archibald, American lawyer and special counsel in Watergate investigation, July 1961, *Obit* Yrbk 2004

Crenshaw, Kimberle Williams, American law professor, May 2011

Cruz, Ted, American state solicitor general, May 2013

Dean, Gordon E., American government official, Sept 1950, *Obit* Nov 1958

Dworkin, Ronald Myles, American law professor, *Obit* Yrbk 2013

Ginsburg, Ruth Bader, American Supreme Court justice, Feb 1994

Goodhart, Arthur L., American lawyer, July 1964, *Obit* Feb 1979

Hill, Anita, American lawyer, Sept 1995

Kelsen, Hans, Austrian-American law professor, Sept 1957, *Obit* June 1973

Kennedy, Anthony M., American Supreme Court justice, July 1988

Kennedy, Randall, American law professor, Aug 2002

Pound, Roscoe, American law professor, May 1947, *Obit* Sept 1964

Reich, Charles A., American law professor, June 1972

Reynolds, Glenn H., American law professor, Oct 2007

S enz Ryan, Maritza, Mar 2013

Tribe, Laurence H., American law professor, July 1988

Warren, Elizabeth, American law professor and consumer rights advocate, Feb 2012

Lawyers

Abbott, Edwin Milton, American lawyer, *Obit* Jan 1941

Abdul Rahman, Malaysian head of state, Yrbk 1957, *Obit* May 1960

Abdul-Razaq, Alhaji, Nigerian lawyer and government official, Jan 2005

Abram, Morris B., American lawyer, Oct 1965, *Obit* July 2000

Abrams, Floyd, American lawyer, July 1999

Abramson, Leslie, lawyer, June 1999

Adams, Alva B., American senator, *Obit* Jan 1942

Addington, David, American lawyer and vice-presidential aide, Jan 2007

Ailes, Stephen, lawyer and secretary of the army, Jan 1965, *Obit* Oct 2001

Al-Yafi, Abdullah Aref, June 1956

Alcorn, Hugh Meade, American lawyer and political party leader, May 1957, *Obit* Mar 1992

Alexander, Clifford, American Secretary of the army, Sept 1977

Alexander, Donald C., American lawyer and tax official, Yrbk 1974, *Obit* Yrbk 2009

Alfonsin, Raul, Argentine president, July 1984, *Obit* Yrbk 2009

Alioto, Joseph L., mayor, Sept 1969, *Obit* Apr 1998

Allen, Florence Ellinwood, American judge, Feb 1941, July 1963, *Obit* Nov 1966

Allen, George E., American lawyer and government official, Mar 1946, *Obit* June 1973

Allen, Leo E., American congressman, June 1948, *Obit* Mar 1973

Alpert, George, railroad executive and lawyer, Sept 1961, *Obit* Oct 1988

Alter, George Elias, American lawyer and state attorney general, *Obit* Oct 1940

Amsterdam, Birdie, judge, Mar 1940, *Obit* Sept 1996

Anderson, John Bayard, American congressman, Sept 1979

Anderson, John Crawford, American state supreme court justice, *Obit* Jan 1940

Anderson, Robert Bernerd, American Secretary of the treasury, June 1953, *Obit* Oct 1989

Andresen, August H., American congressman, Feb 1956, *Obit* Mar 1958

Andrews, Charles O., American senator, *Obit* Nov 1946

Archer, Dennis, American mayor, Feb 1997

Arnall, Ellis Gibbs, governor, Aug 1945, *Obit* Feb 1993

Arnold, George Stanleigh, American lawyer, *Obit* Mar 1942

Ashley, Thomas L., American lobbyist and congressman, May 1979, *Obit* Yrbk 2010

Askew, Reubin, governor, Apr 1973

Aspinall, Wayne N., American congressman, Apr 1968, *Obit* Nov 1983

Atherton, Warren H., American army officer, lawyer and veterans organization official, Yrbk 1943, *Obit* May 1976

Auchincloss, Louis, American novelist, short story writer and lawyer, Yrbk 1954, Aug 1978, *Obit* Apr 2010

Aughinbaugh, William, American lawyer, physician and travel writer, *Obit* Feb 1941

Bacon, Charles L., American lawyer and veterans leader, May 1962

Badillo, Herman, American municipal official and congressman, May 1971

Bailey, Consuelo Northrop, American lawyer and state legislator, June 1954

Bailey, F. Lee, lawyer, Yrbk 1967

Bailey, John Moran, American lawyer and political leader, June 1962, *Obit* June 1975

Bailey, Thomas L., American governor, *Obit* Yrbk 1946

Baker, Howard H., American senator and presidential adviser, Mar 1974, Aug 1987

Baker, Roy, American lawyer, Nov 1948

Baldwin, Tammy, American congresswoman, June 2005

Ball, Stuart S., American retail executive, July 1952

Bankhead, John Hollis, American senator, May 1943, *Obit* July 1946

Banzhaf, John F., law professor, Yrbk 1973

Barber, Anthony, Jan 1971

Barden, Graham Arthur, American congressman, Sept 1949, *Obit* Mar 1967

Barkley, Alben William, American vice-president, May 1941, Jan 1949, *Obit* July 1956

Barnes, Roy E., American governor, Jan 2000

Barnes, Stanley N., American judge, Sept 1953

Barnes, Wendell B., government official and congressman, June 1957, *Obit* Aug 1985

Barnett, Ross Robert, American governor, Sept 1961, *Obit* Jan 1988

Barros Hurtado, Cesar, Argentine lawyer, sociologist and diplomat, Jan 1959

Barry, William Bernard, American congressman, *Obit* Yrbk 1946

Barzel, Rainer, German political leader, May 1967, *Obit* Yrbk 2006

Bates, Sanford, American penologist, Jan 1961, *Obit* Nov 1972

Battle, John S., American lawyer and governor, Nov 1950, *Obit* June 1972

Bayard, Thomas Francis, American senator, *Obit* Sept 1942

Bayh, Birch, American senator and governor, June 1965

Bazelon, David L., American judge, Jan 1971, *Obit* Apr 1993

Becker, Ralph E., lawyer and diplomat, Nov 1948, *Obit* Oct 1994

Becker, William Dee, American judge and mayor, *Obit* Sept 1943

Belli, Melvin M., American lawyer, July 1979, *Obit* Sept 1996

Bennett, Robert LaFollette, American lawyer and government official, Sept 1967

Berge, Wendell, American lawyer and government official, Feb 1946, *Obit* Yrbk 1956

Berger, Sandy, American presidential adviser, Feb 1998

Bergson, Herbert A., American lawyer, Sept 1950

Berman, Emile Zola, American lawyer, June 1972, *Obit* Aug 1981

Bird, Rose Elizabeth, judge, May 1984, *Obit* May 2000

Black, Hugo LaFayette, American Supreme Court justice, Sept 1941, May 1964, *Obit* Nov 1971

Blair, David H., American tax official and lawyer, *Obit* Nov 1944

Blair, James T., American governor, Apr 1958, *Obit* Sept 1962

Bliss, Anthony Addison, lawyer and opera manager, Apr 1979, *Obit* Nov 1991

Boateng, Paul, British cabinet member, Jan 2002

Bolten, Josh, American presidential adviser, July 2006

Booker, Cory, American mayor, Feb 2007

Borah, William Edgar, American senator, Jan 1940

Boras, Scott, American baseball agent, May 2009

Bosone, Reva Zilpha Beck, congresswoman and judge, Jan 1949

Bourne, Jonathan, American senator, *Obit* Oct 1940

Boyle, William Marshall, American political leader and lawyer, June 1949, *Obit* Nov 1961

Bradley, Tom, American lawyer and mayor, Nov 1973, Oct 1992, *Obit* Jan 1999

Brandeis, Louis Dembitz, American Supreme Court justice, *Obit* Nov 1941

Brannan, Charles F., American Secretary of agriculture, Sept 1948

Brentano, Heinrich von, Feb 1955, *Obit* Jan 1965

Brooke, Edward, American senator, Apr 1967

Brookhart, Smith W., American senator, *Obit* Jan 1945

Brooks, Overton, June 1957, *Obit* Yrbk 1961

Brown, Francis Shunk, *Obit* Jan 1940

Brown, Prentiss M., American senator, Jan 1943, *Obit* Feb 1974

Brown, Ron, American Secretary of commerce, July 1989, *Obit* June 1996

Brown, Scott, American senator, Aug 2010

Brown, Virginia Mae, lawyer and government official, July 1970, *Obit* May 1991

Brown, Willie Lewis, American mayor and political leader, Apr 1997

Browne, Edward E., *Obit* Jan 1946

Bruce, David K. E., American diplomat, June 1949, Sept 1961, *Obit* Feb 1978

Brucker, Wilber M., American Secretary of the army, Sept 1955, *Obit* Yrbk 1968

Bryce, Quentin, Australian governor general, Feb 2010

Buckner, Emory Roy, American lawyer, *Obit* May 1941

Bumpers, Dale, American senator, Aug 1979

Burdick, Usher L., American congressman, Apr 1952, *Obit* Nov 1960

Burford, Anne McGill, American regulatory agency official, Sept 1982, *Obit* Yrbk 2004

Burger, Warren E., American Chief Justice of the Supreme Court, Nov 1969, *Obit* Aug 1995

Burke, Thomas A., July 1954, *Obit* Jan 1972

Burke, Yvonne Brathwaite, American lawyer and congresswoman, Oct 1975

Burleigh, George William, *Obit* Apr 1940

Butler, John Marshall, American senator, May 1954, *Obit* May 1978

Butler, Paul M., American political party leader, May 1955, *Obit* Feb 1962

Butler, Sally, Yrbk 1946

Byrnes, John W., American congressman, Oct 1960, *Obit* Mar 1985

Caffrey, James J., June 1947, *Obit* May 1961

Cairns, Huntington, American lawyer, Nov 1940

Campa, Miguel Angel, Sept 1957, *Obit* Nov 1965

Campney, Ralph Osborne, Sept 1955, *Obit* Yrbk 1967

Cannon, Howard W., American senator, Feb 1960, *Obit* Sept 2002

Cao, Joseph, American congressman, June 2009

Carey, Charles Henry, *Obit* Oct 1941

Carroll, John A., American senator, May 1958, *Obit* Oct 1983

Carusi, Ugo, government official, Oct 1948, *Obit* Sept 1994

Case, Clifford Philip, American senator, Mar 1955, *Obit* Apr 1982

Casey, Ralph E., Feb 1966

Casey, William J., American intelligence official, Mar 1972, *Obit* June 1987

Castro, Julian, American mayor, June 2013

Celler, Emanuel, American congressman, Oct 1949, Nov 1966, *Obit* Mar 1981

Chandy, Anna, Apr 1960

Chapman, Oscar L., American Secretary of the interior, Feb 1949, *Obit* Apr 1978

Chaudhry, Iftikhar Mohammad, Pakistani supreme court justice, Jan 2007

Chavan, Yashwantrao Balwantrao, Apr 1963

Chelf, Frank L., June 1952

Chevrier, Lionel, June 1952

Chiperfield, Robert B., Sept 1956, *Obit* May 1971

Church, Frank, American senator, Mar 1958, Mar 1978, *Obit* May 1984

Claxton, Brooke, Yrbk 1947, *Obit* Sept 1960

Clifford, Clark M., American presidential adviser, lawyer and Secretary of defense, Mar 1947, Sept 1968, *Obit* Jan 1999

Cochran, Johnnie, American lawyer, June 1999, *Obit* Oct 2005

Cockrell, Ewing, May 1951, *Obit* Apr 1962

Coffin, Frank M., American judge, Apr 1959, *Obit* Yrbk 2010

Cohen, Manuel F., Apr 1967, *Obit* Aug 1977

Cohen, William S., American Secretary of defense, Apr 1982, Jan 1998

Colby, William E., American intelligence official, Jan 1975, *Obit* July 1996

Cole, Albert M., Jan 1954

Cole, David L., Jan 1949, *Obit* Mar 1978

Coleman, William T., American Secretary of transportation, Mar 1976

Collet, John C., Feb 1946, *Obit* Feb 1956

Collins, LeRoy, American governor, June 1956, Apr 1965, *Obit* May 1991

Collins, Lorin Cone, *Obit* Yrbk 1940

Combs, Bert Thomas, governor and lawyer, June 1960, *Obit* Feb 1992

Connally, Tom, American senator, Yrbk 1941, Apr 1949, *Obit* Jan 1964

Cook, Donald C., May 1952, *Obit* Feb 1982

Cook, Marlow W., Jan 1972

Cooper, Jere, American congressman, Mar 1955, *Obit* Feb 1958

Cooper, John Sherman, American senator and diplomat, June 1950, *Obit* Apr 1991

Corcoran, Thomas, American lawyer, Mar 1940, *Obit* Feb 1982

Cordon, Guy, American senator, Apr 1952, *Obit* July 1969

Corea, Claude, Mar 1961, *Obit* Nov 1962

Costello, John A., Apr 1948, *Obit* Feb 1976

Costle, Douglas M., June 1980

Cothran, James W., Sept 1953

Cotton, Joseph Bell, *Obit* Sept 1940

Coudert, Frederic Rene, American congressman, June 1941, *Obit* July 1972

Cox, E. Eugene, American congressman, Apr 1943, *Obit* Feb 1953

Craig, George North, governor, Feb 1950, *Obit* Feb 1993

Craig, Walter Early, judge, June 1964, *Obit* Sept 1986

Cravath, Paul D., *Obit* Aug 1940

Cripps, C. A., *Obit* Aug 1941

Crosby, Robert, June 1954

Crum, Bartley C., lawyer, May 1947, *Obit* Feb 1960

Culver, John C., Nov 1979

Daley, Richard M., American mayor, Aug 1992

Daley, William, American presidential adviser, Mar 1998

Darden, Christopher, district attorney, Feb 1997

Dati, Rachida, French lawyer and cabinet member, Apr 2009

Davidson, Irwin D., American congressman, Jan 1956

Davies, Clement, Oct 1950, *Obit* May 1962

Davies, Joseph Edward, American lawyer and diplomat, Apr 1942, *Obit* July 1958

Davies, Ronald N., American judge, Sept 1958, *Obit* June 1996

Davis, Artur, American congressman, Feb 2009

Davis, James C., Apr 1957, *Obit* Feb 1982

Davis, John William, American lawyer, congressman and diplomat, Mar 1953, *Obit* May 1955

Davis, William H., June 1941, *Obit* Oct 1964

De Klerk, Frederik Willem, South African president, Feb 1990

De Silva, Desmond, British barrister and United Nations war crimes prosecutor, Jan 2006

DeConcini, Dennis, American senator, Feb 1992

Dean, Arthur Hobson, American lawyer and diplomat, Mar 1954, *Obit* Jan 1988

Deasy, Luere B., *Obit* Apr 1940

Dehler, Thomas, July 1955, *Obit* Oct 1967

Del Ponte, Carla, Swiss war crimes prosecutor, Jan 2002

Denham, R. N., American regulatory agency official, Oct 1947, *Obit* Sept 1954

Denning, Alfred Thompson Denning, British judge, July 1965, *Obit* June 1999

Densen-Gerber, Judianne, American lawyer and psychiatrist, Nov 1983, *Obit* July 2003

Devaney, John Patrick, *Obit* Nov 1941

Dhebar, Uchhrangrai Navalshankar, June 1955

DiSalle, Michael V., American governor, Jan 1951, *Obit* Nov 1981

Dies, Martin, American lawyer and congressman, Apr 1940, *Obit* Jan 1973

Dieterich, William H., *Obit* Yrbk 1940

Dinkins, David, American mayor, Mar 1990

Donlon, Mary H., July 1949, *Obit* May 1977

Donnell, Forrest C., American governor and senator, Sept 1949

Donnelly, Phil M., June 1956, *Obit* Nov 1961

Donovan, James B., American lawyer, June 1961, *Obit* Mar 1970

Douglas, Arthur F., Nov 1950, *Obit* May 1956

Downey, Sheridan, Oct 1949, *Obit* Jan 1962

Dukakis, Michael, American governor, Feb 1978

Eagleton, Thomas F., American senator, Nov 1973, *Obit* Yrbk 2007

Edwards, John, American senator and lawyer, Oct 2004

Edwards, John H., American congressman and government official, *Obit* Yrbk 1945

Ehrlichman, John, American presidential adviser, Oct 1979, *Obit* Apr 1999

Ellison, Keith, American congressman, Apr 2007

Emerson, Lee E., Oct 1953

Engle, Clair, American senator, Mar 1957, *Obit* Oct 1964

Erickson, John Edward, *Obit* June 1946

Erlanger, Mitchell Louis, *Obit* Oct 1940

Ervin, Sam J., American senator, Jan 1955, Oct 1973, *Obit* June 1985

Espy, Mike, American Secretary of agriculture, Oct 1993

Etzel, Franz, German economist and cabinet member, Sept 1957

Ewing, Oscar R., American government official, July 1948, *Obit* Mar 1980

Fairchild, Benjamin Lewis, *Obit* Yrbk 1946

Faricy, William T., June 1948

Farmer, Guy, Feb 1955

Faure, Edgar, French statesman, Feb 1952, *Obit* May 1988

Feingold, Russ, American senator, July 1998

Feith, Douglas J., American military official, July 2008

Felt, W. Mark, American FBI official and Watergate informant Deep Throat, Sept 2005, *Obit* Yrbk 2009

Finnegan, Joseph F., Apr 1959, *Obit* Apr 1964

Fischer, Israel Frederick, judge and congressman, *Obit* Apr 1940

Fitzgerald, Patrick, American district attorney, Jan 2006

Fleischmann, Manly, lawyer, July 1951

Flexner, Bernard, *Obit* June 1945

Fly, James L., lawyer, Sept 1940, *Obit* Feb 1966

Fortas, Abe, American Supreme Court justice, Feb 1966, *Obit* May 1982

Fosdick, Raymond Blaine, Feb 1945, *Obit* Sept 1972

Fowler, R. M., Oct 1954

Frank, Hans, German jurist and Nazi leader, Mar 1941, *Obit* Nov 1946

Frank, Jerome N., American judge, Apr 1941, *Obit* Mar 1957

Frost, Leslie M., Canadian political leader, Oct 1953, *Obit* July 1973

Fuller, Kathryn, conservationist and lawyer, Jan 1994

Gabrielson, Guy George, American lawyer, Oct 1949, *Obit* June 1976

Gamble, Ralph A., Jan 1953, *Obit* May 1959

Gambrell, E. Smythe, June 1956

Gandy, Kim A., American feminist, Oct 2001

Gao Zhisheng, Chinese lawyer and dissident, Jan 2007

Garbus, Martin, American lawyer, Nov 2000

Gardner, O. Max, Jan 1947

Garzon, Baltasar, Spanish judge, Mar 2001

Gates, Ralph F., Sept 1947

Gaud, William S., Jan 1969, *Obit* Feb 1978

George, Walter F., American senator, June 1943, June 1955, *Obit* Oct 1957

Gillibrand, Kirsten, American senator, Oct 2013

Gilpatric, Roswell L., American lawyer and government official, Mar 1964, *Obit* May 1996

Gimlette, John, English travel writer and lawyer, Apr 2012

Giuliani, Rudolph W., American mayor and lawyer, Apr 1988, Jan 2008

Goldman, Frank, Jan 1953, *Obit* Apr 1965

Goldsborough, T. Alan, June 1948, *Obit* July 1951

Gomez, Jean-Jacques, French judge, Jan 2002

Goodell, Charles E., American senator, Yrbk 1968, *Obit* Mar 1987

Goodloe, John D., Apr 1947

Gossett, William T., lawyer and diplomat, July 1969, *Obit* Oct 1998

Granholm, Jennifer M., American governor, Oct 2003

Granik, Samuel Theodore, Yrbk 1952, *Obit* Nov 1970

Gray, C. Boyden, American lawyer and presidential adviser, Aug 1989

Gray, L. Patrick, American FBI director, Sept 1972, *Obit* Yrbk 2005

Green, Dwight H., American governor, Apr 1948, *Obit* Apr 1958

Green, Howard, Jan 1960

Green, Theodore Francis, American senator and governor, Feb 1950, *Obit* June 1966

Greene, Harold H., American judge, Aug 1985, *Obit* May 2000

Griffin, Robert P., American senator, May 1960

Griffiths, Martha Wright, American congresswoman and state official, Oct 1955, *Obit* Yrbk 2003

Grisham, John, American lawyer and novelist, Sept 1993

Gunter, Julius Caldeen, *Obit* Yrbk 1940

Hackworth, Green H., Jan 1958, *Obit* Sept 1973

Hailsham of St. Marylebone, Quintin Hogg, British cabinet member, Sept 1957, *Obit* Feb 2002

Hale, Richard Walden, *Obit* Apr 1943

Haley, Andrew G., lawyer, Oct 1955, *Obit* Nov 1966

Hall, Leonard Wood, American congressman, July 1953, *Obit* July 1979

Hall, William Edwin, Jan 1954, *Obit* Mar 1961

Halley, Rudolph, June 1953, *Obit* Jan 1957

Hallinan, Vincent, American lawyer, Oct 1952, *Obit* Nov 1992

Hand, Learned, American judge, Apr 1950, *Obit* Nov 1961

Hannegan, Robert Emmet, American postmaster general, June 1944, *Obit* Nov 1949

Hanson, Ole, *Obit* Sept 1940

Harlan, John Marshall, American Supreme Court justice, May 1955, *Obit* Feb 1972

Harris, Oren, American congressman and judge, May 1956

Harris, Walter, June 1955

Harrison, Earl G., Aug 1943, *Obit* Oct 1955

Harrison, Pat, American senator, *Obit* Aug 1941

Harron, Marion J., Yrbk 1949

Hart, Edward J., Feb 1953, *Obit* June 1961

Hart, Gary, American senator and lawyer, May 1976

Hart, Merwin K., Oct 1941, *Obit* Jan 1963

Hart, Philip A., American senator, Sept 1959, *Obit* Feb 1977

Hartke, Vance, American senator, Mar 1960, *Obit* Yrbk 2003

Hartzog, George B., American national parks director, July 1970, *Obit* Yrbk 2008

Hastie, William H., American lawyer, Mar 1944, *Obit* June 1976

Hatch, Carl A., senator and judge, Yrbk 1944, *Obit* Nov 1963

Hatch, Orrin G., American senator, Aug 1982

Hay, Charles M., *Obit* Mar 1945

Hayes, Denis, lawyer and environmentalist, Oct 1997

Hayes, Edward W., American lawyer, May 2006

Hayes, Robert M., lawyer, Apr 1989

Hearnes, Warren Eastman, American governor, June 1968

Heeney, A. D. P., June 1953

Heineman, Ben W., lawyer and machine tool executive, Jan 1962, *Obit* Yrbk 2012

Heitkamp, Heidi, state attorney general, Sept 2013

Hennings, Thomas C., American senator, Oct 1954, *Obit* Nov 1960

Hennock, Frieda, lawyer and government official, Nov 1948, *Obit* Sept 1960

Henry, E. William, Feb 1964

Hensel, H. Struve, American lawyer and military official, Yrbk 1948, *Obit* July 1991

Hertz, Emanuel, *Obit* July 1940

Hewart, Gordon Hewart, *Obit* June 1943

Hickenlooper, Bourke B., American senator and governor, May 1947, *Obit* Oct 1971

Hicks, Henry D., Oct 1956

Hiss, Alger, American diplomat and lawyer, Feb 1947, *Obit* Jan 1997

Hodel, Donald Paul, American organization official and Secretary of the interior, June 1987

Hoegh, Leo A., governor and civil defense official, July 1956, *Obit* Yrbk 2000

Hoey, Clyde R., American governor and senator, Oct 1949, *Obit* July 1954

Hoff, Philip H., American governor, Sept 1963

Hogan, Frank S., American district attorney, Sept 1953, *Obit* May 1974

Holaday, William Perry, *Obit* Mar 1946

Holenstein, Thomas, May 1958, *Obit* Jan 1963

Hollister, John B., American lawyer, congressman and government official, Oct 1955

Holt, Harold, Australian prime minister, Oct 1966, *Obit* Feb 1968

Holton, A. Linwood, American lawyer and governor, Feb 1971

Holtz, Jackson J., Mar 1950

Holtzman, Elizabeth, American congresswoman and municipal official, Nov 1973

Hoopes, Darlington, socialist leader, Sept 1952, *Obit* Nov 1989

Hope, Clifford R., American congressman, May 1953, *Obit* July 1970

Hopkins, John Jay, Mar 1954, *Obit* July 1957

Hormel, James C., lawyer, philanthropist and diplomat, Oct 1999

Hoshino, Naoki, Nov 1940

Howrey, Edward F., July 1953

Hruska, Roman Lee, American senator, July 1956, *Obit* July 1999

Hughes, Sarah T., American judge, Nov 1950, *Obit* July 1985

Hull, John Adley, *Obit* June 1944

Humphrey, Helen F., Nov 1952, *Obit* Oct 1963

Hunt, James B., American governor, June 1993

Impellitteri, Vincent R., American mayor, Feb 1951, *Obit* Mar 1987

Inouye, Daniel K., American senator, May 1960, Sept 1987, *Obit* Yrbk 2013

Ireland, Patricia, American lawyer and feminist, June 1992

Iverson, Kenneth R., Apr 1951

Jackson Lee, Sheila, American congresswoman, Nov 2008

Jackson, Maynard H., American mayor, Sept 1976, *Obit* Yrbk 2003

Jackson, Thomas Penfield, judge, June 2001, *Obit* Yrbk 2013

Jackson, William K., July 1946, *Obit* Yrbk 1947

Jahangir, Asma, Pakistani lawyer and feminist, Jan 2003

Jamail, Joseph, American lawyer, Sept 2008

Jameson, William James, judge, July 1954

Javits, Jacob K., American senator, June 1948, Oct 1958, *Obit* Apr 1986

Jaworski, Leon, American lawyer and special prosecutor, June 1974, *Obit* Feb 1983

Jenkins, Hayes Alan, American figure skater and lawyer, May 1956

Jenkins, Ray H., June 1954, *Obit* Feb 1981

Jenner, William E., American senator, June 1951, *Obit* May 1985

Johnson, Daniel, Canadian provincial premier, Nov 1967, *Obit* Nov 1968

Johnson, David M., July 1952

Johnson, Frank M., American judge, Aug 1978, *Obit* Oct 1999

Johnson, Leroy, Sept 1949, *Obit* June 1961

Johnston, Olin D., American senator and governor, Nov 1951, *Obit* June 1965

Jones, James R., Oct 1981

Jones, Marvin, congressman and judge, Aug 1943, *Obit* Jan 1984

Jones, Norman L., *Obit* Jan 1941

Jones, Sam Houston, lawyer and governor, Mar 1940, *Obit* Yrbk 1991

Jordan, Barbara, American lawyer and congresswoman, Sept 1974, Apr 1993, *Obit* Apr 1996

Jowitt, William Allen Jowitt, Aug 1941, *Obit* Nov 1957

Joyce, James Avery, English lawyer, author and pacifist, Mar 1959

Kampelman, Max M., American diplomat, July 1986

Kastenmeier, Robert W., American congressman, July 1966

Kaufman, Irving R., American judge, Apr 1953, *Obit* Apr 1992

Keating, Kenneth Barnard, American congressman, senator and diplomat, Oct 1950, *Obit* June 1975

Kee, John, June 1950, *Obit* June 1951

Keech, Richmond B., Mar 1950

Keenan, Joseph B., Sept 1946, *Obit* Feb 1955

Kem, James P., Oct 1950, *Obit* Apr 1965

Kemmis, Daniel, mayor and public policy analyst, Oct 1996

Kempner, Robert M. W., German lawyer, May 1943, *Obit* Oct 1993

Kennedy, Stephen P., June 1956, *Obit* Jan 1979

Kenyon, Dorothy, American judge, Apr 1947, *Obit* Apr 1972

Kersten, Charles J., Sept 1952

Khan, Muhammad Zafrulla, Yrbk 1947

Kilday, Paul J., Oct 1958, *Obit* Yrbk 1968

Kilgore, Harley Martin, American senator, June 1943, *Obit* May 1956

Kingsland, Lawrence C., Jan 1949

Kinnear, Helen Alice, Canadian judge, Apr 1957

Kintner, Earl W., lawyer and government official, Apr 1960, *Obit* Mar 1992

Kirbo, Charles H., lawyer, Sept 1977, *Obit* Nov 1996

Kirk, Paul, American senator and political party leader, Aug 1987

Kirkpatrick, Miles W., lawyer and government official, Feb 1972, *Obit* July 1998

Koch, Ed, American mayor, Sept 1978, *Obit* Yrbk 2013

Kostunica, Vojislav, Yugoslav president, Jan 2001

Krishna Menon, V. K., Indian lawyer and diplomat, Mar 1953, *Obit* Nov 1974

Kroll, Jules, American lawyer and private detective, Feb 1999

Kross, Anna M., American judge, Nov 1945, *Obit* Oct 1979

Krupp, Frederic D., American lawyer and environmentalist, Sept 2007

Krupsak, Mary Anne, July 1975

Kuhn, Edward W., June 1966

La Roe, Wilbur, Mar 1948, *Obit* July 1957

LaMarsh, Judy, Apr 1968, *Obit* Jan 1981

Lafontaine, Henri Marie, Belgian judge and pacifist, *Obit* July 1943

Lamberton, Robert Eneas, American lawyer, judge and mayor, *Obit* Oct 1941

Landis, James McCauley, American lawyer and regulatory agency official, Mar 1942, *Obit* Oct 1964

Landrieu, Moon, American state legislator, mayor and Secretary of housing and urban development, Jan 1980

Landry, Jeff, American congressman, Jan 2012

Lane, William Preston, June 1949, *Obit* Apr 1967

Langlie, Arthur B., Oct 1950, *Obit* Sept 1966

Lannung, Hermod, Yrbk 1949

Larson, Jess, American government official, June 1951

Latham, Dana, Mar 1959, *Obit* Apr 1974

Lee, Dorothy McCullough, Jan 1949

Lee, Martin, Chinese lawyer and political leader, July 1997

Leedom, Boyd, May 1956, *Obit* Oct 1969

Lefevre, Theo, June 1962, *Obit* Nov 1973

Leibowitz, Samuel Simon, American judge, Jan 1953, *Obit* Mar 1978

Lequerica y Erquiza, Jose Felix de, June 1951, *Obit* July 1963

Levin, Carl, American senator, May 2004

Levinson, Salmon Oliver, lawyer and pacifist, *Obit* Mar 1941

Lewis, Clyde A., Feb 1950

Liebenow, Robert C., May 1956

Lightner, Milton C., Nov 1958, *Obit* May 1968

Liman, Arthur L., lawyer, Jan 1988, *Obit* Oct 1997

Lindsey, Benjamin B., judge, *Obit* May 1943

Linowitz, Sol M., American lawyer and diplomat, Mar 1967, *Obit* Yrbk 2005

Locker, Jesse D., Mar 1955, *Obit* June 1955

Lockwood, Rodney M., Sept 1949

Long, Breckinridge, diplomat, Nov 1943, *Obit* Yrbk 1958

Loomis, Daniel P., Jan 1960

Lopez Obrador, Andres Manuel, Mexican mayor and political leader, Jan 2003

Lucas, Scott W., American senator, Yrbk 1947, *Obit* Apr 1968

Ludwig, Ken, American lawyer and dramatist, May 2004

Luhring, Oscar Raymond, *Obit* Oct 1944

MacDonald, William J., *Obit* May 1946

Machold, Earle J., Nov 1958

Mack, Julian W., American judge, *Obit* Oct 1943

Magnuson, Warren, American senator, Oct 1945, *Obit* July 1989

Mahady, Henry J., July 1954

Mahan, John W., July 1959

Mahon, George H., American congressman, Mar 1958, *Obit* Jan 1986

Maile, Boniface R., Feb 1951

Malone, Ross Lynn, lawyer, Mar 1959, *Obit* Oct 1974

Maloney, Walter E., American lawyer, Oct 1952, *Obit* Yrbk 2007

Mankin, Helen Douglas, congresswoman and lawyer, Apr 1946

Marcantonio, Vito, American congressman, Feb 1949, *Obit* Oct 1954

Marland, William C., Apr 1956, *Obit* Jan 1966

Marshall, David, Singaporean lawyer and political leader, July 1956, *Obit* Feb 1996

Martin, George Brown, *Obit* Yrbk 1945

Martin, Kevin, American lawyer and regulatory official, Aug 2005

Mason, Lowell B., June 1949

Mathias, Charles, American senator, Yrbk 1972, *Obit* Yrbk 2010

Matthews, Burnita Shelton, judge, Apr 1950, *Obit* June 1988

Matthews, Francis P., American Secretary of the navy, Sept 1949, *Obit* Yrbk 1952

Matthews, W. Donald, Sept 1952

Maverick, Maury, American congressman and mayor, Mar 1944, *Obit* Sept 1954

Max, Adolphe, Belgian burgomaster, *Obit* Jan 1940

Maxwell, David Farrow, lawyer and association executive, June 1957

May, Andrew Jackson, American congressman, Apr 1941, *Obit* Nov 1959

McAdoo, William G., American Secretary of the treasury and senator, *Obit* Mar 1941

McCarl, John Raymond, lawyer and government official, *Obit* Sept 1940

McCarran, Pat, American senator, July 1947, *Obit* Yrbk 1954

McCarthy, Leighton, Oct 1942, *Obit* Nov 1952

McClellan, John L., American senator, Apr 1950, *Obit* Feb 1978

McCloskey, Paul N., American congressman and lawyer, Nov 1971

McConnell, Mitch, American senator, Feb 2008

McDaniel, Glen, May 1952

McDonald, Gabrielle, judge, Oct 2001

McIntyre, James T., Jan 1979

McIntyre, Thomas James, American senator, Nov 1963, *Obit* Oct 1992

McKeldin, Theodore R., American governor, Oct 1952, *Obit* Oct 1974

McKellar, Kenneth Douglas, American senator, Jan 1946, *Obit* Jan 1958

McKneally, Martin B., congressman and veterans' leader, Mar 1960, *Obit* Aug 1992

McLachlin, Beverley M., Canadian judge, Sept 2009

McMahon, Brien, American senator, Yrbk 1945, *Obit* Sept 1952

McMillan, John L., American congressman and lawyer, Nov 1956

McNair, Arnold Duncan McNair, Feb 1955

McNary, Charles Linza, American senator, Aug 1940, *Obit* Apr 1944

McNichols, Stephen L. R., American governor, Oct 1958, *Obit* Feb 1998

Meader, George, July 1956

Mechem, Merritt Cramer, *Obit* June 1946

Medina, Harold R., American judge, Apr 1949, *Obit* May 1990

Metcalf, Lee, American senator, Feb 1970, *Obit* Mar 1978

Metzenbaum, Howard M., American senator, July 1980, *Obit* Yrbk 2008

Meyner, Robert Baumle, American governor, Apr 1955, *Obit* July 1990

Mikva, Abner J., American judge, July 1980

Miller, Edward G., June 1951, *Obit* June 1968

Miller, Marshall E., Oct 1953

Miller, William Edward, American congressman and lawyer, Feb 1962, *Obit* Aug 1983

Millikin, Eugene Donald, American senator, Apr 1948, *Obit* Oct 1958

Mills, Wilbur D., American congressman, Nov 1956, *Obit* July 1992

Mink, Patsy T., American congresswoman, Sept 1968, *Obit* Jan 2003

Minow, Newton Norman, American lawyer and regulatory agency official, Oct 1961

Mitchell, Stephen Arnold, American lawyer and political party leader, Oct 1952, *Obit* June 1974

Mitchell, William D., Jan 1946, *Obit* Nov 1955

Monckton of Brenchley, Walter Turner Monckton, British cabinet member, Yrbk 1951, *Obit* Feb 1965

Mondale, Walter F., American vice-president, Jan 1969, May 1978

Monsky, Henry, Nov 1941, *Obit* June 1947

Moore, Michael C., state attorney general, Aug 1997

Moore, Preston J., Apr 1959

Morgenthau, Robert, American district attorney, Jan 1986

Morris, Dave Hennen, *Obit* June 1944

Morris, Earl, American bar association executive, June 1968, *Obit* July 1992

Morris, Newbold, American municipal official, Mar 1952, *Obit* Apr 1966

Morris, Roland Sletor, lawyer and diplomat, *Obit* Jan 1946

Morrison, Frank Brenner, May 1964

Morrison, William Shepherd, British statesman, Jan 1952, *Obit* Apr 1961

Morse, Clarence G., Nov 1957

Mortimer, John, English dramatist, novelist and lawyer, Apr 1983, *Obit* Yrbk 2009

Morton, James Madison, *Obit* Aug 1940

Moss, Frank E., American senator, Yrbk 1971, *Obit* June 2003

Mott, James W., *Obit* Yrbk 1945

Mukhtar, Aloma, Nigerian supreme court justice, Jan 2005

Murphy, Charles S., American lawyer and presidential adviser, Apr 1950, *Obit* Oct 1983

Murphy, Thomas F., police commissioner and judge, Mar 1951, *Obit* Jan 1996

Murray, Tom, Nov 1956, *Obit* Jan 1972

Murrell, Ethel Ernest, Oct 1951

Musmanno, Michael Angelo, June 1967, *Obit* Yrbk 1968

Mwanawasa, Levy, Zambian president, Jan 2003, *Obit* Yrbk 2008

Myers, Francis John, Apr 1949, *Obit* Sept 1956

Nader, Ralph, American consumer rights advocate, Nov 1968, Apr 1986

Neely, Matthew M., Jan 1950, *Obit* Mar 1958

Neumann, Emanuel, Mar 1967, *Obit* Jan 1981

Newbolt, Francis George, *Obit* Jan 1941

Ney, Hubert, Nov 1956

Nizer, Louis, American lawyer, Nov 1955, *Obit* Jan 1995

Noon, Firoz Khan, June 1957

Norris, George William, American senator, *Obit* Oct 1944

Norton, Gale, American Secretary of the interior, June 2001

Nunn, Sam, American senator, Jan 1980

O'Connor, Basil, Sept 1944, *Obit* May 1972

O'Conor, Herbert R., Feb 1950, *Obit* May 1960

O'Dwyer, Paul, American lawyer and municipal official, Sept 1969, *Obit* Sept 1998

O'Gorman, James A., *Obit* July 1943

O'Mahoney, Joseph C., American senator, Oct 1945, *Obit* Jan 1963

O'Melveny, Henry W., *Obit* June 1941

O'Neal, A. Daniel, June 1979

O'Neill, C. William, July 1958

O'Neill, Joseph, American lawyer and novelist, June 2009

Obama, Barack, American president, July 2005, Mar 2009

Ogburn, Charlton, Feb 1955, *Obit* Apr 1962

Olds, Irving S., American lawyer and steel industry executive, Oct 1948, *Obit* Apr 1963

Olson, Theodore B., American lawyer and former Solicitor general, Nov 2010

Osborne, William Hamilton, *Obit* Feb 1943

Ottinger, Nathan, *Obit* Jan 1941

Owens, Clarence Julian, *Obit* Apr 1941

Palme, Olof, Swedish prime minister, May 1970, *Obit* Apr 1986

Palmer, Hazel, June 1958

Palmer, Thomas Waverly, Mar 1949

Parker, Cola G., Sept 1956, *Obit* Sept 1962

Parker, John J., American judge, Yrbk 1955, *Obit* May 1958

Parker, Robert M., American wine critic, May 2005

Pastore, John O., American senator, Apr 1953, *Obit* Yrbk 2000

Pate, Walter L., Mar 1947, *Obit* June 1974

Patman, Wright, American congressman, Feb 1946, *Obit* Apr 1976

Patterson, Robert Porter, American Secretary of war, Oct 1941, *Obit* Mar 1952

Paul, Alice, American lawyer and feminist, Sept 1947, *Obit* Sept 1977

Pena, Federico, American Secretary of transportation, Oct 1993

Percy, William Alexander, American poet and lawyer, *Obit* Mar 1942

Persad-Bissessar, Kamla, Trinidadian prime minister, Jan 2013

Phillips, Lena Madesin, Apr 1946, *Obit* July 1955

Picard, Frank A., Mar 1947, *Obit* Apr 1963

Piccioni, Attilio, Oct 1967, *Obit* May 1976

Pike, Otis, American congressman, Feb 1976

Pine, David A., American judge, June 1952, *Obit* Sept 1970

Pittman, Steuart L., American government official, Jan 1963, *Obit* Yrbk 2013

Podesta, John, American public policy organization official and former presidential adviser, Feb 2010

Pool, Joe, American congressman, Mar 1967, *Obit* Sept 1968

Poole, Franklin Osborne, *Obit* Mar 1943

Porter, Charles O., Sept 1957

Porter, Paul A., American regulatory agency official, Jan 1945, *Obit* Jan 1976

Powell, Lewis F., American Supreme Court justice, Feb 1965, *Obit* Nov 1998

Power, Donald C., Mar 1960, *Obit* May 1979

Pressman, Lee, American labor lawyer, May 1947, *Obit* Jan 1970

Pribichevich, Stoyan, Aug 1944, *Obit* July 1976

Priebus, Reince, American political party leader, May 2012

Prio Socarras, Carlos, Cuban president, May 1949, *Obit* June 1977

Rabaut, Louis Charles, Jan 1952, *Obit* Jan 1962

Radcliffe, Cyril John Radcliffe, British jurist and government official, June 1963, *Obit* May 1977

Ragon, Heartsill, *Obit* Nov 1940

Ralls, Charles C., Jan 1951

Ramspeck, Robert, June 1951, *Obit* Yrbk 1972

Randall, John D., May 1960

Rangel, Charles B., American congressman, Mar 1984

Rankin, J. Lee, American solicitor general, Feb 1959, *Obit* Sept 1996

Rankin, John E., American congressman, Feb 1944, *Obit* Jan 1961

Rawalt, Marguerite, lawyer, Mar 1956

Reed, Daniel A., American congressman, May 1953, *Obit* Apr 1959

Reed, James A., American senator, *Obit* Oct 1944

Reed, Stanley Forman, American Supreme Court justice, Feb 1942, *Obit* May 1980

Rees, Edward H., Jan 1958, *Obit* Yrbk 1969

Reeves, Jesse S., *Obit* Aug 1942

Reid, Frank R., *Obit* Mar 1945

Resor, Stanley R., American Secretary of the army, Sept 1969, *Obit* Yrbk 2012

Reuss, Henry S., American congressman and lawyer, Oct 1959, *Obit* Mar 2002

Revercomb, Chapman, June 1958

Reynolds, Robert Rice, senator, Oct 1940, *Obit* Mar 1963

Reynolds, William Bradford, government official and lawyer, July 1988

Reynoso, Cruz, American lawyer and judge, Mar 2002

Rhyne, Charles S., American lawyer, May 1958, *Obit* Yrbk 2003

Richards, James P., Sept 1951, *Obit* Apr 1979

Richberg, Donald R., American government official, Yrbk 1949, *Obit* Jan 1961

Rifkind, Simon H., lawyer, May 1946, *Obit* Jan 1996

Roberts, Dennis J., governor, Yrbk 1956, *Obit* Sept 1994

Roberts, John G., American Chief Justice of the Supreme Court, Feb 2006

Robertson, A. Willis, American senator, Yrbk 1949, *Obit* Yrbk 1971

Robinson, Elmer E., Nov 1955

Rodriguez Zapatero, Jose Luis, Spanish prime minister, Jan 2004

Rogge, O. John, Feb 1948, *Obit* June 1981

Rooney, John J., American congressman, Yrbk 1964, *Obit* Jan 1976

Roper, Daniel C., *Obit* May 1943

Rosenfeld, Kurt, *Obit* Nov 1943

Rosenfield, Harry N., lawyer, lobbyist and refugee settlement leader, Apr 1952, *Obit* Aug 1995

Rowe, Leo Stanton, director general of the Pan American union, Aug 1945, *Obit* Jan 1947

Ruckelshaus, William D., American government official, July 1971

Rudman, Warren B., senator, Nov 1989, *Obit* Yrbk 2013

Ruiz Guinazu, Enrique, Apr 1942, *Obit* Jan 1968

Ryan, William F., American congressman, May 1967, *Obit* Yrbk 1972

Saakashvili, Mikheil, Georgian president, May 2009

Sabath, Adolph J., American congressman, July 1946, *Obit* Yrbk 1952

Salit, Norman, rabbi and lawyer, Mar 1955, *Obit* Oct 1960

Saltonstall, Leverett, American governor and senator, June 1944, Apr 1956, *Obit* Sept 1979

Sanders, Carl E., American governor, Yrbk 1964

Santa Cruz, Hernan, Yrbk 1949

Santorum, Rick, American lawyer, presidential candidate and former senator, Aug 2011

Satterfield, John C., July 1962

Saund, Dalip Singh, congressman, June 1960, *Obit* June 1973

Saunders, Robert, Yrbk 1951, *Obit* Mar 1955

Saunders, Stuart Thomas, American railroad executive, Apr 1966, *Obit* Mar 1987

Saxon, James J., Yrbk 1963, *Obit* Apr 1980

Sayre, Francis Bowes, American diplomat, Jan 1940, *Obit* May 1972

Scardino, Marjorie, American publishing executive, Apr 2000

Schaffer, Fritz, Mar 1953, *Obit* May 1967

Scheck, Barry, American lawyer, Mar 1998

Scheiberling, Edward N., Yrbk 1944, *Obit* Jan 1968

Schulthess, Edmund, *Obit* June 1944

Scott, Hugh Doggett, American senator, Sept 1948, *Obit* Sept 1994

Scott, John R. K., *Obit* Feb 1946

Scottoline, Lisa, American lawyer and novelist, July 2001

Scribner, Fred C., government official, Yrbk 1958, *Obit* Apr 1994

Sebald, William J., naval officer, lawyer and diplomat, Oct 1951

Segal, Bernard G., law association official, June 1970, *Obit* Aug 1997

Seymour, Whitney North, lawyer, May 1961, *Obit* July 1983

Shea, William Alfred, lawyer, Oct 1965, *Obit* Nov 1991

Shiras, George, American lawyer and naturalist, *Obit* May 1942

Shriver, Sargent, American lawyer and government official, Yrbk 1961, *Obit* Yrbk 2011

Simms, John F., Sept 1956, *Obit* June 1975

Simon, John Allsebrook Simon, British statesman, July 1940, *Obit* Mar 1954

Singh, Swaran, Mar 1971, *Obit* Jan 1995

Singh, Vishwanath Pratap, Indian prime minister, May 1990, *Obit* Yrbk 2009

Sirica, John J., American judge, May 1974, *Obit* Oct 1992

Sklar, Rachel, Media blogger, author and attorney, Mar 2012

Smith, Chesterfield H., American lawyer, Nov 1974, *Obit* Yrbk 2003

Smith, Gerard C., American lawyer and diplomat, Oct 1970, *Obit* Sept 1994

Smith, Gregory White, lawyer and author, Mar 1998

Smith, H. Alexander, American senator, Apr 1948, *Obit* Jan 1967

Smith, Sylvester C., July 1963

Smylie, Robert E., American governor, Feb 1956, *Obit* Yrbk 2004

Sobchak, Anatoly, Russian mayor, July 1992, *Obit* July 2000

Solh, Sami, Feb 1958, *Obit* Jan 1969

Sorensen, Theodore C., American presidential adviser, Yrbk 1961, *Obit* Yrbk 2011

Spangler, Harrison Earl, lawyer, Aug 1943, *Obit* Oct 1965

Spence, Brent, Sept 1952, *Obit* Jan 1968

Spencer, P. C., July 1951, *Obit* Jan 1970

Springer, Adele I., Apr 1947

Squires, Richard Anderson, *Obit* May 1940

Stanley, Winnifred Claire, congresswoman, June 1943

Starr, Louis E., June 1947

Steele, Michael S., American political party leader, July 2004

Steinhardt, Laurence Adolph, lawyer and diplomat, July 1941, *Obit* Apr 1950

Stelle, John, Jan 1946, *Obit* Sept 1962

Stephens, Hubert D., *Obit* Apr 1946

Stepovich, Michael A., Nov 1958

Steuer, Max, *Obit* Oct 1940

Stevenson, Adlai, American senator, Apr 1974

Strauss, J. G. N., Jan 1951

Strauss, Robert S., American political party leader and diplomat, Mar 1974, July 1992

Strijdom, Johannes Gerhardus, May 1956, *Obit* Nov 1958

Sullivan, John L., American Secretary of the navy, Sept 1948, *Obit* Oct 1982

Sulzer, William, *Obit* Jan 1942

Swart, Charles Robberts, June 1960

Sykes, Eugene Octave, *Obit* July 1945

Symington, James W., June 1968

Syran, Arthur George, Mar 1950

Taber, John, American congressman, Feb 1948, *Obit* Jan 1966

Taft, Robert A., American senator, Oct 1967, *Obit* Feb 1994

Teitgen, Pierre-Henri, French political leader, Jan 1953

Thatcher, Margaret, British prime minister, July 1975, Nov 1989, *Obit* Yrbk 2013

Thomas, Albert, American congressman, Oct 1950, *Obit* Mar 1966

Thomas, Elmer, American senator, Yrbk 1949, *Obit* Nov 1965

Thomas, Franklin A., American lawyer and foundation official, Oct 1981

Thompson, James R., American governor and lawyer, Jan 1979

Tice, Merton B., June 1955

Tipton, Stuart G., Mar 1967

Train, Arthur Cheney, lawyer and author, *Obit* Feb 1946

Trevethin and Oaksey, Geoffrey Lawrence, British judge, Jan 1946, *Obit* Yrbk 1991

Trumka, Richard L., labor leader and lawyer, Apr 1986

Tucker, B. Fain, Yrbk 1957

Tunney, John V., June 1971

Turner, Donald Frank, American government official, lawyer and economist, July 1967, *Obit* Sept 1994

Turow, Scott, American lawyer and novelist, Aug 1991

Tweed, Harrison, Jan 1950, *Obit* July 1969

Udall, Morris K., American congressman, Apr 1969, *Obit* Mar 1999

Udall, Stewart L., American Secretary of the interior, May 1961, *Obit* Yrbk 2010

Ulman, Joseph N., *Obit* May 1943

Untermyer, Samuel, American lawyer, Apr 1940

Uribe Velez, Alvaro, Colombian president, Jan 2002

Utterback, Hubert, *Obit* July 1942

Vance, John Thomas, *Obit* May 1943

Vanderbilt, Arthur T., judge, Feb 1947, *Obit* Oct 1957

Vandiver, S. Ernest, American governor, July 1962, *Obit* Yrbk 2005

Verges, Jacques, French lawyer, Jan 2004, *Obit* Yrbk 2013

Veronese, Vittorino, June 1959

Voorhees, Tracy S., Feb 1957, *Obit* Nov 1974

Vorys, John M., American congressman, Sept 1950, *Obit* Nov 1968

Wagner, J. Addington, May 1956

Wagner, Robert F., American senator and judge, May 1941, *Obit* June 1953

Wald, Patricia M., American judge, June 2000

Walker, Daniel, governor, Aug 1976

Walker, Frank Comerford, postmaster general, Oct 1940, *Obit* Nov 1959

Walker, Paul A., May 1952, *Obit* July 1966

Walsh, Joseph, *Obit* Mar 1946

Walsh, Lawrence E., American lawyer, Oct 1991

Walter, Francis E., American congressman, June 1952, *Obit* July 1963

Wapner, Joseph A., judge, Sept 1989

Warburton, Herbert B., Nov 1951

Ward, Christopher L., *Obit* Apr 1943

Waring, Julius Waties, judge, Yrbk 1948, *Obit* Mar 1968

Waring, Roane, Yrbk 1943, *Obit* Yrbk 1958

Warner, Milo J., Nov 1941

Warnke, Paul C., American lawyer and government official, Aug 1977, *Obit* Feb 2002

Warren, Fuller, American governor, Yrbk 1949

Washington, Walter E., American mayor, July 1968, *Obit* Yrbk 2004

Waste, William Harrison, *Obit* July 1940

Watkins, Arthur V., American senator and judge, July 1950, *Obit* Yrbk 1973

Watson, Jack H., Nov 1980

Webb, James E., American NASA official, Oct 1946, May 1962, *Obit* May 1992

Webb, Jim, American senator, Aug 1987, Nov 2007

Webb, William Flood, Yrbk 1948

Weil, Frank L., Feb 1949, *Obit* Jan 1958

Welch, Joseph N., American lawyer, June 1954, *Obit* Yrbk 1960

Welker, Herman, American senator, Feb 1955, *Obit* Jan 1958

Wheeler, Burton K., American senator, Aug 1940, *Obit* Feb 1975

Wherry, Kenneth S., American senator, Apr 1946, *Obit* Jan 1952

White, Byron R., American Supreme Court justice, Yrbk 1962, *Obit* July 2002

White, Kevin H., American mayor, Yrbk 1974, *Obit* Yrbk 2012

White, S. Harrison, *Obit* Feb 1946

White, W. Wilson, Jan 1959, *Obit* Jan 1965

Whitlam, Edward Gough, Jan 1974

Wigglesworth, Richard B., May 1959, *Obit* Yrbk 1960

Wiley, Alexander, American senator, Apr 1947, *Obit* Jan 1968

Wiley, Richard E., American lawyer, Mar 1977

Wilkins, J. Ernest, Yrbk 1954, *Obit* Mar 1959

Williams, Harrison A., American senator, Oct 1960, *Obit* Mar 2002

Wilson, Donald R., Jan 1952

Wiseman, Frederick, American documentary filmmaker, Yrbk 1974

Wofford, Harris, American senator, Apr 1992

Wolcott, Jesse P., American congressman and regulatory agency official, Yrbk 1949, *Obit* Apr 1969

Wood, John S., American congressman, July 1949, *Obit* Nov 1968

Wright, Fielding, American governor, Sept 1948, *Obit* July 1956

Wright, Loyd, July 1955, *Obit* Jan 1975

Yarborough, Ralph W., American senator, Feb 1960, *Obit* Apr 1996

Young, Owen D., lawyer and manufacturing executive, Aug 1945, *Obit* Sept 1962

Youngdahl, Luther W., Mar 1948, *Obit* Aug 1978

Younger, Kenneth Gilmour, Sept 1950

Zoli, Adone, Mar 1958, *Obit* Apr 1960

Zubiria, Alberto F., Yrbk 1956

Zuckert, Eugene Martin, American Secretary of the air force, Apr 1952, *Obit* Yrbk 2000

Lecturers

Alexander, Ruth, American economist and lecturer, Mar 1943

Buscaglia, Leo F., educator and lecturer, Oct 1983, *Obit* Aug 1998

Carnegie, Dale, American self-improvement lecturer and writer, Yrbk 1941, Sept 1955

Carter, Huntly, *Obit* May 1942

Chesser, Elizabeth Sloan, *Obit* Mar 1940

Clapper, Olive Ewing, Sept 1946, *Obit* Jan 1969

Dell, Robert Edward, *Obit* Sept 1940

Greenbie, Sydney, Sept 1941, *Obit* Sept 1960

Holmes, Burton, May 1944, *Obit* Oct 1958

Huckel, Oliver, *Obit* Jan 1940

Kilmer, Aline, *Obit* Yrbk 1941

Kohoutek, Lubos, June 1974

Marquand, Hilary A., Apr 1951

Meerloo, Joost A. M., Jan 1962, *Obit* Feb 1977

Moir, Phyllis, Apr 1942

Ojike, Mazi Mbonu, July 1947

Paton, Stewart, *Obit* Mar 1942

Power, D'Arcy, *Obit* July 1941

Richter, George Martin, *Obit* July 1942

Ross, Edward Denison, *Obit* Nov 1940

Schain, Josephine, July 1945

Shinn, Florence Scovel, *Obit* Yrbk 1940

Smedley, Constance, *Obit* Apr 1941

Stewart, Anna Bird, Yrbk 1948

Toch, Maximilian, *Obit* June 1946

Von Tempski, Armine, *Obit* Jan 1944

Wiggam, Albert Edward, July 1942, *Obit* June 1957

Williamson, Marianne, New Age preacher, Feb 1993

Lexicographers

Barnhart, Clarence Lewis, lexicographer, Sept 1954, *Obit* Jan 1994

Funk, Charles Earle, June 1947, *Obit* July 1957

Gove, Philip Babcock, Oct 1962, *Obit* Jan 1973

Herold, J. Christopher, Yrbk 1959, *Obit* Feb 1965

Nicholson, Margaret, Nov 1957

Simpson, J. A., English editor and lexicographer, Jan 2003

Librarians

Adams, Randolph Greenfield, librarian, Aug 1943

Adkinson, Burton W., American geographer and librarian, June 1959

Babb, James Tinkham, American librarian, July 1955, *Obit* Oct 1968

Beals, Ralph Albert, librarian, Feb 1947, *Obit* Yrbk 1954

Bettmann, Otto L., archivist, Nov 1961, *Obit* July 1998

Blackwell, Earl, society leader and celebrity information service executive, Nov 1960, *Obit* May 1995

Bliss, Henry Evelyn, librarian, Sept 1953, *Obit* Oct 1955

Bostwick, Arthur Elmore, American librarian, *Obit* Apr 1942

Bradshaw, Lillian Moore, American library director, June 1970

Bray, Robert S., Feb 1966, *Obit* Feb 1975

Brode, Mildred H., Sept 1963

Brown, Alberta L., May 1958

Brown, Charles Harvey, librarian, Aug 1941, *Obit* Mar 1960

Budington, William S., June 1964

Bush, Laura, wife of American president George W. Bush, June 2001

Carlton, W. N. C., *Obit* Mar 1943

Castagna, Edwin, librarian, June 1964

Clapp, Verner W., librarian, Mar 1959, *Obit* Sept 1972

Clift, David Horace, librarian, June 1952, *Obit* Yrbk 1973

Colwell, Eileen, British librarian, July 1963

Cory, John Mackenzie, librarian, Sept 1949, *Obit* May 1988

Culver, Essae Martha, American librarian, Sept 1940

Dix, William S., librarian, June 1969, *Obit* Apr 1978

Doms, Keith, June 1971

Downs, Robert B., librarian, Jan 1941, June 1952, *Obit* Apr 1991

Fletcher, Angus, Sept 1946, *Obit* Nov 1960

Flexner, Jennie Maas, librarian, *Obit* Jan 1945

Forsythe, Robert S., *Obit* Aug 1941

Francis, Frank Chalton, British librarian, July 1959, *Obit* Apr 1989

Freehafer, Edward G., librarian, June 1955, *Obit* Feb 1986

Fuller, Margaret H., American librarian, June 1959

Fyan, Loleta Dawson, librarian, Yrbk 1951

Gaver, Mary Virginia, American librarian, June 1966, *Obit* Mar 1992

Gibson, Robert William, May 1969

Gonzalez, Efren W., Jan 1971

Graham, Clarence R., librarian, Nov 1950

Greenaway, Emerson, librarian, July 1958, *Obit* June 1990

Hill, Frank Pierce, librarian, *Obit* Oct 1941

Howard, Alice Sturtevant, *Obit* Nov 1945

Jackson, Eugene B., June 1961

Jones, Clara Stanton, librarian, July 1976

Kaiser, John Boynton, librarian, May 1943

Keck, Lucile L., Mar 1954

Kinder, Katharine L., May 1957

Klahre, Ethel S., May 1962

Koch, Theodore Wesley, librarian, *Obit* May 1941

Laich, Katherine, librarian, June 1972

Lord, Milton Edward, librarian, Feb 1950

Lorenz, John G., Sept 1966

Ludington, Flora Belle, librarian, Nov 1953

Lydenberg, Harry Miller, librarian, Sept 1941, *Obit* June 1960

Martin, Allie Beth, American librarian, June 1975, *Obit* June 1976

McDonough, Roger H., state librarian, June 1968

Mearns, David Chambers, librarian, July 1961, *Obit* July 1981

Milam, Carl Hastings, American librarian, June 1945, *Obit* Oct 1963

Mohrhardt, Foster Edward, American librarian, June 1967

Morsch, Lucile M., librarian, June 1957, *Obit* Nov 1972

Morton, Elizabeth Homer, Canadian librarian, July 1961

Mumford, Lawrence Quincy, American Librarian of Congress, June 1954, *Obit* Jan 1983

Oltman, Florine, May 1970

Otuken, Adnan, Turkish librarian, June 1954

Paradise, Nathaniel Burton, *Obit* June 1942

Parma, V. Valta, *Obit* Nov 1941

Poole, Franklin Osborne, *Obit* Mar 1943

Potter, Alfred Claghorn, *Obit* Yrbk 1940

Powell, Benjamin Edward, librarian, June 1959

Ranganathan, S. R., Indian librarian, Sept 1965, *Obit* Yrbk 1972

Rathbone, Josephine Adams, librarian and educator, *Obit* July 1941

Rice, Paul North, librarian, Nov 1947, *Obit* June 1967

Richards, John Stewart, librarian, June 1955

Rigling, Alfred, *Obit* Jan 1941

Roberts, Kate L., *Obit* Oct 1941

Rogers, Frank Bradway, physician and librarian, June 1962

Rogers, Rutherford David, June 1962

Shaver, Mary, *Obit* Mar 1942

Shaw, Ralph R., American librarian, June 1956, *Obit* Yrbk 1972

Shearer, Augustus Hunt, *Obit* July 1941

Smith, Carleton Sprague, musicologist, Yrbk 1960, *Obit* Nov 1994

Thompson, Alleen, June 1965

Tyler, Alice S., librarian, *Obit* June 1944

Usher, Elizabeth Reuter, May 1967

Utley, George B., librarian, *Obit* Nov 1946

Vail, Robert W. G., librarian and bibliographer, Feb 1945, *Obit* July 1966

Vance, John Thomas, *Obit* May 1943

Vosper, Robert Gordon, librarian, July 1965

Wagman, Frederick H., librarian, July 1963

Warren, Althea, librarian, Feb 1942, *Obit* Feb 1960

Wilson, Margaret Stevens, *Obit* May 1943

Woods, Bill Milton, librarian, May 1966, *Obit* Sept 1974

Wright, Louis B., historian and librarian, Nov 1950, *Obit* June 1984

Wynkoop, Asa, *Obit* Yrbk 1942

Lighting designers

Tipton, Jennifer, American lighting designer, July 1997

Linguists

Bacon, Leonard, poet, critic and translator, June 1941, *Obit* Mar 1954

Berlitz, Charles, American educator and writer on the paranormal, Feb 1957, *Obit* Yrbk 2004

Buber, Martin, Israeli philosopher, June 1953, *Obit* July 1965

Cortazar, Julio, Argentine novelist, Feb 1974, *Obit* Apr 1984

De Onis, Harriet, translator, Apr 1957, *Obit* May 1969

Deutscher, Guy, Feb 2012

Galassi, Jonathan, American editor, poet and translator, Sept 1999

Goetz, Delia, author and translator, Yrbk 1949, *Obit* Sept 1996

Gordon, Jaimy, American novelist, poet and short story writer, July 2011

Heaney, Seamus, Irish poet, Jan 1982, *Obit* Yrbk 2013

Jimenez, Juan Ramon, Spanish poet, Feb 1957, *Obit* Sept 1958

Labov, William, American sociolinguist, Mar 2006

Lin Yutang, Chinese novelist, essayist and translator, May 1940, *Obit* May 1976

McWhorter, John H., American linguist, Feb 2003

Molloy, Robert, author and translator, Yrbk 1948, *Obit* Mar 1977

Ogden, C. K., English linguist, Jan 1944, *Obit* June 1957

Pasternak, Boris Leonidovich, Russian poet and novelist, Feb 1959, *Obit* July 1960

Pei, Mario, linguist, Oct 1968, *Obit* May 1978

Peterson, Virgilia, Yrbk 1953, *Obit* Feb 1967

Quasimodo, Salvatore, Italian poet, Mar 1960, *Obit* Sept 1968

Rexroth, Kenneth, American poet, essayist and translator, Apr 1981, *Obit* Aug 1982

Richards, I. A., English poet, critic and linguist, Yrbk 1972, *Obit* Oct 1979

Simon, Edith, Yrbk 1954

Soueif, Ahdaf, Egyptian-British novelist and short story writer, Jan 2003

Thomas, D. M., English novelist, poet and translator, Nov 1983

Volokhonsky, Larissa, Russian translator, June 2006

Watkins, Shirley, Yrbk 1958

Wilbur, Richard, American poet, Jan 1966

Literary critics

Amis, Martin, English novelist and short story writer, June 1990, Jan 2003

Brantley, Ben, American drama critic, Aug 2011

Cassidy, Claudia, drama and music critic, Sept 1955, *Obit* Oct 1996

Clurman, Harold, theatrical director and critic, Feb 1959, *Obit* Nov 1980

Day Lewis, C., Anglo-Irish poet, critic and mystery writer, Jan 1940, July 1969, *Obit* July 1972

Grossman, Lev, American literary critic and novelist, Apr 2010

Guerard, Albert J., novelist and critic, Yrbk 1946, *Obit* Mar 2001

Hicks, Granville, American literary critic and novelist, May 1942, *Obit* Aug 1982

Johnson, Pamela Hansford, English novelist and critic, Yrbk 1948, *Obit* Aug 1981

Kott, Jan, Polish literary critic, Apr 1969, *Obit* Mar 2002

Lovett, Robert Morss, literary critic and author, Aug 1943, *Obit* Apr 1956

Mantle, Burns, American drama critic, Nov 1944, *Obit* Mar 1948

Nathan, George Jean, drama critic, Apr 1945, *Obit* June 1958

Pound, Ezra, American poet and literary critic, Nov 1942, May 1963, *Obit* Yrbk 1972

Prescott, Orville, literary critic, Mar 1957, *Obit* July 1996

Pritchett, V. S., English short story writer, novelist and critic, Jan 1974, *Obit* June 1997

Ransom, John Crowe, American poet and literary critic, July 1964, *Obit* Sept 1974

Schwartz, Delmore, poet and critic, June 1960, *Obit* Nov 1966

Symons, Arthur, English poet and critic, *Obit* Mar 1945

Tynan, Kenneth, British drama critic, Yrbk 1963, *Obit* Sept 1980

Lithographers

Alechinsky, Pierre, Belgian painter and lithographer, Sept 1988

Benton, Thomas Hart, American painter, Oct 1940, *Obit* Mar 1975

Ganso, Emil, *Obit* June 1941

Goodman, Bertram, May 1954

Grant, Gordon, June 1953, *Obit* July 1962

Wales, George C., *Obit* May 1940

Little people

Dinklage, Peter, American actor, Apr 2013

Lobbyists

Ashley, Thomas L., American lobbyist and congressman, May 1979, *Obit* Yrbk 2010

Barbour, Haley, American governor, Nov 1996

Gore, Tipper, wife of American vice-president Albert Gore, Jr., Oct 2000

Humphry, Derek, English euthanasia advocate, Mar 1995

Norquist, Grover, American economist and tax reform lobbyist, Oct 2007

Rosenfield, Harry N., lawyer, lobbyist and refugee settlement leader, Apr 1952, *Obit* Aug 1995

Yard, Molly, American feminist and social activist, Nov 1988, *Obit* Apr 2006

Local government employees

Biaggi, Mario, congressman, Jan 1986

Reyes, Silvestre, American congressman, Sept 2007

Rizzo, Frank Lazaro, American mayor, Mar 1973, *Obit* Sept 1991

Local government officials

Additon, Henrietta Silvis, American social worker, prison superintendent and police official, Sept 1940

Adebari, Rotimi, Nigerian-Irish mayor, Jan 2007

Ahmadinejad, Mahmoud, Iranian president, Jan 2005

Alioto, Joseph L., mayor, Sept 1969, *Obit* Apr 1998

Badillo, Herman, American municipal official and congressman, May 1971

Bakoyianni, Dora, Greek mayor, Jan 2003

Barry, Marion, American mayor, May 1987

Belton, Sharon Sayles, American mayor, Jan 2001

Bilandic, Michael A., American mayor, Feb 1979, *Obit* Apr 2002

Bono, Sonny, American singer, songwriter and congressman, Feb 1974, *Obit* Mar 1998

Booker, Cory, American mayor, Feb 2007

Briscoe, Robert, Irish member of Parliament and mayor, May 1957, *Obit* July 1969

Brown, Lee Patrick, American mayor, Sept 2002

Brown, Willie Lewis, American mayor and political leader, Apr 1997

Bruckner, Henry, *Obit* June 1942

Bryan, Charles W., governor, *Obit* Apr 1945

Buchanan, Frank, Feb 1951

Burke, Charles H., *Obit* May 1944

Burke, Thomas A., July 1954, *Obit* Jan 1972

Burton, Harold Hitz, American senator and Supreme Court justice, Apr 1945, *Obit* Jan 1965

Byrne, Jane, American mayor, Jan 1980

Cain, Harry P., American senator, Apr 1949, *Obit* May 1979

Calder, William M., *Obit* Apr 1945

Campbell, Bill, American mayor, July 1996

Castro, Julian, American mayor, June 2013

Cavanagh, Jerome P., Apr 1968, *Obit* Jan 1980

Chafee, Lincoln, American senator, Jan 2004

Chelf, Frank L., June 1952

Chirac, Jacques, French president, June 1975, Apr 1993

Christopher, George, mayor, Feb 1958, *Obit* Yrbk 2000

Chu, Shen, *Obit* Aug 1943

Clark, Joseph S., American senator, June 1952, *Obit* Mar 1990

Cobo, Albert E., Nov 1951, *Obit* Yrbk 1958

Cohen, Manuel F., Apr 1967, *Obit* Aug 1977

Coleman, Norman, American senator, Sept 2004

Collins, John F., American mayor, Jan 1965, *Obit* Feb 1996

Cook, Marlow W., Jan 1972

Daley, Richard J., American mayor, Sept 1955, June 1976

Davey, Martin L., American governor, congressman and mayor, *Obit* May 1946

De Castro, Morris F., May 1950

Delanoe, Bertrand, French mayor, Jan 2002

Dinkins, David, American mayor, Mar 1990

Donovan, Shaun, American Secretary of housing and urban development, Mar 2009

Drapeau, Jean, Canadian mayor, Yrbk 1967, *Obit* Oct 1999

Dunbar, P. B., July 1949, *Obit* Nov 1968

Erdogan, Recep Tayyip, Turkish prime minister, Jan 2003

Faurot, Joseph A., *Obit* Jan 1943

Feinstein, Dianne, American senator, June 1979, Aug 1995

Fenty, Adrian, American mayor, Mar 2007

Fitzgibbons, John, *Obit* Oct 1941

Flynn, Raymond, American mayor and diplomat, Oct 1993

Franklin, Shirley, American mayor, Aug 2002

Garza, Ed, American mayor, June 2002

Gibson, Kenneth A., American mayor, May 1971

Gilligan, John J., American governor and congressman, May 1972, *Obit* Yrbk 2013

Goode, W. Wilson, American mayor, Oct 1985

Halley, Rudolph, June 1953, *Obit* Jan 1957

Hanson, Ole, *Obit* Sept 1940

Hartke, Vance, American senator, Mar 1960, *Obit* Yrbk 2003

Harvard, Beverly Joyce, American police chief, Sept 1997

Hatcher, Richard G., American mayor, Feb 1972

Hay, Charles M., *Obit* Mar 1945

Haynes, Roy Asa, *Obit* Yrbk 1940

Hays, Wayne Levere, American congressman, Nov 1974, *Obit* Apr 1989

Helpern, Milton, May 1973, *Obit* June 1977

Henry, E. William, Feb 1964

Hicks, Louise Day, American congresswoman and municipal official, Mar 1974, *Obit* June 2004

Hodson, William, *Obit* Mar 1943

Hoey, Jane M., American social worker and government official, Sept 1950

Hollande, Fran‡ois, French political leader, May 2013

Howrey, Edward F., July 1953

Humphrey, Helen F., Nov 1952, *Obit* Oct 1963

Ingersoll, Raymond Vail, *Obit* Mar 1940

Jackson, Maynard H., American mayor, Sept 1976, *Obit* Yrbk 2003

James, W. Frank, *Obit* Jan 1946

Kastenmeier, Robert W., American congressman, July 1966

Kelley, Clarence M., American FBI director, May 1974, *Obit* Nov 1997

Kelly, Raymond, American police commissioner, Sept 2008

Kennedy, Stephen P., June 1956, *Obit* Jan 1979

Kennelly, Martin H., mayor, Yrbk 1949, *Obit* Jan 1962

Kerlikowske, R. Gil, American law enforcement official, Nov 2009

Kersten, Charles J., Sept 1952

Kilpatrick, Kwame M., American mayor, Apr 2004

Kirk, Ron, American trade represenative, Apr 2010

Kollek, Teddy, Israeli mayor, Oct 1974, Mar 1993, *Obit* Yrbk 2007

Krueger, Wilhelm, *Obit* June 1943

Kucinich, Dennis, American congressman, Mar 1979, July 2008

Landes, Bertha K., mayor, *Obit* Jan 1944

Lanier, Cathy L., American police chief, Mar 2007

Lapham, Roger D., July 1948, *Obit* May 1966

Larson, Jess, American government official, June 1951

Lausche, Frank John, American governor and senator, Apr 1946, Nov 1958, *Obit* June 1990

Lawrence, David Leo, American governor, June 1959, *Obit* Jan 1967

Lee, Dorothy McCullough, Jan 1949

Lee, J. Bracken, American governor and mayor, May 1949, *Obit* Jan 1997

Lee, Richard C., American mayor, Yrbk 1967, *Obit* Yrbk 2003

Lee, Teng-hui, Taiwanese president, Mar 1996

Lindsay, John V., American congressman and mayor, Nov 1962, *Obit* Mar 2001

Lingle, Linda, American governor, June 2003

Livingstone, Ken, British mayor, Jan 2003

Lopez Obrador, Andres Manuel, Mexican mayor and political leader, Jan 2003

Lozovskii, A., Nov 1941

Lugar, Richard G., American senator, Oct 1977

Luzhkov, Yuri, Russian mayor, Nov 1999, Jan 2007

Maloney, Carolyn B., American congresswoman, Apr 2001

Mason, Lowell B., June 1949

Maverick, Maury, American congressman and mayor, Mar 1944, *Obit* Sept 1954

Max, Adolphe, Belgian burgomaster, *Obit* Jan 1940

Maybank, Burnet R., American senator and governor, Apr 1949, *Obit* Nov 1954

McManamy, Frank, *Obit* Nov 1944

Morris, Newbold, American municipal official, Mar 1952, *Obit* Apr 1966

Morrison, DeLesseps S., American mayor and diplomat, Nov 1949, *Obit* July 1964

Murphy, Patrick V., Nov 1972, *Obit* Yrbk 2012

Neely, Matthew M., Jan 1950, *Obit* Mar 1958

Neill, Charles Patrick, *Obit* Nov 1942

O'Dwyer, Paul, American lawyer and municipal official, Sept 1969, *Obit* Sept 1998

O'Dwyer, William, American mayor, Sept 1941, May 1947, *Obit* Jan 1965

Olmert, Ehud, Israeli prime minister, Jan 2006

Owens, Clarence Julian, *Obit* Apr 1941

Palin, Sarah, American governor, Jan 2009

Prouty, Winston L., American senator, July 1960, *Obit* Oct 1971

Quadros, Janio, Brazilian mayor and president, June 1961, *Obit* Apr 1992

Rama, Edi, Albanian artist and mayor, Jan 2005

Ramspeck, Robert, June 1951, *Obit* Yrbk 1972

Rankin, J. Lee, American solicitor general, Feb 1959, *Obit* Sept 1996

Ravenstahl, Luke, American mayor, Aug 2008

Ray, Robert D., governor, Jan 1977

Reed, James A., American senator, *Obit* Oct 1944

Reuter, Ernst, German mayor, Oct 1949, *Obit* Yrbk 1953

Rhodes, James Allen, American governor and political party leader, Mar 1949, Apr 1976, *Obit* July 2001

Rhodes, John J., American congressman, Sept 1976, *Obit* Yrbk 2004

Ribadu, Nuhu, Nigerian law enforcement official, Jan 2006

Rimsza, Skip, American mayor, July 2002

Rincon de Gautier, Felisa, Puerto Rican mayor, Oct 1956, *Obit* Nov 1994

Rooney, John J., American congressman, Yrbk 1964, *Obit* Jan 1976

Ross, C. Ben, American governor, *Obit* May 1946

Rua, Fernando de la, Argentine president, Apr 2001

Sadik-Khan, Janette, American transportation official, Nov 2012

Samuel, Bernard, Sept 1949, *Obit* Mar 1954

Sanders, Bernard, American senator, June 1991

Schaefer, William Donald, American mayor and governor, July 1988, *Obit* Yrbk 2011

Schreiber, Walther, Feb 1954, *Obit* Sept 1958

Scott, Harold, Yrbk 1950

Seger, George N., *Obit* Oct 1940

Sobchak, Anatoly, Russian mayor, July 1992, *Obit* July 2000

Spence, Brent, Sept 1952, *Obit* Jan 1968

Staggers, Harley O., American congressman, Mar 1971, *Obit* Nov 1991

Suhr, Otto, Apr 1955, *Obit* Nov 1957

Swope, Gerard, Sept 1941, *Obit* Feb 1958

Thomas, Albert, American congressman, Oct 1950, *Obit* Mar 1966

Thompson, William Hale, American mayor, *Obit* May 1944

Torp, Oscar, Norwegian prime minister, Yrbk 1952, *Obit* July 1958

Valentine, Lewis J., June 1946, *Obit* Feb 1947

Velazquez, Nydia, American congresswoman, July 1999

Villaraigosa, Antonio R., American mayor, Aug 2007

Voinovich, George, American senator, May 1997

Wagner, Robert Ferdinand, American mayor, Feb 1954, *Obit* Apr 1991

Walker, Paul A., May 1952, *Obit* July 1966

Ward, Benjamin, American police commissioner, Aug 1988, *Obit* Yrbk 2002

Washington, Harold, American mayor, Feb 1984, *Obit* Jan 1988

Washington, Walter E., American mayor, July 1968, *Obit* Yrbk 2004

Webb, Wellington E., American mayor, Aug 1999

Weizsacker, Richard von, German president, Mar 1985

Whalen, Grover A., Sept 1944, *Obit* June 1962

White, Kevin H., American mayor, Yrbk 1974, *Obit* Yrbk 2012

White, Michael R., American mayor, Mar 1999

Whitmire, Kathryn J., mayor, Mar 1988

Wilder, L. Douglas, American governor and mayor, Apr 1990

Williams, Anthony, American mayor, Oct 1999

Woodsmall, Ruth Frances, July 1949, *Obit* July 1963

Wowereit, Klaus, German mayor, Jan 2002

Wu, Kuo-Cheng, Chinese government official, Feb 1953, *Obit* Aug 1984

Yorty, Sam, American mayor, Jan 1967, *Obit* Aug 1998

Young, Coleman, American mayor, Sept 1977, *Obit* Feb 1998

Zeidler, Carl F., July 1940, *Obit* Feb 1943

Zhu Rongji, Chinese prime minister, July 2001

Logicians

Russell, Bertrand, British philosopher, Apr 1940, Jan 1951, *Obit* Mar 1970

Long jumpers

George, Anju Bobby, Indian long jumper, Jan 2005

Jones, Marion, American sprinter, long jumper and basketball player, Oct 1998

Lebedeva, Tatyana, Russian long and triple jumper, Jan 2004

Powell, Mike, American long jumper, Oct 1993

Longshore workers

Bridges, Harry, American labor leader, Nov 1940, May 1950, *Obit* May 1990

Gleason, Thomas W., American labor leader, Oct 1965, *Obit* Mar 1993

Hoffer, Eric, American philosopher and essayist, Mar 1965, *Obit* July 1983

Ryan, Joseph P., American longshore workers union leader, Jan 1949, *Obit* Sept 1963

Luge racers

Hackl, Georg, German luge racer, Jan 2003

Lute players

Bream, Julian, English guitarist, Mar 1968

Liu Fang, Chinese pipa player, Jan 2006

Lyricists

Adams, Stanley, American lyricist, Feb 1954, *Obit* Mar 1994

Cahn, Sammy, American lyricist, Nov 1974, *Obit* Mar 1993

Gershwin, Ira, American lyricist, Jan 1956, *Obit* Oct 1983

Harburg, E. Y., American lyricist, July 1980, *Obit* Apr 1981

Hart, Lorenz, American lyricist, May 1940, *Obit* Feb 1944

Kahn, Gus, American lyricist, *Obit* Yrbk 1941

Latouche, John, dramatist and lyricist, Jan 1940, *Obit* Oct 1956

Mercer, Johnny, American lyricist, June 1948, *Obit* Aug 1976

Meyer, Jean-Luc de, Belgian singer and lyricist, Jan 2006

Sondheim, Stephen, American lyricist and composer, Nov 1973

Stapp, Scott, American singer and lyricist, May 2002

Yorke, Thom, Scottish singer, June 2001

Machinery industry executives

Crompton, Rookes Evelyn Bell, English electrical equipment industry executive, *Obit* Mar 1940

Kirby, Robert E., electrical generating equipment industry executive, Sept 1979, *Obit* Mar 1999

Link, Edwin A., flight simulator industry executive, Jan 1974, *Obit* Yrbk 1983

Rand, James Henry, *Obit* Nov 1944

Swigert, Ernest Goodnough, machinery industry executive, Oct 1957, *Obit* Feb 1987

Magazine editors

Abelson, Philip H., American physicist and periodical editor, Oct 1965, *Obit* Yrbk 2004

Bailey, Glenda, American magazine editor, Oct 2001

Birnie, William A. H., American magazine editor, Sept 1952, *Obit* Oct 1979

Blackwell, Betsy Talbot, American magazine editor, June 1954, *Obit* Apr 1985

Cela, Camilo Jose, Spanish novelist, short story writer, essayist, travel writer and poet, June 1990, *Obit* Apr 2002

Chase, Edna Woolman, magazine editor, Nov 1940, *Obit* June 1957

Fuller, Bonnie, American magazine editor, May 2000

Fuoss, Robert M., Feb 1959, *Obit* Mar 1980

Gould, Beatrice Blackmar, magazine editor, Nov 1947, *Obit* Apr 1989

Grosvenor, Gilbert Hovey, magazine editor, Yrbk 1946, *Obit* Mar 1966

Grosvenor, Melville Bell, periodical editor, Apr 1960, *Obit* June 1982

Hibbs, Ben, magazine editor, July 1946, *Obit* May 1975

Kirchwey, Freda, American magazine editor, Yrbk 1942, *Obit* Feb 1976

Lane, Gertrude Battles, magazine editor, *Obit* Nov 1941

Littledale, Clara Savage, Oct 1946, *Obit* Mar 1956

Michel, Sia, American magazine editor, Sept 2003

Mirabella, Grace, magazine editor, Oct 1991

Monroque, Shala, American magazine editor, Jan 2012

Moss, Adam, American magazine editor, Mar 2004

Myasnikova, Yelena, Russian magazine editor, Jan 2002

Northrop, Peggy, American magazine editor, Nov 2009

Peters, Charles, periodical editor, Aug 1990

Phillips, William, American periodical editor, Oct 1984, *Obit* Yrbk 2002

Ross, Harold Wallace, American periodical editor, May 1943, *Obit* Jan 1952

Rubenstein, Atoosa, American magazine editor, Oct 2004

Schlosser, Alex L., American newspaper and magazine editor, *Obit* Mar 1943

Seymour, Lesley Jane, magazine editor, Nov 2001

Stockbridge, Frank Parker, *Obit* Jan 1941

Tilberis, Liz, British magazine editor, Nov 1998, *Obit* July 1999

Vreeland, Diana, American magazine editor, Feb 1978, *Obit* Oct 1989

Wintour, Anna, British fashion editor, July 1990

Magazine executives

Dennis, Felix, British magazine publisher, Apr 2000

Fairchild, John, American magazine publisher, June 1971

Flynt, Larry, American magazine publisher, Sept 1999

Forbes, Malcolm S., American magazine publisher, May 1996

Guccione, Bob, American magazine publisher, Aug 1994, *Obit* Yrbk 2010

Hammond, Godfrey, Oct 1953, *Obit* Oct 1969

Hecht, George Joseph, magazine publisher, Oct 1947, *Obit* June 1980

Hefner, Christie, American magazine publisher, Oct 1986

Hefner, Hugh, American magazine publisher, Sept 1968

Heiskell, Andrew, American magazine executive, Mar 1966, *Obit* Yrbk 2003

Johnson, John H., American magazine publisher, Oct 1968, *Obit* Yrbk 2005

Lear, Frances, magazine publisher, Apr 1991, *Obit* Jan 1997

McCabe, Gibson, magazine publisher, Feb 1963, *Obit* Yrbk 2000

Moore, Ann, American magazine executive, Aug 2003

Parrish, Wayne W., American magazine and newspaper executive, Nov 1958

Rice, Linda Johnson, American magazine publishing executive, July 2011

Sanchez Junco, Eduardo, Spanish magazine publisher, Jan 2003, *Obit* Yrbk 2010

Smart, David A., magazine publisher, June 1944

Wenner, Jann S., American magazine executive, Jan 1980

Ziff, William B., American magazine executive, Oct 1946, *Obit* Feb 1954

Zuckerman, Mortimer B., American real estate developer and magazine and newspaper publisher, Jan 1990

Magicians

Blaine, David, American magician, Apr 2001

Copperfield, David, American magician, July 1992

Dunninger, Joseph, magician and mind reader, Sept 1944, *Obit* May 1975

Henning, Doug, Canadian magician, Aug 1976, *Obit* Apr 2000

Jay, Ricky, American magician and actor, May 1994

Jillette, Penn, American magician, June 2000

Penn & Teller, American magicians, June 2000

Randi, James, American magician, May 1987

Swiss, Jamy Ian, American magician, Feb 2010

Teller, American magician, June 2000

Makeup artists

Baker, Rick, American makeup artist, Mar 1997

Smith, Dick, makeup artist, Mar 1959

Westmore, Perc, American makeup artist, Oct 1945, *Obit* Nov 1970

Winston, Stan, American special effects technician, July 2002, *Obit* Nov 2008

Mammalogists

Fossey, Dian, American primatologist, May 1985, *Obit* Feb 1986

Galdikas, Birute, Canadian primatologist, Mar 1995

Goodall, Jane, British primatologist, Nov 1967, Nov 1991

Jolly, Alison, American primatologist, Jan 2009

Mayor, Mireya, American primatologist and television personality, Sept 2011

Merriam, C. Hart, American mammalogist, *Obit* May 1942

Patterson, Francine, American psychologist and animal rights activist, Nov 2000

Scheffer, Victor B., marine mammalogist, Apr 1994

Tuttle, Merlin D., mammalogist, June 1992

Waal, Frans de, Dutch primatologist, Mar 2006

Zuberbuhler, Klaus, Swiss psychologist and primatologist, July 2010

Management consultants

Appley, Lawrence A., business consultant, July 1950, *Obit* June 1997

Bernays, Edward L., American public relations consultant, Feb 1942, Sept 1960, *Obit* May 1995

Birdwell, Russell, July 1946, *Obit* Mar 1978

Buckingham, Marcus, American management consultant, Aug 2006

Burke, William R., July 1961

Collins, Jim, American business consultant, Aug 2003

Dalrymple, Jean, theatrical producer, Sept 1953, *Obit* Feb 1999

Deming, W. Edwards, American statistician and business consultant, Sept 1993, *Obit* Mar 1994

Diebold, John, American management consultant, Mar 1967, *Obit* Yrbk 2006

Hoffman, Anna Rosenberg, American public relations executive and government official, Jan 1943, Jan 1951, *Obit* July 1983

Magaziner, Ira C., American business consultant and presidential adviser, Apr 1995

Maney, Richard, July 1964, *Obit* Sept 1968

Soss, Wilma Porter, publicist, Mar 1965, *Obit* Jan 1987

Starch, Daniel, psychologist and marketing analyst, Jan 1963

Wick, Charles Z., American government official, Mar 1985, *Obit* Yrbk 2008

Witt, James Lee, American emergency management official and consultant, Mar 2000

Zelomek, A. Wilbert, Yrbk 1956

Manufacturing executives

Allyn, Stanley C., American cash register company executive, Mar 1956, *Obit* Yrbk 1970

Arnault, Bernard, French manufacturing executive, June 1998

Backstrand, C. J., American manufacturing executive, Feb 1954, *Obit* Yrbk 1968

Barad, Jill E., American toy industry executive, Sept 1995

Barton, Robert B. M., games industry executive, Apr 1959, *Obit* Apr 1995

Batcheller, Hiland Garfield, American steel industry executive, Apr 1949, *Obit* July 1961

Batt, William L., American manufacturing executive, Feb 1942, *Obit* Mar 1965

Bausch, William, *Obit* Yrbk 1944

Biggers, John D., American manufacturing executive, Sept 1941, *Obit* Feb 1974

Blackall, Frederick S., American manufacturing executive, Jan 1953

Block, Joseph L., steel executive, June 1961, *Obit* Feb 1993

Blough, Roger M., American steel industry executive, July 1955, *Obit* Jan 1986

Boeschenstein, Harold, American manufacturing executive, Feb 1961, *Obit* Yrbk 1972

Borch, Fred J., manufacturing executive, Oct 1971

Bosch, Robert, German manufacturing executive, *Obit* Apr 1942

Browdy, Benjamin G., July 1951

Buckley, George W., British manufacturing executive, Sept 2011

Buetow, Herbert P., Mar 1960, *Obit* Mar 1972

Buitoni, Giovanni, June 1962, *Obit* Mar 1979

Bullis, Harry A., Oct 1946, *Obit* Jan 1964

Chapman, Albert Kinkade, photographic industry executive, Sept 1952, *Obit* Yrbk 1984

Chapman, Gilbert W., June 1957, *Obit* Feb 1980

Coleman, John S., American manufacturing executive, Apr 1953, *Obit* July 1958

Cordiner, Ralph, Jan 1951, *Obit* Jan 1974

Dallas, C. Donald, Apr 1949, *Obit* June 1959

Davis, Nathanael V., American aluminum industry executive, Jan 1959, *Obit* Yrbk 2005

Davis, Roy H., Feb 1955, *Obit* Sept 1956

Deripaska, Oleg, Russian aluminum industry executive, Jan 2006

Emanuel, Victor, American manufacturing executive, May 1951, *Obit* Jan 1961

Eyler, John, American toy store chain executive, Aug 2000

Fleming, Arthur Henry, *Obit* Sept 1940

Fruehauf, Roy, Feb 1953, *Obit* Jan 1966

Fuller, Alfred C., brush industry executive, Oct 1950, *Obit* Jan 1974

Gaylord, Robert M., Mar 1944

Girdler, Tom M., American steel executive, Apr 1944, *Obit* Mar 1965

Grace, Eugene G., American steel company executive, Apr 1941, *Obit* Oct 1960

Grede, William J., iron and steel executive, Feb 1952, *Obit* Aug 1989

Gullander, W. P., Oct 1963

Hall, Joyce Clyde, greeting card executive, May 1953, *Obit* Jan 1983

Halligan, William J., Oct 1957

Hardenbrook, Donald J., July 1962, *Obit* Aug 1976

Hassenfeld, Alan Geoffrey, American toy industry executive, July 2003

Heidenstam, Rolf von, Oct 1951, *Obit* Oct 1958

Hill, David G., Apr 1960

Hill, George Washington, June 1946

Homer, Arthur B., July 1952, *Obit* Sept 1972

Hood, Clifford F., Apr 1953, *Obit* Jan 1979

Hope, Stanley C., May 1959, *Obit* Oct 1982

Hughes, Edward Everett, *Obit* Jan 1940

Innocenti, Ferdinando, Feb 1959, *Obit* July 1966

Keegan, Robert J., American manufacturing executive, Jan 2004

Kellems, Vivien, American wire and cable industry executive, Sept 1948, *Obit* Mar 1975

Kestnbaum, Meyer, May 1953, *Obit* Feb 1961

Knoll, Hans G., May 1955

Litchfield, P. W., Yrbk 1950, *Obit* May 1959

Martin, Edmund F., steel executive, Jan 1962, *Obit* Mar 1993

McCaffrey, John L., Nov 1950

McClellan, Harold C., Oct 1954, *Obit* Sept 1979

McColough, C. Peter, American office equipment industry executive, Jan 1981, *Obit* Yrbk 2007

McGovern, John, American rubber company executive, Nov 1961, *Obit* June 1975

Mitarai, Fujio, Japanese photographic and office equipment industry executive, Jan 2002

Mittal, Lakshmi, Indian steel industry executive, Jan 2006

Morgan, Thomas A., Mar 1950, *Obit* Jan 1968

Mosher, Ira, Feb 1945, *Obit* May 1968

Mulcahy, Anne, American office equipment industry executive, Nov 2002

Paepcke, Walter Paul, Apr 1960

Putnam, Claude Adams, Feb 1950

Reynolds, Richard S., American manufacturing executive, May 1967, *Obit* Nov 1980

Reynolds, Richard Samuel, American aluminum industry executive, Feb 1953, *Obit* Oct 1955

Roderick, David M., steel executive, Apr 1987

Ruffin, William H., Feb 1951

Sayre, Morris, Jan 1948, *Obit* Apr 1953

Schneider, Eugene, *Obit* Jan 1943

Sims, William L., Yrbk 1956

Sligh, Charles R., Apr 1953

Stolk, William C., Mar 1953

Straus, Roger W., American metal industry executive, July 1952, *Obit* Oct 1957

Thyssen, Fritz, German industrialist, May 1940, *Obit* Mar 1951

Truitt, Paul T., Sept 1948

Wagner, Richard, Apr 1962

Watson, Thomas J., American office equipment industry executive, Nov 1940, July 1950, *Obit* Sept 1956

Weir, Ernest T., American steel industry executive, June 1941, *Obit* Oct 1957

White, Charles M., June 1950, *Obit* Mar 1977

White, Francis W., Jan 1954, *Obit* June 1957

Whitehead, Edward, British manufacturing executive, Jan 1967, *Obit* June 1978

Wilson, Joseph C., American office equipment industry executive, Oct 1966, *Obit* Jan 1972

Witherow, W. P., Apr 1942, *Obit* Mar 1960

Worthington, Leslie B., steel executive, Oct 1960, *Obit* Oct 1998

Marine biologists

Nachtigall, Paul E., American marine scientist, Jan 2006

Payne, Roger, marine biologist, June 1995

Safina, Carl, American marine conservationist and scientist, Apr 2005

Marine corps officers

Hamblet, Julia E., Oct 1953

Smith, Paul C., Apr 1943, *Obit* Sept 1976

Streeter, Ruth Cheney, marine corps officer, July 1943, *Obit* Jan 1991

Thomason, John W., marine corps officer and author, *Obit* May 1944

Wilson, Rufus H., June 1955

Market researchers

Nielsen, Arthur C., American market research executive, Yrbk 1951, *Obit* July 1980

Yankelovich, Daniel, American sociologist, Mar 1982

Marketing executives

Brophy, Thomas D'Arcy, Sept 1952, *Obit* Oct 1967

Cone, Fairfax, July 1966, *Obit* Aug 1977

Duffy, Bernard C., July 1952, *Obit* Nov 1972

Goshorn, Clarence B., Mar 1950, *Obit* Jan 1951

Kimball, Abbott, May 1949, *Obit* Nov 1968

Mortimer, Charles G., Nov 1955, *Obit* Feb 1979

Roper, Elmo, American public opinion analyst, Jan 1945, *Obit* June 1971

Shelly, Warner S., Feb 1952

Strong, William McCreery, *Obit* May 1941

Marksmen

Bjoerndalen, Ole Einar, Norwegian biathlete, Jan 2003

Lee, Willis A., American admiral and marksman, *Obit* Sept 1945

Marriage counselors

Mudd, Emily, American family and marriage counselor, Nov 1956, *Obit* July 1998

Marshals

Alanbrooke, Alan Francis Brooke, British field marshal, Jan 1941, *Obit* Sept 1963

Auchinleck, Claude John Eyre, British field marshal, Feb 1942, *Obit* May 1981

Bock, Fedor von, German field marshal, Oct 1942, *Obit* June 1945

Brauchitsch, Walther von, German field marshal, Mar 1940, *Obit* Yrbk 1948

Broadhurst, Harry, May 1943

Brooke-Popham, Robert, Oct 1941, *Obit* Jan 1954

Budennyi, Semen M., Soviet field marshal, Sept 1941, *Obit* Yrbk 1973

Cole-Hamilton, J. B., *Obit* Sept 1945

Coningham, Arthur, British air marshal, Nov 1944, *Obit* Feb 1948

De Bono, Emilio, Italian field marshal, *Obit* Feb 1944

Dill, John Greer, British field marshal, Feb 1941, *Obit* Yrbk 1944

Doihara, Kenji, Mar 1942, *Obit* Feb 1949

Douglas of Kirtleside, William Sholto Douglas, British air marshal, June 1943, *Obit* Yrbk 1969

Dowding, Hugh Caswall Tremenheere Dowding, British air marshal, Nov 1940, *Obit* Apr 1970

Franchet d'Esperey, Louis Felix Marie Francois, French field marshal, *Obit* Sept 1942

Goring, Hermann, German Nazi leader, Aug 1941, *Obit* Nov 1946

Harding of Petherton, John Harding, British field marshal, Oct 1952

Ironside, William Edmund Ironside, British field marshal, May 1940, *Obit* Nov 1959

Juin, Alphonse, French field marshal, Aug 1943, *Obit* Mar 1967

Kan-In, Kotohito, *Obit* June 1945

Keitel, Wilhelm, German field marshal, Sept 1940, *Obit* Nov 1946

Kesselring, Albert, German field marshal, Nov 1942, *Obit* Oct 1960

Kleist, Ewald von, German field marshal, July 1943, *Obit* Jan 1955

Konev, Ivan S., Soviet field marshal, Oct 1943, Jan 1956, *Obit* July 1973

Kulik, Grigory, July 1942

Lattre, Jean de, French field marshal, Jan 1945, *Obit* Feb 1952

Manstein, Erich von, German field marshal, Oct 1942, *Obit* Sept 1973

Montgomery of Alamein, Bernard Law Montgomery, British field marshal, Yrbk 1942, *Obit* May 1976

Newall, Cyril Louis Norton, Aug 1940

Peirse, R. E. C., Sept 1941, *Obit* Oct 1970

Portal of Hungerford, Charles Frederick Algernon Portal, British air marshal, Mar 1941, *Obit* June 1971

Prezan, Constantin, *Obit* Oct 1943

Reichenau, Walter von, German field marshal, *Obit* Mar 1942

Rokossovskii, Konstantin K., Soviet field marshal, Jan 1944, *Obit* Oct 1968

Rommel, Erwin, German field marshal, Aug 1942, *Obit* Yrbk 1944

Rundstedt, Karl Rudolf Gerd von, German field marshal, Nov 1941, *Obit* Apr 1953

Shaposhnikov, Boris, Soviet field marshal, Mar 1942, *Obit* May 1945

Slim, William Joseph Slim, British field marshal, June 1945, *Obit* Feb 1971

Sugiyama, Hajime, Japanese field marshal, *Obit* Oct 1945

Tedder, Arthur William Tedder, British air marshal, Jan 1943, *Obit* Oct 1967

Templer, Gerald Walter Robert, British field marshal, July 1952, *Obit* Jan 1980

Thanom Kittikachorn, Thai field marshal and prime minister, Yrbk 1969, *Obit* Yrbk 2004

Timoshenko, Semen Konstantinovich, Soviet field marshal, Aug 1941, *Obit* May 1970

Tolbukhin, Fedor Ivanovich, Soviet field marshal, May 1945, *Obit* Yrbk 1949

Voroshilov, Kliment Efremovich, Soviet field marshal and communist leader, Mar 1941, *Obit* Jan 1970

Wilson, Henry Maitland Wilson, Oct 1943, *Obit* Feb 1965

Zhukov, Georgii Konstantinovich, Soviet field marshal, Feb 1942, Apr 1955, *Obit* Sept 1974

Martial artists

Jones, Jon, American mixed martial artist, Mar 2013

Tamura, Ryoko, Japanese judoist, Jan 2003

Urquidez, Benny, American martial artist, Nov 2001

Mathematicians

Aiken, Howard Hathaway, American mathematician and computer scientist, Mar 1947, *Obit* May 1973

Austin, William Lane, American statistician, Apr 1940

Babson, Roger W., statistician, Feb 1945, *Obit* May 1967

Bartol, William Cyrus, American mathematician, *Obit* Yrbk 1940

Benesh, Rudolf, British mathematician, July 1957

Bombieri, Enrico, Italian mathematician, Jan 2005

Borcherds, Richard, English mathematician, Feb 1999

Brenner, Charles H., forensic mathematician, Oct 2000

Bronowski, Jacob, British mathematician, Sept 1958, *Obit* Oct 1974

Caddell, Patrick, public opinion analyst and presidential adviser, Nov 1979

Carson, John Renshaw, *Obit* Yrbk 1940

Chaddock, Robert Emmet, *Obit* Yrbk 1940

Cherwell, Frederick Alexander Lindemann, British physicist, Mar 1952, *Obit* Sept 1957

Conway, John Horton, British mathematician, Sept 2003

Courant, Richard, mathematician, Sept 1966, *Obit* Mar 1972

D'Ambrosio, Ubiratan, Brazilian mathematician, Jan 2003

Deming, W. Edwards, American statistician and business consultant, Sept 1993, *Obit* Mar 1994

Donaldson, Simon K., English mathematician, Jan 2005

Dublin, Louis Israel, statistician, Oct 1942, *Obit* Yrbk 1991

Eddington, Arthur Stanley, British astronomer, Apr 1941, *Obit* Yrbk 1991

Falkner, Roland Post, *Obit* Jan 1941

Gardner, Martin, American children's author and mathematician, Sept 1999, *Obit* Yrbk 2010

Gavrilovic, Stoyan, May 1946, *Obit* Mar 1965

Gowers, Tim, English mathematician, Jan 2001

Hammond, E. Cuyler, biologist and statistician, June 1957, *Obit* Jan 1987

Hooper, C. E., Apr 1947, *Obit* Feb 1955

Hun, John Gale, *Obit* Nov 1945

James, Bill, American baseball statistician, June 2004

Jeans, James Hopwood, British physicist and mathematician, Apr 1941, *Obit* Oct 1946

Keldysh, Mstislav, Russian mathematician and physicist, Feb 1962, *Obit* Aug 1978

Lax, Peter D., American mathematician, Oct 2005

Mandelbrot, Benoit B., American mathematician, June 1987, *Obit* Yrbk 2010

Milnor, John, American mathematician, July 2011

Montgomery, Deane, mathematician, Nov 1957, *Obit* May 1992

Morse, Marston, Mar 1957, *Obit* Aug 1977

Newell, Homer Edward, physicist and mathematician, Nov 1954, *Obit* Sept 1983

Penney, William George Penney, English physicist, Feb 1953, *Obit* May 1991

Penrose, Roger, British mathematician, Sept 2013

Perelman, Grigori, Russian mathematician, Jan 2006

Picard, Emile, *Obit* Feb 1942

Serre, Jean Pierre, French mathematician, Jan 2003

Silver, Nate, American baseball statistician and pollster, Feb 2013

Smith, Clara E., *Obit* July 1943

Stone, John Charles, *Obit* July 1940

Tanner, John Henry, *Obit* Mar 1940

Tao, Terence, Australian mathematician, Sept 2007

Volterra, Vito, Italian mathematician and physicist, *Obit* Yrbk 1940

Von Neumann, John, American mathematician, July 1955, *Obit* Apr 1957

Werner, Wendelin, German-French mathematician, Jan 2006

Wiener, Norbert, American mathematician, Mar 1950, *Obit* May 1964

Wiles, Andrew, English mathematician, Mar 1996

Mayors

Adebari, Rotimi, Nigerian-Irish mayor, Jan 2007

Barry, Marion, American mayor, May 1987

Belton, Sharon Sayles, American mayor, Jan 2001

Bilandic, Michael A., American mayor, Feb 1979, *Obit* Apr 2002

Briscoe, Robert, Irish member of Parliament and mayor, May 1957, *Obit* July 1969

Brown, Lee Patrick, American mayor, Sept 2002

Buchanan, Frank, Feb 1951

Byrne, Jane, American mayor, Jan 1980

Cain, Harry P., American senator, Apr 1949, *Obit* May 1979

Campbell, Bill, American mayor, July 1996

Cavanagh, Jerome P., Apr 1968, *Obit* Jan 1980

Chafee, Lincoln, American senator, Jan 2004

Christopher, George, mayor, Feb 1958, *Obit* Yrbk 2000

Clark, Joseph S., American senator, June 1952, *Obit* Mar 1990

Cobo, Albert E., Nov 1951, *Obit* Yrbk 1958

Coleman, Norman, American senator, Sept 2004

Collins, John F., American mayor, Jan 1965, *Obit* Feb 1996

Daley, Richard J., American mayor, Sept 1955, June 1976

Drapeau, Jean, Canadian mayor, Yrbk 1967, *Obit* Oct 1999

Erdogan, Recep Tayyip, Turkish prime minister, Jan 2003

Feinstein, Dianne, American senator, June 1979, Aug 1995

Fenty, Adrian, American mayor, Mar 2007

Franklin, Shirley, American mayor, Aug 2002

Garza, Ed, American mayor, June 2002

Gibson, Kenneth A., American mayor, May 1971

Hatcher, Richard G., American mayor, Feb 1972

Hays, Wayne Levere, American congressman, Nov 1974, *Obit* Apr 1989

James, W. Frank, *Obit* Jan 1946

Kennelly, Martin H., mayor, Yrbk 1949, *Obit* Jan 1962

Kilpatrick, Kwame M., American mayor, Apr 2004

Kucinich, Dennis, American congressman, Mar 1979, July 2008

Landes, Bertha K., mayor, *Obit* Jan 1944

Lapham, Roger D., July 1948, *Obit* May 1966

Lee, Richard C., American mayor, Yrbk 1967, *Obit* Yrbk 2003

Lindsay, John V., American congressman and mayor, Nov 1962, *Obit* Mar 2001

Livingstone, Ken, British mayor, Jan 2003

Lugar, Richard G., American senator, Oct 1977

Luzhkov, Yuri, Russian mayor, Nov 1999, Jan 2007

Prouty, Winston L., American senator, July 1960, *Obit* Oct 1971

Ravenstahl, Luke, American mayor, Aug 2008

Reuter, Ernst, German mayor, Oct 1949, *Obit* Yrbk 1953

Rimsza, Skip, American mayor, July 2002

Rincon de Gautier, Felisa, Puerto Rican mayor, Oct 1956, *Obit* Nov 1994

Samuel, Bernard, Sept 1949, *Obit* Mar 1954

Schreiber, Walther, Feb 1954, *Obit* Sept 1958

Seger, George N., *Obit* Oct 1940

Thompson, William Hale, American mayor, *Obit* May 1944

Villaraigosa, Antonio R., American mayor, Aug 2007

Washington, Harold, American mayor, Feb 1984, *Obit* Jan 1988

Webb, Wellington E., American mayor, Aug 1999

White, Michael R., American mayor, Mar 1999

Whitmire, Kathryn J., mayor, Mar 1988

Williams, Anthony, American mayor, Oct 1999

Wowereit, Klaus, German mayor, Jan 2002

Wu, Kuo-Cheng, Chinese government official, Feb 1953, *Obit* Aug 1984

Yorty, Sam, American mayor, Jan 1967, *Obit* Aug 1998

Young, Coleman, American mayor, Sept 1977, *Obit* Feb 1998

Zeidler, Carl F., July 1940, *Obit* Feb 1943

Mechanical engineers

Collyer, John L., Mar 1947

Emerson, Victor Lee, *Obit* July 1941

Flanders, Ralph E., American senator, Jan 1948, *Obit* Apr 1970

Hicks, Beatrice Alice, mechanical engineer, Jan 1957

Keenan, Walter Francis, *Obit* Apr 1940

Newhall, Arthur B., Oct 1942

Norden, Carl Lukas, American mechanical engineer and inventor, Jan 1945, *Obit* Sept 1965

Sillcox, Lewis Ketcham, mechanical engineer, Yrbk 1954, *Obit* May 1989

Sutton, George Paul, July 1958

White, John R., Jan 1956

Medical association officials

Allman, David B., American surgeon and medical association official, Feb 1958, *Obit* May 1971

Alstadt, W. R., American dentist, July 1958

Annis, Edward R., Apr 1964

Appel, James Z., American physician and medical association official, Mar 1966, *Obit* Oct 1981

Askey, E. Vincent, American surgeon, Feb 1961, *Obit* Feb 1975

Bauer, Louis Hopewell, American cardiologist, Oct 1948, *Obit* Mar 1964

Chamberlain, Francis L., July 1959

Cline, John Wesley, June 1951, *Obit* Sept 1974

Due-Gundersen, Gunnar, Feb 1959, *Obit* Aug 1979

Fister, George M., June 1963, *Obit* July 1976

Fitz Gerald, Leslie M., Sept 1954

Frothingham, Channing, Mar 1948, *Obit* Nov 1959

Griffin, John Douglas Morecroft, May 1957

Hammond, Graeme M., *Obit* Yrbk 1944

Henderson, E. L., June 1950, *Obit* Oct 1953

Hess, Elmer, Jan 1956, *Obit* June 1961

Irons, Ernest E., Oct 1949, *Obit* Apr 1959

Jacobs, Philip Peter, *Obit* Aug 1940

Lahey, Frank H., American surgeon, Mar 1941, *Obit* Sept 1953

Larson, Leonard W., American medical association official and pathologist, May 1962, *Obit* Nov 1974

Leech, Paul Nicholas, *Obit* Mar 1941

Lewis, Francis Park, *Obit* Oct 1940

Marshall, C. Herbert, Oct 1949

Martin, Walter B., Nov 1954, *Obit* May 1966

Murray, Dwight H., May 1957, *Obit* Nov 1974

O'Connor, Basil, Sept 1944, *Obit* May 1972

Peters, Le Roy S., *Obit* Feb 1942

Pusey, William Allen, *Obit* Oct 1940

Ridenour, Nina, Apr 1951

Rivers, Thomas M., American virologist, July 1960, *Obit* July 1962

Routley, Thomas Clarence, Jan 1956, *Obit* June 1963

Runyon, Mefford R., May 1949

Sensenich, Roscoe L., June 1949, *Obit* Feb 1963

Shoulders, Harrison H., Nov 1946, *Obit* Jan 1964

Ward, Donovan F., Mar 1965

Whitehouse, Harold Beckwith, *Obit* Sept 1943

Wilbur, Dwight Locke, medical association official and gastroenterologist, July 1969, *Obit* May 1997

Medical historians

Antall, Jozsef, Hungarian prime minister, Sept 1990, *Obit* Feb 1994

Sigerist, Henry Ernest, Swiss medical historian, Sept 1940, *Obit* June 1957

Medical instrument makers

Kamen, Dean, American inventor and medical instrument maker, Nov 2002

Medical physicists

Yalow, Rosalyn S., American medical physicist, July 1978, *Obit* Yrbk 2011

Members of Congress

Aandahl, Fred G., American governor, Sept 1958, *Obit* May 1966

Abraham, Spencer, American Secretary of energy, May 2001

Adams, Alva B., American senator, *Obit* Jan 1942

Adams, Brock, American Secretary of transportation and senator, July 1977, *Obit* Yrbk 2004

Adams, Sherman, American presidential adviser, Nov 1952, *Obit* Jan 1987

Aiken, George D., American senator, June 1947, *Obit* Feb 1985

Albert, Carl, American congressman and Speaker of the House, June 1957, *Obit* June 2000

Aldrich, Richard S., American congressman, *Obit* Feb 1942

Allen, Leo E., American congressman, June 1948, *Obit* Mar 1973

Allott, Gordon, American senator, May 1955, *Obit* Apr 1989

Anderson, Clinton P., American Secretary of agriculture and senator, June 1945, *Obit* Jan 1976

Andresen, August H., American congressman, Feb 1956, *Obit* Mar 1958

Arends, Leslie Cornelius, American congressman, Feb 1948, *Obit* Sept 1985

Aspin, Les, American Secretary of defense, Feb 1986, *Obit* July 1995

Aspinall, Wayne N., American congressman, Apr 1968, *Obit* Nov 1983

Baldwin, Tammy, American congresswoman, June 2005

Bankhead, John Hollis, American senator, May 1943, *Obit* July 1946

Bankhead, William Brockman, American Speaker of the House, Oct 1940, *Obit* Oct 1940

Barbour, W. Warren, American senator, *Obit* Jan 1944

Barden, Graham Arthur, American congressman, Sept 1949, *Obit* Mar 1967

Barkley, Alben William, American vice-president, May 1941, Jan 1949, *Obit* July 1956

Barnes, Wendell B., government official and congressman, June 1957, *Obit* Aug 1985

Barr, Joseph W., American Secretary of the treasury, Jan 1968, *Obit* May 1996

Bartlett, Edward Lewis, American senator, June 1951, *Obit* Mar 1969

Bayard, Thomas Francis, American senator, *Obit* Sept 1942

Bayh, Evan, American senator, Nov 1998

Beall, J. Glenn, American senator, Apr 1955, *Obit* Mar 1971

Bell, Thomas M., *Obit* May 1941

Bellmon, Henry, American governor and senator, July 1963, *Obit* Yrbk 2009

Bender, George H., American congressman and senator, Jan 1952, *Obit* Sept 1961

Bentley, Helen Delich, American congresswoman, Yrbk 1971

Bentsen, Lloyd, American Secretary of the treasury, Sept 1973, Apr 1993, *Obit* Oct 2006

Berry, George L., American labor leader, Jan 1948, *Obit* Jan 1949

Bible, Alan, American senator, Feb 1957, *Obit* Oct 1988

Biden, Joseph R., American vice-president, Jan 1987, Mar 2009

Bilbo, Theodore G., American senator, Apr 1943, *Obit* Oct 1947

Bingham, Jonathan B., congressman, July 1954, *Obit* Aug 1986

Blatnik, John A., American congressman, Feb 1958, *Obit* Feb 1992

Blease, Coleman Livingston, American senator and governor, *Obit* Mar 1942

Blitch, Iris Faircloth, congresswoman, Apr 1956, *Obit* Oct 1993

Blunt, Roy, American senator, Mar 2008

Boehner, John, American congressman and Speaker of the House, Apr 2006

Boggs, Hale, American congressman and political leader, Apr 1958, *Obit* Mar 1973

Boggs, J. Caleb, American governor and senator, July 1956

Boland, Edward P., American congressman, Oct 1987, *Obit* Feb 2002

Bolling, Richard Walker, American congressman, Mar 1960, *Obit* July 1991

Bolton, Frances Payne Bingham, American congresswoman, Mar 1940, Apr 1954, *Obit* May 1977

Bonner, Herbert C., American congressman, July 1956, *Obit* Jan 1966

Borah, William Edgar, American senator, Jan 1940

Bourne, Jonathan, American senator, *Obit* Oct 1940

Boxer, Barbara, American senator, Apr 1994

Brewster, Owen, American senator, May 1947, *Obit* Feb 1962

Bricker, John William, American senator and governor, Apr 1943, July 1956, *Obit* May 1986

Bristow, Joseph Little, *Obit* Sept 1944

Brooke, Edward, American senator, Apr 1967

Brookhart, Smith W., American senator, *Obit* Jan 1945

Brooks, C. Wayland, Sept 1947, *Obit* Mar 1957

Brooks, Jack, congressman, June 1992, *Obit* Yrbk 2013

Brooks, Overton, June 1957, *Obit* Yrbk 1961

Brown, Prentiss M., American senator, Jan 1943, *Obit* Feb 1974

Brownback, Sam, American senator, Apr 2008

Browne, Edward E., *Obit* Jan 1946

Brownson, Charles B., July 1955

Broyhill, Joel T., American congressman, May 1974, *Obit* Feb 2007

Bruckner, Henry, *Obit* June 1942

Budge, Hamer H., American congressman and regulatory agency official, Yrbk 1970, *Obit* Yrbk 2003

Burdick, Quentin, American senator, May 1963, *Obit* Nov 1992

Burke, Charles H., *Obit* May 1944

Burke, Edward Raymond, Sept 1940, *Obit* Yrbk 1968

Burke, Yvonne Brathwaite, American lawyer and congresswoman, Oct 1975

Burris, Roland W., American senator, June 2009

Burton, Dan, American congressman, Sept 1998

Butler, John Marshall, American senator, May 1954, *Obit* May 1978

Byrd, Harry Flood, American senator, Apr 1942, Sept 1955, *Obit* Yrbk 1966

Byrd, Robert C., American senator, Mar 1960, Feb 1978, *Obit* Sept 2010

Byrnes, John W., American congressman, Oct 1960, *Obit* Mar 1985

Byron, William D., *Obit* Apr 1941

Calder, William M., *Obit* Apr 1945

Campbell, Ben Nighthorse, American senator, Oct 1994

Campbell, Philip P., Speaker of the House, *Obit* July 1941

Cannon, Howard W., American senator, Feb 1960, *Obit* Sept 2002

Cantwell, Maria, American senator, Feb 2005

Cao, Joseph, American congressman, June 2009

Capps, Lois, American congresswoman, Mar 2008

Caraway, Hattie Wyatt, American senator, Mar 1945, *Obit* Jan 1951

Carey, Hugh L., American governor, Sept 1965, *Obit* Yrbk 2011

Carlson, Frank, American governor and senator, Apr 1949, *Obit* July 1987

Carroll, John A., American senator, May 1958, *Obit* Oct 1983

Case, Clifford Philip, American senator, Mar 1955, *Obit* Apr 1982

Celler, Emanuel, American congressman, Oct 1949, Nov 1966, *Obit* Mar 1981

Chafee, John, American senator and governor, Nov 1969, *Obit* Jan 2000

Chavez, Dennis, American senator, Mar 1946, *Obit* Jan 1963

Chiles, Lawton, senator and governor, Sept 1971, *Obit* Mar 1999

Chiperfield, Robert B., Sept 1956, *Obit* May 1971

Chisholm, Shirley, American congresswoman, Oct 1969, *Obit* Apr 2005

Church, Frank, American senator, Mar 1958, Mar 1978, *Obit* May 1984

Church, Marguerite Stitt, congresswoman, Feb 1951, *Obit* July 1990

Clark, Bennett Champ, Nov 1941, *Obit* Sept 1954

Clayton, Eva, American congresswoman, June 2000

Cleland, Max, American senator, Feb 1978

Clyburn, James E., American congressman, Oct 2001

Cochran, Thad, American senator, Apr 2002

Coffee, John M., Oct 1946

Cole, Albert M., Jan 1954

Cole, William Sterling, congressman, Mar 1954, *Obit* May 1987

Collins, Cardiss, American congresswoman, Feb 1997, *Obit* Yrbk 2013

Collins, Susan, American senator, May 2000

Connery, Lawrence J., *Obit* Yrbk 1941

Conyers, John, American congressman, Sept 1970

Cooper, Jere, American congressman, Mar 1955, *Obit* Feb 1958

Cordon, Guy, American senator, Apr 1952, *Obit* July 1969

Cotton, Norris, American senator, Feb 1956, *Obit* May 1989

Coudert, Frederic Rene, American congressman, June 1941, *Obit* July 1972

Cox, Christopher, American regulatory agency official, July 1999

Crane, Philip M., American congressman, May 1980

Cranston, Alan, American senator, Feb 1950, Oct 1969, *Obit* Mar 2001

Culkin, Francis D., *Obit* Sept 1943

Cullen, Thomas H., *Obit* Apr 1944

Culver, John C., Nov 1979

Cummings, Elijah E., American congressman, Feb 2004

Curtis, Carl T., American senator, Sept 1954, *Obit* June 2000

Curtis, Thomas B., American congressman, Mar 1965, *Obit* Mar 1993

D'Amato, Alfonse, American senator, Sept 1983

Daniel, Dan, congressman, June 1957

Daschle, Thomas, American senator, Oct 1995

Davis, Artur, American congressman, Feb 2009

Dawson, William Levi, American congressman, Apr 1945, *Obit* Yrbk 1970

DeConcini, Dennis, American senator, Feb 1992

DeLauro, Rosa, American congresswoman, Mar 2000

DeLay, Tom, American congressman, May 1999

Dellums, Ronald V., American congressman, Sept 1972, Sept 1993

Derwinski, Edward J., American Secretary of veterans affairs, Aug 1991, *Obit* Yrbk 2012

Dick, Charles, *Obit* May 1945

Dies, Martin, American lawyer and congressman, Apr 1940, *Obit* Jan 1973

Dieterich, William H., *Obit* Yrbk 1940

Diggs, Charles, American congressman, July 1957, *Obit* Nov 1998

Dingell, John D., American congressman, Mar 1949, *Obit* Yrbk 1956

Dingell, John D., American congressman, Aug 1983

Dirksen, Everett McKinley, American senator, Apr 1941, Sept 1957, *Obit* Nov 1969

Ditter, J. William, *Obit* Jan 1944

Dodd, Thomas, American senator, Sept 1959, *Obit* July 1971

Dole, Robert J., American senator, Apr 1972, Oct 1987

Domenici, Pete, American senator, June 1982

Doughton, Robert L., American congressman, July 1942, *Obit* Yrbk 1955

Douglas, Emily Taft, congresswoman, Apr 1945, *Obit* Mar 1994

Douglas, Lewis W., American government official, Mar 1947, *Obit* May 1974

Downey, Sheridan, Oct 1949, *Obit* Jan 1962

Duff, James Henderson, senator and governor, Apr 1948, *Obit* Feb 1970

Dunn, Jennifer, American congresswoman, Mar 1999, *Obit* Nov 2007

Durbin, Richard J., American senator, Aug 2006

Durenberger, David, American senator, Oct 1988

Eagleton, Thomas F., American senator, Nov 1973, *Obit* Yrbk 2007

Eastland, James O., American senator, Jan 1949, *Obit* Apr 1986

Edwards, Don, American congressman, Mar 1983

Edwards, John, American senator and lawyer, Oct 2004

Edwards, John H., American congressman and government official, *Obit* Yrbk 1945

Ehlers, Vernon J., American congressman, Jan 2005

Ellender, Allen J., American senator, July 1946, *Obit* Oct 1972

Ellison, Keith, American congressman, Apr 2007

Engle, Clair, American senator, Mar 1957, *Obit* Oct 1964

Englebright, Harry L., *Obit* July 1943

Esch, John J., *Obit* June 1941

Exon, J. James, American senator, Nov 1996, *Obit* Yrbk 2005

Fairchild, Benjamin Lewis, *Obit* Yrbk 1946

Fall, Albert B., American Secretary of the interior, *Obit* Jan 1945

Fallin, Mary, American congresswoman, Mar 2011

Fascell, Dante B., congressman, Apr 1960, *Obit* Feb 1999

Fattah, Chaka, American congressman, Sept 2003

Fauntroy, Walter E., American congressman, Feb 1979

Feingold, Russ, American senator, July 1998

Fenwick, Millicent, American congresswoman, Apr 1977, *Obit* Nov 1992

Ferguson, Homer, American diplomat and senator, May 1943, *Obit* Mar 1983

Ferris, Scott, *Obit* July 1945

Fish, Hamilton, American congressman, Jan 1941, *Obit* Mar 1991

Flood, Daniel J., American congressman, Aug 1978, *Obit* Aug 1994

Florio, James J., governor, May 1990

Fogarty, John Edward, congressman, Apr 1964, *Obit* Mar 1967

Foley, Thomas S., American Speaker of the House, Sept 1989

Folger, A. D., *Obit* June 1941

Fong, Hiram, American senator, Feb 1960, *Obit* Yrbk 2004

Ford, Gerald R., American president, Mar 1961, Nov 1975, *Obit* Feb 2007

Frank, Barney, American congressman, Apr 1995

Frist, Bill, American surgeon and senator, Nov 2002

Fulbright, J. William, American senator, Nov 1943, Oct 1955, *Obit* Apr 1995

Gallagher, William J., *Obit* Oct 1946

Gamble, Ralph A., Jan 1953, *Obit* May 1959

Garn, Jake, senator, Aug 1985

Gephardt, Richard A., American congressman, Oct 1987

Gibson, Ernest Willard, American senator, *Obit* Aug 1940

Giffords, Gabrielle, American congresswoman, Mar 2012

Gillette, Guy M., Sept 1946, *Obit* Apr 1973

Gillibrand, Kirsten, American senator, Oct 2013

Gingrich, Newt, American political leader and former Speaker of the House, July 1989

Glass, Carter, American senator, Oct 1941, *Obit* June 1946

Goldsborough, Phillips Lee, *Obit* Yrbk 1946

Goldwater, Barry M., American senator, May 1955, June 1978, *Obit* Aug 1998

Gonzalez, Henry B., American congressman, June 1964, Feb 1993, *Obit* Feb 2001

Goodell, Charles E., American senator, Yrbk 1968, *Obit* Mar 1987

Gordon, Thomas S., American congressman, Apr 1957, *Obit* Apr 1959

Gore, Al, American vice-president, June 1987

Gore, Albert A., American senator and father of Vice-President Albert Gore, Jr., Jan 1952, *Obit* Feb 1999

Gorton, Slade, senator, Aug 1993

Gould, Arthur R., *Obit* Sept 1946

Graham, Bob, American senator, July 1986

Granahan, Kathryn Elizabeth, congresswoman, Oct 1959, *Obit* Sept 1979

Grasso, Ella, American governor, May 1975, *Obit* Mar 1981

Gravel, Mike, American senator, Jan 1972

Green, Edith, American congresswoman, May 1956, *Obit* June 1987

Griffin, Robert P., American senator, May 1960

Griswold, Dwight P., American senator, governor and diplomat, Yrbk 1947, *Obit* June 1954

Gross, H. R., American congressman, Jan 1964, *Obit* Oct 1987

Guffey, Joseph F., Mar 1944, *Obit* May 1959

Guyer, Ulysses Samuel, *Obit* July 1943

Hall, Leonard Wood, American congressman, July 1953, *Obit* July 1979

Halleck, Charles A., American congressman and political leader, Mar 1947, *Obit* Apr 1986

Halsey, Edwin A., *Obit* Mar 1945

Hamilton, Lee H., American congressman, Mar 1988

Hardy, Porter, congressman, May 1957, *Obit* June 1995

Harkin, Tom, American senator, Jan 1992

Harris, Fred R., American senator, Jan 1968

Hart, Edward J., Feb 1953, *Obit* June 1961

Hart, Gary, American senator and lawyer, May 1976

Hart, Philip A., American senator, Sept 1959, *Obit* Feb 1977

Hartley, Fred A., American congressman, June 1947, *Obit* June 1969

Hastert, Dennis, American congressman and Speaker of the House, Apr 1999

Hatch, Orrin G., American senator, Aug 1982

Hatfield, Mark O., American senator, Nov 1959, Mar 1984, *Obit* Yrbk 2011

Hawkins, Augustus F., American congressman, Feb 1983, *Obit* Yrbk 2008

Hawkins, Paula, American senator, Sept 1985, *Obit* Yrbk 2010

Hawley, Willis C., *Obit* Sept 1941

Hayden, Carl Trumbull, American senator, July 1951, *Obit* Mar 1972

Hays, Brooks, American congressman, Jan 1958, *Obit* Jan 1982

Heinz, John, American senator, Apr 1981, *Obit* May 1991

Hendrickson, Robert C., Nov 1952, *Obit* Feb 1965

Hennings, Thomas C., American senator, Oct 1954, *Obit* Nov 1960

Herring, Clyde L., *Obit* Nov 1945

Hicks, Louise Day, American congresswoman and municipal official, Mar 1974, *Obit* June 2004

Hill, J. B. P. Clayton, *Obit* July 1941

Hill, Lister, American senator, Oct 1943, *Obit* Feb 1985

Hillings, Patrick J., congressman, Oct 1957, *Obit* Sept 1994

Hinshaw, Carl, American congressman, July 1951, *Obit* Oct 1956

Hoffman, Clare Eugene, American congressman, Mar 1949, *Obit* Jan 1968

Holaday, William Perry, *Obit* Mar 1946

Holifield, Chet, American congressman, Oct 1955, *Obit* Apr 1995

Hollings, Ernest F., American senator, July 1982

Hollister, John B., American lawyer, congressman and government official, Oct 1955

Hope, Clifford R., American congressman, May 1953, *Obit* July 1970

Hosmer, Craig, congressman, May 1958, *Obit* Mar 1983

Houston, Andrew Jackson, *Obit* Aug 1941

Howell, Charles R., Feb 1954, *Obit* Sept 1973

Hoyer, Steny H., American congressman, Mar 2004

Hughes, Harold E., American governor and senator, June 1963, *Obit* Jan 1997

Hull, William Edgar, *Obit* July 1942

Humphrey, Hubert Horatio, American vice-president, July 1949, Apr 1966, *Obit* Mar 1978

Hutchison, Kay Bailey, American senator, Sept 1997

Hyde, Henry J., American congressman, Oct 1989, *Obit* Yrbk 2008

Ives, Irving M., American senator, Feb 1948, *Obit* Apr 1962

Izac, Edouard V. M., American congressman, Yrbk 1945, *Obit* Mar 1990

Jackson, Henry Martin, American senator, Oct 1953, Oct 1979, *Obit* Oct 1983

Jackson, Jesse L., American congressman, May 1998

Javits, Jacob K., American senator, June 1948, Oct 1958, *Obit* Apr 1986

Jeffords, James, American senator, Sept 2001

Jenner, William E., American senator, June 1951, *Obit* May 1985

Johnson, Ed, American senator and governor, Yrbk 1946, *Obit* July 1970

Johnson, Eddie Bernice, American congresswoman, July 2001

Johnson, Leroy, Sept 1949, *Obit* June 1961

Johnson, Lyndon B., American president, Jan 1951, Mar 1964, *Obit* Mar 1973

Johnson, Paul B., *Obit* Feb 1944

Jones, James R., Oct 1981

Jordan, Barbara, American lawyer and congresswoman, Sept 1974, Apr 1993, *Obit* Apr 1996

Kaptur, Marcy C., American congresswoman, Jan 2003

Kassebaum Baker, Nancy, American senator, Feb 1982

Kasten, Robert W., senator, June 1989

Kee, Elizabeth, Jan 1954

Kee, John, June 1950, *Obit* June 1951

Kefauver, Estes, American senator, Jan 1949, *Obit* Oct 1963

Kelly, Edna Flannery, congresswoman, Mar 1950, *Obit* Feb 1998

Kem, James P., Oct 1950, *Obit* Apr 1965

Kennedy, Edward Moore, American senator, Sept 1963, Oct 1978, *Obit* Oct 2009

Kennedy, John F., American president, June 1950, July 1961, *Obit* Jan 1964

Kerry, John Forbes, American senator, June 1988, Sept 2004

Kilday, Paul J., Oct 1958, *Obit* Yrbk 1968

King, Cecil R., American congressman, Feb 1952, *Obit* May 1974

King, Samuel Wilder, Oct 1953, *Obit* June 1959

Knutson, Coya, congresswoman, Mar 1956, *Obit* Jan 1997

Kowalski, Frank, July 1960, *Obit* Yrbk 1974

Kuchel, Thomas H., American senator, Feb 1954, *Obit* Feb 1995

Kunz, Stanley H., *Obit* June 1946

La Follette, Charles M., Feb 1950

La Follette, Robert M., American senator, May 1944, *Obit* Apr 1953

La Hood, Ray, American Secretary of transportation, Mar 2009

Laird, Melvin R., American Secretary of defense, Nov 1964

Landry, Jeff, American congressman, Jan 2012

Langer, William, American governor and senator, Feb 1952, *Obit* Jan 1960

Langevin, Jim, American congressman, Aug 2005

Lantos, Tom, American congressman, July 2007, *Obit* May 2008

Lea, Clarence F., Nov 1946, *Obit* Sept 1964

Leahy, Patrick J., American senator, Sept 1990

Lee, Barbara, American congresswoman, June 2004

Lee, Blair, *Obit* Feb 1945

Lesinski, John, July 1949, *Obit* July 1950

Levin, Carl, American senator, May 2004

Lewis, Lawrence, *Obit* Jan 1944

Lieberman, Joseph I., American senator, July 1994

Lincoln, Blanche Lambert, American senator, Mar 2002

Lloyd, James T., *Obit* May 1944

Long, Russell B., American senator, Yrbk 1951, Oct 1965, *Obit* Yrbk 2003

Lott, Trent, American senator, Sept 1996

Lowden, Frank O., governor, *Obit* May 1943

Lowey, Nita M., American congresswoman, Sept 1997

Lubke, Heinrich, Jan 1960, *Obit* May 1972

Lucas, Scott W., American senator, Yrbk 1947, *Obit* Apr 1968

Luce, Robert, *Obit* May 1946

Luhring, Oscar Raymond, *Obit* Oct 1944

Lujan, Manuel, American Secretary of the interior, Sept 1989

Lumpkin, Alva M., *Obit* Sept 1941

Lundeen, Ernest, *Obit* Oct 1940

MacDonald, William J., *Obit* May 1946

Madden, Ray J., congressman, Apr 1953, *Obit* Nov 1987

Madigan, Edward R., American Secretary of agriculture, Nov 1992, *Obit* Feb 1995

Magner, Thomas F., *Obit* Feb 1946

Magnuson, Warren, American senator, Oct 1945, *Obit* July 1989

Maloney, Carolyn B., American congresswoman, Apr 2001

Mankin, Helen Douglas, congresswoman and lawyer, Apr 1946

Mansfield, Mike, American senator and diplomat, Apr 1952, Jan 1978, *Obit* Jan 2002

Markey, Edward J., American congressman, Nov 1997

Martin, Edward, governor and senator, Oct 1945, *Obit* May 1967

Mathias, Charles, American senator, Yrbk 1972, *Obit* Yrbk 2010

Matsui, Robert T., American congressman, Oct 1994, *Obit* Apr 2005

May, Andrew Jackson, American congressman, Apr 1941, *Obit* Nov 1959

May, Catherine Dean, congresswoman, Jan 1960

McCain, John S., American senator, Feb 1989, Mar 2006

McCarran, Pat, American senator, July 1947, *Obit* Yrbk 1954

McCarthy, Eugene J., American senator, Nov 1955, *Obit* Mar 2006

McCarthy, Joseph, American senator, Jan 1950, *Obit* July 1957

McClellan, John L., American senator, Apr 1950, *Obit* Feb 1978

McCloskey, Paul N., American congressman and lawyer, Nov 1971

McCormack, John William, American congressman and Speaker of the House, June 1943, Apr 1962, *Obit* Jan 1981

McCormick, Ruth Hanna, congresswoman, *Obit* Feb 1945

McGovern, George S., American senator, Mar 1967, *Obit* Yrbk 2012

McGregor, J. Harry, Oct 1958

McIntyre, Thomas James, American senator, Nov 1963, *Obit* Oct 1992

McKellar, Kenneth Douglas, American senator, Jan 1946, *Obit* Jan 1958

McKinney, Cynthia, American congresswoman, Aug 1996

McKneally, Martin B., congressman and veterans' leader, Mar 1960, *Obit* Aug 1992

McMahon, Brien, American senator, Yrbk 1945, *Obit* Sept 1952

McMillan, John L., American congressman and lawyer, Nov 1956

Mead, James M., July 1944, *Obit* Apr 1964

Meader, George, July 1956

Merritt, Matthew J., *Obit* Nov 1946

Metcalf, Jesse H., *Obit* Yrbk 1942

Metzenbaum, Howard M., American senator, July 1980, *Obit* Yrbk 2008

Michel, Robert H., American congressman and political leader, Sept 1981

Mikulski, Barbara A., American senator, Nov 1985

Miller, George, American congressman, Feb 1964

Miller, William Edward, American congressman and lawyer, Feb 1962, *Obit* Aug 1983

Miller, Zell, American senator, July 1996

Millikin, Eugene Donald, American senator, Apr 1948, *Obit* Oct 1958

Mink, Patsy T., American congresswoman, Sept 1968, *Obit* Jan 2003

Minton, Sherman, American Supreme Court justice, Mar 1941, Yrbk 1949, *Obit* May 1965

Montoya, Joseph M., American senator, Mar 1975, *Obit* July 1978

Moore, R. Walton, *Obit* Apr 1941

Morano, Albert P., congressman, Mar 1952, *Obit* Feb 1988

Morella, Constance A., American congresswoman, Feb 2001

Morgan, Thomas E., American congressman and physician, June 1959, *Obit* Oct 1995

Morton, Thruston Ballard, American senator, Nov 1957, *Obit* Oct 1982

Moseley-Braun, Carol, American senator, June 1994

Moses, George H., *Obit* Feb 1945

Moses, John, *Obit* Apr 1945

Moss, John E., American congressman, Nov 1956, *Obit* Feb 1998

Mott, James W., *Obit* Yrbk 1945

Mundt, Karl E., American senator, July 1948, *Obit* Oct 1974

Murdock, Victor, *Obit* Aug 1945

Murkowski, Frank H., American senator and governor, July 2003

Murray, James E., American senator, Aug 1945, *Obit* May 1961

Murray, Patty, American senator, Aug 1994

Myers, Francis John, Apr 1949, *Obit* Sept 1956

Neuberger, Maurine Brown, American senator, Oct 1961, *Obit* July 2000

Newberry, Truman Handy, *Obit* Nov 1945

Newton, Cleveland Alexander, *Obit* Oct 1945

Nolan, W. I., *Obit* Sept 1943

Norton, Mary Teresa Hopkins, congresswoman, Nov 1944, *Obit* Nov 1959

Nunn, Sam, American senator, Jan 1980

O'Connor, James Francis, *Obit* Mar 1945

O'Daniel, W. Lee, American senator and governor, Oct 1947, *Obit* June 1969

O'Day, Caroline Love Goodwin, American congresswoman, *Obit* Feb 1943

O'Gorman, James A., *Obit* July 1943

O'Leary, James A., *Obit* May 1944

O'Mahoney, Joseph C., American senator, Oct 1945, *Obit* Jan 1963

O'Neill, Tip, American Speaker of the House, Apr 1974, *Obit* Mar 1994

Owen, Ruth Bryan, American congresswoman, Yrbk 1944, *Obit* Oct 1954

Packwood, Robert, American senator, Jan 1981

Parker, Homer Cling, *Obit* July 1946

Partridge, Frank C., *Obit* Apr 1943

Passman, Otto E., American congressman, Oct 1960, *Obit* Sept 1988

Paul, Ron, American congressman, June 2008

Pelosi, Nancy, American congresswoman and former Speaker of the House, Feb 2003

Pepper, Claude, American congressman, Feb 1941, Jan 1983, *Obit* July 1989

Perkins, Carl D., American congressman, Feb 1968, *Obit* Sept 1984

Pfost, Gracie Bowers, congresswoman, May 1955, *Obit* Oct 1965

Phelan, Michael F., *Obit* Yrbk 1941

Pike, Otis, American congressman, Feb 1976

Pine, William B., *Obit* Oct 1942

Pittman, Key, American senator, *Obit* Yrbk 1940

Poage, W. R., American congressman, Yrbk 1969, *Obit* Mar 1987

Pool, Joe, American congressman, Mar 1967, *Obit* Sept 1968

Porter, Charles O., Sept 1957

Potter, Charles E., American senator, Yrbk 1954

Pressler, Larry, senator, Oct 1983

Proxmire, William, American senator, June 1958, Aug 1978, *Obit* Mar 2006

Quayle, Dan, American vice-president, June 1989

Rabaut, Louis Charles, Jan 1952, *Obit* Jan 1962

Rains, Albert McKinley, congressman, Sept 1959, *Obit* May 1991

Randolph, Jennings, American senator, Jan 1962, *Obit* July 1998

Rangel, Charles B., American congressman, Mar 1984

Rayburn, Sam, American congressman and Speaker of the House, Oct 1940, Mar 1949, *Obit* Jan 1962

Reece, Brazilla Carroll, American congressman, May 1946, *Obit* May 1961

Reed, Daniel A., American congressman, May 1953, *Obit* Apr 1959

Reed, Herbert Calhoun, *Obit* Sept 1940

Rees, Edward H., Jan 1958, *Obit* Yrbk 1969

Reid, Charlotte Thompson, congresswoman and regulatory official, Jan 1975

Reid, Frank R., *Obit* Mar 1945

Reid, Harry, American senator, Mar 2003

Reuss, Henry S., American congressman and lawyer, Oct 1959, *Obit* Mar 2002

Revercomb, Chapman, June 1958

Rhodes, John J., American congressman, Sept 1976, *Obit* Yrbk 2004

Riegle, Donald W., senator, Oct 1986

Rivers, L. Mendel, American congressman, Oct 1960, *Obit* Feb 1971

Robb, Charles S., American senator, Apr 1989

Rodino, Peter W., American congressman, Oct 1954, *Obit* Yrbk 2005

Rogers, Edith Nourse, American congresswoman, Apr 1942, *Obit* Nov 1960

Ros-Lehtinen, Ileana, American congresswoman, Aug 2000

Rostenkowski, Dan, American congressman, Jan 1982, *Obit* Yrbk 2010

Roth, William V., American senator, Apr 1983, *Obit* Yrbk 2004

Roudebush, Richard L., congressman and veterans' leader, June 1976, *Obit* Apr 1995

Rowland, John, American governor, Oct 1997

Rubio, Marco, American senator, Apr 2011

Rudman, Warren B., senator, Nov 1989, *Obit* Yrbk 2013

Russell, Richard B., American senator, Nov 1949, *Obit* Mar 1971

Ryan, Paul, American congressman, Jan 2013

Ryun, Jim, American runner and congressman, May 1968

Sackett, Frederic M., senator and diplomat, *Obit* July 1941

Sanders, Jared Young, *Obit* May 1944

Santorum, Rick, American lawyer, presidential candidate and former senator, Aug 2011

Sarbanes, Paul S., American senator, Jan 1997

Sasser, James R., senator and diplomat, July 1993

Satterfield, John C., July 1962

Schakowsky, Jan, American congresswoman, July 2004

Scheel, Walter, Feb 1971

Scheuer, James H., American congressman, Apr 1968, *Obit* Apr 2006

Schoeppel, Andrew Frank, senator and governor, Mar 1952, *Obit* Mar 1962

Schumer, Charles E., American senator, July 1995

Scott, John R. K., *Obit* Feb 1946

Sears, William Joseph, *Obit* May 1944

Sevier, Henry Hulme, *Obit* Mar 1940

Shaheen, Jeanne, American senator, Jan 2001

Simmons, Furnifold McLendel, American senator, *Obit* Jan 1940

Simon, Paul, American senator, Jan 1988, *Obit* Yrbk 2004

Simpson, Alan K., American senator, Oct 1990

Simpson, Kenneth F., *Obit* Mar 1941

Simpson, Milward Lee, governor and senator, Jan 1957, *Obit* Aug 1993

Simpson, Richard M., Yrbk 1953, *Obit* Mar 1960

Sims, Hugo S., Oct 1949

Singh, Swaran, Mar 1971, *Obit* Jan 1995

Slaughter, Louise M., American congresswoman, Apr 1999

Small, John Humphrey, *Obit* Sept 1946

Smathers, George A., American senator, Apr 1954, *Obit* June 2007

Smith, Clyde Harold, *Obit* May 1940

Smith, Ellison DuRant, American senator, *Obit* Jan 1945

Smith, Margaret Chase, American senator, Feb 1945, Mar 1962, *Obit* Aug 1995

Smith, Robert C., American senator, Sept 2000

Smoot, Reed, American senator, *Obit* Mar 1941

Snowe, Olympia J., American senator, May 1995

Snyder, J. Buell, *Obit* Apr 1946

Solarz, Stephen J., American congressman, Nov 1986, *Obit* Yrbk 2011

Sparkman, John J., American senator, Mar 1950, *Obit* Jan 1986

Speaks, John Charles, *Obit* Yrbk 1945

Specter, Arlen, American senator, Aug 1988, Aug 2009, *Obit* Yrbk 2012

St. George, Katharine, congresswoman, Yrbk 1947, *Obit* July 1983

Stabenow, Debbie, American senator, Feb 2006

Stafford, Robert T., American senator, Sept 1960, *Obit* Yrbk 2008

Stanfield, Robert Nelson, *Obit* June 1945

Steagall, Henry Bascom, *Obit* Jan 1944

Stephens, Hubert D., *Obit* Apr 1946

Stephens, William D., *Obit* June 1944

Stevens, Ted, American senator, Oct 2001, *Obit* Yrbk 2010

Stevenson, Adlai, American senator, Apr 1974

Stratton, Samuel S., congressman, Jan 1966, *Obit* Jan 1991

Stratton, William G., American governor, Apr 1953, *Obit* Aug 2001

Sullivan, Leonor K., American congresswoman, Yrbk 1954, *Obit* Oct 1988

Sutherland, George, American Supreme Court justice, *Obit* Sept 1942

Symington, James W., June 1968

Symington, Stuart, American senator, Sept 1945, July 1956, *Obit* Feb 1989

Taber, John, American congressman, Feb 1948, *Obit* Jan 1966

Taft, Robert A., American senator, May 1940, Apr 1948, *Obit* Oct 1953

Taft, Robert A., American senator, Oct 1967, *Obit* Feb 1994

Talmadge, Herman E., American governor and senator, Mar 1947, *Obit* June 2002

Taylor, Edward T., *Obit* Oct 1941

Taylor, Glen Hearst, American senator, Oct 1947, *Obit* July 1984

Teague, Olin E., congressman, Mar 1952, *Obit* Apr 1981

Thomas, Elmer, American senator, Yrbk 1949, *Obit* Nov 1965

Thomas, John W., *Obit* Yrbk 1945

Thompson, Frank, American congressman, July 1959, *Obit* Sept 1989

Thompson, George L., *Obit* Oct 1941

Thompson, Ruth, congresswoman, Nov 1951

Thomson, Vernon Wallace, governor and congressman, July 1958, *Obit* June 1988

Thorkelson, Jacob, *Obit* Jan 1946

Thurmond, Strom, American senator, Sept 1948, Nov 1992, *Obit* Nov 2003

Timberlake, Charles B., American congressman, *Obit* July 1941

Tinkham, George H., Apr 1942, *Obit* Oct 1956

Truman, Harry S., American president, Jan 1942, Apr 1945, *Obit* Feb 1973

Tsongas, Paul, American senator, July 1981, *Obit* Mar 1997

Tunney, John V., June 1971

Tydings, Millard E., American senator, Jan 1945, *Obit* Apr 1961

Ullman, Al, congressman, Aug 1975, *Obit* Jan 1987

Underhill, Charles Lee, *Obit* Mar 1946

Van Nuys, Frederick, *Obit* Mar 1944

Van Zandt, James E., congressman, Nov 1950, *Obit* Mar 1986

Velazquez, Nydia, American congresswoman, July 1999

Velde, Harold H., American congressman, Mar 1953, *Obit* Jan 1986

Vinson, Carl, American congressman, Apr 1942, *Obit* July 1981

Voorhis, Jerry, American congressman, Aug 1941, *Obit* Nov 1984

Vorys, John M., American congressman, Sept 1950, *Obit* Nov 1968

Wadsworth, James W., July 1943, *Obit* Sept 1952

Walter, Francis E., American congressman, June 1952, *Obit* July 1963

Warner, John W., American senator, Nov 1976

Wason, Edward H., *Obit* Apr 1941

Waters, Maxine, American congresswoman, Nov 1992

Watson, Clarence Wayland, *Obit* July 1940

Waxman, Henry Arnold, American congressman, July 1992

Weicker, Lowell P., senator and governor, Jan 1974, May 1993

Weis, Jessica, congresswoman, Yrbk 1959, *Obit* June 1963

Weiss, Ted, congressman, Oct 1985, *Obit* Nov 1992

Welker, Herman, American senator, Feb 1955, *Obit* Jan 1958

Wheat, William Howard, *Obit* Apr 1944

Wherry, Kenneth S., American senator, Apr 1946, *Obit* Jan 1952

White, Wallace H., May 1948, *Obit* May 1952

Wiley, Alexander, American senator, Apr 1947, *Obit* Jan 1968

Williams, Harrison A., American senator, Oct 1960, *Obit* Mar 2002

Williams, Thomas Sutler, *Obit* May 1940

Wilson, Pete, governor, Apr 1991

Wirth, Timothy E., senator, Mar 1991

Wofford, Harris, American senator, Apr 1992

Wolcott, Jesse P., American congressman and regulatory agency official, Yrbk 1949, *Obit* Apr 1969

Woodhouse, Chase Going, congresswoman, Mar 1945, *Obit* Apr 1985

Wright, Jim, American Speaker of the House, Apr 1979

Yates, Sidney, American congressman, Aug 1993, *Obit* Jan 2001

Young, Milton R., American senator, Yrbk 1954, *Obit* July 1983

Young, Stephen M., American senator, Oct 1959, *Obit* Feb 1985

Zablocki, Clement, American congressman, June 1958, June 1983, *Obit* Jan 1984

Members of Parliament

Abe, Shinzo, Japanese prime minister, Jan 2006

Acker, Achille van, Belgian prime minister, May 1958, *Obit* Sept 1975

Acland, Richard, British member of Parliament, Aug 1944

Al-Yafi, Abdullah Aref, June 1956

Alexander, Albert, Yrbk 1940, *Obit* Feb 1965

Allon, Yigal, Israeli political leader, Sept 1975, *Obit* Apr 1980

Almirante, Giorgio, Italian political leader, Jan 1974, *Obit* July 1988

Amery, Leopold Charles Maurice Stennett, British cabinet member, July 1942, *Obit* Yrbk 1956

Angelopoulos-Daskalaki, Gianna, Greek Olympic executive, Jan 2004

Ashdown, Paddy, British political leader, Oct 1992

Ashida, Hitoshi, Japanese prime minister, June 1948, *Obit* Sept 1959

Astor, Nancy Witcher Langhorne, British member of Parliament, Nov 1940, *Obit* July 1964

Atholl, John George Stewart-Murray, British army officer and member of Parliament, *Obit* May 1942

Attlee, C. R., British prime minister, May 1940, Feb 1947, *Obit* Yrbk 1967

Balladur, Edouard, French prime minister, Feb 1994

Barber, Anthony, Jan 1971

Barzel, Rainer, German political leader, May 1967, *Obit* Yrbk 2006

Blair, Tony, British prime minister, Aug 1996, Jan 2005

Blucher, Franz, German cabinet member, Jan 1956, *Obit* June 1959

Braddock, E. M., British labor leader and member of Parliament, July 1957, *Obit* Jan 1971

Broadbent, Edward, Canadian political leader, May 1988

Brown, Gordon, British prime minister, Jan 2002

Butler of Saffron Walden, Richard Austen Butler, British cabinet member, May 1944, Sept 1964, *Obit* May 1982

Callaghan, James, British prime minister, Feb 1968, *Obit* Yrbk 2005

Calwell, A. A., Oct 1947

Cameron, David, British prime minister, Aug 2010

Campney, Ralph Osborne, Sept 1955, *Obit* Yrbk 1967

Caramanlis, Constantinos, Greek prime minister, Jan 2004

Carr, Robert, Jan 1973

Casey, Richard Gardiner Casey, Australian governor-general, Jan 1940, *Obit* Aug 1976

Chamberlain, Neville, British prime minister, *Obit* Yrbk 1940

Chevrier, Lionel, June 1952

Chiappe, Jean, French government official, *Obit* Jan 1941

Clarke, Kenneth H., British political leader, Jan 2002

Coe, Sebastian, British runner, Nov 1980

Coldwell, M. J., Canadian member of Parliament, Sept 1943, *Obit* Oct 1974

Colijn, Hendrikus, Dutch prime minister, *Obit* Jan 1945

Cousins, Frank, English labor leader, Feb 1960, *Obit* July 1986

Crosland, Anthony, British cabinet member, Sept 1963, *Obit* Apr 1977

Cross, Ronald H., June 1941

Cyrankiewicz, Jozef, Feb 1957

Darwin, Leonard, *Obit* May 1943

Davies, Clement, Oct 1950, *Obit* May 1962

De Lille, Patricia, South African political leader, Jan 2004

Devold, Kristin Krohn, Norwegian military official, Jan 2003

Dickinson, Willoughby Hyett Dickinson, British member of Parliament, *Obit* July 1943

Dion, Stephane, Canadian political leader, Jan 2007

Doi, Takako, Japanese socialist leader, July 1992

Douglas, T. C., Canadian political leader, July 1957, *Obit* Apr 1986

Duncan Smith, Iain, British political leader, Jan 2002

Duncan, Andrew Rae, July 1941, *Obit* May 1952

Duncan, Patrick, South African governor-general, *Obit* Sept 1943

Eaton, Charles A., American congressman, May 1945, *Obit* Mar 1953

Eccles, David, British cabinet member, Jan 1952, *Obit* May 1999

Ede, James Chuter, May 1946, *Obit* Jan 1966

Edelman, Maurice, Jan 1954, *Obit* Feb 1976

Fairclough, Ellen Louks, Canadian cabinet member, Oct 1957, *Obit* Yrbk 2005

Fischer, Carlos L., Feb 1959

Fitzroy, Edward Algernon, *Obit* Apr 1943

Fleming, Amalia Koutsouri, Greek legislator, Nov 1972, *Obit* Apr 1986

Flores Nano, Lourdes, Peruvian political leader, Jan 2006

Fogh Rasmussen, Anders, Danish prime minister, Jan 2004

Fremantle, Francis Edward, *Obit* Oct 1943

Gaillard, Felix, French prime minister, Feb 1958, *Obit* Oct 1970

Galloway, George, British member of Parliament, Jan 2005

Gayatri Devi, Mar 1968, *Obit* Yrbk 2009

Geijer, Arne, Swedish labor leader and member of Parliament, July 1964

George-Brown, George Alfred George-Brown, British cabinet member, Yrbk 1963, *Obit* July 1985

Gerstenmaier, Eugen, German political leader, Feb 1958, *Obit* May 1986

Gilani, Yusuf Raza, Pakistani prime minister, Nov 2008

Gilmour, John, British cabinet member, *Obit* Apr 1940

Golding, Bruce, Jamaican prime minister, Mar 2008

Gorbach, Alfons, Oct 1961, *Obit* Oct 1972

Gordon-Walker, Patrick Chrestien Gordon Walker, Jan 1966

Gouin, Felix, French statesman, Mar 1946, *Obit* Oct 1979

Green, Howard, Jan 1960

Grimond, Jo, British political leader, Oct 1963, *Obit* Jan 1994

Gronchi, Giovanni, Oct 1955, *Obit* Jan 1979

Gunter, Ray, July 1967, *Obit* June 1977

Han, Myeong Sook, Korean prime minister, Jan 2006

Hansen, H. C., Mar 1956, *Obit* Apr 1960

Harris, Walter, June 1955

Hees, George, Canadian cabinet member, Oct 1959

Herriot, Edouard, French statesman, Feb 1946, *Obit* June 1957

Heseltine, Michael, British political leader, June 1985

Hesselgren, Kerstin, Swedish sociologist and member of Parliament, Jan 1941, *Obit* Oct 1962

Holland, Sidney, New Zealand prime minister, Jan 1950, *Obit* Nov 1961

Home of the Hirsel, Alexander Frederick Douglas-Home, British prime minister, Feb 1958, *Obit* Jan 1996

Horsbrugh, Florence Gertrude Horsbrugh, British cabinet member, Feb 1952, *Obit* Mar 1970

Howe, Geoffrey, British cabinet member, Oct 1980

Hylton-Foster, Harry, Jan 1961, *Obit* Nov 1965

Johanna Sigurdardottir, Icelandic prime minister, July 2010

Jones, Arthur C., Jan 1948, *Obit* Jan 1965

Jorgensen, Anker, Danish prime minister, Sept 1978

Jowitt, William Allen Jowitt, Aug 1941, *Obit* Nov 1957

Kaiser, Jakob, German labor leader and government official, Feb 1956, *Obit* July 1961

Kaur, Rajkumari Amrit, Oct 1955, *Obit* Mar 1964

Kiesinger, Kurt Georg, German chancellor, Apr 1967, *Obit* Apr 1988

King, William Lyon Mackenzie, Canadian prime minister, Aug 1940, *Obit* Sept 1950

Kirchner, Cristina E. Fernandez de, Argentine president, Jan 2007

Kiviniemi, Mari, Finnish prime minister, Oct 2010

Knuth-Winterfeldt, Kield Gustav, Sept 1959

Kok, Wim, Dutch prime minister, Jan 2003

Kraft, Ole Bjorn, Feb 1953

Lamont, Norman, British cabinet member, Aug 1992

Laniel, Joseph, French prime minister, Feb 1954

Lansbury, George, British socialist leader, *Obit* Jan 1940

Lapointe, Ernest, Canadian political leader, *Obit* Jan 1942

Layton, Jack, Canadian political leader, Nov 2009, *Obit* Yrbk 2012

Lee, Jennie, British member of Parliament, May 1946, *Obit* Jan 1989

Louw, Eric, Mar 1962, *Obit* Sept 1968

MacEachen, Allan Joseph, Canadian political leader, Apr 1983

Macleod, Iain Norman, British cabinet member, Apr 1956, *Obit* Oct 1970

Mandel, Georges, French political leader, Yrbk 1940

Margesson, Henry David Reginald Margesson, Feb 1941, *Obit* Feb 1966

Maudling, Reginald, British cabinet member, May 1960, *Obit* Apr 1979

Maxton, James, British member of Parliament, *Obit* Sept 1946

May, Theresa, British member of Parliament, Jan 2003

Mayer, Rene, French prime minister, May 1948, *Obit* Feb 1973

McAliskey, Bernadette Devlin, Irish political leader, Jan 1970

McLaughlin, Audrey, Canadian political leader, July 1990

Mendes-France, Pierre, French statesman, Oct 1954, *Obit* Jan 1983

Menshikov, Mikhail A., May 1958, *Obit* Sept 1976

Merkel, Angela, German chancellor, Jan 2004

Mikhailov, Nikolai Aleksandrovich, Nov 1958

Mlambo-Ngcuka, Phumzile, South African deputy president, Jan 2005

Morales, Evo, Bolivian president, Jan 2006

Morrison of Lambeth, Herbert Stanley Morrison, British cabinet member, July 1940, Feb 1951, *Obit* Apr 1965

Mosley, Oswald, British political leader, July 1940, *Obit* Feb 1981

Moyo, Jonathan N., Zimbabwean political leader, Jan 2007

Muir, Ramsay, *Obit* June 1941

Muldoon, Robert D., New Zealand prime minister, Feb 1978, *Obit* Sept 1992

Mulroney, Brian, Canadian prime minister, Apr 1984

Nabarro, Gerald, Nov 1963, *Obit* Jan 1974

Nutting, Anthony, British cabinet member, Feb 1955, *Obit* May 1999

Patil, Pratibha, Indian president, Jan 2007

Pflimlin, Pierre, French political leader, Nov 1955, *Obit* Oct 2000

Pickersgill, J. W., Canadian cabinet member, Mar 1968

Pierlot, Hubert, Belgian prime minister, May 1943, *Obit* Feb 1964

Pilot, Sachin, Indian member of Parliament, Jan 2007

Pleven, Rene, French political leader, June 1950, *Obit* Mar 1993

Profumo, John D., British cabinet member, Oct 1959, *Obit* June 2006

Pym, Francis, British cabinet member, Sept 1982, *Obit* Yrbk 2008

Rae, Bob, Canadian political leader, Feb 1991

Rajoy, Mariano, Spanish political leader, Jan 2007

Rapacki, Adam, July 1958, *Obit* Yrbk 1970

Reynaud, Paul, French prime minister, Apr 1940, May 1950, *Obit* Nov 1966

Robens of Woldingham, Alfred Robens, June 1956

Royal, Segolene, French political leader, Jan 2007

Saleh, Allah-Yar, Feb 1953

Salisbury, Robert Arthur James Gascoyne-Cecil, British member of Parliament, Nov 1941, *Obit* Apr 1972

Samuel, Herbert Louis Samuel, British statesman, Apr 1955, *Obit* Mar 1963

Sauve, Jeanne, Canadian government official, Aug 1984, *Obit* Mar 1993

Savage, Michael Joseph, *Obit* Apr 1940

Scarbrough, Roger Lumley, Jan 1958, *Obit* Sept 1969

Shabandar, Musa, Feb 1956

Shehu, Mehmet, Feb 1958, *Obit* Feb 1982

Silva, Benedita da, Brazilian governor and political leader, Jan 2002

Simon, John Allsebrook Simon, British statesman, July 1940, *Obit* Mar 1954

Simpson-Miller, Portia, Jamaican prime minister, Jan 2006

Sinclair, Archibald, British political leader, Sept 1940, *Obit* Oct 1970

Siroky, Viliam, Apr 1957, *Obit* Nov 1971

Skinner, Dennis, British member of Parliament, Jan 2002

Snell, Henry Snell, May 1941

Solh, Sami, Feb 1958, *Obit* Jan 1969

Stanfield, Robert Lorne, Canadian political leader, Yrbk 1958, *Obit* Yrbk 2004

Stanley, Oliver, Apr 1943, *Obit* Jan 1951

Stoica, Chivu, Jan 1959, *Obit* Apr 1975

Stokes, Richard Rapier, British cabinet member, Sept 1951, *Obit* Oct 1957

Strauss, Franz Josef, German political leader, Feb 1957, Feb 1987, *Obit* Nov 1988

Summerskill, Edith, British member of Parliament and physician, Apr 1943, July 1963, *Obit* Apr 1980

Swart, Charles Robberts, June 1960

Takeshita, Noboru, Japanese prime minister, May 1988, *Obit* Nov 2000

Tebbit, Norman, British cabinet member, Nov 1987

Teitgen, Pierre-Henri, French political leader, Jan 1953

Tenby of Bulford, Gwilym Lloyd George, British cabinet member, Nov 1952, *Obit* Apr 1967

Thatcher, Margaret, British prime minister, July 1975, Nov 1989, *Obit* Yrbk 2013

Thorneycroft of Dunston, Peter, British cabinet member, Yrbk 1952, *Obit* Aug 1994

Thorning-Schmidt, Helle, Prime minister of Denmark, May 2012

Thorpe, Jeremy, British member of Parliament, Oct 1974

Trimble, David, Northern Ireland political leader, July 2000

Tryon, George Clement Tryon, British government official, *Obit* Jan 1941

Turner, Ben, *Obit* Nov 1942

Tymoshenko, Yulia, Ukrainian economist and prime minister, Jan 2006

Wallace, Euan, *Obit* Apr 1941

Watkinson, Harold Arthur Watkinson, Mar 1960

Waverley, John Anderson, British statesman, July 1941, *Obit* Mar 1958

Wedgwood, Josiah C., British member of Parliament, Apr 1942, *Obit* Sept 1943

Whitelaw, William Whitelaw, British cabinet member, Mar 1975, *Obit* Nov 1999

Whitlam, Edward Gough, Jan 1974

Wilkinson, Ellen, British cabinet member, July 1941, *Obit* Mar 1947

Williams, Shirley, British political leader, Oct 1976

Wilson, Harold, British prime minister, Feb 1948, May 1963, *Obit* July 1995

Woodsworth, James Shaver, Canadian clergyman and political leader, *Obit* May 1942

Younger, Kenneth Gilmour, Sept 1950

Yui, O. K., May 1955, *Obit* Sept 1960

Zoli, Adone, Mar 1958, *Obit* Apr 1960

Memoirists

Atkinson, Oriana Torrey MacIlveen, author, Yrbk 1953, *Obit* Oct 1989

Beebe, William, American naturalist and author, July 1941, *Obit* Sept 1962

Burroughs, Augusten, American novelist and memoirist, Apr 2004

Calisher, Hortense, American short story writer and novelist, Nov 1973, *Obit* Yrbk 2009

Carey, Ernestine Gilbreth, American memoirist, May 1949, *Obit* Yrbk 2007

Chatwin, Bruce, English memoirist, travel writer and novelist, Jan 1988, *Obit* Mar 1989

Durrell, Lawrence, English novelist, poet and travel writer, July 1963, *Obit* Jan 1991

Fermi, Laura, wife of Enrico Fermi, May 1958

Garland, Hamlin, American novelist and memoirist, Mar 1940

Harris, Mark, American novelist and memoirist, Yrbk 1959, *Obit* Yrbk 2007

Isherwood, Christopher, Anglo-American novelist, Oct 1972, *Obit* Feb 1986

Kazan, Elia, American theatrical and film director, Jan 1948, Oct 1972, *Obit* Yrbk 2004

Luhan, Mabel Ganson Dodge, American patron of the arts and memoirist, Jan 1940, *Obit* Oct 1962

Merrick, Elliott, author, Yrbk 1950, *Obit* July 1997

Monsarrat, Nicholas, English novelist, Yrbk 1950, *Obit* Oct 1979

Patchett, Ann, American novelist, Apr 2003

Pelzer, David J., American self-help writer and motivational speaker, Mar 2002

Ratushinskaya, Irina, Russian poet, July 1988

Rives, Hallie Erminie, American novelist, Yrbk 1956

Settle, Mary Lee, American novelist and memoirist, Yrbk 1959, *Obit* Yrbk 2006

Sinclair, Jo, author, Mar 1946, *Obit* June 1995

White, Edmund, American novelist and biographer, Jan 1991

Mental calculators

Tammet, Daniel, British autistic savant, Jan 2007

Mentally handicapped

Helfgott, David, Australian pianist, Mar 1997

Mentally ill

Helfgott, David, Australian pianist, Mar 1997

Merchant marine officers

Anderson, John W., American merchant marine officer, July 1953

Bisset, James, British ship captain, Yrbk 1946

Manning, Harry, May 1952, *Obit* Oct 1974

McLintock, Gordon, admiral, Nov 1953, *Obit* June 1990

Merchant seamen

Curran, Joseph E., American labor leader, Apr 1945, *Obit* Oct 1981

Merchants

Foyle, Gilbert, June 1954, *Obit* Jan 1972

Foyle, William Alfred, English bookseller, June 1954, *Obit* July 1963

Gimbel, Bernard F., Mar 1950, *Obit* Yrbk 1966

Hitz, Ralph, *Obit* Jan 1940

Igleheart, Austin S., Oct 1950

Johnston, Clement D., May 1955, *Obit* Jan 1980

Josephson, Walter S., *Obit* Mar 1940

Liggett, Louis Kroh, *Obit* July 1946

Marks of Broughton, Simon Marks, English merchant, Nov 1962, *Obit* Feb 1965

Martinez, Rueben, American bookstore owner, June 2005

Perkins, Milo, June 1942

Richards, Wayne E., July 1954

Selfridge, Harry Gordon, American-British merchant, Mar 1941, *Obit* June 1947

Swift, Harold Higgins, Feb 1950, *Obit* Sept 1962

Trefflich, Henry, Jan 1953, *Obit* Sept 1978

Wells, Gabriel, bookseller, *Obit* Yrbk 1946

Metallurgists

Alexander, Harry Held, American metallurgist, *Obit* Feb 1941

Khan, A. Q., Pakistani nuclear scientist, Jan 2004

Metalworkers

Abel, I. W., American labor leader, Nov 1965, *Obit* Sept 1987

Graff, Laurence, British jeweler, Sept 2011

McBride, Lloyd, steelworkers' union leader, Feb 1978, *Obit* Jan 1984

Toussaint, Jeanne, Feb 1955

Winston, Harry, jeweler, Apr 1965, *Obit* Feb 1979

Yellin, Samuel, American metalsmith, *Obit* Nov 1940

Yoshihara, Yoshindo, Japanese swordsmith, Jan 2005

Meteorologists

Bowie, Edward Hall, *Obit* Sept 1943

Devereaux, William Charles, *Obit* Sept 1941

Dunn, Gordon E., meteorologist, May 1966

Emanuel, Kerry A., American meteorologist, Jan 2007

Gray, William M., American meteorologist, Jan 2010

Hansen, James E., American physicist, meteorologist and government official, May 1996

Hayhoe, Katharine, Feb 2012

Houghton, John Theodore, British climatologist, Jan 2004

Howell, Wallace E., meteorologist, July 1950, *Obit* Sept 1999

Kimball, James Henry, *Obit* Feb 1944

Krick, Irving, meteorologist, July 1950, *Obit* Sept 1996

Marvin, Charles F., American meteorologist, *Obit* July 1943

McAdie, Alexander, meteorologist, *Obit* Yrbk 1943

Myers, Joel Norman, American meteorologist, Apr 2005

Orville, Howard T., May 1956, *Obit* July 1960

Reichelderfer, Francis Wilton, meteorologist, May 1949, *Obit* Mar 1983

Schaefer, Vincent J., American chemist and meteorologist, Jan 1948, *Obit* Sept 1993

Scott, Willard, American television weathercaster, July 1989

Spilhaus, Athelstan F., American meteorologist and oceanographer, June 1965, *Obit* June 1998

White, Robert M., American meteorologist, Mar 1964

Microbiologists

Alibek, Ken, Kazakh biological weapons expert, June 2002

Burnet, Frank Macfarlane, Australian bacteriologist, May 1954, *Obit* Oct 1985

Cox, Herald R., Apr 1961

De Kruif, Paul, author and bacteriologist, May 1942, July 1963, *Obit* Apr 1971

Domagk, Gerhard, German bacteriologist, Mar 1958, *Obit* June 1964

Enders, John F., American virologist, June 1955, *Obit* Jan 1986

Evans, Alice Catherine, American bacteriologist, Oct 1943, *Obit* Oct 1975

Fleming, Alexander, British bacteriologist, Apr 1944, *Obit* May 1955

Flexner, Simon, American physician, *Obit* June 1946

Florey, Howard, Australian bacteriologist, Apr 1944, *Obit* Apr 1968

Gurdon, John Bertrand, British microbiologist, Jan 2007

Hill, Justina Hamilton, Apr 1941

Horsfall, Frank L., American virologist, Mar 1941, Jan 1961, *Obit* Apr 1971

Jacob, Francois, French bacteriologist, Yrbk 1966, *Obit* Yrbk 2013

Koprowski, Hilary, Mar 1968, *Obit* Yrbk 2013

Krim, Mathilde, American geneticist and virologist, Aug 1987

Levine, Philip, American bacteriologist, May 1947, *Obit* Nov 1987

Montagnier, Luc, French virologist, Aug 1988

Peiris, Malik, Sri Lankan microbiologist, Jan 2003

Rivers, Thomas M., American virologist, July 1960, *Obit* July 1962

Robbins, Frederick C., American bacteriologist, June 1955, *Obit* Yrbk 2003

Steinhaus, Edward A., Yrbk 1955

Theiler, Max, American microbiologist, Jan 1952, *Obit* Oct 1972

Waksman, Selman Abraham, American microbiologist, May 1946, *Obit* Oct 1973

Weller, Thomas H., American virologist, June 1955, *Obit* Yrbk 2008

Midwives

Gaskin, Ina May, midwife, May 2001

Lubic, Ruth Watson, American nurse and midwife, Sept 1996

Military engineers

Christie, J. Walter, *Obit* Feb 1944

Ljungberg, Ernst Carl, Mar 1955

Moreell, Ben, June 1946, *Obit* Sept 1978

Military historians

Liddell Hart, Basil Henry, British military historian, Jan 1940, *Obit* Mar 1970

Military officials

Ailes, Stephen, lawyer and secretary of the army, Jan 1965, *Obit* Oct 2001

Al-Maktoum, Mohammed bin Rashid, United Arab Emirates prime minister, Apr 2008

Alexander, Clifford, American Secretary of the army, Sept 1977

Auchinleck, Claude John Eyre, British field marshal, Feb 1942, *Obit* May 1981

Campinchi, Cesar, *Obit* Apr 1941

Edison, Charles, July 1940, *Obit* Oct 1969

Feith, Douglas J., American military official, July 2008

Grigg, James, Apr 1942, *Obit* July 1964

Hensel, H. Struve, American lawyer and military official, Yrbk 1948, *Obit* July 1991

Kabila, Joseph, Congolese president, Sept 2001

Lehman, John F., secretary of the navy, Nov 1985

Ljungberg, Ernst Carl, Mar 1955

Moorer, Thomas H., American admiral, Apr 1971, *Obit* Yrbk 2004

Newberry, Truman Handy, *Obit* Nov 1945

Nitze, Paul H., American statesman, Feb 1962, *Obit* Mar 2005

Resor, Stanley R., American Secretary of the army, Sept 1969, *Obit* Yrbk 2012

Sullivan, John L., American Secretary of the navy, Sept 1948, *Obit* Oct 1982

Symington, Stuart, American senator, Sept 1945, July 1956, *Obit* Feb 1989

Warner, John W., American senator, Nov 1976

Zuckert, Eugene Martin, American Secretary of the air force, Apr 1952, *Obit* Yrbk 2000

Milliners

Mr. John, milliner, Oct 1956, *Obit* Sept 1993

Victor, Sally, Apr 1954, *Obit* July 1977

Mimes

Barrault, Jean-Louis, French actor and theatrical director, Mar 1953, *Obit* Mar 1994

Irwin, Bill, American actor and mime, Oct 1987

Marceau, Marcel, French mime, Feb 1957, *Obit* Yrbk 2007

Miners

Boyle, Tony, American labor leader, July 1970, *Obit* July 1985

Church, Sam, American labor leader, Oct 1981, *Obit* Yrbk 2009

Lewis, John L., American labor leader, Mar 1942, *Obit* July 1969

Miller, Arnold R., labor leader, Nov 1974, *Obit* Sept 1985

Murray, Philip, American labor leader, Jan 1941, Feb 1949, *Obit* Yrbk 1952

Scargill, Arthur, English labor leader, Jan 1985

Miniaturists

Baer, William J., American painter, *Obit* Nov 1941

Mining engineers

Beard, James T., American mining engineer, *Obit* Yrbk 1942

Mining executives

Brown, David M., American coal executive and veterans' leader, June 1950

Carroll, Cynthia, American mining executive, May 2011

Jonah, Sam, Ghanaian gold mining executive, Jan 2004

Oppenheimer, Harry Frederick, South African diamond mining executive, Feb 1961, *Obit* Nov 2000

Patino, Simon Iturri, Bolivian mining executive, Oct 1942, *Obit* May 1947

Missing persons

Hearst, Patricia Campbell, American socialite, Aug 1982

Waite, Terry, British church official, Sept 1986

Missionaries

Allan, John J., American Salvation Army leader, Jan 1950, *Obit* Jan 1961

Binder, Theodor, German physician and missionary, Sept 1964

Booth, Ballington, American evangelist and social reformer, *Obit* Nov 1940

Booth, Evangeline C., English evangelist and Salvation Army leader, Feb 1941, *Obit* Sept 1950

Browning, Webster E., *Obit* June 1942

Buchman, Frank Nathan Daniel, missionary, Oct 1940, *Obit* Nov 1961

Daly, Thomas A., *Obit* Mar 1941

Danner, Louise Rutledge, *Obit* Nov 1943

Davis, William Ellsworth, Apr 1940

Dooley, Tom, American physician and missionary, July 1957, *Obit* Mar 1961

Graves, Frederick Rogers, *Obit* July 1940

Keller, James, Oct 1951, *Obit* Apr 1977

Kepler, Asher Raymond, *Obit* Oct 1942

Leger, Paul-Emile, Canadian missionary, May 1953, *Obit* Jan 1992

Leiper, Henry Smith, Nov 1948, *Obit* Mar 1975

McCurdy, William Albert, *Obit* Feb 1942

Mellon, William Larimer, medical missionary, June 1965, *Obit* Oct 1989

Miller, Harry W., Mar 1962, *Obit* Mar 1977

Neill, Stephen, British bishop, Mar 1960

Newell, Horatio B., *Obit* Oct 1943

Seagrave, Gordon S., American physician and missionary, Nov 1943, *Obit* May 1965

Teresa, Yugoslav nun and missionary, Sept 1973, *Obit* Nov 1997

West, Annie Blythe, *Obit* May 1941

Mistresses

Lupescu, Elena, mistress of King Carol II of Romania, Oct 1940, *Obit* Aug 1977

Model and fashion agents

Ford, Eileen, American model agent, Oct 1971

Models (Persons)

Aymar, Luciana, Feb 2013

Brinkley, Christie, American model, Feb 1994

Bruni-Sarkozy, Carla, Italian model, singer and wife of French president Nicolas Sarkozy, Jan 2007

Bundchen, Gisele, Brazilian model, Jan 2007

Campbell, Naomi, British model, Feb 1997

Crawford, Cindy, American model, Aug 1993

Dirie, Waris, Somali model and social activist, Jan 2005

Dixit, Madhuri, Indian actress, Jan 2006

Fawcett, Farrah, American actress, Feb 1978, *Obit* Aug 2009

Hemingway, Margaux, American model and actress, Mar 1978, *Obit* Sept 1996

Herrera, Carolina, Venezuelan model and daughter of fashion designer Carolina Herrera, Mar 1996

Hounsou, Djimon, Beninese model and actor, Aug 2004

Hutton, Lauren, American model and actress, July 1994

Iman, Somali model, June 1995

Johnson, Beverly, American model, Sept 1994

Jones, Grace, American singer and actress, Sept 1987

Kebede, Liya, Ethiopian model and social activist, Jan 2005

Leslie, Lisa, American basketball player, Jan 1998

MacDowell, Andie, American model and actress, Nov 1999

McCrary, Jinx Falkenburg, television performer and model, July 1953

Raut, Ujjwala, Indian model, Jan 2004

Russo, Rene, American model and actress, July 1997

Sevigny, Chloe, American actress, Aug 2000

Seymour, Stephanie, American model, Oct 2002

Shields, Brooke, American model and actress, Oct 1982

Stephanie, Aug 1986

Tiegs, Cheryl, American model, Nov 1982

Twiggy, English model and actress, Oct 1968

Wek, Alek, Sudanese model, June 2001

Molecular biologists

Greider, Carol W., American molecular biologist, Feb 2008

Melton, Douglas, American molecular biologist, June 2008

Sinclair, David, Australian molecular biologist, Sept 2008

Sulston, John, English molecular biologist, Jan 2007

Vogelstein, Bert, molecular biologist, Jan 1996

Monks

Pierre, French abbot, Nov 1955

Monologists

Gray, Spalding, American monologist, Sept 1986, *Obit* Yrbk 2004

Mormon leaders

Benson, Ezra Taft, American Secretary of agriculture and Mormon leader, Feb 1953, *Obit* Aug 1994

Grant, Heber J., *Obit* June 1945

Kimball, Spencer W., American clergyman and Mormon leader, Feb 1979, *Obit* Jan 1986

McKay, David Oman, American Mormon leader, June 1951, *Obit* Mar 1970

Smith, George Albert, Nov 1947, *Obit* May 1951

Motion picture critics

Barrett, Wilton Agnew, American film critic, *Obit* Mar 1940

Crowther, Bosley, motion picture critic, July 1957, *Obit* Apr 1981

Lane, Anthony, British film critic, Nov 2008

Mitchell, Elvis, American film critic, July 2008

Shales, Tom, American television and film critic, Jan 2009

Starr, Cecile, American film critic, Mar 1955

White, Armond, American film critic, Oct 2006

Motion picture directors

Abu-Assad, Hany, Palestinian filmmaker and screenwriter, Jan 2006

Agresti, Alejandro, Argentine film director, Jan 2005

Al-Abnoudi, Attiyat, Egyptian documentary filmmaker, Jan 2005

Alda, Alan, American actor and film director, Jan 1977

Almendros, Nestor, Cuban cinematographer and director, Nov 1989, *Obit* May 1992

Almodovar, Pedro, Spanish film director, Sept 1990

Altman, Robert, American motion picture director and producer, Feb 1974, *Obit* Yrbk 2007

Amari, Raja, Tunisian screenwriter and motion picture director, Jan 2002

Amenabar, Alejandro, Spanish film director, Jan 2005

Anderson, Lindsay, British motion picture and theatrical director, Nov 1975, *Obit* Nov 1994

Anderson, Wes, American film director and screenwriter, May 2002

Angelopoulos, Theodoros, Greek film director and screenwriter, *Obit* Yrbk 2012

Antonioni, Michelangelo, Italian film director, Yrbk 1964, May 1993, *Obit* Yrbk 2007

Apted, Michael, British motion picture director, Feb 2000

Arau, Alfonso, Mexican motion picture director, Jan 2005

Arcand, Denys, Canadian film director, Oct 1990

Armstrong, Gillian, Australian film director, Aug 1995

Aronofsky, Darren, American screenwriter and director, Feb 2009

Arrabal, Fernando, French-Spanish dramatist, Sept 1972

Ataman, Kutlug, Turkish video artist and film director, Jan 2006

Attenborough, Richard, British actor and motion picture director, May 1984

Bakri, Mohammad, Palestinian filmmaker and actor, Jan 2005

Bancroft, Anne, American actress, June 1960, *Obit* Oct 2005

Barmak, Siddiq, Afghan motion picture director and screenwriter, Jan 2005

Baumbach, Noah, American film director and screenwriter, Oct 2010

Beatty, Warren, American actor, producer and director, May 1962, May 1988

Bekmambetov, Timur, Kazakhstani film director, Jan 2006

Benigni, Roberto, Italian actor and filmmaker, June 1999

Benoit-Levy, Jean, Oct 1947, *Obit* Nov 1959

Beresford, Bruce, Australian film director, Mar 1993

Bergman, Ingmar, Swedish film and theatrical director, Apr 1960, Oct 1981, *Obit* Sept 2007

Bertolucci, Bernardo, Italian film director, July 1974

Besson, Luc, French film director, Jan 2002

Bigelow, Kathryn, American film director, Mar 2010

Blackton, James Stuart, American film director and producer, *Obit* Oct 1941

Blier, Bertrand, French motion picture director, Oct 1988

Bogdanovich, Peter, American film director and producer, June 1972

Boll, Uwe, German film director, producer and screenwriter, Sept 2010

Bong, Joon-Ho, Korean film director, Jan 2007

Boorman, John, British film director, June 1988

Borzage, Frank, motion picture director, Yrbk 1946, *Obit* Sept 1962

Bourne, St. Clair, American documentary filmmaker, June 2000, *Obit* Mar 2008

Branagh, Kenneth, Irish actor and director, Apr 1997

Bresson, Robert, French film director, Jan 1971, *Obit* June 2000

Brook, Peter, English director and dramatist, May 1961

Bryan, Julien, American photographer and documentary filmmaker, July 1940, *Obit* Jan 1975

Bunuel, Luis, Mexican film director, Mar 1965, *Obit* Sept 1983

Burns, Ken, American documentary filmmaker, May 1992

Burtt, Ben, American motion picture sound designer, editor and documentary filmmaker, May 2003

Cacoyannis, Michael, Greek film and theatrical director, May 1966, *Obit* Yrbk 2011

Caetano, Adrian, Argentine film director and screenwriter, Jan 2003

Cameron, James, Canadian film director, producer and screenwriter, Jan 1998

Campion, Jane, New Zealand film director, Apr 1994

Capra, Frank, American motion picture director and producer, Apr 1948, *Obit* Oct 1991

Carewe, Edwin, *Obit* Jan 1940

Cassavetes, John, American actor and film director, July 1969, *Obit* Mar 1989

Chabrol, Claude, French film director, Jan 1975, *Obit* Yrbk 2010

Chadha, Gurinder, British motion picture director, Jan 2004

Chaplin, Charlie, English actor, director and producer, Yrbk 1940, Mar 1961, *Obit* Feb 1978

Chen, Joan, Chinese actress, Sept 1999

Chereau, Patrice, French theatrical, opera and film director, Jan 1990

Chopra, Yash, Indian film director and producer, Jan 2006, *Obit* Yrbk 2013

Cimino, Michael, motion picture director, Jan 1981

Clair, Rene, French motion picture director, Nov 1941, *Obit* May 1981

Cohen, Rob, American motion picture director and producer, Nov 2002

Columbus, Chris, American film director and screenwriter, Nov 2001

Coppola, Francis Ford, American film director, May 1974, July 1991

Corbijn, Anton, Dutch photographer, June 2006

Corman, Roger, American motion picture director, producer and screenwriter, Feb 1983

Costa-Gavras, Greek-French motion picture director, Sept 1972

Costner, Kevin, American actor and film director, June 1990

Crichton, Michael, American novelist, screenwriter and film director, Apr 1976, Nov 1993, *Obit* Apr 2009

Cronenberg, David, Canadian motion picture director, May 1992

Crowe, Cameron, American screenwriter and film director, Mar 1996

Cruze, James, motion picture director, *Obit* Sept 1942

Cuaron, Alfonso, Mexican film director, Jan 2003

Cukor, George, American motion picture director, Apr 1943, *Obit* Mar 1983

Dangarembga, Tsitsi, Zimbabwean novelist and film director, Jan 2006

Daniels, Lee, American film director and producer, June 2010

Dardenne, Jean-Pierre, Belgian film director and screenwriter, May 2011

Dardenne, Luc, Belgian film director and screenwriter, May 2011

Dassin, Jules, American film director, Mar 1971, *Obit* Yrbk 2008

Davis, Peter, American film and television producer and director, Feb 1983

De Mille, Cecil B., American motion picture director and producer, May 1942, *Obit* Mar 1959

De Niro, Robert, American actor, Aug 1976, May 1993

De Palma, Brian, American motion picture director, Sept 1982

De Sica, Vittorio, Italian motion picture director, July 1952, *Obit* Jan 1975

DeVito, Danny, American actor and film director, Feb 1988

Demarbre, Lee Gordon, Canadian film director, Jan 2003

Demme, Jonathan, American film director, Apr 1985

Deruddere, Dominique, Belgian motion picture director, Jan 2003

Deschanel, Caleb, American cinematographer and film director, Feb 2008

Dickerson, Ernest, American cinematographer and film director, July 2000

Dieterle, William, motion picture director, Sept 1943, *Obit* Feb 1973

Duras, Marguerite, French novelist, screenwriter and film director, Nov 1985, *Obit* May 1996

Duvall, Robert, American actor and motion picture director, July 1977

Duvivier, Julien, French motion picture director, July 1943, *Obit* Jan 1968

Edwards, Blake, American film director, producer and screenwriter, Jan 1983, *Obit* Yrbk 2011

Egoyan, Atom, Canadian film director and screenwriter, May 1994

Eisenstein, Sergei, Russian theatrical and motion picture director, May 1946, *Obit* Mar 1948

Ejiro, Zeb, Nigerian motion picture producer and director, Jan 2002

El-Tahri, Jihan, French-Egyptian documentary filmmaker, Aug 2009

Emmerich, Roland, German film director, producer and screenwriter, Nov 2000

Everson, Kevin Jerome, American filmmaker and video artist, Nov 2011

Eyre, Chris, Native American motion picture director, May 2003

Farrelly, Bobby, American screenwriter and film director, Sept 2001

Farrelly, Peter, American screenwriter and film director, Sept 2001

Fassbinder, Rainer Werner, German film director and producer, May 1977, *Obit* Aug 1982

Fellini, Federico, Italian motion picture director, June 1957, Oct 1980, *Obit* Jan 1994

Ferrer, Jose, American actor and director, May 1944, *Obit* Mar 1992

Fitzmaurice, George, *Obit* Aug 1940

Ford, John, American film director, Feb 1941, *Obit* Nov 1973

Forman, Milos, Czech film director, Yrbk 1971

Forster, Marc, Swiss film director, Jan 2007

Forsyth, Bill, Scottish motion picture director, Jan 1989

Foster, Jodie, American actress and film director, June 1981, Aug 1992

Fox, Eytan, Israeli motion picture director, Jan 2004

Frankenheimer, John, American film director, Oct 1964, *Obit* Oct 2002

Frears, Stephen, British motion picture director, Apr 1990, Jan 2004

Friedkin, William, American motion picture director, June 1987

Fuller, Samuel, American film director, Aug 1992, *Obit* Jan 1998

Furtado, Jorge, Brazilian film director, Jan 2006

Gentele, Goran, Sept 1972

Gilroy, Frank Daniel, American playwright, screenwriter and filmmaker, Oct 1965

Gimbel, Peter, motion picture director and producer, Jan 1982, *Obit* Aug 1987

Gitai, Amos, Israeli film director, Jan 2003

Godard, Jean Luc, French film director, May 1969, Oct 1993

Gondry, Michel, French film director, May 2007

Gonzalez Inarritu, Alejandro, Mexican film director, Jan 2003

Grant, Lee, actress and director, Mar 1974

Gray, F. Gary, American film director, Mar 2011

Greenaway, Peter, British film director, Feb 1991

Grubin, David, American documentary filmmaker, producer and screenwriter, Aug 2002

Guggenheim, Davis, American film director, Nov 2009

Hall, Peter, British theatrical director, Feb 1962

Hallstrom, Lasse, Swedish motion picture director, Feb 2005

Harron, Mary, Canadian motion picture director, Sept 2000

Hartley, Hal, American motion picture director and screenwriter, Aug 1995

Hawks, Howard, American motion picture director and producer, May 1972, *Obit* Mar 1980

Haynes, Todd, American film director, July 2003

Heckerling, Amy, motion picture director, July 1999

Herzog, Werner, German film director, Aug 1978

Hill, George Roy, American motion picture director, Apr 1977, *Obit* June 2003

Hitchcock, Alfred, Anglo-American motion picture director, Mar 1941, July 1960, *Obit* June 1980

Holland, Agnieszka, Polish film director and screenwriter, Jan 1998

Hong, Sang-Soo, Korean film director, Jan 2006

Hood, Gavin, South African motion picture director, Jan 2006

Hou, Hsiao-hsien, Taiwanese film director, July 1999

Howard, Ron, American actor and film director, Jan 1979, Aug 1995

Hughes, John, American film director, producer and screenwriter, Sept 1991, *Obit* Yrbk 2009

Huston, John, American film director and screenwriter, Feb 1949, Mar 1981, *Obit* Oct 1987

Imamura, Shohei, Japanese motion picture director, Jan 2002, *Obit* CB Int 2006

Itami, Juzo, Japanese actor and motion picture director, May 1990, *Obit* Mar 1998

Ivory, James, American motion picture director, July 1981

Jackson, Peter, New Zealand film director and screenwriter, Jan 2002

Jarecki, Eugene, American film director, May 2006

Jarmusch, Jim, American film director, Apr 1990

Jeunet, Jean-Pierre, French film director, Jan 2005

Jewison, Norman, Canadian motion picture director and producer, June 1979

Jodorowsky, Alejandro, Chilean film director and comic book writer, Jan 2005

Jones, Tommy Lee, American actor, Oct 1995

Jonze, Spike, American video and motion picture director, Apr 2003

Jordan, Neil, Irish film director, screenwriter and novelist, Aug 1993

Kaneko, Shu, Japanese film director, Jan 2007

Kanin, Garson, dramatist and director, Jan 1941, Oct 1952, *Obit* June 1999

Kanwar, Amar, Indian documentary filmmaker, Jan 2005

Kasdan, Lawrence, American film director and screenwriter, May 1992

Kassovitz, Mathieu, French actor and film director, Jan 2005

Kaurismaki, Aki, Finnish screenwriter and director, Jan 2003

Keaton, Diane, American actress and motion picture director, June 1978, May 1996

Keighley, William, motion picture director, Nov 1948, *Obit* Aug 1984

Kentridge, William, South African artist, Oct 2001

Kiarostami, Abbas, Iranian film director, July 1998

Kieslowski, Krzysztof, Polish motion picture director, May 1995, *Obit* May 1996

Kopple, Barbara, American film and television director, July 1998

Korda, Alexander, British film director and producer, Sept 1946, *Obit* Mar 1956

Korine, Harmony, American filmmaker, Feb 2010

Kramer, Stanley, American motion picture producer and director, May 1951, *Obit* May 2001

Kubrick, Stanley, American film director, Feb 1963, *Obit* May 1999

Kunuk, Zacharias, Canadian Inuit film director, Jan 2002

Kurosawa, Akira, Japanese motion picture director, Apr 1965, July 1991, *Obit* Nov 1998

Kurosawa, Kiyoshi, Japanese film director, Jan 2006

La Cava, Gregory, motion picture director, Yrbk 1941, *Obit* Apr 1952

Lang, Fritz, Austrian film director, June 1943, *Obit* Sept 1976

Laporte, Genevieve, French poet and documentary filmmaker, Jan 2005

Lean, David, British film director and producer, May 1953, June 1989, *Obit* June 1991

Leconte, Patrice, French motion picture director, Jan 2004

Lee, Ang, Taiwanese film director, Mar 1997

Leigh, Mike, English dramatist, motion picture director and screenwriter, June 1994

Lelouch, Claude, French motion picture director and producer, Nov 1982

Lester, Richard, British film director, Apr 1969

Levinson, Barry, American film director and screenwriter, July 1990

Loach, Ken, British film and television director, July 1995

Logan, Joshua, American theatrical and motion picture director, Oct 1949, *Obit* Aug 1988

Longo, Robert, American artist, Oct 1990

Losey, Joseph, American motion picture director, Yrbk 1969, *Obit* Aug 1984

Lucas, George, American film director, producer and screenwriter, Apr 1978, May 2002

Luhrmann, Baz, Australian film director, Jan 2002

Lumet, Sidney, American television and film director, Sept 1967, June 2005, *Obit* Yrbk 2011

Lupino, Ida, American actress and film director, Sept 1943, *Obit* Oct 1995

Lyne, Adrian, English motion picture director, Jan 1994

Maddin, Guy, Canadian film director, Jan 2006

Makhmalbaf, Samira, Iranian motion picture director, Jan 2003

Malick, Terrence, American film director, June 1999

Malkovich, John, American actor, May 1988

Malle, Louis, French motion picture director, Feb 1976, *Obit* Feb 1996

Mamet, David, American dramatist, Aug 1978, Mar 1998

Mamoulian, Rouben, Russian-American theatrical and film director, Mar 1949, *Obit* Jan 1988

Mankiewicz, Joseph L., American film director, producer and screenwriter, Sept 1949, *Obit* Apr 1993

Mann, Michael, American motion picture director and television producer, Jan 1993

Marshall, Penny, American actress and motion picture director, Mar 1980, May 1992

Mazursky, Paul, American film director, May 1980

McCarey, Leo, American motion picture director and producer, July 1946, *Obit* Sept 1969

McCarthy, Thomas, American actor and motion picture director, Jan 2012

Medem, Julio, Spanish film director and screenwriter, Jan 2003

Mehta, Deepa, Indian motion picture director, Jan 2002

Mendes, Sam, British theatrical and motion picture director, Oct 2002

Meyers, Nancy, American screenwriter, director and producer, Feb 2002

Miike, Takashi, Japanese motion picture director, Jan 2003

Mikhalkov, Nikita, Russian film director and actor, Oct 1995

Milland, Ray, actor, Feb 1946, *Obit* Apr 1986

Minac, Matej, Czech motion picture director, Jan 2002

Minnelli, Vincente, American film director, May 1975, *Obit* Sept 1986

Moodysson, Lukas, Swedish screenwriter and film director, Jan 2003

Morris, Errol, American documentary filmmaker, Feb 2001

Mungiu, Cristian, Romanian film director, Jan 2007

Nair, Mira, Indian motion picture director, Nov 1993

Nelson, Stanley, American documentary filmmaker, May 2005

Nichols, Mike, American theatrical and motion picture director, Mar 1961, Jan 1992

Nicholson, Jack, American actor, Oct 1974, Apr 1995

Nimoy, Leonard, American actor, Feb 1977

Nolan, Christopher, Anglo-American screenwriter and director, Jan 2005

Nolan, Jonathan, Apr 2013

Norton, Edward, American actor, June 2000

Noujaim, Jehane, Egyptian-American documentary filmmaker, Jan 2005

Nuridsany, Claude, French documentary filmmaker, June 1997

Oest, Paula van der, Dutch motion picture director, Jan 2003

Oliveira, Manoel de, Portuguese film director, Jan 2002

Ophuls, Marcel, motion picture and television director, June 1977

Osawa, Sandy Sunrising, American filmmaker, Jan 2001

Ouedraogo, Idrissa, Burkinabe film director and screenwriter, May 1993

Oz, Frank, puppeteer and motion picture director, Oct 1999

Ozon, Francois, French film director, Jan 2003

Pakula, Alan J., American film director and producer, June 1980, *Obit* Feb 1999

Panahi, Jafar, Iranian film director, Jan 2004

Park, Chan-Wook, Korean screenwriter and film director, Jan 2004

Parke, William, *Obit* Sept 1941

Parker, Alan, English motion picture director, Mar 1994

Pascal, Gabriel, Hungarian-British motion picture producer, Jan 1942, *Obit* Sept 1954

Payne, Alexander, American motion picture director and screenwriter, Feb 2003

Peck, Raoul, Haitian motion picture director and cabinet member, Jan 2002

Peckinpah, Sam, American motion picture director, May 1973, *Obit* Feb 1985

Peirce, Kimberly, American film director and screenwriter, Aug 2008

Peli, Oren, American film director and screenwriter, July 2013

Penn, Arthur, American film, theatrical and television director, Jan 1972, *Obit* Yrbk 2010

Penn, Sean, American actor and film director, June 1993

Perennou, Marie, French documentary filmmaker, June 1997

Perry, Frank, motion picture director and producer, Oct 1972, *Obit* Nov 1995

Petersen, Wolfgang, German motion picture director, July 2001

Poitier, Sidney, American actor and film director, May 1959, Sept 2000

Polanski, Roman, Polish film director, June 1969

Pollack, Sydney, American motion picture director, Sept 1986, *Obit* Sept 2008

Porter, Edwin S., American film director and producer, *Obit* June 1941

Powell, Michael, British screenwriter, film director and producer, Aug 1987, *Obit* Apr 1990

Preminger, Otto, American film director, July 1959, *Obit* June 1986

Quintero, Jose, theatrical director, Apr 1954, *Obit* May 1999

Raimi, Sam, American film director, July 2002

Rapp, Adam, American playwright and novelist, Mar 2011

Ratoff, Gregory, Aug 1943, *Obit* Feb 1961

Ray, Satyajit, Indian motion picture director, Mar 1961, *Obit* June 1992

Redford, Robert, American actor and motion picture director, Apr 1971, Mar 1982

Reed, Carol, British motion picture director and producer, Mar 1950, *Obit* June 1976

Reggio, Godfrey, American motion picture director and foundation official, July 1995

Reiner, Rob, American actor and film director, May 1988

Reitman, Ivan, Canadian film director, Mar 2001

Renoir, Jean, French film director and screenwriter, Yrbk 1959, *Obit* Apr 1979

Resnais, Alain, French film director, Feb 1965

Richardson, Tony, British film and theatrical director, Yrbk 1963, *Obit* Feb 1992

Ritt, Martin, motion picture director, Nov 1979, *Obit* Feb 1991

Robbins, Tim, American actor, July 1994

Roeg, Nicolas, British film director, Jan 1996

Roodt, Darrell, South African film director, Jan 2005

Rossellini, Roberto, Italian film director, July 1949, *Obit* Aug 1977

Rossen, Robert, American motion picture director, producer and screenwriter, Oct 1950, *Obit* Mar 1966

Rotha, Paul, English motion picture producer and director, Apr 1957, *Obit* May 1984

Salle, David, American painter and filmmaker, Sept 1986

Salles, Walter, Brazilian motion picture director, Jan 2004

Salman, Saad, Iraqi documentary filmmaker, Jan 2004

Saura, Carlos, Spanish motion picture director, Sept 1978

Schaefer, George, television director and producer, Feb 1970, *Obit* Jan 1998

Schlesinger, John, British motion picture director, Nov 1970, *Obit* Yrbk 2003

Schlondorff, Volker, German film director and screenwriter, Aug 1983

Schnabel, Julian, American painter and film director, Nov 1983

Schneider, Alan, American theatrical director, Yrbk 1969, *Obit* June 1984

Schrader, Paul, American screenwriter and film director, Aug 1981

Scorsese, Martin, American film director, Feb 1979, June 2007

Scott, Ridley, British film director, Oct 1991

Scott, Tony, British film director, Nov 2004, *Obit* Yrbk 2012

Seidelman, Susan, motion picture director, May 1990

Seitz, George B., *Obit* Aug 1944

Selwyn, Edgar, *Obit* Apr 1944

Sembene, Ousmane, Senegalese novelist and film director, Apr 1994, *Obit* Yrbk 2007

Sen, Ivan, Australian motion picture director and screenwriter, Jan 2002

Shah, Saira, British journalist and documentary filmmaker, Jan 2003

Shyamalan, M. Night, American film director and screenwriter, Mar 2003

Singer, Bryan, American motion picture director, Apr 2005

Singleton, John, American film director and screenwriter, Feb 1997

Sinise, Gary, American actor and director, Apr 1997

Soderbergh, Steven, American film director and screenwriter, Oct 1998

Soldati, Mario, Italian film director, screenwriter, novelist and short story writer, Apr 1958, *Obit* Nov 1999

Solomon, Philip S., American film director, Oct 2007

Sonnenfeld, Barry, American film director, Nov 1998

Spielberg, Steven, American film director and producer, July 1978, Feb 1996

Spurlock, Morgan, American documentary filmmaker, June 2013

Stevens, George, American motion picture director, Apr 1952, *Obit* May 1975

Stone, Oliver, American film director and screenwriter, June 1987

Strand, Paul, American photographer, July 1965, *Obit* May 1976

Sturges, Preston, American screenwriter and film director, Apr 1941, *Obit* Oct 1959

Sucksdorff, Arne, Swedish motion picture director, Apr 1956, *Obit* Sept 2001

Suzuki, Seijun, Japanese film director, Jan 2005

Swanberg, Joe, American film director and screenwriter, Nov 2010

Syberberg, Hans Jurgen, German motion picture producer and director, Apr 1983

Tanner, Alain, Swiss motion picture director, June 1990

Tati, Jacques, French actor and film director, Feb 1961, *Obit* Jan 1983

Tavernier, Bertrand, French film director, June 1988

To, Johnny, Chinese film director, Jan 2007

Toro, Guillermo del, Mexican film director, Jan 2004

Towne, Robert, American screenwriter and film director, June 1989

Townsend, Robert, American actor and motion picture director, May 1994

Trotta, Margarethe von, German film director, Nov 1988

Truffaut, Francois, French film director, Jan 1969, *Obit* Jan 1985

Tsai, Ming-Liang, Taiwanese film director, Jan 2002

Tsui, Hark, Chinese film director, Oct 2001

Ullmann, Liv, Norwegian actress and film director, Yrbk 1973

Vadim, Roger, French motion picture director, Jan 1984, *Obit* Aug 2000

Van Dyke, W. S., American motion picture director, *Obit* Apr 1943

Van Peebles, Mario, American actor and motion picture director, Nov 1993

Van Sant, Gus, American film director, Mar 1992

Varda, Agnes, French film director, July 1970

Vidor, King, motion picture director and producer, Feb 1957, *Obit* Jan 1983

Visconti, Luchino, Italian film director, Jan 1965, *Obit* May 1976

Wachowski, Andy, American film director and screenwriter, Sept 2003

Wachowski, Larry, American film director and screenwriter, Sept 2003

Wajda, Andrzej, Polish motion picture and theatrical director, July 1982

Warhol, Andy, American artist, Feb 1968, July 1986, *Obit* Apr 1987

Washington, Denzel, American actor, July 1992

Watanabe, Shinichiro, Japanese motion picture director, Jan 2006

Waters, John, American film director, June 1990

Wayne, John, American actor, Feb 1951, July 1972, *Obit* Aug 1979

Weir, Peter, Australian motion picture director, Aug 1984

Welles, Orson, American actor, director and producer, May 1941, Feb 1965, *Obit* Nov 1985

Wellman, William Augustus, American motion picture director, June 1950, *Obit* Feb 1976

Wenders, Wim, German film producer and director, July 1984

Wertmuller, Lina, Italian motion picture director, Sept 1976

Whitaker, Forest, American actor and motion picture director, Feb 1997

Wilcox, Herbert, Nov 1945, *Obit* July 1977

Wilder, Billy, Austrian-American film director and screenwriter, Feb 1951, Oct 1984, *Obit* Yrbk 2002

Wilder, Gene, American actor and motion picture director, Apr 1978

Williamson, Kevin, American screenwriter and director, Apr 2000

Wise, Robert, American film director, Sept 1989, *Obit* Apr 2006

Wiseman, Frederick, American documentary filmmaker, Yrbk 1974

Wong, Kar-Wai, Chinese film director and screenwriter, Apr 1998

Woo, John, Chinese motion picture director, Feb 1999

Wood, Sam, Nov 1943, *Obit* Nov 1949

Wyler, William, American film director, Jan 1951, *Obit* Sept 1981

Xie Jin, Chinese film director, Jan 2003

Yates, David, British film director, Apr 2011

Yu, Ronny, Chinese motion picture director, Jan 2004

Yuen, Cory, Chinese actor and motion picture director, Jan 2004

Zaillian, Steven, screenwriter and film director, Oct 2001

Zeffirelli, Franco, Italian director and set designer, Yrbk 1964

Zemeckis, Robert, American motion picture director, Sept 1997

Zhang Yimou, Chinese film director, Aug 1992, Jan 2003

Zinnemann, Fred, motion picture director, Mar 1953, *Obit* June 1997

Motion picture editors

Schoonmaker, Thelma, American film editor, Mar 1997

Wise, Robert, American film director, Sept 1989, *Obit* Apr 2006

Motion picture executives

Balaban, Barney, American motion picture executive, Oct 1946, *Obit* Apr 1971

Cook, Richard, American motion picture executive, July 2003

Eisner, Michael, American motion picture executive, Nov 1987

Geffen, David, American recording and motion picture executive, Jan 1992

Kalmus, Herbert T., American physicist and motion picture executive, Feb 1949, *Obit* Sept 1963

Katzenberg, Jeffrey, American motion picture executive, May 1995

Lansing, Sherry, American motion picture executive, May 1981

Lasky, Jesse Louis, American film producer, Apr 1947, *Obit* Mar 1958

Mayer, Louis B., American motion picture executive, June 1943, *Obit* Jan 1958

Pascal, Amy, American motion picture executive, Mar 2002

Puttnam, David, English motion picture producer, Feb 1989

Rackmil, Milton R., motion picture and recording executive, Nov 1952, *Obit* Jan 1992

Rank, Joseph Arthur Rank, British motion picture executive, Nov 1945, *Obit* May 1972

Shurlock, Geoffrey, Jan 1962, *Obit* June 1976

Skouras, Spyros P., American motion picture executive, June 1943, *Obit* Nov 1971

Snider, Stacey, American motion picture executive, Apr 2008

Warner, Albert, American motion picture executive, Jan 1945, *Obit* Jan 1968

Warner, Harry M., American motion picture executive, Jan 1945, *Obit* Oct 1958

Warner, Jack L., American motion picture executive, Jan 1945, *Obit* Nov 1978

Weinstein, Bob, American motion picture executive, Mar 1997

Weinstein, Harvey, American motion picture executive, Mar 1997

Yates, Herbert J., July 1949, *Obit* Mar 1966

Zanuck, Darryl F., American motion picture producer, Aug 1941, Mar 1954, *Obit* Feb 1980

Motion picture producers

Altman, Robert, American motion picture director and producer, Feb 1974, *Obit* Yrbk 2007

Anderson, Erica Kellner, Feb 1957, *Obit* Nov 1976

Blackton, James Stuart, American film director and producer, *Obit* Oct 1941

Bourne, St. Clair, American documentary filmmaker, June 2000, *Obit* Mar 2008

Brackett, Charles, American screenwriter and motion picture producer, Feb 1951, *Obit* Apr 1969

Bruckheimer, Jerry, American film producer, Mar 1999

Capra, Frank, American motion picture director and producer, Apr 1948, *Obit* Oct 1991

Chodorov, Edward, American dramatist and screenwriter, Apr 1944, *Obit* Nov 1988

Chopra, Yash, Indian film director and producer, Jan 2006, *Obit* Yrbk 2013

Cohen, Rob, American motion picture director and producer, Nov 2002

Daniels, Lee, American film director and producer, June 2010

Davis, Peter, American film and television producer and director, Feb 1983

De Laurentiis, Dino, Italian film producer, May 1965, *Obit* Yrbk 2011

De Mille, Cecil B., American motion picture director and producer, May 1942, *Obit* Mar 1959

De Rochemont, Louis, motion picture producer, Nov 1949, *Obit* Feb 1979

De Rochemont, Richard G., Oct 1945, *Obit* Sept 1982

De Sylva, Buddy, songwriter and motion picture producer, Sept 1943, *Obit* Sept 1950

Douglas, Michael, American actor and motion picture producer, Apr 1987

Dunne, Dominick, American novelist, journalist and true-crime writer, May 1999, *Obit* Yrbk 2009

Ejiro, Zeb, Nigerian motion picture producer and director, Jan 2002

Fletcher, C. Scott, Feb 1953

Ghai, Subhash, Indian motion picture producer, Jan 2003

Gimbel, Peter, motion picture director and producer, Jan 1982, *Obit* Aug 1987

Goldwyn, Samuel, American motion picture producer, Jan 1944, *Obit* Mar 1974

Gordon, Max, Oct 1943, *Obit* Jan 1979

Gordy, Berry, American recording executive, July 1975

Grade, Lew, British film and television producer, Aug 1979, *Obit* Mar 1999

Gregory, Paul, Apr 1956

Harrison, Joan, English screenwriter and producer, May 1944, *Obit* Oct 1994

Hawks, Howard, American motion picture director and producer, May 1972, *Obit* Mar 1980

Hudlin, Warrington, motion picture producer, May 1999

Hunter, Ross, motion picture producer, Yrbk 1967, *Obit* May 1996

Ice Cube (Musician), American rapper and actor, Aug 1995

Jewison, Norman, Canadian motion picture director and producer, June 1979

Kennedy, Kathleen, American film producer, Feb 2009

Korda, Alexander, British film director and producer, Sept 1946, *Obit* Mar 1956

Kramer, Stanley, American motion picture producer and director, May 1951, *Obit* May 2001

Lancaster, Burt, American actor, July 1953, Apr 1986, *Obit* Jan 1995

Lean, David, British film director and producer, May 1953, June 1989, *Obit* June 1991

Lelouch, Claude, French motion picture director and producer, Nov 1982

Levine, Joseph E., American motion picture producer, Oct 1979, *Obit* Sept 1987

Lloyd, Harold, American actor and producer, Sept 1949, *Obit* Apr 1971

McCarthy, Frank, motion picture producer, Sept 1945, *Obit* Feb 1987

Milchan, Arnon, Israeli film producer, Oct 2000

Nair, Mira, Indian motion picture director, Nov 1993

Nelson, Stanley, American documentary filmmaker, May 2005

Obst, Lynda Rosen, American motion picture producer, Oct 2000

Osawa, Sandy Sunrising, American filmmaker, Jan 2001

Osborne, Barrie M., American motion picture producer, Feb 2005

Pakula, Alan J., American film director and producer, June 1980, *Obit* Feb 1999

Parsons, Harriet, motion picture producer, Jan 1953, *Obit* Mar 1983

Pascal, Gabriel, Hungarian-British motion picture producer, Jan 1942, *Obit* Sept 1954

Porter, Edwin S., American film director and producer, *Obit* June 1941

Pressman, Edward, American film producer, Feb 2011

Reed, Carol, British motion picture director and producer, Mar 1950, *Obit* June 1976

Reitman, Ivan, Canadian film director, Mar 2001

Rosenthal, Jane, American film producer, Apr 2011

Rotha, Paul, English motion picture producer and director, Apr 1957, *Obit* May 1984

Schary, Dore, motion picture producer, May 1948, *Obit* Sept 1980

Selznick, David O., motion picture producer, June 1941, *Obit* Sept 1965

Sheehan, Winfield R., *Obit* Aug 1945

Silver, Joel, American motion picture producer, Nov 2003

Spielberg, Steven, American film director and producer, July 1978, Feb 1996

Stigwood, Robert, Australian film, recording and theatrical producer, Oct 1979

Syberberg, Hans Jurgen, German motion picture producer and director, Apr 1983

Talley, Truman H., *Obit* Mar 1942

Todd, Michael, American motion picture producer, Yrbk 1955, *Obit* June 1958

Vidor, King, motion picture director and producer, Feb 1957, *Obit* Jan 1983

Wald, Jerry, American motion picture producer, May 1952, *Obit* Sept 1962

Wanger, Walter, motion picture producer, June 1947, *Obit* Jan 1969

Wenders, Wim, German film producer and director, July 1984

Wilcox, Herbert, Nov 1945, *Obit* July 1977

Wiseman, Frederick, American documentary filmmaker, Yrbk 1974

Wolper, David L., American film and television producer, Oct 1986, *Obit* Yrbk 2010

Ziskin, Laura, American film producer, Oct 1997, *Obit* Yrbk 2011

Motion picture technicians

Armstrong, Vic, British motion picture stunt coordinator, Aug 2003

Motivational speakers

Carnegie, Dale, American self-improvement lecturer and writer, Yrbk 1941, Sept 1955

Marcinko, Richard, motivational speaker, Mar 2001

Robbins, Tony, American motivational speaker and author, July 2001

Motorcycle racers

Rossi, Valentino, Italian motorcycle racer, Jan 2005

Stewart, James, American motorcycle racer, Feb 2005

Mountaineers

Messner, Reinhold, Italian mountaineer, Mar 1980

Miura, Yuichiro, Japanese mountaineer, Jan 2005

Tenzing Norgay, Nepalese mountaineer, Oct 1954, *Obit* July 1986

Murder victims

Fossey, Dian, American primatologist, May 1985, *Obit* Feb 1986

Hearst, Patricia Campbell, American socialite, Aug 1982

Waite, Terry, British church official, Sept 1986

Murderers

Perry, Anne, English mystery novelist, Aug 1996

Museum administrators

Brown, J. Carter, American museum director, Apr 1976, *Obit* Yrbk 2002

Buechner, Thomas S., American painter and museum director, Feb 1961, *Obit* Yrbk 2010

De Montebello, Philippe, American museum director, Apr 1981

Force, Juliana, museum director, Mar 1941, *Obit* Oct 1948

Hightower, John B., July 1970, *Obit* Yrbk 2013

Lordkipanidze, David, Georgian paleontologist, Jan 2005

Martini, Helen, American zookeeper, July 1955

Rich, Daniel Catton, Yrbk 1955, *Obit* Feb 1977

Rorimer, James J., Yrbk 1955, *Obit* June 1966

Saint-Gaudens, Homer Schiff, museum director, Oct 1941, *Obit* Feb 1959

Taylor, Francis Henry, Jan 1940, *Obit* Feb 1958

Washburn, Gordon Bailey, Yrbk 1955

Wetmore, Alexander, ornithologist, Feb 1948, *Obit* Mar 1979

Woodward, Arthur Smith, British paleontologist, *Obit* Oct 1944

Museum personnel

Barton, William H., American astronomer and planetarium curator, *Obit* Aug 1944

Brown, J. Carter, American museum director, Apr 1976, *Obit* Yrbk 2002

D'Harnoncourt, Rene, Sept 1952, *Obit* Oct 1968

De Montebello, Philippe, American museum director, Apr 1981

Force, Juliana, museum director, Mar 1941, *Obit* Oct 1948

Golden, Thelma, American museum curator, Sept 2001

Hightower, John B., July 1970, *Obit* Yrbk 2013

Kellogg, Remington, paleontologist, Nov 1949

Lutz, Frank Eugene, entomologist and museum curator, *Obit* Jan 1944

Noble, G. Kingsley, zoologist and museum curator, *Obit* Jan 1941

Novacek, Michael J., American paleontologist and museum curator, Sept 2002

Rich, Daniel Catton, Yrbk 1955, *Obit* Feb 1977

Rorimer, James J., Yrbk 1955, *Obit* June 1966

Saint-Gaudens, Homer Schiff, museum director, Oct 1941, *Obit* Feb 1959

Sayles, R. W., *Obit* Yrbk 1942

Schuchert, Charles, *Obit* Jan 1943

Taylor, Francis Henry, Jan 1940, *Obit* Feb 1958

Washburn, Gordon Bailey, Yrbk 1955

Wetmore, Alexander, ornithologist, Feb 1948, *Obit* Mar 1979

Music administrators

Bing, Rudolf, British opera manager, Feb 1950, *Obit* Nov 1997

Bliss, Anthony Addison, lawyer and opera manager, Apr 1979, *Obit* Nov 1991

Fox, Carol, July 1978, *Obit* Sept 1981

Gentele, Goran, Sept 1972

Hurok, Sol, concert manager, Sept 1941, Apr 1956, *Obit* Apr 1974

Krainik, Ardis, opera manager, Nov 1991, *Obit* Mar 1997

McLaren, Malcolm, English rock musician, band manager and talent agent, Aug 1997, *Obit* Yrbk 2010

Mortier, Gerard, Belgian opera manager and director, July 1991

Sills, Beverly, American opera singer and manager, Nov 1969, Feb 1982, *Obit* Oct 2007

Stein, Jules, concert and theatrical agent, May 1967, *Obit* June 1981

Winter, Paul, saxophonist, Oct 1987

Zirato, Bruno, Yrbk 1959, *Obit* Jan 1973

Music arrangers

Elfman, Danny, American composer, Jan 2007

Jobim, Antonio Carlos, Brazilian singer and songwriter, July 1991, *Obit* Feb 1995

Jones, Quincy, American composer and record producer, Feb 1977

Kay, Hershy, Mar 1962, *Obit* Feb 1982

Mancini, Henry, American composer, July 1964, *Obit* Aug 1994

Williams, John T., American composer, Oct 1980

Music critics

Colles, H. C., *Obit* Apr 1943

Darrell, R. D., music critic, Sept 1955, *Obit* June 1988

Downes, Olin, music critic and historian, Mar 1943, *Obit* Oct 1955

Elson, Arthur, Mar 1940

Korngold, Julius, *Obit* Oct 1945

Marcus, Greil, American music critic, Oct 1999

Pareles, Jon, American music critic, Nov 2008

Music publishers

Acuff, Roy, singer, June 1976, *Obit* Jan 1993

Daniels, Charles N., composer, *Obit* Mar 1943

Forsyth, Cecil, *Obit* Feb 1942

Jacobi, Victor, European music publisher, *Obit* Nov 1942

Von Tilzer, Harry, American songwriter and music publisher, *Obit* Mar 1946

Music teachers

Allen, Betty, American opera singer, Nov 1990, *Obit* Yrbk 2009

Antoine, Josephine, American opera singer, Aug 1944

Baur, Bertha, American music teacher, *Obit* Nov 1940

Bigelow, William P., American music teacher, *Obit* May 1941

Curtin, Phyllis, American opera singer and teacher, Sept 1964

Dornay, Louis, *Obit* Sept 1940

Duncan, Todd, singer and voice teacher, July 1942, *Obit* May 1998

Flesch, Carl, Hungarian violinist, *Obit* Jan 1945

Haas, Jonathan, American timpanist, June 2003

Lhevinne, Rosina, Russian-American pianist and teacher, Nov 1961, *Obit* Jan 1977

Maddy, Joseph E., musician and educator, Apr 1946, *Obit* May 1966

Marius, Emilie Alexander, *Obit* Apr 1940

Mittell, Philipp, *Obit* Mar 1943

Samaroff, Olga, American pianist and music teacher, Mar 1946, *Obit* June 1948

Schoen-Rene, Anna Eugenie, *Obit* Jan 1943

Singher, Martial, French opera singer and voice teacher, Feb 1947, *Obit* May 1990

Whiteman, Wilberforce James, *Obit* Jan 1940

Zajick, Dolora, American opera singer and teacher, May 2000

Music therapists

Seymour, Harriet Ayer, music therapist, *Obit* Sept 1944

Musicians

3D (Singer), English singer and DJ, June 2004

A-mei, Taiwanese pop singer, Jan 2002

Adamowski, Timothee, Polish violinist, *Obit* May 1943

Adams, Edie, American actress and singer, Feb 1954, *Obit* Yrbk 2008

Adams, Stanley, American lyricist, Feb 1954, *Obit* Mar 1994

Adams, Yolanda, American gospel singer, Mar 2002

Adderley, Cannonball, American jazz saxophonist, July 1961, *Obit* Oct 1975

Ade, King Sunny, Nigerian pop musician, Nov 1994

Adele, British singer, July 2009

Adler, Kurt Herbert, opera director and conductor, Mar 1979, *Obit* Apr 1988

Adler, Larry, American harmonica player, Feb 1944, *Obit* Oct 2001

Aguilera, Christina, American singer, Aug 2000

Akita, Masami, Japanese electronic musician, Jan 2006

Akon, Senegalese-American rap and rhythm and blues singer, Jan 2008

Al-Jazairia, Warda, Algerian singer, Jan 2006

Al-Sahir, Kazem, Iraqi singer, Jan 2003

Alagna, Roberto, French opera singer, July 1997

Albanese, Licia, Italian opera singer, Mar 1946

Alberghetti, Anna Maria, Italian singer, Jan 1955

Allen, J. D., American jazz saxophonist, Nov 2010

Allen, Lily, British pop singer and songwriter, Jan 2007

Allen, Peter, Australian singer and songwriter, Mar 1983, *Obit* Aug 1992

Amato, Pasquale, Italian opera singer, *Obit* Oct 1942

Ameling, Elly, Dutch singer, Oct 1982

Anderson, June, opera singer, May 1991

Anderson, Leroy, American composer, Sept 1952, *Obit* Aug 1975

Anderson, Marian, American opera singer, May 1940, Apr 1950, *Obit* June 1993

Andre 3000, American rapper, Apr 2004

Angeles, Victoria de los, Spanish opera singer, Feb 1955, *Obit* Aug 2005

Anka, Paul, Canadian singer and songwriter, Feb 1964

Ansermet, Ernest, Swiss conductor, July 1949, *Obit* Apr 1969

Antheil, George, American composer, July 1954, *Obit* Apr 1959

Anu, Christine, Australian singer and actress, Jan 2003

Apl. de. Ap (Musician), American singer, Oct 2006

Apple, Fiona, American singer and songwriter, Nov 2006

Argerich, Martha, Argentine pianist, Sept 1999

Armstrong, Billie Joe, American singer and songwriter, Aug 2005

Arnold, Eddy, American country singer, Mar 1970, *Obit* Yrbk 2008

Arrau, Claudio, Chilean pianist, Jan 1942, Nov 1986, *Obit* Aug 1991

Arroyo, Martina, American opera singer, Feb 1971

Ascher, Leo, Austrian composer, *Obit* Apr 1942

Ashanti (Singer), American rhythm and blues singer, Jan 2003

Ashford, Nickolas, American singer and songwriter, Apr 1997, *Obit* Yrbk 2011

Ashkenazy, Vladimir, Russian pianist and conductor, July 1967

Auger, Arleen, American opera singer, Feb 1989, *Obit* Aug 1993

Babbitt, Milton, American composer, Sept 1962, *Obit* Yrbk 2011

Babyface, American singer, songwriter and producer, July 1998

Baccaloni, Salvatore, Oct 1944, *Obit* Feb 1970

Bacharach, Burt, American composer, Oct 1970

Bachauer, Gina, Greek pianist, June 1954, *Obit* Sept 1977

Bada, Angelo, Italian opera singer, *Obit* May 1941

Badu, Erykah, American singer and songwriter, Apr 1998

Bailey, Pearl, American singer and actress, June 1955, Oct 1969, *Obit* Oct 1990

Baker, Anita, American singer, Apr 1989

Baker, Josephine, American actress, singer and dancer, July 1964, *Obit* June 1975

Balsom, Alison, Trumpeter, Mar 2012

Bampton, Rose, American opera singer, Mar 1940, *Obit* Yrbk 2007

Bantock, Granville, English composer, *Obit* Yrbk 1946

Barber, Patricia, American jazz singer and pianist, Sept 2007

Barber, Samuel, American composer, Sept 1944, Sept 1963, *Obit* Mar 1981

Barbieri, Fedora, Italian opera singer, Feb 1957, *Obit* Aug 2003

Barbirolli, John, British conductor, Yrbk 1940, *Obit* Oct 1970

Barker, Travis, American drummer, Aug 2002

Bartok, Bela, Hungarian composer, Sept 1940, *Obit* Oct 1945

Barzin, Leon, conductor, May 1951, *Obit* Aug 1999

Bass, Lance, American singer, Nov 2000

Baum, Kurt, opera singer, Sept 1956, *Obit* Feb 1990

Bax, Arnold, English composer, Sept 1943, *Obit* Jan 1954

Bear, Christopher, American drummer, Sept 2011

Beecham, Thomas, English conductor, Yrbk 1941, Jan 1951, *Obit* May 1961

Behrens, Hildegard, German opera singer, Jan 1985, *Obit* Yrbk 2009

Bennett, Richard Rodney, English composer, Mar 1992, *Obit* Yrbk 2013

Bennett, Tony, American singer, Mar 1965, June 1995

Bennington, Chester, American singer, Mar 2002

Berganza, Teresa, Spanish opera singer, Jan 1979

Bergen, Polly, actress and singer, Sept 1958

Bergonzi, Carlo, Italian opera singer, Nov 1992

Berigan, Bunny, American jazz trumpet player, *Obit* July 1942

Berlin, Steve, American keyboardist and saxophonist, Oct 2005

Berman, Lazar, Russian pianist, Sept 1977, *Obit* Yrbk 2005

Bernstein, Elmer, American composer, June 2003

Berryman, Guy, Scottish bassist, May 2004

Beyonce, American singer and actress, Aug 2001

Bhosle, Asha, Indian singer, Jan 2006

Big Boi, American rapper, Apr 2004

Biggs, E. Power, organist, Nov 1950, *Obit* May 1977

Bing, Rudolf, British opera manager, Feb 1950, *Obit* Nov 1997

Bjork, Icelandic singer, July 2001

Bjorling, Jussi, Swedish opera singer, Sept 1947, *Obit* Nov 1960

Bland, Bobby Blue, singer, *Obit* Yrbk 2013

Blegen, Judith, American opera singer, June 1977

Blythe, Stephanie, American opera singer, Aug 2004

Bohlen, Dieter, German pop singer, songwriter and producer, Jan 2006

Bohm, Karl, Austrian conductor, June 1968, *Obit* Oct 1981

Bolton, Michael, American singer and songwriter, Aug 1993

Bon Jovi, Jon, American singer and actor, Jan 1990

Bonci, Alessandro, Italian opera singer, *Obit* Sept 1940

Bond, Jessie, English singer and actress, *Obit* Aug 1942

Bonynge, Richard, Australian conductor, Feb 1981

Borodina, Olga, Russian opera singer, Feb 2002

Bostic, Onika, Trinidadian singer, Jan 2004

Bostridge, Ian, British classical singer, Jan 2006

Boult, Adrian Cedric, English conductor, Mar 1946, *Obit* Apr 1983

Bourdon, Rob, American drummer, Mar 2002

Boy George, British pop singer and songwriter, Oct 1985

Boyer, Lucien, *Obit* Aug 1942

Brailowsky, Alexander, French pianist, June 1956, *Obit* June 1976

Branch, Michelle, American singer and songwriter, May 2005

Branzell, Karin, Swedish opera singer, Feb 1946, *Obit* Feb 1975

Braxton, Toni, American singer, Sept 2000

Bregovic, Goran, Bosnian composer, Jan 2006

Brel, Jacques, French singer and songwriter, Mar 1971, *Obit* Nov 1978

Bressanutti, Daniel, Belgian rock musician, Jan 2006

Brico, Antonia, conductor, Sept 1948, *Obit* Oct 1989

Bridge, Frank, English composer and conductor, *Obit* Mar 1941

Bridges, Jeff, American actor, Mar 1991

Bridgewater, Dee Dee, American jazz singer, Oct 2008

Britten, Benjamin, English composer, Oct 1942, Apr 1961, *Obit* Feb 1977

Broemel, Carl, American rock guitarist and singer, Nov 2008

Bronfman, Yefim, American pianist, Jan 2007

Brooks, Garth, American country singer, Mar 1992

Brown, Bobby, American singer, Apr 1991

Browne, Jackson, American singer and songwriter, Oct 1989

Browning, John, American pianist, May 1969, *Obit* June 2003

Bruni-Sarkozy, Carla, Italian model, singer and wife of French president Nicolas Sarkozy, Jan 2007

Bryant, Anita, American singer, Nov 1975

Bryson, David, American guitarist, Mar 2003

Buble, Michael, Canadian singer, May 2009

Buck, Gene, Feb 1941, *Obit* May 1957

Buckland, Jon, English guitarist, May 2004

Bumbry, Grace, American opera singer, Mar 1964

Bunton, Jaleel, American drummer, Apr 2009

Burleigh, Harry T., American singer and composer, Aug 1941, *Obit* Oct 1949

Burnett, Carol, American actress, Jan 1962, Nov 1990

Burnside, Jay, Finnish drummer, Jan 2003

Burr, Henry, *Obit* May 1941

Burstyn, Mike, American actor and singer, May 2005

Busch, Fritz, German conductor, Jan 1946, *Obit* Oct 1951

Bush, Kate, English singer and songwriter, Mar 1995

Butler, Win, American singer and songwriter, Jan 2007

Byrne, David, Scottish-American rock singer and songwriter, June 1985

Caballe, Montserrat, Spanish opera singer, June 1967

Cahn, Sammy, American lyricist, Nov 1974, *Obit* Mar 1993

Callas, Maria, American opera singer, Sept 1956, *Obit* Nov 1977

Calleros, Juan, Mexican bassist, Jan 2005

Cam'Ron (Musician), American rapper, Feb 2011

Cameron, Basil, English conductor, Apr 1943

Campora, Giuseppe, Italian opera singer, July 1957

Cantor, Eddie, singer and comedian, Nov 1941, May 1954, *Obit* Jan 1965

Canty, Brendan, American drummer, Mar 2002

Carey, Mariah, American singer, July 1992

Carlos, Wendy, American composer, Sept 2008

Carpenter, John Alden, composer, May 1947, *Obit* May 1951

Carroll, Diahann, American singer and actress, Sept 1962

Carter, Betty, American jazz singer, Mar 1982, *Obit* Jan 1999

Carter, James, American jazz saxophonist, Feb 1997

Carter, Jimmy, American gospel singer, Oct 2001

Carter, Nick, American singer, May 2000

Carter, Regina, American jazz violinist, Oct 2003

Casablancas, Julian, American singer and songwriter, Feb 2007

Casadesus, Robert, French pianist and composer, Jan 1945, *Obit* Nov 1972

Casals, Pablo, Spanish cellist, Nov 1950, Nov 1964, *Obit* Yrbk 1973

Cave, Nick, Australian singer and songwriter, June 2005

Cester, Chris, Australian drummer and singer, Jan 2005

Cester, Nic, Australian guitarist and singer, Jan 2005

Chailly, Riccardo, Italian conductor, June 1991

Chaminade, Cecile, French composer, *Obit* June 1944

Champion, Will, English drummer, May 2004

Chao, Manu, French singer, Jan 2002

Chapman, Steven Curtis, American Christian rock singer and songwriter, Oct 2004

Chapman, Tracy, American singer and songwriter, Aug 1989

Chasez, JC, American singer, Nov 2000

Chassagne, Regine, Canadian singer and instrumentalist, Jan 2007

Chavchavadze, George, Mar 1943, *Obit* Apr 1962

Cher, American singer and actress, Jan 1974, June 1991

Cherkassky, Shura, American pianist, Oct 1990, *Obit* Mar 1996

Chesney, Kenny, American country singer, May 2004

Chestnut, Cyrus, American jazz pianist, July 2009

Chevalier, Maurice, French singer and actor, Jan 1948, Mar 1969, *Obit* Feb 1972

Chicherina, Julia, Russian pop singer, Jan 2006

Chotzinoff, Samuel, pianist, Apr 1940, *Obit* Apr 1964

Chung, Kyung-Wha, Korean violinist, Feb 2007

Chung, Myung-Whun, Korean pianist and conductor, Aug 1990

Clark, Petula, English singer, Feb 1970

Clarkson, Kelly, American singer and contestant on reality TV show American idol, Sept 2006

Claussen, Julia, *Obit* June 1941

Clegg, Johnny, South African singer and songwriter, Jan 2005

Cliburn, Van, American pianist, Sept 1958, *Obit* Yrbk 2013

Cline, Nels, American guitarist, Feb 2010

Clooney, Rosemary, American singer, Feb 1957, *Obit* Nov 2002

Coates, John, *Obit* Oct 1941

Cockburn, Bruce, Canadian singer and songwriter, Jan 2005

Cocker, Jarvis, English rock singer, Nov 1998

Codenys, Patrick, Belgian rock musician, Jan 2006

Cohen, Leonard, Canadian poet, novelist, singer and songwriter, June 1969

Cole, Nat King, American singer and pianist, Feb 1956, *Obit* Mar 1965

Cole, Natalie, American singer, Nov 1991

Coleman, Steve, American jazz saxophonist, July 2004

Collins, Judy, American singer and songwriter, Apr 1969

Collins, Phil, British singer, songwriter and drummer, Nov 1986

Colvin, Shawn, singer, Mar 1999

Common, American rapper, Feb 2012

Como, Perry, American singer, Apr 1947, *Obit* July 2001

Conlee, Jenny, American keyboardist, Aug 2007

Conley, Eugene, July 1954, *Obit* Feb 1982

Conner, Nadine, American opera singer, Jan 1955, *Obit* Aug 2003

Converse, Frederick Shepherd, composer, *Obit* Aug 1940

Cook, Jamie, British rock singer, Jan 2006

Cook, Murray, Australian actor and singer, Jan 2004

Cool, Tre, American drummer, Aug 2005

Coolio, American rapper, Aug 1998

Copland, Aaron, American composer, Sept 1940, Mar 1951, *Obit* Yrbk 1991

Corelli, Franco, Italian opera singer, Feb 1964, *Obit* Mar 2004

Cotrubas, Ileana, Oct 1981

Crandall, Martin, American keyboardist, June 2007

Crawford, Michael, English actor and singer, Jan 1992

Crespin, Regine, French opera singer, Sept 1979, *Obit* Yrbk 2007

Criss, Peter, American drummer, Apr 1999

Crosby, Bing, American singer and actor, Sept 1941, June 1953, *Obit* Jan 1978

Crow, Sheryl, American singer and songwriter, May 1998

Cruz, Celia, Cuban-American singer, July 1983, *Obit* Nov 2003

Cui Jian, Chinese rock musician, Jan 2002

Curran, Pearl G., *Obit* June 1941

Curzon, Clifford, English pianist, May 1950, *Obit* Oct 1982

D'Angelo, American singer, May 2001

DMX, American rapper, Aug 2003

Daddy G (Singer), English singer and DJ, June 2004

Dale, Clamma, Apr 1979

Danforth, William, *Obit* June 1941

Daratista, Inul, Indonesian singer and dancer, Jan 2003

David, Hal, songwriter, Sept 1980, *Obit* Yrbk 2012

Davidovich, Bella, Russian pianist, May 1989

Davies, Dennis Russell, conductor, May 1993

Davis, Andrew, British conductor, May 1983

Davis, Colin, British conductor, Nov 1968, *Obit* Yrbk 2013

Davis, Sammy, American actor and singer, Sept 1956, July 1978, *Obit* July 1990

Day, Doris, American singer and actress, Apr 1954

De Leath, Vaughn, *Obit* July 1943

De Luca, Giuseppe, Italian opera singer, Mar 1947, *Obit* Oct 1950

De Sylva, Buddy, songwriter and motion picture producer, Sept 1943, *Obit* Sept 1950

DeBarge, El, American singer, June 2011

DeGaetani, Jan, opera singer, Oct 1977

DeLonge, Tom, American guitarist, Aug 2002

DePreist, James, conductor, Oct 1990

Dearie, Blossom, American singer, Feb 1989, *Obit* Yrbk 2009

Deasy, Mary, Yrbk 1958

Del Monaco, Mario, Feb 1957, *Obit* Jan 1983

Della Casa, Lisa, Swiss opera singer, July 1956, *Obit* Yrbk 2013

Della Chiesa, Vivian, American opera singer, Nov 1943

Dello Joio, Norman, American composer, Sept 1957, *Obit* Yrbk 2008

Delson, Brad, American guitarist, Mar 2002

Deschanel, Zooey, American actress, Aug 2012

Desplat, Alexandre, French composer, June 2011

Dett, Robert Nathaniel, composer, *Obit* Nov 1943

Diamond, David, American composer, Nov 1966, *Obit* Yrbk 2005

Diamond, Neil, American singer and songwriter, May 1981

Dirnt, Mike, American bassist and singer, Aug 2005

Dixon, Dean, conductor, Apr 1943, *Obit* Jan 1977

Dixon, Willie, American blues singer, May 1989, *Obit* Apr 1992

Dobbs, Mattiwilda, American opera singer, Sept 1955

Dodge, Charles, American composer, Aug 2007

Dohnanyi, Christoph von, German conductor, Oct 1985

Dorough, Howie, American singer, May 2000

Downey, Morton, American singer, July 1949, *Obit* Jan 1986

Drake, Alfred, actor and singer, Apr 1944, *Obit* Sept 1992

Drake, Bobby, American drummer, Sept 2010

Drexler, Jorge, Uruguayan singer and songwriter, Jan 2005

Droste, Ed, American guitarist and singer, Sept 2011

Druckman, Jacob, composer, May 1981, *Obit* Aug 1996

Duff, Hilary, American actress and singer, Feb 2006

Duke, Vernon, American composer, June 1941, *Obit* Mar 1969

Dunmall, Paul, British jazz saxophonist, May 2011

Dunne, Irene, American actress and singer, Aug 1945, *Obit* Nov 1990

Durbin, Deanna, American singer and actress, June 1941, *Obit* Yrbk 2013

Duritz, Adam, American singer and songwriter, Mar 2003

Dyer-Bennet, Richard, singer, June 1944, *Obit* Feb 1992

Eckstine, Billy, American jazz singer, July 1952, *Obit* Apr 1993

Eddy, Nelson, singer and actor, Feb 1943, *Obit* May 1967

Edwards, Clarence, Antiguan keyboardist and singer, Jan 2004

Edwards, David, Antiguan bassist, Jan 2004

Edwards, Gus, songwriter, *Obit* Yrbk 1945

Edwards, Joan, singer and composer, Oct 1953, *Obit* Oct 1981

Edwards, Kathleen, Canadian singer and songwriter, Oct 2012

Edwards, Toriano, Antiguan guitarist and singer, Jan 2004

Eggerth, Marta, Austro-Hungarian singer and actress, Nov 1943

Einem, Gottfried von, Austrian composer, July 1953, *Obit* Sept 1996

Eisler, Hanns, German composer, May 1942, *Obit* Nov 1962

Eldridge, Roy, American trumpet player, Mar 1987, *Obit* Apr 1989

Elias, Rosalind, Jan 1967

Elling, Kurt, American jazz singer, Jan 2005

Elliott, Joe, English singer, Jan 2003

Elman, Mischa, American violinist, Oct 1945, *Obit* June 1967

Elzy, Ruby, *Obit* Aug 1943

Engel, Kurt, *Obit* Mar 1942

Eschenbach, Christoph, German pianist and conductor, Aug 1989

Estefan, Gloria, Cuban-American singer and songwriter, Oct 1995

Estes, Simon, American opera singer, Aug 1986

Evans, Faith, American singer and songwriter, Feb 1999

Eve (Singer), American rapper and actress, July 2003

Ewing, Maria, American opera singer, Apr 1990

Falla, Manuel de, Spanish composer, *Obit* Yrbk 1946

Fals, Iwan, Indonesian singer and songwriter, Jan 2002

Farrell, Eileen, American singer, Feb 1961, *Obit* June 2002

Fassbaender, Brigitte, German opera singer, June 1994

Fatone, Joey, American singer, Nov 2000

Fatt, Jeff, Australian actor and singer, Jan 2004

Faussart, Celia, French singer, Jan 2003

Faussart, Helene, French singer, Jan 2003

Feinstein, Michael, American pianist and singer, Apr 1988

Feist (Musician), Canadian singer and songwriter, June 2008

Feltsman, Vladimir, Russian pianist, Apr 1988

Fenton, George, English composer, July 2010

Fergie, American singer, Oct 2006

Fernandez, Alejandro, Mexican singer, Jan 2005

Ferrier, Kathleen, British opera singer, Oct 1951, *Obit* Yrbk 1953

Fiedler, Arthur, American conductor, Sept 1945, May 1977, *Obit* Sept 1979

Field, Anthony, Australian actor and singer, Jan 2004

Fields, Gracie, English actress and singer, Apr 1941, *Obit* Nov 1979

Finn, Craig, American singer and songwriter, Sept 2010

Firkusny, Rudolf, Czech pianist, Oct 1979, *Obit* Sept 1994

Fischer-Dieskau, Dietrich, German opera singer, Feb 1967, *Obit* Yrbk 2012

Fisher, Eddie, American singer, Oct 1954, *Obit* Yrbk 2010

Fisher, Fred, songwriter and composer, *Obit* Mar 1942

Fishman, Jon, American drummer, July 2003

Fitzgerald, Ella, American singer, Oct 1956, July 1990, *Obit* Aug 1996

Flack, Roberta, American singer, Nov 1973

Flagstad, Kirsten, Norwegian opera singer, May 1947, *Obit* Jan 1963

Flanagan, Tommy, American pianist, Apr 1995, *Obit* Mar 2002

Flansburgh, John, guitarist, Nov 1999

Fleck, Bela, American banjoist, Nov 1996

Fleisher, Leon, American pianist and conductor, Jan 1971

Fleming, Renee, American opera singer, May 1997

Florez, Juan Diego, Peruvian opera singer, Jan 2007

Fodor, Eugene, American violinist, Apr 1976, *Obit* Yrbk 2011

Followill, Caleb, American singer and guitarist, July 2010

Followill, Jared, American bassist, July 2010

Followill, Matthew, American guitarist, July 2010

Followill, Nathan, American drummer, July 2010

Foo, Sharin, Danish singer and bassist, Jan 2004

Ford, Tennessee Ernie, singer, Mar 1958, *Obit* Jan 1992

Forrester, Maureen, Canadian opera singer, July 1962, *Obit* Yrbk 2010

Fou Ts'ong, Chinese pianist, Jan 2003

Fountain, Clarence, American gospel singer, Oct 2001

Fox, Carol, July 1978, *Obit* Sept 1981

Fox, Virgil, Jan 1964, *Obit* Jan 1981

Frager, Malcolm, pianist, Apr 1967, *Obit* Aug 1991

Fraiture, Nikolai, American bassist, Feb 2007

Frampton, Peter, English guitarist and singer, May 1978

Francescatti, Zino, French violinist, Oct 1947, *Obit* Nov 1991

Francis, Connie, singer, July 1962

Franklin, Kirk, American gospel rap singer, Mar 2000

Frehley, Ace, American guitarist, Apr 1999

Froese, Edgar, German electronic musician, Jan 2005

Fuchs, Joseph, violinist, Oct 1962, *Obit* May 1997

Fujii, Satoko, Japanese jazz pianist, June 2010

Funk, Chris, American guitarist and thereminist, Aug 2007

G, Kenny, American saxophonist, Nov 1995

Gara, Jeremy, Canadian drummer, Jan 2007

Garcia, Jerry, American guitarist and singer, May 1990, *Obit* Oct 1995

Garfunkel, Art, American singer and actor, June 1974

Garland, Judy, American singer and actress, Nov 1941, Yrbk 1952, *Obit* Sept 1969

Gary, John, singer and songwriter, July 1967, *Obit* Mar 1998

Gavrilov, Andrei, Russian pianist, Oct 2000

Gayle, Crystal, singer, Mar 1986

Gedda, Nicolai, Swedish opera singer, Nov 1965

George, Zelma Watson, sociologist and opera singer, Oct 1961, *Obit* Sept 1994

Gergiev, Valery, Russian conductor and opera director, Jan 1998

Gershwin, Ira, American lyricist, Jan 1956, *Obit* Oct 1983

Getz, Stan, American jazz saxophonist, Apr 1971, *Obit* Aug 1991

Ghostface Killah, American rapper, June 2008

Gibb, Barry, English singer and songwriter, Sept 1981

Gieseking, Walter, German pianist, Oct 1956, *Obit* Jan 1957

Gilels, Emil, Russian pianist, Oct 1956, *Obit* Jan 1986

Gillingham, Charlie, American keyboardist, Mar 2003

Giordani, Marcello, Italian opera singer, May 2008

Giulini, Carlo Maria, Italian conductor, Mar 1978, *Obit* Yrbk 2005

Glasper, Robert, American jazz pianist, Mar 2011

Gobbi, Tito, Italian opera singer, Jan 1957, *Obit* May 1984

Goerne, Matthias, German opera singer, Jan 2006

Goldman, Edwin Franko, Sept 1942, *Obit* May 1956

Goldovsky, Boris, Russian-American pianist, conductor and opera director, Yrbk 1966, *Obit* Aug 2001

Goldsmith, Jerry, American composer, May 2001, *Obit* Yrbk 2004

Golijov, Osvaldo, Argentine composer, Jan 2006

Gonzalez, Alex, Mexican drummer, Jan 2005

Goode, Richard, American pianist, Nov 1988

Googoosh, Iranian singer and actress, May 2001

Gordon, Mike, American bassist, July 2003

Gordon, Wycliffe, American jazz trombonist, Sept 2009

Gorecki, Henryk, Polish composer, May 1994, *Obit* Yrbk 2011

Gorme, Eydie, singer, Feb 1965, *Obit* Yrbk 2013

Gould, Morton, pianist and composer, Sept 1945, Jan 1968, *Obit* May 1996

Goulet, Robert, American singer and actor, Sept 1962, *Obit* Yrbk 2008

Graffman, Gary, pianist, July 1970

Graham, Ed, British drummer, Jan 2004

Graham, Susan, American opera singer, Oct 2005

Gramm, Donald, opera singer, Nov 1975, *Obit* July 1983

Grappelli, Stephane, French jazz violinist, Aug 1988, *Obit* Feb 1998

Gray, David, British singer and songwriter, Jan 2004

Gray, Macy, American singer and songwriter, May 2000

Grebenshikov, Boris, Russian singer, Jan 2002

Greco, Juliette, French singer, Jan 1992

Green, Martyn, June 1950, *Obit* Apr 1975

Greenberg, Noah, conductor and musicologist, May 1964, *Obit* Feb 1966

Greenwood, Colin, English bassist, June 2001

Greenwood, Jonny, English guitarist, June 2001

Grey, Joel, American actor and singer, Jan 1973

Grimaud, Helene, French pianist, Jan 2007

Groban, Josh, American pop singer, Aug 2009

Grofe, Ferde, July 1940, *Obit* May 1972

Gronemeyer, Herbert, German singer and actor, Jan 2003

Gubaidulina, Sofia Asgatovna, Russian composer, Oct 1999

Gueden, Hilde, Apr 1955

Hackett, Charles, American opera singer, *Obit* Feb 1942

Hadley, Jerry, American opera singer, Nov 1991, *Obit* Yrbk 2007

Hagegard, Hakan, Swedish opera singer, May 1985

Hahn, Hilary, American violinist, Sept 2002

Hahn, Joseph, American DJ, Mar 2002

Haitink, Bernard, Dutch conductor, Nov 1977

Halasz, Laszlo, Hungarian-American conductor and pianist, Jan 1949, *Obit* Feb 2002

Hallahan, Patrick, American rock drummer, Nov 2008

Hallyday, Johnny, French singer, Jan 2003

Hamilton, Tom, American rock bassist, July 2004

Hamlisch, Marvin, American composer and pianist, May 1976, *Obit* Yrbk 2012

Hammer (Musician), American rapper, Apr 1991

Hammond, Albert, American guitarist, Feb 2007

Hampson, Thomas, American opera singer, Mar 1991

Hanley, James Frederick, songwriter, *Obit* Apr 1942

Harbison, John, composer, Feb 1993

Harburg, E. Y., American lyricist, July 1980, *Obit* Apr 1981

Hardy, Francoise, French singer, Jan 2005

Hargrove, Roy, American jazz trumpet player, Apr 2000

Harper, Ben, American singer and guitarist, Jan 2004

Harrington, David, violinist, Nov 1998

Harris, Emmylou, American singer, Oct 1994

Harris, Roy, composer, Aug 1940, *Obit* Nov 1979

Harry, Deborah, American singer, Nov 1981

Hart, Lorenz, American lyricist, May 1940, *Obit* Feb 1944

Hatfield, Juliana, American singer and songwriter, Aug 2011

Hawkins, Dan, British rock guitarist, Jan 2004

Hayes, Isaac, American singer and composer, Oct 1972, *Obit* Yrbk 2008

Hayes, Roland, American singer, May 1942, *Obit* Mar 1977

Heifetz, Jascha, Russian-American violinist, Feb 1944, *Obit* Feb 1988

Helders, Matt, British rock drummer, Jan 2006

Henderson, Florence, American singer and actress, Apr 1971

Hendricks, Barbara, opera singer, Mar 1989

Henze, Hans Werner, German composer, Apr 1966, *Obit* Yrbk 2013

Heppner, Ben, Canadian opera singer, Jan 1997

Hernandez, Dave, American bassist, June 2007

Hess, Myra, English pianist, Sept 1943, *Obit* Jan 1966

Hetfield, James, American singer and guitarist, Jan 2000

Hewitt, Angela, Canadian pianist, Apr 2007

Hildegarde, American singer, Nov 1944, *Obit* Yrbk 2005

Hill, Faith, American country singer, Mar 2001

Hill, Patty Smith, American educator, *Obit* June 1946

Hindemith, Paul, German composer, Oct 1941, *Obit* Feb 1964

Hines, Earl, pianist and band leader, Mar 1967, *Obit* June 1983

Hines, Jerome, American opera singer, Feb 1963, *Obit* June 2003

Hinrichs, Gustav, German-American conductor, *Obit* May 1942

Hirt, Al, trumpet player, Feb 1967, *Obit* July 1999

Hoiby, Lee, American composer, Mar 1987, *Obit* Yrbk 2011

Holliday, Jennifer, American singer, June 1983

Holliger, Heinz, Swiss oboist, Jan 1987

Holloway, Stanley, Feb 1963, *Obit* Mar 1982

Holm, Georg, Icelandic bassist, Jan 2003

Honegger, Arthur, Swiss composer, Apr 1941, *Obit* Feb 1956

Hong, Hei-Kyung, Korean opera singer, Nov 2003

Hook, Peter, British bassist and singer, Jan 2006

Hoppus, Mark, American singer and bassist, Aug 2002

Horne, Lena, American singer, June 1944, Nov 1985, *Obit* Aug 2010

Horne, Marilyn, American opera singer, July 1967

Horner, James, composer, Mar 1997

Horowitz, Vladimir, Russian-American pianist, Sept 1943, Mar 1966, *Obit* Jan 1990

Houston, Whitney, American singer and actress, Nov 1986, *Obit* Yrbk 2012

Hovhaness, Alan, American composer, Apr 1965, *Obit* Oct 2000

Huberman, Bronislaw, Polish violinist, July 1941, *Obit* July 1947

Hudson, Jennifer, American singer and actress, May 2007

Hugo, Chad, American record producer, singer and songwriter, May 2004

Hunt Lieberson, Lorraine, American opera singer, July 2004, *Obit* Yrbk 2006

Hurley, Laurel, American opera singer, June 1957

Hurok, Sol, concert manager, Sept 1941, Apr 1956, *Obit* Apr 1974

Hussain, Zakir, Indian percussionist and composer, Jan 2005

Hutton, Betty, American singer and actress, June 1950, *Obit* Yrbk 2007

Hvorostovsky, Dmitri, Russian opera singer, Jan 2006

Hynde, Chrissie, American singer and songwriter, Apr 1993

Ice-T, American rapper and actor, Sept 1994

Iglesias, Enrique, Spanish singer, Apr 1999

Iglesias, Julio, Spanish singer, June 1984

India.Arie (Singer), American singer, Feb 2002

International, Dana, Israeli singer, Jan 2005

Irimia, Gabriela, Romanian singer, Jan 2003

Irimia, Monica, Romanian singer, Jan 2003

Isaak, Chris, singer, May 1993

Isokoski, Soile, Finnish opera singer, Jan 2006

Istomin, Eugene, American pianist, Oct 1977, *Obit* Feb 2004

Iturbi, Jose, Spanish-American pianist and conductor, Sept 1943, *Obit* Aug 1980

Ives, Charles Edward, American composer, June 1947, *Obit* July 1954

Ivins, Mike, American bassist, Oct 2002

Ja Rule, American rapper, July 2002

Jackson, Alan, American country singer, Apr 2004

Jackson, Janet, American singer, June 1991

Jackson, Joe, English singer and songwriter, Feb 1996

Jackson, Mahalia, American gospel singer, Oct 1957, *Obit* Mar 1972

Jagger, Mick, British singer, Yrbk 1972

Janis, Byron, pianist, June 1966

Jaroussky, Philippe, French countertenor, Mar 2011

Jarreau, Al, American singer, Oct 1992

Jerusalem, Siegfried, German opera singer, Sept 1992

Jett, Joan, American singer and songwriter, Sept 1993

Jo, Sumi, Korean opera singer, Jan 2002

Johannesen, Grant, American pianist, June 1961, *Obit* Yrbk 2005

Johnson, Brian, English singer, Mar 2005

Johnson, Edward, Canadian-American opera singer and director, Mar 1943, *Obit* June 1959

Johnson, Howard E., *Obit* June 1941

Jolson, Al, singer and actor, Nov 1940, *Obit* Yrbk 1950

Jones, Bobby, American gospel singer, June 2002

Jones, George, American country singer, Feb 1995, *Obit* Yrbk 2013

Jones, Norah, American pianist and singer, May 2003

Jones, Rickie Lee, singer and songwriter, May 1990

Jonsi Thor Birgisson, Icelandic singer, Jan 2003

Jordan, Philippe, Swiss opera conductor, Oct 2010

Jorgensen, Mikael, American keyboardist, Feb 2010

Josefowicz, Leila, American violinist, May 2007

Juanes, Colombian singer, Jan 2003

K'naan, Somali rapper, June 2010

Kahal, Irving, *Obit* Apr 1942

Kahn, Gus, American lyricist, *Obit* Yrbk 1941

Kahn, Madeline, American actress and singer, May 1977, *Obit* Mar 2000

Kapell, William, American pianist, May 1948, *Obit* Jan 1954

Karajan, Herbert von, Austrian conductor, Oct 1956, Sept 1986, *Obit* Sept 1989

Kavafian, Ani, American violinist, Oct 2006

Kavina, Lydia, Russian theremin player, Jan 2002

Kay, Hershy, Mar 1962, *Obit* Feb 1982

Kelberine, Alexander, *Obit* Mar 1940

Kelley, Edgar Stillman, composer, *Obit* Jan 1945

Kelly, R., American singer, songwriter and record producer, June 1999

Kelman, Charles D., American ophthalmologist and saxophonist, June 1984, *Obit* Yrbk 2004

Kennedy, English violinist, July 1992

Kern, Jerome, American composer, June 1942, *Obit* Yrbk 1945

Khachaturian, Aram Il'ich, Mar 1948, *Obit* June 1978

Khan, Chaka, American singer, July 1999

Kid Rock, American rapper, Oct 2001

Kiepura, Jan, Nov 1943, *Obit* Nov 1966

King, Carole, American singer and songwriter, Jan 1974

Kipnis, Alexander, opera singer, Yrbk 1943, *Obit* July 1978

Kirkpatrick, Chris, American singer, Nov 2000

Kirsten, Dorothy, American opera singer, Feb 1948, *Obit* Jan 1993

Kissin, Evgeny, Russian pianist, Nov 1997

Kitt, Eartha, American singer and actress, Apr 1955, *Obit* Yrbk 2009

Kjartan Sveinsson, Icelandic keyboardist, Jan 2003

Kleiber, Carlos, German conductor, July 1991, *Obit* Yrbk 2004

Klemperer, Otto, German conductor, Mar 1965, *Obit* Sept 1973

Knight, Gladys, American singer, Feb 1987

Koh, Jennifer, American violinist, Sept 2006

Koite, Habib, Malian guitarist, Jan 2002

Korngold, Erich Wolfgang, Austrian composer, Mar 1943, *Obit* Feb 1958

Kostelanetz, Andre, American conductor, July 1942, *Obit* Mar 1980

Koster, Bo, American rock keyboardist, Nov 2008

Kotche, Glenn, American drummer and percussionist, Feb 2010

Koussevitzky, Serge, Russian conductor, Nov 1940, *Obit* July 1951

Kozena, Magdalena, Czech opera singer, Jan 2005

Krainik, Ardis, opera manager, Nov 1991, *Obit* Mar 1997

Krall, Diana, Canadian singer and pianist, June 2000

Kramer, Joey, American rock drummer, July 2004

Kraus, Alfredo, Spanish opera singer, June 1987, *Obit* Nov 1999

Kraus, Lili, Hungarian pianist, Oct 1975, *Obit* Jan 1987

Kravitz, Lenny, American singer and guitarist, Apr 1996

Kremer, Gidon, Russian violinist, Mar 1985

Krenek, Ernst, American composer, July 1942, *Obit* Feb 1992

Kubelik, Jan, Czech violinist and composer, *Obit* Jan 1941

Kubelik, Rafael, Czech conductor, Feb 1951, *Obit* Oct 1996

Kubler, Tad, American guitarist, Sept 2010

Kullmer, Ann, Feb 1949

Kurenko, Maria, Sept 1944

Kurtz, Efrem, conductor, Feb 1946, *Obit* Sept 1995

Kuti, Femi, Nigerian singer and songwriter, Jan 2002

Kweli, Talib, American rapper, July 2012

Kwiecie?, Mariusz, Polish opera singer, July 2012

LL Cool J, American rapper and actor, Nov 1997

La India, Puerto Rican salsa singer, May 2002

LaBelle, Patti, American singer, July 1986

LaMontagne, Ray, American singer, Oct 2013

Lady Gaga, American pop singer and songwriter, May 2010

Lafourcade, Natalia, Mexican singer and songwriter, Jan 2003

Laine, Cleo, Britlsh singer and actress, Feb 1986

Laine, Frankie, American singer, Nov 1956, *Obit* Yrbk 2007

Lally, Joe, American bassist, Mar 2002

Landowska, Wanda, Polish harpsichordist, Nov 1945, *Obit* Nov 1959

Lane, Burton, American composer, Mar 1967, *Obit* Mar 1997

Lang, David, American composer, Feb 2000

Lang, Lang, Chinese pianist, Jan 2003

Laredo, Jaime, violinist, Sept 1967

Laredo, Ruth, American pianist, Oct 1987, *Obit* Yrbk 2005

Larrocha, Alicia de, Spanish pianist, July 1968, *Obit* Yrbk 2009

Lau, Andy, Chinese singer and actor, Jan 2005

Lauper, Cyndi, American singer and songwriter, Aug 1985

Lavigne, Avril, Canadian singer and songwriter, Apr 2003

Lawrence, Carol, American singer and actress, Nov 1961

Lawrence, Marjorie, Australian opera singer, Apr 1940, *Obit* Mar 1979

Lawrence, Steve, singer, Nov 1964

Lear, Evelyn, American opera singer, Apr 1973, *Obit* Yrbk 2012

Lecuona, Ernesto, Cuban composer, May 1944, *Obit* Jan 1964

Lee, Geddy, Canadian singer, Feb 2001

Lee, Peggy, American singer, Mar 1963, *Obit* May 2002

Legend, John, American singer and pianist, Feb 2007

Lehmann, Lotte, German-American opera singer, May 1941, July 1970, *Obit* Oct 1976

Leinsdorf, Erich, conductor, May 1940, Oct 1963, *Obit* Nov 1993

Lennox, Annie, Scottish singer, May 1988

Lenya, Lotte, German singer and actress, June 1959, *Obit* Jan 1982

Leonard, Eddie, singer and dancer, *Obit* Sept 1941

Lerche, Sondre, Norwegian singer and songwriter, Jan 2004

Lev, Ray, Jan 1949, *Obit* July 1968

Levert, Gerald, American singer and songwriter, Oct 2003, *Obit* Yrbk 2007

Levine, Adam, American rock singer and guitarist, Mar 2013

Levine, James, American conductor, Apr 1975

Levitzki, Mischa, pianist, *Obit* Feb 1941

Lewis, Mary, opera singer, *Obit* Feb 1942

Lewis, Ramsey, American jazz pianist, Oct 1996

Lhevinne, Josef, Russian pianist, *Obit* Jan 1945

Liberace, American pianist, Nov 1954, Mar 1986, *Obit* Mar 1987

Licad, Cecile, Philippine pianist, Jan 2003

Liebermann, Rolf, Swiss composer and opera director, Sept 1973, *Obit* Mar 1999

Lifeson, Alex, Canadian guitarist, Feb 2001

Lightfoot, Gordon, Canadian singer, Aug 1978

Lil' Kim, American rapper, Oct 2000

Lindemann, Till, German singer, Jan 2007

Litton, Andrew, conductor, Sept 1998

Littrell, Brian, American singer, May 2000

Liu Fang, Chinese pipa player, Jan 2006

Lloyd, Alex, Australian singer and songwriter, Jan 2002

Lockhart, Keith, American conductor, Aug 2008

Loewe, Frederick, American composer, July 1958, *Obit* Apr 1988

London, George, Canadian opera singer, Nov 1953, *Obit* June 1985

London, Julie, singer and actress, May 1960, *Obit* Feb 2001

Lopez, Trini, singer, Mar 1968

Loudon, Dorothy, American actress and singer, June 1984, *Obit* Yrbk 2004

Lovano, Joe, American jazz saxophonist, Mar 1998

Love, Courtney, American singer and actress, June 1996

Lowe, Jack Warren, pianist, Jan 1954, *Obit* Aug 1996

Lozano, Conrad, American bassist, Oct 2005

LuPone, Patti, American actress and singer, Apr 1989

Lucia, Paco de, Spanish flamenco guitarist, Jan 2004

Ludacris, American rapper, June 2004

Ludwig, Christa, German opera singer, Mar 1971

Luisi, Fabio, Principal conductor of the Metropolitan Opera, Mar 2012

Lurie, John, American saxophonist and actor, Oct 2010

M. I. A. (Singer), Sri Lankan-British singer and songwriter, May 2009

MacDermot, Galt, Canadian composer, July 1984

MacKaye, Ian, American singer and guitarist, Mar 2002

MacNeil, Cornell, American opera singer, Jan 1976, *Obit* Yrbk 2011

Mackenzie, Gisele, Canadian singer, Nov 1955, *Obit* July 2004

Mackerras, Charles, Australian conductor, Feb 1985

Madeira, Jean, Oct 1963, *Obit* Sept 1972

Maimon, Shiri, Israeli pop singer, Jan 2006

Maines, Natalie, American singer, July 2000

Makeba, Miriam, South African singer, June 1965, *Obit* Yrbk 2009

Malaby, Tony, American jazz saxophonist, Sept 2008

Malbin, Elaine, Feb 1959

Malley, Matt, American bassist, Mar 2003

Malone, Kyp, American guitarist and singer, Apr 2009

Mami, Cheb, Algerian singer, Jan 2005

Mandrell, Barbara, singer, Aug 1982

Mangesakara, Lata, Indian singer, Jan 2003

Manson, Marilyn, American singer, May 1999

Marquardt, Alexandria, *Obit* June 1943

Marriner, Neville, English conductor, Aug 1978

Mars, Bruno, American singer and songwriter, May 2011

Marsalis, Ellis, American jazz pianist, Aug 2000

Marshall, Lois, Canadian singer, June 1960, *Obit* May 1997

Martin, Chris, English singer and guitarist, May 2004

Martin, Dean, American actor and singer, Nov 1964, *Obit* Mar 1996

Martin, Mary, American actress and singer, Jan 1944, *Obit* Jan 1991

Martin, Ricky, Puerto Rican singer and actor, Sept 1999

Martinelli, Giovanni, Italian opera singer, Jan 1945, *Obit* Mar 1969

Martinez, Speedo, Argentine singer, Jan 2003

Marton, Eva, Hungarian opera singer, Apr 1985

Mascagni, Pietro, Italian composer, *Obit* Sept 1945

Mathis, Johnny, American singer, July 1965, Feb 1993

Matisyahu, American Hasidic reggae and rap singer, Mar 2007

Mattila, Karita, Finnish opera singer, Jan 2004

Maxwell, American singer, songwriter and recording producer, July 2011

May, Brian, English rock guitarist, Oct 2008

Maynor, Dorothy, singer, Jan 1940, Yrbk 1951, *Obit* May 1996

McBride, Martina, American country singer, Mar 2004

McCartney, Paul, English singer and songwriter, Nov 1966, Jan 1986

McConnell, Page, American keyboardist, July 2003

McCracken, James, opera singer, Nov 1963, *Obit* June 1988

McDonald, Audra, American singer and actress, Apr 1999

McFerrin, Bobby, American singer and conductor, Aug 1989

McGovern, Maureen, singer, Feb 1990

McGraw, Tim, American country singer, Sept 2002

McLaren, Malcolm, English rock musician, band manager and talent agent, Aug 1997, *Obit* Yrbk 2010

McLean, A. J., American singer, May 2000

McLean, Don, American singer and songwriter, May 1973

McLean, Jackie, American saxophonist, Mar 2001, *Obit* Nov 2006

McNair, Barbara, American singer and actress, Nov 1971, *Obit* Yrbk 2007

McNair, Sylvia, American opera singer, Nov 1997

McNeil, John, American jazz trumpet player, June 2007

McRae, Carmen, American singer, Apr 1983, *Obit* Jan 1995

Mei Lanfang, *Obit* Sept 1943

Melchior, Lauritz, Danish opera singer, Jan 1941, *Obit* May 1973

Mellencamp, John, American singer and songwriter, Mar 1988

Meloy, Colin, American singer and songwriter, Aug 2007

Melton, James, American opera singer, Sept 1945, *Obit* June 1961

Melua, Katie, British singer and songwriter, Jan 2007

Mendez, Kinito, Dominican singer, Jan 2004

Menken, Alan, American composer, Jan 2001

Menuhin, Yehudi, violinist, Feb 1941, May 1973, *Obit* June 1999

Mercer, James, American guitarist and singer, June 2007

Mercer, Mabel, singer, Feb 1973, *Obit* June 1984

Merchant, Natalie, American singer and songwriter, Jan 2003

Merrill, Robert, American opera singer, Mar 1952, *Obit* Feb 2005

Michael, George, English pop singer, Nov 1988

Michele, Chrisette, American singer and songwriter, Apr 2011

Midori, Japanese violinist, June 1990

Milanov, Zinka, Yugoslav-American opera singer, July 1944, *Obit* July 1989

Milhaud, Darius, French composer, June 1941, May 1961, *Obit* Sept 1974

Miller, Mildred, opera singer, June 1957

Millo, Aprile, American opera singer, Apr 1988

Milnes, Sherrill, American opera singer, Nov 1970

Milstein, Nathan, Russian-American violinist, Mar 1950, *Obit* Feb 1993

Minaj, Nicki, American rapper, Oct 2013

Minogue, Kylie, Australian actress and singer, Jan 2003

Misia, Portuguese singer, Jan 2002

Moby, American singer, Apr 2001

Moen, John, American singer and drummer, Aug 2007

Moffo, Anna, American opera singer, May 1961, *Obit* Yrbk 2007

Monheit, Jane, American jazz singer, Feb 2008

Monroe, Lucy, singer, Aug 1942, *Obit* Nov 1987

Montand, Yves, French actor and singer, July 1960, Sept 1988, *Obit* Jan 1992

Montero, Gabriela, Venezuelan pianist, July 2007

Monteux, Pierre, American conductor, Apr 1946, *Obit* Sept 1964

Montoya, Carlos, Spanish guitarist, Mar 1968, *Obit* May 1993

Moore, Douglas, American composer, Nov 1947, *Obit* Oct 1969

Moore, Dudley, English actor, June 1982, *Obit* Yrbk 2002

Moore, Gerald, English pianist, Oct 1967, *Obit* May 1987

Moore, Grace, opera singer, Apr 1944, *Obit* Mar 1947

Moore, Melba, American singer and actress, Jan 1973

Morath, Max, musician, Nov 1963

Moretti, Fabrizio, Brazilian drummer, Feb 2007

Morgan, Lorrie, American country singer, Apr 1999

Morini, Erica, Austrian violinist, Apr 1946, *Obit* Jan 1996

Morissette, Alanis, Canadian singer and songwriter, May 1997

Morris, James, American opera singer, July 1986

Morris, Stephen, British drummer, Jan 2006

Mortier, Gerard, Belgian opera manager and director, July 1991

Mos Def (Singer), American rapper, Apr 2005

Moyet, Alison, British singer, Jan 2003

Mulligan, Gerry, American jazz saxophonist, Yrbk 1960, *Obit* Mar 1996

Muncey, Cameron, Australian guitarist and singer, Jan 2005

Munch, Charles, Yrbk 1947, *Obit* Yrbk 1968

Munn, Frank, singer, May 1944, *Obit* Yrbk 1953

Munsel, Patrice, American opera singer, Mar 1945

Murphy, Mark, American jazz singer, Sept 2004

Murray, Anne, Canadian singer, Jan 1982

Murray, J. Harold, *Obit* Feb 1941

N'Dour, Youssou, Senegalese singer, Jan 1996

Nabors, Jim, American actor and singer, Nov 1969

Narelle, Marie, *Obit* Mar 1941

Nas (Musician), American rapper, Sept 2009

Nelly (Musician), American rapper, Oct 2002

Nelson, Harriet, actress and singer, May 1949, *Obit* Jan 1995

Netrebko, Anna, Russian opera singer, Jan 2005

Neufeld, Sarah, Canadian violinist, Jan 2007

Newman, Randy, American singer and songwriter, Oct 1982

Newton, Wayne, American singer, Feb 1990

Newton-John, Olivia, Australian singer and actress, Nov 1978

Nezet-Seguin, Yannick, Canadian conductor, Nov 2011

Nicholson, Andy, British rock bassist, Jan 2006

Nielsen, Alice, *Obit* Apr 1943

Nilsson, Birgit, Swedish opera singer, May 1960, *Obit* Sept 2006

Nin, Khadja, Burundian singer, Jan 2005

Nixon, Marni, American singer, Oct 2009

Norman, Jessye, American opera singer, Feb 1976

Norrington, Roger, English conductor, Jan 1990

Novaes, Guiomar, Brazilian pianist, June 1953, *Obit* May 1979

Novotna, Jarmila, Czech opera singer, Mar 1940, *Obit* Apr 1994

O'Brien, Ed, English guitarist, June 2001

O'Connor, Sinead, Irish singer, June 1991

O'Day, Anita, American jazz singer, June 1990, *Obit* Jan 2007

O'Hara, Kelli, American actress and singer, Oct 2008

O'Horgan, Tom, American theatrical director and composer, Apr 1970, *Obit* Yrbk 2009

O'Malley, Nick, British rock bassist, Jan 2006

Oberlin, Russell, opera singer, July 1960

Obraztsova, Elena, Russian opera singer, Feb 1983

Odetta, American folk singer, Yrbk 1960, *Obit* Jan 2009

Ohlsson, Garrick, American pianist, June 1975

Oistrakh, David, Russian violinist, Mar 1956, *Obit* Yrbk 1974

Olivero, Magda, Italian opera singer, Apr 1980

Olvera, Fernando, Mexican singer and guitarist, Jan 2005

Omarion (Musician), American singer, Feb 2008

Ono, Yoko, Japanese artist, Nov 1972

Onuki, Ami, Japanese pop singer, Jan 2005

Orff, Carl, German composer, Aug 1976, *Obit* May 1982

Origliasso, Jess, Australian singer, Jan 2006

Origliasso, Lisa, Australian singer, Jan 2006

Ormandy, Eugene, conductor, Jan 1941, *Obit* May 1985

Orri Pall Dyrason, Icelandic drummer, Jan 2003

Osbourne, Ozzy, English singer, Nov 1998

Osmond, Donny, American singer, Feb 1998

Otter, Anne Sofie von, Swedish opera singer, Sept 1995

Page, Greg, Australian singer and actor, Jan 2004

Page, Patti, American singer, Sept 1965, *Obit* Yrbk 2013

Paige, Janis, actress and singer, Jan 1959

Pallett, Owen, Canadian singer and violinist, Jan 2007

Papa Wemba, Congolese singer, Jan 2003

Pape, Rene, German opera singer, Jan 2003

Papi, Gennaro, *Obit* Jan 1942

Paradis, Vanessa, French singer and actress, Jan 2004

Part, Arvo, Estonian composer, Feb 1995

Pasternack, Josef, *Obit* Jan 1940

Patinkin, Mandy, American actor and singer, Jan 1999

Patty, Sandi, American gospel singer, Feb 2004

Paul, Les, American guitarist, Aug 1987, *Obit* Yrbk 2009

Pausini, Laura, Italian singer, Jan 2007

Pavarotti, Luciano, Italian opera singer, June 1973, *Obit* Nov 2007

Payton, Nicholas, American trumpet player, Sept 1999

Pears, Peter, English opera singer, July 1975, *Obit* May 1986

Peart, Neil, Canadian drummer, Feb 2001

Peerce, Jan, opera singer, May 1942, *Obit* Feb 1985

Pelt, Jeremy, American jazz trumpet player, Feb 2009

Penn, Arthur A., *Obit* Apr 1941

Perahia, Murray, American pianist, Mar 1982

Perez, Louis, American drummer, Oct 2005

Perlman, Itzhak, American violinist, May 1975

Peroni, Carlo, *Obit* May 1944

Perry, Joe, American rock guitarist, July 2004

Perry, Katy, American singer and songwriter, Jan 2012

Person, Houston, American saxophonist, June 2003

Peters, Bernadette, American actress and singer, Sept 1984

Peters, Roberta, opera singer, Apr 1954

Petri, Egon, Dutch pianist, Nov 1942, *Obit* July 1962

Petrillo, James C., American labor leader, Yrbk 1940, *Obit* Jan 1985

Pharrell, American record producer, singer and songwriter, May 2004

Phillips, Scott, American drummer, May 2002

Phoenix (Musician), American bassist, Mar 2002

Piaf, Edith, French singer, Yrbk 1950, *Obit* Nov 1963

Pickens, Jane, singer, Yrbk 1949, *Obit* Apr 1992

Pinza, Ezio, Italian opera singer, Feb 1941, Yrbk 1953, *Obit* July 1957

Pires, Maria Joao, Portuguese pianist, Jan 2007

Plant, Robert, British singer, Oct 1998

Podles, Ewa, Polish opera singer, Jan 2006

Pogorelich, Ivo, Yugoslav pianist, Sept 1988

Polivka, Galen, American bassist, Sept 2010

Pollain, Rene, *Obit* Yrbk 1940

Pollini, Maurizio, Italian pianist, Nov 1980

Pons, Lily, French opera singer, Jan 1944, *Obit* Apr 1976

Portuondo, Omara, Cuban singer, Jan 2005

Poullain, Frankie, British rock bassist, Jan 2004

Powell, Jane, American singer and actress, Yrbk 1974

Powers, Marie, Jan 1951, *Obit* Feb 1974

Presley, Elvis, American singer, Sept 1959, *Obit* Oct 1977

Previn, Dory, singer and songwriter, Sept 1975, *Obit* Yrbk 2012

Prey, Hermann, German opera singer, Feb 1975, *Obit* Oct 1998

Price, Leontyne, American opera singer, May 1961, Oct 1978

Price, Margaret, Welsh opera singer, Aug 1986, *Obit* Yrbk 2011

Pride, Charley, American country singer, Apr 1975

Primrose, William, violist, Yrbk 1946, *Obit* July 1982

Prince, American singer and songwriter, Feb 1986

Prokofiev, Sergey, Russian composer, Nov 1941, *Obit* Apr 1953

Pryor, Arthur, trombonist, *Obit* Aug 1942

Pugacheva, Alla, Russian singer, Jan 2004

Punisher (Musician), Finnish bassist, Jan 2003

Putnam, Ashley, Mar 1982

Quasthoff, Thomas, German classical singer, Jan 2005

Queler, Eve, conductor, July 1972

Query, Nate, American bassist, Aug 2007

Racette, Patricia, American opera singer, Feb 2003

Rahman, A. R., Indian composer and singer, June 2009

Rain (Singer), Korean pop singer, Jan 2006

Rakim, American rapper, Aug 2008

Ramazzotti, Eros, Italian singer and songwriter, Jan 2004

Ramey, Samuel, American opera singer, July 1981

Rampal, Jean-Pierre, French flutist, Mar 1970, *Obit* Aug 2000

Raphael, Spanish singer, Aug 1991

Raskin, Judith, American opera singer, Apr 1964, *Obit* Feb 1985

Rava, Enrico, Italian jazz trumpet player, Jan 2006

Rawls, Lou, American singer, Mar 1984, *Obit* Oct 2006

Reardon, John, opera singer, Nov 1974, *Obit* June 1988

Reddy, Helen, American singer, Apr 1975

Redman, Joshua, American jazz saxophonist, Jan 1997

Redpath, Jean, Scottish singer, Feb 1984

Reed, Lou, American singer, July 1989

Reese, Della, American singer and actress, Sept 1971

Reeves, Dianne, American jazz singer, July 2006

Reiner, Fritz, conductor, Apr 1941, Yrbk 1953, *Obit* Jan 1964

Resnik, Regina, opera singer, Jan 1956, *Obit* Yrbk 2013

Reynolds, Debbie, American actress and singer, Yrbk 1964

Richard 23, Belgian percussionist and singer, Jan 2006

Richards, Keith, British guitarist, Feb 1989

Richardson, Kevin, American singer, May 2000

Richter, Sviatoslav, Russian pianist, Feb 1961, *Obit* Oct 1997

Rihanna, Barbadian singer, Nov 2007

Ringling, Robert E., May 1945, *Obit* Feb 1950

Ritchard, Cyril, Jan 1957, *Obit* Feb 1978

Rivers, Larry, American painter and sculptor, Apr 1969, *Obit* Nov 2002

Robison, Paula, flutist, May 1982

Rock, Pete, American record producer and DJ, Aug 2009

Rodgers, Richard, American composer, May 1940, Apr 1951, *Obit* Feb 1980

Rodzinski, Artur, Aug 1940, *Obit* Feb 1959

Rogers, Kenny, American country singer, Jan 1981

Romberg, Sigmund, composer, Mar 1945, *Obit* Yrbk 1951

Rosas, Cesar, American singer and guitarist, Oct 2005

Rose, Arnold, *Obit* Oct 1946

Rosenstock, Joseph, conductor and opera director, Jan 1954, *Obit* Jan 1986

Rosenthal, Moriz, Polish pianist, *Obit* Oct 1946

Ross, Rick, American rapper, June 2012

Rossi, Vasco, Italian rock singer, Jan 2005

Rotten, Johnny, English singer, Nov 1996

Rowland, Kelly, American singer, Aug 2001

Rowntree, Dave, British drummer, Nov 2003

Rubinstein, Artur, Polish-American pianist, Yrbk 1945, Feb 1966, *Obit* Mar 1983

Rudel, Julius, Austrian-American conductor, July 1965

Rysanek, Leonie, Austrian opera singer, Mar 1966, *Obit* May 1998

Sachs, Curt, German musicologist, Aug 1944, *Obit* Apr 1959

Sade, British singer, Sept 1986

Sairam, Aruna, Indian singer, Jan 2006

Salerno-Sonnenberg, Nadja, violinist, Nov 1987

Salonga, Lea, Filipino singer and actress, Jan 2007

Sanchez, David, Puerto Rican jazz saxophonist, Nov 2001

Sandor, Gyorgy, American pianist, July 1947, *Obit* Yrbk 2006

Sandoval, Arturo, Cuban jazz trumpet player, Jan 2003

Sandoval, Jesse, American drummer, June 2007

Sangare, Oumou, Malian singer, Jan 2003

Santaolalla, Gustavo, Argentine composer and record producer, Jan 2007

Sargent, Malcolm Watts, English conductor, Yrbk 1945, *Obit* Jan 1968

Sauer, Emil von, German pianist, *Obit* June 1942

Sayao, Bidu, Brazilian opera singer, Feb 1942, *Obit* June 1999

Scallon, Dana Rosemary, British singer, Jan 2007

Scherman, Thomas, American conductor, Yrbk 1954, *Obit* July 1979

Schiotz, Aksel, Mar 1949, *Obit* June 1975

Schippers, Thomas, American conductor, Apr 1970, *Obit* Feb 1978

Schlamme, Martha, singer, Feb 1964, *Obit* Jan 1986

Schneider, Alexander, violinist, Mar 1976, *Obit* Mar 1993

Schnittke, Alfred, Russian composer, July 1992, *Obit* Oct 1998

Schoenberg, Arnold, Austrian-American composer, Apr 1942, *Obit* Sept 1951

Schorr, Friedrich, Hungarian opera singer, July 1942, *Obit* June 1954

Schwartz, Arthur, composer, Nov 1979, *Obit* Oct 1984

Schwarz, Gerard, trumpet player and conductor, Apr 1986

Schwarzkopf, Elisabeth, German-British opera singer, Yrbk 1955, *Obit* Yrbk 2006

Scott, Christian, American jazz trumpet player, Jan 2008

Scott, George, American gospel singer, Oct 2001, *Obit* Yrbk 2005

Scott, Hazel, American pianist and singer, Aug 1943, *Obit* Nov 1981

Scott, Hillary, American country singer, July 2011

Scott, Tom, American composer and singer, Nov 1946

Scotto, Renata, Italian opera singer, Sept 1978

Seal, English singer, Feb 1997

Sean Paul, Jamaican reggae singer, Jan 2007

Sedaka, Neil, American pop singer and songwriter, Oct 1978

Seefried, Irmgard, German opera singer, Feb 1956, *Obit* Jan 1989

Segovia, Andres, Spanish guitarist, May 1948, June 1964, *Obit* July 1987

Selway, Phil, English drummer, June 2001

Serkin, Peter, pianist, June 1986

Serkin, Rudolf, Czech-American pianist, July 1940, June 1990, *Obit* July 1991

Shaham, Gil, American violinist, Apr 1997

Shakira, Colombian singer, Jan 2002

Shinoda, Mike, American singer, Mar 2002

Shore, Dinah, American singer, June 1942, Yrbk 1966, *Obit* May 1994

Siepi, Cesare, Italian opera singer, Yrbk 1955, *Obit* Yrbk 2010

Simionato, Giulietta, Italian opera singer, Apr 1960, *Obit* Yrbk 2010

Simon, Carly, American singer and songwriter, Aug 1976

Simpson, Valerie, American singer and songwriter, Apr 1997

Sinatra, Frank, American singer and actor, June 1943, Oct 1960, *Obit* July 1998

Singer, Richard, *Obit* Mar 1940

Sitek, David Andrew, American guitarist and record producer, Apr 2009

Slick, Grace, American singer, Apr 1982

Smith, Carleton, musicologist and foundation official, Apr 1961, *Obit* July 1984

Smith, Carleton Sprague, musicologist, Yrbk 1960, *Obit* Nov 1994

Smith, Kate, singer, Yrbk 1940, Nov 1965, *Obit* Aug 1986

Smith, Will, American rapper and actor, Sept 1996

Soderstrom, Elisabeth, Swedish opera singer, Nov 1985, *Obit* Yrbk 2010

Solaar, MC, French rapper, Jan 2002

Solex, Dutch pop singer, Jan 2005

Solti, Georg, Hungarian-British conductor, Mar 1964, Obit Nov 1997

Sothern, Ann, American actress and singer, Yrbk 1956, Obit Aug 2001

Souleyman, Omar, Musician, Aug 2012

Souzay, Gerard, French opera singer, Jan 1966, Obit Yrbk 2004

Spaeth, Sigmund, musicologist, July 1942, Obit Jan 1966

Spalding, Albert, violinist, Jan 1944, Obit July 1953

Spears, Britney, American singer, Apr 2000

Spector, Phil, American record producer, songwriter and arranger, July 1989

Spektor, Regina, Russian-American singer, songwriter and pianist, July 2007

Spivakov, Vladimir, Russian violinist and conductor, Feb 1996

Stader, Maria, Swiss opera singer, July 1958, Obit Aug 1999

Stanley, Paul, American guitarist, Apr 1999

Starker, Janos, Hungarian cellist, May 1963, Obit Yrbk 2013

Starr, Ringo, English drummer, Yrbk 1965

Stebbins, George Coles, Obit Nov 1945

Steber, Eleanor, American opera singer, Mar 1943, Obit Jan 1991

Steinberg, William, American conductor, Sept 1940, Mar 1958, Obit July 1978

Stella, Antonietta, Italian opera singer, Yrbk 1959

Stern, Isaac, American violinist, Apr 1949, Feb 1989, Obit Jan 2002

Stevens, Rise, American opera singer, Nov 1941, Obit Yrbk 2013

Stewart, Rod, English singer, Aug 1979

Stewart, Thomas, American opera singer, May 1974, Obit Yrbk 2007

Stignani, Ebe, Italian opera singer, Feb 1949, Obit Yrbk 1991

Still, William Grant, American composer, Jan 1941, Obit Feb 1979

Stilwell, Richard, American opera singer, Feb 1986

Stipe, Michael, American singer, Apr 1997

Stirratt, John, American bassist, Feb 2010

Stock, Frederick, conductor, Obit Yrbk 1942

Stokowski, Leopold, American conductor, Feb 1941, July 1953, Obit Nov 1977

Stoltzman, Richard, clarinetist, Mar 1986

Stone, Joss, British soul singer, Jan 2005

Strait, George, American country singer, Feb 2000

Stratas, Teresa, Canadian opera singer, Jan 1980

Straus, Oscar, Austrian composer, Mar 1944, Obit Mar 1954

Strauss, Richard, German composer, July 1944, Obit Oct 1949

Stravinsky, Igor, Russian composer, May 1940, Apr 1953, Obit May 1971

Studer, Cheryl, opera singer, Apr 1992

Styne, Jule, composer, May 1983, Obit Nov 1994

Suesse, Dana, composer, May 1940, Obit Jan 1988

Sullivan, Brian, Yrbk 1957

Sumac, Yma, Peruvian singer, Yrbk 1955, Obit Yrbk 2008

Summer, Donna, American singer, July 1979, Obit Yrbk 2012

Sumner, Bernard, British guitarist and singer, Jan 2006

Sutherland, Joan, Australian opera singer, Yrbk 1960, Obit Yrbk 2010

Suzuki, Pat, singer and actress, Jan 1960

Svanholm, Set, Swedish opera singer, Yrbk 1956, Obit Yrbk 1964

Swados, Elizabeth, American composer, Feb 1979

Swann, Donald, English pianist and composer, Jan 1970, Obit May 1994

Swarthout, Gladys, opera singer, Mar 1944, Obit Sept 1969

Swift, Taylor, American singer and songwriter, Jan 2010

Szell, George, American conductor, June 1945, Obit Oct 1970

Szeryng, Henryk, Polish violinist, Jan 1968, Obit Apr 1988

Szigeti, Joseph, Hungarian violinist, May 1940, Mar 1958, Obit Apr 1973

Taboo (Musician), American singer, Oct 2006

Tagliavini, Ferruccio, Italian opera singer, June 1947, Obit Apr 1995

Talvela, Martti, Finnish opera singer, Oct 1983, Obit Sept 1989

Tan Dun, Chinese composer, Jan 2007

Tanon, Olga, Puerto Rican singer, Jan 2005

Tarkan, Turkish pop singer, Jan 2006

Tavares, Sara, Portuguese singer and songwriter, Jan 2007

Tavener, John, English composer, June 1999

Taylor, Chris, American bassist and singer, Sept 2011

Taylor, James, American singer and songwriter, June 1972

Te Kanawa, Kiri, New Zealand opera singer, Nov 1978

Tebaldi, Renata, Italian opera singer, Apr 1955, Obit Apr 2005

Teitur, Danish singer and songwriter, Jan 2004

Templeton, Alec, Mar 1940, Obit May 1963

Tennstedt, Klaus, German conductor, Sept 1983, Obit Mar 1998

Tetrazzini, Luisa, Italian opera singer, Obit Jan 1940

Teyte, Maggie, English opera singer, Yrbk 1945, Obit July 1976

Thalia, Mexican actress and singer, Jan 2004

The Black Keys, Jan 2013

Thebom, Blanche, American opera singer, Oct 1948, *Obit* Yrbk 2010

Theodorakis, Mikis, Greek composer, July 1973

Thomas, Augusta Read, composer, Nov 1999

Thomas, Jess, American opera singer, June 1964, *Obit* Jan 1994

Thomas, John Charles, May 1943, *Obit* Feb 1961

Thorborg, Kerstin, Swedish opera singer, Mar 1940, *Obit* July 1970

Tian, Hao Jiang, Chinese opera singer, Feb 2009

Tibbett, Lawrence, American opera singer, Feb 1945, *Obit* Oct 1960

Timbaland, American hip-hop musician and recording producer, Mar 2003

Timberlake, Justin, American singer, Nov 2000

Tippett, Michael, English composer, Sept 1974, *Obit* Mar 1998

Torme, Mel, singer, Mar 1983, *Obit* Aug 1999

Toscanini, Arturo, Italian conductor, June 1942, May 1954, *Obit* Mar 1957

Tourel, Jennie, American opera singer, Feb 1947, *Obit* Jan 1974

Townshend, Pete, British singer and guitarist, Aug 1983

Tozzi, Giorgio, American opera singer, Oct 1961, *Obit* Yrbk 2011

Trampler, Walter, violist, Nov 1971, *Obit* Jan 1998

Traubel, Helen, American opera singer, Jan 1940, Feb 1952, *Obit* Oct 1972

Travis, Randy, American country singer, Sept 1989

Trevi, Gloria, Mexican pop singer, Jan 2005

Tritt, Travis, American country singer, Feb 2004

Troyanos, Tatiana, opera singer, Aug 1979, *Obit* Oct 1993

Trulock, Mussette Langford, Jan 1957

Tubb, Ernest, singer, Oct 1983, *Obit* Oct 1984

Tucker, Richard, opera singer, Mar 1956, *Obit* Feb 1975

Tucker, Sophie, singer, Apr 1945, *Obit* Mar 1966

Tuckwell, Barry, Australian horn player, July 1979

Tully, Alice, music patron and singer, Jan 1984, *Obit* Feb 1994

Tunstall, KT, Scottish rock singer and songwriter, Jan 2007

Tureck, Rosalyn, American pianist and harpsichordist, Sept 1959, *Obit* Yrbk 2003

Turner, Alex, British rock guitarist and singer, Jan 2006

Turner, Mark, American jazz saxophonist, Nov 2002

Turre, Steve, American jazz trombonist, Apr 2001

Tuzun, Sibel, Turkish pop singer, Jan 2006

Tweedy, Jeff, American singer and songwriter, Feb 2010

Tweet (Singer), American singer and songwriter, Nov 2002

Two-Tone Tommy, American rock bassist, Nov 2008

Tyler, Steven, American rock singer, Aug 1996, July 2004

Tyler, the Creator (Musician), American rapper and record producer, Aug 2011

Uchida, Mitsuko, Japanese pianist, Sept 1991

Uematsu, Nobuo, Japanese composer, Jan 2006

Uggams, Leslie, American singer and actress, Oct 1967

Ullman, Tracey, English actress and singer, Oct 1988

Underwood, Carrie, American singer and contestant on reality TV show American idol, Mar 2007

Upshaw, Dawn, American opera singer, Feb 1990

Usmanova, Yulduz, Uzbek singer, Jan 2004

Valensi, Nick, American guitarist, Feb 2007

Valente, Benita, opera singer, Mar 1988

Vallin, Sergio, Mexican guitarist and singer, Jan 2005

Van Heusen, Jimmy, American composer, June 1970, *Obit* Apr 1990

Vandross, Luther, American rhythm and blues singer and songwriter, Sept 1991, *Obit* Yrbk 2005

Vaness, Carol, American opera singer, Sept 1986

Vanessa-Mae, British violinist, Jan 2002

Varnay, Astrid, American opera singer, May 1951, *Obit* Yrbk 2007

Vaughan Williams, Ralph, English composer, Yrbk 1953, *Obit* Nov 1958

Veloso, Caetano, Brazilian singer and songwriter, Jan 2002

Verrett, Shirley, American opera singer, Apr 1967, *Obit* Yrbk 2011

Vickers, Jon, Canadian opera singer, Mar 1961

Vickrey, Dan, American guitarist, Mar 2003

Voigt, Deborah, American opera singer, Jan 1999

Volkova, Julia, Russian singer, Jan 2003

Vollenweider, Andreas, Swiss harpist, May 1987

Volume, Johnny, Finnish guitarist, Jan 2003

Von Stade, Frederica, American opera singer, Aug 1977

Voorhees, Donald, conductor, Feb 1950, *Obit* Apr 1989

Waart, Edo de, Dutch conductor, Mar 1990

Walton, William, English composer, Mar 1940, *Obit* May 1983

Ward, Robert, composer, July 1963, *Obit* Yrbk 2013

Ware, David S., American jazz saxophonist, Sept 2003, *Obit* Yrbk 2013

Warren, Diane, American songwriter, June 2000

Warren, Leonard, opera singer, Yrbk 1953, *Obit* Apr 1960

Waters, Ethel, American actress and singer, Apr 1941, Mar 1951, *Obit* Oct 1977

Watkins, Rone, Antiguan drummer, Jan 2004

Watts, Andre, American pianist, May 1968

Weede, Robert, Feb 1957, *Obit* Sept 1972

Weill, Kurt, German composer, Yrbk 1941, *Obit* May 1950

Weissenberg, Alexis, Bulgarian pianist, June 1978, *Obit* Yrbk 2012

Welch, Florence, British singer, June 2012

Welitsch, Ljuba, Bulgarian opera singer, May 1949, *Obit* Nov 1996

West, Kanye, American rapper and record producer, Aug 2006

Westenra, Hayley, New Zealand singer, Jan 2006

White, Jack, American singer and guitarist, Sept 2003

White, Meg, American drummer, Sept 2003

White, Portia, Mar 1945

Whitford, Brad, American rock guitarist, July 2004

Whittemore, Arthur Austin, pianist, Jan 1954, *Obit* Feb 1985

Wicker, Ireene, singer and storyteller, Apr 1943, *Obit* Jan 1988

Wiedoeft, Rudy, *Obit* Mar 1940

Wilder, Alec, composer, July 1980, *Obit* Feb 1981

Will. i. Am (Musician), American singer, Oct 2006

Williams of Barnburgh, Thomas Williams, Apr 1946, *Obit* May 1967

Williams, Andy, American singer, Feb 1960, *Obit* Yrbk 2012

Williams, Camilla, opera singer, June 1952, *Obit* Yrbk 2012

Williams, Hank, American country singer, Mar 1998

Williams, Joe, singer, Apr 1985, *Obit* June 1999

Williams, John, Australian guitarist, July 1983

Williams, Lucinda, American singer and songwriter, Mar 1999

Williams, Michelle, American singer, Aug 2001

Williams, Robbie, British pop singer, Jan 2004

Williams, Saul, American rapper and poet, June 2011

Williamson, Nicol, British actor, Jan 1970, *Obit* Yrbk 2012

Williamson, Ski, Finnish guitarist and singer, Jan 2003

Willis, Kelly, singer, Oct 1999

Wilson, Brian, American singer and songwriter, July 1988

Wilson, Cassandra, American jazz singer, Mar 1998

Wilson, Mark, Australian bassist, Jan 2005

Wolfe, Julia, American composer, Oct 2003

Womack, Lee Ann, American country singer, Apr 2010

Wood, Peggy, actress and singer, July 1942, Yrbk 1953, *Obit* May 1978

Wright, Martha, American singer and actress, Feb 1955

Wu Man, Chinese pipa player, Jan 2007

Wynette, Tammy, American country singer, June 1995, *Obit* June 1998

Wynonna, American country singer, May 1996

Xenakis, Iannis, Greek composer, Sept 1994, *Obit* July 2001

Yankovic, Al, American rock music parodist, Feb 1999

Yanni, Greek composer, Jan 2003

Yauch, Adam, American rapper and bassist, *Obit* Yrbk 2012

Yearwood, Trisha, American country singer, July 1998

Yepes, Narciso, Spanish guitarist, Oct 1966, *Obit* July 1997

Yon, Pietro A., Italian-American organist and composer, *Obit* Jan 1944

Yoshimura, Yumi, Japanese pop singer, Jan 2005

Youmans, Vincent, composer, Apr 1944, *Obit* May 1946

ZaBach, Florian, Yrbk 1955

Zandonai, Riccardo, Italian composer, *Obit* Aug 1944

Zimmer, Hans, German composer, Mar 2002

Zirato, Bruno, Yrbk 1959, *Obit* Jan 1973

Zola, South African rapper, Jan 2004

Musicologists

Finscher, Ludwig, German musicologist, Jan 2007

Landsbergis, Vytautas, Lithuanian president, July 1990

Smith, Carleton, musicologist and foundation official, Apr 1961, *Obit* July 1984

Spaeth, Sigmund, musicologist, July 1942, *Obit* Jan 1966

Mystery writers

Ambler, Eric, English mystery novelist, June 1975, *Obit* Jan 1999

Armstrong, Charlotte, author, Yrbk 1946, *Obit* Sept 1969

Baker, Nina Brown, American young adult author, Yrbk 1947, *Obit* Nov 1957

Barton, George, American journalist and mystery writer, *Obit* Apr 1940

Boucher, Anthony, American mystery and science fiction writer, June 1962, *Obit* June 1968

Bramah, Ernest, English author, *Obit* Sept 1942

Bristow, Gwen, author, Yrbk 1940, *Obit* Yrbk 1984

Buchanan, Edna, American journalist and novelist, Sept 1997

Chandler, Raymond, American mystery novelist, Yrbk 1946, *Obit* June 1959

Christie, Agatha, English mystery writer, Sept 1940, July 1964, *Obit* Mar 1976

Clark, Dorothy Park, American novelist, Yrbk 1957

Clark, Mary Higgins, American mystery novelist, Jan 1994

Cornwell, Patricia Daniels, American mystery novelist, May 1997

Creasey, John, English novelist, Sept 1963, *Obit* July 1973

Crispin, Edmund, English novelist and short story writer, Yrbk 1949

Dannay, Frederic, American mystery writer, July 1940, *Obit* Oct 1982

De la Torre, Lillian, author, Yrbk 1949, *Obit* Nov 1993

Dodge, David, author, Yrbk 1956

Eustis, Helen, author, Yrbk 1955

Evanovich, Janet, American mystery novelist, Apr 2001

Freeman, R. Austin, English physician and mystery writer, *Obit* Nov 1943

Gardner, Erle Stanley, American mystery novelist, June 1944, *Obit* Apr 1970

George, Elizabeth, American mystery novelist, Mar 2000

Grafton, Sue, American mystery novelist, Sept 1995

Gruber, Frank, American screenwriter and mystery novelist, Nov 1941, *Obit* Feb 1970

Highsmith, Patricia, American mystery novelist, Jan 1990, *Obit* Apr 1995

Hillerman, Tony, American mystery novelist, Jan 1992, *Obit* Yrbk 2008

Hubbard, Margaret Ann, American young adult mystery writer, Yrbk 1958

Isaacs, Susan, American novelist, Oct 1993

Jakes, John, American novelist, Sept 1988

James, P. D., English mystery novelist, Aug 1980

Jong, Dola de, Dutch-American mystery novelist, Yrbk 1947, *Obit* Yrbk 2004

Kendrick, Baynard Hardwick, author, Feb 1946, *Obit* May 1977

Lawrence, Hilda, author, Yrbk 1947

Leblanc, Maurice, French author, *Obit* Jan 1942

Lee, Manfred, American mystery writer, July 1940

Lehane, Dennis, American mystery novelist, Oct 2005

Lethem, Jonathan, American novelist and short story writer, Mar 2006

Levin, Ira, American novelist, Aug 1991, *Obit* Feb 2008

Lockridge, Richard, American mystery novelist, Oct 1940, *Obit* Oct 1982

MacDonald, John D., American mystery novelist, Oct 1986, *Obit* Feb 1987

Macdonald, Ross, American mystery novelist, Yrbk 1953, Aug 1979, *Obit* Sept 1983

Marcos, Mexican revolutionary, Jan 2002

McGraw, Eloise Jarvis, American children's author, Yrbk 1955, *Obit* Mar 2001

Millar, Margaret, author, Yrbk 1946, *Obit* June 1994

Mosley, Walter, American mystery novelist, Sept 1994

Newman, Bernard, English author, Apr 1959, *Obit* Apr 1968

Oppenheim, Edward Phillips, English mystery novelist, *Obit* Mar 1946

Packard, Frank Lucius, Canadian author, *Obit* Apr 1942

Paretsky, Sara, American mystery novelist, May 1992

Paul, Elliot, author, Feb 1940, *Obit* June 1958

Popkin, Zelda F., author, Yrbk 1951, *Obit* July 1983

Rankin, Ian, Scottish mystery novelist, Jan 2008

Rendell, Ruth, English mystery writer, Apr 1994

Robinson, Peter, English mystery novelist, Sept 2007

Roueche, Berton, American novelist and medical and travel writer, Yrbk 1959, *Obit* July 1994

Saunders, Hilary Aidan St. George, English author, June 1943, *Obit* Feb 1952

Simenon, Georges, Belgian novelist, Apr 1970, *Obit* Nov 1989

Simpson, Helen, Australian author, *Obit* Yrbk 1940

Spillane, Mickey, American mystery novelist, Sept 1981, *Obit* Nov 2006

Steel, Kurt, author, *Obit* June 1946

Stout, Rex, American mystery novelist, Mar 1946, *Obit* Jan 1976

Upfield, Arthur W., Australian author, Yrbk 1948, *Obit* Apr 1964

Waldman, Ayelet, American novelist, Sept 2009

White, Randy Wayne, American mystery writer and fishing guide, Nov 2011

Williams, Jay, American novelist, Yrbk 1955, *Obit* Sept 1978

Mystics

Ammachi, Indian Hindu mystic, Jan 2003

Bhave, Vinoba, Indian mystic and social reformer, Sept 1953, *Obit* Jan 1983

NASA officials

Dryden, Hugh L., American physicist and NASA official, Apr 1959, *Obit* Jan 1966

Fletcher, James C., American physicist and NASA official, May 1972, *Obit* Feb 1992

Jastrow, Robert, American physicist, Jan 1973, *Obit* Yrbk 2008

O'Keefe, Sean, American NASA official, Jan 2003

NATO officials

Fogh Rasmussen, Anders, Danish prime minister, Jan 2004

Narcotic addicts

Gooden, Dwight, American baseball player, Apr 1986

Naturalists

Allen, Arthur Augustus, American ornithologist, Jan 1961, *Obit* Mar 1964

Atwell, Wayne J., American anatomist, *Obit* May 1941

Bailey, Vernon, American naturalist, *Obit* June 1942

Bakker, Robert T., American paleontologist, Aug 1995

Bedford, Herbrand Arthur Russell, English zoologist, *Obit* Oct 1940

Beehler, Bruce McP., American ornithologist and conservationist, Aug 2006

Benyus, Janine M., American environmentalist, naturalist and science writer, Mar 2006

Blakeslee, Albert Francis, American botanist, Oct 1941, *Obit* Jan 1955

Blatchley, W. S., American entomologist and geologist, *Obit* July 1940

Carver, George Washington, American botanist, Nov 1940, *Obit* Feb 1943

Chapman, Frank Michler, American ornithologist, *Obit* Jan 1946

Colbert, Edwin Harris, American paleontologist, Sept 1965, *Obit* Feb 2002

Commoner, Barry, American biologist and environmentalist, Sept 1970, *Obit* Yrbk 2012

Cowdry, E. V., anatomist and gerontologist, Jan 1948

Dart, Raymond A., South African anatomist, Sept 1966, *Obit* Jan 1989

Day, Albert M., biologist, Yrbk 1948

Driesch, Hans, German biologist and philosopher, *Obit* June 1941

Egloff, Gustav, Sept 1940

Espinoza Fuentes, Fernando, Ecuadorian biologist, Jan 2004

Fawcett, Edward, *Obit* Nov 1942

Fay, Michael, American biologist and conservationist, Sept 2001

Fortey, Richard A., British paleontologist, Sept 2005

Frisch, Karl von, German zoologist, Feb 1974, *Obit* Yrbk 1983

Goff, M. Lee, forensic entomologist, June 2001

Hagens, Gunther von, German anatomist, Jan 2005

Haig-Brown, Roderick Langmere, Canadian naturalist, conservationist and author, Yrbk 1950

Hair, Jay D., American zoologist and conservationist, Nov 1993, *Obit* Jan 2003

Hammond, E. Cuyler, biologist and statistician, June 1957, *Obit* Jan 1987

Holman, Eugene, May 1948, *Obit* Oct 1962

Kinsey, Alfred Charles, American zoologist and sex researcher, Jan 1954, *Obit* Oct 1956

Knipling, E. F., entomologist, May 1975, *Obit* Yrbk 2000

Laidlaw, Patrick Playfair, *Obit* Apr 1940

Levi-Montalcini, Rita, Italian biologist, Nov 1989, *Obit* Yrbk 2013

Little, Clarence C., American biologist, Yrbk 1944, *Obit* Feb 1972

Maathai, Wangari, Kenyan biologist and environmentalist, Sept 1993, *Obit* Yrbk 2011

Masursky, Harold, geologist, Aug 1986, *Obit* Oct 1990

Medawar, P. B., British biologist, Apr 1961, *Obit* Nov 1987

Merriam, John C., *Obit* Yrbk 1945

Mittermeier, Russell, biologist and conservationist, Oct 1992

Monod, Jacques, French biologist, July 1971, *Obit* July 1976

Nylander, Olof O., *Obit* Sept 1943

Osborn, Fairfield, American naturalist and conservationist, Sept 1949, *Obit* Nov 1969

Packard, Winthrop, *Obit* May 1943

Pearl, Raymond, American biologist, *Obit* Jan 1941

Peattie, Donald Culross, American naturalist, Oct 1940, *Obit* Jan 1965

Perret, Frank Alvord, *Obit* Mar 1943

Pincus, Gregory, American biologist, May 1966, *Obit* Oct 1967

Profet, Margie, biologist, Nov 1998

Rogers, Lynn L., wildlife biologist, Oct 1994

Schaller, George B., American zoologist, Aug 1985

Scott, Peter Markham, English ornithologist and painter, May 1968, *Obit* Nov 1989

Shiras, George, American lawyer and naturalist, *Obit* May 1942

Shoemaker, Eugene Merle, planetary geologist, June 1967, *Obit* Oct 1997

Simpson, George Gaylord, American paleontologist, Yrbk 1964, *Obit* Jan 1985

Strong, Lee A., *Obit* July 1941

Tewolde Berhan Gebre Egziabher, Ethiopian biologist and government official, Jan 2004

Thompson, Lonnie, American glaciologist, Jan 2004

Vishniac, Roman, American biologist and photographer, Feb 1967, *Obit* Mar 1990

Vogt, William, ornithologist, Mar 1953, *Obit* Sept 1968

Weng Wenhao, Nov 1948

Wilmut, Ian, British embryologist, June 1997

Wright, Berlin H., *Obit* Jan 1941

YamashitaYukiko, Developmental biologist, Mar 2012

Naval architects

Gibbs, William Francis, naval architect, Apr 1944, *Obit* Nov 1967

Naval historians

Morison, Samuel Eliot, American naval historian, Oct 1951, Sept 1962, *Obit* July 1976

Naval officers

Anderson, John W., American merchant marine officer, July 1953

Badger, Oscar C., American admiral, May 1949, *Obit* Feb 1959

Barbey, Daniel E., admiral, Jan 1945, *Obit* June 1969

Beach, Edward Latimer, American naval officer, Oct 1960, *Obit* May 2003

Blandy, W. H. P., American admiral, Nov 1942, *Obit* Mar 1954

Bloch, Claude Charles, American admiral, Feb 1942, *Obit* Yrbk 1967

Boone, J. T., American physician and admiral, Mar 1951, *Obit* June 1974

Bristol, Arthur LeRoy, *Obit* June 1942

Bryant, Benjamin, Nov 1943

Burke, Arleigh A., American admiral, Sept 1955, *Obit* Mar 1996

Byrd, Sam, Nov 1942, *Obit* Jan 1956

Callaghan, Daniel J., American admiral, *Obit* Jan 1943

Cantu, Giuseppe, *Obit* Yrbk 1940

Caperton, William B., American admiral, *Obit* Feb 1942

Cassady, John H., Oct 1952, *Obit* Mar 1969

Castro e Silva, Jose Machado de, *Obit* Aug 1943

Clark, J. J., American admiral, Jan 1954, *Obit* Sept 1971

Cruzen, Richard H., Mar 1947, *Obit* June 1970

Culshaw, John, British recording producer, June 1968, *Obit* June 1980

Cunningham of Hyndhope, Andrew Browne Cunningham,

British admiral, May 1941, *Obit* Sept 1963

Darlan, Francois, French admiral, Mar 1941, *Obit* Feb 1943

Dauser, Sue S., Aug 1944

Davidson, John Frederick, admiral, Nov 1960, *Obit* Apr 1989

Denebrink, Francis C., admiral, Feb 1956, *Obit* June 1987

Denfeld, Louis E., American admiral, Yrbk 1947, *Obit* May 1972

Dennison, Robert L., Apr 1960, *Obit* May 1980

Donitz, Karl, German admiral, Nov 1942, *Obit* Feb 1981

Du Fournet, Louis Rene Marie Charles Dartige, *Obit* Mar 1940

Duerk, Alene, Sept 1973

Fallon, William J., American admiral, July 2007

Fechteler, William M., American admiral, Sept 1951, *Obit* Oct 1967

Field, Frederick Laurence, *Obit* Yrbk 1945

Fiske, Bradley A., *Obit* May 1942

Fraser, Bruce, July 1943, *Obit* Apr 1981

Gallery, Daniel V., Apr 1966, *Obit* Mar 1977

Gardner, Matthias B., June 1952

Ghormley, Robert Lee, admiral, Oct 1942, *Obit* Oct 1958

Granville, William Spencer Leveson-Gower, Sept 1950, *Obit* Sept 1953

Halsey, William Frederick, American admiral, Yrbk 1942, *Obit* Nov 1959

Hamblet, Julia E., Oct 1953

Hancock, Joy Bright, naval officer, Feb 1949, *Obit* Oct 1986

Harp, Edward B., Oct 1953

Hart, Thomas Charles, Jan 1942, *Obit* Sept 1971

Hewitt, H. Kent, American admiral, Apr 1943, *Obit* Nov 1972

Holloway, James, American admiral, Jan 1947

Horthy, Miklos, Hungarian admiral and regent, Oct 1940, *Obit* Apr 1957

Hough, Henry Hughes, *Obit* Oct 1943

Ingersoll, Royal E., Oct 1942, *Obit* July 1976

Jacobs, Randall, Aug 1942, *Obit* Oct 1967

Joy, C. Turner, American admiral, June 1951, *Obit* Sept 1956

Kidd, Isaac Campbell, *Obit* Feb 1942

Kimmel, Husband Edward, admiral, Jan 1942, *Obit* July 1968

King, Ernest Joseph, American admiral, Feb 1942, *Obit* Sept 1956

Kinkaid, Thomas Cassin, American admiral, Yrbk 1944, *Obit* Jan 1973

Koga, Mineichi, *Obit* Oct 1943

Krug, J. A., American Secretary of the interior, Oct 1944, *Obit* May 1970

Laborde, Jean de, Feb 1943

Land, Emory S., Sept 1941, *Obit* Jan 1972

Layton, Geoffrey, British admiral, Feb 1942

Leary, Herbert F., Aug 1942, *Obit* Feb 1958

Lemonnier, Andre, Nov 1952, *Obit* July 1963

Long, Andrew Theodore, *Obit* July 1946

Ma, G. John, July 1953

Manning, Harry, May 1952, *Obit* Oct 1974

Marcinko, Richard, motivational speaker, Mar 2001

McCain, John S., American admiral, June 1970, *Obit* June 1981

McCain, John Sidney, American admiral, Oct 1943, *Obit* Oct 1945

McDonald, David Lamar, admiral, Nov 1963, *Obit* Mar 1998

McIntire, Ross T., Oct 1945, *Obit* Feb 1960

McLintock, Gordon, admiral, Nov 1953, *Obit* June 1990

Meyers, George Julian, *Obit* Jan 1940

Mitscher, Marc Andrew, admiral, Aug 1944, *Obit* Mar 1947

Momsen, C. B., American admiral and inventor, July 1946, *Obit* July 1967

Moore, Henry Ruthven, Sept 1943, *Obit* May 1978

Mountevans, Edward Ratcliffe Garth Russell Evans, British admiral, May 1941, *Obit* Nov 1957

Mullen, Mike, American admiral, Feb 2008

Nagano, Osami, July 1942, *Obit* Feb 1947

Nelles, Percy Walker, Canadian admiral, Feb 1944

Nimitz, Chester W., American admiral, Feb 1942, *Obit* Mar 1966

Orville, Howard T., May 1956, *Obit* July 1960

Osumi, Mineo, *Obit* Apr 1941

Poindexter, John M., American admiral and presidential adviser, Nov 1987

Pound, Dudley, Jan 1941, *Obit* Yrbk 1943

Pride, Alfred Melville, admiral, Nov 1954, *Obit* Feb 1989

Pugh, Herbert Lamont, Mar 1951

Radford, Arthur W., American admiral, Nov 1949, *Obit* Oct 1973

Raeder, Erich, German admiral, Apr 1941, *Obit* Jan 1961

Ramsay, Bertram, British admiral, Mar 1944, *Obit* Feb 1945

Ramsey, Dewitt C., Jan 1953, *Obit* Nov 1961

Rawlings, Bernard, Aug 1945, *Obit* Yrbk 1962

Rickover, Hyman George, American admiral, May 1953, *Obit* Aug 1986

Robert, Georges, June 1943

Robinson, David, American basketball player, July 1993

Robinson, Samuel M., Feb 1942

Royal, Forrest B., American admiral, *Obit* July 1945

Schirra, Wally, American astronaut, June 1966, *Obit* Yrbk 2007

Schofield, Frank H., *Obit* Apr 1942

Sexton, W. R., *Obit* Oct 1943

Sherman, Forrest P., Mar 1948, *Obit* Sept 1951

Sides, John H., Jan 1961, *Obit* June 1978

Small, John D., American admiral and government official, Feb 1946, *Obit* Mar 1963

Smith, William Ward, American admiral, Feb 1948, *Obit* July 1966

Solberg, Thorvald A., American admiral, Yrbk 1948

Somerville, James, British admiral, Apr 1943, *Obit* Apr 1949

Spruance, Raymond Ames, American admiral, Apr 1944, *Obit* Mar 1970

Stark, Harold R., admiral, May 1940, *Obit* Oct 1972

Streeter, Ruth Cheney, marine corps officer, July 1943, *Obit* Jan 1991

Struble, Arthur Dewey, admiral, Nov 1951, *Obit* July 1983

Stump, Felix B., American admiral, Jan 1953, *Obit* Sept 1972

Sueyro, Saba H., Argentine admiral, *Obit* Sept 1943

Suzuki, Kantaro, Japanese admiral, Aug 1945, *Obit* May 1948

Tawresey, John Godwin, American admiral, *Obit* Apr 1943

Tennant, William George, British admiral, Feb 1945, *Obit* Sept 1963

Thach, John Smith, Yrbk 1960

Thomason, John W., marine corps officer and author, *Obit* May 1944

Towers, John Henry, American admiral, Oct 1941, *Obit* June 1955

Turner, Richmond Kelly, admiral, Apr 1944, *Obit* Apr 1961

Van Zandt, James E., congressman, Nov 1950, *Obit* Mar 1986

Vian, Philip, British admiral, Aug 1944, *Obit* Sept 1968

Vickery, H. L., American admiral, Yrbk 1943, *Obit* May 1946

Waesche, Russell Randolph, American Coast Guard admiral, Mar 1945, *Obit* Yrbk 1946

Wagner, J. Addington, May 1956

Wake-Walker, William Frederick, British admiral, *Obit* Oct 1945

Wilcox, J. W., American admiral, *Obit* May 1942

Wilde, Louise K., Apr 1954

Wilson, Rufus H., June 1955

Yamamoto, Isoroku, Japanese admiral, Feb 1942, *Obit* July 1943

Yonai, Mitsumasa, Jan 1940, *Obit* June 1948

Zumwalt, Elmo R., American admiral, June 1971, *Obit* June 2000

Nazi leaders

Abetz, Otto, German diplomat, Feb 1941

Daluege, Kurt, German Nazi leader, *Obit* Yrbk 1946

Darre, R. Walther, German Nazi leader, Nov 1941, *Obit* Jan 1957

Frank, Hans, German jurist and Nazi leader, Mar 1941, *Obit* Nov 1946

Frick, Wilhelm, German Nazi leader, Aug 1942, *Obit* Nov 1946

Goebbels, Joseph, German Nazi leader, Sept 1941, *Obit* Yrbk 1991

Hess, Rudolf, German Nazi leader, Mar 1941, *Obit* Oct 1987

Heydrich, Reinhard, German Nazi leader, *Obit* July 1942, July 1942

Himmler, Heinrich, German Nazi leader, June 1941, *Obit* June 1945

Hitler, Adolf, German dictator, Mar 1942, *Obit* Jan 1957

Kaltenbrunner, Ernst, Austrian Nazi leader, Apr 1943, *Obit* Nov 1946

Keitel, Wilhelm, German field marshal, Sept 1940, *Obit* Nov 1946

Kerrl, Hanns, German cabinet member, *Obit* Feb 1942

Krueger, Wilhelm, *Obit* June 1943

Ley, Robert, German Nazi leader, Sept 1940, *Obit* Yrbk 1945

Mussert, Anton Adriaan, Dutch Nazi leader, Nov 1942

Papen, Franz von, German diplomat, June 1941, *Obit* June 1969

Pavelic, Ante, Croatian Nazi leader, Aug 1942, *Obit* Feb 1960

Raeder, Erich, German admiral, Apr 1941, *Obit* Jan 1961

Reventlow, Ernst, *Obit* Jan 1944

Rosenberg, Alfred, German Nazi leader, Oct 1941, *Obit* Nov 1946

Rust, Bernhard, German Nazi leader, July 1942

Sauckel, Fritz, German Nazi leader, *Obit* Nov 1946

Seyss-Inquart, Artur von, Austrian Nazi leader, May 1941, *Obit* Nov 1946

Strasser, Otto, German Nazi leader, Sept 1940, *Obit* Oct 1974

Streicher, Julius, German Nazi leader, *Obit* Nov 1946

Terboven, Josef, German war criminal, Nov 1941, *Obit* June 1945

Neurologists

Allawi, Iyad, Iraqi interim prime minister and neurologist, Jan 2004

Bannister, Roger, British neurologist and runner, Apr 1956

Brickner, Richard M., Sept 1943

Hall, George W., *Obit* Yrbk 1941

Hammond, Graeme M., *Obit* Yrbk 1944

Head, Henry, British neurologist, *Obit* Yrbk 1940

Levi-Montalcini, Rita, Italian biologist, Nov 1989, *Obit* Yrbk 2013

Prusiner, Stanley, American neurologist, June 1997

Sachs, Bernard, American neurologist, *Obit* Mar 1944

Sacks, Oliver W., American neurologist and medical writer, Feb 1985

Neuroscientists

Davidson, Richard J., American neuroscientist, Aug 2004

Donoghue, John P., American neuroscientist, May 2010

Eagleman, David, American neuroscientist, Jan 2012

Gazzaniga, Michael S., American neuroscientist, Apr 1999

Goldman-Rakic, Patricia S., American neuroscientist, Feb 2003

Greenfield, Susan, British neuroscientist, Jan 2003

Harris, Sam, American neuroscientist, Jan 2012

LeDoux, Joseph E., American neuroscientist, Oct 2010

Milner, Brenda, Canadian neuroscientist, Jan 2006

Sapolsky, Robert M., American neurobiologist, Jan 2004

Schiller, Daniela, Israeli neuroscientist, Mar 2011

Taylor, Jill Bolte, American neuroanatomist, Jan 2009

Volkow, Nora D., American neuroscientist, Oct 2011

Voytek, Bradley, Neuroscientist, May 2012

News agency executives

Howard, Roy Wilson, news agency and newspaper executive, Nov 1940, *Obit* Jan 1965

Newspaper editors

Adzhubei, Aleksei I., Russian newspaper editor and son-in-law of Nikita Sergeevich Khrushchev, Sept 1964, *Obit* May 1993

Catledge, Turner, American newspaper editor, July 1975, *Obit* July 1983

Dennis, Charles H., newspaper editor, *Obit* Nov 1943

Forrest, Wilbur S., May 1948, *Obit* May 1977

Frankel, Max, newspaper editor, Apr 1987

Ghezali, Salima, Algerian newspaper editor, May 1998

Grimes, W. H., June 1947, *Obit* Mar 1972

Haffajee, Ferial, South African newspaper editor, Jan 2004

MacNeil, Neil, American newspaper editor, May 1940

Markel, Lester, newspaper editor, Yrbk 1952, *Obit* Jan 1978

Marshall, Verne, American newspaper editor, Feb 1941, *Obit* May 1965

Meloney, Marie Mattingly, *Obit* Aug 1943

Ramm, Fredrik, *Obit* Jan 1944

Rosenthal, A. M., American newspaper editor, Yrbk 1960, *Obit* Sept 2006

Rowell, Chester Harvey, newspaper editor, Yrbk 1940, *Obit* May 1948

Seltzer, Louis B., Yrbk 1956, *Obit* June 1980

Sey, Abdoulie, Gambian newspaper editor, Jan 2004

Soth, Lauren K., newspaper editor, Yrbk 1956, *Obit* June 1998

Stevenson, E. Robert, Jan 1940

Stout, Wesley Winans, June 1941, *Obit* Jan 1972

Van Doren, Irita, American newspaper editor, Sept 1941, *Obit* Feb 1967

Walker, Stanley, newspaper editor, Nov 1944, *Obit* Jan 1963

Woods, Donald, South African newspaper editor, Feb 1982, *Obit* Nov 2001

Newspaper executives

Abbott, Robert S., American newspaper publisher, *Obit* Mar 1940

Adler, Harry Clay, American newspaper executive, *Obit* Apr 1940

Adler, Julius Ochs, American newspaper executive, June 1948, *Obit* Yrbk 1956

Astor of Hever, John Jacob Astor, British newspaper publisher, May 1954, *Obit* Sept 1971

Beaverbrook, Max Aitken, British newspaper publisher, July 1940, *Obit* Sept 1964

Bingham, Barry, American newspaper publisher, Sept 1949, *Obit* Sept 1988

Block, Paul, American newspaper publisher, *Obit* Aug 1941

Camrose, William Ewert Berry, British newspaper publisher, Oct 1941, *Obit* Sept 1954

Chandler, Dorothy Buffum, American newspaper publisher and patron of the arts, July 1957, *Obit* Sept 1997

Chandler, Norman, American newspaper publisher, July 1957, *Obit* Yrbk 1973

Chandler, Otis, American newspaper publisher, Nov 1968, *Obit* Yrbk 2006

Cowles, John, American newspaper publisher, June 1954, *Obit* Apr 1983

Dryfoos, Orvil Eugene, American newspaper publisher, Jan 1962, *Obit* July 1963

Farrington, Elizabeth Pruett, American newspaper publisher, June 1955, *Obit* Sept 1984

Field, Marshall, American department store executives and newspaper publisher, Apr 1941, Mar 1952, *Obit* Jan 1957

Friendly, Edwin S., American newspaper executive, July 1949, *Obit* Sept 1970

Gannett, Frank Ernest, American newspaper publisher, Mar 1945, *Obit* Feb 1958

Graham, Donald E., American newspaper publisher, May 1998

Graham, Philip Leslie, American newspaper publisher, Feb 1948, *Obit* Oct 1963

Hearst, William Randolph, American newspaper publisher, Oct 1955, *Obit* July 1993

Kalikow, Peter, American real estate developer, Sept 1988

Kann, Peter R., American publishing executive, Mar 2003

Kemsley, James Gomer Berry, British newspaper publisher, Jan 1951, *Obit* Mar 1968

Knight, John Shively, American newspaper publisher, Apr 1945, *Obit* Aug 1981

Kushner, Jared, American newspaper publisher, June 2007

McCarrens, John S., American newspaper publisher, *Obit* Sept 1943

McLean, Robert, American newspaper publisher, Nov 1951, *Obit* Feb 1981

Murphy, Frederick E., American newspaper publisher, *Obit* Mar 1940

Neuharth, Allen, American newspaper publisher, Apr 1986, *Obit* Yrbk 2013

Pape, William Jamieson, American newspaper publisher, Jan 1940, *Obit* Mar 1961

Reid, Helen Rogers, American newspaper publisher, Feb 1941, May 1952, *Obit* Oct 1970

Rivero, Jose Ignacio, Cuban newspaper publisher, *Obit* May 1944

Roberts, C. Wesley, American public relations executive and political party leader, Apr 1953, *Obit* June 1975

Robinson, Janet L., American newspaper executive, Mar 2003

Rothermere, Harold Sidney Harmsworth, British newspaper publisher, *Obit* Jan 1941

Schiff, Dorothy, American newspaper publisher, July 1945, Jan 1965, *Obit* Oct 1989

Sengstacke, John, newspaper executive, Nov 1949, *Obit* Aug 1997

Shannon, William V., newspaper executive, Jan 1979, *Obit* Nov 1988

Smith, Hazel Brannon, American newspaper publisher, Sept 1973, *Obit* July 1994

Springer, Axel, German publishing executive, Yrbk 1968, *Obit* Nov 1985

Stern, Leonard, American real estate executive and newspaper publisher, Mar 1991

Sulzberger, Arthur Hays, American newspaper publisher, Mar 1943, *Obit* Feb 1969

Sulzberger, Arthur O., American newspaper publisher, Jan 1997

Sulzberger, Arthur Ochs, American newspaper publisher, Nov 1966, *Obit* Yrbk 2012

Thomson of Fleet, Roy Herbert Thomson, Canadian newspaper publisher, Jan 1960, *Obit* Sept 1976

Thomson, Kenneth, Canadian newspaper executive, July 1989, *Obit* Yrbk 2006

Wiley, William Foust, American newspaper publisher, *Obit* Oct 1944

Nobel laureates

Abrikosov, Alexei A., Russian-American physicist, Jan 2007

Adrian, Edgar Douglas Adrian, British physiologist, Feb 1955, *Obit* Oct 1977

Agnon, Shmuel Yosef, Israeli novelist and short story writer, Mar 1967, *Obit* Apr 1970

Aleixandre, Vicente, Spanish poet, Mar 1978, *Obit* Mar 1985

Alvarez, Luis W., American physicist, May 1947, *Obit* Oct 1988

Anderson, Carl David, American physicist, Jan 1951, *Obit* Mar 1991

Appleton, Edward Victor, British physicist, Sept 1945, *Obit* June 1965

Arafat, Yasir, Palestinian political leader, Mar 1971, Nov 1994, Jan 2002, *Obit* Feb 2005

Aston, Francis William, British chemist, *Obit* Jan 1946

Asturias, Miguel Angel, Guatemalan novelist, Oct 1968, *Obit* July 1974

Balch, Emily Greene, American economist and pacifist, Jan 1947, *Obit* Mar 1961

Banting, Frederick G., Canadian physician, *Obit* Apr 1941

Beckett, Samuel, Irish playwright and novelist, Feb 1970, *Obit* Feb 1990

Begin, Menachem, Israeli prime minister, Oct 1977, *Obit* Apr 1992

Bellow, Saul, American novelist, Feb 1965, Nov 1988, *Obit* Aug 2005

Benavente, Jacinto, Spanish dramatist, June 1953, *Obit* Sept 1954

Bergson, Henri, French philosopher, *Obit* Feb 1941

Bethe, Hans, German-American physicist, Jan 1940, Apr 1950, *Obit* Aug 2005

Blackett, Patrick M. S., British physicist, Feb 1949, *Obit* Sept 1974

Bloch, Felix, Swiss-American physicist, Sept 1954, *Obit* Nov 1983

Bohr, Niels Henrik David, Danish physicist, Sept 1945, *Obit* Jan 1963

Boll, Heinrich, German novelist and short story writer, July 1972, *Obit* Sept 1985

Born, Max, German physicist, May 1955, *Obit* Feb 1970

Bosch, Carl, German chemist, *Obit* Jan 1940

Bothe, Walther Wilhelm, German physicist, May 1955, *Obit* Apr 1957

Bovet, Daniel, Swiss-Italian pharmacologist, Jan 1958, *Obit* June 1992

Bragg, William Henry, British physicist, *Obit* Apr 1942

Brattain, Walter Houser, American physicist, Sept 1957, *Obit* Nov 1987

Brenner, Sydney, British geneticist, Jan 2007

Bridgman, P. W., American physicist, Apr 1955, *Obit* Nov 1961

Broglie, Louis de, French physicist, Sept 1955, *Obit* May 1987

Calvin, Melvin, American biochemist, Apr 1962, *Obit* Mar 1997

Chadwick, James, British physicist, Nov 1945, *Obit* Oct 1974

Chain, Ernst Boris, British biochemist, Nov 1965, *Obit* Oct 1979

Chamberlain, Owen, American physicist, Mar 1960, *Obit* July 2006

Chandrasekhar, Subrahmanyan, American astrophysicist, Mar 1986, *Obit* Oct 1995

Chauvin, Yves, French chemist, Jan 2007

Ciechanover, Aaron J., Israeli biochemist, Jan 2007

Cockcroft, John, British physicist, Nov 1948, *Obit* Nov 1967

Compton, Arthur Holly, American physicist, Aug 1940, Sept 1958, *Obit* May 1962

Corrigan, Mairead, Irish pacifist, Apr 1978

Crick, Francis, British biochemist, Mar 1983, *Obit* Yrbk 2004

Dalai Lama, Tibetan religious and political leader (deposed 1959), July 1951, June 1982

Dam, Henrik, Danish biochemist, Sept 1949, *Obit* June 1976

Dausset, Jean, French immunologist, May 1981, *Obit* Yrbk 2009

Eccles, John C., Australian physiologist, Oct 1972, *Obit* July 1997

Einstein, Albert, German-American physicist, Nov 1941, May 1953, *Obit* June 1955

Elytes, Odysseus, Greek poet, Sept 1980, *Obit* June 1996

Enders, John F., American virologist, June 1955, *Obit* Jan 1986

Faulkner, William, American novelist, Jan 1951, *Obit* Sept 1962

Fermi, Enrico, Italian-American physicist, Oct 1945, *Obit* Jan 1955

Feynman, Richard Phillips, American physicist, Oct 1955, Nov 1986, *Obit* Apr 1988

Fischer, Hans, German chemist, *Obit* May 1945

Forssmann, Werner, German physician, Mar 1957, *Obit* Aug 1979

Fowler, William A., American physicist, Sept 1974, *Obit* May 1995

Franck, James, German-American physicist, May 1957, *Obit* July 1964

Gabor, Dennis, British physicist, Oct 1972, *Obit* Apr 1979

Garcia Marquez, Gabriel, Colombian novelist and short story writer, July 1973, Jan 2002

Gbowee, Leymah, Liberian peace activist, Oct 2012

Ginzburg, Vitalii L., Russian physicist, Jan 2007, *Obit* Yrbk 2010

Glaser, Donald Arthur, American physicist, Mar 1961, *Obit* Yrbk 2013

Goeppert-Mayer, Maria, American physicist, June 1964, *Obit* Apr 1972

Golding, William, English novelist, Mar 1964, *Obit* Aug 1993

Goldstein, Joseph Leonard, American physician, July 1987

Greider, Carol W., American molecular biologist, Feb 2008

Hahn, Otto, German chemist, Mar 1951, *Obit* Oct 1968

Hansch, Theodor W., German physicist, Jan 2007

Harden, Arthur, British biochemist, *Obit* Aug 1940

Hartwell, Leland, American geneticist, Nov 1999

Heidenstam, Verner von, Swedish poet and novelist, *Obit* July 1940

Heisenberg, Werner, German physicist, Apr 1957, *Obit* Mar 1976

Hench, Philip Showalter, American physician, Yrbk 1950, *Obit* May 1965

Herzberg, Gerhard, Canadian physicist, Feb 1973, *Obit* July 1999

Hess, Victor Francis, American physicist, Oct 1963, *Obit* Feb 1965

Hesse, Hermann, German novelist, Oct 1962

Hevesy, George Charles, Hungarian chemist, Apr 1959, *Obit* Sept 1966

Heyrovsky, Jaroslav, Czech chemist, July 1961, *Obit* May 1967

Hinshelwood, Cyril Norman, British chemist, Apr 1957, *Obit* Yrbk 1967

Hofstadter, Robert, American physicist, Oct 1962, *Obit* Jan 1991

Huggins, Charles B., American surgeon, Feb 1965, *Obit* Mar 1997

Jelinek, Elfriede, Austrian novelist and dramatist, Jan 2005

Joliot-Curie, Frederic, French physicist, Oct 1946, *Obit* Oct 1958

Joliot-Curie, Irene, French physicist, Apr 1940, *Obit* May 1956

Jouhaux, Leon, French labor leader, Jan 1948, *Obit* July 1954

Kahneman, Daniel, Israeli psychologist, Jan 2007

Kapitsa, P. L., Russian physicist, Oct 1955, *Obit* May 1984

Karman, Tawakel, Mar 2013

Kastler, Alfred, French physicist, Yrbk 1967, *Obit* Mar 1984

Kawabata, Yasunari, Japanese novelist and short story writer, Mar 1969, *Obit* June 1972

Kendall, Edward Calvin, American biochemist, Yrbk 1950, *Obit* June 1972

Kim, Dae Jung, South Korean president, Sept 1985, *Obit* Yrbk 2009

Koshiba, Masatoshi, Japanese physicist, Jan 2007

Kusch, Polykarp, American physicist, Mar 1956, *Obit* May 1993

Kuznets, Simon, American economist, May 1972, *Obit* Sept 1985

Lamb, Willis E., American physicist, Mar 1956, *Obit* Yrbk 2008

Landau, Lev Davidovich, Russian physicist, July 1963, *Obit* May 1968

Lawrence, Ernest Orlando, American physicist, Feb 1940, Jan 1952, *Obit* Nov 1958

Laxness, Halldor, Icelandic novelist and essayist, Oct 1946, *Obit* Feb 1999

Le, Duc Tho, Vietnamese communist leader, Mar 1975, *Obit* Jan 1991

Lee, Tsung Dao, American physicist, Nov 1958

Leggett, A. J., Anglo-American physicist, Jan 2007

Leontief, Wassily W., American economist, Jan 1967, *Obit* Apr 1999

Libby, Willard Frank, American chemist, Nov 1954, *Obit* Nov 1980

Lorenz, Konrad, Austrian ethologist, July 1955, Oct 1977, *Obit* Apr 1989

Luthuli, Albert John, South African political leader, Feb 1962, *Obit* Oct 1967

Lynen, Feodor, German biochemist, June 1967, *Obit* Oct 1979

Mahfuz, Najib, Egyptian novelist, May 1989, *Obit* Yrbk 2007

Mansfield, Peter, British physicist, Jan 2007

Martin, Archer, British biochemist, Nov 1953, *Obit* Yrbk 2002

McClintock, Barbara, American geneticist, Mar 1984, *Obit* Nov 1992

Medawar, P. B., British biologist, Apr 1961, *Obit* Nov 1987

Millikan, Robert A., American physicist, Jan 1940, June 1952, *Obit* Feb 1954

Monod, Jacques, French biologist, July 1971, *Obit* July 1976

Montagnier, Luc, French virologist, Aug 1988

Mossbauer, Rudolf L., German physicist, May 1962, *Obit* Yrbk 2012

Mott, John Raleigh, American religious and youth leader, Jan 1947, *Obit* Mar 1955

Muller, Paul Hermann, Swiss chemist, Oct 1945, *Obit* Yrbk 1965

Mullis, Kary B., American biochemist, Feb 1996

Natta, Giulio, Italian chemist, Nov 1964

Nernst, Hermann Walther, German chemist, *Obit* Jan 1942

Nirenberg, Marshall Warren, American biochemist, Apr 1965, *Obit* Yrbk 2010

Oe, Kenzaburo, Japanese novelist, May 1996

Pamuk, Orhan, Turkish novelist, Jan 2007

Pasternak, Boris Leonidovich, Russian poet and novelist, Feb 1959, *Obit* July 1960

Pauli, Wolfgang, German physicist, June 1946, *Obit* Mar 1959

Pearson, Lester Bowles, Canadian prime minister, Nov 1947, Nov 1963, *Obit* Feb 1973

Penzias, Arno Allan, American physicist, Sept 1985

Peres, Shimon, Israeli political leader, Jan 1976, Mar 1995

Perutz, Max, British biochemist, Nov 1963, *Obit* Apr 2002

Pinter, Harold, English dramatist, Nov 1963, *Obit* July 2009

Pire, Georges, Belgian priest, May 1959, *Obit* Mar 1969

Prigogine, Ilya, Russian-Belgian chemist, Feb 1987, *Obit* Yrbk 2003

Prusiner, Stanley, American neurologist, June 1997

Purcell, Edward M., American physicist, Sept 1954, *Obit* May 1997

Quidde, Ludwig, German historian and pacifist, *Obit* Apr 1941

Rabi, Isidor Isaac, American physicist, Apr 1948, *Obit* Mar 1988

Rabin, Yitzhak, Israeli prime minister, Sept 1974, Jan 1995, *Obit* Jan 1996

Raman, Chandrasekhara Venkata, Indian physicist, Nov 1948, *Obit* Jan 1971

Reichstein, Tadeus, Swiss chemist, Feb 1951, *Obit* Oct 1996

Richards, Dickinson W., American physician, Mar 1957, *Obit* Apr 1973

Richter, Burton, American physicist, Sept 1977

Rotblat, Joseph, British physicist and pacifist, July 1997, *Obit* Feb 2006

Rous, Francis Peyton, American pathologist, Mar 1967, *Obit* Apr 1970

Rubbia, Carlo, Italian physicist, June 1985

Ryle, Martin, British physicist and astronomer, Sept 1973, *Obit* Jan 1985

Sabatier, Paul, French chemist, *Obit* Oct 1941

Sachs, Nelly, German poet, Mar 1967, *Obit* July 1970

Sadat, Anwar, Egyptian president, Mar 1971, *Obit* Nov 1981

Sakharov, Andrei Dmitrievich, Russian physicist, July 1971, *Obit* Feb 1990

Salam, Abdus, Pakistani physicist, Apr 1988, *Obit* Jan 1997

Sanger, Frederick, British biochemist, July 1981

Saramago, Jose, Portuguese novelist, June 2002, *Obit* Yrbk 2010

Sato, Eisaku, Japanese prime minister, Yrbk 1965, *Obit* Aug 1975

Schwinger, Julian, American physicist, Oct 1967, *Obit* Sept 1994

Segre, Emilio, American physicist, Apr 1960, *Obit* July 1989

Semenov, Nikolay Nikolayevich, Russian chemist, Mar 1957

Shechtman, Daniel, Scientist and educator, May 2012

Sholokhov, Mikhail Aleksandrovich, Russian novelist, Jan 1942, Feb 1960, *Obit* Apr 1984

Simon, Claude, French novelist, May 1992, *Obit* Yrbk 2005

Solzhenitsyn, Aleksandr, Russian novelist, Feb 1969, July 1988, *Obit* Nov 2008

Sommerfeld, Arnold Johannes Wilhelm, German physicist, Apr 1950, *Obit* May 1951

Sperry, Roger Wolcott, American psychologist, Jan 1986, *Obit* June 1994

Staudinger, Hermann, German chemist, Apr 1954, *Obit* Nov 1965

Steinbeck, John, American novelist, Jan 1940, May 1963, *Obit* Feb 1969

Stigler, George Joseph, American economist and educator, July 1983, *Obit* Feb 1992

Sulston, John, English molecular biologist, Jan 2007

Synge, Richard Lawrence Millington, British biochemist, Nov 1953

Tamm, Igor Evgenievich, Russian physicist, Yrbk 1963, *Obit* June 1971

Tanaka, Koichi, Japanese chemist, Jan 2007

Teresa, Yugoslav nun and missionary, Sept 1973, *Obit* Nov 1997

Theiler, Max, American microbiologist, Jan 1952, *Obit* Oct 1972

Theorell, Hugo, Swedish biochemist, Feb 1956, *Obit* Oct 1982

Thomson, George Paget, British physicist, Mar 1947, *Obit* Oct 1975

Thomson, Joseph John, British physicist, *Obit* Oct 1940

Tiselius, Arne Wilhelm Kaurin, Swedish biochemist, Apr 1949, *Obit* Yrbk 1971

Todd, Alexander R., British chemist, Mar 1958, *Obit* Mar 1997

Townes, Charles H., American physicist, Mar 1963

Transtr"mer, Tomas, Swedish poet, July 2012

Trimble, David, Northern Ireland political leader, July 2000

Undset, Sigrid, Norwegian novelist, Sept 1940, *Obit* July 1949

Vane, John R., British pharmacologist, May 1986, *Obit* Yrbk 2005

Vargas Llosa, Mario, Peruvian novelist, Feb 1976

Von Bekesy, Georg, Hungarian-American physicist, Yrbk 1962, *Obit* Sept 1972

Wagner-Jauregg, Julius, Austrian psychiatrist, *Obit* Nov 1940

Waksman, Selman Abraham, American microbiologist, May 1946, *Obit* Oct 1973

Walton, Ernest T. S., Irish physicist, Mar 1952, *Obit* Sept 1995

Warren, J. Robin, Australian pathologist, Jan 2007

Weller, Thomas H., American virologist, June 1955, *Obit* Yrbk 2008

White, Patrick, Australian novelist, June 1974, *Obit* Nov 1990

Wigner, Eugene P., American physicist, Apr 1953, *Obit* Mar 1995

Williams, Betty, Irish pacifist, Mar 1979

Williams, Jody, American pacifist, Mar 1998

Willstatter, Richard, German chemist, *Obit* Sept 1942

Wilson, Kenneth Geddes, American physicist, Sept 1983, *Obit* Yrbk 2013

Wuthrich, Kurt, Swiss chemist, Jan 2007

Yalow, Rosalyn S., American medical physicist, July 1978, *Obit* Yrbk 2011

Yang, Chen-ning, Chinese-American physicist, Nov 1958

Yukawa, Hideki, Japanese physicist, Jan 1950, *Obit* Nov 1981

Zeeman, Pieter, Dutch physicist, *Obit* Yrbk 1943

Zernike, Frits, Dutch physicist, Feb 1955, *Obit* Apr 1966

Nobel laureates for chemistry

Aston, Francis William, British chemist, *Obit* Jan 1946

Bosch, Carl, German chemist, *Obit* Jan 1940

Chauvin, Yves, French chemist, Jan 2007

Fischer, Hans, German chemist, *Obit* May 1945

Herzberg, Gerhard, Canadian physicist, Feb 1973, *Obit* July 1999

Hevesy, George Charles, Hungarian chemist, Apr 1959, *Obit* Sept 1966

Heyrovsky, Jaroslav, Czech chemist, July 1961, *Obit* May 1967

Hinshelwood, Cyril Norman, British chemist, Apr 1957, *Obit* Yrbk 1967

Joliot-Curie, Frederic, French physicist, Oct 1946, *Obit* Oct 1958

Kobilka, Brian, Apr 2013

Libby, Willard Frank, American chemist, Nov 1954, *Obit* Nov 1980

Natta, Giulio, Italian chemist, Nov 1964

Nernst, Hermann Walther, German chemist, *Obit* Jan 1942

Sabatier, Paul, French chemist, *Obit* Oct 1941

Semenov, Nikolay Nikolayevich, Russian chemist, Mar 1957

Staudinger, Hermann, German chemist, Apr 1954, *Obit* Nov 1965

Tanaka, Koichi, Japanese chemist, Jan 2007

Todd, Alexander R., British chemist, Mar 1958, *Obit* Mar 1997

Willstatter, Richard, German chemist, *Obit* Sept 1942

Wuthrich, Kurt, Swiss chemist, Jan 2007

Nobel laureates for economic sciences

Kuznets, Simon, American economist, May 1972, *Obit* Sept 1985

Leontief, Wassily W., American economist, Jan 1967, *Obit* Apr 1999

Nobel laureates for literature

Agnon, Shmuel Yosef, Israeli novelist and short story writer, Mar 1967, *Obit* Apr 1970

Aleixandre, Vicente, Spanish poet, Mar 1978, *Obit* Mar 1985

Asturias, Miguel Angel, Guatemalan novelist, Oct 1968, *Obit* July 1974

Heidenstam, Verner von, Swedish poet and novelist, *Obit* July 1940

Hesse, Hermann, German novelist, Oct 1962

Kawabata, Yasunari, Japanese novelist and short story writer, Mar 1969, *Obit* June 1972

Mahfuz, Najib, Egyptian novelist, May 1989, *Obit* Yrbk 2007

Mann, Thomas, German novelist, May 1942, *Obit* Oct 1955

Pamuk, Orhan, Turkish novelist, Jan 2007

Saramago, Jose, Portuguese novelist, June 2002, *Obit* Yrbk 2010

Sholokhov, Mikhail Aleksandrovich, Russian novelist, Jan 1942, Feb 1960, *Obit* Apr 1984

Simon, Claude, French novelist, May 1992, *Obit* Yrbk 2005

Solzhenitsyn, Aleksandr, Russian novelist, Feb 1969, July 1988, *Obit* Nov 2008

Transtr"mer, Tomas, Swedish poet, July 2012

Nobel laureates for peace

Arafat, Yasir, Palestinian political leader, Mar 1971, Nov

1994, Jan 2002, *Obit* Feb 2005

Begin, Menachem, Israeli prime minister, Oct 1977, *Obit* Apr 1992

Corrigan, Mairead, Irish pacifist, Apr 1978

Dalai Lama, Tibetan religious and political leader (deposed 1959), July 1951, June 1982

Gbowee, Leymah, Liberian peace activist, Oct 2012

Jouhaux, Leon, French labor leader, Jan 1948, *Obit* July 1954

Le, Duc Tho, Vietnamese communist leader, Mar 1975, *Obit* Jan 1991

Mott, John Raleigh, American religious and youth leader, Jan 1947, *Obit* Mar 1955

Pire, Georges, Belgian priest, May 1959, *Obit* Mar 1969

Rotblat, Joseph, British physicist and pacifist, July 1997, *Obit* Feb 2006

Sato, Eisaku, Japanese prime minister, Yrbk 1965, *Obit* Aug 1975

Williams, Betty, Irish pacifist, Mar 1979

Williams, Jody, American pacifist, Mar 1998

Nobel laureates for physics

Abrikosov, Alexei A., Russian-American physicist, Jan 2007

Alvarez, Luis W., American physicist, May 1947, *Obit* Oct 1988

Anderson, Carl David, American physicist, Jan 1951, *Obit* Mar 1991

Appleton, Edward Victor, British physicist, Sept 1945, *Obit* June 1965

Bethe, Hans, German-American physicist, Jan 1940, Apr 1950, *Obit* Aug 2005

Blackett, Patrick M. S., British physicist, Feb 1949, *Obit* Sept 1974

Bloch, Felix, Swiss-American physicist, Sept 1954, *Obit* Nov 1983

Bohr, Niels Henrik David, Danish physicist, Sept 1945, *Obit* Jan 1963

Born, Max, German physicist, May 1955, *Obit* Feb 1970

Bothe, Walther Wilhelm, German physicist, May 1955, *Obit* Apr 1957

Bragg, William Henry, British physicist, *Obit* Apr 1942

Brattain, Walter Houser, American physicist, Sept 1957, *Obit* Nov 1987

Broglie, Louis de, French physicist, Sept 1955, *Obit* May 1987

Chadwick, James, British physicist, Nov 1945, *Obit* Oct 1974

Chamberlain, Owen, American physicist, Mar 1960, *Obit* July 2006

Cockcroft, John, British physicist, Nov 1948, *Obit* Nov 1967

Einstein, Albert, German-American physicist, Nov 1941, May 1953, *Obit* June 1955

Feynman, Richard Phillips, American physicist, Oct 1955, Nov 1986, *Obit* Apr 1988

Franck, James, German-American physicist, May 1957, *Obit* July 1964

Gabor, Dennis, British physicist, Oct 1972, *Obit* Apr 1979

Ginzburg, Vitalii L., Russian physicist, Jan 2007, *Obit* Yrbk 2010

Hansch, Theodor W., German physicist, Jan 2007

Heisenberg, Werner, German physicist, Apr 1957, *Obit* Mar 1976

Hess, Victor Francis, American physicist, Oct 1963, *Obit* Feb 1965

Hofstadter, Robert, American physicist, Oct 1962, *Obit* Jan 1991

Kapitsa, P. L., Russian physicist, Oct 1955, *Obit* May 1984

Kastler, Alfred, French physicist, Yrbk 1967, *Obit* Mar 1984

Lamb, Willis E., American physicist, Mar 1956, *Obit* Yrbk 2008

Landau, Lev Davidovich, Russian physicist, July 1963, *Obit* May 1968

Mossbauer, Rudolf L., German physicist, May 1962, *Obit* Yrbk 2012

Pauli, Wolfgang, German physicist, June 1946, *Obit* Mar 1959

Penzias, Arno Allan, American physicist, Sept 1985

Purcell, Edward M., American physicist, Sept 1954, *Obit* May 1997

Raman, Chandrasekhara Venkata, Indian physicist, Nov 1948, *Obit* Jan 1971

Richter, Burton, American physicist, Sept 1977

Ryle, Martin, British physicist and astronomer, Sept 1973, *Obit* Jan 1985

Sommerfeld, Arnold Johannes Wilhelm, German physicist, Apr 1950, *Obit* May 1951

Tamm, Igor Evgenievich, Russian physicist, Yrbk 1963, *Obit* June 1971

Thomson, George Paget, British physicist, Mar 1947, *Obit* Oct 1975

Thomson, Joseph John, British physicist, *Obit* Oct 1940

Walton, Ernest T. S., Irish physicist, Mar 1952, *Obit* Sept 1995

Yang, Chen-ning, Chinese-American physicist, Nov 1958

Yukawa, Hideki, Japanese physicist, Jan 1950, *Obit* Nov 1981

Zeeman, Pieter, Dutch physicist, *Obit* Yrbk 1943

Zernike, Frits, Dutch physicist, Feb 1955, *Obit* Apr 1966

Nobel laureates for physiology or medicine

Forssmann, Werner, German physician, Mar 1957, *Obit* Aug 1979

Goldstein, Joseph Leonard, American physician, July 1987

Muller, Paul Hermann, Swiss chemist, Oct 1945, *Obit* Yrbk 1965

Reichstein, Tadeus, Swiss chemist, Feb 1951, *Obit* Oct 1996

Rous, Francis Peyton, American pathologist, Mar 1967, *Obit* Apr 1970

Vane, John R., British pharmacologist, May 1986, *Obit* Yrbk 2005

Von Bekesy, Georg, Hungarian-American physicist, Yrbk 1962, *Obit* Sept 1972

Warren, J. Robin, Australian pathologist, Jan 2007

Yalow, Rosalyn S., American medical physicist, July 1978, *Obit* Yrbk 2011

Nonfiction writers

Abend, Hallett, American journalist, Sept 1942, *Obit* Feb 1956

Achebe, Chinua, Nigerian novelist, Jan 1992, *Obit* Yrbk 2013

Adamic, Louis, author, Yrbk 1940, *Obit* Oct 1951

Adams, Gerry, Irish political leader, Sept 1994

Adams, James Truslow, historian, Nov 1941, *Obit* July 1949

Adams, Joseph H., American inventor, philanthropist and nonfiction writer, *Obit* Apr 1941

Adler, Mortimer J., American philosopher and educator, Apr 1940, Sept 1952, *Obit* Sept 2001

Al-Emam, Mahassen, Jordanian journalist, Jan 2004

Al-Turabi, Hassan, Sudanese political leader, Jan 1999

Aleksievich, Svetlana, Belarusian journalist, Jan 2006

Allegro, John Marco, British paleographer and philologist, Yrbk 1970, *Obit* Apr 1988

Allen, Jay, American journalist, Oct 1941, *Obit* Feb 1973

Allen, Larry, American journalist, July 1942

Alterman, Eric, American journalist, Feb 2007

Andrews, Bert, American journalist, Sept 1948, *Obit* Oct 1953

Andrews, Charles McLean, American historian, *Obit* Oct 1943

Angier, Natalie, American science writer, Aug 1999

Angoff, Charles, American novelist and editor, Yrbk 1955, *Obit* July 1979

Applebaum, Anne, American journalist, Aug 2004

Ardrey, Robert, American playwright and screenwriter, July 1973, *Obit* Mar 1980

Arendt, Hannah, German-American political philosopher, May 1959, *Obit* Feb 1976

Armstrong, Margaret Neilson, author, *Obit* Sept 1944

Arne, Sigrid, American journalist, Oct 1945

Arnow, Harriette Louisa Simpson, American novelist and historian, Yrbk 1954, *Obit* May 1986

Aron, Raymond, French political philosopher and journalist, June 1954, *Obit* Jan 1984

Ashe, Arthur, American tennis player, Nov 1966, *Obit* Mar 1993

Aswell, James, American novelist, Yrbk 1951, *Obit* Apr 1955

Banning, Margaret Culkin, author, May 1940, *Obit* Feb 1982

Barbour, Ralph Henry, author, *Obit* Apr 1944

Barth, John, American novelist and essayist, May 1969

Barth, Karl, Swiss theologian, Nov 1962, *Obit* Feb 1969

Baudrillard, Jean, French social theorist, June 1993, *Obit* Yrbk 2007

Bauer, Erwin A., photographer, Feb 1993

Bauer, Peggy, photographer, Feb 1993

Beals, Carleton, journalist, Yrbk 1942, *Obit* Aug 1979

Bedford, Sybille, English novelist, Feb 1990, *Obit* Yrbk 2006

Beebe, Lucius Morris, journalist, Sept 1940, *Obit* Mar 1966

Beer, Thomas, author, *Obit* May 1940

Bell, Edward Price, American journalist, *Obit* Nov 1943

Belluck, Pam, New York Times science writer and journalist, June 2012

Bemis, Samuel Flagg, historian, June 1950, *Obit* Nov 1973

Bennett, James O'Donnell, American journalist, *Obit* Mar 1940

Berg, Elizabeth, American novelist and short story writer, Nov 1999

Bernstein, Carl, American journalist, Oct 1976

Bertrand, Louis, French novelist and historian, *Obit* Feb 1942

Bess, Demaree, American journalist, Jan 1943, *Obit* Sept 1962

Bettelheim, Bruno, American psychologist, July 1961, *Obit* May 1990

Bigart, Homer, American journalist, June 1951, *Obit* July 1991

Binet-Valmer, Jean, French novelist, *Obit* Sept 1940

Birmingham, Stephen, author, May 1974

Blake, Doris, Canadian journalist, Nov 1941

Blake, Tiffany, American journalist, *Obit* Nov 1943

Booker, Edna Lee, American journalist, Apr 1940

Bowden, Mark, American journalist, Jan 2002

Bowen, Catherine Drinker, American biographer, July 1944, *Obit* Yrbk 1973

Bowman, George Ernest, American historian, *Obit* Nov 1941

Boyd, James, author, *Obit* Apr 1944

Boyle, Kay, American novelist, short story writer and poet, June 1942, *Obit* Feb 1993

Braudel, Fernand, French historian, Apr 1985, *Obit* Jan 1986

Breslin, Howard, Yrbk 1958, *Obit* July 1964

Brogan, Denis William, Scottish political scientist and historian, Yrbk 1947, *Obit* Feb 1974

Bromfield, Louis, novelist, July 1944, *Obit* May 1956

Brooks, Geraldine, Australian journalist, Aug 2006

Browder, Earl, American communist leader, Oct 1944, *Obit* Sept 1973

Brown, Dee Alexander, American historian and novelist, Aug 1979, *Obit* Mar 2003

Buck, Frank, big game hunter, June 1943, *Obit* Apr 1950

Bumiller, Elisabeth, American journalist, Sept 2008

Burke, Thomas, English author, *Obit* Oct 1945

Burns, Cecil Delisle, *Obit* Mar 1942

Burton, Jean, Yrbk 1948

Burtsev, Vladimir L'vovich, Russian revolutionary and journalist, *Obit* Yrbk 1942

Butterfield, Roger Place, journalist, Mar 1948, *Obit* Yrbk 1991

Byas, Hugh, Mar 1943, *Obit* Apr 1945

Caballero, Maria Cristina, Colombian journalist, Jan 2004

Calder, Nigel, English author, June 1986

Calder, Ritchie, Scottish author and journalist, Apr 1963, *Obit* May 1986

Calvino, Italo, Italian novelist and short story writer, Feb 1984, *Obit* Nov 1985

Capote, Truman, American short story writer and novelist, Sept 1951, Mar 1968, *Obit* Oct 1984

Carr, William G., educator, Sept 1952, *Obit* May 1996

Cassidy, Henry Clarence, journalist, Sept 1943

Chadourne, Marc, *Obit* Feb 1941

Champion, Pierre, *Obit* Aug 1942

Chapman, Frank Michler, American ornithologist, *Obit* Jan 1946

Charques, Dorothy, Yrbk 1958

Chase, Stuart, economist, Oct 1940, *Obit* Jan 1986

Chen Guidi, Chinese journalist, Jan 2005

Clampitt, Amy, American poet, Feb 1992, *Obit* Nov 1994

Clapper, Olive Ewing, Sept 1946, *Obit* Jan 1969

Clark, Eugenie, American oceanographer, Sept 1953

Clark, Sydney, Sept 1956

Clendening, Logan, physician, *Obit* Mar 1945

Coit, Margaret L., American biographer, June 1951

Coker, Elizabeth Boatwright, author, Yrbk 1959, *Obit* Nov 1993

Colby, Nathalie S., *Obit* July 1942

Collingwood, R. G., British philosopher and historian, *Obit* Mar 1943

Commager, Henry Steele, historian, Jan 1946, *Obit* May 1998

Cornwell, Patricia Daniels, American mystery novelist, May 1997

Corsi, Jerome R., American political writer, Nov 2008

Counts, George S., author and educator, Yrbk 1941, *Obit* Jan 1975

Cowles, Virginia, author and journalist, May 1942, *Obit* Nov 1983

Coxe, Howard, *Obit* Jan 1941

Creeley, Robert, American poet, novelist, short story writer and essayist, Oct 1988, *Obit* Yrbk 2005

Crum, Bartley C., lawyer, May 1947, *Obit* Feb 1960

Dafoe, John Wesley, *Obit* Feb 1944

Daley, Arthur, sportswriter, Sept 1956, *Obit* Feb 1974

Daniel, Clifton, American journalist, Mar 1966, *Obit* July 2000

Daniell, Raymond, Mar 1944, *Obit* June 1969

Daringer, Helen Fern, Yrbk 1951

Davenport, Marcia, novelist, Jan 1944, *Obit* Mar 1996

Davidson, William L., American physicist, July 1952

Davies, W. H., Welsh poet and author, *Obit* Nov 1940

Davis, Watson, Yrbk 1945, *Obit* Oct 1967

De Luce, Daniel, June 1944

De Roussy de Sales, Raoul, *Obit* Jan 1943

De la Torre, Lillian, author, Yrbk 1949, *Obit* Nov 1993

Deat, Marcel, French political leader, Jan 1942, *Obit* May 1955

Debray, Regis, French political philosopher, novelist and government official, June 1982

Decker, Karl, *Obit* Feb 1942

Deford, Frank, American sportswriter and novelist, Aug 1996

Derounian, Arthur, journalist, Oct 1943

Deuel, Wallace R., Aug 1942

Deutsch, Linda, American court reporter, Apr 2007

Diamant, Gertrude, American novelist and nonfiction writer, Nov 1942

Dietz, David, author and journalist, Oct 1940, *Obit* Apr 1985

Dixon, Jeane, American astrologer and psychic, Feb 1973, *Obit* Mar 1997

Dodge, David, author, Yrbk 1956

Dolci, Danilo, Italian social reformer and author, Sept 1961, *Obit* Mar 1998

Drew, Elizabeth, journalist, Oct 1979

Drew, George A., Canadian political leader, Yrbk 1948, *Obit* May 1984

Drummond, Roscoe, journalist, Nov 1949, *Obit* Nov 1983

Du Maurier, Daphne, English novelist, short story writer and biographer, May 1940, *Obit* June 1989

Du Puy, William Atherton, *Obit* Oct 1941

Dublin, Louis Israel, statistician, Oct 1942, *Obit* Yrbk 1991

Duranty, Walter, Anglo-American journalist, Jan 1943, *Obit* Yrbk 1958

Edwards, India, journalist and political activist, Sept 1949, *Obit* Mar 1990

Egan, Jennifer, American novelist, journalist and short story writer, Mar 2002

Eliot, George Fielding, American journalist, Jan 1940, *Obit* June 1971

Ellis, Bret Easton, American novelist, Nov 1994

Ellroy, James, American novelist, Apr 1998

Elson, Edward L. R., clergyman, Nov 1967, *Obit* Nov 1993

Emery, DeWitt, Oct 1946, *Obit* Oct 1955

Eysenck, H. J., German-British psychologist, Nov 1972, *Obit* Nov 1997

Fast, Howard, American novelist and short story writer, Apr 1943, Apr 1991, *Obit* July 2003

Feininger, Andreas, American photographer, Oct 1957, *Obit* May 1999

Feinstein, John, American sportswriter, July 1998

Fergusson, Erna, Yrbk 1955

Fermor, Patrick Leigh, English travel writer and novelist, Yrbk 1955, *Obit* Yrbk 2011

Ferrero, Guglielmo, Italian historian and author, *Obit* Sept 1942

Ferris, Timothy, American journalist and science writer, Jan 2001

Fielding, Temple Hornaday, travel book author, Apr 1969, *Obit* July 1983

Finney, Gertrude E., Yrbk 1957

Fisk, Robert, British journalist, Jan 2006

FitzGerald, Frances, American journalist, June 1987

Florinsky, Michael T., Russian historian, Oct 1941, *Obit* Jan 1982

Floyd, William, *Obit* Jan 1944

Folliard, Edward T., journalist, Nov 1947, *Obit* Feb 1977

Fong-Torres, Ben, American music journalist, Aug 2001

Foote, Shelby, American novelist and historian, Apr 1991, *Obit* Yrbk 2005

Forsyth, Frederick, English journalist and novelist, May 1986

Fosdick, Harry Emerson, American clergyman, Oct 1940, *Obit* Nov 1969

Foster, Maximilian, *Obit* Nov 1943

Foster, William Zebulon, American communist leader, July 1945, *Obit* Nov 1961

Francis-Williams, Edward Francis, English author and journalist, Mar 1946, *Obit* Sept 1970

Frank, Lawrence K., social scientist, Jan 1958, *Obit* Nov 1968

Frank, Waldo David, American novelist and essayist, Nov 1940, *Obit* Mar 1967

Frankel, Charles, philosopher and educator, Apr 1966, *Obit* July 1979

Freud, Anna, British psychoanalyst, Apr 1979, *Obit* Mar 1983

Fromm, Erich, American psychoanalyst and philosopher, Apr 1967, *Obit* May 1980

Frum, David, Canadian journalist, June 2004

Fyfe, H. Hamilton, Yrbk 1940, *Obit* July 1951

Gage, Nicholas, American journalist, Mar 1990

Gaines, Donna, American sociologist, June 2006

Galloway, Joseph L., American journalist, Sept 2003

Ganim, Sara, Aug 2013

Garcia, Cristina, American novelist and journalist, Aug 1999

Garst, Shannon, Yrbk 1947

Garth, David, Yrbk 1957

Gawande, Atul, American physician and medical writer, Mar 2005

George, Susan, American social scientist, July 2007

Geraud, Andre, Sept 1940, *Obit* Jan 1975

Gervasi, Frank Henry, author and journalist, June 1942, *Obit* Mar 1990

Gesell, Arnold Lucius, American psychologist, Nov 1940, *Obit* Sept 1961

Gessen, Masha, Russian journalist, Nov 2013

Gifford, Sanford R., American ophthalmologist, *Obit* Apr 1944

Gilmore, Eddy, American journalist, June 1947, *Obit* Yrbk 1967

Gimlette, John, English travel writer and lawyer, Apr 2012

Gladwell, Malcolm, Canadian business writer, June 2005

Godwin, Gail, American novelist and short story writer, Oct 1995

Gold, Herbert, American novelist and short story writer, Yrbk 1955

Goldberg, Michelle, American journalist, Jan 2012

Goodall, Jane, British primatologist, Nov 1967, Nov 1991

Goodspeed, Edgar Johnson, biblical scholar, Nov 1946, *Obit* Mar 1962

Gopnik, Alison, American psychologist, Jan 2007

Graebner, Walter, Aug 1943

Green, Constance McLaughlin, historian, Oct 1963

Griffin, John Howard, American novelist and journalist, Nov 1960, *Obit* Nov 1980

Groopman, Jerome E., American physician and medical writer, Oct 2004

Gruenberg, Sidonie Matsner, May 1940, *Obit* May 1974

Guillermoprieto, Alma, Mexican journalist, Sept 2004

Gunther, John, journalist and author, Nov 1941, Feb 1961, *Obit* July 1970

Guthrie, A. B., American novelist, short story writer and poet, July 1950, *Obit* July 1991

Habe, Hans, German author and journalist, Feb 1943, *Obit* Nov 1977

Habermas, Jurgen, German social philosopher, Jan 2007

Hahn, Emily, American novelist and biographer, July 1942, *Obit* Apr 1997

Hancock, Graham, Scottish writer, Feb 2005

Harris, Judith Rich, textbook author, Apr 1999

Harris, Sam, American neuroscientist, Jan 2012

Harrison, Jim, American poet and novelist, July 1992

Harsanyi, Zsolt, *Obit* Apr 1944

Hass, Amira, Israeli journalist, Apr 2009

Heath, S. Burton, Jan 1940, *Obit* Sept 1949

Hedges, Chris, American foreign correspondent, June 2012

Heidegger, Martin, German philosopher, June 1972, *Obit* July 1976

Heiden, Konrad, Mar 1944, *Obit* Sept 1975

Heiser, Victor G., physician, Apr 1942, *Obit* May 1972

Heming, Arthur Henry Howard, *Obit* Yrbk 1940

Hemingway, Mary, wife of American novelist Ernest Hemingway, Sept 1968, *Obit* Jan 1987

Herold, J. Christopher, Yrbk 1959, *Obit* Feb 1965

Hertzberg, Hendrik, American journalist, Mar 2011

Hertzler, Arthur E., American surgeon, *Obit* Oct 1946

Higgins, Marguerite, journalist, June 1951, *Obit* Feb 1966

Hightower, John M., journalist, Nov 1952, *Obit* Apr 1987

Hoagland, Edward, American novelist, essayist and travel writer, Sept 1982

Hocking, William Ernest, American philosopher, Mar 1962, *Obit* July 1966

Hoellering, Franz, Oct 1940

Holt, John Caldwell, American educator, June 1981, *Obit* Nov 1985

Horgan, Paul, author, Feb 1971, *Obit* May 1995

Hours, Madeleine, Apr 1961

Hoyle, Fred, English astronomer and science fiction writer, Apr 1960, *Obit* Jan 2002

Humphry, Derek, English euthanasia advocate, Mar 1995

Infeld, Leopold, May 1941, July 1963, *Obit* Mar 1968

Irving, John, American novelist, Oct 1979

Ivey, John E., educator, July 1960, *Obit* Aug 1992

Jacobs, Philip Peter, *Obit* Aug 1940

Jeans, James Hopwood, British physicist and mathematician, Apr 1941, *Obit* Oct 1946

Jenkins, Jerry B., American sportswriter and novelist, June 2003

Jenkins, Roy, British political leader, Mar 1966, Oct 1982, *Obit* Yrbk 2003

Johnson, Malcolm, June 1949, *Obit* Aug 1976

Jones, Idwal, author, Yrbk 1948, *Obit* Jan 1965

Jones, Rufus Matthew, American Quaker leader, Oct 1941, *Obit* Sept 1948

Jordan, Virgil, Oct 1947, *Obit* June 1965

Jung, C. G., Swiss psychologist, Apr 1943, Oct 1953, *Obit* Sept 1961

Kagawa, Toyohiko, Japanese clergyman and philosopher, Sept 1941, *Obit* June 1960

Kahn, Herman, American physicist and futurist, Oct 1962, *Obit* Aug 1983

Kahn, Roger, American novelist, short story writer and sportswriter, June 2000

Kallen, Horace Meyer, philosopher, Oct 1953, *Obit* Apr 1974

Kane, Joseph Nathan, American historian, Nov 1985, *Obit* Nov 2002

Kaplan, Justin, American biographer, July 1993

Keen, Sam, author and philosopher, Feb 1995

Kempner, Robert M. W., German lawyer, May 1943, *Obit* Oct 1993

Kenny, Elizabeth, Australian nurse, Oct 1942, *Obit* Jan 1953

Kerensky, Aleksandr Fyodorovich, Russian socialist leader, Yrbk 1966, *Obit* Sept 1970

Kernan, W. F., Apr 1942

Keynes, John Maynard, British economist, June 1941, *Obit* May 1946

Kieran, John, sportswriter, Apr 1940, *Obit* Feb 1982

Kilpi, Eeva, Finnish essayist, poet, short story writer and novelist, Jan 2007

Kinkade, Thomas, American painter, June 2000, *Obit* Yrbk 2012

Kirk, Russell, American political philosopher, Sept 1962, *Obit* June 1994

Kirkpatrick, Helen, journalist, May 1941

Klinkenborg, Verlyn, American nonifction writer, July 2006

Knickerbocker, Hubert Renfro, journalist, Sept 1940, *Obit* Sept 1949

Knight, Eric Mowbray, Anglo-American novelist, short story writer and journalist, July 1942, *Obit* Mar 1943

Krishnamurti, J., Indian philosopher, Oct 1974, *Obit* Apr 1986

Kubly, Herbert O., author and dramatist, Feb 1959, *Obit* Oct 1996

Kuhn, Irene Corbally, journalist, Feb 1946, *Obit* Mar 1996

Kung, Hans, Swiss theologian, July 1963

Laidler, Harry Wellington, economist, Feb 1945, *Obit* Oct 1970

Laing, R. D., Scottish psychiatrist, Mar 1973, *Obit* Mar 1989

Laird, Donald Anderson, Sept 1946

Lane, Carl Daniel, Yrbk 1951

Langer, Susanne Katherina Knauth, American philosopher, Nov 1963, *Obit* Sept 1985

Lash, Joseph P., author, Yrbk 1972, *Obit* Oct 1987

Laughlin, Clara Elizabeth, *Obit* Apr 1941

Laurence, William Leonard, journalist, Oct 1945, *Obit* May 1977

Lazareff, Pierre, May 1942, *Obit* June 1972

Le Roy Ladurie, Emmanuel, French historian, July 1984

Leach, Penelope, English child psychologist, Aug 1994

Lee, Andrea, American novelist and short story writer, Sept 2003

Lee, Harper, American novelist, Nov 1961

Leech, Margaret, American historian and novelist, July 1942, Nov 1960, *Obit* Apr 1974

Lengyel, Emil, journalist and author, Feb 1942, *Obit* Apr 1985

Leviero, Anthony, Sept 1952, *Obit* Nov 1956

Levy, Bernard Henri, French philosopher, Nov 1993

Levy, David H., Canadian science writer and amateur astronomer, Jan 1995

Lewis, Willmott, May 1941, *Obit* Feb 1950

Ley, Willy, German-American scientist and author, June 1941, Feb 1953, *Obit* Sept 1969

Leyburn, James Graham, Apr 1943

Lippmann, Walter, American journalist and political philosopher, Sept 1940, Nov 1962, *Obit* Jan 1975

Livingston, M. Stanley, physicist, Feb 1955, *Obit* Nov 1986

Lochner, Louis Paul, journalist, Aug 1942, *Obit* Feb 1975

Lombard, Helen, May 1943

Long, Tania, Anglo-Russian journalist, May 1946, *Obit* June 1999

Lord, Walter, American historian, Oct 1972, *Obit* Yrbk 2002

Louchheim, Katie, government official, June 1956, *Obit* Apr 1991

Lukas, J. Anthony, American journalist, Jan 1987, *Obit* Aug 1997

MacGowan, Gault, Jan 1945

MacLennan, Hugh, Canadian novelist, Yrbk 1946, *Obit* Jan 1991

Mailer, Norman, American novelist, Oct 1948, Feb 1970, *Obit* Jan 2008

Mangione, Jerre, American memoirist, novelist and historian, Mar 1943, *Obit* Nov 1998

Marble, Alice, American tennis player, Nov 1940, *Obit* Mar 1991

Marburg, Theodore, *Obit* Apr 1946

Marcuse, Herbert, American political philosopher, Mar 1969, *Obit* Sept 1979

Maritain, Jacques, French philosopher, May 1942, *Obit* June 1973

Marshall, S. L. A., Nov 1953, *Obit* Mar 1978

Mason, Joseph Warren Teets, American journalist, *Obit* July 1941

Masserman, Jules H., psychiatrist, July 1980, *Obit* Jan 1995

Matthews, Herbert L., American journalist, Nov 1943, *Obit* Sept 1977

Matthews, J. B., American senatorial aide, May 1943

Matthiessen, Peter, American novelist and nature writer, Oct 1975

Mattingly, Garrett, historian, Nov 1960, *Obit* Feb 1963

Maugham, W. Somerset, English novelist, short story writer and playwright, Jan 1963, *Obit* Jan 1966

May, Rollo, psychologist, June 1973, *Obit* Jan 1995

Mayer, Jane, American journalist, Oct 2008

McCann, Colum, Irish novelist and short story writer, Mar 2010

McClinton, Katharine Morrison, author, Mar 1958, *Obit* Mar 1993

McGinniss, Joe, American true crime writer, Jan 1984

McGurn, Barrett, Apr 1965

McLean, Evalyn Walsh, socialite, May 1943, *Obit* May 1947

McMurtry, Larry, American novelist, June 1984

Medvedev, Roy Aleksandrovich, Russian educator and historian, Sept 1984

Menninger, Karl A., American psychiatrist, Oct 1948, *Obit* Sept 1990

Michener, James A., American novelist, June 1948, Aug 1975, *Obit* Jan 1998

Michie, Allan A., Nov 1942, *Obit* Jan 1974

Middleton, Drew, journalist and author, Sept 1943, *Obit* Mar 1990

Millar, Margaret, author, Yrbk 1946, *Obit* June 1994

Miller, Henry, American novelist, Nov 1970, *Obit* July 1980

Miller, Judith, American journalist, Jan 2006

Miller, Max, American journalist, May 1940, *Obit* Feb 1968

Miller, Merle, author, Yrbk 1950, *Obit* July 1986

Miller, Webb, American journalist, *Obit* Jan 1940

Mlodinow, Leonard, American science writer, June 2009

Moats, Alice-Leone, author and journalist, May 1943, *Obit* July 1989

Moen, Lars, May 1941

Montgomery, Elizabeth Rider, author, Yrbk 1952

Moon, Bucklin, American writer, Yrbk 1950

Moore, Marianne, American poet, Yrbk 1952, Apr 1968, *Obit* Mar 1972

Morris, Desmond, British ethologist, Nov 1974

Morris, Edmund, American biographer, July 1989

Morris, Jan, English journalist and travel writer, Jan 1964, June 1986

Morrow, Honore Willsie, author, *Obit* May 1940

Morse, John Lovett, *Obit* May 1940

Morse, Philip McCord, physicist, June 1948, *Obit* Nov 1985

Morton, Henry H., *Obit* July 1940

Mosca, Gaetano, Italian political philosopher, *Obit* Jan 1942

Moulton, Forest Ray, American astronomer, Jan 1946, *Obit* Jan 1953

Moulton, Harold G., Nov 1944, *Obit* Feb 1966

Munro, Alice, Canadian short story writer and novelist, Sept 1990

Murakami, Haruki, Japanese novelist, Sept 1997

Murdoch, Iris, English novelist and philosopher, Yrbk 1958, Aug 1980, *Obit* Apr 1999

Murnane, Gerald, Australian short story writer and essayist, Jan 2007

Murray, Charles A., American social scientist, July 1986

Mydans, Shelley Smith, American journalist and novelist, May 1945, *Obit* Aug 2002

Myers, Norman, English environmentalist, May 1993

Naifeh, Steven W., author, Mar 1998

Naisbitt, John, American social forecaster, Nov 1984

Narayan, R. K., Indian novelist and short story writer, Sept 1987, *Obit* July 2001

Nehru, Jawaharlal, Indian prime minister, Jan 1941, Apr 1948, *Obit* July 1964

Neill, Alexander Sutherland, British child psychologist, Apr 1961, *Obit* Nov 1973

Newell, Homer Edward, physicist and mathematician, Nov 1954, *Obit* Sept 1983

Newman, Bernard, English author, Apr 1959, *Obit* Apr 1968

Nichols, Roy Franklin, historian, July 1949, *Obit* Mar 1973

Nicholson, Margaret, Nov 1957

Niebuhr, Reinhold, American theologian, Mar 1941, Nov 1951, *Obit* July 1971

Nin, Anais, American novelist, Feb 1944, Sept 1975, *Obit* Mar 1977

Nizer, Louis, American lawyer, Nov 1955, *Obit* Jan 1995

Nordmann, Charles, *Obit* Yrbk 1940

Norton, Howard Melvin, June 1947

O'Brian, Patrick, Irish novelist, June 1995, *Obit* Mar 2000

O'Neill, Gerard K., physicist, Feb 1979, *Obit* June 1992

Ogburn, Charlton, Feb 1955, *Obit* Apr 1962

Ojike, Mazi Mbonu, July 1947

Ornish, Dean, American physician, Apr 1994

Ottley, Roi, Oct 1943, *Obit* Yrbk 1960

Oursler, Fulton, editor and author, Oct 1942, *Obit* July 1952

Oz, Amos, Israeli novelist, July 1983

Ozick, Cynthia, American novelist and short story writer, Aug 1983

Packard, Eleanor, Apr 1941, *Obit* June 1972

Packard, Winthrop, *Obit* May 1943

Page, Irvine H., physician, June 1966, *Obit* Aug 1991

Page, Robert Morris, physicist, Nov 1964, *Obit* July 1992

Palast, Greg, American journalist, June 2011

Pares, Bernard, English historian, Jan 1946, *Obit* May 1949

Pearlman, Edith, American short story writer and essayist, June 2011

Peck, M. Scott, American psychiatrist and self-help writer, June 1991, *Obit* Yrbk 2005

Peixotto, Ernest C., *Obit* Jan 1941

Pell, Edward Leigh, American clergyman and religious writer, *Obit* Aug 1943

Percy, Walker, American novelist, Sept 1976, *Obit* July 1990

Perkins, Dexter, historian and educator, Jan 1958, *Obit* July 1984

Piaget, Jean, Swiss psychologist, Yrbk 1958, *Obit* Nov 1980

Pierce, Lorne, Nov 1956

Pierson, Louise Randall, Oct 1943

Pileggi, Nicholas, journalist and author, Jan 1999

Pipher, Mary Bray, psychologist and author, Aug 1999

Pitkin, Walter B., author, Oct 1941, *Obit* Mar 1953

Poliakov, Aleksandr, *Obit* Nov 1942

Pollack, Jack Harrison, American journalist, Yrbk 1957, *Obit* Feb 1985

Pollitt, Katha, American poet and essayist, Oct 2002

Pomeroy, Wardell Baxter, sex researcher, July 1974, *Obit* Yrbk 2001

Poncins, Gontran de, French travel writer, June 1941

Poore, Henry Rankin, *Obit* Oct 1940

Popper, Karl Raimund, Austrian-British philosopher, Jan 1963, *Obit* Nov 1994

Porter, Eliot, American photographer, Nov 1976, *Obit* Jan 1991

Post, Robert P., *Obit* Sept 1943

Potok, Chaim, American novelist and historian, May 1983, *Obit* Yrbk 2002

Pourtales, Guy de, *Obit* Aug 1941

Powell, Anthony, English novelist, Sept 1977, *Obit* Aug 2000

Powys, Llewelyn, English author, Jan 1940

Pyle, Ernie, American journalist, Apr 1941, *Obit* May 1945

Pynchon, Thomas, American novelist, Oct 1987

Quinn, Sally, American journalist, Oct 1988

Radhakrishnan, S., Indian statesman and philosopher, June 1952, *Obit* June 1975

Rahner, Karl, German theologian, July 1970, *Obit* May 1984

Rajagopalachari, C., Indian political leader, July 1942, *Obit* Feb 1973

Rama Rau, Santha, Indian travel writer and novelist, Aug 1945, Yrbk 1959, *Obit* Yrbk 2009

Ramonet, Ignacio, Spanish journalist, June 2008

Rand, Ayn, American novelist, May 1982

Randall, Ruth Painter, Yrbk 1957

Rashid, Ahmed, Pakistani journalist, Jan 2007

Reader, John, British photojournalist and writer, Jan 2007

Reilly, Rick, American sportswriter, Feb 2005

Resnick, Louis, *Obit* May 1941

Ressler, Robert K., American criminologist, Feb 2002

Restrepo, Laura, Colombian novelist and journalist, Jan 2006

Revel, Jean-Francois, French philosopher, Feb 1975, *Obit* Yrbk 2006

Reynolds, Helen Wilkinson, *Obit* Feb 1943

Reynolds, Quentin James, journalist, Mar 1941, *Obit* Apr 1965

Rice, Grantland, American sportswriter, Sept 1941, *Obit* Sept 1954

Ricks, Thomas E., American military writer, Nov 2007

Riesenberg, Felix, Yrbk 1957

Riesman, David, American physician, *Obit* July 1940

Riggs, Austen Fox, *Obit* Mar 1940

Risen, James, American journalist, Aug 2007

Robertson, Ben, American journalist, Nov 1942

Robinson, Marilynne, American novelist, Oct 2005

Ronson, Jon, English journalist, Apr 2012

Ross, Nancy Wilson, author, Yrbk 1952, *Obit* May 1986

Roth, Henry, American novelist and short story writer, Jan 1989, *Obit* Jan 1996

Rothery, Agnes, Yrbk 1946, *Obit* Oct 1954

Rowntree, Cecil, *Obit* Yrbk 1943

Rugg, Harold Ordway, American educator, May 1941, *Obit* July 1960

Rule, Ann, American true-crime writer, Sept 2000

Rushkoff, Douglas, American nonfiction writer and novelist, Nov 2013

Sabin, Albert, American physician, Feb 1958, *Obit* Apr 1993

Salk, Lee, child psychologist, Sept 1979, *Obit* July 1992

Salter, Andrew, psychologist, May 1944, *Obit* Jan 1997

Sandford, John, American crime novelist, Mar 2002

Scheffer, Victor B., marine mammalogist, Apr 1994

Schillebeeckx, Edward, Belgian priest and theologian, June 1983, *Obit* May 2010

Schoonover, Lawrence L., Yrbk 1957, *Obit* Mar 1980

Schultz, Sigrid Lillian, journalist, Apr 1944

Schwartz, Gil, American public relations executive and journalist, Aug 2007

Seabrook, William B., American occultist and travel writer, Nov 1940, *Obit* Oct 1945

Sears, Martha, nurse and writer on health, Aug 2001

Seghers, Anna, German author, Yrbk 1942, *Obit* July 1983

Seibold, Louis, *Obit* June 1945

Selye, Hans, Canadian physician, June 1953, Jan 1981, *Obit* Jan 1983

Severgnini, Beppe, Italian journalist, Jan 2006

Seymour, Flora Warren, historian and author, June 1942

Shah, Idries, Indian author, June 1976, *Obit* Feb 1997

Shamsie, Kamila, Pakistani novelist, Sept 2009

Shapley, Harlow, astronomer, Jan 1941, Yrbk 1952, Yrbk 1972

Shay, Edith, Yrbk 1952

Shay, Frank, Yrbk 1952, *Obit* Mar 1954

Sheehan, Neil, American journalist, Aug 1989

Sheldon, Charles M., clergyman and author, *Obit* Apr 1946

Shellabarger, Samuel, author, May 1945, *Obit* May 1954

Sherard, Robert Harborough, English author and journalist, *Obit* Mar 1943

Shiber, Etta, underground leader, Yrbk 1943, *Obit* Jan 1949

Shilts, Randy, American journalist, Oct 1993, *Obit* May 1994

Shimazaki, Toson, Japanese novelist, poet and essayist, *Obit* Oct 1943

Shinn, Milicent Washburn, author and journalist, *Obit* Oct 1940

Shoemaker, Samuel Moor, clergyman, Apr 1955, *Obit* Yrbk 1963

Shridharani, Krishnalal, Indian journalist and author, Jan 1942, *Obit* Oct 1960

Siddons, Anne Rivers, American novelist, Jan 2005

Siegel, Bernie S., surgeon, June 1993

Silberman, Charles E., American journalist, July 1979, *Obit* Yrbk 2011

Skinner, Quentin, British historian, Jan 2007

Sloane, Eric, painter and author, Sept 1972, *Obit* May 1985

Smedley, Agnes, American journalist, Jan 1944, *Obit* June 1950

Smith, Bruce, Feb 1953, *Obit* Nov 1955

Smith, Gary, American sportswriter, Jan 2009

Smith, Gregory White, lawyer and author, Mar 1998

Smith, Hedrick, American journalist, June 1991

Smith, Merriman, journalist and author, Yrbk 1964, *Obit* Nov 1993

Snow, Edgar, journalist, June 1941, *Obit* Apr 1972

Snow, Edward Rowe, Yrbk 1958

Snyder, Gary, American poet and nature writer, Nov 1978

Solomon, Susan, American atmospheric scientist, July 2005

Sorokin, Pitirim Aleksandrovich, sociologist, July 1942, *Obit* Apr 1968

Spark, Muriel, Scottish novelist, Nov 1975, *Obit* Yrbk 2007

Spence, Hartzell, journalist and novelist, Oct 1942, *Obit* Yrbk 2001

St. John, Robert, American journalist, June 1942, *Obit* Yrbk 2003

St. Johns, Adela Rogers, author and journalist, Aug 1976, *Obit* Sept 1988

Stace, W. T., Apr 1961, *Obit* Oct 1967

Steel, Danielle, American romance novelist, July 1989

Steiner, Walter Ralph, *Obit* Jan 1943

Steptoe, Patrick, British surgeon, Mar 1979, *Obit* June 1988

Stevens, Edmund, American journalist, July 1950, *Obit* July 1992

Stewart, George Rippey, American novelist and nonfiction writer, Jan 1942, *Obit* Nov 1980

Stewart, Kenneth L., Yrbk 1943

Stone, Irving, biographer, Yrbk 1967, *Obit* Oct 1989

Stout, Rex, American mystery novelist, Mar 1946, *Obit* Jan 1976

Streit, Clarence K., journalist, May 1940, May 1950, *Obit* Sept 1986

Stridsberg, Gustaf, *Obit* Yrbk 1943

Strong, Anna Louise, American journalist, Mar 1949, *Obit* May 1970

Sturzo, Luigi, Feb 1946, *Obit* Nov 1959

Styron, William, American novelist, July 1968, June 1986, *Obit* Yrbk 2007

Sugar, Bert Randolph, American sportswriter, Nov 2002, *Obit* Yrbk 2012

Sullivan, Harry Stack, American psychiatrist, Nov 1942, *Obit* Feb 1949

Sulloway, Frank J., science historian, Sept 1997

Suskind, Ron, Feb 2013

Suzuki, Daisetz Teitaro, Japanese philosopher, Oct 1958, *Obit* Nov 1966

Tabouis, Genevieve R., French journalist, Jan 1940

Talese, Gay, American journalist, July 1972

Tallant, Robert, author, Yrbk 1953, *Obit* June 1957

Taylor, A. J. P., British historian, Nov 1983, *Obit* Nov 1990

Taylor, Henry O., *Obit* June 1941

Taylor, Robert Lewis, biographer, Yrbk 1959, *Obit* Jan 1999

Teller, Edward, American physicist, Yrbk 1954, Nov 1983, *Obit* Yrbk 2004

Terhune, Albert Payson, author, *Obit* Apr 1942

Thayer, Ernest Lawrence, American journalist and poet, *Obit* Oct 1940

Theroux, Paul, American novelist and short story writer, Nov 1978

Thomas, Norman, American socialist leader, Sept 1944, July 1962, *Obit* Feb 1969

Thomas, William Sturgis, *Obit* Feb 1942

Thurman, Robert A. F., American Buddhist leader, Sept 1997

Toffler, Alvin, American futurist and writer, Apr 1975

Tolischus, Otto D., Jan 1940, *Obit* Apr 1967

Tolle, Eckhart, German spiritual writer, Feb 2005

Tournier, Michel, French novelist, Apr 1990

Toynbee, Arnold Joseph, British historian, July 1947, *Obit* Jan 1976

Travers, P. L., English children's author, May 1996, *Obit* June 1996

Treanor, Tom, *Obit* Oct 1944

Tregaskis, Richard, author and journalist, Aug 1943, *Obit* Oct 1973

Trotsky, Leon, Soviet communist leader, *Obit* Oct 1940

Troyat, Henri, French novelist and biographer, Mar 1992, *Obit* Yrbk 2007

Trussell, C. P., July 1949, *Obit* Yrbk 1968

Turow, Scott, American lawyer and novelist, Aug 1991

Tuttle, Merlin D., mammalogist, June 1992

Updike, Daniel Berkeley, *Obit* Feb 1942

Uris, Leon, American novelist, Yrbk 1959, Feb 1979, *Obit* Yrbk 2003

Utley, Freda, Yrbk 1958, *Obit* Mar 1978

Valdes-Rodriguez, Alisa, American novelist, Jan 2006

Velikovsky, Immanuel, May 1957, *Obit* Jan 1980

Viereck, Peter, American poet and historian, Apr 1943, *Obit* Yrbk 2006

Vogt, William, ornithologist, Mar 1953, *Obit* Sept 1968

Wallace, Irving, author, Mar 1979, *Obit* Sept 1990

Wallerstein, Judith S., psychologist, Nov 1996

Wallraff, Gunter, German journalist, Jan 2004

Waln, Nora, journalist, Jan 1940, *Obit* Nov 1964

Walsh, George Ethelbert, *Obit* Apr 1941

Walsh, James Joseph, *Obit* Apr 1942

Walworth, Arthur, American biographer, Yrbk 1959, *Obit* Yrbk 2005

Wambaugh, Sarah, authority on plebiscites, Apr 1946, *Obit* Jan 1956

Warren, Rick, American pastor and religious writer, Oct 2006

Watson, Mark Skinner, journalist, Nov 1946, *Obit* Apr 1966

Watts, Alan, American philosopher, Mar 1962, *Obit* Jan 1974

Webb, Beatrice Potter, British sociologist and reformer, *Obit* June 1943

Wedgwood, C. V., English historian, Jan 1957, *Obit* May 1997

Wells, H. G., English science fiction novelist, *Obit* Sept 1946

Wendt, Gerald Louis, scientist, Mar 1940, *Obit* Feb 1974

Werner, Max, Yrbk 1943, *Obit* Feb 1951

Werth, Alexander, English journalist, Apr 1943, *Obit* Apr 1969

Wertham, Frederic, American psychologist, July 1949, *Obit* Jan 1982

West, Rebecca, English novelist and journalist, June 1968, *Obit* May 1983

Whipple, Wayne, *Obit* Yrbk 1942

White, Stewart Edward, author and hunter, *Obit* Nov 1946

Whitehead, Don, journalist, Yrbk 1953, *Obit* Mar 1981

Whitford, Harry Nichols, *Obit* July 1941

Whyte, William H., American journalist and sociologist, Jan 1959, *Obit* Mar 1999

Wiener, Norbert, American mathematician, Mar 1950, *Obit* May 1964

Wiggam, Albert Edward, July 1942, *Obit* June 1957

Wildmon, Donald, clergyman, Jan 1992

Wilkerson, Isabel, American journalist, Oct 2011

Williams, Jay, American novelist, Yrbk 1955, *Obit* Sept 1978

Williams, Wythe, journalist, Oct 1943, *Obit* Sept 1956

Willison, George Findlay, historian, Jan 1946

Wilson, Angus, English novelist and short story writer, Feb 1959, *Obit* Aug 1991

Wilson, Colin, English novelist and nonfiction writer, Apr 1963

Winchester, Simon, Anglo-American journalist, Oct 2006

Winter, Ella, Yrbk 1946, *Obit* Sept 1980

Wolfe, Tom, American journalist and novelist, Jan 1971

Wolfert, Ira, author and journalist, Apr 1943, *Obit* Feb 1998

Woltman, Frederick, July 1947, *Obit* Apr 1970

Woodward, C. Vann, American historian, May 1986, *Obit* June 2000

Woolf, Virginia, English novelist, *Obit* May 1941

Wu Chuntao, Chinese journalist, Jan 2005

Wylie, Max, Jan 1940, *Obit* Nov 1975

Yeats-Brown, Francis, British army officer and author, *Obit* Feb 1945

Zimmer, Carl, American science journalist, Oct 2012

Zolotow, Maurice, author, May 1957, *Obit* May 1991

Novelists

Abdullah, Achmed, British novelist and short story writer, *Obit* June 1945

Abe, Kobo, Japanese novelist, July 1989, *Obit* Mar 1993

Abouet, Marguerite, French comic book writer, Nov 2012

Adamic, Louis, author, Yrbk 1940, *Obit* Oct 1951

Adams, Alice, American short story writer, Aug 1989, *Obit* Aug 1999

Adams, Douglas, English science fiction writer and satirist, July 1993, *Obit* Sept 2001

Adams, Richard, English fantasy novelist, Oct 1978

Aksenov, Vasilii Pavlovich, Russian novelist, Jan 1990, *Obit* Yrbk 2009

Aldrich, Richard, theatrical producer, June 1955, *Obit* June 1986

Aldridge, James, Australian author, Mar 1943

Alegria, Ciro, Peruvian novelist, Yrbk 1941

Alvarez de Toledo, Luisa Isabel, Spanish novelist and social reformer, Apr 1972

Alvtegen, Karin, Swedish novelist, Jan 2007

Amado, Jorge, Brazilian novelist, Mar 1986, *Obit* Oct 2001

Ambler, Eric, English mystery novelist, June 1975, *Obit* Jan 1999

Amichai, Yehuda, Israeli poet, Feb 1998, *Obit* Jan 2001

Anderson, Sherwood, American novelist and short story writer, *Obit* Apr 1941

Arden, John, English playwright and novelist, Sept 1988, *Obit* Yrbk 2012

Armstrong, Charlotte, author, Yrbk 1946, *Obit* Sept 1969

Arriaga, Guillermo, Mexican novelist, short story writer and screenwriter, Jan 2007

Atherton, Gertrude Franklin Horn, American novelist, Nov 1940, *Obit* Sept 1948

Atkinson, Eleanor, author, *Obit* Jan 1943

Atkinson, Kate, English novelist, Feb 2007

Attaway, William, American novelist, Yrbk 1941

Auel, Jean M., American novelist, Feb 1991

Austin, F. Britten, English novelist, dramatist and screenwriter, *Obit* May 1941

Babson, Naomi Lane, American novelist and short story writer, Yrbk 1952

Bailey, Carolyn Sherwin, American children's author, Yrbk 1948

Baker, Dorothy, author, Yrbk 1943, *Obit* Sept 1968

Baker, Frank, English author, Yrbk 1948

Baker, Nicholson, American novelist, Aug 1994

Ball, Zachary, Yrbk 1953

Ballard, J. G., English novelist and short story writer, May 1988, *Obit* Yrbk 2009

Banks, Russell, American novelist and short story writer, Jan 1992

Banville, John, Irish novelist, May 1992

Barnes, Margaret Campbell, English novelist, Yrbk 1953

Barthelme, Donald, American short story writer and novelist, Mar 1976, *Obit* Sept 1989

Bassett, Sara Ware, American novelist, Yrbk 1956

Bates, H. E., English short story writer and novelist, Sept 1944, *Obit* Mar 1974

Baumer, Marie, American screenwriter and novelist, Yrbk 1958

Beach, Edward Latimer, American naval officer, Oct 1960, *Obit* May 2003

Bell, Margaret Elizabeth, Yrbk 1952

Bellamann, Henry, author and poet, Sept 1942, *Obit* July 1945

Benchley, Nathaniel, American novelist, short story writer and children's author, Sept 1953, *Obit* Feb 1982

Benet, Stephen Vincent, American poet, novelist and short story writer, *Obit* Apr 1943

Berg, Elizabeth, American novelist and short story writer, Nov 1999

Berger, Thomas, author, June 1988

Berlin, Ellin, author and wife of Irving Berlin, Aug 1944, *Obit* Sept 1988

Bettelheim, Bruno, American psychologist, July 1961, *Obit* May 1990

Bialk, Elisa, author, Yrbk 1954, *Obit* May 1990

Blakemore, Michael, Australian theatrical director, May 2001

Blaker, Richard, English author, *Obit* Mar 1940

Blatty, William Peter, American novelist, June 1974

Blier, Bertrand, French motion picture director, Oct 1988

Blume, Judy, American young adult novelist, Apr 1980

Boileau, Ethel, English author, *Obit* Mar 1942

Bois, Jules, *Obit* Aug 1943

Boles, Paul Darcy, author, Yrbk 1956, *Obit* June 1984

Borgese, Giuseppe Antonio, Italian-American novelist, Yrbk 1947, *Obit* Jan 1953

Boucher, Anthony, American mystery and science fiction writer, June 1962, *Obit* June 1968

Bower, Bertha Muzzy, American novelist, *Obit* Sept 1940

Boyd, James, author, *Obit* Apr 1944

Boyle, T. Coraghessan, American novelist and short story writer, Jan 1991

Brace, Gerald Warner, author, Yrbk 1947, *Obit* Sept 1978

Brink, Carol Ryrie, American children's author, Yrbk 1946

Briscoe, Connie, American romance novelist, Jan 2000

Bristow, Gwen, author, Yrbk 1940, *Obit* Yrbk 1984

Brockmeier, Kevin, American novelist, short story writer and children's author, May 2010

Bromfield, Louis, novelist, July 1944, *Obit* May 1956

Brown, Dan, American novelist, May 2004

Buechner, Frederick, American novelist and clergyman, Yrbk 1959

Bukowski, Charles, American poet, novelist and short story writer, Apr 1994, *Obit* Apr 1994

Burnett, Hallie Southgate, author and editor, Yrbk 1954, *Obit* Nov 1991

Burroughs, William S., American novelist, Nov 1971, *Obit* Nov 1997

Cadell, Elizabeth, English author, Yrbk 1951

Cain, James M., American novelist, Yrbk 1947, *Obit* Jan 1978

Caldwell, Taylor, author, Jan 1940, *Obit* Oct 1985

Campbell, Grace, Yrbk 1948, *Obit* July 1963

Campbell, Patricia, Yrbk 1957

Canin, Ethan, American novelist, short story writer and physician, Aug 2001

Cannon, LeGrand, author, Mar 1943

Capote, Truman, American short story writer and novelist, Sept 1951, Mar 1968, *Obit* Oct 1984

Carruth, Hayden, American poet, Apr 1992, *Obit* Yrbk 2008

Cartland, Barbara, English romance novelist, Aug 1979, *Obit* Aug 2000

Cary, Joyce, Anglo-Irish novelist, Yrbk 1949, *Obit* June 1957

Caspary, Vera, author, dramatist and screenwriter, Yrbk 1947, *Obit* Aug 1987

Cavanna, Betty, American young adult novelist, Yrbk 1950, *Obit* Oct 2001

Chabon, Michael, American novelist, Nov 2012

Chaon, Dan, American novelist and short story writer, Feb 2012

Chase, Mary Ellen, author, May 1940, *Obit* Oct 1973

Cheever, John, American novelist and short story writer, Sept 1975, *Obit* Aug 1982

Cheney, Brainard, author, Yrbk 1959, *Obit* Mar 1990

Chevalier, Elizabeth Pickett, Jan 1943

Chute, B. J., author, Yrbk 1950, *Obit* Oct 1987

Clancy, Tom, American novelist, Apr 1988

Clark, Dorothy Park, American novelist, Yrbk 1957

Clark, Mary Higgins, American mystery novelist, Jan 1994

Clavell, James, Australian-American novelist and screenwriter, Oct 1981, *Obit* Nov 1994

Cohen, Leonard, Canadian poet, novelist, singer and songwriter, June 1969

Collins, Jackie, English novelist, July 2000

Collins, Suzanne, American young adult fantasy novelist, Sept 2012

Condon, Richard, novelist, Feb 1989, *Obit* June 1996

Conroy, Pat, American novelist, Jan 1996

Cook, Fannie, American novelist and painter, Yrbk 1946, *Obit* Oct 1949

Coolidge, Dane, author, *Obit* Sept 1940

Cooper, Courtney Ryley, author, *Obit* Nov 1940

Cooper, Louise Field, author, Yrbk 1950, *Obit* Jan 1993

Coover, Robert, American novelist, Feb 1991

Corey, Paul, American novelist, Yrbk 1940

Cost, March, Jan 1958, *Obit* Apr 1973

Costain, Thomas B., American novelist and editor, May 1953, *Obit* Yrbk 1965

Cottenham, Mark Everard Pepys, *Obit* Sept 1943

Cotterell, Geoffrey, Yrbk 1954

Cottrell, Dorothy, Yrbk 1955, *Obit* Sept 1957

Cozzens, James Gould, American novelist, June 1949, *Obit* Oct 1978

Creasey, John, English novelist, Sept 1963, *Obit* July 1973

Crispin, Edmund, English novelist and short story writer, Yrbk 1949

Cronin, A. J., Scottish novelist and physician, July 1942, *Obit* Mar 1981

Cullen, Countee, American poet, *Obit* Mar 1946

Cunningham, Michael, American novelist, July 1999

Curry, Peggy Simson, author and poet, Yrbk 1958

Cussler, Clive, American novelist, Nov 2000

Dannay, Frederic, American mystery writer, July 1940, *Obit* Oct 1982

De Chirico, Giorgio, Italian painter, Jan 1956, June 1972, *Obit* Jan 1979

De Hartog, Jan, Dutch novelist, Feb 1970, *Obit* Jan 2003

De Jong, David C., novelist, July 1944, *Obit* Nov 1967

De Lima, Sigrid, novelist, Yrbk 1958, *Obit* Feb 2000

De Sherbinin, Betty, Yrbk 1948

De Vries, Peter, American novelist, Yrbk 1959, *Obit* Jan 1994

De Wohl, Louis, Yrbk 1955, *Obit* Oct 1961

DeLillo, Don, American novelist, Jan 1989

DeMille, Nelson, American novelist, Oct 2002

Deighton, Len, English novelist, Sept 1984

Delafield, E. M., English novelist, *Obit* Jan 1944

Deland, Margaret Wade Campbell, author, *Obit* Mar 1945

Dennis, Patrick, American novelist, May 1959, *Obit* Feb 1977

Desai, Kiran, Indian novelist, Jan 2007

Diamant, Gertrude, American novelist and nonfiction writer, Nov 1942

Disney, Doris Miles, American novelist, Yrbk 1954

Dixon, Thomas, American novelist, *Obit* May 1946

Doctorow, E. L., American novelist, July 1976

Doerr, Anthony, American short story writer and novelist, Oct 2011

Doig, Ivan, American western writer, Feb 2011

Donleavy, J. P., Irish novelist, dramatist and short story writer, July 1979

Donoghue, Emma, Irish novelist and dramatist, Jan 2013

Donoso, Jose, Chilean novelist, Feb 1978, *Obit* Feb 1997

Dos Passos, John, American novelist, Aug 1940, *Obit* Nov 1970

Doyle, Roddy, Irish novelist, Oct 1997

Drabble, Margaret, English novelist and playwright, May 1981

Dreiser, Theodore, American novelist, *Obit* Feb 1946

Du Jardin, Rosamond, Yrbk 1953

Dunne, John Gregory, American novelist and screenwriter, June 1983, *Obit* Yrbk 2004

Edmonds, Walter D., American novelist and children's author, Sept 1942, *Obit* May 1998

Elkin, Stanley, American novelist and short story writer, July 1987, *Obit* Aug 1995

Ellroy, James, American novelist, Apr 1998

Enright, Anne, Irish novelist and short story writer, Jan 2002

Estes, Harlow, Mar 1941

Eugenides, Jeffrey, American novelist, Oct 2003

Eustis, Helen, author, Yrbk 1955

Evanovich, Janet, American mystery novelist, Apr 2001

Everett, Percival L., American novelist, children's author and short story writer, Sept 2004

Exley, Frederick, novelist, Oct 1989, *Obit* Aug 1992

Eyre, Katherine Wigmore, Yrbk 1949, Yrbk 1957

Farley, Walter, American children's and young adult author, Yrbk 1949, *Obit* Feb 1990

Farrell, James T., American novelist and short story writer, Sept 1942, *Obit* Oct 1979

Faust, Frederick, American western novelist, *Obit* July 1944

Fedorova, Nina, Nov 1940

Fermor, Patrick Leigh, English travel writer and novelist, Yrbk 1955, *Obit* Yrbk 2011

Ferris, Joshua, American novelist, Oct 2010

Field, Rachel, American novelist, poet and children's author, *Obit* May 1942

Finney, Gertrude E., Yrbk 1957

Fitzgerald, F. Scott, American novelist and short story writer, *Obit* Feb 1941

Flavin, Martin, dramatist and author, Yrbk 1943, *Obit* Feb 1968

Fleming, Berry, author, Yrbk 1953, *Obit* Nov 1989

Fletcher, Inglis, American children's author and novelist, Yrbk 1947, *Obit* July 1969

Foer, Jonathan Safran, American novelist, Sept 2002

Follett, Ken, Welsh novelist, Jan 1990

Ford, Richard, American novelist and short story writer, Sept 1995

Fossum, Karin, Norwegian novelist, Jan 2007

Fowles, John, English novelist, Mar 1977, *Obit* Apr 2006

Franken, Rose, novelist and playwright, Yrbk 1941, Yrbk 1947, *Obit* Aug 1988

Franzen, Jonathan, American novelist, Sept 2003

Freed, Lynn, South African novelist, Jan 2002

Freedman, Nancy, Sept 1947

Freund, Philip, Canadian novelist and short story writer, Yrbk 1948

Friedman, Bruce Jay, American novelist, short story writer and dramatist, June 1972

Gaddis, William, American novelist, Nov 1987, *Obit* Mar 1999

Gaines, Ernest J., American novelist and short story writer, Mar 1994

Gaither, Frances, author, Yrbk 1950, *Obit* Jan 1956

Gallant, Mavis, Canadian short story writer and novelist, May 1990

Gardner, Erle Stanley, American mystery novelist, June 1944, *Obit* Apr 1970

Garner, Helen, Australian novelist, Jan 2007

Garratt, Geoffrey Theodore, *Obit* June 1942

Garth, David, Yrbk 1957

Genet, Jean, French dramatist, novelist and poet, Apr 1974, *Obit* June 1986

George, Elizabeth, American mystery novelist, Mar 2000

Giles, Janice Holt, author, Yrbk 1958

Gipson, Frederick Benjamin, author, Yrbk 1957

Glasgow, Ellen Anderson Gholson, American novelist, *Obit* Jan 1946

Glyn, Elinor, English novelist, *Obit* Nov 1943

Godwin, Gail, American novelist and short story writer, Oct 1995

Goertz, Arthemise, Yrbk 1953

Gogarty, Oliver St. John, Irish otolaryngologist, poet and novelist, July 1941, *Obit* Yrbk 1957

Gold, Herbert, American novelist and short story writer, Yrbk 1955

Goldman, William, American novelist and screenwriter, Jan 1995

Goodrich, Arthur, *Obit* Aug 1941

Goodrich, Marcus, author, Apr 1941, *Obit* Jan 1992

Gordon, Mary, American novelist, Nov 1981

Goudge, Elizabeth, English novelist, children's author and short story writer, Sept 1940, *Obit* Aug 1984

Grafton, Sue, American mystery novelist, Sept 1995

Graham, Gwethalyn, Canadian novelist, Jan 1945, *Obit* Jan 1966

Graham, Winston, English novelist, Yrbk 1955, *Obit* Yrbk 2003

Grandes, Almudena, Spanish novelist, Jan 2006

Grant, Kay, Yrbk 1959

Grau, Shirley Ann, novelist and short story writer, Yrbk 1959

Gray, Simon, English dramatist and novelist, June 1983, *Obit* Yrbk 2008

Grisham, John, American lawyer and novelist, Sept 1993

Gurney, A. R., American dramatist, July 1986

Guterson, David, American novelist and short story writer, Nov 1996

Hall, Radclyffe, English novelist and poet, *Obit* Nov 1943

Halsey, Margaret, author, Nov 1944, *Obit* Apr 1997

Hamilton, Cosmo, English author and dramatist, *Obit* Yrbk 1942

Hargrove, Marion, American novelist and humorist, June 1946, *Obit* Yrbk 2004

Harris, Bernice Kelly, novelist and dramatist, Yrbk 1949

Harris, E. Lynn, American novelist, June 1996, *Obit* Yrbk 2009

Hauck, Louise Platt, *Obit* Feb 1944

Havill, Edward, Yrbk 1952

Hawley, Cameron, Yrbk 1957

Hazzard, Shirley, Australian novelist and short story writer, Jan 1991

Hedden, Worth Tuttle, American novelist and short story writer, Yrbk 1957, *Obit* Jan 1986

Heinlein, Robert A., American science fiction writer, Mar 1955, *Obit* June 1988

Heller, Joseph, American novelist, Jan 1973, *Obit* Mar 2000

Heym, Stefan, German novelist, Mar 1943, *Obit* Mar 2002

Heyward, DuBose, American novelist and dramatist, *Obit* July 1940

Highsmith, Patricia, American mystery novelist, Jan 1990, *Obit* Apr 1995

Hilton, James, English novelist, Sept 1942, *Obit* Feb 1955

Hobson, Laura Keane Zametkin, author, Sept 1947, *Obit* Apr 1986

Hoffman, Alice, American novelist, Sept 1992

Holt, Isabella, Yrbk 1956, *Obit* May 1962

Hosseini, Khaled, Afghan-American physician and novelist, July 2013

Houellebecq, Michel, French novelist and poet, Jan 2002

Hubbard, Margaret Ann, American young adult mystery writer, Yrbk 1958

Hughes, Langston, American poet, novelist, short story writer and playwright, Oct 1940, *Obit* July 1967

Hull, Helen R., author, May 1940, *Obit* Sept 1971

Hunter, Aislinn, Canadian short story writer, poet and novelist, Jan 2002

Hunter, Evan, American novelist, short story writer and dramatist, Yrbk 1956, *Obit* Yrbk 2005

Hutchinson, R. C., English novelist, Nov 1940

Idell, Albert Edward, author, Oct 1943, *Obit* Oct 1958

Innes, Hammond, English novelist, Yrbk 1954

Ionesco, Eugene, French dramatist, Oct 1959, *Obit* June 1994

Irwin, Margaret, English author, Yrbk 1946, *Obit* Yrbk 1991

Isaacs, Susan, American novelist, Oct 1993

Ishiguro, Kazuo, Japanese-British novelist, Sept 1990

Jackson, Charles, novelist and short story writer, May 1944, *Obit* Nov 1968

Jacobs, W. W., English short story writer and novelist, *Obit* Oct 1943

Jakes, John, American novelist, Sept 1988

James, P. D., English mystery novelist, Aug 1980

Janowitz, Tama, American novelist and short story writer, Aug 1989

Jenkins, Sara, Yrbk 1953

Jennings, John Edward, author, Yrbk 1949

Jhabvala, Ruth Prawer, British screenwriter and novelist, Mar 1977, *Obit* Yrbk 2013

Johnson, Mat, American novelist, Mar 2010

Jones, Edward P., American short story writer and novelist, Mar 2004

Jordan, Mildred, author, Yrbk 1951

Joyce, James, Irish novelist, dramatist and poet, *Obit* Mar 1941

Kadare, Ismail, Albanian novelist, Feb 1992

Karon, Jan, American novelist, Mar 2003

Karp, David, American novelist and screenwriter, Yrbk 1957, *Obit* Feb 2000

Kaufman, Millard, American screenwriter and novelist, Jan 2008, *Obit* Yrbk 2009

Kelly, Judith, Oct 1941, *Obit* July 1957

Keneally, Thomas, Australian novelist, June 1987

Kennelly, Ardyth, Yrbk 1953

Kerouac, Jack, American novelist, Nov 1959, *Obit* Yrbk 1969

Kesey, Ken, American novelist, May 1976, *Obit* Feb 2002

King, Stephen, American novelist and short story writer, Oct 1981

Kingsolver, Barbara, American novelist and short story writer, July 1994

Kinnell, Galway, American poet, Aug 1986

Kirkland, Winifred Margaretta, *Obit* July 1943

Klass, Perri, American pediatrician and novelist, May 1999

Knoblock, Edward, *Obit* Aug 1945

Koch, Kenneth, American poet, Feb 1978, *Obit* Yrbk 2002

Kossak, Zofia, June 1944, *Obit* June 1968

Krantz, Judith, American romance novelist, May 1982

Krauss, Nicole, American novelist, Nov 2010

Kureishi, Hanif, English novelist, dramatist and screenwriter, Feb 1992

L'Amour, Louis, American western novelist, Feb 1980, *Obit* July 1988

LaValle, Victor D., American short story writer and novelist, Jan 2010

Laird, Nick, Irish novelist and poet, Jan 2006

Landon, Margaret, American novelist, Feb 1945, *Obit* Feb 1994

Langley, Adria Locke, Aug 1945

Lardner, Ring, American screenwriter, July 1987, *Obit* Feb 2001

Laughlin, Clara Elizabeth, *Obit* Apr 1941

Lauritzen, Jonreed, Yrbk 1952

Lawrence, Hilda, author, Yrbk 1947

Leblanc, Maurice, French author, *Obit* Jan 1942

Lee, Andrea, American novelist and short story writer, Sept 2003

Lee, Manfred, American mystery writer, July 1940

Lehane, Dennis, American mystery novelist, Oct 2005

Leighton, Margaret Carver, author, Yrbk 1952

Lethem, Jonathan, American novelist and short story writer, Mar 2006

Levin, Meyer, American novelist, Apr 1940, *Obit* Sept 1981

Levy, Andrea, English novelist, Sept 2010

Lewis, Ethelreda, South African author, *Obit* Sept 1946

Lincoln, Joseph C., American short story writer, novelist and poet, *Obit* Apr 1944

Lively, Penelope, English novelist, short story writer and children's author, Apr 1994

Llewellyn, Richard, Welsh author, Apr 1940, *Obit* Jan 1984

Lockridge, Richard, American mystery novelist, Oct 1940, *Obit* Oct 1982

Lockridge, Ross, novelist, Mar 1948

Longfellow, Ki, Novelist, playwright and theater producer and director, July 2012

Loos, Anita, American novelist, dramatist and screenwriter, Feb 1974, *Obit* Oct 1981

Lothar, Ernst, Austrian author, Yrbk 1947

Loveman, Amy, June 1943, *Obit* Feb 1956

Ludlum, Robert, American novelist, Nov 1982, *Obit* July 2001

Lurie, Alison, American novelist, Feb 1986

Lutes, Della T., author, *Obit* Sept 1942

MacDonald, John D., American mystery novelist, Oct 1986, *Obit* Feb 1987

MacInnes, Helen, Scottish-American novelist, Nov 1967, *Obit* Nov 1985

Macdonald, Ross, American mystery novelist, Yrbk 1953, Aug 1979, *Obit* Sept 1983

Mackaye, David L., American novelist, Yrbk 1949

Malamud, Bernard, American novelist and short story writer, Yrbk 1958, July 1978, *Obit* May 1986

Maltz, Albert, screenwriter, Jan 1940, *Obit* July 1985

Manfred, Frederick Feikema, American novelist, Yrbk 1950

Margueritte, Victor, *Obit* May 1942

Marquand, John P., American novelist, Apr 1942, *Obit* Oct 1960

Marshall, Rosamond, author, Aug 1942, *Obit* Feb 1958

Mauriac, Claude, French author, Sept 1993, *Obit* June 1999

Mayer, Jane, American novelist and children's author, Yrbk 1954

McCormick, Jay, Apr 1943

McCracken, Harold, Yrbk 1949

McCullers, Carson, American novelist, Sept 1940, *Obit* Yrbk 1967

McCullough, Colleen, Australian novelist, Apr 1982

McDermott, Alice, American novelist and short story writer, Sept 1992

McEwan, Ian, English novelist and short story writer, July 1993

McGuane, Thomas, American novelist and screenwriter, Nov 1987

McInerney, Jay, American novelist, Nov 1987

McKenney, Ruth, author, Aug 1942, *Obit* Oct 1972

McMeekin, Clark, American novelists, Yrbk 1957

McMinnies, Mary, Yrbk 1959

Mda, Zakes, South African dramatist and novelist, Jan 2005

Merrill, James, American poet, novelist and playwright, Aug 1981, *Obit* Apr 1995

Meyer, Stephenie, American novelist, Oct 2008

Miasha, American novelist, Oct 2009

Michaels, Anne, Canadian poet and novelist, Jan 2002

Michener, James A., American novelist, June 1948, Aug 1975, *Obit* Jan 1998

Millar, George, Scottish author, Yrbk 1949

Miller, Alice Duer, author, Sept 1941, *Obit* Oct 1942

Mirvish, Robert F., Yrbk 1957

Mitchell, David, English novelist, Jan 2011

Molloy, Robert, author and translator, Yrbk 1948, *Obit* Mar 1977

Montero, Mayra, Cuban novelist and short story writer, Jan 2002

Montgomery, L. M., Canadian novelist, *Obit* June 1942

Moody, Ralph, Yrbk 1955

Moon, Bucklin, American writer, Yrbk 1950

Moore, Brian, Canadian novelist, Jan 1986, *Obit* Mar 1999

Moore, Ruth, Yrbk 1954

Mosley, Walter, American mystery novelist, Sept 1994

Mumford, Ethel Watts, *Obit* Jan 1940

Mundy, Talbot, English novelist, *Obit* Sept 1940

Murakami, Haruki, Japanese novelist, Sept 1997

Newby, P. H., English novelist and short story writer, Yrbk 1953

Norman, Marsha, American dramatist, May 1984

Norris, Charles Gilman, author, *Obit* Aug 1945

North, Sterling, author, Nov 1943, *Obit* Feb 1975

O'Brien, Edna, Irish novelist and short story writer, Sept 1980

O'Connor, Edwin, American novelist and short story writer, Nov 1963, *Obit* May 1968

O'Connor, Flannery, American novelist and short story writer, Yrbk 1958, *Obit* Sept 1965

O'Donnell, E. P., *Obit* June 1943

O'Hara, John, American novelist and short story writer, Feb 1941, *Obit* June 1970

O'Neill, Joseph, American lawyer and novelist, June 2009

Ogilvie, Elisabeth, American novelist, Yrbk 1951, *Obit* Yrbk 2007

Oppenheim, Edward Phillips, English mystery novelist, *Obit* Mar 1946

Osborne, William Hamilton, *Obit* Feb 1943

Oxenham, John, English author and poet, *Obit* Mar 1941

Oyeyemi, Helen, Nigerian-British novelist, Jan 2005

Packard, Frank Lucius, Canadian author, *Obit* Apr 1942

Paretsky, Sara, American mystery novelist, May 1992

Parker, Alan, English motion picture director, Mar 1994

Paterson, Katherine, American young adult author, Nov 1997

Patton, Frances Gray, short story writer and novelist, Yrbk 1955, *Obit* Sept 2000

Paul, Elliot, author, Feb 1940, *Obit* June 1958

Pennell, Joseph Stanley, author, Yrbk 1944

Petry, Ann Lane, American novelist, Mar 1946, *Obit* July 1997

Phillips, Thomas Hal, Yrbk 1956

Pinkerton, Kathrene Sutherland, American novelist, Jan 1940, *Obit* Yrbk 1967

Plain, Belva, American novelist, Feb 1999, *Obit* Yrbk 2010

Popkin, Zelda F., author, Yrbk 1951, *Obit* July 1983

Porter, Katherine Anne, American short story writer, May 1940, Mar 1963, *Obit* Nov 1980

Potter, Dennis, English novelist, playwright and screenwriter, July 1994, *Obit* July 1994

Powers, J. F., short story writer and novelist, Jan 1989, *Obit* Sept 1999

Prevost, Marcel, French novelist and playwright, *Obit* June 1941

Price, Richard, American novelist and screenwriter, Jan 1994

Priestley, J. B., English novelist and dramatist, May 1976, *Obit* Oct 1984

Puig, Manuel, Argentine novelist, Jan 1988, *Obit* Sept 1990

Pullman, Philip, English fantasy writer, Jan 2003

Raddall, Thomas Head, Canadian author, Yrbk 1951

Rama Rau, Santha, Indian travel writer and novelist, Aug 1945, Yrbk 1959, *Obit* Yrbk 2009

Rameau, Jean, *Obit* Apr 1942

Rand, Ayn, American novelist, May 1982

Rankin, Ian, Scottish mystery novelist, Jan 2008

Rawlings, Marjorie Kinnan, American novelist and short story writer, July 1942, *Obit* Feb 1954

Renault, Mary, English novelist, Jan 1959, *Obit* Feb 1984

Rendell, Ruth, English mystery writer, Apr 1994

Reuter, Gabriele, German author, *Obit* Jan 1942

Rhys, Jean, English novelist and short story writer, Yrbk 1972, *Obit* July 1979

Ricci, Nino, Canadian novelist, Jan 2007

Rice, Alice Caldwell Hegan, author, *Obit* Apr 1942

Rice, Anne, American novelist, July 1991

Rice, Elmer, American dramatist, Apr 1943, *Obit* July 1967

Richards, Laura Elizabeth Howe, author and poet, *Obit* May 1943

Richardson, Henry Handel, Australian novelist, *Obit* May 1946

Richter, Conrad, American novelist and short story writer, June 1951, *Obit* Yrbk 1968

Ripley, Alexandra, American novelist, Mar 1992, *Obit* Yrbk 2004

Ritner, Ann, Yrbk 1953

Rives, Amelie, American novelist, *Obit* July 1945

Robbins, Harold, American novelist, May 1970, *Obit* Jan 1998

Robbins, Tom, American novelist, June 1993

Roberts, Dorothy James, author, Yrbk 1956, *Obit* June 1990

Roberts, Elizabeth Madox, novelist, short story writer and poet, *Obit* May 1941

Roberts, Nora, American romance novelist, Sept 2001

Robertson, Constance, Yrbk 1946

Robinson, Henry Morton, author and poet, July 1950, *Obit* Mar 1961

Robinson, Kim Stanley, American science fiction writer, Nov 1998

Robinson, Peter, English mystery novelist, Sept 2007

Roncagliolo, Santiago, Peruvian novelist, Jan 2006

Rosten, Norman, poet, playwright and novelist, Apr 1944, *Obit* May 1995

Roth, Philip, American novelist and short story writer, Mar 1970, May 1991

Rothery, Agnes, Yrbk 1946, *Obit* Oct 1954

Russell, Karen, American short story writer and novelist, May 2011

Sagan, Francoise, French novelist and short story writer, Sept 1960, *Obit* Feb 2005

Salinger, J. D., American novelist and short story writer, *Obit* Yrbk 2010

Salverson, Laura Goodman, Canadian author, Yrbk 1957

Sanders, Lawrence, author, Apr 1989, *Obit* May 1998

Santayana, George, Spanish-American philosopher, Apr 1944, *Obit* Nov 1952

Saroyan, William, American short story writer, novelist and dramatist, July 1940, Nov 1972, *Obit* July 1981

Saunders, Hilary Aidan St. George, English author, June 1943, *Obit* Feb 1952

Saxon, Lyle, American novelist, *Obit* May 1946

Schmitt, Gladys, author, Mar 1943, *Obit* Yrbk 1972

Schulberg, Budd, American novelist, playwright and screenwriter, June 1941, May 1951, *Obit* Yrbk 2009

Scottoline, Lisa, American lawyer and novelist, July 2001

Seifert, Elizabeth, author, Yrbk 1951, *Obit* Oct 1983

Seifert, Shirley, Yrbk 1951

Selinko, Annemarie, Jan 1955

Sembene, Ousmane, Senegalese novelist and film director, Apr 1994, *Obit* Yrbk 2007

Senarens, Luis Philip, *Obit* Jan 1940

Seton, Anya, author, Yrbk 1953, *Obit* Jan 1991

Shaw, Bernard, Irish dramatist, June 1944, *Obit* Yrbk 1950

Shaw, Irwin, author and dramatist, Oct 1942, *Obit* July 1984

Sherwood, Robert E., American dramatist, Jan 1940, *Obit* Jan 1956

Shiner, Lewis, American novelist and short story writer, July 2011

Shriver, Lionel, American novelist, Sept 2005

Shulman, Irving, American novelist, Yrbk 1956, *Obit* June 1995

Shulman, Max, humorist, Oct 1959, *Obit* Oct 1988

Shute, Nevil, English novelist, July 1942, *Obit* Mar 1960

Silva, Daniel, American television producer and novelist, Apr 2007

Simenon, Georges, Belgian novelist, Apr 1970, *Obit* Nov 1989

Simpson, Helen, Australian author, *Obit* Yrbk 1940

Simpson, Louis Aston Marantz, poet and educator, Yrbk 1964, *Obit* Yrbk 2012

Simpson, Mona, American novelist, Feb 1993

Sinclair, May, English novelist, *Obit* Yrbk 1946

Sittenfeld, Curtis, American novelist and short story writer, Nov 2008

Skidmore, Hubert Standish, *Obit* Mar 1946

Slaughter, Frank G., American novelist and physician, Oct 1942, *Obit* Yrbk 2006

Smiley, Jane, American novelist and short story writer, Apr 1990

Smith, Ali, Scottish short story writer and novelist, June 2006

Smith, Betty, American novelist, Nov 1943, *Obit* Mar 1972

Smith, Eleanor, English author, *Obit* Nov 1945

Smith, Lillian Eugenia, American novelist and social critic, May 1944, *Obit* Yrbk 1966

Smith, Martin Cruz, American novelist, Nov 1990

Smith, Zadie, English novelist, Aug 2000

Sneider, Vern, Yrbk 1956, *Obit* June 1981

Snow, C. P., British physicist and novelist, Yrbk 1954, Yrbk 1961, *Obit* Aug 1980

Sorensen, Virginia Eggertsen, American children's author, Yrbk 1950

Sorokin, Vladimir, Russian novelist, Jan 2005

Sparks, Nicholas, American novelist, Feb 2001

Speare, Elizabeth George, American children's and young adult author, Yrbk 1959, *Obit* Jan 1995

Spencer, Scott, American novelist, July 2003

Spiegel, Clara E., novelist, Yrbk 1954

Spring, Howard, English author, Jan 1941, *Obit* June 1965

Stafford, Jean, American novelist and short story writer, Yrbk 1951, *Obit* May 1979

Standish, Burt L., American children's author, *Obit* Mar 1945

Steel, Danielle, American romance novelist, July 1989

Steen, Marguerite, English author, Oct 1941, *Obit* Sept 1975

Stolz, Mary, American children's author and young adult novelist, Yrbk 1953, *Obit* Yrbk 2007

Stone, Robert, American novelist, Jan 1987

Storey, David, English dramatist and novelist, Sept 1973

Straub, Peter, American horror novelist, Feb 1989

Street, James, American novelist, Yrbk 1946, *Obit* Nov 1954

Stromberg, Leonard, *Obit* Sept 1941

Stuart, Jesse, author, Aug 1940, *Obit* Apr 1984

Sumner, Cid Ricketts, American novelist and short story writer, Yrbk 1954

Tallant, Robert, author, Yrbk 1953, *Obit* June 1957

Tarkington, Booth, American novelist, *Obit* June 1946

Tartt, Donna, American novelist, Feb 2003

Taylor, Elizabeth, English novelist and short story writer, Yrbk 1948

Taylor, Peter Hillsman, American short story writer and novelist, Apr 1987, *Obit* Jan 1995

Tesich, Steve, American dramatist and screenwriter, Aug 1991, *Obit* Sept 1996

Theroux, Paul, American novelist and short story writer, Nov 1978

Thomas, D. M., English novelist, poet and translator, Nov 1983

Thomson, Rupert, English novelist, Feb 2000

Tietjens, Eunice Hammond, poet and author, *Obit* Nov 1944

Tomasi, Mari, May 1941

Train, Arthur Cheney, lawyer and author, *Obit* Feb 1946

Trevor, William, Irish novelist, short story writer and playwright, Sept 1984

Trollope, Joanna, English novelist, Jan 2006

Trumbo, Dalton, American screenwriter, May 1941, *Obit* Oct 1976

Tweedie, Ethel Brilliana, English author and traveler, *Obit* May 1940

Tyler, Anne, American novelist and short story writer, June 1981

Updike, John, American novelist and short story writer, Feb 1966, Oct 1984, *Obit* Yrbk 2009

Upfield, Arthur W., Australian author, Yrbk 1948, *Obit* Apr 1964

Uris, Leon, American novelist, Yrbk 1959, Feb 1979, *Obit* Yrbk 2003

Urrea, Luis Alberto, Mexican-American novelist and short story writer, Nov 2005

Van Druten, John, English dramatist, Feb 1944, *Obit* Feb 1958

Verghese, Abraham, American physician and novelist, Nov 2011

Viereck, George Sylvester, author and poet, Nov 1940, *Obit* May 1962

Vincent, Leon H., *Obit* Apr 1941

Vining, Elizabeth Gray, American novelist, short story writer and children's author, Sept 1943

Von Arnim, Elizabeth, English novelist, *Obit* Mar 1941

Von Tempski, Armine, *Obit* Jan 1944

Von Ziegesar, Cecily, American young adult novelist, Jan 2008

Wakeman, Frederic, American novelist, Sept 1946

Walden, Amelia Elizabeth, Yrbk 1956

Waldman, Ayelet, American novelist, Sept 2009

Walpole, Hugh, English novelist, *Obit* July 1941

Waltari, Mika, Finnish novelist, Feb 1950, *Obit* Oct 1979

Wambaugh, Joseph, American novelist, Mar 1980

Ward, Mary Jane, author, June 1946

Wasilewska, Wanda, Polish poet and novelist, July 1944, *Obit* Oct 1964

Weidman, Jerome, author and dramatist, Aug 1942, *Obit* Jan 1999

Weiner, Jennifer, American novelist, July 2008

Weld, John, motion picture stunt performer, May 1940

Weldon, Fay, English novelist, short story writer and dramatist, May 1990

Welsh, Irvine, Scottish novelist and short story writer, Nov 1997

Welty, Eudora, American short story writer and novelist, Jan 1942, Oct 1975, *Obit* Nov 2001

West, Keith, Yrbk 1947

West, Morris L., Australian novelist, Jan 1966, *Obit* Feb 2000

West, Nathanael, American novelist and screenwriter, *Obit* Feb 1941

Wheelwright, Jere, Yrbk 1952, *Obit* Mar 1961

Whipple, Maurine, American novelist, Mar 1941

White, Nelia Gardner, author, Yrbk 1950, *Obit* Oct 1957

Whitehead, Colson, American novelist, Nov 2001

Wickham, Madeleine, English novelist, Jan 2004

Wilder, Laura Ingalls, American children's and young adult author, Yrbk 1948, *Obit* May 1957

Wilder, Thornton, American novelist and dramatist, Aug 1943, Nov 1971, *Obit* Feb 1976

Willard, John, *Obit* Nov 1942

Williams, Tad, American science fiction and fantasy writer, Sept 2006

Williams, Tennessee, American dramatist, Jan 1946, Apr 1972, *Obit* Apr 1983

Wilson, Colin, English novelist and nonfiction writer, Apr 1963

Wilson, Dorothy Clarke, Yrbk 1951

Winslow, Anne, Yrbk 1948

Winsor, Kathleen, American novelist, Yrbk 1946, *Obit* Yrbk 2003

Woiwode, Larry, American novelist, Mar 1989

Wolff, Maritta M., American novelist, July 1941, *Obit* Yrbk 2002

Wouk, Herman, American novelist and playwright, Yrbk 1952

Wren, P. C., English historical novelist, *Obit* Jan 1942

Wright, Anna Rose, author, Yrbk 1952

Wright, Harold Bell, American clergyman and novelist, *Obit* July 1944

Yamanaka, Lois-Ann, American novelist and poet, June 1999

Yates, Elizabeth, American children's author, Yrbk 1948, *Obit* Nov 2001

Yazbek, Samar, Aug 2013

Yerby, Frank, American novelist and short story writer, Sept 1946, *Obit* Mar 1992

Nuclear engineers

Hinton of Bankside, Christopher Hinton, British nuclear engineer, June 1957

Numismatists

Newell, Edward Theodore, *Obit* Apr 1941

Nuns

Butler, Marie Joseph, American nun and educator, *Obit* Jan 1940

Kent, Corita, American artist and nun, Feb 1969, *Obit* Nov 1986

Mary Joseph, American nun and educator, Yrbk 1942

Nurses

Blanchfield, Florence Aby, American nurse and army officer, Sept 1943, *Obit* June 1971

Dauser, Sue S., Aug 1944

Deming, Dorothy, nurse and educator, May 1943

Densford, Katharine J., Feb 1947

Flikke, Julia O., July 1942

Galard Terraube, Genevieve de, Oct 1954

Gaskin, Ina May, midwife, May 2001

Lubic, Ruth Watson, American nurse and midwife, Sept 1996

McIver, Pearl L., nurse, Mar 1949

Sleeper, Ruth, nurse and educator, Oct 1952, *Obit* Feb 1993

Stimson, Julia Catherine, nurse, Nov 1940, *Obit* Nov 1948

Wilbur, Bernice M., Sept 1943

Nutritionists

Barber, Mary I., American dietician and home economist, July 1941, *Obit* Apr 1963

Davis, Adelle, nutritionist, Jan 1973, *Obit* July 1974

Metzelthin, Pearl V., Nov 1942, *Obit* Jan 1948

Omichinski, Linda, Canadian dietician, Jan 2004

Pattee, Alida Frances, *Obit* May 1942

Sebrell, W. H., nutritionist, May 1951, *Obit* Nov 1992

Obstetricians

Dickinson, Robert Latou, American gynecologist and obstetrician, Mar 1950, *Obit* Jan 1951

Edwards, Waldo B., American obstetrician, June 1943

Whitehouse, Harold Beckwith, *Obit* Sept 1943

Occultists

Kingsley, Myra, Apr 1943

Seabrook, William B., American occultist and travel writer, Nov 1940, *Obit* Oct 1945

Oceanographers

Ballard, Robert D., American oceanographer, June 1986

Cousteau, Fabien, Aquatic filmmaker and oceanographer, June 2012

Fish, Marie Poland, oceanographer, Oct 1941, *Obit* Apr 1989

Iselin, Columbus O'Donnell, Nov 1948, *Obit* Feb 1971

Piccard, Jacques, Swiss oceanographer, Yrbk 1965, *Obit* Yrbk 2009

Revelle, Roger, American oceanographer, Mar 1957, *Obit* Sept 1991

Spilhaus, Athelstan F., American meteorologist and oceanographer, June 1965, *Obit* June 1998

Stewart, Harris B., oceanographer, Mar 1968

Office workers

Bush, Dorothy Vredenburgh, American political party secretary, July 1948

Olympic athletes

Aamodt, Kjetil Andre, Norwegian skier, Jan 2002

Ahn, Hyun-Soo, Korean speed skater, Jan 2006

Aouita, Said, Moroccan runner, May 1990

Arakawa, Shizuka, Japanese figure skater, Jan 2006

Armstrong, Lance, American cyclist, Sept 1997

Beatty, Jim, American runner, Jan 1963

Blair, Bonnie, American speed skater, July 1992

Boitano, Brian, American figure skater, Nov 1989

Bolt, Usain, Jamaican runner, July 2009

Bonaly, Surya, French figure skater, Jan 2002

Boxx, Shannon, American soccer player, May 2011

Brodeur, Martin, Canadian hockey player, Nov 2002

Bruijn, Inge de, Dutch swimmer, Jan 2004

Brumel, Valerii, Russian high jumper, Apr 1963, *Obit* June 2003

Bubka, Sergei, Ukrainian pole vaulter, July 1996

Camplin, Alisa, Australian skier, Jan 2004

Cohen, Sasha, American figure skater, Feb 2006

Coleman, Georgia, diver, *Obit* Nov 1940

Comaneci, Nadia, Romanian gymnast, Feb 1977

Coughlin, Natalie, American swimmer, July 2012

Curry, John, English figure skater, July 1979, *Obit* June 1994

Curtis, Ann, swimmer, June 1945, *Obit* Yrbk 2012

Davis, Shani, American speed skater, May 2006

De Varona, Donna, American sportscaster and swimmer, Aug 2003

Devers, Gail, American runner and hurdler, July 1996

Du Toit, Natalie, South African swimmer, Jan 2005

Edberg, Stefan, Swedish tennis player, Jan 1994

Edwards, Teresa, American basketball player, Mar 1998

El-Guerrouj, Hicham, Moroccan runner, Jan 2004

Elliott, Herb, Australian runner, July 1960

Evans, Janet, American swimmer, July 1996

Fabris, Enrico, Italian speed skater, Jan 2006

Fleming, Peggy, American figure skater, July 1968

Flowers, Vonetta, American bobsledder, May 2006

Freeman, Cathy, Australian runner, Jan 2002

Fu Mingxia, Chinese diver, Jan 2002

Gable, Dan, wrestler and coach, Aug 1997

Gardner, Rulon, American wrestler, Nov 2004

Gebrselassie, Haile, Ethiopian runner, July 1999

Gehrmann, Don, runner, Oct 1952

George, Anju Bobby, Indian long jumper, Jan 2005

Graf, Steffi, German tennis player, Feb 1989

Granato, Cammi, American hockey player, Apr 1998

Guevara, Ana, Mexican runner, Jan 2004

Hackl, Georg, German luge racer, Jan 2003

Hamill, Dorothy, American figure skater, June 1976

Hamilton, Scott, American figure skater, Apr 1985

Hamm, Mia, American soccer player, Sept 1999

Hamm, Morgan, American gymnast, Nov 2004

Hamm, Paul, American gymnast, Nov 2004

Hannawald, Sven, German ski jumper, Jan 2002

Hasek, Dominik, Czech hockey player, May 1998

Hayes, Bob, American sprinter and football player, Sept 1966, *Obit* Jan 2003

Heiss, Carol, American figure skater, Oct 1959

Holmes, Kelly, British runner, Jan 2004

Holyfield, Evander, American boxer, Aug 1993

Iginla, Jarome, Canadian hockey player, Jan 2004

Jackson, Lauren, Australian basketball player, June 2003

Jazy, Michel, French runner, Apr 1967

Jenner, Bruce, American decathlete, Aug 1977

Johnson, Ben, Canadian runner, June 1988

Johnson, Rafer, American decathlete, June 1961

Jones, Cullen, American swimmer, Aug 2008

Jones, Roy, American boxer, Feb 1999

Joubert, Brian, French figure skater, Jan 2007

Keino, Kip, Kenyan runner, June 1967

Khan, Amir, British boxer, Jan 2006

Khorkina, Svetlana, Russian gymnast, Jan 2003

Killy, Jean Claude, French skier, June 1968

Klitschko, Vitali, Ukrainian boxer, Jan 2003

Klochkova, Yana, Ukrainian swimmer, Jan 2004

Korbut, Olga, Soviet gymnast, July 1973

Kukoc, Toni, Croatian basketball player, July 1997

Kusner, Kathy, American equestrian, Apr 1973

Lagat, Bernard, Kenyan-American runner, Oct 2008

Lebedeva, Tatyana, Russian long and triple jumper, Jan 2004

Leonard, Sugar Ray, American boxer, Feb 1981

Lewis, Denise, British heptathlete, Jan 2004

Lilly, Kristine, American soccer player, Apr 2004

Lindros, Eric, Canadian hockey player, Apr 1998

Lipinski, Tara, American figure skater, Apr 1998

Lobo, Rebecca, American basketball player, Sept 1997

Maier, Hermann, Austrian skier, Jan 2003

Marta, Brazilian soccer player, Apr 2008

Martin, Camilla, Danish badminton player, Jan 2004

Matson, Randy, American shot putter and discus thrower, Sept 1968

May-Treanor, Misty, American volleyball player, June 2013

Mayweather, Floyd, American boxer, Oct 2004

Meyer, Debbie, American swimmer, May 1969

Miller, Shannon, American gymnast, July 1996

Moser-Proell, Annemarie, Austrian skier, Sept 1976

Moses, Edwin, American hurdler, Nov 1986

O'Brien, Dan, American decathlete, July 1996

Ohno, Apolo, American speed skater, Feb 2006

Owens, Jesse, American runner, Nov 1956, *Obit* May 1980

Paddock, Charles W., sprinter, *Obit* Sept 1943

Peirsol, Aaron, American swimmer, June 2010

Phelps, Michael, American swimmer, Aug 2004

Plushenko, Evgeni, Russian figure skater, Jan 2007

Powell, Mike, American long jumper, Oct 1993

Prinz, Birgit, German soccer player, Jan 2005

Radcliffe, Paula, English runner, Jan 2003

Retton, Mary Lou, American gymnast, Feb 1986

Richards, Bob, American pole vaulter and decathlete, June 1957

Rose, Murray, swimmer, June 1962, *Obit* Yrbk 2012

Rudolph, Wilma, American runner, Sept 1961, *Obit* Jan 1995

Sabatini, Gabriela, Argentine tennis player, June 1992

Sacramone, Alicia, American gymnast, Mar 2011

Salazar, Alberto, American marathon runner, May 1983

Sampras, Pete, American tennis player, May 1994

Samuelson, Joan, American marathon runner, Aug 1996

Sanchez Vicario, Arantxa, Spanish tennis player, Aug 1998

Scherbo, Vitaly, Belarusian gymnast, July 1996

Schollander, Don, American swimmer, Sept 1965

Schranz, Karl, Austrian skier, Jan 1971

Scott, Barbara Ann, Canadian figure skater, July 1948, *Obit* Yrbk 2012

Seagren, Bob, American pole vaulter, June 1974

Slaney, Mary Decker, American runner, Oct 1983

Spitz, Mark, American swimmer, Oct 1972

Stenmark, Ingemar, Swedish skier, Apr 1982

Stockton, John, American basketball player, June 1995

Street, Picabo, American skier, Apr 1998

Tarver, Antonio, American boxer, June 2006

Thomas, John, high jumper, July 1960, *Obit* Yrbk 2013

Thompson, Daley, British decathlete, Nov 1986

Thorpe, Jim, American decathlete and pentathlete, Nov 1950, *Obit* May 1953

Tomba, Alberto, Italian skier, May 1993

Torrence, Gwen, American sprinter, July 1996

Vonn, Lindsey, American skier, Feb 2010

Vujanic, Milos, Serbian basketball player, Jan 2004

Waitz, Grete, Norwegian marathon runner, Apr 1981, *Obit* Yrbk 2011

Walsh, Kerri, American volleyball player, June 2013

Wambach, Abby, American soccer player, Mar 2011

Wang Nan, Chinese table tennis player, Jan 2003

Weir, Johnny, American figure skater, Apr 2010

Wickenheiser, Hayley, Canadian hockey player, Jan 2003

Williams, Lauryn, American runner, Sept 2008

Witt, Katarina, German figure skater, July 1988

Yagudin, Aleksei, Russian figure skater, Feb 2004

Yamaguchi, Kristi, American figure skater, June 1992

Zatopek, Emil, Czech runner, Apr 1953, *Obit* Feb 2001

Zorzi, Cristian, Italian cross-country skier, Jan 2006

Olympic executives

Bushnell, Asa S., July 1952, *Obit* May 1975

Rogge, Jacques, Belgian orthopedic surgeon and Olympic executive, Jan 2002

Samaranch, Juan Antonio, Spanish Olympics executive, Feb 1994, *Obit* Yrbk 2010

Oncologists

Ewing, James, *Obit* July 1943

Wynder, Ernst L., American oncologist and foundation official, Nov 1974, *Obit* Sept 1999

Zubrod, Charles Gordon, oncologist, Jan 1969, *Obit* July 1999

Opera directors

Chereau, Patrice, French theatrical, opera and film director, Jan 1990

Corsaro, Frank, American theatrical director and drama teacher, Aug 1975

Cravath, Paul D., *Obit* Aug 1940

D'Oyly Carte, Rupert, Feb 1948

Dexter, John, English theatrical director, July 1976, *Obit* May 1990

Gallo, Fortune, Oct 1949, *Obit* May 1970

Gatti-Casazza, Giulio, opera director, *Obit* Oct 1940

Gobbi, Tito, Italian opera singer, Jan 1957, *Obit* May 1984

Graf, Herbert, May 1942, *Obit* May 1973

Hall, Peter, British theatrical director, Feb 1962

Johnson, Edward, Canadian-American opera singer and director, Mar 1943, *Obit* June 1959

Keller, Marthe, Swiss actress and opera director, July 2004

Mansouri, Lotfi, Iranian opera director, Apr 1990, *Obit* Yrbk 2013

McEwen, Terry A., opera director, July 1985, *Obit* Jan 1999

Ponnelle, Jean-Pierre, French scenic designer and opera director, Mar 1983, *Obit* Sept 1988

Rennert, Gunther, June 1976, *Obit* Sept 1978

Serban, Andrei, Romanian theatrical director, Feb 1978

Taymor, Julie, American theatrical director and designer, Feb 1998

Zambello, Francesca, American opera director, May 2003

Opera singers

Alagna, Roberto, French opera singer, July 1997

Albanese, Licia, Italian opera singer, Mar 1946

Amato, Pasquale, Italian opera singer, *Obit* Oct 1942

Anderson, June, opera singer, May 1991

Anderson, Marian, American opera singer, May 1940, Apr 1950, *Obit* June 1993

Angeles, Victoria de los, Spanish opera singer, Feb 1955, *Obit* Aug 2005

Arroyo, Martina, American opera singer, Feb 1971

Auger, Arleen, American opera singer, Feb 1989, *Obit* Aug 1993

Baccaloni, Salvatore, Oct 1944, *Obit* Feb 1970

Bada, Angelo, Italian opera singer, *Obit* May 1941

Baker, Janet, English opera singer, June 1971

Bampton, Rose, American opera singer, Mar 1940, *Obit* Yrbk 2007

Barbieri, Fedora, Italian opera singer, Feb 1957, *Obit* Aug 2003

Bartoli, Cecilia, Italian opera singer, June 1992

Battle, Kathleen, American opera singer, Nov 1984

Baum, Kurt, opera singer, Sept 1956, *Obit* Feb 1990

Behrens, Hildegard, German opera singer, Jan 1985, *Obit* Yrbk 2009

Berganza, Teresa, Spanish opera singer, Jan 1979

Bergonzi, Carlo, Italian opera singer, Nov 1992

Bjorling, Jussi, Swedish opera singer, Sept 1947, *Obit* Nov 1960

Blegen, Judith, American opera singer, June 1977

Blythe, Stephanie, American opera singer, Aug 2004

Bonci, Alessandro, Italian opera singer, *Obit* Sept 1940

Borodina, Olga, Russian opera singer, Feb 2002

Branzell, Karin, Swedish opera singer, Feb 1946, *Obit* Feb 1975

Bumbry, Grace, American opera singer, Mar 1964

Caballe, Montserrat, Spanish opera singer, June 1967

Callas, Maria, American opera singer, Sept 1956, *Obit* Nov 1977

Campora, Giuseppe, Italian opera singer, July 1957

Claussen, Julia, *Obit* June 1941

Coates, John, *Obit* Oct 1941

Conley, Eugene, July 1954, *Obit* Feb 1982

Corelli, Franco, Italian opera singer, Feb 1964, *Obit* Mar 2004

Cotrubas, Ileana, Oct 1981

Crespin, Regine, French opera singer, Sept 1979, *Obit* Yrbk 2007

Danforth, William, *Obit* June 1941

De Luca, Giuseppe, Italian opera singer, Mar 1947, *Obit* Oct 1950

DeGaetani, Jan, opera singer, Oct 1977

Del Monaco, Mario, Feb 1957, *Obit* Jan 1983

Della Casa, Lisa, Swiss opera singer, July 1956, *Obit* Yrbk 2013

Della Chiesa, Vivian, American opera singer, Nov 1943

Dobbs, Mattiwilda, American opera singer, Sept 1955

Elias, Rosalind, Jan 1967

Estes, Simon, American opera singer, Aug 1986

Ewing, Maria, American opera singer, Apr 1990

Fassbaender, Brigitte, German opera singer, June 1994

Ferrier, Kathleen, British opera singer, Oct 1951, *Obit* Yrbk 1953

Fischer-Dieskau, Dietrich, German opera singer, Feb 1967, *Obit* Yrbk 2012

Flagstad, Kirsten, Norwegian opera singer, May 1947, *Obit* Jan 1963

Fleming, Renee, American opera singer, May 1997

Florez, Juan Diego, Peruvian opera singer, Jan 2007

Forrester, Maureen, Canadian opera singer, July 1962, *Obit* Yrbk 2010

Gedda, Nicolai, Swedish opera singer, Nov 1965

George, Zelma Watson, sociologist and opera singer, Oct 1961, *Obit* Sept 1994

Giordani, Marcello, Italian opera singer, May 2008

Goerne, Matthias, German opera singer, Jan 2006

Graham, Susan, American opera singer, Oct 2005

Gramm, Donald, opera singer, Nov 1975, *Obit* July 1983

Gueden, Hilde, Apr 1955

Hackett, Charles, American opera singer, *Obit* Feb 1942

Hadley, Jerry, American opera singer, Nov 1991, *Obit* Yrbk 2007

Hagegard, Hakan, Swedish opera singer, May 1985

Hampson, Thomas, American opera singer, Mar 1991

Hendricks, Barbara, opera singer, Mar 1989

Heppner, Ben, Canadian opera singer, Jan 1997

Hines, Jerome, American opera singer, Feb 1963, *Obit* June 2003

Hong, Hei-Kyung, Korean opera singer, Nov 2003

Horne, Marilyn, American opera singer, July 1967

Hunt Lieberson, Lorraine, American opera singer, July 2004, *Obit* Yrbk 2006

Hurley, Laurel, American opera singer, June 1957

Hvorostovsky, Dmitri, Russian opera singer, Jan 2006

Isokoski, Soile, Finnish opera
singer, Jan 2006

Jaroussky, Philippe, French
countertenor, Mar 2011

Jerusalem, Siegfried, German
opera singer, Sept 1992

Jo, Sumi, Korean opera singer,
Jan 2002

Kipnis, Alexander, opera singer,
Yrbk 1943, *Obit* July 1978

Kirsten, Dorothy, American
opera singer, Feb 1948, *Obit*
Jan 1993

Kozena, Magdalena, Czech
opera singer, Jan 2005

Kraus, Alfredo, Spanish opera
singer, June 1987, *Obit* Nov
1999

Kurenko, Maria, Sept 1944

Kwiecie?, Mariusz, Polish opera
singer, July 2012

Lawrence, Marjorie, Australian
opera singer, Apr 1940, *Obit*
Mar 1979

Lear, Evelyn, American opera
singer, Apr 1973, *Obit* Yrbk
2012

Lehmann, Lotte,
German-American opera
singer, May 1941, July 1970,
Obit Oct 1976

Lewis, Mary, opera singer, *Obit*
Feb 1942

London, George, Canadian
opera singer, Nov 1953, *Obit*
June 1985

Ludwig, Christa, German opera
singer, Mar 1971

MacNeil, Cornell, American
opera singer, Jan 1976, *Obit*
Yrbk 2011

Madeira, Jean, Oct 1963, *Obit*
Sept 1972

Malbin, Elaine, Feb 1959

Martinelli, Giovanni, Italian
opera singer, Jan 1945, *Obit*
Mar 1969

Marton, Eva, Hungarian opera
singer, Apr 1985

Mattila, Karita, Finnish opera
singer, Jan 2004

McCracken, James, opera
singer, Nov 1963, *Obit* June
1988

McNair, Sylvia, American opera
singer, Nov 1997

Melchior, Lauritz, Danish opera
singer, Jan 1941, *Obit* May
1973

Merrill, Robert, American opera
singer, Mar 1952, *Obit* Feb
2005

Milanov, Zinka,
Yugoslav-American opera
singer, July 1944, *Obit* July
1989

Miller, Mildred, opera singer,
June 1957

Millo, Aprile, American opera
singer, Apr 1988

Milnes, Sherrill, American opera
singer, Nov 1970

Moffo, Anna, American opera
singer, May 1961, *Obit* Yrbk
2007

Moore, Grace, opera singer, Apr
1944, *Obit* Mar 1947

Morris, James, American opera
singer, July 1986

Munsel, Patrice, American opera
singer, Mar 1945

Netrebko, Anna, Russian opera
singer, Jan 2005

Nielsen, Alice, *Obit* Apr 1943

Nilsson, Birgit, Swedish opera
singer, May 1960, *Obit* Sept
2006

Norman, Jessye, American
opera singer, Feb 1976

Novotna, Jarmila, Czech opera
singer, Mar 1940, *Obit* Apr
1994

Oberlin, Russell, opera singer,
July 1960

Obraztsova, Elena, Russian
opera singer, Feb 1983

Olivero, Magda, Italian opera
singer, Apr 1980

Otter, Anne Sofie von, Swedish
opera singer, Sept 1995

Pape, Rene, German opera
singer, Jan 2003

Pavarotti, Luciano, Italian opera
singer, June 1973, *Obit* Nov
2007

Pears, Peter, English opera
singer, July 1975, *Obit* May
1986

Peerce, Jan, opera singer, May
1942, *Obit* Feb 1985

Peters, Roberta, opera singer,
Apr 1954

Pinza, Ezio, Italian opera singer,
Feb 1941, Yrbk 1953, *Obit*
July 1957

Podles, Ewa, Polish opera
singer, Jan 2006

Pons, Lily, French opera singer,
Jan 1944, *Obit* Apr 1976

Powers, Marie, Jan 1951, *Obit*
Feb 1974

Prey, Hermann, German opera
singer, Feb 1975, *Obit* Oct
1998

Price, Leontyne, American
opera singer, May 1961, Oct
1978

Price, Margaret, Welsh opera
singer, Aug 1986, *Obit* Yrbk
2011

Racette, Patricia, American
opera singer, Feb 2003

Ramey, Samuel, American
opera singer, July 1981

Raskin, Judith, American opera
singer, Apr 1964, *Obit* Feb
1985

Reardon, John, opera singer,
Nov 1974, *Obit* June 1988

Resnik, Regina, opera singer,
Jan 1956, *Obit* Yrbk 2013

Rysanek, Leonie, Austrian opera
singer, Mar 1966, *Obit* May
1998

Sayao, Bidu, Brazilian opera
singer, Feb 1942, *Obit* June
1999

Schiotz, Aksel, Mar 1949, *Obit*
June 1975

Schorr, Friedrich, Hungarian
opera singer, July 1942, *Obit*
June 1954

Schwarzkopf, Elisabeth,
German-British opera singer,
Yrbk 1955, *Obit* Yrbk 2006

Scotto, Renata, Italian opera
singer, Sept 1978

Seefried, Irmgard, German
opera singer, Feb 1956, *Obit*
Jan 1989

Siepi, Cesare, Italian opera
singer, Yrbk 1955, *Obit* Yrbk
2010

Simionato, Giulietta, Italian
opera singer, Apr 1960, *Obit*
Yrbk 2010

Soderstrom, Elisabeth, Swedish
opera singer, Nov 1985, *Obit*
Yrbk 2010

Souzay, Gerard, French opera
singer, Jan 1966, *Obit* Yrbk
2004

Stader, Maria, Swiss opera
singer, July 1958, *Obit* Aug
1999

Steber, Eleanor, American
opera singer, Mar 1943, *Obit*
Jan 1991

Stella, Antonietta, Italian opera
singer, Yrbk 1959

Stewart, Thomas, American opera singer, May 1974, *Obit* Yrbk 2007

Stignani, Ebe, Italian opera singer, Feb 1949, *Obit* Yrbk 1991

Stilwell, Richard, American opera singer, Feb 1986

Stratas, Teresa, Canadian opera singer, Jan 1980

Studer, Cheryl, opera singer, Apr 1992

Sutherland, Joan, Australian opera singer, Yrbk 1960, *Obit* Yrbk 2010

Svanholm, Set, Swedish opera singer, Yrbk 1956, *Obit* Yrbk 1964

Swarthout, Gladys, opera singer, Mar 1944, *Obit* Sept 1969

Tagliavini, Ferruccio, Italian opera singer, June 1947, *Obit* Apr 1995

Talvela, Martti, Finnish opera singer, Oct 1983, *Obit* Sept 1989

Te Kanawa, Kiri, New Zealand opera singer, Nov 1978

Tebaldi, Renata, Italian opera singer, Apr 1955, *Obit* Apr 2005

Tetrazzini, Luisa, Italian opera singer, *Obit* Jan 1940

Teyte, Maggie, English opera singer, Yrbk 1945, *Obit* July 1976

Thebom, Blanche, American opera singer, Oct 1948, *Obit* Yrbk 2010

Thomas, Jess, American opera singer, June 1964, *Obit* Jan 1994

Thomas, John Charles, May 1943, *Obit* Feb 1961

Thorborg, Kerstin, Swedish opera singer, Mar 1940, *Obit* July 1970

Tian, Hao Jiang, Chinese opera singer, Feb 2009

Tibbett, Lawrence, American opera singer, Feb 1945, *Obit* Oct 1960

Tourel, Jennie, American opera singer, Feb 1947, *Obit* Jan 1974

Tozzi, Giorgio, American opera singer, Oct 1961, *Obit* Yrbk 2011

Traubel, Helen, American opera singer, Jan 1940, Feb 1952, *Obit* Oct 1972

Troyanos, Tatiana, opera singer, Aug 1979, *Obit* Oct 1993

Tucker, Richard, opera singer, Mar 1956, *Obit* Feb 1975

Upshaw, Dawn, American opera singer, Feb 1990

Valente, Benita, opera singer, Mar 1988

Vaness, Carol, American opera singer, Sept 1986

Varnay, Astrid, American opera singer, May 1951, *Obit* Yrbk 2007

Verrett, Shirley, American opera singer, Apr 1967, *Obit* Yrbk 2011

Vickers, Jon, Canadian opera singer, Mar 1961

Voigt, Deborah, American opera singer, Jan 1999

Von Stade, Frederica, American opera singer, Aug 1977

Warren, Leonard, opera singer, Yrbk 1953, *Obit* Apr 1960

Welitsch, Ljuba, Bulgarian opera singer, May 1949, *Obit* Nov 1996

Williams, Camilla, opera singer, June 1952, *Obit* Yrbk 2012

Ophthalmologists

Bonine, Frederick N., American ophthalmologist, *Obit* Oct 1941

Key, Ben Witt, *Obit* July 1940

Lewis, Francis Park, *Obit* Oct 1940

May, Charles H., *Obit* Jan 1944

Shine, F. W., *Obit* Nov 1941

Optometrists

Lewis, Francis Park, *Obit* Oct 1940

Orators

Alexander, Ruth, American economist and lecturer, Mar 1943

Carter, Huntly, *Obit* May 1942

Dell, Robert Edward, *Obit* Sept 1940

Greenbie, Sydney, Sept 1941, *Obit* Sept 1960

Holmes, Burton, May 1944, *Obit* Oct 1958

Huckel, Oliver, *Obit* Jan 1940

Kohoutek, Lubos, June 1974

Marcinko, Richard, motivational speaker, Mar 2001

Organists

Biggs, E. Power, organist, Nov 1950, *Obit* May 1977

Messiaen, Olivier, French organist and composer, Feb 1974, *Obit* June 1992

Organization officials

Achelis, Elisabeth, June 1954

Allen, Martha F., American social worker and youth leader, Oct 1959

Allman, David B., American surgeon and medical association official, Feb 1958, *Obit* May 1971

Annis, Edward R., Apr 1964

Appel, James Z., American physician and medical association official, Mar 1966, *Obit* Oct 1981

Archer, Glenn L., May 1949

Armstrong, David W., American youth leader, July 1949, *Obit* Mar 1963

Askey, E. Vincent, American surgeon, Feb 1961, *Obit* Feb 1975

Atherton, Warren H., American army officer, lawyer and veterans organization official, Yrbk 1943, *Obit* May 1976

Bacon, Charles L., American lawyer and veterans leader, May 1962

Baden-Powell of Gilwell, Robert Stephenson Smyth Baden-Powell, English Boy Scouts founder, *Obit* Mar 1941

Baden-Powell, Olave St. Clair, British girls association founder, May 1946

Barnett, Eugene Epperson, May 1941

Beck, Mildred Buchwalder, American social worker, June 1950

Belmont, Eleanor Robson, July 1944, *Obit* Jan 1980

Bevis, Palmer, American public relations executive, Apr 1953

Blake, Eugene Carson, American clergyman and church leader, Sept 1955, *Obit* Oct 1985

Blalock, Richard W., American youth organization official, May 1950

Boardman, Mabel Thorp, Red Cross official, Aug 1944, *Obit* Apr 1946

Booth, Arch N., Yrbk 1961

Bowditch, Richard L., July 1953, *Obit* Nov 1959

Boyce, Westray Battle, Sept 1945, *Obit* Mar 1972

Brannaman, Ray H., Nov 1947

Breckinridge, Aida de Costa, American social welfare leader, June 1954, *Obit* July 1962

Brode, Mildred H., Sept 1963

Brooks, D. W., June 1951

Brower, David, American conservationist, June 1973, *Obit* Feb 2001

Brown, Alberta L., May 1958

Brown, Perry J., Apr 1949

Brunner, Jean Adam, Sept 1945, *Obit* June 1951

Buck, Dorothea Dutcher, Sept 1947

Buck, Gene, Feb 1941, *Obit* May 1957

Budington, William S., June 1964

Buford, John Lester, Apr 1956

Burke, William R., July 1961

Burns, John Lawrence, youth organization official, Apr 1960, *Obit* Nov 1996

Butler, Sally, Yrbk 1946

Caldwell, Sarah C., Jan 1953

Cameron, Charles S., Sept 1954

Canada, Geoffrey, American charitable organization official, Feb 2005

Carey, Charles Henry, *Obit* Oct 1941

Carey, Walter F., Feb 1965

Carlyle, A. J., *Obit* July 1943

Carmichael, Oliver C., Jan 1946, *Obit* Yrbk 1966

Carpenter, J. Henry, Feb 1943, *Obit* Sept 1954

Casey, Ralph E., Feb 1966

Cashman, Robert, Nov 1952

Cavert, Samuel McCrea, Jan 1951, *Obit* Mar 1977

Cenerazzo, Walter W., Sept 1955

Chamberlain, Francis L., July 1959

Chamberlin, Georgia Louise, *Obit* Oct 1943

Chapman, Helen B., Apr 1955

Charlesworth, James Clyde, Sept 1954, *Obit* Mar 1974

Christman, Elizabeth, Jan 1947

Clark, Fred G., Oct 1949

Cline, John Wesley, June 1951, *Obit* Sept 1974

Cloninger, Kathy, American Girl Scouts official, Oct 2012

Cocke, Erle, army officer and veterans' leader, Jan 1951, *Obit* Sept 2000

Cockrell, Ewing, May 1951, *Obit* Apr 1962

Colvin, Mamie White, Yrbk 1944, *Obit* Jan 1956

Connell, Arthur J., Feb 1954

Cooke, Leslie E., June 1962, *Obit* Apr 1967

Cortney, Philip, Jan 1958, *Obit* July 1971

Cothran, James W., Sept 1953

Cowan, Minna G., Feb 1948

Cowden, Howard A., Mar 1952

Cunningham, Graham, Sept 1949

Darling, Sharon, American literacy advocate, May 2003

Dearborn, Ned Harland, Jan 1947, *Obit* Oct 1962

Densford, Katharine J., Feb 1947

Dickinson, Lucy Jennings, Nov 1945

Diehl, Frances, Oct 1947

Ditchy, Clair W., Mar 1954, *Obit* Oct 1967

Dodd, Alvin E., Nov 1947, *Obit* July 1951

Dodge, Cleveland E., Mar 1954, *Obit* Feb 1983

Dollard, Charles, Yrbk 1948, *Obit* Apr 1977

Doms, Keith, June 1971

Dorman, Gerald D., June 1970

Dowling, Robert W., Oct 1952, *Obit* Nov 1973

Due-Gundersen, Gunnar, Feb 1959, *Obit* Aug 1979

Dunham, Franklin, Jan 1942, *Obit* Jan 1962

Early, William Ashby, Mar 1954

Edey, Birdsall Otis, *Obit* Aug 1940

Edwards, Charles C., American surgeon and regulatory official, Oct 1973, *Obit* Yrbk 2011

Embree, Edwin R., Yrbk 1948, *Obit* Mar 1950

Empie, Paul C., Oct 1958

Erhard, Werner, self-actualization educator, Apr 1977

Eshelman, W. W., May 1960

Evans, Hugh Ivan, Nov 1950, *Obit* July 1958

Fawcett, Sherwood L., Yrbk 1972

Ferguson, Harriet, Jan 1947, *Obit* Feb 1966

Fisher, Walter C., July 1950

Fister, George M., June 1963, *Obit* July 1976

Fletcher, C. Scott, Feb 1953

Fosdick, Raymond Blaine, Feb 1945, *Obit* Sept 1972

Fowler, R. M., Oct 1954

Fraser, I., Yrbk 1947

Freitag, Walter, Jan 1954, *Obit* Oct 1958

Frothingham, Channing, Mar 1948, *Obit* Nov 1959

Fry, Franklin, June 1946, *Obit* Sept 1968

Fuller, Margaret H., American librarian, June 1959

Gaither, H. Rowan, American foundation official, May 1953, *Obit* June 1961

Galinsky, Ellen, American educator and organization official, Oct 2003

Gambrell, E. Smythe, June 1956

Gargan, William, Jan 1969, *Obit* Apr 1979

Geer, Alpheus, *Obit* Oct 1941

Gibson, Robert William, May 1969

Gillmore, Frank, *Obit* May 1943

Giri, V. Mohini, Indian social activist, Jan 2007

Givens, Willard E., Sept 1948, *Obit* July 1971

Glenn, Mary Willcox, *Obit* Yrbk 1940

Goldman, Frank, Jan 1953, *Obit* Apr 1965

Gonzalez, Efren W., Jan 1971

Gordon, Edmund W., American psychologist, June 2003

Gough, Lewis K., Jan 1953, *Obit* Jan 1968

Griffin, John Douglas Morecroft, May 1957

Gruber, L. Franklin, *Obit* Feb 1942

Guinzburg, Harold K., July 1957, *Obit* Jan 1962

Hall, Florence L., Aug 1943

Hall, Paul, Feb 1966, *Obit* Aug 1980

Hall, William Edwin, Jan 1954, *Obit* Mar 1961
Harrison, Shelby M., Jan 1943
Haskell, William N., Feb 1947, *Obit* Sept 1952
Haskins, Caryl Parker, American biophysicist, Feb 1958, *Obit* Feb 2002
Hauser, Conrad Augustine, *Obit* Apr 1943
Hawkins, Edler G., Jan 1965
Hay, Regina Deem, July 1948
Hayes, A. J., Oct 1953
Hayes, Anna Hansen, Nov 1949
Head, Walter W., Apr 1945, *Obit* June 1954
Henderson, E. L., June 1950, *Obit* Oct 1953
Hess, Elmer, Jan 1956, *Obit* June 1961
Heston, Charlton, American actor, May 1957, July 1986, *Obit* July 2008
Hickman, Emily, June 1945, *Obit* July 1947
Hilton, Frank C., July 1952
Holt, Cooper T., July 1957
Holtz, Jackson J., Mar 1950
Houghton, Dorothy Deemer, Sept 1950
Huck, Arthur, Feb 1957, *Obit* Mar 1973
Hulcy, Dechard A., Sept 1951
Hutton, Ruth Wilson, Feb 1948
Idleman, Finis Schuyler, *Obit* May 1941
Irons, Ernest E., Oct 1949, *Obit* Apr 1959
Irwin, Helen G., Oct 1952
Irwin, Robert B., Mar 1948, *Obit* Jan 1952
Israel, Edward L., *Obit* Yrbk 1941
Jackson, Eugene B., June 1961
Jodoin, Claude, Mar 1956
Johnson, C. Oscar, Feb 1948, *Obit* Jan 1966
Johnson, Roy W., May 1958, *Obit* Oct 1965
Kaur, Rajkumari Amrit, Oct 1955, *Obit* Mar 1964
Kearns, Nora Lynch, Sept 1956
Keck, Lucile L., Mar 1954
Keller, James, Oct 1951, *Obit* Apr 1977
Kenyon, Helen, Oct 1948
Khan, Begum Liaquat Ali, July 1950
Kimball, Lindsley Fiske, American social welfare

leader, July 1951, *Obit* Oct 1992
Kinder, Katharine L., May 1957
Kirk, William T., Feb 1960, *Obit* Mar 1974
Kish, Daniel, Echolation developer and president of World Access for the Blind, Sept 2013
Klahre, Ethel S., May 1962
Kline, Allan B., American agricultural leader, Mar 1948, *Obit* Sept 1968
Kline, Clarice, May 1961
Knight, O. A., June 1952
Knorr, Nathan H., Feb 1957, *Obit* Aug 1977
Knox, Louise Chambers, *Obit* Mar 1942
Kuhn, Edward W., June 1966
Kumm, Henry William, physician and foundation official, June 1955, *Obit* Mar 1991
La Roe, Wilbur, Mar 1948, *Obit* July 1957
Lahey, Frank H., American surgeon, Mar 1941, *Obit* Sept 1953
Larson, Leonard W., American medical association official and pathologist, May 1962, *Obit* Nov 1974
Latham, Harold S., Jan 1950, *Obit* Apr 1969
Layton, Olivia, Jan 1952, *Obit* Jan 1976
Lee, Laurence F., June 1952, *Obit* Oct 1961
Leech, Paul Nicholas, *Obit* Mar 1941
Leiper, Henry Smith, Nov 1948, *Obit* Mar 1975
Leonard, Lucille Putnam, Feb 1953
Lewis, Clyde A., Feb 1950
Lober, Georg John, Nov 1957, *Obit* Feb 1962
Lord, Mary Pillsbury, Oct 1952
Lundeberg, Harry, Nov 1952, *Obit* Mar 1957
MacLeod, Dorothy Shaw, Apr 1949
Macauley, Jane Hamilton, Sept 1949
Macy, Edith Dewing, Yrbk 1952, *Obit* Oct 1967
Magnuson, Paul B., June 1948, *Obit* Jan 1969
Mahady, Henry J., July 1954
Maile, Boniface R., Feb 1951

Malin, Patrick Murphy, Mar 1950, *Obit* Feb 1965
Manson, John T., *Obit* Apr 1944
Marshall, C. Herbert, Oct 1949
Martell, Edward, Nov 1964
Martin, Edgar Stanley, *Obit* Sept 1940
Martin, Walter B., Nov 1954, *Obit* May 1966
Marvel, Elizabeth Newell, American youth leader, Apr 1962
May, Henry John, *Obit* Jan 1940
Mays, Ewing W., Jan 1952
McCarthy, Kenneth C., Nov 1953
McCormack, Emmet J., July 1953, *Obit* Apr 1965
McCune, George Shannon, *Obit* Feb 1942
McDaniel, Glen, May 1952
McDonald, David J., June 1953, *Obit* Oct 1979
McHale, Kathryn, Jan 1947, *Obit* Yrbk 1957
McLean, Alice T., July 1945, *Obit* Yrbk 1968
McNair, Arnold Duncan McNair, Feb 1955
Means, Helen Hotchkin, Jan 1946
Meehan, Thomas F., *Obit* Sept 1942
Michael, Moina, *Obit* June 1944
Milam, Carl Hastings, American librarian, June 1945, *Obit* Oct 1963
Miller, Frieda S., Feb 1945, *Obit* Oct 1973
Miller, Irving, Nov 1952, *Obit* Feb 1981
Miller, J. Cloyd, Yrbk 1951
Miller, Marshall E., Oct 1953
Mohammed, W. Deen, American Islamic leader, Jan 2004, *Obit* Yrbk 2008
Monsky, Henry, Nov 1941, *Obit* June 1947
Moore, Elisabeth Luce, American philanthropist and foundation official, Oct 1960, *Obit* Yrbk 2002
Moore, Preston J., Apr 1959
Morris, Earl, American bar association executive, June 1968, *Obit* July 1992
Morrow, Elizabeth, Apr 1943, *Obit* Mar 1955
Mowrey, Corma, Nov 1950
Murray, Dwight H., May 1957, *Obit* Nov 1974

Murrell, Ethel Ernest, Oct 1951

Neumann, Emanuel, Mar 1967, *Obit* Jan 1981

Newkirk, Ingrid, American animal rights activist, Apr 2008

Nidetch, Jean, American dieting organization founder, Yrbk 1973

Nwuneli, Ndidi O., Nigerian youth organization official, Jan 2007

Nyborg, Victor H., Feb 1954

O'Byrne, Estella, Nov 1948

O'Connor, Basil, Sept 1944, *Obit* May 1972

O'Neil, James F., Nov 1947, *Obit* Sept 1981

O'Neill, J. E., June 1952

Oleson, Lloyd F., June 1947

Oltman, Florine, May 1970

Orr, Louis M., Apr 1960, *Obit* July 1961

Orsborn, Albert, Nov 1946, *Obit* Apr 1967

Ozbirn, Catharine Freeman, Jan 1962, *Obit* Mar 1974

Pacelle, Wayne, American animal rights activist, Jan 2010

Palmer, Hazel, June 1958

Parker, Karla V., Feb 1947

Paterson, Chat, veterans' leader, Mar 1948, *Obit* May 1992

Patterson, Ernest Minor, Oct 1949

Patton, Marguerite Courtwright, women's organization official, May 1950

Peters, Le Roy S., *Obit* Feb 1942

Phelan, Edward, Jan 1947

Phillips, Ruth Schertz, Jan 1959

Pingree, Chellie, American citizen advocacy organization official, Jan 2005

Plumley, H. Ladd, Apr 1963

Poling, Daniel A., Nov 1943, *Obit* Mar 1968

Poole, Dewitt C., Nov 1950, *Obit* Oct 1952

Potter, Dan, Feb 1964

Powers, Bertram A., American labor leader, Jan 1974

Powers, James E., June 1963

Preus, Jacob A. O., clergyman and church official, May 1975, *Obit* Oct 1994

Priest, Ivy Baker, Nov 1952, *Obit* Aug 1975

Pugmire, Ernest I., Apr 1945, *Obit* Sept 1953

Pyle, Howard, American governor and presidential aide, Nov 1955, *Obit* Jan 1988

Ralls, Charles C., Jan 1951

Randall, John D., May 1960

Reading, Stella, Apr 1948, *Obit* July 1971

Reed, Ralph, American political leader, Mar 1996

Reggio, Godfrey, American motion picture director and foundation official, July 1995

Reinartz, F. Eppling, July 1953

Rhyne, Charles S., American lawyer, May 1958, *Obit* Yrbk 2003

Richards, Cecile, American family planning advocate, May 2007

Ridenour, Nina, Apr 1951

Riley, Susan B., Feb 1953

Rittenhouse, Constance, Mar 1948

Roelofs, Henrietta, *Obit* Mar 1942

Rometty, Virginia, American marketing executive, June 2012

Roth, Almon E., Oct 1946

Rouse, Milford O., June 1968

Routley, Thomas Clarence, Jan 1956, *Obit* June 1963

Runyon, Mefford R., May 1949

Rutenberg, Pinhas, *Obit* Mar 1942

Samaranch, Juan Antonio, Spanish Olympics executive, Feb 1994, *Obit* Yrbk 2010

Sayre, Ruth Buxton, May 1949

Scheiberling, Edward N., Yrbk 1944, *Obit* Jan 1968

Schleich, Michel, *Obit* June 1945

Schnitzler, William F., Apr 1965

Schuck, Arthur A., Apr 1950, *Obit* Apr 1963

Sensenich, Roscoe L., June 1949, *Obit* Feb 1963

Sepp Blatter, Joseph, Swiss soccer association executive, Jan 2002

Serratosa Cibils, Joaquin, Feb 1954

Shaver, Erwin L., Mar 1949

Shoulders, Harrison H., Nov 1946, *Obit* Jan 1964

Shull, Martha A., Apr 1957

Shuman, Charles B., American farm organization official, Feb 1956

Siemiller, P. L., Nov 1966

Sink, M. Virginia, Mar 1964

Skinner, Eleanor Oakes, May 1951

Smallwood, Robert B., Mar 1956, *Obit* Sept 1974

Smith, Chesterfield H., American lawyer, Nov 1974, *Obit* Yrbk 2003

Smith, Ida B. Wise, Feb 1943, *Obit* Apr 1952

Smith, John L., June 1952, *Obit* Yrbk 1958

Smith, Sylvester C., July 1963

Smithdas, Robert J., Yrbk 1966

Snow, Glenn E., Nov 1947

Sordoni, Andrew J., July 1956, *Obit* Apr 1963

Sporborg, Constance Amberg, Nov 1947, *Obit* Feb 1961

Springer, Adele I., Apr 1947

Staats, Elmer Boyd, American government official, June 1967, *Obit* Yrbk 2011

Stalnaker, John Marshall, psychologist, July 1958, *Obit* Oct 1990

Stamm, John S., Feb 1949, *Obit* May 1956

Starr, Louis E., June 1947

Steinfeld, Jesse L., Apr 1974

Stephens, John A., Yrbk 1956

Stout, Ruth A., Jan 1959

Strachan, Paul A., Jan 1952

Studebaker, Mabel, Nov 1948

Sues, Ralf, May 1944

Sullivan, Henry J., June 1958

Sutton, George Paul, July 1958

Swift, Ernest John, *Obit* Yrbk 1941

Talbott, Philip M., Apr 1958

Thadden-Trieglaff, Reinold von, July 1959

Thomas, Franklin A., American lawyer and foundation official, Oct 1981

Thomas, R. J., Nov 1942, *Obit* June 1967

Tipton, Stuart G., Mar 1967

Tobias, Channing H., July 1945, *Obit* Jan 1962

Tope, John, Feb 1950

Toy, Henry, May 1952

Turner, Ewald, May 1962

Tweed, Harrison, Jan 1950, *Obit* July 1969

Usher, Elizabeth Reuter, May 1967

Veronese, Vittorino, June 1959
Voris, John Ralph, Yrbk 1948, *Obit* Mar 1968
Wagner, J. Addington, May 1956
Walker, Waurine, Feb 1955
Wallace, Clayton M., Sept 1948
Warburton, Herbert B., Nov 1951
Ward, Donovan F., Mar 1965
Warner, Milo J., Nov 1941
Warren, Harry Marsh, *Obit* Feb 1941
Watt, Donald B., Jan 1958
Weafer, Elizabeth, Jan 1958
Weidlein, Edward R., chemist and foundation official, July 1948, *Obit* Nov 1983
Wells, Agnes, Nov 1949, *Obit* Oct 1959
White, Wilbert Webster, *Obit* Oct 1944
Williams, Preston Warren, American religious official, May 2007
Williams, W. Walter, Nov 1948
Wilson, Donald R., Jan 1952
Wilson, Donald V., Jan 1954
Wilson, Rufus H., June 1955
Wolfe, Hugh C., Feb 1950
Woolley, Mary E., Mar 1942, *Obit* Nov 1947

Ornithologists

Beehler, Bruce McP., American ornithologist and conservationist, Aug 2006

Orthopedists

Albee, Fred H., May 1943, *Obit* Apr 1945

Pacifists

Atyam, Angelina, Ugandan peace activist and children's rights advocate, Jan 2004
Baden-Powell, Olave St. Clair, British girls association founder, May 1946
Catt, Carrie Chapman, American feminist and pacifist, Oct 1940, *Obit* Apr 1947
Coffin, William Sloane, American clergyman and pacifist, July 1968, Apr 1980, *Obit* Yrbk 2006
Hayden, Tom, American state legislator and social activist, Apr 1976

Heymann, Lida Gustava, *Obit* Sept 1943
Levinson, Salmon Oliver, lawyer and pacifist, *Obit* Mar 1941
Sheehan, Cindy, American anti-war activist, May 2007
Taylor, Theodore B., American physicist, Apr 1976, *Obit* Feb 2005

Painters

Aaltonen, Waino, June 1954, *Obit* July 1966
Abts, Tomma, British painter, Jan 2007
Afro, Nov 1958
Albright, Ivan Le Lorraine, American painter, Feb 1944, Yrbk 1969, *Obit* Jan 1984
Alechinsky, Pierre, Belgian painter and lithographer, Sept 1988
Ali, Laylah, American painter, July 2008
Allen, Joel Nott, American painter, *Obit* Mar 1940
Allen, Marion Boyd, American painter, *Obit* Feb 1942
Altenburg, Alexander, American painter, *Obit* Mar 1940
Anderson, Abraham Archibald, American painter, *Obit* Jan 1940
Antes, Horst, German painter, etcher and sculptor, Feb 1986
Anuszkiewicz, Richard Joseph, Oct 1978
Appel, Karel, Dutch painter, Mar 1961, *Obit* Yrbk 2006
Artschwager, Richard, painter and sculptor, July 1990, *Obit* Yrbk 2013
Auerbach-Levy, William, painter and etcher, Feb 1948, *Obit* Sept 1964
Avery, Milton, American painter, June 1958, *Obit* Feb 1965
Baca-Flor, Carlos, Peruvian painter, *Obit* July 1941
Bachrach, Elise Wald, American painter, *Obit* Mar 1940
Bacon, Francis, English painter, Feb 1957, Aug 1985, *Obit* June 1992
Baer, William J., American painter, *Obit* Nov 1941
Balthus, French painter, Nov 1979, *Obit* May 2001

Barclay, McClelland, American illustrator, Sept 1940, *Obit* Yrbk 1946
Barnard, Elinor M., American painter, *Obit* Apr 1942
Barnet, Will, American painter, June 1985, *Obit* Yrbk 2013
Beaux, Cecilia, American painter, *Obit* Nov 1942
Benton, Thomas Hart, American painter, Oct 1940, *Obit* Mar 1975
Berman, Eugene, American painter, June 1965, *Obit* Feb 1973
Biddle, George, American painter and sculptor, Feb 1942, *Obit* Jan 1974
Bishop, Isabel, American painter, Oct 1977, *Obit* Apr 1988
Blanche, Jacques-Emile, French painter, *Obit* Nov 1942
Blume, Peter, American painter, Mar 1956, *Obit* Jan 1993
Bogert, George H., American painter, *Obit* Feb 1945
Bohrod, Aaron, painter, Feb 1955, *Obit* June 1992
Borglum, Gutzon, American sculptor and painter, *Obit* Apr 1941
Botero, Fernando, Colombian painter and sculptor, Mar 1980
Brackman, Robert, painter, July 1953, *Obit* Sept 1980
Braque, Georges, French painter, Nov 1949, *Obit* Oct 1963
Brook, Alexander, painter, Apr 1941, *Obit* Apr 1980
Brooks, James, painter, Feb 1959, *Obit* May 1992
Browne, George Elmer, American painter, *Obit* Sept 1946
Brush, George de Forest, American painter, *Obit* June 1941
Buffet, Bernard, French painter, Apr 1959, *Obit* Feb 2000
Burchfield, Charles Ephraim, American painter, May 1942, May 1961, *Obit* Mar 1967
Burliuk, David Davidovich, Russian painter and poet, Apr 1940, *Obit* Mar 1967
Cadmus, Paul, painter and printmaker, July 1942, *Obit* Mar 2000

Canovas del Castillo, Antonio, Sept 1962

Capogrossi, Giuseppe, Yrbk 1957

Carlson, John F., *Obit* May 1945

Carone, Nicolas, American painter and draughtsman, July 2006, *Obit* Yrbk 2010

Carroll, John, painter, July 1955, *Obit* Jan 1960

Cartotto, Ercole, *Obit* Nov 1946

Celmins, Vija, American painter, Jan 2005

Chagall, Marc, Russian painter, Nov 1943, Nov 1960, *Obit* May 1985

Chapin, James, American painter, Mar 1940, *Obit* Sept 1975

Charles, Michael Ray, American painter, Oct 2005

Charlot, Jean, American painter and illustrator, Sept 1945, *Obit* Yrbk 1984

Cheney, Russell, American painter, *Obit* Aug 1945

Chia, Sandro, Italian painter, June 1990

Chryssa, American sculptor and painter, Nov 1978

Chukwuogo-Roy, Chinwe, Nigerian painter, Jan 2007

Close, Chuck, American painter, July 1983

Coe, Sue, Anglo-American painter and illustrator, Aug 1997

Coffin, Haskell, *Obit* July 1941

Cole, Jessie Duncan Savage, *Obit* Yrbk 1940

Colville, Alex, Canadian painter, Mar 1985, *Obit* Yrbk 2013

Congdon, William, painter, May 1967, *Obit* July 1998

Cox, Allyn, painter, July 1954, *Obit* Jan 1983

Curran, Charles Courtney, American painter, *Obit* Jan 1943

Curry, John Steuart, American painter, Apr 1941, *Obit* Oct 1946

Dardel, Nils von, Swedish painter, *Obit* July 1943

Davis, Gladys Rockmore, painter, Sept 1953, *Obit* Apr 1967

De Kooning, Elaine Marie Catherine, American painter, July 1982, *Obit* Mar 1989

De Kooning, Willem, American painter, June 1955, Sept 1984, *Obit* May 1997

Deming, Edwin Willard, painter and sculptor, *Obit* Yrbk 1942

Dickinson, Edwin Walter, American painter, Sept 1963, *Obit* Feb 1979

Diebenkorn, Richard, American painter, Yrbk 1971, *Obit* May 1993

Dine, Jim, American painter, June 1969

Djanira, Jan 1961

Drouet, Bessie Clarke, *Obit* Oct 1940

Dubuffet, Jean, French painter and sculptor, July 1962, *Obit* July 1985

Duchamp, Marcel, French painter, June 1960, *Obit* Yrbk 1968

Dufy, Raoul, French painter, Mar 1951, *Obit* May 1953

Dumas, Marlene, South African painter, Jan 2010

Eggleston, Edward Mason, *Obit* Mar 1941

Eilshemius, Louis Michel, American painter, Apr 1940, *Obit* Feb 1942

Elisofon, Eliot, American photographer and painter, Jan 1972, *Obit* May 1973

Ensor, James, Belgian painter and engraver, *Obit* Feb 1943

Ernst, Jimmy, painter, Mar 1966, *Obit* Apr 1984

Ernst, Max, German painter, Yrbk 1942, Oct 1961, *Obit* May 1976

Estes, Richard, American painter, Nov 1995

Evergood, Philip, American painter, Oct 1944, Oct 1960, *Obit* Apr 1973

Eves, Reginald Grenville, Sept 1940, *Obit* Aug 1941

Fasanella, Ralph, painter, June 1975, *Obit* Mar 1998

Ferber, Herbert, American sculptor and painter, Nov 1960, *Obit* Oct 1991

Ferren, John, American painter, July 1958, *Obit* Oct 1970

Fiene, Ernest, American painter and printmaker, Aug 1941

Filmus, Tully, painter, Apr 1964, *Obit* June 1998

Fischl, Eric, American painter and sculptor, June 1986

Folon, Jean Michel, Belgian painter and illustrator, Feb 1981, *Obit* Yrbk 2006

Francis, Sam, American painter, Oct 1973, *Obit* Jan 1995

Frankenthaler, Helen, American painter, Apr 1966, *Obit* Yrbk 2012

Fredenthal, David, Sept 1942, *Obit* Jan 1959

Freilicher, Jane, American painter, Nov 1989

Freud, Lucian, British painter, July 1988, *Obit* Yrbk 2011

Gabo, Naum, Russian painter and sculptor, Apr 1972, *Obit* Oct 1977

Gallagher, Ellen, American painter, Feb 2009

Ganso, Emil, *Obit* June 1941

Gatch, Lee, Mar 1966, *Obit* Jan 1969

Gibson, Charles Dana, American illustrator and painter, *Obit* Feb 1945

Giger, H. R., Swiss painter, sculptor and scenic designer, Jan 2002

Goldthwaite, Anne, American painter and printmaker, *Obit* Mar 1944

Golub, Leon Albert, American painter, Aug 1984, *Obit* Yrbk 2004

Goodman, Bertram, May 1954

Gordon, Leon, *Obit* Feb 1944

Gorman, R. C., American painter and sculptor, Jan 2001

Gottlieb, Adolph, American painter, Jan 1959, *Obit* Apr 1974

Gowda, Sheela, Indian artist, Jan 2002

Graves, Michael, American architect and designer, Jan 1989

Graves, Morris, painter, July 1956, *Obit* Sept 2001

Graves, Nancy, American painter and sculptor, May 1981, *Obit* Jan 1996

Green, Florence Topping, *Obit* June 1945

Greene, Balcomb, painter, Nov 1965, *Obit* Jan 1991

Groot, Adriaan M. de, *Obit* Mar 1942

Groth, John, illustrator and painter, Feb 1943, *Obit* Aug 1988

Gruppe, Charles Paul, *Obit* Nov 1940

Guston, Philip, American painter, Feb 1971, *Obit* July 1980

Gwathmey, Robert, American painter, Yrbk 1943, *Obit* Nov 1988

Haacke, Hans, German artist, July 1987

Hammond, Aubrey, English illustrator, *Obit* Apr 1940

Hancock, Trenton Doyle, American painter and performance artist, Apr 2006

Haring, Keith, American artist, Aug 1986, *Obit* Apr 1990

Hartigan, Grace, American painter, Sept 1962, *Obit* Yrbk 2009

Hartung, Hans, French painter, July 1958, *Obit* Feb 1990

Hayter, Stanley William, English painter and engraver, Yrbk 1945, *Obit* June 1988

Held, Al, American painter, Jan 1986, *Obit* Yrbk 2005

Heliker, John, painter, Jan 1969, .*Obit* July 2000

Helion, Jean, French painter, Nov 1943, *Obit* Jan 1988

Hinckley, Robert C., *Obit* July 1941

Hirshfield, Morris, painter, Sept 1943

Hirst, Damien, English artist, Aug 2013

Hockney, David, English painter, July 1972

Hodgkin, Howard, English painter, May 1991

Hopper, Edward, American painter, Yrbk 1950, *Obit* July 1967

Hurd, Peter, American painter, Oct 1957, *Obit* Sept 1984

Indiana, Robert, American painter and sculptor, Mar 1973

Inglis, John J., *Obit* Oct 1946

James, Alexander R., *Obit* Apr 1946

John, Augustus, English painter, Oct 1941, *Obit* Jan 1962

Johns, Jasper, American painter, May 1967, May 1987

Jones, Joe, American painter, Oct 1940, *Obit* June 1963

Kabakov, Ilya, Russian painter and illustrator, Apr 1998

Kainen, Jacob, American painter and printmaker, Feb 1987, *Obit* Aug 2001

Kandinsky, Wassily, Russian painter, *Obit* Feb 1945

Karfiol, Bernard, Nov 1947, *Obit* Oct 1952

Katz, Alex, American painter, July 1975

Keith, Dora Wheeler, American painter, *Obit* Feb 1941

Kelly, Ellsworth, American painter and sculptor, May 1970

Kiefer, Anselm, German painter, June 1988

Kienholz, Edward, American painter and sculptor, Aug 1989, *Obit* Aug 1994

Kingman, Dong, American painter and illustrator, Oct 1962, *Obit* Yrbk 2000

Kitaj, R. B., American painter, Apr 1982, *Obit* Yrbk 2008

Klee, Paul, Swiss painter, *Obit* Aug 1940

Knaths, Karl, painter, July 1953, *Obit* Apr 1971

Knox, Simmie, American painter, May 2009

Koch, John, American painter, May 1965, *Obit* June 1978

Komar, Vitali, Russian painter, Oct 1984

Konijnenburg, Willem Adriaan van, *Obit* Apr 1943

Kramer, Edward Adam, *Obit* Feb 1942

Krasner, Lee, American painter, Mar 1974, *Obit* Aug 1984

Kroll, Leon, American painter, Mar 1943, *Obit* Yrbk 1974

Kruger-Gray, George, *Obit* June 1943

Kuniyoshi, Yasuo, Japanese-American painter, June 1941, *Obit* June 1953

Lalupu Flores, Wilmer, Peruvian painter, Jan 2005

Landau, Jacob, illustrator, Yrbk 1965

Lavery, John, Irish painter, *Obit* Mar 1941

Lawrence, Jacob, American painter and illustrator, July 1965, Sept 1988, *Obit* Aug 2000

LeWitt, Sol, American sculptor, July 1986, *Obit* Yrbk 2007

Lebrun, Rico, Sept 1952, *Obit* July 1964

Lee, Doris Emrick, American painter and illustrator, Jan 1954, *Obit* Jan 1986

Leger, Fernand, French painter, Jan 1943, *Obit* Oct 1955

Levi, Julian, Apr 1943, *Obit* Apr 1982

Levine, Jack, American painter, June 1956, *Obit* Yrbk 2011

Lichtenstein, Roy, American painter, Feb 1969, *Obit* Jan 1998

Linton, Frank B. A., *Obit* Jan 1944

Little, Philip, *Obit* May 1942

Liu Bolin, Chinese painter and photographer, Nov 2013

Llewellyn, William, *Obit* Mar 1941

Long, Richard, English artist, Sept 1995

Lucioni, Luigi, painter, Oct 1943, *Obit* Sept 1988

Lurcat, Jean, French painter and tapestry designer, Sept 1948, *Obit* Feb 1966

MacEwen, Walter, *Obit* May 1943

MacIver, Loren, American painter, Nov 1953, Nov 1987, *Obit* Aug 1998

Magritte, Rene, Belgian painter, Sept 1966, *Obit* Oct 1967

Mahlangu, Esther, South African painter, Jan 2007

Maillol, Aristide, French sculptor and illustrator, May 1942, *Obit* Nov 1944

Manessier, Alfred, French painter, May 1957, *Obit* Oct 1993

Manzu, Giacomo, Italian sculptor, Mar 1961, *Obit* Mar 1991

Marca-Relli, Conrad, American collage artist, Sept 1970, *Obit* Nov 2000

Marden, Brice, American painter and printmaker, Aug 1990

Marin, John, American painter, July 1949, *Obit* Yrbk 1953

Mark, Louis, *Obit* May 1942

Marsh, Reginald, American painter, Sept 1941, *Obit* Sept 1954

Martin, Agnes, American painter, Sept 1989, *Obit* Apr 2005

Masson, Andre, French painter and stage designer, Nov 1974, *Obit* Jan 1988

Matisse, Henri, French painter, May 1943, June 1953, *Obit* Jan 1955

Matta, Chilean painter, Nov 1957, *Obit* Yrbk 2003

Mattson, Henry, Jan 1956, *Obit* Nov 1971

McMein, Neysa, illustrator and painter, Feb 1941, *Obit* June 1949

Mechau, Frank Albert, American painter, *Obit* Apr 1946

Mehretu, Julie, American artist, July 2010

Mehta, Tyeb, Indian painter, Jan 2006

Melamid, Aleksandr, Russian painter, Oct 1984

Merida, Carlos, Mexican painter, Jan 1960

Meyerowitz, William, American etcher and painter, May 1942

Miro, Joan, Spanish painter, May 1940, Nov 1973, *Obit* Feb 1984

Mitchell, Dean, American painter, Aug 2002

Mitchell, Joan, American painter, Mar 1986, *Obit* Jan 1993

Mondrian, Piet, Dutch painter, *Obit* Mar 1944

Mora, Francis Luis, American painter, *Obit* July 1940

Morley, Malcolm, English painter, June 1984

Morris, Robert, American artist, Apr 1971

Moses, Grandma, American painter, Jan 1949, *Obit* Feb 1962

Munch, Edvard, Norwegian painter, Yrbk 1940, *Obit* Mar 1944

Murray, Elizabeth, American painter, Apr 1995, *Obit* Yrbk 2007

Myers, Jerome, *Obit* Aug 1940

Nash, Paul, English illustrator and painter, *Obit* Sept 1946

Neals, Otto, American sculptor and painter, Feb 2003

Neel, Alice, American painter, Aug 1976, *Obit* Jan 1985

Neiman, LeRoy, American painter, July 1996, *Obit* Yrbk 2012

Nevinson, Christopher Richard Wynne, English painter, *Obit* Nov 1946

Newman, Barnett, American painter, Sept 1969, *Obit* Sept 1970

Nicholson, Ben, English painter, Jan 1958, *Obit* Apr 1982

Noland, Kenneth, American painter, Sept 1972, *Obit* Yrbk 2010

O'Keeffe, Georgia, American painter, June 1941, Feb 1964, *Obit* Apr 1986

Olitski, Jules, American painter, Oct 1969, *Obit* Yrbk 2007

Orozco, Jose Clemente, Mexican painter, Sept 1940, *Obit* Oct 1949

Page, Marie Danforth, *Obit* Mar 1940

Palmer, James Lynwood, English painter, *Obit* Aug 1941

Parrish, Maxfield, American illustrator and painter, Nov 1965, *Obit* Apr 1966

Paxton, William McGregor, painter, *Obit* July 1941

Pearlstein, Philip, American painter, Feb 1973

Peirce, Waldo, American painter, Yrbk 1944, *Obit* May 1970

Pereira, Irene Rice, American painter, Nov 1953, *Obit* Feb 1971

Picasso, Pablo, Spanish painter, Jan 1943, Nov 1962, *Obit* May 1973

Piper, John, English painter, Apr 1964, *Obit* Aug 1992

Pippin, Horace, American painter, Aug 1945, *Obit* Yrbk 1947

Pollock, Jackson, American painter, Apr 1956

Poor, Henry Varnum, American ceramist and painter, Apr 1942, *Obit* Jan 1971

Portinari, Candido, Brazilian painter, Yrbk 1940, *Obit* Mar 1962

Pousette-Dart, Richard, painter, Mar 1976, *Obit* Jan 1993

Prellwitz, Henry, *Obit* Apr 1940

Prestopino, Gregorio, painter, June 1964, *Obit* Apr 1985

Rand, Ellen G. Emmet, American painter, *Obit* Feb 1942

Rattner, Abraham, American painter, Mar 1948, *Obit* Apr 1978

Rauch, Neo, German painter, Jan 2007

Ray, Man, American painter and photographer, Yrbk 1965, *Obit* Jan 1977

Redpath, Anne, Jan 1957, *Obit* Mar 1965

Richter, Gerhard, German painter and printmaker, June 2002

Riley, Bridget, English painter, Sept 1981

Riopelle, Jean-Paul, Canadian painter and sculptor, Oct 1989, *Obit* Sept 2002

Rivera, Diego, Mexican painter, July 1948, *Obit* Feb 1958

Rivers, Larry, American painter and sculptor, Apr 1969, *Obit* Nov 2002

Roberts, Goodridge, Canadian painter, May 1955

Robinson, William Heath, English illustrator, *Obit* Nov 1944

Robus, Hugo, Yrbk 1962, *Obit* Feb 1964

Rockwell, Norman, American painter, June 1945, *Obit* Jan 1979

Romano, Emanuel, painter and illustrator, Mar 1940, *Obit* Feb 1985

Romano, Umberto, Mar 1954, *Obit* Nov 1982

Rosenquist, James, American painter, Sept 1970

Roszak, Theodore J., Polish-American painter and sculptor, June 1966, *Obit* Oct 1981

Rothenberg, Susan, American painter and printmaker, Mar 1985

Rothko, Mark, American painter, May 1961, *Obit* Apr 1970

Rouault, Georges, French painter, May 1945, *Obit* Apr 1958

Rubin, Reuven, Apr 1943, *Obit* Jan 1975

Ruscha, Edward, American painter, printmaker and photographer, Oct 1989

Salle, David, American painter and filmmaker, Sept 1986

Samaras, Lucas, American sculptor, painter and photographer, Nov 1972

Sawyer, Helen, painter, Oct 1954

Schapiro, Miriam, American artist, Aug 2000

Scharf, Kenny, American painter, Feb 2012

Schnabel, Julian, American painter and film director, Nov 1983

Scholder, Fritz, American painter, Apr 1985, *Obit* Yrbk 2005

Scudder, Janet, painter and sculptor, *Obit* July 1940

Segal, George, American sculptor, Jan 1972, *Obit* Sept 2000

Sert, Jose Maria, Spanish painter, *Obit* Jan 1946

Shahn, Ben, American painter, Yrbk 1954, *Obit* May 1969

Sheckell, Thomas O., *Obit* Apr 1943

Sheeler, Charles, American painter and photographer, Nov 1950, *Obit* June 1965

Shepard, Ernest H., English painter and illustrator, Yrbk 1963, *Obit* May 1976

Shikler, Aaron, painter, Yrbk 1971

Shinn, Everett, painter, May 1951, *Obit* June 1953

Sickert, Walter, British painter and engraver, *Obit* Mar 1942

Sikander, Shahzia, Pakistani painter, Jan 2002

Siqueiros, David Alfaro, Mexican painter, June 1959, *Obit* Feb 1974

Smith, Kiki, American painter, sculptor and printmaker, Mar 2005

Snell, Henry Bayley, *Obit* Mar 1943

Soto, Jesus Raphael, Venezuelan painter and sculptor, Jan 2004

Soulages, Pierre, French painter, graphic artist and set designer, Apr 1958

Soyer, Isaac, American painter, Mar 1941, *Obit* Sept 1981

Soyer, Moses, American painter, Mar 1941, *Obit* Oct 1974

Soyer, Raphael, American painter, Mar 1941, *Obit* Jan 1988

Speicher, Eugene Edward, American painter, Oct 1947, *Obit* July 1962

Stamos, Theodoros, painter, Jan 1959, *Obit* Apr 1997

Stella, Frank, American artist, Apr 1971, Apr 1988

Stella, Joseph, painter, *Obit* Yrbk 1946

Sterne, Hedda, American painter, Mar 1957, *Obit* Yrbk 2011

Sterne, Maurice, American painter, Apr 1943, *Obit* Oct 1957

Still, Clyfford, American painter, Sept 1971, *Obit* Aug 1980

Stoddard, Frederick Lincoln, *Obit* Mar 1940

Struzan, Drew, American poster artist, Mar 2005

Stuart, James Everett, painter, *Obit* Feb 1941

Sutherland, Graham Vivian, English painter, Jan 1955, *Obit* Apr 1980

Tamayo, Rufino, Mexican painter, Mar 1953, *Obit* Aug 1991

Tapies, Antoni, Spanish painter and sculptor, July 1966, *Obit* Yrbk 2012

Tchelitchew, Pavel, Russian painter, Mar 1943, *Obit* Oct 1957

Tobey, Mark, American painter, Mar 1957, *Obit* June 1976

Tooker, George, American painter, Mar 1958, *Obit* Yrbk 2011

Torrey, George Burroughs, painter, *Obit* June 1942

Townsend, Harry Everett, *Obit* Oct 1941

Tuymans, Luc, Belgian painter, Jan 2007

Twombly, Cy, American painter, Apr 1988, *Obit* Yrbk 2011

Tworkov, Jack, American painter, Mar 1964, *Obit* Oct 1982

Utrillo, Maurice, French painter, Sept 1953, *Obit* Jan 1956

Varian, Dorothy, Jan 1943

Vertes, Marcel, Hungarian painter and illustrator, Apr 1961, *Obit* Jan 1962

Vezin, Charles, *Obit* May 1942

Vieira da Silva, Maria Helena, Portuguese painter, Yrbk 1958, *Obit* May 1992

Villon, Jacques, French painter and engraver, Jan 1956, *Obit* July 1963

Von Wicht, John, Jan 1963, *Obit* Mar 1970

Walker, Kara, American silhouette artist, Mar 2000

Watrous, Harry Willson, painter, *Obit* Jan 1940

Waugh, Frederick Judd, *Obit* Oct 1940

Weber, Max, American painter, June 1941, *Obit* Yrbk 1961

Wenner, Kurt, American street artist, Sept 2011

Werner, Theodor, Yrbk 1958

Wheelock, Warren, Mar 1940, *Obit* Oct 1960

Wiley, Kehinde, American painter, Aug 2007

Winter, Fritz, German painter, Mar 1958

Wood, Grant, American painter, Aug 1940, *Obit* Apr 1942

Woodbury, Charles Herbert, painter, *Obit* Jan 1940

Wyeth, Andrew, American painter, Apr 1955, Nov 1981, *Obit* Yrbk 2009

Wyeth, Jamie, American painter, Jan 1977

Wyeth, N. C., American painter and illustrator, *Obit* Nov 1945

Yarrow, William, *Obit* June 1941

Young, Charles Jac, *Obit* Apr 1940

Youngerman, Jack, painter, Nov 1986

Zao, Wou-ki, French painter, *Obit* Yrbk 2013

Zerbe, Karl, Feb 1959, *Obit* Jan 1973

Zhang Xiaogang, Chinese painter, Jan 2005

Zorach, William, American sculptor and painter, Feb 1943, Feb 1963, *Obit* Jan 1967

Paleontologists

Colbert, Edwin Harris, American paleontologist, Sept 1965, *Obit* Feb 2002

Merriam, John C., *Obit* Yrbk 1945

Parapsychologists

Rhine, J. B., American parapsychologist, Jan 1949, *Obit* Apr 1980

Parents of presidents

Bush, Barbara, wife of American president George Bush, Oct 1989

Carter, Lillian, mother of American president Jimmy Carter, Jan 1978, *Obit* Jan 1984

Kennedy, Rose Fitzgerald, mother of President John F. Kennedy, Nov 1970, *Obit* Mar 1995

Roosevelt, Sara Delano, mother of American President Franklin D. Roosevelt, *Obit* Oct 1941

Parents of prominent persons

Abrams, Benjamin, father of Robert Abrams, Sept 1954, *Obit* Oct 1967

Bush, Barbara, wife of American president George Bush, Oct 1989

Carter, Lillian, mother of American president Jimmy Carter, Jan 1978, *Obit* Jan 1984

Gore, Albert A., American senator and father of Vice-President Albert Gore, Jr., Jan 1952, *Obit* Feb 1999

Kennedy, Rose Fitzgerald, mother of President John F. Kennedy, Nov 1970, *Obit* Mar 1995

Roosevelt, Sara Delano, mother of American President Franklin D. Roosevelt, *Obit* Oct 1941

Pathologists

Cunningham, William Francis, *Obit* Jan 1941

Dandy, Walter E., American neurosurgeon, *Obit* May 1946

Kevorkian, Jack, American pathologist and right to die advocate, Sept 1994, *Obit* Yrbk 2011

Krause, Allen K., *Obit* July 1941

Perla, David, Mar 1940

Slye, Maud, American pathologist, Yrbk 1940, *Obit* Nov 1954

Patriarchs

Aleksii, Mar 1953, *Obit* June 1970

Aleksii, Jan 2003, *Obit* Yrbk 2009

Bartholomeos, Jan 2004

Shenouda, Egyptian patriarch, Jan 2003, *Obit* Yrbk 2013

Patrons of the arts

Coolidge, Elizabeth Sprague, music patron, Aug 1941, *Obit* Jan 1954

Guggenheim, Peggy, American patron of the arts, Oct 1962, *Obit* Feb 1980

Tully, Alice, music patron and singer, Jan 1984, *Obit* Feb 1994

Webb, Aileen Osborn, American art patron, Yrbk 1958, *Obit* Oct 1979

Whitney, Gertrude Vanderbilt, American sculptor and art patron, July 1941, *Obit* Yrbk 1942

Pediatricians

Caldicott, Helen, American pediatrician and anti-nuclear activist, Oct 1983

Elders, Joycelyn, American surgeon general, Mar 1994

Eliot, Martha May, American pediatrician, Oct 1948, *Obit* Apr 1978

Griffith, J. P. Crozer, *Obit* Sept 1941

Jalal, Massouda, Afghan pediatrician, social activist and political leader, Jan 2002

Levine, Melvin D., American pediatrician, Nov 2005

Offit, Paul A., American immunologist, Apr 2009

Schick, Bela, pediatrician, July 1944, *Obit* Feb 1968

Senn, Milton John Edward, pediatrician and psychiatrist, June 1950, *Obit* Aug 1990

Shaw, Henry, American pediatrician, *Obit* May 1941

Penologists

Kirchwey, George W., *Obit* Apr 1942

Van Waters, Miriam, American penologist, Mar 1963, *Obit* Apr 1974

Percussionists

Palmieri, Eddie, American salsa pianist and band leader, June 1992

Richard 23, Belgian percussionist and singer, Jan 2006

Performance artists

Anderson, Laurie, American performance artist and musician, July 1983

Dine, Jim, American painter, June 1969

Emin, Tracey, British performance artist, Nov 2009

Finley, Karen, performance artist, Sept 1998

Jacir, Emily, Palestinian artist, Aug 2009

Oldenburg, Claes, Swedish-American sculptor, Feb 1970

Wilson, Robert, American director, dramatist and artist, Aug 1979

Perfumers

Tonatto, Laura, Italian perfumer, Apr 2009

Pharmacologists

Brodie, Bernard B., American pharmacologist, Sept 1969, *Obit* May 1989

Loewe, Siegfried, American pharmacologist, Jan 1947

Moncada, Salvador, Honduran pharmacologist, Jan 2003

Terrett, Nicholas K., British pharmacologist and co-inventor of Viagra, Jan 2003

Philanthropists

Aoki, Rocky, American restaurant chain executive, June 2005, *Obit* Yrbk 2008

Belmont, Eleanor Robson, July 1944, *Obit* Jan 1980

Bolton, Frances Payne Bingham, American congresswoman, Mar 1940, Apr 1954, *Obit* May 1977

Cherne, Leo, economist and humanitarian, Yrbk 1940, *Obit* Mar 1999

Coolidge, Elizabeth Sprague, music patron, Aug 1941, *Obit* Jan 1954

Delacorte, George T., American publisher and philanthropist, Nov 1965, *Obit* July 1991

Dodge, Cleveland E., Mar 1954, *Obit* Feb 1983

Falk, Maurice, *Obit* Apr 1946

Guggenheim, Florence Shloss, *Obit* July 1944

Guggenheimer, Minnie, Oct 1962, *Obit* June 1966

Hale, Arthur, *Obit* Mar 1940

Horlick, William, *Obit* Apr 1940

Lasker, Mary, American art dealer and philanthropist, Oct 1959, *Obit* May 1994

Maxon, Lou R., Aug 1943, *Obit* July 1971

Meyer, Danny, American restaurateur, July 2007

Moore, Elisabeth Luce, American philanthropist and foundation official, Oct 1960, *Obit* Yrbk 2002

Morgan, Anne Tracy, philanthropist and social worker, Jan 1946, *Obit* Mar 1952

Pierre, French abbot, Nov 1955

Rank, Joseph, *Obit* Jan 1944

Rockefeller, John D., American philanthropist, June 1953, *Obit* Sept 1978

Rockefeller, John D., American philanthropist, July 1941, *Obit* July 1960

Rusesabagina, Paul, Rwandan hotel manager and humanitarian, May 2005

Straus, Percy Selden, American department store executive, *Obit* May 1944

Webb, Aileen Osborn, American art patron, Yrbk 1958, *Obit* Oct 1979

Wenner-Gren, Axel, Oct 1942, *Obit* Jan 1962

Wexner, Leslie H., American fashion chain store executive and philanthropist, Feb 1994

Whitney, Gertrude Vanderbilt, American sculptor and art patron, July 1941, *Obit* Yrbk 1942

Philologists

Barnhart, Clarence Lewis, lexicographer, Sept 1954, *Obit* Jan 1994

Deutscher, Guy, Feb 2012

Funk, Charles Earle, June 1947, *Obit* July 1957

Gove, Philip Babcock, Oct 1962, *Obit* Jan 1973

McWhorter, John H., American linguist, Feb 2003

Ogden, C. K., English linguist, Jan 1944, *Obit* June 1957

Philosophers

Agacinski, Sylviane, Feb 2012

Arendt, Hannah, German-American political philosopher, May 1959, *Obit* Feb 1976

Ayer, A. J., British philosopher, May 1964, *Obit* Aug 1989

Badinter, Elisabeth, French philosopher, Nov 2011

Barrett, William, professor of philosophy, Aug 1982, *Obit* Nov 1992

Bush, Wendell T., *Obit* Mar 1941

Churchland, Patricia Smith, Canadian philosopher, May 2003

Collingwood, R. G., British philosopher and historian, *Obit* Mar 1943

Derrida, Jacques, French philosopher, July 1993, *Obit* Mar 2005

Dewey, John, American philosopher and educator, Aug 1944, *Obit* July 1952

Dooyeweerd, Herman, Dutch philosopher, Sept 1958

Driesch, Hans, German biologist and philosopher, *Obit* June 1941

Dutton, Denis, American philosopher, Aug 2009, *Obit* Yrbk 2011

Glucksmann, Andre, French philosopher, Jan 2006

Habermas, Jurgen, German social philosopher, Jan 2007

Heidegger, Martin, German philosopher, June 1972, *Obit* July 1976

Heller, Agnes, Hungarian philosopher, Nov 2008

Hocking, William Ernest, American philosopher, Mar 1962, *Obit* July 1966

Hook, Sidney, American philosopher, Oct 1952, Apr 1988, *Obit* Sept 1989

Illich, Ivan, American priest and philosopher, Yrbk 1969, *Obit* Yrbk 2003

Kallen, Horace Meyer, philosopher, Oct 1953, *Obit* Apr 1974

Keen, Sam, author and philosopher, Feb 1995

Keyserling, Hermann, German philosopher, *Obit* June 1946

Kimpton, Lawrence A., June 1951, *Obit* Jan 1978

Kripke, Saul A., American philosopher, Oct 2004

Levy, Bernard Henri, French philosopher, Nov 1993

Marcuse, Herbert, American political philosopher, Mar 1969, *Obit* Sept 1979

Maritain, Jacques, French philosopher, May 1942, *Obit* June 1973

Mosca, Gaetano, Italian political philosopher, *Obit* Jan 1942

Nozick, Robert, American political philosopher, June 1982, *Obit* Apr 2002

Plantinga, Alvin, Plantinga, Alvin C(arl) (1932-), Nov 2013

Popper, Karl Raimund, Austrian-British philosopher, Jan 1963, *Obit* Nov 1994

Quine, W. V., American philosopher, Nov 1999, *Obit* Mar 2001

Radhakrishnan, S., Indian statesman and philosopher, June 1952, *Obit* June 1975

Santayana, George, Spanish-American philosopher, Apr 1944, *Obit* Nov 1952

Suzuki, Daisetz Teitaro, Japanese philosopher, Oct 1958, *Obit* Nov 1966

Trout, J. D., American philosopher, July 2009

Warnock, Mary, British philosopher, Jan 2005

Weiss, Paul, American philosopher, May 1969, *Obit* Yrbk 2002

Weizsacker, Carl Friedrich von, German physicist and philosopher, Jan 1985, *Obit* Yrbk 2007

Wilson, George Arthur, *Obit* Nov 1941

Zizek, Slavoj, Slovenian philosopher, Jan 2004

Photographers

Abbott, Berenice, American photographer, July 1942, *Obit* Feb 1992

Adams, Ansel, American photographer, May 1977, *Obit* June 1984

Addario, Lynsey, American photojournalist, Apr 2013

Almendros, Nestor, Cuban cinematographer and director, Nov 1989, *Obit* May 1992

Alvarez Bravo, Manuel, Mexican photographer, Jan 1999, *Obit* Jan 2003

Ammann, Karl, Swiss wildlife photographer, Jan 2002

Anderson, Erica Kellner, Feb 1957, *Obit* Nov 1976

Araki, Nobuyoshi, Japanese photographer, Jan 2003

Arnold, Eve, American photojournalist, Oct 2005, *Obit* Yrbk 2012

Avedon, Richard, American photographer, Feb 1975, *Obit* Mar 2005

Bannister, Constance, American baby photographer, July 1955, *Obit* Yrbk 2005

Black, Alexander, American photographer, *Obit* Jan 1940

Bonney, Therese, Feb 1944

Bourke-White, Margaret, American photographer, Jan 1940, *Obit* Oct 1971

Brandt, Bill, English photographer, Aug 1981, *Obit* Feb 1984

Brenner, Frederic, French photographer, Jan 2004

Burri, Rene, Swiss photojournalist, Jan 2007

Callahan, Harry M., American photographer, Nov 1984, *Obit* July 1999

Calle, Sophie, French artist, May 2001

Capa, Cornell, American photojournalist, July 2005, *Obit* Yrbk 2008

Cartier-Bresson, Henri, French photographer, Mar 1947, May 1976, Jan 2003, *Obit* Yrbk 2004

Colbert, Gregory, Canadian photographer and cinematographer, Sept 2005

Corbijn, Anton, Dutch photographer, June 2006

Corrales, Raul, Cuban photographer, Jan 2003

Cunningham, Bill, American photographer, Aug 2011

DeCarava, Roy, American photographer, Aug 2008, *Obit* Yrbk 2009

Deakins, Roger, British cinematographer, May 2001

Dean, Tacita, English installation artist, May 2010

Demand, Thomas C., German photographer, Mar 2010

Demarbre, Lee Gordon, Canadian film director, Jan 2003

Deschanel, Caleb, American cinematographer and film director, Feb 2008

DiCorcia, Philip-Lorca, American photographer, Apr 2008

Dickerson, Ernest, American cinematographer and film director, July 2000

Dith, Pran, Cambodian photojournalist, Oct 1996, *Obit* Yrbk 2008

Doubilet, David, American underwater photographer, Mar 2003

Doyle, Christopher, Australian cinematographer, Jan 2006

Duncan, David Douglas, American photojournalist, Nov 1968

Eggleston, William, American photographer, Feb 2002

Eisenstaedt, Alfred, American photojournalist, Jan 1975, *Obit* Oct 1995

Elisofon, Eliot, American photographer and painter, Jan 1972, *Obit* May 1973

Evans, Walker, American photographer, Sept 1971, *Obit* June 1975

Faidley, Warren, American photographer and storm chaser, Feb 2008

Frank, Robert, Swiss-American photographer and film director, Aug 1997

Frankel, Felice, American photographer, Apr 1998

Friedlander, Lee, American photographer, May 2006

Frissell, Toni, photographer, June 1947, *Obit* June 1988

Gallagher, William M., Oct 1953, *Obit* Nov 1975

Genthe, Arnold, *Obit* Oct 1942

Goldsworthy, Andy, English photographer and sculptor, Oct 2000

Gursky, Andreas, German photographer, July 2001

Guzy, Carol, American photojournalist, Feb 2000

Hall, Conrad L., American cinematographer, Aug 2000, *Obit* May 2003

Halsman, Philippe, Latvian-American photographer, Mar 1960, *Obit* Aug 1979

Higgins, Chester, American photojournalist, June 2002

Hockney, David, English painter, July 1972

Hondros, Chris, American photojournalist, Nov 2004, *Obit* Yrbk 2011

Horst, photographer, June 1992, *Obit* Mar 2000

Howe, James Wong, cinematographer, Feb 1943, *Obit* Sept 1976

Hudson, Henrietta, *Obit* May 1942

Jaar, Alfredo, Chilean mixed-media and installation artist, Jan 2005

Kamber, Michael, American photojournalist, June 2009

Kaminski, Janusz, Polish cinematographer, Mar 2000

Karsh, Yousuf, Canadian photographer, Yrbk 1952, Feb 1980, *Obit* Nov 2002

Kertesz, Andre, American photographer, Aug 1979, *Obit* Nov 1985

Klein, William, American photographer, Mar 2004

Koltai, Lajos, Hungarian cinematographer, Jan 2003

Kruger, Barbara, American artist, July 1995

LaChapelle, David, American photographer, June 2008

Lanting, Frans, Dutch-American photographer, Nov 1995

Leibovitz, Annie, American photographer, Oct 1991

Link, O. Winston, American photographer, June 1995, *Obit* Apr 2001

Liu Bolin, Chinese painter and photographer, Nov 2013
Long, Richard, English artist, Sept 1995
Lubezki, Emmanuel, Mexican cinematographer, July 2011
MacDonald, Pirie, *Obit* June 1942
Magritte, Rene, Belgian painter, Sept 1966, *Obit* Oct 1967
Mark, Mary Ellen, American photographer, Sept 1999
McCurry, Steve, American photojournalist, Nov 2005
Meiselas, Susan, American photographer, Feb 2005
Michals, Duane, American photographer, Apr 1981
Moffett, Mark W., American ecologist and photographer, Oct 2011
Mydans, Carl, American photojournalist, May 1945, *Obit* Yrbk 2004
Neshat, Shirin, Iranian photographer and video artist, Jan 2002
Newman, Arnold, American photographer, Oct 1980, *Obit* Yrbk 2006
Newton, Helmut, German photographer, Nov 1991, *Obit* Yrbk 2004
Nykvist, Sven, Swedish cinematographer, June 1989, *Obit* Yrbk 2007
Orozco, Gabriel, Mexican conceptual artist, Jan 2004
Papamichael, Phedon, Greek cinematographer, Sept 2012
Pau, Peter, Chinese cinematographer, Feb 2002
Penn, Irving, American photographer, Nov 1980, *Obit* Yrbk 2009
Plowden, David, photographer, Feb 1996
Prieto, Rodrigo, Mexican cinematographer, Jan 2003
Ray, Man, American painter and photographer, Yrbk 1965, *Obit* Jan 1977
Richardson, Robert, American cinematographer, Jan 2010
Rosenthal, Joe, American photojournalist, June 1945, *Obit* Yrbk 2007
Salgado, Sebastiao, Brazilian photographer, Jan 2002

Samaras, Lucas, American sculptor, painter and photographer, Nov 1972
Scavullo, Francesco, American fashion photographer, May 1985, *Obit* Yrbk 2004
Sheckell, Thomas O., *Obit* Apr 1943
Sheeler, Charles, American painter and photographer, Nov 1950, *Obit* June 1965
Sherman, Cindy, American photographer, Oct 1990
Sidibe, Malick, Malian photographer, Jan 2004
Simpson, Lorna, American photographer and video artist, Nov 2004
Snowdon, Antony Armstrong-Jones, English photographer, Oct 1960
Sonnenfeld, Barry, American film director, Nov 1998
Steichen, Edward, American photographer, Oct 1942, Yrbk 1964, *Obit* May 1973
Steinmetz, George, American photographer, July 2013
Strand, Paul, American photographer, July 1965, *Obit* May 1976
Teller, Juergen, German photographer, Jan 2004
Testino, Mario, Peruvian fashion photographer, Jan 2006
Tice, George A., American photographer, Nov 2003
Toland, Gregg, American cinematographer, July 1941, *Obit* Nov 1948
Toscani, Oliviero, Italian photographer, Sept 1998
Underwood, Bert E., *Obit* Feb 1944
Vandivert, William, Mar 1963
Wall, Jeff, Canadian artist and photographer, Jan 2007
Waller, Fred, American inventor of Cinerama, Feb 1953, *Obit* July 1954
West, Levon, Feb 1948, *Obit* June 1968
Weston, Brett, photographer, Feb 1982, *Obit* Mar 1993
Wexler, Haskell, American cinematographer, Aug 2007
Wolfe, Art, American photographer, June 2005
Woodard, Stacy, *Obit* Mar 1942
Zhou Hai, Chinese photographer, Jan 2003

Zsigmond, Vilmos, Hungarian-American cinematographer, Oct 1999

Photojournalists

Addario, Lynsey, American photojournalist, Apr 2013
Arnold, Eve, American photojournalist, Oct 2005, *Obit* Yrbk 2012
Burri, Rene, Swiss photojournalist, Jan 2007
Capa, Cornell, American photojournalist, July 2005, *Obit* Yrbk 2008
Dith, Pran, Cambodian photojournalist, Oct 1996, *Obit* Yrbk 2008
Duncan, David Douglas, American photojournalist, Nov 1968
Eisenstaedt, Alfred, American photojournalist, Jan 1975, *Obit* Oct 1995
Gallagher, William M., Oct 1953, *Obit* Nov 1975
Guzy, Carol, American photojournalist, Feb 2000
Higgins, Chester, American photojournalist, June 2002
Hondros, Chris, American photojournalist, Nov 2004, *Obit* Yrbk 2011
Kamber, Michael, American photojournalist, June 2009
McCurry, Steve, American photojournalist, Nov 2005
Mydans, Carl, American photojournalist, May 1945, *Obit* Yrbk 2004
Rosenthal, Joe, American photojournalist, June 1945, *Obit* Yrbk 2007
Salgado, Sebastiao, Brazilian photographer, Jan 2002

Physical chemists

Chizmadzhev, IUrii Aleksandrovich, Russian physical chemist, Jan 2005
Tizard, Henry Thomas, British physical chemist, Jan 1949, *Obit* Yrbk 1959

Physically handicapped athletes

Scdoris, Rachael, American sled dog racer, July 2005

Physicians

Adair, Frank E., American surgeon, May 1946, *Obit* Feb 1982

Agatston, Arthur, American cardiologist, Mar 2007

Al-Jaafari, Ibrahim, Iraqi prime minister and physician, Jan 2006

Albee, Fred H., May 1943, *Obit* Apr 1945

Alexander, Franz, Austrian psychiatrist, Aug 1942, Sept 1960, *Obit* Apr 1964

Antinori, Severino, Italian physician, Jan 2002

Arsonval, Jacques Arsene d', French physiologist, *Obit* Feb 1941

Bang, Abhay, Indian physician and public health scientist, Jan 2007

Bang, Rani, Indian gynecologist and public health scientist, Jan 2007

Barnard, Christiaan, South African heart surgeon, May 1968, *Obit* Nov 2001

Barringer, Emily Dunning, physician, Mar 1940, *Obit* June 1961

Beers, Clifford Whittingham, American mental hygienist, *Obit* Aug 1943

Begg, Colin Luke, American physician, *Obit* Mar 1941

Benjamin, Regina, American Surgeon general, Jan 2010

Benson, Francis Colgate, American surgeon and radiologist, *Obit* Apr 1941

Bernheim, Bertram M., American surgeon, Sept 1943

Best, Charles Herbert, Canadian physiologist, June 1957, *Obit* May 1978

Blaese, R. Michael, physician, Mar 2000

Blain, Daniel, American psychiatrist, Sept 1947

Blanton, Smiley, June 1956, *Obit* Jan 1967

Bonine, Frederick N., American ophthalmologist, *Obit* Oct 1941

Bortz, Edward Leroy, physician, Sept 1947, *Obit* Apr 1970

Broder, Samuel, physician and government official, Aug 1992

Brodie, Bernard B., American pharmacologist, Sept 1969, *Obit* May 1989

Burney, Leroy E., surgeon general, July 1957, *Obit* Oct 1998

Cameron, Charles S., Sept 1954

Canady, Alexa, neurosurgeon, Aug 2000

Cannon, Walter Bradford, American physiologist, *Obit* Nov 1945

Caturani, Michele Gaetano, *Obit* Mar 1940

Colby, Charles De Witt, *Obit* Nov 1941

Collins, George Lewis, *Obit* Aug 1940

Connell, Karl, *Obit* Yrbk 1941

Cooley, Denton A., American cardiac surgeon, Jan 1976

Cooper, Irving S., neurosurgeon, Apr 1974, *Obit* Jan 1986

Crile, George Washington, American surgeon, *Obit* Feb 1943

Cunningham, William Francis, *Obit* Jan 1941

Dafoe, Allan Roy, *Obit* July 1943

Damadian, Raymond, American physician and inventor, Jan 2000

Dandy, Walter E., American neurosurgeon, *Obit* May 1946

Dawson of Penn, Bertrand Edward Dawson, English physician, *Obit* Apr 1945

DeVries, William C., surgeon, Jan 1985

Demikhov, Vladimir P., Russian surgeon, June 1960, *Obit* Feb 1999

Densen-Gerber, Judianne, American lawyer and psychiatrist, Nov 1983, *Obit* July 2003

Diefendorf, Allen Ross, *Obit* Sept 1943

Dorman, Gerald D., June 1970

Duffy, James J., *Obit* Feb 1942

Dunham, Charles L., Mar 1966

Edwards, Waldo B., American obstetrician, June 1943

Eliot, Martha May, American pediatrician, Oct 1948, *Obit* Apr 1978

Ewing, James, *Obit* July 1943

Exner, Max J., *Obit* Nov 1943

Folkman, Judah, American surgeon, May 1998, *Obit* Yrbk 2008

Frankl, Viktor E., Austrian psychiatrist, July 1997, *Obit* Nov 1997

Gale, Robert Peter, physician, Jan 1987

Gayle, Helene D., American epidemiologist, Jan 2002

Gerberding, Julie, American physician and public health official, Sept 2004

Goddard, James L., American regulatory agency official, Oct 1968, *Obit* Yrbk 2010

Goler, George Washington, American physician, *Obit* Nov 1940

Griffith, J. P. Crozer, *Obit* Sept 1941

Guevara, Ernesto, Argentine-Cuban revolutionary, June 1963, *Obit* Yrbk 1967

Guttmacher, Alan Frank, physician, Oct 1965, *Obit* May 1974

Haddon, William, government official and physician, Feb 1969, *Obit* Apr 1985

Hall, George W., *Obit* Yrbk 1941

Heimlich, Henry J., American surgeon, Oct 1986

Heller, John Roderick, physician, Feb 1949, *Obit* July 1989

Hilleboe, Herman E., June 1955, *Obit* June 1974

Holland, Charles Thurstan, *Obit* Mar 1941

Horder, Thomas Jeeves Horder, English physician, July 1944, *Obit* Oct 1955

Hosseini, Khaled, Afghan-American physician and novelist, July 2013

Hubeny, Maximilian J., *Obit* Sept 1942

Huebner, Robert J., epidemiologist, Sept 1968, *Obit* Nov 1998

Jackson, Chevalier, July 1940

Jacobson, Leon, American physician, Oct 1962, *Obit* Feb 1993

Jaffe, Harold W., epidemiologist, Sept 1992

Jelliffe, Smith Ely, psychiatrist, *Obit* Oct 1945

Jellinek, E. M., May 1947, *Obit* Jan 1964

Jordan, Sara Claudia Murray, gastroenterologist, Mar 1954, *Obit* Jan 1960

Joseph, Stephen C., physician and public health official, Jan 1989

Karadzic, Radovan, Bosnian Serb political leader, Oct 1995

Key, Ben Witt, *Obit* July 1940

Kline, Nathan S., psychiatrist and educator, Oct 1965, *Obit* May 1983

Kolff, Willem J., American physician, May 1983, *Obit* Yrbk 2009

Koop, C. Everett, American surgeon general, Sept 1983, *Obit* Yrbk 2013

Kotb, Heba, Egyptian sex therapist, Jan 2007

Krause, Allen K., *Obit* July 1941

Kuhlmann, Frederick, *Obit* June 1941

Kutchuk, Fazil, Cypriot political leader and physician, Feb 1961, *Obit* Mar 1984

Lambert, Sylvester M., American physician, Oct 1941, *Obit* Feb 1947

Lane, Arbuthnot, British surgeon, *Obit* Mar 1943

Levine, Melvin D., American pediatrician, Nov 2005

Lilly, John Cunningham, American physician, Nov 1962, *Obit* Feb 2002

Loewe, Siegfried, American pharmacologist, Jan 1947

Macartney, William Napier, *Obit* Aug 1940

Magee, James C., May 1943

Magnuson, Paul B., June 1948, *Obit* Jan 1969

Martland, Harrison Stanford, Nov 1940, *Obit* June 1954

Masters, William H., American physician, Nov 1968, *Obit* May 2001

Maung, Cynthia, Burmese physician, Jan 2003

May, Charles H., *Obit* Jan 1944

McCarthy, Kenneth C., Nov 1953

McCormick, Edward James, surgeon, Nov 1953, *Obit* Feb 1975

Moncada, Salvador, Honduran pharmacologist, Jan 2003

Montessori, Maria, Italian educator, Nov 1940, *Obit* June 1952

Neuman, Leo Handel, *Obit* May 1941

Neumann, Heinrich, *Obit* Jan 1940

Ochsner, Alton, surgeon, Oct 1966, *Obit* Nov 1981

Orr, Louis M., Apr 1960, *Obit* July 1961

Paddon, Harry Locke, *Obit* Jan 1940

Pitanguy, Ivo, Brazilian plastic surgeon, Jan 2004

Pritchard, Stuart, *Obit* Sept 1940

Reed, John Howard, *Obit* Mar 1940

Reid, Mont, *Obit* June 1943

Rhoads, Cornelius P., American physician, Mar 1953, *Obit* Nov 1959

Robitzek, Edward Heinrich, physician, Yrbk 1953, *Obit* May 1984

Rock, John Charles, American physician, Yrbk 1964, *Obit* Jan 1985

Rosanoff, Aaron J., *Obit* Feb 1943

Rosen, Samuel, Feb 1974, *Obit* Jan 1982

Rosenberg, Steven A., American surgeon, Feb 1991

Ross, Jerilyn, American psychotherapist, Nov 2009, *Obit* Yrbk 2010

Rouse, Milford O., June 1968

Rusk, Howard Archibald, American physician, Mar 1946, May 1967, *Obit* Jan 1990

Sachs, Bernard, American neurologist, *Obit* Mar 1944

Sakel, Manfred, Jan 1941, *Obit* Feb 1958

Scheele, Leonard Andrew, surgeon general, May 1948, *Obit* Mar 1993

Scheer, Alan Austin, Jan 1964

Schereschewsky, Joseph Williams, *Obit* Sept 1940

Schick, Bela, pediatrician, July 1944, *Obit* Feb 1968

Senn, Milton John Edward, pediatrician and psychiatrist, June 1950, *Obit* Aug 1990

Shaw, Henry, American pediatrician, *Obit* May 1941

Shine, F. W., *Obit* Nov 1941

Siemionow, Maria, Polish plastic surgeon, May 2009

Sigerist, Henry Ernest, Swiss medical historian, Sept 1940, *Obit* June 1957

Slye, Maud, American pathologist, Yrbk 1940, *Obit* Nov 1954

Southworth, James L., American surgeon, June 1943

Starzl, Thomas E., American surgeon, Mar 1993

Stekel, Wilhelm, Austrian psychoanalyst, *Obit* Aug 1940

Stevenson, George S., psychiatrist, Yrbk 1946

Stewart, Alice, British epidemiologist, July 2000, *Obit* Yrbk 2002

Stewart, William H., American surgeon general, Apr 1966, *Obit* Yrbk 2008

Torrey, E. Fuller, psychiatrist, July 1998

Travell, Janet, physician, Yrbk 1961, *Obit* Oct 1997

Trehan, Naresh, Indian cardiologist, Jan 2003

Ulianov, Dmitrii, *Obit* Sept 1943

Volkow, Nora D., American neuroscientist, Oct 2011

Voronoff, Serge, Jan 1941, *Obit* Oct 1951

Walsh, William B., physician, May 1962, *Obit* Mar 1997

Watkins, Levi, American cardiac surgeon, Mar 2003

Wenckebach, Karel Friedrich, Dutch cardiologist, *Obit* Yrbk 1940

Wile, Ira S., *Obit* Nov 1943

Wilgus, Sidney Dean, *Obit* Mar 1940

Wood, Fiona M., Australian plastic surgeon, Jan 2007

Zerhouni, Elias A., Algerian-American radiologist and public health official, Oct 2003

Zilboorg, Gregory, psychiatrist, Sept 1941, *Obit* Nov 1959

Zubrod, Charles Gordon, oncologist, Jan 1969, *Obit* July 1999

Physicists

Abrikosov, Alexei A., Russian-American physicist, Jan 2007

Alcock, Norman Z., Canadian physicist, Mar 1963

Alvarez, Luis W., American physicist, May 1947, *Obit* Oct 1988

Anderson, Carl David, American physicist, Jan 1951, *Obit* Mar 1991

Appleton, Edward Victor, British physicist, Sept 1945, *Obit* June 1965

Astin, Allen Varley, physicist, May 1956, *Obit* Apr 1984

Bacher, Robert F., American physicist, Feb 1947, *Obit* Yrbk 2005

Bethe, Hans, German-American physicist, Jan 1940, Apr 1950, *Obit* Aug 2005

Bhabha, Homi Jehangir, Indian physicist, Sept 1956, *Obit* Feb 1966

Birge, Raymond T., American physicist, Mar 1940

Blackett, Patrick M. S., British physicist, Feb 1949, *Obit* Sept 1974

Bloch, Felix, Swiss-American physicist, Sept 1954, *Obit* Nov 1983

Blodgett, Katharine, American physicist, Jan 1940, May 1952, *Obit* Jan 1980

Bohr, Niels Henrik David, Danish physicist, Sept 1945, *Obit* Jan 1963

Born, Max, German physicist, May 1955, *Obit* Feb 1970

Borst, Lyle B., American nuclear physicist, July 1954, *Obit* Yrbk 2002

Boss, Alan P., American astrophysicist, Apr 2010

Bothe, Walther Wilhelm, German physicist, May 1955, *Obit* Apr 1957

Bowen, Ira S., astrophysicist, June 1951, *Obit* Apr 1973

Bradbury, Norris Edwin, physicist, Apr 1949, *Obit* Nov 1997

Branly, Edouard, French physicist and inventor, *Obit* Apr 1940

Brattain, Walter Houser, American physicist, Sept 1957, *Obit* Nov 1987

Bullard, Edward Crisp, English geophysicist, Sept 1954, *Obit* May 1980

Butler, R. Paul, American astrophysicist, Nov 2002

Chadwick, James, British physicist, Nov 1945, *Obit* Oct 1974

Chamberlain, Owen, American physicist, Mar 1960, *Obit* July 2006

Chang-Diaz, Franklin R., American astronaut and physicist, Aug 2011

Cherwell, Frederick Alexander Lindemann, British physicist, Mar 1952, *Obit* Sept 1957

Christofilos, Nicholas C., Nov 1965, *Obit* Nov 1972

Coblentz, William W., American physicist, Mar 1954, *Obit* Nov 1962

Cockcroft, John, British physicist, Nov 1948, *Obit* Nov 1967

Compton, Karl Taylor, Mar 1941, *Obit* Sept 1954

Crawford, Morris Barker, *Obit* Yrbk 1940

Crewe, Albert, American physicist, Feb 1964, *Obit* Yrbk 2010

Davies, P. C. W., English physicist, Jan 2002

Dryden, Hugh L., American physicist and NASA official, Apr 1959, *Obit* Jan 1966

Dunning, John R., May 1948, *Obit* Oct 1975

Ehlers, Vernon J., American congressman, Jan 2005

Ehricke, Krafft A., physicist and rocket engineer, June 1958, *Obit* Feb 1985

Einstein, Albert, German-American physicist, Nov 1941, May 1953, *Obit* June 1955

Eklund, Sigvard, July 1962

Fawcett, Sherwood L., Yrbk 1972

Fisk, James Brown, Jan 1959, *Obit* Oct 1981

Fleming, John A., May 1940, *Obit* Oct 1956

Fletcher, James C., American physicist and NASA official, May 1972, *Obit* Feb 1992

Foster, John S., Yrbk 1971

Fowler, Alfred, English astrophysicist, *Obit* Aug 1940

Friedman, Herbert, American astrophysicist, Sept 1963, *Obit* Nov 2000

Gabor, Dennis, British physicist, Oct 1972, *Obit* Apr 1979

Garwin, Richard, American physicist, Mar 1989

Gavrilovic, Stoyan, May 1946, *Obit* Mar 1965

Ginzburg, Vitalii L., Russian physicist, Jan 2007, *Obit* Yrbk 2010

Gottlieb, Melvin, physicist, Jan 1974, *Obit* Mar 2001

Goudsmit, Samuel Abraham, American physicist, Oct 1954, *Obit* Feb 1979

Graves, Alvin C., American physicist, Yrbk 1952, *Obit* Oct 1965

Greiner, Markus, Physicist and educator, June 2012

Guth, Alan H., physicist, Sept 1987

Haas, Arthur E., *Obit* Apr 1941

Hafstad, Lawrence R., physicist, Oct 1956, *Obit* Jan 1994

Hansch, Theodor W., German physicist, Jan 2007

Hansen, James E., American physicist, meteorologist and government official, May 1996

Hau, Lene Vestergaard, Danish physicist, Jan 2002

Haworth, Leland J., Yrbk 1950, *Obit* May 1979

Heisenberg, Werner, German physicist, Apr 1957, *Obit* Mar 1976

Herndon, J. Marvin, American geophysicist, Nov 2003

Herzberg, Gerhard, Canadian physicist, Feb 1973, *Obit* July 1999

Hess, Victor Francis, American physicist, Oct 1963, *Obit* Feb 1965

Heuer, Rolf-Dieter, German physicist, Mar 2012

Higgs, Peter, British physicist, Feb 2009

Higinbotham, William A., physicist, Feb 1947, *Obit* Jan 1995

Hirschfelder, Joseph Oakland, physicist, Yrbk 1950, *Obit* May 1990

Hofstadter, Robert, American physicist, Oct 1962, *Obit* Jan 1991

Iijima, Sumio, Japanese physicist, Nov 2009

Infeld, Leopold, May 1941, July 1963, *Obit* Mar 1968

Ives, James E., *Obit* Feb 1943

Jin, Deborah, American physicist, Apr 2004

Joliot-Curie, Frederic, French physicist, Oct 1946, *Obit* Oct 1958

Kantrowitz, Arthur, American physicist, Oct 1966, *Obit* Yrbk 2009

Kapitsa, P. L., Russian physicist, Oct 1955, *Obit* May 1984

Kaplan, Joseph, physicist, Oct 1956, *Obit* Nov 1991

Kastler, Alfred, French physicist, Yrbk 1967, *Obit* Mar 1984

Kelly, Mervin J., physicist and engineer, Oct 1956, *Obit* May 1971

Kerst, Donald William, physicist, Apr 1950, *Obit* Oct 1993

Keyworth, George A., American physicist and presidential adviser, Mar 1986

Kurchatov, Igor Vasilevich, Russian physicist, Nov 1957, *Obit* Apr 1960

Lamb, Willis E., American physicist, Mar 1956, *Obit* Yrbk 2008

Lang, Robert J., American physicist and origami artist, July 2007

Lapp, Ralph Eugene, American physicist, Nov 1955, *Obit* Feb 2005

Lattes, C. M. G., Brazilian physicist, May 1949

Leighton, Robert B., physicist, July 1966, *Obit* May 1997

Liddel, Urner, May 1951

Lisi, Antony Garrett, American physicist, Sept 2012

Livingston, M. Stanley, physicist, Feb 1955, *Obit* Nov 1986

Lodge, Oliver Joseph, English physicist, *Obit* Oct 1940

Lovins, Amory B., American physicist and conservationist, June 1997

Matare, Herbert F., German physicist, Jan 2003

McKay, Christopher P., American astrophysicist, Aug 2009

Meitner, Lise, Austrian physicist, Sept 1945, *Obit* Sept 1968

Menzel, Donald Howard, physicist and astronomer, Apr 1956, *Obit* Mar 1977

Miller, Dayton C., American physicist, *Obit* Apr 1941

Morse, Philip McCord, physicist, June 1948, *Obit* Nov 1985

Mossbauer, Rudolf L., German physicist, May 1962, *Obit* Yrbk 2012

O'Neill, Gerard K., physicist, Feb 1979, *Obit* June 1992

Oberth, Hermann, German physicist and rocket engineer, Apr 1957, *Obit* Mar 1990

Oliphant, Mark, Australian physicist, Yrbk 1951, *Obit* Oct 2000

Oort, Jan Hendrik, Dutch astrophysicist, June 1969, *Obit* Jan 1993

Page, Robert Morris, physicist, Nov 1964, *Obit* July 1992

Panofsky, Wolfgang Kurt Hermann, American physicist, June 1970, *Obit* Yrbk 2007

Pauli, Wolfgang, German physicist, June 1946, *Obit* Mar 1959

Penney, William George Penney, English physicist, Feb 1953, *Obit* May 1991

Penzias, Arno Allan, American physicist, Sept 1985

Perrin, Francis, French physicist, July 1951

Piccard, Auguste, Swiss physicist, Sept 1947, *Obit* May 1962

Pickering, William H., American physicist, Nov 1958, *Obit* Yrbk 2004

Purcell, Edward M., American physicist, Sept 1954, *Obit* May 1997

Queloz, Didier, Swiss astrophysicist, Feb 2002

Raman, Chandrasekhara Venkata, Indian physicist, Nov 1948, *Obit* Jan 1971

Randall, Lisa, American physicist, May 2006

Randers, Gunnar, Jan 1957

Richter, Burton, American physicist, Sept 1977

Singer, S. Fred, American physicist, Yrbk 1955

Smyth, Henry DeWolf, physicist, Yrbk 1948, *Obit* Nov 1986

Snook, H. Clyde, *Obit* Nov 1942

Sperti, George Speri, biophysicist, Jan 1940, *Obit* July 1991

Spiropulu, Maria, Greek physicist, May 2004

Stone, Edward C., American physicist, Feb 1990

Suits, Chauncey Guy, physicist and inventor, Feb 1950, *Obit* Oct 1991

Szilard, Leo, Hungarian physicist, Jan 1947, *Obit* July 1964

Tainter, Charles Sumner, *Obit* May 1940

Tamm, Igor Evgenievich, Russian physicist, Yrbk 1963, *Obit* June 1971

Tarter, Jill Cornell, American astrophysicist, Feb 2001

Taylor, A. H., Sept 1945, *Obit* Jan 1962

Taylor, Theodore B., American physicist, Apr 1976, *Obit* Feb 2005

Teller, Edward, American physicist, Yrbk 1954, Nov 1983, *Obit* Yrbk 2004

Thaler, William J., American physicist, Feb 1960, *Obit* Yrbk 2005

Thomson, George Paget, British physicist, Mar 1947, *Obit* Oct 1975

Thomson, Joseph John, British physicist, *Obit* Oct 1940

Veksler, V. I., Russian physicist, Jan 1965, *Obit* Nov 1966

Volterra, Vito, Italian mathematician and physicist, *Obit* Yrbk 1940

Von Bekesy, Georg, Hungarian-American physicist, Yrbk 1962, *Obit* Sept 1972

Walton, Ernest T. S., Irish physicist, Mar 1952, *Obit* Sept 1995

Wang Yongzhi, Chinese astrophysicist, Jan 2006

Waterman, Alan T., American physicist, June 1951, *Obit* Feb 1968

Weinberg, Alvin M., American physicist, Sept 1966, *Obit* Yrbk 2006

Weizsacker, Carl Friedrich von, German physicist and philosopher, Jan 1985, *Obit* Yrbk 2007

Wheeler, John Archibald, American physicist, Jan 1970, *Obit* Yrbk 2008

Wilkins, T. Russell, *Obit* Feb 1941

Williams, John H., Jan 1960, *Obit* May 1966

Wilson, Robert R., American physicist, Aug 1989, *Obit* May 2000

Wilson, Volney C., June 1958

Witten, Edward, American physicist, June 1997

Wu, Chien Shiung, Chinese-American physicist, Oct 1959, *Obit* Apr 1997

Yang, Chen-ning, Chinese-American physicist, Nov 1958

York, Herbert F., American physicist, Yrbk 1958, *Obit* Yrbk 2009

Yukawa, Hideki, Japanese physicist, Jan 1950, *Obit* Nov 1981

Zacharias, Jerrold R., physicist, Feb 1964, *Obit* Sept 1986

Zeeman, Pieter, Dutch physicist, *Obit* Yrbk 1943

Zernike, Frits, Dutch physicist, Feb 1955, *Obit* Apr 1966

Zinn, Walter H., nuclear physicist, Yrbk 1955, *Obit* Aug 2000

Physiologists

Arnon, Daniel I., American plant physiologist, June 1955, *Obit* Mar 1995

Davis, Adelle, nutritionist, Jan 1973, *Obit* July 1974

Metzelthin, Pearl V., Nov 1942, *Obit* Jan 1948

Omichinski, Linda, Canadian dietician, Jan 2004

Pattee, Alida Frances, *Obit* May 1942

Sebrell, W. H., nutritionist, May 1951, *Obit* Nov 1992

Pianists

Argerich, Martha, Argentine pianist, Sept 1999

Arrau, Claudio, Chilean pianist, Jan 1942, Nov 1986, *Obit* Aug 1991

Ax, Emanuel, American pianist, Mar 1984

Bachauer, Gina, Greek pianist, June 1954, *Obit* Sept 1977

Barenboim, Daniel, Israeli pianist and conductor, Apr 1969

Berman, Lazar, Russian pianist, Sept 1977, *Obit* Yrbk 2005

Bernstein, Leonard, American conductor and composer, Feb 1944, Feb 1960, *Obit* Nov 1990

Blake, Eubie, American pianist and composer, Apr 1974, *Obit* Apr 1983

Bolcom, William, American composer and pianist, Apr 1990

Brailowsky, Alexander, French pianist, June 1956, *Obit* June 1976

Brendel, Alfred, Austrian pianist, July 1977

Carmichael, Hoagy, American songwriter, May 1941, *Obit* Feb 1982

Charles, Ray, American singer and pianist, Apr 1965, June 1992, *Obit* Yrbk 2004

Chavchavadze, George, Mar 1943, *Obit* Apr 1962

Cherkassky, Shura, American pianist, Oct 1990, *Obit* Mar 1996

Chotzinoff, Samuel, pianist, Apr 1940, *Obit* Apr 1964

Cleveland, James, American clergyman and gospel singer, Aug 1985, *Obit* Apr 1991

Cole, Nat King, American singer and pianist, Feb 1956, *Obit* Mar 1965

Coleman, Cy, American composer, Aug 1990, *Obit* Feb 2005

Dallapiccola, Luigi, Italian composer, Feb 1966

Davidovich, Bella, Russian pianist, May 1989

Engel, Kurt, *Obit* Mar 1942

Feinstein, Michael, American pianist and singer, Apr 1988

Feltsman, Vladimir, Russian pianist, Apr 1988

Firkusny, Rudolf, Czech pianist, Oct 1979, *Obit* Sept 1994

Frager, Malcolm, pianist, Apr 1967, *Obit* Aug 1991

Franklin, Aretha, American singer, Yrbk 1968, May 1992

Gavrilov, Andrei, Russian pianist, Oct 2000

Gieseking, Walter, German pianist, Oct 1956, *Obit* Jan 1957

Gilels, Emil, Russian pianist, Oct 1956, *Obit* Jan 1986

Graffman, Gary, pianist, July 1970

Hancock, Herbie, American jazz keyboardist and composer, Apr 1988

Hewitt, Angela, Canadian pianist, Apr 2007

Janis, Byron, pianist, June 1966

Jarrett, Keith, American jazz pianist and composer, May 1985

Joel, Billy, American singer and songwriter, Sept 1979

Johannesen, Grant, American pianist, June 1961, *Obit* Yrbk 2005

John, Elton, English singer and songwriter, Mar 1975

Kapell, William, American pianist, May 1948, *Obit* Jan 1954

Kelberine, Alexander, *Obit* Mar 1940

Kissin, Evgeny, Russian pianist, Nov 1997

Kraus, Lili, Hungarian pianist, Oct 1975, *Obit* Jan 1987

Lennon, John, English singer and songwriter, Yrbk 1965, *Obit* Feb 1981

Levitzki, Mischa, pianist, *Obit* Feb 1941

Lhevinne, Josef, Russian pianist, *Obit* Jan 1945

Liberace, American pianist, Nov 1954, Mar 1986, *Obit* Mar 1987

Little Richard, American singer, Sept 1986

Lowe, Jack Warren, pianist, Jan 1954, *Obit* Aug 1996

Manilow, Barry, American pop singer and songwriter, July 1978

Moore, Gerald, English pianist, Oct 1967, *Obit* May 1987

Novaes, Guiomar, Brazilian pianist, June 1953, *Obit* May 1979

Paderewski, Ignace Jan, Polish pianist and statesman, *Obit* Aug 1941

Perahia, Murray, American pianist, Mar 1982

Petri, Egon, Dutch pianist, Nov 1942, *Obit* July 1962

Pogorelich, Ivo, Yugoslav pianist, Sept 1988

Pollini, Maurizio, Italian pianist, Nov 1980

Rachmaninoff, Sergei, Russian composer and pianist, *Obit* May 1943

Roberts, Marcus, American jazz pianist, Mar 1994

Rosenthal, Moriz, Polish pianist, *Obit* Oct 1946

Sandor, Gyorgy, American pianist, July 1947, *Obit* Yrbk 2006

Sauer, Emil von, German pianist, *Obit* June 1942

Scott, Hazel, American pianist and singer, Aug 1943, *Obit* Nov 1981

Serkin, Peter, pianist, June 1986

Short, Bobby, American singer and pianist, July 1972, *Obit* Nov 2005

Singer, Richard, *Obit* Mar 1940

Tilson Thomas, Michael, American conductor and pianist, May 1971, June 1996

Uchida, Mitsuko, Japanese pianist, Sept 1991

Watts, Andre, American pianist, May 1968

Whittemore, Arthur Austin, pianist, Jan 1954, *Obit* Feb 1985

Plant physiologists

Arnon, Daniel I., American plant physiologist, June 1955, *Obit* Mar 1995

Poets

Bellamann, Henry, author and poet, Sept 1942, *Obit* July 1945

Benet, Stephen Vincent, American poet, novelist and short story writer, *Obit* Apr 1943

Biddle, Katherine Garrison Chapin, poet, Oct 1943, *Obit* Jan 1984

Biermann, Wolf, German poet, Jan 2003

Bishop, Elizabeth, American poet, Sept 1977, *Obit* Nov 1979

Bukowski, Charles, American poet, novelist and short story writer, Apr 1994, *Obit* Apr 1994

Carver, Raymond, American short story writer and poet, Feb 1984, *Obit* Sept 1988

Cohen, Leonard, Canadian poet, novelist, singer and songwriter, June 1969

Copeland, Benjamin, *Obit* Jan 1941

Curry, Peggy Simson, author and poet, Yrbk 1958

Davenport, Russell W., Jan 1944, *Obit* June 1954

Dugan, Alan, American poet, Nov 1990, *Obit* Yrbk 2004

Eberhart, Richard, American poet, Jan 1961, *Obit* Yrbk 2005

Elliot, Kathleen Morrow, Mar 1940

Fowles, John, English novelist, Mar 1977, *Obit* Apr 2006

Frost, Robert, American poet, Sept 1942, *Obit* Mar 1963

Ginsberg, Allen, American poet, Apr 1970, Apr 1987, *Obit* June 1997

Guiterman, Arthur, poet, *Obit* Mar 1943

Gunn, Thom, English poet, Nov 1988, *Obit* Yrbk 2004

Hall, Radclyffe, English novelist and poet, *Obit* Nov 1943

Hecht, Anthony, American poet, May 1986, *Obit* Yrbk 2005

Hillyer, Robert Silliman, poet, July 1940, *Obit* Feb 1962

Hoagland, Tony, American poet, May 2011

Houellebecq, Michel, French novelist and poet, Jan 2002

Hughes, Ted, English poet, June 1979, *Obit* Jan 1999

Hunter, Aislinn, Canadian short story writer, poet and novelist, Jan 2002

Kinnell, Galway, American poet, Aug 1986

Koch, Kenneth, American poet, Feb 1978, *Obit* Yrbk 2002

Kolar, Jiri, Czech poet and artist, Apr 1986, *Obit* Yrbk 2002

Kunitz, Stanley, American poet, Mar 1943, Nov 1959, *Obit* Aug 2006

Laird, Nick, Irish novelist and poet, Jan 2006

Laporte, Genevieve, French poet and documentary filmmaker, Jan 2005

Lleshanaku, Luljeta, Albanian poet, Jan 2002

Lowell, Robert, American poet, July 1947, Jan 1972, *Obit* Nov 1977

Markham, Edwin, poet, Mar 1940

McKenzie, William P., *Obit* Oct 1942

Michaels, Anne, Canadian poet and novelist, Jan 2002

Moore, Ruth, Yrbk 1954

Oxenham, John, English author and poet, *Obit* Mar 1941

Paley, Grace, American short story writer and poet, Mar 1986, *Obit* Yrbk 2007

Percy, William Alexander, American poet and lawyer, *Obit* Mar 1942

Pratt, E. J., Canadian poet, Oct 1946, *Obit* June 1964

Rameau, Jean, *Obit* Apr 1942

Ridge, Lola, poet, *Obit* July 1941

Rivers, Larry, American painter and sculptor, Apr 1969, *Obit* Nov 2002

Roberts, Charles G. D., Canadian poet and short story writer, *Obit* Jan 1944

Roberts, Elizabeth Madox, novelist, short story writer and poet, *Obit* May 1941

Robinson, Henry Morton, author and poet, July 1950, *Obit* Mar 1961

Rukeyser, Muriel, American poet, Mar 1943, *Obit* Apr 1980

Ryan, Kay, American poet, Apr 2012

Salamun, Tomaz, Slovenian poet, Jan 2007

Smith, Patti, American rock singer, songwriter and poet, Apr 1989

Stuart, Jesse, author, Aug 1940, *Obit* Apr 1984

Tietjens, Eunice Hammond, poet and author, *Obit* Nov 1944

Tvardovskii, A., Russian poet, May 1971, *Obit* Feb 1972

Updike, John, American novelist and short story writer, Feb 1966, Oct 1984, *Obit* Yrbk 2009

Valery, Paul, French poet, *Obit* Aug 1945

Van Duyn, Mona, American poet, Jan 1998, *Obit* Nov 2005

Viereck, George Sylvester, author and poet, Nov 1940, *Obit* May 1962

Vilas, Guillermo, Argentine tennis player and poet, Apr 1978

Voznesenskii, Andrei, Russian poet, Mar 1967, *Obit* Yrbk 2010

Wheelwright, John, poet, *Obit* Nov 1940

Wilbur, Richard, American poet, Jan 1966

Yamanaka, Lois-Ann, American novelist and poet, June 1999

Yevtushenko, Yevgeny Aleksandrovich, Russian poet, Feb 1963, Mar 1994

Zamora, Daisy, Nicaraguan poet, Jan 2004

Poets laureate

Hughes, Ted, English poet, June 1979, *Obit* Jan 1999

Van Duyn, Mona, American poet, Jan 1998, *Obit* Nov 2005

Poker players

Brunson, Doyle, American poker player, Sept 2007

Pole vaulters

Bubka, Sergei, Ukrainian pole vaulter, July 1996

Pennel, John, pole vaulter, Nov 1963, *Obit* Jan 1994

Seagren, Bob, American pole vaulter, June 1974

Police

Hayden, Carl Trumbull, American senator, July 1951, *Obit* Mar 1972

Police officials

Chu, Shen, *Obit* Aug 1943

Harvard, Beverly Joyce, American police chief, Sept 1997

Kelly, Raymond, American police commissioner, Sept 2008

Lanier, Cathy L., American police chief, Mar 2007

Murphy, Patrick V., Nov 1972, *Obit* Yrbk 2012

Scott, Harold, Yrbk 1950

Valentine, Lewis J., June 1946, *Obit* Feb 1947

Ward, Benjamin, American police commissioner, Aug 1988, *Obit* Yrbk 2002

Political commentators

Carter, Boake, radio commentator, Jan 1942, *Obit* Yrbk 1947

Chancellor, John, American television news anchor and commentator, Jan 1962, Nov 1988, *Obit* Sept 1996

Frederick, Pauline, American television reporter and commentator, Oct 1954, *Obit* July 1990

Heatter, Gabriel, radio commentator, Apr 1941, *Obit* May 1972

Kaltenborn, H. V., radio commentator, Aug 1940, *Obit* Sept 1965

Lewis, Fulton, radio commentator, Nov 1942, *Obit* Nov 1966

McCrary, Tex, American journalist and talk show host, July 1953, *Obit* Yrbk 2003

McGee, Frank, television commentator and newscaster, June 1964, *Obit* June 1974

Newman, Edwin, American television reporter, commentator and moderator, Sept 1967, *Obit* Yrbk 2010

Schorr, Daniel, American television reporter, Sept 1959, Feb 1978, *Obit* Yrbk 2010

Smith, Howard K., American television newscaster and commentator, Mar 1943, July 1976, *Obit* Aug 2002

Taylor, M. Sayle, *Obit* Mar 1942

Tinney, Cal, Feb 1943

Political consultants

Atwater, Lee, American presidential adviser, June 1989, *Obit* May 1991

Axelrod, David, American presidential adviser, Apr 2009

Brazile, Donna, American political consultant, Mar 2006

Donald, W. H., July 1946

Finkelstein, Arthur, American political consultant, Nov 1999

Garth, Dave, political consultant, Jan 1981

Jordan, Hamilton, American presidential adviser and campaign consultant, Aug 1977, *Obit* Yrbk 2008

Messina, Jim, American presidential adviser and political consultant, Mar 2013

Plouffe, David, American presidential adviser, June 2009

Reed, Ralph, American political leader, Mar 1996

Rollins, Ed, American political consultant, Mar 2001

Sharp, Mitchell, Canadian political adviser, July 1966

Tweed, Thomas Frederic, *Obit* Jan 1940

Verveer, Melanne, Mar 2013

Political leaders

Abbas, Ferhat, Algerian political leader, Mar 1961, *Obit* Feb 1986

Abbas, Mahmoud, Palestinian political leader, June 1999

Abdul Rahman, Malaysian prime minister, Yrbk 1957, *Obit* Mar 1991

Abdullah, Mohammad, Indian political leader, Nov 1952, *Obit* Jan 1983

Aberhart, William, Canadian evangelist and political leader, *Obit* July 1943

Abiola, Moshood Kashimawo, Nigerian political leader, Sept 1998, *Obit* Nov 1998

Acland, Richard, British member of Parliament, Aug 1944

Adami, Edward Fenech, Maltese prime minister, Jan 2003

Adams, Gerry, Irish political leader, Sept 1994

Adams, Grantley Herbert, Barbadian prime minister, Sept 1958, *Obit* Jan 1972

Adenauer, Konrad, German statesman, July 1949, Apr 1958, *Obit* June 1967

Ahern, Bertie, Irish prime minister, July 1998

Ahmadu, Alhaji, Nigerian political leader, July 1957

Al-Dari, Harith, Iraqi Islamic cleric and tribal leader, Jan 2007

Al-Glawi, Thami al-Mezouari, Sept 1954, *Obit* Mar 1956

Al-Hassan, Seif al-Islam, Feb 1957

Al-Husseini, Faisal, Palestinian political leader, Jan 1998

Al-Jamali, Mohammed Fadhel, Iraqi prime minister, Jan 1954, *Obit* Aug 1997

Al-Maliki, Nuri Kamal, Iraqi prime minister, Jan 2006

Al-Said, Nuri, Iraqi prime minister, June 1955, *Obit* Oct 1958

Albert, Carl, American congressman and Speaker of the House, June 1957, *Obit* June 2000

Alcorn, Hugh Meade, American lawyer and political party leader, May 1957, *Obit* Mar 1992

Aldrich, Richard S., American congressman, *Obit* Feb 1942

Aleman Valdez, Miguel, Mexican president, Sept 1946, *Obit* July 1983

Alexander, Albert, Yrbk 1940, *Obit* Feb 1965

Ali, Asaf, June 1947, *Obit* May 1953

Ali, Chaudhri Muhammad, Pakistani prime minister, Feb 1956

Ali, Mohammed, Pakistani prime minister and diplomat, Oct 1952, *Obit* Mar 1963

Alkatiri, Mari, East Timorese prime minister, Jan 2006

Allott, Gordon, American senator, May 1955, *Obit* Apr 1989

Almirante, Giorgio, Italian political leader, Jan 1974, *Obit* July 1988

Alvear, Marcelo Torcuato de, *Obit* May 1942

Amato, Giuliano, Italian prime minister, Sept 1993

Ambedkar, Bhimrao Ramji, Indian statesman and reformer, Nov 1951, *Obit* Feb 1957

Ameringer, Oscar, socialist leader, *Obit* Yrbk 1943

Amini, Ali, Iranian prime minister, Jan 1962

Andreotti, Giulio, Italian prime minister, Feb 1977, *Obit* Yrbk 2013

Aquino, Corazon, Filipino president, Aug 1986, *Obit* Yrbk 2009

Arafat, Yasir, Palestinian political leader, Mar 1971, Nov 1994, Jan 2002, *Obit* Feb 2005

Arbenz Guzman, Jacobo, Guatemalan president, Sept 1953, *Obit* Mar 1971

Arends, Leslie Cornelius, American congressman, Feb 1948, *Obit* Sept 1985

Argeseanu, George, Romanian prime minister, *Obit* Jan 1941

Arias Navarro, Carlos, Spanish prime minister, Oct 1974, *Obit* Jan 1990

Armstrong, Anne, American presidential adviser and diplomat, May 1976, *Obit* Yrbk 2008

Arroyo del Rio, Carlos Alberto, Ecuadorian president, June 1942

Asgeir Asgeirsson, Icelandic president, Sept 1952

Ashdown, Paddy, British political leader, Oct 1992

Ashrawi, Hanan, Palestinian political leader, Mar 1992

Astor, Nancy Witcher Langhorne, British member of Parliament, Nov 1940, *Obit* July 1964

Averoff-Tossizza, Evangelos, Greek political leader, May 1957, *Obit* Mar 1990

Avila Camacho, Manuel, Mexican president, Sept 1940, *Obit* Yrbk 1956

Awolowo, Obafemi, Nigerian prime minister, July 1957, *Obit* July 1987

Ayala, Eusebio, Paraguayan president, *Obit* July 1942

Aylwin, Patricio, Chilean president, Aug 1990

Ayub Khan, Mohammad, Pakistani president, Apr 1959, *Obit* June 1974

Azad, Abulkalam, Indian political leader, July 1942, *Obit* May 1958

Azana, Manuel, Spanish president, *Obit* Yrbk 1940

Azcona Hoyo, Jose, Honduran president, Feb 1988, *Obit* Yrbk 2006

Aznar, Jose Maria, Spanish prime minister, Jan 2002

Bailey, John Moran, American lawyer and political leader, June 1962, *Obit* June 1975

Baker, Roy, American lawyer, Nov 1948

Bakiyev, Kurmanbek, Kirghiz president, Jan 2007

Bakshi, Ghulam Mohammad, June 1956, *Obit* Sept 1972

Balaguer, Joaquin, Dominican president, Nov 1966, *Obit* Yrbk 2002

Baldwin, C. B., American political leader, Nov 1943

Balewa, Abubakar Tafawa, Nigerian prime minister, Sept 1961, *Obit* Feb 1966

Bandaranaike, S. W. R. D., Sri Lankan prime minister, Sept 1956, *Obit* Nov 1959

Bandaranaike, Sirimavo, Sri Lankan prime minister, May 1961, *Obit* Jan 2001

Banerjee, Mamata, Indian political leader, Nov 2011

Bani-Sadr, Abu al-Hasan, Iranian president, Feb 1981

Bankhead, William Brockman, American Speaker of the House, Oct 1940, *Obit* Oct 1940

Barbour, W. Warren, American senator, *Obit* Jan 1944

Barco Vargas, Virgilio, Colombian president, Feb 1990, *Obit* Aug 1997

Barre, Raymond, French prime minister, July 1977, *Obit* Yrbk 2007

Barrette, Antonio, Canadian provincial premier, July 1960, *Obit* Feb 1969

Barrow, Errol W., Barbadian prime minister, Sept 1968, *Obit* July 1987

Bartlett, Edward Lewis, American senator, June 1951, *Obit* Mar 1969

Bauer, Gary L., political activist, Jan 1999

Belaunde Terry, Fernando, Peruvian president, July 1965, *Obit* Sept 2002

Ben Bella, Ahmed, Algerian president, Feb 1963, *Obit* Yrbk 2012

Ben-Gurion, David, Israeli prime minister, Oct 1947, Jan 1957, *Obit* Jan 1974

Bender, George H., American congressman and senator, Jan 1952, *Obit* Sept 1961

Benes, Edvard, Czech statesman, Jan 1942, *Obit* Oct 1948

Bennett, W. A. C., Canadian political leader, May 1953, *Obit* May 1979

Benson, Allan L., American socialist leader, *Obit* Oct 1940

Bentley, Helen Delich, American congresswoman, Yrbk 1971

Berger Perdomo, Oscar, Guatemalan president, Jan 2004

Berlinguer, Enrico, Italian communist leader, July 1976, *Obit* Aug 1984

Berri, Nabih, Lebanese political leader, Nov 1985

Betancourt, Romulo, Venezuelan president, May 1960, *Obit* Nov 1981

Betancur, Belisario, Colombian president, Apr 1985

Bhutto, Benazir, Pakistani prime minister, July 1986, *Obit* Apr 2008

Bhutto, Zulfikar Ali, Pakistani president, Apr 1972, *Obit* May 1979

Bible, Alan, American senator, Feb 1957, *Obit* Oct 1988

Biden, Joseph R., American vice-president, Jan 1987, Mar 2009

Bilbo, Theodore G., American senator, Apr 1943, *Obit* Oct 1947

Bildt, Carl, Swedish prime minister, Jan 1993

Bingham, Jonathan B., congressman, July 1954, *Obit* Aug 1986

Bitar, Salah al-Din, Syrian political leader, Feb 1958, *Obit* Sept 1980

Blair, Tony, British prime minister, Aug 1996, Jan 2005

Blatnik, John A., American congressman, Feb 1958, *Obit* Feb 1992

Blitch, Iris Faircloth, congresswoman, Apr 1956, *Obit* Oct 1993

Blunt, Roy, American senator, Mar 2008

Boehner, John, American congressman and Speaker of the House, Apr 2006

Boggs, Hale, American congressman and political leader, Apr 1958, *Obit* Mar 1973

Boland, Edward P., American congressman, Oct 1987, *Obit* Feb 2002

Bonner, Herbert C., American congressman, July 1956, *Obit* Jan 1966

Bonomi, Ivanhoe, Aug 1944, *Obit* May 1951

Bordaberry, Juan Maria, Uruguayan president, Apr 1975, *Obit* Yrbk 2011

Borno, Louis, *Obit* Sept 1942

Bose, Subhas Chandra, Indian political leader, June 1944, *Obit* Yrbk 1945

Bourassa, Robert, Canadian economist and political leader, Sept 1976, *Obit* Jan 1997

Bourges-Maunoury, Maurice, French political leader, July 1957

Boxer, Barbara, American senator, Apr 1994

Boyle, William Marshall, American political leader and lawyer, June 1949, *Obit* Nov 1961

Brewster, Owen, American senator, May 1947, *Obit* Feb 1962

Brezhnev, Leonid Il'ich, Soviet communist leader, Jan 1963, Nov 1978, *Obit* Jan 1983

Bristow, Joseph Little, *Obit* Sept 1944

Broadbent, Edward, Canadian political leader, May 1988

Brookeborough, Basil Stanlake Brooke, Northern Ireland political leader, June 1948, *Obit* Oct 1973

Brooks, C. Wayland, Sept 1947, *Obit* Mar 1957

Brooks, Jack, congressman, June 1992, *Obit* Yrbk 2013

Brownback, Sam, American senator, Apr 2008

Broyhill, Joel T., American congressman, May 1974, *Obit* Feb 2007

Bruton, John, Irish prime minister, Nov 1996

Bryant, Gyude, Liberian businessman and interim leader, Jan 2005

Budge, Hamer H., American congressman and regulatory agency official, Yrbk 1970, *Obit* Yrbk 2003

Burdick, Quentin, American senator, May 1963, *Obit* Nov 1992

Burke, Edward Raymond, Sept 1940, *Obit* Yrbk 1968

Burnham, Forbes, Guyanese president, Nov 1966, *Obit* Oct 1985

Burton, Dan, American congressman, Sept 1998

Bustamante, Alexander, Jamaican prime minister, May 1965, *Obit* Sept 1977

Buthelezi, Mangosuthu, South African Zulu statesman, Oct 1986

Butler, Paul M., American political party leader, May 1955, *Obit* Feb 1962

Byrd, Robert C., American senator, Mar 1960, Feb 1978, *Obit* Sept 2010

Byron, William D., *Obit* Apr 1941

Caetano, Marcello, Portuguese prime minister, Mar 1970, *Obit* Jan 1981

Cafe Filho, Joao, Jan 1955, *Obit* Apr 1970

Caillaux, Joseph, French statesman, *Obit* Jan 1945

Caldera, Rafael, Venezuelan president, July 1969, *Obit* Yrbk 2010

Calero, Adolfo, Nicaraguan rebel leader, Oct 1987, *Obit* Yrbk 2012

Calwell, A. A., Oct 1947

Cameron, David, British prime minister, Aug 2010

Campbell, Ben Nighthorse, American senator, Oct 1994

Campbell, Philip P., Speaker of the House, *Obit* July 1941

Campora, Hector Jose, Argentine political leader, Oct 1973, *Obit* Feb 1981

Cantwell, Maria, American senator, Feb 2005

Caramanlis, Constantinos, Greek president, May 1956, Apr 1976, *Obit* July 1998

Caramanlis, Constantinos, Greek prime minister, Jan 2004

Caraway, Hattie Wyatt, American senator, Mar 1945, *Obit* Jan 1951

Cardoso, Fernando Henrique, Brazilian president, Oct 1996

Carias Andino, Tiburcio, Honduran president, June 1942, *Obit* Feb 1970

Carlsson, Ingvar, Swedish prime minister, Feb 1988

Carr, Robert, Jan 1973

Carrero Blanco, Luis, Oct 1973, *Obit* Feb 1974

Carstens, Karl, German president, Apr 1980, *Obit* Aug 1992

Castillo Armas, Carlos, Guatemalan president, Jan 1955, *Obit* Sept 1957

Castillo, Ramon S., July 1941, *Obit* Yrbk 1944

Cavaco Silva, Anibal, Portuguese prime minister, Mar 1991

Cerezo Arevalo, Vinicio, Guatemalan president, Mar 1987

Chaban-Delmas, Jacques, French prime minister, July 1958, *Obit* Feb 2001

Chadli, Bendjedid, Algerian president, Apr 1991, *Obit* Yrbk 2012

Chamoun, Camille Nimer, Lebanese president, July 1956, *Obit* Sept 1987

Charles, Eugenia, Dominica prime minister, Oct 1986, *Obit* Yrbk 2006

Chavez, Dennis, American senator, Mar 1946, *Obit* Jan 1963

Chee, Soon Juan, Singaporean political leader, Jan 2004

Chen, Shui-bian, Taiwanese president, Sept 2000

Chernenko, Konstantin Ustinovich, Soviet communist leader, Aug 1984, *Obit* May 1985

Chernomyrdin, Viktor, Russian prime minister, Aug 1998, *Obit* Yrbk 2011

Chiang, Ching-kuo, Taiwanese president, Sept 1954, *Obit* Mar 1988

Chiappe, Jean, French government official, *Obit* Jan 1941

Chiari, Roberto F., Panamanian president, Feb 1961

Chifley, Joseph B., Aug 1945, *Obit* July 1951

Chisholm, Shirley, American congresswoman, Oct 1969, *Obit* Apr 2005

Chretien, Jean, Canadian prime minister, Apr 1990

Chuan Leekpai, Thai prime minister, Nov 1998

Church, Marguerite Stitt, congresswoman, Feb 1951, *Obit* July 1990

Ciller, Tansu, Turkish political leader, Sept 1994

Clark, Bennett Champ, Nov 1941, *Obit* Sept 1954

Clark, Helen, New Zealand prime minister, Nov 2000

Clayton, Eva, American congresswoman, June 2000

Cleland, Max, American senator, Feb 1978

Clyburn, James E., American congressman, Oct 2001

Coates, Gordon, *Obit* July 1943

Cochran, Thad, American senator, Apr 2002

Coffee, John M., Oct 1946

Coldwell, M. J., Canadian member of Parliament, Sept 1943, *Obit* Oct 1974

Cole, William Sterling, congressman, Mar 1954, *Obit* May 1987

Collins, Cardiss, American congresswoman, Feb 1997, *Obit* Yrbk 2013

Collins, Susan, American senator, May 2000

Collor de Mello, Fernando, Brazilian president, Mar 1990

Colombo, Emilio, Apr 1971, *Obit* Yrbk 2013

Connery, Lawrence J., *Obit* Yrbk 1941

Conyers, John, American congressman, Sept 1970

Cosgrave, Liam, Irish prime minister, June 1977

Costello, John A., Apr 1948, *Obit* Feb 1976

Cot, Pierre, French political leader, June 1944, *Obit* Oct 1977

Cotton, Norris, American senator, Feb 1956, *Obit* May 1989

Coty, Rene, French president, Apr 1954, *Obit* Jan 1963

Cox, Christopher, American regulatory agency official, July 1999

Craigavon, James Craig, Northern Ireland political leader, *Obit* Jan 1941

Crane, Philip M., American congressman, May 1980

Cristiani, Alfredo, Salvadoran president, Jan 1990

Crosbie, John Carnell, Canadian political leader, Jan 1990

Culkin, Francis D., *Obit* Sept 1943

Cullen, Thomas H., *Obit* Apr 1944

Cummings, Elijah E., American congressman, Feb 2004

Cunhal, Alvaro, Portuguese communist leader, Sept 1975, *Obit* Yrbk 2005

Curtin, John, Australian prime minister, July 1941, *Obit* Aug 1945

Curtis, Carl T., American senator, Sept 1954, *Obit* June 2000

Curtis, Thomas B., American congressman, Mar 1965, *Obit* Mar 1993

D'Amato, Alfonse, American senator, Sept 1983

D'Aubuisson, Roberto, Salvadoran political leader, July 1983, *Obit* Apr 1992

Daladier, Edouard, French statesman, Apr 1940, *Obit* Yrbk 1970

Daluege, Kurt, German Nazi leader, *Obit* Yrbk 1946

Daniel, Dan, congressman, June 1957

Daschle, Thomas, American senator, Oct 1995

Davidovitch, Ljuba, *Obit* Mar 1940

Davis, William G., Canadian political leader, May 1973

Dawson, William Levi, American congressman, Apr 1945, *Obit* Yrbk 1970

De Bono, Emilio, Italian field marshal, *Obit* Feb 1944

De Maiziere, Lothar, German political leader, Aug 1990

De Quay, Jan Eduard, Dutch prime minister, May 1963, *Obit* Aug 1985

De Sapio, Carmine G., American political leader, Sept 1955, *Obit* Yrbk 2004

De Valera, Eamon, Irish statesman, Nov 1940, Sept 1951, *Obit* Oct 1975

DeLauro, Rosa, American congresswoman, Mar 2000

DeLay, Tom, American congressman, May 1999

Deat, Marcel, French political leader, Jan 1942, *Obit* May 1955

Debre, Michel, French prime minister, May 1959, *Obit* Oct 1996

Dehler, Thomas, July 1955, *Obit* Oct 1967

Dellums, Ronald V., American congressman, Sept 1972, Sept 1993

Deloncle, Eugene, French political leader, *Obit* Feb 1944

Demirel, Suleyman, Turkish prime minister, Feb 1980

Deng Xiaoping, Chinese communist leader, May 1976, June 1994, *Obit* Apr 1997

Dennis, Eugene, American communist leader, May 1949, *Obit* Mar 1961

Desai, Morarji, Indian prime minister, Sept 1958, Jan 1978, *Obit* June 1995

Deuba, Sher Bahadur, Nepalese prime minister, Jan 2002

Deutsch, Julius, Nov 1944, *Obit* Mar 1968

Dick, Charles, *Obit* May 1945

Dickinson, Willoughby Hyett Dickinson, British member of Parliament, *Obit* July 1943

Diefenbaker, John George, Canadian prime minister, May 1957, *Obit* Oct 1979

Diggs, Charles, American congressman, July 1957, *Obit* Nov 1998

Dimitrov, Georgi, Bulgarian prime minister, May 1949

Dingell, John D., American congressman, Mar 1949, *Obit* Yrbk 1956

Dingell, John D., American congressman, Aug 1983

Diogo, Luisa, Mozambican prime minister, Jan 2004

Dirksen, Everett McKinley, American senator, Apr 1941, Sept 1957, *Obit* Nov 1969

Ditter, J. William, *Obit* Jan 1944

Djukanovic, Milo, Montenegrin president, Aug 2001

Dodd, Thomas, American senator, Sept 1959, *Obit* July 1971

Doe, Samuel Kanyon, Liberian president, May 1981, *Obit* Nov 1990

Dole, Robert J., American senator, Apr 1972, Oct 1987

Domenici, Pete, American senator, June 1982

Doriot, Jacques, French political leader and wartime collaborationist, Nov 1940

Dorticos Torrado, Osvaldo, Cuban president, Feb 1963, *Obit* Aug 1983

Doughton, Robert L., American congressman, July 1942, *Obit* Yrbk 1955

Douglas, Denzil, Saint Kitts-Nevis prime minister, Jan 2007

Drees, Willem, Dutch prime minister, Jan 1949, *Obit* July 1988

Drew, George A., Canadian political leader, Yrbk 1948, *Obit* May 1984

Duarte, Jose Napoleon, Salvadoran president, Sept 1981, *Obit* Apr 1990

Dubcek, Alexander, Czech communist leader, Nov 1968

Duclos, Jacques, French communist leader, Feb 1946, *Obit* June 1975

Duncan Smith, Iain, British political leader, Jan 2002

Duncan, Andrew Rae, July 1941, *Obit* May 1952

Duncan, Patrick, South African governor-general, *Obit* Sept 1943

Dunn, Jennifer, American congresswoman, Mar 1999, *Obit* Nov 2007

Duplessis, Maurice LeNoblet, Canadian provincial premier, Oct 1948, *Obit* Nov 1959

Durbin, Richard J., American senator, Aug 2006

Durenberger, David, American senator, Oct 1988

Duvalier, Jean-Claude, Haitian president, June 1972

Duvieusart, Jean, Sept 1950

Eastland, James O., American senator, Jan 1949, *Obit* Apr 1986

Ecevit, Bulent, Turkish prime minister, Jan 1975, *Obit* Yrbk 2007

Ede, James Chuter, May 1946, *Obit* Jan 1966

Edwards, Don, American congressman, Mar 1983

El-Khoury, Beshira, Yrbk 1951, *Obit* Feb 1964

El-Nahas, Mustafa, July 1951, *Obit* Nov 1965

Ellender, Allen J., American senator, July 1946, *Obit* Oct 1972

Endara, Guillermo, Panamanian president, Feb 1991, *Obit* Yrbk 2009

Endeley, E. M. L., July 1959

Enkhbayar, Nambaryn, Mongolian president, Jan 2007

Erhard, Ludwig, German chancellor, Jan 1950, June 1964, *Obit* July 1977

Erlander, Tage F., Swedish prime minister, Oct 1947, *Obit* Aug 1985

Esch, John J., *Obit* June 1941

Eshkol, Levi, Israeli prime minister, Oct 1963, *Obit* Apr 1969

Evren, Kenan, Turkish president, Apr 1984

Exon, J. James, American senator, Nov 1996, *Obit* Yrbk 2005

Eyskens, Gaston, Belgian prime minister, Nov 1949, *Obit* Feb 1988

Fagerholm, Karl August, Finnish prime minister, Oct 1948, *Obit* July 1984

Falldin, Thorbjorn, Swedish prime minister, May 1978

Fallin, Mary, American congresswoman, Mar 2011

Fanfani, Amintore, Italian prime minister, Oct 1958, *Obit* Mar 2000

Farley, James Aloysius, American political leader, Sept 1944, *Obit* Aug 1976

Fascell, Dante B., congressman, Apr 1960, *Obit* Feb 1999

Fatemi, Hossein, May 1953, *Obit* Jan 1955

Fattah, Chaka, American congressman, Sept 2003

Faulkner, Brian, prime minister of Northern Ireland, Feb 1972, *Obit* May 1977

Fenwick, Millicent, American congresswoman, Apr 1977, *Obit* Nov 1992

Ferguson, Howard, *Obit* Apr 1946

Ferris, Scott, *Obit* July 1945

Figueres Ferrer, Jose, Costa Rican president, Oct 1953, *Obit* Aug 1990

Filov, Bogdan, Apr 1941

Fini, Gianfranco, Italian political leader, Jan 2003

FitzGerald, Garret, Irish prime minister, Aug 1984, *Obit* Yrbk 2011

Flandin, Pierre Etienne, French political leader, Jan 1941, *Obit* Oct 1958

Flood, Daniel J., American congressman, Aug 1978, *Obit* Aug 1994

Flores Nano, Lourdes, Peruvian political leader, Jan 2006

Flynn, Edward J., American political leader, Sept 1940, *Obit* Oct 1953

Fogarty, John Edward, congressman, Apr 1964, *Obit* Mar 1967

Folger, A. D., *Obit* June 1941

Fong, Hiram, American senator, Feb 1960, *Obit* Yrbk 2004

Foreman, Clark, Oct 1948, *Obit* Aug 1977

Fox Quesada, Vicente, Mexican president, May 2001

Frank, Barney, American congressman, Apr 1995

Fraser, Malcolm, Australian prime minister, Mar 1976

Fraser, Peter, May 1942, *Obit* Jan 1951

Frei Montalva, Eduardo, Chilean president, Apr 1965, *Obit* Mar 1982

Fremantle, Francis Edward, *Obit* Oct 1943

Frondizi, Arturo, Argentine president, Oct 1958, *Obit* June 1995

Frost, Leslie M., Canadian political leader, Oct 1953, *Obit* July 1973

Fujiyama, Aiichiro, Japanese cabinet member, Apr 1958, *Obit* May 1985

Fukuda, Takeo, Japanese prime minister, June 1974, *Obit* Sept 1995

Fulani, Lenora, American psychologist and political activist, Mar 2000

Fulbright, J. William, American senator, Nov 1943, Oct 1955, *Obit* Apr 1995

Furtseva, Ekaterina A., Soviet communist leader, June 1956, *Obit* Yrbk 1974

Gabrielson, Guy George, American lawyer, Oct 1949, *Obit* June 1976

Gaillard, Felix, French prime minister, Feb 1958, *Obit* Oct 1970

Gallagher, William J., *Obit* Oct 1946

Galloway, George, British member of Parliament, Jan 2005

Gandhi, Indira, Indian prime minister, Oct 1959, June 1966, *Obit* Jan 1985

Gandhi, Sonia, Italian wife of Indian Prime Minister Rajiv Gandhi, May 1998

Garcia Medina, Amalia, Mexican provincial governor, Jan 2004

Garcia Perez, Alan, Peruvian president, Nov 1985

Garcia, Carlos P., Filipino president, June 1957, *Obit* July 1971

Garn, Jake, senator, Aug 1985

Gasperi, Alcide de, Italian statesman, Yrbk 1946, *Obit* Oct 1954

Gatov, Elizabeth Rudel, Yrbk 1961

Gayatri Devi, Mar 1968, *Obit* Yrbk 2009

Gbagbo, Laurent, Ivorian president, Jan 2004

Gemayel, Amin, Lebanese president, Mar 1983

Gephardt, Richard A., American congressman, Oct 1987

Gerhardsen, Einar, Norwegian prime minister, Mar 1949, *Obit* Nov 1987

Gheorghiu-Dej, Gheorghe, Romanian prime minister, Oct 1958, *Obit* May 1965

Gibson, Ernest Willard, American senator, *Obit* Aug 1940

Gierek, Edward, Polish communist leader, May 1971, *Obit* Oct 2001

Giffords, Gabrielle, American congresswoman, Mar 2012

Gillette, Guy M., Sept 1946, *Obit* Apr 1973

Gnassingbe, Faure, Togolese president, Jan 2005

Goebbels, Joseph, German Nazi leader, Sept 1941, *Obit* Yrbk 1991

Golding, Bruce, Jamaican prime minister, Mar 2008

Goldmann, Nahum, Israeli Zionist leader, May 1957, *Obit* Oct 1982

Goldwater, Barry M., American senator, May 1955, June 1978, *Obit* Aug 1998

Gomes, Francisco da Costa, Portuguese president, May 1976

Gomulka, Wladyslaw, Polish communist leader, Jan 1957, *Obit* Oct 1982

Gonzalez Videla, Gabriel, Cuban president, June 1950

Gonzalez, Felipe, Spanish prime minister, Jan 1978

Gonzalez, Henry B., American congressman, June 1964, Feb 1993, *Obit* Feb 2001

Gordon, Thomas S., American congressman, Apr 1957, *Obit* Apr 1959

Gorton, John Grey, Australian prime minister, July 1968, *Obit* Sept 2002

Gorton, Slade, senator, Aug 1993

Gouin, Felix, French statesman, Mar 1946, *Obit* Oct 1979

Goulart, Joao Belchior Marques, Brazilian president, Sept 1962, *Obit* Feb 1977

Gould, Arthur R., *Obit* Sept 1946

Granahan, Kathryn Elizabeth, congresswoman, Oct 1959, *Obit* Sept 1979

Grandi, Dino, Italian political leader, July 1943, *Obit* July 1988

Grau San Martin, Ramon, Cuban president, Oct 1944, *Obit* Oct 1969

Gravel, Mike, American senator, Jan 1972

Green, Edith, American congresswoman, May 1956, *Obit* June 1987

Greenwood, Arthur, Oct 1940, *Obit* Sept 1954

Grimond, Jo, British political leader, Oct 1963, *Obit* Jan 1994

Gross, H. R., American congressman, Jan 1964, *Obit* Oct 1987

Grosz, Karoly, Hungarian prime minister, Sept 1988, *Obit* Mar 1996

Grotewohl, Otto, July 1950, *Obit* Nov 1964

Guardia, Ernesto de la, Panamanian president, Jan 1957

Guardia, Ricardo Adolfo de la, Panamanian president, May 1942, *Obit* Feb 1970

Guffey, Joseph F., Mar 1944, *Obit* May 1959

Gul, Abdullah, Turkish prime minister, Jan 2007

Gusmao, Xanana, East Timorese president, Jan 2002

Guyer, Ulysses Samuel, *Obit* July 1943

Habash, George, Palestinian nationalist leader, Mar 1988, *Obit* Yrbk 2008

Habre, Hissene, Chadian president, Aug 1987

Hacha, Emil, Yrbk 1942, *Obit* Sept 1945

Hadi Awang, Malaysian Islamic leader, Jan 2004

Halim, Mustafa ben, Libyan prime minister, Sept 1956

Hall, Gus, American communist leader, May 1973, *Obit* Jan 2001

Halleck, Charles A., American congressman and political leader, Mar 1947, *Obit* Apr 1986

Halprin, Rose L., June 1950

Halsey, Edwin A., *Obit* Mar 1945

Hamilton, Lee H., American congressman, Mar 1988

Han, Myeong Sook, Korean prime minister, Jan 2006

Haniyeh, Ismail, Palestinian prime minister, Jan 2006

Hansson, Per Albin, Oct 1942, *Obit* Nov 1946

Hardy, Porter, congressman, May 1957, *Obit* June 1995

Hargis, Billy James, American clergyman, Mar 1972, *Obit* Yrbk 2005

Hariri, Saad, Lebanese telecommunications executive and political leader, Jan 2005

Harkin, Tom, American senator, Jan 1992

Hartley, Fred A., American congressman, June 1947, *Obit* June 1969

Hashimoto, Ryutaro, Japanese prime minister, Feb 1998, *Obit* Yrbk 2006

Hastert, Dennis, American congressman and Speaker of the House, Apr 1999

Hatta, Mohammad, Indonesian prime minister, Yrbk 1949, *Obit* Yrbk 1991

Haughey, Charles, Irish prime minister, Feb 1981, *Obit* Yrbk 2006

Hawke, Robert J. L., Australian prime minister, Aug 1983

Hawley, Willis C., *Obit* Sept 1941

Haya de la Torre, Victor Raul, Peruvian political leader, June 1942, *Obit* Sept 1979

Hays, Brooks, American congressman, Jan 1958, *Obit* Jan 1982

Heath, Edward, British prime minister, Oct 1962, *Obit* Yrbk 2005

Hedtoft, Hans, Mar 1949, *Obit* Mar 1955

Heinemann, Gustav Walter, June 1969, *Obit* Aug 1976

Heinz, John, American senator, Apr 1981, *Obit* May 1991

Hendrickson, Robert C., Nov 1952, *Obit* Feb 1965

Henriot, Philippe, French political leader, *Obit* Aug 1944

Hepburn, Mitchell Frederick, Canadian provincial premier, Yrbk 1941, *Obit* Feb 1953

Hermann Jonasson, Aug 1941

Herrera Campins, Luis, Venezuelan president, July 1980, *Obit* Yrbk 2008

Herring, Clyde L., *Obit* Nov 1945

Herriot, Edouard, French statesman, Feb 1946, *Obit* June 1957

Hess, Rudolf, German Nazi leader, Mar 1941, *Obit* Oct 1987

Hesselgren, Kerstin, Swedish sociologist and member of Parliament, Jan 1941, *Obit* Oct 1962

Heuss, Theodor, German president, Nov 1949, *Obit* Jan 1964

Heydrich, Reinhard, German Nazi leader, *Obit* July 1942, July 1942

Hicks, Henry D., Oct 1956

Hill, Lister, American senator, Oct 1943, *Obit* Feb 1985

Hillings, Patrick J., congressman, Oct 1957, *Obit* Sept 1994

Himmler, Heinrich, German Nazi leader, June 1941, *Obit* June 1945

Hinshaw, Carl, American congressman, July 1951, *Obit* Oct 1956

Hitler, Adolf, German dictator, Mar 1942, *Obit* Jan 1957

Ho, Chi Minh, Vietnamese communist leader, Nov 1949, Oct 1966, *Obit* Nov 1969

Hodza, Milan, *Obit* Aug 1944

Hoffman, Clare Eugene, American congressman, Mar 1949, *Obit* Jan 1968

Hoffman, Johannes, Apr 1950

Holifield, Chet, American congressman, Oct 1955, *Obit* Apr 1995

Holland, Sidney, New Zealand prime minister, Jan 1950, *Obit* Nov 1961

Holyoake, Keith Jacka, New Zealand prime minister, Feb 1963, *Obit* Feb 1984

Honecker, Erich, East German communist leader, Apr 1972, *Obit* July 1994

Hore-Belisha, Leslie Hore-Belisha, British political leader, July 1941, *Obit* May 1957

Hosmer, Craig, congressman, May 1958, *Obit* Mar 1983

Hosokawa, Morihiro, Japanese prime minister, May 1994

Houston, Andrew Jackson, *Obit* Aug 1941

Howard, John Winston, Australian prime minister, Mar 1999

Howell, Charles R., Feb 1954, *Obit* Sept 1973

Hoxha, Enver, Albanian communist leader, Jan 1950, *Obit* June 1985

Hoyer, Steny H., American congressman, Mar 2004

Hrawi, Elias, Lebanese president, Feb 1992, *Obit* Yrbk 2006

Hu Yaobang, Chinese communist leader, Nov 1983, *Obit* June 1989

Hua Guofeng, Chinese prime minister, Mar 1977, *Obit* Yrbk 2008

Hull, William Edgar, *Obit* July 1942

Humphrey, Hubert Horatio, American vice-president, July 1949, Apr 1966, *Obit* Mar 1978

Hussein, Saddam, Iraqi president, Sept 1981, Jan 2002, *Obit* Apr 2007

Hutchison, Kay Bailey, American senator, Sept 1997

Huvayda, Amir Abbas, Oct 1971, *Obit* June 1979

Hylton-Foster, Harry, Jan 1961, *Obit* Nov 1965

Iglesias Pantin, Santiago, Puerto Rican labor leader, Jan 1940

Ikeda, Hayato, Japanese prime minister, May 1961, *Obit* Oct 1965

Iliescu, Ion, Romanian president, June 1990

Im, Yong-Sin, Oct 1947, *Obit* Apr 1977

Inonu, Ismet, Turkish president, Mar 1941, Oct 1964, *Obit* Feb 1974

Isaias Afwerki, Eritrean president, Jan 2002

Ishibashi, Tanzan, Mar 1957, *Obit* June 1973

Ives, Irving M., American senator, Feb 1948, *Obit* Apr 1962

Izac, Edouard V. M., American congressman, Yrbk 1945, *Obit* Mar 1990

Izetbegovic, Alija, Bosnian president, Aug 1993, *Obit* June 2004

Jabotinsky, Vladimir, Russian Zionist leader, *Obit* Sept 1940

Jackson, Henry Martin, American senator, Oct 1953, Oct 1979, *Obit* Oct 1983

Jackson, Jesse L., American congressman, May 1998

Jagan, Cheddi, Guyanese president, Apr 1963, *Obit* May 1997

Janson, Paul Emile, *Obit* Aug 1944

Jayewardene, Junius Richard, Sri Lankan president, Jan 1984, *Obit* Jan 1997

Jeffords, James, American senator, Sept 2001

Jiang Qing, Chinese communist leader and wife of Mao Zedong, June 1975, *Obit* Jan 1992

Jinnah, Mohamed Ali, Pakistani political leader, May 1942, *Obit* Oct 1948

Johnson, Daniel, Canadian provincial premier, Nov 1967, *Obit* Nov 1968

Johnson, Eddie Bernice, American congresswoman, July 2001

Johnston, Victor A., July 1949, *Obit* May 1967

Jones, Arthur C., Jan 1948, *Obit* Jan 1965

Jumblatt, Kamal, Lebanese political leader, Jan 1977, *Obit* Jan 1977

Kabbah, Ahmad Tejan, Sierra Leonean president, Jan 2002

Kadar, Janos, Hungarian prime minister, May 1957, *Obit* Yrbk 1989

Kaganovich, L. M., Soviet communist leader, Apr 1942, Oct 1955, *Obit* Sept 1991

Kaifu, Toshiki, Japanese prime minister, June 1990

Kallay, Nicholas, Hungarian prime minister, June 1942, *Obit* May 1967

Kallio, Kyosti, *Obit* Feb 1941

Kaltenbrunner, Ernst, Austrian Nazi leader, Apr 1943, *Obit* Nov 1946

Kampmann, Viggo, Jan 1961, *Obit* July 1976

Kan, Naoto, Japanese prime minister, July 2011

Kania, Stanislaw, June 1981

Kaptur, Marcy C., American congresswoman, Jan 2003

Karadzic, Radovan, Bosnian Serb political leader, Oct 1995

Karami, Rashid, Lebanese prime minister, Nov 1959, *Obit* July 1987

Kardelj, Edvard, Yugoslav communist leader, Yrbk 1949, *Obit* Apr 1979

Karzai, Hamid, Afghan president, May 2002

Kasavubu, Joseph, Congolese president, Mar 1961, *Obit* May 1969

Kassebaum Baker, Nancy, American senator, Feb 1982

Kasten, Robert W., senator, June 1989

Katayama, Tetsu, Jan 1948

Kaunda, Kenneth D., Zambian president, July 1966

Kawakami, Jotaro, Mar 1963, *Obit* Jan 1966

Keating, Paul, Australian prime minister, May 1992

Kee, Elizabeth, Jan 1954

Kefauver, Estes, American senator, Jan 1949, *Obit* Oct 1963

Keita, Modibo, Malian president, Apr 1960, *Obit* July 1977

Kekkonen, Urho, Finnish president, Sept 1950, *Obit* Oct 1986

Kelly, Edna Flannery, congresswoman, Mar 1950, *Obit* Feb 1998

Kelly, Petra, German political leader, Mar 1984, *Obit* Jan 1993

Kennedy, Edward Moore, American senator, Sept 1963, Oct 1978, *Obit* Oct 2009

Kenyatta, Jomo, Kenyan president, Oct 1953, Apr 1974, *Obit* Oct 1978

Kerry, John Forbes, American senator, June 1988, Sept 2004

Khaleda Zia, Bangladeshi prime minister, Jan 2003

Khama, Seretse, Batswana president, May 1967, *Obit* Sept 1980

Khan, Liaquat Ali, June 1948, *Obit* Yrbk 1951

Khomeini, Ruhollah, Iranian religious and political leader, Nov 1979, *Obit* July 1989

Khrushchev, Nikita Sergeevich, Soviet communist leader, July 1954, *Obit* Oct 1971

Kibaki, Mwai, Kenyan president, Jan 2003

Kiesinger, Kurt Georg, German chancellor, Apr 1967, *Obit* Apr 1988

Kiir, Salva, Sudanese rebel and vice-president, Jan 2005

Kim, Il Sung, North Korean head of state, Sept 1951, *Obit* Yrbk 1994, Yrbk 1994

Kim, Jong Il, North Korean head of state, Jan 2002, *Obit* Yrbk 2012

Kim, Young Sam, Korean president, June 1995

King, Cecil R., American congressman, Feb 1952, *Obit* May 1974

King, William Lyon Mackenzie, Canadian prime minister, Aug 1940, *Obit* Sept 1950

Kirchner, Nestor, Argentine president, Jan 2004, *Obit* Yrbk 2010

Kishi, Nobusuke, Japanese prime minister, June 1957, *Obit* Sept 1987

Klaus, Josef, Austrian chancellor, Jan 1965, *Obit* Oct 2001

Knutson, Coya, congresswoman, Mar 1956, *Obit* Jan 1997

Kohl, Helmut, German chancellor, Aug 1977

Koirala, Girija Prasad, Nepalese prime minister, Jan 2006, *Obit* Yrbk 2010

Koivisto, Mauno, Finnish president, Sept 1982

Koizumi, Junichiro, Japanese prime minister, Jan 2002

Kolarov, Vassil, Yrbk 1949, *Obit* Mar 1950

Konare, Alpha Oumar, Malian president, Oct 2001

Konoye, Fumimaro, Japanese prime minister, Sept 1940, *Obit* Feb 1946

Korizis, Alexander, Mar 1941, *Obit* Mar 1941

Kosygin, Aleksei Nikolaevich, Soviet prime minister, Sept 1965, *Obit* Feb 1981

Kotelawala, John Lionel, Sri Lankan prime minister, Oct 1955

Kozlov, Frol R., Nov 1959, *Obit* Mar 1965

Kozlowski, Leon, *Obit* July 1944

Krag, Jens Otto, Danish prime minister, Oct 1962, *Obit* Aug 1978

Kravchuk, Leonid, Ukrainian president, Jan 1993

Kreisky, Bruno, Austrian chancellor, Sept 1960, *Obit* Sept 1990

Krenz, Egon, East German communist leader, Mar 1990

Kubitschek, Juscelino, Brazilian president, Apr 1956, *Obit* Nov 1976

Kuchel, Thomas H., American senator, Feb 1954, *Obit* Feb 1995

Kuchma, Leonid, Ukrainian president, Oct 1997

Kufuor, John, Ghanaian president, Jan 2002

Kumaratunga, Chandrika Bandaranaike, Sri Lankan prime minister, Jan 1996

Kunz, Stanley H., *Obit* June 1946

Kutchuk, Fazil, Cypriot political leader and physician, Feb 1961, *Obit* Mar 1984

Kyprianou, Spyros, Cypriot president, May 1979, *Obit* May 2002

La Follette, Robert M., American senator, May 1944, *Obit* Apr 1953

La Rocque, Francois de, French political leader, *Obit* June 1946

Lange, David, New Zealand prime minister, Sept 1985, *Obit* Yrbk 2005

Langevin, Jim, American congressman, Aug 2005

Largo Caballero, Francisco, Spanish prime minister, *Obit* May 1946

Laurel, Jose P., Filipino president, June 1953, *Obit* Jan 1960

Layton, Jack, Canadian political leader, Nov 2009, *Obit* Yrbk 2012

Le Pen, Jean-Marie, French political leader, Jan 1988

Lea, Clarence F., Nov 1946, *Obit* Sept 1964

Leahy, Patrick J., American senator, Sept 1990

Lee, Barbara, American congresswoman, June 2004

Lee, Blair, *Obit* Feb 1945

Lee, Bum Suk, Jan 1949

Lee, Kuan Yew, Singaporean prime minister, Nov 1959, Jan 1995

Lee, Martin, Chinese lawyer and political leader, July 1997

Lefevre, Theo, June 1962, *Obit* Nov 1973

Lemass, Sean, Irish prime minister, Mar 1960, *Obit* June 1971

Leone, Giovanni, Italian president, May 1972, *Obit* Feb 2002

Leoni, Raul, Venezuelan president, Oct 1964, *Obit* Sept 1972

Lesage, Jean, Canadian government official, Nov 1961, *Obit* Feb 1981

Lescot, Elie, Haitian president, June 1941, *Obit* Yrbk 1974

Lesinski, John, July 1949, *Obit* July 1950

Levy, David, Israeli cabinet member, Mar 1998

Lewis, Lawrence, *Obit* Jan 1944

Ley, Robert, German Nazi leader, Sept 1940, *Obit* Yrbk 1945

Li Peng, Chinese prime minister, Nov 1988

Lieberman, Joseph I., American senator, July 1994

Ligachev, Yegor K., Soviet communist leader, Aug 1990

Limann, Hilla, Ghanaian president, June 1981, *Obit* Apr 1998

Lincoln, Blanche Lambert, American senator, Mar 2002

Liu Shaoqi, Chinese communist leader, Oct 1957, *Obit* Yrbk 1974

Lloyd George, David Lloyd George, British statesman, Nov 1944, *Obit* May 1945

Lloyd, James T., *Obit* May 1944

Loeb, James I., American diplomat and political leader, Jan 1962, *Obit* Mar 1992

Long, Russell B., American senator, Yrbk 1951, Oct 1965, *Obit* Yrbk 2003

Longo, Luigi, Feb 1966, *Obit* Jan 1981

Lopez Mateos, Adolfo, Mexican president, Mar 1959, *Obit* Nov 1969

Lopez Michelsen, Alfonso, Colombian president, Apr 1975

Lopez Portillo, Jose, Mexican president, June 1977, *Obit* Yrbk 2004

Lott, Trent, American senator, Sept 1996

Lougheed, Peter, Canadian political leader, Aug 1979

Lowey, Nita M., American congresswoman, Sept 1997

Luce, Robert, *Obit* May 1946

Lumpkin, Alva M., *Obit* Sept 1941

Lumumba, Patrice, Congolese prime minister, Nov 1960, *Obit* Apr 1961

Lundeen, Ernest, *Obit* Oct 1940

Lynch, John Mary, Irish prime minister, May 1967, *Obit* Feb 2000

Macapagal, Diosdado, Filipino president, Nov 1962, *Obit* July 1997

Macapagal-Arroyo, Gloria, Filipino president, Jan 2002

Macauley, Jane Hamilton, Sept 1949

Machado Ventura, Jose Ramon, Cuban vice-president, Sept 2011

Machado, Bernardino, *Obit* June 1944

Machel, Samora, Mozambican president, Mar 1984, *Obit* Jan 1987

Madden, Ray J., congressman, Apr 1953, *Obit* Nov 1987

Madrid Hurtado, Miguel de la, Mexican president, Apr 1983, *Obit* Yrbk 2012

Magloire, Paul, Haitian president, Feb 1952, *Obit* Nov 2001

Magner, Thomas F., *Obit* Feb 1946

Magsaysay, Ramon, Filipino president, Yrbk 1952, *Obit* May 1957

Mahathir bin Mohamad, Malaysian prime minister, Aug 1988

Maher, Ahmed, *Obit* Apr 1945

Maher, Aly, Mar 1952, *Obit* Nov 1960

Major, John, British prime minister, Oct 1990, Apr 1997

Malan, Daniel Francois, South African prime minister, Apr 1949, *Obit* Apr 1959

Malenkov, Georgi M., Soviet prime minister, June 1952, *Obit* Mar 1988

Malik, Adam, Indonesian statesman and diplomat, Nov 1970, *Obit* Nov 1984

Malvern, Godfrey Martin Huggins, Rhodesian prime minister, Nov 1956, *Obit* June 1971

Mandela, Winnie, South African political leader and wife of Nelson Mandela, Jan 1986

Manley, Michael, Jamaican prime minister, Jan 1976, *Obit* May 1997

Manley, Norman Washington, Jamaican prime minister, Nov 1959, *Obit* Nov 1969

Manning, Ernest, Canadian political leader, Yrbk 1959, *Obit* May 1996

Manning, Patrick A. M., Trinidadian prime minister, Jan 2006

Mao Zedong, Chinese communist leader, Feb 1943, May 1962, *Obit* Oct 1976

Marchais, Georges, French communist leader, June 1976, *Obit* Jan 1998

Marcos, Ferdinand E., Filipino president, Feb 1967, *Obit* Nov 1989

Margai, Milton Augustus Striery, Sierra Leonean prime minister, Feb 1962, *Obit* June 1964

Marie, Andre, French political leader, Sept 1948, *Obit* Sept 1974

Markey, Edward J., American congressman, Nov 1997

Markovic, Ante, Yugoslav prime minister, Nov 1991, *Obit* Yrbk 2012

Marshall, David, Singaporean lawyer and political leader, July 1956, *Obit* Feb 1996

Martens, Wilfried, Belgian prime minister, Feb 1987

Martin, Paul, Canadian prime minister, Jan 2004

Masuku, Mario, Swazi political leader, Jan 2006

Matsui, Robert T., American congressman, Oct 1994, *Obit* Apr 2005

Maurer, Ion Gheorghe, Romanian prime minister, Sept 1971, *Obit* July 2000

Mauroy, Pierre, French prime minister, June 1982, *Obit* Yrbk 2013

Maxton, James, British member of Parliament, *Obit* Sept 1946

May, Catherine Dean, congresswoman, Jan 1960

May, Theresa, British member of Parliament, Jan 2003

Mayer, Daniel, French socialist leader, Nov 1949

Mayes, Rose Gorr, May 1950

Mbeki, Thabo, South African president, Aug 1998

Mboya, Tom, Kenyan political and labor leader, June 1959, *Obit* Sept 1969

McAliskey, Bernadette Devlin, Irish political leader, Jan 1970

McCain, John S., American senator, Feb 1989, Mar 2006

McCarthy, Eugene J., American senator, Nov 1955, *Obit* Mar 2006

McCarthy, Joseph, American senator, Jan 1950, *Obit* July 1957

McCormack, John William, American congressman and Speaker of the House, June 1943, Apr 1962, *Obit* Jan 1981

McCormick, Ruth Hanna, congresswoman, *Obit* Feb 1945

McGovern, George S., American senator, Mar 1967, *Obit* Yrbk 2012

McGregor, J. Harry, Oct 1958

McGuinty, Dalton, Canadian provincial premier, Feb 2013

McKinney, Cynthia, American congresswoman, Aug 1996

McLaughlin, Audrey, Canadian political leader, July 1990

McMahon, William, Australian prime minister, Sept 1971, *Obit* May 1988

Mead, James M., July 1944, *Obit* Apr 1964

Meciar, Vladimir, Slovak prime minister, July 1994

Mende, Erich, July 1966

Menderes, Adnan, Turkish prime minister, Nov 1954, *Obit* Nov 1961

Menem, Carlos Saul, Argentine president, Nov 1989

Mengistu Haile-Mariam, Ethiopian head of state, July 1981

Menocal, Mario Garcia, Cuban president, *Obit* Oct 1941

Menzies, Robert Gordon, Australian prime minister, Feb 1941, Jan 1950, *Obit* July 1978

Merkel, Angela, German chancellor, Jan 2004

Merritt, Matthew J., *Obit* Nov 1946

Meta, Ilir, Albanian prime minister, Feb 2002

Metcalf, Jesse H., *Obit* Yrbk 1942

Michel, Robert H., American congressman and political leader, Sept 1981

Miki, Takeo, Japanese prime minister, Apr 1975, *Obit* Jan 1989

Mikolajczyk, Stanislaw, Polish political leader, Mar 1944, *Obit* Feb 1967

Mikulski, Barbara A., American senator, Nov 1985

Miller, George, American congressman, Feb 1964

Miller, Leszek, Polish prime minister, Jan 2002

Millerand, Alexandre, French president, *Obit* May 1943

Minor, Robert, Apr 1941, *Obit* Jan 1953

Mintoff, Dom, Maltese prime minister, Mar 1984, *Obit* Yrbk 2012

Mirza, Iskander, May 1956, *Obit* Jan 1970

Mitchell, Stephen Arnold, American lawyer and political party leader, Oct 1952, *Obit* June 1974

Mitsotakis, Constantine, Greek prime minister, Nov 1990

Miyazawa, Kiichi, Japanese prime minister, Feb 1992, *Obit* Yrbk 2007

Mlambo-Ngcuka, Phumzile, South African deputy president, Jan 2005

Mogae, Festus G., Batswana president, Jan 2004

Moi, Daniel Arap, Kenyan president, May 1979

Mollet, Guy, French prime minister, Sept 1950, *Obit* Nov 1975

Montoya, Joseph M., American senator, Mar 1975, *Obit* July 1978

Moore, R. Walton, *Obit* Apr 1941

Morano, Albert P., congressman, Mar 1952, *Obit* Feb 1988

Morella, Constance A., American congresswoman, Feb 2001

Morinigo, Higinio, Paraguayan president, June 1942

Moro, Aldo, Italian prime minister, June 1964, *Obit* June 1978

Morton, Thruston Ballard, American senator, Nov 1957, *Obit* Oct 1982

Mosaddeq, Mohammad, Iranian prime minister, May 1951, *Obit* May 1967

Moscoso, Mireya, Panamanian president, Jan 2002

Moses, George H., *Obit* Feb 1945

Mosley, Oswald, British political leader, July 1940, *Obit* Feb 1981

Moss, John E., American congressman, Nov 1956, *Obit* Feb 1998

Motta, Giuseppe, *Obit* Jan 1940

Mousavi, Mir Hossein, Iranian presidential candidate and former prime minister, Sept 2009

Mowinckel, Johan Ludwig, *Obit* Nov 1943

Mubarak, Hosni, Egyptian president, Apr 1982

Mugabe, Robert Gabriel, Zimbabwean president, Apr 1979, Jan 2002

Muir, Ramsay, *Obit* June 1941

Mujibur Rahman, Bangladeshi prime minister and president, Jan 1973, *Obit* Oct 1975

Muldoon, Robert D., New Zealand prime minister, Feb 1978, *Obit* Sept 1992

Mulroney, Brian, Canadian prime minister, Apr 1984

Muluzi, Bakili, Malawian president, Jan 2003

Mundt, Karl E., American senator, July 1948, *Obit* Oct 1974

Murdock, Victor, *Obit* Aug 1945

Murray, James E., American senator, Aug 1945, *Obit* May 1961

Murray, Patty, American senator, Aug 1994

Museveni, Yoweri, Ugandan president, Aug 1990

Mussert, Anton Adriaan, Dutch Nazi leader, Nov 1942

Muti, Ettore, *Obit* Oct 1943

Mwinyi, Ali Hassan, Tanzanian president, June 1995

Nabarro, Gerald, Nov 1963, *Obit* Jan 1974

Nabulsi, Suleiman, Mar 1957

Nakasone, Yasuhiro, Japanese prime minister, June 1983

Namboodiripad, E. M. S., Indian communist leader, Nov 1976

Narain, Jai Prakash, Indian statesman, May 1958, *Obit* Nov 1979

Narasimha Rao, P. V., Indian prime minister, Jan 1992, *Obit* Yrbk 2005

Nasheed, Mohamed, Maldivian president, Aug 2012

Nasrallah, Hassan, Lebanese guerrilla leader, Jan 2006

Nasser, Gamal Abdel, Egyptian president, Nov 1954, *Obit* Nov 1970

Navon, Yitzhak, May 1982

Nazimuddin, Khwaja, Mar 1949, *Obit* Yrbk 1964

Nenni, Pietro, Mar 1947, *Obit* Feb 1980

Neuberger, Maurine Brown, American senator, Oct 1961, *Obit* July 2000

Neumann, Emanuel, Mar 1967, *Obit* Jan 1981

Newton, Cleveland Alexander, *Obit* Oct 1945

Ney, Hubert, Nov 1956

Ngo, Dinh Diem, South Vietnamese president, Mar 1955, *Obit* Jan 1964

Nguyen, Thi Binh, Vietnamese communist leader, July 1976

Niyazov, Saparmurad, Turkmen president, Jan 2003

Nkomo, Joshua, Zimbabwean political leader, Apr 1976, *Obit* Sept 1999

Nkrumah, Kwame, Ghanaian president, July 1953, *Obit* June 1972

Nolan, W. I., *Obit* Sept 1943

Norton, Mary Teresa Hopkins, congresswoman, Nov 1944, *Obit* Nov 1959

Nu, Burmese prime minister, Yrbk 1951, *Obit* Apr 1995

Nujoma, Sam, Namibian president, Feb 1990

Nyerere, Julius K., Tanzanian president, Apr 1963, *Obit* Jan 2000

O'Connor, James Francis, *Obit* Mar 1945

O'Day, Caroline Love Goodwin, American congresswoman, *Obit* Feb 1943

O'Flanagan, Michael, Irish priest and republican, *Obit* Sept 1942

O'Kelly, Sean T., July 1948, *Obit* Jan 1967

O'Leary, James A., *Obit* May 1944

O'Neill of the Maine, Terence Marne O'Neill, prime minister of Northern Ireland, Sept 1968, *Obit* Sept 1990

O'Neill, Tip, American Speaker of the House, Apr 1974, *Obit* Mar 1994

Obote, A. Milton, Ugandan president, Apr 1981, *Obit* Yrbk 2006

Obuchi, Keizo, Japanese prime minister, May 1999, *Obit* Aug 2000

Odria, Manuel Arturo, Peruvian president, Nov 1954, *Obit* Apr 1974

Oduber Quiros, Daniel, Costa Rican president, July 1977

Ohira, Masayoshi, Japanese prime minister, Mar 1964, *Obit* Aug 1980

Ollenhauer, Erich, Jan 1953, *Obit* Feb 1964

Orlando, Vittorio Emanuele, Italian statesman, Feb 1944, *Obit* Jan 1953

Ortega Saavedra, Daniel, Nicaraguan president, Oct 1984

Ortiz, Roberto M., *Obit* Sept 1942

Osmena, Sergio, Filipino president, Sept 1944, *Obit* Yrbk 1961

Ospina Perez, Mariano, Colombian president, Feb 1950, *Obit* June 1976

Owen, Ruth Bryan, American congresswoman, Yrbk 1944, *Obit* Oct 1954

Paasikivi, Juho Kusti, Finnish president, May 1944, *Obit* Feb 1957

Pacciardi, Randolfo, Italian political leader, Mar 1944, *Obit* July 1991

Packwood, Robert, American senator, Jan 1981

Paisley, Ian R. K., Irish clergyman and political leader, Jan 1971, June 1986

Papandreou, Andreas, Greek prime minister, May 1970, Apr 1983, *Obit* Sept 1996

Papandreou, George, Greek political leader, Yrbk 1944, *Obit* Yrbk 1968

Parizeau, Jacques, Canadian economist and political leader, July 1993

Parker, Homer Cling, *Obit* July 1946

Parri, Ferruccio, Nov 1945

Passman, Otto E., American congressman, Oct 1960, *Obit* Sept 1988

Pastora Gomez, Eden, Nicaraguan political leader, July 1986

Pastrana Borrero, Misael, Colombian president, July 1971, *Obit* Nov 1997

Patel, Vallabhbhai, Indian nationalist leader, Mar 1948, *Obit* Jan 1951

Patterson, P. J., Jamaican prime minister, Feb 1995

Pavelic, Ante, Croatian Nazi leader, Aug 1942, *Obit* Feb 1960

Paz Estenssoro, Victor, Bolivian president, May 1953, *Obit* Sept 2001

Peker, Recep, Sept 1947, *Obit* May 1950

Pella, Giuseppe, Nov 1953, *Obit* Aug 1981

Pelosi, Nancy, American congresswoman and former Speaker of the House, Feb 2003

Pendergast, Tom, American political party leader, *Obit* Mar 1945

Pepper, Claude, American congressman, Feb 1941, Jan 1983, *Obit* July 1989

Perez, Carlos Andres, Venezuelan president, Feb 1976, *Obit* Yrbk 2011

Perkins, Carl D., American congressman, Feb 1968, *Obit* Sept 1984

Peron, Isabel, Argentine president, Jan 1975

Peterson, David Robert, Canadian political leader, Feb 1988

Peynado, Jacinto B., *Obit* Mar 1940

Pfost, Gracie Bowers, congresswoman, May 1955, *Obit* Oct 1965

Pham, Van Dong, Vietnamese prime minister, Feb 1975, *Obit* Sept 2000

Phelan, Michael F., *Obit* Yrbk 1941

Phillips, Morgan, British socialist leader, Sept 1949, *Obit* Feb 1963

Pholien, Joseph, Feb 1951, *Obit* Mar 1968

Phoui Sananikone, Laotian prime minister, Sept 1959, *Obit* Feb 1984

Pieck, Wilhelm, Yrbk 1949, *Obit* Nov 1960

Pierlot, Hubert, Belgian prime minister, May 1943, *Obit* Feb 1964

Pilot, Sachin, Indian member of Parliament, Jan 2007

Pindling, Lynden Oscar, Bahamian prime minister, May 1968, *Obit* Yrbk 2000

Pittman, Key, American senator, *Obit* Yrbk 1940

Plastiras, Nicholas, May 1950, *Obit* Oct 1953

Plavsic, Biljana, Bosnian Serb political leader, Feb 1998

Poage, W. R., American congressman, Yrbk 1969, *Obit* Mar 1987

Pohamba, Hifkepunye, Namibian president, Jan 2006

Pol Pot, Cambodian political leader, Apr 1980, *Obit* June 1998

Pollitt, Harry, British communist leader, May 1948, *Obit* Sept 1960

Pompidou, Georges, French president, Nov 1962, *Obit* May 1974

Porras, Belisario, Panamanian president, *Obit* Oct 1942

Potter, Charles E., American senator, Yrbk 1954

Poujade, Pierre, French political leader, Apr 1956, *Obit* Yrbk 2004

Pozsgay, Imre, Hungarian communist leader, Mar 1990

Prado Ugarteche, Manuel, Peruvian president, June 1942, *Obit* Oct 1967

Pressler, Larry, senator, Oct 1983

Preval, Rene, Haitian president, Jan 2006

Price, George C., Belizean prime minister, Aug 1984, *Obit* Yrbk 2012

Priebus, Reince, American political party leader, May 2012

Proxmire, William, American senator, June 1958, Aug 1978, *Obit* Mar 2006

Putin, Vladimir, Russian prime minister, Apr 2000, Jan 2002

Qaddafi, Muammar al-, Libyan dictator, Sept 1973, Mar 1992, *Obit* Yrbk 2011

Quayle, Dan, American vice-president, June 1989

Queuille, Henri, French prime minister, Oct 1948, *Obit* Sept 1970

Quezon, Manuel Luis, Filipino president, Aug 1941, *Obit* Sept 1944

Quirino, Elpidio, Filipino president, Sept 1948, *Obit* May 1956

Quispe Huanca, Felipe, Bolivian Indian leader, Jan 2002

Quwatli, Shukri al-, Syrian president, May 1956, *Obit* Oct 1967

Raab, Julius, Austrian chancellor, Apr 1954, *Obit* Feb 1964

Rae, Bob, Canadian political leader, Feb 1991

Raffarin, Jean-Pierre, French prime minister, Jan 2003

Rafsanjani, Hashemi, Iranian president, Nov 1989

Rahmon, Emomali, Tajik president, Jan 2007

Rains, Albert McKinley, congressman, Sept 1959, *Obit* May 1991

Rajoy, Mariano, Spanish political leader, Jan 2007

Rakosi, Matyas, Hungarian communist leader, Mar 1949, *Obit* Mar 1971

Rakowski, Mieczyslaw F., Polish communist leader, Apr 1989, *Obit* Feb 2009

Ram, Jagjivan, Indian political leader, Oct 1978, *Obit* Aug 1986

Ramaphosa, Cyril, South African political leader and businessman, Sept 1995

Randolph, Jennings, American senator, Jan 1962, *Obit* July 1998

Rau, Benegal Rama, Feb 1949, *Obit* Feb 1970

Rayburn, Sam, American congressman and Speaker of the House, Oct 1940, Mar 1949, *Obit* Jan 1962

Reece, Brazilla Carroll, American congressman, May 1946, *Obit* May 1961

Reid, Harry, American senator, Mar 2003

Relander, Lauri Kristian, *Obit* Apr 1942

Renner, Karl, Austrian president, Sept 1945, *Obit* Jan 1951

Reynolds, Albert, Irish prime minister, Sept 1994

Rhee, Syngman, Korean president, Sept 1947, *Obit* Sept 1965

Rhodes, Edgar Nelson, *Obit* May 1942

Riegle, Donald W., senator, Oct 1986

Rios, Juan Antonio, Chilean president, Apr 1942, *Obit* July 1946

Rivers, L. Mendel, American congressman, Oct 1960, *Obit* Feb 1971

Robarts, John P., Canadian political leader, Yrbk 1962, *Obit* Jan 1983

Robens of Woldingham, Alfred Robens, June 1956

Robichaud, Louis J., Canadian political leader, May 1968

Robles, Marco Aurelio, Panamanian president, June 1968, *Obit* June 1990

Rocard, Michel, French prime minister, Oct 1988

Rodino, Peter W., American congressman, Oct 1954, *Obit* Yrbk 2005

Rogers, Edith Nourse, American congresswoman, Apr 1942, *Obit* Nov 1960

Romero Barcelo, Carlos, Puerto Rican governor, Oct 1977

Ros-Lehtinen, Ileana, American congresswoman, Aug 2000

Rose, Alex, American labor leader, Yrbk 1959, *Obit* Feb 1977

Rosenberg, Alfred, German Nazi leader, Oct 1941, *Obit* Nov 1946

Rostenkowski, Dan, American congressman, Jan 1982, *Obit* Yrbk 2010

Roth, William V., American senator, Apr 1983, *Obit* Yrbk 2004

Roudebush, Richard L., congressman and veterans' leader, June 1976, *Obit* Apr 1995

Roxas y Acuna, Manuel, May 1946, *Obit* May 1948

Rubio, Marco, American senator, Apr 2011

Ruiz Cortines, Adolfo, Mexican president, Sept 1952, *Obit* Jan 1974

Rumor, Mariano, Italian prime minister, July 1969, *Obit* Mar 1990

Sabry, Hassan, *Obit* Yrbk 1940

Saionji, Kimmochi, Japanese statesman, *Obit* Jan 1941

Salinas de Gortari, Carlos, Mexican president, Mar 1989

Salisbury, Robert Arthur James Gascoyne-Cecil, British member of Parliament, Nov 1941, *Obit* Apr 1972

Sanchez de Lozada, Gonzalo, Bolivian president, Jan 2002

Sanjiva Reddy, N., Indian president, Mar 1981, *Obit* Aug 1996

Santos, Jose Eduardo dos, Angolan president, May 1994

Saracoglu, Sukru, June 1942, *Obit* Mar 1954

Sarbanes, Paul S., American senator, Jan 1997

Sarkis, Elias, Lebanese president, Mar 1979, *Obit* Aug 1985

Sarney, Jose, Brazilian president, Mar 1986

Sastroamidjojo, Ali, June 1950, *Obit* May 1975

Sauckel, Fritz, German Nazi leader, *Obit* Nov 1946

Sauve, Jeanne, Canadian government official, Aug 1984, *Obit* Mar 1993

Savimbi, Jonas, Angolan rebel leader, Aug 1986, *Obit* June 2002

Scarbrough, Roger Lumley, Jan 1958, *Obit* Sept 1969

Scelba, Mario, Italian prime minister, May 1953, *Obit* Feb 1992

Schakowsky, Jan, American congresswoman, July 2004

Scheel, Walter, Feb 1971

Scheuer, James H., American congressman, Apr 1968, *Obit* Apr 2006

Schmidt, Fritz, *Obit* Aug 1943

Schroder, Gerhard, German political leader, Yrbk 1962, *Obit* Mar 1990

Schroder, Gerhard, German chancellor, Nov 1998

Schumacher, Kurt, German socialist leader, Feb 1948, *Obit* Oct 1952

Schumer, Charles E., American senator, July 1995

Seaga, Edward P. G., Jamaican prime minister, Apr 1981

Sears, William Joseph, *Obit* May 1944

Senanayake, Don Stephen, Apr 1950, *Obit* May 1952

Senanayake, Dudley, Ceylonese prime minister, Yrbk 1952, *Obit* June 1973

Seyss-Inquart, Artur von, Austrian Nazi leader, May 1941, *Obit* Nov 1946

Shagari, Shehu, Nigerian president, Aug 1980

Shamir, Yitzhak, Israeli prime minister, Feb 1983, Yrbk 1996, *Obit* Yrbk 2012

Sharif, Nawaz, Pakistani prime minister, Sept 1998

Shastri, Lal Bahadur, Indian prime minister, Yrbk 1964, *Obit* Feb 1966

Shazar, Zalman, Feb 1964, *Obit* Nov 1974

Shipley, Jenny, New Zealand prime minister, Mar 2000

Shvernik, Nikolai, Soviet communist leader, Oct 1951, *Obit* Feb 1971

Siles Zuazo, Hernan, Bolivian president, Sept 1958, June 1985, *Obit* Oct 1996

Siles, Hernando, Bolivian president, *Obit* Jan 1943

Silva, Benedita da, Brazilian governor and political leader, Jan 2002

Simmons, Furnifold McLendel, American senator, *Obit* Jan 1940

Simon, Paul, American senator, Jan 1988, *Obit* Yrbk 2004

Simpson, Alan K., American senator, Oct 1990

Simpson, Kenneth F., *Obit* Mar 1941

Simpson, Richard M., Yrbk 1953, *Obit* Mar 1960

Sims, Hugo S., Oct 1949

Sinclair, Archibald, British political leader, Sept 1940, *Obit* Oct 1970

Singh, Manmohan, Indian prime minister, Jan 2005

Skinner, Dennis, British member of Parliament, Jan 2002

Slaughter, Louise M., American congresswoman, Apr 1999

Slim, Mongi, Tunisian political leader, Mar 1958, *Obit* Yrbk 1969

Small, John Humphrey, *Obit* Sept 1946

Smallwood, Joseph R., Canadian political leader, Feb 1953, *Obit* Mar 1992

Smathers, George A., American senator, Apr 1954, *Obit* June 2007

Smetona, Antanas, Lithuanian president, *Obit* Feb 1944

Smith, Alfred Emanuel, American governor, Sept 1944

Smith, Clyde Harold, *Obit* May 1940

Smith, Ellison DuRant, American senator, *Obit* Jan 1945

Smith, Ian Douglas, Rhodesian prime minister, May 1966, *Obit* Feb 2008

Smith, Margaret Chase, American senator, Feb 1945, Mar 1962, *Obit* Aug 1995

Smith, Mary Louise, American political party leader, Oct 1976, *Obit* Nov 1997

Smoot, Reed, American senator, *Obit* Mar 1941

Snell, Henry Snell, May 1941

Snowe, Olympia J., American senator, May 1995

Soekarno, Indonesian president, Sept 1947, *Obit* Sept 1970

Solarz, Stephen J., American congressman, Nov 1986, *Obit* Yrbk 2011

Sophoulis, Themistocles, Nov 1947, *Obit* Sept 1949

Soukup, Frantisek, *Obit* Yrbk 1940

Souvanna Phouma, Nov 1962, *Obit* Mar 1984

Spangler, Harrison Earl, lawyer, Aug 1943, *Obit* Oct 1965

Sparkman, John J., American senator, Mar 1950, *Obit* Jan 1986

Speaks, John Charles, *Obit* Yrbk 1945

Specter, Arlen, American senator, Aug 1988, Aug 2009, *Obit* Yrbk 2012

St. George, Katharine, congresswoman, Yrbk 1947, *Obit* July 1983

St. Laurent, Louis S., Mar 1948, *Obit* Oct 1973

Stalin, Joseph, Soviet dictator, Mar 1942, *Obit* Apr 1953

Stanfield, Robert Lorne, Canadian political leader, Yrbk 1958, *Obit* Yrbk 2004

Stanfield, Robert Nelson, *Obit* June 1945

Stanley, Oliver, Apr 1943, *Obit* Jan 1951

Steagall, Henry Bascom, *Obit* Jan 1944

Steele, Michael S., American political party leader, July 2004

Stevens, Ted, American senator, Oct 2001, *Obit* Yrbk 2010

Stoph, Willi, East German communist leader, Oct 1960, *Obit* Aug 1999

Strasser, Otto, German Nazi leader, Sept 1940, *Obit* Oct 1974

Stratton, Samuel S., congressman, Jan 1966, *Obit* Jan 1991

Streicher, Julius, German Nazi leader, *Obit* Nov 1946

Strijdom, Johannes Gerhardus, May 1956, *Obit* Nov 1958

Suarez, Adolfo, Spanish prime minister, May 1977

Suchocka, Hanna, Polish prime minister, Jan 1994

Suhrawardy, Huseyn Shaheed, Pakistani prime minister, Apr 1957, *Obit* Jan 1964

Sullivan, Gael, May 1947, *Obit* Jan 1957

Sullivan, Leonor K., American congresswoman, Yrbk 1954, *Obit* Oct 1988

Summerfield, Arthur Ellsworth, American postmaster general, Sept 1952, *Obit* June 1972

Sunay, Cevdet, Mar 1969, *Obit* Aug 1982

Sung, Ching-ling, Chinese political leader and wife of stateman Sun Yat-sen, Apr 1944, *Obit* July 1981

Suslov, Mikhail Andreevich, Soviet communist leader, Feb 1957, *Obit* Mar 1982

Suzuki, Zenko, Japanese prime minister, Jan 1981, *Obit* Yrbk 2004

Sveinn Bjornsson, Aug 1944, *Obit* Mar 1952

Svinhufvud, Pehr Evind, *Obit* Apr 1944

Szold, Henrietta, American Zionist leader, Jan 1940, *Obit* Apr 1945

Taft, Robert A., American senator, May 1940, Apr 1948, *Obit* Oct 1953

Talabani, Jalal, Iraqi president, Jan 2005

Tambo, Oliver, South African political leader, Apr 1987, *Obit* June 1993

Tanaka, Kakuei, Japanese prime minister, Yrbk 1972, *Obit* Feb 1994

Taylor, Charles, Liberian president, Sept 1992

Taylor, Edward T., *Obit* Oct 1941

Taylor, Glen Hearst, American senator, Oct 1947, *Obit* July 1984

Teague, Olin E., congressman, Mar 1952, *Obit* Apr 1981

Terboven, Josef, German war criminal, Nov 1941, *Obit* June 1945

Terra, Gabriel, Uruguayan president, *Obit* Nov 1942

Thomas, John W., *Obit* Yrbk 1945

Thompson, Frank, American congressman, July 1959, *Obit* Sept 1989

Thompson, George L., *Obit* Oct 1941

Thompson, Ruth, congresswoman, Nov 1951

Thorning-Schmidt, Helle, Prime minister of Denmark, May 2012

Thorpe, Jeremy, British member of Parliament, Oct 1974

Timberlake, Charles B., American congressman, *Obit* July 1941

Tindemans, Leo, Belgian statesman, Mar 1978

Tinkham, George H., Apr 1942, *Obit* Oct 1956

Tito, Josip Broz, Yugoslav head of state, Nov 1943, Mar 1955, *Obit* June 1980

Togliatti, Palmiro, Italian communist leader, Nov 1947, *Obit* Oct 1964

Tolbert, William R., Liberian president, Mar 1974, *Obit* June 1980

Toure, Ahmed Sekou, Guinean president, June 1959, *Obit* May 1984

Trudeau, Pierre Elliott, Canadian prime minister, Nov 1968, *Obit* Jan 2001

Trygger, Ernst, *Obit* Nov 1943

Tshombe, Moise, Congolese prime minister, Yrbk 1961, *Obit* Sept 1969

Tsongas, Paul, American senator, July 1981, *Obit* Mar 1997

Tsvangirai, Morgan, Zimbabwean prime minister, Jan 2005

Tubman, William Vacanarat Shadrach, Liberian president, Jan 1955, *Obit* Sept 1971

Turbay Ayala, Julio Cesar, Colombian president, July 1979

Turner, John, Canadian prime minister, Nov 1984

Tweed, Thomas Frederic, *Obit* Jan 1940

Tydings, Millard E., American senator, Jan 1945, *Obit* Apr 1961

Ubico, Jorge, Guatemalan president, June 1942, *Obit* July 1946

Ulbricht, Walter, East German communist leader, July 1952, *Obit* Oct 1973

Ullman, Al, congressman, Aug 1975, *Obit* Jan 1987

Underhill, Charles Lee, *Obit* Mar 1946

Unruh, Jesse M., American state legislator and official, Oct 1969, *Obit* Sept 1987

Urrutia Lleo, Manuel, Cuban president, May 1959, *Obit* Aug 1981

Vajpayee, Atal Bihari, Indian prime minister, Aug 2000, Jan 2002

Van Nuys, Frederick, *Obit* Mar 1944

Vargas, Antonio, Ecuadorian Quechua leader, Jan 2004

Vargas, Getulio, Brazilian president, Aug 1940, May 1951, *Obit* Oct 1954

Velasco Ibarra, Jose Maria, Ecuadorian president, Nov 1952, *Obit* May 1979

Velde, Harold H., American congressman, Mar 1953, *Obit* Jan 1986

Venizelos, Sophocles, Yrbk 1950, *Obit* Mar 1964

Verwoerd, Hendrik Frensch, South African prime minister, Mar 1959, *Obit* Nov 1966

Vienot, Pierre, *Obit* Oct 1944

Vigidis Finnbogadottir, Icelandic president, May 1987

Vike-Freiberga, Vaira, Latvian president, Jan 2005

Vinson, Carl, American congressman, Apr 1942, *Obit* July 1981

Voorhis, Jerry, American congressman, Aug 1941, *Obit* Nov 1984

Vorster, B. J., South African prime minister, June 1967, *Obit* Nov 1983

Vukmanovic-Tempo, Svetozar, Yrbk 1958

Wade, Abdoulaye, Senegalese president, Jan 2006

Wadsworth, James W., July 1943, *Obit* Sept 1952

Wallace, Euan, *Obit* Apr 1941

Wang Jingwei, Chinese political leader and collaborationist, May 1940, *Obit* Jan 1945

Warburton, Herbert B., Nov 1951

Wason, Edward H., *Obit* Apr 1941

Waters, Maxine, American congresswoman, Nov 1992

Watkinson, Harold Arthur Watkinson, Mar 1960

Waverley, John Anderson, British statesman, July 1941, *Obit* Mar 1958

Waxman, Henry Arnold, American congressman, July 1992

Weis, Jessica, congresswoman, Yrbk 1959, *Obit* June 1963

Weiss, Ted, congressman, Oct 1985, *Obit* Nov 1992

Wen Jiabao, Chinese prime minister, Jan 2003

Wetter, Ernst, Feb 1942

Wheat, William Howard, *Obit* Apr 1944

White, Wallace H., May 1948, *Obit* May 1952

Williams, Thomas Sutler, *Obit* May 1940

Wilson, Harold, British prime minister, Feb 1948, May 1963, *Obit* July 1995

Wirth, Timothy E., senator, Mar 1991

Wise, Stephen Samuel, American rabbi, July 1941, *Obit* May 1949

Witos, Wincenty, *Obit* Yrbk 1945

Wright, Jim, American Speaker of the House, Apr 1979

Yahya Khan, A. M., Jan 1971, *Obit* Oct 1980

Yamani, Ahmed Zaki, Saudi Arabian cabinet member, Sept 1975

Yaroslavski, Emel'yan Mikhailovich, Soviet communist leader, *Obit* Jan 1944

Yates, Sidney, American congressman, Aug 1993, *Obit* Jan 2001

Yeltsin, Boris, Russian president, Jan 1989, *Obit* June 2007

Yingluck Shinawatra, Thai prime minister, Oct 2011

Yonai, Mitsumasa, Jan 1940, *Obit* June 1948

Youlou, Fulbert, Congolese political leader, Yrbk 1962, *Obit* June 1972

Young, Milton R., American senator, Yrbk 1954, *Obit* July 1983

Young, Stephen M., American senator, Oct 1959, *Obit* Feb 1985

Yui, O. K., May 1955, *Obit* Sept 1960

Yushchenko, Viktor, Ukrainian president, Jan 2005

Zablocki, Clement, American congressman, June 1958, June 1983, *Obit* Jan 1984

Zail Singh, Indian president, Sept 1987, *Obit* Mar 1995

Zamora, Ruben, Salvadoran rebel leader, Sept 1991

Zapotocky, Antonin, June 1953, *Obit* Jan 1958

Zardari, Asif Ali, Pakistani president, Jan 2009

Zeeland, Paul van, Mar 1950

Zhirinovsky, Vladimir, Russian political leader, Nov 1995

Zhivkov, Todor, Bulgarian communist leader, Jan 1976, *Obit* Oct 1998

Zuma, Jacob, South African president, Jan 2006

Zyuganov, Gennady, Russian communist leader, Oct 1996

Political party leaders

Alcorn, Hugh Meade, American lawyer and political party leader, May 1957, *Obit* Mar 1992

Baker, Roy, American lawyer, Nov 1948

Butler, Paul M., American political party leader, May 1955, *Obit* Feb 1962

Duvieusart, Jean, Sept 1950

Endeley, E. M. L., July 1959

Foreman, Clark, Oct 1948, *Obit* Aug 1977

Gatov, Elizabeth Rudel, Yrbk 1961

Grotewohl, Otto, July 1950, *Obit* Nov 1964

Johnston, Victor A., July 1949, *Obit* May 1967

Kawakami, Jotaro, Mar 1963, *Obit* Jan 1966

Longo, Luigi, Feb 1966, *Obit* Jan 1981

Macauley, Jane Hamilton, Sept 1949

Mayes, Rose Gorr, May 1950

Mende, Erich, July 1966

Mitchell, Stephen Arnold, American lawyer and political party leader, Oct 1952, *Obit* June 1974

Ollenhauer, Erich, Jan 1953, *Obit* Feb 1964

Priebus, Reince, American political party leader, May 2012

Rose, Alex, American labor leader, Yrbk 1959, *Obit* Feb 1977

Smith, Mary Louise, American political party leader, Oct 1976, *Obit* Nov 1997

Sullivan, Gael, May 1947, *Obit* Jan 1957

Venizelos, Sophocles, Yrbk 1950, *Obit* Mar 1964

Political prisoners

Bakshi, Ghulam Mohammad, June 1956, *Obit* Sept 1972

Xu Wenli, Chinese dissident, Jan 2003

Political scientists

Al-Baghdadi, Ahmad, Kuwaiti political scientist, Jan 2004

Barnard, James Lynn, American political scientist, *Obit* Oct 1941

Bremmer, Ian, American international relations specialist, Aug 2013

Clark, Evans, Sept 1947, *Obit* Nov 1970

Cordier, Andrew Wellington, Apr 1950, *Obit* Sept 1975

Hadley, Stephen J., American national security adviser, Nov 2006

Khalilzad, Zalmay, Afghan-American diplomat, Aug 2006

Mamdani, Mahmood, Ugandan political scientist, Jan 2010

Scammon, Richard M., political scientist and public opinion analyst, Mar 1971, *Obit* Sept 2001

Shikaki, Khalil, Palestinian political scientist, Jan 2004

Skocpol, Theda, American political scientist, Aug 2000

Tobin, Harold J., *Obit* Aug 1942

Wambaugh, Sarah, authority on plebiscites, Apr 1946, *Obit* Jan 1956

Political workers

Bush, Dorothy Vredenburgh, American political party secretary, July 1948

Hughes, Karen, American diplomat and presidential adviser, Oct 2001

Tijerina, Reies Lopez, American political activist, July 1971

Politicians

Abbas, Ferhat, Algerian political leader, Mar 1961, *Obit* Feb 1986

Abbas, Mahmoud, Palestinian political leader, June 1999

Abdul Rahman, Malaysian prime minister, Yrbk 1957, *Obit* Mar 1991

Abdullah, Mohammad, Indian political leader, Nov 1952, *Obit* Jan 1983

Abiola, Moshood Kashimawo, Nigerian political leader, Sept 1998, *Obit* Nov 1998

Adami, Edward Fenech, Maltese prime minister, Jan 2003

Adams, Grantley Herbert, Barbadian prime minister, Sept 1958, *Obit* Jan 1972

Adenauer, Konrad, German statesman, July 1949, Apr 1958, *Obit* June 1967

Agnew, Spiro, American vice-president, Yrbk 1968, *Obit* Nov 1996

Ahern, Bertie, Irish prime minister, July 1998

Ahmadu, Alhaji, Nigerian political leader, July 1957

Al-Glawi, Thami al-Mezouari, Sept 1954, *Obit* Mar 1956

Al-Husseini, Faisal, Palestinian political leader, Jan 1998

Al-Jamali, Mohammed Fadhel, Iraqi prime minister, Jan 1954, *Obit* Aug 1997

Al-Maliki, Nuri Kamal, Iraqi prime minister, Jan 2006

Al-Said, Nuri, Iraqi prime minister, June 1955, *Obit* Oct 1958

Ali, Chaudhri Muhammad, Pakistani prime minister, Feb 1956

Alkatiri, Mari, East Timorese prime minister, Jan 2006

Ameringer, Oscar, socialist leader, *Obit* Yrbk 1943

Amini, Ali, Iranian prime minister, Jan 1962

Anderson, Sigurd, governor, Sept 1953, *Obit* Mar 1991

Argeseanu, George, Romanian prime minister, *Obit* Jan 1941

Arias Navarro, Carlos, Spanish prime minister, Oct 1974, *Obit* Jan 1990

Ariyoshi, George R., governor, Jan 1985

Ashrawi, Hanan, Palestinian political leader, Mar 1992

Awolowo, Obafemi, Nigerian prime minister, July 1957, *Obit* July 1987

Azad, Abulkalam, Indian political leader, July 1942, *Obit* May 1958

Aznar, Jose Maria, Spanish prime minister, Jan 2002

Bailey, Consuelo Northrop, American lawyer and state legislator, June 1954

Baldwin, C. B., American political leader, Nov 1943

Balewa, Abubakar Tafawa, Nigerian prime minister, Sept 1961, *Obit* Feb 1966

Bandaranaike, S. W. R. D., Sri Lankan prime minister, Sept 1956, *Obit* Nov 1959

Bandaranaike, Sirimavo, Sri Lankan prime minister, May 1961, *Obit* Jan 2001

Banerjee, Mamata, Indian political leader, Nov 2011

Barre, Raymond, French prime minister, July 1977, *Obit* Yrbk 2007

Barrow, Errol W., Barbadian prime minister, Sept 1968, *Obit* July 1987

Bennett, W. A. C., Canadian political leader, May 1953, *Obit* May 1979

Benson, Allan L., American socialist leader, *Obit* Oct 1940

Berlinguer, Enrico, Italian communist leader, July 1976, *Obit* Aug 1984

Berri, Nabih, Lebanese political leader, Nov 1985

Bhutto, Benazir, Pakistani prime minister, July 1986, *Obit* Apr 2008

Bildt, Carl, Swedish prime minister, Jan 1993

Blue, Robert Donald, American governor, Yrbk 1948, *Obit* Feb 1990

Bonomi, Ivanhoe, Aug 1944, *Obit* May 1951

Bordes, Pierre-Louis, *Obit* Sept 1943

Bose, Subhas Chandra, Indian political leader, June 1944, *Obit* Yrbk 1945

Bourassa, Robert, Canadian economist and political leader, Sept 1976, *Obit* Jan 1997

Boyle, William Marshall, American political leader and lawyer, June 1949, *Obit* Nov 1961

Bradford, Robert F., governor, Yrbk 1948, *Obit* May 1983

Brewer, Jan, American governor, Jan 2011

Brookeborough, Basil Stanlake Brooke, Northern Ireland political leader, June 1948, *Obit* Oct 1973

Bruton, John, Irish prime minister, Nov 1996

Bryant, C. Farris, American governor, Sept 1961, *Obit* Yrbk 2002

Bryant, Gyude, Liberian businessman and interim leader, Jan 2005

Burns, John A., American governor, Feb 1972, *Obit* June 1975

Bush, Dorothy Vredenburgh, American political party secretary, July 1948

Bustamante, Alexander, Jamaican prime minister, May 1965, *Obit* Sept 1977

Buthelezi, Mangosuthu, South African Zulu statesman, Oct 1986

Caetano, Marcello, Portuguese prime minister, Mar 1970, *Obit* Jan 1981

Cahill, William Thomas, governor, June 1970, *Obit* Sept 1996

Caillaux, Joseph, French statesman, *Obit* Jan 1945

Calderon, Sila M., Puerto Rican governor, Nov 2001

Caldwell, Millard Fillmore, American governor, Nov 1948, *Obit* Feb 1985

Calero, Adolfo, Nicaraguan rebel leader, Oct 1987, *Obit* Yrbk 2012

Carrero Blanco, Luis, Oct 1973, *Obit* Feb 1974

Carrillo, Santiago, Spanish communist leader, June 1977, *Obit* Yrbk 2012

Cavaco Silva, Anibal, Portuguese prime minister, Mar 1991

Chaban-Delmas, Jacques, French prime minister, July 1958, *Obit* Feb 2001

Charles, Eugenia, Dominica prime minister, Oct 1986, *Obit* Yrbk 2006

Chee, Soon Juan, Singaporean political leader, Jan 2004

Chernomyrdin, Viktor, Russian prime minister, Aug 1998, *Obit* Yrbk 2011

Chifley, Joseph B., Aug 1945, *Obit* July 1951

Chuan Leekpai, Thai prime minister, Nov 1998

Clark, Helen, New Zealand prime minister, Nov 2000

Coates, Gordon, *Obit* July 1943

Cobham, Charles John Lyttelton, Apr 1962

Collins, Martha Layne, governor, Jan 1986

Colombo, Emilio, Apr 1971, *Obit* Yrbk 2013

Colquitt, Oscar Branch, *Obit* Mar 1940

Cosgrave, Liam, Irish prime minister, June 1977

Cotton, Joseph Bell, *Obit* Sept 1940

Craigavon, James Craig, Northern Ireland political leader, *Obit* Jan 1941

Cross, Burton Melvin, governor, Apr 1954, *Obit* Jan 1999

Cunhal, Alvaro, Portuguese communist leader, Sept 1975, *Obit* Yrbk 2005

D'Aubuisson, Roberto, Salvadoran political leader, July 1983, *Obit* Apr 1992

Daluege, Kurt, German Nazi leader, *Obit* Yrbk 1946

Davidovitch, Ljuba, *Obit* Mar 1940

Davis, Gray, American governor, June 1999

Davis, Jonathan M., governor, *Obit* Aug 1943

Davis, William G., Canadian political leader, May 1973

De Maiziere, Lothar, German political leader, Aug 1990

De Quay, Jan Eduard, Dutch prime minister, May 1963, *Obit* Aug 1985

De Sapio, Carmine G., American political leader, Sept 1955, *Obit* Yrbk 2004

Debre, Michel, French prime minister, May 1959, *Obit* Oct 1996

Deloncle, Eugene, French political leader, *Obit* Feb 1944

Demirel, Suleyman, Turkish prime minister, Feb 1980

Dempsey, John Noel, governor, June 1961, *Obit* Sept 1989

Deng Xiaoping, Chinese communist leader, May 1976, June 1994, *Obit* Apr 1997

Desai, Morarji, Indian prime minister, Sept 1958, Jan 1978, *Obit* June 1995

Deukmejian, George, governor, June 1983

Deutsch, Julius, Nov 1944, *Obit* Mar 1968

Dickinson, Luren D., *Obit* June 1943

Diefenbaker, John George, Canadian prime minister, May 1957, *Obit* Oct 1979

Docking, George, governor, June 1958, *Obit* Mar 1964

Doriot, Jacques, French political leader and wartime collaborationist, Nov 1940

Douglas, Denzil, Saint Kitts-Nevis prime minister, Jan 2007

Duclos, Jacques, French communist leader, Feb 1946, *Obit* June 1975

Duplessis, Maurice LeNoblet, Canadian provincial premier, Oct 1948, *Obit* Nov 1959

Dwinell, Lane, governor, June 1956, *Obit* June 1997

Ecevit, Bulent, Turkish prime minister, Jan 1975, *Obit* Yrbk 2007

Egan, William Allen, American governor, Sept 1959, *Obit* July 1984

El-Nahas, Mustafa, July 1951, *Obit* Nov 1965

Ellington, Buford, governor, Sept 1960, *Obit* May 1972

Erlander, Tage F., Swedish prime minister, Oct 1947, *Obit* Aug 1985

Eshkol, Levi, Israeli prime minister, Oct 1963, *Obit* Apr 1969

Fagerholm, Karl August, Finnish prime minister, Oct 1948, *Obit* July 1984

Falldin, Thorbjorn, Swedish prime minister, May 1978

Fanfani, Amintore, Italian prime minister, Oct 1958, *Obit* Mar 2000

Fatemi, Hossein, May 1953, *Obit* Jan 1955

Faubus, Orval, American governor, Oct 1956, *Obit* Feb 1995

Faulkner, Brian, prime minister of Northern Ireland, Feb 1972, *Obit* May 1977

Ferguson, James Edward, governor, *Obit* Nov 1944

Filov, Bogdan, Apr 1941

Fine, John Sydney, governor, Sept 1951, *Obit* July 1978

Fini, Gianfranco, Italian political leader, Jan 2003

Fisher, John Stuchell, governor, *Obit* Aug 1940

FitzGerald, Garret, Irish prime minister, Aug 1984, *Obit* Yrbk 2011

Flynn, Edward J., American political leader, Sept 1940, *Obit* Oct 1953

Folsom, James Elisha, American governor, Sept 1949, *Obit* Jan 1988

Foreman, Clark, Oct 1948, *Obit* Aug 1977

Fraser, Peter, May 1942, *Obit* Jan 1951

Fukuda, Takeo, Japanese prime minister, June 1974, *Obit* Sept 1995

Gabbard, Tulsi, July 2013

Gandhi, Indira, Indian prime minister, Oct 1959, June 1966, *Obit* Jan 1985

Gandhi, Sonia, Italian wife of Indian Prime Minister Rajiv Gandhi, May 1998

Garcia Medina, Amalia, Mexican provincial governor, Jan 2004

Gary, Raymond, governor, Oct 1955, *Obit* Feb 1994

Gasperi, Alcide de, Italian statesman, Yrbk 1946, *Obit* Oct 1954

Gerhardsen, Einar, Norwegian prime minister, Mar 1949, *Obit* Nov 1987

Gilmore, James S., governor, June 2001

Goebbels, Joseph, German Nazi leader, Sept 1941, *Obit* Yrbk 1991

Goodrich, James P., *Obit* Oct 1940

Graham, Horace F., *Obit* Jan 1942

Grandi, Dino, Italian political leader, July 1943, *Obit* July 1988

Grantham, Alexander, May 1954

Graves, Bibb, governor, *Obit* May 1942

Gul, Abdullah, Turkish prime minister, Jan 2007

Habash, George, Palestinian nationalist leader, Mar 1988, *Obit* Yrbk 2008

Hadi Awang, Malaysian Islamic leader, Jan 2004

Haley, Nikki, American governor, Feb 2011

Halim, Mustafa ben, Libyan prime minister, Sept 1956

Hall, Gus, American communist leader, May 1973, *Obit* Jan 2001

Hallinan, Vincent, American lawyer, Oct 1952, *Obit* Nov 1992

Halprin, Rose L., June 1950

Handley, Harold W., July 1960, *Obit* Nov 1972

Haniyeh, Ismail, Palestinian prime minister, Jan 2006

Hansson, Per Albin, Oct 1942, *Obit* Nov 1946

Hashimoto, Ryutaro, Japanese prime minister, Feb 1998, *Obit* Yrbk 2006

Hatta, Mohammad, Indonesian prime minister, Yrbk 1949, *Obit* Yrbk 1991

Haughey, Charles, Irish prime minister, Feb 1981, *Obit* Yrbk 2006

Haya de la Torre, Victor Raul, Peruvian political leader, June 1942, *Obit* Sept 1979

Hedtoft, Hans, Mar 1949, *Obit* Mar 1955

Heitkamp, Heidi, state attorney general, Sept 2013

Henriot, Philippe, French political leader, *Obit* Aug 1944

Henry, Brad, American governor, Jan 2005

Hepburn, Mitchell Frederick, Canadian provincial premier, Yrbk 1941, *Obit* Feb 1953

Hermann Jonasson, Aug 1941

Hernandez-Colon, Rafael, Puerto Rican governor, May 1973

Heydrich, Reinhard, German Nazi leader, *Obit* July 1942, July 1942

Himmler, Heinrich, German Nazi leader, June 1941, *Obit* June 1945

Hodza, Milan, *Obit* Aug 1944

Hoffman, Johannes, Apr 1950

Holmes, Robert D., July 1958

Holyoake, Keith Jacka, New Zealand prime minister, Feb 1963, *Obit* Feb 1984

Hosokawa, Morihiro, Japanese prime minister, May 1994

Howard, John Winston, Australian prime minister, Mar 1999

Hu Yaobang, Chinese communist leader, Nov 1983, *Obit* June 1989

Hull, Jane Dee, American governor, Feb 2002

Hurley, Charles F., American governor, *Obit* May 1946

Huvayda, Amir Abbas, Oct 1971, *Obit* June 1979

Iglesias Pantin, Santiago, Puerto Rican labor leader, Jan 1940

James, Arthur Horace, governor, July 1940, *Obit* June 1973

Janson, Paul Emile, *Obit* Aug 1944

Jiang Qing, Chinese communist leader and wife of Mao Zedong, June 1975, *Obit* Jan 1992

Jinnah, Mohamed Ali, Pakistani political leader, May 1942, *Obit* Oct 1948

Johnson, Sonia, American feminist, Feb 1985

Johnston, Victor A., July 1949, *Obit* May 1967

Jumblatt, Kamal, Lebanese political leader, Jan 1977, *Obit* Jan 1977

Kaganovich, L. M., Soviet communist leader, Apr 1942, Oct 1955, *Obit* Sept 1991

Kaifu, Toshiki, Japanese prime minister, June 1990

Kallay, Nicholas, Hungarian prime minister, June 1942, *Obit* May 1967

Kaltenbrunner, Ernst, Austrian Nazi leader, Apr 1943, *Obit* Nov 1946

Kampmann, Viggo, Jan 1961, *Obit* July 1976

Karami, Rashid, Lebanese prime minister, Nov 1959, *Obit* July 1987

Kardelj, Edvard, Yugoslav communist leader, Yrbk 1949, *Obit* Apr 1979

Katayama, Tetsu, Jan 1948

Kawakami, Jotaro, Mar 1963, *Obit* Jan 1966

Kelly, Petra, German political leader, Mar 1984, *Obit* Jan 1993

Khaleda Zia, Bangladeshi prime minister, Jan 2003

Khan, Liaquat Ali, June 1948, *Obit* Yrbk 1951

Khomeini, Ruhollah, Iranian religious and political leader, Nov 1979, *Obit* July 1989

Kiir, Salva, Sudanese rebel and vice-president, Jan 2005

King, Angus, governor, Apr 2013

Kishi, Nobusuke, Japanese prime minister, June 1957, *Obit* Sept 1987

Klaus, Josef, Austrian chancellor, Jan 1965, *Obit* Oct 2001

Kohl, Helmut, German chancellor, Aug 1977

Koirala, Girija Prasad, Nepalese prime minister, Jan 2006, *Obit* Yrbk 2010

Kolarov, Vassil, Yrbk 1949, *Obit* Mar 1950

Konoye, Fumimaro, Japanese prime minister, Sept 1940, *Obit* Feb 1946

Kotelawala, John Lionel, Sri Lankan prime minister, Oct 1955

Kozlowski, Leon, *Obit* July 1944

Kumaratunga, Chandrika Bandaranaike, Sri Lankan prime minister, Jan 1996

La Rocque, Francois de, French political leader, *Obit* June 1946

Laffoon, Ruby, governor, *Obit* Apr 1941

Lange, David, New Zealand prime minister, Sept 1985, *Obit* Yrbk 2005

Le Pen, Jean-Marie, French political leader, Jan 1988

Leader, George Michael, American governor, Jan 1956, *Obit* Yrbk 2013

Lee, Bum Suk, Jan 1949

Lee, Kuan Yew, Singaporean prime minister, Nov 1959, Jan 1995

Lee, Martin, Chinese lawyer and political leader, July 1997

Lemass, Sean, Irish prime minister, Mar 1960, *Obit* June 1971

Leopold, Alice, government official, Jan 1955

Lesage, Jean, Canadian government official, Nov 1961, *Obit* Feb 1981

Ley, Robert, German Nazi leader, Sept 1940, *Obit* Yrbk 1945

Ligachev, Yegor K., Soviet communist leader, Aug 1990

Liu Shaoqi, Chinese communist leader, Oct 1957, *Obit* Yrbk 1974

Lloyd George, David Lloyd George, British statesman, Nov 1944, *Obit* May 1945

Long, Earl K., American governor, Yrbk 1950, *Obit* Nov 1960

Loomis, Orland S., *Obit* Jan 1943

Lougheed, Peter, Canadian political leader, Aug 1979

Loveless, Herschel Cellel, governor, July 1958, *Obit* July 1989

Lumumba, Patrice, Congolese prime minister, Nov 1960, *Obit* Apr 1961

Lynch, John Mary, Irish prime minister, May 1967, *Obit* Feb 2000

Mahathir bin Mohamad, Malaysian prime minister, Aug 1988

Maher, Ahmed, *Obit* Apr 1945

Maher, Aly, Mar 1952, *Obit* Nov 1960

Malan, Daniel Francois, South African prime minister, Apr 1949, *Obit* Apr 1959

Malvern, Godfrey Martin Huggins, Rhodesian prime minister, Nov 1956, *Obit* June 1971

Mandela, Winnie, South African political leader and wife of Nelson Mandela, Jan 1986

Manley, Michael, Jamaican prime minister, Jan 1976, *Obit* May 1997

Manley, Norman Washington, Jamaican prime minister, Nov 1959, *Obit* Nov 1969

Manning, Ernest, Canadian political leader, Yrbk 1959, *Obit* May 1996

Manning, Patrick A. M., Trinidadian prime minister, Jan 2006

Marchais, Georges, French communist leader, June 1976, *Obit* Jan 1998

Margai, Milton Augustus Striery, Sierra Leonean prime minister, Feb 1962, *Obit* June 1964

Markovic, Ante, Yugoslav prime minister, Nov 1991, *Obit* Yrbk 2012

Marshall, David, Singaporean lawyer and political leader, July 1956, *Obit* Feb 1996

Martz, Judy, American governor, Mar 2005

Masuku, Mario, Swazi political leader, Jan 2006

Maw, Herbert B., governor, Oct 1948, *Obit* Jan 1991

Mayer, Daniel, French socialist leader, Nov 1949

Mboya, Tom, Kenyan political and labor leader, June 1959, *Obit* Sept 1969

McCall, Tom, American governor, June 1974, *Obit* Mar 1983

McGovern, Francis Edward, American governor, *Obit* June 1946

McGuinty, Dalton, Canadian provincial premier, Feb 2013

McMahon, William, Australian prime minister, Sept 1971, *Obit* May 1988

McMath, Sidney Sanders, American governor, Mar 1949, *Obit* Jan 2004

Meciar, Vladimir, Slovak prime minister, July 1994

Menderes, Adnan, Turkish prime minister, Nov 1954, *Obit* Nov 1961

Menzies, Robert Gordon, Australian prime minister, Feb 1941, Jan 1950, *Obit* July 1978

Meta, Ilir, Albanian prime minister, Feb 2002

Miki, Takeo, Japanese prime minister, Apr 1975, *Obit* Jan 1989

Mikolajczyk, Stanislaw, Polish political leader, Mar 1944, *Obit* Feb 1967

Miller, Leszek, Polish prime minister, Jan 2002

Minner, Ruth Ann, American governor, Aug 2001

Mitsotakis, Constantine, Greek prime minister, Nov 1990

Mook, Hubertus J. van, Apr 1942, *Obit* July 1965

Moro, Aldo, Italian prime minister, June 1964, *Obit* June 1978

Mosaddeq, Mohammad, Iranian prime minister, May 1951, *Obit* May 1967

Mousavi, Mir Hossein, Iranian presidential candidate and former prime minister, Sept 2009

Mowinckel, Johan Ludwig, *Obit* Nov 1943

Mulcair, Thomas, Nov 2013

Mussert, Anton Adriaan, Dutch Nazi leader, Nov 1942

Nakasone, Yasuhiro, Japanese prime minister, June 1983

Nasrallah, Hassan, Lebanese guerrilla leader, Jan 2006

Nenni, Pietro, Mar 1947, *Obit* Feb 1980

Nguyen, Thi Binh, Vietnamese communist leader, July 1976

Nice, Harry, *Obit* Apr 1941

Nkomo, Joshua, Zimbabwean political leader, Apr 1976, *Obit* Sept 1999

Nu, Burmese prime minister, Yrbk 1951, *Obit* Apr 1995

O'Flanagan, Michael, Irish priest and republican, *Obit* Sept 1942

O'Neill of the Maine, Terence Marne O'Neill, prime minister of Northern Ireland, Sept 1968, *Obit* Sept 1990

O'Neill, William A., American governor, Feb 1985, *Obit* Yrbk 2008

Ohira, Masayoshi, Japanese prime minister, Mar 1964, *Obit* Aug 1980

Ollenhauer, Erich, Jan 1953, *Obit* Feb 1964

Orlando, Vittorio Emanuele, Italian statesman, Feb 1944, *Obit* Jan 1953

Paisley, Ian R. K., Irish clergyman and political leader, Jan 1971, June 1986

Papandreou, George, Greek political leader, Yrbk 1944, *Obit* Yrbk 1968

Pardee, George C., *Obit* Oct 1941

Parizeau, Jacques, Canadian economist and political leader, July 1993

Parri, Ferruccio, Nov 1945

Pastora Gomez, Eden, Nicaraguan political leader, July 1986

Pataki, George, American governor, Apr 1996

Patel, Vallabhbhai, Indian nationalist leader, Mar 1948, *Obit* Jan 1951

Patterson, John, American governor, Nov 1960

Patterson, P. J., Jamaican prime minister, Feb 1995

Pavelic, Ante, Croatian Nazi leader, Aug 1942, *Obit* Feb 1960

Peterson, David Robert, Canadian political leader, Feb 1988

Peterson, Val, governor and presidential aide, June 1949, *Obit* Jan 1984

Pholien, Joseph, Feb 1951, *Obit* Mar 1968

Phoui Sananikone, Laotian prime minister, Sept 1959, *Obit* Feb 1984

Pindling, Lynden Oscar, Bahamian prime minister, May 1968, *Obit* Yrbk 2000

Pinero, Jesus T., Oct 1946, *Obit* Jan 1953

Pingree, Chellie, American citizen advocacy organization official, Jan 2005

Plaisted, Frederick William, *Obit* Apr 1943

Plastiras, Nicholas, May 1950, *Obit* Oct 1953

Plavsic, Biljana, Bosnian Serb political leader, Feb 1998

Poindexter, Joseph B., Jan 1942, *Obit* Jan 1952

Pollitt, Harry, British communist leader, May 1948, *Obit* Sept 1960

Poujade, Pierre, French political leader, Apr 1956, *Obit* Yrbk 2004

Pozsgay, Imre, Hungarian communist leader, Mar 1990

Price, George C., Belizean prime minister, Aug 1984, *Obit* Yrbk 2012

Quispe Huanca, Felipe, Bolivian Indian leader, Jan 2002

Raab, Julius, Austrian chancellor, Apr 1954, *Obit* Feb 1964

Raffarin, Jean-Pierre, French prime minister, Jan 2003

Rell, M. Jodi, American governor, Sept 2005

Reynolds, Albert, Irish prime minister, Sept 1994

Rhodes, Edgar Nelson, *Obit* May 1942

Richards, John G., *Obit* Yrbk 1941

Robarts, John P., Canadian political leader, Yrbk 1962, *Obit* Jan 1983

Robichaud, Louis J., Canadian political leader, May 1968

Roca, Julio A., *Obit* Nov 1942

Roemer, Buddy, governor, Nov 1990

Rosenberg, Alfred, German Nazi leader, Oct 1941, *Obit* Nov 1946

Ross, Nellie Tayloe, American governor, May 1940, *Obit* Feb 1978

Rounds, M. Michael, American governor, June 2006

Rumor, Mariano, Italian prime minister, July 1969, *Obit* Mar 1990

Ryan, George H., American governor, Sept 2001

Sabry, Hassan, *Obit* Yrbk 1940

Saracoglu, Sukru, June 1942, *Obit* Mar 1954

Sargent, Francis W., governor, June 1971, *Obit* Jan 1999

Sauckel, Fritz, German Nazi leader, *Obit* Nov 1946

Savimbi, Jonas, Angolan rebel leader, Aug 1986, *Obit* June 2002

Schmidt, Fritz, *Obit* Aug 1943

Schulthess, Edmund, *Obit* June 1944

Schumacher, Kurt, German socialist leader, Feb 1948, *Obit* Oct 1952

Scrugham, James Graves, *Obit* July 1945

Seaga, Edward P. G., Jamaican prime minister, Apr 1981

Senanayake, Don Stephen, Apr 1950, *Obit* May 1952

Senanayake, Dudley, Ceylonese prime minister, Yrbk 1952, *Obit* June 1973

Seyss-Inquart, Artur von, Austrian Nazi leader, May 1941, *Obit* Nov 1946

Sharif, Nawaz, Pakistani prime minister, Sept 1998

Shipley, Jenny, New Zealand prime minister, Mar 2000

Shivers, Allan, American governor, Oct 1951, *Obit* Mar 1985

Shoup, Oliver Henry, *Obit* Nov 1940

Slim, Mongi, Tunisian political leader, Mar 1958, *Obit* Yrbk 1969

Smallwood, Joseph R., Canadian political leader, Feb 1953, *Obit* Mar 1992

Smith, Ian Douglas, Rhodesian prime minister, May 1966, *Obit* Feb 2008

Smith, John L., June 1952, *Obit* Yrbk 1958

Smith, Mary Louise, American political party leader, Oct 1976, *Obit* Nov 1997

Sophoulis, Themistocles, Nov 1947, *Obit* Sept 1949

Sordoni, Andrew J., July 1956, *Obit* Apr 1963

Souvanna Phouma, Nov 1962, *Obit* Mar 1984

Spangler, Harrison Earl, lawyer, Aug 1943, *Obit* Oct 1965

Spaulding, Rolland H., *Obit* May 1942

St. Laurent, Louis S., Mar 1948, *Obit* Oct 1973

Stainback, Ingram Macklin, Yrbk 1947, *Obit* June 1961

Stonehaven, John Lawrence Baird, *Obit* Oct 1941

Stoph, Willi, East German communist leader, Oct 1960, *Obit* Aug 1999

Strasser, Otto, German Nazi leader, Sept 1940, *Obit* Oct 1974

Suarez, Adolfo, Spanish prime minister, May 1977

Suchocka, Hanna, Polish prime minister, Jan 1994

Suhrawardy, Huseyn Shaheed, Pakistani prime minister, Apr 1957, *Obit* Jan 1964

Sullivan, Gael, May 1947, *Obit* Jan 1957

Suslov, Mikhail Andreevich, Soviet communist leader, Feb 1957, *Obit* Mar 1982

Sweet, William Ellery, *Obit* July 1942

Talmadge, Eugene, American governor, Sept 1941, *Obit* Feb 1947

Tambo, Oliver, South African political leader, Apr 1987, *Obit* June 1993

Tanaka, Kakuei, Japanese prime minister, Yrbk 1972, *Obit* Feb 1994

Thompson, M. E., Mar 1947

Thomson, Meldrim, governor, Oct 1978, *Obit* Sept 2001

Thore, Wendell Phillips, *Obit* May 1941

Tijerina, Reies Lopez, American political activist, July 1971

Tjarda van Starkenborgh Stachouwer, A. W. L., Feb 1942

Togliatti, Palmiro, Italian communist leader, Nov 1947, *Obit* Oct 1964

Trudeau, Pierre Elliott, Canadian prime minister, Nov 1968, *Obit* Jan 2001

Tshombe, Moise, Congolese prime minister, Yrbk 1961, *Obit* Sept 1969

Tuck, William M., governor, Yrbk 1946, *Obit* Aug 1983

Underwood, Cecil H., American governor, May 1958, *Obit* Yrbk 2009

Unruh, Jesse M., American state legislator and official, Oct 1969, *Obit* Sept 1987

Vajpayee, Atal Bihari, Indian prime minister, Aug 2000, Jan 2002

Van Wagoner, Murray, governor, Nov 1941, *Obit* Aug 1986

Vargas, Antonio, Ecuadorian Quechua leader, Jan 2004

Verwoerd, Hendrik Frensch, South African prime minister, Mar 1959, *Obit* Nov 1966

Vienot, Pierre, *Obit* Oct 1944

Vorster, B. J., South African prime minister, June 1967, *Obit* Nov 1983

Walla, Kah (Edith Kabbang Walla), Aug 2013

Wallace, George Corley, American governor, Yrbk 1963, *Obit* Nov 1998

Wallace, Henry Agard, American vice-president, Aug 1940, Jan 1947, *Obit* Jan 1966

Wallace, Lurleen, governor, Sept 1967, *Obit* July 1968

Wallace, Thomas W., *Obit* Sept 1943

Wallgren, Mon C., Nov 1948, *Obit* Nov 1961

Wang Jingwei, Chinese political leader and collaborationist, May 1940, *Obit* Jan 1945

Weaver, Arthur J., *Obit* Nov 1945

Welsh, Matthew E., governor, June 1962, *Obit* Aug 1995

Wen Jiabao, Chinese prime minister, Jan 2003

White, Mark, governor, Aug 1986

Whitman, Christine Todd, American government official, June 1995

Witos, Wincenty, *Obit* Yrbk 1945

Yaroslavski, Emel'yan Mikhailovich, Soviet communist leader, *Obit* Jan 1944

Yingluck Shinawatra, Thai prime minister, Oct 2011

Youlou, Fulbert, Congolese political leader, Yrbk 1962, *Obit* June 1972

Zamora, Ruben, Salvadoran rebel leader, Sept 1991

Zhirinovsky, Vladimir, Russian political leader, Nov 1995

Zyuganov, Gennady, Russian communist leader, Oct 1996

Pollsters

Buckingham, Marcus, American management consultant, Aug 2006

Caddell, Patrick, public opinion analyst and presidential adviser, Nov 1979

Crossley, Archibald M., public opinion analyst, Yrbk 1941, *Obit* July 1985

Gallup, George Horace, American public opinion analyst, Mar 1940, Yrbk 1952, *Obit* Sept 1984

Harris, Louis, American public opinion analyst, May 1966

Scammon, Richard M., political scientist and public opinion analyst, Mar 1971, *Obit* Sept 2001

Silver, Nate, American baseball statistician and pollster, Feb 2013

Polo players

Cambiaso, Adolfo, Argentine polo player, Jan 2007

Pool players

Hoppe, Willie, June 1947, *Obit* Apr 1959

Lee, Jeanette, American billiards player, Oct 2002

Mosconi, Willie, billiards player, June 1963, *Obit* Nov 1993

O'Sullivan, Ronnie, British snooker player, Apr 2013

Pop musicians

A-mei, Taiwanese pop singer, Jan 2002

Aguilera, Christina, American singer, Aug 2000

Bass, Lance, American singer, Nov 2000

Bjork, Icelandic singer, July 2001

Carter, Nick, American singer, May 2000

Chasez, JC, American singer, Nov 2000

Chicherina, Julia, Russian pop singer, Jan 2006

Clooney, Rosemary, American singer, Feb 1957, *Obit* Nov 2002

Cole, Natalie, American singer, Nov 1991

Como, Perry, American singer, Apr 1947, *Obit* July 2001

Dorough, Howie, American singer, May 2000

Fatone, Joey, American singer, Nov 2000

Fitzgerald, Ella, American singer, Oct 1956, July 1990, *Obit* Aug 1996

Groban, Josh, American pop singer, Aug 2009

Iglesias, Enrique, Spanish singer, Apr 1999

Irimia, Gabriela, Romanian singer, Jan 2003

Irimia, Monica, Romanian singer, Jan 2003

Jackson, Janet, American singer, June 1991

Jackson, Michael, American singer and songwriter, Nov 1983, *Obit* Aug 2009

Kirkpatrick, Chris, American singer, Nov 2000

Laine, Frankie, American singer, Nov 1956, *Obit* Yrbk 2007

Littrell, Brian, American singer, May 2000

Maimon, Shiri, Israeli pop singer, Jan 2006

Mathis, Johnny, American singer, July 1965, Feb 1993

McLean, A. J., American singer, May 2000

Michael, George, English pop singer, Nov 1988

Origliasso, Jess, Australian singer, Jan 2006

Origliasso, Lisa, Australian singer, Jan 2006

Pugacheva, Alla, Russian singer, Jan 2004

Richardson, Kevin, American singer, May 2000

Ross, Diana, American singer and actress, Mar 1973

Sade, British singer, Sept 1986

Solex, Dutch pop singer, Jan 2005

Spears, Britney, American singer, Apr 2000

Tarkan, Turkish pop singer, Jan 2006

Trevi, Gloria, Mexican pop singer, Jan 2005

Tuzun, Sibel, Turkish pop singer, Jan 2006

Volkova, Julia, Russian singer, Jan 2003

Williams, Robbie, British pop singer, Jan 2004

Popes

Benedict, Apr 1986, Sept 2005

Francis, July 2013

John, Feb 1959, *Obit* July 1963

John Paul, Nov 1979, Mar 2000, *Obit* June 2005

John Paul, Nov 1978, *Obit* Jan 1979

Paul, Jan 1956, Nov 1963, *Obit* Sept 1978

Pius, Apr 1941, Mar 1950, *Obit* Yrbk 1958

Porters

Townsend, Willard S., American railroad porter and labor leader, Jan 1948

Postmasters general

Bolger, William F., postmaster general, Oct 1979, *Obit* Oct 1989

Donaldson, Jesse M., American postmaster general, Jan 1948, *Obit* May 1970

Presidential advisers

Berger, Sandy, American presidential adviser, Feb 1998

Card, Andrew H., American presidential adviser, Nov 2003

Eckstein, Otto, American economist, Feb 1967, *Obit* May 1984

Frankfurter, Felix, American Supreme Court justice, June 1941, July 1957, *Obit* Apr 1965

Gray, C. Boyden, American lawyer and presidential adviser, Aug 1989

Hadley, Stephen J., American national security adviser, Nov 2006

Henderson, Loy Wesley, American diplomat, Mar 1948, *Obit* May 1986

Jarrett, Valerie, American presidential adviser, Apr 2009

Keyserling, Leon H., American economist, Jan 1947, *Obit* Sept 1987

Keyworth, George A., American physicist and presidential adviser, Mar 1986

Kirbo, Charles H., lawyer, Sept 1977, *Obit* Nov 1996

McFarlane, Robert C., American presidential adviser, May 1984

McIntyre, James T., Jan 1979

Murphy, Charles S., American lawyer and presidential adviser, Apr 1950, *Obit* Oct 1983

Nourse, Edwin, American economist and presidential adviser, Oct 1946, *Obit* June 1974

Sorensen, Theodore C., American presidential adviser, Yrbk 1961, *Obit* Yrbk 2011

Sperling, Gene, American economist and presidential adviser, Apr 2011

Watson, Jack H., Nov 1980

Presidential aides

Addington, David, American lawyer and vice-presidential aide, Jan 2007

Biffle, Leslie L., American presidential aide, Sept 1946, *Obit* May 1966

Clarke, Richard A., American presidential aide and security consultant, May 2006

Costanza, Midge, American presidential aide, June 1978, *Obit* Yrbk 2010

Currie, Lauchlin Bernard, American economist, May 1941, *Obit* Mar 1994

Favreau, Jonathan, American speechwriter, May 2009

Fitzwater, Marlin, American presidential press secretary, May 1988

Gaspard, Patrick, American presidential aide, July 2010

Gerson, Michael, American presidential speechwriter, Feb 2002

Gibbs, Robert, American presidential press secretary, Apr 2009

Hauge, Gabriel, American economist, Oct 1953, *Obit* Sept 1981

Lawton, Frederick J., government official, Mar 1951

McIntyre, Marvin Hunter, American presidential aide, *Obit* Feb 1944

Myers, Dee Dee, American presidential press secretary and television moderator, Aug 1994

Perino, Dana, American presidential press secretary, Jan 2008

Powell, Jody, American presidential press secretary, July 1977, *Obit* Yrbk 2009

Schoeneman, George J., American government official, Nov 1947

Speakes, Larry Melvin, presidential press secretary, Mar 1985

Steelman, John R., American presidential aide and economist, May 1941, Nov 1952, *Obit* Nov 1999

Presidential candidates

Hallinan, Vincent, American lawyer, Oct 1952, *Obit* Nov 1992

Le Pen, Jean-Marie, French political leader, Jan 1988

Walla, Kah (Edith Kabbang Walla), Aug 2013

Presidents

Kiir, Salva, Sudanese rebel and vice-president, Jan 2005

Nasheed, Mohamed, Maldivian president, Aug 2012

Press secretaries

Fitzwater, Marlin, American presidential press secretary, May 1988

Gibbs, Robert, American presidential press secretary, Apr 2009

Perino, Dana, American presidential press secretary, Jan 2008

Powell, Jody, American presidential press secretary, July 1977, *Obit* Yrbk 2009

Speakes, Larry Melvin,
presidential press secretary,
Mar 1985

Priests

Arrupe, Pedro, Spanish priest,
Feb 1970, *Obit* Apr 1991
Boff, Leonardo, Brazilian
theologian, Jan 1988
Carroll-Abbing, J. Patrick, priest
and social worker, July 1967,
Obit Nov 2001
Corrigan, Joseph M., *Obit* Aug
1942
Crowley, John J., priest, *Obit*
Apr 1940
Daly, Thomas A., *Obit* Mar 1941
Fitzpatrick, George L., *Obit* June
1941
Fox, Robert John, priest and
social welfare leader, May
1970, *Obit* June 1984
Gutierrez, Gustavo, Peruvian
priest and theologian, Jan
2004
Illich, Ivan, American priest and
philosopher, Yrbk 1969, *Obit*
Yrbk 2003
Kolvenbach, Peter-Hans, Dutch
Jesuit leader, May 1984
Leonard, Edward F., *Obit* Jan
1941
Orlemanski, Stanislaw,
Polish-American priest, June
1944
Riggs, T. Lawrason, *Obit* June
1943
Ryan, John A., priest and
theologian, *Obit* Oct 1945
Waring, George J., *Obit* Apr
1943

Primatologists

Galdikas, Birute, Canadian
primatologist, Mar 1995
Jolly, Alison, American
primatologist, Jan 2009

Princes

Abdullah, Yrbk 1947, *Obit* Sept
1955
Albert, Jan 2005
Andrew, Mar 1987
Arthur, *Obit* Mar 1942
Bernhard Leopold, June 1950,
Obit Mar 2005
Boris Vladimirovitch, *Obit* Yrbk
1943

Charles, May 1946, *Obit* July
1983
Charles, Nov 1969
George, *Obit* Oct 1942
Guise, Jean d'Orleans, *Obit* Oct
1940
Juan Carlos, Oct 1964, Jan
2003
Juan Carlos, Oct 1951, *Obit*
June 1993
Kan-In, Kotohito, *Obit* June 1945
Khan, Aly, Pakistani diplomat,
May 1960
Narendra Shiromani, *Obit* Mar
1943
Osman Ali, Oct 1948, *Obit* Apr
1967
Pavle, Apr 1941, *Obit* Oct 1976
Philip, Oct 1947
Rainier, Nov 1955, *Obit* Yrbk
2005
Strathmore and Kinghorne,
Claud George Bowes-Lyon,
Obit Yrbk 1944

Princesses

Anne, Oct 1973
Beatrice, *Obit* Yrbk 1944
Camilla, Jan 2005
Caroline, Nov 1989
Catherine, Aug 2011
Charlotte, Apr 1949, *Obit* Aug
1985
Diana, Jan 1983, *Obit* Nov 1997
Grace, Mar 1955, Oct 1977, *Obit*
Nov 1982
Hohenlohe-Waldenburg-Schillin
gsfurst, Stephanie Juliana,
Austro-Hungarian princess,
Jan 1940
Louise, *Obit* Jan 1940
Margaret, Nov 1953, *Obit* May
2002
Maria Theresa, *Obit* Apr 1944
Ortiz Rocasolano, Letizia,
Spanish television reporter
and wife of Felipe, Prince of
Spain, Jan 2004
Radziwill, Catherine, Russian
biographer, *Obit* July 1941
Sarah, Mar 1987
Schratt, Katharina, *Obit* May
1940
Stephanie, Aug 1986

Principals

Fenimore-Cooper, Susan De
Lancey, *Obit* Mar 1940
Fuller, Clara Cornelia, *Obit* Yrbk
1940

Patri, Angelo, American school
principal, Nov 1940, *Obit* Nov
1965

Printers

Carter, Matthew, British
typographer, Oct 2007
Deviny, John J., Sept 1948, *Obit*
Apr 1955
Gill, Eric, English sculptor,
engraver and typographer,
Obit Jan 1941
Goudy, Frederic W.,
typographer, June 1941, *Obit*
June 1947
McMurtrie, Douglas Crawford,
typographer, July 1944
Powers, Bertram A., American
labor leader, Jan 1974
Rogers, Bruce, American
typographer, Yrbk 1946, *Obit*
July 1957
Rollins, Carl Purington, Sept
1948, *Obit* Jan 1961
Updike, Daniel Berkeley, *Obit*
Feb 1942
Zapf, Hermann, German
typographer and calligrapher,
Jan 1965

Printmakers

Avery, Milton, American painter,
June 1958, *Obit* Feb 1965
Bontecou, Lee, American
sculptor, assemblage artist
and printmaker, Mar 2004
Cadmus, Paul, painter and
printmaker, July 1942, *Obit*
Mar 2000
Catlett, Elizabeth, American
sculptor and printmaker, May
1998, *Obit* Yrbk 2012
Davidson, Jo, American sculptor
and engraver, Apr 1945, *Obit*
Feb 1952
Drake, James, American artist,
July 2005
Evergood, Philip, American
painter, Oct 1944, Oct 1960,
Obit Apr 1973
Fiene, Ernest, American painter
and printmaker, Aug 1941
Frankenthaler, Helen, American
painter, Apr 1966, *Obit* Yrbk
2012
Goldthwaite, Anne, American
painter and printmaker, *Obit*
Mar 1944

Golub, Leon Albert, American painter, Aug 1984, *Obit* Yrbk 2004

Gottlieb, Adolph, American painter, Jan 1959, *Obit* Apr 1974

Gross, Chaim, American sculptor, Nov 1941, Feb 1966, *Obit* July 1991

Hirst, Damien, English artist, Aug 2013

Hodgkin, Howard, English painter, May 1991

Johns, Jasper, American painter, May 1967, May 1987

Kainen, Jacob, American painter and printmaker, Feb 1987, *Obit* Aug 2001

Kandinsky, Wassily, Russian painter, *Obit* Feb 1945

Katz, Alex, American painter, July 1975

Kelly, Ellsworth, American painter and sculptor, May 1970

Kroll, Leon, American painter, Mar 1943, *Obit* Yrbk 1974

Levine, Jack, American painter, June 1956, *Obit* Yrbk 2011

Lichtenstein, Roy, American painter, Feb 1969, *Obit* Jan 1998

Manzu, Giacomo, Italian sculptor, Mar 1961, *Obit* Mar 1991

Marden, Brice, American painter and printmaker, Aug 1990

Marin, John, American painter, July 1949, *Obit* Yrbk 1953

Merida, Carlos, Mexican painter, Jan 1960

Miro, Joan, Spanish painter, May 1940, Nov 1973, *Obit* Feb 1984

Moore, Henry, English sculptor, Feb 1954, Feb 1978, *Obit* Oct 1986

Nevelson, Louise, American sculptor, Oct 1967, *Obit* May 1988

Newman, Barnett, American painter, Sept 1969, *Obit* Sept 1970

Piper, John, English painter, Apr 1964, *Obit* Aug 1992

Riley, Bridget, English painter, Sept 1981

Rosenquist, James, American painter, Sept 1970

Rothenberg, Susan, American painter and printmaker, Mar 1985

Schapiro, Miriam, American artist, Aug 2000

Sickert, Walter, British painter and engraver, *Obit* Mar 1942

Smith, Kiki, American painter, sculptor and printmaker, Mar 2005

Soulages, Pierre, French painter, graphic artist and set designer, Apr 1958

Soyer, Raphael, American painter, Mar 1941, *Obit* Jan 1988

Stella, Frank, American artist, Apr 1971, Apr 1988

Sterne, Maurice, American painter, Apr 1943, *Obit* Oct 1957

Sutherland, Graham Vivian, English painter, Jan 1955, *Obit* Apr 1980

Tapies, Antoni, Spanish painter and sculptor, July 1966, *Obit* Yrbk 2012

Wales, George C., *Obit* May 1940

Walker, Kara, American silhouette artist, Mar 2000

Weber, Max, American painter, June 1941, *Obit* Yrbk 1961

Whiteread, Rachel, English sculptor, Jan 2006

Wood, Grant, American painter, Aug 1940, *Obit* Apr 1942

Prisoners

Cocke, Erle, army officer and veterans' leader, Jan 1951, *Obit* Sept 2000

Mooney, Thomas J., labor leader, *Obit* Apr 1942

Private investigators

Kroll, Jules, American lawyer and private detective, Feb 1999

Stanton, Bill, private detective, May 2001

Prizewinners

Mott, John Raleigh, American religious and youth leader, Jan 1947, *Obit* Mar 1955

Pro-choice activists

Michelman, Kate, American abortion rights activist, Nov 2000

Psychiatrists

Alexander, Franz, Austrian psychiatrist, Aug 1942, Sept 1960, *Obit* Apr 1964

Blain, Daniel, American psychiatrist, Sept 1947

Blanton, Smiley, June 1956, *Obit* Jan 1967

Diefendorf, Allen Ross, *Obit* Sept 1943

Frankl, Viktor E., Austrian psychiatrist, July 1997, *Obit* Nov 1997

Jelliffe, Smith Ely, psychiatrist, *Obit* Oct 1945

Kuhlmann, Frederick, *Obit* June 1941

Sakel, Manfred, Jan 1941, *Obit* Feb 1958

Stekel, Wilhelm, Austrian psychoanalyst, *Obit* Aug 1940

Stevenson, George S., psychiatrist, Yrbk 1946

Torrey, E. Fuller, psychiatrist, July 1998

Wilgus, Sidney Dean, *Obit* Mar 1940

Zilboorg, Gregory, psychiatrist, Sept 1941, *Obit* Nov 1959

Psychics

Geller, Uri, American psychic, Sept 1978

Psychologists

Allport, Gordon, psychologist, Sept 1960, *Obit* Yrbk 1967

Arnett, Jeffrey Jensen, American psychologist, Feb 2011

Baron-Cohen, Simon, British psychologist, Jan 2006

Boring, E. G., American psychologist, Mar 1962, *Obit* Sept 1968

Brigham, Carl C., *Obit* Mar 1943

Bruner, Jerome Seymour, American psychologist and law professor, Oct 1984

Chee, Soon Juan, Singaporean political leader, Jan 2004

Clark, Kenneth B., American psychologist, Sept 1964, *Obit* Sept 2005

Eysenck, H. J., German-British psychologist, Nov 1972, *Obit* Nov 1997

Feifel, Herman, American psychologist, Aug 1994, *Obit* Yrbk 2005

Fisher, Helen E., American anthropologist and psychologist, Oct 2010

Gesell, Arnold Lucius, American psychologist, Nov 1940, *Obit* Sept 1961

Gopnik, Alison, American psychologist, Jan 2007

Hayes, Samuel Perkins, psychologist and teacher of the blind, Sept 1954, *Obit* Sept 1958

Jamison, Kay R., American psychologist, Feb 2009

Janov, Arthur, psychologist, May 1980

Jensen, Arthur Robert, American psychologist, Jan 1973, *Obit* Yrbk 2013

Johnson, Virginia E., American psychologist, Apr 1976, *Obit* Yrbk 2013

Kellogg, Winthrop Niles, Apr 1963

Kelly, Everett Lowell, psychologist, Mar 1955, *Obit* Apr 1986

Koffka, Kurt, German psychologist, *Obit* Jan 1942

Laird, Donald Anderson, Sept 1946

Lecky, Prescott, psychologist, *Obit* July 1941

Loftus, Elizabeth F., American psychologist, Jan 1999

Lorge, Irving, psychologist, July 1959, *Obit* Apr 1961

Martin, Lillien Jane, psychologist, Apr 1942, *Obit* May 1943

May, Rollo, psychologist, June 1973, *Obit* Jan 1995

Milgram, Stanley, American social psychologist, Aug 1979, *Obit* Mar 1985

Miller, Geoffrey F., American psychologist, July 2010

Miller, Neal E., American professor of psychology, July 1974, *Obit* June 2002

Osgood, Charles E., psychologist, Apr 1962

Pennebaker, James W., American social psychologist, Aug 2011

Piaget, Jean, Swiss psychologist, Yrbk 1958, *Obit* Nov 1980

Pintner, Rudolf, Anglo-American psychologist, *Obit* Jan 1943

Pipher, Mary Bray, psychologist and author, Aug 1999

Pratt, J. Gaither, Nov 1964

Rhine, J. B., American parapsychologist, Jan 1949, *Obit* Apr 1980

Riecken, Henry W., social psychologist, Yrbk 1961

Rimm, Sylvia B., American child psychologist, Feb 2002

Rogers, Carl R., American psychologist, Yrbk 1962, *Obit* Mar 1987

Salter, Andrew, psychologist, May 1944, *Obit* Jan 1997

Seabury, David, Sept 1941, *Obit* May 1960

Skinner, B. F., American psychologist, Jan 1964, Nov 1979, *Obit* Oct 1990

Spearman, Charles E., English psychologist, *Obit* Oct 1945

Spelke, Elizabeth S., American psychologist, Apr 2006

Steele, Claude M., American social psychologist, Feb 2001

Thorndike, Edward L., American psychologist, Sept 1941, *Obit* Oct 1949

Wallerstein, Judith S., psychologist, Nov 1996

Watson, John Broadus, American psychologist, Oct 1942, *Obit* Yrbk 1958

Way, Niobe, psychologist, Feb 2012

Wertham, Frederic, American psychologist, July 1949, *Obit* Jan 1982

Wertheimer, Max, Czech psychologist, *Obit* Yrbk 1943

Young, Kimberly S., American psychologist, Jan 2006

Psychotherapists

Beers, Clifford Whittingham, American mental hygienist, *Obit* Aug 1943

Kotb, Heba, Egyptian sex therapist, Jan 2007

Ross, Jerilyn, American psychotherapist, Nov 2009, *Obit* Yrbk 2010

Public health officials

Folks, Homer, Yrbk 1940

Gunn, Selskar M., *Obit* Sept 1944

McCormack, Arthur Thomas, *Obit* Sept 1943

Molloy, Daniel M., *Obit* Mar 1944

Public health scientists

Bang, Abhay, Indian physician and public health scientist, Jan 2007

Public relations consultants

Birdwell, Russell, July 1946, *Obit* Mar 1978

Dalrymple, Jean, theatrical producer, Sept 1953, *Obit* Feb 1999

Maney, Richard, July 1964, *Obit* Sept 1968

Soss, Wilma Porter, publicist, Mar 1965, *Obit* Jan 1987

Public relations personnel

Bevis, Palmer, American public relations executive, Apr 1953

Gehrmann, Don, runner, Oct 1952

Publishing employees

Appleton, Edward Dale, American publishing executive, *Obit* Mar 1942

Appleton, Robert, American publishing executive, *Obit* Mar 1945

Baker, Asa George, American publishing executive, *Obit* Oct 1940

Ballantine, Ian, publisher, May 1954, *Obit* May 1995

Becker, May Lamberton, author and editor, May 1941, *Obit* July 1958

Beecroft, John, American editor, Mar 1954, *Obit* Yrbk 1966

Brett, George Platt, publisher, Yrbk 1948, *Obit* May 1984

Carter, Matthew, British typographer, Oct 2007

Crowell, T. Irving, *Obit* Mar 1942

Dalmia, Ramkrishna, Yrbk 1948

De Graff, Robert F., May 1943

Deviny, John J., Sept 1948, *Obit* Apr 1955

Dodge, John V., July 1960

Farrar, Margaret, crossword puzzle editor, July 1955, *Obit* Aug 1984

Forbes, Bertie Charles, publisher, Mar 1950, *Obit* July 1954

Friedman, Jane, American publisher, Mar 2001

Geis, Bernard, American publisher, Sept 1960, *Obit* Mar 2001

Gollancz, Victor, British publisher, Oct 1963, *Obit* Apr 1967

Goudy, Frederic W., typographer, June 1941, *Obit* June 1947

Hooper, Franklin Henry, *Obit* Oct 1940

Hornblow, Arthur, *Obit* June 1942

Jacobi, Victor, European music publisher, *Obit* Nov 1942

Kanter, Albert Lewis, publisher, July 1953

Knopf, Alfred, American publisher, June 1943, Nov 1966, *Obit* Oct 1984

Knopf, Blanche W., American publishing executive, July 1957, *Obit* July 1966

Lacy, Dan M., publishing executive, Nov 1954, *Obit* Nov 2001

Lane, Allen, British publisher, May 1954, *Obit* Sept 1970

Larsen, Roy, publishing executive, Sept 1950, *Obit* Oct 1979

Lippincott, Joshua Bertram, *Obit* Jan 1940

Longman, Hubert Harry, *Obit* Apr 1940

Lunt, Storer B., Nov 1958

Macrae, John, *Obit* Apr 1944

McGraw, Curtis W., June 1950, *Obit* Nov 1953

McMurtrie, Douglas Crawford, typographer, July 1944

Melcher, Frederic Gershom, American publisher, July 1945, *Obit* Apr 1963

Middelhoff, Thomas, German publishing and recording executive, Feb 2001

Motley, Arthur H., publisher, Jan 1961, *Obit* July 1984

Nast, Conde, publisher, *Obit* Nov 1942

Norton, W. W., *Obit* Yrbk 1945

Onassis, Jacqueline Kennedy, wife of American president John F. Kennedy and Greek-Argentine shipping executive Aristotle Socrates Onassis, Oct 1961, *Obit* July 1994

Patterson, Graham, Mar 1949, *Obit* Jan 1970

Praeger, Frederick A., American publishing executive, Sept 1959, *Obit* Aug 1994

Rigg, Edgar T., June 1961

Rinehart, Stanley M., Yrbk 1954, *Obit* June 1969

Rogers, Bruce, American typographer, Yrbk 1946, *Obit* July 1957

Schiffrin, Andre, American publisher, Jan 2000

Schuster, M. Lincoln, July 1941, *Obit* Feb 1971

Sheed, F. J., American theologian and publisher, Sept 1981, *Obit* Jan 1982

Shimkin, Leon, publisher, May 1954

Shortz, Will, American editor and puzzle maker, Apr 1996

Simon, Richard L., American publisher, July 1941, *Obit* Oct 1960

Skira, Albert, Swiss art publisher, Apr 1967, *Obit* June 1990

Smith, Thomas R., *Obit* June 1942

Straus, Roger W., American publishing executive, Aug 1980, *Obit* Yrbk 2004

Thielen, Gunter, German publishing executive, Jan 2005

Thornhill, Arthur H., Apr 1958, *Obit* Mar 1970

Ullstein, Herman, *Obit* Jan 1944

Unwin, Stanley, British publisher, Mar 1949, *Obit* Yrbk 1968

Wickware, Francis Graham, *Obit* Yrbk 1940

Wilson, Halsey William, publisher, Yrbk 1941, May 1948, *Obit* Apr 1954

Yust, Walter, Apr 1943, *Obit* Apr 1960

Zevin, Ben David, publisher, Sept 1943, *Obit* Feb 1985

Publishing executives

Jacobi, Victor, European music publisher, *Obit* Nov 1942

Skira, Albert, Swiss art publisher, Apr 1967, *Obit* June 1990

Puppeteers

Baird, Bil, puppeteer, Mar 1954, *Obit* May 1987

Baird, Cora, American puppeteer, Mar 1954, *Obit* Feb 1968

Henson, Jim, American puppeteer, Mar 1977, *Obit* July 1990

Lewis, Shari, puppeteer and ventriloquist, Mar 1958, *Obit* Oct 1998

Obraztsov, Sergei, Russian puppeteer, Nov 1964

Oz, Frank, puppeteer and motion picture director, Oct 1999

Tillstrom, Burr, puppeteer, May 1951, *Obit* Feb 1986

Queens

Beatrix, May 1981

Elizabeth, June 1944, June 1955, Jan 2002

Elizabeth, Aug 1981, *Obit* June 2002

Frederika, Queen, consort of Paul I, King Of The Hellenes, Jan 1955, *Obit* Apr 1981

Juliana, Sept 1944, Jan 1955, *Obit* Yrbk 2004

Margrethe, Nov 1972

Nur el Hussein, Apr 1991

Rania, Feb 2001

Salote Tupou, Yrbk 1953, *Obit* Feb 1966

Sirikit, Yrbk 1960

Wilhelmina, Jan 1940, *Obit* Jan 1963

Rabbis

Bernstein, Philip S., American rabbi, Nov 1951, *Obit* Feb 1986

Fredman, Samuel, *Obit* June 1941

Herzog, Isaac, Apr 1959

Jakobovits, Immanuel, British rabbi, June 1988, *Obit* Feb 2000

Klein, Edward E., rabbi, Sept 1966, *Obit* Sept 1985

Levin, Yehuda Leib, Sept 1969, *Obit* Jan 1972

Schindler, Alexander M., American rabbi, Sept 1987, *Obit* Feb 2001

Schneerson, Menachem M., American rabbi, Sept 1983, *Obit* Aug 1994

Werne, Isaac, *Obit* Mar 1940

Radio directors

Granik, Samuel Theodore, Yrbk 1952, *Obit* Nov 1970

Radio personalities

Ace, Jane, radio performer, May 1948, *Obit* Jan 1975

Allen, Mel, sportscaster, Oct 1950, *Obit* Aug 1996

Andrews, Erin, American television sportscaster, Sept 2013

Barber, Red, sportscaster, July 1943, *Obit* Jan 1993

Bell, Art, American radio talk show host, Apr 2000

Bergen, Edgar, American ventriloquist and radio performer, May 1945, *Obit* Nov 1978

Berman, Chris, American television sportscaster, Aug 1998

Bowes, Edward, radio performer, Mar 1941, *Obit* July 1946

Bradley, Ed, American television reporter, May 1988, *Obit* Yrbk 2007

Brown, Cecil, radio newscaster, Mar 1942, *Obit* Jan 1988

Cecil, Mary, *Obit* Feb 1941

Cohn, Linda, American television sportscaster, Aug 2002

Collingwood, Charles, American radio and television reporter, June 1943, *Obit* Nov 1985

Costas, Bob, American sportscaster, Jan 1993

Cronkite, Walter, American television news anchor, Jan 1956, Nov 1975, *Obit* Sept 2009

Cross, Milton, Jan 1940, *Obit* Feb 1975

Daly, John Charles, radio reporter and television moderator, May 1948, *Obit* May 1991

Damerel, Donna, *Obit* Apr 1941

Donahue, Phil, American television talk show host, May 1980

Edwards, Bob, American radio newscaster, Sept 2001

Edwards, Douglas, radio and television newscaster, Aug 1988, *Obit* Jan 1991

Fitzgerald, Edward, radio talk show host, Apr 1947, *Obit* June 1982

Fitzgerald, Pegeen, radio talk show host, Apr 1947, *Obit* Apr 1989

Flannery, Harry W., Oct 1943

Frost, David, English talk show host, July 1969, *Obit* Yrbk 2013

Garrels, Anne, American television and radio reporter, Mar 2004

Godfrey, Arthur, radio and television personality, July 1948, *Obit* May 1983

Graham, Virginia, radio and television talk show host, Oct 1956, *Obit* Mar 1999

Graser, Earle W., *Obit* June 1941

Gray, Jim, American sportscaster, Jan 2011

Gumbel, Greg, American television sportscaster, Sept 1996

Harvey, Paul, American radio reporter, Mar 1986, *Obit* Yrbk 2009

Husing, Ted, sportscaster, June 1942, *Obit* Oct 1962

Inskeep, Steve, American radio reporter, June 2009

Jordan, Marian, radio performer, Nov 1941, *Obit* June 1961

King, Billie Jean, American tennis player, Yrbk 1967

King, Larry, American radio and television talk show host, May 1985

Lampley, Jim, American sportscaster, Oct 2011

Lesueur, Larry, American radio newscaster, June 1943, *Obit* Yrbk 2003

McCarthy, Clem, radio sportscaster, Oct 1941, *Obit* July 1962

McKay, Jim, American television sportscaster, Oct 1973, *Obit* Yrbk 2008

McNeill, Don, radio talk show host, July 1949, *Obit* Aug 1996

McNellis, Maggi, radio and television performer, Jan 1955, *Obit* Aug 1989

Montagne, Renee, American radio reporter, Nov 2009

Moore, Garry, American radio and television personality, Nov 1954, *Obit* Jan 1994

Morgan, Henry, American radio and television personality, Mar 1947, *Obit* July 1994

Myers, Joel Norman, American meteorologist, Apr 2005

Nyad, Diana, American swimmer and sportscaster, Aug 1979

Oliver, Pam, American television sportscaster, July 2009

Phillips, Albert, *Obit* Mar 1940

Pivot, Bernard, French television talk show host, Oct 1990

Raphael, Sally Jessy, television talk show host, Feb 1990

Roberts, Robin, American television news anchor, Feb 2008

Scott, Stuart, American television sportscaster, Jan 2012

Scott, Willard, American television weathercaster, July 1989

Scully, Vin, American television sportscaster, Oct 2001

Seacrest, Ryan, American television personality, Sept 2009

Shaw, Bernard, American television newscaster, Feb 1995

Siegel, Robert, American radio newscaster, July 2008

Stamberg, Susan, American radio newscaster, Oct 2008

Stern, Bill, sportscaster, June 1941, *Obit* Jan 1972

Stern, Howard, American radio personality, Jan 1996

Swenson, Alfred G., *Obit* May 1941

Totenberg, Nina, American radio and television reporter, Mar 1996

Trabert, Tony, American tennis player and sportscaster, July 1954

Trout, Robert, American radio and television reporter, Oct 1965, *Obit* Jan 2001

Visser, Lesley, American television sportscaster, Apr 2007

Von Zell, Harry, June 1944, *Obit* Jan 1982

Walter, Wilmer, *Obit* Oct 1941

Wertheimer, Linda, radio newscaster, Nov 1995

Williams, Wendy, American talk show host, Oct 2009

Wilson, Don, radio and television personality, Aug 1944, *Obit* Yrbk 1991

Yang Lan, Chinese talk show host, Jan 2003

Radio producers

Denny, George V., Sept 1940, Sept 1950, *Obit* Jan 1960

Radio reporters

Nelson, Soraya Sarhaddi, Oct 2013

Radio scriptwriters

Carrington, Elaine, Feb 1944, *Obit* July 1958

Oboler, Arch, radio author and screenwriter, Mar 1940, *Obit* May 1987

Radiologists

Benson, Francis Colgate, American surgeon and radiologist, *Obit* Apr 1941

Holland, Charles Thurstan, *Obit* Mar 1941

Hubeny, Maximilian J., *Obit* Sept 1942

Railroad executives

Armand, Louis, French railroad executive, Sept 1957, *Obit* Oct 1971

Cahill, Michael Harrison, *Obit* Apr 1940

Clement, Martin W., Nov 1946, *Obit* Nov 1966

Debutts, Harry A., Apr 1953

Franklin, Walter S., Feb 1950, *Obit* Oct 1972

Jeffers, William M., Nov 1942, *Obit* Apr 1953

Johnston, Wayne A., American railroad executive, May 1951, *Obit* Feb 1968

Kummant, Alexander, American railroad executive, Jan 2007

Marsh, Ernest Sterling, Feb 1960

McGinnis, Patrick B., Nov 1955, *Obit* Apr 1973

Metzman, G., July 1946, *Obit* June 1960

Pelley, John J., *Obit* Yrbk 1946

Perlman, Alfred E., railroad executive, Apr 1955, *Obit* July 1983

Russell, Donald J., railroad executive, May 1962, *Obit* Feb 1986

Simpson, Howard E., railroad executive, May 1958, *Obit* Apr 1985

Symes, James M., Yrbk 1955, *Obit* Sept 1976

White, William, Jan 1953, *Obit* June 1967

Young, Robert Ralph, railroad executive, Apr 1947, *Obit* Mar 1958

Railroad workers

Johnston, Alvanley, American labor leader, June 1946, *Obit* Nov 1951

Whitney, A. F., American labor leader, Feb 1946, *Obit* Sept 1949

Rap musicians

Akon, Senegalese-American rap and rhythm and blues singer, Jan 2008

Cam'Ron (Musician), American rapper, Feb 2011

Coolio, American rapper, Aug 1998

DMX, American rapper, Aug 2003

Fergie, American singer, Oct 2006

Ghostface Killah, American rapper, June 2008

Hammer (Musician), American rapper, Apr 1991

Ja Rule, American rapper, July 2002

K'naan, Somali rapper, June 2010

Kid Rock, American rapper, Oct 2001

Kweli, Talib, American rapper, July 2012

Lil' Kim, American rapper, Oct 2000

Matisyahu, American Hasidic reggae and rap singer, Mar 2007

Minaj, Nicki, American rapper, Oct 2013

Nas (Musician), American rapper, Sept 2009

Nelly (Musician), American rapper, Oct 2002

Queen Latifah, American rapper and actress, Feb 1997

Rakim, American rapper, Aug 2008

Ross, Rick, American rapper, June 2012

Solaar, MC, French rapper, Jan 2002

Timbaland, American hip-hop musician and recording producer, Mar 2003

Tyler, the Creator (Musician), American rapper and record producer, Aug 2011

West, Kanye, American rapper and record producer, Aug 2006

Zola, South African rapper, Jan 2004

Real estate brokers

Peden, Katherine G., real estate broker and state official, May 1962

Real estate developers

Beban, Gary J., football player and real estate executive, May 1970

Campeau, Robert, Canadian real estate and retail executive, Mar 1989

Dowling, Robert W., Oct 1952, *Obit* Nov 1973

Ghermezian, Eskander, Canadian real estate developer, Jan 2004

Helmsley, Harry B., American real estate executive, June 1985, *Obit* Mar 1997

Jarrett, Valerie, American presidential adviser, Apr 2009

Maenner, T. H., Nov 1949, *Obit* Mar 1958

Paterson, Chat, veterans' leader, Mar 1948, *Obit* May 1992

Reichmann, Paul, Canadian real estate developer, Jan 1991

Rouse, James W., American real estate developer, Feb 1982, *Obit* June 1996

Shepard, Alan B., American astronaut and real estate executive, Yrbk 1961, *Obit* Sept 1998

Speyer, Jerry I., American real estate developer, May 2008

Staubach, Roger, American football player and real estate executive, Apr 1972

Stevens, Roger L., real estate executive and theatrical producer, Yrbk 1955, *Obit* Apr 1998

Taubman, A. Alfred, American real estate executive, Jan 1993

Wu, Gordon, Chinese real estate developer, Aug 1996

Zeckendorf, William, real estate executive, Mar 1952, *Obit* Nov 1976

Zhang Xin, Chinese real estate developer, Jan 2006

Recording industry executives

Cohen, Barbara, American poetry recorder, May 1957

Cohen, Lyor, American recording industry executive, Aug 2012

Davis, Clive, American recording executive, July 2000

Greenwald, Julie, American recording industry executive, Nov 2009

Mantell, Marianne, American recording company executive, May 1957

Phillips, Sam, American record producer, Apr 2001

Rhone, Sylvia, American recording industry executive, June 1998

Rubin, Rick, American recording producer and executive, Sept 2007

Wexler, Jerry, American recording industry executive, Jan 2001, *Obit* Yrbk 2008

Recording producers

Automator (Musician), American recording producer, May 2007

Cowell, Simon, British record producer and talent judge on television program, Jan 2004

Culshaw, John, British recording producer, June 1968, *Obit* June 1980

Epworth, Paul, Aug 2013

Jackson, Michael, American singer and songwriter, Nov 1983, *Obit* Aug 2009

Lanois, Daniel, Canadian record producer, Jan 2005

Luger, Lex (Lexus Arnel Lewis), May 2013

Madonna, American singer, May 1986

Prince, American singer and songwriter, Feb 1986

Spector, Phil, American record producer, songwriter and arranger, July 1989

Stigwood, Robert, Australian film, recording and theatrical producer, Oct 1979

Red Cross officials

Boardman, Mabel Thorp, Red Cross official, Aug 1944, *Obit* Apr 1946

Referees (Sports)

Bavetta, Dick, American basketball referee, Mar 2008

Collina, Pierluigi, Italian soccer referee, Jan 2002

Palmer, Violet, American basketball referee, Nov 2006

Thomas, Sarah, American football referee, Nov 2010

Regents

Charles, May 1946, *Obit* July 1983

Reggae musicians

Sean Paul, Jamaican reggae singer, Jan 2007

Regulatory agency officials

Bacher, Robert F., American physicist, Feb 1947, *Obit* Yrbk 2005

Bair, Sheila C., American regulatory agency official, Feb 2010

Bernanke, Ben, American economist and Federal Reserve chairman, Mar 2006

Burford, Anne McGill, American regulatory agency official, Sept 1982, *Obit* Yrbk 2004

Denham, R. N., American regulatory agency official, Oct 1947, *Obit* Sept 1954

Dixon, Paul Rand, American regulatory agency official, Jan 1968

Landis, James McCauley, American lawyer and regulatory agency official, Mar 1942, *Obit* Oct 1964

Lee, Robert E., American regulatory agency official, July 1967, *Obit* June 1993

Martin, Kevin, American lawyer and regulatory official, Aug 2005

Miller, James C., economist and regulatory official, May 1986

Minow, Newton Norman, American lawyer and regulatory agency official, Oct 1961

Porter, Paul A., American regulatory agency official, Jan 1945, *Obit* Jan 1976

Relief organization officials

Belmont, Eleanor Robson, July 1944, *Obit* Jan 1980

Glenn, Mary Willcox, *Obit* Yrbk 1940

Martin, Edgar Stanley, *Obit* Sept 1940

Swift, Ernest John, *Obit* Yrbk 1941

Religious leaders

Aga Khan, Indian Islamic leader, May 1946, *Obit* Sept 1957

Aked, Charles F., American clergyman, *Obit* Oct 1941

Al-Sadr, Muqtada, Iraqi Islamic cleric, Jan 2007

Al-Sistani, Ali, Iraqi Islamic leader, Jan 2004

Alfrink, Bernard, May 1966, *Obit* Feb 1988

Ammachi, Indian Hindu mystic, Jan 2003

Arrupe, Pedro, Spanish priest, Feb 1970, *Obit* Apr 1991

Asahara, Shoko, Japanese cult leader, Jan 2003

Barnett, Eugene Epperson, May 1941

Barr, Norman B., American clergyman, *Obit* May 1943

Baudrillart, Alfred, *Obit* July 1942

Baum, William W., Oct 1976

Bea, Augustin, Sept 1964, *Obit* Jan 1969

Bell, Rob, American pastor, Mar 2013

Benedict, Apr 1986, Sept 2005

Benelli, Giovanni Cardinal, Sept 1977, *Obit* Jan 1983

Bernardin, Joseph L., Oct 1982, *Obit* Jan 1997

Bertram, Adolf, *Obit* Aug 1945

Blake, Eugene Carson, American clergyman and church leader, Sept 1955, *Obit* Oct 1985

Boff, Leonardo, Brazilian theologian, Jan 1988

Boggiani, Tommaso Pio, *Obit* Apr 1942

Bonnell, John Sutherland, clergyman, June 1945, *Obit* Apr 1992

Brennan, Francis, Oct 1967, *Obit* Sept 1968

Brookes, George S., Aug 1940

Burton, Charles Emerson, *Obit* Oct 1940

Burton, Lewis William, *Obit* Yrbk 1940

Cadle, E. Howard, *Obit* Feb 1943

Carlyle, A. J., *Obit* July 1943

Carpenter, George L., Jan 1943, *Obit* May 1948

Carpenter, J. Henry, Feb 1943, *Obit* Sept 1954

Carroll-Abbing, J. Patrick, priest and social worker, July 1967, *Obit* Nov 2001

Cashman, Robert, Nov 1952

Cattani-Amadori, Federico, *Obit* May 1943

Cavert, Samuel McCrea, Jan 1951, *Obit* Mar 1977

Chamberlin, Georgia Louise, *Obit* Oct 1943

Chase, William Sheafe, *Obit* Sept 1940

Clayton, P. B., May 1955, *Obit* Mar 1973

Clinchy, Everett R., religious leader, Apr 1941, *Obit* Mar 1986

Cody, John Patrick, Nov 1965, *Obit* June 1982

Coffin, Henry S., clergyman and educator, Apr 1944, *Obit* Jan 1955

Cooke, Leslie E., June 1962, *Obit* Apr 1967

Cooke, Terence James, Sept 1968, *Obit* Nov 1983

Crowley, John J., priest, *Obit* Apr 1940

Cushing, Richard James, June 1952, *Obit* Yrbk 1970

Dahlberg, Edwin T., clergyman, May 1958, *Obit* Oct 1986

De Pauw, Gommar A., May 1974

De Wolfe, James P., Aug 1942, *Obit* Mar 1966

Dearden, John, July 1969, *Obit* Sept 1988

Denny, Collins, *Obit* July 1943

Divine, Frank H., *Obit* May 1941

Dodds, Gil, June 1947, *Obit* Apr 1977

Du Bose, Horace M., *Obit* Mar 1941

Dunham, Franklin, Jan 1942, *Obit* Jan 1962

Egan, Edward M., July 2001

Empie, Paul C., Oct 1958

Enrique y Tarancon, Vicente, Oct 1972, *Obit* Feb 1995

Evans, Hugh Ivan, Nov 1950, *Obit* July 1958

Fagnani, Charles P., *Obit* Mar 1941

Farooq, Umar, Kashmiri Islamic leader, Jan 2002

Farrakhan, Louis, American Black Muslim leader, Apr 1992

Fiske, Charles, *Obit* Mar 1942

Fitzpatrick, George L., *Obit* June 1941

Fox, Robert John, priest and social welfare leader, May 1970, *Obit* June 1984

Fry, Franklin, June 1946, *Obit* Sept 1968

Galen, Clemens August von, *Obit* Apr 1946

Glemp, Jozef, Sept 1982, *Obit* Yrbk 2013

Glennon, John Joseph, *Obit* Apr 1946

Goldman, Frank, Jan 1953, *Obit* Apr 1965

Grant, Heber J., *Obit* June 1945

Grey, J. D., clergyman, Sept 1952, *Obit* Sept 1985

Griffin, Bernard, Oct 1946, *Obit* Oct 1956

Gruber, L. Franklin, *Obit* Feb 1942

Guthrie, Charles Ellsworth, *Obit* Sept 1940

Gutierrez, Gustavo, Peruvian priest and theologian, Jan 2004

Hale, Arthur, *Obit* Mar 1940

Hall, Raymond S., Oct 1953

Harp, Edward B., Oct 1953

Harris, James Rendel, *Obit* Apr 1941

Hauser, Conrad Augustine, *Obit* Apr 1943

Hawkins, Edler G., Jan 1965

Herbster, Ben Mohr, clergyman, July 1962, *Obit* Mar 1985

Hering, Hermann S., *Obit* July 1940

Hume, T. C., *Obit* Yrbk 1943

Hyvernat, Henri, *Obit* July 1941

Idleman, Finis Schuyler, *Obit* May 1941

Ironside, H. A., clergyman, Feb 1945, *Obit* Feb 1951

John, Feb 1959, *Obit* July 1963

John Paul, Nov 1979, Mar 2000, *Obit* June 2005

John Paul, Nov 1978, *Obit* Jan 1979

Johnson, C. Oscar, Feb 1948, *Obit* Jan 1966

Johnson, Hewlett, English clergyman, May 1943, *Obit* Yrbk 1966

Jones, J. D., Welsh clergyman, *Obit* June 1942

Kaup, Felix F., *Obit* Apr 1940

Kenyon, Helen, Oct 1948

Kepler, Asher Raymond, *Obit* Oct 1942

Kimball, Spencer W., American clergyman and Mormon leader, Feb 1979, *Obit* Jan 1986

Knorr, Nathan H., Feb 1957, *Obit* Aug 1977

Knox, Louise Chambers, *Obit* Mar 1942

Kolvenbach, Peter-Hans, Dutch Jesuit leader, May 1984

Krol, John, Jan 1969, *Obit* May 1996

Kunz, Alfred A., Yrbk 1941

Lauri, Lorenzo, *Obit* Yrbk 1941

Lauterbach, Jacob Zallel, *Obit* June 1942

Lawrence, William, *Obit* Jan 1942

Ledochowski, Wlodzimierz, *Obit* Jan 1943

Leonard, Edward F., *Obit* Jan 1941

Li Hongzhi, Chinese religious leader, Jan 2002

Libby, Frederick J., Apr 1949, *Obit* Sept 1970

Locke, Charles Edward, *Obit* Mar 1940

Lustiger, Jean Marie, Feb 1984, *Obit* Yrbk 2007

MacLeod, Dorothy Shaw, Apr 1949

Macrossie, Allan, *Obit* Mar 1940

Maglione, Luigi, *Obit* Oct 1944

Maharaj Ji, Indian religious leader, Yrbk 1974

Maier, Walter Arthur, evangelist and theologian, May 1947, *Obit* Feb 1950

Manning, William Thomas, Apr 1940, *Obit* Jan 1950

Manson, John T., *Obit* Apr 1944

Marella, Paolo, Oct 1964

Marshall, Peter, Scottish-American clergyman, Apr 1948, *Obit* Feb 1949

Marvin, Dwight Edwards, American clergyman, *Obit* Mar 1940

Masliansky, Zvi Hirsch, *Obit* Mar 1943

McCune, George Shannon, *Obit* Feb 1942

McCurdy, William Albert, *Obit* Feb 1942

McIntire, Carl, American clergyman, Oct 1971, *Obit* June 2002

McIntyre, James Francis Aloysius, Feb 1953, *Obit* Sept 1979

McKay, David Oman, American Mormon leader, June 1951, *Obit* Mar 1970

Mead, Charles Larew, *Obit* July 1941

Medeiros, Humberto, Nov 1971, *Obit* Nov 1983

Meehan, Thomas F., *Obit* Sept 1942

Mendenhall, Harlan G., *Obit* July 1940

Mikell, Henry Judah, *Obit* Apr 1942

Mindszenty, Jozsef, Jan 1957, *Obit* June 1975

Mohammed, W. Deen, American Islamic leader, Jan 2004, *Obit* Yrbk 2008

Monsky, Henry, Nov 1941, *Obit* June 1947

Montgomery, James Shera, Apr 1948, *Obit* Sept 1952

Moore, T. Albert, *Obit* Apr 1940

Mosher, Gouverneur Frank, *Obit* Sept 1941

Myers, C. Kilmer, Feb 1960

O'Boyle, Patrick, July 1973, *Obit* Sept 1987

O'Connell, William Henry, June 1941, *Obit* June 1944

O'Connor, John Joseph, June 1984, *Obit* July 2000

O'Gorman, Patrick F., *Obit* Apr 1940

O'Malley, Sean Patrick, Jan 2004

Obando y Bravo, Miguel, Mar 1988

Orlemanski, Stanislaw, Polish-American priest, June 1944

Orsborn, Albert, Nov 1946, *Obit* Apr 1967

Osman Ali, Oct 1948, *Obit* Apr 1967

Ottaviani, Alfredo, Yrbk 1966, *Obit* Sept 1979

Paul, Jan 1956, Nov 1963, *Obit* Sept 1978

Pellegrinetti, Ermenegildo, *Obit* May 1943

Phillips, Theodore Evelyn Reece, *Obit* July 1942

Phillips, Ze Barney Thorne, *Obit* July 1942

Pius, Apr 1941, Mar 1950, *Obit* Yrbk 1958

Poling, Daniel A., Nov 1943, *Obit* Mar 1968

Potter, Dan, Feb 1964

Preus, Jacob A. O., clergyman and church official, May 1975, *Obit* Oct 1994

Pruden, Edward Hughes, clergyman, Sept 1950

Pugmire, Ernest I., Apr 1945, *Obit* Sept 1953

Rael, French cult leader, Jan 2002

Ramadan, Tariq, Swiss Islamic leader, Jan 2004

Ray, Randolph, Apr 1945, *Obit* July 1963

Reinartz, F. Eppling, July 1953

Reisner, Christian Fichthorne, *Obit* Sept 1940

Riggs, T. Lawrason, *Obit* June 1943

Ritter, Joseph Elmer, Yrbk 1964, *Obit* Oct 1967

Roy, Maurice, Feb 1958, *Obit* Jan 1986

Rugambwa, Laurean, Sept 1960, *Obit* Feb 1998

Rutenberg, Pinhas, *Obit* Mar 1942

Rutherford, J. F., religious leader, Nov 1940, *Obit* Mar 1942

Ryan, John A., priest and theologian, *Obit* Oct 1945

Sayre, Francis B., American cathedral dean, Yrbk 1956, *Obit* Yrbk 2008

Scherer, Paul, May 1941, *Obit* May 1969

Schiotz, Fredrik Axel, clergyman, Apr 1972, *Obit* May 1989

Schleich, Michel, *Obit* June 1945

Schonborn, Christoph von, Jan 2006

Sergii, *Obit* July 1944

Shaver, Erwin L., Mar 1949

Shehan, Lawrence, Oct 1965, *Obit* Oct 1984

Sherrill, Henry Knox, Mar 1947, *Obit* June 1980

Sin, Jaime, Sept 1995, *Obit* Yrbk 2005

Smith, George Albert, Nov 1947, *Obit* May 1951

Smith, Ida B. Wise, Feb 1943, *Obit* Apr 1952

Sockman, Ralph Washington, clergyman, June 1946, *Obit* Nov 1970

Stepinac, Alojzije, Feb 1953, *Obit* Apr 1960

Stewart, George Craig, *Obit* Jan 1940

Storr, Vernon Faithfull, *Obit* Yrbk 1940

Stott, John R. W., British clergyman and evangelist, May 2005, *Obit* Yrbk 2011

Stritch, Samuel Alphonsus, Apr 1946, *Obit* Sept 1958

Taylor, George Braxton, clergyman, *Obit* Apr 1942

Thadden-Trieglaff, Reinold von, July 1959

Tien, Thomas, May 1946, *Obit* Oct 1967

Tisserant, Eugene, Apr 1963, *Obit* Apr 1972

Upham, Francis Bourne, *Obit* May 1941

Visser 't Hooft, Willem Adolph, Dutch clergyman and

theologian, May 1949, *Obit* Aug 1985

Voris, John Ralph, Yrbk 1948, *Obit* Mar 1968

Warren, Harry Marsh, *Obit* Feb 1941

Watson, Samuel Newell, *Obit* May 1942

Wedel, Cynthia C., religious leader, Mar 1970, *Obit* Oct 1986

Wegner, Nicholas H., Yrbk 1949, *Obit* May 1976

White, Wilbert Webster, *Obit* Oct 1944

Woodcock, Charles Edward, *Obit* Mar 1940

Wright, John J., Feb 1963, *Obit* Oct 1979

Wyszynski, Stefan, Jan 1958, *Obit* July 1981

Yassin, Ahmed, Palestinian Islamic leader, July 1998, *Obit* Yrbk 2004

Yusuf, Hamza, American Islamic leader, Mar 2007

Religious officials

Barnett, Eugene Epperson, May 1941

Carlyle, A. J., *Obit* July 1943

Cashman, Robert, Nov 1952

Gruber, L. Franklin, *Obit* Feb 1942

Hauser, Conrad Augustine, *Obit* Apr 1943

Knox, Louise Chambers, *Obit* Mar 1942

Manson, John T., *Obit* Apr 1944

Meehan, Thomas F., *Obit* Sept 1942

Orsborn, Albert, Nov 1946, *Obit* Apr 1967

Pugmire, Ernest I., Apr 1945, *Obit* Sept 1953

Shaver, Erwin L., Mar 1949

Thadden-Trieglaff, Reinold von, July 1959

Religious scholars

Barth, Karl, Swiss theologian, Nov 1962, *Obit* Feb 1969

Brookes, George S., Aug 1940

Cox, Harvey Gallagher, American theologian, Nov 1968

Holt, Arthur E., *Obit* Mar 1942

Johnson, Elizabeth A., American theologian, Nov 2002

Maynard, John Albert, Oct 1943

Moffatt, James, English theologian, *Obit* Aug 1944

Moore, Edward Caldwell, *Obit* May 1943

Rahner, Karl, German theologian, July 1970, *Obit* May 1984

Smith, George Adam, Scottish biblical scholar, *Obit* Apr 1942

Visser 't Hooft, Willem Adolph, Dutch clergyman and theologian, May 1949, *Obit* Aug 1985

Resort executives

Grossinger, Jennie, American resort owner, Oct 1956, *Obit* Jan 1973

Restaurant employees

Achatz, Grant, American chef and restaurateur, Jan 2011

Adria, Ferran, Spanish chef and restaurateur, Jan 2006

Andr,s, Jos,, Spanish chef and restaurateur, June 2013

Arzak, Juan Mari, Spanish chef and restaurateur, Jan 2007

Billingsley, Sherman, American nightclub owner, Feb 1946, *Obit* Yrbk 1966

Bocuse, Paul, French chef and restaurateur, Jan 1988

Boulud, Daniel, French chef and restaurateur, Jan 2005

Chang, David, American chef and restaurateur, Aug 2010

English, Todd, American chef and restaurateur, Jan 2012

Greenberg, Jack, fast food industry executive, Nov 2001

Hamilton, Gabrielle, American chef and restaurateur, May 2013

Henderson, Fergus, British chef and restaurateur, Feb 2011

Holzen, Heinz von, Swiss chef and restaurateur, Jan 2002

Johnson, Howard B., Sept 1966

Mardikian, George M., Nov 1947

Matsuhisa, Nobu, Japanese chef and restaurateur, Jan 2005

Meyer, Danny, American restaurateur, July 2007

Morimoto, Masaharu, Japanese chef and restaurateur, Jan 2004

Puck, Wolfgang, Austrian-American

restaurateur and chef, Jan 1998

Regine, Belgian nightclub owner, Apr 1980

Robuchon, Joel, French chef and restaurateur, Jan 2003

Sanders, Harland, American restaurateur, Apr 1973, *Obit* Feb 1981

Sardi, Vincent, American restaurateur, May 1957, *Obit* Yrbk 2008

Sardi, Vincent, American restaurateur, May 1957, *Obit* Jan 1970

Schultz, Howard, American coffee chain executive, May 1997

Smith, Orin, American coffee retailer, Nov 2003

Waters, Alice, American chef and restaurateur, Jan 2004

White, Marco Pierre, British chef and restaurateur, Jan 2007

Restaurant industry executives

Ells, Steve, American restaurant chain executive, May 2012

Restaurateurs

Billingsley, Sherman, American nightclub owner, Feb 1946, *Obit* Yrbk 1966

DiSpirito, Rocco, American chef and restaurateur, Feb 2012

Lahlou, Mourad, Chef and restauranteur, May 2012

Mardikian, George M., Nov 1947

Redzepi, Ren,, Danish chef and restaurateur, Apr 2012

Regine, Belgian nightclub owner, Apr 1980

Sanders, Harland, American restaurateur, Apr 1973, *Obit* Feb 1981

Sardi, Vincent, American restaurateur, May 1957, *Obit* Yrbk 2008

Sardi, Vincent, American restaurateur, May 1957, *Obit* Jan 1970

Retail executives

Brennan, Edward A., American retail executive, Nov 1990, *Obit* Yrbk 2008

Custin, Mildred, retail executive, Nov 1967, *Obit* June 1997

Goodman, Andrew, American department store executive, Apr 1975, *Obit* June 1993

Hess, Max, Oct 1961, *Obit* Nov 1968

Houser, Theodore V., Mar 1957, *Obit* Feb 1964

Hoving, Walter, department store executive, Sept 1946, *Obit* Feb 1990

Jones, George L., American bookstore chain executive, Apr 2007

Kamprad, Ingvar, Swedish household furnishings chain executive, June 1998

Lewis, Mary, retail executive, Sept 1940

Marcus, Bernard, American home improvement chain executive, Aug 2007

Marcus, Stanley, American department store executive, June 1949, *Obit* Apr 2002

Marks of Broughton, Simon Marks, English merchant, Nov 1962, *Obit* Feb 1965

McConnell, F. B., July 1952, *Obit* Feb 1962

Meyrowitz, Carol, American retail executive, Nov 2011

Mirvish, Edwin, Canadian theater owner and producer, Apr 1989, *Obit* Yrbk 2007

Ortega Gaona, Amancio, Spanish clothing retailer, Aug 2012

Penney, James Cash, retail executive, Yrbk 1947, *Obit* Mar 1971

Puckett, B. Earl, Sept 1950, *Obit* Apr 1976

Scott, H. Lee, American retail executive, Oct 2006

Shaver, Dorothy, American department store executive, Jan 1946, *Obit* Sept 1959

Shield, Lansing P., June 1951, *Obit* Mar 1960

Sinegal, James D., American warehouse club executive, Aug 2007

Storch, Jerry, American retail executive, June 2007

Stutz, Geraldine, American retail executive, May 1983, *Obit* Yrbk 2005

Vandervelde, Luc, Belgian retail executive, Jan 2002

Vernon, Lillian, American mail order executive, Mar 1996

Walton, Sam, American retail executive, Mar 1992, *Obit* Mar 1992

Weil, Richard, July 1951, *Obit* July 1958

Wood, Robert Elkington, retail executive, May 1941, *Obit* Yrbk 1969

Retail personnel

Kraus, Hans Peter, American rare book dealer, July 1960, *Obit* Jan 1989

Ortega Gaona, Amancio, Spanish clothing retailer, Aug 2012

Revolutionaries

Alley, Rewi, New Zealand revolutionary, Oct 1943, *Obit* Feb 1988

Ayers, William, American educator, Apr 2009

Calero, Adolfo, Nicaraguan rebel leader, Oct 1987, *Obit* Yrbk 2012

Guevara, Ernesto, Argentine-Cuban revolutionary, June 1963, *Obit* Yrbk 1967

Jiang Zuobin, *Obit* Feb 1943

Li Liejun, *Obit* Apr 1946

Lin Sen, *Obit* Sept 1943

Minor, Robert, Apr 1941, *Obit* Jan 1953

Osama bin Laden, Saudi Arabian terrorist, *Obit* Yrbk 2012

Rodriguez, Cecilia, feminist and revolutionary, May 1999

Rodriguez, Nicolas, *Obit* Sept 1940

Savimbi, Jonas, Angolan rebel leader, Aug 1986, *Obit* June 2002

Tresca, Carlo, Italian anarchist, *Obit* Mar 1943

Ulianov, Dmitrii, *Obit* Sept 1943

Yassin, Ahmed, Palestinian Islamic leader, July 1998, *Obit* Yrbk 2004

Zamora, Ruben, Salvadoran rebel leader, Sept 1991

Rhythm and blues musicians

Ashanti (Singer), American rhythm and blues singer, Jan 2003

Baker, Anita, American singer, Apr 1989

Brown, Bobby, American singer, Apr 1991

Charles, Ray, American singer and pianist, Apr 1965, June 1992, *Obit* Yrbk 2004

DeBarge, El, American singer, June 2011

India.Arie (Singer), American singer, Feb 2002

Knight, Gladys, American singer, Feb 1987

LaBelle, Patti, American singer, July 1986

Omarion (Musician), American singer, Feb 2008

Rowland, Kelly, American singer, Aug 2001

Williams, Michelle, American singer, Aug 2001

Rock musicians

Bennington, Chester, American singer, Mar 2002

Bonamassa, Joe, Apr 2013

Bressanutti, Daniel, Belgian rock musician, Jan 2006

Cook, Jamie, British rock singer, Jan 2006

Cui Jian, Chinese rock musician, Jan 2002

Gabriel, Peter, English singer and songwriter, Jan 1990

Grebenshikov, Boris, Russian singer, Jan 2002

Hallyday, Johnny, French singer, Jan 2003

Jagger, Mick, British singer, Yrbk 1972

Joel, Billy, American singer and songwriter, Sept 1979

Jonsi Thor Birgisson, Icelandic singer, Jan 2003

Joplin, Janis, American singer, Mar 1970, *Obit* Mar 1970

Lee, Geddy, Canadian singer, Feb 2001

Lennon, John, English singer and songwriter, Yrbk 1965, *Obit* Feb 1981

Lennox, Annie, Scottish singer, May 1988

Little Richard, American singer, Sept 1986

Manson, Marilyn, American singer, May 1999

Martinez, Speedo, Argentine singer, Jan 2003

Neufeld, Sarah, Canadian violinist, Jan 2007

Osbourne, Ozzy, English singer, Nov 1998

Pallett, Owen, Canadian singer and violinist, Jan 2007

Petty, Tom, American singer and guitarist, Nov 1991

Plant, Robert, British singer, Oct 1998

Reed, Lou, American singer, July 1989

Rossi, Vasco, Italian rock singer, Jan 2005

Rotten, Johnny, English singer, Nov 1996

Shinoda, Mike, American singer, Mar 2002

Slick, Grace, American singer, Apr 1982

Smith, Patti, American rock singer, songwriter and poet, Apr 1989

Stipe, Michael, American singer, Apr 1997

Tyler, Steven, American rock singer, Aug 1996, July 2004

Yankovic, Al, American rock music parodist, Feb 1999

Romance writers

Briscoe, Connie, American romance novelist, Jan 2000

Cartland, Barbara, English romance novelist, Aug 1979, *Obit* Aug 2000

James, E.L., June 2013

Krantz, Judith, American romance novelist, May 1982

Ogilvie, Elisabeth, American novelist, Yrbk 1951, *Obit* Yrbk 2007

Roberts, Nora, American romance novelist, Sept 2001

Rowers

Redgrave, Steven, English rower, Jan 2000

Saville, Curtis, long distance rower, Jan 1986

Saville, Kathleen, long distance rower, Jan 1986

Royal favorites

Lupescu, Elena, mistress of King Carol II of Romania, Oct 1940, *Obit* Aug 1977

Royal pretenders

Juan Carlos, Oct 1951, *Obit* June 1993

Rugby players

Lomu, Jonah, New Zealand rugby player, Sept 2012

Pichot, Agustin, Argentine rugby player, Jan 2004

Runners (Athletes)

Aouita, Said, Moroccan runner, May 1990

Beatty, Jim, American runner, Jan 1963

Bolt, Usain, Jamaican runner, July 2009

Claiborne, Loretta, American runner, July 1996

Clarke, Ron, May 1971

Costa, Ronaldo da, Brazilian marathon runner, Jan 2002

El-Guerrouj, Hicham, Moroccan runner, Jan 2004

Elliott, Herb, Australian runner, July 1960

Freeman, Cathy, Australian runner, Jan 2002

Gebrselassie, Haile, Ethiopian runner, July 1999

Guevara, Ana, Mexican runner, Jan 2004

Holmes, Kelly, British runner, Jan 2004

Jazy, Michel, French runner, Apr 1967

Johnson, July 1996

Johnson, Ben, Canadian runner, June 1988

Keino, Kip, Kenyan runner, June 1967

Lagat, Bernard, Kenyan-American runner, Oct 2008

Mutai, Geoffrey, Long-distance runner, June 2013

Okayo, Margaret, Kenyan marathon runner, Jan 2004

Owens, Jesse, American runner, Nov 1956, *Obit* May 1980

Paddock, Charles W., sprinter, *Obit* Sept 1943

Patton, Mel, June 1949

Radcliffe, Paula, English runner, Jan 2003

Rice, Greg, runner, Yrbk 1941, *Obit* Aug 1991

Rodgers, Bill, American marathon runner, Aug 1982

Rudolph, Wilma, American runner, Sept 1961, *Obit* Jan 1995

Salazar, Alberto, American marathon runner, May 1983

Samuelson, Joan, American marathon runner, Aug 1996

Slaney, Mary Decker, American runner, Oct 1983

Torrence, Gwen, American sprinter, July 1996

Waitz, Grete, Norwegian marathon runner, Apr 1981, *Obit* Yrbk 2011

Williams, Lauryn, American runner, Sept 2008

Zatopek, Emil, Czech runner, Apr 1953, *Obit* Feb 2001

Sailors

Anderson, John W., American merchant marine officer, July 1953

Badger, Oscar C., American admiral, May 1949, *Obit* Feb 1959

Barbey, Daniel E., admiral, Jan 1945, *Obit* June 1969

Bisset, James, British ship captain, Yrbk 1946

Blandy, W. H. P., American admiral, Nov 1942, *Obit* Mar 1954

Bloch, Claude Charles, American admiral, Feb 1942, *Obit* Yrbk 1967

Bristol, Arthur LeRoy, *Obit* June 1942

Bryant, Benjamin, Nov 1943

Burke, Arleigh A., American admiral, Sept 1955, *Obit* Mar 1996

Butterworth, Brad, New Zealand yacht racer, Jan 2007

Callaghan, Daniel J., American admiral, *Obit* Jan 1943

Cantu, Giuseppe, *Obit* Yrbk 1940

Caperton, William B., American admiral, *Obit* Feb 1942

Cassady, John H., Oct 1952, *Obit* Mar 1969

Castro e Silva, Jose Machado de, *Obit* Aug 1943

Clark, J. J., American admiral, Jan 1954, *Obit* Sept 1971

Conner, Dennis, yacht racer, Nov 1987

Coutts, Russell, New Zealand boat racer, Jan 2003

Cruzen, Richard H., Mar 1947, *Obit* June 1970

Culshaw, John, British recording producer, June 1968, *Obit* June 1980

Cunningham of Hyndhope, Andrew Browne Cunningham, British admiral, May 1941, *Obit* Sept 1963

Curran, Joseph E., American labor leader, Apr 1945, *Obit* Oct 1981

Darlan, Francois, French admiral, Mar 1941, *Obit* Feb 1943

Davidson, John Frederick, admiral, Nov 1960, *Obit* Apr 1989

Denfeld, Louis E., American admiral, Yrbk 1947, *Obit* May 1972

Dennison, Robert L., Apr 1960, *Obit* May 1980

Du Fournet, Louis Rene Marie Charles Dartige, *Obit* Mar 1940

Fallon, William J., American admiral, July 2007

Fechteler, William M., American admiral, Sept 1951, *Obit* Oct 1967

Field, Frederick Laurence, *Obit* Yrbk 1945

Fraser, Bruce, July 1943, *Obit* Apr 1981

Gardner, Matthias B., June 1952

Ghormley, Robert Lee, admiral, Oct 1942, *Obit* Oct 1958

Halsey, William Frederick, American admiral, Yrbk 1942, *Obit* Nov 1959

Hancock, Joy Bright, naval officer, Feb 1949, *Obit* Oct 1986

Hart, Thomas Charles, Jan 1942, *Obit* Sept 1971

Hewitt, H. Kent, American admiral, Apr 1943, *Obit* Nov 1972

Holloway, James, American admiral, Jan 1947

Hough, Henry Hughes, *Obit* Oct 1943

Ingersoll, Royal E., Oct 1942, *Obit* July 1976

Jacobs, Randall, Aug 1942, *Obit* Oct 1967

Joy, C. Turner, American admiral, June 1951, *Obit* Sept 1956

Kidd, Isaac Campbell, *Obit* Feb 1942

Kimmel, Husband Edward, admiral, Jan 1942, *Obit* July 1968

King, Ernest Joseph, American admiral, Feb 1942, *Obit* Sept 1956

Kinkaid, Thomas Cassin, American admiral, Yrbk 1944, *Obit* Jan 1973

Koga, Mineichi, *Obit* Oct 1943

Laborde, Jean de, Feb 1943

Layton, Geoffrey, British admiral, Feb 1942

Leary, Herbert F., Aug 1942, *Obit* Feb 1958

Lemonnier, Andre, Nov 1952, *Obit* July 1963

Long, Andrew Theodore, *Obit* July 1946

Ma, G. John, July 1953

Manning, Harry, May 1952, *Obit* Oct 1974

McCain, John S., American admiral, June 1970, *Obit* June 1981

McCain, John Sidney, American admiral, Oct 1943, *Obit* Oct 1945

McDonald, David Lamar, admiral, Nov 1963, *Obit* Mar 1998

Meyers, George Julian, *Obit* Jan 1940

Mitscher, Marc Andrew, admiral, Aug 1944, *Obit* Mar 1947

Moore, Henry Ruthven, Sept 1943, *Obit* May 1978

Mountevans, Edward Ratcliffe Garth Russell Evans, British admiral, May 1941, *Obit* Nov 1957

Mullen, Mike, American admiral, Feb 2008

Nagano, Osami, July 1942, *Obit* Feb 1947

Nelles, Percy Walker, Canadian admiral, Feb 1944

Nimitz, Chester W., American admiral, Feb 1942, *Obit* Mar 1966

Orville, Howard T., May 1956, *Obit* July 1960

Osumi, Mineo, *Obit* Apr 1941

Pound, Dudley, Jan 1941, *Obit* Yrbk 1943

Pride, Alfred Melville, admiral, Nov 1954, *Obit* Feb 1989

Pugh, Herbert Lamont, Mar 1951

Radford, Arthur W., American admiral, Nov 1949, *Obit* Oct 1973

Ramsay, Bertram, British admiral, Mar 1944, *Obit* Feb 1945

Rawlings, Bernard, Aug 1945, *Obit* Yrbk 1962

Rickover, Hyman George, American admiral, May 1953, *Obit* Aug 1986

Robinson, Samuel M., Feb 1942

Royal, Forrest B., American admiral, *Obit* July 1945

Schofield, Frank H., *Obit* Apr 1942

Sexton, W. R., *Obit* Oct 1943

Sherman, Forrest P., Mar 1948, *Obit* Sept 1951

Sides, John H., Jan 1961, *Obit* June 1978

Smith, William Ward, American admiral, Feb 1948, *Obit* July 1966

Solberg, Thorvald A., American admiral, Yrbk 1948

Somerville, James, British admiral, Apr 1943, *Obit* Apr 1949

Spruance, Raymond Ames, American admiral, Apr 1944, *Obit* Mar 1970

Stark, Harold R., admiral, May 1940, *Obit* Oct 1972

Struble, Arthur Dewey, admiral, Nov 1951, *Obit* July 1983

Stump, Felix B., American admiral, Jan 1953, *Obit* Sept 1972

Tawresey, John Godwin, American admiral, *Obit* Apr 1943

Tennant, William George, British admiral, Feb 1945, *Obit* Sept 1963

Thach, John Smith, Yrbk 1960

Towers, John Henry, American admiral, Oct 1941, *Obit* June 1955

Turner, Richmond Kelly, admiral, Apr 1944, *Obit* Apr 1961

Vian, Philip, British admiral, Aug 1944, *Obit* Sept 1968

Vickery, H. L., American admiral, Yrbk 1943, *Obit* May 1946

Wake-Walker, William Frederick, British admiral, *Obit* Oct 1945

Wilcox, J. W., American admiral, *Obit* May 1942

Wilde, Louise K., Apr 1954

Yamamoto, Isoroku, Japanese admiral, Feb 1942, *Obit* July 1943

Zumwalt, Elmo R., American admiral, June 1971, *Obit* June 2000

Salsa musicians

Cruz, Celia, Cuban-American singer, July 1983, *Obit* Nov 2003

La India, Puerto Rican salsa singer, May 2002

Sanitary engineers

Wolman, Abel, sanitary engineer, Feb 1957, *Obit* May 1989

Saxophonists

Coleman, Ornette, American jazz saxophonist, June 1961

G, Kenny, American saxophonist, Nov 1995

Rollins, Sonny, American jazz saxophonist, Apr 1976

Sanborn, David, American saxophonist, Aug 1992

Shorter, Wayne, American jazz saxophonist, Apr 1996

Wiedoeft, Rudy, *Obit* Mar 1940

Zorn, John, American saxophonist, composer and conductor, Aug 1999

Scholars

Agacinski, Sylviane, Feb 2012

Andrews, Charles McLean, American historian, *Obit* Oct 1943

Barnhart, Clarence Lewis, lexicographer, Sept 1954, *Obit* Jan 1994

Bowman, George Ernest, American historian, *Obit* Nov 1941

Brand, Oscar, folklorist, June 1962

Burke, James, British science historian, Jan 2005

Cock, Guillermo A., Peruvian archaeologist, Jan 2007

Commager, Henry Steele, historian, Jan 1946, *Obit* May 1998

Davis-Kimball, Jeannine, American archaeologist, Feb 2006

Dorpfeld, Wilhelm, German archaeologist, *Obit* Jan 1940

Evans, Arthur John, British archaeologist, *Obit* Sept 1941

Fisher, Clarence S., *Obit* Sept 1941

Florinsky, Michael T., Russian historian, Oct 1941, *Obit* Jan 1982

Funk, Charles Earle, June 1947, *Obit* July 1957

Gilder, George F., American economist and forecaster, Oct 1981

Glucksmann, Andre, French philosopher, Jan 2006

Goddio, Franck, French marine archaeologist, Jan 2002

Gove, Philip Babcock, Oct 1962, *Obit* Jan 1973

Keyserling, Hermann, German philosopher, *Obit* June 1946

King, Alexander, Scottish chemist and futurist, Jan 2002

Le Roy Ladurie, Emmanuel, French historian, July 1984

Love, Iris, archaeologist, Aug 1982

Maynard, John Albert, Oct 1943

McWhorter, John H., American linguist, Feb 2003

Moffatt, James, English theologian, *Obit* Aug 1944

Nichols, Roy Franklin, historian, July 1949, *Obit* Mar 1973

Ogden, C. K., English linguist, Jan 1944, *Obit* June 1957

Pares, Bernard, English historian, Jan 1946, *Obit* May 1949

Reich, Nathaniel Julius, *Obit* Nov 1943

Reinhard, Johan, archaeologist, Aug 1999

Romer, John, British Egyptologist, July 2003

Shear, T. Leslie, *Obit* Aug 1945

Skinner, Quentin, British historian, Jan 2007

Smith, George Adam, Scottish biblical scholar, *Obit* Apr 1942

Spaeth, Sigmund, musicologist, July 1942, *Obit* Jan 1966

Thompson, R. Campbell, *Obit* July 1941

Utley, Freda, Yrbk 1958, *Obit* Mar 1978

Wedgwood, C. V., English historian, Jan 1957, *Obit* May 1997

Weizsacker, Carl Friedrich von, German physicist and philosopher, Jan 1985, *Obit* Yrbk 2007

Woodward, C. Vann, American historian, May 1986, *Obit* June 2000

Zizek, Slavoj, Slovenian philosopher, Jan 2004

School administrators

Bestor, Arthur E., American educator, *Obit* Mar 1944

Cartwright, Morse A., Sept 1947, *Obit* June 1974

Collins, Marva, American teacher, Nov 1986

Duggan, Laurence, May 1947, *Obit* Jan 1949

Hansen, Carl F., Oct 1962

Jansen, William, Oct 1951, *Obit* Apr 1968

Newlon, Jesse H., *Obit* Oct 1941

Santos, Rufino J., Yrbk 1960, *Obit* Nov 1973

Shaw, Lloyd, Sept 1943

Taft, Horace D., American school administrator and brother of President William H. Taft, *Obit* Mar 1943

Wanamaker, Pearl A., Sept 1946

Science consultants

Hafstad, Lawrence R., physicist, Oct 1956, *Obit* Jan 1994

Lapp, Ralph Eugene, American physicist, Nov 1955, *Obit* Feb 2005

Swings, Pol, Belgian astronomer, Yrbk 1954

Science fiction writers

Ballard, J. G., English novelist and short story writer, May 1988, *Obit* Yrbk 2009

King, Stephen, American novelist and short story writer, Oct 1981

Robinson, Kim Stanley, American science fiction writer, Nov 1998

Scientific administrators

Haworth, Leland J., Yrbk 1950, *Obit* May 1979

Scientists

Ahmed, Akbar S., Pakistani anthropologist, Jan 2005

Alcock, Norman Z., Canadian physicist, Mar 1963

Alibek, Ken, Kazakh biological weapons expert, June 2002

Anderson, William French, American geneticist, Oct 1994

Astin, Allen Varley, physicist, May 1956, *Obit* Apr 1984

Atwell, Wayne J., American anatomist, *Obit* May 1941

Austin, William Lane, American statistician, Apr 1940

Baekeland, Leo Hendrik, Belgian-American chemist, *Obit* Apr 1944

Bailey, Vernon, American naturalist, *Obit* June 1942

Ballard, Robert D., American oceanographer, June 1986

Baulieu, Etienne-Emile, French biochemist, Nov 1995

Bedford, Herbrand Arthur Russell, English zoologist, *Obit* Oct 1940

Bell Burnell, Jocelyn, British astronomer, May 1995

Benesh, Rudolf, British mathematician, July 1957

Bhabha, Homi Jehangir, Indian physicist, Sept 1956, *Obit* Feb 1966

Blakey, Michael L., biological anthropologist, Sept 2000

Blodgett, Katharine, American physicist, Jan 1940, May 1952, *Obit* Jan 1980

Bombieri, Enrico, Italian mathematician, Jan 2005

Bowie, Edward Hall, *Obit* Sept 1943

Bowman, Isaiah, American geographer, Jan 1945, *Obit* Feb 1950

Branly, Edouard, French physicist and inventor, *Obit* Apr 1940

Brenner, Charles H., forensic mathematician, Oct 2000

Britton, Edgar C., Apr 1952, *Obit* Oct 1962

Burpee, David, Mar 1955, *Obit* Aug 1980

Calderone, Mary Steichen, sexologist, Nov 1967, *Obit* Jan 1999

Cavalli-Sforza, Luigi Luca, Italian geneticist, Aug 1997

Cerf, Vinton G., American computer scientist, Sept 1998

Chizmadzhev, IUrii Aleksandrovich, Russian physical chemist, Jan 2005

Christofilos, Nicholas C., Nov 1965, *Obit* Nov 1972

Clemensen, Erik Christian, *Obit* July 1941

Coblentz, William W., American physicist, Mar 1954, *Obit* Nov 1962

Compton, Karl Taylor, Mar 1941, *Obit* Sept 1954

Cousteau, Fabien, Aquatic filmmaker and oceanographer, June 2012

Curtis, Heber D., American astronomer, *Obit* Mar 1942

D'Ambrosio, Ubiratan, Brazilian mathematician, Jan 2003

Dart, Raymond A., South African anatomist, Sept 1966, *Obit* Jan 1989

Davis, Joseph S., July 1947, *Obit* June 1975

Devereaux, William Charles, *Obit* Sept 1941

Dobzhansky, Theodosius Grigorievich, American geneticist, Sept 1962, *Obit* Feb 1976

Donoghue, John P., American neuroscientist, May 2010

Dow, Willard H., Feb 1944, *Obit* May 1949

Du Pont, Francis Irenee, *Obit* May 1942

Dunn, Gordon E., meteorologist, May 1966

Ellerman, Ferdinand, *Obit* Apr 1940

Emanuel, Kerry A., American meteorologist, Jan 2007

Evans, Alice Catherine, American bacteriologist, Oct 1943, *Obit* Oct 1975

Field, Henry, anthropologist, Mar 1955, *Obit* Mar 1986

Fish, Marie Poland, oceanographer, Oct 1941, *Obit* Apr 1989

Fisk, James Brown, Jan 1959, *Obit* Oct 1981

Foote, H. W., *Obit* Mar 1942

Foster, John S., Yrbk 1971

Freundlich, Herbert, German chemist, *Obit* May 1941

Funk, Casimir, biochemist, May 1945, *Obit* Jan 1968

Galdikas, Birute, Canadian primatologist, Mar 1995

Gallo, Robert C., biochemist, Oct 1986

Garwin, Richard, American physicist, Mar 1989

Gazzaniga, Michael S., American neuroscientist, Apr 1999

Getman, Frederick H., *Obit* Jan 1942

Goldenweiser, Alexander A., American anthropologist, *Obit* Sept 1940

Goldman-Rakic, Patricia S., American neuroscientist, Feb 2003

Gottlieb, Melvin, physicist, Jan 1974, *Obit* Mar 2001

Gray, William M., American meteorologist, Jan 2010

Greenfield, Susan, British neuroscientist, Jan 2003

Gurdon, John Bertrand, British microbiologist, Jan 2007

Haddon, Alfred Cort, British anthropologist, *Obit* May 1940

Hagens, Gunther von, German anatomist, Jan 2005

Hamer, Dean H., geneticist, June 1997

Hammond, John Hays, July 1962, *Obit* Apr 1965

Handler, Philip, biochemist, Feb 1964, *Obit* Feb 1982

Harris, Eva, American geneticist, Mar 2004

Hasegawa, Ichiro, Japanese astronomer, Jan 2004

Haushofer, Karl, German geographer, Apr 1942, *Obit* Sept 1946

Herlin, Emil, *Obit* Feb 1943

Heuer, Rolf-Dieter, German physicist, Mar 2012

Higgs, Peter, British physicist, Feb 2009

Higinbotham, William A., physicist, Feb 1947, *Obit* Jan 1995

Hill, Justina Hamilton, Apr 1941

Hillis, Daniel, American computer scientist, Feb 1995

Hooper, C. E., Apr 1947, *Obit* Feb 1955

Horgan, Stephen H., inventor, *Obit* Oct 1941

Horsfall, Frank L., American virologist, Mar 1941, Jan 1961, *Obit* Apr 1971

Howell, Wallace E., meteorologist, July 1950, *Obit* Sept 1999

Hoxie, Charles A., *Obit* Yrbk 1941

Iijima, Sumio, Japanese physicist, Nov 2009

Ittner, Martin H., Nov 1942, *Obit* May 1945

Johanson, Donald C., American anthropologist, Feb 1984

Johnson, Virginia E., American psychologist, Apr 1976, *Obit* Yrbk 2013

Jolly, Alison, American primatologist, Jan 2009

Jones, Harold Spencer, British astronomer, Mar 1955, *Obit* Jan 1961

Jordan, Frank Craig, *Obit* Apr 1941

Karle, Isabella L., American chemist, Jan 2003

Kaspersky, Eugene, Russian computer scientist, Jan 2005, June 2013

Kelly, Mervin J., physicist and engineer, Oct 1956, *Obit* May 1971

Kimball, James Henry, *Obit* Feb 1944

Knipling, E. F., entomologist, May 1975, *Obit* Yrbk 2000

Koller, Daphne, computer scientist, May 2013

Kozyrev, Nikolai A., Feb 1970

Krick, Irving, meteorologist, July 1950, *Obit* Sept 1996

Kroeber, A. L., American anthropologist, Oct 1958, *Obit* Yrbk 1960

Kurchatov, Igor Vasilevich, Russian physicist, Nov 1957, *Obit* Apr 1960

Lang, Robert J., American physicist and origami artist, July 2007

Langmuir, Arthur Comings, *Obit* July 1941

Lattes, C. M. G., Brazilian physicist, May 1949

Lauger, Paul, Oct 1945

Lee, Henry C., American forensic scientist, Aug 1996

Levene, Phoebus Aaron Theodore, American biochemist, *Obit* Oct 1940

Levine, Philip, American bacteriologist, May 1947, *Obit* Nov 1987

Li, Choh-hao, biochemist, Apr 1963, *Obit* Jan 1988

Lisi, Antony Garrett, American physicist, Sept 2012

Little, Clarence C., American biologist, Yrbk 1944, *Obit* Feb 1972

Lodge, Oliver Joseph, English physicist, *Obit* Oct 1940

Lovell, Bernard, English astronomer, Oct 1959, *Obit* Yrbk 2012

Lovins, Amory B., American physicist and conservationist, June 1997

Marett, Robert R., *Obit* Apr 1943

Marvin, Charles F., American meteorologist, *Obit* July 1943

Marvin, Harry, *Obit* Jan 1940

Massevitch, Alla G., Russian astronomer, Jan 1964

Masursky, Harold, geologist, Aug 1986, *Obit* Oct 1990

Matare, Herbert F., German physicist, Jan 2003

Matzinger, Polly, American immunologist, Oct 1998

Mayor, Michel, Swiss astronomer, Jan 2007

McAdie, Alexander, meteorologist, *Obit* Yrbk 1943

McFate, Montgomery, American cultural anthropologist, Aug 2008

McLurkin, James, American computer scientist, Sept 2005

Meitner, Lise, Austrian physicist, Sept 1945, *Obit* Sept 1968

Melton, Douglas, American molecular biologist, June 2008

Menzel, Donald Howard, physicist and astronomer, Apr 1956, *Obit* Mar 1977

Merriam, C. Hart, American mammalogist, *Obit* May 1942

Miller, Dayton C., American physicist, *Obit* Apr 1941

Miller, William Lash, Canadian chemist, *Obit* Oct 1940

Milner, Brenda, Canadian neuroscientist, Jan 2006

Minsky, Marvin Lee, American computer scientist, Sept 1988

Murayama, Makio, Oct 1974

Murdock, George J., *Obit* Sept 1942

Murdock, George Peter, anthropologist, Mar 1957

Nachtigall, Paul E., American marine scientist, Jan 2006

Norton, Thomas, *Obit* Jan 1942

Osborn, Fairfield, American naturalist and conservationist, Sept 1949, *Obit* Nov 1969

Paabo, Svante, Swedish geneticist, Feb 2007

Panofsky, Wolfgang Kurt Hermann, American physicist, June 1970, *Obit* Yrbk 2007

Peiris, Malik, Sri Lankan microbiologist, Jan 2003

Penney, William George Penney, English physicist, Feb 1953, *Obit* May 1991

Perelman, Grigori, Russian mathematician, Jan 2006

Perkins, C. H., June 1955, *Obit* Apr 1963

Perret, Frank Alvord, *Obit* Mar 1943

Perrin, Francis, French physicist, July 1951

Piccard, Auguste, Swiss physicist, Sept 1947, *Obit* May 1962

Piccard, Jacques, Swiss oceanographer, Yrbk 1965, *Obit* Yrbk 2009

Pincus, Gregory, American biologist, May 1966, *Obit* Oct 1967

Plaskett, John S., Canadian astronomer, *Obit* Yrbk 1941

Powdermaker, Hortense, American anthropologist, Feb 1961, *Obit* Sept 1970

Profet, Margie, biologist, Nov 1998

Randers, Gunnar, Jan 1957

Reichelderfer, Francis Wilton, meteorologist, May 1949, *Obit* Mar 1983

Revelle, Roger, American oceanographer, Mar 1957, *Obit* Sept 1991

Rockley, Alicia Margaret Tyssen-Amherst Cecil, *Obit* Nov 1941

Rogers, Lynn L., wildlife biologist, Oct 1994

Rolland, Michel, American enologist, Jan 2007

Roman, Nancy Grace, astronomer, Yrbk 1960

Rubin, Eddy, American geneticist, Jan 2006

Sager, Ruth, geneticist, July 1967, *Obit* June 1997

Salzano, Francisco M., Brazilian geneticist, Jan 2006

Sandage, Allan, American astronomer, Jan 1999, *Obit* Yrbk 2011

Schaefer, Vincent J., American chemist and meteorologist, Jan 1948, *Obit* Sept 1993

Schiller, Daniela, Israeli neuroscientist, Mar 2011

Schlesinger, Frank, astronomer, *Obit* Aug 1943

Schmelkes, Franz C., *Obit* Feb 1943

Schmidt, Maarten, Dutch astronomer, Sept 1966

Schwarzschild, Martin, astronomer, Feb 1967, *Obit* June 1997

Schwidetzky, Oscar, Yrbk 1943, *Obit* Nov 1963

Shaw, Louis Agassiz, *Obit* Oct 1940

Shiras, George, American lawyer and naturalist, *Obit* May 1942

Shoemaker, Eugene Merle, planetary geologist, June 1967, *Obit* Oct 1997

Shreeve, Herbert Edward, *Obit* June 1942

Silver, Nate, American baseball statistician and pollster, Feb 2013

Sinclair, David, Australian molecular biologist, Sept 2008

Skolnick, Mark H., geneticist, June 1997

Smyth, Henry DeWolf, physicist, Yrbk 1948, *Obit* Nov 1986

Snell, Foster Dee, Jan 1943

Snook, H. Clyde, *Obit* Nov 1942

Snow, Clyde, forensic anthropologist, Apr 1997

Sperti, George Speri, biophysicist, Jan 1940, *Obit* July 1991

Spiropulu, Maria, Greek physicist, May 2004

Stefansson, Kari, Icelandic geneticist, Jan 2003

Stewart, Harris B., oceanographer, Mar 1968

Stine, Charles Milton Altland, Jan 1940, *Obit* Sept 1954

Stone, Edward C., American physicist, Feb 1990

Struve, Otto, astronomer, Oct 1949, *Obit* June 1963

Suits, Chauncey Guy, physicist and inventor, Feb 1950, *Obit* Oct 1991

Suzuki, Umetaro, *Obit* Nov 1943

Sveda, Michael, chemist and inventor, Yrbk 1954, *Obit* Nov 1999

Szilard, Leo, Hungarian physicist, Jan 1947, *Obit* July 1964

Tainter, Charles Sumner, *Obit* May 1940

Telkes, Maria, American chemist, Nov 1950, *Obit* Oct 1996

Thaler, William J., American physicist, Feb 1960, *Obit* Yrbk 2005

Thomas, William Leroy, Mar 1958

Thompson, Kenneth Lane, American computer scientist, Mar 1999

Thompson, Lonnie, American glaciologist, Jan 2004

Tishler, Max, chemist, Mar 1952, *Obit* May 1989

Totty, Charles H., Jan 1940

Van Slyke, Donald D., Jan 1943, *Obit* July 1971

Veksler, V. I., Russian physicist, Jan 1965, *Obit* Nov 1966

Venter, J. Craig, American biochemist, Feb 1995

Vogelstein, Bert, molecular biologist, Jan 1996

Volterra, Vito, Italian mathematician and physicist, *Obit* Yrbk 1940

Voytek, Bradley, Neuroscientist, May 2012

Warner, W. Lloyd, American anthropologist and sociologist, Yrbk 1959, *Obit* July 1970

Waterman, Alan T., American physicist, June 1951, *Obit* Feb 1968

Weinberg, Alvin M., American physicist, Sept 1966, *Obit* Yrbk 2006

Weinberg, Robert A., American biochemist, June 1983

Wells, Spencer, American geneticist, Mar 2008

Wendt, Gerald Louis, scientist, Mar 1940, *Obit* Feb 1974

White, Robert M., American meteorologist, Mar 1964

Wiigh-Masak, Susanne, Swedish ecologist, Jan 2005

Williams, Robert R., Sept 1951, *Obit* Yrbk 1965

Wilmut, Ian, British embryologist, June 1997

Wilson, Robert R., American physicist, Aug 1989, *Obit* May 2000

Wilson, Volney C., June 1958

Worden, Edward Chauncey, *Obit* Nov 1940

Yamanaka, Shinya, Japanese geneticist, June 2013

Yamashita Yukiko, Developmental biologist, Mar 2012

York, Herbert F., American physicist, Yrbk 1958, *Obit* Yrbk 2009

Zinn, Walter H., nuclear physicist, Yrbk 1955, *Obit* Aug 2000

Zuckerman, Solly Zuckerman, English scientist, July 1972, *Obit* May 1993

Zwicky, Fritz, Swiss astronomer, Apr 1953, *Obit* Apr 1974

Scout leaders

Baden-Powell of Gilwell, Robert Stephenson Smyth Baden-Powell, English Boy Scouts founder, *Obit* Mar 1941

Cloninger, Kathy, American Girl Scouts official, Oct 2012

Wood, Louise Aletha, Girl Scouts leader, July 1961, *Obit* July 1988

Screenwriters

Anderson, Robert, American dramatist and screenwriter, Sept 1954, *Obit* Yrbk 2009

Anouilh, Jean, French dramatist, Apr 1954, *Obit* Nov 1987

Benson, Sally, American short story writer, dramatist and screenwriter, Aug 1941, *Obit* Sept 1972

Bolt, Robert, English dramatist and screenwriter, July 1963, *Obit* Apr 1995

Carlino, Lewis John, dramatist and filmmaker, May 1983

Chayefsky, Paddy, American screenwriter and dramatist, Sept 1957, *Obit* Sept 1981

Collison, Wilson, *Obit* July 1941

D'Usseau, Arnaud, dramatist and screenwriter, Mar 1944, *Obit* Apr 1990

Delaney, Shelagh, English playwright and screenwriter, Apr 1962, *Obit* Yrbk 2012

Eszterhas, Joe, American screenwriter, Apr 1998

Frings, Ketti, dramatist and screenwriter, Jan 1960, *Obit* Apr 1981

Fuller, Charles, American dramatist, June 1989

Goldin, Daniel, screenwriter, June 1993

Goldsman, Akiva, American screenwriter, Sept 2004

Goodrich, Frances, American dramatist and screenwriter, Oct 1956, *Obit* Apr 1984

Gow, James Ellis, Mar 1944, *Obit* Mar 1952

Grahame-Smith, Seth, American screenwriter, Nov 2012

Hackett, Albert, American dramatist and screenwriter, Oct 1956, *Obit* May 1995

Henley, Beth, American dramatist, Feb 1983

Inge, William, American dramatist, June 1953, *Obit* July 1973

Johnson, Nunnally, screenwriter, Aug 1941, *Obit* May 1977

Jones, Grover, *Obit* Nov 1940

Kaufman, Charlie, American screenwriter, July 2005

Krasna, Norman, dramatist and screenwriter, May 1952, *Obit* Feb 1985

Logan, John, American screenwriter and playwright, Feb 2011

Marber, Patrick, English dramatist, Jan 2007

Miller, Arthur, American dramatist, Oct 1947, Feb 1973, *Obit* July 2005

Nichols, Dudley, screenwriter, Sept 1941, *Obit* Mar 1960

Odets, Clifford, American dramatist, Nov 1941, *Obit* Nov 1963

Ross, Gary, American screenwriter, May 2004

Saunders, John Monk, screenwriter, *Obit* Apr 1940

Serling, Rod, American television scriptwriter and screenwriter, Yrbk 1959, *Obit* Aug 1975

Simon, Neil, American playwright, Feb 1968, Mar 1989

Sorkin, Aaron, American television scriptwriter, June 2000

West, Claudine, *Obit* May 1943

Whedon, Joss, American film and television scriptwriter, July 2012

Willimon, Beau, American playwright, June 2012

Sculptors

Aaltonen, Waino, June 1954, *Obit* July 1966

Abakanowicz, Magdalena, Polish sculptor, Jan 2001

Adams, Herbert, sculptor, *Obit* June 1945

Andersen, Hendrik Christian, American sculptor, *Obit* Feb 1941

Andre, Carl, American sculptor, May 1986

Archambault, Louis, Sept 1959

Archipenko, Alexander, Russian sculptor, Sept 1953, *Obit* Apr 1964

Armitage, Kenneth, English sculptor, Apr 1957, *Obit* May 2002

Aronson, Naoum, Russian sculptor, *Obit* Nov 1943

Artschwager, Richard, painter and sculptor, July 1990, *Obit* Yrbk 2013

Barney, Matthew, American sculptor and installation and video artist, Aug 2003

Barthe, Richmond, American sculptor, July 1940, *Obit* May 1989

Beuys, Joseph, German artist, July 1980, *Obit* Mar 1986

Biddle, George, American painter and sculptor, Feb 1942, *Obit* Jan 1974

Bontecou, Lee, American sculptor, assemblage artist and printmaker, Mar 2004

Borglum, Gutzon, American sculptor and painter, *Obit* Apr 1941

Botero, Fernando, Colombian painter and sculptor, Mar 1980

Bourgeois, Louise, American sculptor, Oct 1983, *Obit* Yrbk 2010

Brancusi, Constantin, Romanian sculptor, Sept 1955, *Obit* June 1957

Calder, Alexander, American sculptor, Apr 1946, July 1966, *Obit* Jan 1977

Calder, Alexander Stirling, American sculptor, *Obit* Feb 1945

Callery, Mary, July 1955

Caro, Anthony, English sculptor, Nov 1981

Catlett, Elizabeth, American sculptor and printmaker, May 1998, *Obit* Yrbk 2012

Chillida, Eduardo, Spanish sculptor, Sept 1985, *Obit* Yrbk 2002

Chryssa, American sculptor and painter, Nov 1978

Dallin, Cyrus Edwin, sculptor, *Obit* Jan 1945

De Creeft, Jose, sculptor, Yrbk 1942, *Obit* Yrbk 1991

Deming, Edwin Willard, painter and sculptor, *Obit* Yrbk 1942

Der Harootian, Koren, Jan 1955

Di Suvero, Mark, sculptor, Nov 1979

Dubuffet, Jean, French painter and sculptor, July 1962, *Obit* July 1985

Estern, Neil, American sculptor, Nov 2008

Ferber, Herbert, American sculptor and painter, Nov 1960, *Obit* Oct 1991

Fischl, Eric, American painter and sculptor, June 1986

Flannagan, John, American sculptor, *Obit* Mar 1942

Fraser, James Earle, sculptor and medalist, July 1951, *Obit* Jan 1954

Friedman, Tom, American sculptor, Oct 2008

Gabo, Naum, Russian painter and sculptor, Apr 1972, *Obit* Oct 1977

Giacometti, Alberto, Swiss sculptor, Feb 1956, *Obit* Feb 1966

Glicenstein, Enrico, *Obit* Feb 1943

Goldsworthy, Andy, English photographer and sculptor, Oct 2000

Gorman, R. C., American painter and sculptor, Jan 2001

Graves, Nancy, American painter and sculptor, May 1981, *Obit* Jan 1996

Hanson, Duane, American sculptor, Oct 1983, *Obit* Mar 1996

Hawkinson, Tim, American sculptor, Aug 2005

Hayes, David, Apr 1966, *Obit* Yrbk 2013

Hepworth, Barbara, English sculptor, Feb 1957, *Obit* Aug 1975

Hirschhorn, Thomas, Swiss installation artist, Sept 2009

Hoffman, Malvina, American sculptor, Yrbk 1940, *Obit* Sept 1966

Huntington, Anna Hyatt, American sculptor, Oct 1953, *Obit* Yrbk 1973

Indiana, Robert, American painter and sculptor, Mar 1973

Johns, Jasper, American painter, May 1967, May 1987

Kapoor, Anish, Indian-British video artist and sculptor, Sept 2013

Kienholz, Edward, American painter and sculptor, Aug 1989, *Obit* Aug 1994

Koussevitzky, Natalya, *Obit* Mar 1942

Lassaw, Ibram, American sculptor, Jan 1957, *Obit* Yrbk 2004

Laurent, Robert, July 1942, *Obit* June 1970

Lipchitz, Jacques, French sculptor, Nov 1948, Apr 1962, *Obit* July 1973

Lippold, Richard, American sculptor, Nov 1956, *Obit* Yrbk 2002

Lipton, Seymour, American sculptor, Nov 1964, *Obit* Feb 1987

Lober, Georg John, Nov 1957, *Obit* Feb 1962

Manship, Paul, American sculptor, May 1940, *Obit* Mar 1966

Marini, Marino, Italian sculptor, Jan 1954, *Obit* Oct 1980

Marisol, Venezuelan sculptor, Apr 1968

Mastroianni, Umberto, Sept 1960

Mestrovic, Ivan, Yugoslav sculptor, Oct 1940, *Obit* Mar 1962

Milles, Carl, sculptor, Yrbk 1940, Yrbk 1952, *Obit* Nov 1955

Morris, Robert, American artist, Apr 1971

Nakian, Reuben, sculptor, Feb 1985, *Obit* Feb 1987

Neals, Otto, American sculptor and painter, Feb 2003

Neto, Ernesto, Brazilian artist, Oct 2009

Nevelson, Louise, American sculptor, Oct 1967, *Obit* May 1988

O'Connor, Andrew, *Obit* Aug 1941

Pelosini, Paolo, Italian sculptor, Jan 2005

Pevsner, Antoine, Russian sculptor, Mar 1959, *Obit* June 1962

Puryear, Martin, American sculptor, Aug 1999

Rautenberg, Robert, Mar 1940

Richard, Louis, *Obit* Sept 1940

Rickey, George W., American sculptor, Feb 1980, *Obit* Yrbk 2002

Riopelle, Jean-Paul, Canadian painter and sculptor, Oct 1989, *Obit* Sept 2002

Robus, Hugo, Yrbk 1962, *Obit* Feb 1964

Rosenquist, James, American painter, Sept 1970

Roszak, Theodore J., Polish-American painter and sculptor, June 1966, *Obit* Oct 1981

Ruckstull, Frederick Wellington, sculptor, *Obit* July 1942

Savage, Augusta Christine, American sculptor, Jan 1941, *Obit* May 1962

Scudder, Janet, painter and sculptor, *Obit* July 1940

Segal, George, American sculptor, Jan 1972, *Obit* Sept 2000

Serra, Richard, American sculptor, Jan 1985

Soto, Jesus Raphael, Venezuelan painter and sculptor, Jan 2004

Soulages, Pierre, French painter, graphic artist and set designer, Apr 1958

Stankiewicz, Richard, American sculptor, June 1967, *Obit* May 1983

Tinguely, Jean, Swiss artist, Jan 1966, *Obit* Oct 1991

Tsereteli, Zurab, Russian sculptor, Jan 2007

Van Loen, Alfred, Feb 1961

Vangi, Giuliano, Italian sculptor, Jan 2003

Voulkos, Peter, American sculptor and ceramist, Nov 1997, *Obit* Aug 2002

Waugh, Sidney, July 1948, *Obit* Sept 1963

Wheelock, Warren, Mar 1940, *Obit* Oct 1960

Whiteread, Rachel, English sculptor, Jan 2006

Zadkine, Ossip, Russian sculptor, Mar 1957, *Obit* Jan 1968

Zorach, William, American sculptor and painter, Feb 1943, Feb 1963, *Obit* Jan 1967

Secret service agents

Rowley, James Joseph, secret service official, Jan 1963, *Obit* Jan 1993

Secretaries of agriculture

Lyng, Richard E., American Secretary of agriculture, Sept 1986, *Obit* Yrbk 2003

Wickard, Claude Raymond, American Secretary of agriculture, Oct 1940, *Obit* June 1967

Secretaries of commerce

Harrington, Francis Clark, *Obit* Mar 1940

Jones, Jesse Holman, American Secretary of commerce, Oct 1940, *Obit* Sept 1956

Secretaries of defense

Lehman, John F., secretary of the navy, Nov 1985

Secretaries of the interior

Watt, James G., American Secretary of the interior, Jan 1982

Secretaries of the treasury

Morgenthau, Henry, American Secretary of the treasury, Sept 1940, *Obit* Apr 1967

Secretaries of transportation

Lewis, Drew, American Secretary of transportation, Feb 1982

Slater, Rodney, American Secretary of transportation, Jan 1999

Secretaries of veterans affairs

Brown, Jesse, American Secretary of veterans affairs, Nov 1993, *Obit* Yrbk 2002

Securities brokers

Bache, Harold L., American securities broker, May 1959

Boylan, Robert P., Apr 1950

Chadwick, Florence, American swimmer and stockbroker, Oct 1950, *Obit* May 1995

Mehta, Deena, Indian securities broker, Jan 2005

Merrill, Charles Edward, American stockbroker, Apr 1956

Nkontchou, Cyrille, Cameroonian securities broker, Jan 2004

Siebert, Muriel, American stockbroker, Aug 1997, *Obit* Yrbk 2013

Security consultants

Abagnale, Frank, American security consultant and former con artist, Apr 2011

Set designers

Fisk, Jack, American motion picture production designer, June 2011

Geddes, Norman Bel, stage designer and producer, May 1940, *Obit* July 1958

Jones, Robert Edmond, scenic designer, Nov 1946, *Obit* Jan 1955

Lee, Ming Cho, Chinese-American set designer, June 1989

Loquasto, Santo, scenic designer, June 1981

Mielziner, Jo, Mar 1946, *Obit* May 1976

Smith, Oliver, American set designer, Sept 1961, *Obit* Mar 1994

Ter-Arutunian, Rouben, Russian stage designer, June 1963, *Obit* Jan 1993

Throckmorton, Cleon, Sept 1943, *Obit* Yrbk 1965

Sex researchers

Calderone, Mary Steichen, sexologist, Nov 1967, *Obit* Jan 1999

Ship captains

Bisset, James, British ship captain, Yrbk 1946

Shoe designers

Blahnik, Manolo, Spanish shoe designer, Jan 2004

McNairy, Mark, American shoe designer, July 2013

Short story writers

Abdullah, Achmed, British novelist and short story writer, *Obit* June 1945

Abe, Kobo, Japanese novelist, July 1989, *Obit* Mar 1993

Adams, Alice, American short story writer, Aug 1989, *Obit* Aug 1999

Aksenov, Vasilii Pavlovich, Russian novelist, Jan 1990, *Obit* Yrbk 2009

Anderson, Sherwood, American novelist and short story writer, *Obit* Apr 1941

Babson, Naomi Lane, American novelist and short story writer, Yrbk 1952

Baker, Nicholson, American novelist, Aug 1994

Banks, Russell, American novelist and short story writer, Jan 1992

Banville, John, Irish novelist, May 1992

Barthelme, Donald, American short story writer and novelist, Mar 1976, *Obit* Sept 1989

Bates, H. E., English short story writer and novelist, Sept 1944, *Obit* Mar 1974

Beattie, Ann, American novelist and short story writer, Oct 1985

Berlin, Ellin, author and wife of Irving Berlin, Aug 1944, *Obit* Sept 1988

Boles, Paul Darcy, author, Yrbk 1956, *Obit* June 1984

Boyle, T. Coraghessan, American novelist and short story writer, Jan 1991

Carver, Raymond, American short story writer and poet, Feb 1984, *Obit* Sept 1988

Chabon, Michael, American novelist, Nov 2012

Chaon, Dan, American novelist and short story writer, Feb 2012

Cheever, John, American novelist and short story writer, Sept 1975, *Obit* Aug 1982

Condon, Frank, *Obit* Feb 1941

Cooper, Louise Field, author, Yrbk 1950, *Obit* Jan 1993

Coover, Robert, American novelist, Feb 1991

Crawford, Phyllis, author, Nov 1940

De Lima, Sigrid, novelist, Yrbk 1958, *Obit* Feb 2000

DeLillo, Don, American novelist, Jan 1989

Delafield, E. M., English novelist, *Obit* Jan 1944

Doerr, Anthony, American short story writer and novelist, Oct 2011

Elkin, Stanley, American novelist and short story writer, July 1987, *Obit* Aug 1995

Emery, Anne, author, Yrbk 1952

Farrell, James T., American novelist and short story writer, Sept 1942, *Obit* Oct 1979

Forbes, Kathryn, Yrbk 1944, *Obit* June 1966

Ford, Richard, American novelist and short story writer, Sept 1995

Freed, Lynn, South African novelist, Jan 2002

Friel, Brian, Irish short story writer and dramatist, June 1974

Gaither, Frances, author, Yrbk 1950, *Obit* Jan 1956

Gallant, Mavis, Canadian short story writer and novelist, May 1990

Garner, Helen, Australian novelist, Jan 2007

Gordon, Mary, American novelist, Nov 1981

Grandes, Almudena, Spanish novelist, Jan 2006

Grau, Shirley Ann, novelist and short story writer, Yrbk 1959

Guterson, David, American novelist and short story writer, Nov 1996

Havill, Edward, Yrbk 1952

Hawley, Cameron, Yrbk 1957

Hazzard, Shirley, Australian novelist and short story writer, Jan 1991

Hedden, Worth Tuttle, American novelist and short story writer, Yrbk 1957, *Obit* Jan 1986

Heller, Joseph, American novelist, Jan 1973, *Obit* Mar 2000

Hobson, Laura Keane Zametkin, author, Sept 1947, *Obit* Apr 1986

Ishiguro, Kazuo, Japanese-British novelist, Sept 1990

Jackson, Charles, novelist and short story writer, May 1944, *Obit* Nov 1968

Jacobs, W. W., English short story writer and novelist, *Obit* Oct 1943

Janowitz, Tama, American novelist and short story writer, Aug 1989

Jones, Edward P., American short story writer and novelist, Mar 2004

Judson, Clara Ingram, author, Yrbk 1948

Kingsolver, Barbara, American novelist and short story writer, July 1994

L'Amour, Louis, American western novelist, Feb 1980, *Obit* July 1988

LaValle, Victor D., American short story writer and novelist, Jan 2010

Malamud, Bernard, American novelist and short story writer, Yrbk 1958, July 1978, *Obit* May 1986

Mallette, Gertrude E., Yrbk 1950

Montero, Mayra, Cuban novelist and short story writer, Jan 2002

Mundy, Talbot, English novelist, *Obit* Sept 1940

O'Brien, Edna, Irish novelist and short story writer, Sept 1980

O'Connor, Edwin, American novelist and short story writer, Nov 1963, *Obit* May 1968

O'Connor, Flannery, American novelist and short story writer, Yrbk 1958, *Obit* Sept 1965

O'Hara, John, American novelist and short story writer, Feb 1941, *Obit* June 1970

Paley, Grace, American short story writer and poet, Mar 1986, *Obit* Yrbk 2007

Patton, Frances Gray, short story writer and novelist, Yrbk 1955, *Obit* Sept 2000

Porter, Katherine Anne, American short story writer, May 1940, Mar 1963, *Obit* Nov 1980

Powers, J. F., short story writer and novelist, Jan 1989, *Obit* Sept 1999

Raddall, Thomas Head, Canadian author, Yrbk 1951

Reuter, Gabriele, German author, *Obit* Jan 1942

Rhys, Jean, English novelist and short story writer, Yrbk 1972, *Obit* July 1979

Richter, Conrad, American novelist and short story writer, June 1951, *Obit* Yrbk 1968

Ritner, Ann, Yrbk 1953

Roberts, Charles G. D., Canadian poet and short story writer, *Obit* Jan 1944

Roth, Philip, American novelist and short story writer, Mar 1970, May 1991

Russell, Karen, American short story writer and novelist, May 2011

Sagan, Francoise, French novelist and short story writer, Sept 1960, *Obit* Feb 2005

Salinger, J. D., American novelist and short story writer, *Obit* Yrbk 2010

Salverson, Laura Goodman, Canadian author, Yrbk 1957

Seifert, Elizabeth, author, Yrbk 1951, *Obit* Oct 1983

Seifert, Shirley, Yrbk 1951

Shah, Idries, Indian author, June 1976, *Obit* Feb 1997

Shiner, Lewis, American novelist and short story writer, July 2011

Sittenfeld, Curtis, American novelist and short story writer, Nov 2008

Smiley, Jane, American novelist and short story writer, Apr 1990

Smith, Zadie, English novelist, Aug 2000

Spiegel, Clara E., novelist, Yrbk 1954

Stafford, Jean, American novelist and short story writer, Yrbk 1951, *Obit* May 1979

Sumner, Cid Ricketts, American novelist and short story writer, Yrbk 1954

Taylor, Elizabeth, English novelist and short story writer, Yrbk 1948

Taylor, Peter Hillsman, American short story writer and novelist, Apr 1987, *Obit* Jan 1995

Urrea, Luis Alberto, Mexican-American novelist and short story writer, Nov 2005

Walpole, Hugh, English novelist, *Obit* July 1941

Welsh, Irvine, Scottish novelist and short story writer, Nov 1997

Welty, Eudora, American short story writer and novelist, Jan 1942, Oct 1975, *Obit* Nov 2001

Wesker, Arnold, English dramatist, Feb 1962

Wright, Anna Rose, author, Yrbk 1952

Yerby, Frank, American novelist and short story writer, Sept 1946, *Obit* Mar 1992

Singers

Al-Jazairia, Warda, Algerian singer, Jan 2006

Alberghetti, Anna Maria, Italian singer, Jan 1955

Ameling, Elly, Dutch singer, Oct 1982

Andrews, Julie, English actress and singer, July 1956, Apr 1994

Apl. de. Ap (Musician), American singer, Oct 2006

Armstrong, Louis, American trumpet player, Sept 1944, Apr 1966, *Obit* Sept 1971

Aznavour, Charles, French singer and songwriter, Feb 1968

Belafonte, Harry, American singer and actor, Jan 1956

Bennett, Tony, American singer, Mar 1965, June 1995

Berry, Chuck, American singer and guitarist, Apr 1977

Bhosle, Asha, Indian singer, Jan 2006

Boone, Pat, American singer and actor, July 1959

Bostic, Onika, Trinidadian singer, Jan 2004

Bowie, David, English singer and songwriter, Oct 1976, Nov 1994

Braxton, Toni, American singer, Sept 2000

Buble, Michael, Canadian singer, May 2009

Bush, Kate, English singer and songwriter, Mar 1995

Carey, Mariah, American singer, July 1992

Carreras, Jose, Spanish opera singer, June 1979

Chao, Manu, French singer, Jan 2002

Clark, Petula, English singer, Feb 1970

Collins, Judy, American singer and songwriter, Apr 1969

Colvin, Shawn, singer, Mar 1999

Cook, Barbara, American singer, Feb 1963

D'Angelo, American singer, May 2001

Dearie, Blossom, American singer, Feb 1989, *Obit* Yrbk 2009

Domingo, Placido, Spanish opera singer, Mar 1972

Downey, Morton, American singer, July 1949, *Obit* Jan 1986

Dylan, Bob, American folk singer and songwriter, May 1965, Oct 1991

Elzy, Ruby, *Obit* Aug 1943

Faith, Paloma, Aug 2013

Farrell, Eileen, American singer, Feb 1961, *Obit* June 2002

Faussart, Celia, French singer, Jan 2003

Faussart, Helene, French singer, Jan 2003

Fernandez, Alejandro, Mexican singer, Jan 2005

Fisher, Eddie, American singer, Oct 1954, *Obit* Yrbk 2010

Flack, Roberta, American singer, Nov 1973

Francis, Connie, singer, July 1962

Franklin, Aretha, American singer, Yrbk 1968, May 1992

Funicello, Annette, American actress and singer, *Obit* Yrbk 2013

Gil, Gilberto, Brazilian singer and songwriter, Jan 2003

Gorme, Eydie, singer, Feb 1965, *Obit* Yrbk 2013

Greco, Juliette, French singer, Jan 1992

Haggard, Merle, American country singer, Jan 1977

Hardy, Francoise, French singer, Jan 2005

Hayes, Roland, American singer, May 1942, *Obit* Mar 1977

Hildegarde, American singer, Nov 1944, *Obit* Yrbk 2005

Holliday, Jennifer, American singer, June 1983

Iglesias, Julio, Spanish singer, June 1984

International, Dana, Israeli singer, Jan 2005

Isaak, Chris, singer, May 1993

Jarreau, Al, American singer, Oct 1992

Jennings, Waylon, American singer and songwriter, Apr 1982, *Obit* Apr 2002

Jepsen, Carly Rae, Sept 2013

Joel, Billy, American singer and songwriter, Sept 1979

John, Elton, English singer and songwriter, Mar 1975

Jones, Shirley, American singer and actress, Oct 1961

Jones, Tom, Welsh singer, Apr 1970

Joplin, Janis, American singer, Mar 1970, *Obit* Mar 1970

Juanes, Colombian singer, Jan 2003

Khan, Chaka, American singer, July 1999

King, B. B., American blues guitarist and singer, June 1970

LaMontagne, Ray, American singer, Oct 2013

Lang, K. D., Canadian singer, Sept 1992

Lawrence, Steve, singer, Nov 1964

Lopez, Trini, singer, Mar 1968

Lynn, Loretta, American country singer and songwriter, Oct 1973

Mackenzie, Gisele, Canadian singer, Nov 1955, *Obit* July 2004

Madonna, American singer, May 1986

Makeba, Miriam, South African singer, June 1965, *Obit* Yrbk 2009

Mami, Cheb, Algerian singer, Jan 2005

Mangesakara, Lata, Indian singer, Jan 2003

Manilow, Barry, American pop singer and songwriter, July 1978

Marshall, Lois, Canadian singer, June 1960, *Obit* May 1997

Maynor, Dorothy, singer, Jan 1940, Yrbk 1951, *Obit* May 1996

McCartney, Paul, English singer and songwriter, Nov 1966, Jan 1986

McCormack, John, Irish opera singer, *Obit* Oct 1945

McGovern, Maureen, singer, Feb 1990

Meat Loaf (Musician), American singer and songwriter, Nov 2006

Mendez, Kinito, Dominican singer, Jan 2004

Mercer, Mabel, singer, Feb 1973, *Obit* June 1984

Merman, Ethel, American actress and singer, Oct 1941, May 1955, *Obit* Apr 1984

Misia, Portuguese singer, Jan 2002

Monroe, Lucy, singer, Aug 1942, *Obit* Nov 1987

Morrison, Van, Irish singer and songwriter, Sept 1996

Moyet, Alison, British singer, Jan 2003

Munn, Frank, singer, May 1944, *Obit* Yrbk 1953

Murray, Anne, Canadian singer, Jan 1982

N'Dour, Youssou, Senegalese singer, Jan 1996

Narelle, Marie, *Obit* Mar 1941

Nelson, Willie, American country singer and songwriter, Feb 1979

Newton, Wayne, American singer, Feb 1990

Nin, Khadja, Burundian singer, Jan 2005

Nixon, Marni, American singer, Oct 2009

O'Connor, Sinead, Irish singer, June 1991

Osmond, Donny, American singer, Feb 1998

Page, Patti, American singer, Sept 1965, *Obit* Yrbk 2013

Papa Wemba, Congolese singer, Jan 2003

Parton, Dolly, American country singer and songwriter, Aug 1977

Pausini, Laura, Italian singer, Jan 2007

Pears, Peter, English opera singer, July 1975, *Obit* May 1986

Piaf, Edith, French singer, Yrbk 1950, *Obit* Nov 1963

Pickens, Jane, singer, Yrbk 1949, *Obit* Apr 1992

Pop, Iggy, American singer and songwriter, Jan 1995

Portuondo, Omara, Cuban singer, Jan 2005

Prince, American singer and songwriter, Feb 1986

Putnam, Ashley, Mar 1982

Raphael, Spanish singer, Aug 1991

Raven-Symone, American actress, Sept 2008

Rawls, Lou, American singer, Mar 1984, *Obit* Oct 2006

Richie, Lionel, American singer and songwriter, July 1984

Rihanna, Barbadian singer, Nov 2007

Robinson, Smokey, American singer and songwriter, July 1980

Ronstadt, Linda, American singer, Jan 1978

Ross, Diana, American singer and actress, Mar 1973

Sairam, Aruna, Indian singer, Jan 2006

Sangare, Oumou, Malian singer, Jan 2003

Seal, English singer, Feb 1997

Shakira, Colombian singer, Jan 2002

Shore, Dinah, American singer, June 1942, Yrbk 1966, *Obit* May 1994

Short, Bobby, American singer and pianist, July 1972, *Obit* Nov 2005

Smith, Kate, singer, Yrbk 1940, Nov 1965, *Obit* Aug 1986

Souleyman, Omar, Musician, Aug 2012

Springsteen, Bruce, American singer and songwriter, Apr 1978, Aug 1992

Stone, Joss, British soul singer, Jan 2005

Streisand, Barbra, American singer and actress, June 1964, Sept 1992

Sumac, Yma, Peruvian singer, Yrbk 1955, *Obit* Yrbk 2008

Summer, Donna, American singer, July 1979, *Obit* Yrbk 2012

Swift, Taylor, American singer and songwriter, Jan 2010

Taboo (Musician), American singer, Oct 2006

Tanon, Olga, Puerto Rican singer, Jan 2005

Torme, Mel, singer, Mar 1983, *Obit* Aug 1999

Turner, Tina, American singer, Nov 1984

Usmanova, Yulduz, Uzbek singer, Jan 2004

Vaughan, Sarah, American singer, Nov 1957, Apr 1980, *Obit* May 1990

Warwick, Dionne, American singer, Feb 1969

Westenra, Hayley, New Zealand singer, Jan 2006

White, Portia, Mar 1945

Wicker, Ireene, singer and storyteller, Apr 1943, *Obit* Jan 1988

Will. i. Am (Musician), American singer, Oct 2006

Williams, Andy, American singer, Feb 1960, *Obit* Yrbk 2012

Young, Neil, Canadian rock singer and guitarist, Feb 1980, Jan 1998

Sitar players

Shankar, Ravi, Indian sitar player, Apr 1968, *Obit* Yrbk 2013

Skateboarders

Hawk, Tony, American skateboarder, June 2000

Hawkins, Lyn-Z Adams, American skateboarder, Sept 2013

Skiers

Aamodt, Kjetil Andre, Norwegian skier, Jan 2002

Camplin, Alisa, Australian skier, Jan 2004

Greene, Nancy, Mar 1969

Hannawald, Sven, German ski jumper, Jan 2002

Killy, Jean Claude, French skier, June 1968

Loosli, E. Fritz, Jan 1942

Maier, Hermann, Austrian skier, Jan 2003

Moser-Proell, Annemarie, Austrian skier, Sept 1976

Schneider, Hannes, Austrian skier, Mar 1941, *Obit* June 1955

Schranz, Karl, Austrian skier, Jan 1971

Stenmark, Ingemar, Swedish skier, Apr 1982

Street, Picabo, American skier, Apr 1998

Tomba, Alberto, Italian skier, May 1993

Vonn, Lindsey, American skier, Feb 2010

Zorzi, Cristian, Italian cross-country skier, Jan 2006

Sled dog racers

Butcher, Susan, American sled dog racer, June 1991, *Obit* Yrbk 2006

Small business owners

Josephson, Walter S., *Obit* Mar 1940

Liggett, Louis Kroh, *Obit* July 1946

Soccer coaches

Arena, Bruce, American soccer coach, Sept 2010

Beckenbauer, Franz, German soccer player and coach, Jan 2006

Bradley, Bob, American soccer coach, Aug 2010

Cruyff, Johan, Dutch soccer player and manager, Nov 1981

Ferguson, Alex, Scottish soccer manager, June 2010

Heinrichs, April, American soccer player and coach, May 2000

Lippi, Marcello, Italian soccer coach, Jan 2006

Maradona, Diego, Argentine soccer player and coach, Nov 1990, Jan 2006

Scolari, Luiz Felipe, Brazilian soccer coach, Jan 2006

Soccer players

Adriano, Leite Ribeiro, Brazilian soccer player, Jan 2004

Adu, Freddy, Ghanaian-American soccer player, Jan 2005

Akers, Michelle, American soccer player, Nov 2004

Batistuta, Gabriel, Argentine soccer player, Jan 2002

Beckham, David, British soccer player, Jan 2003

Boxx, Shannon, American soccer player, May 2011

Cannavaro, Fabio, Italian soccer player, Jan 2006

Cristiano Ronaldo, Portuguese soccer player, Jan 2007

Donovan, Landon, American soccer player, June 2006

Drogba, Didier, Ivorian soccer player, July 2011

Eto'o, Samuel, Cameroonian soccer player, Feb 2013

Fabregas, Cesc, Spanish soccer player, Jan 2006

Fawcett, Joy, American soccer player, May 2004

Figo, Luis, Portuguese soccer player, Jan 2003

Hamm, Mia, American soccer player, Sept 1999

Howard, Tim, American soccer player, Sept 2005

Kahn, Oliver, German soccer player, Jan 2002

Kaka, Brazilian soccer player, May 2008

Keane, Roy, Irish soccer player, Jan 2006

Keller, Kasey, soccer player, Nov 1998

Lilly, Kristine, American soccer player, Apr 2004

Marta, Brazilian soccer player, Apr 2008

Messi, Lionel, Argentine soccer player, Jan 2007

Milla, Roger, Cameroonian soccer player, Jan 2003

Nakamura, Shunsuke, Japanese soccer player, Jan 2002

Nakata, Hidetoshi, Japanese soccer player, Jan 2002

Nedved, Pavel, Czech soccer player, Jan 2002

Park, Ji-Sung, Korean soccer player, Apr 2010

Pele, Brazilian soccer player, Mar 1967

Prinz, Birgit, German soccer player, Jan 2005

Rivaldo, Brazilian soccer player, Jan 2002

Roberto Carlos, Brazilian soccer player, Jan 2007

Ronaldinho, Brazilian soccer player, Jan 2005

Ronaldo, Brazilian soccer player, Aug 1998

Sissi, Brazilian soccer player, June 2001

Solo, Hope, American soccer player, Aug 2012

Sun Wen, Chinese soccer player, Apr 2001

Taylor, Katie, July 2013

Vieira, Patrick, French soccer player, Jan 2006

Wambach, Abby, American soccer player, Mar 2011

Zidane, Zinedine, Algerian-French soccer player, Jan 2002

Soccer referees

Collina, Pierluigi, Italian soccer referee, Jan 2002

Social activists

Abiola, Hafsat, Nigerian dissident, Jan 2007

Achmat, Zackie, South African AIDS activist, Jan 2003

Ambedkar, Bhimrao Ramji, Indian statesman and reformer, Nov 1951, *Obit* Feb 1957

Banks, Dennis, American Indian leader, June 1992

Barlow, Maude, Canadian environmentalist, Feb 2009

Bearden, Bessye J., American political activist and civic leader, *Obit* Nov 1943

Bhave, Vinoba, Indian mystic and social reformer, Sept 1953, *Obit* Jan 1983

Blatch, Harriot Eaton Stanton, American suffratist, *Obit* Jan 1941

Brady, Sarah, American gun control activist and wife of James S. Brady, Oct 1996

Brueggemann, Ingar, German family planning advocate, Nov 2001

Bukovskii, Vladimir Konstantinovich, Soviet dissident, Mar 1978

Clay, Laura, American suffragist, *Obit* Aug 1941

Clinchy, Everett R., religious leader, Apr 1941, *Obit* Mar 1986

Colvin, Mamie White, Yrbk 1944, *Obit* Jan 1956

Dirie, Waris, Somali model and social activist, Jan 2005

Edelman, Marian Wright, American children's rights advocate, Sept 1992

Elliott, John Lovejoy, social reformer, *Obit* June 1942

Evans, Anne, *Obit* Feb 1941

Feldt, Gloria A., American birth control advocate, July 2000

Flesch, Rudolf Franz, American educational reformer, Apr 1948, *Obit* Nov 1986

Fornos, Werner H., demographer and social reformer, July 1993

Giri, V. Mohini, Indian social activist, Jan 2007

Gmeiner, Hermann, Austrian social worker, May 1963, *Obit* June 1986

Hale, Clara, American child benefactor, July 1985, *Obit* Feb 1993

Hernandez, Aileen C., feminist, July 1971

Honkala, Cheri, American social activist, July 2012

Ibrahim, Saad Eddin, Egyptian sociologist and political dissident, Jan 2003

Johnson, William E., *Obit* Mar 1945

Kebede, Liya, Ethiopian model and social activist, Jan 2005

Lee, Percy Maxim, American civic leader, July 1950, *Obit* Jan 2003

Malcolm, Ellen, American feminist and political activist, Feb 2010

Parsons, Rose Peabody, feminist, Yrbk 1959, *Obit* June 1985

Paya, Oswaldo, Cuban dissident, Jan 2003, *Obit* Yrbk 2012
Pertschuk, Michael, consumer activist and government official, Sept 1986
Rama Rau, Dhanvanthi, Indian social welfare leader and feminist, Apr 1954, *Obit* Sept 1987
Satyarthi, Kailash, Indian social activist, Jan 2007
Sheehan, Cindy, American anti-war activist, May 2007
Smeal, Eleanor, American feminist, Mar 1980
Strauss, Anna Lord, Nov 1945, *Obit* Apr 1979
Street, Jessie M. G., Australian feminist, Sept 1947
Tridish, Pete, American pirate radio broadcaster and social activist, Apr 2004
Tull, Tanya, American social services organization official, Nov 2004
Verveer, Melanne, Mar 2013
Wallace, Clayton M., Sept 1948

Social reformers

Elliott, John Lovejoy, social reformer, *Obit* June 1942
Johnson, William E., *Obit* Mar 1945

Social scientists

Al-Baghdadi, Ahmad, Kuwaiti political scientist, Jan 2004
Allport, Gordon, psychologist, Sept 1960, *Obit* Yrbk 1967
Amin, Samir, Egyptian economist, Aug 2012
Anderson, H. Dewey, American economist, Jan 1950
Andrews, John Bertram, economist, *Obit* Feb 1943
Appiah, Anthony, American professor of African-American studies, June 2002
Bacon, Selden Daskam, sociologist, May 1952, *Obit* Feb 1993
Barnouw, Erik, American sociologist, Nov 1940, *Obit* Oct 2001
Baron-Cohen, Simon, British psychologist, Jan 2006
Bell, Daniel, American sociologist, Yrbk 1973, *Obit* Yrbk 2011

Bigelow, Karl W., economist and educator, Feb 1949, *Obit* June 1980
Brooks, Robert C., *Obit* Apr 1941
Chandrasekhar, S., Indian economist and demographer, Oct 1969, *Obit* Sept 2001
Clark, John Davidson, Jan 1947
Coleman, James Samuel, American sociologist, Oct 1970, *Obit* June 1995
Cordier, Andrew Wellington, Apr 1950, *Obit* Sept 1975
Cortney, Philip, Jan 1958, *Obit* July 1971
Crossley, Archibald M., public opinion analyst, Yrbk 1941, *Obit* July 1985
Daniken, Erich von, Swiss author, May 1976
Dewhurst, J. Frederic, Jan 1948, *Obit* July 1967
Einaudi, Luigi, July 1948, *Obit* Jan 1962
Embree, Edwin R., Yrbk 1948, *Obit* Mar 1950
Feifel, Herman, American psychologist, Aug 1994, *Obit* Yrbk 2005
Felton, Ralph A., Sept 1957
Ferrero, Gina Lombroso, *Obit* May 1944
Gaines, Donna, American sociologist, June 2006
Gallup, George Horace, American public opinion analyst, Mar 1940, Yrbk 1952, *Obit* Sept 1984
Garreton Merino, Manuel A., Chilean sociologist, Jan 2006
George, Susan, American social scientist, July 2007
Glueck, Eleanor Touroff, Oct 1957, *Obit* Nov 1972
Glueck, Sheldon, Oct 1957, *Obit* May 1980
Harris, Louis, American public opinion analyst, May 1966
Harris, Seymour Edwin, American economist, Feb 1965, *Obit* Yrbk 1974
Henderson, Hazel, Anglo-American environmentalist and economist, Nov 2003
Henderson, Leon, American economist and government official, July 1940, *Obit* Jan 1987

Hill, Howard Copeland, *Obit* Aug 1940
Husted, Marjorie Child, American home economist, June 1949, *Obit* Feb 1987
Janov, Arthur, psychologist, May 1980
Kellogg, Winthrop Niles, Apr 1963
Kemmerer, Edwin Walter, Oct 1941, *Obit* Feb 1946
Kirchwey, George W., *Obit* Apr 1942
Koffka, Kurt, German psychologist, *Obit* Jan 1942
Laffer, Arthur B., American economist, Feb 1982
Leyburn, James Graham, Apr 1943
Lorge, Irving, psychologist, July 1959, *Obit* Apr 1961
Marjolin, Robert E., French economist, Yrbk 1948, *Obit* June 1986
Martin, Lillien Jane, psychologist, Apr 1942, *Obit* May 1943
McKenzie, Roderick Duncan, *Obit* Jan 1940
Merton, Robert King, American sociologist, Sept 1965, *Obit* Yrbk 2003
Mills, Frederick Cecil, economist, Nov 1948, *Obit* Apr 1964
Moyo, Dambisa, Zambian economist, Feb 2012
Murray, Charles A., American social scientist, July 1986
Nathan, Robert R., American economist, Sept 1941, *Obit* Nov 2001
O'Neill, Jim, economist, Oct 2013
Ogburn, William Fielding, sociologist, Feb 1955, *Obit* July 1959
Oppenheimer, Franz, German sociologist and economist, *Obit* Nov 1943
Osgood, Charles E., psychologist, Apr 1962
Parsons, Talcott, American sociologist, Jan 1961, *Obit* July 1979
Pasvolsky, Leo, May 1945, *Obit* June 1953
Rhine, J. B., American parapsychologist, Jan 1949, *Obit* Apr 1980

Rimm, Sylvia B., American child psychologist, Feb 2002

Rogers, Carl R., American psychologist, Yrbk 1962, *Obit* Mar 1987

Rueff, Jacques, French economist, Feb 1969, *Obit* June 1978

Sachs, Jeffrey D., American economist, Nov 1993

Scammon, Richard M., political scientist and public opinion analyst, Mar 1971, *Obit* Sept 2001

Seabury, David, Sept 1941, *Obit* May 1960

Shikaki, Khalil, Palestinian political scientist, Jan 2004

Skinner, B. F., American psychologist, Jan 1964, Nov 1979, *Obit* Oct 1990

Sorokin, Pitirim Aleksandrovich, sociologist, July 1942, *Obit* Apr 1968

Soule, George Henry, American economist, Yrbk 1945, *Obit* June 1970

Spearman, Charles E., English psychologist, *Obit* Oct 1945

Sprinkel, Beryl W., American economist and government official, July 1987, *Obit* Yrbk 2009

Sturzo, Luigi, Feb 1946, *Obit* Nov 1959

Taussig, Frank William, economist, *Obit* Yrbk 1940

Thorndike, Edward L., American psychologist, Sept 1941, *Obit* Oct 1949

Thorp, Willard Long, American economist and government official, July 1947, *Obit* July 1992

Venkatesh, Sudhir, American sociologist, May 2010

Wallerstein, Immanuel Maurice, American sociologist, May 2009

Watson, John Broadus, American psychologist, Oct 1942, *Obit* Yrbk 1958

Weidenbaum, Murray L., economist and government official, Mar 1982

Wertheimer, Max, Czech psychologist, *Obit* Yrbk 1943

White, Harry Dexter, American economist and government official, Sept 1944, *Obit* Oct 1948

Wickens, Aryness Joy, economist and government official, Sept 1962, *Obit* Apr 1991

Wilson, Logan, college administrator, Yrbk 1956, *Obit* Jan 1991

Wootton, Barbara, British sociologist, Feb 1964

Yankelovich, Daniel, American sociologist, Mar 1982

Zandi, Mark M., American economist, May 2010

Social welfare leaders

Allen, Martha F., American social worker and youth leader, Oct 1959

Altmeyer, Arthur Joseph, American government official, Nov 1946, *Obit* Yrbk 1972

Anderson, Constance, youth leader, May 1948, *Obit* Apr 2001

Armstrong, David W., American youth leader, July 1949, *Obit* Mar 1963

Berry, Martha, Apr 1940, *Obit* Apr 1942

Blalock, Richard W., American youth organization official, May 1950

Breckinridge, Aida de Costa, American social welfare leader, June 1954, *Obit* July 1962

Burns, John Lawrence, youth organization official, Apr 1960, *Obit* Nov 1996

Canada, Geoffrey, American charitable organization official, Feb 2005

Christman, Elizabeth, Jan 1947

Clayton, P. B., May 1955, *Obit* Mar 1973

Danner, Louise Rutledge, *Obit* Nov 1943

Epstein, Abraham, *Obit* June 1942

Glenn, Mary Willcox, *Obit* Yrbk 1940

Hall, George A., American child welfare leader, *Obit* Nov 1941

Harriman, Florence Jaffray Hurst, social welfare leader, Mar 1940, *Obit* Nov 1967

Lenroot, Katharine F., American government official, May 1940, Nov 1950, *Obit* Yrbk 1991

Mann, Marty, social welfare leader, June 1949, *Obit* Sept 1980

Marvel, Elizabeth Newell, American youth leader, Apr 1962

Mitchell, William L., Nov 1959

Nwuneli, Ndidi O., Nigerian youth organization official, Jan 2007

Pantaleoni, Helenka Adamowska, social welfare leader, Nov 1956, *Obit* Mar 1987

Pickett, Clarence, June 1945, *Obit* May 1965

Rosenfield, Harry N., lawyer, lobbyist and refugee settlement leader, Apr 1952, *Obit* Aug 1995

Rosenman, Dorothy, housing advocate, Apr 1947, *Obit* Mar 1991

Schoff, Hannah Kent, social welfare leader, *Obit* Feb 1941

Tull, Tanya, American social services organization official, Nov 2004

Wegner, Nicholas H., Yrbk 1949, *Obit* May 1976

Social workers

Beck, Bertram M., social worker, May 1961, *Obit* Sept 2000

Beck, Mildred Buchwalder, American social worker, June 1950

Brownson, Josephine, American children's author and social worker, Mar 1940

Chute, Charles Lionel, Sept 1949, *Obit* Jan 1954

Cowan, Minna G., Feb 1948

Deer, Ada, Native American leader and government official, Sept 1994

Dunn, Loula, Mar 1951

Duvall, Evelyn Ruth Millis, Oct 1947

Geer, Alpheus, *Obit* Oct 1941

Hoey, Jane M., American social worker and government official, Sept 1950

Huck, Arthur, Feb 1957, *Obit* Mar 1973

Johnson, Alexander, *Obit* July 1941

Johnson, Thomasina Walker, Mar 1947

Kirk, William T., Feb 1960, *Obit* Mar 1974

Leonard, Lucille Putnam, Feb 1953

MacLeod, Dorothy Shaw, Apr 1949

Magee, Elizabeth S., Oct 1950

McCloskey, Mark A., Nov 1955, *Obit* Jan 1978

Montanari, A. J., Feb 1968

Morgan, Anne Tracy, philanthropist and social worker, Jan 1946, *Obit* Mar 1952

Royden, Agnes Maude, English social worker and evangelist, Apr 1942, *Obit* Oct 1956

Simkhovitch, Mary Melinda Kingsbury, American social worker, Mar 1943, *Obit* Yrbk 1951

Smithdas, Robert J., Yrbk 1966

Weil, Frank L., Feb 1949, *Obit* Jan 1958

Wilson, Donald V., Jan 1954

Socialites

Longworth, Alice Roosevelt, daughter of American president Theodore Roosevelt, June 1943, Aug 1975, *Obit* Apr 1980

McLean, Evalyn Walsh, socialite, May 1943, *Obit* May 1947

Mesta, Perle, society leader and diplomat, Sept 1949, *Obit* May 1975

Radziwill, Lee, American socialite, Apr 1977

Sociologists

Ferrero, Gina Lombroso, *Obit* May 1944

Oppenheimer, Franz, German sociologist and economist, *Obit* Nov 1943

Wootton, Barbara, British sociologist, Feb 1964

Softball players

Finch, Jennie, American softball player, Oct 2004

Soldiers

Boyce, Westray Battle, Sept 1945, *Obit* Mar 1972

Brannaman, Ray H., Nov 1947

Buckner, Simon Bolivar, Oct 1942, *Obit* July 1945

Bunau-Varilla, Philippe, *Obit* July 1940

Cazalet, Victor Alexander, *Obit* Aug 1943

Cordier, Constant, *Obit* Mar 1940

Davenport, Russell W., Jan 1944, *Obit* June 1954

Durning, Charles, American actor, Sept 1997, *Obit* Yrbk 2013

Dutra, Eurico Gaspar, Mar 1946, *Obit* Sept 1974

Fleming, Philip Bracken, Apr 1940, *Obit* Yrbk 1956

Galloway, Irene O., May 1953, *Obit* Feb 1963

Garratt, Geoffrey Theodore, *Obit* June 1942

Hallaren, Mary A., American army officer, Mar 1949, *Obit* Yrbk 2005

Haskell, William N., Feb 1947, *Obit* Sept 1952

Li Liejun, *Obit* Apr 1946

Louis, Joe, American boxer, Oct 1940, *Obit* June 1981

Maxwell, Russell L., Nov 1942, *Obit* Jan 1969

Meyer, Dakota, U.S. soldier and Medal of Honor recipient, Mar 2012

Milligan, Mary Louise, May 1957

Nastase, Ilie, Romanian tennis player, Oct 1974

O'Neil, James F., Nov 1947, *Obit* Sept 1981

Oleson, Lloyd F., June 1947

Rowan, Andrew S., American army officer, *Obit* Mar 1943

Sokolovsky, Vasilii D., Yrbk 1953, *Obit* July 1968

Sturgis, Samuel D., Jan 1956, *Obit* Sept 1964

Vall, Ely Ould Mohamed, Mauritanian head of state, Jan 2006

Solicitors general

Olson, Theodore B., American lawyer and former Solicitor general, Nov 2010

Songwriters

Aznavour, Charles, French singer and songwriter, Feb 1968

Berry, Chuck, American singer and guitarist, Apr 1977

Bowie, David, English singer and songwriter, Oct 1976, Nov 1994

Bush, Kate, English singer and songwriter, Mar 1995

Curran, Pearl G., *Obit* June 1941

David, Hal, songwriter, Sept 1980, *Obit* Yrbk 2012

Dylan, Bob, American folk singer and songwriter, May 1965, Oct 1991

Edwards, Gus, songwriter, *Obit* Yrbk 1945

Franklin, Aretha, American singer, Yrbk 1968, May 1992

Green, Al, American gospel singer and clergyman, Feb 1996

Hanley, James Frederick, songwriter, *Obit* Apr 1942

Jennings, Waylon, American singer and songwriter, Apr 1982, *Obit* Apr 2002

Jepsen, Carly Rae, Sept 2013

Kahal, Irving, *Obit* Apr 1942

Lang, K. D., Canadian singer, Sept 1992

Lynn, Loretta, American country singer and songwriter, Oct 1973

Manilow, Barry, American pop singer and songwriter, July 1978

Morrison, Van, Irish singer and songwriter, Sept 1996

Nelson, Willie, American country singer and songwriter, Feb 1979

Parton, Dolly, American country singer and songwriter, Aug 1977

Richie, Lionel, American singer and songwriter, July 1984

Robinson, Smokey, American singer and songwriter, July 1980

Springsteen, Bruce, American singer and songwriter, Apr 1978, Aug 1992

Warren, Diane, American songwriter, June 2000

Warren, Harry, composer, June 1943, *Obit* Nov 1981

Young, Neil, Canadian rock singer and guitarist, Feb 1980, Jan 1998

Soul musicians

Green, Al, American gospel singer and clergyman, Feb 1996

Sound engineers

Beranek, Leo Leroy, American acoustic engineer, Mar 1963

Bolt, Richard H., American sound engineer, June 1954

Special effects technicians

Armstrong, Vic, British motion picture stunt coordinator, Aug 2003

Fangmeier, Stefen, American special effects technician, Aug 2004

Muren, Dennis, American special effects technician, Mar 1997

Winston, Stan, American special effects technician, July 2002, *Obit* Nov 2008

Speech therapists

Johnson, Wendell, American speech pathologist, Apr 1959, *Obit* Nov 1965

Spies

Quisling, Vidkun, Norwegian traitor, Nov 1940, *Obit* Yrbk 1946

Spiritualists

Wilber, Ken, American spiritualist and author, Apr 2002

Sports agents

Boras, Scott, American baseball agent, May 2009

Rosenhaus, Drew, American sports agent, July 2011

Sports executives

Burke, Michael, sports executive, Apr 1972, *Obit* Mar 1987

Kilpatrick, John Reed, July 1948, *Obit* July 1960

Murphy, Mark, CEO fo Green Bay Packers, Oct 2012

Schultz, Richard D., sports executive, July 1996

Sports promoters

Duva, Lou, American boxing manager and promoter, Nov 1999

King, Don, American boxing promoter, June 1984

McMahon, Vince, American wrestling promoter, Feb 1999

Warren, Frank, British boxing promoter, Jan 2006

Sports trainers

Jacobs, Joe, *Obit* Jan 1940

Sportscasters

Allen, Mel, sportscaster, Oct 1950, *Obit* Aug 1996

Barber, Red, sportscaster, July 1943, *Obit* Jan 1993

Berman, Chris, American television sportscaster, Aug 1998

Cohn, Linda, American television sportscaster, Aug 2002

Costas, Bob, American sportscaster, Jan 1993

Gray, Jim, American sportscaster, Jan 2011

Gumbel, Greg, American television sportscaster, Sept 1996

Husing, Ted, sportscaster, June 1942, *Obit* Oct 1962

Lampley, Jim, American sportscaster, Oct 2011

McCarthy, Clem, radio sportscaster, Oct 1941, *Obit* July 1962

McKay, Jim, American television sportscaster, Oct 1973, *Obit* Yrbk 2008

Oliver, Pam, American television sportscaster, July 2009

Scott, Stuart, American television sportscaster, Jan 2012

Scully, Vin, American television sportscaster, Oct 2001

Stern, Bill, sportscaster, June 1941, *Obit* Jan 1972

Visser, Lesley, American television sportscaster, Apr 2007

Spouses of presidents

Bush, Barbara, wife of American president George Bush, Oct 1989

Carter, Rosalynn, wife of American president Jimmy Carter, Mar 1978

Chiang, Mei-ling, wife of Taiwanse president Chiang Kai-shek, May 1940, *Obit* Mar 2004

Eisenhower, Mamie Doud, wife of American president Dwight D. Eisenhower, May 1953, *Obit* Jan 1980

Ford, Betty, wife of American president Gerald R. Ford, Sept 1975, *Obit* Yrbk 2011

Gorbachev, Raisa Maksimovna, wife of Soviet President Mikhail Gorbachev, May 1988, *Obit* Nov 1999

Hoover, Lou Henry, wife of American president Herbert Hoover, *Obit* Feb 1944

Johnson, Lady Bird, wife of American president Lyndon B. Johnson, Oct 1964, *Obit* Oct 2007

Mandela, Winnie, South African political leader and wife of Nelson Mandela, Jan 1986

Nixon, Patricia, wife of American president Richard M. Nixon, Jan 1970, *Obit* Aug 1993

Peron, Eva, wife of Argentine president Juan Domingo Peron, Mar 1949, *Obit* Sept 1952

Reagan, Nancy, wife of American president Ronald Reagan, May 1982

Sadat, Jehan, wife of Egyptian president Anwar Sadat, Aug 1986

Taft, Helen Herron, wife of American president William H. Taft, *Obit* July 1943

Truman, Bess Wallace, wife of American president Harry S. Truman, Feb 1947, *Obit* Jan 1983

Wyman, Jane, American actress, Mar 1949, *Obit* Yrbk 2007

Spouses of prominent persons

Asquith, Margot, wife of British Prime Minister Herbert Henry Asquith, *Obit* Sept 1945

Carter, Rosalynn, wife of American president Jimmy Carter, Mar 1978

Chiang, Mei-ling, wife of Taiwanse president Chiang Kai-shek, May 1940, *Obit* Mar 2004

Churchill, Clementine, wife of British Prime Minister Sir Winston Churchill, July 1953, *Obit* Mar 1978

Eisenhower, Mamie Doud, wife of American president Dwight D. Eisenhower, May 1953, *Obit* Jan 1980

Ford, Betty, wife of American president Gerald R. Ford, Sept 1975, *Obit* Yrbk 2011

Gandhi, Sonia, Italian wife of Indian Prime Minister Rajiv Gandhi, May 1998

Gorbachev, Raisa Maksimovna, wife of Soviet President Mikhail Gorbachev, May 1988, *Obit* Nov 1999

Gore, Tipper, wife of American vice-president Albert Gore, Jr., Oct 2000

Hawkins, Lyn-Z Adams, American skateboarder, Sept 2013

Hoover, Lou Henry, wife of American president Herbert Hoover, *Obit* Feb 1944

Jagger, Bianca, Nicaraguan actress, Apr 1987

Johnson, Lady Bird, wife of American president Lyndon B. Johnson, Oct 1964, *Obit* Oct 2007

Mondale, Joan, wife of American vice-president Walter F. Mondale, Jan 1980

Nixon, Patricia, wife of American president Richard M. Nixon, Jan 1970, *Obit* Aug 1993

Peron, Eva, wife of Argentine president Juan Domingo Peron, Mar 1949, *Obit* Sept 1952

Presley, Priscilla Beaulieu, American actress, Sept 1990

Sadat, Jehan, wife of Egyptian president Anwar Sadat, Aug 1986

Shriver, Maria, American television newscaster and wife of Arnold Schwarzenegger, Nov 1991

Snowdon, Antony Armstrong-Jones, English photographer, Oct 1960

Taft, Helen Herron, wife of American president William H. Taft, *Obit* July 1943

Truman, Bess Wallace, wife of American president Harry S. Truman, Feb 1947, *Obit* Jan 1983

Windsor, Wallis Warfield, wife of Windsor, Edward, Duke of, Sept 1944, *Obit* June 1986

State government officials

Abbott, Edwin Milton, American lawyer, *Obit* Jan 1941

Allen, James Edward, American government official and educator, June 1969, *Obit* Yrbk 1971

Brown, Francis Shunk, *Obit* Jan 1940

Brown, Virginia Mae, lawyer and government official, July 1970, *Obit* May 1991

Donlon, Mary H., July 1949, *Obit* May 1977

Fleischmann, Manly, lawyer, July 1951

Garvey, Jane F., government official, Sept 2000

Gough, Lewis K., Jan 1953, *Obit* Jan 1968

Houghton, Dorothy Deemer, Sept 1950

Jackson, Lisa P., American government official, Mar 2010

Krupsak, Mary Anne, July 1975

Leopold, Alice, government official, Jan 1955

Mays, Ewing W., Jan 1952

Moore, Michael C., state attorney general, Aug 1997

Parsons, Herbert Collins, *Obit* July 1941

Trigg, Ralph S., Nov 1950

White, Katherine Elkus, diplomat and state official, Feb 1965, *Obit* June 1985

Statesmen

Allen, George Venable, American diplomat, Nov 1948, *Obit* Oct 1970

Allison, John Moore, American diplomat, Mar 1956, *Obit* Feb 1979

Alphand, Herve, French diplomat, Nov 1951, *Obit* Mar 1994

Anderson, Eugenie M., American diplomat, Jan 1950

Andrade, Victor, Bolivian diplomat, Feb 1953

Armitage, Richard L., American government official, Oct 2003

Armour, Norman, American diplomat, Apr 1945, *Obit* Nov 1982

Asakai, Koichiro, Japanese diplomat, Sept 1957

Atcheson, George, American diplomat, Sept 1946, *Obit* Oct 1947

Austin, Margretta, American diplomat, Feb 1954

Barrere, Camille, French diplomat, *Obit* Yrbk 1940

Barshefsky, Charlene, American trade representative, Feb 2000

Beam, Jacob Dyneley, American diplomat, July 1959, *Obit* Oct 1993

Beaulac, Willard Leon, diplomat, Sept 1958, *Obit* Oct 1990

Bebler, Ales, Yugoslav diplomat, Apr 1950

Belt, Guillermo, Cuban diplomat, Nov 1947, *Obit* Sept 1989

Berendsen, Carl August, New Zealand diplomat, Oct 1948, *Obit* Yrbk 1973

Bernadotte, Folke, Swedish diplomat, May 1945, *Obit* Nov 1948

Boheman, Erik, Swedish diplomat, Mar 1951

Bohlen, Charles E., American diplomat, June 1948, May 1960, *Obit* Feb 1974

Bonnet, Henri, French diplomat, Feb 1945, *Obit* Feb 1979

Bonsal, Philip Wilson, diplomat, June 1959, *Obit* Sept 1995

Borberg, William, Nov 1952, *Obit* Sept 1958

Braden, Spruille, American diplomat, Sept 1945, *Obit* Mar 1978

Bruce, James, diplomat, Jan 1949, *Obit* Sept 1980

Brunauer, Esther Caukin, American diplomat, Nov 1947, *Obit* Sept 1959

Buchanan, Wiley T., diplomat, Nov 1957, *Obit* Mar 1986

Bunker, Ellsworth, American diplomat, Apr 1954, Mar 1978, *Obit* Nov 1984

Buthelezi, Mangosuthu, South African Zulu statesman, Oct 1986

Butler, Nevile Montagu, Apr 1941

Byroade, Henry Alfred, diplomat, Feb 1952, *Obit* Mar 1994

Cabot, John M., American diplomat, Sept 1953, *Obit* Apr 1981

Caccia, Harold Anthony, British diplomat, Feb 1957, *Obit* Jan 1991

Caffery, Jefferson, diplomat, Nov 1943, *Obit* June 1974

Campbell, Gerald, Mar 1941, *Obit* Sept 1964

Cannon, Cavendish Welles, diplomat, July 1957, *Obit* Yrbk 1962

Carr, Wilbur J., diplomat, *Obit* Aug 1942

Cartier de Marchienne, Emile de, *Obit* July 1946

Chagla, Mahomed Ali Currim, Indian diplomat, June 1959, *Obit* Jan 1984

Chalmers, Philip O., *Obit* Mar 1946

Chauvel, Jean, French diplomat, Oct 1950, *Obit* July 1979

Clark Kerr, Archibald John Kerr, Yrbk 1942, *Obit* Sept 1951

Cochran, H. Merle, Feb 1950, *Obit* Nov 1973

Colina, Rafael de la, Jan 1951

Concheso, Aurelio Fernandez, May 1942, *Obit* Jan 1956

Craigie, Robert, British diplomat, July 1942, *Obit* July 1959

Crocker, Ryan, American diplomat, Oct 2007

Csaky, Stephen, *Obit* Mar 1941

Cudahy, John, diplomat, *Obit* Oct 1943

Dawson, William, diplomat, Apr 1941, *Obit* Sept 1972

Dayal, Rajeshwar, Feb 1961

Dendramis, Vassili, June 1947, *Obit* July 1956

Des Graz, Charles Louis, *Obit* Yrbk 1940

Des Portes, Fay Allen, *Obit* Nov 1944

Dobrynin, Anatoly F., Soviet diplomat, Sept 1962, *Obit* Yrbk 2010

Donnelly, Walter Joseph, diplomat, Sept 1952, *Obit* Jan 1971

Dowling, Walter, American diplomat, Mar 1963, *Obit* Sept 1977

Duke, Angier Biddle, diplomat, Feb 1962, *Obit* July 1995

Dunn, James Clement, May 1943, *Obit* June 1979

Eban, Abba, Israeli diplomat, Oct 1948, May 1957, *Obit* Mar 2003

Elizalde, Joaquin M., Feb 1948, *Obit* Mar 1965

Erkin, Feridun C., Jan 1952

Ertegun, Mehmet Munir, *Obit* Jan 1945

Fawzi, Mahmoud, Yrbk 1951

Feller, Abraham H., Nov 1946, *Obit* Jan 1953

Fernandes, L. Esteves, Oct 1950

Fernandez de la Vega, Maria Teresa, Spanish vice-president, Jan 2007

Fish, Bert, *Obit* Sept 1943

Gaffney, T. St. John, *Obit* Mar 1945

Garreau, Roger, Apr 1950

Garrels, Arthur, *Obit* Aug 1943

Gauss, Clarence Edward, diplomat, Jan 1941, *Obit* June 1960

Geoffrey-Lloyd, Geoffrey William, British cabinet member, Feb 1956

Gladwyn, Hubert Miles Gladwyn Jebb, British diplomat, Yrbk 1948

Gonzalez, Cesar, Oct 1954

Gork, Haydar, Oct 1956

Grew, Joseph C., American diplomat, Feb 1941, *Obit* July 1965

Groenman, Frans Eyso Henricus, *Obit* Aug 1943

Gunther, Franklin Mott, *Obit* Feb 1942

Gurtner, Franz, German cabinet member, *Obit* Mar 1941

Habib, Philip Charles, American diplomat, Sept 1981, *Obit* July 1992

Hare, Raymond Arthur, American diplomat, July 1957, *Obit* May 1994

Hassel, Kai-Uwe von, May 1963

Hearne, John J., July 1950, *Obit* May 1969

Henderson, Nevile Meyrick, British diplomat, Apr 1940, *Obit* Feb 1943

Henry, Jules, *Obit* Aug 1941

Henry-Haye, Gaston, Nov 1940

Hibbard, Frederick P., *Obit* Oct 1943

Hickerson, John Dewey, diplomat, May 1950, *Obit* Apr 1989

Hill, Robert C., American diplomat, Jan 1959, *Obit* Feb 1979

Holsti, Rudolf, *Obit* Sept 1945

Hoo, Victor, Mar 1947, *Obit* July 1972

Hoppenot, Henri, Mar 1944

Hussein, Ahmed, Egyptian diplomat, Mar 1956, *Obit* Feb 1985

Jarring, Gunnar, Swedish diplomat, Oct 1957, *Obit* Sept 2002

Jarvis, Robert Y., *Obit* Yrbk 1943

Jernegan, John D., Nov 1959

Johnson, Nelson Trusler, diplomat, Jan 1940, *Obit* Feb 1955

Johnson, U. Alexis, American diplomat, Oct 1955, *Obit* June 1997

Johnston, Eric, Apr 1943, Oct 1955, *Obit* Oct 1963

Jooste, Gerhardus Petrus, Apr 1951

Joseph, Keith, British cabinet member, Feb 1975, *Obit* Feb 1995

Karnebeek, Herman Adriaan van, *Obit* May 1942

Katz-Suchy, Juliusz, June 1951, *Obit* Yrbk 1971

Kauffmann, Henrik, Apr 1956, *Obit* July 1963

Kirk, Alexander C., Feb 1945

Kleffens, Eelco Nicolaas van, Oct 1947

Knabenshue, Paul, *Obit* Mar 1942

Knatchbull-Hugessen, Hughe, Mar 1943, *Obit* May 1971

Krekeler, Heinz L., Yrbk 1951

Kurusu, Saburo, Jan 1942, *Obit* May 1954

Lang, Jack, French cabinet member, Aug 1983

Laughlin, Irwin, *Obit* June 1941

Lawson, Edward B., Jan 1956

Lawson, Nigel, British cabinet member, Mar 1987

Lefaucheux, Marie-Helene, French United Nations official, Oct 1947, *Obit* Apr 1964

Leger, Jules, Nov 1976, *Obit* Jan 1981

Lindsay, Ronald, *Obit* Sept 1945

Litvinov, Maxim Maximovich, Soviet diplomat, Yrbk 1941, *Obit* Feb 1952

Lopez Bravo, Gregorio, Spanish diplomat, July 1971, *Obit* Apr 1985

Loudon, Alexander, July 1942, *Obit* Mar 1953

Lucet, Charles, Yrbk 1967

MacArthur, Douglas, American diplomat, Nov 1954, *Obit* Jan 1998

Machado Hernandez, Alfredo, *Obit* Sept 1946

Maddox, William P., Nov 1947, *Obit* Yrbk 1972

Maiskii, I. M., Soviet diplomat, Sept 1941, *Obit* Oct 1975

Makin, Norman J. O., Mar 1946

Mallory, Lester D., diplomat, Sept 1960, *Obit* Sept 1994

Mann, Thomas Clifton, American diplomat, Apr 1964, *Obit* Apr 1999

Martin Artajo, Alberto, Nov 1949

Massigli, Rene, May 1956

Matsui, Keishiro, *Obit* July 1946

Matsuoka, Yosuke, Mar 1941, *Obit* July 1946

Matthews, H. Freeman, American diplomat, Mar 1945, *Obit* Jan 1987

McClintock, Robert Mills, American diplomat, Apr 1955

McDonald, James Grover, diplomat, Apr 1949, *Obit* Yrbk 1964

Mehta, G. L., Nov 1952, *Obit* June 1974

Mello Franco, Afranio de, *Obit* Feb 1943

Menon, K. P. S., Indian diplomat, Mar 1957, *Obit* Yrbk 1983

Merry del Val y Alzola, Alfonso, Nov 1965

Messersmith, George S., American diplomat, Oct 1942, *Obit* Apr 1960

Moffat, Jay Pierrepont, diplomat, *Obit* Mar 1943

Morgenstierne, Wilhelm Thorleif von Munthe af, May 1949, *Obit* Sept 1963

Moyne, Walter Edward Guinness, *Obit* Yrbk 1944

Muccio, John Joseph, American diplomat, Jan 1951, *Obit* July 1989

Muniz, Joao Carlos, Sept 1952, *Obit* Sept 1960

Murphy, Robert D., American diplomat, Feb 1943, Nov 1958, *Obit* Mar 1978

Narain, Jai Prakash, Indian statesman, May 1958, *Obit* Nov 1979

Nehru, B. K., Indian diplomat and government official, Feb 1963, *Obit* Feb 2002

Novikov, Nikolai Vasil'evich, Feb 1947

Nufer, Albert F., Mar 1955, *Obit* Jan 1957

Obaid, Thoraya, Saudi Arabian United Nations official, Jan 2004

Okonjo-Iweala, Ngozi, Nigerian cabinet member, Jan 2006

Paderewski, Ignace Jan, Polish pianist and statesman, *Obit* Aug 1941

Padilla Nervo, Luis, Yrbk 1946

Pant, Govind Ballabh, Indian cabinet member, Jan 1959, *Obit* May 1961

Panyushkin, Aleksandr S., Yrbk 1948, *Obit* Jan 1975

Parodi, Alexandre, French government official and diplomat, June 1946

Pelt, Adrian, Feb 1948

Peurifoy, John Emil, American diplomat, Jan 1949, *Obit* Oct 1955

Phillips, William, American diplomat, July 1940, *Obit* Apr 1968

Politis, Athanase G., Sept 1950, *Obit* June 1968

Politis, Nicolas, *Obit* Apr 1942

Popovic, Vladimir, Feb 1952, *Obit* May 1972

Porter, William James, diplomat, Mar 1974, *Obit* May 1988

Potemkin, Vladimir P., *Obit* Apr 1946

Procope, Hjalman Johan Fredrik, Apr 1940, *Obit* Apr 1954

Pueyrredon, Honorio, *Obit* Oct 1945

Quo, Tai-Chi, May 1946, *Obit* Apr 1952

Rankin, Karl Lott, American diplomat, Apr 1955, *Obit* Apr 1991

Rasmussen, Gustav, Yrbk 1947, *Obit* Nov 1953

Reber, Samuel, Sept 1949, *Obit* Feb 1972

Riddleberger, James W., diplomat, May 1957, *Obit* Jan 1983

Robertson, Norman A., Yrbk 1957, *Obit* Sept 1968

Roijen, Jan Herman van, Dutch diplomat, Yrbk 1953

Rountree, William M., diplomat, June 1959, *Obit* Jan 1996

Rubottom, R. Richard, American diplomat, May 1959, *Obit* Yrbk 2011

Sargeant, Howland Hill, diplomat, Yrbk 1952, *Obit* Apr 1984

Self, Henry, Oct 1942

Sherfield, Roger Mellor Makins, British diplomat, Jan 1953, *Obit* Jan 1997

Shigemitsu, Mamoru, June 1943, *Obit* Mar 1957

Shone, Terence Allen, Nov 1946, *Obit* Yrbk 1965

Sinclair, Adelaide, Canadian government official, Apr 1951, *Obit* Jan 1983

Soheily, Ali, Sept 1943, *Obit* July 1958

Spender, Percy Claude, Mar 1950

Stewart, Michael, British cabinet member, Sept 1965, *Obit* June 1990

Stoessel, Walter J., diplomat, June 1970, *Obit* Feb 1987

Stoltenberg, Gerhard, German cabinet member, Sept 1989, *Obit* Mar 2002

Sullivan, William H., American diplomat, Aug 1979

Tani, Masayuki, May 1956

Tello, Manuel, Yrbk 1959, *Obit* Jan 1972

Thompson, Llewellyn E., American diplomat, Nov 1957, *Obit* Mar 1972

Timberlake, Clare H., Jan 1961

Toon, Malcolm, diplomat, July 1978

Tsarapkin, Semyon K., Soviet diplomat, June 1960, *Obit* Nov 1984

Umanskii, Konstantin Aleksandrovich, Feb 1941, *Obit* Mar 1945

Vassallo, Ernesto, *Obit* Jan 1940

Vaughn, Jack Hood, American diplomat and government official, Apr 1966, *Obit* Yrbk 2013

Vishinski, Andrei IAnuarevich, Soviet diplomat, May 1944, *Obit* Jan 1955

Wadsworth, James J., American diplomat, June 1956, *Obit* May 1984

Wakasugi, Kaname, *Obit* Jan 1944

Wang, Shih-chieh, Sept 1945, *Obit* June 1981

Warren, Avra M., Feb 1955, *Obit* Mar 1957

Warren, Fletcher, diplomat, July 1960, *Obit* Mar 1992

Waterlow, Sydney, *Obit* Jan 1945

Wei, Tao-ming, Yrbk 1942

Wharton, Clifton R., American diplomat, July 1958, *Obit* June 1990

Wilgress, L. Dana, Jan 1954, *Obit* Oct 1969

Wilson, Hugh Robert, diplomat, May 1941, *Obit* Feb 1947

Woodward, Robert F., diplomat, Yrbk 1962, *Obit* Yrbk 2001

Woodward, Stanley, diplomat, June 1951, *Obit* Oct 1992

Wright, Michael, British diplomat, July 1961

Wrong, Hume, Oct 1950, *Obit* Mar 1954

Zarubin, Georgi N., Apr 1953, *Obit* Jan 1959

Stock exchange officials

Abdul-Razaq, Alhaji, Nigerian lawyer and government official, Jan 2005

Boylan, Robert P., Apr 1950

Furse, Clara, British-Canadian stock exchange official, Jan 2006

Grasso, Richard, American stock exchange official, Oct 2002

Haack, Robert, stock exchange official, Mar 1969, *Obit* Aug 1992

McCormick, Edward Theodore, government official and stock exchange executive, May 1951, *Obit* Oct 1991

Mehta, Deena, Indian securities broker, Jan 2005

Okereke-Onyiuke, Ndi, Nigerian stock exchange official, Jan 2005

Schram, Emil, stock exchange official, Oct 1941, May 1953, *Obit* Nov 1987

Stunt performers

Belle, David, French actor and roof jumper, Jan 2007

Knievel, Evel, American motorcycle stunt performer, Feb 1972, *Obit* Yrbk 2008

Knievel, Robbie, American motorcycle stunt performer, Mar 2005

Sultans

Hassanal Bolkiah, Oct 1989

Qabus bin Said, Aug 1978

Said bin Taimur, Oct 1957, *Obit* Aug 1978

Sumo wrestlers

Akebono, American sumo wrestler, Aug 1999

Takanohana, Japanese sumo wrestler, Jan 2002

Supreme Court justices

Alito, Samuel A., American Supreme Court justice, Apr 2006

Blackmun, Harry A., American Supreme Court justice, Oct 1970, *Obit* May 1999

Brandeis, Louis Dembitz, American Supreme Court justice, *Obit* Nov 1941

Brennan, William J., American Supreme Court justice, June 1957, *Obit* Oct 1997

Breyer, Stephen G., American Supreme Court justice, June 1996

Clarke, John Hessin, Supreme Court justice, *Obit* May 1945

Eicher, Edward C., May 1941, *Obit* Jan 1945

Harlan, John Marshall, American Supreme Court justice, May 1955, *Obit* Feb 1972

O'Connor, Sandra Day, American Supreme Court justice, Jan 1982

Rehnquist, William H., American Chief Justice of the Supreme Court, Apr 1972, Nov 2003, *Obit* Yrbk 2005

Roberts, John G., American Chief Justice of the Supreme Court, Feb 2006

Scalia, Antonin, American Supreme Court justice, Nov 1986

Souter, David H., American Supreme Court justice, Jan 1991

Stevens, John Paul, American Supreme Court justice, May 1976

Stewart, Potter, American Supreme Court justice, Yrbk 1959, *Obit* Feb 1986

Thomas, Clarence, American Supreme Court justice, Apr 1992

Van Devanter, Willis, American Supreme Court justice, *Obit* Mar 1941

Wheat, Alfred Adams, *Obit* Apr 1943

Whittaker, Charles Evans, American Supreme Court justice, Yrbk 1957, *Obit* Jan 1974

Surfers

Beachley, Layne, Australian surfer, Jan 2002

Fanning, Mick, Australian surfer, June 2013

Hamilton, Laird, American surfer, Aug 2005

Mulanovich, Sofia, Peruvian surfer, Jan 2004

Occhilupo, Mark, Australian surfer, Jan 2002

Slater, Kelly, American surfer, July 2001

Surgeons

Adair, Frank E., American surgeon, May 1946, *Obit* Feb 1982

Bernheim, Bertram M., American surgeon, Sept 1943

Canady, Alexa, neurosurgeon, Aug 2000

Cooley, Denton A., American cardiac surgeon, Jan 1976

Cooper, Irving S., neurosurgeon, Apr 1974, *Obit* Jan 1986

Crile, George Washington, American surgeon, *Obit* Feb 1943

DeVries, William C., surgeon, Jan 1985

Demikhov, Vladimir P., Russian surgeon, June 1960, *Obit* Feb 1999

Folkman, Judah, American surgeon, May 1998, *Obit* Yrbk 2008

Jackson, Chevalier, July 1940

Lane, Arbuthnot, British surgeon, *Obit* Mar 1943

McCormick, Edward James, surgeon, Nov 1953, *Obit* Feb 1975

Ochsner, Alton, surgeon, Oct 1966, *Obit* Nov 1981

Pitanguy, Ivo, Brazilian plastic surgeon, Jan 2004

Reid, Mont, *Obit* June 1943

Scheer, Alan Austin, Jan 1964

Siemionow, Maria, Polish plastic surgeon, May 2009

Southworth, James L., American surgeon, June 1943

Starzl, Thomas E., American surgeon, Mar 1993

Voronoff, Serge, Jan 1941, *Obit* Oct 1951

Wood, Fiona M., Australian plastic surgeon, Jan 2007

Swimmers

Bell, Marilyn, Canadian swimmer, Sept 1956

Bruijn, Inge de, Dutch swimmer, Jan 2004

Coughlin, Natalie, American swimmer, July 2012

Cox, Lynne, American swimmer, Sept 2004

Curtis, Ann, swimmer, June 1945, *Obit* Yrbk 2012

Evans, Janet, American swimmer, July 1996

Jones, Cullen, American swimmer, Aug 2008

Klochkova, Yana, Ukrainian swimmer, Jan 2004

Meyer, Debbie, American swimmer, May 1969

Peirsol, Aaron, American swimmer, June 2010

Phelps, Michael, American swimmer, Aug 2004

Rose, Murray, swimmer, June 1962, *Obit* Yrbk 2012

Schollander, Don, American swimmer, Sept 1965

Soni, Rebecca, Aug 2013

Spitz, Mark, American swimmer, Oct 1972

Strel, Martin, Slovenian marathon swimmer, Jan 2007

Thorpe, Ian, Australian swimmer, Jan 2002

Swimming coaches

Kiphuth, Robert J. H., swimming coach, June 1957, *Obit* Mar 1967

Table tennis players

Wang Nan, Chinese table tennis player, Jan 2003

Talent agents

Conover, Harry, Feb 1949, *Obit* Oct 1965

Emanuel, Ariel, American talent agent, July 2009

Ford, Eileen, American model agent, Oct 1971

Hayward, Leland, theatrical agent and producer, Feb 1949, *Obit* Apr 1971

Leigh, William Colston, lecture agent, Jan 1942, *Obit* Sept 1992

Powers, John Robert, June 1945, *Obit* Sept 1977

Teachers

Baur, Bertha, American music teacher, *Obit* Nov 1940

Bloch, Ernest, American composer, Sept 1953, *Obit* Oct 1959

Brown, Helen Dawes, *Obit* Nov 1941

Chapman, Helen B., Apr 1955

Cook, W. W., *Obit* Yrbk 1943

Cubberley, Ellwood Patterson, educator, *Obit* Nov 1941

Dahanayake, Wijeyananda, Apr 1960

Dinsmore, Charles Allen, *Obit* Oct 1941

Eklund, John M., labor leader and teacher, Yrbk 1949, *Obit* Mar 1997

Eustis, Oskar, American theatrical director and drama teacher, Oct 2002

Gould, Ronald, English labor leader and teacher, Nov 1952

Guthrie, William Buck, *Obit* Yrbk 1940

Hadid, Zaha M., Iraqi architect, Jan 2003

Hamilton, George Livingston, *Obit* Nov 1940

Hanus, Paul H., *Obit* Feb 1942

Harper, Samuel Northrup, *Obit* Mar 1943

Holden, Louis Edward, *Obit* June 1942

Isozaki, Arata, Japanese architect, Apr 1988

Jewett, James R., *Obit* May 1943

Kahn, Louis I., American architect, Oct 1964, *Obit* May 1974

Kearns, Nora Lynch, Sept 1956

Klenze, Camillo von, *Obit* Apr 1943

Koch, Fred, drama teacher and theatrical director, Oct 1953, *Obit* Yrbk 2000

Koch, Frederick H., *Obit* Oct 1944

Kolbe, Parke Rexford, *Obit* Apr 1942

Marcial Dorado, Carolina, *Obit* Sept 1941

Martin, Percy Alvin, *Obit* Apr 1942

Mearns, Hughes, Jan 1940, *Obit* Apr 1965

Meier, Richard, American architect, Jan 1985

Messiaen, Olivier, French organist and composer, Feb 1974, *Obit* June 1992

Meyer, Albert, Jan 1960, *Obit* May 1965

Moore, Robert Webber, *Obit* Jan 1943

Murray, Arthur, American dance teacher, Apr 1943, *Obit* May 1991

Prall, David Wight, *Obit* Yrbk 1940

Prentiss, Henrietta, *Obit* Jan 1940

Ripley, William Z., *Obit* Oct 1941

Rogers, Robert Emmons, *Obit* July 1941

Schlauch, Margaret, Polish professor of English, Yrbk 1942, *Obit* Sept 1986

Selden, David, teacher and labor leader, July 1974, *Obit* Aug 1998

Shanker, Albert, American labor leader and teacher, Apr 1969, *Obit* May 1997
Shull, Martha A., Apr 1957
Snyder, Alice D., *Obit* Apr 1943
Stout, Ruth A., Jan 1959
Tigerman, Stanley, American architect, Feb 2001
Walker, Waurine, Feb 1955
Wambaugh, Eugene, *Obit* Sept 1940
Watrous, George Dutton, *Obit* Yrbk 1940
Whiteman, Wilberforce James, *Obit* Jan 1940
Young, Karl, *Obit* Jan 1944
Zimbalist, Efrem, American violinist, Mar 1949, *Obit* Apr 1985

Technicians

Fangmeier, Stefen, American special effects technician, Aug 2004
Muren, Dennis, American special effects technician, Mar 1997

Telecommunications executives

Araskog, Rand V., telecommunications executive, Nov 1991
Brown, Charles L., American telephone executive, Sept 1981, *Obit* Yrbk 2004
Cico, Carla, Italian telecommunications executive, Jan 2005
Craig, Cleo F., Sept 1951, *Obit* June 1978
Ebbers, Bernard, American telecommunications executive, Feb 1998
Forsee, Gary, American telecommunications executive, Oct 2005
Griswold, Augustus H., *Obit* Mar 1940
Harrison, William H., Feb 1949, *Obit* July 1956
Ibrahim, Mohamed, Sudanese-British telecommunications executive, Jan 2007
Marshall, Walter P., Apr 1950, *Obit* June 1969
McCaw, Craig, American telecommunications executive, Sept 2001

Wilson, Leroy A., Apr 1948, *Obit* July 1951

Telecommunications workers

Allen, William L., Canadian labor leader, Sept 1953

Telegraphers

Allen, William L., Canadian labor leader, Sept 1953

Telepathists

Dunninger, Joseph, magician and mind reader, Sept 1944, *Obit* May 1975

Television directors

Brownlow, Kevin, English television producer and director, Mar 1992
Burns, Ken, American documentary filmmaker, May 1992
Burrows, James, American television director, Oct 2006
Gondry, Michel, French film director, May 2007
Kopple, Barbara, American film and television director, July 1998
Liebman, Max, television producer and director, Apr 1953, *Obit* Sept 1981
Loach, Ken, British film and television director, July 1995
Lumet, Sidney, American television and film director, Sept 1967, June 2005, *Obit* Yrbk 2011
McCleery, Albert, Feb 1955, *Obit* July 1972
Ophuls, Marcel, motion picture and television director, June 1977
Penn, Arthur, American film, theatrical and television director, Jan 1972, *Obit* Yrbk 2010
Schaefer, George, television director and producer, Feb 1970, *Obit* Jan 1998
Weiner, Matthew, American television producer and scriptwriter, Mar 2012
Westin, Av, Aug 1975
Yates, David, British film director, Apr 2011

Television moderators

Amanpour, Christiane, British television reporter and moderator, Apr 1996
Brinkley, David, American television newscaster and moderator, Mar 1960, Sept 1987, *Obit* Sept 2003
Gregory, David, American television reporter and moderator, Oct 2010
Koppel, Ted, American television newscaster, July 1984
Roberts, Cokie, American television reporter and moderator, May 1994
Susskind, David, American television producer, May 1960, *Obit* Apr 1987
Wallace, Chris, American television reporter and moderator, Feb 2011
Zahn, Paula, American television newscaster, Feb 2002

Television news anchors

Arraras, Maria Celeste, Puerto Rican television news anchor, Aug 2002
Bartiromo, Maria, American television reporter, Nov 2003
Blitzer, Wolf, American television news anchor, Feb 2007
Brokaw, Tom, American television news anchor, May 1981, Nov 2002
Brown, Aaron, American television news anchor, Mar 2003
Brown, Campbell, American television news anchor, Nov 2008
Brzezinski, Mika, American television news anchor, July 2010
Burnett, Erin, American television news anchor, Sept 2012
Cafferty, Jack, American television newscaster, Oct 2008
Chung, Connie, American television newscaster, July 1989

Couric, Katie, American television news anchor, Mar 1993, Apr 2008

Curry, Ann, American television newscaster, June 2004

Dhaliwal, Daljit, English television newscaster, Nov 2000

Dobbs, Lou, American television newscaster, Nov 2006

Gibson, Charles, American television news anchor, Sept 2002

Huntley, Chet, American television news anchor, Oct 1956, *Obit* May 1974

Husain, Mishal, British television news anchor, Jan 2004

Jennings, Peter, Canadian television newscaster, Nov 1983, *Obit* Sept 2005

King, John, American television news anchor, Mar 2010

Kotb, Hoda, American television news anchor, Apr 2011

Lemon, Don, American television news anchor, May 2010

Mudd, Roger, American television newscaster, Jan 1981

O'Brien, Soledad, American television news anchor, Nov 2009

Pelley, Scott, American television news anchor, Aug 2011

Rather, Dan, American television newscaster, May 1975

Reasoner, Harry, American television newscaster, Feb 1966, *Obit* Oct 1991

Savitch, Jessica, television news anchor, Jan 1983, *Obit* Mar 1984

Schieffer, Bob, American television news anchor, Aug 2006

Simpson, Carole, American television newscaster, Nov 1999

Vargas, Elizabeth, American television news anchor, Apr 2006

Wallace, Mike, American television newscaster, July 1957, Nov 1977, *Obit* Yrbk 2012

Williams, Brian, American television news anchor, July 1998

Woodruff, Judy, American television newscaster, Sept 1986

Television personalities

Arnett, Peter, New Zealand television reporter, Nov 1991

Banfield, Ashleigh, Canadian television newscaster, July 2002

Burdett, Winston, radio reporters, Oct 1943, *Obit* July 1993

Chang, Juju, television reporter, Aug 2013

Crowley, Candy, American television reporter, Jan 2011

Dickerson, Nancy, American television reporter, Sept 1962, *Obit* Jan 1998

Donaldson, Sam, American television newscaster, Sept 1987

Downs, Hugh, television personality, Mar 1965

Emerson, Faye, American actress and television personality, Sept 1951, *Obit* May 1983

Florence, Tyler, American chef, Aug 2012

Francis, Arlene, American television personality, May 1956, *Obit* Sept 2001

Francisco, Chilean television personality, Feb 2001

Garroway, Dave, American television personality, May 1952, *Obit* Sept 1982

Hansen, Chris, American television reporter, June 2010

Hartman, David, actor and television personality, June 1981

Judd, Jackie, American television reporter, Sept 2002

Kroft, Steve, American television reporter, Nov 1996

Linkletter, Art, American television personality, Nov 1953, *Obit* Yrbk 2010

Logan, Lara, South African television reporter, July 2006

Lunden, Joan, American television personality, May 1989

McMahon, Ed, American television personality, Apr 1977, *Obit* Yrbk 2009

Parks, Bert, actor and television personality, Feb 1973, *Obit* Apr 1992

Phillips, Kyra, American television reporter, Jan 2013

Safer, Morley, Canadian television newscaster, July 1980

Sanders, Marlene, television newscaster, Feb 1981

Santelli, Rick, American television reporter, July 2010

Simpson, John, British television reporter, June 2010

Stahl, Lesley, television reporter, June 1996

Susskind, David, American television producer, May 1960, *Obit* Apr 1987

Vergara, Sofia, Colombian actress, June 2013

White, Vanna, American television personality, Jan 1988

Television photographers

Salgado, Sebastiao, Brazilian photographer, Jan 2002

Television producers

Bunim, Mary-Ellis, American television producer, May 2002, *Obit* Yrbk 2004

Carsey, Marcy, American television producer, Jan 1997

Coe, Fred, television producer, Jan 1959, *Obit* June 1979

Fager, Jeff, American television producer, Jan 2012

Goodman, Julian, Feb 1967, *Obit* Yrbk 2012

Goodson, Mark, television producer, May 1978, *Obit* Feb 1993

Grade, Lew, British film and television producer, Aug 1979, *Obit* Mar 1999

Hewitt, Don, American television producer, June 1988, *Obit* Yrbk 2009

Jarvis, Lucy, television producer, Apr 1972

Liebman, Max, television producer and director, Apr 1953, *Obit* Sept 1981

Mann, Michael, American motion picture director and television producer, Jan 1993

McCleery, Albert, Feb 1955, *Obit* July 1972

Miner, Worthington C., television producer, Feb 1953, *Obit* Mar 1983

Mol, John de, Dutch television producer, Jan 2004

Murray, Jonathan, American television producer, May 2002

Singer, Bryan, American motion picture director, Apr 2005

Westin, Av, Aug 1975

Wolper, David L., American film and television producer, Oct 1986, *Obit* Yrbk 2010

Television scriptwriters

Mosel, Tad, American dramatist, Nov 1961, *Obit* Yrbk 2008

Nixon, Agnes, American television scriptwriter, Apr 2001

Nolan, Jonathan, Apr 2013

Wilson, Lanford, American playwright, Mar 1979, *Obit* Yrbk 2011

Tennis players

Agassi, Andre, American tennis player, Oct 1989

Austin, Tracy, American tennis player, May 1981

Azarenka, Victoria, Belarusian tennis player, Oct 2013

Baghdatis, Marcos, Cypriot tennis player, Jan 2006

Becker, Boris, German tennis player, Feb 1987

Blake, James, American tennis player, Mar 2006

Borg, Bjorn, Swedish tennis player, Yrbk 1974

Brough, Louise, American tennis player, June 1948

Brown, Dustin, Jamaican tennis player, Oct 2010

Budge, Don, American tennis player, June 1941, *Obit* June 2000

Bueno, Maria, American tennis player, Apr 1965

Capriati, Jennifer, American tennis player, Nov 2001

Chang, Michael, American tennis player, July 1997

Clijsters, Kim, Belgian tennis player, Jan 2004

Connolly, Maureen, American tennis player, Nov 1951, *Obit* Sept 1969

Connors, Jimmy, American tennis player, Sept 1975

Costa, Albert, Spanish tennis player, Jan 2002

Court, Margaret, Australian tennis player, Sept 1973

Dementieva, Elena, Russian tennis player, Jan 2005

Djokovic, Novak, Serbian tennis player, Apr 2012

Edberg, Stefan, Swedish tennis player, Jan 1994

Emerson, Roy, Australian tennis player, June 1965

Evert, Chris, American tennis player, Apr 1973

Federer, Roger, Swiss tennis player, Jan 2004

Gerulaitis, Vitas, American tennis player, June 1979, *Obit* Nov 1994

Gibson, Althea, American tennis player, Oct 1957, *Obit* Feb 2004

Gonzales, Pancho, American tennis player, Oct 1949, *Obit* Sept 1995

Goolagong, Evonne, Australian tennis player, Nov 1971

Graebner, Clark, American tennis player, Feb 1970

Graf, Steffi, German tennis player, Feb 1989

Hard, Darlene, July 1964

Henin, Justine, Belgian tennis player, Jan 2003

Hewitt, Lleyton, Australian tennis player, Oct 2002

Hoad, Lew, Australian tennis player, Sept 1956, *Obit* Sept 1994

Kournikova, Anna, Russian tennis player, Jan 2002

Kramer, Jack, American tennis player, May 1947, *Obit* Yrbk 2009

Kuznetsova, Svetlana, Russian tennis player, Mar 2008

Kvitova, Petra, Czech tennis player, Jan 2012

Laver, Rod, Australian tennis player, Feb 1963

Lendl, Ivan, Czech-American tennis player, Sept 1984

Li Na, Chinese tennis player, Jan 2006

Mandlikova, Hana, Czech tennis player, Jan 1986

McKinley, Chuck, tennis player, Nov 1963, *Obit* Sept 1986

Mirza, Sania, Indian tennis player, Jan 2005

Mulloy, Gardnar, tennis player, Nov 1957

Muster, Thomas, Austrian tennis player, May 1997

Nadal, Rafael, Spanish tennis player, Jan 2005

Navratilova, Martina, Czech-American tennis player, Sept 1977, Feb 2004

Newcombe, John, Australian tennis player, Oct 1977

Noah, Yannick, French tennis player, Aug 1987

Olmedo, Alex, Peruvian tennis player, Yrbk 1959

Parker, Frank, tennis player, Sept 1948, *Obit* Oct 1997

Pate, Walter L., Mar 1947, *Obit* June 1974

Petrova, Nadia, Russian tennis player, Jan 2005

Potro, Juan Martin del, Argentine tennis player, May 2010

Ralston, Dennis, tennis player, Oct 1965

Riggs, Bobby, American tennis player, Sept 1949, *Obit* Jan 1996

Roddick, Andy, American tennis player, Jan 2004

Rosewall, Ken, Australian tennis player, Yrbk 1956

Sabatini, Gabriela, Argentine tennis player, June 1992

Safin, Marat, Russian tennis player, Jan 2003

Sampras, Pete, American tennis player, May 1994

Sanchez Vicario, Arantxa, Spanish tennis player, Aug 1998

Santana, Manuel, Spanish tennis player, Sept 1967

Savitt, Dick, tennis player, June 1952

Schroeder, Frederick R., American tennis player, Oct 1949, *Obit* Yrbk 2006

Sedgman, Frank, Australian tennis player, Nov 1951

Segura, Pancho, Ecuadorian tennis player, Sept 1951

Seixas, Vic, tennis player, July 1952

Seles, Monica, Yugoslav-American tennis player, Nov 1992

Sharapova, Maria, Russian tennis player, Jan 2004

Srichaphan, Paradorn, Thai tennis player, Jan 2004

Talbert, William F., tennis player, Mar 1957, *Obit* June 1999

Wade, Virginia, English tennis player, May 1976

Williams, Serena, American tennis player, Feb 2003

Williams, Venus, American tennis player, Feb 2003

Terrorists

Osama bin Laden, Saudi Arabian terrorist, *Obit* Yrbk 2012

Textile artists

Fassett, Kaffe, American textile designer, June 1995

Liebes, Dorothy, American textile designer, Apr 1948, *Obit* Yrbk 1972

Theater executives

Beck, Martin, American theater owner, *Obit* Jan 1941

Drabinsky, Garth, Canadian theatrical producer, Oct 1997

Frohman, Daniel, *Obit* Feb 1941

Lortel, Lucille, theater owner and producer, Feb 1985, *Obit* July 1999

Nederlander, James Morton, American theater owner, Apr 1991

Theater people

Abraham, F. Murray, American actor, Jan 1991

Abraham, John, Indian actor, Jan 2006

Abril, Victoria, Spanish actress, Jan 2004

Adjani, Isabelle, French actress, Jan 1990

Aghdashloo, Shohreh, Iranian actress, Jan 2005

Aherne, Brian, English actor, Feb 1960, *Obit* Apr 1986

Aiello, Danny, American actor, June 1992

Albee, Edward, American dramatist, Feb 1963, Apr 1996

Albert, Eddie, American actor, Jan 1954, *Obit* Yrbk 2005

Albertson, Jack, American actor, Mar 1976, *Obit* Jan 1982

Aldrich, Richard, theatrical producer, June 1955, *Obit* June 1986

Alexander, Jason, American actor, Jan 1998

Alley, Kirstie, American actress, July 1994

Allyson, June, American actress, Jan 1952, *Obit* Yrbk 2006

Alvarez Quintero, Joaquin, Spanish dramatist, *Obit* Aug 1944

Ameche, Don, actor, May 1965, *Obit* Feb 1994

Anderson, Judith, English actress, Yrbk 1941, Feb 1961, *Obit* Mar 1992

Anderson, Lindsay, British motion picture and theatrical director, Nov 1975, *Obit* Nov 1994

Anderson, Mary, American actress, *Obit* July 1940

Anderson, Maxwell, American dramatist, Nov 1942, Sept 1953, *Obit* May 1959

Andersson, Bibi, Swedish actress, Sept 1978

Andrews, Anthony, English actor, June 1991

Andrews, Dana, actor, Oct 1959, *Obit* Feb 1993

Arden, Eve, actress, Sept 1953, *Obit* Jan 1991

Argento, Asia, Italian actress, Jan 2003

Arkin, Alan, American actor, Oct 1967

Arliss, George, English actor, *Obit* Mar 1946

Armetta, Henry, American actor, *Obit* Nov 1945

Armfield, Neil, Australian theatrical director, Jan 2007

Arness, James, American actor, Nov 1973, *Obit* Yrbk 2011

Arquette, Patricia, American actress, Oct 1997

Arthur, Bea, American actress, Yrbk 1973, *Obit* Yrbk 2009

Arthur, Jean, actress, Mar 1945, *Obit* Aug 1991

Asano, Tadanobu, Japanese actor, Jan 2007

Ashcroft, Peggy, British actress, Sept 1963, Jan 1987, *Obit* Aug 1991

Ashley, Elizabeth, actress, Mar 1978

Asner, Edward, American actor, Aug 1978

Atkins, Eileen, English actress, Jan 2002

Atwill, Lionel, English actor, *Obit* June 1946

Auteuil, Daniel, French actor, Jan 2007

Aykroyd, Dan, Canadian actor, Jan 1992

Ayres, Agnes, American actress, *Obit* Feb 1941

Azmi, Shabana, Indian actress, Jan 2002

Bacall, Lauren, American actress, Mar 1970

Bach, Reginald, British actor and theatrical director, *Obit* Feb 1941

Bachchan, Amitabh, Indian actor, Jan 2002

Bae, Yong Joon, Korean actor, Jan 2005

Baker, Rick, American makeup artist, Mar 1997

Baker, Tom, British actor, Jan 2004

Bakula, Scott, American actor, Feb 2002

Baldwin, Alec, American actor, July 1992

Ball, Lucille, American actress, Sept 1952, Jan 1978, *Obit* June 1989

Ball, William, theatrical director and producer, May 1974, *Obit* Oct 1991

Banderas, Antonio, Spanish actor, Mar 1997

Bankhead, Tallulah, American actress, July 1941, Jan 1953, *Obit* Feb 1969

Bankole, Isaach de, Ivorian actor, Jan 2004

Barbier, George W., American actor, *Obit* Aug 1945

Bardem, Javier, Spanish actor, Jan 2002

Bardot, Brigitte, French actress, Jan 1960

Barfield, Tanya, American playwright, Mar 2011

Barlow, Reginald, American actor, *Obit* Aug 1943

Barrymore, Drew, American actress, Oct 1998

Barrymore, Ethel, actress, Mar 1941, *Obit* Sept 1959

Barrymore, John, American actor, *Obit* July 1942

Barrymore, Lionel, actor, July 1943, *Obit* Jan 1955

Basinger, Kim, American actress, Feb 1990

Bassett, Angela, American actress, May 1996

Bateman, Jason, American actor, Oct 2005

Bates, Alan, English actor, Mar 1969, *Obit* Yrbk 2004

Bates, Blanche, American actress, *Obit* Feb 1942

Bates, Granville, American actor, *Obit* Sept 1940

Baur, Harry, French actor, *Obit* May 1943

Baxter, Anne, actress, May 1972, *Obit* Feb 1986

Beart, Emmanuelle, French actress, Jan 2002

Beck, Martin, American theater owner, *Obit* Jan 1941

Beckinsale, Kate, English actress, Aug 2001

Begley, Ed, American actor, Mar 1956, *Obit* June 1970

Bel Geddes, Barbara, American actress, July 1948, *Obit* Yrbk 2005

Bellamy, Ralph, actor, Nov 1951, *Obit* Jan 1992

Bellucci, Monica, Italian actress, Jan 2003

Belmondo, Jean-Paul, French actor, Yrbk 1965

Belmore, Alice, British actress, *Obit* Sept 1943

Belushi, Jim, American actor, Jan 1995

Bendix, William, American actor, Sept 1948, *Obit* Feb 1965

Bennett, Richard, American actor, *Obit* Yrbk 1944

Bentley, Irene, American actress, *Obit* July 1940

Bergman, Ingmar, Swedish film and theatrical director, Apr 1960, Oct 1981, *Obit* Sept 2007

Bergman, Ingrid, Swedish actress, Jan 1940, Sept 1965, *Obit* Oct 1982

Berry, Halle, American actress, May 1999

Bervoets, Gene, Dutch actor, Jan 2002

Best, Edna, English actress, July 1954, *Obit* Nov 1974

Birkin, Jane, English actress, Jan 2002

Bishop, Andre, American theatrical producer, July 1999

Bisset, Jacqueline, English actress, May 1977

Black, Karen, American actress, Mar 1976, *Obit* Yrbk 2013

Blake, Robert, American actor, Oct 1975

Blakemore, Michael, Australian theatrical director, May 2001

Blanchett, Cate, Australian actress, Aug 1999

Blau, Bela, American theatrical producer, *Obit* Yrbk 1940

Bloom, Claire, English actress, May 1956

Bloom, Orlando, English actor, Jan 2003

Bloomgarden, Kermit, American theatrical producer, Yrbk 1958, *Obit* Nov 1976

Blumenthal, George, American theatrical producer, *Obit* Sept 1943

Bogart, Anne, theatrical director, Feb 1999

Bogart, Humphrey, American actor, May 1942, *Obit* Mar 1957

Bond, Edward, English dramatist, June 1978

Bonham Carter, Helena, English actress, Jan 1998

Booth, Shirley, American actress, Nov 1942, Apr 1953, *Obit* Jan 1993

Borgnine, Ernest, American actor, Apr 1956, *Obit* Yrbk 2012

Bosworth, Hobart, American actor, *Obit* Feb 1944

Bova, Raoul, Italian actor, Jan 2004

Boyd, Stephen, Irish actor, Yrbk 1961, *Obit* Aug 1977

Boyd, William, American actor, Mar 1950, *Obit* Nov 1972

Boyer, Charles, French actor, Feb 1943, *Obit* Oct 1978

Bracken, Eddie, American actor, Oct 1944, *Obit* Feb 2003

Brandauer, Klaus Maria, Austrian actor, July 1990

Brando, Marlon, American actor, Apr 1952, Mar 1974, *Obit* Yrbk 2004

Brazzi, Rossano, Italian actor, May 1961, *Obit* Mar 1995

Brennan, Walter, actor, May 1941, *Obit* Nov 1974

Breuer, Lee, dramatist and director, Oct 1999

Bridges, Lloyd, actor, July 1990, *Obit* May 1998

Broderick, Matthew, American actor, May 1987

Brody, Adrien, American actor, July 2003

Brolin, Josh, American actor, Feb 2008

Bronson, Charles, American actor, Mar 1975, *Obit* Mar 2004

Brooks, Louise, American actress, Apr 1984, *Obit* Oct 1985

Brosnan, Pierce, Irish actor, Jan 1997

Brown, Gilmor, July 1944

Brown, Joe E., American actor, Feb 1945, *Obit* Sept 1973

Browne, Coral, Australian actress, Yrbk 1959, *Obit* July 1991

Brynner, Yul, American actor, Sept 1956, *Obit* Nov 1985

Buchholz, Horst, German actor, Mar 1960, *Obit* Aug 2003

Bullock, Sandra, American actress, Aug 1997

Burr, Raymond, actor, Sept 1961, *Obit* Nov 1993

Burstyn, Ellen, American actress, June 1975

Burton, LeVar, American actor, Mar 2000

Burton, Richard, Welsh actor, Yrbk 1960, *Obit* Sept 1984

Byington, Spring, actress, Sept 1956, *Obit* Oct 1971

Byrne, Gabriel, Irish actor, May 1999

Byron, Arthur, *Obit* Sept 1943

Caan, James, American actor, May 1976

Cage, Nicolas, American actor, Apr 1994

Cagney, James, American actor, Yrbk 1942, *Obit* May 1986

Caine, Michael, English actor, May 1968, Jan 1988

Caldwell, Zoe, Australian actress, Yrbk 1970

Calhern, Louis, July 1951, *Obit* July 1956

Cameron, Hugh, *Obit* Jan 1942

Campbell, Bruce, American actor, May 2013

Campbell, Douglas, Canadian actor and theatrical director, June 1958, *Obit* Yrbk 2009

Campbell, Neve, Canadian actress, Jan 2000

Campbell, Patrick, English actress, *Obit* May 1940

Candy, John, Canadian actor, Feb 1990, *Obit* May 1994

Carle, Richard, *Obit* Aug 1941

Carney, Art, American actor, Apr 1958, *Obit* Yrbk 2004

Carnovsky, Morris, actor, Jan 1991

Carradine, Keith, American actor, Aug 1991

Carroll, Madeleine, actress, Apr 1949, *Obit* Nov 1987

Carroll, Pat, actress, Aug 1980

Cattrall, Kim, Anglo-Canadian actress, Jan 2003

Caulfield, Joan, actress, May 1954, *Obit* Aug 1991

Cavanagh, Tom, Canadian actor, June 2003

Chadwick, Helene, *Obit* Oct 1940

Chaikin, Joseph, American theatrical director and actor, July 1981, *Obit* Yrbk 2003

Chamberlain, Richard, American actor, July 1963, Nov 1987

Channing, Carol, American actress, Sept 1964

Channing, Stockard, American actress, Apr 1991

Chaplin, Geraldine, actress, July 1979

Chapman, Blanche, *Obit* Aug 1941

Charters, Spencer, *Obit* Mar 1943

Chase, Charley, actor, *Obit* Aug 1940

Chase, Ilka, May 1942, *Obit* Apr 1978

Chase, Mary, dramatist, Oct 1945, *Obit* Jan 1982

Cheadle, Don, American actor, Sept 1999

Chereau, Patrice, French theatrical, opera and film director, Jan 1990

Cherry, Addie, American vaudeville actress, *Obit* Yrbk 1942

Chow, Yun Fat, Chinese actor, May 1998

Christensen, Hayden, Canadian actor, Jan 2005

Christians, Mady, May 1945, *Obit* Yrbk 1951

Christie, Julie, English actress, Sept 1966

Churchill, Berton, *Obit* Yrbk 1940

Churchill, Caryl, English playwright, June 1985

Claire, Ina, actress, May 1954, *Obit* Apr 1985

Clark, Marguerite, *Obit* Nov 1940

Clarkson, Patricia, American actress, Aug 2005

Clayburgh, Jill, American actress, Sept 1979, *Obit* Yrbk 2011

Clift, Montgomery, American actor, July 1954, *Obit* Sept 1966

Clive, E. E., *Obit* July 1940

Close, Glenn, American actress, Nov 1984

Cobb, Lee J., Feb 1960, *Obit* Apr 1976

Coburn, Charles, actor, June 1944, *Obit* Nov 1961

Coburn, James, American actor, June 1999, *Obit* Feb 2003

Cochran, Charles Blake, English theatrical producer, Oct 1940, *Obit* Mar 1951

Coco, James, actor, May 1974, *Obit* Apr 1987

Cohen, Alexander H., American theatrical producer, June 1965, *Obit* Aug 2000

Colbert, Claudette, American actress, Jan 1945, May 1964, *Obit* Oct 1996

Collier, Constance, July 1954, *Obit* June 1955

Collier, William, American actor, *Obit* Mar 1944

Collins, Eddie, American actor, *Obit* Oct 1940

Colman, Ronald, English actor, July 1943, *Obit* Sept 1958

Connelly, Jennifer, American actress, June 2002

Connelly, Marc, dramatist, Nov 1969, *Obit* Feb 1981

Connery, Sean, Scottish actor, Jan 1966, June 1993

Conness, Robert, *Obit* Mar 1941

Connolly, Walter, actor, *Obit* July 1940

Conover, Harry, Feb 1949, *Obit* Oct 1965

Conti, Tom, Scottish actor, June 1985

Cook, Donald, July 1954, *Obit* Yrbk 1961

Cooper, Chris, American actor, July 2004

Cooper, Gary, American actor, Yrbk 1941, *Obit* July 1961

Cooper, Gladys, English actress, Feb 1956, *Obit* Jan 1972

Cornell, Katharine, American actress, May 1941, Mar 1952, *Obit* July 1974

Cotten, Joseph, American actor, July 1943, *Obit* Apr 1994

Courtenay, Tom, English actor, May 1964

Cox, Brian, Scottish actor, Jan 2004

Cox, Wally, Feb 1954, *Obit* Apr 1973

Craig, Daniel, British actor, Apr 2007

Crain, Jeanne, American actress, Nov 1951, *Obit* Yrbk 2004

Crawford, Broderick, actor, Apr 1950, *Obit* June 1986

Crawford, Cheryl, American theatrical producer, Yrbk 1945, *Obit* Nov 1986

Crawford, Joan, American actress, Jan 1946, Sept 1966, *Obit* July 1977

Cregar, Laird, *Obit* Jan 1945

Crews, Laura Hope, actress, *Obit* Jan 1943

Cromer, David, American theatrical director and actor, Sept 2011

Cromwell, James, American actor, Aug 2005

Cronyn, Hume, Canadian actor, Mar 1956, June 1988, *Obit* Yrbk 2003

Cross, Ben, English actor, Aug 1984

Crouse, Russel, dramatist, June 1941, *Obit* May 1966

Crowe, Russell, Australian actor, May 2000

Cruise, Tom, American actor, Apr 1987

Cruz, Penelope, Spanish actress, July 2001

Curtin, Jane, actress, Jan 1997

Curtis, Tony, American actor, May 1959, *Obit* Nov 2010

Cusack, Joan, American actress, July 1998

Cusack, John, American actor, June 1996

Cushing, Charles C. S., *Obit* Apr 1941

D'Onofrio, Vincent, American actor, May 2004

Dafoe, Willem, American actor, Apr 1990

Dalton, Charles, *Obit* Aug 1942

Dalton, Timothy, English actor, May 1988

Daly, James, Oct 1959, *Obit* Sept 1978

Daly, Tyne, actress, Mar 1992

Danner, Blythe, American actress, Jan 1981

Danson, Ted, American actor, Oct 1990

Darin, Ricardo, Argentine actor, Jan 2002

Darwell, Jane, June 1941, *Obit* Oct 1967

Dashiell, Willard, *Obit* June 1943

Davidson, Gordon, American theatrical director and producer, Apr 2005

Davis, Bette, American actress, Oct 1941, Mar 1953, *Obit* Nov 1989

Davis, Geena, American actress, Oct 1991

Davis, Judy, Australian actress, Nov 1993

Day, Laraine, American actress, Sept 1953, *Obit* Yrbk 2008

Day-Lewis, Daniel, Anglo-Irish actor, July 1990

De Havilland, Olivia, American actress, May 1944, Nov 1966

Dee, Ruby, American actress, Nov 1970

Del Toro, Benicio, American actor, Sept 2001

Delon, Alain, French actor, Apr 1964

Dench, Judi, English actress, Jan 1999

Deneuve, Catherine, French actress, Feb 1978

Dennehy, Brian, American actor, July 1991

Dennis, Sandy, actress, Jan 1969, *Obit* May 1992

Denniston, Reynolds, *Obit* Mar 1943

Depardieu, Gerard, French actor, Oct 1987

Depp, Johnny, American actor, May 1991

Dern, Bruce, American actor, Oct 1978

Dern, Laura, American actress, Oct 1992

Dewhurst, Colleen, actress, July 1974, *Obit* Oct 1991

Dexter, John, English theatrical director, July 1976, *Obit* May 1990

DiCaprio, Leonardo, American actor, Mar 1997

Diaz, Cameron, American actress, Apr 2005

Dickinson, Angie, American actress, Feb 1981

Dietrich, Marlene, German-American actress, June 1953, Feb 1968, *Obit* June 1992

Diggs, Taye, American actor, Aug 2011

Dillman, Bradford, actor, Jan 1960

Dillon, Matt, American actor, May 1985

Dixey, Henry E., *Obit* Apr 1943

Douglas, Kirk, American actor, Mar 1952

Douglas, Melvyn, actor, May 1942, *Obit* Sept 1981

Dowling, Eddie, Feb 1946, *Obit* Apr 1976

Downey, Robert, American actor, Aug 1998

Drabinsky, Garth, Canadian theatrical producer, Oct 1997

Drescher, Fran, American actress, Apr 1998

Dreyfuss, Richard, American actor, Jan 1976

Dukakis, Olympia, American actress, July 1991

Duke, Patty, American actress, Sept 1963

Dullea, Keir, American actor, June 1970

Dunaway, Faye, American actress, Feb 1972

Duncan, Malcolm, *Obit* June 1942

Duncan, Michael Clarke, actor, Aug 2000, *Obit* Yrbk 2012

Duncan, Sandy, actress, Jan 1980

Dunnock, Mildred, actress, Sept 1955, *Obit* Sept 1991

Dunst, Kirsten, American actress, Oct 2001

Durang, Christopher, American dramatist, June 1987

Edwards, Vince, actor, Oct 1962, *Obit* May 1996

Eisenstein, Sergei, Russian theatrical and motion picture

director, May 1946, *Obit* Mar 1948

Ejiofor, Chiwetel, British actor, Jan 2004

Eldridge, Florence, actress, Mar 1943, *Obit* Sept 1988

Elizondo, Hector, American actor, Jan 1992

Elliott, Maxine, actress, Mar 1940

Eltinge, Julian, *Obit* Apr 1941

Emanuel, Ariel, American talent agent, July 2009

Englund, Robert, actor, Mar 1990

Ensler, Eve, American dramatist, Aug 2002

Evans, Chris, American actor, Aug 2013

Evans, Edith, English actress, June 1956, *Obit* Jan 1977

Evans, Linda, American actress, Mar 1986

Evans, Maurice, English actor, May 1940, June 1961, *Obit* May 1989

Everett, Rupert, English actor, Jan 2005

Ewell, Tom, actor, May 1961, *Obit* Nov 1994

Fairbanks, Douglas, American actor, Jan 1940

Fairbanks, Douglas, American actor, Nov 1941, Feb 1956, *Obit* Aug 2000

Falco, Edie, American actress, Mar 2006

Falk, Peter, American actor, July 1972, *Obit* Yrbk 2011

Falls, Robert, American theatrical director, Jan 2004

Farrell, Colin, Irish actor, Jan 2004

Farrow, Mia, American actress, Apr 1970

Faversham, William, *Obit* May 1940

Ferguson, Elsie, Feb 1944, *Obit* Jan 1962

Fernandel, Oct 1955, *Obit* Apr 1971

Ferrera, America, American actress, Sept 2007

Fichandler, Zelda, American theatrical producer and director, June 1987

Field, Betty, Sept 1959, *Obit* Nov 1973

Field, Sally, American actress, Oct 1979

Fields, Stanley, *Obit* June 1941

Fiennes, Ralph, British actor, Sept 1996

Finch, Peter, English actor, Sept 1972, *Obit* Mar 1977

Finney, Albert, English actor, Oct 1963

Firth, Colin, English actor, Mar 2004

Fishburne, Laurence, American actor, Aug 1996

Fitzgerald, Barry, Feb 1945, *Obit* Feb 1961

Fitzgerald, Cissy, *Obit* July 1941

Fitzgerald, Geraldine, Irish actress and director, Oct 1976, *Obit* Yrbk 2005

Fonda, Bridget, American actress, Jan 1994

Fonda, Henry, American actor, Yrbk 1948, Nov 1974, *Obit* Sept 1982

Fonda, Peter, American actor, Mar 1998

Fontaine, Joan, American actress, May 1944

Fontanne, Lynn, Anglo-American actress, June 1941, *Obit* Sept 1983

Ford, Glenn, American actor, June 1959, *Obit* Yrbk 2007

Ford, Harrison, American actor, Sept 1984, June 2008

Foreman, Richard, American theatrical director and playwright, July 1988

Forrest, Alan, *Obit* Sept 1941

Forsythe, John, American actor, May 1973, *Obit* Yrbk 2010

Fox, Megan, American actress, Feb 2010

Fox, Michael J., Canadian actor, Nov 1987

Fox, Sidney, actress, *Obit* Jan 1943

Franciosa, Tony, American actor, July 1961, *Obit* Yrbk 2006

Franco, James, American actor, Apr 2011

Franklin, Irene, actress, *Obit* Aug 1941

Franz, Dennis, American actor, July 1995

Fraser, Brad, Canadian dramatist, July 1995

Fraser, Brendan, American actor, Feb 2001

Freeman, Martin, British actor, Nov 2013

Freeman, Morgan, American actor, Feb 1991

Fresnay, Pierre, Feb 1959, *Obit* Feb 1975

Frohman, Daniel, *Obit* Feb 1941

Fry, Christopher, English dramatist, Feb 1951, *Obit* Yrbk 2005

Gabin, Jean, French actor, June 1941, *Obit* Jan 1977

Gable, Clark, American actor, May 1945, *Obit* Jan 1961

Gabor, Eva, Hungarian actress, July 1968, *Obit* Sept 1995

Gabor, Zsa Zsa, Hungarian-American actress, Mar 1988

Gallo, Fortune, Oct 1949, *Obit* May 1970

Gandolfini, James, American actor, Feb 2000, *Obit* Yrbk 2013

Ganz, Bruno, Swiss actor, Jan 2006

Garbo, Greta, Swedish-American actress, Apr 1955, *Obit* June 1990

Garcia Bernal, Gael, Mexican actor, Jan 2003

Gardner, Ava, American actress, Mar 1965, *Obit* Mar 1990

Garfield, John, actor, Apr 1948, *Obit* July 1952

Garner, James, American actor, Nov 1966

Garner, Jennifer, American actress, Apr 2008

Garson, Greer, Anglo-Irish actress, Sept 1942, *Obit* June 1996

Gassman, Vittorio, Italian actor and theatrical director, Oct 1964, *Obit* Oct 2000

Gazzara, Ben, American actor, Nov 1967, *Obit* Yrbk 2012

Gere, Richard, American actor, Aug 1980

Gerwig, Greta, American actress, June 2010

Gest, Morris, *Obit* July 1942

Getty, Estelle, American actress, Mar 1990, *Obit* Yrbk 2008

Giamatti, Paul, American actor, Sept 2005

Giannini, Giancarlo, June 1979

Gielgud, John, English actor, director and producer, Apr 1947, Feb 1984, *Obit* Aug 2000

Gingold, Hermione, English actress, Oct 1958, *Obit* July 1987

Gish, Dorothy, American actress, Aug 1944, *Obit* Sept 1968

Gish, Lillian, American actress, Aug 1944, Aug 1978, *Obit* Apr 1993

Glover, Danny, American actor, Apr 1992

Goddard, Paulette, American actress, *Obit* June 1990

Goldblum, Jeff, American actor, July 1997

Gordon, C. Henry, *Obit* Jan 1941

Gordon, Max, Oct 1943, *Obit* Jan 1979

Gordon-Levitt, Joseph, American actor, June 2011

Gosden, Freeman F., actor, Yrbk 1947, *Obit* Feb 1983

Gossett, Louis, American actor, Nov 1990

Gould, Elliott, American actor, Feb 1971

Grammer, Kelsey, American actor, May 1996

Grant, Cary, Anglo-American actor, Sept 1941, Nov 1965, *Obit* Jan 1987

Grant, Hugh, English actor, Sept 1995

Greene, Lorne, actor, Jan 1967, *Obit* Oct 1987

Greenstreet, Sydney, May 1943, *Obit* Mar 1954

Greenwood, Joan, English actress, May 1954, *Obit* Apr 1987

Gregory, Paul, Apr 1956

Grenfell, Joyce, English actress, Mar 1958, *Obit* Feb 1980

Gribble, Harry Wagstaff, Sept 1945, *Obit* Apr 1981

Grier, Pam, American actress, Feb 1998

Griffies, Ethel, Jan 1968, *Obit* Nov 1975

Griffith, Melanie, American actress, Oct 1990

Grimes, Tammy, actress, July 1962

Grizzard, George, American actor, June 1976, *Obit* Yrbk 2008

Grotowski, Jerzy, Polish theatrical director, Yrbk 1970, *Obit* Mar 1999

Guare, John, American dramatist, Aug 1982

Guillaume, Robert, American actor, Apr 2000

Guinness, Alec, English actor, Oct 1950, Mar 1981, *Obit* Oct 2000

Gulpilil, David, Australian actor, Jan 2003

Guthrie, Tyrone, British theatrical producer and director, July 1954, *Obit* July 1971

Gwenn, Edmund, Sept 1943, *Obit* Nov 1959

Hackett, Walter, *Obit* Mar 1944

Hackman, Gene, American actor, July 1972

Hagen, Uta, American actress, May 1944, Oct 1963, *Obit* Yrbk 2004

Hagman, Larry, American actor, Sept 1980, *Obit* Yrbk 2013

Hall, Deidre, American actress, Nov 2002

Hall, James, actor, *Obit* July 1940

Hall, Peter, British theatrical director, Feb 1962

Hamilton, Hale, *Obit* July 1942

Hamilton, Margaret, actress, Apr 1979, *Obit* July 1985

Hamm, Jon, American actor, Mar 2013

Hampden, Walter, American actor, May 1953, *Obit* Sept 1955

Hanks, Tom, American actor, Apr 1989

Hannah, Daryl, American actress, May 1990

Harden, Marcia Gay, American actress, Sept 2001

Hardwicke, Cedric, English actor, Oct 1949, *Obit* Oct 1964

Hare, David, English dramatist and theatrical director, Aug 1983

Harlan, Otis, *Obit* Jan 1940

Harper, Valerie, American actress, Feb 1975

Harrelson, Woody, American actor, Jan 1997

Harris, Barbara, American actress, Apr 1968

Harris, Julie, American actress, Feb 1956, Aug 1977, *Obit* Yrbk 2013

Harris, Naomie, British actress, Sept 2012

Harris, Richard, Irish actor, May 1964, *Obit* Yrbk 2003

Harris, Rosemary, British actress, Sept 1967

Harris, Sam H., American theatrical producer, *Obit* Aug 1941

Harris, William, *Obit* Oct 1946

Harrison, Rex, English actor, Jan 1947, Feb 1986, *Obit* July 1990

Harrower, David, Scottish dramatist, Jan 2007

Hart, Moss, American playwright, July 1940, Nov 1960, *Obit* Feb 1962

Hart, William S., American actor, *Obit* July 1946

Hartman, Paul, American actor, Nov 1942, *Obit* Yrbk 1973

Hartwig, Walter, *Obit* Mar 1941

Harvey, Laurence, British actor, May 1961, *Obit* Jan 1974

Hathaway, Anne, American actress, Feb 2009

Hawkins, Jack, Nov 1959, *Obit* Oct 1973

Hawley, H. Dudley, *Obit* May 1941

Hawn, Goldie, American actress, Yrbk 1971

Hayakawa, Sessue, Japanese actor, Sept 1962, *Obit* Jan 1974

Hayes, Helen, American actress, Jan 1942, Oct 1956, *Obit* May 1993

Hayes, Peter Lind, actor, Mar 1959, *Obit* July 1998

Haysbert, Dennis, American actor, Nov 2006

Hayward, Leland, theatrical agent and producer, Feb 1949, *Obit* Apr 1971

Hayward, Susan, American actress, May 1953, *Obit* May 1975

Hayworth, Rita, American actress, May 1960, *Obit* July 1987

Heche, Anne, American actress, Sept 1998

Heckart, Eileen, American actress, June 1958, *Obit* Mar 2002

Heflin, Van, July 1943, *Obit* Sept 1971

Helburn, Theresa, theatrical producer, Sept 1944, *Obit* Nov 1959

Hemsworth, Chris, Australian actor, Jan 2013

Henry, Martha, Canadian actress and theatrical director, Jan 2006

Hepburn, Audrey, Anglo-Dutch actress, Mar 1954, *Obit* Mar 1993

Hepburn, Katharine, American actress, May 1942, Nov 1969, *Obit* Nov 2003

Hershey, Barbara, American actress, Aug 1989

Hersholt, Jean, American actor, Yrbk 1944, *Obit* Sept 1956

Hill, Abram, theatrical director, producer and dramatist, Aug 1945, *Obit* Nov 1986

Hill, Arthur, Canadian actor, Mar 1977, *Obit* Yrbk 2007

Hill, Dule, American actor, July 2003

Hill, George Roy, American motion picture director, Apr 1977, *Obit* June 2003

Hiller, Wendy, English actress, Oct 1941, *Obit* Yrbk 2003

Hingle, Pat, American actor, Apr 1965, *Obit* Yrbk 2009

Hirsch, John, Canadian theatrical director, Apr 1984, *Obit* Oct 1989

Hirsch, Judd, actor, Mar 1984

Hjejle, Iben, Danish actress, Jan 2003

Hoch, Danny, American actor, Oct 1999

Hochhuth, Rolf, German dramatist, Oct 1976

Hoffman, Dustin, American actor, Yrbk 1969, Jan 1996

Hoffman, Philip Seymour, American actor, May 2001

Holbrook, Hal, American actor, May 1961

Holden, William, actor, June 1954, *Obit* Jan 1982

Holliday, Judy, actress, Apr 1951, *Obit* July 1965

Holm, Celeste, American actress, Apr 1944, *Obit* Yrbk 2012

Holm, Ian, English actor, Mar 2002

Hong, Seok Chon, Korean actor, Jan 2004

Hopkins, Anthony, Welsh-American actor, Feb 1980, Mar 1997

Hopkins, Arthur M., theatrical producer and director, June 1947, *Obit* Apr 1950

Horton, Edward Everett, American actor, Yrbk 1946, *Obit* Nov 1970

Hoskins, Bob, English actor, Sept 1990

Houseman, John, theatrical director, producer and actor, July 1959, Apr 1984, *Obit* Jan 1989

Howard, Cordelia, actress, *Obit* Oct 1941

Howard, Leslie, English actor, *Obit* July 1943

Howard, Terrence, American actor, June 2007

Howard, Trevor, English actor, July 1964, *Obit* Feb 1988

Hudson, Rock, American actor, Oct 1961, *Obit* Nov 1985

Hughes, Barnard, American actor, Sept 1981, *Obit* Yrbk 2006

Hughes, Hatcher, American dramatist, *Obit* Nov 1945

Hull, Josephine, Oct 1953, *Obit* May 1957

Hunt, Helen, Nov 1996

Hunt, Linda, actress, Jan 1988

Hunter, Glenn, American actor, *Obit* Mar 1946

Hunter, Holly, American actress, July 1994

Hunter, Kermit, dramatist, May 1959, *Obit* Sept 2001

Hunter, Kim, American actress, May 1952, *Obit* Yrbk 2002

Huppert, Isabelle, French actress, Nov 1981

Hurt, John, British actor, Jan 1982

Hurt, William, American actor, May 1986

Huston, Anjelica, American actress, July 1990

Huston, Walter, actor, Feb 1949, *Obit* May 1950

Hwang, David Henry, American dramatist, May 1989

Imam, Adel, Egyptian actor, Jan 2002

Innaurato, Albert, dramatist, Mar 1988

Irons, Jeremy, English actor, Aug 1984

Irving, Jules, July 1970, *Obit* Sept 1979

Ivey, Judith, actress, June 1993

Jackman, Hugh, Australian actor, Oct 2003

Jackson, Anne, actress, Sept 1980

Jackson, Samuel L., American actor, Nov 1996

Jacobi, Derek, British actor, May 1981

Janssen, David, American actor, Mar 1967, *Obit* Apr 1980

Jentsch, Julia, German actress, Jan 2006

Johansson, Scarlett, American actress, Mar 2005

Johns, Glynis, Sept 1973

Johnson, Don, American actor, Apr 1986

Johnson, Van, American actor, July 1945, *Obit* Yrbk 2009

Jolie, Angelina, American actress, Oct 2000

Jones, Barry, Mar 1958

Jones, Buck, *Obit* Jan 1943

Jones, Carolyn, American actress, Mar 1967, *Obit* Sept 1983

Jones, Cherry, American actress, May 1998

Jones, James Earl, American actor, Sept 1969, Nov 1994

Jones, Jennifer, American actress, May 1944, *Obit* Yrbk 2010

Jones, Rashida, American actress, Aug 2013

Jourdan, Louis, French actor, Jan 1967

Jouvet, Louis, French actor and theatrical director, Oct 1949, *Obit* Oct 1951

Judd, Ashley, American actress, Feb 2000

Julia, Raul, American actor, Sept 1982, *Obit* Jan 1995

Kaminska, Ida, Polish actress, Nov 1969, *Obit* July 1980

Kapoor, Karisma, Indian actress, Jan 2002

Karloff, Boris, Anglo-American actor, Mar 1941, *Obit* Mar 1969

Kaufman, George S., American dramatist, Aug 1941, *Obit* Sept 1961

Kaufman, Moises, American playwright and theatrical director, Aug 2011

Kavner, Julie, American actress, Oct 1992

Keach, Stacy, American actor, Nov 1971

Keane, Doris, actress, *Obit* Jan 1946

Keaton, Michael, American actor, June 1992

Keener, Catherine, American actress, Oct 2002

Keitel, Harvey, American actor, Mar 1994

Kekilli, Sibel, Turkish-German actress, Jan 2006

Kelly, David, Irish actor, Jan 2005, *Obit* Yrbk 2012

Kelly, Nancy, actress, June 1955, *Obit* Mar 1995

Kennedy, Arthur, American actor, Nov 1961

Kentridge, William, South African artist, Oct 2001

Kerr, Deborah, British actress, Sept 1947, *Obit* Feb 2008

Khan, Aamir, Indian actor, Jan 2002

Kidman, Nicole, Australian actress, Mar 1997

Kier, Udo, German actor, Jan 2005

Kiley, Richard, actor, Apr 1973, *Obit* May 1999

Kilmer, Val, American actor, Jan 1996

Kingsley, Ben, English actor, Nov 1983

Kingsley, Sidney, dramatist, June 1943, *Obit* May 1995

Kinski, Nastassia, German actress, June 1984

Kitchen, Michael, British actor, Nov 2008

Kline, Kevin, American actor, July 1986

Knightley, Keira, English actress, Jan 2005

Knott, Sarah Gertrude, July 1947

Kopit, Arthur L., dramatist, Yrbk 1972

Kotto, Yaphet, American actor, Mar 1995

Kouka, Hone, New Zealand dramatist, Jan 2004

Kozlenko, William, Oct 1941

Kurtz, Swoosie, American actress, Oct 1987

Kushner, Tony, American dramatist, July 2002

LaBeouf, Shia, American actor, Aug 2009

Ladd, Alan, American actor, Sept 1943, *Obit* Mar 1964

Lahr, Bert, actor, Jan 1952, *Obit* Feb 1968

Lanchester, Elsa, English actress, May 1950, *Obit* Feb 1987

Lane, Nathan, American actor, Aug 1996

Lange, Jessica, American actress, May 1983

Langella, Frank, American actor, Sept 1980

Langham, Michael, English theatrical director, Sept 1965, *Obit* Yrbk 2011

Langner, Lawrence, dramatist and producer, Sept 1944, *Obit* Feb 1963

Lansbury, Angela, American actress, Sept 1967

Laughton, Charles, Anglo-American actor, Nov 1948, *Obit* Jan 1963

Lavant, Denis, French actor, June 2013

Lavery, Emmet, July 1947

Lavin, Linda, actress, Nov 1987

Lawford, Ernest, *Obit* Feb 1941

Lawrence, Gertrude, English actress, Aug 1940, Sept 1952

Lawrence, Jennifer, American actress, May 2013

Lawson, Mary, *Obit* July 1941

LeCompte, Elizabeth, American theatrical director, Aug 1997

Leachman, Cloris, American actress, Oct 1975

Ledger, Heath, Australian actor, June 2006, *Obit* Yrbk 2008

Ledoyen, Virginie, French actress, Jan 2002

Lee, Auriol, *Obit* Sept 1941

Lee, Canada, American actor, Yrbk 1944, *Obit* June 1952

Lee, Christopher, English actor, Sept 1975

Leigh, Jennifer Jason, American actress, Aug 1992

Leigh, Vivien, English actress, July 1946, *Obit* Oct 1967

Leigh, William Colston, lecture agent, Jan 1942, *Obit* Sept 1992

Leighton, Margaret, English actress, Mar 1957, *Obit* Mar 1976

Lemmon, Jack, American actor, Feb 1961, Aug 1988, *Obit* Oct 2001

Leo, Melissa, American actress, July 2009

Leon, Kenny, American theatrical director, Nov 2005

Leonidoff, Leon, American theatrical producer, July 1941, *Obit* Oct 1989

Leung, Tony Chiu-wai, Chinese actor, Jan 2006

Lewis, Juliette, American actress, Feb 1996

Li Gong, Chinese actress, May 1997

Liebler, Theodore A., *Obit* June 1941

Lillie, Beatrice, British actress, Feb 1945, Sept 1964, *Obit* Mar 1989

Linden, Hal, actor, Jan 1987

Lindfors, Viveca, Swedish actress, Apr 1955, *Obit* Jan 1996

Lindo, Delroy, American actor, Mar 2001

Lindsay, Howard, dramatist, Apr 1942, *Obit* Apr 1968

Liotta, Ray, American actor, May 1994

Lockhart, Gene, Canadian actor, May 1950, *Obit* June 1957

Lockwood, Margaret, English actress, Sept 1948, *Obit* Sept 1990

Logan, Joshua, American theatrical and motion picture director, Oct 1949, *Obit* Aug 1988

Lohan, Lindsay, American actress, Nov 2005

Lombard, Carole, American actress, *Obit* Mar 1942

Loren, Sophia, Italian actress, Mar 1959

Lortel, Lucille, theater owner and producer, Feb 1985, *Obit* July 1999

Louis-Dreyfus, Julia, American actress, Oct 1995

Lowe, Rob, American actor, July 2000

Lowensohn, Elina, Romanian actress, Jan 2005

Loy, Myrna, American actress, Oct 1950, *Obit* Feb 1994

Lucas, Craig, American dramatist, Sept 1991

Lucci, Susan, American actress, Oct 1989

Lukas, Paul, American actor, Feb 1942, *Obit* Oct 1971

Luna, Diego, Mexican actor, Jan 2002

Lunt, Alfred, American actor, June 1941, *Obit* Sept 1977

Lynch, Jane, American actress, July 2010

Lynn, Diana, actress, Nov 1953, *Obit* Feb 1972

Lyubimov, Yuri, Russian theatrical director, Nov 1988

MacKintosh, Cameron, English theatrical producer, Mar 1991

MacLachlan, Kyle, American actor, Aug 1993

MacMurray, Fred, actor, Feb 1967, *Obit* Feb 1992

Madsen, Michael, American actor, Apr 2004

Magnani, Anna, Italian actress, Apr 1956, *Obit* Nov 1973

Maguire, Tobey, American actor, Sept 2002

Mahoney, John, actor, Aug 1999

Main, Marjorie, actress, Oct 1951, *Obit* June 1975

Malden, Karl, American actor, Apr 1957, *Obit* Yrbk 2009

Malina, Joshua, American actor, Apr 2004

Malina, Judith, American actress and theatrical director, June 2011

Mamoulian, Rouben, Russian-American theatrical and film director, Mar 1949, *Obit* Jan 1988

Mann, Emily, American dramatist and director, June 2002

Mara, Rooney, American actress, Oct 2012

Marais, Jean, French actor, Apr 1962, *Obit* Jan 1999

March, Fredric, American actor, Mar 1943, *Obit* June 1975

Marion, George F., *Obit* Jan 1946

Marsh, Jean, English actress, Nov 1977

Marshall, E. G., actor, June 1986, *Obit* Nov 1998

Marshall, Tully, actor, *Obit* Apr 1943

Martin, Jesse L., American actor, July 2006

Marvin, Lee, American actor, Sept 1966, *Obit* Oct 1987

Mary Alice, actress, Nov 1995

Masina, Giulietta, Italian actress, Apr 1958, *Obit* June 1994

Mason, James, English actor, May 1947, *Obit* Sept 1984

Mason, Marsha, American actress, Apr 1981

Massey, Raymond, Canadian-American actor, Feb 1946, *Obit* Sept 1983

Mastroianni, Marcello, Italian actor, June 1963, *Obit* Feb 1997

Matthau, Walter, American actor, June 1966, *Obit* Sept 2000

Mature, Victor, actor, Yrbk 1951, *Obit* Oct 1999

Maura, Carmen, Spanish actress, Apr 1992

McAdams, Rachel, Canadian actress, May 2009

McBurney, Simon, British actor and theatrical director, Jan 2005

McCambridge, Mercedes, American actress, June 1964, *Obit* Yrbk 2004

McClanahan, Rue, American actress, May 1989, *Obit* Yrbk 2010

McClintic, Guthrie, theatrical director and producer, May 1943, *Obit* Jan 1962

McCormick, Myron, Jan 1954, *Obit* Oct 1962

McCowen, Alec, Oct 1969

McDaniel, Hattie, American actress, Sept 1940, *Obit* Yrbk 1952

McDaniel, James, American actor, Feb 2000

McDonagh, Martin, Irish dramatist, Aug 1998

McDonnell, Mary, American actress, May 1997

McDormand, Frances, American actress, Sept 1997

McDowell, Malcolm, English actor, Yrbk 1973

McGuire, Dorothy, American actress, Sept 1941, *Obit* Nov 2001

McKellen, Ian, English actor, Jan 1984

McKenna, Siobhan, Irish actress, Nov 1956, *Obit* Jan 1987

McNally, Terrence, American dramatist, Mar 1988

McQueen, Steve, American actor, Oct 1966, *Obit* Jan 1981

McShane, Ian, English actor, July 2011

Meadows, Audrey, actress, May 1958, *Obit* Apr 1996

Meadows, Jayne, May 1958

Mendes, Sam, British theatrical and motion picture director, Oct 2002

Menjou, Adolphe, actor, June 1948, *Obit* Jan 1964

Meredith, Burgess, actor, July 1940, *Obit* Nov 1997

Merivale, Philip, *Obit* Apr 1946

Merrick, David, American theatrical producer, Jan 1961, *Obit* July 2000

Messing, Debra, American actress, Aug 2002

Meyer, Jean, Nov 1955

Mifune, Toshiro, Japanese actor, June 1981, *Obit* Mar 1998

Miller, Gilbert, Apr 1958, *Obit* Feb 1969

Mills, Hayley, English actress, Apr 1963

Mills, John, British actor, May 1963, *Obit* Yrbk 2005

Mirren, Helen, English actress, July 1995

Mitchum, Robert, American actor, Sept 1970, *Obit* Sept 1997

Mix, Tom, actor, *Obit* Yrbk 1940

Mnouchkine, Ariane, French theatrical director, Mar 1993

Molina, Alfred, British actor, Feb 2004

Monroe, Marilyn, American actress, July 1959, *Obit* Oct 1962

Montenegro, Fernanda, Brazilian actress, Oct 1999

Moore, Demi, American actress, Sept 1993

Moore, Julianne, American actress, Oct 1998

Moore, Mary Tyler, American actress, Feb 1971

Moore, Raymond, *Obit* Mar 1940

Moore, Roger, English actor, Feb 1975

Moorehead, Agnes, American actress, June 1952, *Obit* June 1974

Moreau, Jeanne, French actress, Yrbk 1966

Moreno, Catalina Sandino, Colombian actress, Jan 2005

Moriarty, Michael, actor, July 1976

Morse, Robert, actor, Nov 1962

Mortensen, Viggo, American actor, June 2004

Morton, Joe, actor, Feb 1999

Moscovitch, Maurice, *Obit* Aug 1940

Moss, Elisabeth, American actress, Nov 2013

Mostel, Zero, American actor, Apr 1943, Nov 1963, *Obit* Nov 1977

Mulligan, Carey, British actress, Oct 2013

Muni, Paul, actor, Jan 1944, *Obit* Nov 1967

Murray, Bill, American actor, Jan 1985, Sept 2004

Murray, Don, actor, Sept 1959

Naish, J. Carrol, actor, Jan 1957, *Obit* Mar 1973

Nares, Owen, *Obit* Sept 1943

Nazimova, Alla, Russian actress, *Obit* Aug 1945

Neagle, Anna, English actress, Nov 1945, *Obit* July 1986

Neal, Patricia, American actress, Sept 1964, *Obit* Yrbk 2010

Nederlander, James Morton, American theater owner, Apr 1991

Neeson, Liam, Irish-American actor, Nov 1994

Nelligan, Kate, Canadian actress, July 1983

Nero, Franco, Italian actor, Jan 2002

Nesbitt, Cathleen, English actress, Nov 1956, *Obit* Sept 1982

Neville, John, Jan 1959, *Obit* Yrbk 2012

Newton, Christopher, Anglo-Canadian theatrical director, Feb 1995

Newton, Thandie, British actress, Jan 2003

Nichols, Mike, American theatrical and motion picture director, Mar 1961, Jan 1992

Nighy, Bill, British actor, Jan 2007

Ninagawa, Yukio, Japanese theatrical director, Jan 2003

Noble, Adrian, English theatrical director, Aug 1999

Nolan, Lloyd, actor, Nov 1956, *Obit* Nov 1985

Nolte, Nick, American actor, Nov 1980

Nottage, Lynn, American dramatist, Nov 2004

Novak, Kim, American actress, Apr 1957

Nunn, Trevor, English theatrical director, Nov 1980

O'Brian, Hugh, actor, July 1958

O'Brien, Pat, American actor, Mar 1966, *Obit* Jan 1984

O'Connell, Hugh, *Obit* Mar 1943

O'Connor, Carroll, American actor, July 1972, *Obit* Sept 2001

O'Connor, Frances, Australian actress, Jan 2002

O'Hara, Maureen, Irish-American actress, Feb 1953

O'Neal, Frederick, actor, Nov 1946, *Obit* Oct 1992

O'Neal, Ryan, American actor, Feb 1973

O'Shea, Milo, June 1982, *Obit* Yrbk 2013

O'Toole, Peter, Irish actor, Sept 1968

Oberon, Merle, English actress, Nov 1941, *Obit* Jan 1980

Obraztsov, Sergei, Russian puppeteer, Nov 1964

Oh, Sandra, Canadian actress, Jan 2005

Okonedo, Sophie, British actress, Jan 2005

Oldman, Gary, English actor, Jan 1996

Olin, Lena, Swedish actress, June 2003

Oliver, Edna May, actress, *Obit* Jan 1943

Olivier, Laurence, English actor, June 1946, Jan 1979, *Obit* Sept 1989

Olsen twins, American actresses, Sept 2010

Olsen, Mary Kate, American actress, Sept 2010

Orbach, Jerry, American actor, May 1970, *Obit* Apr 2005

Ormond, Julia, English actress, Mar 1999

Osborne, John, English dramatist, June 1959, *Obit* Feb 1995

Otto, Miranda, Australian actress, Jan 2003

Pacino, Al, American actor, July 1974

Page, Ellen, Canadian actress, May 2008

Page, Geraldine, actress, Nov 1953, *Obit* Aug 1987

Palance, Jack, American actor, Aug 1992, *Obit* Feb 2007

Palmer, Geoffrey, English actor, Jan 2006

Paltrow, Gwyneth, American actress, Jan 2005

Papp, Joseph, American theatrical producer and director, May 1965, *Obit* Jan 1992

Parker, Mary-Louise, American actress, Apr 2006

Parker, Sarah Jessica, American actress, Sept 1998

Parks, Robert J., Feb 1968

Parsons, Estelle, American actress, Oct 1975

Parsons, Jim, American actor, Sept 2013

Paulus, Diane, American theatrical director, May 2010

Pawley, Edward, Mar 1946

Paxinou, Katina, Oct 1943, *Obit* Apr 1973

Peck, Gregory, American actor, July 1947, Oct 1992, *Obit* Sept 2003

Pemberton, Brock, American theatrical producer and director, Jan 1945, *Obit* Mar 1950

Peppard, George, actor, Yrbk 1965, *Obit* July 1994

Perkins, Anthony, American actor, Sept 1960, *Obit* Nov 1992

Perkins, Elizabeth, American actress, Jan 2007

Perrine, Valerie, actress, Oct 1975

Perry, Antoinette, actress and theatrical director, *Obit* July 1946

Pesci, Joe, American actor, Mar 1994

Pfeiffer, Michelle, American actress, Mar 1990

Piccoli, Michel, French actor, Jan 2002

Pickford, Mary, American actress, Apr 1945, *Obit* July 1979

Picon, Molly, actress, June 1951, *Obit* June 1992

Pidgeon, Walter, actor, Sept 1942, *Obit* Nov 1984

Pierce, David Hyde, American actor, Apr 2001

Pierce, Wendell, American actor, Aug 2010

Pike, Rosamund, British actress, Nov 2012

Piscator, Erwin, German theatrical director, Oct 1942, *Obit* Apr 1966

Pitt, Brad, American actor, Mar 1996

Pleasence, Donald, English actor, June 1969, *Obit* Apr 1995

Plimpton, Martha, American actress, Apr 2002

Plowright, Joan, English actress, Feb 1964

Plummer, Christopher, Canadian actor, July 1956, Aug 1988

Pollock, Allan, *Obit* Apr 1942

Portman, Eric, Mar 1957, *Obit* Feb 1970

Posey, Parker, American actress, Mar 2003

Poston, Tom, American actor, Apr 1961, *Obit* Yrbk 2007

Potente, Franka, German actress, Jan 2003

Powell, William, American actor, Oct 1947, *Obit* May 1984

Power, Tyrone, American actor, Yrbk 1950, *Obit* Jan 1959

Powers, James T., American actor, *Obit* Mar 1943

Powers, John Robert, June 1945, *Obit* Sept 1977

Preston, Robert, American actor, Yrbk 1958, *Obit* May 1987

Price, Vincent, American actor, Nov 1956, *Obit* Jan 1994

Prince, Hal, theatrical producer and director, Apr 1971

Prinze, Freddie, American actor, Jan 2003

Quarshie, Hugh, Ghanaian-British actor, Jan 2004

Quayle, Anthony, English actor and theatrical director, Yrbk 1971, *Obit* Jan 1990

Quinn, Aidan, American actor, Apr 2005

Quinn, Anthony, Mexican-American actor, Yrbk 1957, *Obit* Sept 2001

Quintero, Jose, theatrical director, Apr 1954, *Obit* May 1999

Rabe, David, American dramatist, July 1973

Radcliffe, Daniel, English actor, Nov 2010

Rai, Aishwarya, Indian actress, Jan 2003

Rains, Claude, Anglo-American actor, Nov 1949, *Obit* July 1967

Rampling, Charlotte, English actress, June 2002

Randall, Tony, American actor, Jan 1961, *Obit* Yrbk 2004

Rathbone, Basil, Anglo-American actor, Mar 1951, *Obit* Oct 1967

Rattigan, Terence, English dramatist, Yrbk 1956, *Obit* Feb 1978

Ray, Charles, American actor, *Obit* Jan 1944

Redgrave, Lynn, English actress, Sept 1969, *Obit* Yrbk 2010

Redgrave, Michael, English actor, Feb 1950, *Obit* May 1985

Redgrave, Vanessa, English actress, Yrbk 1966, Sept 2003

Reeves, Keanu, Canadian actor, May 1995

Reid, Kate, Canadian actress, Mar 1985, *Obit* May 1993

Reilly, John C., American actor, Oct 2004

Reinhardt, Max, Austrian theatrical director, *Obit* Yrbk 1943

Remick, Lee, American actress, Oct 1966, *Obit* Sept 1991

Renaud, Madeleine, French actress and theatrical producer, Mar 1953, *Obit* Nov 1994

Rennert, Gunther, June 1976, *Obit* Sept 1978

Rey, Fernando, Spanish actor, Mar 1979, *Obit* May 1994

Reynolds, Burt, American actor, Oct 1973

Reza, Yasmina, French dramatist, Sept 1998

Richardson, Miranda, English actress, Feb 1994

Richardson, Ralph, English actor, Nov 1950, *Obit* Nov 1983

Richardson, Tony, British film and theatrical director, Yrbk 1963, *Obit* Feb 1992

Richman, Charles J., *Obit* Jan 1941

Rigg, Diana, English actress, Oct 1974

Ringwald, Molly, American actress, May 1987

Ritter, John, American actor, June 1980, *Obit* Yrbk 2004

Ritter, Thelma, Yrbk 1957, *Obit* Feb 1974

Robards, Jason, American actor, Oct 1959, *Obit* Mar 2001

Roberts, Florence, *Obit* July 1940

Roberts, Julia, American actress, May 1991

Roberts, Tony, American actor, Oct 2006

Robertson, Cliff, American actor, Yrbk 1969, *Obit* Yrbk 2011

Robinson, Edward G., actor, Jan 1950, *Obit* Mar 1973

Robson, Flora, English actress, Jan 1951, *Obit* Sept 1984

Robson, May, actress, *Obit* Yrbk 1942

Rogers, Paul, Mar 1960

Rooney, Mickey, American actor, Feb 1942, Sept 1965

Rose, George, actor, Sept 1984, *Obit* June 1988

Rourke, Mickey, American actor, Oct 1991

Rowlands, Gena, American actress, Nov 1975

Rubio, Ingrid, Spanish actress, Jan 2002

Rudd, Paul, American actor, Sept 1977, *Obit* Yrbk 2010

Ruhmann, Heinz, Apr 1965

Russell, Kurt, American actor, Nov 2004

Russell, Rosalind, American actress, Jan 1943, *Obit* Feb 1977

Rutherford, Margaret, English actress, Jan 1964, *Obit* July 1972

Ryan, Meg, American actress, May 1999

Ryan, Robert, American actor, Yrbk 1963, *Obit* Sept 1973

Ryder, Winona, American actress, June 1994

Sagnier, Ludivine, French actress, Jan 2004

Saint, Eva Marie, American actress, June 1955

Sanders, George, British actor, June 1943, *Obit* June 1972

Sansa, Maya, Italian actress, Jan 2004

Sarandon, Susan, American actress, Sept 1989

Sass, Katrin, German actress, Jan 2003, *Obit* Mar 1994

Savalas, Telly, actor, Feb 1976

Schell, Maria, Austrian actress, June 1961, *Obit* Yrbk 2005

Schell, Maximilian, Austrian actor, Yrbk 1962

Schildkraut, Joseph, Austrian actor, Apr 1956, *Obit* Mar 1964

Schisgal, Murray, dramatist, Jan 1968

Schneider, Alan, American theatrical director, Yrbk 1969, *Obit* June 1984

Schneider, Romy, Austrian actress, Jan 1965, *Obit* July 1982

Schwartz, Maurice, theatrical director, producer and actor, Feb 1956, *Obit* July 1960

Schwartzman, Jason, American actor, Oct 2009

Schygulla, Hanna, German actress, July 1984

Scofield, Paul, English actor, Mar 1962, *Obit* Yrbk 2008

Scott, George C., American actor, Apr 1971, *Obit* Nov 1999

Scourby, Alexander, actor, July 1965, *Obit* Apr 1985

Seberg, Jean, actress, Apr 1966, *Obit* Oct 1979

Segal, George, American actor, Nov 1975

Seigner, Emmanuelle, French actress, Jan 2006

Sellars, Peter, American theatrical director, Jan 1986

Selleck, Tom, American actor, Nov 1983

Sellers, Peter, English actor, Yrbk 1960, *Obit* Sept 1980

Selznick, Myron, *Obit* May 1944

Sen, Sushmita, Indian actress, Jan 2006

Serban, Andrei, Romanian theatrical director, Feb 1978

Serlin, Oscar, Mar 1943, *Obit* Apr 1971

Shaffer, Peter, English dramatist, May 1967, Nov 1988

Shalhoub, Tony, American actor, Nov 2002

Shannon, Peggy, actress, *Obit* July 1941

Sharif, Omar, Egyptian actor, May 1970

Shatner, William, Canadian actor, July 1987

Sheen, Martin, American actor, June 1977

Sheldon, Edward, dramatist, *Obit* May 1946

Shepherd, Cybill, American actress, Mar 1987

Sherawat, Mallika, Indian actress, Jan 2007

Shetty, Shilpa, Indian actress, Jan 2007

Short, Hassard, Nov 1948, *Obit* Yrbk 1956

Shumlin, Herman, Mar 1941, *Obit* Aug 1979

Sidney, Sylvia, actress, Oct 1981, *Obit* Sept 1999

Silvers, Phil, actor, Yrbk 1957, *Obit* Jan 1986

Simmons, Jean, English actress, Feb 1952, *Obit* Yrbk 2010

Simms, Hilda, actress, Nov 1944, *Obit* May 1994

Sitgreaves, Beverley, *Obit* Sept 1943

Skarsgard, Stellan, Swedish actor, Jan 2002

Skinner, Otis, *Obit* Feb 1942

Slezak, Walter, actor, Mar 1955, *Obit* June 1983

Sloane, Everett, Jan 1957, *Obit* Oct 1965

Smith, C. Aubrey, English actor, Sept 1944, *Obit* Jan 1949

Smith, Charles, American playwright, May 2011

Smith, Dick, makeup artist, Mar 1959

Smith, Maggie, English actress, June 1970, July 2002

Smits, Jimmy, American actor, May 2006

Snipes, Wesley, American actor, Sept 1993

Sorvino, Mira, American actress, Aug 1998

Spacek, Sissy, American actress, Jan 1978

Spanic, Gabriela, Venezuelan actress, Jan 2004

Spencer, John, American actor, Jan 2001, *Obit* Yrbk 2006

Spottswood, James, *Obit* Yrbk 1940

Stanley, Kim, American actress, May 1955, *Obit* Jan 2002

Stanwyck, Barbara, American actress, July 1947, *Obit* Mar 1990

Stapleton, Jean, actress, Yrbk 1972, *Obit* Yrbk 2013

Stapleton, Maureen, American actress, May 1959, *Obit* Nov 2006

Staunton, Imelda, English actress, Jan 2005

Steiger, Rod, American actor, June 1965, *Obit* Yrbk 2002

Stephenson, James, British actor, *Obit* Sept 1941

Stevens, Roger L., real estate executive and theatrical producer, Yrbk 1955, *Obit* Apr 1998

Stevenson, McLean, actor, June 1980, *Obit* Apr 1996

Stewart, Ellen, American theatrical producer, June 1973, *Obit* Yrbk 2011

Stewart, James, American actor, Apr 1941, Yrbk 1960, *Obit* Sept 1997

Stewart, Patrick, British actor, Aug 1994

Stigwood, Robert, Australian film, recording and theatrical producer, Oct 1979

Stockwell, Dean, actor, Feb 1991

Stone, Emma, American actress, Feb 2013

Stone, Sharon, American actress, Apr 1996

Stoppard, Tom, English dramatist, July 1974

Strasberg, Susan, actress, May 1958, *Obit* Apr 1999

Streep, Meryl, American actress, Aug 1980, Mar 1997

Strehler, Giorgio, Italian theatrical director, Mar 1991, *Obit* Mar 1998

Stritch, Elaine, American actress, June 1988

Struthers, Sally, American actress, Jan 1974

Sullavan, Margaret, actress, July 1944, *Obit* Feb 1960

Sullivan, Daniel, American theatrical director, Feb 2003

Sullivan, Francis L., June 1955, *Obit* Jan 1957

Summerville, Slim, actor, *Obit* Feb 1946

Sutherland, Donald, Canadian actor, Feb 1981

Sutherland, Kiefer, Canadian actor, Mar 2002

Suzman, Janet, May 1976

Swank, Hilary, American actress, Sept 2000

Swanson, Gloria, actress, Sept 1950, *Obit* May 1983

Swinton, Tilda, Scottish actress, Nov 2001

Sydow, Max von, Swedish actor, Apr 1967

Tandy, Jessica, Anglo-American actress, Mar 1956, Aug 1984, *Obit* Nov 1994

Tautou, Audrey, French actress, Jan 2002

Taylor, Charles A., *Obit* May 1942

Taylor, Elizabeth, Anglo-American actress, July 1952, Oct 1985, *Obit* Yrbk 2011

Taylor, Laurette, American actress, July 1945, *Obit* Jan 1947

Taylor, Lili, American actress, July 2005

Taylor, Robert, American actor, May 1952, *Obit* July 1969

Tempest, Marie, English actress, *Obit* Yrbk 1942

Terrell, St. John, actor, Feb 1966, *Obit* Jan 1999

Theron, Charlize, South African actress, Nov 2004

Thomas, Richard, American actor, Nov 1975

Thompson, Emma, British actress, Mar 1995

Thompson, John Douglas, Canadian actor, Sept 2010

Thompson, Sada, American actress, Mar 1973, *Obit* Yrbk 2011

Thorndike, Sybil, English actress, Yrbk 1953, *Obit* Aug 1976

Thurman, Uma, American actress, Aug 1996

Tipton, Jennifer, American lighting designer, July 1997

Todd, Michael, American motion picture producer, Yrbk 1955, *Obit* June 1958

Todd, Richard, British actor, Yrbk 1955, *Obit* Yrbk 2010

Tone, Franchot, actor, May 1940, *Obit* Nov 1968

Torn, Rip, American actor, Apr 1977

Tracy, Spencer, American actor, Apr 1943, *Obit* Oct 1967

Travolta, John, American actor, Oct 1978, May 1996

Trintignant, Jean-Louis, French actor, July 1988

Truex, Ernest, Jan 1941, *Obit* Sept 1973

Turner, Kathleen, American actress, June 1986

Turner, Lana, American actress, June 1943, *Obit* Sept 1995

Turturro, John, American actor, Oct 1996

Tushingham, Rita, Oct 1965

Tyson, Cicely, American actress, Aug 1975

Van Dyke, Dick, American actor, Mar 1963

Vanbrugh, Violet, British actress, *Obit* Jan 1943

Vaughn, Robert, American actor, Sept 1967

Vaughn, Vince, American actor, Sept 2006

Veidt, Conrad, German actor, *Obit* May 1943

Veiller, Bayard, dramatist, *Obit* Aug 1943

Velez, Lupe, Mexican actress, *Obit* Feb 1945

Vilar, Jean, French actor and director, Apr 1962, *Obit* Sept 1971

Visconti, Luchino, Italian film director, Jan 1965, *Obit* May 1976

Voight, Jon, American actor, Apr 1974

Wagner, Robert, American actor, June 1984

Wajda, Andrzej, Polish motion picture and theatrical director, July 1982

Walken, Christopher, American actor, Oct 1990

Walker, Nancy, actress, Feb 1965, *Obit* May 1992

Wallach, Eli, American actor, May 1959

Ward, Lem, *Obit* Jan 1943

Watanabe, Ken, Japanese actor, Jan 2004

Waterston, Sam, American actor, Sept 1985

Watson, Emily, British actress, May 2007

Watson, Lucile, actress, Yrbk 1953, *Obit* Sept 1962

Watts, Naomi, Australian actress, Mar 2007

Wayans, Shawn, American actor, May 2001

Wayne, David, actor, June 1956, *Obit* Apr 1995

Weaver, Affie, *Obit* Jan 1941

Weaver, Dennis, American actor, Nov 1977, *Obit* Yrbk 2006

Weaver, Fritz, Jan 1966

Weaver, Sigourney, American actress, Mar 1989

Weber, L. Lawrence, *Obit* Mar 1940

Webster, Margaret, American actress and theatrical director, May 1940, Sept 1950, *Obit* Jan 1973

Weitzenkorn, Louis, *Obit* Mar 1943

Welch, Raquel, American actress, May 1971

Weld, Tuesday, American actress, July 1974

Weller, Michael, American dramatist, May 1989

Werner, Oskar, Austrian actor, June 1966, *Obit* Jan 1985

Westley, Helen, actress, *Obit* Feb 1943

Westmore, Perc, American makeup artist, Oct 1945, *Obit* Nov 1970

White, Betty, American actress, June 1987

Whitford, Bradley, American actor, Apr 2003

Whitmore, James, American actor, Sept 1976, *Obit* Yrbk 2009

Whitty, May, English actress, Yrbk 1945, *Obit* July 1948

Widmark, Richard, American actor, Apr 1963, *Obit* Yrbk 2008

Wiest, Dianne, actress, Mar 1997

Williams, Billy Dee, American actor, Apr 1984

Williams, John D., *Obit* May 1941

Willis, Bruce, American actor, Feb 1987

Wilson, Luke, American actor, Feb 2005

Wiman, Dwight Deere, June 1949, *Obit* Feb 1951

Windust, Bretaigne, Mar 1943, *Obit* May 1960

Winger, Debra, American actress, July 1984

Winters, Shelley, American actress, Apr 1952, *Obit* Apr 2006

Witherspoon, Reese, American actress, Jan 2004

Wolfe, George C., American dramatist and director, Mar 1994

Wolfit, Donald, Mar 1965, *Obit* Apr 1968

Wood, Elijah, American actor, Aug 2002

Wood, Evan Rachel, American actress, June 2009

Wood, John, English actor, Apr 1983, *Obit* Yrbk 2011

Wood, Natalie, American actress, Apr 1962, *Obit* Jan 1982

Woodard, Alfre, American actress, Feb 1995

Woods, James, American actor, Nov 1989

Woodward, Joanne, American actress, June 1958

Woolley, Monty, July 1940, *Obit* June 1963

Worth, Irene, American actress, May 1968, *Obit* Aug 2002

Wray, John, *Obit* May 1940

Wright, Jeffrey, American actor, May 2002

Wright, Teresa, American actress, May 1943, *Obit* Yrbk 2005

Wyatt, Jane, American actress, May 1957, *Obit* Yrbk 2006

Yeoh, Michelle, Chinese actress, Jan 1998

York, Michael, English actor, Apr 1976

Yorke, Oswald, *Obit* Mar 1943

Young, Alan, Anglo-Canadian actor, June 1953

Young, Loretta, American actress, Mar 1948, *Obit* Nov 2000

Young, Robert, actor, July 1950, *Obit* Sept 1998

Zellweger, Renee, American actress, Feb 2004

Zeta-Jones, Catherine, Welsh actress, Apr 2003

Zhang Ziyi, Chinese actress, Jan 2005

Zimbalist, Efrem, American actor, Feb 1960

Theatrical directors

Agresti, Alejandro, Argentine film director, Jan 2005

Al-Abnoudí, Attiyat, Egyptian documentary filmmaker, Jan 2005

Almodovar, Pedro, Spanish film director, Sept 1990

Amenabar, Alejandro, Spanish film director, Jan 2005

Anderson, Lindsay, British motion picture and theatrical director, Nov 1975, *Obit* Nov 1994

Antonioni, Michelangelo, Italian film director, Yrbk 1964, May 1993, *Obit* Yrbk 2007

Apted, Michael, British motion picture director, Feb 2000

Arcand, Denys, Canadian film director, Oct 1990

Armfield, Neil, Australian theatrical director, Jan 2007

Armstrong, Gillian, Australian film director, Aug 1995

Ataman, Kutlug, Turkish video artist and film director, Jan 2006

Ball, William, theatrical director and producer, May 1974, *Obit* Oct 1991

Beresford, Bruce, Australian film director, Mar 1993

Bergman, Ingmar, Swedish film and theatrical director, Apr 1960, Oct 1981, *Obit* Sept 2007

Bertolucci, Bernardo, Italian film director, July 1974

Blackton, James Stuart, American film director and producer, *Obit* Oct 1941

Bogart, Anne, theatrical director, Feb 1999

Bong, Joon-Ho, Korean film director, Jan 2007

Boorman, John, British film director, June 1988

Borzage, Frank, motion picture director, Yrbk 1946, *Obit* Sept 1962

Bresson, Robert, French film director, Jan 1971, *Obit* June 2000

Brown, Gilmor, July 1944

Bunuel, Luis, Mexican film director, Mar 1965, *Obit* Sept 1983

Burrows, James, American television director, Oct 2006

Campion, Jane, New Zealand film director, Apr 1994

Capra, Frank, American motion picture director and producer, Apr 1948, *Obit* Oct 1991

Carewe, Edwin, *Obit* Jan 1940

Chabrol, Claude, French film director, Jan 1975, *Obit* Yrbk 2010

Chadha, Gurinder, British motion picture director, Jan 2004

Chopra, Yash, Indian film director and producer, Jan 2006, *Obit* Yrbk 2013

Clair, Rene, French motion picture director, Nov 1941, *Obit* May 1981

Cohen, Rob, American motion picture director and producer, Nov 2002

Costa-Gavras, Greek-French motion picture director, Sept 1972

Cravath, Paul D., *Obit* Aug 1940

Cronenberg, David, Canadian motion picture director, May 1992

Cruze, James, motion picture director, *Obit* Sept 1942

Cuaron, Alfonso, Mexican film director, Jan 2003

Cukor, George, American motion picture director, Apr 1943, *Obit* Mar 1983

D'Oyly Carte, Rupert, Feb 1948

Daniels, Lee, American film director and producer, June 2010

Davidson, Gordon, American theatrical director and producer, Apr 2005

De Mille, Cecil B., American motion picture director and producer, May 1942, *Obit* Mar 1959

De Palma, Brian, American motion picture director, Sept 1982

De Sica, Vittorio, Italian motion picture director, July 1952, *Obit* Jan 1975

Demme, Jonathan, American film director, Apr 1985

Deruddere, Dominique, Belgian motion picture director, Jan 2003

Dexter, John, English theatrical director, July 1976, *Obit* May 1990

Dieterle, William, motion picture director, Sept 1943, *Obit* Feb 1973

Duvivier, Julien, French motion picture director, July 1943, *Obit* Jan 1968

Eisenstein, Sergei, Russian theatrical and motion picture director, May 1946, *Obit* Mar 1948

Ejiro, Zeb, Nigerian motion picture producer and director, Jan 2002

El-Tahri, Jihan, French-Egyptian documentary filmmaker, Aug 2009

Everson, Kevin Jerome, American filmmaker and video artist, Nov 2011

Eyre, Chris, Native American motion picture director, May 2003

Falls, Robert, American theatrical director, Jan 2004

Fellini, Federico, Italian motion picture director, June 1957, Oct 1980, *Obit* Jan 1994

Fichandler, Zelda, American theatrical producer and director, June 1987

Ford, John, American film director, Feb 1941, *Obit* Nov 1973

Forman, Milos, Czech film director, Yrbk 1971

Forsyth, Bill, Scottish motion picture director, Jan 1989

Fox, Eytan, Israeli motion picture director, Jan 2004

Frankenheimer, John, American film director, Oct 1964, *Obit* Oct 2002

Frears, Stephen, British motion picture director, Apr 1990, Jan 2004

Friedkin, William, American motion picture director, June 1987

Furtado, Jorge, Brazilian film director, Jan 2006

Gallo, Fortune, Oct 1949, *Obit* May 1970

Gatti-Casazza, Giulio, opera director, *Obit* Oct 1940

Gimbel, Peter, motion picture director and producer, Jan 1982, *Obit* Aug 1987

Gitai, Amos, Israeli film director, Jan 2003

Godard, Jean Luc, French film director, May 1969, Oct 1993

Gonzalez Inarritu, Alejandro, Mexican film director, Jan 2003

Graf, Herbert, May 1942, *Obit* May 1973

Gray, F. Gary, American film director, Mar 2011

Greenaway, Peter, British film director, Feb 1991

Gregory, Paul, Apr 1956

Grotowski, Jerzy, Polish theatrical director, Yrbk 1970, *Obit* Mar 1999

Guggenheim, Davis, American film director, Nov 2009

Guthrie, Tyrone, British theatrical producer and director, July 1954, *Obit* July 1971

Hallstrom, Lasse, Swedish motion picture director, Feb 2005

Harron, Mary, Canadian motion picture director, Sept 2000

Hartwig, Walter, *Obit* Mar 1941

Hawks, Howard, American motion picture director and producer, May 1972, *Obit* Mar 1980

Haynes, Todd, American film director, July 2003

Heckerling, Amy, motion picture director, July 1999

Herzog, Werner, German film director, Aug 1978

Hill, George Roy, American motion picture director, Apr 1977, *Obit* June 2003

Hirsch, John, Canadian theatrical director, Apr 1984, *Obit* Oct 1989

Hitchcock, Alfred, Anglo-American motion picture director, Mar 1941, July 1960, *Obit* June 1980

Hong, Sang-Soo, Korean film director, Jan 2006

Hopkins, Arthur M., theatrical producer and director, June 1947, *Obit* Apr 1950

Hou, Hsiao-hsien, Taiwanese film director, July 1999

Imamura, Shohei, Japanese motion picture director, Jan 2002, *Obit* CB Int 2006

Ivory, James, American motion picture director, July 1981

Jarmusch, Jim, American film director, Apr 1990

Jeunet, Jean-Pierre, French film director, Jan 2005

Jewison, Norman, Canadian motion picture director and producer, June 1979

Jonze, Spike, American video and motion picture director, Apr 2003

Kaneko, Shu, Japanese film director, Jan 2007

Kanwar, Amar, Indian documentary filmmaker, Jan 2005

Keighley, William, motion picture director, Nov 1948, *Obit* Aug 1984

Kiarostami, Abbas, Iranian film director, July 1998

Kieslowski, Krzysztof, Polish motion picture director, May 1995, *Obit* May 1996

Knott, Sarah Gertrude, July 1947

Korda, Alexander, British film director and producer, Sept 1946, *Obit* Mar 1956

Kramer, Stanley, American motion picture producer and director, May 1951, *Obit* May 2001

Kubrick, Stanley, American film director, Feb 1963, *Obit* May 1999

Kunuk, Zacharias, Canadian Inuit film director, Jan 2002

Kurosawa, Akira, Japanese motion picture director, Apr 1965, July 1991, *Obit* Nov 1998

Kurosawa, Kiyoshi, Japanese film director, Jan 2006

La Cava, Gregory, motion picture director, Yrbk 1941, *Obit* Apr 1952

Lang, Fritz, Austrian film director, June 1943, *Obit* Sept 1976

Langham, Michael, English theatrical director, Sept 1965, *Obit* Yrbk 2011

LeCompte, Elizabeth, American theatrical director, Aug 1997

Lean, David, British film director and producer, May 1953, June 1989, *Obit* June 1991

Leconte, Patrice, French motion picture director, Jan 2004

Lee, Ang, Taiwanese film director, Mar 1997

Lelouch, Claude, French motion picture director and producer, Nov 1982

Leon, Kenny, American theatrical director, Nov 2005

Lester, Richard, British film director, Apr 1969

Logan, Joshua, American theatrical and motion picture director, Oct 1949, *Obit* Aug 1988

Longfellow, Ki, Novelist, playwright and theater producer and director, July 2012

Longo, Robert, American artist, Oct 1990

Lyne, Adrian, English motion picture director, Jan 1994

Lyubimov, Yuri, Russian theatrical director, Nov 1988

Maddin, Guy, Canadian film director, Jan 2006

Makhmalbaf, Samira, Iranian motion picture director, Jan 2003

Malick, Terrence, American film director, June 1999

Malle, Louis, French motion picture director, Feb 1976, *Obit* Feb 1996

Mamoulian, Rouben, Russian-American theatrical and film director, Mar 1949, *Obit* Jan 1988

Mansouri, Lotfi, Iranian opera director, Apr 1990, *Obit* Yrbk 2013

McClintic, Guthrie, theatrical director and producer, May 1943, *Obit* Jan 1962

McEwen, Terry A., opera director, July 1985, *Obit* Jan 1999

Mehta, Deepa, Indian motion picture director, Jan 2002

Mendes, Sam, British theatrical and motion picture director, Oct 2002

Miike, Takashi, Japanese motion picture director, Jan 2003

Miller, Gilbert, Apr 1958, *Obit* Feb 1969

Minac, Matej, Czech motion picture director, Jan 2002

Minnelli, Vincente, American film director, May 1975, *Obit* Sept 1986

Mnouchkine, Ariane, French theatrical director, Mar 1993

Moore, Raymond, *Obit* Mar 1940

Morris, Errol, American documentary filmmaker, Feb 2001

Nair, Mira, Indian motion picture director, Nov 1993

Nelson, Stanley, American documentary filmmaker, May 2005

Newton, Christopher, Anglo-Canadian theatrical director, Feb 1995

Nichols, Mike, American theatrical and motion picture director, Mar 1961, Jan 1992

Ninagawa, Yukio, Japanese theatrical director, Jan 2003

Noble, Adrian, English theatrical director, Aug 1999

Noujaim, Jehane, Egyptian-American

documentary filmmaker, Jan 2005

Nunn, Trevor, English theatrical director, Nov 1980

Nuridsany, Claude, French documentary filmmaker, June 1997

Oest, Paula van der, Dutch motion picture director, Jan 2003

Oliveira, Manoel de, Portuguese film director, Jan 2002

Osawa, Sandy Sunrising, American filmmaker, Jan 2001

Ozon, Francois, French film director, Jan 2003

Pakula, Alan J., American film director and producer, June 1980, *Obit* Feb 1999

Panahi, Jafar, Iranian film director, Jan 2004

Papp, Joseph, American theatrical producer and director, May 1965, *Obit* Jan 1992

Parks, Robert J., Feb 1968

Pascal, Gabriel, Hungarian-British motion picture producer, Jan 1942, *Obit* Sept 1954

Paulus, Diane, American theatrical director, May 2010

Peckinpah, Sam, American motion picture director, May 1973, *Obit* Feb 1985

Pemberton, Brock, American theatrical producer and director, Jan 1945, *Obit* Mar 1950

Perennou, Marie, French documentary filmmaker, June 1997

Petersen, Wolfgang, German motion picture director, July 2001

Piscator, Erwin, German theatrical director, Oct 1942, *Obit* Apr 1966

Polanski, Roman, Polish film director, June 1969

Porter, Edwin S., American film director and producer, *Obit* June 1941

Prince, Hal, theatrical producer and director, Apr 1971

Quintero, Jose, theatrical director, Apr 1954, *Obit* May 1999

Raimi, Sam, American film director, July 2002

Reed, Carol, British motion picture director and producer, Mar 1950, *Obit* June 1976

Reinhardt, Max, Austrian theatrical director, *Obit* Yrbk 1943

Reitman, Ivan, Canadian film director, Mar 2001

Rennert, Gunther, June 1976, *Obit* Sept 1978

Resnais, Alain, French film director, Feb 1965

Richardson, Tony, British film and theatrical director, Yrbk 1963, *Obit* Feb 1992

Ritt, Martin, motion picture director, Nov 1979, *Obit* Feb 1991

Roeg, Nicolas, British film director, Jan 1996

Roodt, Darrell, South African film director, Jan 2005

Rossellini, Roberto, Italian film director, July 1949, *Obit* Aug 1977

Salles, Walter, Brazilian motion picture director, Jan 2004

Salman, Saad, Iraqi documentary filmmaker, Jan 2004

Saura, Carlos, Spanish motion picture director, Sept 1978

Schlesinger, John, British motion picture director, Nov 1970, *Obit* Yrbk 2003

Schneider, Alan, American theatrical director, Yrbk 1969, *Obit* June 1984

Scorsese, Martin, American film director, Feb 1979, June 2007

Scott, Ridley, British film director, Oct 1991

Scott, Tony, British film director, Nov 2004, *Obit* Yrbk 2012

Seidelman, Susan, motion picture director, May 1990

Seitz, George B., *Obit* Aug 1944

Sellars, Peter, American theatrical director, Jan 1986

Selwyn, Edgar, *Obit* Apr 1944

Serban, Andrei, Romanian theatrical director, Feb 1978

Serlin, Oscar, Mar 1943, *Obit* Apr 1971

Solomon, Philip S., American film director, Oct 2007

Spielberg, Steven, American film director and producer, July 1978, Feb 1996

Spurlock, Morgan, American documentary filmmaker, June 2013

Stevens, George, American motion picture director, Apr 1952, *Obit* May 1975

Stewart, Ellen, American theatrical producer, June 1973, *Obit* Yrbk 2011

Strehler, Giorgio, Italian theatrical director, Mar 1991, *Obit* Mar 1998

Sucksdorff, Arne, Swedish motion picture director, Apr 1956, *Obit* Sept 2001

Sullivan, Daniel, American theatrical director, Feb 2003

Suzuki, Seijun, Japanese film director, Jan 2005

Syberberg, Hans Jurgen, German motion picture producer and director, Apr 1983

Tanner, Alain, Swiss motion picture director, June 1990

Tavernier, Bertrand, French film director, June 1988

To, Johnny, Chinese film director, Jan 2007

Toro, Guillermo del, Mexican film director, Jan 2004

Trotta, Margarethe von, German film director, Nov 1988

Tsai, Ming-Liang, Taiwanese film director, Jan 2002

Tsui, Hark, Chinese film director, Oct 2001

Vadim, Roger, French motion picture director, Jan 1984, *Obit* Aug 2000

Van Dyke, W. S., American motion picture director, *Obit* Apr 1943

Van Sant, Gus, American film director, Mar 1992

Varda, Agnes, French film director, July 1970

Vidor, King, motion picture director and producer, Feb 1957, *Obit* Jan 1983

Visconti, Luchino, Italian film director, Jan 1965, *Obit* May 1976

Wajda, Andrzej, Polish motion picture and theatrical director, July 1982

Ward, Lem, *Obit* Jan 1943

Warhol, Andy, American artist, Feb 1968, July 1986, *Obit* Apr 1987

Watanabe, Shinichiro, Japanese motion picture director, Jan 2006

Weir, Peter, Australian motion picture director, Aug 1984

Wellman, William Augustus, American motion picture director, June 1950, *Obit* Feb 1976

Wenders, Wim, German film producer and director, July 1984

Wilcox, Herbert, Nov 1945, *Obit* July 1977

Williams, John D., *Obit* May 1941

Woo, John, Chinese motion picture director, Feb 1999

Wood, Sam, Nov 1943, *Obit* Nov 1949

Wyler, William, American film director, Jan 1951, *Obit* Sept 1981

Xie Jin, Chinese film director, Jan 2003

Yu, Ronny, Chinese motion picture director, Jan 2004

Zambello, Francesca, American opera director, May 2003

Zemeckis, Robert, American motion picture director, Sept 1997

Zhang Yimou, Chinese film director, Aug 1992, Jan 2003

Zinnemann, Fred, motion picture director, Mar 1953, *Obit* June 1997

Theatrical producers

Ball, William, theatrical director and producer, May 1974, *Obit* Oct 1991

Bishop, Andre, American theatrical producer, July 1999

Bloomgarden, Kermit, American theatrical producer, Yrbk 1958, *Obit* Nov 1976

Blumenthal, George, American theatrical producer, *Obit* Sept 1943

Brown, Gilmor, July 1944

Bruckheimer, Jerry, American film producer, Mar 1999

Bunim, Mary-Ellis, American television producer, May 2002, *Obit* Yrbk 2004

Carsey, Marcy, American television producer, Jan 1997

Cochran, Charles Blake, English theatrical producer, Oct 1940, *Obit* Mar 1951

Coe, Fred, television producer, Jan 1959, *Obit* June 1979

Cohen, Alexander H., American theatrical producer, June 1965, *Obit* Aug 2000

Crawford, Cheryl, American theatrical producer, Yrbk 1945, *Obit* Nov 1986

Davidson, Gordon, American theatrical director and producer, Apr 2005

De Laurentiis, Dino, Italian film producer, May 1965, *Obit* Yrbk 2011

De Rochemont, Louis, motion picture producer, Nov 1949, *Obit* Feb 1979

De Rochemont, Richard G., Oct 1945, *Obit* Sept 1982

Fager, Jeff, American television producer, Jan 2012

Fichandler, Zelda, American theatrical producer and director, June 1987

Gest, Morris, *Obit* July 1942

Ghai, Subhash, Indian motion picture producer, Jan 2003

Goldwyn, Samuel, American motion picture producer, Jan 1944, *Obit* Mar 1974

Goodman, Julian, Feb 1967, *Obit* Yrbk 2012

Goodson, Mark, television producer, May 1978, *Obit* Feb 1993

Gordon, Max, Oct 1943, *Obit* Jan 1979

Guthrie, Tyrone, British theatrical producer and director, July 1954, *Obit* July 1971

Harris, Sam H., American theatrical producer, *Obit* Aug 1941

Harris, William, *Obit* Oct 1946

Helburn, Theresa, theatrical producer, Sept 1944, *Obit* Nov 1959

Hewitt, Don, American television producer, June 1988, *Obit* Yrbk 2009

Hopkins, Arthur M., theatrical producer and director, June 1947, *Obit* Apr 1950

Hudlin, Warrington, motion picture producer, May 1999

Hunter, Ross, motion picture producer, Yrbk 1967, *Obit* May 1996

Jarvis, Lucy, television producer, Apr 1972

Kennedy, Kathleen, American film producer, Feb 2009

Leonidoff, Leon, American theatrical producer, July 1941, *Obit* Oct 1989

Levine, Joseph E., American motion picture producer, Oct 1979, *Obit* Sept 1987

Liebler, Theodore A., *Obit* June 1941

MacKintosh, Cameron, English theatrical producer, Mar 1991

McCarthy, Frank, motion picture producer, Sept 1945, *Obit* Feb 1987

McClintic, Guthrie, theatrical director and producer, May 1943, *Obit* Jan 1962

Merrick, David, American theatrical producer, Jan 1961, *Obit* July 2000

Milchan, Arnon, Israeli film producer, Oct 2000

Miller, Gilbert, Apr 1958, *Obit* Feb 1969

Miner, Worthington C., television producer, Feb 1953, *Obit* Mar 1983

Mol, John de, Dutch television producer, Jan 2004

Murray, Jonathan, American television producer, May 2002

Obst, Lynda Rosen, American motion picture producer, Oct 2000

Osborne, Barrie M., American motion picture producer, Feb 2005

Papp, Joseph, American theatrical producer and director, May 1965, *Obit* Jan 1992

Parsons, Harriet, motion picture producer, Jan 1953, *Obit* Mar 1983

Pemberton, Brock, American theatrical producer and director, Jan 1945, *Obit* Mar 1950

Piscator, Erwin, German theatrical director, Oct 1942, *Obit* Apr 1966

Pressman, Edward, American film producer, Feb 2011

Prince, Hal, theatrical producer and director, Apr 1971

Rosenthal, Jane, American film producer, Apr 2011

Selznick, David O., motion picture producer, June 1941, *Obit* Sept 1965

Selznick, Myron, *Obit* May 1944

Serlin, Oscar, Mar 1943, *Obit* Apr 1971

Sheehan, Winfield R., *Obit* Aug 1945

Short, Hassard, Nov 1948, *Obit* Yrbk 1956

Shumlin, Herman, Mar 1941, *Obit* Aug 1979

Silver, Joel, American motion picture producer, Nov 2003

Stevens, Roger L., real estate executive and theatrical producer, Yrbk 1955, *Obit* Apr 1998

Stewart, Ellen, American theatrical producer, June 1973, *Obit* Yrbk 2011

Talley, Truman H., *Obit* Mar 1942

Todd, Michael, American motion picture producer, Yrbk 1955, *Obit* June 1958

Wanger, Walter, motion picture producer, June 1947, *Obit* Jan 1969

Weber, L. Lawrence, *Obit* Mar 1940

Williams, John D., *Obit* May 1941

Wiman, Dwight Deere, June 1949, *Obit* Feb 1951

Ziskin, Laura, American film producer, Oct 1997, *Obit* Yrbk 2011

Theologians

Moffatt, James, English theologian, *Obit* Aug 1944

Therapists

Seymour, Harriet Ayer, music therapist, *Obit* Sept 1944

Theremin players

Kavina, Lydia, Russian theremin player, Jan 2002

Tourist trade executives

Binns, Joseph Patterson, American hotel executive, June 1954, *Obit* Mar 1981

Hilton, Conrad N., American hotel executive, Yrbk 1949, *Obit* Mar 1979

Wilson, Kemmons, American hotel chain executive, Sept 1973, *Obit* Yrbk 2003

Tourist trade personnel

Clark, Sydney, Sept 1956

Fergusson, Erna, Yrbk 1955

Fielding, Temple Hornaday, travel book author, Apr 1969, *Obit* July 1983

Poncins, Gontran de, French travel writer, June 1941

Toy industry executives

Fong, Dennis, American computer game player and executive, Aug 2012

Track athletes

Clarke, Ron, May 1971

Costa, Ronaldo da, Brazilian marathon runner, Jan 2002

Johnson, July 1996

Okayo, Margaret, Kenyan marathon runner, Jan 2004

Patton, Mel, June 1949

Pennel, John, pole vaulter, Nov 1963, *Obit* Jan 1994

Rice, Greg, runner, Yrbk 1941, *Obit* Aug 1991

Rodgers, Bill, American marathon runner, Aug 1982

Translators

De Onis, Harriet, translator, Apr 1957, *Obit* May 1969

Volokhonsky, Larissa, Russian translator, June 2006

Transportation executives

Franklin, John M., Sept 1949, *Obit* Aug 1975

Greenebaum, Leon C., Jan 1962, *Obit* May 1968

Hill, Arthur M., Oct 1948, *Obit* Nov 1972

Slater, John E., Nov 1951

Transportation officials

Garvey, Jane F., government official, Sept 2000

Sadik-Khan, Janette, American transportation official, Nov 2012

Transportation workers

Beck, Dave, American labor leader, May 1949, *Obit* Feb 1994

Carey, Ron, American labor leader, May 1992, *Obit* Yrbk 2009

Fitzsimmons, Frank Edward, American labor leader, May 1971, *Obit* July 1981

Guinan, Matthew, labor leader, Sept 1974, *Obit* May 1995

Johnston, Alvanley, American labor leader, June 1946, *Obit* Nov 1951

Lawe, John, labor leader, Jan 1984, *Obit* Apr 1989

Presser, Jackie, labor leader, Sept 1983, *Obit* Aug 1988

Quill, Mike, American labor leader, Aug 1941, Mar 1953, *Obit* Mar 1966

Whitney, A. F., American labor leader, Feb 1946, *Obit* Sept 1949

Travelers

Bancroft, Ann, American adventurer, July 2000

Tweedie, Ethel Brilliana, English author and traveler, *Obit* May 1940

Tribal leaders

Begaye, Kelsey, Navajo leader, Jan 2000

Bruce, Louis Rooks, American government official, May 1972, *Obit* July 1989

Hall, Tex G., Native American leader, May 2005

Seboko, Mosadi, Botswanan tribal chief, Jan 2004

Trombonists

Pryor, Arthur, trombonist, *Obit* Aug 1942

Truck drivers

Beck, Dave, American labor leader, May 1949, *Obit* Feb 1994

Carey, Ron, American labor leader, May 1992, *Obit* Yrbk 2009

Fitzsimmons, Frank Edward, American labor leader, May 1971, *Obit* July 1981

Presser, Jackie, labor leader, Sept 1983, *Obit* Aug 1988

Trumpet players

Balsom, Alison, Trumpeter, Mar 2012

Twins

Soyer, Moses, American painter, Mar 1941, *Obit* Oct 1974

Typographers

Carter, Matthew, British typographer, Oct 2007

Goudy, Frederic W., typographer, June 1941, *Obit* June 1947

McMurtrie, Douglas Crawford, typographer, July 1944

Rogers, Bruce, American typographer, Yrbk 1946, *Obit* July 1957

Underground leaders

Shiber, Etta, underground leader, Yrbk 1943, *Obit* Jan 1949

Urban planners

Tange, Kenzo, Japanese architect, Sept 1987, *Obit* Yrbk 2005

Veterans

Bacon, Charles L., American lawyer and veterans leader, May 1962

Brown, Perry J., Apr 1949

Brunner, Jean Adam, Sept 1945, *Obit* June 1951

Connell, Arthur J., Feb 1954

Cothran, James W., Sept 1953

Fraser, I., Yrbk 1947

Lewis, Clyde A., Feb 1950

Mahady, Henry J., July 1954

Maile, Boniface R., Feb 1951

Miller, Marshall E., Oct 1953

Paterson, Chat, veterans' leader, Mar 1948, *Obit* May 1992

Powers, James E., June 1963

Ralls, Charles C., Jan 1951

Wilson, Donald R., Jan 1952

Vice-presidents

Cavero, Salvador, Peruvian vice-president, *Obit* Mar 1940

Video artists

Aitken, Doug, American multimedia artist, Apr 2007

Barney, Matthew, American sculptor and installation and video artist, Aug 2003

Chan, Paul, American video artist, Mar 2011

Ciocci, Jessica, American video and installation artist, Apr 2010

Collins, Phil, English video artist, Jan 2007

Kapoor, Anish, Indian-British video artist and sculptor, Sept 2013

Neshat, Shirin, Iranian photographer and video artist, Jan 2002

Rist, Pipilotti, Swiss video artist, Jan 2005

Simpson, Lorna, American photographer and video artist, Nov 2004

Viola, Bill, American video artist, May 1998

Video directors

Gray, F. Gary, American film director, Mar 2011

Jonze, Spike, American video and motion picture director, Apr 2003

Violinists

Bell, Joshua, American violinist, July 2000

Elman, Mischa, American violinist, Oct 1945, *Obit* June 1967

Fuchs, Joseph, violinist, Oct 1962, *Obit* May 1997

Harrington, David, violinist, Nov 1998

Heifetz, Jascha, Russian-American violinist, Feb 1944, *Obit* Feb 1988

Huberman, Bronislaw, Polish violinist, July 1941, *Obit* July 1947

Kennedy, English violinist, July 1992

Kreisler, Fritz, Austrian violinist, July 1944, *Obit* Mar 1962

Laredo, Jaime, violinist, Sept 1967

Maazel, Lorin, American conductor, Yrbk 1965

Meyers, Anne Akiko, (1970-), Aug 2013

Midori, Japanese violinist, June 1990

Milstein, Nathan, Russian-American violinist, Mar 1950, *Obit* Feb 1993

Morini, Erica, Austrian violinist, Apr 1946, *Obit* Jan 1996

Mutter, Anne-Sophie, German violinist, Jan 1990

Oistrakh, David, Russian violinist, Mar 1956, *Obit* Yrbk 1974

Rose, Arnold, *Obit* Oct 1946

Schneider, Alexander, violinist, Mar 1976, *Obit* Mar 1993

Spalding, Albert, violinist, Jan 1944, *Obit* July 1953

Szeryng, Henryk, Polish violinist, Jan 1968, *Obit* Apr 1988

Szigeti, Joseph, Hungarian violinist, May 1940, Mar 1958, *Obit* Apr 1973

Zimbalist, Efrem, American violinist, Mar 1949, *Obit* Apr 1985

Zukerman, Pinchas, Israeli violinist and conductor, Nov 1978

Zwilich, Ellen Taaffe, American composer, Jan 1986

Violists

Primrose, William, violist, Yrbk 1946, *Obit* July 1982

Trampler, Walter, violist, Nov 1971, *Obit* Jan 1998

Volleyball players

May-Treanor, Misty, American volleyball player, June 2013

Walsh, Kerri, American volleyball player, June 2013

Webcasters

Ezarik, Justine, American webcaster, Mar 2013

Western writers

Bower, Bertha Muzzy, American novelist, *Obit* Sept 1940

Doig, Ivan, American western writer, Feb 2011

Faust, Frederick, American western novelist, *Obit* July 1944

Wine critics

Robinson, Jancis, British wine critic, Jan 2007

Wrestlers

Akebono, American sumo wrestler, Aug 1999

Asashoryu, Mongolian sumo wrestler, Jan 2005

Flair, Ric, wrestler, Mar 2000

Foley, Mick, American wrestler, Sept 2001

Gardner, Rulon, American wrestler, Nov 2004

Goldberg, wrestler, Apr 2001

Hogan, Hulk, American wrestler, Nov 1998

Takanohana, Japanese sumo wrestler, Jan 2002

Writers on crime

Rule, Ann, American true-crime writer, Sept 2000

Writers on science

Calder, Nigel, English author, June 1986

Whitford, Harry Nichols, *Obit* July 1941

Writers on the military

Werner, Max, Yrbk 1943, *Obit* Feb 1951

Yogis

Choudhury, Bikram, Indian yogi, Jan 2004

Iyengar, B. K. S., Indian yogi, June 2007

Young adult authors

Caudill, Rebecca, author, Yrbk 1950, *Obit* Jan 1986

Fox, Genevieve, Yrbk 1949, *Obit* Yrbk 1959

Howard, Elizabeth, Yrbk 1951

Kahmann, Chesley, Yrbk 1952

Lambert, Janet, Yrbk 1954

Latham, Jean Lee, American children's author, Yrbk 1956

Lindgren, Astrid, Swedish children's author, Oct 1996, *Obit* Apr 2002

Neilson, Frances Fullerton, Yrbk 1955

Paterson, Katherine, American young adult author, Nov 1997

Von Ziegesar, Cecily, American young adult novelist, Jan 2008

Youth leaders

Anderson, Constance, youth leader, May 1948, *Obit* Apr 2001

Armstrong, David W., American youth leader, July 1949, *Obit* Mar 1963

Baden-Powell of Gilwell, Robert Stephenson Smyth Baden-Powell, English Boy Scouts founder, *Obit* Mar 1941

Blalock, Richard W., American youth organization official, May 1950

Burns, John Lawrence, youth organization official, Apr 1960, *Obit* Nov 1996

Cloninger, Kathy, American Girl Scouts official, Oct 2012

Marvel, Elizabeth Newell, American youth leader, Apr 1962

Nwuneli, Ndidi O., Nigerian youth organization official, Jan 2007

Wood, Louise Aletha, Girl Scouts leader, July 1961, *Obit* July 1988

Zionist leaders

Goldmann, Nahum, Israeli Zionist leader, May 1957, *Obit* Oct 1982

Jabotinsky, Vladimir, Russian Zionist leader, *Obit* Sept 1940

Szold, Henrietta, American Zionist leader, Jan 1940, *Obit* Apr 1945

Zoologists

Rockley, Alicia Margaret Tyssen-Amherst Cecil, *Obit* Nov 1941

Totty, Charles H., Jan 1940

Wiigh-Masak, Susanne, Swedish ecologist, Jan 2005